Dictionary Catalog
of the Library

BERNICE P. BISHOP
MUSEUM

Honolulu, Hawaii

Volume 3

COU - FIS

G. K. HALL & CO., 70 LINCOLN STREET, BOSTON, MASSACHUSETTS

1964

This publication is printed on Permalife paper, developed by W. J. Barrow under a grant from the Council on Library Resources.

QL
Crus
Pam
#64

Couch, Jonathan

Discovery of Alpheus Edwardsii on the Coast by Cornwall.

[Jrnl. Nr. 18] Read April 4th 1860.

Source ? — — 8vo. pp. 209-212.

FEB 23 1911

QL
681
C85

Coues, Elliott

Key to North American birds containing a concise account of every species of living and fossil bird at present known from the continent north of the Mexican and United States boundary.

Salem, Naturalist Agency, 1872. 361p.

missing march, 1934, 1935.

QK
1
B3

Coulter, John Merle, 1851-   ed.

The Botanical gazette. v. 1–
Nov. 1875–
Hanover, Ind. [etc.] 1875–96; Chicago, University of Chicago, 1896–19
v. illus, plates, ports. 24cm. monthly.
No numbers were issued in Nov. and Dec. 1877.
Published by the University of Chicago from Mar. 1896.
Title varies: Nov. 1875–Oct. 1876, Botanical bulletin.
Nov. 1876–   The Botanical gazette.
Editors: 1875–19   J. M. Coulter (with M. S. Coulter, 1876-82; J. C. Arthur, 1883-1900; C. R. Barnes, 1883-1910)
Published in Hanover, Ind., 1875-77; Logansport, Ind. [etc.] 1878; Madison, Ind., 1878-79; Crawfordsville, Ind., 1880-83; Indianapolis, Ind., 1883-85; Crawfordsville, Ind., 1886-91; Bloomington, Ind., 1892-93; Madison, Wis., 1894-96; Chicago, Ill., 1896-19
I. Coulter, John Merle, 1851-   ed. II. Coulter, M.S., ed. III. Barnes, Charles Reid, 1858-1910, ed. IV. Arthur, Joseph Charles, 1850- ed. v. Chicago. University. Library of Congress   QK1.B3
          (2)   19–16845

AS
720.T
R 88

Couchman, L. E.

A catalogue of the Tasmanian Lepidoptera-Rhopalocera.

(Papers and Proc. of the R. Soc. of Tasmania Vol. 90:1-33, 1956)

AS
36
S1

Coues, Elliott, 1842–1899.

... List of birds ascertained to inhabit the District of Columbia, with the times of arrival and departure of such as are non-residents, and brief notices of habits, etc. By Elliott Coues and D. Webster Prentiss.

(*In* Smithsonian institution. Annual report. 1861. Washington, 1862. 23½cm. p. [399]-421)

1. Birds—District of Columbia. I. Prentiss, Daniel Webster, 1843-1899, joint author.
          S 15-123
Library of Congress   Q11.S66 1861
Library, Smithsonian   Institution

QK
1
U

Coulter, John Merle, 1851-

... Botany of western Texas; a manual of the phanerogams and pteridophytes of western Texas. By John M. Coulter ... Washington, Govt. print. off., 1891–94.

3 pt. in 1 v. 3 pl. 24cm. (U. S. Dept. of agriculture. Division of botany. Contributions from the U. S. National herbarium. vol. II)

Paged continuously.

1. Botany—Texas.
          8–10558
Library of Congress   QK1.U5 vol. 2

AS
36
S5

Coues, Elliott.

Avifauna Columbiana: being a list of birds ascertained to inhabit the District of Columbia, with the times of arrival and departure of such as are non-residents, and brief notices of habits, etc. ... Second edition revised to date and ... rewritten; by Elliott Coues ... and D. Webster Prentiss ... Washington, Govt. print. off., 1883.

133 p. front., illus. 23cm. (U. S. National museum, Bulletin, no. 26)

1. District of Columbia—Birds. I. Prentiss, Daniel Webster, ed.
Birds — District of Columbia   W 6-68
Washington, D.C.   Public Library

AS
36
A 65-n

Couffer, Jack C.

Galápagos adventure.

(Natural History, Vol. LXV(3):140-145, March, 1955)

QK
980
C85

Coulter, John Merle

Evolution of sex in plants.

Chicago, 1914, 8vo. pp 140. illus.

QH
199.K
K 47

Coues, Elliott

Kidder, Jerome Henry
Contributions to the natural history of Kerguelen Island...1874-75
I. Ornithology, ed. by Elliott Coues.

(Bull. U. S. Nat. Mus., Nos. 2, 1875)

DS
525
C 85

Coughlin, Richard J.

Double identity, the Chinese in modern Thailand. Hong Kong University Press. 1960. 8vo. xi + 222 pp.

QK
1
U

Coulter, John Merle, 1851-
Hesperogenia, a new genus of *Umbelliferae* from Mount Rainier. By John M. Coulter and J. N. Rose.

(*In* U. S. Dept. of agriculture. Division of botany. Contributions from the U. S. National herbarium. Washington, 1897-1901. 23cm. vol. V, no. 4, p. 203, pl. XXVII)

Issued October 31, 1899.

1. Hesperogenia. I. Rose, Joseph Nelson, 1862- joint author.
          8–10553
Library of Congress   QK1.U5 vol. 5

QL
677.N
C85

Coues, [Elliott]

The Coues check list of North American birds: with a dictionary of the etymology, orthography, and orthoepy of the scientific names.

Boston, Estes, 1882. 2nd edition. 165p.

GN
2.S
S 72

Coulborn, Rushton

Note on method in anthropology.

(Southwestern Jour. of Anthropology, 1(3):311 to 317, 1945)

QK
1
U

Coulter, John Merle, 1851-
Leibergia, a new genus of *Umbelliferae* from the Columbia River region. By John M. Coulter and J. N. Rose.

(*In* U. S. Dept. of agriculture. Division of botany. Contributions from the U. S. National herbarium. Washington, 1892-96. 24cm. vol. III, no. 9, p. 575-576. pl. XXVII)

Issued August 5, 1896.

1. Leibergia. I. Rose, Joseph Nelson, 1862- joint author.
Umbelliferae   8–10560
Library of Congress   QK1.U5 vol. 3

QL
715
C85

Coues, Elliott

Fur-bearing animals: a monograph of North American mustelidae in which an account of the wolverine... various other kinds of weasels... land and sea otters... contributed to the history of North American mammals. Department of Int., U. S. Geological Survey of the Territories, Misc. Publ. 8, Washington, 1877.

DU
12
C 85
locked
case

Coulter, John

Adventures on the western coast of South America, and the interior of California: including a narrative of incidents at the Kingsmill Islands, New Ireland, New Britain, New Guinea, and other islands in the Pacific Ocean; with an account of the natural productions, and the manners and customs, in peace and war, of the various savage tribes visited. In two volumes (2 v. in 1). London. Longman, Brown...1847. 8vo. pp.xxiv+288 xii+278.

QK
139
C 85

Coulter, John M.

Manual of the botany(Phaenogamia and Pteridophyta) of the Rocky Mountain region, from New Mexico to the British boundary. New York... American Book Company. 1885c. 8vo. xvi + 452 + 28 pp.

QL
681
C 85

Coues, Elliott, 1842–1899.
Key to North American birds. Containing a concise account of every species of living and fossil bird at present known from the continent north of the Mexican and United States boundary, inclusive of Greenland and Lower California, with which are incorporated General ornithology ... and Field ornithology ... The 5th ed. (entirely rev.) exhibiting the nomenclature of the American ornithologists' union ... By Elliott Coues ... Boston, Dana Estes and company, 1903. Page Co. (c1882-1903
2 v.   ts, illus, port. 26cm. 2 vols. Paged continuously.
"In memoriam: Elliott   Coues," by D. G. Elliott: p. [xxxvi]-xli.
1. Birds—Collection and   2. Birds—North America.
preservation.
Library of Congress   QL681.C867   3-32820/3
Copyright
598   P2

DU
12
C 85
locked
case

Coulter, John

Adventures in the Pacific; with observations on the natural productions, manners and customs of the natives of the various islands; together with remarks on missionaries, British and other residents, etc... Dublin. William Curry. 1845. 8vo. xi+290 pp.

over

QK
1
U

Coulter, John Merle, 1851-
... Monograph of the North American *Umbelliferae*. By John M. Coulter and J. N. Rose. Washington, Govt. print. off., 1900.

256, vii p. illus, IX pl. 24cm. (U. S. Dept. of agriculture. Division of botany. Contributions from the U. S. National herbarium. vol. VII, no. 1)

Issued December 31, 1900.
Bibliography: p. 10-11.

1. Umbelliferae. 2. Botany—North America. I. Rose, Joseph Nelson, 1862- joint author.
          8–10529
Library of Congress   QK1.U5 vol. 7

QK 643 C 85

Coulter, John M. & Chamberlain, C. J.

Morphology of Gymnosperms, by John M. Coulter and Charles J. Chamberlain. Rev. ed.

Univ. of Chic.press, (1917). 466p. illus.

QK 1 U

Coulter, John Merle, 1851–

Report on Mexican *Umbelliferæ*, mostly from the state of Oaxaca, recently collected by C. G. Pringle and E. W. Nelson. By John M. Coulter and J. N. Rose.

(*In* U. S. Dept. of agriculture. Division of botany. Contributions from the U. S. National herbarium. Washington, 1895. 24ᵐ. vol. III, no. 5, p. 289-309. pl. V-X)

Issued December 14, 1895.

1. Botany—Mexico. 2. Umbelliferae. I. Rose, Joseph Nelson, 1862–

8—22680

Library of Congress   QK1.U5 vol. 3

G 3 A 1

Coulter, John Wesley

The Bikinians.

(Geogr. Rev., Vol. 40(4):670-671, 1950)

QK 1 U

Coulter, John Merle

Manual of the Phanerogams and Pteridophytes of western Texas.

(Contributions of the U. S. National Herbarium, Vol. 2, 1891-1894.) Published as Botany of western Texas IN title-page for the volume.

AS 36 S1

Coulter, John Merle, 1851–

The social, educational, and scientific value of botanic gardens. By Prof. John Merle Coulter.

(*In* Smithsonian institution. Annual report. 1917. Washington, 1919. 23½ᵐ. p. 463-468)

"Reprinted ... from Science, June 29, 1917, n. s., vol. 45, no. 1174."

1. Botanical gardens.

Library of Congress   Q11.S66 1917   20-5160
[9]

AS 763 U

Coulter, John Wesley

Chinese rice farmers in Hawaii, by John Wesley Coulter and Chee Kwon Chun.

(Univ. of Hawaii Research publications, no.16. March 1937. 72 pp.)

QK 1 U

Coulter, John M.

Phanerogams and pteridophytes of Western Texas.

U.S. Nat. Herb. II, Wash. 1894.

QK 1 U

Coulter, John Merle, 1851–

Supplement to the Monograph of the North American *Umbelliferæ*. By John M. Coulter and J. N. Rose.

(*In* Smithsonian institution. United States national museum. Contributions from the United States national herbarium. Washington, 1903-24½ᵐ. vol. XII, pt. 10, p. 441-451. pl. LXXXII-LXXXIII)

"Issued July 21, 1909."
Bibliography: p. 441-442.

1. Umbelliferae. I. Rose, Joseph Nelson, 1862– joint author.

Botany — United States   Agr 9-1873

Library, U. S. Dept. of   Agriculture 450C76 vol. 12, pt. 10
[519c]

G 55 F 65

Coulter, John Wesley

Eastern Melanesia.

IN

Freeman, Otis W. Geography of the Pacific. N.Y. 1951. pp. 173-204.

QK Pam #680 4to

Coulter, John M.

The phylogeny of Angiosperms, ex Decennial Pub., vol. X, 1903.

QK 150 Co

Coulter, John M. & Porter, T. C.

Synopsis of the flora of Colorado. (U.S. geological & geographical survey of the territories: Miscellaneous publications, no. 4).

Washington, 1874.

and

QK Botany Pam 137?

G 7 S 43

AND

DU Pac.Pam. 712

Coulter, John Wesley

Environment, race and government in South Sea Islands.

(Scottish Geographical Magazine, Vol. 63: 49-56, 1947)

QK 53 C 85

Coulter, John M.

Plant relations: a first book of botany. Third edition revised. New York. D. Appleton and Company. 1905   8vo. viii + 348 pp.

QK 47 Co C85

Barnes + Cowles.

Coulter, John Merle, and others

A textbook of botany for colleges and universities, Volume II, Ecology. Chicago, 1911 (?), 8vo, pp. x 485-964 q.

JAN 23 '14

DU 600 C 85

Coulter, John Wesley

Fiji: little India of the Pacific. University of Chicago Press. 1942c. 8vo. xiii + 156 pp.

QK 1 U

Coulter, John Merle, 1851–

... Preliminary revision of the North American species of *Cactus, Anhalonium*, and *Lophophora*. By John M. Coulter ... Washington, Govt. print. off., 1894.

iii, 91-132, ii p. 24ᵐ. (U. S. Dept. of agriculture. Division of botany. Contributions from the U. S. National herbarium. vol. III, no. 2)

Issued June 10, 1894.

1. Botany—North America. 2. Cactaceae.

8—22683

Library of Congress   QK1.U5 vol. 3

QK 1 U

Coulter, John Merle, 1851–

... Upon a collection of plants made by Mr. G. C. Nealley in the region of the Rio Grande, in Texas, from Brazos Santiago to El Paso County. By John M. Coulter ... Washington, Gov't print. off., 1890.

iii, 29-65 p. 23ᵐ. (U. S. Dept. of agriculture. Division of botany. Contributions from the U. S. National herbarium. vol. I) no. 11)

Issued July 18, 1890.

1. Botany—Texas—Rio Grande.

8-10536

Library of Congress   QK1.U5 vol. 1

DU 622 C 85

AS 763 U

Coulter, John Wesley

A gazetteer of the Territory of Hawaii.

(University of Hawaii Research Publications No. 11, 1935. pp. 1-241)

QK 1 U

Coulter, John Merle, 1851–

... Preliminary revision of the North American species of *Echinocactus, Cereus,* and *Opuntia*. By John M. Coulter. Washington, Govt. print. off., 1896.

iii, 355-462, iv p. 24ᵐ. (U. S. Dept. of agriculture. Division of botany. Contributions from the U. S. National herbarium. vol. III, no. 7)

Issued April 1, 1896.

1. Botany—North America. 2. Cactaceae.

8-10565

Library of Congress   QK1.U5 vol. 3

S 399 E 6

Coulter, John Wesley

Agricultural land-use planning in the Territory of Hawaii.

(Univ. of Hawaii, Agric Ext. Service, Ext. Bulletin 36, 1940)

DU 622 C 85

Coulter, John Wesley

Hawaiian toponymy.
Coulter, John Wesley
A gazetteer of the Territory of Hawaii.

(University of Hawaii Research Publications, No. 11, 1935. pp. 231-237)

G
3
A 1

Coulter, John Wesley

Impact of the war on South Sea islands.

(Geographical Review, Vol. 36 (3):409-419, 1946)

and
DU
Pac.Pam.
694

DU
Pac.Pam.
492

Coulter, John Wesley

Manoa Valley, Honolulu: A study in economic and social geography.

(Reprinted from The Bulletin of the Geographical Society of Philadelphia, Vol. XXX, No. 2, April, 1932.) 109-130 pp. 8vo.

GN
Ethn. Pam.
3143

Coulter, John Wesley

Small farming on Kauai: Hawaiian islands.

(Economic Geography, October, 1935, pp. 401-409)

DU
Pac.Pam.
506

Coulter, John Wesley

The Island of Hawaii.

(The Journal of Geography, Vol. 31, 1932, pp. 225-236)

QE
Geol.Pam.
1036
1037

Coulter, John Wesley   and others

Meteorological reports of the Mauna Kea Expedition, 1935, (1-2)

(Bull. American Meteorological Society, Vol. 19, 1939, pp. 349-351; Vol. 20, 1939, pp. 97-105)

G
Geogr.
Pam.
45

Coulter, John Wesley

Wings over the Atlantic—the time place factor in geography.

(Journal of Geography, Vol. 47(8):313-325, 1948)

DU
620
H 4

Coulter, John Wesley

The journal of Nelson Haley, a whaler.

(Haw. Hist. Soc., Ann. Rept. 49th, 1940, pp. 40-41)

DU
Pac.Pam.
505

Coulter, John Wesley

The Oahu Sugar Cane Plantation, Waipahu.

(Economic Geography, Vol. IX, Jan. 1933, pp. 60-71)

QH
48
C85

Coulter, Merle C.

Outline of genetics with special reference to plant material.

Chicago, Univ. Press, [1923].   211p.

Q
101
P 18

Coulter, John Wesley

Land utilization by Fijians and East Indians in Fiji.

IN Proc. Sixth Pac. Sci. Congress, 1939 (California), Vol. 4, 1940, pp. 29-38.

DU
12
C 85

Coulter, John Wesley

The Pacific dependencies of the United States.   The Macmillan Company.   New York. 1957 8vo.   xv + 388 pp.

QK
1
B3

Coulter, M.S., ed.

The Botanical gazette. v. 1–
Nov. 1875–
Hanover, Ind. [etc.] 1875–96; Chicago, University of Chicago, 1896–19
v. illus., plates, ports. 24ᶜᵐ. monthly.
No numbers were issued in Nov. and Dec. 1877.
Published by the University of Chicago from Mar. 1896.
Title varies: Nov. 1875–Oct. 1876, Botanical bulletin.
Nov. 1876–   The Botanical gazette.
Editors: 1875–19   J. M. Coulter (with M. S. Coulter, 1876–82; J. C. Arthur, 1883–1900; C. R. Barnes, 1883–1910)
Published in Hanover, Ind., 1875–77; Logansport, Ind. [etc.] 1878; Madison, Ind., 1878–79; Crawfordsville, Ind., 1880–83; Indianapolis, Ind., 1883–85; Crawfordsville, Ind., 1886–91; Bloomington, Ind., 1892–93; Madison, Wis., 1894–96; Chicago, Ill., 1896–19
i. Botany—Period.   i. Coulter, John Merle, 1851–   ed.
ii. Coulter, M.S., ed. iii.   Barnes, Charles Reid, 1858–1910, ed.
iv. Arthur, Joseph Charles,   1850–   ed. v. Chicago. University.
Library of Congress   QK1.B3   19–16845
                          (2)

DU
Pac.
Pam.
643

Coulter, John Wesley

Land utilization in American Samoa.

(Bernice P. Bishop Museum, Bulletin 170, 1941)

DU
Pac.Pam.
480

Coulter, John Wesley

Population and Utilization of Land and Sea in Hawaii, 1853.

(Bernice P. Bishop Museum Bulletin 88, 1931)

AM
Mus.Pam.
195

Council for British Archaeology.

Notes for the guidance of archaeologists in regard to expert evidence.   7 pp.

Q
101
P 18

Coulter, John Wesley

Land utilization in the Hawaiian islands.

IN Proceedings of the Fifth Pacific Science Congress, Vol. 2, 1933, pp. 1351-1356

G
Geogr.
Pam. 40

Coulter, John Wesley

Le rapport entre la densité de la population et le mode d'utilisation (ou exploitation) du sol dans les régions coloniales.

(C. R. du Congres Intern. de Geographie, Amsterdam, 1938, Tome 2, pp.149-162)

GN
492
S 34

COUNCIL HOUSES   MICRONESIA

Schlesier, Erhard

Die Erscheinungsformen des Mannerhauses und das Klubwesen in Mikronesien.   Eine ethno-soziologische untersuchung.   Mouton and Co. 's-Gravenhage.   1953. 8vo.

[review by S.H.Riesenberg IN Am. Anthropologist, 57:1081-3, 1955]

DU
627.6
C 85

Coulter, John Wesley

Land Utilization in the Hawaiian Islands.

(University of Hawaii, Research Publication, 8, 1933)

Q
101
P 18

Coulter, John Wesley

The relation of soil erosion to land utilization in the Territory of Hawaii.

IN Proc. Sixth Pac. Sci. Congress, 1939, (California), Vol. 4, 1940, pp. 897-904.

QK
Pam
#422

Councilman, W. T.

The root system of Epigaea Repens and its relation to the fungi of the Humus, ex Proc. N. A. S., vol. 9, 1923.

GN
1
Z 50

Count, Earl W.

The "Australoid" in California.

(Zeitschrift f. Rassenkunde, Vol. 8, 1938, pp. 62-95)

see review by Carl C. Seltzer IN Am. Jour. of Phys. Anthrop., Vol. 1, N.S., 1943, p. 111-113

GN
320
C 85

Coupin, Henri

Les Bizarreries des Races Humaines. Paris. Vuibert et Nony. 1905. R8vo. 285 pp.

GC
57
C 86

Cousteau, Jacques-Yves

The living sea. By Jacques-Yves Cousteau with James Dugan. New York. Harper & Row. 1963. 325 pp. 4to.

GN
370
C 85

Count, Earl W., editor

This is race: an anthology selected from the international literature on the races of man. Selected, edited, and with an introduction by Earl W. Count. New York. R8vo. 1950c xxviii +747 pp.

AS
162
P 23

Cour, P.

Identification de quelques plantes critiques de la flore de l'Archipel des Kerguelen.

(Bull. Mus. Nat. d'Hist. Nat., ser. 2, Tome 33:221-223, 1961)

GN
2.1
E
20

Couteaud, Dr.

Les origines de l'île de Pâques. In Revue, Ecole d'anthrop. de Paris, Vol. 1910, pp 86 - 97.

GN
1
A-j

Count, Earl W.

REVIEW of
Ackernecht, Erwin H.
Rudolf Virchow: doctor, statesman, anthropologist. Madison. 1953. U. of Wisconsin Press

(Am. Jour. of Phys. Anthropology, ns vol. 12 pp. 623-627, 1954)

QH
1
M 17 b

Cours, G.

Le manioc à Madagascar.

(Mem. Inst. Sci. de Madagascar, Ser. B., Tome 3(2):203-400, 1951)

[Manihot esculenta]

GN
Ethn.
Pam.3418

Couteaud, P.

Mariage royal à Borabora. pamphlet, unbound, 12 pp.

GN
2.5
P 76

COUNTING KEWA
Franklin, Karl

The Kewa counting systems. By Karl and Joice Franklin.

(Jour. Poly. Soc., 71(2):188-191, 1962)

[southern highlands of Papua]

GN
22
B 61

Courses toward urban life; archaeological considerations of some cultural alternates.

Braidwood, Robert J.

GN
Ethn.
Pam.
3417

Couteaux, P.

Voyage à l'Archipel Dangereux.

File on Upper Floor of Library

Country Club Organized

in Haw. Gazette 1916. April 6. p. 1, & p. 7.

GN
855.1
B 95

Cousens, Henry
Burgess, James

Architectural antiquities of northern Gujarat ... by James Burgess and Henry Cousens. London. 1903. 4to.

(Archaeological Survey of Western India, Vol. IX).

AP
2
A 5

Couthouy, Capt.

Volcanic phenomena in Hawaii. Extract from his letter dated Honolulu, Oahu, Oct. 24, 1840. in Am. Journ. of Sc. XL, No. 1, 1st ser. 1841, p. 200.
(Sent to the editor by D. H. Storer.)

QE
342
N 56 p

Couper, R. A.

New Zealand Mesozoic and Cainozoic plant microfossils.

(New Zealand Geol. Survey, Paleontological Bull. 32, 1960)

DU
12
C 86

Cousins, George

The story of the South Seas. With maps and many illustrations. London. London Missionary Society. 1894. 8vo. viii + 246 pp.

(missionary)

AP
2
A 5

Couthouy, J. P.
Dana, James D.

(Acknowledgments of J. D. Dana and J. P. Couthouy, relative to a charge of plagiarism)

(Am. Jour. Sci., Ser. 1, Vol. 47, 1844, pp. 122-126)

AS
36
S1

Coupin, Henri Eugène Victor, 1868-
Animals that hunt. By Henri Coupin.

(In Smithsonian institution. Annual report. 1903. Washington, 1904. 234... p. 567-571)

"Translated from the Revue scientifique (Paris), August 29, 1903, pp. 274-277."

1. Animals, Food habits of.

S 15-1206

Library of Congress   Q11.S66 1903
Library, Smithsonian   Institution

G
3
N 27

Cousteau, Jacques-Yves

Calypso Explores an undersea canyon.

(Nat. Geogr., 113(3):373-396, 1958)

AS
36
B

Couthouy, Joseph P.

Remarks upon coral formations in the Pacific with suggestions as to the causes of their absence in the same parallels of latitude on the coast of South America.

(Boston Journal of Natural History, Vol. 4, 1843-44, pp. 66-105, 137-162)

AP
2
A 5

Couthouy, Joseph P.

　　　Reply of J. P. Couthouy to the accusations of J. D. Dana, geologist of the Exploring Expedition, contained on pp. 130 and 145 of this Volume.

　　　(Am. Jour. of Sci., Ser. 1, Vol. 45, 1843, pp. 378-389)

Picture albums

Looked Case

Covarrubias, Miguel

　　　Pageant of the Pacific.
　　　Six murals for Pacific House, San Francisco
　　　Native means of transportation
　　　The fauna and flora
　　　Native dwellings
　　　Art forms
　　　Economy
　　　Peoples
folio. in color.　1943

AS
36
S1

Coville, Frederick Vernon, 1867–

　　　Desert plants as a source of drinking water. By Frederick V. Coville.

　　　(*In* Smithsonian institution. Annual report. 1903. Washington, 1904. 23½ᵐ. p. 499-505. illus., II pl. on 1 l.)

　　　1. Desert flora.　I. Title.　Flora—desert

Library of Congress
Library, Smithsonian　　　Q11.S66 1903　　　Institution　　　S 15-1201

QL
444.D3
C87

Coutière, Henri

　　　... Les "Alpheidae", morphologie externe et interne, formes larvaires, bionomie ... (Thèses présentées a la faculté des sciences de Paris, Ser.A no.321)

　　　Paris, Masson, 1899.　559p.,6pls.

Covarrubias, M.

　　　Pageant of the Pacific.　1943.

　　　UH has

AS
36
S5

Coville, Frederick Vernon, 1867–

　　　... Directions for collecting specimens and information illustrating the aboriginal uses of plants. By Frederick V. Coville ... Washington, Govt. print. off., 1895.

　　　8 p. 24½ᵐ. (Part J of Bulletin of the United States National museum, no. 39)

　　　At head of title: Smithsonian institution. United States National museum.

　　　1. Plants—Collection and preservation.　2. Indians—Medicine.　3. Indians—Implements.
Collecting plants

Library, Smithsonian　　　Institution Q11.U6　　　S 13-149

QL
Crustacea
Pam. 496

Coutière, Henri.

　　　The American Species of Snapping Shrimps of the genus Synalpheus.

　　　(Proc. of the U. S. Nat'l. Museum, Vol. XXXVI, 1909, pp. 1-93)

AS
36
A 16

Coventry, G. Ayres

　　　Crustacea. (eastern Pacific, shores of Mexico, Central and South America, Tres Marias I.)
IN
　　　Results of the Fifth George Vanderbilt Expedition (1941)...
　　　(Acad. Nat. Sci., Philadelphia, Monograph 6, 1944, pp. 531-544)

AS
36
S1

Coville, Frederick Vernon, 1867–

　　　The formation of leafmold. By Frederick V. Coville.

　　　(*In* Smithsonian institution. Annual report. 1913. Washington, 1914. 23½ᵐ. p. 333-343)

　　　"Reprinted ... from the Journal of the Washington academy of sciences, vol. 3, pp. 77 to 89, Feb. 4, 1913."

　　　1. Leaf-mold.

　　　　　　15-1741

Library of Congress　　　Q11.S66 1913

AS
36
S4

Coutière, Henri i. e. François Louis Henri, 1869–
　　　The snapping shrimps (*Alpheidæ*) of the Dry Tortugas, Florida.　By Henri Coutière ...

　　　(*In* U. S. National museum. Proceedings. Washington, 1910. 23½ᵐ. vol. 37, p. 485-487. illus.)

　　　1. Shrimp.

　　　　　　11-9680

Library of Congress　　　Q11.U55 vol. 37

QK
1
U

Coville, Frederick Vernon, 1867–
　　　... Botany of the Death Valley expedition. Report on the botany of the expedition sent out in 1891 by the U. S. Department of agriculture to make a biological survey of the region of Death Valley, California. By Frederick Vernon Coville ... Washington, Govt. print. off., 1893.

　　　viii, 363 p. front., 21 pl. (part fold.) fold. map. 24ᵐ. (U. S. Dept. of agriculture. Division of botany. Contributions from the U. S. National herbarium. vol. IV)

　　　Issued November 29, 1893.
　　　Bibliography. By Josephine A. Clark: p. 284-300.

　　　1. Botany—California—Death Valley.　I. Clark, Josephine Adelaide.

　　　　　　8–10557

Library of Congress　　　QK1.U5 vol. 4

AS
36
S1

Coville, Frederick Vernon, 1867–
　　　The influence of cold in stimulating the growth of plants. By Frederick V. Coville.

　　　(*In* Smithsonian institution. Annual report. 1919. Washington, 1921. 23½ᵐ. p. 281-291. 27 pl. on 14 l.)

　　　"Reprinted from the Journal of agricultural research, vol. 20, pp. 151 to 160, 1920."

　　　1. Plants, Effect of temperature on.　2. Growth (Plants)

　　　　　　22-309

Library of Congress　　　Q11.S66 1919
[10]

QL
401
J 85

Couturier, M.

　　　Etude sur les mollusques Gastropodes recueillés par M. L.-G. Seurat dans les archipels de Tahiti, Paumotu et Gambier.

　　　(Journal de Conchyliologie, Tome 55:123-178, 1907)

QK
1
U

Coville, Frederick Vernon, 1867–
　　　[Botany of Yakutat Bay, Alaska] II. Botanical report. By Frederick Vernon Coville.

　　　(*In* U. S. Dept. of agriculture. Division of botany. Contributions from the U. S. National herbarium. Washington, 1895. 24ᵐ. vol. III, no. 6, p. 334-353)

　　　Issued January 15, 1896.

　　　1. Botany—Alaska—Yakutat Bay.

　　　　　　8–22677

Library of Congress　　　QK1.U5 vol. 3
[21f1]

QK
1
U

Coville, Frederick Vernon, 1867–
　　　... Notes on the plants used by the Klamath Indians of Oregon. By Frederick V. Coville. Washington, Gov't print. off., 1897.

　　　v, 87-108, ii p. 23ᵐ. (U. S. Dept. of agriculture. Division of botany. Contributions from the U. S. National herbarium. vol. v, no. 2)

　　　Issued June 9, 1897.

　　　1. Botany, Economic.

　　　　　　8–10555

Library of Congress　　　QK1.U5 vol. 5

GN
662
L 76

Covarrubias, Miguel

Linton, Ralph

　　　Arts of the South Seas, by Ralph Linton and Paul S. Wingert... The Museum of Modern Art. Simon and Schuster. New York. 1946. sm4to. 199 pp.　Color illustrations by Miguel Covarrubias.

QK
1
U

Coville, Frederick Vernon, 1867–
　　　Crepis occidentalis and its allies.　By Frederick V. Coville.

　　　(*In* U. S. Dept. of agriculture. Division of botany. Contributions from the U. S. National herbarium. Washington, 1892-96. 24ᵐ. vol. iii, no. 9, p. 559-565. xxi-xxvi pl.)

　　　Issued August 5, 1896.

　　　1. Crepis occidentalis.

　　　　　　8–10562

Library of Congress　　　QK1.U5 vol. 3

AS
36
S3

Coville, Frederick Vernon, 1867–
　　　Wokas, a primitive food of the Klamath Indians. By Frederick Vernon Coville ...

　　　(*In* U. S. National museum. Annual report. 1902. Washington, 1904. 23½ᵐ. p. 725-739. 13 pl. (2 col., incl. double front.))

　　　Half-title.

　　　1. Klamath Indians.　2. Indians of North America—Food.　I. Title.
　　　　　　14-19919

Library of Congress　　　Q11.U5 1902
———— Copy 2.
———— Separate.　　　E99.K7C6

DS
647.B2
C 87

Covarrubias, Miguel

　　　Island of Bali.　With an album of photographs by Rose Covarrubias.　New York. Alfred A. Knopf. 1942. R8vo. xxv + 417 + x pp.

QK
78
C87

Coville, Frederick Vernon, 1867–
　　　Desert botanical laboratory of the Carnegie institution, by Frederick Vernon Coville and Daniel Trembly Macdougal. Washington, U. S. A., The Carnegie institution, 1903.

　　　vi, 58 p. illus. (maps, diagr.) xxix pl. (incl. front.) 25½ᵐ.

　　　"Carnegie institution of Washington. Publication no. 6."
　　　"Bibliography. By William Austin Cannon": p. 46-58.

　　　1. Botanical laboratories.　2. Carnegie institution of Washington. Desert botanical laboratory.　I. Macdougal, Daniel Trembly, 1865–　joint author.

　　　　　　4–19091

Library of Congress　　　QK78.C2C8
———— Copy 2.　　　[s19g2]

Coville, Frederick V
QK
78
C　*and Macdougal*
Desert Botanical Laboratory of the Carnegie Institution. Pub. 6

127
Carnegie Institution Washington　*1903. 8° pl. 58.*
Bound
AUG 1 1907

QK
110
N 56

Coville, Frederick Vernon

    Grossulariaceae, by Frederick Vernon Coville and Nathaniel Lord Britton.

    IN North American flora, Vol. 22, Part 3, 1908, pp. 193-225.

GN
1
O 15

Cowan, H. K. J.

    A large Papuan language phylum in West New Guinea.

    (Oceania, 28(2):159-166, 1957)

QK
1
B 97-b3
and
QK
Bot.Pam.
1972

Cowan, J. M.

    The Malaysian species of Wendlandia (Rubiac

    (Bull.du Jardin Batanique de Buitenzorg. Series III, vol.XIV¹. 1936. pp.8-46)

DU
870
C 87

Covit, Bernard

    Official directory and guide book for Tahiti. Marshall-Adams Printing Corp. San Francisco. 1951. 8vo. 136 pp.

    Revised edition. Ye Olde Printerie, Ltd. Hong Kong. 1962. 160 pp. 8vo.

GN
2.S
N 67

Cowan, Dr. H. K. J.

    Linguistic research in Netherlands New Guinea.

    (New Guinea Studien, Vol. 3(3):196-206, July 1959)

GN
2.S
P 76

Cowan, James

    The breadfruit-tree in Maori tradition.

    (Journal of the Polynesian Society, 19: 94-96, 1910.)

GN
700
C 97

COWA Surveys and Bibliographies
Council for Old World Archaeology

    Area 1:²   British Isles *1958-1960*
    " 2:1   Scandinavia
    " 3:1   Western Europe

    9:1   N.E. Africa
    19:1   S.E. Asia
    30:1   Indonesia
    Cambridge   Mass. 4to

PL
1
B 59

Cowan, H. K. J.

    Nadere gegevens betreffende de verbreiding der West-Papoease taalgroep (Vogelkop, Nieuw-Guinea)

    (Bijdragen tot de Taal-, Land- en Volkenkunde, Deel 116(3):350-364, 1960)

GR
Folklore
Pam.
123

Cowan, James

    The Caltex book of Maori lore. Illustrated by Dennis Turner. A. H. and A. W. Reed. sm4to. 1959. 63 pp.

DU
400
Rec
Pam
#4
N.Z.

Cowan, Frank

    Fact and fancy in New Zealand. The terraces of Rotomahana; a poem to which is prefixed a paper on Geyser eruptions and terrace formations by Josiah Martin. Auckland, 1885, 8vo, pp.61.

GN
1
O 15

Cowan, H. K. J.

    Notes on Windesi grammar.

    (Oceania, Vol. XXVI(1):42-58, 1955)

    [geographical area outlined]

GN
2.S
P 76

Cowan, J(ames)

    The Canoe of Maui.

    (Journal of the Polynesian Society, 14: 161-2, 1905.)

DU
620
M 67

Cowan, Frank

    Visit in verse to Halemaumau. Honolulu, 1885, 4vo. pp. 2.
    Also in Miscell. Pams.Haw. II, pp. 167-196.

GN
2.S
N 67

Cowan, H. K. J.

    Een tweede grote Papoea-taalgroepering in Nederlands-Nieuw-Guinea.

    (Nieuw Guinea Studiën, Jaargang 1, Nr. 2: 106-117, April, 1957)

    [Two Papuan language groups in Netherlands New Guinea]

GN
2.S
P 76

Cowan, J.

    The cave dwellings at Te Pehu. (The story of a stone axe.)

    (Journal of the Polynesian Society, 17: 222-226, 1908.)

    Maori text: "The story of Te Pehu pa" as told by Waharoa, of Utuhina, Rotorua (1907). (ibid, pp. 227-228)

GN
1
A 63

Cowan, H. K. J.

    La classification des langues papoues.

    (Anthropos, 54:973-981, 1959)

GN
1
O 15

Cowan, H. K. J.

    Variability in New Guinea languages.

    (Oceania, 25(3):208-215, 1955)

GN
2.S
P 76

Cowan, James

Smith, S. Percy

    Clairvoyance among the Maoris. With notes by James Cowan.

    (Journal of the Polynesian Society, 29: 149-161, 1920; 30: 119-120, 1921)

GN
1
O 15

Cowan, H. K. J.

    Ethnolinguistics and "Papuan" etymology.

    (Oceania, 26(4):54-60, 1954)

AS
42
V 64

Cowan, Ian McTaggart

    The mammals of British Columbia. By Ian McTaggart Cowan and Charles J. Guiguet.

    (British Columbia Provincial Museum, Handbook No. 11 2nd edition, 1960)

GR
375
C 87

Cowan, James

    Hero stories of New Zealand. Harry H. Tombs Limited. Wellington. 1935. sm8vo. xv + 288 pp.

GN 2.S P 76   Cowan, J(ames)

The last of the Ngati-Mamoe. Some incidents of southern Maori history.

(Journal of the Polynesian Society, 14: 193-199, 1905.)

DU 406 C 87   Cowan, James

The Maoris of New Zealand; with numerous illustrations from photographs and drawings. Christchurch, Whitcombe and Tombs, Ltd., 1910. 8vo. pp. ix + 356.

DU Pac.Pam 803   Cowan, James

Tales of our coral lands and pearlshell lagoons.

(Brett's Christmas Annual, 1928, pp. 22-24)

[Penrhyn, Rakahanga, Pukapuka, Rarotonga]

GR 375 P 78   Cowan, James

Legends of the Maori, by Sir Maui Pomare and James Cowan, in collaboration. Illustrations by Stuart Peterson. Wellington. Fine Arts. (N.Z.) Ltd. 1930-34. R8vo. Vol. 1-2. Vol.2. Maori-Polynesian Historical Traditions Folk-lore, and Stories of Old New Zealand...edited by James Cowan... Wellington. H. H. Tombs,Ltd (1934).

GN 2.S P 76   Cowan, James

Miru, of the Reinga.

(Journal of the Polynesian Society, 21: 104, 1912.)

QH 1 P 11   Cowan, Richard S.

A taxonomic revision of the genus Neraudia (Urticaceae).

(Pacific Science, Vol. 3:231-270, 1949)

and QK Bot.Pam. 2559

DU Pac.Pam 527   (Cowan, James)

The Maori. (New Zealand Government Publicity Production. 1926). 32 pp.

GN 2.S P 76   Cowan, James

"Ngau-Taringa."

(Journal of the Polynesian Society, 29: 204-206, 1920.)

[transference of wisdom by biting the ear of a tohunga in "articulo mortis"]

Carter Coll. 7-E-4

Cowan, Robert Ernest

A bibliography of the history of California and the Pacific West 1510-1906. San Francisco The Book Club of California. 1914 xxxi + 318pp.

GN Pam #498   Cowan, James, & Best, Elsdon

Maori children playing knucklestones (typewritten copy).

QL Bird Pam #11   Cowan, J(ames)

Our New Zealand Birds, ex Illustrated Magazine, April, 1920.

QK Bot.Pam. 2814   Cowan, R. S.

Tinian plants collected by author.

(Bull. of the Torrey Botanical Club, Vol. 73(6); 1946)

AS 750 N   *Cowan, James*

Maori Place Names, with special reference to the Great Lakes & Mountains of the South Island

N.Z.I. Trans. & Proc. Vol. XXXVIII, 1905 pp. 113-120

GN 2.S P 76   Cowan, James

The Patu-Paiarehe; Notes on Maori folk-tales of the fairy people.

(Journal of the Polynesian Society, 30: 96-102, 142-151, 1921.)

COWBIRDS.

AS 36 S3   Bendire, Charles Emil, 1836-1897.

The cowbirds. By Major Charles Bendire ...

(*In* U. S. National museum. Annual report. 1893. Washington, 1895, 23½cm. p. 587-624. 3 pl.)

Half-title.

1. Cowbirds.

Library of Congress   Q11.U5 1893   14-19795
———— Copy 2.
———— Separate.   QL696.P2B4

GN 2.S P 76   Cowan, James

Maori tattooing survivals, some notes on Moko.

(Journal of the Polynesian Society, 30: 241-245, 1921)

DU 406 C87   Cowan, James   comp.

Sketches of old New Zealand: Maori biographies. Descriptive catalogue of M Maori portraits painted by Herr G.Lindauer Auckland, 1901.

(Photographs of the paintings are fastened to the pages by clips)

COWBIRDS.

QL 1 C15   Grinnell, Joseph, 1877-

A new cowbird of the genus *Molothrus*, with a note on the probable genetic relationships of the North American forms, by Joseph Grinnell. Berkeley, The University press, 1909.

cover-title, p. (275)-281. illus. 27cm. (University of California publications in zoology, vol. 5, no. 5)

"Contribution from the Museum of vertebrate zoology of the University of California."

1. Cow-bird.

Title from Univ. of Calif.   Library of Congress   A 11-2223

Cowan, J.

The Maori yesterday and today. 1930.

UH has

GN 2.S P 76   Cowan, James

Nihoniho, Tuta

Story of the "Takitimu" canoe; a Hawaikian Maori epic. Collected by James Cowan. Translated by Hare Hongi. Parts I-II.

(Jour. Poly. Soc., 16:220-225, 1907; 17:93-107, 1908)

QH 309 C87   Cowdry, Edmund V

Human biology and racial welfare. New York, Hoeber, 1930. 612p.

PL
615
C 87

Cowell, Reid

The structure of Gilbertese. Rongorongo Press. Beru, Gilbert Islands. 1951. 8vo. (8)1-59(L2-L7, P1-P3, EV1-EV18, GV1-GV14) pp.

2 copies

QH
P 11

Cox, Doak O.

Emery, K. O.

Beach rock in the Hawaiian Islands. By K. O. Emery and Doak C. Cox.

(Pacific Science, 10:382-402, 1956)

QC
Physics
and
Meteoro-
logy
Pam.
33

Cox, Doak C.

Shepard, F. P.

The tsunami of April 1, 1946. By F. P. Shepard, G. A. Macdonald, and D. C. Cox.

(Bull. of the Scripps Inst. of Oceanography, Univ. of Calif., Vol. 5(6):391-470, 1950)

QK
358
C 87

Cowen, D. V.

Flowering trees and shrubs in India. Thacker and Co., Ltd. Bombay. sm4to. (1950) xvi + 137 pp. [59 color plates]

QE
1
H 38

Cox, Doak C.

MacDonald, G. A.

Geology and ground-water resources of the island of Kauai, Hawaii, by G. A. MacDonald, D. A. Davis and D. C. Cox.

(Hawaii division of Hydrography, Bull. 13: 1-212 (map); 1960)

AS
763
I. 38

Cox, Doak C.

Variation of intensity of the 1946 tsunami on Hawaiian shores.

(Proc. Hawaiian Acad. of Sci., 22nd Ann. Meeting, 1946/47:8)

GC
21
C 87

Cowen, Robert C.

Frontiers of the sea; the story of oceanographic exploration. Introduction by Roger R. Revelle. Drawings by Mary S. Cowen. Doubleday and Company, Inc. Garden City. 8vo. 1960. 307 pp.

QH
11
P 11

Cox, Doak C.

The hydrology of Arno atoll, Marshall Islands.

(Scientific Investigations in Micronesia, Pac. Sci. Board, NRC, No. 9, March 1951)

Z
6011
C 87

Cox, Edward Godfrey

A reference guide to the literature of travel, including voyages, geographical descriptions, adventures, shipwrecks, and expeditions. Volume one: The Old World; Volume two: the New World. Vol. 3:Great Britain.

(Univ. of Washington Pub. in Language and Lit., Vol. 9, 1935; Vol. 10, 1938) Vol. 12,1949

PL
61.B
C 87

Cowie, Andson

English-Sulu-Malay vocabulary, with useful sentences, tables, etc. Edited by Wm. Clark Cowie. Grammatical introduction by the editor. London. 1893. 8vo. 288 pp.

QH
1
A 88

Cox, Doak C.

The hydrology of Arno Atoll, Marshall Islands. Scientific Investigations in Micronesia.

(Atoll Research Bulletin, No. 8, pp. 1-29, Dec. 15, 1951)

DU
Pac.
Pam.
1066

Cox, H. H.

Melbourne: a garden of a city.

(Airways, Vol. 29(11):1-17, 1963)

QK
157.C
C 87

Cowles, Henry C.

The plant societies of Chicago and vicinity.

(The Geographic Society of Chicago, Bull. 2, n.d.)

QE
1
G 3

Cox, Doak C.

Shepard, Francis P.

Recent tsunami in the Hawaiian islands. By F. P. Shepard, G. A. Macdonald and Doak C. Cox.

(Bull. Geol. Soc. Amer., 57:1230, 1947)

DU
620
P 22

Cox, Halley J.

Are these the menehunes?

(Paradise of the Pacific, 72(10):52-53; 1960)

COWRY

See

CYPRAEIDAE

QH
1
P 11

Cox, Doak C.

Research in ground-water hydrology in Hawaii.

(Pacific Science, 8(2):230-231, 1954)

QL
430.7.P3
C 87

Cox, Ian   editor

The scallop, studies of a shell and its influences on humankind. By eight authors. Published in London by the "Shell" Transport and Trading Company, Limited. 1957 4to. 135 pp.

AS
540
P

Cox, Alvin

Composition of fine ejecta and a few other inorganic factors of Taal volcano. In Phil. Jour. Sc. A. VII pp 93-97.

QH
1
P 11

Cox D(oak) C.

MacDonald, G(ordon) A.

The tsunami of April 1, 1946, in the Hawaiian islands. By G. A. MacDonald, F. P. Shepard and D. C. Cox.

(Pacific Science, Vol. 1(1):21-37, 1946)

DU
620
P

Cox, J. Halley

The Maoris had a word for it...tiki

(Paradise of the Pacific, Holiday Annual, pp. 48-49, 1956)

DU 629.H3k N 28
Cox, J. Halley

Natural and cultureal history report, Kalapana Extension, Hawaii National Park. Vol. I. Cultural history report, by Kenneth P. Emory, J. Halley Cox, and others.

Prepared by Bernice P. Bishop Museum for the Hawaii National Park Service. Honolulu, 1959. 4to. mimeographed.

QL Mol Pam #109
Cox, James C.

Distribution of Australasian Volutes. Sydney, 1872. 8vo. 23 pp.

and
QL 402 G 23

(Garrett collection of Papers on conchology, Vol. 21)

locked case

GN 2.S T
COX, JOHN HENRY

Cottez, J.

Recherches historiques sur une expedition militaire suedoise en Océanie, a la fin du XVIII siècle.

(Bull. Soc. des Etudes Oceaniennes, No. 94, March 1951, pp. 173-179)

QL Mol Pam #107
Cox, James C.

Catalogue of Australian land shells, Sydney, 1864. 8vo. pp. 44

QL 402 G 23
Cox, James C.

Exchange list of land and marine shells from Australia and the adjacent islands. Sydney. 1868. 81 pp. 12mo.

(Garrett collection of papers on conchology, Vol. 8)

locked case

Cox, L. M.

THE ISLAND OF GUAM. Partially rewritten by Captain E. J. Dorn, U.S.N. Revised by Paymaster K. C. McIntosh, U.S.N. (4) 77 pp. Wrs. (Agana, Guam) 1911.

UH has

QL 402 G 23
Cox, James C.

A monograph of Australian land shells. Illustrated by 20 plates. Sydney. William Maddock. 1868. 8vo. 111 pp.

(Garrett collection of papers on conchology, Vol. 12)

locked case

QL Pam #120
Cox, J.C. M.D., F.L.S.

Notes on two wax figures from aboriginal camp near Rockhampton Q.

Ethn. Dept. Pam box DE Petroglyphs

Aug 20th 79?

QL 401 M 23
Cox, L. R.

Thoughts on the classification of the Bivalvia.

(Proc. Malac. Soc. London, 34(2):60-87, 1960)

AS 750 D-mi
(Cox, J. C.)

Catalogue of the Land Mollusca of New Zealand, with Descriptions of the Species.(By J. C. Cox and A. W. Scott). Collected from Various Authors. Published by Command. Colonial Museum and Geological Survey Department. Wellington. 1873. 8vo. xxvii pp.

IN:
Colonial Museum Miscellaneous Publications...

QL Mol Pam #108
Cox, James C.

Observations on a Cytherea, Sydney, 1895.

C

QK Botany Pam 1511
Cox, Oscar P

Copy of a letter to George R. Carter on various kinds of Awa root. 1930.

1 typed sheet.

QL 402 G 23
Cox, James C.

Catalogue of the specimens of the Australian land shells in the collection of James C. Cox. Sydney. John Alex. Engel. 1864. 12mo. 46 pp.

(Garrett collection of papers on conchology, Vol. 8)

locked case

AS 720.N L
Cox, J. C.

On the stone implements of Australia and the South Sea Islands.

(Linn. Soc. N.S.W., Proc., vol. 1, pp. 21-29, 1875-6)

Cox, Ross

Carter Coll. 2-C-20

Adventures on the Columbia River, including the narrative of a residence of six years on the western side of the Rocky Mountains, among various tribes of Indians, hitherto unknown; together with a journey across the American continent. Vol. I-II. London. Henry Colburn and Richard Bentley. 1831 xxiv + 368 pp. 8vo.

QL 401 J 85
Cox, J. C.

Description d'espèces nouvelles provenant d'Australie et des Îles Salomon et Norfolk.

(Jour. de Conchyl., 14:45-48, 1866)

DU 12 M 88
Cox, John Henry (commander, Mercury)

Mortimer, George

Observations and remarks made during a voyage to the islands of Teneriffe, Amsterdam, Maria's Islands near Van Dieman's Land; Otaheite, Sandwich Islands; Owhyhee, the Fox Islands on the north west coast of America, Tinian, and from thence to Canton, in the brig Mercury, commanded by John Henry Cox. London. 1791

AS 36 S1
Cox, Samuel Sullivan, 1824-1889.

Eulogy of Hon. Stephen Arnold Douglas. Prepared ... by Hon. Samuel S. Cox ...

(In Smithsonian institution. Annual report. 1861. Washington, 1862. 23½cm. p. 117-122)

1. Douglas, Stephen Arnold, 1813-1861.

Library of Congress Library, Smithsonian   Q11.S66 1861 Institution

S 15-103 b

QL 402 G 23
Cox, James

Descriptions of new species of land and marine shells from Australia and the Solomon Islands and Louisiade Islands.
(Proceedings of the Zool. Soc. of London, June 17 1873, pp. 146-152; 564-569)

(Garrett collection of papers on conchology, Vol. 19)

locked case

GN 2.S T
COX, J. H. (JOHN HENRY)

Cootes, J.

Histoire d'une expédition militaire Suédoise dans le Pacifique à la fin du XVIIIme siècle

(Bull. Soc. des Etudes Océaniennes, Tome VIII(1):425-453, 1952)

GN 2.1 A-M
Cox, W. H.

New Ireland (New Mecklenburg) myths.

(Man, vol. 13, 1913, no. 106, pp. 195-199)

DU
620
H 4

COXE, JOHN

Barry, J. Neilson

An interesting Hawaiian in old Oregon.

(Ann. Rept., Haw. Hist. Soc., Vol. 38, 1929, pp. 20-24)

QL
458.A2
b 16

Crabill, R. E., Jr.

Baker, E. W.

Guide to the families of mites. With contributions by R. E. Crabill, Jr.

(Inst. Acarology, Dept. Zool., Univ. of Maryland, Contrib. 3, 1958)

GN
Ethn.
Pam.
4072

CRAFTS JAPAN

Yanagi, Sōetu

Folk-crafts in Japan. The Society for International Cultural Relations. Tokyo. 1956. 8vo. 53 pp.

Coxe, M.   Carter Coll. 10-C-23

Les Nouvelles Découvertes des Russes, entre l'asie et l'amérique, avec l'histoire de la conquête de la Sibérie, and du Commerce de Russes et des chinois. Paris. Rue des poitevins. 1781. 314 pp. 4to.

QL
461
P 11

Crabill, R. E., Jr.

A new centipede from Okinawa.

(Pacific Insects, 1(2/3):173-176, 1959)

GN
Ethn.
Pam.
4160

CRAFTS PACIFIC

Tovey, Gordon

Art and craft for the South Pacific. Islands Education Division of the Department of Education, New Zealand. (rec'd 1959) 8vo. 68 pp.

QL
Birds
Pam.
337

Coy, Roy E.

The net and the goose.

(Museum Graphic, Vol. 5(3):10-15,1953)

[Canada goose]

QL
461
P 11

CRABRONINAE HAWAII

Yoshimoto, Carl M.

Revision of Hawaiian Crabroninae with synopsis of Hawaiian Spheeidae (Hym.)

(Pacific Insects, 2(3):301-338, 1960)

DU
1
P

Crago, L. P.

Spotlight on Emirau. Incidents in the patchy history of a remote island.

(Pacific Islands Monthly, Vol. 17 (10): 38; 1947)

QL
Birds
Pam.
490

Coy, Roy E.

The White Pelican: the fisherman's best friend.

(Museum Graphic, Vol. 15(3):13-14, 1963)

CRABS

See also

BRACHYURA
CRUSTACEA   and sub-divisions such as
CRYPTOCHIRUS
BIRGUS LATRO   (coconut crab)
GRAPSIDAE

DU
1
P 10

Craib, Ralph

The Pacific's best goes to Chicago.

(Pacific Isl. Monthly, 30(1):77-79, 1959)

(A. W. F. Fuller collection to Chicago Natural History Museum)

Coyer, G. F.

A supplement to Lord Anson's Voyage round the world, containing a discovery and description of the island of Frivola.   1752

[A take-off on Lord Anson's voyage]

UH

AS
36
S3

CRADLES.

Mason, Otis Tufton, 1838-1908.

Cradles of the American aborigines. By Otis T. Mason.

(In U. S. National museum. Annual report. 1887. Washington, 1889. 22½ᶜᵐ. p. 161-212. illus.)

Bibliographic foot-notes, relating especially to the artificial deformation of children in North America.

1. Cradles. 2. Indians of North America — Children. 3. Indians of North America — Soc. life & cust. 4. Deformities, Artificial.

Library of Congress   Q11.U5 1887
———— Copy 2.   14-19253
———— ———— Separate.   GN415.C8M3

QK
1
Ke

Craib, William G.

Contributions to the flora of Siam.

(Bulletin of Miscellaneous Information, Kew, 1911:7,385; Additamenta, 1912:144,264,397; 1913:65,193; 1914:4,122,279; 1915:419; 1916:259; 1918:362;1920:300; 1922:165,225; 1924:81; 1925: 7,404; *[handwritten notes]*

(pages not inclusive, first page only given in each case)

DU
625
K 87

CRACROFT, SOPHIA

Korn, Alfons L.

The Victorian visitors; an account of the Hawaiian kingdom, 1861-1866, including the journal letters of Sophia Cracroft, extracts from the journals of Lady Franklin, and diaries and letters of Queen Emma of Hawaii. University of Hawaii Press. Honolulu 1958. sm4to. (9)+ 351 pp.

DU
623
C 88

Craft, Mabel Clare

Hawaii nei. Illustrated. William Doxey, at the sign of the lark. San Francisco. 1899. sm8vo. (1)viii-ix(1)2-197 pp.

QK
364
C 88

Craib, W. G.

Florae Siamensis Enumeratio. A List of the Plants Known from Siam, with Records of Their Occurrence. Volumes 1- 2:1-5   1931- 1939 Siam Society. Bangkok. 8vo. *[handwritten]*

[handwritten notes]

DU
620
P

Crabbe, Horace G.

A reminiscence. (of Honolulu, time of Kam. III)
(Paradise of the Pacific, Vol. 13, No. 12, 1900)

GN
391
M 41

CRAFTS

Mason, Otis T.

The origins of invention; a study of industry among primitive peoples. With illustrations. Walter Scott, Ltd. London. 1895. 419 pp.

GN
Pam
#137

Craig, Eric

Catalogue of curiosities in the private collection of Eric Craig, of Princes Street, Auckland, New Zealand, 1889.

DU
400
T 25

Craig, Elsdon

Mormon Maoris build their way to education.

(Te Ao Hou, The New World, Vol. 3(4), no. 12,
pp.14-16, 1955)

Craighead, John (and Frank)

We survive on a Pacific atoll.

(National Geographic Magazine, Vol. 93; 73-
94, Jan. 1948)

Am
101
A 71
(5)

CRAMPTON, HENRY EDWARD, 1875-
Sherwood, George H

... The big tree and its story ... [New York, The
Museum] 1915.

cover-title, 23 p. incl. illus., pl. 25^cm. (American museum of natural
history ... Guide leaflet series no. [42])
"The greater part of this leaflet was written by George H. Sherwood
and appeared in Leaflet no. 8, The sequoia. Additions and changes have
been made by Henry E. Crampton and F. A. Lucas. The label is by Miss
M. C. Dickerson."
Guide leaflet series incorrectly numbered 41.

1. Sequoia. I. Crampton, Henry Edward, 1875- II. Lucas,
Frederic Augustus, 1852- III. Dickerson, Mary Cynthia, 1866-
IV. Title.

16-23574

Library of Congress   QK495.S5S4

GC
Oceano-
graphy
Pam.
48

Craig, H.

A critical evaluation of radiocarbon techniques for determining mixing rates in the ocean
and the atmosphere.   Second U. N. Int. Conference on the peaceful uses of atomic energy.
June 1958 mimeogr. 4to   14 pp.

AS
36
A 91-m

Craigie, E. Horne   trans.

Recollections of my life. Santiago Ramón
y Cajal.

(Memoirs of the Amer.Philos.Soc. vol.8,
1937)

F
Central
&
S.America
Pam
No. 16

Crampton, Henry E.(dward)

British Guiana and Brazil to Mount
Roraima. From Am. Mus. Nat. Hist. Journ.
Vol. XI, No.8, Dec. 1911.

AP
2
O 96

Craig, Hugh

Hawaiian cable.

(Overland Monthly, Vol. 25, No. 150, 1895,
pp. 653-660)

DU
406
C89

[Craik, G.L.].

The New Zealanders. (The library of
entertaining knowledge).

London, Charles Knight, 1830. 424p.
map.

QL
Mollusks
Pam.
280

Crampton, Henry E.(dward)

The coincident production of dextral
and sinistral young in the land- gaster-
opod Partula. Reprinted from Science
June 20, 1924, p 558.

AS
763
H 38

Craig, Robert S.

The need for development of Hawaii's resources and current progress.

(Haw. Acad. Sci., Proceedings, Ann. Meeting
1954/55, p. 10, 1955)

AS
36
S6

Cramer, Frank.

... On the cranial characters of the genus *Sebastodes*
(rock-fish). By Frank Cramer ... Palo Alto, Cal., Leland Stanford jr. university, 1895.

2 p. l., [573]-610 p. LVII-LXX pl. 24½^cm. (Leland Stanford junior university publications. Contributions to biology from the Hopkins seaside
laboratory. II)
Reprint from the Proceedings of the California academy of sciences,
series 2, vol. v.

1. Skull. 2. Rockfish.

Library of Congress   QL1.L53   7-10276
———— Copy 2.   Library of Congress QL638.S36C8

QL
Moll.
Pam.
278

Crampton, Henry Edward

Contemporaneous organic differentiati
on in the species of Partula living in
Moorea, Society Islands.   From American
Naturalist, Vol 59, pp 5- 35, 1925.

QL
Insects
Pam.
1113

Craighead, F. C.

Contributions toward a classification and
biology of the North American Cerambycidae.
Larvae of the Prioninae.

(U. S. Department of Agriculture, Office
of the Secretary, Report No. 107, 1915)

AS
182
L

Cramer, M

Beitrage zur Kenntnis der Polydaktyl
und Syndaktylie beim Menschen und einigen Haustieren. K. Leop.- Carol.Deutsche
Akademie..BdXCIII,1. Halle, 1910, pp
1- 40

QH
367
C88

Crampton, Henry Edward

The doctrine of evolution; its basis and its
scope.

New York, Columbia, 1924.   320p.

QL
573
B 78

Craighead, F. C.
Böving, Adam G.

An illustrated synopsis of the principal larval forms of the order Coleoptera. By Adam G.
Böving and F. C. Craighead.

(Entomologica Americana, XI n.s., 1930)

DU
1
P

Cramer, P. J. S.

Institutes for research work in the
interest of Agriculture in the Netherlands Indies. In Journ. Pan- Pacific Research Institution, Vol. I, No. 2, April-
July, 1926.

AS
36
A 5

Crampton, Henry E.(dward)

A journey to the Mariana islands-Guam and
Saipan.

(Natural History, Vol. 21, 1921, pp. 126-
145)

QL
463
C 88

Craighead, F.C.

Insect enemies of eastern forests.

(U. S. Dept. of Agric., Misc. Pub., 657,
1950)

QL
Fish
Pam
257

Cramer, Rudolf

Ueber mene rhombeus (Volta sp.).
Inaugural dissertation... Friedrich-
Wilhelms Univ. zu Berlin, 1906.

QL
1
U

Crampton, Henry E.
Lundman, Bertil

Maps of the racial geography of some Par-
tulae of the Society Islands based upon the
material published by H. E. Crampton.

(Zoologiska Bidrag, Uppsala, Festskrift,
Nils von Hosten; Bd. 25:517-533, 1947)

QL
Mollusks
Pam
279

Crampton, Henry Edward

New and significant species of Partula from Moorea, Society Islands. Reprinted from The Nautilus , Vol. 37, April, 1924.

QL
430.5B8
C 88

Crampton, Henry Edward

Studies on the variation, distribution and evolution of the genus Partula: The species of the Mariana Islands, Guam and Saipan. Carnegie Inst. Washington, Pub. 228, A, 1925, 116 pp., 14 pls.

Crandall, L. S.   (see S.)

Paradise quest; a naturalist's experiences in New Guinea. 1931c

UH

AS
36
A 65-no

Crampton, Henry E.

New species of land snails of the genus Partula from Raiatea, Society Islands.

(American Museum Novitates, No. 1761, Mar. 8, 1956)

QL
430.5.B8
C 88

Crampton, Henry Edward

Studies on the variation, distribution and evolution of the genus Partula, the species inhabiting Tahiti. Car. Inst. Wash. Pub. 228, 1916.

MAR 16 '47

Crane, E. A.

King Cakobau's government; or, an experiment in government in Fiji: 1871-1874. Complete. Ph.D., University of New Zealand (Wellington?), 1938.

microfilm in Inst. Adv. Studies, Dept. of Pac. Hist., Austr. Nat. Univ. (Harry Maude)

QL
Moll
Pam
649

AS
763
B-4

Reading
Room

Crampton, Henry E(dward)

Cooke, C. Montague Jr., and Crampton, Henry E.

New species of Partula. Bernice P. Bishop Museum, Occasional papers, vol. IX, no. 11. 1930. 9p. 1pl.

QL
430.5B9
C 88

Crampton, Henry Edward

Studies on the Variation, Distribution, and Evolution of the Genus Partula: the Species Inhabiting Moorea. Carnegie Institution of Washington, Publication No. 410. 1932. vi + 335 pp. 24 pl. 4to.

DU
620
P

Crabbe, Horace G.

Half a century ago.

(Paradise of the Pacific, Vol. 15, 1902, No. 12, p. 55-56)

QL
Mollusca
Pam
936

Crampton, Henry E.

New species of Partula from southeastern Polynesia. By Henry E. Crampton and C. Montague Cooke, Jr.

(Occ. Papers, Bernice P. Bishop Museum, Vol. 21(8):135-159, 1953)

AS
36
35

Crampton, Henry E. (dward)

Two active volcanoes of the south seas. in Am. Mus. Journ. X. no. 6. 1910. pp. 141-146, illus. (Savaii & Kilauea)

AP
2
S 35

Crane, H. R.

University of Michigan radiocarbon dates III. by H. R. Crane and J. B. Griffin.

(Science, 128(3332):1117-1123, 1958)

QL
Insects
Pam
442

Crampton, Henry Edward

On a general theory of adaptation and selection . Reprinted from the Journ. Exper. Zool. Vol. II, No.3, Baltimore, 1905.

QL
401
H 39

CRAMPTON, HENRY E.

Kondo, Yoshio

Henry E. Crampton, 1875-1956.

(Hawaiian Shell News, Vol. 4(7):70, 1956)

QL
1
N 6-s

Crane, Jocelyn

Brachygnathous crabs from the Gulf of California and the west coast of Lower California. Templeton Crocker Expedition (1936), III.

(Zoologica, 22, 1937, pp. 47-78)

AP
2
S 35

Crampton, Henry E. (dward)

On the differential effects of the influenza epidemic among native peoples of the Pacific islands.

(Science, N. S. Vol. 55, 1922, pp. 90-92)

QB
81
C 89

Cranbrook Institute of Science

Planetaria and their use for education; papers from a symposium held September 7-10, 1958.

(Bull. 38, Cranbrook Institute of Science, 1959)

QL
1
N 6-s

Crane, Jocelyn

Crabs of the genus Uca from the west coast of Central America. Eastern Pacific Exp. of the N. Y. Zool. Soc., XXVI.

(Zoologica, Vol. 26, 1941, pp. 145-208)

AS
36
A5

and
GN
Ethn.Pam.
319

Crampton, Henry E(dward)

The songs of Tahiti. In Am. Mus. Journ. Vol.12, 1912, pp 141- 144, illus.

DU
490
C 89

Crandall, Lee S.

Paradise quest; a naturalist's experiences in New Guinea. Charles Scribner's Sons. New York and London. 1931. 8vo. xvii + 226 pp.

QL
1
N -6 s

Crane, Jocelyn

Intertidal Brachygnathous crabs from the west coast of tropical America, with special reference to ecology.

(Zoologica, Vol. 32:69-95, 1947)

QL 1 N 6-z
Crane, Jocelyn

On the growth and ecology of Brachyuran crabs of the genus Ocypode. Eastern Pacific Expeditions of the New York Zoological Society, 29.

(Zoologica, Vol. 26, 1941, pp. 297-310)

QL 1 F
CRANE PACIFIC EXPEDITION

Herre, Albert W.

New fishes obtained by the Crane Pacific Expedition.

(Field Museum, Publ. 335, Zool. Ser., Vol. XVIII, No. 12, 1935, pp. 383-438)

GN Ethn. Pam. 3395
CRANIA-EVOLUTION

Weidenreich, Franz

The torus occipitalis and related structures and their transformations in the course of human evolution.

(Bull. Geological Soc. of China, 19, 1940, pp. 479-544, pls. 1-6)

QL 1 N 6-z
Crane, Jocelyn

On the post-embryonic development of Brachyuran crabs of the genus Ocypode. Eastern Pacific Expedition of the New York Zoological Society, XVIII.

(Zoologica, 25, 1940, pp. 65-82).

QL 1 F
CRANE PACIFIC EXPEDITION

Mayr, Ernst

Birds of the Crane Pacific Expedition, by Ernst Mayr and Sidney Camras.

(Field Museum of Nat. Hist., Zool. Ser., Vol. 20, No. 34, 1938, pp. 453-473)

GN 2.S Z 78
CRANIA MALEKULA

Hasebe, Kotondo

A portrait skull from the island of Malekula

(Zinruigaku Zassi, Vol. 56:240-244, 1941)

QL 1 N 6-z
Crane, Jocelyn

Oxystomatous and Dromiaceous crabs from the Gulf of California and the west coast of Lower California. The Templeton Crocker Expedition (1936), VI.

(Zoologica, 22, 1937, pp. 97-108).

QL 1 F
CRANE PACIFIC EXPEDITION

Schmidt, Karl P.

Notes on New Guinean Crocodiles. Reports on Results of the Crane Pacific Expedition.
(Field Museum of Natural History, Zoological Series, Publication, Vol. XVIII, pp. 167-172, Plate VII, 1932)

AS 720.N L
CRANIA MELANESIA

Macintosh, N. W. G.

Crania in the Macleay Museum.

(Proc. Linnean Soc. of New South Wales, 74:161-191, 1949)

QL 1 N 6-z
Crane, Jocelyn

Uca Schmitti, a new species of brachyuran crab from the west coast of Central America. Eastern Pacific Expeditions of the New York Zoological Society, XXXI.

(Zoologica, Vol. 28, 1943, pp. 31-32)

QL 1 F
CRANE PACIFIC EXPEDITION

Schmidt, Karl P.

Reptiles and Amphibians from the Solomon Islands. Reports on Results of the Crane Pacific Expedition.

(Field Museum of Natural History, Zoological Series, Volume XVIII, No. 9 (pp. 175-190),1932)

GN Ethn. Pam. 3878
CRANIA MELANESIA

Schlaginhaufen, Otto

Kunstliche Defekte an menschlichen Schadeln aus Melanesien.

(Bull. Schweizerischen Gesellschaft fur Anthrop. und Ethn., 28:19-23, 1951/52)

Q 115 C1
Crane, Walter

Challenger expedition reports.

Portraits of the contributors, reproduced from the photographs presented by them to John Murray, with facsimiles of the designs for the cover and dedication of the album containing them, by Walter Crane.
London, Dulau & co., 1897. 19p.

CRANGONIDAE

Bannder, Albert Henry

The Hawaiian Crustacea of the family Crangonidae. (Thesis...University of Hawaii, January, 1940) manuscript

UH

QH 301 B
CRANIA-MORIORI

Pearson, Karl

Was the skull of the Moriori artificially deformed?

(Biometrika, Vol. 13, 1921, pp. 338-346)

CRANE-FLIES

see

TIPULIDAE

QH 1 P 11
CRANGONIDAE HAWAII

Banner, Albert H.

The Crangonidae, or snapping shrimp, of Hawaii.

(Pacific Science, 7:3-144, 1953)

Q 115 G 76
CRANIA NEW GUINEA

Pycraft, W. P.
Report on the human crania collected by the British Ornithologists' Union Expedition and the Wollaston Expedition in Dutch New Guinea.

Grant, William R. Ogilvie
Reports on the collections made by the British Ornithologists' Union Expedition and the Wollaston Expedition in Dutch New Guinea, 1910-1913. Vols. I-II. London. 1916.
Vol. 1, No. 1. 34 pp. 5 pl.

QL 1 F
Crane Pacific Expedition

Herre, Albert W.

Fishes of the Crane Pacific Expedition.

(Field Museum of Natural History, Zool. Ser. Vol. 21, 1936)

GN Ethn. Pam. 3406
CRANIA

Weidenreich, Franz

The brain and its role in the phylogenetic transformation of the human skull.

(Trans. Am. Phil. Soc., N. S. Vol. 31, 1941, pp. 321-442)

GN 1 A-j
CRANIA SIAM

Schlaginhaufen, Otto

Skulls from northwestern Siam.

(Am. Jour. of Phys. Anthrop., Vol. 26, 1940, pp. 367-381. 6 pl.)

GN
Pam
#461

Crania Ethnica Philippinica

by Dr J. D. E. Schmeltz and
G. A. Koeze

D E

JUN - 1906

Leide 1906. 8 44 24

GN
Pam
2295

CRANIOLOGY

Angelotti, Guido

   Intorno a du tipi cranici del territorio etrusco. From Atti. Soc. Romana di Antrop. v.15, fasc.3, 1910.

GN
73
D26

CRANIOLOGY

Davis, Joseph Barnard

   Thesaurus craniorum: catalogue of the skulls of the various races of man, in the collection of Joseph Barnard Davis.

London, n.p., 1867. 374p.

GN
73
D26

——— Supplement. 1875. 101p.

GN
103.S2
R 44

Crania Suecica Antiqua

Retzius, Gustaf

GN
Pam
2493

CRANIOLOGY

Angelotti, Guido

   Variazioni e lacune nella "Pars tympanica" del temporale. From Atti Soc. Romana d. antrop. v.15, fasc. 1, 1909.

GN
22
D 85

CRANIOLOGY

Duckworth, W.L.H.

   Studies from the Anthropological Laboratory, the Anatomy School, Cambridge. Cambridge. 1904.

GN
Pam
2314

CRANIOLOGY

Aeby, Ch

   Bemerkungen uber die bildung des schadels und der extremitaten im menschen schlechte. From Verh. Nat. Gesell. Basel, Theil 3, heft 4, 1863.

GN
Pam
2597

CRANIOLOGY

Buschan, Georg

   Chirurgisches aus der volkerkunde.

Leipzig, Konegen, 1902. 46p.

GN
Pam
757

CRANIOLOGY

Ecker, Alexander

   Crania Germaniae meridionalis occidentalis.

Freiburg, Wagner, 1863. 18p. pls.

GN
Pam
763

CRANIOLOGY

Albrecht, Paul

   Sur le crane remarquable d'une idiote de 21 ans... communication faite a la Societe d'Anthropologie de Bruxelles dans la seance du 26 fevrier 1883.

Bruxelles, Manceaux, 1883. 58p. pls.

GN
Pam
472
4to
28-1

Craniology

Caleri, Cav. Luigi

Sopra un cranio scafoideo

Bologna, 1871. 4° pp. 30. pl. I- V.

GN
Pam
1929

CRANIOLOGY

Flower, William Henry

   Description of two skeletons of Akkas, a pygmy race from Central Africa. From Anthrop. Inst. Journ. Great Britain and Ireland.

GN
Pam.
2001

CRANIOLOGY

Alsberg, Moritz

   Schädelform und Umwelt einflusse.

   (Arch.Rass.-u. Gesells.-Biol, 1912, heft 2, pp. 175-184)

GN
Pam
2392

CRANIOLOGY

Canestrini, Giovanni

   Sopra due teschi umani scavati nelle terremare del modenese.

[1864]

GN
Pam
2630

CRANIOLOGY

Friedemann, Max

   Ueber den bau des gesichtsskelettes in seiner beziehung zur prognathie. Inaugural dissertation... Georg Augusts Univ. Gottingen, 1905.

GN
Pam
1894

CRANIOLOGY

Angelotti, Guido

   Di alcune critiche al mio studio sulla base del cranio. From Rivista di Antrop. v.17, fasc.1-2, 1912.

GN
Pam
2071

CRANIOLOGY

Danielli, Jacopo

   Studio sui crani Bengakesi con appunti d'etnologia indiana, From Arch. Antrop e etnol. v.22, fasc. 2-3, 1892.

GN
Pam
2293

CRANIOLOGY

Fürst, Carl M.

   Skelettfynd i jamtlandska grafvar fran den yngre jarnaldern. From Ymer, 1905, heft 4.

GN
Pam
2296

CRANIOLOGY

Angelotti, Guido

   Crani del monte Amiata. From Atti Soc. Romana di antrop. v.14, fasc.3, 1908

GN
71
D 26

CRANIOLOGY

Davis, J. B.

   Collection of papers on craniology, by various authors. In 8 volumes. Index at beginning of each volume.

   (Only checked articles are catalogued)

GN
Pam
473
434

CRANIOLOGY

Gaddi, Paolo

   Cranio ed encefalo di un idiota.

Modena, 1867.

GN
Pam.
426

CRANIOLOGY

Gaddi, Paolo

Dimostrazione anatomica intorno alla maggiore perfezione della mano dell'uomo confrontata con quella delle scimie.

Modena, 1866.

CRANIOLOGY *Indian Museum Calcutta*

GN
Ethn.
Pam.
462

Ethnogr. Survey of India
Craniological Data from the Indian Museum

Calcutta, 1909. 4°. p. 1-70

GN
71
K91

CRANIOLOGY

Krause, W

Ossa leibnitii. From Anhang zu d. abh d. k. Akad. d. Wissen. zu Berlin, 1902.

GN
Pam
1869

CRANIOLOGY

Giuffrida-Ruggeri, V

Un cranio Guayachi e un cranio fuegino. From Soc. Romana d. Antrop. atti, v.12, fasc.3, 1906.

GN
Ethn.Pam.
2840

CRANIOLOGY

Imbelloni, J.

Die Arten der kunstlichen Schädeldeformation.

Anthropos, Tome XXV, 1930 pp. 801-830

GN
75
L77

CRANIOLOGY

Lissauer,

Alt-Pommerellische schadel: ein beitrag zur germanischen urgeschichte.

Danzig, Kafemann, 1872. 24p. pls. (From Schriften der nat. Gesell. Danzig n.f. bd.3, heft 1).

GN
71
G 67

CRANIOLOGY

Gosse, L. A.

Essai sur les déformations artificielles du crâne, par L. A. Gosse, de Geneve...Paris. 1855.

GN
Pam
2552

CRANIOLOGY

Jacoby, Willy

Unterschiede am schadel des schimpansen, gorilla und orang-utan. Inaugural dissertation... Univ. Bern, 1903.

GN
Pam
#536
38-7
Pam.67

Craniology

Luschan, F. von.

Ein neanderthaloider Ungar-Schädel. Mittheil. der Anthropolog. Gesellsch. in Wien Bd. III, 7, 1873, 8vo. pp. 12.

GN
Pam
2484

CRANIOLOGY

Haferland, R

Einen schadel mit einem processus asteriacus. From Zeit. d. Ethnol. heft1, 1905.

GN
125 P
K 77

CRANIOLOGY

Koeze, G. A.

Crania Ethnica Philippinica. Ein Beitrage zur Anthropologie der Philippinen. Beschreibung der Schädelsammlung von Dr. A.Schadenberg. Mit Einleitung und unter Mitwirkung von J. Kollmann. Mit 25 Tafeln.

(Veröffentlichungen des Niederländischen Reichsmuseums fur Völkerkunde, Series II, No. 3, 1901-1904. Haarlem)

AS
36
S1

CRANIOLOGY.

Macnamara, Nottidge Charles, 1834–
The craniology of man and anthropoid apes. By N. C. Macnamara ...

(In Smithsonian institution. Annual report. 1902. Washington, 1903. 23½ cm. p. 431-449. VI pl. on 3 L)

1. Craniology.

Library of Congress   Q11.S66 1902   S 15-1159
Library, Smithsonian   Institution

GN
Pam
2265

CRANIOLOGY

Hoelder, H. v

Zusammenstellung der in Wurttemberg vorkommenden schadelformen.

GN
Pam
822

CRANIOLOGY

Koganei,

Cribia cranii und cribra orbitalia. From Mittheil d. med. fakultat d. k. Univ. zu Tokyo, bd. 10, heft 2, 1911.

GN
73
MS1

CRANIOLOGY

Meigs, J. Aitken

Catalogue of human crania in the collection of the Academy of Natural Sciences of Philadelphia.

Philadelphia, n.p., 1857. 103p.

GN
Ethn.
Pam.
476

CRANIOLOGY

Housselle, Carolus

Descriptio duorum craniorum rariorum e gente puriana.

Berlin. 1822, 4to pp. 18. Pl. I.

GN
Pam
2550

CRANIOLOGY

Kollmann, J

Neue gedaken uber das alte problem von der abstammung des menschen. From Corresp-blatt d. Deutschen anthrop. Gesell. n.2-3, 1905.

GN
Pam
2429

CRANIOLOGY

Mollison, Th

Die abstammung des menschen. From Naturwissenschaften, jahrg. 9, heft 8, Berlin, 1921.

AS
36
84

CRANIOLOGY

Hrdlicka, Ales

Catalogue of human crania in the U.S.Nat. Mus collections: The Algonkin and related Iroquois; Siouan, Caddoan, Salish and Sahaptin, Shoshonean and Californian Indians.

(In Proc. U.S.Nat. Mus., Vol. 69, Art. 5, 1927)

GN
Pam
1866

CRANIOLOGY

Kollmann, Julius

Schädel aus alten grabern bei Genf. (Corsier, Vernier, La Cluse, Petit-Sacconez). From Verh. d. Nat. Gesell. in Basel, Theil 8, heft 1, 1886.

GN
Pam
#469

CRANIOLOGY

Nicolucci, Giustiniano

Peso del cervello dell'uomo.

Napoli, 1881. 4to pp. 29.

AS 36 A6

CRANIOLOGY

Oetteking, Bruno

Craniology of the north Pacific coast. N. Y. Stechert, 1930. Memoir of the Amer. museum of nat. hist., vol. XV.

Publications of the Jesup north Pacific expedition. vol. XI, part I.

GN Pam #461

Schmeltz Dr J.D.E.
und G. A. Koeze.

Crania Ethnica Philippinia

(See Koeze ebbay 3 8##01) ?

DE

Leiden 1906   8° pl 24

GN Pam 1675 1532

Craniology

Ujfalvy, Charles de

Memoire sur les Huns blancs et sur la deformation de leurs cranes. From L'Anthropologie, 1898.

GN 550 .I-1(m)

CRANIOLOGY

Oetteking, Bruno

Skeletal remains from Santa Barbara, California. I. Craniology. New York, Mus. A. Indian, Indian Notes and M., Misc No. 39, 1925, 168 pp 32 pls.

GN Pam 842

CRANIOLOGY

Schultz, Adolf

From, grosse, und lage der squama temporalis des menschen. From Zeit. f. Morphol. und anthrop. bd. 19, heft 2, 1915.

GN Pam 532

CRANIOLOGY

Virchow, (Prof.)

Schädel aus dem altgermanischen Gräberfeld am Schieriteiner Wege bei Wiesbaden.

no.data, 4to. pp. 11-58.

GN 73 Q93

CRANIOLOGY

Quatrefages, A de & Hamy, Ernest T.

Crani ethnica les cranes des races humaines.

Paris, Baillier, 1873.

Library has

Liv.2, feuilles 7-11, pl.11-20.

GN Pam 2386

CRANIOLOGY

Schultz, C. J.

Bemerkungen ueber den bau der normalen menschenschaedel nebst einer nachlese.

St. Petersburg, n.p., 1852.

GN Pam #534

CRANIOLOGY

Virchow

Über mikronesische Schädel

Pam-box Anthrop.

DE

1881.

aug 26th '99

GN 120.E R19

CRANIOLOGY

Randall-Maciver, David

The earliest inhabitants of Abydos. (a craniological study).

Oxford, Clarendon Press, 1901.

GN 71 S48

CRANIOLOGY

Sera, G. L.

Sui rapporti della conformazione dell base del cranio colle forme craniensi e colle strutture della faccia nelle razzi umane.

Pavia, Fusi, 1920.
(Mem. d. Soc. Ital. d. Sci. Nat. Milano, v.9, fasc.11.)

GN Pam 2405

CRANIOLOGY

Virchow,

Unter vorlegung einiger specimina uber gold-schadel. From Verh. d. Berl. Anthrop. Gesell. 1873.

AS 36 S1

CRANIOLOGY

Retzius, Anders Adolf, 1796-1860.
Present state of ethnology in relation to the form of the human skull. By Professor Anders Retzius ...
(*In* Smithsonian institution. Annual report. 1859. Washington, 1860. 23½ᶜᵐ. p. (251-270))
"Translated for the Smithsonian institution from the Archives des sciences physiques et naturelles, Geneva, 1860, by C. A. Alexander."

1. Craniology. I. Alexander, Charles Armistead, d. 1869? tr.
           S 15-80

Library of Congress   Q11.S66 1859
Library, Smithsonian   Institution

AS 36 S2

Craniology

Sergi, Giuseppe, 1841-
... The varieties of the human species: principles and method of classification, by Giuseppe Sergi ... City of Washington, Smithsonian institution, 1894.
61 p. illus. 24ᶜᵐ. (Smithsonian miscellaneous collections. [vol. XXXVIII, art. 1])
Publication 969.
Prefatory note by D. G. Brinton.

GN Pam 770   Separate in Italian

1. Anthropology—Classification. 2. Craniology. I. Title.
         4-34152 Revised
Library of Congress   Q11.S7 vol. 38, art. 1
———— Copy 2. 23½ᶜᵐ.   GN34.S48
———— Copy 3. 24½ᶜᵐ.   Q11.S7 2d set

GN 71 V78

CRANIOLOGY

Vogt, Carl

Vorlefungen uber den menschen seine stellung in der schopfung und in der geschichte der erde.

Giessen, Richer, 1863.   2v.in 1.

GN Pam 2143

CRANIOLOGY

Russell, Frank

Studies in cranial variation. From Amer. Naturalist, v.34, n.405, 1900.

GN Eth. Pam. 2863

CRANIOLOGY

Shapiro, H. L.

A Correction for Artificial Deformation of Skulls.

(From Anthropological Papers of the American Museum of Natural History, Vol. XXX, Part I, Pages 5-36).

GN Pam #477 4to # 455 and

CRANIOLOGY

Weisbach, ...

Der deutsche Weiberschädel, ex Archiv für Anthropologie. Bd.III, Heft II.

GN Pam #458 4to

CRANIOLOGY

Schaaffhausen, Hermann

Über die Urform des Menschlichen Schädels.

Abdruck aus Festschrift der Nieder-Rheinischen Gesell. für Natur u. Heilkung zu 50 jährigen Jubelfeier der Universität, Bonn 1868.

GN Pam 1975

CRANIOLOGY

Thurnam, John

On synostosis of the cranial bones, especially the parietals regarded as a race character in one class of ancient British and in African skulls. From Nat. Hist. Rev. n.18, 1865.

GN Pam #531 4to and # 456

CRANIOLOGY

Weisbach, A.

Vier Schädel aus alten Grabstätten in Böhmen, ex Archiv für Anthropologie Bd. II, Heft III.

GN
Pam
#530
4 to

CRANIOLOGY

Wittwer? , Carolus Ludovicus

De varia humani cranii forma.

Berlin, 1825. 4º. pp. 24. Pl. 2.

GN
Pam
1973

CRANIOLOGY - AFRICA, SOUTH

Shrubsall, Frank C.

Notes on some Bushman crania and bones from South African Museum, Cape Town. From Ann. South African Mus. v.5, 1907.

AS
122
E

CRANIOLOGY AUSTRALIA

Berry, Richard J. A.
Sectional anatomy of the head of the Australian aboriginal . . . .
in Roy. Soc. Edin. Proc. XXXI, 1910-1911, pp. 604-624.

GN
Pam
2804

CRANIOLOGY.

Jones, Frederic Wood-

The non-metrical morphological characters of the skull as criteria for racial diagnosis. Pt.I. General discussion of the Morphological characters employed in racial diagnosis. Cambridge, Univ. pr., n.d.

Reprinted from the Journal of anatomy, v.LXV, pt.II, January 1931.

GN
Pam
1895

CRANIOLOGY - AFRICA, WEST

Passavant, Carl

Craniologische untersuchung der neger und der negervölker: nebst einem bericht über meine erste reise nach Cameroons (West Africa) im jahre 1883.

Basel, Georg, 1884.   94p.   pls.

AS
122
E

Crania? Australia

Berry, Richard J. A.
Sectional anatomy of the head of the Australian aboriginal. . . . .
in Roy. Soc. Edin. Proc. XXXI, 1910-1911, pp. 604-624.

GN
Ethn.Pam
2804a

CRANIOLOGY

Wood-Jones, Frederic   .

The Non-Metrical Morphological Characters of the Skull as Criteria for Racial Diagnosis. Part II. The Non-Metrical Morphological Characters of the Hawaiian Skull.

(Reprinted from the Journal of Anatomy, Vol. LXV, Part III, April, 1931. Cambridge. pp. 368-378)

AS
182
Dr

GN
Pam
2250

CRANIOLOGY - ALASKA

Oetteking, Bruno

Ein beitrag·zur kraniologie der Eskimo. Abh. und Ber. d. k. Zoologischen und anthropologische ethno. Mus. zu Dresden, bd.12, n.3, 1908.

separate

GN
Pam
1930
2214

CRANIOLOGY - AUSTRALIA

Brackebusch, Karl

Die Australierschädel der sammlung des anatomischen instituts zu Göttingen. Inaugural dissertation... Georg-Augusts Univ. zu Göttingen. 1905.

CRANIOLOGY

see also

PHYSICAL ANTHROPOLOGY

GN
Ethn.Pam
3021

CRANIOLOGY AMERICA

Sera, G. L.

L'altezza del cranio in America...Firenze.
1913.

(Archivio per l'Antropologia e la Etnologia, Vol. XLII-XLIII, 1912-1913)

GN
Pam
2486

CRANIOLOGY - AUSTRALIA

Ecker, A

Ueber den queren hinterhauptswulst (Torus occipitalis transversus) am schadel vershierdener aussereuröpaische volker.

GN
Ethn.
Pam.
462

CRANIOLOGY -- COLLECTIONS

Indian museum, Calcutta.
... Craniological data from the Indian museum, Calcutta. Pub. by permission of the trustees of the Indian museum. Calcutta, Superintendent government printing, India, 1909.

3 p. l., 70 p. 32ᶜᵐ.

At head of title: Ethnographic survey of India.
Comp. by B. A. Gupte, assistant director of ethnography for India.

1. Craniology—Collections.   i. Gupte, B. A., comp.   ii. India. Ethnographic survey.

Library of Congress   ◊ ✚ GN113.I 4A4
——— Copy 2.   10-17943

AS
36
S1

CRANIOLOGY - AMERICA

Wilson, *Sir* Daniel, 1816-1892.
... Physical ethnology. By Daniel Wilson ...
(*In* Smithsonian institution. Annual report. 1862. Washington, 1863. 23½ᶜᵐ. p. [240]-302. illus., tables)

1. Craniology—America. 2. Ethnology—America.   i. Title.

                                                          S 15-126
Library of Congress   ◊ ✚ Q11.S66 1862
Library, Smithsonian   Institution

AS
36
S 4

CRANIOLOGY AUSTRALIA

Hrdlicka, Ales

Catalogue of human crania in the United States National Museum collections: Australians, Tasmanians, South African Bushmen, Hottentots and Negro.

(In Proc. U. S. Nat. Mus., Vol. 71, Art. 24, 1928)

GN
Pam
2356

CRANIOLOGY - AFRICA

Poch, Rudolf

Untersuchung v. Buschmann: schadeln und skeletten aus dem Transvaal Museum. From Annals Transvaal Museum, 1909.

GN
90
V1
over
size

CRANIOLOGY -- AMERICA (North &South)

Virchow, Rudolf

Crania ethnica Americana. Sammlung auserlesener Americanischer Schädel-typen.

Berlin, 1892, 34 pp 26 pls., folio.

[Listed as a supplement to Zeitschrift für Ethnologie   ]

GN
Pam
1871

CRANIOLOGY - AUSTRALIA

Miklouho-Maclay, N. de

Remarks on a skull of an Australian aboriginal from the Lachlan district. From Linnean Soc. Proc. 1883.

GN
123.A
S 49

CRANIOLOGY AFRICA

Sergi, Sergio

Crania habessinica:...Roma. 1912.

GN
29
B 18

CRANIOLOGY AUSTRALIA

Balfour, Henry, and others

Anthropological essays...Oxford. 1907. 4to. pp. 85-80. The Australian Forehead, by D. J. Cunningham.

AS
122
E

CRANIOLOGY AUSTRALIA

Robertson, A. W. D.
Craniological observations on the lengths, breadths, and heights of a hundred Australian aboriginal crania. in Roy. Soc. of Edinburgh Proc. XXXI, 1910-1911. pp. 1-16.

QH
301
L

CRANIOLOGY   AUSTRALIA

Shellshear, Joseph L.

The brain of the aboriginal Australian; a study in cerebral morphology.

(Philosophical Transactions of the Royal Society of London, Series B, Vol. 227, pp. 293-409)

AS
36
S1

CRANIOLOGY-CALIFORNIA
Whitney, Josiah Dwight, 1819-1896.
Cave in Calaveras County, California. By J. D. Whitney.

(*In* Smithsonian institution. Annual report. 1867. Washington, 1868. 23½ᵗʰ. p. 406-407)

1. Craniology—California. 2. California—Antiq.

S 15-227

Library of Congress   Q11.S66 1867
Library, Smithsonian   Institution

GN
Pam
2486

CRANIOLOGY - CHINA

Ecker, A

Ueber den queren hinterhauptswulst (Torus occipitalis transversus) am schadel verschiedener aussereuropaischer volker.

GN
Ethn.Pam.
3046

GN
2.M
M 60

CRANIOLOGY AZTECS

De La Borbolla, D. F. Rubin

Crania Azteca. 1933.

(Anales del Museo Nacional de Arquelogie, Historia y Etnografia, Tome VIII, No. 1, Epoca 4a, 1933, pp. 96-106)

GN
Pam
2301

CRANIOLOGY - CANARY ISLANDS

Kalkhof, J

Beschreibung einer schadelserie von den Canarischen inseln. From Ber. Nat. Gesell. Freiburg, bd.20, 1913.

GN
2.I
R 93

CRANIOLOGY EASTER ISLAND

Imbelloni, J.

Craneología de la Isla de Pascua.

(Runa, IV:223-281, 1951)

GN
564
C 52

CRANIOLOGY BOLIVIA

Chervin, Arthur

Anthropologie Bolivienne. 3 volumes. Paris, 1907-1908. 4to.

Tome III. Craniologie. 151 pp.

(Mision Scientifique, G. De Créqui Montfort et E. Senéchal de la Grange.)

GN
Pam
1801

CRANIOLOGY   CAROLINE ISLANDS

Davis, J. B.   (Joseph Barnard)

The skulls of the inhabitants of the Caroline islands. From Anthrop. Review, v.4.

GN
2.S
V

CRANIOLOGY   EASTER ISLAND

Petri, H.

Eine Schadelserie von der Osterinsel.

(Mitt. Anthropologishhen Gesellschaft, Wien, Bd. 66, 1936, pp. 17-29)

GN
Pam
2557

CRANIOLOGY - BORNEO

Hrdlicka, Ales

Anatomical observations on a collection of orang skulls from western Borneo; with a bibliography. From Proc. U. S. Nat. Mus. v.31, 1906.

GN
Pam
2034

GN 71
D 26

CRANIOLOGY CAROLINE ISLANDS

Hoeven, J. van der

Beschrijving van schedels van inboorlingen der Carolina-eilanden.

(Vers. K. Adak. van Wetenschappen, Afd. Natuurkunde, 2 Reeks, Deel 1, 1865)

(English translation, by J. B. Davis, in his Collection of papers on craniology, Vol. 1, No.20)

GN
Pam
1917

CRANIOLOGY - EGYPT

Schmidt, Emil

Ueber alt und neu Aegyptische schädel formen...

Leipzig, Metzger, 1885.   64p.

GN
Pam
2220

CRANIOLOGY - BUENOS AIRES

Imbelloni, Jose

Habitantes neoliticos del lago Buenos Aires. From Revista Mus. de La Plata, v.27, 1923.

GN
2.I
A-4

CRANIOLOGY   CHATHAM ISLANDS

Duckworth, W.L.H.

On a collection of crania, with two skeletons of the Mori-ori, or aborigines of the Chatham Islands. With a note on some crania from the same islands now in the Museum of the Royal College of surgeons.

(Journ. Anthrop. Inst. of Great Britain and Ireland, Vol. 30, 1900, pp. 141-152)

GN
120
S78

CRANIOLOGY - EGYPT

Stahr, Hermann

Die rassenfrage im antiken Ägypten.

Berlin, Brandus, 1907.   164p.   pls.

GN
Ethn.Pam.
4269

CRANIOLOGY   BRITISH COLUMBIA

van Bork-Feltkamp, A. J.

Some remarks on skulls and skull fragments of the Fraser middens (British Columbia) Nederlandsch Museum voor Anthropologie. Amsterdam. 1960. 8vo. 32 pp.

GN
2.I
A-4

CRANIOLOGY   CHATHAM ISLANDS

Flower, W. H.

Note on a Moriori skull from Waitangi West, Chatham Islands.

(Journ. Anthrop. Inst. of Great Britain and Ireland, Vol. 26, 1896-7, pp. 295-296)

GN
2.I
A-4

CRANIOLOGY   FIJI

Flower, William Henry

On the cranial characters of the natives of the Fiji Islands.

(Journ. Anthrop. Inst. of New Britain and Ireland, Vol. 10, 1880-1, pp. 153-174, pls. 12-14)

GN
2 I
Ca

CRANIOLOGY - CALIFORNIA
Hrdlička, Alěs i. e. Alois Ferdinand, 1869-

... Contribution to the physical anthropology of California, based on collections in the Department of anthropology of the University of California and in the U. S. National museum, by Ales Hrdlicka. Berkeley, The University press, 1906.

cover-title. [49]-64 p. 6 pl. (incl. map) 5 tab. (4 fold.) 27ᵐᵐ. (University of California publications. American archaeology and ethnology, vol. 4, no. 2)

GN
Pam
780

separate

Descriptions of 47 skulls from various localities in California.

1. Craniology—California.

Library of Congress   E51.C15   6-25633
——— Copy 2.   E78.C15H8

GN
Pam
834

CRANIOLOGY - CHINA

Bartels, Paul

Ueber ein os praebasiocipitale, Sergi (Os basioticum, Albrecht) an eimem Chinesenschadel. From Zeit. f. Ethnol. heft 1, 1904.

GN
Pam
2596

CRANIOLOGY - FRANCE

Broca, Paul

Sur le capacite des cranes parisiens des diverses epoques. From Bull. d. Soc d'anthrop. d. Paris, v.3, fasc.1, 1861.

GN
71
D 26
CRANIOLOGY GREAT BRITAIN

Davis, Joseph Barnard

Crania Britannica. Delineations and Descriptions of the skulls of the early inhabitants of the British Islands...by Joseph Barnard Davis and John Thurnam. London. 1856-1860. folio.

AS
36
A1
CRANIOLOGY HAWAII

Peirce, C. N.

Remarks on Hawaiian Skulls.

(Acad. Nat. Sc. of Phil. Proc. 1893, pp. 224-225)

GN
Ethn.Pam.
3331
CRANIOLOGY MELANESIA

Schlaginhaufen, Otto

Ein Melanesierschädel mit Parietalia bipartita und anderen Nahtvariationene.

(Kultur und Rasse, Festschrift 60 Geburtstag Otto Reches, 1939, pp. 200-207)

GN
801.1
S 46
CRANIOLOGY GUATEMALA

Seler, Eduard

Die alten Ansiedelungen von Chacula im... der Republik Guatemala, I..., pp. 207-213: Schädel aus Chacula und Guatemala, by Felix von Luschan. Berlin. 1901.

GN
1
Z
CRANIOLOGY HAWAII

Virchow, Rudolf

Schädel- und Tibiaformen von Südsee-Insulanern...

(Zeit. f. Ethn., 12: (112)-(119), 1880)

GN
Pam
2237
CRANIOLOGY - MEXICO

Batres, Leopold

Osteologie: Anthropologie Mexicaine. Congres Pan Americain de medecine, 1896.

AS
36
W1
GN
Pam
1375
437
662
CRANIOLOGY HAWAII

Allen, Harrison

Study of Hawaiian Skulls.

(Wagner Free Inst. Sci., Trans., Vol. 5, (no. 1, 1898, pp. 1-55, 12 pl.)

AS
36
B2
CRANIOLOGY HAWAII

Wyman, Jeffries

Observations on Crania.

(Boston Soc. Nat. Hist. Proc. XI, 1868, pp. 440-462. See especially pp. 447-451)

GN
2.1
A-M
CRANIOLOGY MORIORI

Keith, Arthur

Moriori in New Zealand.

(Man, vol. 13, 1913, no. 97, pp. 171-172, figs. 1-3)

AS
36
B2
CRANIOLOGY HAWAII

Brigham, W. T.

Short reference to distorted skull of a child.

(Boston Soc. Nat. Hist. Proc. XI, 1866-1868. P. 70)

GN
103.H9
L56
CRANIOLOGY - HUNGARY

Lenhossek, Joseph Edlen v.

Die ausgrabungen zu Szeged-Othalom in Ungarn.

Budapest, K. Ungar. Univ., 1884. 251p.pls

GN
2M
Pe
and
GN
Ethn.Pam.
416
CRANIOLOGY - NEW BRITAIN

MacCurdy, George Grant, 1863-

... Human skulls from Gazelle Peninsula, by George Grant MacCurdy. Philadelphia, University museum, 1914.

21 p. x pl. 27½ᶜᵐ. (University of Pennsylvania. The University museum. Anthropological publications. vol. vi, no. 1)

1. Craniology—Gazelle Peninsula.

Library of Congress   GN128.G3M3

14-18011

GN
71
R 44
CRANIOLOGY HAWAII

Retzius, Anders

Ethnologische schriften...nach dem tode des verfassers gesammelt. Stockholm. 1864.

(Contains chapter: Ueber schadel von Sandwich Insulaner).

GN
Ethn.
Pam.
462
CRANIOLOGY INDIA

Indian museum, *Calcutta.*

... Craniological data from the Indian museum, Calcutta. Pub. by permission of the trustees of the Indian museum. Calcutta, Superintendent government printing, India, 1909.

3 p. l., 70 p. 32ᶜᵐ.

At head of title: Ethnographic survey of India.
Comp. by B. A. Gupte, assistant director of ethnography for India.

1. Craniology—Collections. I. Gupte, B. A., comp. II. India. Ethnographic survey.

Library of Congress   GN113.I 4A4   10-17943

————— Copy 2.

GN
Ethn.Pam.
3024
415
CRANIOLOGY NEW BRITIAN

Müller, Wilhelm

Beiträge zur Kraniologie der New-Britannier, ...

(Beiheft 5, Hamburgischen Wissenschaftlichen Anstalten, Jahrbuch XXIII, 1905)

GN
Pam
2486
CRANIOLOGY - HAWAII.

Ecker, A

Ueber den queren hinterhauptswulst (Torus occipitalis transversus) am schadel verschiedener aussereuropaischer volker.

GN
.550
S
Craniology. INDIANS

Hrdlička, Aleš

Physical anthropology of the Lenape or Delawares, and of the eastern Indians in general.
Bur. of Am. Ethn. Bull. 62. (also)
Mus. of Am. Indian Contributions. III,1916

GN
2.1
A-4
CRANIOLOGY NEW CALEDONIA

Waterson, David

Skulls from New Caledonia.

(Journ. Anthrop. Inst. of Great Britain and Ireland, Vol. 38, 1908, pp. 36-46, with pls. 6-7)

AS
36
B2
CRANIOLOGY HAWAII

Mann, Horace

(Short References to Hawaiian Skulls.)

(Boston Soc. Nat. Hist. Proc. X, 1864-1866, pp.229-230.)

(sand burial at Diamond Head, Oahu)

GN
Pam
1685
CRANIOLOGY - MAORI

Mollison, Th.

Beitrag zur kraniologie und osterologie der Maori. From Zeit. f. Morphol. und Anthrop. bd.11, heft 3, 1908.

GN
671.N5
N
Craniology New Guinea

Broek, A. J. P. v. d.

in "Nova Guinea" VII, pp. 103-232.

GN
2M
FI

CRANIOLOGY - NEW GUINEA
Dorsey, George Amos, 1868-
... Observations on a collection of Papuan crania, by
George A. Dorsey ... With notes on preservation and
decorative features, by William H. Holmes ... Chicago,
1897.
48 p. illus. XI pl. 24½ᶜᵐ. (Field Columbian museum. Publication 21.
Anthropological series. vol. II, no. 1)

1. Craniology—New Guinea. I. Holmes, William Henry, 1846-

Library of Congress   GN2.F4   4-12212
——— Copy 2.   GN128.N5D8

GN
571.S 9
K 64

CRANIOLOGY NIAS
Kleiweg de Zwaan, J. P.

Die Insel Nias bei Sumatra. Martinus Nijhof
Haag. R8vo. 1913-1915
I: Uatersuchungen
II: Anthropologische Untersuchungen
III: Kraniologische Untersuchungen

GN
2.I
A-4

CRANIOLOGY PALAU ISLANDS
Clapham, Crochley

On the brainweights of some Chinese and
Pelew islanders.

(Journ. Anthrop. Inst. of Great Britain and
Ireland, Vol. 7, 1877-8, pp. 89-94)

GN
125.N
H 37

CRANIOLOGY NEW GUINEA
Hauser, Karl

Das kraniologischen material der Neu-Guinea
...Berlin. 1906

GN
Pam.
2002

GN
71
D 26

CRANIOLOGY PACIFIC
Davis, J. B.

Collection of papers on craniology, Vol. 2,
No. 6: On the peculiar crania of the inhabitants
of certain groups of islands in the western Pacific, with review by J. Van der Hoeven, ibid. No.5)

(Natuurkundige Verhandelingen, Deel 24, 1866)

GN
Pam
2486

CRANIOLOGY - PAPUA
Ecker, A

Ueber den queren hinterhauptswulst
(Torus occipitalis transversus) am
schadel verschiedener aussereuropaischer
volker.

GN.
Ethn
Pam.
No.636

CRANIOLOGY - NEW GUINEA
Krämer, Augustin

Zwei sehr kleine Pygmaenschadel von
Neuguinea und meine Messungen an Busch-
mannern in Sudafrika, 1906. Aus Archiv
fur Anthrop. 1914 (?).

GN
1
Z

Craniology. Pacific.
Virchow, Rud.
Schädel und Tibiaformen von Sudsee-In-
sulaner
Zeit. für Ethn., vol.12,Berlin,1880
pp.(112)-(119).

GN
Pam
2483

CRANIOLOGY - PERU
Luschan, Felix v.

Defecte des os tympanicum an kunst-
lich deformirten schadeln von Peruanern.
From Verh. d. Berliner anthrop. Gesell.
1896.

GN
Pam
No.631

CRANIOLOGY - NEW GUINEA
Mantegazza, Paolo

Nuovi studi craniologici sulla Nuova
Guinea . Estratto dall' Archivio per l'
antrop. e la etnol. Vol. XI, 1881.

Florence, n.d.

GN
125.Pa
W 13

CRANIOLOGY PACIFIC
Wagner, K.

The craniology of the Oceanic races.
With 22 figures in the text and 31 plates.

(Skrifter utgit av Det Norske Videnskaps-
Akademi i Oslo, I. Math.-Naturv. Klasse, 1937,
No. 2)

GN
125P
Ko

Craniology-Philippine Islands
Koeze, G.A.

Crania ethnica Philippinica...

Haarlem, 1901-1904.

GN
2.I
A4

CRANIOLOGY NEW HEBRIDES
Busk, George
Notes on a collection of skulls from
the islands of Mallicollo and Vanikoro in
the New Hebrides group. In Jour. Anthr.
Inst. VI , 1876-'77. pp. 200-208.
pls. IX - XII.

CRANIOLOGY PACIFIC
Wagner, Konrad Adolf
The craniology of the Oceanic races.

(Skrifter utgitt av de Norske Videnskapsakademi i Oslo. I. Math. Nat. Klasse, 1937, No. 2)

UH has ·

GN
2.M
Bæ-v

Craniology-Polynesia
Luschan, F. von.

Sammlung Baessler, Schadel von
Polynesischen.Inseln. Berlin. Mus. fur
Volkerkunde Band XII, 1907.
Berlin, 1907, pp 256. 33 pls.

GN
2.I
A4

Crania - New Hebrides.
Flower, William Henry.
On a collection of monumental heads
and artificially deformed crania from the
island of Mallicollo in the New Hebrides.
In Jour. Anthr. Inst. XI, 1881 - '82.
pp. 75-81. pl. VI.

Q
115
W 95
looked
case

CRANIOLOGY PACIFIC
Wüllerstorf-Urbair, Bernhard
Reise der Oesterreichischen Fregatte Novara
um die Erde...1857-1859.
Anthropologischer Theil, Abt. I. 1875. von
E. Zuckerkandl. Wien. 4to

(New Zealand, Tahiti, Tuamotus, Australia,
Malay, Marquesas, New Caledonia, Chatham Is.)

GN
2.I
A.m

Craniology - Pitcairn Islanders.
Keith, Arthur
Physical characteristics of two
Pitcairn islanders. In Man, XVII, 1917,
No. 88.

GN
Pam
2009

CRANIOLOGY - NEW HEBRIDES
Krause, Rudolph

Ueber macrocephale schadel von den
N. Hebriden. From Verh. Vereins f. natur.
Unterhaltung, bd. 4, 1877.

CRANIOLOGY -- PACIFIC ISLANDERS

See also

Spengel, J. W.

AS
36
S2

CRANIOLOGY-PERU.
Hrdlička, Aleš i. e. Alois Ferdinand, 1869-
... Some results of recent anthropological exploration
in Peru, with four plates, by Dr. Aleš Hrdlička ... Washington, Smithsonian institution, 1911.
1 p. l., 16 p. 4 pl. (2 col.) 24½ᶜᵐ. (Smithsonian miscellaneous collections. v. 56, no. 16)
Publication 2005.
"Bibliography of the physical anthropology of Peru": p. 13-16.

1. Peru—Antiq. 2. Craniology—Peru.
11-16461

Library of Congress   Q11.S7 vol. 56, no. 16

GN
93.P
R 37

CRANIOLOGY PERU

Reiss, Johann Wilhelm

Das Todtenfeld von Ancon in Peru: ein beitrag zur kenntniss der kultur und industrie des Incareiches, nach den ergebnissen eigener ausgrabungen von W. Reiss und A. Stübel. Mit unterstützung der generalverwaltung der Königlichen Museen. Berlin. A. Asher. n.d. Folio. (19) pp. + pls.

AS
182
H

CRANIOLOGY POLYNESIA

Spengel, Johann Wilhelm

Ein Beitrag sur Kenntnis der Polynesier-Schädel.

(Jour. Mus. Godeffroy, Heft 12, 1876, pp. 116-158, Tafeln 4-8)

GN
103.S
P 68

CRANIOLOGY SWITZERLAND

Pittard, Eugène

Anthropologie de la Suisse:...Genève. 1909-1910.

GN
Pam
823

CRANIOLOGY - PERU

Sergi, Sergio

Canalis intrasquamosis e processus parietalis sulci exocranici arteriae meningeae mediae nel temporale dei crani deformati del Peru. From Rivista d. Antrop. v.17, fasc.3, 1912.

GN
125
Pol

Craniology-Polynesia.

Spengel, J.W.

Ein Beitrag zur Kenntnis der Polynesier-Schadel   im Mus.Godeffroy Journ.,pp. 554-596. Heft XII Tafeln 4-8.

AS
36
S1

CRANIOLOGY - SWITZERLAND

Troyon, Frédéric, 1815?-1866?
On the crania helvetica. By Frederick Troyon.
(*In* Smithsonian institution. Annual report. 1864. Washington, 1865. 23½ᶜᵐ. p. [282]-284. illus.)

1. Craniology—Switzerland.

Library of Congress   Q11.S66 1864
Library, Smithsonian   Institution

S 15-167

GN
Pam
2015

CRANIOLOGY - PERU

Tschudi, J. J. v.

Ueber die ureinwohner von Peru. From Muller's Archiv, 1844.

GN
Pam
833

CRANIOLOGY - RUSSIA

Sergi, G

Di quanto il tipo del cranio della presente popolazione della Russia centrale differisce dal tipo antico dell' epoca dei Kurgani ? Al congresso internaz. di medicino a di antropologica. From Atti Soc. Romana di Antrop. v.5, fasc.1.

AS
720.V
R

Crania Tasmanian

Berry, Richard J.A.
Dioptrographic tracings in four Normae of fifty-two Tasmanian crania.
Roy. Soc. of Victoria Trans. V, Part I, 1909.

GN
125 P
K 77

CRANIOLOGY PHILIPPINE ISLANDS

Koeze, G. A.

Crania Ethnica Philippinica...

(Veröffentlichungen des Niederländischen Reichsmuseums fur Volkerkunde, Serie II, No. 3, 1901-1904. Haarlem)

GN
802
P 85

CRANIOLOGY SOUTH AMERICA

Posnansky, Arthur

Eine praehistorische metropole in Südamerika Band I, mit 88 tafeln, zahlreichen textbildern und einem kraniologischen beobachtungsblatt. Berlin. 1914. 4to.

(German and Spanish)

GN
Pam
2038

CRANIOLOGY - TASMANIA

Büchner, L. W. G.

A study of the curvatures of the Tasmanian aboriginal cranium. From Proc. Royal Soc. Edinburgh, v.34, pt. 2.

GN
Pam
2012

CRANIOLOGY - POLAND

Kopernicki, Isidor

On the scaphoid skull of a Pole. From Journ. Anthrop. Instit. v.6.

GN
Pam
1808

CRANIOLOGY - SPAIN

Sainz, Luis de Hoyos

Craneo foguino del Museo Antropologico de Madrid. From Rev. d. Acad. d. Ciencias Exactas, Fisicas y Nat. d. Madrid, 1911.

GN
71
D 26

CRANIOLOGY TASMANIA

Davis, J. B.

Collection of papers on craniology...Vol. 2, No. 7: On the osteology and peculiarities of the Tasmanians, by J. B. Davis.

(Nat. Verh. der Hollandsche Maatschappij der Wetenschappen, 3rd Reeks, Deel II, No. 4, pp.3-19 Tafel 1-4. 1874)

GN
Pam
1852

CRANIOLOGY - POLAND

Loth, Edward

Beitrage zur kraniologie der Polen. From Zeit. f. Morphol. und Anthrop. bd. 14, heft 2, 1911.

GN
Pam
1982

CRANIOLOGY - SUMATRA

Giuffrida-Ruggeri, V

Crani e mandibole di Sumatra. From Soc. Romana d. antro. atti, v.9, fasc. 3, 1903.

AS
36
S 4

CRANIOLOGY TASMANIA

Hrdlicka, Ales

Catalogue of human crania in the United States National Museum collections: Australians Tasmanians, South African Bushmen, Hottentots, and Negro.

(In Proc. U. S. Nat. Mus., Vol. 71, Art. 24, 1928)

GN
1
A-j
and
GN
Ethn.
Pam.
4059

CRANIOLOGY - POLYNESIA

Marshall, D.S.

An evaluation of Polynesian craniology. By Donald Stanley Marshall and Charles Ernest Snow.

(American Journal of Physical Anthropology, n.s., Vol. 14(3):405-427, September, 1956)

GN
103.S2
R 44

CRANIOLOGY SWEDEN

Retzius, Gustaf

Crania Suecica Antiqua: eine darstellung der Schwedischen menschen-schädel aus steinzeitalter, dem bronzezeitalter und dem eisenzeitalter sowie ein blick auf die forschungen über die rassencharaktere der Europäischen völker...Stockholm. 1900. Folio. iii + 182 pp. + pls.

DS
615
F 69

CRANIOLOGY-TIMORLAUT

Forbes, H. O.

A Naturalist's Wanderings in the Eastern Archipelago...On the Cranial Characters of the Natives of Timor-Laut, by J. G. Garson, pp. 340-355. 1885. 8vo.

CRANIOLOGY--U. S.
GN
550 Hrdlička, Aleš, 1869-
S   ... Skeletal remains suggesting or attributed to early
man in North America, by Aleš Hrdlička. Washington,
Govt. print. off., 1907.

113 p. illus. xxi pl. 23ᶜᵐ. (Smithsonian institution. Bureau of
American ethnology. Bulletin 33)

1. Man, Prehistoric--U. S. 2. U. S.--Antiq. 3. Craniology--U. S.

(Name originally: Alois Ferdinand Hrdlička)

Library of Congress   E51.U6 no. 33   7-35430 Revised
——— Copy 2.   GN70.5.U6H7 1907
——— Another issue.   59th Cong., 2d sess. House. Doc. 816.
               GN70.5.U6H7 1907a
               (r20g2)

GN
2.M
F 45 CRANIOMETRY

Hambly, Wilfrid D.

Cranial capacities, a study in methods.

(Fieldiana. Anthropology, Vol. 36 (3):25-
75, 1947)

GN
649 CRANIOMETRY AFRICA (NORTH)
B 54 Bertholon, L.

Recherches anthropologiques dans la Berbérie
Orientale: Tripolitaine, Tunisie, Algérie, par L.
Bertholon et E. Chantre... 2 vols. Lyon. 1912-1913
4to.

Tome premier: Anthropométrie, Craniométrie,
Ethnographie...
Tome deuxième: Album de 174 portraits
ethniques.

CRANIOLOGY

See also

SKULLS

GN
Pam
2545 CRANIOMETRY

Hambruch, Paul

Beitrage zur untersuchung uber die
langskrummung des schadels beim menschen.
From Korresp-blatt d. Gesell. Anthrop.
jahrg. 38, n.3, 1907.

GN
2.M
F 45 CRANIOMETRY AMBRYM ISLAND

Hambly, Wilfrid D.

Craniometry of Ambrym Island.

(Fieldiana, Anthropology, Vol. 37 (1), 1946,
pp. 1-150)

GN
Pam
2539 CRANIOMETRY

Bartels, Paul

Ueber vergleichbarkeit kraniometris-
cher reihen. From Zeit. f. Ethnol. heft
6, 1903.

GN
125
K91 CRANIOMETRY

Krause, R.

Ein beitrage... von J.D.E. Schmeltz
und R. Krause. Schädel und skelete bes-
chreiben von... R. Krause.

Hamburg, Friederichsen, 1881.   119p.

GN
125.H
U 29 CRANIOMETRY HAWAII

Uhde, C. W. F.

Uber die Schädelform der Sandwich-Insulaner.
...Jena. 1861

GN
Pam.
533

GN
Pam
2226 CRANIOMETRY

Broca, Paul

Memoire sur le craniographie et sur
quelques unes de ses applications. From
Mem. Soc. d'anthrop. Paris, 1863.

GN
Pam
2542 CRANIOMETRY

Reche, Otto

Langen breitenindex und schadellange.
From Arch. f. Anthrop. n.f. bd.10, heft
1, 1911.

GN
58.I
R59 CRANIOMETRY INDIA

Risley, H. H.

The tribes and castes of Bengal.

Calcutta, Bengal Sec. Press, 1891.   2v.

GN
Pam
2234 CRANIOMETRY

Broca, Paul

Sur le sterographie: nouvel instru-
ment craniographique destire a dessiner
tous les details du relief des corps
solides. From Mem. Soc. anthrop. Paris,
1865.

GN
181
S 46 CRANIOMETRY

Sergi, Sergio

Cerebra hererica.

(Jenaische Denkschriften, XV, 1909)

AS
36
C8 CRANIOMETRY. INDIANS OF NORTH AMERICA
Knight, Marian Vera.
... The craniometry of southern New England Indians,
by Marian Vera Knight, A. M., with an introduction by
Harris Hawthorne Wilder ... New Haven, Conn., Yale
university press, 1915.

36 p., 6 l. x pl., 2 fold. tab., diagrs. 30 x 24½ᶜᵐ. (Memoirs of the Connecticut academy of arts and sciences ... vol. IV, July, 1915)

1. Craniometry. 2. Indians of North America — New England.
I. Wilder, Harris Hawthorne, 1864-

                         16-5113

Library of Congress   Q11.C85 vol. 4

GN
Pam
2543 CRANIOMETRY

Czekanowski, Jan

Untersuchungen uber das verhaltnis
der kopfmasse zu den schadelmassen. From
Arch. f. Anthrop. n.f. bd.6, heft 1,1907.

GN
Pam
2509 CRANIOMETRY

Spengel, J. W.

Zur craniometrie. From Zeit. f.
Ethnol. 1877.

GN
Ethn.Pam.
3657 CRANIOMETRY MELANESIA

Schlaginhaufen, Otto

Ein Melanesierschädel von ungewöhnlich
kleiner Kapazität.

(Bull. der Schweizerischen Gesellschaft für
Anthropologie und Ethnologie, 27 Jahrg., 1950/51
pp. 26-37)

GN
71
D 26 CRANIOMETRY

Davis, J. B.

Collection of papers on craniology...Vol. 2,
GN   No. 12: Contributions towards determining the
Pam   weight of the brain in different races of man,
424   by J. B. Davis. 1868.

GN
Ethn.Pam.
3018 CRANIOMETRY

Szombathy, Josef

Tabellen zur Umrechnung der Schädelmasse auf
ounen Rauminhalt von 1000 Kubikzentimetern...
Wein. 1918.

GN
2.M
F 45 CRANIOMETRY NEW GUINEA

Hambly, Wilfrid D.

Craniometry of New Guinea.

(Field Mus. of Nat. Hist., Anthrop. Ser.,
Vol. 25, No. 3, 1940, pp. 81-290)

GN
Pam
1998

Du craniophore

Topinard, Paul

QK
Bot.Fam
3293

Cranwell, Lucy M.

Endemism and isolation in the Three Kings'
Islands, New Zealand- with notes on pollen and
spore types of the endemics.

(Records of the Auckland Institute and Museum, Vol. 5(5/6):215-232, 1962)

Q
101
P 18

and

QK
Bot. Pam.
3167

Cranwell, Lucy M.

A mid-Pacific coal and its microfossils.

Abstract: Pollen Symposium, "Pollen clues
to ancient Pacific floras." Tenth Pacific Science
Congress, Honolulu Aug. 23, 1961. mimeographed.
3 pp.

AM
41
M 98-h

Cranstone, B. A. L.

Ethnography.

IN

Handbook for Museum Curators, The Museums
Association, Part C, Section 4, 1958. London

AS
750
A 89

Cranwell, L(ucy) M.

Flora of Manihiki, Cook Group.

(Records of the Auckland Institute and
Museum, Vol. 1, No. 4, 1933, pp. 169-171)

QK
Bot.Pam.
2089

Cranwell, Lucy M.

New plant records from the Poor Knights
Islands, with special reference to Todea barbara.

(Records of the Auckland Institute Museum,
Vol. 2, 1937, pp. 101-110)

GN
2.I
A 62-m

Cranstone, B. A. L.

Review of
Fragments of Hawaiian History...

(Man,71, art. 130, May 1961)

AP
2
A 28

Cranwell, Lucy M.

Fossil pollen from Seymour Island, Antarctica.

(Nature, Vol. 184, No. 4701, Dec. 5, 1959,
pp. 1782-1785)

QK
Bot.Pam.
2348

Cranwell, Lucy M.

New Zealand pollen studies.

(Records Auckland Institute Museum, Vol.
2, 1942, no. 6, pp. 280-308)

GN
668
C 89

Cranstone, B. A. L.

Melanesia, a short ethnography.
Published by the Trustees of the British Museum.
London. sm4to. 1961 115 pp.

QK
Bot.Pam.
2128

2 copies

Cranwell, Lucy M.

Fossil pollens, the key to the vegetation
of the past.

(New Zealand Journal of Science and Technology, Vol. 19, 1938, pp. 628-645)

AS
750
A 89-b

and

QK
Bot.Pam
2771

OVER

Cranwell, Lucy M.

New Zealand pollen studies: the Monocotyle-
dons; a comparative account.

(Bull. Auckland Institute and Museum, No. 3,
1952. Published by Harvard University Press, for
Auckland Institute and Museum, 1953)

Q
101
P 18

and

QK
Bot.Pam
3168

Cranwell, Lucy M.

Antarctica: cradle or grave for Nothofagus?

Abstract: Pollen Symposium, "Pollen clues to
ancient Pacific floras." Tenth Pacific Science
Congress, Honolulu, Aug. 23, 1961. mimeographed.
3 pp.

AS
750
A 89

Cranwell, Lucy M.

Moore, L. B.

Induced dominance of Microlaena avenacea
(Raoul) Hook. f. in a New Zealand rain-forest
area. By L. B. Moore and Lucy M. Cranwell.

(Rec. Auckland Inst. and Mus., I:219-238,
1934)

QK
Bot.Pam.
2781

Cranwell, Lucy M.

An outline of New Zealand peat deposits.
With notes on the condition of the rain-fed
cushio bogs.

(Seventh Pacific Science Congress, New Zealand, Vol. VI:1-23, 1953)

QK
Bot.Pam.
2144

Pam.
2144

Wall, Arnold

The botany of Auckland, by Arnold Wall and
Lucy M. Cranwell. Dedicated to the memory of
the late Mr. T. F. Cheeseman. 1936.

(Reprinted from "The New Zealand Herald",
1936. 47 pp.)
Second edition, revised and enlarged, 1943.
43 pp.

QK
Bot.Pam.
2129

Cranwell, Lucy M.

Intertidal communities of the Poor Knights
Islands, N. Z., by L. M. Cranwell and L.B. Moore.

(Transactions of the R. Soc. of New Zealand,
Vol. 67, 1938, pp. 375-406)

QK
Bot.Pam.
2302
2318

Cranwell, Lucy M.

Pollen grains of the New Zealand conifers.

(New Zealand Journal of Science and Technology, Vol. 22, No. 1b, 1940, pp. 1-17)

QK
Bot.Pam.
3178

Cranwell, Lucy M.

Coniferous pollen types of the southern
hemisphere. 1. Aberration in Camopyle and Podo-
carpus dacrydioidea.

(Journal of the Arnold Arboretum, 42:416-
423, 1961)

QK
Bot.Pam.
3126

Cranwell, Lucy M.

Lower Tertiary microfossils from McMurdo
Sound, Antarctica. By Lucy M. Cranwell, H. J.
Harrington and I. G. Speden.

(Nature, 184(4726):700-702, 1960)

Q
101
P 18

Cranwell, Lucy M.

Pollen Symposium Abstracts: "Pollen clues
to ancient Pacific floras." Tenth Pacific
Science Congress, Honolulu, 1961.

(Nouvelles et Revuew, n.d. 4 pp.)

QK
Bot.Pam.
2086

Cranwell, Lucy M.

Post-Pleistocene pollen diagrams from the southern hemisphere. I. New Zealand, by Lucy M. Cranwell and Lennart von Post.

(Geografiska Annaler, 1936, pp. 309-347)

QH
Nat.Hist.
Pam.
193

CRASSOSTREA

Colwell, R. R.

Microbiology of shellfish; bacteriological study of the natural flora of Pacific oysters Crassostrea gigas).

(Applied Microbiology, 8(2):104-109, 1960)

AS
619
S

Crassulaceae

Schönland, S.

In Annals S. African Mus.
IX 2 pp. 46-57.

GN
2.S
P 76

CRANWELL, LUCY

Pearson, Richard

Some bases for ecological inferences about the aboriginal population of the Hanapepe Valley, Kauai.

(Jour. Poly. Soc., 71(4):379-385, 1962)

QL
1
A 84

CRASSOSTREA

Thomson, J. M.

The naturalization of the Pacific oyster in Australia.

(Australian Journal of Marine and Freshwater Research, 10(2):144-149, 1969)

[Japanese oysters successfully planted in Australia and Tasmania]

QE
1
G 3 m

CRATERS

Jaggar, Thomas A.

Origin and development of craters.

(Geol. Soc. of America, Mem. 21, 1947)

AS
750
A 89

and

QK
Bot.Pam.
2251

Cranwell, Lucy M.

Southern-beech pollens.

(Records of the Auckland Institute and Museum, Vol. 2, No. 4, 1939:175-196)

QK
110
N 56

CRASSULACEAE

Britton, Nathaniel Lord

Crassulaceae, by Nathaniel Lord Britton and Joseph Nelson Rose.

IN North American flora, Vol. 22, Part 1, 1905, pp. 7-74

DU
Pac.
Pam.
1023

CRATERS

Scrope, G. Poulett

On the formation of craters, and the nature of the liquidity of lavas.

(From Jour. Geol. Soc., 12(326):346-359, no date)

QK
Bot.Pam.
3173

Cranwell, Lucy M.

Subantarctic pollen and spores. I. Lyallia of Kerguelen.

(Mus. National d'Hist. Nat., Paris, Publ. semestrielle, Vol. III(1):11-20; reissued as Contrib. No. 42, Geochronology Laboratories, University of Arizona)

AS
36
S2

CRASSULACEAE

Britton, Nathaniel Lord, 1859–

... *Lenophyllum,* a new genus of *Crassulaceæ,* by N. L. Britton and J. N. Rose.

(*In* Smithsonian institution. Smithsonian miscellaneous collections. Washington, 1905. 24½ᶜᵐ. vol. XLVII (Quarterly issue, vol. II) p. 159-162. illus., pl. XX (col.))

Publication 1479.
Originally published October 10, 1904.

1. Lenophyllum. ɪ. Rose, Joseph Nelson, 1862– joint author.

Library of Congress   Q11.S7 vol. 47   16-10999
—— Copy 2.

G
7
R 91

Crawford, Allan

Map making on Tristan da Cunha.

(Geographical Journal, Vol. 94, 1939, p. 410-413)

QE
Bot.Pam.
1801

Cranwell, L. M.

The vegetation of Maungapohatu, by L. M. Cranwell, and L. B. Moore.

(Rec. Auck. Inst. Mus., Vol. 1, No. 2, pp.71-80, Nov., 1931)

QK
1
U

CRASSULACEAE

Britton, Nathaniel Lord, 1859–

Thompsonella, a new genus of *Crassulaceae* from Mexico. By N. L. Britton and J. N. Rose.

(*In* Smithsonian institution. United States national museum. Contributions from the United States national herbarium. Washington, 1903-24½ᶜᵐ. vol. XII, pt. 9, p. 391-392. pl. XLIV-XLV)

"Issued May 10, 1909."

1. ¡Thompsonella¡ ɪ. Rose, Joseph Nelson, 1862– joint author.

Agr 9-1501
Library, U. S. Dept. of   Agriculture 450C76 vol. 12, pt. 9

QL
671
E 55

Crawford, Allan B.

The birds of Marion Island, South Indian Ocean. With annotations by D. L. Serventy.

(The Emu, 52:73-85, 1952)

QL
Fish
Pam.
#16

CRAPPIE

Pearse, A. S.

Habits of the black crappie in inland lakes of Wisconsin, ex Bur. of Fisheries, doc. no. 867, 1919.

QK
1
U

CRASSULACEAE

Rose, Joseph Nelson, 1862–

Five new species of *Crassulaceae* from Mexico. By J. N. Rose.

(*In* Smithsonian institution. United States national museum. Contributions from the United States national herbarium. Washington, 1903-24½ᶜᵐ. vol. XII, pt. 10, p. 439-440. pl. LXXVII-LXXXI)

"Issued July 21, 1909."

1. Crassulaceae.

Agr 9-1872
Library, U. S. Dept. of   Agriculture 450C76 vol. 12, pt. 10

QL
461
H 1

and

QL
Insects
Pam.
473

Crawford, D. L. (David Livingston)

The Bishop Museum collection of Psyllidae. In Proc. Hawaii. Ent. Soc. Vol V, pp 369 – , 1924.

Q
115
S 56

CRASPEDOTA

Maas, Otto
Die Craspedoten Medusen der Siboga-Expedition

Weber, Max
Uitkomsten...Nederlandsch Oost-Indie 1899-1900...Siboga...Monographie X (livr.26). 1905 84 pp., 14 pl.

QK
1
U

CRASSULACEAE

Rose, Joseph Nelson, 1862–

Three new species of *Crassulaceae* from Guatemala. By J. N. Rose.

(*In* Smithsonian institution. United States national museum. Contributions from the United States national herbarium. Washington, 1903-24½ᶜᵐ. vol. XII, pt. 9, p. 395-396. pl. XLVII-XLVIII)

"Issued May 10, 1909."

1. Crassulaceae.

Agr 9-1503
Library, U. S. Dept. of   Agriculture 450C76 vol. 12, pt. 9

Crawford, David Livingston

Carter Coll.
12-B-26

Can nations be neighbors? Internationalism in four dimensions. Boston. The Stratford Co. 1933. iii + 120 pp. sm8vo.

QL
Insects
Pam.
467

Crawford, D. L. (David Livingston)

Ceylonese and Philippine Psyllidae (Homoptera). From Philippine Journ. Sc. Vol. X, 1915,

Homoptera

QL
Insects
Pam. 997

Crawford, D. L. (David Livingston)

The three musketeers, by D. L. Crawford and Edwin H. Bryan, Jr.

(Reading course in Science and Natural History, April 21, 1922)

AS
750
N

Crawford, J. C.

The Orthography of the Maori language.

(New Zealand, Inst., Trans. & Proc. I, 1868, pp. 40-43).

AS
36
S4

Crawford, David Livingston, 1889–

A contribution toward a monograph of the homopterous insects of the family *Delphacidæ* of North and South America. By David L. Crawford ...

(*In* U. S. National museum. Proceedings. Washington, 1914. 23½ᶜᵐ. v. 46, p. 557-640. pl. 44-49)

Bibliography: p. 634-635.

1. Delphacidae. 2. Hemiptera—America.

14-10997 Revised

Library of Congress   Q11.U55 vol. 46

DU
1
S 72 t

Crawford, H. E. and others

Ophthalmological survey of the Trust Territory of the Pacific Islands. By H. E. Crawford, Grace C. Hamman and Isaac Lanwi.

(South Pacific Commission, Tech. Pap. No. 67, 1954)

AS
750
N

Crawford, James Coutts

The Maori Language with Remarks on the Reform of English Spelling.

Trans. + Proc. N. Z. I. Vol. XVIII. 1885. pp. 46-68.

QK
473.H
C 89

Crawford, David Livingston

Hawaii's crop parade. A review of useful products derived from the soil in the Hawaiian Islands, past and present. Honolulu. 1937. Advertiser Publishing Co., Ltd. 8vo. 305 pp.

AS
36
S4

Crawford, James Chamberlain, 1880–

Hymenoptera, superfamilies *Apoidea* and *Chalcidoidea*, of the Yale Dominican expedition of 1913. By J. C. Crawford ...

(*In* U. S. National museum. Proceedings. Washington, 1915. 23½ᶜᵐ. v. 47, p. 131-134)

1. Hymenoptera—Dominica.   I. Yale Dominican expedition, 1913.

15-14946

Library of Congress   Q11.U55 vol. 47

AS
750
N

Crawford, James Coutts

On Maori Ancestry

Trans. + Proc. N. Z. I. Vol. XX 1887. pp. 414-418.

QL
Ins
Pam
#321

Crawford, David L (ivingston)

The jumping plant lice of the Palaeotropics and the South Pacific Islands. ex Philippine Journ. of Sc., vol. XV, No. 2, 1919.

AS
36
S4

Crawford, James Chamberlain, 1880–

New *Hymenoptera* from the Philippine Islands. By J. C. Crawford ...

(*In* U. S. National museum. Proceedings. Washington, 1911. 23½ᶜᵐ. vol. 38, p. 119-133)

1. Hymenoptera— Philippine Islands.

11-15594

Library of Congress   Q11.U55 vol. 38

GN
2.I
A-1

Crawford, John

On Cannibalism in relation to ethnology.

(Trans. Ethnol. Soc. of London, N.S., Vol. 4, 1866, pp. 105-124)

AS
36
S5

Crawford, David Livingston, 1889–

... A monograph of the jumping plant-lice, or *Psyllidæ*, of the New World, by David L. Crawford ... Washington, Govt. print. off., 1914.

ix, 186 p. 30 pl. 24½ᶜᵐ. (Smithsonian institution. United States National museum. Bulletin 85)

Bibliography: p. 161-169.

1. Psyllidae.

14-30483 Revised

Library of Congress   Q11.U6
——— Copy 2.   QL523.P8C7

AS
36
S4

Crawford, James Chamberlain, 1880–

New South American parasitic *Hymenoptera*. By J. C. Crawford ...

(*In* U. S. National museum. Proceedings. Washington, 1911. 23½ᶜᵐ. v. 30, p. 235-239. illus.)

1. Hymenoptera—South America. 2. Parasites.

11—21202

Library of Congress   Q11.U55 vol. 39

GN
2.I
A

Crawford, John

On the Malayan and Polynesian languages and races.

(Journal Ethnol. Soc. of London, Vol. 1, 1848, pp. 330-374)

QL
Insects
Pam.
466

Crawford, D. L. (David Livingston)

New genera and species of Psyllidae from the Philippine Islands. Reprinted from Philippine Journ. Sc. Vol. VIII, No. 4 Sec. D. Aug., 1913.

AS
36
S4

Crawford, James Chamberlain.

Three new genera and species of parasitic *Hymenoptera*. By J. C. Crawford ...

(*In* U. S. National museum. Proceedings. Washington, 1911. 23½ᶜᵐ. vol. 38, p. 87-90. illus.)

1. Hymenoptera. 2. Parasites.

11-15591

Library of Congress   Q11.U55 vol. 38

GN
2.M
A

Crawford, M. D. C. (Morris De Camp)

Peruvian fabrics. In Anthr. Papers Am. Mus. of Nat. Hist. XII, part IV. pp. 107-191.

QL
Insects
Pam.
461

Crawford, D. L. (David Livingston)

Philippine and Asiatic Psyllidae. Fr. Philippine Journ. Sc. Vol. XII, No.3, May, 1917.

AS
750
N

Crawford, J. Coutts

On the geology of the North Island of New Zealand.

(Trans. and Proc. New Zealand Institute, 1, Pt III. 27 pp. 1868)

DU
623
C 89

Crawford, M. Leola

Seven weeks in Hawaii, by an American Girl. With fifty-four illustrations. John J. Newbegin San Francisco. 1917. 8vo. 113 pp.

Crawford, M. Leola   Carter Coll. 1-B-15

Seven weeks in Hawaii, with fifty-four illustrations. San Francisco. John J. Newbegin. 1917 112 pp.

GN 2.I A4 and GN Pam #401

Crawley, A. E.

Sexual taboo: a study in the relations of the sexes. In Journ. Roy. Anth. Inst. XXIV, 1894-1895, pp 116-235, 430-446.
Also separate.

QL 225 P 36

Creaser, Edwin P.

Pearse, A. S.

The cenotes of Yucatan, a zoological and hydrographic survey, by A. S. Pearse, Edwin P. Creaser, F. G. Hall, and others.

(Carnegie Institution of Washington, publication 457, 1936)

GN 2M A

Crawford, Morris De Camp, 1882-

... Peruvian textiles. By M. D. C. Crawford. New York, The Trustees, 1915.

1 p. l, p. 53-104. illus. 24½ᶜᵐ. (Anthropological papers of the American museum of natural history. vol. XII, pt. III)
Bibliography: p. 104.

1. Indians of South America—Textile industry and fabrics. 2. Textile industry and fabrics—Peru.
         17-28726

Library of Congress   GN2.A27 vol. 12, pt. 3

GN 479 C 91

Crawley, Ernest

Studies of savages and sex. Edited by Theodore Besterman. London. Methuen & Co. (1929) 8vo. ix + 300 pp.

CREATION MYTHS

See

MYTHS CREATION
KUMULIPO

QL Insect Pam. 1778

Crawford, R.

Some anopheline pupae of Malaya, with a note on pupal structure. Published by the Government of the Straites Settlements and the Malaria Advisory Board, Fed. Malay States. 1938 8vo. 110 pp.

CRAYFISH

see

ASTACIDAE
CAMBARUS
PROCAMBARUS
PARASTACIDAE
EUASTACUS
PALINURUS

GN 2M X

CREE INDIANS.

Goddard, Pliny Earle, 1869-

... Notes on the sun dance of the Sarsi. By Pliny Earle Goddard. The sun dance of the Plains-Cree. By Alanson Skinner. Notes on the sun dance of the Cree in Alberta. By Pliny Earle Goddard. The sun dance of the Canadian Dakota. By W. D. Wallis. Notes on the sun dance of the Sisseton Dakota. By Alanson Skinner. New York, The Trustees, 1919.

1 p. l., p. 271-385. illus. 24½ᶜᵐ. (Anthropological papers of the American museum of natural history. vol. XVI, pt. IV)
"The sun dance of the Plains-Ojibway, by Alanson Skinner": p. 311-315.
1. Sun-dance. 2. Sarsi Indians. 3. Cree Indians. 4. Chippewa Indians. 5. Dakota Indians. I. Skinner, Alanson Buck, 1886- II. Wallis, Wilson Dallam, 1886-
     20-16350

Library of Congress   GN2.A27 vol. XVI, pt. IV
     [81]

DU Hist. Pam. 292

Crawford, Will C.

The sugar industry in Hawaii. [signed by Will C. Crawford, ..."preparation of the first half"...by Thomas Vance.] Dept. of Public Instruction, T. H., Honolulu, 1933. 8vo. 67 pp.

PL Phil. pam. 345

(Creagh, S. M. tr?)

Evangelia hnei Ioane hma xiwamomone. Translated by S. M. Creagh and J. Jones? Nengone. Mission Press. 1861) 102 pp. 8vo.

(Nengone (Maré) Loyalty Is., Gospel of John)

GN 2.M A

CREE INDIANS.

Skinner, Alanson Buck, 1886-

... Notes on the eastern Cree and northern Saulteaux. By Alanson Skinner. New York, The Trustees, 1911.

1 p. l., p. 1-177. illus., 2 pl. 24ᶜᵐ. (Anthropological papers of the American museum of natural history. vol. IX, pt. I)
Bibliography: p. 176-177.

1. Cree Indians. 2. Chippewa Indians.
     15-3020 Revised

Library of Congress   GN2.A27 vol. 9, pt. 1
———— Copy 2.   E99.C88S7
     [r21c2]

PL Pam #44

Crawfurd

An inscription from the Kawi or ancient Javanese language.
extract, n.d.

PL Phil. pam. 346

(Creagh, S. M. tr.)

Evangelia hnei Mathiu hna xiwamomone. (Translated by S. M. Creagh and J. Jones. Nengone. Mission Press. 186-?) 73 pp. 8vo.

(Nengone (Maré) Loyalty Is., Gospel of Matthew)

GN 2.M A

CREE INDIANS.

Skinner, Alanson Buck, 1886-

... Political organization, cults, and ceremonies of the Plains-Ojibway and Plains-Cree Indians. By Alanson Skinner. New York, The Trustees, 1914.

1 p. l, p. 475-542. illus. 24½ᶜᵐ. (Anthropological papers of the American museum of natural history. vol. XI, pt. VI)

1. Chippewa Indians. 2. Cree Indians. 3. Indians of North America—Soc. life & cust.
     15-3023 Revised

Library of Congress   GN2.A27 vol. 11, pt. 6
     [r21c2]

DS 603 C89

Crawfurd, John

History of the Indian archipelago: Containing an account of the manners, arts, languages, religions, institutions, and commerce of its inhabitants. By John Crawfurd....With maps and engravings. in three volumes.
Edinburgh,   Archibald Constable. 1820. 8vo.

GN Pam #341

Creagh, S. M.

Notes on the Loyalty Islands, ex Australasian Ass. for Advancement of Sc. ~~Provxxxxixxxxxxxx~~ 1892 pp. 680-688, Rept. of the 4th meeting.

GN 2 S A 22

CREEK INDIANS

Speck, Frank Gouldsmith, 1881-

... The Creek Indians of Taskigi town, by Frank G. Speck. Lancaster, Pa., The New Era printing company, 1907.

cover-title, p. 99-164. v pl. (incl. fold. map) diagr. 25½ᶜᵐ. (Memoirs of the American anthropological association. vol. II, pt. 2)

1. Creek Indians. 2. Taskigi, Okl.
     8-10851 Revised

Library of Congress   GN2.A22 vol. 2, pt. 2
     [r19d2]

GN 29 B 18

Crawley, A. E.

Exogamy and the mating of cousins.

Balfour, Henry, and others

Anthropological essays...Oxford. 1907. 4to. pp.51-64.

Creak

Q 115 .C

Creak, E. W.

Challenger Expedition

Physics & Chemistry Vol. II Pt. III

G 13. 14.   *Magnetic Results*

AM Mus. Pam. 221

Creighton, Harriet B.

Political control of science in the U. S. S. R. A lecture delivered on the Nellie Heldt Lecture Fund. Oberlin College. 1950. 12mo. 27 pp.

RC
Pathol.
Pam. 2

Creighton, Robert J.

Dedication of the Kapiolani Home for girls, the offspring of leper parents, at Kakaako, Oahu, by Their Majesties King Kalakaua and Queen Kapiolani. (with article on Molokai; description of the leper colony on this island; social condition of the lepers...by Robert J. Creighton.) Honolulu. 1885. 8vo.

QL
Mollusca
Pam. 884

CREPIDULA   GROWTH

Gould, Harley N.

Growth and sex development in the slipper limpet Crepidula plana.

(Reprinted from Bios, Vol. 20(3):173-176, 1949)

CRESCENT   ISLAND

See

TEMOE

DU
621
H 77

locked
case

Creighton, Robert J.

The leper settlement on Molokai.

(Honolulu Almanac and Directory, 1886, pp. 90-96)

QL
Mollusca
Pam. 884

CREPIDULA   SEX DEVELOPMENT

Gould, Harley N.

Growth and sex development in the slipper limpet Crepidula plana.

(Reprinted from Bios, Vol. 20(3):173-176, 1949)

QK
Bot.Pam.
3148

CRESCENTIA

Neubauer, H. F.

Uber die Blattbuschel von Crescentia cujete L.

(Osterreichischen Bot. Zeit., 106(6):551-555, 1959)

QL
1
H-1

Creighton, William Steel

The ants of North America.

(Bull. Mus. of Comp. Zool, Harvard College, Vol. 104, 1950)

AS
720.S
S 72

CREPIPODA   AUSTRALIA

Cotton, Bernard C.

The correlation of recent and fossil Crepipoda (Mollusca) of the Australian sub-region. By Bernard C. Cotton and Benjamin J. Weeding.

(Records of the South Australian Museum, Vol. VI (4):435-450, 1941)

GN
Ethn.Pam.
3371

Cressman, L. S.

Early man in Oregon: archaeological studies in the northern Great Basin. By L. S. Cressman, Howel Williams, and Alex D. Krieger. University of Oregon. Eugene, 1940. 8vo. 78 pp 16 pl.

AS
36
S4

CREMASTINI.

Cushman, Robert Asa.

A revision of hymenopterous insects of the tribe *Cremastini* of America north of Mexico. By R. A. Cushman ...

(*In* U. S. National museum. Proceedings. Washington, 1917. 23½ᶜᵐ. v. 53, p. 503-551)

1. Cremastini.

18-14645

Library of Congress   Q11.U55 vol. 53

QK
495.C91
B 11

CREPIS

Babcock, E(rnest) B.

The American species of Crepis, their interrelationships and distribution as affected by polyploidy and apomixis, by E. B. Babcock and G. L. Stebbins jr. Carnegie Institution of Washington, Publication No.504, 1938, pp. 1-199, 12 tables + 1 p. supplement. R8vo.

QL
563
C 92

Cresson, E. T.

Synopsis of the Families and Genera of the Hymenoptera of America, North of Mexico, together with a catalogue of the described species, and bibliography.

(Transactions of the American Entomological Society, Supplementary volume,. 1887. 350 pp. 8vo)

GN
2 S
P 76

CREMATION   MAORI

Campbell, R. E. M.

Cremation amongst the Maoris.

(Journal of the Polynesian Society, Vol.3, 1894, pp. 134-135)

QK
495.Y6
B 11

CREPIS

Babcock, Ernest B.

The genus Youngia, by Ernest B. Babcock and G. Ledyard Stebbins, Jr. Carnegie Institution of Washington, Publication No. 484, 1937. 8vo. 106 pp.

GC
1
M 33

Cresswell, M.

Open boat voyages.

(The Marine Observer, Vol. 16, No. 134, 1939, pp. 55-58)

QL
958
C 75

Crepidula

Conklin, Edwin Grant, 1863-

The embryology of Crepidula: a contribution to the cell lineage and early development of some marine gasteropods; by Edwin Grant Conklin ... Boston, Ginn & company, 1897.

1 p. l., 226 p. illus., 9 pl. (part col.) 25½ᶜᵐ. (Contributions from the Zoölogical laboratory of the University of Pennsylvania)

Reprinted from Journal of morphology, vol. XIII, no. 1.

Embryology   2. Crepidula.

3—16270

Library of Congress   QL958.C7

QK
101
G 65

CREPIS

Babcock, E. B.

The origin of Crepis and related genera, with particular reference to distribution and chromosome relationships.

Goodspeed, T. H.
Essays in geobotany...Setchell. 1936. pp. 9-53.

Cressy, George B.

China's Geographic Foundations

UH has

AS
36
A5

CREPIDULA

Dahlgren, B   E.

The development of a mollusk. A guide to the series of models illustrating the development of *Crepidula* in the Department of invertebrate zoölogy, by B. E. Dahlgren ... New York, The Museum, 1906.

32 p. incl. front., illus., plan, diagrs. 25ᶜᵐ. (Guide leaflet. no. 21)

Double pagination.

"Reprinted from the American museum journal, vol. VI, no. 1, January, 1906."

1. Mollusks—Embryology. 2. Crepidula.

7-37574

Library of Congress   QL431.D13

QK
1
U

CREPIS OCCIDENTALIS

Coville, Frederick Vernon, 1867-

Crepis occidentalis and its allies. By Frederick V. Coville.

(*In* U. S. Dept. of agriculture. Division of botany. Contributions from the U. S. National herbarium. Washington, 1892-96. 24ᶜᵐ. vol. iii, no. 9, p. 559-565. xxi-xxvi pl.)

Issued August 5, 1896.

1. Crepis occidentalis.

8-10562

Library of Congress   QK1.U5 vol. 3

PL
48
C 92

Creswell, H. T.

A dictionary of military terms, English-Japanese; Japanese-English. By H. T. Creswell, J. Hiraoka and R. Namba. American edition. University of Chicago Press. 8vo ob (1943) 175 pp.

AS
36
S

Cretaceous reptiles of U.S.

Leidy, J.

Smithsn. Contr. to Knowl, vol. 14, art. 6

QK
Bot.Pam.
3226

Cribb, A. B.

Records of marine Algae from South-eastern Queensland, I

(Univ. of Queensland, Dept. Bot., 3(3), 1954)

GN
Ethn.Pam.
3312

CRIME AND PUNISHMENT　NEW GUINEA

Hogbin, H. Ian

Social reaction to crime: law and morals in the Schouten Islands, New Guinea.

(Journal of the R. Anthrop. Inst. Great Britain and Ireland, Vol. 68, 1938, pp. 223-262)

CRETE　ARCHAEOLOGY

see

ARCHAEOLOGY　CRETE

AM
101.F4
(5)

CRICKETS

Laufer, Berthold

Insect musicians and cricket champions of China. Field Mus. Nat. His. Anthrop. Leaflet 22, 1927.

GN
2.1
A-M

CRIME AND PUNISHMENT　NEW GUINEA

Lyons, A.P.

Harina, or punishment by substitute - a custom amongst the Kiwai and kindred peoples of Western Papua.

(Man, vol. 21, 1921, no. 12, pp. 24-27)

CRETE　MOLLUSCA

See

MOLLUSCA　CRETE

QE
349.F
L 15

Crickmay, Geoffrey W.

Chemical composition of limestones, by J.W. Sanders, Jr. and Geoffrey W. Crickmay.

IN
Ladd, Harry S.
Geology of Lau, Fiji, by Harry S. Ladd and J. Edward Hoffmeister, pp. 251-259.

(Bernice P. Bishop Museum, Bull. 181, 1944)

GN
1
O 15

CRIME AND PUNISHMENT　NEW GUINEA

Todd, J. A.

Native offences and European law in southwest New Britain.

(Oceania, Vol. 5, No. 4, 1935, pp. 437-460)

QL
336
Ru 92

Cretzschmar, J

Säugethiere. Atlas zu der Reise im nordlichen Afrika von Eduard Rüppelt, pp 1- 78.

Frankfurt, 1826, folio.

See Ruppell for detail

QE
349.F
L 15

Crickmay, Geoffrey W.

Petrography of limestones.

IN
Ladd, Harry S.
Geology of Lau, Fiji, by Harry S. Ladd and J. Edward Hoffmeister, pp. 211-250.

(Bernice P. Bishop Museum, Bull. 181, 1944)

GN
Ethn.Pam.
3058

CRIME & PUNISHMENT　QUEENSLAND

Roth, Walter E.

Notes on government, morals, and crime (in Queensland). Brisbane. 1906. 4to.

(North Queensland Ethnography: Bulletin No. 8, No., 1905.)

QL
336
R 7

Cretschmar, J.

Vogel: Atlas zu der Reise im nordlichen Afrika von Eduard Rüppell, pp 1-55.

Frankfurt, 1826, folio.

[See Rüppell]

QE
1
G 3

and
QE
Geol.Pam.
1072

Crickmay, G. W.

Shallow-water Globigerina sediments, by G.W. Crickmay, H. S. Ladd, and J. E. Hoffmeister.

(Bull. Geological Soc. of America, Vol. 52, 1941, pp. 79-106)

AS
36
A 9

CRIMINAL ANTHROPOLOGY

Hooton, Earnest A.

Preliminary Remarks on the Anthropology of the American Criminal.

(Proceedings of the American Philosophical Society, Vol. 71, pp. 349-356, 1932)

Creuss, W. V.

Commercial fruit and vegetable products.

UH

QK
Bot.Pam.
1662

Crié, L(ouis)

Coup d'Oeil sur la Végétation Fongine de la Nouvelle-Calédonie.

(Bull. de la Soc. Linn. de Normandie, Ser. 2, Vol. 8, 1873-1874, pp. 442-451)

GN
270
M13

CRIMINAL ANTHROPOLOGY

MacDonald, Arthur

Abnormal man, being essays on education and crime and related subjects. Bureau of Ed. Cir. of Information, no.4, 1893.

Washington, Govt. Print., 1893.

AS
720.T
R 88

Cribb, A. B.

Notes on marine Algae from Tasmania.

(Papers and Proc. of the R. Soc. of Tasmania, Vol. 90:183-188, 1956)

GN
495.4
M 25

CRIME and PUNISHMENT

Malinowski, Bronislawa

Crime and custom in savage society. London. Routledge and Kegan Paul, Ltd. 8vo. 7th impression, 1961. x ii + 132 pp.

AS
36
S1

CRIMINAL ANTHROPOLOGY

Wilson, Thomas, 1832-1902.

Criminal anthropology. By Thomas Wilson, LL. D.

(In Smithsonian institution. Annual report. 1890. Washington, 1891. 25¹ᵐ. p. 617-686)

"A report on the Second international congress of criminal anthropology, held at Paris, August, 1889."

1. Criminal anthropology.

S 15-746

Library of Congress　　Q11.S65 1890
Library, Smithsonian　　Institution

CRINOIDEA

QL 1 H2 Agassiz, Alexander, 1835–1910.

... *Calamocrinus diomedæ*, a new stalked crinoid, with notes on the apical system and the homologies of echinoderms, by Alexander Agassiz ... Cambridge, Printed for the Museum, 1892.

95 p. XXXII pl. (part fold.) 29ᶜᵐ. (Memoirs of the Museum of comparative zoölogy at Harvard college, vol. XVII, no. 2)

Each plate accompanied by leaf with descriptive letterpress.
Reports on an exploration off the west coasts of Mexico, Central and South America, and off the Galapagos Islands ... by the U. S. Fish commission steamer "Albatross," during 1891 ... I.

1. Crinoidea. 2. Echinodermata. 3. Albatross (Steamer) I. Title.

A 19-1036

—— Another copy. QL384.C8A3
Title from Univ. of Chicago QL1.H375 vol. 17, no. 2
Printed by L. C. [3]

CRINOIDEA

QL 1 H2 Agassiz, Alexander, 1835–1910.

... *Echini*, crinoids, and corals, by Alexander Agassiz and L. F. de Pourtalès ... Cambridge, University press, Welch, Bigelow, & co., 1874.

[3], 54 p. illus., x pl. 30ᶜᵐ. (Memoirs of the Museum of comparative zoölogy at Harvard college, v. 4, no. 1)

At head of title: Illustrated catalogue of the Museum of comparative zoölogy at Harvard college. no. VIII.
Zoological results of the Hassler expedition. I.

1. Sea-urchins. 2. Crinoidea. 3. Corals. 4. Hassler expedition. I. Pourtalès, Louis François de, 1824–1880.

A 19-1038

Title from Univ. of Chicago QL1.H375 vol. 4, no. 1
Printed by L. C. [3]

QL 385.5 I CRINOIDEA

Clark, Austin Hobart, 1880–

... The crinoids of the Indian Ocean, by Austin Hobart Clark ... Calcutta, Printed by order of the Trustees, 1912.

1 p. l., iii, 325 p. illus. 31½ᶜᵐ. (Echinoderma of the Indian museum, pt. VII)

1. Crinoidea. I. Indian museum, Calcutta.

13-17440

Library of Congress QL384.C8C54

AS 36 S4 CRINOIDEA

Clark, Austin Hobart, 1880–

The crinoids of the Museum fuer naturkunde, Berlin. By Austin Hobart Clark ...

(*In* U. S. National museum. Proceedings. Washington, 1913. 23½ᶜᵐ. vol. 43, p. 381–410)

"List of papers containing references to the crinoids in the collection of the Museum fuer naturkunde": p. 409–410.

1. Crinoidea. I. Berlin. Universität. Museum für naturkunde.

13-13121

Library of Congress QL11.U55 vol. 43

AS 36 S2 CRINOIDEA

Clark, Austin Hobart, 1880–

... The crinoids of the Natural history museum at Hamburg, by Austin H. Clark ... Washington, Smithsonian institution, 1912.

1 p. l., 33 p. 24½ᶜᵐ. (Smithsonian miscellaneous collections, v. 60, no. 10)

Publication 2150.
"List of the published papers dealing wholly or in part with the crinoids in the collection of the Hamburg museum": p. 33.

1. Crinoidea. 2. Hamburg. Naturhistorisches museum.

12-29067

Library of Congress QL11.S7 vol. 60, no. 10
—— Copy 2. QL384.C8C53

AS 36 S2 CRINOIDEA

Clark, Austin Hobart, 1880–

Five new recent crinoids from the north Pacific Ocean, by Austin Hobart Clark.

(*In* Smithsonian institution. Smithsonian miscellaneous collections. Washington, 1908. 24½ᶜᵐ. vol. L (Quarterly issue, vol. IV) p. 337–342. illus.)

Publication 1777.
Originally published October 29, 1907.

1. Crinoidea. 2. Echinodermata—Pacific Ocean.

16-11647

Library of Congress QL11.S7 vol. 50
—— Copy 2.

AS 36 S4 CRINOIDEA

Clark, Austin Hobart, 1880–

Five new species of recent unstalked crinoids. By Austin Hobart Clark ...

(*In* U. S. National museum. Proceedings. Washington, 1910. 23½ᶜᵐ. vol. 37, p. 29–34)

1. Crinoidea.

11-9661

Library of Congress QL11.U55 vol. 37

AS 36 S5 CRINOIDEA

Clark, Austin Hobart, 1880–

... A monograph of the existing crinoids, by Austin Hobart Clark ... Washington, Govt. print. off., 1915–

v. illus., pl. 31ᶜᵐ. (Smithsonian institution. United States National museum. Bulletin 82

1. Crinoidea.

15-26419

Library of Congress QL11.U6 no. 82
—— Copy 2. QL384.C8C57

AS 36 S4 CRINOIDEA

Clark, Austin Hobart, 1880–

A new Australian crinoid. By Austin H. Clark ...

(*In* U. S. National museum. Proceedings. Washington, 1911. 23½ᶜᵐ. vol. 38, p. 275–276)

1. Crinoidea. 2. Echinodermata—Australia.

11-15729

Library of Congress QL11.U55 vol. 38

AS 36 S4 CRINOIDEA

Clark, Austin Hobart, 1880–

A new European crinoid. By Austin Hobart Clark ...

(*In* U. S. National museum. Proceedings. Washington, 1911. 23½ᶜᵐ. vol. 38, p. 329–333)

1. Crinoidea. 2. Echinodermata—Europe.

11-15735

Library of Congress QL11.U55 vol. 38

QL Protozoa to Polyzoa Pam. 185 CRINOIDEA

Clark, Austin Hobart

A new species of crinoid (Ptilocrinus from the Pacific coast with a note on Bathycrinus.)

(Proc. U. S. Nat. Mus. Vol. XXXII, pp. 551–554, 1907)

AS 36 S4 CRINOIDEA

Clark, Austin Hobart, 1880–

A new unstalked crinoid from the Philippine Islands. By Austin Hobart Clark ...

(*In* U. S. National museum. Proceedings. Washington, 1912. 23½ᶜᵐ. v. 41, p. 171–173)

1. Crinoidea. 2. Echinodermata—Philippine Islands.

12-17771

Library of Congress QL11.U55 vol. 41

AS 36 S2 CRINOIDEA

Clark, Austin Hobart, 1880–

... Notes on the recent crinoids in the British museum, by Austin Hobart Clark ... Washington, Smithsonian institution, 1913.

1 p. l., 89 p. 24½ᶜᵐ. (Smithsonian miscellaneous collections. v. 61, no. 15)

Publication 2242.

1. Crinoidea. I. British museum (Nat. hist.) Dept. of zoology.

14-30048

Library of Congress QL11.S7 vol. 61
—— Copy 2. QL384.C8C69

AS 36 S4 CRINOIDEA

Clark, Austin Hobart, 1880–

... On a collection of unstalked crinoids made by the United States fisheries steamer "Albatross" in the vicinity of the Philippine Islands. By Austin Hobart Clark ...

(*In* U. S. National museum. Proceedings. Washington, 1911. 23½ᶜᵐ. v. 39, p. 529–563)

Scientific results of the Philippine cruise of the fisheries steamer "Albatross," 1907–10.—no. 8.

1. Crinoidea. 2. Echinodermata — Philippine Islands. 3. Albatross (Steamer)

11–21253

Library of Congress QL11.U55 vol. 39 [s20g2]

AS 36 S4 CRINOIDEA

Clark, Austin Hobart, 1880–

On the inorganic constituents of the skeletons of two recent crinoids. By Austin Hobart Clark ...

(*In* U. S. National museum. Proceedings. Washington, 1911. 23½ᶜᵐ. v. 39, p. 487–488)

1. Crinoidea.

11-21250

Library of Congress QL11.U55 vol. 39

AS 36 S4 CRINOIDEA

Clark, Austin Hobart, 1880–

On the origin of certain types of crinoid stems. By Austin Hobart Clark ...

(*In* U. S. National museum. Proceedings. Washington, 1911. 23½ᶜᵐ. vol. 38, p. 211–216)

1. Crinoidea.

11-15726

Library of Congress QL11.U55 vol. 38

AS 36 S4 CRINOIDEA

Clark, Austin Hobart, 1880–

The phylogenetic interrelationships of the recent crinoids. By Austin H. Clark ...

(*In* U. S. National museum. Proceedings. Washington, 1911. 23½ᶜᵐ. vol. 38, p. 115–118)

1. Crinoidea.

11-15593

Library of Congress QL11.U55 vol. 38

AS 36 S2 CRINOIDEA

Clark, Austin Hobart, 1880–

... A phylogenetic study of the recent crinoids, with special reference to the question of specialization through the partial or complete suppression of structural characters, by Austin H. Clark ... Washington, Smithsonian institution, 1915.

1 p. l., 67 p. 24½ᶜᵐ. (Smithsonian miscellaneous collections. v. 65, no. 10)

Publication 2369.

1. Crinoidea.

15-26530

Library of Congress QL11.S7
—— Copy 2. QL384.C8C64

AS 36 S2 CRINOIDEA

Clark, Austin Hobart, 1880–

Preliminary notice of a collection of recent crinoids from the Philippine Islands, by Austin Hobart Clark.

(*In* Smithsonian institution. Smithsonian miscellaneous collections. Washington, 1910. 24½ᶜᵐ. vol. LII (Quarterly issue, vol. V) p. 199–234)

Publication 1820.
Originally published December 23, 1908.

1. Crinoidea. 2. Echinodermata—Philippine Islands.

16-12710

Library of Congress QL11.S7 vol. 52
—— Copy 2.

AS 36 S4 CRINOIDEA

Clark, Austin Hobart, 1880–

The recent crinoids of the coasts of Africa. By Austin Hobart Clark ...

(*In* U. S. National museum. Proceedings. Washington, 1911. 23½ᶜᵐ. v. 40, p. 1–51)

1. Crinoidea. 2. Echinodermata—Africa.

11-31588

Library of Congress QL11.U55 vol. 40

AS 36 S2 CRINOIDEA

Clark, Austin Hobart, 1880–

... Sea-lilies and feather-stars (with 16 plates) by Austin H. Clark ... Washington, Smithsonian institution, 1921.

1 p. l., 43 p. 16 pl. on 9 l. 24½ᶜᵐ. (Smithsonian miscellaneous collections, v. 72, no. 7)

Publication 2620.

1. Crinoidea. I. Smithsonian institution. Publication 2620. II. Title.

21-26376

Library of Congress QL11.S7 vol. 72, no. 7 [7]

QL
636
A
CRINOIDEA

Clark, Hubert Lyman
Report on the sea-lilies, starfishes
brittle-stars and sea-urchins, in Australia
"Fisheries" Zool. Results of F. I. S.
"Endeavour" Vol. IV. pp. 1-123, pls.I-XLIV
Sydney 1916.

AS
36
S5
and
QL
Prot.-
Poly.Pam
186
CRINOIDEA   HAWAII

Clark, A. H.
Descriptions of new species of crinoids ....
from collections made by .. U.S. Fisheries
steamer "Albatross" at Hawaiian Islands ......
in U.S. Nat. Mus. Proc. xxxiv, pp. 209-239.
Washington, 1908.

QE
782
A762
CRINOIDEA, FOSSIL

Springer, Frank
American silurian crinoids.
Washington, Smithsonian Inst., 1926.
(publication 2871, 228p. pls.)

QL
1
U
and
QL
Prot.to
Polyzoa
Pam. 576
CRINOIDEA

Gislen, Torsten
Echinoderm studies. Academical Dissertation.
(Zool. Bidrag fron Uppsala, IX, 1924)

QL
5
M 98
CRINOIDEA   INDIAN OCEAN

Clark, Austin H.
Crinoidea.
IN The John Murray Expedition, 1933-34.
Sci. Repts., Vol. IV, no. 4, 1936, pp. 87-108.

QL
1
H2
CRINOIDEA FOSSIL

Springer, Frank, 1848-
... Cleiocrinus. By Frank Springer ... Cambridge,
Printed for the Museum, 1905.
(9)1-114 p. pl. 36cm. (Memoirs of the Museum of comparative zoölogy at Harvard college, vol. XXV, no. 2)

1. Crinoidea, Fossil.   1. Title.
A 19-1076
Title from Univ. of Chicago   QL1.H375 vol. 25, no. 2
Printed by L. C.   (3)

Q
115
M 46
CRINOIDEA

John, D. Dilwyn
Crinoidea.
Mawson, Sir Douglas   leader
British, Australian, and New Zealand
Antarctic Research Expedition, 1929-31
Reports, Series B, Vol. IV, Part 6, pp. 191-212.
1939.

AS
244
D
CRINOIDEA   JAPAN

Gislén, Torsten
Japanese Crinoids.
(Vid. Med. Dansk Nat. For. Kobenhavn, Bd. 83
1927.-Papers from Dr. Th. Mortensen's Pacific
Expedition 1914-16, No. 37)

AS
36
S4
CRINOIDEA FOSSIL

Springer, Frank, 1848-
The crinoid fauna of the Knobstone formation. By
Frank Springer ...
(In U. S. National museum. Proceedings. Washington, 1912. 23½cm.
v. 41, p. 175-208)

1. Crinoidea, Fossil.
12-17772
Library of Congress   Q11.U55 vol. 41

Q
115
M 46
CRINOIDEA   ANTARCTIC

Clark, Austin H.
Crinoidea.
Mawson, Sir Douglas   leader
Australasian Antarctic Expedition, 1911-14.
Scientific Reports, Series C, Vol. 8, Part 4,
1937.

AS
244
D
CRINOIDEA

Gislén, Torsten
Two new stalked Crinoids from the Kei
Islands.
(Vid. Med. Dansk Nat. For. Kobenhavn, Bd. 79
1925.-Papers from Dr. Th. Mortensen's Pacific Ex-
pedition, 1914-16, No. 26)

QE
782
S76
CRINOIDEA, FOSSIL

Springer, Frank
The crinoidea flexibilia.
Washington, Smithsonian Inst., 1920. 2v.
(publication 2501, with atlas, 76pls.)

GC
63
D 61
CRINOIDEA   ANTARCTIC

John, D. Dilwyn
Crinoidea
Discovery Committee
Discovery Reports, Vol. 18, 1940, pp. 125-
222. (published 1938)

QH
301
C3
CRINOIDEA.

Mortensen, Theodor, 1868-
... Studies in the development of crinoids, by Th. Mortensen ... Washington, Carnegie institution of Washington, 1920.
v, 94 p. illus., xxviii pl. 29cm. (On verso of t.-p.: Carnegie institution of Washington. Publication no. 294)
At head of title: Department of marine biology of the Carnegie institution of Washington, Alfred G. Mayor, director. Papers from the Department of marine biology of the Carnegie institution of Washington,
vol. XVI.
1. Crinoidea.
20-18049
Library of Congress   QH301.C3 vol. XVI
———— Copy 2.   QH301.C3 2d set
(9)

QE
782
S76
CRINOIDEA, FOSSIL

Springer, Frank
On the crinoid genus scyphocrinus
and its bulboud root camarocrinus.
Washington, Smithsonian Inst., 1917.
(publication 2440, 58p. pls.)

Q
115
S 56
CRINOIDEA   DUTCH EAST INDIES

Clark, Austin H.
The unstalked Crinoids of the Siboga Expedition.
Weber, Max
Uitkomsten...Nederlandsch Oost Indie, 1899-
1900...Siboga...Monographie XLIIb (livr. 83)
1918. 300 pp., 28 pl.

AS
36
S4
CRINOIDEA

Springer, Frank
Unusual forms of fossil crinoids.
Proc. U. S. Nat. Mus. Vol. 67, 1926, Art.
9.

QL
1
H2
CRINOIDEA, FOSSIL

Springer, Frank, 1848-
... Some new American fossil crinoids. By Frank
Springer ... With six plates. Cambridge, U. S. A.,
Printed for the Museum, 1911.
1 p. l., p. (117)-161. vi pl. 34cm. (Memoirs of the Museum of com-
parative zoology at Harvard college. vol. XXV, no. 3)
Each plate preceded by leaf with descriptive letterpress.

1. Crinoidea, Fossil.
A 21-448
Title from Univ. of Chicago   QL1f.H375 vol. 25
Printed by L. C.   (3)

Q
115
S 56
CRINOIDEA   DUTCH EAST INDIES

Döderlein, L.
Die gestielten Crinoiden der Siboga-Expedition.
Weber, Max
Uitkomsten...Nederlandsch Oost Indie, 1899-
1900...Siboga...Monographie XLIIa (livr. 37)
1907. 52 pp., 23 pl.

QE
1
F4
CRINOIDEA, FOSSIL

Slocom, Arthur Ware, 1860-
... New crinoids from the Chicago area. By Arthur
Ware Slocom ... Chicago, 1907.
1 p. l., p. 273-306. pl. LXXXII-LXXXVII, diagrs. 24½cm. (Field Columbian museum. Publication 123. Geological series. vol. II, no. 10)
Plates LXXXIV-LXXXVII preceded by guard sheet with descriptive letterpress.

1. Crinoidea, Fossil. 2. Paleontology—Illinois.

Library of Congress   QE1.F4   8-9042
(a20f2)

QL
1
H2
CRINOIDEA, FOSSIL

Springer, Frank, 1848-
... Uintacrinus: its structure and relations. By Frank
Springer ... Cambridge, Printed for the Museum, 1901.
(1), 89 p. viii pl. 35½cm. (Memoirs of the Museum of comparative
zoölogy at Harvard college, vol. XXV, no. 1)
Each plate accompanied by leaf with descriptive letterpress.

1. Crinoidea, Fossil.   1. Title.
A 19-1077
Title from Univ. of Chicago   QL1.H375 vol. 25, no. 1
Printed by L. C.   (3)

QL
1
H2

Crinoidea , Fossil

Wachsmuth, Charles, 1829–1896.

... The North American *Crinoidea camerata.* By Charles Wachsmuth and Frank Springer ... Cambridge, U. S. A., Printed for the Museum, 1897.

2 v. illus., tables, diagr. *and atlas of* LXXXIII pl. 35½ᶜᵐ. *(Added t.-p.:* Memoirs of the Museum of comparative zoology at Harvard college, vol. XX–XXI)

Each plate accompanied by leaf with descriptive letterpress.
Series title also at head of t.-p.

1. Crinoidea, Fossil. 2. Echinodermata—North America. I. Springer, Frank, 1848– joint author.

—— Another copy. QE782.W2

Title from Univ. of Chicago. QL1.H375 vol. 20–21
Printed by L. C. [3]

A 19–1079

AS
36
A6

CRINOIDEA, FOSSIL

Whitfield, Robert Parr, 1828–1910.

... Republication of descriptions of lower Carboniferous *Crinoidea* from the Hall collection now in the American museum of natural history, with illustrations of the original type specimens not heretofore figured. By R. P. Whitfield. [New York?] 1893.

cover-title, 37 p. illus., III pl. 36ᶜᵐ. (Memoirs of the American museum of natural history. vol. I, pt. I)

Each plate is accompanied by leaf with descriptive letterpress.
Issued September 15, 1893.

1. Crinoidea, Fossil. 2. Paleontology—Carboniferous.

* Library of Congress QH1.A43   6—322
—— —— Copy 2.

AS
36
S5

CRINOIDEA, FOSSIL

Wood, Elvira.

... A critical summary of Troost's unpublished manuscript on the crinoids of Tennessee, by Elvira Wood ... Washington, Govt. print. off., 1909.

xi, 150 p. front. (port.) 15 pl., diagr. 25ᶜᵐ. (Smithsonian institution. United States national museum. Bulletin 64)

Each plate preceded by leaf with letterpress.
Presented as thesis (M. A.) Columbia university, 1908. *cf.* p. vi.
"Literature": p. 113–115.

1. Crinoidea, Fossil. 2. Paleontology—Tennessee. I. Troost, Gerard, 1776–1850.   9—35535

Library of Congress Q11.U6 no. 64
—— —— Copy 2. QE782.T8
—— —— Copy 3.

AS
36
S2

CRINOIDEA, FOSSIL

Wood, Elvira.

On new and old Middle Devonic crinoids, by Elvira Wood.

(*In* Smithsonian institution. Smithsonian miscellaneous collections. Washington, 1905. 24½ᶜᵐ. vol. XLVII (Quarterly issue, vol. II) p. 56–84, illus., pl. XV–XVI)

Publication 1471.
Originally published August 6, 1904.

1. Crinoidea, Fossil. 2. Paleontology—Devonian.

Library of Congress Q11.S7 vol. 47   16–10993
—— —— Copy 2.
—— —— Separate. QE782.W7

AS
244
D

CRINOIDEA ST. HELENA

Gislén, Torsten

A small collection of Crinoids from St. Helena.

(Vid. Med. Dansk nat. For. i Kobenhavn, Bd. 93, 1932/33, pp. 475–485. Papers from Dr. Th. Mortensen's Pacific Expedition, 1914–16, No. 67)

QK
Bot.Pam.
1614

CRINUM ASIATICUM L.

Koshimizu, Takuji

Carpobiological Studies of Crinum asiaticum L. var. japonicum Bak.

(Reprinted from the Memoirs of the College of Science, Kyoto Imperial University, Series B. Vol. V, No. 2 (Article 9) 1930

Microfilm
No. 119

CRIOCERINAE

Heinze, E.

Ueber bekannte und neue Criocerinen.

(Stettiner Ent. Zeit., 104:101–109, 1943)

G
R 91

Crisp, D. J.

The influence of climatic changes on animals and plants.

(Geogr. Journal, 125(1):1–19, 1959)

[based on European studies]

QL
1
W 31

and

Z
7996.B61
C 93

Crispens, Charles G., Jr.

Quails and partridges of North America; a bibliography.

(University of Washington Publications in Biology, Vol. 20, 1960)

QL
1
C15

CRISSIIDAE.

Robertson, Alice, 1859–

... Embryology and embryonic fission in the genus *Crisia.* By Alice Robertson. Berkeley, The University press, 1903.

cover-title, p. 115–156. pl. XII–XIV (2 fold.) 27ᶜᵐ. (University of California publications. Zoology, v. I, no. 3)
Thesis (PH. D.)—Univ. of Calif.

1. Crissiidae. 2. Embryology—Polyzoa. 3. Fission.

A 11–2274

Title from Univ. of Calif.   Library of Congress

DU
Pac.Pam.
474

Criswell, Howard

Hawaii. A series of brief talks on the Territory radiocast from the University of Kentucky extension studio of radio station WHAS...as part of the general educational program of the University of Kentucky for 1931. 44 pp. mimeographed. 1931.

G
51
W 17

Critchley, L. G.

The explorations of von Mueller.

(Walkabout, Vol. 19(9):18–20, 1953)

QL
1
C 15

CRITHIDIA

McCulloch, Irene Agnes, 1886–

... A comparison of the life cycle of *Crithidia* with that of *Trypanosoma* in the invertebrate host, by Irene McCulloch. Berkeley, University of California press, 1919.

cover-title, p. [135]–190. illus., pl. 2–6. 27½ᶜᵐ. (University of California publications in zoology. v. 19, no. 4)
"Literature cited": p. 180–181.

1. [Crithidia] 2. Trypanosoma. I. Title.

A 19–1358

Title from Univ. of Calif.   Library of Congress
[s20b3]

QL
1
C 15

CRITHIDIA EURYOPHTHALMI

McCulloch, Irene Agnes, 1886–

... *Crithidia euryophthalmi,* sp. nov., from the hemipteran bug, *Euryophthalmus convivus* Stål, by Irene McCulloch ... Berkeley, University of California press, 1917.

cover-title, p. [75]–88. illus., 27½ᶜᵐ. (University of California publications in zoology. v. 18, no. 5)
"Literature cited": p. 88.

1. Crithidia euryophthalmi.

A 18–124

Title from Univ. of Calif.   Library of Congress

QL
1
C 15

CRITHIDIA LEPTOCORIDIS

McCulloch, Irene Agnes, 1886–

... An outline of the morphology and life history of *Crithidia leptocoridis,* sp. nov., by Irene McCulloch. Berkeley, University of California press, 1915.

cover-title, p. [1]–22. illus., pl. 1–4. 27ᶜᵐ. (University of California publications in zoology. v. 16, no. 1)
"Literature cited": p. 14.

1. Crithidia leptocoridis. 2. Box-elder bug. I. Title.

A 15–2125

Title from Univ. of Calif.   Library of Congress

QK
1
Jo

CRITHMUM MARITIMUM

Seemann, Berthold

On the estivation of Crithmum maritimum. In Journ. Bot. Vol. II, 1864, pp 5–8.

QL
Crus
Pam
#272

Crivelli, G. Balsamo, junk. author

Sui Crustacei etc.

See Taramelli, T.

QK
573
J 73

Croall, Alexander

Johnstone, William Grosart

The nature-printed British sea-weeds: a history, accompanied by figures and dissections, of the algae of the British Isles. By William Grosart Johnstone and Alexander Croall. Nature-printed by Henry Bradbury. In four volumes. London. Bradbury and Evans. 1859–1860. 8vo.

QL
1
T 64

CROCIDURA

Tokuda, M.

A bat and a new shrew from Koto-Sho (Botel-Tobago). By M. Tokuda and T. Kano.

(Ann. Zool. Japonenses, 15:427–432, 1936)

QK
Botany
Pam.1627

Crocker, A. A., Jr.

Fungoid Growths - The Science of Mycology. Compiled by the Junior Society of Natural Sciences, Cincinnati. 16 pp. 12mo.

DU
628.8
C 93

Crocker, Henry J.

Hawaiian Numerals: a Compilation of Unofficial Data Relating to the Type-set Stamps of the Kingdom of Hawaii, with a short history of the... stamps...1851–1866... San Francisco. Published by the Author. 1909. 108 pp. R8vo.

AS
36
A 65
CROCKER, TEMPLETON

Armstrong, John C.

The Caridea and Stomatopoda of the Second
Templeton Crocker-American Museum Expedition
to the Pacific Ocean.

(American Mus. Novitates, No. 1137, 1941)

QL
1
F
CROCODILES NEW GUINEA

Schmidt, Karl P.

Notes on New Guinea Crocodiles. Reports on
Results of the Crane Pacific Expedition.

(Field Museum of Natural History, Publication, Zoological Series, Vol. XVIII, pp. 167-172,
Plate VII, 1932)

QK
1
A 75
Croizat, Leon

New species of Croton L. from New Guinea.

(Jour. Arnold Arboretum, Vol. 23, 1942, p.
369-376)

AP
2
S 35
Crocker, Templeton

Kuns, A. H.

The Crocker Expedition of the American
Museum of Natural History.

(Science, vol.84, pp. 220-221. 1936)

QL
Amphibia
and
Reptilia
Pam
79
CROCODILIA PALAU ISLANDS

Motoda, Shigeru

On crocodiles of Pelew.

(In Japanese, pp. 131-138 from ?)

QK
Bot.Fam.
2396
Croizat, Leon

Notes on Fijian Euphorbiaceae.

(Occ. Papers, Bernice P. Bishop Museum, Vol.
18, No. 3, 1944, pp. 69-71)

AS
36
C 3
"Crocker, Templeton"

The Templeton Crocker Expedition of the
California Academy of Sciences, 1932.

(California Academy of Sciences, Proceedings
Fourth Series, Vol. 21, Nos. 1-7, 1937)

GN
2.I
A 62
Crocombe, R. G.

A modern Polynesian cargo cult.

(Man, Vol. 61, No. 28, 1961)

[in the Cook Islands]

QK
Bot.
Pam.
2359
Croizat, Leon

Notes on Polynesian Glochidion and Phyllanthus.

(Occ. Papers, Bernice P. Bishop Museum, Vol.
17, 1943, No. 16, pp.207-214)

Crocker, Templeton

See

Templeton Crocker Expedition, 1933 (on board
yacht Zaca)

DU
1
H 67
Crocombe, Ron

Early Polynesian authors - the example of
Ta'unga. By Ron and Marjorie Crocombe.

(Historical Studies, Australia and New
Zealand, Vol. 10(37), 1961:92-93)

QH
84
C 94
Croizat, Léon

Panbiogeography, or an introductory synthesis of zoogeography, phytogeography, and geology;
with notes on evolution, systematics, ecology,
anthropology, etc. Vols. I, IIa, IIb. 1958
8vo. Wheldon and Wesley. Codicote, England.
[vols. IIa and IIb published by the author at
Caracas, Venezuela] 1018; 1731 pages.

CN
671.M5
C 93
Crockett, Charis

The house in the rain forest. With illustrations. Houghton Mifflin Company. Boston.
1942c. 8vo. x + 300 pp.

GN
477.4
C 93
Crocombe, Ronald Gordon

Land tenure in the Cook Islands. A thesis
submitted for the degree of Doctor of Philosophy
in the Australian National University. July
1961. folio mimeographed. 366 pp.

QK
1
B 97-b 3
Croizat, L.

A significant new species from New Guinea:
Euphorbia euonymoclada Croiz., n. sp.

(Bull. Jardin Bot., Buitenzorg, Ser. 3, Vol
16, 1940, pp. 351-357)

QL
Rept.&
Batrach.
Pam
#22
CROCODILES,FOSSIL

Mook, Charles C.

A new Crocodilian from Mongolia. Am.
Mus. Nat. His. Nov. #117. 1924.

Croizat, L.

Manual of phytogeography or an account
of plant dispersal throughout the world.
The Hague. 1952. 587 pp. cloth,$11.85

UH has

no need for second copy

QL
Fishes
Pam.
457
Croker, Richard S.

Glossary of Japanese fisheries terms.

(General Headquarters, Supreme Commander
for the Allied Powers, Natural Resources Section
Report No. 83, Tokyo, 1946)

QL
Amphib.
and
Reptilia
Pam.
72
CROCODILIA BORNEO

Raven, Harry C.

Crocodiles in Borneo.

(The Chicago Naturalist, Vol. 9:12-16, 1946)

QK
936
T 85
Croizat, Leon

New Euphorbiaceae from the Island of Mauritius.

(Tropical Woods, No. 77, 1944, pp. 13-18)

QC
884
Or
C 94
Croll, James.

Climate and Time in their Geological
relations. A theory of secular changes
of the Earth's climate.

London:Daldy,Isbister. 1875. pp.577.
charts and plates,8.

QC
884
C 94

Croll, James.

Discussions on Climate and Cosmology

N.Y.:Appleton. 1886. pp.327. 1 chart.

G
161
H

Crone, G. R.   translator

The voyages of Cadamosto and other documents on western Africa in the second half of the fifteenth century.

(Works issued by the Hakluyt Society, Second Series, No. 80, 1937)

GN
Ethn.Pam.
2894

Crook, A.R.

The origin of the Cahokia mounds

(Bulletin Illinois State Museum) 1922. 26 pp.

QE
Geology
Pam
749

Croll, James

On ocean currents. III. On the physical cause of ocean-currents. From Philosophical Mag. Oct. 1871.

G
51
W 17

Cronin, Bernhard

Pariah of our wild creatures.

(Walkabout, 15(1):11-14, 1953)

[the dingo, or Australian dog]

AM
Mus.Pam.
346

Crook, A. R.

Scientific activities of the Illinois State Museum of Natural History.

(Trans. Ill. State Acad. of Sci, 2nd ann. meeting, Feb. 20, 1909. pp. 77-82)

Cromar, J.

Jook of the islands; early days in the South Seas. 1935.

UH has

F
856
C 94

Cronise, Titus Fey.

The natural wealth of California...A detailed description of each county ...by Titus Fey Cronise.

San Francisco, H.H. Bancroft & co., 1868. 696p.

1. Arrow-heads. 2. Indians of North America—Soc. life & cust.

S 15-326 a

Library of Congress   Q11.S66 1871
Library, Smithsonian   Institution

AS
36
S1

Crook, George, 1828-1890.

Indian mode of making arrow-heads and obtaining fire. Extract of a letter from General George Crook ...

(In Smithsonian institution. Annual report. 1871. Washington, 1873. 231ᵈ. p. 420)

AP
2
N 4

Crombie, A. C.

Rat plagues in western Queensland.

(Nature, 155:803-804, 1945)

QC
721
C 94

Cronkite, E. P.   and others

Some effects of ionizing radiation on human beings: a report on the Marshallese and Americans accidentally exposed to radiation from fallout and a discussion of radiation injury in the human being. U. S. Atomic Energy Commission. July 1956. 106 pp. 4to.

QE
1
N 54

Crook, Keith A. W.

Burial metamorphic rocks from Fiji.

(N.Z. Jour. of Geol. and Geophysics, Vol. 6(5):681-704, 1963)

QL
5
B 61

Cromwell, Townsend

Circulation in a meridional plane in the Central Equatorial Pacific.

(Journal of Marine Research, Vol. 12(2):196-213, 1953)

QC
1
B 87

Cronkite, E. P.   and others

Twelve-month postexposure survey on Marshallese exposed to fallout radiation.

(Brookhaven National Laboratory... BNL 384 (T-71) August, 1955)

GN
671.M3
S 54

Crook, William Pascoe

(manuscript on the Marquesas, "original manuscript, writier unknown" in the Mitchell Library. The handwriting does not seem to be that of Rev. Crook... says George M. Sheahan, Jr. IN
Sheahan, George M., Jr.
Marquesan source materials. Part II: pp. 114-183

QL
752
U 58

Cromwell, Townsend

Mid-Pacific oceanography, January through March, 1950.

(Fish and Wild Life Service, U.S.Dept. Int. Special Sci. Rept.-Fisheries, No. 54, 1951)

AM
101
I
N. 17.

Crook, A. R

A History of the Illinois State Museum of Natural History
Springfield 1907.

Crook, William Pascoe

(Marquesan dictionary and grammar) Compiled in the 18th century (1897-1899) 91 pages.

London Missionary Society

AP
2
S 41

CROMWELL CURRENT

Knauss, John A.

The Cromwell current...

(Scientific American, 204:105-116, 1961)

AM
Mus
Pam
97

Crook, A   R

Its fifty years of service. Illinois State Museum, 1877-1927. Springfield, 1927.

Crook, William Pascoe

[The Marquesas Islands]

Ms, a copy in Mitchell Library, Sydney

GN
635.1
C 94

Crooke, W.

     The popular religion and folk-lore of northern India. In two volumes. A new edition, revised and illustrated. Westminster. Archibald Constable & Co. 1896. 8vo. pp.viii + 294;359.

QR
41
Cr
C95

Crookshank, Edgar M.

     A text-book of bacteriology including the etiology and prevention of infective diseases and a short account of yeast and moulds, haematozoa, and psorosperms. Fourth edition.

London, 1896. ppxxx, 715.

GN
Pam
1774

Cross, K. Stuart

     On a numerical determination of the relative positions of certain biological types in the evolutionary scale and of the relative values of various cranial measurements and indices as criteria. From Proc. Royal Soc. Edinburgh, v.31, pt.1, n.4.

GN
Eth
Pam
#604

Crooke, W.

     Rites at the accession of a Raja in India, ex Man, no. 3, Jan., 1921.

QH
104
U-b

CROP ZONES
Merriam, Clinton Hart.

     ... Life zones and crop zones of the United States. By C. Hart Merriam ... Washington, Govt. print. off., 1898.
79 p. front. (double map) 23cm. (U. S. Dept. of agriculture. Division of biological survey. Bulletin 10)

1. Crop zones. 2. Life zones.

Agr 6-832 Revised

Library, U. S. Dept. of   Agriculture

QH
205
C95

Cross, M. I and Cole, Martin J.

Modern microscopy. A handbook for beginners. London 1895 8vo. pp 182

P. 14.

Oct.3.96

QK
531
C 94

Crookes, Marguerite

     New Zealand ferns. Incorporating illustrations and original work by H. B. Dobbie. 6th edition. Auckland. Whitcombe and Tombs Ltd. 1963. xxiv + 407 pp. 8vo.

QK
1
L 2

Crosby, Charles Steele
Burkill, I. H.

     Flora of Vavau, one of the Tonga Islands, by I. H. Burkill; with a short account of its vegetation by Charles Steele Crosby.

(Jour. Linn. Soc., Botany, 35:20-65, 1901)

vegetation, by Crosby, pp. 21-24

QE
76

Cross, Whitman, 1854–

     ... Lavas of Hawaii and their relations, by Whitman Cross. Washington, Govt. print. off., 1915.
97 p. plates, fold. map, fold. diagr. 29cm. (U. S. Geological survey. Professional paper 88)

1. Lava.

G S 15-339

Library, U. S. Geological   Survey (200) B no. 88
——— Copy 2.

QK
520
A 51

Crookes, Marguerite

     On the lava fields of Rangitote.

(American Fern Journal, 50(4):257-263, 1960)

DU
Missions
Pam. 5

Crosby, E. Theodora

     A Day in Kusaie. Woman's Board of Missions, Leaflet, No. 3. Issued by Committee on Junior Work. 1891. 16mo. 15 pp.

QE
Geol.Pam
307

Cross, Whitman

     An occurence of Trachyte on the island of Hawaii.

(Journal of Geology, Vol. XII, No. 6, Sept.-Oct., 1904, pp.510-523)

QE
76
B

(U.S.Geol. Survey, Professional Papers)

AS
750
N 56

Crookes, Marguerite W.

     A revised and annotated list of New Zealand Filicinae.

(Trans. and Proc. of the R. Soc. of New Zealand, Vol. 77:209-225, 1949)

AM
101
NY

CROSBY BROWN COLLECTION
New York Metropolitan Museum

     Hand-book No. 13. Catalogue of the Crosby Brown collection of musical instruments of savage tribes and semi-civilized peoples. Part 2. Oceania.

New York, 1907, pp 71.

QE
461
C95

Cross, Whitman and others

     Quantitative classification of igneous rocks based on chemical and mineral characters with a systematic nomenclature.....

Chicago, 1903. 8vo. pp 286.

AS
36
B1
566

Crookes, *Sir* William, 1832–
Diamonds. By William Crookes, F. R. S.

(*In* Smithsonian institution. Annual report. 1897. Washington, 1898. 23½cm. p. 219-235)

"Printed in Nature, no. 1449, vol. 56, August 5, 1897."

1. Diamonds.

S 15-954

Library of Congress   Q11.S66 1897
Library, Smithsonian   Institution

DU
Pac.Pam.
291

Crosby, E. E.

     The persecutions in Tonga, as narrated by onlookers and now taking place, 1886. (compiled from various newspapers and magazines, 1885-86) 74 pp. 8vo. (Printed in London)

AS
36
S2

CROSSBILLS
Bent, Arthur Cleveland, 1866–

     ... A new subspecies of crossbill from Newfoundland, by A. C. Bent ... Washington, Smithsonian institution, 1912.
1 p. l., 3 p. 24½cm. (Smithsonian miscellaneous collections, v. 60, no. 15) Publication 2158.

1. Crossbills. 2. Birds—Newfoundland.

12-29926

Library of Congress   Q11.S7 vol. 60, no. 15

AS
36
S1

Crookes, *Sir* William, 1832–
Sir William Crookes on psychical research. By Sir William Crookes.

(*In* Smithsonian institution. Annual report. 1899. Washington, 1901. 23½cm. p. 185-205)

"From Report of the British association for the advancement of science, 1898. Bristol meeting."

1. Psychical research. 2. Thought transference.

S 15-1025

Library of Congress   Q11.S66 1899
Library, Smithsonian   Institution

DU
Pac
Pam
#237

Crosby, E. Theodora

     The Caroline Islands and their people extract, (no name given) 1899, pp. 10-19

AS
36
S1

CROSSBOW
Balfour, Henry, 1863–

     The origin of West African crossbows ... By Henry Balfour, M. A.

(*In* Smithsonian institution. Annual report. 1910. Washington, 1911. 23½cm. p. 635-650. illus, pl.)

"Reprinted ... from the Journal of the African society, London; no. 32, vol. 8, July, 1909."

GN
Pam
783

separate

1. Crossbow.

11-31585

Library of Congress   Q11.S66 1910

GN
Ethn.
Pam.
3732

CROSS-CULTURE SURVEY

Murdock, George P.

The cross-cultural survey.

(Reprinted from American Sociological Review,
Vol. V(3):361-370, 1940)

QL
401
J 85

Crosse, Joseph Charles Hippolyte

Description d'un Helix de la Nouvelle-
Calédonie. By H. Crosse and S. Marie.

(Jour. de Conchyl., 15:58-60, 1867)

QL
Mollusk
Pam
517

(Joseph Charles Hippolyte)

Crosse, H.   and Fischer, P

Etude sur la machoire et l'armature linguale
des cylindrellidae et de quelques genres voisins
sous le rapport conchyliologique.

QL
401
J 85

Crosse, Hippolyte

Additions à la faune malacologique de la
Nouvelle-Calédonie et ses dépendances.

(Jour. de Conchyl., Tome 43:79-82, 1895;
Tome 44:48-50, 1896; Tome 46:20-21, 1898)

QL
401
J 85

Crosse, Joseph Charles Hippolyte

Description d'espèces nouvelles des archipels
Samoa et Viti.

(Jour. de Conchyl., 15:297-302, 1867)

QL
Mollusk
Pam
515

(Joseph Charles Hippolyte)

Crosse, H

Faune malacologique du lac tanganyika. From
Jour. d. Conch. 1881.

QL
Mol
Pam
#113
C

Crosse, H.

Description de Coquilles fossiles ...
ex (?) Paris, Impreimerie de Mme. Ve
Bouchard-Huzard, due de l'Eperon, 5.
pp.369-376, n.d.

QL
401
J 85

Crosse, H.   (Joseph Charles Hippolyte)

Descriptions d'espèces nouvelles de l'Archipel calédonien.

(Jour. de Conchyl., 10:405-408, 1862)

also 11:178-224, 1863

QL
401
J 85

Crosse, Hippolyte

Faune malacologique terrestre et fluviatile
de la Nouvelle-Calédonie et de ses dépendances.

(Jour. de Conchyl., Tome 42:161-473, 1894;
Vol. 43:79-82, 1896; 44:48-50, 1896; 46:20-21,
1898)

partial copies also at QL Moll. Pam 812 and
Bibliofilm 47

QL
401
J 85

Crosse, Joseph Charles Hippolyte

Description de coquilles terrestres nouvelles.

(Jour. de Conchyl., 14:53-61, 1866)

doubtful provenance- Solomon Islands?

QL
401
J 85

Crosse, H.

Description d'un Placostylus inédit, provenant de la Nouvelle-Calédonie.

(Jour. de Conchyl., Tome 34:163-165, 1886)

QL
Mollusk
Pam
530

(Joseph Charles Hippolyte)

Crosse, H

Faune malacologique terrestre et fluviatile
de l'île de Saint Domingue.

Paris, Crosse, 1891.   143p. pls.
[Jour. d. Conchyliologie, 1891]

QL
401
J 85

Crosse, H.   (Joseph Charles Hippolyte)

Description d'espèces nouvelles provenant
des îles Gambier.

(Jour. de Conchyl., 13:217-224, 1865)

QL
401
J 85

Crosse, H.   (Joseph Charles Hippolyte)

Description d'un Rimula de la Nouvelle-Calédonie, accompagnée d'observations sur la valeur
du genre, et du catalogue des espèces vivantes.

(Jour. de Conchyl., 14:167-212, 1866)

QL
401
J 85

Crosse, H.

Note préliminaire sur la faune malacologique
terrestre et fluviatile de la Nouvelle-Zélande
et sur ses affinités.

(Jour. de Conchyl., Tome 41:209-219, 1893)

QL
401
J 85

Crosse, Joseph Charles Hippolyte

Description d'un genre nouveau et de plusieurs espèces inédites provenant de la Nouvelle-
Calédonie.

(Jour. de Conchyl., 15:312-321, 1867)

QL
401
J 85

Crosse, H.   (Joseph Charles Hippolyte)

Description d'une Columbelle de la Nouvelle-
Calédonie.

(Jour. de Conchyl., 13:164-208, 1865)

QL
Mollusk
Pam
513

(Joseph Charles Hippolyte)

Crosse, H

Note sur le nouveau genre livinhacia. From
Jour. d. Conch. 1889.

QL
401
J 85

Crosse, Joseph Charles Hippolyte

Description d'un genre nouveau et de plusieurs espèces inédites provenant de la Nouvelle-
Calédonie.

(Jour. de Conchyl., 15:177-194, 1867)

QL
401
J 85

Crosse, H.

Diagnoses molluscorum Novae Caledoniae inco-
larum.

(Jour. de Conchyl., Vol. 35:303-305, 1887)

QL
401
J 85

Crosse, Joseph Charles Hippolyte

Note sur les mollusques operculés terrestres
des îles Pelew ou Palaos.

(Jour. de Conchyl., 14:346-350, 1866)

QL
401
J 85

Crosse, H(ippolyte)

    Note sur quelques mollusques terrestres des Iles Philippines, encore peu répandus dans les collections.

    (Jour. de Conchyl. Tome 46:5-19, 1898)

AP
2
N 4

Crossland, Cyril

    Barrier reefs of Tahiti and Moorea.

    (Nature, Tome 120, 1927, pp. 618-619)

DT
39
C 95

Crossland, Cyril

    Desert and water gardens of the Red Sea, being an account of the natives and the shore formations of the coast. Cambridge. University Press. 1913. R8vo. pp.xv+158.

QL
Mollusk
Pam
511

(Joseph Charles Hippolyte)
Crosse, H

    Note sur une deformation d'helix pomatia, Linne, recemment observee.

QE
Geology
Pam
708

Crossland, Cyril

    The coral reefs of Pemba Island and of the East African mainland. From Proc. Cambridge Philo. Soc., v.12, pt.1.

QL
Protozoa
to
Polyzoa
Pam
213

Crossland, Cyril

    The ecology and deposits of the Cape Verde marine fauna. From Proc. Zool. Soc. London, 1905.

QL
Mol
Pam
#112

(Joseph Charles Hippolyte)
Crosse, H. and Fischer, P.

    L'etude des Mollusques ....., ex Journ. de Conch., Paris, le 1er janvier, 1867.

G
7
R 91

Crossland, Cyril

    The Coral Reefs of Tahiti Compared with the Great Barrier Reefs.

    (In The Geographical Journal, Vol. 77, pp. 395-396, April, 1931)

GC
Oceanography
Pam. 27

Crossland, Cyril

    The Expedition to the South Pacific of the S. Y. "St. George": Marine ecology and coral formations in the Panama region, the Galápagos and Marquesas Islands, and the atoll of Napuka.

    (Trans. Roy. Soc. Edinburgh, Vol. 55, 1927, pp. 531-554)

QL
402
G 23
locked
case

(Joseph Charles Hippolyte)
Crosse, H.

    Notice sur les Bulimes de la Nouvelle-Calédonie et description de deux espèces nouvelles. (Extrait de la Revue et Magasin de Zoologie, No. 2, 1855.)

    (Garrett collection of papers on conchology, Vol. 19)

QL
1
L-j

over

Crossland, Cyril

    Coral Reefs of Tahiti, Moorea, and Rarotonga.

    (IN The Journal of the Linnean Society: Zoology, Vol. 36, No. 248, 1928) pp 577-620

QL
1
L-j
and
QE
Geol.Pam
1025

Crossland, Cyril

    Further notes on the Tahitian Barrier Reef and lagoons.

    (Journal of the Linnean Society of London, Zoology, Vol.XL, 1939, pp. 459-474.)

QL
402
G 23
locked
case
QL
Mollusca
Pam
114

(Joseph Charles Hippolyte)
Crosse, H.

    Observations sur le genre Cone et description de trois especes nouvelles avec un catalogue alphabetique des cones actuellement connus. (Extrait de la Revue et Magasin de Zoologie, 1858, Nos. 3-4, 32 pp.)

    (Garrett collection of papers on conchology, Vol. 19)

GN
2.S
T 12
and
QL
Prot.-Poly
Pam
197

Crossland, Cyril

    The corals of the Papeete Museum.

    (Bull. Soc. d'Etudes Oceaniennes, No. 16: 147-152, 1926)

AS
122
L-p

over

Crossland, Cyril

    Further notes on the Tahitian barrier reef and lagoons.

    (Proc. of the Linnean Soc. of London, 150th Session, 1937/38, pp. 77v)

AS
122
E

Crosse, Rosalind

    Studies on Periodicity in plant growth. Pt. 2. Correlation in root and shoot growth. in Roy. Soc. Edin. Proc. XXXIV, pp. 85-102; XXXV, pp. 46-63, illus.

GN
2.S
T 12

Crossland, Cyril

    Croissance des coraux.

    (Bull. Soc. d'Etudes Oceaniennes, No. 12: 41-42, 1926)

    [effect of fresh water on corals]

G
7
R91

Crossland, Cyril

    The island of Tahiti. In Geographical Journal, v. 71, n.6, 1928. pp. 561-585

QL
1
Z 88 t

Crosskey, R. W.

    A revision of the genus Pygophora Schiner (Diptera: Muscidae)

    (Trans. of Zool. Soc. of London, Vol. 29 (6):393-551, 1962)

QL
1
A 94

Crossland, Cyril

    The cultivation of the mother-of-pearl oyster in the Red Sea.

    (Australian Jour. of Marine and Freshwater Research, Vol. 8(2):111-130, 1957)

QL
Prot. to
Poly.613

Crossland, Cyril

    Marine ecology and coral formations in the Panama region, the Galapagos and Marquesas Islands, and the atoll of Napuka. (The Expedition to the South Pacific of the S. Y. "St. George")

    (Trans. of the R. Soc. of Edinburgh, Vol. 55, 1927, pp. 531-554)

QL
Protozoa
to
Polyzoa
Pam
209

Crossland, Cyril

The marine fauna of Zanzibar and British East Africa, from collections made by Cyril Crossland in the years 1901 and 1902. - The Polychaeta. Part III. With which is incorporated the account of Stanley Gardiner's collection made in the Maldive archipelago in the year 1899. From Proc. Zool. Soc. London, 1904.

QL
Protozoa
to
Polyzoa
Pam
208

Crossland, Cyril

Polychaeta of tropical east Africa, the Red Sea, and Cape Verde islands collected by Cyril Crossland, and of the Maldive archipelago collected by Professor Stanley Gardiner. From Proc. Zool. Soc. London, 1924.

QL
Protozoa
to
Polyzoa
Pam
212

Crossland, Cyril

Reports on the marine biology of the Sudanese Sea, from collections made by Cyril Crossland, communicated ... by W. A. Herdman. From Linnean Soc. Journ. Zool. v.31, n.203, 1907.

QK
Botany
Pam
1363

Crossland, Cyril

Note on the dispersal of mangrove seedlings. From Annals of Botany, v.17, n. 55, 1903.

QE
Geology
Pam
707

Crossland, Cyril

A privately printed supplement to the "Physical description of Khor Dongonab, Red Sea." From Linn. Soc. Journ. Zool. v.31, p. 208, 1911.

DU
Pac.Pam.
483

Crossland, Cyril

Tahiti.

(Blackwood's Magazine, Vol. 225, pp. 126-33, January, 1929)

QL
1
Z

Crossland, Cyril

Notes on the Ecology of Reef Builders of Tahiti.

(In Proceedings of the Zoological Society of London, 1928, pp. 717-736)

AP
2
N 4

Crossland, Cyril

Recession and age of the Tahitian coral reefs.

(Nature, Vol. 124, 1929, p. 576)

QL
Mollusk
Pam
495

Crossland, Cyril

Warning coloration in a nudibranch mollusc and in a chameleon. From Proc. Zool. Soc. London, 1911.

QL
Prot.-
Poly.
Pam.667

Crossland, C(yril)

On Forskal's collection of corals in the Zoological Museum of Copenhagen.

(Spolia Zoologica Musei Hauniensis I; Skrifter Univ. Zool. Mus., København, I, 1941)

AP
2
N 4

Crossland, Cyril

Recession of the Tahitian coral reefs.

(Nature, Vol. 119, 1927, p. 597)

AS
244
D 19

CROSSLAND, CYRIL

Kramp, P. L.

Medusae collected in the eastern tropical Pacific by Cyril Crossland in 1924-1925.

(Videnskabelige Meddelelser, Bind 118:1-6, 1956)

Crossland, Cyril

On Forskal's collection of corals in the Zoological Museum of Copenhagen.   1941

UH has

QL
1
Z
and also
QL Pam
Prot.Poly.
561

Crossland, Cyril

The Reduced Building- power and other Variation in the Astrean Corals of Tahiti, with a Note on Herpetolitha limax and Fungia spp.

(In Proceedings of the...Zoological Society of London, 1931, Part II, pp. 351-392, plates I-XXII)

DU
620
P 22

Crossley, Randolph

The ride of the paniolos. (as told by Len Hughes)

(Paradise of the Pacific, 69th Holiday edition, for 1958; issued 1957:48-49)

QL
Protozoa
to
Polyzoa
Pam
211

Crossland, Cyril

On the marine fauna of Zanzibar and British East Africa, from collections made by Cyril Crossland in the years 1901 and 1902 - Polychaeta Part II. From Proc. Zool. Soc. London, 1903.

AS
618
N

Crossland, Cyril

Reef corals of the South African coast.

(Annals of the Natal Museum, Vol. XI(2):169-205, pl. 5-14, 1948)

QK
110
N 56

CROSSOMATACEAE

Small, John Kunkel

Crossosomataceae.

IN North American flora, Vol. 22, Part 3, 1908, pp. 231-232.

QL
Protozoa
to
Polyzoa
Pam
210

Crossland, Cyril

Polychaeta of the Maldive archipelago from the collections made by J. Stanley Gardiner in 1899. From Proc. Zool. Soc. London, 1904, vol. i.

QE
Geology
Pam
713

Crossland, Cyril

Reports on the marine biology of the Sudanese Red Sea - XVIII. A physical description of Khor Dongonab, Red Sea... suppl. to "Recent History of the Coral Reefs of the Red Sea". From Linnean Soc. Journ. Zool, v.31, n.208, 1911.

DU
620
P

The crossroads of the Pacific.

(Paradise of the Pacific, Vol. 32, No. 10, 1919, pp. 5-9)

AS 36
C 53

CROTALIDAE

Gloyd, Howard K.

A new Crotalid snake from Kume Shima, Riu Kiu Islands.

(Bull. of the Chicago Academy of Sciences, Vol. 10(8):123-134, 1955)

GN 2.M
A

CROW INDIANS.

Lowie, Robert Harry, 1883–

... Social life of the Crow Indians. By Robert H. Lowie. New York, The Trustees, 1912.

1 p. l., 179-253. 24ᶜᵐ. (Anthropological papers of the American museum of natural history. vol. IX, pt. II)

Bibliography: p. 247.

1. Crow Indians. 2. Indians of North America—Soc. life & cust.

15-3019

Library of Congress   GN2.A27 vol. 9, pt. 2

G 3
N 27

Crowder, William

Crabs and crablike curiosities of the sea.

(National Geographic Magazine, 54:55-72,1928)

QK 1
A 75

CROTON

Croizat, Leon

New species of Croton L. from New Guinea.

(Jour. Arnold Arboretum, Vol. 23, 1942, p. 369-376)

GN 2.M
A

CROW INDIANS.

Lowie, Robert Harry, 1883–

... Societies of the Crow, Hidatsa and Mandan Indians. By Robert H. Lowie. New York, The Trustees, 1913.

2 p. l., p. 145-358. illus. 24ᶜᵐ. (Anthropological papers of the American museum of natural history. vol. XI, pt. III)

1. Indians of North America — Soc. life & cust. 2. Crow Indians. 3. Hidatsa Indians. 4. Mandan Indians.

15-3010

Library of Congress   GN2.A27 vol. 11, pt. 3

QL 362
C 95

Crowder, William

Dwellers of the Sea and Shore. Drawings and Photographs by the Author. New York, The Macmillan Company. 1923. 8vo. xv + 333 pp.

AS 162
M 36

CROTON

Leandri, M. J.

Les "Croton" de Madagascar et des iles voisines.

(Annales du Musee Colonial de Marseille, Annee 47, Ser. 5, Vol. 7, 1939, pp. 1-100)

GN 2.M
A

CROW INDIANS.

Lowie, Robert Harry, 1883–

... The sun dance of the Crow Indians. By Robert H. Lowie. New York, The Trustees, 1915.

1 p. l., p. 1-50. illus. 24ᶜᵐ. (Anthropological papers of the American museum of natural history. vol. XVI, pt. I)

1. Sun-dance. 2. Crow Indians.

17-28722

Library of Congress   GN2.A27 vol. 16, pt. 1

QE 1
J 85

Crowell, John C.

Submarine canyons bordering central and southern California.

(Journal of Geology, Vol. 60:58-83, 1952)

DU 620
P

CROTONS

Neal, Marie C.

Fascinating crotons. Watercolor by Marian Mastick.

(Paradise of the Pacific, pp. 55, 102, Annual Holiday Edition 1955)

GN 2m
A

CROW INDIANS.

Lowie, Robert Harry, 1883–

... The Tobacco society of the Crow Indians, by Robert H. Lowie. New York, The Trustees, 1919.

1 p. l., p. 101-200. illus. 24ᶜᵐ. (Anthropological papers of the American museum of natural history. vol. XXI, pt. II)

Bibliography: p. 200.

1. Crow Indians. 2. Tobacco. 3. Indians of North America—Societies. I. Title.

20-16771

Library of Congress   GN2.A27 vol. XXI, pt. II.

[8]

GN Pam
1343

Crowfoot, J. W.

Survivals among the Kappadokian Kizilbash (Bektash). From Anthrop. Instit. Journ. v. 30, 1900. 14p.

GN 1
An

Crotty, John

First dictionary of Tchaga language, Central Highlands, New Guinea.

(Anthropos, 46:933-963, 1951)

GN 2M
FI

CROW INDIANS

Simms, Stephen Chapman, 1864–

... Traditions of the Crows, by S. C. Simms ... Chicago, 1903.

2 p. l., [281]-324 p. 24½ᶜᵐ. (Field Columbian museum. Publication 85. Anthropological series. vol. II, no. 6)

1. Crow Indians. 2. Indians of North America—Legends.

4-6731

Library of Congress   GN2.F4

QL 671
I

Crowfoot, W. M.

Notes on the breeding habits of certain sea birds frequenting Norfolk Island and the adjoining islets.

(Ibis, Ser. 5, Vol. 3, 1885, pp. 263-270)

AP 2
S 41

Crow, James F.

Ionizing radiation and evolution.

(Scientific American, 201(3):138-176, 1959)

CROW INDIANS   LEGENDS

see

LEGENDS   CROW INDIANS

Crowl, Philip A. and Edmund G. Love.

United States Army in World War II: The war in the Pacific: seizure of the Gilberts and Marshalls. Office of the Chief of Military History, Department of the Army. Washington. 1955.

UH has ?

GN 2M
A

CROW INDIANS.

Lowie, Robert Harry, 1883–

... Myths and traditions of the Crow Indians, by Robert H. Lowie ... New York, The Trustees, 1918.

1 p. l., 308 p. 24½ᶜᵐ. (Anthropological papers of the American museum of natural history, vol. XXV, pt. I)

Bibliography: p. 305-306.

1. Crow Indians. 2. Indians of North America—Legends. I. Title.

19-6009

Library of Congress   GN2.A27 vol. XXV, pt. I.

[5]

DU Pac.Pam.
830

Crowder, Roy V.

Hawaii that has all things, age cannot wither her, nor custom stale her infinite variety.

(Nature Magazine, Vol. 13(6):363-370, 1929)

G 51
W 17

Crowley, F. K.

The further settlement of Australia.

(Australian Geographical Walkabout Magazine, Vol. 21(10):10-18, October, 1955)

[climatic and geographic conditions]

QL
1
M 62

Crowley, T. E.

A monograph of the African land snails of the genus Limicolariopsis d'Ailly. (Mollusca, Achatinidae) By T. E. Crowley and T. Pain.

(Zoologische Wetenschappen, K. Mus. voor Midden Afrika, No. 101, 1961)

AS
720.T
R

Crowther, W. E. L. H.

The development of the guano trade from Hobart Town in the fifties and sixties.

(R. Soc. of Tasmania, Papers and Proc., 1938, pp. 213-220)

G
7
R 91

CROZET ISLANDS

Tilman, H. W.

Voyage to the Iles Crozet and Iles Kerguelen.

(The Geographical Journal, 127(3):310-316, 1961)

DU
Hist.Pam.
303

CROWN HAWAII

The story of the stolen royal crown: revelation of a colorful incident in Hawaiian history by one of the participants.

(Honolulu Advertiser, July 18,1948)

GN
2.8
P 76

Crowther, W.E.L.H.

Method of migration of the extinct Tasmanian race.

(Journal of the Polynesian Society, Vol. 46, 1937, pp. 225-231)

also
GN
Ethn.Pam.
3805

QK
9
C 95

Crozier, A. A.

Dictionary of botanical terms.   New York. Henry Holt. 1892. 8vo. v + 202 pp.

Hms
M10

CROWN LANDS.

Kalanianaole.

Accounts and mele.

Storage
Case
4

List of Crown lands at end of book. Medicines near last page.

GN
Ethn.Pam.
3839

Crowther, W. E. L. H.

The passing of the Tasmanian race.

(Reprinted from The Medical Journal of Australia, Feb. 3, 1924:147-160) The Halford Oration.

QL
Mollusca
Pam.
735

Crozier, W. J.

Evidence of assortive mating in a Nudibranch.

(Proc. of the National Academy of Sciences, Vol. III, No. 8.)

DU
620
M 67

Crowning of the dead king.
Stewart, C. W.
Honolulu, 1843, 1°. pp. 32.
in Miscell. Pams. Haw. III. pp. 1-32.

AS
720.T
R

Crowther, W. L.

Notes on Tasmanian whaling.

(Papers and Proc. R. Soc. of Tasmania, 1919: 130-151)

QL
Protozoa
to
Polyzoa
Pam.
369

Crozier, W. J.

A Note on the physiology of the cuvierian organs of holothuria captiva ludw.   From The Am. Jour. of Physiology, v.36, n.2, 1915.

AM
101
P 35

CROWNINSHIELD, GEORGE

Peabody Museum, Salem, Mass.

One hundred anniversary of the building of "Cleopatra's Barge" 1816-1916. Catalog of the commemorative exhibition held at the Peabody Museum, Salem, Massachusetts, July 17-September 30, 1916. Salem. 8vo. 36 pp.

DU
12
R 68

looked
case

CROZET, Monsieur   ?   (name unknown)

(Rochon, A. M. de)

Nouveau voyage a la mer du sud, commencé sous les ordes de M. Marion...achevé, après la mort de cet officier, sous ceux de M. de Chevalier Duclesmeur...cette relation a été rédigée d'après les plans & journaux de M. Crozet...Paris. 1783. 8vo.

QL
1
M4

Crozier, W. J. and Snyder, L. H.

Selective coupling of gammarids. Biological Bull., Marine Biological Laboratory, vol. XLV, No. 2, 1923. Woods Hole, Mass.

DU
Hist.Pam.
398

CROWNINSHIELD, GEORGE

Whitehill, Walter Muir

George Crowninshield's yacht Cleopatra's Barge.

(Reprinted from The American Neptune, Vol. 13(4), 1953. 19 pp.)

DU
12
R 68

looked
case

Crozet's Voyage to Tasmania, New Zealand, the Ladrone Islands, and the Philippines...

(Rochon, A. M. de)

QK
97
E 58

CRUCIFERAE

Engler, Adolf

Das Pflanzenreich...IV. 105. 1919. (Heft 70). Cruciferae-Brassiceae, by O. E. Schulz. Subtribus I et II.

QH
104
U-b

CROWS

Barrows, Walter Bradford.

... The common crow of the United States. By Walter B. Barrows and E. A. Schwarz. General report: Walter B. Barrows. Report on insect food: E. A. Schwarz. Washington, Govt. print. off., 1895.

98 p. front., illus. 23cm. (U. S. Dept. of agriculture. Division of ornithology and mammalogy. Bulletin 6)

1. Crows. 1. Crow 1. Schwarz, Eugene Amandus.

Agr 6-828

Library, U. S. Dept. of   Agriculture

AS
162
P 23

CROZET ISLANDS

de Rue, Edgar Aubert

Notes sur les Iles Crozet.

(Bull. Mus. Nat. d'Hist. Nat., Paris, Ser. 2, Tome 22(2):197-203, 1950)

QK
97
E 58

CRUCIFERAE

Engler, Adolf

Das Pflanzenreich...IV. 105. 1923. (Heft 84.) Cruciferae-Brassiceae, by O. E. Schulz. Subtribus III-VII.

QK
97
E 58   CRUCIFERAE

Engler, Adolf

    Das Pflanzenreich...IV. 105. 1924. (Heft 86.) Cruciferae-Sisymbrieae, by O. E. Schulz.

DU
12
C 80   Cruise of the "Alert".

Coppinger, R. W.

QL
561.N7
C 95   Crumb, S. E.

    The larvae of the Phalaenidae.

    (U. S. Dept. Agric., Technical Bull. 1135, 1956)

QK
97
E 58   CRUCIFERAE

Engler, Adolf

    Das Pflanzenreich...IV. 105. 1927. (Heft 89.) Cruciferae-Draba et Erophila, by O. E. Schulz.

DU
Pac.Pam.
714   Cruise of the Kon-tikis modern Vikings sail a raft 101 days across the open Pacific.

    (Life, Oct. 20, 1947, pp. 113-122)

G
3
N 27   CRUSOE, ROBINSON

Schmitt, Waldo L.

    A voyage to the island home of Robinson Crusoe.

    (National Geographic Magazine, 54:353-370, 1928)

QK
1
E 58   CRUCIFERAE

Schulz, O. E.

    Eine Crucifere der Karolinen.

Diels, L.
    Beiträge zur Flora von Mikronesien und Polynesien. II. No. 6.

    (Bot. Jahrb. Bd. 56, 1921, p. 507.)

DU
760
M34   *Cruise of the Rosario*

   Markham. A. H.

   Note See also Palmer, Kidnapping

QE
1
G 3 s   Crust of the earth (a symposium).

Poldervaart, Arie

    (Geological Society of America, Special Paper 62, 1955)

QK
Bot.Pam.
2382   CRUCIFERAE   HAWAII

St. John, Harold

    Revision of Cardamine and related Cruciferae in Hawaii, and Nasturtium in Polynesia. Pacific plant studies 3.

    (Occ. Papers, Bernice P. Bishop Mus., 18, no. 5, 1945, pp. 77-83)

DU
12
F99   *Cruise of the St. George (1891-'92)*

   Tybe, George.

BERNICE P. BISHOP MUSEUM LIBRARY
THE KAIULANI COLLECTION

QE
Geol.Pam.
1044   The crust of the earth and its relation to the interior.

Washington, H. S.

QL
684.N
C 95   Cruickshank, Allan D.

    Birds around New York City; where and when to find them...

    (Am. Mus. of Nat. Hist., Handbook Series, No. 13, 1942)

QK
Botany
Pam.
3146   Crum, Howard

    Bryophytes from Guadalupe Island, Baja California, By Howard Crum and Harvey A. Miller

    (The Southwestern Naturalist, 1(3):116-120, 1956)

Q
101
P 16   The crust of the Pacific basin.

Macdonald, Gordon A.   and others

    10th Pac. Sci. Congress

DU
406
C95   *Cruise, Richard A.*

   Journal of a ten months' residence in New Zealand. 2d. ed.

   London, 1824. 8°. pp. 327.

AS
75
J 27   Crum, Howard

    A survey of the moss flora of Jamaica. By Howard Crum and Edwin B. Bartram.

    (Bull. Inst. of Jamaica, Sci. Series No. 8, pp. 1-90, 1958)

QL
1
H 2   CRUSTACEA

Agassiz, Alexander

    Selections from embryological monographs... I.- Crustacea, by Walter Faxon.

    (Memoirs of the Museum of Comparative Zoology at Harvard, Vol. 9, No. 1, 1882.)
    ---Bibliography:Bull. MCZH, Vol. IX:6

DU
12
A 97   Cruise in the Pacific, from the log of a naval officer

Aylmer, Fenton

QL
Insects
Pam.
1089   Crumb, S. E.

    The European earwig, by S. E. Crumb, P. M. Eide, and A. E. Bonn.

    (U. S. Dept. of Agriculture, Technical Bulletin, No. 766, 1941)

AS
472
A   CRUSTACEA

Alcock, Alfred William

    Natural history notes from the Royal Indian Marine Survey Ship "Investigator", Ser. III, No. 3: On some notable and rare species of Crustacea.

    (Journal Asiatic Soc. Bengal, Vol. 68, Part 2, [1899], 1900, pp. 111-119)

QL
430.6
A 88

CRUSTACEA

Atwood, W. G.

Marine structures, their deterioration and preservation. Report of the Committee on Marine Piling Investigations of the Division of Engineering and Industrial Research of the National Research Council, by William G. Atwood, and A. A. Johnson...Washington. c1924. 8vo.

QL
435
B 25

CRUSTACEA

Barnard, J. Laurens   and others

Abyssal Crustacea. By J. Laurens Barnard, Robert J. Menzies and Mihai C. Bacescu. Columbia University Press. New York and London. 1962 4to. ix + 222 pp.

QL
Crust.Pam.
31

CRUSTACEA

Bouvier, E. L(Eugene Louis)

Les pargurines des mers d'Europe crustacés tableaux dichotomiques des genères et des espèces (La Feuille III serie, 26 annee, Nos. 308 et 309 1896 pp. 125-128, 149-155)

QL
Crust
Pam
No.332

CRUSTACEA

Balss, Heinrich

Decapoden von Juan Fernandez . Ex Nat. Hist. Juan Fernandez (Skottsberg , ed.) , Vol. III, 1922.

QL
444.A5
Ba
B32

CRUSTACEA

Bate, C. Spence

Catalogue of the specimens of amphibious Crustacea in the collection of the British Museum.

London, British Mus., 1862, pp iv, 399, pls. lviii.

QL
Crus
Pam
#27

Crustacea.

Bouvier, E. L

Em les Janthes des Mers d'Europe Extrait de La Feuille des Jeunes Naturalistes Juin 1878 III° Serie 28° Annee

Rennes 1893   8° pp. 5

QL
Crust.
Pam.
No.330

CRUSTACEA

Balss, Heinrich

Ostasiatische Stomatopoden ... Munchen, 1910.

QL
Crust.Pam.
292

CRUSTACEA

Bate, C. Spence

A history of British sessile-eyed crustacea.

(REVIEW ONLY, from Natural History Review, pp. 130-135. date?)

QL
434
B86Br

CRUSTACEA

British Museum

Guide to the Crustacea, Arachnida, Onychophora and Myriopoda exhibited in the department of Zoology, British Museum.

London, 1910, pp 133

QL
Crust.
Pam
No. 329

CRUSTACEA

Balss, Heinrich

Potamoniden.. 1914 .

(See author card for detail)

QL
Crustacea
Pam
355
and
AS
36
S4

CRUSTACEA

Benedict, James E.

Description of a new genus + forty six new species of Crustaceans of the family Galatheridae with a list of the known marine species Proc. U.S. N. Mus. Vol. XXVI pp. 243-264. Wash. 1902   8° pp. 243-394.
FEB 22 1911

QL
435
C 16

CRUSTACEA

Calman, W. T.

The life of Crustacea. With thirty-two plates and eighty-five figures. Methuen and Co., Ltd. London. (1911). sm8vo. xvi + 289 pp.

QL
Crust.
Pam.
Pam.
No.331

CRUSTACEA

Balss, Heinrich

Stomatopoden des Rothen Meeres.... Expeditionen ... "Pola"... 1895/96 - 1897/98. ... Wien, 1910.

(See author card for detail)

QL
Crustacea
Pam
#352
and
AS
36
S4

Crustacea.

Bigelow, Robert Payne

Scientific Results of Explorations no. XXXII by the U. S. Fish Com. S.S. Albatross Report upon the Crustacea of the order Stomatopoda collected by the S.S. Albatross between 1885-1891 + oth other specimens in the U. S. Nat. Museum Proc. U.S.N.M.   Vol. XVII. Wash. 1894   8° pp. 485-550. pl. XX-XXII
FEB 22 1911

GC
63
D 61

CRUSTACEA

Cannon, H. Graham

Nebaliacea.

Discovery Committee
Discovery Reports, Vol. 3, 1931, p.199-222

QL
Crust.
Pam.
332

CRUSTACEA

Balss, Heinrich

Stomatopoda, Macrura , Paguridea, und Galatheidea. Dr. E. Mjoberg's Swedish Scientific Expeditions to Australia, 1910 - 13, no. xxix. Stockholm, 1921.

(See author card for detail.)

QL
309
G

Crustacea.

Borradaile, L. A.

Land crustaceans, in Fauna and Geog. of the Maldive and Laccadive groups.

(Gardiner ed.)I. pp. 64-100.

QL
Crust
Pam
374

CRUSTACEA

Chamberlin, Joseph C. and Carl D. Duncan.

Notes on lepidurus glacialis kroyer crustacea, branchiopoda, apodidae. 1926.

QL
Crust.
Pam.
No.335

CRUSTACEA

Balss, Heinrich

Uber einige Pontoniiden. Sonderabdruck aus Zool. Anzeig. Bd. 45, Nr.2, 1914.

QL
1
H2

CRUSTACEA - (MACRURA)

Bouvier, E. L.

Les Macroures marcheurs. Harvard Mus. Comp. Zool. Mem. Vol. 47, No.5, 1925.

QL
Crus.
Pam.
#55

CRUSTACEA, Charles

Chilton, Charles

On Cercaria in the Cockle

Trans of N.Z. Inst. Vol. XXXVII 1914

Wellington 1905. 8° pp. 323-326. pl. XIX

QL Crus. Pam. 65
AS 36 S4

CRUSTACEA

Cushman, Joseph A.

Fresh Water Crustacea from Labrador and Newfoundland.

Proc. U.S.N. Mus. Vol. XXXIII.

(Washington 1908, 8vo. pp. 700-713, Plates LVIII - LXII.)

QL Crust. Pam. 151

CRUSTACEA

Edwards, Alphonse Milne-

Sur les Modifications que subissent les pagures suivant l'enroulement de la coquille qu'ils habitent, by Alphonse Milne-Edwards and E. L. Bouvier.

(Ex. Bull Société Philomatique de Paris. 1891, pp. 151-153)

QL Crust. Pam. # 365
and AS 36 S4

CRUSTACEA

Hansen, H. J. (Hans Jacob)

The Euphausiacean crustaceans of the "Albatross" Expedition to the Philippines From Proc. U. S. Nat. Mus. Vol. 49, pp. 635- 654. 1916.

QL Crust. Pam. No.340

CRUSTACEA

Doflein , F. und Balss, H.

Die Dekapoden und Stomatopoden der Hamburger Magalhaensischen Sammelreise 1893/93. Aus Mitt Natur.Mus. Hamburg Bd. XXIX, 1912.

QL 1 H2

CRUSTACEA
Faxon, Walter, 1848-

... The stalk-eyed *Crustacea*. By Walter Faxon ... Cambridge, Printed for the Museum, 1895.

292 p. plates (part col.) fold. map. 29ᶜᵐ. (Memoirs of the Museum of comparative zoölogy at Harvard college, vol. XVIII.)

Reports on an exploration off the west coasts of Mexico, Central and South America, and off the Galapagos Islands ... by the U. S. Fish commission steamer "Albatross," during 1891 ... xv.

1. Crustacea. 2. Albatross (Steamer) I. Title.
A 19-1056

Title from Univ. of Chicago   QL1.H375 vol. 18 Printed by L. C.
[3]

QL Crust. Pam. 554

CRUSTACEA

Hay, W. P.

The life history of the blue crab (Callinectes sapidus).

(U. S. Bureau of Fisheries Report, 1904, pp. 397-413)

QL Crustacea Pam 399
AS 763 B-4
Reading Room

CRUSTACEA

Edmondson, Charles Howard

Effect of ultraviolet rays in regeneration Chelipeds. Bernice P. Bishop Museum, Occasional Papers, vol. IX, no.7. 1930. 7p.

QL Crus. Pam. 216

CRUSTACEA

Fritsch, Anton

Ueber das Vorkommen von Apus und Branchipus in Böhmen.

(Wien, Zool. Bot. Verhandl., XVI, 1866, (Abh.), pp. 557-562)

QL Crus. Pam. 110

CRUSTACEA

Hay, William Perry

Observations on the Crustacean Fauna of Nickajack Cave, Tennessee, and vicinity.

(Proc.U.S.Nat.Mus.,Vol.XXV. 1902. pp. 417-439)

AS 182 H

Crustacea

Edwards, A.Milne

Description de quelques Crustacés, Nouveaux ou peu connus, in Mus.Godeffroy Journal, pp.255-266. Heft IV Tafel 12 and 13. Hamburg, 1873.

QL 402 G 23
looked case

CRUSTACEA

Gray, John Edward

List of the specimens of crustacea in the collection of the British Museum. London. Order of the Trustees. 1847. 143 pp.

(Bound with Cox, James C. Exchange list of land and marine shells... Garrett collection of papers on conchology, Vol. 8)

QL Crus. Pam. 108

CRUSTACEA

Hay, William Perry

Observations on the Crustacean Fauna of the region about Mammoth Cave, Kentucky.

(Proc.U.S.Nat.Mus.,Vol.XXV. 1902. pp.223-236)

QL 1 H2

CRUSTACEA
Milne-Edwards, Alphonse, 1835-1900.

... Description des crustacés de la famille des galatheidés recueillis pendant l'expédition. Par Alphonse Milne-Edwards et E. L. Bouvier ... Cambridge, Printed for the Museum, 1897.

[3]-141 p. XII pl. 29ᶜᵐ. (Memoirs of the Museum of comparative zoölogy at Harvard college, vol. XIX, no. 2)

Each plate accompanied by leaf with descriptive letterpress.

Reports on the results of dredging ... in the Gulf of Mexico (1877-78) in the Caribbean Sea (1878-79) and along the Atlantic coast of the United States (1880) by the U. S. Coast survey steamer "Blake" ... xxxv.

1. Galatheidae. 2. Crustacea. 3. Blake (Steamer) I. Bouvier, Eugène Louis, 1856-   joint author.
A 19-1070

Title from Univ. of Chicago   QL1.H375 vol. 19, no. 2
Printed by L. C.   [3]

QH 11 G 78

CRUSTACEA

Gurney, Robert

The larvae of the decapod Crustacea; Palaemonidae and Alpheidae.

IN Great Barrier Reef Expedition, 1928-29, Scientific Repts., Vol. 6, no. 1, pp. 1-60, 1938 British Mus. of Nat. Hist.

QL 435 H

CRUSTACEA
Crustaceen beschrieben von Camil Heller Reise der Fregatte Novara 1857-1859. (Zool. Th, 2ᵗᵉ Band, 3ᵗᵉ Abt.)

QL 435 E 26
looked case

CRUSTACEA

Edwards, (Henri) Milne

Histoire Naturelle des Crustacés, comprenant l'Anatomie, la Physiologie et la Classification de Ces Animaux. Tomes 1-3, and atlas of 42 pl. Paris. Roret. 1834-1840. 8vo.

QL Crust. Pam. # 366
and AS 36 S4

CRUSTACEA
Hansen, H. J.(Hans Jacob)

The Crustacea Euphausiacea of the United States National Museum. From Proc. U. S. Nat. Mus. Vol. 48, 1915, pp 59 - 114.

QL Crust. Pam. 365

CRUSTACEA

Heller, Cam

Neue crustaceen gesammelt wahrend der weltumseglung der k.k. fregatte Novara. From Verh. k.k. zool-bot. Gesell. Wien, 1862.

QL Bibliofilm 66

CRUSTACEA

Edwards, Alphonse Milne-

Etude zoologique des Crustacés récents.

(Nouv. Archives du Musée d'Histoire Naturelle, Paris, I:177-308, 1865)

QL Crus. Pam. 96

CRUSTACEA

Hansen, H. J. (Hans Jacob)

The Crustaceans of the Genera Petalidium and Sergestes from the 'Challenger' with an account of Luminous Organs in Sergestes Challengeri, n. sp.

(Proc.Zoo.Soc.of London. 1903. pp.51-79)

QL Crust. Pam 384

CRUSTACEA

Heller, Cam

Vorlaufiger bericht uber die wahrend der weltumseglung der k.k. fregatte Novara gesammelten crustaceen. From Verh. der k.k. zool-bot. Gesell. Wien, 1861.

QL
444.D3
H 53
locked case

CRUSTACEA

Herbst, Johann Friedrich Wilhelm

Versuch einer Naturgeschichte der Krabben und Krebse, hebst einer Systematischen Beschreibung ihrer Verschiedenen Arten. Bd. 1-3. Berlin und Stralsund. (Heft 1, Bd. 1 publ in Zürich) Joh. Caspar Fuessly. 1782-1804. 4to. with atlas of 62 plates, bound separately.

AS
36
C9

Crustacea.
Kunkel, B. W. The Arthrostraca of Connecticut. Hartford, 1918.

261 pp., 84 figs., 25cm.

(Bulletin no. 26, Connecticut geological and natural history survey.)

Bibliography, p. 258-261.

QL
Crust.Pam.
150

CRUSTACEA

Miers, E. J. (Edward John)

On Actaeomorpha erosa, a new species and genus of Crustacea.

(Linn. Soc. Journ. Zool. Vol. XIII, 1876, pp. 183-185)

QL
627
U -b

CRUSTACEA

Herrick, Francis Hobart

The American lobster; a study of its habits and development. U.S.Bur.Fish. Bul Vol. XV for 1895, 1896. pp 5 - 252, pls. 1-54.

QL
Crustacea
Pam.
638

CRUSTACEA

Lang, Karl

Leptognathia paramanca n. sp.

(Arkiv f. Zool., K. Svenska Vetenskapsakad., Stockholm, s2, Bd. 11 (25), 1958

[Tanaidaceae]

AS
36
S1

CRUSTACEA
Minkevich, Romūal'd Kasimīrovich.

The instinct of self-concealment and the choice of colors in the *Crustacea*. By Romuald Minkiewicz.

(*In* Smithsonian institution. Annual report. 1909. Washington, 1910. 23½cm. p. 465-485. illus.)

Tr. from Rev. générale des sciences pures et appliquées, Paris, 20th year, no. 3, Feb. 15, 1909.

1. Crustacea.   11-9831

Library of Congress   Q11.S66 1909

CRUSTACEA
QL
444.D3
H56

Herrick, Francis Hobart, 1858–

Natural history of the American lobster ... [By Francis Hobart Herrick] Washington, Govt. print. off., 1911.

1 p. l., p. 149-408. illus., pl. xxviii-xlvii (part col.) 28cm. ([U. S.] Bureau of fisheries. Doc. 747)

From Bulletin of the Bureau of fisheries, vol. xxix, 1909. Bibliography: p. 384-408.

1. Lobster. 2. Crustacea. 3. ~~Lobster-fisheries~~ U. S. 4. Crayfish.

P 11-278

Library, U. S. Bur. of   Fisheries

QL
Crust.
Pam.
No.
338

CRUSTACEA

Lenz, H.

Crustaceen von Madagaskar, Ostafrika und Ceylon..... 1910

See author card for detail.

QL
441.5
N 74

CRUSTACEA

Nobili, G.

Crustacés decapodes et stomatopodes. Mission J. Bonnier et Ch. Perez (Golfe Persique) 1901.

(Bull. Sci. France et Belgique, Vol. 40, 1906, pp. 1-157, pl. 2-7)

QL
Crust
Pam
375

CRUSTACEA

Hilgendorf, Franz.

Crustaceen. Bd III, Abt/1, Von der Decken's Reisen in Ost Afrika, 1859-61.

QL
Crus
Pam
#135

CRUSTACEA

Lenz, H.

Ergebnisse einer Reise nach dem Pacific Schauinsland 1896 – 1897. Crustaceen

Abdruck aus d. Zool. Jahrbüchern Bd. 14. Abth. f. Syst.

Jena 1901   8vo pp. 429-492
Tafel 32

QL
Crust.
Pam. 157

CRUSTACEA

Nordquist, Oscar

Om forekomsten af Ishafscrustaceer uti mellersta Finlands sjoar.

(Fauna och Flora Fennica, Medd. 11, 1885, p. 28-32)

QL
Crust.
Pam.
339

CRUSTACEA

Hilgendorf F.

Die von Hrn. W. Peters in Mocambique gesammelten Crustaceen.... Berlin, 1878, pp 782- 850.

AS
182
Se

CRUSTACEA

Lenz, H.

Ostafrikanische Dekapoden und Stomatopoden gesammelt von ....Voeltzow.... Aus Abh. Senck. nat. Gesell. Bd. XXVII, Heft iv, 1905.

QL
Crust.
Pam.
No. 344

CRUSTACEA

Odhner, Teodor

Monographierte Gattungen der Krabbenfamilie. Xanthidae. Goteborg, 1925.

See author card for detail.

Q L
1
C

CRUSTACEA
Holmes, Samuel J[ackson]

... On some new or imperfectly known species of west American *Crustacea*. By Samuel J. Holmes. With three plates ... San Francisco, The Academy, 1904.

1 p. l., 307-330 p. xxxv-xxxvii pl. 25½cm. (Proceedings of the California academy of sciences. Third series. Zoology. vol. III, no. 12)

"Issued October 11, 1904."

1. Crustacea.

Library of Congress   Q11.C25   4-30945

QL
444.D3
& S8
Ma

CRUSTACEA

Man, J. G.

Die von Herrn Professor Kukenthal im Indischen Archipel gesammelten Dekapoden und Stomatopoden. Senckenberg. Nat. Ge Gesell. Abhand. Bd. 25, Heft 3, 1902, 4to

---

QL
Crus. Pam.
161

CRUSTACEA

Ouchakoff, N.

Pontie de Wacarino.

(?   pp. 245-250, 1855)

QL
1
Liv

CRUSTACEA

Jackson, H. G.

Eupagarus : Liverpool Biol. Soc. Proc and Trans. Vol. XXVII, 1913, pp 495-573. 1913.

AS
36
34

CRUSTACEA
Marsh, Charles Dwight, 1855–

A new crustacean, *Diaptomus virginiensis*, and a description of *Diaptomus tyrelli* Poppe. By C. Dwight Marsh.

(*In* U. S. National museum. Proceedings. Washington, 1916. 23½cm. v. 49, p. 457-462. illus.)

"Literature cited": p. 462.

1. Diaptomus.   16-11798

Library of Congress   Q11.U55 vol. 49
—— Copy 2.   Q11.U55 vol. 49 2d set

QL
Crus
Pam
#325

Crustacea

Paper in Italian - title page missing. Published in Torino, before 1911, pp. 17-58.

CRUSTACEA

QL
Crust. Pam.
131

Paulmier, Frederick C.

Higher Crustacea of New York City. New York State Mus. Bull. No. 91, 1905. 189 pp.

CRUSTACEA

QL
435
.St S84

Stebbing, Thomas Roscoe Rede, 1835–

... A history of Crustacea; recent Malacostraca, by the Rev. Thomas R. R. Stebbing ... with numerous illustrations. New York, D. Appleton and company, 1893.
Lond., Paul, Trench, Trübner & Co.

xvii, 466 p. illus., xix pl. 19½ᶜᵐ. (The international scientific series [v. 74])

1. Crustacea.

3-19005

Library of Congress   QL435.S81

CRUSTACEA

AS
36
C8

Verrill, Addison Emory, 1839–

... Decapod *Crustacea* of Bermuda; I.—*Brachyura* and *Anomura*. Their distribution, variations, and habits.

(*In* Connecticut academy of arts and sciences. Transactions. New Haven, Conn., 1908. 23ᶜᵐ. v. 13, p. [299]-474. illus., pl. IX-XXVIII)

Bibliography: p. 458-464.

1. Decapoda (Crustacea)   I. Title.

A 17-911

Library of Congress   Q11.C9   vol. 13
Yale University   A53n.366.13

CRUSTACEA

QL
Crust. Pam
#373

Pickering, Charles and James D. Dana.

Description of a species of caligus.

CRUSTACEA

QL
Crusta-
cea
Pam.
253

Stebbing, Thomas Roscoe Rede

Marine investigations in South Africa, South African crustacea, Part IV.

(Annals of the South African Museum, Vol. 6:1-88, 1908)

CRUSTACEA

AS
36
San

Vodges, Anthony Wayne

Palaeozoic Crustacea. San Diego Soc. Nat. Hist. Trans. Vol. IV, 1925, 154 pp. 2 pls.

CRUSTACEA

QL
Crus
Pam
#190

Pilsbry, Henry A.

Crustacea of the Cretaceous formation of New Jersey.

Proc. Acad. Nat. Sci. Phila. 1901

Phila. 1901, 8ᵛᵒ pp. 111-210
Plates 5.

CRUSTACEA

QL
Crust. Pam.
253

Stebbing, Thomas R.R. (Roscoe Rede)

Marine Investigations in South Africa.

(Annals of S.Afr.Mus.,Vol.VI, Pt.1, 1908, pp. 1-88)

CRUSTACEA

QL
Crust. Pam.
283

Walter, Alfred

Anceus (Praniza) Torpedinis. n. sp. aus Ceylon.

(Jenaische Zeitschrift, Bd. 18, 1884, p. 445-451)

CRUSTACEA

GC
63
D 61

Rayner, G. W.

The Falkland species of the crustacean genus Munida.

Discovery Committee
Discovery Reports, Vol. 10, 1935, p. 209-245

CRUSTACEA

AS
244
D

Stephensen, K.

Crustacea from the Auckland and Campbell Islands.

(Vid. Med. Dansk Nat. For. Kobenhavn, Bd. 83 1927,– Papers from Dr. Th. Mortensen's Pacific Expedition 1914-16, No. 40)

CRUSTACEA

QL
Crust. Pam.
284

Walker, Alfred O.

Hippolyte fascigera, Gosse, and H. gracillis (Heller)

(Annals and Magazine of Natural History, Ser. 7, Vol. iii, 1899)   pp. 147-150

CRUSTACEA

QL
441.4
S 24

Sars, George Ossian

An account of the Crustacea of Norway, with short descriptions and figures of all the species. Vols. 1-9, 1893-1928. Published by the Bergen Museum, Bergen. R8vo.

CRUSTACEA– (North Pacific Explor. Exped.)
See
Stimpson, W.

CRUSTACEA

QL
Crust. Pam.
285

Walker, Alfred

Note on some habits of Crustacea.

(Liverpool Biol. Soc., Proc. and Trans., Vol. 4, 1890, pp. 84-86)

CRUSTACEA

QL
Crus. Pam.
242

Scott, Thomas

On some rare and interesting Crustacea from the Dogger Bank collected by Ernest W. L. Holt.

(Ann. and Mag. Nat. Hist., 13, 1894, pp. 412-420)

Crustacea

AS
122
E

Tait, John

Experiments and observations on Crustacea. In Roy. Soc. Edinburgh Proc. XXXVII, Pt.1, 1916-'17 pp 50-94. XXXVII, Pt.3, 1916-'17 pp 246-304.

CRUSTACEA

AS
36
S2

Weymouth, Frank Walter.

... Observations on the habits of the crustacean *Emerita analoga*, with one plate, by Frank Walter Weymouth and Charles Howard Richardson, jr. ... Washington, Smithsonian institution, 1912.

1 p. l., 13, [1] p. illus., pl. 24½ᶜᵐ. (Smithsonian miscellaneous collections, v. 59, no. 7)

Publication 2082.
Bibliography: p. 12-13.

1. Emerita analoga.   I. Richardson, Charles Howard, jr., joint author.

12—35744

Library of Congress   Q11.S7   vol. 59, no. 7

CRUSTACEA

QL
Crust. Pam.
249

Stebbing, Thomas Roscoe Rede

Gregarious Crustacea from Ceylon.

(Rep. from "Spolia Zeylanica", Vol. II, Pt.V, 1904, pp. 1-28)

CRUSTACEA

QL
Crust. Pam.
272

Taramelli, Torquato

Sui Crostacei di forme marine viventi nelle Acque dolci e specialmente sul Palaemon Palustris di Martens by Torquato Taramelli...G. Balsamo Grivelli.

(Atti. Soc. Ital. Milano, VI, 1864, pp. 363-371)

CRUSTACEA

QL
Crustacea
Pam.
626

Wiersma, C. A. G.

Further functional differences between fast and slow contractions in certain crustacean muscles. By C. A. G. Wiersma and S. H. Ripley.

(Physiologia Comp. et Oecologia, III(4): 327-336, 1954)

Q
115
W 95
looked
case

CRUSTACEA

Müllerstorf-Urbair, Bernhard

Reise der Oesterreichischen Fregatte Novara
um die Erde...1857-1859.
Zoologischer Theil, Bd. 2, Abt. 3. Crustacea
von C. Heller. Wien. 1865. 4to.

QL
Crustacea
Pam.
630

CRUSTACEA   BIOLOGY

Schwabe, Calvin W.   and others

The molt cycle in Panulirus japonicus. Pt.
2 of the hormonal regulation of metabolism in
crustaceans. By Calvin W. Schwabe, Bradley T.
Scheer, and Marlin Ann Ray Scheer.

(Physiologia Comparata et Oecologia, 2(4):
310-320, 1952)

QL
Crustacea
Pam.
633

CRUSTACEA   FOSSIL

Imaizumi, Rikizo

A Miocene crab, Tymolus kamadai n.sp. from
the Numanouchi Formation of the Joban coal-
field.

(Trans. Proc. Pal. Soc. Japan. n.s. No. 7,
pp. 201-204, 1952)

QL
Crust.Pam.
289

CRUSTACEA

Williamson, W. C.

On some histological features in the shells
of Crustacea.

(Micr. Journ. Vol. VIII, 1760, pp. 35-50)

QL
Crustacea
Pam.
629

CRUSTACEA   BIOLOGY

Wiersma, C. A. G.

Innervation patterns of Crustacean limbs.
By C. A. G. Wiersma and S. H. Ripley.

(Physiologia Comp. et Oecologia, 2(4):391-
405, 1952)

QL
Crustacea
Pam.
631

CRUSTACEA   FOSSIL

Imaizumi, Rikizo

Trachycarcinus huziokai n.sp. from Yamagata
prefecture.

(Short Papers, IGPS, No. 3:33-40, 1951)

[other papers by this author fastened with
this paper]

QL
Crust.Pam.
282

CRUSTACEA

Woodward, Henry

Further remarks on the Relationship of the
Xiphosura to the Eurypterida and to the
Trilobita and Arachnida.

(Quarterly Journal of the Geological Society
1872, pp. 46-63)

QL
1
I-r

CRUSTACEA DECAPODA

Kemp, S.

See author card for detail

AS
36
S 19

and
QL
Crust.
Pam.
356

CRUSTACEA   FOSSIL

Vodges, Anthony Wayne

Paleozoic Crustacea. The publications
and notes on the genera and species during the
past twenty years, 1895-1917.

(Trans. San Diego Soc. Nat. Hist., 3(1),
1917)

AS
122
E

Crustacea Anatomy

Paul, J. Herbert

Comparative study of the reflexes of
autotomy in decapod crustacea.

in Roy. Soc. of Edinburgh Proc. XXXV, 3, 1915, pp. 252-262.

AS
750
N

CRUSTACEA-DISPERSAL

Chilton, Charles

Dispersal of marine Crustacea by means of
ships.

(Trans. New Zealand Inst., Vol. 43, 1910,
pp. 131-133)

QE
349.F
L 15

CRUSTACEA   FOSSIL   FIJI

Rathbun, Mary J.
Decapod Crustacea.

IN
Ladd, Larry S.
Geology of Lau, Fiji, by Harry S. Ladd and
J. Edward Hoffmeister. pp. 373-383

(Bernice P. Bishop Museum, Bull. 181, 1944)

QL
Crustacea
Pam.
605

CRUSTACEA   ANATOMY

Wiersma, C. A. G.

Further functional differences between fast
and slow contractions in certain crustacean
muscles. By C. A. G. Wiersma and S. H. Ripley.

(separate from Physiologie Comparata et
Oecologia, an international journal of comparative physiology and ecology, III(4):327-336, 1954)

AP
2
S 35

CRUSTACEA   FOOD HABITS

Bonnet, David D.

The Portuguese man-of-war as a food source
for the sand crab (Emerita pacifica).

(Science, Vol. 103:148-149, 1946)

AS
36
C1

CRUSTACEA, FOSSIL - BIBLIOGRAPHY

Vogdes, Anthony W.

A classed and annotated bibliography
of the palaeozoic crustacea 1898-1892
to which is added a catalogue of North
American species. California Academy of
Sci. Occasional Papers, v.4, 1893.

CRUSTACEA   BIBLIOGRAPHY

Holthuis, L. B.

A bibliography of some groups of the higher
Crustacea. 1953. 8 vol.

UH has

QH
1
P 11

CRUSTACEA   FOOD HABITS

Matthews, Donald C.

Feedings habits of the sand crab Hippa
pacifica (Dana).

(Pacific Science, Vol. IX(4):382-386, 1955)

AS
36
W 2

CRUSTACEA   NOMENCLATURE

Chace, Fenner A., Jr.

The number of species of decapod and stoma-
toped Crustacea.

(Jour. Washington Acad. of Sci., 41(11):
370-372, 1951)

QL
Crustacea
Pam.
628

CRUSTACEA   BIOLOGY

Scheer, Bradley T., and others

Tissue oxidations in crustaceans. Part III
of the hormonal regulation of metabolism in
crustaceans.

QL
Mollusca
Pam.
632

CRUSTACEA   FOSSIL

Imaizumi, Rikizo

A Miocene crab, Hyas tsuchidai n.sp. from
the Wakkanai formation of Teshio Province, Japan.
Hokkaido.

(Trans. Proc. Pa. Sco. Japan, n.s. No. 5:179-
183, 1952)

QL
Crust.
Pam.
593

CRUSTACEA   PARASITIC

Pearse, A. S.

Parasitic Crustacea from the Texas Coast.

(Inst. of Marine Sci., Port Aransas, Texas
Dec. 1952. 42 pp.

QL
Crustacea
Pam.
592

CRUSTACEA   PARASITIC

Pearse, A. S.

     Parasitic crustaceans from Alligator Harbor, Florida.

     (The Quarterly Journal of the Florida Acad. of Sci., Vol. 15(4):187-243, 1952)

QL
406
R 93

CRUSTACEA   AMBOINA

Rumpf, George Eberhard

     D'Amboinsche Rariteitkamer, Behelzende eene Beschryvinge van allerhande zoo weeke als harde Schaalvisschen, te weenten raare Krabben, Kreeften... T'Amsterdam. 1705. folio.

AS
36
S4

CRUSTACEA--ARGENTINE REPUBLIC

Richardson, Harriet.

     Descriptions of a new genus and species of isopod crustacean of the family *Idotheidæ* from the mouth of the Rio de La Plata, Argentina, South America. By Harriet Richardson ...

     (*In* U. S. National museum. Proceedings. Washington, 1911. 23¾ᶜᵐ. v. 40, p. 169-171. Illus.)

     1. Idotheidae. 2. Crustacea—Argentine Republic.

     11-31591

Library of Congress   Q11.U55   vol. 40

QL
445
W 32

CRUSTACEA   PHYSIOLOGY

Waterman, Talbot H.   editor

     The physiology of Crustacea. Vol. I: Metabolism and growth. Vol. II: Sense organs, intergration, and behavior.

     (Academic Press. New York and London. 1960 R8vo.)

QL
5
S 47

locked
case

CRUSTACEA   AMBOINA

Seman, Richard

     Zoologische Forschungsreisen in Australien und dem Malayischen Archipel...1891-1893. Bd. 5, Lief. 1, pp. 3-80, 1894: Crustaceen, by A. Ortmann.

QL
Crustacea
Pam.
656

CRUSTACEA   ATLANTIC

Manning, Raymond B.

     Stomatopod Crustacea from the Atlantic coast of northern South America.

     (Allan Hancock Atlantic Expedition, Report No. 9, 1961)

QL
Crustacea
Pam.
571

CRUSTACEA   **RESPIRATION**

Kawaguti, Siro

     On the respiration of Branchiura Sowerbyi.

     (Memoirs of the Faculty of Science and Agric. Taihoku Univ., Vol. 14(4):91-115 [Zool. No. 6], 1936)

QL
441.1
H29

Crustacea-Alaska

Harriman Alaska series, v. 10.

     Crustaceans, by Mary J. Rathbun, Harriet Richardson, S.J. Holmes, and Leon J. Cole.

     Washington, 1910. 337p. illus. pls.

QL
Crus.Pam.
48

CRUSTACEA   AUSTRALIA

Chilton, Charles

     Notes on a few Australian Edriophthalmata.

     (Linnean Society of N.S.W. Proceedings Vol. IX. Part 4, 8vo. pp. 1-10, PL. 46-47)

QH
1
P 11

CRUSTACEA   SPERMATOPHORES

Matthews, Donald C.

     Further evidences of Anomuran non-pedunculate Spermatophores.

     (Pacific Science, XI:380-385, 1957)

QH
1
M 17

CRUSTACEA   AMSTERDAM ISLAND

Chappius, P.A.

     Crustacés des eaux douces de l'ile Amsterdam: Protochoraon antarctica, n.sp.

     (Mem. Insti Sci. de Madagascar, Tome 12:13-24, 1958)

QL
Crus.Pam.
87

CRUSTACEA   AUSTRALIA

Grant, F. E.

     Crustacea dredged off Port Jackson in deep water.

     (Proc. Linnean Soc. of N.S.Wales, 1905, pp. 312-324)

AS
619
S

CRUSTACEA   AFRICA   (south)

Barnard, K. H.

     Contributions to the crustacean fauna of South Africa.

     (Annals, South African Museum, Vol. 20: 1-100, 1924)

Q
115
M 46

CRUSTACEA   ANTARCTIC

Brady, G. Stewardson
Cladocera and Halocypridae.

Mawson, Sir Douglas   leader
     Australasian Antarctic Expedition, 1911-14.
Scientific Reports, Series C, Vol. 5, Part 4, 1918.

QL
Crust.Pam.
86

CRUSTACEA   AUSTRALIA

Grant, F. E.

     On a collection of Crustacea from the Port Curtis District, Queensland, by F. E. Grant and Allan R. McCulloch.

     (Proc. Linn. Soc. N.S.Wales, Vol. 31, 1906, pp. 1-54)

QL
441.6
H54

CRUSTACEA -- AFRICA

Herklots, J. A.

     Additamenta ad fauna carcinologicam Africae occidentalis .....

     Lugdoni - Batavorum, 1851, 27 pp., 2 pls.

Q
115
M 46

CRUSTACEA   ANTARCTIC

Calman, W. T.
Cumacea and Phyllocarida.

Mawson, Sir Douglas   leader
     Australasian Antarctic Expedition, 1911-14,
Scientific Reports, Series. C., Vol. 5, Part 6, 1918.

QH
197
S 72

CRUSTACEA   AUSTRALIA

Hale, Herbert M.
     The Crustaceans of South Australia, Parts I-II
     IN
South Australian Branch of the British Science Guild... Handbook of the flora and fauna of South Australia... Adelaide, 1927, 1929.

CRUSTACEA -- AFRICA

     See also

CRUSTACEA -- RED SEA

Q
115
M 46

CRUSTACEA   ANTARCTIC

Hale, Herbert M.
Decapod Crustacea.

Mawson, Sir Douglas   leader
     British, Australian, and New Zealand Antarctic Research Expedition, 1929-31. Reports, Ser. B, Vol. IV, Part 9, 1941

AS
720.S
S 72

CRUSTACEA   AUSTRALIA

Hale, Herbert M.

     Notes on Australian Crustacea, I, IV.

     (Records of the South Australian Museum, Vol. 2, 1921-24, pp. 491-502 [pub. Apr. 30,1924], Vol. 4:33-34, 1925)

QL
441.7
H 35
CRUSTACEA' AUSTRALIA

Haswell, William A.

Catalogue of the Australian stalk- and sessile-eyed crustacea. The Australian Museum. Sydney. Catalogue No. 5. F. W. White. 1882. 8vo. xxiv + 324 pp.

AS
36
C8
and
QH
Nat.Hist.
Pam. 91
CRUSTACEA BERMUDA

Verrill, Addison Emory, 1839–

... Additions to the *Crustacea* and *Pycnogonida* of the Bermudas.

(*In* Connecticut academy of arts and sciences. Transactions. New Haven, 1899-1900. 25ᶜᵐ. v. 10, p. (573)-582. illus., pl. LXX)

1. Crustacea—Bermuda Islands. 2. Pycnogonida. I. Title.

A 17-886

Library of Congress   Q11.C9 vol. 10
Yale University   A53n.366.10

AS
36
C8
CRUSTACEA–BRAZIL

Smith, Sidney Irving, 1843–

... Notice of the *Crustacea* collected by Prof. C. F. Hartt on the coast of Brazil in 1867.

(*In* Connecticut academy of arts and sciences. Transactions. New Haven, 1871-73. 25ᶜᵐ. v. 2, p. 1-42. pl. I)

1. Crustacea—Brazil. I. Hartt, Charles Frederick, 1840-1878. II. Title.

A 17-763

Library of Congress   Q11.C9 vol. 2
Yale University   A53n.366.2

AS
719
A
Crustacea, Studies in Australian

McCulloch, Allan R.
no. 1

(in Rec. Aus. Mus. VII. 1908. p. 31–)

QL
Crus.Pam.
280
CRUSTACEA BERMUDA

Verrill, A. E. (Addison Emory)

Crustacea of Bermuda; Schizopoda, Cumacea, Stomatopoda and Phyllocarida.

Trans. (Connecticut Academy of Arts and Sciences. Vol.26, 1923. pp. 181-211)

QL
5
Br.
CRUSTACEA' BRITISH ANTARCTIC EXPED.

See

Tattersall, W. M.

AS
719
A
Crustacea, Studies in Australian

McCulloch, Allan R.
no. 2

(in Rec. Aus. Mus. VII. 1908 p. 305–)

QL
Crustacea
Pam.
487
CRUSTACEA - BERMUDA

Verrill, A. E. (Addison Emory)

Decapod Crustacea of Bermuda I-II.

(Trans. Conn. Acad. Arts and Sci. Vol. 13, 1908. pp. 299-474 and Vol. 26, 1922, pp. 1-179).

QL
1
C 15
CRUSTACEA & CALIFORNIA

Barrows, Albert Lloyd, 1883–

... The occurrence of a rock-boring isopod along the shore of San Francisco Bay, California, by Albert L. Barrows. Berkeley, University of California press, 1919.

cover-title, p. (299)–316. pl. 15-17. 27½ᶜᵐ. (University of California publications in zoology. v. 19, no. 9)

Bibliography: p. 310-311.

1. Isopoda. 2. Crustacea—California. I. Title.

Title from Univ. of Calif.   Library of Congress   A 19-1526
                              (a20b3)

QL
636.5N
Og
CRUSTACEANS - AUSTRALIA.

Ogilby, J. Douglas

Edible fishes and crustaceans of New South Wales.

Sydney, 1893, pp 212, 51 pls.

Ql
Crust
Pam
346
CRUSTACEA -BERMUDA

Verrill, A. E.

Crustacea of Bermuda .....
Conn. Acad. Sc. Trans. Vol. 26, 1923, pp 181- 211.

AS
36
C1
CRUSTACEA - CALIFORNIA

Holmes, Samuel J.

Synopsis of California stalk-eyed crustacea. California Academy of Sci. Occasional Papers, v.7, 1900.

AS
182
H
Crustacea - Australia.

Richters, F.

Branchipus Australiensis, nov. spec. In
(Mus. Godeffroy Journ. Heft XII. Tafel 3.
pp. 181-482XX 43-44
Hamburg, 1876.)

Z
7996.C95
G 98
CRUSTACEA BIBLIOGRAPHY

Gurney, Robert

Bibliography of the larvae of Decapod Crustacea. London. Printed for the Ray Society. 1939. 8vo. vi + 123 pp.

QL
1
C15
CRUSTACEA - CALIFORNIA

Schmidt, Waldo L.

Marine decapod crustacea of California Univ. of Calif. Zool. Vol. 23. 1921.

QL
1
L-J
CRUSTACEA BERMUDA

Gurney, Robert

On the larvae of certain Crustacea Macrura, mainly from Bermuda. By Robert Gurney and Marie V. Lebour.

(Journal of the Linnean Soc. of London, Vol. 41, 1941, pp. 89-180)

QL
Crust
Pam
386
CRUSTACEA - BORNEO

Nobili, Giuseppe

Contributo alla fauna carcinologica di Borneo. Bollettino Mus. Zool.-Anat. d. R. Univ. Torino, v.18, n.447, 1903.

AS
36
S7
CRUSTACEA - CALIFORNIA - MONTEREY BAY

Weymouth, Frank Walter.

... Synopsis of the true crabs (*Brachyura*) of Monterey Bay, California, by Frank Walter Weymouth, with plates I–XIV. Stanford University, Cal., The University, 1910.

64, (2) p., 13 l. XIV pl. 26ᶜᵐ. (Leland Stanford junior university publications. University ser. no. 4)

Each plate accompanied by leaf with descriptive letterpress.
Bibliography: p. 64.

1. Crabs. 2. Crustacea—California—Monterey Bay.

11—1825

Library of Congress   QL444.D3W5

AS
36
C8
CRUSTACEA--BERMUDA ISLANDS.

Richardson, Harriet.

... The marine and terrestrial isopods of the Bermudas, with descriptions of new genera and species.

(*In* Connecticut academy of arts and sciences. Transactions. New Haven, 1901-03. 25ᶜᵐ. v. 11, p. (277)-310. pl. XXXVII-XL)

1. Isopoda. 2. Crustacea—Bermuda Islands. I. Title.

A 17-899

Library of Congress   Q11.C9 vol. 11
Yale University   A53n.366.11

QL
Crust.Pam.
155
CRUSTACEA BORNEO

Nobili, Giuseppe

Note intorno ad una collezione di Crostacei di Sarawak (Borneo).

(Boll. Mus. Zool. ed Anat. comp. della R. Universita di Torino. Vol. XVI, 1901, pp. 1-14)

QH
1
A 88
CRUSTACEA CANTON ISLAND

Van Zwaluwenburg, R. H.

The insects and certain other arthropods of Canton Island.

(Atoll Research Bulletin, No. 42, 1955)

QL
1
A 93

CRUSTACEA   CAPRICORN GROUP

McNeill, Frank A.

    Biology of Northwest Islet, Capricorn Group.
Crustacea.

    (The Australian Zoologist, 4:299-318, 1926)

QL
Crust.Pam.
135

CRUSTACEA   CLIPPERTON ISLAND

Lenz, H.

    Ergebnisse einer Reise nach dem Pacific
(Schauinsland 1896-1897) Crustaceen.

    (Aus.Zool.Jahr. 1901, Bd. 14, pp. 429-482)

    (Laysan, Samoa, New Zealand, Chatham Is.,
Hawaii, Clipperton Island)

QL
Crus.Pam.
109

CRUSTACEA   CUBA

Hay, William Perry

    On a small collection of Crustaceans from
the island of Cuba.

    (Proc.U.S.Nat.Mus., Vol.XXVI. 1903. pp.429-
435)

QL
1
A 93

CRUSTACEA   CAPRICORN GROUP

Ward, Melbourne

    The Crustacea of the Capricorn and Bunker
Groups, Queensland.

    (The Australian Zoologist, 5:241-246, 1928)

AS
522.S
R 13

CRUSTACEA-COCOS KEELING ISLANDS

Tweedie, M. W. F.

    Crustacea (Brachyura and Stomatopoda).

    IN
Papers on the fauna of the Cocos-Keeling
Islands...1940...1941

    (Bull. Raffles Museum, No. 22:105-148, 1950)

Q
115
S 56

CRUSTACEA   DUTCH EAST INDIES

Leigh-Sharpe, W. Harold

    The Copepoda of the Siboga Expedition.

    (Siboga-Expeditie, Livr. CXXIII. 1934)

QL
Crus.Pam.
521

CRUSTACEA CARIBOU STREAM

Nylander, Olof O.

    The Crustacea and Mollusca of Caribou stream.

    Nylander Museum, Caribou, Maine, 1938, 4to.
12 pp. mimeographed.

AS
36
S4

CRUSTACEA--COLOMBIA
Pearse, Arthur Sperry, 1877-
    An account of the *Crustacea* collected by the Walker
expedition to Santa Marta, Colombia. By A. S. Pearse...
    (*In* U. S. National museum. Proceedings. Washington, 1916. 23½ᶜᵐ.
v. 49, p. 531-556. illus., pl. 70-73)
    Bibliography: p. 555-556.

    1. Crustacea—Colombia.

Library of Congress   Q11.U55 vol. 49   16-11804
—— —— Copy 2.   Q11.U55 vol. 49 2d set

Q
115
S 56

CRUSTACEA   DUTCH EAST INDIES

Pirlot, Jean M.

    Les Amphipodes de l'Expedition du Siboga.

    (Siboga-Expeditie, Livr. CXX, 1933; Livr.
CXXVI, 1936)

QL
Crust.
Pam
381

CRUSTACEA - CELEBES

Schenkel, E

    Beitrag zur kenntnis der dekapoden-
fauna von Celebes. Naturf. Ges. Basel.
cerh. v.13, Basel, 1902.   100p. pls.

AS
36
S4

CRUSTACEA--COLORADO
Dodds, Gideon Stanhope, 1880-
    Altitudinal distribution of *Entomostraca* in Colorado.
By Gideon S. Dodds...
    (*In* U. S. National museum. Proceedings. Washington, 1919. 23½ᶜᵐ.
v. 54, p. 59-87. illus. (incl. maps) pl. 13-14, fold. tab., diagrs.)
    Bibliography: p. 87.

    1. Entomostraca.   2. Crustacea—Colorado.

Library of Congress   Q11.U55 vol. 54   19-20009
    [6]

AS
36
S4

CRUSTACEA--ECUADOR

Richardson, Harriet.
    Description of a new species of isopod belonging to the
genus *Apseudes* from Ecuador. By Harriet Richardson...
    (*In* U. S. National museum. Proceedings. Washington, 1912. 23½ᶜᵐ.
vol. 42, p. 583-585)
    "List of references": p. 585.

    1. Apseudes.   2. Crustacea—Ecuador.

                                 13-9547
Library of Congress   Q11.U55 vol. 42

QL
Crust.Pam.
135

CRUSTACEA   CHATHAM ISLAND

Lenz, H.

    Ergebnisse einer Reise nach dem Pacific
(Schauinsland 1896-1897) Crustaceen.

    (Aus.Zool.Jahr. 1901, Bd. 14, pp. 429-482)

    (Laysan, Samoa, New Zealand, Chatham Is.,
Hawaii, Clipperton Island)

AS
36
S4

CRUSTACEA--COLORADO
Dodds, Gideon Stanhope, 1880-
    Descriptions of two new species of *Entomostraca* from
Colorado, with notes on other species. By G. S. Dodds...
    (*In* U. S. National museum. Proceedings. Washington, 1916. 23½ᶜᵐ.
v. 49, p. 97-102. illus.)

    1. Entomostraca.   2. Crustacea—Colorado.

Library of Congress   Q11.U55 vol. 49   16-11777
—— —— Copy 2.   Q11.U55 vol. 49 2d set

QH
1
P 11

CRUSTACEA   ENIWETOK

Held, Edward E.

    Land crabs and fission products at Eniwetok
Atoll.

    (Pacific Science, 14(1):18-27, 1960)

QL
Crustacea
Pam
484

CRUSTACEA- CHINA

Kellogg, C. R.

    Crustacea of Fukien province.   From Lingnan
science journal, vol. 5, no. 4, 1928.   p. 551 -
356.

AS
36
S4

CRUSTACEA -- COSTA RICA
Richardson, Harriet.
    Terrestrial isopods collected in Costa Rica by J. F.
Tristan, with descriptions of a new genus and species.
By Harriet Richardson...
    (*In* U. S. National museum. Proceedings. Washington, 1911. 23½ᶜᵐ.
v. 39, p. 93-95. illus.)

    1. Isopoda.   2. Crustacea—Costa Rica.   I. Tristan, J. F.

Library of Congress   Q11.U55 vol. 39   11-20926
    [a19e2]

QL
Crustacea
Pam
288
342

CRUSTACEA ELLICE ISLANDS

Whitelegge, Thomas

    The Crustacea of Funafuti.

AS
719
A-me

    (Australian Museum, Memoirs, Vol. III, Pt. 2,
pp. 127-151, 1896-97)

AS
36
S 66 p

CRUSTACEA   CLIPPERTON ISLAND

Chace, Fenner A., Jr.

    The non-Brachyuran decapod crustaceans of
Clipperton Island.

    (Proc. U. S. Nat. Mus., Vol. 113:605-635,
1962)

AS
36
S4

CRUSTACEA- COSTA RICA
Richardson, Harriet.
    Terrestrial isopods collected in Costa Rica by Mr.
Picado, with the description of a new genus and species.
By Harriet Richardson...
    (*In* U. S. National museum. Proceedings. Washington, 1913. 23½ᶜᵐ.
v. 44, p. 337-340. illus.)

    1. Isopoda.   2. Crustacea—Costa Rica.

                               13-20864
Library of Congress   Q11.U55 vol. 44

AS
763
B-b

QL
Crustacea
Pam
493

Reading
Room

CRUSTACEA FANNING ISLAND

Edmondson, Charles H.

    Crustacea from Palmyra and Fanning Islands,
with descriptions of new species of crabs from
Palmyra Island by Mary J. Rathbun.

    (Bull. No. 5, Bernice P.Bishop Museum, 1923)

QL
Crustacea
Pam
348

CRUSTACEA FANNING ISLAND

Streets, T. H.

Contributions to the Natural History of the Hawaiian and Fanning Islands...U. S. North Pacific surveying expedition, 1873-1875. pp.103-141.

AS
36
S 5

AS
36
S 2

(U. S. Nat'l Mus., Bull. No. 7, 1877; Smithsonian Misc. Coll., Vol. XIII, art. 7, publ. no. 303)

AS
36
S4

CRUSTACEA- Galapagos islands

Richardson, Harriet.

Descriptions of two new isopods, an *Apseudes* and a *Munnopsis*, both from the Galapagos Islands. By Harriet Richardson ...

(*In* U. S. National museum. Proceedings. Washington, 1913. 23½ᶜᵐ. vol. 43, p. 159-162. illus.)

"List of references": p. 162.

1. Isopoda. 2. Crustacea—Galápagos Islands.

Library of Congress   Q11.U55 vol. 43   13-13112

CRUSTACEA   HAWAII

Banner, Albert Henry

The Hawaiian Crustacea of the family Crangonidae. (Thesis...University of Hawaii, January, 1940) manuscript

UH

QL
Crustacea
Pam.510

CRUSTACEA   FIJI

Edmondson, C. H.

Quantitative studies of Copepods in Hawaii with brief surveys in Fiji and Tahiti.

AS
763
B-4

Reading
Room

(B.P.Bishop Museum. Occasional Papers, vol. XIII, no. 12. 1937. pp.131-146)

AS
36
S 2

CRUSTACEA   GALAPAGOS ISLANDS

Schmitt, Waldo L.

Decapod and other Crustacea collected on the Presidential Cruise of 1938...

(Smithsonian Misc. Coll., Vol. 98, 1939, No. 6, pp. 29)

Q
115
U 68

CRUSTACEA   HAWAII

Dana, James Dwight
Crustacea

United States Exploring Expedition, during the years 1838, 1839, 1840, 1841, 1842, under the command of Charles Wilkes. Vols. 13-14: Crustacea, by James D. Dana. With a folio atlas of 96 plates. 1852-53.

QL
Crust.
Pam.
592

CRUSTACEA   FLORIDA

Pearse, A. S.

Parasitic crustaceans from Alligator Harbor, Florida.

(The Quarterly Journal of the Florida Acad. of Sci., Vol. 15(4):187-243, 1952)

AS
36
S 2

CRUSTACEA   GALAPAGOS ISLANDS

Tattersal, W. M.

Euphausiacea and Mysidacea collected on the Presidential Cruise of 1938.

(Smith. Misc. Coll., Vol. 99, No. 13, 1941, pp. 1-7)

QK
Crustacea
Pam.
660

CRUSTACEA   HAWAII

Edmondson, Charles Howard

Hawaiian Crustacea: Goneplacidae, Pinnotheridae, Cymopoliidae, Ocypodidae, and Gecarcinidae.

(Bernice P. Bishop Museum, Occ. Papers, Vol. 23, No. 1, 1962)

QL
Crustacea
Pam
288
342

CRUSTACEA   FUNAFUTI

Whitelegge, Thomas

The Crustacea of Funafuti.

(Australian Museum, Memoirs, Vol. III, Pt. 2, pp. 127-151, 1896-97)

AS
719
A-me

QL
437
W58

CRUSTACEA - GREAT BRITAIN

White, Adam

A popular history of British crustacea; comprising a familiar account of their classification and habits.

London, Reeve, 1857.   358p.   pls.

AS
763
B-o

CRUSTACEA - Hawaii

Edmondson, Charles H.

Hawaiian Dromiidae

In Occasional Papers Bernice P. Bishop Museum Vol. VIII, No. 2, 1922

QL
1
N 6-z

CRUSTACEA   GALAPAGOS ISLANDS

Boone, Lee

The Littoral Crustacean Fauna of the Galapagos Islands. Part II.—Anomura.

(Zoologica, Volume XIV:1, 1932)

QL
Crustacea
Pams.
561
562

CRUSTACEA   GREENLAND

Stephensen, K.

The Zoology of east Greenland; Marine Ostracoda, parasitic and semi-parastic Copepoda and Cirripedia; Leptostraca, Mysidacea, Cumacea Tanaidacea, Isopoda and Euphausiacea.

(Meddelelser om Gronland, Bd. 121, No. 9, 10, 1943)

QL
Crustacea
Pam.
596

CRUSTACEA   HAWAII

Edmondson, Charles Howard

Hawaiian Portunidae.

(Occasional Papers of B. P. Bishop Museum Vol. XXI(12):217-274, 1954)

QH
1
P 11

CRUSTACEA   GALAPAGOS ISLANDS

Garth, John S.

Pinnixa darwini, a new species of pinnotherid crustacean from the Galápagos Islands.

(Pacific Science, 14(1):39-42, 1960)

DU
647
G 91

CRUSTACEA   GUAM

(Linsley, Leonard Noel)

Curious things about Guam, by L. N. L. (the coconut crab).

(The Guam Recorder, 1934, Sept., pp. 115-116)

QL
Prot. to
Poly.
Pam.
571

CRUSTACEA   HAWAII

Edmondson, Charles Howard

New Crustaceans from Kauai, Oahu and Maui.

(Bernice P. Bishop Museum, Occasional Paper, Vol. IX, No. 17, 1931)

QL
Crust.
Pam.
534
527

CRUSTACEA   GALAPAGOS ISLANDS

Hult Jöran

Crustacea Decapoda from the Galapagos Island collected by Mr. Rolf Blomberg.

(Arkiv f. Zoologi, Svenska Vetenskapsakad. Bd. 30 A, No. 5, 1938, pp. 1-18)

AS
36
S4

CRUSTACEA--GUATEMALA

Richardson, Harriet.

Description of a new terrestrial isopod from Guatemala. By Harriet Richardson ...

(*In* U. S. National museum. Proceedings. Washington, 1910. 23½ᶜᵐ. vol. 37, p. 495-497. illus.)

1. Isopoda. 2. Crustacea—Guatemala.

Library of Congress   Q11.U55 vol. 37   11-9682

QL
Crustacea
Pam
485

AS
763
B-4

Reading
Room

CRUSTACEA   HAWAII

Edmondson, Charles Howard

New Hawaiian Crustacea. Bernice P. Bishop Museum Occasional papers, vol. 9, no. 10. 1930.

Card 1

QL
Crustacea
Pam.510

CRUSTACEA HAWAII

Edmondson, C.H.

Quantitative studies of Copepods in Hawaii with brief surveys in Fiji and Tahiti.

AS
763
B-4

(B.P. Bishop Museum. Occasional Papers, vol. XIII, no.12. 1937. pp.131-146)

Reading
Room

Card 2

QL
Crust.
Pam.
536

CRUSTACEA HAWAII

Miller, Milton A.

The Isopod Crustacea of the Hawaiian islands II. Asellota.

(Bernice P. Bishop Museum, Occ. Papers, Vol. 16, No. 13, pp. 305-320, 1941)

Card 3

AS
36
S4

CRUSTACEA -- Hawaiian Islands.

Richardson, Harriet

Description of a new parasitic isopod from the Hawaiian Islands. By Harriet Richardson ...

(*In* U. S. National museum. Proceedings. Washington, 1911. 23½ᶜᵐ. vol. 38, p. 645-647. illus.)

1. Isopoda. 2. Crustacea—Hawaiian Islands.

Library of Congress   Q11.U55 vol. 38   11-16456

Card 4

Q
101
P 18

CRUSTACEA HAWAII

Edmondson, C. H.
The shellfish resources of Hawaii, by C. H. Edmondson and I. H. Wilson.

IN Proc. Sixth Pac. Sci. Congress, 1939, (California), Vol. 3, 1940, pp. 241-244.

also
QL
Moll.
Pam. 926

Separate.

Card 5

QL
Crustacea
Pam.
No.341
and
QL
1
C15

CRUSTACEA - Hawaii

Miller, Robert Cunningham

Wood-boring Crustacea from Hawaii and Samoa. Univ. Calif. Pub. Zool. Vol. 26, No.8, 1924.

Card 6

QL
627
U-b

CRUSTACEA HAWAII

Richardson, Harriet

Isopods collected at the Hawaiian Islands by the U.S. Fish Commission Steamer "Albatross". in U. S. Fish Com. Bull. XXIII, Part III, pp. 817-816

Card 7

QL
Crust.Pam.
71
72
494

CRUSTACEA HAWAII

Edmondson, Charles H.

Stomatopoda in the Bernice P.Bishop Museum.

(Bernice P.Bishop Museum, Occasional Papers, Vol.7, No.13, 1921, pp. 281-302)

Card 8

QL
1
C15

CRUSTACEA - HAWAII AND SAMOA

Miller, Robert Cunningham

Wood-boring Crustacea from Hawaii and Samoa. Univ. Calif. Pub. Zool. Vol 26, pp 145-164. 1924.

Card 9

AS
36
S 5

AS
36
S 2

QL Crust.
Pam 348

CRUSTACEA HAWAII

Streets, T. H.

Contributions to the natural history of the Hawaiian and Fanning Islands...U. S. North Pacific surveying expedition, 1873-1875. pp. 103-141.

(U. S. Nat'l Mus., Bull. No. 7, 1877; Smithsonian Misc. Coll., Vol. XIII, art. 7, publ. no. 303)

Card 10

AS
182
H

Crustacea - Hawaiian Islands, Samoa etc

Edwards, A. Milne

Description de quelques Crustacés. In Journ. Mus. Godeffroy. Heft IV. 1873. pp. 76-88. (B. P. Mus. pagination pp. 255-270)

Card 11

QL
627
U-a
and
Crustacea
Pam.
467

CRUSTACEA HAWAII

Ortmann, A.E.

Schizopoda of the Hawaiian Islands collected by the Albatross in Haw. in U.S. Fish Com. Bull. XXIII Part III, pp. 963-974

Card 12

CRUSTACEA HAWAII

Townsley, Sidney Joseph

Adult and larval stomatopod crustaceans occuring in Hawaiian waters. Univ. of Hawaii thesis for Master of Science degree, 1950.

UH Library   (typed copy)

Card 13

QH
1
P 11

CRUSTACEA HAWAII

Hiatt, Robert W.

Records of rare Hawaiian decapod Crustacea.

(Pacific Science, Vol. 2;78-80, 1948)

Card 14

QL
Crustacea
Pam. 488

CRUSTACEA HAWAII

Pesta, Otto

Marine Harpacticiden aus dem Hawaiischen Inselgebiet. I. Beitrag.

(Abdruck aus Zoologische Jahrbucher, Abt. f. Systematik, Okologie und Geographie...Bd. 63, Heft 2, 1932, pp. 145-162, Taf. 4)

Card 15

QL
Crustacea
Pam.
508

AS
763
B-4

CRUSTACEA HAWAII

Ueno, Masuzo

Cladocera of Mauna Kea, Hawaii.

(B. P. Bishop Mus., Occ. Papers, vol. XII, no. 11, 1936, 9 pp. 3 figs.)

Card 16

QL
Crust.Pam.
135

CRUSTACEA HAWAII

Lenz, H.

Ergebnisse einer Reise nach dem Pacific (Schauinsland 1896-1897) Crustaceen.

(Aus. Zool. Jahr. 1901, Bd. 14, pp. 429-482)

(Laysan, Samoa, New Zealand, Chatham Is. Hawaii, Clipperton Island)

Card 17

AS
36
A 16

CRUSTACEA HAWAII

Randall, John W.

Catalogue of the Crustacea brought by Thomas Nuttall and J. K. Townsend from the West Coast of North America and the Sandwich Islands, with descriptions of such species as are apparently new.

(Acad. Nat. Sci., Philadelphia, Journal, Vol. 8:106-147, 1839-1942)

Card 18

QL
627
U-b

QL
Crustacea
Pam
400

CRUSTACEA HAWAII BIBLIOGRAPHY

Rathbun, Mary J(ane)

Brachyura and Macrura of the Hawaiian Islands.

(U. S. Fish Commission, Bull. XXIII, Pt.III, pp. 929-930) 1903

Card 19

QL
Crust.
Pam.530

CRUSTACEA HAWAII

Miller, Milton A.

The isopod Crustacea of the Hawaiian Islands (Chelifera and Valvifera).

(Occ. Papers, Bernice P. Bishop Museum, Vol. 15, No. 26, 1940, pp. 295-321)

Card 20

QL
627
U-b
and
Crustacea
Pam.
400

AS
36
S4

CRUSTACEA HAWAII

Rathbun, Mary J. (Mary Jane)

Brachyura and Macrura of the Hawaiian Islands. in U.S. Fish Com. Bull. XXIII, Part III, pp. 829-930, 24 pls. 1906.

U.S. Nat'l Museum Bur. XXI, XXVI

Card 21

QL
Crust.Pam.
291

CRUSTACEA HUNGARY

Szilády, Zoltán

A retyezati tavak alsobrendu rakjai. (The crustacea of Retyezat)

(Math. Termt. Ertes. XVIII, 1901, pp. 1-24; a reprint, first printed in 1900)

QL
444.D3
A 35

CRUSTACEA   INDIA

Alcock, Alfred William

Catalogue of the Indian Decapod Crustacea
in the collection of the Indian Museum.
Part I, Fasc. 1-2, 1901, 1910
"   II, Fasc. 1, 1905
"   III, Fasc. 1, 1906

Indian Museum.   Calcutta.   4to.

QL
5
M 98

CRUSTACEA   INDIAN OCEAN

Calman, W. T.
Crustacea: Caridea.

IN The John Murray Expedition, 1933-34,
Sci. Repts., Vol. VI, no. 4, 1939, pp. 183-224.

QL
Crustacea
Pam.
603

CRUSTACEA   JAPAN

Motoda, Sigeru

Observations on diurnal migration of plankton crustaceans in lakes Shikotsu, Hokkaido, and
Tsugarujuni, Aomori, and some experiments on
photo- and geotropism.

(Mem. Fac. of Fisheries, Hokkaido Univ.,
Vol. 1(1):1-56, 1953)

QL
444.D3
A 35

CRUSTACEA   INDIA

Alcock, Alfred William

A descriptive catalogue of the Indian deep-
sea Crustacea, Decapoda, Macrura and Anomala,
in the Indian Museum, being a revised account of
the deep-sea species collected in the Royal Indian Marine Survey ship Investigator. Indian
Museum. Calcutta. 1901.

QH
1
M 45

CRUSTACEA   INDIAN OCEAN

Ward, Melbourne

Notes on the Crustacea of the Desjardins
Museum, Mauritius Institute, with descriptions
of new genera and species.

(Mauritius Institute Bulletin, Vol. 2, 1942,
pp. 49-108)

QL
Crust.Pam.
489

CRUSTACEA - JAPAN

Pearse, A. S.

The Ecology of Certain Crustaceans of the
Beaches at Misaki, Japan, with Special Reference
to Migrations from Sea to Land.

(Journal of the Elisha Mitchell Scientific
Society, Vol. 46, No. 2, 1931)

AS
472
A

Crustacea - India.

Alcock, A.
Materials for a Carcinological Fauna
of India. No. 5. In Journ. As. Soc. of
Bengal, Vol. LXVIII, pp 123-169.

AS
122
L-p

CRUSTACEA   INDO-PACIFIC

Gordon, Isabella

Notes on some Indo-Pacific crabs (Crustacea,
Decapoda).

(Linnean Soc. of London, Proc., 153rd
Session, 1940-41, Pt. 1, pp. 123-140, 15 figs.)

QL
Crus.Pam.
207

CRUSTACEA   JAPAN

Rathbun, Mary J(ane)

Japanese Stalk-Eyes Crustaceans.

(Proc.U.S.Nat.Mus.,Vol.XXVI. 1902. pp23-55)

AS
472
A

Crustacea - India.

Alcock, A.
Materials for a Carcinological Fauna
of India. No. 6. In Journ. As. Soc. of
Bengal, Vol. LXIX, pp 280-456.

QL
Crustacea
Pam.
No. 345

CRUSTACEA -   INDO'- PACIFIC

Odhner, Teodor

Indopazifische Stomatopoden . Fran
Med. Goteborgs Musei Zoolog. Avdelning.
30, 1923.

AS
36
S4

CRUSTACEA--JAPAN
Richardson, Harriet

Description of a new species of isopod of the genus
Cleantis from Japan. By Harriet Richardson ...

(*In* U. S. National museum. Proceedings. Washington, 1912. 23½ᵐᵐ.
vol. 42, p. 27-29. 1 illus.)

"List of references": p. 29.

1. Cleantis. 2. Crustacea—Japan.

13-9512

Library of Congress   Q11.U55 vol. 42

QL
Crustacea
Pam.
650

CRUSTACEA   INDIA

Kemp, Stanley

Crustacea Decapoda of the Inlé Lake Basin.

(Records of the Indian Museum, Vol. 14:81-
102, 1918)

QL
1
1 - M

Crustacea Stomatopoda) Indo- Pacf

Kemp, Stanley
Crustacea Stomatopoda of the
Indo-Pacific region.   Ind. Mus.Mem.IV,1
4to. pp. 217, pls. IX.
Calcutta, 1913.

S
303
T 64

CRUSTACEA   JAPAN

Yokoya, Yu

On the distribution of decapod crustaceans
inhabiting the continental shelf around Japan,
chiefly based upon materials collected by S. S.
Soyo-Maru, during the years 1923-1930.

(Jour. College of Agric., Tokyo Imp. Univ.,
12 (1):1-226, 1933)

QL
Crustacea
Pam.
649

CRUSTACEA   INDIA

Kemp, Stanley

Crustacea Decapoda of the Siju Cave, Garo
Hills, Assam.

(Records of the Indian Museum, 26(1):41-48,
1924)

QL
444
M 46

CRUSTACEA   ITALY

Mayer, Paul

Die Caprelliden des Golfes von Neapel und der
Angrenzenden Meeres-Abschnitte: Eine Monographie
& Nachtrag zur Monographie Derselben... Leipzig
and Berlin. 1882; 1890. 4to.2 pts.

(Zoologischen Station zu Neapel, Monographie,
VI and XVII)

QL
Crustacea
Pam.486

CRUSTACEA - JAVA.

Pesta, Otto.

Zur kenntnis der land- und süsswasserkrabben
von Sumatra und Java.

Sonder-abdruck aus dem Archiv für hydrobiologie. 1930. Suppl.-bd. VIII. S.92-108.

QL
Crust
Pam
388

CRUSTACEA - INDIA

Nobili, Giuseppe

Crostacei di Pondichery, Mahe, Bombay
etc. Bollettino Mus. Zool.-Anat. R. Univ.
Torino, v.18, n.452, 1903.

AS
36
S4

CRUSTACEA - JAMAICA
Richardson, Harriet.

Marine and terrestrial isopods from Jamaica. By
Harriet Richardson ...

(*In* U. S. National museum. Proceedings. Washington, 1912. 23½ᵐᵐ.
vol. 42, p. 187-194. illus.)

1. Isopoda. 2. Crustacea—Jamaica.

13-9522

Library of Congress   Q11.U55 vol. 42

AS
750
N

CRUSTACEA-KERMADEC ISLANDS

Chilton, Charles

The Crustacea of the Kermadec Islands,

(Trans. New Zealand Institute, Vol. 43,
1910, pp. 544-573)

QL
461
H 38

CRUSTACEA   KURE ISLAND

Butler, George D. Jr.

     Insects and other arthropods from Kure Island. By George D. Butler Jr. and Robert L. Usinger.

     (Proc. Haw. Ent. Soc., Vol. 18(2):237-244, 1963)

QL
444.D3
M 26

CRUSTACEA   MALAY ARCHIPELAGO

Man, J. G. de

     Die von Herrn Professor Kükenthal im Indischen Archipel gesammelten Dekapoden und Stomatopoden von Dr. J. G. de Man. Mit neun tafeln. Frankfurt. 1902. 4to.

AS
182
S

     (Abh. Senck. Naturforsch. Gesellschaft, Bd. 25, Heft 3, pp. 467-929)

Biblio-
film
67

CRUSTACEA   MEXICO

Edwards, Alphonse Milne-

     Etudes sur les Ziphosures et les Crustacés de la Région Mexique. (Part 5 of Recherches Zoologiques, Mission Scientifique au Mexique et dans l'Amerique Centrale)

AS
36
S2

CRUSTACEA - LIBERIA

Richardson, Harriet.

     Terrestrial isopods of the family *Eubelidæ*, collected in Liberia by Dr. O. F. Cook, by Harriet Richardson.

     (*In* Smithsonian institution. Smithsonian miscellaneous collections. Washington, 1908. 24½cm. vol. L (Quarterly issue, vol. IV) p. 219-247. illus.)

Publication 1733.
Originally published September 12, 1907.
"List of references": p. 219-220.

1. Eubelidae. 2. Crustacea—Liberia. I. Cook, Orator Fuller, 1867–

Library of Congress   Q11.S7 vol. 50   16-11643
———— Copy 2.

QL
Crustacea
Pam. 509

CRUSTACEA   MALAYSIA

Jackson, H.G.

     Terrestrial isopods from Malaysia.

     (Bull. of the Raffles Museum, Singapore, Straits Settlements. no.12. 1936. pp.77-87. 4 figs.)

AS
36
S4

CRUSTACEA--MEXICO

Richardson, Harriet.

     Description of a new species of the isopod genus *Cassidinidea* from Mexico. By Harriet Richardson ...

     (*In* U. S. National museum. Proceedings. Washington, 1912. 23½cm. vol. 42, p. 107-108. illus.)

1. Cassidinidea. 2. Crustacea—Mexico.

Library of Congress   Q11.U55 vol. 42   13-9515

QL
5
O 55

CRUSTACEA   LYBIA   (Oasis)

Omer-Cooper, J.

     Results of the Armstrong College Zoological Expedition to Siwa Oasis (Libyan Desert) 1935. Crustacea (Copepoda), by Friedrich Kiefer. (Proc. IV:62-112, 1949)

QK
371
M 26

CRUSTACEA   MANCHOUKUO

Tokunaga, Shigeyasu   leader

     Report of the first scientific expedition to Manchoukuo...

     (Section V, Division I, Part II: Crustacea of Jehol, by Masuzô Ueno, Tune Sakai, Hajime Uchida. 1935.

AS
36
S4

CRUSTACEA--MEXICO, GULF OF

Pearse, Arthur Sperry, 1877–

     Notes on certain amphipods from the Gulf of Mexico, with descriptions of new genera and new species. By Arthur S. Pearse ...

     (*In* U. S. National museum. Proceedings. Washington, 1913. 23½cm. vol. 43, p. 369-379. illus.)

1. Amphipoda. 2. Crustacea—Mexico, Gulf of.

13-13120

Library of Congress   Q11.U55 vol. 43

QL
Crust
Pam
378

CRUSTACEA - MADAGASCAR

Hoffmann, C   K

     Crustaces et echinodermes de Madagascar et de l'ile de la Reunion.

Leyde, 1874.   58p.   10pls.

QL
1
T 64
and
QL Crust.
Pam.
531

CRUSTACEA   MARIANAS ISLANDS   (Saipan)

Gurney, Robert

     A description of the adult and larval stages of a new species of Palaemonetes from the Marianne Islands. (Res. Prof. Esaki's Micronesian Expeditions, 1936-1938, No. 26.)

     (Annotations Zool. Japonenses, 18:145-150, 1939) and vol. 19, 1940, p. 80

AS
162
P 23

CRUSTACEA   NEW CALEDONIA

Remy, J. M.

     Sur les crabes sub-fossiles de Nouvelle-Caledonie.

     (Bull. Mus. Nat. d'Histo. Nat., Paris, ser. 2, Tome 24(1):114-117, 1952)

QH
1
M 17 a

CRUSTACEA   MADAGASCAR

Lindberg, K.

     Cyclopides (Crustaces Copépodes) de Madagascar.

     (Mem. Inst. Sci. de Madagascar, Ser. A., Tome 5:187-195, 1951)

AS
36
S4

CRUSTACEA--MASSACHUSETTS

Sharpe, Richard Worthy, 1869–

     Notes on the marine *Copepoda* and *Cladocera* of Woods Hole and adjacent regions, including a synopsis of the genera of the *Harpacticoida*. By Richard W. Sharpe ...

     (*In* U. S. National museum. Proceedings. Washington, 1911. 23½cm. vol. 38, p. 405-436. illus.)

Bibliography: p. 435-436.

1. Entomostraca. 2. Crustacea—Massachusetts.

11-15889

Library of Congress   Q11.U55 vol. 38

AS
28
E 85

CRUSTACEA   NEW CALEDONIA

Risbec, Jean

     Simples remarques sur la biologie des colonies de crabes de Magenta (New Caledonia).

     (Etudes Mélanesiennes, n.s. Année 1(3):61-66, 1948)

QL
444.D3
M 26

CRUSTACEA   MALAY ARCHIPELAGO

Man, Jan Govert de

     Bericht über die von Herrn Dr. J. Brock im indischen Archipel gesammelten Decapoden und Stomatopoden.

     (Archiv für Naturgeschichte, Jahrg. 53:215-600, pl. 7-22,22a, 1887.   separate)

QH
1
M 45

CRUSTACEA   MAURITIUS

Ward, Melbourne

     Notes on the Crustacea of the Desjardins Museum, Mauritius Institute, with descriptions of new genera and species.

     (Mauritius Institute Bulletin, Vol. 2, 1942, pp. 49-108)

AS
36
S4

CRUSTACEA -- NEW ENGLAND

Doolittle, Alfred A.

     Descriptions of recently discovered *Cladocera* from New England. By Alfred A. Doolittle ...

     (*In* U. S. National museum. Proceedings. Washington, 1912. 23½cm. v. 41, p. 161-170. pl. 13-19)

1. Cladocera. 2. Crustacea—New England.

12-17770

Library of Congress   Q11.U55 vol. 41

QL
444.D3
M 26

CRUSTACEA   MALAY ARCHIPELAGO

Man, J. G. de

     Decapoden des Indischen Archipels.

     (Zoologische Ergebnisse einer reise in Niederländisch Ost-Indien, Bd. II, Mit tafel XV-XXIX. Leiden. 1892. 4to. pp. 266-527)

QH
301
T 92

CRUSTACEA   MEDITERRANEAN

Heldt, Henri

     Les crustacés comestibles des mers Tunisiennes et leur pêche. Par Henri Heldt et Jeanne H. Heldt.

     (Station Oceanographique de Salammbo, Tunis, Annales No. IX, Mars., 1954)

AS
773
N 53 z

CRUSTACEA   NEW GUINEA

Holthuis, L. B.

     Contributions to New Guinea carcinology, parts I-IV.

     (Nova Guinea, Vol. 7(1):123-137, 1956; Vol. 9(2):231-234, 1958; Vol. 10(2):303-309, 1959; Vol. 10(18):355-359, 1963)

AS
36
S4

CRUSTACEA - NEW MEXICO

Richardson, Harriet

    Description of a new crustacean of the genus sphaeroma from a warm spring in New Mexico. Proc. U. S. Nat. Mus. v.20, pp. 465-466.

and

QL
Crustacea
Pam
390   separate

QH
1
T 88

CRUSTACEA   NEW ZEALAND

Richardson, L. R.

    A guide to the natant decapod crustacea (shrimps and prawns) of New Zealand, by L. R. Richardson and J. C. Yaldwyn.

    (Tuatara, 7(1):17-41; 1958)

AS
36
S4

CRUSTACEA -- NORTH AMERICA

Wilson, Charles Branch, 1861-

    North American parasitic copepods.—Part 9. The *Lernæopodidæ*. By Charles Branch Wilson ...

    (*In* U. S. National museum. Proceedings. Washington, 1911. 23½ᶜᵐ. v. 39, p. 189-226. pl. 29-36)

    Bibliography: p. 224.

    1. Lernaeopodidae. 2. Crustacea—North America.

    Library of Congress   Q11.U55 vol. 39   11-21199

QL
Crustacea
Pam.
No. 131

CRUSTACEA - NEW YORK

Paulmier, Frederick C.

    Higher Crustacea of New York city. New York State Mus. Bull. No. 91, 1905. 189 pp.

AP
2
N 54

CRUSTACEA   NEW ZEALAND

Thomson, George M.

    The Crustacea of New Zealand.

    (The New Zealand Journal of Science and Technology, Vol. XIV, pp. 55-57, 1932)

AS
36
S4

CRUSTACEA--NORTH AMERICA

Wilson, Charles Branch, 1861-

    North American parasitic copepods belonging to the *Lernaeopodidae*, with a revision of the entire family. By Charles Branch Wilson ...

    (*In* U. S. National museum. Proceedings. Washington, 1915. 23½ᶜᵐ. v. 47, p. 565-729. illus, pl. 25-56)

    Bibliography: p. 717-721.

    1. Lernaeopodidea. 2. Crustacea—North America.

    Library of Congress   Q11.U55 vol. 47   15-14961

QL
Crus.Pam.
54

CRUSTACEA   NEW ZEALAND

Chilton, Charles

    Note on some Crustacea from the Freshwater Lakes of New Zealand.

    (Proc. of Zool. Soc. of London, 1906. 8vo. pp. 702-705)

QL
441.1
P 11

CRUSTACEA NORTH AMERICA

Packard, A. S.

    A monograph of North American phyllopod crustacea.

    (12th Ann. Rept. of the U. S. Geological Survey, 1883, pp. 295-526, pl. 6-39.)

AS
36
S4

CRUSTACEA -- NORTH AMERICA

Wilson, Charles Branch, 1861-

    North American parasitic copepods belonging to the family *Ergasilidæ*. By Charles Branch Wilson ...

    (*In* U. S. National museum. Proceedings. Washington, 1911. 23½ᶜᵐ. v. 39, p. 263-400. illus, pl. 41-60)

    Bibliography: p. 393-395.

    1. Ergasilidae. 2. Crustacea—North America.

    Library of Congress   Q11.U55 vol. 39   11-21204

QL
Crus.Pam.
47

CRUSTACEA   NEW ZEALAND

Chilton, Charles

    Report of some Crustacea dredged of the Coast of Auckland.

    (Trans. of N.Z.Inst. Vol. XXXVIII. 1905. Wellington, 1906, 8vo. pp.265-268)

AS
36
R4

CRUSTACEA--NORTH AMERICA.

Rathbun, Mary Jane, 1860-

    Description of three species of crabs (*Osachila*) from the eastern coast of North America. By Mary J. Rathbun ...

    (*In* U. S. National museum. Proceedings. Washington, 1916. 23½ᶜᵐ. v. 50, p. 647-652. pl. 36)

    1. Crabs. 2. Crustacea—North America.

    Library of Congress   Q11.U55 vol. 50   16-19497
    —— Copy 2.   Q11.U55 vol. 50 2d set

QL
Crust.
Pam.
553

CRUSTACEA   PACIFIC (northeast)

Banner, Albert Henry

    The Crustacea of the orders Mysidacea and Euphausiacea of the northeastern Pacific.

    (University of Washington, Abstracts of Theses and Faculty Bibliography, 1943-44, Vol. 9, pp. 33-34, 1946)

QL
Crust
Pam
377

CRUSTACEA - NEW ZEALAND

Filhol, Henri

    Considerations relatifs a le faune des crustaces de la Nouvelle-Zelande.

    Paris, 1885. 60 p.

AS
36
C8

CRUSTACEA-NORTH AMERICA

Smith, Sidney Irving, 1843-

    ... The stalk-eyed crustaceans of the Atlantic coast of North America north of Cape Cod.

    (*In* Connecticut academy of arts and sciences. Transactions. New Haven, 1878-82. 23ᶜᵐ. v. 5, p. (27)-138. pl. VIII-XII)

    1. Crustacea—North America.   I. Title.

     A 17-796

    Library of Congress   Q11.C9 vol. 5
    Yale University   A53n.366.5

QL
Crustacea
Pam.
604

CRUSTACEA   PACIFIC

Banner, Albert H.

    Some "Schizopod" crustaceans from the deeper water off California.

    (Allan Hancock Foundation Publ., Univ. of Southern California, Occ. Paper No. 13:1-48, 1954)

QL
Crust.Pam.
135

CRUSTACEA   NEW ZEALAND

Lenz, H.

    Ergebnisse einer Reise nach dem Pacific (Schauinsland 1896-1897) Crustaceen.

    (Aus. Zool. Jahr. 1901, Bd. 14, pp. 429-482)

    (Laysan, Samoa, New Zealand, Chatham Is., Hawaii, Clipperton Island)

AS
36
S2

CRUSTACEA--NORTH AMERICA.

Smithsonian institution.

    ... Circular of inquiries relative to the natural history of the American crawfish and other fresh water *Crustacea*. [Washington, Smithsonian institution, 1878]

    8 p. illus. 24ᶜᵐ. (Smithsonian miscellaneous collections. [vol. XV, art. X])

    Publication 319.
    Caption title.
    Signed: Joseph Henry, secretary.
    Contains 72 questions.

    1. Crayfish. 2. Crustacea—North America.   I. Henry, Joseph, 1799-1878. II. Title.

    Library of Congress   Q11.S7 vol. 15, art. 10   16-6372
    —— Copy 2.   Q11.S7 2d set

QL
Crustacea
Pam.575

CRUSTACEA   PACIFIC

Banner, Albert H.

    A taxonomic study of the Mysidacea and Euphausiacea (Crustacea) of the northeastern Pacific, I-III.

    (Reprinted, Trans. R. Canadian Inst., Vol. 26:345-399, 1947; 27:65-125, 1948; 28:1-62, 1950)

QL
438
M 63

CRUSTACEA   NEW ZEALAND

Miers, E. J.

    Catalogue of the Stalk and Sessile-eyed Crustacea of New Zealand. Colonial museum and geological survey department.

2 cops.

    London. 1876. pls. 3.

AS
36
S4

CRUSTACEA--NORTH AMERICA.

Wilson, Charles Branch, 1861-

    North American parasitic copepods belonging to the *Lernaeidae*; with a revision of the entire family. By Charles Branch Wilson ...

    (*In* U. S. National museum. Proceedings. Washington, 1917. 23½ᶜᵐ. v. 53, p. 1-150. pl. 1-21)

    Bibliography: p. 127-144.

    1. Lernaeidae. 2. Crustacea—North America.

     18-14620

    Library of Congress   Q11.U55 vol. 53

GC
1
W 31c

CRUSTACEA   PACIFIC

Banner, Albert H.

    A taxonomic study of the Mysidacea and Euphausiacea (Crustacea) of the northeastern Pacific.

    (Trans. Roy. Canadian Inst., 26:345-399, Y) being Contribution 132, Univ. of Washington, Pubs. in Oceanography

CRUSTACEA PACIFIC

QL
618
V 22

Boone, Lee

Crustacea: Stomatopoda and Brachyura.
Scientific results of the world cruise of the
yacht "Alva", 1931, William K. Vanderbilt, commanding. 1934. 8vo. 210 pp. 109 plates.

(Bulletin of the Vanderbilt Museum, Vol. V)

CRUSTACEA PACIFIC

Q
115
U 58

Dana, James Dwight
Crustacea.

United States Exploring Expedition, during
the years 1838, 1839, 1840, 1841, 1842, under
the command of Charles Wilkes. Vols. 13-14:
Crustacea, by James D. Dana. With a folio atlas
of 96 plates. 1852-53.

CRUSTACEA PACIFIC

AS
122
L-p

Gordon, Isabella

Notes on some Indo-Pacific crabs (Crustacea,
Decapoda).

(Linnean Soc. of London, Proc., 153rd
Session, 1940-41, Pt. 1, pp. 123-140, 15 figs.)

CRUSTACEA PACIFIC

QL
618
V 22

Boone, Lee

Scientific results of the world cruise of
the yacht "Alva", 1931, William K. Vanderbilt,
commanding. Crustacea: Anomura, Macrura,
Euphausiacea, Isopoda, Amphipoda, and
Echinodermata: Asteroidea and Echinoidea.

(Bulletin of the Vanderbilt Marine Museum,
Vol. 6, 1935, 264 pp., 96 pl.)

CRUSTACEA PACIFIC

QL
Crustacea
Pam.
590

Edmondson, Charles Howard

Additional central Pacific Crustaceans.

(Occ. Papers, Bernice P. Bishop Museum, Vol.
21(6):67-86, 1952)

Crustacea - Pacific

QL
5
D /

Jacquinot, Honoré and Lucas, M. H.
Description des crustacées, in Voyage
au Pole Sud.....l'Astrolabe et la Zélée...
Dumont-d'Urville.
Zoologie III. Crustacées. pp. 1-105

Crustacea. - Pacific.

QL
Crus
Pam
#26

Borradaile, L. A.

On some Crustaceans from
the South Pacific. Collections of
Mr. J. S. Gardiner of Gonville + Caius
College, Cambridge, + of F. Wiley.
P.G.S. 1898 Part I. Stomatopoda pp. 8-39. Pl. V-VI.
" II Macrura anomala. 457-468 " XXVII
" III " } pp. 1001-1010. Pl. LXIX-LXV
1900 " IV Quills intersexnabrinals. Crabs
" V

CRUSTACEA PACIFIC

QL
Crust.
Pam.
545

Edmondson, Charles Howard

Callianassidae of the Central Pacific.

(Occ. Papers, Bernice P. Bishop Museum,
Vol. 18, No. 2, pp. 35-61, 1944)

CRUSTACEA PACIFIC

QL
Crustacea
Pam.
582

Johnson, Martin W.

A giant Phyllosoma Larva of a Loricate
Crustacean from the tropical Pacific.

(Trans. Am. Microscopical Society, Vol. 70
(3):274-278, 1951)

CRUSTACEA PACIFIC

AS
36
S 4

Chace, Fenner A., Jr.

The oceanic crabs of the genera Planes and
Pachygrapsus.

(U. S. Nat. Mus., Proc., 101 (3272):65-103,
1951)

CRUSTACEA PACIFIC

QL
138
E 24

AS
763
B-b

Reading
Room

Edmondson, C. H. and others
Marine zoology of tropical central Pacific:
Crustacea, by Charles Howard Edmondson, pp. 3-62.

(Bernice P. Bishop Museum, Bulletin No. 27,
1925; Tanager Expedition Publication No. 1)

CRUSTACEA PACIFIC

DU
12
J 94

locked
case

Jukes, J. B.

Narrative of the surveying voyage of H.M.S.
Fly,...in Torres Strait, New Guinea, and other
islands of the eastern archipelago, during...1842
-1846...Vol. 2. London. 1847. 8vo. 2 vols.

CRUSTACEA PACIFIC (eastern)

AS
36
A 16

Coventry, J. Ayres
Crustacea (eastern Pacific, shores of Mex-
ico, Central and South America, Tres Marias Is.)
IN
Results of the Fifth George Vanderbilt Expe-
dition (1941)...
(Acad. Nat. Sci., Philadelphia, Monograph 6,
1944, pp. 531-544)

CRUSTACEA PACIFIC

QL
Crustacea
Pam. 583

Edmondson, Charles Howard

Some central Pacific crustaceans.

(Occ. Papers, Bernice P. Bishop Museum,
Vol. 20, No. 13, 1951)

CRUSTACEA PACIFIC

QL
1
In-m

Kemp, Stanley

An account of the Crustacea Stomatopoda of
the Indo-Pacific region, based on the collection
in the Indian Museum, with which are issued illustrations of the zoology of the R.I.M.S.S. "Investigator"...Crustacea Stomatopoda, Plates I-X,
issued by order of Captain Walter Lumsden.

(Memoirs, Indian Museum, Vol. IV, 1913)
[New Zealand   Australia,Hongkong,
Singapore,   Mauritius]

CRUSTACEA-PACIFIC

QL
1
N 6-z

Crane, Jocelyn

On the growth and ecology of Brachyuran
crabs of the genus Ocypode. Eastern Pacific
Expeditions of the New York Zoological Society,
29.

(Zoologica, Vol. 26, 1941, pp. 297-310)

Crustacea - Pacific

AS
182
H

Edwards A. Milne
Description de quelques Crustacés.
In Journ. Mus. Godeffroy. Heft IV. 1873.
pp. 76-88. (B. P. Mus. pagination pp. 255-
270) 77

CRUSTACEA-PACIFIC

QL
1
C 2-b

MacKay, Donald C. G.

The growth of the Pacific edible crab,
Cancer magister Dana, by Donald C. G. MacKay and
Frank W. Weymouth.

(Journal Biol. Board of Canada, 1, No. 3,
pp. 191-212, 1935)

CRUSTACEA PACIFIC

AP
2
A 5

and
AS
36
A 25

Dana, James Dwight

Conspectus Crustaceorum in orbis terrarum
circumnavigatione, C. Wilkes e classe Reipublicae
Foederatae duce, collectorum auctore J. D. Dana.

(Proc. Am. Acad. Arts and Sci., I, 1846-48,
149-155; II, 9-61, 201-220; Am. Jour. Sci., Ser.
2, Vol. VIII, 1849, 424-428; IX, 1850, 129-133;
XI, 1851, 268-274)

CRUSTACEA PACIFIC

QL
1
H2

Faxon, Walter

The stalk-eyed Crustacea. Reports on
an exploration ..... "Albatross", 1891...
Harvard Mus. Comp. Zool. Vol. XVIII.
1895.

CRUSTACEA PACIFIC

QL
Crus.Pam.
519,
528

Schellenberg, A.

Litorale Amphipoden des tropischen Pazifiks,
nach Sammlungen von Prof. Bock (Stockholm), Prof.
Dahl+(Berlin) und Prof. Pietschmann (Wien)

(Kungl. Svenska Vetenskapsakadem.Handlingar,
III Series, Vol. 16, No. 6, 1938)

AS
36
A-1

CRUSTACEA   PACIFIC

Stimpson, William

Prodromus descriptionis animalium evertebratorum quae in Expeditione ad Oceanum Pacificum ...missa...Pars III-VIII.

Proc. Acad. Nat. Sci., Philadelphia, 1857, pp. 216-221; 1858, 31-40, 93-110, 159-163, 225-252, 1860, pp. 22-47.)

Q
115
U 58

looked
case

CRUSTACEA   PACIFIC

United States Exploring Expedition...1838-1842, under the command of Charles Wilkes. Vols. 13-14: Crustacea by James D. Dana. Philadelphia. 1852-53. 4to with folio atlas of 96 plates.

AS
719
A-m

CRUSTACEA   PACIFIC

Ward, Melbourne

The crab in medicine, magic and myth.

(Australian Museum Magazine. Vol.VI. 1937. pp.211-216)

QH
1
M 45

CRUSTACEA   PACIFIC

Ward, Melbourne

Notes on the Crustacea of the Desjardins Museum, Mauritius Institute, with descriptions of new genera and species.

(Mauritius Institute Bulletin, Vol. 2, 1942, pp. 49-108)

QL
1
T 64

CRUSTACEAE   PALAU ISLANDS

Ueno, Masuzo

Cladocera of lake Ngardok in Babelthaop of the Palau islands.

(Annotationes Zoologicae Japonensis, Vol.15, 1936, pp. 514-519)

AS
763
B-b

QL
Crustacea
Pam
493

Reading
Room

CRUSTACEA   PALMYRA

Edmondson, Charles H.

Crustacea from Palmyra and Fanning Islands, with descriptions of new species of crabs from Palmyra Island by Mary J. Rathbun.

Bull. No. 5, Bernice P. Bishop Museum, 1923

AS
36
S2

CRUSTACEA--PANAMA.

Marsh, Charles Dwight, 1855-

... Report on fresh-water *Copepoda* from Panama, with descriptions of new species (with five plates) by C. Dwight Marsh ... Washington, Smithsonian institution, 1913.

1 p. l., 30 p. incl. 4 pl. pl. 24½ᶜᵐ. (Smithsonian miscellaneous collections. v. 61, no. 3)

Publication 2182.
Bibliography: p. 20-21.

1. Copepoda. 2. Crustacea—Panama.

Library of Congress   Q11.S7   13-35484
———— Copy 2.   QL444.C7M33

AS
36
S5

CRUSTACEA--PANAMA

Rathbun, Mary Jane, 1860-

... Decapod crustaceans from the Panama region. By Mary J. Rathbun ... Washington, Govt. print. off., 1918.

1 p. l., 123-184, iii p. pl. 54-66. 24½ᶜᵐ. (Smithsonian institution. United States National museum. Bulletin 103 (pt. 7₁)

At head of title: Contributions to the geology and paleontology of the Canal Zone, Panama, and geologically related areas in Central America and the West Indies.
"Extract from Bulletin 103, pages 123-184, with plates 54-66."

1. Decapoda (Crustacea) 2. Crustacea—Panama.

Library, Smithsonian   Institution   S 21-7
          (s21b5)

AS
36
S2

CRUSTACEA-PANAMA.

Rathbun, Mary Jane, 1860-

... New decapod crustaceans from Panama, by Mary J. Rathbun ... Washington, Smithsonian institution, 1912.

1 p. l., 3 p. 24½ᶜᵐ. (Smithsonian miscellaneous collections, v. 59, no. 13)

Publication 2090.

1. Decapoda (Crustacea) 2. Crustacea—Panama.

Library of Congress   Q11.S7 vol. 59, no. 13   12-35780
———— Copy 2.   QL441.2.R3

AS
36
S4

CRUSTACEA- PANAMA

Richardson, Harriet.

Description of a new isopod crustacean belonging to the genus *Livoneca* from the Atlantic coast of Panama. By Harriet Richardson ...

(In U. S. National museum. Proceedings. Washington, 1912. 23½ᶜᵐ. vol. 42, p. 173-174. 1 illus.)

1. Livoneca. 2. Crustacea—Panama.

Library of Congress   Q11.U55 vol. 42   13-9520

AS
36
S4

CRUSTACEA- PANAMA

Richardson, Harriet.

Description of a new terrestrial isopod belonging to the genus *Cubaris* from Panama. By Harriet Richardson ...

(In U. S. National museum. Proceedings. Washington, 1912. 23½ᶜᵐ. vol. 42, p. 477-479. illus.)

1. Cubaris. 2. Crustacea—Panama.

Library of Congress   Q11.U55 vol. 42   13-9540

AS
36
S4

CRUSTACEA - PANAMA

Richardson, Harriet.

Descriptions of two new parasitic isopods belonging to the genera *Palægyge* and *Probopyrus* from Panama. By Harriet Richardson ...

(In U. S. National museum. Proceedings. Washington, 1912. 23½ᶜᵐ. vol. 42, p. 521-524. illus.)

1. Isopoda. 2. Crustacea—Panama.

Library of Congress   Q11.U55 vol. 42   13-9543

AS
36
S4

CRUSTACEA--PATAGONIA

Richardson, Harriet.

Description of a new isopod of the genus *Notasellus* from the east coast of Patagonia. By Harriet Richardson ...

(In U. S. National museum. Proceedings. Washington, 1910. 23½ᶜᵐ. vol. 37, p. 649-650. illus.)

1. Notasellus. 2. Crustacea—Patagonia.

Library of Congress   Q11.U55 vol. 37   11-9684

AS
36
C51

CRUSTACEA--PENNSYLVANIA

Ortmann, Arnold Edward, 1863-

... The crawfishes of the state of Pennsylvania. By Arnold E. Ortmann, PH. D.

(In Pittsburg. Carnegie museum. Memoirs. Pittsburgh, 1906. 33½ x 26¾ᶜᵐ. vol. ii, no. 10, p. 343-533. plates (partly col.) maps)

A continuation of, and an enlargement upon "The crawfishes of Western Pennsylvania" pub. in the Annals of the Carnegie museum, vol. III, 1905, p. 387 et seq. cf. p. 343.
Publications of the Carnegie museum. Serial no. 44.
Bibliography: p. 513-517.

1. Crayfish. 2. Crustacea—Pennsylvania.

Library of Congress   QH1.P57   7-13498
———— Copy 2.

AS
36
S4

CRUSTACEA -- PERU

Rathbun, Mary Jane, 1860-

The stalk-eyed *Crustacea* of Peru and the adjacent coast. By Mary J. Rathbun ...

(In U. S. National museum. Proceedings. Washington, 1911. 23½ᶜᵐ. vol. 38, p. 531-620. illus., pl. 36-56)

"List of the principal works relating to the stalk-eyed crustacean fauna of the Peruvian province": p. 566-569.

1. Crustacea—Peru.

Library of Congress   Q11.U55 vol. 38   11-15897

AS
36
S4

CRUSTACEA--PERU

Richardson, Harriet.

Report on isopods from Peru, collected by Dr. R. E. Coker. By Harriet Richardson ...

(In U. S. National museum. Proceedings. Washington, 1911. 23½ᶜᵐ. v. 38, p. 79-85. illus.)

1. Isopoda. 2. Crustacea—Peru. I. Coker, Robert Ervin, 1876-

Library of Congress   Q11.U55 vol. 38   11-15590

AS
36
S4

CRUSTACEA -- PERU

Walker, Alfred O.

Marine amphipods from Peru. By Alfred O. Walker ...

(In U. S. National museum. Proceedings. Washington, 1911. 23½ᶜᵐ. vol. 38, p. 621-622. illus.)

1. Amphipoda. 2. Crustacea—Peru.

Library of Congress   Q11.U55 vol. 38   11-15898

AS
36
S4

CRUSTACEA -- PERU

Weckel, Ada L.

Fresh-water amphipods from Peru. By Ada L. Weckel ...

(In U. S. National museum. Proceedings. Washington, 1911. 23½ᶜᵐ. vol. 38, p. 623-624. illus.)

1. Amphipoda. 2. Crustacea—Peru.

Library of Congress   Q11.U55 vol. 38   11-16464

AS
540
P

CRUSTACEA   PHILIPPINE ISLANDS

Blanco, Guillermo J.

Four new Philippine species of fresh-water shrimps of the genus Caridina.

(Phil. Jour. of Sci., Vol. 70, 1939, pp. 389-393)

QL
Crustacea
Pam. 498

AS
763
B-4

Reading
Room

CRUSTACEA   POLYNESIA

Edmondson, Charles Howard

New and rare Polynesian crustacea. Honolulu. 1935.

(Bernice P. Bishop Museum, Occ. Papers, vol. 10, no. 24)

QL
Crustacea
Pam. 518

AS
763
B-4

Reading
Room

CRUSTACEA   POLYNESIA

Jackson, Harold Gordon

Terrestrial Isopods of Southeastern Polynesia.

(Bernice P. Bishop Museum, Occasional Papers, Vol. 14, No. 10, pp. 167-192. Mangarevan Expedition Publication 26. 1938)

QL
Crustacea
Pam. 518

CRUSTACEA POLYNESIA

Jackson, Harold Gordon

Terrestrial Isopoda of Southeastern Polynesia.

(Bernice P. Bishop Museum, Occasional Papers Vol. 14, No. 10, pp. 167-192. Mangarevan Expedition Publication 26. 1938)

QL
Crust.
Pam
576

CRUSTACEA - RODRIGUEZ

Miers, Edward J.

Zoology of Rodriguez-Crustacea. London, 1879, 12p.

QL
Crustacea
Pam.
656

CRUSTACEA SOUTH AMERICA

Manning, Raymond B.

Stomatopod Crustacea from the Atlantic coast of northern South America.

(Allan Hancock Atlantic Expedition, Report No. 9, 1961)

Biblio-
film
No. 54

CRUSTACEA POLYNESIA

Nobili, Giuseppe

Ricerche sui crostacei della Polinesia, Decapodi, Stomatopodi, Anisopodi e Isopodi.

(Mem. R. Accad. Sci., Torini, ser. 2, vol. 57:351-430, 1907)

QL
Crust.
Pam.618

(also photostat - pp.384-385, and pl.2: Thalamita)

QL
Crust.Pam.
135

CRUSTACEA SAMOA

Lenz, H.

Ergebnisse einer Reise nach dem Pacific (Schauinsland 1896-1897) Crustaceen.

(Aus. Zool. Jahr. 1901, Bd. 14, pp. 429-482)

(Laysan, Samoa, New Zealand, Chatham Is. Hawaii, Clipperton Island)

AS
36
S4

CRUSTACEA - SOUTHAMERICA

Richardson, Harriet.

Descriptions of a new genus of isopod crustaceans, and of two new species from South America. By Harriet Richardson ...

(*In* U. S. National museum. Proceedings. Washington, 1913. 23½ᶜᵐ. vol. 43, p. 201-204. illus.)

"List of references": p. 204.

1. Isopoda. 2. Crustacea—South America.

Library of Congress   Q11.U55 vol. 43   13-13113

QH
109.P
N 53

CRUSTACEA PORTO RICO

Schmitt, Waldo L.

Crustacea Macrura of Porto Rico and the Virgin Islands.

IN Scientific survey of Porto Rico and the Virgin Islands. Vol. 15, Part 2, pp. 125-227. 1935.

QL
Crustacea Pam.
34

CRUSTACEA SAMOA

Miller, Robert Cunningham

Wood-boring Crustacea from Hawaii and Samoa.

(Univ. Calif. Pub. in Zool. Vol. 26, 1924)

AS
750
D 67 c

CRUSTACEA SUBANTARCTIC ISLANDS

Yaldwyn, J. C.

Decapod Crustacea from Subantarctic seal and shag stomachs.

(Cape Exp., Sci. Res. of the New Zealand Subantarctic Exp., 1941-45, No. 23, 1958)

AS
36
S4

CRUSTACEA--PRIBILOF ISLANDS

Pearse, Arthur Sperry, 1877-

Notes on a small collection of amphipods from the Pribilof Islands, with descriptions of new species. By A. S. Pearse ...

(*In* U. S. National museum. Proceedings. Washington, 1913. 23½ᶜᵐ. v. 45, p. 571-573. illus.)

1. Amphipoda. 2. Crustacea—Pribilof Islands.

Library of Congress   Q11.U55 vol. 45   14-4155

Q
115
R 29

CRUSTACEA SAMOA

Pesta, O.

Crustacea, Teil I-II. (Samoa)

Rechinger, Karl
Botanische und zoologische Ergebnisse einer Wissenschaftlichen Forschungsreise nach den Samoainseln dem Neuguinea-Archipel und den Salomonsinseln...1905. Teil IV:4,pp.36-65,1911 and Teil V:pp.231-240. 1913.

QL
Crustacea
Pam. 495

CRUSTACEA-SUMATRA

Man, J. G. de

Decapoda and Stomatopoda from Pulau Berhala.

(Miscellanea Zoologica Sumatrana, XXXVI,1929)

QL
636
Q 3

CRUSTACEA QUEENSLAND

Marshall, T.C.

Know your fishes; an illustrated guide to the principal commercial fishes and crustaceans of Queensland. By T.C.Marshall, E.M.Grant and N.M.Haysom

(Ichthyological Notes, Vol.1(4), 1959)

QL
1
C 1

CRUSTACEA - SAN FRANCISCO BAY

Schmitt, Waldo Lasalle, 1887-
The marine decapod *Crustacea* of California, with special reference to the decapod *Crustacea* collected by the United States Bureau of fisheries steamer "Albatross" in connection with the biological survey of San Francisco Bay during the years 1912-1913, by Waldo L. Schmitt ... Berkeley, University of California press, 1921.

cover-title, 1 p. l., 470 p. illus., 50 pl. (incl. maps; part fold.) 27½ᶜᵐ. (University of California publications in zoology. v. 23)

Published by permission of the secretary of the Smithsonian institution and of the United States commissioner of fisheries.

1. Crustacea—San Francisco Bay. 2. Decapoda (Crustacea)   I. Albatross (Steamer)

Title from Univ. of Calif   Library of Congress   A 21-878
[5]

QL
Crustacea
Pam.486

CRUSTACEA - SUMATRA.

Pesta, Otto.

Zur kenntnis der land- und süsswasserkrabben von Sumatra und Java.

Sonder-abdruck aus dem Archiv für hydrobiologie. 1930. Suppl.-bd. VIII. S.92-108.

QL
Crustacea
Pam.
347

CRUSTACEA -- RED SEA

Heller, Camil

Synopsis der im Rothen Meere vorkommenden Crustaceen. Ex Zool.-Bot. Ges. Wien. Abh. XI, 1861. 32 pp.

QL
Crust
Pam
389

CRUSTACEA - SINGAPORE

Nobili, Giuseppe

Crostacei di Singapore. Bollettino Mus. Zool.-Anat. R. Univ. Torino, v.18, n.455, 1903.

AS
496
F 29

CRUSTACEA SUMATRA

Rothschild, N. Charles   and others
Invertebrates collected in Korinchi...

IN Results of an expedition to Korinchi Peak, Sumatra (1914). Part III, 1919-1931, pp. 166-167. 1925.
(Jour. Fed. Malay States Mus., Vol. 8, Part III, 1919-1931, pp. 166-167)

QL
1
T 64

CRUSTACEA RIUKIU ISLANDS

Shiino, Sueo M.

Further notes on Bopyrids from Kyûsyû and Ryûkyû.

(Annotationes Zoologicae Japonenses, Vol. 20(3):154-158, 1941)

AS
619
S 72

CRUSTACEA SOUTH AFRICA

Barnard, K. H.

Additions to the fauna-list of South African Crustacea and Pycnogonida. (With fifty-three text-figures).

(Annals of the South African Museum, Part I, pp. 1-107, December, 1955)

QL
Crustacea
Pam.510

AS
763
B-4

Reading
Room

CRUSTACEA TAHITI

Edmondson, C. H.

Quantitative studies of Copepods in Hawaii with brief surveys in Fiji and Tahiti.

(B.P.Bishop Museum. Occasional Papers, vol. XIII, no.12. 1937. pp.131-146)

CRUSTACEA   TAHITI

QL
441.8
S 61

Forest, Jacques

Crustacés Décapodes Brachyoures de Tahiti et des Tuamotu. Par Jacques Forest et Danièle Guinot. Paris. Éditions de la Fondation Singer-Polignac. 1961. xi + 195 pp. + 18 plates. folio.

CRUSTACEA   THURSDAY ISLAND

QL
5
S 47

locked
case

Semon, Richard

Zoologische Forschungsreisen in Australien und dem Malayischen Archipel...1891-1893. Bd. 5, Lief. 1, pp. 3-80, 1894: Crustaceen, by A. Ortmann.

CRUSTAL STRUCTURE   HAWAII

QE
Geol.Pam.
1339

Eaton, J. P.

Crustal structure and volcanism in Hawaii.

(Reprint, Crust of the Pacific Basin, Monograph 6:13-29, 1962)

CRUSTACEA   TASMANIA

AS
720.T
R

Clark, Ellen

Tasmanian Parastacidae.

(Papers and Proc. R. Soc. Tasmania, 1938: 117-128)

CRUSTACEA   TUAMOTUS

QL
441.8
S 61

Forest, Jacques

Crustacés Décapodes Brachyoures de Tahiti et des Tuamotu. By Jacques Forest and Danièle Guinot. Paris. Éditions de la Fondation Singer-Polignac. 1961. xi + 195 pp. + 18 plates. Folio.

AS
80 Ins
A. 14.

Cruz, O. G.

Dos Accidentes em Sorotherapia

Rio de Janeiro, 1902. 8°. p. 65.

CRUSTACEA   TASMANIA

QK
Crustacea
Pam.
x585
AS
720.T
Q 3

Guiler, Eric R.

A list of the Crustacea of Tasmania.

(Records of the Queen Victoria Museum, Launceston, Vol. 3(3):15-44, 1952)

supplement, ibid, n.s. No. 5, 1956

CRUSTACEA   VIRGIN ISLANDS

QH
109.P
N 53

Schmitt, Waldo, L.

Crustacea Macrura of Porto Rico and the Virgin Islands.

IN Scientific survey of Porto Rico and the Virgin Islands, Vol. 15, Part 2, pp. 125-227. 1935.

AS
80 Ins
A. 14.

Cruz, O. G.

Uma nova especie do genero Borophora

Rio de Janeiro, 1907. 8°. p. 9.

CRUSTACEA   TASMANIA

AS
720.T
R

Hickman, V. V.

The embryology of the Syncarid crustacean, Anaspides tasmaniae.

(Papers and Proc. R. Soc. Tasmania, 1936: 1-36)

CRUSTACEA--VIRGINIA

AS
36
S4

Embody, George Charles, 1876–

A new fresh-water amphipod from Virginia, with some notes on its biology. By George C. Embody ...

(In U. S. National museum. Proceedings. Washington, 1911. 23½ᶜᵐ. vol. 38, p. 299-305. illus.)

1. Amphipoda. 2. Crustacea—Virginia.

11-15732

Library of Congress   Q11.U55 vol. 38

AS
80
A. 14
Ins

Cruz, O. G.

Um nova genero brazileiro da sub-familia "Anophelinae"

Rio de Janeiro, 1907. 8°. p. 10.

CRUSTACEA   TEXAS

QL
Crust.
Pam.
593

Pearse, A. S.

Parasitic Crustacea from the Texas Coast.

(Inst. of Marine Sci., Port Aransas, Texas Dec. 1952. 42 pp.)

CRUSTACEA--WEST INDIES

AS
36
S4

Rathbun, Mary Jane, 1860–

Additions to West Indian Tertiary decapod crustaceans. By Mary J. Rathbun ...

(In U. S. National museum. Proceedings. Washington, 1921. 23½ᶜᵐ. v. 58, p. 381-384. pl. 25)

"Additions to the bibliography of West Indian Tertiary Decapoda": p. 384.

1. Decapoda (Crustacea) 2. Crustacea—West Indies.

21-21446

Library of Congress   Q11.U55 vol. 58
[5]

AS
80 Ins
A. 14

Cruz, O. G.

Peste

Rio de Janeiro, 1906. 8°. p. 37.

CRUSTACEA   THAILAND

AS
145
B

Jackson, H.G.

A new terrestrial isopod from Siam, collected by H.R.H. The Price Leopold of Belgium in the Far East in the year 1932.

(Bull. Musée royal d'Histoire naturelle de Belgique. vol.XIII, 1937. pp.1-4. 2 figs.)

CRUSTACEA--WEST INDIES. I. TITLE.

AS
36
S4

Wilson, Charles Branch, 1861–

Crustacean parasites of West Indian fishes and land crabs, with descriptions of new genera and species. By Charles Branch Wilson ...

(In U. S. National museum. Proceedings. Washington, 1913. 23½ᶜᵐ. v. 44, p. 189-277. pl. 18-53)

1. Parasites—Fishes. 2. Parasites—Crustacea. 3. Crustacea—West Indies. I. Title.

13-20860

Library of Congress   Q11.U55 vol. 44

AS
80
Ins

Cruz, Oswaldo.

Prophylaxia da Febre Amarella. Memoria apresentada ao 4° Congresso Medico Latino-Americano

Rio Janeiro 1909. pp. 158. 1910

CRUSTACEA   THAILAND

QL
Fish
Pam.
352

Pearse, A. S.

Parasites of Siamese Fishes and Crustaceans.

(Jour. of the Siam Soc., Nat. Hist. Supp., Vol. IX, No. 2, 1933.)

CRUSTACEA - ZANZIBAR

QL
Crust
Pam
387

Nobili, Giuseppe

Crostacei di Zanzibar. Bollettino Mus. Zool.-Anat. R. Univ. Torino, v.20, n.506, 1905.

CRYOLITE--[GREENLAND]

AS
36
S

[Quale, Paul]

An account of the cryolite of Greenland. Communicated by Messrs. Lewis & sons.

(In Smithsonian institution. Annual report. 1866. Washington, 1867. 23½ᶜᵐ. p. [398]-401)

Signed: Paul Quale.

1. Cryolite—[Greenland]

S 15-200

Library of Congress   Q11.S66 1866
Library, Smithsonian   Institution

QL
Insects
Pam.
1110

CRYPHALINAE

Hopkins, A. D.

Classification of the Cryphalinae, with descriptions of new genera and species.

(U. S. Dept. of Agric., Office of the Secretary, Report no. 99, 1915)

QK
Bot.Pam.
2854

CRYPTOCORYNE

Wit, H. C. D. de

Spicilegium Malaianum II.

(Webbia, vol. IX(2):455-464, 1954)

Q
115
W.95

locked
case

CRYPTOGAMIA PACIFIC

Wüllerstorf-Urbair, Bernhard

Reise der Oesterreichischen Fregatte Novara um die Erde...1857-1859.
Botanischer Theil, Heft 1-4, redigirt von E. Fenzl. 1868-70. Wien. 4to.

QL
Insect
Pam.
1799

CRYSOMELIDAE

Gressitt, J. Linsley

Hispine beetles from the South Pacific (Coleoptera: Chrysomelidae)

(Nova Guinea, n.s. Vol. 8(2):205-324, 1957)

AS
36
S1

CRYPTOGAMIA

Reichardt, Heinrich Wilhelm, 1835-
On the present state of our knowledge of cryptogamous plants. Lecture delivered before the Vienna society for the diffusion of scientific knowledge, by Heinrich Wilhelm Reichardt.

(*In* Smithsonian institution. Annual report. 1871. Washington, 1873. 23⅜ᵐᵒ. p. (249)-260)

"Translated for the Smithsonian institution by Professor C. F. Kroeh."

1. Cryptogams. I. Kroeh, Charles Frederick, 1846-

Library of Congress   Q11.S66 1871
Library, Smithsonian Institution

S 15-319

QK
368
C 78

CRYPTOGAMIA PHILIPPINE ISLANDS

Copeland, E. B.

QK
Bot.Pam.
216

I. The Polypodiaceae of the Philippine Islands. II. New species of edible Philippine fungi. Manila. 1905.

(Dep't Interior, Bur. Gov't Laboratories, no. 28, July 1905, pp. 1-138)

QK
1
T 69 m

CRYSOPTERIS

Blasdell, Robert F.

A monographic study of the fern genus Cystopteris.

(Memoirs of the Torrey Botanical Club, Vol. 21(4):1-102, 1963)

AS
142
V

CRYPTOGAMIA

Zahlbruckner, A.

Schedae ad Kryptogamas exsiccatas editae a Museo Palatino Vindobonensi.
Aus K. K. Natur histor. Hofmuseum in Wien. Band —
Index to Century I - XX in Band XXVI Heft-1-2. pp. 183 — 247.

QK
5
H 78

locked
case

The Cryptogamic Botany of the Antarctic Voyage of H. M. ships Erebus and Terror in the years 1839-1843... London. 1845

Hooker, Joseph Dalton

QK
Bot.Pam.
3037

CRYPTOCARYA

Kosterman, Andre J. G. H.

Le genre Cryptocarya R. Br. (Lauracées) à Madagascar.

(Bull. Jardin Bot. de l'Etat, Bruxelles, 27(2):173-188, 1957)

QK
5
Nov

CRYPTOGAMIA

Novara Voyage . 8.Botanischer Theil:

Sporenpflanzen.

See Novara

AS
36
A25

Cryptogamie laboratories Harvard Contributions from

In Am. Acad. Arts + Sc. Proc. XLVII. 7. 10 - 26.

QL
Insects
Pam.
1716

CRYPTOCEPHALINAE

Chujo, Michio

A taxonomic study on the Chrysomelidae (Insecta-Coleoptera) from Formosa, Part VII. Subfamily Cryptocephalinae.

(Quarterly Journal of the Taiwan Museum, 7(3/4), 1954)

AS
720.V
R

Cryptogamia- Australia.

Stirling, James
Cryptogamia of the Australian Alps.
In Roy. Soc. Victoria Trans. & Proc. XXII. 1886. pp. 49-56

QK
1
C 2

CRYTOGAMIA - ALASKA

Setchell, William Albert, 1864-
... Some unreported Alaskan *Sphagna*, together with a summary of the cryptogamic work of the University of California botanical expedition to Alaska in 1899. By William Albert Setchell. Berkeley, The University press, 1907.

cover-title, p. (309)-315. 27ᶜᵐ. (University of California publications in botany, vol. 2, no. 14)

1. Sphagnaceae. 2. Cryptogams—Alaska.

A 11-746

Title from Univ. of Calif.   Library of Congress

AS
36
A 25

CRYPTOCERCUS

Cleveland, L. R.

The wood-feeding roach Cryptocercus, its protozoa, and the symbiosis between protozoa and roach, by L. R. Cleveland, in collaboration with S. R. Hall, Elizabeth P. Sanders, and Jane Collier.

(Memoirs of Amer. Acad. of Arts and Sciences, Vol. 17, No. 2, 1934, pp. 187-342. 4to. pls.1-60)

DU
620
I 82

locked
case

CRYPTOGAMIA HAWAII

Bailey, Edward

Hawaiian Cryptogams

(Islander, I, 1875, pp. 43, 50, 57-58)

QK
Bot.
Pam.
2971

CRYPTOGAMS KAPINGAMARANGI

Miller, Harvey Alfred

Cryptogams of Kapingamarangi Atoll, Caroline Islands I.Bryophyta, by Harvey Alfred Miller. II. Ecology and phytogeography, by W. A. Niering and H. A. Miller.

(The Bryologist, Vol. 59(3):167-180, 1956)

QL
Crustacea
Pam. 491

CRYPTOCHIRUS PACIFIC

Edmondson, Charles Howard

Cryptochirus of the Central Pacific.

(Bernice P. Bishop Museum, Occasional Papers, Vol. X, No. 5, 1933)

QK
5
H 78

locked
case

CRYPTOGAMIA ANTARCTIC

Hooker, Joseph Dalton

The Cryptogamic Botany of the Antarctic Voyage of H.M. ships Erebus and Terror in the years 1839-1843, under the command of Captain Sir James Clark Ross. London. Reeve Brothers. 1845. 258 pp. pl. 57-80, 151-198.

QK
Bot.Pam.
2163

CRYPTOMERIA JAPONICA

Forestry of the "Sugi"(Cryptomeria Japonica, don) and the "Karamatsu"(Larix Leptolepis,Gord.)

Japan, Department of Forestry, Ministry of Agriculture and Forestry, 85 pp., + 3 plates, + 3 maps, 1926, 8vo.

Card 1 (row 1, col 1)

AS
720.S
S 72

CRYPTORHYNCHIDAE

Lea, Arthur Mills

Cryptorhynchides (Curculionidae), mostly
from Australia.

(Records from the South Australian Museum,
Vol. 4, 1928-1932, pp. 49-90) [pub. Sept. 30,
1928]

Card (row 1, col 2)

QK
Bot.Pam.
2617

CRYPTOTERMES

Wolcott, George N.

An index to the termite-resistance of woods.

(Univ. of Puerto Rico, Agric. Exp. Station,
Bull. No. 85, 1950)

Card (row 1, col 3)

QL
473
J 95

Csiki, E.

Mordellidae
IN

Junk, W.
Coleopterorum catalogus...Pars 63, 1915.

Card (row 2, col 1)

QL
Insect
Pam. 973

CRYPTORHYNCHINAE

Zimmerman, Elwood C.

Cryptorhynchinae of Rapa.

(Bernice P. Bishop Museum, Bulletin No. 151,
1938)

Card (row 2, col 2)

AS
36
S1

CRYSTALLIZATION

Gaubert, Paul *i. e.* Marie Benoit Paul, 1865-
The formation, growth, and habit of crystals. By Paul
Gaubert.

(*In* Smithsonian institution. Annual report. 1909. Washington, 1910.
23½ᶜᵐ. p. 271-278)
"Translated ... from Revue scientifique, Paris, 48th year, no. 3, January
15, 1910."

1. Crystallization.

11-9868

Library of Congress   Q11.S66 1909

Card (row 2, col 3)

AS
472
A-jp

Csoma (Körösi), Sándor, 1784?-1842.
Tibetan studies: being a reprint of the articles contributed to the Journal of the Asiatic society of Bengal
by Alexander Csoma de Körös. Ed. by E. Denison Ross.
Calcutta, Printed at the Baptist mission press, 1912.
3 p. l., 172 p. front. (port.) 24½ᶜᵐ. (*On cover:* Journal & proceedings
of the Asiatic society of Bengal. vol. VII, extra no. 1911)
CONTENTS.— Geographical notice of Tibet.— Translation of a Tibetan
fragment.— Note on the origin of the Kala-Chakra and Adi-Buddha systems.— Translation of a Tibetan passport, dated A. D. 1688.— Origin of the
Shakya race translated from the ... (La), or the 26th volume of the mDo
class in the Kâ-gyur, commencing on the 161st leaf.— Tibetan symbolical
(Continued on next card)
15-12140

Card (row 3, col 1)

QL
Insects
Pam. 987

CRYPTORHYNCHINAE

Zimmerman, Elwood C.

Idosaulus, a new genus of Fijian Cryptorhynchinae (Coleoptera, Curculionidae)

(The Pan-Pacific Entomologist, Vol. 14, 1938
pp. 158-160)

Card (row 3, col 2)

AS
36
S1

CRYSTALLOGRAPHY

Brezina, Aristides *i. e.* Maria Aristides Severin Ferdinand, 1848-
Explanation of the principles of crystallography and
crystallophysics. By Aristides Brezina.
(*In* Smithsonian institution. Annual report. 1872. Washington, 1873.
23½ᶜᵐ. p. (233)-266. diagrs.)
"Translated ... by Professor T. Egleston."

1. Crystallography.   I. Egleston, Thomas, 1832-1900, tr.

S 15-338

Library of Congress   Q11.S66 1872
Library, Smithsonian   Institution

Card (row 3, col 3)

AS
472
A-jp

Csoma (Körösi), Sándor, 1784?-1842.   Tibetan studies
... 1912. (Card 2)
CONTENTS—Continued.
names, used as numerals.— Extracts from Tibetan works.— Analysis of a
Tibetan medical work.— Interpretation of the Tibetan inscription on a
Bhotian banner, taken in Assam, and presented to the Asiatic society by
Captain Bogle.— Note on the white satin-embroidered scarfs of the Tibetan
priests. By Major T. H. A. Lloyd. With a translation of the motto on
the margin of one presented to the Asiatic society.— Notices on the different systems of Buddhism, extracted from the Tibetan authorities.— Enu-
meration of historical and grammatical works to be met with in Tibet.—
Remarks on Trans-Himalayan Buddhist amulets.— A brief notice of the
Subháshita Ratna Nidhi of Saskya Pandita, with extracts and translations.
1. Tibet. 2. Tibetan literature (Collections) 3. Buddha and Buddhism.
I. Ross, Edward Denison, 1871-   ed. II. Title.

Library of Congress   AS472.B33 vol.7   15-12140

Card (row 4, col 1)

QL
461
H 1

CRYPTORHYNCHINAE

Zimmerman, Elwood C.

On Chaenosternum with a key to the genera
of Hawaii Cryptorhynchinae (Col., Curculionidae)

(Haw. Ent. Soc., Pro., Vol. 10, 1938, pp.
134-136)

Card (row 4, col 2)

QD
931
D 27

CRYSTALLOGRAPHY

Day, Arthur Louis, 1869-
The isomorphism and thermal properties of the feld-
spars. Part I— Thermal study (by) Arthur L. Day and
E. T. Allen. Part II— Optical study (by) J. P. Iddings.
With an introduction by George F. Becker. Washington,
D. C., Carnegie institution of Washington, 1905.
95 p. illus., XXVI (i. e. 27) pl. 26½ᶜᵐ. (Carnegie institution of Wash-
ington. Publication no. 31)

1. Crystallography. 2. Feldspar.   I. Allen, Eugene Thomas, 1862-
joint author. II. Iddings, Joseph Paxson, 1857-   joint author. III. Becker, George Ferdinand, 1847-

5—32416

Library of Congress   QD931.D27

Card (row 4, col 3)

QL
Mammals
Pam.
157

Csordas, S. E.

The Kerguelen fur seal on Macquarie Island.

(Reprint, The Victorian Naturalist, Vol.
79(8):4 pp. unnumbered, 1962)

Card (row 5, col 1)

QL
Insect Pam.
915

AS
763
B-4

CRYPTORRHYNCHINAE   AUSTRAL ISLANDS

Zimmerman, Elwood C.

Cryptorrhynchinae of the Austral Islands.
(Coleoptera, Curculionidae).

(Bishop Museum Occasional Papers, vol.XII,
no.17. 1936. 19 pp., 2 figs.)

Card (row 5, col 2)

AS
36
S1

CRYSTALLOGRAPHY

Judd, John Wesley, 1840-
The rejuvenescence of crystals. By Prof. John W.
Judd ...
(*In* Smithsonian institution. Annual report. 1892. Washington, 1893.
23½ᶜᵐ. p. 281-288)
"From Nature, May 28, 1891; vol. XLIV, pp. 83-86."

1. Crystallography.   I. Title.

S 15-790

Library of Congress   Q11.S66 1892
Library, Smithsonian   Institution

Card (row 5, col 3)

QL
Mammals
Pam.
144

Csordas, S. E.

Leopard seals on Macquarie Island.

(Reprint, Victoria National Mus., Vol. 79:
358-362, 1963)

Card (row 6, col 1)

QL
Insect
Pam.
1525

CRYPTOSTEMMATIDAE

Linnavuori, R.

Studies on the family Cryptostemmatidae.
On some new or lesser known Heteroptera. Calli-
gypona leptosoma Fl. and C. albofimbriata (Sign.)
Fieb. (Hom. Delphacidae)

(Reprint: Suomen Hyonteistieteellinen Aika-
kauskirja: Annales Ent. Fennici, 17:92-110,1951)

Card (row 6, col 2)

AS
36
S1

CRYSTALLOGRAPHY

Liveing, George Downing, 1827-
Crystallization. By G. D. Liveing ...
(*In* Smithsonian institution. Annual report. 1892. Washington, 1893.
23½ᶜᵐ. p. 269-280. diagrs.)
"From Nature, June 18, 1891; vol. XLIV, pp. 156-160."

1. Crystallography.

S 15-789

Library of Congress   Q11.S66 1892
Library, Smithsonian   Institution

Card (row 6, col 3)

QH
Nat.
Hist.
Pam.
244

Csordas, S. E.

Sea lions on Macquarie Island.

(Victoria Nat. Mus., Vol. 80:32-35, 1963)

Card (row 7, col 1)

QL
Insect
Pam.
1836

and

AS
720.S
S 72

CRYPTOSTEMMATIDAE   AUSTRALIA

Gross, Gordon F.

On a new species of Cryptostemmatidae (Hemiptera-Heteroptera) from Australia.

(From Records of the South Australian Museum,
Vol. IX(3):327-329, June, 1950)

Card (row 7, col 2)

Q
115
R 29

Csiki, E.
Carabidae der Samoainseln.

Rechinger, Karl
Botanische und Zoologische Ergebnisse einer
Wissenschaftlichen Forschungsreise nach den Sa-
moainseln dem Neuguinea-Archipel und den Salo-
monsinseln...1905. Teil VI:pp. 25-26. 1914.
Nachtrage, pp. 163-164, 1914.

Card (row 7, col 3)

QL
1
N 6-z

CTENOCHAETUS

Randall, John E.

A revision of the surgeon fish genus Ctenochaetus, family Acanthuridae, with descriptions
of five new species.

(Zoologica, Vol. 40:149-166, 1955)

AS 36 A25-M

CTENOPHORA

Agassiz, Louis *i. e.* Jean Louis Rodolphe, 1807–1873.
... Contributions to the natural history of the *Acalephæ* of North America. By L. Agassiz ...

(*In* American academy of arts and sciences, Boston. Memoirs. Cambridge and Boston, 1850. n. s., vol. IV, pt. II, p. [221]–374. illus, 16 pl. (partly col.))

p. *313–316* inserted after p. 312.

CONTENTS.—pt. I. On the naked-eyed *Medusæ* of the shores of Massachusetts, in their perfect state of development.—pt. II. On the beroid *Medusæ* of the shores of Massachusetts, in their perfect state of development.

1. Hydromedusæ. 2. Ctenophora. 3. Marine fauna—Massachusetts.

Library of Congress   Q11.B68   11–8019
—— Copy 2, detached.   QL376.1.A3

Q 115 S 56

CTENOPHORA   DUTCH EAST INDIES

Moser, Fanny
Die Ctenophoren der Siboga-Expedition.

Weber, Max
Uitkomsten...Nederlandsch Oost-Indie, 1899–1900...Siboga...Monographie XIII (livr. 11). 1903
28 pp., 4 pl.

CUBA   BOTANY

see

BOTANY   CUBA

QL 1 C1

CTENOPHORA

Esterly, Calvin Olin, 1879–
... A study of the occurrence and manner of distribution of the *Ctenophora* of the San Diego region, by Calvin O. Esterly. Berkeley, University of California press, 1914.

cover-title, p. [21]–38 incl. tables. 27cm. (University of California publications in zoology, v. 13, no. 2)

Contribution from the Scripps institution for biological research.
Bibliography: p. 38.

1. Ctenophora.

A 14–1002 Revised

Title from Univ. of Calif.   Library of Congress

QL Prot.-Poly. Pam. 756

CTENOPHORA   HAWAII

Matthews, Donald C.

Records of Hawaiian Ctenophora.

(Reprinted from Transactions of the American Microscopical Society, Vol. LXXIII(3):282–284, 1954)

CUBA   BUFO MARINUS

see

BUFO MARINUS   CUBA

AS 36 S5

CTENOPHORA

Bigelow, Henry Bryant, 1879–
... Hydromedusae, siphonophores, and ctenophores of the "Albatross" Philippine expedition, by Henry B. Bigelow ... Washington, Govt. print. off., 1919.

1 p. l., 279–362 p., 1 l. pl. 39–43. 25cm. (Smithsonian institution. United States National museum. Bulletin 100, v. 1, pt. 5)

At head of title: Contributions to the biology of the Philippine archipelago and adjacent regions.
Bibliography: p. 355–360.

1. Hydromedusae. 2. Siphonophora. 3. Ctenophora.

19–26511

Library of Congress   Q11.U6   no. 100, vol. 1, pt. 5
—— Copy 2.   QL376.5.P6B5
[9]

QK 1 F 45

Cuatrecasas, José

Contributions to the Flora of South America. Studies on Andean Compositae -I; Studies in South American plants-II.

(Fieldiana: Botany, Vol. 27(1), 1950)

CUBA   ECHINODERMATA

See

ECHINODERMATA   CUBA

QL 1 C15

CTENOPHORA

Esterly, Calvin Olin, 1879–
... A study of the occurrence and manner of distribution of the *Ctenophora* of the San Diego region, by Calvin O. Esterly. Berkeley, University of California press, 1914.

cover-title, p. [21]–38 incl. tables. 27cm. (University of California publications in zoology, v. 13, no. 2)

Contribution from the Scripps institution for biological research.
Bibliography: p. 38.

1. Ctenophora.

A 14–1002 Revised

Title from Univ. of Calif.   Library of Congress

QL 1 H1

CUBA

Agassiz, Alexander Emmanuel Rudolph, 1835–1910.
... A reconnoissance of the Bahamas and of the elevated reefs of Cuba in the steam yacht "Wild duck," January to April, 1893. By Alexander Agassiz. With forty-seven plates. Cambridge, Mass., Printed for the Museum, 1894.

1 p. l., 203 p. illus., XLVII pl. (incl. fold. maps, fold. diagrs.) 24cm. (Bulletin of the Museum of comparative zoology at Harvard college. vol. XXVI, no. 1)

1. Geology—Bahamas. 2. Geology—Cuba. 3. Bahamas—Descr. & trav. 4. Cuba—Descr. & trav. I. "Wild duck" (Steamer)

Library, U. S. Geol.   survey S(214) H29 vol. 26, no. 1   G S 12–1
—— Copy 2.   502(390) Ag16
—— Copy 3.

CUBA   ECHINOIDEA

See

ECHINOIDEA   CUBA

QL 377.C8 M

CTENOPHORA (COELENTERATA)

Mayer, Alfred Goldsborough, 1868–
Ctenophores of the Atlantic coast of North America, by Alfred Goldsborough Mayer ... Washington, D. C., Carnegie institution of Washington, 1912.

1 p. l., 58 p. illus., 17 pl. (16 col.) 25½cm. (On verso of t.-p.: Carnegie institution of Washington. Publication no. 162)

Colored plates accompanied by guard sheets with descriptive letterpress.

1. Ctenophora (Coelenterata) 2. Coelenterata—Atlantic coast.

Library of Congress   QL377.C8M4   12—6814
—— Copy 2.

F 1761 B 23

CUBA

Barbour, Thomas

A naturalist in Cuba.
Little, Brown and Company. Boston. 1945. 8vo.
x + 317 pp.

CUBA   FAUNA

See

FAUNA   CUBA

AS 244 D

CTENOPHORA

Mortensen, Th.

Two New Ctenophores.

(Vid. Med. Dansk Nat. For. Kobenhavn, Bd. 83 1927,- Papers from Dr. Th. Mortensen's Pacific Expedition, 1914-16, No. 39)

CUBA   ALGAE

see

ALGAE   CUBA

CUBA   FISHES

see

FISHES   CUBA

QL 1 C15

CTENOPHORA.

Torrey, Harry Beal, 1873–
... The ctenophores of the San Diego region. By Harry Beal Torrey. [Berkeley, The University press] 1904.

p. [45]–50. pl. 27cm. (University of California publications. Zoology. vol. 2, no. 2)

At head of title: Contributions from the laboratory of the Marine biological association of San Diego. II.
Issued in single cover with vol. 2, no. 1 of the series.
Bibliography: p. 49.

1. Ctenophora.

A 11–2280

Title from Univ. of Calif.   Library of Congress

CUBA   BATRACHIA

see

BATRACHIA   CUBA

QE 75 B

CUBA   GAZETTEERS

Gannett, Henry, 1846–
... A gazetteer of Cuba, by Henry Gannett. Washington, Govt. print. off., 1902.

112 p. maps. 23cm. (U. S. Geological survey. Bulletin no. 192. ser. F, Geography, 29)

57th Cong. 1st sess. House. Doc. no. 474.

1. Cuba—Descr. & trav.—Gazetteers. I. Title.

Library of Congress   QE75.B9   3–5819
—— Copy 2.   F1754.G9

CUBA   GRAMINEAE
 	
see
 	
GRAMINEAE   CUBA
	AS
	36
	S4
	CUBARIS
	Richardson, Harriet.
	   Description of a new terrestrial isopod belonging to the genus *Cubaris* from Panama. By Harriet Richardson ...
	   (In U. S. National museum. Proceedings. Washington, 1912. 23½ᶜᵐ. vol. 42, p. 477–479. illus.)
	
	1. Cubaris. 2. Crustacea—Panama.
	                13–9540
	Library of Congress Q11.U55 vol. 42
		AS
		720.N
		L
		Cucujidae. Australia
		Olliff, A. Sidney
		List of the Cucujidae of Australia with notes and descriptions of new species.
		in Linn. Soc. N.S.W. Proc. 10, 1885–86, pp. 203–214.

CUBA   HELICINIDAE
 	
See
 	
HELICINIDAE   CUBA
	F
	1211
	C 96
	Cubas, Antonio Garcia
	   Mexico, its trade, industries and resources; translated by William Thompson, assisted by Charles B. Cleveland. Mexico, 1893. 8vo. xviii + 436 pp.
		QK
		1
		M 1
		CUCURBITA
		Whitaker, Thomas W.
		   American origin of the cultivated cucurbits.
		   (Annals Miss. Botanical Garden, 34 (2):101–111, 1947)

CUBA   INSECTS
 	
see
 	
INSECTS   CUBA
	QH
	301
	J 71-m
	The Cubomedusae
	Conant, Franklin Story
	   (Memoirs from the Biological Laboratory of Johns Hopkins University, IV:1, 1898, 4to.)
		QK
		495.C96
		B 15
		CUCURBITACEAE
		Bailey, L(iberty) H(yde)
		   The garden of gourds; with decorations. The Macmillan Company. New York. 1937. 8vo. 4 + 134 pp.

CUBA   MARINE FLORA
 	
see
 	
MARINE FLORA   CUBA
	G
	51
	W 17
	CUBOMEDUSAE
	Pope, Elizabeth C.
	   Venomous jelly-fish- the sea wasps.
	   (Walkabout, 23(12):40–41, 1957)
		QK
		97
		C 21
		CUCURBITACEAE
		Candolle, A.L.P.P. de, and Candolle, A.C.P. de
		   Monographiae Phanerogamarum...Vol. 3: Philydraceae, Alismaceae, Butomaceae, Juncagineae, Commelinaceae, Cucurbitaceae cum tabulis VIII. Paris. 1881. 8vo. pp. 325–951.
		   Cucurbitaceae by Alfred Cogniaux.

CUBA   MOLLUSCA
 	
see
 	
MOLLUSCA   CUBA
	Q
	115
	H 23
	Cuckler, Ashton C.
	   Nematode parasites of the Galapagos land Iguana.
	   (The Hancock Pacific Expeditions, Vol.2, No.9, 1938, pp. 137–162)
		QK
		97
		E
		CUCURBITACEAE
		Cogniaux, A. und Harms, A.
		   Cucurbitaceae..... Engler, Pflanzenreich IV, 275, II (Heft 88) 1924, 246 pp.

CUBA   PALEONTOLOGY
 	
see
 	
PALEONTOLOGY   CUBA
	AS
	36
	S1
	CUCKOOS
	Barrett, C L.
	   The origin and development of parasitical habits in the *Cuculidæ* ... By C. L. Barrett ...
	   (In Smithsonian institution. Annual report. 1909. Washington, 1910. 23½ᶜᵐ. p. 487–492. 2 pl.)
	   Reprinted by permission of the Emu, Melbourne, vol. 6, 1906–7, p. 55–60.
	
	1. Cuckoos.
	               11–9883
	Library of Congress Q11.S66 1909
		QK
		97
		E 58
		CUCURBITACEAE
		Engler, Adolf
		   Das Pflanzenreich...IV. 275. I. 1916. (Heft 66.) Cucurbitaceae-Fevilleae et Melothrieae, by A. Cogniaux.

CUBA   REPTILIA
 	
see
 	
REPTILIA   CUBA
	QH
	104
	U-b
	CUCKOOS
	Beal, Foster Ellenborough Lascelles, 1840–1916.
	   ... Cuckoos and shrikes in their relation to agriculture. The food of cuckoos, by F. E. L. Beal. The food of shrikes, by Sylvester D. Judd ... Washington, Govt. print. off., 1898.
	   26 p. front. illus. 23ᶜᵐ. (U. S. Dept. of agriculture. Division of biological survey. Bulletin 9)
	
	1. Cuckoos. [1. Cuckoo] 2. Shrikes. [2. Shrike] I. Judd, Sylvester Dwight, 1871–1905.
	            Agr 6–831
	Library, U. S. Dept. of Agriculture
		QK
		97
		E 58
		CUCURBITACEAE
		Engler, Adolf
		   Das Pflanzenreich...IV. 275. II. 1924. (Heft 88.) Cucurbitaceae-Cucurbiteae-Cucumerinae, by A. Cogniaux und H. Harms.

QK
1
S 67

CUCURBITACEAE

Guillaumin, A.

Matériaux pour la flore de la Nouvelle-Calédonie. XLIV. Revision des Cucurbitacées.

and

QK
Bot.Pam
1999

(Soc. Botanique de France, Bull. vol.84. 1937. pp.98-100)

QK
Bot.Pam.
3121

CUCURBITACEAE   AFRICA

Fernandes, Rosette

Cucurbitaceae africanae novae - 1

(Boletim da Sociedade Broteriana, 33, 1959: 189-195)

AS
36
S1

Culbertson, Thaddeus A.

... Journal of an expedition to the Mauvaises Terres and the upper Missouri in 1850; by Thaddeus A. Culbertson.

(*In* Smithsonian institution. Fifth annual report. 1850. Washington, 1851. 24ᶜᵐ. p. 84-145)

At head of title: Appendix—No. iv.

Discovery + Exploration   *Discovery + Exploration*
1. Missouri Valley—Descr. & trav. 2. South Dakota—Descr. & trav.
3. Indians of North America—Missouri Valley.

Library of Congress   Q11.S66   7-13558
——— Copy 2, detached   Library of Congress F597.C96

QK
Pam
945

CUCURBITACEAE

Lloyd, Francis E.

The pollen tube in the Cucurbitaceae and Rubiaceae. From Columbia Univ. Dept. Bot., Contrib. Vol. I , No. 210, 1904.

QK
Bot.Pam
2850

CUCURBITACEAE   MALAYSIA

Jacobs, M.

Notes on some Malaysian Cucurbitaceae.

(Blumea, Vol. 7(3):617-622, 1954)

QL
1
A 93

CULCITA

Livingstone, Arthur A.

Notes on some representatives of the Asteroid genus Culcita.

(The Australian Zoologist, 7:265-273, 1932)

QK
Botany
Pam
1441

CUCURBITACEAE

McAtee, W   L

Gourds for bird houses and other purposes. U. S. Department Agriculture, leaflet 36, 1929

QK
Bot.Pam.
3054

CUCURBITACEAE   PALAU

Fosberg, F. Raymond

A new Trichosanthes (Cucurbitaceae) from Palau.

(Bernice P. Bishop Museum, Occ. Papers, Vol. 22(6), 1958)

QL
Insects
Pam.
1795

CULCOIDES   NEW BRITAIN

Laird, Marshall

A Ceratopogonine midge (Culicoides anophelis Edwards, 1922) sucking engorged blood from a mosquito (Armigeres lacuum Edwards, 1922) at Palmalmal, New Britain.

(Reprint, Trans. R. Soc. New Zealand, 76(2): 158-161, 1946)

QK
1
F 29-b

CUCURBITACEAE

Neitsch, E.

Die morphologische Natur der Ranken der Cucurbitaceen.

(Report. Spec. Nov. Reg. (Fedde), Beihefte, Bd. 18, 1923)

AS
36
A 65

CUCURBITACEAE   PERU

Whitaker, Thomas W.

Identification and significance of the cucurbit materials from Huaca, Prieta, Peru. By Thomas W. Whitaker and Junius Bird.

(Am. Mus. Novitates, No. 1246, 1949)

QL
Insects
Pam
181

Hurst, C. Herbert

On the life-history and development of a Gnat (culex).

Pam box   (Reprinted from Trans. of Manchester Microscopical
Diptera   Society, 1890, 1ᵛᵒ. pp. 14, 2 pls.)

CULEX

QK
495.C9
W 74

CUCURBITACEAE

Wilson, Eddie W.

The gourd in folk literature. The Gourd Society of America, Inc. 1947c. Boston. 120 pp. 8vo.

QK
1
Jo

CUCURBITACEAE -- POLYNESIA

Seemann, Berthold

The Cucurbitaceae of tropical Polynesia
In Journ. Bot. Vol. II, 1864, pp 47 - 52.

QL
Insect
Pam.
1382

CULEX

Mosquitoes and their relation to disease; their life-history, habits and control. British Museum (Natural History), Economic Series, No. 4. 1949. London. 5th edition. 17 pp.

QK
Bot.Pam.
2516

CUCURBITACEAE

Wilson, Katherine S.

Vitamin patterns in the development of cucurbit fruits.

(American Journal of Botany, Vol. 34:469-483, 1947)

Q
115
R 29

CUCURBITACEAE   SAMOA

Cogniaux, A.

Cucurbitaceae.

Rechinger, Karl
Botanische und Zoologische Ergebnisse einer Wissenschaftlichen Forschungsreise nach den Samoainseln, dem Neu-guinea-Archipel und den Salomoninseln...1915. Teil III: pp. 205-214, 1910.

AS
36
W 2

CULICIDAE

Belkin, John N.

A new species of Anopheles from the Solomon Islands, by John N. Belkin and Ralph J. Schlosser

(Journal of the Washington Acad. of Sci., Vol. 34, 1944, pp. 268-273)

QK
495.C96
Z 73

CUCURBITACEAE

Zimmermann, A.

Die Cucurbitaceen. Beiträge zur Anatomie, Morphologie, Biologie, Pathologie und Systematik. Hefte 1-2. Jena. Gustav Fischer. 1922. 205+186 pp.

AS
36
S1

Cuénot, Lucien Claude Marie Julien, 1866–
Heredity. By L. Cuénot ...

(*In* Smithsonian institution. Annual report. 1906. Washington, 1907. 23½ᶜᵐ. p. 335-344. diagrs.)

"Translation ... of a public lecture given March 17, 1906, at the University of Nancy, under the auspices of the Réunion biologique, printed in the Revue scientifique, Paris, April 28, 1906."

1. Heredity.

S 15-1319

Library of Congress   Q11.S66 1906
Library, Smithsonian   Institution

QL
Insects
Pam.
1022

CULICIDAE

Bishopp, F. C.

Domestic mosquitoes.

(U. S. Dept. of Agric. Leaflet, No. 186, 1939)
Pam.1426   revised edition, 1951

QL
536
B 88

CULICIDAE
British museum, London.

A monograph of the Culicidae or mosquitoes. Bry Fred V. Theobald. 2 vols. of text, 1 vol. of plates.

London, 1901.

AS
36
S2

CULICIDAE
Dyar, Harrison Gray, 1866-

Descriptions of some new species and a new genus of American mosquitoes, by Harrison G. Dyar and Frederick Knab.

(*In* Smithsonian institution. Smithsonian miscellaneous collections. Washington, 1910. 24¼cm. vol. LII (Quarterly issue, vol. V) p. 253-266. illus.)

Publication 1822.
In continuation of a paper by the same authors, "Descriptions of some new mosquitoes from tropical America," pub. in the Proceedings of the U. S. National museum, v. 35, 1908, p. 53-70.
Originally published January 12, 1909.

1. Mosquito.   I. Knab, Frederick, 1865-   joint author.

Library of Congress   Q11.S7 vol. 52   16-12712
——— Copy 2.

QL
Insect
Fam.
1964

CULICIDAE
Grant, C. Donald   editor

Proceedings and Papers of the 28th Annual Conference of the California Mosquito Control Association, Inc. Jan. 25-27, 1960. 4to.

QL
1
I -r

CULICIDAE
Brunetti, E.
Annotated catalogue of Oriental Culicidae.
in Records Indian Mus. I pp. 297-377. Supplement in Records IV pp. 403-516.

QL
536
D99

CULICIDAE
Dyar, Harrison G

The mosquitoes of the Americas.

Washington, Carnegie Institution, 1928.

QL
Insects
Pam
443

CULICIDAE
Grunberg, K.

Zur Kenntnis der Culiciden -fauna von Samoa. From Ent. Rundschau. Jahrgang 30, No. 22, Nov. 1913.

AS
36
S2

CULICIDAE .
Busck, August, 1870-

Report on a trip for the purpose of studying the mosquito fauna of Panama, by August Busck.

(*In* Smithsonian institution. Smithsonian miscellaneous collections. Washington, 1910. 24¼cm. vol. LII (Quarterly issue, vol. V) p. 49-77.)

Publication 1795.
Originally published May 1, 1908.

1. Mosquito. 2. Panama Canal Zone—Sanit. affairs.

Library of Congress   Q11.S7 vol. 52   16-12735
——— Copy 2.

AS
36
S2

CULICIDAE
Dyar, Harrison Gray, 1866-

... The species of mosquitoes in the genus *Megarhinus*, by Harrison G. Dyar and Frederick Knab.

(*In* Smithsonian institution. Smithsonian miscellaneous collections. Washington, 1907. 24¼cm. vol. XLVIII (Quarterly issue, vol. III) p. 241-258. illus.)

Publication 1657.
Originally published September 27, 1906.

1. Mosquito.   I. Knab, Frederick, 1865-   joint author.

Library of Congress   Q11.S7 vol. 48   16-12731
——— Copy 2.

QL
Insect
Pam
#519

CULICIDAE
Hill, Gerald F.

The distribution of Anopheline mosquitoes in the Australian region, with notes on some culicine species.

Reprinted from Proc. Roy. Soc. Victoria, May, 1925.

QL
1
C 42

CULICIDAE
Carter, H. F.

The genus Taeniorhynchus Lynch Arribalzaga (Diptera Culicidae) with special reference to the bionomics and relation to disease of the species occurring in Ceylon.

(Ceylon Journal of Science, Sect. B. Zool., Vol. 24(1):1-26, 1950)

QL
536
E 26

CULICIDAE
Edwards, F. W.

A synopsis of adult oriental Culicine mosquitoes.

(Indian Journal of Medical Research, Vol. 10:249-293; 430-475, 1922)

S
21
A45

CULICIDAE
King, W. V. and Bradley, G. H.

Airplane dusting in the control of mosquitoes. U. S. Dept. Agric., Dept. Circ., 367, 1926.

QL
Insect
Pam.
849

CULICIDAE -
Cavanaugh, William J.

Algal Food, Feeding and Case-Building Habits of the Larva of the Midge Fly. Tanytarsus Dissimilis by W.J.Cavanaugh and Josephine Tilden

Reprinted from Ecology, Vol.XI, No. 2, 1930

QH
1.S
W 31

CULICIDAE
Farner, D. S.

A new species of Aedes from the Caroline Islands. (Diptera, Culicidae)

(Proc. Biol. Soc. Washinton, 58:59-62, 1945)

QL
Insects
Pam.1019

CULICIDAE
King, W. V.

The mosquitoes of the southeastern states, by W. V. King, G. H. Bradley and T. E. McNeel.

(U. S. Dept. of Agric., Misc. Pub., No. 336, June, 1939)

QL
536
C 93

CULICIDAE
Christophers, Sir S. Rickard

Aedes Aegypti (L.); the yellow fever mosquito, its life history, bionomics and structure Cambridge. At the University Press. 1960. 4to. xii + 739 pp.

QL
536
F 68

CULICIDAE
Foote, Richard H.

Mosquitoes of medical importance. By Richard H. Foote and David R. Cook.

(U. S. Dept. of Agriculture, Agriculture Handbook No. 152, 1959)

AS
36
S2

CULICIDAE .
Knab, Frederick, 1865-
Observations on the mosquitoes of Saskatchewan, by Frederick Knab.

(*In* Smithsonian institution. Smithsonian miscellaneous collections. Washington, 1908. 24¼cm. vol. L (Quarterly issue, vol. IV) p. 540-547)

Publication 1787.

1. Mosquito. 2. Insects—Saskatchewan.

Library of Congress   Q11.S7 vol. 50   16-11653
——— Copy 2.

AM
101
A71
(5)

CULICIDAE
Dahlgren, B   E.
The malaria mosquito; a guide leaflet explanatory of a series of models in the American museum of natural history, by B. E. Dahlgren ... New York, The Museum, 1908.

48 p. incl. front., illus. 25cm. (Guide leaflet series, no. 27)
"Literature on mosquitoes": p. 47-48.

1. Mosquitoes.   I. Title.

Library of Congress   RC116.D25   20-23774
(2)

AS
80
P1

CULICIDAE
Göldi, Emilio Augusto

Os mosquitos no Pará

In Mem. Museu Goeldi IV Para, 1905 4º pp. 154 Pl. 2-V.
3

QL
Insects
Pam.
1338

CULICIDAE
Knight, Kenneth L.

A new nomenclature for the Chaetotaxy of the mosquito pupa, based on a comparative study of the genera: (Diptera:Culicidae). By Kenneth L. Knight and Roy W. Chamberlain.

(Proc. of the Helminthological Soc. of Washington, Vol. 15(1):1-10, figs. 1-35, 1948)

CULICIDAE

QL
536
M 36

Marshall, J. F.

The British mosquitoes. The British Museum, London, 1938. R8vo. 341 pp. + 20 plates.

CULICIDAE

AS
36
S1

Sternberg, George Miller, 1838–
Transmission of yellow fever by mosquitoes. By George M. Sternberg ...

(*In* Smithsonian institution. Annual report. 1900. Washington, 1901. 231ᵛⁱⁱ· p. 657-673)

1. Mosquito. 2. Yellow fever.

S 15-1085

Library of Congress   Q11.S66 1900
Library, Smithsonian   Institution

CULICIDAE

QL
345.N 6
S 24

Theobald, Fred. V.

Culicidae from New Caledonia and the Loyalty Islands.

Sarasin, Fritz
Nova Caledonia...A. Zoologie, Vol. 1, Livr. 3, 1913, No. 3.

CULICIDAE

QL
Insect
Pam 834

The Mosquito: Its Life-history and Control in Hawaii. Published by the Anti-Mosquito League, a project of the Chamber of Commerce of Honolulu. Honolulu. 16 pp. (1931) 8vo.

CULICIDAE

QL
536
S 87

Stone, Alan and others

A synoptic catalog of the mosquitoes of the world (Diptera, Culicidae). By Alan Stone, Kenneth L. Knight and Helle Starcke. The Thomas Say Foundation, Vol. VI, 1959. Publ. by Ent. Soc. America. 8vo. (6) + 358 pp.

CULICIDAE

QL
I
I-r

Theobald, Fred V.

Second report on the collection of Culicidae in the Indian Museum, Calcutta, with descriptions of new genera and species.

(Records Indian Museum, IV, pp. 1-33)

CULICIDAE

AS
750
N

Robertson, Ernest
Malaria + mosquitoes.
In T. P. New Z. Inst. XXXV. 1902.
pp 225-289.

CULICIDAE

QL
489.G
I 59

Swezey, Otto H.
Culicidae of Guam
IN
Swezey, Otto H. and others
Insects of Guam-I, pp. 199-200.

(Bernice P. Bishop Museum, Bull. 172, 1942)

CULICIDAE

RC
690
L

Wise, K. S.

An examination of the city of Georgetown, British Guiana for breeding places of mosquitoes. In Annals Trop. Med. V.3 pp 485-441.

CULICIDAE

QL
627
U-b

Seal , William P.
Fishes in their relation to the mosquito problem. In Bul. Bur. of Fish.xxviii p 831-838.
Also separate.

CULICIDAE

QL
Insect
Pam. 182

Symons, Thos. B. and others

The Mosquito, by Thos. B. Symons, T. H. Coffin, and A. B. Gahan.

(The Maryland Agric. Exp. Station, Bull.No. 109, 1906)

CULICIDAE

QL
Insect
Pams.
1905-1908

World Health Organization Technical Report Series

No. 132: Malaria conference for the eastern Mediterranean and European regions. 1956. Report
No.133: Expert Committee on Health Statistics. Fifth report. 1957
No. 135: Joint ILO/WHO Committee on Occupational Health. Third report. 1957
No. 136: Expert Committee on Yellow Fever Vaccine. First Report. 1957

CULICIDAE

QL
Fish
Pam
130

Sewell, R. B. Seymour + Chaudhuri
Indian fish of proved utility as mosquito-destroyers.
Indian Mus. 1912 (Miscell.)

CULICIDAE

AS
720.N
L

Taylor, Frank H.

The Diptera of the Territory of New Guinea. I. Family Culicidae.

(Proc. Linn. Soc. New South Wales, Vol. 59: 229-236, 1934)

CULICIDAE

See also

AEDES

CULICIDAE

QL
Ins.Pam.
184

Smith, J. B. (John Bernhard)

Common Mosquitoes of New Jersey.

(N. J. Agr. Exp. Stat. Bull. 171, 1904)

CULICIDAE

QL
Insects
Pam.
1188

Taylor, Frank H.

Mosquitoes.

(Australian Museum Magazine, Vol. 8, 1942, 57-60)

CULICIDAE ANATOMY

QL
Insects
Pam.
1321

Marshall, Wm. S.

The rectal glands of mosquitoes.

(Trans. Wisconsin Acad. Sci., Arts and Letters, Vol. 37:149-155, 1945)

CULICIDAE

QL
536
S 65

Smith, John B.

Report of the New Jersey State Agricultural Experiment Station upon the mosquitoes occurring within the State, their habits, life history, etc. Trenton. 1904. 482 pp. 8vo.

CULICIDAE

QL
Insects
Pam.
1184

Taylor, Frank H.

The tiger mosquito (Aedes [Stegomyia] aegypti) and dengue fever.

(Australian Journal of Science, Vol. 4, 1942 pp. 171-172)

CULICIDAE BREEDING

QL
461
H-1

Bonnet, David D.

The distribution of mosquito breeding by type of container in Honolulu, T. H.

(Proc. Haw. Ent. Soc., 13:43-49, 1947)

AS
36
S 66 m Snodgrass, R .E.

CULICIDAE ANATOMY

The anatomical life of the mosquito.

(Smithsonian Misc. Collections, Vol.139(8), 1959)

QL
Insect
Pam 369

and
RA
789
Aus

CULICIDAE AUSTRALIA

Cooling, L. E.

A Synonymic List of the Most Important Species of Culicidae of the Australian Region.

(Service Publication, (Tropical Division) Commonwealth of Australia, Department of Health, No. 2, 1924)

AS
720.N
L

CULICIDAE AUSTRALIA

Taylor, Frank H.

Contributions to a knowledge of Australian Culicidae. I- VI

and sops.
of some
QL   (Proc. Linn. Soc. N.S.Wales, 39,1914:454-
  468; 40, 1915:176-184; 41, 1910:564-574; 43,
Ins. Pams.1918:826-843; 47, 1942:277-278; 48, 1943: 153-
505,506, 157)
506 a,b

QL
Insect
Pam.
1959

CULICIDAE DISTRIBUTION

Macdonald, W. W.

Some ecological factors influencing the distribution of Malayan mosquitoes.

(Proc. of the Centenary and Bicentenary Congress of Biology, Singapore, 1958:117-122)

AS
720.N
L 75

CULICIDAE AUSTRALIA

Dobrotworsky, N. V.

Notes on Australian mosquitoes (Diptera, Culicidae). IV. Aedes alboannulatus complex in Victoria.

(Proc. Linn. Soc. N. S. Wales, Vol. 84(1): 131-145, 1959

QL
Insects
Pam.841

CULICIDAE - AUSTRALIA.

Taylor, Frank H

Notes on Australian culicidae (dipt.)

Reprinted from the Bulletin of entomological research, v.XX, pt.3, October 1929.

QL
Insect
Pam.
2123

CULICIDAE REPELLENTS

Smith, Carroll N.   and others

Factors affecting the protection period of mosquito repellents.

(U.S.D.A., Agricultural Res. Ser., Tech. Bull. No. 1285:1-36, 1963)

QL
Insect
Pam.
2098

CULICIDAE AUSTRALIA

Lee, D. J.   and others

The blood sources of some Australian mosquitoes. By D. J. Lee, K. J. Clinton, and A. K. O'Gower.

(Austalian Journal of Biological Sciences, 7(3):282-301, 1954)

AS
720.N
L

CULICIDAE BORNEO

Colless, Donald H.

The Anopheline mosquitoes of north-west Borneo.

(Proc. Linn. Soc. New South Wales, Vol. 73:71-119, 1948)

QL
Insect.
Pam.
1971

CULICIDAE ALASKA

Gjullin, C. M.

The mosquitoes of Alaska. By C. M. Gjullin, R. I. Sailer, Alan Stone, and B. V. Travis.

(U.S.D.A. Agriculture Handbook No. 182, 1961)   Agriculture Reasearch Service.

AS
720.N
L

CULICIDAE AUSTRALIA

Mattingly, P. F.

Some Australasian mosquitoes (Diptera, Culicidae) of the subgenera Pseudoskusea and Neoculex. By P. F. Mattingly and Elizabeth N. Marks.

(The Proc. of the Linnean Society of New South Wales, Vol. LXXX(2):163-176, 1955)

QL
Insect
Pam.
1670

CULICIDAE BRAZIL

Grjebine, A.

Moustiques du Moyen-Congo.

(Institut d'Etudes Centrafricaines, extrait du Bulletin, No. 1, Nouvelle série, pp. 25-48, 1950)

QL
1
S 98

CULICIDAE AUSTRALASIA

Lee, David J.

The Anopheline mosquitoes of the Australasian region. By David J. Lee and A.R.Woodhill.

(Monographs, Dept. of Zool., Univ. of Sydney, 2, 1944)

QL
Insect
Pam.
2097

CULICIDAE AUSTRALIA

O'Gower, A. K.

The mosquitoes of north western Australia.

(Australia. School of Public Health and Tropical Medicine, Service Publication, no. 7, 1958)

QL
536
P 49

CULICIDAE - BRAZIL

Peryassu, Antonio Goncalves

Os Culicideos do Brazil

(Trabalho do Instituto de Manguinhos, Rio de Janeiro, 1908, Tipographia Leuzinger. vi + 407 pp. 8vo.)

QL
Insect
Pam 367

and
RA
789
Aus

CULICIDAE AUSTRALIA

Cooling, L. E.

The larval stages and biology of the commoner species of Australian mosquitoes.

(In Service Publication, (Tropical Division) Commonwealth of Australia, Department of Health, No. 8, 1924)

QL
Insects
Pam.842

CULICIDAE - AUSTRALIA.

Taylor, Frank H

The anopheles of the Australian region, their bionomics and their distribution.

Reprinted from v.III, Transactions of the F.E.A.T.M. 7th congress ... Dec. 1927.

QL
536
H. 85

CULICIDAE CENTRAL AMERICA

Howard, Leland Ossian.

The mosquitoes of North America and Central America and the West Indies, by L.O.Howard, H.G. Dyar and F. Knab. 4 vols.

Carnegie inst. of Washington, 1912-1917. Pub. #159.

QL
Insects
Pam
#390

CULICIDAE - AUSTRALIA

Cooling, L. E.

Seven common species of mosquitoes described for purposes of identification. Australia Dept. Health,Service Publ. [Tropical Div.] No.1. Melbourne, n.d. 1924.

RA
789
A 93

CULICIDAE AUSTRALIA

Taylor, Frank H.

A check list of the Culicidae of the Australian region.

(Service Publication (School of Public Health and Tropical Medicine), Commonwealth of Australia, No. 1, 1934)

QL
Insects
Pam.
1743

CULICIDAE ELLICE ISLANDS

Laird, Marshall

Notes on the mosquitos of the Gilbert, Ellice and Tokelau Islands, and on filariasis in the latter group.

(Bull. Ent. Research, 46(2):291-300, 1955)

QL
461
Q 3

CULICIDAE   AUSTRALIA

Marks, Elizabeth B.

    The subgenus Ochlerotatus in the Australian region (Diptera:Culicidae) I.

    (Univ. of Queensland Papers, Dept. of Ent. I(5), 1957)

QL
Insects
Pam.
1743

CULICIDAE   GILBERT ISLANDS

Laird, Marshall

    Notes on the mosquitos of the Gilbert, Ellice and Tokelau Islands, and on filariasis in the latter group.

    (Bull. Ent. Research, 46(2):291-300, 1955)

QL
Insects
Pam.
1203

CULICIDAE   HAWAII

Usinger, Robert L.

    Entomological phases of the recent dengue epidemic in Honolulu.

    (Reprint No. 2548 from the Public Health Reports, Vol. 59, No. 13, Mch. 31, 1944, pp. 423-430)

QL
536
H 79

CULICIDAE   ETHIOPIA

Evans, Alwen M.

    Mosquitoes of the Ethiopian Region. II: Anophelini, adults and early stages. London. 1938.

QL
Ins
Pam
540

Insect
Pam. 899

CULICIDAE   GREAT BRITIAN

Edwards, F. W. and James, S. P.

    British mosquitoes and their control. 1925.

    ---second edition, revised, London, 1934.

S
399
E8

CULICIDAE   HAWAII

Van Dine, D. L.

    Introduction of top-minnows (natural enemies of mosquitoes) into the Hawaiian Islands. Haw. Agric. Exper. Sta. Press Bul. No. 20. 1907

QL
536
H 79

CULICIDAE   ETHIOPIA

Edwards, F. W.

    Mosquitoes of the Ethiopian Region. III: Culicine adults and pupae. Oxford Univ. Press, 1941. 8vo. pp. 1-499. 184 figs., 4 colored plates.

QL
461
J 86

CULICIDAE   GUAM

Bailey, S. F.

    A mosquito survey and control program in Guam. By S. F. Bailey and R. M. Bohart.

    (Journal of Economic Ent., 45(6):947-952, 1952)

QL
461
P 11

CULICIDAE   INDIA

Qutubuddin, M.

    Mosquito studies in the Indian subregion. Part I: Taxonomy, a brief review.

    (Pacific Insects, 2(2):133-148, 1960)

QL
536
H 79

CULICIDAE   ETHIOPIA

Hopkins, G. H. E.

    Mosquitoes of the Ethiopian region. I-Larval bionomics of mosquitoes and taxonomy of Culicine larvae. Oxford Univ.Press, 1936. 8vo. 250 pp., 158 figs.

    also 2nd edition, with notes and addenda by P. F. Mattingly. 1952

QL
Insects
Pam.
1265

CULICIDAE   HAWAII

Bonnet, David D.

    The dispersal of Aedes albopictus in the Territory of Hawaii. By David D. Bonnet and Douglas J. Worcester.

    (The American Journal of Tropical Medicine, Vol. 26 (4): 465-476, 1946)

QL
536
M 44

CULICIDAE   INDOMALAYA

Mattingly, P. F.

    The Culicine mosquitoes of the Indomalayan area. Parts I-
    Part I.   Genus Ficalbia Theobald.
    " II.   Genus Heizmannia Ludlow.
    " III. Genus Aedes Meigen...

    British Museum (Natural History) sm4to. 1957-

QL
Insect
Pam.
2024

CULICIDAE   HOKKAIDO

Asanuma, Kiyoshi

    Notes on Culicidae of Hokkaido, I. Descriptions on the male terminalia of subgenus Ochlerotatus Arrib, (Aedes, Culicidae) By Kiyoshi Asanuma and Rokubo Kano, and Hirosi Takahasi.

    (source? 6 pp.)

QL
461
H-1

CULICIDAE   HAWAII

Bonnet, David D.

    The distribution of mosquito breeding by type of container in Honolulu, T. H.

    (Proc. Haw. Ent. Soc., 13:43-49, 1947)

AS
73
J 27

CULICIDAE   JAMAICA

Hill, Rolla B.

    The mosquitoes of Jamaica. By Rolla B. Hill and Claire McDowell Jill.

    (Bull. Institute of Jamaica, No. 4, 1948)

QL
Insects
Pam.
1197

CULICIDAE   FIJI

Amos, David W.

    Mosquito control, Suva, Fiji. Training manual. 1944. 43 pp.

QL
461
H-1

CULICIDAE   HAWAII

Bonnet, David D.

    The introduction of Toxorhynchites brevipalpis Theobald into the Territory of Hawaii. By David D. Bonnet and Stephen M. K. Hu.

    (Proc. Haw. Entomological Soc., 14(2):237-242, 1951)

QL
Insects
Pam
1264

CULICIDAE   JAPAN

Hsiao, Tsai-Yu

    The mosquitoes of Japan and their medical importance. By Tsai-Yu Hsiao and Richard M. Bohart. Bureau of Medicine and Surgery, Navy Department. Washington. 8vo. 44 pp. 1946 NAVMED 1095

QL
Insects
Pam. 966

CULICIDAE   FIJI

Paine, R. W.

    An introduction to the mosquitoes of Fiji, descriptive notes on the commoner species; together with simplified keys for distinguishing the adults and larvae of Fijian mosquitoes. Deaprtment of Agriculture, Fiji. 1935. 29 pp.

QL
Insect
Pam 834

CULICIDAE   HAWAII

    The Mosquito: Its Life-history and Control in Hawaii. Published by the Anti-Mosquito League, a project of the Chamber of Commerce of Honolulu. Honolulu. 16 pp. (1931) 8vo.

QL
536
L 12

CULICIDAE   JAPAN

LaCasse, Walter J.

    Mosquito fauna of Japan and Korea. By Walter J. LaCasse and Satyu Yamaguti. Prepared under direction and distributed by Office of the Surgeon, HQ I Corps, APO 301. 4to. 189 + 273 pp., 78 pl. 1948
    ...3rd revision, viii+268; 212 pp., 95 pl. (1950)

QL
536
L 12
CULICIDAE   KOREA

LaCasse, Walter J.

Mosquito fauna of Japan and Korea. By Walter J. LaCasse and Satyu Yamaguti. Prepared under direction and distributed by Office of the Surgeon, HQ I Corps, APO 301. 4to. 189 + 273 pp., 78 pl. 1948
...3rd revision, viii+268; 212 pp., 95 pl. (1950)

QL
595. Mi
I 59
CULICIDAE   MICRONESIA

Bohart, Richard M.

Insects of Micronesia, Diptera: Culicidae. IN

Insects of Micronesia, Vol. 12, No. 1, 1956. Bishop Museum Press.   Honolulu

---

QH
1.S
W 31
CULICIDAE   NEW GUINEA

King, Willard V.

The New Guinea species of Culex (Culiciomyia), with descriptions of two new species. By Willard V. King and Harry Hoogstraal

(Proc. Biol. Soc. of Washington, Vol. 59: 143-154, 1946)

AS
28
E 85
CULICIDAE   LOYALTY ISLANDS

Rageau, J.

Recherches sur les moustiques (Diptères, Culicidae) des Iles Loyauté. By J. Rageau and G. Vervent.

(Etudes Melanesiennes, n.s., Nr. 12?13;50-63, 1961)

AS
720.N
L 75
CULICIDAE   NEW CALEDONIA

Marks, Elizabeth N.

Culex pipens australicus Dobrotworsky and Drummond in New Caledonia. By Elizabeth N. Marks and J. Rageau.

(Proc. Linn. Soc. New South Wales, 82(383): 156, 1957)

AS
36
W 2
CULICIDAE   NEW GUINEA

King, Willard V.

New Guinea species of mosquitoes of the genus Aedes, subgenus Aedes. By Willard V. King and Harry Hoogstraal.

(Journal of the Washington Acad. of Sci., Vol. 37:113-134, 1947)

QL
Insect
Pam.
1960
CULICIDAE   MALAYA

Macdonald, W. W.

A new species of Udaya from Malaya and a description of the early stages of U. argyrurus (Edwards, 1934) (Diptera: Culicidae)

(Proc. R. Ent. Soc. London, ser. B. Taxonomy, Vol. 29(1/2):22-29, 1960)

DU
1
S 72 t
CULICIDAE   NEW CALEDONIA

Rageau, Jean

La repartition geographique des moustiques en Nouvelle-Caledonie et dependances, avec des clés pour leur indentification.

(Tech. Paper No. 117, South Pacific Commission, 1958)

QH
1
P 11
CULICIDAE   NEW GUINEA

Penn, George Henry

The pupae of the mosquitoes of New Guinea.

(Pacific Science, Vol. 3:3-85, 1949)

QL
Insect
Pam.
1959
CULICIDAE   MALAYA

Macdonald, W. W.

Some ecological factors influencing the distribution of Malayan mosquitoes.

(Proc. of the Centenary and Bicentenary Congress of Biology, Singapore, 1958;117-122)

S
17.H3
S 3
CULICIDAE   NEW CALEDONIA

Williams, Francis X.

Mosquitoes and some other noxious flies that occur in New Caledonia.

(Hawaiian Planters' Record, Vol. 47, 1943, pp. 205-222)

RA
789
A 93
CULICIDAE   NEW GUINEA

Taylor, Frank H.

Mosquito intermediary hosts of disease in Australia and New Guinea.

(Australia, Dept. of health, Service Pub., School of Public Health and Tropical Med., No. 4, 1943)

QL
536
M 44
CULICIDAE   MALAYA

Mattingly, P. F.

The Culicine mosquitoes of the Indomalayan area. Parts I-
Part I.   Genus Ficalbia Theobald.
"   II.   Genus Heizmannia Ludlow.
"   III.   Genus Aedes Meigen...

British Museum (Natural History) sm4to. 1957-

QH
1
P 11
CULICIDAE   NEW GUINEA

Bick, George H.

The ecology of the mosquito larvae of New Guinea.

(Pacific Science, Vol. 5:392-431, 1951)

QL
Insects
Pam.
1337
CULICIDAE   NEW HEBRIDES

Belkin, John N.

Anopheline mosquitoes of the Solomon Islands and New Hebrides. By John N. Belkin, Kenneth L. Knight, and Lloyd E. Rozeboom.

(Journal of Parasitology, 31:241-265, 1945)

QL
Insect
Pam.
2099
CULICIDAE   MARQUESAS ISLANDS

Stone, Alan

A new species of Culex from the Marquesas Islands and the larva of Culex atriceps Edwards (Diptera, Culicidae). By Alan Stone and Leon Rosen.

(Journal of the Washington Academy of Sciences, 43(11):354-358, 1953)

QL
1
B 93
CULICIDAE   NEW GUINEA   (Dutch)

Bonne-Wepster, J.

Diptera Culicidae. Notes on the mosquitoes collected by the Netherlands Indian-American Expedition to Central and North New Guinea. Results of the Third Archbold Expedition 1938-1939.

(Treubia, Vol. 19:305-322, 1948)

QL
Insects
Pam.
1744
CULICIDAE   NEW HEBRIDES

Laird, Marshall

Mosquitos and malaria in the hill country of the New Hebrides and Solomon Islands.

(Bull. Ent. Research, Vol. 46(2):275-289, 1956)

QH
1
P 11
CULICIDAE   MELANESIA

Belkin, John N.

The Tripteroides caledonica complex of mosquitoes in Melanesia (Diptera:Culicidae).

(Pacific Science, 9(2):221-246, 1955)

DU
1
S 72t
CULICIDAE   NEW GUINEA

Iyengar, M. O. T.

Distribution of mosquitoes in the South Pacific region.

(South Pacific Commission, Technical Paper No. 86, 1955)

QL
Insects
Pam.
184
CULICIDAE   NEW JERSEY

Smith, John B.

The common mosquitoes of New Jersey.

New Jersey Agric. Exper. Stations Bull. 171
New Brunswick 1904.

QL
Insects
Pam.
2030

CULICIDAE   NEW ZEALAND

Miller, D.

Identification of New Zealand mosquitoes.
By D. Miller and W. J. Phillipps. Cawthron
Institute. New Zealand. 28 pp. Issued by the
New Zealand Department of Health. no date

DU
1
S 72 t

CULICIDAE   PACIFIC

Iyengar, M. O. T.

Annotated bibliography on filariasis. Part
2. Studies on mosquitoes of the South Pacific
region.

(South Pacific Commission, Technical Paper
No. 88, January, 1956)

QL
1
S 98

CULICIDAE   PACIFIC   (western)

Lee, David J.

The Anopheline mosquitoes of the Australasian region. By David J. Lee and A.R. Woodhill.

(Monographs, Dept. of Zool., Univ. of Sydney, 2, 1944)

QL
Insects
Pam.
1204

CULICIDAE   NEW ZEALAND

Miller, David

Mosquitoes, malaria, and New Zealand.

(Cawthron Institute, Publication 60, 1944:
Reprinted from "The New Zealand Science Review"
March-June, 1944. 10 pp.)

DU
1
S72t

CULICIDAE   PACIFIC

Iyengar, M. O. T.

Distribution of mosquitoes in the South
Pacific region.

(South Pacific Commission, Technical Paper
No. 86, 1955)

QH
1
P 11

CULICIDAE   PACIFIC

Mattingly, P. F.

Culex (Culex) iyengari n.sp., a new species
of mosquito (Diptera, Culicidae) from the South
Pacific. By P. F. Mattingly and J. Rageau.

(Pacific Science, 12(3):241-250, 1958)

QL
536
H 85

CULICIDAE   NORTH AMERICA

Howard, Leland Ossian, 1857-

The mosquitoes of North and Central America and the
West Indies, by Leland O. Howard, Harrison G. Dyar,
and Frederick Knab ... Washington, D. C., Carnegie institution of Washington, 1912-17.

4 v. in 3. illus. plates. 25ᶜᵐ. (On verso of t.-p.: Carnegie institution
of Washington. Publication no. 159)
Bibliography: v. 1, p. 451-488.
CONTENTS.—v. 1. A general consideration of mosquitoes, their habits,
and their relations to the human species.—v. 2. Plates.—v. 3-4. Systematic
description.
1. Mosquito.   I. Dyar, Harrison Gray, 1866-   joint author. II.
Knab, Frederick, 1865-   joint author.

Library of Congress   QL536.H85   13—6044

———— Copy 2.

QL
InsectPam.
1968

CULICIDAE   PACIFIC

Iyengar, M. O. T.

A review of the mosquito fauna of the South
Pacific. (Diptera: Culicidae)

(South Pacific Commission, Tech. Paper, No.
130, 1960)

AP
2
S 35

CULICIDAE-PACIFIC

Mumford, Edward Philpot

Mosquitoes, malaria and the war in the
Pacific.

(Science, Vol. 96, 1942, pp. 191-194)

AS
36
W 2

CULICIDAE   OKINAWA

Bohart, Richard M.

Four new species of mosquitoes from Okinawa
(Diptera: Culicidae). By Richard M. Bohart and
Robert L. Ingram.

(Jour. Washington Acad. Sci., Vol. 36 (2):
46-52, 1946)

AS
36
W 2

CULICIDAE   PACIFIC

Knight, Kenneth L.

The Aedes (Mucidus) mosquitoes of the
Pacific (Diptera: Culicidae).

(Journal of the Washington Acad. Sci., Vol.
37:315-324, 1947)

AS
36
S 2

CULICIDAE   PANAMA

Busck, August

Report on a trip for the purpose of studying
the mosquito fauna of Panama.

(Smith. Misc. Coll., Vol. 52, 1908, pp. 49-
77)

QL
536
B 43

CULICIDAE   PACIFIC

Belkin, John N.

The mosquitoes of the South Pacific (Diptera, Culicidae). Volumes I-II. University of
California Press. Berkeley. 4to. 1962

CULICIDAE   PACIFIC

Knight, K. L.   and others

Key to the mosquitoes of the Australasian
region. 1944.

UH

Supply exhausted at NRC, no reprint
contemplated June 1953

QL
Insect
Pam
879

CULICIDAE   PAPUA

Taylor, Frank H.

A new species of Finlaya (Order Diptera:
Family Culicidae) from Papua.

(Australian Zoologist, Vol. VII, Pt. V, Aug.
22, 1933. 1 p.)

QL
536
F 23

locked
case

CULICIDAE   PACIFIC

Farner, D. S.   and others

The distribution of mosquitoes of medical
importance in the Pacific area. Prepared by
Lieut. D.S.Farner, Lieut. R.J.Dicke, G.Sweet,
L. Isenhour and T.Y.Hsiao. Bureau of Medicine
and Surgery. Navy Department, Washington. March
1946. obfolio. 64 pp.

GN
2.S
E 47

CULICIDAE   PACIFIC

Laird, M.

Mosquito research in the South Pacific.

(Trans. and Proc. of the Fiji Society, Vol.
5:79-88, 1953)

QL
1
F 45

CULICIDAE   PHILIPPINE ISLANDS

Baisas, Francisco E.

Notes on Philippine mosquitoes, XIII. Four
new species of Zeugnomyia and Topomyia. By
Francisco E. Baisas and Pablo Feliciano. Philippine Zoological Expedition, 1946-1947.

(Fieldiana: Zoology, Vol. 33(3):163-179,
1953)

QH
1.S
W 31

CULICIDAE   PACIFIC

Farner, D. S.

Three new species of Australasian Aedes
(Diptera, Culicidae). By D.S.Farner and R.M.
Bohart.

(Proc. Biol. Soc. of Washington, 57:117-
122, 1944)

[from Guam, New Hebrides, Solomon Is.]

AS
750
N 56-b

CULICIDAE   PACIFIC

Laird, Marshall

Studies of mosquitoes and freshwater ecology
in the South Pacific.

(Royal Society of New Zealand, Bulletin No.
6, January, 1956)

QL
Insects
Pam.
1349

CULICIDAE   PHILIPPINE ISLANDS

Bick, George H.

Notes on mosquitoes from Leyte, Philippine
Islands (Diptera, Culicidae).

(Natural History Miscellanea, No. 41, 1949)

QH
1.8
W 31
CULICIDAE PHILIPPINE ISLANDS

Bohart, R. M.

New Culicine mosquitoes from the Philippine
Islands. By R. M. Bohart and D. S. Farner.

(Proc. Biol. Soc. Washington, Vol. 57:69-
74, 1945)

QL
Insects
Pam.
1406
CULICIDAE POLYNESIA

Marks, Elizabeth N.

Mosquitoes from southeastern Polynesia.

(Bernice P. Bishop Museum, Occ. Papers, Vol.
20(9), 1951; Mangarevan Expedition, Pub. No.
40)

AS
36
N 4
CULICIDAE SOLOMON ISLANDS

Belkin, John N.

Mosquitoes of the genus Tripteroides in the
Solomon Islands.

(Proc. U. S. Nat. Museum, Vol. 100:201-274,
1950)

AS
540
P 55j
CULICIDAE PHILIPPINE ISLANDS

Delfinado, M. D.

A checklist of Philippine mosquitoes with
a larval key to genera (Diptera, Culicidae).
By M. D. Delfinado, G. B. Viado, and L. T.
Coronel.

(The Philippine Jour. of Science, Vol. 91
(4):433-457, 1962)

QL
Insect
Pam.
2100
CULICIDAE POLYNESIA

Rosen, Leon

Morphologic variations of larvae of the
Scutellaris group of Aedes (Diptera, Culicidae)
in Polynesia. By Leon Rosen and Lloyd E. Rozeboom.

(Am. Jour. of Tropical Medicine and Hygiene,
3(3):529-538, 1954)

QH
1
P 11
CULICIDAE SOLOMON ISLANDS

Belkin, John N.

Mosquitoes of the genus Uranotaenia in the
Solomon Islands (Diptera:Culicidae).

(Pacific Science, 7:312-391, 1953)

QL
1
F 45
CULICOIDES PHILIPPINE ISLANDS

Delfinado, Mercedes D.

The Philippine biting midges of the genus
Culicoides (Diptera:Ceratopogonidae).
Philippine Zoological Expedition, 1946-1947.

(Fieldiana;Zoology, Vol. 33(7), 1961)

AS
36
W 2
CULICIDAE PONAPE

Knight, Kenneth L.

The mosquitoes of Ponape Island, eastern
Carolines. By Kenneth P. Knight and Herbert S.
Hurlburt.

(Journal of the Washington Academy of Sciences, Vol. 39:20-34, 1949)

QL
Insects
Pam.
1744
CULICIDAE SOLOMON ISLANDS

Laird, Marshall

Mosquitos and malaria in the hill country
of the New Hebrides and Solomon Islands.

(Bull. Ent. Research, Vol. 46(2):275-289,
1956)

AS
36
W 2
CULICIDAE PHILIPPINE ISLANDS

King, Willard V.

Descriptions of three new species of mosquitoes of the genus Aedes, subgenus Finlaya,
from New Guinea. By Willard V. King and
Harry Hoogstraal.

(Journal of the Washington Acad. Sci., Vol.
36:305-313, 1946)

AS
720.Q
R
CULICIDAE QUEENSLAND

Roberts, F. H. S.

The distribution and seasonal prevalence
of anopheline mosquitoes in North Queensland.

(Proc. R. Soc. Queensland, for 1947, Vol.
59(2):93-100, 1948)

S
398.F
A j
CULICIDAE SUVA

Lever, R. J. A. W.

Entomological notes: 1. Some common mosquitoes of the Suva area; 2. Insects from cave
deposits of bat guano.

(Agricultural Journal, Fiji, Vol. 14, 1943,
no. 4, pp. 101-102)

QH
1
P 11
CULICIDAE PHILIPPINE ISLANDS

Knight, Kenneth L.

The Aedes mosquitoes of the Philippines, I:
keys to species. Subgenera Mucidus, Ochlerotatus
and Finlaya (Diptera, Culicidae). By Kenneth L.
Knight and William B. Hull.

(Pacific Science, Vol. 5:211-251, 1951)

QL
Insects
Pam.
501
CULICIDAE ----- SAMOA

Buxton, P. A. and Hopkins, G. H. E.

The early stages of Samoan mosquitoes
Reprinted from Bull. Ent. Research, Vol.
XV, 1925, pp 295 - 301.

GN
2.8
T 12
CULICIDAE TAHITI

Buxton, Patrick A.

Sur les moustiques de Tahiti er du Groupe
des Iles de la Société. Translated by M. Barrier.

(Bull. Soc. d'Etudes Oceaniennes, No. 21:
306-308, 1927)

QH
1.8
W 31

and

QL
Insects
Pam.
1333
CULICIDAE PHILIPPINE IS.

Knight, Kenneth L.

A new species of Aedes (Christophersiomyia)
from the Philippines (Diptera-Culicidae).

(Proc. Biol. Soc. Washington, Vol. 60:73-
76, 1947)

QL
489.8
P 11

AS
763
B-b

Reading
Room
CULICIDAE SOCIETY ISLANDS

Lamb, C.G.

Dolichopodids from the Society Islands.

Society Islands Insects. Pacific Entomological Survey Publication 6, pp. 71-73 (Art.13),
1935.

(Bernice P. Bishop Museum, Bulletin 113)

QH
181.T
T 13
CULICIDAE TAIWAN

Chow, C. Y.

Collection of Culicine mosquitoes (Diptera,
Culicidae) in Taiwan (Formosa), China, with
description of a new species.

(Quarterly Journal of the Taiwan Museum,
Vol. III(4):281-287, 1950)

QH
1
P 11
CULICIDAE-PHILIPPINE ISLANDS

Knight, Kenneth L.

Three new speices of Aedes from the Philippines (Diptera, Culicidae). By Kenneth L.
Knight and William B. Hull.

(Pacific Science, V:197-203, 1951)

QL
Insects
Pam.
1337
CULICIDAE SOLOMON ISLANDS

Belkin, John N.

Anopheline mosquitoes of the Solomon Islands and New Hebrides. By John N. Belkin,
Kenneth L. Knight, and Lloyd E. Rozeboom.

(Journal of Parasitology, 31:241-265, 1945)

AS
720.T
Q3
CULICIDAE TASMANIA

Lee, David J.

Mosquitoes (Diptera, Culicidae) recorded
from Tasmania.

(Records of the Queen Victoria Mus.,
Launceston, Tasmania, Vol. 2:53-56, 1948)

Q
101
P 18

CULICIDAE   THAILAND

Thurman, Ernestine B.

The mosquito dauna of Thailand (Diptera:
Culicidae)
IN
Proc. of the 9th Pac. Sci. Congress, Bangkok, 1957, Vol. 17:144-158, 1962.

QL
461
T 86

CULICOIDES

Dorsey, C. K.

Population and control studies of the Palau
gnat on Peleliu, Western Caroline Islands.

(Journal of Economic Entomology, Vol. 40:
805-814, 1947)

AS
36
S3

Culin, Stewart *i. e.* Robert Stewart, 1858–
Chinese games with dice and dominoes. By Stewart
Culin ...

(*In* U. S. National museum. Annual report. 1893. Washington, 1895.
23½ᶜᵐ. p. 489-537. illus, 12 pl. (1 col.))

Half-title.
Prepared to illustrate a portion of the collection of games in the U. S.
National museum, and enlarged from a preliminary study published in
1889 with title: Chinese games with dice.

1. Games, Chinese. 2. Dice. 3. Dominoes. I. Title.

Library of Congress   Q11.U5 1893   14-19793
———— Copy 2.
———— Separate.   GV1303.C96 1895

QL
Insects
Pam.
1743

CULICIDAE   TOKELAU ISLANDS

Laird, Marshall

Notes on the mosquitos of the Gilbert, Ellice and Tokelau Islands, and on filariasis in
the latter group.

(Bull. Ent. Research, 46(2):291-300, 1955)

QL
Insect
Pam.
1614

CULICOIDES

Fox, Irving

Hoffmania, a new subgenus in Culicoides
(Diptera:Ceratopogonidae)

(Proceedings of the Biological Society of
Washington, Vol. 61:21-28, 1948)

GN
Pam
#12

Culin, Stewart.

H. 18 The Gambling Games of the Chinese
in America. Fan t'an & Pak Kop Piu
(Publications of University of Pennsylvania Vol. I No.4)

Philadelphia 1891   8vo   pp17.

N.5.

6/10/99

QL
Insect
Pam.
1604

CULICIDAE   UNITED STATES

Stage, H. H.   and others

Mosquitoes of the northwestern states.

(U. S. Dept. of Agric., Agriculture Handbook No. 46, 1952)

QL
461
M 62

CULICOIDES   JAPAN

Arnaud, Paul

The heleid genus Culicoides in Japan, Korea,
and Ryukyu Islands (Insects: Diptera)

(Microentomology, Vol. 21(3), 1956)

GN
550
S

Culin, Stewart *i. e.* Robert Stewart, 1858–
Games of the North American Indians, by Stewart
Culin.

(*In* U. S. Bureau of American ethnology. Twenty-fourth annual report
... 1902-1903. Washington, 1907. 29¼ᶜᵐ. p. 1-846. illus., XXI (*i. e.* 24) pl.
(2 col.))

1. Indians of North America—Games.

Library of Congress   E51.U55   7-35262
———— Copy 2.   GN2.U5

QL
537
W 54

CULICIDAE   UNITED STATES

King, W. V. and others

A handbook of the mosquitoes of the southeastern United States. By W. V. King, G. H.
Bradley, carroll N. Smith and W. C. McDuffie.

(U. S. D. A. Agriculture Handbook, No. 173,
1960)

QL
461
M 62

CULICOIDES   RYUKYU ISLANDS

Arnaud, Paul

The heleid genus Culicoides in Japan, Korea,
and Ryukyu Islands (Insects: Diptera)

(Microentomology, Vol. 21(3), 1956)

GN
454
C 96

Culin, Stewart

Games of the Orient: Korea, China, Japan.
Charles E. Tuttle Company. Rutland, Vt.; Tokyo
8vo.   xxxvi + 177 pp.

QL
461
H-1

CULICIDAE   WAKE ISLAND

Rosen, L.

Aedes Aegypti on Wake Island. By L. Rosen,
W. C. Reeves and T. Aarons.

(Haw. Ent. Soc., Proc., 13(2):255, 1948)

QL
461
P 11

CULICOIDES   TAIWAN

Wirth, W. W.

New species and records of Taiwan Culicoides (Diptera: Ceratopogonidae). By W. W. Wirth
and A. A. Hubert.

(Pacific Insects, 3(1):11-26, 1961)

Gn
1
A

Culin, Stewart

Hawaiian games.. In Am. Anthrop. Vol.
I, pp 201-250. 1899

QL
536
H 85

CULICIDAE   WEST INDIES

Howard, Leland Ossian, 1857–
The mosquitoes of North and Central America and the
West Indies, by Leland O. Howard, Harrison G. Dyar,
and Frederick Knab ... Washington, D. C., Carnegie institution of Washington, 1912-17.
4 v. in 3. illus., plates. 25ᶜᵐ. (*On verso of t.-p.:* Carnegie institution
of Washington. Publication no. 159)
Bibliography: v. 1, p. 451-488.
Contents.—v. 1. A general consideration of mosquitoes, their habits,
and their relations to the human species.—v. 2. Plates.—v. 3-4. Systematic
description.
1. Mosquito. I. Dyar, Harrison Gray, 1866–   joint author. II.
Knab, Frederick, 1865–   joint author.

Library of Congress   QL536.H85   13-6044
———— Copy 2.

GN
1
A

Culin, Stewart

American Indian Games (1902)

(American Anthropologist, N. S. Vol. 5,
1903, pp. 58-64)

GN
635.K
C 96

Culin, Stewart

Korean games, with notes on the corresponding
games of China and Japan. Philadelphia. University of Pennsylvania. 1895. R8vo. xxxvi +
177 pp.

AS
122
E 23

CULICOIDES

Campbell, J. Allan

A taxonomic review of the British species of
"Culicoides" Latreille (Diptera, Ceratopogonidae)

R. Soc. Edinburgh, Proc., 67(3):181-302,
1959-60)

GN
Pam
#258

Culin, Stewart

American Indian Games, ex Univ. of
Penn. Mus. Bull., vol. 1, no. 3, 1898.

AS
36
S3

Culin, Stewart *i. e.* Robert Stewart, 1858–
Mancala, the national game of Africa. By Stewart
Culin ...
(*In* U. S. National museum. Annual report. 1894. Washington, 1896.
23½ᶜᵐ. p. 595-607. illus., 5 pl.)
Half-title.
Read before the Oriental club of Philadelphia, May 10, 1894.

1. Games, African. I. Title.

14-19602

Library of Congress   Q11.U5 1894

GN
Pam
#381

Culin, Stewart

The origin of Ornament, ex Univ.
of Penn. Mus., Bull. no. 4, vol. 2,
1900.

GN
2.M
A 85

CULTS   ADMIRALTY ISLANDS

Schwartz, Theodore

The Paliau Movement in the Admiralty Islands, 1946-1954.

(Anthrop. Papers, Am. Mus. Nat. Hist.
49(2), 1962)

GN
Ethn.
Pam.
4458

CULTS   NEW GUINEA

Van Baal, J.

The cult of the bull-roarer in Australia.
and southern New Guinea.

(Reprint, Bijdragen tot de Taal, Land en
Volkenkunde, Deel 119(2):201-214, 1963)

GN
1
A

Culin, Stewart

Philippine Games.

(American Anthropologist, N. S. Vol. 2,
1900, pp. 643-656)

GN
Ethn.
Pam.
4458

CULTS   AUSTRALIA

Van Baal, J.

The cult of the bull-roarer in Australia
and southern New Guinea.

(Reprint, Bijdragen tot de Taal, Land en
Volkenkunde, Deel 119(2):201-214, 1963)

CULTS

See also under

HERO CULTS
CARGO CULTS

Culin, Stewart

The Wreck of the Wakamiya Maru.

(Asia, 1920, pp. 365-372, 436)

(Japanese survivors touched at Sandwich Islands in 1804)

AM
101
F 45-n

CULTS   MALEKULA

South Pacific tribe has '4-H Club'.

(Chicago Nat. Hist. Mus. Bull. 28(8):5, 1957)

GN
400
K 26

Cultural anthropology; the science of custom.

Keesing, Felix M.

QL
671
I 12

Cullen, J. M.

The Black Noddy, Anous tenuirostris, on
Ascension Island. Part 2: behaviour. By
J. M. Cullen and N. P. Ashmole.

(Ibis, Vol. 103b(3):423-446, 1963)

(Centenary Expeditions Volume)

CULTS   MELANESIA

Harwood, R.

The Tamberan cult as found in Melanesia and
the tropical forest of South America. M.A.
Columbia Univ., 1950

Microfilm copy in Dept. Pac. Hist., Inst.
Adv. Studies, Australian Nat. Univ.

GN
1
C 97

CULTURAL DRIFT

Eggan, Fred

Cultural drift and social change.

(Current Anthropology, Vol. 4(4):347-355,
1963)

QK
Bot.Pam.
2944

CULLENIA   INDONESIA

Kostermans, A. J. G. H.

The genus Cullenia Wight (Bombacaceae).

(Communication (Pengumuman) of the Forest
Research Institute, Bogor, Nr. 51, July, 1956)

GN
1
O 15

CULTS   NEW GUINEA

Berndt, Ronald M.

A cargo movement in the eastern Central
Highlands of New Guinea.

(Oceania, 23:40-65, 137-158, 202-234, 1953)

GN
2.S
P 76

CULTURAL EVOLUTION   PACIFIC

Goodenough, Ward H.

Oceania and the problem of controls in the
study of cultural and human evolution.

(Jour. Poly. Soc., 66(2):146-155, 1957)

QL
461
P 11

CULOIDES   NEW GUINEA

Tokunaga, M.

Biting midges of the genus Culicoides from
New Guinea (Diptera:Ceratopogonidae)

(Pacific Insects, 4(2):457-516, 1962)

GN
Ethn. Pam.
#391

CULTS   NEW GUINEA

Bühler, Alfred

Kultkrokodile vom Korewori (Sepik-Distrikt,
Territorium Neuguinea)

1961 (Zeit. für Ethnologie, 86(2):183-207,

GN
Ethn.
Pam.
4097

CULTURE   EVOLUTION   (PACIFIC)

Schricke, B.

The evolution of culture in the Pacific in
relation to the theories of the "Kulturhistoris-
che" and the "Manchester" schools of social anthropology.

(Reprinted from the Proceedings of the
Third Pan-Pacific Science Congress, Tokyo, 1926;
pp. 2423-2441)

[Translation: Miss A. Adriani.]

QK
Bot.Pam.
2172

Culpepper, C. W.

Composition of the rhizome, stem, and leaf
of some horticultural forms of Canna in relation
to their possible use, by C.W.Culpepper and H.H.
Moon.

(United States, Dept. of Agriculture, Circular
No.497, 1938, 21 pp.)

GN
1
O 15

CULTS   NEW GUINEA

Read, K. E.

Nama cult of the central highlands, New
Guinea.

(Oceania, 23(i):1-25, 1952)

GN
2.S
P 76

CULTURAL EVOLUTION   POLYNESIA

Goldman, Irving

Cultural evolution in Polynesia: a reply to
criticism.

(Jour. Poly. Soc., 66(2):156-164, 1957)

GN
23
M 48   Cultural patterns and technical change.

Mead, Margaret

GN
400
K 26   CULTURE

Keesing, Felix M.

     Cultural anthropology; the science of custom. With illustrations by the author. Rinehart and Company, Inc. New York. R8vo. 1958c xxv + 477 pp.

P
121
S 24   CULTURE

Sapir, Edward

     Selected writings of Edward Sapir in language, culture, and personality. Edited by David G. Mandelbaum. University of California Press. 1949. R8vo. xv + 617 pp. Berkeley and Los Angeles

---

GN
22
B 26   CULTURE

Barnouw, Victor

     Culture and personality. Homewood, Ill. Dorsey Press, Inc. 1963 xi + 410 pp. R8vo.

GN
2.M
P 35   CULTURE

Kroeber, A. L.

     Culture, a critical review of concepts and definitions. By A. L. Kroeber and Clyde Kluckhohn, with the assistance of Wayne Untereiner and appendices by Alfred G. Meyer.

     (Papers of the Peabody Museum of Am. Arch. and Ethn., Harvard, Vol. 47(1), 1952)

GN
451
S 24   CULTURE

Sargent, S. Stansfeld   editor

     Culture and personality. Edited by S. Stansfeld Sargent and Marian W. Smith. Proceedings of an Interdisciplinary Conference held under auspices of the Viking Fund, Nov. 7 and 8, 1947. Published by the Viking Fund. 1949. 8vo. vi + 219 pp.

GN
Ethn.
Pam.
3699   CULTURE

Bateson, Gregory

     Sex and culture.

     (Reprinted from the Annals of The New York Academy of Sciences Vol. 47(5):647-660, 1947)

GN
405
K 93   CULTURE

Kroeber, A. L.

     The nature of culture. The University of Chicago Press. (Chicago) (1952) R8vo. x + (1-2)3-437 pp. + index

---

GN
Ethn.
Pam.
4277   CULTURE

Schmitz, Carl A.

     Historische Volkerkunde; Aufgaben und Möglichkeiten in der Gegenwart. 1961. Univ. of Basel. mimeographed. Folio. 16 pp.

GN
4
D 53   CULTURE

Diamond, Stanley   editor

     Culture in history; essays in honor of Paul Radin. Published for Brandeis University, by Columbia University Press. New York. 1960 R8vo. xxiv + 1014 pp.

GN
2.F
V 69   CULTURE

Kroeber, A.

     A roster of civilizations and culture.

     (Viking Fund, Publ. 30, 1962, 96 pp.)

GN
400
S 49   CULTURE

Service, Elman R.

     A profile of primitive culture. Harper and Brothers. New York. 1958c R8vo. xiv + 474 pp.

     (For revision see "Profiles in ethnology")

GN
22
D 66   CULTURE

Dole, Gertrude E.

     Essays in the science of culture, in honor of Leslie A. White, in celebration of his sixtieth birthday and his thirtieth year of teaching at the University of Michigan. By Gertrude E. Dole and Robert L. Carneiro. Thomas Y. Crowell Company. New York. 1960c R8vo. xlvi + 509 pp.

GN
22
M 25   CULTURE

Malinowski, Bronislaw

     A scientific theory of culture and other essays. With a preface by Huntington Cairns. Univ. of North Carolina Press. Chapel Hill. 1944. 8vo. ix + 228 pp.

GN
22
S 52   CULTURE

Shapiro, H.L.

     Aspects of culture. Rutgers University Press. New Brunswick, N.J. sm8vo. (1957c) 147 pp.

GN
400
H 77   CULTURE

Honigmann, John J.

     Understanding culture. New York. Harper & Row. 1963. viii + 468 pp. R8vo.

GN
478
M 25   CULTURE

Malinowski, Bronislaw

     Sex, culture, and myth. London. Rupert Hart-Davis. 1963. vi + 346 pp.

GN
22
S 52   CULTURE

Shapiro, Harry L.   Editor

     Man, culture, and society. Oxford University Press. New York. 1956. 8vo. xiii + 380 pp.

AS
36
S1   CULTURE.

Jacob, Georg, 1862-
   Oriental elements of culture in the Occident. By Dr. Georg Jacob.
     (*In* Smithsonian institution. Annual report. 1902. Washington, 1903. 23½ᶜᵐ. p. 509-529)

   1. Culture.   I. Title.

                       S 15-1165

Library of Congress   Q11.S66 1902
Library, Smithsonian   Institution

GN
2.I
A-n   CULTURE

Murphy, John

     Racial crossing and cultural efflorescence.

     (Man, Jan.-Feb. 1941, No. 2)

GN
400
S 75   CULTURE

Spier, Leslie and others, editors

     Language, culture, and personality; essays in memory of Edward Sapir. Menasha. 1941.

AP
2
S 41

CULTURE

Steward, Julian H.

Cultural evolution; the 19th century idea
that cultures evolve in the same was asplants
and animals was abandoned when anthropologists
found that it did not jibe with their observations. Now the evolutionary approach is revived.

(Scientific American, May 1950:69-80)

CULTURE CHANGE   PONAPE

Coale, G. L.

Study of chieftainship, missionary contact
and culture change on Ponape, 1852-1900. Complete. M.A., University of Southern California,
1951.

microfilm in Inst. Adv. Studies, Dept. of
Pac. Hist., Austr. Nat. Univ. (Harry Maude)

GN
2.I
A 52

CULTURE   NEW GUINEA

Wirz, Paul

Kunst und Kult des Sepik-Gebietes [Neu-
Guinea].

(K. Instituut voor de Tropen-Amsterdam,
Mededeling No. 133, 1959.)

GN
22
W 58

CULTURE

White, Leslie A.

The evolution of culture; the development
of civilization to the fall of Rome. McGraw-
Hill Book Company, Inc. 1959. New York...8vo.
xi + 378 pp.

GN
635.B7
G 29

CULTURE   DAYAKS

Geddes, W. R.

Nine Dayak nights.   Oxford University
Press Melbourne.   1957.   8vo xxxi + 134 pp.

GN
Ethn.
Pam.
4285

CULTURE   PHILIPPINE ISLANDS

Philippine Islands cultural-linguistic
groups. map. Philippine Studies program,
University of Chicago. May 1955.

GN
Ethn.
Pam.
3722

CULTURE

White, Leslie A.

History, evolutionism, and functionalism:
three types of interpretation of culture.

(Reprinted from Southwestern Journal of
Anthropology, Vol. 1(2): 221-248, 1945)

GN
671.H2
B 27

CULTURE   HAWAII

Barrère, Dorothy B.

Summary of Hawaiian history and culture.
Prepared for the National Park Service, Region
Four, by Bernice P. Bishop Museum. Honolulu
1961. Typed 4ro. 106 pp.

GN
635.B7
G 29

CULTURE   SARAWAK

Geddes, W. R.

Nine Dayak nights.   Oxford University
Press Melbourne.   1957.   8vo xxxi + 134 pp.

GN
Ethn.
Pam.
3992
8993
GN
308
M 97

CULTURE   CLASSIFICATION

Murdock, George P.

Outline of world cultures. Behavior Science
Outlines. Human Relations Area Files. Yale
University. New Haven. 1954. mimeographed
4to. 180 pp.

[two copies]

Q
101
P 18

CULTURE   EFFECT OF ISOLATION

Vayda, Andrew P.
Island cultures. By Andrew P. Vayda and
Roy A. Rappaport.

IN
Fosberg, F. Raymond   editor
Man's place in the island ecosystem, a
symposium. pp. 133-144. Honolulu. 1963.
Tenth Pacific Science Congress.

GN
323
S 74

CULTURE   AREAS

Spencer, R.F.   (compiler)

An ethno-atlas (a student's manual of tribal, linguistic and racial groupings). William
C. Brown Company. Dubuque, Iowa. 4to. 1956c
iii + 42 pp.

DU
1
P

CULTURE   EXPERIMENTS IN

Population of Moturiki, Fiji, will be "mass
educated" next year.

(Pac. Islands Monthly, 20(5):61-62, 1949)

GN
Ethn.
Pam.
4278

CULTURE   HAWAII

Taylor, Clarice B.

Hawaiian Almanac. 2nd printing, 1960.
Tongg Publishing Company, Ltd. Honolulu 8vo.
64 pp.

AS
36
S 1

AREAS -
CULTURE   DUTCH EAST INDIES

Kennedy, Raymond

Contours of culture in Indonesia.

(Ann. Rept. Smithsonian Institution, 1943:
513-522)

GN
24
K 93

CULTURE   HISTORY

Kroeber, Alfred L.

Configurations of culture growth.
University of California Press. Berkeley. 1944.
R8vo.   x + 882 pp.

GN
2.I
A 62 j

CULTURE   MARQUESAS

Suggs, R. C.

The derivation of Marquesan culture.

(Jour. R. Anthrop. Inst. of Great Britain
and Ireland, Vol. 91(1):1-10, 1961)

DU
Pac.
Pam.
34

CULTURE AREAS   NEW ZEALAND

Skinner, H. D.

Culture areas in New Zealand.

(Jour. Poly. Soc., 30:71-78, 1921)

GN
635.B7
G 29

CULTURE   BORNEO

Geddes, W. R.

Nine Dayak nights.   Oxford University
Press Melbourne.   1957.   8vo xxxi + 134 pp.

GN
Ethn.
Pam.
4271

CULTURE   MELANESIA

Schmitz, Carl A.

Das Problem der austro-melaniden Kultur.

(Acta Tropica, 18(2):97-141, 1961)

GN
323
S 74

CULTURE AREAS - PACIFIC

Spencer, R.F.   (compiler)

An ethno-atlas (a student's manual of tribal, linguistic and racial groupings). William
C.Brown Company. Dubuque, Iowa. 4to. 1956c
iii + 42 pp.

GN
2.S
P 76

CULTURE AREAS POLYNESIA

Burrows, Edwin G.

Culture areas in Polynesia.

(Journal of the Polynesian Soc., Vol. 49,
1940, pp. 349-363)

GN
2.S
S 72

CULTURE CHANGE PAPUA

Maher, Robert P.

Varieties of change in Koriki culture.

(Southwestern Jour. of Anthropology, 17:
26-39, 1961)

[Purari River, Papua]

Z
Biblio-
graphy
Pam.
173

Culture and personality in the Pacific
Islands: a bibliography.

Howard, Irwin compiler, and others

GN
22
O 61

CULTURE TRUK

Gladwin, Thomas

Culture and individual personality inte-
gration on Truk. By Thomas Gladwin and Seymour
B. Sarason.
IN
Opler, Marvin K. editor
Culture and mental health. Cross-culture
studies. Macmillan. New York. R8vo. 1959.

[based on "Truk: Man in Paradise"]

GN
2.S
P 76

CULTURE CHANGE POLYNESIA

Hawthorn, H. B.

Cultural evolution or cultural change?
The case of Polynesia. By H. B. Hawthorn and
C. S. Belshaw.

(Jour. Poly. Soc., 66(1):18-35, 1957)

GN
Ethn.
Pam.
4043

Culture and the structural evolution of the
neural system

Mettler, Fred A.

GN
400
B 26

CULTURE CHANGE

Barnett, H. G.

Innovation, the basis of cultural change.
first edition. McGraw-Hill Book Co., Inc.
New York. 1953. 8vo. xi and 462 pp.

GN
Ethn.Pam.
3529

CULTURE CHARTS

[Chronological charts for world cultures.]
University of Chicago, Dept. of Anthropology.
3 charts.

QH
1
N 28

La culture du caoutchouc aux îles Hawaii.

(Le Naturaliste, 2 série, No.452,1906, pp.
13-14)

GN
2.1
S 78

CULTURE CHANGE

Keesing, Felix M.

Culture change, an analysis and bibliography
of anthropological sources to 1952.

(Stanford Anthropological Series, No. 1,
1953)

GN
1
Ar-s

CULTURE COMPLEXES -- NEW HEBRIDES

Speiser, Felix

Kultur-Komplexe in den Neuen Hebriden,
.... In Archiv Suisses d'Anthrop. Gen.
Vol. III, 1919, pp 300 - 319 : IV, 1920-
22, pp 18- 77, 207- 232.

CULTURE HEROS

SEE

HERO CULTS

GN
Ethn.
Pam.
3707

CULTURE CHANGE

Mead, Margaret

The implications of culture change for
personality development.

(Reprinted from The American Journal of
Orthopsychiatry Vol. XVII(4):633-646, 1947)

CULTURE CONTACT

See under

CONTACT

GN
Ethn.Pam.
3005

The Culture of the Maya:
Excavations at Uaxactun, by Oliver G.
Ricketson, Jr., The Maya and Modern Civilization,
by Robert Redfield, The Calakmul Expedition, by
Sylvanus G. Morley.

(Carnegie Institution of Washington, Supplementary Publication, No. 6, 1933- reprinted from
Scientific Monthly, 1933, Vol. 37, pp. 72-86,
110-123, 193-206)

GN
400
S 85

CULTURE CHANGE

Steward, Julian H.

Theory of culture change: the methodology
of multilinear evolution. Univ. of Illinois
Press. Urbana. 1955. 8vo. (6) + 244 pp.

GN
488
K 66

Culture and behavior.

Kluckhohn, Clyde

GN
400
S 64

Culture: the diffusion controversy

Smith, G. Elliot

DU
1
P 9

CULTURE CHANGE FIJI

Watters, R. F.

Sugar production and culture change in
Fiji: A comparison between peasant and
plantation agriculture.

(Pacific Viewpoint, Vol. 4(1):25-52,
1963)

GN
488.3
H 19

Culture and experience

Hallowell, A. Irving

PL
8
H 71

CULTURE CONTENT IN LANGUAGE

McQuown, Norman A.

Analysis of the cultural content of language
materials.
IN
Hoijer, Harry editor

Language in culture. Conference on the in-
terrelations of language and other aspects of
culture. The University of Chicago Press.
Chicago. (1955) 8vo. pp. 20-31

GN
Ethn.Pam.
4264

CULTURE EXCHANGE TONGA

Koch, Gerd

Das gegenwartige Ergebnis des Kulturwandels bei den Tonganern und die Ursachen dieser Entwicklung.

(Zeit. f. Ethnologie, 79(2):165-174, 1954)

QL
441.4
S 24

CUMACEA

Sars, George Ossian

An account of the Crustacea of Norway... Vol. 3, 1899-1900. Bergen. R8vo.

DU
1
S 72 q

Cumber, R. A.

Rhinoceros beetle investigations in Western Samoa.

(South Pacific Commission, Quarterly Bulletin, Vol. 5(2):2-4, 1955)

AM
Mus.Pam.
399

Culture of the Kamehameha Kingdom; Hawaiian art exhibition, at Tokyo, August 11-23, and Nagoya, Sept. 1-6, Fukuoka, Hiroshima, August-October, 1959. Grouping and display in charge of Yoshihiko Sinoto. 32 pp. R8vo.

[many objects loaned by Bishop Museum]

AS
720.S
S 72

CUMACEA AUSTRALIA

Hale, Herbert M.

Australian Cumacea, Nos. 7

(Records of the South Australian Mus., Vol. 8:63-142, 1944)

(papers on Cumacea preceding this are in vols. 4:549-550, 1928, Vol. 5:395-403, 404-438, 1936) others?

DU
1
S 72 t

Cumber, R. A.

The Rhinoceros beetle in Western Samoa.

(South Pacific Commission, Tech. Paper, no. 107, 1957)

GN
550
B32

Die culturlander des alten America.

Bastian, Adolf

2 vols.

AS
720.S
S 72

CUMACEA AUSTRALIA

Hale, Herbert M.

Australian Cumacea, 8

(Trans. R. Soc. S. Australia, 63:225-285, 1944)

G
3
A 1

Cumberland, Kenneth B.

Aotearoa Maori: New Zealand about 1780.

(Geographical Review, Vol. 39:401-424, 1949)

AS
36
S4

CUMACEA

Calman, William Thomas, 1871–

The *Crustacea* of the order *Cumacea* in the collection of the United States national museum. By William T. Calman ...

(*In* U. S. National museum. Proceedings. Washington, 1912. 23½ᶜᵐ. v. 41, p. 603-676. illus.)

"Bibliography of American *Cumacea*": p. 675-676.

1. Cumacea.   12-17797

Library of Congress   Q11.U55 vol. 41

AS
720.S
S 72

CUMACEA AUSTRALIA

Hale, Herbert M.

Australian Cumacea, 9.

(Records of the South Australian Museum, Vol. 8:145-218, 1945)

G
3
A 1

Cumberland, Kenneth B.

Contrasting regional morphology of soil erosion in New Zealand.

(Geographical Review, Jan. 1944, Vol. 34, pp. 77-95)

Q
115
M 46

CUMACEA

Calman, W. T(William Thomas)
Cumacea and Phyllocarida.

Mawson, Sir Douglas   leader
Australasian Antarctic Expedition, 1911-14, Scientific Reports, Series. C, Vol. 5, Part 6, 1918.

AS
720.S
S 72

CUMACEA AUSTRALIA

Hale, Herbert M.

Australian Cumacea. No. 12, 15-16

(Records of the South Australian Museum, Vol. 8 (3):357-444, 1946)

GN
2.S
P 76

Cumberland, Kenneth B.
The future of Polynesia.

(Jour. Polynesian Society, 71(4):386-396, 1962)

Q
115
M 46

CUMACEA

Hale, H. M.
Cumacea and Nebaliacea.

Mawson, Sir Douglas   leader
British, Australian, and New Zealand Antarctic Research Expedition, 1929-31. Reports, Series B, Vol. IV, Part 2. 1937. pp. 39-56.

QL
Insect
Pam.
2115

Cumber, R. A.

The interaction of native and introduced insect species in New Zealand.

(Reprint, Proc. of the N.Z. Ecological Soc., 8:55-60, 1961)

G
7
N 56

Cumberland, Kenneth B.

Man in nature in New Zealand.

(New Zealand Geographer, 17(2):137-154, 1961)

GC
63
D 61

CUMACEA

Jones, N. S.

Cumacea of the Benguela current.

(Discovery Reports, Vol. XXVII:279-292, 1955)

QL
Insect
Pam.
2077

Cumber, R. A.

Notes on the biology of Melampsalta cruentata Fabricius (Hemiptera-Homoptera:Cicadidae), with special reference to the nymphal stages.

(Trans. of the R. Entomological Soc. of London, 103(6):219-238, 1952)

Q
101
P 18

Cumberland, Kenneth B.
Man's role in modifying island environments in the southwest Pacific: with special reference to New Zealand.

IN
Fosberg, F. Raymond, editor
Man's place in the island ecosystem, a symposium. pp. 187-206. Honolulu. 1963. Tenth Pacific Science Congress.

G
7
S 43

Cumberland, Kenneth

New Zealand and the South West Pacific.

(The Scottish Geographical Magazine, Vol. 66:14-16, 1950)

Q
Biography
Pam. 47

Cuming, Hugh

Biographical notes.

QK
Bot.Pam.
2273

CUMING, HUGH

St. John, Harold

Itinerary of Hugh Cuming in Polynesia.

(Occ. Papers, B. P. Bishop Museum, Vol. 16, No. 4, 1940, pp. 81-90)

G
7
N 56

Cumberland, Kenneth B.

Problem and prospect in Fiji.

(New Zealand Geographer, 16(2):214-217, 1960)

QK
1
H

and

QK
1
H 78

Cuming, Hugh

Hooker, William Jackson

Contributions towards a flora of South America and the islands of the Pacific, by W. J. Hooker and G. A. W. Arnott.
(Hooker, Bot. Misc. III: 1833, pp. 129-211, 302-367; Hooker's Journal of Botany, I, 1834, pp. 276-296; III, pp. 19-47, 310-348; Hooker, Comp. Bot. Mag. I, 1835, pp. 29-38, 102-111, 234-244; II, pp. 41-52, 250-254)
Note, Library lacks the references underlined in red.

QK
Bot.Pam.
2683

CUMINIA

Skottsberg, Carl

An unnecessary name change.

(Svensk Bot. Tidskrift, Bd. 45(1):1-3, 1951)

GN
2.S
F 47

Cumberland, Kenneth B.

Soil erosion and the world food situation.

(Trans. and Proc. of the Fiji Society, 1948-1950, Vol. 4:1-8, 1953)

GN
2/S
T 12

Cuming, Hugh

L'identité de l'ile Grimwood.

(Bull. Soc. Etudes Oceaniennes, 127/128: 46-48, 1959)

DU
600
C97

Cumming, C. F. Gordon

At home in Fiji.
New York, 1882. pp x, 365, illus., map.

G
55
C 96

Cumberland, Kenneth B.

Southwest Pacific, a geography of Australia, New Zealand and their Pacific island neighbourhoods. Whitcombe and Tombs, Ltd. Christchurch. 1954. 8vo. xviii + 365 pp.

DU
Pac.Pam.
597

Cuming, H(ugh)

Excerpt from letter written to Dr. (Joseph Dalton) Hooker by H. Cuming, dated "London, March 21st, 1832".

(Voyage was in 1828,- stopped at Easter Island, Mangareva, Crescent, Rurutu, Tubuai, Ducie, Tuamotus, Rapa)

DU
623
C97

Cumming, C. F. Gordon

Fire fountains; the kingdom of Hawaii, its volcanoes and the history of its missions.

Edinburgh & London, 1883. 8vo pp. VII, 297 illus. maps. 2 vols.

DU
12
F 62
locked
case

CUMBERLAND (SHIP)

Flinders, Matthew

Voyage to Terra Australis; undertaken for the purpose of completing the discovery of that vast country, and prosecuted in the years 1801-1803, in His Majesty's ship the Investigator, and subsequently in the armed vessel Porpoise and Cumberland schooner. With an account of the shipwreck of the Porpoise, arrival of the Cumberland at Mauritius...2 vols. and atlas. London. 1814. 4to.

AS
540
P

Cuming, Hugh

Merrill, Elmer D.

Hugh Cuming's letters to Sir William J. Hooker.

(Phil. Jour. Sci. 30:153-184. 1926)

DU
12
C 97

Cumming, C. F. Gordon

A Lady's Cruise in a French Man-of-War. In two volumes. Volumes 1-2. With Map and Illustrations. Edinburgh and London. William Blackwood and Sons. 1882. xi +304, vii + 309 pp. 8vo.

GN
2.S
P 11

CUMBERLAND (SHIP)

Maude, Harry W.

Rarotonga sandalwood; the visit of Goodenough to Rarotonga in 1814. By H. E. Maude and Marjorie Tuainekore Crocombe.

(Jour. Poly. Soc., 71(1):32-56, 1962)

[presented in abstract at 10th Pac. Science Congress]

QL
401
H 33

CUMING, HUGH

Clench, William J.

Some notes on the life and explorations of Hugh Cuming.

(Occ. Papers on Mollusks, Dept. of Mollusks, Mus. of Comp. Zool., Harvard Univ., Vol. 1, No. 3, 1945)

DU
Hist.Pam.
266

Cumming, C. F. Gordon

The last king of Tahiti.

(Contemporary Review, Vol. 41, 1882, pp. 821-836)

QK
936
T 85

Cumbie, Billy G.

Anatomical studies in the Leguminosae.

(Tropical Woods, No. 113:1-47, 1960)

QK
1
L 23

CUMING, HUGH

Howell, John Thomas

Hugh Cuming's visit to the Galapagos Islands.

(Lloydia, Vol. 4(4):291-292, 1947)

RC
Leprosy
Pam. 27

Cumming, H. S.

Care and Treatment of Leprous Persons in Hawaii. Letter from the Secretary of the Treasury transmitting a report from the Surgeon General of the United States Public Health Service, authorizing a survey to be made as to existing facilities for the protection of the public health in the care and treatment of leprous persons in the Territory of Hawaii.
(72nd Congress, 2nd Session, House Doc. 470, Washington, 1933. 35 pp. 14 pl. 2 maps.)

DU
626
C 97

(Cummings. (Mrs.) A.P.)

The Missionary's Daughter: A Memoir of Lucy Goodale Thurston, of the Sandwich Islands. New York. American Tract Society. 1842. 209pp. 12mo.

DU
12
B 93

locked case

Cummins, John

Bulkeley, John

A Voyage to the South-Seas, in the years 1740-1...Containing a faithful narrative of the loss of His Majesty's Ship the Wager...compiled by persons concerned in the facts related, viz John Bulkeley and John Cummins, late gunner and carpenter of the Wager. London. 1743. sm8vo.

QK
1
H 78

Cunningham, Allan (editor)

Florae insularum Novae Zelandiae precursor; or a speciment of the botany of the islands of New Zealand.

(Comp. Bot. Mag. (Hooker), Vol. II, 1836, pp. 222-233; 327-336, 358-378)

(Continued in Annals and Mag. Nat. Hist. which is at HSPA Library)

GN
Ethn.Pam.
3031

Cummings, Byron

Cuicuilco and the Archaic Culture of Mexico.

(University of Arizona, Bulletin,-Social Science Bulletin No. 4, Nov. 1933)

Storage
Case
1

Cummins, John A.

Portrait. In charcoal, done by A.A.Montano, Honolulu. Sanfrancisco, 1878. Loaned by Hawaiian Contracting Company.

GN
635.S
C 97

Cunningham, Clark E.

The postwar migration of the Toba-Bataks to east Sumatra.

(Yale Univ., Southeast Asia Studies, Cultural Report Series, 1958)

AS
36
B 92

Cummings, Carlos Emmons

East is East and West is West; some observations on the World's Fairs of 1939 by one whose main interest is in museums.

(Bull. Buffalo Society of Natural Sci., Vol. 20, 1940)

DU
Hist.
Pam. 181

Cummins, John A.

Queen Emma's Tour of Oahu in 1875.

(Honolulu Star Bulletin, July 22, 1933)

QL
483.I
C 97

Cunningham, D. D.

Plagues and pleasures of life in Bengal. With illustrations. London. John Murray. 1907. 8vo. xi + 385 pp.

DU
12
C 97

locked case

Cummings, Henry

A synopsis of the cruise of the U. S. S. "Tuscarora" from the date of her commission to her arrival in San Francisco, Cal., Sept. 2d, 1874. Compiled by Henry Cummings. San Francisco. Cosmopolitan Steam Printing Co. 1874. 8vo. 61 pp.

Q
101
P 18

Cumpston, J. H. L.

A cooperative epidemiological intelligence service in the south Pacific.

(Proc. Pac. Sci. Congress, 6th, 1939, Vol.5 (pub. in 1942), pp. 429-432)

GN
Pam
2300

Cunningham, D. J (Daniel John) and others

Anthropometric investigation in the British Isles. Report of committee consisting of Cunningham and others.

(Report...British Ass'n for the Adv. of Science, York, 1906, Section H, pp. 349-369)

2 copies

DU
620
P

Cummings, Margaret Kamm

All aboard for the Bishop Museum...and a non-stop ride by silver bus any week day morning you choose!

(Paradise of the Pacific, Vol. 67(10):12-13, October, 1955)

CUNA INDIANS SONGS

See

SONGS CUNA INDIANS

GN
29
B 18

Cunningham, D. J. (Daniel John)

The Australian Forehead

Balfour, Henry, and others

Anthropological essays...Oxford. 1907. 4to pp. 65-80.

DU
Pac.Pam.
645

Cummings, Philip H.

One time consul in Samoa. (William Churchill)

(The log of the Circumnavigators' Club, Vol. 28, 1940, No. 4, pp. 39-50; Vol. 29, 1941, No. 1, pp. 34-42)

GN
2M
Pe-1

CUNEIFORM INSCRIPTIONS.

Pennsylvania. University. *University museum. Babylonian section.*
... Publications of the Babylonian section. v. 1–

Philadelphia, Pub. by the University museum, 1911–

v. plates. 27½ᶜᵐ.

At head of title: University of Pennsylvania. The museum. "Eckley Brinton Coxe junior fund." Continues the series published 1893-1911 under title: The Babylonian expedition of the University of Pennsylvania, ed. by H. V. Hilprecht.

1. Babylonia—Antiq. 2. Cuneiform inscriptions.

18-5956

Library of Congress   PJ3711.P5

Q
115
C43

G 2.7

Cunningham D. J (Daniel John)

Challenger Expedition

Zoology V. Pt XIV. Marsupialia.

Hns
M46

Storage
case
4

Cummins,

Name songs. (Inoa.)

GR
885
C 97

Cunha, A. R.

Famous Hawaiian Songs. Arranged by A. R. Cunha. Translations by W. H. Coney and Solomon Mehuela. Published by Bergstrom Music Co., Ltd. Honolulu. 1914c. 4to. 96 pp.

QM
23
C97

Cunningham, Daniel John, 1850-1909, ed.

Cunningham's Text-book of anatomy, ed. by Arthur Robinson ... Rev. 5th ed., illustrated by 1124 figures, 637 of which are printed in colors, and two plates. New York, W. Wood and company, 1916. 1919. 5th ed.

xxvii, 1593 p. illus. (part col.) II pl. 26ᶜᵐ.

1. Anatomy, Human. I. Robinson, Arthur, 1862- ed.

17-7199

Library of Congress   QM23.C97 1916

AS 750 N 56 — Cunningham, G. H.

Additions to the rust fungi of New Zealand, I.

(Trans. R. Soc. of New Zealand, Vol. 75(3): 324-327, 1945)

...II, by Shirley D. Baker.
(ibid, Vol. 83(3):453-463, 1956)

GN 2.I A 62 — Cunnington, W. A.

String figures and tricks from Central Africa.

(Jour. R. Anthropological Institute, Grt. Britain and Ireland, Vol. 36:121-131, 1906)

QK Bot. am. 1770 — CUPANIA

Radlkofer, Ludwig

Ueber Cupania und damit verwandte Pflanzen.

(Sitzungsber. Bayer. Akad. Wissen. Vol. 9, 1879, pp. 457-678)

G 1 C 16 — Cunningham, Glenn

Faleapuna: a Samoan village.

(The California Geographer, Vol. 4:23-34, 1963)

QK 110 N 56 — CUNONIACEAE

Britton, Nathaniel Lord

Cunoniaceae, Iteaceae, Hamamelidaceae.

IN North American flora, Vol. 22, Part 2, 1905, pp. 179-180, 185-187.

QL 573 J 95 s — CUPESIDAE

Janssens, Em.

Cupesidae, Paussidae

IN

Hincks, W. D.   editor

Coleopterorum catalogus, Supplementa, Pars 5 (nd ed.), 1953.

GN 658 C 97 — Cunningham, J. F.

Uganda and its peoples: notes on the Protectorate of Uganda, especially the anthropology and ethnology of its indigenous races. With a preface by Sir Harry Johnston. With a map and 212 illustrations, including a coloured plate. London. Hutchinson & Co. 1905. R8vo.   xxix + 370 pp.

GN 2.S P 76 — CUNONIACEAE   FIJI

Smith, Albert C.

Studies of Pacific Island plants, XII: The Cunoniaceae of Fiji and Samoa.

(Journal of the Arnold Arboretum, 33:119-149, 1952)

GC 1 S 43 — Cupp, Easter E.

Marine plankton diatoms of the west coast of North America.

(Bull. Scripps Institution of Oceanography, Vol. 5, No1, 1943, pp. 1-238)

QK 1 Com — CUNNINGHAM, RICHARD

Hooker, W. J.

A brief biographical sketch of the late Richard Cunningham , colonial botanist in New South Wales. In Companion Bot. Mag. Vol. II, 1836, pp 210 - 221.

GN 2.S P 76 — CUNONIACEAE   SAMOA

Smith, Albert C.

Studies of Pacific Island plants, XII: The Cunoniaceae of Fiji and Samoa.

(Journal of the Arnold Arboretum, 33:119-149, 1952)

GC Oceanography Pam. 31 — Cupp, Easter Ellen

Allen, Winfred Emory

Plankton diatoms of the Java Sea, by Winfred Emory Allen and Easter Ellen Cupp.

(Annales du Jardin Bot. de Buitenzorg. Vol. 44, 1935, pp. 101-174)

QH 111 C973 — Cunningham, Robert O.

Notes on the natural history of the Strait of Magellan and west coast of Patagonia made during the voyage of H. M. S. 'Nassau' in the years 1866, 67, 68 and 69.   Edinburgh, Edmonston, 1871.   517p. pls.

GN Pam 1913 — Cunow, Heinrich

Religionsgeschichtliche streiszuge. From Neue Zeit, n.21, bd.1, 1911.

QK 1 O 11 — CUPRESSINOXYLON

Lutz, H. J.

A New Species of Cupressinoxylon (Goeppert) Gothan from the Jurassic of South Dakota.

Contributions from the Osborn Botanical Laboratory, Yale University, IX. (Reprinted from the Botanical Gazette, Vol. XC, No. 1, September, 1930

DU 620 P 22 — Cunningham, Steve

Fresh water "tropical" fish off the beaten track, sparkling gems abound.

(Paradise of the Pacific, Sept. 1956:9-11)

GN 2.I A4 — *Cup and ring markings: their origin + significance.*

Astley, H. J.

In R. Anthro. Inst. XLI pp 83-99.

1911

DU 12 B 83 looked case — CURAÇOA (SHIP)

Brenchley, J. L.

Jottings during the cruise of H. M. S. Curaçoa among the South Sea Islands in 1865... London. 1873. R8vo.

AP 2 A5 — Cunningham, W. C.

Temperature of the air and surface of the sea, taken on a voyage from Samoa to Valparaiso, in 1841.

(Am. Jour. Sci., Ser. 2, Vol. 15, 1853, pp. 66-67)

QK 1 P 23   AND   QK Bot.Pam. 1278 — CUPANIA

Radlkofer, L.

Sur le Cupania collina Panch. et Séb.

(Notulae Systematicae, Vol. 2, pp. 9-11, 1911)

DU 400 M 48 — CURACOA (ship)

Meade, Herbert

A ride through the disturbed districts of New Zealand; together with some account of the South Sea islands. Being selections from the journals and letters of Lieut. the Hon. Herbert Meade. Edited by his brother.   Second edition. With maps and illustrations from the author's sketches. London.   John Murray. 1871. 8vo. xi + 375 pp.

CURACAO   MOLLUSCA

see

MOLLUSCA   CURACAO

QL
461
B 93   Marshall, Sir Guy A. K.

Some injurious Curculionidae (Col.) from New Guinea.

(Bull. Ent. Research, Vol. 48(1):1-7, 1957)

QL
461
H 1   Zimmerman, Elwood C.

A second species of Elytroteinus (Col., Curculionidae).

(Haw. Ent. Soc., Proc., Vol. 10, 1938, pp. 155-157)

AM
101
E 45 n   Curator appointed to Oceanic post. (Roland W. Force)

(Chicago Nat. Hist. Mus. Bull. Aug. 1956, p. 2)

QL
489.G
I 59   Zimmerman, Elwood C.
Curculionidae of Guam
IN
Swezey, Otto H. and others
Insects of Guam-I, pp. 73-146.

(Bernice P. Bishop Museu, Bull. 172, 1942)

QL
Insects
Pam.
1174   Zimmerman, Elwood C.

Some Curculionidae from Rotuma Island (Coleoptera).

(Occ. Papers, Bernice P. Bishop Museum, Vol. 17, 1943, No. 14, pp. 183-189)

CURATORS' HANDBOOKS

See

MUSEUMS   TECHNIQUE

QH
1
P 11   Zimmerman, Elwood C.

Description of a new species of Elytrurus and a catalogue of the known species (Coleoptera: Curculionidae: Otiorhynchinae).

(Pacific Science, Vol. X(3):286-295, July, 1956)

QL
461
H 1   Zimmerman, Elwood C.

The status of Acalles wilkesii (Col. Curculionidae).

(Haw. Ent. Soc., Proc., Vol. 10, 1938, pp. 150-151)

DU
1
P 10   Curb wanted on native NG bird of paradise hunters.

(Pac. Islands Monthly, 28(5):69, 1957)

QL
461
H 1   Zimmerman, Elwood C.

Four new Solomon and Caroline Island Deretiosus (Col. Curculionidae).

(Haw. Ent. Soc., Proc., Vol. 10, 1938, pp. 159-164)

QL
461
J 86   Zimmerman, Elwood C.

Synonymy of the Euscepes sweetpotato weevil (Coleoptera, Curculionidae).

(Journ. Econ. Ent., 31(2):323, 1938)

GN
2.S
M 26   Austen, Leo

Notes on the food supply of the Turamarubi of western Papua.

(Mankind, Vol. 3 (8):227-230, 1946)

QL
461
H 1   Zimmerman, Elwood C.

Heteramphus of Oahu (Col., Curculionidae).

(Haw. Ent. Soc., Proc., Vol. 10, 1938, pp. 139-142)

QL
461
H 1   Zimmerman, Elwood C.

Teleodactylus in the Solomon Islands (Col. Curculionidae).

(Haw. Ent. Soc., Proc., Vol. 10, 1938, pp. 157-159)

QL
Insect
Pam.
1380   Günther, Klaus

Über einige Curculionidae von den Salomon-Inseln. (Col.).

(Mitt. der Deutschen Ent. Gesell., Jahrg. 8 (3):37-43, 1937)

QL
461
H 1   Zimmerman, Elwood C.

Idotasia in New Ireland (Col. Curculionidae)

(Haw. Ent. Soc., Proc., Vol. 10, 1938, pp. 148-150)

AS
36
S 66 p   Anderson, Donald M.

The weevil genus Smicronyx in America north of Mexico (Coleoptera: Curculionidae).

(Proc. U. S. Nat. Mus., No. 3456, Vol. 113: 185-372, 1962)

CURCULIONIDAE

Marshall, G. A. K.

Coleoptera. Rhynchophora: Curculionidae. Vol. 1, 1916.

UH has

QL
461
H 1   Zimmerman, Elwood C.

Orochlesis in the Solomon Islands (Col., Curculionidae).

(Haw. Ent. Soc., Proc., Vol. 10, 1938, pp. 185-186)

QL
Insect
Pam.
915

AS
763
B-4   Zimmerman, Elwood C.

Cryptorrhynchinae of the Austral Islands. (Coleoptera, Curculionidae).

(Bishop Museum Occasional Papers, vol.XII, no.17. 1936. 19 pp., 2 figs.)

AS
720.S
S 72

CURCULIONIDAE   AUSTRALIA

Lea, Arthur Mills

Cryptorhynchides (Curculionidae), mostly from Australia.

(Records from the South Australian Museum, Vol. 4, 1928-1932, pp. 49-90) [pub. Sept. 30, 1928]

QL
Insect
Pam.930

AS
763
B-44
Reading
Room

CURCULIONIDAE   FIJI

Zimmerman, Elwood C.

On Lea's Fijian Deretiosus (Coleoptera, Curculionidae).

(B. P. Bishop Mus., Occ. Papers, vol. XIII, Reading no. 7, May 17, 1937. pp. 67-73, 1 fig.)

QL
461
H-1

CURCULIONIDAE   MARIANAS

Zimmerman, Elwood C.

Notes on Marianas Islands Curculionidae (Coleoptera).

(Haw. Ent. Soc., Proc. 13(2):305-315, 1948)

QL
461
H-1

and
QL
Insects
Pam.
1258

CURCULIONIDAE   BORNEO

Zimmerman, Elwood C.

New Usingerius from the Philippines and Borneo (Coleoptera: Curculionidae).

(Proc. Haw. Ent. Soc., 12 (3):653-655, 1946)

AS
763
B-4
QL
Ins.Pam.
1001

Reading
Room

CURCULIONIDAE   FIJI

Zimmerman, Elwood C.

Revision of the Fijian Ottistirini (Coleoptera, Curculionidae).

QL
461
I 59

CURCULIONIDAE   MICRONESIA

Kono, Hiromichi

Die Rüsselkäfer auf den Micronesien.

(Insecta Matsumurana, XVI (1/2):13-21, 1942)

AS
222
G

CURCULIONIDAE   BURMA

Faust, Johannes

Viaggio di Leonardo Fea in Birmania e regioni vicine, LX:Curculionidae.

(Annali del Mus. Civico di Storia Nat. di Genova, Ser. 2, Vol. 14 (34), May 15, 1894, pp. 153-370)

AS
122
L 75

CURCULIONIDAE   GOUGH ISLAND

Kuschel, G.

The Curculionidae of Gough Island and the relationships of the weevil fauna of the Tristan da Cunha group.

(Proc. of the Linnean Soc. of London, Vol. 173(2): 69-78, 1960/61)

QL
461
H-1

CURCULIONIDAE   NEW CALEDONIA

Zimmerman, Elwood C.

New Ampagia weevils from New Caledonia and the Philippines. (Coleoptera, Curculionidae).

(Proc. Haw. Ent. Soc., Vol. 12:453-460, 1946)

AS
763
B-4

CURCULIONIDAE   CAROLINE ISLANDS

Zimmerman, Elwood C.

Four New Microcryptorhynchus from the New Hebrides and Caroline Islands (Coleoptera, Curculionidae).

(B. P. Bishop Mus., Occ. Papers, 15(15): 167-173, 1939)

QL
461
H-1

CURCULIONIDAE   HAWAII

Zimmerman, Elwood C.

A new Rhyncogonus from Oahu, Hawaii (Coleoptera: Curculionidae).

(Proc., Hawaiian Entomological Society, Vol. XVI(1):165-169, July, 1956)

AS
763
B-4

CURCULIONIDAE   NEW CALEDONIA

Zimmerman, Elwood C.

New Caledonia Microcryptorhynchus (Coleoptera, Curculionidae).

(B. P. Bishop Mus., Occ. Papers, 17(8):85-89, 1942)

AS
763
B-4

CURCULIONIDAE   FIJI

Zimmerman, Elwood C.

Apioninae and Brachyderinae of Fiji.

(B. P. Bishop Mus., Occ. Papers, 17(11):152-170, 1943)

QL
Insect
Pam.951

CURCULIONIDAE   JAPAN

Kono, Hiromichi

Die Japanischen Hylobiinen (Col. Curc.)

(Journal, Faculty of Agric., Hokkaido Imp. Univ., Sapporo, Japan, Vol. 35, 1934, pp. 223-248)

AS
763
B-4

CURCULIONIDAE   NEW HEBRIDES

Zimmerman, Elwood C.

Four New Microcryptorhynchus from the New Hebrides and Caroline Islands (Coleoptera, Curculionidae).

(B. P. Bishop Mus., Occ. Papers, 15(15): 167-173, 1939)

QL
461
H-1

CURCULIONIDAE   FIJI

Zimmerman, Elwood C.

The genus Ossesteris in Fiji (Coleoptera, Curculionidae).

(Proc. Haw. Ent. Soc., 9(3):449-452, 1937)

QL
Insect
Pam.945

CURCULIONIDAE   JAPAN

Kono, Hiromichi

Kurzrüssler aus dem japanischen Reich.

(Jour. Faculty of Agric. Hokkaido Imp. Univ. Sapporo, Japan. Vol. 24, 1930, pp. 153-242)

QL
461
H-1

CURCULIONIDAE   NEW HEBRIDES

Zimmerman, Elwood C.

A new Phanerostethus from the New Hebrides (Coleoptera: Curculionidae).

(Proc. Haw. Ent. Soc., Vol. 13:193-198, 1947)

QL
461
H-1

CURCULIONIDAE   FIJI

Zimmerman, Elwood C.

A new Chaetectetorus from Fiji (Coleoptera, Curculionidae).

(Proc. Haw. Ent. Soc., 9(3):447-449, 1937)

AS
222
G

CURCULIONIDAE - MALAY-ARCHIPELAGO

Pascoe, Francis P.

List of the Curculionidae of the Malay Archipelago collected by Dr. Odoardo Beccari, L.M. d'Albertis, and others.

(Annali del Museo Civico di Storia Naturale. Genova. 1885. no. 12. 135 pp.)

QL
461
I 59

CURCULIONIDAE   OGASAWARA

Kono, Hiromichi

Die Rüsselkäfer auf den Ogasawara-Inseln.

(Insecta Matsumurana, XVI(1/2):31-33, 1942)

QL
461
D 48a

CURCULIONOIDEA   PAPUA

Heller, K.M.

Neue Papuanische Rüsselkäfer aus der Sammlung des Deutschen Entomologischen Institutes.

(Arbeiten uber morphologische und taxonomische Entomologie, Bd. 9(4):209-214, 1942)

CURÉ   (Island in Hawaiian group)

See

KURE

QL
Insects
Pam. 993

Curran, C(harles) Howard

African Syrphidae collected by J.C.Bridwell by C. Howard Curran and E.H.Bryan, Jr.

(Annals of the Ent. Soc. of America, Vol. 19, 1926, pp. 82-84)

QL
461
H-1

CURCULIONIDAE   PHILIPPINE ISLANDS

Zimmerman, Elwood C.

New Ampagia weevils from New Caledonia and the Philippines. (Coleoptera, Curculionidae).

(Proc. Haw. Ent. Soc., Vol. 12:453-460, 1945)

AS
36
S1

Curie, E.

Radium. By E. Curie ...

(*In* Smithsonian institution. Annual report. 1903. Washington, 1904. 23½ᶜᵐ. p. 187-198. illus.)

"Translated from a lecture delivered by Prof. E. Curie before the Royal institution of London, as printed in the Revue scientifique, February 13, 1904."

1. Radium.

Library of Congress
Library, Smithsonian

Q11.S66 1903
Institution

S 15-1182

AS
36
C 3

Curran, C. H.   (Charles Howard)

Diptera (Templeton Crocker Expedition of the California Academy of Sciences, 1932, No. 13)

(Proc. of Calif. Acad. of Sciences, 4th ser., Vol. 21, No. 13, pp. 147-172. March 27, 1934).

QL
461
H-1

and
QL
Insects
Pam.
1258

CURCULIONIDAE   PHILIPPINE ISLANDS

Zimmerman, Elwood C.

New Usingerius from the Philippines and Borneo (Coleoptera:Curculionidae).

Proc. Haw. Ent. Soc., 12 (3):653-655, 1946)

GN
Pam
#553

CURIOS   HAWAII

Rare and unique display of Hawaiian curios, newspaper clipping, May 29,1885.

AS
36
C 3

Curran, C. H.   (Charles Howard)

Diptera (Templeton Crocker Expedition to Western Polynesian and Melanesian Islands, 1933, no. 30)

(Proc. of Calif. Acad. of Sciences, 4th ser. vol.22, no.1, pp.1-66. December 18, 1936).

QL
461
H-1

CURCULIONIDAE   SAMOA

Zimmerman, Elwood C.

A new genus of Samoan Curculionidae (Coleoptera).

(Proc. Haw. Ent. Soc., 9(3):452-455, 1937)

G
159
C 97

A curious collection of voyages, selected from the writers of all nations. In which the conjectures and interpolations of several vain editors and translators are expunged...illustrated and embellished with variety of maps and prints ...10 volumes. London. J. Newbery. 1761. 16mo.

Curran, C. H.

Families and genera of North American Diptera. 1934. $7.50

HSPA has

QL
Insect
Pams.
1289

CURCULIONIDAE   SOLOMON ISLANDS

Zimmerman, Elwood C.

A new Telephae from the Solomon Islands. (Coleoptera, Curculionidae).

(Proc. New England Zoological Club, Vol. 23:17-20, 1944)

GN
Ethn.Pam
3934

Curious legend tells how secret of making fire was discovered by Hawaiians.
IN Collection of clippings made by Martha W. Beckwith, pp. 35

Curran, C. H.   (Charles Howard)

The families and genera of North American Diptera.

E. H. Bryan has copy

QL
596.C9
F 45

CURCULIONIDAE   SOUTH AMERICA

Fiedler, Karl

Monograph of the South American weevils of the genus Conotrachelus.   London. By Order of the Trustees of the British Museum. 1940. R8vo. 365 pp.

AS
36
S1

CURLEWS.

Swenk, Myron Harmon, 1883–

The Eskimo curlew and its disappearance. By Myron H. Swenk.

(*In* Smithsonian institution. Annual report. 1915. Washington, 1916. 23½ᶜᵐ. p. 325-340. pl)

"Reprinted ... from the Proceedings of the Nebraska ornithologists' union, vol. 6, pt. 2, Feb. 27, 1915."

1. Curlews.   I. Title.

16-16017

Library of Congress
——— Copy 2.

Q11.S66 1915
Q11.S66 1915 2d set

AS
36
A65

Curran, C(harles) H(oward)

Four new American diptera. Am. Mus. Nov. n. 275, 1927.

AS
122
L 75

CURCULIONIDAE   TRISTAN DA CUNHA

Kuschel, G.

The Curculionidae of Gough Island and the relationships of the weevil fauna of the Tristan da Cunha group.

(Proc. of the Linnean Soc. of London, Vol. 173(2):69-78, 1960/61)

GN
665
C 95

Curr, Edward M.

The Australian race: its origin, languages, customs, place of landing in Australia, and the routes by which it spread itself over that continent...In four volumes. Melbourne. John Ferres. 1886. 8vo.   Vols. 1-4.
Volume 4. Folio.   1887.

Oversize
case

QL
489
C 97

Curran, Charles Howard

Insects of the Pacific world. The Macmillan Company. New York. 1945. 8vo. xv + 317 pp.

AM
101
A 51
(5)

Curran, C. H.

Insects, ticks and human diseases, by C.H. Curran and Frank E. Lutz.

(Guide Leaflet, American Museum of Natural History, No. 113, 1942)

AS
36
A65

Curran, C(harles) H(oward)

Undescribed asilidae from the Belgian Congo. Am. Mus. Nov. n. 272, 1927.

QC
Physics
and
meteoro-
logy
Pam.
37

CURRENTS, AIR

Mintz, Yale

The observed mean field of motion of the atmosphere. By Yale Mintz and Gordon Dean.
IN Investigation of the general circulation of the atmosphere, by Jacob Bjerknes. Univ. of California, Los Angeles, March 15, 1951. 4to. 55 pp.

QL
Insects
Pam. 985

Curran, C(harles) Howard

New Australian Syrphidae (Diptera) in the Bishop Museum, by C. Howard Curran and E. H. Bryan, Jr.

(Proc. of the Linnean Soc. of New South Wales, Vol. 51, Part 2, 1926, pp.129-133)

CURRENCY HAWAII

see

MONEY HAWAII

QC
885
P 17

CURRENTS (AIR)

Palmer, C. E.

Synoptic analysis over the southern Oceans.

(New Zealand Meteorological Office, Professional Note, no. 1, 1942. Air Department)

AS
36
A65

Curran, C. H. (Charles Howard)

New diptera from the West Indies. Am. Mus. Nat. His. Nov. 220, 1926.

GN
22
T 46

Current anthropology...

Thomas, William L., Jr.

Q
115
C 26

CURRENTS (air) PACIFIC

Thomson, Andrew

Upper-wind observations and results obtained on cruise VII of the Carnegie.

IN Scientific results of cruise VII of the Carnegie... Meteorology II. Carnegie Inst. of Washington Pub. 547, 1943.

AS
36
A 65

Curran, C. H.

New species of Volucella from Hawaii and the United States (Syrphidae, Diptera).

(American Museum Novitates, No. 1361,1947)

DU
1
S 72

Current research in the South Pacific in the field of economic development.

(South Pacific Commission, Technical Paper No. 29, July 1952)

QC
993
N 56

CURRENTS (AIR ROSS SEA)

Ramage, C. S.

The atmospheric circulation of the Ross Sea area.

(New Zealand Meteorological Office, Air Department, Professional Note No. 2, 1944)

AS
36
A 65

Curran, C. H.

Syrphidae from Sarawak and the Malay Peninsula (Diptera)

(American Museum Novitates, No. 1216, 1942)

AS
36
S1

AIR CURRENTS.   (air)

Colding, Ludvig August, 1815–1888.

Some remarks concerning the nature of currents of air. By A. Colding.

(In Smithsonian institution. Annual report. 1877. Washington, 1878. 23½ᵐ. p. 447–462. diagrs.)

"Translated by Cleveland Abbe and H. L. Thomas, from the Oversigt over det K. Danske videnskabernes selskabs, aaret 1871, page 89, with occasional reference to Hann in Zeitschrift Oest. met. ges., vol. x."

1. Storms.   i. Abbe, Cleveland, 1838– tr. ii. Thomas, Henry L., joint tr.   S 15–475

Library of Congress   Q11.S66 1877
Library, Smithsonian   Institution

Small
Map
Case

CURRENTS AIR

Wind and Current charts for Pacific, Atlantic and Indian Oceans. Published and issued by Hydrographer of the Navy. London. 1872 -1900, Four charts, Nos. 2640, 2932-2934. folio

---

AS
36
A 65

Curran, C. H.

The Syrphidae of Guadalcanal, with notes on related species.

(American Museum Novitates, No. 1364, 1947)

QE
Geol.
Pam.
1075
and
Q
101
P 18

CURRENTS (air)

Giovanelli, J. L.

Atmospheric currents in French Oceania.

(Proc. Sixth Pacific Science Congress, 1939, pp. 697-705)

CURRENTS, AIR

see also

ATMOSPHERE

WIND

AS
36
B4

Curran, C(harles) H(oward)

Two undescribed syrphid flies from New England.

Bos. Soc. of Nat. Hist., Occ. Pap, vol. 5, pp 65-67, 1923.

QE
Geol.Pam.
1059

CURRENTS (air)

Giovanelli, J. L.

Les courants aériens et la pression atmosphérique en Océanie Francaise.

(Annales de Physique du Globe de la France d'Outre-Mer. Année 6, 1939, No. 36, pp. 168-191)

DU
620
F

CURRENTS OCEAN

Bishop, S(ereno) E.

A big stick - ocean currents.

(The Friend, Oct. 1, 1862, p. 76)

(a log of wood from the Northwest, one of "the immense body of timber launched into the Pacific during the great floods of last winter upon the American coasts...")

AP
2
A 5

CURRENTS   OCEAN

Dana, James Dwight

Note on the currents of the oceans.

(Am. Jour. of Sci., Ser. 2, Vol. 26, 1858, pp. 231-233)

QH
301
S

Currents   OCEAN

McEwen George F.

Oceanic circulation and its bearing upon attempts to make seasonal weather forecasts: A sketch of observational methods and explanations.   Scripps Inst for Biol. Res. Univ. of Calif. Bul. No. 7. 1918.

GC
1
S 43-p

CURRENTS OCEAN

Munk, W. H.

The wind-driven circulation in ocean basins of various shapes. By W. H. Munk and G. F. Carrier.

(Univ. of Calif., Scripps Inst. of Oceanography, Oceanographic Report No. 18; reprint from Tellus, Vol. 2, no. 3, pp. 158-167, 1950)

GC
231
E 37

CURRENTS OCEAN

Ekman, V. W.

Studies on ocean currents; results of a cruise on board the "Armauer Hansen" in 1930 under the leadership of Bjorn Helland-Hansen.

(Geofysiske Publikasjoner, Norske Videnskapsakademi i Oslo, Vol. 19(1), 1953. Text and plates)

G
3
A 1

CURRENTS OCEAN

Marmer, H.A.

The Peru and Nino currents.

(Geogr. Review, 41(2):337-338, 1951)

GC
Oceano.
Pam. 5

CURRENTS OCEAN

Niblack, A. P.

Ocean currents in relation to oceanography, marine biology, meteorology and hydrography. Int. Hydrographic Bureau, spec. publ. 19, Monaco, 1927.

GC
1
M 73-a

CURRENTS OCEAN

Idrac, Pierre

Le nouvel enrigistreur de courants sousmarins de M. Pierre Idrac; les premiers résultats qu'il a permis d'obtenir en océanographie.

(Ann. Inst. Océanographique, N. S. Tome 10, fasc. 4, 1931, p. 101-116)

G
Pam.
3

and
AS
36
A 9

CURRENTS OCEAN

Mayer, Alfred Goldsborough

Detecting ocean currents by observing their hydrogen-ion concentration, ex Am. Phil. Soc. Proc., vol. LVIII, No. 2, 1919.

GC
1
G 59

CURRENTS OCEAN

Riedel, W. R.

Tertiary radiolaria in western Pacific sediments. With a note by Hans Pettersson: Current observations close to the ocean bottom.

(Göteborgs Kungl. Vetenskaps- och Vitterhets samhälle, 6th Foljden, Ser. B, Bd. 6(3), 1952) Being Medd. Oceanografiska Inst. i Goteborg, 19.

Q
101
P 18

CURRENTS OCEAN

Kamenovich, V. M.

On the theory of the Antarctic circumpolar current.

(Akad. Nauk, SSSR, Trudy Inst. Okeanolochi, Tome 56:241-293, 1962)

AS
36
W 2

CURRENTS OCEAN

Mears, Eliot G.

Boundaries of the Humboldt Current.

(Journal of the Washington Acad. of Sci., Vol. 33, 1943, pp. 125-130)

GC
1
M 73

CURRENTS OCEAN

Saint-Guily, Bernard

Les méandres des veines de courant dans les océans.

(Bull. Inst. Oceanographique, No. 1108, Dec. 1957)

AP
2
S 41

CURRENTS OCEAN

Knauss, John A.

The Cromwell current...

(Scientific American, 204:105-116, 1961)

AS
36
S 1

CURRENTS OCEAN

Mears, Eliot G.

The ocean current called "The Child".

(Ann. Rept. Smithsonian Inst.,1943:245-251)

[El Niño]

GC
Ocean.
Pam. 40

CURRENTS OCEAN

(Schureman, Paul)

Manual of current observations.

(U.S. Coast and Geodetic Survey, Special Publication No. 215, 1938)

AP
2
N 28

CURRENTS OCEAN

Knauss, John A.

Measurements of the Pacific equatorial countercurrent. By John A. Knauss and Robert Pepin.

(Nature, Vol. 183(4658):380, 1959)

QL
5
B 61

CURRENTS OCEAN

Montgomery, R. B.

Contribution to the question of the equatorial counter current, by R. B. Montgomery and E. Palmen.

(Journal of Marine Research, Vol. III,1940, pp. 112-133)

AS
122
L-p

CURRENTS OCEAN

Sewell, R. B. Seymour

The extent to which the distribution of marine organisms can be explained by and is dependent on the hydrographic conditions present in the great oceans, with special reference to the plankton.

(Proc. Linnean Society of London, 152nd session, 1939-40, pp. 256-286)

AS
36
A 9

CURRENTS OCEAN

McEwen, George F.

Modern dynamical oceanography: an achievement of applications to ocean observations of principles of mechanics and heat.

(Proc. of the Am. Philosophical Soc., Vol. 79, 1938, pp. 145-166)

QK
396
U 58

CURRENTS OCEAN

Muir, John

The seed-drift of South Africa and some influences of ocean currents on the strand vegetation.

(Union of South Africa, Dept. of Agric. and Forestry, Botanical Memoir, No. 16, 1937)

AS
36
S 1

CURRENTS OCEAN

Smith, F. G. Walton

Rivers in the sea.

(Ann. Rept. of the Smithsonian Institution for 1956; pp. 431-441)

AP
2
S 35

CURRENTS   OCEAN

Sverdrup, H. U.

The Pacific ocean.

(Science, Vol. 94, 1941, pp. 287-293)

GC
Oceano-
graphy
Pam.
57

CURRENTS   OCEAN   ARGENTINE

Balech, Enrique

Estudio critico de las corrientes marinas del littoral Argentino.

(Physis, Tome 20:159-164, 1949)

GN
2.S
P 76

CURRENTS   OCEAN   NEW GUINEA

Sinoto, Yosihiko H.

Drifting canoe prows.

(Jour. Poly. Soc., 68:354-356, 1959)

GC
Oceanogr.
Pam.
49

CURRENTS   OCEAN

Takenouti, Y.   and others

The deep-current in the sea east of Japan. By Y. Takenouti, T. Nan'niti and M. Yasui.

(Oceanographical Mag., 13(2):89-101, 1962)

QL
636
A 93 c

CURRENTS   OCEAN   AUSTRALIA

Hamon, B. V.

The structure of the East Australian current.

(CSIRO, Div. of Fisheries and Oceanography Technical Paper No. 11, 1961)

GC
1
M 33

CURRENTS   OCEAN   PACIFIC

Barlow, E. W.

The 1910 to 1937 survey of the currents of the south Pacific Ocean.

(Marine Observer, Vol. 15, 1938, No. 132, pp. 140-149)

GC
1
M 73-a

CURRENTS   OCEAN

Thoulet, J.

Notes d'oceanographie abyssale.

(Ann. Inst. Oceanographique, N. S. Tome.12, fasc. 7, 1932, pp. 385-407)

QE
Geol.
Pam.
1215

CURRENTS   OCEAN   JAPAN

Hishida, Kozo

Studies on the current along the coast in the Japan Sea.

(Memoirs of the College of Agriculture, Kyoto University, No. 62(Fisheries Series No. 2) March, 1952)

DU
12
B 41

looked
case

CURRENTS   OCEAN   PACIFIC

Beechey, F. W.

Narrative of a Voyage to the Pacific and Beering's Strait...in...Ship Blossom, under the command of Captain F. W. Beechey...in...1825-28. Vol. 2, pp. 395-440. London. 1831. 8vo.

The same... New Edition.   London. 1831. 8vo.

Small
Map
Case

CURRENTS   OCEAN

Wind and Current charts for Pacific, Atlantic and Indian Oceans.   Published and issued by Hydrographer of the Navy. London. 1872-1900. Four charts, No. 2640, 2932-2934.   folio

---

GC
Oceanogr.
Pam.
49

CURRENTS   OCEAN   JAPAN

Takenouti, Y.   and others

The deep-current in the sea east of Japan. By Y. Takenouti, T. Nan'niti and M. Yasui.

(Oceanographical Mag., 13(2):89-101, 1962)

DU
Pac.Pam.
77

CURRENTS   OCEAN   PACIFIC

Bishop, Sereno Edwards

The cold-current system of the Pacific, and source of the Pacific coast current.

(Science, Vol. 20, 1904, no. 506, pp. 338-340)

(article of same title in Haw. Ann., 1905, pp. 74-79)

GC
63
D 61

CURRENTS   OCEAN   ANTARCTIC

Deacon, G. E. R.

Note on the dynamics of the Southern ocean.

Discovery Committee
Discovery Reports, Vol. 15, 1937, p. 125-152

GC
Oceanogr
Pam. 56

CURRENTS   OCEAN   MARSHALL ISLANDS

Barnes, C. A.

Ocean circulation in Marshall Islands area. By C. A. Barnes, D. F. Bumpus, and John Lyman.

(Trans. Am. Geophysical Union, Vol. 29(6): 871-875, 1948)

Q
115
H 39

looked
case

CURRENTS   OCEAN   PACIFIC

Hawks, Francis L.

Narrative of the expedition of an American squadron to the China Seas and Japan...1852-54... Vol. II, pp. 363-370: Report made to Commodore M. C. Perry upon the Kuro Siwo, or Gulf Stream of the North Pacific Ocean, by Silas Bent.

Q
101
P 18

CURRENTS   ANTARCTIC

Kamenovich, V. M.

On the theory of the Antarctic circumpolar current.

(Acad. Nauk, SSSR, Trudy Inst. Okeanolochi. Tome 56:241-293, 1962)

G
3
A 11

CURRENTS   OCEAN   MARSHALL ISLANDS

Laubenfels, M. W. de

Ocean currents in the Marshall Islands.

(Geographical Review, Vol. 40(2):254-259, 1950)

GC
Oceano-
graphy
Pam. 20

CURRENTS- OCEAN   PACIFIC

Kishindo, Saburo

Chart showing the drift of ocean currents (by bottles), in the seas adjacent to the Caroline and Marshall Islands. (In Japanese, title translated)

GC
63
D 61

CURRENTS   OCEAN   ANTARCTIC

Sverdrup, H. U.

On vertical circulation in the ocean due to the action of the wind with application to conditions within the Antarctic circumpolar current.

Discovery Committee
Discovery Reports, Vol. 7, 1933, p.139-170

GC
1
S 43-t

CURRENTS   OCEAN   MARSHALL ISLANDS

Mao, Han-Lee

Physical oceanography in the Marshall Islands area. By Han-Lee Mao and Kozo Yoshida.

(SIO Reference 53-27, 15 April 1953, Scripps Institution of Oceanography, Univ. of Calif.)

Chart
Case 2

Folder
14

Currents, OCEAN   PACIFIC

Maps and Charts. Pacific Ocean, General. North Pacific Ocean, South Pacific Ocean, Pilot Charts

GC
Oceano-
graphy
Pam.45
49

CURRENTS OCEAN PACIFIC

Mears, Eliot G.

New evidence regarding deep-water flow in the eastern Pacific.

(Trans. Am. Geophical Union, 1943, pp. 242-244)

AP
2
S 35

CURRENTS OCEAN PACIFIC

Sverdrup, H. U.

The currents of the Pacific Ocean and their bearing on the climates of the coasts.

(Science, Vol. 91, 1940, p. 273-282)

Q
115
U 58
locked
case

DU
12
U 58
locked
case

CURRENTS OCEAN PACIFIC

United States Exploring Expedition...1838-1842, under the command of Charles Wilkes. Volume V, pp. 485-533. Philadelphia. C.Sherman. 4to. 1844

(Short comments on currents about the islands throughout the work)
...Vol. 23:Hydrography...pp. 484-504
...Narrative, Vols. 1-5 and atlas. Phila. 1845. R8vo. Vol. V, pp. 457-502.

Q
101
P 18

CURRENTS- OCEAN PACIFIC

Ocean Currents.

(Pan-Pacific Scientific Congress, 1st, Honolulu, 1920, pp. 487-636)

Q
115
C 26

CURRENTS OCEAN PACIFIC

Sverdrup, H. U. and others
Observations and results in physical oceanography, by H. U. Sverdrup, J. A. Fleming, F.L. Soule and C. C. Ennis.

IN Scientific Results of Cruise VII of the Carnegie during 1928-1929...Oceanography-1A. Carnegie Inst. of Washington, Pub. no.545,1944.

Q
101
P 18

CURRENTS OCEANIC PACIFIC

Wyrtki, K.

The flow of water into the deep sea basins of the western south Pacific ocean.

(Reprinted from the Australian Jour. of Marine and Freshwater Research, Vol. 12(1):1-16, 1961)

AP
2
A 5

CURRENTS OCEAN PACIFIC

The Pacific Gulf Stream, or oceanic current flowing northward along the Asiatic continent.

(Am. Jour. of Sci., Ser. 3, Vol. 3, 1872, pp. 394-395)

AP
2
S 35

CURRENTS- OCEAN PACIFIC

Sverdrup, H. U.

Water masses and currents of the North Pacific Ocean.

(Science, Vol. 93, 1941, pp. 436)

QL
5
B 61

CURRENTS PACIFIC

Yoshida, Kozo and others

Circulation in the upper mixed layer of the equatorial North Pacific.

(Journal of Marine Research, Vol. 12(1):99-120, 1953)

Q
101
P 18

CURRENTS OCEAN PACIFIC

Pacific Science Association. Proceedings of the Fifth Pacific Science Congress...Vol. 1, pp. 643-712, 1933

GC
1
M 73-a

CURRENTS OCEAN PACIFIC

Thoulet, J.

Contributions à l'étude de la circulation océanique.

(Ann. Inst. Océanographique, N. S., Tome 2, fasc. 4, 1925, pp. 409-423)

AS
36
A 4

CURRENTS OCEAN PANAMA (bight)

Nichols, John Treadwell

A collection of fishes from the Panama bight, Pacific Ocean, by John Treadwell Nichols and Robert Cushman Murphy.

(Bull. Am. Mus. of Nat. Hist., Vol. 83(4): 217-260, 1944)

AP
2
A 5

CURRENTS OCEAN PACIFIC

Redfield, W. C.

Remarks on tides and the prevailing currents of the ocean and atmosphere.

(Am. Jour. Sci., Ser. 1, Vol. 45, 1843, pp. 293-309)

QL
628
Ca-b

CURRENTS OCEAN PACIFIC

Tibby, Richard B.

Report on returns of drift bottles released off Southern California, 1937.

(California, Division of Fish and Game, Bureau of Marine Fisheries, Fish Bulletin No. 55, 1939)

QH
1
P 11

CURRENTS OCEAN PERU

Bieri, Robert

The Chaetognath fauna off Peru in 1941.

(Pacific Science, Vol. XI(3):255-364, 1957)

GC
1
S 43-c

CURRENTS OCEAN PACIFIC

Reid, Robert O.

The equatorial currents of the eastern Pacific as maintained by the stress of the wind.

(Journal Marine Research, 7:74-99, 1948; reprinted as Scripps Inst. of Oceanography, Contribution, No. 393, 1948)

GC
1
S 43-c

CURRENTS- OCEAN PACIFIC

Tibby, Richard B.

The water masses off the west coast of North America.

(Scripps Inst. of Oceanography, Contrib. 141; and Journal of Marine Research, Sears Foundation, 1941, pp. 112-121)

GC
63
D 61

CURRENTS OCEAN PERU

Gunther, E. R.

A report on oceanographical investigations in the Peru coastal current.

Discovery Committee
Discovery Reports, Vol. 13, 1936, p.107-276

AS
122
L-p

CURRENTS OCEAN PACIFIC

Sewell, R. B. Seymour

The extent to which the distribution of marine organisms can be explained by and is dependent on the hydrographic conditions present in the great oceans, with special reference to the plankton.

(Proc. Linnean Soc. of London, 152nd session 1939-40, pp. 256-286)

GC
Oceanogr.
Pam.
38

CURRENTS OCEAN PACIFIC

Udintsev, G. B.

Discovery of a deep-sea trough in the western part of the Pacific Ocean.

(typed translation by Olga Jones, Scripps Institution, from PRIRODA, July 1958:85-88)

QL
5
B 61

CURRENTS PERU

Morrow, James E.

Studies in ichthyology and oceanography off coastal Peru. By James E. Morrow and Gerald S. Posner.

(Bull. Bingham Oceanographic Collection, Peabody Mus. Nat. Hist., Yale Univ., 16(2), 1957

QK 925
G 97

CURRENTS   OCEAN   WEST INDIES

Guppy, H. B.

Plants, seeds and currents in the West Indies and Azores.

London, Williams and Norgate, 1917. pp. viii, maps 3, pp. 531, frontis-piece.

QL 671
E 39

Curry, Haskell B.

Bird observations in the Hawaiian Islands, February 1962.

(The Elepaio, Vol. 23(12):61-63, 1963)

QK Pam #864

Curtis, Carlton C.

The evolution of assimilating tissue in Sporophytes, ex Columbia Univ. Dept. of Bot. Contr., vol. VI, no. 130, 1898.

QE Geol.Pam. 1098

CURRENTS   OCEAN   DAVIDSON

Mears, Eliot G.

Counterpart of the Davidson current.

(Nature, 153, Mch. 18, 1944)
pp. 346-7

G 7
N 56

Curry, Leslie

Atmospheric circulation in the southern South Pacific.

(New Zealand Geographer, 16:71-83, 1960)

QK Pam #982

Curtis, Carlton C.

Forestry and Columbia, ex Columbia Univ. Dept. of Bot. Contr., vol. X, no. 248, 1910.

GC 63
D 61

CURRENTS   OCEAN   HUMBOLDT

Gunther, E. R.

A report on oceanographical investigations in the Peru coastal current.

Discovery Committee
Discovery Reports, Vol. 13, 1936, p.107-276

Curry, Leslie

The physical geography of Western Samoa.

(The New Zealand Geographer, 11(1):28-52, 1955)

UH has

QK Pam #926

Curtis, Carlton C.

Some observations on transpiration, ex Columbia Univ. Dept. of Bot. Contr., vol. VIII, no. 191, 1902.

QE Geol. Pam. 1097

CURRENTS   OCEAN   HUMBOLDT

Mears, Eliot G.

Humboldt current in 1941.

(Science, 95 (2469), Apr. 24, 1942)
pp. 433-34

GN 500
S

Curtin, Jeremiah, 1840-1906, comp.
Seneca fiction, legends, and myths ... Collected by Jeremiah Curtin and J. N. B. Hewitt; ed. by J. N. B. Hewitt.

(*In* U. S. Bureau of American ethnology. Thirty-second annual report, 1910-1911. Washington, 1918. 30°°. p. 37-819)

1. Seneca Indians—Legends. 2. Seneca Indians—Religion and mythology. 1. Hewitt, John Napoleon Brinton, 1859-

Library of Congress   E51.U55 32d   19-11817
[9]

QK Pam #902

Curtis, Carlton C.

Turgidity in Mycelia, ex Columbia Univ. Dept. of Bot. Contr., vol. VII, no. 168, 1900.

GC 1
M 73-a

CURRENTS   OCEAN   HUMBOLDT

Thoulet, J.

Le courant de Humboldt et la mer de l'île de Pâques.

(Ann. Inst. Océanographique, N. S., Tome 5, fasc. 2, 1929, pp. 1-12)

AS 492
S 6

Curtis, C.

A catalogue of the flowering plants and ferns found growing wild in the Island of Penang.

(R. Asiatic Society, Straits Branch, Journal, Vol. No. 25, 1894, pp. 67-167)

QK Pam #918

Curtis, Carlton C.

The work performed in transpiration and the resistance of stems, ex Columbia Univ. Dept. of Bot. Contr., vol. VIII, no. 183, 1901.

GC 1
M 73-a

CURRENTS   OCEAN   KURO SIWO

Thoulet, J.

Volcanicité abyssale et courant Kuosio-Oysaio (Pacifique nord)

(Ann. Inst. Océanographique, N. S., Tome 7, fasc. 2, 1929, pp. 25-51)

QK Pam #971

Curtis, Carlton C.

Botany at Columbia, ex Columbia Univ. Dept. of Bot. Contr., vol. X, no. 237, 1908.

GN Ethn.Pam. 3498

Curtis, Caroline

Pukui, Mary Kawena

Hawaii long ago. By Mary Kawena Pukui and Caroline Curtis. mimeographed. Kamehameha Schools, Preparatory Department. 1946. 4to. 44 pp.

AM Mus. Pam. 281

Currier, Margaret

The Peabody Museum library.

(Offprint from Harvard Library Bulletin, Vol. III(1):94-101, 1949)

QK Pam #795

Curtis, Carlton C.

A contribution to the history of the formation of the lichen Thallus, ex Columbia Coll. Herb. Contr., vol. III, no. 58, 1894.

GR Folklore Pam. 77

Curtis, Caroline

Pukui, Mary Kawena

Legends of Hawaii, by Mary Kawena Pukui and Caroline Curtis. Kamehameha Schools, Preparatory Department. mimeographed. 4to. rec'd Aug. 1946. 108 pp.

GR
Folklore
Pam.
76

Curtis, Caroline

Pukui, Mary Kawena

Legends of Oahu, by Mary Kawena Pukui and Caroline Curtis. mimeographed. Kamehameha Schools, Preparatory Department. (1946) 71 pp. 4to

---

AS
36
S1

Curtis, Heber Doust, 1872–

Modern theories of the spiral nebulae. By Heber D. Curtis ...

(*In* Smithsonian institution. Annual report. 1919. Washington, 1921. 23½ᶜᵐ. p. 123-132)

"Abstract of a lecture given on Mar. 15, 1919, at a joint meeting of the Washington academy of sciences and the Philosophical society of Washington ... Reprinted ... from the Journal of the Washington academy of sciences, vol. 9, no. 8, Apr. 19, 1919."

1. Nebulae.

Library of Congress   Q11.S66 1919   22-301
[9]

QL
47
C 98

Curtis, Winterton C.

General zoology. By Winterton C. Curtis and Mary J. Guthrie. 4th edition. John Wiley and Sons, Inc. New York. 1947. xx + 794 pp. R8vo

---

GN
Ethn.Pam.
3501

Curtis, Caroline

Pukui, Mary Kawena

The makahiki; fishing and farming. By Mary Kawena Pukui and Caroline Curtis. Kamehameha Schools, Preparatory Department. mimeographed. rec'd Aug. 1946. 50 pp. 4to.

AP
2
A 5

Curtis, M. A.

Berkeley, M. J.

Descriptions of new species of fungi collected by the U. S. Exploring Expedition under C. Wilkes, U. S. N. Commander, by Rev. M. J. Berkeley and Rev. M. A. Curtis.

(Am. Jour. Sci., Ser. 2, Vol. XI, 1851, pp. 93-95)

QL
345.S
C 98

Curtiss, Anthony

A short zoology of Tahiti in the Society Islands. (Brooklyn). 1938. 8vo. xvi + 193 pp

---

GR
385.H
C 97

Curtis, Caroline

Pikoi and other legends of the island of Hawaii. Collected or suggested by Mary Kawena Pukui; retold by Caroline Curtis; illustrated by Robert Lee Eskridge. Printed and published by Kamehameha Schools Press. 1949c. 8vo. 282 pp.

DU
621
H3

Curtis, Mattoon M.

Ancient Hawaiian theories as to the nature and origin of things. In Haw. Annual for 1919, pp 79-96.

AS
36
S1
and
G
Geog
Pam
#6

Curtiss, Ralph Hamilton, 1880–

An account of the rise of navigation. By R. H. Curtiss.

(*In* Smithsonian institution. Annual report. 1918. Washington, 1920. 23½ᶜᵐ. p. 127-138)

"Reprinted ... from Popular astronomy, vol. xxvi, no. 254, April 1918."

1. Navigation.

Library of Congress   Q11.S66 1918   20-18963
[9]

GR
385.H
C 97

Curtis, Caroline

Pikoi and other legends of the island of Hawaii. Collected or suggested by Mary Kawena Pukui; retold by Caroline Curtis; illustrated by Robert Lee Eskridge. Printed and published by Kamehameha Schools Press. Honolulu c1949. 282 pp. 8vo.

G
51
W 17

Curtis, R. Emerson

[New Guinea drawings]

(Walkabout, Vol. 11, 1945—various issues, usually at center of the issue)

DU
870
C 98

Curton, E. de

Tahiti: terre francaise combattante. Publications de La France Combattante. Londres. Brochure 101. 1942. R8vo. 103 pp.

GR
385.H
C 97

Curtis, Caroline

The water of Kane, and other legends of the Hawaiian Islands. Collected or suggested by Mary Kawena Pukui; retold by Caroline Curtis; illustrated by Richard Goings. Printed and published by The Kamehameha Schools Press. c1951 249 pp. 8vo. [Honolulu]

AS
36
S1

Curtis, Thomas E.

The Zeppelin air ship. By Thomas E. Curtis.

(*In* Smithsonian institution. Annual report. 1900. Washington, 1901. 23½ᶜᵐ. p. 217-222. VI pl.)

"Reprinted ... from the Strand magazine, September, 1900."

1. Aeronautics. 2. Air-ships. 3. Zeppelin, Ferdinand Adolf August Heinrich, graf von, 1838–

Library of Congress   Q11.S66 1900   S 15-1056
Library, Smithsonian   Institution

GN
424
C 98

Curwen, E. Cecil

Plough and pasture, the early history of farming. Part I. Prehistoric farming of Europe and the near East by E. Cecil Curwen. Part II. Farming of non-European peoples by Gudmund Hatt. Henry Schuman, Inc. New York. 1953. 8vo. xii + 3-329(2) pp.

[Chap. 13: Plowless agriculture in Oceania]

AP
2
S35

Curtis, Geo. Carroll

Work going on at Kilauea Volcano.

(Science N. S. XXXVIII, 1913, pp. 355-358.)

G
440
A 16

Curtis, William E.

Ackermann, Jessie A.

The World Through a Woman's Eyes. Introduction by William E. Curtis. Illustrated.

Chicago. (Privately printed), 1896, 325 pp. 8vo

QK
1
T 1

CUSCUTA

Yuncker, Truman George

The genus Cuscuta.

(Memoirs of the Torrey Botanical Club, Vol. 18, No. 2, 1932)

AS
36
S1

Curtis, George Edward.

Progress of meteorology in 1889. By George E. Curtis.

(*In* Smithsonian institution. Annual report. 1889. Washington, 1890. 23½ᶜᵐ. p. 205-285. tables, diagrs.)

"Bibliography of meteorology for 1889. By O. L. Fassig": p. 271-285.

1. Meteorology—Hist.   1. Fassig, Oliver Lanard, 1860–

S 15-695
Library of Congress   Q11.S66 1889
Library, Smithsonian   Institution

QK
457
C 98

Curtis, Winifred M.

The student's flora of Tasmania, parts 1 and 2. Tasmania. L. G. Shea, Govt. Printer. 1956. xlvii + 475 pp.

Part 1: Gymnospermae; Angiospermae: Ranunculaceae to Myrtaceae.
Part 2: Angiospermae: Lythraceae to Epacridaceae.

G
51
W 17

Cusec

Surf fishing on New Zealand's Ninety Mile Beach.

(Walkabout, Vol. 11, No. 12 [Oct., 1945], pp. 29-30)

QL
463
C 98

Cushing, Emory C.

History of entomology in World War II.
Smithsonian Institution. Washington, D. C. 1957.
8vo. vi + 117 pp.

AM
Mus.Pam.
302

Cushing, Harvey

The binding influence of a library on a
subdividing profession.

(Science, 70(1821):485-493, 1929)

AS
36
S5

Cushman, Joseph Augustine.
... *Foraminifera* of the Philippine and adjacent seas
by Joseph A. Cushman ... Washington, Govt. print.
off., 1921.

608 p. illus., 100 pl. 24½ᶜᵐ. (Smithsonian institution. United States National museum. Bulletin 100, v. 4)
At head of title: Contributions to the biology of the Philippine Archipelago and adjacent regions.

1. Foraminifera.
Library of Congress   Q11.U6 Bull. 100, vol. 4   21-26712
———— Copy 2.   QL368.F6C75
[6]

AS
36
A9

Cushing, Frank Hamilton

DEC -8 1900   *Exploration of ancient key-dweller
remains on the gulf coast of Florida*
41-2   *(P. Am. Philosophical Society, Nov 6 1896)*
Pam.box   Vol. XXXV, No. 153, pp 329-448.
N. America
            Philadelphia 1897. 8vo pp 120 pl xxv - xxxv.

N.5

Given by Stewart Culin.

Q
101
P 18

Cushing, John E.   and others, Chairmen
A symposium on immunogenetic concepts
in marine population research.   Tenth Pacific Science Congress of the Pacific Science
Association...1961

(American Naturalist, 96(889):193-246,
1962)

AS
36
S 5

Cushman, Joseph Augustine
The Foraminifera of the Tropical Pacific
Collections of the "Albatross", 1899-1900.
Part I:Astrorhizidae to Trochamminidae.
  "   II:Lagenidae to Alveolinellidae.
  "   III:Heterohelicidae and Buliminidae.

(Bulletin United States National Museum,
161, 1932-194?)   to be complete in 4 pts.

GN
550
S

Cushing, Frank Hamilton, 1857-1900.
Outlines of Zuñi creation myths, by Frank Hamilton
Cushing.
(In U. S. Bureau of American ethnology. Thirteenth annual report,
1891-92. Washington, 1896. 29½ᶜᵐ. p. 321-447)

1. Zuñi Indians—Religion and mythology.
                                  16-5518 Revised
Library of Congress   E51.U55 13th

QD
11
Cu
C98

Cushman, Allerton S.

Chemistry and civilization, by
Allerton S. Cushman.

Boston, Badger, [1920]. 151p. (Half-
title:Chemistry and civilization:
Lectures delivered under the Richard B.
Westbrook free lectureship foundations
at the Wagner Free institute of science,
Philadelphia)

QL
138
E 24

Cushman, Joseph Augustine
Foraminifera (Pacific)

Edmondson, C. H.   and others

AS
763
B-b   Marine zoology of tropical central Pacific
...pp. 121-144. Honolulu. 1925.

Reading   (Bernice P. Bishop Museum, Bulletin No. 27,
Room   1925; Tanager Expedition, Publication No.1)

GN
550
S

Cushing, Frank Hamilton, 1857-1900.
... A study of Pueblo pottery as illustrative of Zuñi
culture growth. By Frank Hamilton Cushing.
(In U. S. Bureau of American ethnology. Fourth annual report, 1882-
83. Washington, 1886. 30ᶜᵐ. p. 467-521. illus.)

1. Zuñi Indians. 2. Indians of North America—Pottery.
                                  16-5493
Library of Congress   E51.U55 4th

Q
Gen Sc
Pam
#2

Cushman, Joseph A.
Foraminifera, ex Rept. of Canadian
Arctic Expedition 1913-18, vol. IX,
pt. M, 1920.

QL
368.F6
C-s

Cushman, Joseph A.
Foraminifera: Their Classification and Economic Use. Sharon, Cushman Laboratory... 401 pp.
8vo.

(Special Publication, Cushman Laboratory for
Foraminiferal Research, No. 1, 1928)

GN
550
S

Cushing, Frank Hamilton, 1857-1900.
... Zuñi fetiches. By Frank Hamilton Cushing.
(In U. S. Bureau of American ethnology. Second annual report, 1880-
81. Washington, 1883. 29½ᶜᵐ. p. 3-45. illus., pl. I-XI (part col.))

1. Zuñi Indians—Religion and mythology.
                                  16-5480
Library of Congress   E51.U55 2d

AS
36
C3

Cushman, Joseph A. and Hanna, G. Dallas
Foraminifera from the eocene near
Coalinga, California. Proc. Calif. Acad.
Sci. 4 ser. v.16, n.8, 1927.

QL
Crus
Pam
#65

Cushman, Joseph A.

*Fresh Water Crustacea from
Labrador and Newfoundland.*

AS
36
S4   *Proc. U. S. N. Mus. Vol. XXXIII.*

Washington 1908. 8vo pp. 700-713
Plates LXVIII - LXIX.
                              FEB   1911

GR
102.Z
C 98

Cushing, Frank Hamilton
Zuñi Folk Tales. With an Introduction by
J. W. Powell. New York and London. G. P. Put-
nam's Sons. 1901. 8vo. xvii + 474 pp.

AS
36
S5

Cushman, Joseph Augustine.
...(The) *Foraminifera* of the Atlantic Ocean ... By
Joseph Augustine Cushman ...
Washington, Govt. print. off., 1918-
     v.   pl. 24½ᶜᵐ. (Smithsonian institution. United States
National museum. Bulletin 104)

1. Foraminifera.
Library of Congress   Q11.U6 no. 104   18-26668
———— Copy 2.   QL368.F6C7

AS
36
S2

Cushman, Joseph A.
(An) introduction to the morphology
and classification of the Foraminifera.
Smith. Miscell. Coll. Vol. 77, No. 4, 1925

QE
Pam
#42

Cushing, H. P. & Bowen N. L.
Structure of the Anorthosite body
in the Adirondacks, and
Adirondack intrusives, ex Journ.
of Geol., vol. XXV, no. 6, Sept.-Oct.,
1917.

QE
Geology
Pam
622

Cushman, Joseph A.
Foraminifera of the genus Ehrenbergina
and its species. From Proc. U. S. Nat.
Mus. v.70, art.16, 1927.

AS
36
S5

Cushman, Joseph Augustine.
...L.The larger fossil *Foraminifera* of the Panama Canal
Zone. By Joseph Augustine Cushman ... Washington,
Govt. print. off., 1918.

1 p. l., p. 89-102, 1 l. pl. 34-45. 24½ᶜᵐ. (Smithsonian institution.
United States National museum. Bulletin 103 (pt. 4))
At head of title: Contributions to the geology and paleontology of the
Canal Zone, Panama, and geologically related areas in Central America and
the West Indies.
"Extract from Bulletin 103, pages 89-102, with plates 34-45."

1. Foraminifera, Fossil. 2. Paleontology—Panama.
Library, Smithsonian   Institution   S 21-4
                              [s21b5]

AS
36
S4
Cushman, Joseph Augustine.
... A monograph of the *Foraminifera* of the north Pacific Ocean ... By Joseph Augustine Cushman ... Washington, Govt. print. off., 1910–17.
6 v. illus., plates. 24½ cm. (Smithsonian institution. United States national museum. Bulletin 71.)
CONTENTS.—pt. I. *Astrorhizidæ* and *Lituolidæ.*—pt. II. *Textulariidæ.*—pt. III. *Lagenidæ.*—pt. IV. *Chilostomellidæ, Globigerinidæ, Nummulitidæ.*—pt. V. *Rotaliidæ.*—pt. VI. *Miliolidæ.*

1. Foraminifera.   Protozoa

Library of Congress   Q11.U6 no. 71   10–35869 Revised
———— Copy 2.   Q1.368.F6C8

AS
36
S 4
Cushman, Joseph A.
    Recent foraminifera from off Juan Fernandez Islands, by Joseph A. Cushman and R. Wickenden.
    (In Proc. U. S. Nat. Mus., Vol. 75, Art. 9, 1929)

QE
1
S78
Cushman, Joseph A. and Valentine, William W.
    Shallow-water foraminifera from the Channel islands of southern California. Stanford Univ. Pub. Cont. Dept. Geol. Vol. I, no.1, 1930.

QE
75
P
Cushman, Joseph A.
    A monograph of the foraminiferal family Nonionidae.
    (U. S. Geol. Survey, Prof. Paper, 191, 1939)

AS
36
S4
Cushman, Joseph Augustine.
    Recent *Foraminifera* from off New Zealand. By Joseph A. Cushman.
    (In U. S. National museum. Proceedings. Washington, 1920. 23½ cm. v. 56, p. 593–640. pl. 74–75 on 1 l.)

1. Foraminifera.
Library of Congress   Q11.U55 vol. 56   20–9679
———— Copy 2.   Q11.U55 vol. 56 2d set

QH
301
C 3
Cushman, Joseph Augustine
    Shallow-water Foraminifera of the Tortugas Region.
Carnegie Institution of Washington, Papers from the Tortugas Laboratory, Vol. 17, 1922. (Carnegie Institution of Washington Publication No. 311 8vo. pp. 85)

AS
36
S4
Cushman, Joseph Augustine.
    ... New arenaceous *Foraminifera* from the Philippines. By Joseph Augustine Cushman ...
    (In U. S. National museum. Proceedings. Washington, 1911. 23½ cm. vol. 38, p. 437–442. illus.)
    "Scientific results of the Philippine cruise of the fisheries steamer 'Albatross,' 1907–10.—no. 6."

1. Foraminifera. 2. Protozoa—Philippine Islands. 3. Albatross (Steamer)
                11–15890
Library of Congress   Q11.U55 vol. 38

AS
36
S 2
Cushman, Joseph A.
    Recent Foraminifera from Old Providence Island collected on the Presidential Cruise of 1938.
    (Smith. Misc. Coll., Vol. 99, No. 9, 1941, pp. 1–14, 2 pl.)

QE
349.F
L 13

Ladd

AS
763
B-b

Reading
Room
Cushman, Joseph A.
    Smaller Foraminifera from Vitilevu, Fiji.
Ladd, Harry S., and others
    Geology of Vitilevu, Fiji...Honolulu. 1934. R8vo. pp. 102–140.
    (Bernice P. Bishop Museum, Bull. 119, 1934.)

AS
36
S4
Cushman, Joseph Augustine.
    ... New arenaceous *Foraminifera* from the Philippine Islands and contiguous waters. By Joseph A. Cushman ...
    (In U. S. National museum. Proceedings. Washington, 1912. 23½ cm. vol. 42, p. 227–230. pl. 28)
    "Scientific results of the Philippine cruise of the fisheries steamer "Albatross,' 1907–1910.—no. 17."

1. Foraminifera. 2. Protozoa—Philippine Islands. 3. Albatross (Steamer)
                13–9526
Library of Congress   Q11.U55 vol. 42

QE
75
P
Cushman, Joseph A. and others
    Recent Foraminifera of the Marshall Islands. [Bikini and nearby atolls, Part 2, Oceanography, (Biologic)]
    (U. S. Geol. Survey, Prof. Paper 260-H, 1954)

AS
36
S5
Cushman, Joseph Augustine.
    ... The smaller fossil *Foraminifera* of the Panama Canal Zone. By Joseph Augustine Cushman ... Washington, Govt. print. off., 1918.
    1 p. l., 45–87, ii p. pl. 19–33. 24½ cm. (Smithsonian institution. United States National museum. Bulletin 103 (pt. 3).)
    At head of title: Contributions to the geology and paleontology of the Canal Zone, Panama, and geologically related areas in Central America and the West Indies.
    "Extract from Bulletin 103, pages 45–87, with plates 19–33."
    Stamped on t.-p.: Issued Feb. 18, 1919.

1. Foraminifera, Fossil. 2. Paleontology—Panama. I. Title.
                                        S 21–3
Library, Smithsonian   Institution

AS
36
S4
Cushman, Joseph Augustine.
    A new foraminifer commensal on *Cyclammina*. By Joseph A. Cushman ...
    (In U. S. National museum. Proceedings. Washington, 1920. 23½ cm. v. 56, p. 101–102. pl. 25)

1. Iridia convexa. 2. Cyclammina.   Foraminifera
Library of Congress   Q11.U55 vol. 56   20–9667
———— Copy 2.   Q11.U55 vol. 56 2d set

AS
36
S 4
Cushman, Joseph A.
    Recent foraminifera from the west coast of South America, by Joseph A. Cushman and Betty Kellett.
    (In Proceedings of the U. S. Nat. Mus., Vol. 75, Art. 25, 1929)

Q
115
H 23
Cushman, Joseph A.
    Some Lagenidae in the collections of the Allan Hancock Foundation. By Joseph A. Cushman and Irene McCulloch.
    (Allan Hancock Pacific Expeditions, Vol. 6(6), 1950)

AS
36
S4
Cushman, Joseph Augustine.
    ... New species and varieties of *Foraminifera* from the Philippines and adjacent waters. By Joseph A. Cushman ...
    (In U. S. National museum. Proceedings. Washington, 1917. 23½ cm. v. 51, p. 651–662)
    "Scientific results of the Philippine cruise of the fisheries steamer 'Albatross,' 1907–1910.—no. 35."

1. Foraminifera. 2. Albatross (Steamer)
                17–23862
Library of Congress   Q11.U55 vol. 51
———— Copy 2.   Q11.U55 vol. 51 2d set

QE
75
P
Cushman, Joseph A.
    Recent foraminifera of the Marshall Islands. By Joseph A. Cushman, Ruth Todd, and Rita J. Post. Bikini and nearby atolls, Part 2, Oceanography (Biologic).
    (U. S. Geol. Survey Prof. Paper 260-H, 1954)

Q
115
H 23
Cushman, Joseph A.
    Some Nonionidae in the collections of the Allan Hancock Foundation. By Joseph A. Cushman and Irene McCulloch.
    (Allan Hancock Pacific Expeditions, Vol. 6, No. 5, pp. 145–178, 1940)

AS
36
S4
Cushman, Joseph Augustine.
    ... New *Textulariidæ* and other arenaceous *Foraminifera* from the Philippine Islands and contiguous waters. By Joseph A. Cushman ...
    (In U. S. National museum. Proceedings. Washington, 1913. 23½ cm. v. 44, p. 633–638. pl. 78–80)
    "Scientific results of the Philippine cruise of the fisheries steamer 'Albatross,' 1907–1910.—no. 25."

1. Foraminifera. 2. Protozoa—Philippine Islands. 3. Albatross (Steamer)
                13–20883
Library of Congress   Q11.U55 vol. 44

QH
301
C3
Cushman, Joseph Augustine
    Samoan foraminifera. Dept. Marine Biology, Carnegie Inst. vol. XXI, 1924. Publication 342

QE
75
B
Cushman, Joseph Augustine.
    ... Some Pliocene and Miocene *Foraminifera* of the coastal plain of the United States; papers by Joseph Augustine Cushman. Washington, Govt. print. off., 1918.
    100 p. xxxi pl. 23½ cm. (U. S. Geological survey. Bulletin 676)
    At head of title: Department of the interior.
    Most of the plates printed on both sides of leaf.

1. Foraminifera, Fossil.
                                        G S 19–40
Library, U. S. Geological   Survey (200) E no. 676

Q 115 H 23 — Cushman, Joseph A.

Some Virgulininae in the collections of the Allan Hancock Foundation. By Joseph A. Cushman and Irene McCulloch.

(Allan Hancock Pacific Expeditions, Vol. 6, No. 4, pp. 179-230, 1942)

AS 36 S4 — Cushman, Robert Asa.

North American ichneumon-flies, new and described, with taxonomic and nomenclatorial notes. By R. A. Cushman ...

(*In* U. S. National museum. Proceedings. Washington, 1921. 23½ᶜᵐ. v. 58, p. 251-292. 1 illus.)

1. Ichneumonidae.

Library of Congress   Q11.U55 vol. 58   21-21437

PL Pam #40 — Cust, Robert Needham

On the origin of the Indian alphabet, ex Roy. Asiatic Soc. Journ., vol. XVI. n.s., 1884, pp. 325-360

AS 36 S4 — Cushman, Robert Asa.

Descriptions of new North American ichneumon-flies. By R. A. Cushman ...

(*In* U. S. National museum. Proceedings. Washington, 1920. 23½ᶜᵐ. v. 55, p. 517-543. illus.)

1. Ichneumonidae.

Library of Congress   Q11.U55 vol. 55   20-5875

AS 36 S 4 — Cushman, Robert Asa

The North American ichneumon-flies of the tribes Lycorini, Polysphinctini, and Theroniini. By R. A. Cushman...

(In U. S. National museum. Proceedings. Washington, 1921. v. 58, p. 7-48. illus., pl.2)

PL Pam #41 — Cust, Robert Needham

The origin of the Phenician and Indian alphabets. ex Roy. Asiatic Soc. Journ., 1897, pp. 49-80

AS 36 S4 — Cushman, Robert Asa.

Descriptions of six new species of ichneumon-flies. By R. A. Cushman ...

(*In* U. S. National museum. Proceedings. Washington, 1915. 23½ᶜᵐ. v. 48, p. 507-513)

1. Ichneumonidae.   15-24789

Library of Congress   Q11.U55 vol. 48

AS 36 S 4 — Cushman, Robert Asa

Notes on certain genera of ichneumon-flies, with descriptions of a new genus and four new species. By R. A. Cushman...

(In U. S. National museum. Washington, 1920. v. 56, p. 373-382. illus.)

CUSTOMS

see

MANNERS & CUSTOMS
RITES & CEREMONIES
SOCIAL LIFE
ETHNOLOGY

AS 36 S4 — Cushman, Robert Asa.

Eight new species of reared ichneumon-flies, with notes on some other species. By R. A. Cushman ...

(*In* U. S. National museum. Proceedings. Washington, 1917. 23½ᶜᵐ. v. 53, p. 457-469)

1. Ichneumonidae.   18-14642

Library of Congress   Q11.U55 vol. 53

AS 36 S4 — Cushman, Robert Asa.

A revision of hymenopterous insects of the tribe *Cremastini* of America north of Mexico. By R. A. Cushman ...

(*In* U. S. National museum. Proceedings. Washington, 1917. 23½ᶜᵐ. v. 53, p. 503-551)

1. Cremastini.   18-14645

Library of Congress   Q11.U55 vol. 53

AS 492 S 61 m — CUSTOMS MALAYA

Wilkinson, R. J.

Malay customs and beliefs. (Monographs on Malay Subjects, No. 4)

(Jour. of the Malayan Branch Royal Asiatic Soc., Vol. 30(4):1-87, 1957)

QL Insect Pam.1040 — Cushman, R. A.

H. Sauter's Formosa collection: Ichneumonidae

(Arbeiten uber morphologische u. taxonomische Ent. aus Berlin-Dahlem, Bd. 4, 1937, pp. 283-311)

AS 763 B-b — Cushman, R. A (Robert Asa)

Two new species of Barichneumon (Hymenoptera: Ichneumonidae) from the Society Islands.

(Bernice P. Bishop Museum, Bull. 142, pp. 169-170. Issued February 28, 1938. Pacific Entomological Survey Publication 8, Article 16)

GN 1 A — Cutler, J. Elbert

Tropical Acclimatization.

(American Anthropologist, N. S. Vol. 4, 1902, pp. 421-440)

QL 461 H-1 — Cushman, R. A.

The Hawaiian species of Enicospilus and Abanchogastra (Hymenoptera: Ichneumonidae).

(Proc. of the Haw. Entomological Soc. Vol. 12, 1944, pp. 39-56)

PL Pam #4 — Cust, Robert Needham

Language as illustrated by Bible-translation.

London, 1886.

AS 36 A25 — Cutler, Manasseh, 1742-1823.

... An account of some of the vegetable productions, naturally growing in this part of America, botanically arranged by the Rev. Manasseh Cutler ... Cincinnati, O., J. U. & C. G. Lloyd, 1903.

(3)-8, (1), 396-493 p. front. (port.) 26ᶜᵐ. (Bulletin of the Lloyd library of botany, pharmacy and materia medica, no. 7. Reproduction series, no. 4)

A reprint of the original article in Memoirs of the American academy of arts and sciences, 1785, v. 1.

1. U. S. Botany.   Agr 5-659

Library, U. S. Dept. of   Agriculture 396.8L77

AS 763 B-b — Cushman, R. A (Robert Asa)

A new species of Echthromorpha (Hymenoptera: Ichneumonidae) from the Marquesas Islands)

(Bernice P. Bishop Museum, Bull. 142, pp. 171. Issued Feb. 28, 1938. Pacific Entomological Survey Publication 8, Article 17)

PL II Philo- Papers — Cust, Robert Needham

Language map of the East Indies I. British India and its border states, ex. Geog. Magazine, Vol. V., No. I, pp. 1-28.

QL Prot.- Poly. Pam. 770 — Cutress, Charles E.

An interpretation of the structure and distribution of Cnidae in Anthozoa.

(Systematic Zoology, 4(3):120-137, 1955)

QH 1 P 11
Cutress, Charles E.
Three new species of Zoantharia from California. By Charles E. Cutress and Willis E. Pequegnat.
(Pacific Science, 14:89-100, 1960)

Cuvier, G. and Valenciennes, A.
Histoire naturelle des poissons. planches
4 vol. 1828-1849.
UH

DU 890 C 99
Cuzent, G(ilbert)
[Archipel des Pomotu (Paumotu-Tuamotu).
(Bull. de la Soc. Académique de Brest. 2 Ser. tome IX. 1883-1884. pp.49-90)

Z 696 C 98
Cutter, Charles Ammi, 1837-1903.
... Three-figure alphabetic-order table. [Boston, Library bureau, 1902]
2 v. 33 x 18½ᶜᵐ.
1. Alphabeting.
5-35431
Library of Congress / Z696.C9892

QL 615 C 99
Cuvier, G. L. C. F. D.
Histoire Naturelle des Poissons, by Cuvier and Valenciennes. Plates only, incomplete,—not certain the plates are from this work.

GN 2.S T
Cuzent, G.
Du kava ou ava (Piper Methysticum).
(Journal de Pharmacie, T. XII, 1826, p. 122-Reprinted in the Bull. Soc. Etudes Oceaniennes, Tome 6, No. 6, 1939, pp. 240-245; No. 7, pp. 276-283)
and translation, GN Ethn. Pam. 3384
* This seems to be an error for 1862.

AS 36 S1
Cutts, J B.
Ancient relics in northwestern Iowa. By J. B. Cutts.
(In Smithsonian institution. Annual report. 1872. Washington, 1873. 23½ᶜᵐ. p. 417)
1. Iowa—Antiq. 'Archaeology - Iowa
S 15-350
Library of Congress Q11.S66 1872
Library, Smithsonian Institution

AS 36 S1
Cuvier, Georges i. e. Jean Léopold Nicolas Frédéric, baron, 1769-1832.
Memoir of Haüy. Read before the French Academy of sciences, by Baron Cuvier ... Tr. ... by C. A. Alexander.
(In Smithsonian institution. Annual report. 1860. Washington, 1861. 23½ᶜᵐ. p. [376]-392)
1. Haüy, René Just, 1743-1822. I. Alexander, Charles Armistead, d. 1869? tr.
S 15-92
Library of Congress Q11.S66 1860
Library, Smithsonian Institution

QK Botany Pam. 1734
Cuzent, Gilbert
Études sur Quelques Végétaux de Tahiti. Typed copy by Martin L. Grant of original published in Tahiti, 1857, Imprimeur du Gouvernment.

QL Insects Pam. 1117
CYLAS
Reinhard, H. J.
The sweet potato weevil.
(Texas Agric. Exp. Station, Bull. 308, 1923)

AS 36 S1
Cuvier, Georges i. e. Jean Léopold Nicolas Frédéric, baron, 1769-1832.
Memoir of Priestley. Read before the National institute of France by M. Cuvier, June 27, 1805.
(In Smithsonian institution. Annual report. 1858. Washington, 1859. 23½ᶜᵐ. p. [138]-152)
"Translated by C. A. Alexander."
1. Priestley, Joseph, 1733-1804. I. Alexander, Charles Armistead, d. 1869? tr.
S 15-58
Library of Congress Q11.S66 1858
Library, Smithsonian Institution

DU 605 C 99
Cuzent, G(ilbert)
Voyage aux Iles Gambier (Archipel de Manga-Reva).
(Extrait de la Soc. Académique de Brest. 1871. pp.237-385. 6 illus.)

S 17 H3 S 44
CUTWORMS
Swezey, Otto Herman, 1869-
... Army worms and cut worms on sugar cane in the Hawaiian Islands, by O. H. Swezey. Honolulu, Hawaii, 1909.
32 p. III pl. 22½ᶜᵐ. (Report of work of the Experiment station of the Hawaiian sugar planters' association. Division of entomology. Bulletin no. 7)
The verso of pl. I-II contains letterpress description of plate opposite.
1. Army-worms. 2. Cutworms. 3. Sugar-cane—[Diseases and] pests.
Agr 9-3202 Revised
Library, U. S. Dept. of Agriculture 420H31 no. 7
[r20f5]

QL 431 C99
Cuvier, M.
Mémoires pour servir à l'histoire et l'Anatomie des Mollusques.
Paris, 1817. 4°. plts 35.

DU 870 C99
Cuzent, [M] G(ilbert)
Tahiti: considerations geologiques, meteorologiques et botanique sur l'ile-etat moral actuel des Tahitiens, traits caracteristiques de leurs moeurs...
Rochefort, Theze, 1860. 275p.

GN 370 C 85
Cuvier, Georges
The animal kingdom.
IN
Count, Earl W. ed.
This is race... pp. 44-50. New York. 1950

AS 36 S1
CUVIER, GEORGES....
Flourens, Pierre i. e. Marie Jean Pierre, 1794-1867.
History of the works of Cuvier. By M. Flourens.
(In Smithsonian institution. Annual report. 1868. Washington, 1869. 23½ᶜᵐ. p. [141]-165)
"Translated ... by C. A. Alexander."
1. Cuvier, Georges i. e. Jean Léopold Nicolas Frédéric, baron, 1769-1832. 2. Zoology. 3. Anatomy. I. Alexander, Charles Armistead, d. 1869? tr.
S 15-245
Library of Congress Q11.S66 1868
Library, Smithsonian Institution
[s19d2]

GN Pam 964
Cvijic, J
Die ethnographische abgrenzung der völker auf der Balkanhabinsel. From Petermann's Mitt. 1913, Mai heft. 33p.

QL 45 C995
Cuvier, Georges i. e. Jean Léopold Nicolas Frédéric, baron, 1769-1832.
The animal kingdom arranged in conformity with its organization, by the Baron Cuvier ... The Crustacea, Arachnides and Insecta, by P. A. Latreille ... Tr. from the French, with notes and additions, by H. M'Murtrie ... New York, G. & C. & H. Carvill, 1831.
Vol. 3, 4 1834
4 v. plates 22½ᶜᵐ. 1, 2, 3, 4.
"Catalogue of authors": v. 4, p. [429]-493.
1. Zoology. I. M'Murtrie, Henry, 1793-1865, tr. II. Latreille, Pierre André, 1762-1833.
QL 45 C995 pls 4 vols pls (vols 1-4 plts)
6-14945
Library of Congress QL45.C945

AS 36 S1
CUVIER, GEORGES i.e. JEAN LEOPOLD.....
Flourens, Pierre i. e. Marie Jean Pierre, 1794-1867.
Memoir of Cuvier. By M. Flourens.
(In Smithsonian institution. Annual report. 1868. Washington, 1869. 23½ᶜᵐ. p. [121]-140)
"Translated ... by C. A. Alexander."
1. Cuvier, Georges i. e. Jean Léopold Nicolas Frédéric, baron, 1769-1832. I. Alexander, Charles Armistead, d. 1869? tr.
S 15-244
Library of Congress Q11.S66 1868
Library, Smithsonian Institution

DU 1 S 72 q
CYAMOPSIS
Barrau, Jacques
A useful plant grown in Fiji.
(South Pacific Commission Quarterly Bull. 8(2):39, 1958)
[Guar, or cluster bean: Cyamopsis psoralioides D. C. ...]

QK
Bot.Pam.
2099

CYANEA

Hosaka, Edward Y.

A new species of Phyllostegia and two new varieties of Cyanea of the Hawaiian Islands, by E. Y. Hosaka and Otto Degener.

(Occ. Papers, Bernice P. Bishop Museum, Vol. 14, No. 3, pp. 27-30)

AS
540
P

CYATHEA

Copeland, Edwin Bingham

Cyathea in New Guinea.

(Philippine Journal of Science, Vol. 77 (2): 95-125, 1947)

QK
495.C11
C44

CYCADACEAE

Chamberlain, Charles Joseph

The living cycads.

Chicago, Univ. Press, [1919] 168p. pls.

QK
Bot.Pam
3270

CYANEA

Rock, Joseph F.

Hawaiian Lobelioids.

(Occ. Papers, Bernice P. Bishop Mus., 23(5), 1962)

QK
Botany
Pam.
3320

CYATHEA

Holttum, R. E.

Morphology and classification of the tree ferns. By R. E. Holttum and U. Sen.

(Reprint, Phytomorphology, Vol. 11(4): 406-420, 1961)

QK
97
E 58

CYCADACEAE

Engler, Adolf

Das Pflanzenreich...IV.1, 1932. (Heft 99): Cycadaceae, by J. Schuster.

QK
Bot.Pam
138
139
140

CYANEA

Rock, Joseph F.

A new Hawaiian Cyanea. In Torrey Bot. Club Bul. 42, pp. 77-78, 1915

3 copies

QK
Bot. Pam.
3282

CYATHEA

Holttum, R. E.

New species of tree ferns (Cyathea Sm. and Dicksonia L'Herit.)

(Kew Bulletin, 16(1):51-64, 1962)

QE
976
W 64

CYCADACEAE

Wieland, C. R.

Fossil Cycads, with special reference to Raumeria Reichenbachiana Goeppert Sp. of the Zwinger of Dresden. With 30 figures in text, and 12 plates.

(Palaeontographica, Bd. 79, Abt. B. 1934)

G
3
N 27

CYANEA

Zahl, Paul A.

Glass menageries of the sea; a jellyfish may be a poisonous monster with 100-foot long tentacles or a fragile, pink-petaled rose growing in a tide pool.

(National Geographic Magazine, Vol. 107(6): 797-822, 1955)

AS
262
M

CYATHODES IMBRICATA

Stschegleow, S.

Cyathodes imbricata m. Insulae Sandwicenses in Bull. de la Soc.Imp. des.Nat. XXXII 1, p. 10, Moscow, 1859.

QE
976
W 4

CYCADACEAE, FOSSIL

Wieland, George Reber, 1865–
American fossil cycads, by G. R. Wieland. [Washington, D. C.] Carnegie institution of Washington, 1906–16.
2 v. front., illus., 112 pl. (1 fold.) 29½ x 23½ᶜᵐ. (On verso of t.-p.: Carnegie institution of Washington. Publication no. 34)

Vol. II, "Taxonomy."
Bibliography: vol. [1] p. 249–256; vol. II, p. 239–248.

1. Cycadaceae, Fossil.

Library of Congress   QE976.W64   6–34020 Revised
———— Copy 2.

QK
Botany
Pam.
1247

CYANOPHYCEAE

Esmarch, Ferdinand

Beitrag zur Cyanophyceenflora unsrer Kolonien.

(Hamburg. Wissens. Anstalt. Jahrb. XXVII, 1910, Beiheft 3, pp. 63-82)

QL
401
M 23

CYATHOPOMA

Preston, H. B.

Descriptions of two new species of Cyathopoma.

(Proc. Mal. Soc. London, Vol. 5, 1943, pp. 340)

AS
36
S2

CYCADOFILICES

White, David, 1862–
Fossil plants of the group *Cycadofilices*, by David White.

(In Smithsonian institution. Smithsonian miscellaneous collections. Washington, 1905. 24½ᶜᵐ. vol. XLVII (Quarterly issue, vol. II) p. 377–390, pl. LIII-LV)

Publication 1557.
Each plate is preceded by a leaf with descriptive letterpress.

1. Cycadofilices.
[Full name: Charles David White]

Library of Congress   Q11.S7 vol. 47   16–11015
———— Copy 2.
———— Separate.   QE989.C8W6

QK
1
C 2

CYANOPHYCEAE

Gardner, Nathaniel Lyon, 1864–
... Cytological studies in *Cyanophyceae*, by Nathaniel Lyon Gardner. Berkeley, The University press, 1906.
cover-title, p. [237]–296. pl. 21–26 (5 col.) 27ᶜᵐ. (University of California publications in botany, vol. 2, no. 12)
Bibliography: p. 283–284.

1. Cytology. 2. Cyanophyceae.

A 11–728

Title from Univ. of Calif.   Library of Congress

QL
401
M 23

CYATHOPOMA

Sykes, Ernest Ruthven

Notes on Ceylon land-shells, with descriptions of new species of Cyathopoma and Thysanota.

(Proc. Malacological Soc. of London, Vol. 3, 1898-99, pp. 159-161)

QK
Bot.Pam.
2220

CYCAS

Kanehira, Ryozo

On the Micronesian species of Cycas.

(Journal of Japanese Botany, Vol. 14, No. 9, 1939, pp. 579-588)

QK
567
S 64

CYANOPHYTA

Drouet, Francis

Cyanophyta.
IN
Smith, Gilbert M.   editor
Manual of phycology; an introduction to the Algae and their biology. 1951. 159-166.

QL
627
P 11

CYBIIDAE

Kishinouye, Kamkichi

A study of the mackerels, Cybiids and tunas.

(Suisan Gakkai, Vol. 1(1):1-24, My 1915)

[Pacific Oceanic Fishery Investigations, Translation No. 25]

AS
36
S4

CYCLAMMINA

Cushman, Joseph Augustine.
A new foraminifer commensal on *Cyclammina*. By Joseph A. Cushman ...

(In U. S. National museum. Proceedings. Washington, 1920. 23½ᶜᵐ. v. 56, p. 101-102. pl. 25)

1. Iridia convexa. 2. Cyclammina.

Library of Congress   Q11.U55 vol. 56   20-9667
———— Copy 2.   Q11.U55 vol. 56 2d set
[6]

CYCLOBOTHRA

QK U

Painter, Joseph Hannum, 1879–1908.

A revision of the subgenus *Cyclobothra* of the genus *Calochortus*. By Joseph H. Painter.

(*In* Smithsonian institution. United States national museum. Contributions from the United States national herbarium. Washington, 1903–24⁺. v. 13, pt. 10, p. 343–350)
"Issued June 8, 1911."

1. Cyclobothra.

Agr 11–1161

Library, U. S. Dept. of   Agriculture 450C76 vol. 13, pt. 10

CYCLOCLYPEUS

QE 1 S 47-s

Hanzawa, S.

Recent and fossil Cycloclypeus from the Ryukyu Islands and their adjacent sea.

(Short Papers from the Institute of Geology and Paleontology, Tohoku Univ., Sendai, No. 3; 1–12, 1951)

CYCLOGASTERIDAE.

AS 36 S4

Burke, Charles Victor.

A new genus and six new species of fishes of the family *Cyclogasteridæ*. By Charles Victor Burke ...

(*In* U. S. National museum. Proceedings. Washington, 1913. 23½⁺. vol. 43, p. 567–574)

1. Cyclogasteridae.

13–13125

Library of Congress   Q11.U55 vol. 43

CYCLONES

QE Geol. Pam. 954

Cline, Isaac Monroe

A century of progress in the study of cyclones; aids in forecasting movements and destructive agencies in tropical cyclones. New Orleans. 1935. 8vo. 29 pp.

CYCLONES

QC 948 C 64

Cline, Isaac Monroe

Tropical cyclones, comprising an exhaustive study along entirely new lines of the distribution of wind directions and velocities, clouds, precipitation, and other features observed and recorded in sixteen tropical cyclones...1900–1924 inclusive... New York. The Macmillan Company. 1926. 8vo. 301 pp.

CYCLONES

QL Birds Pam. 356

Goddard, M. T.

Sea-birds and cyclones: some interesting New South Wales records. By M. T. Goddard and K. A. Hindwood.

(The Emu, Vol. 51:169–171, 1951)

CYCLONES

AS 36 S1

Pike, Nicholas, *U. S. consul, Port Louis, Mauritius.*

An account of a cyclone, January 6 and 7, 1867, encountered by the United States steamer Monocacy, while on her passage from Simon's Bay to Mauritius, in the Indian Ocean. By Nicholas Pike ...

(*In* Smithsonian institution. Annual report. 1867. Washington, 1868. 23½⁺. p. 477–481)

1. Cyclones.

S 15–241

Library of Congress
Library, Smithsonian   Q11.S66 1867 Institution

CYCLONES MAURITIUS

QE Geol. Pam. 1327

Sauer, Jonathan D.

Effects of recent tropical cyclones on the coastal vegetation of Mauritius.

(Jour. of Ecology, Vol. 50:275–290, 1962)

CYCLONES PACIFIC

AP 2 A 5

Redfield, William C.

On the cyclones or typhoons of the north Pacific Ocean, with a chart, showing their course of progression.

(Am. Jour. of Sci., Ser. 2, Vol. 24, 1857, pp. 21–38)

CYCLONES PACIFIC

QE Geol. Pam. 996

Visher, Stephen Sargent

Tropical cyclones and the dispersal of life from island to island in the Pacific.

(American Naturalist, Vol. 59, 1925, pp. 70–78)

CYCLONES PACIFIC

QC 948 V 82

Visher, S. S.

Tropical cyclones of the Pacific. Honolulu. 1925.

(Bernice P. Bishop Museum, Bulletin 20)

AS 763 B-b Reading Room

CYCLONES

AP 2 A 5

Visher, Stephen S.

Sun spots and the frequency of tropical cyclones.

(Am. Jour. of Sci., Ser. 5, Vol. 8, 1924, pp. 312–316)

CYCLONES PACIFIC

QE Geol. Pam. 1055

Giovanelli, J. L.

Les cyclones en Océanie Française: caractères généraux des cyclones tropicaux.

(Bull. Soc. des Etudes Océaniennes, No. 68, Mars, 1940, pp. 250–267)

CYCLONES PACIFIC

Q 115 H 39 locked case

Hawks, Francis L.

Narrative of the expedition of an American squadron to the China Seas and Japan...1852–54... Vol. II, pp. 337–359: Observations in relation to the cyclones of the Pacific, by William C. Redfield.

CYCLONES PACIFIC

Hutchings, J. W.

Tropical cyclones in the southwest Pacific.

(New Zealand Geographer, Vol. 9(1):37–57, maps, 1953)

CYCLOPAEDIA

AH 4 Na READING ROOM

The **National** cyclopædia of American biography, being the history of the United States as illustrated in the lives of the founders, builders, and defenders of the republic, and of the men and women who are doing the work and moulding the thought of the present time; edited by distinguished biographers, selected from each state, revised and approved by the most eminent historians, scholars, and statesmen of the day. v. 1–
New York, J. T. White & company, 1893–19
v. fronts., illus., ports. 28½⁺.
Copyright

(Continued on next card)
(s19g2)   6—38537

CYCLOPAEDIA

AH 4 Na Reading Room

The **National** cyclopædia of American biography ... 1893–19 (Card 2)
A conspectus of American biography; being an analytical summary of American history and biography, containing also the complete indexes of The national cyclopædia of American biography. [v. 1–13] Comp. by George Derby ... New York, J. T. White & company, 1906.
4 p. l., 752 p. 28½⁺.
"Character lessons in American biography. Adapted for the use of the public schools. By James T. White": p. 717–752.
Copyright A 144371

(Continued on next card)
(s19g2)   6—38537

Cyclopaedia of American Biography

see

National Cyclopaedia.

QK 7 B †

Cyclopedia of American Horticulture by L. H. Bailey assisted by Wilhelm Miller. In 4 volumes New York 1900. 4to Vol. I. A-D. pp XVII 509 "II E-N. pp XIV. 511–1002"

K. 11. 14 to 17.
C.

CYCLOPHORIDAE

QL 406 B78

British museum (*Nat. hist.*) *Dept. of zoology.*

Catalogue of *Phaneropneumona*, or terrestrial operculated *Mollusca*, in the collection of the British museum. London, Printed by order of the Trustees [by Woodfall and Kinder] 1852.
2 p. l., 324 p. 18½⁺.
Prepared by Dr. L. Pfeiffer.

1. Cyclophoridae. 2. Helicinidae.   I. Pfeiffer, Ludwig Georg Karl, 1805–1877.

8–21403

Library of Congress   QL406.B78

CYCLOPHORIDAE

QL Mollusca Pam. 869

Clench, William J.

Cyclophoridae and Pupinidae of Caroline, Fijian, and Samoan Islands.

(Bernice P. Bishop Museum, Bull. 196, 1949)

QL
430.5.C 9
K 75

CYCLOPHORIDAE

Kobelt, Wilhelm

Cyclophoridae. Mit 110 Abbildungen und 1
Landkarte.
(Das Tierreich...In Verbindung mit der Deut-
schen Zoologischen Gesellschaft...Lieferung 16,
Mollusca. Berlin. R. Friedlander und Sohn. 1902
R8vo. 662 pp.)

QL
537.N4
E 26

CYCLORRHAPHA

Edwards, F. W. and others

British blood-sucking flies, by F. W. Edwards, H. Oldroyd, and J. Smart. Printed by
order of the Trustees, British Museum. 1939.
London. R8vo. vii + 156 pp. 45 pl.

QL
1
H1

CYCLURA

Barbour, Thomas, 1884–

... A revision of the lizards of the genus *Cyclura*. By
Thomas Barbour and G. K. Noble. With fifteen plates.
Cambridge, Mass., The Museum, 1916.

p. [137]–164. 15 pl. 24½ᶜᵐ. (Bulletin of the Museum of comparative
zoology at Harvard college. vol. LX, no. 4)

Each plate accompanied by leaf with descriptive letterpress.

1. Cyclura.   i. Noble, G. Kingsley, joint author.

17–31390

Library of Congress   QL1.H3 vol. 60, no. 4

QL
401
M 23

CYCLOPHORIDAE

Smith, Edgar A.

Descriptions of three new species of Opis-
thostoma from Sarawak, North Borneo.

(Proc. Mal. Soc. London, Vol. 6, 1905, pp.
189–190)

QL
Moll.
Fam.
370

CYCLOSTOMA

Garnault, Paul

Recherches anatomiques et histologiques sur
le Cyclostoma elegans. Thèse présenté à la
Faculté des Sciences de Paris...1887. Bordeaux
1887. R8vo. pp. 1–152, 9 plates.

AS
36
S 66 p

CYDNIDAE

Froeschner, Richard C.

Cydnidae of the western hemisphere.

(Proc. of the U. S. National Mus., Vol. 111:
337–680, 1960)

QL
1
H 33 br

CYCLOPHORIDAE

Thompson, Fred G.

Systematic notes on the land snails of
the genus Tomocyclus (Cyclophoridae).

(Breviora, No. 181, 1963)

QL
401
C 44

CYCLOSTOMACEA

Martens, Eduard von

Cyclostomacea in insulis Moluccis lecta.

(Malakozoologische Blätter, Bd. 10, 1862,
pp. 83–87)

Q
115
C 28

CYEMA

Bertin, Léon

Les poissons abyssaux du genre Cyema Günther
(anatomie, embryologie, bionomie.)

(Carlsberg Foundation's Oceanographical
Expedition round the world, 1928–30...Dana
Reports...No. 10. 1937)

QL
Crustacea
Pam. 78

CYCLOPIDAE

Forbes, Ernest B.

A contribution to a knowledge of North American fresh-water Cyclopidae.

(Bull. Ill. State Laboratory of Natural
History, Vol. 5, 1897, pp. 27–82)

QL
398.C9
B 97

CYCLOSTOMATA

Busk, George

Catalogue of the Cyclostomatous Polyzoa in
the collection of the British Museum. London.
Printed by order of the Trustees. 1875. 8 vo.
viii + 29 pp., 34 pl. [Catalogue of marine
Polyzoa in the collection of the British Museum,
Part III. Cyclostomata.]

QL
Insect
Pam.
1859

CYLAS

The sweet potato-weevil; how to control it.

(U. S. Dept. Agric., Leaflet No. 431, 1958)

[Cylas formicarius elegantulus]

QH
1
M 17a

CYCLOPIDAE

Lindberg, K.

Cyclopides des Iles Kerguelen (Crustacés
Copépodes).

(Mémoires de l'Institut Scientifique de
Madagascar, Série A, Tome VIII, fasc. 1:19–24,
1953)

QL
Mol
Pam
#287
4to

F.1 16

CYCLOSTOMATA

Lelapanède, René Eduard

Cyclostomatis elegantis anat-
ome. Berlin, 1857 46 pp. 26
pl. 11

QK
1
U

CYMBIA

Standley, Paul Carpenter, 1884–

A revision of the cichoriaceous genera *Krigia, Cynthia,*
and *Cymbia*. By Paul C. Standley.

(*In* Smithsonian institution. United States national museum. Contributions from the United States national herbarium. Washington, 1903–
24½ᶜᵐ. v. 13, pt. 10, p. 351–357)

"Issued June 8, 1911."

1. Krigia.   2. Cynthia.   3. Cymbia.

Agr 11–1170

Library, U. S. Dept. of   Agriculture 450C76 vol. 13, pt. 10

QL
1
T 64

CYCLOPIDAE FORMOSA

Harada, I.

Studien uber die Susswasserfauna Formosas.
IV. Cyclopiden.

(Ann. Zool. Japonenses, 13:149–168, 1931)

QL
430.5C9
G 23

CYCLOSTOMA

Garnault, Paul

Recherches anatomiques et histologiques sur
le Cyclostoma elegans. Bordeaux, 1887. R8vo.
pp. 1–152, 9 pl.

(Thèse présenté à la Faculté des Sciences
de Paris...1887)

AS
763
B-b

CYNIPIDAE MARQUESAS

Kinsey, Alfred C.

New Figitidae from the Marquesas Islands.

(Bull. Bernice P. Bishop Museum, No. 142,
pp. 193–197. Issued October 20, 1938. Pac. Ent.
Survey Publication 8, Art. 21)

AS
36
S2

CYCLOPTERUS

Gill, Theodore Nicholas, 1837–1914.

The lumpsucker; its relationship and habits, by Theodore Gill.

(*In* Smithsonian institution. Smithsonian miscellaneous collections.
Washington, 1908. 24½ᶜᵐ. vol. L (Quarterly issue, vol. IV) p. 175–194.
illus.)

Publication 1728.
Originally published July 10, 1907.

1. Lump-fish.

16–11639

Library of Congress   Q11.S7 vol. 50
— Copy 2.

QL
1
C1

CYCLOSTOMATA

Robertson, Alice, 1859–

... The cyclostomatous *Bryozoa* of the west coast of
North America. By Alice Robertson. Berkeley, The
University press, 1910.

cover-title, p. [225]–284. pl. 18–25. 27ᶜᵐ. (University of California publications in zoology, vol. 6, no. 12)

Bibliography: p. 265–268.

1. Cyclostomata.

A 11–171

Title from Univ. of Calif.   Printed by L. C.

QL
Insect
Pam
878-a

CYNIPIDAE PACIFIC

Weld, Lewis H.

Check list of the Cynipidae of Oceania.

14 pp.

AS
36
S4
CYNIPOIDEA
Rohwer, Sievert Allen, 1887–

Additions and corrections to "The type-species of the genera of the *Cynipoidea* or the gall wasps and parasitic cynipoids." By S. A. Rohwer and Margaret M. Fagan ...

(*In* U. S. National museum. Proceedings. Washington, 1920. 23½ᶜᵐ. v. 55, p. 237–240)

1. Gall-flies.   I. Fagan, Margaret Mary, 1887–   joint author.

Library of Congress   Q11.U55 vol. 55   20–5857
                                                   [5]

AS
36
S4
CYNIPOIDEA.
Rohwer, Sievert Allen, 1887–

The type-species of the genera of the *Cynipoidea*, or the gall wasps and parasitic cynipoids. By S. A. Rohwer and Margaret M. Fagan ...

(*In* U. S. National museum. Proceedings. Washington, 1917. 23½ᶜᵐ. v. 53, p. 357–380)

1. Gall-flies.   I. Fagan, Margaret Mary, 1887–   joint author.

Library of Congress   Q11.U55 vol. 53   18–14634

QL
596.C9
W 44
CYNIPOIDEA
Weld, Lewis H.

Cynipoidea (Hym.) 1905–1950, being a supplement to the Dalla Torre and Kieffer monograph the Cynipidae in Das Tierreich, Lieferung 24, 1910, and bringing the systematic literature of the world up to date, including keys to families and subfamilies and lists of new genera, specific and variety names. Ann Arbor, Mich. Privately printed. 1952. 4to. 351 pp.

QL
461
P 11
CYNIPOIDEA   POLYNESIA
Yoshimoto, Carl M.

Synopsis of Polynesian Cynipoidea (Hymenoptera: Eucoilinae)

(Pacific Insects, Vol. 5(2):433–443, 1963)

QL
568.C9
K 56
CYNIPS
Kinsey, Alfred C.

The gall wasp genus Cynips: a study in the origin of species.

(Indiana University Studies, nos. 84,85,86, 1929)

QK
Botany
Pam
No.1207
CYNOMETRA
Harms, H.

Einige neue Arten der Gattungen Cynometra und Maniltoa. From Notizbl. K. bot. Garten, Berlin, No. 29, 1902.

QK
1
U
CYNTHIA
Standley, Paul Carpenter, 1884–
A revision of the cichoriaceous genera *Krigia, Cynthia,* and *Cymbia.* By Paul C. Standley.

(*In* Smithsonian institution. United States national museum. Contributions from the United States national herbarium. Washington, 1903–24½ᶜᵐ. v. 13, pt. 10, p. 351–357)
"Issued June 8, 1911."

1. Krigia. 2. Cynthia. 3. Cymbia.

Library, U. S. Dept. of   Agriculture 450C76 vol. 13, pt. 10   Agr 11–1170

QK
495.074
A 31
CYPERACEAE
Akiyama, Shigeo

Carices of the far eastern region of Asia. (Hokkaido University) Sapporo, Japan. March 1955. Text, 257 pp.; plates, 1–248. smfolio.

QK
1
S 46
CYPERACEAE
Barros, M.

Las Ciperaceas del Estado de Santa Catalina.

(Sellowia, No. 12 (cont.), Dec. 1960)

QK
495.C99
C 59
CYPERACEAE
Clarke, Charles Baron

Illustrations of Cyperaceae. Prepared under the direction of the late Charles Baron Clarke. London. Williams & Norgate. 1909. 8vo. 144 pls.

QK
97
E 58
CYPERACEAE
Engler, Adolf

Das Pflanzenreich...IV.20, 1909. (Heft 38)
Cyperaceae-Caricoideae, by Georg Kükenthal.

QK
Bot. Pam.
2912
CYPERACEAE
Kern, J. H.

Florae Malesianae Precursores X. Notes on Malaysian and some S. E. Asian Cyperaceae III[1].

(Reprinted from Blumea, Vol. VIII, No. 1:110–169, 1955)

[1) I in Reinwardtia 2, 1952, pp. 97–130; II In Reinwardtia , III, 1954, pp. 27–66]

QK
Bot. Pam.
3256
CYPERACEAE
Kern, J. H.

New look at some Cyperaceae mainly from the tropical standpoint.

(Advancement of Science, July 1962:141–148)

QK
Bot. Pam.
3061
CYPERACEAE
Kern, J.H.

Notes on Malaysian and some S. E. Asian Cyperaceae V. Florae Malesianae Precursores XVII.

(Reprint: Blumea, 9(1):215–236, 1958)

...3066   [ibid. VI. Florae...XIX IN Blumea, Suppl. IV:162–169, 1958]

QK
1
T 64
CYPERACEAE
Koyama, T.

Classification of the family Cyperaceae (1).

(Jour. Fac. Sci., Univ. Tokyo. Sect. 3; Botany, 8(1–3):37–148, 1961)

QK
1
E 58
CYPERACEAE
Kükenthal, G(eorg)

Beiträge zur Cyperaceenflora von Mikronesien
Diels, L. Beiträge zur Flora von Mikronesien und Polynesien, III. No. 2.

(Bot. Jahrb. Bd. 59, 1925, pp. 2–10.)

QK
97
E 58
CYPERACEAE
Kükenthal, Georg

Cyperaceae-Scirpoideae-Cypereae.

(Das Pflanzenreich...von A.Engler. 101. (Heft IV. 20) 4.Lieferung. 1936)

QK
97
E
Heft 38
Cyperaceae-Caricoideae
Kükenthal, Georg

Pflanzenreich, Das   Heft 38 IV. 20.

Leipzig, Wilhelm Engelmann, 1909, pp 824, Figs. 128.

AS
36
S2
CYPERACEAE.
Mackenzie, Kenneth Kent, 1877–
... Two new sedges from the southwestern United States, by Kenneth K. Mackenzie ... Washington, Smithsonian institution, 1915.

1 p. l., 3 p. 24½ᶜᵐ. (Smithsonian miscellaneous collection. v. 65, no.7) Publication 2364.

1. Cyperaceae. 2. Botany—Southwest, New.   15–26310

Library of Congress   Q11.S7 vol. 65, no. 7
——— Copy 2.   QK495.C997M2

QK
1
M 96
CYPERACEAE
Merxmüller, H.

Eine neue Gattung der Cyperaceen. By H. Merxmüller and G. Czech.

(Mitt. der Bot. Staatssammlung München, Heft 8, 1953)

QK
Botany
Pam.
1224
CYPERACEAE
Palla, Ed.
II
Neue Cyperaceen./From Oesterreichischen Bot. Zeit. Vol. 57, 1907, pp 424–425.

[Description of plants collected on the volcano Maunga-afi on Savaii, Samoa.

QK
Bot. Pam.
3076

CYPERACEAE

Raymond, Marcel

Carices Indochinenses neonon Siamenses.

(Mem. Jardin Bot. de Montreal, No. 53, 1959)

QK
1
B 97b

CYPERACEAE BORNEO

Kükenthal, Georg

Oreobolus ambiguus Kükenthal et van Steenis, eine neue Art der Cyperaceen Gattung Oreobolus aus Brisisch Nord Borneo.

(Bull. Jardin Bot. de Buitenzorg, Ser. III, vol. XIV. 1936. pp. 47-49)

QK
Bot.Pam.
2004

CYPERACEAE PACIFIC

Benl, Gerhard

Eigenartige Verbreitungseinrichtungen bei der Cyperaceengattung Gahnia Forst. (Die Befestigung der Früchte an den persistierenden Filamenten.)

(Flora, oder allgemeine botanische Zeitung. Neue Folge. 31 Bd. 1937. pp.369-386)

QK
1
F

CYPERACEAE

Standley, Paul C.

The Cyperaceae of Central America.

(Pub. Field Mus. of Nat. Hist., Bot. Ser., Vol. 8, No. 4, 1931, pp. 239-292)

AS
552
K

CYPERACEAE JAPAN

Ohwi, Jisaburo
                    -II
Cyperaceae Japonicae I. A synopsis of the Caricoideae of Japan, including the Kuriles, Saghalin, Korea, and Formosa.

(Memoirs of the College of Science, Kyoto Imperial University, Series B, Vol. XI, 1936, pp. 229-530. 21 figs., 10 pl.) ibid, Vol. 18 (1) pp. 1-182, 1944

Q
115
R 29

CYPERACEAE SAMOA

Palla, E.

Cyperaceae.

Rechinger, Karl
    Botanische und Zoologische Ergebnisse einer Wissenschaftlichen Forschungsreise nach den Samoainseln...1905. Teil II:3, pp. 66-71,1908; Teil V:pp56-59, 265, 1913.

QK
495.G74
St
984

CYPERACEAE

Steudel, E. G.

Synopsis plantarum graminearum: Pars I, Gramineae: pars II, Cyperaceae.

Stuttgart, 1855.

QK
Bot.
Pam.
3223

CYPERACEAE MALAYSIA

Kern, J. H.

Florae Malesianae precursores XXI: Notes on Malaysian and some S. E. Asian Cyperaceae, VII

(Acata Botanica, 7:786-800, 1958)

Q
115
R 29

CYPERACEAE SOLOMON ISLANDS

Palla, E.

Cyperaceae,

Rechinger, Karl
    Botanische und Zoologische Ergebnisse einer Wissenschaftlichen Forschungsreise nach den Samoainseln...1905. Teil II: 3, pp. 66-71, 1908; Teil IV: pp. 265, 1913; Teil V: pp. 56-59, 1913.

QK
495.C99
S 96

CYPERACEAE

Suringar, J. Valckenier

Het Geslacht Cyperus (sensu amplo) in den Maleischen Archipel, benevens een overzicht van de Geschiedenis der Systematiek van de familie der Cyperaceen. Leeuwarden. Hugo Suringar. 1898. sm 4to. xv + 185 pp.

QK
Bot.Pam.
3012

CYPERACEAE MALAYSIA

Kern, J. H.

Notes on Malaysian and some S. E. Asian Cyperaceae.

(Teinwardtia, 4(1):89-97, 1956)

[Florae Malesianae Praecursores, XIII]

QK
396
S 36

CYPERACEAE SOUTH AFRICA

Schönland, S.

South African Cyperaceae.

(Botanical Survey of South Africa. Memoir No. 3, 1922.)

AS
36
C 3

CYPERACEAE

Svenson, H. K.

The Cyperaceae. (Galapagos, Cocos Island and Mexico). The Templeton Crooker Expedition of the California Academy of Sciences, 1932, No. 37.

(Proc. California Acad. of Sci., Ser. 4, Vol. 22, 1939, pp. 187-193)

QK
1
A 75

CYPERACEAE NEW GUINEA

Blake, S. F.

The Cyperaceae collected in New Guinea by L. J. Brass, I, II

(Journal of the Arnold Arboretum, Vol. 28:99-116; 207-229, 1947)

QK
Bot.Pam.
3310

CYPERACEAE - THAILAND

Kern, J. H.

Cyperaceae of Thailand (Excl. Carex)

(Reinwardtia, Vol. 6(1):25-83, 1961. Reprint)

QK
Bot.Pam.
1835

CYPERACEAE

Svenson, H. K.

Monographic studies in Eleocharis, II-V

(Contributions from the Brooklyn Botanic Garden, No. 65, 1932; 68, 1934; 77, 1937; 86, 1939)

(Note: No. 1 is Contrib. Gray Harbarium, Harvard University, No. 86, 1929, pp. 121-242)

Q
115
R 29

CYPERACEAE NEW GUINEA

Palla, E.

Cyperaceae.

Rechinger, Karl
    Botanische und Zoologische Ergebnisse einer Wissenschaftlichen Forschungsreise nach den Samoainseln...1905. Teil II: 3, pp. 66-71, 1908; Teil IV: pp. 265, 1913; Teil V: pp. 56-59, 1913.

QK
Bot.
Pam.
2334

CYPERUS

Scanlan, Sister Grace Margaret

A study of the genus Cyperus in the Hawaiian Islands. A dissertation submitted to the faculty of the graduate school of Arts and Sciences of the Catholic University of America in partial fulfillment of the...doctor of philosophy. The Catholic Univ. of America Press. Washington. 1942. 8vo. 62pp. (Biological Series, no. 41)

QK
Bot.
Pam.
3197

CYPERACEAE ASIA

Kern, J. H.

Florae Malesianae precursores XXV: Notes on Malaysian and some S. E. Asian Cyperaceae VIII

(Blumea, 10(2), 1960)

QK
1
A 75

CYPERACEAE NEW GUINEA

Uittien, H.

New Cyperaceae from New Guinea.

(Journal of the Arnold Arboretum,Vol.XX,1939, pp. 213-215)

AS
750
D 67 a

CYPHOPHTHALMI

Forster, R. R.

The sub-order Cyphophthalmi Simon in New Zealand.

(Dominion Museum Records in Entomology, Vol. 1 (7):79-119, 1948)

QL
401
C 87

CYPRAEA

The Cowry

Vol. 1, Dec. 1960 -

AS
763
B-4

QL
Moll.Pam.
780

Reading
Room

CYPRAEA HAWAII

Ingram, William M.

Endemic Hawaiian Cowries.

(Bernice P.Bishop Museum Occasional Papers,
Vol.XIV, No.19, March6,1939,pp. 327-333)

QL
Mollusca
Pam. 639

CYPRAEACEA HAWAII

Schilder, F. A.

Cypraeacea from Hawaii.

(Occasional Paper, Bernice P. Bishop Museum,
Vol. X, No. 3, 1933)

QL
401
J 85

CYPRAEA

Dautzenberg, Ph.

Sur quelques déformations chez des Cypraea
de la Nouvelle-Caledonie.

(Jour. de Conchyliologie, Vol. 53:263-266,
1906)

QL
Mollusca
Pam.
1037

CYPRAEA HAWAII

Kay, Alison

On Cypraea tigris schilderiana Cate.

(The Veliger, Vol. 4(1):36-40, 1961)

QL
430.4 C9
A 41

CYPRAEIDAE

Allan, Joyce

Cowry shells of world seas. Illustrations
by the author.. Georgian House. Melbourne.
R8vo. (1956) x + 170 pp.

QL
401
N

CYPRAEA

Harris, Wray

Cypraea Tigris Linné in the Hawaiian Islands

(The Nautilus, Vol. 49, No. 2, 1935, pp.
39-41)

QL
401
H 39

CYPRAEA HAWAII

Ostergaard, J. M.

Check list of Hawaiian Cypraea.

(Hawaiian Shell News, Vol. III(2):15, 1954;
(4):35-37, 1955)

QL
Mol
Pam
#197
189
190
198
151

CYPRAEIDAE

Garrett, Andrew

Annotated catalogue of the species
of Cypraeidae collected in the South Sea
Islands, in Journ. of Conch., April,1879.

QL
Insect
Pam.
626

CYPRAEA

Melvill, James Cosmos

A Catalogue of the species and varieties of
Cypraea...Manchester Lit. & Philo. Soc., Mem.-
Proc., ser. 4, v. 1, n. 5, pp. 238-252, 1888.

QL
401
N

CYPRAEA HAWAII

Ostergaard, Jens M.

A new species of Cypraea from Hawaii.

(Nautilus, Vol. 63(4):111-112, 1950)

QL
401
N

CYPRAEIDAE

Helfer, Jacques R.

The classification of Cypraeidae.

(The Nautilus, Vol. 60:49-53, 1946)

QL
Insect
Pam.
626

CYPRAEA

Melvill, James Cosmos

A survey of the genus Cypraea (Linn.), its
Nomenclature, Geographical Distribution, and
Distinctive Affinities;..Manchester Lit. &
Philo. Soc., Mem.-Proc., ser. 4, v. 1, n. 5, pp.
184-237, 1888.

QL
401
J 85

CYPRAEA NEW CALEDONIA

Bouge, L. J.

Malformations et colorations specifiques
chez plusieurs Cypraea de la Nouvelle-Caledonie
et de la Polynesie francaise.

(Journal de Conchyliologie, 101(1):3-6,
1961)

QL
401
N

CYPRAEIDAE

Ingram, William Marcus

Cypraeidae from Christmas, Palmyra, Washington, and Fanning Islands.

(The Nautilus. Vol.51. 1937. pp.1-3)

QL
Mollusca
Pam.
1036

CYPRAEA CLIPPERTON ISLAND

Hertlein, Leo G.

Species of the genus Cypraea from Clipperton
Island.

(The Veliger, 2(4):94-95, 1960)

QL
401
N

CYPRAEA PACIFIC

Ingram, William Marcus

A new cowry Cypraea jensostergaardi.

(The Nautilus, Vol.52, 1939, pp. 122-123 +
1 plate)

AS
763
B-4

QL
Moll.Pam.
779

Reading
Room

CYPRAEIDAE

Ingram, William M.

Cypraeidae from Makatea Island, Tuamotu Archipelago.

(Bernice P.Bishop Museum Occasional Papers,
Vol.XIV, No.18, March 6,1939, pp. 323-325)

QL
Mollusca
Pam.
1022

CYPRAEA HAWAII

Cate, Crawford N.

A new Hawaiian subspecies of Cypraea cernica
Sowerby.

(The Veliger, Vol. 3:3-7, 1960)

QL
401
J 85

CYPRAEA SOCIETY ISLANDS

Boullaire, Aiu

Observations sur Cypraea capu-serpentis
Linné en Océanie francaise.

(Journal de Conchyliologie, 97(4):150; 1957)

QL
Mollusca
Pam.
778

CYPRAEIDAE

Ingram,William Marcus

Notes on the cowry, Cypraea spadicea,
Swainson.

(The Nautilus, Vol.52, 1938, pp.1-4)

QL
Mollusca
Pam.901

CYPRAEIDAE

Ingram, William W.

The living Cypraeidae of the western hemisphere.

(Bull. Am. Paleontology, Vol. 33, No. 136, 1951)

QL
401
N

CYPRAEIDAE   ADMIRALTY IS.

Ingram, William Marcus

Cypraeidae from the Admiralty Islands with therapy notes on their uses. By William Marcus Ingram and Karl W. Kenyon.

(The Nautilus, Vol. 58, pp. 129-134, 1945)

QL
401
N

CYPRAEIDAE   HAWAII

Demond, Joan

A key to the Hawaiian Cypraeidae.

(The Nautilus, Vol. 67(3):86-90, 1954)

QL
Mollusk
Pam
435

CYPRAEIDAE

Kenyon, Agnes F.

On two new cypraeidae.   From Proc. Malacological Soc. Vol. 4, pt. 2, 1900.

QL
402
G 23
locked
case

CYPRAEIDAE   AUSTRALASIA

Brazier, J. W.   (John William)

Distribution and Geographical Range of Cowries in Australasia. 8vo. 44 pp.

(Garrett collection of papers on conchology, vol. 21)

QL
401
N

CYPRAEIDAE   HAWAII

Ingram, William M.

The family Cypraeidae in the Hawaiian Islands.

(The Nautilus. vol.50. 1937. pp.77-82)

QL
Mollusk
Pam
440

CYPRAEIDAE

Kenyon, Agnes F.

On species of cypraea. From Proc. Malacological Soc. v.3, pt. 2, 1898.

QL
1
A 93

CYPRAEIDAE   AUSTRALIA

Iredale, Tom

Australian cowries, I-II

(The Australian Zoologist, 8:96-135, 1935; 9:297-323, 1939)

QL
Mollusca
Pam.
851

CYPRAEIDAE   HAWAII

Ingram, William Marcus

Hawaiian Cypraeidae.

(Occ. Papers, Bernice P. Bishop Museum, Vol. 19 (1):1-23, 1947)

QL
402
G 23
locked
case
AS
720.N
L

CYPRAEIDAE

Rossiter, Richard C.

A list of the Cypraeidae found on the coast of New Caledonia and Loyalty Islands.
(Proc. Linnean Soc. of New South Wales, vol. 6, 1881, pp. 817-831)

(Garrett collection of papers on conchology, vol. 18)

QL
Crustacea
Pam.
623

CYPRAEIDAE   COSTA RICA

Ingram, William Marcus

Two new cypraeas from Costa Rica.

(Jour. of Paleontology, 14(5):505-506, 1940)

QL
401
M 23

CYPRAEIDAE   HAWAII

Kenyon, Mrs. A. F.

On two new Cypraeidae.

(Proc. of the Malacological Soc. of London, Vol. 4, 1900-1901, pp. 68-69)

QL
401
M 23

CYPRAEIDAE

Schilder, F. A.

The cowries of Mauritius.

(Proc. Malacological Soc. of London, 34(1): 52-53, 1960)

AS
720.S
S 72

CYPRAEIDAE   FIJI

Steadman, W. R.

The cowries (Cypraeidae) of Fiji. By W.R. Steadman and Bernard C. Cotton.

(Records of the South Australian Museum, Vol. 7 (4), pp. 309-336, 1943)

AS
145
B 91

CYPRAEIDAE   HAWAII

Schilder, F. A.

Ph. Dautzenberg's collection of Cypraeidae. By F. A. Schilder and M. Schilder.

(Inst. R. des Sci. Nat. de Belgique, Mem. Ser. 2, Fasc. 45, 1952)

QL
Mollusca
Pam.
832
720.Cg
S 33

CYPRAEIDAE

Schilder, F. A.

Prodrome of a monograph on living Cypraeidae by F. A. Schilder and M. Schilder.

(Proc. Malacological Society, Vol. 23 (4), pp. 119-231, 1939)

QL
Mollusca
Pam.
778

CYPRAEIDAE   GUAM

Ingram, William Marcus

Cypraeidae from Guam.

(Nautilus, Vol. 52,1938, pp.5-7)

QL
401
J 85

CYPRAEIDAE   NEW CALEDONIA

Dautzenberg, Ph.

Revision des Cypraeidae de la Nouvelle-Calédonie.

(Jour. de Conchyl. Vol. 50:291-384, 1902)

AS
720.S
S 72

CYPRAEIDAE

Steadman, W. R.

A key to the classification of the cowries (Cypraeidae). By W. R. Steadman and Bernard C. Cotton.

(Records of the South Australian Museum, Vol. 8 (3):503-530, pl. 8-12, 1946)

QL
401
H 39

CYPRAEIDAE   HAWAII

Brock, Vernon E.

Hawaiian tiger cowries.

(Hawaiian Shell News, Vol. II(6):32-33, 1954)

QL
401
N

CYPRAEIDAE   PACIFIC

Ingram, William Marcus

Tropical central Pacific Cypraeidae.

(The Nautilus, Vol. 57, 1944, pp. 81-86)

[Mortlock Islands, Pukapuka, Nassau, Jarvis, Baker, Howland]

AS
145
B 91

CYPRAEIDAE PACIFIC

Schilder, F. A.

Ph. Dautzenberg's collection of Cypraeidae.
By F. A. Schilder and M. Schilder.

(Inst. R. des Sci. Nat. de Belgique, Mem.
Ser. 2, Fasc. 45, 1952)

AS
36
S2

CYPRINIDAE
Gill, Theodore Nicholas, 1837–1914.
The family of cyprinids and the carp as its type, by
Theodore Gill.

(*In* Smithsonian institution. Smithsonian miscellaneous collections.
Washington, 1907. 24½ᶜᵐ. vol. XLVIII (Quarterly issue, vol. III) p. 195-217.
pl. XLV-LVIII)

Publication 1591.
Originally published September 8, 1905.
Part of the plates are preceded by leaves with descriptive letterpress.

1. Cyprinidae. 2. Carp.

Library of Congress   Q11.S7 vol. 48   16–11339
———— Copy 2.

AS
36
A 65

and

QL
Fishes
Pam.
362

CYPSELURUS

Nichols, J. T. (John T.)

New Pacific flying-fishes collected by
Templeton Crocker, by J. T. Nichols and C. M.
Breder, Jr.

(American Museum Novitates, no. 821, 1935)

AS
145
B 91

CYPRAEIDAE POLYNESIA

Schilder, F. A.

Ph. Dautzenberg's collection of Cypraeidae.
By F. A. Schilder and M. Schilder.

(Inst. R. des Sci. Nat. de Belgique, Mem.
Ser. 2, Fasc. 45, 1952)

AS
36
S2

CYPRINIDAE
Gill, Theodore Nicholas, 1837–1914.
Some noteworthy extra-European cyprinids, by Theodore Gill.

(*In* Smithsonian institution. Smithsonian miscellaneous collections.
Washington, 1907. 24½ᶜᵐ. vol. XLVIII (Quarterly issue, vol. III) p. 297-340.
illus.)

Publication 1662.

1. Cyprinidae.

Library of Congress   Q11.S7 vol. 48   16–11619
———— Copy 2.

AS
36
S2

CYRENIDAE.
Prime, Temple, 1832–1903.
... Monograph of American *Corbiculadæ*. (Recent and
fossil.) Prepared for the Smithsonian institution. By
Temple Prime. Washington, Smithsonian institution,
1865.

xi, 80 p. illus. 23½ᶜᵐ. (Smithsonian miscellaneous collections. ₍vol.
VII, art. VI₎)

Publication 145.

1. Cyrenidae.

Library of Congress   Q11.S7 vol. 7, art. 5   16–5462
———— Copy 2.   Q11.S7 2d set

QL
401
N

CYPRAEIDAE SAMOA

Ingram, William Marcus

Cypraeidae from American Samoa with notes
on species from Palmyra Islands.

(The Nautilus, Vol. 52, 1939, pp. 103-105)

QL
1
H2

CYPRINODONTIDAE
Garman, Samuel, 1846–
... The cyprinodonts. By S. Garman ... Cambridge,
Printed for the Museum, 1895.

179 p. XII pl. 29ᵐᵐ. (Memoirs of the Museum of comparative zoölogy
at Harvard college, vol. XIX, no. 1)
Each plate accompanied by leaf with descriptive letterpress.
"Literature": p. ₍161₎-171.

1. Cyprinodontidae.   A 19–1057

Title from Univ. of Chicago   QL1.H375 vol. 19, no. 1
Printed by L. C.   ₍3₎

QL
483.I
C 35

CYRINOIDEA INDIA

Ochs, Georg

Gyrinoidea.

(Catalogue of Indian Insects, Part 19, 1930)

QL
401
J 86.1

CYPRAEIDAE TOKELAU GROUP

Ingram, William Marcus

Cypraeidae from Atafu Island, Union Group,
[Tokelau]

(Journal of Conchology, Vol. 21:213-214,
1938-1942)

AS
36
S2

CYPRINOID FISH
Jordan, David Starr, 1851–
Description of a new cyprinoid fish, *Hemibarbus joiteni*, from the Pei Ho, Tientsin, China, by David Starr
Jordan and Edwin Chapin Starks.

(*In* Smithsonian institution. Smithsonian miscellaneous collections.
Washington, 1903. 24½ᶜᵐ. vol. XLV (Quarterly issue, vol. 1) p. 241-242.
pl. LXIV)

Publication 1448.
Originally published April 11, 1904.
Vol. 45 (Quarterly issue, v. 1) with t.-p. dated 1903, was issued 4 parts
in 2, with covers dated 1904.

1. Hemibarbus joiteni. I. Starks, Edwin Chapin, 1867– joint author.

Library of Congress   Q11.S7 vol. 45   16–11324
———— Copy 2.

QL
1
C15

CYROCOTYLE.
Watson, Edna Earl, 1882–
... The genus *Gyrocotyle*, and its significance for problems of cestode structure and phylogeny, by Edna Earl
Watson. Berkeley, The University press, 1911.

cover-title, p. ₍353₎-468. pl. 33-48. 27ᶜᵐ. (University of California
publications in zoology, v. 6, no. 15)

The author's doctoral dissertation, University of California, 1910, but
not published as a thesis.
Thesis note is a foot-note on p. ₍353₎
"Literature cited": p. 434-437.

1. Gyrocotyle.

A 11–2021 Revised

Title from Univ. of Calif.   Library of Congress

AS
36
A 65

CYPRAEIDAE TONGAREVA

Ingram, William Marcus

Additions to the knowledge of the Cypraeidae based on the collections of the American
Museum of Natural History.

(American Museum Novitates, No. 1366, 1947)

GN
815.C
G53

CYPRUS

Gjerstad, Einar

Studies on prehistoric Cyprus.

Uppsala, n.p., 1926.   342p.

QK
358
C 59

looked
case

CYRTANDRA
Clarke, Charles Baron

Commelynaceae et Cyrtandraceae Bengalenses.
(Paucis aliis ex terris adjacentibus additis)
Calcutta. 1874. folio. 93 plates with descriptive text.

AS
36
A 65

CYPRAEIDAE TUAMOTUS

Ingram, William Marcus

Additions to the knowledge of the Cypraeidae based on the collections of the American
Museum of Natural History.

(American Museum Novitates, No. 1366, 1947)

CYPRUS ETHNOLOGY

see

ETHNOLOGY CYPRUS

QK
Bot.Pam.
2244 b

CYRTANDRA
Rock, Joseph F.

Cyrtandreae Hawaiienses, sect. Crotonocalyces Hillebr.

(Am. Journal of Botany, 5:259-277, 1918)

AS
540
P 55

CYPRINIDAE

Brittan, Martin R.

A revision of the Indo-Malayan fresh-water
genus Rasbora.

(Philippine Island, Nat. Inst. Sci. and Tech.
Monograph no. 3, 1954)

QL
Fish
Pam.
560

CYPSELURUS
Hubbs, Carl L.

The flight of the California flying-fish
(Cypselurus californicus).

(Copeia, No. 62, pp. 85-88, Oct., 1918)

QK
Bot.Pam.
2244d

CYRTANDRA
Rock, Joseph F.

Cyrtandreae Hawaiienses, sect. Microcalyces
Hillebr.

(Am. Journal of Botany, 6:203-216, 1919)

QK
Bot.Pam.
2244 c

CYRTANDRA

Rock, Joseph F.

Cyrtandreae Hawaiienses, sections Schizo-
calyces Hillebr. and Chaetocalyces Hillebr.

(Am. Journal of Botany, 6:47-68, 1919)

QK
97
C 21

CYRTANDREAE

Candolle, Alphonse et Casimir de

Monographiae Phanerogamarum: Prodromi nunc
continuatio, nunc revisio. Vol. 5: Cyrtandreae
by C. B. Clarke...Paris. G. Masson. 1883-87.
8vo. 303 pp. 32 plates. pp. 1-303.

QL
461
H 1

CYRTORHINUS

Usinger, Robert L.

Distribution and host relationships of Cyrtorhinus (Hemiptera: Miridae).

(Proc. Haw. Ent. Soc., Vol. 10, 1939, pp.
271-273)

QK
Bot.Pam.
2244 a

CYRTANDRA

Rock, Joseph F.

Revision of the Hawaiian species of the
genus Cyrtandra, section Cylindrocalyces Hillebr.

(Am. Journal of Botany, 4:604-623, 1917)

QK
Bot.Pam.
1668

CYRTANDROPSIS

Hochreutiner, B. P. G.

Un Cyrtandropsis nouveau dans les Iles
Hawaï.

(Archives des Sciences Physiques et Naturelles de Genève, Série 5, Tome X, suppl. C. R.
de la Soc. de Physique, pp. 76-77, 1928)

QL
1
C 15

CYSTOFLAGELLATA

Kofoid, Charles Atwood, 1865-
... A new morphological interpretation of the structure
of *Noctiluca*, and its bearing on the status of the *Cystoflagellata* (Haeckel), by Charles A. Kofoid. Berkeley,
University of California press, 1920.

cover-title, p. [317]-334. illus. pl. 18. 27¹ᵐ. (University of California
publications in zoology. v. 19, no. 10)
"Literature cited": p. 331-332.

1. Noctilucidae. I. Title.

Title from Univ. of Calif.   Library of Congress   A 20-302
[5]

QK
Bot.Pam.
2601

CYRTANDRA

St. John, Harold

Diagnoses of new species of Cyrtandra (Ges-
neriaceae) from Oahu, Hawaiian Islands. Hawaiian
Plant Studies 20. By Harold St. John and
William Bicknell Storey

(Bernice P. Bishop Museum, Occ. Papers,
Vol. 20(6), 1950)

QL
535.3
B 86

CYRTIDAE

British Museum of Natural History.

Diptera of Patagonia and South Chile...Part
V, fasc. 2, by F. W. Edwards. London, 1930.

QK
1
C 2

CYSTOSEIRA

Estee, Lula May.
... Fungus galls on *Cystoseira* and *Halidrys*, by Lula
May Estee. Berkeley, University of California press,
1913.

cover-title, p. [305]-316. pl. 35. 27ᵐ. (University of California publications in botany. vol. 4, no. 17)
"Originally presented as a thesis ... Master of science ... Univ. of California, May, 1912, but as published somewhat enlarged and changed."
"Literature cited": p. 314-315.

1. Galls (Botany) 2. Cystoseira. 3. Halidrys.

A 13-1010

Title from Univ. of Calif.   Library of Congress

QK
Bot.Pam.
2870

CYRTANDRA

St. John, Harold

New species of Cyrtandra (Gesneriaceae) from
the Austral Islands. Pacific Plant Studies 14.

(Occ. Papers, Bernice P. Bishop Museum, Vol.
21, No. 13, 1955. pp. 275-283)

QH
1
P 11

CYRTIDAE NEW ZEALAND

Paramonov, S. J.

New Zealand Cyrtidae (Diptera) and the problem of the Pacific Island fauna.

(Pacific Science, Vol. IX(1):16-25, 1955)

QK
567
S 64

CYTOLOGY ALGAE

Bold, H. C.

Cytology of Algae.
IN

Smith, Gilbert M. editor
Manual of phycology; an introduction to the
Algae and their biology. 1951. pp. 203-227

QK
1
A 75

CYRTANDRA

Smith, Albert C.

Studies of Pacific Island plants, XIV: Notes
on the Fijian species of Cyrtandra.

(Journal of the Arnold Arboretum, 34(1):37-
51, 1953)

AS
763
B-b

CYRTOPELTIS

Knight, Harry H.

Four new species of Cyrtopeltis (Hemiptera:
Miridae) from the Marquesas Islands.

(Bernice P. Bishop Museum Bull. 142, pp.173-
177. Issued April 18, 1938. Pacific Entomological Survey Publication 8, article 18)

QK
1
C 2

CYTOLOGY

Gardner, Nathaniel Lyon, 1864-
... Cytological studies in *Cyanophyceae*, by Nathaniel
Lyon Gardner. Berkeley, The University press, 1906.

cover-title, p. [237]-296. pl. 21-26 (5 col.) 27ᵐ. (University of California publications in botany, vol. 2, no. 12)
Bibliography: p. 283-284.

1. Cytology. 2. Cyanophyceae.

A 11-728

Title from Univ. of Calif.   Library of Congress

QK
Bot.Pam.
2810

CYRTANDRA FIJI

Smith, A. C.

Studies of Pacific Island Plants, XIV:
Notes on the Fijian species of Cyrtandra.

(Journal of the Arnold Arboretum, Vol. 34,
pp. 37-51, 1953)

QL
461
H 38

CYRTOPELTIS HAWAII

Carvalho, J. C. M.

New species of Cyrtopeltis from the Hawaiian
Islands with a revised key (Hemiptera:Miridae)
By J. C. M. Carvalho and Robert L. Usinger.

(Proc. Haw. Ent. Soc. 17:249-254, 1960)

QK
Pam
991

Cytology of the Hymenomycetes

Levine, Michael

Studies in the cytology of the
Hymenomycetes, especially the Boleti,
ex Columbia Univ. Dept. of Bot. Contr.,
vol. XI, no. 257, 1913.

See author card

QK
Bot.Pam.
2884

CYRTANDRA HAWAII

St. John, Harold

Cyrtandra nutans (Gesneriaceae) from the
Island of Maui. Hawaiian Plant Studies 24.

(Occ. Papers, Bernice P. Bishop Museum, Vol.
21(15), 1955)

QL
Amphib.
and
Reptilia
Pam.
95

CYRTORHINUS

Bufo stars in Hollywood move; Cyrtorhinus
fights in Mauritius.

(Hawaii's Sugar News, June, 1956)

QP
1
C

CYTOLYSIS

Robertson, Thorburn Brailsford, 1884-
... On the cytolytic action of ox-blood serum upon sea-
urchin eggs, and its inhibition by proteins (preliminary
communication) by T. Brailsford Robertson. Berkeley,
University of California press, 1912.

cover-title, p. [79]-88. 27ᵐ. (University of California publications in
physiology. v. 4, no. 3)
"From the Herzstein research laboratory and the Rudolph Spreckels
physiological laboratory of the University of California."

1. Cytolysis. 2. Fertilization (Biology) 3. Sea-urchins. 4. Proteids.

A 12-402

Title from Univ. of Calif.   Library of Congress
[s19c2]

QK
861
Cs
C99

Czapek, Friedrich, 1868–

Biochemie der pflanzen, von dr. phil. et med. Friedrich Czapek ... 2., umgearb. aufl. Jena, G. Fischer, 1913–

3 v. illus. 25ᶜᵐ.

Bibliographical foot-notes.

1. Botany—Physiological. (1. Botany, Physiological and structural; 2. Botany—Anatomy. 3. Botanical chemistry. (3. Chemistry, Vegetable;

Agr 13–2017

Library, U. S. Dept. of   Agriculture   463.2C99

GN
2.I
P89

Czechoslovak Oriental Institute [Prague]

Archiv Orientalni: journal of the Czechoslovak Oriental Institute.

Vol. I, 1929 –

see serial file

CZECHOSLOVAKIA   BOTANY

see

BOTANY   CZECHOSLOVAKIA

CZECHOSLOVAKIA   ETHNOLOGY

see

ETHNOLOGY   CZECHOSLOVAKIA

QL
Insect
Pam.
2128

Czeczuga, Bazyli

Ecological-physiological aspects of the distribution of some species of Tendipedidae (Diptera) larvae in water reservoir. (Title also in Polish)

(Roczniki Akademii Medycznej im. Juliana Marchlewskiego w Bialymstoku, Suplement 8:1-99, 1962)

GN
Pam.
2168

Czekanowski, Jan

Die anthropologisch ethnologischen arbeiten der expedition S. H. des herzogs Adolf Friedrich zu Mecklenburg für den zeitraum vom 1, Juni 1907 bis 1 August 1908. From Zeit. f. Ethnologie, jahrg. 1909. heft 5.

GN
Pam.
980

Czekanowski, Jan

Beitrage zur anthropologie von Polen. From Arch. f. Anthrop. bd.10, heft 2-3, 1911. 8p.

GN
651
C 99

Czekanowski, Jan

Forschungen im Nil-Kongo-Zwischengebiet von Dr. Jan Czekanowski: Dritter band: Ethnographisch-anthropologischer atlas. Zwischenseen-Bantu, Pygmäen und Pygmoiden. Urwaldstämme. Mit 139 tafeln in lichtdruck. Leipzig, Klinkhardt & Biermann. 1911. 4to. 43 pp.

2 copies

(Wissenschaftliche Ergebnisse der Deutschen Zentral-Afrika-Expedition 1907-1908 unter führung Adolf Friedrichs, Herzogs zu Mecklenburg, Band VII)

GN
Pam.
1212

Czekanowski, Jan

Objektive kriterien in der ethnologie. From Korresp-blatt der deutschen gesell. f. anthrop. ethnol. und urgeschichte, jahrg. 42, n.8-12, 1911. 5p.

GN
Pam.
2543

Czekanowski, Jan

Untersuchungen uber das verhaltnis der kopfmasse zu den schadelmassen. From Arch. f. Anthrop. n.f. bd. 6, heft 1, 1907.

GN
Pam.
850

Czekanowski, Jan

Zur frage der correlationen der muskelvarietäten. From Boas Mem. vol. New York, 1906.

GN
Pam.
1035

Czekanowski, Jan

Zur Höhenmessung des schädels. From Arch. f. Anthrop. n.f., bd.1, heft 4, 1904. 5p.

QE
502
N 56 i

D.S.I.R. handbook, 1960 edition.

(New Zealand, Dept. Sci. and Ind. Research, Information Series No. 26, 1960)

QL
Insect
Pam.
1263

DDT

DDT and other insecticides and repellents developed for the armed forces.*

(U. S. Dept. Agric., Misc. Pub. 606, 1946)

*Interim Report No. O-100 (NRC Insect Control Committee Report No. 100.) Prepared by the Orlando, Fla. Laboratory of the Bureau of Entomology and Plant Quarantine.

QL
Insect
Pam.
1263

DDT and other insecticides and repellents developed for the armed forces.*

(U. S. Dept. Agric., Misc. Pub. 606, 1946)

*Interim Report No. O-100 (NRC Insect Control Committee Report No. 100.) Prepared by the Orlando, Fla. Laboratory of the Bureau of Entomology and Plant Quarantine.

QK
455
D 11
locked
case

D., F. E.

Wild Flowers of South Australia.   Plates 1-20, with descriptive text. Adelaide. 1861. 4to.

DU
Hist.
Pam.
6

8vo.

D., F. R.

The Late Revolution in Hawaii.

(From The California) 1893. pp. 633-642.

QK
495.G 68
D 11

Dabney, Charles W.   and others

The cotton plant: its history, botany, chemistry, culture, enemies, and uses. Prepared under the supervision of A. C. True..., with an introduction by Charles W. Dabney.

(U.S.Dept. of Agric., Office of Exp. Sta., Bull. 33, 1896)

QL
Prot.-
Poly.
-am.
679

Dach, Herman von

Factors which affect the growth of a colorless flagellate, Astasia Klebsii, in pure cultures.

(Ohio Journal of Science, Vol. 40, no. 1, 1940, pp. 37-48)

QH
1
P 11

DACINI

Hardy, D. Elmo

Studies in the fruit flies of the Philippine Islands, Indonesia, and Malaya. Part L. Dacini (Tephritidae-Diptera). By D. Elmo Hardy and Marian S. Adachi.

(Pacific Science, 8:147-208, 1954)

AS
36
S2

Da Costa, Jacob Mendes, 1833-1900.

... On strain and over-action of the heart. By J. M. Da Costa ... Washington, Smithsonian institution, 1874.

iii, 28 p. 2 illus. 24ᶜᵐ. (Smithsonian miscellaneous collections. (vol. XV, art. IV))

Publication 279.
The Toner lectures, III.
Delivered May 14, 1874.

1. Heart. I. The Toner lectures, III. II. Title.

Library of Congress   Q11.S7 vol. 15, art. 4   16-6367

——— Copy 2.   Q11.S7 2d set

QL 461
H 38

DACNE

Boyle, W. Wayne

Dacne picta Crotch in Hawaii, with notes on morphology and mode of entry from Japan (Coleoptera: Erotylidae)

(Proc. Haw. Ent. Soc., Vol. 18(2):235-236, 1963)

S 17.H3
H 38

DACUS

Illingworth, J. F.

Fruit flies of Fiji.

(Haw. For. and Agric., Vol. 10, 1913, pp. 366-370)

DU 12
M 26

looked case

DAEDALUS   (ship)

Manby, Thomas

Journal of Vancouver's voyage (1791-1793); and The Massacre of Lieutenant Hergest of the Navy, Mr. Gooch, appointed Astronomer of the Discovery, and one seaman.

From the logbook of the Daedalus, store ship.

(Copied from a copy made in England by Donald Angus)

QL 1
C

DACTYLOPINAE

Coleman, George Albert, 1866–

... The redwood mealy bug (*Dactylopius sequoiæ*, sp. nov.) By George A. Coleman ... San Francisco, The Academy, 1901.

1 p. l., p. 409-420. pl. xxvii. 25½ᶜᵐ. (Proceedings of the California academy of sciences. 3d ser. Zoology. vol. ii, no. 11)
"Issued May 29, 1901."

1. Dactylopius sequoiae.

16-22022

Library of Congress   Q11.C25   vol. 2, no. 11

S 17.H3
S 3

DACUS

Pemberton, C. E.

A new fruit fly in Hawaii.

(The Hawaiian Planters' Record, Vol. 50:53-55, 1946)

AS 322
Z-v

Däniker, A. U.

Ergebnisse der Reise von Dr. A. U. Däniker nach Neu-Caledonien und den Loyalitäts-Inseln (1924/25)
1. Neu-Caledonische Flechten, von Edw. A. Wainio. ...Laubmoose von J. Thériot,...Ferns by Carl Christensen and...Orchidaceen von Fr. Kränzlin.

(Vierteljahrsschrift der Nat. Ges. Zürich, Jahrg. 74, 1929, pp. 50-98)

QL Ins. Pam. 191

DACTYLOPINAE

Quekett, John

Observations on the structure of the white filamentous substance surrounding the so-called Mealy bug (Coccus vitis) of the vine.
(From Micr. Soc. Trans. II, 1856, pp. 4, pl. I.)

QL 461
J 86

DACUS

Steiner, Loren F.

Fruit fly control in Hawaii with poison-bait sprays containing protein hydrolysates.

(Journal of Economic Entomology, Vol. 45(5): 838-842, 1952)

AS 322
Z-v

over and QKPam 2249

Däniker, A. U.

Ergebnisse der Reise von Dr. A. U. Däniker nach Neu-Caledonien und den Loyalitäts-Inseln (1924/25).
2. Neue Phanerogamen von Neu-Caledonien und den Loyalitäts-Inseln, von A. U. Däniker

(Vierteljahrsschrift der Naturforschenden Gesellschaft in Zürich, Jahrgang 76, 1931, Heft 3-4, pp. 160-213, being also Mitt. aus dem Bot. Mus. der Univ. Zurich, 137:III, 1931)

S 17.H3
H 38

and QL Insect Pam.216

DACTYLOPINAE

Whitney, L. A.

Mealybugs intercepted at quarantine.

(Hawaiian Forester and Agriculturist, vol. 20, no. 3, 1923, pp. 90-95)

GN 2.S
F 47

DACUS FIJI

Krauss, N. H. L.

Fruit flies and biological control in the Pacific.

(Trans. and Proc. of the Fiji Society, Vol. 5:169-172, 1951)

QK Bot.Pam. 2249

Däniker, A. U.

Ergebnisse der Reise von Dr. A. U. Däniker nach Neu-Caledonien und den Loyalitäts-Inseln. (1924/25)
3. Die Loyalitats-Inseln und ihre Vegetation. By A. U. Däniker.

(Mitt. Bot. Mus. Univ. Zürich, 137, 1931, pp. 133-213)

QL 461
J 85

DACUS

Clancy, D. W.

Importation of natural enemies to control the oriental fruit fly in Hawaii. By D. W. Clancy, P. E. Marucci and E. Dresner.

(Journ. Economic Ent., 45(1):85-90, 1952)

DU 400
D 12

Dadelszen, E. J. von

Report on the results of a census of the colony of New Zealand taken for the night of the 29th of April, 1906. pp. 163. Summary.

Wellington, 1908

AS 322
Z-v

Däniker, A. U.

Ergebnisse der Reise von Dr. A.U.Däniker nach Neu-Caledonien und den Loyalitäts-Inseln (1924/25). 4. Katalog der Pteridophyta und Embryophyta siphonogama, Teil I-V.
(Vierteljahrsschrift Nat. Ges. Zürich, Jahrg 77,1932; 78; 1933: Beiblatt 19, pp. 1-507)

(Being Mitt. Bot. Mus. Univ. Zurich, 142)

QL Insect Pam. 1703

DACUS

Hardy, D. Elmo

The Dacus (Afrodacus) Bezzi of the world (Tephritidae, Diptera)

(Reprinted from the Jour. Kansas Entomological Society, 28(1):1-15, 1955)

QK 936
T 85

Dadswell, H. E.

Timbers of the New Guinea region.

(Tropical Woods, No. 83, 1945, pp. 1-14)

QK Bot.Pam. 2249

Däniker, A. U.

Ergebnisse der Reise von Dr. A. U. Däniker nach Neu-Caledonien und den Loyailtäts-Inseln (1924/26)
5. Beitrag zur Kenntnis von Callitropsis araucarioides Compton, by Werner Schmid.

(Mitt. Bot. Mus. Univ. Zürich, 153, 1937, pp. 124-159)

QL Insect Pam. 1360

DACUS

A host list of Dacus dorsalis Hendel. mimeographed. 3 pp. rec'd from U. S. Dept. Agric., Bur. Ent. and Plant Quarantine, P. O. Box 340, Honolulu. 1949.

(a fruit fly)

DU 12
E 12
l.c.

DAEDALUS (SHIP)

Earnshaw, John (introduced...by)

A letter from the South Seas, by a voyager on the 'Daedalus', 1792. Introduced and annotated by John Earnshaw. Talkarra Press. Cremorne, N.S.W. 1957. 8vo. [no. 49 of limited edition] 41 pp. unnumbered.

QL Mollusca Fam. 788

Däniker, A. U.

Ergebnisse der Reise von Dr. A. U. Däniker nach Neu-Caledonien und den Loyalitäts-Inseln. (1924/26)
No. 6. Beiträge zur Kenntnis der Anatomie von Nautilus macromphalus G. B. Sow. By Franz Mugglin.

(Naturforschenden Gesell. Zürich, Vierteljahrsschrift, 84, 1939, pp. 25-118)

QK
Bot.Pam.
2250

Däniker, A. U.

Ergebnisse der Reise von D. A. U. Däniker nach Neu-Caledonien und den Loyalitäts-Inseln. (1924/26)
Nr. 7. Purpureostemon gen. nov. By Karl Gugerli.

(Fedde, Repertorium, Bd. 46, 1939, pp. 228-230)

QL
671
Co

DAFILA

Lincoln, Frederick C.

American pintail on Palmyra Island.

(Condor, Vol. 45, 1943, pp. 232)

DU
Missions
Pam.16

Dahl, I.

Der Stand der Evangelischen Heidenmission in den Jahren 1845 und 1890. Eine vergleichende missionsgeschichtliche und missionsstatistiche Rundschau. Gütersloh. 1892. C. Vertelsmann. 8vo. 136 pp.

QK
Bot.Pam.
2249

Däniker, A. U.

Die Loyalitäts-Inseln und ihre Vegetation. Ergebnisse der Reise von Dr. A. U. Däniker nach Neu-Caledonien und den Loyalitäts-Inseln,(1924-1926), Nr. 3.

(Mitt. Bot. Mus. Univ. Zürich, 137, 1931)

AS
719
A 93-m

DAGGER AUSTRALIA

McCarthy, Drederick D.

A werpoo, or bone dagger, from South Australia.

(Australian Museum Magazine, 10(9):290-292, 1952)

QK
1
F 45-1

Dahlgren, B. E.

Coffee.

(Field Museum of Natural History, Botany Leaflet, No. 22, 1938)

QK
Bot.Pam.
2258

Däniker, A. I.

Neu-Caledonien.

(Vegetationsbilder, Reihe 25, Heft 6, 1939, 9 pp., Tafel 31-36)

DU
Hist.Pam
516

Dagger said to be the one used in killing Captain Cook. IN Provincial Museum, Victoria B. C. typed copy and photo.

AS
36
A5

Dahlgren, B   E.
The development of a mollusk. A guide to the series of models illustrating the development of *Crepidula* in the Department of invertebrate zoölogy, by B. E. Dahlgren ... New York, The Museum, 1906.

32 p. incl. front., illus., plan, diagrs. 25ᶜᵐ. (Guide leaflet. no. 21)

Double pagination.
"Reprinted from the American museum journal, vol. vi, no. 1, January, 1906."

1. Mollusks—Embryology. 2. Crepidula.

7-37574

Library of Congress   QL431.D13

QK
Bot.Pam.
2249

Däniker, A. U.

Neue Phanerogamen von Neu-Caledonien und den Loyalitäts-Inseln. Ergebnisse der Reise von Dr. A. U. Däniker nach Neu-Caledonien und den Loyalitäts-Inseln, 1924/26, Nr. 2.

(Mitt. Bot. Mus., Univ. Zurich, 137, 1931 pp. 160-170)

GR
385.H
K 14

Daggett, R. M.

Kalakaua

The Legends and Myths of Hawaii...Edited and with and Introduction by R. M. Daggett. New York. 1888.

QK
936
T 85

Dahlgren, B. E.

Economic products of palms.

(Tropical Woods, No. 78, 1944, pp. 10-35)

QK
Bot.Pam.
2248

Däniker, A. U.

Die Pflanzengesellschaft, ihre Struktur und ihr Standort.

(Berichte der Schweizerischen Bot. Gesell., 1939, Bd. 49, pp. 522-540)

QL
461
A 51

Daggy, Richard H.

The biology and seasonal cycle of Anopheles farauti on Espiritu Santo, New Hebrides.

(Annals of the Entomological Soc. of America, Vol. 38:1-13, 1945)

QK
1
F 45

Dahlgren, B. E.

Index of American palms: fossil palms by A. C. Noé.

(Field Museum of Natural History, Botanical Series, Vol. 14, 1936)

Plates published in 1959.

AS
36
A 5

Daets, Gary

Meet and eat the octopus.

(Natural History, 64(4):210-213, 1955)

QL
Crustacea
Pam.
570

Dahl, Erik

Amphipoda of the family Ampeliscidae from Professor Sixten Bock's expedition to Japan 1914.

(Arkiv för Zoologi, Bd. 36 A, N:o 1, pp. 1-18, 1944)

AM
101
A 71

Dahlgren, B. E.

The Malaria Mosquito.

(Am. Mus. of Nat. Hist., Guide Leaflet, No. 27, 1908. 48 pp.)

GN
Ethn.Pam
3019

Daffner, Franz

Das Wachstum des Menschen, anthropologische studie. Leipzig. 1897. 129 pp.

GN
Pam
1753

Dahl, E

Termini technici der rinderzucht treibenden watusi in Deutsch-Ostafrika. From Mitt. Seminars f. Orientalische sprachen zu Berlin, jahr. 10, abt.3, 1907

QK
1
F 45-1

Dahlgren, B. E.

Tropical and subtropical fruits. Drawings by Albert Frey.

(Chicago Natural History Museum, Popular Series, Botany, No. 26, 1947)

Dahlgren, E. W.

Discovery of the Hawaiian Islands.

(Kgl. Svenska Vetenskapsakademiens Handlingar, Bd. 57, No. 4.   Uppsala) 1917

HHS has

QL
Insects
Pam.
1456

Dahms, R. G.

Preventing greenbug outbreaks.

(U. S. D. A. Leaflet, No. 309, 1951)

DU
620
P 22

Daingerfield, Lawrence Hite

The wettest spot on earth.

(Paradise of the Pacific, Vol. 34(12):68-71, December, 1921)

DU
12
D 13
locked
case

Dahlgren, E. W.

Les relations commerciales et maritimes entre La France et les côtes de l'océan Pacifique (commencement du XVIII° siècle). Tome Premier: Le commerce de la mer du sud jusqu'à la paix d'Utrecht. Paris. Honoré Champion. 1909. 8vo. xvi+740 pp.

Daiber, A.

Eine Australien- und Südseefahrt. 1902.

UH has

QE
33
D 13

Dake, C. L. and Brown, J. S.

Interpretation of topographic and geologic maps with special reference to determination of structure. 1st ed.

New York, 1925, pp x, 355.

DU
Pac.Pam
528

Dahlgren, Eric W.

Voyages Français à destination de la mer du sud avant Bougainville (1695-1749).

(Nouvelles Archives des Missions Scientifiques et Litteraires...Tome XIV, Fasc. 4. Paris. 1907. pp.423-568)

QK
70
D 13

Dailey, Gardner A.

Memorial gardens for the Manila Cemetery. Prepared for the American Battle Monuments Commission, by Gardner A. Dailey. San Francisco.   (1956) 4to ob. 74 pp.

QL
362
D 13

Dakin, William J.

Australian seashores; a guide for the beach-lover, the naturalist, the shore fisherman and the student. By...assisted by Isobel Bennett and Elizabeth Pope. Angus and Robertson Sydney... Reprint of 1956. R8vo. xii + 372 pp.

Dahlgren, E. W.

Voyages français à destination de la mer du Sud avant Bougainville (1695-1749) 1907

UH has

Storage
Case
5

(Misc.)

Card 1

Daily logs of parties left by the Bureau of Air Commerce on Howland, Baker and Jarvis Islands

Baker, June 19-Sept. 18, 1935
Howland, June 19-Sept. 18, 1935
Jarvis, March 25-June 15 and June 15-Sept. 14, 1935. (2 books)

Presented to the Museum on October 1, 1935, by W.T. Miller, Airways Superintendent.
  also Sept. 1935-Mch. 1936 (rec'd Mch.1936.)
                                        over

See next card

QL
1
L-J

Dakin, W. J.

General description of the coral islands forming the Houtman Abrolhos Group- the formation of the islands : Percy Sladen Trust Exped.to the Abrolhos Islands , Report 1. In Linn. Soc. Journ. Vol. XXXIV, No. 226, 1919.

DU
12
D 13

Dahlgren, Eric W.

Were the Hawaiian Islands visited by the Spaniards before their discovery by Captain Cook in 1778? A contribution to the geographical history of the North Pacific Ocean, especially of the relations between America and Asia in the Spanish period.

(Kungl. Svenska Vetenskapsakademiens, Bd. 57 No. 4, 1916)

Storage
Case
5

(Misc.)

Card 2

Daily logs of parties left by the Bureau of Air Commerce on Howland, Baker and Jarvis Islands.

Baker, June 18-August 4, 1936
Howland, June 18-August 5, 1936
Jarvis, June 13-August 2, 1936

QH
197
D 13

Dakin, William J.

Great Barrier Reef and some mention of other Australian coral reefs. Australian Travel Association. 1955 repr. Melbourne. R8vo. 133 + (2) pp.

over

Dahlgren, Eric W.

Were the Hawaiian Islands visited by the Spaniards before their discovery by Captain Cook in 1778?... (K. Svenska Vetenskaps-Akademiens Handlingar, Bd. 57, No. 4, 1916.   Stockholm)

HMCS

Q
101
P 18

Daingerfield, Lawrence H.

Kona Storms.

(Monthly Weather Review, June, 1921, pp. ?)

U. S. Weather Bureau at Honolulu must have

Noted in Pan-Pacific Scientific Congress, 1st, Honolulu, 1920, p. 437.

QL
1
A 93

Dakin, William John

Migrations and productivity in the sea. A study of the factors controlling marine organisms with some reference to New South Wales fishing problems.

(The Australian Zoologist, 7:15-33, 1931)

Dahlgren, Madeleine Vinton

South Sea Sketches. Boston: James R. Osgood & Co. 1881.

The lady went from New York to South America but never got into the South Seas!

Honolulu Academy of Arts

DU
621
H3

Daingerfield, L.H.

Some phases of the Hawaiian climate. Thrum's Hawaiian Annual. 1920, p.43-5.

QL
1
S 98

Dakin, William J.

The plankton of the Australian coastal waters off New South Wales, Part 1 By William J. Dakin and Alan N. Colefax.

(Publications of the University of Sydney, Department of Zoology, Monograph 1, 1940)

G
51
W 17

Dakin, William J.

The story of Nauru.

(Walkabout, Vol. 1 (5):33-36, 1935)

GN
550
S

DAKOTA INDIANS.
Densmore, Frances.

... Teton Sioux music, by Frances Densmore. Washington, Govt. print. off., 1918.

xxviii, 561 p. illus. (incl. music) 82 pl. on 66 l. (incl. front.) 24ᶜᵐ. (Smithsonian institution. Bureau of American ethnology. Bulletin 61)

Issued also as House doc. 853, 64th Cong., 1st sess.

1. Indians of North America—Music. 2. Dakota Indians.   1. Title.

Library of Congress   E51.U6 no. 61   18—26735
ₜₛ19f3₎

DAKOTA INDIANS · MUSIC

see

MUSIC   DAKOTA INDIANS

G
51
W 17

Dakin, William J.

The story of the Great Barrier Reef.

(Walkabout, Vol. 16(9):10-17, 1950; ibid, no. 10:29-37; (12):10-20, 1950; vol. 17(1):29-33, 1951)

GN
2.M
A

DAKOTA INDIANS.
Lowie, Robert Harry, 1883–

... Dance associations of the Eastern Dakota. By Robert H. Lowie. New York, The Trustees, 1913.

1 p. l., p. 101–142. 24½ᶜᵐ. (Anthropological papers of the American museum of natural history. vol. XI, pt. II)

1. Dakota Indians. 2. Indians of North America—Dances.

15–3012

Library of Congress   GN2.A27 vol. 11, pt. 2

DAKOTA INDIANS · MYTHS

see

MYTHS   DAKOTA INDIANS

AS
719
A-m

Dakin, William J.

The true sea-slug- Onchidium.

(The Australian Museum Magazine, Vol. 9: 141-144, 1947)

DAKOTA INDIANS

see also

SIOUAN INDIANS

QK
1
L 2

DALBERGIEAE
Bentham, George

A synopsis of the Dalbergieae, a tribe of the Leguminosae.

(Linnean Soc. of London, Supplement to Vol. 4, 1860. 134 pp.)

G
51
W 17

Dakin, William J.

Sea waves and surf beaches. A short story (with Australian examples) of the application of scientific observation to sea waves and the changes they undergo as they approach shallow water and sea shores.

(Walkabout, Vol. 15 (10):29-31, 1949)

AS
36
S

DAKOTA INDIANS   DICTIONARIES
Riggs, Stephen Return, 1812–1883, ed.
Grammar and dictionary of the Dakota language. Collected by the members of the Dakota mission. Ed. by Rev. S. R. Riggs ... Under the patronage of the Historical society of Minnesota. ₜWashington, Smithsonian institution, 1852₎

2 p. l., ₍xiii₎–xix, ₍1₎, 64, 338 p. 31ᶜᵐ. (Added t.-p.: Smithsonian contributions to knowledge, vol. IV)

Smithsonian institution publication 40.
"Dakota bibliography": verso of p. xix.

1. Dakota language — Grammar. 2. Dakota language — Dictionaries—English. 3. English language—Dictionaries—Dakota.   1. Minnesota historical society.

S 13–20

Library, Smithsonian   Institution Q11.S68

QK
936
T 85

DALBERGIA
Record, Samuel J. and Garratt, George A.

Cocobolo

(Yale University, School of Forestry, Bull. 8, 1923)

QL
737.C4
D 13

Dakin, William John

Whalemen adventurers. The story of whaling in Australian waters and other southern seas related thereto, from the days of sails to modern times. Angus and Robertson, Ltd. Sydney. 1934. R8vo. (i-vii)viii-xx + (1)2-263 pp.

AS
36
S

DAKOTA INDIANS   GRAMMAR
Riggs, Stephen Return, 1812–1883, ed.
Grammar and dictionary of the Dakota language. Collected by the members of the Dakota mission. Ed. by Rev. S. R. Riggs ... Under the patronage of the Historical society of Minnesota. ₜWashington, Smithsonian institution, 1852₎

2 p. l., ₍xiii₎–xix, ₍1₎, 64, 338 p. 31ᶜᵐ. (Added t.-p.: Smithsonian contributions to knowledge, vol. IV)

Smithsonian institution publication 40.
"Dakota bibliography": verso of p. xix.

1. Dakota language — Grammar. 2. Dakota language — Dictionaries—English. 3. English language—Dictionaries—Dakota.   1. Minnesota historical society.

S 13–20

Library, Smithsonian   Institution Q11.S68

DU
740
D8

D'Albertis , L. M.

See

Albertis, L.M. d'

QK
70
A 45

Dakkus, P. M. W.

An alphabetical list of plant species cultivated in the Hortus Botanicus Bogoriensis. (Published by) Foundation for Nature Research (Botanic Gardens of Indonesia) (Lembaga Pusat Penjelidikan Alam, Kebun Raya Indonesia) with the support of the Council for Sciences of Indonesia (Madjelis Ilmu Pengetahuan Indonesia) Bogor. 1957. 8vo. xxiii + 256 pp. (revision of "An alphabetical list..." by P.M.W. Dakkus, 1930)

AS
36
S

DAKOTA INDIANS   LANGUAGE
Riggs, Stephen Return, 1812–1883.

... Grammar and dictionary of the Dakota language. Collected by the members of the Dakota mission. Ed. by Rev. S. R. Riggs ... Under the patronage of the Historical society of Minnesota. Washington City, Smithsonian institution; New York, G. P. Putnam, 1852.

xi, ₍1₎, 64, 338 p. 32½ x 24½ᶜᵐ. (Smithsonian contributions to knowledge)

"Dakota bibliography": p. ₍xii₎

1. Minnesota historical society.

8–27015

Library of Congress

QL
951
D 13

Dalcq, A. M.

Introduction to general embryology. Translated by Jean Medawar. Oxford University Press 1957. 8vo. vii + 177 pp.

AS
36
S1

DAKOTA INDIANS
Brackett, Albert Gallatin, 1829–1896.
The Sioux or Dakota Indians. By Col. Albert G. Brackett ...

(In Smithsonian institution. Annual report. 1876. Washington, 1877. 23½ᶜᵐ. p. 466–472)

1. Dakota Indians.

S 15–435

Library of Congress   Q11.S66 1876
Library, Smithsonian   Institution

AS
36
S1

DAKOTA INDIANS   LANGUAGE
Roehrig, Frederic Louis Otto, 1819–1908.
On the language of the Dakota or Sioux Indians. By F. L. O. Roehrig.

(In Smithsonian institution. Annual report. 1871. Washington, 1873. 23½ᶜᵐ. p. ₍434₎–450)

1. Dakota language.

S 15–330

Library of Congress   Q11.S66 1871
Library, Smithsonian   Institution

QE
Geol.Pam.
1175

Dale, T. Nelson

The granites of Connecticut. By T. Nelson Dale and Herbert E. Gregory.

(U. S. Geol. Survey, Bull. 484, 1911)

MS
Case
3

Dale, W. C.
 Collection of stone and shell, implements and weapons, and pottery fragments. Collected on Guam in the years 1925-1926.
IN
Hornbostel, Hans G.
 Marianas...

QL
Insect
Pam.
2092b

Dalenius, Per
 Studies on the Oribatei (Acari) of the Tornetr\u00e4sk Territory in Swedish Lapland, IV: Aspects on the distribution of the moss-mites and the seasonal fluctuations of their populations.

 (Lunds Universitets Arsskrift, N.F., Avd. 2, Bd. 59(2):1-33, 1963)

Storage
Case
4

Misc.
Hms
54

Dall, William Healey
 Catalog of the Garrett Collection of Mollusca in the Bernice Pauahi Bishop Museum, arranged generally after the order of Tryon's "Systematic conchology". Prepared by the Curator, 1894. 4to notebook of 405 pp. ms. With annotations by William Healey Dall.

G
1
M 23

Dale, W. L.
 The rainfall of Malaya. I-II.

 (Journal of Tropical Geography, Vol. 13-14, 1959-60)

QL
Insect
Pam.
2092c

Dalenius, Per
 Studies on the Oribatei (Acari) of the Tornetr\u00e4sk Territory in Swedish Lapland, V: Some interesting species.

 (Arkiv F\u00f6r Zoologi, Serie 2, Band 16(1): 1-8, 1963)

QE
74
U

Dall, W. H.
 Tribes of the extreme Northwest, in Contributions to N. American Ethnology, Vol. I, pp 1-156. 1877 (U.S.Geog. & Geol. Survey of the Rocky Mt. region)

QL
1
S 96

also
QL
Insect
Pam.
2093

Dalenius, Per
 On the soil fauna of the Antarctic and of the Sub-Antarctic Islands. The Oribatidae (Acari).

 (Arkiv for Zoologi, 2nd Ser., Bd. 11:393-425, 1958)

QL
1
Z

Dales, R. Phillips
 The distribution of some heteropod molluscs off the Pacific coast of North America.

 (Proc. Zool. Soc. London, Vol. 122(4):1007-1015, 1953)

QL
Mol
Pam
#119
D

Dall, William H(ealey)
 American work on recent mollusca in 1881. ex American Naturalist, Dec., 1882.

QL
Insect
Pam.
2092a

Dalenius, Per
 Studies on the Oribatei (Acari) of the Tornetr\u00e4sk Territory in Swedish Lapland. (Thesis). Uppsala. Almqvist & Wiksells Boktryckeri Ab. 1963. 9 pp.

GC
1
S 43 b

Dales, R. Phillips
 Pelagic polychaetes of the Pacific Ocean.

 (Bull. Scripps Inst. of Oceanography, Univ. of Calif., Vol. 7(2), 1957)

QL
Mol
Pam
#367

Dall, William H(ealey)
 American work on recent mollusca in 1881, ex Am. Naturalist, Nov., 1882.

QL
Insect
Pam.
2091

Dalenius, Per
 Studies on the Oribatei (Acari) of the Tornetr\u00e4sk Territory in Swedish Lapland, I: A list of the habitats...

 (Oikos, Acta Oecologica Scandinavica, Vol. 11(1):80-123, 1960)

QH
Nat.Hist.
Pam.
#222

Dall, W.
 A bibliography of the marine invertebrates of Queensland. By W. Dall and W. Stephenson. and
 Queensland faunistic records, III:Echinodermata (excluding Crinoidea) By R. Endean.

 (Univ. of Queensland, Dept. of Zool., Papers, Vol. 1(2/3), 1953)

Storage
Case
4

Misc.
Hms
52

Dall, William Healey
 Catalog of the Garrett Collection of Mollusca in the Bernice Pauahi Bishop Museum, arranged generally after the order of Tryon's "Systematic conchology". Prepared by the curator 1894. 4to.notebook of 405 pp. (ms.) With annotations by William Healey Dall.

QL
Insect
Pam.
2092

Dalenius, Per
 Studies on the Oribatei (Acari) of the Tornetr\u00e4sk territory in Swedish Lapland, II: Some notes concerning the microclimate of the habitats.

 (Arkiv for Zoologi, s. 2, Band 15(nr 20), 1962. pp. 317-346)

QL
1
A 94

Dall, W.
 A revision of the Australian species of Penaeinae (Crustacea Decapoda: Penaeidae)

 (Australian Journal of Marine and Freshwater Research, Vol. 8(2):136-231, 1957)

AS
36
S4

and
QE
Pam
No.10

Dall, William Healey, 1845-
 A contribution to the invertebrate fauna of the Oligocene beds of Flint River, Georgia. By William Healey Dall.

 (In U. S. National museum. Proceedings. Washington, 1917. 23½ᶜᵐ. v. 51, p. 487-524. pl. 83-88)

 1. Invertebrates, Fossil. 2. Paleontology—Oligocene. 3. Paleontology—Georgia.

 Library of Congress Q11.U55 vol. 51 17-23852
  ——— Copy 2. Q11.U55 vol. 51 2d set

QL
Insect
Pam.
2092

Dalenius, Per
 Studies on the Oribatei (Acari) of the Tornetr\u00e4sk territory in Swedish Lapland, III. The vertical distribution of the moss mites.

 (Kungl. Fysiografiska S\u00e4llskapets i Lund Forhandlingar, Bd 32, Nr. 10, 1962: 105-129)

AS
36
S 2

DALL, WILLIAM HEALEY
Bartsch, Paul
 A bibliography and short biographical sketch of William Healey Dall. By Paul Bartsch, Harald Alfred Rehder and Beulah E. Shields.

 (Smithsonian Misc. Coll., Vol. 104, (15), pp. 1-97, 1946)

QE
75
P

Dall, William Healey, 1845-
 ... Contributions to the Tertiary paleontology of the Pacific coast. I. The Miocene of Astoria and Coos Bay, Oregon, by William Healey Dall. Washington, Govt. print. off., 1909.
 278 p. incl. 22 pl. illus., fold. map. 29½ x 23ᶜᵐ. (U. S. Geological survey. Professional paper 59)
 "A further account of the fossil sea lion *Pontolis magnus*, by F. W. True": p. 143-148.
 Appendices: I. Fossil shells from Tertiary deposits on the Columbia River near Astoria, by T. A. Conrad. II. Fossils from northwestern America, by J. D. Dana. III. Notes on shells, with descriptions of new species, by T. A. Conrad. IV. Descriptions of new fossil shells of the United States, by T. A. Conrad. V. Notes on shells, with descriptions of species, by T. A. Conrad. VI. Descriptions of fossil shells from the Eocene and Miocene

  (Continued on next card)
      G S 9—99

QE 75 P

Dall, William Healey, 1845–   ... Contributions to the Tertiary paleontology of the Pacific coast ... 1909. (Card 2)

formations of California, by T. A. Conrad. VII. Note on the Miocene and Post-Pliocene deposits of California, with descriptions of two new fossil corals, by T. A. Conrad. VIII. Descriptions of new genera and new species of fossils from California and Texas, by T. A. Conrad. IX. Description of the Tertiary fossils collected on the Pacific railroad survey, by T. A. Conrad. X. Report on the paleontology of the Pacific railroad survey, by T. A. Conrad. XI. Descriptions of certain fossils collected by Dr. John Evans, by B. F. Shumard. XII. On the Pleistocene fossils collected by Col. E. Jewett at Santa Barbara, Cal., by P. P. Carpenter. XIII. Material toward a bibliography, by W. H. Dall.

Appendices I–XII are reprints.
1. Paleontology—Tertiary. 2. Paleontology—Oregon. I. True, Frederick William, 1858–1914. II. Conrad, Timothy Abbot, 1803–1877. III. Dana, James Dwight, 1813–1895. IV. Shumard, Benjamin Franklin, 1820–1869. V. Carpenter, Philip Pearsall, 1819–1877.

—— Copy 2.   G S 9–99
Library, U. S. Geological   Survey (200) B no. 59
(a19c2)

AS 36 S4

Dall, William Healey, 1845–
    Diagnoses of new species of marine bivalve mollusks from the northwest coast of America in the collection of the United States national museum. By William Healey Dall ...

(*In* U. S. National museum. Proceedings. Washington, 1917. 23½ᶜᵐ. v. 52, p. 393–417)

1. Lamellibranchiata. 2. Mollusks—Pacific coast.

18–15658
Library of Congress   Q11.U55 vol. 52

QL Mol Pam #118 D

Dall, William Healey
    An index to the Museum Boltenianum, Smithsonian Inst. Pub. 2360, 1915.

QL 1 F

Dall, William Healey, 1845–
    ... Description of two new pulmonate mollusks, with a list of other species from the Solomon Islands, collected by Dr. George A. Dorsey. By William Healey Dall ... Chicago, 1910.

2 p. l., p. 215–221. pl. 24½ᶜᵐ. (Field museum of natural history. Publication 139. Zoölogical series. vol. VII, no. 8)

1. Mollusks—Solomon Islands.

10–8262
Library of Congress   QL1.F4 vol. 7, no. 8

AS 36 S4

Dall, William Healey, 1845–
    Diagnoses of new shells from the Pacific Ocean. By William Healey Dall ...

(*In* U. S. National museum. Proceedings. Washington, 1913. 23½ᶜᵐ. v. 45, p. 587–597)

1. Mollusks—Pacific Ocean.

14–4159
Library of Congress   Q11.U55 vol. 45

AS 36 S2

Dall, William Healey, 1845–
    Index to the names which have been applied to the subdivisions of the class *Brachiopoda* excluding the *Rudistes* previous to the year 1877. By W. H. Dall ... Washington, Govt. print. off., 1877.

88 p. 24½ᶜᵐ. (*Added t.-p.:* ... Bulletin of the United States National museum. no. 8)

AS 36 S5

Issued also as vol. XIII, art. 8 of the Smithsonian miscellaneous collections.
Smithsonian institution publication 304.

1. Brachiopoda—Nomenclature.

S 13–120
Library, Smithsonian   Institution Q11.U6

QL Mol Pam #120

Dall, Willaim Healey.
    Description of New Species of Chitons from the Pacific Coast of America.

Reprint No. 2383. Nat. Mus. Proc. Vol. 55. pp. 499–516.

Wash. Gov. Pr. 1919.

QL Mollusk Pam 434

Dall, William Healey
    Diagnoses of undescribed new species of mollusks in the collection of the United States National Museum. From Proc. U. S. Nat. Mus. v.70, art.19, Washington, 1927.

AS 36 S5

Dall, William Healey, 1845–
    ... Instructions for collecting mollusks, and other useful hints for the conchologist. By William H. Dall ... Washington, Govt. print. off., 1892.

56 p. illus. 24½ᶜᵐ. (Part G of Bulletin of the United States National museum, no. 39)

At head of title: Smithsonian institution. United States National museum.
"Books of reference": p. 54–56.

1. Mollusks—Collection and preservation.

S 13–146
Library, Smithsonian   Institution Q11.U6

AS 36 S4

Dall, William Healey, 1845–
    Descriptions of new species of chitons from the Pacific coast of America. By William Healey Dall ...

(*In* U. S. National museum. Proceedings. Washington, 1920. 23½ᶜᵐ. v. 55, p. 499–516)

1. Chiton. 2. Mollusks—Pacific coast.

20–5874
Library of Congress   Q11.U55 vol. 55
(5)

AS 36 S1

Dall, William Healey, 1845–
    Explorations on the western coast of North America. By William H. Dall ...

(*In* Smithsonian institution. Annual report. 1873. Washington, 1874. 23½ᶜᵐ. p. (417)–418)

1. Aleutian Islands.

S 15–374
Library of Congress   Q11.S66 1873
Library, Smithsonian   Institution

QL 407 H 29

Dall, William H
    Land and fresh water mollusks. Harriman Alaska expedition, Washington, 1905.

2 copies

AS 36 S4

Dall, William Healey, 1845–
    Descriptions of new species of mollusks of the family *Turritidae* from the west coast of America and adjacent regions. By William Healey Dall ...

(*In* U. S. National museum. Proceedings. Washington, 1920. 23½ᶜᵐ. v. 56, p. 1–86. 24 pl. on 12 l.)

1. Turritidae. 2. Mollusks—America.

Library of Congress   Q11.U55 vol. 56   20–9665
—— Copy 2.   Q11.U55 vol. 56 2d set
(6)

QE Geology Pam 763

Dall, William H
    Fossils of the Bahama islands, with a list of the non-marine mollusks. From Geog. Soc. of Baltimore, 1905.

AS 36 S2

Dall, William H.
    Landshells from Panama Canal Zone (new species)
    In Smith. Mis. Coll. Vol. 59 no 18. Washington 1912

AUG 28 1912

AS 36 S4

Dall, William Healey, 1845–
    Descriptions of new species of *Mollusca* from the north Pacific Ocean in the collection of the United States National museum. By William Healey Dall ...

(*In* U. S. National museum. Proceedings. Washington, 1920. 23½ᶜᵐ. v. 56, p. 293–371)

1. Mollusks—Pacific Ocean.

Library of Congress   Q11.U55 vol. 56   20–9672
—— Copy 2.   Q11.U55 vol. 56 2d set
(5)

AS 36 S2

Dall, William Healey, 1845–
    An historical and systematic review of the frog-shells and tritons, by William Healey Dall.

(*In* Smithsonian institution. Smithsonian miscellaneous collections. Washington, 1905. 24½ᶜᵐ. vol. XLVII (Quarterly issue, vol. II) p. 114–144)

Publication 1475.
Originally published August 6, 1904.
Synonymic history of the subdivisions of the family *Septidae*: p. 138–144.

1. Tritonidae. I. Title: Frog-shells and tritons.

Library of Congress   Q11.S7 vol. 47   16–10997
—— Copy 2.
—— Separate.   QL430.5.T7D2

QL 1 F

Dall, William Healey, 1845–
    ... List of a collection of shells from the Gulf of Aden. Obtained by the museum's East African expedition, by Dr. W. H. Dall ... Chicago, 1898.

1 p. l., p. 187–189. 24½ᶜᵐ. (Field Columbian museum. Publication 26. Zoological series. vol. I, no. 9)

1. Mollusks—Aden, Gulf of.

Library of Congress   QL1.F4   4–10466
—— Copy 2.   QL418.9.D14

AS 36 S2

Dall, William Healey, 1845–
    Descriptions of new species of shells, chiefly *Buccinidæ*, from the dredgings of the U. S. S. "Albatross" during 1906, in the northwestern Pacific, Bering, Okhotsk, and Japanese seas, by William Healey Dall.

(*In* Smithsonian institution. Smithsonian miscellaneous collections. Washington, 1908. 24½ᶜᵐ. vol. L (Quarterly issue, vol. IV) p. 139–173)

Publication 1727.
Originally published July 9, 1907.

1. Buccinidae. 2. Mollusks—Pacific Ocean. I. Albatross (Steamer)

Library of Congress   Q11.S7 vol. 50   16–11637
—— Copy 2.

AS 36 S4

Dall, William Healey
    Illustrations of unfigured types of shells in the collection of the United States National Museum. Proc. U.S. Nat. Mus. Vol. 66 , pp 1–41, pls 1–36, 1925. (Art. 17).

QL Mollusk Pam 618

separate

QE 75 B

Dall, William Healey, 1845–
    ... List of marine *Mollusca*, comprising the Quaternary fossils and recent forms from American localities between Cape Hatteras and Cape Roque, including the Bermudas, by William Healey Dall. Washington, Govt. print. off., 1885.

336 p. 23½ᶜᵐ. (U. S. Geological survey. Bulletin no. 24)

Bibliography: p. 9–17.

1. Mollusks. 2. Paleontology—Quaternary. 3. Paleontology—U. S.

G S 5–611
Library, U. S. Geological   Survey 654(200) D16

QL
Mollusk
Pam
464

Dall, W. H(William Healey)

List of species collected at Bahia,
Brazil. From Nautilus, v.10, n.11, 1897.

AS
36
S2

Dall, William Healey, 1845–

... New landshells from the Smithsonian African expedition, by William Healey Dall ... Washington, Smithsonian institution, 1910.

1 p. l., 3 p. illus. 24½ᶜᵐ. (Smithsonian miscellaneous collections.
v. 56, no. 10)

Publication 1945.

1. Mollusks—Africa, British East.

Library of Congress   Q11.S7 vol. 56, no. 10   11–21562

AS
36
S4

Dall, William Healey, 1845–

Notes on *Chrysodomus* and other mollusks from the
north Pacific Ocean. By William Healey Dall ...

(*In* U. S. National museum. Proceedings. Washington, 1919. 23½ᶜᵐ.
v. 54, p. 207–234)

1. Mollusks—Pacific Ocean.

Library of Congress   Q11.U55 vol. 54   19–20017
[4]

QL
430.6
D 14

Dall, William Healey, 1845–1927.

A manual of the recent and fossil marine pelecypod mollusks
of the Hawaiian islands, by William Healy [!] Dall, Paul
Bartsch [and] Harald Alfred Rehder ... Honolulu, Hawaii,
The Museum, 1938.

1 p. l., iv, [3]–233 p. illus. 58 pl. on 29 l. 25½ᶜᵐ. (Bernice P. Bishop
museum. Bulletin 153)

1. Lamellibranchiata. 2. Mollusks—Hawaiian islands. i. Bartsch,
Paul, 1871– joint author. ii. Rehder, Harald Alfred, 1907– joint
author. iii. Title: Pelecypod mollusks of the Hawaiian islands.

Library of Congress   GN670.B4 no. 153   39–13601
[3]   (572.996) 594.100069

AS
36
S2

Dall, William Healey, 1845–

A new species of *Cavolina* with notes on other ptero-
pods, by Wm. H. Dall.

(*In* Smithsonian institution. Smithsonian miscellaneous collections.
Washington, 1908. 24½ᶜᵐ. vol. L (Quarterly issue, vol. IV) p. 501–502)

Publication 1785.

1. Cavolinia. 2. Pteropoda.

Library of Congress   Q11.S7 vol. 50   16–12779
———— Copy 2.

AS
36
S2

Dall, William Healey, 1845–

Notes on *Gonidea angulata* Lea, a fresh-water bivalve,
with description of a new variety, by Wm. H. Dall.

(*In* Smithsonian institution. Smithsonian miscellaneous collections.
Washington, 1908. 24½ᶜᵐ. vol. L (Quarterly issue, vol. IV) p. 499–500)

Publication 1784.

1. Gonidea.

Library of Congress   Q11.S7 vol. 50   16–12734
———— Copy 2.

AS
36
A

Dall, William Healey

Mollusk fauna of North-
west America
in Phil. Acad. Nat. Sc. Journ. XV
pp. 241–248.

AS
36
S2

Dall, William Healey, 1845–

... New species of fossil shells from Panama and Costa
Rica, collected by D. F. MacDonald, by William Healey
Dall ... Washington, Smithsonian institution, 1912.

1 p. l., 10 p. 24½ᶜᵐ. (Smithsonian miscellaneous collections, v. 59, no. 2)

Publication 2077.

1. Mollusks, Fossil. 2. Paleontology—Panama. 3. Paleontology—Costa
Rica.

Library of Congress   Q11.S7 vol. 59, no. 2   12–35446

AS
36
S2

Dall, William Healey, 1845–

... Notes on some upper Cretaceous *Volutidæ*, with descriptions of new species and a revision of the groups to
which they belong, by William Healey Dall.

(*In* Smithsonian institution. Smithsonian miscellaneous collections.
Washington, 1908. 24½ᶜᵐ. vol. L (Quarterly issue, vol. IV) p. 1–23. illus.)

Publication 1704.
Originally published March 7, 1907.

1. Volutidae, Fossil. 2. Paleontology—Cretaceous.

Library of Congress   Q11.S7 vol. 50   16–11625
———— Separate.   QE809.V7D2

QL
Mollusk
Pam
506

Dall, William H(ealey)

The mollusk fauna of the Pribilof islands.
From Fur seals and fur-seal islands of the
North Pacific ocean, Washington, 1899.

AS
36
S2

Dall, William Healey, 1845–

... New species of landshells from the Panama Canal
Zone, with two plates, by William H. Dall ... Washington, Smithsonian institution, 1912.

1 p. l., 3 p. 2 pl. 24½ᶜᵐ. (Smithsonian miscellaneous collections, v.
59, no. 18)

Publication 2134.

1. Mollusks—Panama.

Library of Congress   Q11.S7 vol. 59, no. 18   12–35966
———— Copy 2.   QL422.D3

AS
36
S4

Dall, William Healey, 1845–

Notes on the nomenclature of the mollusks of the family *Turritidae*. By William Healey Dall ...

(*In* U. S. National museum. Proceedings. Washington, 1919. 23½ᶜᵐ.
v. 54, p. 313–333)

1. Turritidae. 2. Mollusks—Nomenclature.

Library of Congress   Q11.U55 vol. 54   19–20021
[6]

AS
36
S5

Dall, William Healey, 1845–

... A monograph of the molluscan fauna of the *Orthau-
lax pugnax* zone of the Oligocene of Tampa, Florida, by
William Healey Dall ... Washington, Govt. print. off.,
1915.

xv, 173 p. 26 pl. 24½ᶜᵐ. (Smithsonian institution. United States National museum. Bulletin 90)

1. Mollusks, Fossil. 2. Paleontology—Oligocene. 3. Paleontology—
Florida—Tampa.

Library of Congress   Q11.U6 no. 90   15–26062
———— Copy 2.   QE801.D18

AS
36
S4

Dall, William Healey, 1845–

New species of shells from Bermuda. By William
Healey Dall and Paul Bartsch ...

(*In* U. S. National museum. Proceedings. Washington, 1911. 23½ᶜᵐ.
v. 40, p. 277–288. pl. 35)

1. Mollusks—Bermuda. i. Bartsch, Paul, 1871– joint author.

Library of Congress   Q11.U55 vol. 40   11–31519

QL
Mol
Pam
#115
D

Dall, William Healey

Notes on the nomelclature of the
Mollusks of the family Turritidae, ex
U. S. Nat. Mus., vol. 54, 1918.

AS
36
S5

Dall, William Healey, 1845–

... A monograph of West American pyramidellid mollusks, by William Healey Dall and Paul Bartsch ...
Washington, Govt. print. off., 1909.

xii, 258 p., 30 pl. 24½ᶜᵐ. (Smithsonian institution. United States national museum. Bulletin 68)

1. Pyramidellidae. i. Bartsch, Paul, 1871– joint author.

Library of Congress   Q11.U6 no. 68   9–35951
———— Copy 2.   QL430.5.P95D2
[s19.2]

QL
430.5.P95
D 14

QL
401
M 23

Dall, W. H.

Note on the Oligocene of Tampa, Florida,
Panama, and the Antillian Region.

(Proc. Malac. Soc. London, Vol. 12, 1916,
pp. 38–40)

QL
Mollusks
Pam.
No.405

Dall, William Healey

Notes on the paleontological publications of Professor William Wagner.
Ex Wagner Free Inst. Trans. Vol. V

AS
36
S2

Dall, William Healey, 1845–

A new genus and several new species of land-shells collected in Central Mexico by Doctor Edward Palmer, by
William Healey Dall.

(*In* Smithsonian institution. Smithsonian miscellaneous collections.
Washington, 1907. 24½ᶜᵐ. vol. XLVIII (Quarterly issue, vol. III) p. 187–194.
illus., pl. XLIII–XLIV)

Publication 1590.
Originally published July 1, 1905.

1. Mollusks—Mexico.

Library of Congress   Q11.S7 vol. 48   16–11338
———— Copy 2.
———— Separate.   QL421.D2

QL
Mollusk
Pam
476

Dall, William Healey

Notes on American species of mactrel-
la. From Nautilus, v.29, n.6, 1915.

AS
36
S4

Dall, William Healey, 1845–

Notes on the shells of the genus *Epitonium* and its allies of the Pacific coast of America. By William Healey
Dall ...

(*In* U. S. National museum. Proceedings. Washington, 1917. 23½ᶜᵐ.
v. 53, p. 471–488)

1. Epitonium.

Library of Congress   Q11.U55 vol. 53   18–14643

AS
36
S4

Dall, William Healey, 1845–
Notes on the species of the molluscan subgenus *Nucella* inhabiting the northwest coast of America and adjacent regions. By William Healey Dall ...

(*In* U. S. National museum. Proceedings. Washington, 1916. 23½ᶜᵐ. v. 49, p. 557-572. pl. 74-75)

1. Nucella.

16-11805

Library of Congress   Q11.U55 vol. 49
——— Copy 2.   Q11.U55 vol. 49 2d set

AS
36
S4

Dall, William Healey, 1845–
On some generic names first mentioned in the "Conchological illustrations." By William Healey Dall ...

(*In* U. S. National museum. Proceedings. Washington, 1913. 23½ᶜᵐ. v. 48, p. 437-440)

1. Mollusks.

15-24783

Library of Congress   Q11.U55 vol. 48

AS
36
S1

Dall, William Healey, 1845–
Professor Baird in science. By Mr. Wm. H. Dall ...

(*In* Smithsonian institution. Annual report. 1888. Washington, 1890. 23½ᶜᵐ. p. 731-738)

1. Baird, Spencer Fullerton, 1823-1887.

S 15-687

Library of Congress
Library, Smithsonian   Q11.S66 1888 Institution

QE
Pam
#271

Dall, W. H.
Notes on the tertiary geology of Oahu, ex Geol. Soc. of America Bull., vol. 11, Feb., 1900.

AS
36
S4

Dall, William Healey, 1845–
On some land shells collected by Dr. Hiram Bingham in Peru. By William Healey Dall ...

(*In* U. S. National museum. Proceedings. Washington, 1911. 23½ᶜᵐ. vol. 38, p. 177-182. illus.)

1. Mollusks—Peru. 1. Bingham, Hiram, 1875–

11-15723

Library of Congress   Q11.U55 vol. 38

AS
36
S

Dall, W. H.(William Healey)
Remains of later Prehistoric Man.
(Smith. Cont. To Know. XXII, Art. VI. pp. 1-44. Wash. 1878.)

AS
36
S4

Dall, William Healey, 1845–
On a brackish water Pliocene fauna of the southern coastal plain. By William Healey Dall ...

(*In* U. S. National museum. Proceedings. Washington, 1914. 23½ᶜᵐ. v. 46, p. 225-237. pl. 20-22)

and

QL
Mol
Pam
116

1. Paleontology—U. S. 2. Paleontology—Pliocene.

14-10980

Library of Congress   Q11.U55 vol. 46

AS
36
S1

Dall, William Healey, 1845–
On the preservation of the marine animals of the northwest coast. By Wm. H. Dall.

(*In* Smithsonian institution. Annual report. 1901. Washington, 1902. 23½ᶜᵐ. p. 683-688)

1. Marine fauna—Northwest coast.

S 15-1136

Library of Congress
Library, Smithsonian   Q11.S66 1901 Institution

AS
36
S4

Dall, William Healey, 1845–
Report on a collection of shells from Peru, with a summary of the littoral marine *Mollusca* of the Peruvian zoological province. By William Healey Dall ...

(*In* U. S. National museum. Proceedings. Washington, 1910. 23½ᶜᵐ. v. 37, p. 147-294. pl. 20-28)

"List of the principal works relating to the molluscan fauna of the Peruvian zoological province": p. 182-185.

1. Mollusks—Peru.

11-9668

Library of Congress   Q11.U55 vol. 37

AS
36
A

Dall, William H(ealey)
On the extrusion of the seminal products in Limpets, with some remarks on the phylogeny of Docoglossa.
(Extract from Acad. Nat. Sc. Phil. Proc. 1876) in Conch. Papers. Vol. I. pp. 151-159.

AS
36
S

Dall, William Healey, 1845–
... On the remains of later prehistoric man obtained from caves in the Catherina Archipelago, Alaska Territory, and especially from the caves of the Aleutian Islands. By W. H. Dall. Washington city, Smithsonian institution, 1878.

2 p. l., 40 p. 10 pl. 32½ᶜᵐ. (Smithsonian contributions to knowledge. [vol. XXII, art. 6])

Smithsonian institution publication 318.

1. Indians of North America—Mortuary customs. 2. Indians of North America—Alaska.

S 13-94 Revised

Library, Smithsonian   Institution Q11.S68

AS
36
S2

Dall, William Healey, 1845–
Report on land and fresh water shells collected in the Bahamas in 1904, by Mr. Owen Bryant and others. By William Healey Dall.

(*In* Smithsonian institution. Smithsonian miscellaneous collections. Washington, 1905. 24½ᶜᵐ. vol. XLVII (Quarterly issue, vol. II) p. 433-452. pl. LVIII-LIX)

Publication 1566.

1. Mollusks—Bahamas.

16-11022

Library of Congress   Q11.S7 vol. 47
——— Copy 2.
——— Separate.   QL423.B2D2

QL
402
C 71

Dall, William H(ealey)
On the genus Pompholyx and its allies, with a revision of the Limnaeidae of authors.
Reprinted from Annals of Lyceum of Nat. Hist. IX, 1870. in Conch. Papers I, pp. 124-150.

AS
36
S5

Dall, William Healey, 1845–
A preliminary catalogue of the shell-bearing marine mollusks and brachiopods of the south-eastern coast of the United States, with illustrations of many of the species. By William Healey Dall ... Washington, Govt. print. off., 1889.

221 p. LXXIV pl. 24ᶜᵐ. (*Added t.-p.:* ... Bulletin of the United States National museum. no. 37)

Smithsonian institution publication 682.
"List of works referred to": p. 14-25.

1. Mollusks—Catalogs and collections. 2. Mollusks—U. S. 3. Brachiopoda.

S 13-142

Library, Smithsonian   Institution Q11.U6

QL
Mol
Pam
#375

and

AS
36
S2

Dall, William Healey
Report on landshells collected in Peru in 1911 by the Yale expedition under Professor Hiram Bingham, with descriptions of a new subgenus, a new species, and new varieties, ex Smithsonian Misc. Collections, vol. 59, no. 14, 1912.

AP
2
A 5

Dall, William H(ealey)
On the Geology of the Hawaiian Islands.
(American Journal of Science, Series IV, Vol. 17, 1904, p. 177)

AS
36
C3

Dall, William Healey, 1845–
... Preliminary descriptions of new species of *Pulmonata* of the Galapagos Islands, by William Healey Dall. San Francisco, The Academy, 1917.

cover-title, p. [375]-382. 25½ᶜᵐ. (Proceedings of the California academy of sciences. 4th ser., vol. II, pt. I, no. 11)

Expedition of the California academy of sciences to the Galapagos Islands, 1905-1906. XI.

1. Pulmonata.

19-2675

Library of Congress   Q11.C253 vol. II, pt. I, no. 11
[4]

AS
36
S4

and

QL
Crustacea
Pam. 66

Dall, William H(ealey)
Report on mollusca and brachiopoda dredged in deep water, chiefly near the Hawaiian Islands......... In U. S. Nat. Mus. Proc. 1894. pp. 675-733. illus.

GN
550
S

Dall, William Healey, 1845–
... On masks, labrets, and certain aboriginal customs, with an inquiry into the bearing of their geographical distribution. By William Healey Dall ...

(*In* U. S. Bureau of American ethnology. Third annual report, 1881-82. Washington, 1884. 29½ᶜᵐ. p. 67-202. illus., pl. V-XXIX)

Relates mainly to the North American Indians.

1. Masks (Sculpture) 2. Labrets. 3. Indians of North America—Religion and mythology.

16-5487

Library of Congress   E51.U55 3d

QL
Fish
Pam
293

Dall, W   H
Preliminary descriptions of three new species of cetacea, from the coast of California. From Proc. California Acad. Sci., 1879.

AS
36
S2

Dall, William Healey, 1845–
A review of the American *Volutidæ*, by William Healey Dall.

(*In* Smithsonian institution. Smithsonian miscellaneous collections. Washington, 1907. 24½ᶜᵐ. vol. XLVIII (Quarterly issue, vol. III) p. 341-373)

Publication 1663.

1. Volutidae. 2. Mollusks—America.

16-11620

Library of Congress   Q11.S7 vol. 48
——— Copy 2.

QL
402
C

Dall, W. H. (William Healey)

Revision of the mollusca of Massachusetts.

in Conch. Papers. Vol. I, pp. 101-120, pl. II.

QL
Mol
Pam
#117
D

Dall, William Healey

Summary of the mollusks of the family Alectrionidae of the west coast of America. U. S. Nat. Mus., Proc. vol. 51, 1917.

TORRE Y HUERTA, CARLOS de la

Sociedad Cubana de Historia Natural "Felipe Poey"

Carlos de la Torre y Huerta (datos biograficos) Homenaje en el primer centenario de su nacimiento, 1858-1958. Univ. de la Habana. 1958 8vo. 39 pp.

QL
Mollusk
Pam
444

Dall, William H(ealey)

Small shells from dredgings off the southeast coast of the United States by the United States fisheries steamer "Albatross" in 1885 and 1886. From Proc. U. S. Nat. Mus. v.70, art.18, 1927.

QL
Mollusk
Pam
589

Dall, William Healey

Synopsis of the genera, subgenera and section of the family pyramidellidae. From Proc. Biol. Soc. Wash. v.17, 1904.

AS
36
S1

Dallas, George Mifflin, 1792-1864.

Address delivered on the occasion of the laying of the corner stone of the Smithsonian institution, May 1, 1847.

(*In* Smithsonian institution. Annual report. 1847. Washington, 1848. 23½ᶜᵐ. p. 139-143)

1. Smithsonian institution—Hist.

Library of Congress   Q11.S66 1847
Library, Smithsonian Institution   S 14-5

AS
36
S2

Dall, William Healey, 1845-

Some new South American land shells, by William H. Dall ...

(*In* Smithsonian institution. Smithsonian miscellaneous collections. Washington, 1910. 24½ᶜᵐ. vol. LII (Quarterly issue, vol. v) p. 361-364. illus., pl. XXXVII)

Publication 1866.
Originally published May 11, 1909.

1. Mollusks—South America.

Library of Congress   Q11.S7 vol. 52   16-12717
—— Copy 2.

AS
36
S1

Dall, William Healey, 1845-

Theodore Nicholas Gill. By William Healey Dall.

(*In* Smithsonian institution. Annual report. 1916. Washington, 1917. 23½ᶜᵐ. p. 579-586. port.)

"Reprinted ... from Biographical memoirs, vol. 8, National academy of sciences, July, 1916."

1. Gill, Theodore Nicholas, 1837-1914.

Library of Congress   Q11.S66 1916   18-3079

GN
22
B 92

Dallas, W. S. (Translator)

Buchner, L.

Man in the past, present, and future...a popular account of the results of recent research.... London, 1872.

Q
143.8
D 14

Dall, William Healey.

Spencer Fullerton Baird: A biography

Philadelphia. 1915. pp 462; illustratio

QL
Mollusk
Pam
470

Dall, William Healey

Two undescribed California shells. From Nautilus, v.19, n.2, 1905.

QL
520
D 14

Dallas, William Sweetland

List of the specimens of Hemipterous insects in the collection of the British Museum. Parts I-II, London. Printed by order of the Trustees. 1851, 1852. sm8vo. 592 pp., 15 pl.

QL
417
D.14

Dall, William Healey, 1845-

... Summary of the marine shellbearing mollusks of the northwest coast of America, from San Diego, California, to the Polar Sea, mostly contained in the collection of the United States National museum, with illustrations of hitherto unfigured species, by William Healey Dall ... Washington, Govt. print. off., 1921.

iii, 217 p. 22 pl. on 11 l. 24½ᶜᵐ. (Smithsonian institution. United States National museum. Bulletin 112)

"Bibliography of works referred to": p. 209-212.

1. Mollusks—North America.

Library of Congress   Q11.U6 no. 112   21-26208
—— Copy 2.   QL411.D2
[6]

AS
36
S2

DALL, WILLIAM HEALEY,

Stearns, Mary Roberta, 1853-

... Bibliography of the scientific writings of R. E. C. Stearns, by Miss Mary R. Stearns, with one plate; with biographical sketch by William H. Dall ... Washington, Smithsonian institution, 1911.

1 p. l., 15 p. port. 25ᶜᵐ. (Smithsonian miscellaneous collections. v. 56, no. 18)

Publication 2007.

1. Stearns, Robert Edwards Carter, 1827-1909—Bibl.   i. Dall, William Healey, 1845-

Library of Congress   Q11.S7 vol. 56, no. 18   11-10086
—— Copy 2.   Z8836.S7
—— Copy 3.   Q11.S7 2d set

Dalle-Torre, C. G and Harms, H.

Genera Siphonogamarum ad systema Englerianum conscripta.

Leipzig, 1900 - 1907, 921 pp.

In Library of Board of Agriculture and Forestry

AS
36
S4

Dall, William Healey, 1845-

Summary of the mollusks of the family *Alectrionidae* of the west coast of America. By William Healey Dall ...

(*In* U. S. National museum. Proceedings. Washington, 1917. 23½ᶜᵐ. v. 51, p. 575-579)

1. Alectrionidae. 2. Mollusks—Pacific coast.

Library of Congress   Q11.U55 vol. 51   17-23856
—— Copy 2.   Q11.U55 vol. 51 2d set

QL
566
D 14

Dalla Torre, Dr. C. G. de

Catalogus Hymenopterum Lipsie 8°.

Vol. 1. 1894. pp. vii. 459. Vol. II. 1893. pp. vii. 140
— III 1901-2 pp. vii. 141. Vol. IV 1898 pp. vii. 323
— V 1898. pp. 598. Vol. VI 1892. pp. vii 118
— VII 1895. pp. vii 209 Vol. VIII. 1897. pp. 749
— IX 1894 pp. vii 81 Vol X. 1896. pp. 643
— I-X - Bound

L. 2.

APR 26 1904

Dallimore, William and Jackson, A. Bruce.

Handbook of coniferae,... New York, Longmans, Green & co., 1923.

UH

AS
36
S4

Dall, William Healey, 1845-

Summary of the shells of the genus *Conus* from the Pacific coast of America in the U. S. National museum. By William Healey Dall ...

(*In* U. S. National museum. Proceedings. Washington, 1911. 23½ᶜᵐ. vol. 38, p. 217-228)

1. Conus. 2. Mollusks—Pacific coast.

Library of Congress   Q11.U55 vol. 38   11-15727

QK
10
Do D14

(de) Dalla Torre & Harms H.

Genera Siphonogamarum ad Systema Englerianum conscripta.

Leipzig 1900-192

AS
36
S 2

Dalmat, Herbert T.

The black flies (Diptera, Simuliidae) of Guatemala and their role as vectors of Onchocerciasis.

(Smithsonian Misc. Coll. Vol. 125(1), 1955)

G
159
D 15
Dalrymple, Alexander

An Historical Collection of the Several Voyages and Discoveries in the South Pacific Ocean. Being Chiefly a Literal Translation from the Spanish Writers. Vol. I-II.   London. Printed for the Author. 1770.   xxx + 24 + 24 +; 204 +.(3); 84 pp.   4to.

GN
1
Ar
Dalton, O. M.

Notes on an ethnographical collection from the West coast of North America, Hawaii + Tahiti formed during the voyage of Captain Vancouver 1790-95 + now in the British Museum. In Archiv für Ethnog. X, 1897 pp. 225-245.

QE
Pam
#457
and
AP
2
A 5
Daly, Reginald A.

The coral reef zone during and after the glacial period, ex Am. Jour. of Sc., vol. XLVIII, Aug. 1919, pp. 136-159.

Dalrymple, A.

A letter from Mr. Dalrymple to Dr. Hawkesworth. 1773.

UH has

GN
Pam
#551
4to
Dalton, O. M.

On an inscribed wooden tablet from Easter Island, ex Man, no. 1, 1906.

QE
Geol.
Pam.
1132
Daly, Reginald A.

Coral reefs- a review.

(Am. Jour. Sci., Vol. 246:193-207, 1948)

DU
406
S 26
Dalrymple, Alexander

Plan for benefiting distant unprovided countries, by Dr. Benjamin Frnaklin and Mr. Alexander Dalrymple.
IN
McKinlay, A. D.
Savage's account of New Zealand in 1805, together with schemes of 1771 and 1824 for commerce and colonization. Wellington, 1939, pp. 171-180.

GN
Pam
#138
E.17
D'Alviella, G.

De la croix gammée au svastika Etude de symbolique comparée

Bruxelles 1889. 8°. pp. 291-346.

DEC 14 190?

QE
Geol.Pam
906
Daly, Reginald A.

The depths of the earth.

(Bull. of the Geological Soc. of Amer., Vol. 44, pp. 243-264, Apr. 30, 1933).

DU
12
A 33
Dalton, John Neale

Albert Victor C. Edward, Prince, and George E. Frederick E. Albert, Prince of Wales

Cruise of Her Majesty's ship "Bacchante" 1879-1882. Compiled from the private journals, letters, and note-books...with additions by John N. Dalton. London. 1886. 8vo. Vols. 1-2.

GN
Pam
#138
D'Alviella, Le Comte Goblet

Etude de symbolique comparée .

Bruxelles, 1889.

QE
Geol.Pam.
864
Daly, Reginald A.

Dolerites Associated with the Karroo System, South Africa, by Reginald Daly and Tom F.W.Barth

Extracted from the Geological Magazine Vol. LXVII, No. 789, pp. 97-110, 1930

GN
653
R 28

oversize
Dalton, Ormonde Maddock

Read, Charles Hercules

Antiquities from the city of Benin and from other parts of West Africa in the British Museum by Charles Hercules Read...and Ormonde Maddock Dalton...London. 1899. Folio.

GN
460
Da
E.12
D'Alviella, Goblet

La Migration des Symboles

Paris 1891. 8°. pp. 343. DEC 14 190?

QE
Geology
Pam
692
Daly, Reginald A.

The earth's crust and its stability: decrease of the earth's rotational velocity and its geological effects. From Amer. Jour. Sci., v.5, 1923.

GN
2.I
A-m
Dalton, O. M.

Easter Island script.

(Man, Vol. 4, pp. 77-78. 1904).

(Bibliography relating to script).

G
Geogr.
Pam. 32
Daly, Charles P.

The Geographical Work of the World in 1872. Annual address before the American Geographical Society, 1873, by Chief Justice Daly, the President. New York. Printed for the Society. 1873. 8vo. 60 pp.

QE
Geol.Pam.
863
Daly, Reginald A.

The Effective Moduli of Elasticity in the Outer Earth-Shells (Second Paper)

Reprinted from "Gerlands Beiträge zur Geophysik" - Vol. XXII. pp. 29-40, 1929.

AM
101
B 81
Dalton, O.M.

Read, Charles H.

Handbook to the ethnographical collections. British Museum. With 15 plates, 275 illustrations and 3 maps. Printed by order of the Trustees. 1910. 8vo. xv + 304 pp. (Oxford)

AP
2
A 5
Daly, Reginald A.

Comments on "Geology of Lau, Fiji."

(American Journal of Science, Vol. 243, pp. 565-571, 1945)

QH
91
D 15
Daly, Reginald Aldworth

The floor of the ocean: new light on old mysteries. The Page-Barbour Lectures at the University of Virginia, 1941. Chapel Hill. The University of North Carolina Press, 1942. 8vo. x + 177 pp.

QE
Geology
Pam.
701

Daly, Reginald A.

The geology of American Samoa. Carnegie Institution of Washington, Publication no. 340, 1924.

AS
36
A25

QE
Geology
Pam
689

Daly, Reginald A.

The geology of Saint Helena island. In Proc. Amer. Acad. Arts and Sci., v.62, n.2, March, 1927.

separate

AS
36
A25-p

QE
Geology
Pam
690

Daly, Reginald Aldworth, 1871-

... The nature of volcanic action. By Reginald A. Daly. With five plates.

(*In* American academy of arts and sciences. Proceedings. Boston, 1911. 23½ᶜᵐ. v. 47, no. 3, 1 p. L, p. [47]-122, 5 L. ▽ pl., diagrs.)

separate

I. Volcanoes.

G S 13-137

Library, U. S. Geol. survey   S(214) Am36

QE
Geol.Pam.
867
691

AS
36
A 25

Daly, Reginald A.

The Geology of Ascension Island.

(Proceedings of the American Academy of Arts and Sciences Vol. 60, No. 1, 1925   80 pp. 21 plates)

AS
36
A 25
and
QE
Geol.Pam
18

Daly, Reginald A.

The glacial control theory of coral reefs.

(Proc. Amer. Acad. Arts and Sci., 51:158-251, 1915)

[see also review by the author, "Coral reefs-a review", in Am. J. Sci., 246:193-207, 1948 and QE Geol. Pam. 1132]

QE
Geol.
Pam.
429

Daly, Reginald A.

A new test of the subsidence theory of coral reefs.

(Proc. Nat. Acad. Sci., 2:664-670, 1916)

QE
Geol.Pam.
700

Daly, Reginald A.

The geology of Ascension and St. Helena islands.

(Geological Mag., Vol. 59, no.694, pp.146-56, April, 1922)

AP
2
N 4

Daly, Reginald A.

Glaciation and submarine valleys.

(Nature, Vol. 149, pp. 156-160)

QE
Geology
Pam
696

Daly, Reginald A.

Origin of beach-rock. From Carnegie Instit. Washington Year Book, n.18, 1919.

QE
Pam
#92

428

Daly, Reginald A.

A general sinking of sea-level in recent time, ex Nat. Acad. of Sc. Proc., vol. 6, no. 5, May, 1920.

QE
Geology
Pam
699

Daly, Reginald A.

Low-temperature formation of alkaline feldspars in limestone. From Proc. Nat. Acad. Sci., v.3, pp. 695-665, 1927.

QE
Geology
Pam
709

Daly, Reginald A.

Origin of the coral reefs: a suggestion bearing on the question of the former mobility of the earth's crust under the deep oceans. From Science Conspectus, v.1, n.4, 1911.

QE
Geology
Pam
697

Daly, Reginald A.

Genesis of the alkaline rocks. From Journ. Geology, v.26, n.2, 1918.

QE
Geol.Pam
305

Daly, Reginald A.

Magmatic differentiation in Hawaii.

(Journal of Geology, Vol. XIX, No. 4, May-June, 1911, pp. 289-316)

QL
Protozoa
Polyzoa
23

Daly, Reginald A.

Origin of the living coral reefs.

(Scientia, Vol. XXII, Sept. 1917, pp. 188-199)

QE
Geology
Pam
701

Daly, Reginald A.

The geology of American Samoa. From Carnegie Instit. Washington Publ. n.340, 1924.

QE
Geol.Pam.
1117

Daly, Reginald A

The mystery of the submarine "canyons".

(Harvard Alumni Bulletin, Apr. 24,1936)

QE
Pam
#90

Daly, Reginald A.

Oscillations of level in the belts peripheral to the Pleistocene ice-caps, ex Geol. Soc. of America Bull., vol. 31, June, 30, 1920.

QE
815
M

Daly, Reginald Aldworth

Geology of the North American Cordillera at the forty-ninth parallel. Geological Survey of Canada, Memoir 38. Parts I-III. Ottawa, 1912, 8vo.

QE
Geol.Pam.
869

Daly, Reginald A.

Nature of Certain Discontinuities in the Earth.

Reprinted from Bulletin of the Seismological Soc. of America, Vol. 20, No. 2, pp. 1-52, 1930.

QE
26
N 15

Daly, Reginald Aldworth

Our mobile earth. New York. Charles Scribner's sons, 1926. 8vo. 342 pp., 187 figs.

QE
Pam
#391

Daly, Reginald A.

Petrography of the Pacific Islands,
ex Geol. Soc. of America Bull., vol.
27, June 3, 1916. pp. 325-344

QE
Geol. Pam.
1024

Daly, Reginald A.

The roots of volcanoes.

(Trans. Am. Geophysical Union, 19th Annual
Meeting, 1938, pp. 35-39)

QE
1
C 3

and

QE
Geol. Pam
1116

Daly, Reginald A.

Volcanism and petrogenesis as illustrated
in the Hawaiian Islands.

(Bulletin of the Geological Society of
America, 55:1363-1400, 1944)

QE
Pam
#91

Daly, Reginald A.

The planetesimal hypothesis in
relation to the earth, ex Scientific
Monthly, May, 1920.

QE
Pam
#205

and

DU
Pac
Pam
359

Daly, Reginald A.

A season in Samoa, ex Havard Alumni
Bull. Feb. 5, 1920.

PL
Phil.
Pam.
571

Damais, L. C.

Le malais moderne ou langue indonésienne et
son rôle dans l'Indonésie nouvelle.

(L'Education, No. 15, Mars/Avril, 1949, pp.
1-15)

QE
Geology
Pam
695

Daly, Reginald A.

Pleistocene changes of level. From Amer.
Jour. Sci., v.10, n. 58, 1925.

QE
Pam
#104

Daly, R. A.

Some chemical conditions in the pre-
Cambrian Ocean, extrait du Compte Rendu
u XI:e Congrès Géologique International

GN
Ethn.
Pam.
3711

Damais, Louis C.

Les formes de politesse en Javanais moderne.

(Bull. Soc. des Etudes Indochinoises, n.s.
Vol. 25(3):2-20, 1950)

AP
2
A 5

and

QE
Geol. Pam.
693

Daly, Reginald A.

Pleistocene glaciation and the coral reef
problem.

(Am. Jour. of Sci., Ser. 4, Vol. 30, 1910,
pp. 297-308)

QE
Geology
Pam
694

Daly, Reginald A., and Molengraff, Gustaf A.F.

Structural relations of the Bushveld
igneous complex, Transvaal: Shaler Mem. Exped.
Rept. n.13. From Jour. Geology, v.32, n.1, 1924.

AS
36
S1

Damas, Désiré, 1877-
The oceanography of the Sea of Greenland ... (A
résumé of the observations made during the expedition
of the Belgica, in 1905.) By D. Damas.

(*In* Smithsonian institution. Annual report. 1909. Washington, 1910.
23½ᶜᵐ. p. 369-383. illus., 2 pl.)

Tr. from La Géographie, Paris, vol. 19, no. 6, June 15, 1909.

1. Greenland Sea. 2. Belgica (Ship)

11-9875

Library of Congress   Q11.S66 1909

QE
Geol. Pam.
868

Daly, Reginald A.

Post-Glacial Warping of Newfoundland and
Nova Scotia.

From The American Journal of Science,
Vol. 1, pp 381-391, 1921.

Q
101
P 18

and

QE
Geol. Pam.
963

Daly, R. A. (Reginald A.)

The sub-Pacific crust.

(Proc. of the Fifth Pacific Science Congress,
Vol. 3, pp. 2503-2510, 1933)

Q
115
C 28

Damas, H.

La collection de Pelagosphaera du "Dana".

(Carlsberg Foundation's Dana-Report No.
59: pp. 1-20, 1962)

QE
Pam
171
21
AP
2
A 5

Daly, Reginald A.

Problems of the Pacific Islands.

(Amer. Journ. of Sci., Vol. XLI, Feb. 1916,
pp. 153-186. pl. 3)

QE
Geol. Pam.
865

Daly, Reginald A.

Swinging Sealevel of the Ice Age

Reprinted from the Bulletin of the
Geological Soc. of Am., Vol 40, pp. 721-734.1929.

QL
401
M 23

DAMAYANTIA

Godwin-Austen, H. H.

Further description of Damayantia carinata,
Cllge., with remarks on that genus and on Col-
lingea and Isselentia.

(Proc. Mal. Soc. London, Vol. 5, 1903, pp.
311-316)

QE
Geol.
Pam.
540

Daly, Reginald A.

Relation of mountain-building to
igneous action. From Am. Philos. Soc.
Proc. Vol LXIV, 1925.

QE
Geology
Pam
698

Daly, Reginald A.

Thirteen-foot model of the world's most
active volcano, faithful reproduction of of the
Kilauea district in Hawaii on a scale of 1-1500.
From Scientific American, Feb.9, 1918.

G
161
H
v.44,49

Dames, Mansel Longworth, tr.

Book of Duarte Barbosa: an account
of the countries bordering on the Indian
Ocean ..... written by Duarte Barbosa:....
about 1518. Translated from the
Portuguese ..... Vol I Hakluyt Society
Ser. II Vol. XLIV, 1918.

G
161
H
v.44,49
Dames, Mansel Longworth, tr.

Book of Duarte Barbosa: an account of the countries bordering on the Indian Ocean ..... written by Duarte Barbosa ... about 1518. Translated from the Portuguese ..... Vol. I Hakluyt Society Ser. II Vol. XLIV, 1918

Carter Coll.
11-C-10

DAMIEN, FATHER

Caudwell, Irene

Damien of Molokai, 1840-1889. New York The Macmillan Co. 1932. xi + 203 pp. 8vo.

RC
Path. Pam.
7

and

DU
Missions
Pam. 20

DAMIEN, FATHER (JOSEPH DAMIEN DE VEUSTER)

Hyde, C. M.

Father Damien and his work for the Hawaiian lepers, a careful and candid estimate.

(The Congregationalist, Aug. 7, 1890)

Corridor
case
43
Damien, Daniel

Kamapuaa, ka moopuna a Kamaunuaniho.

(Buke Moolelo Aekai o Hawaii, III, 3, pp. 9-16)

DU
625.4
C 63
DAMIEN, FATHER (JOSEPH DAMIEN DE VEUSTER)

Clifford, Edward

Father Damien. A Journey from Cashmere to his home in Hawaii. London. MacMillan and Co. 1889. 176 pp. 8vo. .

DU
625.4
M 14
DAMIEN, FATHER

McGaw, Martha Mary

Stevenson in Hawaii. By Sister Martha Mary McGaw. University of Hawaii Press. Honolulu. 1950. xviii + 182 pp.

Corridor
case
43
Damien, Daniel

Keiki kaukau'lii o na Pali Koolau o Maui.

(Buke Moolelo Aekai o Hawaii, III, 3, pp. 1-8)

DU
Pac.Pam.
45
DAMIEN, FATHER (JOSEPH DAMIEN DE VEUSTER)

Clifford, Edward

A few more words on the Hawaiians and Father Damien.

(Nineteenth Century, June, 1889)

DU
625.4
M 92
DAMIEN, FATHER

Mouly, R. P., SS. CC.

Le Père Damien; Chevalier de la lèpre; son heroisme, son auréole, sa survie. 3d edition. Librairie Catholique Emmanuel Vitte. Lyon-Paris. 1945. 8vo. 177 pp.

Damien, Father

The heart of Father Damien. 1955. By Father Damien and V. Jourdan.

UH has

DU
625.4
C 77
DAMIEN, FATHER

Cooke, Frances E.

The story of Father Damien. Written for young people. London. Swan Sonnenschein & Co. 1889. 16mo. 127 pp.

Carter Coll.
4-C-20

DAMIEN, FATHER

Mouritz, A. A. St. M.

"The path of the destroyer," a history of leprosy in the Hawaiian islands and thirty years research into the means by which it has been spread. Four maps and sixty nine illustrations. Honolulu. Honolulu Star-Bulletin 1916 424 pp. 8vo.

DU
625.4
D 15
Damien, Father (Joseph Damien de Veuster)

Life and Letters of Father Damien, the Apostle of the Lepers. Edited, with Introduction by His Brother, Father Pamphile. London. The Catholic Truth Society. 1889. sm8vo. 151 pp.

Carter Coll.
6-A-9

DAMIEN, FATHER

Donahue, G. J.

Damien and Reform. Boston. The Stratford Co. 1921. 86 pp. sm8vo.

DU
Missions
Pam. 57

DU
625.4
S 84
DAMIEN, FATHER (JOSEPH DAMIEN DE VEUSTER)

Stevenson, Robert Louis

Father Damien: an open letter to the Reverend Dr. Hyde of Honolulu. Sydney. 1890. 8vo. 32 pp.

The same...(with extracts from three private letters) and an introduction by Edwin Osgood Grover. Boston. 1900. sm8vo. 23 pp.

DU
623
B 97
DAMIEN, FATHER

Bushnell, O. A.

Molokai.   New York.   World Publishing Co.   c1963.   539 pp.   8vo.

fiction

Carter Coll.
11-C-11

DAMIEN, FATHER

Dutton, Charles J.

The Samaritans of Molokai, the lives of Father Damien and Brother Dutton among the lepers. New York. Dodd, Mead and Co. 1932. xiv + 286 pp. 8vo.

Carter Coll.
4-E-24

DAMIEN, FATHER

Tauvel, Philibert

Le P. Damien, apotr des Lepreux 1870-1889.

(Les Contemporains)

Carter Coll.
6-F-4

DAMIEN, FATHER

Case, Howard D. editor

Joseph Dutton, (His memoirs); The story of forty-four years of service among the leapers of Molokai, Hawaii. Honolulu. The Honolulu Star-Bulletin. 1931 242 pp. 8vo.

DU
Missions
Pam. 18
DAMIEN, FATHER (JOSEPH DAMIEN DE VEUSTER)

Father Damien . Many clippings from old Hawaiian newspapers.

DU
Pac.
Pam.
1043
DAMIEN, FATHER

Woods, G. W.

Reminiscences of a visit in July, 1876, to the leper settlement of Molokai, having special reference to Rev. Father J. Damien Deveuster. No place. No date. 15 pp.

GN
2.M
L 53

Damm, Hans

Alte Steingeräte aus Melanesien und von den
Samoa-Inseln.

(Jahrbuch des Museums für Völkerkunde zu
Leipzig, 19:8-26, 1962)

GN
4
F 72

Damm, Hans

Keule von den Banks-Inseln oder Götterstab
der Maori.

IN Von fremden Völkern und Kulturen...Hans
Plischke...pp. 215-221, 1955

Z
Bib. Pam.
53

Damm, Hans

Südsee. (Bibliography of South Seas ethnological issues)

(Ethnologischen Anzeiger, 1928:154-169;
Bd. II, 2/3, 1930: 79-103; Bd. III, 2/3, 1933:
118-168)

how many other issues appeared?

AM
Mus.Pam.
244

Damm, Hans

Die Erforschung ozeanischer Kulturen durch
das Bernice Pauahi Bishop-Museum in Honolulu
1936 und 1937.

(Ethnologischer Anzeiger, Bd. IV(5):238-
239, 1939)

GN
Pam
2735

Damm, Hans

Kreiselspiele bei den Indonesiern und
Sudseevölkern. From In Memoriam Karl Weule,
Leipzig, 1929.

GN
1
Z 65

Damm, Hans

Die Süsskartoffel (Batate) im Leben der
Völker Neuguineas.

(Zeitschrift f. Ethnologie, 86(2):208-223,
1961)

GN
663
T 44

Damm, H.

Thilenius, G.

Ergebnisse der Südsee Expedition, 1908-1910.
II. Ethnographie: B. Mikronesien, Bd. 6, Inseln
im Truk, 1935, Halbband 2 von H. Damm und E. Sarfert.

GN
663
T 44

Damm, H.

Luangiua und Nukumanu, von E. Sarfert und
H. Damm.

Thilenius, G.
Ergebnisse der Sudsee Expedition, 1908-1910.
II. Ethnographie: B. Mikronesien, Bd. 12, 1929,
1931.

GN
Ethn.
Pam.
4437

Damm, Hans

Temes nevinbur aus Süd-Malekula (Neue
Hebriden).

(Leipzig. Museums für Völkerkunde.
Jahrbuch, Band 18:87-96 + 1 plate, 1959)

GN
2.M
L 53

Damm, Hans

Ethnographische Materialien aus dem Küsten-
gebiet der Gazelle-Halbinsel (Neubritannien).

(Jahrbuch des Museums f. Völkerkunde zu
Leipzig, Bd. XVI: 110-152, 1959)

GN
662
B 29

Damm, Hans

Methoden der Feldbewässerung in Ozeanien.

IN Basel. Museum f. Volkerkunde, und
Schweizerischen Museum f. Volkskunde Basel:
Südseestudien, pp. 1-10, 1951.

GN
1
B

and
GN
Ethn.Pam.
3334

Damm, Hans

Das Tika-Spiel der Polynesier.

(Baessler-Archiv. Beiträge zur Völkerkunde,
Bd.XIX, heft 1-2, 1936, pp.5-15)

GN
Ethn.
Fam.
4058

Damm, Hans

Form und Anwendung der Feldgeräte beim
pfluglosen Anbau der Ozeanier.

(Ethnographisch-Archaeologische Forschungen
No. 2, 1954: 18-99)

[Form and use of agricultural implements
among the plowless Pacific Islanders]

GN
2.M
L 53

Damm, Hans

Mikronesische Kultboote, Schwebealtäre und
Weihegabenhänger.

(Jahrbuch des Museums f. Volkerkunde zu
Leipzig, Bd. 13:45-72, 1954)

GN
2.M
L 53

Damm, Hans

Eine "Totenfigur" aus dem Gebiete der Jatmül
(Sepik, Neuguinea).

(Jahrbuch des Museums für Völkerkunde zu
Leipzig, Band XI, pp. 91-99, 1952)

GN
662
D 16

Damm, Hans

Die gymnastischen spiele der Indonesier und
Südseevölker. 1. Teil: Die Zweikampfspiele. Mit
7 Karten. Leipzig. Otto Spamer. 1922. 4to.
vii + 133 pp.

(Staatliche Forschungsinstitute in Leipzig,
Institut für Völkerkunde. Erste Reihe: Ethnographie und Ethnologie, Fünfter Band).

"Bd.2 has not yet appeared" 3/10/59 reports the
Deutsche Hochschule für Körperkultur

DS
Asia
Pam.
79

Damm, Hans

Ein "Schiffstuch" aus Süd-Sumatra.

(Leipzig. Museums für Völkerkunde.
Jahrbuch, Bd. 17:67-72 + 1 plate, 1958)

GN
Ethn.
Pam.
4435

Damm, Hans

Versuch einer Deutung der sog. Fetische
von den Anachoreten-Inseln (Kaniet), Bismarckarchipel.

(Ethnologica, Neue Folge, Band 2:146-153,
1960)

[experiment in interpreting the so-called
fetishes of the Anachoreten Islands, Bismarck
Archipelago]

GN
2.M
L 53

Damm, Hans

Hacken- und beilartige Geräte mit Schildkrot-
klinge und ihre Bedeutung im Wirtschaftsleben der
Ozeanier.

(Jahrbuch des Museums für Völkerkunde zu
Leipzig, Band XI, pp. 64-90, 1952)

GN
Ethn.
Pam.
4436

Damm, Hans

Die sogenannten Haarkörbchen und verwand-
ter kopfputz in Melanesien.

(Acta Ethnographica, Vol. 8(1-2):63-83,
1959)

GN
Ethn.
Pam.
4434

Damm, H.

Vom Wesen sog. Leibesübungen bei Naturvölkern.

(Studium Generale, Jahrg. 13, Heft 1:1-10,
1960)

GN
2.M
L 53

Damm, Hans

　　Wie die Südsee-Insulaner Stoff aus Baum-
winnen und Verarboiten.

　　(Mitt. Mus. f. Völkerkunde zu Leipzig, Nr.
3, 1960:1-4)

QL
1
B 93

Dammerman, K. W.

　　On the zoogeography of Java.

　　(Treubia, Vol. XI:1-88, 1929)

DU
623
D 16

Damon, Ethel M(osely)

　　Father Bond of Kohala, a chronicle of pioneer life in Hawaii. Published by The Friend.
Honolulu. 1927. R8vo. ix + 284 pp.

GN
663
T 44

Damm, Hans

　　Zentralkarolinen

Thilenius, Georg   editor

　　Ergebnisse der Südsee-Expedition,1908-1910.
II. Ethnographie :. Micronesien, Band 10. 1938.
4to. 379pp.

QH
186
D 16

Dammerman, K. W.

　　Preservation of Wild Life and Nature Reserves in the Netherlands Indies.　Fourth
Pacific Science Congress, Java, 1929. (Weltevreden).

DU
Missions
Pam. 68

Damon, Ethel M(osely)

Paris, John Davis

　　Fragments of Real Missionary Life...The arrangement of the account in its present form is
the contribution of Mary C. Porter, assisted by
Ethel M. Damon. Honolulu. 1926. 63 pp. 8vo.

GN
Ethn.Pam.
3337

Damm, Hans

　　Zeremonialschemel vom Sepik ("aiser Wilhelms
land).

　　(Kultur und Rasse, Festschrift 60 Geburtstag
Otto Reches, 1939, pp. 274-289)

QL
Insects
Pam.
1162

Dammerman, K. W.

　　De rijsthoorderplaag op Java.
(with a summary in English)

　　(Mededeelingen van het Lab. voou Plantenziekten, Inst. voor Plantenziekten en Cultures,
Soerabaia, No. 16, 1915.)

DU
620
H 4

Damon, Ethel M(osely)

　　From Manoa to Punahou.

　　(Haw. Hist. Soc., 49th Ann. Rept., 1940,
pp. 5-11)

QE
301
M 71

DAMMER ISLAND

Molengraaff, Gustaaf Adolf Friederik

　　Nederlandsche Timor-Expeditie, 1910-1922...
Leiden. E. J. Brill. 1915-1922. Vols. I-III
R8vo.

QL
1
B 93

Dammerman, K. W.

　　Second contribution to a study of the
tropical soil and surface fauna.

　　(Treubia. Deel 16. 1937. pp.121-147)

DU
Missions
Pam. 63

Damon, Ethel Moseley

　　Hawaiian Mission Centennial Historical
Pageant. Text by Ethel Moseley Damon. Music by
Jane Lathrop Winne. 1921c.　8vo.　39 pp.

2 copies

Dammermann, K. W.

　　Agricultural zoology of the Malay Peninsula.
(includes Philippines)   Amsterdam. 1929
Debussy (publisher)

　　　　HSPA   has

DU
Hist. Fam.
318

Damon, Ethel M.

　　Art at Lahainaluna.

　　(The Friend, July 1931:153-155)

DU
620
F

Damon, Ethel M(osely)

　　A historical view of the Kamehameha Schools,
prepared for the Fortieth Anniversary at the request of President Frank E. Midkiff, by Ethel M.
Damon and Josephine Sullivan.

　　(The Friend, Vol. 98, 1928, No. 12)

AS
522
N 28

Dammerman, K. W.

　　Geschiedenis van de Natuurbescherming in
Indonesia.

　　(Chronica Naturae, 106(5):216-228, 1950)

Hma.
La11.
La 11

Storage
Case
5

Damon, Ethel M(osely)

　　Copy of interleaves in Hawaiian dictionary of Rev. Elias Bond, missionary at
Kohala, Hawaii, 1841- 1896. To accompany
corresponding emendations and key letters
copied from Mr. Bond's dictionary into the
Kaiulani copy, Andrews 1865, belonging to
the Bernice P. Bishop Museum [in 9 note
books and accompanied by emended copy of
Andrews' Dictionary (B.Mus. "Kaiulani"
copy)]

DU
623
D 16

Damon, Ethel M(osely)

　　Koamalu: A Story of Pioneers on Kauai and of
What They Built in That Island Garden. In two
volumes. Volumes 1-2. Honolulu. Privately
Printed. 1931. 493 + 976 pp. 8vo.

Q
101
P 18

Dammerman, K. W.

　　Krakatau's New Fauna.

Krakatau. Part 3. (Fourth Pacific Science Congress, 1929)　pp. 83-118

DU
Hist.
Pam.
406

Damon, Ethel M.   editor

　　Early Hawaiian churches and their manner of
building.　(Honolulu, April, 1924) 8vo. 51 pp

　　[this is second edition; first ed. was 1920]

DU
620
F

Damon, Ethel M(osely)

　　Legends of Ka-Puna-Hou, by Ethel M. Damon and
Joseph S. Emerson.

　　(Friend, March 1924, pp. 73-74)

DU
625.4
W 66

Damon, Ethel M., editor

Wilcox, Abner   and others

Letters from the life of Abner and Lucy Wilcox, 1836-1869. Edited by Ethel M. Damon. Waioli sketch book by Juliette May Fraser. Privately printed. Honolulu, 1950. 8vo. (10)+ 402 pp.

DU
623
D 16

Damon, Ethel M.

The stone church at Kawaiahao, 1820-1944. Published by the Trustees of Kawaiahao Church. Honolulu, 1945. 8vo. (6) + 152 pp.

DU
620
F

Damon, Samuel Chenery

Kings of Hawaii. (with illustrations)

(The Friend, Feb. 1, 1876, pp. 9-12.)

DU
Hist.Pam
7

(Illus. Christian Weekly, Vol. 5, No. 2, p.14, 1875. Article condensed from above)

DU
Missions
Pam. 69

Damon, Ethel M(osely)

Lyman House Memorial. David Belden Lyman, Sarah Joiner Lyman.

2 copies

DU
Missions
Pam.
86

Damon, Ethel M.

The story of founding of Kawaiahao Church; struggles of early days...

(The Honolulu Advertiser, July 22, 1942)

G
7
A 51

Damon, S. C.

Lahaina Chaplaincy. U. S. Hospital.

(Sailor's Magazine. Vol. 21, 1849. pp. 216-217).

PL
Phil. Pam.
467

Damon, Ethel M(osely)

Na Himeni Hawaii, a record of hymns in the Hawaiian language. Honolulu, 1935, 38 pp.

DU
620
F

Damon, F. W.

A sheaf of old letters. (1815, 1818).

(Friend, October 1906, pp. 6-8)

(Information about Obookiah)

DU
620
F

(Damon, Samuel Chenery)

Morning Star Papers: or, Glimpses and glances at the sights, scenes and people of Micronesia, seen and sketched by the editor during the fifth trip of the "Morning Star".

(Friend, Sept.,1861, pp.42-45; 50-55; Oct.,pp. 58-63; 66-71; Nov.,pp.74-78).

DU
Missions
Pam 72

DU
Hist.
Pam. 9

Damon, Ethel Moseley

One Hundred Years of Christian Civilization in Hawaii. A Historical Pageant Commemorating the Arrival of the First Missionaries on Hawaiian Shores. Text by Ethel Moseley Damon, Music by Jane Lathrop Winne. 1920. Honolulu. 24 pp. 8vo.

DU
620
F

[Damon, S. C.   editor]

Andrew Garrett, American naturalist.

(Friend, Oct. 13, 1858, p. 76; and Aug. 1863, p. 57)

DU
Missions
Pam. 6

Damon, Samuel C.

Puritan Missions in the Pacific: a Discourse delivered at Honolulu, (S. I.) on the Anniversary of the Hawaiian Evangelical Association, June 17, 1866. First American Edition, Edited by H. Bingham. New Haven. J. Hunnewell. 1869. 48 pp. 12mo.

(Also 1866 edition, Honolulu. Printed for the Hawaiian Evangelical Association)

over

DU
625.4
D 16

Damon, Ethel M.

Sanford Ballard Dole and his Hawaii. With an analysis of Justice Dole's legal opinions, by Samuel B. Kemp. Published for the Hawaiian Historical Society, by Pacific Books. Palo Alto R8vo. 1957c   xiv + 394 pp.

DU
620
F

Damon, Samuel Chenery

Ascent of Haleakala.

(Friend, August, 1847, pp.116-117)

DU
620
F

looked case.

Damon, Samuel Chenery   editor

The Temperance Advocate and Seamen's Friend. Edited and published by Samuel C. Damon. Honolulu. 1843-

Continued as the Friend.

DU
625
D 16

Damon, Ethel M.

The seventy-fifth anniversary pageant, Punahou. Illustrated by J. May Fraser and Jessie C. Shaw. June 21, 1916. R8vo. 77 pp.

DU
625.4
D 16

Damon, Samuel Chenery

Damon Memorial; or Notices of Three Damon Families who came from Old England to New England in the XVIIth Century. Honolulu. 1882. xii + 146 pp. 8vo.

DU
620
F

Damon, Samuel Chenery

To the memory of the Rev. William Ellis and Mrs. Sarah S. Ellis...

(Friend, August 1872, pp. 65-67)

DU
Missions
Pam.
91

Damon, Ethel M.

Siloama, the church of the healing spring; the story of certain almost forgotten Protestant churches. Gathered together by Ethel M. Damon, and due in part to the prompting of the Woman's Board of Missions for the Pacific Islands. Published by the Hawaiian Board of Missions. Honolulu. 1948. 8vo. 104 pp.

G
7
A 51

Damon, S. C. (Samuel Chenery)

Honolulu Chaplaincy, Interesting Journal.

(Sailor's Magazine,Vol. 21, 1849, pp. 197-200, 232-236)

DU
620
F

Damon, Samuel Chenery

Tribute to the memory of Rev. Artemas Bishop.

(Friend, Jan.,1873, pp.1-3)

Card 1 (row 1, col 1):

DU
Hist.
Pam.
23

Damon, S. C.

　　A Tribute to the memory of Hon. William L.
Lee, late Chief Justice of the Hawaiian kingdom.
Honolulu. H.M.Whitney's Press. 1857. 21 pp.
8vo.

and
DU
620
M 67

　　(Misc. Pams. Haw. II: 1-21)

Card 2 (row 1, col 2):

G
159
D 16

Dampier, William

　　A collection of voyages, in four volumes...
Illustrated with maps and draughts: also several
birds, fishes, and plants, not found in this
part of the world: curiously engraven on copper-
plates. London, James and John Knapton. 1729.
8vo.

Card 3 (row 1, col 3):

QE
526
D2

AP
2
A5

Dana, Edward S.

　　Petrography of the Sandwich Islands.
From the Am. Journ. Sc. XXXVII, 1889.
pp. 441-467. (Bound with James Dana's paper
on the Hawaiian Volcanoes) Pl. XIV.

Card 4 (row 2, col 1):

DU
620
F

DAMON, SAMUEL CHENERY

　　Editorial tribute on the death of S. C. Damon

　　(Friend, March 1885, pp. 4-8)

Card 5 (row 2, col 2):

Dampier, William

　　Dampier's Voyages. Edited by John
Masefield. Two Vols. London: E. Grant
Richards. 1906.

Honolulu Academy of Arts

Card 6 (row 2, col 3):

Dana, E. S.　　and others

　　A century of science in America, with special
reference to the American Journal of Science,
1818-1918. (Silliman Mem. Lectures, Vol. XIV)
1918. Yale Univ. Press.

UH

Card 7 (row 3, col 1):

DU
12
W 29

DAMON, SAMUEL C.

Warinner, Emily V.

　　Voyager to destiny. The amazing adventures
of Manjiro, the man who changed worlds twice...
The Bobbs-Merrill Company, Inc. Indianapolis,
New York. 8vo. (1956c) 267 pp.

Card 8 (row 3, col 2):

G
159
C 15

Dampier, William

Callander, John

　　Terra Australis Cognita...Vol. 2, pp. 556-
673: William Dampier, to Magellanica and Polynesia. Edinburgh. 1768.

　　and Vol. 3, pp. 66-143: William Dampier's
last voyage to Australasia.

Card 9 (row 3, col 3):

AP
2
A 5

Dana, Edward S.

　　Contributions to the petrography of the
Sandwich Islands.

　　(Amer. Journ. Science, Vol. 37, 1889, 3rd
series, pp. 441-467)

Card 10 (row 4, col 1):

Z
Bib. Pam.
67

DAMON, S. M.

　　Books of Hawaiian or Pacific interest in
the library of S. M. Damon, Moanalua, Oahu.

Card 11 (row 4, col 2):

DU
12
A 43

DAMPIER, WILLIAM

　　Allgemeine Historie der Reisen zu Wasser und
zu Lande; oder Sammlung aller Reisebeschreibungen
...in Europa, Asia, Africa und America...Bd. 12.
Leipzig. 1754. R8vo. pp. 222-253; 343-447.

Card 12 (row 4, col 3):

GH
Pam
#577

Dana, Francis Marion

　　The ritual significance of yellow
among the Romans.

　　Philadelphia, 1919,

Card 13 (row 5, col 1):

DU
625.4
D 16

DAMON FAMILY

Damon, Samuel Chenery

　　Damon Memorial; or Notices of Three Damon
Families who came from Old England to New England
in the XVIIth Century. Honolulu. 1882. xii +
146 pp. 8vo.

Card 14 (row 5, col 2):

DU
12
B 96
looked
case

DAMPIER, WILLIAM

Burney, James

　　Chronological history of the discoveries in
the South Sea or Pacific Ocean...London. 1803-
1817.　4to. 5 vols.
　　Vol. 4, pp. 389-448.

Card 15 (row 5, col 3):

AP
2
A 5

Dana, James D(wight)

　　(Acknowledgments of J. D. Dana and J. P.
Couthouy, relative to a charge of plagiarism)

　　(Am. Journal of Sci., Ser. 1, Vol. 47,1844,
pp. 122-126)

Card 16 (row 6, col 1):

AM
101
H 77

DAMPIER, ROBERT

　　New light on Dampier.

　　(Honolulu Academy of Arts, News Bull. and
Calendar, XIII(4):6, 1951)

　　[notes sent in by Ray Jerome Baker]

Card 17 (row 6, col 2):

DAMPIER, WILLIAM

　　Lives and voyages of Drake, Cavendish and
Dampier... Edinburgh. Oliver and Boyd... 1831
12mo. 461 pp.

Card 18 (row 6, col 3):

QE
526
D16

Dana, James Dwight.

　　Characteristics of volcanoes with
contributions of facts and principles
from the Hawaiian Islands.

　　New York. 1891. pp xvi, 399.

Card 19 (row 7, col 1):

AM
101
H 77

DAMPIER, ROBERT

(Griffing, Robert P., Jr.)

　　Two royal portraits.

　　(Honolulu Academy of Arts, News Bull. and
Calendar, XIII(2):1-3, 1951)

　　[Prince Kauikeaouli and Princess Nahienaena,
by Robert Dampier (1825)]

Card 20 (row 7, col 2):

AP
2
N 4

DAMPIER, WILLIAM

Matthews, L. Harrison

Dampier: Pirate and Naturlist.

　　(Nature, Vol. 170 (4323):408-409)1952.

Card 21 (row 7, col 3):

AP
2
A 5
and
AS
36
A 25
over

Dana, James Dwight

　　Conspectus Crustaceorum in orbis terrarum
circumnavigatione, C. Wilkes e classe Reipublicae
Foederatae duce, collectorum auctore J. D. Dana.
　　(Proc. Am. Acad. Arts and Sci., I, 1846-48,
149-155; II, 9-61,201-220; Am.J.Sci., Ser. 2,Vol.
VIII,1849,424-428;IX,1850,129-133; XI,1851,268-
274)
　　(QL Crustacea Pam. no. 67 is a separate of
the Isopoda, A.J/S.A., Ser. 2, Vol. 8,1849:424-
427)

QE
565
D16

Dana, James Dwight, 1813-1895.
Corals and coral islands. By James D. Dana ... New York, Dodd & Mead, 1872.

398 p. col. front., illus., plates, maps (part fold.) 25½ᵐ.
"List of works and memoirs referred to": p. [389]-390.

1. Coral reefs and islands. 2. Corals.
Title
6—13394

Library of Congress   QE565.D15

AS
36
A3

Dana, J. D. (James Dwight)
Isolation of volcanic action in Hawaii
In Am .Assoc. Adv. Sc. Proc. II for 1849, pp. 95 - 100. Boston, 1850, Reprinted Salem , Mass, 1885.

[See Wilkes Exped. Dana for fuller report]

AP
2
A 5

Dana, James Dwight
Note on the eruption of Mauna Loa, (February, 1852)
(Am. J. of Sci., Ser. 2, Vol. 14, 1852, pp. 254-257)

Q
115
U 58

locked
case

Dana, James Dwight
Crustacea
United States Exploring Expedition, during the years 1838, 1839, 1840, 1841, 1842, under the command of Charles Wilkes. Vols: 13-14:Crustacea, by James D. Dana. With a folio atlas of 96 plates. 1852-53.

QE
Geol.
Pam.1058

Dana, James Dwight
Hoffmeister, J. Edward
James Dwight Dana's studies of volcanoes and of coral islands.
(Proc. of the Am. Philosophical Soc., Vol. 82, 1940, pp. 721-732)

AP
2
A 5

Dana, James Dwight
On a new genus of Crustacea in the collections of the U. S. Exploring Expedition under Capt. C. Wilkes, U. S. N.
(Am. J. of Sci., Ser. 2, Vol. XI, 1851, pp. 223-224)

AP
2
A 5

Dana, James Dwight
A dissected volcanic mountain; some of its revelations.
(Am. Jour. of Sci., Ser. 3, Vol. 32, 1886, pp. 247-255)

QE
Geol.
Pam.
279

Dana, James D.
Kilauea after the eruption of March, 1886; communications to Prof. W. D. Alexander, Surveyor General of the Hawaiian Islands, by...J.S.Emerson, L. L. Van Slyke and F. S. Dodge.
(American Jour. of Science, 33:87-115, 1887)

AP
2
A 5

Dana, James Dwight
On an isothermal oceanic chart, illustrating the geographical distribution of marine animals.
(Am. Jour. Sci., Ser. 2, Vol. 16, 1853, pp. 153-167, 314-327)

AP
2
A 5

Dana, James Dwight
Eruption at Kilauea, Hawaii, in March, 1886.
(Am. Jour. of Sci., Ser. 3, Vol. 31, 1886, pp. 397-398)

QE
26
D16

Dana, James D(wight)
Manual of geology: treating of the principles of the science with special reference to American geological history.
New York, American Book Company, 1895.   1087p.

QE
565
D 16

Carter
Coll.
10-C-4
4-B-22

Dana, James D(wight)
On coral reefs and islands. By James D. Dana...
N.Y. Putnam, 1853. 143p. illus. map.

1872 Edition
1875

AP
2
A 5

Dana, James Dwight
Eruption of Mauna Loa, Hawaii.
(Am. Jour. Sci., Ser. 2, Vol. 27, 1859, pp. 410-415)

AS
36
S1

Dana, James Dwight, 1813-1895.
A memoir of Asa Gray. By James D. Dana.
(In Smithsonian institution. Annual report. 1888. Washington, 1890. 23½ᵐᵐ. p. 745-762)
"From the American journal of science, March 1, 1888, vol. xxxv."

1. Gray, Asa, 1810-1888.
S 15-689

Library of Congress   Q11.S66 1888
Library, Smithsonian   Institution

AP
2
A 5

Dana, James Dwight
On labradorite from the island of Maui, Hawaiian group.
(Am. J. Sci., Ser. 2, Vol. XI, 1851, pp. 121)

AP
2
A 5

Dana, James Dwight
Historical account of the eruptions on Hawaii.
(Am. Jour. Sci., Ser. 2, Vol. 9, 1850, pp. 347-364; Vol. 10, 1850, pp. 235-244)
(extracted and condensed from the author's Exp. Expd. Geological Report)

AP
2
A 5

Dana, James Dwight
Note on the characters and mode of formation of the coral reefs of the Solomon Islands, being results of observations made in 1882-1884, by H. B. Guppy, during the surveying cruise of the "Lark".
(Am. Jour. of Sci., Ser. 3, Vol. 34, 1887, pp. 229-230)

AP
2
A 5

Dana, James Dwight
On changes of level in the Pacific Ocean.
(Am. Jour. of Sci., Ser. 2, Vol. 15, 1853, pp. 157-175)
(from U. S. Expl. Exp. Geological Report)

AP
2
A 5

Dana, James Dwight
History of the changes in the Mt Loa craters
(Am. Jour. of Sci., Ser. 3, Vol. 33, 1887, pp. 433-451; 34, 1887, pp. 81-97, 349-364; 35, 1888, pp. 15-34, 213-228, 282-289; 36, 1888, pp. 81-112, 167-175)

AP
2
A 5

Dana, James Dwight
Note on the currents of the oceans.
(Am. Jour. Sci., Ser. 2, Vol. 26, 1858, pp. 231-233)

AP
2
A 5

Dana, James Dwight
On coral reefs and islands. (from the Report on geology of the Exploring Expedition under Captain Wilkes)
(Am. J. of Sci., Ser. 2, Vol. XI, 357-372; XII, 25-51,165-186,329-338; XIII, 34-41, 185-195 339-350, XIV, 76-84)

AP
2
A 5

Dana, James Dwight

On denudation in the Pacific.

(Am. Journ. Sci., Ser. 2, Vol. 9, 1850, pp. 48-62)

("extracted from different chapters in the Geological Report of the Exploring Expedition under Captain Wilkes")

AP
2
A 5

Dana, James Dwight

On Zoophytes. (abstracted and reprinted from U. S. Exploring Expedition report by Dana)

(Am. J. of Sci., Ser 2, Vol. 2, 1846, pp. 64-69, 187-202; Vol. 3, 1847, pp. 1-24, 160-163, 337-347)

AP
2
A 5

and
QE
Pam.
270

Dana, James Dwight

Volcanic action.

(Am. Jour. of Sci., Ser. 3, Vol. 33, 1887, pp. 102-115)

AP
2
A 5

Dana, James D(wight)

On the areas of subsidence in the Pacific, as indicated by the distribution of coral islands.

(American Journal of Science, Ser. 1, Vol. 45, 1843, pp. 131-135)

AP
2
A5

Dana, James D(wight)

Origin of Coral Reefs and Islands.

In Am. Journ. Sc. 3rd Ser Vol. XXX pp. 89-104. New Haven 1880. - 169-189

AP
2
A 5

Dana, James Dwight

The volcanic nature of a Pacific island not an argument for little or no subsidence.

(Am. Jour. of Sci., Ser. 3, Vol. 30, 1885, pp. 158-159)

AP
2
A 5

Dana, James D(wight)

On the origin of the deep troughs of the oceanic depression; are any of volcanic origin?

(Am. Jour. Sci., Ser. 3, Vol. 37, 1889, pp. 192-202)

AP
2
A 5

Dana, James D(wight)

Origin of the grand outline features of the earth.

(Am. Jour. Sci. and Arts, 2d series, Vol. 3, pp. 381-398, 1847)

AP
2
A 5

DANA, JAMES D(WIGHT)

Couthouy, Joseph P.

Reply of J. P. Couthouy to the accusations of J. D. Dana, geologist of the Exploring Expedition, contained on pp. 130 and 145 of this Volume.

(Am. Jour. Sci., Ser. 1, Vol. 45, 1843, pp. 378-389)

AP
2
A 5

Dana, James D(wight)

On the temperature limiting the distribution of corals.

(Am. Jour. of Sci., Ser. 1, Vol. 45, 1843, pp. 130-131)

AP
2
A 5

Dana, James D(wight)

Points in the geological history of the islands of Maui and Oahu.

(Amer. Journ. of Science, Vol. 37, Feb., 1889, pp. 81-102)

QE
526
D2
D16

Dana, James D(wight)

Volcanoes and volcanic phenomena of the Hawaiian Islands. From the Am. Journ. of Science XXXIII-XXXVII, 1887-1889. 10 papers. Also a paper on the petrography of the islands by Edward S. Dana, bound in one.

JAN 4 '17

AS
36
A 3

Dana, James D(wight)

On the Trend of Islands and Axis of Subsidence in the Pacific.

(Proceedings of the American Association for the Advancement of Science, 2nd Meeting, 1849, pp. 321-325)

AP
2
A 5

Dana, James Dwight

Recent eruption of Mauna Loa and Kilauea, Hawaii.

(Am. J. of Sci., Ser. 2, Vol. 46, 1868, pp. 105-123)

AP
2
A5

Dana, James Dwight

Dana, Edward S.

James Dwight Dana. in Am. Journ. of Sc. XLIX, 1895, Ser. III. pp. 329-356. Bibliography of his writings. pp. 349-356.

AP
2
A 5

Dana, James D(wight)

On the volcanoes of the moon.

(Am. Jour. Sci. and Arts, 2d series, Vol. 2, 1846, pp. 335-348)

(comparison with Kilauea)

QE
Pam
#272
and
AP
2
A 5

Dana, James D(wight)

Recent observations of Mr. Frank S. Dodge, of the Hawaiian Government Survey on Halema'uma'u and its debris-cone, ex Am. Journ. of Sc., Ser. 3, Vol. 37, 1889, pp. 48-50)

QE
22.D 26
G 48

DANA, JAMES DWIGHT

Gilman, Daniel C.

The life of James Dwight Dana, scientific explorer, mineralogist, geologist, zoologist, Professor in Yale University. Harper & Brothers, New York, 1899, 8vo. pp. 1-409.

AP
2
A 5

Dana, James Dwight

On volcanic action at Mauna Loa.

(Am. Jour. Sci., Ser. 2, Vol. 21, 1856, pp. 241-244)

Q
115
U 58
locked
case

2 copies
of Vol. 7

Dana, James D(wight)

United States Exploring Expedition...1838-1842. Vol. 7: Zoophytes, by James D. Dana. 1846. 4to. With a folio atlas of 61 plates.

...Vol. 10: Geology...with a folio atlas of 21 plates. 1849.

...Vols. 13-14: Crustacea...with a folio atlas of 96 plates. 1853, atlas, 1855.

AS
36
A 9

DANA, JAMES DWIGHT

Hoffmeister, J. Edward

James Dwight Dana's studies of volcanoes and of coral islands.

IN

Centenary celebration; the Wilkes Exploring Expedition...1940, pp. 721-732.

(Proc. Am. Philosophical Soc., 82:721-732, 1940)

AS 36 A25

Dana, James Freeman, 1793–1827.
Outlines of the mineralogy and geology of Boston and its vicinity, with a geological map. By J. F. Dana, M. D. and S. L. Dana, M. D.
(*In* American academy of arts and sciences, Boston. Memoirs. Boston, 1818. 29 x 24ᶜᵐ. v. 4, p. [129]–223. fold. map)
Q11.B68
—— Outlines of the mineralogy and geology of Boston and its vicinity, with a geological map. By J. Freeman Dana, M. D. and Samuel L. Dana ... Boston, Cummings and Hillard, 1818.
108 p. front. (fold. map) 26½ᶜᵐ.
"List of the authors and editions of the works consulted": p. [7]
1. Mineralogy—Massachusetts. 2. Geology—Massachusetts. I. Dana, Samuel Luther, 1795–1868, joint author.
5—15478–9
Library of Congress   QE375.D19

DU 620 H41

Dana, Richard
Towse, E.J.
"Some Hawaiians abroad." in Haw. Hist. Soc. Paper no. 11, 1904, pp. 3-22.

GN Ethn. Pam. 4387

DANCES ELLICE ISLANDS
Koch, Gerd

Polynesier-Niutao (Ellice Islands) fakanau-Tänze. Gottingen. Institut für den Wissenschaftlichen Film. Text only - to a accompany the film. 1962

AM 151 D16

Dana, John Cotton

Installation of a speaker; and accompanying exhibits. Woodstock, Elm Tree Press, 1919.

(No. 3 of the New Museum Series)

QE Geol. Pam. 806

DANA EXPEDITION, 1928–1930
Schmidt, Johannes

Oceanographical Expedition of the "Dana" 1928–1930.

Reprint from Nature, March 21, and 28, 1931

R8vo.

GN 2.S P 76

DANCES GILBERT ISLANDS
Laxton, P. B.

"Ruoia". A Gilbertese dance. By P. B. Laxton and Te Kautu Kamoriki.

(Jour. Polynesian Soc., 62(1):57-72, 1953)

AM 5 D 16

Dana, John Cotton

New Museum. New Mus. Ser. I.

Woodstock, Elm Tree Press, 1917, pp. 52.

Q 115 C 28

DANA (SHIP)

Carlsberg Foundation's Oceanographical Expedition round the world, 1928–1930 and previous "Dana" Expeditions under the leadership of Professor Johannes Schmidt.

Dana Reports, 1-7   1932-7

AS 36 A 65 J

DANCES - JAPAN

The Bon Dance.

(Junior Natural History, Oct. 1959:18)

AM Mus Pam #40 and # 39

Dana, John Cotton

The new relations of museums and industries.

Newark, N. J. ; 1919.

QL 1 Z

DANAIDAE

Carpenter, G. D. Hale

The genus Euploea (Lep. Danaidae) in Micronesia, Melanesia, Polynesia and Australia. A zoo-geographical study.

(Transactions of the Zoological Society of London, Vol. 28(1):1-184, 1953)

GN 2.S T

DANCES MANGAREVA
Laguesse, Jean

La légende du requin, pei Mangarévien.

(Bull. Soc. des Etudes Océaniennes, No. 113: 481-484, Dec. 1955)

[a legend, acted out]

DU 12 D 16

Dana, Julian

Gods who die: the story of Samoa's greatest adventurer. As told to Julian Dana.   New York. The Macmillan Company. 1935. 8vo.   xvi + 320 pp.

(George Westbrook)

AS 182 H

DANAIS

Semper, G(eorg)

Die Wanderung von Danais Erippus, Cramer, nach den Südsee-Inseln, Australien und Celebes.

(Jour. Mus. Godeffroy, Heft IV, 1873, pp. 117-119 [293-295])

DU 400 T 25

DANCES MAORI

The poi dance.

(Te Ao Hou, The New World, Vol. 3(4), no. 12 pp. 32-34, 1955)

AG 519.S Da D 17

Dana, R. H.

The seamen's friend: containing a treatise on practical seamanship ... a dictionary of sea terms ....

Boston, 1865, 11th ed. pp 225.

Hms M24

Storage Case 4

Dance chants.

Extracts from various sources.

GN 2.M S 93

and GN Ethn. Pam. 4242

DANCES POLYNESIA
Hye-Kerkdal, K. J.

Tanz als Akkulturationsproblem (Polynesien).

(Tribus, 9:153-163, 1960)

Carter Coll. 2-D-20

Dana, R. H., Jr.

Two years before the mast; a personal narrative of life at sea. New York International Book Co. 1840 362 pp. 8vo.

1841 edition 1-A-25
1851 "   11-A-27
1878 "   1-A-23
1930 "   10-C-1

DU 620 P 22

Dance - Tahitians - dance:

(Paradise of the Pacific, Holiday ed., 1957: 60-61)

AS 36 P 41-e

DANCES - TIWI
Goodale, Jane C.

The Tiwi dance for the dead.

(Expedition, Vol. 2(1):3-13, 1959)

[Tiwi: people of Melville Island, Australia]

DANCING HAWAII

See also

HULA HAWAII

GN
2M
A
DANCING BLACKFOOT INDIANS

Wissler, Clark, 1870–

... The sun dance of the Blackfoot Indians, by Clark Wissler. New York, The Trustees, 1918.

1 p. l., p. 223-270. 1 illus. 24½ᶜᵐ. (Anthropological papers of the American museum of natural history, vol. XVI, pt. III)

1. Siksika Indians. 2. Sun-dance.

Library of Congress　　　GN2.A27 vol. XVI, pt. III
19–10681

G
1
As
and
DU
Pac.Fam.
100
DANCING GILBERT ISLANDS

Farrell, Andrew

Micronesia under the moon.

(Asia, 1921, April, 312-315)

DU
620
P
DANCING HAWAII

Hula past and present.

(Paradise of the Pacific, Vol. 41, No. 4, 1928, p. 6)

DU
400
T 25
DANCING BORABORA

Harrison, Rangi

My visit to kinsmen of ancient days.

(Te Ao Hou, No. 15:28-31, 1956)

[Tahiti]

DANCING HAWAII

See

HULA

GN
2.1
A-M
DANCING ADMIRALTY ISLANDS

Hardy, H.N.M.

Note on native dance in the Admiralty Islands.

(Man, vol. 16, 1916, no. 69, pp. 121-122)

GN
2.M
Dr
DANCING BUKA

Foy, W.

Tanzobjecte vom Bismarck Archipel, Nissan und Buka.

(Publ. Kgl. Ethnographisches Museum, Dresden Bd. 13, 1900)

GN
2.M
F1

N.2
DANCING – INDIANS OF NORTH AMERICA

Dorsey, George A.

The Arapaho Sun Dance: the ceremony of the Offerings Lodge.

v. Field Columbian Museum. Anthropological Series Vol IV.

APR 2? 1904

GN
2M
Pe
DANCING ALASKA

Hawkes, Ernest William.

... The dance festivals of the Alaskan Eskimo, by E. W. Hawkes. Philadelphia, University museum, 1914.

4 l., 1) p., 3 l. pl. XI-XV. 26½ᶜᵐ. (University of Pennsylvania. The University museum. Anthropological publications. vol. VI, no. 2)

1. Indians of North America—Dances. 2. Eskimos—Alaska.
15-3050

Library of Congress　　　E99.E7H39

G
51
W 17
DANCING CAPE YORK PENINSULA

Thomson, Donald F.

The masked dancers of I'wai'i; a remarkable hero cult which has invaded Cape York Peninsula.

(Walkabout, 22(12):17-20, 1956)

GN
2.M
A
DANCING – INDIANS OF NORTH AMERICA.

Wissler, Clark, 1870–

... Societies and ceremonial associations in the Oglala division of the Teton-Dakota, by Clark Wissler. New York, The Trustees, 1912.

2 p. l., p. 3-99. illus. 24½ᶜᵐ. (Anthropological papers of the American museum of natural history. vol. XI, pt. I)

1. Oglala Indians. 2. Indians of North America—Soc. life & cust.
3. Indians of North America—Dances.
15-3011

Library of Congress　　　GN2.A27 vol. 11, pt. 1

G
51
W 17
DANCING AUSTRALIA

Carell, Beth Dean

In search of Stone-Age dance.

(Walkabout, 25(5):15-20, 1955)

[Arnhem Land]

GN
635.D9
K 21
DANCING CELEBES

Kaudern, Walter

Ethnographical studies in Celebes: results of the author's expedition to Celebes 1917-1920. I. Structures and settlements in Central Celebes; II. Migrations of the Toradja in Central Celebes; III. Musical instruments in Celebes; IV. Games and dances in Celebes. With...plates...maps...figures. 1925-1929. 8vo. Göteborg.

GN
2.M
A
DANCING – INDIANS OF NORTH AMERICA

Wissler, Clark, 1870– ed.

... Societies of the Plains Indians, ed. by Clark Wissler. New York, The Trustees (1912)–16.

13 pt. in 1 v. illus., fold. tab. 24½ᶜᵐ. (Anthropological papers of the American museum of natural history, vol. XI)
Paged continuously.
Bibliography: p. 13, p. 987-992.
CONTENTS.—pt. I. Societies and ceremonial associations in the Oglala division of the Teton-Dakota, by C. Wissler. 1912.—pt. II. Dance associations of the eastern Dakota, by R. H. Lowie. 1913.—pt. III. Societies of the Crow, Hidatsa and Mandan Indians, by R. H. Lowie. 1913.—pt. IV. Societies and dance associations of the Blackfoot Indians, by C. Wissler. 1913.—pt. V. Dancing societies of the Sarsi Indians, by P. E. Goddard.

(Continued on next card)
19-13711

GN
2.M
Dr
DANCING BISMARK ARCHIPELAGO

Foy, W.

Tanzobjecte vom Bismarck Archipel, Nissan und Buka. Mit 17 (darunter 3 Doppel-) Tafeln in Lichtdruck und 2 Textillustrationen in Autotypie.

(Publ. Kgl. Ethnographisches Museum, Dresden, Bd. XIII, 1900)

GN
1
An
DANCING FIJI

Rougier, Emmanuel

Danses et jeux aux Fijis (Iles de l'Océanie)

(Anthropos. Bd.VI. 1911. pp.466-484)

GN
2.M
A
DANCING – INDIANS OF NORTH AMERICA.

Wissler, Clark, 1870– ed. ... Societies of the Plains Indians ... (1912)–16. (Card 2)

CONTENTS—Continued.
1914.—pt. VI. Political organizations, cults, and ceremonies of the Plains-Ojibway and Plains-Cree Indians, by A. Skinner. 1914.—pt. VII. Pawnee Indian societies, by J. R. Murie. 1914.—pt. VIII. Societies of the Arikara Indians, by R. H. Lowie. 1915.—pt. IX. Societies of the Iowa, Kansa, and Ponca Indians, by A. Skinner. 1915.—pt. X. Dances and societies of the Plains Shoshone, by R. H. Lowie. 1915.—pt. XI. Societies of the Kiowa, by R. H. Lowie. 1916.—pt. XII. General discussion of shamanistic and dancing societies, by C. Wissler. 1916.—pt. XIII. Plains Indian age-societies: historical and comparative summary, by R. H. Lowie. 1916.
1. Indians of North America—Secret societies. 2. Indians of North America—Societies. 3. Indians of North America—Soc. life & cust. 4. Indians of North America—Dances. I. Title.
19-13711
Library of Congress　　　GN2.A27 vol. 11
——— Copy 2.　　　E98.S75W8

GN
2.M
A
DANCING – BLACKFOOT INDIANS.

Wissler, Clark, 1870–

... Societies and dance associations of the Blackfoot Indians, by Clark Wissler ... New York, The Trustees, 1913.

1 p. l., p. 359-460. illus. 24½ᶜᵐ. (Anthropological papers of the American museum of natural history. vol. XI, pt. IV)

1. Siksika Indians. 2. Indians of North America—Soc. life & cust.
3. Indians of North America—Dances.
15-3014

Library of Congress　　　GN2.A27 vol. 11, pt. 4

GN
2.S
F 47
DANCING FIJI

Rougier, E(mmanuel)

Fijian dances and games.

(Trans. of the Fijian Society. 1915. pp. 16-36)

AS
36
M64
DANCING – INDIANS OF NORTHERN WISCONSIN.

Barrett, S. A.

The dream dance of the Chippewa and Menomiee Indiand of northern Wisconsin. Milwaukee Mus. Bull. Vol. I, Art. IV, 1911.

GN
2.1
A-m

DANCING   MALEKULA

Layard, John

Song and dance in Malekula.

(Man, Vol. 44, 1944, No. 97)

AS
28
E 85

DANCING   NEW CALEDONIA

"Bebenod", dance de Mare.

(Etudes Mélanésiennes, n.s., 3rd yr., No. 5:
145-146, 1951)

GN
Ethn.Pam.
3655

DANCING   SAMOA

Dunlap, Helen L.

Games, sports, dancing, and other vigorous
recreational activities and their function in
Samoan.

(reprint, The Research Quarterly of the
American Association for Health, Physical Education, and Recreation, 22:298-311, 1951)

GN
2.S
T

DANCING   MANGAREVA

Mordvinoff, Nicholas

Ru a kipo: pei Mangarevien.

(Bull. Soc. d'Etudes Oceaniennes, No. 75
[Tome 6, no. 4], Dec. 1945, pp. 131-140)

GN
1
An

DANCING   NEW GUINEA

Vormann, Franz

Tänze und Tanzfestlichkeiten der Monumbo-
Papua (Deutsch-Neuguinea).

(Anthropos. Bd.VI. 1911. pp.411-427)

GN
2.M
E 85

DANCING   SANTA CRUZ ISLANDS

Foy, Willy

Zur Geschichte der Tanzkeulen von den Santa-
Cruz-Inseln.

(Ethnologica, 2(2):215-238, 1916)

DU
400
T 25

DANCING   MAORI

A haka to honour Te Rangihiroa.

(Te Ao Hou, The New World, Vol. 3(1), no. 9:
15-16, 1954)

GN
1
F

DANCING   NEW HEBRIDES

Layard, John

Maze-dances and the ritual of the labyrinth
in Malekula.

((Folk-Lore. Vol. 47. 1936. pp.123-170)

DANCING   SOCIETY ISLANDS

Costa, M. K.

Dance in the Society and Hawaiian islands
as presented by the early writers, 1767-1842.

(Hawaii. University of   Thesis for degree
of Master of Arts. 1951)

UH has

DU
1
P

DANCING   MELANESIA

On with the dance! Novel features of village
life in Melanesia, by C. W. W. A.

(Pacific Islands Monthly, Vol. 12, No. 12,
1942, pp. 24-26)

GN
Ethn.
Pam.
201

DANCING   PAPUA

Haddon, Alfred C.

Papuan dances.

n.p.n.d.4to. pp.16.(typewritten)

DU
12
F 74
looked
case

DANCING   SOCIETY ISLANDS

Forster, J. R.

Observations made during a voyage round the
world, on physical geography, natural history,
and ethic philosophy... London. 1778. 4to.
pp. 465-467; 476.

GN
1
O 15

DANCING   NEW BRITAIN

Poole, Jean (Mrs.)

Still further notes on a snake dance of the
Baining.

(Oceania, Vol. 13, 1943, pp. 224-227)

GN
2.1
A-M

DANCING   PAPUA

Humphries, A. R.

The Gulf Division Ehalo dance.

(Man, vol. 31, 1931, no. 165, pp. 159-163)

GN
2.1
T 69

DANCING   SOLOMON ISLANDS

Paravicini, Eugen

Die speere der Salomons Inseln.

(Revista del Instituto de Etnologia, Universidad de Tucuman, Tomo II, 1932, pp. 481-491)

GN
1
O 15

DANCING   NEW BRITAIN

Read, W. J.

A snake dance of the Baining.

(Oceania, Vol. 2, 1931-1932, pp. 232-236,
pls. 1,2)

---Further notes on a snake dance of the
Baining, by Gregory Bateson. (ibid, Vol. 2,
1931-1932, pp. 334-341) and Still further notes
on a snake dance of the Baining, by Jean Poole,
(ibid, Vol. 13,   1943, pp. 224-227)

GN
2.S
P 76

DANCING   POLYNESIA

Burrows, Edwin B.

Polynesian music and dancing.

(Journal of the Polynesian Soc., Vol. 49,
1940, pp. 331-346)

GN
2.S
T 12

DANCING   TAHITI

Chants, dances et costumes anciens au 14
Juillet.   (at Tahiti)

(Bull. Soc. d'Etudes Oceaniennes, No. 20:
277, 1927)

(complaint of the editor that the old are
not being used, and cheap innovations are
introduced)

GN
1
O 15

DANCING   NEW BRITAIN

Bateson, Gregory

Further notes on a snake dance of the Baining

(Oceania, Vol. 2, 1931-1932, pp. 334-341,
pl. 1)

(See also "A snake dance of the Baining", by
W.J. Read. (ibid, Vol. 2, 1931-1932, pp. 232-236)

GN
2.M
Be

DANCING   PONAPE

Hahl

Feste und Tänze der Eingeborenen von Ponape.

(Ethnologisches Botizblatt, Bd. III, Heft
2, 1902, pp. 95-102)

DU
620
P 22

DANCING   TAHITI

Dance - Tahitians - dance!

(Paradise of the Pacific, Holiday ed., 1957:
60-61)

DU
400
T 25

DANCING TAHITI

Harrison, Rangi

My visit to kinsmen of ancient days.

(Te Ao Hou, No. 15:28-31, 1956)

[Tahiti]

DU
Pac
Pam
No.12

Danes, J. V.

Australia in Czechoslovak literature.
n.p. 1922.

GN
Ethn.Pam.
2961

Dangel, Richard

Quechua und Maori.

(Mitteilungen der Anthropologischen Gesellschaft in Wien, Bd. LX, 1930.343-351 pp.)

G
51
W 17

DANCING TORRES STRAITS

Church, A. E.

Ballet at Badu.

(Walkabout, Vol. XI, no. 9, pp. 33-34)

QE
Pam
#62

Danes, J. V.

Das Karstgebiet Goenoeng Sewoe in
Java, ex Sitzungsberichten der Konigl.
Bohm. Gesells. der Wissens. in Prag,
1915.

F
821
J 54

DANGER CAVE

Jennings, Jesse D.

Danger Cave; with a chapter on textiles by
Sara Sue Rudy and six appendices by Charles B.
Hunt and others. Robert Anderson, Editor.

(Anthropolo-ica Papers, University of Utah,
No. 27, 1957)

GN
1
Z

DANCING YAP

Born

Einige Bemerkungen uber Musik, Dicht unst,
und Tanz der Yapleute.

(Zeit. f. Ethnologie, 35, 134-42, 1903)

DU
Pac
Pam
No.11

Danes, J. D.

Gross-Australian. np. nd.

DANGER ISLAND

See

PUKA PUKA ISLAND

GN
Pam
2499

Danckelman,

Aus dem schutsgebiete Togo. From
Mittheil. v. forsch. und gelehrten aus
den Deutschen Schutsgebieten, heft 1,1888

QE
Pam
#61

Danes, J. V.

Karststudien in Jamaica, ex Sitzungsberichten der Konigl. Bohm. Gesells.
der Wissens. in Prag, 1914.

DANGER ISLANDS   CICADELLIDAE

See

CICADELLIDAE   DANGER ISLANDS

DU
Hist.
Pam.
906

Dandy Ioane.

(Daily Pacific Advertiser, Feb. 27, 1883)

QE
Pam
#337

Danes, J. V.

Karststudien in Australien.

Prag, 1916.

QL
Fish
Pam
#209

Danglade, Ernest

The flatworm as an enemy of
Florida oysters, ex App. V to Rept.
of U. S. Comm. of Fish. for 1918,
Bur. of Fish. doc. no. 869.

AS
36
S1

Dane, John M.
The problem of color vision. By John M. Dane.
(*In* Smithsonian institution. Annual report. 1907. Washington, 1908.
23½ᵐ. p. 613-625. illus.)
"Reprinted ... from the American naturalist, vol. XLI, no. 486, June 1907."

1. Color sense.

Library of Congress   S 15-1355
Library, Smithsonian   Q11.S66 1907
                                Institution

QE
Pam
#384

Danes, J. V.

Physiography of some limestone areas
in Queensland. Roy. Soc. Queensland
Proc., Vol. XXIII.

GN
740
D 18

Daniel, Glyn E.

A hundred years of archaeology. Gerald
Duckworth and Co., Ltd. London. (1952) 8vo.
5-343(1) pp.

QK
495.S68
D 17

Danert, Siegfried

Zur Systematik von Nicotiana tabacum L.

(Die Kulturpflanze, Band 9:287-363, 1961)

QL
Bird
Pam
162

Danforth, Stuart T   & Emlen, John T

A new agelaius from Haiti. From Proc.
Biological Soc. Washington, v. 40, pp. 147-148,
1927.

DU
12
D 18

Daniel, Hawthorne

Islands of the Pacific.   G.P.Putnam's
Sons. New York. 1943c. 8vo. xi +228 pp.

QL 1 C15
Daniel, John Frank, 1873–
... The anatomy of *Heterodontus francisci*, i–
By J. Frank Daniel.
(*In* University of California publications in zoology. Berkeley, 1914–27. v. 13, p. (147)–166; plates)
Bibliographies.

1. Heterodontus francisci. 2. Fishes—California. i. Title.
A 14–1336
Title from Univ. of Calif.   Library of Congress

Q Gen.Sci. Pam. 132
Danielsen, Edwin F. and others
Intensity and frequency of severe storms in the Gulf of Alaska.
(Trans. Am. Geophysical Union, Vol. 38(1): pp. 44–49, 1957)

Danielsson, Bengt
Economy of Raroia Atoll, Tuamotu archipelago.
See his
QH 11 P 11   Raroian culture.
(The issue has one title in the list of contents, another title on the commencing page of the article.)

Daniel, John Franklin, 1873–
... The anatomy of *Heptanchus maculatus:* the endoskeleton, by J. Frank Daniel. Berkeley, University of California press, 1916.
cover-title, p. (349)–370. illus. pl. 27–29. 27cm. (University of California publications in zoology. v. 16, no. 18)
"Literature cited": p. 364.
1. Heptanchus maculatus. i. Title.
A 17–45
Title from Univ. of Calif.   Library of Congress

QL Protozoa to Polyzoa Pam 309
Danielssen, D C and Koren, J
Fra den norske nordhavsexpedition. From Nyt Magazin f. Natur., Kristiania, 1880.

DU 700 D 18
Danielsson, Bengt
Forgotten islands of the South Seas. Translated by F. H. Lyon. George Allen and Unwin Ltd. 8vo. (1957) London. 204 pp.

QL 1 C 15
Daniel, John Franklin, 1873–
... The subclavian vein and its relations in elasmobranch fishes, by J. Frank Daniel. Berkeley, University of California press, 1918.
cover-title, p. (479)–484. illus. 27cm. (University of California publications in zoology. v. 18, no. 16)
"Literature cited": p. 484.
1. Subclavian vein. 2. Fishes—Veins.
A 18–903
Title from Univ. of Calif.   Library of Congress

QL Protozoa to Polyzoa Pam 469
Danielssen, D C
Fra den norske nordhavsexpedition. From Nyt Magazin for naturv, 25 binds, 2 hefte, 1879.

DU 890 D 18
Danielsson, Bengt
The happy island. Translated from the Swedish by F. H. Lyon. George Allen and Unwin Ltd. London. 8vo. 252 pp.

QL 1 C15
Daniel, J. Frank and Stoker, Edith
The relations and nature of the cutaneous vessels in selachian fishes. Calif. Univ. Publ. Zool. v.31, n.1, 1927.

GN 479 D 18
Danielsson, Bengt
L'amour dans les mers du Sud. Roman, traduit de l'anglais par Evelyn Mahyère, et revu par l'auteur. Librairie Stock. Paris. 8vo. 231 pp.
[French edition of "Love in the South Seas"]

DU 890 D 18
Danielsson, Bengt
L'ile du "Kon-Tiki" (den lyckliga ön). Traduit du suédois par Marguerite Gay et Gerd de Mautort. Editions Albin Michel. Paris. (1953) 8vo. (1–7)8–332 pp.

GL Pam 110 *Danielli, Dr Jacopo.*
Contributo allo Studio del Tatuaggio negli Antichi Peruviani.
Firenze 1894.

Danielsson, Bengt
Anthropometrical data on the Jibaro Indians.
(Ethnos, 24(1–2), 1959)
[review in Humanitas, II:2, 1961, pp. 80–81]

GN 479 D 18
Danielsson, Bengt
Love in the South Seas. Translated by F. H. Lyon. Reynal and Co. New York. 1956. 8vo. (1–9)10–240 pp.

GN Pam 1990
Danielli, Iacopo
Crani ed ossa lunghe di abitanti dell isola d'engano. From Arch. per antrop. e etnol. v.23, fasc.3, 1893.

GN 2.S P 76
Danielsson, Bengt
Contributions to Marquesan archaeology.
(Jour. Poly. Soc. 63(1):75–76, 1954)

GN 2.S T 12
Danielsson, Bengt
Nouvelle lumière sur la préhistoire polynesienne.
(Bull. Soc. Etudes Oceaniennes, 127/128, 1959:42–45)

GN Pam 2071
Danielli, Jacopo
Studio sui crani Bengakesi con appunti d'etnologia indiana. From Arch. Antrop. e etnol. v. 22, fasc. 2–3, 1892.

GN 2.S T
Danielsson, Bengt
Dernières recherches scientifiques à Raroia.
(Bull. Soc. des Etudes Oceaniennes, No. 105, pp. 139–141, 1953)
(report of 1952 expedition, from Hawaii...)

GN 2.S T
Danielsson, Bengt
Quelques observations meteorologiques faites a Raroia (Tuamotu) Jan. 1–Dec. 31, 1950.
(Bull. Soc. des Etudes Océaniennes, Nos. 94–95, 1951)

QH
11
P 11

Danielsson, Bengt

    Raroian culture. By Bengt Danielsson and
Aurora Natua.

      Part 1. Economy; Part 2. Native topographi-
cal terms, Part 3. Native terminology of the
coconut palm, Part 4. Bird names, Part 5. Check
list of the native names of fishes.

    (Atoll Research Bull. No. 32, 1954)

over

QH
11
G 14

Danish Deep-Sea Expedition Round the
World 1950-1952.

    Galathea report: Scientific results of the
Danish Deep-Sea Expedition ...

      Vol. 1, 1957-

DU
1
S 72 t

Danks, K. H.

    Industrial activity in selected areas of the
South Pacific.

    (South Pacific Commission, Technical Paper
No. 90, March, 1956)

GN
2.S
P 76

Danielsson, Bengt

    A recently discovered marae in the Tuamotu
Group.

    (Jour. Poly. Soc., 61(3/4):222-229, 1952)

QL384.E2
M88
QL377.C6
J95

Danish Ingolf-Expedition.

    Vol. IV:1-2. Echinoidea, by Th. Mortensen.

    " V:1. Pennatulida, by Hector F.E.Junger-
sen.

QE
Geology
Pam.
1248

Danner, Wilbert R.

    Geology of Olympic National Park. Published
in cooperation with the Olympic Natural History
Association. University of Washington Press.
Seattle. 1955. 5-68 pp. 8vo.

GN
2.S
P 76

Danielsson, Bengt

    A unique Tahitian stone figure.

    (Jour. Poly. Soc., 66(4):396-397)

AG
41
D26

DANISH LANGUAGE - DICTIONARIES

Davis, J. R. Ainsworth

    Burt's Danish-Norwegian-English
dictionary.. new edition and improved.

New York, Burt, n.d.   433p.

GN
Pam
1952

Dannert,

    Ueber die sitte der Zahnverstummelung
bei den Ovaherero. From Zeit. f. Ethno.
heft 6, 1907.

DU
12
D 18

Danielsson, Bengt

    What happened on the Bounty. Translated
from the Swedish by Alan Tapsell. London.
George Allen & Unwin, Ltd. 1962. 230 pp.
8vo

DU
1
P 10

    Danish scientists in the Pacific.

    (Pacific Islands Monthly, 31(12):23, 1961)

    [Monnberg going to Rennell and Bellona...]

QL
636
A

Dannevig, H. C. In Memoriam
Lockyer, N.
in Biol. Results of Fishing Experiments
carried on by F.I.S. "Endeavour" 1909-'14.
Australia Commonwealth Dept. of Trade & Customs.
Fisheries III, pp. I-XIV.

GN
671.T8
B 18

Danielsson, Bengt

    Work and life on Raroia. An acculturation
study from the Tuamotu group, French Oceania.
Almqvist and Wiksells Boktryckeri Ab. Uppsala.
1955. 8vo. 244 pp. + maps

GN
2.1
A

Danks, B.

    Burial customs of New Britain.

    (J. R. Anthrop. Inst. Grt. Brit. and Ire-
land, Vol. 21, 1891/2, p. 348-358)

QK
Bot. Pam.
1862

Danser, B. H.

Mekel, J. C.

    Der Blütenstand und die Blüte von
Korthasella Dacryii. (Description from notes of
Mekel arranged for publication by B. H. Danser)

    (Blumea, Vol. I, No. 2, 1935, pp. 312-319)

AS
162
P

Danis, V.

    Etude d'une nouvelle collection d'oiseaux
de l'ile Bougainville.

    (Bull. Mus. Nat. d'Hist. Nat., Ser. 2,
Tome 9, 1937, pp. 119-123, 362-365)

AS
701
A

Danks, B.

    New Britain and its people.

    (Austr. Ass'n for the Adv. of Sci., 1892
(2nd meeting) pp. 614-620)

QK
1
B 65

Danser, B. H.

    The Cornaceae, Sensu Stricto, of the Nether-
lands Indies.

    (Blumea, Vol. 1, No. 1, 1934, pp.46-74).

QK
Bot. Pam.
1860

AG
41
R82

DANISH ... DICTIONARY

Rosing, S

    English-Danish ordbog.

    Kobenhavn, Hegel, 1863.   566p.

GN
Ethn.
Pam .2158

Danks, Benjamin

    On the shell money of New Britain.

    (Jour. R. Anthrop. Inst. of Grt. Britain and
Ireland, 17:305-317, 1888)

QK
1
B 65

Danser, B. H.

    Grammatical objections to the international
rules of botanical nomenclature, adopted at
Cambridge in 1930

and
QK
Bot.Pam.
1861

    (Blumea, Vol. 1, No. 2, 1935, pp.295-304)

QK
Bot. Pam.
1857

Danser, B. H.

Loranthaceae collected in the Solomon Islands by L. J. Brass and S. F. Kajewski, on the Arnold Arboretum Expedition 1930-1932.

(Journal of the Arnold Arboretum, Vol. 16, 1935. pp. 206-209)

QK
Bot. Pam.
2123

Danser, B. H.

Miscellaneous notes on Loranthaceae, 16-18.

(Blumea, Vol. III, 1938, pp. 34-59)

QK
Bot. Pam.
1852

Danser, B. H.

On some Rumex and Polygonum hybrids from Java.

(Bulletin du Jardin Botanique de Buitenzorg, Serie III, Vol. 12, Livr. 1, 1932. pp.65-70)

QK
1
B 97-b3

and

QK
Bot.Pam.
1966

Danser, B. H.

The Loranthaceae Loranthoideae of the tropical archipelagos east of the Philippines, New Guinea, and Australia.

(Bull.du Jardin Botanique de Buitenzorg. Series III, vol.XIV¹. 1936. pp.73-98)

QK
Bot. Pam.
1849

Danser, B. H.

Nepenthaceae.

(Mitteilungen aus dem Institut für allgemeine Botanik in Hamburg, 7. Band, Heft 3. 1931. pp. 217-221)

QK
Bot. Pam.
1851

Danser, B. H.

On the taxonomy and the nomenclature of the Loranthaceae of Asia and Australia.

(Bulletin du Jardin Botanique de Buitenzorg, Serie III, Vol. 10, Livr. 3, 1929, pp. 291-373)

QK
Bot. Pam.
1853

Danser, B. H.

The Loranthaceae of the Netherlands Indies.

(Bulletin du Jardin Botanique de Buitenzorg, Serie III, Vol. 11, Livr. 3-4, 1931. pp.233-519)

QK
1
N 53

Danser, B. H.

A new Papuan Didisous.

(Brittonia, Vol. 2, 1936, pp. 135-136)

QK
1
B 65

Danser, B. H.

On two Loranthaceae from the Solomon Islands Miscellaneous notes on Loranthaceae, 19.

(Blumea, Vol. 3 (3), pp. 389-391,1940)

QK
Bot. Pam.
1855

Danser, B. H.

The Loranthaceae of the Oxford University Expedition to Sarawak in 1932.

(Recueil des Travaux Botaniques Néerlandais, Vol. 31, 1934. pp. 237-247)

QK
1
N 53

and

QK
Bot.Pam.
1774

Danser, B. H.

New Papuan Loranthaceae. Botanical results of the Archbold Expedition, No. 2.
(Brittonia, Vol. 2, 1936, pp. 131-134)

QK
Bot. Pam.
1848

Danser, B. H.

Polygonaceae

(Nova Guinea. Résultats de l'expédition scientifique néerlandaise a la Nouvelle-Guinée Vol. XIV, Botanie, Livr. 2. 1927. pp. 333-336)

QK
Bot. Pam.
1854

Danser, B. H.

Miscellaneous notes on Loranthaceae 1-6.

(Recueil des Travaux Botaniques Néerlandais Vol. 31, 1934. pp.223-236)

QK
Bot. Pam.
1847

Danser, B. H.

A new system for the genera of Loranthaceae Loranthoideae, with a nomenclator for the old world species of this subfamily.

(Verhandelingen der Koninklijke Akademie van Wetenschappen te Amsterdam. Afdeeling natuurkunde. Tweede sectie, Deel XXIX, No. 6 1933. 128 pp.)

QK
Bot. Pam.
2011

and

QK
1
B 97-a

Danser, B. H.

A revision of the genus Korthalsella.

(Bull. du Jardin Botanique de Buitenzorg. Ser.III, vol.XIV. pp.115-159) 1937

QK
Bot. Pam.
1856

Danser, B. H.

Miscellaneous notes on Loranthaceae 7-8.

(Recueil des Travaux Botaniques Néerlandais, Vol. 31, 1934. pp. 752-760)

QK
Bot. Pam.
1922

Danser, B. H.

Note on a number of New Guinea Polygonaceae, mainly collected by L. J. Brass in Papua on the 1933 New Guinea Expedition of Natural History

(Bull. du Jardin Botanique de Buitenzorg, Ser. 3, Vol. 13, Livr. 3, 1935, pp. 429-431)

over

QK
Bot. Pam.
1923

Danser, B. H.

A revision of the Philippine Loranthaceae.

(The Philippine Jour. Sci., Vol. 58, No. 1, 1935, pp. 1-151)

QK
1
B 65

and

QK
Bot. Pam.
1967

Danser, B. H.

Miscellaneous notes on Loranthaceae, 9-15.

(Blumea, vol.II. 1936. pp.34-59)

QK
Bot. Pam.
1921

Danser, B. H.

Note on few Nepenthes.

(Bull. du Jardin Botanique de Buitenzorg, Ser. 3, Vol. 13, Livr. 3, 1935, pp. 465-469)

QK
1
B 97-b3

Danser, B. H.

A supplement to the revision of the genus Korthalsella (Lor.)

(Bull. Jardin Bot., Buitenzorg, Ser. 3, Vol. 16, 1940, pp. 329-342)

QK
Bot. Pam.
2900
Danser, B. H.

Supplementary notes on the Santalaceous genera Dendromyza and Cladomyza (with pictures of these genera and of Hylomyza).

(From: Nova Guinea, new ser., Vol. 6(2):261-277, Dec., 1955)

QK
Botany
Pam.
3295
Dansereau, Pierre

New Zealand revisited. 28 pp.

(Reprint, The Garden Journal), 12(1): 12-16; (2):55-58; (3):108-113; (4):144-147; (5):185-189; (6):217-219, 227. 1962)

GN
Pam
1098
Danzel, Theodor-Wilhelm

Babylon und Altmexiko. From El Mexico antiguo, tomo 1, n.9, 1921. 25p.

QK
Bot. Pam.
1859
Danser, B. H.

Thaumasianthes, eine neue Loranthaceengattung aus den Philippinen.

(Recueil des Travaux Botaniques Néerlandais, Vol. 30, 1933. pp. 464-481)

GN
Ethn.
Pam.
4402
Dansereau, Pierre

Research program in the biological sciences at the Seventh Pacific Science Congress, New Zealand, 1949.

(Northwest Science, Vol. XXIII, No. 4, 1949, pp.147-153)

GN
Pam
2469
Danzel, Th.W.

Magisches und litteilendes Zeichnen. From Globus, bd. 98, n.23, 1910.

QK
Bot. Pam.
1920
Danser, B. H.

Vernacular names of Loranthaceae in the Malay Peninsula and the Netherlands Indies.

(Bull. du Jardin Botanique de Buitenzorg, Ser. 3, Vol. 13, Livr. 3, 1935, pp. 487-496)

QK
Bot.Pam.
2875
Dansereau, Pierre

Structural units of vegetation in tropical and temperate climates with special reference to areas.

(Seventh Pacific Science Congress, Vol. V: reprint, 13 pp. 1953)

GR
380.1
D 19
Danzel, Theodor Wilhelm

Danzel, Hedwig

Sagen und Legenden der Südsee-Insuler (Polynesien). Herausgegeben von Hedwig und Theodor Wilhelm Danzel.

Schriften-Reihe, Kulturen der Erde... Abteilung: Textwerke...Folkwang verlag. Hagen u. Darmstadt. 1923. 4to. 81 pp.

QK
Bot. Pam.
1850
2301
Danser, B. H.

Über die Niederlandisch-Indischen Stachytarpheta-Arten und ihre Bastarde, nebst Betrachtungen über die Begrenzung der Arten im Allgemeinen.

(Annales du Jardin Botanique de Buitenzorg, Vol. XL, pp. 1-44, 10 pl. 1929)

QH
Nat. Hist.
Pam.
167
Dansereau, Pierre

The varieties of evolutionary opportunity.

(Reprinted from Revue Canadienne de Biologie, 11(4):305-388, 1952)

AS
36
C 81
DAPHNIA

Brooks, John Langdon

The systematics of North American Daphnia.

(Mem. Conn. Acad. Arts and Sci., Vol. 13, 1957)

QK
Bot. Pam.
1858
Danser, B. H.

Zur Polymorphie des Polygonum Lapathifolium.

(Overgedrukt uit het Nederlandsch Kruidkundig Archief, Jaarg. 1931, Afl. 1. pp.100-125)

DU
406
D 19
Dansey, H. D. B.

How the Maoris came to Aotearoa. A.H.Reed Wellington. sm8vo. 1947. 115 pp.

QL
Crus.Pam.
126
DAPHNIA

Kerhervé, L.B. de

De L'Apparition Provoquée Des Mâles Chez Les Daphnies (Daphnia Psittacea).

(Mémoires de la Société Zoologique de France, Tome VIII,1895. pp-200-211)

QH
541
D 19
Dansereau, Pierre

Biogeography; an ecological perspective. The Ronald Press Company. New York. R8vo. 1957c xiii + 394 pp.

QL
523.C7
D 19
Dantec, F le & Berard, L.

Les sporozoaires et particulierment les Coccidies pathogenes.

Paris, n.d.

QL
Crus.Pam.
128.
DAPHNIA

Leydig, Franz

Naturgeschichte der Daphniden (Crustacea Cladocera). Tübingen, 1860.

REVIEW ONLY, by sir John Lubbock.

(Natural History Review, London, Vol. 1, 1861, pp. 22-43)

2 copies

QH
Nat.Hist.
Pam.
186
Dansereau, Pierre

Contributions to the "Encyclopedia Americana", 1957 on Tundra, Taiga, Acclimatization, Adaptation, etc.

GR
380.1
D 19
Danzel, Hedwig

Sagen und Legenden der Südsee-Insulaner (Polynesien). Herausgegeben von Hedwig und Theodor Wilhelm Danzel.

Schriften-Reihe, Kulturen der Erde... Abteilung: Textwerke...Folkwang verlag. Hagen u. Darmstadt. 1923. 4to. 81 pp.

QL
Crus.Pam.
143
DAPHNIA

Lubbock, J.

Leydig's Natural History of the Daphnidae.

(Nat.His.Review 1861. pp. 1-12)

QL
Crus.Pam.
241

DAPHNIA

Schouteden, H.

Le phototropisme de Daphnia Magna Straus (Crust.)

(Annales de la Société entomologique de Belgique, Tome XLVI, 1902. pp. 352-362)

Q
115
B

Nat. Hist.

Darbyshire, Otto Vernon

Lichens. In Nat. Antarctic Exped., 1901-1904. Nat. Hist. Vol. 5, zool. and botany, pp. 1-11, pl.1.

PL
870
D 25

Darling, D.

Davies, John

A Tahitian and English dictionary...by John Davies and D. Darling. Tahiti. London. Missionary Society. 1851. 314 + 7 pp. 8vo.

QL
Crus.Pam.
271

DAPHNIA

Scourfield, D. J.

A Hyaline Daphnia.

(Annual of Microscopy. 1900. pp. 1-12)

AS
162
P 23

DARDANUS

Forest, J.

Sur un Dardanus des Hawaii et de Madagascar, D. brachyops sp. nov. (Crustacea Paguridea Diogenidae)

(Bull. Mus. Nat. d'Hist. Nat., ser.2, Tome 34(5):365-370, 1962)

GN
2.S
T

Darling, David

Extrait du Journal du Révérend David Darling à Vaitahu, Tahuata, Décembre 1834- Septembre 1835. (signed Colin Newbury- translator?)

(Bull. Soc. des Etudes Océaniennes, No. 113, Tome IX(12):476-480, 1955)

[religion, social organization, tabu...]

QL
Crus.Pam.
265

DAPHNIA

Scourfield, D. J.

The swimming peculiarities of Daphnia, with an account of a new method of examining living Entomostraca and similar organisims.

(Jour. Quekett Micro. Club. Ser. 2, VII, 1900, pp. 395-404)

QH
1
P 11

DARDANUS

Matthews, Donald C.

The probable method of fertilization in terrestrial hermit crabs based on a comparative study of spermatophores.

(Pacific Science, Vol. X(3):303-309, July, 1956)

GN
23
D 22

Darling, F. Fraser

West highland survey; an essay in human ecology. Edited by F. Fraser Darling. Oxford Univ. Press. London. 1955. R8vo.   xvi + 438 pp.

QK
97
E 58

DAPHNIPHYLLACEAE

Engler, A.

Das Pflanzenreich, Heft 68 (IV. 147a),1919, by Käthe Rosenthal.

QH
1
P 11

DARDANUS   HAWAII

Matthews, Donald C.

The development of the pedunculate spermatophore of a hermit crab, Dardanus asper (De Haan).

(Pacific Science, 7:255-266, 1953)

GN
Ethn.Pam.
3210

Darlington, H. S.

The confession of sins.

(The Psychoanalytic Review. vol.24. 1937. pp.150-164)

QL
Mollusk
Pam
478

Darbishire, A. D.

Professor Lang's breeding experiments with Helix hortensis and H. nemoralis: an abstract and review. From Journ. of Conchology, v.2, n.7, 1905.

DU
Pac.
Pam.
973

Darden, T. F.

Administration of the Government of American Samoa, 1900-1951.   Department of the Navy. (U.S.) Washington. (1952) 4to.   39 pp.

QL
1
H 33 br

Darlington, P. J., Jr.

Australian carabid beetles VIII. Leiradira, especially the tropical species.

(Breviora, No. 147, 1961)

Also, XIII (part)

(Breviora, No. 183:pp. 1-10, 1963)

QK
5
Br

Darbishire, O. V. (Otto Vernon)

British Antarctic ("Terra Nova") Expedition, 1910. Natural history report : Botany, Part III (of vol. I) Lichens. 1923 , pp 29 - 76.

DU
110
D 22

Dark, Eleanor

The timeless land.   The Macmillan Company. New York. 1941. 8vo. ix +499 pp.

[fiction, based on the history of the first settlement of Sydney]

QL
461
P 11

Darlington, P. J., Jr.

The Bembidion and Trechus (Col.; Carabidae) of the Malay Archipelago.

(Pacific Insects, 1(4):331-346, 1959)

GN
Ethn.Pam
3070

Darby, George E.

Gates, R. R.

Blood groups and physiognomy of British Columbia coastal Indians, by R. Ruggles Gates, and Geo. E. Darby.

(Journal of Royal Anthropological Institute, Vol. LXIV, pp. 23-44, pls. I-V. Jan.-June, 1934)

QK
Pam
973

Darling, Chester Arthur

Sex in dioecious plants, ex Columbia Univ. Dept. of Bot. Contr., vol. X, no. 239, 1909.

QL
1
H 33 b

Darlington, P. J., Jr.

The carabid beetles of New Guinea, Part 1. Cicindelinae, Carabinae, Harpalinae through Pterostichini.

(Bull. Mus. of Comp. Zool., Harvard, Vol. 126(3), 1962)

QL 1 H 33 b   Darlington, P. J., Jr.

The Carabid beetles of New Guinea, Part 2. The Agonini.

(Bull. Mus. of Comp. Zool., Harvard College, Vol. 107(3):89-252, 1952)

GN Ethn. Pam No.692   Dart, Raymond A.

"The newly discovered man-ape skull". Science supplement, p viii, (separate sheet - not dated) JUN 11 '36

DU 12 D 22 locked case   Darwin, Charles

Journal of researches into the natural history and geology of the countries visited during the voyage of H.M.S. Beagle round the world, under the command of Capt. Fitz Roy, R.N. London. John Murray. 1860. 8vo. xv+519 pp.

The same...new edition, with illustrations of the places visited and described by R.T.Pritchett. London. John Murray. 1890. 8vo. 538 pp.

DU 12 K 54   The same...Vol.III of Narrative of the Surveying Voyage...of Adventure and Beagle, by King and others. London. 1839. Fitzroy

---

QH Nat.Hist. Pam. 226   Darlington, P. J., Jr.

The origin of the fauna of the Greater Antilles, with discussion of dispersal of animals over water and through the air.

(Quarterly Rev. of Biology, 13(3):274-300, 1938)

QH 1 A 88   Darwin, Charles

Coral Islands, with introduction, map and remarks, by D. R. Stoddart.

(Atoll Research Bull., No. 88, 1962)

QL 444.C5 D 22   Darwin, Charles

A monograph on the sub-class Cirripedia, with figures of all the species: The Lepadidae; or pedunculated Cirripedes, (Vol. 2) The Balanidae. (or sessile cirripedes); the Verrucidae. London. Printed for the Ray Society. 1851, 1854. 8vo.

QL 72 D 22   Darlington, Philip J., Jr.

Zoogeography: the geographical distribution of animals. New York. John Wiley and Sons, Inc. 8vo. xi + 675 pp.

QH 365 D22   Darwin, Charles

The descent of man, and selection in relation to sex.

New York, Appleton, 1871. 2v.

DU Hist.Pam. 261   Darwin, Charles

Staley, Thomas Nettleship

Notes on kahunas and priestcraft in Hawaii, sent to Charles Darwin at his request by Bishop Staley in 1864.

(Hawaiian Church Chronicle, Dec. 1935 and August, 1938)

AS 36 S   DARLINGTONIA CALIFORNICA

Torrey, John, 1796-1873.

... On the *Darlingtonia californica,* a new pitcher-plant, from northern California. By John Torrey ... [Washington, Smithsonian institution, 1853]

7, [1] p. pl. 32½ᶜᵐ. (Smithsonian contributions to knowledge. [vol. VI, art. 4])

Smithsonian institution publication 61.

1. Darlingtonia californica. I. Smithsonian institution. Publication 61.

Library of Congress   Q11.S68 vol. 6   5-37965 Revised

———— Copy 2.   QK495.D22T7

QK 840 D22   Darwin, Charles

The different forms of flowers on plants of the same species.

London, Murray, 1877. 352p. pls.

GN 370 C 65   Darwin, Charles

On the races of man.

IN

Count, Earl W. ed. This is race... pp. 133-144. New York. 1950

Pediculidae—Hawaii, p. 135

Darnand, J.

Aux Iles Samoa; la foret qui s'illume. 1934.

UH has

QH 365 D 22   Darwin, Charles

Evolution by natural selection, by Charles Darwin and Alfred Russel Wallace. With a foreword by Sir Gavin de Beer. Published for the XV International Congress of Zoology and the Linnean Society of London. Cambridge University Press. 1958. 8vo. viii + 288 pp.

QE 565 D22   Darwin, Charles

On the structure and distribution of coral reefs; and geological observations on the volcanic islands and parts of South America visited during the voyage of H.M.S. Beagle.

London, Ward, Lock, 1890. 549p.

see also Darwin, Charles The structure and distribution... 1962 edition. ed. by H.W. Menard

---

GN 470 D 66   Darnell, N., translator

Döllinger, John J. I.

The Gentile and the Jew, in the courts of the Temple of Christ: an introduction to the history of Christianity, from the German...(translated) by N. Darnell. Second edition. London. 1906. 2 vols.

QE 499 D 22   Darwin, Charles

The formation of vegetable mould, through the action of worms with observations on their habits. With illustrations. Sixth thousandth (corrected.) London. John Murray. 1882. 8vo. vii + 328 pp.

QE 565 D 22   Darwin, Charles

On the Structure and Distribution of Coral Reefs, with an introduction by Joseph W. Williams. London. Walter Scott. 12mo. xxiv + 278 pp. n.d.

QK 1 K 44   Darnell-Smith, G. P.

The Kentia palm seed industry, Lord Howe Island.

(Bull. Misc. Inf., Kew, 1931, pp. 1-4)

QP 401 D 22   Darwin, Charles

The expression of the emotions in man and animals. With photographic and other illustrations. With a preface by Margaret Mead. Philosophical Library. New York. 8vo. xi + 372 pp. 1955c.

QK Pam #522   Darwin, Charles

On the two forms or dimorphic conditions, in the species of Primula and on their remarkable sexual relations, ex Nat. Hist. Review, 1862.

QH
365
D 22

Darwin, Charles Robert, 1809–1882.
    The origin of species by means of natural selection, or The preservation of favoured races in the struggle for life. By Charles Darwin ... London, J. Murray, 1897.
    2 v. front. (port.) fold. diagr. 19½ᶜᵐ.
    "First edition, November 24th, 1859; sixth edition, Jan. 1872."

    1. Species, Origin of. 2. Natural selection.
                    Evolution   4–1283

    Library of Congress   QH365.O 1897

Q
Biogr.
Pam.
125

DARWIN, CHARLES

Castellanos, Telasco Garcia

    Darwin, homenaje en el Centenario de la primera manifestacion cientifica sobre el origen de las especies.

    (Cordoba, Acad. Nac. de Ciencias, Misc. No. 36, 1958)

QH
325
T 23

DARWIN, CHARLES

Tax, Sol.   editor

    Evolution after Darwin.
        Vol. I: The evolution of life: its origin history and future.
        Vol. II: The evolution of man: man, culture and society.
        Vol. III: Issues in evolution.
    The University of Chicago Press. R8vo. 1960.
    Edited by Sol Tax and Charles Callender

AS
36
S1

Darwin, Charles Robert, 1809–1882.
    Queries about expression for anthropological inquiry. By Charles Darwin ...
    (*In* Smithsonian institution. Annual report. 1867. Washington, 1868. 23½ᶜᵐ. p. [324])

    1. Expression.
                                    S 15–216

    Library of Congress   Q11.S66 1867
    Library, Smithsonian   Institution

Q
Biog
Pam
#16

DARWIN, CHARLES

    Commemoration of the centenary of Charles Darwin's birth and the fifteenth anniversary of the publication of the "Origin of Species".

AS
36
S1

DARWIN, CHARLES ROBERT, 1809–1882

Weismann, August, 1834–
    Charles Darwin. By August Weismann.
    (*In* Smithsonian institution. Annual report. 1909. Washington, 1910. 23½ᶜᵐ. p. 431–452)
    "Reprinted ... from the Contemporary review July, 1909."

    1. Darwin, Charles Robert, 1809–1882.
                                    11–9879

    Library of Congress   Q11.S66 1909

QE
565
M 53

Darwin, Charles
    The structure and distribution of coral reefs. Foreword by H. W. Menard. University of California Press. 1962. sm8vo. xii + 214; maps.

        see also by Darwin, Charles On the structure... 1890

QH
Nat.Hist.
Pam.
179

DARWIN, CHARLES

Darwin-Wallace Centenary.

    (Journal of the Linnean Soc. of London, Botany, Vol. 56, No. 365:pp. 1–152, 1958)

Q
Gen Sc
Pam
#36

Darwin, Francis
    Address of the President of the British Association for the Advancement of Science, ex Sc., vol. XXVIII, no. 716, Sept. 18, 1908.

QL
1
H 33 b

Darwin, Charles

Barrett, Paul H.   editor

    A transcription of Darwin's first notebook on "Transmutation of species".

QH
366
E 36

DARWIN, CHARLES

Eiseley, Loren

    Darwin's century; evolution and the men who discovered it. Doubleday Anchor Books. 1958. New York. 8vo. xvii + 378 pp.

AS
36
S1

Darwin, (Sir) George Howard, 1845–1912.
    The evolution of satellites. By G. H. Darwin.
    (*In* Smithsonian institution. Annual report. 1897. Washington, 1898. 23½ᶜᵐ. p. 109–124)
    "Reprinted from the Atlantic monthly of April, 1898."

    1. Satellites. I. Title.
                                    S 15–947

    Library of Congress   Q11.S66 1897
    Library, Smithsonian   Institution

QL
5
D 22

Looked
case

Darwin, Charles
    The Zoology of the Voyage of H.M.S.Beagle, under the command of Captain Fitzroy, during the years 1832 to 1836. Edited and superintended by Charles Darwin. In five parts. Parts 1–5. (in 3) London. Smith, Elder and Co. 1839–1843. 4to.
    Part I:Fossil Mammalia, by Richard Owen; Part II:Mammalia by George Waterhouse; Part III: Birds, by John Gould; Part IV:Fishes, by Leonard Jenyns; Part V:Reptiles, by Thomas Bell.

AS
719
A 93-m

DARWIN, CHARLES

Evans, J. W.

    The life and work of Charles Darwin.

    (Australian Mus. Mag., 13(4):105–114, 1959)

Q
Gen.Sci.
Pam
90

Darwin, G. H.
    First part of address to be delivered at Cape Town, Tuesday August 15, 1905, British Assn. Advancement of Sci., South Africa.

QH
9
B 32

DARWIN, CHARLES

Bates, Marston,   ed.

    The Darwin reader.   Edited by Marston Bates and Philip S. Humphrey.   Charles Scribner's Sons, New York. R8vo. ix + 470 pp. (1956c)

GN
22
M 41

DARWIN, CHARLES

    Man, race and Darwin; papers read at a joint conference of the R. Anthropological Inst. of Great Britain and Ireland and the Inst. of Race Relations. With an introduction and epilogue by Philip Mason. Oxford Univ. Press. 1960. vii + 151 pp.

QH
367
D22

Darwin, Leonard
    Organic evolution; outstanding difficulties and possible explanations. Cambridge, University press, 1921.

AS
322
Z 96 n

DARWIN, CHARLES R.

Burla, Hans

    Darwin und sein Werk.

    (Neujahrsblatt Gesellschaft in Zurich, 1959, 161 Stück)

QH
26
O 81

DARWIN, CHARLES

Osborn, Henry Fairfield

    Impressions of great naturalists; reminiscences of Darwin, Huxley, Balfour, Cope and others. Illustrated with portraits. Charles Scribner's Sons New York...1925. 8vo. xxviii + 212 pp.

    [also James Bryce, Louis Pasteur, Joseph Leidy, Theodore Roosevelt, John Muir, John Burroughs]

QH
367
R75

Darwin and after Darwin. 1896–7.

Romanes, George John.

QH
Nat.Hist.
Pam.
179

Darwin-Wallace Centenary.

(Journal of the Linnean Soc. of London, Botany, Vol. 56, No. 365:pp. 1-152, 1958)

AS
36
S1

Dastre, Albert *i. e.* Jules Albert Frank, 1844–
A new theory of the origin of species. By A. Dastre.

(*In* Smithsonian institution. Annual report. 1903. Washington, 1904. 23½ᶜᵐ. p. 507-517)

"Translated from the Revue des deux mondes for July, 1903, pp. 207-219."

1. Species, Origin of.

Library of Congress   Q11.S66 1903   S 15-1202
Library, Smithsonian   Institution

QL
Fishes
Pam.
518

DASYATIDAE

Halstead, Bruce W.

Stingray attacks and their treatment. By Bruce W. Halstead and Norman C. Bunker.

(Am. Jour. of Trop. Med. and Hygiene, Vol. 2(1):115-128, 1953)

QH
366
G 32

DARWINISM

Genetics and twentieth century Darwinism.

(Cold Spring Harbor Symposia on Quantitative Biology, vol. 24, 1959)

AS
36
S1

Dastre, Albert *i. e.* Jules Albert Frank, 1844–
Salt and its physiological uses. By M. A. Dastre.

(*In* Smithsonian institution. Annual report. 1901. Washington, 1902. 23½ᶜᵐ. p. 561-574)

"Translated and condensed from the Revue des deux mondes for 1901, vol. 1, pp. 197-227."

1. Salt.

Library of Congress   Q11.S66 1901   S 15-1125
Library, Smithsonian   Institution

AS
719
A 93-m

DASYURUS

Troughton, Ellis

Our marsupial "native cat".

(Austr. Mus. Mag., 11(3):90-92, 1953)

DU
Pac.
Pam.
886

Das, Florentino

[Voyage across the Pacific solo, 1955/56, stopping at various islands.]

(Honolulu Star-Bulletin, May 1-4,6-8,12; August 8; Honolulu Advertiser, July 31, 1956)

AS
36
S1

Dastre, Albert *i. e.* Jules Albert Frank, 1844–
The stature of man at various epochs. By A. Dastre.

(*In* Smithsonian institution. Annual report. 1904. Washington, 1905. 23½ᶜᵐ. p. 517-532)

"Translated from Revue des deux mondes. Paris, September 1, 1904."

1. Anthropometry.   I. Title.

Library of Congress   Q11.S66 1904   S 15-1260
Library, Smithsonian   Institution

Z
696
U 58

DATA PROCESSING

Handbook on data processing methods. Part 1. Provisional edition.

Food and Agriculture Organiation of the United Nations, Rome 1959. 4to. 111 pp.

AP
2
S 35

DAS, UPENDRA KUMAR

Borden, Ralph J.

Upendra Kumar Das

(Science, Vol. 87:58, 1938)

QK
358
D 23

Dastur, J. F.

Medicinal plants of India and Pakistan, a concise work describing plants used for drugs and remedies according to Ayurvedic, Unani, Tibbi systems and mentioned in British and American Pharmacopoeias. D. B. Taraporevala Sons and Co., Ltd. Bombay. n.d. cr8vo. vi + (1)2-317 pp.

QK
1
U

Date Palm
Cook, O. F.
Relationships of the false Date Palm of the Florida keys with a synoptical key to the families of American Palms.   U. S. Nat. Herb. XVI, 8, 1913, pp. 243-254, pls. 74-75.

S
21
A35

Dasheen: its uses and culture.
Young, Robert A.

Dasheen: its uses and culture. In U. S. Dept. Agric. Yearbook, 1916, pp 200-208.

QK
358
D 23

Dastur, J. F.

Useful plants of India and Pakistan, a popular handbook of trees and plants of industrial, economic and commercial utility. With 66 illustrations D. B. Taraporevala Sons and Co., Ltd. Bombay. n.d. cr8vo. vi + 260 pp.

G
3
A1

DATE-PALM

Poponoe, Paul

The distribution of the date-palm. In Geog. Rev. Vol. XVI, 1926, pp 117 - 121.

QL
401
H 39

Dashwood, R. Julian

Shell news from the Cook Islands.

(Hawaiian Shell News, Vol. IV(11):116, September, 1956)

QL
1
N 6-z

DASYATIDAE

Beebe, William

Fishes from the tropical eastern Pacific... Part 3. Rays, Mantas and Chimeras, by William Beebe and John Tee-Van. Eastern Pacific Exp. of the New York Zool. Soc., XXVIII.

(Zoologica, Vol. 26, 1941, pp. 245-280)

QK
Bot.Pam.
1599

DATES

Mason, S.C.

The Saidy Date of Egypt: A Variety of the First Rank Adapted to Commercial Culture in the United States

U.S.D.A. Bulletin No. 1125, 1923

Q
101
P 18

Dasmann, Raymond F.

Mule deer in relation to a climatic gradient. By Raymond F. Dasmann and William P. Dasmann.

(Reprint, Jour. of Wildlife Management, Vol. 27(2):196-202, 1963)

QL
Fishes
Pam.
439

DASYATIDAE

Gudger, Eugene W.

Is the sting ray's sting poisonous? A historical resumé showing the development of our knowledge that it is poisonous.

(Bull. History of Medicine, Vol. 14, No. 4, Nov. 1943 [issued Jan. 27, 1944], pp. 467-504)

S
Agric.
Pam.
92

DATES

Nixon, R. W.

Growing dates in the United States.

(USDA Bull. 207:1-50; 1959)

GN
855.1
D 23
Datta-Majumder, Nabendu

The Santal, a study in culture-change.

(Department of Anthropology, Government of India, Memoir No. 2, 1955)

AM
7
D23
Daukes, S   H

The medical museum; modern developments, organisation and technical methods, based on a new system of visual teaching.

London, Wellcome Foundation,[1929]   183p.

QL
401
J 85
Dautzenberg, Ph.

Description d'une espèce nouvelle du genre Cyrena, provenant des Nouvelles-Hébrides.

(Jour. de Conchyl., Vol. 48:105-108, 1900)

QK
1
H 33
DATURA

Barclay, Arthur S.

New considerations in an old genus: Datura.

(Bot. Mus. Leaflets, Harvard Univ., 18(6), pp. 245-327, 1959)

DU
740
D24
Dauncey, H. M.

Papuan Pictures.

London, 1913. PP 184 illus.

QL
Mollusk
Pam
595
Dautzenberg, Ph.

Dragages effectués par l'Hirondelle et par laPrincesse-Alice. Extrait des memoires de la Soc. Zool. de France, 1896.

QE
521
D 23
Daubeny, C.

Description of active and extinct volcanos of earthquakes and of thermal springs; with remarks on causes of these phaenomena, character of their respective products and influence on past and present condition of the globe.

London, 1848,   2nd. ed. 8vo. pp. 830. illus.

QL
401
J 85
Dautzenberg, Ph.

Contribution à la faune malacologique de l'Indochine. By Ph. Dautzenberg and H. Fischer.

(Jour. de Conchyl., Tome 54:145-226, 1906)

QL
Mollusk
Pam
596
Dautzenberg, Ph.

Dragages effectués par L'Hirondelle et la Princesse-Alice. From Société Zool. deFrance, 1897.

AS
36
S1
Daubrée, Auguste i. e. Gabriel Auguste, 1814-1896.
Deep-sea deposits. By A. Daubrée.

(*In* Smithsonian institution. Annual report. 1893. Washington, 1894. 23½ᶜᵐ. p. 545-566. pl. XXXV-XXXVI)
"Translated from Journal des savants, December, 1892, pp. 733-743, January, 1893, pp. 37-54."

1. Challenger expedition, 1872-1876. 2. Deep-sea deposits.

S 15-842

Library of Congress
Library, Smithsonian   Q11.S66 1893
Institution

QL
Mollusk
Pam
593
Dautzenberg, Ph.

Contribution a la faune malacologique de Sumatra (recoltes de M. J.-L. Weyers). From Annales de la Soc. Royale Malacologique de Belgique. Tome 34. 1899.

AS
145
B
Dautzenberg, Ph.

Gastéropodes marins: Famille Conidae.

Van Straelen, V.
Résultats scientifiques du voyage aux Indes Orientales Néerlandaises...Léopold de Belgique. Vol. 2, Fasc. 18, 1937, pp. 1-284

(Mem. hors ser. Mus. Roy. d'Hist. Nat., Belgique)

AS
36
S1
Daubrée, Auguste i. e. Gabriel Auguste, 1814-1896.
Synthetic experiments relative to meteorites—approximations to which these experiments have lead. By M. Daubrée ...

(*In* Smithsonian institution. Annual report. 1868. Washington, 1869. 23½ᶜᵐ. p. (312)-341)
From Annales des mines, Paris, 1868.

1. Meteorites.

S 15-254

Library of Congress
Library, Smithsonian   Q11.S66 1868
Institution

QL
401
J 85
Dautzenberg, Ph.

Bavay, A.

Description de coquilles nouvelles de l'Indochine. By A. Bavay and Ph. Dautzenberg. (Parts) 1-8
(Jour. de Conchyl., Tome 47:28-55,276-296, 1899; 48:435-460, 1900; 51:201-236, 1903; 57:81-105, 163-206, 279-288, 1909; 60:1-54, 1912; 62:147-153, 1914/15)

Parts 7-8 also in QL Moll. Pams. 260-261

AS
145
B
Dautzenberg, Ph.

Gastéropodes marins; 1. Famille Terebridae; 2. Famille Mitridae.

Van Straelen, V.
Résultats Scientifiques du Voyage aux Indes Orientales Néerlandaises... Vol. 2, Fasc. 17, 1935. 208 pp. (being Mem. hors ser. Mus. R. d'Hist. Nat., Belgique)

AS
36
S1
Daubrée, Auguste i. e. Gabriel Auguste, 1814-1896.
Synthetical studies and experiments on metamorphism and on the formation of crystalline rocks. By M. Daubrée.

(*In* Smithsonian institution. Annual report. 1861. Washington, 1862. 23½ᶜᵐ. p. (228)-304)
"Translated by T. Egleston ..."
"Annales des mines, 5 series, vol. 16, pp. 155-393."

1. Rocks, Crystalline and metamorphic. 1. Egleston, Thomas, 1832-1900.

S 15-111

Library of Congress
Library, Smithsonian   Q11.S66 1861
Institution

QL
401
J 85
Dautzenberg, Ph.

Description d'un Bulimide nouveau, provenant de la Nouvelle-Caledonie. By Ph. Dautzenberg and J. Bernier.

(Jour. de Conchyl., Vol. 49:215-216, 1900)

Q
115
S 56
Dautzenberg, Ph.

Les Lamellibranches de l'expedition du Siboga...Partie systematique, I: Pectinides by Ph. Dautzenberg...

Weber, Max
Uitkomsten...Nederlandsch Oost Indie, 1899-1900...Siboga...Mon. LIIIb (livr. 63), 1912.

QK
Bot.Pam.
2317
Daugherty, Lyman H.

The Upper Triassic flora of Arizona, with a discussion of its geologic occurrence, by Howard R. Stagner. (Carnegie Institution of Washington, Pub. no. 526) 1941. 4to. 108 pp., 34 pl.

QL
401
J 85
Dautzenberg, Ph.

Description d'un Bulimidé nouveau provenant de Lifou.

(Jour. de Conchyliologie, Vol. 67: 260-261, 1922)

QL
Moll.
Pam.
263
Dautzenberg, Ph.

Liste des mollusques rapportés de la Nouvelle- Zemble par M. Serge Ivanoff. Extrait Journ.de Conchyl. Vol 59, 1911 pp. 297-310

QL
401
J 85

Dautzenberg, Ph.

Liste préliminaire des mollusques marins de Madagascar et description de deux espèces nouvelles.

(Journal de Conchyliologie, Tome 68:21-74, 1923)

QL
401
J 85

Dautzenberg, Ph.

Mollusques testacés marins de Madagascar.- Supplement.

(Jour. de Conchyliologie, Vol. 76:5-119, 1932)

QL
Mollusca
Pam.
567

Dautzenberg, Ph.

Sur quelques types de Garidés de la collection de Lamarck existant au Muséum de Paris. By Ph. Dautzenberg and H. Fischer
(Jour. de Conchyl., 61:215-228, 1913)

QL
401
J 85

Dautzenberg, Ph.

Mitridés de la Nouvelle-Calédonie et de ses dépendances. By Ph. Dautzenberg and L.J. Bouge.

(Jour. de Conchyl., Tome 67:179-259, 1922)

QL
428.5
D 24

Dautzenberg, Ph.

Les Mollusques Testacés Marins des Établissements Français de l'Océanie, par Ph. Dautzenberg et J. L. Bouge.

(Extrait du Journal de Conchyliologie, Vol. 77, 1933, pp. 41-469)

D'Auvergne collection of shells

QL
406
F27

Favanne de.

Catalogue systematique et raisonne...
Paris, 1784.

QL
Mollusk
Pam
603

Dautzenberg, Ph.

Les mollusques de la baie de Saint-Malo. Extrait de la 'Feuille des jeunes naturalistes, 1913.

QL
401
J 85

Dautzenberg, Ph.

Olividés de la Nouvelle-Calédonie et de ses dépendances.

(Jour. de Conchyl. vol. 71:1-72; 103-147, 1927)

GN
2.S
O 15

Dauvergne, Robert

Les debuts du Papeete francais:1843-1863.

(Jour. de la Soc. des Océanistes, 15:113-145, 1959)

QL
Mollusk
Pam
520

Dautzenberg, Ph   and Fischer, H

Mollusques et brachiopodes recueillis en 1908 par la mission Benard dans les mers du nord. Paris, 1911. From Jour. de Conch. v. 59, 1911.   pp. 1-51

QL
Mollusca
Pam. 69

Dautzenberg, Ph.

Bouge, L. J.

Les Pleurotomides de la Nouvelle Calédonie et de ses dependances.

(Journal de Conch., Vol. 61, 1913, pp. 123-214)

AS
36
A 25

and
GN
Ethn.Pam
3764

Davenport, Charles Benedict

Critical examination of physical anthropometry on the living, by C. B. Davenport, Morris Steggerda and William Drager.

(Proc. of Amer. Acad. of Arts and Sciences, Vol. 69, No. 6, Feb., 1934.   pp. 265-284)

QL
Mollusk
Pam
548

Dautzenberg, Ph   and Fischer, P   H

Les mollusques marins du Finistere et en particulier de la region de Roscoff. From Travaux de la station biologique de Roscoff, fasc.3, 1925.

QL
401
J 85

Dautzenberg, Ph.

Revision des Cypraeidas de la Nouvelle-Calédonie.

(Jour. de Conchyl, Vol. 50:291-384, 1902)

QH
351
D24

Davenport, Charles Benedict

Experimental morphology

New York, Macmillan, 1899.

Library has Part 2 - Effect of chemical and physical agents upon growth

---

QL
Mollusk
Pam
549

Dautzenberg, Ph

Mollusques nouveaux provenant des croisieres du Prince Albert Monaco. From Bull. L'institute Oceanographique, n.457, 1925.

QL
Mollusk
Pam
578

Dautzenberg, Ph

Sinistrorsites et dextrorsites teratologiques chez les molusques gasteropodes. From Bull. Soc. Zool. France, v.39, n.2, 1914.

QH
431
D24

Davenport, Charles Benedict, 1866-

The feebly inhibited; Nomadism, or the wandering impulse, with special reference to heredity, Inheritance of temperament, by Charles B. Davenport ... Washington, D. C., Carnegie institution of Washington, 1915.

1 p. l., 158 p. diagrs. 25½ᶜᵐ. (On verso of t.-p.: Carnegie institution of Washington. Publication no. 236)

Paper no. 24 of the Station for experimental evolution at Cold Spring Harbor, New York.

"Literature cited": p. 26, 123-124.

1. Heredity. 2. Temperament. I. Title. II. Title: Nomadism.

Library of Congress   QH431.D214   16—780
———— Copy 2.

QL
345.N 6
S 24

Dautzenberg, Ph.

Mollusques terrestres de la Nouvelle-Calédonie et des Iles Loyalty.

Sarasin, Fritz
Nova Caledonia...A. Zoologie, Tome III, Livr. 1, pp. 135-156. 1923.

QL
401
J 85

Dautzenberg, Ph.

Sur quelques déformations chez des Cypraea de la Nouvelle-Calédonie.

(Jour. de Conchyliologie, Vol. 53:263-266, 1906)

GN
51
D24

Davenport, Charles B

Guide to physical anthropometry and anthroposcopy.   Cold Spring Harbor, 1927.   55 p.

QH
431
De-
D24
Davenport, Charles Benedict, 1866–
Heredity of skin color in negro-white crosses, by Charles B. Davenport ... with appendix, being abridgement of field-notes, chiefly of Florence H. Danielson ... Washington, D. C., Carnegie institution of Washington, 1913.
2 p. l., 106 p. incl. tables, diagrs. 4 pl. 25½ᶜᵐ. (On verso of t.-p.: Carnegie institution of Washington, Publication no. 188)
Paper no. 20 of the Station for experimental evolution at Cold Spring Harbor, New York.
Plates accompanied by guard sheets with descriptive letterpress.
1. Heredity. 2. Color of man. 3. Miscegenation. I. Danielson, Florence Harris, 1886–

Library of Congress   QH431.D25
——— Copy 2.   (s21f2)   13—24763

GN
1
A51
Davenport, Charles B.
Physical Anthropology of Australian Aborigines.
(American Journal of Physical Anthropology, Vol. 8, 1925, pp. 73–94.)

GN
1
A 51
Davenport, William
Nonunilinear descent and descent groups.
(Am. Anthrop., 61(4):557–572, 1959)

QH
431
D1
D24
457
Davenport, Charles, B.
Inheritance in Canaries.
Carnegie Inst. 8° pp. 26. plts 1–3.
Wash. 1908. Publ. 95.

GN
237
D24
Davenport, Charles Benedict, and Morris Steggerda
Race crossing in Jamaica. Carnegie institution of Washington, 1929. 516 p. pl.
Carnegie Pub. 395

GN
1
J
Davenport, William H.
Fourteen Marshallese riddles.
(Journal of American Folklore, Vol. 65(257): 265–266, 1952)

QH
431
C35
Davenport, C. B.
Inheritance in Poultry. (Paper No. 7, Stn. Exp. Evolution.) Carnegie Institution of Washington Publication No. 52. Washington 1906. 8vo. 141 pp.

GN
1
A-J
Davenport, Charles Benedict
Some principles of anthropometry.
(American Journal of Physical Anthrop., Vol. 23, 1937, pp. 91–99)

QK
477
D 24
Davey, John
The tree doctor; a book on tree culture, illustrated profusely with photographs. Published by the Author. Akron. 1902. R8vo. 88 pp.

QH
431
D24
Davenport, Ch. B.
Inheritance of characteristics in domestic fowl.
Wash. 1909. Carn. Inst. Publ. 121.
4°. p. 100. plts. 1–12.

AS
36
A9
Davenport, George E.
Some comparative tables showing the distribution offerns in the United States of North America. In Proc. Amer. Phil. Soc. XX, 1883, pp. 605–612.

QL
Mol
Pam
#121½
D
David, A.
Sur Les Mollusques des Parties Centrales de L'Asie (Chine et Thibet)
ex (?), 1882.

QH
431
D 24
Davenport, Charles Benedict, 1866–
Naval officers, their heredity and development, by Charles Benedict Davenport ... assisted by Mary Theresa Scudder ... Washington, Carnegie institution of Washington, 1919.
iv p., 1 l., 236 p. diagrs. 25½ᶜᵐ. (On verso of t.-p.: Carnegie institution of Washington. Publication no. 259)
Paper no. 29 of the Station for experimental evolution at Cold Spring Harbor, New York.
Includes bibliographies.
1. Heredity. 2. U. S.—Navy—Officers. 3. Gt. Brit.—Navy—Officers. I. Scudder, Mary Theresa. II. Title.

Library of Congress   V61.D3
——— Copy 2.   (s19j5)   19—6421

AP
2
S 41
Davenport, William
Red-feather money.
(Scientific American, 206(3):95–104, 1962)

DU
590
D 24
David, (Mrs.) Edgeworth
Funafuti, or Three Months on a Coral Island: an Unscientific Account of a Scientific Expedition. With Portraits, Map, and Illustrations. London. John Murray. 1899. 8vo. xiii + 318 pp.

Q
Gen So
Pam
#26
Davenport, C. B.
The new views about reversion, ex Am. Phil. Soc. Proc., 49, 1910.

Newspaper closet
Davey and Company.
Photographs, Portraits, Landscapes, Views of buildings. etc. taken chiefly on Oahu and Hawaii by Davey and Company. In 9 folio volumes.
(see correspondence files, R. J. Baker. Dates of Davey's work are within 1898-1908)

GC
63
D 61
David, P. M.
The distribution of Sagitta gazellae Ritter-Zahony.
(Discovery Reports, Vol. XXVII:235–278, 1956)

QL
Protozoa
to
Polyzoa
Pam
343
Davenport, C B
On the variation of the statoblasts of pectinatella magnifica from Lake Michigan, at Chicago. From American Naturalist, v. 34, n. 408.

GN
1
J 86
Davenport, William
Marshallese folklore types.
(Jour. Am. Folklore, 66(261):219–237, 1953)

GC
63
D 61
David, P. M.
The distribution of the Chaetognatha of the Southern Ocean.
(Discovery Reports, Vol. 29:199–228, 1958)

Q 115
S47
Ba

David, T. W. Edgeworth

Geology I, British Antarctic expedition, 1907-9 under the command of Sir E. H. Shackleton, C. V. O. ......

London, 1914, pp xiv, 319, 4to.

(Geology of South Victoria Land)

AS
36
A 9

Davidson, Daniel Sutherland

Aboriginal Australian string figures.

(Proc. Am. Phil. Soc., 84, 1941, pp. 763-901)

GN
1
A

Davidson, D. S. (Daniel Sutherland)

The Family Hunting Territory in Australia.

(American Anthropologist, N. S. Vol. 30, 1928, pp. 614-631)

QE
Geol.Pam.
1120

David, T. W. Edgeworth

Geology of the Commonwealth (Australia). Reprinted from the Federal Handbook on Australia, issued in connexion with the visit of the British Association for the Advancement of Science to Australia, 1914. Government Printer. Melbourne. (1915?) 8vo pp.241-325

GN
775
M 13

Davidson, Daniel Sutherland

The antiquity of man in the Pacific and the question of trans-Pacific migrations.

MacCurdy, George Grant

Early man as depicted by leading authorities at the international symposium...Philadelphia, 1937. pp. 269-276.

AS
36
A 9
and
GN
Ethn.Pam.
3310

Davidson, D. Sutherland

An ethnic map of Australia.

(Proc. Am. Philosophical Society, Vol. 79, 1938, pp. 649-679)

DU
155
J 83

David, T. W. Edgeworth, editor

Jose, A. W.

New South Wales: Historical, physiographical and economic, by A. W. Jose, T. Griffith Taylor, and W. G. Woolnough. Edited by T. W. Edgeworth David. Melbourne, Whitcombe & Toombs, n.d. vii + 372 pp. illus, maps.

GN
2.S
P 76

Davidson, D. S.

Australian netting and basketry techniques.

(Journal of the Polynesian Society, 42: 257-299, 1933.)

GN
2.S
S 72

Davidson, D. S.

Footwear of the Australian aborigines: environmental vs. cultural determination.

(Southwestern Jour. of Anthropology, Vol. 3(2):114-123, 1947)

QE
Geol.Pam.
907

David, T. W. Edgeworth

Sussmilch, C. A.

Sequence, glaciation and correlation of the carboniferous rocks of the Hunter River District, New South Wales. By C. A. Sussmilch and T. W. Edgeworth David.

(Journal and Proc. of the R. Soc. of N. S. Wales, Vol. 53, 1920, pp. 245-338.)

GN
2.S
P 76
and
GN
Ethn.Pam.
3773

Davidson, D. S. (Daniel Sutherland)

Australian spear-traits and their derivations.

(Journ. Polyn. Soc., Vol. 43, No. 3, Sept., 1934, pp. 143-162)

GN
2.S
M 26

Davidson, D. S.

The interlocking key design in aboriginal Australian decorative art.

(Mankind, Vol. 4:85-98, 1949)

GN
470.B
D 25

Davids, Rhys (Mrs.)

Buddhism: a Study of the Buddhist Norm. New York. Henry Holt and Company. ND 255 pp. 12mo.

GN
1
A

Davidson, D. S. (Daniel Sutherland)

Australian throwing-sticks, throwing-clubs, and boomerangs.

(American Anthropologist, N. S., Vol. 38, 1936, pp. 76-100)

GN
1
A
and
GN
Ethn.Pam.
3095

Davidson, D. S. (Daniel Sutherland)

Knotless netting in America and Oceania.

(American Anthropologist, Vol. 37, No. 1, pt. 1, Jan.-Mar., 1935, pp. 117-134)

QK
Pam
#420

Davidson, A.

New California Plants, Extract, n.p; n.d.

GN
1
A
and
GN
Pam.766

(Daniel)
Davidson, D. Sutherland

The Basis of Social Organization in Australia.

(American Anthropologist, N. S. Vol. 28, 1926, pp. 529-548)

GN
2.S
A 51
and
GN
Ethn.Pam.
3774

Davidson, D. S (Daniel Sutherland)

Northwestern Australia and the question of influences from the near east.

(Journal of the Am. Oriental Soc., Vol. 58, 1938, pp. 61-80)

AS
36
A 91-m

Davidson, Daniel S.

Aboriginal Australian and Tasmanian rock carvings and paintings.

(Mem. Am. Philosophical Society, 5, 1936, pp.)

GN
Pam
2683

Davidson, Daniel Sutherland

The chronological aspects of certain Australian social institutions: as inferred from geographical distribution.

[a thesis in anthropology.. University of Pennsylvania, Philadelphia, 1928]

GN
Ethn.
Pam.
3530

Davidson, D. Sutherland

Oceania: The oceanic collections of the University Museum.

(University Museum Bull., Vol. 12, Nos. 3-4, June, 1947) University of Pennsylvania

GN
2.S
P 76
Davidson, D. S. (Daniel Sutherland)

The Pacific and circum-Pacific appearances of the dart-game.

(Jrl. of the Polynesian Soc., vol.45, 1936, pp.99-114; vol.46, 1937, pp.1-23)

GN
Ethn.Pam.
3893
Davidson, George

Mesh-knot of the Tchin-cha-au Indiands, Port Simpson, British Columbia.

(Calif. Acd. Sci., Proceedings, Oct. 19, 1874)

AS
36
C 3
Davidson, M. E. McLellan

Templeton Crocker Expedition to western Polynesian and Melanesian Islands, 1933, No. 16: Notes on the birds, by M. E. McLellan Davidson.

(Proc. Calif. Acad. of Sci., Vol. 21, no. 16, pp. 189-198. Oct. 16, 1934)

AS
36
A 9-m
Davidson, Daniel Sutherland

A preliminary consideration of aboriginal Australian decorative art.

(Mem. American Philosophical Soc., Vol. 9, 1937. pp. xi + 147)

F
856
D25
Davidson, George
Origin and meaning of the name California. In Geog. Soc. of the Pacific, Trans. and Proc. 2d ser. Vol. VI, pt.1. [San Francisco], 1910.

QL
1
C 15
Davidson, Pirie, 1892-
... The musculature of *Heptanchus maculatus*, by Pirie Davidson. Berkeley, University of California press, 1918.

cover-title, p. [151]-170. illus. 27½ᶜᵐ. (University of California publications in zoology. v. 18, no. 10)
"Literature cited": p. 170.

1. Heptanchus maculatus. 2. Fishes—Anatomy. i. Title.
A 18-455

Title from Univ. of Calif.   Library of Congress

GN
Ethn.Pam.
3313
Davidson, Daniel Sutherland

A preliminary register of Australian tribes and hordes. American Philosophical Society, Philadelphia, 1938, 130 pp. 4to.

QL
Insect
Pam
876
Davidson, J.

The "Lucerne Flea" Smynthurus viridis L. (Collembola) in Australia. Melbourne. 1934. 66 pp. 5 pls.

(Commonwealth of Australia, Council for Scientific and Industrial Research, Bulletin No. 79, 1934).

Q
115
C43

G.2.3.

Davidson Thomas

Challenger Expedition

Zoology. Part 1. Brachiopoda.

GN
1
A

and
GN
Ethn.Pam.
3772
Davidson, D. S. (Daniel Sutherland)

Question of relationship between the cultures of Australia and Tierra del Fuego.

(American Anthropologist, Vol. 39, 1937, pp. 229-243)

DU
1
A 93
Davidson, J. W.

The literature of the Pacific Islands.

(The Australian Outlook, Vol. 1:63-79, 1947)

QL
Protozoa
to
Polyzoa
Pam
312
Davidson, Th

Qu'est-ce qu'un brachiopode. Bruxelles, 1875

AS
36
A 9
Davidson, D. S. (Daniel Sutherland)

The spearthrower in Australia.

(Proc. of the American Philosophical Soc., vol.76, 1936, pp.445-483)

DU
Pac.Pam.
849
Davidson, J. W.
Spate, O. H. K.

Notes on New Guinea. October-November, 1951. By O. H. K. Spate, J. W. Davidson and Raymond Firth. typed, folio. 3+13+18+10 pp. (from The Australian National University)

[studies of history, government, social and economic change, etc.]

GN
Ethn.Pam.
2982
Davies, E. Harold

Aboriginal Songs of Central and Southern Australia.

(Oceania, Vol. II, 1932, pp. 454-467)

GN
2.S
P 76
Davidson, D. S. (Daniel Sutherland)

Transport and receptacles in aboriginal Australia.

(Journal of the Polynesian Society, Vol. 46, 1937, pp. 175-205)

GN
2.S
O 15
Davidson, J. W.

Peter Dillon and the discovery of sandalwood in the New Hebrides.

(Jour. Soc. des Océanistes,12:99-106, 1956)

QL
Fishes
Pam.
452
Davies, D. H.

A new Goby from the Knysna River.

(Annals and Mag. Nat. Hist., s 12, vol. 1: 375, 1948)

Q
101
P 18
Davidson, F. A.

Age, growth, and seasonal time of migration of the Pacific salmon as an indication of environmental conditions in the sea.

IN Proc. Sixth Pac. Sci. Congress, 1939, (California), Vol. 3, pp. 533-534, 1940.

AS
36
C 3

and
QL
Birds
Pam.
244
Davidson, M. E. McLellan

On a small collection of birds from Torres Strait Islands, and from Guadalcanar Island, Solomon Group.

(Proc. Calif. Acad. Sci., Fourth Ser., Vol. 18, 1929, pp. 245-260)

GN
Pam
2732
Davies, E   Harold

Adelaide University field anthropology: Central Australia - No. 4. Aboriginal songs. From Trans. Royal Soc. South Australia, v.51, 1927.

GN
2.S
P 76

Davies, G. H.

Tuhoto-Ariki

An ancient Maori poem. Translated and paraphrased by G. H. Davies and J. H. Pope.

(Jour. Poly. Soc., 16:43-53, 1907)

PL 870E11

Davies, John   translator of

Te mau epistole a te aposetola ra a Paulo, Ta'na i papai adu i to Galatia...Tahiti. 1824.

DU
Hist.Pam.
152

Davies, Theo. H.

Correspondence with Reference to Pearl Harbor. 29 pp. 8vo.

(Reprinted from the Hawaiian Gazette for Mr. Theo. H. Davies. November, 1892) (For Private Circulation)

GN
2.S
P 76

Davies, G. H.

Maori star names.

(Journal of the Polynesian Society, Vol. 20, 1911, pp. 10-11)

AP
2
N 4

Davies, John D. Griffith

Sir Joseph Banks, P. C., K. C. B., F. R. S. (1743-1820)

(Nature, Vol. 151, 1943, pp. 181-183)

DU
Pacific
Pam
2787

Davies Theophilus Harris

The Hawaiian situation. From North American Review, May 1893.

QL
1
C 23

Davies, D. H.

Preliminary investigations on the foods of South African fishes. (With notes on the general fauna of the area surveyed).

(Union of South Africa, Dept. of Commerce and Industries, Fisheries and Marine Biological Survey Division, Investigational Report No. 11, 1949.)

QK
451
Ew 3
E94

Davies, Olive B   joint author.

Ewart, Alfred J

Flora of the Northern territory, by Alfred J. Ewart and Olive B. Davies ... Melbourne, McCarron, Bird & co., 1917.
387p. illus.

DU
Hist.Pam.
170

Davies, Theo. H.

The Kingdom of Hawaii. A lecture delivered by Mr. Theo. H. Davies before the Members of the Southport Literary and Philosophical Society, on Friday evening, December 4th, 1891. Southport 1891. Robert John and Co., Limited. 22 pp. 8vo.

G
3
A 51

Davies, J. L.

The Pinnepedia: an essay in zoogeography.

(Geographical Review, 48(4):474-493, 1958)

QL
464
R 51

Davies, R. G.

Imms, A. D.

A general textbook of entomology, including the anatomy, physiology, development and classification of insects. Ninth edition, entirely revised by O. W. Richards and R. G. Davies. Methuen and Co., Ltd. London. R8vo. 1957. x + 886 pp.

DU
620
H 4

Davies, Theo. H.

The Last Hours of Liholiho and Kamamalu: Copy of a letter sent to H. R. H. Princess Liliuokalani, presented to the Hawaiian Historical Society by the author, Theo. H. Davies.

(Annual Report of the Hawaiian Historical Society, 4th, 1896, pp. 30-32)

PL
870
G 74

and

PL
Phil.Pams.
208,268

PL
870
T 25

(Davies, John)

A grammar of the Tahitian dialect of the Polynesian language. Burder's Point, Tahiti. Mission Press. 1823. 43 pp. 8vo. contains also Dictionary from A through Arapoa. 49 pp.

(Bound with 33 other pamphlets: Te evanelia a to tatou ... no. 8)

QL
BirdsPam
479

Davies, S. J. J. F.

Aspects of the behaviour of the magpie goose, Anseranas semipalmata.

(Ibis, 105:76-98, 1963)

DU
Hist.Pam.
170

Davies, Theo. H.

A lecture delivered by Mr. Theo. H. Davies before the Members of the Southport Literary and Philosophical Society, On Friday evening, December 4th, 1891. Southport. 1891. Robert John and Co., Limited.

G
151
H 15

over

Davies, John

The history of the Tahitian Mission, 1799-1830, written by John Davies, missionary to the South Sea Islands, with supplementary papers from the correspondence of the missionaries. Edited by C. W. Newbury.

(Works issues by the Hakluyt Society, 2nd ser., No. 116, issued for 1959)

DU
Hist.Pam.
146

Davies, Theo. H.

Closing letter from Mr. T. H. Davies to Mr. C. J. Lyons.

IN Final correspondence resulting from the open letter...by Curtis J. Lyons, pp. 7-10.

DU
Missions
Pam 24

Davies, Theo. H.

Letter to His Grace the Archbishop of Canterbury in response to the appeal of the Bishop of Honolulu. Honolulu. 1886. 8vo. 95 pp.

PL
870
D 25

2 copies.

(Davies, John)

A Tahitian and English dictionary with introductory remarks on the Polynesian and a short grammar of the Tahitian dialect with an appendix containing a list of words used in the Tahitian Bible, in commerce, etc. with the sources from which they have been derived, by John Davies and E. Taplin. Tahiti. London Miss. Soc., 1851. 314 + 7 pp.

DU
Hist.Pam.
144

Davies, Theo. H.

Correspondence resulting from the Open Letter addressed to the Honolulu "Bulletin". Printed for Private Circulation. San Francisco, 1893. 8vo. 9 pp.

DU
Hist.Pam.
71

Davies, Theo. H.

Letters upon the Political Crisis in Hawaii January, 1893, to January, 1894. (Reprinted) Honolulu. 1894. 8vo. 68 pp.

Also Second Series, 1894 (Reprinted)

DU
Hist.Pam.
148

and

DU
620
M 67

Davies, Theo. H.

Open letter to the Right Reverend Alfred Willis, Bishop of Honolulu, and President of the Cathedral Building Committee. 9 pp. 1886. 8vo.

(Misc. Pams. Haw. 1:565-574)

DU
Hist.Pam.
80

Davies, Theo. H. (& Co.)

The Shone Sewerage System as Applied to Honolulu. Honolulu. Hawaiian Gazette Co. 1892. sm8vo. 14 pp.

QL
Insects
Pam.
1200

Davis, A. C.

The mushroom mite (Tyrophagus lintneri (Osborn)) as a pest of cultivated mushrooms.

(Tech. Bull., U. S. D. A., 879, 1944)

DU
Hist.Pam.
143

Davies, Theo. H.

Open Letter upon the Hawaiian Crisis. Written for publication in the "Hawaiian Gazette" and "Bulletin". Printed for Private Circulation. Southport, 1893. 8vo. 11 pp.

Davies, W. L.

David Samwell (1751-1798). Surgeon of the "Discovery", London-Welshman and poet. 1928.

UH has

QK
Botany
Pam.
1204

Davis, A. R.

Enzyme action in the marine Algae. Reprinted from Ann. Missouri Botanical Gard. Vol. 2, pp 771- 836, 1915.

DU
Hist.Pam.
147

Davies, Theo. H.

Willis, Alfred

Open Reply to Theo. H. Davies (in re Davies standing in the Anglican Church and disagreements about moneys of the church). 1886. 8vo. 13 pp.

QK
473.N
D 25

Davies, William C.

New Zealand native plant studies.   A. H. and A. W. Reed. Wellington. sm4to. 328 pp. (1956)

QK
Botany
Pam.
1200

and

AP
2
S35

Davis, A. R. and others

The feeding power of plants. Reprint from Science, Vol. 57, pp 299- 301, 1923.

DU
623
D 25

Davies, Theo. H.

Personal recollections of Hawaii,
Early recollections of Honolulu, written in 1885, of the days of 1857-1862.
An account of the first visit to the island of Hawaii, between August 3 and Sept. 15, 1859.
An account of the first visit to the island of Kauai, in Sept. 1860.
An account of a visit to Hawaii from England, Nov. 20, 1880-March 20, 1881.
Letter from Honolulu, July 11, 1861.
Privately issued.   94 pp. 1959. By T.H. Davies Company.   Honolulu.

AM
MUS
Pam
100

Davies, William C

Photography as an aid to the study of plants and plant problems.   From Jour. of N. Z. Inst. of horticulture, 1929. vol. 1, pp. 5-14.   pl.

QK
Botany
Pam.
1202

Davis, A. R.

The variability of plants grown in water cultures. Reprinted from Soil Sc. Vol. 11, Jan.,1921.

DU
Hist.Pam.
145

Davies, Theo. H.

The Relation of Christian Societies to the Hawaiian Revolution. Letters in reply to an anonymous correspondent. Southport. 1894. 8vo. 16 pp.

QK
Bot.Pam.
2494

Davies, William C.

Some salient features of the New Zealand native flora.

(Bulletin of the Royal New Zealand Institute of Horticulture, Banks Lecture, 1947)

AS
36
A25-P

Davis, Andrew MacFarland, 1833–

... Ancient Chinese paper money as described in a Chinese work on numismatics. By Andrew McF. Davis. [Boston, 1918]

1 p. l., p. [467]-647. front., illus. 23½ᶜᵐ. (Proceedings of the American academy of arts and sciences, v. 53, no. 7.—June, 1918)

CONTENTS.—Foreword, by Andrew McF. Davis.—Introduction by the translator, Kojiro Tomita.—Translation of the Ch'üan Pu T'ung Chih.—Appendix: Translations from other sources.

1. Paper money—China.   I. Ch'üan Pu T'ung Chih.   II. Tomita, Kojiro.   III. Title. Chinese paper money.

CA 18-1757 Unrev'd

Library of Congress   Q11.B7 vol. 53
——— Copy 2.   Q11.B7 vol. 53 2d set

DU
620
M 67

Also
DU
Pac.
Pam.
1045

Davies, Theo. H.

Second open letter to the Right Reverend Alfred Willis, Bishop of Honolulu. Honolulu. 1886. 8vo. 6 pp.

(Misc. Pams. Haw. 1: 591-596)

QL
406
D 25

Davila, M. de

Catalogue systematique et raisonne des curiosites de la nature et de l'art qui composent le cabinet.

Paris, 1767. 3 vols.

GN
550
D 26

Davis, Andrew McFarland

Indian Games: an Historical Research; (and) a Few Additional Notes Concerning Indian Games.

(Bulletin of the Essex Institute, Vol. 17, 1886, pp. 89-147; Volume 18, 1887, pp. 168-191)

DU
Hist.Pam.
175

Davies, Theo. H.

To the Hawaiian People; Honolulu. 1898. 2 pp.   (in re annexation)

QK
16V.
M 68

DA VINCI, LEONARDO

McMurrich, J. Playfair

Leonardo DA Vinci the anatomist (1452-1519). Carnegie Institution of Washington, publication 411, 1930.

GN
Pam
#391

Davis, B. J.

On some of the bearings of ethnology upon archaeological science
Edinburg, 1856, pp. 13. 8vo.

QL
627
U-b

Davis, B. M.

General characteristics of the Algal vegetation of Buzzards Bay and Vineyard Sound in the vicinity of Woods Hole. in U.S. Bur. of Fish. Bull. XXXI, 1911, Sec. II, Bot. pp. 443-544. illus. 4to.

QL
1
W 31

Davis, Charles C.

The pelagic Copepoda of the northeastern Pacific Ocean.

(Univ. of Washington Pubs. in Biology, Vol. 14, pp. 1-118, 1949)

QE
1
H 38

Davis, D. A.   (Dan A. Davis)

MacDonald, G. A.

Geology and ground-water resources of the island of Kauai, Hawaii, by G. A. MacDonald, D. A. Davis and D. C. Cox.

(Hawaii division of Hydrography, Bull. 13: 1-212 (map); 1960)

QL
1
C1

Davis, Benjamin Marshall, 1867-

... The early life-history of *Dolichoglossus pusillus* Ritter. By B. M. Davis. Berkeley, The University press, 1908.

p. [187]-226. pl. 4-8 (1 col.) 27cm. (University of California publications in zoology, vol. 4, no. 3)

Contributions from the laboratory of the Marine biological association of San Diego, XIX.
Originally submitted in 1907 as thesis (PH. D.)—University of California.
Bibliography: p. 216.

1. Dolichoglossus.

Title from Univ. of Calif.   Printed by L. C.   A 10-1050

GC
1
S 43-c

Davis, Charles C.

The pelagic copepoda of the northeastern Pacific Ocean.

(Contributions, Scripps Inst. of Oceanography, No. 430, 1949)

QE
Geol.
Pam.
1245

Davis, Dan A.

Wentworth, Chester K.

Salt-water encroachment as induced by sea-level excavation on Angaur Island. By Chester K. Wentworth, Atnold C. Mason, and Dan A. Davis.

(Economic Geology, 50(7):669-680, 1955)

QK
Pam
#663
4to

Davis, Bradley Moore

Oogenesis in Saprolegnia, ex The Decennial Publications, vol. X, 1903.

QL
461
H-1

Davis, C. J.

Host records of Philaenus spumarius (Linn.) at Kilauea, Hawaii National Park. (Homoptera: Cercopidae), by C. J. Davis and A. L. Mitchell.

(Haw. Ent. Soc., Proc., 12(3):515-516, 1946)

AS
522.S
R 13

Davis, D. Dwight

Mammals of the lowland rain-forest of North Borneo.

(Bulletin of the National Museum, State of Singapore, No. 31, 1962)

Q
Gen Sc
Pam
#19

Davis, Bradley Moore

Species, pure and impure, ex Science vol. LV, no. 1414, Feb. 3, 1922.

DU
406
D26

Davis, C.O.

The life and times of Patuone, the celebrated Ngapuhi chief, by C.O. Davis.

Auckland, N.Z., 1876. 141p. front.

Cost, May, 1947

GN
2.S
E 96

Davis, E. Mott, Jr.

The archaeology of northeastern Asia.

(Papers of the Excavators' Club, Vol. 1, No. 1, 1940, pp. 1-58)

Q
101
P 18

Davis, C. J.

Recent developments in the biological control of weed pests in Hawaii. By C. J. Davis and N. L. H. Krauss.

(Proc. Haw. Ent. Soc., 1962:65-67)

QL
123
D 26

Davis, Charles C.

The marine and fresh-water plankton. Michigan State University Press. 8vo. 1955. xi + 562 pp. no place

---

GN
550
I-C

Davis, Edward H.

... The Diegueño ceremony of the death images, by Edward H. Davis. New York, Museum of the American Indian, Heye foundation, 1919.

1 p. l., 7-33 p. illus. (incl. plan) v pl. 25½cm. (Contributions from the Museum of the American Indian, Heye foundation. v. 5, no. 2)

Rites: ceremonies

1. Diegueño Indians—Religion and mythology. I. Title.

Library of Congress   E11.N52 vol.5   19-13933
[3]

QL
461
H-1

Davis, C. J.

Some recent Lepidopterous outbreaks on the island of Hawaii.

(Proc. Haw. Ent. Soc for 1954; Vol. 15(3); 401-403, 1955)

G
3
A-1

Davis, Charles M.

Coconuts in the Russell Islands.

(Geographical Review, Vol. 37:400-413, 1947)

DU
620
H 42

Davis, Eleanor H.

The Norse migration: Norwegian labor in Hawaii.

(Hawaiian Hist. Soc., 71st Ann. Rept.: 28-35, 1962)

QL
Insect
Pam
725

Davis, C   Abbott

Instructions for collecting and mounting insects.

AS
36
S

Davis, Charles Henry, 1807-1877.

... The law of deposit of the flood tide: its dynamical action and office. By Charles Henry Davis ... [Washington, Smithsonian institution, 1852]

13 p. 32½cm. (Smithsonian contributions to knowledge, vol. III, art. 6)
Smithsonian institution publication 33.

1. Sedimentation and deposition. I. Title.

Library, Smithsonian   Institution Q11.S68   S 13-17

DU
406
D 26

Davis, Eliot R.

A link with the past. Oswald-Sealy. Auckland. 1948. 8vo. 283 + (10) pp.

GR 340 D 26 — Davis, F. Hadland

Myths and legends of Japan. With 32 full-page illustrations by Evelyn Paul. London. Harrap & Co. (1912-1920). 8vo. xx + 21-432 pp.

QH 1 T 88 — Davis, John H.

Evidences of trans-oceanic dispersal of plants to New Zealand.

(Tuatara, 3(3):87-97; 1950)

GN Pam 468 — Davis, Joseph Bernard

Account of the skull of a Chiliak, ex Anthr. Soc. London Mem. vol. iii, 1870.

AM 7 D 26 — Davis, Helen Miles   editor

Exhibit techniques. Science Service. Washington. 1951. sm8vo. 112 pp.

QL Poly-Prot. Pam. 809 — Day, J. H.

The Polychaet fauna of South Africa. Part 6. Sedentary species dredged off Cape coasts with a few new records from the shore.

(Jour. Linn. Soc. of London, 44(299):463-560, 1961)

GN Pam 424 — Davis, Joseph Barnard

Contributions towards determining the weight of the brain in different races of man, ex publication of some scientific Soc., London, 1868.

DU 12 C 18 — DAVIS, ISAAC

Campbell, Archibald

looked case

A Voyage round the world, from 1806 to 1812; in which...the Sandwich Islands were visited... Edinburgh. 1816. 8vo. pp. 135-151.

QH 301 C 3 — Davis, J. H., Jr.

The ecology and geologic role of mangroves in Florida.

(Papers from Tortugas Laboratory, Vol. 32, 1940, pp. 303-412)

GN 71 D 26 — Davis, Joseph Barnard

Collection of papers on craniology, by various authors. In 8 volumes. Index at beginning of each volume.

(only the checked articles are catalogued)

DU 620 P — DAVIS, ISAAC

Cooper, Bryant

Kiilae.

(Paradise of the Pacific, Vol. 45(3):29-31, 1933)

[land given to Isaac Davis]

G 51 W 17 — Davis, J. K.

Kerguelen Island: lashed by almost fabulous excess of storm.

(Walkabout, Vol. 9 (6):4-12, 1943)

GN 71 D 26 — Davis, Joseph Barnard

Contributions towards determining the weight of the brain in different races of man. 1868.

GN Pam 424 — Davis, J. B.

Collections of papers on craniology...Vol. 2 No. 12.

DU 620 P — DAVIS, ISAAC

Westervelt, William Drake

Life of Kamehameha, John Young and Isaac Davis.

(Paradise of the Pacific, Vol. 25, 1912, No. 10, p. 16-18)

DU 200 V — Davis, J. K.

Magellan (1480-1521) and the first voyage round the world by the "Victoria", by Captain J. K. Davis. (Read to the Historical Society of Victoria, 18th April, 1951)

(The Victorian Historical Magazine, Vol. XXIV:2, 52-71 pp. Sept. 1951)

GN 71 D 26 — Davis, Joseph Barnard

Crania Britannica. Delineations and descriptions of the skulls of the early inhabitants of the British Islands, together with notices of their other remains, by Joseph Barnard Davis and John Thurnam. London. Printed for the author. 1856-1860. folio.

GN Pam 1801 — Davis, J. B. (Joseph Barnard)

The skulls of the inhabitants of the Caroline Islands. From Anthrop. Review, v.4.

AG 41 D26 — Davis, J. R. Ainsworth

Burt's Danish-Norwegian-English dictionary... new edition and improved.

New York, Burt, n.d.   433p.

GN 2.1 A-4 — Davis, J. Barnard

A few notes upon the hair and some other peculiarities of oceanic races.

(Journ. Anthrop. Inst. of Great Britain and Ireland, Vol. 2, 1873, pp.95-101)

DU Missions Pam. 3 — Davis, J. E.

An Armstrong Pilgrimage. (Samuel Chapman Armstrong)
(The Southern Workman, October, 1927, pp. 453-460)

GN 2.1 A-3 — Davis, J. Barnard

Welch, E. A.

An account of the Chatham Islands, their discovery, inhabitants, conquest by the Maoris, and the fate of the aborigines, by E.A. Welch and J. Barnard Davis.

(The Anthrop. Review, Vol. 8, 1870-1, pp. xcvii-cviii)

GN 2.1 A-3 — Davis, J. Barnard

Oceanic races, their hair, etc., and the value of skulls in the classification of man.

(The Anthrop. Review, Vol. 8, 1870, pp. 183-196)

GN
71
D 26

Davis, Joseph Barnard

On the Osteology and peculiarities of the Tasmanians.

(Nat. Verh. der Hollandsche Maatschappij der Wetenschappen, 3rd Reeks, Deel II, No. 4, pp. 3-19, Tafel 1-4. 1874.)

Davis, Joseph Barnard
Collection of papers on craniology, Vol. 2, No. 7.

GN
71
D 26

Davis, Joseph Barnard

On the peculiar crania of the inhabitants of certain groups of islands in the western Pacific. (Natuurkundige Verhandelingen, Deel 24,1866)

Davis, Joseph Barnard
Collection of papers on craniology. Vol. 2, No. 6.
(with review by J. Van der Hoeven,ibid. No. 5)

GN
73
D26

Davis, Joseph Barnard

Thesaurus craniorum: catalogue of the skulls of the various races of man, in the collection of Joseph Barnard Davis

London,n.p., 1867.　　374p.

GN
73
D26

_____　Supplement. 1875.　101p.

QE
Geol.
Pam.
1307

Davis, L. E.

The mineral industry of Hawaii. By L.E. Davis and R. Y. Ashizawa.

(Bureau of Mines. Minerals Yearbook, 1959. 9 pp.)

Davis, L. E.

Mineral industry of Hawaii. By L.E.Davis and R. Y. Ashizawa.

(Reprint from Mines Minerals Yearbook, Vol. 111, 1960?)

at
Library, Dole Corporation, Honolulu office

QK
96
T 23

Davis, Mervyn T.

A guide and an analysis of Engler's "Das Pflanzenreich"

(Taxon, Vol. 6(6):161-184, 1957)

Davis, Oscar King　　　Carter Coll.
　　　　　　　　　　　　　4-A-2

Our conquests in the Pacific. Illustrated. New York Frederick A. Stokes Co; 1899 iv + 352 pp. 8vo.

QK
495.0 64
D 26

Davis, Reg S.

Philippine orchids, a detailed treatment of some one hundred native species. By Reg S. Davis and Mona Lisa Steiner. The William-Frederick Press. New York. 1952. 8vo. 270 pp.

QE
Geol.
Pam.
1256

Davis, S. G.

Geological problems in relation to building-sites and foundations in Hong Kong. (Read before the Engineering Society of Hong Kong on the 6th April 1955)

(The Engineering Society of Hongkong, Session 1954-1955, April, Vol. VIII(7):177-202, 1955)

QE
Geol.
Pam.
1336

Davis, S. G.

The geology and structure of the Lion Rock Tunnel, Hong Kong.

(The Engineering Soc. of Hong Kong, Session 1962-63: pp. 6.1- 6.26, 1963)

QE
301.H
D 26

Davis, S. G.

The geology of Hong Kong. Government Printer. Hong Kong. R8vo. (1962) iv + 210 pp.

QE
Geol.
Pam.
1295

Davis, S. G.

Geology of the Lin Ma Hang lead mine, New Territories, Hong Kong. By S.G.Davis and A.K. Snelgrove.

(Reprinted from the Mining Magazine, Feb. 1956)

Q
101
P 18

Davis, S. G.

Mineralogy and genesis of the wolframite ore deposits, Needle Hill,Mine, New Territories, Hong Kong.

(Economic Geology, 56(7):1238-1249, 1961)

[Symposium paper, 10th Pac. Sci. Congress: Earth's crust in the Pacific basin]

QE
Geol.
Pam.
1313

Davis, S. G.

Mineralogy of theMa Pm Shan iron mine, Hong Kong

(Economic Geology,56(3):592-602, 1961)

Davis, S. G.
Geol.Pam.
1337

The rural-urban migration in Hong Kong and its new territories.

(Reprint, The Geographical Jour., Vol.128 (Part 3):328-333, 1962)

QK
Bot.Pam.
2075

Davis, Spencer

Hillebrand's masterpiece; magnificent Foster garden where jungle'sfinest mark the genius and foresight of noted scientist.

(Honolulu Advertiser, January 2, 1938)

GN
2.S
P 76

Davis, T. R.A.

Rarotonga today.

(Journal of the Polynesian Society, Vol. 56: 197-218, 1947)

DU
570
D 26

Davis, Tom and Lydia

Doctor to the Islands. With illustrations by Tom Davis. Little, Brown and Company. Boston 8vo.　(8) + 331 pp.　1954.

[Cook Islands and neighboring islands]

Davis, Tom

Doctor to the islands.

331 p. ill. 1954

Davis, W. H.

Sixty Years in California, personal, political and military, under the Mexican regime, quasi-military government of the territory by the U.S. and after the admission of the state into the Union, 8vo, pp. 659, San Francisco, 1889.

HMCS

AP
2
N 4

Davis, William Morris

Barrier reefs of Tahiti and Moorea.

(Nature, Vol. 120, 1927, pp. 330-331)

QE
565
D26

Davis, William Morris

The coral reef problem.

New York, Amer. Geographical Soc., 1928. 596p.
[American Geographical Soc., Spec. Publ. n.9]

AP
2
A 5

Davis, William Morris

The Great Barrier Reef of Australia.

(Am. Jour. of Sci., Ser. 4, Vol. 44, 1917,
pp. 339-350)

HEG
has copy

Davis, William Morris

Subsidence of reef encircled islands.

(Bull. Geol. Soc. of America, 29, 1919,
pp. 489-574)

QE
Pam
#19

Davis, W. M. (William Morris)

Coral reefs of the Louisiade archipelago, ex Washington Acad. of Sc.
Journ., vol. 13, no. 7.

G
3
A

Davis, W. M. (William Morris)

The home study of coral reefs.

in Am. Geog. Soc. Bull. XLVI, 8, pp. 561-577, XLVI, pp.
641-654. 721-739, 1914.

GN
Ethn.
Pam. 3523

DU
Pac. Pam.
401

GN...
3523 a

Davison, Charles

Hawaiian medicine.

(The Medical Age, May, 1899:373-381)

reprinted in the Queen's Hospital Bull.,
Vol. 4, Nos. 3 and 4, 1927.

QE
Geol.Pam
921

AP
2
S 35

Davis, W. M. (William Morris)

Coral reefs of Tutuila, Samoa.

(Science, Vol. LIII, No. 1382, June 24, 1921,
pp. 559-565)

G
7
R 91

Davis, W. M.

The islands and coral reefs of Fiji.

(Geogr. Journal, 55, 1920, pp. 34-45, 200-
220, 377-388)

QE
529
D 26

Davison, Charles

Studies on the periodicity of earthquakes.
With 14 illustrations. London. Thomas Murby
& Co. 1938. sm8vo. ix + 107 pp.

QE
Geol
Pam
671

Davis, W(illiam) M(orris)

Les cotes et les recifs coralliens de
la Nouvelle Caledonie.

Paris, Colin, 1926. 118p. pls.
(Annales de geographie, t.34, 1925)

F
2001
D 26

Davis, William Morris

The Lesser Antilles.

(American Geographical Society, Publication
2, 1926)

QK
490
D 26

Davy, J. Burtt

Check-lists of the forest trees and shrubs
of the British Empire. Edited by J. Burtt Davy
and A. C. Hoyle. No. 4: Draft of first descriptive check-list for Ceylon. Compiled by L.A.J.
Abeyesundere and R. A. De Rosayro...Imperial
Forestry Institute, Oxford. 1939. R8vo. 115 pp

AP
2
A 5

Davis, W. M. (William Morris)

Dana's confirmation of Darwin's theory of
coral reefs.

(Am. Jour. of Sci., Ser. 4, Vol. 35, 1913,
pp. 173-188) (also note, p. 334)

QE
Pam
#449
and
AP
2
A 5

Davis, W. M. (William Morris)

The marginal belts of the coral
seas, ex Nat. Acad. of Sc. Proc.,
vol. 9, 1923.

(Am. Jour. of Sci., Ser. 5, Vol. 6, 1923,
pp. 181-195)

QK
Pam
#393

Davy, Joseph Burtt

The native vegetation and crops of
the Colorado Delta in the Salton basin.
Extract, 1902.

AS
36
N1

Davis, W. M. (William Morris)

Exploration of the Pacific.

(Nat. Acad. of Sc. Proc. II, 1916, pp. 391-
394)

AP
2
A 5

Davis, W. M. (William Morris)

A migrating anticline in Fiji.

(Am. Jour. of Sci., Ser. 5, Vol. 14, 1927,
pp. 333-351)

QH
1
T 88

Dawbin, W. H.

A guide to the Holothurians of New Zealand.

(Tuatara, 3(1):33-41; 1950)

G
62
D26

Davis, William Morris.

Geographical essays, by William
Morris Davis. Edited by Douglas Wilson
Johnson.

Bost. Ginn & co., [1909] 777p. illus.

AP
2
A 5

Davis, W. M. (William Morris)

Shaler memorial study of coral reefs.

(Am. Jour. of Sci., Ser. 4, Vol. 40, 1915,
pp. 223-271)

DU
1
P 12

Dawbin, W. H.

The Maori went a whaling- and became one of
the world's best whalemen.

(Pacific Discovery, Vol. 7(4):18-22, 1954)

AP
2
E 56

Dawbin, W. H.

The tuatara in its natural habitat.

(Endeavour, Vol. 21(81):16-24, 1962)

QH
1
P 10

Dawson, E. Yale

Changes in Palmyra atoll and its vegetation through the activities of man, 1913-1958.

(Pacific Naturalist, Vol. 1(2), 1959)

QH
1
L 87

Dawson, E. Yale

Marine algae from the 1958 cruise of the Stella Polaris in the Gulf of California.

(Contributions in Science, Los Angeles County Museum, No. 27, pp. 3-39, 1959)

AS
719
A 93 m

Dawbin, W. H.

Whales and the Antarctic.

(Australian Mus. Mag., 12(8):264-267, 1957)

Q
115
H 24-o

Dawson, E. Yale

Contributions toward a marine flora of the Southern Californian Channel Islands, I-III.

(Allan Hancock Foundation Publications, Occasional Papers, No. 8, 1949)

QH
1
L 87

Dawson, E. Yale

Marine Algae from the Pacific Costa Rican gulfs.

(Los Angeles County Museum, Contributions in Science, No. 15, 1957)

GN
308
P 63

The dawn of civilization.

Piggott, Stuart   editor

Q
115
H 23

Dawson, Elmer Yale

Field observations on the Algae of the Gulf of California.

(Allan Hancock Pacific Expeditions, Vol. 3, no. 7, pp. 115-119, 1941)

Q
115
H 23

Dawson, Elmer Yale

The marine Algae of the Gulf of California.

(Allan Hancock Pacific Expeditions, Vol. 3, No. 10: 189-453, 1944)

DU
620
H 42

Daws, Alan Gavan

Evangelism in Hawaii: Titus Coan and the Great Revival of 1837.

(Haw. Hist. Soc., Ann. Rept. 1960:20-34)

QK
567
D 27

Dawson, E. Yale

A guide to the literature and distributions of the marine algae of the Pacific coast of North America.

(Mem. Southern Calif. Acad. Sci., Vol. 3 (1):1-134, 1946)

Q
115
H 23

Dawson, E. Yale

Marine red Algae of Pacific Mexico, Part I: Bangiales to Corallinaceae Subf. Corallinoideae. Part II: Cryptonemiales (cont.)
(Allan Hancock Pacific Expeditions, Vol. 17 (1):1-171, pl. 1-33, 1952; Vol. 17(2):241-397, 1954)

G
51
W 17

Dawson, C. St. M.

Legends of Yarrabah.

(Walkabout, Vol. 21(7):20, 1955)

QH
1
P 11

Dawson, E. Yale

A guide to the literature and distributions of Pacific Benthic Algae from Alaska to the Galapagos Islands.

(Pacific Science, Vol. 15(3):370-461,1961)

QH
1
P 10

Dawson, E. Yale

Marine red Algae of Pacific Mexico, Part 3: Cryptonemiales, Corallinaceae subf Melobesioideae.

(Pacific Naturalist, Vol. 2(1), 1960)

...Part 4:Gigartinales, by E. Yale Dawson
...Part 5:The genus Polysiphonia, by G.J. Hollenberg, in collaboration with E. Yale Dawson (ibid, 2(5/6), 1961)

AS
36
S 19

Dawson, Elmer Yale

An annotated list of the marine Algae and marine grasses of San Diego County, California.

(Occ. Papers, San Diego Soc. of Nat. Hist., No. 7, 1945)

AS
36
S 55

Dawson, Elmer Yale

Marine Algae associated with upwelling along the northwestern coast of Baja California, Mexico.

(Bull. So. Calif. Acad. Sci., Vol. 44:57-71, 1945)

QK
Bot.Pam.
3336

Dawson, E. Yale

Marine red Algae of Pacific Mexico, part 6: Rhodymeniales.

(Reprint, Nova Hedwigia, Band V(3-4):437-476, 1963)

GN
2.S
P 76

Dawson, Elliot Watson

Excavation of a Maori burial, at Longbeach, Otago; with notes on associated artifacts.

(Jour. Poly Soc., Vol. 58(2):58-63, 1949)

Q
115
H 24-o
and
QK
Bot.Pam.
2863

Dawson, E. Yale

Marine Algae from Palmyra Island with special reference to the feeding habits and toxicology of reef fishes. By E. Yale Dawson, A.A. Aleem and Bruce W. Halstead.

(Allan Hancock Foundation Publications, Occ. Papers No. 17, 1955)

Q
115
H 23

Dawson, E. Yale

Marine red algae of Pacific Mexico. Part 7: Ceramiales: Ceramiaceae, Delesseriaceae.

(Allan Hancock Pacific Expeditions, Vol. 26(1), 1962)

QH
1
P 10

Dawson, E. Yale

A new gigartinoid Grateloupia (red alga) from Hawaii.

(Pacific Naturalist, Vol. 1(1), 1958)

Q
115
H 23

Dawson, Elmer Yale

A review of the genus Rhodymenia with descriptions of new species.

(Allan Hancock Pacific Expeditions, Vol. 3, No. 8, pp. 123-181, 1941)

QL
Prot.
to
Poly.
Pam
254

Dawson, George M

On some Canadian species of spongillae. From Canadian Nat. and Geol. Sept., 1875.

QH
1
P 10

Dawson, E. Yale

New records of marine Algae from the Galapagos Islands.

(Pacific Naturalist, 4(1):1-23, 1963)

AS
36
A 65 n

Dawson, E. Yale

The rim of the reef. Calcareous algae occupy a major role in the growth of atolls.

(Natural History, 70(6):8-17, 1961)

QH
1
T 88

Dawson, J. W.

Interrelationships of the Australasian and South American floras.

(Tuatara, 7(1):1-6; 1958)

QH
1
L 87

Dawson, E. Yale

Notes on Eastern Pacific insular marine Algae.

(Los Angeles County Museum, Contributions in Science, No. 8, 1957)

[Galapagos Islands, Clipperton, San Benedicto Island, Alijos Rocks]

QH
1
A 88

Dawson, E. Yale

Some marine Algae from Canton Atoll.

(Atoll Research Bull. No. 65, 1959)

QC
Physics
Pam
1

Dawson, W. Bell

Temperatures and densities of the Waters of Eastern Canada. Canada, Naval Service. Ottawa, 1922.

AS
36
S 55

Dawson, E. Yale

Notes on Pacific coast marine Algae.

(Bull. Southern Calif. Acad. Sci., 44:22-27, 1945)

QH
1
P 11

Dawson, E. Yale

Some marine algae of the southern Marshall islands.

(Pacific Science, Vol. X(1):25-66, Jan.,1956)

GN
2.1
A-4

Dawson, Warren R.

Mummification in Australia and in America.

(Journ. R. Anthrop. Inst. of Great Britain and Ireland, Vol. 58, 1928, pp. 115-138, pls. 8-13)

AS
36
S 55

Dawson, E. Yale

Notes on tropical Pacific marine algae.

(Bull. of the Southern California Academy of Sciences, Vol. 53(1):1-7, 1954)

QH
1
P 10

Dawson, E. Yale

Some Algae from Clipperton Island and the Danger Islands.

(Pacific Naturalist, Vol. 1(7), 1959)

QL
684.C15
D 27

Dawson, William Leon

The birds of California: a complete, scientific and popular account of the 580 species and subspecies of birds found in the state. Illustrated by...photogravures...plates...cuts... with drawings...by Allan Brooks. Format de luxe, Santa Barbara edition. In four volumes. Vols. 1-4. South Moulton Co. San Diego... 1923. 4to. (Copy no. 31)

AP
2
S 35

Dawson, E. Yale

Oceanographic Institute of Nhatrang, Viet Nam.

(Science, 118(3053):3, 1953)

QH
1
P 10

Dawson, E. Yale

Una clave ilustrada de los generos de algas del Pacifico de la America Central. (Illustrated Key to the Genera of Pacific Central American Benthic Algae)

(Pacific Naturalist, 3(4), 1962)

DU
Missions
Pam. 71

The Day is Breaking; or, Light in Dark Lands. Prepared for Contributors for Mission Schools. Boston. Am. Board of Com. for Foreign Missions. 1870. 96 pp. 12mo.

QK
Bot.Pam.
2543

Dawson, E. Yale

Review of Echinocereus pacificus (Englm.) B. and R.

(Reprinted without change of paging, Desert Plant Life, Dec. 1948:151-159)

QH
1
P 10

Dawson, E. Yale

William H. Harvey's report on the marine Algae of the United States North Pacific Exploring Expedition of 1853-1856.

(Pacific Naturalist, Vol. 1(5), 1959)

QC
801
57-5-

Day, Arthur L.

Annual report of the Director of the Geophysical Laboratory. Carn. Inst. Wash.

DU
620
P

Day, A. Grove

The first printers of Hawaii.

(Paradise of the Pacific, pp. 33-36, 101, Annual Holiday Edition 1955)

DU
Hist.Pam
310

Day, A. Grove

Ka Palapala Hemolele.

(Reprinted from Kokua, Nov. 1949)

AS
36
W1
11-6

Day, Arthur L. and Shepherd, E. S.
Geophysics.- Water and the magmatic gases. in Washington Acad. of Sciences Journal III. 1913, pp. 457-463.

DU
625
K 97

Day, A. Grove

Kuykendall, Ralph S.

Hawaii: a history from Polynesian kingdom to American Commonwealth. By Ralph S. Kuykendall and A. Grove Day. Prentice-Hall, Inc. New York. 1948c. 8vo. x + 331 pp.

DU
Hist.
Pam.
384

Day, A. Grove

Pioneer presses of Hawaii.

(Reprinted from The Journal of the American Institute of Graphic Arts, Vol. IV(5):33-40, 1952)

QE
528
A 42

Day, Arthur L.

Allen, E. T.

Hot springs of the Yellowstone National Park, by E. T. Allen and Arthur L. Day.

(Carnegie Institution of Washington, 1935, publication no. 466)

DU
625
K 97

Day, A. Grove

Kuykendall, Ralph S.

Hawaii: a history, from Polynesian kingdom to American state. Revised edition. By Ralph S. Kuykendall and A. Grove Day. Prentice-Hall, Inc. Englewood Cliffs, N. J. 8vo. 1961 x + 331 pp.

[first published in 1948]

DU
12
S 92

Day, A. Grove

Stroven, Carl

The spell of the Pacific: an anthology of its literature. Selected and edited by Carl Stroven and A. Grove Day. With an introduction by James A. Michener. The Macmillan Company. New York. 1949. 8vo. xx + 940 pp.

QD
931
D27

Day, Arthur Louis, 1869-
The isomorphism and thermal properties of the feldspars. Part I— Thermal study (by) Arthur L. Day and E. T. Allen. Part II— Optical study (by) J. P. Iddings. With an introduction by George F. Becker. Washington, D. C., Carnegie institution of Washington, 1905.

95 p. illus. xxvi (i. e. 27) pl. 26½cm. (Carnegie institution of Washington. Publication no. 31)

1. Crystallography. 2. Feldspar. I. Allen, Eugene Thomas, 1862- joint author. II. Iddings, Joseph Paxson, 1857- joint author. III. Becker, George Ferdinand, 1847-

5—32416

Library of Congress   QD931.D27

DU
625
D 27

Day, A. Grove

Hawaii and its people. With illustrations by John V. Morris. Duell, Sloan and Pearce. New York. 1955. 8vo. (1-3)4-338 pp.

DU
Pac.Pam
794

Day, A. Grove

Strong man of the Saginaw; shipwreck off Ocean Island provides a saga of indomitable courage.

(American Heritage, Vol. 2(3), n.s.: 13-15, 1951)

QE
Pam
#474

Day, Arthur L.

Possible causes of the volcanic activity at Lassen Peak, ex Journ. of Franklin Inst., vol. 194, november, 1922.

Day, A. Grove

Hawaii and its people.   Honolulu. U. of H. Press. 1955

UH has ...

Pam (?)

AP
2
A5
10-6
Pam by
Museum.

Day, Arthur L., Sosman, and Hostetter.
The determination of mineral and rock densities at high temperatures.   From the American Journal of Science, Vol. XXXVII, January, 1914.

Given by the authors.

QC
801
Ca

and

QC
801
Ca

Day, Arthur L.

Some causes of volcanic activity. Carnegie Inst. Geophysic. Lab. Pub. 572. 1925, 24 pp. extracted from yearbook 20.

DU
623
D 27

Day, A. Grove

A Hawaiian reader; selected and edited by A. Grove Day and Carl Stroven. With an introduction by James A. Michener. Appleton-Century-Crofts, Inc. New York. 8vo. xvii + 361 pp. (1959)

QE
Pam
#106

Day, Arthur L.

Geophysical research, ex Smithsonian Rept. for 1912.

QE
Geol.
Pam.
No. 537

Day, Arthur L. and Allen, E. T.

The source of the heat and the source of the water in the hot springs of the Lassen National Park. From Journ. Geol. XXXII, No.3, 1924.

DU
623
D 27

Day, A. Grove

A Hawaiian reader, selected and edited by A. Grove Day and Carl Stroven. With an introduction by James A. Michener. Popular Library New York. paperbd. 12mO

AS
36
S1

Day, Arthur Louis, 1869-
Geophysical research. By Arthur L. Day.
(In Smithsonian institution. Annual report, 1912. Washington, 1913. 23½cm. p. 359-369)
"Reprinted ... from Journal of the Washington academy of sciences, vol. 1, no. 9, December 4, 1911, pp. 247-260."

1. Geophysics.
2. Earth

13—25684

Library of Congress   Q11.S66 1912

QE
524
D27

Day, Arthur L.

The volcanic activity and hot springs of Lassen Peak, by A.L. Day and E. T. Allen. Carnegie Institution of Washington, Pub. 360. Washington, 1925. 4to. X + 190 pp.

2 copies

AS
36
S1

and

QE
Pams
158
278

Day, Arthur Louis, 1869–
Water and volcanic activity. By Arthur L. Day and
E. S. Shepherd ...

(*In* Smithsonian institution. Annual report. 1913. Washington, 1914.
23½ᶜᵐ. p. 275–305. 9 pl. on 5 L)

"Reprinted ... from Bulletin of the Geological society of America. vol.
24, pp. 573–606."

1. Volcanoes. I. Shepherd, Earnest Stanley, 1879–   joint author.
II. Title.
15–1738

Library of Congress   Q11.S66 1913

Day, F.

The fishes of Malabar.   1865.

UH

QL
Prot.Poly.
822

Day, J. H.

Polychaeta from several localities in the
western Indian Ocean.

(Reprint, Proc. Zool. Soc. Lond, Vol 139
(Part 4):627–656, 1962)

QE
Pam
#105

Day, A. L; Sosman, R. B. & Hostetter, J. C.
The determination of mineral and
rock densities at high temperatures,
ex Am. Journ. of Sc., vol. XXXVII,
January, 1914.

Day, Francis Rooke

See also

D., F. R.

(These may be the same)

QL
Prot.-
Poly.
Pam.
800

Day, J. H.

A small collection of Polychaeta from Gough
Island.

(Annals and Mag. Nat. Hist., s 13, volume
1:787–790, 1958)

Day, C. D.

British Tachinid flies. Tachinidae (Larvae-
voridae and Calliphoridae). A key for the identification of the genera and species... (Illustrated)

(Reprinted from the Northwestern Naturalist,
Vols. 21–22, for 1946–47. Arbroath (England), 1948.
8vo. 150 pp.)

HSPA

GR
385.H
D 27

Day, Mrs. Frank R.
The princess of Manoa and other romantic
tales from the folk-lore of old Hawaii. Illustrated by D. Howard Hitchcock. Paul Elder and
Company. San Francisco and New York. R8vo.
1906c.

AS
36
C8

Day, Jeremiah, 1773–1867.
... A statement of the quantity of rain which falls, on
different days of the moon ...

(*In* Connecticut academy of arts and sciences. Memoirs. New Haven,
1810. 22½ᶜᵐ. v. 1, p. (125)–127)

1. Rain and rainfall. I. Title. Meteorology
A 17–743

Library of Congress   Q11.C85 vol. 1
Yale University   A53n.365.1

Day, C. D.

British Tachinid flies (Tachinidae- Lar-
vaevoridae and Claiphoridae)

T. Buncle and Co. Ltd. (Market Place, Arbroath,
Scotland)

HSPA ?

QH
Nat.Hist.
Pam.
148

Day, J. H.

The ecology of South African estuaries.
Part I. A review of estuarine conditions in
general.

(Trans. R. Soc. of South Africa, 33(1):52–
91, 1951)

QK
Pam
#1081

Day, R. N.
The forces determining the position
of dorsiventral leaves, ex Minn. Bot.
Studies I, Minn. Geol. & Nat. Hist.
Sur. Bull. no. 9.

Day, D. E.

Tahiti: a chapter in Pacific imperialism.
Complete. M.A., University of California, Berkeley, 1933.

microfilm in Inst. Adv. Studies, Dept. of
Pac. Hist., Austr. Nat. Univ. (Harry
Maude)

Q
Gen.Sci.
Pam.
127
128

Day, J. H.

Scott, K. M. F.

The ecology of South African Estuaries, Part
II. The Klein River Estuary, Hermanus, Cape.
By K. M. F. Scott, A. D. Harrison, and W. Macnae.
Part III. Knysna, a clear open estuary. By J.H.
Day, N. A. H. Millard, and A. D. Harrison.

(Trans. R. Soc. of South Africa, 33:283–331;
367–413, 1952)

GN
Ethn.
Pam.
3977

DAYAKS

Geddes, W. R.

The Land Dayaks of Sarawak. A report on a
social economic survey of the Land Dayaks of
Sarawak presented to the Colonial Social Science
Research Council. Published by Her Majesty's
Stationery Office for the Colonial Office, London.
1954. folio. 113 pp.

Day, Emily Foster

The Menehunes. San Francisco: Paul
Elder & Co. N. D.

Honolulu Academy of Arts

QL
Prot.-
Poly.
Pam.
738

Day, J. H.

The Polychaet fauna of South Africa, Part I:
The intertidal and estuarine Polychaeta of Natal
and Mosambique. Part 2: Errant species from Cape
Shores and Estuaries.

(Annals of the Natal Museum, 12(1):1–67, 1951;
12(3):397–441, 1953)

Part 4, ibid, 14(1):59–129, 1957

DAYAKS   CULTURE

See

CULTURE   DAYAKS

QL
634.1
D 27
locked
case

Day, Francis, 1829–1889.
The fishes of India; being a natural history of the fishes
known to inhabit the seas and fresh waters of India,
Burma, and Ceylon ... London, B. Quaritch, 1875–78.

4 pt. cxcv (i. e. 198) pl. 32 x 26ᶜᵐ.

—— Supplement to the Fishes of India ... By Francis
Day ... London (etc.) Williams and Norgate, 1888.

1 p. l., p. (779)–816. illus. 31½ x 25½ᶜᵐ.

—— One hundred and ninety-eight plates to illustrate
Francis Day's work on the Fishes of India. (London,
G. Norman and son, printers) 1889.

11 p. cxcv (i. e. 198 pl.) 32½ x 26ᶜᵐ.

Plates are the same as those issued with the work.
1. Fishes—India.
A 18–1868

Title from Harvard Univ.   Printed by L. C.

QL
1
L 75

Day, J. H.

The Polychaet fauna of South Africa, Part
3.

(Jour. Linn. Soc. London, Zool., 42 (287),
Oct. 1955)

DAYAK   DEATH CUSTOMS

see

DEATH CUSTOMS   DAYAK

AS
522.B
Sa

DAYAKS VOCABULARY

Buok, W. S. B.

Vocabulary of Land Dayak as spoken in Kampong Boyan, Upper Sarawak.

(Sarawak Museum Journal, Vol. 4, 1933 (no. 13), pp. 187-192)

G
7
R 91

Deacon, G. E. R.

The Antarctic voyages of R.R.S. Discovery II and R.R.S. William Scoresby, 1935-37.

(The Geographical Journal, Vol. 93, 1939, pp. 185-209)

DU
Hist.Pam.
382

The dead king. (King Kalakaua).
Typed copy of pamphlet loaned to Kennth P. Emory in 1953.

AS
522.B
Sa

DAYAKS VOCABULARY

Elam, E. H.

Slakow and Larah Land Dyaks of Lundu.

(Sarawak Museum Journal, Vol. 4, 1935, [no. 14], pp. 241-251)

GC
63
D 61

Deacon, G. E. R.

A general account of the hydrology of the South Atlantic Ocean.

Discovery Committee
Discovery Reports, Vol. 7, 1933, p. 171-238

DU
1
P 11

Deadly coconut pest found in the Tokelaus.

(Pacific Islands Monthly, 34(3):55-57, 1963)

De

Foreign names beginning with this prefix will be found under the latter part of the name, except when compounded with the name.

GC
63
D 61

Deacon, G. E. R.

The hydrology of the Southern Ocean

Discovery Committee
Discovery Reports, Vol. 15, 1937, p. 1-124

DU
625
D 28

Dean, Arthur L.

Alexander and Baldwin, Ltd. and the predecessor partnerships. Alexander and Baldwin, Ltd. Honolulu. 1950. 8vo. xii+ 3-245 pp.

GN
Pam
2661

and
GN
1
F

Deacon, A   B

The Kakihan society of Ceram and New Guinea initiation cults. From Folk-lore, v.36, n.4, 1925.

AP
2
N 28

Deacon, G. E. R.

Marine science in the Pacific area.

(Nature, Vol. 177(4504):353-355, 1956)

[UNESCO; Interim Advisory Committee; meeting of Oct. 1955 in Tokyo...]

Dean, A. L.

Cooperation in the Sugar Industry of Hawaii.
Institute of Pacific Relations.

Institute of Pacific Relations Library

GN
2.I
A-4

Deacon, A. Bernard

Geometrical drawings from Malekula and other islands of the New Hebrides. Edited by Camilla H. Wedgwood, with notes by A. C. Haddon.

(Journal Royal Anthr. Inst., Vol.LXIV, 1934, pp. 129-175. 90 figs. pl.XIII)

GC
63
D 61

Deacon, G. E. R.

Note on the dynamics of the Southern ocean.

Discovery Committee
Discovery Reports, Vol. 15, 1937, p. 125-152

AS
763
U

Dean, Arthur Lyman

Historical sketch of the University of Hawaii. Univ. Hawaii Occa. Papers n.5, 1927.

GN
671.N55
D 27

Deacon, Arthur Bernard

Malekula, a vanishing people in the New Hebrides. Edited by Camilla H. Wedgwood. With a preface by A. C. Haddon. London. George Routledge & Sons. 1934. 8vo. pp.xxxviii +(5) + 789.

G
7
R 91

Deacon, G. E. R.

The Sargasso Sea.

(Geographical Journal, Vol. 99, 1942, pp. 16-28)

DU
Pac.Pam.
748

Dean, Arthur L.   editor

Issues in Micronesia. Tenth Conference of the Institute of Pacific Relations. Stratford-upon-Avon, England. Sept. 1947. United States Paper No. 5. 41 pp. mimeographed.

Contents: Physical geography, climate, vegetation, fauna, history, native population, resources, education, Christian missions, administration, future program, health.

GN
2.1
A-4

Deacon, A. Bernard

Notes on some islands of the New Hebrides. (Edited by Camilla H. Wedgwood).

(Journ. R. Anthrop. Inst. of Great Britain and Ireland, Vol. 59, 1929, pp. 461-515)

Q
101
P 18

Deacon, G. E. R.

The work of the "Discovery" committee in the South Pacific Ocean.

IN Proc. Sixth Pacific Science Congress, 1939, (California), Vol. 3, pp. 139-142.

MSS
Storage
Files

Dean, Arthur Lyman

Treatment of leprosy.

Z
5971
.D35
Dean, Bashford, 1867–
A bibliography of fishes, by Bashford Dean; enl. and ed. by Charles Rochester Eastman ... New York, The Museum, 1916– 1923
3 v. 25½ᶜᵐ.
Seal of the American museum of natural history on t.-p.

1. Fishes—Bibl.   ɪ. Eastman, Charles Rochester, 1868–   ed.
ɪɪ. American museum of natural history, New York.

17–12736

Library of Congress   Z5971.D35

QL
615
G 89
"Dean, Bashford"
Gregory, William K.
Memorial of Bashford Dean.
(The Bashford Dean Memorial Volume: Archaic Fishes, Edited by Eugene Willis Gudger, Article I, 1930. pp. 1–42, VIII plates)

AS
36
S
Dean, John, 1831–1888.
... The gray substance of the medulla oblongata and trapezium. By John Dean ... ₍Washington, Smithsonian institution, 1864₎
2 p. l., 75 p. illus. xvɪ pl. 32½ᶜᵐ. (Smithsonian contributions to knowledge. ₍vol. xvɪ, art. 2₎)
Smithsonian institution publication 173.

1. Medulla oblongata. 2. Trapezium (Anatomy)

S 13–71

Library, Smithsonian   Institution Q11.S68

QL
9 b9
D28
Dean, Bashford, 1867–
Chimæroid fishes and their development, by Bashford Dean ... Washington, D. C., Carnegie institution of Washington, 1906.
2 p. l., 194 p. illus. xɪ pl. (10 col. 1 fold.) 29ᶜᵐ. (On verso of t.-p.: Carnegie institution of Washington. Publication no. 32)
Each plate preceded by a leaf with descriptive letterpress.
"Literature list": p. 159–172.

1. Embryology—Fishes. 2. Chimeridae.

6–45312

Library of Congress   QL959.D28
———— Copy 2.

QL
615
G 89
"DEAN, BASHFORD"
Gudger, Eugene Willis   editor
The Bashford Dean Memorial Volume: Archaic Fishes. Article I-VIII.   New York, American Museum of Natural History, 1930– 1942. 4to

---

AS
145
B
Dean, L. M. I.
Alcyonaria
Van Straelen, V.
Résultats scientifiques du voyage aux Indes Orientales Néerlandaises...Léopold de Belgique. Vol. 2, Fasc. 11, 1932, pp. 1–24.
(Mem. hors ser. Mus. Roy. d'Hist. Nat. Belgique)

QL
Fish
Pam
298
Dean, Bashford
The Egg of the hag-fish, myxine glutinosa. From Mem. N. Y. Acad. Sci., v.2, part 2, 1900.

G
51
W 17
Dean, Beth
Exotic New Guinea. By Beth Dean and Victor Carell.
(Walkabout, 23(7):10–14, 1957)

GN
2.8
F 47
Deane, W.
Fijian Fishing and its Superstitions.
(Trans. Fijian Society, 1908–1910, pp. 57–61)

Q
GenSc
Pam
#4
Dean, Bashford
The marine biological stations of Europe, ex Smithsonian Rept. for 1893.

G
51
W 17
Dean, Beth
Maori life on the east coast.
(Walkabout, Vol. 19(6):35–37, 1953)

GN
671.F1
D 28
Deane, W.
Fijian Society, or the Sociology and Psychology of the Fijians.   London.   Macmillan. 1921. 8vo.   xv + 255 pp.

AS
36
S1
Dean, Bashford, 1867–
The marine biological stations of Europe. By Bashford Dean ...
(In Smithsonian institution. Annual report. 1893. Washington, 1894, 23½ᶜᵐ. p. 505–519. illus, pl. xxvɪ-xxxɪv)
"In the main as published in the Biological lectures, 1893, of the Woods Holl marine laboratory. (Boston: Ginn & co.)"

1. Biological laboratories.   ɪ. Title.

S 15–840

Library of Congress   Q11.S66 1893
Library, Smithsonian   Institution

GN
671.N5
D 28
Dean, Beth
Softly, wild drums. By Beth Dean and Victor Carell. Sydney. Ure Smith Pty. Ltd. 1958. 8vo. 200 pp.

DU
600
B 97
Deane, Wallace
Burton, J. W.
A hundred years in Fiji. By J. W. Burton and Wallace Deane. London. The Epworth Press. (1936) sm8vo. 144 pp.

QL
615
G 89
Dean, Bashford
Gudger, Eugene Willis
The Segmentation of the Egg of the Myxinoid, Bdellostoma stouti, Based on the Drawings of the Late Bashford Dean. By Eugene Willis Gudger and Bertram G. Smith.
(The Bashford Dean Memorial Volume: Archaic Fishes, Edited by E. W. Gudger, Article II, New York, Am. Mus. of Nat. Hist. 1931, pp. 47–57, 2 plates. 4to)

AS
36
S1
Dean, C   K.
Mound in Wisconsin. By C. K. Dean ...
(In Smithsonian institution. Annual report. 1872. Washington, 1873, 23½ᶜᵐ. p. 415)

1. Mounds—Wisconsin.

S 15–348

Library of Congress   Q11.S66 1872
Library, Smithsonian   Institution

QL
671
F4
Dearborn, Ned, 1865–
... Catalogue of a collection of birds from British East Africa, by Ned Dearborn ... Chicago, 1909.
1 p. l., p. 141–190. front. (map) 24½ᶜᵐ. (Field museum of natural history. Publication 135. Ornithological series. vol. ɪ, no. 4)
Bibliography: p. 141–143.

1. Birds—Catalogs and collections. 2. Birds—Africa, British East.

9–17311

Library of Congress   QL671.F4 vol. 1, no. 4
₍s20f2₎

AS
36
A6
Dean, Bashford, 1867–
... Studies on fossil fishes (sharks, chimæroids, and arthrodires). By Bashford Dean. ₍Cambridge, Mass., E. W. Wheeler, printer₎ 1909.
cover-title, p. 209–287. illus, pl. xxvɪ-xLɪ. 36ᶜᵐ. (Memoirs of the American museum of natural history. vol. ɪx, pt. v)

1. Fishes, Fossil.

11–14268

Library of Congress   QH1.A43 vol. 9
———— Copy 2.   QE851.D4

PL
Phil.Pam
624
Dean, James
The phonemes of Bilaan. by James and Gladys Dean.
(Phil. Jour. Sci., 84(3):311–322, 1955)

QL
671
F4
Dearborn, Ned, 1865–
... Catalogue of a collection of birds from Guatemala, by Ned Dearborn ... Chicago, 1907.
1 p. l., p. 69–138. ɪv pl. (incl. front., maps) 24½ᶜᵐ. (Field museum of natural history. Publication 125. Ornithological series. vol. ɪ, no. 3)

1. Birds—Guatemala. 2. Birds—Catalogs and collections.

8–9039

Library of Congress   QL671.F4

QU
104
U-G

Dearborn, Ned.

... Seed-eating mammals in relation to reforestation. By Ned Dearborn ... (Washington, Govt. print. off.) 1911.

5 p. illus. 23ᶜᵐ. (U. S. Dept. of agriculture. Bureau of biological survey. Circular no. 78)

1. Reforestation. 2. Rodentia. (2. Rodents) I. Title.

Agr 11—486

Library, U. S. Dept. of   Agriculture 1B52C no.78

GN
451
M 91

DEATH   MALAYSIA

Moss, Rosalind

The life after death in Oceania and the Malay Archipelago. Oxford University Press. 1925. 8vo. xii + 247 pp. 1 map, folded.

GN
Ethn.Pam.
3958

DEATH CUSTOMS   NEW BRITAIN

Goodenough, Ward

The pageant of death in Nakanai: a report of the 1954 expedition to New Britain.

(Bull. Univ. Museum, Univ. of Pennsylvania, Vol. 19(1):19-43, 1955)

QK
Bot.Pam.

Dearness, J.

Ellis, J. B.

New species of Canadian Fungi, by J. B. Ellis and J. Dearness.

(Canadian Record of Science, January, 1893, pp. 267-272)

GN
451
M 91

DEATH   PACIFIC

Moss, Rosalind

The life after death in Oceania and the Malay Archipelago. Oxford University Press. 1925. 8vo. xii + 247 pp., 1 map, folded.

AS
28
E 85

DEATH CUSTOMS   NEW CALEDONIA

Turpin, de Morel

Moeurs et coutumes canaques (extraits).

(Etudes Mélanesiennes, n.s. Année 2 (4):32-36, 1949)

DU
620
H 4

The death of Dr. Gregory.

(Haw. Hist. Soc., Ann. Rept., 60th, 1951:26)

GN
Ethn.
Pam.
3741

DEATH CUSTOMS

Gabus, Jean

L'homme face a la mort; l'homme primitif devant la mort. (sent from Musee d'Ethnographie, Neuchâtel, Switzerland) pp. 27-46. Received Nov. 1952. (no date)

GN
1
An

DEATH CUSTOMS   NEW GUINEA

Luzbetak, Louis J.

Worship of the dead in the Middle Wahgi (New Guinea).

(Anthropos, Vol. 51(1-2):81-96, 1956)

DU
1
P

Death of James Norman Hall. End of Tahiti's famous literary partnership.

(Pacific Islands Monthly, Vol. 21(12):9, 1951)

GN
2.M
E 85

DEATH CUSTOMS   DAYAK

Stöhr, Waldemar

Das Totenritual der Dajak.

(Ethnologica, Neue Folge, Bd. 1, 1959)

GN
Ethn.
Pam.
4164

CUSTOMS -
DEATH   POLYNESIA

Schoch, Alfred

Rituelle Menschentötungen in Polynesien. Ulm (Donau) 1954/55. 8vo. 95 pp.

AN
2.E
P 78

Death of Keolaokalani Paki Bishop. Aug. 29, 1864, only son of Her Excellency Luka Keelikolani, Governess of Hawaii and Hon. Isaac Y. Davis, and adopted son of Mr. and Mrs. C. R. Bishop; the deceased was 6 months and 29 days old.

(The Polynesian, Aug. 29, 1864)

GN
486
B 78

DEATH CUSTOMS   HAWAII

Bowen, Robert N.

Hawaiian disposal of the dead. A thesis submitted to the Graduate School of the University of Hawaii in partial fulfillment of the requirements for the degree of Master of Arts, June, 1961. typed copy. 266 pp. 3 figs.

QU
104
U-B

... The **Death Valley** expedition. A biological survey of parts of California, Nevada, Arizona, and Utah. Part II ... Washington, Govt. print. off., 1893.

402 p. front., illus., xiv pl., 5 maps. 23ᶜᵐ. (U. S. Dept. of agriculture. Division of ornithology and mammology. North American fauna no. 7)

Pt. i not yet published (May 1910)

CONTENTS.—1. Report on birds. By A. K. Fisher.—2. Report on reptiles and batrachians. By Leonhard Stejneger.—3. Report on fishes. By Charles H. Gilbert.—4. Report on insects. By C. V. Riley.—5. Report on mollusks. By R. E. C. Stearns.—6. Report on desert trees and shrubs. By C. Hart Merriam.—7. Report on desert cactuses and yuccas. By C. Hart Merriam.—8. List of localities. By T. S. Palmer.

1. Zoology—Pacific states. 2. Botany—Pacific states. i. Fisher, Albert Kenrick. ii. Stejneger, Leonhard Hess. iii. Gilbert, Charles Henry. iv. Riley, Charles Valentine. v. Stearns, Robert Edwards Carter. vi. Merriam, Clinton Hart. vii. Palmer, Theodore Sherman.

Library, U. S. Dept. of   Agriculture   Agr 6-1192

PL
1
B 59

DEATH   BORNEO

Harrisson, Tom.

Borneo death.

(Bijdragen tot de Taal-, Land- en Volkenkunde, Deel 118:1-41, 1962)

GN
2.S
P 76

DEATH CUSTOMS   MAORI

Beaglehole, Ernest

Contemporary Maori death customs. By Ernest and Pearl Beaglehole.

(Journal of the Polynesian Society, Vol. 54, no. 2, pp. 91-116, 1945)

QK
1
U

DEATH VALLEY, CALIFORNIA - BOTANY

Coville, Frederick Vernon, 1867–

... Botany of the Death Valley expedition. Report on the botany of the expedition sent out in 1891 by the U. S. Department of agriculture to make a biological survey of the region of Death Valley, California. By Frederick Vernon Coville ... Washington, Govt. print. off., 1893.

viii, 363 p. front., 21 pl. (part fold.) fold. map. 24ᶜᵐ. (U. S. Dept. of agriculture. Division of botany. Contributions from the U. S. National herbarium. vol. iv)

Issued November 29, 1893.

Bibliography. By Josephine A. Clark: p. 284-300.

1. Botany—California—Death Valley. i. Clark, Josephine Adelaide.

8—10557

Library of Congress   QK1.U5 vol. 4

GN
485
S 46

DEATH   INDONESIA

Sell, Hans Joachim

Der Schlimme Tod bei den Volkern Indonesiens Mouton and Co. 's-Gravenhage. 1955. R8vo. viii + 337 pp.

GN
Ethn.Pam.
3599

DEATH CUSTOMS   MELANESIA

Speiser, Felix

Uber Totenbestattungen in Insel Melanesien.

(Internationales Archiv f. Ethnographie, Bd. 40(5/6):125-174, 1942)

AS
145
B

Debauche, H.

Geometridae de Celebes (Lepidoptera Heterocera).

(Mem. Musée R. d'Hist. Nat. de Belgique, S 2, Fasc. 22, 1941)

GN
802
D 28

Debenedetti, Salvador

    Exploración Arqueológica en los Cementerios Prehistóricos de la Isla de Tilcara (Quebrada de Humahuaca, Provincia de Jujuy) Campaña de 1908, por el Dr. Salvador Debenedetti. Homenaje al XVII Congreso Internacional de Americanistas. Buenos Aires. Alsina. 1910. R8vo. 263 pp.

    (Facultad de Filosofia y Letras, Pub. de la Sección Antropológica, No. 6).

QL
Crust.
Pam.
No. 334

DECAPODA

Balss, Heinrich

    Diagnosen neuer Macruren der Valdivi aexpedition. Sonderabdruck aus dem Zool. Anzeig. Bd. 44, Nr.13, 1914.

GC
63
D 61

DECAPODA

Fraser, F. C.

    On the development and distribution of the young stages of krill (Euphausia superba)

Discovery Committee
    Discovery Reports, Vol. 14, 1936, p.1-192

G
161
H

Debenham, Frank   Editor

Bellingshausen, Thaddeus

    The voyage of Captain Bellingshausen to the Antarctic Seas, 1819-1821. Translated from the Russian. Edited by Frank Debenham. Vols 1-2.

    (Works issued by the Hakluyt Society, Ser. 2, Vols. 91-92, 1945.)

QL
Crust.
Pam.
No. 336

DECAPODA

Balss, Heinrich

    Uber eine neue Pontiniide aus dem Golf von Neapel. Aus Mitt. Zool. Sta. NeapelBd.22, Nr. 15, 1921.

QL
Crust.Pam.
85

DECAPODA

Girard, Maurice

    Note monographique sur les genres Crabe Platycarcin, avec indication d'espèces nouvelles. Famille des Cancerides.- Ordre des Decapodes.- Section des Brachyures.- Classe des Crustacés.

    (Ann. Soc. Ent., Paris, VII, 1859, p. 142-162)

DU
1
P 10

DE BISSCHOP, ERIC

    Spontaneous combustion began it all.

    (Pacific Islands Monthly, 12(5):65-67, 1959)

    [biography of Eric de Bisschop, and review of his "Tahiti Nui"]

GC
63
D 61

DECAPODA

Bargmann, Helene E.

    The development and life-history of adolescent and adult krill, Euphausia superba.

IN
Discovery Reports, Vol. 23, pp. 103-176, Cambridge, 1945

QL
8
Br

DECAPODA (- LARVAE)

Gurney, Robert

    Decapod larvae. British Mus. Brit. Antarc. Exped 1910, Zool. Vol. VIII, No. 2, Crustacea Part IX. London, 1924.

AS
162
P

Decaisne, Joseph

    Description d'un herbier de l'ile de Timor.

    (Nouv. Annales Mus. Hist. Nat., Paris, 3: 333-501, 1834. pl. 16-21)

GC
63
D 61

DECAPODA

Bargmann, Helene E.

    The reproductive system of Euphausia superba

Discovery Committee
    Discovery Reports, Vol. 14, 1937, p. 325-350

GC
63
D 61

DECAPODA

Gurney, Robert

    Larvae of Decapod Crustacea, I-III; IV; V

Discovery Committee
    Discovery Reports, Vol. 12, 1936, p.377-440 and Vol. 14, 1937, p.351-404; Vol. 17, 1938, p. 291-344

Q
115
D 93

locked
case

Decaisne, J(oseph)

Du Petit-Thouars, Abel A.

    Voyage autour du monde sur la frégate La Venus, pendant les années 1836-1839... Botanique par J. Decaisne. 1864, with atlas of 23 plates, 1846. Paris. 8vo. and folio.

Q
115
C 28

DECAPODA

Bernard, F.

    Decapoda Eryonidae (Eryoneicus et Willemoesia).

    (The Carlsberg Foundation's Oceanographical Expedition round the world 1928-1930 and previous Dana Expeditions, Dana Report No. 37, 1953)

QL
Crust.Pam.
100

DECAPODA

Hansen, H. J.

    On a new species of Sergestes obtained by Mr. George Murray during the cruise of the Oceana, in 1898.

    (Ann. and Mag. Nat. Hist., Ser. 7, Vol. 11, 1903, pp. 479-481)

AS
36
S4

DECAPODA (CRUSTACEA)

Andrews, Ethan Allen, 1859-

    Sperm transfer in certain decapods. By E. A. Andrews ...

    (In U. S. National museum. Proceedings. Washington, 1911. 23½ᶜᵐ. v. 39, p. 419-434. illus.)

    1. Decapoda (Crustacea)

    11-21246

Library of Congress   Q11.U55 vol. 39

QL
Crustacea
Pam.
625

DECAPODA

Coffin, Harold G.

    A new southern form of "Pagurus hirsutiusculis" (Dana) (Crustacea, Decapoda)

    (Walla Walla College Pub. of the Dept. of Biol. Sci...No. 21, 1957)

XXX
XXXXX
Pam.
X520X

GC
1
M 73-a

DECAPODA

Heldt, Jeanne H.

    La reproduction chez les crustacés décapodes de la famille des Pénéides.

    (Annales de l'Inst. Océanographique, N. S. Tome 18, Fasc. 2, 1938, pp. 31-206)

QL
Crust.
Pam.
No. 337

DECAPODA

Balss, Heinrich

    Diagnosen neuer japanischer Decapoden, Sonderabdruck aus Zool.Anzeig. Bd. 54, Nr. 1/2, 1922.

QL
1
H2

DECAPODA

Faxon, W.

    Notes on the crayfishes in the U.S. National Museum and the Museum of Comparative Zoology with descriptions of new species and subspecies to which is appended a catalogue of the known species and subspecies. in Mus. Comp. Zoology Mem. XL, 8, pp. 351-427, 13 pls. Cambridge, 1914.

AS
36
C1

DECAPODA

Holmes, Samuel J.

    Synopsis of California stalk-eyed crustacea. California Academy of Sci. Occasional Papers, v.7, 1900.

QL 1 Liv

DECAPODA (Crustacea)

Jackson, H. G.

Eupagarus. In Liverpool Biol. Soc. Proc. & Trans. Vol. XXVII, 1913. pp 495-573, 6 pls.

QL Crust.Pam. 246

DECAPODA

Nobili, Giuseppe

Decapodi raccolti dal Dr. Filippo Silvestri nell'America meridionale.

(Bollettino dei Musei di Zoologia ed Anatomia comparata...Torino, Vol. 16, 1901. pp. 1-16)

DECAPODA (CRUSTACEA).

Rathbun, Mary Jane, 1860-

... New decapod crustaceans from Panama, by Mary J. Rathbun ... Washington, Smithsonian institution, 1912.

1 p. l., 3 p. 24½ᶜᵐ. (Smithsonian miscellaneous collections, v. 59, no. 13) Publication 2090.

1. Decapoda (Crustacea) 2. Crustacea—Panama.

Library of Congress   Q11.S7 vol. 59, no. 13   12-35780
—— Copy 2.   QL441.2.R3

GC 63 D 61

DECAPODA

John, D. Dilwyn

The southern species of the genus Euphausia.

Discovery Committee
Discovery Reports, Vol. 14, 1936, p. 193-324.

QL Crus.Pam. 156

DECAPODA

Nobili, Giuseppe

Decapodi e Stomatopodi(Viaggio...Ecuador...)

(Boll. d. Musei di Zool. Anat. comparata R. Universita di Torino. Vol. XVI, 1901, pp. 1-16)

QL 435 S 32

DECAPODA

Schellenberg, Adolf

Krebstiere oder Crustacea, II: Decapoda, Zehnfüsser (14. Ordnung). [Die Tierwelt Deutschlands...Teil 10] 1928. iv + 146 pp.

QL Crus.Pam. 127

DECAPODA

Kinahan, John Robert

On Xantho Rivulosa and other decapod crustacean occurring at Valentia Island, Co. Kerry.

(Proc. Dublin Nat. Hist. Soc., II, 1856-1859, pp. 9-17)

QL Crus.Pam. 153

DECAPODA

Nobili, Giuseppe

Intorno ad alcuni Crostacei Decapodi del Brasile.

(Bollettino dei Musei di Zoologia ed Anatomia comparata della R. Universith di Torino.Vol. XIV, 1899, pp. 1-6)

QL Crust Pam 381

DECAPODA (CRUSTACEA)

Schenkel, E

Beitrag zur kenntnis der dekapodenfauna von Celebes. Naturf. Ges. Basel. verh. v.13, Basel, 1902. 100p. pls.

QL Crus.Pam. 128

DECAPODA

Kinahan, John Robert

Report on Crustacea of Dublin District. Part I Decapoda Podophthalmata.

(Report of the British Association for Advancement of Science for 1858.(1859) pp. 262-268)

QL Crust.Pam. 298

DECAPODA

Pfeffer, Georg

Beiträge zur Morphologie der Dekapoden und Isopoden.

(Hamb. Nat. Ver., Abh. 10, 1887, No. 11, 10 pp.)

QL 1 C 1

DECAPODA (CRUSTACEA)

Schmitt, Waldo Lasalle, 1887-

The marine decapod *Crustacea* of California, with special reference to the decapod *Crustacea* collected by the United States Bureau of fisheries steamer "Albatross" in connection with the biological survey of San Francisco Bay during the years 1912-1913, by Waldo L. Schmitt ... Berkeley, University of California press, 1921.

cover-title, 1 p. l., 470 p. illus., 50 pl. (incl. maps; part fold.) 27½ᶜᵐ. (University of California publications in zoology. v. 23)

Published by permission of the secretary of the Smithsonian institution and of the United States commissioner of fisheries.

1. Crustacea—San Francisco Bay. 2. Decapoda (Crustacea) I. Albatross (Steamer)

Title from Univ. of Calif   Library of Congress   A 21-878
[5]

AS 244 D

DECAPODA

Man, J. G. de

On a small collection of Decapoda, one of which, a *Crangon*, caught by the Danish Pacific Expedition at the Jolo Islands, is new to science.

(Vid. Med. Dansk Nat. For. Kobenhavn, Bd. 87 1929-30, Papers from Dr. Th. Mortensen's Pacific Expedition 1914-16, No. 50).

AS 36 S4

DECAPODA (CRUSTACEA)

Rathbun, Mary Jane, 1860-

Additions to West Indian Tertiary decapod crustaceans. By Mary J. Rathbun ...

(In U. S. National museum. Proceedings. Washington, 1921. 23½ᶜᵐ. v. 58, p. 381-384. pl. 25)

"Additions to the bibliography of West Indian Tertiary *Decapoda*": p. 384.

1. Decapoda (Crustacea) 2. Crustacea—West Indies.

Library of Congress   Q11.U55 vol. 58   21-21446
[5]

QL Crus.Pam. 245

DECAPODA

Siebold, Carl Theodor Ernst von

Ueber die in Munchen gezuchtete Artemia Fertilis aus dem grossen Salzsee von Utah.

(Verhandl. der schweiz. naturf. Gesell. in Basel, 59th Jahr., 1876, pp. 267-280)

QL Crustacea Pam. 657

DECAPODA

Miller, Paul Emanuel

A laboratory study of the developmental stages of Haplogaster mertensii (Brandt), (Crustacea, Decapoda). By Paul Emanuel Miller and Harold G. Coffin.

(Walla Walla College Publications of the Department of Biological Science...No. 30, 1961)

AS 36 S5

DECAPODA (CRUSTACEA)

Rathbun, Mary Jane, 1860-

... Decapod crustaceans from the Panama region. By Mary J. Rathbun ... Washington, Govt. print. off., 1918.

1 p. l., 123-184, iii p. pl. 54-66. 24½ᶜᵐ. (Smithsonian institution. United States National museum. Bulletin 103 [pt. 7])

At head of title: Contributions to the geology and paleontology of the Canal Zone, Panama, and geologically related areas in Central America and the West Indies.

"Extract from Bulletin 103, pages 123-184, with plates 54-66."

1. Decapoda (Crustacea) 2. Crustacea—Panama.

Library, Smithsonian   Institution   S 21-7
[s21b5]

AS 36 C8

DECAPODA (CRUSTACEA)

Smith, Sidney Irving, 1843-

... Occasional occurrence of tropical and subtropical species of decapod *Crustacea* on the coast of New England.

(In Connecticut academy of arts and sciences. Transactions. New Haven, 1877-82. 25ᶜᵐ. v. 4, p. [254]-267)

1. Decapoda (Crustacea) I. Title.

Library of Congress   Q11.C9 vol. 4   A 17-791
Yale University   A53n.366.4

QL Crus.Pam. 154

DECAPODA

Nobili, Giuseppe

Crustacei Decapodi. (Viaggio...Argentina e Paraguay)

(Boll. Mus. Zool. ed Anat. Compar. della R. Universita di Torino. Vol. XI, 1896, pp. 1-14)

QL Crus.Pam. 191

DECAPODA

Rathbun, Mary J(ane)

The Decapod Crustaceans of West Africa.

(Proc.U.S.Nat.Mus.Vol.XXIV,1900. pp.271-316)

AS 36 S2

DECAPODA (CRUSTACEA)

Stimpson, William, 1832-1872.

... Report on the *Crustacea* (Brachyura and Anomura) collected by the North Pacific exploring expedition, 1853-1856. By William Stimpson ... Washington, Smithsonian institution, 1907.

240 p. xxvi pl. 25ᶜᵐ. (Smithsonian miscellaneous collections. Part of vol. XLIX, no. 1717)

1. Decapoda (Crustacea) I. North Pacific exploring expedition, 1853-1856.

Library of Congress   Q11.S7 vol. 49   7—34605
—— Copy 2.   QL444.D3S85

DECAPODA(CRUSTACEA).
AS
36
C8
Verrill, Addison Emory, 1839-

... Decapod *Crustacea* of Bermuda; I.—*Brachyura and Anomura*. Their distribution, variations, and habits.

(In Connecticut academy of arts and sciences. Transactions. New Haven, Conn., 1908. 25ᵐ. v. 13, p. (299)-474. illus., pl. IX-XXVIII)

Bibliography: p. 458-464.

1. Decapoda (Crustacea) I. Title.

A 17-911

Library of Congress   Q11.C9 vol. 13
Yale University   A53n.366.13

DECAPODA   DUTCH EAST INDIES
Q
115
S 56
Holthuis, L. B.
The Decapoda of the Siboga-Expedition, Part X: The Palaemonidae...with remarks on other species, I. Subfamily Palaemoninae; II...Pontoniinae
IN
Weber, Max   and L. F. de Beaufort
Uitkomsten op zoologisch, botanisch, oceanographisch en geologisch Gebied...1899-1900...
Monographie XXXIXa⁹, Leiden, 1950. 4to.
"   XXXIXa¹⁰. "   1952   "

DECAPODA   GALAPAGOS ISLANDS
QL
Crust.
Pam.
534
527
Hult, Jöran

Crustacea Decapoda from the Galapagos Islands collected by Mr. Rolf Blomberg.

and
QL
1
S 96
(Arkiv f. Zoologi, Svenska Vetenskapsakad. Bd. 30 A, No. 5, 1938, pp. 1-18)

DECAPODA   BIBLIOGRAPHY
Z
7996.C95
G 98
Gurney, Robert

Bibliography of the larvae of Decapod Crustacea. London. Printed for the Ray Society. 1939. 8vo. vi + 123 pp.

DECAPODA   DUTCH EAST INDIES
Q
115
S 56
Man, Jan Govert de
The Decapoda of the Siboga Expedition, Parts I-VII.   (Part 8 by Anna J. van Dam.)

Weber, Max
Uitkomsten...Nederlandsch Oost Indie, 1899-1900...Siboga...Monographie XXXIXa, a¹-a⁹ (livr. 55, 60, 76, 87, 93, 102, 109). 1911-1928.

DECAPODA   GALAPAGOS ISLANDS
AS
36
S 2
Schmitt, Waldo L.

Decapod and other Crustacea collected on the Presidential Cruise of 1938...

(Smithsonian Misc. Coll., Vol. 98, 1939, No. 6, pp. 29)

DECAPODA   ANTARCTIC
GC
63
D 61
Dennell, Ralph

On the structure of the photophores of some Decapod Crustacea.

IN
Discovery Committee...Reports, Vol.20, 1940 pp. 309-382.

DECAPODA   DUTCH EAST INDIES
Q
115
S 56
Holthus, L. B.
The Decapoda of the Siboga-Expedition, Part IX: The Hippolytidae and Rhynchocinetidae collected by the Siboga and Snellius Expeditions with remarks on other species.
IN
Weber, Max   and L. F. de Beaufort
Uitkomsten op zoologisch, botanisch...
Gebied...1899-1900. Monographie XXXIXa⁸ Leiden. 1947.

DECAPODA   HAWAII
QL
Crustacea
Pam.
566
MacKay, Donald C. G.

A survey of the Decapod Crustacea of Wailupe commercial fish pond near Honolulu, Hawaii.

(reprint: Canadian Field Naturalist, Vol. 61:134-140,1947)

DECAPODA   ANTARCTIC
GC
63
D 61
Gurney, R.

Larvae of Decapod Crustacea, Part VI. The Genus Sergestes, by R. Gurney and M. V. Lebour. 1940.

IN
Discovery Committee...Reports, Vol. 20, 1940 pp. 3-67.

DECAPODA   DUTCH EAST INDIES
AS
145
B
Roux, Jean
Crustacés Décapodes d'eau douce.

Van Straelen, V.

Résultats scientifiques du voyage aux Indes Orientales Néerlandaises...Léopold de Belgique. Vol. 3, Fasc. 14, 1933, pp. 1-18.

(Mem. hors ser. Mus. Roy. d'Hist. Nat. Belgique)

DECAPODA   INDIA
QL
444.D3
A 35
Alcock, Alfred William
A descriptive catalogue of the Indian deep-sea Crustacea, Decapoda, Macrura and Anomala, in the Indian Museum, being a revised account of the deep-sea species collected in the Royal Indian Marine Survey ship Investigator. Indian Museum. Calcutta. 1901. 4to.

DECAPODA   ASIA, EAST
QL
444.D3
B 19
Balss, Heinrich

Ostasiatische Decapoden.
I: Die Galatheiden und Paguriden
II: Die Natantia und Reptantia.
Beitrage zur Naturgeschichte Ostasiens.
(Abh. der math-phys. Kl. der K. Bayer. Akad. der Wissenschaften, Suppl. Bd. II, Abhandl. 9-10, 1913-1914)

DECAPODA   DUTCH EAST INDIES
Q
115
S 56
Van Dam, Anna J.
Die Decapoden des Siboga-Expedition,
Part VIII: Galatheidea: Chirostylidae

Weber, Max
Uitkomsten...Nederlandsch Oost Indie, 1899-1900...Siboga...Monographie XXXIXa⁷ (livr. 119) 1933. 46 pp.

DECAPODA   INDIA
QL
444.D3
K 32
Kemp, Stanley

Notes on Crustacea Decapoda in the Indian Museum.
1. (Rec. Indian Mus., 5:175-182, 1910)
2. ("   "   " 6:5-12, 1911)
3. ("   "   " 7:15-32, 1912)
4.("   "   " 7:113-122, 1912)
5.17(" "   "   " 15:27, 1914-25)

DECAPODA   ANTARCTIC
Q
115
M 46
Bage, Freda
Crustacea Decapoda

Mawson, Sir Douglas   leader
Australasian Antarctic Expedition, 1911-14. Scientific Reports, Series C, Vol. 2, Part 6, 1938.

DECAPODA   FIJI
QE
349.F
L 13   Ladd, Harry S., and others

Geology of Vitilevu, Fiji...Honolulu. 1934.
AS   Fossil Decapod Crustaceans from Vitilevu, Fiji,
763   by Mary J. Rathbun. pp. 238-241. pl. 44. R8vo.
B-b
        (Bernice P. Bishop Museum, Bull. 119, 1934.)
Reading
Room

DECAPODA   MALAY ARCHIPELAGO
QL
444.D3
M 26
Man, Jan Govert de

Bericht über die von Herrn Dr. J. Brock im indischen Archipel gesammelten Decapoden und Stomatopoden.

(Archiv für Naturgeschichte, Jahrg. 53:215-600, pl. 7-22,22a, 1887. separate)

DECAPODA   AUSTRALIA
QL
Crustacea
Pam.
591 a,b
Hess, Wilhelm

Beitrage zur Kenntniss der Decapoden-Krebse Australiens.

(Archiv f. Naturgeschichte, 31:127-173, taf. 6-7, 1865)

DECAPODA   GALAPAGOS ISLANDS
AS
182
S 47   Bott, R.

Decapoden von den Galapagos-Inseln.

(Senckenbergiana, Biologica, Bd. 39(3/4): 209-211, 1958)

DECAPODA   MALAY ARCHIPELAGO
QL
444.D3
M 26   Man, J. G. de

Decapoden des Indischen Archipels.

(Zoologische Ergebnisse einer reise in Niederländisch Ost-Indien, Bd. II, Mit tafel XV-XXIX. Leiden. E. J. Brill. 1892. 4to. pp. 266-527)

QL
444.D3
M 26

DECAPODA   MALAY ARCHIPELAGO

Man, J. G. de

Die von Herrn Professor Kükenthal im Indischen Archipel gesammelten Dekapoden und Stomatopoden von Dr. J. G. de Man. Mit neun tafeln. Frankfurt. 1902. 4to.

AS
182
S

(Abh. Senck. Naturforsch. Gesellschaft. Bd. 25, Heft 3, pp. 467-929)

QL
1
N 6-z

DECAPODA   PACIFIC

Robson, G.C.

The Cephalopoda Decapoda of the Arcturus Oceanographic Expedition, 1925. By the late G. C. Robson.

(Zoologica, Vol. 33:115-132, 1948)

QE
349.F
L 13

DECAPODA   VITILEVU

Ladd, Harry S., and others

Geology of Vitilevu, Fiji...Honolulu. 1934.

AS
763
B-b

Fossil Decapod Crustaceans from Vitilevu, Fiji, by Mary J. Rathbun. pp. 238-241. pl. 44. R8vo.

Reading
Room

(Bernice P. Bishop Museum, Bull. 119, 1934.)

AS
36
S 4

DECAPODA   MARSHALL ISLANDS

Chace, Fenner A., Jr.

Notes on shrimps from the Marshall Islands.

(Proc. of the United States National Museum, Vol. 105(3349):1-22, 1955)

QL
Crus.Pam.
196

DECAPODA   PACIFIC COAST

Rathbun, Mary J.

Descriptions of new Decapod Crustaceans from the West Coast of North America.

(Proc.U.S.Nat.Mus., Vol. XXIV,1902. pp.885-905)

AS
36
A 65

DECAPTERUS

Nichols, John Treadway

East Indian mackerel scads (Decapterus) described and differentiated. (Notes on Carangin fishes, VI)

(American Museum Novitates, 1196, 1942)

QL
5
M 62

DECAPODA   MICRONESIA

Miyake, Sadayoshi
Notes on Decapod Crustaceans collected by Prof. Teiso Esaki from Micronesia. (Ann. Zool. Japonenses, 17, 1938, p. 107-112)

Esaki, Teiso
Results of the Micronesian Expedition, 1937-1938, No. 14.

AS
540
P

DECAPODA   PHILIPPINE ISLANDS

Estampador, Eulogio P.

A check list of Philippine crustacean decapods.

(Philippine Journal of Science, Vol. 62, 1937, pp. 465-599)

QL
Fishes
Pam.479

DECAPTERUS

Nichols, John Treadwell

Notes on Carangin fishes.

(Am. Mus. Novitates, No. 1527, Jl 16, 1951)

AS
162
P 23

DECAPODA   NEW CALEDONIA

Remy, J. M.

Sur les crabes sub-fosslies de Nouvelle-Calédonie.

(Bull. Mus. Nat. d'Histo. Nat., Paris, ser. 2, Tome 24(1):114-117, 1952)

QL
Crustacea
Pam.
621

DECAPODA   RED SEA

Balss, H(einrich)

Decapoden des Roten Meeres. Photostat, pp. 10-11 only, for description of Cestopagurus Helleri.
IN
Balss, Heinrich
Die Dekapoda Brachyura von Dr. Sixten Bock's Pazifik-Expedition 1917-1918.

(K. Vet. och   Vitterhets Samh., Handl. Ser B. 5(7):1-85, 1938)

QH
195.M
D 29

Decary, Raymond

La faune malgache, son role dans les croyances et les usages indigènes. Avec 22 figures. Payot. Paris. 1950. 8vo. 236 pp.

QL
345.N 6
S 24

DECAPODA   NEW CALEDONIA

Roux, J(ean)

Crustacés décapodes d'eau douce de la Nouvelle-Calédonie.

Sarasin, Fritz
Nova Caledonia...A. Zoologie, Vol. IV, L.II, pp. 182-240. 1926

QL
1
L 52

DECAPODA   SURINAM

Holthuis, L. B.

Scientific results of the Surinam Expedition 1948-1949. Part II. Zoology, No. 1. Crustacea Decapoda Macrura.

(Zool. Mededelingen, Deel 31(3):25-37, 1950)

Decary, R.

La faune malgache. 1950.

UH has

QL
Crustacea
Pam.
560

DECAPODA   PACIFIC

Balss, Heinrich

Die Dekapoda Brachyura von Dr. Sixten Bocks Pazifik-Expedition, 1917-1918.

(Meddelanden fran Goteborgs Musei Zoologiska Avdelning, 75, 1938) 85 pp., 2 pl.

(Fiji, Gilberts, Marshalls, Niue, Ellice, Rotuma)

AS
162
P 23

DECAPODA   TAHITI

Forest, J.

Crustacés Décapodes marcheurs des iles de Tahiti et des Tuamotu.

(Bull. Mus. Nat. d'Hist. Nat., Paris, s 2, vol. 26:345-352, 1954)

AS
162
M 36

Decary, Raymond

Plantes et animaux utiles de Madagascar.

(Annales du Musée Colonial de Marseille, ser. 6, vol. 4:9-234, 1946)

QH
1
A 88

DECAPODA   PACIFIC

Holthuis, L. B.

Enumeration of the Decapod and Stomatopod Crustacea from Pacific coral islands.

(Atoll Research Bulletin, No. 24, 1-66 pp., 1953)

AS
162
P 23

DECAPODA   TUAMOTU ISLANDS

Forest, J.

Crustacés Décapodes marcheurs des iles de Tahiti et des Tuamotu.

(Bull. Mus. Nat. d'Hist. Nat., Paris, s 2, vol. 26:345-352, 1954)

AS
162
S 67

Dechambre, Ed.

Origine des animaux domestiques de Madagascar.

(La Terre et la Vie, 1951(4):185-196)

G
104
U-d

Decisions on names in Hawaii.

(U. S. Board on Geographic Names, Dept. of Interior, Cumulative decision list No. 5403, July, 1954)

G
104
U-d

Decisions on names in the Trust Territory of the Pacific Islands and Guam, Part I: The Caroline Islands. Cumulative decision list no. 5501. U. S. Board on Geographic Names. Dept. of the Interior. Jan. 1955. 8vo. 120 pp.

GN
2.S
P 76

Deck, Norman C.

A grammar of the language spoken by the Kwara'ae people of Mala, British Solomon Islands.

(Journal of the Polynesian Society, Vol. 42, No.2, pp. 33-48; No.3, pp.133-144; No. 4, pp.241-256; Vol. 43, No. 1, pp. 1-16;Vol. 43, No. 2, pp. 85-100;No.3, pp.163-70;No.4,pp.246-57;1933-1934.)

G
7
R 91

(Deck, Northcote)

Rennell Island.

(The Geographical Journal, Vol. 57, 1921, pp. 474-476)

Deck and port

DU
12
~~075~~
C 72

Colton, Rev. Walter.

Deck and port...[1850].

For fuller entry see main card

GN
658
K 39

Decken, Carl Claus von der

Kersten, Otto

Baron Carl Claus von der Decken's reisen in Ost-Afrika in den jahren 1859 bis 1961. Bearbeitet von Otto Kersten...Mit einem vorworte von Dr. A. Petermann. Die Insel Zanzibar. Reisen nach dem Niassasee und dem Schneeberge Kilimandscharo. Erläutert durch 13 tafeln, 25 eingedruckte holzschnitte und 3 karten. Leipzig. Winter. 1869. R8vo. pp. xxi 336 (15). pls. Erster band.

G
159
C 15

Decker, Adolph

Callander, John

Terra Australis Cognita...Vol. 2, pp. 286-334; Jacques Le Hermite, to Polynesia and Australasia. Edinburgh. 1768. (the author of this judicious journal was Adolph Decker)

QL
461
C 15 v

Decker, George C.

Pesticide-wildlife relationships.

(California Vector Views, Vol. 10(7), 1963)

Q
101
P 18

Decker, John L.

Gout and hyperuricemia in a Pacific population group.

(Eugenics Quarterly, Vol. 9(1):54-58, 1962)

(Paper read at symposium on medical genetics, Tenth Pacific Science Congress, 1961)

DU
406
N 56

DECLARATION OF INDEPENDENCE (NEW ZEALAND)

(New Zealand)

Fac-similes of the Declaration of Independence and the Treaty of Waitangi. Wellington, 1892. Folio.

GN
Ethn
Pam.
635

DECORATION PALAU ISLANDS

Krämer, Augustin

Ornamentik und Mythologie von Palau. 1908. (Sonderabdruck aus dem Korrespondenz-Blatt der Deutschen Gesell. Anthrop. Ethnol. und Urgeschichte. Jahrg. 39, Nr. 9-12, Sept.-Dec. 1908.)

GN
550
S

DECORATION AND ORNAMENT--HIST.

Holmes, William Henry, 1846-

... Origin and development of form and ornament in ceramic art. By William H. Holmes.

(*In* U. S. Bureau of American ethnology. Fourth annual report, 1882-83. Washington, 1886. 30ᶜᵐ. p. 437-465. illus.)

1. Pottery—Hist. 2. Decoration and ornament—Hist.

Library of Congress   E51.U56 4th
          [a20f2]   12--8583

GN
550
S

DECORATION AND ORNAMENT.

Holmes, William Henry, 1846-

A study of the textile art in its relation to the development of form and ornament, by William H. Holmes.

(*In* U. S. Bureau of American ethnology. Sixth annual report, 1884-85. Washington, 1888. 30ᶜᵐ. p. 189-252. illus.)

Mainly a study of the textile art of the American Indians.

1. Textile industry and fabrics. 2. Decoration and ornament. 3. Indians—Textile industry and fabrics.

Library of Congress   E51.U55 6th   16-5499

VALLEY

AS
36
A6

DECORATION AND ORNAMENT--AMUR RIVER &

Laufer, Berthold, 1874-

... The decorative art of the Amur tribes. By Berthold Laufer. [New York] 1902.

cover-title, p. 1-86. illus., pl. I-XXXIII (partly col.) 36ᶜᵐ. (Memoirs of the American museum of natural history. vol. VII. Anthropology. vol. VI, [pt.] 1)

Publications of the Jesup north Pacific expedition. vol. IV, pt. I.

1. Decoration and ornament—Amur River and Valley.

Library of Congress   QH1.A43 vol. 7   11-14264

GN
419
S46

DECORATION & ORNAMENT

Selenka, Emil

Der schmuck des menschen.

Berlin, Vita, 1900.   72p.   pls.

GN
Ethn
Pam.
718

and
GN
2.I
A4

DECORATION OF BOATS

Hornell, James

Survivals of the use of oculi in modern boats. Reprint from Journ. Anthrop. Inst. Vol. 53, July- Dec. 1923.

DECORATIONS OF HONOR

see

ROYAL ORDERS

DECORATIVE ART

See

Art, Decorative

Decoux, J.

Sillages dans les Mers du Sud. 1953.

UH has

QK
Botany
Pam.
1235

Decrock, E.

Recherches morphologiques et anatomiques sur la graine des Ravenala. Ex Ann. Mus. Col. Marseille, Vol.9, 1911.

[Bound with papers by Cordemoy and Planchon.]

GN
Pam
2241

De Cunha, Gerson

On amulets. In Journ. Anthrop. Soc. Bombay, v.1, n.6, 1888.

RC
Path. Pam.
2

Dedication of the Kapiolani Home for girls, the offspring of leper parents, at Kakanko, Oahu, by Their Majesties King Kalakaua and Queen Kapiolani. Description of the Leper Settlement on the island of Molokai. Honolulu. 1885. 42 pp. 8vo.

(contains address by Walter M. Gibson and article on the leper settlement by Robert J. Creighton)

AS
36
S5

DEEP-SEA DEPOSITS

Flint, James Milton, 1838–

A contribution to the oceanography of the Pacific, compiled from data collected by the United States steamer Nero while engaged in the survey of a route for a trans-Pacific cable. By James M. Flint ... Washington, Govt. print. off., 1905.

v, 62 p. incl. tables. v pl., 9 fold. diagr. 23ᶜᵐ. (*Added t.-p.:* ... United States National museum. Bulletin ... no. 55)

1. Pacific Ocean. 2. Deep-sea deposits.

Library of Congress   Q11.U6
                               [s19c2]   6–7327

GC
380
T 77

DEEP SEA DEPOSITS

Trask, Parker D.

Recent marine sediments; a symposium, prepared under the direction of a subcommittee... National Research Council, Washington, D. C... Published by the American Association of Petroleum Geologists. Tulsa. Thomas Murby. London. 8vo. 1939. vi, 736 pp.

DU
563
D 31

Deeken, Richard

Die Karolinen: Nach eigenen Reisebeobachtungen älteren Monographien und den neuesten amtlichen Berichten. Mit 24 Vollbildern, meistens nach Photographien des Verfassers. Wilhelm Süsserott. Berlin. nd. 8vo. 140 pp.

GC
63
D 61

DEEP-SEA DEPOSITS

Matthews, L. Harrison

The marine deposits of the Patagonian continental shelf.

Discovery Committee
Discovery Reports, Vol. 9, 1934, p. 175–206

Q
115
S 56

DEEP SEA DEPOSITS   DUTCH EAST INDIES

Boggild, O. B.
Meeresgrundproben der Siboga-Expedition.

Weber, Max
Uitkomsten...Nederlandsch Oost Indie, 1899–1900...Siboga...Monographie LXV (livr. 79), 1916
50 pp. 1 pl., 1 chart

DU
810
De
D31

Deeken, Richard

Manuia Samoa: Samoanische Reiseskizzen und Beobachtungen.

Oldenburg [1901] , 240 pp.

GC
63
D 61

DEEP-SEA DEPOSITS

Moore, Hilary B.

Faecal pellets from marine deposits.

Discovery Committee
Discovery Reports, Vol. 7, 1933, p. 17–26

GC
380
T 77

DEEP SEA DEPOSITS   INDIAN OCEAN

Schott, W.
Deep-sea sediments of the Indian Ocean.

IN
Trask, Parker D.
Recent marine sediments...London, 1939, pp. 396–408.

QL
1
H1

DEEP-SEA DEPOSITS

Agassiz, Alexander, 1835–1910.

A contribution to American thalassography. Three cruises of the United States Coast and geodetic survey steamer "Blake," in the Gulf of Mexico, in the Caribbean Sea, and along the Atlantic coast of the United States, from 1877 to 1880. By Alexander Agassiz ... Boston and New York [etc.] Houghton, Mifflin and company, 1888.

2 v. illus, plates, fold. maps, diagrs. 26ᶜᵐ.

Published also as Bulletin of the Museum of comparative zoology at Harvard college, v. 14 and 15.

1. Marine fauna—Atlantic Ocean. 2. Ocean. 3. Blake (Steamer) 4. Deep-sea deposits.   I. U. S. Coast and geodetic survey. II. Title: Three cruises of the "Blake."

[*Full name:* Alexander Emmanuel Rodolphe (originally Alexandre Rodolphe Albert) Agassiz]

Library of Congress   QH93.A26   11–4261 Revised 2
—— Copy 2.
Copyright 1888: 8244   [r20c2]

QL
1
H2

DEEP SEA DEPOSITS.

Murray, Sir John, 1841–1914.

... The depth and marine deposits of the Pacific. By John Murray and G. V. Lee ... Cambridge, Printed for the Museum, 1909.

[3]–169, [1] p. 5 pl, [1] fold. maps. 31 x 26ᶜᵐ. (Memoirs of the Museum of comparative zoology at Harvard college, vol. xxxviii, no. 1)

Each plate and map accompanied by leaf with descriptive letterpress.

Reports on the scientific results of the expedition to the tropical Pacific ... on the U. S. Fish commission steamer "Albatross" from August 1899 to March 1900 ... xii.

Reports on the scientific results of the expedition to the eastern tropical Pacific ... by the U. S. Fish commission steamer "Albatross" from October 1904 to March 1905 ... xvii.

1. Pacific Ocean. 2. Ocean bottom. 3. Deep sea deposits. 4. Albatross (Steamer)   I. Lee, G. V., joint author.

                               A 19–1074

Title from Univ. of Chicago   QL1.H375 vol. 38, no. 1
Printed by L. C.   [3]

DEEP SEA DEPOSITS   PHILIPPINE ISLANDS

Selga, Miguel

Marine deposits in the Philippines.

(Publications of the Manila Observatory 3(7):177–186, 1931)

POFI has

AS
36
S

DEEP SEA DEPOSITS

Bailey, Jacob Whitman, 1811–1857.

... Microscopical examination of soundings, made by the U. S. Coast survey off the Atlantic coast of the U. S. By Prof. J. W. Bailey ... [Washington, Smithsonian institution, 1851]

15 p. pl. 31½ᶜᵐ. (Smithsonian contributions to knowledge. vol. ii, art. 3)

Smithsonian institution publication 20.

1. Deep sea deposits.   I. U. S. Coast and geodetic survey.

Library, Smithsonian   Institution Q11.S68   S 13–4

GC
63
D 61

DEEP-SEA   DEPOSITS

Neaverson, E.

The sea-floor deposits, I: General characters and distribution.

Discovery Committee
Discovery Reports, Vol. 9, 1934, p.295–350

AP
2
A 5

A deep-sea depression in the Pacific near Tongatabu.

(Am. Jour. Sci., Ser. 3, Vol. 37, 1889, p. 420)

Q
115
C

Deep-sea deposits

Challenger expedition.

Report on the scientific results of the voyage of H.M.S. Challenger during the years 1873–76...

London, 1881–1895.

For fuller entry see main card

GC
Oceanography
Pam. 28

DEEP-SEA DEPOSITS

Revelle, Roger

Preliminary remarks on the deep-sea bottom samples collected in the Pacific on the last cruise of the Carnegie.

(Journal of Sedimentary Petrology, Vol. 5, pp. 37–39, 1935)

Deep-Sea Research

An international research journal, edited by L. Fage, Paris, C. D. Ovey, Cambridge, Mary Sears, Woods Hole, Mass. Pergamon Press. Lond.

Vol. 1, 1961 +   ($12.60 per vol.)

UH

AS
36
S1

DE PSEA DEPOSITS

Daubrée, Auguste *i. e.* Gabriel Auguste, 1814–1896.

Deep-sea deposits. By A. Daubrée.

(*In* Smithsonian institution. Annual report. 1893. Washington, 1894. 23½ᶜᵐ. p. 545–566. pl. xxxv–xxxvi)

"Translated from Journal des savants, December, 1892, pp. 733–743, January, 1893, pp. 37–54."

1. Challenger expedition, 1872–1876. 2. Deep-sea deposits.

                               S 15–842

Library of Congress
Library, Smithsonian   Q11.S66 1893
                        Institution

QL
121
Th

Deep-sea deposits

Thomson, Sir Charles Wyville.

The depths of the sea...

London, 1873.

For fuller entry see main card

Deep-sea Research.

"Established under the instigation of the Joint Commission on Oceanography, of the International Council on Scientific Unions. Pergamon Press Ltd. (Distributed by Lange, Maxwell and Springer, Ltd. 242 Marylebone Road, London, N.W.1 Subscription, $12.50)"

UH has

AP
2
S 35

DEEP-SEA SEDIMENTS

Riedel, W. R.

"Pliocene-Pleistocene" boundary in deep-sea sediments. By W. R. Riedel, M. N. Bramlette, and F. L. Parker.

(Science, Vol. 140(3572):1238-1240, 1963)

QL
Mammals
Pam. 70

DEER

Johnson, F. W.

Deer kill records- a guide to management of deer hunting.

(California Fish and Game, Vol. 25, No. 2, 1939,- reprint)

DU
600
M 62

Defnign, Fran

The rai of Yap.

(Micronesian Reporter, 9(2):16-18, 1961)

GC
63
D 61

DEEP-SEA SOUNDINGS

Herdman, H. F. P.

Report on soundings taken during the Discovery investigations, 1926-1932.

Discovery Committee
Discovery Reports, Vol. 6, 1932, p.205-236

QL
Mammals
Pam.
107

DEER   CALIFORNIA

Sheldon, H. H.

The deer of California.

(Santa Barbara Museum of Natural History, Occasional Papers, No. 3, 1933)

GN
Ethn.
Pam.
3896

DEFORMATION   HAWAII

Stokes, John G.

Artificial deformations in Hawaii. 3 typewritten pages.

GC
Oceano-
graphy
Pam. 84

DEEP-SEA SOUNDINGS   PACIFIC

Gaskell, T. F.   and others

Seismic measurements made by H.M.S. Challenger in the Atlantic, Pacific and Indian Oceans and in the Mediterranean Sea, 1950-1953. By T. F. Gaskell, M. N. Hill and J. C. Swallow.

(Phil. Trans. R. Soc. London, Series A. No. 988, Vol. 251:23-83, 1958)

S
17.H3
S 41

Deerr, Noël.

... A theory of the extraction of sugar from massecuites, by Noël Deerr. Honolulu, T. H., 1907.

29 p. illus, tables. 23ᶜᵐ. (Report of work of the Experiment station of the Hawaiian sugar planters' association. Division of agriculture and chemistry. Bulletin no. 20)

1. Sugar. Manufacture. 2. Masse cuite.

Agr 7-2296

Library, U. S. Dept. of   Agriculture 100H31B no. 20

CH
71
C 67

DEFORMITIES   ARTIFICIAL

Gosse, L. A.

Essai sur les déformations artificielles du crâne, par L. A. Gosse, de Genève...Paris. 1855.

QL
121
Th

Deep sea temperature

Thomson, Sir Charles Wyville.

The depths of the sea...

London, 1873.

For fuller entry see main card

QK
Bot
Pam
#1025

Deerr, Noel & Bokart, C. F.

Varieties of cane with special reference to nomenclature, Division of Agr. and Chem. of Hawaiian Sugar Planters' Ass Bull. no. 26, 1908.

AS
36
S3

DEFORMITIES, ARTIFICIAL.

Mason, Otis Tufton, 1838-1908.

Cradles of the American aborigines. By Otis T. Mason.

(*In* U. S. National museum. Annual report. 1887. Washington, 1889. 22½ᶜᵐ. p. 161-212. illus.)

Bibliographic foot-notes, relating especially to the artificial deformation of children in North America.

1. Cradles. 2. Indians of North America—Children. 3. Indians of North America—Soc. life & cust. 4. Deformities, Artificial.

14-19253

Library of Congress   Q11.U5 1887

————— Copy 2.

————— Separate.   GN415.C8M3

QL
1
C 1

DEEP SEA TEMPERATURE

Sumner, Francis Bertody

A report upon the physical conditions in San Francisco Bay, based upon the operations of the United States fisheries steamer "Albatross" during the years 1912 and 1913...

(Univ. of Calif., Pubs. in Geology, Vol. 14, pp. 1-198, 1914)

AP
2
S 41

Deevey, Edward S., Jr.

The end of the moas...

(Scientific American, 190(2):84-90, 1954)

AS
36
S3

DEFORMITIES, ARTIFICIAL.

Porter, John Hampden.

Notes on the artificial deformation of children among savage and civilized peoples. ⟨With a bibliography.⟩ By Dr. J. H. Porter.

(*In* U. S. National museum. Annual report. 1887. Washington, 1889. 22½ᶜᵐ. p. 213-235)

Running title: Artificial deformation of children.

"The accompanying notes are collected from various sources as a supplement to Professor [O. T.] Mason's paper on 'The cradles of the American aborigines.'"—p. 213.

Bibliographic notes: p. 220-235.

"Most of the bibliography relating to the artificial deformation of children in North America is embodied in Professor Mason's work."—Footnote, p. 213.

1. Deformities, Artificial. 2. Deformities, Artificial—Bibl.   I. Title: Artificial deformation of   children.

14-19254

Library of Congress   Q11.U5 1887

————— Copy 2.

————— Separate.   GN477.5.P8

QH
104
V-Q

DEER

... Regulation for the protection of deer in Alaska. [Washington, Govt. print. off.] 1912.

1 p. 23ᶜᵐ. (U. S. Dept. of agriculture. Bureau of biological survey. Circular no. 86)

1. Deer.

Agr 12-2220

Library, U. S. Dept. of   Agriculture 1B52C no. 86

QH
431
E 79

DEFECTIVE AND DELINQUENT CLASSES

Estabrook, Arthur Howard, 1885-

The Jukes in 1915, by Arthur H. Estabrook ... Washington, The Carnegie institution of Washington, 1916.

vii, 85 p. fold. diagrs. 29½ᶜᵐ. (*On verso of t.-p.:* Carnegie institution of Washington. Publication no. 240)

Paper no. 25 of the Station for experimental evolution at Cold Spring Harbor, New York.

"Historical note [sketch of Richard L. Dugdale]": p. v-vi.

"Literature cited": p. 85.

1. Defective and delinquent classes. 2. Heredity. 3. Juke family. 4. Dugdale, Richard Louis, 1841-1883. The Jukes.   I. Title.

16—18515

Library of Congress   HV6125.E8

————— Copy 2.

GN
Ethn.
Pam.
3878

DEFORMITIES — ARTIFICIAL

Schlaginhaufen, Otto

Kunstliche Defekte an menschlichen Schadeln aus Melanesien.

(Bull. Schweizerischen Gesellschaft fur Anthrop. und Ethn., 28:19-23, 1951/52)

QL
1
F

DEER

Elliot, Daniel Giraud, 1835-1915.

... Remarks upon two species of deer of the genus *Cervus* from the Philippine archipelago, by D. G. Elliot ... Chicago, 1897.

2 l. xvi-xxxix pl. (part fold.) 24½ᶜᵐ. (Field Columbian museum. Publication 20. Zoological series. vol. l, no. 7)

1. Deer.

4—10864

Library of Congress   QL1.F4

————— Copy 2.   QL701.E46

QE
727
B 76

Defense des colonies

Barrande, Joachim, 1799-1883.

Défense des colonies ... Par Joachim Barrande ... Prague [etc.] L'auteur, 1861-81.

5 v. in 4. 4 fold. pl. (3 col.) 23ᶜᵐ.

CONTENTS.—I. Groupe probatoire comprenant: La colonie Haidinger, la colonie Krejčí et la coulée Krejčí. 1861.—II. Incompatibilité entre le système des plis et la réalité des faits matériels. 1862.—III. Etude générale sur nos étages G-H, avec application spéciale aux environs de Hlubočep, près Prague. 1865.—IV. Description de la colonie d'Archiac. Paix aux colonies. 1865.—V. Apparition et réapparition de M. M. Krejčí et Lipold. Caractères généraux des colonies, dans le bassin silurien de la Bohême. 1870.—V. Apparition et réapparition en Angleterre et en Ecosse des espèces coloniales Siluriennes de la Bohême. D'après les documents anglais les plus authentiques et les plus récents. 1881.

1. Paleontology—Bohemia. 2. Paleontology—Silurian.   I. Title.

12-11456 Revised

Library of Congress   QE727.B22

————— Copy 2. v. 1-4.

GN
477.6
S 48

DEFORMITIES   ARTIFICIAL

Schröder, Hermann

Die Kunstliche Deformation des Gebisses. Eine zahnarztlich-ethnologische studie. Mit 23 bildern und 3 tafeln in vierfarbendruck. Griefswald. Julius Abel. 1906. 4to. 116 pp.

GN
2.1
T 89

DEFORMITIES--ARTIFICIAL

Speiser, Félix

Note À propos des dents de cochon déformées dans les mers du sud et en Indonésie (1)

(Revista del Instituto de Etnologia, Universidad de Tucumán, Tomo II, 1932, pp. 441-444)

GN
2.1
A-4

DEFORMITIES. ARTIFICIAL   NEW HEBRIDES

Flower, W. H.

Exhibition of an artificially deformed skull from Mallicollo.

(Journ. Anthrop. Inst. of Great Britain and Ireland, Vol. 19, 1889-90, pp. 52-54)

AH
20
We

Degener, Hermann A. L.

Unsere Zeitgenossen "Wer ist's?" Zeitgenossen-Lexikon
III Ausgabe, 8... ff XII. 1574
V   " " L. 1698.
VII   " ja 1914 Apr 1674

Leipzig 1908 c1911, 8vo.

GN
161
V 81

GN
Pam
400

DEFORMITIES ARTIFICIAL

Virchow, Hans

Des fuss der Chinesin; anatomische untersuchung...Bonn. 1913. Ob4to.

GN
Ethn.Pam
3317

DEFORMITIES ARTIFICIAL PACIFIC

Söderstrom, Jan

Die rituellen Fingerverstümmelungen in der Südsee und in Australien.

(Zeitschrift für Ethnologie, 70 Jahrgang, 1938, pp. 24-47)

DU
1
P

Degener and de Bisschop; new phase in the long war of the junk Cheng Ho.

(Pacific Islands Monthly, vol. 22(10):20, 132-k33m 1952)

AS
720.N
R

DEFORMITIES-ARTIFICIAL · AUSTRALIA

Bancroft, T. L.

Note on mutilations practised by Australian aborigines.

(R. Soc. New South Wales, Journal, Vol. 31, 1897, pp. 25-28)

GN
Ethn.Pam.
2987

DEFORMITIES - ARTIFICIAL - SOUTH AMERICA

Imbelloni, J.

Deformaciones Intencionales del Cráneo en Sud América.

(Revista del Museo de La Plata, Tomo XXVIII, pp. 329-407, 1925)

QH
1
A 88

Degener, Otto

Canton Island, South Pacific. By Otto Degener and Edwin Gillaspy.

(Atoll Research Bulletin, No. 41, 1955)

GN
2 S
P 76

DEFORMITIES ARTIFICIAL   EASTER ISLAND

Rutland, Joshua.

The big-ears.

(Journal of the Polynesian Society, Vol.5, 1896, pp. 213-215)

GN
Ethn.Pam.
2986

DEFORMITIES - ARTIFICIAL - SOUTH AMERICA

Imbelloni, J.

Sur un appareil de déformation de crâne des anciens Humahuacas.

(Congrès International des Americanistes, XXI, Session de Goteborg, 1924, pp. 607-618)

QH
1
A 88

Degener, Otto

Canton Island, South Pacific (resurvey of 1958). By Otto and Isa Degener.

(Atoll Research Bull., No. 64, 1959)

AS
701
A

DEFORMITIES ARTIFICIAL   FIJI

Corney, Bolton S.

On Certain Mutilations Practised by Natives of the Viti Islands.

(Report of the Meeting of the Australasian Association for the Advancement of Science, No. 2, 1890, pp. 646-653)

GN
2.1
A-4

DEFORMITIES - CRANIAL - NEW BRITAIN

Blackwood, Beatrice

A study of artificial cranial deformity in New Britain. By Beatrice Blackwood and Mrs.P. N.Danby.

(Jour. R.Anthrop. Inst. Great Britain and Ireland, 85:173-191, 1955)

QK
Bot.Pam.
2753

Degener, Otto

Die Flora des Canton Atolls im Stillen Ozean. By Otto Degener and William Hatheway.

(Revista Sudamericana de Botanica, 10(2):33-42, pl. 3-5, n.d. 1952? 1953?)

GN
1
A

DEFORMITIES ARTIFICIAL HAWAII

Stokes, John G.

Artificial Deformations in Hawaii.

(American Journal of Physical Anthropology, Vol. 3, 1920, pp. 489-491)

GN
Genea-
logy
Fam. 5

Defries, Emma

Genealogy of Emma Defries, by Emma Defries. From the Honolulu Advertiser, Feb. 28, 1901. 1 typed page and two pages of charted names, Hon. Adv., Nov. 7, 1901.

QK.H
473.H
D 31

2 copies

up to date file in Herbarium

OVER

Degener, Otto

Flora Hawaiiensis or the new illustrated flora of the Hawaiian islands. Books 1- 6 1932-63. 8vo. Privately printed.

(loose-leaf compilation, no pagination, order is by taxonomy, by family numbers and alphabetically by genus names, in upper right corner of each sheet)
Second edition, 1946
(Published by the author. Honolulu.)

GN
Ethn.
Pam.
3450

DEFORMITIES ARTIFICIAL   NEW BRITAIN

Ford, Edward

Artificial cranial deformation in New Britain.

(The Medical Journal of Australia, Oct. 29, 1938, p. 729)

QE
Geol.Pam.
850

De Geer, Gerard

Geochronology as Based on Solar Radiation, and its Relation to Archeology

From the Smithsonian Report, pp. 687-696; 1928.

DU
1
M 6

Degener, Otto

The Flora Hawaiiensis or New Illustrated Flora of the Hawaiian Islands. (Prospectus)

(Journal of the Pan-Pacific Research Institution, Vol. 7, No. 4, 1932. IN Mid-Pacific Magazine, Vol. 44, 1932, No. 4)

QK
Botany
Pam.
1361
1169

Degener, Otto

Four new stations of lycopodium prothallia.
From Botanical Gazette, v. LXXVII, n.1, 1924.

QK
Bot.Pam.
1692

Degener, Otto

Kokoolau, the Hawaiian tea (illustrated),
with specimen pages of the Flora Hawaiiensis or
New illustrated flora of the Hawaiian Islands.

(Journal of the Pan-Pacific Research Institution, Volume VII, No. 2, 1932)

QK
1
B 51 m

Degener, Otto

Nutzpflanzen der Eingeboren von Fidschi.

(Botanischen Garten und Museum Berlin-Dahlem,
Mitteilungen, Bd. 1, Heft 1, pp. 131-150, 1953)

and
QK
Botany
Pam.
2779

QK
1
H 38

Degener, Otto

Franz Elfried Wimmer, 1881-1961. By Otto
And Isa Degener.

(Hawaiian Botanical Society Newsletter,
1(8), 1962)

DU
Pac.Pam.
664

Degener, Otto

The last cruise of the "Cheng-Ho". Parts 1-
2.
(Journal of the New York Botanical Garden,
Vol. 44, 1943, Nos. 525-526, pp. 197-213; 221-
232)

QK
Bot.Pam.
2961

Degener, Otto H.

Plant explorer in Fiji.

(Through the Garden Gate, Vol. 1, No. 4,
1946, N. Y. Botanical Garden)

QK
Botany
Pam.
1285
1360

Degener, Otto

The gametophyte of Lycopodium cernuum of Hawaii. Reprinted from Bot. Gaz.
Vol. 80, pp 26 - 47, 1925, pls iv- vi.

DU
600
D 31

Degener, Otto

Naturalist's South Pacific expedition: Fiji.
Paradise of the Pacific, Ltd.   Honolulu. 1949.
8vo. (8)+301 pp.

QK
473.H
D 31

Degener, Otto

Plants of Hawaii National Park illustrative
of plants and customs of the South Seas. (First
photo-lithoprint edition of "Ferns and flowering
plants of Hawaii National Park...") * no place.
1945c. 8vo. xv + 314 pp.

*The title begins, "Illustrated guide to
the more common or noteworthy ferns or flowering
plants..."

QK
Bot.
Pam.
3261

Degener, Otto and Isa

Gouldia in Hawaii.

(Phytologia, 7(9):465-467, 1961)

QL
Bot.Pam.
3261

(Otto and Isa)
Degener, O. and I.

A new Dodonaea from Molokai, Hawaii

(Phytologia, 7(9):465, 1961)

QK
1
N 53

and

QK
Bot.Pam.
2372

Degener, Otto

Stenogyne Sherfii Degener, a new mint from
Hawaii.

(Brittonia, Vol. 5, 1943, pp. 58-59)

QK
473.H
D 31

Degener, Otto

Illustrated Guide to the More Common or Noteworthy Ferns or Flowering Plants of Hawaii National Park. With Descriptions of Ancient Hawaiian Customs and an Introduction to the Geologic History of the Islands.

Honolulu, Honolulu Star-Bulletin, Ltd.,
(1930c), xv,312 pp. 8vo

[also a photolithoprint edition entitled "Plants
of Hawaii National Park..." 1945c]

QK
1
N 53

Degener, Otto

A new Hawaiian species of Rutaceae, by Otto
Degener and Carl Skottsberg.

(Brittonia. Vol.2. 1937. p.362)

QK
1
T 1

Degener, Otto

Straussia sessilis, a new species from
Hawaii, by Otto Degener and E. Y. Hosaka.

(Bull. Torrey Bot. Club, Vol. 67, 1940,
pp. 301)

QK
1
H 38

Degener, Otto

Kaena Point, Oahu. By Otto and Isa Degener.

(Newsletter, Hawaiian Botanical Soc.,
Vol. 2(6):77-80, 1963)

QK
Bot.Pam.
2099

Degener, Otto

Hosaka, Edward Y.

A new species of Phyllostegia and two new
varieties of Cyanea of the Hawaiian Islands,
by E. Y. Hosaka and Otto Degener.

(Occ. Papers, Bernice P. Bishop Museum, Vol.
14, No. 3, pp. 27-30)

QK
474.5
D 31

Degener, Otto

Tropical plants the world around, I- IV

(Reprints from Journal of the New York
Botanical Garden, April, May, June July, (1945)

QK
Bot.Pam.
1943

Degener, Otto

Kokoolau, the Hawaiian tea. Printed by
the Honolulu Star-Bulletin, 1932.

QK
Bot.Pam.
2643

Degener, Otto

A new variety of Perrottetia (Celastraceae)
from the Hawaiian Islands. By O. Degener and
A. B. H. Greenwell.

(Revista Sud Americana Botanica, 10(1):
p. 25, Apr. 1951)

QK
Bot.Pam.
2744

Degener, Otto

William Hillebrand, 1821-1886.

(Honolulu Advertiser, Nov. 18, 1951)

[also copy of the Asa Gray Bulletin, n.s.
Vol. III(2), 1957] original source?

DU
1
P

DEGENER, OTTO

Cheng Ho still at anchor; Mr. Otto Degener is married.

(Pacific Islands Monthly, Vol. 23(10):115, 1953)

QK
1
A 75

DEGENERIACEAE

Swamy, B. L.

Further contributions to the morphology of the Degeneriaceae.

(Journal of the Arnold Arboretum, Vol. 30: 10-38, 1949)

AS
36
S 2

Deichmann, Elisabeth

A new holothurian of the genus Thyone collected on the Presidential Cruise of 1938.

(Smithsonian Misc. Coll., Vol. 98, No. 12, 1938, pp. 1-7)

DU
1
P

DEGENER, OTTO

Claim for possession of the "Cheng Ho".

(Pacific Islands Monthly, 22(11):59, 1962)

AS
36
S 2

Deichmann, Elisabeth

Coelenterates collected on the Presidential Cruise of 1938.

(Smithsonian Misc. Coll., Vol. 99, No. 10, 1941, pp. 1-17, pl. 1)

AS
244
D

Deichmann, Elizabeth

On some cases of multiplication by fission and of coalescence in Holothurians; with notes on the synonymy of Actinopyga parvula (Sel).

(Vid. Med. Dansk Nat. For. Kobenhavn, Bd.73 1922,- Papers from Dr. Mortensen's Pacific Expedition, 1914-1916, No. 9)

DU
1
P

DEGENER, OTTO

Degener and de Bisschop; new phase in the long war of the junk Cheng Ho.

(Pacific Islands Monthly, vol. 22(10):20, 132-k33m 1952)

AS
618
N

Deichmann, Elisabeth

The Holothurian fauna of South Africa.

(Annals of the Natal Museum, Vol. XI(2): 325-376, 1948)

AS
36
S 5

Deignan, H. G.

The birds of northern Thailand.

(Bull. U. S. Nat. Mus., 186, 1945)

QL
401
H 39

DEGENER, OTTO

Bryan, E. H., Jr.

Marine shells collected by Otto Degener on Canton Island.

(Hawaiian Shell News, Vol. III(12):126-127, October, 1955)

QL
1
N 6-z

Deichmann, Elizabeth

Holothurians from the Gulf of California and the west coast of Lower California and Clarion Island. The Templeton Crocker Expedition (1936), IX.

(Zoologica, 22, 1937, pp. 161-176).

GN
2.I
S 66

Deignan, H. G.

Burma- gateway to China.

(War Background Studies, No. 17, 1943, Smithsonian Institution)

AM
101
F 45-n

DEGENER, OTTO

Sherff, Earl E.

With thanks to all who aid research.

(Bulletin, Chicago Natural History Museum, Vol. 26(10):10-11, October, 1955)

QL
1
N 6-z

Deichmann, Elisabeth

Holothurians from the western coasts of Lower California and Central America, and from the Galapagos Islands. Eastern Pacific Expeditions of the New York Zoological Society, XVI.

(Zoologica, 23, 1938, pp. 361-388).

AS
36
A 16 n

Deignan, H. G.

Notes on birds of northern Siam.

(Notulae Naturae, No. 173, 1946)

QK
1
A 75

DEGENERIA

Smith, Albert C.

Additional notes on Degeneria vitiensis.

(Journal of the Arnold Arboretum, Vol. 30:1-9, 1949)

QL
1
H 33 br

Deichmann, Elisabeth

The Holothurians of Clipperton Island in the eastern tropical Pacific.

(Breviora, No. 170, 1963)

QL
671
A

Deignan, H. G.

Occurrence of certain birds of the Southern Ocean in the tropical Atlantic.

(The Auk, Vol. 56, 1939, p. 326-327)

QK
1
A 75

DEGENERIACEAE

Bailey, I. W.

Degeneriaceae, a new family of flowering plants from Fiji. By I.W. Bailey and A.C.Smith.

(Journal of the Arnold Arboretum, Vol. 23, 1942, pp. 356-365)

Q.
115
H 23

Deichmann, Elisabeth

The Holothurioidea collected by the Velero III during the years 1932 to 1938, Part 1, Dendrochirota. Part II. Aspidochirota.

(Allan Hancock Pacific Expeditions, Vol. 8, No. 5, pp. 61-195, 1941) ibid, Vol. 11(2), 1958

QL
GN
A

Deignan, H. G.

Short notes on some New Zealand birds.

(Auk, Vol. LI, No. 4, Oct., 1934, pp. 487-92)

AS
36
S 66 b

Deignan, Herbert G.

Type specimens of birds in the United States National Museum.

(Smithsonian Institution, U. S. National Museum, Bull. 221, 1961)

GN
635.D9
D 32

De Josselin de Jong, J. P. B.

Studies in Indonesian culture. I-

(Verhandelingen der K. Akad. van Wetenschappen te Amsterdam, Afd. Lotterkunde, Nieuwe Reeks, Deel 39, 1937; 50 (2), 1947

GN
Ethn.Pam.
3217

de la Condamine

Observations de Mr. de la Condamine sur l'insulaire de la Polynésie, amené de lisle de Tayti en France par Mr. de Bougainville.

(Photostat copy of ms in the Bibliothèque Nationale, Paris, with transcription by André Ropiteau. 8 pages and a map)

PL
Philology
Pam
144

Deighton, S.

Moriori vocabulary. 1st part. In Report to New Zealand General Assembly 1889.

Wellington. 1889. f. pp5.

QL
195
D32

De Kay, James E

Zoology of New York, or the New York fauna; comprising detailed descriptions of all the animals hitherto observed within the state of New York.

Library has Plates only

---

de la Corte y Ruano Calderon, Felipe

See

Corte y Ruano Calderon, Felipe de la

GN
Ethn.Pam.
2967

Deihl, Joseph R.

Kava and Kava-Drinking

(Primitive Man, Vol. V, No. 4, 1932, pp. 61-67)

QL
Birds
Pam
446

Dekeyser, P. L.

Etude d'un type d'oiseau Ouest-Africain; Corvus albus. By P. L. Dekeyser and J. Derivot.

(Inst. Fr. d'Afrique Noire, Initiations Africaines, 16, 1955)

DS
659
D 33

de la Costa, H.

The Jesuits in the Philippines, 1581-1768. Harvard University Press. Cambridge. 1961 R8vo. xiii + 702 pp.

GN
Ethn.Pam.
2958

Deihl, Joseph

The Position of Woman in Samoan Culture.

(Primitive Man, Vol. V, 1932, pp. 21-26)

G
112
D 33

De la Blache, P. Vidal

Principles of human geography; edited by Emmanuel de Martonne; translated from the French by Millicent Todd Bingham. New York, Henry Holt, (c1926). 8vo. xv + 511 pp.

QL
691.M
D 33

Delacour, Jean

Birds of Malaysia. With line drawings by Earl L. Poole and Alexander Seidel. The Macmillan Company. New York. 1947. 8vo. xvi + 382 pp.

PL
Philo
Pam
23

Deissmann, Adolf

Die sprache der griechischen Bibel. From Theologische Rundschau, jahrg. 15, heft 10.

GN
Ethn.Pam.
3047

De La Borbolla, D. F. Rubin

Contribucion a la antropologia fisica de Mexico. 15 pp. 12 tables. Mexico. 1933.

(Publicaciones del Museo Nacional de Arqueologia, Historia y Etnografia, 1933).

QL
694.P1
D 33

Delacour, Jean

Birds of the Philippines, by Jean Delacour and Ernst Mayr. With line drawings by Earl L. Poole and Alexander Seidel. The Macmillan Company. New York. 1946. 8vo. xv + 309 pp.

QL
573
D32

Dejean, [Pierre Francois Auguste], M. Le Compte

Catalogue des coléoptères de la collection de M. Le Compte Dejean. Troisième edition, revue, corigée, et augmentée

Paris, 1837, 503 pp

GN
Ethn.
Pam
3046

De La Borbolla, D. F. Rubin

Crania Azteca. 10 pp. 1933.

(Anales del Museo Nacional de Arqueologie, Historia y Etnografia, Tome VIII, No. 1, Epoca 4a, 1933, pp. 96-106)

GN
2.M
M 60

QL
Bird Pam.
191

Delacour, J.

Description de neuf oiseaux nouveaux de Madagascar.

(L'Oiseau et la Revue Française d'Ornithologie, no. 8-9, 1931) pp. 475-486

QL
573
D 32

Dejean, (Pierre Francois Marie Auguste)

Iconographie et histoire naturelle des Coléoptères d'Europe par M. Le Comte Dejean et M. J. A. Boisduval. Tomes 1-5. Chez Mequignon-Marvis Paris. 1832-1837. R8vo.

GN
Pam
3091

De La Borbolla, D. F. Rubin

Grupos sanguineos y metabolismo basal. Dos nuevos metodos antropologicos. Mexico. 1934.

(Publicaciones del Museo Nacional de Mexico, Anales, no. 1, tomo 1, Epoca 5a)

Delacour, J.

Les oiseaux des iles Hawaii.

(L'Oiseau, 9:1-30, 1928)

Reviewed by editor of Ibis, s. 12, vol. 5:159, 1929.
"brief but useful account of the birds of Hawaii"

QL
671
I

Delacour, Jean

    Note on the names and geographical distribution of the red junglefowl Gallus gallus.

    (Ibis, 90:462-464, 1948)

S
Agri
Pam
#43

DELACROIX, G.

    Les Maladies et les ennemis des caféiers.

    Paris, 1900. 8vo. pp. 212.

K.13.25

P

PL
711
D 33

Delaporte, Philip A.

    Buch n Lesen n Kakairun Nauru. 1900. 8vo. 34 pp.

    Nauru, primer

QL
1
N 6-z

Delacour, Jean

    Notes on the taxonomy of the birds of Malaysia.

    (Zoologica, Vol. 31 (1):1-8, 1946)

QL
45
De P33

Delage, Yves & Herouard, Edgard

    Traite de zoologie concrete.

    Library has:
    v.1 La cellule et les protozoaires. Par. Reinwald, 1896. 584p.

PL
711
D 33

Delaporte, Philip A.   translator

    Deutsches Liederbuch fuer Schule und Kirche. Ausgewaehlt und herausgegeben von Philip A. Delaporte. Missions-Druckerei. Nauru 1906 12mo no pagination

    Nauru - hymn book

QL
1
N 6-z

Delacour, Jean

    Notes on the taxonomy of the birds of the Philippines. By Jean Delacour and Ernst Mayr.

    (Zoologica, 30 (3):105-117, 1945)

AS
36
S1

DELAMBRE, JEAN BAPTISTE JOSEPH, 1749-1822

Fourier, Jean Baptiste Joseph, baron, 1768-1830.

    Memoir of Delambre. By Joseph Fourier ...

    (In Smithsonian institution. Annual report. 1864. Washington, 1865. 234ᵐ. p. (125)-134)

    "Translated ... by C. A. Alexander."

    1. Delambre, Jean Baptiste Joseph, 1749-1822.   i. Alexander, Charles Armistead, d. 1869? tr.

                                 S 15-155

    Library of Congress   Q11.S66 1864
    Library, Smithsonian   Institution

PL
711
D 33

Delaporte, Philip A.   translator

    Etoronab inon nana re mek iat testament obwe me testament etsimeduw. Nauru. Mission-Druckerei. 1903. 8vo. 31 pp.

    Nauru, Bible stories

QL
691 A3-I
D 33

Delacour, J.

    Les Oiseaux de l'Indochine Francaise, par J. Delacour and P. Jabouille. (In four volumes.) Tome 1-4. Paris. Exposition Coloniale Internationale. Indochine Francaise. 1931. lvi + 279 + xlvi, 338 + lxi, 296 + lxvi, 348 + lxxiii pp. R8vo.

G
51
S

Deland, Charles C.

    The isle of Bougainville.

    (Proc. R. Geogr. Soc. of Australasia, South Australian Branch, Vol. 37, 1935/36, pp. 91-95)

    (part of the Australian Mandated Territory)

PL
711
D 33

Delaporte, Philip A.

    Etoronab it ekalesia, mu urien ada itueb n protestant. Uebersetzt und herausgegeben von Ph. A. Delaporte. Nauru Missions-Druckerei. 1903. 8vo. 39 pp.

    Nauru- church history, Protestant vs. Catholic discussion

---

QL
Bird Pam.
190

Delacour, J.

    Les oiseaux de la mission zoologique Franco-Anglo-Américaine a Madagascar

    (Extrait de L'Oiseau et la Revue Francaise d'Ornithologie, vol. II, no. 1. 1932) pp. 1-96

DU
12
D 33

looked
case

Carter
Coll.
10-D-17

Delano, Amasa

    Narrative of voyages and travels, in the northern and southern hemispheres: comprising three voyages round the world; together with a voyage of survey and discovery, in the Pacific Ocean and Oriental islands, by Amasa Delano. Boston. E. G. House. 1817. 8vo. 594 pp.

    1818 2nd edition

PL
711
D 33

Delaporte, Ph. A.   translator

    Irian it taramawir me Psalmen. Missions-Druckerei. Nauru 1911 8vo. 155 pp.

    Nauru, hymns and psalms

AM
36
A 65 no

Delacour, Jean

    Preliminary note on taxonomy of Canada geese, Branta canadensis.

    (Am. Mus. Novitates, no. 1537, Nov. 12, 1951)

DU
12
D 34

looked
case

Delaporte,

    Le Voyageur François ou la connoissance de l'ancien et du nouveau monde, mis au jour par M. l'Abbé Delaporte. Nouvelle edition. Tome IV. Paris. L. Cellot. 1774. 18mo. 548 pp.

PL
711
D 33

Delaporte, Philip A.

    Irian it taramawir me baibait ecclesia. A gadauw iow iturin Ph. A. Delaporte. Missions-Druckerei. Nauru 1909 8vo. 107 pp.

    Nauru, hymnbook

QL
673
D 33

Delacour, Jean

    The waterfowl of the world. With...plates in colour by Peter Scott, and ...distribution maps.
        Vol. 1: The magpie goose, whistling ducks, swans and geese.
        Vol. 2: The dabbling ducks.
        Vol. 3: Eiders, Pochards, Perching ducks; Scoters, Golden-eyes and Mergansers, Stiff-tailed ducks.

    1954, 1956, 1959 Country Life Limited. London. sm4to

PL
Phil.pam.
318

Delaporte, Ph. A.

    Buch in drian nea wanara buch Kristian n tsitan Gott. Kusaie. Missions-Druckerei. 1902.

    (Gilbert Is., hymn book)
    Nauru

PL
Phil.Pam
339

(Delaporte, Ph. A.   tr.)

    Iain Neues Testament, oa berith etsimeduw won wora temoniba ma amen katsimor nea Jesu Kristo. Teil des Neuen Testaments in der Nauru Sprache. Kusaie. Missions-Druckerei. 1902. (157 pp.) 12mo.

    [New Testament in Nauru dialect]

PL
711
D 33

Delaporte, Philip A.

Markus, Lukas ma aura makur apostel. Preliminary edition. Mission Mimeograph. 1906.
8vo. 191 pp.

Nauru, Scriptures.

QE
Geol.Pam.
948

de la Rue, E. Aubert

L'Archipel de Kerguelen.

(Association Française pour l'Avancement
des Sciences, 1932, pp. 11-17)

QE
308.K
D 33

de la Rue, Edgar Aubert

Etude Géologique et Géographique de l'Archipel de Kerguelen.

(Revue de Géographie Physique et de Géologie
Dynamique, Vol. V, Fasc. 1-2, 1932)

PL
711
D 33

Delaporte, Philip A.   translator

Oat eonin oa katechismus n Bibel. ... Mission-Mimeograph. Nauru. 1905. 8vo. 136 pp.

Nauru,   catechism

DU
Pac.Pam.
590

de la Rüe, Edgar Aubert

Aux Nouvelles-Hébrides: la colonisation et
le régime du Condominium.

(La Geographie, Tome 68, 1937, pp. 193-207)

QE
Geol.Pam.
944

de la Rue, E. Aubert

Une expédition au Yurumangui et au Naya,
fleuves de la Cordillère occidentale des Andes
de Colombie.

(La Géographie, Tome 61, 1934, pp. 1-29)

PL
711
D 33

Delaporte, Ph. A.   translator

Toronab in Bibel (Altes Testament)
Nauru. Missions-Druckerei 1906 8vo. 131 pp.

Nauru - Old Testament

QE
Geol. Pam.
946

de la Rue, E. Aubert

La constitution géologique des Iles Wallis
et Futuna.

(Comptes-Rendus des séances de l'Académie
des Sciences, Tome 200, 1935, p. 328)

AS
162
P

de la Rue, Edgar Aubert

Fischer, P. H.

Gasteropodes marins recueillis au Nouvelles-
Hebrides par E. E. Aubert de la Rue. Par P. H.
Fischer adn E. Fischer-Piette.

(Bull. Mus. Nat. Hist. Nat. Paris, Ser. 2,
Tome XI, 1939, pp. 263-266)

PL
711
D 33

Delaporte, Philip A.

Wanara Buch n Kereri ran protestantischen
Schulen. A Gadauw Eow Iturin Ph. A. Delaporte.
Mission-Mimeograph. Nauru. 1904. 8vo. 138 pp.

Nauru, comprehensive book of stories, geography, dictionary- German-Nauru, German school
songs.

QE
Geol. Pam.
941

de la Rue, E. Aubert

Contribution a l'étude géologique de la
Cordillere occidentale des Andes de Colombie.

(Comptes-Rendus des séances de l'Académie
des sciences, Tome 197, p. 991, 1933)

GN
2.S
O 15

de la Rue, Edgar Aubert

La géologie des Nouvelles-Hébrides

(Jour. Soc. des Océanistes, 12:63-98, 1956)

DU
620
F

Delaporte, Philip H.

Nauru as it was, and as it is now, by Rev.
Philip H. Delaporte.

(Friend, June 1907, pp.6-7; July, pp.13-14;
Aug., pp.7-8; Sept., pp.9-11).

QE
Geol.Pam.
1002

de la Rüe, Edgar Aubert

Contribution à l'étude géologique des Nouvelles-Hébrides.

(Comptes Rendus des Seances de l'Acad. des
Sciences, Tome 204, p. 1880, 1937)

GN
2.S
O 15

and

QE
Geol.
Pam.
1272

de la Rue, Edgar Aubert

La géologie des Nouvelles-Hébrides.

(Journal de la Soc. des Océanistes, Tome
12:63-98, 1956)

GN
2.S
T

de la Roche, Jean

Glyptique Océanienne avant l'histoire.
des Etudes
(Bull. Soc. Océaniennes, Vol.VI, 1939, p.
209-218)

DU
950.K3
D 33

de la Rüe, E. Aubert

Deux ans aux iles de la désolation (archipel
de Kerguelen). Photographies de l'auteur.
René Julliard. Paris. 1954. 8vo. 8-316 pp.

QE
Geol.
Pam. 1008

de la Rüe, Edgar Aubert

Les Gisements d'Or de la Mélanésie.

(Sciences, Mai, 1937, pp. 183-192. Is this
reference correct? Typed on p. 183)

AS
36
S1

De La Rue, Warren, 1815-1889, *comp.*
Abbreviations used in England in 1867. Comp. by
W. De La Rue.

(*In* Smithsonian institution. Annual report. 1867. Washington, 1868.
23½ᵐ. p. (485)-488)

1. Abbreviations, English.

S 15-243

Library of Congress   Q11.S66 1867
Library, Smithsonian   Institution

AS
162
P 23

de la Rue, E. Aubert

L'enigme géologique du Mont Campbell (Archipel de Kerguelen).

(Bull. Mus. National d'Hist. Nat., Paris,
Ser. 2, Tome 34:333-335, 1962)

DU
12
D 33.1

De La Rue, E. Aubert

L'homme et les iles. Paris. Librairie
Gallimard. 1935. 194 pp. 8vo.

DU Pac.Pam. 544 2 copies	de la Rue, E. Aubert Les îles Wallis et Futuna, le pays et les habitants. (La Terre et la Vie, 1935, No. 2, pp. 51-66)
QE Geol. Pam. 1271	de la Rue, Edgar Aubert Une mission geologique en Polynésie française. no place no date, no source. (1956) 6 pp. 4to [author writes that it is Chroniques d'Outre Mer, No. 25:3-8, June 1956]
DU Pac.Pam. 916	de la Rue, Edgar Aubert La Polynesie francaise. (Larousse Mensuel, No. 1957:364-366)

QL Fishes Pam. 358	de la Rue, E. Aubert Informations sur les pêches étrangères et coloniales: la pêche aux îles Saint-Paul et Amsterdam. (Revue des Travaux de l'Office des Pêches Maritimes, Tome V, Fasc. 1, No. 17, nd, pp. 83-109)
AS 162 P 23	de la Rue, Edgar Aubert Notes sur les Iles Crozet. (Bull. Mus. Nat. d'Hist. Nat., Paris, Ser. 2, Tome 22(2):197-203, 1950)
GN Ethn.Pam. 3226	de la Rüe, Edgar Aubert **Les populations des Nouvelles-Hébrides et leur civilisation.** (La Terre et la Vie, Année 7, 1937, pp. 129-158)

DU Pac. Pam. 550	de la Rue, E. Aubert Une journee sur l'île Walpole. (La Geographie, Vol. 43, No. 2, 1935. pp.102-116)
DU 760 D 33	de la Rüe, Edgar Aubert Les Nouvelles Hebrides:iles de cendre et de corail. Photographies et dessins de l'auteur. Collection "France Forever". Les Editions de l'Arbre. Montreal. 1945c. sm8vo. 252 + (2) pp.
DU 1 Re QE Geol.Pam. 940	De la Rue, Edgar Aubert Premiers résultats d'une mission Géologique aux Nouvelles-Hébrides. (La Revue du Pacifique, 15° Année, 1936, pp. 379-381)

QE Geol.Pam. 1276	de la Rüe, Edgar Aubert Le Manganese aux Nouvelles Hébrides (Mélanésie) (Excerpt from XX Congreso Geol. Int., Symposium sobre yacimientos de Manganeso, Tomo IV, Oceania. pp. 331-332, 1956)
QE Geol.Pam. 949	de la Rue, E. Aubert Nouvelles observations sur la météorologie des îles Kerguelen. (Revue de Geographie Physique et de Geologie Dynamique, nd. pp. 1-32, 197-200)
QE 349 D 33	de la Rue, Aubert Recherche géologique et minérale en Polynésie française. Publié par l'Inspection Générale des Mines et de la Géologie. Paris. 1959. 4to. 60 pp. 1 map

QE Geol.Pam. 1006	de la Rüe, Edgar Aubert **Les manifestations actuelles de l'activité volcanique aux Nouvelles-Hébrides.** (C. R. S. de la Soc. GEol. de France, No. 11 1937, p. 149-150)
QE Geol.Pam. 945	de la Rue, E. Aubert Observations géologiques sur les vallées du Yurumangui et du Naya (Cordillère occidentale des Andes de Colombie). (Revue de Geographie Physiques et de Géologie Dynamique, Vol. VI, Fasc. 3, 1933, pp. 191-200, pl. 10-13)
QE Geol. Pam. 1274	de la Rüe, E. Aubert Sur la géologie des Etablissements francais d'Océanie. (C. R. Soc. Biogéogr., 287, pp. 38-45, 1956)

QE Geol. Pam. 1278	de la Rüe, E. Aubert Les minéraux des Nouvelles Hébrides. (Bulletin du Muséum, 2° s., t. XI, n°3, pp. 342-348, 1939?)
QE Geol.Pam. 943	de la Rue, E. Aubert Observations sur la geologie de l'Île Saint-Paul (Océan Indien). (Comptes Rendus de la Soc. Geol. de France, No. 14, 1931, pp. 206-208)
QE Geol. Pam. 942	de la Rue, E. Aubert Sur l'existence de l'agate et du spath d'Islande dans l'archipel de Kerguelen. (Comptes-Rendus des séances de l'Académie des sciences, Tome 188, 1929, p. 1421)

AS 162 P	de la Rüe, Edgar Aubert Les minereaux des Nouvelles Hebrides. (Bull. Mus. Nat. d'Hist. Nat., Ser. 2, Tome 11, 1939, pp. 342-348)
DU Pac.Pam. 917	de la Rüe, Edgar Aubert La Polinesia francese. (Le Vie del Mondo, Rivista Mensile del Touring Club Italiano, 19(7):769-784, 1957)
QE Geol. Pam. 951	de la Rue, E. Aubert Sur la nature et l'age probable de l'ile Walpole (Océan Pacifique Austral) (C. R. S. de la Société Géologique de France, No. 4, 1935. pp.48-49)

GN
A 62
Aubert de la Rüe, Edgar

Sur la nature et l'origine probable des pierres portées en pendentifs à l'ile Tanna (Nouvelles-Hébrides)

(L'Anthropologie, Tome 48, Nos. 3-4, 1938, pp. 249-260)

QE
Geol.Pam.
1028
de la Rüe, Edgar Aubert

Le volcanisme aux Nouvelles Hébrides(Mélanésie).

(Bulletin Volcanologique. Série II, Vol.II, 1937, pp. 79-142 + 18 plates and 1 map)

QL
464
D 34
de la Torre-Bueno, J. R.

A glossary of entomology. Smith's "An explanation of terms used in entomology", completely revised and rewritten. Published by Brooklyn Entomological Society. The Science Press. Lancaster, Penna. 1937. 8vo. 336 pp., 9 pl.

QE
Geol.Pam.
1003
de la Rüe, Edgar Aubert

Abrard, René

Sur l'existence du Néogène supérieur à Cycloclypeus aux îles Epi et Malekula (Nouvelles-Hébrides), by René Abrard et Edgar Aubert de la Rüe.

(Comptes Rendus des séances de l'Acad. des Sciences, Tome 204, 1937, p. 1951- ?)

QE
Geol.Pam.
950
de la Rue, E. Aubert

Voyage d'exploration a l'Ile Heard. Comité de l'Afrique Française. Paris. 1930. sm8vo. 42 pp.

GN
Pam
2195
Delattre, A. J.

L'Assyriologie depuis onze ans. From Rev. des questions scientifiques, 1891.

QE
Geol.Pam.
1275
de la Rüe, Edgar Aubert

Sur la présence du manganèse à Rurutu (Iles Australes), Etablissements Francais d'Océanie

(Excerpt from XX Congreso Geol. Int., Symposium sobre yacimientos de Manganeso, Tomo IV. Oceania. 1 page, unnumbered)

QH
1
M 17 b
DE LA RUE, EDGAR AUBERT

Tardieu-Blot, Mme.

Sur les Fougères récoltées par Aubert de la Rue aux îles Kerguelen et Amsterdam.

(Mémoires de l'Institut Scientifique de Madagascar, série B. Biologie, Tome V:59-64, 1954)

Delattre, C.

Voyages et naufrages curieux en Océanie. 1837.

UH has

QE
Geol.Pam.
1004
de la Rüe, Edgar Aubert

Abrard, René

Sur la présence du Pliocène à l'île Malekula (Nouvelles-Hébrides). By René Abrard et Edgar de la Rue.

(Comptes Rendus des Seances de l'Academie des Sciences, Tome 205, 1937, p. 290-?)

AS
36
S 4
de la Torre, Carlos

The Cuban operculate land shells of the subfamily Chondropominae, by Carlos de la Torre and Paul Bartsch.

(Proc. of the U. S. Nat. Mus., Vol. 85, pp. 193-423) 1938

DU
623
D 34
de la Vergne, George H.

Hawaiian sketches. H. S. Crocker Company. San Francisco. 12 mo. 1878. 112 pp.

DU
870
D 33
de la Rüe, Edgar Aubert

Tahiti et ses archipels; Polynesie francaise Horizons de France. Paris. 8vo. 158 pp.

QL
464
D 34
De la Torre-Bueno, J. R.

A glossary of entomology. Smith's "An Explanation of terms used in entomology". Completely revised and rewritten. Published by Brooklyn Entomological Society. Science Press. Lancaster. 1937. 8vo. ix + 336 pp. IX pl.

over

Supplement A. July 1960 36 pp.

GR
385.H
D 57
De La Vergne, George H.

A Legend of Haleakala.

Dillingham, Emma L. and others
Six Prize Hawaiian Stories of the Kilohana Art League...A Legend of Haleakala, by George H. De La Vergne, pp. 24-43.

DU
12
D 33
de la Rue, Edgar Aubert

Terres francaises.Paysages, scenes et types de la France d'Outre-Mar. 116 photographies, avec une preface du Paul Rivet. Paris.(1950) 4to. 96 pp. Société Parisienne d'Edition.

De Laet, Sigfried J.

See

Laet, Sigfried J. De

DELAWARE   INSECTS, INJURIOUS AND BENEFICIAL

See

INSECTS, INJURIOUS AND BENEFICIAL   DELAWARE

QE
Geol.Pam.
1277
de la Rüe, E. Aubert

Le volcanisme aux Nouvelles Hébrides (Mélanésie)

(Extrait du Bulletin Volcanologique Organe de l'Association de Volcanologie de l'Union géodésique et géophysique internationale, Série II- Tome II, pp.79-142 and XVIII pl. and map)

QH
Nat.Hist.
Pam.
182
de la Torre, Luis

Name changes and nomenclatureal stability. By Luis de la Torre and Andrew Starrett.

(Nat. Hist. Miscellanea, No. 167, 1959)

GN
550
S
DELAWARE INDIANS.

Hrdlička, Aleš, 1869-

... Physical anthropology of the Lenape or Delawares, and of the eastern Indians in general, by Aleš Hrdlička. Washington, Govt. print. off., 1916.

130 p. incl. map. 29 pl. (incl. fold. map, plan) 24cm. (Smithsonian institution. Bureau of American ethnology. Bulletin 62)

1. Delaware Indians. I. Title.

(Name originally: Alois Ferdinand Hrdlička)

Library of Congress   E51.U6 no. 62   16-26533

GN
550
I-C

DELAWARE INDIANS

Hrdlička, Aleš, 1869–

... Physical anthropology of the Lenape or Delawares, and of the eastern Indians in general, by Aleš Hrdlička. New York, The Museum of the American Indian, Heye foundation, 1916.

3 p. l., 3–130 p. xxix pl. (incl. fold. map, plan) 25ᶜᵐ. (Contributions from the Museum of the American Indian, Heye foundation, vol. III)
A copy of Bulletin 62 of the Bureau of American ethnology, with new t.-p. and prefatory note prefixed.
"Based largely on a collection of skeletal remains recovered ... in a cemetery associated with the site of an historic Munsee settlement near Montague ... northwestern New Jersey."—Note.
1. Delaware Indians. 2. Munsee Indians. 3. Indians of North America—Physical characteristics.
(Name

originally: Alois Ferdinand Hrdlička)

Library of Congress   E11.N56 vol. 3
16–23257

AS
122
L-p

Delf, E. Marion

The significance to the exposure factor in relation to zonation.

(Proc. Linn. Soc. of London, 154th Session, pp. 234–239, 1941/42)

QL
1
C 74

Delkeskamp, Kurt

Beitrag zur Kenntnis der Erotyliden. Revision der afrikanischen Gattung Palaeolybas Crotch (Coleoptera Erotylidae), 17

(Ann. Mus. R. du Congo Belge, s in 8, Sci. Zool., Vol. 44, 1956)

GN
2.S
P
37–6

Del Campana, Domenico

Notizie intorno all'uso della "Siringa" o "Flauto di pane!" in Archivio per l'Antrop. e la Etnol. xxxix, 1909, pp. 46–60, illus.

Note— Concerning the use of the "Pipes of Pan."

AS
540
P 55 j

Delfinado, M. D.

A checklist of Philippine mosquitoes with a larval key to genera (Diptera, Culicidae). By M. D. Delfinado, G. B. Viado, and L. T. Coronel.

(The Philippine Jour. of Science, Vol. 91 (4):433–457, 1962)

QL
1
C 74

Delkeskamp, Kurt

Revision der afrikanischen Gattung Palaeolybas Crotch (Coleoptera Erotylidae). 17. Beitrag zur Kenntnis der Erotyliden.

(Zoologische Wetenschappen, Deel 44, 1956; Annalen van het K. Mus. van Belgisch-Congo, Tervuren, Ser. in 8°)

QK
98
D 34

locked
case

Delessert, Benjamin

Icones Selectae Plantarum Quas in Systemate universali, ex herbariis Parisiensibus praesertim ex Lessertiano, descripsit Aug. Pyr. de Candolle, ex archetypus speciminibus a P.J.F.Turpin delineatae et Editae a Benj. DeLessert. (In five volumes, 1820–1846). Vol. 1, 1820 only. Parisiis. folio.

(Ranunculaceae, Dilleniaceae, Magnoliaceae, Anonaceae, Menispermeae)

QL
1
F 45

Delfinado, Mercedes D.

On some parasitic laelaptoid mites (Acarina) of the Philippines.   (Philippine Zoological Expedition, 1946–47)

(Fieldiana-Zoology, Vol. 42(8), 1960)

QE
502
N 56

Dell, R. K.

Chatham Island marine Mollusca based upon the collections of the Chatham Islans Expedition 1954.
IN
Biological Results of the Chatham Islands 1954 Expedition, Part 4:141–157, 1960

QL
406
D 34

Delessert, Benj(amin)

Recueil de Coquilles décrites par (J.B.P. A. de M. de) Lamarck, dans son Histoire Naturelle des Animaux sans Vertèbres, et non figurées. Paris. Fortin, Masson et Cie. 1841. folio. 40 plates, with descriptive letterpress.

QL
1
F 45

Delfinado, Mercedes D.

The Philippine biting midges of the genus Culicoides (Diptera:Ceratopogonidae). Philippine Zoological Expedition, 1946–1947.

(Fieldiana:Zoology, Vol. 33(7), 1961)

AS
750
N 56

Dell, R. K.

The fresh-water mollusca of New Zealand. Part I-The genus Hyridella. Part II-The species previously assigned to...Limnaea and Myxas. Part III-The genus Physastra.
(Transactions of the Royal Society of New Zealand, Vol. 81(2):221–237, 1953)
ibid, 84(1):71–90, 1956

DU
12
D 35

locked
case

Delessert, Eugène

Voyages dans les deux oceans Atlantique et Pacifique, 1844 a 1847. Brésil, États-Unis, Cap de Bonne-Espérance, Nouvelle Hollande, Nouvelle-Zélande, Taiti, Philippines, Chine, Java, Indes Orientales, Égypte, par M. Eugène Delessert. Paris. A. Franck. 1848. 4to. 326 pp. Maps.

DU
12
S 52

DELIA BYRD (ship)

Shaler, William

Journal of a voyage between China and the Northwestern Coast of America, made in 1804 by William Shaler. Introduction by Lindley Bynum. Illustrations by Ruth Saunders. Saunders Studio Press. Claremont. 1935. 8vo. 109 pp. (limited edition, copy 205)

QH
1
T 88

Dell, R. K.

A key to the common chitons of New Zealand.

(Tuatara, 4(1):4–12; 1951)

Delessert, E.

Voyages dans les deux oceans, Atlantique et Pacific, 1844 a 1847.   1848

UH has

QL
561.P6
T 13

DELIAS

Talbot, G.

A monograph of the Pierine genus Delias. Trustees of the British Museum. London. 1928–1937. R8vo. Issued in 6 parts.   Parts 1–6.

QH
1
P 11

Dell, R. K.

The land mollusca of Nissan Island, Solomon Islands.

(Pacific Science, Vol. IX(3):324–331, 1955)

AP
2
N 6

Delf, E. Marion

Nature and uses of seaweeds.

(Nature, Vol. 152, 1943, pp. 149–153)

AS
36
S 1

Delitzsch, Friedrich

Discoveries in Mesopotamia.

(Smithsonian Inst., Ann. Rept., 1900, pp. 435–549, 10 pls.)

QH
1
P 11

Dell, R. K.

The land mollusca of the Treasury Islands, Solomon Islands.

(Pacific Science, Vol. IX(4):423–429, 1955)

AS
750
D 67 r

Dell, R. K.

The littoral marine Mollusca of the Snares Islands.

(Records of the Dominion Museum, Vol. 4(15), 1963)

QH
1
P 11

Dell, R. K.

A Tornatellinid land mollusk from the Solomon Islands.

(Pacific Science, Vol. IX(3):357-358, 1955)

DU
Pacific
Pam
No. 130

Delmas, Siméon (Rev.Père)

Lettre du R.P. Siméon Delmas, missionaire à l'île Nukuhiva. Taiohae ,23 juillet, 1920.

QE
502
N 56

Dell, R. K.

Marine Mollusca.
IN
Biological Results of the Chatham Islands 1954 Expedition. Part 4:pp. 141-157, 1960
title: Chatham Island marine Mollusca based upon the collections of the Chatham Islands Expedition, 1954.

GN
Ethn.Pam.
3012

Dellenbach, Marguerite

Begouen, Comte

Deux modèles de tatouage pyrogravés sur bambou, provenant des îles Marquises, par Comte Begouen et Marguerite Dellenbach.

(Archives suisses d'Anthropologie générale, Tome VI, 1932/33, pp. 191-200)

GN
2.S
T 12

Delmas, Simeon

(letter) to R. P. Hervé Audran. (in re Marquesan forms of words for moon)

(Bull. Soc. d'Etudes Oceaniennes, No. 14: 90-91, 1926)

QH
1
T 88

Dell, R. K.

The New Zealand cephalopoda.

(Tuatara, 4(3):91-102; 1952)

GN
2.I
T 89

also
GN
Ethn.Pam.
3735

Dellenbach, Marguerite

Un manteau de plumes ancien inédit des îles Hawaï.

(Revista del Instituto de Etnología, Universidad de Tucumán, Tomo II, 1932, pp. 539-541)

GN
671.L3
D 35

2 copies

Delmas, (P.)Siméon

La religion ou le paganisme des Marquisiens. D'après les notes des anciens missionnaires, collationnées par le Rév. P. Siméon Delmas. Paris. Gabriel Beauchesne. 1927. 8vo. 198 pp.

AS
750
D 67-s

Dell, R. K.

Papers on Mollusca.

(Dominion Museum Records in Zoology, Vol. 1(3-6):21-58, 1950)

QH
1
P 11

Dellow, Vivienne

Inter-tidal ecology at Narrow Neck Reef, New Zealand (Studies in Inter-tidal zonation, 3).

(Pacific Science, Vol. IV(4):355-374, 1950)

AS
36
S 66 r

DeLong, Dwight M.

Man in a world of insects.

(Ann. Rept. Smithsonian Inst. for 1962:423-440, 1963)

AS
750
D

Dell, R. K.

The recent Cephalopoda of New Zealand.

(Dominion Museum Bull. No. 16, 1952)

DU
406
D35

Del Mar, Frances

A year among the Maoris: a study of their arts and customs.

London, Benn, 1924. 176 pp.

AS
36
O 3

DeLong, Dwight M.

Modern Buildings and the Termite Problem.

(In The Ohio Journal of Science, Vol. XXXI, No. 3, pp. 177-180, May, 1931)

QL
1
V 64

Dell, R. K.

Some additional New Zealand Cephalopods from Cook Strait.

(Zoology Publications from Victoria Univ. of Wellington, No. 25, 1959)

GR
Folklore
Pam.
87

Del Re, Arundel

Creation myths of the Formosan natives. The Hokuseido Press. 75 pp. 12mo. (Tokyo)

GN
2.S
P 76

Delph, L. W.

Cave drawings near Tongaporutu, Taranaki.

(Jour. Poly. Soc., Vol. 48, 1939, p. 116-121)

AS
750
D 67r

Dell, R. K.

Some new off-shore mollusca from New Zealand.

(Records of the Dominion Museum, Vol. 3(1): 27-59, April, 1956)

DU
700
D 26
35

Delmas, (le R. P.)Siméon

Essai d'histoire de la Mission des Iles Marquises, depuis les origines jusqu'en 1881.

(Extrait des Annales des Sacrés-Coeurs, 1905-1911) Au Bureau des Annales des Sacres-Coeurs, Paris, 1929, 358 pp. 8vo

---

AS
750
A 89

and
GN
Ethn.Pam
3778

Delph, L. W.

The Piraunui Pa at Matawhana, Waikato, by L. W. Delph and Gilbert Archey.

(In Records of the Auckland Institute and Museum, Vol. 1, No. 1, 1930, pp. 57-69)

AS
33
S4

DELPHACIDAE

Crawford, David Livingston, 1889–

A contribution toward a monograph of the homopterous insects of the family *Delphacidæ* of North and South America. By David L. Crawford ...

(*In* U. S. National museum. Proceedings. Washington, 1914. 23½ᶜᵐ. v. 46, p. 557–640. pl. 44–49)

Bibliography: p. 634–635.

1. Delphacidae. 2. Hemiptera—America.

14-10997 Revised

Library of Congress   Q11.U55 vol. 46

QL
461
H-1

DELPHACIDAE   HAWAII

Zimmerman, Elwood C.

A new Nesosydne from Chenopodium on Hawaii (Hemiptera-Homoptera:Delphacidae)

(Proc. Haw. Ent. Soc. Vol. 14(3):433-435, 1951)

DU
646.7
D 36

(Delprat, D. A.)   editor

Vademecum voor Nederlands-Nieuw-Guinea. 1956 In Samenwerking met het Ministerie van Overzeese Rijksdelen, uitgegeven door her Nieuw-Guinea Instituut te Rotterdam. H. C. de Boer Jr.-Den Helder. 4to. (rec'd 1957, Dec.) 216 pp. and folded map.

QL
Insect
Pam.
1818

DELPHACIDAE

Linnavuori, R.

Remarks on some Italian Delphacidae (Hemiptera Homoptera)

(Boll. Soc. Ent. Italiana, 87 (3/4):49-52, 1957)

QL
461
H-1

DELPHACIDAE   KAUAI

Beardsley, John W., Jr.

A new Dictyophorodelphax from Kauai (Homoptera: Delphacidae).

(Proc., Hawaiian Entomological Society, Vol. XVI(1):21-23, July, 1956)

GR
335.T
D 36

Del Re, Arundel

Creation myths of the Formosan natives. The Hokuseido Press. sm8vo. no date. 75 pp

---

QL
Insect
Pam
320

and

S
17H3
S44

DELPHACIDAE

Muir, F.

Contribution to our knowledge of South American fulgoroidea (homoptera). H.S.P.A. bull. 18, 1926.

duplicate

AS
182
H

DELPHINIDAE   PACIFIC

Gray, John Edward

Feresa attenuata.

(Jour. Mus. Godeffroy, Heft 8, 1875, p.52)

AS
540
P

del Rosario, F.

Philippine Psychodidae (Diptera), I.

(Philippine Journal of Science, Vol.59, 1936, pp.553-572)

QL
Insects
Pam #
322

DELPHACIDAE

Muir F. & Gifford W. M.

Studies in North American Delphacidae U. S. P. A. Entom. ser. Bull. 15, 1924.

AS
36
A 5

DELPHINIDAE   PACIFIC

Grey, Zane

Dolphin at Tahiti.

(Natural History, Vol. 32, pp.300-302, 1932)

QL
319
D 36

Delsman, H. C.

Dierenleven in Indonesië. N.V. Uitgeverij W. van Hoeve. 's-Gravenhage-Bandung. 1951 R8vo. 348 pp.

AS
619
S 72-q

DELPHINIDAE

Barnard, K. H.

A guide book to South African whales and dolphins.

(South African Mus. Capetown, Guide No. 4, 1954)

DU
1
P 12

DELPHINIDAE   PACIFIC

Scheffer, Victor B.

Dolphins- little-known mammals of the Pacific

(Pacific Discovery, 2(4):18-22, 1949)

QL
B 93

Delsman, H. C.

Preliminary plankton investigations in the Java Sea.

(Treubia, Deel 17, 1939, pp. 139-173)

AS
36
S5

DELPHINIDAE

True, Frederick William, 1858–

Contributions to the natural history of the cetaceans. A review of the family *Delphinidæ*. By Frederick W. True ... With forty-seven plates. Washington, Govt. print. off., 1889.

191 p. xlvii pl. 24ᶜᵐ. (*Added t.-p.:* ... Bulletin of the United States National museum. no. 36)

Smithsonian institution publication 681.

1. Dolphins.

S 13–141

Library, Smithsonian   Institution   QH.U6

AS
720.T
R

DELPHINIDAE   TASMANIA

Pearson, Joseph

The whales and dolphins of Tasmania, Part 1: external characters and habits.

(Papers and Proc. R. Soc. Tasmania, 1935: 163-192)

QE
Geol. Pam
883

DELTAS

Hubbard, George D.

The Pearl river Delta

(Lingnan Science Journal, vol. 7, 1929, pp. 23-34)

AS
36
S 5

DELPHINIDAE

True, Frederick W.(illiam)

A review of the family Delphinidae. (Contributions to the natural history of the cetaceans)

(Bull. U. S. Nat. Mus., No. 36, 1889.)

QK
1
U

DELPHINIUM

Piper, Charles Vancouver, 1867–

Delphinium simplex and its immediate allies. By Charles V. Piper.

(*In* Smithsonian institution. United States national museum. Contributions from the United States national herbarium. Washington, 1903-24½ᶜᵐ. v. 16, pt. 5, p. 201-203)

"Issued February 11, 1913."

1. Delphinium.

Agr 13–245

Library, U. S. Dept. of   Agriculture   450C76   vol. 16, pt. 5

S
Agri
Pam
65

Delteil, A

La vanille: sa culture et sa preparation.

Paris, Challamel, 1897.   64p. pls. (Bibliotheque d'agriculture Coloniale)

QL
523.H7
L 75   DELTOCEPHALINAE

Linnavuori, Rauno

Revision of the neotropical Deltocephalinae
and some related subfamilies (Homoptera).

(Annaels Zoologici Societatis Zool. Bot.
Fennica "Vanamo", Tom. 20, No. 1, 1959)

DU
620
P 22   Demigod Maui and his great Hawaiian feats.

(Paradise of the Pacific, Vol. 68(7):2,7,
July, 1956)

GN
738
D27   De Morgan, Jacques

Prehistoric man: a general outline
of prehistory.

London, Kegan Paul, 1924.   304p.

GN
635.C1
D 36   Delvert, Jean

Le paysan Cambodgien.

(Le Monde d'Outre Mer, Passe et Present,
Ser. 1: Etudes X;   Ecole Pratique des Hautes
Etudes, Sorbonne; Sciences Economiques et
Sociales. 1961. Paris)

AS
36
A 65   DEMIGRETTA

Mayr, Ernst

Birds collected during the Whitney South
Sea Expedition, XLVI: Geographical variation in
Demigretta sacra (Gmelin), by Ernst Mayr and
Dean Amadon.

(Am. Mus. Novitates, No. 1144, 1941)

Dempwolff, O.

Grammatik der Jabem-sprache auf Neuguinea. 1939

UH has

AP
2
E 56   Delvingt, W.

The sense of direction in migratory
birds. By W. Delvingt and J. Leclercq.

(Endeavour, 22:27-30, 1963)

QL
401
N   Demond, Joan

A key to the Hawaiian Cypraeidae.

(The Nautilus, Vol. 67(3):86-90, 1954)

and
QL
Mollusca
Pam.
977

Dempwolff, O.

Die Lautentsprechungen der indonesischen
Lippenlaute in einigen anderen austronesischen
Südseesprachen. 1920.

UH has

G
1
As   Demaitre, Edmond

Those South Sea women.

(Asia, vol.36, pp.670-675. 1936)

QL
1
P 11   Demond, Joan

Micronesian reef-associated gastropods.

(Pacific Science, 11(3):275-341, 1957)

GN
1
B   Dempwolff, Otto

Sagen und Märchen aus Bilibili.
in Baessler-Archiv. I, 2, 4to. pp. 63-102.

Sent
to
Univ.
of
Hawaii   Deman, Esther Boise Van

The Atrium Vestae
Carnegie Inst. Wash. Pub. 108. 1909

QL
541
C 68   DEMOGRAPHY

Cold Spring Harbor Symposia on quantitative
biology, Vol. XXII:

Population studies: animal ecology and
demography. The Biological Laboratory, Cold
Spring Harbor, L. I., New York. 1957. sm4to
xiv + 437 pp.

GN
2.I
Ha   Dempwolff, Otto

Die Sandawe. Hamburgischen Kolonial-
instituts, abh. bd.34, 1916.

GN
2.M
H   Demandt, E.

Die Fischerei der Samoaner: Eine Zusammenstellung der bekanntesten Methoden des Fanges der
Seetiere bei den Eingeborenen.

(Mus. für Volkerkunde III, 1. 1913. Hamburg
142 pp. 4to. pls.)

DEMOGRAPHY

See under

POPULATION

PL
22
D 38   Dempwolff, Otto

Vergleichende Lautlehre des Austronesischen
Wortschatzes. Bd. 1:Induktive Aufbau einer Indonesischen Ursprache; Bd. 2:Deduktive Anwendung
des Urindonesischen auf austronesische Einzel-
sprachen; Bd. 3:Austronesisches Wörterverzeichnis.

(Beihefte zur Zeitschrift f. Eingeborenen-
Sprachen, Hefte 15,17,19, 1934-1938)

See also
PL
60
D 38

AS
162
P 23   Demange, J. M.

Myriapodes récoltés en Nouvelle-Calédonie
par M. Y. Plessis et description d'un cas
tératologique.

(Bull. Mus. Hist. Nat., Vol. 35(1):85-89,
1963)

GN
2.S
P 76   DEMOGRAPHY   MAORI

Maxwell, Gabrielle M.

Some demographic indications of population
movement among New Zealand Maoris.

(Jour. Poly. Soc., 70(1):31-42, 1961)

Dempwolff, Otto

Vergleichende Lautlehre des Austronesischen
Worterschatzes. Berlin, 1934-38. Volumes 1-3.
(Supplements, Zeit. f. Eingeborenensprachen)
(Beihefte 15, 1934, 17,1937, 19, 1938)
        UH has

(Malay-Polynesian language,- Proto-Polynesian, etc.)

Pub. by Dietrich Reimer, Berlin; Friederichsen,
        de Gruyter, Hamburg.

QK
Bot.Fam.
2007

den Berger, Ir L. G.

Determinatietabel voor houtsoorten van Malesie tot op familie of geslacht naar voor de loep (10 X en 20 X) zichtbare kenmerken. Publicatie can de Stichting "Fonds Landbouw Exportbureau 1916-1918" Wageningen, No. 34, 1949. R8vo. 82 pp.

QL
Protozoa
to
Polyzoa
Pam.
268

DENDROCERATIDA

Topsent, E(mile)

Etude sur les Dendroceratida.
(Archives de Zool. expérimentale et générale,
(4). v.3, Notes et Revue, no. 8, 1905.)

QK
Bot.Pam.
3032

DENDROLOGY   JAPAN

Hamaya, Toshio

A dendrological monograph on the Thymelaeaceae plants of Japan.

(Reprint: Bull. Tokyo Univ. Forests, No. 50:47-96, 1955)

Denburgh, Van

see

Van Denburgh

GN
2.1
N

Dendroglyphs

Etheridge, R. Junr.

The dendroglyphs, or "carved trees" of New South Wales. Mem. Geol. Survey of N. S. W. Ethnol. Ser. No. 3. 1918.

AS
720.V
R

Dendy, Arthur

Anatomy of an Australian land Planarian.

(Roy. Soc. Victoria Trans. I, Part II, 1889, pp. 50-95)

QL
5
Br

Denby, Arthur

Porifera. Part 1. Non- Antarctic sponges. British Mus. British Antarctic Exped. 1910 , Zool. Vol. VI, No.3, 1924.

GN
2.S
P 76

DENDROGLYPHS   CHATHAM ISLANDS

Jefferson, Christina

The dendroglyphs of the Chatham Islands.

(The Journal of the Polynesian Society, Vol. 64(4):367-441, December, 1955)

Q
115
C
v.20

G. 1. 4.

Dendy, Arthur.

Dendy, Arthur
and Ridley, Stuart O.
Challenger Expedition
Zoology. XX.

Monaxonida.

AS
720-V
R

Denby, Arthur

Anatomy of an Australian land Planarian. in Roy. Soc. Victoria Trans. I, Part II, 1889, pp. 50-95. pls. IV-V.

91
1
C15

DENDROICA.

Taylor, Walter Penn, 1888-

... An apparent hybrid in the genus *Dendroica*, by Walter P. Taylor. Berkeley, The University press, 1911.

p. [173]-177. 27ᵐ. (University of California publications in zoology. v. 7, no. 3)

Caption title.
Contribution from the Museum of vertebrate zoology of the University of California.
"Literature cited": p. 177.

1. Dendroica. 2. Hybridization.

――― Copy 2.   QL696.P2T2   A 11-934

Title from Univ. of Calif.   Library of Congress
Library of Congress   {   QL1.C15
                                         [a20c2]

QL
Crustacea
Pam. 68

Dendy, Arthur

Note from the biological laboratory of the Melbourne University: On a crayfish with abnormally developed appendages.

(R. Soc. Victoria, Proceedings, Vol. 6, 1894 pp. 160-161)

Q
115
M 46

Denby, Arthur

Calcareous sponges.

Mawson, Sir Douglas
Australasian Antarctic Expedition, 1911-14, Scientific Reports, Ser. C., Vol. 6, Part 1,1918.

GN
2.S
P 76

DENDROCHRONOLOGY   NEW ZEALAND

Cameron, R. J.

Dendrochronology in New Zealand.

(Jour. Poly. Soc. 69(1):37-38, 1960)

QL
1
L-1

Dendy, Arthur

On a collection of sponges from the Abrolhos islands, Western Australia. In Linnean Soc. London, Journ. Vol. XXXV, 1924, pp 477 - 519. Zoology

---

AS
720-V
R

Denby, Arthur

Monograph of the Victorian Sponges. Part I.- Organization and classification of the Calcarea Homocoela, with descriptions of the Victorian species. Roy. Soc. Victoria. Trans. III, Part I, 1891, pp. 1-81. pls. I-XI.

QL
Insect
Pam.941

DENDROLIMUS

Matsumura, S.

On the Five Species of Dendrolimus, injurious to Conifers in Japan, with their Parasitic and Predaceous Insects.

(Jour. College of Agric., Hokkaido Imp.Univ. Sapporo, Japan, Vol. 18, 1926, pp. 1-42)

AS
750
N

Dendy, Arthur

On some relics of the Maori race.

In J. + P. New Z. Inst. XXXV, 1901 pp. 123-134.

AS
720-V
R

Denby, Arthur

On the Victorian land Planarians. in Roy. Soc. Victoria Trans. II, Part I, 1890, pp. 65-80. pl. VII.

Z
5351
R 34

Reading
Room

DENDROLOGY BIBLIOGRAPHY

Rehder, Alfred

Bradley Bibliography: a guide to the literature of the woody plants of the world published before the beginning of the twentieth century. Compiled at the Arnold Arboretum of Harvard University under the direction of Charles Sprague Sargent... Volumes 1-5. Cambridge. 1901-1918. 4to. Vols. I and II: Dendrology.
(Publications of the Arnold Arboretum, No. 3)

AS
720.V
R

Denby, Arthur

On the Victorian land Planarians.

(Roy. Soc. Victoria, Trans. II, Part I,1890, pp. 65-80)

GN
Pam.
2380

DENE INDIANS

Morice, A. C.

The great Dene race.

(Anthropos, Bd. 1, Heft 2)

QK
Botany
Pam.
1261

DENHAM,   CAPTAIN

Milne, William

On some of the plants used for food
by the Feejee islanders. By Mr. William
Milne, late Botanical Collector in Cap-
tain Denham's Expedition to the   South
Seas. From Trans. Bot. Soc. Edinburgh,
Vol. VI, 1850, pp 263 - 265.

GN
22
D 39

Deniker, J(oseph)

The races of man; an outline of anthropology
and ethnography, with 176 illustrations and 2
maps. London. Walter Scott. 1900. 8vo. xxiii+
611 pp.

GN
2.S
T

DENGUE

Historique de la dengue à Tahiti.

(Bull. Soc. Etudes Oceaniennes, No. 72
[Tome VII(1)], pp. 40-41, 1945)

Q
Gen.Sci.
Pam. 113

Denham, H. G.

Science as an aid to world culture and
civilization. Cawthron Lecture, 1937. The
Cawthron Institute, New Zealand. 8vo. 22 pp.

(chiefly the pure sciences...)

GN
370
C 85

Deniker, J.

The races of man.

IN
Count, Earl W. ed.
This is race... pp. 207-221. New York. 1950

RA
789
A 93

DENGUE

Lumley, George F.

Dengue: Part I, Medical, by George F. Lumley
Part II, Entomological by Frank H. Taylor.

(Service Pub. (School of Public Health and
Tropical Medicine), Commonwealth of Australia,
No. 3, 1943)

GN
2.S
P 76

Dening, G. M.

The geographical knowledge of the Polynesians and the nature of inter-island contact.
IN
Polynesian Navigation, pp. 81-101,1962

QL
401
J 86

Denis, M.

Catalogue des Achatininae existant au Museum de Paris.

(Journal de Conchyliologie, 95(4):127-159,
1956)

AS
540
P 55

DENGUE

Siler, J. F.

Dengue: Its History, Epidemiology, Mechanism of Transmission, Etiology, Clinical Mani-
festations, Immunity and Prevention, by J. F.
Siler, Milton W. Hall, and A. Parker Hitchens.

(Monograph, Bureau of Science, Philippine
Islands, No. 20, 1926)

DU
40
H 67

Dening, G. M.   and others

Review of

Sharp, Andrew
Ancient voyagers in the Pacific.

(Historical Studies, Australia and New Zealand, Vol. 8(31):322-328, 1958)

Carter Coll.
6-A-23
Denison, Charles W.   editor

Old Slade, or fifteen years adventures of
a sailor: including a residence among cannibals or
Wallace Islands, and sketches of other parts of
the North and South Pacific oceans. With a likeness of the narrator. Boston. John Putnam
(1844) 104 pp.

[lacks "likeness of the narrator" and pp.
101-104.]

AS
540
P 55

DENGUE

Simmons, James Stevens,

Experimental Studies of Dengue, by James
Stevens Simmons, Joe H. St.John, and Francois
H. K. Reynolds.

(Monograph, Bureau of Science, Philippine
Islands, No. 29, 1931)

GN
Pam
2117

Deniker, J. et Bonifacy,

Les annamites et les cambodgiens.
From Soc. Anthrop. Paris, bull.et mem.

Carter Coll.
6-A-23
Denison, Charles W.   editor

Stories of the sea, number 1; Old Slade,
fifteen years adventures of a sailor...
Boston. John Putnam. 1844 100 pp. sm8vo.

QL
Insects
Pam.
1184

DENGUE

Taylor, Frank H.

The tiger mosquito (Aedes [Stegomyia]
aegypti) and dengue fever.

(Australian Journal of Science, Vol. 4, 194?
pp. 171-172)

QH
1
N 28

Denikar, J(oseph)

Collections ethnographiques rapportées de
Mélanésie par le Dr François.

(Le Naturaliste,Vol.6, 1891, pp. 227-229;
243-247)

F
1435
R 94

Denison, John, Jr.

Ruppert, Karl

Archaeological reconnaissance in Campeche,
Quintana Roo, and Peten. By Karl Ruppert and
John Denison, Jr. Carnegie Inst. of Washington
Publication 543, 1943. 4to. vii + 156 pp.
Washington.

QL
Insects
Pam.
1203

DENGUE   HONOLULU

Entomological phases of the recent dengue
epidemic in Honolulu.

(Reprint No. 2548 from the Public Health
Reports, Vol. 59, No. 13, Mch. 31, 1944, pp.
423-430)

GN
562
F 81

Deniker, Joseph

(France.) Ministères de la Marine et de l'Instruction Publique

Mission Scientifique du Cap Horn, 1882-1883.
Tome VII. Anthropologie, Ethnographie (de Tierra
del Fuego) par P. Hyades et J. Deniker. Paris
1891. 4to.

AS
36
A 16 n

DENISON CROCKETT EXPEDITION

Dunn, Emmett Reid

Zoological results of the Denison-Crockett
Expedition to the south Pacific for the Academy
of Natural Sciences of Philadelphia, 1937-1938.
Part II.- Amphibia and Reptilia.

(Notulae Naturae, Acad. Nat. Sci. Philadelphia, No. 14, 1939)

AS
36
A 16

DENISON CROCKETT EXPEDITION

Fowler, Henry W.

Zoological results of the Denison Crockett
South Pacific Expedition for the Academy of
Natural Sciences of Philadelphia, 1937-1938.
Part III. The fishes.

(Proc. Acad. Nat. Sci., Phil., Vol. 91, 1939,
pp. 77-96)

QL
Birds
Pam. 222

DENISON CROCKETT EXPEDITION

Mayr, Ernst

Zoological results of the Denison-Crockett
Expedition to the South Pacific for the Academy
of Natural Sciences of Philadelphia, 1937-1938.
Part I: The birds of the island of Biak...

(Proc. of the Acad. of Nat. Sci., Philadelphia, Vol. 91, 1939, pp. 1-37)

QL
Birds
Pam. 222

DENISON CROCKETT EXPEDITION

Mayr, Ernst

Zoological results of the Denison-Crockett
Expedition to the South Pacific for the Academy
of Natural Sciences of Philadelphia, 1937-1938.
Part IV: Birds from northwest New Guinea, by
Ernst Mayr and Rodolphe Meyer de Schauensee.

(Proc. Acad. Nat. Sci., Philadelphia, Vol.
91, 1939, pp. 97-144)

QL
Birds
Pam. 222

DENISON CROCKETT EXPEDITION

Mayr, Ernst

Zoological results of the Denison-Crockett
Expedition to the South Pacific for the Academy
of Natural Sciences of Philadelphia, 1937-1938.
Part V: Birds from the western Papuan Islands,
by Ernst Mayr and Rodolphe Meyer de Schauensee.

(Proc. Acad. Nat. Sci., Philadelphia, Vol.
91, 1939, pp. 145-163)

DU
744
R 58

DENISON CROCKETT EXPEDITION

Ripley, Dillon

The trail of the money bird; 30,000 miles
of adventure with a naturalist. Harper and
Brothers. New York and London. Second edition.
1942c. 8 vo. xii + 305 pp.

AS
36
A 16 n

DENISON CROCKETT EXPEDITION

Schauensee, Rodolphe Meyer de

On a collection of birds from Waigeu.

(Notulae Naturae, Acad. Nat. Sci., Phil.,
No. 45, 1940, pp. 1-10)

AS
36
A 16 n

DENISON CROCKETT EXPEDITION

Ulmer, Frederick, A., Jr.

Zoological results of the Denison-Crockett
South Pacific Expedition for the Academy of
Natural Sciences of Philadelphia, 1937-38. Part
VI: A new race of the New Guinea short-headed
flying phalanger from Biak Island.

(Notulae Naturae, Acad. of Nat. Sci., Philadelphia, No. 52, 1940)

DENMARK BOTANY

see

BOTANY DENMARK

DENMARK DIPTERA

see

DIPTERA DENMARK

DENMARK EXPEDITIONS

See

EXPEDITIONS DENMARK

GC
63
D 61

Dennell, Ralph

On the structure of the photophores of some
Decapod Crustacea.

IN
Discovery Committee...Reports, Vol. 20, 1940
pp. 309-382.

GN
654
D 39

Dennett, R. E.

At the back of the black man's mind, or,
Notes on the kingly office in west Africa.
London. Macmillan. 1906. 8vo. xv + 288 pp.

GN
653
D39

Dennett, R   E

Nigerian studies, or, the religious and
political system of the Yoruba.   With illustrations.
London, Macmillan, 1910.   8vo. xvii + 232 pp.
map.

DU
620
P 22

Dennis, Hope

Napoopoo lad's dream comes true; the story
of how Christianity came to the Islands.

(Paradise of the Pacific, June 1956:24-25)

QL
671
E 39

Dennis, Virginia

Happy Birthday, George Munro.

(reprinted in The Elepaio, 22(12), 1962,
from Hawaiian Life, Aug. 8, 1959)

QK
524
D71
Co

DENNSTAEDTIA PUNCTILOBULA
Conard, Henry Shoemaker, 1874–
The structure and life-history of the hay-scented fern.
By Henry Shoemaker Conard, PH. D. Washington, D. C.,
Carnegie institution of Washington, 1908.

56 p. 25 pl. 25½ᶜᵐ. (*On verso of t.-p.*: Carnegie institution of Washington. Publication no. 94)

Johns Hopkins university. Botanical laboratory. Contribution no. 7.
cf. Pref.
Bibliography: p. 48-50.

1. Dennstaedtia punctilobula.

Library of Congress   QK524.D5C7   8–21810
—— —— Copy 2.

DU
Hist.Pam.
129

Denny, George P.

A Report on the Hawaiian Treaty, Presented
to the National Board of Trade, at Its Annual
Meeting, held at Washington in January, 1883, by
George P. Denny and Edward Kemble. Boston, 1883.
8vo. 13 pp.

GC
1
M 73-a

DENSITY

Thoulet, J.

Etude desimétrique des eaux océaniques
abyssales.

(Ann. Inst. Océanographiques, N. S. Tome 8,
fasc. 3, 1930, pp. 187-213)

AP
2
A 5

and

QE
Geol.Pam.
784

2 copies

DENSITY HAWAII

Goranson, Roy W.

The density of the island of Hawaii, and
density of distribution in the earth's crust.

(Am. Jour. of Sci., Ser. 5, Vol. 16, 1928,
pp. 89-120)

DENSITY PACIFIC

Kuwahara, S.

Correction the echo-depth for the density of
water in the Pacific Ocean.

(Japanese Journal of Astronomy and Geophysics,
Vol. 16, 1939, pp. 43-78)

Q
115
C 26

DENSITY PACIFIC

Sverdrup, H. U. and others
Observations and results in physical ocean-
ography, by H. U. Sverdrup, J. A. Fleming, F. M.
Soule and C. C. Ennis.

IN Scientific Results of Cruise VII of the
Carnegie during 1928-1929...Oceanography-1A.
Carnegie Inst. of Washington, Pub. no. 545, 1944.

GC
1
M 73-a
DENSITY PACIFIC

Thoulet, J.

Etude densimétrique dans le Pacifique.

(Ann. Inst. Océanographique, N. S., Tome 4, fasc. 7, 1927, p. 261-273)

GN
1
A
Densmore, Frances

The Music of the Filipinos.

(American Anthropologist, N. S. Vol. 8, 1906, pp. 611-632)

GN
Ethn.Pam
3393
Dental health education and dental health service in Hawaii: a survey.

Millberry, Guy S.

GC
1
M 73-a
DENSITY PACIFIC

Thoulet, J.

Densimétrie et volcanicité abyssale dans le Pacifique.

(Ann. Inst. Océanographique, N. S., Tome 4, fasc. 2, 1927, p. 25-45)

GN
1
A
Densmore, Frances

The Native Music of American Samoa.

(American Anthropologist, Vol. 34, 1932, pp. 415-417)

DU
1
S 72 ti
DENTAL HYGIENE PACIFIC

Cadell, P. B.

Notes on dental hygiene for persons engaged in health education in the South Pacific.

(South Pacific Commission, Technical Information Circular No. 60:1-3, 1963)

GC
1
M 73-a
DENSITY PACIFIC

Thoulet, J.

Essai d'une densimétrie des océans.

(Ann. Inst. Océanographique, N. S., Tome, fasc. 3, 1926, pp. 137-158)

GN
1
A
Densmore, Frances

Scale Formation in Primitive Music.

(American Anthropologist, N. S. Vol. 11, 1909, pp. 1-12)

QL
Mollusca
Pam.
824
DENTITION

Kondo, Yoshio

Dentition of six Syncerid genera, Gasteropoda, Prosobranchiata, Synceridae: (Assimineidae).

(Occ. Papers, Bernice P. Bishop Museum, Vol. 17, no. 23, 1944, pp. 313-318)

GN
550
S
Densmore, Frances.

... Chippewa music, by Frances Densmore. Washington, Govt. print. off., 1910-13.

2 v. front. (vol. II) illus., plates. 24½ᶜᵐ. (Smithsonian institution. Bureau of American enthnology. Bulletin 45, 53)

Issued also as House doc. 417, 61st Cong., 2d sess. and House doc. 1232, 62d Cong., 3d sess.
Contains music.

1. Indians of North America—Music. 2. Chippewa Indians. I. Title.

Music — Chippewa Indians

10—36111

Library of Congress   E51.U6 no, 45, 53
——— Copy 2.   E99.C6D4

GN
550
S
Densmore, Frances.

... Teton Sioux music, by Frances Densmore. Washington, Govt. print. off., 1918.

xxviii, 561 p. illus. (incl. music) 82 pl. on 66 l. (incl. front.) 24ᶜᵐ. (Smithsonian institution. Bureau of American ethnology. Bulletin 61)

Issued also as House doc. 853, 64th Cong., 1st sess.

1. Indians of North America—Music. 2. Dakota Indians. I. Title.

Music — Dakota Indians

18—26735

Library of Congress   E51.U6 no. 61
    [s19f3]

GN
2.S
P 76
DENTITION MAORI

Taylor, R. M. S.

Non-metrical studies in the human palate and ditition in Moriori and Maori skulls. Parts 1-2.

(Jour. Poly. Soc., Vol. 71(1-2), 1962)

GN
550
S
Densmore, Frances

Chippewa customs. U. S. Bur. Amer. Ethn. Bull. 86, 1929.

GN
Pam
#22
Densmore, Frances

Teton Sioux music, review of, ex Journ. of Am. Folk-Lore, vol. XXXII, no. CXXVI, October-December, 1919.

GN
2.S
P 76
DENTITION MORIORI

Taylor, R. M. S.

Non-metrical studies in the human palate and dentition in Moriori and Maori skulls. Parts 1-2.

(Jour. Poly. Soc., Vol. 71(1-2), 1962)

GN
550
S
Densmore, Frances

Mandan and Hidatsu music: Bur. Am. Ethn. Bul. 80 , 1923.

QK
1
C 2
Densmore, Hiram Delos, 1862-

... The origin, structure and function of the polar caps in *Smilacina amplexicaulis*, Nutt. By Hiram D. Densmore. Berkeley, The University press, 1908.

cover-title, p. [303]-330. pl. 4-8. 27ᶜᵐ. (University of California publications in botany, v. 3, no. 2)

"Literature cited": p. 320.

1. Karyokinesis. 2. Cells. 3. Smilacina amplexicaulis, Nutt.

Title from Univ. of Calif.   Library of Congress   A 11-727
    [s19d1]

GN
Ethn
Pam.
$ 712
aboriginal

Dentition and palate of the Australian

Campbell, T. D,

AS
36
S5
Densmore, Frances

United States National Museum

Handbook of the collection of musical instruments in the United States National Museum. By Frances Densmore, Bull. 136, 1927.

RC
Pathology
Pam.
76
DENTAL CARIES JAPANESE

Yanagi, Kintaro

Dental caries and nutrition among Japanese.

(The Bulletin of Tokyo Med. and Dental Univ., Vol. 9(1):45-50, 1962)

QL
Ins.
Pam.
149.
Denton Brothers.

Butterfly hunter's guide.

D'Entrecasteaux , Joseph Antoine Bruni

See

d'Entrecasteaux, Joseph Antoine Bruni d'

D'ENTRECASTEAUX ISLANDS   PETROGLYPHS

See

PETROGLYPHS   D'ENTRECASTEAUX ISLANDS

GN
Pam
1112

Deonna, Waldemar

Quelques remarques sur la stylisation. From Rev. d'ethnog. et sociol. Paris, 1913.

D'ENTRECASTEAUX

Hulot, E. G. J.

D'Entrecasteaux, 1737 - 1793. 1894

UH has

AS
36
B3

DENUDATION   HAWAII

Mann, Horace

Denudation observed in the rocks of the Hawaiian Islands.
in Boston Soc. Nat. Hist. Proc. X, 1864-1866, pp. 232-237.

Department of Commerce and Labor, U.S.

Bureau of Fisheries

See

U. S. Bureau of Fisheries

DU
580
Je

D'ENTRECASTEAUX ISLANDS

Jenness, D. and Ballantyne, A.

The northern D'Entrecasteaux, with a preface by R. R. Marett. Oxford, Clarendon, 1920, pp. 219.

QE
75
P

DENUDATION AND EROSION .....

Glenn, Leonidas Chalmers, 1871–

... Denudation and erosion in the Southern Appalachian region and the Monongahela basin, by Leonidas Chalmers Glenn.   Washington, Govt. print. off., 1911.

1 p. l., 137 p. illus., xxi pl. (part fold., incl. maps) 29ᶜᵐ. (U. S. Geological survey. Professional paper 72)

Issued also as House doc. no. 1267, 61st Cong., 3d sess.

1. Erosion. 2. Appalachian Mountains, Southern.   I. Title.

                                    G S 11-54

Library, U. S. Geol.   survey (200) B no. 72

Hawaii

Corridor
Case
4o

Depew. —

Report from the Committee on Pacific Islands and Porto Rico, amending the organic act of Hawaii.
61st Cong. 2ᵈ Sess. Senate Report no. 126, Jan. 31, 1910

DU
740
H7
M84

D'Entrecasteaux Islands

Moresby, John.

Discoveries and surveys in New Guinea and the D'Entrecasteaux Islands.. London, 1876. 327p. maps.

QL
430
D41

Denys de Montfort, [Pierre]
De Montfort, Denys

Conchyliologie Systematique.

Vols. I-II.

Paris, 1808-10. Schoell

QK
Bot.Pam.
1658

DEPLANCHEA

Vieillard, Eugène

Etudes sur les Genres Oxera et Deplanchea.
(Bulletin de la Société Linnéenne de Normandie, Vol. 7, 1861-62, pp. 88-98)

GN
2.S
M 26

D'ENTRECASTEAUX ISLANDS

Róheim, Géza

Cannibalism in Duau, Normanby Island, D'Entrecasteaux Group, Territory of Papua.

(Mankind, Vol. IV(12):487-495, 1954)

QL
403
D39

F.7

Denys de Montfort, [Pierre]
de Denys- Montfort, Paris

Histoire naturelle des Mollusques.
vols. I - VI.
continué par Felix de Roissy
see vols. V + VI.

QL
Mollusk
Pam
508

Depontaillier, J

Diagnose d'une nouvelle espece de Nassa des argiles bleues de biot pres antibes. From Jour. d. Conch. 1878.

D'ENTRECASTEAUX ISLANDS   BIRDS

see

BIRDS   D'ENTRECASTEAUX ISLANDS

GN
Pam
1079

Deonna, Waldemar

Etudes d'art compare. From Revue d'ethnog. et socio. Paris, 1913. 10p.

GN
1
O 15

DEPOPULATION

Pentony, B.

Psychological causes of depopulation of primitive groups.

(Oceania, Vol. XXIV(2):142-145, 1953)

DENTRECASTEAUX ISLANDS   HEALTH

See

HEALTH   DENTRECASTEAUX ISLANDS

GN
Pam
843

Deonna, W.

L'influence de la technique sur l'oeuvre d'art. From Revue Archeol. Paris 1913. 27p.

GN
1
O 15

DEPOPULATION

Williams, F. E.

Depopulation and Administration.

(Oceania, Vol. III, 1932, pp. 218-226)

DEPOPULATION

see also

POPULATION

GN
1
A62
DEPOPULATION MARQUESAS

Tautain

Étude sur la dépopulation de l'archipel des marquises.

(L'Anthropologie, Tome 9, 1898, pp. 298-318; 418-436)

GN
2.S
F 47
DEPOPULATION NEW HEBRIDES

Frater, A. S.

Depopulation in the New Hebrides.

(Transactions of the Fiji Society of Science and Industry, Vol. 3(3):166-185, 1947)

GN
Ethn.Pam.
68
DEPOPULATION FIJI

Triggs, Oscar Lovell

The Decay of Aboriginal Races.

(The Open Court...[Chicago], Vol. 26, pp. 584-603, 1912)

GN
Pam
3081
DEPOPULATION MELANESIA

Buxton, P. A.

Depopulation of the New Hebrides and other parts of Melanesia. And discussion.

(Trans. Royal Soc. of Tropical Medicine and Hygiene, Vol. XIX, No. 8, 1926, pp. 420-458)

GN
1
O 15
DEPOPULATION NEW ZEALAND

Repa, T. Wi

Depopulation in New Zealand.

(Oceania, Vol. III, 1932, pp. 227-234)

DU
620
H 5

locked
case
DEPOPULATION HAWAII

Bishop, Artemas

An inquiry into the causes of decrease in the population of the Sandwich Islands.

(Hawaiian Spectator, Vol. 1, No. 1, 1838, pp. 52-66)

GN
Ethn.Pam.
3296
DEPOPULATION MELANESIA

Hamlin, H(annibal)

The problem of depopulation in Melanesia.

(Yale Journal of Biology and Medicine, Vol. 4, 1932, pp. 301-321)

GN
2.S
P 76
DEPOPULATION ONGTONG JAVA

Hogbin, H. Ian

The problem of depopulation in Melanesia as applied to Ontong Java.

(Journal of the Polynesian Society, Vol. 39: 43-66, 1930)

DU
620
F
DEPOPULATION HAWAII

Bishop, Sereno E.

Why are the Hawaiians dying out?

(Friend, March 1889, pp. 18-20; April, pp. 26-27.)

GN
2.S
P 76
DEPOPULATION MELANESIA

Hogbin, H. Ian

The problem of depopulation in Melanesia as applied to Ontong Java.

(Journal of the Polynesian Society, Vol. 39, pp. 43-66, 1930)

DU
12
D 90
DEPOPULATION PACIFIC

Dunbabin, Thomas

Slavers of the south seas.

Sydney. Angus & Robertson, Ltd. 1935. sm8vo. xiv + 308 pp.

DU
620
H 5

locked
case
DEPOPULATION HAWAII

Malo, David

On the decrease of population of the Hawaiian Islands. Translated by L. Andrews.

(Hawaiian Spectator, Vol. 2, No. 2, 1839, pp. 121-130)

GN
1
O 15
DEPOPULATION NEW GUINEA

Chinnery, E. W. P.

Census and Population.

(Oceania, Vol. III, 1932, pp. 214-217)

DU
12
E 47

DU 12
E 47
locked
case
DEPOPULATION PACIFIC

Ellis, William, 1794-1872

Polynesian Researches...2 vols. London. 1829. 8vo. Vol. 2, pp. 26-36.

The same...1830. 2 vols. 8vo.

DU
620
F
DEPOPULATION HAWAII

Notes.

(Friend, March 1849, p. 20)

GN
2.1
A-4
DEPOPULATION NEW HEBRIDES

Baker, John R.

Depopulation in Espiritu Santo, New Hebrides.

(Journ. R. Anthrop. Inst. of Great Britain and Ireland, Vol. 58, 1928, pp. 279-303, pl. 24)

G
1
A s
DEPOPULATION PACIFIC

Greene, M. T.

Twilight of the sailing-gods.

(Asia, Vol. 35, No. 3, Mar. 1935, pp. 133-38)

AP
2
N 54
DEPOPULATION MAORI

Buller,

The decrease of the Maori race.

(New Zealand Jour. of Sci., 1884, vol. 2, no. 2, pp. 55-59)

GN
Pam
3081
DEPOPULATION NEW HEBRIDES

Buxton, P. A.

Depopulation of the New Hebrides and other parts of Melanesia. And discussion.

(Trans. Royal Soc. of Tropical Medicine and Hygiene, Vol. XIX, No. 8, 1926, pp. 420-458)

DU
620
F
DEPOPULATION PACIFIC

Notes.

(Friend, March 1849, p. 20)

GN
669
C 77   DEPOPULATION PACIFIC
      Peabody Museum, Harvard University

      The Micronesians of Yap and their depopulation. Report of the Peabody Museum Expedition to Yap Island, Micronesia, 1947-1948.

      (Coordinated Investigation of Micronesian Anthropology, Pacific Science Board)

AP
2
N 4   DEPTH PACIFIC
      Carruthers, J. N.

      The deepest oceanic sounding. By J. N. Carruthers and A. L. Lawford.

      (Nature, Vol. 169(4302):601-603, 1952)

      [greatest ocean depth, Mariana Trench]

Q
115
C 26   DEPTH PACIFIC
      Sverdrup, H. U. and others

      Observations and results in physical oceanography, by H. U. Sverdrup, J. A. Fleming, F. M. Soule and C. C. Ennis.

      IN Scientific Results of Cruise VII of the Carnegie during 1928-1929...Oceanography-1A. Carnegie Inst. of Washington, Pub. no. 545,1944.

GN
1
O 15   DEPOPULATION PAPUA
      Murray, Hubert

      Depopulation in Papua.

      (Oceania, Vol. III, 1932, pp. 207-213)

AP
2
A 5   DEPTH PACIFIC
      Dana, James D.

      On the origin of the deep troughs of the oceanic depression; are any of volcanic origin?

      (Am. Jour. of Sci., Ser. 3, Vol. 37, 1889, pp. 192-202)

QE
1
G 3   DEPTH PACIFIC ALEUTIAN TRENCH
      Murray, Harold W.

      Profiles of the Aleutian trench.

      (Bull. Geol. Soc. Amer., Vol. 56:757-782, 1945)

G
3r
A   DEPOPULATION POLYNESIA
      Churchill, William

      The dying people of Tauu.

      (Bulletin of the American Geographical Society, Vol. 41, 1909, pp. 86-92)

AP
2
A 5   DEPTH PACIFIC
      A deep-sea depression in the Pacific near Tongatabu.

      (Am. Jour. of Sci., Ser. 3, Vol. 37, 1889, p. 420)

GC
Oceanography
Pam.
64   DEPTH PACIFIC JAPAN
      Ogura, Sinkiti

      On the depths of the adjacent seas of Japan. 2 pp. no place, no date; accompanied papers of the 1926 Pacific Science Congress, Tokyo.

DU
620
F   DEPOPULATION POLYNESIA
      Depopulation of Polynesia. Editorial.

      (Friend, August 1873, p. 70)

GC
Oceanography
Pam.
63   DEPTH PACIFIC
      Depths of the adjacent seas of Japan. Hydrographic Department, Imperial Japanese Navy. August 1926. (one map)

GC
Oceanography
Pam.
63   Depths of the adjacent seas of Japan. Hydrographic Department, Imperial Japanese Navy. August 1926. (one map)

G
1
As   DEPOPULATION - TUAMOTUS
      Gessler, Clifford

      "Aita Fanau"

      "Asia, Vol. 35, 1935, pp. 551-555)

AP
2
A 5   DEPTH PACIFIC
      Great depth in the South Pacific Ocean.

      (Am. Jour. of Sci., Ser. 3, Vol. 39, 1890, pp. 412-413)

QL
Insects
Pam.
1116   DERAEOCORIS
      Knight, Harry H.

      Monograph of the North American species of Deraeocoris-Heteroptera, Miridae.

      (Univ. of Minn. Agric. Exp. Station, Tech. Bull. 1, 1921)

DU
Pac.Pam.
864   DEPOPULATION ULITHI
      Lessa, William A.

      Depopulation on Ulithi.

      (Reprint from Human Biology, Vol. 27(3):161-183, Sept., 1955)

GC
Oceanogr.
Pam.
38   DEPTH PACIFIC
      Hanson, P. P. and others

      Maximum depths of the Pacific Ocean. By P. P. Hanson, N. L. Zenkevich, U.V.Sergeev and G. B. Udintsev.

      (Trans. Priroda, No. 6, June, 1959)

QL
634.C
D 42   Deraniyagala, P. E. P.

      A colored atlas of some vertebrates from Ceylon. Vol. 1:Fishes, Vol. 2: Tetrapod Reptilia.
      Illustrated by the author. Ceylon National Museums Publication. Ceylon Government Press. 1952. ob-4to. 149 pp., 34 pl.; 101 pp. 35 pl.

AP
2
N 4   DEPTH OCEAN MARIANAS
      Carruthers, J. N.

      The deepest oceanic sounding. By J. N. Carruthers and A. L. Lawford.

      (Nature, Vol. 169(4302):601-603, 1952)

      [greatest ocean depth, Mariana Trench]

Q
101
P 18   DEPTH PACIFIC
      Masuzawa, Jotaro

      The deep water in the western boundary of the north Pacific.

      (Jour. of the Oceanographical Soc. of Japan, 20th Anniversary Volume, 1962:279-285)

AM
Mus.Pam.
465   Deraniyagala, P. E. P.

      A general guide to the Colombo Museum. With ten plates. Geology, Paleontology, Zoology, Prehistory, Anthropology, Archaeology and Art. 12mo. 1961 45 pp.

AS 474 S

Deraniyagala, P. E. P.

The Istiophoridae and Xiphiidae of Ceylon.

(Spolia Zeylanica, vol. 26(2):137-142,1951)

QL Insects Pam. 1080

DERETIOSUS

Zimmerman, Elwood C.

A revision of the genus Deretiosus (Coleoptera, Curculionidae).

(Bernice P. Bishop Museum, Occ. Papers, Vol. 16, 1941, No. 8, pp. 177-214)

QL Insect Pam. 1682

DERMAPTERA

Hincks, W. D.

The Dermaptera of Sumba and Flores.

(Verh. Naturf. Ges. Basel, Vol. 65(1):9-23, 1954)

AS 474 S 76

Deraniyagala, P. E. P.

Mass mortality of the fish? Lutianus marginatus.

(Spolia Zeylanica, 27(2):239, 240, 1955)

QL 345.N 6 S 24

DERMAPTERA

Burr, M.

Les Dermaptères de la Nouvelle-Calédonie et des Iles Loyalty.

Sarasin, Fritz
Nova Caledonia...A. Zoologie, Tome I, Livr. 4, 1914, No. 7.

QL Insect Pam. 1684

DERMAPTERA

Hincks, W. D.

Dermaptères. IN La Reserve Naturelle Intégrale du Mont Nimba, Fasc. II.

(Mémoires de l'Institut Français d'Afrique Noire, No. 40:161-121, 1954)

CE 696 D 42

Deraniyagala, P. E. P.

The Pleistocene of Ceylon. Ceylon National Museums, Natural History Series. 1958. 4to. 164 pp. 58 pl. Colombo National Museum

---

QL Insect Pam. 1804

DERMANYSSUS

Laird, Marshall

Notes on the infestation of man by the chicken mite Dermanyssus Gallinae (de Geer) in New Zealand.

(reprint, New Zealand Medical Journal, 49 No. 269, pp. 22-23, 1950)

QL Insect Pam. 1652

DERMAPTERA

Hincks, W. D.

The male genital armature of some primitive earwigs (Dermaptera, Diplatyinae).

(Reprinted from: Trans. of the IXth International Congress of Ent., Vol. 2:3-6, 1953)

QL 737.U8 D 42

Deraniyagala, P. E. P.

Some extinct elephants, their relatives and the two living species. Ceylon National Museums Publication. Published August, 1955. 4to. 153 pp. + 48 plates and 13 text figures

---

QL Insects Pam. 1089

DERMAPTERA

Crumb, S. E.

The European earwig, by S. E. Crumb, P. M. Eide, and A. E. Bonn.

(U. S. Dept. of Agriculture, Technical Bull. No. 766, 1941)

QL Insect Pam. 1681

DERMAPTERA

Hincks, W. D.

Notes on Dermaptera.

(Proc. R. Soc. of London, Ser. B. Taxonomy, Vol. 23(9/10):159-163, 1954)

GN Ethn. Pam. 4220

Deraniyagala, P. E. P.

Some Sinhala combative field and aquatic sports and games.
Published by the National Museums of Ceylon. 4to. July 30, 1959

QL 489 B 91

DERMAPTERA

Hebard, Morgan

Dermaptera and Orthoptera.

Bryan, Edwin H., Jr.
Insects of Hawaii, Johnston Island ...

(Bernice P. Bishop Museum, Bull. 31, 1926, pp. 82-88. Tanager Expedition Publication 3.)

QL 508.F7 H 66

DERMAPTERA

Hincks, W. D.

A systematic monograph of the Dermaptera of the world, based on material in the British Museum (Natural History). Parts 1-2, 1955-1959. British Mus. (Nat. Hist.). London. R8vo.

QL 321.C D 43

Deraniyagala, P. E. P.

Some vertebrate animals of Ceylon.
Vol. 1   1949.   folio. The National Museums of Ceylon Pictorial Series.

QL Insects Pam. 1680

DERMAPTERA

Hincks, W. D.

Additions to the Belgian Congo Dermaptera.

(Ann. Mus. Congo Tervuren, Zool. 1:387-389, 1954)

QL 505 W 17

DERMAPTERA

Walker, Francis

Catalogue of the specimens of Dermaptera saltatoria and supplement to the Blattariae in the collection of the British Museum. Printed for the Trustees of the British Museum. Parts 1-5. London. 1869-1870. 8vo.

DU 621 H3

Derby, Charles.

List of Hawaiian ferns.   Thrum's Hawaiian Annual.   1875, pp. 16-18.

QL Insect Pam. 2080

DERMAPTERA

Hincks, W. D.

Dermaptera

(Boletim do Museu Municipal do Funchal, No. 14, Art. 45:17-20, 1961)

QL Insect Pam. 1862

DERMAPTERA   AFRICA

Hincks, W. Douglas

Dermaptera.

(Exploration Hydrobiologique du Lac Tanganika (1946-1947), Resultats Scientifiques, III, Fasc. 6:41-42, 1957)

QL
Insect
Pam.
1772

DERMAPTERA   AFRICA

Hincks, Walter D.

Dermaptera.

(In Parc National de L'Upemba, I. Mission G. F. de Witte... Fasc. 35(1):1-15, 1955)

QL
Insect
Pam.
1668

DERMAPTERA   AUSTRALIA

Hincks, W. D.

Report from Prof. T. Gislen's expedition to Australia in 1951-1952, No. 8: Dermaptera.

(Lunds Univ. Arsskrift, n.f. Avd. 2, Bd. 50 Nr. 4, 1954)

AS
763
B-b

DERMAPTERA   MARQUESAS

Hebard, Morgan

Additional notes on the Dermaptera and Orthoptera of the Marquesas.

(Bernice P. Bishop Museum, Bull. 142, pp. 143-148. Issued Sept. 29, 1935. Pacific Ent. Survey Publication 8, Art. 12)

QL
Insect
Pam.
1771

DERMAPTERA   AFRICA

Hincks, Walter D.

Dermaptera. Contributions à l'étude de la faune entomologique du Ruanda-Urundi (Mission P. Basilewsky 1953). LIV.

(Ann. Mus. Congo Tervuren, Zool. 40, 1955: 73-81)

QL
Insects
Pam.
1766

DERMAPTERA   AFRICA

Hincks, W. D.

Results from the Danish Expedition to the French Cameroons 1949-50, V. Dermaptera

(Bulletin de l'I. F. A. N., T. 18, Ser. A, No. 2, 1956:597-606)

QL
Insects
Pam.
1522

DERMAPTERA   MELANESIA

Rehn, James A. G.

Dermaptera records from various Pacific islands.

(Trans. Amer. Ent. Soc., 74:165-171, 1949)

QL
Insect
Pam.
1868

DERMAPTERA   AFRICA (SOUTH)

Hincks, W. D.

Dermaptera; the earwigs of South Africa.

(South African Animal Life; Results of the Lund University Expedition in 1950-51, Vol. 4 pp. 33-94, 1957)

QL
Insects
Pam.
1522

DERMAPTERA   CAROLINE ISLANDS

Rehn, James A. G.

Dermaptera records from various Pacific islands.

(Trans. Amer. Ent. Soc., 74:165-171, 1949)

QL
461
M 98

and
QL
Insects
Pam.
1088

DERMAPTERA   MICRONESIA

Menozzi, Carlo

Dermatteri della Micronesia.

(Mushi, Vol. 13:73-80, 1941)

[Results of Prof. T. Esaki's Micronesia Expeditions 1936-1939, No. 42]

QL
1
D 95

DERMAPTERA   AFRICA

Hincks, W. D.

Notes on some South African Dermaptera.

(Durban Museum Novitates, Vol. IV(II):25-29, 1952)

QL
Insects
Pam.
1521

DERMAPTERA   GUAM

Rehn, James A. G.

Dermaptera records from Guam.

(Trans. Am. Ent. Soc., 75:109-111, 1949)

QL
Insect
Pam.
1636

DERMAPTERA   NEW HEBRIDES

Hincks, W. D.

The Dermaptera of the New Hebrides.

(Annals and Magazine of Natural History, Ser. 12, Vol. 5:200, February, 1952)

QL
Insect
Pam.
1643

DERMAPTERA   AFRICA

Hincks, W. D.

Some Dermaptera from Sierra Leone.

(From the Proceedings of the Royal Entomological Soc. of London, Ser. B. Taxonomy, Vol. 21(1-2):19-26, 1952)

AS
763
B-4

&
QL
Ins.Pam.
285

DERMAPTERA   HAWAII

Hebard, Morgan

Dermaptera and Orthoptera of Hawaii.

(Bernice P. Bishop Museum, Occasional Papers, Vol. 7, 1922, pp. 305-378)

AS
496
F 29

DERMAPTERA   PACIFIC

Hincks, W. D.

The Dermaptera of Oceania.

(Journal of the Federated Malay States, Museums, Vol. 18, 1938, pp. 299-318)

QL
Insect
Pam.
2082

DERMAPTERA   AFRICA

Hincks, W. D.

Two new species of Diplatys Serville (Dermaptera:Pygidioranidae) from West Africa, with a note on a recently described Carcinophorine (Dermaptera:Labiduridae)

(Bull. de l'I. F. A. N., 23, Ser. A., No. 1, 1961, pp. 25-29)

QL
Insect
Pam.
1687

DERMAPTERA   MADAGASCAR

Hincks, W. D.

Liste préliminaire des Dermaptères de Madagascar.

(Mem. Inst. Sci. de Madagascar, ser. E, Tome IV:361-380, 1953)

QL
Insects
Pam.
1522

DERMAPTERA   PACIFIC

Rehn, James A. G.

Dermaptera records from various Pacific islands.

(Trans. Amer. Ent. Soc., 74:165-171, 1949)

QL
Insect
Pam.
1637

DERMAPTERA   AUSTRALIA

Hincks, W. D.

A new Australian species of the genus Antisolabis (Dermaptera, Labiduriiae).

(Reprinted from The Entomologist's Monthly Magazine, Vol. 88:214-215, Sept., 1952)

QL
Insects
Pam.
1522

DERMAPTERA   MANGAREVA

Rehn, James, A. G.

Dermaptera records from various Pacific islands.

(Trans. Amer. Ent. Soc., 74:165-171, 1949)

QL
Insects
Pam.
1266

DERMAPTERA   PACIFIC

Rehn, James A. G.

Five new species of earwigs of the Indo-Pacific genus Nesogaster (Dermaptera:abiidae: Nesogastrinae).

(Proc. Acad. Nat. Sci. Philadelphia, Vol. 98:219-239, 1946)

QH
1
P 11

DERMATITIS

Chu, George W.T.C.

    Pacific area distribution of fresh-water and marine cercarial dermatitis.

    (Pacific Science, 12(4): 299-312, 1958)

GN
2.S
F 47

Derrick, R. A.

    The early days of Levuka.

    (Trans. and Proc. of the Fiji Soc., Vol. 2, 1940-44: 49-58, 1953)

GN
2.S
P 76

Derrick, R. A.

    Notes on Fijian clubs, with a system of classification.

    (Jour. Poly. Soc., 66(4):391-395, 1958)

GN
Ethn.
Pam.
4429

DERMATOGLYPHICS   AINU

Kimura, Kunihiko

    Dermatoglyphics in Ainu of Tokachi province, Hokkaido. By Kunihiko Kimura and Yukitaka Terakado.

    (Reprint, Osaka City Medical Jour., Vol. 1(1):15-27, 1954)

DU
600
D 43

Derrick, R. A.

    The Fiji Islands, a geographical handbook. Government Printing Department. Suva, Fiji. R8vo. xviii+334+xix pp. (1951)

QL
671
I

Derscheid, J. M.

    An unknown species—the Tahitian goose (?).

    (Ibis, Ser. 14, Vol. 3:756-760, 1939)

QL
Insect
Pam.
1814

and

QH
541
E 17

DERMESTIDAE

Fosberg, F. R.

    Ants and dermestids on a mountain top.

    (Reprinted from Ecology, Vol. 36(2):367-368, April, 1955)

GN
2.S
F 47

Derrick, R. A.

    The Fiji Museum.

    (Trans. and Proc. of the Fiji Society, Vol. 6:153-156, 1957)

AS
162
P

des Abbayes, H.

    Contribution à l'étude des lichens des iles Hawaii: Cladonia récoltés en 1909-1910 par l'abbé Faurie.

    (Bull. Mus. Nat. d'Hist. Nat., Paris, Ser. 2, Tome 19:105-117, 1947)

QL
Insects
Pam
1176

DERMESTIDAE

Rees, Bryant E.

    Classification of the Dermestidae (larder, hide, and carpet beetles) based on larval characters, with a key to the North American genera.

    (U. S. Department of Agriculture, Misc., Pub. 511, 1943)

GN
2.S
F 47

Derrick, R. A.

    Fijian warfare.

    (Trans. and Proc. of the Fiji Soc., Vol. 2, 1940-44:137-146, 1953)

Q
101
P 18

Desai, R. G.

    Blood groups, secretor phenomenon, and gastric cancer in various ethnic groups (abstract) By R. G. Desai and W. P. Creger.

    (Eugenics Quarterly, Vol. 9(1):44, 1962)

    (Paper read at symposium on medical genetics, Tenth Pacific Science Congress, 1961)

QL
595.Mi
I 59

DERMESTIDAE   MICRONESIA

Beal, R. S. Jr.

    Coleoptera:Dermestidae
IN
Insects of Micronesia, Vol. 16(3), 1961.

GN
2.S
F 47

Derrick, R. A.

    Fiji's darkest hour— an account of the measles epidemic of 1875.

    (Trans. and Proc. Fiji Society, Vol. 6:3-16, 1955-57)

QL
Insects
Pam.
1169

Desbrochers des Loges, Jules

    Opuscules entomologiques (Coléoptères). Cahier 1, 1874-1875. Gannat. 8vo. pp. 1-56.

DU
700
R12

Les derniers sauvages

Radiguet, Max

DU
600
D 43

Derrick, R. A.

    The geography of the Fiji Islands, historical, physical, and political. First edition. Printed at Davuilevu Technical School. Fiji. 1938. R8vo.(5)+183 pp.

GN
1
A62

Descamps, Paul

    Le Cannibalisme -- ses causes et ses modalites.

    (L'Anthropologie, Tome 35, 1925. pp. 321-344)

GN
Ethn.
Pam.
4168

Derrick, R. A.

    A collection of sketches of Fijian artifacts Made by R.A.Derrick, Curator of the Fiji Museum, Suva, for identification purposes; copy made at Bishop Museum, 1959. 9 mimeo. pp.

DU
600
D 43

Derrick, R. A.

    A history of Fiji. Vol. 1 School edition. Printed and published by the Printing and Stationery Department, Suva, Fiji. (1946). R8vo. vii + 250 + VIII + ix-xxviii pp.

GN
1
A62

Descamps, Paul

    Le role social de la Pirogue.

    (L'Anthropologie, Tome 33, 1923, pp. 127-145)

GN 1 A 61   DESCENT
Davenport, William

Nonunilinear descent and descent groups.

(Am. Anthrop., 61 (4):557-572, 1959)

Deschanel, P. E. L.

Les intérêts français dans l'océan Pacifique.
1888.

UH has

QE Geol.Pam. 1206   DESERT
Smith, J. Russell

The desert's edge.

(Bull. Am. Geogr. Soc., 47(11):813-831, 1915)

GN 2.1 A 62 m   DESCENT
Leach, Edmund R.

On certain unconsidered aspects of double descent systems.

(Man, Vol. 72, no. 214, 1962)

AS 36 S1
De Schweinitz, Emil Alexander, 1866-1904.
The war with the microbes. By E. A. de Schweinitz.
(*In* Smithsonian institution. Annual report. 1896. Washington, 1898. 23½ᶜᵐ. p. 485-496)
"Printed in Science, vol. v, no. 119, pages 561-570."

1. Bacteriology.   I. Title.   S 15-933

Library of Congress   Q11.S66 1896
Library, Smithsonian   Institution

QK 938.D4 C22   DESERT FLORA
Cannon, William Austin, 1870-
Botanical features of the Algerian Sahara, by William Austin Cannon. Washington, D. C., Carnegie institution of Washington, 1913.

vi, 81 p. 36 pl. (incl. front.) fold. map. 25½ᶜᵐ. (*On verso of t.-p.:* Carnegie institution of Washington. Publication no. 178)

1. Botany—Sahara. 2. Desert flora. 3. Roots (Botany)

Library of Congress   QK922.C3   13-17680
————— Copy 2.

GN 1 E 85   DESCENT   AUSTRALIA
Lane, Barbara S.

Implicit double descent in South Australia and the northeastern New Hebrides. By Barbara S. Lane and Robert B. Lane.

(Ethnology, 1(1):46-52, 1962)

QE Pam #107
Descloiseaux, A.

Observations physiques et geologiques sur les principaux geysirs d'Islande, extrait des Annales de Chimie et de Physique, 3e serie, t. XIX.

QK 101 G 65   DESERT FLORA
Clements, Frederic E.

The origin of the desert climax and climate.

Goodspeed, T. H.
Essays in geobotany...Setchell. 1936.
pp. 87-140.

GN 1 E 85 and Q 101 P 18   DESCENT   NEW HEBRIDES
Lane, Barbara S.

Implicit double descent in South Australia and the northeastern New Hebrides. By Barbara S. Lane and Robert B. Lane.

(Ethnology, 1(1):46-52, 1962)

Presented at the 10th Pac. Sci. Congress, Honolulu, 1961

Descole, H. R.

Genera et species plantarum argentinarum. Vol. 1-3, 1943-45.

UH

AS 36 S1   DESERT FLORA.
Coville, Frederick Vernon, 1867-
Desert plants as a source of drinking water. By Frederick V. Coville.
(*In* Smithsonian institution. Annual report. 1903. Washington, 1904. 23½ᶜᵐ. p. 499-505. illus., II pl. on 1 L)

1. Desert flora.   I. Title.
     S 15-1201

Library of Congress   Q11.S66 1903
Library, Smithsonian   Institution

GN 1 O 15   DESCENT   SAMOA
Ember, Melvin

The nonunilinear descent groups of Samoa.

(American Anthropologist, 61:573-577, 1959)

DESCRIPTION AND TRAVEL

See under the name of the place

QK 922 C22   DESERT FLORA
Cannon, William Austin, 1870-
The root habits of desert plants, by William Austin Cannon. Washington, D. C., Carnegie institution of Washington, 1911.

96 p. illus., 23 pl. 25½ᶜᵐ. (*On verso of t.-p.:* Carnegie institution of Washington. Publication no. 131)

1. Desert flora. 2. Roots (Botany)

Library of Congress   QK922.C22   11-8150
————— Copy 2.

DU 870 D 29
Deschamps, Hubert

Tahiti (La Polynesie française).
Editions Berger-Levrault. Paris. 1957. 8vo. 92 pp. L'Union Française...

[contains also: Nouvelle-Caledonie, Nouvelles-Hebrides, by Jean Guiart. pp. 93-311]

AM Mus. Pam # 38
Deseret Museum
Bulletin, Final number. Feb. 15, 1919

The passing of the Deseret Museum, by James E. Talmage, Director.
Salt Lake City. pp 4.

QK 882 C3   DESERT FLORA
Cannon, William Austin

The typography of the chlorophyll apparatus in desert plants. Carnegie Inst Washington. Pub. 98, pt.1, 1908.

QK 1 T 1   DESCHAMPSIA
St. John, Harold

Dryopteris, Deschampsia, Portulaca, Lupinus, Fagara, Stenogyne, and Dubautia. Hawaiian Plant Studies 12.

(Bul., Torrey Botanical Club, Vol. 72, pp. 22-30, 1944)

DT 12 Cr
Desert and water gardens of the Red Sea

Crossland, Cyril

QK 938 D4 M13   DESERT FLORA
Macdougal, Daniel Trembly, 1865-
Botanical features of North American deserts, by Daniel Trembly MacDougal. Washington, D. C., Carnegie institution of Washington, 1908.

2 p. l., 111 p. illus. (maps) 62 pl. (incl. front., 3 fold. maps) diagrs. 25½ᶜᵐ. (*On verso of t.-p.:* Carnegie institution of Washington. Publication no. 99)

1. Desert flora. 2. Botany—The West.

Library of Congress   QK903.M2   8-26864
————— Copy 2.

QK 873 Mc M13
DESERT FLORA
Macdougal, Daniel Trembly, 1865–
 The water-balance of succulent plants, by D. T. Macdougal and E. S. Spalding. Washington, D. C., Carnegie institution of Washington, 1910.
 iii, 77 p. incl. tables, diagrs. 8 pl. (incl. front.) 25½ᶜᵐ. (On verso of t.-p.: Carnegie institution of Washington. Publication no. 141)

 1. Desert flora. 2. Botany—Ecology. 3. Cactaceae. I. Spalding, E. S., joint author. II. Title.
 Library of Congress   QK922.M3   11–1316

QE Geol. Pam. # 544 # 548 #549 # 566 & 4 dups. 739
Desert strip of west Molokai
Wentworth, Chester K.

GN Ethn.Pam 3934
Desha, Stephen L.
 Thomas Square is sacred ground. IN Collection of clippings gathered by Martha W. Beckwith, pp. 39-

---

QK 873 Sh S56
DESERT FLORA
Shreve, Edith Bellamy.
 The daily march of transpiration in a desert perennial, by Edith Bellamy Shreve. Washington, D. C., Carnegie institution of Washington, 1914.
 64 p. incl. illus., tables, diagrs. pl. 25½ᶜᵐ. (On verso of t.-p.: Carnegie institution of Washington. Publication no. 194)

 1. Desert flora. 2. Plants, Transpiration of.
 Library of Congress   QK922.S5   14–8111
 ——— Copy 2.

QK 1 B 97-b and QK Bot.Pam. 1969
DESERTS
Van Steenis, C.G.G.J.
 Cycles of drought and reafforestation in the U.S.A. seen in the light of a new botanical hypothesis on the origin of deserts in general.
 (Bull. du Jardin Bot. de Buitenzorg, Ser. III, vol. XIV. 1936. pp. 50-55)

QL 426 D 45 also QL 402 G 23 locked case
Deshayes, G(erard) P(aul)
 Catalogue des Mollusques de l'Ile de la Réunion (Bourbon). (Being) Annexe E de l'Ouvrage Intitulé: Notes sur l'Ile de la Réunion, par L. Maillard.   Paris. 1862. 8vo. 144 pp.
 (Garrett collection of papers on conchology, Vol. 11)

QK Bot.Pam. 1930
DESERT FLORA
Shreve, Forrest
 The plant life of the Sonoran Desert.
 (Carnegie Institution of Washington, Supplementary Publications, no. 22, 1936. Reprinted from The Scientific Monthly, 1936, vol. XLII, pp. 195-213)

QK Bot.Pam. 3052
DESERTS   AUSTRALIA
Chippendale, G. M.
 Notes on the vegetation of a desert area in central Australia.
 (Trans. R. Soc. of South Australia, 81:31-41, 1958)

QL 406 B P346
Deshayes, Gerard Paul
British museum (*Nat. hist.*) Dept. of zoology.
 Catalogue of the *Conchifera* or bivalve shells in the collection of the British museum ... London, Printed by order of the Trustees (by Taylor and Francis) 1853-54.
 2 v. 18½ᶜᵐ.
 Paged continuously.
 Title of v. 2 reads: Catalogue of the *Conchifera* ... By Monsieur Deshayes ...
 No more published.
 Contents.—pt. I. *Veneridæ, Cyprinidæ* and *Glauconomidæ.*—pt. II. *Petricoladæ* (concluded) *Corbiculadæ.*
 1. Lamellibranchiata. I. Deshayes, Gerard Paul, 1795-1875.
 Library of Congress   QL406.B75   6—29450

QK 938.D4 sh S56
DESERT FLORA
Shreve, Forrest, 1878–
 The vegetation of a desert mountain range as conditioned by climatic factors, by Forrest Shreve. Washington, D. C., Carnegie institution of Washington, 1915.
 112 p. incl. tables, diagrs. 36 pl., map. 25½ᶜᵐ. (On verso of t.-p.: Carnegie institution of Washington. Publication no. 217)

 1. Desert flora.
 Library of Congress   QK938.D4S5   15–24561
 ——— Copy 2.

DU Pac.Fam. 631
Desfontaines, Jules
 Autour de l'hémisphère austral, Deuxième partie: Les iles enchantées de la Polynésie, légendes inédites, récits de voyage faits à la Société de Géographie de Nantes le 16 Avril, et le 21 Mai, 1891. Nantes, 1891. pp. 113-196. 8vo.

QL Mol Pam #121
Deshayes,
 Conchyliologie, colored plates XXVIII-XLI, np. nd.

QK 922 Sp S73
DESERT FLORA
Spalding, Volney Morgan, 1849–
 Distribution and movements of desert plants, by Volney M. Spalding. Washington, D. C., Carnegie institution of Washington, 1909.
 v, 144 p. illus., plates (part fold.) maps, diagrs. 25½ᶜᵐ. (On verso of t.-p.: Carnegie institution of Washington. Publication no. 113)
 "Literature cited": p. 143-144.

 1. Desert flora. 2. Botany—Geographical distribution.
 Library of Congress   QK903.S7   9—28159
 ——— Copy 2.   (s19e2)

DU 700 V 76
Desgraz, C.
Vincendon-Dumoulin, A.C.
 Iles Marquises, ou, Nouka-Hiva. Histoire, geographie, moeurs et considerations generales... par MM. Vincendon-Dumoulin et C. Desgraz. Paris, Arthus Bertrand, 1843. 362 pp. map. pls.

QL 403 F 41
Deshayes, G. P.
Ferussac, (J. B. L. d'A.) de
 Histoire Naturelle Générale et Particulière des Mollusques Terrestres et Fluviatiles...par D. de Forussac et G. P. Deshayes. Accompagnée d'un Atlas de 247 Planches Gravées. Text, Tome 1-2, Atlas, Tomes 1-2. 1820-1851. Paris, J.-B. Baillière. folio.

QK Bot.Pam. 2910
DESERT PLANTS
Hertrich, William
 A guide to the desert plant collection in the Huntington Botanical Gardens. Henry E. Huntington Library and Art Gallery. San Marino, California. 1940. 8vo. 5-32 pp.

DU 870 V 76
Desgraz, C.
Vincendon-Dumoulin, Adrien Clément
 Iles Taïti, Esquisse historique et géographique, précédée de considerations générales sur la colonisation Francaise dans l'Océanie. Par Vincendon-Dumoulin et C. Desgraz. Paris. Parties 1-2. 1844.

QL Mol Pam #68 B
Deshayes and others
 Lucinidae, Kellidae, Solenomyadae, Arcacea, Mollusca Monomyaria. Ex (?) date (?), n.p.

AS 36 S1
DESERT PLANTS AS A SOURCE OF DRINKING WATER.
Coville, Frederick Vernon, 1867–
 Desert plants as a source of drinking water. By Frederick V. Coville.
 (In Smithsonian institution. Annual report. 1903. Washington, 1904. 23½ᶜᵐ. p. 499-505. illus., II pl. on 1 l.)

 1. Desert flora. I. Title.
 Library of Congress   Q11.S66 1903   S 15–1201
 Library, Smithsonian   Institution

QL 1 E 38 and GR Folklore Pam. 98
Desha, Stephen
 The legend of the Naha stone. Recorded in Hawaiian and translated by Stephen Desha, Sr., adapted by L. W. de Vis-Norton.
 (Hawaii Nature Notes, Vol. 4(3), 1952)

QL Mollusk Pam 510
Deshayes, G   P
 Observations sur les animaux de deux nayades asiatiques. From Jour. d. Conch. 1875.

AS
36
S4

DESIGN

Krieger, Herbert W.

Design Areas in Oceania, based on Specimens in the United States National Museum.

(Proceedings of the United States National Museum, Vol. 79, Art. 30, 1932).

DU
Pac.Pam.
456

DESIGN HAWAII

Jones, Stella M.

Hawaiian quilts.   Honolulu Academy of Art.
1930. Honolulu.

AS
763
B-b

GN
670
G 82

Reading
Room
GN
Pam.
622

DESIGN MARQUESAS

Greiner, Ruth H.

Polynesian decorative designs. Honolulu.
1923. pp. 4-34

(Bernice P. Bishop Museum, Bulletin 7, 1923)
2 copies

GN
Ethn.Pam.
3623

DESIGN

Wirz, Paul

Über die Bedeutung der Fledermaus in Kunst,
Religion und Aberglauben der Völker.

(Geographica Helvetica, III(3):267-278,
1948)

GN
2.S
P 76

DESIGN MAORI

Archey, Gilbert

Evolution of certain Maori carving patterns.

(Journal of the Polynesian Society, 42:
171-190, 1933.)

GN
Ethn.Pam.
3491

DESIGN MARSHALL ISLANDS

Krämer, Augustin

Die Ornamentik der Kleidmatten und der Ta-
tauierung auf den Marshallinseln nebst techno-
logischen, philologischen und ethnologischen Notizen.

(Archiv f. Anthropologie, 30:1-28,1904.
Braunschweig)

DS
Asia
Pam.
79

DESIGN SHIPS

Damm, Hans

Ein "Schiffstuch" aus Süd-Sumatra.

(Leipzig. Museums für Völkerkunde.
Jahrbuch, Bd. 17:67-72 + 1 plate, 1958)

AS
719
A-m

DESIGN MAORI

Bramell, Elsie

Maori carving (exhibit of the Auckland
Museum to illustrate theory of Gilbert Archey
that Maori design is based on the human figure.)

(The Australian Museum Magazine, Vol. 7,
1940, pp. 121-124)

GN
668
R 34

DESIGN MELANESIA

Reichard, Gladys A.

Melanesian design...2 volumes. New York.
Columbia University Press. 1933. 4to. pp. 172;
14 pls. CLI.

GN
2.M
F 45 d

DESIGN BATIK

Lewis, Albert Buell

Javanese Batik designs from metal stamps.

(Field Mus., Anthrop. Design ser. No. 2,
1924)

AS
750
N

DESIGN MAORI

Buck, Peter Henry

Maori decorative art: No. 1, House-panels
(Arapaki, Tuitui, or Tukutuku)

(Trans. New Zealand Institute, Vol. 53:
452-470, 1921)

GN
Ethn.
Pam.
4354

DESIGN MELANESIA

Schuster, Carl

An ancient Chinese mirror design reflected
in modern Melanesian art.

(Far Estern Quarterly, 11(1):53-66, 1951)

GN
2.S
P 76

DESIGN COOK ISLANDS

Gudgeon, W.E.

The origin of the Ta-Tatau or heraldic
marks at Aitutaki Island.

(Journal of the Polynesian Society, 14:
217-18, 1905.)

AS
763
B-b

GN
670
G 82

Reading
Room
GN
Pam.622

DESIGN MAORI

Greiner, Ruth H.
Polynesian decorative designs. Honolulu.
1923. pp. 77-80.

(Bernice P. Bishop Museum, Bulletin 7, 1923)
2 copies

GN
2.M
S 93

DESIGN NEW CALEDONIA

Lobsiger-Dellenbach, M. et G.

Les bambous gravés de Nouvelle-Calédonie
du Linden-Museum de Stuttgart.

(Tribus, Nr. 10:115-130, 1961)

GN
2.S
P 76

DESIGN FIJI

Surridge, Margaret N.

Decoration of Fiji water-jars.

(Journal of the Polynesian Society, Vol.
53, No. 1, pp. 17-36, 1944)

GN
Ethn.
Pam.
3458

Pam.
3717

DESIGN MAORI

Phillipps, W. J.

Maori designs.   Harry H. Tombs, Limited.
Wellington. pamphlet. n.d. 8vo. 24 pp.

1941 issue

GN
2.S
O 15

DESIGN NEW CALEDONIA

Lobsiger-Dellenbach, Marguerite et Georges

Description de trois bambous gravés de
Nouvelle-Calédonie. Collection de M. Ratton.

(Journal de la Soc. des Oceanistes, 7:165-121
1951)

AS
763
B-b

GN
670
G 82

Reading
Room
Pam.
GN
622

DESIGN HAWAII

Greiner, Ruth H.

Polynesian decorative designs. Honolulu. 1923.
pp. 35-36.
(Bernice P. Bishop Museum, Bulletin 7, 1923)
2 copies

GN
2.S
P 76

DESIGN MAORI

Rowe, W. Page

The origin of the Maori spiral.

(Journal of the Polynesian Society, Vol. 27,
pp. 129-133, 1938)

GN
662
B 29

DESIGN NEW CALEDONIA

Lobsiger-Dellenbach, Marguerite

Dessins réalistes et motifs symboliques
gravés sur les bambous de Nouvelle-Calédonie.

IN Südseestudien, pp. 318-330, Basel, 1951

GN
Ethn.Pam.
3587

DESIGN   NEW GUINEA

Bodrogi, T.

Yabim drums in the Biró collection.

(Folia Ethnographica, I (2-4):205-222, 1949)

GN
670
C 56

DESIGN POLYNESIA

Churchill, William

Club types of nuclear Polynesia. Washington.
1917. R8vo.

(Carnegie Institution of Washington, Publication No. 255.)

DS
Asia
Pam.
79

DESIGN   SUMATRA

Damm, Hans

Ein "Schiffstuch" aus Süd-Sumatra.

(Leipzig. Museums für Völkerkunde.
Jahrbuch, Bd. 17:67-72 + 1 plate, 1958)

AS
28
E 85

DESIGN   PACIFIC

Guiart, Jean

Etude du symbolisme des croix de fil (1)

(Etudes Melanésiennes, n.s. 4th (yr), No.
6:50-55, 1952)

[the thread ___ cross]

AS
763
B-b

GN
670
G 82

Reading
Room
GN
Pam.
622

DESIGN POLYNESIA

Greiner, Ruth H.

Polynesian decorative designs. Honolulu.1923.

(Bernice P. Bishop Museum. Bulletin 7, 1923)

2 copies

Storage
Case
1

DESIGN   TAIWAN

Hsiao, Erika Karawina

Taiwan design: 4 small rubbings of native
combs in Taiwan Museum; 1 large roll, rubbing
from specimen in Museum of Department of Archaeology of National Museum of Taiwan. Figure,
"ancestral deity", is of unknown age. Made by
Erika K. Hsiao in 1955.

GN
1
An

DESIGN   PACIFIC

Schuster, Carl

V-shaped chest-markings: distribution in
and around the Pacific.

(Anthropos, Vol. 47:99-118, 1952)

GN
2.S
P 76

DESIGN-POLYNESIA

March, H. Colley

Polynesian ornament a mythography, or symbolism of origin and descent.

(Jour. of the R. Anthrop. Inst. of Great
Britain and Ireland, Vol. 22, 1893, pp. 307-333)

AS
763
B-b

GN
670
G 82

Reading
Room
GN
Pam.622

DESIGN TONGA

Greiner, Ruth H.

Polynesian decorative designs. Honolulu.
1923. pp. 69-76.

(Bernice P. Bishop Museum, Bulletin 7, 1923)

2 copies

AM
101
F 45-n

DESIGN   PACIFIC

Tardy, Christine

Modern design is "old stuff" to South Sea
islanders.

(Chicago Natural Hist. Mus. Bull. 23(3):6-7,
1952)

GN
2.S
P 76

DESIGN   POLYNESIA

Taylor, Donna

The relation of matplaiting to barkcloth
decoration in Polynesia.

(Jour. Poly. Soc., 69(1):43-53, 1960)

GN
2.1
A-m

DESIGN   TROBRIAND ISLANDS

Salisbury, Richard F.

A Trobriand medusa?

(Man, March 1959, No. 66)

GN
Ethn.Pam.
3349

DESIGN   PACIFIC

Tichelman, G. L.

Dr. Carl Schuster on bird-designs in the
western Pacific: Indonesia, Melanesia, Polynesia.

(Cultureel Indie, Jaarg. 1, 1939, pp. 232-235)

AS
763
B-b

GN
670
G 82

Reading
Room
GN
Pam.
6

DESIGN   SAMOA

Greiner, Ruth H.

Polynesian decorative designs. Honolulu.
1923. pp. 57-68

(Bernice P. Bishop Museum, Bulletin 7, 1923)

2 copies

GN
Ethn.Pam.
3587

DESIGN   YABIM

Bodrgi, T.

Yabim drums in the Biró collection.

(Folia Ethnographica, I (2-4):205-222, 1949)

GN
Ethn.Pam.
3549

DESIGN   PACIFIC   INDONESIA AMERICA

Schuster, Carl

Joint-marks a possible index of cultural
contact between America, Oceania and the Far
East.

(K. Inst. voor de Tropen, Mededeling No.
94, 1951)

GN
2.1
A-M

DESIGN   SOLOMON ISLANDS

Balfour, Henry

Bird and human designs from the Solomon Islands, illustrating the influence of one design
over another.

(Man, vol. 5, 1905, no. 50, pp. 81-83, pl.F)

also

(Records of the Past, vol. 4, 1905, 253-255)

Am
101
A 71
(5)

DESIGN, DECORATIVE

Mead, Charles Williams, 1845-
... Peruvian art; a help for students of design, by
Charles W. Mead ... [New York] 1917.
cover-title, 16 p. illus., pl. 24½ᶜᵐ. (American museum of natural history ... Guide leaflet no. 46)
Bibliography: p. 15-16.

1. Art—Peru. 2. Design, Decorative. 3. Indians of South America—Art. I. Title.

Library of Congress   F3429.3.A7M4
                          [5]

19-4698

AS
720.S
S 72

DESIGN   PAPUA

Berndt, R. M.

The evolution of the human motif in Papuan
arrow designs.

(Records of the South Australian Museum,
Vol. 6, 1939, pp. 297-308)

[Gulf of Papua, - Toaripi, Nekeo, Central
District and Pt. ___ Moresby]

GN
2.1
A-m

DESIGN   SOLOMON ISLANDS

Joyce, T. A.

Forehead ornaments from the Solomon Islands.

(Man, Vol. 35, 1935, No. 108)

GN
2.1
W3

and

GN
Ethn.
Pam.
719

DESIGN, DECORATIVE

Spier, Leslie

An analysis of Plains Indians parfleche decoration. In Univ. Washington
Pub. in anthrop. Vol. I, pp 89 - 112, 1925

GN
1
An

DESIGN, DECORATIVE   INDONESIA

Vroklage, B. A. G.

Das Schiff in den Megalithkulturen Südostasiens und der Südsee.

(Anthropos, Bd. XXXI, pp. 712-757. 1936)

QK
923
S 64

DESMIDIACEAE

Smith, Gilbert Morgan

Phytoplankton of the inland lakes of Wisconsin. Part II: Desmidiaceae.

(Wisconsin Geological and Natural History Survey, Bull. 57, Part II, 1924)

DU
600
D 47

Destable, R. P.

La croix dans l'Archipel Fidji (de 1844 à nos jours.) by R. P. Destable and J. M. Sedes. Editions Spes. Paris. sm8vo. (1944), 222 pp.

GN
1
An

DESIGN, DECORATIVE   MELANESIA

Vroklage, B. A. G.

Das Schiff in den Megalithkulturen Südostasiens und der Südsee.

(Anthropos, Bd. XXXI, pp. 712-757. 1936)

QH
188
K 99

DESMIDIACEAE   JAPAN

Hirano, Minoru

Flora desmidiarum japonicarum.

(Contributions from the Biological Laboratory, Kyoto University, Nos. 1,2,4,5,7,9,11 1955-1960)

Destable, R. P. and Sedes, J. M.

La croix dans l'archipel Fidji. 1944

UH has

AS
182
Dr

DESIGN, DECORATIVE   NEW GUINEA

Schlaginhaufen, Otto

Verzierte Schädel aus Neuguinea und Neumecklenburg.

(Abhandlungen u.Berichte d.Kgl.Zool.u. Anthr.Ethnogr.Mus.z.Dresden, Bd.13, no. 4, 1910-1911)

S
399
E-7

DESMODIUM

Hosaka, Edward Y.

Kaimi Spanish clover for humid lowland pastures of Hawaii.

(Hawaii. Agric. Exp. Station, Circ. 22, 1945)

AM
101
M 98

Destrem, Jean

Catalogue raisonné du Musée de Marine, par Jean Destrem and G. Clerc-Rampal. Paris. Imprimerie Française. 1909. sm8vo. xiii + 517 pp (Musées Nationaux)

GN
Ethn.Pam.
3903

DESIGN   PRIMITIVE

Bühler, A.

Primitive Stoffmusterungen. Führer durch das Museum f. Volkerkunde, Basel. (1953)

[some Melanesian, no Polynesian]

QK
1
U

DESMODIUM

Rose, Joseph Nelson, 1862-
The American species of *Meibomia* of the section *Nephromeria*. By J. N. Rose and Paul C. Standley.

(*In* Smithsonian institution. United States national museum. Contributions from the United States national herbarium. Washington, 1903-24½ᶜᵐ. v. 16, pt. 5, p. 211-216. pl. 51)

"Issued February 11, 1913."

1. Desmodium.   I. Standley, Paul Carpenter, 1884-   joint author.

Agr 13-249

Library, U. S. Dept. of   Agriculture   450C76   vol. 16, pt. 5

DESVENTURADAS ISLANDS   FAUNA

See

FAUNA   DESVENTURADAS ISLANDS

DU
620
P

A desirable bird.

(Paradise of the Pacific, 17 (11):18, 1904)

[Asks for importation of Geococcyx to kill the mongoose.]

QL
1
C 15

DESMOPTERIDAE

Essenberg, Christine Elizabeth, 1879-
... The pteropod *Desmopterus pacificus* sp. nov., by Christine Essenberg. Berkeley, University of California press, 1919.

cover-title, p. 185-88. illus. 27½ᶜᵐ. (University of California publications in zoology. v. 19, no. 2)

"Literature cited": p. 88.

1. (Desmopteridae)   I. Title.

A 19-460

Title from Univ. of Calif.   Library of Congress
(4)

QL
401
H 39

Details of death from cone sting.

(Hawaiian Shell News, 9(5), 1961)

QL
435
D44

Desmarest, Anselme-Gaëtan

Considérations générales sur la classe des Crustacés et description des espèces de ces animaux qui vivent dans la mer, sur les côtes, ou dans les eaux douces de la France.

Paris, Lebrault, 1825.   432p. pls.

QL
381
A 26

Desor, Édouard

Agassiz, Louis i. e. Jean Louis Rodolphe, 1807-1873.
Monographies d'échinodermes, vivans et fossiles, par Louis Agassiz ... Neuchâtel, L'auteur, 1838-(42)
(490) p. 63 pl. (partly col.) 31½ᶜᵐ.
Various paging.
Issued in parts.
CONTENTS.—Échinites. Famille des cidarides. 1. monographie. Des salénies.—Observations sur les progrès récens de l'histoire naturelle des échinodermes. — Échinites. Famille des clypéastroides. 2. monographie. Des scutelles. 1841.—Échinites. Famille des clypéastroides. 3. monographie. Des galérites. Par Ed. Desor. 1842.—Échinites. Famille des clypéastroides. 4. monographie. Des *Dysaster*. Par Ed. Desor. 1842.—Anatomie des échinodermes. 1. monographie. Anatomie du genre *Echinus*. Par G. Valentin. 1841.
1. Echinodermata. 2. Echinodermata, Fossil.   I. Desor, Édouard i. e. Pierre Jean Édouard, 1811-   1882. II. Valentin, Gabriel Gustav, 1810-1883.

6-17840

Library of Congress   QL381.A3

QK
425
D

Detlefsen, J. A.

Genetic studies on a cavy species cross.

Carnegie institution of Washington, 1914. Pub. no. 205.

GN
2.S
B 91

Desmedt, G. Maurice

Les funérailles et l'exposition des morts à Mangareva (Gambier).

(Bull. Soc. des Americanistes de Belgique, Dec. 1932:128-136)

(Reviewed by K. P. Emory, in Jour. Poly. Soc. 42:125-127, 1933) see also ibid, p. 335

AS
36
S 1

Desor, Édouard i. e. Pierre Jean Édouard, 1811-1882.
Palafittes, or Lacustrian constructions on the Lake of Neuchatel. By E. Desor: with designs by Prof. A. Favre-Guillarmod.

(*In* Smithsonian institution. Annual report. 1865. Washington, 1866. 23½ᶜᵐ. p. (347)-409. illus.)

"Translated with the author's recent additions (by C. A. Alexander)"

1. Lake-dwellers and lake-dwellings—Switzerland.   I. Alexander, Charles Armistead, d. 1869? tr. II. Title.

S 15-181

Library of Congress   Q11.S66 1865
Library, Smithsonian   Institution

De Toni, G. B.

Sylloge algarum hucusque cognitarum. Vols. 1-5 Patavii (Padova) 1889-1907

UH has

(expensive)

GN
Ethn.Pam.
4004
Detwiler, Richard M.

Dog tooth money.   (Pacific)

(Frontiers, The Acad. of Nat. Sciences of Philadelphia, Vol. 19(3):67-69, February, 1955)

GN
651
D48
Deutschen Zentral-Afrika expedition 1907-1908
Wissenschaftliche ergebnisse unter fuhrung Adolf Friedrichs, Herzogs zu Mecklenburg.

Library has

Bd. VII.- Forschungen im Nil-Kongo-zwischengebiet. By Jan Czekanowski.,

---

DA
28.4
C 12
DEVEREAUX, ROBERT, EARL OF ESSEX

Cadwallader, Laura Hanes

The career of the Earl of Essex, from the islands voyage in 1597 to his execution in 1601. A thesis in history... Philadelphia. Univ. of Penn. 1923. 8vo. (xi)+128 pp.

DU
740
D 48
Detzner, Hermann

Vier Jahre unter Kannibalen, von 1914 bis zum Waffenstillstand unter deutscher Flagge im unerforschten Innern von Neuguinea. 3rd edition. Berlin. August Scherl. 1921. 8vo. 341 pp.

Atlas
Case
Deutscher Kolonial-Atlas

× Richard Kupert.

Berlin 1893. f

a. 11. 7

GN
22
W 31
Devereux, George

Normal and abnormal: the key problem of psychiatric anthropology.
IN

Some uses of anthropology...Anthropological Society of Washington, D. C. 1956 pp. 23-48

GN
Pam
2641
Deubner, Ludwig

Lustrum. From Arch. f. Religions-wissen. bd. 16, 1913.

DU
12
A 65
Deux océans   vols. 1 and 2

Arago, M. Jacques

AS
36
S 2
DEVIL FISH

Gill, Theodore

The story of the devil-fish.

(Smithsonian Misc. Coll., Vol. 52, 1910, pp. 155-180)

Deutsch Ost Africa

GN
653
F95
v. 9. Fülleborn, Friedrich. Deutsche Njassa und Ruwuma gebeit, land und leute.

QK
401
S93
v. 10. Stuhlmann, Franz. Beiträge zur kulturgeschichte von Ostafrica.

GN
2.S
T 12
Deuxieme fete du folk-lore tahitien, 11 septembre 1927.

(Bull. Soc. d'Etudes Oceaniennes, No. 21: 289-304, 1927)

[includes "Les marae de Papara, leur histoire", by Marau Taaroa i Tahiti; "Legende de Honoura i te pii marina", by Teraitua...]

Deville, Charles Sainte-Claire

See

Sainte-Claire, Deville, Charles

PL
711
D 48
Deutsche Lieder für die Nauru protestan-tische Schule. Drian in Deutsch. Kusaie. Missions Druckerai. 1903. sm8vo.

Nauru, hymns

DU
1
S 72 q
Devambez, Louis

A cruise in Orsom III. A first-hand account of a brief cruise ...recently commissioned oceanographic research vessel of the French Institute of Oceania, Noumea.

(South Pac. Commission Quarterly, 6(4):25-27, 1956)

Devins, John Bancroft   Carter 7-B-9   7-B-9

An observer in the Philippines or life in our new possessions. Boston... American Tract Society 416pp. 1905. r8vo.

DS 659
D 49
also copy in Bishop Museum Library

another in   HMCS

DU
10
D 48
Reading Room
Deutsche Seewarte

Segelhandbuch für den Stillen Ozean. Mit einem atlas von 31 karten. Herausgegeben von der Direktion (der Deutschen Seewarte) Mit 32 in den text gedruckten figuren und 9 steindrucktafeln. Hamburg. L. Friederichsen & Co. 1896-1897. xii + 916 pp. 4to and folio. Atlas in map case.

DEVELOPMENT MOLLUSCA

See

MOLLUSCA DEVELOPMENT

QK
1000
Ar
A66
DEVONIAN FLORAS

Arber, E. A. Newell

Devonian floras: a study of the origin of Cormophyta.

Cambridge Univ. Press, 1921, 100 pp. illus.

Deutsche Tiefsee-Expedition

See

Chun, Carl

Development of international cooperation in science. A symposium held in conjunction with the 3rd Ann. Meeting of the Executive Board, International Council of Scientific Unions. Oct. 18, 1951. Washington, D. C.   1952. 4to. 27 pp.

Pac. Sci. Association has

GN
2.S
P 76
Devonshire, C. W.

Rarotongan string figures.

(Jour. Polynesian Soc., Vol. 58(3):112-123, 1949)

De Vries, J. L.

See

Vries, J. L. de

DU
12
D51

Dewar, Thomas R.

Ramble round the globe.

London, 1894. 8vo. pp. 316.

Given by Mr. J. W. Waldron.

sco 2 '46

QL
596.B9
D 52

Deyrolle, Henri

Description des Buprestides de la Malaisie recueillis par L. Wallace pendant son voyage dans cet archipel.

(Annales de la Soc. Ent. de Belgique, Tome 8:1-172, 1864)

QL
1
A 94

Dew, Barbara

Observations on periodicity in marine invertebrates. By Barbara Dew and E. J. Ferguson Wood.

(Australian Journal of Marine and Freshwater Research, Vol. 6(3):469-478, 1955)

DU
12
D 51

D'Ewes, J.

China, Australia and the Pacific Islands in the years 1855-56. London, Richard Bentley, 1857. 8vo. 340 pp.

QL
403
D 53

Dezallier d'Argonville, Antoine Joseph

La conchyliologie, ou Histoire Naturelle des coquilles de mer, d'eau douce, terrestres et fossiles; avec un Traité de la Zoomorphose... Troisieme edition. 2 volumes and atlas of 80 plates. Paris, Guillaume De Bure, 1780. 4o.

QH
1
P 11

DEW

Leopold, Luna B.

Dew as a source of plant moisture.

(Pacific Science, 6:259-261, 1952)

GN
662
L 76

d'Harnoncourt, Rene

Linton, Ralph

Arts of the South Seas, by Ralph Linton and Paul S. Wingert... The Museum of Modern Art. Simon and Schuster. New York. 1946c. sm4to. 199 pp.

PL
Pam
#30

Dezeimeris, Reinhold

Remarques sur des inscriptions antiques recemment decouvertes a Bordeaux.

Bordeaux, 1880.

AS
36
S1

Dewar, Douglas, 1875–
The birds of India. By Douglas Dewar ...

(*In* Smithsonian institution. Annual report. 1908. Washington, 1909. 23½ᵐ. p. 617-639)

"Reprinted ... from Journal of the Royal society of arts, London, no. 2927, vol. LVII, December 25, 1908."

1. Birds—India.   15-21178

Library of Congress   Q11.S66 1908

Z
Bibliog
Pam No
40

Dewey, Melvil

A selection of cataloguers reference books in New York State Library. Univ. State of New York Bull. 302, pp 416,

---

GN
550
S

DHEGIHA LANGUAGE ✓

Dorsey, James Owen

Omaha and Ponka letters. Washington, 1891. 8vo. pp [Smithsonian Bur. Ethn. Bull. 11

E.14.

AP
2
N 4

Dewar, E. T.

International seaweed symposium.

(Nature, Vol. 170(4325):478-480, 1952)

Chart
No.
483
World

On wall

DeWit, A. F.

Nova orbis tabula in lucem edita.

No place, no date [1660 (?)]

An early map of the World 24 x20 in.

QL
1
B 93

Diakonoff, A.

Fauna buruana. Lepidoptera, Fam. Tortricidae

(Treubia, Vol. 18:213-216, pl. 7,8, 1941)

DU
12
D 51

Dewar, J. Cumming

Voyage of the Nyanza, R.N.Y.C.; Being the record of a three years' cruise in a schooner yacht in the Atlantic and Pacific, and her subsequent shipwreck. With a map and illustrations. London. William Blackwood. 1892. 8vo. xviii+ 466 pp.

PL
Pam
#29

Dewulf, E.

Inscriptions trouvées dans le cercle d'Ain - Beida pendant l'annee 1866. ex Annuaire de ? , 1867.

QL
546
D 53

Diakonoff, A.

Microlepidoptera of New Guinea. Results of the Third Archbold Expedition (American-Netherlands Indian Expedition 1938-1939)

Parts 1-5

(Verhandlingen K. Nederlandse Akad. van Wetenschappen, Afd. Natuurkunde, 2 Reeks, Deel 49(1,3,4), 50(1,3), 1952-1955)

---

also
IN
HMCS

Dewar, James Cumming.
Voyage of the Nyanza, R. N. Y. C., being the record of a three years' cruise in a schooner yacht in the Atlantic and Pacific, and her subsequent shipwreck. By J. Cumming Dewar ... Edinburgh and London, W. Blackwood and sons, 1892.

xviii, 466 p. front., illus., plates, fold. map. 22ᵐ.

1. Nyanza (Yacht) 2. Voyages and travels.

5—22524

Library of Congress   G463.D51

Deyrolle, Ach.

Coléoptères, being Annexe H of Maillard, L. Notes sur l'Ile de la Réunion.

HSPA

Micro-
film
142

Diakonoff, A.

Microlepidoptera. (New Guinea)

(Wissenschatliche Ergebnisse...Sumba Exp. in Mus. f. Volkerkunde u.des Naturhist. Mus., Basel, 1949:138-152)

Diakonoff, A.

Microlepidoptera of New Guinea. Pt. 1.
1952.

and probably the continuation also, as
does Bishop Museum

UH has

AS
36
S1

DIAMOND AND OTHER PRECIOUS STONES
Babinet, Jacques, 1794–1872.
The diamond and other precious stones. By M. Babinet ...

(*In* Smithsonian institution. Annual report. 1870. Washington, 1871.
23½ᶜᵐ. p. (333)–363)

"Translated ... by John Stearns, M. D."

1. Precious stones.   I. Stearns, John, tr. II. Title.

S 15–288

Library of Congress   Q11.S66 1870
Library, Smithsonian   Institution

QK
495.L 72
S 34

DIANELLA

Schlitter, Jakob

Monographie der Liliaceengattung Dianella
Lam. Inaugural-Dissertation...Universität
Zürich. Zurich, 1940. 8vo. 284 pp., 35 Tafeln

QL
Insects
Pam.
2110-
2111

Diakonoff, A.

Microlepidoptera from Sumba, parts I-II.

(Reprint, Verh. Naturf. Ges. Basel, Vol.
63(1):137-152, 1952; Vol. 67(1):55-61, 1956)

Title of part I omits "from Sumba".

QL
671
E 39

DIAMOND HEAD

Munro, George C.

Leahi Native Garden.

(Elepaio, Vol. XI(7):37-39, 1951)

AS
162
P 23

DIAPRIINAE

Kelner-Pillault, S.

Les Diapriinae (Hym. Proctotrupidae) des
Iles Philippines provenant de la collection de
L'Abbé J.-J. Kieffer.

(Bull. du Muséum National d'Histoire
Naturelle, Paris, Tome XXX(5):418-421, 1958)

Micro-
film
142

Diakonoff, A.

New Guinean Microlepidoptera, I-IV

(K. Nederlandse Akad. van Wetenschappen,
Amsterdam, Ser. C.:Biol. and Med., Vol. 55:383-
393; 394-406; 644-655; Vol. 56:474-485, 1952-53)

QE
Geol.Pam.
1008

DIAMOND HEAD

Wentworth, Chester K.

The Diamond Head black ash.

(Journal of Sedimentary Petrology, Vol. 7,
1937, pp. 91-103)

QP
1
C

DIAPTOMUS

Moore, Arthur Russell, 1882–
... Negative phototropism in *Diaptomus* by means of
strychnine, by A. R. Moore. [Berkeley, University of
California press] 1912.

p. (185)–186. 27ᶜᵐ. (University of California publications in physiology. vol. 4, no. 17)

"From the Rudolph Spreckles physiological laboratory of the University
of California."

1. Phototropism. 2. Diaptomus.

A 13–590

Title from Univ. of Calif.   Library of Congress

AS
222
G 33 d

Diakonoff, A.

A new species of Tortricidae from New
Guinea, collected by O. Beccari. (Lepidoptera
Tortricidae)

(Doriana, Vol. III, No. 105, 1960)

DU
620
P

DIAMOND HEAD

Why we call it Diamond Head.

(Paradise of the Pacific, Vol. 48(10):24-25,
1936)

AS
552
I

DIAPTOMUS FORMOSA

Kikuchi, Kenzo

A new species of Diaptomus from Formosa.

(Proc. of the Imperial Academy, Tokyo, vol.
12, 1936, pp. 198-199)

QL
461
B 86

Diakonoff, A.

A revision of the family Ceracidae (Lepidoptera Tortricoidea).

(Bull. Brit. Mus. (Nat. Hist.): Ent., Vol.
1(2):173-219, 1950)

AS
36
S1

DIAMONDS.
Crookes, *Sir* William, 1832–
Diamonds. By William Crookes, F. R. S.
(*In* Smithsonian institution. Annual report. 1897. Washington, 1898.
23½ᶜᵐ. p. 219–235)
"Printed in Nature, no. 1449, vol. 56, August 5, 1897."

1. Diamonds.

S 15–954

Library of Congress   Q11.S66 1897
Library, Smithsonian   Institution

QL
523.H7
S 35

DIASPIDIDAE

Schmutterer, Heinrich

Schildläuse oder Coccoidea. I. Deckel-
schildläuse oder Diaspididae.
IN
Die Teirwelt Deutschlands...van Friedrich
Dahl. 45. Teil, 1959. Gustav Fischer. Jena.

QL
461
B 86

Diakonoff, A.

The type specimens of certain Oriental Eucosmidae and Carposinidae (Microlepidoptera),
described by Edward Meyrick, together with descriptions of new Eucosmidae and Carposinidae in
the British Museum (Natural History).

(Bull. Brit. Mus. (Nat. Hist.): Entomology,
Vol. (4):275-300, 1950)

GN
2M
FI

DIAMONDS

Laufer, Berthold, 1874–
... The diamond; a study in Chinese and Hellenistic
folk-lore, by Berthold Laufer ... Chicago, 1915.

75 p. 24½ᶜᵐ. (Field museum of natural history. Publication 184. Anthropological series. vol. xv, no. 1)

1. Diamonds. 2. Folk-lore—China.

16–910

Library of Congress   GN2.F4 vol. 15, no. 1
(s19e1)

QL
Insect
Pam.
1822

DIASPIDIDAE

Takahashi, R.

Dimorphism in some species of Chionaspis
or Phenacaspis (Diaspididae, Coccoidea, Homoptera)

(Boll. Lab. di Zoo. Gen. e Agraria "Filippo
Silvestri", Portici, 33:48-56, 1953)

GN
4
D 53

Diamond, Stanley   editor

Culture in history; essays in honor of Paul
Radin. Published for Brandeis University, by
Columbia University Press. New York 1960.
R8vo. xxiv + 1014 pp.

AS
36
S1

DIAMONDS

Williams, Gardner Fred, 1842–
The genesis of the diamond. By Gardner F. Williams
...
(*In* Smithsonian institution. Annual report. 1905. Washington, 1906.
23½ᶜᵐ. p. 193-209. Illus., map)
"Reprinted ... from Transactions American institute of mining engi-
neers, 1905 ..."

1. Diamonds.

S15–1287

Library of Congress   Q11.S66 1905
Library, Smithsonian   Institution

QL
461
B 86

DIASPIDIDAE   INDO-MALAYA

Hall, W. J.

New Diaspididae (Homoptera:Coccoidea) from
the Indo-Malayan region. By W. J. Hall and D. J.
Williams.

(Bull. British Mus. (Nat. Hist.), Entomology
13(2); 1962)

QL
Insects
Pam.
1868

DIASPIDIDAE   JAPAN

Takahashi, Ryoichi

Descriptions of five new species of Diaspididae from Japan, with notes on dimorphism in Chionaspis or Phenacaspis (Coccoidea, Homoptera)

(Reprint, Misc. Reports of the Res. Inst. for Nat. Resources, No. 27:7-15, 1952)

QL
Prot.-
Poly. Pam.
99

DIATOMACEAE

Allen, Winfred Emory

Some tide-water collections of marine diatoms taken at half-hour intervals near San Diego, California.

(Univ. of California, Pubs. in Zool., Vol. 22, 1923, pp. 413-416)

GC
63
D 61

DIATOMACEAE

Hart, T. John

On the diatoms of the skin film of whales, and their possible bearing on problems of whale movements.

Discovery Committee
    Discovery Reports, Vol. 10, 1935, p. 247-282

QL
Insect
Pam.
1846

DIASPIDIDAE   JAPAN

Takahashi, Ryoichi

A new genus of Diaspididae from Japan (Coccoidea, Homoptera)

(Kontyu, 1957:102-105)

QL
Prot.-
Poly.
Pam.
98

and

QL
1
C 15

DIATOMACEAE

Allen, Winfred Emory

Statistical studies of marine diatoms of the San Diego region collected by U. S. S. Pioneer in midwinter 1923.

(Univ. Calif. Pub. Zool., Vol. 22, pp. 445-448, 1923)

AS
36
S2

DIATOMACEAE

Mann, Albert, 1853–

Diatoms, the jewels of the plant-world, by Albert Mann.

(*In* Smithsonian institution. Smithsonian miscellaneous collections. Washington, 1907. 24½ᶜᵐ. vol. XLVIII (Quarterly issue, vol. III) p. 50-58. illus., pl. XXII-XXV)

Publication 1578.
Originally published May 23, 1905.
Plates accompanied by two leaves with descriptive letterpress.
Lecture delivered at the U. S. National museum, Washington, D. C., March 18, 1905, under the auspices of the Washington Biological society.

1. Diatomaceae.   I. Title.

Library of Congress   Q11.S7 vol. 48   16-11028
———— Copy 2.
———— Separate.   QK569.D54M3

QL
Insect
Pam.
1847

DIASPIDIDAE   JAPAN

Takahashi, Ryoichi

Some Japanese species of Diaspididae (Coccoidea, Homoptera)

(Trans. Shikoku Ent. Soc., 5(7):104-111, 1957)

QL
Prot.-
Poly.
Pam.
200

DIATOMACEAE

Allen, Winfred Emory

Statistical studies of surface catches of marine diatoms and dinoflagellates made by the yacht "Ohio" in tropical waters in 1924.

(Trans. Amer. Microso. Soc., 1925, pp. 24-30)

(coast San Diego to Peru and Canal Zone, and Galapagos Islands)

AS
36
S1

DIATOMACEAE

Mann, Albert, 1853–

The economic importance of the diatoms. By Albert Mann.

(*In* Smithsonian institution. Annual report. 1916. Washington, 1917. 23½ᶜᵐ. p. 377-386. 6 pl. on 3 l.)

1. Diatomaceae.

                                           18-3069
Library of Congress   Q11.S66 1916

QL
Insects
Pam.
1734

DIASPIDIDAE   JAPAN

Takahashi, Ryoichi

Some new and little-known species of Diaspididae from Japan (Coccoidea, Homoptera)

(Annotationes Zool. Japonenses, 29(1):57-61, 1956)

QL
1
C 15

and

QL
Protozoa
Pam.100

DIATOMACEAE

Allen, Winfred Emory

Studies on marine diatoms and dinoflagellates caught by aid of the Kofoid bucket in 1922.

(Univ. of California, Pubs. in Zool., Vol. 22, No. 11, 1923, pp. 435-445)

QK
1
U

DIATOMACEAE

Mann, Albert.

... Report on the diatoms of the Albatross voyages in the Pacific Ocean, 1888-1904. By Albert Mann ⟨Assisted in the bibliography and citations by P. L. Ricker⟩ Washington, Govt. print. off., 1907.

v, 221-442, vii-viii p. xliv-liv pl. 24½ᶜᵐ. (Smithsonian institution. United States national museum. Contributions from the United States national herbarium. vol. x, pt. 5)
"Bulletin of the United States National museum. Issued July 11, 1907."

1. Albatross (Ship) 2. Diatomaceae.   I. Ricker, Percy Leroy, 1878–
                                               Agr 7-2037
Library, U. S. Dept. of   Agriculture 450C76 vol. 10, pt. 5

QL
Insects
Pam.1030

DIATHETES

Zimmerman, Elwood C.

A new Fijian Diathetes injurious to Pandanus (Coleoptera: Curculionidae).

(Proc. Haw. Ent. Soc., Vol. 10, pp. 335-338, 1939)

QL
Prot.-
Poly.
Pam.
129

DIATOMACEAE

Allen, Winfred Emory

Surface catches of marine diatoms and dinoflagellates made by the U.S.S. Pioneer between San Diego and Seattle in 1923.

(Univ. Calif. Pub. Zool., Vol. 26, pp. 243-248, pl. 25, 1924)

AS
182
V-s1

DIATOMACEAE

Richter, Oswald

Zur Physiologie der Diatomeen. In Akad. Wissens. Wien, Sitzungsb. math.-nat.Klasse, Bd. 115, pp 27- 119, 6 pls., 1906.

QK
Pam.
512

DIATOMACEAE

Allen, W. E.

Observations on surface distribution of marine diatoms between San Diego and Seattle.

(Ecology, Vol. III, No. 2, April 1922, pp. 140-145)

GC
1
S 43

DIATOMACEAE

Allen, Winfred Emory

Surface catches of marine diatoms and dinoflagellates made by U.S.S. "Pioneer" in Alaskan waters in 1923.

(Bull. Scripps Inst. Oceanography, vol. 1, No. 4, Berkeley, 1927, pp. 39-48, Tech. Ser.)

QL
5
B 61

DIATOMACEAE

Sverdrup, H. U.

Distribution of diatoms in relation to the character of water masses and currents off southern California in 1938, by H. U. Sverdrup and W. E. Allen

(Journal of Marine Research, Vol. II, 1939, pp. 131-144)

GC
1
S 43

DIATOMACEAE

Allen, Winfred Emory

Quantitative studies on inshore marine diatoms and dinoflagellates of southern California in 1921 and 1922.

(Bull. Scripps Instit. Oceanography, Vol. 1, No. 2-3, Tech. Ser., Berkeley, 1927, pp. 19-38)

QK
569.D54
B 79

DIATOMACEAE

Boyer, Charles S.

The Diatomaceae of Philadelphia and vicinity Illustrated with seven hundred drawings by the author. J. B. Lippincott Company. Philadelphia 1916. 4to. 143 pp., 40 pl.

QK
Bot.Pam.
2851

DIATOMACEAE

van der Werff, A.

Diatoms as a means for identifying the origin of aquatic plants.

(Blumea, Vol. VII(3):599-601, 1954)

QL
Prot.-Poly
Pam. 729

DIATOMACEAE

van der Werff, A.

On a characteristic diatom from the skin film of whales.

(The Amsterdam Naturalist, I:91-93, 1950)

QK
Botany
Pam.
1259

DIATOMACEAE   PACIFIC

Greville, R. K.

Descriptions of new genera and species of diatoms from the south Pacific from Trans. Bot. Soc. Edinburgh, Vol.7, 1863 and Vol. 8, 1866. 3 pls.

Q
115
R 29

DIATOMACEAE   SOLOMON ISLANDS

Peragallo, H.

Diatomaceae marinae, von H. u. M. Peragallo.

Rechinger, Karl
Botanische und Zoologische Ergebnisse einer Wissenschaftlichen Forschungsreise nach den Samoainseln, dem Neuguinea-Archipel und den Salomon inseln...1905. Teil IV: 1, pp. 3-11, 1911.

Q
115
M 46

DIATOMACEAE   ANTARCTIC

Mann, Albert
Diatoms

Mawson, Sir Douglas   leader
Australasian Antarctic Expedition, 1911-14.
Sci. Reports, Series C, Vol. 1, Part 1, 1937.

Q
115
S 97

DIATOMACEAE PACIFIC

Kolbe, R. W.

Diatoms from equatorial Pacific cores.
IN
Pettersson, Hans
Reports of the Swedish Deep-Sea Expedition, 1947-1948. Vol. VI: Sediment cores from the west Pacific, Fasc. 1, 1955

QL
Prot.-
Poly.
Pam.
768

DIATOMITE   PACIFIC   (COAST)

Mulryan, Henry

Fresh-water Diatomite in the Pacific Coast region.

(American Institute of Mining and Metallurgical Engineers, Technical Publication No. 1057, pp. 1-8, 1939)

QK
1
E 58

DIATOMACEAE   HAWAII

Lemmermann, E.

Die Algenflora der Sandwich-Inseln.

(Bot. Jarhbucher, Bd. 34, 1905:607-663)

AS
182
H

DIATOMACEAE   PACIFIC

Witt, Otto N.

Ueber Südsee Diatomaceen, II Folge.

(Jour. Mus. Godeffroy, Heft IV, 1873, pp. 111-118 [287-292])

G
161
H
v.40

Diaz del Castillo, Bernal

The true history of the conquest of New Spain. Ed. and published in Mexico by Genaro Garcia. Translated into English ......by Alfred Percival Maudslay. Vol.V, Hakluyt Society - Series II, Vol. XL.

Q
115
R 29

DIATOMACEAE   HAWAII

Peragallo, H. & M.

Diatomaceae marinae. Hawaii-Inseln.

(Rechinger's Bot.--zool.Ergebnisse von den Samoa- u. Salomonsinseln. Teil IV, 1911, pp. 9-11)

AS
182
H

DIATOMACEAE   PACIFIC

Witt, Otto N.

Untersuchungen Über Diatomaceen-Gemische; ein Beitrag zur Flora der Südsee.

(Jour. Mus. Godeffroy, Heft 1, 1873, pp. 63-70)
(title on p. 63: Bericht uber die Untersuchung zweier Diatomaceen-Gemische, ein Beitrag...)

GN
Ethn.Pam.
3665

Diaz Vial, Carlos

Asociacion de suelos de la Isla de Pascua.

(Agricultura Tecnica, Ano IX, Dec. 1949, No. 2:pp. 115-126)

Q
115
S 97

DIATOMACEAE   INDIAN OCEAN

Kolbe, R. W.

Diatoms from equatorial Indian Ocean cores.
IN
Pettersson, Hans
Reports of the Swedish Deep-Sea Expedition, 1947-1948, Vol. 9(1):1-50, 1957)

GC
1
S 43

DIATOMACEAE   PACIFIC COAST

Cupp, Easter E.

Marine plankton diatoms of the west coast of North America.

(Bull. Scripps Institution of Oceanography, Vol. 5, No. 1, 1943, pp. 1-238)

GN
Ethn.Pam.
3666

Diaz Vial, Carlos

Posibilidades agricolas de la Isla de Pascua.

(Geochile, Vol. 1(1):16-23, 1951)

GC
Oceano-
graphy
Pam. 31

DIATOMACEAE   JAVA

Allen, Winfred Emory

Plankton diatoms of the Java Sea, by Winfred Emory Allen and Easter Ellen Cupp.

(Annales du Jardin Bot. de Buitenzorg, Vol. 44, 1935, pp. 101-174)

AS
36
S5

DIATOMACEAE   PHILIPPINE ISLANDS

Mann, Albert

Marine diatoms of the Philippine Islands. U. S. Nat. Mus. Bull. 100, Vol. 6. Part 1, 1925, 182 pp, 39 pls.

S
Agric. Pam
54

Diaz Vial, Carlos

Los suelos y la agricultura de la Isla de Pascua.

Reprinted from Simiente, Vol. 17:213-219, 1947.

AS
540
P

DIATOMACEAE   NEW ZEALAND

Skvortzow, B. W.

Notes on the algal flora of New Zealand, I. Fresh-water diatoms from New Zealand.II. Fresh-water algae from Napier.
(Philippine Journal of Science, Vol. 67,1938, pp. 167-174: pp. 411-418 + 1 plate)

Q
115
R 29

DIATOMACEAE   SAMOA

Peragallo, H.

Diatomaceae marinae, von H. u. M. Peragallo.

Rechinger, Karl
Botanische und Zoologische Ergebnisse einer Wissenschaftlichen Forschungsreise nach den Samoainseln, dem Neuguinea-Archipel und den Salomon inseln...1905. Teil IV: 1, pp. 3-11, 1911.

PL
Phil.
Pam.
605

Dibabaon-Mandayan vocabulary.
Published by the Summer Inst. of Linguistics, in cooperation with the Bur. of Public Schools and the Inst. of National Language, Dept. of Education, Manila. Philippines. 1954. 8vo. 67 pp.

DU
625
D44

Dibble, Sheldon

History of the Sandwich Islands. Lahainaluna, Press of the Mission Seminary. 1843. 8 vo.
viii, 464 pp. 2 copies.

Over
Carter
Coll.
2-A-20

Also 1909 edition. Honolulu, Thos.G.Thrum.
428 pp. Appendices.

~~1839 edition~~
~~One copy of the~~ 1843 edition is in Locked Case

PL
Phil.
Pam.
662

Dibshu, I.　　Inibaloi.(dialect).
Summer Institute of Linguistics.　38 pp.

QK
Bot.Pam.
3015

DICHAPETALUM　MELANESIA

Leenhouts, P. W.

Some notes on the genus Dichapetalum (Dich-
apetalaceae) in Asia, Australia, and Melanesia.

(Reinwardtia, 4(1):75-87, 1956)

[Florae Malesianae Praecursores XII]

PL
623
G 16

Dibble, S.　　(Sheldon)

Gallaudet, T. H.

Hoike akua, he palapala ia e hoike ana ma na
mea i hanaia aia no he akua, he mana loa kona a
me ka ike kapanaha. Na T. H. Gallaudet i kakau.
Na S. Dibble hoi i unuhi. Lahainaluna. 1840.
178 pp. 12mo.

also 1842 ed. 174 pp.

(Natural theology, in Hawaiian)

QH
541
D 54

Dice, Lee R.

The biotic provinces of North America.
University of Michigan Press. Ann Arbor. 1943.
R8vo. viii + 78 pp.

QK
9
Don
D67

DICHLAMYDEOUS PLANTS

Don, G.

A general history of the dichlamydeous plants..... 4 vols.

London, 1831- 1838, 4to.

[Binder's title - "Don's Gardener's
Dictionary"]

PL
Phil.Pam.
395

(Dibble, Sheldon)

He hoikeholoholona na na kamalii. (Explanation of the animals that walk,- for children.)
Ekolu pai ana (3rd edition) Oahu. Mea pai palapala a na misionari. 1 37. 12mo. 76 pp.

Bound with "O ka ikemua he palapala..."

QH
549
D 54

Dice, Lee R.

Natural communities. University of Michigan
Press. Ann Arbor. 1952. R8vo. x + 547 pp.

QL
461
H-1

DICHROMOTHRIPS　HAWAII

Sakimura, K.

A revision of the genus Dichromothrips
Preisner.

(Proc. Haw. Ent. Soc. for 1954, Vol. 15(3):
583-600, 1955)

DU
620
H 5

Dibble, Sheldon　compiler

Lahainaluna School

Ka Mooolelo Hawaii: Hawaiian history, written by scholars at the High School, and corrected
by one of the instructors (Sheldon Dibble). Lahainaluna. 1838. (Edited by Reuben Tinker)

AN
2.E
P 78

(Hawaiian Spectator, Vol. 2, Nos. 1-4, pp.
58-77, 211-231, 334-340, 438-447,. Continued in
the Polynesian, Vol. 1, 1840, pp. 29,33,37,41)

QL
1
C 15

Dice, Lee Raymond, 1887-
... Distribution of the land vertebrates of southeastern
Washington, by Lee Raymond Dice. Berkeley, University of California press, 1916.
cover-title, p. (293)-348 incl. maps, tables. pl. 24-26. 27½ᶜᵐ. (University of California publications in zoology. v. 16, no. 17)
"Literature cited": p. 341-342.

1. Vertebrates—Washington (State)　i. Title.

A 16-878

Title from Univ. of Calif.　　Library of Congress

QC
Physics
Pam.
No. 4

Dickerson, Edward N.

Joseph Henry and the magnetic telegraph. An address delivered at Princeton
College, June 16, 1885.

New York, Scribner, 1885. pp 65.

PL
623
A 73

Dibble, Sheldon

Armstrong, Richard

Ka wehewehehala, oia hoi ka hulikanaka. Na
Limakaika (Armstrong) i kakau, na laua me Dibela
(Dibble) e hooponopono hou. Honolulu, Oahu.
Mea pai palapala a na misionari. 1847. sm8vo.
208 pp.

GN
488.2
D 54

Dice, Lee R.

Man's nature, and nature's man. The ecology
of human communities. The Univ. of Michigan Press
Ann Arbor. 1955. 8vo. 329 pp.

AS
36
S 4

and
QL
Fishes
Pam.
280
365

Dickerson, Mary Cynthia

Jordan, David Starr

On a collection of fishes from Fiji...

(Proc. U.S.Nat. Mus., 34, 1908, pp. 603-617)

Dibble, Sheldon　　Carter Coll.
1-B-19

Voice from abroad, or thoughts on missions,
from a missionary to his classmates. Lahainaluna
Press of the Mission Seminary. 1844. 130 pp.
sm4to

AS
36
S3

DICE

Culin, Stewart i. e. Robert Stewart, 1858-
Chinese games with dice and dominoes. By Stewart
Culin ...

(In U. S. National museum. Annual report. 1893. Washington, 1895.
23½ᶜᵐ. p. 489-537. illus. 12 pl. (1 col.))
Half-title.
Prepared to illustrate a portion of the collection of games in the U. S.
National museum, and enlarged from a preliminary study published in
1889 with title: Chinese games with dice.

1. Games, Chinese. 2. Dice. 3. Dominoes.　i. Title.

14-19793

Library of Congress　　Q11.U5 1893
---- Copy 2.
---- Separate.　　GV1303.C96 1895

Am
101
A 71
(5)

Dickerson, Mary Cynthia.
Trees and forestry: an elementary treatment of the
subject based on the Jesup collection of North American
woods in the American museum of natural history. By
Mary Cynthia Dickerson ... New York, The Museum,
1910.
104 p. incl. front., illus. 24½ᶜᵐ. (On verso of t.-p.: Guide leaflet series
of the American museum of natural history ... no. 32)
"Some books on trees and forestry": p. (7)

1. Trees—North America. 2. Forests and forestry—North America.
3. American museum of natural history, New York. Jesup collection of
North American trees.

11-16781

Library of Congress　　SD391.D6

DU
620
F

DIBBLE, SHELDON

Clark, E. W.

Brief notice of the life and labors of Rev.
Sheldon Dibble...

(The Friend, Mar. 1, 1845, pp. 33-36.)

QK
Bot.Pam.
3015

DICHAPETALUM　AUSTRALIA

Leenhouts, P. W.

Some notes on the genus Dichapetalum (Dich-
apetalaceae) in Asia, Australia, and Melanesia.

(Reinwardtia, 4(1):75-87, 1956)

[Florae Malesianae Praecursores XII]

---

quarto Dickerson, Mary Cynthia
see also
David Starr Jordan
On a collection of Fishes &

AS
36
C3

Dickerson, Roy Ernest, 1877–
... VI. Climate and its influence upon the Oligocene faunas of the Pacific coast, with descriptions of some new species from the *Molopophorus lincolnensis* zone. VII. Climatic zones of Martinez Eocene time. VIII. Ancient Panama canals. By Roy E. Dickerson ... San Francisco, The Academy, 1917.
cover-title, p. [157]–205. illus. (map) pl. 27–31. 25½ᶜᵐ. (Proceedings of the California academy of sciences. 4th ser. vol. VII, no. 6–8)
"Printed from the John W. Hendrie publication endowment."
1. Paleontology—Oligocene. 2. Paleontology—Pacific coast. 3. Paleoclimatology. 4. Paleontology—Eocene. 5. Geology—Panama.
18-11958
Library of Congress   Q11.C253 vol. 7, no. 6-8

QE
Geol.
Pam.
546

Dickerson, Roy E.
Review of Philippine paleontology. Reprint from Philippine Journ. Sc. Vol. 20, 1922.

QK
1
L2

Dickie, G.
Notes on Algae from the Island of Mangaia, South Pacific. Extract from (Linnean Soc. Journ- Botany, Vol.XV. pp 30-33. 1877)

(collected by W. W. Gill)

AS
36
C3

Dickerson, Roy Ernest, 1877–
... The fauna of a medial Tertiary formation and the associated horizons of northeastern Mexico, by Roy E. Dickerson and William S. W. Kew ... San Francisco, The Academy, 1917.
cover-title, p. [125]–156. pl. 17–26, fold. map, fold. tab. 25½ᶜᵐ. (Proceedings of the California academy of sciences. 4th ser. vol. VII, no. 5)
"Printed from the John W. Hendrie publication endowment."
1. Paleontology—Tertiary. 2. Paleontology—Mexico. I. Kew, William Stephen Webster, 1890– joint author.
18-11960
Library of Congress   Q11.C253 vol. 7, no. 5

QE
Geol.
Pam.
No.522

Dickerson, Roy E.
Tertiary and quaternary history of the Potaluma, Point Reyes and Santa Rosa Quadrangles, ex California Acad. of Sc. Proc., vol. XI, no. 19, 1922.

GN
2.S
P 76

Dickie, J.
Note on a salt substitute used by one of the inland tribes of New Guinea. By J. Dickie and D. S. Malcolm.

(Journal of the Polynesian Society, Vol. 49, 1940, p. 144-147)

QH
187
D49

Dickerson, Roy E
Distribution of life in the Philippines. Manila, Bureau of Printing, 1928.   322 p. pl.

(Monograph, Bureau of Science, Manila, Philippine Islands, No. 21)

DU
Hist.Pam.
67

Dickey, Charles H.
Ainokea. A Camping Trip on Haleakala, In the Hawaiian Islands, The Largest Extinct Crater in the World. Ottawa. (Illinois) Wm. Osman & Son. 1883. 8vo. 35 pp.

AS
36
S1

Dickinson, Andrew B.
Account of an eruption of a volcano in Nicaragua, Nov. 14, 1867. By A. B. Dickinson ...
(*In* Smithsonian institution. Annual report. 1867. Washington, 1868. 23½ᶜᵐ. p. 467-470)

1. Volcanoes—Nicaragua.
Library of Congress   Q11.S66 1867
Library, Smithsonian   Institution   S 15-238

AS
36
C3

Dickerson, Roy Ernest, 1877–
... The fauna of the *Siphonalia sutterensis* zone in the Roseburg quadrangle, Oregon, by Roy E. Dickerson ... San Francisco, The Academy, 1914.
cover-title, p. [113]–128. pl. 11–12. 25½ᶜᵐ. (Proceedings of the California academy of sciences. 4th ser. vol. IV [no. IV])
1. Paleontology—Oregon. 2. Paleontology—Eocene. I. Title: Siphonalia sutterensis zone.
17-1218
Library of Congress   Q11.C253 vol. 4, no. 4

QL
1
F

Dickey, Donald R.
The birds of El Salvador, by Donald R. Dickey and A. J. Van Rossem.
(Field Museum of Nat. Hist., Zool. Ser., Vol. 23, 1938)

QK
573
D 55

Dickinson, Carola I.
British seaweeds. Colour illustrations by Ernest V. Petts. Text illustrations by Ernest V. Petts and Lura M. Ripley. London. Eyre and Spottiswoode. 1963.   232 pp. sm8vo.

AS
36
C3

Dickerson, Roy Ernest, 1877–
... Fauna of the type Tejon: its relation to the Cowlitz phase of the Tejon group of Washington, by Roy E. Dickerson ... San Francisco, The Academy, 1915.
cover-title, p. [33]–98. pl. 1–11, 2 maps. 25½ᶜᵐ. (Proceedings of the California academy of sciences. 4th ser. vol. V, no. 3)
1. Paleontology—Pacific coast. 2. Paleontology—Eocene.
17-1223
Library of Congress   Q11.C253 vol. 5, no. 3

Dickey, Florence V. V.
Familiar birds of the Pacific southwest.
$4.50   1956?

?   (Californian Pacific?)

sent postal to Librarian, Los Angeles County Museum, for information: Pacific or Calif.?

QK
936
T 85

Dickinson, Fred E.
Properties and uses of tropical woods, I. By Fred E. Dickinson, Robert W. Hess, and Frederick F. Wangaard; II, by Robert W. Hess...
(Tropical Woods, No. 95, 1949) and No. 97, 1950

QE
Geol.
Pam.
#569

Dickerson, Roy E
Floristic and faunistic provinces and subprovinces of the Philippines. Geologic aspects of Philippine hydrography. Overdruk uit Handelingen van het Derde Nederl.-Indisch natuurwetenschappelijk Congres. 1924   28p., 7pls.

DU
620
H 4

Dickey, Lyle A.
Stories of Wailua, Kauai.
(Haw'n. Hist. Soc., 25th Annual Report, 1916, pp. 14-36)

DU
620
P

Dickson, Dickson
Wake Island
(Paradise of the Pacific,Vol.51, No.4, p.6, 1938)

AS
36
C3

Dickerson, Roy Ernest, 1877–
... Notes on a fauna of the Vigo group and its bearing on the evolution of marine molluscan faunas, by Roy E. Dickerson ... San Francisco, The Academy, 1921.
cover-title, p. 1–26. 25½ᶜᵐ. (Proceedings of the California academy of sciences. 4th ser. vol. XI, no. 1)
1. Paleontology—Tertiary. 2. Paleontology—Philippine Islands. 3. Mollusks, Fossil.
21-16428
Library of Congress   Q11.C253 vol. 11, no. 1
—— Copy 2.   QE736.D5
[7]

GN
671.H2
D 55

AS
763
D-b
Reading
Room

Dickey, Lyle A.
String figures from Hawaii, including some from New Hebrides and Gilbert Islands. Honolulu. 1928. R8vo.   168 pp. 2 pls.

(Bernice P. Bishop Museum, Bull. 54. 1928).

GN
Ethn.Pam.
2824

Dickson, Don F.
Dicksons Mound Builders Tomb, Lewistown, Illinois. (Lewistown, privately printed, ND, pamphlet of 8 pages and book of postcard views)

DU
850
D55

Dickinson, Joseph H   C

    A trader in the savage Solomons: a record of romance and adventure.

London, Witherby, 1927.   218p.   pls.

GN
Pam
196

Dickson, Oscar

    Expédition polaire Suédoise de 1878.
Passage du Nord-Est.

Upsala, 1879.

QL
Insect
Pam.
2069

DICRANOCEPHALUS

Linnavuori, R(auno)

    A new Dicranocephalus species from the Near East, D. pilicornis n. sp. (Het. Stenocephalidae)

    (Ann. Ent. Fenn. 27, 1962:83-89)

Q
115
H 23

Dickinson, Malcolm Gibson

    Sponges of the Gulf of California.

    IN Allan Hancock Pacific Expeditions, Vol. 11, No. 1, 1945. 55 pp., 97 pl.

GN
2.I
A-m

Dickson, T. Elder

    Ceremonial lime spatulae from British New Guinea.

    (Man, Vol. 43, 1943, No. 15)

QK
477
L 55

Dictionnaire descriptif et synonymique des genres de plantes phanérogames.

Lemée, Albert

DU
Pac.Pam
756

Dickinson, Sidney

    A trip to the Antipodes. No. 1.
(description of a trip from San Francisco to Hawaii)

    (what newspaper?, July 14, 1888)

GN
2.I
A-m

Dickson, T. Elder

    An unusual ceremonial lime-spatula from British New Guinea. By T. Elder Dickson and Ernest Whitehouse.

    (Man, Vol. 42, 1943, No. 29)

PL
63
Gr

Dictionnaire futunien-français.

Grezel, (Le Pere).

QL
Amphib.
and Rep-
tilia
Pam.
76

Dickinson, W. E.

    Field guide to the lizards and snakes of Wisconsin.

    (Milwaukee Public Museum, Popular Science Handbook Series, No. 2, 1949)

QK
Bot.Pam.
1768

DICKSONIA

Conard, Henry Shoemaker

    The Structure and Life-History of the Hay-scented Fern.

    (Carnegie Institution of Washington, Publication No. 94, 1908)

AH
Gn
A.6.

Dictionnaire International des Écrivains du Monde Latin par Angelo de Gubernatis

JAN 21 1907

Given by Dr. Brigham

DU
620
P

Dickson, Donald

    Wake Island.

    (Paradise of the Pacific, Vol. 51, No. 4, 1939, p. 6)

QK
Botany
Pam.
3320

DICKSONIA

Holttum, R. E.

    Morphology and classification of the tree ferns. By R. E. Holttum and U. Sen.

    (Reprint, Phytomorphology, Vol. 11(4): 406-420, 1961)

PL
92
P

Dictionaire Latin - Uvea à l'usage des eleves du College de Lano.

Paris, 1886. 185 pp.

DU
620
P

Dickson, Donald

    Hull Island.

    (Paradise of the Pacific, Vol. 51, No. 10, 1939, p.13,14)

AS
765
B b

QK
471
B 87

Reading
Room

DICOTYLEDONS

Brown, Forest B. H.

    Flora of southeastern Polynesia. III. Dicotyledons, by Forest B. H. Brown. Bayard Dominick Expedition, publication no. 22. Honolulu. 1935. 386 pp. 9 pl. 62 fig.

    (Bernice P. Bishop Museum, Bulletin 130)

DICTIONARIES

Trubner (publishing firm)

    Catalogue of dictionaries and grammars of the principal languages and dialects of the world. 2nd ed. 1882.

    UH has

AS
36
S1

Dickson, Henry Newton, 1866–
    The redistribution of mankind. By Prof. H. N. Dickson ...

    (In Smithsonian institution. Annual report. 1913. Washington, 1914. 23½ᶜᵐ. p. 553-569)

    "Reprinted ... from Report of the British association for the advancement of science, Birmingham, 1913, pp. 536-546. London, 1914."

    1. Anthropo-geography. 2. Natural resources. i. Title. Man

    15-1753

Library of Congress   Q11.S66 1913

QK
N 53

DICOTYLEDONS HAWAII

Sherff, Earl E.

    A name for the "Alpha" variety or forma of miscellaneous Dicotyledonous plants.

    (Brittonia, Vol. 6:332-342, 1948)

DU
621
H 39

Dictionary English-Hawaiian.

    (Hawaiian Tourfax Annual, Vol. 1, 1937,
pp. 52-62)

AG
5.
W 38   DICTIONARY

Webster's

Dictionary of synonyms. First edition.
A Merriam-Webster. A dictionary of discrimi-
nated synonyms with antonyms and analogous and
contrasted words. G. and C. Merriam Co. Springfield. R8vo. 1942c. xxxiv + 907 pp.

DICTIONARY   CELEBES

see

CELEBES   DICTIONARY

DICTIONARY   FRANCE

see

FRANCE   DICTIONARY

Front
Hall   DICTIONARY

Macmillan's modern dictionary. Compiled and
edited under the supervision of Bruce Overton.
The Macmillan Company, New York, 1938. xiii,
1466 pp. R8vo.

DICTIONARY   CHILE

see

CHILE   DICTIONARY

DICTIONARY   FUTUNA

see

FUTUNA   DICTIONARY

Director's   DICTIONARY
Office

Webster, (Noah)

Webster's new international dictionary of
the English language. Second edition, unabridged
An entirely new book...William Allan Neilson,
editory in chief, and others. G.C.Merriam Co.
Springfield, Mass. 1941. folio.

DICTIONARIES   DAKOTA INDIANS

see

DAKOTA INDIANS   DICTIONARIES

DICTIONARY   GAELIC

see

GAELIC   DICTIONARY

AH
5
Gu   DICTIONARY - BIOGRAPHICAL

Gubarnatis, A.

Dictionnaire international des ecri-
vains du monde Latin.

Rome and Florence, 1905 - 1906.

Library has Parts 1-3, 5,6.

Reading   DICTIONARY   DUTCH-ENGLISH
Room

Prick van Wely, F. P. H.

Kramers' Dutch dictionary. English-Dutch
and Dutch-English. 15th revised edition.
London. Bailey Bros... (1940.)   sm8vo. 1236
pp.

DICTIONARY   GERMANY

see

GERMANY   DICTIONARY

AH
25
am   DICTIONARY - BIOGRAPHICAL.

Who's who in America; a biographical dictionary of
notable living men and women of the United States,
vol. [1]-   1899/1900-
Founded, 1899. Rev. and reissued biennially. Chicago,
A. N. Marquis & company; [etc., etc., °1899-°19
v. 20ᶜᵐ. $5.00
Advertising matter included in paging at end of each volume.
Vol. 9 covers the years 1916-1917.
Editors: 1899-1907, John W. Leonard.—1907-   Albert Nelson Marquis.
1. U. S.—Biog.—Dictionaries. 1. Leonard, John William, 1849-   ed.
11. Marquis, Albert Nelson, ed.
                                        4—16934
Library of Congress   E663.W56
——— 2d set.
Copyright
920   [a19s20m3]   E83

DICTIONARY   EASTER ISLAND

see

EASTER ISLAND   DICTIONARY

DICTIONARY   GILBERT ISLANDS

see

GILBERT ISLANDS   DICTIONARY

DICTIONARY   ANEITYUM

see

ANEITYUM   DICTIONARY

Editor's   DICTIONARY   ENGLISH
Office

Fowler, H(enry) W(atson)

A dictionary of modern English usage.
Oxford. At the Clarendon Press. sm8vo. 1961
viii + 742 pp.

DICTIONARY   GREECE

see

GREECE   DICTIONARY

DICTIONARY   BRAZIL

see

BRAZIL   DICTIONARY

DICTIONARY   FIJI

see

FIJI   DICTIONARY

DICTIONARY   HAWAII

see

HAWAII   DICTIONARY

DICTIONARY HEBREW

see

HEBREW DICTIONARY

DICTIONARY MALAY

see

MALAY DICTIONARY

DICTIONARY NIUE

see

NIUE DICTIONARY

DICTIONARY HORNE ISLANDS

see

HORNE ISLANDS DICTIONARY

DICTIONARY MANGAREVA

see

MANGAREVA DICTIONARY

DICTIONARY PALAU

See

PALAU DICTIONARY

DICTIONARY HOLLAND

see

HOLLAND DICTIONARY

DICTIONARY MAORI

see

MAORI DICTIONARY

PL
490.NG
K 44

DICTIONARY PAPUA

Keysser, Christian

Worterbuch der Kate-Sprache gesprochen in Neuguinea: Dictionary of the Kate-Language as spoken in New-Guinea.

(Beihefte zur Zeitschrift für Eingeborenen-Sprachen 7th Heft, 1925)

DICTIONARY ITALY

see

ITALY DICTIONARY

DICTIONARY MARQUESAS

see

MARQUESAS DICTIONARY

DICTIONARY PHILIPPINE ISLANDS

see

PHILIPPINE ISLANDS DICTIONARY

DICTIONARY JAPAN

See

JAPAN DICTIONARY

DICTIONARY
DICTIONARIES MARSHALL ISLANDS

See

MARSHALL ISLANDS DICTIONARY

DICTIONARY POLYNESIA

see

POLYNESIA DICTIONARY

DICTIONARY KAPINGAMARANGI

See

KAPINGAMARANGI DICTIONARY

DICTIONARY MOTA ISLAND

see

MOTA ISLAND DICTIONARY

DICTIONARY PORTUGAL

see

PORTUGAL DICTIONARY

DICTIONARY MADAGASCAR

see

MADAGASCAR DICTIONARY

DICTIONARY NEW HEBRIDES

see

NEW HEBRIDES DICTIONARY

DICTIONARY ROTUMA

See

ROTUMA DICTIONARY

DICTIONARY ROVIANA

see

ROVIANA DICTIONARY

DICTIONARY SPAIN

see

SPAIN DICTIONARY

GR
35
L 43

Dictionary of folklore, mythology and legend.

Leach, Maria   editor

DICTIONARY RUSSIA

see

RUSSIA DICTIONARY

DICTIONARY TAGALOG

see

TAGALOG DICTIONARY

AG
100
H

Dictionary of scientific terms

Henderson, I. F.

Dictionary of scientific terms.

Edinburgh, 1920.

DICTIONARY SAMOA

see

SAMOA DICTIONARY

DICTIONARY TAHITI

see

SOCIETY ISLANDS DICTIONARY

AG
519.S
Da

DICTIONARY OF SEA TERMS

Dana, R. H.

The seamen's friend .....

Boston, 1865.

Q
123
T 97

DICTIONARY SCIENCE

Tweney, C. F.   editor

Chambers' technical dictionary, comprising terms used in pure and applied science, medicine, the chief manufacturing industries,..with definitions. Edited by C.F.Tweney and L.E.C.Hughes. New York. The Macmillan Company. 1940. 8vo. (8) + 957 pp.

DICTIONARY TONGA

see

TONGA DICTIONARY

AS
36
A 65-b

DICTYNIDAE

Chamberlin, Ralph V.

The spider family Dictynidae in America north of Mexico. By Ralph V. Chamberlin and Willis J. Gertsch.

(Bull. Am. Mus. of Nat. Hist., 116(1), 1958)

AG
192
F 63

DICTIONARY SCIENTIFIC WORDS

Flood, W. E.

Scientific words, their structure and meaning. Duell, Sloan and Pearce. New York 8vo. 1960c xix + 220 pp.

DICTIONARY TUAMOTUS

see

TUAMOTUS DICTIONARY

E
105 oP5
J73

Did the Phoenicians discover America?

Johnston, T. C.

DICTIONARY SOCIETY ISLANDS

See

SOCIETY ISLANDS DICTIONARY

DICTIONARY UVEA

see

UVEA DICTIONARY

AM
145.T
D 55

Didier, R.

L'art de la taxidermie au XXe siécle. Recueil de technique pratique de taxidermie pour naturalistes, professionnels, amateurs et voyageurs. Par R. Didier et A. Boudarel. Introduction pr le Dr. E. L. Trouessart. 57 fig 49 planches. Deuxieme tirage.

(Encyclopédie Biologique, XXX, 1948)

DICTIONARY SOLOMON ISLANDS

see

SOLOMON ISLANDS DICTIONARY

Ref.
Shelf

Reading
Room

DICTIONARY OF ENGLISH SYNONYMS.

Soule, Richard

A dictionary of English synonyms and synonymous or parallel expressions designed as a practical guide to aptness and variety of phraseology. New edition, revised and enlarged, by George H. Howison. Boston, Little, Brown and Company. 1899. 8 vo. vi + 488 pp.

QK
1
N 53

DIDISCUS PAPUA

Danser, B. H.

A new Papuan Didiscus.

(Brittonia, Vol. 2, 1936, pp. 135-136)

Dido (Ship)

DS
646.3
K38

Keppel, Henry.

The expedition to Borneo of H.M.S.
Dido...2 vols. 8vo.

London, 1847. illus.

DIEGUENO INDIANS RITES & CEREMONIES

see

RITES & CEREMONIES DIEGUENO INDIANS

QK
520
A 51

DIELLIA

Wagner, W. H., Jr.

The habitat of Diellia.

(American Fern Journal, Vol. 40(1):21-32,
1950)

G
7
R8

Dieffenbach, E.

Description of the Chatham Islands.
In Journ. Roy. Geog. Soc. , Vol. 11, p.
195; 12, p 142, 1840.

GN
Ethn.Pam.
3479

Diehl, Walter H.

Oceanic culture; a survey of Pacific island
culture illustrative of a special exhibition of
oceanic art, The City Art Museum of Saint Louis.
Nov.-Dec. 1945. 8vo. no pagination

[a few good pictures, text faulty]

QK
Bot.Pam.
1794

AS
763
B-4

Reading
Room

DIELLIA HAWAII

Smith, Frances Grace

Diellia and its variations. Honolulu. 1934

(Bernice P. Bishop Museum, Occasional Papers
Vol. X, No. 16. 1934.)

DU
406
D55

Dieffenbach, Ernest.

Travels in New Zealand; with contributions to the geography, geology,
botany, and natural history of that
country...2 vols.

London, John Murray, 1843. illus.

DU
620
H5

looked
case

Diell, John.

Oahu Charity School,

(Hawaiian Spectator I, 1838.pp.22-35.)

QK
520
A 51

DIELLIA HAWAII

Wagner, W. H., Jr.

A new species of Diellia from Oahu.

(American Fern Journal, Vol. 41(1):9-13,
1951)

QK
97
E 58

DIEFFENBACHIEAE

Engler, A.

Das Pflanzenreich, Heft 64 (IV. 28Dc), 1915.
Dieffenbachieae, by A. Engler.

DU
620
H 5

looked
case

Diell, John

Sketch of Honolulu, Oahu.

(Hawaiian Spectator, Vol. 1, No. 2, 1838,
pp. 83-93)

DIELLIA HAWAII

see also

FERNS HAWAII

DIEGO ALVAREZ (island)

See

GOUGH ISLAND

QK
Bot.Pam.
2762

DIELLIA

Wagner, Warren H. Jr.

An Asplenium prototype of the genus Diellia.

(Bulletin of the Torrey Botanical Club, Vol.
80(1):76-94, 1953)

GN
Pam
917

Diels, Hermann

Parmenides lehrgedicht Griechisch und
Deutsch.

Berlin, Reimer, 1897. 161p.

GN
2 I
Ca

PL
Pam
50

DIEGUENO INDIANS LANGUAGE

Kroeber, Alfred Louis, 1876–

... Phonetic elements of the Diegueño language, by
A. L. Kroeber and J. P. Harrington. Berkeley, University of California press, 1914.

cover-title, p. [177]-188. 27½ᵐᵐ. (University of California publications
in American archaeology and ethnology. v. 11, no. 2)

Bibliographical foot-notes.

separate

1. Diegueño language. I. Harrington, John Peabody, joint author.
II. Title.

A 16-596

Title from Univ. of Calif.   Library of Congress

QK
1
Ca

and
QK
524.D5
W 13

DIELLIA

Wagner, Warren H., Jr.

The fern genus Diellia, its structure, affinities and taxonomy.

(Univ. of California Pub. in Botany, 26(1):
1-212, pl. 1-21, 1952)

QK
1
E 58

Diels, L(udwig)

Anonaceae.

Volkens, G.
Beiträge zur Flora von Mikronesien. I.(Be-
ing part 1. of work continued by L.Diels,Beiträge
...)
(Bot. Jahrb. Bd. 52, 1915, pp. 16-18.)

DIEGUENO INDIANS RELIGION

see

RELIGION DIEGUENO INDIANS

QK
Bot.Pam.
2765

DIELLIA

Wagner, Warren H. Jr.

The genus Diellia and the value of characters
in determing fern affinities.

(Reprinted from The American Journal of
Botany, Vol. 40(1):34-40, 1953)

QK
1
E 58

Diels, Ludwig

Beiträge zur flora des Saruwaged-gebirges.

(Bot. Jahrb. Engler, 62:452-501, 1929)

QK
1
E 58

Diels, L(udwig)

Beiträge zur Flora von Mikronesien und Polynesien. I - V

(Botanische Jahrbücher, Bd. 52, 1915, pp.1-18; Bd. 56, 1921, pp. 429-577; Bd. 59, 1924, pp. 1-29; Bd. 63, 1930, pp. 271-323; Bd. 69, 1938, pp. 395-400;

over

QK
97
E 58

Diels, L(udwig)

Menispermaceae

Engler, Adolf

Das Pflanzenreich...IV. 94. 1910. (Heft 46.)

QK
1
P63

Diels, Ludwig

Die Pflanzenareale ... unter mitwirkung von Ludwig Diels und G. Samuelsson. Jena. 4to. 1926-

For current volumes see serial file

QK
410.S5
D 56

Diels, L(udwig)

Beiträge zur Kenntnis der Vegetation und Flora der Seychellen.

(Wissenschaftliche Ergebnisse der Deutschen Tiefsee-Expedition auf dem Dampfer 'Valdivia' 1898-1899...herausgegeben von Carl Chun, Bd. II, Teil 1, Lieferung 3, IV, Jena, Gustav Fischer, 1932. 4to. pp. 409-466, 1 karte, Tafeln 28-44)

Q
115
R 29

Diels, L(udwig)

Menispermaceae.

Rechinger, Karl
Botanische und Zoologische Ergebnisse einer Wissenschaftlichen Forschungsreise nach den Samoainseln dem Neuguinea-Archipel und den Salomonsinseln...1905. Teil V; pp. 110-112. 1913.

QK
Botany
Pam
1256

Diels, Ludwig

Die primitivste Form von Lygodium. Sonderabdruck aus Hedwigia, Band XLIV, pp 133 - 136, 1905.

QK
1
E 58

Diels, L(udwig)

Lauterbach, C. , . and others

Beiträge zur Flora von Papuasien. I- 26
(Bot. Jahrbücher, Bd. 49, 1913- 1922, 1942)

(for pages, see author card)

QK
1
E 58

Diels, L(udwig)

Die Moraceen von Mikronesien.

Diels, L.
Beiträge zur Flora von Mikronesien und Polynesien, V. No. 2.

(Bot. Jahrb. Bd. 69, 1938, pp. 397-400.)

QK
1
E 58

Diels, L(udwig)

Eine Scaevola von Mikronesien.

Diels, L.
Beiträge zur Flora von Mikronesien und Polynesien. II. No. 20.

(Bot. Jahrb. Bd. 56, 1921, pp.561.)

QK
266
D 56

Diels, Ludwig

Beiträge zur Kenntnis der Vegetation und Flora von Ecuador.

(Bibliotheca Botanica, Heft 116, 1937. 190 pp. Stuttgart)

QK
1
E 58

Diels, L(udwig)

Die Myrtaceen Mikronesiens.

Diels, L.
Beiträge zur Flora von Mikronesien und Polynesien. II. No. 15.

(Bot. Jahrb., Bd. 56, 1921, pp. 529-534.)

QK
1
E 58

Diels, L(udwig)

Die Theaceen Mikronesiens.

Diels, L.
Beiträge zur Flora von Mikronesien und Polynesien. II. No. 13.

(Bot. Jahrb. Bd. 56, 1921, p. 526.)

QK
266
D 56

Diels, Ludwig,

Contribuciones al conocimiento de la vegetacion y de la flora del Ecuador. Version castellana del Reinaldo Espinosa, de la edicion de Stuttgart, 1937. Quito, Imp. de la Univ. Central. 1939. 364 pp. R8vo.

QK
1
E 58

Diels, L(udwig)

Eine neue Menispermacee der Palau-Inseln.

Diels, L.
Beiträge zur Flora von Mikronesien und Polynesien. II. No. 5.

(Bot. Jahrb. Bd. 56, 1921, p.507.)

QK
Bot-Pam.
2578

DIELS, LUDWIG

Milbraed, J.

Ludwig Diels.

(Botanische Jarhbucher, Bd. 74(2):173-198, 1948)

QK
97
E 58

Diels, L(udwig)

Droseraceae

Engler, Adolf

Das Pflanzenreich...IV. 112. 1906. (Heft 26.)

QK
1
A 75

Diels, L(udwig)

New Guinea records of Annonaceae and Menispermaceae. Botanical results of the Archbold expeditions. (not numbered)

(Journal of the Arnold Arboretum, Vol. XX, 1939, pp. 73-74)

QL
391.T9
D 56

Diesing, K(arl) M(oritz)

Revision der Turbellarien. Abtheilung: Dendrocoelen, Rhabdocoelen, and Nächträge.

(Sitz. math. nat. classe, K. Akad. der wiss., Wien, Bd. 44, 1861, pp. 485-578; Bd. 45, 1862, pp. 191-318; Bd. 46, pp. 1-16.)

QK
101
G 65

Diels, Ludwig

The genetic phytogeography of the southwestern Pacific area, with particular reference to Australia.

Goodspeed, T. H.
Essays in geobotany...Setchell. 1936. pp. 189-194

QK
97
E 58

Diels, L(udwig)

Engler, Adolf

Das Pflanzenreich...Fortgesetzt von L. Diels (Heft 98a-h). 1934...

QL
Protozoa
to
Polyzoa
Pam
462

Diesing, K   M

Vortrāge. Revision der myzhelminthen. Abtheilung: Trematoden. (Vorgelegt in der Sitzung vom 24, 1858.

AS
36
S7   DIET

Slonaker, James Rollin, 1866–

... The effect of a strictly vegetable diet on the spontaneous activity, the rate of growth, and the longevity of the albino rat, by James Rollin Slonaker ... with one plate and fifteen text figures. Stanford University, Cal., The University, 1912.

36 p. incl. tables. pl., diagrs. 26ᵐᵐ. (Leland Stanford junior university publications. University series)

"References": p. [35]-36.

1. Diet. 2. Rat. 3. Vegetarianism.

Library of Congress   12-14518
———— Copy 2.   TX392.S5
             AS36.L5

DU
1
S 72 t   DIET   SAMOA

Malcolm, Sheila

Diet and nutrition in American Samoa, a survey.

(South Pac. Commission, Tech. Paper, No. 63, 1954)

GN
Ethn.Pam.
3622   Dietschy, Hans

Felix Speiser, 1880-1949.

(Verhandlungen der Schweizer. Naturf. Gesell. Lausanne, 1949:408-410)

GN
2.S
P 76   DIET   ELLICE ISLANDS

Turbott, I. G.

Diets, Gilbert and Ellice Islands Colony.

(Jour. of the Poly. Soc., 58:36-46, 1949)

QE
Pam
#236   Dietrich

L'Eruption du Krakatau,

Paris, 1884.

GN
662
B 29   Dietschy, Hans

Verwandtschaft und Freundschaft. Analytische Bemerkungen zur Socialstruktur der Melanesier von Südwest Malekula.
IN

Also
GN
Ethn.
Pam.
4414

Südseestudien, pp. 358-412, Basel, 1951.

GN
2.S
P 76   DIET   GILBERT ISLANDS

Turbott, I. G.

Diets, Gilbert and Ellice Islands Colony.

(Jour. of the Poly. Soc., 58:36-46, 1949)

Q
143.G5
S 76   DIETRICH, AMALIE

Spoehr, Florence Mann

White falcon: the House of Godeffroy and its commercial and scientific role in the Pacific. Palo Alto, Calif. Pacific Books. xiii + 120 pp. sm8vo.

QL
Insects
Pam.No
385   Dietz, Harry Frederic

Biological notes on the termites of the Canal Zone and adjoining parts of the Republic of Panama. Reprint from Journ. of Agric. Research Vol.XXVI, No. 7, Nov. 1923.

GN
407
P 85   DIET   INDONESIA

Postmus, S. and others

Nutrition bibliography of Indonesia. Compiled and annotated by S. Postmus, R. Luyken, and P. J. Van der Rijst. University of Hawaii Press. Honolulu. 1955. 8vo. ix + 135 pp.

QE
Geol.
Pam.
236   Dietrich ————

Les premières nouvelles concernant l'éruption du Krakatau en 1883. Dans les journaux de l'Insulinde. Extrait de la Revue Géographique Internationale (No.102, Avril 1884)
Paris, 1884, roy. 8vo, pp. 23, 1 map.

QL
Insects
Pam.
1149   Dietz, Harry F.

The Coccidae or scale insects of Indiana. By Harry F. Dietz and Harold Morrison. Office of State Entomologist, Indianapolis, Indiana. 1916. 8vo. pp. 195-321 (from Annual Report, 1916)

DU
80
A 93   DIET   NEW GUINEA

Hamilton, Lucy

Dietary survey in Malaguna Village, Rabaul. By Lucy Hamilton and Winifred Wilson.

(South Pacific, Vol. 9(3):400-406, 1957)

QK
97
D56   Dietrich, D. N.F.

Synopsis plantarum seu enumeratio systematica plantarum plerumque adhuc cognitarum cum differentiis specificis et synonymis ad modum Persoonii elaborata.

Vimariae, 1839- 1852, 5 vols.

QE
1
G 3   Dietz, R. S. and others

Phosphorite deposits on the sea floor off southern California.

(Bull. Geol. Soc. America, Vol. 53, 1942, pp. 815-848)

DU
Pac.
Pam.
977
739   DIET   PACIFIC

Buchanan, J. C. R. compiler

A guide to Pacific Island dietaries. On behalf of the South Pacific Board of Health 1947. 12mo. 75 pp.

GC
11
D 56   Dietrich, Günter

Allgemeine Meereskunde; eine Einführung in die Ozeanographie. Mit Beiträgen von Kurt Kalle. Gebruder Borntraeger. Berlin-Nikolassee R8vo. viii + 492 pp.

QE
1
J 85   Dietz, Robert S.

Hawaiian swell, deep, and arch, and subsidence of the Hawaiian Islands. By Robert S. Dietz and H. W. Menard.

(The Journal of Geology, Vol. 61(2):99-113, 1953)

DU
1
S 72 q   DIET   PACIFIC

Oomen, H. A. P. C.

Maternal and infant diets in the South Pacific.

(South Pacific Commission Quarterly Bulletin Vol. 6(2):6-9,56, April, 1956)

QL
401
N   Dietrich, Richard V.

Mollusks from Kwajalein. By Richard V. Dietrich and Percy A. Morris.

(Nautilus, 67(1):13-18, 1953)

QE
1
G 3   Dietz, Robert S.

Marine geology of northwestern Pacific: description of Japanese bathymetric chart 6901.

(Bull. Geol. Soc. of America, 65 (No. 12, Part 1), pp. 1199-1224, 1954)

[the chart placed in map collection, under Maps-Western Pacific]

GC
1
S 43

Dietz, Robert

The Pacific floor.

(Scripp Inst. of Oceanography, Contrib., 1952
No. 564; from Sci. American, 186(4):5 pp. unnumbered, 1952)

GN
775
M 13

DIFFUSION

Merrill, Elmer Drew

Domesticated plants in relation to the diffusion of culture.
IN
MacCurdy, George Grant   editor
Early man as depicted by leading authorities
at the international symposium...1937. Philadelphia. pp. 277-284.

GN
2.S
P 76

DIFFUSION   MELANESIA AMERICA

Emory, Kenneth Pike

Oceanian influence on American Indian culture.

(Journal of the Pllynesian Society, Vol.
51, 1942, pp. 126-135)

AP
2
A 5

Dietz, Robert S.

Carsola, Alfred J.

Submarine geology of two flat-topped northeast Pacific seamounts. By Alfred J. Carsola
and Robert S. Dietz.

(Am. Jour. Sci., Vol. 250:481-497, 1952)

GN
451
R 62

DIFFUSION

Rivers, W. H. R.

Psychology and Ethnology...London...1926.

GN
Ethn.Pam.
3892

DIFFUSION   OLD WORLD   NEW WORLD

Seder, Theodore A.

Old world overtones in the new world; some
parallels with North American Indian musical instruments.

(University Museum Bulletin, Univ. of Penn.,
Vol. 16(4); 1952)

G
3
N 27

Diffenderfer, Hope A.

Okinawa, the island rebuilt.

(The National Geographic Magazine, Vol.
CVII(2):265-288, February, 1955)

GN
400
S 64

DIFFUSION

Smith, G. Elliot

Culture: the diffusion controversy...London
1928.

GN
2.I
A-m

DIFFUSION   PACIFIC

Hedley, Charles

Transport of the coco-nut across the Pacific. Ocean.

(Man, Vol. 17, 1917, No. 6, pp. 12-13)

GN
1
A

DIFFUSION

Boas, Franz

Evolution or Diffusion?

(American Anthropologist, N. S.,
Vol. 26, 1924, pp. 340-344)

DIFFUSION

See also

CONTACT

GN
1
F

and
EthnPam. 232)
646

DIFFUSION   PACIFIC

Hocart, A. M.

The convergence of customs.

(Folk-lore, vol. 34, Sept. 1923, pp. 224-

GN
320
D 62

DIFFUSION

Dixon, Roland B.

The building of Cultures. New York. 1928.

QK
Bot.
Pam.
2709

DIFFUSION

Merrill, E. D.

Domesticated plants in relation to the
diffusion of culture.

(Reprinted from Botanical Review, 4:1-20,1938

GN
1
A

GN
Ethn.Pam.
3095

DIFFUSION - PACIFIC - AMERICA

Davidson, D. S.

Knotless netting in America and Oceania.

(American Anthropologist, vol. 37, no. 1,
pt. 1, Jan.-Mar., 1935, pp. 117-134)

AS
522.S
R 13

DIFFUSION

Evans, Ivor H. N.

"Melanesoid" culture in Malaya.

(Bulletin of the Raffles Museum, Ser. B,
Vol. 1:141-146, 1937)

GN
Ethn.Pam.
3107

DIFFUSION   AUSTRALIA-AMERICA

Rivet, P.

Les Australiens en Amerique.

(Bulletin de la Société de Linguistique de
Paris, Tome 26, 1925, pp. 23-63)

AS
36
S 2

DIFFUSION   PACIFIC   AMERICA

Hrdlicka, Ales

Melanesians and Australians and the peopling
of America.

(Smithsonian Miscellaneous Collections,
Vol. 94, No. 11, 1935)

GN
Ethn.Pam.
2841

DIFFUSION

Imbelloni, J.

El Toki Magico - La fórmula de encantamiento
del carpintero Maori al derribar un árbol,
conservada textualmente en el cuento chileno del
viejo Tatrapay

De los Anales de las Soc. Científica de
Santa Fe, tomo III, pag. 128 y sig. (24 pp.)
1931. 8vo.

GN
Ethn. Pam.
3124

DIFFUSION   EASTER ISLAND-ASIA

Hevesy, Guillaume de

Océanie et Inde Préaryenne:Mohgenjo Daro et
L'Ile de Paques.

(Bulletin de L'Association Française des
Amis de l'Orient, No. 14-15, 1933, pp. 29-50)

Q
101
P 18

DIFFUSION   PACIFIC   AMERICA

Merrill, E. D.(Elmer Drew)

The problem of economic plants in relation
to man in pre-Columbian America.

(Proc. of the Fifth Pacific Science Congress, vol. 1, pp. 759-767, 1933)

GN
2 S
P 76

DIFFUSION PACIFIC ASIA

Tregear, Edward

Asiatic Gods in the Pacific.

(Journal of the Polynesian Society, Vol.II,
1893, pp. 129-146)

QL
Mollusca
Pam. 774

DIFFUSION - POLYNESIA - AMERICA

Hertlein, Leo George

A note on some species of marine mollusks
occuring in both Polynesia and the western
Americas.

(Proc. Am. Philosophical Soc., Vol. 78, 1937,
pp. 303-312)

QK
495.D5
H 51

DIGITARIA

Henrard, J. Th.

Monograph of the genus Digitaria.

Universitaire Pers Leiden. Leiden. 1950. R8vo.
xxi + 999 pp.

AP
2
N 4

DIFFUSION-PACIFIC-ASSAM

Hutton, J. H.

Assam origins in relation to Oceania.

(Nature, Vol. 140, 1937, pp. 487-469)

GN
2.S
P 76

DIFFUSION POLYNESIAN ARYAN

Smith, S. Percy

Aryan and Polynesian points of contact. The
Story of Te Niniko.

(Journal of the Polynesian Society, 19:
84-88, 1910.)

also
GN
2.S
P 76

The Fatherland of the Polynesians. No. 4

(Jour. of the Poly. Soc.:28:18-30, 1919)

QK
1
E 58

DIGITARIA

Mez, C.

Digitaria marianensis.

Diels, L.
Beiträge zur Flora von Mikronesien und Polynesien, III.

(Bot. Jahrb., Bd. 59, 1925, p. 1.)

GN
1
M 26

DIFFUSION PACIFIC INDIA

Handy, E.S. Craighill

Indian cultural influence in Oceania.

(Man in India, vol. 8, no. 1, 1928, pp. 1-5)

GN
775
M 13

DIFFUSION TRANS-PACIFIC

Davidson, Daniel Sutherland
The antiquity of man in the Pacific and the
question of trans-Pacific migrations.
MacCurdy, George Grant
Early man as depicted by leading authorities
at the international symposium, the Academy of
Natural Sciences, Philadelphia, March, 1937...
Philadelphia, 1937.   pages 269-276

QK
Bot.Pam.
2598

DIGITARIA JAPAN

Tuyama, Rakesi

Notes on Japanese Digitaria.

(Syokubutu Kenkyu Zassi (Journal of Japanese
Botany, Vol. 18(1):6-21, 1942)

[translated by G. Luhrs Stroud; edited by F.
Raymond Fosberg]

GN
1
M 26

DIFFUSION PACIFIC INDIA

Hutton, J. H.

Assam and the Pacific.

(Man in India, vol. 4, nos. 1,2, 1924, pp.
1-13)

GN
22
S 64

The Diffusion of Culture.

Smith, G. Elliot

QK
368
D 57

Diguangco, Jose

Notes on Philippine medicinal plants.
University of Sto. Tomas Press.   Manila. 1950.
8vo.   146 pp.

GN
Ethn. Pam.
3125

DIFFUSION PACIFIC-SOUTH AMERICA

Imbelloni, Jose

Toki: La primera cadena isoglosematica es-
tablecida entre las islas del Oceano Pacifico
y el Continente Americano.

(Revista de la Sociedad "Amigos de la Arqueologia", Tomo 5, 1931, pp. 1-25)

GN
2.I
A-m

Digby, Adrian

Origin of the Double Stabilizer on Canoes.

(Man, Vol. 33, 1933, No. 147)

QH
11
L97

Dijmphna-togtets zoologisk-botaniske Udbytte

Lutken, Chr   Fr

GN
Ethn.Pam.
3411

DIFFUSION POLYNESIA   (western)

Buck, Peter H.

Pan-pipes in Polynesia.

(Jour. Polynesian Soc., Vol. 50, 1941, pp.
173-184)

GN
2.I
A-m

Digby, Adrian

Shark-tooth wristlets in Oceania.

(Man, 48, No. 54, 1948)

DU
12
D57

Dilke, Charles Wentworth

Greater Britain: a record of travel in
English-speaking countries during 1866 & 1867.
2 vols.
London, 1868, 8vo. pp. 402, + 426, illus., maps.

GN
2.S
P 76

DIFFUSION POLYNESIA AMERICA

Emory, Kenneth Pike

Oceanian influence on American Indian culture.

(Journal of the Polynesian Society, Vol.
51, 1942, pp. 126-135)

GN
Ethn.
Pam.
4085

[Digest of material culture. Ryukyu Government Committee on Preservation of Material Culture. 1957.]

entirely in Japanese. unbound. sm4to.

AS
36
A5

Dill, H. R. (Homer R.)

The albatrosses of Laysan island.
in Am. Mus. Journ., XIII, 4, 1913, pp. 185-192.

AM
Mus.
Pam.
492

Dill, Homer R.

The correlation of art and science in the museum.

(Museum Graphic, Vol. 15(4):10-12, 1963)

GN
Pam
1819

Dillenius, J. A.

Observaciones arqueologicas sobre alfareria funeraria de la "poma". From Rev. d. la Univ. Buenos Aires, 1909.

AG
100
U

Dillingham, William P.

Dictionary of races or peoples: Report of the Immigration Commission, 61st Congress, 3d Sess. Doc. No. 662, Washington, 1911. pp 150.

QH
104
U-b
and
QL
Birds
Pam.
126

Dill, Homer R.

... Report of an expedition to Laysan Island in 1911 under the joint auspices of the United States Department of agriculture and University of Iowa, by Homer R. Dill ... and Wm. Alanson Bryan ... Washington, Govt. print. off., 1912.

30 p. incl. map. ix pl. on 5 l. 23ᵐᵐ. (U. S. Dept. of agriculture. Biological survey. Bulletin no. 42)

1. Hawaiian Islands reservation. 2. Birds, Protection of. ι2. Bird protection\3. Birds—Hawaiian Islands.\4. Laysan (Island) \ι. Bryan, William Alanson, 1875— joint author.

Agr 12-991 Revised

Library, U. S. Dept. of   Agriculture 1B52B no. 42
ιr20h7ι

DU
Hist.
Pam.
614

DILLINGHAM, BENJAMIN F.

(Wright, John)

Benjamin Franklin Dillingham, 1844-1918. IN
Oahu Railway and Land Company, 69th Ann. Rept., 1959:1-3

QL
595.F
D 57

Dillon, Elizabeth S.

Dillon, Lawrence S.

Cerambycidae of the Fiji Islands. By Lawrence S. Dillon and Elizabeth S. Dillon.

(Bernice P. Bishop Museum, Bulletin 206, 1952)

QH
104
U-b

Dill, Homer R.

Report on conditions on Laysan, with recommendations for protecting the Hawaiian Islands Reservation. By Homer R. Dill and W. A. Bryan.

(U. S. Dept. Agric., Biol. Survey, Bull. 42, 1912.)

Q
Biogr.
Pam.
115

DILLINGHAM, BENJAMIN FRANKLIN

Oahu Railway and Land Company, 69th Ann. Report, 1959; contains biography of Benjamin Franklin Dillingham. 20 pp.

QL
581
D 57

Dillon, Elizabeth S.

A manual of common beetles of Eastern North America. By Elizabeth S. Dillon and Lawrence S. Dillon. Row, Peterson and Company. Evanston Illinois. 8vo. 1961c viii + 884 pp., 544 figs. 4 colored plates.

QL
Birds
Pam.
394

Dill, Homer R.

Skinning a bird for taxidermy.

(Museum Graphic, Vol. 9(1):18-20, 1957)

GR
385.H
D 57

Dillingham, Emma L.   and others

Six Prize Hawaiian Stories of the Kilohana Art League. Honolulu Gazette Company. 1899. 12mo. 123 pp.
Kalani-Emma L. Dillingham
A Legend of Haleakala-Geo. H. De La Vergne
Peleg Chapman's Sharks-W. N. Armstrong
'Twas Cupid's Dart-J.W.Girvin
Legend of Hiku i Kanahele-Mauricio
The Story of a Brave Woman-A Native

QK
495.O 64
D 57

Dillon, Gordon W.

Proceedings of the Second World Orchid Conference, September 19-23, 1957, Honolulu, Hawaii. Printed...by Harvard University Printing Office. Cambridge, Massachusetts. 1958. xii + 253 pp.

QH
Nat.Hist.
Pam.
228

Dill, Homer R.

Taxidermy for the tyro: mounting a squirrel.

(Museum Graphic, St. Joseph Museum, Mo., 14(4), 1962)

DU
620
P 22

Dillingham, Harold G., Jr.

Hawaii's scientists look west.

(Paradise of the Pacific, Oct. 1957:22-23)

QL
595.F
D 57

Dillon, Lawrence S.

Cerambycidae of the Fiji Islands. By Lawrence S. Dillon and Elizabeth S. Dillon.

(Bernice P. Bishop Museum, Bulletin 206, 1952)

QK
1
B 65

DILLENIA

Hoogland, R. D.

A revision of the genus Dillenia.

(Blumea, Vol. 7(1):1-145, 1952)

DU
Pac.Pam.
1000

Dillingham, Lowell S.

Art at Ala Moana; shopping center of the Pacific. Hawaiian Land Company, Limited. 8vo. ob Jan. 1963 16 pp.

DU
12
D 57
looked
case

Dillon, Peter

Narrative and successful result of a voyage in the South Seas, performed by order of the government of British India, to ascertain the actual fate of La Pérouse's Expedition, interspersed with accounts of the religion, manners, customs, and cannibal practices of the South Sea Islanders, by the Chevalier Capt. P. Dillon...In two volumes London. Hurst, Chance. 1829. 8vo. pp.lxix + 302; (5)+436.

QK
Bot.Pam.
3119

DILLENIACEAE

Hoogland, R. D.

Additional notes on Dilleniaceae 1-9.

(Blumea, 9(2):579-589, 1959)

DU
620
P 22

DILLINGHAM, WALTER FRANCIS

Hogue, C.E.

Walter Francis Dillingham. Code of master builder: do better than was promised.

(Paradise of the Pacific, Vol. 69(2): 25, 32, February, 1957)

DU
12
D 57
looked
case

Dillon, Peter

Voyage aux iles de la mer du sud, en 1827 et 1828, et relation de la découverte du sort de La Pérouse. Dédié au roi, par le Capitaine Peter Dillon...Tome Premier; Tome Second. Paris. Pillet. 1830. 8vo. pp.lx+294; 361.

GN
2.S
O 15

DILLON, PETER

Davidson, J. W.

Peter Dillon and the discovery of sandalwood in the New Hebrides.

(Jour. Soc. des Océanistes, 12:99-106, 1956)

AS
36
S4

DIMETRODON GIGAS.
Gilmore, Charles Whitney, 1874–

A mounted skeleton of *Dimetrodon gigas* in the United
States National museum, with notes on the skeletal anatomy. By Charles W. Gilmore ...

(*In* U. S. National museum. Proceedings. Washington, 1920. 23½°°.
v. 56, p. 525-539. illus., pl. 70-73 on 2 l.)

1. Dimetrodon gigas.

Library of Congress   Q11.U55   vol. 56   20-9677

————— Copy 2.   Q11.U55   vol. 56   2d set

[5]

Ding Hou

See

Hou, Ding

GN
2.S
O 15

DILLON, PETER

Davidson, J. W.

Peter Dillon and the discovery of sandalwood
in the New Hebrides.

(Jour. Soc. des Océanistes, 12:99-106, 1956)

QL
Insect
Pam.
735

Dimmock, George

The anatomy of the mouth-parts and of the
sucking apparatus of some diptera. Dissertation
...Leipzig University, 1881.

Z
4001
S 91

Dinginger, P. Johannes

Striet, P. Robert

Bibliotheca missionum. Begonnen von P.
Robert Streit, fortgeführt von P. Johannes Din-
dinger. Bd. 21:Missionsliteratur von Australien
und Oceanien, 1525-1950. Verlag Heider. Freiburg. 1955. 8vo. xv + 796 pp.

Q
Biography
Pam. 76

Dillon, Richard H.

"And did a gunner kill..."

(Sutro Library Notes, Vol. 2(2):2-9, 1956)

[biography of Captain William Kidd]

DU
Hist.Pam.
26

Dimond, E. H.

The Subject of the Time according to Justice
and Law.   (anti-annexation statement)

G
51
W 17

DINGO

Cronin, Bernhard

Pariah of our wild creatures.

(Walkabout, 15(1):11-14, 1953)

[the dingo, or Australian dog]

DU
Hist.Pam.
407

Dillon, Richard H.

Kanaka colonies in California.

(Pacific Historical Review, February, 1955:
17-23, 1955)

QK
Bot.
Pam.
3198

DIMORPHANTHERA

Sleumer, H.

Florae Malesianae precursores XXVI, the
genus Dimorphanthera F. V. M.

(Nova Guinea, Botany, No. 7, 1961)

GN
2.1
N

DINGO

Etheridge, R. Junr.

Warrigal, or "Dingo," introduced or
indigenous?. in N.S.Wales Geol. Survey
Mem. Ethn. Ser. no. 2. pp. 43-51, pls. X-XII.
no Date!

QL
402
G 23

[Vol.
5-6]

locked
case

Dillwyn, Lewis Weston, 1778–1855.

A descriptive catalogue of recent shells, arranged according to the Linnæan method; with particular attention
to the synonymy. By Lewis Weston Dillwyn ... London, Printed for J. and A. Arch, 1817.

2 v. in 1. 22°°.

Paged continuously; v. 1: xii, 580 p.; v. 2: 2 p. l., [581]-1092, [29] p.

*of the Garrett collection

*1. Shells. 2. Mollusks. Mollusca

Library of Congress   QL403.D57   6-41364†
———— Copy 2.
In 2 vol., bound   separately.
Vol. 2 imperfect;   half-title wanting.

QL
1
C15

DIMORPHISM, SEXUAL.

Torrey, Harry Beal, 1873–

... Sexual dimorphism in *Aglaophenia*. By Harry Beal
Torrey and Ann Martin. [Berkeley, The University
press] 1906.

p. [47]-52. illus. 27°°. (University of California publications. Zoology. v. 3, no. 4)

At head of title: Contributions from the laboratory of the Marine bio-
logical association of San Diego. XI.
Issued in single cover with v. 3, no. 3 of the series.
Bibliography: p. 52.

1. Aglaophenia. [2. Dimorphism, Sexual] 3. Sex (Biology) I. Martin, Ann, joint author. II. Title.

Title from Univ. of Calif.   Library of Congress   A 11-2285

AS
719
A 93 m

DINGO

Marlow, B. J.

Dingoes.

(Australian Natural History, 14(2):61-63,
1962)

QK
Bot.Pam.
2279

2253

DILLWYNIA

Blakely, W. F.

A key to the New South Wales species of
Dillwynia.

(The Australian Naturalist, Vol. 10, Part 5,
1939, pp. 157-168; 181-187)

AS
36
S4

DIMYA.

Bartsch, Paul, 1871–

... The Philippine mollusks of the genus *Dimya*. By
Paul Bartsch ...

(*In* U. S. National museum. Proceedings. Washington, 1913. 23½°°.
v. 45, p. 305-307. pl. 27-28)

"Scientific results of the Philippine cruise of the fisheries steamer 'Albatross,' 1907-1910.—no. 27."

1. Dimya. 2. Mollusks—Philippine Islands. 3. Albatross (Steamer)

      14-4141

Library of Congress   Q11.U55   vol. 45

G
51
W 17

DINGO

Murray, A. G.

Trapping dingoes- a dying art.

(Walkabout, vol. 26(6): 32-34, 1960)

QK
Bot.
Pam.
3210

Dilmy, Anwari

A new species of Anisoptera (Dipterocarpaceae)II.

(Reinwardtia, 5(3):267, 1960)

PL
Phil.pam.
452

Dina, J. H.

Ka elele euanelio. He buke e hoakaka
pokole ana i na kumu manaoio o ka ekalesia o
Iesu Kristo o ka poe hoano o na la hope nei. He
kuhikuhi pauku Baibala no hoi, me kekahi mau mea
hoomanao e ae. Honolulu. Press Publishing
Company Steam Print. 1888. 54 pp. 12mo.

(Bible teachings of the Latter Day Saints,
in Hawaiian)

G
51
W 17

DINGO

Parsons, A. D.

The phantom band; theories and misconcep-
tions about the dingo.

(Walkabout, Vol. 22(1):15-17, 1956)

S 393 Jo — DINGO

Tomlinson, A. R.

On the trail of the Dingo, by A. R. Tomlinson and A. C. Moore.

(The Journal of Agriculture, Western Australia, Vol. 1(3):277-285, 1952)

QL 363.DC K 78 — DINOFLAGELLATA

Kofoid, Charles Atwood

The Free-Living Unarmored Dinoflagellata, by Charles Atwood Kofoid and Olive Swezey.

(Memoirs of the University of California, Volume 5, 1921.)

DINOSAURIA.

AS 36 S2 — Gilmore, Charles Whitney, 1874–

... A new dinosaur from the Lance formation of Wyoming, by Charles W. Gilmore ... Washington, Smithsonian institution, 1913.

1 p. l., 5 p. illus. 24½ᶜᵐ. (Smithsonian miscellaneous collections. v. 61, no. 5)

Publication 2184.

1. Dinosauria. 2. Paleontology—Wyoming.

Library of Congress   Q11.S7   13–35412
———— Copy 2.   QE862.D5G5

QL Prot.- Poly. Pam. 720 — DINOFLAGELLATA

Balech, Enrique

Estudio de "Ceratocorys horrida" Stein, var. "extensa" Pavillard.

(Physis, Tome 20:165-173, 1949)

QL 1 A 94 — DINOFLAGELLATA   AUSTRALIA

Wood, E. J. F.

Dinoflagellates in the Australian region.

(Australian Jour. of Marine and Freshwater Research, Vol. 5(2):171-351, 1954)

DINOSAURIA

AS 36 S5 — Gilmore, Charles Whitney, 1874–

... Osteology of the armored *Dinosauria* in the United States National museum, with special reference to the genus *Stegosaurus*, by Charles Whitney Gilmore ... Washington, Govt. print. off., 1914.

xi, 143 p. illus. 37 (i. e. 36) pl. (2 fold.) 31ᶜᵐ. (Smithsonian institution. United States National museum. Bulletin 89)

One plate printed on both sides.
"List of works cited": p. 127–130.

1. Dinosauria. 2. Stegosaurus. 3. U. S. National museum—Collections.

Library of Congress   Q11.U6 no. 89   15–26063
———— Copy 2.   QE862.D5G55

QL 1 H 1 — DINOFLAGELLATA

Kofoid, Charles Atwood

The Dinoflagellata: the family Heterodiniidae of the Peridinioidae, by Charles Atwood Kofoid and Alastair Martin Adamson. Reports on the scientific results of the expedition to the eastern tropical Pacific, in charge of Alexander A. assiz...U.S. Fish Com. steamer "Albatross"...1904...1905...XXXVI.

(Mem. Mus. of Comp. Zool., Harvard College, Vol. 54, 1933,   pp. 1-136, pl. 1-22)

AS 36 C8 — DINOPHILUS

Verrill, Addison Emory, 1839–

... *Dinophilidæ* of New England.

(*In* Connecticut academy of arts and sciences. Transactions. New Haven, 1888-92. 25ᶜᵐ. v. 8, p. (457)-458. illus.)

1. Dinophilus.   I. Title.

Library of Congress   Q11.C9 vol. 8   A 17–859
Yale University   A53n.366.8

DINOSAURIA

AS 36 S5 — Gilmore, Charles Whitney, 1874–

... Osteology of the carnivorous *Dinosauria* in the United States National museum, with special reference to the genera *Antrodemus* (*Allosaurus*) and *Ceratosaurus*, by Charles Whitney Gilmore ... Washington, Govt. print. off., 1920.

xi, 159 p. illus. 36 pl. on 19 l. (1 fold.) 31ᶜᵐ. (Smithsonian institution. United States National museum. Bulletin 110)

"List of works cited": p. 147–148.

1. Dinosauria.

Library of Congress   Q11.U6 Bull. 110   20–26775
———— Copy 2.   QE862.D5G58
(7)

DINOFLAGELLATA.

QL 1 C15 — Kofoid, Charles Atwood, 1865–

... *Dinoflagellata* of the San Diego region ...   I–
By Charles Atwood Kofoid.

(*In* California. University. Publications. Zoology. Berkeley, 1906-27ᶜᵐ. v. 2, p. (341)-368;   illus., plates)

Contributions from the laboratory of the Marine biological association of San Diego.
Bibliographies.

1. Dinoflagellata.

A 11–2261

Title from Univ. of Calif.   Library of Congress

QL Prot.- Poly. Pam. 739 — DINOPHYSIS

Balech, Enrique

Sobre dos variedades de Dinophysis caudata Kent.

(Comunicaciones Zool. del Museo de Hist. Nat. de Montevideo, Nr. 60, Vol. 3, 1951. pp. 1-9, 4 pl.)

DINOSAURIA.

AS 36 C8 — Lull, Richard Swann, 1867–

... The sauropod dinosaur *Barosaurus* Marsh, redescription of the type specimens in the Peabody museum, Yale university, by Richard Swann Lull ... New Haven, Conn., Connecticut academy of arts and sciences (1919)

42 p. illus., vii pl. (1 fold.) 30½ᶜᵐ. (Memoirs of the Connecticut academy of arts and sciences, vol. vi)

Each plate accompanied by guard sheet with descriptive letterpress, plates ii–v, by duplicates in outline.
"Contributions from the Othniel Charles Marsh publication fund, Peabody museum, Yale university, New Haven, Conn."

1. Dinosauria.

Library of Congress   Q11.C85 vol. vi   20–7852
———— Copy 2.   (3)

QL Prot.-Poly. Pam. 596 — DINOFLAGELLATA   PACIFIC

Böhm, Anton

Dinoflagellates of the coastal waters of the western Pacific.

(B. P. Bishop Mus. Bull. 137, 1936, 54 pp.)

DINORNIS MAXIMUS

See

MOA

DINOSAURIA.

AS 36 S1 — Lucas, Frederick Augustus, 1852–

The dinosaurs or terrible lizards. By F. A. Lucas.

(*In* Smithsonian institution. Annual report. 1901. Washington, 1902. 23½ᶜᵐ. p. 641-647. IV pl.)

1. Dinosauria.

S 15–1131

Library of Congress   Q11.S66 1901
Library, Smithsonian   Institution

GC 1 S 43 — DINOFLAGELLATA

Allen, Winfred Emory

Surface catches of marine diatoms and dinoflagellates made by the U.S.S. "Pioneer" in Alaskan waters in 1923.

(Bull. Scripps Inst. Oceanography, Vol. 1, No. 4, Tech. Ser., Berkeley, 1927, pp. 39-48.)

AS 36 A7 — DINOSAUR EGGS

American Museum of Natural History

Third Asiatic Expedition. In Nat. Hist., Vol. 25. Nov.- Dec. 1925, pp 622- 623.

QE 862 D5 M43 — DINOSAURIA

Matthew, William Diller, 1871–

Dinosaurs with special reference to the American museum collections, by W. D. Matthew ... New York, American museum of natural history, 1915.

162 p. incl. front., illus., diagrs. 20ᶜᵐ. (American museum of natural history. Handbook series no. 5)

"This volume is in large part a reprint of various popular descriptions and notices in the American museum journal and elsewhere by Professor Henry Fairfield Osborn, Mr. Barnum Brown, and the writer ... In reprinting it seemed best to combine and supplement them so as to make a consecutive and intelligible account of the dinosaur collections in the museum."—Pref.

"References": p. 160-162.

1. Dinosauria.   I. Osborn, Henry Fairfield, 1857–   II. Brown, Barnum, 1873–

G S 17–233

Library, U. S. Geological   Survey S(221) Am488 no. 5

QL Prot.- Poly. Pam. 769 — DINOFLAGELLATA

Balech, E.

Etude des Dinoflagellés du sable de Roscoff.

(Revue Algologique, n.s., Tome II:29-52, 1956)

QE 862.D5 C 68 — DINOSAURIA

Colbert, Edwin H.

The dinosaur book: the ruling reptiles and their relatives. Illustrated by John C. Germann; with additional illustrations, previously published, by Charles R. Knight and others. Man and Nature Publications, Am. Mus. of Nat. Hist. Handbook No. 14, 1945. sm4to. 156 pp.

DINOSPHAERA.

QL 1 C15 — Kofoid, Charles Atwood, 1865–

... On the structure and relationships of *Dinosphaera palustris* (Lemm.) by Charles Atwood Kofoid and Josephine Rigden Michener. Berkeley, University of California press, 1912.

cover-title, p. (21)-28. 8 illus. 27ᶜᵐ. (University of California publications in zoology. vol. 11, no. 2)

"Literature cited": p. 28.

1. Dinosphaera.   I. Michener, Josephine Rigden, joint author.

A 13–754

Title from Univ. of Calif.   Library of Congress

Z
929
D5
D57
Reading
Room

Dinse, Paul

    Katalog der Bibliothek der Gesellschaft für Erdkunde zu Berlin : Versuch einer Systematik des geographischen Literatur.

    Berlin, 1903, pp xxvii, 925.

QL
671
A

DIOMEDEA

Anthony, A. W.

    Habits of the gooney.

    (Auk, 18:189, 1901)

QL
671
A

DIOMEDEA

Fisher, Walter Kenrick

    On the habits of the Laysan albatross.

    (Auk, 21:8-20, pl. 2-7, 1904)

QK
1
F 29-b

Dinter, Kurt

    Botanische Reisen in Deutsch-Sud-west Afrika.

    (Repert. Spec. Nov. (Fedde), Beihefte 3, 1921)

QH
P 11

DIOMEDEA

Austin, Oliver L., Jr.

    The status of Steller's albatross.

    (Pacific Science, Vol. 3:283-295, 1949)

    [Diomedea albatrus] now extinct?

G
51
W 17

DIOMEDEA

Green, R. H.

    Albatross Island. (off Tasmania)

    (Walkabout, Jan. 1961:31-35, 1961)

QK
97
Fe

Dinter, Kurt

    Succulentenforschungen in Sudwestafrika . Fedde, Rep.spec.nov. reg.. Beihefte , Band XXIII, 1923, 64 pp., 3 pls.

QL
Birds
Pam.
331

DIOMEDEA

Bailey, Alfred M.

    Laysan and Black-footed albatrosses.

    (Museum Pictorial, Denver Museum of Natural History, No. 6, pp. 2-79, 1952)

QL
1
A 93

DIOMEDEA

Horton-Smith, C.

    Theories on the effect of certain physical conditions on the distribution of Diomedea exulans.

    (The Austr. Zool., 3:119-122, 1923)

AS
719
A 53 m

DIODONTIDAE   AUSTRALIA

Whitley, Gilbert P.

    Porcupine fishes.

    (Australian Mus. Magazine, Vol. 10(11):353-360, 1952)

QL
Birds
Pam.
451

DIOMEDEA

Carrick, R. and others

    Fact and fiction on the breeding of the Wandering Albatross. By R. Carrick, K, Keith and A. M. Gwynn.

    (Nature, vol. 188(4745:112-114, 1960)

    [Diomedea exulans]

QL
694.D5
J 31

DIOMEDEA

Jameson, William

    The wandering albatross. Foreword by Robert Cushman Murphy. With drawings by Peter Shepheard. William Morrow and Company. New York. 1959. 8vo. 128 pp.

QL
Moll.
Pam.
938

DIODORA

Kanakoff, George P.

    A new fossil shell from the Palos Verdes sand.

    (Bull., So. Calif. Academy of Sciences, Vol. 52(2):67-70, 1953)

QL
671
Co

DIOMEDEA

Fisher, Harvey I.

    Black-footed albatrosses eating flying fish.

    (Condor, 47:128-129, 1945)

QL
671
Co

DIOMEDEA

Kenyon, Karl W.

    Distribution of albatrosses in the north Pacific and adjacent waters.

    (Condor, Vol. 52:97-103, 1950)

AS
162
P 23

DIOGENIDAE   HAWAII

Forest, J.

    Sur un Dardanus des Hawaii et de Madagascar, D. brachyops sp. nov. (Crustacea Paguridae Diogenidae)

    (Bull. Mus. Nat. d'Hist. Nat., ser 2, Tome 34(5): 365-370, 1962)

QL
671
Co

DIOMEDEA

Fisher, Walter Kenrick

    The albatross dance at sea.

    (Condor, 6:78, 1904)

QL
Birds
Pam.
450

DIOMEDEA

Kenyon, Karl W.

    Homing of Laysan albatrosses. By Karl W. Kenyon and Dale W. Rice.

    (Condor, 60:3-6, 1958)

    [Diomedea mutabilis]

AS
162
P 23

DIOGENIDAE   MADAGASCAR

Forest, J.

    Sur un Dardanus des Hawaii et de Madagascar, D. brachyops sp. nov. (Crustacea Paguridae Diogenidae)

    (Bull. Mus. Nat. d'Hist. Nat., ser. 2, Tome 34(5):365-370, 1962)

QH
1
P 11

DIOMEDEA

Fisher, Harvey I.

    Laysan albatross nesting on Moku Manu Islet, off Oahu, T. H.

    (Pacific Science, Vol. 2:66, 1948)

QH
1
P 11

DIOMEDEA

McHugh, J. L.

    Distribution of Black-footed Albatross, Diomedea nigripes, off the West Coast of North America, 1949 and 1950.

    (Pacific Science, Vol. IX(4):375-381, October, 1955)

QL
671
Co

DIOMEDEA

Miller, Love

    Some tagging experiments with black-footed albatrosses.

(The Condor, Vol. 44, 1942, pp. 3-9)

QL
Birds
Pam.
287

DIOMEDEA

Richdale, L. E.

    Photographs of the Royal Albatross. Otago Daily Times... Dunedin. 8vo. pp. 121-136. n.d. rec'd July 21, 1949.

QL
671
A 92

DIOMEDEA

Slipp, J. W.

    A record of the Tasmanian white-capped Albatross, Diomedea cauta cauta, in American North Pacific waters.

(The Auk, 69(4):458-459, 1952)

QL
671
E 39

DIOMEDEA

Moir, Sandie

    Dance of the Laysan albatross.

(The Elepaio, 6(12), 1946, pp. 80-81)

QL
Birds
Pamphlet
304

DIOMEDEA

Richdale, L. E.

    The pre-egg stage in the albatross family. Biological Monographs, No. 3 (of the author). Otago Daily Times, Dunedin. 1950. 8vo. 92 pp

---

QL
671
Co

DIOMEDEA

Starrett, William C.

    The scarcity of the black-footed albatross in parts of its known range. By William C. Starrett and Keith L. Dixon.

(The Condor, Vol. 48:268-271, 1946)

QL
671
E 39

DIOMEDEA

Munro, George C.

    The Laysan albatross on Kauai.

(The Elepaio, Vol. 5, no. 11, 1945, pp. 70)

G
51
W 17

DIOMEDEA

Richdale, L. M.

    The royal albatross.

(Walkabout, Vol. 10 (11):4-8,1944)

QL
693.Nz
N 91

DIOMEDEA

Westerskov, Kaj

    Field identification and sex of the Royal Albatross.

(Notornis, 9(1):6, 1960)

QL
671
E 39

DIOMEDEA

Munro, George C.

    Notes on the black-footed and Laysan albatrosses.

(The Elepaio, Vol. 7 (4):28-29, 1946)

QL
Birds
Pam.
317

DIOMEDEA

Richdale, L. E.

    The royal Albatross, Diomedea epomophora sandfordi.

(Otago University Library exchange publication No. 20. 1942) 16 pp.

    also
QL
Birds
Pam. 246

QL
671
E 39

DIOMEDEA

Wilder, Howard

    The black-footed albatross.

(The Elepaio, Vol. 10(1):3-4, 1949)

QL
1
A 93

DIOMEDEA

Paradice, W. E. J.

    Some recent natural history observations.

(The Australian Zoologist, 4:319-322, pl. 43-44, 1926)

QL
Birds
Pam.
239

DIOMEDEA

Richdale, L. E.

    Supplementary notes on the Royal Albatross.

(The Emu, Vol. 41, 1942, part 3, p. 169-264)

QL
671
Co

DIOMEDEA

Wilson, Rowland Steele

    The summer bird life of Attu.

(Condor, Vol. 50:124-129, 1948)

QL
671
A 92

DIOMEDEA

Rice, Dale W.

    Breeding distribution, history, and populations of North Pacific albatrosses. By Dale W. Rice and Karl W. Kenyon.

(The Auk, 79(3):365-386, 1962)

QL
Birds
Pam. 246

DIOMEDEA

Richdale, L. E.

    The Royal Albatross: Diomedea epomophora sandfordi. 1942. Dunedin. Otago Daily Times... 16 pp.

QL
671
C 74

DIOMEDEA   BEHAVIOR   EGG-LAYING

Frings, Carl

    Egg sizes of Laysan and black-footed albatrosses.

(Condor, 63(3):263, 1961)

QL
671
Co

DIOMEDEA

Richards, T. W.

    Nesting of Diomedea nigripes and D. immutabilis on Midway Islands.

(Condor, 11:122-123, 1909)

QL
677
B 86

DIOMEDEA

Salvin, Osbert

    [Species of Diomedea.] IN Cat. Birds Brit. Mus., 25:440-448, 1895.

QL
671
Co

DIOMEDEA   CALIFORNIA

McHugh, J. L.

    Increasing abundance of albatrosses off the Coast of California.

(Condor, Vol. 52:153-156, 1950)

AS
750
D 67 o

DIOMEDEA   CAMPBELL ISLAND

Sorensen, J. H.

The royal albatross.

(Cape Exp. Sci. Results of the New Zealand Sub-antarctic Exp., 1941-45, Bull. 2, 1950)

QL
671
C 74

DIOMEDEA   MIDWAY

Howell, Thomas R.

Temperature regulation in Layson and Black-footed albatrosses.

(Condor, 63(3):185-197, 1961)

QK
211
B 74

DIOSCOREA

Morton, C. V.

Notes on Dioscorea, with special reference to the species of the Yucatan Peninsula.

IN
Botany of the Maya area, Miscellaneous Papers, No. 11, 1936.

QL
671
C 74

DIOMEDEA   EGGS

Frings, Carl

Egg sizes of Laysan and black-footed albatrosses.

(Condor, 63(3):263, 1961)

QL
671
A

DIOMEDEA   PACIFIC

Yocom, Charles

Notes on behavior and abundance of the black-footed albatrosses in the Pacific waters off the continental North American shores.

(Auk, Vol. 64:507-523, 1947)

QK
1
C 14

DIOSCOREA

Prain, D.

An account of the genus Dioscorea in the East, Part I: the species which twine to the left, by D. Frain and I. H. Burkill. With 85 plates. 4to.

(Annals of the R. Bot. Garden, Calcutta, Vol. 14, Part I, 1936)

QL
671
E 39

DIOMEDEA   KAUAI

Munro, George C.

The Laysan Albatross on Kauai.

(The Elepaio, Vol. 5(11):70, 1945)

See
Moir, Sandie

Dance of the Laysan Albatross.

(The Elepaio, Vol. 6(12):80-81,1946)

QL
671
C 74

DIOMEDEA   TEMPERATURE REGULATION

Howell, Thomas R.

Temperature regulation in Layson and Black-footed albatrosses.

(Condor, 63(3):185-197, 1961)

GN
2.S
P 76

and

QK
Bot.Pam.
2871

DIOSCOREA   HAWAII

St. John, Harold

The Hawaiian variety of Dioscorea pentaphylla, an edible yam. Hawaiian plant studies 22.

(Journal of the Poly. Soc., 63(1):27-34, 1954)

AS
36
A 5

DIOMEDEA   LAYSAN ISLAND

Dill, Homer R.

The albatrosses of Laysan Island.

(Am. Mus. Journal, 13(4):185-192, 1913)

DIOMEDEA
DIOMEDEIDAE

See Also

ALBATROSSES

GN
2.S
P 76

and

QK
Bot.Pam.
2871

DIOSCOREA   PACIFIC

St. John, Harold

The Hawaiian variety of Dioscorea pentaphylla, an edible yam. Hawaiian plant studies 22.

(Journal of the Poly. Soc., 63(1):27-34, 1954)

QL
Birds
Pam.
368

DIOMEDEA   LAYSAN

DuMont, Philip A.

Gooneys sit out second battle of Midway, 4 mimeographed pages. (rec'd Feb. 1955) 4 pp.

QK
Bot.Pam.
2642

DIOSCOREA

Burkill, I. H.

The rise and decline of the greater yam in the service of man.

(The Advancement of Science, Vol. VII, No. 28, 1951, pp. 443-448)

QK
1
L 75

DIOSCOREACEAE

Burkill, I. H.

Organography and evolution of Dioscoreaceae, the family of the Yams.

(The Jour. of the Linn. Soc., London, Botany, Vol. 66(367):319-412, 1960)

QL
671
A 92

DIOMEDEA   LAYSAN

McAllister, Tom

The Laysan albatross (Diomedia immutabilis) on the Oregon Coast.

(The Auk, Vol. 71(2):211, 1954)

QH
1
T 88

DIOMEDEIDAE   NEW ZEALAND

Moreland, J.

A guide to the larger oceanic birds (albatrosses and giant petrel) of New Zealand waters.

(Tuatara, 6(3):99-107, 1957)

QK
97
E 58

DIOSCOREACEAE

Engler, Adolf

Das Pflanzenreich...IV. 43. 1924. (Heft 87) Dioscoreaceae, by K. Knuth.

QL
671
C 74

DIOMEDEA   MIDWAY

Frings, Hubert

Some biometric studies on the albatrosses of Midway Atoll. By Hubert and Mable Frings.

(Condor, 63(4):304-312, 1961)

GN
2.I
R 93

DIOSCOREA

Frau, Salvador Canals

Las dioscoreas cultivadas (Names) y su introducción en el nuevo mundo.

(Runa, 8(1):26-42, 1958)

QK
1
F

DIOSCOREACEAE

Uline, Edwin Burton, 1867–
...Studies in the herbarium. I. *Higinbothamia*, a new genus, and other new *Dioscoreaceæ*. New *Amaranthaceæ*. By Edwin B. Uline ... Chicago, 1899.

1 p. l., p. 413-422. pl. xxii-xxiv. 24½ᵐᵐ. (Field Columbian museum. Publication 39. Botanical series. vol. I, no. 5)

Each plate preceded by guard sheet with brief explanation.

1. Dioscoreaceae. 2. Amarantaceae.

Library of Congress   QK1.F4

———— Copy 2.   QK99.U4

4—10574

QK
Bot.Pam.
2214

DIOSPYROS

Fosberg, F. Raymond

Diospyros ferrea (Ebenaceae) in Hawaii.

(Occ. Papers, Bernice P. Bishop Museum, Vol. 15, 1939, No. 10, pp. 119-131)

QL
401
J 85

DIPLOMPHALUS

Franc, A.

Diplomphatus Fischeri, mollusque terrestre nouveau de Nouvelle-Calédonie.

(Jour. de Conchyliologie, Vol. XCIII(3): 81-82, 1953)

QL
449.D
S 93

DIPLOPODA

Stoljalowska, Wanda

Krocionogi (Diplopoda) Polski. Instytut Zoologiczny, Polska Akad. Nau. Warszawa, 1961. R8vo. 215 pp.

S
17.H3
H 38

DIOSPYROS EBENASTER

MacCaughey, Vaughan

A rare fruit tree of Hawaii: the black persimmon or Guayu-bota, Diospytos Ebenaster Retz.

(Haw. For. and Agric., Vol. 14, 1917) pp. 97-98

QL
461
P 11

DIPLONYCHUS

Menke, A. S.

A new species of Diplonychus from Thailand, and notes concerning the identity of Diplonychus stali (Mayr) (Hemiptera:Belostomatidae)

(Pacific Insects, 4(1): 115-118, 1962)

AS
36
A 65

DIPLOPODA DUTCH EAST INDIES

Chamberlin, Ralph V.

On some Diplopods from the Indo-Australian Archipelago.

(American Museum Novitates, No. 1282, 1945)

AS
36
A 65

DIPHYLLODES

Rand, A. L.

Breeding habits of the birds of paradise: Macgregoria and Diphyllodes. (Rex. of the Archbold Expeditions. No. 26)

(American Museum Novitates, No. 1073, 1940)

AS
36
S 5

DIPLOPODA

Chamberlin, Ralph V.

Checklist of the millipeds of North America. By Richard V. Chamberlin and Richard L. Hoffman.

(U. S. Nat. Mus., Bull. 212, 1958)

QL
245.N 6
S 24

DIPLOPODA LOYALTY ISLANDS

Carl, J.

Diplopoden von Neu-Caledonien und den Loyalty-Inseln.

Sarasin, Fritz
Nova Caledonia...A. Zoologie, Vol. IV, Livr. III, 1926.

QL
1
C15

DIPLODINIUM ECAUDATUM.

Sharp, Robert G   1883-

... *Diplodinium ecaudatum*; with an account of its neuromotor apparatus, by Robert G. Sharp ... Berkeley, University of California press, 1914.

cover-title, p. [43]-122. 7 pl. (part col. part fold.) 27ᶜᵐ. (University of California publications in zoology. v. 13, no. 4)

Thesis (PH. D.)—University of California, 1914.
Bibliography: p. 110-112.

1. Diplodinium ecaudatum.

Library of Congress   QL1.C15 vol. 13, no. 4
Univ. of California Libr.   14-9951

QL
Crus.Pam.
62

DIPLOPODA

Cook, O.F. (Orator Fuller)

African Diplopoda of the family Gomphodesmidae.

(Proc.U.S.Nat.Mus.Vol.XXI. pp.677-739. Pl.LV-LXi. Washington, 1899. 8vo)

QL
345.N 6
S 24

DIPLOPODA NEW CALEDONIA

Carl, J.

Diplopoden von Neu-Caledonien und den Loyalty-Inseln.

Sarasin, Fritz
Nova Caledonia...A. Zoologie, Vol. IV, Livr. III, 1926.

QK
Bot.
Pam.
3209

DIPLODISCUS

Kostermans, A. J. G. H.

A monograph of the genus Diplodiscus Turcz. (Tiliaceae).

(Reinwardtia, 5(3): 255-265, 1960)

QL
Crus.Pam.
61

DIPLOPODA

Cook, O.F. (Orator Fuller)

African Diplopoda of the Genus Pachybolus.

(Proc.U.S.Nat.Mus.Vol.XXI pp.657-666.Pl.L-LII. Washington 1899. 8vo.)

AS
36
A 65

DIPLOPODA NEW GUINEA

Chamberlin, Ralph V.

On some Diplopods from the Indo-Australian Archipelago.

(American Museum Novitates, No. 1282, 1945)

DIPLOMATIC & CONSULAR SERVICE HAWAII

see

HAWAII DIPLOMATIC & CONSULAR SERVICE

QL
Crus.Pam.
60

DIPLOPODA

Cook, O.F. (Orator Fuller)

American Oniscoid Diplopoda of the order Merocheta.

(Proc. U.S.N.Mus. Vol. XXI pp.451-468. Pl.XXIX-XXXII)

QL
Insect
Pam.
2026
and
QH
181.T
T 13

DIPLOPODA PHILIPPINE ISLANDS

Wang, Yu-hsi Moltze

The Diplopoda of the Philippine Islands. A revision of the Myriapoda of the Philippine Islands.

(Quarterly Jour. of the Taiwan Museum, Vol. 14, Nos. 1/2:89-140, 1961)

QL
401
N

DIPLOMORPHA

Kondo, Yoshio

Anatomy of Diplomorpha delatouri (Hartman) and four species of Placostylus (Pulmonata, Bulimulidae).

(Nautilus, Vol. 61:119-126, pl. 9-10, 1948)

QL
Crus.Pam.
63

DIPLOPODA

Cook, O.F. (Orator Fuller)

The Diplopod family Striariidae.

(Proc. of U.S.Nat. Mus. Vol. XXI. pp.667-676 Washington, 1899. 8vo. pp.10. Pl.LIV.)

AS
750
N 56 b

DIPLOPODA TONGA

Schubart, Otto

Two new Sphaerotrhchopids from Tonga (Diplopoda, Proterospermophora)

(Trans. R. Soc. of New Zealand, Zoology, Vol. 3(10), 1963)

AS
36
A 35-b　DIPLOTAXIS

Vaurie, Patricia

A revision of the genus Diplotaxis (Coleoptera, Scarabaeidae, Melolonthinae)
Part I -II

(Bull. Am. Mus. of Nat. Hist., 115(5), 1958
Vol. 120(2), 1960)

QL
Insects
Pam.　DIPTERA
423　Alexander, Charles P.

The Blepharocerid genus Bibiocephala
Osten Sacken in Japan. . Reprinted from
Insecutor Inscitiae Menstruus, Vol. X,
Nos. 4-6, 1922.

QL
Insects
pam.　DIPTERA
417　Alexander, Charles P.

New or little-known species of Australian Tipulidae (Diptera). From Proc.
Linnean Society N.S.W. Vol.XLVII, 1922.

QK
Bot. Pam.　DIPLYCOSIA
3060
Sleumer, H.

A revision of the genus Diplycosia (Ericaceae).

(Reinwardtia, 4(2):119-161, 1957)

QL
Indects　DIPTERA
Pam
427　Alexander, Charles P.

The crane- flies. 1920.

QL
Insects　DIPTERA
Pam.　Alexander, Charles P.
409　New or little-known Tipulidae.- XIX
Australasian species . From Annals and
Mag. Nat/ Hist. Jan. 1924.

AS
302　DIPTERA
B36
Abreu, Elias Santos

Monografia de los Liminodos de las
Islas Canarias: R. Acad. de Cien. y Arte
de Barcelona 3d epoca Vol. XVIII, Num.4,
1923.

QH
104　DIPTERA
U-b
Alexander, Charles Paul

Diptera of the Pribilof Islands, Alaska
(Tipulidae and Rhyphidae).

(North Amer. Fauna, No. 46, 1923, pp. 159-
169)

QL
Insects　DIPTERA
Pam.
410　Alexander, Charles P.

New or little-known Tipulidae.- XX,
Australasian species. From Annals and
Mag. Nat. Hist. 1924.

QL
595.M1　DIPTERA
I 59
Aczel, Martin L.

Diptera: Neriidae and Micropezidae.

IN
Insects of Micronesia, Vol. 14(3), 1959
pp. 47-90, figs. 1-12.

AS
36　DIPTERA
S4
Alexander, Charles Paul, 1889-
Diptera of the superfamily *Tipuloidea* found in the
District of Columbia.　By C. P. Alexander ... and W. L.
McAtee ...

(In U. S. National museum. Proceedings. Washington, 1921. 23½ᶜᵐ.
v. 58, p. 385-435. pl. 26)

Bibliography: p. 433-435.

1. Crane-flies.　i. McAtee, Waldo Lee, 1883-　joint author.

Library of Congress　（　）Q11.U55　vol. 58
　　　　　　　　　　　　　　　　21-21447
　　　　　　　　　　　　　　　　(5)

QL
Insects　DIPTERA
Pam.
411　Alexander, Charles P.

New or little-known Tipulidae.- XXI,
Australasian species. From Annals and Ma
Nat. Hist. April, 1924.

QL
568.09　DIPTERA
A 23　Adler, H.

Alternating generations, a biological
Study of Oak Galls and Gall Flies.

Oxford, 1894.

QL
Insect　DIPTERA
Pam.
25　Alexander, Charles P.

Four undescribed species of Limnobia from
the Oriental region.　(Diptera, Tipulidae) reprinted from Insecutor Inscitiae Menstruus, Vol.
X, No. 4-6, 1922. pp. 75-80.

QL
Insects　DIPTERA
Pam
412　Alexander, Charles P.

New or little-known Tipulidae .-XXII,
Australasian species. From Annals and Mag
Nat. Hist. May, 1924.

AS
36　DIPTERA
S4　Aldrich, J. M.
and　New Diptera or two-winged flies in
QL　the U. S. National Museum. In U.S.Nat.
Insects　Mus. Proc. Vol. 66 Art 18, 1925.
Pam.
400
589

QL
Insects　DIPTERA
Pam.　Alexander, Charles P.
424　New or little-known crane flies from
northern Japan (Tipulidae, Diptera) . Se
from Philippine Journ Sc. Vol.24, 1924.

QL
Insects　DIPTERA
Pam.　Alexander, Charles P.
413
New or little- known Tipulidae(Dipter
.- XXIII. Australasian species. Ex Annals
and Mag. Nat.Hist. June, 1924.

QL
Insect　DIPTERA
Pam
832　Aldrich, John Merton.

New two-winged flies of the family Calliph-
oridea from China.　From Proc. U. S. Nat. Mus.,
v. 78, art. 1.　pp. 1-5, 1927

QL
Insects　DIPTERA
Pam.　Alexander, Charles P.
425
Two new crane-flies from the Philippin
Islands. Reprinted from Insec. Insc. Mens
Vol.5, 1917.

QL
Insects　DIPTERA
Pam.　Alexander, Charles P.
#414
New or little-known Tipulidae .- XXIV,
Australasian species . 1924.

QL
IInsects
Pam.
415

DIPTERA
Alexander, Charles P.

New or little- known Tipulidae.- XXV
Palaearctic. From Annals and Mag. Nat.
Hist. 1924.

QL
Insects
Pam.
428

DIPTERA
Alexander, Charles P.

An undescribed species of Dixa from
New Zealand 1922.

AS
36
C3

DIPTERA
Cole, Frank R.

A study of the terminal abdominal
structures of male diptera (two-winged
flies). Proc. Calif. Acad. Sci. 4th ser.
v. 16, n.14, 1927.

QL
Insect
Pam.
419

DIPTERA
Alexander, Charles P.

Notes on the crane- flies of the
Hawaiian islands . Reprinted from Annals
Ent. Soc. America, Vol. XII, No.1, 1919.

QL
Insects
Pam.
420

DIPTERA
Alexander, Charles P.

Undescribed species of crane-flies
from New Zealand. Reprinted from Insecutor
Inscitiae Menstruus, Vol. X, Nos.10 - 12,
1922.

AS
36
A65

DIPTERA
Curran, C   H

Four new American diptera. Am. Mus.
Nov. n. 275, 1927.

QL
Insects
Pam.
418

DIPTERA
Alexander, Charles P.

On a collection of crane-flies....
from the Fiji islands. 1914.

QL
Insects
Pam.
429

DIPTERA
Alexander, Charles P.

Two undescribed species of Tanyderus
from the Australasian region . 1924.

AS
36
B4

DIPTERA
Curran, C. Howard

Two undescribed flies (syrphid) from
New England.

Bos. Soc. of Nat. Hist. Occ. Pap. Vol. 5,
pp. 65-7, 1923.

QL
Insects
Pam.
422

DIPTERA
Alexander, Charles P,

Studies on the crane-flies of New
Zealand, Part 1: Order Diptera, Super-
family Tipuloidea. From Trans New Zealand
Inst. Vol 55, 1924.

QL
Insect
Pam.
2079

DIPTERA
Brindle, Allan

Taxonomic notes on the larvae of British
Diptera, I-IV.

(The Entomologist, 1961:122-124, 144-148,
202-205, 218-220)

AS
3C
S4

DIPTERA
Cushman, Robert Asa.
The North American ichneumon-flies of the tribes *Lycorini*, *Polysphinctini*, and *Theroniini*. By R. A. Cushman ...
(*In* U. S. National museum. Proceedings. Washington, 1921. 23½ᵐ.
v. 58, p. 7-48. illus., pl. 2)

1. Ichneumonidae.

Library of Congress   Q11.U55 vol. 58   21-21430

QL
Insects
Pam.
416

DIPTERA
Alexander, Charles P.

Undescribed or little-known crane-
flies from the Pacific islands ...
Brooklyn Ent. Soc. Vol.XVI, 1921.

QL
489
B 91

DIPTERA
Bryan, Edwin H., Jr.

Diptera.

Bryan, Edwin H., Jr.
Insects of Hawaii, Johnston Island ...

(Bernice P. Bishop Museum, Bull. 31, 1926,
pp. 67-71. Tanager Expedition Publication 3.)

QL
Insect
Pam.
2055

DIPTERA
Dyce, A. L.

Blood-sucking flies (Diptera) and Myxomatosis transmission in a mountain environment in
New South Wales. II. Comparison of the use or
man and rabbit as bait animals in evaluating
vectors of Myxomatosis. By A. L. Dyce and D. J.
Lee.

(Reprint, Australian Journal of Zoology,
Vol. 10(1):84-94   1962)

QL
Insects
Pam.
431
430

DIPTERA
Alexander, Charles P.

Undescribed species of Anisopodidae
from New Zealand. 1923.

QL
Insect
Pam.
849

DIPTERA
Cavanaugh, William J.

Algal Food, Feeding and Case-Building Habits
of the Larva of the Midge Fly, Tanytarsus
Dissimilis by W.J.Cavanaugh and Josephine Tilden.

Reprinted from Ecology, Vol. XI, No. 2, 1930.

QL
537.N4
E 26

DIPTERA
Edwards, F. W.   and others

British blood-sucking flies, by F. W.
Edwards, H. Oldroyd, and J. Smart. London.
Printed by order of the Trustees, British
Museum. 1939. Aug. 23, R8vo. viii + 156 pp.,
45 pl.

QL
Insects
Pam.
421

DIPTERA
Alexander, Charles P.

Undescribed species of crane-flies
from New Zealand. Reprinted from Annals
Entom. Soc. America, Vol. XV, No.3, 1922.

AS
36
S4

DIPTERA.
Cockerell, Theodore Dru Alison, 1866–
Some *Diptera* (*Microdon*) from nests of ants. By
T. D. A. Cockerell and Hazel Andrews ...
(*In* U. S. National museum. Proceedings. Washington, 1917. 23½ᵐ.
v. 51, p. 53-56. illus.)

1. Microdon. 1. Andrews, Hazel.

Library of Congress   Q11.U55 vol. 51   17-23831
—— Copy 2.   Q11.U55 vol. 51 2d set

QL
531
E 56

DIPTERA
Encyclopedie Entomologique, Serie B:II.
Diptera: Recueil d'Etudes Biologiques et Systema-
tiques sur les Diptères du Globe, par M. Bezzi,
E. Brunetti, F. W. Edwards...reunies par E.Séguy.
Tome 1-5, 1924-1929. Paris. Paul Lechevalier
(Editeur). 1924-29. 201,208,205,204 and 169 pp.
8vo.

DIPTERA

QL
431
H 1

Felt, E. P.

A new species of gall midge predacious on mealybugs (Dipt.).

(Haw. Ent. Soc., Proc., Vol. 10, 1938, pp. 43)

DIPTERA

QL
489.G
I 59

Johannsen, O(skar) A.
Some new species of nemocerous Diptera from Guam
IN
Swezey, Otto H. and others
Insects of Guam-II, pp. 187-193.

(Bernice P. Bishop Museum, Bull. 189, 1946)

DIPTERA

AS
36
34

Malloch, John Russell, 1875–
One new genus and eight new species of dipterous insects in the United States national museum collection. By J. R. Malloch ...

(*In* U. S. National museum. Proceedings. Washington, 1913. 23½ᵐᵐ. vol. 43, p. 649-658. pl. 46)

1. Diptera.

13-13129

Library of Congress   Q11.U55 vol. 43

DIPTERA

QL
Insect
Pam
#530

Ferris, G.F.

Report upon a collection of insect Ectoparasites from Australian and Tasmanian mammals. Am. Mus. Nat. His. Nov. 110, 1924.

DIPTERA

AS
36
B4

Johnson, Charles W.

List of the Diptera or two-winged flies. Boston Soc. Nat. Hist., Occ. Papers VII, 1925. 326 pp.

DIPTERA

AS
36
34

Malloch, John Russell, 1875–
Three new species of *Anthomyiidæ* (*Diptera*) in the United States national museum collection. By J. R. Malloch ...

(*In* U. S. National museum. Proceedings. Washington, 1913. 23½ᵐᵐ. v. 45, p. 603-607)

1. Anthomyiidæ.

14-4161

Library of Congress   Q11.U55 vol. 45

DIPTERA

QL
Insect
Pam
543

Greene, Charles T.

Descriptions of larvae and pupae of two-winged flies belonging to the family Leptidae. From Proc. U. S. Nat. Mus. vol. 70, art. 2, pp. 1-20, pls. 1926.

DIPTERA

AS
36
34

Malloch, John Russell, 1875–
Descriptions of new species of American flies of the family *Borboridæ.* By J. R. Malloch ...

(*In* U. S. National museum. Proceedings. Washington, 1913. 23½ᵐᵐ. v. 44, p. 361-372)

1. Flies.

13-20868

Library of Congress   Q11.U55 vol. 44

DIPTERA

QL
Insect
Pam. 978

Malloch, John R.

Trypetidae of the Mangarevan Expedition (Diptera). Mangarevan Exp. Pub. 24.

(Bernice P. Bishop Museum, Occ. Paper, Vol. 14, No. 7, 1938 (July 11) pp. 11-116)

Diptera

AS
182
Dr

Vol.14
No.3

Handel, Friedrich

Die Bohrfliegen Südamerikas Übersicht und Katalog der bisher aus der neotropischen Region beschriebenen Tephritinen.

DIPTERA

AS
36
34

Malloch, John Russell, 1875–
Flies of the genus *Agromyza*, related to *Agromyza virens*. By J. R. Malloch ...

(*In* U. S. National museum. Proceedings. Washington, 1916. 23½ᵐᵐ. v. 49, p. 103-108. 1 illus., pl. 36)

1. Agromyzidae.

Library of Congress   Q11.U55 vol. 49   16-11778
——— Copy 2.   Q11.U55 vol. 49 2d set

DIPTERA

QL
489.G
I 59

Malloch, J. R.
Trypetidae, Otitidae, Helomyzidae, and Clusiidae of Guam (Diptera)
IN
Swezey, Otto H. and others
Insects of Guam-I, pp. 201-210.

(Bernice P. Bishop Museum, Bull. 172, 1942)

DIPTERA

QL
595.Mi
I 59

Hardy, D. Elmo

Omphralidae (Scenopinidae), and Sarcophagidae, by H. de Souza Lopes.

IN
Insects of Micronesia, 13, No. 2, 1958

DIPTERA

AS
36
34

Malloch, John Russell, 1875–
The genera of flies in the subfamily *Botanobiinæ* with hind tibial spur. By J. R. Malloch ...

(*In* U. S. National museum. Proceedings. Washington, 1914. 23½ᵐᵐ. v. 46, p. 239-266. pl. 23-24)

1. Botanobiinae.

14-10981

Library of Congress   Q11.U55 vol. 46

DIPTERA

AS
36
34

Malloch, John Russell, 1875–
Two new species of *Diptera* in the United States National museum collection. By J. R. Malloch ...

(*In* U. S. National museum. Proceedings. Washington, 1913. 23½ᵐᵐ. v. 44, p. 461-463)

1. Diptera.

13-20872

Library of Congress   Q11.U55 vol. 44

DIPTERA

AS
36
1

Illinois state laboratory of natural history, *Urbana.* Bulletin ... 1876–1918. (Card 15)

CONTENTS—Continued.

Equipment for maintaining a flow of oxygen-free water, and for controlling gas content, by V. E. Shelford.—art. X. A collecting bottle especially adapted for the quantitative and qualitative determination of dissolved gases, particularly very small quantities of oxygen, by E. B. Powers. May 1918.

vol. XII, art. I. The relation of evaporation and soil moisture to plant succession in a ravine, by F. T. Ullrich. Sept. 1915.—art. II. A classification of the *Lepidoptera* based on characters of the pupa, by Edna Mosher. Mar. 1916.—art. III. A preliminary classification of *Diptera*, exclusive of *Pupipara*, based upon larval and pupal characters, with keys to imagines in certain families. pt. I. By J. R. Malloch. Mar. 1917.—art. IV. The *Zygoptera*, or damsel-flies, of Illinois, by Philip Garman. June 1917.

1. Natural history—Societies, etc.

12-33598 Revised

Library of Congress   QH1.I 25
[r19d3]

DIPTERA

AS
36
34

Malloch, John Russell, 1875–
The insects of the dipterous family *Phoridæ* in the United States national museum. By J. R. Malloch ...

(*In* U. S. National museum. Proceedings. Washington, 1913. 23½ᵐᵐ. vol. 43, p. 411-529. pl. 35-41)

1. Phoridæ.

13-13122

Library of Congress   Q11.U55 vol. 43

DIPTERA

QL
535.4
Me

Meigen, J. W.

Systematische Beschreibung der bekannten Europaischen zweiflugeligen insekten.

Hamm and Halle , 1822 - 1851, 7 vols.

See author card for detail

DIPTERA

QL
Insects
Pam.
1309

James, Maurice T.

The flies that cause myiasis in man.

(U. S. Dept. of Agriculture, Misc. Pub. 631, 1947)

DIPTERA

AS
36
34

Malloch, John Russell, 1875–
Notes on some American *Diptera* of the genus *Fannia*, with descriptions of new species. By J. R. Malloch ...

(*In* U. S. National museum. Proceedings. Washington, 1913. 23½ᵐᵐ. v. 44, p. 621-631. pl. 77)

1. Fannia.

13-20882

Library of Congress   Q11.U55 vol. 44

DIPTERA

QL
Insect Pam.
850

Miller, David Franklin

Determining the Effects of Change in Temperature upon the Locomotor Movements of Fly Larvae.

Reprinted from the Journal of Experimental Zoology, Vol. 52, No. 2, 1929.

DIPTERA
Muesebeck, C.F.W.

QL
Ins
Pam
#55
65
and
AS
36
S4

A revision of the North Am. species of Ichneumon-flies belonging to the genus Apanteles; ex Proc. U.S.Nat. Mus. vol. 58, pp. 483-576.

AS
36
S2

DIPTERA
Ritter, Wolfgang.

... The flying apparatus of the blow-fly; a contribution to the morphology and physiology of the organs of flight in insects, with twenty plates, by Dr. Wolfgang Ritter ... Washington, Smithsonian institution, 1911.

1 p. l., 76 p. illus., 19 (i. e. 20) pl. 24½ᶜᵐ. (Smithsonian miscellaneous collections. v. 56, no. 12)

Publication 1947.
At head of title: Hodgkins fund.
"Literature": p. [36]-37.

1. Blow-flies. 2. Flight.

11-13126

Library of Congress   Q11.S7 vol. 56, no. 12

Q
115
V 81
locked
case

DIPTERA

Thomson, C. G.
Diptera. Species novas descripsit C.G.Thomson.

Virgin, Christian Adolf
Kongliga Svenska Fregatten Eugenies Resa omkring jorden under befal af C. A. Virgin, aren 1851-1853. Del II;1,pp. 443-614. 1 pl. 1869.

AS
36
S1

DIPTERA
Osten-Sacken, Carl Robert, *freiherr von der*, 1828-1906.
The so-called bugonia of the ancients, and its relation to a bee-like fly—*Eristalis tenax.* By C. R. Osten Sacken.

(*In* Smithsonian institution. Annual report. 1893. Washington, 1894. 23½ᶜᵐ. p. 487-500)

"Extracts from articles in Bullettino della Societa entomologica italiana, 1893."

1. Bugonia. 2. Eristalis tenax.

S 15-838

Library of Congress   Q11.S66 1893
Library, Smithsonian   Institution

QL
Insect
Pam.
1952

DIPTERA

Seevers, Charles H.

New termitophilous Diptera from the neotropics.

(Field Mus. Nat. Hist., Zool. Ser. 24(18), 1941)

QL
461
T 31

DIPTERA

Tokunaga, Massaki

Biting midges from Japan and neighboring countries, including Micronesian Islands, Manchuria, North China and Mongolia (Diptera, Ceratopogonidae).

(Tenthredo, Vol. 3, 1940, p. 58-100)

121-165

QL
Insects
Pam.
377
and
378

Diptera

Ostensacken, R.

See author card

QL
Insect
Pam.
584

DIPTERA

Shannon, Raymond C.

A review of the South American two-winged flies of the family syrphidae.

(Proc. U. S. Nat. Mus. v.70, art. 9, Washington, 1927)

QL
531
W 64

DIPTERA

Wiedemann, Christian Rudolph Wilhelm

Aussereuropaische zweiflügelige Insekten. Als Fortsetzung des Meigenschen Werkes. Theile 1-2. Mit sieben und fünf Steintafeln. Hamm. Schulzischen Buchhandlung. 1828, 1830. 8vo.

AS
36
I 4

DIPTERA
Peterson, Alvah.
The head-capsule and mouth-parts of *Diptera*, with twenty-five plates, by Alvah Peterson ... [Urbana, University of Illinois, 1916]

112 p. xxv pl. 27ᶜᵐ. (Added t.-p.: Illinois biological monographs. vol. III, no. 2. Oct. 1916] $2.00
Thesis (PH. D.)—University of Illinois, 1915.
Thesis note on verso of t.-p.
"Contributions from the Entomological laboratories of the University of Illinois, no. 52."
Bibliography: p. 57-60.

1. Diptera.

Library of Congress   QL538.P5
——— Copy 2.
Copyright A 453727   17-2691 Revised

QL
Insects
Pam.
1602

DIPTERA

Steyskal, George C.

The genus Sepedon Latreille in the Americas (Diptera: Sciomyzidae)

(The Wasmann Journal of Biology, Vol. 8(3): 271-297, 1950)

QL
461
H 1

DIPTERA

Williams, Francis Xavier

Biological studies in water-loving insects, Part I, Coleoptera or Beetles; Part II, Odonata or Dragon flies; Part III, Diptera.

(Haw. Ent. Soc., Proc. Vol. 9, 1936, pp. 235-249; Vol. 10, 1938-39, pp. 85-119)

QL
Insect
Pam.
1903

DIPTERA

Rageau, Jean

Note sur les Phlebotomes d'Evodoula (Cameroun francais). By Jean Rageau et J.P. Adam.

(Bull. Soc. Pathologie exotique, 46:587-594, 1953)

QL
537
S93

DIPTERA

Sturtevant, A. H.

Contributions to the genetics of drosophila simulans and drosophila melanogaster. Carnegie Institution of Washington, 1929. 296 p.

Publication no. 399

AS
36
C8

DIPTERA
Williston, Samuel Wendell, 1852-
... Some interesting new *Diptera.*

(*In* Connecticut academy of arts and sciences. Transactions. New Haven, 1877-82. 25ᶜᵐ. v. 4, p. [243]-246. illus.)

1. Diptera. I. Title.

A 17-789

Library of Congress   Q11.C9 vol. 4
Yale University   A53n.366.4

QL
Insect
Pam.
1902

DIPTERA

Rageau, J.(ean)

Phlebotomes du Cameroun.

(Bull. Soc. de Pathologie exotique, 44:793-800, 1951)

AS
36
S4

DIPTERA

Sturtevant, Alfred Henry, 1891-
The dipterous genus *Zygothrica* of Wiedemann. By A. H. Sturtevant ...

(*In* U. S. National museum. Proceedings. Washington, 1921. 23½ᶜᵐ. v. 58, p. 155-158. illus.)

1. Zygothrica.

Library of Congress   Q11.U55 vol. 58
21-21433

AS
36
S5

DIPTERA

Williston, Samuel W.
Synopsis of the North American Syrphidae. U. S. Nat. Mus. Bul. No. 31. Washington, 1886.

QL
1
C 15

DIPTERA
Reeves, Edna Mary, 1882-
... The inheritance of extra bristles in *Drosophila melanogaster* Meig., by Edna M. Reeves. Berkeley, University of California press, 1916.

cover-title, p. [495]-515 incl. tables, diagr. 27½ᶜᵐ. (University of California publications in zoology. v. 13, no. 13)
"Literature cited": p. 515.

1. Heredity. 2. Variation (Biology) 3. Flies. I. Title.

A 16-1547

Title from Univ. of Calif.   Library of Congress

QL
489.G
I 59

DIPTERA

Swezey, Otto H.
Some miscellaneous Diptera of Guam
IN
Swezey, Otto H. and others
Insects of Guam-II, pp. 195-200.

(Bernice P. Bishop Museum, Bull. 189, 1946)

Q
115
M 46

DIPTERA

Womersley, H.
Diptera.

Mawson, Sir Douglas   leader
British, Australian, and New Zealand Antarctic Research Expedition, 1929-31. Reports, Series B, Vol. IV, Part 3, pp. 59-79. 1937.

QL
431
H 1

DIPTERA

Zimmerman, Elwood C.

Two insect immigrants new to the Hawaiian (Diptera, Col.)

(Haw. Ent. Soc. Proc., Vol. 10, 1938, pp. 131-132)

QL
1
A 93

DIPTERA   AUSTRALIA

Bezzi, M.

Note on the Australian genus Tapeigaster Macq. (Diptera) with descriptions of new species.

(The Australian Zoologist, Vol. 3:72-8, 1923)

QL
1
A 93

DIPTERA   AUSTRALIA

Malloch, J. R.

Notes on Australian Diptera with descriptions of thirteen new species.

(The Australian Zoologist, 3:322-338) 1924

QL
535.9
L 74

DIPTERA   FOSSIL

Lindner, Erwin

Die Fliegen der Palaearktischen Region

See author card

AS
720.N
L

DIPTERA   AUSTRALIA

Fuller, Mary E.

Notes on the biology of Scaptia Auriflua Don. (Diptera, Tabanidae).

(Proc. of the Linnean Soc. of New South Wales, vol. LXI, 1936, pp. 1-9)

QL
Insect
Pam.
1442

DIPTERA   AUSTRALIA

Paramonov, S. J.

Review of Australian Mydaidae (Diptera).

(Bull. No. 255, Commonwealth Scientific and Industrial Research Organization, Australia, 1950)

AS
619
S 72

DIPTERA   AFRICA

Hesse, A. J.

A revision of the Bombyliidae (Diptera) of southern Africa. Parts I-II.

(Annals S. African Museum, Vol. 35, 1956)

AS
720.N
L

DIPTERA   AUSTRALIA

Malloch, John R.

Notes on Australian Diptera. XXXV.

(Proc. of the Linnean Soc. of New South Wales, vol. LXI, 1936, pp. 10-26)

QL
Insect
Pam
666

DIPTERA - AUSTRALIA

Taylor, Frank H.

Notes on Australian tabanidae (diptera). From Bull. Entomolog. Research, v.17, pt.2, 1926.

QH
11
G 74

DIPTERA   ANTARCTIC

Richards, O. W.

Sphaeroceridae (Diptera)

IN British Graham Land Expedition, 1934-37. Scientific Reports, Vol. 1, no. 7, pp. 323-326. 1941. British Museum (Natural History).

AS
720.T
R

DIPTERA   AUSTRALIA

Hardy, G. H.

Australian Bombyliidae and Cyrtidae.

(Papers and Proc. R. Soc. Tasmania, 1921: 41-83)

QL
Insect
Pam
665

DIPTERA - AUSTRALIA

Taylor, Frank H.

Two new species of Australian culicidae (diptera) and a note on simulium bancrofti, Taylor, with the description of a new species of simulium (diptera). From Bull. Entomolog. Research, v.18, pt. 1, 1927.

QL
535.9
L 74

DIPTERA   ARCTIC

Lindner, Erwin

Die Fliegen der Palaearktischen Region.

See author card

AS
720.T
R

DIPTERA   AUSTRALIA

Hardy, G. H.

Australian Rhyphidae and Leptidae (Diptera).

(Papers and Proc. R. Soc. of Tasmania, 1919:117-129)

QL
1
A 93

DIPTERA   AUSTRALIA

Tillyard, R. J.

Australian Blepharoceridae. (Order Diptera). I-III. By R.J.Tillyard, A. Tonnoir

(The Australian Zoologist, Vol. 2:159-172, 1922; 3:47-59,1923; ibid, pp. 135-142)

QL
535.9
L 74

DIPTERA   ARCTIC   (Palaearctic)

Lindner, Erwin

Die Fliegen der Palaearktischen Region.

Lief. 1-239
(Still being issued, 1963)

Stuttgart. E. Schweizerbart'sche Verlagsbuchhandlung.   1928 +   R8vo.

QL
1
A 93

DIPTERA   AUSTRALIA

Hardy, G. H.

The geographical distribution of genera belonging to the Diptera Brachycera of Australia.

(The Australian Zoologist, Vol. 2:143-147, 1922)

AS
720.T
R

DIPTERA   AUSTRALIA

Tonnoir, A. L.

Australian Dixidae [Dipt.].

(Papers and Proc. R. Soc. Tasmania, 1923: 58-71)

QL
Insect
Pam.
2023

DIPTERA   ASIA (SOUTH)

van der Wulp, F. M.

Catalogue of the described Diptera from South Asia. Published by the Dutch Entomological Society. The Hague. Martinus Nijhoff. 1896. 8vo. 220 pp.

AS
719
A 92

DIPTERA   AUSTRALIA

McAlpine, David K.

A key to the Australian families of Acalyptrate Diptera (Insecta).

(Records of the Australian Museum, Vol. 24 (12), 1958)

AS
36
W 2

DIPTERA   BOUGAINVILLE

Roback, Selwyn S.

New species of Sarcophagini (Diptera: Sarcophagidae).

(Jour. Washington Acad. Sci., 42(2):45-49, 1952)

QL
535.41
C 72

DIPTERA   BRITISH ISLES

Colyer, Charles N.

Flies of the British Isles. By Charles N.
Colyer in collaboration with Cyril O. Hammond,
with 48 plates in colour, 55 half-tone plates
and numerous text figures and diagrams depicting
286 representative species from original enlarged
microscope drawings by Cyril O. Hammond. Frederick Warne and Co. Ltd. London... sm8vo.
(1951) 383 pp.

AS
36
C3

DIPTERA--CALIFORNIA.

Malloch, John Russell, 1875–

... New species of flies (*Diptera*) from California, by
J. R. Malloch ... San Francisco, The Academy, 1919.

cover-title, p. [297]–312. 25½ᶜᵐ. (Proceedings of the California academy
of sciences. 4th ser. vol. IX, no. 11)

"Printed from the John W. Hendrie publication endowment."

1. Diptera—California.

20-3211

Library of Congress   Q11.C253 vol. 9, no. 11

[5]

QL
535.3
B 86

DIPTERA CHILE

British Museum of Natural History

Diptera of Patagonia and South Chile; based
mainly on material in the British Museum.
London, British Museum. 1929–> 8vo

Parts 1 –>

See main card for full information

QL
535.4
L 98

DIPTERA .. DENMARK

Lundbeck, William

Diptera Danica, genera and species of flies hitherto found in Denmark.
London, Wesley, 1907. 5 vols.

AS
145
B

DIPTERA   DUTCH EAST INDIES

Goetghebuer, M.
Diptera, I-II.

Van Straelen, V.
Résultats scientifiques du voyage aux Indes
Orientales Néerlandaises...Léopold de Belgique,
Vol. 4, Fasc. 7, 1932, pp. 1-38; Fasc. 10, 1934,
pp. 1-27.

(Mem. hors ser. Mus. Roy. d'Hist. Nat.
Belgique)

QH
138.J
S 62

DIPTERA   EASTER ISLAND

Enderlein, Günther

Die Dipterenfauna der Juan-Fernandez-Inseln
und der Oster-Insel.

IN
Skottsberg, Carl   editor
The natural history of Juan Fernandez and
Easter Island, Vol. III. Zoology, Art. 60, pp.
643-680. Uppsala, 1940.

QL
535.4
K 47

DIPTERA   ENGLAND

Kidd, L. N.

The Diptera of Lancashire and Cheshire,
Part I By L. N. Kidd and A. Brindle.
Lancashire and Cheshire Fauna Committee.
T. Buncle and Co., Ltd. Arbroath. 8vo. 136 pp.

QL
535.8
B 57

DIPTERA   FIJI

Bezzi, Mario

Diptera Brachycera and Athericera of the
Fiji Islands, based on material in the British
Museum (Natural History).   London. 1928. 219p

AS
36
C 3

DIPTERA GALAPAGOS

Bequaert, Joseph C.

The Hippoboscidae of the Galapagos Archipelago...

(Proc. of the Calif. Acad. of Sciences, 4th
Series, Vol. 21, No. 11, pp. 131-138, 1933)

AS
36
C 3

DIPTERA GALAPAGOS

Curran, C. H.

Diptera. (Templeton Crocker Expedition of the
California Academy of Sciences, 1932, No. 13)
(Proc. of Calif. Acad. of Sciences, 4th Ser.,
Vol. 21, No. 13, pp. 147-172. March 27, 1934)

QL
489.G
B 67

DIPTERA GUAM

Bohart, George E.

Filth-inhabiting flies of Guam. By George
E. Bohart and J. Linsley Gressitt.

(Bernice P. Museum, Bull. 204, 1951)

AS
36
S 4

DIPTERA GUAM

Bohart, G. E.

The phorid flies of Guam.

(Proc. U. S. Nat. Mus., Vol. 96:397-416,
1947)

QH
1
P 11

DIPTERA-GUAM

James, Maurice T.

Some Stratiomyidae (Diptera) from Okinawa
and Guam.

(Pacific Science, Vol. 4:184-187, 1950)

AS
36
S 2

DIPTERA GUATEMALA

Dalmat, Herbert T.

The black flies (Diptera, Simuliidae) of
Guatemala and their role as vectors of Onchocerciasis.

(Smithsonian Misc. Coll. Vol. 125(1), 1955)

QL
Insects
Pam.
474

and

QL
461
H1

DIPTERA   HAWAII

Aldrich, J. M. (John Merton)

Descriptions of lantana gall-fly and
lantana seed-fly.

(Proc. Hawaii. Ent. Soc., Vol. V, 1923,
pp. 261-263)

QL
Ins.
Pam.
160

and

AS
36
S 4

DIPTERA   HAWAII

Aldrich, John Merton

Two-winged flies of the genera Dolichopus
and Hydrophorus collected in Alaska in 1921,
with new species of Dolichopus from North
America and Hawaii.

(Proc. U. S. Nat. Mus., 1922, Vol. 61,
No. 2446: 1-18)

QL
Insects
Pam. 986

2 copies

DIPTERA   HAWAII

Bryan, Edwin H., Jr.

A review of the Hawaiian Diptera, with descriptions of new species.

(Haw. Ent. Soc., Proc., VIII, 1934, p. 399-
468)

AS
36
A 65

DIPTERA   HAWAII

Curran, C. H.

New species of Volucella from Hawaii and
the United States (Syrphidae, Diptera).

(Am. Mus. Novitates, No. 1361, 1947) 6pp.

QL
461
H 1

DIPTERA   HAWAII

Hardy, D. Elmo

Additions and corrections to Bryan's check
list of the Hawaiian Diptera (Presidential address).

(Proc. Haw. Ent. Soc., Vol. 14(3):443-484,
1951)

QL
489.H
Z 73

DIPTERA   HAWAII

Hardy, D. Elmo
Diptera: Nematocera-Brachycera

IN
Zimmerman, Elwood C.
Insects of Hawaii, Vol. 10, 1960

.QL
461
H-1

DIPTERA   HAWAII

Hardy, D. Elmo

Flies collected in bait traps.

(Proc. Haw. Ent. Soc., Vol.14(3):407-409,
1951)

QL
461
H-1

DIPTERA   HAWAII

Hardy, D. Elmo

     Studies in Hawaiian Dorilaidae (Diptera)
Part I

(Proc. of the Hawaiian Entomological Society
for 1952, Vol. XV(1):59-73, 1953)

QL
Insect
Pam.
2025

DIPTERA   JAPAN

Kano, Rokuro

     Notes on the flies of medical importance
in Japan. (Parts 1-6).

(Japanese Journal of Experimental Medicine,
Vol. 20-22, 1950-1952)

QL
489.M
P 11

DIPTERA   MARQUESAS

Malloch, John R.
     New species and other records of Otitidae
(Ortalidae), Piophilidae, Clusiidae, Chloropidae,
and Drosophilidae from the Marquesas.
IN
Marquesan Insects-I, pp. 205-224. (Art. 22)

(Bernice P. Bishop Museuj, Bulletin 98,1932.
Pacific Entomological Survey Publication 1)

QL
461
H-1

DIPTERA   HAWAII

Jensen, D. D.

     The identity and host plants of blossom
midge in Hawaii. (Diptera:Cecidomyiidae:Conta-
rinia).

(Proc. Haw. Ent. Soc., Vol. 12(3):525-534,
1946)

QL
136.J
S 62

DIPTERA JUAN FERNANDEZ

Enderlein, Günther

     Die Dipterenfauna der Juan-Fernandez-Inseln
und der Oster-Insel.

IN

Skottsberg, Carl   editor
     The natural history of Juan Fernandez and
Easter Island, Vol. III. Zoology, Art. 60. pp.
643-680.   Uppsala, 1940.

QL
489.M
P 11

DIPTERA MARQUESAS

Malloch, John R.
Two new species of Astiidae (Diptera) from
the Marquesas.
IN
Marquesan Insects-I, pp. 115-116 (Art. 11)

(Bernice P. Bishop Museum, Bulletin 98,1932.
Pacific Entomological Survey Publication 1)

QL
461
H-1

DIPTERA   HAWAII

Quate, Larry W.

     A revision of the Psychodidae of the Hawaiian
Islands (Diptera).

(Proceedings of the Hawaiian Entomological
Society for 1953, Vol. XV(2):335-356)

QL
345.N 6
S 24

DIPTERA   LOYALTY ISLANDS

Falcoz, L.

     Diptères Pupipares de la Nouvelle-Caledonie
et des Iles Loyalty (Streblidae et Nycteribiidae)

Sarasin, Fritz
     Nova Caledonia...A. Zoologie, Tome III, Livr
1, 1923, pp. 83-96.

QL
489.M
P 11

DIPTERA MARQUESAS

Malloch, John R.
Two Trypetidae from the Marquesas Islands,
with on new species (Diptera).
IN
Marquesan Insects-I, pp. 145-147. (Art. 14)

(Bernice P. Bishop Museum, Bulletin 98,1932.
Pacific Entomological Survey Publication 1)

QL
Insects
Pam. 999

AS
763
B-4

Reading
Room

DIPTERA   HAWAII

Souza Lopes, H. de

     On the genus Goniophyto Townsend, 1927, with
description of a new species from Hawaii.

(Bernice P. Bishop Museum, Occasional Papers,
Vol. 14, No. 11, pp. 193-197, 1938)

QL
Insects
Pam
No 377
&
378

DIPTERA - MALAY ARCHIPELAGO

Osten- Sacken, C. R. (Baron) von
     Enumeration of the Diptera of the
Malay Archipelago collected by Prof.
Odoardo Beccari ....   Genova 1881 - 1882
Also supplement.

AS
36
C 3

DIPTERA MELANESIA

Curran, C. H.

     Diptera (Templeton Crocker Expedition to
Western Polynesian and Melanesian Islands, 1933,
no. 30)

(Proc. of Calif. Acad. of sciences, 4th ser.
vol.22, no. 1, pp.1-66. Dec.18,1936)

QL
461
H-1

DIPTERA   HAWAII

Williams, Francis X.

     Psychoda Pseudalternata n.sp. Diptera:
Psychodiidae.

(Haw. Ent. Soc., Proc., 12(3):637, 1946)

QL
489.M
P 11

DIPTERA MARQUESAS

Edwards, F. W.

     Marquesan Simuliidae.
IN
Marquesan Insects-I, pp. 103-109. (Art. 9)

(Bernice P. Bishop Museum, Bulletin 98, 1932
Pacific Entomological Survey Publication 1.

QL
Insects
Pam.
1066

DIPTERA MICRONESIA

Tokunaga, Masaaki

     Biting midges from the Micronesian Islands,
with biological notes by Teiso Esaki.

(Tenthredo, Vol. III, No. 2, 1940, pp. 166-
186)

QL
531
B 89

DIPTERA   INDIA

Brunetti, E.

     Diptera Brachycera. Vol.1

IN
Fauna of British India, including Ceylon
and Burma... London,1920.

QL
489.M
P 11

DIPTERA MARQUESAS

Malloch, John R(ussell)

     New Species of Calliphora from the Marquesas
with notes on Sarcophaga taitensis Schiner.
IN
Marquesan Insects-I, pp. 13-16. (Art. 2)

(Bernice P. Bishop Museum, Bulletin 98,1932
Pacific Entomological Survey Publication 1)

AS
773
N 53 z

DIPTERA MOLUCCAS

Paramonov, S. J.

     Some new species of Euphumosia Mall. and
Hemipyrellia Towns. from the Moluccas and New
Guinea (Diptera, Calliphorida).

(Nova Guinea, Zoology, No. 12, 1961)

[Results of the Archbold Expedition]

QL
531
B 89

DIPTERA   INDIA

Brunetti, E.

     Diptera.   Vol.III. Pipenculidae, Syrphidae,
Conopidae, Oestridae.

IN
Fauna of British India... London,1923.

QL
489.M
P 11

DIPTERA MARQUESAS

Malloch, John R(ussell)

     New Species of Sapromyzidae from the Mar-
quesas.
IN
Marquesan Insects-I, pp. 3-12. (Art. 1)

(Bernice P. Bishop Museum, Bulletin 98,
1932) Pacific Entomological Survey Publication 1

QL
345.N 6
S 24

DIPTERA   NEW CALEDONIA

Falcoz, L.

     Diptères Pupipares de la Nouvelle-Caledonie
et des Iles Loyalty (Streblidae et Nycteribiidae)

Sarasin, Fritz
     Nova Caledonia...A. Zoologie, Tome III, Livr.
1, 1923. pp. 83-96

AS
36
W 2

DIPTERA   NEW CALEDONIA

James, Maurice T.

The Stratiomyidae (Diptera) of New Caledonia and the New Hebrides with notes on the Solomon Islands forms.

(Journal of the Washington Academy of Sciences, Vol. 40:248-260, 1950)

RC
1
S 98

DIPTERA   NEW GUINEA

Malloch, J. R.

III. Families Muscidae and Tachinidae.

(Sydney University, School of Public Health and Tropical Medicine, Collected Papers, No. 1, Article 28)

QL
Insect
Pam.
1371

DIPTERA   NEW GUINEA

Parent, O.

The Diptera of the Territory of New Guinea. VIII. Dolichopodidae.

(Proc. Linn. Soc. New South Wales, Vol. 64: 155- 168, 1939)

AS
720.N
L

DIPTERA   NEW GUINEA

Alexander, Charles P.

Contribution to a knowledge of Papuan Tipulidae (Diptera).

(Proceedings of the Linnean Society of N.S.W., vol. LXI, 1936, pp. 122-127)

QL
Insect
Pam.
1371

DIPTERA   NEW GUINEA

Malloch, John R.

VII. Family Otitidae (Ortalidae).

(Proc. Linn. Soc. New South Wales, Vol. 64: 97-154, 1939)

AS
36
W 2

DIPTERA   NEW GUINEA

Roback, Selwyn S.

New species of Sarcophagini (Diptera: Sarcophagidae).

(Jour. Washington Acad. Sci., 42(2):45-49, 1952)

AS
720.N
L

DIPTERA   NEW GUINEA

Alexander, Charles P.

The Diptera of the Territory of New Guinea. Family Tipulidae. Parts, I, II, III.

(Proc. of the Linnean Soc. of New South Wales, vol. LX, 1935, pp. 51-70; vol. LXI, 1936, pp. 169-183; pp.322-340)

AS
763
B-4

QL
Insect
Pam 875

Reading
Room

DIPTERA   NEW GUINEA

Malloch, John R.

A new Chaetomosillus from New Guinea(Diptera Ephydridae.) Honolulu. May. 12, 1934.

(Bernice P. Bishop Museum, Occasional Papers Vol. X, No. 17. 1934.)

QL
Insects
Pam.
1601

DIPTERA   NEW GUINEA

Steyskal, George C.

Notes and records of Phytalmiidae (Diptera: Acalyptratae)

(The Wasmann Journal of Biology, Vol. 8(1): 93-96, 1950)

QL
Insects
Pam.
1374

DIPTERA   NEW GUINEA

Alexander, Charles P.

The Diptera of the Territory of New Guinea, XII. Family Tipulidae, Part 4.

(Proc. Linn. Soc. New South Wales, Vol. 66: 138-144, 1941)

QL
Insect
Pam.
1371

DIPTERA   NEW GUINEA

Malloch, John R.

IX. Family Phytalmiidae.

(Proc. Linn. Soc. New South Wales, Vol. 64:169-180, 1939)

AS
720.N
L

DIPTERA   NEW GUINEA

Taylor, Frank H.

The Diptera of the Territory of New Guinea. I. Family Culicidae.

(Proc. Linn. Soc. New South Wales, Vol. 59: 229-236, 1934)

Q
115
G 76

DIPTERA   NEW GUINEA

Edwards, F. W.

Report on the Diptera collected by the British Ornithologists' Union Expedition and the Wollaston Expedition in Dutch New Guinea. With a section on the Asilidae by E. E. Austen.
Grant, William R. Ogilvie
Reports on the collections made by the British Ornithologists' Union Expedition and the Wollaston Expedition in Dutch New Guinea..no.XI, pp. 391-424,   Trans. Zool. Soc. London, Vol. 20, 1915.

QL
Insect
Pam.
1373

DIPTERA   NEW GUINEA

Malloch, John R.

Diptera of the Territory of New Guinea, XI. Family Trypetidae.

(Proc. Linn. Soc. of New South Wales, Vol. 64:409-465, 1939)

RC
1
S 98

DIPTERA   NEW GUINEA

Taylor, F. H.

The Diptera of the Territory of New Guinea, I. Family Culicidae.

(Sydney University, School of Public Health and Tropical Medicine, Collected Papers, No. 1, Article 46, 1937)

QL
Insect
Pam.
1370

DIPTERA   NEW GUINEA

Lindner, Erwin

VI. Family Stratiomyiidae.

The Diptera of the Territory of New Guinea.

(Proc. Linn. Soc. of New South Wales, Vol. 63:431-436, 1938)

QL
Insect
Pam.
1376

DIPTERA   NEW GUINEA

Oldroyd, H.

The Diptera of the Territory of New Guinea, XIV. Family Tabanidae, Part II. Pangoniinae, except the genus Chrysops.

(Proc. Linn. Soc. New South Wales, Vol. 72: 125-142, 1947)

QL
Insect
Pam.
1375

DIPTERA   NEW GUINEA.

Taylor, Frank H.

The Diptera of the Territory of New Guinea, XIII. Family Tabanidae, Part I. The genus Chrysops.

(Proc. Linn. Soc. of New South Wales, Vol. 70:328-332, 1946)

QL
Insect
Pam.
1372

DIPTERA   NEW GUINEA

Macfie, J. W. S.

The Diptera of the Territory of New Guinea, X. Family Ceratopogonidae.

(Proc. Linnean Soc. of New South Wales, Vol. 64:367-368, 1939)

AS
773
N 53 z

DIPTERA   NEW GUINEA

Paramonov, S. J.

Some new species of Euphumosia Mall. and Hemipyrellia Towns. from the Moluccas and New Guinea (Diptera, Calliphorida).

(Nova Guinea, Zoology, No. 12, 1961)

[Results of the Archbold Expedition]

AS
36
W 2

DIPTERA   NEW HEBRIDES

James Maurice T.

The Stratiomyidae (Diptera) of New Caledonia and the New Hebrides with notes on the Solomon Islands forms.

(Journal of the Washington Academy of Sciences, Vol. 40:248-260, 1950)

AS 36 S4
DIPTERA—NEW MEXICO
Walton, William Randolph, 1873–
Report on some parasitic and predaceous *Diptera* from northeastern New Mexico. By W. R. Walton ...
(*In* U. S. National museum. Proceedings. Washington, 1915. 23½cm. v. 48, p. 171-186. pl. 6-7)
1. Diptera—New Mexico.
15-24774
Library of Congress   Q11.U55 vol. 48

AS 720.N L
DIPTERA NEW SOUTH WALES
Malloch, John R.
The Diptera of the Territory of New Guinea. III. Families Muscidae and Tachinidae.
(Proc. Linn. Soc. New South Wales, Vol. 60: 74-78, 1935)

AS 750 N 56
DIPTERA NEW ZEALAND
Dumbleton, L. J.
Notes on New Zealand Diptera.
(Transactions of the Royal Society of New Zealand, Vol. 81(2):239-244, 1953)

AS 750 N 56
DIPTERA - NEW ZEALAND
Harrison, Roy A.
The Diptera of the Antipodes and the Bounty Islands.
(Transactions of the Royal Society of New Zealand, Vol. 81(2):269-282, 1953)

QL 461 D 48 b
DIPTERA NEW ZEALAND
Hennig, Willi
Die Dipteren-fauna von Neuseeland als systematisches und tiergeographisches Problem.
(Beitrage zur Entomologie, Bd. 10:221-329, 1960)

QL Insect Pam 26 and AS 750 D-m
Diptera-New Zealand
Hutton, Frederick Wollaston, 1836–1905.
... Catalogues of the New Zealand *Diptera, Orthoptera, Hymenoptera;* with descriptions of the species. By Frederick Wollaston Hutton ... Wellington, G. Didsbury, government printer, 1881.
x, 132 p. illus. 24½cm.
At head of title: Colonial museum and geological survey of New Zealand. James Hector ... director.
Published by command.
1. Diptera—New Zealand. 2. Orthoptera—New Zealand. 3. Hymenoptera—New Zealand. I. New Zealand. Geological survey dept. II. Wellington, New Zealand. Colonial museum.
8-6744
Library of Congress   QL487.N5H9

QL Insects Pam 172 and #170
Diptera-New Zealand
Hutton, Frederick W.
Synopsis of the Diptera brachycera of New Zealand. (Transactions of the New Zealand institute, 1900).

QL Ins Pam #168
Diptera New Zealand
Kirby, W.F.
Notes on the Diptera of New Zealand supplementary to Prof. Hutton's catalogue of 1881
(from Ent. Soc. Trans. 1884. pt. III. pp. 269-275)

AS 36 S2
Diptera.- North American
Aldrich, J. M.
A catalogue of North American Diptera.
In Smithsonian Mis. Col. XLVI. Art. II.
Washington. 1905. pp. 680.

AS 36 S2
DIPTERA-NORTH AMERICA.
Aldrich, John Merton, 1866–
... A catalogue of North American *Diptera* (or two-winged flies) by J. M. Aldrich ... Washington, Smithsonian institution, 1905.
1 p. l., 680 p. 25cm. (Smithsonian miscellaneous collections. vol. XLVI. (no. III.))
Publication no. 1444.
"Based upon Osten Sacken's Catalogue of North American *Diptera,* second edition, 1878," published as Smithsonian miscellaneous collections, v. 16, article II.
Bibliography: p. 7-75; appendix: p. 659-665.
1. Diptera—North America. I. Osten-Sacken, Carl Robert, freiherr von der, 1828-1906.
5-26783
Library of Congress   Q11.S7 vol. 46 no. 2
—— Copy 2.   QL535.1.A36

AS 36 S4
DIPTERA--NORTH AMERICA.
Aldrich, John Merton, 1866–
The dipterous genus *Symphoromyia* in North America. By John Merton Aldrich ...
(*In* U. S. National museum. Proceedings. Washington, 1916. 23½cm. v. 49, p. 113-142. illus.)
1. Symphoromyia. 2. Diptera—North America.
16-11780
Library of Congress   Q11.U55 vol. 49
—— Copy 2.   Q11.U55 vol. 49 2d set

AS 36 S4
DIPTERA--NORTHAMERICA
Coquillett, Daniel William, 1856–
The type-species of the North American genera of *Diptera.* By D. W. Coquillett ...
(*In* U. S. National museum. Proceedings. Washington, 1910. 23½cm. vol. 37, p. 499-647)
1. Diptera—North America.
11-9683
Library of Congress   Q11.U55 vol. 37

DIPTERA NORTH AMERICA
Curran, C. H.
Families and genera of North American Diptera. 1934. $7.50
HSPA has

AS 36 S2
DIPTERA--NORTH AMERICA.
Loew, Hermann, 1807–1879.
... Monographs of the *Diptera* of North America. Prepared for the Smithsonian institution ... Washington, Smithsonian institution, 1862-73.
4 v. illus, 15 pl. 24cm. (Smithsonian miscellaneous collections. (vol. VI, art. I-II; vol. XI, art. III; vol. VIII, art. II))
Publications 141, 171, 256, and 219.
Part I: By H. Loew, ed. with additions, by R. Osten Sacken. 1862.
Part II: By H. Loew, ed. by R. Osten Sacken. 1864.
Part III: By H. Loew. 1873.
Part IV: By R. Osten Sacken. 1869.
CONTENTS.—pt. I. *Trypetidæ, Sciomyzidæ, Ephydrinidæ, Cecidomyidæ.*—pt. II. *Dolichopodidæ.*—pt. III. *Ortalidæ.* Review of North American *Trypetina,* with appendices.—pt. IV. *Tipulidæ.* pt. I: *Tipulidæ brevipalpi.*
1. Diptera—North America. I. Osten-Sacken, Carl Robert, freiherr von der, 1828-1906. II. Osten-Sacken, Carl Robert, freiherr von der, 1828-1906, ed.
5-5456
Library of Congress   Q11.S7 vol. 6, art. 1-2; vol. 11, art. 3; vol. 8, art. 1
—— Copy 2.   Q11.S7 2d set

AS 36 S4
DIPTERA--NORTH AMERICA
Malloch, John Russell, 1875–
New American dipterous insects of the family *Pipunculidæ.* By J. R. Malloch ...
(*In* U. S. National museum. Proceedings. Washington, 1913. 23½cm. vol. 43, p. 291-299. illus.)
1. Pipunculidæ. 2. Diptera—North America.
13-13118
Library of Congress   Q11.U55 vol. 43

AS 36 S2
DIPTERA-NORTH AMERICA
Osten-Sacken, Carl Robert, *freiherr* von der, 1828–1906.
... Catalogue of the described *Diptera* of North America. Prepared for the Smithsonian institution by R. Osten Sacken. Washington, Smithsonian institution, 1858.
2 p. l, (vii)-xx, 95 p. 23½cm. (Smithsonian miscellaneous collections. (vol. III, art. I))
Publication 102.
Appendix, p. (93)-95, pub. October, 1859.
Authorities: p. (xi)-xviii.
1. Diptera—North America.
6-44420 Revised
Library of Congress   Q11.S7 vol. 3, art. 1
—— Copy 2.   QL535.1.O8
Appendix wanting.
—— Copy 3.   Q11.S7 2d set

AS 36 S2
DIPTERA - NORTH AMERICA
Osten-Sacken, Carl Robert, *freiherr* von der, 1828–1906.
... Catalogue of the described *Diptera* of North America. By C. R. Osten Sacken. <2d ed.> Washington, Smithsonian institution, 1878.
xlvi, (2), 276 p. 24cm. (Smithsonian miscellaneous collections. (vol. XVI, art. II))
Publication 270.
"... Not merely a new edition ... but an entirely new work."—Advertisement.
Authorities: p. (xxvii)-xlvi.
1. Diptera—North America.
16-10043
Library of Congress   Q11.S7 vol. 16, art. 2

AS 36 S5
DIPTERA - NORTH AMERICA
Williston, Samuel Wendell, 1852–
... Synopsis of the North American *Syrphidæ.* By Samuel W. Williston ... With twelve plates. Washington, Govt. print. off., 1886.
xxx, 335 p. XII pl. 24cm. (*Added t.-p.:* ... Bulletin of the United States National museum. no. 31)
Smithsonian institution publication 653.
1. Syrphidæ. 2. Diptera—North America.
S 13-136
Library, Smithsonian   Institution Q11.U6

QL 537.M6 S93
Diptera-North America
Sturtevant, Alfred Henry.
The North American species of Drosophila, by A. H. Sturtevant.
Carnegie institution of Washington, 1921. Publication no. 301.

AS 36 C3
DIPTERA - NORTH AMERICA
Van Duzee, M. C.
A contribution to our knowledge of the North American conopidae (diptera). Proc. Calif. Acad. Sci. 4 ser. v.16, n.18, 1927.

AS 36 S5
DIPTERA - NORTH AMERICA
Van Duzee, Millard C.
... The dipterous genus *Dolichopus* Latreille in North America, by M. C. Van Duzee, F. R. Cole and J. M. Aldrich. Washington, Govt. print. off., 1921.
iv, 304 p. 1 illus., 16 pl. on 8 l. 25cm. (Smithsonian institution. United States National museum. Bulletin 116)
"Bibliography of genus *Dolichopus* Latreille": p. 8.
1. Dolichopus. 2. Diptera—North America. I. Cole, Frank R., joint author. II. Aldrich, John Merton, 1866– joint author.
21-26209
Library of Congress   Q11.U6 no. 116
—— Copy 2.   QL537.D7V27

AS 36 0 2
DIPTERA - OHIO
Metcalf, Clell Lee.
... The *Syrphidae* of Ohio, by C. L. Metcalf. Columbus, The Ohio state university, 1913.
122, [1] p. illus., diagrs. 25cm. (Ohio biological survey. vol. 1. Bulletin 1)
On cover: The Ohio state university bulletin. vol. XVII, no. 31. Bibliography: p. 99–100.

1. Syrphidae. 2. Diptera—Ohio. A 14–169
Title from Ohio State Library of Congress   Univ. Printed by L. C.   QL537.S8M4
[a21c1]

AS S2
DIPTERA-PANAMA
Malloch, John Russell, 1875–
... Three new species of *Pipunculidæ* (*Diptera*) from Panama, by J. R. Malloch ... Washington, Smithsonian institution, 1912.
1 p. l., 4 p. illus. 24½cm. (Smithsonian miscellaneous collections, v. 60, no. 1)
Publication 2141.

1. Pipunculidae. 2. Diptera—Panama.
Library of Congress   Q11.S7 vol. 60, no. 1   12–24426
——— Copy 2.   Q1.537.P6M3

AS 36 S 4
DIPTERA PHILIPPINES
Malloch, J. R.
Notes on some Oriental sapromyzid flies (diptera), with particular reference to the Philippine species.
(In Proc. U. S. Nat. Mus., Vol. 74, Art. 6, 1929)

QH 1 P 11
DIPTERA OKINAWA
James, Maurice T.
Some Stratiomyidae (Diptera) from Okinawa and Guam.
(Pacific Sicence, Vol. 4:184–187, 1950)

AS 720.N L
DIPTERA PAPUA
Alexander Charles P.
Contribution to a knowledge of Papuan Tipulidae (Diptera).
(Proceedings of the Linn. Soc. of N.S.Wales, vol. LXI, 1936, pp. 122–127)

AS 36 C 3
DIPTERA POLYNESIA
Curran, C. H.
Diptera (Templeton Crocker Expedition to Western Polynesian and Melanesian Islands, 1933, no. 30)
(Proc. of Calif. Acad. of Sciences, 4th ser. vol.22, no.1, pp.1-66. Dec.18,1936),

---

AS 36 C3
DIPTERA—OREGON.
Cole, Frank R.
... New Oregon *Diptera*, by F. R. Cole ... and A. L. Lovett ... San Francisco, The Academy, 1919.
cover-title, p. [221]–255. pl. 14–19. 25½cm. (Proceedings of the California academy of sciences. 4th ser., vol. IX, no. 7)
"Printed from the John W. Hendrie publication endowment."

1. Diptera—Oregon. I. Lovett, Arthur Lester, joint author.
Library of Congress   Q11.C253 vol. IX, no. 7   19–15472
[5]

AS 720.N L
DIPTERA PAPUA
Malloch, John Russell
Description of a new genus and two new species from Papua. Family Pyrgotidae (Diptera).
(Proceedings, Linnean Society of New South Wales, Vol. LXIV, 1939, pp. 51-53)

QL 489.S P 11

AS 763 B-b
Reading Room
DIPTERA SOCIETY ISLANDS
Edwards, F. W.
Some Tahitian Mycetophilidae and Chironomidae.
Society Islands Insects. Pacific Entomological Survey Publication 6, pp. 85-86 (Art.16), 1935.
(Bernice P. Bishop Museum, Bulletin 113)

QL Insect Pam.929

AS 763 B-84
Reading Room
DIPTERA PACIFIC
Barnes, H. F.
Check list of the Cecidomyidae of Oceania.
(B.Mus.Occasional Papers, vol.XIII, no.6. 1937. pp.61-66)

AS 720.N L
DIPTERA PAPUA
Malloch, John Russell
Papuan Diptera.I. Family Diopsidae.
(Proceedings, Linnean Society of New South Wales, Vol. LXIII, 1938, pp. 437-438)

QL 489.S P 11

AS 763 B-b
Reading Room
DERMAPTERA SOCIETY ISLANDS
Hebard, Morgan
Demaptera and Orthoptera from the Society Islands.
Society Islands Insects. Pacific Entomological Survey Publication 6, pp. 57-65 (Art.11), 1935.
(Bernice P. Bishop Museum, Bulletin 113)

QL 461 H-1
DIPTERA PACIFIC
Sabrosky, Curtis W.
The Muscid genus Ophyra in the Pacific region (Diptera).
(Proc. Haw. Ent. Soc., 13:423-432, 1949)

QL 535.3 B 86
DIPTERA PATAGONIA
British Museum of Natural History.
Diptera of Patagonia and South Chile; based mainly on material in the British Museum. London, British Museum. 1929- > 8vo
Part 1 —>
See main card for full information

QL 489.S P 11

AS 763 B-b
Reading Room
DIPTERA SOCIETY ISLANDS
Malloch, John R(ussell)
An aberrant Scaptomyza from the Society Islands (Diptera, Drosophilidae).
Society Islands Insects. Pacific Entomological Survey Publication 6, pp. 95-96 (Art. 20), 1935.
(Bernice P. Bishop Museum, Bulletin 113)

QL 537.B6 A 93
DIPTERA PALESTINE
Austen, E. E.
Bombyliidae of Palestine...London. 1937. Printed by order of the Trustees of the British Museum.

AS 36 S 4
DIPTERA PHILIPPINES
Aldrich, J. M.
New species of two-winged flies of the family Cyrtidae, with a new genus from the Philippines.
(In Proc. U. S. Nat. Mus., Vol. 72, Art. 9, 1927)

QL 489.S P 11

AS 763 B-b
Reading Room
DIPTERA SOCIETY ISLANDS
Malloch, John R(ussell)
Asteia societas, new species, from Tahiti (Diptera, Asteidae).
Society Islands Insects. Pacific Entomological Survey Publication 6, p. 91 (Art. 18), 1935.
(Bernice P. Bishop Museum, Bulletin 113)

AS 36 S2
DIPTERA-PANAMA.
Malloch, John Russell, 1875–
. ... New *Diptera* from Panama, by J. R. Malloch ... Washington, Smithsonian institution, 1912.
1 p. l., 8 p. 24½cm. (Smithsonian miscellaneous collections, v. 59, no. 17)
Publication 2133.

1. Diptera—Panama.
Library of Congress   Q11.S7 vol. 59, no. 17   12–35967
——— Copy 2.   QL535.2.M3

AS 540 P
DIPTERA PHILIPPINE ISLANDS
del Rosario, F.
Philippine Psychodidae (Diptera), I.
(Philippine Journal of Science, Vol. 59, 1936, pp. 563–572)

QL 489.S P 11

AS 763 B-b
Reading Room
DIPTERA SOCIETY ISLANDS
Malloch, John R(ussell)
Species of Arnomyia from the Society Islands (Diptera, Sapromyzidae).
Society Islands Insects. Pacific Entomological Survey Publication 6, p. 93, (Art. 19), 1935.

QL
Insects
Pam.
429

DIPTERA   SOLOMON ISLANDS

Alexander, Charles Paul

Two undescribed species of Tanyderus from the Australasian region...

(Insector Inscitiae Menstruus, Vol. XII, Nos. 7-9, 1924, pp. 141-143)

QL
461
D 48 b

DIPTERA   SUNDA ISLANDS

Hardy, D. E.

Dipteren von den Kleinen Sunda-Inseln, V. Bibionidae.

(Beiträge zur Entomologie, Bd 2(4/5):425-434, 1952)

AS
36
A65

DIPTERA-WEST INDIES

Curran, C. H.

New Diptera from the West Indies. Am. Mus. Nat. His. Nov. 220, 1926.

AS
36
S 4

DIPTERA SOLOMON ISLANDS

James, Maurice T.

Flies of the family Stratiomyidae of the Solomon Islands.

(Proc. of the U. S. Nat. Mus., Vol. 98:187-213, 1948)

QL
461
D 48-a

DIPTERA SUNDA ISLANDS

Hennig, W.

Diptera von den Kleinen Sunda-Inseln, I-II.

(Arbeiten uber morphologische und taxonomische Entomologie, B d. 8:16-45, 1941)

QL
535.4
L 96

Diptera Danica...

Lundbeck, William

Diptera Danica, genera and species of flies hitherto found in Denmark. Parts I-V

London. William Wesley & Son. 1907-1916.

AS
36
W 2

DIPTERA SOLOMON ISLANDS

James, Maurice T.

The Stratiomyidae (Diptera) of New Caledonia and the New Hebrides with notes on the Solomon Islands forms.

(Journal of the Washington Academy of Sciences, Vol. 40:248-260, 1950)

QL
461
D 48-b

DIPTERA   SUNDA ISLANDS

Hennig, Willi

Dipteren von den Kleinen Sunda-Inseln. IV. Fam. Muscidae.

(Beiträge zur Entomologie, Bd. 2(1):55-93, 1952)

QK
1
S 61

DIPTEROCARPACEAE   BORNEO

Ashton, P. S.

Some new Dipterocarpaceae from Borneo.

(The Gardens' Bulletin, 19(2):253-320, 1962)

QL
Insect
Pam.
757

DIPTERA   SOUTH AMERICA

Aldrich, John Merton

New diptera or two-winged flies from South America.

(Proc. U. S. Nat. Mus., Vol. 74, 1928, pp. 1-25, Art. 2746).

QL
461
D 48 e

DIPTERA TAIWAN

Hennig, Willi

Verzeischnis der Dipteren von Formosa.

(Entomologische Beihefte aus Berlin-Dahlem, Bd. 8, 1941)

QK
Bot.Pam.
3095

DIPTEROCARPACEAE   THAILAND

Smitinand, Tem

Identification keys to the Dipterocarpaceae of Thailand.

(Repr. Nat. Hist. Bull. of the Siam Society, Vol. 19,1958: 57-83)

AS
36
S4

DIPTERA--SOUTH AMERICA.
Alexander, Charles Paul.
A revision of the South American dipterous insects of the family *Ptychopteridæ*. By Charles P. Alexander ...

(*In* U. S. National museum. Proceedings. Washington, 1913. 23½ᶜᵐ. v. 44, p. 331-335. illus.)

1. Ptychopteridae. 2. Diptera—South America.

13-20863

Library of Congress   Q11.U55 vol. 44

AS
720.T
R

DIPTERA TASMANIA

Hardy, G. H.

Notes on Tasmanian Diptera and descriptions of new species.

(Papers and Proc. R. Soc. Tasmania, 1916: 267-272) and 1917:60-66

QK
364
S 64

DIPTEROCARPUS

Smitinand, Tem

The genus Dipterocarpus, Gaertn. F. in Thailand.

(Thai Forest Bull. (Bot.) No.4, 1958)

QL
535.3
B86

DIPTERA. SOUTH AMERICA

British Museum of Natural History

Diptera of Patagonia and South Chile; based mainly on material in the British Museum.

Part I   Crane flies.   Alexander
Part II, Fasc. 1, Psychodidae.   Tonnoir
Part II. Fasc. 2, Blepharoceridae.   Edwards.
Part III
London, British Museum, 1929 →

see main card for full information

AS
720.T
R

DIPTERA TASMANIA

White, Arthur

The Diptera-Brachycera of Tasmania, Parts 1-3.

(Papers and Proc. R. Soc. of Tasmania, 1914:35-74; 1915:1-59; 1916:267-272)

AS
36
C8

DIPTEROUS LARVAE FROM THE WESTERN...
Williston, Samuel Wendell, 1852-
... Dipterous larvæ from the western alkaline lakes and their use as human food.

(*In* Connecticut academy of arts and sciences. Transactions. New Haven, 1882-85. 25ᶜᵐ. v. 6, p. 187-90. illus.)

1. Diptera—U. S. 2. Insects as food. i. Title.

A 17-802

Library of Congress   Q11.C9 vol. 6
Yale University   A53n.366.6

AS
750
D 67 c

DIPTERA SUBANTARCTIC ISL. (NZ)

Harrison, Roy A.

Report on Diptera of Auckland and Campbell Islands. By Roy A. Harrison and others.

(Cape Exp., Sci. Res. of the New Zealand Subantarctic Exp., 1941-45, No. 2, 1955)

AS
36
C8

DIPTERA-U.S.
Williston, Samuel Wendell, 1852-
... Dipterous larvæ from the western alkaline lakes and their use as human food.

(*In* Connecticut academy of arts and sciences. Transactions. New Haven, 1882-85. 25ᶜᵐ. v. 6, p. 187-90. illus.)

1. Diptera—U. S. 2. Insects as food. i. Title.

A 17-802

Library of Congress   Q11.C9 vol. 6
Yale University   A53n.366.6

QH
431
K46

The direction of hair in animals and man.

Kidd, Walter

QK
Pam
163

Directions for Collecting.

Directions for collecting and preparing Herbarium specimens for the Philadelphia Museums.

Philadelphia: 1899.

Z
222
C1

DIRECTORY - BOOKSELLERS

Clegg, James

The international directory of booksellers.....

London, 1914, pp 644.

AH
20 Ca
1905

Directory, Naturalists Universal.

Cassino, Samuel Edson.

Salem, 1905, pp 208.

AS
36
S 5

and

AM
Mus.Pam.
14

Directions for collecting and preserving specimens. (birds by Ridgway; reptiles by Stejneger, insects by Riley, etc)

(Bulletin, U. S. National Museum, No. 39, 1911)

AM
Mus.
Pam.
442

DIRECTORY BOTANISTS

Moore, Raymond J.

A directory of botanists in Canada. Published by Plant Research Institute, Research Branch, Canada Department of Agriculture, Ottawa 1959. 8vo. 99 pp.

DIRECTORY OCEANOGRAPHERS

Emery, K. O.

An international directory of oceanographers. 2nd edition. 1955.

UH has

GN
Pam
#61

Directions for collecting

Hrdlička, Aleš

Directions for collecting information and specimens for physical anthropology, ex U. S. Nat. Mus. Bull. no. 39, pt. R., 1904.

See author card

AM
11
C 55

DIRECTORY MUSEUMS

Christensen, Erwin O.

Museums directory of the United States and Canada. American Association of Museums. Smithsonian Institution. Washington, D. C. sm4to. 1961. xx + 567 pp.

AS
522
N 28-b

DIRECTORY SCIENTISTS INDONESIA

Guide of scientists in Indonesia. Third edition.

(Bull. Organization for Sci. Research, Djakarta, No. 11, Jan. 1952)

QL
Ins.
Pam.
34

DIRECTIONS FOR COLLECTING INSECTS

Cockerell, T. D. A.

Directions for collecting and preserving scale insects (Coccidae)

(U.S.Nat.Mus. Pt.L, Bul.39, 1897)

AS
36
B 92

DIRECTORY (AMERICAN) MUSEUMS

Rea, Paul Marshall

A directory of American museums of art, history, and science.

(Bull. Buffalo Society of Natural Sciences, Vol. X, pp. 1-360, 1910)

Reading
Room

Directory of agencies and officers of the Territory of Hawaii.   Sixth edition. Legislative Reference Bureau, University of Hawaii. November, 1951.

QK
Pam.
162

and

AS
36
S5

DIRECTIONS TO COLLECTORS

Knowlton, F. H.

Directions for collecting recent and fossil plants. In U.S.Nat. Mus. Bul. no. 39, part B, Washington, 1891.

DIRECTORY MUSEUMS

See also

MUSEUMS DIRECTORY

Reading
Room

Directory of Conchologists, 1949. John Q. Burch. Los Angeles. 4to. 21 pp. mimeographed.

Reading
Room
Ref.
Shelf

DIRECTORY ANTHROPOLOGICAL INSTITUTIONS

Thomas, William L., Jr. editor

International directory of anthropological institutions. Edited by William L. Thomas, Jr. and Anna M. Pikelis. Wenner-Gren Foundation for Anthropological Research, Inc. New York. 1953. xii + 468 pp. 4to.

AH
25.Am
1925

DIRECTORY -- NATURALISTS -- AMERICA

Cassino, Samuel E.

The naturalists' directory...... of the United States and Canada.

Salem, 1925.

QH
104
U -d

Directory of field activities of the Bureau of Biological Survey, 1939.

(Misc. Pub. No. 343, U. S. Dept. Agric., 1939)

DIRECTORY HONOLULU

see

HONOLULU DIRECTORY

DU
1
P

Honolulu.
DIRECTORY -- Scientific institutions

Pan- Pacific Research Institution

Institutions for research work in the Territory of Hawaii. Journ.Pan-Pacific Research Inst. Vol. I, No.3, July - Sept. 1926.

AM
11
S 53

Directory of historical societies and agencies in the United States and Canada.

Silvestro, Clement M. compiler

DU
622
P 72

Directory of Honolulu and the Territory of Hawaii,1918. Vol. XXV. Honolulu. Polk-Husted Directory Co. (1918) 1290 pp. R8vo.

... Vol. 38, 1931/32

Carter
Coll.
7-C-21   Directory of 1902

AS
522
I 41-h   Directory of Scientific Institutions in Indonesia.

(Bull. Madjelis Ilmu Pengetahuan Indonesia, No. 1, 1959)

DU
Hist.
Pam.
553

Disappearing Honolulu architecture. (Explanation of an exhibition, Honolulu Academy of Arts, Nov. 29-Dec. 30, 1962) 2 pp. mimeographed.

Reference
Shelf

Directory of International Scientific Organizations. UNESCO, Paris. 8vo. 1950c. xiii + 224 pp.

QL
26
B 63   Directory of zoological taxonomists.

Blackwelder, Richard E.   and Ruth M.

DU
1
P 12

Discombe, Reece

Voyage to Vanikoro, by Reece Discombe and Pierre Anthonioz.

(Pacific Discovery, 13(1):4-15, 1960)

[finding evidence, remains of the ships of La Perouse' voyage]

Z
3301
N 27

Directory of Japanese Learned Periodicals. 1957:
     Natural and medical sciences.
     Applied Sciences - Fine Arts
     Generalities and Social Sciences.

Compiled by National Diet Library. Tokyo. Tokyo Library Bureau. 1957-58.

Hms
M48

Dirge. (Kanikau, Uwe.)
Extracts from various sources.

Storage
Case
4

QK
Bot.Pam.
2092

DISCOMYCETES

Cash, Edith K.

New records of Hawaiian Discomycetes.

(Mycologia, Vol. 30, 1039,pp. 97-107)

QL
627
P 11

A directory of Japanese marine biologists and scientists in related fields.

(Pacific Oceanic Fishery Investigations, U. S. Fish and Wildlife Service, Dept. of the Interior, Honolulu 1949)

Storage
Case
4

Hms
68
a,b,c

Dirges for Albert, Prince of Hawaii. (printed, clippings from newspapers, sources not always given; 11 items, one dated Mei 1, 1862)

(includes memorabilia, and Kanikau no ka moi Alexander Kalanikualiholiho Maka o Iouli, Kunuiakea o Kukailimoku, Kamehameha IV, by W. L. Moehonua. 1864)

AS
244
D

DISCOPHORA

Stiasny, Gustav

Die Scyphomedusen-Sammlung von Dr. Th. Mortensen nebst anderen Medusen aus dem zoologischen Museum der Universität in Kopenhagen.

(Vid. Med. Dansk Nat. For. Kobenhavn, Bd. 73, 1922,- Papers from Dr. Mortensen's Pacific Expedition 1914-16, No. 13)

AM
213
H 85

Directory of Museums

Howarth E. and Platnauer, H. M.

Directory of museums in Great Britain & Ireland together with a section on Indian and Colonial museums.

Museums Assoc. [London], 1911, 312 pp.

GN
Pam
1408

Dirr, A

Uber die klassen in den Kaukasischen sprachen. From Int. Arch. f. Ethnog. bd. 18.

DU
Pac.Pam.
522

Discoveries and Acquisitions in the Pacific. Handbooks prepared under the direction of the Historical section of the Foreign Office (London) No. 139. H. M. Stationery Office. 1920. 8vo. 35 pp. 8vo.

AM
213
M

Directory of Museums

Merrill, Frederick J. H.

Natural history museums of the of the United States and Canada. New York State Mus. Bull. No. 62. , 1903.

QL
461
B 86

Dirsh, V. M.

The Acridoidea (Orthoptera) of Madagascar. I. Acrididae (except Acridinae).

(Bull. British Mus. (Nat. Hist.), Entomology, 12(6), 1962)

DU
96
H 45
l.c.

DISCOVERIES, DUTCH

Heeres, J. E.

Part borne by the Dutch in the discovery of Australia 1606-1765...(In Dutch and in English) London, Luzac & Co., 1899. xvii + 106 pp. sm folio

---

Ref.
Shelf
Reading
Room

Directory of New Zealand science.

Bastings, Lyndon   editor

DISCOBOLI

QL Garman, Samuel, 1846-
1   The *Discoboli. Cyclopteridæ, Liparopsidæ,* and *Liparididæ.* By S. Garman ... Cambridge, Printed for the
H2   Museum, 1892.

96 p. XIII pl. 29ᶜᵐ. (Memoirs of the Museum of comparative zoölogy at Harvard college, vol. XIV, no. 2)

1. Discoboli.   A 19-1058

Title from Univ. of Chicago   QL1.H375   vol. 14, no. 2
Printed by L. C.   [3]

G
159
H 44

DISCOVERIES (IN GEOGRAPHY)

Heawood, Edward

A history of geographical discovery in the 17th and 18th centuries. Cambridge, 1912.

G 161 H
DISCOVERIES ‑(in geography) ‑ SPANISH
Queiros, Pedro Fernandes de, *d.* 1615.
The voyages of Pedro Fernandez de Quiros, 1595 to 1606. Tr. and ed. by Sir Clements Markham ... London, Printed for the Hakluyt society, 1904.

2 v. fold. maps in pocket. 22½ᵐᵐ. (*Half-title:* Works issued by the Hakluyt society ... 2d ser., no. xiv‑xv)

Paged continuously.
The first and third narratives are translations of the "Historia del descubrimiento de las regiones australes," first published at Madrid in 1876 by Zaragoza, who ascribes the authorship to Luis de Belmonte Bermudez.

(Continued on next card)
5—20290

G 161 H
DISCOVERIES (IN GEOGRAPHY) ‑ SPANISH
Queiros, Pedro Fernandes de, *d.* 1615.   The voyages of Pedro Fernandez de Quiros ... 1904.   (Card 2)
CONTENTS.—v. 1. Introduction. Comparative list of maps of the New Hebrides, etc., 1570‑1904 by B. H. Soulsby. Bibliography. Narrative of the second voyage of the adelantado Alvaro de Mendaña, by the chief pilot, Pedro Fernandez de Quiros. Narrative of the voyage of the adelantado Alvaro de Mendaña de Neira for the discovery of the Islands of Solomon. Written by ... Pedro Fernandez de Quiros, for Dr. Antonio de Morga. Narrative of the voyage of Pedro Fernandez de Quiros in 1606, for the discovery of the austrial regions.—v. 2. True account of the events of the voyage that the Captain Pedro Fernandez de Quiros made by order of His Majesty to the southern unknown land, by Gaspar Gonzalez de Leza. Torquemada's Voyage of Quiros; translation, with notes, from the "Monarquia indiana." Letter from Luis Vaez de Torres ... to the
(Continued on next card)
5—20290

G 161 H
DISCOVERIES ‑ (IN GEOGRAPHY) ‑ SPANISH
Queiros, Pedro Fernandes de, *d.* 1615.   The voyages of Pedro Fernandez de Quiros ... 1904.   (Card 3)
CONTENTS—Continued.
king of Spain, giving an account of his voyage to Manilla after parting company with Quiros. Legends on the four maps signed Diego de Prado y Tobar, illustrating the discoveries of Quiros and Torres. Appendix. I. Eighth memorial of Quiros, 1606. II‑III. Memorials of Quiros, 1609. IV. Memorial of Don Fernando de Castro, 1608. v. Letters from Don Diego de Prado y Tobar, 1613. IV. Note on the Memorial of Captain Quiros to the Council of the Indies, 1610. VII. Memorial touching papers printed by Quiros, 1610. VIII. Memorial by Juan Luis Arias.
1. Oceanica—Disc. & explor. 2. Discoveries (in geography)—Spanish. 3. Mendaña de Neira, Alvaro, d. 1595. 4. Cartography. 5. Maps, Early. I. Markham, Sir Clements Robert, 1830‑1916, ed. II. Soulsby, Basil Harrington. III. Belmonte y Bermudez, Luis de, 17th cent. IV. Gonzalez de Leza, Gaspar, 17th cent. V. Torquemada, Juan de, fl. 1600. VI. Torres, Luis Vaez de, fl. 1606. VII.   Prado y Tobar, Diego de, 17th cent. VIII. Castro, Fernando   de, fl. 1590‑1609. IX. Arias, Juan Luis.

Library of Congress   G161.H2 .
5—20290

DISCOVERIES (IN GEOGRAPHY)

See also

under names of countries, regions, etc., as Pacific-Discovery and Exploration.

DU 1 Pa
Discoveries in New Guinea. Centre of Main Island is Rich, Temperate Densely Populated Plateau.

(The Pacific Islands Monthly, Vol. 4, No. 5, 1933, pp. 11-15)

QH 301 L
DISCOVERY COMMITTEE
Mackintosh, N. A.
The work of the Discovery Committee.

(Proc. Roy. Soc., London, Ser. B., No. 867, Vol. 137, pp. 137-152, 1950)

GC 63 D 61
Discovery Committee
Discovery Reports, issued by the Discovery Committee, Colonial Office, London, on behalf of the Government of the Dependencies of the Falkland Islands.
    Vol. I: Station List, 1925-1927. (1929)
        Discovery Investigations: objects, equipment and methods, by S. Kemp, A.C. Hardy, and N. A. Mackintosh. (1929)
        The natural history of the elephant seal, by L. H. Matthews. (1929)

    continued on next card
(Card 1)

GC 63 D 61
Discovery Committee
    Discovery Reports...
        Vol. I (cont.) Southern blue and fin whales, by N. A. Mackintosh and J. F. G. Wheeler. (1929)
        Parasitic Nematoda and Acanthocephala, collected in 1925-1927, by H. A. Baylis. (1929)
        The birds of South Georgia, by L.H. Matthews. (1929)
        Vol. II: Polychaete worms, by C. C. A. Monro (1930)
        Thoracic Cirripedes collected in 1925-27. (1930), by C.A. Nilsson-Cantell.

        continued on next card
Card 2

GC 63 D 61
Discovery Committee
    Discovery Reports...
        Vol. II (cont.) Oceanic fishes and flatfishes collected in 1925-1927, by J. R. Norman. (1930)
        Cephalopoda, I: Octopoda, by G.C. Robson (1930).
        The age of fin whales at physical maturity with a note on multiple ovulations (1931) by J. F. G. Wheeler.
        On the anatomy of a marine Ostracod, Cypridina (Doloria) levis Skogsberg, by H.Graham Cannon. (1931)

        Continued on next card
Card 3

GC 63 D 61
Discovery Committee
    Discovery Reports ...
        Vol. III: Station List 1927-1929. (1930)
        The South Sandwich Islands, by Stanley Kemp and A.L.Nelson and G.W.Tyrrell. (1931)
        Nebaliacea by H.Graham Cannon(1931)
        Cephalodiscus by C.C.John (1931)
        Spiders collected by the Discovery Expedition with a description of a new species from South Georgia, by W.S.Bristowe (1931)
        Narrative of hydrographic survey... 1926-1930 by J.M.   Chaplin. (1932)

card 4

GC 63 D 61
Discovery Committee
    Discovery Reports ...
        Vol. IV: Station List 1929-1931. (1932)
        Oligochaeta, Part I: Microdrili (mainly Enchytraeidae) , by J. Stephenson. (1932)
        Oligochaeta, Part II: Earthworms, by Grace E.Pickford. (1932)
        Foraminifera. Part I: The ice-free area of the Falkland Islands...by Edward Heron-Allen and Arthur Earland. (1932)

card 5

GC 63 D 61
Discovery Committee
    Discovery Reports...
        Vol. V: Amphipoda, by K.H.Barnard (1932)
        The vascular networks (Retia Mirabilia) of the fin whale (Balaenoptera Physalus) by F.D. Ommanney. (1932)
        The urino-genital system of the fin whale (Balaenoptera Physalus), by F.D. Ommanney. (1932)
        Lobster-krill: Anomuran Crustacea that are the food of whales, by L. Harrison Matthews. (1932)

        continued on next card
Card 6

GC 63 D'61
Discovery Committee
    Discovery Reports...
        Vol. VI: Pycnogonida, by Isabella Gordon ('32)
        Report on penguin embryos collected during the Discovery investigations, by C.W. Parsons. (1932)
        On the distribution and movements of whales on the South Georgia and South Shetland whaling grounds, by Stanley Kemp and A.G.Bennett. (1932)
        On the development of Cephalodiscus, by C.C.John.   (1932)

        continued on next card
Card 7

GC 63 D 61
Discovery Committee
    Discovery Reports...
        Vol. VI (cont) Report on soundings taken during the Discovery investigations, 1926-1932, by N. F. P. Hardman. (1932)
        Sponges, by M. Burton (1932)
        A list of worms parasitic in Cetacea by H. A. Baylis (1932).
        Vol. VII: Fossil Foraminifera from the Burdwood Bank and their geological significance, by W. A. Macfadyen (1933).

        continued on next card
Card 8

GC 63 D 61
Discovery Committee
    Discovery Reports...
        Vol. VII (cont) Faecal pellets from marine deposits, by Hilary B. Moore (1933).
        Foraminifera, Part II: South Georgia, by Arthur Earland (1933).
        On the vertical circulation in the ocean due to the action of the wind with application to conditions within the Antarctic Circumpolar Current, by H. U. Svordrup (1933)

        continued on next card
Card 9

GC 63 D 61
Discovery Committee
    Discovery Reports...
        Vol. VII (cont) A general account of the hydrology of the South Atlantic Ocean, by G.E.R. Deacon (1933).
        Whaling in the Dominion of New Zealand, by F. D. Ommanney. (1933).
        Isopod Crustacea, Part I: The family Serolidae, by Edith M. Sheppard (1933).
        Some aspects of respiration in blue and fin whales, by Alec H. Laurie (1933).

        continued on next card
Card 10

GC 63 D 61
Discovery Committee
    Discovery Reports...
        Vol. VIII: On the phytoplankton of the South-west Atlantic and the Bellingshausen Sea, 1929-1931, by T. J. Hart (1934).
        The southern sea lion, Otaria byronia (De Blainville), by J. E. Hamilton (1934)
        On a new species of mite of the family Halarachnidae from the southern sea lion, by Susan Finnegan (1934).

        continued on next card
Card 11

GC 63 D 61
Discovery Committee
    Discovery Reports...
        Vol. VIII (cont) Scyphomedusae, by G.Stiasny (1934).
        Vol. IX: Hydrology of the Bransfield Strait, by A. Clowes. (1934).
        Distribution of the macroplankton in the Atlantic sector of the Antarctic, by N. A. Mackintosh (1934)
        The sub-Antarctic forms of the Great Skua, (Catharacta skua skua), by J. E. Hamilton. (1934)

        continued on next card
Card 12

GC 63 D 61
Discovery Committee
    Discovery Reports...
        Vol. IX: (cont) The marine deposits of the Patagonian Continental Shelf, by L. Harrison Matthews (1934).
        The development of Rhincalanus, by Robert Gurney (1934).
        Nemerteans from the South Atlantic and Southern Oceans, by J.F.G.Wheeler (1934).
        The sea-floor deposits: I. General characters and distribution, by E. Neaverson ('34)

        continued on next card
Card 13

GC 63 D 61
Discovery Committee
    Discovery Reports...
        Vol. IX (cont) On the stock of whales at South Georgia, by J. F. G. Wheeler (1934)

        continued on next card
Card 14

GC 63 D 61
Discovery Committee
    Discovery Reports ...
        Vol. X: Foraminifera. Part III: The Falkland sector of the Antarctic (excluding South Georgia), by Arthur Earland. (1934)
        The Falkland species of the crustacean genus Munida, by G.W.Rayner (1935)
        On the diatoms of the skin film of whales...and on problems of whale movements, by T.John Hart. (1935)
        The South Orkney Islands, by James W. S.Marr. (1935)

        continued on next card
Card 15

Card 16

GC
63
D 61
    Discovery Committee

      Discovery Reports ...

        Vol.X: Report on rocks from the South Orkney Islands, by C.E.Tilley.(1935)

Card 23

GC
63
D 61
    Discovery Committee

      Discovery Reports ...

        Vol.XVI: Coast Fishes.Part II:The Patagonian region,by J.R.Norman.(1937)
          The plankton diatoms of the Southern Seas, by N.Ingram Hendey.(1937)
          The seasonal circulation of the Antarctic microplankton, by N.A.Mackintosh, (1937)
          Rhizosolenia curvata Zacharias,an indicator species in the Southern Ocean,by T.John Hart.(1937)

---

card 30

GC
63
D 61
    Discovery Committee

      Discovery Reports...

        Vol. 20: Larvae of Decapod Crustacea, Part VI. The genus Sergestes, by R. Gurney and M.V. Lebour. (1940)
        Asteroidea, by Walter K. Fisher. (1940)
        On the structure of the photophores of some Decapod Crustacea, by Ralph Dennell. (1940)

Card 17

GC
63
D 61
    Discovery Committee

      Discovery Reports...

        Vol. XI: The plankton of the South Georgia whaling grounds and adjacent waters, 1926-27('35) by A. C. Hardy and E. R. Gunther.
        The continuous plankton recorder, by A. C. Hardy. With an appendix: a test of the validity of the continuous plankton recorder method, by A. C. Hardy and N. Ennis. (1936)
        Observations on the uneven distribution of oceanic plankton, by A. C. Hardy (1936).

        continued on next card

Card 24

GC
63
D 61
    Discovery Committee

      Discovery Reports ...

        Vol.XVII: On the histological structure of Cetacean lungs,by F.Haynes and Alec H.Laurie(1937)
        The humpback whale,Megaptera nodosa,by L.Harrison Matthews.(1937)
        The sperm whale,Physeter catodon, by L.Harrison Matthews.(1938)
        Notes on the Southern right whale Eubalaena australis, by L.Harrison Matthews.(1938)

        continued on next card

---

card 31

GC
63
D 61
    Discovery Committee

      Discovery Reports...

        Vol. 21: Station list, 1931-1933;
        A rare porpoise of the south Atlantic, Phocaena dioptrica (Lahille, 1912), by J.E.Hamilton (1941).
        The Echiuridae, Sipunculidae and Priapulidae collected by the ships of the Discovery Committee...1926-1937, by A. C. Stephen.
        Phytoplankton periodicity in Antarctic surface waters. by T.John Hart.

Card 18

GC
63
D 61
    Discovery Committee

      Discovery Reports...

        Vol. XII: Coast fishes, Part I: The south Atlantic, by J. R. Norman.(1935)
        Polychaete worms, Part II, by C.C.A Monro.(1936)
        Echinoidea and Ophiuroidea, by T. Mortensen.(1936).
        The birds of the South Orkney Islnads, by R.A.B. Ardley.(1936).
        Larvae of Decapod Crustacea, by Robert Gurney,   (1936)

        continued on next card

---

card 25

GC
63
D 61
    Discovery Committee

      Discovery Reports ...

        Vol.XVII: The Sei whale,Balaenoptera borealis, by L.Harrison Matthews.(1938)
        Larvae of Decapod crustacea.Part V: Nephropsidea and Thalassinidea,by Robert Gurney. (1938)

---

card 32

GC
63
D 61
    Discovery Committee

      Discovery Reports...
        Vol. 22: Station list, 1933-1935;
        The southern stocks of whalebone whales, by N. A. Mackintosh.
        Polyzoa (Bryozoa), by Anna B. Hastings.

Card 19

GC
63
D 61
    Discovery Committee

      Discovery Reports...

        Vol. XIII: Foraminifera, Part IV. Additional records from the Weddell Sea sector from material obtained by the S. Y. Scotia, by A. Earland. With a report on some crystalline components of Weddell Sea deposits, by F. A. Bannister, with chemical analyses by M.H.Hey. (1936)
        The Royal research ship, Discovery, II, by R.A.B. Ardley and N.A.Mackintosh (1936)

        continued on next card

Card 26

GC
63
D 61
    Discovery Committee

      Discovery Reports...

        Vol. XVIII: Coast fishes. Part III. The Antarctic zone, by J. R. Norman. (1938)
        On the operation of large plankton nets, by James W. S. Marr. (1938)
        Crinoidea, by D. Dilwyn John. (1938)
        Thoracic Cirripedes collected in 1925-1936, by C. A. Nilssen-Cantell. (1939)

        continued on next card

---

card 33

GC
63
D 61
    Discovery Committee

      Discovery Reports...
        Vol. 23: The gut of Nebaliacea, by Helen G. Q. Rowett (pp. 1-18, 1943); On a specimen of the southern bottle-nosed whale, Hyperoodon planifrons. By F. C. Fraser. (pp. 19-36,1945); Report on rocks from west Antarctica and the Scotia arc. By G. W.Tyrrell (pp. 37-102, 1945); The development and life-history of adolescent and adult krill, Euphausia superba, by Helen E. Bargmann (pp. 103-176, 1945).

Card 20

GC
63
D 61
    Discovery Committee

      Discovery Reports...

        Vol. XIII:(cont) A report on oceanographical investigation in the Peru Coastal Current, by E. R. Gunther.(1936)
        Rhincalanus Gigas (Brady), a Copepod of the southern microplankton, by F.D. Ommanney. (1936).

        continued on next card

---

card 27

GC
63
D 61
    Discovery Committee

      Discovery Reports...

        Vol. XVIII (continued)
        The leopard seal Hydrurga Leptonyx (de Blainville), by J. E. Hamilton. (1939)
        Hydromedusae from the Falkland Islands, by Edward T. Browne and P. L. Kramp. (1939)
        Madreporarian corals, with an account of variation in Caryophyllia, by J. Stanley Gardiner (1939).

---

card 34

GC
63
D 61
    Discovery Committee

      Discovery Reports... **Vol 23 (continued): The Antarctic convergence and the distribution of surface temperatures in Antarctic waters. By N. A. Mackintosh (pp. 177-212, 1946)**
        Vol. 23, pp. 213-222. Nebaliopsis typica, by H. Graham Cannon. 1946.
        Vol. 23, pp. 223-408. Report on trawling surveys on the Patagonian continental shelf, by T. John Hart. 1946.
        Title-page   and contents. 1947.

Card 21

GC
63
D 61
    Discovery Committee

      Discovery Reports...

        Vol. XIV: On the development and distribution of the young stages of krill (Euphausia Superba), by F. C. Fraser. (1936)
        The southern species of the genus Euphausia, by D. D. John.(1936)
        The reproductive system of Euphausia Superba, by H. E. Bargmann, (1937)
        Larvae of Decapod Crustacea, Part IV: Hippolytydae, by R. Gurney. (1937)

        continued on next card

---

card 28

GC
63
D 61
    Discovery Committee

      Discovery Reports...

        Vol. XIX: Phosphate and silicate in the southern ocean, by A. J. Slowes. (1938)
        A second report on the southern sea lion, Otaria Byronia (de Balinville), by J.E.Hamilton. (1939)
        Macrobertson Land and Kemp Land, 1936. By George W. Rayner. (1940).

---

cd. 35

GC
63
D 61
    Discovery Committee

      Discovery Reports...
        Vol. 24: Station list, 1935-1937; 1937-39 title-page and contents, 1947
        Vol. 25:Antarctic pyrenocarp lichens, by L. Mackenzie Lamb. pp. 1-30, 1948
        ...Whale marking II, by G. W. Rayner.pp. 31-38, 1948
        ...Soundings taken during the Discovery investigations, 1932-39, by H.F.P.Herdman. 1948. pp. 39-106

Card 22

GC
63
D 61
    Discovery Committee

      Discovery Reports...

        Vol. XV: The hydrology of the southern ocean, by G.E.R.Deacon. (1937)
        Note on the dynamics of the southern ocean, by G.E.R.Deacon. (1937)
        New species of marine Mollusca from New Zealand, by A.W.B. Powell. (1937)
        The age of female blue whales and the effect of whaling on the stock, by A.H.Laurie. (1937)

        continued on next card

---

card 29

GC
63
D 91
    Discovery Committee

      Discovery Reports...

        Vol. XIX(continued)
        On the anatomy of Gigantocypris mülleri, by H. Graham Cannon. (1940)
        Whale marking: progress and results to December 1939. By George W. Rayner. (1940)
        Distribution of the pack-ice in the southern ocean, by N. A. Mackintosh. (1940)

---

cd. 36

GC
63
D 61
    Discovery Committee

      Discovery Reports...
        Vol. 25:On the reproductive organs of Holozoa cylindriva Lesson. by A. A. Christie-Linde. pp. 107-112, 1949.
        ...The habits of fin whales, by E. R. Gunther. pp. 113-142, 1949.
        ...Station list, 1931-38. pp. 143-280,1949
        ...Ellobiopsidae, by H. Boschma. pp. 281-314, 1949
        Title-page and list of contents. 1953.

GC
63
D 61

cd
37

Discovery Committee

Discovery Reports...
Vol. 26: The bathypelagic angler fish Ceratias holbölli Kröyer, by Robert Clarke.
pp. 1-32, 1950
...Stylasteridae (Hydrocorals) from Southern seas, by Hjalmar Broch. pp. 33-46, 1950
...Antarctic and subantarctic mollusca: Pelecypoda and Gastropoda. By A.W.B. Powell. pp. 47-196, 1951.

---

card 38

GC
63
D 61

Discovery Committee

Discovery Reports...
Vol. 26: The Vampyromorpha of the Discovery expeditions, by Grace E. Pickford. pp. 197-210. 1952
Station list, R. R. S. 'William Scoresby' 1950. Issued 1953 pp. 211-258
A preliminary report on the Ostracoda of the Benguela current. By E. J. Iles. pp. 259-290 1953
Open boat whaling in the Azores, the history and present methods of a relic industry. By Robert Clarke. pp. 281-354, 1954.

Card 39

GC
63
D 61

Discovery Committee

Discovery Reports...
Vol. 26: Dispersal in blue and fin whales by S.G. Brown. pp. 355-384, 1954
Vol. 27: Siphonophora of the Indian Ocean together with systematic and biological notes on related specimens from other oceans. By A. K. Totton. pp. 1-162, 1954
The pelagic mollusca of the Benguela current. Part 1. First survey, R.R.S. 'William Scoresby', March. 1950...by J.E. Morton. pp. 163-200

Card 40

GC
63
D 61

Discovery Committee

Discovery Reports...
Vol. 27: The circumpolar continuity of Antarctic plankton species by A. de C. Baker. pp. 201-218. 1954
Vol. 27: The planktonic decapod crustacea and stomatopoda of the Benguela current. Part I. First survey, R.R.S. 'William Scoresby', March, 1950 by Marie V. Lebour. pp. 219-234. 1954.
Vol. 27: The distribution of Sagitta gazellae Ritter-Zahony by P. M. David. pp. 235-278. 1955.

Card 41

GC
63
D 61

Discovery Committee

Discovery Reports...
Vol. 27: Cumacea of the Benguela current by N. S. Jones. pp. 279-292. 1955.
27: The wax plug in the external auditory meatus of the Mysticeti by P.E. Purves. pp. 293-302. 1955.
27: Alepisauroid fishes by N.B. Marshall pp. 303-336. 1955
27: Euphausiacea of the Benguela current first survey, R.R.S. "William Scoresby", March 1950 by Brian P. Boden. pp. 337-376. 1955

Card 42

GC
63
D 61

Discovery Committee

Discovery Reports...
Vol. 27: Cestodes of whales and dolphins from the Discovery collections by S. Markowski. pp. 377-395. 1955. TPI, 1956
Vol. 28: Mysidacea by Olive S. Tattersall. pp. 1-190. 1955
Vol. 28: The distribution of the standing crop of zooplankton in the southern ocean. By P. Foxton pp. 191-236. 1956

Card 43

GC
63
D 61

Discovery Committee

Discovery Reports...
Vol. 28: Sperm whales of the Azores. By Robert Clarke. pp. 237-298. 1956 TPI
Vol. 28: Station list, 1950/51. 1957 TPI

Vol. 29: Hydromedusae from the Discovery collections, by P. L. Kramp. pp. 1-128, 1957
Vol. 29: New observations on the aberrant Medusae Tetraplatia volitans Busch. By William J. Rees and Ernest White. pp. 129-140. 1957

see next card

Card 44

GC
63
D 61

Discovery Committee

Discovery Reports...
Vol. 29: Isopod Crustacea, Part II: The suborder Valvifera... By Edith M. Sheppard. pp. 141-198, 1957
Vol. 29: The distribution of the Chaetognatha of the Southern Ocean, by P. M. David. pp. 199-228, 1958
Vol. 29: The reliability of deep-sea reversing thermometers. By H.F.P.Herdman and L.H. Pemberton. pp. 229-244. 1958

cont. on next card

Card 45

GC
63
D 61

Discovery Committee

Discovery Reports...
Vol. 29: pp. 245-280. Octocorals, Part I. Pennatularians, by Hjalmar Broch. 1958.
... pp. 281-308. The foetal growth rates of whales with special reference to the fin whales, Balaenoptera physalus Linn. by R.M.Laws. 1959.
... pp. 309-340: Distribution and life history of Euphausia triacantha Holt and Tattersall. By A. de C. Baker. 1959
Title page and Contents 1959

Card 46

GC
63
D 61

Discovery Committee

Discovery Reports...
Vol. 30:1-160. Ascidiacea, by R. H. Millar, 1960
Vol. 30:161-300. The Distribution of Pelagic Polychaetes in the South Atlantic Ocean, by Norman Tebble, 1960
Vol. 30:301-408. Studies on Physalia physalis (L.), Part I. Natural history and morphology, by A. K. Totton; Part II. Behavior and histology, by G.O.Mackie. 1960
Cambridge. At the University Press. 4to.
TPI received.

Card 47

GC
63
D 61

Discovery Committee

Discovery Reports...
Vol. 31:1-122. Swimbladder structure of deep-sea fishes in relation to their systematics and biology. By N. B. Marshall 1960
Vol. 31: 123-298. The Benguela current. By T. John Hart and Ronald I. Currie. 1960
Vol. 31:299-326. The appendages of the Halocyprididae. By E.J.Iles. 1961
Vol. 31:327-486. Reproduction, growth and age of southern fin whales. By R.M.Laws. 1961
TPI received. cont. next card

Card 48

GC
63
D 61

Discovery Committee

Discovery Reports...
Vol. 32:1-32. Salpa fusiformis cuvier and related species. By P. Foxton.
Vol. 32:33-464. The natural history and geography of the Antarctic krill (Euphausia superba Dana) By J. W. S. Marr. 1962.

Card 49

GC
63
D 61

Discovery Committee

Discovery Reports...
Vol. 33:1-54. The movements of fin and blue whales within the Antarctic Zone. By S. G. Brown. 1962
Vol. 33:55-94. Rhizocephala, by H. Boschma. 1962

GC
63
D 61

Discovery Committee

Report on the progress of the Discovery Committee's investigation. Issued by the Discovery Committee, Colonial Office, London. (1937) sm 4to. 52 pp.

QL
Crus.Pam.
64

Discovery of Alpheus Edwardsii on the Coast of Cornwall.

(Read April 5, 1860, 8vo. pp. 209-212)

Micro-
film
100

DISCOVERY (SHIP)

Burney, James

Journal of the Proceedings of his Majs. Sloop the Discovery, Chas. Clerke, Commander, in company with the Resolution, Captn. James Cook, from Feb. 10, 1776, to Aug. 24, 1779. 4 vols. IN Mitchell Library, Sydney.

Bishop Museum has microfilm of pp. 1, 1779, at the Sandwich Islands, to p. 10, 1779, March, towards Kamschatka.

DU
12
C 77-3
1st ed.
locked
case

2d ed.

DISCOVERY (SHIP)

Cook, James

Voyage to the Pacific Ocean...for making discoveries in the northern hemisphere...performed by Captains Cook, Clerke and Gore...in the Resolution and Discovery. In the years 1776-80. 3 vols. Vols. I and II written by James Cook; Vol. III by James King... London. 1784. 4to. Atlas of plates. Folio. Index.
The same...Second edition. London. 1785. 4to. 3 vols. (No atlas)

Q
101
P 18

DISCOVERY (ship)

Deacon, G. E. R.
The work of the "Discovery" committee in the South Pacific Ocean.

IN Proc. Sixth Pacific Science Congress, 1939, (California), Vol. 3, pp. 139-142.

GC
63
D 61

DISCOVERY (ship)

Discovery Committee

Report on the progress of the Discovery Committee's investigation. Issued by the Discovery Committee, Colonial Office, London. (1937) sm 4to. 52 pp.

GC
63
D 61

DISCOVERY (ship)

Discovery Committee

Discovery Reports...

DU
12
E 47
locked
case

DISCOVERY (SHIP)

Ellis, William,

Authentic narrative of a voyage performed by Captain Cook and Captain Clerke, in...Resolution and Discovery...1776-1780...2 vols. London. 1782. 8vo.

Second edition...1783.

AP
2
E 56

DISCOVERY (ship)

Holmes, Sir Maurice

Captain James Cook, R. N., F. R. S.

(Endeavour, Vol. 8:11-17, 1949)

AS
36
S1

DISCOVERY (SHIP)

Zimmermann, Maurice, 1869–

The Antarctic land of Victoria. From the voyage of the "Discovery." By Maurice Zimmermann.

(*In* Smithsonian institution. Annual report. 1909. Washington, 1910. 23½ᶜᵐ. p. 331–353)

"Translated ... from Annales de géographie, Paris, no. 98, 18th year, March 15, 1909."

1. Antarctic regions. 2. Discovery (Ship)

11–9873

Library of Congress   Q11.S66 1909

DISCOVERY & EXPLORATION   AMERICA

see

AMERICA   DISCOVERY & EXPLORATION

QH
11
G 74

DISCOVERY (ship)

Harding, J. P.

Lower Crustacea.

IN British Graham Land Expedition, 1934–37 Scientific Reports, vol. 1, no. 6, pp. 319–322, 1941. British Museum (Natural History).

[Entomostraca from the Discovery expedition included.]

GC
63
D 61

DISCOVERY II (ship)

Ardley, R. A. B.

The royal research ship "Discovery II" by R. A. B. Ardley and N. A. Mackintosh.

Discovery Committee
Discovery Reports, Vol. 13, 1936, p.77–106

DISCOVERY AND EXPLORATION   ANTARCTIC

see

ANTARCTIC   DISCOVERY AND EXPLORATION

Micro-
film
99

DISCOVERY (SHIP)

Journal of the sloop Discovery. Original in Mitchell Library, Sydney.

At Bishop Museum : pp. headed 1778 November towards Sandwich Islands to end of volume.

G
7
R 91

DISCOVERY II (ship)

Deacon, G. E. R.

The Antarctic voyages of R. R. S. Discovery II and R. R. S. William Scoresby, 1935–37.

(The Geographical Journal, Vol. 93, 1939, pp. 185–209)

G
680
G 79

Locked
Case

DISCOVERY AND EXPLORATION   ARCTIC REGIONS

see

ARCTIC REGIONS   DISCOVERY AND EXPLORATION

AS
36
S1

DISCOVERY (SHIP).

Markham, *Sir* Clements Robert, 1830–

The first year's work of the National antarctic expedition. By Sir Clements R. Markham ...

(*In* Smithsonian institution. Annual report. 1903. Washington, 1904. 23½ᶜᵐ. p. 459–465. fold. map)

"Read at the Royal geographical society, June 10, 1903 ... Reprinted from the Geographical journal, London, July, 1903, vol. XXII, no. 1, pp. 13–20."

1. Antarctic regions. 2. Discovery (Ship)

S 15–1198

Library of Congress   Q11.S66 1903
Library, Smithsonian   Institution

G
7
R 91

DISCOVERY II   (SHIP)

Herdman, H. F. P.

The voyage of Discovery II, 1950–1951.

(Geogr. Journal, 118(4):429–442, 1952)

DISCOVERY AND EXPLORATION   AUSTRALIA

see

AUSTRALIA   DISCOVERY AND EXPLORATION

AP
2
N 4

DISCOVERY (ship)

Rayner, George W.

Preliminary results of the marking of whales by the Discovery Committee.

(Nature, Vol. 144, 1939, pp. 99–1002)

AP
2
N 4

DISCOVERY II   (ship)

Mackintosh, N. A.

Voyage of the Discovery II.

(Nature, vol. 196 (4289):52–53, 1952)

DISCOVERY & EXPLORATION   BISMARCK ARCHIPELAGO

see

BISMARCK ARCHIPELAGO   DISCOVERY & EXPLORATION

DU
12
V 22

locked
case

DISCOVERY (SHIP)

Vancouver, George

Voyage of discovery to the north Pacific Ocean and round the world...1790–1795, in the Discovery...and Chatham, under the command of Captain George Vancouver. 3 vols. London. 1798. 4to. Folio atlas.

...new edition, with corrections...6 vols. London. 1801. 8vo.

GC
1
M 73

DISCOVERY II (ship)

Vallaux, Camille

Recherches du Discovery II sur la dynamique de l'Ocean Austral.

(Bull. de l'Inst. Oceanographique (Monaco), No. 751, 1938)

DISCOVERY & EXPLORATION   BONIN ISLANDS

see

BONIN ISLANDS   DISCOVERY & EXPLORATION

AP
2
N 4

DISCOVERY (ship)

The voyages of the Discovery.

(Nature, Vol. 140, p. 529–532. signed DWT)

DISCOVERY AND EXPLORATION

see under name of locality, as

SAMOA   DISCOVERY AND EXPLORATION

DISCOVERY & EXPLORATION   CAROLINE ISLANDS

see

CAROLINE ISLANDS   DISCOVERY & EXPLORATION

DISCOVERY & EXPLORATION   CENTRAL AMERICA
see
CENTRAL AMERICA   DISCOVERY & EXPLORATION

DISCOVERY AND EXPLORATION   HAWAII
see
HAWAII   DISCOVERY AND EXPLORATION

DISCOVERY & EXPLORATION   OREGON
see
OREGON   DISCOVERY & EXPLORATION

DISCOVERY & EXPLORATION   CLIPPERTON ISLAND
see
CLIPPERTON ISLAND   DISCOVERY & EXPLORATION

DISCOVERY & EXPLORATION   HORNE ISLANDS
see
HORNE ISLANDS   DISCOVERY & EXPLORATION

DISCOVERY & EXPLORATION   PACIFIC
see
PACIFIC   DISCOVERY & EXPLORATION

DISCOVERY & EXPLORATION   COCOS ISLAND
see
COCOS ISLAND   DISCOVERY & EXPLORATION

DISCOVERY AND EXPLORATION   MAKATEA
see
MAKATEA   DISCOVERY AND EXPLORATION

DISCOVERY & EXPLORATION   PALAU ISLANDS
see
PALAU ISLANDS   DISCOVERY & EXPLORATION

DISCOVERY & EXPLORATION   EASTER ISLAND
see
EASTER ISLAND   DISCOVERY & EXPLORATION

DISCOVERY & EXPLORATION   MALAY STATES
see
MALAY STATES   DISCOVERY & EXPLORATION

DISCOVERY & EXPLORATION   PHILIPPINE ISLANDS
see
PHILIPPINE ISLANDS   DISCOVERY & EXPLORATION

DISCOVERY & EXPLORATION   FIJI
see
FIJI   DISCOVERY & EXPLORATION

DISCOVERY & EXPLORATION   MARQUESAS
see
MARQUESAS   DISCOVERY & EXPLORATION

DISCOVERY & EXPLORATION   POLYNESIA
see
POLYNESIA   DISCOVERY & EXPLORATION

DISCOVERY & EXPLORATION   GALAPAGOS ISLANDS
see
GALAPAGOS ISLANDS   DISCOVERY & EXPLORATION

DISCOVERY & EXPLORATION   NEW ZEALAND
see
NEW ZEALAND   DISCOVERY & EXPLORATION

DISCOVERY & EXPLORATION   PONAPE
see
PONAPE   DISCOVERY & EXPLORATION

DISCOVERY & EXPLORATION   GUAM
see
GUAM   DISCOVERY & EXPLORATION

ONGTONG JAVA
DISCOVERY & EXPLORATION   LORD HOWE ISLAND
see
ONGTONG JAVA
LORD HOWE ISLAND   DISCOVERY & EXPLORATION

DISCOVERY & EXPLORATION   PUKAPUKA
see
PUKAPUKA   DISCOVERY & EXPLORATION

DISCOVERY & EXPLORATION   REUNION ISLAND

see

REUNION ISLAND   DISCOVERY & EXPLORATION

DISCOVERY AND EXPLORATION   SWAIN'S ISLAND

see

SWAIN'S ISLAND   DISCOVERY AND EXPLORATION

DISCOVERY & EXPLORATION   MONGOLIA

see

MONGOLIA   DISCOVERY & EXPLORATION

DISCOVERY & EXPLORATION   RIU KIU ISLANDS

see

RIU KIU ISLANDS   DISCOVERY & EXPLORATION

DISCOVERY AND EXPLORATION   TAFAHI

see

TAFAHI   DISCOVERY AND EXPLORATION

DISCOVERY & EXPLORATION   NEW GUINEA

see

NEW GUINEA   DISCOVERY & EXPLORATION

DISCOVERY AND EXPLORATION   SAMOA

see

SAMOA   DISCOVERY AND EXPLORATION

DISCOVERY & EXPLORATION   JUAN FERNANDEZ IS.

see

JUAN FERNANDES ISLANDS   DISCOVERY & EXPLORATION

DISCOVERY & EXPLORATION   NEW HEBRIDES

see

NEW HEBRIDES   DISCOVERY & EXPLORATION

DISCOVERY AND EXPLORATION   SANTA CRUZ IS.

see

SANTA CRUZ ISLANDS   DISCOVERY AND EXPLORATION

DISCOVERY & EXPLORATION   KERGULEN ISLAND

see

KERGULEN ISLAND   DISCOVERY & EXPLORATION

DISCOVERY AND EXPLORATION   TAHITI

see

TAHITI   DISCOVERY AND EXPLORATION

DISCOVERY AND EXPLORATION   SOCIETY ISLANDS

see

SOCIETY ISLANDS   DISCOVERY AND EXPLORATION

DISCOVERY & EXPLORATION   MANCHURIA

see

MANCHURIA   DISCOVERY & EXPLORATION

DISCOVERY & EXPLORATION   TIBET

see

TIBET   DISCOVERY & EXPLORATION

DISCOVERY AND EXPLORATION   SOLOMON ISLANDS

see

SOLOMON ISLANDS   DISCOVERY AND EXPLORATION

DISCOVERY & EXPLORATION   MARIANAS

see

MARIANAS   DISCOVERY & EXPLORATION

DISCOVERY & EXPLORATION   TIKOPIA

see

TIKOPIA   DISCOVERY & EXPLORATION

DISCOVERY AND EXPLORATION   SOUTH AMERICA

see

SOUTH AMERICA   DISCOVERY AND EXPLORATION

DISCOVERY & EXPLORATION   MISSOURI

see

MISSOURI   DISCOVERY & EXPLORATION

DISCOVERY & EXPLORATION   TASMANIA

see

TASMANIA   DISCOVERY & EXPLORATION

DISCOVERY & EXPLORATION   TUAMOTUS

see

TUAMOTUS   DISCOVERY & EXPLORATION

GN
Ethn.
Pam.
4327

DISEASE

Norman-Taylor, W.

Witchcraft, sorcery and mental health.

(Health Education Journal, March, 1961.
9 pp.)

RC
Pathology
Pam.
69

DISEASES   AUSTRALIA

Mann, Ida

Opthalmic survey of the south-west portion
of Western Australia.   Government Printer.
Perth.   1956.   folio.   35 pp.

DISCOVERY & EXPLORATION   UNITES STATES,
NORTHWEST

see

UNITED STATES, NORTHWEST   DISCOVERY & EXPLORATION

DISEASE

See also under

MALARIA
YAWS

etc.

DU
Missions
Pam.
1

DISEASES   CAROLINE ISLANDS

Wetmore, C. H.

Report of a visit to the mission of the
Marshall and Caroline Islands.   1886.   8vo.   19 pp

DISCOVERY & EXPLORATION   TONGA

see

TONGA   DISCOVERY & EXPLORATION

QL
497
S 63

DISEASE   INSECTS AS CARRIERS

Smart, John

A handbook for the identification of insects
of medical importance.   With chapters on fleas,
by Karl Jordan, and on arachnids by R.J. Whittick
Printed by order of the Trustees, British Museum,
London.   1943.   R8vo.   x + 269 pp.

RB
151
H66

DISEASES - CAUSES & THEORIES OF
CAUSATION

Hirsch, August

Die allgemeinen acuten infections-
krankheiten vom historisch-geographischen
standpunkte.

Stuttgart, Enke, 1881-1886.   3v.
(Handbuch der historisch-geographischen
pathologie)

DU
96
C7\

DISCOVERY OF AUSTRALIA

Collingridge, George.

Discovery of Australia.

Sydney, 1895.

QL
461
H-1

DISEASE TRANSMISSION   PLANTS

Sakimura, K.

Thrips in relation to gall-forming and
plant disease transmission; a review.   (Presidential address).

(Proc. Haw. Ent. Soc., 13:59-95, 1947)

RB
601
F 23

DISEASES   DUTCH EAST INDIES

Farner, D. S.

Epidemiology of diseases of military importance in the Netherlands Indies, including the
identification and distribution of arthropods of
medical importance.   Washington.   Government
Printing Office.   (Navmed 133)   1944.   sm8vo.
250 pp.

AM
101
A 51
(5)

DISEASE

Curran, C. H.

Insects, ticks and human diseases, by C. H.
Curran and Frank E. Lutz.

(Guide Leaflet, American Museum of Natural
History, No. 113,   1942)

QL
Insect
Pam.
1972

DISEASES   AFRICA

Kurk, R.

African Leishmaniasis.

(Central African Journal of Medicine, 2:199-
203, 1956)

RA
789
A 93

DISEASES   DUTCH EAST INDIES

Taylor, Frank H.

The intermediary hosts of malaria in the
Netherlands Indies.

(Service publications, School of Public
Health and Tropical Medicine, No. 5, 1943)

QH
548
F 26

DISEASE

Faust, Ernest Carroll

Animal agents and vectors of human disease.
216 text figures, 9 plates... Lea and Febiger
Philadelphia.   R8vo.   1955c.   660 pp.

RC
Pathol.
Pam.
42

DISEASES   AUSTRALIA

Ford, Edward

A destructive skin disease of the face in
natives of Papua and north Australia.

(The Medical Journal of Australia, 1940,
pp. 668-670)

GN
2.S
F 47

DISEASES   FIJI

Derrick, R. A.

Fiji's darkest hour-an account of the
measles epidemic of 1875.

(Trans. and Proc. Fiji Society, Vol. 6:3-
16, 1955-57)

RB
541
M 46

DISEASE

May, Jacques M.

The ecology of human disease.   Foreword
by Félix Marti-Ibanez.   MD Publications, Inc.
New York.   R8vo.   1958c   xxiv + 327 pp.

RC
Pathology
Pam.
68

DISEASES   AUSTRALIA

Mann, Ida

Opthalmic survey of the Kimberley Division
of Western Australia.   Gov. Printer, Perth,
Western Australia.   1954.   folio.   43 pp.

GN
2.S
F 47

DISEASE   FIJI

Hemming, G. R.

Social conditions in relation to disease
in Fiji.

(Trans. and Proc. Fiji Society, 6:85-89,
1956)

GN
671.F1
S 74

DISEASES   FIJI

Spencer, Dorothy M.

Disease, religion and society in the Fiji Islands.

(Monographs of the American Ethnological Society, II, 1941)

DU
620
H 5

locked case

DISEASES HAWAII

Chapin, Alonzo

Remarks on the Sandwich Islands; their situation, climate, diseases, and their suitableness as a resort for individuals affected with or predisposed to pulmonary diseases.

(Hawaiian Spectator, Vol. 1, No. 2, 1838, pp. 248-267)

GN
Ethn.
Pam.
4302

DISEASES KURU

Gajdusek, D. Carleton

Studies on Kuru.
I. The ethnologic setting of Kuru by D. Carleton Gajdusek and Vincent Zigas.
II. Serum proteins in natives from the Kuru region of New Guinea. By C. C. Curtain, S. C. Gajdusek and V. Zigas.

(Reprint, Am. Jour. of Tropical Med. and Hygiene, Vol. 10 (10:80-91;92-109, 1961)

GN
1
N 27

DISEASES FIJI

Vakatawa, Lanuve T.

What the Fijians believe as the cause of disease.

(Native Medical Practitioner, Vol. 3, 1940 pp. 522-524)

DU
Pacific
Pam
263

DISEASES HAWAII

*Gulick, Luther H.
Climate, diseases, and materia medica of the Hawaiian Islands. (from the New York of Medicine for March, 1855.) New York, 1855, 8vo. pp. 46.*

C.M. Hyde Coll.

G
1
M 23

DISEASES MALAYA

Hodder, B. W.

Biogeographical aspects of settlement in Malaya.

(The Malayan Journal of Tropical Geography, Vol. 5:12-19, 1955)

RC
Pathology
Pam.
82

DISEASES FRENCH OCEANIA

Rosen, Leon

Observations on Dirofilaria immitis in French Oceania.

(Annals of Tropical Medicine and Parasitology, 48(3):318-328, 1954)

RB
Tropical
Diseases
Pam 15

DU
Pac.Pam.
640

DISEASES-HAWAII

Halford, F. J.

Tuberculosis in the Hawaiian Islands; a Study of School-Children of Hawaiian Blood.

(The American Review of Tuberculosis, Vol. 28, No. 3, September, 1933) pp 370-380.

G
1
M 23

DISEASES MALAYA

Ooi, Jin-bee

Rural development in tropical areas, with special reference to Malaya.

(Journal of Tropical Geography, Vol. 12, 1959)

RC
Pathology
Pam.
81

DISEASES FRENCH OCEANIA

Rosen, Leon

Observations on the epidemilogy of human filariasis in French Oceania.

(The Am. Jour. of Hygiene, 61(2):219-248, 1955)

Storage
Case
4

K 31

DISEASES HAWAII

Livermore, Katherine

Diseases, Hawaii; remedies.

[about 80 pages, uncounted; list made up during her work with E.S.C. Handy]

AS
36
S 1

DISEASE MALAYA

Watson, Sir Malcolm

The geographical aspects of malaria.

(Annual Report, Smithsonian Institution, for 1942 (published 1943), pp. 339-350)

RC
Pathology
Pam.
86

DISEASES FRENCH OCEANIA

Rosen, Leon

Poliomyelitis in French Oceania... by Leon Rosen and George Thooris.

(Am. Jour. of Hygiene, 57(2):237-252, 1953)

DU
12
S 19

locked case

DISEASES HAWAII

Samwell, David

A narrative of the death of Captain James Cook. To which are added some particulars, concerning his life and character and observations respecting the introduction of the venereal disease into the Sandwich Islands... London. 1786. R8vo.

GN
Ethn.
Pam.
4306

DISEASE MARIANAS ISLANDS

Kurland, Leonard T.

Epidemiologic investigations of amyotrophic lateral sclerosis. I. A Preliminary report on geographic distribution, with special reference to the Mariana Islands,...By Leonard T. Kurland and Donald W. Mulder.

(reprinted from Neurology, 4:355-448, 1954)

RC
Pathology
Pam.
83

DISEASES FRENCH OCEANIA

Thooris, G.

Aspect clinique d'une epidemie de polio-myelite en Océanie Française et importance des injections introvmusculaires dan l'etiologie des paralysies. By G. Thooris and L. Rosen.

(La Presse Medicale, 60 Année, No. 80:1712-1714, 1952)

DU
Pac.
Pam.
173

DISEASES HAWAII

Woods, Dr. George W.

The Democratico effects of introduced Diseases, and especially leprosy, upon the Hawaiian people. 1887.

GN
Ethn.
Pam.
4310

DISEASE MARIANAS

Sanford, Skelton

Tuberculosis in the northern Marianas. By Skelton P. Sanford and Murdock S. Bowman.

(U. S. Armed Forces Medical Journal, 3(5): 709-720, 1952)

DU
657
G 91

DISEASES GUAM

McMillan, C. H.

Guahan the healthful.

(The Guam Recorder, vol.13, no.5, 1936, pp.5, 22A)

Q
101
P 18

DISEASES KURU

Gajdusek, D. Carleton

Kuru: an appraisal of five years of investigation.

(Eugenics Quarterly, Vol. 9(1):69-74, 1962)

(Paper read at symposium on medical genetics, Tenth Pacific Science Congress, 1961)

RC
Pathology
Pam.
87

DISEASES MARQUESAS ISLANDS

Rosen, Leon

Human filariasis in the Marquesas Islands

(Am. Jour. of Tropical Med. and Hygiene, 3(4):742-745, 1954)

RC
Pathology
Pam.
33

DISEASES MELANESIA

Ford, Clellan S.   editor

Distribution of diseases in Melanesia.
Compiled by the Cross-Cultural Survey, Inst. of
Human Relations, Yale University. Strategic
Bulletins of Oceania, No. 6, 1943. 26 pp.

RC
Pathology
Pam.
70

DISEASES NEW GUINEA

Mann, Ida

Opthalmic survey of the Territories of
Papua and New Guinea, 1955. By Ida Mann and J.
Loschdorfer. Government Printer. Port Moresby.
folio. June 1956. 53 pp.

QL
Insects
Pam.
1204

DISEASE NEW ZEALAND

Miller, David

Mosquitoes, malaria, and New Zealand.

(Cawthron Institute, Publication 60, 1944:
Reprinted from "The New Zealand Science Review"
March-June, 1944. 10 pp.)

RC
Pathology
Pam.
59

DISEASE MICRONESIA

Colby, E.

Medical and sanitary data on Micronesia.
By Col. E. Colby, Office Surgeon, CPA and Elwood
C. Zimmerman. Mch. 1944. 11 pp. mimeographed.

RA
Pathology
Pam.
74 a,b

AND
GN
Ethn.
Pam.
4330

DISEASES NEW GUINEA

Simmons, Roy T. and others

Studies on kuru.
V. A blood group genetical survey of the
Kuru Region and other parts of Papua-New Guinea.
VI. Blood groups on Kuru.

(American Journal of Tropical Med. and Hygiene, 10(4):639-664, 665-668, 1961)

DU
1
S 72ti

DISEASES NIUE

Loschdorfer, J. J.

General survey on eye diseases in Niue Island, American Samoa and Western Samoa. With an
introduction on some ophthalmological conditions
in the South Pacific islands by Dr. Guy Loison.

(South Pacific Commission, Technical Information, Circular No. 13, August, 1955)

RC
Path.Pam.
62

DISEASES MICRONESIA

Alicata, Joseph E.

Leptospiral infection among rodents in
Micronesia.

(Science, Vol. 105, no. 2722:236, 1947)

RA
789
A 93

DISEASE NEW GUINEA

Taylor, Frank H.

Mosquito intermediary hosts of disease in
Australia and New Guinea.

(Australia, Dept. of Health, Service Pub.,
School of Public Health and Tropical Med., No.
4, 1943)

G
51
A 93

DISEASES PACIFIC

Black, Robert H.

The geographical distribution of malaria in
the South-West Pacific.

(The Australian Geographer, Vol. VI(4):32-
35, January, 1955)

AP
2
S 35

DISEASE NEW GUINEA

Blake, Francis G. and others

Trombicula fletcheri Womersley and Heaslip
1943, a vector of Tsutsugamushi disease (scrub
typhus) in New Guinea.

(Science, Vol. 102, no. 2638, pp. 61-64,
1945)

GN
1
O 15

DISEASE NEW GUINEA

Ward, Hugh

Infectious disease in the western highlands
of New Guinea.

(Oceania, 28(3):199-203, 1958)

DISEASES PACIFIC

See bibliography of

Bushnell, O. A.
(his work in process on disease in
Hawaii and the rest of the Pacific)

UH; BM, etc.

GN
Ethn.
Pam.
4302

DISEASE NEW GUINEA

Gajdusek, D. Carleton

Studeis on Kuru.
I. The ethnologic setting of Kuru by D.
Carleton Gajdusek and Vincent Zigas.
II. Serum proteins in natives from the
Kuru region of New Guinea. By C. C. Curtain,
D. C. Gajdusek and V. Zigas.

(Reprint, Am. Jour. of Tropical Med. and
Hugiene, Vol. 10   (1):80-91; 92-109, 1961)

GN
2.I
A-4

DISEASE NEW HEBRIDES

McNabb, D.

(Journ. Anthrop. Inst. of Great Britain and
Ireland, Vol. 23, 1893-4, pp. 393-395)

QH
1
P 11

DISEASES PACIFIC

Chu, George W.T.C.

Pacific area distribution of fresh-water
and marine cercarial dermatitis.

(Pacific Science, 12(4): 299-312,1958)

GN
1
O 15

DISEASES NEW GUINEA

Glasse, R. M.

A kuru bibliography. [a recently discovered disease of the people of the Eastern
Highlands, New Guinea.]

(Oceania, 31(4):294-295, 1961)

DU
1
A 72-t

DISEASES NEW HEBRIDES

Rageau, Jean

Enquete entomologique sur le paludisme aux
Nouvelles-Hebrides. Par Jean Rageau et Guy
Vervent.

(South Pacific Commission, Technical Paper
no. 119, 1959)

AP
2
S 35

DISEASES PACIFIC

Crampton, Henry E.

On the differential effects of the influenza
epidemic among native peoples of the Pacific
islands.

(Science, N. S. Vol. 55, 1922, pp. 90-92)

DU
1
P 10

DISEASE NEW GUINEA

Inder, Stuart

Five years have not found cause of kuru;
black magic or heredity?

(Pacific Islands Monthly, 28(5):49-51, 1957)

RB
Trop.
Diseases
Pam.
19

DISEASES NEW ZEALAND

Hercus, C. E.

Goitre in the light of recent research.
Cawthron Institute Lecture, 1930. 8vo. 22 pp.

Q
101
P 18

DISEASE-PACIFIC

Cumpston, J. H. L.

A cooperative epidemiological intelligence
service in the south Pacific.

(Proc. Pac. Sci. Congress, 6th, 1939, Vol.5
(pub. in 1942), pp. 429-432)

DU
12
F 74
locked
case

DISEASES PACIFIC

Forster, J. R.

Observations made during a voyage round the world, on physical geography, natural history, and ethic philosophy...London. 1778. 4to. pp. 477-500.

S
115
W 95
locked
case

DISEASES PACIFIC

Wüllerstorf-Urbair, Bernhard

Reise der Oesterreichischen Fregatte Novara um die Erde...1857-1859. Medizinischer Theil, von E. Schwarz. 1861. Wien. 4to.

G
7
R 8

DISEASES POLYNESIA

Waldegrave, W.

Extracts from a private journal kept on board H. M. S. Seringapatam, in the Pacific, 1830. (Marquesas, Society Islands, Tonga)

(Journal of the R. Geogr. Soc., London, 3, 1883, pp. 168-196)

Q
101
P 18

DISEASES PACIFIC

Herms, W. B.
Some entomological problems of the Pacific area with which medical entomologists should be concerned.

IN Proc. Sixth Pac. Sci. Congress, 1939, (California), Vol. 4, 1940, pp. 429-432.

RC
Pathol.
Pam.
42

DISEASES PAPUA

Ford, Edward

A destructive skin disease of the face in natives of Papua and north Australia.

(The Medical Journal of Australia, 1940, pp. 668-670)

RC
Path.Pam.
63

DISEASES PONAPE

Alicata, Joseph E.

Helminthic infection among natives of the islands of Ponape and Truk, Eastern Carolines.

(Journal of Parasitology, Vol. 32, sect. 2, page ?, 1946)

Q
101
P 18

DISEASES PACIFIC

Kimura, Noboru

Symposium on nutrition and cardio-vascular disease for the Tenth Pacific Science Congress. [6 papers printed in the Japanese Heart Journal, March 1962]

RC
Pathology
Pam.
70

DISEASES PAPUA

Mann, Ida

Opthalmic survey of the Territories of Papua and New Guinea, 1955. By Ida Mann and J. Loschdorfer. Gov. Printer. Port Moresby. folio. June 1956. 53 pp.

DU
1
S 72ti

DISEASES SAMOA

Loschdorfer, J. J.

General survey on eye diseases in Niue Island, American Samoa and Western Samoa. With an introduction on some ophthalmological conditions in the South Pacific islands by Dr. Guy Loison.

(South Pacific Commission, Technical Information, Circular No. 13, August, 1955)

AP
2
N 28

DISEASES PACIFIC

Manson-Bahr, Sir Philip

The fight against filariasis in the Pacific.

(Nature, Vol. 171(4348):368-371, 1953)

AS
540
P 55

DISEASES PHILIPPINE ISLANDS

McKinley, Earl Baldwin

Filterable Virus and Rickettsia Diseases.

(Monograph, Bureau of Science, Philippine Islands, No. 27, 1929)

RC
Pathology
Pam.
80

DISEASES SOCIETY ISLANDS

Rosen, Leon

Dengue antibodies in residents of the Society Islands, French Oceania.

(Am.Jour. of Tropical Med and Hygiene,Vol. 7(4):403-405, 1958)

AP
2
S 35

DISEASE-PACIFIC

Mumford, Edward Philpot

Mosquitoes, malaria and the war in the Pacific.

(Science, Vol. 96, 1942, pp. 191-194)

AS
540
P 55

DISEASES PHILIPPINE ISLANDS

Simmons, James Stevens

Experimental Studies of Dengue, by James Stevens Simmons, Joe H. St. John and Francois H. K. Reynolds.

(Monograph, Bureau of Science, Philippine Islands, No. 29, 1931)

RC
Pathology
Pam.
89

DISEASES TAHITI

Black, Francois L.

Patterns of measles antibodies in residents of Tahiti and their stability in the absence of re-exposure. By Francois L. Black and Leon Rosen.

(reprint. Jour. of Immunology, 88(6):725-731, 1962)

DISEASES PACIFIC

Strong, R. P.

Stitt's diagnosis, prevention and treatment of tropical diseases. Vols. 1,2, and 1 6th Edition. The Blakiston Company, Philadelphia. 1942.

Where in Honolulu?

RC
Pathology
Pam.
84

DISEASES POLYNESIA

Rosen, Leon   and others

The transmission of dengue by Aedes Polynesiensis Marks. By Leon Rosen, Lloyd E. Rozeboom, Benjamin H. Sweet and Albert B. Sabin.

(Am. Jour. of Tropical Medicine and Hygiene, Vol. 3(5):878-882, 1954)

DU
621
H 39

DISEASE TAHITI

Greer, Richard A.

The Deadley Don.

(Hawaii Historical Review, I(3):52-54, 1963)

Q
101
P 18

DISEASES PACIFIC

Symposium on present status of our scientific knowledge of rodent pest in the Pacific area with special reference to the control of rats and the plague.
IN
Proc. of the 9th Pac. Sci. Congress, Bangkok, 1957, Vol. 19, Zoology, pp. 12-54, 1962

GN
Ethn.Pam.
3304

DISEASES POLYNESIA

Villaret, Bernard

Climatologie médicale des Etablissements Francais d'Océanie. Paris, 1936. 48 pp.

2 copies

GN
2.8
T

DISEASES TAHITI

Historique de la dengue à Tahiti.

(Bull. Soc. Etudes Oceaniennes, No. 72 [Tome VII(1)], pp. 40-41, 1945)

RC Pathology Pam. 88

DISEASE TAHITI

Rosen, Leon and others

Eosinophilic meningoencephalitis caused by a metastrongylid lung-work of rats.

(Jour. Am. Med. Association, 179:620-624, 1962)

AS 763 B-4 and QL Mammals Pam. 115

DISEASES - DOGS

Svihla, Arthur

Dental caries in the Hawaiian dog.

(Occ. Papers, Bernice P. Bishop Museum, Vol.22, no.2, 1957)

GN Ethn. Pam. 4331

Diskul, Subhadradis

Ayudhya art. With 22 illustrations. Publ. by the Fine Arts Department. Bangkok. 1956
12 pp. 22 figs.

RC Pathology Pam. 78

DISEASES TAHITI

Rosen, Leon

Measles on Tahiti.

(Am. Jour. of Diseases of Children, Vol. 103:254-255, 1962)

DU 1 S 72 t

DISEASES PLANTS PACIFIC

Dumbleton, L. J.

A list of plant diseases recorded in South Pacific territories.

(South Pacific Commission, Technical Paper No. 78, 1954)

[title and text also in French]

AS 750 N

DISPERSAL-CRUSTACEA

Chilton, Charles

Dispersal of marine Crustacea by means of ships.

(Trans. New Zealand Inst., Vol. 43, 1910, pp. 131-133)

RC Pathology Pam. 79

DISEASES TAHITI

Rosen, Leon and others

Observations on an outbreak of Eosinophilic meningitis on Tahiti, French Polynesia. By Leon Rosen, Jacques Laigret and Serge Bories.

(Am. Jour. of Hygiene, Vol. 74(1):26-42, 1961)

GN 2.I C 14

DISEASES PRIMITIVE CONCEPTS

Clements, Forrest E.

Primitive concepts of disease.

(Univ. California Pub. Am. Archaeology and Ethnology, Vol. 32, No. 2, 1932)

AS 36 A 4

DISPERSAL FAUNA

Mayr, Ernst

The birds of Timor and Sumba.

(Bull. Am. Mus. of Nat. Hist., Vol. 83, 1944, Art. 2, pp. 129-194)

RC Path.Pam. 63

DISEASES TRUK

Alicata, Joseph E.

Helminthic infection among natives of the islands of Ponape and Truk, Eastern Carolines.

(Journal of Parasitology, Vol. 32, sect. 2, page ?, 1946)

DISEASES TROPICS

See

TROPICS DISEASES AND HYGIENE

AS 763 B 62 p

DISPERSAL NEW GUINEA

Robbins, R. G.

Correlations of plant patterns and population migration into the Australian New Guinea Highlands.

IN
Barrau, Jacques editor
Plants and the migrations of Pacific peoples; a symposium. Bishop Museum Press. 1963. Tenth Pacific Science Congress, Honolulu, 1961 ( ) pp. 45-59.

DU 1 S 72 t

DISEASES ANIMALS PACIFIC

Dumbleton, L. J.

A list of communicable diseases and parasites of domestic and some other animals recorded in South Pacific territories.

(South Pacific Commission, Technical Paper No. 77, 1954)

[title also in French]

DISEASES TROPICS

Strong, R. P.

Stitt's diagnosis, prevention and treatment of tropical diseases. Vols. 1,2, and ? 6th edition. The Blakiston Company. Philadelphia. 1942.

in Honolulu?

AS 36 A 4

DISPERSAL PACIFIC

Mayr, Ernst

The birds of Timor and Sumba.

(Bull. Am. Mus. of Nat. Hist., Vol. 83, 1944 Art 2, pp. 129-194)

QL Insect Pam. 2125

DISEASES ANIMAL PACIFIC

Lee, D. J.

"Sandflies" as possible vectors of disease in domesticated animals in Australia. By D. J. Lee, E. J. Reye and A. L. Dyce.

(Reprint, Proc. of the Linnean Soc. of New South Wales, Vol. 87(3):364-376, 1962)

DISEASES

See also

TUBERCULOSIS

DISPERSAL

See also under

BOTANY SEEDS DISPERSAL
INSECTS DISPERSAL

RA 47 G 13

DISEASES DISTRIBUTION

Geigy, R.

Erreger und Uberträger tropischer Krankheiten. By R. Geigy and A. Herbig. Verlag für Recht und Gesellschaft ag. Basel. R8vo. xxiv + 472 pp. 1955.

Diseases of plants

See

Botany-Pathology

QH Nat.Hist. Pam. 105

DISPERSAL PACIFIC

Adamson, A. Martin

Review of the fauna of the Marquesas Islands and discussion of its origin.(Published May 24, 1939)
(Bernice P. Bishop Museum, Bulletin 159, 1939, pp. 1 - 93)
Pacific Entomological Survey, Publication 10.

GN 2.S P 76

DISPERSAL POLYNESIA

Emory, Kenneth P.

East Polynesian relationships.

(Jour. of the Polynesian Soc., Vol. 72 (2):78-100, 1963)

QL 556.M D 61

Distant, William Lucas

Rhopalocera Malayana: a description of the butterflies of the Malay Peninsula. With 46 colored plates and 129 woodcuts. London; Penang 1882-1886. 4to. xvi + 481 pp.

AS 162 P 23

DISTENIINAE PACIFIC

Villiers, A.

Notes sur les Disteniinae de la region indo-pacifique (Col. Cerambycidae).

(Bull. Mus.Nat. d'Hist.Nat.,Paris,30:262-270, 1958)

GN 1 C 97

DISPERSAL POLYNESIA

Emory, Kenneth P.

Society Islands Archaeological discovery.

(Current Anthropology, Vol. 4(4):357-358, 1963)

QL Ins. Pam. 205

Distant, W. L.

Rhynchota from the Australian and Pacific Regions.

(Trans. Ent.Soc. 1881)

AS 36 S1

Distinction between tornadoes and tempests.

(*In* Smithsonian institution. Annual report. 1871. Washington, 1873. 23½ᶜᵐ. p. 455-456)

1. Tornadoes. 2. Storms.

Library of Congress
Library, Smithsonian

Q11.S66 1871
Institution

S 15-330 c

QK 929 R 54

The Dispersal of Plants throughout the World... 1930 Ashford, Kent. 8vo

Ridley, Henry N.

QL 345.N 6 S 24

Distant, W. L.

Rhynchota from New Caledonia and the surrounding islands.

Sarasin, Fritz
Nova Caledonia...A. Zoologie, Tome I, Livr. IV, 1914, No. 10.

QL 1 C 15

DISTOME

Cort, William Walter, 1887-

... A new distome from *Rana aurora*, by William W. Cort. Berkeley, University of California press, 1919.

cover-title, p. [283]-298, illus. 27ᶜᵐ. (University of California publications in zoology. v. 19, no. 8)

Bibliography: p. 298.

1. Margeana californiensis. I. Title.

Title from Univ. of Calif. Library of Congress
[5]

A 19-1504

G 109 U.S. Reading Room

DISTANCES

U. S. Hydrog. Office

Table of distances between ports via the shortest navigable routes....

Washington, 1923.

QL 1 Z and QL Insects Pam # 201

Distant, W. L.

Some undescribed Cicadidae from the Australian and Pacific regions. in Ted. Soc. of London 1881, pp. 125-134, 1 pl.

also separate

AS 36 S4

DISTOMUM.

Linton, Edwin, 1855-

Notes on a viviparous distome. By Edwin Linton ...

(*In* U. S. National museum. Proceedings. Washington, 1914. 23½ᶜᵐ. v. 46, p. 551-555. pl. 43)

"References": p. 555.

1. Distomum.

Library of Congress Q11.U55 vol. 46

14-10996

QL Insects Pam 455

Distant, W. L.

Contributions to a knowledge of the Rhynchota. Soc. Ent. Belgique , Tome 47, pp 43 - 65, 1903.

QL 523.H7 D61

Distant, W. L.

A synonymic catalogue of Homoptera. Part 1. Cicadidae.
London, British Mus. 1906, pp 207.

QK 922 Sp S73

DISTRIBUTION AND MOVEMENTS OF DESERT...

Spalding, Volney Morgan, 1849-

Distribution and movements of desert plants, by Volney M. Spalding. Washington, D. C., Carnegie institution of Washington, 1909.

v, 144 p. illus., plates (part fold.) maps, diagrs. 25½ᶜᵐ. (On verso of t.-p.: Carnegie institution of Washington. Publication no. 113)

"Literature cited": p. 143-144.

1. Desert flora. 2. Botany—Geographical distribution.

Library of Congress QK903.S7
——— Copy 2. [s19e2]

9—28159

QL 318 An

Distant, W. L.

ide Fasciculi Malayenses

E.11.27.

MAR 15 1904

QL Insect Pam 687

Distant, W L

Synonymical notes on some recently described Australian cicadidae. From Proc. Linnean Soc. N.S.W., v. 37, pt. 4, 1912.

Distribution of Animals & Plants

See

Geographical Distribution of Animals & Plants.

Q 115 G 76

Distant, W. L.

Report on the Rhynchota collected by the British Ornithologists' Union Expedition and the Wollaston Expedition in Dutch New Guinea.

Grant, William R. Ogilvie
Reports on the collections made by the British Ornithologists' Union Expedition...Vol. II, no. XIII, pp. 335-360, from Trans. Zool. Soc. of London, Vol. 20, 1914.

AS 162 P 23

DISTENIINAE INDO-PACIFIC

Villiers, A.

Notes sur les Disteniinae de la region indo-Pacific (Col. Cerambycidae).

(Bull. Mus. Nat. d'Hist. Nat., Paris, 30: 262-270, 1958)

AP 2 N 4

Distribution of marine organisms.

(Nature, Vol. 145, 1940, p. 732-734)

QE
75 QD10 *District of Columbia, Geologic Atlas.*
U A Folio 70 *Washington.*
152 *Patuxent.*

AS
36
A5 **Ditmars, Raymond Lee,** 1876–

The batrachians of the vicinity of New York city, with reference to the collection in the American museum of natural history, by Raymond L. Ditmars ... With illustrations from photographs taken from life, by Herbert Lang ... New York, The Museum, 1905.

52 p. incl. front., illus. 25ᶜᵐ. (Guide leaflet. no. 20)

Reprinted from the American museum journal, vol. v, no. 4, October, 1905.

1. Batrachia—New York (State)

7-37573

Library of Congress   QL653.N7D6

GN
Pam
735 Divination – Chinese in America

Culin, Stewart

Divination and Fortune-telling among the Chinese in America.
(from Overland Monthly, Feb.1895.pp.165-172

DISTRICT OF COLUMBIA BIRDS

see

BIRDS   DISTRICT OF COLUMBIA

AS
36
A5 **Ditmars, Raymond Lee,** 1876–

The reptiles of the vicinity of New York city, with reference to the collection in the American museum of natural history. By Raymond L. Ditmars ... New York, The Museum, 1905.

v, 93-140 p. incl. front., illus. 25ᶜᵐ. (Guide leaflet. no. 19)

Reprinted from the American museum journal. vol. v, no. 3, July, 1905.

1. Reptiles—New York (State)

7-37572

Library of Congress   QL653.N7D7

DU
568.U 1
D 61 Divine, David

The king of Fassarai. The Macmillan Company. New York. 1950. 296 pp. 8vo.

DISTRICT OF COLUMBIA BOTANY

see

BOTANY   DISTRICT OF COLUMBIA

QL
641
D61 Ditmars, Raymond L(ee)

Reptiles of the World: tortoises and turtles, crocodilians, lizards and snakes of the eastern and western hemispheres.

New York, Macmillan, 1922, 373 pp.

QL
671
E 39 DIVING

Cornelison, A. H.

Aqualung diving.

(The Elepaio, Vol. 18(11):72-75, 1958)

DISTRICT OF COLUMBIA CLIMATE

see

CLIMATE   DISTRICT OF COLUMBIA

Dittmar

Q
115
C *Dittmar Prof Wm.*
Challenger Expedition
Physics & Chemistry. Vol 1. Pt 1.
G. 13. 16   *Composition of Oceanwater*

AM
Mus.Pam.
282 DIVING   TUAMOTUS

Smithsonian's intensive exploration of coral atoll of Raroia bags curiosities.

(The Explorers Journal, 31(1/2)16-17, 1953)

QL
Insect
Pam.
2071 DISTYLIUM

Takahashi, Ryoichi

Aphids causing galls on Distylium racemosum in Japan, with descriptions of two new related species(Aphididae, Homoptera).

(Bull. Univ. Osaka Pref., Ser. B, 13:1-11, 1962)

GR
375
D 61 Dittmer, Wilhelm

Te Tohunga: Alte Sagen aus Maoriland, in Bild und Wort. Hamburg. Verlag Alfred Janssen n.d. 4to. (8) + 119 pp.

GC
Oceano-
graphy
Pam. 21 DIVING APPARATUS

Camara, Antonio Alves

Analyse dos Instrumentos de Sondar e Perscrutar os segredos da Natureza Submarinha... Rio de Janeiro. G. Leuzinger and Filhos. 1878. 8vo. 130pp

---

AS
244
D Ditlevsen, Hjalmar

Marine free-living Nematodes from New Zealand.

(Vid. Med. Dansk Nat. For. Kobenhavn, Bd. 87 1929-30,- Papers from Dr. Th. Mortensen's Pacific Expedition 1914-16, No. 52)

AS
36
S1 DIVERGENT EVOLUTION THROUGH CUMULATIVE SEGREGATION.
Gulick, J. T. (Rev) (Comm. by Wallace, A. R.)
Divergent evolution through cumulative segregation. in Journ. Linn. Soc. vol XX, 1890, pp. 189-274.

GN
2.8
P 76 DIVINING   CAROLINE ISLANDS

Lessa, William A.

Divining by knots in the Carolines.

(Jour. Poly. Soc. 68(3):188-204, 1959)

AS
244
D Ditlevsen, Hjalmar

Marine freeliving Nematodes from the Auckland and Campbell Islands.

(Vid. Med. Dansk Nat. For. Kobenhavn, Bd. 73, 1922,- Papers Mortensen Pac. Exp. No. 3)

GN
451
L 66 DIVINATION

Lévy-Bruhl, Lucien

Primitive Mentality...London. (1923).

2 copies

QE
75
W
and
QE
Geol.
Pam.
461 DIVINING ROD

Ellis, Arthur Jackson, 1885–

... The divining rod, a history of water witching, with a bibliography, by Arthur J. Ellis. Washington, Govt. print. off., 1917.

59 p. illus. 23½ᶜᵐ. (U. S. Geological survey. Water-supply paper 416)

At head of title: Department of the interior.

1. Divining-rod.

——— Copy 2.   G S 17-226

Library, U. S. Geological   Survey (200) G no. 416

QE
Geol.Pam.
840

DIVINING-ROD

Gregory, J.W.

Water Divining

From the Smithsonian Report for 1928,
Pub.2992, pp. 325-348, 1929.

AS
36
S1

Dixon, Henry Horatio.

Transpiration and the ascent of sap. By Henry H. Dixon ...

(*In* Smithsonian institution. Annual report. 1910. Washington, 1911. 23½ᶜᵐ. p. 407-425. illus.)

"Reprinted ... from Progressus rei botanicæ. Herausgegeben von der Association internationale des botanistes, redigiert von dr. J. P. Lotsy. Dritter band."

1. Sap.

11-31571

Library of Congress Q11.S66 1910

QK
1
J 86

Dixon, H. N. (Hugh Neville)

New and Rare Species of New Zealand Mosses, by H. N. Dixon and G.O.K.Sainsbury.

(Journal of Botany British and Foreign, Vol. 71, 1933, pp. 213-220, 244-251)

DU
12
D62

Dix, William C. od.

Wreck of the Glide with recollections of the Fijiis, and of Wallis Island. (1829-) New York, 1848. 8vo. pp 203. front.

ref. to Hawaii pp. 172-183.

Note. The above was compiled from manuscrip by James Oliver written chiefly in Oahu.

AS
496
F 29

Dixon, H. N.
Bryophyta.
IN Results of an expedition to Korinchi Peak, Sumatra (1914). Part IV:Botany by H.N.Ridley H.N.Dixon and A. Lorrain Smith.

(Jour. of the Fed. Malay States Mus, Vol. 8, Part IV, 1917)

[Bryophyta, by H.N.Dixon, pp. 137-138]

QK
1
L2

Dixon, H. N. (Hugh Neville)

On a collection of Bornean Mosses made by the Rev. C. H. Binstead. In Journ. Linn. Soc. Bot. Vol. XLIII. pp. 291-323. Pls. 26 - 27.

QH
1
C 13

[Dixième]

Xe Congrès du Pacifique.

(Cahiers du Pacifique, No. 4, Juin, 1962: 111-144, 1962)

QK
1
J 86

Dixon, H. N.

Madagascar mosses.

(Journal of Botany, British and Foreign, Vol. 80, 1942, pp. 41-50)

QK
534
V 48

Dixon, H. N.(Hugh Neville)

On a small collection of mosses from New Guinea, with a revision of the genus Spiridens by W. R. Sherrin.

(Annales Bryologici, Vol. 10, 1937, p. 16-19)

QL
Prot.
to
Poly.
Pam
237

Dixon, Francis

On the arrangement of the mesenteries in the genus sagartia, Gosse. From Sci. Proc. Roy. Dublin Soc. [n.s. v.6]

Q
115
M 46

Dixon, H. N.

Mosses, by H. N. Dixon and W. Walter Watts.

Mawson, Sir Douglas leader
Australasian Antarctic Expedition, 1911-14.
Scientific Reports, Ser. C., Vol. 7, Part 1,1918.

QK
1
L2

Dixon, H. N. (Hugh Neville)

On some Mosses of New Zealand.

(In Linn. Soc. Journ. Bot. XL, pp. 433-459. pls. 20 & 21.)

QL
Protozoa
to
Polyzoa
Pam
301

Dixon, G. Y

Remarks on Sagartia venusta and sagartia nivea. From Sci. Proceedings of the Royal Dublin Soc., 1888.

AS
36
S2

Dixon, Hugh Neville, 1861-
... The mosses collected by the Smithsonian African expedition, 1909-10 (with two plates) by H. N. Dixon ... Washington, Smithsonian institution, 1918.

1 p. l., 28 p. 2 pl. 24½ᶜᵐ. (Smithsonian miscellaneous collections. v. 69, no. 2)

Publication 2494.
Bibliography: p. 26-27.

1. Mosses—Africa.

18-26892

Library of Congress Q11.S7 vol. 69, no. 2
———— Copy 2. QK546.A3D5

QK
1
J 86

Dixon, H. N.

Papuan mosses.

(Journal of Botany, Brit. and For., Vol. 80, 1942, pp. 1-11, 25-35

DU
12
D 62

looked
case

Dixon, George

A Voyage Round the World; but more particularly to the north-west coast of America: performed in 1785, 1786, 1787, and 1788, in the King George and Queen Charlotte, Captains Portlock and Dixon. ...by Captain George Dixon. London. Goulding. 1789. 4to. xxxi+360+47 pp. Maps.

Second edition. 1789. 4to.

QK
1
J 86

Dixon, H. N. (Hugh Neville)

New and rare Bornean mosses.

(Journal of Botany, British and Foreign, Vol 99, No. 940, 1941, pp. 57-62)

AS
36
S5

Dixon, Hugh Neville, 1861-
... Reports upon two collections of mosses from British East Africa (with two plates) by H. N. Dixon ... City of Washington, Smithsonian institution, 1920.

1 p. l., 20 p. 2 pl. 24½ᶜᵐ. (Smithsonian miscellaneous collections. v. 72, no. 3)

"Publication 2583."

1. Mosses—Africa, British East. 1. Smithsonian institution. Publication 2583.

20-26774

Library of Congress Q11.S7 vol. 72, no. 3
———— Copy 2. QK546.B7D5

DU
12
P 85

looked
case

DIXON, GEORGE

Portlock, Nathaniel

Voyage round the world; but more particularly to the north-west coast of America: performed in 1785-1788, in the King George and Queen Charlotte Captains Portlock and Dixon . London. 1789. 4to.

QK
Bot.Pam.
1579

Dixon, H. N. (Hugh Neville)

The Mosses of Fiji.

(From the Proceedings of the Linnean Society of New South Wales, Vol. 55, Part 3, 1930, pp. 261-302, plates viii-ix)

AS
122
L-p

Dixon, H. N.

A note on the phytogeographical relations of Sumatran and other alpine mosses.

(Proc. Linn. Soc. of London, 156th Session (2):91-94, 1943/44)

Dixon, H. N.

Student's handbook of British mosses. London. 1924.

UH

QL Mammal Pam 61

Dixon, Joseph

Rodents and reclamation in the Imperial Valley. From Jour. of mammalogy, v.3, no.3, 1922. Pp. 136-46.

E 58 J 54

also

GN Ethn. Pam. 2956

Dixon, Roland B(urrage)

Contacts with America Across the Southern Pacific.

Jenness, Diamond

The American Aborigines...pp. 313-354

QK 548.N D 61

Dixon, Hugh Neville

Studies in the bryology of New Zealand, with special reference to the herbarium of Robert Brown, of Christchurch, New Zealand. Parts 1-6

(New Zealand Institute, Bull. 3, 1913-1929)

QL 671 A 92

Dixon, Keith L.

Offshore observations of tropical sea birds in the western Pacific. By Keith L. Dixon and William C. Starrett.

(The Auk, Vol. 69(3):266-272, 1952)

GN Pam #162

Dixon, Roland B (urrage)

The Huntington California Expedition Maidu Myths.

Bulletin of the American Museum of Natural History. Vol XVII. Pt II. pp. 35-118.

New York 1902. 8°.

DE 4.

NOV - 1 1933

AS 36 S2

Dixon, Hugh Neville, 1861–

... Uganda mosses collected by R. Dümmer and others (with one plate) by H. N. Dixon ... Washington, Smithsonian institution, 1918.

1 p. l., 10 p. pl. 24½ᶜᵐ. (Smithsonian miscellaneous collections. v. 69, no. 8)

Publication 2522.

1. Mosses—Uganda.

18-26893

Library of Congress   Q11.S7 vol. 69, no. 8

GN Pam 1923

Dixon, Roland B (urrage)

Achomawi and Atsugewi tales. From Journ. Amer. Folk-lore, v.21, n.81, 1908.

GN 2 I Ca

Dixon, Roland Burrage, 1875–

... Linguistic families of California, by Roland B. Dixon and A. L. Kroeber. Berkeley, University of California press, 1919.

cover-title, p. [47]-118. col. map, diagr. 27½ᶜᵐ. (University of California publications in American archaeology and ethnology. v. 16, no. 3)

Bibliographical foot-notes.

1. Indians of North America—California. 2. Indians of North America—Languages. I. Kroeber, Alfred Louis, 1876– joint author. II. Title.

Title from Univ. of Calif.   Library of Congress   A 19-1254

[s20b3]

AN 2.S W 51

Dixon, J. B.

Our "Little Brother", the Kona "Nightingale" has interesting history.

(West Hawaii News, 1:26, Mch 25, 1953)

GN Pam #175

Dixon, Roland B (urrage)

Basketry designs of the Indians of Northern California, ex Am. Mus. of Nat. Hist. Bull., vol. XVII, pt. 1, February, 12, 1902.

GN Pam 1702

Dixon, Roland (Burrage)

Linguistic relationships within the Shasta-Achomawi stock. From Mem. et Deliberations d. XV Congres des Amer. Quebec, 1906.

QL C15

Dixon, Joseph.

... A new harvest mouse from Petaluma, California, by Joseph Dixon. Berkeley, The University press, 1909.

cover-title, p. [271]-273. 27ᶜᵐ. (University of California publications in zoology, vol. 5, no. 4)

"A contribution from the Museum of vertebrate zoology of the University of California."

Muridae
1. Harvest-mice. 2. Mammals—California.

A 11-2218

Title from Univ. of Calif.   Library of Congress

GN Pam #174

Dixon, Roland B (urrage)

Basketry Designs of the Maidu Indians of California.

(From American Anthropologist (N.S) Vol 2.)

DE 4.

New York 1900   8°   NOV - 1 1933

AS 36 A 9

and

GN Ethn. Pam. 3704

Dixon, Roland B (urrage)

The Long Voyages of the Polynesians.

(Proc. of American Philosophical Society, Vol. LXXIV, No. 3, July, 1934, pp.167-75).

Separate.

QL 1 C15

Dixon, Joseph.

... A northern coast form of the California gray fox. By Joseph Dixon. [Berkeley, The University press] 1910.

p. [303]-305. 27ᶜᵐ. (University of California publications in zoology, vol. 5, no. 7)

"Contribution from the Museum of vertebrate zoology of the University of California."

Issued in single cover with vol. 5, no. 6 of the series.

1. Gray fox. 2. Mammals—California.

A 11-2219

Title from Univ. of Calif.   Library of Congress

GN 520 D 62

Dixon, Roland B (urrage)

The building of cultures. New York. Scribner. 1928. 8vo. x + 312 pp.

GN Pam 1445

Dixon, Roland B (urrage)

The mythology of the Shasta-Achomawi. From Amer. Anthrop. v.7, n.4, 1905.

QL 1 C 15

Dixon, Joseph, 1884–

... Notes on the natural history of the bushy-tailed wood rats of California, by Joseph Dixon. Berkeley, University of California press, 1919.

cover-title, p. [49]-74. illus., pl. 1-3. 27½ᶜᵐ. (University of California publications in zoology. v. 21, no. 3)

"Contribution from the Museum of vertebrate zoology of the University of California."

"Literature cited": p. 68-69.

Muridae
1. Wood rats. 2. Mammals—California. I. Title.

Title from Univ. of Calif.   Library of Congress   A 19-1527

[s20b3]

GN 2 I Ca

Dixon, Roland Burrage, 1875–

... The Chimariko Indians and language. By Roland B. Dixon. Berkeley, The University press, 1910.

cover-title, p. [293]-380. 27ᶜᵐ. (University of California publications in American archaeology and ethnology, v. 5, no. 5)

1. Chimariko Indians—Language. 2. Indians of North America—Languages.

A 10-1222 Revised

Title from Univ. of Calif.   Library of Congress

PL Philo Pam 16

and

GN Pam 163

Dixon, Roland B (urrage) and Kroeber, Alfred L.

The native languages of California. From Amer. Anthrop. n.s. v.5, 1903.

pp. 1-16

AS 36 A 9

Dixon, Roland B(urrage)

A new theory of Polynesian origins.

(Proc. American Philosophical Society, Vol. 59, 1920, pp. 261-267)

GN 2.S P 76

(see also review by editor of the Polynesian Society, Jour. Poly. Soc. 30:79-90, 1921)

GN Pam 1243

Dixon, Roland B(urrage)

The Shasta-Achomawi: a new linguistic stock, with four new dialects, ex Am. Anthrop., vol. 7, 1905.

DU Pac.Pam. 515

Dixon, W. S.

Notes on the Zoology of Caroline Island.

(Memoir, National Academy of Sciences, II, 1884, pp. 90-96)

(Report of the Eclipse Expedition to Caroline Island, May, 1883)

PL Philo Pam 15

(urrage)
Dixon, Roland B, and Kroeber, A. L.

Numeral systems of the languages of California. From Amer. Anthrop. n.s. v.9, n.4, 1907.

GN Pam 1783

Dixon, Roland B(urrage)

Some aspects of North American archeology. From Amer. Anthrop. n.s. v.15, n.4, 1913.

HA 29 D 61

Dixon, Wilfred J.

Introduction to statistical analysis. By Wilfred J. Dixon and Frank J. Massey, Jr. First edition. McGraw-Hill Book Company, Inc. 1951 x + 370 pp. 8vo.

GR 15 M 99

Dixon, Roland B(urrage)

Oceanic (Mythology)

The Mythology of All Races...Vol. 9, 1916. 364 pp....

GN 29 B 27
GN Ethn.Pam 690

Dixon, Roland B(urrage)

The Swan Maiden Theme in the Oceanic Area.

Barrett, S. A., and others.

Holmes Anniversary Volume: Anthropological Essays presented to William Henry Holmes... Washington. 1916. pp. 80-87.

QL 1 N 6-z

DIXONIA

Beebe, William

Atlantic and Pacific fishes of the genus Dixonia. Eastern Pacific Expeditions of the New York Zoological Society, XXX.

(Zoologica, Vol. 27, 1942, pp. 43-48)

GN Ethn.Pam 3187

Dixon, Roland Burrage

The peopling of the Pacific.

(Philippine Magazine, Vol. 26, 1929, pp. 195 to 197, 244)

GN 2 I Ca

DIXON, ROLAND BURRAGE

Sapir, Edward.

... Yana texts, by Edward Sapir, together with Yana myths collected by Roland B. Dixon. Berkeley, The University press [1910]

cover-title, 235 p. 27ᶜᵐ. (University of California publications in American archeology and ethnology. v. 9, no. 1)

Yana text, with English translation.

1. Yana Indians. 2. Folklore, Indian. 3. Indians of North America— Legends. 4. Yana language—Texts. I. Dixon, Roland Burrage.

Library of Congress   E51.C15   vol. 9, no. 1   10-11176
———— Copy 2.

PL 62 D 62

Dixon, N. C.

Dictionary in English, Tagalog, Ilocano and Visayan, and a brief Tagalog grammar, written in English and translated in Ilocano and in Visayan. Published by Juan de la Cruz Book Room, Honolulu. 8vo. 182 pp. (1948)

GN 1 A
and
GN Ethn.Pam 2885

Dixon, Roland B(urrage)

The Problem of the Sweet Potato in Polynesia

(American Anthropologist, New Series, Vol. 34, No. 1, 1932. pp. 40-66)

GN 2.M P 35

DIXON, ROLAND BURRAGE

Coon, Carleton S.   ... editor

Studies in the anthropology of Oceania and Asia, presented in memory of Roland Burrage Dixon, by James M. Andrews, IV, Gordon T. Bowles, Carleton S. Coon...and others. [contains bibliography of Dixon]

(Papers of the Peabody Mus. of Am. Archaeology and Ethnology, Harvard University, Vol. 20, 1943)

GN 480 D 62

Djamour, Judith

Malay kinship and marriage in Singapore.

(London School of Economics, Monographs on Social Anthropology, No. 21, 1959)

PL Philo Pam 63

Dixon, Roland B(urrage)

The pronominal dual in the languages of California. From Boas Mem. Vol. 1906.

AP 2 S 35

DIXON, ROLAND BURRAGE

Hooton, Ernest A.

Roland Burrage Dixon.

(Science, vol. 81:166-167, 1935)

GN 667.A B 52

Djanggawul: an aboriginal religious cult of north-eastern Arnhem Land.

Berndt, Ronald M.

GN 22 B4 D62

Dixon, Roland B(urrage)

The racial history of man.

New York, Scribner, 1923. -- pp. xvi, 583. pls. 44...

AS 720.N R

Dixon, W. A.

Notes on the meteorology, natural history etc. of a guano island; and guano and other phosphatic deposits.

(Journal and Proc. of the R. Soc. of New South Wales, 1877, Vol. XI, pp. 165-181)

QH 326 H 97

DNA

Hutchins, Carleen Maley

Life's key-DNA; a biological adventure into the unknown. Illustrated with 27 drawings and photographs. Coward-McCann, Inc. New York 1961. R8vo. 64 pp.

QE 349.M4 D 63

Doan, David B.

    Military geology of Tinian, Mariana Islands. Part I. Description of terrain and environment; Part II. Engineering aspects. By David B. Doan, Harold W. Burke, Harold G. May, Carl H. Stensland; and Climate by David I. Blumenstock. Prepared...Chief of Engineers, U. S. Army...Intelligence Divison, Office of the Engineer...U.S.Army Pacific, with the personnel of the U. S. Geological Survey. Tokyo. 1960. folio. 149 pp; maps.

    [Part III, confidential; sent to military libraries only]

AS 720.N R

PL Pam #132

Doane, E. T.

    A comparison of the languages of Hawaii and Ponape. Additional notes and illustrations by Sidney H. Ray. In Roy. Soc. N.S.W, Journ. Vol. XXIX, 1895, pp 420 - 453.

Also separate

Storage Case 5

Hms La 19

Doane, E. T.

    The Rarotongan and Hawaiian languages compared. ("written on the voyage from Panama to California, in 1858")

QE 349.Ry D 63

Doan, David B. and others

    Military geology of the Miyako Archipelago, Ryukyu-Retto. By David B. Doan, James E. Paseur, and F. Raymond Fosberg. Prepared under the direction of the Chief of Engineers, U.S.Army, by the Intelligence Division, Office of the Engineer, U. S. Army Pacific, with the personnel of the U. S. Geological Survey. 1960. folio. 214 pp.; maps.

DU 620 F

Doane, E. T.

    Dialects of Micronesia.

    (Friend, March 1882, p. 26).

Storage Case 5

Hms La 20

Doane, E. T.

    Remarks on the dialects of the islands of Ponape and Ebon, Micronesia, as related to the Malay language. ms. or a copy of an ms. 32 pp.

PL Phil.Pam 761

Doane, E. T.

    Buk in Bwinbwin. By E. T. Doane and H.Asa. Marshall Islands primary arithmetic. Honolulu 1863 edition, 24 pp.

Storage Case 5

Hms La 18

Doane, E. T.

    Letters to Prof. W. D. Alexander, dated Feb. 2, 1884, with a postcript of Feb. 28, 1884; Sept. 27, 1884 and Feb. 9, 1885, concerning Micronesian dialects.

QL 461 J 86

Doane, R. W.

    Notes on insects affecting the cocoanut trees in the Society Islands.

    (Jour. of Economic Entomology, Vol. 2:220-

PL Phil.pam. 298

(Doane, E. T.)

    Buk in bwinbwin mokta. (By Rev. E. T. Doane and Rev. H. Asa) Marshall Islands. Primary arithmetic. San Francisco. Hicks-Judd Co. n.d. 32 pp. 16mo.

    (also Phil. pam. 299, Buk in bwinbwin, 1888 edition (3rd. edition) Honolulu. 31 pp., and Phil. pam. 300, Buk in bwinbwin, 1873 edition. Honolulu. 24 pp. 18mo.) by E. T. Doane and H. Asa.

DU 620 F

Doane, E. T.

    A lost people. (Tinian, in the Ladrones)

    (Friend, July 1880, p. 54)

QK 531 C 94

Dobbie, H. B.

Crookes, Marguerite

    New Zealand ferns. Incorporating illustrations and original work by H. B. Dobbie. 6th edition. Auckland. Whitcombe and Tombs Ltd. 1963. xxiv + 407 pp. 8vo.

PL Phil.Pam. 489

Doane, E. T.

    A comparative vocabulary of the Malay language and dialect of Ponape. (8) pages. n.d.

DU 620 F

Doane, E. T.

    New explorations in Micronesia: the Mortlock group.

    (Friend, June 1874, pp. 42-43)

QL 634.Ma K 42

Dobby, E. H. G.

    The geographic setting of Malayan fisheries.

    IN
Kesteven, G. L.
    Malayan fisheries...Singapore, 1949. pp. 25-32.

PL Phil. Pam. 490

Doane, E. T.

    A comparative vocabulary of the Malay language and Ebon dialect. (3 pages) n.d.

Ms C1

Storage Case 5

Doane, Rev. E. T.

    New testament in the Ponape language.

G 1 M 23

Dobby, E. H. G.

    Padi landscapes of Malaya.

    (The Malayan Journal of Tropical Geogr., Vol. 10, June 1957)

PL Phil.Pam. 488

Doane, E. T.

    A comparative vocabulary of the Ponape dialect...and the dialect of Mortlook... 4 pp and (1) page, entitled "examples of the Ponape and Mortlock suffix and prefix." n.d.

Storage Case 5

Hms La 17

Doane, E. T.

    Notes on Micronesian dialects:-
Vocabulary: English-Ebon-Bonabe-Kusaie-Apaian
Pronouns compared.- Indo-Malay, Polynesian, Micronesian, Melanesian
The Lord's Prayer in Micronesian Languages
Notes on the grammar of the Kusaien language
Sketch of the grammar of the Gilbert Is.language.

G 7 R 91

Dobby, E.H.G.

    Settlement and land utilization, Malacca.

    (Geographical Journal, Vol. 94, 1939, pp. 466-478)

G
3
A 1

Dobby, E. H. G.

    Settlement patterns in Malaya.

    (Geographical Review, Vol. 32, 1942, pp. 211-232)

QE
1
G 3

Dobrin, M. B.

    Subsurface constitution of Bikini Atoll as indicated by a seismic refraction survey. By M. B. Dobrin, Beauregard Perkins and B.L. Snavely.

    (Geol. Soc. America, Bull., Vol. 60:807-828, 1949)

Q
101
P 18

Dobzhansky, Theodosius
Biological evolution in island populations.

    IN
Fosberg, F. Raymond   editor
    Man's place in the island ecosystem, a symposium. pp. 65-74. Honolulu. 1963. Tenth Pacific Science Congress.

DS
505
D 63

Dobby, E. H. G.

    Southeast Asia. 2nd edition. New York. John Wiley and Sons, Inc. (1950) pp. (1-4) 5-415. 8vo.

AS
720.N
L 75

Dobrotworsky, N. V.

    Notes on Australian mosquitoes (Diptera, Culicidae). IV. Aedes alboannulatus complex in Victoria.

    (Proc. Linn. Soc. N. S. Wales, Vol. 84(1): 131-145, 1959)

QL
537.M 6
S 93

Dobzhansky, T.   joint author
Sturtevant, A. H.

    Contributions to the Genetics of Certain Chromosome Anomalies in Drosophila Melanogaster, by A. H. Sturtevant and T. Dobzhansky. Carnegie Institution of Washington Publication No. 421. 1931. 81 pp. 8vo.

DS
707
D 63

Dobel, Pierre

    Sept annees en Chine. Nouvelles observations sur cet empire, l'Archipel Indo-Chinois, les Philippines et les Iles Sandwich, par Pierre Dobel...traduit du Russe par le Prince Emmanuel Galitzin. Paris. Gide. 1838. 8vo. pp. x+358.

GN
2.I
A-m

Dobson, Jessie

    Frederic Wood Jones, F. R. S.: 1879-1954.

    (Man, 56, Art. 79, 1956)

QH
366
D 63

Dobzhansky, Theodosius

    Evolution, genetics, and man. John Wiley and Sons, Inc. New York. 1955. 8vo. ix + 398 pp.

GN
2.S
N 67

Doble, Marion

    Essays on Kapauku grammar (Part 1-3)

    (Nieuw-Guinea Studien, 6(2):152-155, 1962)
    6(3): 211-218,1962; 6(4):279-248,1962
    to be continued

GN
2.S
P 76

DOBU

Fortune, R. F.   translator

    Dobuans abroad; letters from the Dobuan Islands.

    (Jour. Poly. Soc. 70(3):314-320, 1961)

AP
2
A 52

Dobzhansky, Theodosius

    Evolution in the tropics.

    (American Scientist, Vol. 38:209-221, 1950)

and
QH
Nat. Hist.
141

PL
22
D 63

Doble, Marion

    Kapauku - Malayan - Dutch - English dictionary. Publication...by the Government of Netherlands New Guinea. Koninklijk voor Taal,-Land- en Volkenkunde. The Hague. Martinus Nijhoff. 1960. 8vo. 156 pp.

GN
668
F 74

DOBU ISLANDS

Fortune, Raoul F.

    Sorcerers of Dobu. The Social Anthropology of the Dobu Islanders of the Western Pacific. With an Introduction by Bronislaw Malinowski. London. George Routledge & Sons, Ltd. 1932. xxviii + 318 pp. 8vo.

QH
366
D 63

Dobzhansky, Theodosius

    Genetics and the origin of species. New York. Columbia University Press. 8vo. xvi + 364 pp. (Columbia Biological Series, No. XI) 1939

QE
75
P

Dobrin, M. B.

    Seismic studies of Bikini Atoll. By M.B. Dobrin and Beauregard Perkins, Jr. [Bikini and nearby atolls, Part 3. Geophysics]
    (U. S. Geological Survey Prof. Paper, 260-J 1954)

DOBU ISLANDS   ETHNOLOGY

    see

ETHNOLOGY   DOBU ISLANDS

QH
366
D 63

Dobzhansky, Theodosius

    Mankind evolving: the evolution of the human species. Yale University Press. New Haven... 1962 8vo. xiii + 381 pp.

QE
1
G 3

Dobrin, Milton B.

    Submarine geology of Bikini Lagoon as indicated by dispersion of water-borne explosion waves.

    (Bull. Geol. Soc. America, 61(10):1091-1118, 1950)

DOBU ISLANDS   SOCIAL ANTHROPOLOGY

    see

SOCIAL ANTHROPOLOGY   DOBU ISLANDS

AP
2
A 52

Dobzhansky, Th.

    On methods of evolutionary biology and anthropology.
    Part I, Biology, by Th. Dobzhansky
    "   II, Anthropology, by Joseph B. Birdsell

    (American Scientist, Vol. 45:381-400, 1957)

QH
431
S 61   Dobzhansky, Th.
Sinnott, Edmund W.

Principles of genetics. By Edmund W. Sinnott
L. C. Dunn and Th. Dobzhansky. 4th Edition, 2nd
impression. McGraw-Hill Book Company, Inc.
New York, Toronto, London. 1950. R8vo. xiv +
505 pp.

GN
2.S
P 76   Dr. Felix von Luschan and Polynesian origins.

(Journal of the Polynesian Society, 33: 78-
79, 1924.)

Q
101
P 18   Docters van, Leeuwen, W. M.

Krakatau's New Flora.

Krakatau. Part 2. (Fourth Pacific Science
Congress, 1929) pp. 57-79

AP
2
S 35   Dobzhansky, Th.

Race and humanity.

(Science, 113:264-266, 1951)

Q
Biogr.
Pam.
88   Dr. Harold Lyon was a great pioneer in
sugar and reforestation of Hawaii's watersheds.

(Hawaii's Sugar News, Vol. 7(6):3, 1957)

AS
522
N 29   Docters van Leeuwen, W. M.

Die vegetation der insel Toppers Hoedje
in der Sunda-Strasse.

(Natuurkundig Tijdschr. Nederland-Indie,
94: 149-169, 1934)

Q
Gen.Sci.
Pam.
115   Dobzhansky, Theodosius

The raw materials of evolution

(Carnegie Institution of Washington,Suppl.
Publ. No. 38. pp.5. 1938)

GN
2.S
H 38-n   Dr. Herbert E. Gregory.

(News from the Pacific, vol. 3(2):1, 1952)

QL
568.C3
D 63   Docters van Leeuwen, W. M.
Docters van Leeuwen-Reijnvaan, Mrs. J.

The Zoocecidia of the Netherlands East
Indies. By Mrs. J. Docters van Leeuwen-Reijnvaan
and W. M. Docters van Leeuwen. [published by]
'sLands Plantentuin- Botanic Gardens- Buitenzorg
Java. Batavia, 1926. 601 pp. R8vo.

QH
401
P 83   Dobzhansky, Theodosius

A review of some fundamental concepts and
problems of population genetics.
IN
Population genetics: the nature and causes
of genetic variability in populations, pp. 1-15

(Cold Spring Harbor Symposia on Quantitative
Biology, Vol. XX, 1955)

QL
568.C3
D 63   Docters van Leeuwen-Reijnvaan, Mrs. J.

The Zoocecidia of the Netherlands East
Indies. By Mrs. J. Docters van Leeuwen-Reijnvaan
and W. M. Docters van Leeuwen. [published by]
'sLands Plantentuin- Botanic Gardens- Buitenzorg
Java. Batavia, 1926. 601 pp. R8vo.

DOCTORS

See

SURGEONS

AS
122
L 75   Dobzhansky, Theodosius

Species in Drosophila. (The Hooker Lecture)

(Proc. of the Linnean Soc. of London, 174th
session (1961-62), Vol. 174(1):1-12, 1963)

QK
1
B97-b3   Docters van Leeuwen, W. M.

Beitrag zur kenntnis der gipfelvegetation
der in Mittel-Java gelegenen vulkane Soembing
und Sindoro.

(Bull. Jard. Bot. Buitenz., Ser. III, Vol.
11:28-56, 1930)

Q
101
P 18   DOCUMENTATION
Hirayama, Kenzo

Time required cost, and personnel for
documentation.

(American Documentation, Vol. 13(3):313-319
1962)

QL
461
P 11   Dobzhansky, T.
Mather, W. B.

Two new species of Drosophila from New
Guinea (Diptera: Drosophilidae). By W. B.
Mather and T. Dobzhansky.

(Pacific Insects, 4(1):245-249, 1962)

QK
1
B 65   Docters van Leeuwen, W. M.

Botanical results of a trip to the Salajar
Islands. (between Celebes and Flores)

(Blumea, 2:239-277, 1937; Addenda et corri-
genda, ibid, 3:236-237, 1939)

Q
101
P 18   DOCUMENTATION INDIA
Parthasarathy, Seringapatam

Insdoc and its regional activities.

(American Documentation, 13(3):334-337, 1962)

DU
1
P   Dr. F. E.Williams killed in plane accident.

(Pacific Islands Monthly, Vol. 13, 1943, p.
10)

QK
367
V 25   Docters van Leeuwen, W. M.

Krakatau, 1883-1933, A: Botany, with a
frontispiece, ten text-figures, sixty photographs on thirty-six plates, and a map of the
islands of the Krakatau Group.
Leiden. E. J. Brill. R8vo. 1936. 506 pp.

QL
121
C 53   Documentos, actas y trabajos del primer congreso Latinoamericano de oceanografia, biologia
marina y pesca. Part 1.

(Revista de Biologia Marina, Valparaiso,
August, 1954, Vol. 4(1-3), 1951)

GN
2.S
T

Documents pour servir à l'histoire de Tahiti
(1):
Document fourni par Tefaaora sur le Gou-
vernement des îles Sous-le-Vent(2).
Parole concernant la conduite de Pomare va-
hine aus Iles Sous-le-Vent...
L'histoire de l'Ile de Borabora et la genea-
logie de notre famille du marae VAIOTAHA, par Tati
Salmon 1904.
(Bull. Soc. des Etudes Océaniennes, Tome 8,
No. 8, 1951:306-330)

DU
Hist.Pam.
55

DOCUMENTS - HAWAII

Knight, Clarence W. de

Claim of Liliuokalani, before Committee on
Pacific Islands and Porto Rico, United States
Senate. Argument on Behalf of Claimant. 45 pp.
8vo. ND

G
7
S 43

Dodd, S.

Formosa.

(The Scottish Geographical Magazine, XI:
553-70, 1895)

Documents

See also

Treaties

DU
Hist.Pam.
5

DOCUMENTS HAWAII

Liliuokalani

The Queen's Speech at the Opening of the
Legislature, May 28th, 1892.

DU
647
G 91

Dodane, Robert

Midshipman William Edwin Safford, Naval Officer and botanist. Excerpt from the U. S.
Naval Academy Log, issue of April 21, 1939.

(Guam Recorder, Vol. 16, No. 12, 1940, p.
491-492)

DU
Hist.Pam.
44

DOCUMENTS - HAWAII

Documents Relating to the Restoration of the
Sandwich Islands Flag:
Declaration of Rear Admiral Thomas...
Articles agreed to...Kamehameha III and
Rear Admiral Thomas...
An Act of Grace accorded by His Majesty
King Kamehameha III...upon ...resuming the reins
of government.
23 pp. 1843. 12mo. English and Hawaiian
text.

DU
Hist.Pam.
44

Documents Relating to the Restoration of the
Sandwich Islands Flag:
Declaration of Rear Admiral Thomas...
Articles agreed to...Kamehameha III and
Rear Admiral Thomas...
An Act of Grace accorded by His Majesty King
Kamehameha III...upon...resuming the reins of
government.
23 pp. 1843. 12mo.
English and Hawaiian text.

Q
115
S1
46

Doderlein, L.

Die Asteriden der Siboga-Expedition,
1899-1900. I. Die Gattung Astropecten
und Ihre Stammesgeschichte, Livr. LXXXI
II. die Gattung Luida,... Livr.LXXXVIII
Siboga Exped. Monog. XLVI.
Leiden, Brill, 1917, pp. 191, pl. 17,
fig. 20.

DU
Hist.Pam.
53

DOCUMENTS - HAWAII

The Land Registration Act of Hawaii, enacted
as Act 56 of the Session Laws of 1903, with the
Decisions Declaring its Constitutionality, some
Introductory Notes, Simple Forms of Conveyance,
Table of Costs and an Index. Honolulu. Robert
Grieve Printing Company, Limited. 1904. 8vo.
98 pp.

AS
719
C 85

Dodd, A. P.

The biological control of prickly-pear in
Australia.

(Bull. 34, 1927, Council for Sci. and Ind.
Res., Australia)

Doderlein, L. H. F.

Die Korallengattung Fungia. 1902.

UH has

DU
Hist.Pam.
40

DOCUMENTS - HAWAII

Order in Council of His Hawaiian Majesty,
prescribing a Code of Etiquette. June 29th,
1844. Honolulu. Polynesian Press. sm8vo.

S
Agric.
Pam.
82

Dodd, Alan P.

The progress of biological control of
prickly pear in Australia. Published under the
authority of the Commonwealth Prickly-pear Board.
Brisbane, 1929. R8vo. 44 pp.

AS
36
I 4

DODDER

Yuncker, Truman George.
Revision of the North American and West Indian spe-
cies of *Cuscuta*, with thirteen plates, by Truman George
Yuncker. [Urbana, Ill., University of Illinois, 1921]
141 p. XIII pl. 27½ᶜᵐ. (*Added t.-p.:* Illinois biological monographs,
vol. VI, nos. 2 and 3, April-July, 1920)
Thesis (PH. D.)—University of Illinois, 1919.
Thesis note on verso of t.-p.
Bibliography: p. 79-91.

1. Dodder.

Library of Congress   QK495.C98Y8   21-5489
———— Copy 2.
Copyright A 611346   [6]

DU
Hist.Pam.
91

DOCUMENTS - HAWAII

Special Report of the Committee on Foreign
Relations in reference to an appropriation for
the preservation and arrangement of the Government Archives and the preparation of a Bibliography of the Hawaiian Islands. Honolulu.
Elele Publishing Co. Print. 1892. 33 pp. 12mo.

AS
492
S 6

Dodd, John

A few ideas on the probable origin of the
Hill Tribes of Formosa,I,II.

(Journal of the Straits Branch of the Royal
Asiatic Society, No. IX, pp. 68-84, Vol. X:195-
221, 1882)

AS
36
S4

Dodds, Gideon Stanhope, 1880–
Altitudinal distribution of *Entomostraca* in Colorado.
By Gideon S. Dodds ...
(*In* U. S. National museum. Proceedings. Washington, 1919. 23½ᶜᵐ.
v. 54, p. 59-87. illus. (incl. maps) pl. 13-14, fold. tab., diagrs.)
Bibliography: p. 87.

1. Entomostraca. 2. Crustacea—Colorado.

Library of Congress   Q11.U55 vol. 54   19-20009
[6]

DU
Hist.Pam.
100

DOCUMENTS - HAWAII

Kalakaua

Provisional Convention between Portugal
and the Hawaiian Islands. 4 pp. 12mo.

(Department of Foreign Affairs, Honolulu,
August 26th, 1882.)

2 copies - (one) English
(one) Hawaiian

AS
492
S 6

Dodd, John

A glimpse at the manners and customs of the
Hill Tribes of North Formosa.

(Journal of the Straits Branch of the Royal
Asiatic Society, No. 15, pp. 69-78, 1885)

AS
36
S4

Dodds, Gideon Stanhope, 1880–
Descriptions of two new species of *Entomostraca* from
Colorado, with notes on other species. By G. S. Dodds ...
(*In* U. S. National museum. Proceedings. Washington, 1916. 23½ᶜᵐ.
v. 49, p. 97-102. illus.)

1. Entomostraca. 2. Crustacea—Colorado.

Library of Congress   Q11.U55 vol. 49   16-11777
———— Copy 2.   Q11.U55 vol. 49 2d set

GN
2.S
F 47
Dodds, K. S.

Banana breeding.

(Transactions of the Fiji Society of Science and Industry, Vol. 3(1):45-56, 1945)

S
Agri
Pam
64
Dodge, Charles Richards

A report on the cultivation of ramie in the United States... preparation of the fiber for manufacture. From U. S. Dept. Agri. Fiber investigations, n.7, 1895.

QK
Bot
Pam
#1094
Dodge, Charles Richards

A report on sisal hemp culture in the United States, with statements relating to the industry in Yucatan and the Bahama islands, and brief considerations upon the question of machinery for extracting the fiber, ex Dept. of Agr. Div. of Statistics Fiber Investigations, Rept. no. 3.

QK
Botany
Pam
#1190
Dodge, Bernard O.

Methods of culture and the morphology of the archicarp in certain species of the Ascobolaceae. Torrey Bot. Club Bull., Vol. 39, No.4, 1912.

S
Agri
Pam
60
Dodge, Charles Richards

A report on the culture of hemp in Europe including a special consular report on the growth of hemp in Italy. From U. S. Dept. Agri. Fiber Investigations, n.11, 1898.

S
Agri
Pam
59
Dodge, Charles Richards

A report on the uncultivated bast fibers of the United States... allied species produced commercially in the Old World. From U. S. Dept. Agri. Fiber Investigations, Rept. 6, 1894.

QK
Pam
#988
Dodge, Bernard O.

Methods of culture and the morphology of the Archicarp in certain species of the Ascobolaceae, ex Columbia Univ. Dept. of Bot. Contr., vol. XI, no. 254, 1912.

S
Agri
Pam
63
Dodge, Charles Richards

A report on the culture of hemp and jute in the United States... preparation of the fiber for market. From U. S. Dept Agri Fiber Investigations, n.8, 1896

QH
317
D64
Dodge, Charles Wright

Introduction to elementary practical biology: a laboratory guide for high-school and college students.

New York, Harpers, 1894.   422p.

QK
Pam
#995
Dodge, B. O.

The morphological relationships of the Florideae and the Ascomycetes, ex Columbia Univ. Dept. of Bot. Contr., vol. XI, no. 261, 1914.

S
Agri
Pam
54
Dodge, Charles Richard

A report on flax culture for fiber in the United States including special reports on flax culture in Ireland, in Belgium, and in Austria with statements relative to the industry in Russia. From U. S. Dept. Agri. Fiber Investigations, n.4, 1892.

AM
Mus.Pam.
272
Dodge, Charlotte Peabody

Hawaiian Mission Children's Society, 1852-1952. Published by the Society. 1952. Honolulu 8vo. (4),42 pp.

AP
2
S 35
Dodge, B. O.

Some problems in the genetics of the Fungi.

(Science, Vol. 90:379-385, 1939)

S
Agri
Pam
61
Dodge, Charles Richard

A report on flax culture for seed and fiber in Europe and America. From U. S. Dept. Agri. Fiber Investigations, n.10, 1898.

DU
625
A 37
Dodge, Charlotte Peabody

Aldexander, Mary Charlotte

Punahou, 1841-1941. My Mary Charlotte Alexander and Charlotte Peabody Dodge. University of California Press. Berkeley... 1941 R8vo. xiii + 577 pp.

Dodge, Carroll William

Medical Mycology.   St. Louis. 1935

UH

QK
Bot
Pam
#1093
Dodge, Charles Richards

A report on flax, hemp, ramie, and jute, with considerations upon flax and hemp culture in Europe, a report on the ramie machine trials of 1889 in Paris, and present status of fiber industries in the United States, Dept. of Agr. Div. of Statistics n.s. Rept. no. 1.

GN
2.S
P 76

and
DU
Pac.Pam.
806
Dodge, Ernest S.(tanley)

An account of the Marquesas Islands in 1825.

(Journal of the Polynesian Society, Vol. 49, 1940, pp. 382-392)

[From a journal kept by Capt. James D. Gillis, in the Endeavour, from Salem]

QK
494
Do
Dodge, Chas. Richards

A descriptive catalogue of useful fiber plants of the world, including the structural and economic classification of fibers. U. S. Dept. of Agric. Fiber Investigations Report No. 9, 1897.

QK
Bot
Pam
#1098
Dodge, Chas. Richards

A report on the leaf fibers of the United States detailing results of recent investigations relating to Florida sisal hemp, the false sisal hemp plant of Florida and other fiber-producing Agaves; bowstring hemp, pineapple fiber, New Zealand flax, and bear-grass, ex U. S. Dept. of Agr. Fiber Investigations, Rept. no. 5.

GN
2.S
P 76
Dodge, Ernest S.

The acoustics of three Maori flutes. By Ernest Dodge and Edwin T. Brewster.

(Journal of the Polynesian Society, Vol. 54, pp.39-61, 1945)

GN
2.S
P 76
and
GN
Ethn.Pam
3812

Dodge, Ernest S(tanley)

    Austral Islands tapa.

    (Jour. Poly. Soc., Vol. 50, No. 3, 1941, pp. 107-113)

GN
Ethn.Pam
3340

Dodge, Ernest Stanley

    The Marquesas Islands Collection in the Peabody Museum of Salem. Salem. Peabody Museum. 1939. R8vo. vii, 38 pp., 20 pl.

AP
2
A 5

Dodge, Frank S.

    Kilauea in August, 1892.

    (Am. Jour. Sci., Ser. 3, Vol. 45, 1893, pp. 241-246)

GN
Ethn.
Pam.
3723

Dodge, Ernest S.

    Captain collectors. The influence of New England shipping on the study of Polynesian material culture.

    (Reprinted from the Essex Institute Historical Collections, Vol. LXXXI, 1-8, 1945)

GN
Ethn.
Fam.3401

Dodge, Ernest Stanley

    The New Zealand Maori collection in the Peabody Museum of Salem. Salem. 1941. R8vo. 56 pp., 24 pl.

AP
2
A 5

Dodge, Frank S.

    Report to Prof. W. D. Alexander or Frank S.Dodge, Assistant Survey or and Draught-man, made Nov. 15, on the Survey of Kilauea in the last week of Sept. and first of Oct. 1886.

    (Am. Journ. of Sc. XXXIII, Ser. III. pp. 98-101.)

AS
36
A 91 p

Dodge, Ernest S.

    Early American contacts in Polynesia and Fiji.

    (Proc. of the Am. Philosophical Soc., Vol. 107(2):102-106, 1963)

AM
Mus.Pam.
472

(Dodge, Ernest S.)

    A special exhibition of the Saltonstall family portraits. Nov. 15- Dec. 31, 1962 at the Peabody Museum of Salem. 12 pp. (16) pl.

Card 1

AS
36
A 65

Dodge, Henry

    A historical review of the mollusks of Linnaeus. Part 1. The classes Loricata and Pelecypoda. Part 2. The class Cephalopoda and the genera Conus and Cypraea of the class Gastropoda.

    (Bull. Am. Mus. of Nat. Hist., 100(1):1-264, 1952; 103(1):1-134, 1953)

GN
2.S
P 76
and
GN
Ethn.Pam
3760

Dodge, Ernest S(tanley)

    Four Hawaiian implements in the Peabody Museum of Salem.

    (Journal of the Poly. Soc., Vol. 48, 1939, pp. 156-157)

GN
1
A 93

Dodge, Ernest S.

    An unusual Easter Island Carving.

    (Journal of Austronesian Studies, Vol. 1(3): 18-26, 1958)

AS
36
A 65-b

Dodge, Henry

    A historical review of the mollusks of Linnaeus, Part 3. The genera Bulla and Voluta of the class Gastropoda.

    (Bull. Am Mus. of Nat. Hist., 107(1):1-155, 1955)

GN
446.51
D 64

Dodge, Ernest S.

    Gourd growers of the south seas: an introduction to the study of the Lagenaria gourd in the culture of the Polynesians.

    (The Gourd Society of America, Ethnographical Series 2, 1943) Peabody Museum, Salem, Mass.

GN
Ethnol
Pam
#755

Dodge, F. H.

    The Brazilian Indian. Pan Am. Mag. & N. World Rev. (London) XXXVI, no. 3.

AS
36
A 65-b

Dodge, Henry

    A historical review of the mollusks of Linnaeus, Part 4: The genera Buccinum and Strombus of the class Gastropoda.

    (Bull. Am. Mus. of Nat. Hist., Vol. 111(3): 157-312, 1956)

AM
Mus.Pam.
204

Dodge, Ernest S.

    Handbook to the collections of the Peabody Museum of Salem. By Ernest S. Dodge and Charles H. P. Copeland. Salem. 1949. 62 pp. 8vo.

AP
2
A 5

Dodge, F. S. (Frank S.)

    The condition of Kilauea, March 20th, 1892.

    (Am. Jour. Sci., Ser. 3, Vol. 48, 1894, pp. 78-79)

AS
36
A 65-b

Dodge, Henry

    A historical review of the mollusks of Linnaeus, Part 5. The genus Murex of the class Gastropoda.

    (American Museum of Natural History, Vol. 113(2), 1957)

GN
Ethn.Pam.
3224

Dodge, Ernest Stanley

    The Hervey Islands adzes in the Peabody Museum of Salem. Salem. Peabody Museum. 1937. 8vo. 16 pp. 8 pl.

AP
2
A 5

Dodge, F. S. (Frank S.)

Emerson, Joseph S.

    Kilauea after the eruption of March 1886... by J.S. Emerson, L.L. Van Slyke, and F.S. Dodge.

    (Am. Jour. of Sci., Ser. 3, Vol. 33, 1887, pp. 87-101) illustration pp. 239-240)

    (ibid, Vol. 34, 1887, pp. 70-71)

AS
36
A 65

Dodge, Henry

    A historical review of the mollusks of Linnaeus, Part 6. The genus Trochus of the class Gastropoda.

    (Bull. Am. Mus. Nat. Hist.,116(2), 1958)

    Part 7. Certain species of the genus Turbo of the class Gastropoda.
    (ibid, Vol. 118(3), 1959)

QL
Mollusca
Pam.
930

Dodge, Henry

Suggested substitutes for the terms "lunule and "escutcheon" in Pelecypoda.

(Journal of Paleontology, Vol. 24(4), 1950)
1 page, unnumbered

QK
Bot.Pam.
2492

DODONAEA

Sherff, Earl Edward

Some new or otherwise noteworthy dicotyledonous plants.

(American Journal of Botany, Vol. 33 (6):
499-510, 1946)

GN
470
D 66

Döllinger, John J. I.

The Gentile and the Jew, in the courts of the Temple of Christ; an introduction to the history of Christianity, from the German...(translated) by N. Darnell. Second edition. 2 volumes. London. Gibbings & Co. 1906. 8vo. pp. xvii + 519; xv + 463.

QH
531
D 64

Dodge, Raymond

Conditions and Consequences of Human Variability. Institute of Human Relations. New Haven. Yale University Press. 1931c. 8vo. x + 162 pp.

QL
Bot. Pam.
3261

DODONARA MOLOKAI
(Otto and Isa)

Degener, D. and I.

A new Dodonaea from Molokai, Hawaii

(Phytologia, 7(9):465, 1961)

AH
30
D 65

Dörfler, I.

Botaniker-Adressbuch.Sammlung von Namen und Adressen der lebenden Botaniker aller Länder, der botanischen Garten und die Botanik pflegenden Institute,Gesellschaften und periodischen Publikationen. Dritte...Auflage. Wien. 1909. 8vo.

Dodman, G. Sutherland   Carter Coll.
                               7-A-23

A voyage round the world in 500 days, with details, compiled and arranged by G. Sutherland Dodman, giving an account of the principal parts to be visited, with a brief description of the scenery and all particulars connected with the undertaking; with illustrations and map and chart of the Route. 2nd Ed. London. Mackie, Brewinall and Co. 1880 xii + 173 pp. 8vo.

DU
623
B 65

DOEDALUS (ship)

Bloxam, Andrew

Diary of Andrew Bloxam, naturalist of the Blonde on her trip from England to the Hawaiian Islands, 1924-25.
(Note relative to the deaths of Hergest and Gooch) p. 96

(Bernice P. Bishop Museum, Special Pun., No. 10, 1925)

GN
1
B

Doering, H. U.

Altperuanische Hausposten und eine Melanesische Parallele.

(Baessler-Archiv. Beiträge zur Völkerkunde, Bd.XIX, heft 1-2, 1936, pp.22-27)

QL
1
J 35

DODO

Hachisuka, Marquess Masauji

The dodo of Mauritius.

(Bulletin of the Biogeographical Society of Japan, Vol. 9, No. 9, 1939, pp. 177-180. colored plate of the dodo, "by G. Edwards, 1759" which is "Keuleman's Dodo")

Q
115
S 56

Döderlein, L.

Die Asteriden der Siboga-Expedition,I:Porcellanasteridae, Astropectinidae, Benthopectinidae. II:Pentagonasteridae; III:Oreasteridae.

Weber, Max
Uitkomsten...Nederlandsch Oost Indie, 1899-1900...:Siboga...Monographie XLVI¹- XLVI⁵ (livr. 91, 98, 125) 1921, 1924, 1935. 110 pp. 27 pl.

GN
Pam
2205
2269

Döring,

Anthropologisches von der deutschen Togo-expedition. From Verh. d. Berliner Anthrop. Gesell. 1896.

G
3
N 27

DODO

Keynes, Quentin

Mauritius, island of the dodo.

(National Geographic Mag., 109(1):80-104, 1956)

Q
115
S 56

Döderlein, L.

Die Asteriden der Siboga Expedition. I:Der Gattung Astropecten und ihre Stammesgeschichte; II:Die Gattung Luidia und ihre Stammesgeschichte. III:Die Unterfamilie Oreasterinae.

Weber, Max
Uitkomsten...Nederlandsch Oost Indie, 1899-1900...Siboga...Monographie XLVIa,b,c (livr. 61, 88, 126) 1917, 1920, 1936. pp. 1-368 pl. 1-32

GN
Pam
1126

Doering,

Uber die herstellung von seise in Togo. From Globus, bd. 86, n.17, 1904. 2p.

QK
Bot.Pam.
2489

DODONEA

Sherff, Earl Edward

Further studies in the genus Dodonaea.

(Field Museum, Nat. Hist., Bot. Ser., Vol. 23(6), 1947)

Q
115
S 56

Döderlein, L.

Die gestielten Crinoiden der Siboga-Expedition.

Weber, Max
Uitkomsten...Nederlandsch Oost Indie, 1899-1900...Siboga...Monographie XLIIa (livr. 37) 1907. 52 pp., 23 pl.

Doering, Heinrich Ubbelohde-

See

Ubbelohde-Doering, Heinrich

QK
Bot.Pam.
2411

DODONAEA

Sherff, Earl Edward

Some additions to the genus Dodonaea L. (Fam. Sapindaceae).

(Am. Jour. of Botany, 32:202-214,1945)

GN
470
D 66

Döllinger, John J. I.

The first age of Christianity and the church. translated by Henry Nutcombe Oxenham. Fourth edition. London. Gibbings & Co. 1906. 8vo. xxv + 448 pp.

GN
Pam
2391

Dörler, Adolf Ferdinand

Schatze und schatzhuter in Tirol. From Zeit. f. osterr. volkskunde, v.IV, heft 9-10, 1898.

AP
2
S 42

Doerr, Arthur H.

Karst landscapes of Cuba, Puerto Rico, and Jamaica. By Arthur H. Doerr and Don R. Hoy.

(Sci. Monthly, 85(4):178-187, 1957)

DOGS

Colbert, Edwin Harris

The origin of the dog; wild dogs and tame, past and present. New York. 1939

Univ. of Clif. Library,
Biology Branch

QL
733
L 63

DOGS   AUSTRALIA

Le Soeuf, A. S.

The wild animals of Australasia, embracing the mammals of New Guinea and the nearer Pacific Islands. By A.S. Le Souef and Harry Burrell, with a chapter on the bats of Australia and New Guinea by Ellis Le G. Troughton. George G. Harrap and Company, Ltd. London... 8vo. (1926) 388 pp.

GN
1
An
765)

Doerr, Erich

Bestattungsformen in Ozeanien.

(Anthropos, Bd. 30, 1935, pp. 369-420, 727-765)

GN
700
A 62

DOGS

Hilzheimer, Max

Dogs.

(Antiquity, Dec. 1932:411-419. Translated by Roland G. Austin from original paper in German IN Zeit. F. Hundeforschung, 1931, Apr., pp. 3-14)

Dogs—Australian native
see also
Warrigal

QH
1
H 38

Doerr, John E., Jr.

Pulu

(Hawaii National Park, Nature Notes, Vol. II No. 2, 1932)

GN
Ethn.
Pam.
1548

DOGS

Hilzheimer, Max

Variationen des candidengebisses mit besonderer berucksichtigung des Haushundes.

(Zeit. f. Morphol. und Anthrop., Bd. 9; ? 1905)

GN
2.1
T 13

DOGS   CHINA

Shun-Sheng, Ling

Dog sacrifice in ancient China and the Pacific area.

(Bull. Inst. of Ethnology, Acad. Sinica, No. 3:37-40 (summary, 1957)

QL
Crust.
Pam.
No. 330

Doflein, F. (ed)

Beiträge zur Naturgeschichte Ostasien Band II, No. 11 (Balss , Stomatopoden)

[Find complete list of contents of the whole series on the inside covers of this paper.]

DOGS

Langkavel, Bernhard August, 1825-1902.
Dogs and savages. By Dr. B. Langkavel ...

(*In* Smithsonian institution. Annual report. 1898. Washington, 1899, 23½"". p. 651-675)

"Translated from the Internationales archiv für ethnographie, bd. VIII, pp. 109-149."

1. Dog. 2. Savages.

S 15-1016

Library of Congress   Q11.S66 1898
Library, Smithsonian   Institution

AS
763
B-4

and

QL
Mammals
Pam.
115

DOGS - HAWAII

Svihla, Arthur

Dental caries in the Hawaiian dog.

(Occ. Papers, Bernice P. Bishop Museum, Vol. 22, no. 2, 1957)

QL
Crustacea
Pam.
No.
340

Doflein, F.   und Balss , H.

Die Dekapoden und Stomatopoden der Hamburger Magalhaenaischen Sammelreise 1892/93. Aus Mitt. Nat.Mus. XXIX, Hamburg, 1912, pp 25 - 44.

DOGS

Tatham, Julie Campbell

World book of dogs; illustrated by Edwin Megargee. Cleveland World Pub. Co. 1st ed. 1953

?

QL
Mammals
Pam 54

DOGS HAWAII

Wood-Jones, Frederic

The Cranial Characters of the Hawaiian Dog.

(Reprinted from Journal of Mammalogy, Vol. 12, No. 1, February, 1931, pp. 39-41)

AP
2
N 28

DOGS

The African wild dog.

(Nature, No. 4526, p. 191, 1956)

QL
Mammals
Pam.80

DOGS

Yeatter, Ralph E.

Bird dogs in sport and conservation.

(Illinois Natural History Survey, Circular 42, 1948)

AS
162
S 67

DOGS MADAGASCAR

Dechambre, Ed.

Origine des animaux domestiques de Madagascar.

(La Terre et la Vie, 1951(4):185-196)

QL
1
H-1

DOGS

Allen, Glover M.

Dogs of the American aborigines.

(Bull. Mus. Comp. Zool., Harvard, Vol. 63, no. 9, 1919-1920, pp. 431-517, pl. 1-12)

Q
115
E 96

DOGS   AFRICA

Philo, Walter

A basenji from the Ituri.

(Explorers Journal, 36(2):18-20, 1958)

DU
400
T 25

DOG   MAORI

Barrow, T.

A rare sculpture (a Maori dog).

(Te Ao Hou, March, 1960, p. 38)

AS 750 N 56 — DOGS MAORI
Colenso, William
Notes on the ancient dog of the New Zealanders.
(Trans. and Proc. of the New Zealand Inst., 10:135-155, 1877)

GN Ethn.Pam. 4004 — DOGS PACIFIC
Detwiler, Richard M.
Dog tooth money. (Pacific)
(Frontiers, The Acad. of Nat. Sciences of Philadelphia, Vol. 19(3):67-69, February, 1955)

AS 763 H 38 — DOG-TOOTH ORNAMENTS
Buck, Peter Henry
Hawaiian dog-tooth ornaments.
(Haw. Acad. Sci., Proc., 21st Ann. Meeting, 1945/46, p. 9)

AS 750 N 56 — DOGS MAORI
Hutton, Frederick W.
Note on the ancient Maori dog.
(Trans. N. Z. Inst., Vol. 30, pp. 151-155, 1897) and plate XV
[measurements of specimens found with moa bones, and a plate, photo of 3 dog skulls]

GN Ethn.Pam. 4029 — DOGS POLYNESIA
Lang, Werner
Der Hund als Haustier der Polynesier.
(Sonderabdruck aus "Von fremden Völkern und Kulturen" Hans Plischke zim 65. Geburtstag. 1955. pp. 227-236)

GN Pam 2308
Doheny Scientific expedition.
Discoveries relating to prehistoric man by the Doheny Scientific expedition in the Hava Supai canyon, Northern Arizona: with supplement; October & November, 1924.

GN 2.S P 76 — DOGS MAORI
The kuri Maori, or native dog.
(Jour. Poly. Soc., 21:137-138, 1912)

GN 2.S T — DOGS POLYNESIA
Lescure, Rey
Le chien en Polynésie.
(Bull. de la Soc. des Etudes Oceaniennes, Vol. 7 (5):266-272, 1946)

GN 2.S S 72
Dohrenwend, Bruce P.
Toward a theory of acculturation. By Bruce P. Dohrenwend and Robert J. Smith.
(Southwestern Journal of Anthropology, Vol. 18(1):30-39, 1962)

GN 2.S P 76 — DOGS MAORI
Skinner, W.H.
The ancient Maori dog.
(Journal of the Polynesian Society, 23: 173-175, 1914.)

GN 4 D 53 — DOG POLYNESIA
Luomala, Katharine
The native dog in the Polynesian system of values.
IN
Diamond, Stanley editor
Culture in history; essays in honor of Paul Radin; pp. 190-240. New York. 1960

AS 182 H
Dohrn, C. A.
Ueber australische Paussiden.
(Jour. Mus. Godeffroy, Heft 12, 1876, pp. 48-55)

GN 2.S P 76 — DOGS MAORI
Smith, W. W.
The native dog (kuri Maori).
(Jour. Poly. Soc., 22:43, 1913)

GN Folklore Pam. 120 — DOGS POLYNESIA
Luomala, Katharine
Polynesian myths about Maui and the dog.
(Sonderabdruck aus Fabula 2:139-162, 1958)

QL Mol Pem #122 D
Dohrn, H.
Australian specimens of mollusca ex (?), np. nd., pp. 366-368.

GN 2.S P 76 — DOGS MAORI
Wilson, Amdrew
The native dog (kuri Maori)
(Jour. Poly. Soc., 22:42, 1913)

GN 2.S P 76 — DOGS POLYNESIA
Mahony, B. G.
The native dog of western Polynesia.
(Jour. Poly. Soc., 24:69, 1915)

QL 401 C 44
Dohrn, H.
Ueber einige Leptopomen der Philippinen.
(Malakozoologischen Blätter, Bd. 9, 1862, pp. 91-94)

QL 733 L 63 — DOGS NEW GUINEA
Le Soeuf, A. S.
The wild animals of Australasia, embracing the mammals of New Guinea and the nearer Pacific Islands. By A.S. Le Soeuf and Harry Burrell, with a chapter on the bats of Australia and New Guinea by Ellis Le G. Troughton. George G. Harrap and Company, Ltd. London... 8vo. (1926) 388 pp.

GN 426 U 73 — DOG POLYNESIA
Urban, Manfred
Die Haustiere der Polynesier; ein Beitrag zur Kulturgeschichte der Südsee.
(Völkerkundliche Beiträge zur Ozeanistik, Bd. 2, 1961)

QK Pam #596 4to
Doi, T.
Uber die Sonnen-und Schattenblatter einiger Baume, ex Jour. of Coll. of Sc., Imp. Univ. of Tokyo, vol. XL, art. 1, 1917.

QK 1 B 74

Doidge, Ethel M.

The South African Fungi and Lichens to the end of 1945.

(Bothalia, Vol. 5, 1950)

DU 620 H 41

Dole, Charles S.

The Hui Kawaihau.

(Haw. Hist. Soc. Papers, No. 16, 1929, pp. 8-15)

GN Eth Pam #589 & 590

Dole, Sanford B(allard)

Evolution of Hawaiian land tenures. Haw. Hist. Soc. Pap. no. 3. 1892.

and
DU 620 H41

2d and 3d copies

Also
DU Pacific Pam.63

4th cop.

QL Mollusca Pam. 1028

DOLABELLA

Hertlein, Leo G.

Description of a new species of Gastropod from Easter Island.

(Bull. Southern Calf. Acad. Sci., 59(1): 19-21, 1960)

DU 620 F

Dole, Daniel   tr.

see

Barrot, Adolphe

Visit of the .....''Bonite''.....

DU Hist.Pam. 94

AP 2 O 96

Dole, Sanford B(allard)

Evolution of Hawaiian Land Tenures.

(From the Overland Monthly, Vol. XXV.- Second Series. January-June, 1895. San Francisco. Overland Monthly Publishing Company. 1895. 565-579 pp. 8vo.)

QL 1 H2

DOLABELLINAE

MacFarland, Frank Mace, 1869-
... The *Dolabellinae*. By F. M. MacFarland. With ten plates ... Cambridge, U. S. A., Printed for the Museum, 1918.
2 p. l., p. [301]-348, 1 l. 10 pl. (1 col.) 30ᶜᵐ. (Memoirs of the Museum of comparative zoölogy at Harvard college. vol. xxxv, no. 5)
Each plate preceded by leaf with descriptive letterpress.
"Reports on the scientific results of the expedition to the tropical Pacific ... by the U. S. Fish commission steamer 'Albatross,' from August, 1899, to June, 1900 ... xix."
"Published by permission of H. M. Smith, U. S. commissioner of fish and fisheries."
"Literature": p. 346-348.
1. [Dolabellinae] 2. Albatross (Steamer)   A 21-458
Title from Univ. of Chicag   QL1l.H375 vol. 35
Printed by L. C.
[2]

Dole, Edmund P.   Carter Coll. 2-B-9

Hiwa, a tale of ancient Hawaii. New York... Harper and Brothers. 1900 108 pp. 4to.

DU 620 H 4

Dole, Sanford B(allard)

The general meeting.

(Haw'n. Hist. Soc., 27th Annual Report, 1918, pp. 12-18)

AS 36 A 16-p

and
QL Prot.- Poly. Pam. 760

Dolan, Thomas, IV

Studies relative to the presence of minute particles in sea water.

(Proc. Acad. Nat. Sci. Philadelphia, Vol. 106:13-44, 1954)

GN 22 D 66

Dole, Gertrude E.

Essays in the science of culture, in honor of Leslie A. White, in celebration of his sixtieth birthday and his thirtieth year of teaching at the University of Michigan. By Gertrude E. Dole and Robert L. Carneiro. Thomas Y. Crowell Company. New York. 1960c R8vo.   xlvi + 509 pp.

DU 620 H 4

Dole, Sanford B(allard)

The Hawaiian Body Politic.

(Haw'n. Hist. Soc., 28th Annual Report, 1919, pp. 29-38)

AS 36 S5

DOLATOCRINUS

Springer, Frank, 1848-
... The fossil crinoid genus *Dolatocrinus* and its allies, by Frank Springer ... Washington, Govt. print. off., 1921.
v, 78 p. illus. 16 pl. on 8 l. 24½ᶜᵐ. (Smithsonian institution. United States National museum. Bulletin 115)

1. Dolatocrinus.
Library of Congress   Q11.U6   21-26377
———— Copy 2.   ♦ ♦   QE782.S73
[6]

DU Pac. Pam. 1052

Dole, James D.

Impressions of five months in Washington, August, 1933 to January, 1934.

(Reprint from New York Herald-Tribune, April, 1934. 32 pp.)

DU Hist.Pam. 101

Dole, Sanford B(allard)

The Hawaiian Crisis. (Inner title is "The Hawaiian Question") Correspondence between President Dole and U. S. Minister Willis, December, 1893. Honolulu. Star Publishing Co., Ltd. 1893 13 pp. 8vo.

GN Pam 2182

Dolby-Tyler and Giglioli, Enrico H.

Di alcuni strumenti litici tuttora in uso presso certe tribu del rio Napo. From Arch. per l'antro. e l'etnol. v.25, fasc. 3, 1895.

Q Biography Pam. 89

DOLE, JAMES D.

White, Henry A.

James D. Dole, industrial pioneer of the Pacific, founder of Hawaii's pineapple industry. The Newcomen Society in North America. New York, San Francisco, Montreal. 8vo. 32 pp.

DU 620 P

Dole, Sanford B(allard)

A Hawaiian heroine.

(Paradise of the Pacific, Vol. 29, 1916, No. 12, pp. 55-56)

Dole, Charles F.   Carter Coll. 10-B-21

My eighty years. New York E. P. Dutton and Co. 1927 xvi + 469 pp. 8vo.

DU 620 P

Dole, Sanford B.

Aquamarine

(Paradise of the Pacific, Vol. 27, 1914, No. 12, p. 41-44)

DU 621 H3

Dole, S.B.   (Sanford Ballard)

Hawaiian land policy. Thrum's Hawaiian Annual, 1898 pp.125-8.

DU
Hist.Pam.
34

Dole, (Sanford Ballard)

    The Hawaiian Question. A Letter of President Dole to U. S. Minister Willis. An Indictment of American Diplomacy in Hawaii. Honolulu. 1894. 8vo. 11 pp.

2 copies

DU
Hist.
Pam.
494

Dole, Sanford L.

Dutton, Meiric K.   (commentator)

    A most extraordinary correspondence. Loomis House Press. Honolulu. 1958. 28 pp.

    (between President Grover Cleveland and Sanford B. Dole)

    (annexation period)

QL
Bird
Pam
#99
and
AS
36
B3

Dole, Sanford B(allard)

    A synopsis of the birds of the Hawaiian Islands, ex Boston Soc. of Nat. Hist. Proc., vol. XII, Feb. 17, 1869.

DU
620
H 4

Dole, Sanford B(allard)

    A hookupu.

    (Haw. Hist. Soc. Rept., 1915, pp. 18-20)

AS
36
B 2

Dole, Sanford B.

Wyman, Jeffries

    Observations on Crania.

    (Proc. Boston Soc. of Nat. Hist., Vol. XI, 1866-1868, pp. 440-462)

    (Letter from Dole to Wyman in re Kauai dune burial, pp. 447, 450)

DU
620
H 4

Dole, Sanford B(allard)

    Thirty days of Hawaiian history (The accession of Lunalilo to the throne).

    (Haw'n. Hist. Soc., 23d Annual Report, 1914, pp. 28-49)

DU
625.4
B 62

Dole, Sanford B.

    Impressions of Bernice Pauahi Bishop, an address, Dec. 13, 1925...
    IN
    Bernice Pauahi Bishop [privately printed, no date, a collection of tributes and data] 57pp.

DU
620
H 4

Dole, Sanford B(allard)

    Old Fish Market.

    (Haw'n. Hist. Soc., 29th Annual Report, 1920, pp. 19-25)

DU
620
M 67

(Dole, Sanford B(allard)

    Vacuum, a farce in three acts.

    (Miscellaneous pamphlets, III)

DU
621
H3

Dole, S.B.   (Sanford Ballard)

    List of birds at the Hawaiian Islands, Thrum's Hawaiian Annual. 1879, p.41-58.

DU
620
P

Dole, Sanford B.

    Overthrow of the Monarchy.

    (Paradise of the Pacific, Vol. 38, No. 12, 1925, pp. 37-40)

DU
620
H 3
locked
case

Dole, Sanford B(allard)

    Voyages of the ancient Hawaiians.

    (Hawaiian Club Papers, 1868, pp. 4-7)

QL
Bird
Pam
#58

Dole, S. B. (Sanford Ballard)

    List of Hawaiian birds prepared by S. B. Dole for the American Centennial, Honolulu, 1876.

Local
Newspapers

Upper
Floor
in
Closet

Dole, Sanford B(allard)

    Political importance of small land holdings for the Hawaiian Islands. in Haw. Gazette 1891, Aug. 14, p. 5.

QL
671
E 39

DOLE, SANFORD BALLARD

Amadon, D.

    Sanford Ballard Dole: early Hawaiian ornithologist.

    (The Elepaio, Vol. 5(3):12-13, 1944)

DU
625
D 66

Dole, Sanford B.

    Memoirs of the Hawaiian revolution. Edited by Andrew Farrell. Honolulu. Advertising Publishing Co., Ltd. 1936. xxiii + 188 pp.

DU
620
H 3
locked
case

GR
Pam
33

Dole, Sanford B(allard)

    Story of Paao.

    (Hawaiian Club Papers, 1868, pp. 13-17)

DU
625.4
D 16

DOLE, SANFORD BALLARD

Damon, Ethel M.

    Sanford Ballard Dole and his Hawaii. With an analysis of Justice Dole's legal opinions, by Samuel B. Kemp. Published for the Hawaiian Historical Society, by Pacific Books. Palo Alto R8vo. 1957c xiv + 394 pp.

Dole, Sanford B.   and Thurston, Lorrin

    Memoirs of the Hawaiian revolution.

LH
UH

QL
Bird Pam.
99
56
47
AS46B3
and
DU
620
M 67

Dole, Sanford Ballard

    A synopsis of the birds of the Hawaiian islands. (native names given)

    (Proc. Boston Soc. of Nat. Hist., Vol. 12, pp. 294-309. 1869)

    (Misc. Pams. Haw. II: 631-646)

QL
671
E 39

DOLE, SANFORD B.

Peppin, Hazel

    Hawaiian ornithologist, Sanford B. Dole.

    (The Elepaio, Vol. 16(10):50-51, 1956)

CR
385.H
D 66
Dole, Edmund P.

Hiwa, a tale of ancient Hawaii. Harper and Bros. New York and London. 1900. 8vo. 108 pp.

QL
1
C
DOLICHOPODIDAE

Wheeler, William Morton, 1865–
... A genus of maritime *Dolichopodidæ* new to America. By William Morton Wheeler ... San Francisco, The Academy, 1897.

1 p. l., p. 145-152. pl. iv. 25½ᶜᵐ. (Proceedings of the California academy of sciences. 3d ser. Zoology. vol. i, no. 4)

"Issued July 10, 1897."

1. Dolichopodidae.

Library of Congress   Q11.C25 vol. 1, no. 4   16-22009
———— Separate.   QL537.D7W5

QL
461
C 21
DOLICHOPODIDAE SOLOMON ISLANDS

Robinson, H.

A new species of Acropsilus from the Solomon Islands (Diptera: Dolichopodidae)

(Canad. Ent., Vol. 95(8):830-831, 1963)

QL
1
C1
DOLICHOGLOSSUS

Davis, Benjamin Marshall, 1867–
... The early life-history of *Dolichoglossus pusillus* Ritter. By B. M. Davis. Berkeley, The University press, 1908.

p. [187]-226. pl. 4-8 (1 col.) 27ᶜᵐ. (University of California publications in zoology, vol. 4, no. 3)

Contributions from the laboratory of the Marine biological association of San Diego, xix.
Originally submitted in 1907 as thesis (PH. D.)—University of California.
Bibliography : p. 216.

1. Dolichoglossus.

Title from Univ. of Calif.   Printed by L. C.   A 10-1050

QL
1
C
DOLICHOPODIDAE

Wheeler, William Morton, 1865–
... New species of *Dolichopodidae* from the United States. By William Morton Wheeler. With four plates ... San Francisco, The Academy, 1899.

1 p. l., 84 p. iv pl. 25½ᶜᵐ. (Proceedings of the California academy of sciences. 3d ser. Zoology. vol. ii, no. 1)

"Issued September 29, 1899."

1. Dolichopodidæ.

Library of Congress   Q11.C25   13-17442
———— Copy 2.   QL537.D7W6

QL
1
C 78
DOLICHOPTERYX

Grey, Marion

First record of the deep-sea fish Dolichopteryx longipes from the Pacific, with notes on Ophthalmopelton macropus.

(Copeia, 1952(2):87-90, 1952)

QL
53&3
B 86
DOLICHOPODIDAE

British Museum of Natural History.

Diptera of Patagonia and South Chile...Part V, Fasc. 1, by M. C. Van Duzee. London, 1930

QL
461
H 1
DOLICHOPODIDAE

Williams, Francis Xavier

Asyndetus carcinophilus Parent (Diptera, Dolichopodidae).

(Haw. Ent. Soc., Proc., Vol. 10, 1938, pp. 126-129)

QL
Ins.
Pam.
160

and

As
36
S 4
DOLICHOPUS

Aldrich, John Merton

Two-winged flies of the genera Dolichopus and Hydrophorus collected in Alaska in 1921, with new species of Dolichopus from North America and Hawaii.

(Proc. U. S. Nat. Mus., 1922, Vol. 61, No. 2446, pp. 1-18)

QL
489.S
P 11

AS
763
B-b

Reading
Room
DOLICHOPODIDAE

Lamb, C. G.

Dolichopodids from the Society Islands.

Society Islands Insects. Pacific Entomological Survey Publication 6, pp. 71-73 (Art.13), 1935.

(Bernice P.Bishop Museum, Bulletin 113)

QL
461
H 1
DOLICHOPODIDAE

Williams, Francis Xavier

Campsicnemus fumipennis Parent (Diptera, Dolichopodidae).

(Haw. Ent. Soc. Proc., Vol. 10, 1938, pp. 120-126)

AS
36
S5
DOLICHOPUS

Van Duzee, Millard C.
... The dipterous genus *Dolichopus* Latreille in North America, by M. C. Van Duzee, F. R. Cole and J. M. Aldrich. Washington, Govt. print. off., 1921.

iv, 304 p. 1 illus. 16 pl. on 8 l. 25ᶜᵐ. (Smithsonian institution. United States National museum. Bulletin 116)

"Bibliography of genus *Dolichopus* Latreille": p. 8.

1. Dolichopus. 2. Diptera—North America. i. Cole, Frank R., joint author. ii. Aldrich, John Merton, 1866– joint author.

Library of Congress   Q11.U6 no. 116   21-26209
———— Copy 2.   QL537.D7V27
191

QL
Insect
Pam.
1371
DOLICHOPODIDAE

Parent, O.

The Diptera of the Territory of New Guinea. VIII. Dolichopodidae.

(Proc. Linn. Soc. New South Wales, Vol. 64: 155-168, 1939)

QL
461
H 1
DOLICHOPODIDAE

Zimmerman, Elwood C.

Emperoptera from Maui (Diptera, Dolichopodidae).

(Haw. Ent. Soc., Proc., Vol. 10, 1938, pp. 145-148)

QL
461
H 38
DOLICHOTHRIPS CEYLON

Stannard, E. J., Jr.

A new species of Dolichothrips s. str. from Guam and Ceylon.

(Proc. Haw. Ent. Soc., 17(3):457-460, 1960)

QL
461
H 1
DOLICHOPODIDAE

Parent, (Abbé) O.

(Dolichopodides des Iles Hawaii, recueillis par Monsieur F. X. Williams, principalement au cours de l'année 1936.

(Proc. Haw. Ent. Soc., Vol. 10, 1939, pp. 225-249)

QL
1
A 93
DOLICHOPODIDAE AUSTRALIA

Hardy, G. H.

Australian Dolichopodidae (Diptera).

(The Australian Zoologist, 6:124-134, 1930)

QL
461
H 38
DOLICHOTHRIPS GUAM

Stannard, E. J., Jr.

A new species of Dolichothrips s. str. from Guam and Ceylon.

(Proc. Haw. Ent. Soc., 17(3):457-460, 1960)

QL
1
C
DOLICHOPODIDAE

Snodgrass, Robert E.
... The hypopygium of the *Dolichopodidæ*. By Robert E. Snodgrass. With four plates ... San Francisco, The Academy, 1904.

1 p. l., 273-294 p. xxx-xxxiii pl. 25½ᶜᵐ. (Proceedings of the California academy of sciences. Third series. Zoology. vol. iii, no. 10)

"Issued September 28, 1904."

1. Dolichopodidae.

Library of Congress   Q11.C25   4-30944

QL
489.M
P 11
DOLICHOPODIDAE—MARQUESAS

Lamb, C. G.
A new species of dolichopodid from the Marquesas.
IN
Marquesan Insects-I, pp. 233-234. (Art. 24)

(Bernice P. Bishop Museum, Bulletin 98,1932. Pacific Entomological Survey Publication 1)

AS
540
P
DOLIIDAE

Alcasid, Godofredo L.

Philippine recent shells, I.

(Philippine Jrl. of Science, vol. 61, 1936, pp. 489-500)

QH
1
P 11

also
QL
Mollusca
Pam.
873

DOLIIDAE

Tinker, Spencer

The Hawaiian tun shells.

(Pacific Science, Vol. 3(4):302-306, 1949)

QL
Crus
Pam
#210

Dollfus, Adrien

Isopodes Terrestres Recueillis aux
Açores en 1887-1889 par MM. Barrois et Chaves

Revue Biologique du Nord de la France
Tome I. 1888-1889.

Lille 1889   8vo pp. 1-3, 391-2
FEB 23 1911

AM
Mus.
Pam.
109

DOLLS

Native dolls in the Transvaal Museum.
From Ann. Transvaal Mus., v.11, pt.2, 1925

QL
Prot. to
Poly.
Pam. 597

DOLIOLIDAE

Neumann, Günther

Doliolidae.

(from Bronn, H. G.   Klassen und Ordnungen
des Tierreichs, Bd. III, Supplement Tunikaten,
Abt. II, Buch 2, Lief. 1, 1935. 67 pp.)

QL
Crus
Pam
#209

Dollfus, Adrien,

On West Indian Terrestrial Isopod
Crustaceans.

(Zoological Society of London, Proc., Vol.
for 1896, pp. 388-400. (p. 388 not present here))

FEB 23 1911

— 1896   pp. 389-400.

GN
2.8
O 15

DOLLS SOLOMON ISLANDS

Masson-Detourbet, Annie

Poupées des Iles Salomon.

(Journal de la Soc. des Océanistes, Vol. 3:
123-126, 1947)

QH
1
P 11

DOLIOLIDS PACIFIC

Tokioka, Takasi

Two new doliolids from the eastern Pacific
Ocean. By Takasi Tokioka and Leo Berner.

(Pacific Science, 12(2):135-138, 1958)

QL
Crustacea
Pam. 516

Dollfus, Adrien

Sur quelques isopodes du Musée de Leyde.
(Notes from the Leyden Museum, Vol. XI,
1889, pp. 91-94)

GN
806
B 73

Dolmens of Ireland...

Borlase, W. C.

DOLLAR, ROBERT   Carter Coll.
                        10-D-3

Memoirs of Robert Dollar. San Francisco
W. S. van Cott and Co. 1921 144 pp. 8vo.

QL
Crustacea
Pam. 213

Dollfus, Adrien

Voyage de M. Ch. Alluaud dans le térritoire
d'Assinie (Afrique occidentale) en juillet et
août 1886, Mem. 12: Crustaces Isopodes terrestres

(Annales de la Société Ent. de France, Vol.
61, 1892, pp. 385-390)

AP
2
A 5

and
QE
Pam.
93

DOLOMITE

Skeats, Ernest W.

The formation of dolomite and its bearing on
the coral reef problem.

(Am. Jour. of Sci., Ser. 4, Vol. 45, 1918,
pp. 185-200)

GN
451
D 66

Dollard, John   and others

Frustration and aggression, by John Dollard
and others, in collaboration with Clellan S. Ford
and others.   Inst. of Human Relations, Yale
University Press. 1939. 8vo. (8) + 209 pp.

QL
Crustacea
Pam. 211

Dollfus, Adrien

Voyage de M. E. Simon au Venezuela (Decembre 1887-Avril 1888) 25th Mem.:Isopodes Terrestre

(Ann. Soc. Ent. Fr., 1893, Vol. 62, pp.
339-346)

AP
2
A5

Dolomite.

Van Tuyl, Francis M.
New points on the origin of dolomite.
In American Journ. of Science. 4th Series.
XLII. pp. 249-260.

QL
Protozoa
& Poly
Pam #39

Dolley, Charles S.

The planktonokrit, a centrifugal
apparatus for the volumetric estimation of the food-supply of oysters
and other aquatic animals, ex Acad.
of Nat. Sc. of Philidelphia Proc.,
May, 1896.

QE
524
D 66

Dollfus, A(uguste)

Voyage Géologique dans les Republiques de
Guatemala et de Salvador, par A. Dollfus et E. de
Mont-Serrat. Paris. Imprimerie Impériale.
1868.   ix + 539 pp. 18 pl. 4to.
(Mission Scientifique au Mexique et dans
L'Amerique Centrale:Géologie)

AS
182
S 471

DOLOMITIZATION

Reuling, H. T.

Der Sitz der Dolomitisierung. Versuch einer
neuen Auswertung der Bohr-Ergebnisse von Funafuti.
Frankfurt. 1934.

(Abh. der Senckenbergischen Naturforschenden
Gesellschaft, 428. 44 pp.)

QL
Crus
Pam
#69

Dollfus, Adrien

Description d'un Isopode Fluviatile
du genre Jaera, provenant de l'Ile
de Flores.
Extrait du Bull Soc. Zool. de France 1889.

Paris 1889   8vo pp. 1-10
FEB 23 1911

AS
145
B

Dollfus, Robert Ph.

Trématodes.

Van Straelen, V.
Résultats scientifiques du voyage aux Indes
Orientales Néerlandaises...Léopold de Belgique.
Vol. 2, Fasc. 10, 1932, pp. 1-13

(Mem. hors ser. Mus. Roy. d'Hist. Nat.
Belgique)

DU
12
B 99

DOLPHIN (SHIP)

(Byron, John)

Voyage round the world, in His Majesty's ship
the Dolphin, commanded by...Byron...London. 1767.
8vo.

DU
12
H 39
locked
case

DOLPHIN (SHIP)

Hawkesworth, John

An account of the voyages undertaken...for making discoveries in the Southern Hemisphere, and successively performed by Commodore Byron, Captain Wallis, Captain Carteret, and Captain Cook, in the Dolphin, the Swallow, and the Endeavor... 3 vols.   London.   1773. 4to.
    Vol. 1, pp. 3-522.
    ...Fourth edition, Vol. 1, pp. 1-132. Perth. 1789. 12mo.

GC
57
L 48
locked
case

DOLPHIN (SHIP)

Lee, S. P.

Reports and charts of the cruise of the U.S. brig Dolphin, made under the direction of the Navy Department...Washington. 1854. 8vo.

G
161
H

DOLPHIN (ship)

Robertson, George

The discovery of Tahiti: a journal of the second voyage of H. M. S. Dolphin round the world under the command of Captain Wallis...1766, 1767, and 1768, written by her master. Edited by Hugh Carrington.

(Works issued by the Hakluyt Society, Ser. 2, No. 98, 1948).

DOLPHINS

see

DELPHINIDAE

AS
540
P 55 j

Domantay, Jose S.

A brief summary of the Pacific and Atlantic Holothurioidea of the Allan Hancock Foundation collections.

(The Philippine Jour. of Science, Vol. 82(2): 133-140, 1953)

AS
540
P

Domantay, Jose S.

The catching of live bait for tuna fishing in Mindanao.

(Phil. Jour. Sci., 73:337-342, 1940)

QL
Prot.-
Poly.
Pam.
812

Domantay, Jose S.

Littoral Holothurioidea of Port Galera Bay and adjacent waters.

(Contrib. from the Dept. of Zoology, College of Liberal Arts, University of the Philippines, Vol. 3:41-101, 1953)

AS
540
P

Domantay, Jose S.

Tuna fishing in southern Mindanao.

(Philippine Journal of Science, Vol. 73, 1940, pp. 423-436)

GN
662
R1
c.7

Domeny de Rienzi, G. L.

Océanie ou cinquième partie du monde de la Malaisie de la Micronésie de la Polynésie et de la Mélanisie.
3 vols.   Paris 1836/37.

GN
2.I
G 59

DOMESTIC ANIMALS

Lang, Werner

Probleme der völkerkundlichen Haustier-Forschung.

(Göttinger Völkerkundliche Studien, Bd. II: 7-26, 1957)

GN
2.M
F 45

DOMESTIC ANIMALS   ORIGIN

Angress, Shimon

An annotated bibliography on the origin and descent of domestic animals, 1900-1955. By Shimon Angress and Charles A. Reed.

(Fieldiana: Anthropology, Vol. 54(1), 1962)

AS
750
N

DOMESTIC ANIMALS   POLYNESIA

Tregear, Edward

Knowledge of cattle amongst the ancient Polynesians.

(Trans. New Zeal. Inst. XXI, 1888, pp. 447-476)

DU
620
P

Domesticating island quail.

(Paradise of the Pacific, 20 (4):18, 1907)

QL
1
Z

DOMICELLA

Finsch, Otto

On a very rare parrot from the Solomon Islands: Domicella cardinalis.

(Proc. Zool. Soc. London, 1869, pp. 126-129)

QK
1
B 748

Domin, Karel   editor
    SEE
Acta Botanica Bohemica.

QK
Bot.Pam.
1986

Domin, Karel

Generis Verbasci L. specierum et hybridarum in Czechoslovakia sponte crescentium enumeratio.

(Z Vestniku Kral. Ces. Spol. Nauk, Tr.11, Roc.1935)

QK
Bot.Pam.
1737

Domin, Karel

Humifuse Forms of Some Species and Their Ecological Signification.

(Preslia, Vol. XI, 1932, pp. 1-6)

Qk
Botany
Pam
1539

Domin, Karel.

Hybrids and Garden forms of the Genus Pityrogramma (Link).   From the Rospr. II. tř. Česká Akademie, vol. XXXVIII, no. 4. 1929. pls.

QK
Bot.Pam.
1736

Domin, Karel

A Monographic Study of the Czechoslovak Plantains of the Group Plantago major L. (translated title, original in Czech. Summary in English)

(Z Vestniku Kralovske Ceske Spolecnosti Nauk, Roc 1932, II, pp. 1-47)

QK
Bot.Pam.
1735

Domin, Karel

A Monographic Synopsis of the Czechoslovak Plantago species.
(translated title, original in Czech. Summary in English)

(Z Vestniku Kralovske Ceske Spolecnosti Nauk, Roc 1933, II, pp. 1-51)

Qk
Botany
Pam
1540

Domin, Karel.

New additions to the flora of Western Australia. Zvlastni Otisk Z Vestnika Kral. Ces. Spole Nauk tr. II Roč. 1921-1922.

QK
526D2
D67

Domin, Karel.

    Pteridophyta of the island of Dominica with notes on various ferns from tropical America. Praha, Royal Society of Sciences, Memoir, new series no. 2 1929.

DOMINICA FUNGI

    See

FUNGI DOMINICA

DOMINICA TREES

    See

TREES DOMINICA

QK
Bot.Pam.
1738

Domin, Karel

    Sempervivum L., Subgenus Jovisbarba Koch.

    (Bulletin international de l'Académie des Sciences de Bohême, 1932, pp. 1-9, pl.1-3)

DOMINICA GEOLOGY

    see

GEOLOGY DOMINICA

DOMINICA ZOOLOGY

    see

ZOOLOGY DOMINICA

QK
Botany
Pam
1537

Domin, Karel

    Some problems of plant ecology. From Proceedings of the International Congress of Plant Sciences I; 497-524, 1929.

DOMINICA HYMENOPTERA

    see

HYMENOPTERA DOMINICA

Carter
Safe

Dominis, John O.

    Marriage certificate.

    [Placed in Carter safe]

QK
Pam
Botany
1538

Domin, Karel.

    Virgin Forest of Boubin with Geobotanical remarks on the Sumava Mountains. Bulletin international de l'Académie des Sciences de Bohême 1927, pls.

DOMINICA LEPIDOPTERA

    see

LEPIDOPTERA DOMINICA

DU
Pac.Pam.
486

DOMINIS, JOHN OWEN

Boyer, Frank Norton

    One-Time Co-Ruler of Hawaii Native of This City (Schenectady, N.Y.)

    (From Schenectady Gazette, August 27, 1932, pages 6-7)

    (About John Owen Dominis)

E
North
America
Pam.
17

DOMINICA

Pan-American Union

    Dominion Republic: General descriptive data.

Washington, 1920, 31 pp.

DOMINICA MOLLUSCA

    see

MOLLUSCA DOMINICA

DU
620
F

DOMINIS, JOHN OWEN

    Death of H. R. H. John O. Dominis, Prince Consort.

    (Friend, Sept., 1891, p. 67)

DOMINICA BIRDS

    see

BIRDS DOMINICA

DOMINICA ORTHOPTERA

    see

ORTHOPTERA DOMINICA

Hms
Misc18

Storage
Case
4

DOMINIS, JOHN OWEN

    Documentary record of the family connections and standing of Governor Dominis.

DOMINICA BOTANY

    See

BOTANY DOMINICA

DOMINIQUE PIPERACEAE

    See

PIPERACEAE DOMINIQUE

DU
620
P

DOMINIS, JOHN OWEN

Taylor, Albert Pierce

    Dalmatian lady, heir to Hawaiian Prince?

    (Paradise of the Pacific, Vol. 40, No. 6, 1927, pp. 12,13)

DU
620
H 3
locked
case

Dominis, Lilia K.

He Mele Lahui Hawaii. (Hawaiian National Hymn)

(Hawaiian Club Papers, 1868, pp. 116-117)

QK
9
Don

Don, G.

A general history of the dichlamydeous plants, comprising complete descriptions of the different orders, together with the characters of the genera and species and an enumeration of the cultivated varieties. 4 vols. 4to.

London, 1831- 1838.

[Binder's title -- Don's Gardener's Dictionary]

QL
671
E 39

Donaghho, Walter

Bird notes from Guadalcanal.

(The Elepaio, 3:32-33,35-36,40-41; Vol. 4: 1-2, 14, 18-20, 1943-1944)

QK
Bot.
Pam.
2881

Domke, Walter

Untersuchungen über die systematische und geographische Gliederung der Thymelaeaceen nebst einer Neubeschreibung ihrer Gattungen.

(Bibliotheca Botanica, Heft 111, Stuttgart 1934)

DU
621
H 39

DON QUIXOTE (SHIP)

Greer, Richard A.

The Deadley Don.

(Hawaii Historical Review, I(3):52-54, 1963)

QL
671
E 39

Donaghho, Walter

A bird walk in New Caledonia.

(The Elepaio, Vol. 5(5):28-30, 1944)

QL
1
B 93

Domrow, R.

The Asian species of Whartonia (Acarina, Trombiculidae).

(Treubia, 26(1):1-10, 1963)

QK
9
Don
D67

Don's Gardener's Dictionary

See

Don, G.

QL
671
E 39

Donaghho, Walter

A birding trip to Tulagi.

(The Elepaio, Vol. 5(1):1-3, 1944)

QL
461
P 11

Domrow, Robert

The genus Guntherana (Acarina, Trombiculidae).

(Pacific Insects, 2:195-238, 1960)

QL
Insect
Pam.
1893

DONACIINAE

Chen, Sicien H.

Notes on Donaciine beetles.

(photostat, Sinensia, 12:1-17, 1941)

QL
671
E 39

Donaghho, Walter

A journal of ornithological work during the summer of 1937, Hawaii National Park.

(The Elepaio, Vol. 7(10):56-57, (11):64-66, (12):69-70, 1947; 11(9):50-52; (10):56-58; (11):62-65; (12):72-73, 1951; 12(7):46-48, 1952)

QL
461
P 11

Domrow, Robert

Halarachne miroungae Ferris redescribed (Acarina:Laelapridae).

(Pacific Insects, 4(4):859-863, 1962)

QL
Insect
Pam.
2059

DONACIINI

Schaeffer, Charles

Revision of the New World species of the tribe Donaciini of the Coleopterous family Chrysomelidae.

(Brooklyn Museum Science Bull., 3(3), 1925)

QL
671
Co

Donaghho, Walter R.

Observations of some birds of Guadalcanal and Tulagi.

(Condor, Vol. 52:127-132, 1950)

QL
1
A 93

Domrow, R.

Mammals of Innisfail,II. Their mite parasites.

(Australian Journal of Zoology, Vol. 10: 268-306, 1962)

Donagho, Walter

See

Donaghho, Walter

QL
671
E 39

Donaghho, Walter

Ornithological notes, Midway Islands, 1940.

(Elepaio, Vol. 14(2):8-11, (3):18-21, (5): 30-31,(6):41-43, 1953)

QL
1
B 93

Domrow, R.

Seven new Oriental-Australasian chiggers (Acarina, Trombiculidae).

(Treubia, 26(1):39-56, 1963)

QL
671
E 39

Donaghho, Walter

A bird day in New Zealand.

(The Elepaio, Vol. 5(10):66-68, 1945)

QL
671
E 39

Donaghho, Walter

A trip up a jungle river. (New Hebrides)

(The Elepaio, Vol. 3, 1943, No. 12; and Vol. 4(1): 1943)

QL
871
E 39

Donaghho, Walter

A visit to Moku Manu.

(The Elepaio, Vol. 7(12):72-73, 1947)

AS
36
S3

Donaldson, Thomas Corwin, 1843-1898.

... The George Catlin Indian gallery in the U. S. National museum (Smithsonian institution) with memoir and statistics. By Thomas Donaldson.

(*In* U. S. National museum. Annual report. 1885. Washington, 1886. 23½ᶜᵐ. app. (pt. V) 1 p. l., vii, 3-939 p. 144 pl. (incl. ports, maps (part fold.) facsims.))

Half-title.
Includes many extracts from the writings of George Catlin.
Memoir of George Catlin (with three portraits: p. 701-718.
Bibliography of George Catlin (1838-1871): p. 779-793.
1. Indians of North America. 2. Catlin, George, 1796-1872. 3. U. S. National museum. Catlin collection.

Library of Congress   Q11.U5 1885   14-19246
———— Copy 2.

QL
577
W 74

Doner, L. H.

Wilson, H. F.

The historical development of insect classification, by H. F. Wilson and M. H. Doner. Planographed by John S. Swift Co., Inc., St. Louis, Chicago,... 4to. ii + 133 pp. 1937

Carter Coll.
6-A-9

Donahue, G. J.

Damien and Reform. Boston. The Stratford Co. 1921 86 pp. sm8vo

---

AS
720.N
L

Donat

Sur quelques similitudes des langues et des coutumes des indigènes de Funafuti (Ellice Group) et des indigènes des Iles de la Société, de l'Archipel des Tuamotu, etc., par MM. Donat et Seurat.

(Proc. Linn. Soc. N. S. Wales, Vol. 28, 1903, pp. 926-931)

Donisthorpe, Horace

List of the type species of the genera and subgenera of the Formicidae.

(Ann. and Mag. Nat. Hist., Ser. 11, Vol. 10, pp. 617, 649, 721,   1943)

(617 -?, 649 ?, 721 ?)
HSPA

DU
1
P 10

Donald McLeod defended on "piracy" charge.

(Pacific Islands Monthly, 26(2):86-90, 1955)

QL
Prot. to
Poly.
Pam.
694

DONATIA

Edmondson, Charles Howard

Reproduction in Donatia deformis (Thiele).

(Occasional Papers, Bernice P. Bishop Museum, Vol. 18, no. 18, 1946)

QK
1
B 97-b

Donk, M. A.

Nomenclatural notes on generic names of agarics (Fungi:Agaricales).

(Bull. Bot. Gardens, Buitenzorg, Ser. 3. Vol. 18(3):271-402, 1949)

QL
Fish Pam.
585

Donaldson, Lauren R.

Effects of radiation on aquatic organisms. By Lauren R. Donaldson and Richard F. Foster.

(Reprint from "The effects of atomic radiation on oceanography and fisheries", Publ. 551, Nat. Acad. Sci.- Nat. Res. Council, pp. 96-102, 1956)

QH
431
D67

Doncaster, L

Heredity in the light of recent research. Cambridge, University press, 1921.   161 p. pl.

Donn and Miller

Atlantic hurricanes.   Louisiana State University Press. 1960

recommended by UH 1963

QL
Prot.-
Poly.
Pam.
814

Donaldson, Lauren R.

Radiobiological studies at the Eniwetok test site and adjacent areas of the Western Pacific.

(Reprinted from the Trans. of the Second Seminar on Biological Problems in Water Pollution, Apr. 20-24, 1959, U. S. Public Health Service, Cincinnati. (7) pp.

AS
36
S1

Doncaster, Leonard, 1877-

Recent work on the determination of sex. By Leonard Doncaster ...

(*In* Smithsonian institution. Annual report. 1910. Washington, 1911. 23½ᶜᵐ. p. 473-485)

"Reprinted ... from Science progress, London, no. 13. July 1909, pp. 90-104."

1. Sex—Cause and determination.

Library of Congress   Q11.S66 1910   11-31575

DU
623
D63

Donne, M. A.

Sandwich Islands and their people.

London, 1866 ?,   pp 188

QL
Fish Pam.
584

Donaldson, L.R.

Return of silver salmon, Oncorhynchus kisutch (Walbaum) to point of release. By Lauren R. Donaldson and George H. Allen.

(Reprint: Trans. Amer. Fish. Soc., vol. 87, 1957:13-22)

DU
Hist.Pam.
508

Dondo, Mathurin

La Perouse in Maui. Maui Publishing Company, Ltd.   Wailuku. 1959. sm8vo. 62 pp.

DU
423
D68

Donne, T   E

The Maori, past and present: an account of a highly attractive, intelligent people, their doubtful origin, their customs and ways of living, art, methods of warfare, hunting, and other characteristics, mental and physical.

London, Seeley Service, 1927.   284p. pls.

QC
1
W 31

Donaldson, Lauren R.   and others

Survey of radioactivity in the sea near Bikini and Eniwetok atolls June 11-21, 1956. By Lauren R. Donaldson, Allyn H. Seymour, etc...

[Health and Safety, UWFL-46, U. S. Atomic Energy Comm. Applied Fisheries Laboratory, Univ of Washington. July 23, 1956]

GN
2.1
A-M

Done, J.

A girl's puberty custom in Boigu.

(Man, vol. 23, 1923, no. 94, p. 150)

QL
L- J

Donoghue, Chas. H.

Opisthobranchiata from the Abrolhos Islands with description of a new parasitic Copepod. In Linnean Soc. London, Journ Zool. Vol. XXXV, PP 521 - 579, 1924.

Donovan, E(dward)

The insects of New Holland, New Zealand, New Guinea, Otaheite, and other Islands in the Indian, Southern and Pacific Oceans. R4to. 41 colored plates. 1805. London.

HSPA

QL
401
M 23

DORCASIA

Pilsbry, Henry A.

Anatomical and systematic notes on Dorcasia, Trygonophrus, n. gen., Corilla, Thersites, and Chloritis.

(Proc. Mal. Soc. London, Vol. 6, 1905, pp. 286-291)

PL
Phil.
Pam. 487

(Dordillon, Rene Ildefonse)

Mou tekao ke. (Elementary statements on geography, astronomy, geometry, physics, chemistry, etc.) Bar-le-Duc. 1886. 85 pp. 12mo.

Marquesas

AS
244
D

Dons, Carl

Notes sur quelques Protozoaires marins.

(Vid. Med. Dansk Nat. For. Kobenhavn, Bd. 73 1922.- Papers from Dr. Mortensen's Pacific Expedition, No. 5)

AS
763
B-4

QL
Insect
Fam.932

Reading
Room

d'Orchymont, Armand

Check list of the Palpicornia of Oceania (Coleoptera, Polyphaga).

(B.P.Bishop Museum Occasional Papers, vol. XIII, no.13. 1937. pp.147-160)

QL
Protozoa
to
Polyzoa
Pam.
No. 88

Dore, Walter

The digestion of wood by Teredo navalis. Univ. Calif. Pub. Zool. Vol. 22, pp 383- 400, 1923.

AS
36
S4

Doolittle, Alfred A.
Descriptions of recently discovered *Cladocera* from New England. By Alfred A. Doolittle ...

(*In* U. S. National museum. Proceedings. Washington, 1912. 23½ᶜᵐ. v. 41, p. 161-170. pl. 13-19)

1. Cladocera. 2. Crustacea—New England.

12-17770

Library of Congress   Q11.U55 vol. 41

Dordick, I. L.

Climate and human welfare in Australian New Guinea. Ph.D., Johns Hopkins Unic. 1951

microfilm in Dept. of Pac. Hist., Inst. of Adv. Studies, Australian Nat. Univ.

QL
595.Mi
I 59

DORILAIDAE

Hardy, D. Elmo

Insects of Micronesia, Diptera: Dorilaidae (Pipunculidae).
IN
Insects of Micronesia, Vol. 13(1), 1956. Bernice P. Bishop Museum. Honolulu

---

AS
36
S4

Doolittle, Alfred Abel, 1870-
Notes on the occurrence of the crustacean *Alonopsis* in America, with description of a new species. By Alfred A. Doolittle ...

(*In* U. S. National museum. Proceedings. Washington, 1913. 23½ᶜᵐ. vol. 43, p. 561-565. pl. 42-43)

1. Alonopsis.

13-13124

Library of Congress   Q11.U55 vol. 43

Dordick, Isadore L.

Climate and work in Australian New Guinea.

(Acta Tropica, 10:233-250, 1953)

Reviewed in Geogr. Rev., 45:123, 1955.
Hawaii Med. Soc. Library has

QL
461
H-1

DORILAIDAE

Hardy, D. Elmo

Studies in Hawaiian Dorilaidae (Diptera) Part I

(Proc. of the Hawaiian Entomological Society for 1952, Vol. XV(1):59-73, 1953)

QL
Mollusca
Pam.
764

Doornink, H. W.

Tertiary Nummulitidae from Java.

(Geologisch Inst., Univ. van Amsterdam, Mededeeling no.34 . 1932)

PL
Phil.Pam.
493

(Dordillon, Rene Ildefonse)

Essai de grammaire de la langue des Iles Marquises, par un pretre de la Société de Picpus Missionaire aux Iles Marquises. Valparaiso. 1857. sm8vo. 120 pp.

GC
1
S43

Dorman, Henry P.

Quantitative studies on marine diatoms and dinoflagellates at four inshore stations on the coast of California in 1923. Bull. Scripps Institution Oceanography, v.1, n.7, Berkeley, 1927.

QH
1
A 88

Doran, Edwin, Jr.   convener

Land tenure in the Pacific: a symposium of the Tenth Pacific Science Congress.

(Atoll Research Bulletin, No. 85, 1961)

PL
700
D 69

Dordillon, I. R.   (René Ildefonse)

Grammaire et dictionnaire de la langue des Iles Marquises. (Marquesan-French and French-Marquesan) Imprimerie Belin Freres. Paris. 1904. sm8vo. pp. 1-294; 1-204 + (1)

[2 copies; in the back inside cover of one copy is a handwritten statement about Rene Ildefonse Dordillon,- from which it may be assumed that the initials I. R. should be R. I.]

GC
1
S43

Dorman, Henry P.

Studies on marine diatoms and dinoflagellates caught with the Kofoid bucket in 1923. Bull. Scripps Instit. Oceanography, v.1, n.5, Berkeley, 1927.

QH
1
A 88

Doran, Edwin Jr.

Report on Tarawa atoll, Gilbert Islands.

(Atoll Research Bull. 72:1-54, appendix A-E; 1960)

PL
700
D 69

Dordillon, René Ildefonse

Grammaire et dictionnaire de la langue des Iles Marquises. Marquisien-Francais.

(Travaux et Mémoires de l'Institut d'Ethnologie, XVII, 1931. R8vo. vi + 446 pp.)

GN
Pam
939

Dorpfeld, W.

Verbrennung und bestattung der Toten im alten Griechenland. From Melan. Nicole. 1905. 9p.

GN
Pam
1762

Dörpfeld, Wilhelm

Zu den altgriechischen bestattungs-sitten. From Neuen Jahrbuchern, 1912, abt. 1, bd. 29, heft 1, Teubner, Leipzig.

QL
461
T 86

Dorsey, C. K.

Population and control studies of the Palau gnat on Peleliu, Western Caroline Islands.

(Journal of Economic Entomology, Vol. 40: 805-814, 1947)

GN
Pam
#46

Dorsey, George A(mos)

The department of anthropology of the field Columbian Museum - a review of six years, ex Am. Anthropologist, vol. 2, April-June, 1900.

DU
700
R 12

Dorsenne, Jean

Radiguet, Max

Les Derniers Sauvages: la Vie et les Moeurs aux Iles Marquises (1842-1859). Illustrations inedites de l'Auteur. Avant-propos de Jean Dorsenne. Paris. Editions Duchartre et Van Buggenhoudt. 1929c 8vo.

GN
Pam
1876

Dorsey, George A(mos)

Anthropology. From The Amer. Naturalist, 1897.

Contains:
Observations on the scapulae of northwest coast Indians.

GN
Pam
1443

Dorsey, George A(mos)

How the Pawnee captured the Cheyenne medicine arrows. From Amer. Anthrop. v.5, n.4, 1903.

GN
671.S 5
F 41

Dorsenne, Jean

Fesche, C. F. P.

La Nouvelle Cythère (Tahiti). Journal de Navigation Inédit. Écrit à bord de la frégate du Roy la Boudeuse, commandée par M. le Chevalier de Bougainville. Avant-propos de Jean Dorsenne. Paris. Editions Duchartre et Van Buggenhoudt. 1929c. 8vo.

GN
2M
FI

Dorsey, George Amos, 1868–

... The Arapaho sun dance; the ceremony of the Offerings lodge, by George A. Dorsey ... Chicago, 1903.

xii, 228 p. cxxxvii pl. (part col.) 24½ᶜᵐ. (Field Columbian museum. Publication 75. Anthropological series. vol. iv)

Each plate preceded by guard sheet with brief explanation.
Bibliography: p. 5.

1. Arapaho Indians. 2. Sun-dance.

4—7725

Library of Congress   GN2.F4

GN
Pam
2178

Dorsey, George A(mos)

The lumbar curve in some American races. From Bull. Essex Instit. v.27, 1895.

Dorsenne, J.

Polynésie. 1929.

UH has

GN
2M
FI

Dorsey, George Amos, 1868–

... Archæological investigations on the island of La Plata, Ecuador. By George A. Dorsey ... Chicago, 1901.

1 p. l., 247–280 p. front., plates, maps, diagrs. 24½ᶜᵐ. (Field Columbian museum. Publication 56. Anthropological series. vol. ii, no. 5)

1. La Plata Island, Ecuador—Antiq.

4—13949

Library of Congress   GN2.F4

GN
2M
FI

Dorsey, George Amos, 1868–

... The Mishongnovi ceremonies of the snake and antelope fraternities, by George A. Dorsey ... and H. R. Voth. The Stanley McCormick Hopi expedition. Chicago, U. S. A., 1902.

2 p. l., p. [161]–261. pl. lxxv–cxlvii (partly col.) 24½ᶜᵐ. (Field Columbian museum. Publication 66. Anthropological series. vol. iii, no. 3)

Each plate accompanied by guard sheet with descriptive letterpress.
"Summary statement of previous accounts of Hopi snake ceremonies": p. 167–168.

1. Hopi Indians—Religion and mythology. 2. Snake dance.   i. Voth, Henry R., 1855–   joint author.

4—12213

Library of Congress   GN2.F4
———— Copy 2.   E99.H7D71

DU
12
D 71

Dorsenne, Jean

La vie de Bougainville. Paris. Librairie Gallimard. 1930. 8vo. 259 pp.

GN
Pam
1444

Dorsey, George A(mos)

An Arikara story-telling contest. From Amer. Anthrop. v.6, n.2, 1904.

GR
102.W
D 71

Dorsey, George A(mos)

The Mythology of the Wichita. Collected under the Auspices of the Carnegie Institution of Washington. 1904. 8vo. 351 pp.

(Carnegie Institution of Washington, Publication No. 21)

QL
Mammals
Pam.
97

Dorsett, Edward Lee

Hawaiian whaling days.

(Reprinted from The American Neptune, Vol. XIV(1):42-46, 1954)

GN
2M
FI

Dorsey, George Amos, 1868–

... A bibliography of the anthropology of Peru. By George A. Dorsey ... Chicago, U. S. A., 1898.

2 p. l., p. 55–206. 24½ᶜᵐ. (Field Columbian museum. Publication 23. Anthropological series. vol. ii, no. 2)

1. Ethnology—Peru—Bibl. 2. Anthropology—Bibl. 3. Peru—Antiq.—Bibl.

4—12214

Library of Congress   GN2.F4
———— Copy 2.   Z5114.D71

GN
2M
FI

Dorsey, George Amos, 1868–

... Observations on a collection of Papuan crania, by George A. Dorsey ... With notes on preservation and decorative features, by William H. Holmes ... Chicago, 1897.

48 p. illus., xi pl. 24½ᶜᵐ. (Field Columbian museum. Publication 31. Anthropological series. vol. ii, no. 1)

1. Craniology—New Guinea.   i. Holmes, William Henry, 1846–

4—12212

Library of Congress   GN2.F4
———— Copy 2.   GN138.N5D8

Dorsett, E. L.

Hawaiian whaling days. 1954.

UH has

GN
2M
FI

Dorsey, George Amos, 1868–

... The Cheyenne, by George A. Dorsey ... Chicago, 1905.

2 v. illus., lxviii pl. (partly col.) 24½ᶜᵐ. (Field Columbian museum. Publication 99, 103. Anthropological series. vol. ix, no. 1-2)

Each plate preceded or accompanied by a guard sheet, with descriptive letterpress.

Contents.—i. Ceremonial organization.—ii. The sun dance.

1. Cheyenne Indians. 2. Sun-dance.

5—33518

Library of Congress   GN2.F4

GN
Pam
2026

Dorsey, George A(mos)

Observations on a collection of Papuan crania. From Field Columbian Mus. publ. 21, anthrop. ser. v.2, n.1, 1897.

GN 2M FI

Dorsey, George Amos, 1868–

   ... The Oraibi Soyal ceremony, by George A. Dorsey ... and H. R. Voth ... The Stanley McCormick Hopi expedition. Chicago, U. S. A., 1901.

   59 p. xxxvii pl. (incl. front.) 24½ᶜᵐ. (Field Columbian museum. Publication 55. Anthropological series. vol. iii, no. 1)

   Each plate accompanied by guard sheet with descriptive letterpress.

   1. Hopi Indians—Religion and mythology. i. Voth, Henry R., 1855– joint author.

Library of Congress   GN2.F4   4–12216
——— Copy 2.   E99.H7D74
——— Copy 3.   E51.F45

GN 2M FI

Dorsey, George Amos, 1868–

   ... Traditions of the Arapaho, collected under the auspices of the Field Columbian museum and of the American museum of natural history, by George A. Dorsey ... and Alfred L. Kroeber ... Chicago, 1903.

   x, 475 p. 24½ᶜᵐ. (Field Columbian museum. Publication 81. Anthropological series. vol. v)

   1. Arapaho Indians. 2. Indians of North America—Legends. i. Kroeber, Alfred Louis, 1876– joint author.

Library of Congress   GN2.F4   4–12211
——— Copy 2.   E99.A7D7

GN 550 S

Dorsey, James Owen, 1848–1895.

   ... Omaha and Ponka letters, by James Owen Dorsey. Washington, Govt. print. off., 1891.

   127 p. 24½ᶜᵐ. (U. S. Bureau of American ethnology. (Bulletin, no. 11))

   At head of title: Smithsonian institution. Bureau of ethnology ...

   1. Omaha Indians. 2. Ponca Indians. 3. Dhegiha language.

Library of Congress   E51.U6 no. 11   2–14652
——— Copy 2.   E99.O4D6
   (a19c2)

GN Pam 1446

Dorsey, George A(mos)

   The Osage mourning-war ceremony. From Amer. Anthrop. v.4, July–Sept. 1902.

GR 102.A D 71

Dorsey, George Amos

   Traditions of the Caddo... Carnegie Inst. of Washington Publication No. 41. 1905.
BOUND WITH
Dorsey, George Amos
   Traditions of the Arikara...

GN 550 S

Dorsey, James Owen, 1848–1895.

   Omaha dwellings, furniture and implements, by James Owen Dorsey.

   (*In* U. S. Bureau of American ethnology. Thirteenth annual report, 1891–92. Washington, 1896. 29½ᶜᵐ. p. 263–288. illus.)

   1. Omaha Indians.

   16–5516

Library of Congress   E51.U55 13th

GR 102.P D 71

Dorsey, George A(mos)

   The Pawnee: Mythology (Part 1). Collected under the Auspices of the Carnegie Institution of Washington. 1906. R8vo. 546 pp.

   (Carnegie Institution of Washington, Publication No. 59)

GN Pam #140

Dorsey, George A(mos)

   Traditions of the Osage, ex Field Columbian Mus. Pub. no. 88, 1904.

GN 550 S

Dorsey, James Owen, 1848–1895.

   ... Omaha sociology. By Rev. J. Owen Dorsey.

   (*In* U. S. Bureau of American ethnology. Third annual report, 1881–82. Washington, 1884. 29½ᶜᵐ. p. 205–370. illus., pl. xxx–xxxiii (incl. map))

   1. Omaha Indians. 2. Indians of North America—Soc. life & cust. i. Title.

   16–5488

Library of Congress   E51.U55 3d

GN Pam 1451

Dorsey, George A(mos)

   The photograph and skeleton of a native Australian. From Bull. Essex Instit. v. 28, 1896.

GN Pam 1927

Dorsey, George A(mos)

   Wichita tales. From Journ. Amer. Folk-lore, v.15, n.59, 1902.

GN 550 S

DORSEY, JAMES OWEN, 1848–1895.
U. S. *Bureau of American ethnology.*

   ... Illustration of the method of recording Indian languages. From the manuscripts of Messrs. J. O. Dorsey, A. S. Gatschet, and S. R. Riggs.

   (*In* U. S. Bureau of American ethnology. First annual report, 1879–80. Washington, 1881. 29½ᶜᵐ. p. 579–589)

   1. Indians of North America—Languages. i. Dorsey, James Owen, 1848–1895. ii. Gatschet, Albert Samuel, 1832–1907. iii. Riggs, Stephen Return, 1812–1883. iv. Title.

   16—5479

Library of Congress   E51.U55 1st
   (s20f2)

GN 2M FI

Dorsey, George Amos, 1868–

   ... The Ponca sun dance, by George A. Dorsey ... Chicago, 1905.

   1 p. l., (61)–88 p. illus., xxxv pl. (part col.) 24½ᶜᵐ. (Field Columbian museum. Publ. no. 102. Anthropological ser. vol. vii, no. 2)

   1. Ponca Indians. 2. Sun-dance.

Library of Congress   GN2.F4   6–13436
——— Copy 2.   E99.P7D7
——— Copy 3.   E51.F45

GN Pam 814

Dorsey, George A(mos)

   Wormian bones in artificially deformed Kwakiutl crania. From Amer. Anth. June, 1897. 13p.

AS 36 S1

Dorsey, James Owen, 1848–1895.

   On the comparative phonology of four Siouan languages. By Rev. J. Owen Dorsey ...

   (*In* Smithsonian institution. Annual report. 1883. Washington, 1885. 23½ᶜᵐ. p. 919–929. tables)

   1. Siouan languages.

   S 15–622

Library of Congress   Q11.S66 1883
Library, Smithsonian   Institution

GN 29 K 93

Dorsey, George A(mos)

Kroeber, F. W.   and others

   Putnam anniversary volume: Anthropological Essays, presented to Frederic Ward Putnam, in honor of his seventieth birthday, April 16, 1909 by his friends and associates. New York. Stechert. 1909. 4to. 627 pp.

   A visit to the German Solomon Islands, by George A. Dorsey. pp. 521–544.

GN 550 S

Dorsey, James Owen, 1848–1895.

   ... A dictionary of the Biloxi and Ofo languages, accompanied with thirty-one Biloxi texts and numerous Biloxi phrases, by James Owen Dorsey and John R. Swanton. Washington, Govt. print. off., 1912.

   v, 340 p. 23½ᶜᵐ. (Smithsonian institution. Bureau of American ethnology. Bulletin 47)

   1. Biloxi language. 2. Ofogoula language. i. Swanton, John Reed, 1873–

   12–35595

Library of Congress   E51.U6 no. 47
——— Copy 2.   PM702.D6
———(Another issue)   PM702.D7
61st Cong., 2d sess.   House. Doc. no. 419.

GN 550 S

Dorsey, James Owen, 1848–1895.

   ... Osage traditions. By Rev. J. Owen Dorsey.

   (*In* U. S. Bureau of American ethnology. Sixth annual report, 1884–85. Washington, 1888. 29½ᶜᵐ. p. 373–397. illus.)

   1. Osage Indians—Legends. 2. Osage language—Texts.

   16–5501

Library of Congress   E51.U55 6th
   (s19c2)

GR 102.A D 71

Dorsey, George A(mos)

   Traditions of the Arikara. Collected under the Auspices of the Carnegie Institution of Washington. Washington, D. C. 1904. 8vo. 136 pp.

   (Carnegie Institution of Washington, Publication No. 17)

GN 550 S

Dorsey, James Owen

The Cegiha language. Washington, 1890. 4t. pp. xviii. 794

[Contrib. to N. A. Ethn. vol. VI]

E.1. 11

GN 550 S

Dorsey, James Owen, 1848–1895.

   Siouan sociology, a posthumous paper, by James Owen Dorsey.

   (*In* U. S. Bureau of American ethnology. Fifteenth annual report, 1893–94. Washington, 1897. 29½ᶜᵐ. p. 205–244. illus.)

   1. Siouan Indians.

   16–5523

Library of Congress   E51.U55 15th

GN
550
S

Dorsey, James Owen, 1848–1895.
... A study of Siouan cults. By James Owen Dorsey.

(*In* U. S. Bureau of American ethnology. Eleventh annual report, 1889–90. Washington, 1894. 29¹ᵐ. p. 351–544. illus., pl. XLIV–L (part col., part double))

"Authorities": p. 361–363.

Religion —
1. Siouan Indians—Religion and mythology.

16-5511

Library of Congress   E51.U55 11th

AS
162
S 67

Dorst, J.
L'exploitation du guano au Pérou.

(La Terre et la Vie, Annee 103(2):49–63, 1956)

AS
162
P

Dorst, Jean
Les chauves-souris de la faune Malgache.

(Bull. Mus. Nat. d'Hist. Nat., Ser. 2; Tome 19:306–313, 1947)

QH
1
M 17 a

Dorst, Jean
Essai d'une clef de determination des chauves souris Malgaches.

(Inst. Sci. de Madagascar, Mem., Ser. A, Vol. 1:81–88, 1948)

Q
101
P 18

Also
AS
36
C 15 o

Dorst, Jean
Future scientific studies in the Galápagos Islands.

(Occ. Papers of the Calif. Acad. of Sciences, No. 44:147–154, 1963)

(Presented at a symposium: Galápagos Islands: a unique area for scientific investigations, Tenth Pacific Science Congress, Honolulu, 1961. Robert I. Bowman, convener)

QL
671
A 71

Dorst, Jean
Secrets of migration. (Nonstop migration record may be the golden plover's 2,065 miles from Alaska to Hawaii.)

(Audubon, Vol. 65(4):240–243, 1963)

QL
671
I 12

Dorward, D. F.
Behaviour of boobies Sula spp.

(Ibis, 103b:22;–234, 1962)

QL
671
I 12

Dorward, D. F.
The Fairy Tern, Gygis alba, on Ascension Island.

(Ibis, Vol. 103b(3):365–378, 1963)

(Centenary Expeditions Volume)

QL
671
I 12

Dorward, D. F.
Notes on the biology of the Brown Noddy, Anous stolidus, on Ascension Island. By D. F. Dorward and N. P. Ashmole.

(Ibis, Vol. 103b(3):447–457, 1963)

(Centenary Expeditions Volume)

QK
1
G 77

DORYOPTERIS
Tryon, R. M., Jr.

A revision of the genus Doryopteris.

(Contributions from the Gray Herbarium of Harvard University, 143, 1942)

Q
Biog.
Pam.
136

Dossier de la succession: Paul Gauguin. Papeete, Tahiti.   Société des Études Océaniennes.   1957.   (1)–43 pp.

GN
625
E 53

Dotson, Lillian Ota
Embree, John F.

Bibliography of the peoples and cultures of mainland southeast Asia. By John F. Embree and Lillian Ota Dotson. New Haven. 1950.

AM
101
U 56

Dottrens, Robert
The primary school curriculum.

(Monographs on Education, 2, 1962, UNESCO)

QH
1
P 11

Doty, Maxwell S.
Acanthophora, a possible invader of the marine flora of Hawaii.

(Pacific Science, 15(4):547–552, 1961)

AS
763
H 38

Doty, Maxwell S.

Aspects of oceanic productivity in the eastern Tropical Pacific.   By Maxwell S. Doty, Mikihiko Oguri, and Robert Pyle.

(Haw. Acad. Sci., Proc. 31:20, 1956)

QH
1
A 88

Doty, Maxwell S.
Miller, Harvey Alfred

Bryophytes from Arno Atoll, Marshall Islands. By Harvey Alfred Miller and Maxwell S. Doty.

(Atoll Research Bulletin, No. 25, pp. 1–10, 1953)

QL
121
H 38

Doty, Maxwell S.
An enumeration of the hypothetical roles of algae in coral atolls.

(Hawaii Marine Laboratory, Contrib. 1958: no. 54, Proc. 8th Pac. Sci. Congress.)

Doty, Maxwell S.
An experimental test of the tide factor hypothesis. By Maxwell S. Doty and Justine G. Archer.

(American Jour. of Botany, 37:458–464, 1950)

Forest Brown has

QH
1
A 88

and

QK
Bot.Pam.
2985

Doty, Maxwell S.   and others
Floristics and plant ecology of Raroia Atoll, Tuamotus.
Part 1. Floristic and ecological notes, by Maxwell S. Doty; Part 2. Ecological and floristic notes on the Myxophyta, by Jan Newhouse; Part 3. Ecological and floristic notes on the Bryophyta, by Harvey A. Miller and Maxwell S. Doty; Part 4. Ecological and floristic notes on the Pteridophyta by Kenneth Wilson.

(Atoll Research Bull., No. 33, 1954)

AS
763
H 38

Doty, Maxwell S.
The hypothetical role of algae in atoll structure.

(Proceedings of the Hawaiian Academy of Science...Twenty-Seventh annual meeting...page 7 1951–1952)

QH
1
A 88

Doty, Maxwell S.
Instructions for collecting Algae.
IN
Fosberg, F. Raymond
Handbook for atoll research (second preliminary edition), pp. 62.

(Atoll Research Bull., No. 17, 1953)

QH
1
A BB
Doty, Maxwell S.

Interrelationships of the organisms on
Raroia aside from man. By Maxwell S. Doty and J.
P. E. Morrison.

(Atoll Research Bull., No. 35, 1954)

S
17.Ha
S 3
Doty, R. E.

Rat control on Hawaiian sugar can plantations.

(The Haw. Planters' Record, 49 (2):71-239,
1945)

QL
Insects
Pam.
1287
Doucette, Charles F.

The lily weevil, a potentially serious pest
in the Pacific Northwest. by Charles F. Doucette and Randall Latta.

(U. S. Dept. Agric., Circular No. 746, 1946)

QK
567
S 64
Doty, Maxwell S.

Smith, Gilbert M. editor
Manual of phycology; an introduction to the
Algae and their biology. 1951.

pp. 313-334: Ecology of marine Algae, by
Jean Feldmann are translated by Maxwell S. Doty

Doty, W. L.

Hawaiian medicine. 1950.

(source?)

UH has

DU
Pac. Pam.
983
Doue, Stephen M.

Some questions and answers on Act 187 or
the State Zoning Law.

(University of Hawaii, Cooperative Ext.
Service, Public Affairs Series No. 9, 1962)

Q
101
P 18
Doty, Maxwell S.   editor

Proceedings of the conference on primary
productivity measurement, marine and fresh-
water.   Tenth Pacific Science Congress.
Univ. of Hawaii.   1961.   ix + 237 pp.

(Financially supported by Contract AT-
(04-3)-15 between the Botany Dept. of the
Univ. of Hawaii and the U. S. Atomic Energy
Commission)

PL
760
D 72

also
PL
Pams
463
486
Douceré, Victor

Curiosités linguistiques. Les langues indigènes des Nouvelles-Hébrides seraient-elles
étroitement apparentées à nos langues indo-
européennes? Paris. Librairie Emmanuel Vitte.
1936. 8vo. 94 pp.

DU
620
P
Dougherty, Henry E.

The cruise of the Itasca.

(Paradise of the Pacific, Vol. 47(3):21-25,
1935)

AS
763
H 38
Doty, Maxwell   and others

The productivity of the inshore waters in
Hawaii.

(Proc. Haw. Acad. Sci., Ann. Meeting, 1954-
55, p. 15, 1955)

DU
760
D 72
Douceré, Victor

La Mission Catholique aux Nouvelles-Hébrides.
D'après des documents écrits et les vieux souvenirs de l'auteur, par Mgr. Victor Doucere, S.M.,
Vicaire apostolique.   Lyon. Emmanuel Vitte.
1934. 8vo. 481 pp.

Dougherty, H. E.

The volcanologist of Kilauea. 1934.

UH has

QH
1
P 11
Doty, Maxwell S.

Structure and reproduction of Cottoniella
hawaiiensis n.sp. By Maxwell S. Doty and M. Ruth
Wainwright.

(Pacific Sci., 12(3):229-235, 1958)

Doucere, V.

Notes ethnologiques sur les populations indigènes des Nouvelles-Hébrides. 1924.

UH has

QC
1090
De
D 73
Douglas, A.E.

Climatic cycles and tree-growth.

Carnegie institution of Washington,
1919. Pub. no. 289.

(Vol. II, out of print; HSPA has Vol. III)

QL
121
H 38
Doty, Maxwell S.

Structure and reproduction of Cottoniella
hawaiiensis n. sp. (Rhodophyta) By Maxwell S.
Doty and M. Ruth Wainwright.

(Hawaiian Marine Laboratory Contrib. 1958:
no. 106. Pacific Sci. 12(3):251-254)

GN
1
A62
Doucere, V.

Les populations indigènes des Nouvelles
Hébrides. Review by Daniel Real.

(L'Anthropologie, Tome 32, 1922, pp. 577-
578)

QL
Mammals
Pam.
148
Douglas, A. M.

Macroderma gigas saturata (Chiroptera,
Megadermatidae): a new subspecies from the
Kimberley Division of Western Australia.

(Reprint, The Western Aus. Naturalist,
Vol. 8(3):59-61, 1962)

QH
1
P 11
Doty, Maxwell S.

Studies in the Helminthocladiaceae (Rhodophyta):Helminthocladia. Maxwell S. Doty and
and Isabella A. Abbott.

(Pacific Science, 15(1):56-63, 1961)

QL
537.A
D 72
Doucet, J.

Les anophélinés de la région malgache.
Publications de l'Institut de Recherche Scientifique. Tananarive-Tsimbazaza. 1951. 8vo.
198 pp.

DU
12
D 73
Douglas, A. J. A.

The South Seas of today, being an account
of the cruise of the yacht St. George to the
south Pacific, by Major A. J. A. Douglas and
P. H. Johnson. With thirty-nine illustrations
and three charts. London.   Cassell and Company
Ltd. (1926)   xiv + 296 pp.

GN
Ethn.Pam.
3619

Douglas, Clementine

Survey of Hawaiian handicrafts. IRAC Project No. 23, June, 1951. 4to. 61 pp.

QK
1
H 78

DOUGLAS, DAVID

Hooker, William Jackson

A Brief Memoir of the Life of Mr. David Douglas, with Extracts from his Letters. (Accompanied by a portrait)

(Companion to the Botanical Magazine, Vol. II, 1836, pp. 79-82)

AS
36
S1

Douglas, James, 1837–

Conservation of natural resources. By James Douglas ...

(*In* Smithsonian institution. Annual report. 1909. Washington, 1910. 23½ᶜᵐ. p. 317-329)

"Reprinted ... from Bulletin of the American institute of mining engineers, New York, no. 29, May, 1909, pp. 439-451."

1. Natural resources.

11-9872

Library of Congress   Q11.S66 1909

DU
620
H 5
locked
case

Douglas, David

The great crater of Mauna Loa, Hawaii. Extracts from the unpublished correspondence of the late David Douglas, Esq.

(Hawaiian Spectator, Vol. 1, No. 2, pp. 98-103. 1838)

DU
620
H 41

DOUGLAS, DAVID

Morgan, Margaret K.

David Douglas - botanist.

(Haw. Hist. Soc. Papers, No. 16, 1929, pp. 33-44)

GN
2.S
P 76

Douglas, R.

Blood groups in Maoris. By R. Douglas and J. M. Staveley.

(Jour. Poly. Soc., 69(1):34-36, 1960)

QK
5
D 73
locked
case

Douglas, David

Journal kept by David Douglas during his travels in North America, 1823-1827, together with a particular description of thirty-three species of American oaks and eighteen species of Pinus; with appendices containing a list of the plants introduced by Douglas and an account of his death in 1834. Published under the direction of the Royal Horticultural Society. London. William Wesley & Son. 1914. 8vo. 364 pp.

DU
Hist.Pam.
251

DOUGLAS, DAVID

Newspaper account of the death of Professor (David?) Douglas. Hilo Tribune, Aug. 22, 1896. (Photostat copy).

GN
2.S
P 76

Douglas, R.

The blood groups of Cook Islanders. By R. Douglas and J. M. Staveley.

(Jour. Poly. Soc., 68(1): 14-20, 1959)

G
7
R8

Douglas, David

Letter to Captain Sabine. Oahu May 3, 1834 in Journ. Roy. Geogr. Soc. Lond. IV, 1834, pp. 333-344.

QK
Bot.Pam.
1778

DOUGLAS, DAVID

Wilson, W. F.

David Douglas, Botanist at Hawaii. Honolulu, 1919. 83pp. 8vo.

AS
36
S1

DOUGLAS, STEPHEN ARNOLD, 1813-1861

Cox, Samuel Sullivan, 1824-1889.

Eulogy of Hon. Stephen Arnold Douglas. Prepared ... by Hon. Samuel S. Cox ...

(*In* Smithsonian institution. Annual report. 1861. Washington, 1862. 23½ᶜᵐ. p. 117-122)

1. Douglas, Stephen Arnold, 1813-1861.

S 15-103 b

Library of Congress   Q11.S66 1861
Library, Smithsonian   Institution

QK
1
H 78

Douglas, David

A Sketch of Journey to the North-western Parts of the Continent of North America, during the years 1824, 5, 6, and 7.

(Companion to the Botanical Magazine, Vol. II, 1836, pp. 82-98)

(by way of the Horn, stopping at Juan Fernandez and Gallapagos)

S
17.H3
H 38

DOUGLAS, DAVID

The late David Douglas.

(Haw. For. and Agric., Vol. 2, 1905, pp. 372-374)

QL
Insects
Pam.
1158

Douglas, W. A.

Rice-field insects, by W. A. Douglas and J. W. Ingram.

(U. S. Department of Agriculture, Circ., No. 632, 1942)

QK
31.D7
H 34

DOUGLAS, DAVID

Harvey, Athelstan George

Douglas of the fir: a biography of David Douglas, botanist. Harvard University Press. Cambridge. 1947. 8vo. x + 290 pp.

G
7
R 91

Douglas, H. P.

Cook as an hydrographical surveyor.

(Geogr. Journal, Vol. 73, 1929, p. 110-116)

QK
Pam.
#441

Douglass, A. E.

Evidence of climatic effects in the annual rings of trees, ex Ecology, vol. I., no. 1, January, 1920.

DU
620
H 5
locked
case

DOUGLAS, DAVID

Hooker, W. J.   compiler

A brief memoir of the life of Mr. David Douglas, with extracts from his letters.

(Hawaiian Spectator, Vol. 2, Nos. 1-4, 1839, pp. 1-49, 131-180, 276-333, 396-437)

DU
Pac.Pam.
273

Douglas, J.

Notes on a recent cruise through the Louisiade Group of islands.

(Royal Geogr. Soc. of Australasia, Victorian Branch, 1887 meeting, Vol. 7 pp. 46-59)

QK
Pam.
#489

Douglass, A. E.

Evidence of climatic effects in the annual rings of trees. Extract, n.p; n.d.

QK
Bot.Pam.
2467

Douglass, A. E.

Precision of ring dating in tree-ring chronologies.

(University of Arizona Bulletin, Vol. 17:no. 3, 1946; Laboratory of Tree-ring Research, Bull. no. 3)

PL
52.A
D 73

Dournes, Jacques

Dictionnaire Srê (Köho) - Français. Recueil de 8.000 mots et expressions du dialecte pémsien Srê, populations montagnardes du Sud-Indochinois, tribu des Srê. Publié grâce aux subventions... accordées par M. le Haut Commissaire de France en Indochine... 8vo. xxx+269 + (13) + (13) pp. (1950)

DOVE

BARRED DOVE, see GEOPELIA
LACE-NECKED of SPOTTED DOVE, see STREPTOPELIA

QK
Bot. Pam.
2181

Douglass, A. E.

Tree rings and chronology.

(University of Arizona Bulletin, Physical Science Bulletin, No.1, Vol.VIII, 1937, pp. 5-36, 8 plates, 3 figs.)

AS
36
I 4

Douthitt, Herman, 1886-
Studies on the cestode family, *Anoplocephalidæ*, with six plates, by Herman Douthitt ... [Urbana, University of Illinois, 1915]

96 p. vi pl, diagr. 27ᶜᵐ. (*Added t.-p.:* Illinois biological monographs. vol. i, no. 3) $0.80

On cover: University of Illinois bulletin, vol. xii, no. 27. "Contributions from the Zoological laboratory of the University of Illinois under the direction of Henry B. Ward, no. 38." Bibliography: p. 81-84.

~1. Anoplocephalidæ. i. Title. Cestodes

Library of Congress   QL391.C4D7   15-6476

——— Copy 2.

Copyright A 397236

DOVE, MOURNING

See

ZENAIDURA

DS
485.P2
D73

Douie, Sir James

The Panjab, North-west frontier province and Kashmir. Cambridge, University press, 1916. 8vo. xiv+373 pp.

QL
595.Mi
I 59

Doutt, Richard L.

Insects of Micronesia, Hymenoptera: Trichogrammatidae and Mymaridae.

IN

Insects of Micronesia, Vol. 19(1), 1955

Dovey, J. W.

The gospel in the South Pacific. 1960.

UH has

AP
2
S 41

Doumani, G.

The ancient life of the Antarctic. By G. Doumani and W. Long.

(Scientific American, 207(3):168-185,1962)

QL
461
A 51

DOUTTIA

Zimmerman, Elwood C.

Douttia, a new genus of New Hebridean Curculionidae (Coleoptera:Cryptorhynchinae)

and
QL
Insects
Pam.
1191

(Annals of the Ent. Soc. of America, Vol. 37 1944, pp. 193-197)

DU
Pac.Pam.
945

Dovey, J. Whitsed

Ship letters of the south Pacific, with an introduction by H. M. Campbell. The hawthorn Press. Melbourne. 1955. 4to. 24 pp.

Doumengue, Francois

L'economie de la Grande Terre caledonienne.

(Les Cahiers d'Outre Mer, 14 annee, No. 50, July-Sept. 1961. pp. 229-254)

?

Douveré, V.

Curiosités linguistiques: les langues indigènes des Nouvelles-Hébrides. 1936.

UH has

G
545
Do
D74

Dow, George Francis

Whale ships and whaling: a pictorial history of whaling during three centuries with an account of the whale fishery in colonial New England. Introduction by Frank Wood... Marine Research Soc. Salem Pub. No.10, 1925.

Salem , 1925, pp xi, 446

DU
12
K 81
looked
case

DOURGA (SHIP)

Kolff, D. H.

Voyages of the Dutch brig of war Dourga through the southern and little-known parts of the Moluccan Archipelago, and along the previously unknown southern coast of New Guinea...1825-1826... Translated from the Dutch... London. 1840. 8vo.

DU
620
P

[Douvile, Robert]

Was there a Pacific continent?

(Paradise of the Pacific, Vol. 24, 1911, No. 7, p. 21-22)

GN
2.S
P 76

Downes, T. W.

Additional stone-cut artifacts from Waverly.

(Journal of the Polynesian Society, 41: 312-316, 1932.)

QK
1
P 41

Dourley, John

The medicinal garden (Morris Arboretum, Chestnut Hill, Pennsylvania)

(Morris Arboretum Bull.,

32? + final art. is in Vol 13(3) 1962 :54-56
in which issues are -- ?

QL
Birds
Pam.
351

Dove, R. S.

Field notes on local bird records. By R. S. Dove and H. J. Goodhart.

(Memoirs of the Hong Kong Biological Circle, No. 1, February, 1953)

GN
2.S
P 76

Downes, T. W.

Bird-snaring, etc., in the Whanganui River district.

(Journal of the Polynesian Society, 37: 1-29, 1928.)

GN
2.S
P 76
Downes, T. W.

The game of koruru, or knuckle-bones, as played by the upper Whanganui River Maori girls.

(Journal of the Polynesian Society, 37: 136-138, 1928)

GN
2.S
P 76
Downes, T. W.

Maruiwi, Maori and Moriori.

(Journal of the Polynesian Society, 42: 156-166, 1933.)

GN
2.S
P 76
Downes, T.W.

On the Whatu-kura.

(Journal of the Polynesian Society, 19: 218-221, 1910.)

DU
406
D 74
Downes, T. W.

History of and guide to the Wanganui River. With preface by J. H. Burnet. 2nd edition, 1923. Wanganui. 99 pp. 8vo.

AS
750
N2
Downes, T. W.

Notes on eels and eel-weirs (Tuna and Patuna). In Trans. New Zeal. Inst. Vol.L 1917, pp 296- 316. illus.

GN
2.S
P 76
Downes, T. W.

Pelorus Jack (Tuhi-rangi), as told by a chief of the Ngati-Kahu-ngunu tribe...

(Journal of the Polynesian Society, 23: 176-180, 1914.)

GN
2.S
P 76
Downes, T.W.

History of Ngati-Kahu-ngunu

(Journal of the Polynesian Society, 23: 28-33, 111-125, 219-225, 1914; 24: 57-61, 77-85, 121-129, 1915; 25: 1-8, 33-43, 77-88, 1916.)

GN
2.S
P 76
Downes, T. W.

Notes on incised designs seen in a cave near Waverley.

(Journal of the Polynesian Society, 34: 252-258, 1925.)

GN
2.S
P 76
Downes, T. W.

Triangular teeth among the Maori.

(Journal of the Polynesian Society, 34: 182-184, 1925.)

GN
2.S
P 76
Downes, T. W.

The lament of Huarau of Whanganui for his son Te Apaapa-O-Te-Rangi.

(Journal of the Polynesian Society, 29:29-33, 1920.)

GN
2.S
P 76
Downes, T. W.

Notes on the moa, as contributed by natives of the Wai-rarapa district.

(Journal of the Polynesian Society, 35: 36-37, 1926.)

GN
2.S
P 76
Downes, T. W.

A tuahu on the Whanganui River.

(Journal of the Polynesian Society, 37: 165-168, 1928.)

GN
2.S
P 76
Downes, T. W.

Maori etiquette.

(Journal of the Polynesian Society, 38: 148-168, 1929.)

GN
2.S
P 76
Downes, T. W.

The Ohura fight of 1864.

(Journal of the Polynesian Society, 35: 223-227, 1926.)

GN
2.S
P 76
Downes, T. W.

Tutae-Poroporo.

(Journal of the Polynesian Society, Vol. 46, 1936, pp. 1-4)

GN
2.S
P 76
Downes, T. W.

Maori mentality regarding the lizard and Taniwha in the Whanganui River area.

(Journal of the Polynesian Society, Vol. 46, 1937, pp. 206-224)

GN
2.S
P 76
Downes, T. W.

Old native stone-cut artifacts from Waverly.

(Journal of the Polynesian Society, 41: 50-58, 1932.)

AS
750
N2
Downes, Thomas W.

Some historic Maori personages. In Trans. New Zeal. Inst. xxxviii, 1906, pp120-127.

GN
2.S
P 76
Downes, T. W.

Maori rat-trapping devices.

(Polynesian Soc. Jour., Vol. 35, 1926, pp. 228-234)

DU
406
D 74
Downes, T. W.

Old Whanganui. W. A. Parkinson and Co.,Ltd Hawera. 1915. R8vo. xiv + 334 pp.

QH
53
D74
Downing, Elliot R.

A field and laboratory guide in biological nature-study.

Chicago, Univ. Press,[1918]. 120p.

QH
47
D75

Downing, Elliot Rowland

Our living world: a source book of biological nature-study.

Chicago, Univ. Press, [1926]. 503p.

DU
625.4
D 75

Doyle, Emma Lyons

Makua Laiana: the story of Lorenzo Lyons lovingly known to Hawaiians as Ka Makua Laiana, Paku Mele o ka Aina Mauna (Father Lyons, Lyric Poet of the Mountain Country). Compiled from manuscript journals 1832-1886, by his granddaughter. Privately printed. Honolulu, 1945. 8vo. ix + 259 pp.

also revised and enlarged edition of 1953. Advertiser Publishing Company. ix + 278 pp. 8vo.

QK
545
D 75

Dozy, Franz

Bryologia Javanica seu descriptio muscorum frondosorum Archipelagi Indici iconibus illustrata Auctoribus F. Dozy et J. H. Molkenboer, post mortem auctorum edentibus R. B. Van Den Bosch et C. M. Van Der Sande Lacoste. Vols. I-II cum tabulis I-CCCXX, in 2 vols. Lugduni-Batavorum. E. J. Brill. 1855-1870. 4to.

DU
810
D 75

Downs, Evelyn A.

Daughters of the islands. (Samoa) Foreword by Dr. Basil Yeaxlee. The Religious Education Press, Limited. Wallington, Surrey. sm4to. 1944. 78 pp.

DU
620
P 22

Doyle, Genevieve

Hawaii salutes her royal hero: King Kamehameha the Great and his successors.

(Paradise of the Pacific, June, 1956:15-19)

[photos of Kamehameha I-V; Lunalilo, Kalakaua and Liliuokalani]

GN
1
O 15

Drabbe, P.

Folk-tales from Netherlands New Guinea.

(Oceania, Vol. 18 (3):248-270, 1948)

18(3): 157-175, 1947; vol 19: 75-90, 1948; 20: 16-79, 1949; vol. 20: 224-240 1950

G
161
H

Downton, Nicholas

The voyage of Nicholas Downton to the East Indies, 1614-14, as recorded in contemporary narratives and letters. Edited by Sir William Foster. London. Printed for the Hakluyt Society.

(Works issued by the Hakluyt Society, Ser. II, Vol. 82, 1939)

DU
620
P 22

Doyle, Genevieve

Lanai, cinderella and pineapple island.

(Paradise of the Pacific, Oct. 1957:16-17)

GN
1
An

Drabbe, P.

Talen en dialecten van Zuid-West Nieuw-Guinea I.

(Anthropos, Vol. 45(4-6):545-574, 1950)

Jélmek, Maklew en Mombum

DU
Pacific
Pams
460
461

DOWSETT REEF

King, R. D.

Index to the islands of the Territory of Hawaii, including other islands...in the North Pacific Ocean. 1931. p. 17.

DU
620
P 22

Doyle, Genevieve

The magic of Kona coast.

(Paradise of the Pacific, 69th Holiday edition, for 1958; issued 1957:p. 22-41)

[photographs by George Logue]

QK
Pam
#677
4to

Drabble, Eric

On the anatomy of the roots of palms, ex Linn. Soc. Trans., 2nd. ser. vol. VI, pt. 10, 1904. pp. 427-490

Storage
Case
4

Hms
H 27

DOWSETT, SAMUEL J.

Appleton

Journal of a cruise in the Waverly also called the Kaahumanu), Capt. Cathcart, for the search for Capt. Dowsett, lost in the South Seas, told by Mr. Appleton, second mate of the brig Waverly...1834.

Also a memorandum of an interview with Mr. Appleton by Mr. Henry A. Pierce in San Francisco in 1849, giving further details of the search and Appleton's own experiences after being parted from Waverly.

DU
620
P 22

Doyle, Genevieve

Maui.

(Paradise of the Pacific, Vol. 68(7):9-13, July, 1956)

[island of Maui]

QK
1
J 86

DRACAENA

Baker, J. G.

Synopsis of the East Indian species of Dracaena and Cordyline.

(Jour. Bot. Brit. and For., vol. 11, pp. 261-266, 1873)

DU
620
P

Doyle, Emma Lyons

Hanaiakamalama.

(Paradise of the Pacific, Holiday Annual, 1956: 60-61)

[Queen Emma Museum]

AS
36
A 35

Doyle, Winfield G.

Co-operative development of popular publications among museums.

(The Museum News, Vol. 27(13):7-8, 1950)

Bibliofilm
25

DRACAENAE

Göppert, Heinrich Robert

Beiträge zur Kenntniss der Dracaeneen.

(Nova Acta Acad. Caes. Leop., Vol. 25, 1855, pp. 41-60)

DU
620
P 22

Doyle, Emma Lyons

The little Prince of Hawaii.

(Paradise of the Pacific, 70(5):22-24, 1958)

QL
Insect
Pam.
1987

Dozier, H. L.

Two new aleyrodid (citrus) pests from India and the South Pacific.

(Jour. Agric. Research, 36(12):1001-1005, 1928)

AS
36
SG

and

QL
1
C

DRACISCUS

Jordan, David Starr, 1851–

... Description of two new genera of fishes (*Ereunias* and *Draciscus*) from Japan. By David Starr Jordan and John Otterbein Snyder.

(In Leland Stanford junior university. Hopkins seaside laboratory. Contributions to biology. Stanford university, Cal., 1901. 24¹ᶜᵐ. ma. XXIV, 377-380 p. xviii-xix fold. pl.)

Reprinted from the Proceedings of the California academy of sciences. 3d ser., Zoology, vol. II.

1. Ereunias. 2. Draciscus. I. Snyder, John Otterbein, 1867-   joint author.

Library of Congress   QL1.L53 no. 24

—— Copy 2.   Library of Congress   QL634.J3J72

9-637

DU
623
D 75

Drage, Una Hunt

    Hawaii deluxe. Compiled from her own diary and letters in 1901. (Honolulu) Copy No. 100. 139 pp.

AS
36
S 66 p

Drake, Carl J.

    Lace-bug genera of the world (Hemiptera: Tingidae)

    (Proc. U. S. Nat. Mus., Vol. 112:1-105, 1960)

AS
36
I 63

Drake, C. J.   **(Carl J.)**

    Some Tingitidae (Hemiptera) from Oceania. By C. J. Drake and M. E. Poor.

    (Iowa State College Journal of Science, Vol. XI:397-404, 1937)

AS
36
A 25

Drager, Wm.

Davenport, Charles Benedict

    Critical examination of physical anthropometry on the living, by C. B. Davenport...and William Drager.

    (Proc. of Amer. Acad. of Arts and Sciences, Vol. 69, No. 6, Feb., 1934. pp. 265-284)

QL
1
F 45

Drake, Carl J.

    A new genus and species of Cantacaderine lace-bug from the Philippines (Hemiptera:Tingidae). Philippine Zoological Expedition, 1946-1947)

    (Fieldiana: Zoology, Vol. 42(9), 1961)

QL
461
H-1

Drake, C. J.   **(Carl J.)**

    Some Tingitidae (Hemiptera) from the eastern hemisphere, by C. J. Drake and M. E. Poor.

    (Haw. Ent. Soc. Proc., Vol. 10, 1939, pp. 203-208)

DU
Pac
Pam
#247

Drago, Giovanni del

    Vingt jours a Honolulu, ex d'un journal de voyage autour de monde. Rome, 1888

QL
461
M 98

AND

QL
Insects
Pam.
1076

Drake, Carl J.

    A new Tingitid from Palau Islands (Hemiptera).

    (Mushi, Vol. 12:102-103, 1939)

    [Results of Prof. T. Esaki's Micronesia Expeditions, 1936-1938, No. 29]

QL
461
H-1

Drake, Carl J.

    Synonomy and distribution of the Lantana lace bug (Hem: Tingitidae), by Carl J. Drake and D. M. Frick.)

    (Proc. Haw. Ent. Soc., Vol. 10, 1939, pp. 199-202)

DRAGONFLIES

    see

ANISOPTERA
ODONATA

QL
5
M 62

and
QL
461
M 98

Drake, Carl J.

    A new tingid from Yap Island.

    (Mushi, Vol. 17(6):27-28, 1946)

    IN Esaki, Teizo Results of the Micronesian Expeditions, 1936-1940, No. 76

QL
461
P 11

Drake, Carl J.

    The Tingidae of Amboina, Larat, and Kai Islands (Hemiptera). By Carl J. Drake and Florence A. Huhoff.

    (Pacific Insects, Vol. 4(4):729-736, 1962)

QL
Insects
Pam
1173

Drake, C. J.

    Fijian Tingitidae (Hemiptera), by C. J. Drake and M. E. Poor.

    (Occ. Papers, Bernice P. Bishop Museum, Vol. 17, no. 15, 1943, pp. 191-205)

AS
720.Q
R

Drake, Carl J.

    A new Saldid from Samoa (Hemiptera).

    (Proc. R. Soc. Queensland, 68:29-30, 1957)

QL
461
P 11

Drake, Carl J.

    Tingidae of New Guinea (Hemiptera)

    (Pacific Insects, 2(3):339-380, 1960)

QL
595.Mi
I 59

Drake, Carl J.

    Hemiptera:Saldidae
    IN

    Insects of Micronesia, Vol. 7(6), 1961

QL
461
H-1

Drake, C. J.   **(Carl J.)**

    Notes on two Fijian Tingitids (Hemiptera) by C. J. Drake and M. Poor Hurd.

    (Proc. Haw. Ent. Soc., Vol. 12:287-289, 1945)

QH
1.S
W 31

Drake, Carl J.

    Two new species of shore-bugs (Hemiptera) (Saldidae: Leptopodidae).

    (Proc. of the Biological Society of Washington, Vol. 68:109-112, October, 1955)

QL
595.Mi
I 59

Drake, Carl J.

    Insects of Micronesia, Hemiptera: Tingidae. IN

    Insects of Micronesia, Vol. 7, No. 2, 1956. Published by the Museum. Honolulu (Bishop Museum)

AS
540
P 55 j

Drake, C. J.

    Saldoidea of the Philippines (Hemiptera). By C. J. Drake and G. B. Viado.

    (Philippine Journal of Science, Vol. 80(3): 339-343, 1952)

G
159
C 15

Drake, Sir Francis

Callander, John

    Terra Australis Cognita...Vol. 1, pp. 285-321: Sir Francis Drake to Magellanica and Polynesia. Edinburgh. 1766.

    and Lopez Vaz's account of Drake's voyage to Magellanica, ibid, Vol. 1, pp. 355-362.

DU
12
B 96
locked
case

DRAKE, SIR FRANCIS

Burney, James

Chronological history of the discoveries in the South Sea or Pacific Ocean... London. 1803-1817. 4to. 5 vols.
Vol. 1, pp. 304-369.

QK
471/
D76

K. 3. 13.

Drake del Castillo, E(mmanuel)

Flore de la Polynésie française Description des plantes vasculaires qui croissent spontanément ou qui sont généralement cultivées aux îles de la Société, Marquise, Pomotou, Gambier et Wallis. Paris, 1893 my 8vo pp.
XXIV. 352

Uct. 3. 96

GN
2 S
P 23

Drapkin, I(srael)

Contribución al estudio antropológico y demográfico de los Pascuenses.

(Journal de la Société des Américanistes, N.S., Tome XXVII, 1935, pp.266-302)

DRAKE, SIR FRANCIS   Carter Coll.
5-A-32

Lives and voyages of Drake, Cavendish, and Dampier...Edinburgh. Oliver and Boyd... 1831 12mo. 461 pp.

QK
471
D76
locked
case

Drake del Castillo, E (mmanuel)

Illustrationes florae insularum maris Pacifici.   Paris, 1886-92. 7 fasc. 50 pl. 458 pp.

[dates of publication of the parts noted in Stearn, William Thomas Drake del Castillo's "Illustationes..." (Jour. Soc. Bibl. Nat. Hist., 1, 1939, 202)]

GN
Ethn.
3116

GN
2.S
B 91

Drapkin, I(srael)

Contribution to the demographic study of Easter Island.

(Occ. Papers, Bernice P. Bishop Museum, Vol. XI, No. 12, 1935)

French edition: Contribution à l'étude démographique de l'île de Pâques. (Bull. Soc. Amer. Belgique, No. 18, 1935, pp. 137-158)

DU
12
M 31
locked
case

DRAKE, FRANCIS

Marchand, Étienne

Voyage autour du monde...1790-1792...précédé d'une introduction historique...Recherches sur les Terres Australes de Drake...Tomes 1-4. Paris. 1796-1800. 4to. Tome 3, pp. 223-273.

QK
Botany
Pam
619

K. 1. 11.

Drake del Castillo, E(mmanuel)

Remarques sur la flore de la Polynésie et sur ses rapports avec celle des terres voisines. Paris, 1890. 4to pp. 52

Oct. 3. 96

QL
Protozoa
to
Polysoa
Pam
495

Drasche, Richard Freiherrn

Ueber einige moIguliden der adria. From Versammlung am 2, 1884.

G
161
H

DRAKE, SIR FRANCIS, 1540? 1596

Nuttall, *Mrs. Zelia, ed. and tr.*
New light on Drake; a collection of documents relating to his voyage of circumnavigation, 1577-1580, tr. and ed. by Zelia Nuttall ... London, Printed for the Hakluyt society, 1914.

lvi, 443, [1] p. front., ports., maps (1 fold.) facsims. (part fold.) 22ᵐᵐ. (*Half-title:* Works issued by the Hakluyt society ... 2d ser. no. xxxiv)

CONTENTS.—Introduction.—pt. I. Testimony of English captives in America.—pt. II. Narrative of Pedro Sarmiento de Gamboa.—pt. III. Spanish official documents.—pt. IV. Depositions of fifteen prisoners taken by Drake between February 5th and April 4th, 1579.—pt. V. Official reports

(Continued on next card)

14-17144

QK
Bot.Pam.
1568a

Drake del Castillo, E(mmanuel)

Sur la géographie botanique des Îles de la Société.

(Bull. Soc. Philom. Paris. 7th Ser. Vol. II, pp.146-155, 1887)

AS
36
C8

DRASSIDAE

Emerton, James Henry, 1847-

... New England spiders of the families *Drassidæ, Agalenidæ* and *Dysderidæ.*

(*In* Connecticut academy of arts and sciences. Transactions. New Haven, 1888-92. 25ᶜᵐ. v. 8, p. [165]-206. pl. III-VIII)

1. [Drassidae] 2. [Agalenidae] 3. [Dysderidae] 4. Spiders—New England. I. Title.

Library of Congress   Q11.C9 vol. 8
Yale University   A53n.366.8

A 17-847

QL
Mollusca
Pam.
1038

Drake, Robert J.

Molluscs in archaeology and the recent, 2. Dept. Zoology, Univ. of British Columbia. Dec. 15, 1960. mimeogr.

GN
2.S
P 76

DRAMA   SOLOMON ISLANDS

Kuper, Henry

A Solomon Islands historical drama.

(Journal of the Polynesian Society, 33: 162-165, 1924)

AM
Mus.Pam.
144

DRAWING

Misonne, Leonard

Photo-drawing.

(American Annual of Photography, Vol. 52, 1932, pp. 187-191)

G
161
H

DRAKE, SIR FRANCIS, 1540? 1596

Nuttall, *Mrs. Zelia, ed. and tr.* New light on Drake ... 1914. (Card 2)

CONTENTS—Continued.
to viceroy and king of Spain relating to Drake's entry into the port of Guatulco.—pt. VI. First depositions of prisoners released at Guatulco and official reports.—pt. VII. The log-book of Nuño da Silva.—pt. VIII. Documents relating to Nuño da Silva's trial by the Inquisition.—pt. IX. English documents relating to the cargo of Nuño da Silva's ship, and its restitution.—pt. X. Spanish documents relating to Nuño da Silva after his release from the Inquisition.—pt. XI. First official reports concerning Drake's voyage received by King Philip II.—pt. XII. Charges against Drake formulated in Spain but written in English.—pt. XIII. False charges against Drake and their refutation.—Index.

1. Drake, Sir Francis, 1540?-1596. I. Sarmiento de Gamboa, Pedro, 1532?-1608. II. Silva, Nuno da. III. Title.

14-17144

Library of Congress   G161.H2 no. 34

QL
401
H 39

DRANGA, TED

Dranga died of heartfailure.

(Hawaiian Shell News, Vol. 5(5):49, 1957)

Q
181
M 94

DRAWING

Mueller, Justus F.

A manual of drawing for science students. New York. Farrar & Rinehart. sm8vo. 1935c. xiii + 122 pp.

QK
Pam
#620

Drake del Castillo, E(mmanuel)

Famille des composées: Fitchia Hook. F. et Remy Hillebr, ex Centenaire de la Société Philomatique.

Paris, 1888 (?)/

DU
1
P 12

Draper, Benjamin

Canoes, campfires and carbon 14.

(Pacific Discovery, 13(3):14-20, 1960)

AM
153
R 36

DRAWING

Reinhardt, Charles W.

The technic of mechanical drafting; a practical guide to neat, correct and legible drawing. New York. Engineering News Co. 1904. 8vo. ob.

Reference Shelf	DRAWING
	
	Ridgway, John L.
	
	    Scientific illustration. Stanford University Press. Stanford University. R8vo. 1938c. xiv + 173 pp.
		GN 1
		A 93
			Draws-Tychsen, Hellmut
			
			    Das Mangaianische Innerhalb und Ausserhalb seiner Sprachumwelten.
			
			    (Jour. Austronesian Studies, 2(1):12-50, 1960)
				GN 2.S
				S 72
					DREAMS NEW GUINEA
					
					Meggitt, M. J.
					
					    Dream interpretation among the Mae Enga of New Guinea.
					
					    (Southwestern Journal of Anthropology, Vol. 18(3):216-299, 1962)

GN 2.1
A-4
	DRAWING MALEKULA
	
	Deacon, A. Bernard
	
	    Geometrical drawings from Malekula and other islands of the New Hebrides. Edited by Camilla H. Wedgwood, with notes by A. C. Haddon.
	
	    (Journal Roy. Anthr. Inst., vol. LXIV, 1934, pp. 129-175. 90 figs. pl. XIII.)
		GN 1
		A 93
			Draws-Tychsen, Hellmut
			
			    Memorial for a Maori.
			
			    (Jour. of Austronesian Studies, 2(2):33-44, 1961)
			
			    [Sir Apirana Ngata]
				GN 2.S
				M 26
					DREAMS NEW GUINEA
					
					Reay, Marie
					
					    The sweet witchcraft of Kuma dream experience.
					
					    (Mankind, 5(11):459-463, 1962)

GN 2.1
A-4
	DRAWING NEW HEBRIDES
	
	Deacon, A. Bernard
	
	    Geometrical drawings from Malekula and other islands of the New Hebrides. Edited by Camilla H. Wedgwood, with notes by A. C. Haddon.
	
	    (Jour. Roy. Anthrop. Inst., vol. LXIV, 1934, pp. 129-175. 90 figs. pl. XIII.)
		GN 2.M
		E 84
			Draws-Tychsen, Hellmut
			
			    Probleme der Ornamentik und Bilderschrift der Polynesier.
			
			    (Ethnos, 1941:1-24)
				GN 295.D7
				T 52
					DREAMS
					
					Thrupp, Sylvia L. editor
					
					    Millennial dreams in action: essays in comparative study.
					
					    (Comparative Studies in Society and History, Suppl. II:139-143, 1962)

GN 2.1
A-4
	DRAWING NEW HEBRIDES
	
	Rowe, W. Page
	
	    A study of the geometrical drawings from the New Hebrides.
	
	    (Journal of the Royal Anthropological Institute, vol. 66, pt. 1, 1936. pp. 117-128)
		GR Folklore
		Pam. 100
			Draws-Tychsen, Hellmut
			
			    Three Polynesian tales about the South Seas.
			
			    (Int. Anthropological and Linguistic Review Vol. 1(4):239-242, 1954)
			
			    (Maori, Tonga, Easter Is.)
				GN 2.S
				M 26
					DREAMS PAPUA
					
					Williams, F. E.
					
					    Papuan dream interpretations.
					
					    (Mankind, vol.2, 1936, pp.29-39)

GN 1
A
	Drawings, Primitive
	
	Kootenay group-drawings by Alexander Francis Chamberlain
	
	In Am. Anthrop. III 2. pp. 248-256. figs.
		GN Ethn.
		Pam.
		3971
			DREAMS
			
			Larsen, Nils P.
			
			    The men with deadly dreams.
			
			    (Saturday Evening Post, Dec. 3, 1955, pp. 20, 21, 140, 142, 143)
				GN 2.1
				A-m
					DREAMS TANGU
					
					Burridge, Kenelm O. L.
					
					    A note on Tangu dreams.
					
					    (Man, Vol. 56, Art. 130, 1956)

GN 2.M
E 84
	Draws-Tychsen, Hellmut
	
	    Einer bisher unbekannt gebliebene Legende vom Ursprunge der Samoaner.
	
	    (Ethnos, 1947:137-146)
		GN Ethn.Pam.
		3637
			DREAMS AUSTRALIA
			
			Lommel, Andreas
			
			    Traum und Bild bei den Primitiven in Nordwest-Australien.
			
			    (Psyche, Jahrg. 5(3):187-209, 1951)
					Dredging (Albatross at Haw. Ilds.)
					
					    see
					
					Albatross.

GN 2.M
L 53
	Draws-Tychsen, Hellmut
	
	    Die Herren der Fische; eine sprachmetrisch und tanzmimisch überlieferte mangaianische Naturmythe.
	
	    (Jahrbuch des Museums f. Völkerkunde zu Leipzig, Bd. 13:147-158, 1954)
		GN 22
		K 93
			DREAMS HAWAII
			
			Handy, Edward Smith Craighill
			
			    Dreaming in relation to spirit kindred and sickness in Hawaii.
			
			    IN Essays in anthropology presented to A.L. Kroeber in celebration of his sixtieth birthday, June 11, 1936. Univ. of Calif., Berkeley. 1936. pp. 119-127.
				AS 36
				C8
					DREDGING (BIOLOGY)
					
					Smith, Sidney Irving, 1843-
					
					    ... Report on the dredgings in the region of St. George's Banks, in 1872. By S. I. Smith and O. Harger.
					
					    (In Connecticut academy of arts and sciences. Transactions. New Haven, 1874-78. 25cm. v. 3, p. 1-57. pl. I-VIII)
					
					    1. Dredging (Biology) I. Harger, Oscar, 1843-1887.
					
					Library of Congress Q11.C9 vol. 3
					Yale University A53n.366.3
					                      A 17-777

QL 1
C 15

DREDGING (BIOLOGY)

California. University. *Scripps institution for biological research, San Diego.*

... Hydrographic, plankton, and dredging records of the Scripps institution for biological research of the University of California, 1901 to 1912, 1913-1915; comp. and arranged under the supervision of W. E. Ritter, by Ellis L. Michael ... [and] George F. McEwen ... Berkeley, University of California press, 1915-16.

cover-title, 254 p. incl. tables, diagrs. fold. map. 27ᶜᵐ. (University of California publications in zoology. v. 15, nos. 1-2)

"Literature cited": p. 43-44, 254

1. Hygrography—California. 2. Plankton—California coast. 3. Dredging (Biology) 4. Marine fauna—Pacific Ocean. I. Ritter, William Emerson, 1856-   ed. II. Michael, Ellis Le Roy, 1881-   III. McEwen, George Fran-   cis. IV. Title.

A 15-1643 Revised

Title from Univ. of Calif.   Library of Congress

QL 671
Co

DREPANIDAE

Bryan, William Alanson

Notes on Loxioides bailleui Oust. from Hawaii.

(Condor, 5:80, 1903)

Dresden

Kgl. Ethnographisches Museum
Dresden

D.7.
GN
2.M
Dr

vol. *IV*
Alterthümer aus dem ostindischen Archipel
von Dr. A. B. Meyer, Leipzig 1884
fol. vol. pp 24 text + 15 plts.

QL 1
C1

DREDGING

Sumner, Francis Bertody, 1874-

... A report upon the physical conditions in San Francisco Bay, based upon the operations of the United States fisheries steamer "Albatross" during the years 1912 and 1913 ... by Francis B. Sumner, George D. Louderback, Waldo L. Schmitt, and Edward C. Johnston. Berkeley, University of California press, 1914.

cover-title, p. [1]-198. incl. tables, pl. 1-13 (incl. 5 maps) diagrs. 27ᶜᵐ. (University of California publications in zoology. v. 14, no. 1)

Published by permission of the United States commissioner of fisheries

1. San Francisco Bay. 2. Hydrography—San Francisco Bay. 3. Dredging (Biology) 4. Deep-sea temperature. 5. Albatross (Steamer) I. Louderback, George Davis, 1874-   joint author. II. Schmitt, Waldo Lasalle, joint author. III. Johnstor, Edward C., joint author.

A 14-1593

Title from Univ. of Calif.   Library of Congress

QL 671
C 74

DREPANIDAE

Richards, Lawrence P.

Recent records of some Hawaiian honeycreepers. By Lawrence P. Richards and Paul H. Baldwin.

(Condor, 55:221-222, 1953)

Dresden

Kgl. Ethnographisches Museum,
Dresden

D.7.
GN
2.M
Dr

vol. *V.*
Seltene Waffen aus Afrika,
Asien und America.
von Dr. A. B. Meyer + Dr. M. Uhle.
fol. vol.   Leipzig 1885.
pp. 6. text + 10 plts.

Q
Gen Sc
Pam
#29

DREDGING--FRANCE

Koehler, M. R.

Dragages profonds exécutés,
à bord du Caudan, dans le
golfe de Gascogne pendant le
mois d' Août 1895.

Paris. Acad. des Sc. n. d. 4ᵗᵒ pp 1-8.

QL
Birds
Pam. 218

DREPANIDAE

Sushkin, Peter P.

On the systematic position of the Drepanidae.

(Verhandl. VI Intern. Orn. Kongress, 1926, (published, 1929) pp. 379-381)

Kgl. Ethnographisches Museum
Dresden.

D.7.
GN
2.M
Dr

vol. *VI.*
Holz- und Bambusgeräte aus
Nord West Neu Guinea
von Dr. M. Uhle. Leipzig 1886.
fol. vol.
pp. 13 text   7. plts.

DU
Hist.Pam
369

Dreier, Thomas

Building materials needed management. (story of Lewers and Cooke firm, Honolulu)

(The Hawaiian Trustees, Vol. 21(3), 1953)

QL 1
Z

DREPANIS

Newton, A.

On a new species of Drepanis discovered by Mr. R. C. L. Perkins.

(Proc. Zool. Soc. London, 1893:690, 1893)

[Drepanis funerea from Molokai]

GN
2.M
Dr

Kgl. Ethnographisches Museum
Dresden.

D.7.

vol. *VII. Masken von Neu Guinea und*
dem Bismarck Archipel. von
A. B. Meyer.
Dresden, 1889. fol. vol. pp. 1- 14.
plts. I- XV.

DU
Hist.Pam
371

Dreier, Thomas

(The Outdoor Circle)

(The Hawaiian Trustee, Vol. 21, No. 5, May, 1953)

Dresden

GN
2.M
Dr

Kgl. Ethnographisches Museum
Dresden.

D.7.

(oversize but in proper place)

vol. *I.*
Bilderschriften des ostindisch
Archipels der Südsee.
von Dr. A. B. Meyer, Leipzig 1881.
fol. vol.
pp. text. 8   plts. 1-6.

GN
2.M
Dr

Kgl. Ethnographisches Museum
Dresden.

D.7.

VIII. Die Philippinen I. Nord Luzon
etc. von A. B. Meyer + A. Schaden-
berg. pp. - 24. plts I - XIII.
Dresden, 1890. fol. vol.

AS 36
A 4

and
QL
Birds
Pam. 311

DREPANIDAE

Amadon, Dean

The Hawaiian honeycreepers (Aves, Drepaniidae).

(Bull. Am. Mus. of Nat. Hist., 95(4), 1950)

review: Nature, 4252, p. 677-78, 1951

Dresden

Kgl. Ethnographisches Museum
Dresden.

D.7.
GN
2.M
Dr

vol. *II. + III.*
Jadeit- und Nephrit- Objekte.
A. Amerika und Europa.
von Dr. A. B. Meyer, Leipzig 1882
pp 1-36 text   1-2 plts.

GN
2.M
Dr

Kgl. Ethnographisches Museum
Dresden.

D.7.

IX. Die Philippinen. II. Die Negritos
von A. B. Meyer
Dresden, 1893. fol. vol. p. 92. plts. I- X.

QL 1
C 15

DREPANIDAE

Baldwin, Paul H.

Annual cycle, environment and evolution in the Hawaiian honeycreepers (Aves: Drepaniidae).

(Univ. of Calif. Pubs. in Zoology, Vol. 52 No. 4, pp. 285-398, 1953)

Dresden

Kgl. Ethnographisches Museum,
Dresden

D.7.
GN
2.M
Dr

vol. *III.   B*
Jadeit- und Nephrit- Objekte.
B. Asien Oceanien und Afrika
von Dr. A. B. Meyer, Leipzig 1883.
pp 37-65 text   3- 6. plts.

Dresden

GN
2.M
Dr

Kgl. Ethnographisches Museum
Dresden.

D.7.

X. Schnitzereien und Masken
vom Bismarck- Archipel +
Neu Guinea. von Meyer + Parkinson
Dresden 1895. fol. vol. p. 25.
plts. I - XIX.

3

Row 1

GN 2.M Dr
Dresden
D.7 H
Kgl. Ethnographisches Museum
Dresden
XI. *Bronzepauken aus Süd-Ost-Asien. von A. B. Meyer & W. Foy.*
Dresden, 1897, fol. vol. p. 24, pl.s I-VII.

AS 182 Dr
Over
Dresden. Museen für Tierkunde und Völkerkunde zu Dresden.
Abhandlungen und Berichte
Band I-   1886-

For current volumes see serial file

Dresden. 4to. 1887-

GN 671.N56 H 21
DRESS MAORIS
Hamilton, Augustus
The art workmanship of the Maori race in New Zealand: a series of illustrations from specially taken photographs, with descriptive notes and essays on the canoes, habitations, weapons, ornaments, and dress of the Maoris, together with lists of the words in the Maori language used in relation to the subjects. Parts 1-5. pp. 271-363. Dunedin. (New Zealand Institute). 1896-1900. 4to. 438 + vii pp. 55 pls.
(Title on   back: "Maori art")

Row 2

GN 2.M Dr
Dresden
D.7 H
Kgl. Ethnographisches Museum
Dresden
XII. *Schwerter von der Celebes-See. Anhang über den Namen Celebes. von W. Foy.*
Dresden, 1899. fol. vol. p. 1-17. pl.ts. 1-III.

AS 182 D77f
Dresden. Museum für Völkerkunde zu Dresden
1875 - 1925. Funfzig Jahre. Museum fur Volkerkunde zu Dresden. By A. Jacobi
Dresden, 1925, 79 pp.

[A history of the Dresden Museum from its foundation]

Dress - Maori
See also
Clothing - Maori
(Change all to Dress some day)

Row 3

GN 2.M Dr
Dresden
D.7 H
Kgl. Ethnographisches Museum
Dresden
XIII. *Tanzobjecte vom Bismarck-Archipel Nissan & Buka. von W. Foy.*
Dresden, 1900. fol. vol. p. 1-40. pl.ts. I-XVIII.

AS 182 Dr-s
Dresden. Staatlichen Sammlungen fur Kunst und wissenschaft zu Dresden.
Berichte
1927-

For current volumes see serial file

Dresden. 8vo. 1927-

GN 671.M3 L 76
AS 763 B-m
Reading Room
GN 700 L 76
DRESS MARQUESAS
Linton, Ralph
The material culture of the Marquesas islands, pp. 411-440. Honolulu. 1923. 4to.
(Bernice P. Bishop Museum, Memoirs, Vol. VIII, No. 5, pp. 263-471. Pls. XL-LXXXIV. Bayard Dominick Expedition, Pub. No. 5)

Row 4

GN 2.M Dr
Dresden
Kgl. Ethnographisches Museum
Dresden
XIV. *I Sammlung Dr. P. und F. Sarasin aus den Jahren 1893-96. Anhang: Bogen-Strich-Punkt & Spiralornamentik von Celebes. von A. B. Meyer & O. Richter*
Dresden, 1903. fol. vol. p. 140.
XX
Nr. 5-   pl.ts. I-XXIX.
1912-1914   on Deutsch-Neuguinea
Rec'd DEC 27 MS

DRESS
See also
ADORNMENT

GN 1 An
DRESS NEW GUINEA
Eschlimann, Henri
L'enfant chez les Kuni (Nouvelle Guinée anglaise).
(Anthropos. Bd.VI. 1911. pp.260-275)

Row 5

AS 182 Dr
Dresden. K. Zoologisch und anthropologisch ethnographisches Museum.
Abhandlungen und Berichte
Library has
Bd.III,6.Wigglesworth, Aves Polynesiae, 1891. (Filed as separate)
and
Band X- XIV; 1902- 1914
"   XV, 1917 - 1923
Name changed   to Museen fur Tierkunde und Volkerkunde.
See serial file
Dresden

GN Ethn. Pam. 3852
DRESS CAROLINE ISLANDS
Riesenberg, Saul H.
Caroline Island belt weaving. By Saul H. Riesenberg and A. H. Gayton.
(Southwestern Journal of Anthropology, Vol. 8(3):342-375, 1952)

GN 662 E 23
DRESS PACIFIC
Edge-Partington, James
An album of the weapons, tools, ornaments, articles of dress, etc. of the natives of the Pacific Islands; drawn and described from examples in public and private collections in England...Manchester. Ser. 1-Ser. 2. (in Boxes) 1890;1895. Ob4to. Ser. 3...drawn and described from examples...in Australasia. 1898. Ob4to.

Row 6

Dresden. K. Zoologisch und anthropologisch ethnographisches Museum zu Dresden
SEE
Dresden. Museen für Tierkunde und Völkerkunde zu Dresden

GN 671.N56 R 84
DRESS MAORIS
Roth, H. Ling
The Maori Mantle, and some comparative notes on N. W. American twined work. With over 250 line illustrations and diagrams and 22 collotype plates. Halifax. Bankfield Museum. 1923. R 8vo. 120 pp.

GN 2.S V
DRESS PAPUA
Finsch, Otto
Ueber bekleidung, Schmuck, und Tätowirung der Papuas der Südostküste von Neu-Guinea.
(Mitt. der Anthropologischen Gesellschaft in Wien, 1885, pp. 12-33)

Row 7

QL 694 W1
P
Dresden
Königliche Zoologischen und Anthropologisch-Ethnographisches Museum zu Dresden.
Abhandlungen und Berichte des -
#6. Aves Polynesiae. A catalogue of the birds of the Polynesian subregion (not including the Sandwich Islands) by Lionel W. Wiglesworth.
Berlin,1891. 4th pp X 92.

AS 750 N
DRESS MAORI
Best, Elsdon
The art of the Whare Pora: Notes on the clothing of the ancient Maori, their knowledge of preparing, dyeing, and weaving various fibres, together with some account of dress and ornaments and the ancient ceremonies and superstitions of the Whare Pora.
(New Zealand Institute, Vol. 31, 1898, pp. 625-658)

DU 12 E 47
DU 12 E 47 looked case
DRESS POLYNESIA
Ellis, William, 1794-1872
Polynesian Researches...2 vols. London. 1829. 8vo. Vol. 2, pp. 122-138; 498-501.
The same...1830. 2 vols. 8vo.

GN
Ethn.Pam.
2744

DRESS   POLYNESIA

Plischke, Hans

Gürtelinvestitur polynesischer Oberhäuptlinge.

(Anthropos, Bd. 25, 1930, pp. 147-162)

QK
1
H 33

Dressler, Robert L.

The pre-Columbian cultivated plants of
Mexico.

(Botanical Museum Leaflets, Vol. 16(5):115-
172, 1953)

QH
301
J-71-m

Drew, Gilman A.

Yoldia Limatula

(Memoirs from the Biological Laboratory
Johns Hopkins University, IV:3. 1899. 4to.)

GN
2.S
P 76

DRESS SAMOA

Mead, Margaret

Samoan kilt.

(Jour. Poly. Soc., 38:239, 1929)

QK
1
M 64

Dressler, Robert L.

A synopsis of Poinsettia (Euphorbiaceae).

(Missouri Botanical Garden, Annals, 48(4):
329-341, 1961)

QK
567
S 64

Drew, Kathleen M.

Rhodophyta.
IN

Smith, Gilbert M.   editor
Manual of phycology; an introduction to the
Algae and their biology. 1951. 167-191.

GN
2.1
A-m

DRESS--SOLOMON ISLANDS

Joyce, T. A.

Forehead ornaments from the Solomon Islands.

(Man, Vol. 35, 1935, No. 108)

QL
53
D77

Drew, Gilman A

A laboratory manual of invertebrate zoology.

Philadelphia, Saunders, 1907.   201p.

GN
Pam
1851

Drews, A.

Die grundlagen des neunzehnten jahr-
hunderts. From Grundlagen der geistigen
und materiellen kultur der gegenwart, Munchen, 1899.

DU
12
H 39

locked
case

DRESS TAHITI

Hawkesworth, John

An account of the voyages...performed by...
Byron, Wallis, Carteret, and Cook...drawn up from
Journals... 3 vols. London. 1773. 4to.
Vol. 2, pp. 191-194.

...Fourth edition. 4 vols. Perth. 1789.
12mo.

QL
Mollusk
Pam
598

Drew, Gilman Arthur

The Habits, anatomy, and embryology of the
giant scallop, (pecten tenuicostatus, mighels).
From the University of Maine studies. 1906.

GN
1
A

Drews, Robin A.

A Gilbert Island canoe.

(Am. Anthropologist, n.s. 47, pp. 471-474,
1945)

G
51
W 17

DRESS TROBRIAND ISLANDS

Hall, Basil

The well-dressed man (Trobriand Islands).

(Walkabout, 23(2):41-44, 1957)

QL
Mollusk
Pam
599

Drew, Gilman A.

Abdruck aus dem anatomischen anzeiger,
Centralblatt für die gesamte wissenschaftliche
anatomie. Amtliches organ der anatomischen Gesell
schaft. Herausgegeben von Prof. Dr. Karl von
Bardeleben in Jena. 1899.

GN
1
A

Drews, Robin A.

Notes on Gilbert Island houses and house
construction.

(Amer. Anthropologist, 48 (2):284-289, 1946)

GN
Ethn.Pam.
3370

The dress of the inhabitants of Otaheite.

(Lady's Magazine, 1773, p. 345-346)

QL
Mollusk
Pam
591

Drew, Gilman A.

Abdruck aus dem anatomischen anzeiger. Centralblatt für die gesamte wissenschaftliche anatomie. Amtliches organ der anatomischen gesselschaft. Herausgegeben von Prof. Dr. Karl von
Bardeleben in Jena. 17.Band. 1900. Verlag von
Gustav Fischer in Jena

AP
2
N 4

(Dreyer, T. F.)

The Bushman skull.

(Nature, vol.139, 1937, p.37. Review in
same issue, p.20)

QK
1
G 77

Dressler, Robert L.

The genus Pedilanthus (Euphorbiaceae).

(Contributions from the Gray Herbarium
of Harvard Univ., No. 182, 1957)

QL
Mollusk
Pam
528

Drew, Gilman A

The physiology of the nervous system of the
razor-shell clam (ensis directus, con.) From
Jour. Exper. Zool. v. 5, n.3, 1908.

DU
620
F

DRIFT LOGS

Bishop, S(ereno) E.

A big stick - ocean currents.

(The Friend, Oct. 1, 1862, p. 76)

(a log of wood from the Northwest, one of
"the immense body of timber launched into the
Pacific during the great floods of last winter
upon the American coasts...")

AP
2
N 28

DRIFT-LOGS

Strong, C. C.

Origin of drift-logs on the beaches of Hawaii. By C. C. Strong and R. Skolmen.

(Nature, 197(4780):890, 1963)

GN
Ethn.Pam.
2987

DRINK

Deihl, Joseph R.

Kava and Kava-Drinking.

67) (Primitive Man, Vol. V, No. 4, 1932, pp. 61-

QL
1
M 4

Drisko, Richard W.

Amino acid content of marine borers. By Richard W. Drisko and Harry Hochman

(Biol. Bull. 112(3):325-329, 1957)

DRIFT LOGS

Strong, C. C.

Pacific floats logs to Hawaiian shores. By C. C. Strong and R. Skolmen.

(Western Conservation Journal, 19(4/5): 24-25, 32-33, 1962)

GN
2.8
P 76

DRINK HAWAII

Titcomb, Margaret

Kava in Hawaii

(Jour. Poly. Soc., 57(2):105-171, 329, 1948)

PL
Pam
#46

Drival, E. van

De l'origine de l'écriture.

Paris, 1879.

QH
1
A 88

DRIFT SUBSTANCES   ATOLLS

Sachet, M.-H.

Pumice and other extraneous volcanic materials on coral atolls.

(Atoll Research Bull., No. 37, 1955)

GN
Ethn.
Pam.
4061

DRINK - MEXICO

Goncalves de Lima, Oswaldo

Alimentos e bebidas no Mexico prehispanico, segundo os manuscritos de Sahagún.

(Instituto Joaquim Nabuco de Pesquisas Sociais, Pub. Avulsas No.2, Recife, 1958)

GN
Ethn.Pam.
3664

Driver, Harold E.

Hoof rattles and girls' puberty rites in North and South America. By Harold E. Driver and S. H. Riesenberg.

(Suppl. to Int. Jour. of Am. Linguistics, Vol. 16(4): Indiana Univ. Pub. in Anthrop. and Linguistics, Mem. 4, 1950)

DU
1
P 10

Drilhon, Freddy

A legend that's become big business.

(Pacific Islands Monthly, 28(7):84-85, 1958)

GN
Ethn.
Pam.
3979

DRINK   MEXICO

Lima, Oswaldo Goncalves de

Alimentos e bebidas no México prehispanico, segundo os manuscritos de Sahagún. Prefácio de Gilberto Freyre.

(Instituto Joaquim Nabuco de Pesquisas Sociais, Publicacoes Avulsas No. 2, Recife, Brazil, 1955)

GN
Ethn.
Pam.
4314

Driver, Harold and others

Indian tribes of North America.

(Int. Jour. of Am. Linguistics, suppl. to Vol. 19(3), 1953. Indiana Univ. Publ. in Anthrop. and Linguistics, Mem. 9, 1953)

AS
36
S3

DRILLING AND BORING.

McGuire, Joseph Deakins, 1842–

A study of the primitive methods of drilling. By J. D. McGuire.

(*In* U. S. National museum. Annual report. 1894. Washington, 1896. 23½ᶜᵐ. p. 623-756. illus.)

Half-title.

1. Drilling and boring.   I. Title : Primitive methods of drilling.

Library of Congress   Q11.U5 1894   14-19806
————— Separate.   GN447.D77M2

GN
2.8
P 76

DRINKING CUP   MAORI

Phillipps, W. J.

A Maori drinking cup.

(Jour. Poly. Soc., 63(2):167-169, 1954)

GN
2.1
W 64

Drobec, Erich

Heilkunde bei den Eingeborenen Australiens.

(Wiener Beiträge, Bd. 9:280-307, 1952)

AS
36
S1

DRILLING AND BORING

Rau, Charles, 1826–1887.

Drilling in stone without metal. By Charles Rau.

(*In* Smithsonian institution. Annual report. 1868. Washington, 1869. 23½ᶜᵐ. p. (392)-400. illus.)

1. Stone implements. 2. Drilling and boring.

Library of Congress   Q11.S66 1868   S 15-259
Library, Smithsonian   Institution

Drioult Gerard, R. H.

La civilisation des Iles Marquises. 1940

UH has

GN
2.8
T

Drollet, Alexandre

De l'emploi des possessifs (adjectifs ou pronoms) dans la langue tahitienne.

(Bull. de la Soc. des Etudes Océaniennes, No. 63, 1938, pp. 34-38)

GN
2.8
P 76

DRILLING AND BORING

Steele, R. H.

Experiments in Kaitahu (Ngai-Tahu) methods of drilling.

(Journal of Polynesian Society, 39: 181-188, 1930)

DU
Pac.Pam
663

Driscoll, Joseph

Samoa pledges firm alliance.

(Honolulu Advertiser, Dec. 21, 1943)

GN
2.8
T

Drollet, Alexandre   (translator)

Legends du morae de "Arahrahu".

(Bull. Soc. des Etudes Oceaniennes, No. 169: 336-345, 1954)

QL
444.D3
A 35
DROMIACEA

Alcock, Alfred William
Catalogue of the Indian Decapod Crustacea
in the collection of the Indian Museum.
Part I. Brachyura; Fasc. 1, Introduction
and Dromides or Dromiacea (Brachyura primigenia).
1901.

Indian Museum.   Calcutta.   4to.

QL
461
H 1
DROSOPHILA

McBride, O. C.

Response of the Mediterranean fruit fly to
its environmental factors.

(Proceedings of the Hawaiian Entomological
Society for the year 1934, Vol. IX, 1935,
pp. 99-108)

QL
537.M6
S 93
DROSOPHILA

Sturtevant, Alfred Henry, 1891–
The North American species of *Drosophila*, by A. H.
Sturtevant. Washington, The Carnegie institution of
Washington, 1921.

iv, 150 p. illus., 3 pl. (2 col.) 25½ᶜᵐ. (*On verso of t.-p.:* Carnegie
institution of Washington. Publication no. 301)

Bibliography: p. 134-141.

1. Drosophila.

Library of Congress   QL537.M6S7   21-5169
———— Copy 2.   [4-4]

GN
Pam.
1165
Drontschilow, Krum

Beiträge zur anthropologie der Bulgaren.
Inaugural dissertation...Friedrich-Wilhelms Univ.
Berlin, 1914. 4to. 77 pp.

2 copies

QH
431
M 84
DROSOPHILA

Morgan, Thomas Hunt

Contribution to the Genetics of Drosophila
Melanogaster. I-III. By T. H. Morgan, C. B.
Bridges and A. H. Sturtevant.

(Carnegie Institution of Washington, Publication No. 278, 1919)

QL
Insect
Pam
810
DROSOPHILA

Willard, H. F., and T. L. Bissell

Parasitism of the Mediterranean fruit fly in
Hawaii, 1922-1924. U. S. Dept. of Agriculture
circular no. 109. March 1930. 12 p.

QL
Insect
Pam.
1774
DROSOPHILA

Braver, Norma B.

The mutants of Drosophila melanogaster,
classified according to body parts affected.

(Carnegie Inst. of Washington Publication
552A, 1956, v + 36 pp.

Q
111
J 23
DROSOPHILA

[Morgan, Thomas Hunt]
The fruit fly, Drosophila, becomes the bio-
logical Cinderella...researches..school of..
IN
Jaffe, Bernard
Outposts of science; a journey to the work-
shops of our leading men of research. N.Y. 1935
pp. 3-46

QL
461
H-1
DROSOPHILA

Zimmerman, Elwood C.

Immigrant species of Drosophila in Hawaii
(Diptera: Drosophilidae)

(Proc. Haw. Ent. Soc., Vol. 11, 1942, pp.
345-350, issued in 1943)

QL
535
B 85
DROSOPHILA

Bridges, Calvin B.

The mutants of Drosophila melanogaster, by
Calvin B. Bridges, completed and edited by
Katherine S. Brehme. Carnegie Institution of
Washington Publication 552, 1944. 252 pp. R8vo.

QH
431
M
DROSOPHILA

Morgan, Thomas Hunt, 1866–
Sex-linked inheritance in *Drosophila*, by T. H. Morgan
and C. B. Bridges. Washington, Carnegie institution of
Washington, 1916.

87, [1] p. incl. illus., tables. II col. pl. 25½ᶜᵐ. (*On verso of t.-p.:* Carnegie institution of Washington. Publication no. 237)

Bibliography: p. 86-87.

1. Heredity. 2. Drosophila. I. Bridges, Calvin Blackman, joint author. II. Title.

Library of Congress   QH431.M87   16—11397
———— Copy 2.

QL
461
P 11
DROSOPHILA   NEW GUINEA

Mather, W. B.

Two new species of Drosophila from New
Guinea (Diptera:Drosophilidae). By W. B. Mather
and T. Dobzhansky.

(Pacific Insects, 4(1):245-249, 1962)

QL
Insect
Pam.
1485
DROSOPHILA

Calaby, J. H.

Adenosine triphosphate from insect muscle.

(Archives of Biochemistry and Biophysics,
31(2):294-299, 1951)

[from Drosophila melanogaster]

QL
Ins
Pam
#158
DROSOPHILA

Severin, H. P.

5 papers on the Mediterranean Fruit-
fly.... from the Journal of Econ. Ent.,
Vol. 5, no.6, Vol.6, nos.1,4,& 5....and
from the Annals Ent. Soc. Am., Vol.5,no.4
1912-13, 8vo.

QH
371
L97
DROSOPHILA   AMPELOPHILA

Lutz, Frank Eugene, 1879–
Experiments with *Drosophila ampelophila* concerning
evolution. By Frank E. Lutz. Washington, D. C., Carnegie institution of Washington, 1911.

iii, 40 p. incl. tables, diagrs. 25ᶜᵐ. (*On verso of t.-p.:* Carnegie institution of Washington. Publication no. 143)

Bibliography: p. 40.
Paper no. 16, of the Station for experimental evolution at Cold Spring
Harbor, New York.

CONTENTS.—The inheritance of abnormal venation.—The effect of sexual
selection.—Disuse and degeneration.

1. Evolution. 2. Heredity. 3. Drosophila ampelophila.

Library of Congress   QH371.L8   11—8151
———— Copy 2.   [s20k3]

AS
122
L 75
DROSOPHILA

Dobzhansky, Theodosius

Species in Drosophila. (The Hooker Lecture)

(Proc. of the Linnean Soc. of London,
174th session (1961-62), Vol. 174(1):1-12,
1963)

AS
36
A 65-b
DROSOPHILA

Spieth, Herman T.

Mating behavior within the genus Drosophila
(Diptera)

(Bull. Am. Mus. of Nat. Hist., 99(7), 1952)

QL
461
H 1
DROSOPHILIDAE

Bryan, Edwin H., Jr.,

Key to the Hawaiian Drosophilidae, with description of new species (Dipt.)

(Haw. Ent. Soc., Proc., Vol. 10, 1937, pp.
25-42)

QK
97
E 58
DROSERACEAE

Engler, Adolf

Das Pflanzenreich...IV. 112. 1906. (Heft
26.) Droseraceae, by L. Diels.

QL
537.M 6
S 93
DROSOPHILA

Sturtevant, A. H.

Contributions to the Genetics of Certain
Chromosome Anomalies in Drosophila Melanogaster,
by A. H. Sturtevant and T. Dobzhansky. Carnegie
Institution of Washington Publication No. 421.
1931. 81 pp. 8vo.

S
399
A 72
and
QL
Insects
Pam.161
DROSOPHILIDAE

Ehrhorn, Edward M.

Mediterranean fruit-fly.

(Bd. Agric. & For. Div., Ent. Circ. 3)

QL
459.S
P 11

AS
763
B-b

Reading
Room

DROSOPHILIDAE

Malloch, John R(ussell)

An aberrant Scaptomyza from the Society Islands (Diptera, Drosophilidae).

Society Islands Insects. Pacific Entomological Survey Publication 6, pp. 95-96 (Art. 20), 1935.

(Bernice P. Bishop Museum, Bulletin 113)

QL
535.M6
O 41

DROSOPHILIDAE   JAPAN

Okada, Toyohi

Systematic study of Drosophilidae and allied families of Japan. Gihodo Co., Ltd. Tokyo. 1956. R8vo. 183 pp.

GN
Eth.
Han.
421

Drucker, Philip

Anthropology in Trust Territory administration.

(Scientific Monthly, 72(5):306-312, 1951)

QL
461
H 1

DROSOPHILIDAE

Malloch, J. R.

Two genera of Hawaiian Drosophilidae (Dipt.)

(Haw. Ent. Soc., Proc., Vol. 10, 1938, pp. 53-56)

QL
461
H-1

DROSOPHILIDAE   PACIFIC

Wheeler, Marshall R.

A key to the genera of Drosophilidae of the Pacific Islands (diptera).

(Proc. Haw. Ent. Soc, Vol. 14(3):421-423, 1951)

DU
500
T 87

Drucker, P.

Family and community in Micronesia.
IN
Trust Territory of the Pacific Islands. Basic Information. 1 July 1951. pp. 101-104

QL
Insect
Pam
230

DROSOPHILIDAE

Willard, H. F. and Theodore L. Bissell.

Work and parasitism of the Mediterranean fruit fly in Hawaii in 1921. From Agri. Research Journ. vol. 33, no. 1, 1926.

Drost, R.

Forced labor in the South Pacific. Complete. Ph.D., State University of Iowa, 1935.

microfilm in Inst. Adv. Studies, Dept. of Pac. Hist., Austr. Nat. Univ.   (Harry Maude)

GN
550
D 79

Drucker, Philip

Indians of the northwest coast. Anthropological Handbook No. 10. Published for The American Museum of Natural History. McGraw-Hill Book Co., Inc. New York. 1955. xii + 208 pp.

QL
1
Po
and
S
399
A

DROSOPHILIDAE   AFRICA

Silvestri, F.

Viaggio in Africa per cercare parassiti di mosche dei fruti.

(Boll. Lab. di Zool. Gen. e Agraria, Portici VIII, 1914, pp. 1-164)

QK
567
S 64

Drouet, Francis

Cyanophyta.
IN

Smith, Gilbert M.   editor
Manual of phycology; an introduction to the Algae and their biology. 1951. 159-166.

QK
101
Dr D79

Drude, Oscar

Manuel de géographie botanique
Paris, 1897, roy. 8vo. pp. 1-552, 4 col. maps and 3 fig. in text.   ju 27 m

(Georges Poirault, Trans.).

S
17.H3
H 38

DROSOPHILIDAE   HAWAII

Dwight, J. L.

The Mediterranean fruit fly in Hawaii.

(Hawaiian Forester and Agriculturist, vol. 26, no. 3, 1929, pp. 113-116)

QL
Mollusca
Pam. 692

Drouet, Henri

Essai sur les mollusques terrestres et fluviatiles de la Guyane Francaise.

(Mem.Soc.Acad.Aube, Tome 23, 1859, Paris. 116 pp. 8vo.)

QK
Botany
Pam.
No 1307

Drude, O.

Pritchardia Thurstoni F.v.M. et Dr. Ex. Gartenflora, Vol. 36, pp 486 - 490, 1887.

DU
620
P
Corridor
Case

DROSOPHILIDAE   HAWAII

Fullaway, D(avid) T.

Hawaii's fruit fly problem.

(Paradise of the Pacific, vol. 49, no. 2, 1937. pp. 23, 31-32)

QL
Mol
Pam
#395
4to

Drouet, Henri

Mollusques marins des Iles Acores.

Paris, 1858.

Drug-plants

See

Medicinal plants

QL
461
H-1

DROSOPHILIDAE   HAWAII

Wirth, Willis W.

Two new spider egg predators from the Hawaiian Islands (Diptera: Drosophilidae)

(Proc. Haw. Ent. Soc, Vol. 14(3):415-417, 1951)

AS
36
S 1

Drowned ancient islands of the Pacific basin.

Hess, H. H.

(Smithsonian Report for 1947:281-300)

Drum,   TREE DRUM

See

Lali.

QL
693
H 98   Drummond, James

Hutton, F. W.

The animals of New Zealand, an account of
the Dominion's air-breathing vertebrates. By
Captain F. W. Hutton and James Drummond. Whitcombe and Tombs, Ltd. Auckland... 1923. 8vo.
(1-5) 6-434 pp.

AS
720.V
M 51-m   DRUMS   NEW GUINEA

Massola, Aldo

Drum types of eastern New Guinea.

(Mem. Nat. Mus. of Victoria, Melbourne,
No. 22(7), 1957)

and
GN
Ethn.
Pam.
4087

QH
Nat.Hist.
Pam.
135   Drury, Newton B.

The National Park Service. Prepared for
the Committee on Interior and Insular Affairs,
of the U. S. Senate. Jan. 7, 1949. 20 pp.

DU
1
M 6   Drummond, James

The Fauna of New Zealand.

(The Mid-Pacific Magazine, Vol. XLIV, pp. 19-
23, 1932)

GN
2.I
A-m   DRUMS   RAIVAVAE

Sheppard, T.

A carved drum from Raivavae (high island).
(with note by P. H. Buck)

(Man, Vol. 39, 1939, No. 93)

QK
Bot.Pam.
3134   DRY FORESTS   MOKULEIA, OAHU

Hatheway, William H.

Composition of certain native dry forests:
Mokuleia, Oahu, T. H.

(Ecological Monographs, 22:153-168, 1952)

DU
406
D79   Drummond, James., comp.

Nature in New Zealand, compiled by
James Drummond and edited by Captain
F.W. Hutton.

Christchurch, Whitcombe & Tombs, n.d.
188p. illus.

GN
Ethn. Pam.
3587   DRUMS YABIM

Bodrogi, T.

Yabim drums in the Biró collection.

(Folia Ethnographica, I (2-4):205-222, 1949)

QL
671
E 39   DRY LAND PLANTS   HAWAII

Munro, Hector G.

Report on plants endemic to Hawaii now
growing at Ke Kua'aina.

(The Elepaio, Vol. 24(1):1-2, 1963)

DU
620
P   DRUMS   HAWAII

The legend of Ai'anaka.

(Paradise of the Pacific, Vol. 26, 1913,No.
12, p. 27-29)

QL
401
N   DRUPA

Pilsbry, Henry A.

Notes on some Hawaiian species of Drupa and
other shells, by Henry A. Pilsbry and Elizabeth
L. Bryan.
(Nautilus, Vol. 31, 1918, pp. 99-102)

QK
5
D 79

locked
case   Drygalski, Erich von

Deutsche Südpolar-Expedition, 1901-1903...
Bd. 8: Botanik. (complete in 5 hefte)
Heft 1-5   1906- 1928

Berlin. Georg Reimer. 4to.

GN
2.S
Po   DRUMS-HAWAII

Skinner, H.D.

Three Polynesian Drums.

(Journal of the Polynesian Society, Vol.42
pp. 308-309)

QL
Mollusca
Pam.
1038
1040   DRUPINAE   PACIFIC

Hertlein, Leo G.

The subfamily Drupinae (Gastropoda) in the
Eastern Pacific.

(Veliger, 3(1), 1960)

DRYINIDAE

Perkins R. C. L.

S
17.H3
S44   Leap Hoppers & their Natural Enemies.

Ide Bulletin 1. Hawaiia Sugar
Planters' Association.
Division of Entomology

L.3.

JUN 30 1905

GN
1
An   DRUMS   NEW BRITAIN

Eberlein, P.J.

Die Trommelsprache auf der Gazellehalbinsel
(neupommern).

(Anthropos. Bd.V. 1910. pp.635-642)

Drury, Clifford Merrill   (editorial notes by)

The diaries and letters of Henry H. Spalding
and Asa Bowen Smith relating to the Nez Perce
Mission, 1838-1842.

(Northwest Historical Series, IV, 1958.
published by The Arthur H. Clark Co., Glendale 4,
Calif.)

UH?

S
17 H3
S 44   DRYINIDAE

Perkins, Robert C   L.

... Parasites of the family Dryinidae. By R. C. L. Perkins. Honolulu, Hawaii, 1912.

20 p. IV pl. 23cm. (Hawaiian sugar planters' association. Experiment
station. Division of entomology. Bulletin no. 11)

1. Dryinidae. 2. Parasitic and predaceous insects.

Agr 12-2048

Library, U. S. Dept. of   Agriculture 420H31 no. 11

GN
Ethn.Pam.
3587   DRUMS   NEW GUINEA

Bodrgi, T.

Yabim drums in the Biró collection.

(Folia Ethnographica, I (2-4):205-222, 1949)

QK
358
D 79   Drury, Heber

The useful plants of India; with notices of
their chief value in commerce, medicine, and the
arts. Second edition, with additions and corrections. London, William H. Allen & Co. 1873
8vo. xvi + 512 pp.

QL
Insect
Pam.
1401   DRYINIDAE   HAWAII

Lindberg, Hakan

Notes on the biology of Dryinids.

(Commentationes Biologicae, Soc. Sci.,
Fennica, X. 15, 1950)

AS
36
S4
DRYOBATES SCALARIS
Oberholser, Harry Church, 1870–

A revision of the forms of the ladder-backed wood-pecker (*Dryobates scalaris* <Wagler>). By Harry C. Oberholser ...

(*In* U. S. National museum. Proceedings. Washington, 1912. 23½ᶜᵐ. v. 41, p. 139–159. fold. map)

1. Dryobates scalaris.

12–17769

Library of Congress   Q11.U55 vol. 41

GN
477
D 81
Dubos, Rene

Mirage of health; Utopias, progress, and biological change. New York. Harper and Brothers Publishers. sm8vo. 1959c xv + 236 pp.

[World Perspectives, Vol. 22, edited by Ruth Nanda Anshen]

QK
1
S67
Dubard, M.

Revision du genre Oxera (Verbenacees) Soc. Bot. France Bull. v.53, pp.705–717, 1906.

AS
36
S4
DRYOBATES VILLOSUS
Oberholser, Harry Church, 1870–

A revision of the forms of the hairy woodpecker (*Dryobates villosus* <Linnaeus>). By Harry C. Oberholser ...

(*In* U. S. National museum. Proceedings. Washington, 1911. 23½ᶜᵐ. v. 40, p. 595–621. fold. map)

1. Dryobates villosus.

11–31537

Library of Congress   Q11.U55 vol. 40

GN
Pam
2410
Du Nord,

Abriss der geschichte von Bosnien und der Herzegovina. From Organ d. Militar-wissen. vereine, bd. 12, heft 6–7, Wien, 1876.

QK
Botany
Pam.
1246

and

AS
162
M
Dubard, Marcel

Les Sapotacées du groupe des Sideroxylinées . From Mus. Col. Marseille, Ann. 2d ser. vol. X, 1912, pp 1– 90.

QL
1
A 93
DRYOPIDAE   AUSTRALIA
Carter, H. J.

Four new species of Australian Dryopidae by H. J. Carter and E. H. Zeck.

(The Australian Zoologist, 9:170–172, 1938)

Du Petit Thouars
see
Dupetit Thouars

AS
162
M
Dubard, Marcel

Sur un Pittosporum nouveau de Nouvelle Caledonie. In Ann. Mus. Col. Marseille, Vol. 19, 1911,pp.51 – 55, illus.

and

QK
Botany
Pam.
1234

QL
1
A 93
DRYOPIDAE   AUSTRALIA
Carter, H. J.

A monograph of the Australian Dryopidae; order- Coleoptera. By H.J.Carter and E.H.Zeck.

(The Australian Zoologist, 6:50–72, 1929)

AP
2
N 4
Du Toit, Alex. L.

Antarctica and glacial ages.

(Nature, Vol. 143, 1939, pp. 242–243)

GC
1
M 73-a
du Baty, Rallier

Quinze mois aux iles Kerguelen.

(Annales de l'Institut Oceanographique, (Monaco), Tlme III, Fasc. 3, 1911, 47 pp., 2 pl)

AS
36
S2
DRYOPTERIS.
Christensen, Carl Frederik Albert, 1872–

The American ferns of the group of *Dryopteris opposita* contained in the U. S. National museum, by Carl Christensen ...

(*In* Smithsonian institution. Smithsonian miscellaneous collections. Washington, 1910. 24½ᶜᵐ. vol. LII, (Quarterly issue, vol. V) p. 365–396)

Publication 1867.
Originally published July 12, 1909.

1. Dryopteris. 2. Ferns—America. ɪ. U. S. National museum.

Library of Congress   Q11.S7 vol. 52   16–12774 Revised
———— Copy 2.

---

du Toit, Alex L.

Our wandering continents: an hypothesis of continental drifting.

First publ.1937; reprint 1957 (30s), NY; repr. for private circulation from The Journal of Geology, Vol. 66, No. 3, 1958.

UH and
GS have Jour. of Geol.

QK
1
T 1
DUBAUTIA
St. John, Harold

Dryopteris, Deschampsia, Portulaca, Lupinus, Fagara, Stenogyne, and Dubautia.   Hawaiian Plant Studies 12.

(Bul., Torrey Botanical Club, Vol. 72, pp. 22–30, 1944)

QK
1
T 1
DRYOPTERIS
St. John, Harold

Dryopteris, Deschampsia, Portulaca, Lupinus, Fagara, Stenogyne, and Dubautia. Hawaiian Plant Studies 12.

(Bul., Torrey Botanical Club, Vol. 72, pp. 22–30, 1944)

G
161
H
Duarte Barbosa

Book of Duarte Barbosa: an account of the countries bordering on the Indian Ocean ..... written by Duarte Barbosa; ..... about 1518. Translated from the Portuguese by Mansel Longworth Dames. Vol. I Hakluyt Society, Ser. II, Vol. XLIV, 1918.

QK
1
P 11
DUBAUTIA
St. John, Harold

The subgenera of Dubautia (Compositae): Hawaiian Plant Studies 18.

(Pacific Science, Vol. 1V(4):339–345, 1950)

AS
36
S1
Du Bois-Reymond, Emil Heinrich, 1818–1896.

On the relation of natural science to art. By Dr. E. du Bois-Reymond ...

(*In* Smithsonian institution. Annual report. 1891. Washington, 1893. 23½ᶜᵐ. pp. 661–682)

"From Nature, December 31, 1891, and January 7, 1892; vol. XLV, pp. 200–204, and 224–227."

1. Art and science.

S 15–777

Library of Congress   Q11.S66 1891
Library, Smithsonian   Institution

QK
1
P 23
Dubard, M.

Description de quelques espèces de Planchonella (sections Burckiiplanchonella et Egassia) d'après les documents de L. Pierre.

(Notulae Systematicae, Vol. 2, pp. 81–84,1911)

GN
2.8
N 67
Dubbeldam, L. F. B.

Traditionele elite in West-Nieuw-Guinea.

(Nieuw-Guinea Studien, 6(2):132–151, 1962)

GN
2 I
Ca

Du Bois, Constance Goddard.

... The religion of the Luiseño Indians of southern California, by Constance Goddard Du Bois. Berkeley, The University press [1908]

cover-title, [69]-186 p., 1 l. 4 pl. 27^{cm}. (University of California publications in American archaeology and ethnology, v. 8, no. 3 ... June 27, 1908)

"Editor's note [signed: A. L. Kroeber]": p. 70-72.
"Appendix I. Games, arts, and industries of the Diegueños and Luiseños. By Constance Goddard Du Bois": p. 167-173.
"Appendix II. Notes on the Luiseños. By A. L. Kroeber": p. 174-186.

1. Luiseño Indians—Religion. 2. Diegueño Indians. 3. Kroeber, Alfred Louis, 1876–

Library of Congress   E51.C15 vol. 8   8—23147
———— Copy 2.   E99.L9D8

AS
36
S1

Dubois, Eugène *i. e.* Marie Eugène François Thomas, 1858–

Pithecanthropus erectus—a form from the ancestral stock of mankind. By Eugene Dubois.

(*In* Smithsonian institution. Annual report. 1898. Washington, 1899. 23½^{cm}. p. 445-459. 3 pl., diagrs.)

"Translated from the Anatomischer anzeiger, vol. XII, pp. 1-22."

1. Pithecanthropus erectus. 2. Man, Origin of.

                S 15-1004

Library of Congress   Q11.S66 1898
Library, Smithsonian   Institution

GN
2.S
O 15

Dubois, Marie-Joseph

Mythes et récits Maréens.

(Jour. de la Soc. des Océanistes, Vol. 4:5-28, 1948)

GN
479
H 28

Du Bois, Cora

Attitudes toward food and hunger in Alor.
IN

Haring, Douglas G.
Personal character and cultural milieu.
Syracuse University Press. 1956.
pp. 241-253

QL
Prot.-
Poly.
Pam.
780

Dubois, Georges

Notocotylus lopezneyrai n.sp. (Trematoda, Notocotylidae), parasito del intestino del Rosthramus sociabilis Levis friedman (Aves).

(Mem. Soc. Cubana de Hist. Nat., 22.V.1953: 251-253)

GN
2.S
O 15

Dubois, M. -J.

Les plantes cultivées dans le folklore maréen.

(Journal de la Soc. des Océanistes, 7:253-258, 1951)

GN
Ethn.Pam.
3359

du Bois, Cora

The feather cult of the middle Columbia.

(General Series in Anthropology, No. 7, 1938. edited by Leslie Spier.)

AS
28
E 85

Dubois, M.

Sorcelleries maréennes: le kaze et le paace.

(Etudes Melanesiennes, No. 4.(Ser. 2), 1949: 5-15)

AS
28
E 85

Dubois, M. J. s.m.

La propriété foncière maréenne au temps du paganisme. By M. J. Dubois and F. Beaulieu.

(Etudes Mélanésiennes, n.s., 3rd yr., No. 5: 69-78, 1951)

GN
635.D9
D 81

Du Bois, Cora

The people of Alor: a social-psychological study of an East Indian island. With analyses by Abram Kardiner and Emil Oberholzer. University of Minnesota Press, Minneapolis. R8vo. 1944c. xvi + 654 pp.

over

GN
2.S
O 15

Dubois, le R. P. Marie-Joseph

Les mythes de Maré: 1. Mythes et récits Maréens, par le R. P. Marie-Joseph Dubois; 2. Sens et rôle du mythe en ethnologie, par Jean Poirier.

(Journal de la Soc. des Océanistes, Tome 4: 5-47, 1948)

AN
28
E 85

Dubois, R.P. (Catholic missionary)

Les "Electoke" de Maré (Loyalty).

(Etudes Mélanésiennea, n.s., Année 1(3):18-28, 1948)

QL
Mammals
Pam.
134

Dubois, Eug.

Hat sich das Gehirn beim Haushunde, im Gergleich mit Wildhundartern, vergrossert, oder verkleinert?

(Bijdragen tot de Dierkunde...K. Zool. Genootschap...Amsterdam, Aflevering 22, pp. 315-320. no date)

GN
1
An

Dubois, (R.P.) H. M. (Soc. Jesus)

Les origines des Malgaches.

(Anthropos, 21:72-126; 1926; Vol. 22:80-124, 1927)

AS
28
E 85

Dubois, R. P. (Catholic Missionary)

Sorcelleries Maréennes: le Kaze et le Paace.

(Etudes Mélanésiennes, n.s., Année 2(4): 5-15, 1949)

GN
2 I
A m

and

GN
Ethn.Pam
4155

Dubois, Eugène

On the fossil human skulls recently discovered in Java, and Pithecanthropus Erectus.

(Man, Vol.37, pp.1-7. 1937.)

AS
28
E 85

Dubois, Marie-Joseph

Les classes d'âge à Maré au temps du paganisme.

(Etudes Mélanésiennes, No. 8, pp. 33-38, Dec. 1954)

DU
Pac.Pam.
294

Dubouzet, E.

Iles Foutouna et Allofa.

(Revue de l'Orient, Bull. n.d. about 1843)

GN
Pam
2516

Dubois, Eugen

Ueber die abhangigkeit des hirngewichtes von der korpergrosse bei den saugethieren. From Arch. f. Anthrop. bd. 25, heft 1-2, 1897.

AS
28
E 85

Dubois, M. J.

Contes Maréens, I. Tojerine et Hamararene.

(Etudes Melanesiennes, n.s. 4th (yr), No. 6:5-14, 1952)

QK
Bot.
Pam.
3191

Dubuy, Father Jules

The giant Pandanus of New Guinea.

(Bulletin, Fairchild Tropical Garden, 10(3), 1954)

GN
575
D 82

DuChaillu, Paul Belloni

The Viking Age: The early history, manners, and customs of the ancestors of the English-speaking nations. Illustrated from the antiquities discovered inmounds, cairns, and bogs as well as from the ancient sagas and eddas...with 1366 illustrations and map. In two volumes. New York. Scribner. 1890. 8vo. pp. xix + 591; viii + 562.

DU
12
M 69

locked
case

DUCIE ISLAND

Moerenhout, J. A.

Voyages aux îles du grand océan...2 vols. Paris. 1837. 8vo. Tome 1, pp. 29-30; Tome 2, p. 280.

GN
Pam
794

Duckworth, W.L.H.

Description of a human cranium from Walfisch bay, S.W. Africa. From Journal of Anatomy and Physiology, v.41. 4p.

QL
377.C5
D 82

Duchassaing de Fonbressin, P(lacide)

Mémoire sur les Coralliaires des Antilles, par P. Duchassaing de Fonbressin et Gioanni (Jean) Michelotti. Turin. Imprimerie Royale. 1860. 4to. 89 pp. 10 pl.

DUCIE ISLAND

DU
12
1852

Pitcairn, Henderson, Ducie and Oeno islands. Laws, statutes, etc. Ordinances, 1952. no. 1-4

UH has

GN
22
Du
D 53

Duckworth, W.L.H.

Morphology and anthropology: A handbook for students, by W.L.H. Duckworth. 2nd ed. vol. 1.

Cambridge: At the Univ. press, 1915. xiv, 504p. illus.

QL
372.4
D 82

Duchassiang de Fonbressin, P(lacide)

Spongiaires de la Mer Caraibe, par P. Duchassaing de Fonbressin et Giovanni Michelotti.

(Mem. Soc. Hollandaise des Sciences à Harlem, 1864)

DUCIE ISLAND   BOTANY

see

BOTANY   DUCIE ISLAND

GN
Pam
797

Duckworth, W.L.H.

Notes on the anatomy of an eunuchoid man dissected at the anatomy school, Cambridge, 1905. From Journ. Anatomy & Physiology, v.41. 4p. pl.

DU
Pac.Pam.
597

DUCIE

Cuming, H(ugh)

Excerpt from letter written to Dr. (Joseph Dalton) Hooker by H. Cuming, dated "London, March 21st. 1832".

(Voyage was in 1828, - stopped at Easter Islands, Mangareva, Crescent, Rurutu, Tubuai, Ducie, Tuamotus, Rapa.)

QL
Birds
Pam.
334

DUCKS

Bellrose, Frank C.

Housing for wood ducks.

(Illinois Nat. Hist. Survey, Circ. 45, 1953)

GN
Pam
795

Duckworth, W.L.H.

Note on an unusual anomaly in crania from the island of Kwaiawata, New Guinea. From Journ. Anatomy & Physiology, bd.41. 5p.

DU
12
B 41

locked
case

DUCIE ISLAND

Beechey, F. W.

Narrative of a Voyage to the Pacific and Beering's Strait...in...Ship Blossom, under the command of Captain F. W. Beechey...in...1825-28. Vol. 1, pp. 59-61. London. 1831. 8vo.

The same...New edition. London. 1831. 8vo.

QL
Bird
Pam.
494

DUCKS

Hines, Bob

Ducks at a distance: a waterfowl identification guide.

(U.S.D.I., Fish and Wildlife Ser., 23 pp. 1963)

GN
2.1
A-4

Duckworth, W.L.H.

On a collection of crania, with two skeletons of the Mori-ori, or aborigines of the Chatham Islands. With a note on some crania from the same islands now in the Museum of the Royal College of surgeons.

(Journ. Anthrop. Inst. of Great Britain and Ireland, Vol. 30, 1900, pp. 141-152)

DU
12
I 31

DUCIE ISLAND

Im Thurn, Sir Everard

Thoughts, talks and tramps: pp. 237-250: Some less-known islands in the Pacific. 1913.

(Proceedings of the Royal Colonial Institute, 1913)

QH
104
U-C

DUCKS--FOOD.

McAtee, Waldo Lee.

... Three important wild duck foods. By W. L. McAtee ... [Washington, Govt. print. off.] 1911.

19 p. illus. 23ᶜᵐ. (U. S. Dept. of agriculture. Bureau of biological survey. Circular no. 81)

1. Ducks—Food.

Agr 11-1540

Library, U. S. Dept. of   Agriculture 1B52C no.81

GN
Pam
#372

Duckworth, W. L. H.

On the brains of aboriginal natives of Australia in the anatomy school, Cambridge University., ex ? vol. 42, 1907.

QL
671
I

DUCIE ISLAND

MacFarlane, J. R. H.

Notes on birds in the western Pacific, made in H. M. S. "Constance", 1883-1885.

(Ibis, Ser. 5, Vol. 5, 1887, pp. 201-215)

DUCKS

See also under

ANAS
ANATIDAE
DAFILA

GN
775
D85

Duckworth, W. L. H.

Prehistoric Man.

Cambridge, University Press, 1912. 18mo. viii + 156 pp.

GN
Pam
796

Duckworth, W.L.H.

   Report on a cranium with greatly reduced irregular dentition. From Journ. Anatomy & Physiology, v.41. 3p.

QL
671
I 12

DUCULA

Lysaght, Averil

   The name of the giant pigeon of the Marquesas Islands.

   (Ibis, 99:118, 1957)

   see also correction by Ernst, Mayr, idem, p. 521, 1957

   [Ducula (Serresius) galenta Bonaparte 1855]

DU
620
H 4

DUDOIT, JULES

Jore, Léonce A.

   Captain Jules Dudoit, the first French consul in the Hawaiian Islands, 1837-1867, and his brig schooner, the Clementine. Translated by Dorothy Brown Aspinwall.

   (Hawaiian Historical Soc. Ann. Rept. 64, for 1955, pp. 21-36, 1956)

GN
2.1
A-4

Duckworth, W.L.H.

   Rotuma: physical anthropology.

   (Journ. Anthrop. Inst. of Great Britain and Ireland, Vol. 30, 1900, note 46 (p. 37))

AM
139
D 84

Dudley, Dorothy H.

   Museum registration methods. By Dorothy H. Dudley and Irma Bezold. The American Association of Museums. Washington, D. C. 1958 R8vo. xi + 225 pp.

QL
Protozoa
to
Polyzoa
Pam
461

Duerden, J   E

   The actiniaria around Jamaica.

GN
22
Bul
D 83

Duckworth, W.L.H.

   Studies from the Anthropological Laboratory, the Anatomy School, Cambridge.

   Cambridge: Univ. Press, 1904. pp 291, illus

AS
36
S1

Dudley, Timothy.

   The earthquake of 1811 at New Madrid, Missouri. (From the narrative of an eye-witness.) · By Timothy Dudley ...

   (*In* Smithsonian institution. Annual report. 1858. Washington, 1859. 23½ᶜᵐ. p. 421-424)

   1. New Madrid, Mo.—Earthquake, 1811.

                                      S 15-68

Library of Congress   Q11.S66 1858
Library, Smithsonian   Institution

QL
Protozoa
& Poly
Pam #78

Duerden, J. E.

   The antiquity of the Zoanthid Actinians, ex Sixth Ann. Rept. of Michigan Acad.. of Sc..

DU
12
R 68

looked
case

DUCLESMEUR, (CAPTAIN)

(Rochon, A. M. de)

   Crozet's voyage to Tasmania, New Zealand, the Ladrone Islands, and the Philippines in the years 1771-1772...translated by H. Ling Roth... London. 1891. 8vo.

AS
36
S7

DUDLEY, WILLIAM RUSSEL, 1849-1911

   ... **Dudley** memorial volume, containing a paper by William Russel Dudley and appreciations and contributions in his memory by friends and colleagues ... Stanford University, Cal., The University, 1913.

   137 p. front. (mounted port.) illus, plates. 26ᶜᵐ. (Leland Stanford junior university publications. University ser. (11))

   CONTENTS. — William Russel Dudley. — Memorial addresses (by): J. C. Branner, D. H. Campbell. — Appreciations (by): D. S. Jordan, Le Roy Abrams, G. J. Peirce, J. T. Newman, W. F. Wight.—List of publications of W. R. Dudley.—List of Cornell university pupils of W. R. Dudley.—List of Stanford university pupils of W. R. Dudley.—Scientific papers: The vitality of *Sequoia gigantea* (by) W. R. Dudley. The morphology and systematic position of *Calycularia radiculosa* (Steph.) (by) D. H. Campbell.

   (Continued on next card)   13—11057

                               [s19c]

QL
Protozoa
& Poly
Pam #49

Duerden, J. E.

   The antiquity of the Zoanthid actinians, ex Sixth Ann. Rept. of Michigan Acad. of Sc.

DU
12
R 68

looked
case

DUCLESMEUR, CAPTAIN

(Rochon, A. M. de)

   Nouveau voyage a la mer du sud, commencé les ordes de M. Marion...& achevé, après la mort de cet officier, sous ceux de M. de Chevalier Duclesmeur...cette relation a été rédigée d'après les plans & journaux de M. Crozet... Paris. 1783. 8vo.

AS
36
S7

DUDLEY, WILLIAM RUSSEL, 1849-1911

   ... **Dudley** memorial volume ... 1913. (Card 2)

           CONTENTS—Continued.

   Studies of irritability in plants, III, The formative influence of light (by) G. J. Peirce. The gymnosperms growing on the grounds of Stanford university (by) Le Roy Abrams. The *Synchytria* in the vicinity of Stanford university (by) James McMurphy. The law of geminate species (by) D. S. Jordan. Some relations between salt plants and salt-spots (by) W. A. Cannon. North American species of the genus *Amygdalus* (by) W. F. Wight.

   1. Dudley, William Russel, 1849-1911. 2. Botany—Collected works.

Library of Congress   QK3.D8   13—11057

                                  [s19c]

QL
Protozoa
to
Polyzoa
Pam
401

Duerden, J. E.

   Contributions to the natural history of Jamaica. From the Jour. of the Institute of Jamaica, v.2, p.3, 1896.

DU
Missions
Pam. 104

(Duclos, Father)

   Trois mois a Fidji. Impressions and souvenirs. Fasc. 1-2, 1904. 8vo. 59 pp. Loreto. Fidji. Imprimerie de la Mission.

   ["Fasc. 3 printed at Sydney, Fasc. 4 in France"]

AS
36
S7

   ... **Dudley** memorial volume, containing a paper by William Russel Dudley and appreciations and contributions in his memory by friends and colleagues ... Stanford University, Cal., The University, 1913.

   137 p. front. (mounted port.) illus, plates. 26ᶜᵐ. (Leland Stanford junior university publications. University ser. (11))

   CONTENTS. — William Russel Dudley. — Memorial addresses (by): J. C. Branner, D. H. Campbell. — Appreciations (by): D. S. Jordan, Le Roy Abrams, G. J. Peirce, J. T. Newman, W. F. Wight.—List of publications of W. R. Dudley.—List of Cornell university pupils of W. R. Dudley.—List of Stanford university pupils of W. R. Dudley.—Scientific papers: The vitality of *Sequoia gigantea* (by) W. R. Dudley. The morphology and systematic position of *Calycularia radiculosa* (Steph.) (by) D. H. Campbell.

   (Continued on next card)   13—11057

                               [s19c]

QL
378
Du
D 5

Duerden, J.E.

   The coral Siderastrea Radians and its postlarval development.

   Carnegie institution of Washington, 1904. Pub. # 20.

QL
408
D 83

Duclos, P. L.

   Histoire Naturelle générale et particulière de tous les genres de coquilles univalves marines, à l'Etat vivant et Fossile...Genre Olive. Paris. Firmin Didot Freres. 1835. folio. 48 pls. 4pp. (index)

AS
36
S7

   ... **Dudley** memorial volume ... 1913. (Card 2)

           CONTENTS—Continued.

   Studies of irritability in plants, III, The formative influence of light (by) G. J. Peirce. The gymnosperms growing on the grounds of Stanford university (by) Le Roy Abrams. The *Synchytria* in the vicinity of Stanford university (by) James McMurphy. The law of geminate species (by) D. S. Jordan. Some relations between salt plants and salt-spots (by) W. A. Cannon. North American species of the genus *Amygdalus* (by) W. F. Wight.

   1. Dudley, William Russel, 1849-1911. 2. Botany—Collected works.

Library of Congress   QK3.D8   13—11057

                                  [s19c]

QL
Protozoa
to
Polyzoa
Pam
402

Duerden, J. E.

   The Geographical distribution of the Actinaria of Jamaica. From Natural Sci., v.12, n.72, 1898.

DU
Pac
Pam
#76

Duerden, J. E.

Marine zoology in the Hawaiian Islands, ex Science, vol. XXI, no. 545, June 9, 1905.

QH
301
J 71-m

Duerden, James Edwin

West Indian Madreporarian Polyps

(Mem.Biol.Lab.Johns Hopkins Univ.,V:2,1903, 4to.)

(Reprinted from Memoirs of the National Academy of Science.)

GN
2.S
P 76

Duff, Roger (S.)

First records of the maro in the New Zealand area.

(Journal of the Polynesian Society, Vol. 52, 1943, pp. 212-215)

QL
Protozoa
& Poly
Pam
#74

" 74a

Duerden, J. E.

The morphology of the Madreporaria V. Septal sequence, ex Biol. Bull. vol. VII, no. 2, July, 1904.

The Morphology of the Madreporaria, VI: The Fossula in Rugose Corals. (Reprinted from Biological Bulletin, Vol. IX, No. 1, June,'05)

Duff, C.

How to learn a language.   1948

UH

AS
750
C 22m

and

GN
Ethn.Pam
3837

Duff, Roger S.
Duff, R. S.

A Maori amulet from Kaikoura.

(Records of the Canterbury Museum, Vol.5, 1939, pp. 254-258, 1 pl.)

QL
Protozoa
& Poly
Pam #b1

Duerden, J. E.

The morphology of the Madreporaria V. Septal sequence, ex Biol. Bull., vol. VII, no. 2, July, 1904.

The morphology of the Madreporaria,VI... see previous card

QK
Bot.Pam.
3109

Duff, J.

Report on the present state and future prospects of Lord Howe Island. Government Printer, Sydney, 1882.

[J. Duff sent to J. Bowie Wilson his second report, "new and most interesting plants..." C(has.) Moore forwarded the report for Wilson to the Principal Under Secretary]

AS
750
C 22 m

and

GN
Ethn.Pam
3818

Duff, Roger S.
Duff, R. S.

Maori stone "axes".

(Records of the Canterbury Museum, Vol.5, 1939, pp. 249-253, 1 pl.)

AS
36
S1

Duerden, James Edwin, 1869–

The plumages of the ostrich ... By Prof. J. E. Duerden ...

(*In* Smithsonian institution. Annual report. 1910. Washington, 1911. 23½ᶜᵐ. p. 561-571. 8 pl. on 4 l.)

"Reprinted ... from the Agricultural journal of the Union of South Africa ... vol. 1, no. 1, February, 1911."

1. Ostrich.

Library of Congress   Q11.S66 1910

11-31580

GN
2.S
P 76

and
GN
Ethn.Pam
3817

Duff, R(oger) S.
Duff, R. S.

A cache of adzes from Motukarara.

(Journal of the Polynesian Soc., Vol. 49, 1940, pp. 285-293)

GN
975.N4
D 85

Duff, Roger (S.)

The moa-hunter period of Maori culture. With a foreword by H. D. Skinner. Department of Internal Affairs. Wellington. 1950. R8vo. (16)+405+(3)pp.

and 2nd edition, 1956

reviewed by J. M. McEwen, in JPS 59(1),1950 and by Linton in Am. Anthrop. 53:264,1951

AS
36
S2

Duerden, James Edwin, 1869–

Recent results on the morphology and development of coral polyps, by J. E. Duerden.

(*In* Smithsonian institution. Smithsonian miscellaneous collections. Washington, 1905. 24½ᶜᵐ. vol. XLVII (Quarterly issue, vol. II) p. 93-111. illus.)

Publication 1473.
Originally published August 6, 1904.

1. Corals.

Library of Congress   Q11.S7 vol. 47

16-10995

——— Copy 2.
——— Separate.   QL377.C5D8

GN
2.I
A-m

Duff, Roger (S.)

Digging up the moa-hunters: an earlier phase of Maori culture.

(Man, Vol. 48, Art. 77, 1948)

AS
750
C-22 m

and
GN
Ethn.
Pam.
4345

Duff, Roger (S.)

Moa-hunters of the Wairau.

(Records of the Canterbury Museum, Vol. V, No. 1, pp. 1-42, pl. 1-16)

QL
Protozoa
& Poly
Pam #50

Duerden, J. E.

Recent results on the morphology and development of coral polyps, ex Smithsonian Misc. Coll. vol. 47.

GN
2.S
M 26

Duff, Roger S.

The evolution of native culture in New Zealand: moa hunters, Morioris, Maoris.

(Mankind, Vol. 3 (10):281-291, 1947)
"   "   " :313-322, 1947

GN
700
A 62

Duff, Roger S.
Duff, R. S.

Moas and man.

(Antiquity, Vol. 23(92):172-179, 1949; Vol. 24 (no. 94):72-83, 1950)

QL
Protozoa
& Poly
Pam #b2

Duerden, J. E.

Recent results on the morphology and development of coral polyps, ex Smithsonian Misc. Coll. vol. 47.

AS
750
C 22 m

pa,

302,

Duff, Roger

Excavation of house-pits at Pari Whakatau Claverley, Marlborough.

(Records of the Canterbury Museum, 7(4):269-302, 1961)

QL
Birds
Pam.
401

Duff, Roger (S.)

Moas and moa-hunters. Gov. Printer. Wellington. (1957)   8vo.   36 pp.

AS
750
D 67

Duff, Roger (S.)

　　A Moriori plaited textile.

and
GN
Ethn.Pam.
3771

　　(Records of the Dominion Museum, Vol. 1,
1942, pp. 61-67)

AS
750
C 22 m

Duff, Roger

　　The Waitara swamp search.

　　(Records of the Canterbury Museum, Vol.
7(4):303-325, 1961)

AS
36
S1

Dufour, Charles, 1827-1903.
　　Directions for observing the scintillation of the stars.
By Ch. Dufour ...
　　(*In* Smithsonian institution. Annual report. 1861. Washington, 1862.
23½ᶜᵐ. p. (220)-227. tab.)
　　Note by L. F. Kämtz, editor of the Repertorium at the end.
"Translated from the 'Repertorium für meteorologie,' etc. Dorpat, 1859."

　　1. Stars—Observations.　ɪ. Kämtz, Ludwig Friedrich, 1801-1867.

S 15-110

Library of Congress　　　Q11.S66 1861
Library, Smithsonian　　　Institution

GN
2.S
P 76

Duff, Roger (S.)

　　A Ngati Raukawa canoe stern-post.

　　(Jour. Poly. Soc., 59(4):368-375, 1951)

GN
2.S
P 76

DUFF, ROGER (S.)

　　Roger Duff, M. A., D. Sc.

　　(Jour. Poly. Soc., 60(2/3):162-163, 1951)

QH
104
U 58-c

Dufresne, Frank

　　Mammals and birds of Alaska.

　　(Circ. 3, 1942, Fish and Wildlife Service,
U. S. Dept. Interior)

GN
2.S
P 76

Duff, Roger

　　Pacific adzes and migrations; a reply to
Andrew Sharp.

　　(Jour. Poly. Soc., 69(3):276-282, 1960)

AM
Mus.Pam.
348

Duff, Wilson

　　Thunderbird park. Victoria, British Columbia
Canada. Photographs by B. C. Government Travel
Bureau. This booklet is compiled and issued by
The British Columbia Government Travel Bureau.
Dept. of trade and industry and printed by The
Printer to the Queen's Most Excellent Majesty.
30 pp.

DUFRESNE, MARION

Kelly, L. G.

1951

　　Marion Dufresne at the Bay of Islands.

UH has

GN
Ethn.
Pam.
3727

Duff, Roger (S.)

　　The Polynesian adze succession. Manuscript,
17 pages.

DU
12
W 74

3 copies
2 in
locked
case.

DUFF (SHIP)

Wilson, James

　　A missionary voyage to the southern Pacific
Ocean, performed in...1796-1798 in the ship Duff,
commanded by Captain James Wilson. Compiled from
journals of the officers and the missionaries...
London. 1799. 4to.

DU
647
G 91

Dugan, Paul F.

　　Historic documents.

　　(Guam Recorder, Vol. 15, No. 3, 1938, pp.
7-9, 36)

GN
2.S
P 76

Duff, Roger (S.)

　　Recent Maori occupation of Notornis Valley,
Te Anau.

　　(Poly. Soc. Journal, 61(1/2):90-119, 1952)

GN
Pam
#342

Duffield, A.J.

Notes on Inhabitants of New Ireland

1884.

Duggar, Benjamin M.

　　Biological effects of radiation. 1936.

UH

GN
2.S
P 76

Duff, Roger (S.)

　　A revised typology of (southern) New Zealand
adzes.

　　(Journal of the Polynesian Society, 54:147-
159, 1945)

QH
11
B 86

Duffy, E. A. J.

　　Cerambycidae.

　　(British Museum (Nat. Hist.), Ruwenzori
Expedition 1934-5, Vol. III(12):165-174, 1953)

QK
603
Du
D86

Duggar, Benjamin Minge

Fungous Diseases of Plants with
chapters on Physiology, Culture Methods
& Technique.

Boston 1909　8ᵛᵒ pp. 508.

DU
Hist.
Pam.
346
a,b,c

Duff, Roger(S.)

　　Unveiling New Zealand's past: background to
the Wairau burials.

　　(The New Zealand Science Review, Vol. 2(1):
8; 1945; Vol. 2(2-3): 13-14, 1944; Vol.3(1):
10-12, 1945)

QL
596.C4
D 85

Duffy, E. A. J.

　　A monograph of the immature stages of Bri-
tish and imported timber beetles (Cerambycidae).
Printed by order of the Trustees of the British
Museum. London. 1953. R8vo. viii +350 pp. +
VIII pl.

G
51
W 17

DUGONG

Church, A. E.

　　The dugong hunt.

　　(Walkabout, XI:no. 7, 1945, pp. 29-30)

QL
733
L 63

DUGONG

Le Soeuf, A. S.

The wild animals of Australasia, embracing the mammals of New Guinea and the nearer Pacific Islands. By A.S.Le Souef and Harry Burrell, with a chapter on the bats of Australia and New Guinea by Ellis Le G. Troughton. George G. Harrap and Company, Ltd. London... 8vo. (1926) 388 pp.

DU
1
P 12

DUGONG   PALAU

Harry, Robert R.

"Eugenie" the dugong mermaid.

(Pacific Discovery, Vol. IX(1):21-27, 1956)

DU
12
L 56

DUHAUT-CILLY, A.

Le Netrel, Edmond

Voyage of the Héros around the world with Duhaut-Cilly in the years 1826, 1827, 1828 and 1829. Translated by Blanch Collet Wagner. Glen Dawson. Los Angeles. 12mo. 1951. (8)+64 pp.

G
51
W 17

DUGONG

Macmillan, L.

The dugong.

(Walkabout, 21(2):17-20, 1955)

AS
540
P

DUGONG PHILIPPINE ISLANDS

Seale, Alvin

Note regarding the dugong in the Philippine Islands.

(Philippine Journal of Sci., X, D:215,1915)

AS
720.V
R 88

Duigan, Suzanne L.

Studies of the pollen grains of plants native to Victoria, Australia, I. Goodeniaceae (including Brunonia).

(Proc. of the R. Soc. of Victoria, New Series, Vol. 74(2):87-109, 1961)

DU
12
J 94

locked
case

DUGONG

Owen, Richard
Notes on the character of the skeleton of a dugong(Helicore Australis) from the North Coast of Australia...
IN
Jukes, Joseph Beete
Narrative of the surveying voyage of H.M.S. Fly...Torres Strait, New Guinea...1842-46... London. 1847. pp. 323-331.

GN
423
D 86

(Duhamel du Monceau, Henry Louis)

Abhandlung von den Fischereien und Geschichte der Fische, oder derer Thiere, die im Wasser leben. Zweeter Abschnitt. Leipzig und Konigsberg, Johann Jacob Kanter. 1773. 4to. 438 pp. pls.

(Schauplatz der Künste und Handwerke...herausgegeben von Daniel Gottfried Schreber...)

QK
9
Du D87
+
K. 11. 4.

Dujardin-Beaumetz and Égasse, E.

Les plantes médicinales indigènes et exotiques, leurs usages thérapeutiques, pharmaceutiques et industriels. Paris 1889. 45 pp. VIII-845

Oct 8 96

G
51
W 17

DUGONG

Patterson, Ewen K.

The dugong hunters.

(Walkabout, Vol. 5(12)43-44,1939)

DU
620
H 4

Dunaut-Cilly, A.

Alexander, W(illiam) D(ewitt)

Incidents of the voyage of the "Heros".

(Hawaiian His. Soc., Fourth Annual Rept., 1896, pp. 26-29)

GN
2.I
A-4

DUK DUK

Pfeil, Graf von

Duk duk and other customs as forms of expression of the Melanesians' intellectual life.

(Journ. Anthrop. Inst. of Great Britain and Ireland, Vol. 27, 1897-8, pp. 181-191)

G
51
W 17

DUGONG

Smart, Peter

The dugong.

(Walkabout, 17(11):34-35, 1951)

DU
12
D 86

locked
case

Duhaut-Cilly, A.

Voyage autour du monde, principalement a la Californie et aux Iles Sandwich, pendant les années 1826, 1827, 1828, et 1829; par A. Duhaut-Cilly...Tomes 1-2. Paris. Bertrand. 1834-1835. 8vo. pp.(11)+409; 439.

over

DU
12
C 78

locked
case

DUKE (SHIP)

Cooke, Edward

Voyage to the south sea and round the world performed in...1708-1711, by the ships Duke and Dutchess of Bristol... 2 vols. London. 1712. 8vo.

DUGONG

See also

SIRENIA

Carter Coll.
6-B-21/22

Duhaut-Cilly, A.

Viaggio intorno al globo principalemente alla California ed alle Isole Sandwich, negli anni 1826, 1827, 1828 e 1829. Con ...osservazioni di Paolo Emilio Botta. Traduzione dal francese nell' italiano di Carlo Botta...Torino Stabilimento Tipografico Fonatan. 1841. Vols. 1-2. 8vo.

DU
12
R 73

Locked
case

DUKE (ship)

Rogers, Woodes

A cruising voyage round the world: first to the South Seas...1708...1711. London. 1712. sm8vo.

QL
1
C 42

DUGONG   TEETH

Fernand, V. S. V.

The teeth of the dugong.

(Ceylon, Jour. of Sci., Sec. B. Zoology, Vol. XXV(2):139-148, 1953)

Duhaut-Cilly, A.

Viaggio intorno al globo principalemente alla California ed alle Isole Sandwich, negli anni 1826, 1827, 1828 e 1829. Con l'aggiunta delle osservazioni sugli abitanti di quei paesi di Paolo Emilio Botta. Traduzione dal francese nell' italiano di Carlo Botta... Torino. Stabilimento tipografico fonatan, 1841. Vols. 1-2 (in one). xvi+296; 392 pp. 22.5 cm.
HMCS

over

G
51
W 77

DUKE OF YORK ISLANDS

Barrett, Charles

Canoeing in tropic seas.

(Walkabout, Vol. 16(8):29-31, 1950)

G
7
R 8

DUKE OF YORK ISLANDS (NEW GUINEA)

Brown, George

Notes on the Duke of York Group, New Britain and New Ireland.

(Journal of the Roy. Geogr. Soc., London, Vol. 47, 1877) pp. 137-150

DUKE OF YORK ISLAND   MYRIAPODA

See

MYRIAPODA   DUKE OF YORK ISLAND

PL
810
D 88

Dumas, Alexandre

O le tulipe uliuli. Faamatalaina e Fanaafi Ma'ia'i mai le tusi a Alexandre Dumas. Published by the Islands Education Section, Dept. of Education, N.Z., for the Dept. of Island Territories, Wellington. sm8vo. 1957. 86 pp.

[The black tulip, translated by Fanaafi Ma'ia'i]

DU
12
C 78

DUKE OF YORK (BISMARCK ARCHIPELAGO)

Cooke, G. A.

New and authentic system of universal geography...pp. 258-59. London. n.d.

DUKE OF YORK ISLANDS   RITES AND CEREMONIES

see

RITES AND CEREMONIES   DUKE OF YORK ISLANDS

QL
461
P 11

Dumbleton, L. J.

Aberrant head-structure in larval Simuliidae (Diptera).

(Pacific Insects, 4(1):77-86, 1962)

DU
550
P7

Duke of York (Island).

Powell, Wilfred.

Wanderings in a wild country.

ref. to New Britain and Duke of York.

DUKE OF YORK ISLANDS   TATTOOING

see

TATTOOING   DUKE OF YORK ISLANDS

AS
36
N 54

Dumbleton, L. J.

Aleyrodidae (Hemiptera: Homoptera) from the South Pacific.

(New Zealand Jour. of Science, 4(4):770-774, 1961)

[Fiji, Rarotonga, Society Islands]

G
13
D

Duke of York Island

Ribbe, C.

Sammelaufenthalt in Neu-Lauenburg.
in Ver. für Erdk. zu Dresden, d[...] 1910-1912.
pp 73-150; 163-222; 273-384;

Note. Contains descriptions and illustrations of fauna, flora and ethnology specimens.

GN
470
D 87

Dulaure, J. A.

Des Divinités Génératrices, chez les anciens et les modernes, avec un chapitre complémentaire par A. Van Gennep. Troisième édition. Paris. Société du Mercure de France. 1905. 12mo. 338 pp.

QH
1
P 11

Dumbleton, L. J.

The Aleyrodidae (Hemiptera-Homoptera) of New Caledonia.

(Pacific Science, Vol. 15(1):114-136, 1961)

DUKE OF YORK ISLANDS   BIRDS

see

BIRDS   DUKE OF YORK ISLANDS

Dulles, Foster Rhea   Carter Coll.
                             10-C-25

The old China trade. Boston...
Houghton Mifflin Co. 1930   228 pp. 8vo.

DU
1
S 72 q

Dumbleton, L. J.

Biological control of the Rhinoceros beetle.

(South Pacific Commission, Quarterly Bull. 5(1):18-19, 1955)

DUKE OF YORK ISLAND   FAUNA

See

FAUNA   DUKE OF YORK ISLAND

GN
2 S
A 22

Dumarest, Noël, 1868-1903.

Notes on Cochiti, New Mexico, by Father Noël Dumarest, with a preface by Stewart Culin; tr. and ed. by Elsie Clews Parsons. Lancaster, Pa., Pub. for the American anthropological association [1919]

cover-title, 1 p. l., p. 137-236. illus., 3 pl. (2 col.) 25ᵉᵐ. (Memoirs of the American anthropological association. vol. VI. no. 3. July-Sept., 1919)

1. Keresan Indians. 2. Cochiti, N. M.   I. Parsons, Mrs. Elsie Worthington (Clews) II. Culin, Stewart i. e. Robert Stewart, 1858-   ed.

Library of Congress   {   }   GN2.A22 vol. VI
                                                    20-23196
                       [9]

AS
36
N 54

Dumbleton, L. J.

The classification and distribution of the Simulidae (Diptera) with particular reference to the genus Austrodimulium.

(New Zealand Journal of Science, 6(3):320-357, 1963)

DUKE OF YORK   LEPIDOPTERA

See

LEPIDOPTERA   DUKE OF YORK

DU
12
D 88

Dumas, Alexandre

The journal of Madame Giovanni. Translated from the French edition (1856) by Marguerite E. Wilbur. With a foreword by Frank W. Reed. Liveright Publishing Corporation. New York. 8vo. xxvii + 404 pp. 1944c.

[material drawn perhaps from some journal, actual source not given by Dumas]

QL
Insect
Fam.
2076

Dumbleton, L. J.

Contribution to the physical ecology of Tortrix postvittana, Walk. (Lep.)

(Bull. Ent. Research, Vol. 30(3):309-319, 1939)

QK
Bot.Pam.
2866

Dumbleton, L. J.

Digest of plant quarantine regulations - second supplement- South Pacific Commission area. Food and Agriculture Organization of the United Nations. Rome, Italy. R8vo. Sept., 1956. 20 mimeographed pp.

AS
36
N 54

Dumbleton, L. J.

New Zealand Blepharoceridae (Diptera: Nematocera)

(New Zealand Jour. of Science, Vol. 6(2): 234-258, 1963)

AS
750
D 67 c
and
QL
Insect
Pam
2061

Dumbleton, L. J.
(Ixodoidea)
The ticks of the New Zealand sub-region.

(Cape Expedition, Sci. Res. of the New Zealand Sub-antarctic Exp., 1941-45, Bull. 14, 1953).

DU
1
S 72 t

Dumbleton, L. J.

A list of communicable diseases and parasites of domestic and some other animals recorded in South Pacific territories.

(South Pacific Commission, Technical Paper No. 77, 1954)

[title also in French]

AS
750
N 56

Dumbleton, L. J.

Notes on New Zealand Diptera.

(Transactions of the Royal Society of New Zealand, Vol. 81(2):239-244, 1953)

AS
36
N 54

Dumbleton, L. J.

The ticks (Acarina:Ixodoidea) of sea birds in New Zealand waters.

(New Zealand Jour. of Science, 4(4):760-769, 1961)

DU
1
S 72t

Dumbleton, L. J.

A list of insect pests recorded in South Pacific territories.

(South Pacific Commission, Technical Paper No. 79, December, 1954)

DU
1
S 72 t

Dumbleton, L. J.

Parasites and predators introduced into the Pacific islands for the biological control of insects and other pests. Corrected and brought up to date by C. P. Hoyt.
(South Pacific Commission, Tech. Paper, No. 101, 1957)

DU
12
H 27

Dumke, Glenn S.

Hardy, Osgood

A history of the Pacific area in modern times. By Osgood Hardy and Glenn S. Dumke. Houghton Mifflin Company. Boston... 1949c R8vo. 752 pp.

DU
1
S 72 t

Dumbleton, L. J.

A list of plant diseases recorded in South Pacific territories.

(South Pacific Commission, Technical Paper No. 78, 1954)

[title and text also in French]

DU
1
S 72 q

Dumbleton, L. J.

Rat poisoning in French Oceania.

(South Pacific Commission, Quarterly Bull. 5(2):15-16, 1955)

QL
Birds
Pam.
368

DuMont, Philip A.

Gooneys sit out second battle of Midway. Fish and Wildlife Service, Washington, D. C. 1954. 4 mimeographed pp.

QH
1
P 11

Dumbleton, L. J.

A new genus of seed-infesting Micropterygid moths.

(Pacific Science, 6(1):17-29, 1952)

DU
1
S 72

Dumbleton, L. J.

Rhinoceros beetle in the Kingdom of Tonga. A report on a visit to Vavau in August, 1952.

(South Pacific Commission, Technical Paper, No. 34:1-6, 1952)

QH
1
A 88

DuMont, Philip A.

Neff, Johnson A.

A partial list of the plants of the Midway Islands. By Johnson A. Neff and Philip A. DuMont

(Atoll Research Bulletin, No. 45, 1955)

AS
36
N 54

Dumbleton, L. J.

A new parasitic mite (Acarina:Trombidiidae) on Orthoptera.

(New Zealand Journal of Science, Vol. 5(1): 8-12, 1962)

DU
1
S 72q

Dumbleton, L. J.

Rhinoceros beetle quarantine and control problems.

(South Pacific Commission Quarterly Bulletin 3(3):2-4, 1953)

PL
Pam
#31

Dumont, Albert

Inscriptions et monuments figures de la Thrace.ex Miss. Scient. III.

QL
461
H-1

Dumbleton, L. J.

A new sub-species of Lallemandana fenestrata (F.) (Homoptera: Cercopidae)

(Proc. Haw. Ent. Soc., 14(1):59-61, 1950)

QH
1
T 88

Dumbleton, L. J.

A synopsis of the ticks (Acarina: Ixodoidea) of New Zealand.

(Tuatara, Vol. 2(2):72-77, 1963)

QK
Bot.Pam.
2655

Dumont D'Urville
D'Urville, Dumont and others

[Descriptions of Carex from various sources] D'Urville, Dumont Flore des Malouines. (Mem. Soc. Linn., Paris, 4:592-621, 1826. pp. 598-9 only are here.

...see under CAREX for full list of these references.

DU 12 D 89 Dumont d'Urville, J. S. C.

New Zealand, 1826-1827. (From the French of Dumont d'Urville, an English translation... by Olive Wright...) Printed by the Wingfield Press for Olive Wright. R8vo. (1950) 251 pp.

DU Pac. Pam. 999 Dumont d'Urville, Jules Sebastian César

Sur les iles du grand océan.

(Bull. Soc. de Géographie (Paris, Tome 17 (105):1-21, 1832)

[within, d'Urville splits up the Pacific into Melanesia, Micronesia, Polynes- the first to do so?]

DU 12 D 89 Dumont d'Urville, Jules Sébastian César

Voyage de découvertes autour du monde et a la recherche de La Pérouse, par M.J. Dumont d'Urville, capitaine de vaisseau, exécuté sous son commandement et par ordre du gouvernement, sur la corvette l'Astrolabe, pendant les années 1826, 1827, 1828, et 1829. Histoire du voyage. 5 vols. in 10 pts. Paris. Roret. 1832-1834. 8vo.

Dumont d'Urville, Jules Sebastian César

Voyage de la corvette l'Astrolabe, exécuté par ordre du Roi, pendant les années 1826-1827-1828-1829...

DU12D89   Histoire du voyage, Tomes 1-5, 1830-1833, with folio atlas, Vols. 1-2.

Q115D89   Botanique: (1 volume)
Part I. Essai d'une flore de la Nouvelle-locked Zélend, par M. A. Richard. 1832-1833.
case   Part II. Sertum Astrolabianum...par M. Lesson et M. A. Richard. 1833-1834
(plates for botany included with those for entomology in 1 atlas)   continued on next card

---

Card 2

Dumont d'Urville, Jules Sebastian César

Voyage de la corvette l'Astrolabe, exécuté par ordre du Roi, pendant les années 1826-29...

Q115D89   Faune Entomologique de l'Océan Pacifique... par...Boisduval: Lépidoptères et Coléoptères. 1832,1835. (plates for entomology and botany are included in one folio atlas)
locked case   Zoologie, par Quoy et Gaimard: Tome 1, L'Homme-Mammifères-Oiseaux, 1830-33; Tome 2-3, Mollusques-Poissons, 1832-35; Tome 4, Zoophytes, 1833-34. Folio atlas, Vols 1-2.
Continued on next card

Card 3

Dumont d'Urville, Jules Sebastian César

Voyage de la corvette l'Astrolabe, exécuté par ordre du Roi, pendant les années 1826-29...

Q115D89   Philologie, par d'Urville. Tomes 1-2, 1833-1834.
locked case
Paris. J. Tastu. 8vo and folio. 1830-35.

Card 1

Dumont d'Urville, Jules Sébastian César

Voyage au Pôle Sud et dans l'Océanie sur les corvettes L'Astrolabe et la Zélée; exécuté... pendant...1837-1840, sous le commandement de M.J. Dumont-d'Urville...publié...sous la direction supérieure de (C.H.) Jacquinot...
locked case   Histoire du voyage, par M.Dumont d'Urville.
DU 12 D89   Texte, Tomes 1-10, 1841-1846; Atlas, 1846.
Q115D89   Anthropologie, par M. Dumoutier. Texte, 1 Tome, 1854; Atlas, 1842-1847.
OVER   continued on next card

Card 2

Q 115 D 39 locked case Dumont d'Urville, Jules Sébastien César

Voyage au Pôle Sud...
Botanique. Atlas only, incomplete.
HAVE plates. Monocotyledones Cryptogames, Nos. 3bis, 4-5; Monocotyledones Phanérogames, Nos 4,6. Dicotyledones Phanérogames, Nos. 1-5,7-16, 19-22, 22bis, 23. Cryptogamie, Nos. 6-10, 12-20.

Paris. Gide et Baudry. 8vo. and folio. 1852
Continued on next card

Card 3

Q 115 D 89 locked case Dumont d'Urville, Jules Sébastien César

Voyage au Pôle Sud...
Géologie, Minéralogie et Géographie Physique du Voyage, par M. J. Grange. Texte, 2 tomes in 1, 1848-1854. Atlas, 1847.
Zoologie, par Hombron et H.Jacquinot. Texte, Tomes 1-5, 1846-1854. Atlas, Tomes 1-2, 1842-1853.

Paris. Gide et Baudry. 8vo. and folio.

Q 115 D 92 locked case Duperrey, Louis Isadore

Voyage autour du monde, exécuté par ordre du Roi, sur la corvette...La Coquille, pendant les années 1822-1825...
Botanique, par d'Urville, Bory de St. Vincent et A. Brongniart. With atlas, 1827-1834. Paris. 4to and folio.

Dumont d'Urville, J. S. C.

Voyage de l'Astrolabe...pendant...1826-29... atlas, Vols. 1-2, Paris, 1830

HHS also has

(aud text?)

G 159 D 89 Dumont d'Urville, Jules Sébastien César

Voyage pittoresque autour du monde; resumé général des voyages de découvertes de Magellan, Tasman, Dampier, Anson...Accompagné de cartes et de nombreuses gravures en taille-douce sur acier, d'après les dessins de M. De Sainson...2 vols. 4to. Paris. L. Tenré. 1834-1835. viii + 576; 581 pp.

AS 750 N DUMONT D'URVILLE

Visit to Tolaga Bay - 1927 (N.Z.J. 1906)
Exploration of Tasman Bay (1907)
Visit to Whangarei, Waitemata & the Thames - 1827 - (N.Z.J. 1909)
(Trans. from the French by S. Percy Smith.)

DU 12 L 52 locked case Dumont d'Urville, Jules Sébastien César

Le Guillou, Élie

Voyage autour du monde de l'Astrolabe et de la Zélée, sous les ordres du contre-amiral Dumont d'Urville, pendant...1837-1840...Vols. 1-2. Paris. 1842. 8vo.

QK Bot. Pam. 2700 DUMONT D'URVILLE, JT

Chevalier, Auguste

Numéro spécial consacré au souvenir de l'Amiral J. Dumont d'Urville, prospecteur de la flore de l'Océanie et de l'Hémisphère austral de 1822 à 1840.

(Revue Internationale de Botanique Appliquee et d'Agriculture Tropicale, Annee 31(339-340):1-136, 1951)

Q 115 D 89 Dumoutier,(Pierre Marie Alexandre)

Anthropologie

Dumont d'Urville, Jules Sébastien César

Voyage au Pôle Sud et dans l'Océanie sur les corvettes l'Astrolabe et la Zélée... Anthropologie Texte (in 1 tome), 1854 and Atlas, 1842-47.

DU 700 V 76 Dumoutier, P. M. A.

Notice phrénologique sur les naturels de l'archipel Nouka-Hiva

Vincendon-Dumoulin, A. C., and Desgraz, C.

Iles Marquises, ou, Nouka-Hiva... Paris. 1843. pp. 292-304.

Z 671 S 74 Dun, G. S.

Rhinoceros beetle control in Papua and New Guinea.

(South Pacific Commission Quarterly Bulletin, Vol. 3(4):12, 1954)

DU 719 A Dun, W. S.

Robert Etheridge, Junior. Obituary. In Australian Mus. Rec. Vol. XV, pp 1-27, port., 1926.

[Bibliography compiled by W. A. Rainbow, pp 5 - 27]

DU 12 D89. Dunbabin, Thomas

The making of Australasia. A brief history of the origin and development of the British dominions in the South Pacific.

London, Black, 1922, 258 pp.

DU .12 D 90 Dunbabin, Thomas

Slavers of the south seas. Sydney. Angus & Robertson, Ltd. 1935. sm8vo. xiv + 308 pp.

DU
Pacific Dunbabin, Thomas
Pam.
No.149   White Japanese . Britain's lost colony
of the Bonins . From The Sun, Aug. 26,
1923.

[Newspaper clipping]

QL   Dunbar, M. J.
C 2-bu   The Pinnipedia of the Arctic and Subarctic.

(Bull. Fisheries Research Board of Canada,
No. 85, 1949)

QL   Duncker, Georg
Ham
Die Fische der Südsee-Expedition der Hamburgischen Wissenschaftlichen Stiftung, 1908-1909,
von Georg Duncker und Erna Mohr. Teil 1-3

(In Mitteilungen Zool. Staatsinst. und Zool
Mus. Hamburg, Bd. 41:93-112, 1925, Bd. 42:126-
136, 1926, Bd. 44:57-84 pp., 1931 — ?)

QL
Prot.-   Dunbar, Carl O.
Poly.Pam.
784   Fusuline Foraminifera.

(Geol. Soc. Amer., Mem. 67:753-54 (of Vol.
2), 1957)

Duncan, David D.

Yap meets the Yanks.

(National Geographic Magazine, 89:364-372,
March, 1946)

QN   Dundas, Charles
Pam
2710   The organization and laws of some Bantu
tribes in East Africa. From _____

QE
Geology   Dunbar, Carl O.   & Condra, G   E
Pam
721   The fusulinidae of the Pennsylvanian system
in Nebraska. From Nebraska Geological Survey,
Bull. 2, second ser., 1927.

QC
Physics   Duncan, J. F.
and
Meteoro-   Radioactivity in the service of man.
logy   Thomas Cawthron Memorial Lecture, No. 34, 1959
Pam.   Cawthron Institute, Nelson, New Zealand. 43 pp.
50

QK   DUNES
Bot.Pam.
2561   Chapman, Valentine Jackson

The stabilization of sand-dunes by vegetation.
(Proc. Conference on Biol. and Civil Engineering, Institution of Civil Engineers, Sept.
1948, 4th session, pp. 142-157)
[reprinted, Auckland Univ. College Reprints
Bor. ser. No. 7]

QL
Mollusca   Dunbar, Carl O.
Pam.
668   New Fusulinid Genera from the Permian of
West Texas by Carl O.Dunbar and John Skinner.

(From American Journal of Science, Vol. XXII,
Sept. 1931, pp. 252-268, 3 plates).

QL
383.9   Duncan, P   Martin
D91   A memoir on the echinodermata of the
Arctic Sea to the west of Greenland.

London, Van Voorst, 1881.   80p.   pls.

QK   DUNES
101
G 65   Cooper, W. S.

The strand and dune flora of the Pacific
coast of North America: a geographic study.

Goodspeed, T. H.
Essays in geobotany...Setchell. 1936.
pp. 141-187

AM
Mus. Pam.   Dunbar, Carl O.
376   Yale's Peabody Museum.

(Yale Alumni Magazine, Oct. 1956:10-24)

QE
778   Duncan, P   Martin
D91   A monograph of the fossil corals and
alcyonaria of Sind, collected by the geological
survey of India.

London, Taylor and Francis, 1880.   110p. pls.
(Palaeontologia Indica, ser. 14.)

QK   DUNES
915
M 37   Martin, Emmett V.

Adaptation and origin in the plant world.
1. Factors and functions in coastal dunes, by
Emmett V. Martin and Frederic E. Clements.
(Carnegie Institution of Washington Publication
No. 521, 1939)

AM
Mus.   Dunbar, Ruth
Pam.384   The story of a state museum: State Capitol
Museum, Olympia, Washington. 8vo. 20 pp.

QD   Duncan, Robert Kennedy
453
D 91   The New Knowledge: A popular account
of the new physics and the new chemistry in
their relation to the new theory of matter.
New York, 1906, 8vo. pp. 263, illustr.

Bingham Coll.

QK   DUNES
Bot.Pam.
2561   van der Burgt, Johan Henri

The use of vegetation to stabilize sand-
dunes. By Johan Henri van der Burgt and Leonard
van Bendegom.
(Proc. Conference on Biol. and Civil Engineering, Institution of Civil Engineers, Sept.
1948, 4th session, pp. 158-180)
[reprinted, Auckland Univ. College Reprints,
Bot. ser. No. 7]

G
7   Duncan, David
N 17   Directions for Tongataboo Anchorage, Friendly Islands.

(Nautical Magazine, Vol. II, 1833, pp. 503-
504)

Duncker, G.

Die Fische der malayischen Halbinsel. n.d.

UH

QE
Geology   DUNES   NEW ZEALAND
Pam.
1349   Cockayne, L.(eonard)

Report on the dune-areas of New Zealand,
their geology, botany, and reclamation. New
Zealand. Department of Lands. Wellington.
1911. folio. 76 pp. numbered C-13.

QL
752
U 58

Dung, Dorothy I. Y.

Morphometric measurements of Pacific scombrids. By Dorothy I. Y. Dung and William F. Royce.

(U. S. Dept. of the Interior, Fish and Wild. Service; Special Sci. Rept.:Fisheries No. 95, 1953)

Dunlop, W. R.

Poisonous fishes in the West Indies.

(West Indian Bulletin, Vol. 16, 1917, pp. 159-167)

UH

AS
36
A65

Dunn, Emmett Reid

Lizards from the East Indies. Am. Mus. Nov. 288, 1927.

(Results of the Douglas Burden expedition to the island of Komodo. III).

QE
Geol.
Pam.
1046

Dunham, Franklin P.   and others

Frontiers of geology. Pamphlet published by the Geol. Soc. of America. Dec. 1939, 8vo. 48 pp.
[Introduction by Charles P. Berkey; Geology and the layman, by George F. Kay; Submarine canyons, by Paul A. Smith; Shifting ocean levels, by Douglas Johnson; Origin of mountains...by Chester R. Longwell; Deep earthquakes, by L. B. Slichter; The role of minerals...by C.K.Leith; Geology in engineering, by Charles P. Berkey...]

G5
A
1

Dunlop, W. R.

Queensland and Jamaica: A comparative study in geographical economics. In Am. Geog. Rev. Oct. 1926.

AS
36
A65

Dunn, Emmett Reid

Notes on varanus komodoensis. Am. Mus. Nov. 286, 1927.

(Results of the Douglas Burden expedition to the island of Komodo. n.1)

QL
402
G 23

locked
case

Dunker, Guil.

Mollusca nova Musei Godeffroy Hamburgensis. (Malakozoologische Blätter, Bd. 18, 1871, pp. 150-175)

(Garrett collection of papers on conchology, Vol. 19)

AG
150
D92

Dunman, Thomas

A glossary of biological, anatomical, and physiological terms.

New York, Appleton, 1879.   161p.

AS
36
A 25

Dunn, Emmett Reid,

The salamanders of the family Hynobiidae. Proc. Am. Academy of Arts and Sciences, Vol. 58, No. 13, pp.445-523.1923

QL
401
C 44

Dunker, W.

Beschreibung einiger von Herrn Dr. v. Hochstetter auf Neuseeland gesammelten Susswasser-Mollusken.

(Malakozoologische Blätter. Bd. 8, 1862, p. 150-154)

QL
671
E 39

Dunmire, William W.

Bird populations in Hawaii Volcanoes National Park.

(The Elepaio, Vol. 22(9), 1962)

AS
36
S4

Dunn, Emmett Reid.

The salamanders of the genera *Desmognathus* and *Leurognathus*. By Emmett R. Dunn ...

(In U. S. National museum. Proceedings. Washington, 1917. 23½ᵐ. v. 53, p. 393-433. illus. (incl. maps))

Bibliography: p. 429-433.

1. Salamanders.

18-14637

Library of Congress   Q11.U55 vol. 53

Q
115
H 23

Dunkle, Meryl Byron

Plant ecology of the Channel Islands of California.

Reports
(Allan Hancock Pacific Expeditions, Vol. 13(3), 1950)

QL
671
E 39

Dunmire, William W.

Peregrine falcon in Hawaii National Park.

(The Elepaio, 21(11):80-81, 1961)

[Falco peregrinus]

AS
36
A 16 n

Dunn, Emmett Reid

Zoological results of the Denison-Crockett Expedition to the south Pacific for the Academy of Natural Sciences of Philadelphia, 1937-1938. Part II.- Amphibia and Reptilia.

(Notulae Naturae, No. 14, 1939, Acad. Nat. Sci. Philadelphia)

QK
1
O 11

Dunlap, Albert A.

The Total Nitrogen and Carbohydrates, and the Relative Rates of Respiration, in Virus-Infected Plants.

Contributions from the Osborn Botanical Laboratory, Yale University, V. (American Journal of Botany, XVII: 348-357, May, 1930)

GN
1
O 15

Dunn, Diane   and others

The blood groups of a third series of New Guinea natives from Port Moresby. By Diane Dunn, Olga Kooptzoff, A.V.G.Price and R. J. Walsh.

(Oceania, 27(1):56-63, 1956)

AS
36
A 16 n

Dunn, Emmett Reid

Zoological results of the George Vanderbilt South Pacific Expedition of 1937. Part III. The lizards of Malpelo Island, Colombia.

(Notulae Naturae, No.4,1939,pp. 1-8)

GN
Ethn.Pam.
3655

Dunlap, Helen L.

Games, sports, dancing, and other vigorous recreational activities and their function in Samoan culture.

(reprint, the Research Quarterly of the American Association for Health, Physical Education, and Recreation, 22:298-311, 1951)

GN
432
D92

Dunn, Eliza

Rugs in their native land.

New York, Prang,[1903].   155p.   pls.

GN
2.M
P

Dunn, Leslie C

An anthropometric study of Hawaiians of pure and mixed blood: based upon data collected by Alfred M. Tozzer. Papers of Peabody Mus. Of Arch. & Ethno. v.XI, n.3, 1928.

GN
Pam
2665   separate

QH
368
D 92

Dunn, L. C.

Heredity and evolution in human populations.
Harvard University Press. Cambridge, Mass.
1959. sm8vo. viii + 157 pp.

QL
Mammals
Pam.
156

Dunnet, G. M.

A population study of the quokka, Setonix
brachyurus Quoy & Gaimard (Marsupialia), part
III.

(Reprint, C.S.I.R.O. Wildlife Research,
Vol. 8(1):78-117, 1963)

DU
12
D 93

locked
case

Q
115
D 93

locked
case

Du Petit-Thouars, Abel (Aubert)

Voyage autour du monde sur la frégate La
Venus, pendant les années 1836-1839...
(Relation), Tomes 1-4 (in 2), 1840-45, with
Atlas Pittoresque, 1841.   1864
Botanique, par J. Decaisne, 34 pp. with
atlas of 28 plates, 1846.
Zoologie...1855, 351 pp. with atlas, 1846.

Paris, Gide et J. Baudry. 1840-55. 8vo and
folio.

 over

QH
431
S 61

Dunn, L. C.
Sinnott, Edmund W.

Principles of genetics. By Edmund W. Sinnott,
L. C. Dunn and Th. Dobzhansky. 4th Edition, 2nd
impression. McGraw-Hill Book Company, Inc.
New York, Toronto, London. 1950. R8vo. xiv +
505 pp.

QC
721
D 92

and
QC
Physics
and
Meteorol-
Pam.
43

Dunning, Gordon M.   editor

Radioactive contamination of certain areas
in the Pacific Ocean from nuclear tests; a summary of the data from the radiological surveys
and medical examinations. U. S. Atomic Energy
Commission. August 1957. 4to.vii + 53 pp.

DU
50
E 96

Du Petit-Thouars, L. M. A. A.

Sa Campagne dans les Mers du Sud (1879-1881)

Etablissements Francais du Pacifique Austral...
pp. i-iv (Annexe).

AS
720.V
M

Dunn, R. A.

New Pedipalpi from Australia and the Solomon Islands.

(Memoirs of the National Museum of Victoria,
No. 16, 1949:7-15)

DU
12
D 92

locked
case

see next
card

Card 1

Duperrey, Louis Isadore

Voyage autour du monde, exécuté par ordre du
Roi, sur la Corvette...La Coquille, pendant les
années 1822, 1823, 1824 et 1825...
Partie Historique, with atlas. (1826)

(see also natural history volumes,-
Q 115 D 92 locked case)   and
(Lesson, P. Voyage autour du monde sur la
la corvette La Coquille...) DU 12 L 64 l.c.)

GN
2.8
O 15

Dupeyrat, André

Essai de classification des peuplades de
Papouasie.

(Jour. de la Soc. des Océanistes, Tome
18(18):21-68, 1962)

QK
1
Ke

Dunn, Stephen Troyte, and Tutcher, W. J.

Flora of Kwantung and Hongkong (China); being
an account of the flowering plants, ferns and fern
allies together with keys for their determination.
London, Royal Botanic Gardens, Kew, 1912.
370 p.
Bulletin of Miscellaneous Information,
Additional series, X.

Q
115
D 92

locked
case

see also DU12D92 l.c.

Card 2

Duperrey, L(ouis) I(sadore)

Voyage autour du monde, exécuté par ordre du
Roi, sur la Corvette...La Coquille, pendant les
années 1822, 1823, 1824 et 1825...
Zoologie, par Lesson et Garnot. 2 Tomes (in
4) and atlas, Tomes 1-3. 1826-1831.
Botanique, par D'Urville...Cryptogamie par
Bory de St. Vincent; Phanerogamie par A.Brongni-
art, with atlas. 1827-1834.
Hydrographie, par L.I.Duperrey, with atlas.
1829; and Physique, par L.I.Duperrey. 1829.
Paris. Arthus Bertrand. 4to and folio.
Partie Historique.

Dupeyrat, A.

Mitsinari; twenty-one years among the Papuans. 1954.

UH has

QK
1
Ke

and

QK
Bot.Pam.
1601

Dunn, Stephen Troyte

The Hongkong Herbarium.

(Bulletin of Miscellaneous Information,Kew.
1910, pp. 188-192)

QL
435
C 95

Duperry, L. I.

Voyage autour du monde...Coquille.

Holthuis, L. B.
On the dates of publication of the crustacean plates in Duperry's "Voyage autour du
monde...Coquille."

(Crustaceana, 3(2):168-9, 1961)

Dupeyrat, A.

Papuan conquest.   1948

UH

AS
36
A65

Dunn, Emmett Reid

Snakes from the East Indies. Am. Mus. Nov.
287, 1927.

(Results of the Douglas Burden expedition to
the island of Komodo. II).

Duperry, M. L. I.

Voyage autour du monde...sur...la Coquille
pendant...1822-1925...
B

HHS has atlas, Zoologie, and text, 2 vols.
by Lesson and Garnot, Paris, 1826.

GN
2.8
O 15

Dupeyrat, R. P. André

Les races de la Papouasie.

(Journal de la Soc. des Oceanistes, 7:247-
249, 1951)

QL
461
P 11

Dunnet, G. M.

Insects of Macquarie Island. Siphonaptera.

(Pacific Insects, 4(4):972, 1962)

Corridor
Case
40

Du Petit Thouars

French government and the islands in
the Pacific. from "Le Semeur" April 5, 1843.
Paris. In the Eclectic Museum, June, 1843.
pp. 165-269. Separate.

DU
740
D 93

Dupeyrat, André

Le sanglier de Kouni: Pere Chabot, missionaire en Papouasie. Dillen et Cie. Issoudun
(Indre). 1951. 8vo. 211 pp.

DU 740 D 93 — Dupeyrat, André

    Savage Papua, a missionary among cannibals. Translated from the French by Erik and Denyse Demauny. Preface by Paul Claudel. With illustrations and endpaper map. E. P. Dutton and Company, Inc. New York 1954. 8vo. 256 pp.

DU 623 D 94 — Du Puy, William Atherton

    Hawaii and its race problem. U.S. Dept. of the Interior. Washington. 1932. 8vo. x + 131 pp.

GN Pam 1712 — Durand, J. P.

    Questions anthropologiques et zoologiques. From Soc. d'anthrop. d. Paris, bull. 1895.

DS Asia Pam. 55 — du Plantier, Nicolas

    La Grande Comore : sa colonisation.

    (Revue Coloniale. 1904: 61 pp.)

QK Bot.Pam. 2816 — Durairatnam, M.

    Ceylon's red seaweed resources. By M. Durairatnam and J. C. Medcof.

    (The Ceylon Trade Journal, Vol. XIX(4), 1954)

Durand, M.

    Le système tonal du Tahitien. 1951.

    UH has

AS 145 B — Dupond, Charles

    Contribution à l'étude de la faune ornithologique des Iles Philippines et des Indes Orientales Néerlandaises.

    (Mem. Musée R. d'Hist. Nat. de Belgique, 82, Fasc. 23, 1942)

QK Bot. Pam. 3222 — Durairatnam, M.

    Contribution to the study of the marine algae of Ceylon.

    (Dept. of Fisheries, Ceylon, Fisheries Research Station, Bull. no. 10, 1961)

QK 1 B 91 — Durand, Th.

    Matériaux pour la flore du Congo, by Th. Durand and Em(ile) de Wildeman.

    (Bull. de la Soc. Royale de Botanique de Belgique, Vol.36, 1897, Part 2,fasc2,pp.47-97; Vol.37,1898,Part 1,fasc1, pp.44-128;Vol.38,1899, Part 2,fasc.2,pp.9-74;78-116,120-168,171-220;Vol. 39,1900,Part 2,fasc.1,pp.24-37,fasc.2,pp.53-82, 93-112; Vol.40, 1901,Part 1,fasc.1,pp.7-41,Part2 fasc.3, pp.62-74)

Dupeyrat, A.

    Vingt et un ans chez les Papous. Nouv. ed. 1952.

    UH has

QK Bot.Pam. 3299 — Durairatnam, M.

    Some marine algae from Ceylon, I.

    (Fisheries Research Station, Ceylon, Bull. 15:1-16, 1962)

AS 36 S1 — Durand, William Frederick, 1859–
Robert Henry Thurston. By Prof. W. F. Durand.
    (*In* Smithsonian institution. Annual report. 1903. Washington, 1904. 23½ᶜᵐ. p. 843-849. front. (port.))

    1. Thurston, Robert Henry, 1839-1903.

    S 15-1226

Library of Congress   Q11.S66 1903
Library, Smithsonian   Institution

AS 145 B — Dupond, Ch.

    Oiseaux

Van Straelen, V.
    Résultats scientifiques du voyage aux Indes Orientales Néerlandaises...Léopold de Belgique, Vol. 5, Fasc. 4, 1937, pp. 1-63.

    (Mem. hors ser. Mus. Roy. d'Hist. Nat. Belgique)

AS 36 A-93 — Durand, Elias *i. e.* Élie Magloire, 1794-1873.
    A sketch of the botany of the basin of the Great Salt Lake of Utah. (*In* Transactions of the American philosophical society. Philadelphia, 1860. 29ᶜᵐ. new ser. vol. XI, p. 155-180)

    1. Botany—Utah.

Library of Congress   Q11.P6   5-23750†
—— Copy 2, de-   tached.
Library of Congress   QK189.D9

GN 470 D 94 — Durandus, William

    The symbolism of churches and church ornaments: a translation of the first book of the Rationale Divinorum Officiorum...with an introductory essay and notes by the Rev. John Mason Neale and the Rev. Benjamin Webb. Third edition. London. Gibbings & Co. 1906. 8vo. xvii + 195 pp.

QL 597 D 93 — du Porte, E. Melville

    Manual of insect morphology. Reinhold Publishing Corporation. New York. R8vo. 1959c xi + 224 pp.

DU Pac.Fam. 842 — Durand, John D.

    The population of Western Samoa.

    (Reports on the Population of Trust Territories, No. 1, 1948. United Nations, Dept. of Social Affairs, Population Division)

AM Mus.Pam. 197 — Durban Museum

    General guide to the Durban Museum, with three plans and 24 photographic illustrations. 4th edition. 1948. 62 pp. by E.C.Chubb.

HC 106 W 66 — Du Puy, William Atherton

Wilbur Ray Lyman
    Conservation in the Department of the Interior, by Ray Lyman Wilbur and William Atherton Du Puy. Washington. 1931. U.S. Gov't Printing Office. 8vo. 253 pp.

Durand, Jules

    Chez les Ouebias, en Nouvelle Caledonie.

    (Tour du monde, 6, 1900, 493-516)

QK Bot. Pam. 1869 — Du Rietz, G. Einar

    Classification and nomenclature of vegetation.

    (Svensk Botanisk Tidskrift, Bd. 24, H. 4, 1930, pp.489-503)

QK
Bot. Pam.
1871

Du Rietz, G. Einar

The fundamental units of biological taxonomy.

(Svensk Botanisk Tidskrift, Bd. 24, H. 3, 1930, pp. 333-428)

AS
36
C 15 p

Durham, J. Wyatt

Corals from the Galapagos and Cocos Islands. Scientific Results of the Galapagos Expedition, 1953-54 of the International Institute for Submarine Research...

(Proc. Calif. Acad. Sci., ser. 4, Vol. 32(2) 41-56, 1962)

QK
Bot.Pam.
2867

DURIO BORNEO

Kostermans, A. J. G. H.

Beberapa keterangan tentang djenis durian dalam hutan dekat Samarinda (Kalimantan Timur) (Some notes on Durio spp. found in the forests near Samarinda, Eastern Borneo. Summary)

(Rimba Indonesia, Th. II(4):164-169,

QK
Bot. Pam.
1870

Du Rietz, G. Einar

The long-tubed New Zealand species of Euphrasia (Siphonidium Armstr.) .

(Svensk Botanisk Tidskrift, Bd. 25, H. 1, 1931, pp. 108-125)

QE
G 3 m

Durham, J. Wyatt

Corals from the Gulf of California and the North Pacific coast of America.

(Geol. Soc. Amer., Memoir 20, 1946)

GN
470
D 96

Durkheim, Émile

The elementary forms of the religious life, a study in religious sociology. Translated from the French by Joseph Ward Swain. London. Allen & Unwin. n.d. vo. xi + 456 pp.

QK
Bot. Pam.
1868

Du Rietz, G. Einar

On Domatia in the genus Nothofagus.

(Svensk Botanisk Tidskrift, Bd. 24, H. 4, 1930, pp. 504-510)

Q
115
H 23

Durham, J. Wyatt

Stony corals of the eastern Pacific collected by the Velero III and Velero IV. By J. Wyatt Durham and J. Laurens Barnard.

(Allan Hancock Pacific Expeditions, Vol. 16:1, 1952)

DUROUR ISLAND

See

AUA ISLAND

QK
1
U69

Du Reitz, G. Einar

Problems of bipolar plant distribution.

(Acta Phytogeographica Suecica, XIII, 1940, pp. 215-282)

QR
101
M 92

Durham, Oren C.

Air-borne Fungus spores as allergens.

Moulton, Forest Ray   editor
Aerobiology, pp. 32-47. Washington, 1942.

GN
668
R 62

2 copies

Durrad, W. J.

The Depopulation of Melanesia.

Rivers, W. H. R.

Essays on the depopulation of Melanesia... pp. 3-24. Cambridge. 1922.

QK
Bot. Pam.
1872

Du Rietz, G. Einar

Two new species of Euphrasia from the Philippines and their phytogeographical significance.

(Svensk Botanisk Tidskrift, Bd. 25, H. 4, 1931, pp. 500-542)

QK
Bot.
Pam.
3211

DURIO

Kostermans, A. J. G. H.

The genus Durio Adans. (Bombac.)

(Reinwardtia, 4(3):47-153, 1958)

GN
1
O 15

Durrad, W. J.

Notes on the Torres Islands.

(Oceania, Vol. X, 1940, pp. 389-403; Vol. XI, 1940, pp. 75-109; 186-201

Durham, Bill

Canoes and kayaks of Western America. Copper Canoe Press. Seattle. 1960 $5.00

QK
Bot.
Pam.
3097

DURIO

Kostermans, A.J.G.H.

A monograph of the genus Durio Adans. (Bombacaceae), Part I, Bornean species. By A.J. G.H. Kostermans and W. Soegeng Reksodihardjo.

(Communication of the Forest Research Institute, Indonesia, Nr. 61, Apr. 1958)

GN
2,S
P 76

Durrad, W. J.

A Tikopian vocabulary. Edited by Herbert W. Williams, compiled mainly from materials collected by the Rev. W. J. Durrad.
(Journal of the Polynesian Society, 35: 267-289, 1926; 36: 1-20, 99-117, 1927.)

QE
1
G 3

Durham, J. Wyatt

Cenozoic marine climates of the Pacific coast.

(Bull. Geol. Soc. America, Vol. 61:1243-1264, 1950)

QK
Bot.Pam.
2798

DURIO

Kostermans, A. J. G. H.

Notes on durian (Durio) species of East Borneo.

(Reprint from De Tropische Natuur, 33. 1., pp. 31-35, 1953)

D'Urville

See

Dumont-d'Urville

3

GN
2.S
P 76

Durward, Elizabeth W.

The Maori population of Otago.

(Journal of the Polynesian Society, 42: 49-82, 1933.)

QE
Geol.
Pam.
1089

DUST VOLCANIC

Arctowski, Henryk

Volcanic dust veils and climatic variations.

(Annals of the New York Acad. of Sci., Vol. 26:149-174, 1915)

DS
615
B 87

DUTCH EAST INDIES

Brown, J. M.

The Dutch East. Sketches and pictures...
London. 1914. 8vo.

QL
Birds
Pam.
442

Dury, Charles

The passenger pigeon, Ectopistes migratorius, Linn.

(The Journal of the Cincinnati Soc. of Nat. Hist., 21(2):52-56, 1910)

GN
Ethn.Pam.
2920

Dustin, Fred

Report on Indian Earthworks in Ogemaw County, Michigan.

(Cranbrook Institute of Science, Bloomfield Hills, Michigan. Scientific Publication No.1, September 1932. viii + 25 pp. 8vo.)

QH
186
D 16

DUTCH EAST INDIES

Dammerman, K. W.

Preservation of Wild Life and Nature Reserves in the Netherlands Indies. Fourth Pacific Science Congress, Java, 1929. (Weltevreden).

QL
Insect
Pam.
1973

Dury, Charles

Synopsis of the coleopterous family Cisidae (Cioidae) of America north of Mexico.

(Cincinnati Soc. Nat. Hist., Journal, Vol. 22(2):1-27, 1917)

AG
19
Ho

DUTCH DICTIONARY

Holtzer, Otto (Nachfolger)

A new pocket- dictionary of the English and Dutch languages.

Leipzig, 1899.

G
161
H

DUTCH EAST INDIES

Fryer, John

A new account of East India and Persia, being nine years' travels, 1672-1681. Edited with notes and an introduction by William Crooke. Vol. II. (Vol. I lacking)

(Works issued by the Hakluyt Society, Ser. II. No. 20, 1912)

Q
115
P 29

Dusén, Per

Bryophyta.

Princeton University
Reports of the Princeton University Expeditions to Patagonia, 1896-1899. Vol. VIII:Botany, Part III. 1903.

QH
186
N-57

transferred
to
Reading
Room
Map
Case

DUTCH EAST INDIES

Atlas van tropisch Nederland.
Uitgegeven door het Koninklijk Nederlandsch Aardrijkskundig Genootschap...met dan Topografischen Dienst in Nederlandsch-Indie. 1938. folio. 31 blad.

Q
125. NI
H 77

DUTCH EAST INDIES

Honig, Pieter editor

Science and scientists in the Netherlands Indies. Edited by Pieter Honig and Frans Verdoorn. Board for the Netherlands Indies, Surinam and Curacao. New York. 1945. R8vo. xxii + 491 pp.

Q
115
P 29

Dusén, Per joint author

Revision of Flora Patagonica by George Macloskie and Per Dusén. With further notes by Carl Skottsberg.

Princeton University
Reports of the Princeton University Expeditions to Patagonia, 1896-1899, Vol. VIII: Botany, Supplement. 1914.

DU
12
B 21

DUTCH EAST INDIES

Banks, Sir Joseph

Journal...during Captain Cook's first voyage in 1768-71...edited by Sir Joseph D. Hooker. London. 1896. 8vo. pp. 331-417.

DS
Asia Pam.
40

DUTCH EAST INDIES

Indonesia, History and growth.

(Netherlands News Letter, Vol. 2, No. 5, 1947)

Q
115
P 29

Dusén, Per

The Vegetation of Western Patagonia.

Princeton University
Reports of the Princeton University Expeditions to Patagonia, 1896-1899. Vol. VIII: Part 1, pp. 1-33. 1903.

G
161
H

DUTCH EAST INDIES

Best, Thomas

The voyage of Thomas Best to the East Indies, 1612-14. London.

(Works of the Hakluyt Society, Ser. II, Vol. 75, 1934)

DS
615
K 36

DUTCH EAST INDIES

Kennedy, Raymond

The ageless Indies. The John Day Company. New York. 1942c. 8vo. xvi + 208 pp.

GN
Pam.
#70

Dussaud, Rene

Les sacrifices humains chez les Cananéens.

Paris, 1910.

DS
615
B 57

DUTCH EAST INDIES

Bezemer, T. J.

Door Nederlandsch Oost-Indie: schetsen van land en volk. Met een inleiding van J. F. Niermeyer. En ongeveer 300 illustraties en kaarten. n.p. 1906. R8vo. xv + 640 pp.

GN
2.I
S 66

DUTCH EAST INDIES

Kennedy, Raymond

Islands and peoples of the Indies.

(War Background Studies, Smithsonian Institution, No. 14, 1943)

DS
614
N 37

DUTCH EAST INDIES

Nederlandsch-Indië

Jaarverslag van den Topographischen Dienst.

Jaargang 15, Deel I, II.   1919-20.
"   16.

Batavia. Topographische Inrichting. 1920-
4to.   21

DUTCH EAST INDIES

see also

NETHERLANDS EAST INDIES

DUTCH EAST INDIES   AMPHINEURA

see

AMPHINEURA   DUTCH EAST INDIES

DS
615
R37

DUTCH EAST INDIES

Reinwardt, C.G.C.

Reis naar het oostelijk gedeelte
van den Indischen Archipel, in het
jaar 1821; door C.G.C. Reinwardt...

Amsterdam, 1858.   646p.

DUTCH EAST INDIES   ACARINA

see

ACARINA   DUTCH EAST INDIES

DUTCH EAST INDIES   AMPHIPODA

see

AMPHIPODA   DUTCH EAST INDIES

G
161
H

DUTCH EAST INDIES

Rodrigues, Fancisco

The Suma Oriental of Tome Pires: an account
of the East, from the Red Sea to Japan, written
in Malacca and India in 1512-1515, and the book
of Francisco Rodrigues...before 1515. Translated
from the Portuguese ms... Vols. 1-2.
(Works issued by the Hakluyt Society, Ser.
2, Vol. 89-90, 1944)

DUTCH EAST INDIES   ACTINARIA

See

ACTINARIA   DUTCH EAST INDIES

DUTCH EAST INDIES   ANGUILLA

See

ANGUILLA   DUTCH EAST INDIES

Q
101
P 18

DUTCH EAST INDIES

Rutten, L. M. R.   editor

Science in the Netherlands East Indies, by
L. F. de Beaufort, L. de Blieck, C. Brakk, and
others. Prepared...for the Fourth Pacific
Science Congress. Koninklijke Akademie van
Wetenschappen. Amsterdam. R8vo. 432 pp.
(Congress held in Batavia, 1929)

DUTCH EAST INDIES   ALANGIUM

see

ALANGIUM   DUTCH EAST INDIES

DUTCH EAST INDIES   ANOMURA

See

ANOMURA   DUTCH EAST INDIES

DS
615
A 62

DUTCH EAST INDIES

van Anterson, Jean Peter

Fataler Schiffs-Capitain, Oder: Merckwürdige
und besondre Erzehlung dessen unvermutheter ers-
terer und andrer Reise nach denen bis dato noch
unbekannten Südl. Welt-Theilen, Nebst andern cu-
rieusen Merckwurdigkeiten...und herausgegeben dur-
durch Monsieur de Blancard. Theil 1º2. Dritte
auflage. 1745. Erfurt. 12mo. (12) + 366; 123
pp.

DUTCH EAST INDIES   ALCYONACEA

See

ALCYONACEA   DUTCH EAST INDIES

DUTCH EAST INDIES   ANNELIDA

see

ANNELIDA   DUTCH EAST INDIES

DS
Asia Pam.
39

DUTCH EAST INDIES

Van Helsdingen, W. H.   editor

Cultural treasures of the East Indies.
Five chapters reprinted from "Mission Inter-
rupted..." a symposium... Amsterdam, 1945.
The Netherlands Information Bureau. New York.
1946. 66 pp.

DUTCH EAST INDIES   ALCYONARIA

see

ALCYONARIA   DUTCH EAST INDIES

DUTCH EAST INDIES   ANOPHELES

See

ANOPHELES   DUTCH EAST INDIES

AS
145
B

DUTCH EAST INDIES

Van Straelen, V.   publisher

Résultats scientifiques du voyage aux Indes
Orientales Néerlandaises, de...Léopold de Bel-
gique.   Vol. 1;Introduction, par V. Van Strae-
len, pp. 1-222, pl. 1-91
(Mem. hors série, Musée Roy. d'Hist. Nat.
Belgique.- Vol. 1, 1930)

DUTCH EAST INDIES   ALGAE

See

ALGAE   DUTCH EAST INDIES

DUTCH EAST INDIES   ANTHROPOLOGY

see

ANTHROPOLOGY   DUTCH EAST INDIES

DUTCH EAST INDIES   ARANEAE

see

ARANEAE   DUTCH EAST INDIES

GN
2.1
Y 19-s   Kennedy, Raymond

DUTCH EAST INDIES   BIBLIOGRAPHY

Bibliography of Indonesian peoples and
cultures.

(Yale Anthropological Studies, Vol. 4, 1945)

Z
3262   Revised edition; editors, Thomas W. Maretzky
K 36   and H. Th. Fischer. Vols. I-II. Human Relations
Area Files, Inc. Yale Univ. 1955.

DUTCH EAST INDIES   CECIDIA

See

CECIDIA   DUTCH EAST INDIES

DUTCH EAST INDIES   ARCHAEOLOGY

See

ARCHAEOLOGY   DUTCH EAST INDIES

DUTCH EAST INDIES   BIRDS

see

BIRDS   DUTCH EAST INDIES

DUTCH EAST INDIES   CEPHALOPODA

See

CEPHALOPODA   DUTCH EAST INDIES

DUTCH EAST INDIES   ART

See

ART   DUTCH EAST INDIES

DUTCH EAST INDIES   BOTANY

see

BOTANY   DUTCH EAST INDIES

DUTCH EAST INDIES   CERATIUM

See

CERATIUM   DUTCH EAST INDIES

DUTCH EAST INDIES   ASCIDEAE

see

ASCIDEAE   DUTCH EAST INDIES

DUTCH EAST INDIES   BRACHIOPODA

see

BRACHIOPODA   DUTCH EAST INDIES

DUTCH EAST INDIES   CETACEA

See

CETACEA   DUTCH EAST INDIES

DUTCH EAST INDIES   ASTEROIDEA

See

ASTEROIDEA   DUTCH EAST INDIES

DUTCH EAST INDIES   BRACHYURA

See

BRACHYURA   DUTCH EAST INDIES

DUTCH EAST INDIES   CHAETOGNATHA

See

CHAETOGNATHA   DUTCH EAST INDIES

DUTCH EAST INDIES   BATRACHIA

see

BATRACHIA   DUTCH EAST INDIES

DUTCH EAST INDIES   CAMACEA

See

CAMACEA   DUTCH EAST INDIES

DUTCH EAST INDIES   CHILOPODA

See

CHILOPODA   DUTCH EAST INDIES

Z
4501
A 43   Allied Geographical Section, Southwest Pacific
Area.

DUTCH EAST INDIES - BIBLIOGRAPHY

An annotated bibliography of the southwest
Pacific and adjacent areas.
Vol. I. The Netherlands and British East
Indies and the Philippine Islands, II. The mandated Territory of New Guinea, Papua, the British Solomon Islands, the New Hebrides and Micronesia, III. Malaya, Thailand, Indo China, the
China Coast and the Japanese Empire, 1944, no
place, sm 4to.

DUTCH EAST INDIES   CAPRELLIDAE

See

CAPRELLIDAE   DUTCH EAST INDIES

DUTCH EAST INDIES   CHITONIDAE

See

CHITONIDAE   DUTCH EAST INDIES

DUTCH EAST INDIES   CHRYSOMELIDAE

See

CHRYSOMELIDAE   DUTCH EAST INDIES

DUTCH EAST INDIES   CORAL REEFS

See

CORAL REEFS   DUTCH EAST INDIES

DUTCH EAST INDIES   DECAPODA

See

DECAPODA   DUTCH EAST INDIES

DUTCH EAST INDIES   CIRRIPEDIA

See

CIRRIPEDIA   DUTCH EAST INDIES

DUTCH EAST INDIES   CORALS

see

CORALS · DUTCH EAST INDIES

DUTCH EAST INDIES   DEEP SEA DEPOSITS

See

DEEP SEA DEPOSITS   DUTCH EAST INDIES

DUTCH EAST INDIES   CLIMATE

see

CLIMATE   DUTCH EAST INDIES

DUTCH EAST INDIES   CORNACEAE

see

CORNACEAE   DUTCH EAST INDIES

DUTCH EAST INDIES   DIPLOPODA

See

DIPLOPODA   DUTCH EAST INDIES

DUTCH EAST INDIES   COELENTERATA

see

COELENTERATA   DUTCH EAST INDIES

DUTCH EAST INDIES   CRINOIDEA

See

CRINOIDEA   DUTCH EAST INDIES

DUTCH EAST INDIES   DIPTERA

see

DIPTERA   DUTCH EAST INDIES

DUTCH EAST INDIES   COLEOPTERA

see

COLEOPTERA   DUTCH EAST INDIES

DUTCH EAST INDIES   CRUSTACEA

see

CRUSTACEA   DUTCH EAST INDIES

DUTCH EAST INDIES   DISEASES

See

DISEASES   DUTCH EAST INDIES

DUTCH EAST INDIES   CONSERVATION

See

CONSERVATION   DUTCH EAST INDIES

DUTCH EAST INDIES   CTENTOPHORA

See

CTENTOPHORA   DUTCH EAST INDIES

DUTCH EAST INDIES   ECHINODERMATA

see

ECHINODERMATA   DUTCH EAST INDIES

DUTCH EAST INDIES   COPEPODA

see

COPEPODA   DUTCH EAST INDIES

DUTCH EAST INDIES   CULTURE

See

CULTURE DUTCH EAST INDIES

DUTCH EAST INDIES   ECHINOIDEA

See

ECHINOIDEA   DUTCH EAST INDIES

DUTCH EAST INDIES   ECHIURIDAE

See

ECHIURIDAE   DUTCH EAST INDIES

DUTCH EAST INDIES   FISHES

See

FISHES   DUTCH EAST INDIES

DUTCH EAST INDIES   GORGONACEA

See

GORGONACEA   DUTCH EAST INDIES

DUTCH EAST INDIES   ECOLOGY

See

ECOLOGY   DUTCH EAST INDIES

DUTCH EAST INDIES   FORAMINIFERA

See

FORAMINIFERA   DUTCH EAST INDIES

DUTCH EAST INDIES   HETEROPODA

See

HETEROPODA   DUTCH EAST INDIES

DUTCH EAST INDIES   ENTEROPNEUSTA

See

ENTEROPNEUSTA   DUTCH EAST INDIES

DUTCH EAST INDIES   FORESTS AND FORESTRY

See

FORESTS AND FORESTRY   DUTCH EAST INDIES

DUTCH EAST INDIES   HIRUDINEA

see

HIRUDINEA   DUTCH EAST INDIES

DUTCH EAST INDIES   ERIOCAULACEAE

see

ERIOCAULACEAE   DUTCH EAST INDIES

DUTCH EAST INDIES   GASTROPODA

See

GASTROPODA   DUTCH EAST INDIES

QH Dutch East Indies. History etc.
Nat.
Hist.   The history and present state of
Pam   scientific medical research in the
63   Dutch East Indies. K. Akad. Van Weten.

DUTCH EAST INDIES   ETHNOLOGICAL RESEARCH

See

ETHNOLOGICAL RESEARCH   DUTCH EAST INDIES

DUTCH EAST INDIES   GEOGRAPHY

See

GEOGRAPHY   DUTCH EAST INDIES

DUTCH EAST INDIES   HOLOTHUROIDEA

See

HOLOTHUROIDEA   DUTCH EAST INDIES

DUTCH EAST INDIES   ETHNOLOGY

see

ETHNOLOGY   DUTCH EAST INDIES

DUTCH EAST INDIES   GEOLOGY

see

GEOLOGY   DUTCH EAST INDIES

DUTCH EAST INDIES   HYDROCORALLINAE

See

HYDROCORALLINAE   DUTCH EAST INDIES

DUTCH EAST INDIES   FISHERIES

See

FISHERIES   DUTCH EAST INDIES

DUTCH EAST INDIES   GEPHRYEA

See

GEPHRYEA   DUTCH EAST INDIES

DUTCH EAST INDIES   HYDROGRAPHY

See

HYDROGRAPHY   DUTCH EAST INDIES

DUTCH EAST INDIES   HYDROIDEA

See

HYDROIDEA   DUTCH EAST INDIES

DUTCH EAST INDIES   LAMELLIBRANCHIATA

See

LAMELLIBRANCHIATA   DUTCH EAST INDIES

DUTCH EAST INDIES   MARINE FAUNA

See

MARINE FAUNA   DUTCH EAST INDIES

DUTCH EAST INDIES   HYDROMEDUSAE

See

HYDROMEDUSAE   DUTCH EAST INDIES

DUTCH EAST INDIES   LEPIDOPTERA

see

LEPIDOPTERA   DUTCH EAST INDIES

DUTCH EAST INDIES   MEDICINAL PLANTS

See

MEDICINAL PLANTS   DUTCH EAST INDIES

DUTCH EAST INDIES   HYMENOPTERA

see

HYMENOPTERA   DUTCH EAST INDIES

DUTCH EAST INDIES   LORANTHACEAE

see

LORANTHACEAE   DUTCH EAST INDIES

DUTCH EAST INDIES   MEDICINE

see

MEDICINE   DUTCH EAST INDIES

DUTCH EAST INDIES   INSECTS

see

INSECTS   DUTCH EAST INDIES

DUTCH EAST INDIES   MADREPORARIA

See

MADREPORARIA   DUTCH EAST INDIES

DUTCH EAST INDIES   METEOROLOGY

see

METEOROLOGY   DUTCH EAST INDIES

DUTCH EAST INDIES   INVERTEBRATA

See

INVERTEBRATA   DUTCH EAST INDIES

DUTCH EAST INDIES   MAMMALS

see

MAMMALS   DUTCH EAST INDIES

DUTCH EAST INDIES   MOLLUSCA

See

MOLLUSCA   DUTCH EAST INDIES

DUTCH EAST INDIES   ISOPODA

See

ISOPODA   DUTCH EAST INDIES

Q
115
S 56   DUTCH EAST INDIES   MAPS

Tydeman, G. F.
Hydrographic results of the Siboga-Expedition 1899-1900.

Weber, Max
Uitkomsten...Nederlandsch Oost-Indie, 1899-1900...Siboga...Mongr. III(livr. 13) 93 + (2) pp., 24 pl. 3 charts, 1927, 1930.

DUTCH EAST INDIES   NATURE - PROTECTION

See

NATURE - PROTECTION   DUTCH EAST INDIES

DUTCH EAST INDIES   LAMELLIBRANCHIA

see

LAMELLIBRANCHIA   DUTCH EAST INDIES

Q
115
S 56   DUTCH EAST INDIES   MAPS

Hickson, Sidney J.
The pennatulacea of the Siboga Expedition, with a general survey of the order.

Weber, Max
Uitkomsten...Nederlandsch Oost-Indie, 1899-1900...Siboga...Monographie SIV(livr. 77). 1916. 265 pp., 10 pl. 1 chart

---

DUTCH EAST INDIES   NEMERTINI

See

NEMERTINI   DUTCH EAST INDIES

DUTCH EAST INDIES   NEUROPTERA

see

NEUROPTERA   DUTCH EAST INDIES

DUTCH EAST INDIES   OPILIONES

see

OPILIONES   DUTCH EAST INDIES

DUTCH EAST INDIES   PENNATULACEA

See

PENNATULACEA   DUTCH EAST INDIES

DUTCH EAST INDIES   NYSSACEAE

see

NYSSACEAE   DUTCH EAST INDIES

DUTCH EAST INDIES   OPISTHOBRANCHIATA

See

OPISTHOBRANCHIATA   DUTCH EAST INDIES

DUTCH EAST INDIES   PLANT NAMES

see

PLANT NAMES   DUTCH EAST INDIES

DUTCH EAST INDIES   OCEANOGRAPHY

See

OCEANOGRAPHY   DUTCH EAST INDIES

DUTCH EAST INDIES   ORCHIDACEAE

see

ORCHIDACEAE   DUTCH EAST INDIES

DUTCH EAST INDIES   POISONOUS PLANTS

See

POISONOUS PLANTS   DUTCH EAST INDIES

DUTCH EAST INDIES   ODONATA

see

ODONATA   DUTCH EAST INDIES

DUTCH EAST INDIES   ORTHOPTERA

see

ORTHOPTERA   DUTCH EAST INDIES

DUTCH EAST INDIES   POLYCHAETA

See

POLYCHAETA   DUTCH EAST INDIES

DUTCH EAST INDIES   OLIGOCHAETA

see

OLIGOCHAETA   DUTCH EAST INDIES

DUTCH EAST INDIES   OSTRACODA

See

OSTRACODA   DUTCH EAST INDIES

DUTCH EAST INDIES   POLYPODIACEAE

see

POLYPODIACEAE   DUTCH EAST INDIES

DUTCH EAST INDIES   OPHIDIA

See

OPHIDIA   DUTCH EAST INDIES

DUTCH EAST INDIES   PALEONTOLOGY

See

PALEONTOLOGY   DUTCH EAST INDIES

DUTCH EAST INDIES   POLYZOA

See

POLYZOA   DUTCH EAST INDIES

DUTCH EAST INDIES   OPHIUROIDEA

See

OPHIUROIDEA   DUTCH EAST INDIES

DUTCH EAST INDIES   PANTOPODA

See

PANTOPODA   DUTCH EAST INDIES

DUTCH EAST INDIES   PORIFERA

See

PORIFERA   DUTCH EAST INDIES

DUTCH EAST INDIES   PROSOBRANCHIA

See

PROSOBRANCHIA   DUTCH EAST INDIES

DUTCH EAST INDIES   RUBIACEAE

see

RUBIACEAE   DUTCH EAST INDIES

DUTCH EAST INDIES   SIPUNCULIDAE

See

SIPUNCULIDAE   DUTCH EAST INDIES

DUTCH EAST INDIES   PROTOZOA

see

PROTOZOA   DUTCH EAST INDIES

DUTCH EAST INDIES   SCAPHOPODA

See

SCAPHOPODA   DUTCH EAST INDIES

DUTCH EAST INDIES   SOCIAL ORGANIZATION

See

SOCIAL ORGANIZATION   DUTCH EAST INDIES

DUTCH EAST INDIES   PTEROBRANCHIA

See

PTEROBRANCHIA   DUTCH EAST INDIES

DUTCH EAST INDIES   SCHIZOPODA

See

SCHIZOPODA   DUTCH EAST INDIES

DUTCH EAST INDIES   SOILS

See

SOILS   DUTCH EAST INDIES

DUTCH EAST INDIES   PTEROPODA

See

PTEROPODA   DUTCH EAST INDIES

DUTCH EAST INDIES   SCIENTISTS

See

SCIENTISTS   DUTCH EAST INDIES

DUTCH EAST INDIES   SOLENOGASTRES

See

SOLENOGASTRES   DUTCH EAST INDIES

DUTCH EAST INDIES   REPTILIA

see

REPTILIA   DUTCH EAST INDIES

DUTCH EAST INDIES   SCYPHOMEDUSAE

See

SCYPHOMEDUSAE   DUTCH EAST INDIES

DUTCH EAST INDIES   STOMATOPODA

See

STOMATOPODA   DUTCH EAST INDIES

DUTCH EAST INDIES   RHIZOCEPHALA

see

RHIZOCEPHALA   DUTCH EAST INDIES

DUTCH EAST INDIES   SERGESTIDAE

See

SERGESTIDAE   DUTCH EAST INDIES

DUTCH EAST INDIES   TERMITIDAE

See

TERMITIDAE   DUTCH EAST INDIES

DUTCH EAST INDIES   RHIZOPHORACEAE

see

RHIZOPHORACEAE   DUTCH EAST INDIES

DUTCH EAST INDIES   SIPHONOPHORA

See

SIPHONOPHORA   DUTCH EAST INDIES

DUTCH EAST INDIES   TIPULIDAE

see

TIPULIDAE   DUTCH EAST INDIES

DUTCH EAST INDIES TREMATODA

see

TREMATODA DUTCH EAST INDIES

DUTCH EAST INDIES ZOOLOGY

see

ZOOLOGY DUTCH EAST INDIES

DT
African
Fam.
20

du Toit, Alex. L.

The Kalahari and some of its problems.

(reprinted from South African Journal of Science, 24:88-101, 1927)

DUTCH EAST INDIES TUNICATA

See

TUNICATA DUTCH EAST INDIES

DUTCH WEST INDIES UMBELLIFERAE

See

UMBELLIFERAE DUTCH WEST INDIES

Q
101
P 18

Du Toit, Alex. L.

Observations on the evolution of the Pacific Ocean.

IN Proc. Sixth Pac. Sci. Congress, 1939, (California), Vol. 1, 1940, pp. 175-184.

DUTCH EAST INDIES UMBELLIFERAE

See

UMBELLIFERAE DUTCH EAST INDIES

DUTCH GUIANA

See

SURINAM

Du Toit, Alex. L.

Our wandering continents: an hypothesis of continental drifting. Edinburgh and London. 1937. 18s

UH has (sufficient)

Review in Geogr. Journal, Vol. 95, 1940, p. 469-470. and in Jour. of Geol. 66(3):388-9, 1958
by Fairbridge

DUTCH EAST INDIES VERBENACEAE

see

VERBENACEAE DUTCH EAST INDIES

DU
12
C 78

locked
case

DUTCHESS (SHIP)

Cooke, Edward

Voyage to the south sea and round the world performed in... 1708-1711, by the ships Duke and Dutchess of Bristol... 2 vols. London. 1712. 8vo.

GN
2.S
P 76

du Toit, Brian M.

Structural looseness in New Guinea.

(Jour. of the Polynesian Soc., 71(4): 397-398. 1962)

DUTCH EAST INDIES VOYAGES

see

VOYAGES DUTCH EAST INDIES

DU
12
H 73

locked
case

DUTCHESS (ship)

Rogers, Woodes

A cruising voyage round the world: first to the South Seas...1708...1711. London. A. Bell 1712. sm8vo.

AP
2
N 28

Dutt, Mridula

Dividing nuclei in coconut milk.

(Nature, Vol. 171(4357):799-800, 1953)

DUTCH EAST INDIES WOODS

See

WOODS DUTCH EAST INDIES

DU
623
D 97

Duthie, D. Wallace

A bishop in the rough. With a preface by the Lord Bishop of Norwich. Illustrated. London. Smith, Elder & Co. 1909. 8vo. xxxvii, 386 pp.

Dutton, Charles J.

Carter Coll.
11-C-11

The Samaritans of Molokai, the lives of Father Damien and Brother Dutton among the lepers. New York. Dodd, Mead and Co. 1932 xiv + 286 pp. 8vo.

DUTCH EAST INDIES

See also

INDONESIA

QE
Geol.Pam.
1039

Duthie, D. Wallace

Sheepshanks, John (Bishop of Norwich)

A bishop in the rough, edited by D. Wallace Duthie. London, 1909. (typed copy of pp. 184-192 only. A copy is at the Volcano House, Kilauea.) (A journal written in April, 1866)

JE
534
D 98

Dutton, Clarence Edward

Earthquakes in the light of the new seismology.

New York. 1904 8vo pp. 314, illus.

AUG 15 1912

DU
Pac.Pam.
257

Dutton, C. E(Clarence Edward)

The Hawaiian islands and people. A lecture delivered at the U. S. National Museum...February 9th, 1884. Washington. 1884. 8vo. 32 pp.

and
DU
620
M 67

(Misc. Pams. Haw. II: 467-518)

DU
Hist.
Pam.
511

Dutton, Meiric K.

The case of the elusive hubs and dies.

Loomis House Press, Honolulu. 1959. 8vo. 11 pp.

DU
Hist.Pam.
444

Dutton, Meiric K.

Love's; a century of one family's enterprise. Love's Biscuit and Bread Co., Ltd. Honolulu. 1952. 8vo. vi + 39 pp.

QE
526
D 98

Dutton, Clarence Edward

Hawaiian volcanoes. Washington. Gov't. Printing Office. 1884. 219 pp. Maps. 4to.

QE
75
A

(Fourth Annual Report of the Director, U. S. Geological Survey)

DU
Hist.
Pam.
424

Dutton, Meiric K.

Final years of the Sandwich Islands Mission Press, including a brief description of its assimilation by Henry M. Whitney's Advertiser Press. Loomis House Press. Honolulu. 1956. 8vo. 9 pp. and 8 pp. of letter, reproduced, E. W. Clark to Rev. R. Anderson, 1858.

DU
Hist.
Pam.
494

Dutton, Meiric K.   (commentator)

A most extraordinary correspondence. Loomis House Press. Honolulu. 1959. 28 pp.

[between President Grover Cleveland and Sanford B. Dole]

(annexation period)

QE
75
D 98

Dutton, Clarence E(dward)

Physical geology of the Grand Canon District. Washington. 1882. 113 pp. R8vo.

QE
75
A

(2d Annual Report U. S. Geological Survey, 1880-1881, pp. 44-166)

DU
Pac.Pam.
939

Dutton, Meiric K.

Financing Hawaii; an account of Hawaii's banks and trust companies. 13 pp.

(Reprint: Honolulu Advertiser, Oct. 3,1954)

DU
Hist.Pam.
311

Dutton, Meiric

Kamehameha IV

Preface to the Book of Common Prayer. (Hawaiian and English text; preface by M. K. D.) 15 pp. 8vo. 1949. Privately printed by Eugenie and Meiric Dutton.

AP
2
A 5

Dutton, Clarence Edward

Recent exploration of the volcanic phenomena of the Hawaiian Islands.

(Am. Jour. of Sci., Ser. 3, Vol. 25, 1883, pp. 219-226)

DU
Hist.Pam.
521

Dutton, Meiric K.

Hawaii's great seal and coat of arms, State of Hawaii. Loomis House Press. Honolulu. 1960. 19 pp.

DU
Hist.
Pam.
433

Dutton, Meiric K.

The succession of King Kamehameha V to Hawaii's throne, including a recently discovered private memorandum written by Attorney-General C. C. Harris. Loomis House Press. Honolulu 1957. 8vo. 20 pp.

DU
620
M 67

Dutton, C. E.

Silver question. Read before the Philosophical Society of Washington. January 31, 1880. (Extract from Bull. of the Sea.) Philadelphia, 1880, 8vo. pp. 28. in Miscell. Pams. Haw. II. pp. 488-880.

DU
Hist.Pam.
412

Dutton, Meiric

Henry M. Whitney, Pioneer Printer-Publisher and Hawaii's First Postmaster. Loomis House Press. Honolulu. 1955. 12mo. (2)+20 pp.

DU
Pac.Pam.
841

Dutton, Meiric K.   translator

Skogman, C.

His Swedish Majesty's frigate Eugenie at Honolulu, June 22-July 2, 1852, being a reprint of seventeen pages from "Fregatten Eugenies Resa omkring jorden, aren 1851-1853..." Translated from the original Swedish by Meiric K. Dutton. Loomis House Press. Honolulu. (21 pp), 1 map.

Carter Coll.
6-F-4

DUTTON, JOSEPH

Case, Howard D. editor

Joseph Dutton, (His memoirs): The story of forty-four years of service among the lepers of Molokai, Hawaii. Honolulu. The Honolulu Star-Bulletin. 1931. 242 pp. 8vo.

DU
Hist. Pam.
325

Dutton, Meiric K.

Ka Haku o Hawaii (His Royal Highness the Prince of Hawaii). Honolulu. 1951. Eugenie and Meiric Dutton. 12mo 32 pp.

DU
Hist.Pam.
381

Dutton, Meiric K.

William L. Lee: his address at the opening of the first term of the Superior Court held in the new courthouse, Honolulu, July 5, 1852; to which is added a biographical note by Meiric K. Dutton. Loomis House Press. Honolulu. 1953. 12mo. 46 pp.

DUTTON, JOSEPH

Lemon, A. M.

Joseph Dutton of Molokai. 1952

UH has

DU
Hist.
Pam.
363

Dutton, Meiric K.

A letter from King Kamehameha V to the Bishop of Honolulu, Honolulu Palace, 24 September 1867, with a note on the Reciprocity Treaty of 1867. Loomis House Press. 1952. Honolulu. 8vo. (14) pp.

Dutton, Sydney Wm.

Bibliography of the Pacific islands. [In preparation]

See his letter of Jan.19, 1925.

QL
Prot.-
Poly.
Pam.
774

Duxbury, A. C.

Plankton pigment nomographs. By A. C. Duxbury and Charles S. Yentsch.

(Sears Foundation: Jour. of Marine Research Vol. 15(1):92-101, 1956)

AS
36
A65

Dwight, Jonathan and Griscom, Ludlow

A new and remarkable flycatcher from Guatemala. Amer. Mus. Nov. 254, 1927.

QL
Bird
Pam
175

separate

QL
401
M 23

DYAKIA

Gude, G. K.

Description of a new species of Dyakia.

(Proc. Mal. Soc. London, Vol. 11, 1915, pp. 321)

QK
100
D 98

Duyster, M.

Giftige Indische planten en plantenbestanddeelen. Visser and Co., Bandoeng. 8vo. 143 + xiv pp. 1927

AS
36
C8

Dwight, Nathaniel, 1770-1831.

... An account of the American cantharis, or *Meloe americae* ...

(*In* Connecticut academy of arts and sciences. Memoirs. New Haven, 1810. 22½ᶜᵐ. v. 1, p. 99:-102)

1. Cantharides.   Title: Meloe americae

A 17-739

Library of Congress   Q11.C85 vol. 1
Yale University   A53n.365.1

QK
401
M 23

DYAKIA

Sykes, Ernest Ruthven

On three species of Dyakia from Western Sumatra.

(Proc. Mal. Soc. London, Vol. 6, 1905, pp. 227-228)

DWARFS

See

PYGMIES

[Note: dwarfish implies small in a teratological sense; do not use this term when pygmy is meant]

AS
36
C8

Dwight, Sereno Edwards, 1786-1850.

... A dissertation on the origin of springs ...

(*In* Connecticut academy of arts and sciences. Memoirs. New Haven, 1813. 22½ᶜᵐ. v. 1, p. (311)-328)

1. Springs.   I. Title.

A 17-751

Library of Congress   Q11.C85 vol. 1
Yale University   A53n.365.1

DS
646.3
B 66

DYAKS

Book, Carl

The head-hunters of Borneo: a narrative of travel up the Mahakkam and down the Barito... London. 1882.

QL
362
C 95

Dwellers of the Sea and Shore.

Crowder, William

AS
36
C8

Dwight, Timothy, 1752-1817.

... Observations on language ...

(*In* Connecticut academy of arts and sciences. Memoirs. New Haven (1816) 22½ᶜᵐ. v. 1, p. (125 i. e. 365)-386)

1. Language and languages.   I. Title.

A 17-755

Library of Congress   Q11.C85 vol. 1
Yale University   A53n.365.1

DS
646.3
B 66

DYAKS   VOCABULARY

Book, Carl

The head-hunters of Borneo: a narrative of travel up the Mahakkam and down the Barito... London. 1882. App. 4: A short vocabulary of the Long Wai (Dyak) dialect. pp. 334-335.

DU
625.4
D 99

Dwight, E. W.

Memoir of Henry Obookiah; a native of the Sandwich Islands, who died at Cornwall, Connecticut, February 17, 1818, Aged 26. (Title-page missing. Date and place of publication unknown) 104 pp. 16mo.

A Sermon delivered at the funeral of Henry Obookiah...by Lyman Beecher. Elizabeth-town, N.J. Edson Hart. 1819. The banner of Christ is set up, a sermon delivered at the inauguration of the Rev. Hermon Daggett...by Joseph Harvey...Bound together, with the above.

QH
1
T 88

Dwyer, P. D.

New Zealand bats.

(Tuatara, 8(2):61-71; 1960)

AS
36
S4

Dyar, Harrison Gray, 1866-

Descriptions of new *Lepidoptera*, chiefly from Mexico. By Harrison G. Dyar ...

(*In* U. S. National museum. Proceedings. Washington, 1913. 23½ᶜᵐ. v. 44, p. 279-324)

1. Lepidoptera—Mexico.

13-20861

Library of Congress   Q11.U55 vol. 44

DU
625.4
D 99

Dwight, E. W.

Memoir of Henry Obookiah; A native of the Sandwich Islands, who died at Cornwall, Connecticut, February 17, 1818, Aged 26. New York. American Tract Society. No date. 12mo. Revised edition.

QL
1
V 64

Dwyer, P. D.

Studies on the two New Zealand bats.

(Zoology Publ. Victoria Univ. of Wellington, No. 28, 1962)

[Chiroptera: Mystacina]

AS
36
S4

Dyar, Harrison Gray, 1866-

Descriptions of new *Lepidoptera* from Mexico. By Harrison G. Dyar ...

(*In* U. S. National museum. Proceedings. Washington, 1919. 23½ᶜᵐ. v. 54, p. 335-372) & v. 51, p. 1-37,

1. Lepidoptera—Mexico.

19-20022

Library of Congress   Q11.U55 vol. 54

S
17.H3
H 38

Dwight, J. L.

The Mediterranean fruit fly in Hawaii.

(Hawaiian Forester and Agriculturist, vol. 26, no. 3, 1929, pp. 113-116)

QL
401
M 23

DYAKIA

Godwin-Austen, H. H.

On a species of the land molluscan genus Dyakia from Siam.

(Proc. Mal. Soc. London, Vol. 7, 1906, pp. 93-96)

AS
36
S4

Dyar, Harrison Gray, 1866-

Descriptions of new species and genera of *Lepidoptera*, chiefly from Mexico. By Harrison G. Dyar ...

(*In* U. S. National museum. Proceedings. Washington, 1912. 23½ᶜᵐ. vol. 42, p. 39-106)

1. Lepidoptera—Mexico.

13-9514

Library of Congress   Q11.U55 vol. 42

AS
36
S4
Dyar, Harrison Gray, 1866–
    Descriptions of new species of saturnian moths in the collection of the United States National museum. By Harrison G. Dyar ...
        (*In* U. S. National museum. Proceedings. Washington, 1913. 23½ᶜᵐ. v. 44, p. 121-134)

1. Moths.

Library of Congress   13–20857
                         Q11.U55 vol. 44

AS
36
S4
Dyar, Harrison Gray, 1866–
    The noctuid moths of the genera *Palindia* and *Dyomyx*. By Harrison G. Dyar ...
        (*In* U. S. National museum. Proceedings. Washington, 1915. 23½ᶜᵐ. v. 47, p. 95-116)

1. Moths.

Library of Congress   15–14944
                         Q11.U55 vol. 47

QL
Insect
Pam.
2056
Dyce, A. L.
    Blood-sucking flies (Diptera) and Myxomatosis transmission in a mountain environment in New South Wales. II. Comparison of the use of man and rabbit as bait animals in evaluating vectors of Myxomatosis. By A. L. Dyce and D. J. Lee.

(Reprint, Australian Journal of Zoology, Vol. 10(1):84-94, 1962)

AS
36
S4
Dyar, Harrison Gray, 1866–
    Descriptions of some new species and genera of *Lepidoptera* from Mexico. By Harrison G. Dyar ...
        (*In* U. S. National museum. Proceedings. Washington, 1911. 23½ᶜᵐ. vol. 38, p. 229-273)

1. Lepidoptera—Mexico.

Library of Congress   11–15728
                         Q11.U55 vol. 38

AS
36
S4
Dyar, Harrison Gray, 1866–
    Report on the *Lepidoptera* of the Smithsonian biological survey of the Panama Canal Zone. By Harrison G. Dyar ...
        (*In* U. S. National museum. Proceedings. Washington, 1915. 23½ᶜᵐ. v. 47, p. 139-350)

1. Lepidoptera—Panama Canal Zone.

Library of Congress   15–14948
                         Q11.U55 vol. 47

GN
2.I
A-m
DYEING   NEW GUINEA
Blackwood, Beatrice M.
    Reserve dyeing in New Guinea.

(Man, Vol. 50, Art. 68, p. 53-55, 1950)

Ramu River

AS
36
S4
Dyar, Harrison Gray, 1866–
    Descriptions of new species and genera of *Lepidoptera* from Mexico. By Harrison G. Dyar ...
        (*In* U. S. National museum. Proceedings. Washington, 1915. 23½ᶜᵐ. v. 47, p. 365-409)

1. Lepidoptera—Mexico.

Library of Congress   15–14952
                         Q11.U55 vol. 47

QL
536
Ho
Dyar, Harrison Gray, joint author
Howard, Leland Ossian.
    The mosquitoes of North America and Central America and the West Indies, by L.O. Howard, H.G. Dyar and F. Knab.   4 vols.

Carnegie inst. of Washington, 1912-1917. Pub. #159.

PL
Phil.
Pam.
682
Dyen, Isidore
    Language distribution and migration theory.

(Language, 32(4):611-626, 1956)

AS
36
S2
Dyar, Harrison Gray, 1866–
    Descriptions of some new species and a new genus of American mosquitoes, by Harrison G. Dyar and Frederick Knab.
        (*In* Smithsonian institution. Smithsonian miscellaneous collections. Washington, 1910. 24½ᶜᵐ. vol. LII (Quarterly issue, vol. V) p. 253-266. illus.)
    Publication 1822.
    In continuation of a paper by the same authors, "Descriptions of some new mosquitoes from tropical America," pub. in the Proceedings of the U. S. National museum, v. 35, 1908 p. 53-70.
    Originally published January 12, 1909.
    1. Mosquito.   I. Knab, Frederick, 1865–   joint author.

Library of Congress   16–12712
                         Q11.S7 vol. 52
—— Copy 2.

QL
536
Ho
Dyar, Harrison Gray
Howard, Leland Ossian, 1857–
    The mosquitoes of North and Central America and the West Indies, by Leland O. Howard, Harrison G. Dyar, and Frederick Knab ... Washington, D. C., Carnegie institution of Washington, 1912-17.
        4 v. in 3. illus., plates. 25ᶜᵐ. (*On verso of t.-p.:* Carnegie institution of Washington. Publication no. 159)
    Bibliography: v. 1, p. 451-488.
    CONTENTS.—v. 1. A general consideration of mosquitoes, their habits, and their relations to the human species.—v. 2. Plates.—v. 3-4. Systematic description.
    1. Mosquito.   I. Dyar, Harrison Gray, 1866–   joint author. II. Knab, Frederick, 1865–   joint author.

Library of Congress   QL536.H85   13–6044
—— Copy 2.

PL
Phil.
Pam.
689
Dyen, Isidore
    The lexicostatistical classification of the Malayopolynesian languages.

(Language, 38(1):38-46, 1962)

AS
36
S4
Dyar, Harrison Gray, 1866–
    Lepidoptera of the Yale Dominican expedition of 1913. By Harrison G. Dyar ...
        (*In* U. S. National museum. Proceedings. Washington, 1915. 23½ᶜᵐ. v. 47, p. 423-426)

1. Lepidoptera—Dominica.   I Yale Dominican expedition, 1913.

Library of Congress   15–14954
                         Q11.U55 vol. 47

AS
36
S2
Dyar, Harrison Gray, 1866–
    ... The species of mosquitoes in the genus *Megarhinus*, by Harrison G. Dyar and Frederick Knab.
        (*In* Smithsonian institution. Smithsonian miscellaneous collections. Washington, 1907. 24½ᶜᵐ. vol. XLVIII (Quarterly issue, vol. III) p. 241-258. illus.)
    Publication 1657.
    Originally published September 27, 1906.

1. Mosquito.   I. Knab, Frederick, 1865–   joint author.

Library of Congress   16–12731
                         Q11.S7 vol. 48
—— Copy 2.

PL
Phil.
Pam.
690
Dyen, Isidore
    The lexicostatistically determined relationship of a language group.

(International Jour. of Am. Linguistics, 28(3):153-161, 1962)

AS
36
S5
Dyar, Harrison Gray, 1866–
    A list of the North American *Lepidoptera* and key to the literature of this order of insects. By Harrison G. Dyar ... assisted by C. H. Fernald, PH. D., the late Rev. George D. Hulst, and August Busck. Washington, Govt. print. off., 1902.
        xix, 723 p. 24½ᶜᵐ. (*Added t.-p.:* ... United States National museum. Bulletin ... no. 52)
    "List of works quoted": p. ix-xix.

1. Lepidoptera—North America.   2. Lepidoptera—Bibl.   I. Fernald, Charles Henry, 1838–   II. Hulst, George D.   III. Busck, August, 1870–

Library of Congress   6–27693
—— Copy 2.   Q11.U6
                 QL545.D98
                 [s19e1]

QL
Mol
Pam
#123
Dybowski, W.
    Studien über die Zahnplatten der Gattung Limnaea Lam., ex (?) np., Bul. 1884, pp. 256-264, pl.V.

PL
Phil.
Pam.
616
Dyen, Isidore
    The Proto-Malayo-Polynesian laryngeals. William Dwight Whitney linguistic series. Published for Yale Univ. by The Linguistic Society of America. Baltimore. 1953. 8vo. viii + 65 pp.

QL
536
D99
Dyar, Harrison G
    The mosquitoes of the Americas.

Washington, Carnegie Institution, 1928.

QL
Ins.
Pam.
36
Dybowski, W.
    Über die Zahnplatten der gattung Limnaea Lam.

(Bul.Soc.Imp.Nat.Moscow, 1885)

GN
2.S
P 76
Dyen, Isidore
    Review of
Grace, George William
    The position of the Polynesian languages within the Austronesian (Malayo-Polynesian) language family.

(Jour. Poly. Soc., 69(2):180-182, 1960)

GN
2.S
A 51

Dyen, Isidore

Some new proto-Malayopolynesian initial phonemes.

(Jour. Am. Oriental Society, Vol. 82(2): 214-215, 1962)

Z
Bibliography
Pam.106

DYES AND DYEING HAWAII

Hawaiian dyes- list of references.

GN
Pam
2230

DYES & DYEING TASMANIA

Noetling, Fritz

Red ochre and its use by the aborigines of Tasmania. Roy. Soc. Tasmania, May,1909

GN
2.S
F 47

Dyer, Ralph W.

Forecasting problems in Fiji. By Ralph W. Dyer and F. O. Ramage

(Trans. and Proc. of the Fiji Soc., Vol. 2, 1940-44:254-267, 1953)

AS
750
N

DYES AND DYEING MAORI

Walsh, Archdeacon

On the Maori method of preparing and using kokowai.

(Trans. and Proc. New Zealand Inst., vol. 36, 1903, pp. 4-10)

QL
Protozoa
and
Polyzoa
Pam.
103

Dyke, W.

The cucumber and tomato eelworm, ex Journ. of Micros. 3d ser. vol. 7,

---

GN
2.S
F 47

Dyer, W. R.

Hurricanes.

(Trans. and Proc. of the Fiji Soc., Vol. 2, 1940-1944:89-96, 1953)

GN
Pam
398

DYES & DYEING - MEXICO

Nuttall, Zelia.

A curious survival in Mexico of the use of the Purpura shell-fish for dyeing, by Zelia Nuttall. From the Putnam anniversary volume.

Cedar Rapids, Iowa Torch press, 1909. pages 368-384, plates.

QL
Mollusca
Pam.677

DYKIA

Sykes, E. R.

On three species of Dyakia from western Sumatra.

(Proc. of the Malac. Soc., Vol. 6, 1905, pp. 227-228)

Dyer, Sir William Turner Thiselton-

see also

Thiselton-Dyer, W. T.

AS
36
S1

DYES AND DYEING NAVAHO INDIANS

Matthews, Washington, 1843-1905.
Navajo dye stuffs. By Dr. Washington Matthews ...

(In Smithsonian institution. Annual report. 1891. Washington, 1893. 234ᵐᵐ. p. 613-615)

"Navajo weavers: Third annual report, Bureau of ethnology, 1881-'82, p. 375."

1. Navaho Indians. 2. Dyes and dyeing.

S 15-774

Library of Congress   Q11.S66 1891
Library, Smithsonian   Institution

QL
596.D9
C 28

DYNASTINAE AUSTRALIA

Carne, P. B.

Systematic revision of the Australian Dynastinae. Division of Entomology, Commonwealth Scientific and Industrial Research Organization. Australia. Melbourne. 1957. R8vo. 284 pp.

GN
Ethn.Fam.
3635

DYES AND DYEING

Bühler, A.

Dyeing among primitive peoples.

(Reprint from Ciba Review, No. 68, Je. 1948, pp. 2478-2512)

GN
Pam
#169

DYES & DYEING NAVAHO INDIANS

Pepper, George H.

Native Navajo Dyes.

Reprinted from The Papoose. Feb. 1903

N. Am

♦E

Gr. the author.

DU
1
P

DYNASTINAE SAMOA

Fighting rhinoceros beetle in W. Samoa; entomologists and wasps play their part.

(Pacific Islands Monthly, 22(7):116, 1952)

AS
36
S1

DYES AND DYEING

Purple dyeing, ancient and modern.

(In Smithsonian institution. Annual report. 1863. Washington, 1864. 234ᵐᵐ. p. (385-403)

"Translated ... from the German periodical, 'Aus der natur,' etc."

1. Dyes and dyeing. 2. Purple.

S 15-152

Library of Congress   Q11.S66 1863
Library, Smithsonian   Institution

DU
12
E 47

DYES AND DYEING POLYNESIA

Ellis, William, 1794-1872
Polynesian Researches...2 vols. London, 1829. 8vo. Vol. 2, pp. 175-176.

DU 12
E 47
locked
case

The same...1830. 2 vols. 8vo.

AS
36
C8

DYSDERIDAE

Emerton, James Henry, 1847-
... New England spiders of the families *Drassidæ, Agalenidæ* and *Dysderidæ*.

(In Connecticut academy of arts and sciences. Transactions. New Haven, 1888-92. 25ᵐᵐ. v. 8, p. (165)-206. pl. III-VIII)

1. [Drassidæ] 2. [Agalenidæ] 3. [Dysderidæ] 4. Spiders—New England. I. Title.

A 17-847

Library of Congress   Q11.C9 vol. 8
Yale University   A53n.366.8

DYES AND DYEING

see also

TAPA

DU
12
H 39
locked
case

DYES AND DYEING TAHITI

Hawkesworth, John

An account of the voyages...performed by... Byron, Wallis, Carteret and Cook...drawn up from Journals... 3 vols. London. 1773. 4to. Vol. 2, pp. 210-216.

...Fourth edition. 4 vols. Perth. 1789. 12mo.

RC
Pathol.
Pam.
53

DYSENTERY

Sawers, W. C.

The epidemiology of bacillary dysentery.

(Med. Jour. of Australia, 1943, pp. 160-162)

G
7
R 91

Dyson, Frank

Captain Cook as an astronomer.

(Geogr. Journal, Vol. 73, 1929, p. 115-122)

PL
Phil.Pam
705

E aratai no te feia i roto i te ekalesia. Huahine. Printed at the Leeward Mission Press. 1840. sm8vo. 23 pp.

PL
870
B 93

E buka himene, i faaauhia e te mau oromotua; no te haamaitairaa i te atua, i te haamoriraa. Lonedona. 1882. 347 hymns. no pagination.

Tahiti, hymns

QL
Insects
Pam.
1196

DYTISCIDAE

Balfour-Browne, J.

Aquatic Coleoptera of Oceania (Dytiscidae, Gyrinidae, and Palpicornia).

(Occ. Papers, Bernice P. Bishop Museum, Vol. 18, No. 7, 1945, pp. 103-132)

PL
Phil.pam.
266

E aronga imene; koia oki te tuatua akamoitaki i te atua. Rarotonga. Mission Press. 1843. 154 pp. 16mo.

(Rarotonga. Hymn book)

PL
850
E 11

E fai tatalofa diena, mala Lau. The four Gospels in the language of Lau, Mala, Solomon Islands. Sydney. New South Wales Auxiliary to the British and Foreign Bible Society. 1910. 12mo. 278 pp.

Solomon Islands, Mala, Lau, New Testament

QL
Insects
Pam.
1193

DYTISCIDAE

Balfour-Browne, J.

New and interesting Dytiscidae (Coleoptera) from Fiji.

(Proceedings of the R. Ent. Soc. of London, Ser. B. Taxonomy, Vol. 13, Parts 9-10, 1944, pp. 97-100)

PL
605
A 88

E Atoga no te ao hepereo i hakapoto hia ra na te mau perepitero no te kaiga i uri i te reo Magareva. Braine-le-Comte. 1908. 12mo. 415 pp.

(Bible stories in Mangarevan)

PL
Phil.
Pam. 496
Duc.

E Haatoitoi. V.C.I.S. I oomi ia i Braine-le-Comte. 1886. 12mo. 131 pp.

(Explanation of the Christian doctrine preceded by moral poetry. In Marquesan)

QL
1
C 74

DYTISCOIDEA   AFRICA

Guignot, Félix

Revision des Hydrocanthares d'Afrique (Coleoptera Dytiscoidea). 3 me Partie.

(Annales du Musee R. du Congo Belge. Sci. Zoologiques, Vol. 90, 1961)

(parts 1-2 in Vols. 70, 78)

PL
605
A 88

E Atoga no te Hu-peata (vies des saints) huri hia ei rakao Magareva (en Mangarévien), par les missionnaires catholiques de cet Archipel...Sacres-Coeurs de Picpus. Puputakao I. Januario...Junio. Braine-le-Comte. ...no Zech. 1908 12mo 519 pp.

Mangarevan- life of the saints

PL
700
E 33

E haatoitoi ia i te ui katolika. I oomi tia i Paris, io Belin. 1903. 12mo. 499 pp.

Marquesas, catechism

QL
Insects
Pam.
1667

DYTISCIDAE   SOUTH AFRICA

Omer-Cooper, Joyce

Some new species of Dytiscidae (Coleoptera) from the Cape Province of South Africa.

(Proc. of Royal Ent. Soc. London, series B. Taxonomy, Vol. 22(1-2):23-31, 1953)

PL
605
A 88

E atoga no te hu-peata (Vies des saints) huri hia ei takao Magareva (en Mangarévien) Par les Missionnaires catholiques de cet Archipel. Puputakao I... Braine-le-Comte. 1908. 12mo. 519 pp.

PL
700
E 34

E hamani haatuhuna i te tekao taitohu. Paris. Simon Raçon et Cie. n.d. 412 pp. 16mo.

(Marquesan prayer book)

GN
2.S
T

E. A.

La Legende de Monoihere et de Tafai.

(Bull. de la Société des Études Océaniennes, Vol. 5, No. 8, Dec. 1933, pp.264-266)

PL
870
T 25

and

PL
Phil.pam.
275

E bue raa himene. Oia hoi te parau haamaitai i te atua. Tahiti. (Mission Press) 1827. 143 pp. 8vo.

(Tahitian hymns)

(Bound with 33 other pamphlets: Te evanelia a to tatou ... no. 9)

PL
Phil.Pam.
223

E hamani pure. V.C.J.S. I Vaiparaiho. P. Ezquerra. 1857. 16mo. 63 pp. (Marquesan prayer book)
(contains also E hamani himene i una he tekao kiritiano. 1857. (hymn book) and E tekao haapoto tia no to tatou haapohoe no ietu-kirito. V.C.J.S. 1857. (discourse on the life of Christ).

PL
870
T 25

E ao raa, ia imi te taata i te maitai. Tahiti. 1833. 4 pp. 8vo.

(Bound with 33 other pamphlets: Te evanelia a to tatou ... no's. 28 and 33)

PL
870
T 25

E buka hakaite i te A, B. E. i te takau Tahuata. Mission Press. Tahiti. 1854. 12 pp. 8vo.
Adjacent, following, is "E ui, i te tekau Tahuata." 8 pp.

(Bound with 33 other pamphlets: Te evanelia a to tatou... no. 3)

PL
700
E 11

E hamani pure ao te vikariato apotoliko Marquises. I oomi ia i Braine-le-Comte. Io Zech et Fils. 1910. 12mo. 647 pp.

PL
Phil.Pam.
224

E hamani pure me te ui i una he teao kiritiano. V.C.J.S. I Patua i Vaiparaino, i te puni. 1845. 16mo. 104 pp.

(Marquesan prayerbook and catechism)

PL
870
G 74

E mau piti na te mau haapii raa, no roto i te parau iriti tahito hia o te ore i faatitiaifaro hia ra.

IN (bound at end of)

Grammaire et dictionnaire de la langue Maori, dialect Tahitien...(1864).

PL
870
E 11

placed
in
Safe
Ms
Room

(labelled "First native prayerbook")

E parau bure. Ahio na, Iaito. Tahiti. Mission Press. 1828. 24 pp. 8vo.

contains also Te mau episetole a te aposetolo ra a Paulo. Tatna i papai adu i i Galatia, Ephesia, Philipi, Colosa, Tesalonia, ia Timoteo hoi, Tito, e Philomona. Tahiti. Windward Mission Press. 1824. 71 pp.

and E parau no te au maitai raa, o ta te mau papai evanelia toomaha ra, faaite raa i te evanelia a Iesu Mesia ra; ei ite ra no te taata atoa. Tahiti. (Mission Press) 1829. 31 pp.

over

PL
700
E 33

E hamani pure me te ui i una he tekao kiritiano. V.C.I.S. I Patua a i Paris. 1868. 582 pp. 16mo.

(Marquesan prayer book)

PL
Phil.Pam.
226

Duc.

E mou kaoha. V.C.I.S. I oomi ia i Bar-le-Duc. 1883. 35 pp. 16mo.

(Marquesan)

PL
870
T 25

E parau faaite i te mau ecclesia atoa i te ienoi mao fenua, i te tere o dareni; i te uta raa i te mau oromedua i matuita. Tahiti. (Mission Press) 1831. 11 pp. 8vo.

(Bound with 33 other pamphlets: Te evanelia a to tatou ... no. 14)

PL
700
E 35-a

E hamani pure no te vikariato apotoliko Marquises. I oomi ia i Braine-le-Comte. Io Zech et fils. 1910. 18mo.

PL
Phil.Pam.
497

E Mou Tekao Ke. V.C.I.S. I Bar-le-Duc. Mei te oomi ia hamani pauro peato. 1886. 12mo. 57 pp.

(Various teaching in verse. In Marquesan)

PL
870
T 25

E parau iti aroha, e te faaitoito i te feia e parahi noa, aore e imi te ora e ora'i to ratou varua. Tahiti. Mission Press. 1827. 8 pp. 8vo.

(Bound with 33 other pamphlets: Te evanelia a to tatou ... no. 31)

PL
700
E 35

E hamani pure no te vikariato apotoliko Marquises me te ui katoliliko. I oomi ia i Paris. 1892. 526 + 29 pp. 16mo.

(Marquesan prayer book and catechism.)

GN
671.N5
C 53

E MIRA

Chinnery, E. W. Pearson

Notes on the Natives of E. Mira and St. Matthias.

(Anthropological Report, Territory of New Guinea, No. 2, Melbourne, ND)

PL
870
T 25

E parau iti faaitoito, na te feia fanau tama ra; no ta ratou haapao raa i ta ratou mau tamarii ra. Tahiti. Mission Press. 1827. 8 pp. 8vo.

(Bound with 33 other pamphlets: Te evanelia a to tatou ... no.'s. 11 and 25)

PL
700
E 32

E hatu evanerio no te tau tominika no titahi a tapu ke, me ko koika ma te ehua. I oomi ia i Paris. Io Belin Freres. 1894. 12mo. 363 pp.

Marquesas, hymn.

E MIRA ETHNOLOGY

see

ETHNOLOGY E MIRA

PL
Phil.Pam.
706

E parau na te mau oromatua porotetani. Printed by the Avondale Press, Cooranbong, New South Wales. 1912.

(A letter to the Protestant Ministers- Tahitian)

2 copies

PL
Phil.Pam.
498

E Himene a Maria Peatu. Magnificat. Me e mou himene a Tavite. V. C. I. S. I Bar-le-Duc. Mei te oomi ia hamani pauro peato. 1886. 12mo. 32 pp.

(The Magnificat, in Marquesan)

PL
870
T 25

E parau A, B, D. Tahiti. Mission Press. 1829. 8 pp. 8vo.

(Bound with 33 other pamphlets: Te evanelia a to tatou ... no. 21)

PL
870
T 25

E parau no te au maitai raa, o ta te mau papai evanelia toomaha ra, faaite raa i te evanelia a Iesu Mesia ra; ei ite ra no te taata atoa. Tahiti. (Mission Press) 1829. 31 pp. 8vo.

(Bound with 33 other pamphlets: Te evanelia a to tatou ...no. 12)

(another copy bound with "E parau bure... PL 870 E 11)

PL
870
T 25

E hitu seremone, no te tahi mau parau tumu, no roto i te parau a te atua, no Iesu Mesia, e no tana mau ohipa. E tia ia taiohia e te taata toa, i haapachia ra no te tahi oromedua ore. Tahiti. (Mission Press) 1832. 59 pp. 8vo.

(Bound with 33 other pamphlets: Te evanelia a to tatou ... no. 27)

PL
870
T 25

E parau bure. A hio na, iaite. Tahiti. Mission Press. 1828. 24 pp. 8vo.

(Bound with 33 other pamphlets: Te evanelia a to tatou ... no. 24)

PL
870
T 25

E parau, no te haapao raa a te hoe tamaiti John Knill te ioa. I pohe oia i te mai rahi buai i parauhia e colera. Tahiti. Windward Mission Press. 1834. 12 pp. 8vo.

(Bound with 33 other pamphlets: Te evanelia a to tatou ... no. 29)

over

PL
870
T 25

E parau ui na to mau taata faaroo; iritihia ei parau Tahiti. Talaa. Leeward Mission Press. 1826. 24 pp. 8vo.

(Bound with 33 other pamphlets: Te evanelia a to tatou ... no. 17)

PL
Phil.Pam.
499

E tekao mea hukuko. Hoa haa meitai i te huna moi. V. C. I. S. I. Bar-le-Duc. Loi te oomi ia hamani pauro peato. 1886. 12mo. 62 pp.

(Moral poetry, in Marquesan)

PL
870
T 25

E ui tumu no te mau parau a te atua; e tia ia faaroo paantoahia, e te taata toa nei. Tahiti. (Mission Press) 1827. 19 pp. 8vo.

(Bound with 33 other pamphlets: Te evanelia a to tatou ... nos. 13 and 16)

PL
870
T 25

E parau ui na te tamarii. n.d. 8 pp. 8vo.

(Bound with 33 other pamphlets: Te evanelia a to tatou ... no. 19)

DU
Pac.
Pam.
914

E. Thomas Gilliard in New Guinea. Prepared especially for the Explorers Journal by the National Geographic.

(The Explorers Journal, Vol. XXXV(1):2-6, Spring, 1957)

EAGLE--PHILIPPINES

QL   Shufeldt, R. W.,
Bird
Pam   Osteological and other notes on
#25   the monkey-eating eagle of the
       Philippines, Pithecophaga Jefferyi
       Grant. ex Philippine Jour. of Sc.
       Vol. XV, pp. 31-58. pls.

PL
870
T 25

E piti himene no te faa arii raa ia Pomare III. n.d. 2 pp. 8vo.

(2 hymns, in Tahitian dialect)

(Bound with 33 other pamphlets: Te evanelia a to tatou ... no. 26)

PL
Phil.pam.
264

E tuatua enua, te mea ia e takai te tu o te au enua katoa nei. E te au mea i rungaō. I kiritia mei roto i te Tuatua Enua a Pinnock. Rarotonga. (Mission press) 1840. 46 pp. 8vo.

(Rarotonga. Geography)

GN
665
M42

Eaglehawk and crow.

Mathew, John

PL
605
P 98

E pupu-takao no te mau evagerio o ha. Braine-Io-Comte...Zech... 1908. 12mo. 544 pp.

Mangareva, New Testament

PL
870
T 25

E ture na Tahiti, e Moorea, e na Meetia, Ana, Auura, Mapoa, e tetiaroa hoi. Tahiti. (Mission Press) 1825. 36 pp. 8vo.

(Bound with 33 other pamphlets: Te evanelia a to tatou ...no. 22)

DU
1
M 6

"Eakle, Arthur Starr"

Stearns, Harold T.

Memorial to Dr. Arthur Starr Eakle.

(Journal of the Pan-Pacific Research Institution, Vol. VI, No. 4. IN Mid-Pacific Magazine Vol. 42, No. 4, 1931) pp. 2-3

PL
Phil.Pam
785

E rine goro ana Luke na usa. ini haatee ni wano. The Gospel according to St. Luke, San Cristoval, Solomon Islands. Melanesian Mission Press. 1905. sm8vo. 72 pp.

Solomon Islands, San Cristoval, St. Luke

PL
870
T 25

E ui, e parau aai; no roto i te mau buka matamua o to baibara, o tei papaihia e Mose. n.d. 12 pp. 8vo.

(Bound with 33 other pamphlets: Te evanelia a to tatou ...no. 20)

DU
1
M 6

Eakle, Arthur S.

The Minerals of Oahu

(The Mid-Pacific Magazine, Vol. 42, No. 4, pp. 341-343, 1931)

PL
850
E 65

E rine, inia haatee rihinai rago rai rihunai mani dani... [Order for morning and evening prayer, and for administration of sacraments of baptism and of the Lord's supper, in the Wano language.] London. Society for Promoting Christian Knowledge. 1901. 12mo. 64 pp

Solomon Islands, Wano, prayers...

PL
870
T 25

E ui, i te tekau tahuata. 8 pp. no date no place.

(A catechism, in Marquesan.)

(Bound with other pamphlets, No. 3 a)

AS
36
A 25

Eakle, Arthur S.

Petrographical notes on some rocks from the Fiji Islands.

(Proc. Amer. Acad. of Arts and Sci., Vol. 34, 1899, pp. 579-595)

PL
870
T 25

E tala A, E, F. Huahine. Mission Press. 11 pp. 8vo.

(Bound with 33 other pamphlets: Te evanelia a to tatou ... no.5)

PL
870
T 25

E ui na te tamarii. Tahiti. Mission Press. 1823. 12 pp. 8vo.

(Catechism, in Tahitian dialect)

(Bound with 33 other pamphlets: Te evanelia a to tatou ...no. 15)

QL
1
B 86

Eales, N. B.

Revision of the world species of Aplysia (Gastropoda, Opisthobranchia)

(Bull. Brit. Mus. (Nat. Hist.), Zoology, Vol. 5(10), 1960)

QL
5
M 98

Eales, N. B.

A systematic and anatomical account of the Opisthobranchia.

IN The John Murray Expedition, 1933-34,
Sci. Repts., Vol. V, no. 4, 1938, pp. 77-122.

QK
641
E 12

Eames, Arthur J.

Morphology of Vascular plants: lower groups.
First edition. McGraw-Hill Book Company., Inc.
New York...1936 8vo. xviii + 433 pp.

DU
12
K 81

locked
case

Earl, George Windsor   translator

Kolff, D. H.

Voyages of the Dutch brig of war Dourga...
1825-1826...Translated from the Dutch by George
Windsor Earl. London. 1840. 8vo.

QL
5
Br

Eales, Nellie B.

Mollusca. British Antarctic Exped.
1910, Natural history report, Zool. Vol.
VII, 1923 -

Note .- Vol. VII, No.1 = Mollusca Part V
Anatomy of Gastropoda (except the Nudi-
branchs)

Eames, Arthur J.

Morphology of vascular plants. New York. 1936
Lower groups (Psilophytales to Filicales)

UH
Miss Neal
HSPA

QL
Birds
Pam.
326

Earl, Marjorie

The world's most ardent birdwatcher. The
gifted son of Scott of the Antarctic will fly
anywhere to gaze lovingly at rare wildfowl. And
when he coveted some trumpeters for his own collection the Queen herself wheedled five from
Canada.

(Maclean's, Canada's National Magazine,
Dec. 1, 1952:24-25, 39, 42, 43)

AS
36
A 65 n

Ealey, E. H. M.

Kangaroo cave life; cool daytime havens
often obviate the euro's need for water.

(Natural History, 72(10):42-49, 1963)

QP
1
C

EAR

Maxwell, Samuel Steen.

... Experiments on the functions of the internal ear.
By S. S. Maxwell ...

(*In* University of California publications in physiology. Berkeley, 1910.
27½ᵐᵐ. vol. 4, no. 1, p. [1]-4)

From the Hertzstein research laboratory of the University of California.

1. Ear.

A 10-1124

Title from Univ. of Calif.   Library of Congress

DU
406
E 12

Earle, Augustus

Narrative of a nine months' residence in
New Zealand in 1827; together with a journal of
a residence in Tristan D'Acunha...London, Longman, 1832. 8vo. 371 pp.

QK
Bot.Fam.
2364

Eames, Arthur J.

The botanical identity of the Hawaiian ipu
nui or large gourd. By Arthur J. Eames and
Harold St. John.

(American Journal of Botany, Vol. 30, no. 3,
1943, pp. 255-259)

2 copies

DU
12
E 13

locked
case

Eardley-Wilmot, Saint-Hill   editor

Our journal in the Pacific. By the officers
of H.M.S. Zealous. Arranged and edited by Lieutenant S. Eardley-Wilmot. With a map and numerous
illustrations. London. Longmans, Green. 1873.
8vo. xiv+333+xx pp.

Carter Coll.
6-F-7

GN
2.I
V 64

Earle, Margaret Jane

Rakau children from six to thirteen years.

(Victoria Univ. of Wellington, Publ. in
Psychology, No. 11, 1958)

[Maori]

QK
47
E12

Eames, Arthur J   and MacDaniels, Laurence H

An introduction to plant anatomy.

New York, McGraw-Hill. 1925, 264p.   pls.

DU
12
B 82

locked
case

Eardley-Wilmot, Sainthill   editor

Brassey, Thomas

Voyages and travels of Lord Brassey, from
1862 to 1894. Arranged and edited by Captain S.
Eardley-Wilmot. 2 vols. London. 1895. 8vo.

GC
63
D 61

Earland, Arthur

Heron-Allen, E.

Foraminifera, Part I-IV, by E. Heron-Allen
and Arthur Earland.

Discovery Committee
Discovery Reports, Vol. 4,1932,p.291-460;
Vol. 7, 1933,p.27-138; Vol. 10, 1934,p.1-208; Vol.
13, 1936,p.1-76.

Eames, Arthur Johnson, 1881-   and MacDaniels,
Lawrence H.
An introduction to plant anatomy. 1st ed.
New York, McGraw-Hill Book company, 1925.

UH has also

DU
620
P

Earl, David

Termites on the wing.

(Paradise of the Pacific, Vol. 41, No. 6,
1928, p. 5-9)

G
51
W 17

Earle, R. Vigors

The bird catchers of Nauru.

(Walkabout, Vol. 7 (11):20, 1941)

QK
641
E 12

Eames, Arthur J.

Morphology of the angiosperms. New
York. McGraw-Hill Book Co. 1961. xiii
+ 518 pp. R8vo.

GN
671.N5
E 12

Earl, George Windsor

Native races of the Indian Archipelago;
Papuans. London. Bailliere. 1853. 8vo. xiv +
239 pp.

(Ethnographical Library, conducted by Edwin
Norris, Vol. 1)

GN
2 S
A 22

An early account of the Choctaw Indians, by John R.
Swanton. Lancaster, Pa., Pub. for the American
anthropological association [1918]

cover-title, 1 p. l., p. 53-72. 25½ᶜᵐ. (Memoirs of the American anthropological association. vol. v, no. 2. April-June, 1918)

A translation of chapters relating to the Choctaw Indians, from a
French manuscript narrative of Louisiana, in the Edward E. Ayer collection in the Newberry library, Chicago, entitled: Relation de la Louisianne.

1. Choctaw Indians. 2. Swanton, John Reed, 1873-   tr.

Library of Congress   GN2.A22 vol. 5   19—4307
[a20c2]

DU
647
G 91

The Early American occupation of Guam.

(The Guam Recorder, vol.13, no.1, 1936, pp.5, 42)

QC
801
Ca
and
AS
36
S1

EARTH

Adams, L. H. and Williamson, E. D.

The composition of the earth's interior. From Smithson. Report for 1923, pp 241 - 260. Papers Geo. Lab.Carnegie Inst. No. 560, 1925.

QE
Geol.Pam.
1044

EARTH

Washington, H. S.

The crust of the earth and its relation to the interior.

(Reprinted from "Physics of the earth, VII, Internal constitution of the earth", by Beno Gutenberg, pp. 91-123. Papers from the Geophysical Laboratory, Carnegie Inst. of Washington, No. 1008, 1939.)

GN
22
G 61

Early civilization

Goldenweiser, A. A.

QE
Geol.
Pam.
1045

EARTH

Adams, L. H.

Elastic properties of materials of the earth's crust.

(Reprinted from "Physics of the earth-VII, Internal constitution of the earth", by Beno Gutenberg, pp. 71-89. Papers from the Geophysical Laboratory, Carnegie Inst. of Washington, No. 1007, 1939)

AS
36
S1

EARTH

Wiechert, Emil, 1861–

Our present knowledge of the earth. By E. Wiechert ...

(*In* Smithsonian institution. Annual report. 1908. Washington, 1909. 23½ᶜᵐ. p. 431-449)

"Translated ... from Deutsche rundschau, band CXXXII (September 1907), Berlin, pp. 376-394."

1. Earth. 2. Geophysics.

{Full name: Johann Emil Wiechert}

15-21172

Library of Congress   Q11.S66 1908

GN
Ethn
Pam
100

Early discoveries of Hawi. Ilds.

Peirce, Henry A

AS
36
S1

EARTH

Chamberlin, Thomas Chrowder, 1843–

The future habitability of the earth. By Thomas Chrowder Chamberlin ...

(*In* Smithsonian institution. Annual report. 1910. Washington, 1911. 23½ᶜᵐ. p. 371-389)

1. Earth.

11-31569

Library of Congress   Q11.S66 1910

AS
36
S1

EARTH

Woodward, Robert Simpson, 1849–

The mathematical theories of the earth. By Robert Simpson Woodward.

(*In* Smithsonian institution. Annual report. 1890. Washington, 1891. 23½ᶜᵐ. p. 183-200)

"From the Proceedings Am. assoc. adv. sci., vol. XXXVIII."

1. Earth.

S 15-723

Library of Congress   Q11.S66 1890
Library, Smithsonian   Institution

DU
620
P

Early grass churches.

(Paradise of the Pacific, Vol. 15, 1902, No. 8, p. 21)

QE
Geol.Pam.
906

EARTH

Daly, Reginald A.

The depths of the earth.

(Bull. of the Geological Soc. of Amer., Vol. 44, pp. 243-264, Apr. 30, 1933)

QE
Geol.
Pam.
1082

EARTH AGE

Becker, George F.

The age of the earth.

(Smithsonian Miscellaneous Collections, Vol. 56, no. 6, 1910, pp. 1-28)

AP
2
N 4

Early Knowledge of Iron in the Pacific.

(Nature, Vol. 129, No 3247, 1932, pp. 124)

AS
36
S1
10-6
Bm.Pub.Wash.
Geology
miscell.

EARTH

Day, A.L.

Geophysical research. from Smith. Report for 1912, 8 vo. pp. 359-369.

Wash., 1913.

AS
36
S1

EARTH, AGE OF

Joly, John, 1857–

The age of the earth. By J. Joly ...

(*In* Smithsonian institution. Annual report. 1911. Washington, 1912. 23½ᶜᵐ. p. 271-293. diagr.)

"Reprinted ... from the Philosophical magazine, London, s. 6, vol. 22, no. 122, September, 1911, pp. 358-370."

1. Earth, Age of.

13-3781

Library of Congress   Q11.S66 1911

Early Migrations

See.

Brooks, Emerson, Garnier
Peirce, Brown (N.Z.J. XLIV), Best.

QE
501
J 47

EARTH

Jeffreys, Sir Harold

The earth, its origin, history and physical constitution. Fourth edition. Cambridge. At the University Press. 1959. R8vo. xvi + 420 pp.

AS
36
S1

EARTH, AGE OF.

Joly, John, 1857–

An estimate of the geological age of the earth. By J. Joly ...

(*In* Smithsonian institution. Annual report. 1899. Washington, 1901. 23½ᶜᵐ. p. 247-288. tables)

"Reprinted from Scientific transactions of the Royal Dublin society, n. s., vol. VII, part III, 1899."

1. Earth, Age of.

S 15-1028

Library of Congress   Q11.S66 1899
Library, Smithsonian   Institution

DU
12
E 12
1.c.

Earnshaw, John   (introduced...by)

A letter from the South Seas, by a voyager on the 'Daedalus', 1792. Introduced and annotated by John Earnshaw. Talkarra Press. Cremorne, N.S.W. 1957. 8vo. [no. 49 of limited edition] 41 pp. unnumbered.

QE
26
K 96

EARTH

Kummel, Bernhard

History of the earth; an introduction to historical geology. Drawings by Evan L. Gillespie. San Francisco and London. 1961 c sm4to. xii + 610 pp.

AS
36
S1

EARTH, AGE OF

King, Clarence, 1842-1901.

The age of the earth. By Clarence King.

(*In* Smithsonian institution. Annual report. 1893. Washington, 1894. 23½ᶜᵐ. p. 335-352. pl. XVII-XVIII, diagr., tables)

"From American journal of science, January, 1893; 3d series, vol. XLV, pp. 1-20."

1. Earth, Age of.   I. Title.

S 15-831

Library of Congress   Q11.S66 1893
Library, Smithsonian   Institution

AS 36 S1

EARTH, AGE OF

Walcott, Charles Doolittle, 1850–

Geologic time, as indicated by the sedimentary rocks of North America. By Charles D. Walcott.

(*In* Smithsonian institution. Annual report. 1893. Washington, 1894. 23½ᶜᵐ. p. 301–334. pl., tables)

1. Earth, Age of.   I. Title.

S 15–830

Library of Congress   Q11.S66 1893
Library, Smithsonian   Institution

QE Geology Pam 662

EARTH – INTERNAL STRUCTURE

Washington, Henry S.

La costituzione della terra. From Bull. Volcanologique, n.5–6, tri. 3–4, 1925.

QH 366 P45

The earth before history.

Perrier, Edmond

AS 36 S1

EARTH, DENSITY OF

Wilsing, Johannes, 1856–

Determination of the mean density of the earth by means of a pendulum principle. By J. Wilsing. Tr. and condensed by Prof. J. Howard Gore ...

(*In* Smithsonian institution. Annual report. 1888. Washington, 1890. 23½ᶜᵐ. p. 635–646. diagr.)

"From Publicationen des Astrophysikalischen observatoriums zu Potsdam, vol. VI, Potsdam, 1887, 1888."

1. Earth, Density of.   2. Pendulum.   I. Gore, James Howard, 1856–   tr.

S 15–681

Library of Congress   Q11.S66 1888
Library, Smithsonian   Institution

QB 506 C44

EARTH–ROTATION

... The Tidal and other problems, by T. C. Chamberlin, F. R. Moulton, C. S. Slichter, W. D. MacMillan, Arthur C. Lunn, and Julius Stieglitz. Washington, D. C., Carnegie institution of Washington, 1909.

2 p. l., iii–iv, 3–264 p. illus. fold. chart, diagrs. 25½ᶜᵐ. (*On verso of t.-p.*: Carnegie institution of Washington. Publication no. 107)

At head of title: Contributions to cosmogony and the fundamental problems of geology.

CONTENTS.—I. The tidal problem: The former rates of the earth's rotation, by T. C. Chamberlin. The rotation-period of a heterogeneous spheroid, by C. S. Slichter. On the loss of energy by friction of the tides, by W. D. MacMillan. On certain relations among the possible changes in the

(Continued on next card)

9—9962

[a20m3]

AS 36 S1

EARTH MOVEMENTS

Blytt, Axel Gudbrand, 1843–1898.

On the movements of the earth's crust. By A. Blytt. Tr. by W. S. Dallas ...

(*In* Smithsonian institution. Annual report. 1889. Washington, 1890. 23½ᶜᵐ. p. 325–375. tables, diagr.)

"From the London, Edinburgh, and Dublin, philosophical magazine, May and June, 1889, vol. XXVII, pp. 405–429, and 487–519."

1. Earth movements.   I. Dallas, William Sweetland, 1824–1890, tr.

S 15–698

Library of Congress   Q11.S66 1889
Library, Smithsonian   Institution

AS 36 S1

EARTH, FIGURE OF.

Gregory, John Walter, 1864–

The plan of the earth and its causes. By J. W. Gregory ...

(*In* Smithsonian institution. Annual report. 1898. Washington, 1899. 23½ᶜᵐ. p. 363–388. diagrs.)

"From the Geographical journal no. 3, March, 1899, vol. XIII, pp. 225–251."

1. Geology, Structural.   2. Earth, Figure of.

S 15–1000

Library of Congress   Q11.S66 1898
Library, Smithsonian   Institution

QB 506 C44

EARTH–ROTATION

... The Tidal and other problems ... 1909. (Card 2)

CONTENTS—Continued.

motions of mutually attracting spheres when disturbed by tidal interactions, by F. R. Moulton. Notes on the possibility of fission of a contracting rotating fluid mass, by F. R. Moulton. The bearing of molecular activity on spontaneous fission in gaseous spheroids, by T. C. Chamberlin.—II. Geophysical theory under the planetesimal hypothesis, by A. C. Lunn.—III. Relations of equilibrium between the carbon dioxide of the atmosphere and the calcium sulphate, calcium carbonate, and calcium bicarbonate of water solutions in contact with it, by J. Stieglitz.

1. Tides.   2. Earth—Rotation.   3. Rotating masses of fluid.   4. Cosmogony.   5. Geophysics.   6. Chemical equilibrium.   I. Chamberlin, Thomas Chrowder, 1843–   II. Moulton, Forest Ray, 1872–   III. Slichter, Charles Sumner, 1864–   IV. MacMillan, William Duncan.   V. Lunn, Arthur Constant, 1877–   VI. Stieglitz, Julius Oscar, 1867–

Library of Congress   QB415.T5
——— Copy 2.   QE511.T5   9—9962
[a20m3]

AS 36 S1

EARTH MOVEMENTS

Gilbert, Grove Karl, 1843–

Modification of the Great Lakes by earth movement. By G. K. Gilbert ...

(*In* Smithsonian institution. Annual report. 1898. Washington, 1899. 23½ᶜᵐ. p. 349–361. diagrs.)

"Reprinted from the National geographic magazine, vol. VIII, no. 9, September, 1897."

1. Great Lakes.   2. Earth movements.   I. Title.

S 15–999

Library of Congress   Q11.S66 1898
Library, Smithsonian   Institution

AS 36 C8

EARTH, FIGURE OF.

Mansfield, Jared, 1759–1830.

... Of the figure of the earth ...

(*In* Connecticut academy of arts and sciences. Memoirs. New Haven, 1810. 22½ᶜᵐ. v. 1, p. [111]–118)

1. Earth, Figure of.   I. Title.

A 17–741

Library of Congress   Q11.C85 vol. 1
Yale University   A53n.365.1

QE Geology Pam 694

EARTH – SURFACE

Bucher, Walter H.

The pattern of the earth's mobile belt. From Journ. Geology, v.32, n.4, 1924.

AS 36 S1

EARTH MOVEMENTS.

Le Conte, Joseph, 1823–1901.

Earth-crust movements and their causes. By Joseph Le Conte.

(*In* Smithsonian institution. Annual report. 1896. Washington, 1898. 23½ᶜᵐ. p. 233–244)

"Printed in Science, vol. v, no. 113, pp. 321–330."

1. Geology, Structural.   2. Earth movements.   I. Title.

S 15–923

Library of Congress   Q11.S66 1896
Library, Smithsonian   Institution

AS 36 S1

EARTH, FIGURE OF

Merino, Miguel.

Figure of the earth. By Sr. Miguel Merino.

(*In* Smithsonian institution. Annual report. 1863. Washington, 1864. 23½ᶜᵐ. p. [306]–330. tables)

"Anuario del Real observatorio de Madrid; cuarto año; 1863. Translated ... by C. A. Alexander."

1. Earth, Figure of.   I. Alexander, Charles Armistead, d. 1869? tr.

S 15–145

Library of Congress   Q11.S66 1863
Library, Smithsonian   Institution

QE 1 G 3s

EARTH SURFACE

Poldervaart, Arie   editor

Crust of the earth (a symposium).

(Geological Society of America, Special Paper 62, 1955)

QC Physics Pam 12

EARTH TEMPERATURE

Kerner, A

Ueber wanderungen des maximums der bodentemperatur. From Zeit. d. osterreich Gesell. f. meterologie.

AS 36 S1

EARTH-CRUST MOVEMENTS AND THEIR CAUSES.

Le Conte, Joseph, 1823–1901.

Earth-crust movements and their causes. By Joseph Le Conte.

(*In* Smithsonian institution. Annual report. 1896. Washington, 1898. 23½ᶜᵐ. p. 233–244)

"Printed in Science, vol. v, no. 113, pp. 321–330."

1. Geology, Structural.   2. Earth movements.   I. Title.

S 15–923

Library of Congress   Q11.S66 1896
Library, Smithsonian   Institution

AS 36 S1

The earth: its figure, dimensions, and the constitution of its interior. By T. C. Chamberlin, Harry Fielding Reid, John F. Hayford, and Frank Schlesinger.

(*In* Smithsonian institution. Annual report. 1916. Washington, 1917. 23½ᶜᵐ. p. 225–254)

"Reprinted ... from Proceedings of the American philosophical society, September and October–December, 1915."

1. Earth.   I. Chamberlin, Thomas Chrowder, 1843–   II. Reid, Harry Fielding, 1859–   III. Hayford, John Fillmore, 1868–   IV. Schlesinger, Frank, 1871–

18—3061

Library of Congress   Q11.S66 1916

AS 36 S1

EARTH TEMPERATURE

Schott, Charles Anthony, 1826–1901.

On underground temperature. By Charles A. Schott ...

(*In* Smithsonian institution. Annual report. 1874. Washington, 1875. 23½ᶜᵐ. p. [249]–253)

1. Earth temperature.

S 15–384

Library of Congress   Q11.S66 1874
Library, Smithsonian   Institution

QE Geol. Pam 1017

EARTH INTERNAL STRUCTURE

Adams, Leason H.

The earth's interior, its nature and composition. Being a lecture...Carnegie Institution of Washington, Oct. 27, 1936.

(Carnegie Inst. of Washington, Supplementary Publications, No. 27, 1937)

QH 84.6 M 36

The earth as modified by human action...

Marsh, George P.

QE 75 B

EARTH TEMPERATURE

Darton, Nelson Horatio, 1865–

... Geothermal data of the United States, including many original determinations of underground temperature, by N. H. Darton. Washington, Govt. print. off., 1920.

97 p. illus. fold. map, diagrs. 23ᶜᵐ. (U. S. Geological survey. Bulletin 701)

At head of title: Department of the interior ... United States geological survey.

1. Earth temperature.   I. Title.

——— Copy 2.   G S 20–337

Library, U. S. Geological   Survey (200) E no. 701
[8]

AP
2
N 4
Earthquake in Solomon Islands of April 30, 1939.

(Nature, Vol. 143, 1939, p. 891)

QE
529
D 26
EARTHQUAKES

Davison, Charles

Studies on the periodicity of earthquakes. With 14 illustrations. London. Thomas Murby & Co. 1938. sm8vo. ix + 107 pp.

AP
2
C 35
EARTHQUAKES

Gutenberg, B(eno)

Magnitude and energy of earthquakes.

(Science, 83(2147):163-185, 1936)

GN
1
A 63
EARTHQUAKE BELIEFS

Aufenanger, H.

The earthquake: beliefs and practices in the Central Highlands, New Guinea.

(Anthropos, Vol. 57:170-176, 1962)

QE
521
D23
Earthquakes

see

Daubeny, C.

Description of active and extinct volcanoes, of earthquakes and of thermal springs; with remarks on causes of these phaenomena... London, 1848. 2nd ed. 8vo. 830 pp.

QE
529
H 44
EARTHQUAKES

Heck, Nicholas Hunter

Earthquakes. Princeton University Press. 1936. 8vo. xi + 222 pp.

QE
539
R
Earthquake Registers, 1895 -1901.

R. Ufficio Centrale di Meteorologia etc.

QE
534 529
D 98
Earthquakes

Dutton, Clarence Edward.

Earthquakes in the light of the new seismology.

New York, 1904. 314p. illus.

AS
36
S2
Earthquakes.

Holden, E. S.

Catalogue of earthquakes on the Pacific coast.

In Smith. Mis. Col. XXXVII, Art V, pp. 1-253.

AM
Mus.Pam.
476
Earthquake Research Institute.

Outline of the Earthquake Research Institute, University of Tokyo. 1962. pp.1-26.

QE
Geol.
Pam.
#565
EARTHQUAKES.

Earthquake studies. (Transactions of the Commonwealth club of Calif. v.XX no. 6)

QE
Geology
Pam.
874
EARTHQUAKES

Imamura, A.

The World-Shaking Earthquake of August 10, 1930, as Observed with a Three-Minute Horizontal Pendulum.

(From Japanese Journal of Astronomy and Geophysics, Vol. IX, No. 1, 3 pages, 1 plate, 1931).

QE
Geol.
Pam.
#565
Earthquake studies. (Transactions of the Commonwealth club of Calif. v.XX no.6.)

QC
801
Oa
C28
EARTHQUAKES

Fenner, Clarence N.

Earth movements accompanying the Katmai eruption. Geophysical Lab. Carnegie Inst. Wash. Paper No. 562, 1925.

QE
531
I
Earthquakes

Japan. *Imperial earthquake investigation committee.* Bulletin. Tokyo, 1907-

no. in   v. illus., plates, fold. map, charts (partly fold.) diagrs. 26⅓ᶜᵐ.

Vol. I by F. Omori and A. Imamura.

See serial file

1. Earthquakes. I. Omori, Fusakichi, 1868-   II. Imamura, A.

10-1033†

Library of Congress   QE531.J17

QE
Pam
#238
Earthquakes

Brigham, W. T.

Earthquakes

ext. Am. Naturalist Vol. II n.d. pp 539-547.

QE
Pam
245
EARTHQUAKES

Flamsteed, John

Letter concerning earthquakes written in the year 1693 ..... to a gentleman ... at Turin in Savoy on the occasion of the destruction of Catanea --- in Sicily in 1692

London 1750   OCT 2013 10 12

QE
Pam
#248
EARTHQUAKES

Liersch, B. M.

Ueber die Ursachen der Erdbeben.

Köln u. Leipzig 1879. 8ᵛᵒ pp. 28

OCT 2013 10 12

QE
521
C 52
Earthquakes

Chevalier, Marcel

Cataclysmes terrestres.

QE
536
G 92
Earthquakes.

Gunther, R. T.

Contributions to the study of earth-movements in the bay of Naples.

QE
Geol.
Pam.
249
Earthquakes

Mallet, M. R.

Sur l'observation des tremblements de terre.

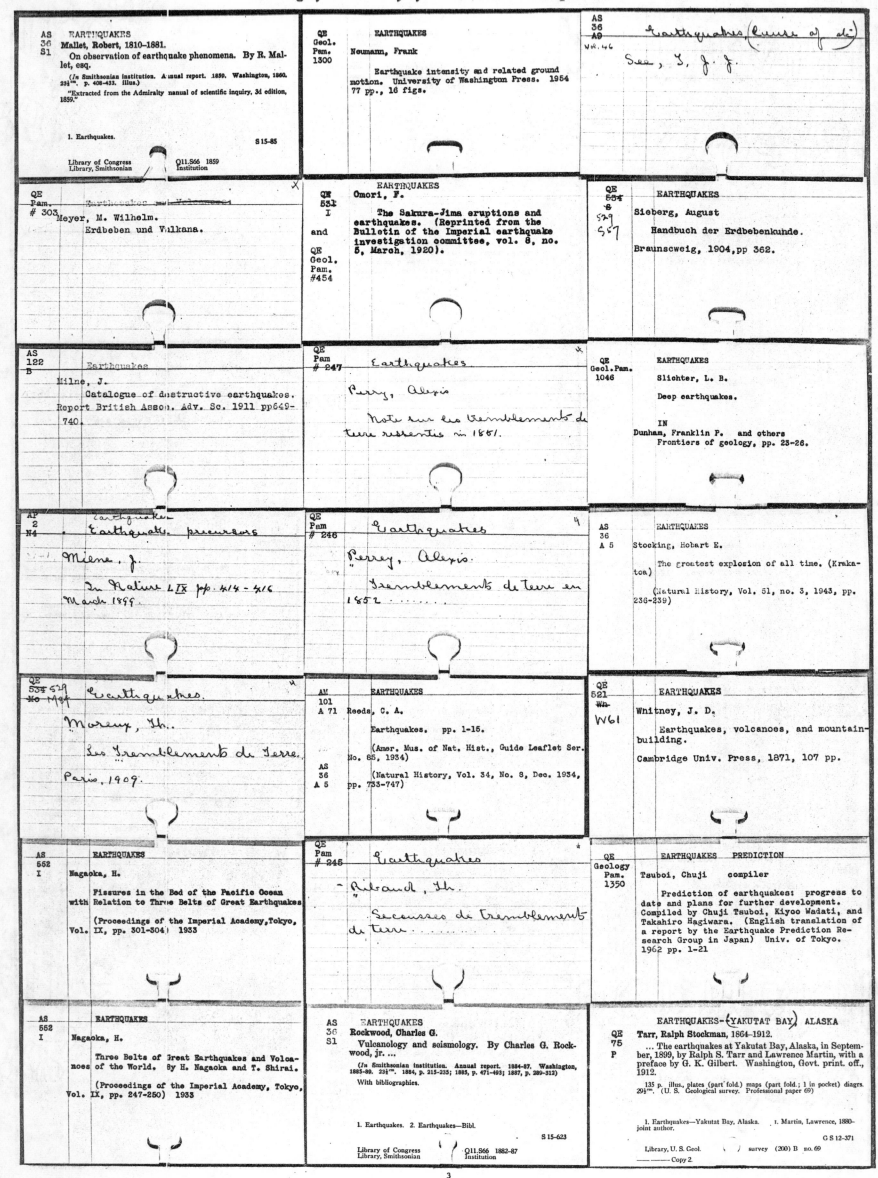

Card 1:

AS
36
S1

EARTHQUAKES
Mallet, Robert, 1810-1881.
   On observation of earthquake phenomena. By R. Mallet, esq.
   (In Smithsonian institution. Annual report. 1859. Washington, 1860. 23½ᶜᵐ. p. 408-433. illus.)
   "Extracted from the Admiralty manual of scientific inquiry, 3d edition, 1859."

1. Earthquakes.   S 15-85

Library of Congress   Q11.S66 1859
Library, Smithsonian   Institution

Card 2:

QE
Geol.
Pam.
1300

EARTHQUAKES
Neumann, Frank
   Earthquake intensity and related ground motion. University of Washington Press. 1954
   77 pp., 16 figs.

Card 3:

AS
36
A9
Vol. 46

Earthquakes (cause of etc)

See, S. J. J.

Card 4:

QE
Pam.
303

Earthquakes and Volcanoes
Meyer, M. Wilhelm.
Erdbeben und Vulkane.

Card 5:

QE
551
I
and
QE
Geol.
Pam.
#454

EARTHQUAKES
Omori, F.
   The Sakura-Jima eruptions and earthquakes. (Reprinted from the Bulletin of the Imperial earthquake investigation committee, vol. 8, no. 5, March, 1920).

Card 6:

QE
554
S
529
S57

EARTHQUAKES
Sieberg, August
   Handbuch der Erdbebenkunde.
   Braunscweig, 1904, pp 362.

Card 7:

AS
122
B

Earthquakes
Milne, J.
   Catalogue of destructive earthquakes.
   Report British Assoc. Adv. Sc. 1911 pp649-740.

Card 8:

QE
Pam
247

Earthquakes

Perry, Alexis

Note sur les tremblements de terre ressentis in 1851.

Card 9:

QE
Geol. Pam.
1046

EARTHQUAKES
Slichter, L. B.
   Deep earthquakes.

IN
Dunham, Franklin P. and others
Frontiers of geology, pp. 23-26.

Card 10:

AP
2
N4

Earthquakes
Earthquake precursors
Milne, J.
In Nature LIX pp. 414-416
March 1899.

Card 11:

QE
Pam
246

Earthquakes

Perrey, Alexis.

Tremblements de terre en 1852........

Card 12:

AS
36
A 5

EARTHQUAKES
Stocking, Hobart E.
   The greatest explosion of all time. (Krakatoa)
   (Natural History, Vol. 51, no. 3, 1943, pp. 236-239)

Card 13:

QE
554 529
Mo M9t

Earthquakes.

Moreux, Th.

Les Tremblements de Terre.

Paris, 1909.

Card 14:

AM
101
A 71

EARTHQUAKES
Reeds, C. A.
   Earthquakes. pp. 1-15.
   (Amer. Mus. of Nat. Hist., Guide Leaflet Ser. No. 85, 1934)

AS
36
A 5
   (Natural History, Vol. 34, No. 8, Dec. 1934, pp. 733-747)

Card 15:

QE
521
Wh
W61

EARTHQUAKES
Whitney, J. D.
   Earthquakes, volcanoes, and mountain-building.
   Cambridge Univ. Press, 1871, 107 pp.

Card 16:

AS
552
I

EARTHQUAKES
Nagaoka, H.
   Fissures in the Bed of the Pacific Ocean with Relation to Three Belts of Great Earthquakes
   (Proceedings of the Imperial Academy, Tokyo, Vol. IX, pp. 301-304) 1933

Card 17:

QE
Pam
245

Earthquakes

Ribaud, Th.

Secousses de Tremblement de terre.

Card 18:

QE
Geology
Pam.
1350

EARTHQUAKES PREDICTION
Tsuboi, Chuji compiler
   Prediction of earthquakes: progress to date and plans for further development. Compiled by Chuji Tsuboi, Kiyoo Wadati, and Takahiro Hagiwara. (English translation of a report by the Earthquake Prediction Research Group in Japan) Univ. of Tokyo. 1962 pp. 1-21

Card 19:

AS
552
I

EARTHQUAKES
Nagaoka, H.
   Three Belts of Great Earthquakes and Volcanoes of the World. By H. Nagaoka and T. Shirai.
   (Proceedings of the Imperial Academy, Tokyo, Vol. IX, pp. 247-250) 1933

Card 20:

AS
36
S1

EARTHQUAKES
Rockwood, Charles G.
   Vulcanology and seismology. By Charles G. Rockwood, jr. ...
   (In Smithsonian institution. Annual report. 1884-87. Washington, 1885-89. 23½ᶜᵐ. 1884, p. 215-235; 1885, p. 471-493; 1887, p. 289-312)
   With bibliographies.

1. Earthquakes. 2. Earthquakes—Bibl.
              S 15-623

Library of Congress   Q11.S66 1882-87
Library, Smithsonian   Institution

Card 21:

QE
75
P

EARTHQUAKES-(YAKUTAT BAY) ALASKA
Tarr, Ralph Stockman, 1864-1912.
   ... The earthquakes at Yakutat Bay, Alaska, in September, 1899, by Ralph S. Tarr and Lawrence Martin, with a preface by G. K. Gilbert. Washington, Govt. print. off., 1912.
   135 p. illus., plates (part fold.) maps (part fold.; 1 in pocket) diagrs. 29½ᶜᵐ. (U. S. Geological survey. Professional paper 69)

1. Earthquakes—Yakutat Bay, Alaska. I. Martin, Lawrence, 1880- joint author.
              G S 12-371

Library, U. S. Geol. survey (200) B no. 69
———— Copy 2.

QE Geol.Pam. 1023 — EARTHQUAKES CALIFORNIA Benioff, Hugo The determination of the extent of faulting with application to the Long Beach earthquake. (Bull. of the Seismological Soc. of America, Vol. 28, 1938, pp. 77-84)	DU 647 G 91 — EARTHQUAKES GUAM Repetti, W. C. Extracts from catalogue of earthquakes felt in Guam, 1825-1938. (Guam Recorder, Vol. 17, 1940, No. 1, p. 25, 26, 38, 39)

AS 36 W 2 — EARTHQUAKES HAWAII

Jones, Austin E.

Earthquakes associated with the 1934 eruption of Kilauea, Hawaii.

(Journal of the Washington Academy of Sciences, Vol. 25, 1935, pp. 429-435)

QE Geol.Pam. 1038 — EARTHQUAKES CALIFORNIA

Benioff, H.

The mammoth "earthquake fault" and related features, by H. Benioff and B. Gutenberg.

(Bull. Seismological Soc. of America, Vol. 29, 1939, pp. 333-340)

AP 2 A 5 — EARTHQUAKES HAWAII

Alexander, William DeWitt

On the earthquake at Oahu, Hawaiian Islands on Feb. 18. (From a letter to J. D. Dana, dated Oahu College, Feb. 28, 1871.)

(Am. Journ. of Sc. 3d Ser. I, 1871, pp. 469-471)

QE Geol.Pam. 937 — EARTHQUAKES HAWAII

Jones, Austin E.

Hawaiian travel times.

(Bulletin of the Seismological Society of America, Vol. 25, 1935, pp. 33-61)

QE 535 C3 — EARTHQUAKES - CALIFORNIA

California. *State earthquake investigation commission.*
The California earthquake of April 18, 1906. Report of the State earthquake investigation commission ... Washington, D. C., Carnegie institution of Washington, 1908-10.

2 v. illus., plates (incl. maps) plans, diagrs. (1 fold.) 29½ x 23cm. and atlas. 61 x 49cm. (On verso of t.-p.: Carnegie institution of Washington. Publication no. 87)

Andrew C. Lawson, chairman of the commission.
Vol. 2: The mechanics of the earthquake, by Harry Fielding Reid.

1. San Francisco—Earthquake and fire, 1906. 2. Earthquakes—California. I. Lawson, Andrew Cowper, 1861- II. Reid, Harry Fielding, 1859-

Library of Congress QE535.C3   8—26871
———— Copy 2.

Local Newspapers Upper Floor in Closet — Hawaii

Earthquake, April 1868

Hawaiian Gazette editorial. April 15, 1868.

AP 2 A 5 — EARTHQUAKES HAWAII

Lyman, Chester S.

A record of earthquakes, kept at Hilo, Hawaii, by S. C. Lyman. (this transposition of initials is probably an error, MT)

(Am. Jour. of Sci., Ser. 2, Vol. 27, 1859, pp. 264-266)

GC Oceanography Pam. 53 — EARTHQUAKES CALIFORNIA

Clements, Thomas

Seismic activity and topography of the sea floor off southern California.

(Bull. Seismological Soc. of America, Vol. 37:307-313, 1947)

Local Newspapers Upper Floor in Closet

Earthquake Hawaiian Islands

Hawaiian Gazette Editorial and letter from J.S. Green. in Haw. Gazette 1930, Aug. 17, p.2.

DU 620 P — EARTHQUAKES HAWAII

Westervelt, W. D. (William Drake)

Kai mimiki.

(Paradise of the Pacific, Vol. 15, 1902, No. 6, p. 15)

QE Geol. Pam. 962 — EARTHQUAKES CALIFORNIA

Wood, Harry O.

Earthquake study in southern California.

(Carnegie Institution of Washington, Supplementary Publications No. 12, 1935, 22 pp.)

QE Geol. Pam. 243 — EARTHQUAKES HAWAII

Hitchcock, C. H.

Hawaiian earthquakes of 1868.

(Seis. Soc. of America, Bull., Vol. II, no. 3, Sept. 1912).

QE Pam. # 252 — EARTHQUAKES -- HAWAIIAN ISLANDS

Wood, Harry O.

On the Earthquakes of 1868 in Hawaii. Re. from Bull. of Seismological Soc. of America. V. 4, 1914, pp. 169-203.

QE Geol.Pam. 902 — EARTHQUAKES CALIFORNIA

Wood, Harry O.

Preliminary Report on the Long Beach Earthquake.

(Bulletin of the Seismological Society of American, Vol. 23, 1933, pp. 43-56)

QE 526 Ha-v — EARTHQUAKES HAWAII

Macdonald, Gordon A.

The Kona earthquake of August 21, 1951. By Gordon A. Macdonald and Chester K. Wentworth.

(The Volcano Letter, No. 513:1-4, J1/S,195?)

QE Geol. Pam. 1252 — EARTHQUAKES HAWKE'S BAY

Hawke's Bay earthquake.

(Auckland Weekly News, vol. 67, no. 3401, Feb. 11, 1931)

QE 535 W73 — EARTHQUAKES - CHILE

Willis, Bailey

Earthquake conditions in Chile. Carnegie Institution of Washington, Publication 382, 1929.

AS 36 W 2 / QE Geol.Pam. 936 / QE Pam .917 — EARTHQUAKES HAWAII

Jones, A. E.

Earthquakes associated with the 1933 eruption of Mauna Loa, Hawaii.

(Journ. of Wash. Acad. of Sciences, Vol. 24, No. 10, Oct. 15, 1934, pp.413-418)

AS 36 S1 — EARTHQUAKES - ICELAND

Thoroddsen, Þorvaldur, 1855-
Volcanic eruptions and earthquakes in Iceland within historic times. Tr. by George H. Boehmer.

(*In* Smithsonian institution. Annual report. 1885. Washington, 1886. 23½cm. p. 495-513)

"Translation of the résumé of 'Oversigt over de islandske vulkaners historie af Th. Thoroddsen ...'"

1. Volcanoes—Iceland. 2. Earthquakes—Iceland. I. Boehmer, George Hans, tr.

Library of Congress Q11.S66 1885   S 15-630-4
Library, Smithsonian Institution

AS
36
S1
EARTHQUAKES - ICELAND - BIBL.

Boehmer, George Hans.

Bibliography of the volcanoes, earthquakes, and geysers of Iceland.

(*In* Smithsonian Institution. Annual report. 1885. Washington, 1886. 23½ᶜᵐ. p. 513-541)

1. Volcanoes—Iceland—Bibl. 2. Earthquakes—Iceland—Bibl. 3. Geysers—Iceland—Bibl.

S 15-632 a

Library of Congress   Q11.S66 1885
Library, Smithsonian   Institution

QE
Geol.Pam.
838

Imamura, A.

A Seismometric Study of the Destructive North Idu Earthquake of November 26, 1930

From Japanese Journal of Astronomy and Geophysics, Vol. VIII, No. 2, 1931

EARTHQUAKES - JAPAN

QE
Geol.
Pam.
No.501
and #52

EARTHQUAKE - KURRAJONG

Cotton, Leo A.

The Kurrajong earthquake of August 15 1919. Reprint. Roy. Soc. N.S.W. Vol. LV 1921.

QE
537
I

Earthquake-India.

Oldham, R. D.

Report on great earthquake of 12th June 1897. Mem. Geol. Survey India XXIX.

QE
Geol.
Pam.
1081

EARTHQUAKES JAPAN

Kuwana, Shinkai Inokiohi

(Concerning the earthquake of 1924, Japan) In Japanese.

AS
36
S1

EARTHQUAKES--MEXICO

Sartorius, Christian i. e. Carl Christian Wilhelm, 1796-1872.

The earthquake in eastern Mexico of the second of January, 1866. By Dr. Charles Sartorius ...

(*In* Smithsonian Institution. Annual report. 1866. Washington, 1867. 23½ᶜᵐ. p. (432)-434. illus.)

"From a letter addressed to the Smithsonian Institution."

1. Earthquakes—Mexico.

S 15-203

Library of Congress   Q11.S66 1866
Library, Smithsonian   Institution

QC
875.B
M 58 e

EARTHQUAKES INDONESIA

Earthquakes in Indonesia for the years 1948-1955

(Djakarta, Ministry of Communications, Meteorological and Geophysical Institute, Ser. A: Nr. 45, 1957)

QE
531
T 64

and
QE
Geol.Pam.
1201

EARTHQUAKES JAPAN

Tsuya, H.   Editor

The Fukui earthquake of June 28, 1948. Report of the Special Committee for the study of the Fukui earthquake. Tokyo. Published by the Committee. 1950, v + 197 pp.

QE
75
B

EARTHQUAKES - MISSOURI

Fuller, Myron Leslie, 1873-

... The New Madrid earthquake, by Myron L. Fuller. Washington, Govt. print. off., 1912.

119 p. x pl., fold. map, diagrs. 23½ᶜᵐ. (U. S. Geological survey. Bulletin 494)

"Bibliography of New Madrid earthquake": p. 111-115.

1. New Madrid, Mo.—Earthquake, 1811-1812.

G S 12-194 Revised

Library, U. S. Geological   Survey (200) E no.494

———— Copy 2.

QE
Geol.Pam.
849

EARTHQUAKES - JAPAN

Imamura, Akitune

Further Studies on the Chronic Block Movements in the Kyoto-Osaka District

From the Proceedings of the Imperial Academy. VII (1931) No. 3.

QE
Geol.Pam.
1020

Yasuda, T.

EARTHQUAKES JAPAN

Earthquakes observed in Tokyo during the period from September, 1872, to December, 1923. By T. Yasuda and T. Kodaira.

QE
536
M 25

EARTHQUAKES NAPLES

Mallet, Robert

Great Neapolitan Earthquake of 1857. The First Principles of Observational Seismology...Expedition...Kingdom of Naples to Investigate the Circumstances of the Great Earthquake of December 1857. In two volumes. London. 1862. R8vo.

QE
Geol.Pam.
848

EARTHQUAKES - JAPAN

Imamura, A.

On the Block Movements that Preceded and Accompanied the Severe Tokyo Earthquake of May 21, 1928 -- Active Faults across the City of Tokyo.

From the Japanese Journal of Astronomy and Geophysics, Vol. VIII, No. 3, 1931.

QE
526
Ha-v

EARTHQUAKES KILAUEA

Macdonald, Gordon A.

The Kilauea earthquake of April 22, 1951, and its aftershocks.

(The Volcano Letter, No. 512, Ap/Je 1951)

QE
Pam
487

Earthquakes - New England.

Brigham, W. T.

Historical notes on the earthquakes of New England. 1688-1869. Jr. Mem. Boston Society Nat. Hist. II. 1. Boston 1871.

Gift of the author

QE
Geology
Pam.
876

EARTHQUAKES - JAPAN

Imamura, Akitune

On the Crustal Deformations that Preceded and Accompanied the Severe Haneda Earthquake of August 3, 1926,.

(From the Proceedings of the Imperial Acad. VII, (1931) no. 7, 4 pages).

QH
1
P 11

EARTHQUAKES KONA

Macdonald, Gordon A.

The Kona earthquake of August 21, 1951, and its aftershocks. By Gordon A. Macdonald and Chester K. Wentworth.

(Pacific Science, 6(4):269-287, 1952)

DU
1
P

EARTHQUAKES NEW HEBRIDES

Eurption: two days of terror in New Hebrides

(Pacific Islands Monthly, Vol. 10, 1939, p. 23-24)

QE
Geol
Pam
No.507

EARTHQUAKE- JAPAN

Imamura, A.

Preliminary note on the great earthquake of S. E. Japan on Sept. 1, 1923. Imp. Earthquake Com. Seis.Notes No.6; Tokyo, July, 1924.

AS
763
H 38

EARTHQUAKES KONA

Wentworth, Chester K.

Earthquake of August 21, 1951, at Kona, Hawaii. By Chester K. Wentworth and Gordon A. Macdonald.

(Proc. Haw. Acad. Sci., 27th Meeting, p. 7, 1951/52)

AS
36
S1

EARTHQUAKE (1811)-NEW MADRID, Mo.

Dudley, Timothy.

The earthquake of 1811 at New Madrid, Missouri. (From the narrative of an eye-witness.) By Timothy Dudley ...

(*In* Smithsonian Institution. Annual report. 1858. Washington, 1859. 23½ᶜᵐ. p. 421-424)

1. New Madrid, Mo.—Earthquake, 1811.

S 15-68

Library of Congress   Q11.S66 1858
Library, Smithsonian   Institution

QE
75
B

EARTHQUAKES -- NEW MADRID

Fuller, Myron

New Madrid Earthquake

U. S. Geol. Survey Bull. 494. 1912

Q
101
P 18

EARTHQUAKES   PACIFIC

Hayes, R. C.
The deep-focus earthquakes of the southwest Pacific.

IN Proc. Sixth Pac. Sci. Congress, 1939, (California), Vol. 1, 1940, pp. 131-134.

QE
75
B

EARTHQUAKE -- SAN FRANCISCO 1906

Gilbert, Grove Karl, 1843-1918.
... The San Francisco earthquake and fire of April 18, 1906, and their effects on structures and structural materials; reports by Grove Karl Gilbert, Richard Lewis Humphrey, John Stephen Sewell, and Frank Soulé, with preface by Joseph Austin Holmes ... Washington, Govt. print. off., 1907.

xii, 170, i p. illus., LVII pl. (part fold, incl. maps) diagrs. 23½ᶜᵐ. (U. S. Geological survey. Bulletin no. 324)

Subject series: R, Structural materials, 1.
"List of papers relating to the earthquake and fire": p. 159-161.

(Continued on next card)

G S 7-1565

(a20f2)

QE
Geol.
Pam.
1252

EARTHQUAKES   NEW ZEALAND

Hawke's Bay earthquake.

(Auckland Weekly News, vol. 67, no. 3401, Feb. 11, 1931)

[The Napier earthquake]

AS
750
N

EARTHQUAKES   PACIFIC

Hogben, G.

Earthquake-origins in the south-west Pacific in 1910.

(New Zealand Inst., Trans. and Proc., Vol. 44, 1911, pp. 139-142)

AP
2
N 4

EARTHQUAKES   SOLOMON ISLANDS

Earthquake in Solomon Islands of April 30, 1939.

(Nature, Vol.143, 1939, p. 891)

AP
2
N 54 b

EARTHQUAKES   NEW ZEALAND

Hayes, R. C.

Earthquakes in New Zealand during the year 1941.

(The New Zealand Journal of Science and Technology, B. Gen. Section, Vol. 23, 1942, pp. 210-211)

AS
36
S2

EARTHQUAKES - PACIFIC COAST

Holden, Edward Singleton, 1846-
... A catalogue of earthquakes on the Pacific coast 1769-1897, by Edward S. Holden ... City of Washington, Smithsonian institution, 1898.

2 p. l., 253 p. illus., 2 pl., 3 maps (incl. front.) 24ᶜᵐ. (Smithsonian miscellaneous collections. (vol. XXXVII, art. vi)

Publication 1087.
"Bibliography of works relating to earthquake phenomena on the Pacific coast": p. 3-6.

1. Earthquakes—Pacific coast.

16-6880

Library of Congress   Q11.S7 vol. 37, art. 5
———— Copy 2.   QE535.H73
———— Copy 3.   Q11.S7 2d set

Q
101
P 18

EARTHQUAKES   TAHITI

Ravet, J.
Remarques sur quelques enregistrements d'ondes a tres courte periode au cours de tremblements de terre eloignes a l'observatoire du Faiere, Papeete, Tahiti.

IN Proc. Sixth Pac. Sci. Congress, 1939, (California), Vol. 1, 1940, pp. 127-130.

DU
400
N 56

EARTHQUAKES   NEW ZEALAND

Henderson, J.

Earthquakes (in New Zealand), by J. Henderson and R. C. Hayes.

(New Zealand Official Year-Book, 1942, pp. 7-10)

(reviewed in Nature, Vol. 150, 1942, p. 554)

AS
36
S2

EARTHQUAKES-PACIFIC COAST

McAdie, Alexander George, 1863-
... Catalogue of earthquakes on the Pacific coast, 1897 to 1906; by Alexander G. McAdie... Washington, Smithsonian institution, 1907.

64 p. 25ᶜᵐ. (Smithsonian miscellaneous collections. Part of vol. XLIX. no. 1721)

1. Earthquakes—Pacific coast.

7-25092

Library of Congress   Q11.S7
———— Copy 2.   QE535.M12

QE
Geol
Pam
590

EARTHQUAKES--UNITED STATES (EASTERN)

Hobbs, William Herbert

The cause of earthquakes:especially those of the eastern United States. From Papers of Michigan Academy of Sci..... vol.5, 1925.

AS
36
S1

EARTHQUAKES - NORTH CAROLINA

Du Pre, Warren.
On a series of earthquakes in North Carolina, commencing on the 10th of February, 1874. By Professor Warren du Pré ...

(In Smithsonian institution. Annual report. 1874. Washington, 1875. 23½ᶜᵐ. p. [254]-260)

1. Earthquakes—North Carolina.

S 15-385

Library of Congress
Library, Smithsonian   Q11.S66 1874
Institution

AS
36
S1

EARTHQUAKES-PERU

Campbell, John V.
The earthquake in Peru, August 13, 1868. ⟨Extract from letters of John V. Campbell ...⟩

(In Smithsonian institution. Annual report. 1870. Washington, 1871. 23½ᶜᵐ. p. [421]-425)

1. Earthquakes—Peru.

S 15-305

Library of Congress
Library, Smithsonian   Q11.S66 1870
Institution

AS
36
S1

EARTHQUAKES-WEST INDIES

Latimer, George A.
Observations regarding the earthquakes which occurred in St. Thomas and neighboring islands, commencing Nov. 18, 1867. By George A. Latimer.

(In Smithsonian institution. Annual report. 1867. Washington, 1868. 23½ᶜᵐ. p. 465-466)

1. Earthquakes—West Indies.

S 15-236

Library of Congress
Library, Smithsonian   Q11.S66 1867
Institution

QE
1
G 3

EARTHQUAKES   PACIFIC

Gutenberg, B.

Depth and geographical distribution of deep-focus earthquakes (second Paper), by B. Gutenberg and C. F. Richter.

(Bulletin of the Geol. Soc. of America, Vol. 30, 1939, pp. 1511-1528)

G
1
G 56

EARTHQUAKES   SAMOA

Bülow, Werner von

Der vulkanische Ausbruch auf der Insel Savaii.(Deutsch-Samoa)

(Globus, Bd. 83, 1903, pp. 108-109)

AS
36
S1

EARTHQUAKES-WEST INDIES

Rojas, Arístides, 1826-
An opinion on the maritime disasters of the Antilles.

(In Smithsonian institution. Annual report. 1867. Washington, 1868. 23½ᶜᵐ. p. 466-467)

First published in the Federalista of Caracas.

1. Earthquakes—West Indies.

S 15-237

Library of Congress
Library, Smithsonian   Q11.S66 1867
Institution

AP
2
S 35

EARTHQUAKES   PACIFIC

Gutenberg, B(eno)

The structure of the Pacific basin as indicated by earthquakes.

(Science, Vol. 90, 1939, pp. 456-458)

QE
75
B

EARTHQUAKE -- SAN FRANCISCO 1906

Gilbert, Grove Karl, 1843-1918. ... The San Francisco earthquake and fire of April 18, 1906... 1907. (Card 2)

CONTENTS.— Preface, by J. A. Holmes.—The earthquake as a natural phenomenon, by G. K. Gilbert.—The effects of the earthquake and fire on various structures and structural materials, by R. L. Humphrey.—The effects of the earthquake and fire on buildings, engineering structures, and structural materials, by J. S. Sewell.—The earthquake and fire and their effects on structural steel and steel-frame buildings, by Frank Soulé.

1. San Francisco — Earthquake and fire, 1906. 2. Building materials. I. Holmes, Joseph Austin, 1859-1915. II. Humphrey, Richard Lewis, 1869- III. Sewell, John Stephen, 1869- IV. Soulé, Frank, 1845-

G S 7-1565

Library, U. S. Geological   Survey   QE535.G5
Library of Congress

(a20f2)

QC
875.B
M 58 e

Earthquakes in Indonesia for the years 1948-1955

(Djakarta, Ministry of Communications, Meteorological and Geophysical Institute, Ser. A: Nr. 45, 1957)

(See also serial file)

QE
520
A 51   Earthquakes in March and April 1946.

    (Trans. Am. Geophysical Union, Vol. 27, pp. 452-453, 1946)

AS
36
A 5   East, Ben

    Sea bird cities of the Aleutians.

    (Natural History, Vol. 51, 1943, pp. 64-71)

G
181
H   The East and West Indian mirror...

    Villiers, J. A. J. de   translator

    The East and West Indian mirror, being an account of Joris van Speilbergen's voyage around the world (1614-1617), and the Australian navigations of Jacob Le Maire.

    (Works issued by the Hakluyt Society, Ser. II, No. XVIII, 1906)

    EARTHWORMS

    see

    CHAETOPODA
    PHEERTIMA

QK
Botany
Pam.
No.1107   East, E. M.

    The Harvard Botanical Garden in Cuba. Science May 16, 1924.

AM
Mus.Pam.
366   EAST INDIA MARINE SOCIETY

    Goodspeed, Charles E.

    Nathaniel Hawthorne and the Museum of the Salem East India Marine Society, or the gathering of a virtuoso's collection. Peabody Museum Salem. 1946. 8vo.

QL
461
H-1   EARWIGS   HAWAII

    Marucci, Philip E.

    Notes on the predatory habits and life cycle of two Hawaiian earwigs.

    (Proc. Haw. Ent. Soc. for 1954, Vol. 15(3): 565-569, 1955)

QK
Botany
Pam.
No 118   East, E. M. and Mangelsdorf, A. J.

    A new interpretation of the hereditary behaviour of self-sterile plants. Ex Proceedings Nat. Acad. Sc. Vol. II, 1925, pp 166. - 171.

AM
101
P 35   EAST INDIA MARINE SOCIETY

    Whitehill, Walter Muir

    The East India Marine Society and the Peabody Museum of Salem: a sesquicentennial history. Salem. Peabody Museum. 1949. R8vo. xvi + 242 pp.

DU
1
S 72-q   Easily-grown semi-aquatic vegetable is highly edible.

    (South Pacific Commission, Quarterly Bull., Vol. 5(3):19-20, July, 1955)

    [Ipomoea aquatica]

GN
22
E 13   East, Edward M.

    Mankind at the crossroads. With maps and diagrams. New York. Scribner. 1923. 8vo. ix + 360 pp.

Q
101
P 18   EAST INDIANS IN FIJI

    Coulter, John Wesley

    Land utilization by Fijians and East Indians in Fiji.

    IN Proc. Sixth Pac. Sci. Congress, 1939, (California), Vol. 4, 1940, pp. 29-38.

GN
2.S
F 47   Eason, W. J.

    Rotuma and the Rotumans.

    (Transactions of the Fiji Society of Science and Industry, Vol. 3(3):145-151, 1947)

AM
111
E 13   East, Marjorie

    Display for learning; making and using visual materials. Edited by Edgar Dale. Publ. by the Dryden Press. New York. 8vo. vii + 306 pp. 1952c

---

AS
763
B-s

GN
Ethn.
Pam.
3308
Reading
Room   EAST INDIANS IN FIJI

    Lambert, S. M.

    East Indian and Fijian in Fiji: their changing numerical relation.

    (Bernice P. Bishop Mus., Special Publication 32, 1938)

DU
802
E 11   Eason, W. J. E.

    A short history of Rotuma. Printed and published by the Govt. Printing Dept., Suva, Fiji R8vo. ix + 127 + iii pp. nd (preface, 1951)

G
440
V87   EAST (FAR EAST)

    Vogel, Karel

    Aloha around the world. New York, Putnam, 1922. 274p.

AS
771
F 47   EAST INDIANS IN FIJI

    Parham, B. E.

    Minor food plants of the Fijian and Indian.

    (Fiji Society of Sci. and Industry, Trans. and Proc., 1940, pp. 12-18)

DU
802
E 13   Eason, W. J. E.

    A short history of Rotuma. Printed and published by the Govt. Printing Dept. Suva, Fiji (1951) R8vo. (i-ii)iii-ix + (1)2-127 + index (i)ii-iii pp.; 22 plates.

    [contains map of Rotuma, and profile]

QE
537
W 73   East African plateaus and rift valleys.

    Willis, Bailey

    EAST INDIES

    See under

    INDONESIA

AP
2
S 35

EAST PACIFIC RISE

Menard, H. W.

The east Pacific rise; recent marine geophysical measurements have shed some light on processes acting in the earth's mantle.

(Science, 132(3441):1838-1746, 1960)

MS
E 2

Storage
Case
5

EASTER ISLAND

Alexander, W. W.

Genealogy of the kings of Rapanui.

G
27
M-s

EASTER ISLAND

Beltrán y Rozpide, Ricardo

La Isla Pascua.

(Boletín de la Sociedad Geográfica de Madrid, Tomo XV, 1883, pp. 153-166)

AM
Mus.Pam.
466

The East-West Center. 12mo. 16 pp. 1962

DU
Pac.Pam.
700

EASTER ISLAND

Artensen S., Sigurd

Un viaje a Rapa-nui.

(Simiente, 14 (3/4:11-14, 1944)

DU
12
M 64

locked
case

EASTER ISLAND

Bernizet
Geographical memoir on Easter Island.

La Pérouse, Jean Francois de Galaup de
The voyage of La Pérouse round the world...
London, 1798. Vol. 2, pp. 248-260

DU
Pac.Pam.
564

(Easter Island) copies of documents in the Archives of the Chilean Government relating to the official status of Easter Island. 35 pp. In Spanish.

GN
1
F

Easter Island

Balfour, Henry

Some ethnological suggestions in regard to Easter Island. In Folk-Lore XXVIII, 4 Dec. 1917. pp 336-381.

GN
Ethn.Pam
3065
2381

GN
2.M
S 23

EASTER ISLAND

Bienvenido de Estella, P.

Isla de Pascua. Santiago de Chile. 1920.

(Publicaciones del Museo de Etnología y antropología de Chile, Tomo II, Num. 1, 1920, pp. 45-113).

DU
620
F

EASTER ISLAND

(Friend, July 1856, p. 49; October 1856, pp. 74-75)

G
51
S

EASTER ISLAND

Barclay, H. V.

Easter Island and its colossal statues.

(Proc. of the R. Geogr. Soc. of Australasia, South Australian Branch, Vol. III, 11th Session, 1897-8, pp. 127-137)

DU
950.E2
B 58

EASTER ISLAND

Bienvenido de Estella, R. P.

Los Misterios de la Isla de Pascua, por el R. P. Bienvenido de Estrella. Santiago de Chile Cervantes. 1920. 8vo. 132 pp.

GN
2.S
T

EASTER ISLAND

Adam, Paul

A propos de l'Expédition Archéologique de Thor Heyerdahl à l'Ile de Pâques.

(Bull. Soc. des Etudes Océaniennes, No. 115 June 1956, pp. 565-571)

GN
2.M
S 93

EASTER ISLAND

Barthel, Th. S.

Hauptlingsgenealogien von der Osterinsel.

(Tribus, Nr. 8:67-82, 1959)

PL
Pam
178

EASTER ISLAND

Bienvenido de Estrella, R. P.

Mis Viajes a Pascua. Santiago de Chile. Imprenta Cervantes. 1921. 8vo. 132 pp.

QL
1
H2

Easter Island

Agassiz, Alexander
in his Report on the scientific results of the expedition to the Eastern Tropical Pacific... in Mus. Comp. Zool. Mem. XXXIII, 1906, pp. 53-62, pls. 13, 16-49.

DU
12
B 41

locked
case

EASTER ISLAND

Beechey, F. W.

Narrative of a Voyage to the Pacific and Beering's Strait...in...Ship Blossom, under the command of Captain F. W. Beechey...in...1825-28. Vol. 1, pp. 40-59. London. 1831. 8vo.

The same...New edition.. London. 1831. 8vo.

GN
2.1
R.93

EASTER ISLAND

Bórmida, Marcelo

Algunas luces sobre la penumbrosa historia de Pascua antes de 1722.

(Runa, Archivo para las Ciencias del Hombre, Vol. 4:5-62, 1951)

GN
2.S
T

EASTER ISLAND

Ahnne, E.

Les Hieroglyphes de l'Ile de Pâques.

(Soc. des Etudes Oceaniennes, Bulletin, Tome 5, No. 6, (whole No. 47), Juin, 1935, pp. 185-193)

DU
12
B 42

locked
case

EASTER ISLAND

(Behrens, Carl Friedrich)

Histoire de l'Expedition de Trois Vaisseaux, envoyés par la Compagnie des Indes Occidentales des Provinces-Unies, aux Terres Australes en 1721 par Monsieur De B****. 2 vols. La Haye. 1739. 18mo. Vol. 1, p. 121-

---

DU
950.E2
B 81

EASTER ISLAND

Branchi, E. C.

L'Isola di Pascua, impero degli Antipodi. Edizioni dell'Istituto di Cultura Italiana. Santiago del Chile. 1934. R8vo. 192 pp.

DU
Pam No.
#228

Easter Island.
Brown, J.Macmillan.

Easter Island. 5 articles clipped from The Press ,Christchurch, New Zealand September 9 - Oct 7, 1922.

DU
12
C 55
looked
case

EASTER ISLAND

Choris, Louis

Voyage pittoresque autour du monde, avec des portraits de sauvages...des paysages, des vues maritimes, et plusieurs objets d'histoire naturelle; accompagné de descriptions...Paris. 1822. Folio. 2 plates (see contents)

G
7
R 91

Easter Island.

Corney, B. Glanvill

Notes on Easter Island. In Geographical Journal. Vol. L, July-Dec. 1917. pp. 57-68. Illus.

DU
950. E2
B37

EASTER ISLAND

Brown, J. Macmillan

The riddle of the Pacific.

London, 1924, 312 pp.

DU
12
C 55
looked
case

EASTER ISLAND

Choris, Louis

Vues et paysages des régions équinoxiales recueillis dans un voyage autour du monde... Plate 9, pp. 17-18. Paris. 1826. Folio.

G
161
H
V.13

EASTER ISLAND

Corney, Bolton Glanvill, 1851- ed.
The voyage of Captain Don Felipe González in the ship of the line San Lorenzo, with the frigate Santa Rosalia in company, to Easter Island in 1770-1: preceded by an extract from Mynheer Jacob Roggeveen's official log of his discovery of and visit to Easter Island, in 1772. Transcribed, translated, and edited by Bolton Glanvill Corney ... Cambridge, Printed for the Hakluyt society, 1908. lxxvii, 176 p. front., plates, 3 maps (in pocket) facsim. 23ᶜᵐ. (Half-title: Works issued by the Hakluyt society ... Second ser., no. XIII) The first article is an extract from Roggeveen's "Dagverhaal der ont-dekkings-reis van Mr. J. Roggeveen mit den schepen Den Arend, Thien-hoven ... en de jaren 1721 en 1722." Te Middelburg. 1838.
(Continued on next card)
9-2606

DU
Pac.Pam.
871

EASTER ISLAND

Burke, Malcolm K.

The world's most durable mystery.

(Reader's Digest, pp. 123-126, December, 1955)

[Easter Island]

PL
950.E2
C 56

GN
671.E2
C 56

EASTER ISLAND

Churchill, William

Easter Island: the Rapanui speech and the peopling of southeast Polynesia. Washington. Carnegie Institution. 1912. R8vo.

(Carnegie Institution of Washington, Pub. No. 174)

G
161
H

EASTER ISLAND

Corney, Bolton Glanvill, 1851- ed. The voyage of Captain Don Felipe González ... 1908. (Card 2)

Appendix I is translated from Behrens' "Der wohlversuchte Süd-Lander" ... Leipzig, 1739.
CONTENTS.—Introductory note by Admiral Sir C. A. G. Bridge.—Introduction.—I. Extract from the official log of Mr. Jacob Roggeveen, in so far as it relates to Easter Island.—II. Journals, royal commands, minutes, and despatches, relating to the voyage of the San Lorenzo under the command of Don Felipe González y Haedo and Santa Rosalia to Easter Island in 1770.—III. Journal of the principal occurrences during the voyage of the frigate Santa Rosalia from El Callao de Lima to the Island of David, and thence to San Carlos de Chiloe, in the year 1770; by an officer of the said frigate (probably Don Francisco Antonio de Agüera y Infanzon,
(Continued on next card)
9-2606

DU
950.E2
C 53

EASTER ISLAND

Casey, Robert J.

Easter Island, home of the scornful gods. New York. 1931c. 8vo.

G
51
S

EASTER ISLAND

Clark, Bouverie F.

Reporting calling at Sala-y-Gomez and Easter Islands. (Letter from the Commander of the Sappho to Rear-Admiral Algernon Lyons, June 20, 1882)

(Proc. of the R. Geogr. Soc. of Austral-asia, South Australian Branch, Vol. III, 11th Session, 1897-8, pp. 143-146)

G
161
H

EASTER ISLAND

Corney, Bolton Glanvill, 1851- ed. The voyage of Captain Don Felipe González ... 1908. (Card 3)
CONTENTS—Continued.
chief pilot)—IV. Narrative of the expedition undertaken by order of His Excellency Don Manuel de Amat, viceroy of Peru, in the ship San Lorenzo and the frigate Santa Rosalia, from the harbour of El Callao de Lima to the Island of David, in 1770 (probably from the pen of Sub-Lieut. Don Juan Hervé, first pilot, or senior navigating officer, of the San Lorenzo)—Appendices: I. Behrens' narrative of Roggeveen's visit to Easter Island. II. Note on Don Manuel de Amat's successor as viceroy of Peru. III. Extract from a contemporary (unsigned) letter relating to Don Felipe González's voyage. IV. Extract from an autograph journal by Lieut. George Peard of H. M. S. Blossom, 1825. Bibliography (p. (145)-158).—Index.
1. Easter Island. 2. America—Disc. & explor. 3. Pacific Ocean. 4. Voyages and travels. I. González y Haedo, Felipe, d. 1792. II. Roggeveen, Jacob, 1659-1729. III. Hervé, Juan, fl. 1770. IV. Agüera y Infanzon, Francisco Antonio de, fl. 1770.
v. Behrens, Karl Friedrich.

Library of Congress   G161.H2 2d ser. vol. 13
9-2606

EASTER ISLAND

Casey, Robert Joseph

Easter Island, home of the scornful gods. Indianapolis (1931) 337 pp. plates.

Library of Hawaii has

DU
12
C 77-2
2d ed.
looked
case

EASTER ISLAND

Cook, James

Voyage towards the South Pole, and round the world...in Resolution and Adventure, in...1772-1775...2 vols. 2d ed. London. 1777. 4to. Vol. 1 (see index)

Atlas of 63 plates. Folio.

GN
2.1
E

Easter Island.

Canteaud, - (Dr.)

Ses origines de l'île de Pâques Revue école d'Anthr. 20 An. 1910 pp. 86-97

DU
12
C 44

EASTER ISLAND

Chamisso, Adelbert von

Reise um die Welt mit der Romanzossischen Entdeckungs-Expedition in den Jahren 1815-18 auf der Brigg Rurik, Kapitain Otto v. Kotzebue. Berlin. 1864. 2 vols. in 1. 8vo.

DU
12
C 78

EASTER ISLAND

Cooke, G. A.

Modern and authentic system of universal geography...pp. 279-85. London. n.d.

AS
36
C3

Easter Island.

Croft, Thomas.

Letter to Prof. George Davidson on the hyloglyphs of Easter Island In Proc. Cal. Acad. Sc. V. pp. 317-323

AS
36
A5

EASTER ISLAND

Chapin, James P.

Through southern Polynesia: exploring some rarely visited islands of the South Seas, including Pitcairn and Easter- the second stage of the Templeton Crocker Expedition.

(Natural History, Vol.37,1936, pp. 287-308)

AS
36
C3

EASTER ISLAND.

Cooke, George Henry, 1836-
Te Pito te Henua, known as Rapa Nui; commonly called Easter Island, South Pacific Ocean. Latitude 27° 10' S., longitude 109° 26' W. By George H. Cooke ...
(In U. S. National museum. Annual report. 1897. Washington, 1899, 29½ᶜᵐ. pt. 1, p. 689-723)
Half-title.
Cruise of the U. S. S. Mohican.
Language of the Rapa Nuiis: p. 720-723.
"In the preparation ... of the glossary the writer has been ably assisted by Lieut. William E. Safford."—p. 691.
1. Easter Island. 2. Rapanui language. 3. Mohican (Steamer) I. Safford, William Edwin, 1859— II. Title.

Library of Congress   Q11.U5 1897   14-19894
———— Copy 2.
———— Separate.   F3169.C77

DU
Pac.Pam.
597

EASTER ISLAND

Cuming, H(ugh)

Excerpt from letter written to Dr. (Joseph Dalton) Hooker by H. Cuming, dated "London, March 21st, 1832".

(Voyage was in 1828, - stopped at Easter Islands, Mangareva, Crescent, Rurutu, Tubuai, Ducie, Tuamotus, Rapa)

DU
12
D 33 Delano, Amasa

locked
case   **Narrative of voyages and travels, in the northern and southern hemispheres...together with a voyage of survey and discovery in the Pacific Ocean and Oriental islands.** Boston. 1817. pp. 355-356.

DU
12
En4   Easter Island.
Enoch, C. Reginald.
    in his Secret of the Pacific pp 257-266

G
51
A 93   EASTER ISLAND
Gosset, Ralph M.

  Easter Island

    (The Australian Geographer, Vol. 3:3-13, 1939) No. 6

DU
12
D 51   EASTER ISLAND
Dewar, J. Cumming

    Voyage of the Nyanza, R.N.Y.C.: being the record of a three years' cruise in a schooner yacht...and her subsequent shipwreck. London. 1892.

      pp. 155-166

DU
Pac.Pam.
596   EASTER ISLAND
Byrand, R. Eugenio

    (Letter (in Spanish) written in 1864 of a sojourn in Easter Island. Santiago de Chile, 1918. pp. 23-48)

GN
Ethn.Pam.
3935   EASTER ISLAND
Günther, Klaus

    Zur Frage der Typologie und Chronologie der grossen Steinbilder auf der Osterinsel.

    (Wissenschaftliche Zeitschrift der Friedrich-Schiller-Universität Jena, Jahrgang 3, pp. 81-107, 1953/54)

G
159
D 89   EASTER ISLAND
Dumont d'Urville, J. S. C.

    Voyage pittoresque autour du monde; resumé général des voyages de découvertes de Magellan, Tasman, Dampier, Anson...Vols. 1-2. Paris. 1834-1835. 4to. Vol. 1, pp. 503-512.

DU
12
F 73   EASTER ISLAND
Forster, George

locked
case   **Voyage round the world, in...Resolution, commanded by Capt. James Cook, during the years 1772-75... 2 vols.** London. 1777. 4to. Vol. 1, pp. 551-602.

GN
2.I
R 93   EASTER ISLAND
Gundian, Daniel Camus

    Salubridad y morbilidad en la Isla de Pascua.

    (Runa, Vol. 4:78-88, 1951)

    [health and mortality...]

DU
12
D 93   EASTER ISLAND
Du Petit-Thouars, Abel A.

locked
case   **Voyage autour du monde sur la frégate La Venus, pendant les années 1836-1839...** (Rélation), Vol. 2, pp. 222-254. Paris. 1841. 8vo and folio. (Atlas Pittoresque)

AM
Mus.Pam.
173   EASTER ISLAND
Fuenzalida Villegas y Dra., Humberto

    La isla de Pascua. Museo Nacional de Historia Natural (Santiago de Chile), Seccion cultura y publicaciones del Ministerio de Educacion. June 25 - July 6, 1946) Santiago. R8vo. 18pp.

GN
2.M
S 23   EASTER ISLAND
    (R)
Gusinde, Martin

    Catálogo de los objetos originarios de la Isla de Pascua conservados en este Museo.

    (Publ. del Museo de Etnología y Antropología de Chile, Tomo III, Num. 1, 1922, pp. 200-244)

GN
Ethn.
Pam.3078   EASTER ISLAND

    Easter Island: photographs (13) of 4 tablets from Easter Island. Tablets now at Braine-le-Comte, Belgium. Ms. by Mgr. Jaussen, giving interpretation of these tablets is in the library of the Papeete Museum. (See Bull. Soc. Etudes Oceaniennes, No. 47, p. 189). Original plates are with Lulu Spitz, Papeete. In Bishop Museum are casts of 2 of the tablets. (See data on back of photographs)

DU
950.E2
G 19   EASTER ISLAND
Gana, Ignacio L.

    La Isla de Pascua. (By) Ignacio L. Gana, Julian Viaud (Pierre Loti), J. R. Ballesteros. Santiago de Chile. 1903. 16mo. 161 pp.

GN
2.S
V   EASTER ISLAND
    (R)
Gusinde, M(artin)

    Mutterrechtliche Eigentumskunde von der Osterinsel.

    (Mitteilungen der Anthropologischen Gesellschaft in Wien, Bd. LX, pp. 352-355, 1930)

DU
Pac. Pam.
555
532   EASTER ISLAND
Edwards, Rafael

    La Isla de Pascua. Consideraciones expuestas acerca de ella por Rafael Edwards, que la visito en Julio de 1916 y Junio de 1917. Santiago de Chile. 1918. 8vo. 26 pp.

GN
Ethn.Pam.
347   EASTER ISLAND
Geiseler, (Kapitänlieutenant)

    Die Oster-Insel. Eine Stätte prähistorischer kultur in der Südsee. Bericht des Kommandanten S.M.K. "Hyäne", Kapitänlieutenant Geiseler, über die ethnologische untersuchung der Oster-Insel (Rapanui)...Berlin. 1883. 54 pp.

DU
12
H 33   EASTER ISLAND
Hartwig, Georg

locked
case   **Die Inseln des grossen Oceans im Natur- und Völkerleben...pp. 90-98.** Wiesbaden. 1861. 8vo.

DU
950.E2
E 58   EASTER ISLAND
Englert, P. Sebastian

    La Tierra de Hotu Matu'a. Historia, etnologia y lengua de la Isla de Pascua. Imprenta y edit. "San Francisco". Padre las Casas. 1948. 4to. 533 pp. + map

---

G
161
H   EASTER ISLAND
Gonzalez y Haedo, Felipe

    The voyage of Captain Don Felipe Gonzalez in the ship of the line San Lorenzo...to Easter Island in 1770-71... Cambridge. Printed for the Hakluyt Society. 1908.

    (Works issued by the Hakluyt Society, Ser. 2, Volume 13, 1908)

GN
2.M
P 11   EASTER ISLAND
Heine-Geldern, Robert

    Politische Zweiteilung, Exogamie und Kriegsursachen auf der Osterinsel.

    (Ethnologica, n.f., Bd. 2:241-273, 1960)

DU
950.E2
H 61

EASTER ISLAND

Heyerdahl, Thor

Aku-Aku: le secret de l'Île de Pâques.
Traduit du norvégien par Marguerite Gay et
Gerd de Mautort. Paris. Éditions Albin
Michel. 1958. 345 pp. 8vo.

GN
Ethn.
Pam.
4205

EASTER ISLAND

Keller R., Carlos

La Isla de Pascua.

(Geochile, Dec. 1951, Vol. 1, No. 1)

DU
12
K 87

locked
case

EASTER ISLAND

Kotzebue, Otto von

Voyage of discovery, into the South Sea and
Beering's Straits...1815-1818...in the ship
Ruriok...(Translation of German edition...1821)
3 vols. London. 1821. 8vo.
Vol. 3, pp. 224-227.

GN
671.E2
H 97

EASTER ISLAND

Hussem, W.

Het Paascheiland, zijn voorouder- en vogel-
cultus. Geillustreerd met 12 foto's.
's Graveland. G. W. Breughel. n.d. 8vo.
81-136 pp.

G
29
S

Easter Island

Knapp, C.

Deux statuettes de l'ile de Pâques.
in Bull. de la Soc. Neuchâteloise de Géographie
XX. 1909-1910, 8vo. pp. 465-466, ph. I.II.

DU
12
L 28

locked
case

EASTER ISLAND

Langsdorff, G. H. von

Voyages and travels in various parts of the
world...1803-1807...Vol. 1, pp. 84-86. London.
1813-1814. 4to.

AP
2.N4

EASTER ISLAND

Im Thurn, Everard (Sir)

Island of stone statues . In Nature,
Vol. 105, pp 583 - 4, July, 1920.

[A review of "Mystery of Easter Island"
by Mrs. Routledge]

GN
1
Z

EASTER ISLAND

Knoche, Walter

Ein atypischer Kopf aus Pechstein von der
Osterinsel.

(Zeitschrift für Ethnologie, 60 Jahrgang,
1928, Heft 4/6, p. 386)

G
3
N 27

EASTER ISLAND

Lafay, Howard

Easter Island and its mysterious monuments.

(National Geographic Magazine, 121(1):90-
117, 1962)

GN
2.S
F 47

EASTER ISLAND

Jaussen, Tepano

Easter Island (history, description, etc.)
translated from the French by George Mackay.

(Trans. Fijian Society, 1920, pp. 20-28)

GN
Pam
#349

EASTER ISLAND

Knoche, Walter

(Die) Osterinsel : Beobachtungen und
Erkunligungen auf der Osterinsel. Aus
Deutsch. Wissen. Verein in Santiago Bd.
VII, Verhandlungen. pp 64
Santiago, 1921

GN
1
A 93

EASTER ISLAND

Lanyon-Orgill, P. A.

A catalog of the inscribed tablets and other
artifacts from Easter Island.

(Journal of Austronesian Studies, 1(2):20-
39, 1956)

GN
Ethn.Pam.
2751

EASTER ISLAND

Jaussen, Tepano

L'Île de Pâques

(Cahiers d'Art, Année 4, 1929, pp. 109-115)

DU
950.E2
K 72

EASTER ISLAND

Knoche, Walter

Die Osterinsel: eine Zusammenfassung der
chilenischen Osterinselexpedition, des Jahres
1911. Concepcion. Soc. Imp. y Lit. 1925.
sm8vo. (8) + 320 pp.

DU
Pac.Pam.
563

EASTER ISLAND

Lapelin, T. de

L'Ile de Pâques (Rapa-nui)

(Revue maritime et coloniale, Tome 35, 1872,
pp. 105-125; 526-544)

GN
Ethn.Pam.
123

EASTER ISLAND

Jaussen, Tepano

L'Île de Pâques. Historique--écriture
et répertoire des signes des tablettes ou bois
d'hibiscus intelligents. Paris, 1893. 32 pp.

GN
1
Z

Easter Island

Knoche, Walter

Vorläufige Bemerkung über
die Entstehung der Standbilder
auf der Osterinsel.
in "Zeitschrift" 44.6 pp 873 - 877.

DU
12
M 64

locked
case

EASTER ISLAND

La Pérouse, Jean Francois de Galaup de

Voyage of La Pérouse round the world...1785-
1788...translated from the French...2 vols.
London. 1798. 8vo. Vol.1, pp. 59-83; Vol. 2,
pp. 238-241; 248-260; 310.

...the same...2 vols. London. 1799. 4to.
Vol. 1, pp. 312-334; Vol. 2, pp. 332-335; 342-353;
401. Atlas, folio.

AP
2
N 4

EASTER ISLAND

Juan Fernandez and Easter Island (declared
national parks by Chilean government)

(Nature, Vol. 135, No. 3408, Feb. 23, 1935,
p. 299)

D
1
P 10

EASTER ISLAND

Kon-Tiki debate moves to Easter Island.

(Pacific Islands Monthly, 26(1):61, 1955)

[Dr. Alex Spoehr quoted: Saipan settlement
radio-carbon dated 1375 BC]

GN
700
A 62

EASTER ISLAND

Lavachery, Henri

Easter Island, Polynesia.

(Antiquity, Vol. 10, No. 37, 1936, pp. 54-60)

EASTER ISLAND

AS 36 S 1
Lavachéry, Henri

Easter Island, Polynesia.

(Ann. Report...Smithsonian Institution,1936 pp.391-396)

EASTER ISLAND

QL 570
L 64 Lesson, Pierre Adolphe

Les Polynésiens, leur origine, leur migration leur langage...ouvrage rédigé d'après le manuscrit de l'auteur par Ludovic Martinet... Paris. Leroux. 1880-1884... Vol. 2, pp. 275-309. 8vo. Maps.

(Index-Tome 4).

EASTER ISLAND

QL 671 I
MacFarlane, J. R. H.

Notes on birds in the western Pacific, made in H. M. S. "Constance", 1883-1885.

(Ibis, Ser.5 Vol. 5, 1887, pp. 201-215)

EASTER ISLAND

DU 950.E2
L 39 Lavachery, Henri

Ile de Paques. Orné de 32 pages hors texte d'illustrations en héliogravure. Paris. Bernard Grasset. 1935c. sm8vo. 299 pp.

EASTER ISLAND

DU 12
L 76 Lisiansky, Urey

locked case
A voyage round the world...1803-1806...in the ship Neva...pp. 51-61. London. 1814. 4to.

EASTER ISLAND

DU Pac.Pac. 523
Malpelo, Cocos and Easter Islands...London. H. M. Stationery Office. 1920.

8vo. 62 pp.

EASTER ISLAND

GN Ethn. Pam.3220
Lavachéry, Henri

L'Ile de Paques, Ile polynésienne.

(Revue de Cercle des Alumni de la Fondation Universitaire, Tome 7, No. 3, 1936. 10 pp.)

EASTER ISLAND

GN Ethn.Pam. 2882
Loppé, Etienne

Note sur une Sculpture en Pierre de L'Ile de Pâques.

(L'Homme préhistorique, Année 15, No. 6-8, 1928, pp. 172-174)

EASTER ISLAND

DU 12
M 35 (Marra, John)

locked case
Journal of the Resolution's voyage in 1772-1775. On discovery to the Southern Hemisphere... also a Journal of the Adventure's voyage in 1772-1774...with historical and geographical descriptions of the islands and countries discovered in the course of their respective voyages... London. 1775. 8vo. pp. 137-149.

EASTER ISLAND

GN 2.M
B 91 Lavachery, Henri

La mission Franco-Belge dans l'Ile de Paques (Juillet 1934-Avril, 1935).

(Bulletin des Musées Royaux d'art et d'Histoire, Ser. 3, 1935, Année 7, No. 3, pp. 50-63; No. 4, pp. 81-91)

EASTER ISLAND

DU Pac.Pam. 573
Loti, Pierre

Expedition der Fregatte "La Flore" nach der Osterinsel, 1872, aud dem Tagebuche des Schiffsfähnrichs Julien Viaud.

(photostat copy from Globus, Bd. 23, 1873, Nos. 5-6)

EASTER ISLAND

AS 36 S 1
Metraux, Alfred

Easter Island.

(Ann. Rept. Smithsonian Institution, 1944: 435-452)

EASTER ISLAND

GN 2.S
B 91 Lavachery, Henri

Notes sur l'Ile de Pâques. L'Ile de Pâques et les Iles Marianes.

(Bulletin de la Société des Américanistes de Belgique, Aout, 1933, pp. 96-104)

EASTER ISLAND

DU 950.E2
L 88 Loti, Pierre

Reflets sur la sombre route. Paris. Calmann-Lévy, Editeurs. n.d. 355 pp. 8vo.

EASTER ISLAND

DU 950.E2
M 59 Métraux, Alfred

L'Ile de Pâques. Seize planches photographiques. Edition revue et augmentée. Gallimard. (Paris?) 1941c. 8vo. 193 pp.

EASTER ISLAND

GN 1 An
Lehmann, Walter

Essai d'une monographie bibliographique sur l'île Pâques. in Anthropos II. 1907, pp. 141-151, 257-268.

EASTER ISLAND

G 7
R 91 Luke, Sir Harry

Easter Island.

(Geographical Journal, 120(4):422-432, 1954)

EASTER ISLAND

DU Pac. Pam. 547
Métraux, A.

Introduction a la connaissance de l'Ile de Pâques. Preface de Paul Morand. A propos d'une exposition au Musée d'Ethnographie du Trocadero, Paris, 1935. sm8vo. (38) pp.

2 copies

EASTER ISLAND

DU Pac Pam 334
Lehmann, W

Die Osterinsel. From Der Tag, April 3, 1904.

EASTER ISLAND

GN Ethn. Pam. 4202
Luke, Sir Harry

Paskeøen.

(Naturen, Nr. 12:363-376, 1955)

EASTER ISLAND

GN Ethn.Pam 3146a
Métraux, Alfred

Introduction a la connaissance de l'Ile de Paques. Préface de Paul Morand. A propos d'une exposition au Musée d'Ethnographie du Trocadéro (Muséum National d'Histoire Naturelle). 1935.

DU
Pac.Pam.
593

EASTER ISLAND

Métraux, Alfred

    Island of mystery. Easter Island, the enigma of the Pacific, is described by Dr. Alfred Métraux, visiting lecturer at the University (of California)...

DU
12
M 69

locked
case

EASTER ISLAND

Moerenhout, J. A.

    Voyages aux îles du grand océan...2 vols. Paris. 1837. 8vo. Tome 1, pp.23-28; Tome 2, pp. 267-280.

GN
2.S
B91

EASTER ISLAND

    Note sur l'Ile de Pâques. Perruque de la statuette Pinart (Tracadero).

    (Bulletin de la Société des Americanistes de Belgique, Decembre, 1932)

GN
2.S
P 76

EASTER ISLAND

Métraux, Alfred

    The kings of Easter Island.

    (Jrl. of the Polynesian Society. Vol.46. 1937. pp.41-62)

GN
Pam
2791

EASTER ISLAND

Mok, Michel

    Explore weird island of the dead. From Popular Science Monthly, April, 1930. 2 p. pl.

DU
Pac.
Pam.
1018

EASTER ISLAND

Ordonez, Miguel

    Figuras y misterio. (Translated into English by Mrs. W. W. Laury)

    (Neuropsiquiatria, Vol. 2(4):51-62, 1963)

GN
Ethn.Pam.
3338

EASTER ISLAND

Métraux, Alfred

    Mysteries of Easter Island.

    (Yale Review, Vol. 28, pp. 758-779, 1939)

DU
950. E2
M 92

EASTER ISLAND

Mouly, R. P., SS. CC.

    Ile de Pâques; ile de mystère et d'héroisme. Ouvrage couronné par l'Academie Française. Librairie Lemiale. Tours. (1948) 12mo. 173 pp.

GN
2.I
R 93

EASTER ISLAND

    Otra vez sobre Pascua. By J.I. (J.Imbelloni)

    (Runa...5(1/2):204-210, 1952)

GN
2.I
A-m

EASTER ISLAND

Métraux, Alfred

    Numerals from Easter Island.

    (Man, vol.36, Nov.1936, pp.190-191)

DU
950. E2
M 92

EASTER ISLAND

Mouly, R. Père

    Ile de Pâques, Ile de Mystere? Librairie de L'Oeuvre St. Charles. Bruges. (1935) 8vo. 168 pp.

GN
2.I
A
1868-9

EASTER ISLAND

Palmer, J. Linton

    Observations on the inhabitants and the antiquities of Easter Island. In Journ Ethn. Soc. n.s. Vol. I, 1869, pp 371- 377.

GN
671.E2
M 59

EASTER ISLAND

Métraux, Alfred

    Die Oster-Insel. W. Kohlhammer Verlag. (Stuttgart. 1957) 8vo. 223 pp., 36 pl.

DU
Pac.Pam.
892

EASTER ISLAND

Mulloy, William

    The island of monster idols. By Dr. William Mulloy as told to William J. Barker. [clipping, donated, from what paper?]

    [Easter Island]

G
7
R 8

EASTER ISLAND

Palmer, J. Linton

    A visit to Easter Island, or Rapa Nui, in 1868.

    (Journal of the R. Geographical Society, London, Vol. 40, 1870, pp. 167-181)

GN
2.S
B 91

EASTER ISLAND

Métraux, Alfred

    Polynesian traditions of voyages to Easter Island.

    (Bull. Soc. des Americanistes de Belgique, No. 24, 1937, pp. 129-138)

AM
Mus.Pam.
370

EASTER ISLAND

    The Museum of Primitive Art; selected works from the collection. Spring 1957. [Introduction by Robert Goldwater] 4to. 39 photos

    [9. Easter Island ceremonial paddle; 14,15. Easter Island ancestral figure.]

DU
12
L122

Easter Island
(Rapanui)

Perouse,J.F.G.de la

    in his voyage autour du monde,Paris, 1797,pp.73-104,Vol.II,and pp.21-35,Vol.IV. in the English translation,vol.I.pp. 312-334,vol.II,pp332-335 and 342-353.

GN
Ethn. Pam.
3162

EASTER ISLAND

Métraux, Alfred

    Voyage autour de l'Ile de Pâques.

    (La Revue de Paris, 42d année, no. 14, July 15, 1935, pp. 372-399)

DU
12
N 64

locked
case

EASTER ISLAND

Nicoll, Michael J.

    Three voyages of a naturalist. Being an account of many little-known islands in three oceans visited by the "Valhalla" R.Y.S. ... Second edition. pp. 191-206. London. 1909. 8vo.

GN
Ethn.Pam
3068

EASTER ISLAND

Philippi, Rudolfo A.

    La Isla de Pascua... Santiago de Chile. 1873.

    (Anales de la Universidad de Chile, Memorias Cientificas i literarias, May 1873, pp. 365-434).

DU
Pac.Pam.
574

EASTER ISLAND

Pinart, Alphonse

Voyage à l'Ile de Pâques, 1877.

(Le Tour du Monde, Tome 36, 1878, pp. 225-240. copied in longhand by Miss Yvette Oddon, Librairie de Museum du Trocadero, Paris)

G
159
C 15

EASTER ISLAND

Roggeveen, Jacob

Callender, John

Terra Australis Cognita... Vol. 3, pp. 584-641: Roggewein, to Polynesia and Australia. Edinburgh. 1768.

Q
115
C 26

EASTER ISLAND

Scientific results of Cruise VII of the Carnegie during 1928-1929...

Carnegie Institution of Washington Publications 536,537,542,544,547,555
1942-1943

G
51
S

EASTER ISLAND

Powell, W. Ashmore

Detailed report upon Easter Island, or Rapa Nui. (Letter from the Commodore of the Topaze to the Lords Commissioners of the Admiralty, December 3, 1868)

(Proc. of the R. Geogr. Soc. of Australasia, South Australian Branch, Vol. III, 11th Session, 1897-8, pp. 138-142)

GN
1
F

Easter Island

Routledge, Mrs. Scoresby

Bird cult of Easter Island. In Folk-Lore XXVIII, 4 Dec. 1917. pp 337-335.

GN
2.M
P 95

EASTER ISLAND

Selected works from the collection, Museum of Primitive Art. Spring 1957. Summer, 1957

[An Easter Island paddle, Easter Island head (stone)], Mangareva, New Guinea...

DU
Pac.Pam.
561

EASTER ISLAND

Prat, Agustin

La Isla de Pascua. (typed copy from newspaper "La Tarde" (Chile), Jan. 7,10, 1903)

G
7
R91

Easter Island.

Routledge, Mrs. Scoresby

Easter Island. In Geog. Journ. Jan.-June 1917. pp. 321-349. Illus.

GN
671.E2
R 93

[EASTER ISLAND]

[several articles (all cataloged) on Easter Island]

(Runa, Archivio para las Ciencias del Hombre Vol. IV, Partes 1º2, 1951)

DU
950.E2
R 17

EASTER ISLAND

Ramirez, J. T.

"El Conquistador de Pascua"; biografia del Hermano Eugenio Eyraud, de los Sdos. Corazones. Tomo I-II. San Jose. (Santiago de Chile). 1944. sm8vo.

DU
950.E2
R86

Easter Island

Routledge, Mrs. Scoresby.

The mystery of Easter Island...

London, 1919. 404p. illus. R8vo

AS
36
A 5

EASTER ISLAND

Shapiro, Harry L.

Mystery Island of the Pacific. An account of an extraordinary island and its strange civilization visited recently by the Crocker Pacific Expedition.

(Natural History, Vol. 35, 1935, pp. 365-377)

DU
950.E2
R 17

EASTER ISLAND

Ramirez O., Julio T.

Navegando a Rapa-Nui. Notas de viaje de la Corbeta General Baquedano en su 30 expedicion a la Islan de Pascua el ano 1934. Santiago, 1939. R8vo. 187 pp.

EASTER ISLAND

Routledge, Mrs. Scoresby

The Mystery of Easter Island.

(National Geographic Magazine, Vol. 40, 1921, pp. 628-646)

GN
2.S
P 76

EASTER ISLAND

Skinner, H. D.

Gilbert's account of Easter Island.

(Journal of the Polynesian Society, 28:178-179, 1919)

GN
2.I
A-4

EASTER ISLAND

Reed, Edwyn

The Easter islanders (extracted and translated by Edwyn Reed from work on Easter Island by A. Rodulpho Phillipi).

(Journ. Anthrop. Inst. of Great Britain and Ireland, Vol. 5, 1876, pp. 111-114)

DU
Pac. Pam.
557

EASTER ISLAND

Sandberg, Sir Harry O.

La Isla de Pascua, el misterio del Pacifico.

(Boletin de la Union Panamericana, Vol. 36, 1913, pp. 2-? - incomplete copy)

(Reference in English edition is Vol. 35, 1912, pp. 897-908)

DU
Pac.Pam
229

EASTER ISLAND

Skottsberg, Carl

Den Engelska Expeditionen till Paskon, 1913-1916.

(Ymer, Tidskrift utgiven av Svenska Sallskapet f. Anthr. och Geogr., 1921, H 2)

GN
2.I
R 93

EASTER ISLAND

Rodriguez, Gregorio

Paisaje natural y cultural de la isla de Pascua.

(Runa, Archivo para las Ciencias del Hombre, Vol. 4(1/2):63-77, 1951)

DU
950.E2
S 38

EASTER ISLAND

Schulze-Maizier, Friedrich

Die Osterinsel. Mit 23 Tafeln und 6 Abbildungen im Text. Leipzig. Insel-Verlag. 8vo. n.d. 238 pp.

QH
138.J
S 62

EASTER ISLAND

Skottsberg, Carl
Notes on a visit to Easter Island.

IN

Skottsberg, Carl
Natural History of Juan Fernandez and Easter Island, Vol. 1, Part I, 1920

F
3171
S 62

EASTER ISLAND

Skottsberg, Carl

Till Robinson-ön och världens ände.
Med 20 plancher, 102 textfigurer och 3 kartor.
Stockholm. Albert Bonniers Förlag. 1918. R8vo.
208 pp.

GN
2.S

PQ
P 76

Easter Island

Tregear, E.

in Journ. of Polyn. Soc. I., 1892, pp. 95-102.

EASTER ISLAND   ADORNMENT

See

ADORNMENT   EASTER ISLAND

DU
Pac.Pam.
844

EASTER ISLAND

Sleight, H. D.

History of Sag Harbor Whale Fisheries, compiled from the original logs, etc. by H. D.
Sleight. Published in the Sag Harbor Corrector.

1855. Whaling bark Prudent, James A. Hamilton, Master.

(an excerpt relating to the loss of a man
at Easter Island)

DU
1
P

EASTER ISLAND

United States seeks base on Easter Island.

(Pacific Islands Monthly, 22(2):85, 1952)

EASTER ISLAND   AGRICULTURE

See

AGRICULTURE   EASTER ISLAND

GN
2.S
P 76

EASTER ISLAND

Smith, S. Percy

Easter Island (Rapa-Nui) and Rapa-(Rapa-Iti
island.

(Journal of the Polynesian Society, 19:
171-175, 1910.)

[review of Dr. Couteaud's paper, and mention
of some other notes on Easter Island, source of
its people, etc.]

DU
12
J 86
looked
case

EASTER ISLAND

Voyage round the world, in the years 1772-
1775, by Captain James Cook, commander of His
Majesty's bark the Resolution...Drawn up from
authentic papers by an officer on board. London.
1781. 4to. pp. 61-62.
IN Journal of a voyage round the world...in
1768-1771...London. 1771.

EASTER ISLAND   AHUS

See

AHUS   EASTER ISLAND

DU
950.E 2
S 93

EASTER ISLAND

Stephen-Chauvet

L'Ile de Paques et ses mystères. La première étude réunissant tous les documents connus
sur cette ile mystérieuse. Preface du E. Loppé.
Paris. Aux éditions "Tel". 86 pp. 68 pl. (7)
pp.

G
51
W 17

EASTER ISLAND

Waterworth, J. Y.

Mystery island of the Pacific. (Easter Is.)

(Walkabout, 19(5):39-41, 1953)

EASTER ISLAND   ALGAE

See

ALGAE   EASTER ISLAND

GN
1
A62

EASTER ISLAND

Tepano, Jaussen

L'île de Pâques. Historique et
écriture. Review by F. Delisle.

(L'Anthropologie, Tome 5, 1894,
pp. 247)

DU
Pac. Pam.
548

EASTER ISLAND

Wilhelm, Ottmar

La isla de Pascua.

(Revista de Marina, Vol. 51, No. 464, 1935.
pp. 1-21)

EASTER ISLAND   AMPHINEURA

see

AMPHINEURA   EASTER ISLAND

DU
950.E2
T48

AS
36
S 3

EASTER ISLAND

Thomson, W. J.

Te Pito te Henua, or Easter Island.

(Report of the U. S. National Museum, 1889,
pp. 447-552)

EASTER ISLAND

see also

CONTACT EASTER ISLAND-CHILE

EASTER ISLAND   AMULET

See

AMULET   EASTER ISLAND

GC
1
M 73-a

EASTER ISLAND

Thoulet, J.

Le courant de Humboldt et la mer de l'île
de Pâques.

(Ann. Inst. Océanographique, N. S., Tome 5,
fasc. 2, 1928, pp. 1-12)

EASTER ISLAND   ACCULTURATION

See

ACCULTURATION   EASTER ISLAND

EASTER ISLAND   ARCHAEOLOGY

See

ARCHAEOLOGY   EASTER ISLAND

EASTER ISLAND   ART

See

ART   EASTER ISLAND

EASTER ISLANDS   BIRDS

See

BIRDS   EASTER ISLANDS

EASTER ISLAND   CONTACT

see

CONTACT   EASTER ISLAND

G
161
H

EASTER ISLAND   BIBLIOGRAPHY

Corney, B. G.

Voyage of Captain Don Felipe Gonzalez ... to Easter Island in 1770-71 ... pp. 147-158. Cambridge. Hakluyt Society. 1908.

(Works issued by the Hakluyt Society ... Second series, No. XIII)

EASTER ISLAND   BLOOD GROUPS

See

BLOOD GROUPS   EASTER ISLAND

EASTER ISLAND   CORALLINACEAE

See

CORALLINACEAE   EASTER ISLAND

GN
2.I
Am

EASTER ISLAND   BIBLIOGRAPHY

Dalton, O. M.

Easter Island script.

(Man, Vol. 4, pp. 77-78. 1904.)

(Bibliography relating to script)

EASTER ISLAND   BOTANY

see

BOTANY   EASTER ISLAND

EASTER ISLAND   CRANIOLOGY

See

CRANIOLOGY   EASTER ISLAND

GN
Ethn.Pam.
3063
3064
2382
2383

GN
2.M
S 23

EASTER ISLAND   BIBLIOGRAPHY
(P.)

Gusinde, Martin

Bibliografia de la Isla de Pascua. Santiago de Chile. 1920-1922.

(Publicaciones del Museo de Etnologia y Antropologia de Chile, Tomo II, Num. 2, 1920, pp. 201-260; Tomo II, Num. 3, 1922, pp. 261-283)

EASTER ISLAND   CARVING

See

CARVING   EASTER ISLAND

EASTER ISLAND   DEFORMITIES ARTIFICIAL

See

DEFORMITIES ARTIFICIAL   EASTER ISLAND

GN
1
An

EASTER ISLAND   BIBLIOGRAPHY

Lehmann, Walter

Essai d'une monographie bibliographique sur l'Isle de Pâques.

GN
Ethn.Pam
1996

(Anthropos, Vol. II, 1907, pp. 141-151; 257-268)

EASTER ISLAND   CHANTS

See

CHANTS EASTER ISLAND

PL
950.E2
E 57

EASTER ISLAND   DICTIONARY

Englert, P. Sebastian

Diccionario Rapanui-Español. Prensas de la Universidad de Chile. 1938. sm8vo. 139 pp.

DU
Pacific
pam.
538

EASTER ISLAND- BIBLIOGRAPHY

Ojeda, Carlos Charlin

Ensayo bibliografico sobre la Isla de Pascua

(Anexo No. 1 al Boletin del Seminario de Derecho Público. Isla de Pascua. Santiago de Chile. n.d. 34 pp.)

EASTER ISLAND   COLEOPTERA

See

COLEOPTERA   EASTER ISLAND

PL
Phil.
Pam. 511

EASTER ISLAND   DICTIONARY

Englert, P. Sebastian

Diccionario Rapanui-Espanol, redactado en la Isla de Pascua. Univ. de Chile. 1938. 12mo. 139 pp.

EASTER ISLAND   BIRD CULT

See

BIRD CULT   EASTER ISLAND

EASTER ISLAND   COLLEMBOLA

See

COLLEMBOLA   EASTER ISLAND

PL
950.E2
F 95

EASTER ISLAND   DICTIONARY

Fuentes, Jordi

Diccionario y gramatica de la lengua de la Isla de Pascua. Pascuense-Castellano; Castellano-Pascuense. Editorial Andres Bello. 1960. 8vo. 1082 pp.

PL
950.E2
F 94

EASTER ISLAND   DICTIONARY

Fuentes, Jordi

Dictionary and grammar of the Easter Island language. Editorial Andres Bello. Santiago de Chile. 1960. 8vo. 1082 pp.

title also in Spanish.
Pascuense-Castellano; Castellano-Pascuense; Pascuense-English; English-Pascuense.

EASTER ISLAND   FISHES

See

FISHES   EASTER ISLAND

EASTER ISLAND   HEADDRESSES

See

HEADDRESSES   EASTER ISLAND

EASTER ISLAND   DIFFUSION

see

DIFFUSION   EASTER ISLAND

EASTER ISLAND   FOLKLORE

see

FOLKLORE   EASTER ISLAND

EASTER ISLANDS   HEALTH

See

HEALTH   EASTER ISLANDS

EASTER ISLAND   DIPTERA

See

DIPTERA   EASTER ISLAND

EASTER ISLAND   GASTROPODA

See

GASTROPODA   EASTER ISLAND

EASTER ISLAND   HEPATICAE

See

HEPATICAE   EASTER ISLAND

DU
12
B 96

looked
case

EASTER ISLAND   DISCOVERY & EXPLORATION

Burney, James

Chronological history of the discoveries in
the South Sea or Pacific Ocean... London. 1803-
1817. 4to. 5 vols.
Vol. 4, pp. 206-210; 560-566.

EASTER ISLANDS   GEOGRAPHY

see

GEOGRAPHY   EASTER ISLANDS

EASTER ISLAND   HOUSES

see

HOUSES   EASTER ISLAND

DU
12
M 31

looked
case

EASTER ISLAND DISCOVERY AND EXPLORATION

Marchand, Étienne

Voyage autour du monde...1790-1792...précédé
d'une introduction historique; auquel on a joint
...un examen critique du voyage de Roggeween...
Tomes 1-4. Paris. 1796-1800. 4to.
Tome 3, pp. 291-298. See also index, Tome 3

EASTER ISLANDS   GEOLOGY

see

GEOLOGY   EASTER ISLANDS

EASTER ISLAND   IMAGES

see

IMAGES   EASTER ISLAND

EASTER ISLAND   ETHNOLOGY

See

ETHNOLOGY   EASTER ISLAND

EASTER ISLAND   GODS

See

GODS   EASTER ISLAND

EASTER ISLAND   IMPLEMENTS & UTENSILS

see

IMPLEMENTS & UTENSILS   EASTER ISLAND

EASTER ISLAND   FILICES

See

FILICES   EASTER ISLAND

PL
950.E2
F 95

EASTER ISLAND   GRAMMAR

Fuentes, Jordi

Diccionario y gramatica de la lengua de
la Isla de Pascua. Pascuense-Castellano; Castellano-Pascuense. Editorial Andres Bello. 1960.
8vo. 1082o pp.

EASTER ISLAND   INSCRIPTIONS

see

INSCRIPTIONS   EASTER ISLAND

PL
950.E2
C 56

EASTER ISLAND LANGUAGE

Churchill, William

Easter Island: the Rapanui speech and the peopling of southeast Polynesia. Washington. Carnegie Institution. 1912. R8vo.

GN
671.E2
C 56

(Carnegie Institution of Washington. Pub. No. 174)

EASTER ISLAND LEPIDOPTERA

See

LEPIDOPTERA EASTER ISLAND

EASTER ISLAND MOLLUSCA

See

MOLLUSCA EASTER ISLAND

AS
36
S 3

EASTER ISLAND LANGUAGE

Cooke, G. H.

Te Pito te Henua, known as Rapa Nui; commonly called Easter Island, South Pacific Ocean...

(U.S. National museum. Annual report, 1897. pt. 1, pp. 689-723)

DU
Pac
Pam
226

Separate

EASTER ISLAND MARAE

see

MARAE EASTER ISLAND

EASTER ISLANDS NATURAL HISTORY

see

NATURAL HISTORY EASTER ISLANDS

GN
2.S
B 91

EASTER ISLAND LANGUAGE

Ross, Alan S.C.

Fontes linguae Paschalis saec. XVIII.

(Bull. de la Soc. des Américanistes de Belgique. no. 22. March 1937. pp. 15-39)

EASTER ISLAND MARINE FAUNA

see

MARINE FAUNA EASTER ISLAND

EASTER ISLAND NEUROPTERA

See

NEUROPTERA EASTER ISLAND

GN
2.I
A-m

EASTER ISLAND LANGUAGE

Ross, Alan S. C.

Preliminary notice of some late eighteenth century numerals from Easter Island.

(Man, Vol. 36, 1936, Art. No. 120, pp. 94-95)

EASTER ISLAND MATERIAL CULTURE

See

MATERIAL CULTURE EASTER ISLAND

EASTER ISLAND NUMERALS

see

NUMERALS EASTER ISLAND

PL
Pam
179

EASTER ISLAND LANGUAGE

Solar, José Ignacio Vives

Te Poki Rapanui (El Nino Pascuense). Te puka mohakamaa e ma oriai ite tagnata honui o Rapa Nui (haka rivariva o). Libro de lectura y conocimientos útiles para el uso de los habitantes de la isla de Pascua... Santiago de Chile Imprenta Cervantes. 1923. 12mo. 49 pp.

(Parallel text,-Spanish-Easter Island)

EASTER ISLAND MATRIARCHY

See

MATRIARCHY EASTER ISLAND

EASTER ISLAND OLIGOCHAETA

See

OLIGOCHAETA EASTER ISLAND

AS
36
S 3

EASTER ISLAND LANGUAGE

Thomson, W. J.

Te Pito te Henua; or, Easter Island...

(U. S. National museum. Annual report, 1889, pp. 447-552)

DU
950.E2
T 48

Separate

EASTER ISLAND METEOROLOGY

See

METEOROLOGY EASTER ISLAND

EASTER ISLAND PADDLES

See

PADDLES EASTER ISLAND

EASTER ISLAND LAVA

see

LAVA EASTER ISLAND

EASTER ISLAND MIGRATIONS

See

Migrations Easter Island

EASTER ISLAND PETROGRAPHY

See

PETROGRAPHY EASTER ISLAND

EASTER ISLAND   PETROGLYPHS

See

PETROGLYPHS   EASTER ISLAND

EASTER ISLAND   PLACE NAMES

See

PLACE NAMES   EASTER ISLAND

EASTER ISLAND   SOILS

See

SOILS   EASTER ISLAND

EASTER ISLAND   PETROLOGY

See

PETROLOGY   EASTER ISLAND

EASTER ISLAND   POPULATION

see

POPULATION   EASTER ISLAND

EASTER ISLAND   SOMATOLOGY

See

SOMATOLOGY   EASTER ISLAND

EASTER ISLAND   PETROGLYPHS

See

PETROGLYPHS   EASTER ISLAND

EASTER ISLAND   RACE

see

RACE   EASTER ISLAND

EASTER ISLAND   STONEWORK

See

STONEWORK   EASTER ISLAND

EASTER ISLAND   PHALLIC STONES

see

PHALLIC STONES   EASTER ISLAND

EASTER ISLAND   REPTILIA

see

REPTILIA   EASTER ISLAND

EASTER ISLAND   TATTOOING

see

TATTOOING   EASTER ISLAND

EASTER ISLAND   PHANEROGAMAE

See

PHANEROGAMAE   EASTER ISLAND

Easter Island—Routledge expedition to

see

Routledge expedition

GR
385.E
E 58

EASTER ISLAND   TEXTS

Englert, P(ater) Sebastian

   Tradiciones de la Isla de Pascua, en idioma rapanui y castellano. Publicaciones de la Comision de Estudios sobre la Isla de Pascua, Universidad de Chile. Imprenta "San Francisco" Padre Las Casas. 1939. R8vo. 85 pp.

EASTER ISLAND   PHOTOGRAPHS

   See album (Easter Island—Métraux), photograph file (pictures without negatives) and folder in DU Locked Case.

EASTER ISLAND   SCULPTURE

See

SCULPTURE   EASTER ISLAND

GN
2.8
T

EASTER ISLAND   TEXTS

Jaussen, Tepano

   Les bois parlants de l'Ile de Pâques (Manuscrit de 1890).

   (Bulletin de la Société des Etudes Océaniennes, Tome 5, No. 14, 1935, pp. 537-542; Vol. 5, No. 15, pp. 583-588, 1936)

EASTER ISLAND   PHYSICAL ANTHROPOLOGY

see

PHYSICAL ANTHROPOLOGY   EASTER ISLAND

EASTER ISLAND   SOCIAL ORGANIZATION

see

SOCIAL ORGANIZATION   EASTER ISLAND

PL
Pam
178

EASTER ISLAND   VOCABULARY

Bienvenido de Estkella, R. P.

   Mis Viajes a Pascua. Santiago de Chile. Imprenta Cervantes. 1921. 8vo. 132 pp.
   Vocabulary: pp. 74-132.

GN
670
B 64

EASTER ISLAND VOCABULARY

Brigham, William Tufts

Ka hana kapa, the making of bark-cloth in Hawaii.

(Bernice P. Bishop Museum, Memoirs, Vol. III, 1911, iv + pp. 1-273, 49 plates and atlas of 27 colored plates)

p. 224, Easter Island

PL
950.E2
M 38

EASTER ISLAND VOCABULARY

Martinez, Edgardo

Vocabulario de la Lengua Rapa-nui, isla de Pascua, por Edgardo Martinez. Santiago de Chile Seccion Impresiones del Instituto Meteorológico. 1913. 8vo. 47 pp.

GN
2.I
A-m

EASTER ISLANDS VOCABULARY

Métraux, Alfred

Numerals from Easter Island

(Man, Vol.36, Nov.1936, pp.190-191)

PL
950.E2
R 86

EASTER ISLANDS VOCABULARY

Roussel, Hippolyte

Vocabulaire de la langue de l'Ile-de-Paques ou Rapanui. Extrait du Muséon, Nos. 2-3, 1908, pp. 159-254. Louvain. J. B. Istas. 1908. 8vo.

(Français-Rapanui)

PL
950.E2
R 86

EASTER ISLANDS VOCABULARY

Roussel, Hippolyte

Vocabulario de la lengua de la Isla de Pascua o Rapanui compuesto por el P. Hipolito Roussel de los SS. CC., y ordenado con la versión castellana por el P. Félix Jaffuel... Santiago de Chile. Imprenta de San José. 1917. R8vo. 189 pp.

(Spanish-Rapanui)

AS
36
S3

and
DU
950.E2
T 48

EASTER ISLANDS VOCABULARY

Thomson, William Judah, 1841-1909.

Te Pito te Henua; or, Easter Island. By Paymaster William J. Thomson ...

(*In* U. S. National museum. Annual report. 1889. Washington, 1891. 23½ᶜᵐ. p. 447-552. illus., pl. XII-LX (incl. front.: map))

On the written language, with translation of Easter Island tablets: p. 513-526.
Language-vocabulary: p. 546-552.

1. Easter Island. 2. Ethnology—Easter Island. 3. Rapanui language. 1. Title.

Library of Congress   Q11.US 1889   14-19269
———— Copy 2.
———— Separate.   F3169.T48

EASTER ISLAND WEAPONS

see

WEAPONS EASTER ISLAND

EASTER ISLAND WRITING

see

WRITING EASTER ISLAND

EASTER ISLAND ZOOLOGY

see

ZOOLOGY EASTER ISLAND

GN
Pam
#348

Easter island tablets, editorial, ex Geog. Mag. April 1, 1876.

Q
Gen
So
Pam
#9

Easterfield, Thomas Hill

The aims and ideals of the Cawthron Institute.

Nelson, 1921.

Card 1

QL
1
N 6-z

Eastern Pacific Expeditions of the New York Zoological Society.
I-XIII See
The Templeton Crocker Expedition (1936)

XIV. Introduction, itinerary, list of stations, nets and dredges of the Eastern Pacific Zaca Expedition, 1937-1938. By William Beebe. (Zoologica, 23, 1938, pp. 287-298)
XV. Seven new marine fishes from Lower California. By William Beebe and John Tee Van. (ibid, 23, 1938, pp. 299-312)

Card 2

QL
1
N 6-z

Eastern Pacific Expeditions of the New York Zoological Society.

XVI. Holothurians from the western coasts of Lower California and Central America, and from the Galapagos Islands. By Elisabeth Deichmann. (ibid, 23, 1938, 361-388)
XVII. A review of the American fishes of the family Cirrhitidae. By John Tee Van. (ibid, 25, 1940, 53-64)
XVIII. On the post-embryonic development of Brachyuran crabs of the genus Ocypode. By Jocelyn Crane. (ibid, 25, 1940, 65-82)

Card 3

QL
1
N 6-z

Eastern Pacific Expeditions of the New York Zoological Society.

XIX. Actiniaria from the Gulf of California by Oskar Carlgren. (ibid, 25, 1940, 211-220)
XX. Medusae of the Templeton Crocker and Eastern Pacific Zaca Expeditions, 1936-1938. By Henry B. Bigelow. (ibid, 25, 1940, 281-322)
XXI. Notes on Echinoderms from the west coast of Central America, by Hubert Lyman Clark. (ibid, 25, 1940, 331-352)

Card 4

QL
1
N 6-z

Eastern Pacific Expeditions of the New York Zoological Society.

XXII. Mollusks from the west coast of Mexico and Central America. Part I. By Leo George Hertlein and A. M. Strong. (ibid, 25,1940,369-432)
XXIII. Polychaetous Annelids from the west coast of Mexico and Central America, by Aaron L. Treadwell. (ibid, 26, 1941, 17-24)
XXIV. Fishes from the tropical eastern Pacific...Part 1. Lancelets and hag-fishes. By William Beebe and John Tee Van. (ibid,26,1941, 89-92)

Card 5

QL
1
N 6-z

Eastern Pacific Expeditions of the New York Zoological Society.

XXV. Fishes from the tropical eastern Pacific...Part 2. Sharks. By William Beebe and John Tee Van. (ibid, 26, 1941, 93-122)
XXVI. Crabs of the genus Uca from the west coast of Central America, by Jocelyn Crane.(ibid, 26, 1941, 145-208)
XXVII. A study of young sailfish (Istiophorus), by William Beebe. (ibid, 26, 1941,209-228)

Card 6

QL
1
N 6-z

Eastern Pacific Expeditions of the New York Zoological Society

XXVIII. Fishes from the tropical eastern Pacific...Part 3. Rays, Mantas and Chimeras, by William Beebe and John Tee-Van. (ibid, 26,1941, pp. 245-280.)
XXIX. On the growth and ecology of Brachyuran crabs of the genus Ocypode. By Jocelyn Crane. (ibid, 26,1941,pp. 297-310)
XXX. Atlantic and Pacific fishes of the genus Dixonia. By William Beebe. (ibid,27,1942,pp. 43-48)

Card 7

QL
1
N 6-z

Eastern Pacific Expeditions of the New York Zoological Society.

XXXI. Uca schmitti, a new species of Brachyuran crab from the west coast of Central America. (ibid, 28, 1943, pp. 31-32)
XXXII. Mollusks from the west coast of Mexico and Central America. by Leo George Hertlein and A. M. Strong. (ibid, 29,1943,pp.149-168)
XXXIII. Pacific Myctophidae (Fishes). By William Beebe abd Mary Vander Pul. (ibid, 29, 1944, pp. 59-95)

Card 8

QL
1
N 6-z

Eastern Pacific Expeditions of the New York Zoological Society.

XXXIV. Mollusks from the west coast of Mexico and Central America. III. By Leo George Hertlein and A. M. Strong (ibid, 31:50-76,1946)
XXXV. Mollusks from the west coast of Mexico and Central America. (IV.) By Leo George Hertlein and A. M. Strong. (ibid, 31:93-120,1946)

Card 9

QL
1
N 6-z

Eastern Pacific Expeditions of the New York Zoological Society.

XXXVI.Mollusks from the West Coast of Mexico and Central America. Part V. By Leo George Hertlein and A. M. Strong. (ibid, 31:129-150, 1947)
XXXVII. Deep-sea Ceratioid fishes. By William Beebe and Jocelyn Crane. (ibid, 31:151-182, 1947)

Card 10

QL
1
N6 -z

Eastern Pacific Expeditions of the New York Zoological Society.

XXXVIII. Intertidal Brachygnathous crabs from the west coast of tropical America, with special reference to ecology. By Jocelyn Crane.

(Zoologica, Vol. 32:69-95, 1947)

QL
1
N 6-z

Card 11

Eastern Pacific Expeditions of the New York Zoological Society.

XXXIX. Mollusks from the West Coast of Mexico and Central America, VI. By Leo George Hertlein and A. M. Strong. (ibid, 33:163-198, 1948)
XL. Mollusks from the West Coast...VII. By Leo George Hertlein and A.M.Strong. (ibid,34 (2):63-97, 1949)
XLI. Mollusks from the West Coast...VIII. By Leo George Hertlein and A.M.Strong. (ibid, 34 (3):239-258, 1949)

PL
500
E 13

Eastman, G. H.

An English--Gilbertese vocabulary of the most commonly used words. Compiled by Rev. G. H. Eastman. Printed at The London Mission Press. Rongorongo, Beru, Gilbert Islands. 1948. 8vo. (3)2-224 pp.

QK
1
Ca

Eastwood, Alice, 1859–
... Some new species of Pacific Coast *Ribes*. By Alice Eastwood ... With 2 plates ... San Francisco, The Academy, 1902.

1 p. l., 241-254 p. xxiii–xxiv pl. 25½ᶜᵐ. (Proceedings of the California academy of sciences. 3d series. Botany. vol. ii, no. 7)
Issued April 14, 1902.
Bibliographical references given with the Key to species: p. 249-251.

1. Ribesieæ. 2. Botany—Pacific states.

Library of Congress   Q11.C24   7-23276

QL
1
N 6-z

Eastern Pacific Expeditions of the New York Zoological Society.

XIIV.Non-intertidal Brachygnathous crabs from the West Coast of Tropical America. Part I. Brachygnatha Oxyrhyncha. By John S. Garth. (Zoologica, 44(3):105-126, 1959)
XLV. ibid, Part II. By John S. Garth. ibid, 46(3):133-160, 1961)

QE
Pam
#433

and

471

Easton, N. wing & Kemmerling, G.L.L.

vulcanology.

Amsterdam, 1923.

QK
1
Ca

Eastwood, Alice, 1859–
... Studies in the herbarium and the field. I–[II] By Alice Eastwood ... With ... plates ... San Francisco, The Academy, 1897-1898.

1 p. l., p. 71-88, 1 l., p. 89-146. pl. vi–xi (part fold.) 25ᶜᵐ. (Proceedings of the California academy of sciences. 3d series. Botany. vol. i, no. 2-3)
i. Issued November 27, 1897; ii, Sept. 24, 1898.
CONTENTS.—I. 1. Report on a small collection of plants from the White Sands of New Mexico. 2. On spurless forms of *Aquilegia*. 3. Three undescribed Californian plants. 4. The manzanitas of Mt. Tamalpais.—II. 1. Notes on the plants of San Nicolas Island. 2. New species of *Cnicus* from southern Colorado and Utah. 3. The Colorado Alpine species of *Synthyris*. 4. Further observations on the manzanitas of Mt. Tamalpais. 5. Two species of *Eriodictyon* heretofore included under *Eriodictyon tomentosum*. 6. New species of Pacific coast plants.
1. Botany—U.S.—Western states.

A 13-1764

Title from Univ. of Calif.   Library of Congress

AS
36
S4

Eastman, Charles Rochester, 1868–
Fossil fishes in the collection of the United States national museum. By Charles R. Eastman ...

(*In* U. S. National museum. Proceedings. Washington, 1917. 23½ᶜᵐ. v. 52, p. 235-304. illus, pl. 1-23)

1. Fishes, Fossil.

18-15652

Library of Congress   Q11.U55 vol. 52

QE
770
E 13

Easton, W. H.

Invertebrate paleontology. Harper and Brothers. New York. R8vo xii + 701 pp. (1959)

QK
Bot.Pam.
1745

EATON, AMOS

Ricketts, Palmer C.

Amos Eaton, Author, Teacher, Investigator: The First Laboratories for the Systematic Individual Work of Students in Chemistry, Physics and Botany...Rensselaer Polytechnic Institute. Troy, 1933. 32pp.

AS
36
S1

Eastman, Charles Rochester, 1868–
Olden time knowledge of *Hippocampus*. By Charles R. Eastman ...

(*In* Smithsonian institution. Annual report. 1915. Washington, 1916. 23½ᶜᵐ. p. 349-357. 4 pl. on 2 l.)

1. Hippocampus.

16-16019

Library of Congress   Q11.S66 1915
—— Copy 2.   Q11.S66 1915 2d set

QL
461
P 11

Eastop, V. F.

Insects of Macquarie Island. Hemiptera: Homoptera: Aphididae.

(Pacific Insects, 4(4):937-938, 1962)

AS
36
A25

Eaton, Daniel C.

Characters of some new filices, from Japan and adjacent regions, collected by Charles Wright in the North Pacific exploring expedition under Captain John Rodgers. In Amer. Acad. Arts & Sc. Proc. IV. pp.110-111. (1860)

QL
1
H2

Eastman, Charles Rochester, 1868–1918.
... Sharks' teeth and cetacean bones from the red clay of the tropical Pacific. By C. R. Eastman ... Cambridge, Printed for the Museum, 1903.

1 p. l., [179]-189, [1] p. illus. 2 pl., fold. map. 29ᶜᵐ. (Memoirs of the Museum of comparative zoölogy at Harvard college, vol. xxvi, no. 4)
Reports on the scientific results of the expedition to the tropical Pacific ... in the U. S. Fish commission steamer "Albatross," from August 1899 to March 1900 ... v.

1. Sharks, Fossil. 2. Cetacea, Fossil. 3. Albatross (Steamer)

A 19-1053

Title from Univ. of Chicago   QL1.H375 vol. 26, no. 4
Printed by L. C.   [3]

QK
484
E 13

AS
36
C 1

Eastwood, Alice

Handbook of the trees of California. San Francisco. 1905. 8vo.

(Calif. Acad. of Sciences, Occas. Papers, Vol. IX)

QK
525
C46

Eaton, Daniel C.

Ferns.

in Chapman's Flora of Southern United States. pp. 515-599.

QL
6
D

Eastman, Charles Rochester, ed.

Dean, Bashford, 1867–
A bibliography of fishes, by Bashford Dean; enl. and ed. by Charles Rochester Eastman ... New York, The Museum, 1916–

v. 25½ᶜᵐ.
Seal of the American museum of natural history on t.-p.

1. Fishes — Bibl. I. Eastman, Charles Rochester, 1868– ed. II. American museum of natural history, New York.

17-12736

Library of Congress   Z5971.D39

QK
1
Ca

Eastwood, Alice, 1859–
... New species from the Sierra Nevada Mountains of California. By Alice Eastwood ... San Francisco, The Academy, 1902.

1 p. l., 285-293 p. 25½ᶜᵐ. (Proceedings of the California academy of sciences. 3d series. Botany. vol. ii, no. 9)
Issued June 3, 1902.

1. Botany—California—Sierra Nevada Mountains.

7-23278

Library of Congress   Q11.C24

QK
525
E 14

Eaton, Daniel Cady

The Ferns of North America. Salem 1879-80 4to 2vols pp XIV, 344 + XXXI, 280 Col. Pl.

K 1 17/16

for conspectus see QK Pam. 612

AS
36
C51

EASTMAN, CHARLES ROCHESTER, 1868
Pittsburgh. Carnegie institute. *Museum.*
... Catalog of fossil fishes in the Carnegie museum. pt. i–
... By Charles R. Eastman. Pittsburgh, Board of trustees of the Carnegie institute, 1911–

v. illus, plates. 33½ᶜᵐ. (Memoirs of the Carnegie museum. vol. iv. no. 7   W. J. Holland, ed.)
Cover-title.
Publications of the Carnegie museum, serial no. 65.

1. Fishes, Fossil. I. Eastman, Charles Rochester, 1868–

11-25030

Library of Congress   AS36.P75 vol. 4, no. 7

AS
36
C5

Eastwood, Alice

New species of ceanothus. Proc. Calif Acad. Sci. 4th ser. v.16, n.11, 1927.

AS
36
C8

Eaton, Daniel Cady, 1834–1895.
... List of marine *Algæ* collected near Eastport, Maine, in August and September, 1873, in connection with the work of the U. S. Fish commission under Prof. S. F. Baird.

(*In* Connecticut academy of arts and sciences. Transactions. New Haven, 1871-73. 25ᶜᵐ. v. 2, p. [343]-350)

1. Algae—Maine. I. U. S. Bureau of fisheries. II. Title.

A 17-774

Library of Congress   Q11.C9 vol. 2
Yale University   A53n.366.2

AS 36 C8

Eaton, George Francis, 1872–

... The collection of osteological material from Machu Picchu, by George F. Eaton ... New Haven, Conn. (The Tuttle, Morehouse & Taylor company) 1916.

96 p., 39 l., illus., xxxix pl., fold. map, 11 fold. tab. 31 x 24ᶜᵐ. (Memoirs of the Connecticut academy of arts and sciences ... vol. v)

GN 802 E 14

1. Peru—Antiq. 2. Machu Picchu, Peru.

16-14320

Library of Congress   Q11.C85 vol. 5

QE 75 B

Eaton, Jerry P.

Macdonald, Gordon A.

Hawaiian volcanoes during 1954. By Gordon A. Macdonald and Jerry P. Eaton. Contributions to general geology. A report of the Hawaiian Volcano Observatory.

(U. S. G. S. Bulletin 1061-B, 1957)

Q 115 C 28

Ebeling, Alfred W.

Melamphaidae I: systematics and zoogeography of the species in the bathypelagic fish genus Melamphaes Günther.

(Carlsberg Foundation's Dana-Report No. 58: pp. 1-164, 1962)

QE Pam #98 and AP 2 A5

Eaton, George F.

Vertebrate fossils from the Mina Eruption, ex Am. Journ. of Sc., vol. VI, Sept., 1923.

AP 2 S 35 and QE Geol. Pam. 1294

Eaton, J. P.

How volcanoes grow: geology, geochemistry, and geophysics disclose the constitution and eruption mechanism of Hawaiian volcanoes, by J. P. Eaton and K. J. Murata.

(Science, 132(3432):925-938, 1960)

Q 115 C 28

Ebeling, Alfred W.

Melamphaidae III: systematics and distribution of the species in the bathypelagic fish genus Scopelogadus Vaillant. By Alfred W. Ebeling and Walter H. Weed III.

(Carlsberg Foundation's Dana-Report No. 60: pp. (1)-58, 1963)

QK Pam #546 and DS 681.5 Ph

Eaton, J. J.

Partial report of the work of Mr. J. J. Eaton, preparer of wood sections in the Bureau of Government Laboratories for use of the Bureau of Forestries, ex Rept. of Philippine Comm. for 1903.

QE 526 H 38 s

Eaton, Jerry P.

Summary of volcanic conditions. By G. A. Macdonald and J. P. Eaton.

(Hawaiian Volcano Observatory Summary, 1-1956-   )

GN Pam 916

Ebeling, Erich

Das verbum der el-Amarna-briefe. Inaugural dissertation ... Friedrich-Wilhelms-Univ. zu Berlin. 1909.

QE Geol.Pam. 1339

Eaton, J. P.

Crustal structure and volcanism in Hawaii.

(Reprint, Crust of the Pacific Basin, Monograph 6:13-29, 1962)

QE Geol. Pam. 1288

Eaton, Jerry P.

Fraser, George D.

The tsunami of March 9, 1957 on the island of Hawaii. By G. D. Fraser, Jerry P. Eaton, and Chester K. Wentworth.

(Bull. Seism. Soc. of America, 49:79-90, 1959)

QK 1 A 75

EBENACEAE

Bakhuizen van den Brink, R. C.

Notes on some of the Ebenaceae and Verbenaceae of the Solomon Islands collected on the Arnold Arboretum Expedition, 1930-1932. With plates 120-122.

(Journal of the Arnold Arboretum, Vol. XVI, No. 1, Jan. 1935, pp. 68-75)

QH 1 P 11

Eaton, Jerry P.

Wentworth, Chester K.   and others

Feasibility of a lava-diverting barrier at Hilo, Hawaii. By C. K. Wentworth, H. A. Powers and J. P. Eaton

(Pacific Science, Vol. 15(3):352-357, 1961)

QE Geol. Pam. 1299

Eaton, Jerry P.   and others

The Tsunami of May 23, 1960, on the island of Hawaii. By J.P.Eaton, D.H.Richter, and W.U. Ault.

(Bull. Seismological Soc. of America, Vol. 51(2):135-157, 1961)

QK Bot.Pam. 2214

EBENACEAE

Fosberg, F. Raymond

Diospyros ferrea (Ebenaceae) in Hawaii.

(Occ. Papers, Bernice P. Bishop Museum, Vol. 15, 1939, No. 10, pp. 119-131)

QE Geol.Pam. 1341

Eaton, J. P.

The Hawaiian Volcano Observatory. By J. P. Eaton and C. K. Wentworth.

(Reprint, Thrum's *All About Hawaii*, pp. 35-43, 1962)

QL Amphib.-Reptilia Pam. 101

Eaton, Theodore H., Jr.

The ancestry of modern Amphibia; a review of the evidence.

(Univ. of Kansas, Mus. of Nat. Hist., Publications, Vol. 12(2):155-180, 1959)

QK 495.E15 H63

EBENACEAE

Hiern, W. P.

A monograph of the Ebenaceae. Trans. Cambridge Phil. Soc. Vol. XII, 1873, pp 27 - 300, pls. 1-11.

[Bound as a separate]

QE 75 B and QE Geology Pam. 1244

Eaton, Jerry P.

Macdonald, Gordon A.

Hawaiian volcanoes during 1953. A contribution to general geology. By Gordon A. Macdonald and Jerry P. Eaton.

(U. S. Geological Survey Bulletin 1021-D, 1955. A report of the Hawaiian Volcano Observatory)

DU 12 S84

The ebb-tide.

Stevenson, Robert Louis

QK 1 J 86

EBENACEAE

Hiern, W. P.

Third notes on Ebenaceae; with description of a new species.

(Jour. Bot. and For., vol. 15, pp. 97-101, 1877)

QK
1
B 97b
and
QK
Bot.Pam.
1983

EBENACEAE MALAYSIA

Bakhuizen, R. C. van den Brink

Revisio Ebenacearum Malayensium.

(Bull. du Jardin Bot. de Buitenzorg, Ser. III, vol. XV. 1936. pp. 1-49)

GN
Ethn.Pam
3552

EBON

Bemerkungen über den Atoll von Ebon in Mikronesien.

(Zeit. f. Erdkunde, n. s.XI:216-218, 1861)

QK
1
U

ECHEVERIA

Rose, Joseph Nelson, 1862–

... Three new species of *Echeveria* from southern Mexico, by J. N. Rose and J. A. Purpus. Washington, Govt. print. off., 1910.

v. p. 45-46. pl. 10-14. 24½ᶜᵐ. (Smithsonian institution. United States national museum. Contributions from the United States national herbarium. vol. 13, pt. 2)

"Bulletin of the United States national museum: issued February 21, 1910."

1. Echeveria. 2. Mexico. Botany. I. Purpus, J. A., joint author.

Agr 10-440

Library, U. S. Dept. of) Agriculture 450C76 vol. 13, pt. 2

GN
Pam
#49

Eberhard, Ernst, Friedrich

Die Menschenrassen

Koburg 1842. 8° pp. 48.

AS
182
H

EBON

Graeffe, E.

Die Lagune von Ebon, nach brieflichen Mitteilungen von J. Kubary.

(Jour. Mus. Godeffroy, Heft 1, 1873, pp. 33-47)

QK
1
U

ECHEVERIA CARNICOLOR

Rose, Joseph Nelson, 1862–

Rediscovery of *Echeveria carnicolor*. By J. N. Rose.

(*In* Smithsonian institution. United States national museum. Contributions from the United States national herbarium. Washington, 1903– 24½ᶜᵐ. vol. XII, pt. 9, p. 393. pl. XLVI)

"Issued May 10, 1909."

1. Echeveria carnicolor.

Agr 9-1502

Library, U. S. Dept. of) Agriculture 450C76 vol. 12, pt. 9

AS
36
S2

Eberhardt, Charles Christopher, 1871–

Indians of Peru, by Charles C. Eberhardt ...

(*In* Smithsonian institution. Smithsonian miscellaneous collections. Washington, 1910. 24½ᶜᵐ. vol. LII (Quarterly issue, vol. V) p. 181-194. pl. XIII-XIV (ports.))

Publication 1817.
Originally published October 24, 1908.

1. Indians of South America—Peru.

Library of Congress   Q11.S7 vol. 52   16-12701
——— Copy 2.

EBON ETHNOLOGY

See

ETHNOLOGY EBON

ECHINI

also
See under

ECHINOIDEA

GN
1
An

Eberlein, P. J.

Die Trommelsprache auf der Gazellehalbinsel (Neupommern).

(Anthropos. Bd.V. 1910. pp.635-642)

Storage
Case
5

Hms La
20

EBON LANGUAGE

Doane, E.T.

Remarks on the dialects of the islands of Ponape and Ebon, Micronesia, as related to the Malay language. mx. or a copy of an ms. 32 pp.

Q
115
H 23

ECHINI PACIFIC

Clark, Hubert Lyman

A report on the Echini of warmer eastern Pacific, based on the collections of the Velero III.

IN Allan Hancock Pacific Expeditions, Vol. 8(5), 1948. pp. xii + 225-351

Z
Bibl.Pam.
89

Eberstadt, Edward   and Sons

The Northwest Coast: personal narratives of discovery, conquest and exploration. (bookdealers catalog, no. 119, (1941))

PL
Phil.Pam.
490

EBON VOCABULARY

Doane, E. T.

A comparative vocabulary of the Malay language and Ebon dialect. (3 pages) n.d.

QK
Bot.Pam.
2543

ECHINOCEREUS

Dawson, E. Yale

Review of Echinocereus pacificus (Englm.) B. and R.

(Reprinted without change of paging, Desert Plant Life, Dec. 1948:151-159)

QE
75
W

EBERT, FRED CHARLES

McGlashan, Harry Deyoe, 1879–

... Southern California floods of January, 1916, by H. D. McGlashan and F. C. Ebert; prepared in cooperation with the state of California. Washington, Govt. print. off., 1918.

80 p. xvii pl. (incl. fold. map in pocket) 23½ᶜᵐ. (U. S. Geological survey. Water-supply paper 426)

At head of title: Department of the interior.

1. Floods—California. I. Ebert, Fred Charles, 1881– joint author.

——— Copy 2.   G S 18-159
Library, U. S. Geological   Survey (200) G no. 426

AS
36
W 2

ECHELIDAE PACIFIC

Schultz, Leonard P.

Keys to the genera of echelid eels and the species of Muraenichthys of the Pacific, with two new species. By Leonard P. Schultz and Loren P. Woods.

(Jour. Washington Acad. Sci., 39:169-174, 1949)

QL
Prot.-
Polyzoa
Pam.
764

ECHINODERES

Karling, Tor G.

Echinoderes levanderi n. sp. (Kinorhyncha) aus der Ostsee.

(Arkiv för Zoologi, Serie 2 Band 7 Nr. 10: 189-192, 1954)

QL
Crust.
Pam. 215

Ebner, Victor von

Helleria, eine neue Isopoden-Gattung aus der Familie der Oniscoiden.

(Wien, Zool. Bot. Verhandl, XVIII, 1868, (Abh.), pp. 95-114)

AS
122
L-p

ECHENEIDIDAE

Norman, J. R.

The Remoras or shark-suckers(Echeneididae).

(Proceedings of the Linnean Society of London, 151st Session (1938-39) pp. 24-29)

Q
115
M 46

ECHINODERIDA

Johnston, T. Harvey
EChinoderida

Mawson, Sir Douglas   leader
Australasian Antarctic Expedition, 1911-14.
Scientific Reports, Series C, Vol. 10, Part 7, 1938.

AS
750
D 67 r

ECHINODERMA

Fell, H. Barraclough

Echinoderms from the Subantarctic Islands of New Zealand: Asteroidea, Ophiuroidea, and Echinoidea.

(Records of the Dominion Museum, Vol. 2(2): 73-111, 1953)

QL
382
Be

ECHINODERMATA

Bell, F. Jeffrey.

Catalogue of the British echinoderms in British Museum.

London, 1892.

AS
36
35

Echinodermata, Crinoidea

Clark, Austin Hobart

Monograph of the existing crinoids.
U.S. Nat. Mus. Bull. 82, pp. 406, pls. 1-17.

QL
1
H2

ECHINODERMATA

Agassiz, Alexander, 1835-1910.

... *Calamocrinus diomedæ*, a new stalked crinoid, with notes on the apical system and the homologies of echinoderms, by Alexander Agassiz ... Cambridge, Printed for the Museum, 1892.

95 p. XXXII pl. (part fold.) 29ᶜᵐ. (Memoirs of the Museum of comparative zoölogy at Harvard college, vol. XVIII, no. 2)

Each plate accompanied by leaf with descriptive letterpress.
Reports on an exploration off the west coasts of Mexico, Central and South America, and off the Galapagos Islands ... by the U. S. Fish commission steamer "Albatross," during 1891 ... I.

1. Crinoidea. 2. Echinodermata. 3. Albatross (Steamer) I. Title.

A 10-1036

Another copy.   QL384.C8A3
Title from Univ. of Chicago   QL1.H375 vol. 17, no. 2
Printed by L. C.   [3]

QL
Mollusca
Pam. 682

ECHINODERMATA

British Museum (Nat. Hist.)

Guide to the Shell and Starfish Galleries... in the Department of Zoology...1888.

For fuller entry see main card.

QL
384.E2
C59

ECHINODERMATA

Clark, Hubert Lyman

A catalogue of the recent sea-urchins (Echinoidea) in the collection of the British Museum.

London, 1925, 250 pp., 12 pls.

QL
45
L 28

ECHINODERMA

Bather, F. A. and others

The Echinoderma

Lankester, Sir Edwin Ray   editor
A treatise on zoology, Part III, 1900

QL
381
L 94

ECHINODERMATA

Bronn, Heinrich Georg

Die Klassen und Ordnungen des Their-Reichs.. Bd. 2, Abt. 3, Echinodermen. Buche 1-3, 1889-1901. By Hubert Ludwig and Otto Hamann.

QH
301
C3
Vol X

ECHINODERMATA

Clark, Hubert Lyman

Echinoderm fauna of Torres Strait: its composition and its origin. Car. Inst. Wash. Pub. 214, 1921.

QL
Crust.
Pam. 1

ECHINODERMATA

Agassiz, Alexander

List of the Echinoderms sent to different institutions in exchange for other specimens, with annotations.

(Bull. Mus. of Comp. Zool., Harvard, I, 1863, pp. 17-28)

AS
36
A 65 n

ECHINODERMATA

Burnett, Allison L.

Enigma of an Echinoderm.

(Natural History, 70(9):11-19, 1961

QL
Protozoa
& Poly
Pam #46

Proto-
P-y

QL
19

Echinodermata

Clark, Hubert Lyman

Echinoderms from Lower California, with descriptions of new species.

in Am. Mus. Nat. Hist. Bull. XXXII, 1913, pp. 185-236, pls. XLIV-XLVI.
Also Separate.

QL
381
A 26

ECHINODERMATA

Agassiz, Louis i. e. Jean Louis Rodolphe, 1807-1873.
Monographies d'échinodermes, vivans et fossiles, par Louis Agassiz ... Neuchâtel, L'auteur, 1838-[42]
[490] p. 63 pl. (partly col.) 31½ᶜᵐ.
Various paging.
Issued in parts.
CONTENTS.—Échinites. Famille des cidarides. 1. monographie. Des salénies—Observations sur les progrès récens de l'histoire naturelle des échinodermes.—Échinites. Famille des clypéastroides. 2. monographie. Des scutelles. 1841.—Échinites. Famille des clypéastroides. 3. monographie. Des galérites. Par Ed. Desor. 1842.—Échinites. Famille des clypéastroides. 4. monographie. Des *Dysaster*. Par Ed. Desor. 1842—Anatomie des échinodermes. 1. monographie. Anatomie du genre *Echinus*. Par G. Valentin. 1841.
1. Echinodermata. 2. Echinodermata, Fossil. I. Desor, Édouard i. e. Pierre Jean Édouard, 1811- 1882. II. Valentin, Gabriel Gustav, 1810-1883.

6-17840

Library of Congress   QL381.A3

QL
Moll
Pam
#427

ECHINODERMATA

Bush, Katherine J.

Catalogue of mollusca and echinodermata dredged on the coast of Labrador... From Proc. U.S. Nat. Mus. 1883.

QH
301
J-71-m

ECHINODERMATA

Clark, Hubert Lyman

Synapta Vivipara

(Memoirs from the Biological Laboratory Johns Hopkins University, IV:2, 1898. 4to.)

QL
1
H1

ECHINODERMATA

Agassiz, Alexander, 1835-1910.

... Preliminary report on the echini and star-fishes dredged in deep water between Cuba and the Florida Reef, by L. F. de Pourtales ... prepared by Alexander Agassiz ...

(In Harvard university. Museum of comparative zoölogy. Bulletin. Cambridge, Mass., 1863-69. 24ᶜᵐ. vol. I, p. 253-308)

Echinodermata

1. Sea-urchins. 2. Starfishes.

8-21386 Revised

Library of Congress   QL1.H3
——— Copy 2, detached.   QL383.2.A2

QL
Prot.-
Poly.
Pam.
826

ECHINODERMATA

Clark, Ailsa M.

Starfishes and their relations. London. British Museum (Nat. Hist.) 1962. 119 pp. 8vo.

AS
36
C9

Echinoderms.

Coe, W. R. Echinoderms of Connecticut. Hartford, 1912.

152 pp., 32 pl., 29 figs. 23ᶜᵐ.

(Bulletin no. 19, Connecticut geological and natural history survey.)

QL
1
H 2

ECHINODERMATA

Agassiz, Alexander and others

Selections from embryological monographs. II. Echinodermata, by Alexander Agassiz.

(Mem. Mus. Comp. Zool. Harvard, Vol. 9, 1883, part 2.)

----Bibliography:Bull MCZH, Vol. X:No. 2

AS
36
S2

ECHINODERMATA

Clark, Austin Hobart, 1880-

... The echinoderms as aberrant arthropods, by Austin H. Clark ... City of Washington, The Smithsonian institution, 1921.

1 p. l., 20 p. 24½ᶜᵐ. (Smithsonian miscellaneous collections. v. 72, no. 11)
Publication 2653.

1. Echinodermata.

21-12897

Library of Congress   Q11.S7 vol. 72, no. 11
[71]

QL
Prot. to
Polyzoa
Pams
279
279a
280
281
314
316
327
413
415

ECHINODERMATA

Bather, F. A.

Echinoderma. (Zool. Record excerpts)

ECHINODERMATA

QL
Protozoa
to
Poly.
Pam.
150
and
QL
1
Au

Coleman, Hedley L.

Echinodermata (supplement). From Mem.
Australian Mus. Vol. iv, pp 699 -701, 1
pl. 1911.

ECHINODERMATA

QH
301
J 71-m

Grave, Caswell

Ophiura Brevispina

[Memoirs from the Biological Laboratory of
Johns Hopkins University, IV:5, 4to. 1900.]

ECHINODERMATA

QP
C

Loeb, Jacques, 1859–

... The fertilization of the egg of the sea-urchin (*Strongylocentrotus purpuratus* and *Strongylocentrotus franciscanus*) by the sperm of the starfish (*Asterias ochracea*)
by Jacques Loeb. Berkeley, The University press, 1903.

cover-title, p. [39]–53. 27ᵐᵐ. (University of California publications. Physiology. vol. 1, no. 6)

"Address delivered before Sigma Xi scientific society at Stanford university, Oct. 13, 1903."

1. Fertilization (Biology) 2. Echinodermata. 3. Embryology, Experimental. 4. Sea-urchins.

A 11–1269

Title from Univ. of Calif.   Library of Congress

ECHINODERMATA

QL
Prot-
Poly.
Pam.
722

Engel, H.

Ophioteresis beauforti nov. spec.

(Bijdragen tot de Dierkunde, Vol. 28:140-
145, 1949)

ECHINODERMATA

QL
Prot. to
Poly.
567

Gray, John Edward

Synopsis of the Species of Starfish in the
British Museum...London. J. Van Voorst, 1866.
iv + 17 + (1) pp. 4to.

ECHINODERMATA

QP
1
C

Loeb, Jacques, 1859–

... Further experiments on the fertilization of the egg
of the sea-urchin (*Strongylocentrotus purpuratus*) with
sperm of various species of starfish and a holothurian
(*Cucumaria*) By Jacques Loeb. Berkeley, The University press, 1904.

cover-title, p. [83]–85. 27ᵐᵐ. (University of California publications. Physiology. vol. 1, no. 11)

1. Fertilization (Biology) 2. Echinodermata. 3. Embryology, Experimental. 4. Sea-urchins.

A 11–1271

Title from Univ. of Calif.   Library of Congress

ECHINODERMATA

QL
Prot.
to
Poly.
Pam.
#196
AS
36
S4

Fisher, W. K.

A new sea star of the genus Evasterias. From Proc. U. S. Nat. Mus. vol. 69,
art. 6, pp. 1-5. 1926.

ECHINODERMATA

QL
Crust
Pam
378

Hoffmann, C   K

Crustaces et echinodermes de Madagascar et de l'ile de la Reunion.

Leyde, 1874.   58p.   10pls.

ECHINODERMATA

QP
1
C

Loeb, Jacques, 1859–

... Further experiments on heterogeneous hybridization in echinoderms ... By Jacques Loeb (tr. from Pflüger's Archiv, 1904, v. 104, p. 325, by John Bruce MacCallum) (Berkeley, The University press) 1904.

p. [5]–30. illus. 27ᵐᵐ. (University of California publications. Physiology. vol. 2, no. 2)

Issued in single cover with v. 2, no. 3-4, of the series.

1. Echinodermata. 2. Fertilization (Biology) 3. Embryology, Experimental. I. MacCallum, John Bruce, 1876-1906, tr.

A 11–1270

Title from Univ. of Calif.   Library of Congress

ECHINODERMATA

AS
36
S4

Fisher, Walter Kenrick, 1878–

... Four new genera and fifty-eight new species of
starfishes from the Philippine Islands, Celebes, and the
Moluccas. By Walter K. Fisher ...

(*In* U. S. National museum. Proceedings. Washington, 1913. 23½ᵐᵐ. v. 43, p. 599-648)

"Scientific results of the Philippine cruise of the fisheries steamer 'Albatross,' 1907-1910.—no. 23."

1. Starfishes. 2. Echinodermata — Philippine Islands. 3. Echinodermata—Dutch East Indies. 4. Albatross (Steamer)

13–13128

Library of Congress   Q11.U55 vol. 43

ECHINODERMATA

QL
Prot.and
Polyzoa
Pam.567

Inaba, Densaburo

Notes on the Development of a Holothurian
Caudina chilensis (J. Müller)

Reprinted from the Science Reports of the
Tohuku Imperial University, 4th Series, Biol.,
Vol. V, No. 2, 1930 pp. 215-248, pl. ix-xiv

ECHINODERMATA

QP
1
C

Loeb, Jacques, 1859–

... On a method by which the eggs of a sea-urchin
(*Strongylocentrotus purpuratus*) can be fertilized with
the sperm of a starfish (*Asterias ochracea*). By Jacques
Loeb. Berkeley, The University press, 1903.

cover-title, 3 p. 27ᵐᵐ. (University of California publications. Physiology. v. 1, no. 1)

1. Fertilization (Biology) 2. Echinodermata. 3. Embryology, Experimental. 4. Sea-urchins.

A 11–1275

Title from Univ. of Calif.   Library of Congress

ECHINODERMATA

AS
36
S4

Fisher, Walter Kenrick, 1878–

... New starfishes from the Philippine Islands, Celebes,
and the Moluccas. By Walter K. Fisher ...

(*In* U. S. National museum. Proceedings. Washington, 1914. 23½ᵐᵐ. v. 46, p. 201-224)

"Scientific results of the Philippine cruise of the fisheries steamer 'Albatross,' 1907-1910.—no. 30."

1. Starfishes. 2. Echinodermata—Philippine Islands. 3. Echinodermata—Dutch East Indies. 4. Albatross (Steamer)

14–10979

Library of Congress   Q11.U55 vol. 46

ECHINODERMATA

QL
383.5
I 39

Indian Museum. Calcutta

Echinoderma of the Indian museum. Parts
1-10, 1899-1927.

Collections of the Royal Indian marine
survey ship Investigator.

For complete entry see
main card.

ECHINODERMATA

QL
381
L 87

Loriol, Percival de

Notes pour servir a l'etude des Echinodermes.
Series I: fasc. 9-10, 1901-1902.
" II: " 1-2, 1902, 1904.

(Ser. II reprinted from Mem. Soc. de Phys. et
d'Hist. Nat., Geneva, Suppl. Vol., 1891; Tome 32:
II:9. Series I sources listed in Fasc. 10)

ECHINODERMATA

GC
1
S 43-c

Fox, Denis L.

Comparative studies of the pigments of some
Pacific coast echinoderms, by Denis L. Fox and
Bradley T. Scheer.

and
QL
1
M 4

(Biological Bull. 80, 1941, pp. 441-455;
also Scripps Inst. of Oceanography, Contribution
no. 132)

Echinodermata

AS
36
S5

Koehler, René

Contribution to study of ophiurans of
U. S. Nat. Mus. Bull. 84, 4to. pp. 173, pls. 18.
Washington, 1914.

Note.—Bibliographical references, pp. 141-142.

ECHINODERMATA

QL
Protozoa
to
Polyzoa
Pam.
182

Rankin, Walter M.

Echinoderms collected off the west
coast of Greenland by the Princeton Arctic Expedition of 1899. From Acad. Nat.
Sc. Philadelphia , 1901.

ECHINODERMATA

QL
1
U

Gislen, Torsten

Echinoderm studies. Academical Dissertation.

and

QL
Prot. to
Polyzoa
Pam. 576

(Zool. Bidrag from Uppsala, IX, 1924.

ECHINODERMATA

QL
384.E2
K 77

Koehler, Rene

Echinides et Ophiures. Expedition Antarctique Belge. Resultats du Voyage de S. Y.
Belgica en 1897-1898-1899...Rapports Scientifiques, Zoologie. Anvers. 1901. 4to. 42 pp.
8 plates.

ECHINODERMA

QL
Prot.Poly.
Pam.570

Süssbach, S.

Die Seeigel, Seesterne und Schlangensterne
der Nord- und Ostsee, von S. Süssbach und A.
Breckner.

(Wiss. Meeresuntersuchungen...Abt. Kiel, N.F.
Bd. 12, pp. 169-300, taf. I-III, Kiel, 1910)

AS
36
C8

ECHINODERMATA
Verrill, Addison Emory, 1839-
... Notes on the *Radiata* in the Museum of Yale college, with descriptions of new genera and species.

(*In* Connecticut academy of arts and sciences. Transactions. New Haven, 1866-71. 25ᶜᵐ. v. 1, p. [247]-613. pl. IV-X)

CONTENTS.—Descriptions of new starfishes from New Zealand.—Notes on the echinoderms of Panama and west coast of America, with descriptions of new genera and species.—On the geographical distribution of the echinoderms of the west coast of America.—Comparison of the tropical echinoderm faunæ of the east and west coasts of America.—Notice of the corals and echinoderms collected by Prof. C. F. Hartt, at the Abrolhos

(Continued on next card)

A 17-762

AS
244
D

ECHINODERMATA AFRICA, SOUTH

Mortensen, Th.

Echinoderms of S. Africa (Asteroidea and Ophiuroidea).

(Vid. Med. Dansk nat. For. i Kobenhavn, Bd. 93, 1932/33, pp. 215-400. Papers from Dr. Th. Mortensen's Pacific Exp., 1914-16, No. 65)

QL
383.7
C 59

ECHINODERMATA AUSTRALIA

Clark, Hubert Lyman

The Echinoderm fauna of Australia; its composition and its origin. Carnegie Institution of Washington Publication 566. 1946. R8vo. iv + 567 pp.

AS
36
C8

ECHINODERMATA
Verrill, Addison Emory, 1839-   ... Notes on the
Radiata ... 1866-71. (Card 2)
CONTENTS—Continued.

reefs, Province of Bahia, Brazil, 1867.—Notice of a collection of echinoderms from La Paz, Lower California, with descriptions of a new genus.—Supplementary note on echinoderms of the west coast of America.—Review of the corals and polyps of the west coast of America.—On the geographical distribution of the polyps of the west coast of America.—Additional observations on echinoderms, chiefly from the Pacific coast of America.—On the echinoderm-fauna of the Gulf of California and Cape St. Lucas.

1. Corals. 2. Echinodermata. 3. Marine fauna—Abrolhos Bank. 4. Marine fauna—California, Lower. I. Title.

A 17-762

Library of Congress   Q11.C9 vol. 1
Yale University   A53n.366.1

QL
1
Proto.-
Poly.Pam.
684

ECHINODERMATA AMBOINA

Loriol, Perceval de

Echinodermes de la Baie d'Amboine.

(Revue Suisse de Zool., 1:359-426, 1893)

QL
1
H 2

ECHINODERMATA AUSTRALIA

Clark, Hubert Lyman

Echinoderms from Australia, an account of collections made in 1929 and 1932. With 28 plates... and 64 textfigures.

(Memoirs of the Museum of Comparative Zoology at Harvard Coolege, Vol. 55, 1938)

QL
1
N 6-z

ECHINODERMATA
Zeisenhenne, Fred C.

Echinoderms from the West Coast of Lower California, the Gulf of California and Clarion Island. The Templeton Crocker Expedition (1936), X.

(Zoologica, 22, 1937, pp. 209-240).

Q
115
M 46

ECHINODERMATA ANTARCTIC
Koehler, Réné
Echinodermata Asteroidea.

Mawson. Sir Douglas
Australasian Antarctic Expedition, 1911-14. Scientific Reports, Series C, Vol. 8, Part 1, 1920.

QL
1
L-j

ECHINODERMS - Australia
Clark, Hubert Lyman

Some echinoderms from West Australia In Linn. Soc. Journ. Vol XXXV, 1923, pp 229- 253.

QL
Proto.-
Poly.
Pam. 761

ECHINODERMATA
Ziesenhenne, Fred C.

A review of the genus Ophioderma M. and T.
IN
Essays in the natural sciences in honor of Captain Allan Hancock, on the occasion of his birthday July 26, 1955. Los Angeles. Univ. of Southern California Press. pp. 185-201

Q
115
M 46

ECHINODERMATA ANTARCTIC
Koehler, Réné
Echinodermata Echinoidea.

Mawson, Sir Douglas   leader
Australasian Antarctic Expedition, 1911-14. Scientific Reports, Series C, Vol. 8, Part 3, 1926.

AS
720.S
S 72

ECHINODERMATA AUSTRALIA
Cotton, Bernard C.

Echinodermata of the Flindersian region, southern Australia. By Bernard C. Cotton and Frank K. Godfrey.

(Rec. South Australian Mus., Vol. VII (2): 193-233, 1942)

QC
M 73

ECHINODERMATA DISTRIBUTION
Tortonese, Enrico

La distribution bathymétrique des Echinodermes et particulièrement des espèces mediterranéennes.

(Bull. Inst. Oceanogr. de Monaco, No. 956, 1949)

Q
115
M 46

ECHINODERMATA ANTARCTIC
Koehler, Réné
Echinodermata Ophiuroidea.

Mawson, Sir Douglas   leader
Australasian Antarctic Expedition, 1911-14. Scientific Reports, Series C, Vol. 8, Part 2, 1922.

QL
383.7
R 17

ECHINODERMATA AUSTRALIA
Ramsay, Edward Pierson

Catalogue of the Echinodermata in the Australian Museum. Part I: Echini. Desmoticha and Petalosticha. Australian Museum, Sydney (Catalogue no. 10). F. W. White. 1885. 8vo. ii + 54 pp.

AS
71
C 96

ECHINODERMATA FOSSIL
Sanchez Roiz, Mario

Nuevos generos y especies de equinodermos fosiles cubanos.

(Mem. Soc. Cubana de Hist. Nat., 21(1):1-30, pl. 1-15, 1952)

QL
383.9
D91

ECHINODERMATA - ARCTIC
Duncan, P   Martin

A memoir on the echinodermata of the Arctic Sea to the west of Greenland.

London, Van Voorst, 1881.   80p. pls.

QL
1
H-1

ECHINODERMATA-BERMUDA
Clark, Hubert Lyman

The Echinoderm fauna of Bermuda.

(Bull. Mus. of Comparative Zool., Harvard College, Vol. 89, No. 8, 1942, pp. 367-391)

AS
36
S4

ECHINODERMATA-- AFRICA
Clark, Austin Hobart, 1880-
The recent crinoids of the coasts of Africa. By Austin Hobart Clark ...
(*In* U. S. National museum. Proceedings. Washington, 1911. 23½ᶜᵐ. v. 40, p. 1-51)

1. Crinoidea. 2. Echinodermata—Africa.

11-31588

Library of Congress   Q11.U55—vol. 40

AS
36
S4

ECHINODERMATA--AUSTRALIA
Clark, Austin Hobart, 1880-
A new Australian crinoid. By Austin H. Clark ...
(*In* U. S. National museum. Proceedings. Washington, 1911. 23½ᶜᵐ. vol. 38, p. 275-276)

1. Crinoidea. 2. Echinodermata—Australia.

11-15729

Library of Congress   Q11.U55 vol. 38

AS
36
C8

and

QH
Nat.Hist.
Pam. 91

ECHINODERMATA BERMUDA
Verrill, Addison Emory, 1839-
... Additions to the echinoderms of the Bermudas.
(*In* Connecticut academy of arts and sciences. Transactions. New Haven, 1899-1900. 25ᶜᵐ. v. 10, p. [383]-587)

1. Echinodermata—Bermuda Islands. I. Title.

A 17-887

Library of Congress   Q11.C9 vol. 10
Yale University   A53n.366.10

AS
36
W 2

ECHINODERMATA BIAK

Clark, Austin H.

     Some echinoderms form Biak, Schouten Islands.
By Austin H. Clark and Frederick M. Bayer

     (Journal of the Washington Acad. Sci., Vol.
38: 143-144, 1948)

GN
2.M
R 13

ECHINODERMATA- COCOS KEELING ISLANDS

Clark, Austin H.

     Echinodermata.

     IN
     Papers on the fauna of the Cocos-Keeling
Islands...collected...1940...1941

     (Bull. Raffles Museum, No. 22: 29-52, 1950)

QL
Protozoa
to
Polyzoa
Pam 27
109

AS
719
A-me

ECHINODERMATA ELLICE ISLANDS

Whitelegge, Thomas

     Echinodermata of Funafuti.

     (Australian Museum, Memoirs, Vol. III, 2,
pp. 155-162. 1896-97)

AS
36
C8

ECHINODERMATA-BRAZIL

Rathbun, Richard, 1852-

     ... A list of the Brazilian echinoderms, with notes on
their distribution, etc.

     (*In* Connecticut academy of arts and sciences. Transactions. New
Haven, 1878-82. 25ᶜᵐ. v. 5, p. [139]-158)

     1. Echinodermata—Brazil. 1. Title.

                              A 17-797

Library of Congress   Q11.C9 vol. 5
Yale University   A.53n.366.5

AS
36
C9

ECHINODERMATA CONNECTICUT

Connecticut. State geological and natural history survey.
Bulletin no. 19. Echinoderms of Connecticut. By
W. R. Coe. Hartford, 1912.

     152 pp., 32 pl., 29 figs. 23ᶜᵐ.

AS
36
S4

ECHINODERMATA--EUROPE

Clark, Austin Hobart, 1880-

     A new European crinoid. By Austin Hobart Clark ...

     (*In* U. S. National museum. Proceedings. Washington, 1911. 23½ᶜᵐ.
vol. 38, p. 329-333)

     1. Crinoidea. 2. Echinodermata—Europe.

                              11-15735

Library of Congress   Q11.U55 vol. 38

AS
36
A4
and
QL
Proto
to
Poly.
Pam.
46

ECHINODERMATA - CALIFORNIA

Clark, Hubert Lyman

     Echinoderms from Lower California,
with descriptions of new species.

in Am. Mus. Nat. Hist. Bull. XXXII, 1913, pp. 185-236,
pls. XLIV - XLVI. Also separate.

Separate given by Dr. C.M. Cooke, 1916.

AS
71
C 96

ECHINODERMATA CUBA

Sanchez Roig, Mario

     Nuevos generos y especies de equinodermos
fosiles cubanos.

     (Mem. Soc. Cubana de Hist. Nat., 21(1):1-30,
pl. 1-15, 1952)

QL
Protozoa
Polyzoa
Pam. 540

ECHINODERMATA FRANCE

Koehler, Rene

     Recherches sur les echinides des cotes de
Provence.

     (Annales d. Mus. d'Hist. Nat. Marseille -
Zool. v.1, 1883. Memoire No. 3)

AS
36
C8

ECHINODERMATA-CALIFORNIA, LOWER

Verrill, Addison Emery, 1839-

     ... Notice of a collection of echinoderms, from La Paz,
Lower California, with descriptions of a new genus ...

     (*In* Connecticut academy of arts and sciences, New Haven. Transac-
tions. New Haven, 1866-   24ᶜᵐ. v. 1, p. 371-376. pl.)

     Running title: Verrill, Notes on *Radiata*.
     Published April, 1868."

     1. Echinodermata—California, Lower.
                              CA 7-2900 Unrev'd
Library of Congress   Q11.C9 vol. 1
—— Copy 2, separate.   QL383.1.V55
Imperfect: plate wanting.

QL
Crust.
Pam.
588

ECHINODERMATA CUBA

Sanchez Roig, Mario

     Nuevos generos y especies de equinoideos
fosiles cubanos.

     (Torreia, Num. 17, Oct. 20, 1952)

QL
Protozoa
to
Polyzoa
Pam 27
109

AS
719
A-me

ECHINODERMATA FUNAFUTI

Whitelegge, Thomas

     Echinodermata of Funafuti.

     (Australian Museum, Memoirs, Vol. III,
2, pp. 155-162. 1896-97)

AS
36
W 2

ECHINODERMATA CANTON ISLAND

Ely, Charles A.

     A new brittle-star (Ophiocoma anaglyptica)
from Canton Island.

     (Jour. Washington Acad. Sci., 34:373-375,
1944)

AS
36
S5

ECHINODERMATA--DUTCH EAST INDIES

Fisher, Walter Kenrick, 1878-
     ... Starfishes of the Philippine seas and adjacent
waters, by Walter K. Fisher ... Washington, Govt. print.
off., 1919.
     xi, 712 p. 156 pl. 24ᶜᵐ. (Smithsonian institution. United States
National museum. Bulletin 100, v. 3)
     At head of title: ... Contributions to the biology of the Philippine Archi-
pelago and adjacent regions.
     On verso of t.-p.: Bulletin of the United States National museum.
     Plates printed on both sides.
     Bibliography: p. 541-546.
     Report based upon a collection made by the United States Fisheries
steamer Albatross, 1907-1910, in the region of the Philippine Islands,
Celebes and Molucca Islands.
     1. Starfishes. 2. Echinodermata — Philippine Islands. 3. Echinoder-
mata—Dutch East Indies.
     Library of Congress   Q11.U6 no. 100 vol.3 19-26691
     —— Copy 2.   QL384.A8F7
                      [8]

AS
36
S 2

ECHINODERMATA GALAPAGOS ISLANDS

Clark, Austin H.

     Echinoderms (other than Holothurians) col-
lected on the Presidential cruise of 1938.

     (Smithsonian Misc. Coll., Vol. 98, No. 11,
1939, pp. 1-18)

AS
474
S

ECHINODERMATA-CEYLON

Clark, Hubert Lyman

     Echinoderms of Ceylon other than
Holothurians.

in Spolia Zeylanica, Colombo Mus. Ceylon,
Vol. X, Part 37, pp. 83-102, illus.

AS
36
S4

ECHINODERMATA -- EAST INDIES

Clark, Austin Hobart, 1880-
     ...Thalassocrinus, a new genus of stalked crinoids from
the East Indies. By Austin Hobart Clark ...

     (*In* U. S. National museum. Proceedings. Washington, 1911. 23½ᶜᵐ.
v. 39, p. 473-476)

     Scientific results of the Philippine cruise of the fisheries steamer "Alba-
tross," 1907-10.—no. 7.

     1 Thalassocrinus. 2. Echinodermata — East Indies. 3. Albatross
(Steamer)

     Library of Congress   Q11.U55 vol. 39   11—21248
                           [s20h2]

QL
383.4
M 88

ECHINODERMATA GREAT BRITAIN

Mortensen, Th(eodor)

     Handbook of the Echinoderms of the British
Isles. Humphrey Milford. Oxford University Press
1927. 8vo. ix + 471 pp.

AS
36
S 2

ECHINODERMATA CLIPPERTON ISLAND

Clark, Austin H.

     Echinoderms (other than Holothurians) col-
lected on the Presidential cruise of 1938.

     (Smithsonian Misc. Coll., Vol. 98, 1939, pp.
1-18, No. 11)

QL
383.5
H 33

ECHINODERMATA DUTCH EAST INDIES

Hartlaub, Charles

     Beitrag zur Kenntniss der Comatulidenfauna
des Indischen Archipels.

     (Nova Acta der K. Leop.-Carol. Deutschen
Akad. der Naturf., Bd. 58, 1891:1-120 pp., 5
tafeln)

AS
36
S4

ECHINODERMATA--HAWAIIAN ISLANDS.

Fisher, Walter Kenrick, 1878-
     Hyalinothrix, a new genus of starfishes from the Ha-
waiian Islands. By Walter K. Fisher ...

     (*In* U. S. National museum. Proceedings. Washington. 1911. 23½ᶜᵐ.
v. 39, p. 659-664. pl. 69-71)

     1. Hyalinothrix. 2. Echinodermata—Hawaiian Islands.

     Library of Congress   Q11.U55 vol. 39   11-21561

QH
1
P 11

ECHINODERMATA   INDO-PACIFIC REGION

Clark, Austin H.

Records of Indo-Pacific Echinoderms.

(Pacific Science, Vol. 8(3):243-263, 1954)

QL
693
H 98

ECHINODERMATA   NEW ZEALAND

Hutton, Frederick Wollaston

Catalogue of the Echinodermata of New Zealand, with Diagnoses of the Species. Colonial Museum and Geological Survey Department. Wellington. 1872. 17 + (1) pp. 8vo.

IN:
Hutton, Frederick Wollaston
Catalogue of the Birds of New Zealand...

QL
1
H2

ECHINODERMATA--NORTH AMERICA

Agassiz, Alexander, 1835-1910.

... North American starfishes. By Alexander Agassiz ... Cambridge, Welch, Bigelow, and company, University press, 1877.

iv, (1, 136, (1) p. illus., xx pl. 30cm. (Memoirs of the Museum of comparative zoology at Harvard college, vol. v, no. 1)

1. Starfishes. 2. Echinodermata—North America.

A 19-1043

Title from Univ. of Chicago   QL1.H375 vol. 5, no. 1
Printed by L. C.   (3)

AS
750
N

ECHINODERMATA   KERMADEC ISLANDS

Benham, W. B.

Stellerids and Echinids from the Kermadec Islands.

(Trans. New Zealand Inst., Vol. 43, 1910, pp. 140-163)

AS
750
D

Echinodermata - NEW ZEALAND
Hutton, Frederick Wollaston
Catalogue of the Echinodermata of
New Zealand. - - - -

QL
1
H2

ECHINODERMATA- NORTH AMERICA

Wachsmuth, Charles, 1829-1896.

... The North American *Crinoidea camerata*. By Charles Wachsmuth and Frank Springer ... Cambridge, U. S. A., Printed for the Museum, 1897.

2 v. illus., tables, diagr. *and atlas of* LXXXIII pl. 35½cm. (*Added t.-p.*: Memoirs of the Museum of comparative zoölogy at Harvard college, vol. XX-XXI)

Each plate accompanied by leaf with descriptive letterpress.
Series title also at head of t.-p.

1. Crinoidea, Fossil. 2. Echinodermata—North America.   I. Springer, Frank, 1848-   joint author.

———— Another copy.   QE782.W2

A 19-1079

Title from Univ. of Chic   QL1.H375 vol. 20-21
Printed by L. C.   (3)

AS
36
S 4

ECHINODERMATA   MARSHALL ISLANDS

Clark, Austin H.

Echinoderms from the Marshall Islands.

(Proc. U. S. Nat. Mus., 102(3302):265-303, 1952)

QL
693
H 98

ECHINODERMATA   NEW ZEALAND

Hutton, Frederick Wollaston

Catalogue of the Echinodermata of New Zealand, with Diagnoses of the Species. Colonial Museum and Geological Survey Department. Wellington. 1872.

IN:
Hutton, Frederick Wollaston
Catalogue of the Birds of New Zealand...

AS
36
S 2

ECHINODERMATA   PACIFIC

Clark, Austin H.

Echinoderms (other than holothurians) collected on the Presidential cruise of 1938.

(Smithsonian Miscellaneous Collections, Vol. 98, No.11, 1939, pp. 1-18 + 5 plates)

QL
Protozoa
Polyzoa
Pam. 540

ECHINODERMATA   MEDITERRANEAN

Koehler, Rene

Recherches sur les echinides des cotes de Provence.

(Annales d. Mus. d'Hist. Nat. Marseille - Zool. v. 1, 1883. Memoire No. 3)

AS
244
D

ECHINODERMATA   NEW ZEALAND

Mortensen, Th.

Echinoderms of New Zealand and the Auckland Campbell Islands, 3-4: Asteroidea, Holothurioidea and Crinoidea.

(Vid. Med. Dansk Nat. For. Kobenhavn, Bd.79 1925,- Papers from Dr. Th. Mortensen's Pacific Expedition, 1914-16, No. 29)

QL
1
N 6-z

ECHINODERMATA   PACIFIC

Clark, Hubert Lyman

Notes on the Echinoderms from the West Coast of Central America. Eastern Pacific Expeditions of the New York Zoological Society, XXI.

(Zoologica, Vol. 25, 1940, pp. 331-352)

GC
1
M 73

ECHINODERMATA   MONACO

Belloc, Gérard

Catalogue des types d'echinodermes du Musée Oceanographique de Monaco.

(Bull. Inst. Oceanographique, Monaco, No. 976, 1950)

AS
244
D

ECHINODERMATA   NEW ZEALAND

Mortensen, Th.

Echinoderms of New Zealand and the Auckland-Campbell Islands. I. Echinoidea.

(Vid. Med. Dansk Nat. For. Kobenhavn, Bd. 73, 1922,-Papers from Dr. Mortensen's Pacific Expedition, No. 8)

QL
384.A8
F 53

ECHINODERMATA   PACIFIC

Fisher, Walter Kenrick

Asteroidea of the North Pacific and Adjacent Waters. Part 1: Phanerozonia and Spinulosa.

(Bull. U.S.Nat.Mus., 76, 1911, Part I.)

QL
1
V 64

ECHINODERMATA   NEW ZEALAND

Fell, H. Barraclough

Deep-sea echinoderms of New Zealand.

(Zool. Publ., Victoria Univ. of Wellington, No. 24, 1958)

AS
244
D

ECHINODERMATA   NEW ZEALAND

Mortensen, Th.

Echinoderms of New Zealand and the Auckland Campbell Islands, II. Ophiuridea.

(Vid. Med. Dansk Nat. For. Kobenhavn, Bd.77 1924, -Papers from Dr. Th. Mortensen's Pacific Expedition 1914-16, No. 20)

QL
1
H2

ECHINODERMATA--PACIFIC OCEAN.

Agassiz, Alexander, 1835-1910.

... Hawaiian and other Pacific *Echini* ... By Alexander Agassiz and Hubert Lyman Clark ... Cambridge, Printed for the Museum, 1907-

v. plates. 31 x 25½cm. (Memoirs of the Museum of comparative zoölogy at Harvard college, vol. XXXIV)

Each plate accompanied by leaf with descriptive letterpress.

CONTENTS.—no. 1. The *Cidaridæ.*—no. 2. The *Salenidæ, Arbaciadæ, Aspidodiadematidæ* and *Diadematidæ.*—no. 3. The *Echinothuridæ.*

1. Sea-urchins. 2. Echinodermata—Pacific Ocean.   I. Clark, Hubert Lyman, 1870-   joint author.

A 19-1040

Title from Univ. of Chicago   QL1.H375 vol. 34
Printed by L. C.   (3)

QL
1
V 64

ECHINODERMATA   NEW ZEALAND

Fell, H. Barraclough

Echinoderms from southern New Zealand.

(Victoria University College, Zool. Pub. No. 18, 1952)

AS
36
S 4

ECHINODERMATA   NIUAFOU

Clark, Austin H.

Echinoderms from the Islands of Niuafoou and Nukualofa, Tonga Archipelago, with the Description of a New Genus and Two New Species.

(Proceedings of the U. S. National Museum, Vol. 80, Art. 5, pp. 1-12, 1931)

QL
618
V 22

ECHINODERMATA   PACIFIC

Boone, Lee

Scientific results of the world cruise of the yacht "Alva", 1931, William K. Vanderbilt, commanding. Crustacea: Anomura, Macrura, Euphausiacea, Isopoda, Amphipoda, and Echinodermata: Asteroidea and Echinoidea.

(Bulletin of the Vanderbilt Marine Museum, Vol. 6, 1935, 264 pp., 96 pl.)

ECHINODERMATA--PACIFIC OCEAN.

AS
36
S2

Clark, Austin Hobart, 1880–

Five new recent crinoids from the north Pacific Ocean, by Austin Hobart Clark.

(*In* Smithsonian institution. Smithsonian miscellaneous collections. Washington, 1908. 24½ᶜᵐ. vol. L (Quarterly issue, vol. IV) p. 337–342. illus.)

Publication 1777.
Originally published October 29, 1907.

1. Crinoidea. 2. Echinodermata—Pacific Ocean.

Library of Congress   Q11.S7 vol. 50   16-11647
—— Copy 2.

AS
36
S4

ECHINODERMATA -- PHILIPPINE ISLANDS

Clark, Austin Hobert, 1880–

… On a collection of unstalked crinoids made by the United States fisheries steamer "Albatross" in the vicinity of the Philippine Islands. By Austin Hobart Clark …

(*In* U. S. National museum. Proceedings. Washington, 1911. 23½ᶜᵐ. v. 39, p. 529–563)

Scientific results of the Philippine cruise of the fisheries steamer "Albatross," 1907–10—no. 8.

1. Crinoidea. 2. Echinodermata — Philippine Islands. 3. Albatross (Steamer)

Library of Congress   Q11.U55 vol. 39   11—21253
[s20g2]

AS
750
D 67 c

ECHINODERMATA SUBANTARCTIC ISL. (NZ)

Fell, H. Barraclough

Echinoderms from the Subantarctic Islands of New Zealand: Asteroidea, Ophiuroidea, and Echinoidea.

(Cape Exp., Sci. Res. New Zealand Subantarctic Exp., 1941-45, No. 18, 1953)

QL
138
E 24

ECHINODERMATA -- PACIFIC

Edmondson, C. H.   and others

Marine zoology of tropical central Pacific… Echinoderms other than sea stars, by Hubert Lyman Clark, pp. 89-111. Honolulu. 1925.

AS
763
B-b

Reading
Room

(Bernice P. Bishop Museum, Bulletin No. 27, 1925; Tanager Expedition, Publication No. 1)

ECHINODERMATA--PHILIPPINE ISLANDS.

AS
36
S2

Clark, Austin Hobart, 1880–

Preliminary notice of a collection of recent crinoids from the Philippine Islands, by Austin Hobart Clark.

(*In* Smithsonian institution. Smithsonian miscellaneous collections. Washington, 1910. 24½ᶜᵐ. vol. LII (Quarterly issue, vol. V) p. 199–234)

Publication 1820.
Originally published December 23, 1908.

1. Crinoidea. 2. Echinodermata—Philippine Islands.

Library of Congress   Q11.S7 vol. 52   16-12710
—— Copy 2.

QL
Protozoa
Pam. 601

ECHINODERMATA TIMOR

Jansen, H.

Die Variationsstatistische Methode angewandt auf ein groszes Material von Schizoblastus aus dem Perm von Timor und einige neue Anomalien dieser Gattung.

(Geologisch Inst., Univ. van Amsterdam, Mededeeling no. 54. 1934)

QL
1
H2

ECHINODERMATA--PANAMA

Agassiz, Alexander, 1835-1910.

… The Panamic deep sea *Echini*. By Alexander Agassiz … Cambridge, Printed for the Museum, 1904.

2 v. in 1. 112 pl. (part col., incl. fold. map) diagrs. 30½ x 25½ᶜᵐ. (Memoirs of the Museum of comparative zoology at Harvard college, vol. XXXI)

Each plate accompanied by leaf with descriptive letterpress.
Reports on an exploration off the west coasts of Mexico, Central and South America, and off the Galapagos Islands … by the U. S. Fish commission steamer "Albatross" during 1891 … XXXII.
[Vol. 1] text; [v. 2] plates.
1. Sea-urchins. 2. Echinodermata—Panama. 3. Albatross (Steamer)

                                          A 19-1044
Title from Univ. of Chicago   QL1.H375 vol. 31
Printed by L. C.   [3]

AS
36
S4

ECHINODERMATA--PHILIPPINE ISLANDS

Fisher, Walter Kenrick, 1878–

… New genera of starfishes from the Philippine Islands. By Walter K. Fisher …

(*In* U. S. National museum. Proceedings. Washington, 1911. 23½ᶜᵐ. v. 40, p. 415–427)

"Scientific results of the Philippine cruise of the fisheries steamer 'Albatross,' 1907–10—no. 10."

1. Starfishes. 2. Echinodermata — Philippine Islands. 3. Albatross (Steamer)

Library of Congress   Q11.U55 vol. 40   11-31526

QL
303.8
CL

Echinodermata--Torres Strait

Clark, Hubert Lyman, 1870–

… The echinoderm fauna of Torres Strait: its composition and its origin, by Hubert Lyman Clark … Washington, D. C., Carnegie institution of Washington, 1921.

viii, 223 p. front, 1 illus., 38 pl. (part col.) fold. map. 29½ x 22½ᶜᵐ. (*On verso of t.-p.:* Carnegie institution of Washington. Publication no. 214)

At head of title: Department of marine biology of the Carnegie institution of Washington, Alfred G. Mayor, director; volume x.
Bibliography: p. 213–218.

1. Echinodermata—Torres Strait.

Library of Congress   QH301.C3 vol. x   21-7575
—— Copy 2.   [4]

QL
Poly.Prot
Pam. 574

ECHINODERMATA PEARL AND HERMES REEF

Holly, Maximilian

Echinodermata from Pearl and Hermes Reef.

(Bernice P. Bishop Museum, Occ. Papers, Volume X, No. 1, 1932)

AS
36
S5

ECHINODERMATA--PHILIPPINE ISLANDS

Fisher, Walter Kenrick, 1878–

… Starfishes of the Philippine seas and adjacent waters, by Walter K. Fisher … Washington, Govt. print. off., 1919.

xi, 712 p. 156 pl. 24½ᶜᵐ. (Smithsonian institution. United States National museum. Bulletin 100, v. 3)
At head of title: … Contributions to the biology of the Philippine Archipelago and adjacent regions.
On verso of t.-p.: Bulletin of the United States National museum.
Plates printed on both sides.
Bibliography: p. 541–546.
Report based upon a collection made by the United States Fisheries steamer Albatross, 1907–1910, in the region of the Philippine Islands, Celebes and Molucca Islands.
1. Starfishes. 2. Echinodermata — Philippine Islands. 3. Echinodermata—Dutch East Indies.

Library of Congress   Q11.U6 no. 100 vol. 3 19-26691
—— Copy 2.   QL384.A8F7
                              [8]

QH
109.P
N 53

ECHINODERMATA VIRGIN ISLANDS

Clark, Hubert Lyman

A handbook of the littoral echinoderms of Porto Rico and the other West Indian islands.

IN Scientific survey of Porto Rico and the Virgin Islands, Vol. 16, Part 1, 1933

QL
H1

ECHINODERMATA--PERU

Clark, Hubert Lyman, 1870–

… The echinoderms of Peru. By Hubert Lyman Clark … Cambridge, 1910.

p. 321-358. 14 pl. 23ᶜᵐ. (Bulletin of the Museum of comparative zoology at Harvard college, vol. LII, no. 17)

"Literature cited": p. 355-358.

1. Echinodermata—Peru.

                                          F 20-20
Library, U. S. Bur. of   Fisheries

QH
109.P
N 53

ECHINODERMATA PORTO RICO

Clark, Hubert Lyman

A handbook of the littoral echinoderms of Porto Rico and the other West Indian islands.

IN Scientific survey of Porto Rico and the Virgin Islands, Vol. 16, Part 1, 1933

QL
Prot. to
Polyzoa
Pam
589

ECHINODERMA WASHINGTON (STATE)

Bush, Mildred

Revised key to the Echinoderms of Friday Harbor. 12 pp.

(Publ. Puget Sound Biol. Sta. 2: 17-44, 1918)

AS
36
S 4

ECHINODERMATA PHILIPPINE ISLANDS

Clark, Austin H.

Echinoderms from the Islands of Niuafoou and Nukualofa, Tonga Archipelago, with the Description of a New Genus and Two New Species.

(Proceedings of the U. S. National Museum, Vol. 80, Art. 5, pp. 1-12, 1931)

QH
Nat. Hist.
Pam.
222

ECHINODERMATA QUEENSLAND

Dall, W.

A bibliography of the marine invertebrates of Queensland. By W. Dall and W. Stephenson. and
Queensland faunistic records, III: Echinodermata (excluding Crinoidea) By R. Endean.

(Univ. of Queensland, Dept. of Zool., Papers, Vol. 1(2/3), 1953)

QH
109.P
N 53

ECHINODERMATA WEST INDIES

Clark, Hubert Lyman

A handbook of the littoral echinoderms of Porto Rico and the other West Indian islands.

IN Scientific survey of Porto Rico and the Virgin Islands, Vol. 16, Part 1, 1933

AS
36
S4

ECHINODERMATA--PHILIPPINE ISLANDS

Clark, Austin Hobart, 1880–

A new unstalked crinoid from the Philippine Islands. By Austin Hobart Clark …

(*In* U. S. National museum. Proceedings. Washington, 1912. 23½ᶜᵐ. v. 41, p. 171–173)

1. Crinoidea. 2. Echinodermata—Philippine Islands.

                                          12-17771
Library of Congress   Q11.U55 vol. 41

AS
244
D

ECHINODERMATA ST. HELENA

Mortensen, Th.

The Echinoderms of St. Helena (other than Crinoids).

(Vid. Med. Dansk nat. For. i Kobenhavn, Bd. 93, 1932/33, pp. 401-472. Papers from Dr. Th. Mortensen's Pacific Expedition, 1914-16, No. 66)

AS
36
S5

ECHINODERMATA-- WEST INDIES

Mortensen, Theodor

On some West Indian Echinoids. U. S. Nat. Mus. Bul. 74. pp. 31. pls. 17.

Also separate

AS 36 C8

ECHINODERMATA--OPHIUROIDEA.

Verrill, Addison Emory, 1839-

... North American *Ophiuroidea*. I.—Revision of certain families and genera of West Indian ophiurans. II.—A faunal catalogue of the known species of West Indian ophiurans.

(*In* Connecticut academy of arts and sciences. Transactions. New Haven, 1899-1900. 25ᶜᵐ. v. 10, p. (301)-386. pl. XLII-XLIII)

Bibliography: p. 383-385.

1. Ophiuroidea. I. Title.

A 17-878

Library of Congress QI1.C9 vol. 10
Yale University A53n.366.10

ECHINODERMATA

See also

Crinoidea; Holothurians; Ophiuroidea; Pelmatozoa; Sea-urchins; Starfishes

---

Echinodermata or Echnoderms

see also
Crinoids (feather-stars or sea-lilies)
Echini (sea-urchins)
Asteroids (starfishes)
Holothurians (sea-cucumbers)
Ophiurans (sand-stars or brittle-stars)
Echinoids

QL 1 H2

ECHINOIDEA

Agassiz, Alexander

Revision of the Echini.

(Mem. Mus. of Comp. Zool., Harvard, Vol. III No. 7, 1872-74)

QL. Prot.-Poly. Pam. 826

ECHINOIDEA

Clark, Ailsa M.

Starfishes and their relations. London. British Museum (Nat. Hist.) 1962. 119 pp. 8vo.

QL 636 A

ECHINOIDEA

Clark, Hubert Lyman

Report on the sea-lilies, starfishes brittle-stars and sea-urchins, in Australia "Fisheries" Zool. Results of F. I. S. "Endeavour" Vol. IV. pp. 1-123. pls. I-XLIV. Sydney 1916.

QL 1 S 96

ECHINOIDEA

Hagström, N.E.

Studies on polyspermy in sea urchins.

(Arkiv för Zoologi. Bd. 10, nr 2:pp.307-315,1957)

QL 384.E2 H 34

ECHINOIDEA

Harvey, Ethel Browne

The American Arbacia and other sea urchins. Princeton University Press. Princeton. 1956. R8vo. xiv + (10) pp. XVI plates; 298 pp.

DU 1 P 12

ECHINOIDEA

Irwin, Margaret

Science looks into it; steel-boring sea urchins.

(Pacific Discovery, 6(2):26-27, 1953)

AS 36 S5

ECHINOIDEA

Jackson, Robert Tracy, 1861-

... Fossil *Echini* of the Panama Canal Zone and Costa Rica. By Robert Tracy Jackson ... Washington, Govt. print. off., 1918.

1 p. l., p. 103-116, 1 l. illus., pl. 46-52. 24½ᶜᵐ. (Smithsonian institution. United States National museum. Bulletin 103 (pt. 5))

At head of title: Contributions to the geology and paleontology of the Canal Zone, Panama, and geologically related areas in Central America and the West Indies.
"Extract from Bulletin 103, pages 103-116, with plates 46-52."
Stamped on t.-p.: Issued Feb. 19, 1919.

1. Sea-urchins, Fossil. 2. Paleontology—Panama.

S 21-5

Library, Smithsonian Institution
(s21b5)

AS 36 B2

ECHINOIDEA

Jackson, Robert Tracy

Phylogeny of the Echini, with a revision of Palaeozoic species. Bost. Soc. Nat. Hist. Mem. VII, 1912. 4to. pp. 491, 76 pls.

QL 385.5 I

ECHINOIDEA

Koehler, René i. e. Jean Baptiste François René, 1860-

Échinides du Musée indien à Calcutta, par René Kœhler ...
Calcutta, 1914-

v. pl. 32ᶜᵐ. (Added t.-p.: Echinoderma of the Indian museum, pt. VIII. Echinoidea I-)
"Liste des ouvrages cités": v. 1, p. (237)-238.

1. Sea-urchins.

14-20956

Library of Congress QL384.E2K6
——— Copy 2. QL383.5.I 6

QP 1 C

ECHINOIDEA

Loeb, Jacques, 1859-

... On an improved method of artificial parthenogenesis, by Jacques Loeb, (I-III) Berkeley, The University press, 1905.

cover-titles, p. (83)-86, (89)-92, (113)-123. 27ᶜᵐ. (University of California publications. Physiology. v. 2, no. 9, 11 and 14)
From the Rudolph Spreckles physiological laboratory of the University of California.

1. Parthenogenesis (Animals) 2. Sea-urchins.

A 11-1276

Title from Univ. of Calif. Library of Congress

QP 1 C

ECHINOIDEA

Loeb, Jacques, 1859-

... On fertilization, artificial parthenogenesis, and cytolysis of the sea urchin egg. By Jacques Loeb ... (tr. by John Bruce MacCallum from Pflüger's Archiv, v. 103, p. 257, 1904) (Berkeley, The University press) 1905.

p. (73)-81. 27ᶜᵐ. (University of California publications. Physiology. v. 2, no. 8)
From the Rudolph Spreckles physiological laboratory of the University of California.
Issued in single cover with v. 2, no. 7, of the series.

1. Fertilization (Biology) 2. Parthenogenesis (Animals) 3. Cytolysis. 4. Sea-urchins. I. MacCallum, John Bruce, 1876-1906, tr.

A 11-1278

ECHINOIDEA

Agassiz, Alexander, 1835-1910.

... *Echini*. The genus *Colobocentrotus*. By Alexander Agassiz ... Cambridge, Printed for the Museum, 1908.

(7), 33, (1) p. 46 (i. e. 49) pl. 31 x 26ᶜᵐ. (Memoirs of the Museum of comparative zoology at Harvard college, vol. XXXVII (i. e. XXXIX) no. 1)
Each plate accompanied by leaf with descriptive letterpress.
Reports on the scientific results of the expedition to the tropical Pacific ... by the U. S. Fish commission steamer "Albatross," from August 1899 to March 1900 ... XI.

1. Sea-urchins. 2. Albatross (Steamer)

A 19-1039

Title from Univ. of Chicago QL1.H375 vol. 39, no. 1
Printed by L. C. (3)

QL 1 H2

ECHINOIDEA

Agassiz, Alexander, 1835-1910.

... *Echini*, crinoids, and corals, by Alexander Agassiz and L. F. de Pourtalès ... Cambridge, University press, Welch, Bigelow, & co., 1874.

(3), 54 p. illus., x pl. 30ᶜᵐ. (Memoirs of the Museum of comparative zoology at Harvard college, v. 4, no. 1)
At head of title: Illustrated catalogue of the Museum of comparative zoology at Harvard college. no. VIII.
Zoological results of the Hassler expedition. I.

1. Sea-urchins. 2. Crinoidca. 3. Corals. 4. Hassler expedition. I. Pourtalès, Louis François de, 1824-1880.

A 19-1038

Title from Univ. of Chicago QL1.H375 vol. 4, no. 1
Printed by L. C. (3)

QL 1 H2

ECHINOIDEA

Agassiz, Alexander, 1835-1910.

... The Panamic deep sea *Echini*. By Alexander Agassiz ... Cambridge, Printed for the Museum, 1904.

2 v. in 1. 112 pl. (part col., incl. fold. map) diagrs. 30¼ x 25¼ᶜᵐ. (Memoirs of the Museum of comparative zoology at Harvard college, vol. XXXI)
Each plate accompanied by leaf with descriptive letterpress.
Reports on an exploration off the west coasts of Mexico, Central and South America, and off the Galapagos Islands ... by the U. S. Fish commission steamer "Albatross" during 1891 ... XXXII.
(Vol. 1) text; (v. 2) plates.

1. Sea-urchins. 2. Echinodermata—Panama. 3. Albatross (Steamer)

A 19-1044

Title from Univ. of Chicago QL1.H375 vol. 31
Printed by L. C. (3)

QL 1 H2

ECHINOIDEA

Agassiz, Alexander, 1835-1910.

... Report on the *Echini*. By Alexander Agassiz ... With thirty-two plates. Cambridge, Printed for the Museum, 1883.

viii, (9)-94 p. XXVIII (i. e. 32) pl. 29¼ᶜᵐ. (Memoirs of the Museum of comparative zoology at Harvard college. vol. X, no. 1)
Each plate preceded by leaf with descriptive letterpress.
"Reports on the results of dredging ... in the Gulf of Mexico (1877-78), in the Caribbean Sea (1878-79), and along the Atlantic coast of the United States (1880), by the U. S. Coast survey steamer 'Blake' ... XXIV, pt. 1."

1. Sea-urchins.

A 21-442

Title from Univ. of Chicago QL.1f.H375 vol. 10
Printed by L. C. (3)

QL 1 H2

QP 1 C

ECHINOIDEA

Loeb, Jacques, 1859-

... On the counteraction of the toxic effect of hypertonic solutions upon the fertilized and unfertilized egg of the sea-urchin by lack of oxygen. By Jacques Loeb ... (Berkeley, The University press) 1906.

p. (49)-56. 27ᶜᵐ. (University of California publications. Physiology. v. 3, no. 7)
From the Herzstein research laboratory at New Monterey.

1. Sea-urchins. 2. Embryology, Experimental.

A 11-1280

Title from Univ. of Calif. Library of Congress

QP 1 C

ECHINOIDEA

Loeb, Jacques, 1859-

... On the necessity of the presence of free oxygen in the hypertonic sea-water for the production of artificial parthenogenesis. By Jacques Loeb ... (Berkeley, The University press) 1906.

p. (39)-47. 27ᶜᵐ. (University of California publications. Physiology. v. 3, no. 6)
From the Herzstein research laboratory at New Monterey.

1. Parthenogenesis. 2. Sea-urchins.

A 11-1282

Title from Univ. of Calif. Library of Congress

QP 1 C

ECHINOIDEA

Loeb, Jacques, 1859-

... On the production of a fertilization membrane in the egg of the sea-urchin with the blood of certain gephyrean worms. <A preliminary note.> By Jacques Loeb. (Berkeley, The University press) 1907.

p. (57)-58. 27ᶜᵐ. (University of California publications. Physiology. v. 3, no. 8)

1. Fertilization (Biology) 2. Sea-urchins.

A 11-1283

Title from Univ. of Calif. Library of Congress

QP
1
C

ECHINOIDEA

Loeb, Jacques, 1859–

... On the toxicity of atmospheric oxygen for the eggs of the sea-urchin ⟨Strongylocentrotus purpuratus⟩ after the process of membrane formation. By Jacques Loeb ... ⟨Berkeley, The University press⟩ 1906.

p. ₍33₎–37. 27ᶜᵐ. (University of California publications. Physiology. v. 3, no. 5)

From the Herzstein research laboratory at New Monterey.

1. Sea-urchins. 2. Embryology, Experimental.

A 11-1287

Title from Univ. of Calif.   Library of Congress

QL
384.E2
M 88

ECHINOIDEA

Mortensen, Theodore

Echinoidea...Copenhagen...1903, 1907.

(Over)

QL
Prot.Poly.
Pam.570

ECHINOIDEA

Süssbach, S.

Die Seeigel, Seesterne und Schlangensterne der Nord- und Ostsee, von S. Süssbach und A. Breckner.

(Wiss. Meeresuntersuchungen...Abt. Kiel, N.F. Bd. 12, pp. 169-300, taf. I-III, Kiel, 1910)

QL
381
L 89

ECHINOIDEA

Loven, S(ven) L(udvig)

Etudes sur les Echinoidées.

(K. Svenska Vetenskaps Akad., Handlingar, N. F. 11(7), 1874-75. 91 pp.)

GC
63
D 61

ECHINOIDEA

Mortensen, Th.

Echinoidea and Ophiuroidea.

Discovery Committee

Discovery Reports, Vol. 12, 1936, p. 199-348

QL
1
H2

ECHINOIDEA

Westergren, A   Magnus.

... Echini. Echinonëus and micropetalon. By A. M. Westergren ... ⟨Pub. by permission of George M. Bowers, U. S. commissioner of fish and fisheries⟩ Cambridge, Printed for the Museum, 1911.

3 p. l., ₍4₎-68, ₍1₎ p. 31 pl. 31 x 26ᶜᵐ. (Memoirs of the Museum of comparative zoölogy at Harvard college. vol. xxxix, no. 2)

Each plate preceded by leaf with descriptive letterpress.

Reports on the scientific results of the expedition to the tropical Pacific ... by the U. S. Fish commission steamer "Albatross," from August 1899 to March 1900 ... xv.

1. Sea-urchins. 2. Albatross (Steamer)

Title from Univ. of Chicago   QL1.H375 vol. 39, no.2   A 21-14

Printed by L. C.

₍2₎

QL
384.P8
L 91

ECHINOIDEA

Loven, Sven

On Pourtalesia, a Genus of Echinoidea.

(K. Svenska Vet. Akad. Handl., Bd. 19, Nr. 7, 1883)

ECHINOIDEA

Mortensen, T.

A monograph of the Echinoidea. 10 vols. 1928-43.

UH

QL
1
T 64

ECHINOIDEA   BONIN ISLANDS

Ikeda, H.

Coptopleura serna, a new genus and new species of the temnopleurid from the Ogasawara Islands (Echinoidea).

(Annotations Zool. Japonenses, 19:93-96, 1940)

QP
1
C

ECHINOIDEA

Moore, Arthur Russell, 1882–

... A new method of heterogeneous hybridization in echinoderms, by A. R. Moore. ⟨Berkeley, University of California press⟩ 1912.

p. ₍109₎-110. 27ᶜᵐ. (University of California publications in physiology. vol. 4, no. 14)

"From the Herzstein research laboratory of the University of California, New Monterey, California."

Issued in single cover with v. 4, no. 15, of the series.

1. Hybridization. 2. Fertilization (Biology) 3. Sea-urchins.

A 12-768

Title from Univ. of Calif.   Library of Congress

QL
384.E
Mo

ECHINOIDEA

Mortensen, Theodor.

... On some West Indian echinoids, by Theodor Mortensen ... Washington, Govt. print. off., 1910.

v, 31 p. 17 pl. 31ᶜᵐ. (Smithsonian institution. United States National museum. Bulletin 74)

1. Sea-urchins.

Library of Congress   Q11.U6 no. 74   10–36045

—— Copy 2.   QL384.E2M7

QL
Prot-Poly.
Pam.
748

ECHINOIDEA   CUBA

Sanchez Roig, Mario

Algunos Equinoideos fosiles Cubanos.

(Revista de Agricultura, 1953:53-67)

QP
1
C

ECHINOIDEA

Moore, Arthur Russell, 1882–

... On the nature of the cortical layer in sea urchin eggs, by A. R. Moore. ⟨Berkeley, University of California press⟩ 1912.

p. ₍89₎-90. 27ᶜᵐ. (University of California publications in physiology. vol. 4, no. 9)

From the Rudolph Spreckels physiological laboratory of the University of California.

Issued in single cover with vol. 4, no. 10, of the series.

1. Sea-urchins. 2. Fertilization (Biology)

A 12-400

Title from Univ. of Calif.   Library of Congress

QL
Prot.-
Poly.Pam.
655

ECHINOIDEA

Motomura, Isao

Studies of cleavage, 1. Changes in surface area of different regions of eggs of a sea urchin in the course of the first cleavage.

(Science Reports of the Tohoku Imp. Univ., Ser. 4, Biology, Vol. 15, 1940, pp. 121-130)

AS
71
C 96

ECHINOIDEA   CUBA

Sanchez Roig, Mario

Dos nuevos generos de Equinoideos cubanos, Lambertona y Neopatagus.

(Mem. Soc. Cubana de Hist. Nat., 21(3):257-262, 1953)

QP
1
C

ECHINOIDEA

Moore, Arthur Russell, 1882–

... On the sensitization of sea urchin eggs by strontium chloride, by A. R. Moore. ⟨Berkeley, University of California press⟩ 1912.

p. ₍91₎-93. 27ᶜᵐ. (University of California publications in physiology. vol. 4, no. 10)

From the Rudolph Spreckels physiological laboratory of the University of California.

Issued in single cover with vol. 4, no. 9, of the series.

1. Sea-urchins. 2. Fertilization (Biology)

A 12-401

Title from Univ. of Calif.   Library of Congress

QP
1
C

ECHINOIDEA

Robertson, Thorburn Brailsford, 1884–

... On the cytolytic action of ox-blood serum upon sea-urchin eggs, and its inhibition by proteins (preliminary communication) by T. Brailsford Robertson. Berkeley, University of California press, 1912.

cover-title, p. ₍79₎-88. 27ᶜᵐ. (University of California publications in physiology. v. 4, no. 8)

"From the Herzstein research laboratory and the Rudolph Spreckels physiological laboratory of the University of California."

1. Cytolysis. 2. Fertilization (Biology) 3. Sea-urchins. 4. Proteids.

A 12-402

Title from Univ. of Calif.   Library of Congress

₍s19c2₎

QL
Prot-Poly.
Pam.
749

ECHINOIDEA   CUBA

Sanchez Roig, Mario

I. La geofisica en su relacion con la paleontologia; II. Nuevos equinidos fosiles de la fauna Cubana.

(Anales de la Acad. de Ciencias Medicas, Fisicas y Naturales de La Habana, 91(2):119-176, 1953)

[article on   equinoids, pp. 135-176]

QL
5
M 98

ECHINOIDEA

Mortensen, Th.

Report on the Echinoidea of the Murray Expedition, Part II.

IN John Murray Expedition, 1933-34, Sci. Repts., Vol. IX, No. 1, 1948.

QP
1
C

ECHINOIDEA

Robertson, Thorburn Brailsford, 1884–

... On the extraction of a substance from the sperm of a sea urchin (Strongylocentrotus purpuratus) which will fertilize the eggs of that species, by T. Brailsford Robertson. ⟨Berkeley, University of California press⟩ 1912.

p. ₍103₎-105. 27ᶜᵐ. (University of California publications in physiology. v. 4, no. 12)

From the Rudolph Spreckels physiological laboratory of the University of California.

Issued in single cover with v. 4, nos. 11 and 13 of the series.

1. Fertilization (Biology) 2. Sea-urchins. I. Title.

A 12-493

Title from Univ. of Calif.   Library of Congress

Q
115
S 56

ECHINOIDEA   DUTCH EAST INDIES

Meijere, J. C. H. de
Die Echinoidea der Siboga-Expedition.

Weber, Max
Uitkomsten...Nederlandsch Oost Indie, 1899-1900...Siboga...Monographie SLIII (livr. 14) 1904. 251 pp. 23 pl.

QE
349.F
L 13

ECHINOIDEA   FIJI

Ladd, Harry S., and others

AS
763
B-b

Reading
Room

Geology of Vitilevu, Fiji...Honolulu. 1934.
Fossil Echinoidea from Vitilevu, Fiji, by Herbert
L. Hawkins. pp. 158-161. R8vo.

(Bernice P. Bishop Museum, Bull. 119, 1934.)

QL
1
H 2

ECHINOIDEA   HAWAII

Agassiz, Alexander

Hawaiian and other Pacific Echini; 1.
Cidaridae; 2, Salenidae, Arbaciadae, Aspidodia-
dematidae, Diadematidae, 3. Echinothuridae, 4.
Pedinidae, Phymosomatidae... By Alexander
Agassiz and Hubert Lyman Clark.

(Mem. Mus. Comp. Zool., 34, 1907-1912, pp.
1-383.)

QE
75
P

ECHINOIDEA   OKINAWA

Cooke, C. Wythe

Pliocene echinoids from Okinawa; a shorter
contribution to general geology. Descriptions
and illustrations of five new species and one
new subspecies.

(Prof. Paper, U. S. Geological Survey, No.
264-C, 1954)

AS
36
S4

ECHINOIDEA   FOSSIL.

Jackson, Robert Tracy, 1861-

Fossil *Echini* of the Panama Canal Zone and Costa
Rica. By Robert Tracy Jackson ...

(*In* U. S. National museum. Proceedings. Washington, 1917. 23½ᶜᵐ.
v. 53, p. 489-501. illus., pl. 62-68)

1. Sea-urchins, Fossil.

Library of Congress   Q11.U55 vol. 53   18-14644

QL
1
H2

ECHINOIDEA   HAWAII

Agassiz, Alexander, 1835-1910.

... Hawaiian and other Pacific *Echini* ... By Alexander Agassiz and Hubert Lyman Clark ... Cambridge,
Printed for the Museum, 1907–

v. plates. 31 x 25½ᶜᵐ. (Memoirs of the Museum of comparative
zoölogy at Harvard college, vol. xxxiv)
Each plate accompanied by leaf with descriptive letterpress.
CONTENTS.—no. 1. The *Cidaridæ*.—no. 2. The *Salenidæ, Arbaciadæ,
Aspidodiadematidæ and Diadematidæ*.—no. 3. The *Echinothuridæ*.

1. Sea-urchins. 2. Echinodermata—Pacific Ocean. I. Clark, Hubert
Lyman, 1870- joint author.

Title from Univ. of Chicago   QL1.H375 vol. 34   A 19-1040
Printed by L. C.   [3]

QL
1
H 2

ECHINOIDEA   PACIFIC

Agassiz, Alexander

Hawaiian and other Pacific Echini; 1,
Cidaridae; 2, Salenidae, Arbaciadae, Aspidodia-
dematidae, Diadematidae, 3, Echinothuridae; 4,
Pedinidae, Phymosomatidae... by Alexander
Agassiz and Hubert Lyman Clark.

(Mem. Mus. Comp. Zool., 34, 1907-12, pp.
1-383)

AS
36
S5

ECHINOIDEA   FOSSIL

Jackson, Robert Tracy, 1861-

... Fossil *Echini* of the Panama Canal Zone and Costa
Rica. By Robert Tracy Jackson ... Washington, Govt.
print. off., 1918.

1 p. l., p. 103-116, 1 l. illus., pl. 46-52. 24½ᶜᵐ. (Smithsonian institution.
United States National museum. Bulletin 103 (pt. 5))
At head of title: Contributions to the geology and paleontology of the
Canal Zone, Panama, and geologically related areas in Central America and
the West Indies.
"Extract from Bulletin 103, pages 103-116, with plates 46-52."
Stamped on t.-p.: Issued Feb. 19, 1919.

1. Sea-urchins, Fossil. 2. Paleontology—Panama.

Library, Smithsonian   Institution   S 21-5
[s21b5]

QL
1
H1

ECHINOIDEA   HAWAII

Agassiz, Alexander and Clark, H. L.

Preliminary report on the Echini col-
lected in 1902 among the Hawaiian Islands
by the U. S. Fish Commission Steamship
Albatross.... Museum of comparative
Zoölogy Bull. L, 8, pages 231-259.
Cambridge, 1907.

AS
36
A1

ECHINOIDEA   PACIFIC

Agassiz, Alexander

Synopsis of the Echinoids collected by
Dr. W. Stimpson on the North Pacific Exploring
Expedition...

(Acad. Nat. Sci., Phil. Proc., 1863, pp. 352-
361)

QE
1
C

ECHINOIDEA   FOSSIL

Merriam, John Campbell, 1869-

... The Tertiary sea-urchins of middle California. By
John C. Merriam. With two plates. Issued March 6,
1899. San Francisco, The Academy, 1899.

1 p. l., p. 161-174. pl. xxi-xxii. 25ᶜᵐ. (Proceedings of the California
academy of sciences. 3d series. Geology. vol. 1, no. 5)
Issued in single cover with vol. 1, no. 6.

1. Sea-urchins, Fossil. 2. Paleontology—California.

Title from Univ. of Calif.   Library of Congress   A 13-1886

AS
36
A1

ECHINOIDEA   HAWAII

Agassiz, Alexander

Synopsis of the Echinoids collected by Dr.
W. Stimpson on the North Pacific Exploring
Expedition...

(Acad. Nat. Sci., Phil., Proc. 1863, pp.
352-361)

AS
36
W 2

ECHINOIDEA   PHILIPPINE ISLANDS

Clark, Austin H.

Some littoral sea-urchins from the Philippines.

(Jour. Washington Acad. Sci., 39:271-272,
1949)

QL
Prot.-
Poly.
Fam.
779

ECHINOIDEA   FOSSIL

Sanchez Roig, Mario

Dos nuevos generos de Equinoideos Cubanos.
Lambertona y Neopatagus.

(Mem. Soc. Cubana de Hist. Nat., 22, V, 1953:
257-262)

QL
5
M 98

ECHINOIDEA   INDIAN OCEAN

Mortensen, Th.
Report on the Echinoidea of the Murray
Expedition, Part 1.

IN The John Murray Expedition, 1933-34,
Sci. Repts., Vol. VI, no. 1, 1939, pp. 1-28

AS
36
S 5

ECHINOIDEA   PHILIPPINE ISLANDS

Mortensen, Theodor

Report on the Echinoidea collected by the
United States Fisheries Steamer "Albatross"
during the Philippine Expedition, 1907-1910.
Part 1: The Cidaridae; Part 2: The Echinothuridae
Saleniidae, Arbaciidae, Aspidodiadematidae...

(U. S. Nat. Mus., Bull. 100, Vol. 6, Part 4,
1927, pp. 243-312; Bull. 100, Vol. 14, Part 1,
1940, pp. 1-52)

QE
1
F4

ECHINOIDEA   FOSSIL

Slocom, Arthur Ware.

... New echinoids from the Ripley group of Mississippi,
by Arthur Ware Slocom ... Chicago, 1909.

1 p. l., 16 p. illus., iii pl. 24½ᶜᵐ. (Field museum of natural history.
Publication 134. Geological series. vol. iv, no. 1)
Each plate preceded by leaf with letterpress.

1. Sea-urchins, Fossil.

Library of Congress   QE1.F4 vol. 4, no. 1   9-17312

QL
1
Z 82

ECHINOIDEA   JAPAN

Hama, Tadao   and others

Inhibition of cell division of sea urchin
egg by hypertonic solutions.

(The Zool. Mag. (Japan), Vol. 49, 1937, p.
74-75)

AS
36
S 5

ECHINOIDEA   PHILIPPINE ISLANDS

Mortensen, Theodor

Report on the Echinoidea collected by the
United States Fisheries Steamer "Albatross"
during the Philippine Expedition, 1907-1910.
Part 3:The Echinoneidae, Echinolampadidae...

(U. S. Nat. Mus., Bull. 100, Vol. 14, Pt. 3,
1948)

QE
349.F
L 15

ECHINOIDEA   FOSSIL   FIJI

Clark, Hubert Lyman
Echinoidea.
IN
Ladd, Harry S.
Geology of Lau, Fiji, by Harry S. Ladd and
J. Edward Hoffmeister. pp. 312-326

(Bernice P. Bishop Museum, Bull. 181, 1944)

QH
1
T 88

ECHINOIDEA   NEW ZEALAND

Fell, H. Barraclough

A key to the sea urchins of New Zealand.

(Tuatara, 1(3):6-13, 1948)and ibid, 3(1):
42, 1950)

AS
540
P

ECHINOIDEA   PHILIPPINE ISLANDS

Roxas, Hilario A.

Philippine littoral Echinoida.

(Philippine Jour. Sci., 36(2):243-270,1928)

QL
1
T 64   ECHINOIDEA   RUYKYU ISLANDS

Ikeda, Hayato

     Preliminary report on Chorocidaris micoa gen. et sp. nov., from the Ryukyu Islands (Echinoidea, Cidaridae)

     (Annotationes Zoologicae Japonenses, Vol. 20(2):85-88, 1941)

QH
1
P 11   ECHIURIDAE   HAWAII

Fisher, Walter K.

     A new Echiuroid worm from the Hawaiian islands and a key to the genera of Echiuridae.

     (Pacific Science, Vol. 2:274-277, 1948)

QL
461
H-1   ECHTHROMORPHA

Perkins, J. F.

     Echthromorpha from the Marquesas and Society Islands (Hymenoptera:Ichneumonidae).

     (Proc. Haw. Ent. Soc, Vol. 14(3):533-536, 1951)

AS
720.T
R 88   ECHINOIDEA   TASMANIA

Hickman, V. V.

     Parasitic Turbellaria from Tasmanian Echinoidea.

     (Papers and Proc. R. Soc. of Tasmania, Vol. 90:169-181, 1956)

QL
5
M 98   ECHIURIDAE   INDIAN OCEAN

Stephen, A. C.
     Sipunculids and Echiurids of the John Murray Expedition to the Red Sea and Indian Ocean, 1933-34.
     IN The John Murray Expedition, 1933-34, Sci. Repts., Vol. VII, no. 4, 1941, pp. 401-409.

DU
1
C 56   Eckardt, M.

     The Archipelago of the New Hebrides. From Verhandlungen des Vereins fuer naturwissenschaftliche Unterhaltung zu Hamburg, 1877, pp. 7

     (Polynesian Papers, V, pp. 94-104)

QE
349.F
L 13   ECHINOIDEA   VITILEVU

Ladd, Harry S., and others

AS
763
B-b

Reading
Room

     Geology of Vitilevu, Fiji...Honolulu. 1934. Fossil Echinoidea from Vitilevu, Fiji, By Herbert L. Hawkins. pp. 158-161. R8vo.

     (Bernice P. Bishop Museum, Bull. 119, 1934.)

AS
162
P 23   ECHIURIDAE   PACIFIC

Wesenberg-Lund, E.

     Sipunculids and Echiurids collected by Mr. G. Ranson in Oceania in 1952.

     (Bull. Mus. Nat. d'Hist. Nat., Paris, Ser. 2, Vol. 26:376-384, 1954)

     [Tuamotus and Tahiti]

QL
Reptiles
Pam.
No. 31   Eckel, Edwin C. and Paulmier, F.C.

     Catalogue of New York reptiles and batrachians, New York State Mus. Bull. No. 51, 1902.

AS
36
S5
and
QL
Protozoa
to
Poly
Pam.
#.81   Echinoidea - West Indies

Mortensen, Theodor
     On some West Indian Echinoids.
     U. S. Nat. Mus. Bul. 74. pp. 31. pls. 17. Washington, 1910.

     Also separate.

QL
Prot.Poly
620   ECHIUROIDEA

Sato, Hayao

     Sipunculoidea and Echiuroidea of the West Caroline Islands.

     (Science Reports of the Tohoku Imperial University, IV Series, Vol.X, 1935, pp. 299-329 + 4 Plates)

QE
75
B   ECKEL, EDWIN CLARENCE, 1875.

Burchard, Ernest Francis.

     ... Iron ores, fuels, and fluxes of the Birmingham district, Alabama, by Ernest F. Burchard and Charles Butts, with chapters on the origin of the ores, by Edwin C. Eckel. Washington, Govt. print. off., 1910.

     204 p. illus., XVII pl. (part fold, incl. maps, tab.) diagrs. 23½ᶜᵐ. (U. S. Geological survey. Bulletin 400)

     Folded map in pocket.
     Issued also as House doc. no. 99, 61st Cong., 1st sess.

     1. Iron ores—Alabama. 2. Coal mines and mining—Alabama. I. Butts, Charles, 1863– II. Eckel, Edwin Clarence, 1875–

     G S 10-56

     Library, U. S. Geological   Survey (200) E no. 400

QL
1
C 15   ECHINOSTOMA REVOLUTUM   (FROELICH)

Johnson, John Christopher, 1891–
     ... The life cycle of *Echinostoma revolutum* (Froelich), by John C. Johnson. Berkeley, University of California press, 1920.

     cover-title, p. [335]–388 incl. illus. pl. 19–25. 27½ᶜᵐ. (University of California publications in zoology. v. 19, no. 11)
     "Literature cited": p. 373–374.

     1. Echinostoma revolutum (Froelich) I. Title.

     Title from Univ. of Calif.   Library of Congress   A 20-743
     [5]

QL
Prot-
Poly.
Pam. 754   ECHIUROIDEA   SOUTH AFRICA

Jones, C. M.
     A new species of echiuroid worm (Ochetostoma capensis) from the Cape Province, South Africa. By C. M. Jones and A. C. Stephen.

     (Trans. R. Soc. South Africa, 34(2):273-278, 1954)

QL
671
C 74   Eckelberry, Don R.

     Laysan Duck, a painting.

     (Condor, Vol. 65(1):opposite p. 3, 1963)

GC
63
D 61   ECHIURIDAE

Stephen, A. C.

     The Echiuridae, Sipunculidae and Priapulidae collected by the ships of the Discovery Committee during the years 1926 to 1937.
     IN
     Discovery Reports, Vol. 21, pp. 235-260, 1941.

AS
36
S 4   ECHIURIDAE   PACIFIC

Fisher, Walter Kenrick

     Additions to the Echiuroid fauna of the North Pacific Ocean.

     (Proc. U. S. Nat. Mus., Vol. 99, No. 3248, 1949)

GN
Pam
#452
4to   Ecker, Alexanxder

     Catalog der Anthropologischen Sammlungen der Universität, nach dem Stande vom 1. April 1878.

     Freiburg i.B.

Q
115
S 56   ECHIURIDAE   DUTCH EAST INDIES

Sluiter, C. Ph.
     Die Sipunculiden und Echiuriden der Siboga-Expedition, nebst Zusammenstellung der Ueberdies aus dem Indischen Archipel Bekannten Arten.

Weber, Max
     Uitkomsten...Nederlandsch Oost Indie 1899-1900...Siboga...Monographie XXV (livr. 8). 1902. 53 pp., 4 pl.

AS
36
S 4   ECHIUROIDEA   PACIFIC   (north)

Fisher, Walter Kenrick

     Echiuroid worms of the north Pacific ocean.

     (Proc. U. S. Nat. Mus., Vol. 96:215-292, 1946)

GN
Pam
#448
4to   Ecker, Alexander

     Die Berechtigung und die Bestimmung des Archivs, ex Archiv. für Anthropologie. Heft I.

GN Pam 757

Ecker, Alexander

Crania Germaniae meridionalis occidentalis.

Freiburg, Wagner, 1865. 18p. pls.

QL Fishes Pam. 458

Eckles, Howard H.

Fishery exploration in the Hawaiian Islands (August to October 1948, by the vessel Oregon of the Pacific Exploration Company)

(U. S. D. Int., Fish and Wildlife Service, Sep. No. 251. Vol. 11, No. 6, 1949) (Commercial Fisheries Review, June 1949:1-9)

AM Mus. Pam. 298

ECOLE FRANCAISE d'EXTREME-ORIENT

Cinquantenaire de la fondation de l'Ecole Francaise d'Extreme-Orient. Séance du 21 Mars 1952. Institut de France, Académie des Inscriptions et Belles-Lettres. 39 pp. Paris. 1952 4to.

GN Pam 2486

Ecker, A

Ueber den queren hinterhauptswulst (Torus occipitalis transversus) am schadel vershiedener aussereuropaischer volker.

QL 627 U-b

Eckles, Howard H.

Observations on juvenile oceanic skipjack (Katsuwonus pelamis) from Hawaiian waters and Sierra mackerel (Scomberomorus sierra) from the Eastern Pacific.

(Fishery Bulletin, U. S. Fish and Wildlife Service, Vol. 51, 1949)

Ecological Monographs.   Vol. 1, 1931-

The Ecological Society of America, Duke University Press. Durham, North Carolina.

AHPC has

GN Pam 984

and

GN Pam 449

Ecker, Alexander

Ueber die verschiedene krümmung des des schädelrohres und uber die stellung des schädels auf der wirbelsaule beim neger und beim Europäer. From Arch. f. Anthrop. bd.4, heft 4, 1871. 24p. pls.

second copy

QB 541 O 62

ECLIPSES

Oppolzer, Theodor Ritter von

Canon of eclipses (Canon der Finisternisse) Translated by Owen Gingerish. With a preface by Donald H. Menzel and Owen Gingerich. Dover Publications, Inc. New York. sm4to. 1962c lxx + 376 pp.

QH 541 E

Ecology. continuing the Plant world

Vols I-   . 1920 - date

Published quarterly in cooperation with the Ecological society of America by the Brooklyn Botanic Garden. Brooklyn, N.Y.

For current volumes see serial file

GN Pam #446 4to

Ecker, A.

Zur Entwicklungsgeschichte der Furchen und Windungen der Grosshirn-Hemisphären im Foetus des Menschen, ex Archiv für Anthropologie. Bd. III, Heft 3.

AN 2.E H 38

ECLIPSES   HAWAII

Alexander, W. D.

Eclipse of the sun, January 1, 1889. (at Honolulu)

(Hawaiian Gazette, 1889, Jan. 1, p. 5)

1 paragraph only.

QK Pam #527

and

AS 36 O 2

ECOLOGY

Braun, E. Lucy

The physiographic ecology of the Cincinnati region, Ohio Biol. Survey, Bull. 7, vol. II, no. 3, 1916.

GN Pam #450 4to

Ecker, Alexander

Zur Kenntniss der Wirkung der Skoliopädie des Schädels auf volumen, Lage und Gestalt des Grosshirns und seiner einzelnen Theile.

Braunschweig, 1876.

AN 2.E H 38

ECLIPSES   HAWAII

Alexander, W. D.

Letter to Editor of Hawaiian Gazette in regard to solar eclipse of June 5, 1872, and elevations of Haleakala and West Maui.

(Hawaiian Gazette, Jan. 31, 1872, p. 2)

AS 222 Z

ECOLOGY

Brockmann-Jerosch, H.

Die südpolar Baumgrenze.

(Vierteljahrsschrift der Naturforschenden Gesellschaft in Zurich, Beiblatt for Jahrg. 73, 1928, pp. 358-381)

GN 1 A n

Eckert, Georg

Der Einfluss der Familienorganisation auf die Bevölkerungsbewegung in Ozeanien.

(Anthropos, Bd. XXXI, 1936. pp.789-799)

GN Pam #39

Ecole d'Anthropologie de Paris

Rapports prealables.

Paris, 1919.

QH 541 C 61

ECOLOGY

Clarke, George L.

Elements of ecology. John Wiley and Sons, Inc. New York. 8vo. 1954c xiv + 534 pp.

QK 1 U

Eckfeldt, John W.

List of lichens from California and Mexico, collected by Dr. Edward Palmer from 1888 to 1892. By J. W. Eckfeldt.

(In U. S. Dept. of agriculture. Division of botany. Contributions from the U. S. National herbarium. Washington, 1890-95. 23ᶜᵐ. vol. i, no. 8, p. 291-292)

Issued October 31, 1893.

1. Lichens—California.

8-10532

Library of Congress   QK1.U5 vol. 1

GN 2.1 E

Ecole d'Anthropologie de Paris

See

Paris. Ecole ......

QH 541 D 19

ECOLOGY

Dansereau, Pierre

Biogeography; an ecological perspective. The Ronald Press Company. New York. R8vo. 1957c xiii + 394 pp.

QH
549
D 54
ECOLOGY

Dice, Lee R.

Natural communities. University of Michigan
Press. Ann Arbor. 1952. R8vo. x + 547 pp.

QK
930
L 78
ECOLOGY

Livingston, Burton E.

The water-relation between plant and soil;
by B. E. Livingston, and L. A. Hawkins: The water
supplying power of the soil as indicated by osmo-
meters, by Howard E. Pulling and Burton E. Livingston. Washington. 1915.

(Carnegie Institution of Washington, Publ.
no. 204)

QK
1
B 97-b
and
QK
Bot.Pam.
1969
ECOLOGY

Van Steenis, C.G.G.J.

Cycles of drought and reafforestation in
the U.S.A. seen in the light of a new botanical
hypothesis on the origin of deserts in general.

(Bull. du Jardin Bot. de Buitenzorg, Ser.
III, vol. XIV. 1936. pp. 50-55)

QK
Botany
Pam.
1537
ECOLOGY

Domin, Karel.

Some problems of plant ecology. From Proceedings of the International Congress of plant
Sciences I; 497-527. 1929.

QK
Botany
Pam.
1543
ECOLOGY

Nichols, George Elwood.

Plant associations and their classification.
From Proc. International Congress Plant Sciences
1, pp. 629-641. 1929.

ECOLOGY

see also

MARINE ECOLOGY
BOTANY ECOLOGY
ZOOLOGY ECOLOGY
PLANT ASSOCIATIONS
PLANT COMMUNITIES
ANIMAL ASSOCIATIONS
ANIMAL COMMUNITIES
BIOME
SOIL ECOLOGY

QH
Nat.Hist.
Pam.
173
ECOLOGY

Fosberg, F. Raymond

The community ecologist.

(Audubon Magazine, 59(5):197-198, 209,
1957)

QH
541
O 27
ECOLOGY

Odum, Eugene P.

Fundamentals of ecology. By Eugene P. Odum
in collaboration with Howard T. Odum. Second
edition. W. B. Saunders Company. Philadelphia
and London. R8vo. xvii + 546 pp.

QK
965
A 22
ECOLOGY AFRICA, SOUTH

Adamson, R. S.

The vegetation of South Africa. With 23
figures and 12 maps...and 17 photographs...
British Empire Vegetation Committee, Monographs. London, 1938, 235 pp. 8vo.

QE
1
G 3 m
ECOLOGY

Hedgpeth, Joel W.

Ecology
IN

Hedgpeth, Joel W.
Treatise on marine ecology and paleoecology. Vol. 1, 1957.

(Mem. Geol. Soc. of America, 67, 1957)

QH
Nat.Hist.
Pam.
83
ECOLOGY

Pearce, A. S.

Ecological Segregation.

(Science, February 23, 1934, Vol. 79,
No. 2043, pp. 167-172.)

QK
965
C 22
ECOLOGY AFRICA, SOUTH

Cannon, William Austin

General and physiological features of the
vegetation of the more arid portions of
southern Africa, with notes on the climatic envir-
-onment. Carnegie Inst. Wash. Pub. 354, Aug.1924

QC
983
H8
ECOLOGY

Huntington, Ellsworth
Climatic factor, as illustrated in arid
America.
Carnegie Inst. Wash. Pub. 192, 4to, pp. 341.
Wash., 1914.

QH
302
S 74
ECOLOGY

Spector, William S. editor

Handbook of biological data. Prepared
under the direction of the Committee on the Handbook of Biological Data, Div. of Biology and
Agriculture, The National Acad. of Sci., The
Nat. Res. Council. W. B. Saunders Company.
Philadelphia and London. 4to. 1956c xxxvi +
584 pp.

QK
Bot.Pam.
2921
ECOLOGY AFRICA

Lauer, W.

Hygrische Klimate und Vegetationszonen der
Tropen mit besonderer Berücksichtigung Ostafrikas.

(Erdkunde, Band V, Lfg. 4:284-293, 1951)

QH
541
J
ECOLOGY

Journal of Ecology

Vol. I, 1913 - *date*

See serial file

QE
1
G 3 m
ECOLOGY

Treatise on marine ecology and paleoecology.
Vol. 1: Ecology. Joel W. Hedgpeth, Editor

(Geol. Soc. America, Mem. 67, Vol. 1, 1957)

QK
Botany
Pam.
3135
ECOLOGY AFRICA

Shantz, H. L.

Photographic documentation of vegetational
changes in Africa over a third of a century.
By H. L. Shantz and B. L. Turner.

(University of Arizona, College of Agriculture, Report No. 169, August 1958)

QH
Nat.Hist.
Pam.
185
ECOLOGY

Ladd, Harry S.

Ecology, paleontology and stratigraphy.
Understanding the habits of living organisms
aids interpretations of fossiliferous sediments.

(Science, 129, No. 3341:69-78, 1959)

G
1
M 23
ECOLOGY

Troll, C.

Landscape ecology and land development
with special reference to the tropics.

(Jour. of Tropical Geography, Vol. 17:
1-11, 1963)

AS
618
N
ECOLOGY AFRICA, SOUTH

Stephenson, T. A.

The constitution of the intertidal fauna
and flora of South Africa.

(Annals of the Natal Museum, Vol. XI(2):
207-324, 1948)

QH 1 P 11

ECOLOGY   ALEUTIAN ISLANDS

Bank, Theodore P.

Biological succession in the Aleutians.

(Pacific Science, Vol. VII(4):493-503, 1953)

Q 115 H 23

ECOLOGY   CHANNEL ISLANDS

Dunkle, Meryl Byron

Plant ecology of the Channel Islands of California.

Reports

(Allan Hancock Pacific Expeditions, Vol. 13(3), 1950)

AS 763 H 38

ECOLOGY   GILBERT ISLANDS

Banner, Albert H.

The coral atoll project for 1951: Onotoa, Gilbert Islands.

(Proceedings of the Hawaiian Academy of Science...Twenty-Seventh annual meeting...page 6, 1951-1952)

Q 115 A 74

ECOLOGY   ARNHEM LAND

Specht, R.L. Editor

Botany and plant ecology.
IN

Records of the American-Australian Scientific Expedition to Arnhem Land, Vol.3, Edited by R.L.Specht and C.P.Mountford. Melbourne University Press.   1958.

QK Bot.Pam. 2243

ECOLOGY   CHILE

Miller, D.

Chiefly on Chilean forests.

(New Zealand Jour. of Forestry, Vol. 4, 1938, pp. 161-172)

QH 1 A 88

ECOLOGY   GILBERT ISLANDS

Cloud, Preston E., Jr.

Preliminary report on geology and marine environments of Onotoa Atoll, Gilbert Islands.

(Atoll Research Bull., No. 12, 1952)

QH 11 P 11

ECOLOGY   ARNO ATOLL

Hatheway, William H.

The land vegetation of Arno Atoll, Marshall Islands.

(Scientific Investigations in Micronesia, Report No. 15, 1953)

QK Bot.Pam. 2268

ECOLOGY   DUTCH EAST INDIES

van Steenis, C. G. G. J.

Het Danoe-Meer: rapport van een dienstreis naar het Natuur-monument Danoe-meer of Danoe-moeras in Bantam.

(Indisch Natuurleven, Jar. 3, 1936/38, pp. 214-222)

QL 1 A 94

ECOLOGY   GREAT BARRIER REEF

Endean, R. and others

The ecology and distribution of intertidal organisms on certain islands off the Queensland coast.

(Australian Jour. of Marine and Freshwater Research, 7(3):317-342, 1956)

[a study of intertidal organisms of the continental islands off   the Queensland coast]

G 51 W 17

ECOLOGY   AUSTRALIA

Gentilli, J.

The Australian plant landscape.

(Walkabout, 25(4):8-13, 1959)

QH 1 A 88

ECOLOGY   CLIPPERTON ISLAND

Sachet, Marie-Hélène

Geography and land ecology of Clipperton Island.

(Atoll Research Bulletin, No. 86, 1962)

QL Birds Pam 278 279

ECOLOGY   HAWAII

Amadon, Dean

Ecology and the evolution of some Hawaiian birds.

(Evolution, 1:63-68, 1947)

QH 541 K 25

ECOLOGY   AUSTRALIA

Keast, A. and others, editors

Biogeography and ecology in Australia. Edited by A. Keast, R. L. Crocker and C. S. Christian. W. Junk. Den Haag. 1959. R9vo. 1959c. 640 pp.

QK Bot.Pam. 2266

ECOLOGY   DUTCH EAST INDIES

Van Steenis, C. G. G. J.

Klimplantsluiers en plantendekens als typen van inzakkende vegetatie.

(De Tropische Natuur, Jrg., 28, Afl. 9, 1939, pp. 141-149)

QH 541 E

ECOLOGY   HAWAII

Campbell, Douglas H(oughton)

Some botanical and environmental aspects of Hawaii.

(Ecology, Vol. 1, 1920, pp. 257-269)

QL 1 A 93

ECOLOGY   AUSTRALIA   (zones of the
                          Australian region)

Whitley, Gilbert P. and others

The Middleton and Elizabeth reefs, South Pacific Ocean. p. 199

(The Australian Zoologist, 8:199-273, 1937)

QL 671 E 39

ECOLOGY   FIJI

Hinckley, Alden D.

Ecological notes on common birds in Fiji.

(The Elepaio, Vol. 23, Nos. 4, 5, 1962)

QH 541 E
&
QK Bot.Pam. 2259

ECOLOGY   HAWAII

Hartt, Constance E.

The plant ecology of Mauna Kea, Hawaii. By Constance E. Hartt and Maire C. Neal.

(Ecology, Vol. 21, 1940, pp. 237-266)

(2 copies)

QH 197 S 72

ECOLOGY   AUSTRALIA

Wood, J. G.
The vegetation of South Australia.

IN
South Australian Branch of the British Science Guild... Handbook of the flora and fauna of South Australia... Adelaide, 1937.

G N 1 A
and
GN Ethn.Pam. 3557

ECOLOGY   FIJI

Thompson, Laura

The relations of men, animals and plants in an island community (Fiji).

(American Anthropologist, Vol. 51(2):253-267, 1949)

QK 1 E 58
and
QK Bot.Pam. 184

ECOLOGY   HAWAII

Hillebrand, (William)

Die Vegetationsformationen der Sandwich-Inseln.

(Botanische Jahrb., (Engler) Bd. 9, 1888, pp. 305-314)

QK Bot.Pam. 2016
ECOLOGY HAWAII
Hosaka, Edward Y.
Ecological and floristic studies in Kipapa Gulch, Oahu.
(Occ. Pap., Bernice P. Bishop Museum, Vol. 13, 1937, pp. 175-232)

QL Crust.Pam. 489
ECOLOGY - JAPAN
Pearse, A. S.
The Ecology of Certain Crustaceans of the Beaches at Misaki, Japan, with Special Reference to Migrations from Sea to Land.
(Journal of the Elisha Mitchell Scientific Society, Vol. 46, No. 2, 1931)

DU 1 P 9
ECOLOGY MALAYA
Jin-bee, Ooi
The nature and distribution of the natural vegetation of Malaya.
(Pacific Viewpoint, 1(2):183-204, 1960)

QK Bot.Pam. 2361
ECOLOGY HAWAII
Hosaka, Edward Y.
Vegetation zones of Hawaii.
(Haw. Agric. Exp. Station, Bull. 89, 1942)

Q Bot.Pam. 2017
ECOLOGY JUAN FERNANDES ISLANDS
Skottsberg, Carl
Notes on the vegetation in the Cumberland Bay caves, Masatierra, Juan Fernandez Islands.
(Ecology, Vol. 16, 1935, pp. 364-374)

AS 522.B Sa
ECOLOGY MALAYSIA
Banks, E.
The change in climate and fauna with ascending altitude in Malaysia.
(Sarawak Museum Journal, Vol. 4 [no. 14], 1935, pp. 343-356)

QK 1 H 38
ECOLOGY HAWAII
Krajina, Vladimir J.
Biogeoclimatic zones on the Hawaiian Islands.
(Newsletter of the Haw. Bot. Soc., Vol. 2(7):93-98, 1963)

QH 11 P 11 and QH 1 A 88
ECOLOGY KAPINGAMARANGI
Niering, William A.
Bioecology of Kapingamarangi Atoll, Caroline Islands: terrestrial aspects.
(Scientific Investigations in Micronesia 1949- , Report No. 22, March, 1956)
(Atoll Research Bull., No. 49, 1956)

QK Bot.Pam. 2855
ECOLOGY MALAYSIA
van Steenis, C. G. G. J.
On the hierarchy of environmental factors in plant ecology.
(reprint, 7th Int. Bot. Congress, Stockholm, 1950, pp. 637-644)

QK Botany Pam. 56 and 29
ECOLOGY HAWAII
MacCaughey, Vaughan
The phytogeography of Manoa Valley, Hawaiian Islands.
(Am. Jour. Botany, 4:561-603, 1917)

QK 1 A 75
ECOLOGY KAUAI
Moomaw, J. C.
Vegetation on gibbsitic soils in Hawaii. By J. C. Moomaw and M. Takahashi.
(Journal of the Arnold Arboretum, Vol. 41: 391-411, 1960)

AP 2 S 35
ECOLOGY MARSHALL ISLANDS
Project atoll. (F. Stearns MacNeil, F. R. Fosberg and Theodore Arnow...Marshall Islands, Taongi and Bikar, November 1951-February, 1952.)
(Science, Vol. 114 (2970):568, 1951)
(Pacific Science, 6(1):77, 1952)

QK Bot.Pam. 2241
ECOLOGY HAWAII
Robyns, W.
Preliminary ecological survey of the island of Hawaii, by W. Robyns and Samuel H. Lamb.
(Bulletin du Jardin Botanique de l'Etat, Bruxelles, Vol. 15, Fasc. 3, 1939, pp. 241-293)

QH 1 P 11
ECOLOGY KERMADEC ISLANDS
Chapman, V. J.
A contribution to the ecology of the Kermadec Islands.
(Pacific Science, Vol. 15(3):347-351, 1961)

QH 1 A 88
ECOLOGY MARSHALL ISLANDS
Wiens, Harold J.
Field notes on atolls visited in the Marshalls, 1956.
(Atoll Research Bull., No. 54, 1957)

QH Nat. Hist. Pam. 205
ECOLOGY JAPAN
Masamune, G. and others
Ecological studies of Hakusan quasi-National Park. Nature Conservation Society of Japan. University of Kanazawa. 4to.

QK Bot.Pam. 2080
ECOLOGY KURILE ISLANDS
Tatewaki, Misao
The phytogeography of the middle Kuriles.
(Journal, Faculty of Agric., Hokkaido Imp. Univ., Sapporo, Japan, Vol. 29, 1933, pp.191-363)

AS 36 S 2
ECOLOGY MEXICO
Goldman, Edward Alphonso
Biological investigations in Mexico.
(Smithsonian Misc. Coll., Vol. 115, 1951, pp. xiii + 476 pp.

QH NatHis. Pam. 84
ECOLOGY JAPAN
Okada, Y. and Koba, Kazuo.
Notes on the mixed fauna of tropical and boreal animals in Honsyû, Japan. By Y. Okada and K. Koba.
(Proc. of the Imperial Acad., IX (1933), No. 8.)

QK Bot.Pam. 2691
ECOLOGY KWAJALEIN ISLAND
Fosberg, F. Raymond
Plants suitable for Naval Station, Kwajalein and suggestions on their cultivation.
(Memorandum, F4/RBM:dz, 29 Jan. 1952, From Dr. F. R. Fosberg to Commanding Officer, U. S. Naval Station, Navy Number 824) mimeographed, 7 + 2 pp.

QL 1 T 35
ECOLOGY MEXICO (GULF OF)
Hedgpeth, Joel W.
An introduction to the zoogeography of the northwestern Gulf of Mexico with reference to the invertebrate fauna.
(Publications of the Institute of Marine Science, Vol. III(1):107-224, 1953)

QL
595.Mi
I 59

ECOLOGY   MICRONESIA

Gressitt, J. Linsley
Insects of Micronesia, Introduction.

IN
Insects of Micronesia, Vol. I. Bernice P.
Bishop Museum. 1954. R8vo.

QL
1
L-j

ECOLOGY   NEW HEBRIDES

Baker, John R.

The seasons in a tropical rain-forest (New
Hebrides).   Parts 1-

(Journal of the Linnean Soc. of London,
Zool., Vol. 39, 1937-   )

for full reference, see main author cards

QK
Bot.Pam.
2521

ECOLOGY   NEW ZEALAND

Chapman, V. J.

Some vegetational changes on a shingle off-
shore bar at Thornham.

(Auckland University College reprint, 1948.
source?)

QH
1
K 99

ECOLOGY   MICRONESIA

Hosokawa, Takahide

A synchorological study of the swamp forests
in the Micronesian Islands.

(Memoirs of the Faculty of Science, Kyushu
University, Series E Biology, Vol. 1(2):101-123,
pl. IV, 1952)

QK
Bot.Pam.
2166
2167

ECOLOGY   NEW SOUTH WALES

Fraser, Lilian

The ecology of the upper Williams river and
Barrington Tops districts. I-II   by Lilian
Fraser and Joyce W. Vickery.

(Proceedings of the Linnean Society of New
South Wales, Vol. 62, 1937, pp. 269-283; Vol. 63,
1938, pp. 139-184;

QK
Bot.Pam.
2494

ECOLOGY   NEW ZEALAND

Davies, William C.

Some salient features of the New Zealand
native flora.

(Bull. R. New Zealand Inst. of Horticulture,
Banks Lecture, 1947)

GN
2.S
O 15

ECOLOGY   NEW CALEDONIA

Virot, R.

Associations végétales de la Nouvelle-Calédonie et leur protection.

(Journal de la Soc. des Océanistes, 7:263-269
1951)

QK
Bot.Pam.
2037

ECOLOGY   NEW ZEALAND

Allan, H. H.

A consideration of the "biological spectra"
of New Zealand.

(Journal of Ecology, Vol. 25, 1937, pp. 116-
152)

QH
1
P 11

ECOLOGY   NEW ZEALAND

Dellow, Vivienne

Inter-tidal ecology at Narrow Neck Reef. New
Zealand (Studies in Inter-tidal zonation, 3).

(Pacific Science, Vol. IV(4):355-374, 1950)

AS
36
A 4

ECOLOGY-BOTANY-NEW GUINEA

Archbold, Richard

Summary of the 1938-1939 New Guinea Expedi-
tion, by Richard Archbold, A. L. Rand and L. J.
Brass. (Results of the Archbold Expeditions,
No. 41) (maps)

(Bull. Am. Mus. of Nat. Hist., Vol. 79,
Art. 3, 1942, pp. 197-288)

QK
Bot.Pam.
2041

ECOLOGY   NEW ZEALAND

Allan, H. H.

Indigene versus alien in the New Zealand
plant world.

(Ecology, Vol. 17, 1935, pp. 187-193)

QK
Bot.Pam.
3046

ECOLOGY   NEW ZEALAND

Teixeira, Alcides Ribeiro

A questo florestal na Nova Zelandia e na
Australia. Secretaria da Agricultura do Estado
de Sao Paulo. 1956. 51 pp.

QK
.1
A 75

ECOLOGY   NEW GUINEA

Brass, L. J.

The 1938-39 expedition to the Snow Mountains, Netherlands New Guinea.

(Journal of the Arnold Arboretum, Vol. 22,
1941, pp. 271-295) and pp. 297-342, pl. 1-7.

QK
Bot.Pam.
2040

ECOLOGY   NEW ZEALAND

Allan, H. H.

Indigenous grasslands of New Zealand.

(Extract from the Handbook prepared for the
Auckland Meeting of the Australian and New
Zealand Association for the Adv. of Sci., 1937,
pp. 92-97)

GC
Oceano-
graphy
Pam.
45

ECOLOGY   OCEAN

Morgans, J. F. C.

The sea we fish in.

(East African Agric. Jour., 25(2):91-96,
1959)

QL
461
H-1

ECOLOGY   NEW GUINEA

Gressitt, J. L.

Entomological investigations in New Guinea
mountains.

(Proc. Hawaiian Entomological Society,
Vol. XVI(1):47-69, July, 1956)

QK
Bot.Pam.
2038

ECOLOGY   NEW ZEALAND

Allan, H. H.

Some ecological features of the main islands.

(Extract from the Handbook prepared for the
Auckland Meeting of the Australian and New
Zealand Association of the Adv. of Sci., 1937,
pp. 36-42)

Q
101
P 18

ECOLOGY   PACIFIC

Fosberg, F. Raymond
The island ecosystem.

IN
Fosberg, F. Raymond   editor
Man's place in the island ecosystem, a
symposium. pp. 1-6. Honolulu. 1963.
Tenth Pacific Science Congress.

QK
Bot.Pam.
2858

ECOLOGY   NEW GUINEA

van Steenis, C. G. G. J.

Vegetatie en flora...

[reprint from Nieuw Guinea... edited by W.C
Klein, Deel II, pp. 218-275, 1954]

(summary in English)

QK
Bot.Pam.
2677

ECOLOGY   NEW ZEALAND

Baylis, G. T. S.

Vegetation of Great Island, Three Kings
Group.

(Rec. Auck. Inst. Mus., Vol. 3(4/5):239-
252, 1948)

AS
763
B 62 p

Q
101
P 18

ECOLOGY   PACIFIC

Fosberg, F. Raymond   editor

Man's place in the island ecosystem; a
symposium. Bishop Museum Press 1963. Tenth
Pacific Science Congress, Honolulu, Hawaii,
1961

ECOLOGY   PACIFIC

Q
101
P 18

Gourou, Pierre
Pressure on island environment.

IN
Fosberg, F. Raymond   editor
Man's place in the island ecosystem, a
symposium. pp. 207-225. Honolulu. 1963.
Tenth Pacific Science Congress.

ECOLOGY   PHILIPPINE ISLANDS

AS
540
P

McGregor, Richard C.

Some features of the Philippine ornis; with
notes on the vegetation in relation to the avifauna.

(The Philippine Journal of Science, Vol. 16,
pp. 361-437, pl. 1-35, 1920)

ECOLOGY—SEYCHELLES ISLANDS

QH
541
J

Vesey-Fitzgerald, Desmond

On the vegetation of Seychelles.

(Jour. of Ecology, Vol. 28, 19 , pp. 465-
483)

ECOLOGY   PACIFIC

QL
627
U 58 b

Iverson, Robert T. B.

Food of Albacore Tuna, Thunnus Germo
(Lacépède), in the central and northeastern
Pacific.

(Fishery Bulletin 214, U. S. Fish and
Wildlife Service, Vol. 62, 1962)

ECOLOGY   QUEENSLAND

QH
197
C 65

Coaldrake, J. E.

Ecosystem of the coastal lowlands, Southern
Queensland.

(Bull. Commonwealth Sci. and Ind. Research
Organization, Australia, No. 283, 1961)

ECOLOGY   SOCIETY ISLANDS

QL
401
J 85

Fischer, P(aul) H(enrique)

Observations d'écologie littorale aux Iles
de la Société.

(Journal de Conchyliologie, Vol. 92(4):186-
194, 1952)

ECOLOGY   PACIFIC

QL
627
U 58 b

King, Joseph E.

Midwater trawling for forage organisms
in the central Pacific, 1951-1956. By
Joseph E. King and Robert T. B. Iversen.

(Fishery Bulletin 210, U. S. Fish and
Wildlife Service, Vol. 62, 1962)

ECOLOGY   RAROIA

GN
2.8
T

Danielsson, Bengt

Dernières recherches scientifiques à Raroia.

(Bull. Soc. des Etudes Oceaniennes, No. 105,
pp. 139-141, 1953)

(report of 1952 expedition, from Hawaii...)

ECOLOGY   SOUTH AFRICA

Q
Gen.Sci.
Pam.
127
128

Scott, K. M. F.

The ecology of South African Estuaries, Part
II. The Klein River Estuary, Hermanus, Cape.
By K. M.F. Scott, A. D Harrison, and W. Macnae.
Part III. Knysna, a clear open estuary. By J.H.
Day, N. A. H. Millard, and A. D. Harrison.

(Trans. R. Soc. of South Africa, 33:283-331;
367-413, 1952)

ECOLOGY   PACIFIC

AS
750
N 56-b

Laird, Marshall

Studies of mosquitoes and freshwater ecology
in the South Pacific.

(Royal Society of New Zealand, Bulletin No.
6, January, 1956)

ECOLOGY   RAROIA

QH
1
A 88

Doty, Maxwell S.   and others
Floristics and plant ecology of Raroia Atoll,
Tuamotus. Parts 1-4

(Atoll Research Bull., No. 33, 1954)

ECOLOGY   SOUTH AMERICA

QK
241
R 81

Roseveare, G. M.

The grasslands of Latin America.

(Bulletin 36, 1948, Imperial Bureau of Pastures and Field Crops, Aberystwyth, Great Britain)

ECOLOGY   PACIFIC (SOUTH)

QH
84.3
P 19

Pantin, C. F. A

A discussion on the biology of the southern
cold temperate zone. Under the leadership of
C. F. A. Pantin. Discussion held...1950-1960

(Proceedings R. Society of London, Ser. B.
Biol. Sciences, Vol. 152, No. 949, 1960)

ECOLOGY   RAROIA

QH
1
A 88

Doty, Maxwell S.

Interrelationships of the organisms on
Raroia aside from man. By Maxwell S. Doty and J.
P. E. Morrison.

(Atoll Research Bull., No. 35, 1954)

ECOLOGY   SUMATRA

QK
Bot.Pam.
2267

van Steenis, C. G. G. J.

Ecological observations on the genus Pleio-
craterium in Gajoland, Sumatra.

(Recueil des Travaux Botaniques Néerlandais
Vol. 36, 1939, pp. 446-448)

ECOLOGY   PACIFIC ISLANDS (NORTH)

QK
938.P7
T 21

Tatewaki, Misao

Forest ecology of the islands of the North
Pacific Ocean.

(Jour. Fac. of Agric., Hokkaido Univ.,
Vol. 50(4), 1968)

ECOLOGY   RAROIA

QH
1
A 88

Harry, Robert R.

Ichthyological field data of Raroia Atoll,
Tuamotu Archipelago.

(Atoll Research Bulletin, No. 18, July, 1953)

ECOLOGY   TAHITI

GN
2.8
T

Papy, H. René

Sur un probleme ecologique posé par la
végétation des hauts sommets de Tahiti et du
plateau Temehani a Raiatea (Océanie Francaise)

(Bull. Soc. des Etudes Oceaniennes, No. 94,
pp. 183-191, 1951)

ECOLOGY   PALMYRA

QH
1
P 10

Dawson, E. Yale

Changes in Palmyra atoll and its vegetation
through the activities of man, 1913-1958.

(Pacific Naturalist, Vol. 1(2), 1959)

ECOLOGY   RAROIA

QH
1
A 88

Morrison, J. P. E.

Animal ecology of Raroia Atoll, Tuamotus.
Part 1. Ecological notes on the mollusks and
other animals of Raroia. Part 2. Notes on the
birds of Raroia.

(Atoll Research Bulletin, No. 34, 1954)

ECOLOGY   THAILAND

QK
364
S 64

Smitinand, Tem

The genus Dipterocarpus, Gaertn. F. in
Thailand.

(Thai Forest Bull.(Bot.) No. 4, 1958)

G
3
A 51 g

ECOLOGY   TROPICS

Fosberg, F. Raymond   and others

Delimitation of the humid tropics. By
F. R. Fosberg, B. J. Garnier, and A. W. Küchler

(The Geogr. Rev., 51(3):333-347, 1961)

QL
751
K 33

ECOLOGY ANIMAL

Kendeigh, S. Charles

Animal ecology. Prentice-Hall, Inc.
Englewood Cliffs, New Jersey. sm4to. 1961
x + 468 pp.

QH
Nat.
Hist.
Pam.
218

ECOLOGY   CORAL REEFS AND ISLANDS

Fosberg, F. Raymond

Coral atoll symposia: Basic information on
the present status of scientific knowledge pertaining to atoll ecology...Prepared...Pac. Sci.
Board of the National Research Council...1951

QH
84.5
R 51

ECOLOGY   TROPICS

Richards, P. W.

The tropical rain forest, an ecological
study. At the University Press. Cambridge.
1952. R8vo. xviii + 450 pp.

QH
1
A 51

ECOLOGY ASSOCIATIONS

Emerson, Alfred E.

Social coordination and the superorganism.

(The American Midland Naturalist, Vol.21,
1939, pp. 182-209)

QH
1
A 88

ECOLOGY   CORAL REEFS

Fosberg, F. Raymond

Qualitative description of the coral atoll
ecosystem.

(Atoll Research Bulletin, No. 81, 1961)

QH
1
P 11

ECOLOGY   TRUK

Hill, Peter J. R.

The vegetation of Yanagi Islet, Truk,
Caroline Islands. By Peter J. R. Hill and
Benjamin C. Stone.

(Pacific Science, 15(4):561-562, 1961)

ECOLOGY   ATOLLS

See also

ECOLOGY   CORAL REEFS AND ISLANDS

QH
1
A 88

ECOLOGY   CORAL REEFS

Gerlach, Sebastian A.

The tropical reef as a biotope.

(Atoll Research Bulletin, No. 80, 1961)

ECOLOGY   TUAMOTUS

See also

ECOLOGY   RAROIA

QL
671
E 55

ECOLOGY   BIRDS

Marshall, A. J.

Food availability as a timing factor in the
sexual cycle of birds.

(The Emu, 59(4):267-282, 1951)

AP
2
S 35

ECOLOGY   CORAL REEFS AND ISLANDS

Project atoll. (F. Stearns MacNeil, F. R.
Fosberg and Theodore Arnow...Marshall Islands,
Taongi and Bikar, November 1951-February, 1952.)

(Science, Vol. 114 (2970):568, 1951)
(Pacific Science, 6(1):77, 1952)

QK
Bot.
Pam.
3186

ECOLOGY   ALGAE

Chapman, V. J.

L'ecologie d'Hormosira Banksii. By V. J.
Chapman and C. B. Trevarthes.

(Colloques Int. du Centre Nat. de la
Recherche Scientifique, LXXXI. Evologie des
Algues Marine, Dinard, 1957. pp. 231-248)

AS
36
A 4

and
QL
Birds
Fam. 311

ECOLOGY   BIRDS   HAWAII

Amadon, Dean

The Hawaiian honeycreepers (Aves, Drepaniidae).

Bull. Am. Mus. of Nat. Hist., 95(4), 1950)

review: Nature, 4252, p. 677-78, 1951

Z
4501
S 12

ECOLOGY   CORAL REEFS AND ISLANDS
ECOLOGY   CORAL ATOLLS

Sachet, Marie-Hélène

Island bibliographies: Micronesian botany,
land environment and ecology of coral atolls,
vegetation of tropical Pacific islands. Compiled
under the offices of the Pacific Science Board.
By Marie-Hélène Sachet and F. Raymond Fosberg.

(Nat. Acad. of Sci.-Nat. Research Council,
Publication 335.   v + 577 pp.   1955)

QL
541
C 68

ECOLOGY   ANIMAL

Cold Spring Harbor Symposia on quantitative
biology, Vol.XXII:
Population studies: animal ecology and
demography. The Biological Laboratory, Cold
Spring Harbor, L. I., New York. 1957. sm4to
xiv + 437 pp.

QH
Nat.Hist.
Pam.
242

ECOLOGY   BOTANY

van Steenis, C. G. G. J.

An attempt towards an explanation of the
effect of mountain mass elevation.

(Reprint, Koninkl. Nederl. Akademie van
Wetenschappen, Proc., Series C, Vol. 64(3):
435-442, 1961)

QL
1
A 93

ECOLOGY   CORAL REEFS and ATOLLS

Ward, Melbourne

The Crustacea of the Capricorn and Bunker
Groups, Queensland.

(The Australian Zoologist, 5:241-246, 1928)

QH
541
E 51

ECOLOGY   ANIMALS

Elton, Charles S.

The ecology of invasions by animals and
plants. Methuen and Co. Ltd.   London. 8vo
181 pp. (1958)

QK
101
G 65

ECOLOGY   CLASSIFICATION

Rübel, Eduard

Plant communities of the world.

Goodspeed, T. H.
Essays in geobotany...Setchell.   1936.
pp. 263-290

QL
1
A 93

ECOLOGY   CORAL REEFS AND ISLANDS

Ward, Melbourne

The true crabs of the Capricorn Group,
Queensland.

(The Australian Zoologist, 7:237-255, 1932)

ECOLOGY   CORAL REEFS AND ISLANDS

See also

ECOLOGY   ATOLLS

ECOLOGY   FOREST

See

FOREST ECOLOGY

GN
23
D 22   Darling, F. Fraser

West highland survey; an essay in human
ecology. Edited by F. Fraser Darling. Oxford
Univ. Press. London. 1955. R8vo. xvi + 438
pp.

QH
Nat.Hist.   ECOLOGY-ESTUARIES
Pam.   Day, J. H.
148
The ecology of South African estuaries.
Part I. A review of estuarine conditions in
general.

(Trans. R. Soc. of South Africa, 33(1):52-
91, 1951)

QH
541   ECOLOGY   GLOSSARY
C 29   Carpenter, J. Richard

An ecological glossary. University of
Oklahoma Press. Norman, 1938. 8vo. ix + 306
pp. maps.

GN
1   ECOLOGY   HUMAN
A 51
Ecology and anthropology: a symposium.

(Am. Anthropologist, 64(1):15-165, 1962)

Q
Gen.Sci.   ECOLOGY   ESTUARIES
Pam.   Scott, K. M. F.
127
128   The ecology of South African Estuaries, Part
II. The Klein River Estuary, Hermanus, Cape.
By K. M. F. Scott, A. D. Harrison, and W. Macnae.
Part III. Knysna, a clear open estuary. By J.H.
Day, N.A. H. Millard, and A. D. Harrison.

(Trans. R. Soc. of South Africa, 33:283-331;
367-413, 1952)

ECOLOGY   GRAMINEAE

See

GRAMINEAE   ECOLOGY

GN
468.2   ECOLOGY   HUMAN
R 31   Redfield, Robert

The little community; viewpoints for the
study of a human whole. University of Chicago
Press. (1955) First published in Sweden as
Vol. 5 of the Gottesman Lectures, Uppsala University.

QH
Nat.Hist.   ECOLOGY   EVOLUTION
Pam.   Dansereau, Pierre
167
The varieties of evolutionary opportunity.

(Reprinted from Revue Canadienne de Biologie, 11(4):305-388, 1952)

QE
1   ECOLOGY   PALAEOECOLOGY
G 3 m   Treatise on marine ecology and paleoecology.
Vol. 2: Paleoecology, by Harry S. Ladd, editor.
Prepared under the direction of a Committee of
the Division of Earth Sciences, Nat. Res. Council
Nat. Acad. Sci., Washington. 1957

(Mem. Geol. Soc. America, No. 67, 1957)

QH
Nat.Hist.   ECOLOGY   HUMAN
Pam.   Thornthwaite, C. W.
109
The relation of geography to human ecology.

(Ecological Monographs, Vol. 10, 1940,
pp. 343-348)

QL
751   ECOLOGY   FAUNA
A 42   Allee, W. C.

Ecological animal geography. second edition
An authorized edition, rewritten and revised.
Based on "Tiergeographie auf oekologischer
Grundlage." By the late Richard Hesse. John
Wiley and Sons, Ltd. New York. (1937, 1951)
8vo. xii + 3-714 pp.

QK
Bot.Pam.   ECOLOGY   SALT MARSHES
3113   Chapman, V. J.

Les "sociétés" des algues des marais salés
et des mangroves.

(Coloques Internationaux du Centre Nat. de
la Recherche Scientifique, LXXXI: Ecologie des
Algues Marines. Dinard, 20-28 Sept. 1957.
Extrait. 1959. pp.153-165)

GN
Ethn.Pam.   ECOLOGY, HUMAN   AUSTRALIA
4259   Birdsell, Joseph B.

Some enviromental and cultural factors influencing the structuring of Australian aboriginal populations.

(The American Naturalist, Vol. 87, pp. 171-
207, 1953)

QL
45   ECOLOGY   FAUNA
L 14   Lack, David

The natural regulation of animal numbers.
Clarendon Press. Oxford, England. 1954. 8vo.
viii+343 pp.

[populations, breeding seasons, food, preda-
tion, disease, migration...]

QL
1   ECOLOGY   SEA BIRDS
C 23   Rand, R. W.

The biology of guano-producing sea-birds.
3. The distribution, abundance and feeding habits of cormorants Phalacrocoracidae off
the South West Coast of the Cape Province.

(Union of South Africa, Investigational
Report 42, 1960)

GN
125.S   ECOLOGY   HUMAN   BOUGAINVILLE
O 48   Oliver, Douglas L.

Somatic variability and human ecology on
Bougainville, Solomon islands. Harvard University
168 mimeographed pp. 4to.

QH
541   ECOLOGY   FISHES
E 17 m   Hiatt, Robert E.

Ecological relationships of the fish fauna
on coral reefs of the Marshall Islands. By
Robert W. Hiatt and Donald W. Strasburg.

(Ecological Monographs, Vol. 30(1):65-127,
1960)

QH
Nat.Hist.   ECOLOGY   ZONATION
Pam.   Chapman, V. J.
160
General schemes of classification in relation
to marine coastal zonation. By V. J. Chapman
and C. B. Trevarthen.

(Journal of Ecology, Vol. 41(1):198-204,
1953)

GN
1   ECOLOGY   HUMAN   FIJI
A   Thompson, Laura

The relations of men, animals and plants in
an island community (Fiji).

and   (American Anthropologist, Vol. 51(2):253-
GN   267, 1949)
Ethn.Pam
3557

QH
1
A 88

ECOLOGY HUMAN GILBERT ISLANDS

Catala, René L. A.

Report on the Gilbert Islands: some aspects of human ecology.

(Atoll Research Bulletin, No. 59, 1957)

QH
1
P 11

ECOLOGY LITTORAL

Carnahan, J. A.

Inter-tidal zonation at Rangitoto Island, New Zealand. (Studies in Inter-tidal Zonation, 4).

(Pacific Science, 6(1):35-46, 1952)

QK
Bot.Pam.
2501

ECOLOGY MOUNTAIN REGIONS MALAYASIA

van Steenis, C. G. G. J.

Vegetatieschetsen van her Idjen-Hoogland.

(De Tropische Natuur, Jrg. 20, afl. 10-12, pp. 157-184, 1940)

G
7
N 56

ECOLOGY HUMAN MAORI

Cumberland, Kenneth B.

Man in nature in New Zealand.

(New Zealand Geographer, 17(2):137-154, 1961)

G
51
W 17

ECOLOGY MANGROVE SWAMP

Patterson, Ewen K.

Where fish climb trees.

(Walkabout, Vol. 5(2):50-56,1938)

QH
Nat.Hist.
Pam.
166

ECOLOGY PHYSIOLOGICAL VARIABILITY

Clausen, Jens

The ecological race as a variable biotype compound in dynamic balance with its environment.

(Reprinted from : I.U.B.S. Symposium on Genetics of Population Structure, Pavia, Italy, August 20-23, 1953. pp. 105-113)

QH
1
A 88

ECOLOGY HUMAN MARSHALL ISLANDS

Mason, Leonard
A quantitative study of certain aspects of the man-land relationship in Marshallese economy at Arno Atoll. By Leonard Mason and Harry Uyehara.
IN
Fosberg, F. Raymond
Handbook for atoll research, 2nd ed., pp. 116-121.

(Atoll Research Bull., No. 17, 1953)

QH
1
A 88

ECOLOGY MARINE

Hiatt, Robert W.
Instructions for marine ecological work on coral atolls.
IN
Fosberg, F. Raymond
Handbook for atoll research, 2nd...ed., pp. 100-108.

(Atoll Research Bull., No. 17, 1953)

QH
Nat.Hist.
Pam.146

ECOLOGY PLANT DISTRIBUTION

Boyko, H.

On climatic extremes as decisive factors for plant distribution.

(Palestine Journal of Botany, Rehovot series Vol. 7, 1949:41-52)

G
7
R 91

ECOLOGY HUMAN NEW GUINEA

Brookfield, H. C.

The Highland peoples of New Guinea: a study of distribution and localization.

(Geographical Journal, 127(4):436-448,1961)

QH
91
M 82

ECOLOGY MARINE

Moore, Hilary B.

Marine ecology. New York. John Wiley and Sons, Inc. 1958c 8vo. xi + 493 pp.

QH
541
E 51

ECOLOGY PLANTS

Elton, Charles S.

The ecology of invasions by animals and plants. Methuen and Co. Ltd. London, 8vo 181 pp. (1958)

E
77
K 93

ECOLOGY, HUMAN NORTH AMERICA

Kroeber, A(lfred) L(ouis)

Cultural and natural areas of native North America. University of California Press. Berkeley. 1939. R8vo. xi + 242 pp.

AS
36
Na

ECOLOGY MARINE

Report of the Committee on Marine Ecology as related to Paleontology, 1941-1942; Harry S. Ladd, Chairman. Presented at the Annual Meeting of the Division of Geology and Geography, National Research Council, May 2, 1942. 58 pp. 4o. Pamphlet, mimeographed.

QH
1
A 51

ECOLOGY POPULATION

Park, Thomas

Analytical population studies in relation to general ecology.

(The American Midland Naturalist, Vol.21, 1939, pp. 235-255)

QH
550
T 68

ECOLOGY INSECTS

Torii, Torizo

The stochastic approach in field population ecology, with special reference to field insect populations. Japan Society for the Promotion of Science. Ueno. Tokyo. 1956. R8vo. 27 pp.

QK
Bot.Pam.
2511

ECOLOGY METHODS OF STUDY

Chapman, V. J.

The application of aerial photography to ecology as exemplified by the natural vegetation of Ceylon.

(Indian Forester, Vol. 73(7):287-314,1947)

QH
Nat.Hist.
Pam.
115

ECOLOGY-SAND BEACHES

Pearse, A. S.

Ecology of sand beaches at Beaufort, North Carolina. By A. S. Pearse, H. J. Humm, and G. W. Wharton.

(Ecological Monographs, 12:135-190, 1942)

QH
1
P 11

ECOLOGY INTER-TIDAL AREA

Dellow, Vivienne

Inter-tidal ecology at Narrow Neck Reef, New Zealand (Studies in Inter-tidal zonation, 3).

(Pacific Science, Vol. 1V(4):355-374, 1950)

QH
1
A 88

ECOLOGY METHODS OF STUDY

Hiatt, Robert W.
Instructions for marine ecological work on coral atolls.
IN
Fosberg, F. Raymond
Handbook for atoll research, 2nd...ed., pp. 100-108.

(Atoll Research Bull., No. 17, 1953)

QH
541
E 17

ECOLOGY SWAMPS

Taylor, B. W.

The classification of lowland swamp communities in northeastern Papua.

(Ecology, 40(4):703-711, 1959)

QH
Nat.Hist.
Pam.
163

ECOLOGY   TERMINOLOGY

Chapman, V. J.

    Problems in ecological terminology. (Pre-
sidential address)

    (Reprinted from Rept. of the Australian and
New Zealand Assn. for the Adv. of Sci., 29th
Meeting, Sydney, pp. 259-279, August, 1952)

QK
Bot.Pam.
2921

ECOLOGY   TROPICS

Lauer, W.

    Hygrische Klimate und Vegetationszonen der
Tropen mit besonderer Berücksichtigung Ostafrikas.

    (Erdkunde, Band V, Lfg. 4:284-293, 1951)

GN
1
A 51

    Ecology and anthropology: a symposium.

    (Am. Anthropologist, 64(1):15-165, 1962)

RB
541
M 46

    The ecology of human disease.

May, Jacques M.

DU
80
A 93

    Economic and political developments in
Western Samoa.

    (South Pacific, Vol. 7(13):955-957, 1954)

G
142
H 94

    Economic and Social Geography

Huntington, Ellsworth

GN
25
H 57

    Economic anthropology; a study in compara-
tive economics.

    Herskovits, Melville J.

QK
Bot.Pam.
2662

ECONOMIC BOTANY

Fosberg, F. Raymond

    Economic botany- a modern concept of its
scope.

    (Economic Botany, Vol. 2(1):3-14, 1948)

SB
107
H 64

    Economic botany, a textbook of useful plants
and plant products.

Hill, Albert F.

    First edition. McGraw-Hill Book Company,
Inc. New York and London. 1937. R8vo. x+ 592 pp.

QK
Bot.Pam.
3101

ECONOMIC BOTANY   PACIFIC

Maclet, Jean-Noël

    Catalogue des plantes utiles aujourd'hi
presentes en Polynésie Francaise. By Jean-Noël
Maclet and Jacques Barrau.

    (Jour. d'Agric. Tropicale et de Bot. Appli-
que, Tome VI(1-3):1-184, 1959)

GN
25
B 34

ECONOMIC CONDITIONS

Bauer, Peter T.

    The economics of under-developed countries.
By Peter T. Bauer and Basil S. Yamey. The University of Chicago Press. sm8vo. 1957 xiii +
271 pp.

GN
406
T 54

ECONOMIC CONDITIONS

Thurnwald, Richard

    Economics in Primitive Communities. London.
International Institute of African Languages and
Cultures. Oxford University Press. 1932. 8vo.
xiv +314 pp.

ECONOMIC CONDITIONS   BANTU

    see

BANTU   ECONOMIC CONDITIONS

ECONOMIC CONDITIONS   FORMOSA

    See

FORMOSA   ECONOMIC CONDITIONS

ECONOMIC CONDITIONS   HAWAII

    see

HAWAII   ECONOMIC CONDITIONS

ECONOMIC CONDITIONS   HONOLULU

    See

HONOLULU   ECONOMIC CONDITIONS

ECONOMIC CONDITIONS   MELANESIA

    See

MELANESIA   ECONOMIC CONDITIONS

ECONOMIC CONDITIONS   MICRONESIA

    See

MICRONESIA   ECONOMIC CONDITIONS

ECONOMIC CONDITIONS   NEW CALEDONIA

    See

NEW CALEDONIA   ECONOMIC CONDITIONS

ECONOMIC CONDITIONS   NEW GUINEA

    SEE

NEW GUINEA   ECONOMIC CONDITIONS

ECONOMIC CONDITIONS   PACIFIC

    see

PACIFIC   ECONOMIC CONDITIONS

ECONOMIC CONDITIONS   SIAM

See

SIAM   ECONOMIC CONDITIONS

GN
671.S6
B 45   Belshaw, Cyril S.

An economic development of a Melanesian economy (A study of Gela, British Solomon Islands). Thesis presented for the degree of M.A. in the University of New Zealand, Nov. 1945. carbon copy, typed. folio. 124 pp.

ECONOMIC LIFE   SOLOMON ISLANDS

GN
25
H 57   Herskovits, Melville F.

Economic anthropology. A study in comparative economics. Originally published in 1940 as The economic life of primitive peoples. Alfred A. Knopf. New York. 1952. 8vo. xiii + 3-547 (4)+xxiii pp.

ECONOMICS

ECONOMIC CONDITIONS   SOLOMON ISLANDS

see

SOLOMON ISLANDS   ECONOMIC CONDITIONS

ECONOMIC PLANTS

See

PLANTS   ECONOMIC

GN
Ethn.Pam.
3242   Thurnwald, Richard

Ein vorkapitalistisches Wirtschaftssystem in Buin. Ein Beitrag zur Kenntnis primitiver Wirtschaft und von Frühgeld.

(Archiv fur Rechts- und Sozialphilosophie, Bd. 31, Heft 1, 1937 (?), pp. 1-37)

ECONOMICS

ECONOMIC CONDITIONS   THAILAND

See

THAILAND   ECONOMIC CONDITIONS

DU
Pac.Pam.
959   Frankel, S. Herbert

The concept of colonization. An inaugural lecture...University of Oxford, June 1949. 8vo. Oxford. At the Clarendon Press. 24 pp.

ECONOMIC EVOLUTION

G
113
W 93   Woytinsky, W. S.

World population and production; trends and outlook. By W. S. and E. S. Woytinsky. The Twentieth Century Fund. New York. 1953. R8vo. lxxii + 1268 pp.

ECONOMICS

ECONOMIC CONDITIONS   TRUK

See

TRUK   ECONOMIC CONDITIONS

GN
665
T 48   Thomson, Donald F.

Economic structure and the ceremonial exchange cycle in Arnhem Land. MacMillan and Co., Ltd. Melbourne. 1949. 8vo. 106 pp.

ECONOMIC STRUCTURE   ARNHEM LAND

GN
Ethn.Pam.
4258   Boeke, J. H.

Three forms of disintegration in dual societies.

(Indonesië ('sGravenhage), n.d., pp. 278-295)

[Lecture given to the Course on Co-operative Education of the I. L. O. Asian Co-operative Field Mission,   Oct. 1953]

ECONOMICS   ASIA

S
142
W 57   Whitbeck, R. H., and Finch, V. C.

Economic geography

QL
44
T 38   Theobald, Fred. V.

First report on economic zoology. British Museum (Natural History). Printed by order of the Trustees. London. 1903. 8vo. xxxiv + 192 pp., 18 figs.

ECONOMIC ZOOLOGY

GN
2.S
P 76   Pitt, David

Some obstacles to economic development in Fiji and Island Polynesia.

(Jour. Poly. Soc., 71(1): 110-116, 1962)

ECONOMICS   FIJI

QE
75
B   Darton, Nelson Horatio, 1865-

... Economic geology of Richmond, Virginia, and vicinity, by N. H. Darton. Washington, Govt. print. off., 1911.

48 p. illus. x pl. (incl. fold. map) 23½ᶜᵐ. (U. S. Geological survey. Bulletin 483)

1. Geology—Virginia. 2. Geology, Economic—Virginia. I. Title.

G S 11-561

Library, U. S. Geological   Survey (200) E no. 483

——— Copy 2.

ECONOMIC GEOLOGY OF RICHMOND, VA.

GN
22
B 66   Boas, Franz   and others

General anthropology. Boston. 1938. (Chapter VIII: The economic organization of primitive peoples, pp. 327-408, by Ruth Bunzel)

ECONOMICS

GN
3
I 61   Sahlins, Michael D.

Production, distribution and power in a primitive society. pp. 495-500 [Moala, Fiji] IN

Wallace, Anthony F. C.
Men and cultures: selected papers of the Fifth International Congress of Anthropological and Ethnological Sciences, Philadelphia, Sept. 1-9, 1956. Univ.   of Penn. Press. R8vo. xxxi+ 810 pp.

ECONOMICS   FIJI

Economic geology

See

Geology, Economic

GN
25
H 29   Hazlewood, Arthur

The economics of 'under-developed' areas; and annotated reading list of books, articles, and official publications. 2nd enlarge edition. Oxford University Press. 1959. 8vo. xii + 156 pp.

ECONOMICS

DU
1
S 72t   Belshaw, Cyril S.

Small scale industry for the South Pacific-preliminary papers.

(South Pacific Commission, Technical Paper No. 89, March, 1956)

ECONOMICS   PACIFIC

DU
1
S 72 t

ECONOMICS PACIFIC

Danks, K. H.

Industrial activity in selected areas of the South Pacific.

(South Pacific Commission, Technical Paper No. 90, March, 1956)

QL
Birds Pam.
442

ECTOPISTES

Dury, Charles

The passenger pigeon, Ectopistes migratorius Linn.
(The Journal of the Cincinnati Soc. of Nat. Hist., 21(2):52-56, 1910)

ECUADOR BOTANY

see

BOTANY ECUADOR

GN
2.S
P 76

ECONOMICS PACIFIC

Pitt, David

Some obstacles to economic development in Fiji and Island Polynesia.

(Jour. Poly. Soc., 71(1):110-116, 1962)

QL
Insect
Pam.
1783

ECTOPARASITES

Hubbard, C. Andresen

Ectoparasites of Western Lagomorpha. Parts I-II.

(Pacific Univ. Bull., 37(8), 1941. 8 pp.)

[found on conies and rabbits]

GN
550
I-C

ECUADOR - HISTORY

Saville, Marshall Howard, 1867-
... A letter of Pedro de Alvarado relating to his expedition to Ecuador. By Marshall H. Saville. New York, Museum of the American Indian, Heye foundation, 1917.

cover-title, 6 p. facsim. 25½ᶜᵐ. (Contributions from the Museum of the American Indian, Heye foundation. vol. v, no. 1)

Alvarado's letter appears in facsimile, and is repeated as text on p. 5-6. Bibliography: p. 6.

1. Ecuador—Hist.—To 1809. I. Alvarado, Pedro de, 1485?-1541.

Library of Congress   E11.N52 vol. 5

—— Copy 2.   F3733.A47

[3]

20-5616

GN
489
U 21

ECONOMICS PACIFIC

Udy, Stanley H., Jr.

Organization of work; a comparative analysis of production among nonindustrial peoples. With an introduction by George P. Murdock. HRAF Press. New Haven. 1959. sm8vo. 12 + 182 pp.

QL
Insect
Pam.
1786

ECTOPARASITES

Hubbard, C. Andresen

West Coast Catallagias (three new species)

(Pacific Univ. Bull., 37(3), 1940. 4 pp. unnumbered)

PL
Philology
Pam.
146

ECUADOR- LANGUAGE

Imbelloni, J

Kichua
L'idioma nel sistema linguistico dell'Oceano Pacifico. Estratto del XXII congresso internaz degli Americanisti. Sept., 1926. p. 495-509

GN
1
O 15

ECONOMICS PRIMITIVE

Walker, K. F.

The study of primitive economics.

(Oceania, Vol. 13, No. 2, 1942, pp. 131-142)

QL
Protozoa
to
Polyzoa
Pam.
358

ECTYONINAE

Topsent, E(mile)

Heteroclathria hallezi type d'un genre nouveau d'ectyonines.
(Archives de zool. expérimentale et générale (4) v.2, Notes et Revue no. 6, 1904.)

ECUADOR MAMMALS

see

MAMMALS ECUADOR

GN
Ethn.
Pam.
4404

ECONOMICS TIKOPIA

Firth, Raymond

Work and community in a primitive society.

(H.R.H. The Duke of Edinburgh's Study Conference, X, 1956) 12pp.

QL
Insects
Pam 24

Rocafuerte
Ecuador. Colegio Nacional Vicente .

Revista
Setiembre de 1921 Num.5
Ano IV, Num.7 - Marzo de 1922.

ECUADOR MOLLUSCA

see

MOLLUSCA ECUADOR

AS
36
A 1
and
QL
Moll.
Pam.
305

ECPHORA

Pilsbry, H. A.

A New Ecphora of the Chesapeake Miocene
in Proc. Acad. Nat. Sc. Phil. May, 1911. pp. 438-439.

Given by author

ECUADOR ARCHAEOLOGY

see

ARCHAEOLOGY ECUADOR

ECUADOR ORCHIDACEAE

See

ORCHIDACEAE ECUADOR

AS
36
S4

ECPHYLUS

Rohwer, Sievert Allen, 1887-
Descriptions of thirteen new species of parasitic *Hymenoptera* and a table to certain species of the genus *Ecphylus*. By S. A. Rohwer ...

(*In* U. S. National museum. Proceedings. Washington, 1913. 23½ᶜᵐ. v. 45, p. 533-540)

1. Hymenoptera. 2. Ecphylus.

Library of Congress   Q11.U55 vol. 45

14-4148

ECUADOR BIRDS

see

BIRDS ECUADOR

AS
36
S1

Eddington, Arthur Stanley, 1882-
Sir David Gill (1843-1914). By A. S. Eddington.

(*In* Smithsonian institution. Annual report. 1915. Washington, 1916. 23½ᶜᵐ. p. 511-522)

"Reprinted ... from Monthly notices of the Royal astronomical society, London, Feb., 1915."

1. Gill, Sir David, 1843-1914.

Library of Congress   Q11.S66 1915

—— Copy 2.   Q11.S66 1915 2d set

16-16027

GN
2.1
A-4   EDDYSTONE ISLAND

Hocart, A.M.

The canoe and the bonito in Eddystone Island

(Jour. R. Anthropological Institute of Great Britain and Ireland, Vol. 65, 1935, pp. 97-111)

AS
36
S4   EDESTUS

Hay, Oliver Perry, 1846-

On an important specimen of *Edestus;* with description of a new species, *Edestus mirus*. By Oliver Perry Hay ...

(*In* U. S. National museum. Proceedings. Washington, 1912. 23½ᶜᵐ. vol. 42, p. 31-38. 2 pl.)

1. Edestus.

13-9513

Library of Congress   Q11.U55 vol. 42

GN
2.1
A-M   Edge-Partington, J.

Ancient Maori houses: their use and abuse.

(Man, vol. 2, 1902, no. 99, pp. 137-138)

S
591
E 22   Edelman, C. H.

Studien over de bodemkunde van Nederlandsch-Indie.

(Publicatie van de Stichting "Fonds Landbouw Export Bureau 1916-1918", No. 24, 1941)

AS
36
S4   EDESTUS

Hay, Oliver Perry, 1846-

On the nature of *Edestus* and related genera, with descriptions of one new genus and three new species. By Oliver P. Hay ...

(*In* U. S. National museum. Proceedings. Washington, 1910. 23½ᶜᵐ. vol. 37, p. 43-61. illus, pl. 12-15)

1. Edestus.

11-9663

Library of Congress   Q11.U55 vol. 37

AM
Mus
Pam
#53   Edge-Partington, James

Australasian Prints, drawings, etc.. in the collection of J. Edge-Partington, Esg., Beaconsfield. 1926.

QP
1
C   EDEMA

Moore, Arthur Russell, 1882-

... Can the presence of acid account for the oedema of living muscle? By A. R. Moore. (Berkeley, University of California press) 1912.

p. (111)-113. 27ᶜᵐ. (University of California publications in physiology. vol. 4, no. 15)

"From the Rudolph Spreckels physiological laboratory of the University of California."
Issued in single cover with vol. 4, no. 14, of the series.

1. Edema. 2. Muscle.

A 12-767

Title from Univ. of Calif.   Library of Congress

DU
623
C 77   Edgar, Thomas

Remarks off Sandwich Islands. ms copy. III

Cook collection, Nos. 111 and 113.

AM
133
P 27   Edge Partington, James

Catalogue of the Australasian collection of books and pictures fromed by the late James Edge Partington; with a memoir by Harry G. Beasley. Francis Edwards Ltd. London. 1934.

DU
1
S 72 q   Eden, D. R. A.

The cocoa industry in Fiji.

(South Pacific Bull. 10(3):59-62, 74, 1960)

AG
25
Ed
Reading
Room   Edgren, Hjalmar and Burnett, Percy

A French and English dictionary with indication of pronounciation, etymologies, and dates of earliest appearance of French words in the language.

New York, 1901, pp xvi, 1252.

GN
2.1
A-M   Edge-Partington, J.

Decorated shields from the Solomon Islands.

(Man, vol. 6, 1906, no. 86, pp. 129-130, pl. I-J)

DU
1
S 72 t   Eden, D. R. A.

The management of coconut plantations in western Samoa.

(South Pacific Commission, Technical Paper No. 48, September, 1953)

Pe
Tr   EDITING

Trelease, Sam and Yule, Emma Sarepta

Preparation of scientific and technical papers.

Baltimore, Williams & Wilkins, 1925.

GN
2.1
A-M   Edge-Partington, J.   (James)

A "Domestic Idol" from Easter Island (Rapa Nui).

(Man, vol. 4, 1904, no. 46, pp. 73-74)

DU
1
S 72 q   Eden, D. R. A.

The quest for the home of the coconut.

(South Pacific Bull., Vol. 13(3):39-42, 1963)

AS
36
S1   Eddy, William Abner, 1850-
The Eiffel tower.

(*In* Smithsonian institution. Annual report. 1889. Washington, 1890. 23½ᶜᵐ. p. 736-743)

"From the Atlantic monthly, June 1889; vol. LXIII, pp. 721-727."

1. Eiffel tower, Paris.

S 15-718

Library of Congress   Q11.S66 1889
Library, Smithsonian   Institution

GN
2.S
P 76

and
DU
Pac.Pam.
51   Edge Partington, James

Extracts from the diary of Dr. Samwell.

(Journal of the Polynesian Society, Vol. 8, 1899, pp. 250-263)

QL
Mollusca
Pam.903   EDENTULINA

Kondo, Yoshio

Report to Invertebrate Consultants Committee for the Pacific (Pacific Science Board) on Gonaxis Kibweziensis and Edentulina affinis. mimeo. 7 pp. June 1951.

GN
662
E 23
(Locked case)   Edge-Partington, James

An album of the weapons, tools, ornaments, articles of dress, etc. of the natives of the Pacific Islands; drawn and described from examples in public and private collections in England...Issued for private circulation by James Edge-Partington and Charles Heape. Manchester. Series 1-Series 2 (in boxes). 1890;1895. Ob4to.
Series 3...drawn and described from examples ...in Australasia. 1898. Ob4to.

GN
Eth
Pam
#503   Edge-Partington, J.

Fishing appliance from Ysabel Island (Bugotu), ex Man, no. 84, Oct. 1915.

GN
Pam
#219

Edge-Partington, J.

Food trough from Rubiana, New Georgia, ex Man, no. 91, 1903.

GN
Pam
2198

Edge-Partington, James

New Zealand Kotahas or whip slings for throwing arts, in the British Museum. Anthrop. Instit. Journ. v.2.

GN
2.1
A-M

Edge-Partington, J.

Solomon Island Basket.

(Man, vol. 6, 1906, no. 46, pp. 73-74, figs. 1,2)

GN
2.1
A-M

Edge-Partington, J.

Hawaiian squid-hook sinkers and slingstones.

(Man, Vol. XVII, 1917, No. 57).

(Short note on mistake made by Captain Cook)

GN
Pam
1631

Edge-Partington, J.

Note on an object of unknown use from the Solomon islands: probably a "tindalo" emblem. Anthropological rev. and misc. n.45, 49, 1900.

GN
2.1
A-M

Edge-Partington, J.

Stone-headed clubs from Malaita, Solomon Islands.

(Man, vol. 8, 1908, no. 90, pp. 164-165, figs. 1,2)

GN
2.1
A-M

Edge-Partington, T. W.

Kite fishing by the salt-water natives of Mala or Malaita Island, British Solomon Islands.

(Man, vol. 12, 1912, no. 4, pp. 9-11)

GN
Pam
2328

Edge-Partington, James

Note on a pataka in the Auckland Mus; note on the genesis of the Maori scroll-pattern. Journ. Anthrop. Instit. v.30.

GN
2.1
A-M

Edge-Partington, J.

Stone-headed clubs from the Outer Coast of British New Guinea.

(Man, vol. 2, 1902, no. 44, pp. 58-59)

GN
2.1
A-M

Edge-Partington, J.

Maori burial chests (Atamira or Tupa-Pakau).

(Man, vol. 9, 1909, no. 18, pp. 36-37, with figure).

GN
Pam
2457

Edge-Partington, J

Note on a shell adze from Ambrym Island, New Hebrides. From Anthrop.Inst. Journ. v.30, (misc). 1900, p. 49.

GN
2.S
P 76

EDGE-PARTINGTON, JAMES

Obituary, James Edge-Partington, Feb. 6, 1854-November 4, 1930.

(Jour. Poly. Soc., 40:247, 1931)

GN
Pam
#228

Edge-Partington, J.

Maori scroll patterns, ex Man no. 21, 1903.

GN
Pam
2329

Edge-Partington, James

Note on a stone battle-axe from New Zealand. Journ. Anthrop. Inst. v.2, n.3-4

AP
2
N 4

Edgell, J. A.

Vertical section of a coral atoll.

(Nature, Vol. 153:680, 1944)

GN
2.1
A-M

Edge-Partington, J.

A New Zealand box (Waka).

(Man, vol. 7, 1907, no. 23, p. 33, and fig.)

GN
2.1
A-M

Edge-Partington, J.   (James)

Note on funerary ornaments from Rubiana and a coffin from Sta. Anna, Solomon Islands. By J. Edge-Partington and T.A. Joyce.

(Man, vol. 4, 1904, no. 86, pp. 129-131, figs. 1-9)

GN
2.S
A 51

Edgerton, Franklin

Sanskrit historical phonology: a simplified outline for the use of beginners in Sanskrit.

(Journal of the Am. Oriental Soc., Suppl. no. 5, 1946)

GN
2.1
A-M

Edge-Partington, J.   (James)

A New Zealand flageolet.

(Man, vol. 3, 1903, no. 106, p. 186, illus.)

GN
Pam
#240

Edge-Partington, J.

On the origin of the stone figures or incised tablets from Easter Island, ex Man, no. 7, 1901.

AG
25
Ed

Edgren, Hjalmar

A French and English dictionary, by Hjalmar Edgren and Percy B. Burnett. New York. 1901. Henry Holt & Co. 8vo. xvi + 1252 pp.

AG
35
Ed
Edgren, Hjalmar

An Italian and English dictionary. New York. 1904. Henry Holt & co. 4vo. 452 pp.

Editor's Shelf

EDITING

Skillin, Marjorie E. and others

Words into type: a guide in the preparation of manuscripts; for writers, editors, proofreaders and printers. Based on studies by Marjorie E. Skillin, Robert M. Gay, and other authorities. Appleton-Century-Crofts, Inc. New York. 8vo. 1948c xx + 585 pp.

QL
Crust.
Pam.
545
Edmondson, Charles Howard

Callianassidae of the Central Pacific.

(Occ. Papers, Bernice P. Bishop Museum, Vol. 18, No. 2, pp. 35-61, 1944)

QL
Amph.-
Reptiles
75
Edgren, Richard A.

Notes on the neotropical population of Hemidactylus frenatus Schlegel.

(Natural History Miscellanea, 55, 1950)

GN
z.S
F 47
Edmonds, A. R.

Medical education with particular reference to the Pacific.

(Trans. and Proc. Fiji Society, 6:134-143, 1957)

Z
Bibliography
Pam. 1251
Edmondson, Charles Howard

Charles Howard Edmondson, Bibliography 1906-1951. 5 typed pages.

AS
36
C 53 s
Edgren, Richard A.

The physiology of reproduction in birds;... symposium, Chicago Acad. Sci...

(Chicago Acad. Sci.,Sp. Publ. No. 14, 1959)

QL
Crustacea
Pam.
590
Edmondson, Charles Howard

Additional central Pacific Crustaceans.

(Occ. Papers, Bernice P. Bishop Museum, Vol. 21(6):67-86, 1952)

QL
138
E 24
Edmondson, Charles Howard

Crustacea (Pacific)

Edmondson, C. H. and others

Marine zoology of tropical central Pacific ...pp. 3-62.

AS
763
B-b

(Bernice P. Bishop Museum, Bulletin No. 27, 1925; Tanager Expedition Publication No. 1)

Reading Room

QL
Botany
Pam.
3128
EDIBLE PLANTS MALAYA

Iconograph of edible wild plants of Malaya. (Botanic Gardens and Natural History Museum, Singapore. Publ. by Military Administration, Japanese Military Forces, Singapore, 1944. R8vo. in Japanese. illustrated.

GN
671.H2
H 23
Edmondson, Charles Howard

Animal Life (Hawaii)

Handy, E. S. C.

Ancient Hawaiian Civilization...by Handy, Emory, Bryan, Buck...and others. pp. 283-290. 1933

AS
763
B-b
Edmondson, Charles H.

Crustacea from Palmyra and Fanning Islands, with descriptions of new species of crabs from Palmyra Island by Mary J. Rathbun

QL
Crustacea
Pam. 493

(Bull.No. 5, Bernice P. Bishop Museum, 1923)

Reading Room

QL
708
T95
Edinburgh. University. Anatomical museum.

The marine mammals in the Anatomical museum of the University of Edinburgh...

London, 1912.

AS
763
B 4
Edmondson, Charles Howard

Atyidae of Southern Polynesia. Honolulu. 1935. 19 pp.

QL
Crust.
Pam.
502

(Bernice P. Bishop Museum, Occasional Papers, Vol. XI, No1 3)

Reading Room

QL
Crustacea
Pam. 491
Edmondson, Charles Howard

Cryptochirus of the Central Pacific.

(Bernice P. Bishop Museum, Occasional Papers, Vol. X, No. 5. 1933)

AS
36
S1
Edinger, Ludwig, 1855–
Have fishes memory? By L. Edinger.

(*In* Smithsonian institution. Annual report. 1899. Washington, 1901. 23½ᶜᵐ. p. 375-394)

"Translated from the Supplement to the Allgemeine zeitung, nos. 241 and 242, October 21 and 23, 1899."

\1. Memory. 2. Fishes.

S 15-1035

Library of Congress   Q11.S66 1899
Library, Smithsonian   Institution

AS
763
B 4
Edmondson, Charles Howard

Autotomy and regeneration in Hawaiian starfishes. Honolulu. 1935. 20 pp.

QL
Protozoa
to Polyzoa
Pam.
594
Reading Room

(Bernice P. Bishop Museum, Occasional Papers, Vol. XI, No. 8)

QL
Mollusca
Pam.
845
Edmondson, Charles Howard

Dispersal of shipworms among central Pacific islands, with descriptions of new species.

(Bernice P. Bishop Mus., Occ. Papers, Vol. 18 (15):211-224, 1946)

[Samoa, Canton, Christmas, Palmyra, Wake, Midway, Hawaii]

AG
511
Ed
Edison's handy encyclopaedia.

Chicago. 1891. 16vo. pp 512.

QL
Prot. to
Poly.
Pam.
693
Edmondson, Charles Howard

Behavior of coral planulae under altered saline and thermal conditions.

(Occasional Papers, Bernice P. Bishop Museum, Vol. 18, no. 19, 1946)

QL
401
N
Edmondson, C. H. (Charles Howard)

Dispersal of shipworms in the Pacific.

(The Nautilus, Vol. 60,(2):53-54, 1946)

AS
763
B-b

QK
473.H
S 62

Reading
Room

Edmondson, Charles Howard

The ecology of an Hawaiian coral reef.

(B.P.Bishop Museum, Bulletin 45, 1928.)

AS
763
B-b

QL
376.8
E24

Reading
Room

Edmondson, Charles Howard

Growth of Hawaiian corals. B. P. Bishop Museum Bull. 58, 1929.

QL
Crust.
Pam.
544

Edmondson, Charles Howard

Incidence of fouling in Pearl Harbor.

(Occasional Papers, Bernice P. Bishop Museum Vol. 18, No. 1, pp. 1-34, 1944)

AS
763
B-o
and

QL
Moll
Pam
125

Edmondson, Charles Howard.

... Edible *Mollusca* of the Oregon coast. By Charles Howard Edmondson. Honolulu, Bishop museum press, 1920.

p. 179-201. 4 pl. 24½ᶜᵐ. (Occasional papers of the Bernice Pauahi Bishop museum of Polynesian ethnology and history. vol. VII, no. 9)

1. Mollusca—Oregon.

Library, U. S. Bur. of   Fisheries   F 21-167
(2)

AS
763
B-b

QL
Crustacea
Pam
481

Reading
Room

Edmondson, Charles Howard

Hawaiian Atyidae. (B. P. Bishop Mus., Bull. 66, 1929. 36 pp. + 1 plate.)

QK
936
T 85

Edmondson, Charles Howard

Marine borer resistance of Syncarpia laurifolia.

(Tropical Woods, No. 92, 1947:44-47)

QL
Crustacea
Pam
399

AS
763
B-4

Reading
Room

Edmondson, Charles Howard

Effect of ultraviolet rays in regeneration of Chelipeds. Bernice P. Bishop Museum, Occasional paper, vol. IX, no. 7. 1930. 7p.

QL
Crustacea
Pam.
567

Edmondson, Charles H.

Hawaiian Caprellidae. By C. H. Edmondson and G. S. Mansfield.

(Occasional Papers, Bernice P. Bishop Museum, Vol. 19, No. 10, 1948). pp. 201-218

QL
Prot-Poly
Pam.
714

Edmondson, Charles E.

Marine wood borers of the Pacific.

(Proc. of "A symposium on wood", Washington June 16/17, 1949; co-sponsored by Nat. Res. Council and Office of Naval Research. 14 pp.)

QL
Crustacea
Pam.
506

AS
763
B-4

Reading
Room

Edmondson, Charles Howard, 1876-

Effect of X-rays on regeneration of chelipeds of *Atya bisulcata*, by Charles Howard Edmondson ... Honolulu, Hawaii, The Museum, 1936.

15 p. illus. 23½ᶜᵐ. (Bernice P. Bishop museum. Occasional papers. vol. XI, no. 16)

"Literature cited": p. 13-14.

1. Regeneration (Biology) 2. X-rays—Physiological effect. 3. Atya bisulcata.   36-33709

Library of Congress   GN670.B6 vol. 11, no. 16
————— Copy 2.   QH499.E35
(3)   (572.996)   591.179

QK
Crustacea
Pam.
660

Edmondson, Charles Howard

Hawaiian Crustacea: Goneplacidae, Pinnotheridae, Cymopoliidae, Ocypodidae, and Gecarcinidae.

(Bernice P. Bishop Museum, Occ. Papers, Vol. 23, No. 1, 1962)

QL
138
E 24

AS
763
B-b

Reading
Room

Edmondson, Charles Howard   and others

Marine zoology of tropical central Pacific, by Charles Howard Edmondson, W. K. Fisher, Hubert Lyman Clark, A. L. Treadwell, Joseph Augustine Cushman. Honolulu. 1925.

(Bernice P. Bishop Museum, Bulletin No. 27, 1925; Tanager Expedition Publication No. 1)

Storage
Case
3

Edmondson, C. H.

1 field note book: Christmas, Jarvis, Palmyra, Washington. Whippoorwill expedition. 1924.

Report on Christmas, Jarvis, and Washington islands: Whippoorwill expedition. 1924.

AS
763
B-o
and

QL
Crustacea
Pam. 492
and 70

Edmondson, Charles H(oward)

Hawaiian Dromiidae

In Occasional Papers Bernice P. Bishop Museum Vol. VIII, No. 2, 1922.

QL
Mollusca
Pam.
831

Edmondson, Charles Howard

Natural enemies of shipworms in Hawaii.

(Trans. Am. Microscopical Soc., 64 (3):220-224, 1945)

AS
763
B-4

QL
Crust.
Pam.
524

Reading
Room

Edmondson, Charles Howard

Fouling organisms in Hawaii, by Charles Howard Edmondson and William Marcus Ingram.

(Bernice P. Bishop Museum, Occasional Papers, Vol. 14, No. 14, March, 1939, pp. 251-300, 9 plates)

QL
Crustacea Pam.
641

Edmondson, Charles Howard

Hawaiian Grapsidae.

(Occasional Paper, Bishop Museum, Vol. 22(10)

1959)

QL
Crustacea
Pam
498

AS
763
B-4

Reading
Room

Edmondson, Charles Howard

New and rare Polynesian crustacea. Honolulu. 1935. 40 pp. 2 pls.

(Bernice P. Bishop Museum, Occasional Papers, Vol. X, No. 24)

QL
Crust.
Pam.490

Edmondson, Charles Howard

A Giant Latreillopsis from Hawaii.

(Bernice P. Bishop Museum, Occasional Papers Vol. IX, No. 24, 1932)

QL
Crustacea
Pam.
596

Edmondson, Charles Howard

Hawaiian Portunidae.

(Occasional Papers of B.P.Bishop Museum, Vol. XXI(12):217-274, 1954)

QL
Crustacea
Pam
485

AS
763
B-4
Reading
Room

Edmondson, Charles Howard

New Hawaiian Crustacea. Bernice P. Bishop Museum Occasional Papers, vol. 9, no 10. 1930.

QL
Prot.
to
Poly
Pam
567

AS
763
B4

Reading
Room

Edmondson, Charles Howard

New Hawaiian Medusae. Bernice p. Bishop Museum Occasional papers, vol. 9, no. 6. 1930. 16p.

Q
101
P 18

Edmondson, Charles Howard

Quantitative studies of copepods about the shores of Oahu.

IN Proceedings of the Fifth Pacific Science Congress, Vol. III, pp. 1997-2002, 1933.

AS
763
B 38

Edmondson, Charles H.(oward)

The resistance of woods to the action of Teredo.

(Proc. Haw. Acad. Sci., 14th Ann. Meeting, 1938/1939, p. 23-24. Bernice P. Bishop Museum, Spec. Pub., 34, 1939)

QL
Prot. to
Poly.Pam.
571

Edmondson, Charles Howard

New Crustaceans from Kauai, Oahu and Maui.

(Bernice P. Bishop Museum, Occasional Paper, Vol. IX, No. 17, 1931.)

Q
101
P 18

and
QL
Prot.Poly
Pam.
659

Edmondson, C. H. (Charles Howard)

A recent shipworm survey in Hawaii.

IN Proc. Sixth Pac. Sci. Congress, 1939, (California), Vol. 3, 1940, pp. 245-250.

QL
122
E 24

Edmondson, Charles Howard

Seashore treasures. Pacific Books. Palo Alto. 1949c 8vo. 144 pp.

QK
936
T 85

Edmondson, Charles Howard

Note on resistance of species of Antidesma to marine borers.

(Tropical Woods, No. 79, 1944, pp. 15)

QL
345.H
E 24

AS
763
B-s

Reading
Room

Edmondson, Charles Howard

Reef and Shore Fauna of Hawaii.

(Bernice P. Bishop Museum, Special Publication, 22, 1933)

---revised edition, 1946. iii + 381 pp., illus. This edition augmented by a section on fishes.

Q
101
P 18

also
QL
Moll.
Pam. 926

Edmondson, C. H.(Charles Howard)

The shellfish resources of Hawaii, by C. H. Edmondson and I. H. Wilson.

IN Proc. Sixth Pac. Sci. Congress, 1939, (California), Vol. 3, 1940, pp. 241-244.

Separate.

QL
Crust.
Pam.
546

Edmondson, Charles H.

Occurrence of Lernaea carassii Tidd in Hawaii. ms. 1 page. given to Library Oct. 30, 1945.

[parasitic on goldfish and tadpoles, on the island of Maui]

QL
Mol
Pam
#124
209

Edmondson, Charles Howard

The reformation of the crystalline style in Mya arenaria after extraction, ex Journ. of Experimental Zoology, vol. 30, No. 3, April 1920.

QL
Mol
Pam
#126
232

Edmondson, Charles Howard

Shellfish resources of the northwest coast of the United States, ex Dept. of Comm. Bur. of Fisheries, Doc. No. 920, 1922.

Q
101
P 18

Edmondson, Charles Howard

Oceanographic activities of the Bernice P. Bishop Museum, Honolulu, Hawaii.

IN Proc. Sixth Pacific Science Congress, 1939, (California), Vol. 3, 1940, pp. 111-112.

Q
101
P 18

QH
Nat.Hist.
Pam.
112

Edmondson, C. H. (Charles Howard)

The relation of the marine fauna of Hawaii to that of other sections of the Pacific area.

IN Proc. Sixth Pac. Sci. Congress, 1939, (California), Vol. 3, 1940, pp. 593-598.

QL
Crust.
Pam. 569

Edmondson, Charles Howard

Some Brachyuran megalopa.

(Occ. Papers, Bernice P. Bishop Museum, Vol. 19, No. 12, pp. 233-246, 1949)

QL
Protozoa
& Poly
Pam #83

Edmondson, C. H.

Protozoa of Devil's Lake complex, North Dakota, ex Am. Microscopical Soc. Trans., vol. XXXIX, no. 3, 1920.

QL
Prot. to
Poly.
Pam.
694

Edmondson, Charles Howard

Reproduction in Donatia deformis (Thiele).

(Occasional Papers, Bernice P. Bishop Museum, Vol. 18, no. 18, 1946)

QL
Crustacea
Pam.
583

Edmondson, Charles Howard

Some central Pacific crustaceans.

(Occ. Papers, Bernice P. Bishop Museum, Vol. 20, No. 13, 1951)

QL
Crustacea
Pam.510

AS
763
B-4

Reading
Room

Edmondson, C. H.

Quantitative studies of Copepods in Hawaii with brief surveys in Fiji and Tahiti.

(B.P.Bishop Museum. Occasional Papers, vol. XIII, no.12. 1937. pp.131-146)

QK
Bot.Pam.
2888

Edmondson, Charles Howard

Resistance of woods to marine borers in Hawaiian waters.

(Bernice P. Bishop Museum, Bull. 217, 1955)

QL
Crustacea
Pam. 494
and 72
71

Edmondson, Charles H.(oward)

Stomatopoda in the Bernice P. Bishop Museum.

(Bernice P. Bishop Museum, Occasional Paper, Vol. VII, No. 13, 1921. pp. 281-302)

QL
401
H 39

Edmondson, Charles H.

Teredinidae and its associates.

(Hawaiian Shell News, Vol. II(9):53, 1964)

[excerpts of Dr. Edmondson's talk at the June meeting of the Hawaiian Malacological Society]

Q
Biogr.
Pam.
121

EDMONDSON, CHARLES H.

Naming ceremonies, Charles H. Edmondson Hall. October 25, 1962. University of Hawaii 8vo. 4 pp.

AM
101
U 56

EDUCATION

Dottrens, Robert

The primary school curriculum.

(Monographs on Education, 2, 1962, UNESCO)

QL
Mollusca
Pam.
807

Edmondson, Charles Howard

Teredinidae of Hawaii.

(Occ. Papers, Bernice P. Bishop Museum, Vol. 17, 1942, No. 10, pp. 97-150)

Mss.
Case
4
Hms H
41

EDMONDSON, CHARLES H.

Record of the trip of the GALATHEA, Danish exploratory vessel, 1952, and medals awarded by the Royal Danish Consul at Honolulu, Mr. Frank E. Midkiff.

[medals awarded to C. H. Edmondson and to E. H. Bryan, Jr., among others]

in three folders

GN
400
H 19

EDUCATION

Hambly, W. D.

Origins of education among primitive peoples ...London. 1926.

QL
Mollusca
Pam.
1044

Edmondson, Charles Howard

Teredinidae, ocean travelers.

(Bishop Museum, Occ. Papers, Vol. 23(3), 1962)

GN
488.1
E 24

Edmondson, Munro S.

Status terminology and the social structure of North American Indians. Seattle. Univ. of Washington Press. 1958. vii + 84 pp. sm8vo.

GN
Ethn.Pam.
3180

EDUCATION

Jones, Thomas Jesse

Universality of educational objectives. (Seminar conference on education in Pacific countries, University of Hawaii, July-Aug., 1936. 6 mimeographed pages)

QL
Mollusca
Pam.
1018

Edmondson, Charles Howard

Two new species of Teredo, subgenus Teredothyra, from the western Pacific.

(Occ. Papers, Bernice P. Bishop Museum, Vol. 22, No. 11, 1959)

QH
308.1
W 25

Edmondson, W. T. editor

Ward, Henry Baldwin

Fresh-water biology. By the late Henry Baldwin Ward and the late George Chandler Whipple Second edition. Edited by W. T. Edmondson. New York. John Wiley and Sons, Inc. R8vo. 1959. xx + 1248 pp.

GN
Ethn.Pam.
3874

EDUCATION

Mayhew, Arthur I.

British Colonial Policy in its Educational Aspects. 9 pp. mimeographed

---

QL
401
N

Edmondson, Charles Howard

Vertical distribution of shipworms in Hawaiian waters.

(Nautilus, Vol. 58, 1944, pp. 55-56)

DU
1
P

Education in Pacific countries. Summary of proceedings at Honolulu conference.

(Pacific Islands Monthly, vol.VII, no.2, 1936. pp.15-16)

GN
Ethn.Pam.
3960

EDUCATION

Read, Margaret

The contribution of social anthropologists to educational problems in underdeveloped territories.

(Fundamental and Adult Education, April 1955 pp. 74-79)

QK
Bot.Pam.
2324

Edmondson, Charles Howard

Viability of coconut seeds after floating in sea.

(B. P. Bishop Mus., Occ. Papers, Vol. 16, No. 12, pp. 293-304, 1941.)

GN
Ethn.Pam.
3174

EDUCATION

Adams, Romanzo

Toward a philosophy of education. (Seminar conference on education in Pacific countries, University of Hawaii, July-Aug., 1936). 2 mimeographed pages.

GN
33
S 75

EDUCATION

Spindler, George D. editor

Education and anthropology. Edited and with a foreword by George D. Spindler. Preface by Lawrence K. Frank. Stanford Univ. Press. Stanford, California. 1955. 8vo. xviii+ 302 pp.

QL
Crustacea
Pam.
659

Edmondson, Charles Howard

Xanthidae of Hawaii.

(Bernice P. Bishop Museum, Occ. Papers, Vol. 22(13), 1962)

AM
Mus.Pam.
408

EDUCATION

Conant, James B.

The American high school today. McGraw-Hill Book Company, Inc. New York...sm8vo. 1959. xiii + 140 pp.

Q
Gen/Sc
Pam
No.70

EDUCATION

Thurber, Clarence H.

Fiscal support of state universities .....U.S,Bur. Educ. Bull 1924, No. 28, Washington, 1925.

GN
2.I
P 21 | EDUCATION
Williams, F. E.

The blending of cultures: an essay on the aims of native education.

(Anthropology Report, No. 16, 1935, Territory of Papua)

GN
2.S
F 47 | EDUCATION FIJI
Edmonds, A. R.

Medical education with particular references to the Pacific.

(Trans. and Proc. Fiji Society, 6: 134-143, 1957)

GN
Ethn.Pam.
3165 | EDUCATION GILBERT ISLANDS
Maude, H. E.

Culture change and education in the Gilbert and Ellice Islands. (Seminar conference on education in Pacific countries, Univ. of Hawaii, July-Aug., 1936. 10 mimeographed pages)

GN
Ethn.Pam.
3175 | EDUCATION
Williams, F. E.

Rival aims of education. (Seminar conference on education in Pacific countries, University of Hawaii, July-Aug., 1936. 2 mimeographed pages)

DU
1
M 6 | EDUCATION FIJI
Griffin, A. M.

Education of girls in Fiji.

(Mid-Pacific, Vol. 47, No. 4, April-June 1934, pp. 349-52)

DU
12
B 64 | EDUCATION GUAM
Blauch, Lloyd E.

Public education in the territories and outlying possessions. By Lloyd E. Blauch, assisted by Charles F. Reid. Prepared for the Advisory Committee on Education Staff Study No. 16, 1939. U. S. Gov. Printing Office. Washington, 1939. 8vo. 242 pp.

GN
Ethn. Pam.
3148 | EDUCATION
Lehmann, Fr. Rud.

Die Erziehung bei schriftlosen Völkern.

(Zeit. f. Pädagogische Psychologie u. Jugendkunde, Jahrg. 36, 1935?)
pp. 225-241

GN
2.S
F 47 | EDUCATION FIJI
Lewis-Jones, W. W.

A historical survey of the development of education in Fiji.

(Trans. and Proc. of the Fiji Society, Vol. 6:109-123)

DU
Pac.
Pam.
787 | EDUCATION GUAM
United States Navy Department

Advisory Committee on Education for Guam and the Trust Territory of the Pacific Islands.

Report and recommendations of the Second Field Conference, held in the Marshall Islands, August 9-23, 1949   31 pp.

mimeographed. 4to.

Ao
U.S
Ed | EDUCATION
See also

U. S. Bureau of Education

DU
1
P | EDUCATION FIJI

Population of Moturiki, Fiji, will be "mass educated" next year.

(Pac. Islands Monthly, 20(5):61-62, 1949)

GN
Ethn.Pam.
3176 | EDUCATION HAWAII
Adams, Romanzo

The education of part-Hawaiians. (Seminar conference on education in Pacific countries, July-Aug., 1936, university of Hawaii. 3 mimeographed pages)

DT
524
M 96 | EDUCATION AFRICA
Mumford, W. Bryant

Africans learn to be French. A review of educational activities in...French West Africa, based upon a tour...undertaken in 1935. By W. Bryant Mumford, in consulation with Major G. St. J. Orde-Brown. London. Evans Brothers Limited. n.d. 8vo. 174 pp., 23 pl.

GN
Ethn.Pam.
3166 | EDUCATION FIJI
Russell, James

Education in Fiji. (Seminar conference on education in Pacific countries, University of Hawaii, July-Aug., 1936. 15 pp. mimeographed)

DU
620
F | EDUCATION HAWAII
Alexander, William DeWitt

The development of education in Hawaii.

(The Friend, December 1902, pp. 22-24.)

GN
Ethn.Pam.
3171 | EDUCATION AUSTRALIA
Elkin, A. P.

Australian native policies in relation to education. (Seminar conference on education in Pacific countries, Univ. of Hawaii, July-Aug., 1936. 7 mimeographed pages)

GN
Ethn.Pam.
3178 | EDUCATION FIJI
Russell, James

Education of Indians in Fiji. (Seminar conference on education in Pacific countries, University of Hawaii, July-Aug., 1936. 7 mimeographed pages)

DU
620
F | EDUCATION HAWAII
Alexander, William DeWitt

Early industrial teaching of Hawaiians.

(The Friend, December 1902, pp. 9-11.)

DU
621
H 3 | (Thrum's Annual, 1895, pp. 91-100.)

GN
Ethn.Pam.
3165 | EDUCATION ELLICE ISLANDS
Maude, H. E.

Culture change and education in the Gilbert and Ellice islands. (Seminar conference on education in Pacific countries, Univ. of Hawaii, July-Aug., 1936. 10 mimeographed pages)

AS
36
S1 | EDUCATION - GERMANY.
Virchow, Rudolf Ludwig Karl, 1821-1902.
Study and research. By Rudolf Virchow.

(*In* Smithsonian institution. Annual report. 1894. Washington, 1896. 23½cm. p. 653-655)

"Translation of an address by Rudolph Virchow on assuming the rectorship of the Friedrich-Wilhelm university, at Berlin, October 15, 1892."

1. Education—Germany.

Library of Congress
Library, Smithsonian Institution | Q11.S66 1894 | S 15-880

DU
621
H 3 | EDUCATION HAWAII
Alexander, W. D.

Education in Hawaii.

(Thrum's Annual, 1898, pp. 76-80)

DU
620
M67

EDUCATION   HAWAII

Alexander, W. D.

Historical sketch of education in the Hawaiian Islands, by W. D. Alexander and Alatau T. Atkinson.

(Misc. Pams. Haw. II: 91-102)

DU
620
H 5
locked
case

EDUCATION   HAWAII

Green, J. S.

Female education at the Sandwich Islands.

(Hawaiian Spectator, Vol. 1, No. 1, 1838. pp. 35-48)

DU
Hist.Pam.
112

EDUCATION   HAWAII

U. S. Department of the Interior. Bureau of Education.

A survey of education in Hawaii, made under the direction of the Commissioner of Education. Washington. Government Printing Office. 1920. (Bulletin, 1920, No. 16.)

Also Preliminary edition, containing Chapters I to IV of final report.

GN
Ethn.Pam.
2928

EDUCATION HAWAII

Allen, Riley H.

Education and Race Problems in Hawaii.

(Reprinted from The American Review of Reviews. December, 1921. pp. 613-624. 8vo.)

DU
625.4
G 97

EDUCATION   HAWAII

Gulick, Rev. and Mrs. Orramel Hinckley

The pilgrims of Hawaii, their own story of their pilgrimage from New England and life work in the Sandwich Islands, now known as Hawaii... Introduction by James L. Barton. Illustrated. New York...Fleming H. Revell Company. 8vo. 1918c 351 pp.

DU
627.2

EDUCATION HAWAII

See also

Hawaii. Administrative Reports. Education

DU
12
B 64

EDUCATION   HAWAII

Blauch, Lloyd E.

Public education in the territories and outlying possessions. By Lloyd E. Blauch, assisted by Charles F. Reid. Prepared for the Advisory Committee on Education, Staff Study No. 16, 1939. U. S. Gov. Printing Office. Washington, 1939. 8vo. 242 pp.

GN
671.H2
H 23

EDUCATION HAWAII

Handy, E. S. C., and others

Ancient Hawaiian Civilization, pp.43-57: Religion and Education, by E. S. C. Handy.

DU
Pac.Pam.
566

EDUCATION   HAWAII

Rodgers, C. T.

Education in the Hawaiian Islands. A brief statement of the present condition of the public and private schools of the Republic. n.d. no place. 8vo. 10 pp.

DU
Pac.Pam.
572

EDUCATION   HAWAII

Cook, Katherine M.

Public Education in Hawaii.

(U.S. Department of the Interior, Office of Education, Bulletin no. 10, 1935)

Local
News-
papers

EDUCATION HAWAII

Hawaiian Public Schools.

(New Era and Weekly Argus, I, 1853, Nov. 3, p. 3, Nov. 17, p. 1).

DU
625.3
H 38

EDUCATION   HAWAII

Survey of schools and industry in Hawaii. Honolulu.   1931.   156 pp.

DU
620
H 5
locked
case

EDUCATION HAWAII

Diell, John

Oahu Charity School

(Hawaiian Spectator, Vol. 1, 1838, pp.22-35)

DU
Hist.Pam.
111

EDUCATION - HAWAII

Moore, J. A.

A Paper on Methods of Teaching: the studies of the Primary Course in the Public English Schools in the Hawaiian Kingdom prepared for the Teachers' Convention, held in Honolulu in April, 1889. Honolulu. 1889. Hawaiian Gazette Publishing Co. Print. 51 pp. 8vo.

Du
620
H4

EDUCATION HAWAII

Westervelt, W. D.
The first twenty years of education in the Hawaiian Islands.
x Haw. Hist. Soc. Rep. 1911, pp. 16-26.

DU
Hist.Pam.
90

EDUCATION - HAWAII

First Pan-Pacific Educational Conference, Honolulu, August 11-24, 1921.

Program and Proceedings. Official Bulletin, 1st ed., August 8th.

DU
620
F

EDUCATION HAWAII

Public and private schools in Honolulu.

(Friend, Dec. 15, 1846, pp. 188-89).

DU
625.3
W 81

EDUCATION   HAWAII

Wist, Benjamin O.

A century of public education in Hawaii: October 15, 1840 - October 15, 1940. Honolulu. Hawaii Educational Review. xi + 221 pp. 1940. 8vo.

DU
625.3
F 56

EDUCATION   HAWAII

Fitzsimmons, Lorraine

Hawaii for today's children. A resource unit for grades 4,5, and 6. Univ. of Hawaii. Education Dept. Honolulu. 1954. 4to. v+65 pp.

DU
Hist.Pam.
274

EDUCATION   HAWAII

Taylor, Clarice B.

Wahapaa- a Kauai kua'aina.

(Honolulu Star-Bulletin, May 25, 1940)

GN
Ethn.
Pam.
4023

EDUCATION   INDIA

Lakshmipathy, V.

Memorandum on the need to introduce Polynesian studies in an Indian university.

(Reprinted from Mysindia, pp. 1-4, March 20, 1955)

GN
Ethn.Pam.
3179

EDUCATION INDO-CHINA

Ner, Marcel

Essay on the philosophy of education in French Indo-China. (Seminar conference on education in Pacific countries, University of Hawaii, July-Aug., 1936. 5 mimeographed pages)

DU
406
J 13

EDUCATION MAORI

Jackson, Patrick M.

Maori and education; or the education of natives in New Zealand and the Dependencies. Ferguson and Osborn Ltd. Wellington. 1931 8vo xxxi + 481 pp.

F
1211
M 61

EDUCATION MEXICO

Mexico. Secretaria de educacion

La educacion publica en Mexico a traves de los mensajes presidenciales des de la consumacion de la independencia hasta nuestras dias. Mexico, 1926.

GN
Ethn.Pam.
3170

EDUCATION MALAYA

Keir, Alexander

Native and western elements in the educational systems of British Malaya. (Seminar conference in education in Pacific countries, Univ. of Hawaii, July-Aug., 1936. 11 mimeographed pages)

AM
Mus. Pam.
464

EDUCATION MAORI

Maxwell, Gabrielle M.

Research needed in the education of Maori children.

(Proceedings of a Conference held in Sept. 1961. New Zealand Council for Education Research Bull. no. 9, 1962)

F
1211
M 61

EDUCATION MEXICO

Mexico. Secretaria de educacion

Las escuelas al aire libre en Mexico. Mexico, 1927.

GN
671.N5
M 48

EDUCATION MANUS ISLAND

Mead, Margaret

Growing up in New Guinea, a comparative study of primitive education. London. George Routledge and Sons. 1931. 8vo. xi + 285 pp.

GN
2.S
P 76

EDUCATION MAORI

Parr, C. J.

A missionary library; printed attempts to instruct the Maori, 1815-1945.

(Poly. Soc., Journal, Vol. 70(4):429-450, 1961)

F
1211
M 61

EDUCATION MEXICO

Mexico. Secretaria de educacion

El sistema de escuelas rurales en Mexico. Mexico, 1927.

GN
671.N5
M 48

EDUCATION MANUS ISLAND

Mead, Margaret

New lives for old; cultural transformation-Manus, 1928-1953. William Morrow and Company. New York. 1956. 8vo. xxi + 548 pp.

GN
2.S
P 76

EDUCATION MAORI

Parsonage, E. W.

The education of Maoris in New Zealand.

(Polynesian Society, Journal, Vol. 65(1): 5-11, 1956)

DU
Pac.
Pam.
792

EDUCATION MICRONESIA

Taylor, J. L.

A Pacific island adaptation of American public schools.

(School and Society, 73(1899):292-294, 1951)

GN
23
A 93

EDUCATION MAORI

Ausubel, David P.

Maori youth.

(Victoria University of Wellington, Publication in Psychology, No. 14, 1961)

GN
2.S
P 76

EDUCATION MAORI

Powell, Guy

The Maori school - a cultural dynamic?
(The Journal of the Polynesian Society, Vol. 64(3):259-266, Sept., 1955)

AS
28
E 85

EDUCATION NEW CALEDONIA

Guiart, Jean

Sociologie et administration, Nouvelle-Caledonia, 1959.

(Etudes Melanesiennes, n.s. Nr. 12/13: 7-19, 1958/59)

GN
2.S
P 76

EDUCATION MAORI

Cowan, James

"Ngau-Taringa."

(Journal of the Polynesian Society, 29: 204-206, 1920.)

[transference of wisdom by biting the ear of a tohunga in "articulo mortis"]

DU
Hist.
Pam.
538

EDUCATION MARIANAS

Vandam, I. K.

Second Commander Marianas Military Government Area Education Conference. Report of Proceedings. 7 June 1947. mimeographed. 12 pp

---

DU
1
A 94

EDUCATION NEW GUINEA

Adult education in Papua and New Guinea.

(Austral. Territories, Vol. 3(5):26-28, 1963)

GN
2.S
P 76

EDUCATION MAORI

Hongi, Hare

Concerning Whare-kura; its philosophies and teachings.

(Journal of the Poly. Soc., Vol. 7:35-41, 1898)

DU
Pac.
Pam.
787

EDUCATION MARSHALL ISLANDS

United States Navy Department

Advisory Committee on Education for Guam and the Trust Territory of the Pacific Islands.

Report and recommendations of the Second Field Confrence, held in the Marshall Islands, August 9-23, 1949 31 pp. mimeographed. 4to.

GN
Ethn.Pam.
3169

EDUCATION NEW GUINEA

Groves, William C.

Education and the New Guinea background. (Seminar conference on education in Pacific countries, University of Hawaii, July-Aug., 1936. 6 mimeographed pages)

GN
Ethn.Pam.
3177

EDUCATION   NEW GUINEA

Groves, William C.

The thesis of the "scientific" approach to native education, special reference to the Territory of New Guinea. (Seminar conference on education in Pacific countries, Univ. of Hawaii, July-Aug., 1936.   4 pp. mimeographed)

DU
80
A 93

EDUCATION   NEW GUINEA

McCarthy, Dudley

Education in Papua and New Guinea.

(South Pacific, Vol. 9(10):517-521, 1958)

GN
671.N5
M 48

EDUCATION   NEW GUINEA

Mead, Margaret

Growing up in New Guinea, a comparative study of primitive education.   London. George Routledge & Sons. 1931. 8vo. xi + 285 pp.

DU
1
P

EDUCATION   NEW GUINEA

Native education in New Guinea.

(Pacific Islands Monthly, Vol.VII, no.2, 1936. pp.33-36)

DU
1
S 72q

EDUCATION   NEW GUINEA

van Baal, Jan

Educating the Netherlands New Guinea village.
(South Pacific Commission Quarterly Bull., 3(3):18-22, 1953)

GN
2.S
N 67

EDUCATION - NEW GUINEA

Voors, A.W.

Health education in Netherlands New Guinea.

(Nieuw Guinea Studien, 1(1):24-30, 1957)

GN
Ethn.Pam.
3181

EDUCATION   NEW ZEALAND

(Ball, D. G.)

Education of native children (New Zealand). Report of inspector of native schools...1934. (Seminar conference on education in Pacific countries, Univ. of Hawaii, July-Aug., 1936. 12 pp. folio.)

GN
Ethn.Pam.
3167

EDUCATION   NEW ZEALAND

Ball, D. G.

Native education in New Zealand.
Seminar conference on education in Pacific countries, Univ. of Hawaii, July-Aug., 1936. 18 mimeographed pages)

GN
Ethn.Pam.
2890

ONGTONG JAVA
EDUCATION - SOLOMON ISLANDS

Hogbin, H. Ian

Education at Ongtong, Java, Solomon Islands

(American Anthropologist, vol. 33, no. 4) pp. 601-614. 1931

QH
53
B 63

EDUCATION   PACIFIC

Blanc, R. R. V.

Nature study; a handbook for Pacific Island teachers. Islands Education Division, Dept. of Education, New Zealand. For the Department of Island Territories, Wellington. 1958. R8vo. xi + 261 pp.

DU
1
P

EDUCATION   PACIFIC

Education in Pacific countries. Summary of proceedings at Honolulu conference.

(Pacific Islands Monthly, vol.VII, no.2, 1936. pp.15-16)

GN
1
O 15

EDUCATION   PACIFIC

Elkin, A. P.

Education of native races in Pacific countries.

(Oceania, vol.VII, 1936. pp.145-168)

GN
488.5
K 26

EDUCATION   PACIFIC

Keesing, Felix M.

Education in Pacific countries, interpreting a Seminar-Conference of Educators and Social Scientists conducted by the University of Hawaii and Yale University, Honolulu, Hawaii, 1936. Kelly and Walsh, Limited. Shanghai... 1937. 8vo. viii + 226 pp.

DU
29
P 18

EDUCATION   PACIFIC

Pan Pacific Conference, First, On Education, Rehabilitation, Reclamation and Recreation, Honolulu, April 11 to 16, 1927.

Report of the Proceedings. Washington, 1927.

DU
Pac.Pam.
588

EDUCATION   PACIFIC

Reid, Charles Frederick

The status of Federal control over education in the territories and outlying possessions of the United States. Delivered before the American Ass'n for the Adv. of Sci. Dec. 29, 1934 mimeographed. 8 folio pp.

DU
1
P

EDUCATION   PACIFIC

South Pacific's number one problem- native education system.

(Pacific Islands Monthly, 22(9):9-10,1952)

DU
Pac.Pam.
587

EDUCATION   PANAMA

Reid, Charles Frederick

Paradox in the Panama Canal Zone. mimeographed. 2 pp. folio.

DU
1
A 94

EDUCATION   PAPUA

Adult education in Papua and New Guinea.

(Austral. Territories, Vol. 3(5):26-28, 1963)

GN
1
O 15

EDUCATION   PAPUA

Capell, A.

The future of education in Papua.

(Oceania, 15:277-295, 1945)

GN
2.I
P 21

EDUCATION   PAPUA

Williams, F. E.

Native Education: The Language of Instruction and Intellectual Education.

(Territory of Papua, Anthropology Report No. 9, 1928)

GN
Ethn.Pam.
3173

EDUCATION   PHILIPPINE ISLANDS

McCormick, J. Scott

The language problem in Philippine education. (Seminar conference on education in Pacific countries, University of Hawaii, July-Aug., 1936. 26 mimeographed pages)

DU
Pac.Pam.
481

EDUCATION . POLYNESIA

Buck, Peter Henry (Te Rangi Hiroa)

Polynesian education, I: a story of virile training and swift reactions; II: adolescence and manhood.

(The Friend, Oct. 1928:226-228; March, 1931: 56-58)

[a duplicate of Part I is DU Pac.Pam. 381]

DU
M 6

EDUCATION SAMOA

Keesing, Felix M.

Language Change in Relation to Native Education in Samoa.

(Mid-Pacific Magazine, Vol. 44, pp. 303-313, 1932)

DU
1
S 72 q

EDUCATION TRUST TERRITORY

Gibson, Robert E.

Education in the Trust Territory of the Pacific Islands. A review of the educational system...

(South Pacific Commission Quarterly Bull., 3(1):6, 1953)

Z
Bibliography
Pam.
104

EDUCATION POLYNESIA

Keesing, Marie

Education in Polynesia.

IN
Luomala, Katharine
Specialized studies in Polynesian anthropology.
(Bull. Bernice P. Bishop Museum, No. 193, 1947)

DU
Pac.Pam.
902
a,b

EDUCATION SAMOA

Samoa. Government of American Samoa

Regulation No. 5, 1926
" No. 3, 1933

[in re education]

DU
Pac.
Pam.
786

EDUCATION TRUST TERRITORY

Taylor, J. L.

Schools of the Trust Territory, a challenging venture in education.

(Reprinted from Hawaii Educational Review, 4 pages, February, 1951)

GN
2.S
T

EDUCATION POLYNESIA

Platten, G. J. and others

L'emploi des langues vernaculaires comme moyen d'enseignment scolaire et extra scolaire et les problemes que pose l'enseignement en langues autres que vernaculaires dans le Pacifique du Sud. (Extraits...Rapport...Commission du Pacifique Sud...sur la demande de l'UNESCO)

(Bull. Soc. des Etudes Oceaniennes, Tome 8(8) Whole no. 97, 1951:pp. 293-305)

GN
2.S
O 15

EDUCATION SAMOA

Schwehr, Louis

L'orateur Samoan.

(Journ. de la Soc. des Océanistes, Tome 8: 117-136, 1952)

DU
Pac.
Pam.
787

EDUCATION TRUST TERRITORY

United States Navy Department

Advisory Committee on Education for Guam and the Trust Territory of the Pacific Islands.

Report and recommendations of the Second Field Conference, held in the Marshall Islands, August 9-23, 1949 31 pp.

mimeographed.4to.

DU
1
P

EDUCATION POLYNESIA

Thornton, Jack

School journals for Polynesia.

(Pacific Islands Monthly, 22(6):66-67, 1952)

GN
2.S
O 15

EDUCATION TAHITI

Rulon, Henri Ch.

Organization, programmes et livres de l'École des Freres à Papeete, lors de sa fondation en 1860.

(Jour. de la Soc. des Océanistes, Tome 18(18):120-123, 1962)

AS
36
S1

EDUCATION--STUDY AND TEACHING.

Armstrong, Henry Edward.
The place of research in education. By H. E. Armstrong.

(In Smithsonian institution. Annual report. 1895. Washington, 1896. 23½ᶜᵐ. p. 743-758)

"Reprinted from Science progress, vol. IV, no. 23, January, 1896."

1. Research. 2. Education—Study and teaching. I. Title.

Library, Smithsonian
Library of Congress   Q11.S66 1895

Institution
[a19d2]

S 15-911

DU
12
B 64

EDUCATION SAMOA

Blauch, Lloyd E.

Public education in the territories and outlying possessions. By Lloyd E. Blauch, assisted by Charles F. Reid. Prepared for the Advisory Committee on Education, Staff Study No. 16, 1939. U. S. Gov. Printing Office. Washington, 1939. 8vo. 242 pp.

GN
2.S
O 15

EDUCATION TAHITI

Rulon, Henri-Charles

Les premiers temps de l'instruction publique à Papeete.

(Jour. de la Soc. des Océanistes, 16:9-27, 1960)

GN
270
M13

EDUCATION AND CRIME

MacDonald, Arthur

Abnormal man, being essays on education and crime and related subjects. Bureau of Ed. Cir, of Information, no.4, 1893.

Washington, Govt.Print., 1893. 445p.

GN
Ethn.Pam.
3172

EDUCATION SAMOA

Brown, G. Gordon

Education in American Samoa.

(Seminar conference on education in Pacific countries, University of Hawaii, July-Aug., 1936. 7 mimeographed pages)

DU
626
M 74

EDUCATION TAHITIANS

Lecure, Ph. Rey

Education de Tahitiens en France il y a 100 ans.

(La Terre et la Vie, 43/44:266-273, 1957)

AH
30
Ed

Educational Directory

U. S. Bureau of Education

Bulletin 1925, No.1. Educational directory : 1925. 201 pp.

DU
Pac.Pam.
482

EDUCATION SAMOA

Buck, Peter H.

Samoan Education.

(The Friend, 1932: pp. 346-348,361,404-406)

GN
1
H 91 c

EDUCATION TRUK

Fischer, J. L.

The Japanese schools for the natives of Truk, Caroline Islands.

(Human Organization, 20(2):83-88, 1961)

AH
30
Ed

Reading
Room

Educational Directory
Bureau of Education, Bulletin, 1919, No 71. Part 6. — Libraries and Museums.

AS
36
S5

Educational Institutions

Goode, George Brown

    Origin of the National Scientific
and Educational Institutions of the
United States. In U.S. Nat. Mus. Report
1897, pp. 265-354

QL
1
H2

Milne-Edwards, Alphonse, 1835-1900.

    ... Description des crustacés de la famille des gala-
theidés recueillis pendant l'expédition. Par Alphonse
Milne-Edwards et E. L. Bouvier ... Cambridge, Printed
for the Museum, 1897.

[3]-141 p. xii pl. 29ᶜᵐ. (Memoirs of the Museum of comparative
zoölogy at Harvard college, vol. xix, no. 2)
Each plate accompanied by leaf with descriptive letterpress.
Reports on the results of dredging ... in the Gulf of Mexico (1877-78)
in the Caribbean Sea (1878-79) and along the Atlantic coast of the United
States (1880) by the U. S. Coast survey steamer "Blake" ... xxxv.

    1. Galatheidae. 2. Crustacea. 3. Blake (Steamer)   i. Bouvier, Eugène
Louis, 1856-   joint author.   A 19-1070

Title from Univ. of Chicago   QL1.H375   vol. 19, no. 2
Printed by L. C.   [3]

QL
1
A

Edwards - *A. Milne.*

*Note sur l'appareil gastro-
vasculaire de quelques acalèphes
Sténophores.*

*In An. d. Sc. Nat. 1ᵉ An. 4ᵉ Série
Vol. VII. no 5   pp. 285-298. pl. xv*

AM
101
Miscel.
Guides
A-K

Educational Museum. St. Louis.

    Catalogue of the Educational Museum
of the St. Louis Public Schools.

    n.p.; n.d., pp 126

QL
1
H2

Milne-Edwards, Alphonse, 1835-1900.

    ... Les dromiacés et oxystomes, par Alphonse Milne
Edwards et E. L. Bouvier ... Cambridge, Printed for
the Museum, 1902.

127 p. xxv pl. 31ᶜᵐ. (Memoirs of the Museum of comparative zoölogy
at Harvard college, vol. xxvii, no. 1)

Each plate accompanied by leaf with descriptive letterpress.
Reports on the results of dredging ... in the Gulf of Mexico (1877-78)
in the Caribbean Sea (1878-79) and along the Atlantic coast of the United
States (1880) by the U. S. Coast survey steamer "Blake" ... xxxix.

    1. Crabs. 2. Blake (Steamer)   i. Bouvier, Eugène Louis, 1856-
joint author.   A 19-1072

Title from Univ. of Chicago   QL1.H375   vol. 27, no. 1
Printed by L. C.   [3]

QL
1
H2

Milne-Edwards, Alphonse, 1835-1900.

    ... Les pénéides et sténopides, par Alphonse Milne-
Edwards et E. L. Bouvier ... With nine plates. Cambridge, U. S. A., Printed for the Museum, 1909.

1 p. l., p. 179-274. illus., ix pl. 30ᶜᵐ. (Memoirs of the Museum
of comparative zoölogy at Harvard college. vol. xxvii, no. 3)
Each plate preceded by leaf with descriptive letterpress.
"Reports on the results of dredging ... in the Gulf of Mexico (1877-
78), in the Caribbean Sea (1878-79), and along the Atlantic coast of the
United States (1880) by the U. S. Coast survey steamer 'Blake' ... xliv."
"Index bibliographique": p. 270-274.
"Published by permission of Carlile P. Patterson and Otto H. Tittmann,
superintendents of the U. S. Coast and geodetic survey."

    1. Penæidæ. 2. Stenopidæ. 3. Blake (Steamer)   i. Bouvier, Eu-
gène Louis, 1856-   joint author.   A 21-452

Title from Univ. of Chicago   QL1f.H375   vol. 27
Printed by L. C.   [3]

AM
MUSEUM
Pam
#41

Educational Value of Museums

Newark Association Publication.

By Louse Connolly

Biblio-
film
66

Edwards, Alphonse Milne-

    Etude zoologique des Crustacés récents.

    (Nouv. Archives du Musée d'Histoire Nat-
urelle, Paris, I:177-308, 1865)

QL
1
H2

Edwards, Alphonse Milne, and Bouvier, E. L.

    Les Porcellanides et des Brachyures.
Harvard Museum Comp. Zool. Mem. Vol.
XLVII, No.4, 1923. (Reports of dredging
under Agassiz.... U. S. S. "Blake" 1877-
1880.)

Q
115
M 46

Edwards, A. B.

    Tertiary lavas from the Kerguelen Archipela-
go.

Mawson, Sir Douglas   leader
British, Australian and New Zealand Antarc-
tic Research Expedition, 1929-31. Reports, Ser.
A, Vol. II, Part 5. 1938. pp. 72-100

Biblio-
film
67

Edwards, Alphonse Milne-

    Etudes sur les Ziphosures et les Crustacés
de la Région Mexique.   (Part 5 of Recherches
Zoologiques, Mission Scientifique au Mexique
et dans l'Amerique Centrale.)

AS
162
P

Edwards, Alphonse Milne

    Recherches sur la faune carcinologique de
la Nouvelle-Calédonie.

    (Paris, Mus. d'Hist. Nat., Nouvelles Arch.
8:229-267, 1872; 9:155-332, 1873; 10:39-58,
1874)

QL
1
H2

Milne-Edwards, Alphonse, 1835-1900.

    ... Les bathynomes, par Alphonse Milne Edwards et
E. L. Bouvier ... Cambridge, Printed for the Museum,
1902.

2 p. l., [133]-174, [1] p. 8 pl. 31 x 26ᶜᵐ. (Memoirs of the Museum of
comparative zoölogy at Harvard college, vol. xxvii, no. 2)

Each plate accompanied by leaf with descriptive letterpress.
Reports on the results of dredging ... in the Gulf of Mexico (1877-78)
in the Caribbean Sea (1878-79) and along the Atlantic coast of the United
States (1880) by the U. S. Coast survey steamer "Blake" ... xl.
"Index bibliographique": 1 leaf at end.

    1. Isopoda. 2. Blake (Steamer)   i. Bouvier, Eugène Louis, 1856-
joint author.   ii. Title.   Bathynomes   A 19-1069

Title from Univ. of Chicago   QL1.H375   vol. 27, no. 2
Printed by L. C.   [3]

Biblio-
film
69

Edwards, Alphonse Milne-

    Etudes zoologiques sur les Crustacés recents
des Portuniens.

    (Arch. Mus. Nat. d'Hist. Nat., Paris, 10:
309-430, and accompanying plates, 1861)

QL
Crus
Pam
#151

Edwards, Alphonse Milne-

Milne- Edwards & E. L. Bouvier

*Sur les Modifications que subissent
les pagures suivant l'enroulement
de la coquille qu'ils habitent.*

Ex. Bull. Soc. Philomatique de Paris

Paris 1891.   8ᵛᵒ pp. 151-153

AS
182
H

Edwards, A. Milne

    Description de quelques Crustacés.
In Journ. Mus. Godeffroy. Heft. IV. 1873.
pp. 76-88. (B. P. Mus. Pagination pp. 255-
270)

QL
5
M 65

Edwards, A. Milne-

    Expeditions scientifiques de "Travailleur"
et du "Talisman" pendant les annees 1880, 1881,
1882, 1883... sous la direction de A. Milne-
Edwards, continué par Edmond Perrier.
    Annélides et Géphyriens, par L. Roule;
Coelentérés atlantiques, par A. F. Marion; Hydro-
droides par Armand Billard; Ophiures par R. Koehler; Cephalopodes par L. Fischer et L. Joubin;
Bryozoaires, par L. Calvet. Paris. Masson et
Cie. 1906. 4to. 495 pp.

DU
10
E 26

Edwards, B. B.   editor

    The Missionary Gazetteer; comprising a geo-
graphical and statistical account of the various
stations of the American and Foreign Protestant
Missionary Societies of all denominations, with
their Progress in Evangelization and Civilization.
Illustrated with engravings.   Boston. William
Hyde & Co. 1832. sm8vo. 431 pp.

AS
182
H

Edwards, A. Milne

    Descriptions de quelques Crustaces,
Nouveaux ou peu connus, (in Mus. Godeffroy
Journ., pp. 255-266. Heft IV Tafeln 12 and
13. Hamburg, 1873.)

QE
816
E26

Edwards, Alphonse Milne

    Histoire des crustaces podophthalmaires
fossiles, monographies Des portuniens et des
thalassiniens.

    Paris, Masson, 1861.   222p.   pls.

QH
Nat.
Hist
Pam
#23

Edwards, Charles Lincoln

    The sex-chromosomes in Ascaris felis,
ex Archiv fur Zellforschung. 7 Bd. 3
Heft.

    Leipzig. 1911.

AS
36
S1

Edwards, Charles Lincoln, 1863–

The abalones of California. By Professor Charles Lincoln Edwards ...

(*In* Smithsonian institution. Annual report. 1913. Washington, 1914.
23½ᶜᵐ. p. 429-438. 10 pl. on 5 l.)

"Reprinted ... from the Popular science monthly, June, 1913."

Rhipidoglossa
1. Abalones.

15-1747

Library of Congress　　Q11.S66 1913

QL
537.N4
E 26

Edwards, F. W.　　and others

British blood-sucking flies, by F. W. Edwards, H. Oldroyd, and J. Smart. London.
Printed by order of the Trustees, British Museum.
1939. Aug. 23.　R8vo. viii +156 pp., 45 pl.

QL
536
E 26

Edwards, F. W.

A synopsis of adult oriental Culicine mosquitoes.

(Indian Journal of Medical Research, Vol. 10:249-293; 430-475, 1922)

GN
Ethn.Pam
3375

Edwards, David J.

Polynesian navigation.

(United States Naval Inst. Proceedings,
Vol. 66, 1940, pp. 1284-1288)

QL
Insect
Pam. 899
and 540

Edwards, F. W.

British mosquitoes and their control. By
F. W. Edwards and S. P. James. (British Museum
(Natural History) Economic Series No. 4a). London. 1934. Second (revised) edition. With four
figures. 30 pp.

QL
489.S
P 11

AS
763
B-b

Reading
Room

Edwards, F. W.

Tahitian Simuliidae.

Society Islands Insects. Pacific Entomological Survey Publication 6, pp. 35-38 (Art. 7),1935.

(Bernice P. Bishop Museum, Bulletin 113)

AS
36
A 5

Edwards, Dorothy L.

A miniature Melanesia. A new exhibition
model at the American Museum shows in miniature
how the manus of the South Seas construct the
necessities of life in their water domain.

(Natural History, Vol. XXXI(5):549-557,
1931)

QL
489.M
P 11

Edwards, F. W.

Marquesan Simuliidae.
IN
Marquesan Insects-I, pp. 103-109. (Art. 9)

(Bernice P. Bishop Museum, Bulletin 98,1932)
Pacific Entomological Survey Publication 1.

QL
435
E 26

locked
case

Edwards, (Henri) Milne

Histoire Naturelle des Crustacés, comprenant l'Anatomie, la Physiologie et la Classification de Ces Animaux. Tomes 1-3, and atlas of 42
pl. Paris. Roret. 1834-1840. 8vo.

DU
12
E 26
2 cops.

Edwards, Edward

Voyage of H.M.S. "Pandora", despatched
to arrest the mutineers of the "Bounty" in
the South Seas, 1790-91. Being the narratives of Captain Edward Edwards, R.N., the
commander and George Hamilton, the surgeon. With introduction and notes by
Basil Thomson. London. Francis Edwards.
1915. 8vo. 177 pp.

QL
536
H 79

Edwards, F. W.

Mosquitoes of the Ethiopian Region. III:
Culicine adults and pupae. Oxford Univ. Press.
1941. 8vo. pp. 1-499. 184 figs., 4 colored
plates.

AS
36
S1

EDWARDS, HENRI MILNE

Berthelot, Marcellin Pierre Eugène, 1827-1907.

Biographical sketch of Henry Milne-Edwards, member
of the Academy of sciences. By M. Berthelot ...

(*In* Smithsonian institution. Annual report. 1893. Washington, 1894.
23½ᶜᵐ. p. 709-727)

"Translated from Annales des sciences naturelles, 1892, tome XIII,
pp. 1-30."

1. Milne-Edwards, Henri, 1800-1885.

S 15-848

Library of Congress　　Q11.S66 1893
Library, Smithsonian　　Institution

QL
686
E 26

Edwards, Ernest Preston

Finding birds in Mexico. Illustrated by
Frederick K. Hilton and the author. Amherst,
Va. E. P. Edwards and Co. 1955. xix+ 101 pp.
8vo

QL
489.M
P 11

AS
763
B-b

Reading
Room

Edwards, F. W.

Mycetophilidae, Culicidae, and Chironomidae
and additional records of Simuliidae, from the
Marquesas Islands.

Marquesan Insects-II. Pacific Entomological
Survey Publication 7, pp. 85-92 (Article 6) 1935.

(Bernice P. Bishop Museum, Bulletin 114)

AS
36
S5

Edwards, Henry, 1830-1891.

Bibliographical catalogue of the described transformations of North America *Lepidoptera*. By Henry Edwards. Washington, Govt. print. off., 1889.

147 p. 24ᶜᵐ. (*Added t.-p.:* ... Bulletin of the United States National
museum. no. 35)

A leaf of errata is inserted between p. 8 and 9.
Smithsonian institution publication 680.
"Principal authors and publications quoted": p. 7-8.

1. Lepidoptera—North America—Bibl.　2. Insects—Development.

S 13-140

Library, Smithsonian　　Institution Q11.U6

QL
535.3
B 86

Edwards, F. W.

Blepharoceridae

(In British Museum of Natural History, Diptera of Patagonia and South Chile...Part II,
Fasc. 2, 1929)

Q
116
G 76

Edwards, F. W.

Report on the Diptera collected by the British Ornithologists' Union Expedition and the Wollaston Expedition in Dutch New Guinea. With a section on the Asilidae by E. E. Austen.

Grant, William R. Ogilvie
Reports on the collections made by the British Ornithologists' Union Expedition and the Wollaston Expedition in Dutch New Guinea. App. pp. 391-424, Trans Zool. Soc. London, Vol. 20, 1915.

G
51
W 17

Edwards, Hugh

The Australian scene: tragedy of the
happy people.

(Walkabout, Vol. 29(10):27-30, 1963)

QL
535.3
B 86

Edwards, F. W.

Bombyliidae, Nemestrinidae, Cyrtidae.

(In British Museum of Natural History, Diptera of Patagonia and South Chile...Part V, Fasc.
2, London, 1930)

QL
489.S
P 11

AS
763
B-b

Reading
Room

Edwards, F. W.

Some Tahitian Mycetophilidae and Chironomidae.

Society Islands Insects. Pacific Entomological Survey Publication 6, pp. 85-86 (Art.16),1935.

(Bernice P. Bishop Museum, Bulletin 113)

QL
Geology
Pam
817

Edwards, Ira

The volcanoes of Hawaii. From Yearbook
Public Museum, Milwaukee, vol. VIII, 1928. pp.
42-64.

Edwards, Milne-

See

Edwards, Alphonse Milne-

AS
36
A 5

EELS

Schultz, Leonard P.

At grips with a giant moray eel.

(Natural History, Vol. 58(1):42-43, 1949)

DU
1
P 12

EELS   MAORI

Hobbs, Derisely F.

How they caught Tangaroa's eels.

(Pacific Discovery, Vol. 7(4):23-28, 1954)

DU
Pac.Pam.
555
532

Edwards, Rafael

La Isla de Pascua. Consideraciones expuestas acerca de ella por Rafael Edwards, que la visito en Julio de 1916 y Junio de 1917. Santiago de Chile. 1918. 8vo. 26 pp.

AS
36
A 16p

and

QL
Fishes
Pam.
574

EELS   ATLANTIC

Böhlke, James

On the occurrence of garden eels in the western Atlantic, with a synopsis of the Heterocongrinae.

(Proc. of the Acad. of Nat. Sci. of Phila., Vol. CIX:59-79, 1957)

QH
1
P 11

EELS   PACIFIC

Gosline, William A.

Central Pacific eels of the genus Uropterygius, with descriptions of two new species.

(Pacific Science, 12(3):221-228, 1958)

GN
Pam
1722

Edwards, T. R.

The juggernath festival in Bengal. From Wide World Magazine, v.4, n.4.

AS
719
A-m

EELS   AUSTRALIA

Whitley, Gilbert

Australian marine eels.

(Australian Museum Magazine, Vol. 9 (2): 60-65, 1946)

Q
115
H 23

EELS   PACIFIC (southeastern coast)

Myers, George S.

Four new genera and ten new species of eels from the Pacific Coast of tropical America. By George S. Myers and Charles B. Wade.

(Allan Hancock Pacific Expeditions, Vol. 9, No. 4, 1941, pp. 65-111)

AS
122
V

Eells, M(yron)

The worship and traditions of the aborigines of the islands of the Pacific Ocean.

(Victoria Inst., or Philosophical Society of Great Britain, Journal of the transactions, Vol. 32, 1900, pp. 58-75; Discussion and comments, pp. 76-86)

QL
Fishes
Pam.
605

EELS   CHINA

Chen, Johnson

A review of the Apodal fishes of Kwangtung.

(Bull. Biol. Dept., Science College, Sun Yat-Sen University, Vol. 1(1), 1929)

EELS

See also

ANGUILLA
OPHICHTHINAE
GYMNOTHORAX (Moray)

QL
838.A55
B 54

EELS

Bertin, Léon

Les anguilles, variation, croissance, eurhylinité, toxicité, hermaphrodisme, juvénile et sexualité, migrations, métamorphoses. Avec 54 figures dans le texte et 8 planches hors texte. Payot. Paris. 1942. 8vo. 218 pp.

QL
1
C 78

EELS   HAWAII

Gosline, William A.

The Hawaiian fishes of the family Moringuidae: another eel problem. By William A. Gosline and Donald W. Strasburg.

(Copeia, 1956, No. 1, pp. 9-18.)

EFATE   LANGUAGE

See

NEW HEBRIDES   GRAMMAR
"   "   DICTIONARY

AS
36
W 2

EELS

Gosline, William A.

Notes on the systematic status of four eel families.

(Journal of the Washington Academy of Sciences, Vol. 42:130-135, 1952)

QH
1
P 11

EELS   HAWAII

Gosline, William A.

The osteology and relationships of the echelid eel, Kaupichthys diodontus.

(Pacific Science, Vol. 4:309-314, 1950)

F
So. Amer.
and
Central
Amer.
Pam. 3

Effler, Louis R.

My flight to Maya-land: a tourist guide. A souvenir booklet. 3rd ed. 1937. Toledo. 63 pp.

AS
36
S 4

EELS

Kanazawa, Robert H.

A revision of the eels of the genus Conger with descriptions of four new species.

(Proc.U.S.Nat.Mus., 108:219-267, 1958)

QL
Fishes
Pam.
576

EELS   JAPAN

Matsubara, Kiyomatsu

On the conger eels related to Arisoma nystromi (Jordan and Snyder) found in the waters of Japan and China. By... and Akira Ochiai.

(Mem. Coll. of Agric., Kyoto Univ., Fisheries Series, No. 1, 1951)

QK
Bot. Pam.
3284

EGERIA

St. John, Harold

Monograph of the genus "Egeria" Planchon.

(Darwiniana, Tome 12(2):293-307, 1961)

QK
Bot. Pam.
3287

EGERIA

St. John, Harold

Note on the fruit of Egeria Naias Planchon.

(Darwiniana 12(3):523, 1962)

GN
1
C 97

Eggan, Fred

Cultural drift and social change.

(Current Anthropology, Vol. 4(4):347-355, 1963)

GN
490
E 30

Eggan, Fred   editor

Social anthropology of North American tribes. Enlarged edition. The University of Chicago Press. Chicago. (1955) 8vo. xv +574 pp.

QK
9
Du

Egasse, E

See Dujardin-Beaumetz

K. 11. A

QK
9
Du

GN
1
A 62

Eggan, Fred

John Fee Embree, 1908-1950.

(American Anthropologist, 53(3):376-382, 1951)

AS
36
S5

AS
36
S2

Eggers, Heinrich Franz Alexander, *baron von*, 1844-1903.
The flora of St. Croix and the Virgin Islands, by Baron H. F. A. Eggers. Washington, Govt. print. off., 1879.

3 p. l., 133 p. 24ᵐᵐ. (*Added t.-p.:* ... Bulletin of the United States National museum. no. 13)

Issued also as vol. XXIII, art. 3 of the Smithsonian miscellaneous collections.
Smithsonian institution publication 313.

1. Botany—St. Croix, West Indies. 2. Botany—Virgin Islands.

S 13-122

Library, Smithsonian   Institution Q11.U6

Q
115
C 28

Ege, Vilh.

Chauliodus Schn., bathypelagic genus of fishes, a systematic, phylogenetic and geographical study. The Carlsberg Foundation's Oceanographical Exp. ...1928-1930...Dana Report No. 31. 1948.

GN
1
I 88

Eggan, Fred

The ninth Pacific Science Congress.

(Items, Social Sci. Research Council, 12(2): 13-15, 1958)

DU
Pac.Pam.
683

Eggleston, F. W.

Data paper on mandates. Institute of Pacific Relations, Second Session, 1927. Mandated Territory of New Guinea, Statistics, 1925-6. 8 pp. 4to. mimeographed.

Q
115
C 28

Ege, Vilh.

The genus Stomias Cuv., taxonomy and biogeography (based on adolescent and adult specimens)

Carlsberg Foundation's Oceanographical Expedition round the world 1928-1930...Report No.5. 1934.

GN
2.8
V 69

Eggan, Fred

The Sagada Igorots of Northern Luzon.

Murdock, George Peter
Social structure in southeast Asia.

(Viking Fund Publications in Anthropology, No. 29:2400 50, 1960)

DU
870
E 30

Eggleston, George T.

Tahiti; voyage through paradise. The story of a small boat passage through the Society Islands. With a photographic log by the author. The Devin-Adair Co. New York. 1953. 9-10(11-14)15-252 pp.

QL
Fishes
Pam.
572

Ege, Vilh.

Paralepididae II (Macroparalepis), taxonomy, ontogeny, phylogeny and distribution.

(Dana Report No. 43, 1957)

GN
2.S
S 72

Eggan, Fred

The Sapilada religion: reformation and accommodation among the Igorots of Northern Luzon. By Fred Eggan and Alfredo Pacyaya.
(Southwestern Journal of Anthropology, Vol. 18(2):95-113, 1962)

QK
Pam
#751

Eggleston, W. W.

The Crataegi of Mexico and Central America, ex New York Bot. Garden Contr. no. 127, 1909.

Q
115
C 28

Ege, Vilh.

A revision of the genus Anguilla Shaw, a systematic, phylogenetic and geographical study.

Dana Report No. 16, 1939.

Z
3291
E 30

2 copies

Eggan, Fred

Selected bibliography of the Philippines, topically arranged and annotated. Prepared by Philippine Studies Program, University of Chicago, Fred Eggan, Director; E. D. Hester, Associate Director. Preliminary Edition. Human Relations Area Files, Behavior Science Bibliographies. Yale University. 1956. 8vo. vi + 138 +(12)pp.

QH
1
A 51

Eggleton, Frank E.

Fresh-water communities.

(The American Midland Naturalist, Vol.21, 1939, pp. 56-74)

QK
1
Ca

Egerod, Lois Eubank

An analysis of the siphonous Chlorophycophyta, with special reference to the Siphonocladales Siphonales, and Dasycladales of Hawaii.

(University of Calif. Pub. in Botany, 25(5) 1952)

GN
490
E 30

Eggan, Fred

Social anthropology methods and results.

IN

Eggan, Fred   editor

Social anthropology of North American tribes. Enlarged edition. The University of Chicago Press. Chicago. (1955) 8vo. pp. 485-551

AS
36
S

EGGS AND NESTS OF BIRDS

Bendire, Charles Emil, 1836-1897.
... Life histories of North American birds with special reference to their breeding habits and eggs, with twelve lithographic plates. By Charles Bendire ... Washington, Govt. print. off., 1892.

x, 446 p. XII col. pl. 33ᵐᵐ. (Smithsonian contributions to knowledge. [vol. XXVIII])

Smithsonian institution publication 840.
Issued also as a Special bulletin of the United States National museum. Published at the joint expense of the Smithsonian institution and the United States National museum.

1. Birds—North America. 2. Birds—Eggs and nests. I. Title.

S 13-106

Library, Smithsonian   Institution Q11.S68

QL
675
·Ca·
C 18

EGGS AND NESTS OF BIRDS
Campbell, Archibald James.
Nests and eggs of Australian birds, including the geographical distribution of the species and popular observations thereon, by Archibald James Campbell ... With map, 28 coloured plates and 131 photographic illustrations. Sheffield, Printed for the author by Pawson & Brailsford, 1901. 1900
2 v. front. (port.) pl. (partly col.) map. 26½ᶜᵐ.

Paged continuously.

1. Birds—Australia. 2. Eggs. 3. Nests.

3-7889

Library of Congress   QL675.✶C18

QK
Bot.Pam.
2520

Egler, Frank E.
Arid southeast Oahu vegetation, Hawaii.

(Ecological Monographs, 17:383-435, 1947)

AP
2
S 35

and

QE
Geol.Pam
1076

Egler, Frank E.
Unrecognized arid Hawaiian soil erosion.

(Science, Vol. 94, 1941, pp. 513-514)

AS
36
S

AS
36
S5

EGGS OF BIRDS
Bendire, Charles Emil, 1836-1897.
... Life histories of North American birds, from the parrots to the grackles, with special reference to their breeding habits and eggs, by Charles Bendire ... with seven lithographic plates. Washington, Smithsonian institution, 1895.
ix, 518 p. vii col. pl. 31½ᶜᵐ. (Smithsonian contributions to knowledge. [vol. XXXII])
Smithsonian institution publication 985.
Each plate preceded by leaf with descriptive letterpress.
Issued also as a Special bulletin of the United States National museum.
Published at the joint expense of the Smithsonian institution and the United States National museum.
1. Birds—North America. 2. Birds—Eggs and nests.

3-18191

Library of Congress   Q11.S68 vol. 32
——— Reissue.   (U. S. National museum. Special
bulletin. no.1)   Q11.U7 no.1
——— Copy 2.   QL698.B45

QH
541
E

and

QK
Bot.Pam
2347

Egler, Frank E.
Indigene versus alien in the development of arid Hawaiian vegetation.

(Ecology, Vol. 23, No. 1, 1942, pp. 14-23)

QK
Bot.Pam.
2227

over

Egler, Frank E.
Vegetation zones of Oahu, Hawaii.

(Empire Forestry Journal, Vol. 18, 1939, pp. 44-57)

QL
Birds
Pam.
466

EGGS PENGUIN
Budd, G. M.
A dwarf egg of the Emperor penguin.

(The Emu, 61:203-208, 1961)

QK
Bot.Pam.
2245

Egler, Frank E.
A key to the common Leguminosae of the Hawaiian Islands, based upon characters of fruit and leaf. mimeographed at the New York State College of Forestry, January, 1940. 4to. iv + 42 pp.

2 copies

AS
36
S5

Egleston, Thomas, 1832-1900.
Catalogue of minerals and synonyms. By T. Egleston ... Washington, Govt. print. off., 1887.
6, 6a-6d, 7-198 p. 24ᶜᵐ. (Added t-p.: ... Bulletin of the United States National museum. no. 33)
Smithsonian institution publication 674.

1. Mineralogy—Nomenclature.

S 13-138

Library, Smithsonian   Institution Q11.U6

GN
1
An

Egidi, V. M.
Casa e villagio, sottotribù e tribù dei Kuni (Nuova Guinea Inglese).

(Anthropos. Bd.IV. 1909. pp.387-404)

QK
Bot.Pam.
2001

AS
763
B-4

Reading
Room

Egler, Frank E.
A new species of Hawaiian Portulaca.

(B.P.Bishop Museum Occ.Papers, vol.XIII, no.15. August 1, 1937. pp.167-170)

AS
36
S2

Egleston, Thomas, 1832-1900.
... Catalogue of minerals, with their formulas, etc. Prepared for the Smithsonian institution. By T. Egleston. Washington, Smithsonian institution, 1863.
xiii, 42 p. 23½ᶜᵐ. (Smithsonian miscellaneous collections. [vol. VII, art. IX])
Publication 156.

1. Mineralogy—Classification.

16-5466

Library of Congress   Q11.S7 vol. 7, art. 9
——— Copy 2.   Q11.S7 2d set

GN
1
An

Egidi, V. M.
Mythes et légendes des Kuni, British New Guinea. Anthropos, Bd. VIII. 1913. pp. 978-1009; Bd.IX. 1914, pp.81-97, 392-404)

QK
1
F 29

and

QK
Bot.Pam.
2226

Egler, Frank E.
Reduction of *Portulaca caumii* F. Brown to *P. villosa* Chamisso.

(Repertorium spec. nov. regni veg. (Fedde) Vol. 44, 1938, pp. 264-265)

AS
36
S1

Egleston, Thomas, 1832-1900.
Scheme for the qualitative determination of substances by the blow-pipe. By T. Egleston, E. M.
(*In* Smithsonian institution. Annual report. 1872. Washington, 1873. 23½ᶜᵐ. p. [219]-222)

1. Blowpipe.

S 15-336

Library of Congress   Q11.S66 1872
Library, Smithsonian   Institution

GN
1
An

Egidi, P. V. M.
Questioni riguardanti la costituzione fisica dei Kuni (Nuova Guinea Inglese).

(Anthropos. Bd.V. 1910. pp.748-755)

QK
Bot.Pam.
2180

Egler, Frank E.
Santalum ellipticum, a restatement of Gaudichaud's species.

(Bernice P.Bishop Museum, Occasional Papers, Vol.14, 1939, pp. 349-357)

QK
Bot.Pam.
3268

EGREGIA
Chapman, V. J.
A contribution to the ecology of Egregia laevigata Setchell. 1. Taxonomic status and morphology. II. Desiccation...III. Photosynthesis and respiration; conclusions.

(Botanica Marina, 3(3/4):33-55;101-122, 1962)

GN
1
An

Egidi, V. M.
La religione e le conoscenze naturali dei Kuni (Nuova Guinea Inglese).

(Anthropos. vol.VIII. 1913. pp.202-218)

QK
Bot.Pam.
2741

Egler, Frank E.
The terminology of floral types.

(Biologia II, 1950/51; Chron. Bot. 12(4/6), 1951:169-173)

EGRET, CATTLE
See
BUBULCUS
CATTLE EGRET

QL
1
P 15
    Eguchi, M.

        A systematic study of the reef-building corals of the Palao Islands.

        (Palao Tropical Biological Station Studies, No. 3, 1938, pp. 325-390)

Z
3651
C 77
  EGYPT BIBLIOGRAPHY

    Cook, William Burt   Jr.

        Catalogue of the Egyptological library and other books from the collection of the late Charles Edwin Wilbour. Brooklyn Museum. Brooklyn. 1924. R8vo. vi + 795 pp.

  EGYPT STONE IMPLEMENTS

    see

STONE IMPLEMENTS EGYPT

QL
1
P 15
    Eguchi, Motoki

    Abe, Noboru

        Preliminary survey of the coral reef of Iwayama Bay, Palao, by Noboru Abe, Motoki Eguchi and Fujio Hiro.

        (Palao Tropical Biological Station Studies, No.1, 1937. pp.17-35)

  EGYPT CRANIOLOGY

    see

CRANIOLOGY EGYPT

  EGYPT TRANSPORTATION

    see

TRANSPORTATION EGYPT

QL
377.C 5
Y 11
    Eguchi, Motoki

    Yabe, Hisakatsu

        Recent reef-building corals from Japan and the South Sea Islands under the Japanese Mandate, by Hisakatsu Yabe, Toshio Sugiyama and Motoki Eguchi.

        (Science Repts, Tohoku Imp. Univ., Ser. 2, Special Vol. No. 1, 1936)

  EGYPT ETHNOLOGY

    see

ETHNOLOGY EGYPT

GN
865.E
M 64
  Egyptological Researches

    Müller, W. M.

GN
865.N
E 32
  Egypt, Ministry of Finance. Survey Department

    Archaeological Survey of Nubia.
    Vol.I. Report for 1908-1909, by C. M. Firth.
        Plates and plans accompanying Vol. I.
    Vol.II. Report for 1907-1908: Report on the human remains, by G. Elliot Smith and F. Wood Jones.
        Plates accompanying Vol. II.
    Cairo. Government Press. 1910-1912. Folio.
    4 vols.

  EGYPT HORSES

    see

HORSES EGYPT

QL
691
E 33
  EHA

        The common birds of India. 3rd edition. Edited with notes by Salim Ali, and a biographical sketch of the author by W. T. Loke. Thacker and Co., Ltd. Bombay. 8vo. 1947. xvii + 93 pp.

  EGYPT ANTHROPOMETRY

    see

ANTHROPOMETRY EGYPT

  EGYPT INSCRIPTIONS

    see

INSCRIPTIONS EGYPT

QE
501
E 33
  Ehara, Shingo

        Geotectonics of the Pacific... By S.Ehara and S. Sawata.

        (various articles from various Japanese geological journals.)

  EGYPT ARCHAEOLOGY

    see

ARCHAEOLOGY EGYPT

PL
Philo
Pam
93
  EGYPT - LANGUAGE

    Erman, Adolf v.

        Bericht uber das worterbuch der Aegyptischen sprache. From Sitz. d. k. Akad. d. Wissen. bd. IV, 1919.

DU
12
E 33
  (Ehlers, Louis A. B.)

        Log of the Anemone, June eleventh to August twenty-ninth, 1906. Colorado Springs. 1907. [dedicatory letter signed by the author] 8vo. (2) + 76 pp.

  EGYPT ART

    see

ART EGYPT

PL
Philo
Pam
95
  EGYPT - LANGUAGE

    Erman, Adolf

        Die flexion des aegyptischen verbums From Sitz. d. k. Akad. d. Wissen. zu Berlin, v.XIX, 1900.

DU
620
P 22
  Ehlers, Sabine

        Pearl Harbor, multi-million dollar enterprise

        (Paradise of the Pacific, Vol. 66(6):13-14, 23, June, 1954)

QL
377.C5
Ehr
E 23

Ehrenberg, C.

    Beiträge zur physiologischen Kenntniss der Corallenthiere im allgemeinen und besonders des rothen Meeres, nebst einem Versuche zur physiologischen Systematik derselben. Abhandl. k.Akad. Wiss. Berlin, for 1832, pp 225 -380.

    [Note. Bound with this - at the back-is Ehrenberg's paper "Über die Natur und Bildung der Coralleninseln .... "]

QL
Insect
Pam
808

Ehrhorn, Edward M.

    Some observations on insect pests, plant diseases, and other agricultural problems, made while in a trip through Fiji, New Zealand, Australia, and Samoa .

(Undated. Trip was made in the summer of 1923.)

    10 typed pages

GN
1
B

Eichhorn, August

    Hawaiische Baststoffe(Kapa) und Werkzeuge zu ihrer Herstellung. In Baessler-Archiv Band VI, pp 176- 203,1922.

QL
377.C5
Ehr
E33

Ehrenberg, C.G.

    Über die Natur und Bildung der Coralleninseln und Corallenbanke im Rothen Meere. Abhandl. k.Akad. Wiss. Berlin, for 1832. Berlin, 1834. 58 pp.,

Note.- This is bound at the back of the volume containing Ehrenberg's "Beiträge zur physiologischen Kenntniss der Corallen thiere.. 1833

DU
M 6

Ehrhorn, E. M. (Edward M.)

    Termites in Hawaii.

    (The Mid-Pacific Magazine, Vol. 42, No. 4, pp. 331-332, 1931)

GN
1
B 1

Eichhorn, August

    Die Herstellung von Muschelperlen aus Conus auf der Insel Ponam und ihre Verwendung im Kunstwerk der Admiralitats-insulaner.

    (In Baessler-Archiv Band V, pp. 257-283, 1916.)

GR
60
E 67

Ehrenreich, Paul

    Die allgemeine Mythologie und ihre ethnologischen Grundlagen. Leipzig. J.C.Hinrichs' sche Buchhandlung. 1910. (Mythologische Bibliothek IV, 1)

GN
Ethn.Pam
3477

Ehrsam, Frederick

    Living in the jungle with U. S. Army knife LC-14-B. (The woodman's pal.) Monograph no. 8, 1943. The Victor Tool Co., Reading, Pa. 16mo. 16 pp.

GN
1
B

Eichhorn, August

    Neuhebridische Spinngewebsmasken mit Rudimenten eines Wangenschmuckes und dessen Verbreitung in Melanesien. In Baessler- Archiv Band V, pp 284- 292, 1916.

GN
Pam
982

Ehrenreich, Paul

    Die ethnographie Südamerkias im beginn des XX jahrhunderts unter besond. berucksichtigung der naturvölker. From Arch. f. Anthrop. bd.3, heft 1, 1904. 15p.

QL
458.A2
P 78

Eibl, Alena   translator

Pomerantzev, B. I.

    Arachnida, Vol. IV, no. 2. Ixodid ticks [Ixodidae] Fauna of U. S. S. R. Translated by Alena Eibl, edited by George Anastos. Published by the American Institute of Biological Sciences. Washington, D. C. R8vo. 1959. 199 pp.

QK
653
E4
E34

Eichler, A. W.

    Bluthendiagramme construirt und erlautert von A. W. Eichler. 2 parts bound in one.

Leipzig, 1875- 78, pp 347, 575.

GR
Ethn.
Pam.
No. 37

and

GN
Pam
1493

Ehrenreich, Paul

    Die Mythen und Legenden der Sudamerikanischen Urvolker und ihre Beziehungen zu den Nordamerikas und der alten Welt. Zeitschrift fur Ethnol. Suppl. 1905, 106 pp.

    v. Luschan copy

DU
Pac.Pam.
933

Eibl-Eibesfeldt, Irenäus

    Survey on the Galapagos Islands. Survey carried out jointly by UNESCO and the International Union for the Conservation of Nature and Natural Resources. Brussels, Belgium. 4to. 1959. 31 pp.

GN
6
B97

Eickhoff, Heinrich

    Die kultur der Pueblos in Arizona und New Mexico. Studien und forschungen zur menschen und volkerkunde,.. Buschan

Stuttgart, Strecker, 1908.   77p.

GN
Pam
1062

Ehrenreich, Paul

    Uber einige altere bildnisse sud-amerikanischer Indianer. From Globus, bd.64, n.6, 1894.

GN
Ethn.Pam.
2751

Eichhorn, A.

    L'Art Chez les Habitants du Fleuve Sépik. (Nouvelle Guinée)

    (Cahiers d'Art, Année 4, pp. 73-78, 1929)

GN
Pam
1101

Eicksted, E. V.

    Die "rasse" beim menschen. From die Umschau, n. 1., Jan., 1921.

QL
Ins.
Pam.
161
and
S
399
A72

Ehrhorn, E. M. (Edward M.)

    Mediterranean Fruit-fly (Ceratitis capitata Wied.)

    (Hawaii Agr.& For.Circ.3.) 7pp. n.d.

GN
1
B

Eichhorn, Aug.

    Alt-Hawaiische Kultobjeckte und Kultgeräte.

    (Baessler-Archiv, Bd. XIII, Heft 1, 1929, pp. 1-30)

GN
Pam
1499

Eickstedt, Egon v.

    Raum und rasse. From Zeitschrift der Gesell. f. Erdkunde zu Berlin, n.8-10, 1921.

AS 36 A 5

Eifert, Virginia S.

The story of spices.

(Natural History, Vol. 41, 1938, pp. 214-222)

AS 36 C 51

Eigenmann, Carl H.

The fishes of western South America, Part I. The fresh-water fishes of northwestern South America, including Colombia, Panama, and the Pacific slopes of Ecuador and Peru, together with an appendix upon the fishes of the Rio Meta in Colombia.

(Mem. Carnegie Mus., Vol. 9(1):1-378, 39 pl. 1922)

AS 36 C51

Eigenmann, Carl H · 1863-

... The *Pygidiidae*, a family of South American cat-fishes, by Carl H. Eigenmann. Pittsburgh, Pub. by the authority of the Board of trustees of the Carnegie institute, 1918.

cover-title, p. 259-398. illus. pl. XXXVI-LVI. 33½ᶜᵐ. (Memoirs of the Carnegie museum, vol. VII, no. 5)

Publications of the Carnegie museum, serial no. 101.
Contribution from the Zoological laboratory of Indiana university, no. 164.

1. Catfishes.

18—27479

Library of Congress ⌣ AS36.P75 vol. 7, no. 5
(s19e1)

QL 1 H 2

Eigenmann, Carl H.

The American Characidae. Parts I-V.

(Mem. Mus. of Comparative Zoology, Harvard, Vol. 43, 1917-1925)

AS 36 C51

Eigenmann, Carl H 1863-

... The freshwater fishes of British Guiana, including a study of the ecological grouping of species, and the relation of the fauna of the plateau to that of the lowlands. By C. H. Eigenmann, PH. D. Pittsburgh, Pub. by the authority of the Board of trustees of the Carnegie institute, 1912.

cover-title, xx, 578 p. front., illus., CIII pl. (1 col., incl. 33 maps) 33½ᶜᵐ. (Memoirs of the Carnegie museum. vol. v)

Publications of the Carnegie museum, serial no. 67.
Bibliography: p. 530-554.

1. Fishes—British Guiana. 2. Fishes—South America—Bibl.

12—23721

Library of Congress ⌣ QL632.B9E5
———— Copy 2. AS36.P75

AS 36 C1

Eigenmann, Carl H. and Eigenmann, Rosa S.

A revision of the South American nematognathi or cat-fishes. California Academy of Sci. Occasional Papers, v.1, 1890.

QL Fish Pam 409

Eigenmann, Carl H.

A catalogue of the fishes of the Pacific Coast of American north of Cerros Island.

(New York Academy of Sciences, Annals, Vol. 6, 1892, pp. 349-358)

QL Fishes Pam. 403

Eigenmann, Carl H.

The fresh-water fishes of Panama east of longitude 80° W; The Magdalena basin and the horizontal and vertical distribution of its fishes.

(Indiana University Studies, 47 A and B., 1920)

QL Fish Pam. 399 400 401

Eigenmann, Carl H.

Some results from an ichthyological reconnaissance of Colombia, South America.

(Indiana University Studies, 16, 18, 20, 1912, -1914: Contributions from the Zoological Laboratory, 127, 131, 135)

QL 117 E34

Eigenmann, Carl H 1863-

Cave vertebrates of America; a study in degenerative evolution, by Carl H. Eigenmann ... Washington, D. C., Carnegie institution of Washington, 1909.

ix, 241 p. front., illus., 29 (i. e. 30) pl. (1 col.) 29½ x 23ᶜᵐ. (On verso of t.-p.: Carnegie institution of Washington. Publication no. 104)

This work forms no. 97 of the Contributions from the Zoological laboratory of the Indiana university. cf. p. ix.

1. Cave fauna. 2. Heteropygii. I. Title.

9—19158

Library of Congress ⌣ QL117.E4
———— Copy 2.

AS 36 S2

Eigenmann, Carl H 1863-

New genera of South American fresh-water fishes, and new names for some old genera, by Carl H. Eigenmann.

(In Smithsonian institution. Smithsonian miscellaneous collections. Washington, 1903. 24½ᶜᵐ. vol. XLV (Quarterly issue, vol. 1) p. 144-148)

Publication 1431.
Vol. 45 (Quarterly issue, v. 1) with t.-p. dated 1903, was issued 4 parts in 2, with covers dated 1904.

1. Fishes—South America.

16—11316

Library of Congress ⌣ Q11.S7 vol. 45
———— Copy 2.

QL 1 H1

Eigenmann, Carl H 1863-

... Zoological results of the Thayer Brazilian expedition. Preliminary descriptions of new genera and species of tetragonopterid characins, by Carl H. Eigenmann. Cambridge, Mass. ... Printed for the museum, 1908.

p. (91)-106. 24ᶜᵐ. (Bulletin of the Museum of comparative zoology at Harvard college. vol. LII, no. 6)

1. Characinidae. 2. Fishes—Brazil.

F 11-173

Library, U. S. Bur. of ⌣ Fisheries

AS 36 C51

Eigenmann, Carl H 1863-

... The *Cheirodontinæ*, a subfamily of minute characid fishes of South America, by Carl H. Eigenmann. Pittsburgh, Pub. by the authority of the Board of trustees of the Carnegie institute, 1915.

cover-title, 99 p. illus., XVII pl. (incl. fold. map) 33½ᶜᵐ. (Memoirs of the Carnegie museum. vol. VII, no. 1)

Publications of the Carnegie museum, serial no. 87.
Contributions from the Zoological laboratory of Indiana university, no. 150.

1. Chirodontinae. 2. Fishes—South America.

16-4874

Library of Congress AS36.P75 vol. 7, no. 1

QL Fish Pam #4.

Eigenmann, Carl H.

On a collection of fishes from Buenos Aires, ex Washington Acad. of Sc. Proc., vol. VIII, March 4, 1907.

QL Fish Pam #5

Eigenmann, C. H. & Ward, David Perkins

The Gymnotidae, ex Washington Acad. of Sc. Proc., vol. VII, June 20, 1905.

QL Fish Pam 300

Eigenmann, Carl H

The Eyes of the blind vertebrates of North America. V. The History of the eye of the blind fish amblyopsis from its appearance to its disintegration in old age. From Mark Anniversary Vol. Article 9, 1903.

QL Fish Pam. 402

Eigenmann, Carl H.

On new species of fishes from the Rio Meta.. Colombia, and on albino fishes from near Bogota.

(Indiana University Studies, 23, 1914)

DU 1 P 16

Eighth Pacific Science Congress.

(Pacific Science Association, Information Bulletin, PS/53/8, 1953)

QL 632 E 34

Eigenmann, Carl H.

Fishes of western South America. I. The intercordilleran and Amazonian lowlands of Peru; II. The high pampas of Peru, Bolivia, and northern Chile. With a revision of the Peruvian Gymnotidae, and of the genus Orestias. The University of Kentucky. Lexington. 1942. 4to. xv + 494 pp.

AS 36 C51

Eigenmann, Carl H 1863-

... *Pimelodella* and *Typhlobagrus*, by Carl H. Eigenmann. Pittsburgh, Pub. by the authority of the Board of trustees of the Carnegie institute, 1917.

cover-title, p. 229-258. illus., pl. XXIX-XXXV. 34ᶜᵐ. (Memoirs of the Carnegie museum. vol. VII. no. 4)

Publications of the Carnegie museum, serial no. 94.
Contribution from the Zoological laboratory of Indiana university, no. 154.

1. Pimelodella. 2. Typhlobagrus.

17-17210

Library of Congress AS36.P75 vol. 7, no. 4

Q 101 P 18

Eighth Pacific Science Congress and the Fourth Far-Eastern Prehistory Congress, November 16-28, 1953, Diliman, Quezon City, Philippines. (popular description) 4to. 77 pp.

Q
101
P 18

Eighth Pacific Science Congress and the Fourth Far-Eastern Prehistory Congress.

Proceedings
Part I: Prehistory, archaeology and physical anthropology, fasc. 1, 1956

Nat. Res. Council, Philippines. Diliman, Quezon City. 1956   8vo

---

Q
115
C 28

Einarsson, Hermann

Euphausiacea, 1. Northern Atlantic species. Dana Report No. 27, 1945.

QK
495.M8
E 34

Eisen, Gustav

The fig: its history, culture, and curing, with a descriptive catalogue of the known varieties of figs.

(U. S. Department of Agriculture, Div. of Pomology, Bull. 9, 1901. 317 pp.)

AP
2
N 28

Eighth Pacific Science Congress: meeting in the Philippines.

(Nature, Vol. 171(4360):913-914, 1953)

AS
36
C8

EINSTEIN, ALBERT, 1879

Page, Leigh.
... The principle of general relativity and Einstein's theory of gravitation, by Leigh Page ... New Haven, Conn., Connecticut academy of arts and sciences [1920]

p. [383]-416. 24½ᵐ. (Transaction of the Connecticut academy of arts and sciences, v. 23)

1. Relativity (Physics) 2. Einstein, Albert, 1879–   I. Title.

Title from Yale Univ.   Printed by L. C.   A 21-519

161

AS
36
C

Eisen, Gustav, 1847–
... On California *Eudrilidæ*. By Gustav Eisen. San Francisco, Cal., 1894.

cover-title, p. [21]-62. pl. XII-XXIX. 30½ x 24½ᵐ. (Memoirs of the California academy of sciences. vol. II, no. 3)
Papers referred to: p. 57.

1. Eudrilidæ.   *Vermes*   2. Worms—California.

Library of Congress   Q11.C17 vol. 2, no. 3   13-24575

Q
101
P 18

Eighth Pacific Science Congress of the Pacific Science Association and the Fourth Far-Eastern Prehistory Congress. Abstracts of papers Published by the Organizing Committee. Quezon City. 1953. 8vo. 559 pp.

...Abstracts of papers supplement. 89 pp.

EIPHOSOMA

AS
36
S4

Cockerell, Theodore Dru Alison, 1866–
New parasitic *Hymenoptera* of the genus *Eiphosoma* ...

(*In* U. S. National museum. Proceedings. Washington, 1914. 23½ᵐ. v. 46, p. 61-64)

1. Eiphosoma.

Library of Congress   Q11.U55 vol. 46   14-10967

AS
36
C

Eisen, Gustav, 1847–
On some ancient sculptures from the Pacific slope of Guatemala. By Gustav Eisen. San Francisco, Cal., 1888.

cover-title, p. [9]-20. pl. I-XI. 30½ x 24½ᵐ. (Memoirs of the California academy of sciences. vol. II, no. 2)

1. Archaeology—Guatemala   1. Guatemala—Antiq.

Library of Congress   Q11.C17   vol. 2, no. 2   13-24574

Q
101
P 18

Eighth Pacific Science Congress of the Pacific Science Association. Campus of the University of the Philippines, November 16 to 28, 1953
Circular of information, July, 1953

8vo. 77 pp.

QH
366
E 36

Eiseley, Loren

Darwin's century: evolution and the men who discovered it. Doubleday Anchor Books. 1958. New York. 8vo. xvii + 378 pp.

AS
36
C

Eisen, Gustav, 1847–
... On the anatomy of the *Sutroa rostrata*, a new annelid of the family of *Lumbriculina*. By Gustav Eisen. San Francisco, Cal., 1888.

cover-title, 8 p. II col. pl. 30½ x 24½ᵐ. (Memoirs of the California academy of sciences. vol. II, no. 1)

1. Sutroa-rostrata. 2. Worms—Anatomy.   *Annelida*

Library of Congress   Q11.C17   vol. 2, no. 1   13-24573

GN
663
T 44

Eilers, Anneliese

Inseln um Ponape

Thilenius, G.

Ergebnisse der Südsee Expedition, 1908-1910, II. Ethnographie: B. Mikronesien, Bd. 8. 1934.

GN
663
T 44

MS. Translation, typed, 103 pp. excerpts
Kapingamarangi,   Nukuoro

Q
171
E 36

Eiseley, Loren

The immense journey. London. Victor Gollancz Ltd. 1958. sm8vo. 210 pp.

AS
36
C

Eisen, Gustav, 1847–
... Pacific coast *Oligochæta* ... By Gustav Eisen. San Francisco, Cal., 1895-96.

cover-title, p. [63]-198. pl. XXX-LVII (part col., part fold.) 2 fold. tab. 30½ x 24½ᵐ. (Memoirs of the California academy of sciences. vol. II, no. 4 and 5)
Literature: p. 84 and 174.
CONTENTS.—I. *Phænicodrilus taste; Pontodrilus Michælseni; Eclipidrilus frigidus.*—II. *Benhamia, Acanthodrilus, Alcodrilus, Sparganophilus, Deltania, Phænicodrilus.*

1. Oligochæta.   *Vermes*   2. Worms—Pacific coast.

Library of Congress   Q11.C17   vol. 2, no. 4-5   13-24576

GN
663
T 44

Eilers, Anneliese
West-Karolinen.

Thilenius, Georg (editor)

Ergebnisse der Südsee Expedition, 1908-1910. II. Ethnographie: B. Mikronesien, Bd. 9: West-karolinen von Anneliese Eilers. Halbband I-II. 1935-1936.

QL
Protozoa
to
Polyzoa
Pam
348

Eisen, Gustaf

Bidrag till kannedomen om pennatulidslagtet Renilla Lamk. From K. Svenska Vet. Akad. Hand., v.13, n.1.

QL
1
C

Eisen, Gustav, 1847–
... Plasmocytes; the survival of the centrosomes and archoplasm of the nucleated erythrocytes, as free and independent elements in the blood of *Batrachoseps attenuatus* Esch. By Gustav Eisen ... San Francisco, The Academy, 1897.

72 p. illus., II col. fold. pl. 25½ᵐ. (Proceedings of the California academy of sciences. 3d ser. Zoology. vol. I, no. 1)
"Issued April 1, 1897."
Bibliography: p. 64-65.

1. Blood—Corpuscles and platelets. 2. Batrachoseps.   I. Title.

Library of Congress   Q11.C25 vol. 1, no. 1   16-22007
———— Separate.   QP91.E36

Q
Bird
Pam
#68
4to

Eimer, Th. und Fickert, C.

Die Artbildung und Verwandtschaft bei den Schwimmvögeln nach deren Zeichnung dargestellt.

Halle, 1899.

(Nova Acta, Abh. der K. Leop.-Carol. Deutschen Akad. der Natur., Bd LXXVII, Nr. 1)

QL
Protozoa
to
Polyzoa
Pam
513

Eisen, Gustaf

Bidrag till skandinaviens oligochaetfauna. From K. Vet. Akad. Forh., 1870; n.10.

QL
1
C
and
QL
391.O 4
E 36

Eisen, Gustav, 1847–
... Researches in American *Oligochæta*, with especial reference to those of the Pacific coast and adjacent islands. By Gustav Eisen ... San Francisco, The Academy, 1900.

1 p. l., p. 85-276. illus., pl. V-XIV (fold., 9 col.) fold. tab. 25½ᵐ. (Proceedings of the California academy of sciences. 3d ser. Zoology. vol. II, no. 2)
"Issued January 20, 1900."
Bibliography: p. 251-253.

1. Oligochæta.   2. Worms—North America.

Library of Congress   Q11.C25 vol. 2, no. 2   16-22015

GN
Ethn.Pam.
3509

Eisenhart, Otto

    Acht Monate unter den Eingeborenen auf Ailu (Marshalls-Gruppe).

    (Aus Allen Welttheilen, XIX:207-8, 223-6, 250-2, 1888)

QE
201
P

Ejutla, Oaxaca, México.—Estudio de una muestra de Grafita de Ejutla, Oaxaca, por el Ingeniero Juan D. Villarello.—*Parergones del Instituto Geológico de México.* Tomo I, núm. 7, págs. 213–228. 1904. 8?

N.16   JUN 30 1905

PL
670
E 36

    Ekonejeu kabesi ni dokuj Iesu Keriso, hna ureie wene ri pene eleni jeu' o re pene nengone. London. 1870. 399 pp. 8vo.

    (Mare, Loyalty Is. New Testament)

QL
671
C 74

Eisenmann, Eugene

    Galapagos penguin in Panama.

    (The Condor, Vol. 58(1):74-75, 1956)

QE
Geol.Pam.
818

Ekblaw, George E.

    Typical Rooks and Minerals in Illinois, by George E. Ekblaw and Don L. Carroll; 79 pp., sm. 8vo.

    State of Illinois Dept. of Registration & Education - State Geological Survey. Educ. Series No. 3, 1931

G
3
A 1

EL NINO

Marmer, H. A.

    The Peru and Nino currents.

    (Geogr. Review, 41(2):337-338, 1951)

QL
671
E 39

Eisenmann, Eugene

    Observations on birds on the island of Hawaii.

    (The Elepaio, 21(9):66-70, 1961)

AS
36
A 5

Ekholm, Gordon F.

    Is American Indian culture Asiatic?

    (Natural History, 59(8):344-351, 1950)

GN
Ethn.
Pam.
738
to
741

El Palacio

    See

New Mexico Museum

QP
84
E 36

Eisenstadt, S. N.

    From generation to generation; age groups and social structure. The Free Press. Glencoe, Illinois. 8vo. 1956c 357 + (6) pp.

AS
36
A 5

Ekholm, Gordon F.

    review of "Kon tiki". By Gordon F. Ekholm and Junius B. Bird.

    (Natural History, Vol. 59(10):437, 1950)

QK
1
S 67
and
QK
Bot.Pam.
1959

ELAEOCARPACEAE

Guillaumin, A.

    Matériaux pour la flore de la Nouvelle-Calédonia. XLI. Revision des Elaeocarpacées.

    (Soc. Botanique de France, Bull. vol. 83, nos. 6-7, 1936. pp. 485-488)

QH
351
E36

Eisler, P

    Die homologie der extremitaeten; morphologische studien. From Abh. der Nat Gesellschaft zu Halle, Bd. XIX.

    Halle, Niemeyer, 1895. 258p. pls.

QK
228
U 73

Ekman, Er. L.

Urban, Ign(atius)

    Plantae Haitienses novae vel rariores, I-X a ol. Er. L. Ekman 1917-1920 lectas.

    (Arkiv för Botanik, Bk. 17, No. 7, 1921; 20A No. 5, 15,1926; 21A, No. 5, 1927, 22A, No. 8 1928; 22A, No. 10,17, 1929; 23A, No. 5,11,1931; 24A, No. 4, 1931)

QK
1
E 58

ELAEOCARPACEAE

Schlechter, R.

    Die Elaeocarpaceen von Mikronesien.

Diels, L.

    Beiträge zur Flora von Mikronesien und Polynesien. II. No. 21.

    (Bot. Jahrb., Bd. 56, 1921, pp. 562-564.)

QL
Fish Pam.
582

Eisler, R.

    Some effects of artificial light on salmon eggs and larvae.

    (Reprint: Trans. Amer. Fisheries Soc., vol. 87, 1957:151-162)

QL
124
E 36

Ekman, Sven

    Zoogeography of the sea. Translated from the Swedish by Elizabeth Palmer. Sidgwick and Jackson Limited. London. (1953). xiv + 417 pp. 8vo.

over

QK
Bot.Pam.
2715

ELAEOCARPUS

Tuyama, Takasi

    Phytogeographical consideration on the genus Elaeocarpus of the Volcano and Bonin Islands.

    (Natural Science Report of the Ochanomizu University, Vol. 3:68-70, 1952)

AP
2
S 41

Eisley, Loren C.

    Alfred Russel Wallace...

    (Science, Vol. 200(2):70-84, 1959)

GC
231
E 37

Ekman, V. W.

    Studies on ocean currents; results of a cruise on board the "Armauer Hansen" in 1930 under the leadership of Bjorn Helland-Hansen.

    (Geofysiske Publikasjoner, Norske Videnskaps-akademi i Oslo, Vol. 19(1), 1953. Text and plates)

QK
1
U

ELAEOCARPUS   FIJI

Smith, A. C.

    Studies of Pacific Island plants, XV. The genus Elaeocarpus in the New Hebrides, Fiji, Samoa, and Tonga.

    (Contributions from the United States National Herbarium, Vol. 30(5):523-573, 1953)

QK
1
U

ELAEOCARPUS   NEW HEBRIDES

Smith, A. C.

     Studies of Pacific Island plants, XV. The genus Elaeocarpus in the New Hebrides, Fiji, Samoa, and Tonga.

     (Contributions from the United States National Herbarium, Vol. 30(5):523-573, 1953)

QL
461
H-1

ELAPHRIA

Swezey, Otto H.

     Elaphria nucicolora (Guenee), a recent immigrant to Hawaii (Lepidoptera: Agrotidae: Acronictinae).

     (Proc. Haw. Ent. Soc., 13:99-100, 1947)

QL
489
B 91

ELATERIDAE

Van Zwaluwenburg, R. H.

     Itodacnus novicornis, a new elaterid species.

Bryan, Edwin H., Jr.
Insects of Hawaii, Johnston Island ...

     (Bernice P. Bishop Museum, Bull. 31, 1926, pp. 50-52. Tanager Expedition Publication 3.)

QK
1
U

ELAEOCARPUS   SAMOA

Smith, A. C.

     Studies of Pacific Island plants, XV. The genus Elaeocarpus in the New Hebrides, Fiji, Samoa, and Tonga.

     (Contributions from the United States National Herbarium, Vol. 30(5):523-573, 1953)

AS
36
A 65

ELAPIDAE

Bogert, Charles M.

     A review of the Elapid genus Ultrocalamus of New Guinea. By Charles M. Bogert and Bessie L. Matalas. (Results to the Archbold Expeditions, No. 53)

     (American Museum Novitates, No. 1284, 1945)

QL
461
H 1

ELATERIDAE

van Zwaluwenburg, R. H.

     Larvae of Hawaiian Elaterid beetles.

     (Proc. Haw. Ent. Soc., Vol. 10, 1939, pp. 275-279)

QK
1
U

ELAEOCARPUS   TONGA

Smith, A. C.

     Studies of Pacific Island plants, XV. The genus Elaeocarpus in the New Hebrides, Fiji, Samoa, and Tonga.

     (Contributions from the United States National Herbarium, Vol. 30(5):523-573, 1953)

AS
162
L

ELAPIDAE

Hoffstetter, Robert

     Contribution a l'etude des Elapidae actuels et fossiles, et de l'osteologie des Ophidiens.

     (Archives du Mus. d'Hit. Nat., Lyons, 15, 1939, Mem. 3:1-82)

     [pp. 39-75: Les Elapidae actuels.]

QL
461
H-1

ELATERIDAE

Van Zwaluwenburg, R. H.

     Some Elaterid beetles from Australia and New Guinea.

     (Proc. Haw. Ent. Soc., Vol. 13:109-115, 1947)

AS
522.B
Sa

Elam, E. H.

     Slakow and Larah Land Dyaks of Lundu.

     (Sarawak Museum Journal, Vol. 4, 1935, [no. 14], pp. 241-251)

QL
Mollusca
Pam.
818

ELASMIAS

Cooke, Charles Montague, Jr.

     A new species of Elasmias from Rurutu, Austral Islands. By C. Montague Cooke, Jr. and Yoshio Kondo.

     (Bernice P. Bishop Museum, Occ. Papers, Vol. 17, 1943, No. 21, pp. 263-265) Mangarevan Exp. Pub. No. 37.

AS
720.V
M

ELATERIDAE   AUSTRALIA

Neboiss, Arturs

     A check list of Australian Elateridae (Coleoptera).

     (Nat. Mus. of Victoria, Melbourne, Mem. No. 22, Part 2, 1956)
     Additions and corrections...ibid, No. 22(3), 1961

AS
552
K 98

ELAPHOGLOSSUM   JAPAN

Tagawa, M.

     Elaphoglossum of Japan, Ryukyu, and Formosa.

     (Mem. Kyoto Univ., College of Science, Ser. B., 20, no. 1, art. 5, 1951)

QE
Geol.Pam
1045

Elastic properties of materials of the earth's crust.

Adams, L. H.

QL
489.M
P11

ELATERIDAE   FIJI

Van Zwaluwenburg, R. H.
Elateridae of the Marquesas, with a new species from Fiji.
IN
Marquesan Insects-I, pp. 129-144. (Art. 13)

     (Bernice P. Bishop Museum, Bulletin 98, 1932. Pacific Entomological Survey Publication 1)

AS
552
K 98

ELAPHOGLOSSUM   RYUKYU

Tagawa, M.

     Elaphoglossum of Japan, Ryukyu, and Formosa.

     (Mem. Kyoto Univ., College of Science, Ser. B., 20, no. 1, art. 5, 1951)

QL
Insect
Pam.
1864

ELATERIDAE

Hincks, W. D.

     Notes on the Elateridae (Col.) of the "British List".

     (Jour. Soc. for British Ent., 5(6):197-8, 1956)

QL
Insects
Pam.
1166

ELATERIDAE-FIJI

Veitch, Robert

     The Sugar cane wireworm in Fiji.

     (Agricultural Report No. 1, Sydney, 1916.)

AS
552
K 98

ELAPHOGLOSSUM   TAIWAN

Tagawa, M.

     Elaphoglossum of Japan, Ryukyu, and Formosa.

     (Mem. Kyoto Univ., College of Science, Ser. B., 20, no. 1, art. 5, 1951)

AS
3C
S4

ELATERIDAE

Hyslop, James Augustus, 1884–
     Genotypes of the elaterid beetles of the world. By J. A. Hyslop ...
     (*In* U. S. National museum. Proceedings. Washington, 1921. 23½ᶜᵐ. v. 58, p. 621-673)

     1. Elateridae.

Library of Congress   Q11.U55 vol. 58   21-21456
     [4]

QL
Insect Pam.
892

ELATERIDAE   JAPAN

Miwa, Yūshirō

     The fauna of Elateridae in the Japanese empire.

     (Report, Department of Agriculture, Government Research Institute, Formosa, Japan, No. 65, October, 1934)

QL 489.M P 11

ELATERIDAE MARQUESAS

Van Zwaluwenburg, R. H.
Elateridae of the Marquesas, with a new species from Fiji.
IN
Marquesan Insects-I, pp. 129-144. (Art. 13)

(Bernice P. Bishop Museum, Bulletin 98, 1932. Pacific Entomological Survey Publication 1)

QL 461 H-1

ELATERIDAE PACIFIC

Van Zwaluwenburg, R. H.

New species and new records of Elaterid Beetles from the Pacific-IV.

(Proc. Haw. Ent. Soc, Vol. 14(3):437-441, 1951)

Q 115 E 37

Elbert, Johannes

Die Sunda-Expedition des Vereins für Geographie und Statistik zu Frankfurt am Main. Fest-shhrift zur Feier des 75jahrigen Bestehens des Vereins. Bde. I-II, 1911-1912. Frankfurt am Main. 4to. xxv + 274 pp., 29 pl., 3 maps and xv + 373 pp., 31 pl., 7 maps. Druck und Verlag con Hermann Minjon.

QL Ins.Pam. 1011

ELATERIDAE MELANESIA

Van Zwaluwenburg, R. H.

New Elateridae (Col.) from Melanesia.

(Stylops: A Journal of Taxonomic Entomology, Vol.2, Part 8, 1933, pp. 176-185)

AS 773 N 53 z

ELATERIDAE PAPUA

Van Zwaluwenburg, R. H.
Some Elateridae from the Papuan region (Coleoptera).

(Nova Guinea, Vol. 10(16):303-346, 1963)

QK 1 L 52

Elbert, J. E. W.

Ueber die zonare verbreitung der vegetation auf den Lawu-vulkan Mittel-Javas.

(Meded. Rijks Herb. Leiden, No. 12, 1912.)

QL Insects Pam. 1981

ELATERIDAE MELANESIA

van Zwaluwenburg, R. H.

New records and new species of Elaterid beetles from Melanesia. II.

(Annals and Mag. Nat. Hist., ser. 10, vol. 17:368-376, 1936)

QL Insects Pam. 1194

ELATERIDAE SAMOA

van Zwaluwenburg, R. H.

Notes on Samoan Elaterid beetles with descriptions of two new species.

(Occ. Papers, Bernice P. Bishop Museum, Vol. 18, No. 6, 1945, pp. 95-101)

GN Pam 1374

Elbert, Joh.

Die kunst bei den Maronene und ihren nachbarstammen auf der insel Celebes. From "Die Sunda-expedition", bd. 2, 1912.

QL 461 H-1

ELATERIDAE NEW GUINEA

van Zwaluwenburg, R. H.

Some elaterid beetles from New Guinea.

(Proc. Haw. Ent. Soc., 14(2):323-326, 1951)

QL 461 P 11

ELATERIDAE PACIFIC

van Zwaluwenburg, R. H.

Some type designations with notes on Pacific Elateridae (Coleoptera).

(Pacific Insects, 1(4):347-414, 1959)

DU 620 P

Elbert, Samuel H.

Art and language in Hawaii.

(Paradise of the Pacific, Holiday Annual, pp. 34-35, 100, 1956)

QL Insect Pam.862

ELATERIDAE PACIFIC

Van Zwaluwenburg, R. H.

Check List of the Elateridae of Oceania.

(Occasional Paper, Bernice P. Bishop Museum, Vol. IX, No. 23, 1932. Pacific Entomological Survey Publication 3)

Micro-film 98

ELATOSTEMA

Schröter, Hilde

Monographie der Gattung Elatostema s l. By Hilde Schroter and Hubert Winkler.

(Fedde, Repertorium novarum regni vegetabilis, 83(2), 1936)

GN 2.S P 76

Elbert, Samuel H.

Chants and love songs of the Marquesas Islands, French Oceania.

(Journal of the Polynesian Soc., Vol. 50, 1941, pp. 53-91)

QL Insects Pam. 1047

ELATERIDAE PACIFIC

van Zwaluwenburg, R. H.

New species and new records of Elaterid beetles from the Pacific. (I)

(Bernice P. Bishop Museum Occ. Papers, Vol. 16, no. 5, 1940, pp. 91-130)

QL 461 H-1
---II. (Proc. Haw. Ent. Soc., Vol. 11, 1942, pp. 289-300) published 1943

GN Pam 2197

Elbert, Johannes

Die entwicklung des Bodenreliefs von Vorpommern und Rugen. From Deutschen Anthrop. Gesell. Freifswald, 1904.

GN 1 J 86

Elbert, Samuel H.

The chief in Hawaiian mythology.

(Journal of American Folklore, Vol. 69, No. 272, pp. 99-113, April-June, 1956) also pp. 341-355; Vol. 70:264-276, 1957)

QL 461 H-1

ELATERIDAE PACIFIC

van Zwaluwenburg, R. H.

New species and new records of Elaterid beetles from the Pacific-III.

(Haw. Ent. Soc., Proc., 13(2):265-276, 1948)

QK 1 L 52

Elbert, Johannes

Die botanischen Ergebnisse der Elbert'schen Sunda-Expedition des Frankfurter Vereins für Geographie und Statistik, von Hans G. Hallier.

(Mededeelingen, Rijks Herbarium, Leiden Nos. 14, 22, 37, 1912-1918)

GN Ethn.Pam 4133

Elbert, Samuel H.

The chief in Hawaiian mythology.

(Journal of American Folklore, Vol. 69:99-113, 341-355, 1956; Vol. 70:264-276, 1957)

PL
Phil.Pam
580

...Pam.
620

PL623E37

Elbert, Samuel H.

　　Conversational Hawaiian. University of Hawaii. Honolulu. 1951. 4to. vi + 98 pp.

　　second edition, 1955. 4to. viii + 131 pp. By Samuel H. Elbert and Samuel A. Keala. Illustrations by Jean Charlot.
　　third edition. 1961

PL
Phil.Pam.
547

Elbert, Samuel H.

　　Kapingamarangi and Nukuoro word list, with notes on linguistic position, pronunciation, and grammar. mimeographed, U. S. Military Government. (Hawaii). December 1946. 81 pp.

GN
2.S
P 76

Elbert, Samuel H.

　　Phonetic expansion in Rennellese.

　　(Jour. Poly. Soc., 71(1):25-31, 1962)

　　[presented in abstract at 10th Pac. Sci. Congress]

GN
669
C 77

Elbert, Samuel H.

　　Grammar and comparative study of the language of Kapingamarangi; texts and word lists.

　　(Coordinated Investigation of Micronesian Anthropology. Pacific Science Board. Aug. 1948)

DU
500
T 87

Elbert, Samuel H.

　　Language as an aid to understanding.
　　IN

　　Trust Territory of the Pacific Islands. Basic Information. 1 July 1951. pp. 82-96

GR
385.H
F 72

Elbert, Samuel H.

Fornander, Abraham

　　Selections from Fornander's "Hawaiian antiquities and folk-lore". Edited by Samuel H. Elbert; illustrations by Jean Charlot. Univ. of Hawaii Press. Honolulu. 4to 297 pp.

PL
950.K
E 37

Elbert, Samuel H.

　　Grammar and comparative study of the language of Kapingamarangi; texts and word lists. Submitted as the Final Report to Pacific Science Board, National Research Council (CIMA Project) August 31, 1948. mimeographed. 288 pp. 4to.

GN
1
A 62

Elbert, Samuel H.

　　Hawaiian literary style and culture.

　　(American Anthropologist, 53(3):345-354, 1951)

PL
Phil.
Pam.
603

Elbert, Samuel H.

　　Tentative percentages of basic vocabulary in common (Polynesian dialects).

PL
623
P 98

Elbert, Samuel H.

Pukui, Mary Kawena

　　Hawaiian-English dictionary. By Mary Kawena Pukui, associate in Hawaiian culture/B. P. Bishop Museum and Samuel H. Elbert, associate professor of Pacific languages and linguistics/University of Hawaii. University of Hawaii Press. 1957. 8vo. xxx + 362 pp.

2 copies

Storage
Case
5

Ms M 7

Elbert, Samuel H.

　　Marquesan legends. 341 typed pages

PL
568.T8
E 37

Elbert, Samuel H.

　　Trukese-English and English-Trukese dictionary, with notes on pronunciation, grammar, vocabularies, phrases. U. S. Naval Military Government. Pearl Harbor. 1947. 337 pages, 1 map.

PL
Phil.Pam
596

Elbert, Samuel H.

　　The Hawaiian language and its relatives. mimeographed. 2 pp. Jan. 1953. 2nd edition

---

AP
2
N 28

Elbert, Samuel H.

　　Linguistic studies in Polynesia. By Samuel H. Elbert and Alexander Spoehr.
　　(Nature, 174(4427):471, 1954)

　　[an answer to Prof. Alan S.C.Ross IN Nature, Oct. 10, 1953]

GN
Ethn.
Pam.
4131

Elbert, Samuel H.

　　?Ukulele. By Samuel H. Elbert and Edgar C. Knowlton, Jr.

　　(American Speech, Dec. 1957:307-310)

DU
620
P

Elbert, Samuel H.

　　Hawaiian language- "handle with care."

　　(Paradise of the Pacific, 64(2):34-35, 1952)

PL
710
D 61

(Elbert, Samuel H.)

　　Marshallese-English and English-Marshallese Dictionary, with notes on pronunciation and grammar. Prepared by District Intelligence Office, 14th Naval District in cooperation with Commander Marshalls-Gilberts Area, U. S. Pacific Fleet and Pacific Ocean Areas. June 1945. folio. 135 and 121 pp. mimeographed.

PL
Phil.Pam.
546

Elbert, Samuel H.

　　Ulithi-English and English-Ulithi word lists with notes on linguistic position, pronunciation, and grammar. mimeographed, U. S. Military Government. (Hawaii). January 1947. 91 pp.

GN
2.S
S 76

Elbert, Samuel H.

　　Internal relationships of Polynesian languages and dialects.

　　(Southwestern Journal of Anthropology, Vol. 9(2):147-173, 1953)

QH
Nat.Hist
Pam.
128

Elbert, Samuel H. (collector)

　　Native names of fish and marine invertebrates, Truk, Caroline Islands.
　　4 pp. ms. collected 1946

GN
2.S
P 76

Elbert, Samuel H.

　　The unheroic hero of Hawaiian tales.

　　(Jou. Poly. Soc., 69(3):266-275, 1960)

GN
1
J
Elbert, Samuel H.

Uta-matua and other tales of Kapingamarangi.

(Journal of American Folklore, Vol. 62:240-246, 1949)

QL
671
E 39
Elder, William H.

Report on the nene. [reported by Edwin H. Bryan, Jr.]
(The Elepaio, Vol. 18(4), Oct. 1957)

GN
671.N5
W 72
ELEMA

Williams, Francis E.

Drama of Orokolo: the social and ceremonial life of the Elema. Oxford, Clarendon Press. 1940. 8vo. xxiv + 464 pp.

PL
Phil.Pam
563
Elbert, Samuel H.

Yap-English and English-Yap word lists; with notes on pronunciation and grammar. Prepared for Military Government, February,1946. mimeographed. 129 pp.

QL
Birds
Pam.
408
Elder, William H.

A report on the nene. July 1958. Typed, 26 pp. of text; 9 tables

---

QC
20
E 3
Elements of Natural Philosophy.

Haven, _____

(Title page missing).

DU
620
P 22
ELBERT, SAMUEL H.

Morris, Aldyth

The Pukui-Elbert Hawaiian-English dictionary the culmination of efforts covering a period of 180 years.

(Paradise of the Pacific, January 1958:22-23)

AS
720.S
R
ELDER SCIENTIFIC EXPEDITION

Helms, Richard

Anthropology.

(Transactions of the Royal Society of South Australia. Vol. XVI, 1896, pp. 238-332)

QK
Bot.Pam.
1835
ELEOCHARIS

Svenson, H. K.

Monographic studies in Eleocharis-II-V

(Contributions from the Brooklyn Botanic Garden, No. 65, 1932; 68, 1934; 77, 1937; 86, 1939)
(Note: No. 1 is Contrib. Gray Herbarium, Harvard University, No. 86, 1929, pp. 121-242)

DU
870
E 22
Elder, (James)

Periodical accounts relative to the Baptist Missionary Society, Vol. 1, pp. 57-66: A journal of Brothers (Henry) Nott and (James) Elder's journey round Otaheite...1802.

QH
325
Eld
E 38
Eldridge, Seba

The organization of life: a revaluation of evidence relative to the primary factors in the activity and evolution of living organisms, including a factorial analysis of human behaviour and experience

New York, 1925, pp ix, 470.

AS
540
P 55 j
ELEOTRIDAE PACIFIC

Herre, Albert W. C. T.

The tropical Pacific Electridae with vomerine teeth with descriptions of two new genera and two new species from the Marshall Islands.

(The Philippine Jour. of Science, Vol. 82(2): 189-192, 1953)

DU
406
M 36
Elder, John Rawson   editor

Marsden, Samuel

The Letters and Journal of Samuel Marsden, 1765-1838. Edited by John Rawson Elder. Dunedin. Coulls Somerville Wilkie, Ltd. 1932. 580 pp. 8vo

---

DU
620
H 4
ELEANORA (SHIP)

Howay, F. W.

Captain Simon Metcalf and the brig "Eleanora

(Ann. Rept., Haw Hist. Soc., Vol. 34, 1925, pp. 33-39)

ELEPAIO

See

CHASIEMPIS

S
Agric.
Pam. 86
Elder, Noll B.

Sugar in Hawaii.

(Dept. of Public Instuction, Hawaii Economic Education Series, Instructional Booklet No. 1, 1955)

DU
623
C 77
ELEANORA (ship)

News from the Southern Ocean.(an account by one of the crew)

(Cook collection of copies of articles and ms. in the Archives of Hawaii, No. 8) From the Columbian Centinel, Nov. 30, 1791. Boston.

DU
12
L 22
ELEPHANTIASIS

Lambert, S. M.

A Yankee doctor in Paradise. Boston, 1941.

pp. 168-169

QL
671
E 39
Elder, William H.

Objectives of the nene study.

(Elepaio, 17(7):47-48, 1957)

ELECTIONS HAWAII

see

HAWAII ELECTIONS

DU
1
S 72t
ELEPHANTIASIS BIBLIOGRAPHY

Iyengar, M. O. T.

Annotated bibliography on Filariasis and Elephantiasis. Parts 1-3

(South Pacific Commission, Technical Papers 65, 88, 109, 1957)

QL
737.U8
D 42

ELEPHANTS

Deraniyagala, P. E. P.

    Some extinct elephants, their relatives and the two living species. Ceylon National Museums Publication. Published August, 1955. 4to. 153 pp. + 48 plates and 13 text figures

---

QL
Mollusk
Pam
551

Eliot, Charles

    Nudibranchiata, with some remarks on the families and genera and description of a new genus, doridomorpha. From Fauna and Geography of the Maldive and Laccadive archipelagoes, v.2, pt.1.

QL
Insects
Pam.
1288

Eliahewitz, H.

    The ticks of the Pacific region. Research Project NMRI-19. Naval Medical Research Institute, National Naval Medical Center, Bethesda, Maryland. Nov. 17,1943. 39 pp. photostat.

ELEPHANTS

SEE ALSO

PROBOSCIDEA

QL
Moll.
Pam
210

Eliot, Charles (Sir)

    Nudibranchs from the Indo-Pacific: Notes on a collection dredged near Karachi and Maskat, ex Journ. of Conch. Vol. XI, pp. 237-256;298-316; pls.V,VI 1905.

DU
620
H 4

ELIZA (SHIP)

Howay, F. W.

    The Ship "Eliza" at Hawaii in 1799. Honolulu. 1934.

    (Hawaiian Historical Society, 42nd Annual report, 1933, pp. 103-113.)

QE
75
B

Elevations. Hawaii

U.S. Geological Survey, Bull. 561.
Results of spirit leveling in Hawaii 1910-1913, inclusive.

QL
Mollusk
Pams
491
492
493

Eliot, Charles

    On some nudibranchs from East Africa and Zanzibar. Pts. 4-6. From Proc. Zool. Soc. London, 1904-5.

DU
800
M 98

ELIZABETH ISLAND

Murray, Thomas Boyles

    Pitcairn: the island, the people, and the pastor... Fifth ed. London, 1855. pp. 266-7

ELGIN CAPE   FEATHER CAPES

See

FEATHER CAPES ELGIN CAPE

QL
Mollusk
Pam
611

Eliot, C N E

    On Doridiidae. From Proceedings of the Malacological Soc. v.5, part 5, 1903.

ELIZABETH ISLAND BOTANY

see

BOTANY ELIZABETH ISLAND

see Henderson I. (Pitcairn group)

GN
295.D7
T 52

Eliade, Mircea

    "Cargo-cults" and cosmic regeneration.

IN

Thrupp, Sylvia L.   editor
Millennial dreams in action: Essays in comparative study.

    (Comparative Studies in Society and History: Suppl. II:139-143, 1962)

DU
Pac.
Pam.
240

Eliot, E.C.

    A model protectorate: Gilbert and Ellice Islands. (Extracted from the United empire: The Royal colonial institute journal, Vol. VI, n.s. No. 12, Dec. 1915)

QL
1
A 93

ELIZABETH REEF

Whitley, Gilbert P.   and others

    The Middleton and Elizabeth reefs, South Pacific Ocean.

    (The Australian Zoologist, 8:199-273, 1937)

QL
Mollusk
Pam
494

Eliot, Charles

    Chromodorids from the Red Sea, collected and figured by Cyril Crossland. From Proc. Zool. Soc. London, 1911.

QL
461
B 86

Eliot, J. N.

    New or little known butterflies from Malaya.

    (Bull. British Mus. (Nat. Hist.), Entomology Vol. 7(8), 1959)

QH
104
U-b

ELK

Preble, Edward Alexander.

    ... Report on condition of elk in Jackson Hole, Wyoming, in 1911 by Edward A. Preble ... Washington, Govt. print. off., 1911.

    23 p. VII pl. (incl. front., 2 maps) 23ᵐ. (U. S. Dept. of agriculture. Biological survey. Bulletin no. 40)

    1. Elk.

                  Agr 11-2387

    Library, U. S. Dept. of   Agriculture 1B52B no. 40

QL
Mollusk
Pam
490

Eliot, Charles

    Notes on a collection of nudibranchs from the Red Sea: Reports on the marine biology of the Sudanese Red Sea XI. From Linnean Soc. Journ. Zool. v. 31, 1908.

QL
1
H 77

Eliot, J. N.

    New records and a check list of butterflies from Hong Kong.

    (Memoirs of the Hong Kong Biological Circle, No. 2, 1963)

GN
1
O 15

Elkin, A. P.

    A. R. Radcliffe-Brown, 1880-1955.

    (Oceania, 26(4):239-251, 1956)

GN
Ethn.
Pam.4321

Elkin, A. P.

The aboriginal Australians. Illustrated by Pamela Johnston. Longmans. 8vo. no date. 56 pp.

GN
665
E 42

Elkin, A. P.

The Australian aborigines, how to understand them. Angus & Robertson. Sydney and London. 1938. 8vo. xiv, 262 pp.

also Third Edition, 1954. Angus and Robertson. xvii + 349 pp.

GN
2.1
A-4

Elkin, A. P.

The Dieri kinship system.

(Journ. R. Anthrop. Inst. of Great Britain and Ireland, Vol. 61, 1931, pp. 493-498)

GN
1
O 15

Elkin, A. P.

Anthropological research in Australia and the western Pacific, 1927-1937.

(Oceania, Vol. 8, 1937-1938, pp. 306-327)

GN
1
O 15

Elkin, A. P.

Australian and New Guinea musical records.

(Oceania, 27(4):313-319, 1957)

GN
1
O 15

Elkin, A. P.

Education of native races in Pacific countries.

(Oceania, vol. VII, 1936, pp. 145-168)

GN
1
O 15

Elkin, A. P.

Anthropology and the future of the Australian aborigines.

(Oceania, Vol. 5, No. 1, 1934, pp. 1-17)

GN
Ethn. Pam
3171

Elkin, A. P.

Australian native policies in relation to education. (Seminar conference on education in Pacific countries, Univ. of Hawaii, July-Aug., 1936. 7 mimeographed pages)

GN
1
O 15

Elkin, A. P.

F. E. Williams- Government Anthropologist, Papua.

(Oceania, Vol. 14, pp. 91-103, 1944)

GN
1
O 15

Elkin, A. P.

Anthropology and the peoples of the southwest Pacific: the past, present and future.

(Oceania, Vol. 14, 1943, pp. 1-19)

OVER

GN
1
O 15

Elkin, A. P.

Captain Cook's Journal, Vol. II: a review.

(Oceania, Vol. 32(3):191-197, 1962)

QH
197
E 44

Elkin, A. P.   editor

A goodly heritage; ANZAAS Jubilee; Science in New South Wales. ...36th Meeting of the Australian and New Zealand Association for the Advancement of Science. Sydney, 1962 R8vo. xiii + 170 pp.

DU
1
S 72q

Elkin, A. P.

Belshaw, C. S.

Anthropology in Oceania; a review of two reports on research needs in social anthropology in the Pacific, just published for the Commission by Oxford University Press (Elkin, Social anthropology in Melanesia, and Keesing, Social anthropology in Polynesia.)

(South Pacific Com., Quarterly Bull. 3(3): 31-32, 43, 1953)

GN
1
O 15

Elkin, A. P.

Cave-paintings in southern Arnhem Land.

(Oceania, 22(4):245-255, 1952)

GN
1
O 15

Elkin, A. P.

The Kopara: the settlement of grievances.

(Oceania, Vol. 2, 1931-1932, pp. 191-198)

GN
1
O 15

Elkin, A. P.

Arnhem Land music.

(Oceania, 24:81-109, 1953; 25:74-121, 1954; 25:293-342, 1955; 26:59-70, 127-152, 1955; 26:214-230, 1956)

(concluded by Trevor I. Jones, ibid, 26:252-339; 28:1-30, 1957)

GN
2.S
S 72

Elkin, A. P.

The complexity of social organization in Arnhem Land.

(Southwestern Journal of Anthropology, 6(1): 1-20, 1950)

GN
1
O 15

Elkin, A. P.

Marriage and descent in East Arnhem Land.

(Oceania, Vol. 3, No. 4, 1933, pp. 412-416)

GN
665
E 43

Elkin, A. P.

Art in Arnhem Land. By A. P. Elkin and Catherine and Ronald Berndt. The University of Chicago Press. Chicago. (1950) R8vo. xii + 123 pp. 22 pl. (some in color)

GN
1
O 15

Elkin, A. P.

Delayed exchange in Wabag sub-district, Central Highlands of New Guinea, with notes on social organization.

(Oceania, Vol. 23(3):161-201, 1953)

GN
1
O 15

Elkin, A. P.

Malinowski: man and culture; a review article.

(Oceania, 29(3):218-226, 1959)

GN
Ethn.
Fam.
4362

Elkin, A. P.

"The Natural History of Man". Presidential address to the second Science Congress, Pan Indian Ocean Science Association. Perth, 1954. 16 pp.

AS
719
A 93

Elkin, A. P.

Peoples of New Guinea.

(Australian Mus. Mag., 12:406-408, 1958)

GN
1
O 15

Elkin, A. P.

The secret life of the Australian aborigines.

(Oceania, Vol. 3, 1932, pp. 119-138, pls. 1-5)

GN
1
O 15

Elkin, A. P.

The nature of Australian languages.

(Oceania, Vol. 8, 1937, pp. 127-169)

GN
Ethn.Fam.
3497

Elkin, A. P.

Post-war and the aborigines. The National Missionary Council of Australia. Sydney. 8vo. 20 pp. (1946)

GN
668
E 43

Elkin, A. P.

Social anthropology in Melanesia; a review of research. Published under the auspices of the South Pacific Commission. Oxford University Press. London... 1953. 8vo. xiii + 186 pp.

GN
1
O 15

Elkin, A. P.

Notes on the social organization of the Worimi, a Kattang-speaking people.

(Oceania, Vol. 2, 1931-1932, pp. 359-363)

GN
1
O 15

Elkin, A. P.

The rainbow-serpent myth in northwest Australia.

(Oceania, Vol. 1, 1930-1931, pp. 349-352)

GN
1
O 15

Elkin, A. P.

Social organization in the Kimberley Division, Northwestern Australia.

(Oceania, Vol. 2, 1931-1932, pp. 296-333)

GN
1
O 15

Elkin, A. P.

Obituary: Sir Peter Buck.

(Oceania, 22(2):162-163, 1951)

GN
2.S
M 26

Elkin, A. P.

Reconstruction and the native peoples of the south-west Pacific.

(Mankind, Vol. 3, 1943, pp. 133-135)

GN
1
O 15

Elkin, A. P.

Social organization of Arnhem Land. By A. P. Elkin, R. M. Berndt and C. H. Berndt.

(Oceania, Vol. 21(4):253-301, 1951)

*not complete
to be continued*

GN
1
O 15

Elkin, A. P.

The origin and interpretation of petroglyphs in south-east Australia.

(Oceania, Vol. 20:119-157, 1959)

GN
1
O 15

Elkin, A. P.

Research in Arnhem Land.

(Oceania, 22(4):290-298, 1952)

GN
1
O 15

Elkin, A. P.

The social organization of South Australian tribes.

(Oceania, Vol. 2, 1921-1932, pp. 44-73, pls. 1,2)

Q
101
P 18

AS
763
B 62 s

Reading
Room

Elkin, A. P.

Pacific Science Association; its history and role in international cooperation.

(Bernice P. Bishop Museum, Special Publication No. 48, 1961)

GN
1
O 15
1937

Elkin, A. P.

Research in Australia and the Pacific, 1927-1937.

(Oceania, Vol. 8, 1938, 306-317)

GN
1
O 15

Elkin, A. P.

Studies in Australian totemism. The nature of Australian totemism.

(Oceania, Vol. 4, No. 2, 1933, pp. 113-131)

GN
1
O 15

Elkin, A. P.

Pacific Science Association 1962 congress.

(Oceania, 32(3):226-230, 1962)

GN
1
O 15

Elkin, A. P.

Rock-paintings of North-west Australia.

(Oceania, Vol. 1, 1930-1931, pp. 257-279, pls. 1-3)

GN
1
O 15

Elkin, A. P.

Studies in Australian totemism. Sub-section, section and moiety totemism.

(Oceania, Vol. 4, No. 1, 1933, pp. 65-90)

GN 1 O 15	Elkin, A. P. Totemism in North-western Australia. (Oceania, Vol. 3, 1933, pp. 257-296, pls. 1,2; pt. 2, Vol. 3, No. 4, pp. 435-481, pls. 1,2; Vol. 4, No. 1, 1933, pp. 54-64)
GN 2.S P 76	Ella, Samuel The Samoan "taumua-lua". (Samoan long boat) (Journal of the Polynesian Society, Vol. 7:247, 1898)
QL 729.A3M E 45	Ellerman, J. R. Supplement to Chasen (1940) A handlist of Malaysian mammals, containing a generic synonymy and a complete index. By J. R. Ellerman and T. C. S. Morrison-Scott. British Museum (Natural History). London. 1955. R8vo. 66 pp.

GN 2.S M 26	ELKIN, A. P. Berndt, Ronald M. Professor A. P. Elkin- an appreciation. (Mankind, Vol. 5(3):89-101, 1956)
DU Pac Pam #281 S and AS 701 A	Ella, S. (Rev.) Samoa. ex Proc. Australasian Assn. for the advancement of Sci., Sec. G. 1892, pp. 620-645.
AS 36 S	Ellet, Charles, 1810-1862. ... Contributions to the physical geography of the United States. Part I. Of the physical geography of the Mississippi Valley, with suggestions for the improvement of the navigation of the Ohio and other rivers. By Charles Ellet, jr. ... [Washington, Smithsonian institution, 1850] 64 p. diagrs. (1 fold.) 31½ᶜᵐ. (Smithsonian contributions to knowledge, vol. II, art. 4) No more published. Smithsonian institution publication 13. 1. Physical geography—Mississippi Valley. 2. Ohio River—Navigation. S 13-5 Library, Smithsonian Institution Q11.S68

DU 12 E43	Elkington, E. Way. The savage South Seas, painted by Norman H. Hardy; described by E. Way Elkington. London, A. & C. Black, 1907. 211p. illus.
DU Pac Pam No.52	Ella, Rev. S. The war of Tonga and Samoa and origin of the name Malietoa. ex Polynesian Soc. Journal, 1899, vol. 8, pp. 231-234
AP 2 A 5	ELLICE ISLANDS Agassiz, Alexander Explorations of the Albatross in the Pacific ocean... (Am. Jour. Sci., Ser. 4, Vol. 9, 1900, pp. 369-74)

AS 701 A	Ella, Samuel The ancient Samoan government. (Australasian Association for the Adv. of Sci., Proc., Vol. 6, 1895, pp. 596-603)
QK Bot.Pam 3170	Ellender Reforestation in Hawaii. (Reprint, Senate Report, 85th Congress, Rept. 2415. 5 pp.)
AS 719 X-me	ELLICE ISLANDS Australian Museum The atoll of Funafuti, Ellice Group: its zoology, botany, ethnology, and general structure based on collections made by Mr. Charles Hedley ...Sydney. 1896-1900. (Australian museum, Sydney. Mem.III. Issued in 10 parts.)

PL Phil. Pam 153	Ella, Samuel Dialect changes in the Polynesian languages. Ex Jour. Anthropological Inst., vol. II, p. 154-180.
AS 763 B-s	Eller, Willard K. Beach, Arthur R. A Study of the magnetic properties of Kilauea rock, by Arthur R.Beach and Willard H.Eller. (Proc. Haw. Acad. Sci., 13th Meeting, 1937-38. B.P.B.Mus. Sp.Pub. 33, 1939, p. 16)
AS 719 A-me	ELLICE ISLANDS - (FUNAFUTI) Australian museum, *Sydney* ... Scientific results of the trawling expedition of H. M. C. S. "Thetis," off the coast of New South Wales, in February and March, 1898 ... Pub. by order of the Trustees ... Sydney, F. Cunninghame & co., printers, 1899-1914. 2 v. illus., XCII pl. (part col.) fold. map. 25ᶜᵐ. (Australian museum, Sydney. Memoir IV) Issued in parts. Each plate preceded by leaf with descriptive letterpress. (Continued on next card) 9-13339 Revised

GN 2 S P 76	Ella, Samuel O le tala ia taema ma na-fanua. (Journal of the Polynesian Society, Vol. 6, 1897, pp. 152-155) (see also: ibid.Fraser,John:Some folk songs and myths from Samoa. Vol.5,1896, pp. 171-183; Vol.6,1897,pp. 19-36,67-76,107-122; Vol.7,1898, pp. 15-29;Vol.9,1900,125-134)
QL 737.R6 E 45	Ellerman, J. R. The families and genera of living rodents. With a list of named forms (1758-1936) by R. W. Hayman and G. W. C. Holt. Vol. I: Rodents other than Muridae; Vol. II. Family Muridae. Printed by order of the Trustees, British Museum (Natural History). London. 1940, 1941. R8vo. xxvi +689 pp; xii + 690 pp. **Vol. III:1, 1949**
AS 719 A-me	ELLICE ISLANDS - (FUNAFUTI) Australian museum, *Sydney*. ... Scientific results of the trawling expedition of H. M. C. S. "Thetis" ... 1914. (Card 2) CONTENTS.—pt. 1. Introduction by E. R. Waite. Fishes by E. R. Waite.—pt. 2-4. *Crustacea*, pt. I-III, by T. Whitelegge.—pt. 5-6. *Mollusca*, pt. I-II, by C. Hedley.—pt. 7. *Crustacea*, pt. IV, by T. Whitelegge.—pt. 8. The anatomy of *Megalatractus*, by H. L. Kesteven.—pt. 9-10. Sponges, pt. I-II, by T. Whitelegge.—pt. 11. *Echinodermata*, by H. L. Clark.—pt. 12. *Crustacea*, pt. V. *Amphipoda*, by the Rev. T. R. R. Stebbing.—pt. 13. *Alcyonaria*, by J. A. Thomson and D. L. Mackinnon.—pt. 14. *Echinodermata* (supplement) by H. L. Coleman.—pt. 15. Recent crinoids of Australia, by A. H. Clark.—pt. 16. *Hydrozoa* (hydroid zoophytes and *Stylasterina*) of the "Thetis" expedition. By J. Ritchie.—pt. 17. The *Tunicata* of the "Thetis" expedition, by W. A. Herdman ... and W. Riddell.—pt. 18. Title pages, contents and index. 1. Thetis (Ship) 2. Ma- rine fauna. 9-13339 Revised Library of Congress QL138.A8

GN 2.S P 76 and GN Ethn.Pam. 3806	Ella, Samuel Polynesian native clothing. (Journal of the Poly. Soc., Vol. 8:165-170, 1899)
QL 1 Z	Ellerman, J. R. Key to the rodents of south-west Asia in the British Museum collection. (Proc. of the Zool. Soc. of London, Vol. 118:765-816, 1948)
DU Pac.Pam. 521	ELLICE ISLANDS British Possessions in Oceania...(London). H. M. Stationery Office. 1920. 8vo. 126 pp.

RB
1
L84

ELLICE ISLANDS

Buxton, Patrick A. and Hopkins, G.H.E.

Researches in Polynesia and Melanesia an account of investigations in... Ellice group... 1924, 1925. Pt. 1-4, (relating to entomology), London School of Hygiene and Tropical Medicine, Mem. 1, 1927.

DU
Pacific
Pam. No.
299

ELLICE ISLANDS

Hedley, Charles

General account of the atoll of Funafuti, Ellice Group.

(Australian Mus. Mem. Vol. III, 1896-7, pp. 1-71.)

DU
1
S 72t

ELLICE ISLANDS

Maude, H. E.

The cooperative movement in the Gilbert and Ellice Islands. A paper read to the Seventh Pacific Science Congress, Auckland, New Zealand, February, 1949.

(South Pacific Commission, Technical Paper No. 1, 1-12 pp., 1949)

DU
80
A 93

ELLICE ISLANDS

Cooper, H. R. R. L.

Co-operative development in the Gilbert and Ellice Islands.

(South Pacific, 9(7):447-450, 1957)

DU
Pac.Pam.
239

ELLICE ISLANDS

Hutson, Eyre

Gilbert and Ellice Islands protectorate.

(Colonial Annual Reports, 1915-1916, No. 884, 17 pp. London, 1916)

GN
Ethn.Pam.
3165

ELLICE ISLANDS

Maude, H. E.

Culture change and education in the Gilbert and Ellice islands. (Seminar conference on education in Pacific countries, Univ. of Hawaii, July-Aug., 1936. 10 mimeographed pages)

DU
Pac
Pam
#240

ELLICE ISLANDS

Eliot, E. C.

A model protectorate: Gilbert and Ellice Islands, Central Pacific. n.p., n.d. pp. 878-882.

See author card

DU
590
I 66

ELLICE ISLANDS

Iremonger, Lucille

It's a bigger life. With illustrations by the author. Hutchinson and Co., Ltd. London, New York... R8vo. (1948?) no date 191 pp.

G
3
A 1

ELLICE ISLANDS

A note on the annexation of Gilbert and Ellice groups to Great Britain, November, 1915.

(Geog. Rev., 1916, p. 145)

DU
12
F 41
locked
case

ELLICE ISLANDS

Festetics de Tolna, Rodolphe

Chez les cannibales. Huit ans de croisiere dans l'Ocean Pacifique a bord du yacht "Le Tolna"...Paris. 1903. 4to. pp. 147-164.

DU
12
J 52
locked
case

ELLICE ISLANDS

Jenkins, J. S.

Recent exploring expeditions to the Pacific, and to the South Seas, under the American, English and French governments. London. 1854. sm8vo. pp. 404-408.

DU
Pac.Pam.
476

Ellice Islands

Pease, Henry

An Account of an Adventure of Henry Pease 2nd of Edgartown, Mass.- Capt. of Ship Planter of Nantucket, on August 18, 1853, on St. Augustine Island, Lat. 5 35 South, Lon 176 - 12 East, near Ellice Group. MS, typed copy.

DU
12
G 47
locked
case

ELLICE ISLANDS

Gill, W. W.

Jottings from the Pacific, pp. 11-27. (London). 1885. sm8vo.

GN
2.S
P76

ELLICE ISLANDS

Kennedy, Donald Gilbert

Field Notes on the Culture of Vaitupu, Ellice Islands.

(Memoirs of the Polynesian Society, Vol. 9, 1931)

GN
2.S
P 76

ELLICE ISLANDS

Roberts, R. G.

Te Atu Tubalu, a short history of the Ellice Islands.

(Journal of the Polynesian Society, Vol. 67, 394-423, 1958)

DU
12
H 33
locked
case

ELLICE ISLANDS

Hartwig, Georg

Die Inseln des grossen Oceans im Natur- und Völkerleben...pp. 430-436. Wiesbaden. 1861. 8vo.

DU
12
L 22

ELLICE ISLANDS

Lambert, S. M.

A Yankee doctor in Paradise. Boston, 1941.

pp. 177-180

DU
590
R83

Ellice Islands(Funafuti)

Royal society of London.

The atoll of Funafuti...

London, 1904. 428p. maps.

DU
615
H 33

ELLICE ISLANDS

Hartzer, (Le Père) Fernand

Les Iles Blanches des Mers du Sud. Histoire du Vicariat Apostolique des Archipels Gilbert et Ellice. Paris. Charles Amat. 1900. 8vo. xii + 345 pp.

DU
12
L 57

ELLICE ISLANDS

Lenwood, Frank

Pastels from the Pacific. With illustrations in colours and in black and white.

(Oxford: Oxford Univ. Press, 1917, 8vo. pp. xii + 224)

GN
2 S
P 76

ELLICE ISLANDS

Smith, S. Percy

The first inhabitants of the Ellice Group.

(Journal of the Polynesian Society, Vol.5, 1896, pp. 209-210)

Q
115
U 58
locked
case

DU
12
U 58
locked
case

ELLICE ISLANDS

United States Exploring Expedition...1838-1842, under the command of Charles Wilkes. Vol. V, pp. 39-47. Philadelphia. C. Sherman. 1844. 4to.
Vol. 23:Hydrography...pp. 253-257
...Narrative, Vols. 1-5 and atlas. Phila. 1845. R8vo. Vol. V, pp. 37-44.

ELLICE ISLANDS   CHILDREN

See

CHILDREN   ELLICE ISLANDS

ELLICE ISLANDS   ENTEROPNEUSTA

see

ENTEROPNEUSTA   ELLICE ISLANDS

Ellice Islands

See also

Gilbert and Ellice Islands

ELLICE ISLANDS   CRUSTACEA

see

CRUSTACEA   ELLICE ISLANDS

ELLICE ISLANDS   ETHNOLOGY

see

ETHNOLOGY   ELLICE ISLANDS

ELLICE ISLANDS   ALCYONARIA

see

ALCYONARIA   ELLICE ISLANDS

ELLICE ISLANDS   CULICIDAE

See

CULICIDAE   ELLICE ISLANDS

ELLICE ISLANDS   FISHES

see

FISHES   ELLICE ISLANDS

ELLICE ISLANDS   BELIEFS

See

BELIEFS   ELLICE ISLANDS

ELLICE ISLANDS   DANCES

See

DANCES   ELLICE ISLANDS

ELLICE ISLANDS   FISHING

See

FISHING   ELLICE ISLANDS

ELLICE ISLANDS   BIRDS

see

BIRDS   ELLICE ISLANDS

ELLICE ISLANDS   DIET

See

DIET   ELLICE ISLANDS

ELLICE ISLANDS   FOODS

See

FOODS   ELLICE ISLANDS

ELLICE ISLANDS   BRACHYURA

see

BRACHYURA   ELLICE ISLANDS

ELLICE ISLANDS   ECHINODERMATA

see

ECHINODERMATA   ELLICE ISLANDS

ELLICE ISLANDS   GEOLOGY

see

GEOLOGY   ELLICE ISLANDS

ELLICE ISLANDS   CEPHALOPODA

See

CEPHALOPODA   ELLICE ISLANDS

ELLICE ISLANDS   EDUCATION

see

EDUCATION   ELLICE ISLANDS

G
7
R7

Ellice Islands - Government

Eliot, E. C.

Model protectorate. In United Empire VI, 12 (Dec.) 1915, pp 878-882.

ELLICE ISLANDS   HEALTH

See

HEALTH   ELLICE ISLANDS

Z
7111
K 96   ELLICE ISLANDS   LANGUAGE

Kunz, E. F.

     An annotated bibliography of the languages of the Gilbert Islands, Ellice Islands, and Nauru. Published by the Trustees of the Public Library of New South Wales. 1959. Sydney. ix + 202 pp. 4to. mimeogr.

ELLICE ISLAND   TRADE

See

TRADE   ELLICE ISLAND

ELLICE ISLANDS   INSECTS

see

INSECTS   ELLICE ISLANDS

ELLICE ISLANDS   MISSIONS

see

MISSIONS   ELLICE ISLANDS

ELLICE ISLANDS   ZOOLOGY

see

ZOOLOGY   ELLICE ISLANDS

ELLICE ISLAND   ISOPODA

See

ISOPODA   ELLICE ISLAND

ELLICE ISLANDS   PORIFERA

see

PORIFERA   ELLICE ISLANDS

QL
1
F   Elliot, Daniel Giraud, 1835–

     ... The caribou of the Kenai Peninsula, Alaska. By D. G. Elliot ... Chicago, 1901.

     1 p. l., p. 59-62. pl. XI–XIII (1 fold.) 24½ᶜᵐ. (Field Columbian museum. Publication 59. Zoological series. vol. III, no. 5)

     1. Caribou.

Library of Congress   QL1.F4   4–10473

ELLICE ISLANDS   ISOPTERA

see

ISOPTERA   ELLICE ISLANDS

ELLICE ISLANDS   SOCIAL ORGANIZATION

see

SOCIAL ORGANIZATION   ELLICE ISLANDS

QL
671
F4   Elliot, Daniel Giraud, 1835–1915.

     ... Catalogue of a collection of birds obtained by the expedition into Somali-land. By D. G. Elliot ... Chicago, 1897.

     1 p. l., 29-67 p. 25ᶜᵐ. (Field Columbian museum. Publication 17. Ornithological series. vol. I, no. 2)

     1. Birds—Somaliland.

Library of Congress   QL671.F4   4–10464
—— Copy 2.   QL692.E44
     ra19d1₁

ELLICE ISLANDS   KIDNAPPING

See

KIDNAPPING & ELLICE ISLANDS

ELLICE ISLANDS   TALES

See

TALES   ELLICE ISLANDS

QL
1
F   Elliot, Daniel Giraud, 1835–

     ... Catalogue of mammals collected by E. Heller in Southern California. By D. G. Elliot ... Chicago, 1904.

     1 p. l., 271-321 p. XXXVIII–XLIX pl., fold. map. 24ᶜᵐ. (Field Columbian museum. Publication 91. Zoological series. vol. III, no. 16)

     1. Mammals—California.

Library of Congress   QL1.F4   4–11561
—— Copy 2.   QL719.C2E4

ELLICE ISLANDS   LAND TENURE

See

LAND TENURE   ELLICE ISLANDS

PL
Phil.
Pam.
515   ELLICE ISLANDS   TEXTS

Iremonger, Thomas Lascelles (Mrs)

     Our daily bread and fifty recipes in Gilbertese, Ellice and English. Government Press, Suva. (1941) 12mo. iv + 38 pp.

QL
1
F   Elliot, Daniel Giraud, 1835–1915.

     ... Catalogue of mammals from the Olympic Mountains, Washington, with descriptions of new species, by D. G. Elliot ... Chicago, 1899.

     1 p. l., p. 241-276. illus., pl. XLI–LXII. 24½ᶜᵐ. (Field Columbian museum. Publication 32. Zoological series. vol. I, no. 13)

     1. Mammals—Washington (State)

Library of Congress   QL1.F4   4–10866
—— Copy 2.   QL717.E32

PL
590
K 35   ELLICE ISLANDS   LANGUAGE

Kennedy, Donald Gilbert

     Te Ngangana a te Tuvalu. Handbook on the language of the Ellice Islands. Suva. 1945. 82 pp.

AN
3.G
G 46 e   ELLICE ISLANDS   TEXTS

Tala o Tuvalu   [News from the Ellice Islands]

Nos. 14-   Jan. 1947-

folio. mimeographed

QL
1
F   Elliot, Daniel Giraud

     A check list of mammals of the North American continent, the West Indies and the neighboring seas, Chicago, 1905.

     (Field Columbian museum. Publication 105. Zoological ser. vol. VI.)

QL
708
E 46   Supplement. N. Y., 1917.

AS
36
S

Elliot, Daniel Giraud, 1835–

... A classification and synopsis of the *Trochilidæ*. By Daniel Giraud Elliot ... [Washington, Smithsonian institution, 1879]

xii, 277 p. illus. 32ᶜᵐ. (Smithsonian contributions to knowledge. [vol. XXIII, art. 5])

Smithsonian institution publication 317.

1. Birds. 2. Humming-birds. Trochilidæ

S 13–97

Library, Smithsonian   Institution Q11.S68

QL
1
F

Elliot, Daniel Giraud, 1835–1915.

... Descriptions of apparently new species and subspecies of mammals from California, Oregon, the Kenai peninsula, Alaska, and Lower California, Mexico. By D. G. Elliot ... Chicago, 1903.

1 p. l., p. 153–173. illus. 25½ᶜᵐ. (Field Columbian museum. Publication 74. Zoological series. vol. III, no. 10)

The forms described in this paper, with a few exceptions, were obtained by Mr. Edmund Heller. *cf.* Introd. note.

1. Mammals—North America. I. Heller, Edmund, 1875–

Library of Congress   QL1.F4   3–22905 Revised
[r21c1]

QL
1
F

Elliot, Daniel Giraud, 1835–

... List of mammals from Somali-land obtained by the museum's East African expedition. By D. G. Elliot ... Chicago, 1897.

1 p. l., 109–155 p. 24½ᶜᵐ. (Field Columbian museum. Publication 19. Zoological series. vol. I, no. 6)

1. Mammals—Somaliland.

4–10568

Library of Congress   QL1.F4
—— Copy 2.   QL701.E4¹

QL
1
F

Elliot, Daniel Giraud, 1835–1915.

... Description of apparently new species and subspecies of mammals from Oklahoma Territory. By D. G. Elliot ... Chicago, 1899.

1 p. l., p. 279–282. 24½ᶜᵐ. (Field Columbian museum. Publication 37. Zoological series. vol. I, no. 14)

1. Mammals—Oklahoma.

4–10567

Library of Congress   QL1.F4
—— Copy 2.   QL719.O5E4

AS
36
S4

Elliot, Daniel Giraud, 1835–

Descriptions of some new species of monkeys of the genera *Pithecus* and *Pygathrix* collected by Dr. W. L. Abbott and presented to the United States national museum. By D. G. Elliot.

(*In* U. S. National museum. Proceedings. Washington, 1911. 23½ᶜᵐ. vol. 38, p. 343–352)

1. Monkeys. I. Abbott, W. L.

11–15737

Library of Congress   Q11.U55 vol. 38

OL
1
F

Elliot, Daniel Giraud, 1835–

... A list of mammals obtained by Edmund Heller, collector for the museum, from the coast region of northern California and Oregon, by D. G. Elliot ... Chicago, 1903.

1 p. l., p. 175–197. 25½ᶜᵐ. (Field Columbian museum. Publication 76. Zoological series. vol. III, no. 11)

1. Mammals—U. S.

3–22906

Library of Congress   QL1.F4

AS
36
S2

Elliot, Daniel Giraud, 1835–

... Description of a new subspecies of African monkey of the genus *Cercopithecus*, by D. G. Elliot. Washington, Smithsonian institution, 1910.

2 l. 24ᶜᵐ. (Smithsonian miscellaneous collections. v. 56, no. 7)

1. Monkeys.

10–35871

Library of Congress   Q11.S7 vol. 56, no. 7

OL
1
F

Elliot, Daniel Giraud, 1835–

... Descriptions of twenty-seven apparently new species and subspecies of mammals. All but six collected by Edmund Heller. By D. G. Elliot ... Chicago, 1903.

1 p. l., [239]–261 p. illus. 24½ᶜᵐ. (Field Columbian museum. Publication no. 87. Zoological series. vol. III, no. 14)

1. Mammals.

4–2637

Library of Congress   QL1.F4
—— Copy 2.   Library of Congress QL738.E46

QL
1
F

Elliot, Daniel Giraud, 1835–1915.

... A list of the land and sea mammals of North America north of Mexico. Supplement to the Synopsis. By D. G. Elliot ... Chicago, 1901.

2 p. l., p. 477–522. pl. L–LVI. 24½ᶜᵐ. (Field Columbian museum. Publication 57. Zoological series. vol. II, no. 2)

1. Mammals—North America.

4–10565

Library of Congress   QL1.F4
—— Copy 2.

QL
1
F

Elliot, Daniel Giraud, 1835–1915.

... Description of apparently new species and subspecies of mammals from the Indian Territory. By D. G. Elliot ... Chicago, 1899.

1 p. l., p. 285–288. 24½ᶜᵐ. (Field Columbian museum. Publication 38. Zoological series. vol. I, no. 15)

1. Mammals—Indian Territory.

4–10566

Library of Congress   QL1.F4

QL
1
F

Elliott, Daniel G.

The Land & Sea Mammals of Middle America & the W. Indies.

vide Field Columbian Publication Zool. Series Vol 10. pts 1 & 2.

N. 2.

DEC 31 1904

QL
1
F

Elliot, Daniel Giraud, 1835–

... List of mammals obtained by Thaddeus Surber, collector for the museum, chiefly in Oklahoma and Indian territories. By D. G. Elliot ... Chicago, 1899.

1 p. l., 291–303 p. 4 pl. 24½ᶜᵐ. (Field Columbian museum. Publication 40. Zoological series. vol. I, no. 16)

1. Mammals—Oklahoma. 2. Mammals—Indian Territory.

4–10877

Library of Congress   QL1.F4
—— Copy 2.   QL717.E36

QL
1
F

Elliot, Daniel Giraud, 1835–

... Description of an apparently new species of mountain goat ... By D. G. Elliot ... Chicago, 1900.

5 p. illus. IV fold. pl. 24½ᶜᵐ. (Field Columbian museum. Publication 46. Zoological series. vol. III, no. 1)

1. Oreamnus.

4–10474

Library of Congress   QL1.F4

OL
1
F

Elliot, Daniel Giraud, 1835–

... A list of a collection of Mexican mammals, with descriptions of some apparently new forms. By D. G. Elliot ... Chicago, 1903.

1 p. l., 141–149 n. 25½ᶜᵐ. (Field Columbian museum. Publication 71. Zoological ser. vol. III, no. 8)

1. Mammals—Mexico.

4–2293

Library of Congress   QL1.F4
—— Copy 2.   QL723.E4

QL
1
F

Elliot, Daniel Giraud, 1835–

... List of mammals obtained by Thaddeus Surber, collector for the museum, in the provinces of New Brunswick and Quebec, Canada. By D. G. Elliot ... Chicago, 1901.

1 p. l., 15–29 p. 24½ᶜᵐ. (Field Columbian museum. Publication 54. Zoological series. vol. III, no. 3)

Bibliographical references.

1. Mammals—Canada.

4–10915

Library of Congress   QL1.F4

OL
1
F

Elliot, Daniel Giraud, 1835–

... Description of an apparently new subspecies of marten from the Kenai Peninsula, Alaska. By D. G. Elliot ... Chicago, 1903.

1 p. l., 151–152. pl. 25½ᶜᵐ. (Field Columbian museum. Publication 72. Zoological ser. vol. III, no. 9)

With his List of a collection of Mexican mammals ... Chicago, 1903.

1. Martens.

4–2291

Library of Congress   QL1.F4
—— Copy 2.   QL737.E44

AS
36
S2

Elliot, Daniel Giraud, 1835–1915.

... List of described species of humming birds. By Daniel Giraud Elliot ... Washington, Smithsonian institution, 1879.

iii, 17 p. 24ᶜᵐ. (Smithsonian miscellaneous collections. [vol. XVI, art. VI])

Publication 334.

"... Reprinted with some changes from the Classification and synopsis of the *Trochilidæ* ... published in the Smithsonian contributions to knowledge," v. 23, art. 5.

1. Humming-birds. Trochilidæ

16–6377

Library of Congress   Q11.S7 vol. 16, art. 6

QL
1
F

Elliot, Daniel Giraud, 1835–

... A list of mammals obtained by Thaddeus Surber, in North and South Carolina, Georgia and Florida. By D. G. Elliot ... Chicago, 1901.

1 p. l., 31–57 p. v–x pl. 24½ᶜᵐ. (Field Columbian museum. Publication 58. Zoological series. vol. III, no. 4)

Bibliographical references.

1. Mammals—U. S.

4–10878

Library of Congress   QL1.F4

QL
1
F

Elliot, Daniel Giraud, 1835–

... Descriptions of apparently new species and subspecies of mammals, and a new generic name proposed, by D. G. Elliot ... Chicago, 1904.

1 p. l., p. 263–270. 24½ᶜᵐ. (Field Columbian museum. Publication no. 90. Zoological series. vol. III, no. 15)

1. Mammals. 2. Moschophoromys.

4–8703

Library of Congress   QL1.F4

OL
1
F

Elliot, D[aniel] G[iraud] 1835–

... A list of mammals collected by Edmund Heller, in the San Pedro Martir and Hanson Laguna Mountains and the accompanying coast regions of Lower California, with descriptions of apparently new species. By D. G. Elliot ... Chicago, 1903.

1 p. l., 199–232 p. 5 pl., map. 24½ᶜᵐ. (Field Columbian museum. Publication 79. Zoological series. vol. III, no. 12)

1. Mammals—California, Lower.

4–8945

Library of Congress   QL1.F4

QL
1
F

Elliot, Daniel Giraud, 1835–

... List of species of mammals, principally rodents, obtained by W. W. Price, Dr. S. E. Meek, G. K. Cherrie, and E. S. Thompson in the states of Iowa, Wyoming, Montana, Idaho, Nevada and California, with descriptions of new species, by D. G. Elliot ... Chicago, 1898.

1 p. l., 193–221 p. 24½ᶜᵐ. (Field Columbian museum. Publication 27. Zoological series. vol. I, no. 10)

1. Mammals—U. S. 2. Rodentia.

4–10876

Library of Congress   QL1.F4
—— Copy 2.   QL717.E4

QL
1
F
Elliot, Daniel Giraud, 1835–
... On sundry collections of mammals, by D. G. Elliot ... Chicago, 1896.

1 p. l., 67–82 p. vi–xiii pl. (1 fold.) 24½ᶜᵐ. (Field Columbian museum. Publication 11. Zoological series. vol. I, no. 3)
Collected from different localities, with descriptions of supposed new species and subspecies.
Each plate accompanied by guard sheet with brief explanation.

1. Mammals.   4–10918

Library of Congress   QL1.F4
—— Copy 2.   QL701.E464

QH
308
E 46
Elliott, Alfred M.
Biology. By Alfred M. Elliott and Charles Kay, Jr. New York. Appleton-Century-Crofts, Inc. R8vo. 1960c ix + 723 pp.

DU
711
E 47
Ellis, Albert F.
Ocean Island and Nauru. Their story. Sydney. Angus and Robertson Ltd. 1936. 8vo. xvi + 319 pp. 49 illus., 3 maps.

QL
1
F
Elliot, Daniel Giraud, 1835–
... Preliminary descriptions of new rodents from the Olympic Mountains, by D. G. Elliot ... Chicago, 1899.

1 p. l., p. 225–228. 24½ᶜᵐ. (Field Columbian museum. Publication 30. Zoological series. vol. I, no. 11)

1. Rodentia.   4–10875

Library of Congress   QL1.F4
—— Copy 2.   QL737.R6E4

QL
611
I 12
Elliott, H. F. I.
A contribution to the ornithology of the Tristan da Cunha group.

(Ibis, 99(4):545–586, 1957)

QE
75
W
and
QE
Geol.
Pam.
461
Ellis, Arthur Jackson, 1885–
... The divining rod, a history of water witching, with a bibliography, by Arthur J. Ellis. Washington, Govt. print. off., 1917.

59 p. illus. 23½ᶜᵐ. (U. S. Geological survey. Water-supply paper 416)
At head of title: Department of the interior.

1. Divining-rod.

—— Copy 2.   G S 17–226
Library, U. S. Geological   Survey (200) G no. 416

QL
1
F
Elliot, Daniel Giraud, 1835–1915.
... Remarks upon two species of deer of the genus *Cervus* from the Philippine archipelago, by D. G. Elliot ... Chicago, 1897.

2 l. xvi–xxxix pl. (part fold.) 24½ᶜᵐ. (Field Columbian museum. Publication 20. Zoological series. vol. I, no. 7)

1. Deer.   4–10864

Library of Congress   QL1.F4
—— Copy 2.   QL701.E46

QL
638.32
U
Elliott, Henry Wood
U.S. Treasury dept. Special agents div.
Seal and salmon fisheries and general resources of Alaska...1898.
For fuller entry see main card

QE
75
W
ELLIS, E. E.
Gregory, Herbert Ernest, 1869–
... Underground water resources of Connecticut, by Herbert E. Gregory, with a study of the occurrence of water in crystalline rocks, by E. E. Ellis. Washington, Govt. print. off., 1909.

200 p. illus., v pl (incl. fold. map) diagrs. 23ᶜᵐ. (U. S. Geological survey. Water-supply paper 232)

1. Water, Underground—Connecticut. 2. Rocks, Crystalline and metamorphic. I. Ellis, Edwin E.
G S 9–361
Library, U. S. Geological   Survey (200) G no. 232

QL
1
F
Elliot, Daniel Giraud, 1835–
A synopsis of the mammals of North America and the adjacent seas, by Daniel Giraud Elliot ... Chicago (Field Columbian museum) 1901.

xiv p., 1 l., 471 p. illus. xlix pl. (part fold.) 25ᶜᵐ. (Added t.-p.: Publication of the Field Columbian museum. Zoological series, vol. II)

1. Mammals—North America.   3–16833

Library of Congress   QL715.E45
—— Copy 2.   QL1.F4

GN
655
E 47
Ellis, A. B.
The Ewe-speaking peoples of the Slave Coast of West Africa: their religion, manners, customs, laws, languages, etc... London. Chapman and Hall. 1890. 8vo. xiii + 331 pp.

AS
36
S1
Ellis, Havelock i. e. Henry Havelock, 1859–
Mescal: a new artificial paradise. By Havelock Ellis.
(In Smithsonian institution. Annual report. 1897. Washington, 1898, 23½ᶜᵐ. p. 537–548)
"Reprinted from the Contemporary review, January, 1898."

1. Mescal.   S 15–974

Library of Congress   Q11.S66 1897
Library, Smithsonian   Institution

QL
737.P9
F
E46
Elliot, Daniel Giraud, 1835–
A review of the *Primates*, by Daniel Giraud Elliot ... New York, American museum of natural history, 1912.

3 v. fronts. (v. 1,3) plates (part col.) 27½ᶜᵐ. (On cover: Monographs of the American museum of natural history. Monograph series no. 1; vol. 1–III)
"The date 1912 on the title-pages ... should be corrected to June, 1913. Although all the text, except the Appendix in volume III, was printed in 1912, unexpected delay in the preparation of the colored plates prevented the issue of the work till June 15, 1913." cf. 1 l. of "Correction" inserted in each vol.
CONTENTS.—I. Lemuroidea, Daubentonia to Indris; Anthropoidea, Seniocebus to Saimiri.—II. Anthropoidea, Aotus to Lasiopyga.—III. Anthropoidea. Miopithecus to Pan.
1. Primates.   14–362

Library of Congress   QL737.P9E7

GN
653
E47
Ellis, A. B.
The Tshi-speaking peoples of the Gold Coast of West Africa; their religion, manners, customs, laws, language, etc.
London, Chapman, 1887. 8vo. vii + 343 pp.

GN
668
M 25
Ellis, Havelock
Malinowski, Bronislaw
The sexual life of savages in north-western Melanesia: an ethnographic account of courtship, marriage, and family life among the natives of the Trobriand Islands, British New Guinea...with a preface by Havelock Ellis. With 96 full-page plates and figures. London. George Routledge. 1929. 8vo. xxiv + 506 pp.

AS
36
A 5
Elliot, Edith
Its mouth is its nursery and its adaptability is making the Largemouth Kurper a promising source of revenue in Hawaii.

(Natural History, 64(6):330–331, 1955)

GN
655
E 47
Ellis, A. B.
The Yoruba-speaking peoples of the Slave Coast of West Africa, their religion, manners, customs, laws, language, etc. With an appendix containing a comparison of the Tshi, Gã, Ewe, and Yoruba languages. London. Chapman and Hall. 1894. 8vo. vii + 402 pp.

QK
Pam
#649
4to
Ellis, Job Bicknell & Everhart, B. M.
Fungi, ex Bull. of Torrey Bot. Club. vol. 22, no. 7, August, 1895.

QH
194
E46
Elliot, G. F. Scott
Naturalist in mid-Africa. London, Innes, 1896.

DU
711
E 47
Ellis, Sir Albert (F.)
Mid-Pacific outposts. With an introduction by J. R. Stevenson...In Command of the Nauru and Ocean Island Expedition. New Zealand Brown and Stewart Limited. Auckland. 1946. 8vo (16) + 303 pp.

QK
Bot.Pam.
2019
Ellis, J. B. (Job Bicknell)
New Fungi, mostly Uredineae and Ustilagineae from various localities, and a new fomes from Alaska, by J. B. Ellis and B. M. Everhart.

(The Bulletin of the Torrey Botanical Club, Vol. 22, 1895, pp. 362–364)

QK
Bot.Pam.
649

Ellis, J. B.(Job Bicknell)

New species of Canadian Fungi, by J. B. Ellis and J. Dearness.

(Canadian Record of Science, January, 1893, pp. 267-272)

DU
625.4
E 47

ELLIS, MARY MERCY

Ellis, William , 1794-1872

Memoir of Mrs. Mary Mercy Ellis, missionary in the South Seas, and Foreign Secretary of the London Missionary Society...With an introductory essay on the marriage of missionaries, by Rufus Anderson. Boston. Crocker and Brewster. 1836. xxii + 286 pp. 8vo.

DU
Missions
Pa. 23

Ellis, William, 1794-1872

The American Mission in the Sandwich Islands a Vindication and an Appeal, in Relation to the Proceedings of the Reformed Catholic Mission at Honolulu. Honolulu. Reprinted from the London edition, by H. M. Whitney. 1866. 8vo. 77 pp.

Carter Coll. 1-C-21, 6-A-16, 6-C-8

Also copy of the London edition. 108 pp.

QK
Pam
#427

(Job Bicknell)
Ellis, J. B. & Everhart, B. M.

New species of fungi from various localities with notes on some published species, ex Bull. of the Torrey Bot. Club, vol. 27, Feb., 1900.

AS
36
S4

Ellis, Max Mapes, 1887-

The branchiobdellid worms in the collections of the United States National museum, with descriptions of new genera and new species. By Max M. Ellis ...

(*In* U. S. National museum. Proceedings. Washington, 1920. 23½ᵐᵐ. v. 55, p. 241-265. illus., pl. 10-13)

1. Branchiobdellidae.

Library of Congress   Q11.U55 vol. 55   20-5858
                                                    (5)

GN
Pam
2769

Ellis, William , 1794-1872

Extracts from William Ellis regarding the use and significance of feathers. Compiled by J. F. G. Stokes.

26 typed pages.

QK
Pam
#428

(Job Bicknell)
Ellis, J. B. & Everhart, B. M.

New species of fungi, I. Sandwich Island fungi, ex Torrey Bot. Club. Bull. vol. 22, no. 10, Oct., 1895, pp. 434-436; Florida fungi and Mexican fungi, pp. 436-440.

AS
36
C51

Ellis, Max Mapes, 1887-

... The gymnotid eels of tropical America, by Max Mapes Ellis. Pittsburgh, Board of trustees of the Carnegie institute, 1913.

cover-title, p. 109-204. illus., pl. XV-XXIII. 23½ᵐᵐ. (Memoirs of the Carnegie museum. vol. VI. no. 3)

Publications of the Carnegie museum, serial no. 77.

1. Gymnotidae. 2. Fishes—South America.

                                                    13-21896
Library of Congress   AS36.P75

DT
469.M2
E 47

Ellis, William , 1794-1872

History of Madagascar. Comprising also the progress of the Christian Mission established in 1818; and an authentic account of the recent martyrdom, and of the persecution of the native Christians. Compiled chiefly from original documents, by the Rev. William Ellis...In two volumes London. Fisher. (1838). 8vo. pp.xv+617;xi+537.

QL
375
E 47

Ellis, John

An Essay Towards a Natural History of the Corallines, and other Marine Productions of the like Kind, commonly found on the Coasts of Great Britain and Ireland. To which is added The Description of a large Marine Polype taken near the North Pole, by the Whale-fishers, in the Summer 1753. London. Printed for the Author. 1755. sm 4to. xvii + (10) + 103 pp., xxxviii pl.

DU
620
F

ELLIS, MRS. SARAH S.

Damon, S. C.

To the memory of the Rev. William Ellis and Mrs. Sarah S. Ellis...

(Friend, August 1872, pp. 65-67)

DU
623
E 47

2 cops.

Ellis, William, 1794-1872

Journal of a tour around Hawaii, the largest of the Sandwich Islands. By a deputation from the Mission on those islands. Boston. Crocker & Brewster. 1825. 12mo. xii+264 pp.

DU
625.4
E 47

Ellis, John Eimeo

Life of William Ellis, missionary to the South Seas and to Madagascar. With a supplementary chapter containing an estimate of his character and work, by Henry Allon, D. D. London. John Murray. 1873. xxiv + 310 pp. 8vo.

DU
620
H 41

Ellis, Thomas W.

A tapa book.

(Haw. Hist. Soc. Paper No. 15, 1928:46-50)

Carter Coll.
5-A-5, 2-A-5

Ellis, William .

A journal of a tour around Hawaii, the largest of the Sandwich Islands. Boston. Crocker and Brewster. 1825 pp. 264 sm8vo

---

QL
379
E47

Ellis, John and Solander, Daniel

The natural history of many curious and uncommon zoophytes collected from various parts of the globe by the late John Ellis.... systematically arranged and described by the late Daniel Solander... with 62 plates engraven by principal artists.

London, 1786, 208 pp, 63 pls. 4to.

DU
12
E 47
locked
case

card 2

Ellis, William ,   (surgeon)

An authentic narrative of a voyage performed by Captain Cook and Captain Clerke... Second edition. 2 vols. London. G. Robinson, J. Sewell... 1785. 8vo.

HAWAII   Carter Coll.
                         5-A-5,2-A-5

Ellis, William .

A journal of a tour around Hawaii, the largest of the Sandwich Islands. Boston. Crocker and Brewster. 1825. pp. 264. sm8vo.

GN
Pam
#155

Ellis, M.

Idolatry among the Indians of Puget Sound, Washington Territory, ex The Museum, vol. I, no. 1, 1917.

DU
12
E 47
locked
case

card 1

Ellis, William ,   (surgeon)

An authentic narrative of a voyage performed by Captain Cook and Captain Clerke, in His Majesty's Ships Resolution and Discovery during the years 1776-1780; in search of a north-west passage between the continents of Asia and America. Including a faithful account of all their discoveries, and the unfortunate death of Captain Cook. Illustrated with a chart and a variety of cuts. By W. Ellis, assistant surgeon to both vessels. 2 volumes. London. G. Robinson, J. Sewell... 1782. 8vo. pp.(7)+358; (5)+347.

                        see next card

DU
Pac.Pam.
253

Ellis, William

Journal of a tour around Hawaii...

Sanders, Mrs. E.

Remarks on the "Tour Around Hawaii" by the missionaries, Messrs. Ellis, Thurston, Bishop, and Goodrich, in 1823. Salem. 1848.

DU
623
384

Ellis, William, 1794-1872

Stewart, C. S.

Journal of a residence in the Sandwich Islands during the years 1823, 1824, and 1825: including remarks on the manners and customs of the inhabitants; an account of Lord Byron's visit in H.M.S. Blonde...With an introduction, and occasional notes by William Ellis. London. H.Fisher 1828.

Also third   edition, with a map and plates. 1830.   2 copies. 8 vo. 407 pp.

Carter Coll.
1-B-9

Ellis, William .

Reife burch Hawaii ober Owhyhee. (Eine der Sandwichs-Infeln.) Rebft Bemerfungen über bie Gefchichte, Cagen, Fitten und Gebrauche ber Ginmohner ber Gandwichs-Infeln. Hamburg . August Campe. 1827 vi + 258 pp. 8vo.

QH
1.S
W 31

ELLISELLIDÁE   PACIFIC

Bayer, Frederick M.

The Ellisellidae (Octocorallia) and their bearing on the zoogeography of the eastern Pacific by Frederick M. Bayer and Elizabeth Deichmann.

(Proc. Bio. Soc. Washington, 73:175-182, 1960)

DU
625.4
E 47

Ellis, William, 1794-1872

Memoir of Mrs. Mary Mercy Ellis, missionary in the South Seas, and Foreign Secretary of the London Missionary Society. Including notices of Heathen Society, of the details of missionary life, and the remarkable display of divine goodness in severe and protracted afflictions. With an introductory essay on the marriage of missionaries, by Reverend Rufus Anderson. Boston. Crocker And Brewster. 1836. xxii + 286 pp. 8vo.

DT
469.M2
E 47

Ellis, William

Three visits to Madagascar during the years 1853-1854-1856, including a journey to the capital, with notices of the natural history of the country and of the present civilisation of the people. Illustrated by woodcuts from photographs. London. John Murray. 1858. R8vo. xvii + 470 pp.

DU
Pac.Pam.
642
736

Ellison, Joseph W.

Opening and penetration of foreign influence in Samoa to 1880. Oregon State College, Corvallis. Studies in History, 1, 1938. 108 pp. R8vo.

DU
623
E 47

Ellis, William, 1794-1872

Missionsreise durch Hawaii, eine der Sandwichs-Inseln, von William Ellis. Aus dem Ethnographischen Archiv besonders abgedruckt. Jena. Bran'schen. 1827. 8vo. 176 pp.

DU
Missions
Pam. 14

Ellis, William, 1794-1872

A Vindication of the South Sea Missions from the Misrepresentations of Otto von Kotzebue, with an Appendix. London. Frederick Westley and A. H. Davis. 1831. 8vo. iv +63 pp.

AS
162
P 23

ELLOBIIDAE   NEW CALEDONIA

Franc, A.

Revision des Ellobiidae (Pulmones Basommatophores) de l'Archipel neo-calédonien.

(Bull. Mus. Nat. d'Hist. Nat., s.2, vol. 26 (4):515-518, 1954)

DU
623
E 47

Ellis, William, 1794-1872

Narrative of a tour through Hawaii, or, Owhyhee; with remarks on the history, traditions, manners, customs, and language of the inhabitants of the Sandwich Islands. London. H. Fisher. 1826. 8vo. (9)+442 pp.

2 cops.   Second edition, enlarged...with observations on the natural history of the Sandwich Islands...London. H. Fisher. 1827. 8vo. (7)+480 pp.

Fourth edition...1828. London

DU
12
S 85

Ellis, William, 1794-1872   editor

Stewart, C. S.

Visit to the South Seas, in the U. S. ship Vincennes, during...1829-1830...edited and abridged by William Ellis. London. 1832. 18mo.

GC
63
D 61

ELLOBIOPSIDAE

Boschma, H.

Ellobiopsidae.

IN Discovery Reports, Vol. 25:281-314, 1949

DU
623
E 47

Ellis, William, 1794-1872

Narrative of a tour through Hawaii, or Owhyhee; with remarks on the history, traditions, manners, customs and language of the inhabitants of the Sandwich Islands. (Reprint of the London 1827 edition). With an introduction by Lorrin A. Thurston. Honolulu. Hawaiian Gazette. 1917. 8vo. 367 pp.

DU
620
F

ELLIS, WILLIAM, 1794-1872

Bishop, Artemas

Some recollections of the Rev. William Ellis.

(Friend, August 1872, p. 68)

DU
Pac.Pam.
938

Ellsworth, S. George

Zion in Paradise; early Mormons in the South Seas. Twenty-first Faculty Honor Lecture Utah State University, Logan, 1959. 8vo. 34 pp

---

card 1

DU
12
E 47

Ellis, William, 1794-1872

Polynesian Researches, during a residence of nearly six years in the South Sea islands; including descriptions of the natural history and scenery of the islands--with remarks on the history, mythology, traditions, government, arts, manners, and customs of the inhabitants. In two volumes. London. Fisher, Jackson. 1829. 8vo. pp.xvi+536

DU 12
E 47
locked
case

viii+576.

The same...1830.   8vo. 2 vols.

see next card

DU
620
F

ELLIS, WILLIAM, 1794-1872

Damon, S. C.

To the memory of the Rev. William Ellis and Mrs. Sarah S. Ellis...

(Friend, August 1872, pp. 65-67)

QK
1
P 56

Elmer, A. D. E.

A century of Philippine Meliaceae.

(Leaflets of Philippine Botany. vol.IX. Art.128. 1937. 122 pp.)

---

card 2

DU
12
E 47
locked
case

Ellis, William, 1794-1872

Polynesian Researches during a residence of nearly eight years in the Society and Sandwich Islands. Second edition, enlarged and improved. In four volumes. London. Fisher, Jackson. (1831)-1839. 18mo.

DU 12
E 47

The same. (1831)-1842. 12mo.   4 vols.

DU 12E47   Index to 2d edition. 2 copies.

DU
625.4
E 47

ELLIS, WILLIAM, 1794-1872

Ellis, John Eimeo

Life of William Ellis, missionary to the South Seas and to Madagascar. With a supplementary chapter containing an estimate of his character and work, by Henry Allon, D. D. London. John Murray. 1873. xxiv + 310 pp. 8vo.

QK
1
P 56

Elmer, A. D. E.

See

Leaflets of Philippine Botany

Vol. 1, 1907 -

QK
Bot.Pam
1797

Elmer, A. D. E.

New Plants from Mount Pinatubo (Philippine Islands). 47 pp.

(Leaflets of Philippine Botany, Vol. IX, Art. 126. May 5, 1934. pp. 3179-3226).

AS
36
W 2

ELOPS

Hildebrand, Samuel F.

Notes on the affinity, anatomy, and development of Elops saurus Linnaeus.

(Journal of the Washington Acad. of Sci., Vol. 33, 1943, pp. 90-94)

QH
541
E 51

Elton, Charles

The Ecology of Animals. Methuen and Co., Ltd. London. 12mo. reprint:1957   97 pp.

QK
1
P 96

Elmer, A. D. E.

New Symplocos from Mindanao, ex Leaflets of Philippine Bot., vol. VII, art. 109.

Manila, August, 1914.

QL
Protozoa
to
Polyzoa
Pam
377

Elrington, George A

Some points in the structure of the larva of lanice conchilega.   From Review La Cellule, 25, 1er, fascicule, 1908.

Q
101
P 18

Elton, Charles

The natural control of rodent populations.

(Proc. Pac. Sci. Congress, 6th, Vol. 5, 1942, pp. 109-114) (Date of congress, 1939)

QK
1
P 96

Elmer, A. D. E.

New Urticaceae and Rubiaceae (Philippine Islands).   45 pp.

(Leaflets of Philippine Botany, Vol. IX, Art. 127, June 14, 1934. pp. 3227-3272).

EL SALVADOR   BIRDS

See

BIRDS   EL SALVADOR

QH
541
E 51

Elton, Charles S.

The ecology of invasions by animals and plants.   Methuen and Co Ltd.   London. 8vo 181 pp. (1958)

QK
1
P 96

Elmer, A. D. E.

Six new Myrsinaceae, ex Leaflets of Philippine Botany, vol. II, art. 22, November, 1908.

DU
711
H14
E 49

Elschner, Carl

Corallogene Phosphat-Inseln Austral-Oceaniens und ihre produkte. Lubeck: 1913, 4to, pp 118.

[Nauru, Ocean, Angaur, Baker, Makatea, Howland, Phoenix, Malden, Equatorial Is., Johnston, Clipperton]

reviewed by Wm. Churchill in Bull. Am. Geog. Soc. 46:691, 1914

GN
2.1
A-4

Elton, F.

Notes on natives of Solomon Islands.

(Journ. Anthrop. Inst. of Great Britain and Ireland, Vol. 17, 1887-8, pp. 90-99)

QL
Insect
Pam.
1483

Elmore, J. C.

The pepper weevil.   By J. C. Elmore and Roy E. Campbell.

(U. S. Dept. of Agric, Leaflet No. 226, Rev. ed. 1951)

Anthonomus eugenii Cano.

QE
Pam
#60

Elschner, Carl

Kolloide phosphate, ex der Kolloid-Zeitschrift, XXXI. Band 1922, Heft 2.

QL
464
E 51

Eltringham, H.

Histological and illustrative methods for entomologists.   With a chapter on mounting whole insects by H. Britten.   Oxford.   At the Clarendon Press.   1930.   8vo. ix + 139 pp.

QL
Insect
Pam. 961

Elmore, J. C.

The tomato pinworm.

(Circular, U. S. D. A., No. 440, 1937)

DU
Pacific
Pam
#69

Elschner, Carl

The Leeward islands of the Hawaiian group. Contribution to the knowledge of the Islands of Oceania. Honolulu, 1915, 8vo. pp. 68.

[Nihoa, Necker, French Frigate, Laysan, Lisianski, Pearl and Hermes, Midway]

Given by the author   Nov. 16, 1915.

GN
Ethn.Pam.
2829

Eluard, Paul

Breton, André

Collection André Breton et Paul Eluard. Scuptures d'Afriques, d'Amérique, d'Océanie. Paris, 1931, 51 pp. xxiv plates.

QK
Bot. Pam.
3285

ELODEA

St. John, Harold

Monograph of the genus Elodea (Hydrocharitaceae), Part I:The species found in the Great Plains, the Rocky Mountains, and the Pacific states and provinces of North America.

(Research Studies, Washington State University, 30(2):19-44, 1962)

AS
36
S1

Elsdale, Henry, 1843-
Scientific problems of the future. By Lieut. Col. H. Elsdale.

(*In* Smithsonian institution. Annual report. 1894. Washington, 1896. 23½cm. p. 667-679)

"From the Contemporary review, March 1894."

1. Science.

S 15-881

Library of Congress   Q11.S66 1894
Library, Smithsonian   Institution

DU
400
E 52

Elvy, W. J.

Kaikoura coast, the history, traditions and Maori place-names of Kaikoura.   Christchurch. Whitcombe and Tombs, Ltd.   1949.   vii + 103 pp.; illustrated + 1 map.   sm8vo.

GN
2.S
P 76
Elvy, W. J.

    Te Rae o Te Karaka, a pa or fortified village in Queen Charlotte Sound.

    (Journal of the Polynesian Society, 36: 367-368, 1927.)

AS
36
S7
Ely, Leonard Wheeler, 1868-

    ... Bone and joint studies ... by Leonard W. Ely ... and John Francis Cowan ... Stanford University, Cal., The University, 1916-

    v. illus. 26ᶜᵐ. (Leland Stanford junior university publications. University series. i25

    "From the Laboratory of surgical pathology, Stanford medical school."

    1. Bones. 2. Joints. 3. Surgery, Experimental.   i. Cowan, John Francis, 1880-   joint author.

                           17-194

    Library of Congress   RD61.E5

Editor's
Room
Emberger, Meta Riley

    Scientific writing. By Meta Riley Emberger and Marian Ross Hall; general editor: W. Earl Britton. Harcourt, Brace and Company. New York 8vo. 1955c xii + 468 pp.

GN
2.S
P 76
Elvy, W. J.

    Supposed pit-dwellings in Queen Charlotte Sound.

    (Journal of the Polynesian Society, 35: 329-332, 1926.)

QL
461
H 1
ELYTROTEINUS

Zimmerman, Elwood C.

    A second species of Elytroteinus (Col., Curculionidae).

    (Haw. Ent. Soc., Proc., Vol. 10, 1938, pp. 155-157)

AS
763
B 4
EMBIIDAE

Friederichs, Karl

    Check list of the Embiidae (Embioptera) of Oceania. Honolulu. 1935. 4 pp.

QL
Insect
Pam.
893

Reading
Room
    (Bernice P. Bishop Museum, Occasional Papers, Vol. XI, No. 7)

DU
12
ELG
E52
Elwes, Robert.

    A sketcher's tour round the world. By Robert Elwes. With illustrations from original drawings, by the author.

    London, Hurst & Blackett, 1854.
        411p. illus.

QH
1
P 11
ELYTRURUS

Zimmerman, Elwood C.

    Description of a new species of Elytrurus and a catalogue of the known species (Coleoptera: Curculionidae: Otiorhynchinae).

    (Pacific Science, Vol. X(3):286-295, July, 1956)

QL
595.Mi
I 59
EMBIOPTERA

Ross, Edward S.

    Insects of Micronesia, Embioptera.
    IN

    Insects of Micronesia, Vol. 8(1), 1955

QK
Bot.Pam.
2444
Elwin, Verrier

    The sago palm in Bastar State.

    (Journal of the Royal Asiatic Society, Bombay Branch, N.S. Vol. 18, pp. 69-78, 1942)

QL
Mammals
Pam.281
EMBALLONURA

Sanborn, Colin Campbell

    Notes on the Caroline sheath-tailed bat. (Emballonura sulvata Miller)

    (Natural History Miscellanea, No. 49, 1949)

QL
598.Mi
I 59
EMBIOPTERA   MICRONESIA

Ross, Edward S.

    Insects of Micronesia; Embioptera.
    IN

    Insects of Micronesia, Vol. 8(1), 1955. Bishop Museum Press. Honolulu.

AS
36
W 2
Ely, Charles A.

    A new brittle-star (Ophiocoma anaglyptica) from Canton Island.

    (Jour. Washington Acad. Sci., 34:373-375, 1944)

QL
1
F 45
EMBALLONURA

Sanborn, Colin Campbell

    The sheath-tailed bat of the Palau and Marshall Islands.

    (Fieldiana. Zoology, Vol. 31 (8):59-61, 1947)

QL
461
H-1
EMBIOPTERA   PACIFIC

Ross, Edward S.

    A new species of Embioptera from Oceania.

    (Haw. Ent. Soc., Proc., 14(2):307-310, 1951)

QL
383.8
E 52
Ely, Charles A.

    Shallow-water Asteroidea and Ophiuroidea of Hawaii.

    (Bernice P. Bishop Museum, Bull. 176, 1942)

GN
1
O 15
Ember, Melvin

    The nonunilinear descent groups of Samoa.

    (American Anthropologist, 61:573-577, 1959)

QK
Bot.Pam.
2835
EMBIOPTERA   TRINIDAD

McC. Callan, E.

    Embioptera of Trinidad with notes on their parasites.

    (Reprinted from Trans. Ninth Int. Congr. Ent. Vol. 1:483-489, 1952)

DU
620
M 27
Ely, James

    Letter of Mr. Ely to the corresponding Secretary, Kaavaloa, Nov. 23, 1826.

    (Missionary Herald, Vol. 23, 1827, pp. 209-211)

    (Notes on some of the chiefs, population estimates, printing of large editions of the gospel urged so that it may be an object of trade, a writing school established)

GN
1
A 51
Ember, Melvin

    Political authority and the structure of kinship in aboriginal Samoa.

    (Am. Anthropologist, Vol. 64:964-971, 1962)

QL
Fishes
Pam.
573
EMBLEMARIIDAE

Böhlke, James

    The Bahaman species of emblemariid blennies.

    (Proc. of the Academy of Natural Sci. of Phila., Vol. CIX:25-57, 1957)

DU
620
P 22
Emblems of royalty; a magnificent display awaits tourists in the kahili room of Bishop Museum.

(Paradise of the Pacific, 70(4):9-11, 1958)

GN
625
E 53
Embree, John F.
Bibliography of the peoples and cultures of mainland southeast Asia. By John F. Embree and Lillian Ota Dotson. Yale University, Southeast Asia Studies. New Haven. 1950. xxxiii + 821 + XII pp.

DS
Asia
Pam. 42
Embree, John F.
Maspero, Georges
The kingdom of Champa [Le royaume du Champa] Paris. Van Oest. 1928.
Translation by John F. Embree, Southeast Asia Studies, Yale University. 1949. 56 pp. mimeographed.

AS
36
S4
Embody, George Charles, 1876–
A new fresh-water amphipod from Virginia, with some notes on its biology. By George C. Embody ...
(*In* U. S. National museum. Proceedings. Washington, 1911. 23½ᶜᵐ. vol. 38, p. 299-305. illus.)

1. Amphipoda. 2. Crustacea—Virginia.

11–15732

Library of Congress   Q11.U55 vol. 38

GN
Ethn.Pam.
3676
Embree, John F.
A bibliography of the physical anthropology of Indo-China, 1938-1947.

(Reprint, Am. Jour. Physical Anthrop., ns vol. 7(1):39-51, 1949)

DU
I 59
Embree, John F.
Micronesia: The Navy and democracy.

(Far Eastern Survey, Vol. 15, No. 11, pp. 161-164, 1946)

DU
Hist.Pam.
183
Embree, Edwin R.
A New School in American Samoa. Published by the Julius Rosenwald Fund, 1932. 20 pp.

GN
1
A
Embree, John F.
Community analysis- an example of anthropology in government.

(American Anthropologist, Vol. 46, 1944, pp. 277-291)

GN
Ethn.Pam.
3677
Embree, John F.
Military government in Saipan and Tinian.

(Applied Anthropology, Vol. 5(1):1-39, 1946)

GN
Ethn.Pam.
3548
Embree, Edwin R.
Peoples of the earth. Hinds, Hayden and Eldredge. New York; Philadelphia. 4to. 73 pp. 1948c

---

GN
635.S2
E 53
Embree, John F.
Ethnic groups of northern southeast Asia. By John F. Embree and William L. Thomas, Jr. Yale Univ., Southeast Asia Studies. New Haven. 1950. 175 pp. unbd. 4to.

GN
2.S
A 51
Embree, John F.
Notes on the Indian god Gavagriva (Godzu Tenno) in contemporary Japan.

(Jour. of the Am. Oriental Soc., Vol. 59, 1939, pp. 67-70)

DU
12
I 92
Embree, Ella (translator)
Iuzhnyi Polius iz zapisok byvshago morskago ofitsera...(The South Pole: memoirs of an ex-naval officer) St. Petersburg. 1853. 8vo. 94 pp. (and English abstract by Mrs. Ella Embree)

(written by one of the officers accompanying Bellinghausen)

DU
Pac.Pam.
648
Embree, John F.
Field report on trip to Micronesia. Dec. 14, 1945 to Jan. 5, 1946. typed copy. 121 pp.

GN
1
A
Embree, John F.
New and local kin groups among the Japanese farmers of Kona, Hawaii.

(American Anthropologist, N. S. 1939, Vol. 41, pp. 400-407)

GN
2.S
A 22

and
GN
Ethn.Pam.
3408
Embree, John F.
Acculturation among the Japanese of Kona, Hawaii.

(Memoirs of the American Anthropological Association, No. 59, 1941)

GN
1
J
Embree, John F.
Japanese peasant songs. Compiled and annotated by John F. Embree with the assistance of Ella Embree and Yukuo Uyehara.

(American Folklore Society, Memoirs, Vol. 38, 1943)

AS
36
W 2
Embree, John F.
The relocation of persons of Japanese ancestry in the United States: some causes and effects.

(Journal of the Washington Academy of Sci., Vol. 33, 1943, pp. 238-242)

GN
1
A
Embree, John
Applied anthropology and its relationship to anthropology.

(American Anthropologist, n.s. 47:635-637, 1945)

GN
Ethn.Pam
3675
Embree, John F.
Kickball and some other parallels between Siam and Micronesia.

(Jour. of the Siam Society, 37(1):33-38, 1948)

GN
Ethn.
Pam.
3460
Embree, John F.
Resistance to freedom, an administrative problem.
(Applied Anthropology, Vol. 2, No. 4, pp. 10-14, 1943)

AS
36
W 2
Embree, John F.

Sanitation and health in a Japanese village.

(Jour. Washington Acad. of Sci., 34:97-108, 1944)

GN
1
J 35
EMBREE, JOHN F(EE)

Yamamoto, Tadashi

Bibliography of Professor John F. Embree.

(The Japanese Jour. of Ethnology, 17(2): 84-86, 1952)

QL
971
F95
EMBRYOLOGY

Foster, M   and Balfour, Francis M

The elements of embryology.

London, Macmillan, 1902.   486p.

GN
635.J 3
E 53
Embree, John F.

Suye Mura, a Japanese village.
University of Chicago Press. Chicago. 8vo.
xxvii + 354 pp.

QL
1
H 2
EMBRYOLOGY

Agassiz, Alexander   and others

Selections from embryological monographs.
I-III.

(Mem. Mus. Comp. Zool. Harvard, Vol. 9, 1882-1884)
-----Bibliography: Bull. Mus. Comp. Zool.
Harvard, Vol. 9, No. 6; X, No. 2; XI, No. 10.

QM
601
K 27
EMBRYOLOGY.

Keibel, Franz and Mall, Franklin P.

Manual of human embryology.   2 Vols.

London. 1910 - 1912.

GN
1
A
Embree, John F.

Thailand- a loosely structured social system.

(American Anthropologist, Vol. 52(2):181-193, 1950)

AS
36
S
EMBRYOLOGY

Agassiz, L.

Classification of Insects from Embryological data.

in Smith. Cont. to Know. II Art VI, pp. 1-28, pls. I.

Wash., 1851.

QL
3
M 7
EMBRYOLOGY

Mark anniversary volume; to Edward Laurens Mark,
Hersey professor of anatomy and director of the zoölogical laboratory at Harvard university, in celebration of twenty-five years of successful work for the
advancement of zoölogy, from his former students,
1877-1902. New York, H. Holt and company, 1903.
2 p. l., (iii)-xiii, 513 p. front. (port.) xxxvi pl. (partly col.) 31 x 24½ᵐ.
Edited by George Howard Parker.
Contains bibliographies.
CONTENTS.—Goto, S. The craspedote medusa *Olindias* and some of its
natural allies.—Pratt, H. S. Descriptions of four distomes.—Locy, W. A.
A new cranial nerve in selachians.—Reighard, J. The natural history of
Amia calva Linnaeus.—Kofoid, C. A. On the structure of *Protophrys*
ovicola, a ciliate infusorian from the brood-sac of *Littorina rudis* Don.—
                                    (Continued on next card)
                                            4-2336

GN
1
A
Embree, John F.

University of Hawaii research in Micronesia.

(American Anthropologist, n.s. 48:476-77, 1946)

QL
955
Ag
A26
EMBRYOLOGY

Agassiz, Louis *i. e.* Jean Louis Rodolphe, 1807-1873.
   Twelve lectures on comparative embryology, delivered
before the Lowell institute, in Boston, December and January, 1848-9, by Louis Agassiz ... Phonographic report,
by James W. Stone ... Originally reported and published
in the Boston daily evening traveller. Boston, Redding
& co.; New York, Dewitt & Davenport; [etc., etc.] 1849.
   104 p. illus. 23ᵐ.

   [XXXV-XXXI] **Embryology**

                                            6-32067

Library of Congress   QL955.A26

QK
Botany
Pam.
1310
EMBRYOLOGY

Stenar, A. Helge S:son

Embryologische Studien: I, Zur Embryologie einiger Columniferen; II, Die Embryologie der Amaryllideen. Akademische
Abhandlung....

Uppsala, 1925, 195 pp.

AS
36
W 2
Embree, John

A visit to Laos, French Indo-China.

(Journal of the Washington Academy of Sci.,
Vol. 39:149-157, 1949)

Sent
to
Univ.
of
Hawaii

EMBRYOLOGY

Carnegie institution of Washington.
   Contributions to embryology. vol. I, no. 1–
Washington, D. C., Carnegie institution of Washington,
1915–
   v. illus., plates (part col.) 29½ᵐ. (*On verso of t.-p.*: Carnegie institution of Washington. Publication no. 221–

   1. Embryology.   I. Title.
                                            15-16335
Library of Congress   {   } QM601.C3
                                 [a20h3]

EMBRYOLOGY -- BOTANY

See

BOTANY -- EMBRYOLOGY

GN
1
A 62
EMBREE, JOHN FEE

Eggan, Fred

John Fee Embree, 1908-1950.

(American Anthropologist, 53(3):376-382, 1951)

QL
958
Co
C7S
EMBRYOLOGY

Conklin, Edwin Grant, 1863–
   The embryology of Crepidula: a contribution to the
cell lineage and early development of some marine gasteropods; by Edwin Grant Conklin ... Boston, Ginn &
company, 1897.
   1 p. l., 226 p. illus., 9 pl. (part col.) 25½ᵐ. (Contributions from the
Zoölogical laboratory of the University of Pennsylvania)
   Reprinted from Journal of morphology, vol. XIII, no. 1.

   Embryology   2. Crepidula.

                                            3-16270
Library of Congress   QL958.C7

QM
601
K 28
Embryology, Human

Keith, Arthur.
   Human embryology and morphology, by Arthur Keith
... 4th ed., rev. and enl., illustrated with 449 figures in
the text, of which 126 are new in this edition. London,
E. Arnold, 1913.
   viii, 475 p. illus. 22ᵐ.
   441

   1. Embryology, Human.   I. Title.   A 15-689

Title from Leland Stan-   ford Jr. Univ. Printed by L. C.

GN
2.I
A-m
EMBREE, JOHN FEE

Radcliffe-Brown, A. R.

John Fee Embree, 26 August, 1908-22 December 1950.

(Man, No. 233, Oct. 1951)

QL
951
D 13
EMBRYOLOGY

Dalcq, A. M.

Introduction to general embryology. Translated by Jean Medawar. Oxford University Press
1957, 8vo. vii + 177 pp.

QL
958
B74
EMBRYOLOGY - AMPHIBIA

Bosaeus, Wilhelm

Beitrage zur kenntnis der genese der ovarial
embryone: experimentelle untersuchungen uber
parthenogenetische ovarialgraviditat bei amphi-
bien.

Uppsala, Almquist, 1926.   303p.   pls.
(Akademische abhandlung)

EMBRYOLOGY--ECHINODERMATA

QL
1
H2

Agassiz, Alexander, 1835–1910.

... Selections from embryological monographs. Comp. by Alexander Agassiz, Walter Faxon, and E. L. Mark ... Cambridge, Printed for the Museum, 1882–84.

3 v. in 1. 42 pl. 29ᶜᵐ. (Memoirs of the Museum of comparative zoology at Harvard college, vol. IX)

CONTENTS.—I. Crustacea, by Walter Faxon.—II. Echinodermata, by Alexander Agassiz.—III. Acalephs, by J. W. Fewkes; and Polyps, by E. L. Mark.

1. Embryology—Echinodermata. 2. Embryology—Crustacea. 3. Embryology—Coelenterata. I. Faxon, Walter, 1848– II. Mark, Edward Laurens, 1847– III. Fewkes, Jesse Walter, 1850–

Another copy.   QL951.A26   A 19-1047
Title from Univ. of Chicago   QL1.H375 vol. 9
Printed by L. C.   (3)

EMBRYOLOGY--POLYZOA.

QL
1
C15

Robertson, Alice, 1859–

... Embryology and embryonic fission in the genus *Crisia*. By Alice Robertson. Berkeley, The University press, 1903.

cover-title, p. 115–156. pl. XII–XIV (2 fold.) 27ᶜᵐ. (University of California publications. Zoology, v. 1, no. 3)

Thesis (PH. D.)—Univ. of Calif.

1. Crissiidae. 2. Embryology—Polyzoa. 3. Fission.

A 11-2274

Title from Univ. of Calif.   Library of Congress

EMBRYOLOGY, EXPERIMENTAL

QP
1
C

Bullot, Georges.

... Artificial parthenogenesis and regular segmentation in an annelid (*Ophelia*), by G. Bullot. Berkeley, The University press (1904)

cover-title, p. (165)–174. illus. 27ᶜᵐ. (University of California publications. Physiology. vol. 1, no. 19)

From the Rudolph Spreckels physiological laboratory of the University of California.

Reprinted, in part, from the Archiv für entwicklungs-mechanik der organismen. vol. 18, 1904, p. 161–

1 Parthenogenesis (Animals) 2. Fertilization (Biology) 3. Embryology, Experimental.

A 11-1255

Title from Univ. of Calif.   Library of Congress

EMBRYOLOGY, EXPERIMENTAL

QP
1
C

Loeb, Jacques, 1859–

... Artificial parthenogenesis in molluscs, by Jacques Loeb. Berkeley, The University press, 1903.

cover-title, p. (7)–9. 27ᶜᵐ. (University of California publications. Physiology. vol. 1, no. 3)

1. Mollusks. 2. Parthenogenesis (Animals) 3. Embryology, Experimental.

A 11-1265

Title from Univ. of Calif.   Library of Congress

EMBRYOLOGY, EXPERIMENTAL

QP
1
C

Loeb, Jacques, 1859–

... The fertilization of the egg of the sea-urchin (*Strongylocentrotus purpuratus* and *Strongylocentrotus franciscanus*) by the sperm of the starfish (*Asterias ochracea*) by Jacques Loeb. Berkeley, The University press, 1903.

cover-title, p. (39)–53. 27ᶜᵐ. (University of California publications. Physiology. vol. 1, no. 6)

"Address delivered before Sigma Xi scientific society at Stanford university, Oct. 13, 1903."

1. Fertilization (Biology) 2. Echinodermata. 3. Embryology, Experimental. 4. Sea-urchins.

A 11-1269

Title from Univ. of Calif.   Library of Congress

EMBRYOLOGY, EXPERIMENTAL

QP
1
C

Loeb, Jacques, 1859–

... Further experiments on the fertilization of the egg of the sea-urchin (*Strongylocentrotus purpuratus*) with sperm of various species of starfish and a holothurian (*Cucumaria*) By Jacques Loeb. Berkeley, The University press, 1904.

cover-title, p. (83)–85. 27ᶜᵐ. (University of California publications. Physiology. vol. 1, no. 11)

1. Fertilization (Biology) 2. Echinodermata. 3. Embryology, Experimental. 4. Sea-urchins.

A 11-1271

Title from Univ. of Calif.   Library of Congress

EMBRYOLOGY, EXPERIMENTAL

QP
1
C

Loeb, Jacques, 1859–

... Further experiments on heterogeneous hybridization in echinoderms ... By Jacques Loeb (tr. from Pflüger's Archiv, 1904, v. 104, p. 325, by John Bruce MacCallum) (Berkeley, The University press) 1904.

p. (5)–30. illus. 27ᶜᵐ. (University of California publications. Physiology. vol. 2, no. 2)

Issued in single cover with v. 2, no. 3–4, of the series.

1. Echinodermata. 2. Fertilization (Biology) 3. Embryology, Experimental. I. MacCallum, John Bruce, 1876–1906, tr.

A 11-1270

Title from Univ. of Calif.   Library of Congress

EMBRYOLOGY, EXPERIMENTAL

QP
1
C

Loeb, Jacques, 1859–

... On a method by which the eggs of a sea-urchin (*Strongylocentrotus purpuratus*) can be fertilized with the sperm of a starfish (*Asterias ochracea*). By Jacques Loeb. Berkeley, The University press, 1903.

cover-title, 3 p. 27ᶜᵐ. (University of California publications. Physiology. v. 1, no. 1)

1. Fertilization (Biology) 2. Echinodermata. 3. Embryology, Experimental. 4. Sea-urchins.

A 11-1275

Title from Univ. of Calif.   Library of Congress

EMBRYOLOGY, EXPERIMENTAL

QP
1
C

Loeb, Jacques, 1859–

... On the counteraction of the toxic effect of hypertonic solutions upon the fertilized and unfertilized egg of the sea-urchin by lack of oxygen. By Jacques Loeb ... (Berkeley, The University press) 1906.

p. (49)–56. 27ᶜᵐ. (University of California publications. Physiology. v. 3, no. 7)

From the Herzstein research laboratory at New Monterey.

1. Sea-urchins. 2. Embryology, Experimental.

A 11-1280

Title from Univ. of Calif.   Library of Congress

EMBRYOLOGY, EXPERIMENTAL

QP
1
C

Loeb, Jacques, 1859–

... The toxicity of atmospheric oxygen for the eggs of the sea-urchin (*Strongylocentrotus purpuratus*) after the process of membrane formation. By Jacques Loeb ... (Berkeley, The University press) 1906.

p. (33)–37. 27ᶜᵐ. (University of California publications. Physiology. v. 3, no. 5)

From the Herzstein research laboratory at New Monterey.

1. Sea-urchins. 2. Embryology, Experimental.

A 11-1287

Title from Univ. of Calif.   Library of Congress

EMBRYOLOGY HUMAN

QM
601
K 28

Keith, Arthur

Human embryology and morphology. 4th ed. rev. and enlarged. illustrated. London. E.Arnold. 1921

EMBRYOLOGY INSECTA

QL
494
J 65

Johannsen, Oskar A.

Embryology of insects and myriapods: the developmental history of insects, centipedes, and millepedes from egg deposition to hatching. By Oskar A. Johannsen and Ferdinand H. Butt. First edition. McGraw-Hill Book Company, Inc. New York and London. 1941. R8vo. xi + 462 pp.

EMBRYOLOGY MYRIAPODA

QL
494
J 65

Johannsen, Oskar A.

Embryology of insects and myriapods: the developmental history of insects, centipedes, and millepedes from egg deposition to hatching. By Oskar A. Johannsen and Ferdinand H. Butt. First edition. McGraw-Hill Book Company, Inc. New York and London. 1941. R8vo. xi + 462 pp.

G
51
W 17

Embury, E. M.

Sea-birds of the Great Barrier reef.

(Walkabout, Vol. 5 (4):13-16, 1939)

(picture and text about sooty tern; text about other sea birds, mutton bird (shearwater) etc.)

QL
461
D 48-a

Emden, F. van

Neue und bekannte Carabidae aus Java. (Coleoptera).

(Deutsche Entom.Institut, Arbeiten über morphologische und taxonomische Entomologie aus Berlin-Dahlem. Bd.3, 1936. pp.268-280; Bd.4, 1937. pp.112-125)

GN
490
Y 73

Emerick, Richard G.

Land tenure in the Marianas.

Young, John de   and others
Land tenure patterns, Trust Territory of the Pacific Islands. Volume 1, Part 4, 1958

EMERITA

AP
2
S 35

Bonnet, David D.

The Portuguese man-of-war as a food source for the sand crab (Emerita pacifica).

(Science, Vol. 103:148-149, 1946)

EMERITA ANALOGA

QL
1
C 15

Mead, Harold Tupper.

... Notes on the natural history and behavior of *Emerita analoga* (Stimpson) by Harold Tupper Mead. Berkeley, University of California press, 1917.

cover-title: p. (431)–438. illus. 26½ᶜᵐ. (University of California publications in zoology. v. 16, no. 23)

"Contribution from the Scripps institution for biological research, La Jolla, California."
"Literature cited": p. 438.

1. (Sand-crabs)   I. Title.

A 17-442

Title from Univ. of Calif.   Library of Congress

EMERITA ANALOGA.

AS
36
S2

Weymouth, Frank Walter.

... Observations on the habits of the crustacean *Emerita analoga*, with one plate, by Frank Walter Weymouth and Charles Howard Richardson, jr. ... Washington, Smithsonian institution, 1912.

1 p. l., 13, (1) p. illus., pl. 24½ᶜᵐ. (Smithsonian miscellaneous collections, v. 59, no. 7)

Publication 2082.
Bibliography: p. 12-13.

1. Emerita analoga.   I. Richardson, Charles Howard, jr., joint author.

12—35744

Library of Congress   Q11.S7 vol. 59, no. 7

AP
2
S 35

Emerson, Alfred E.

Distribution of termites.

(Science, 83(2157):410-11, 1936)

AS
36
A 65-b

Emerson, Alfred E.

The neotropical genera Procornitermes and Cornitermes (Isoptera, Termitidae)

(Bull. Am. Mus. of Nat. Hist., 99(8), 1952)

QL
751
A 42

Emerson, Alfred E.

Allee, W. C. and others

　Principles of animal ecology. By W. C.
Allee, Orlando Park, Alfred E. Emerson, Thomas
Park, and Karl P. Schmidt. W. B. Saunders Com-
pany. Philadelphia and London. R8vo. 1949c
Reprinted 1951, 1955. xii + 827 pp.

DU
620
H4

Emerson, Joseph Swift

　The bow and arrow in Hawaii. In Haw.
Hist. Soc. Report 1915. pp. 52-55.

GR
Pam
#9

GR
Pam
48

and
GN
Ethn.Pam.
4152

Emerson, Joseph Swift

　Hawaiian string games. Edited by
Martha Warren Beckwith.

New York, Vassar, 1924. 18p.

(Publication Folk-lore Foundation, Vassar
College, No. 5)

CH
1
A 51

Emerson, Alfred E.

　Social coordination and the superorganism.

(The American Midland Naturalist, Vol.21,
1939, pp.182-209).

Hms
Misc.2

Storage
Case
4

Emerson, J. S. (Joseph Swift)

　Cats' cradles. (Hei.)

GR
385.H
E 53

Emerson, J. S. (compiler) (Joseph Swift)

　Hawaiian traditions,-scrap-book of clippings
from Hawaiian newspapers.

QL
1
N16

Emerson, Alfred Edwards

　The termites of Kartabo. Bartica
district, British Guiana. In Zoologica,
Vol. VI, pp 293- 459, 1925.

GN
Pam
2771

Emerson, J. S. (Joseph Swift)

　Disposal of the umbilical cord in Hawaiian
Islands.

　Note made by J. S. Emerson and copied by Miss
Beckwith. 1914.

　2 copies.

PL
623
E 53

Emerson, J. S. (Joseph Swift)

　He hoakaka olelo no na huaolelo Beretania,
i mea kokua i na kanaka Hawaii e ao ana ia olelo.
Lahainaluna. 1845. 184 pp.

(Hawaiian-English dictionary)
2 copies,- 1 contains also "A Vocabulary of Words in the
Hawaiian Language". Lahainaluna. date destroyed.
(1836)

GN
Ethn.Pam
3352

Emerson, Arthur T.

　Native craft of Samoa.

(U. S. Naval Institute Proceedings, Vol.
60, 1934, No. 381, pp. 1549-1552, illustrated)

GN
Ethn.Pam
3934

Emerson, Joseph S.

　Eminent white kahuna exposes secret sites and
practices dread brotherhood. Delivered before
the Pan Pacific Union, April 9, 1926.
　IN Collection of clippings made by Martha W.
Beckwith, pp. 9-12

DU
Hist.Pam
230

Emerson, Joseph Swift

　Historical notes: Coronation times; Kamehameha I, genealogy; Battle of Kuamoo;
Kalele-alua-kaa; Kalakaua's call to arms; Genealogical notes; Death of Waikea. ms. typed
pages.

GR
Pam
#10

Emerson, B. K.

　Medieval creation myths, ex Pop.
Sc. Monthly, Dec., 1909.

Storage
Case
1

Emerson, Joseph S.

　Fish classed as kuku. ms. note.
(Hawaiian ethnological notes, ms. I:728)

DU
1
M6

and
GN
Ethn.Pam
3517

Emerson, Joseph Swift

　Kahunas and kahunaism . In Mid-Pacific
Vol. XXXI, 1926, pp 503 - 516.

CE
Pam
#2

Emerson, B. K.

　Plumose diabase and Palagonite
from the Holyoke trap sheet, ex Geol.
Soc. of America, Bull. vol. 16, March,
1905.

DU
620
P

Emerson, Joseph Swift

　The four greater gods of Polynesia.

(Paradise of the Pacific, Vol. 36, No. 5,
1923, pp. 5-7)

GN
Ethn.Pam
3934

Emerson, Joseph S.

　Kahunas masters of black art...
IN
Book of clippings gathered together by
Martha W. Beckwith, pp. 4-8.

DU
Hist.Pam
332

Emerson, John S.

　Extracts from a letter from him, May 18,
1832. 1 typed page.

　(relates his meeting with Kauikeaouli, Boki,
Kaahumanu, etc.)

GR
Folklore
Pam
46

Emerson, J. S. (Joseph Swift)

　The four greater gods of Polynesia.

　Read before Social Science Assn., Feb.
5, 1923, 2 copies. Typewritten .19 p.

S
17.H3
H

Emerson, J. S. (Joseph Swift)

MacCaughey, Vaughan

　Kalo in Hawaii, by Vaughan MacCaughey and
J. S. Emerson.

(Hawaiian Forester and Agriculturist, Vol.
10:186-192,225-231, 280-288, 315-323, 349-358,
371-375; Vol. XI:17-23, 44-51, 111-122, 201-216,
1913-1914)

DU
620
F

Emerson, Joseph Swift

Kekela, an Hawaiian hero.

(Friend, May 1920, pp.142-46; 150)

Manu-
script
shelf

(top)

recatalog some day
when space for mss is extended

Emerson, J. S.

Letters to, and lists of shells loaned, received, given, to various collections, etc., as Bardwell, Dranga, Hargreaves, Bucknill, et.

(Received from office of Charles Montague Cooke, Jr. April, 1956)

DU
620
H 5

locked
case

Emerson, J. S. (Joseph Swift)

The shipwrecked Japanese.

(Hawaiian Spectator, Vol. 1, No. 3, 1838, pp. 296-300)

AP
2
A 5

Emerson, Joseph Swift

Kilauea after the eruption of March, 1886... by J. S. Emerson, L. L. Van Slyke and F. S. Dodge

(Am. Jour. of Sci., Ser. 3, Vol. 33, 1887, pp. 87-101)   illustration p. 239-240

(ibid. Vol. 34, 1887, pp. 70-71)

DU
621
H3

Emerson, J.S. (Joseph Swift)

The Myth of Hiku and Kawelu.   Thrum's Hawaiian Annual.   1883, p.36-9.

AP
2
A 5

Emerson, J. S. (Joseph Swift)

Some characteristics of Kau.

(Am. Jour. Sci., Ser. 4, Vol. 14, 1902, pp. 431-439)

GN
Ethn.Pam
3908

Emerson, Joseph S. (wift)

Kite-flying.   2pp.   typed.

GN
Ethn.Pam
3112

Emerson, J. S.   (Joseph Swift)

The origin of the coconut,- a Gilbert Islands myth.

Hms
La4

Storage
Case
5

Emerson, Joseph Swift

Some features of the Polynesian language.

Gift of Emma Lyons Dole.

DU
620
H 4

Emerson, J. S. (Joseph Swift)

Legends and cradle song, a story of the Hawaiian god Kane.
(Haw'n. Hist. Soc., 27th Annual Report, 1918, pp. 31-35)

PL
Pam
#47

Emerson, J. S. (Joseph Swift)

Report of the president of Hawaiian Historical Society on Polynesian Dialects, Ex Haw. Hist. Soc Rept. for1920.

DU
620
H 4

Emerson, J(oseph) S(wift)

Some Hawaiian beliefs regarding spirits.

(Hawaiian Hist. Soc., Ninth Ann. Rept., 1902, pp. 10-17)

DU
620
F

Emerson, Joseph Swift

Damon, Ethel M.

Legends of Ka-Puna-Hou, by Ethel M. Damon and Joseph S. Emerson.

(Friend, March 1924, pp. 73-74)

QE
Geol.Pam
955

Emerson, J. S. (Joseph Swift)

Report to Prof. W. D. Alexander: Crater of Kilauea. n.d. ms. 22 pp.

Storage
Case
4
Misc.
Hms 53

also
GN
Ethn.Pam
3518

Emerson, Joseph Swift

Some of the old Hawaiian games. ms. written in 1927.   7 pp.

GN
Ethn.Pam
3833

WITHDRAWN
and placed
with
Letters
Carter
Mss
Room

Emerson, Joseph S.

Letters to Martha Warren Beckwith, 1913, 1914, 1921.

(various matters: breeding stones, the singing snail, sayings and riddles, comments on the new dictionary, on Lyle Dickey's string figures)

S
17.H3
H 38

Emerson, Joseph S. (wift)

MacCaughey, Vaughan

A revised list of Hawaiian varietal names for kalo, by Vaughan MacCaughey and Joseph S. Emerson.

(Haw. For. and Agric., Vol. 11, 1914, pp. 338-341)

Hms
K10

Storage
Case
4

Emerson, J. S. (Joseph Swift)

Stone gods, prayers.

DU
620
H4

GN
Pam
306
332
338
588

Emerson, J. S. (Joseph Swift)

Lesser Hawaiian gods. Haw. Hist. Soc. Paper No. 2, pp 1-24 read April 7, 1892.

DU
620
H 4

and
GN
Ethn.Pam.
517
2793

Emerson, Joseph Swift

Selections from a kahuna's book of prayers.

(Haw. Hist. Soc., Report for 1917:17-37)

DU
1
M 6

Emerson, Joseph Swift

The story of a cowry, an Hawaiian legend.

(Mid-Pacific Magazine, vol. 19:237-241, 1920)

Hms
Misc.3

Emerson, J.S. (Joseph Swift)

Tapa beater patterns.

Storage
Case
4

DU
620
F

Emerson, Nathaniel Bright.

The causes of the decline of ancient Hawaiian
sports.

(Friend, August 1892, pp.57-60)

DU
620
H 4

Emerson, N. B. (Nathaniel Bright)

Mamala-hoa.

(Annual Report, Hawaiian Historical Society,
10th, 1902, pp. 15-29)

QL
401
N

EMERSON, JOSEPH SWIFT

Cooke, Charles Montague, Jr.
Joseph Swift Emerson.
(Nautilus, Vol. 44, 1931, pp. 94-95)

GN
671.H2
M 25
2 copies

AS
763
B-s
1903.

Reading
Room

Emerson, Nathaniel Bright, trans.

Malo, David

Hawaiian antiquities (Moolelo Hawaii) by
David Malo; translated from the Hawaiian by Dr.
N. B. Emerson. Honolulu. Hawaiian Gazette.
1903. 8vo. 366 pp.

(Bernice P. Bishop Museum, Spec. Pub. No. 2)

DU
Hist.Pam.
63

also
AP
2
O 96
and
Corridor
Case
40

Emerson, N. B. (Nathaniel Bright)

Pakua the Outlaw: a Peep into Ancient Hawaii

(Overland Monthly, April, 1893, pp. 638-644)

DU
620
F

EMERSON, JOSEPH SWIFT, 1800-1867

Memorial.

(Friend, April 1867, p. 28-29).

Hms
Misc. 8

Emerson, Nathaniel B.(right)

Hawaiian Chap-book: a Collection of Proverbs.
34 typed pages. Received Dec. 20, 1922.

GR
385.H
E 53

over

Emerson, Nathaniel B(right)

Pele and Hiiaka: a Myth from Hawaii. Honolulu. Honolulu Star-Bulletin Limited. 1915.
8vo.   xvi + 250 pp.

QK
Pam
4737

Emerson, Julia T. & Welker, William H.

Some notes on the chemical composition and toxicity of Ibervillea sonorae,
ex New York Bot. Garden Contr. no. 113,
1908.

DU
620
H 4

Emerson, N. B. (Nathaniel Bright)

The Honolulu Fort.

(Annual Report, Hawaiian Historical Society,
8th, 1900, pp. 11-25)

DU
620
H 4

Emerson, N. B.(Nathaniel Bright)

The Poetry of Hawaii.

(Annual Report, Hawaiian Historical Society,
11th, 1903, pp. 12-22)

DU
620
F

Emerson, Nathaniel Bright

Ancient Hawaiian house.

(Friend, April 1902, p. 9)

DU
Hist.Pam.
63

Emerson, N. B. (Nathaniel Bright)

Kamehameha the Great.

(Overland Monthly, April, 1893, pp. 629-638)

DU
620
H 4

Emerson, N. B. (Nathaniel Bright)

A Preliminary Report on a Find of Human
Bones Exhumed in the Sands of Waikiki.

(Annual Report, Hawaiian Historical Society,
9th, 1901, 18-20)

DU
620
F

Emerson, Nathaniel Bright

Biography of Oliver Pomeroy Emerson.

(Friend, November 1906, pp.11-12)

DU
Pac.Pam.
578

Emerson, N. B.(Nathaniel Bright)

Life on a Guano island. January and February
1869. Typed extracts from (?)

DU
620
H 4

Emerson, N. B. (Nathaniel Bright)

(Rediscovery of heiau of Kupopolo,Waialua)

(Annual Report of the Hawaiian Historical
Society, 13th, 1906, pp. 11-13)

DU
621
H3

Emerson, N.B.(Nathaniel Bright)

The bird hunters of ancient Hawaii.
Thrum's Hawaiian Annual, 1895. p.101-11

DU
620
H 4

DU
Pac.Pam
73.

Emerson, Nathaniel Bright, 1839-
The long voyages of the ancient Hawaiians, read before the Hawaiian historical society, May 18, 1893, by
Dr. N. B. Emerson ... (Honolulu, Hawaiian gazette company, printers, 1893?)

cover-title, 34 p. 25cm. (Papers of the Hawaiian historical society,
no. 5)

1. Hawaiian Islands—Hist. 2. Polynesia—Hist. 3. Voyages and travels.

                                                13-11118

Library of Congress   DU626.E5

DU
620
H 4

Emerson, N. B.(Nathaniel Bright)

Regarding Ho-ao, Hawaiian Marriage.

(Annual Report of the Hawaiian Historical
Society, 6th, 1898, pp. 16-22)

DU
621
H3

Emerson, N.B. (Nathaniel Bright)

The story of Kalelealuaka. Thrum's Hawaiian Annual. 1885, p.30-46.

AP
2
A 5

Emerson, O. H. (Oliver Pomeroy)

The formation of aa and pahoehoe.

(Am. Jour. of Sci., Ser. 5, Vol. 12, 1926, pp. 109-114)

AS
36
A 65-n

Emerson, William K.

A new Scaphopod Mollusk, Dentalium (Tesseracme) hancocki, from the Eastern Pacific.

(Am. Mus. Novitates, No. 1787, Sept. 1956)

[from islands off California and Mexico]

GN
550
S

and

GR
385.H
E 53
3 cops.

Emerson, Nathaniel Bright, 1839-1915.

... Unwritten literature of Hawaii; the sacred songs of the hula collected and tr. with notes and an account of the hula, by Nathaniel B. Emerson ... Washington, Govt. print. off., 1909.

288 p. illus., xxiv pl. (incl. front.) 25ᶜᵐ. (Smithsonian institution. Bureau of American ethnology. Bulletin 38)

U. S. 60th Cong., 2d sess. House. Doc. no. 1501. Contains music.

1. Songs, Hawaiian. 2. Hawaiian language—Texts. 3. Folk-lore—Hawaiian Islands.

Library of Congress   E51.U6 no. 38   (over)
——— Copy 2.

9—35871

QL
Mollusca
Pam. 874

also
Storage
Case
3

Emerson, Oliver P.

The gay Achatinellidae and their habits. Lecture, no date. manuscript. 24 pp.

2 copies

AS
36
A 65-no

Emerson, William K.

Remarks on some eastern Pacific muricid gastropods.

(American Museum Novitates, No. 2009, 1960)

GN
1
A

Emerson, Nathaniel Bright

Unwritten Literature of Hawaii.

(American Anthropologist, N. S. Vol. 8, 1906, pp. 271-275)

Storage
Case
4

Hms
Misc. 56

Emerson, Oliver (?)

The gay Achatinellidae and their habitats. Lecture, no date. copy of a ms. 25 pp.

AS
36
C8

Emerton, James Henry, 1847–

... Canadian spiders ...

(*In* Connecticut academy of arts and sciences. Transactions. New Haven, 1892-95. 25ᶜᵐ. v. 9, p. (400)-429. pl. I-IV (i. e. IV-VII))

Araneae
1. ~~Spiders~~—Canada. i. Title.

Library of Congress   Q11.C9 vol. 9
Yale University   A53n.366.9

A 17-867

GN
2.S
P 76

Emerson, N.B.

"Unwritten literature of Hawaii: the sacred songs of the Hula."

(Journal of the Polynesian Society, 19: 137-141, 1910.)

REVIEW by the Editor

DU
625
E53

Emerson, Oliver Pomeroy

Pioneer days in Hawaii. Garden City, Doubleday, Doran, 1928. 8 vo. 257 pp.

AS
36
C8

Emerton, James Henry, 1847–

... Canadian spiders, II.

(*In* Connecticut academy of arts and sciences. Transactions. New Haven, Conn., 1916. 25ᶜᵐ. v. 20, p. (145-160) pl. II-III)

Supplements a paper by Emerton published in the Transactions in 1894.

1. Spiders—Canada. i. Title. *Arachnida – Canada*

Library of Congress   Q11.C9 vol. 20
Yale University   A53n.366.20

A 17-945

DU
620
H4

EMERSON N. B. (NATHANIEL BRIGHT)

Westervelt, W. D.

Dr. N. B. Emerson. (Obituary) In Haw. Hist. Society Rept. 1915. pp. 16-17. Port.

AP
2
A 5

Emerson, O. H. (Oliver Pomeroy)

Finch, R. H.

Sulphate deposits in lava tubes, by R. H. Finch and O. H. Emerson.

(Am. Jour. of Sci., Ser. 5, Vol. 10, 1925, pp. 38-40)

QL
457.1
E 53

Emerton, James H.

The common spiders of the United States. With a new key to common groups of spiders by S. W. Frost. Dover Publications, Inc. New York. sm8vo. xx + 227 pp.

DU
621
H3

Emerson, O.P. (Oliver Pomeroy)

The Awa habit of the Hawaiians. Thrum's Hawaiian Annual. 1903, p.130-40.

DU
620
F

EMERSON, OLIVER POMEROY

Emerson, Nathaniel Bright

Biography of Oliver Pomeroy Emerson

(Friend, November 1906, pp. 11-12.)

QL
362
E53

Emerton, James H (enry)

Life on the seashore or animals of our coasts and bays. Salem, Bates, 1880. (Naturalist's handy series).

DU
620
H 4

Emerson, O. P. (Oliver Pomeroy)

Bad boy of Lahaina, the goblin-killer of Lanai.

(Haw'n. Hist. Soc., 29th Annual Report, 1920, pp. 16-19)

DU
12
E 53

Emerson, Rupert   and others

America's Pacific dependencies; a survey of American colonial policies and of Administration and Progress toward self-rule in Alaska, Hawaii, Guam, Samoa and the Trust Territory. American Institute of Pacific Relations. New York. 1949 4to. 134 pp.

AS
36
C8

Emerton, James Henry, 1847–

... New England *Lycosidæ*.

(*In* Connecticut academy of arts and sciences. Transactions. New Haven, 1882-85. 25ᶜᵐ. v. 6, p. (481)-505. pl. XLVI-XLIX)

1. Lycosidae.

Library of Congress   Q11.C9 vol. 6
Yale University   A53n.366.6

A 17-812

AS 36 C8

Emerton, James Henry, 1847–
... New England spiders identified since 1910 ...

(*In* Connecticut academy of arts and sciences. Transactions. New Haven, Conn., 1914. 25^{cm}. v. 18, p. (209)-224. 2 pl.)

Each plate accompanied by leaf with descriptive letterpress.

Araneae
1. Spiders—New England. I. Title.

A 17-938

Library of Congress   Q11.C9 vol. 18
Yale University   A53n.366.18

AS 36 C8

Emerton, James Henry, 1847–
... New spiders from New England ...

(*In* Connecticut academy of arts and sciences. Transactions. New Haven, Conn., 1911. 25^{cm}. v. 16, p. (383)-407. VI pl.)

Each plate accompanied by leaf with descriptive letterpress.

Araneae
1. Spiders—New England. I. Title.

A 17-932

Library of Congress   Q11.C9 vol. 16
Yale University   A53n.366.16

QH 1 P 11

Emery, K. O.
Beach rock in the Hawaiian Islands. By K. O. Emery and Doak C. Cox

(Pacific Science, 10:382-402, 1956)

AS 36 C8

Emerton, James Henry, 1847–
... New England spiders of the families *Drassidæ, Agalenidæ* and *Dysderidæ*.

(*In* Connecticut academy of arts and sciences. Transactions. New Haven, 1888-92. 25^{cm}. v. 8, p. (166)-206. pl. III-VIII)

Araneae
1. (Drassidæ) 2. (Agalenidæ) 3. (Dysderidæ) 4. Spiders—New England. I. Title.

A 17-847

Library of Congress   Q11.C9 vol. 8
Yale University   A53n.366.8

AS 36 C8

Emerton, James Henry, 1847–
... New spiders from New England, XI.

(*In* Connecticut academy of arts and sciences. Transactions. New Haven, Conn., 1915. 25^{cm}. v. 20, p. (133-144) illus., pl. I)

Araneae
1. Spiders—New England. I. Title.

A 17-944

Library of Congress   Q11.C9 vol. 20
Yale University   A53n.366.20

QH 1 A 88

Emery, K. O.
Tracey, J. I. Jr.

Conspicuous features of organic reefs. By J. I. Tracey, Jr., P. E. Cloud, Jr. and K. O. Emery.

(Atoll Research Bulletin, No. 46, 1955)

AS 36 C8

Emerton, James Henry, 1847–
... New England spiders of the family *Attidæ*.

(*In* Connecticut academy of arts and sciences. Transactions. New Haven, 1888-92. 25^{cm}. v. 8, p. (220)-252. pl. XVI-XXI)

Araneae
1. Attidæ. 2. Spiders—New England.

A 17-850

Library of Congress   Q11.C9 vol. 8
Yale University   A53n.366.8

AS 36 C8

Emerton, James Henry, 1847–
... Supplement to the New England spiders, by J. H. Emerton. Pub. under the auspices of Yale university. New Haven, Conn., 1909.

1 p. l., p. (173)-236, 12 l. xii pl. 24^{cm}. (Transactions of the Connecticut academy of arts and sciences ... v. 14 (art. III))

Supplementing a series of papers by the author published in the Transactions of the Connecticut academy of arts and sciences, 1882-92.

Araneae
1. Spiders—New England.

Library of Congress   Q11.C9 vol. 14   12-31559
——— Copy 2.

QE 1 G 3

Emery, K. O.
Continental shelf sediments of Southern California.

(Geol. Soc. of America, Bull. Vol. 63:1105-1108, 1952)

AS 36 C8

Emerton, James Henry, 1847–
... New England spiders of the family *Ciniflonidæ*.

(*In* Connecticut academy of arts and sciences. Transactions. New Haven, 1885-88. 25^{cm}. v. 7, p. (443)-458. pl. IX-XI)

Araneae
1. (Ciniflonidæ) 2. Spiders—New England. I. Title.

A 17-836

Library of Congress   Q11.C9 vol. 7
Yale University   A53n.366.7

QL 1 Po

Emery, Carlo
Formiche d'Australia e di Samoa, raccolte dal Prof. Silvestri nel 1913.

(Boll. Lab. Zool. So.Agric. Portici, Vol. 8, 1914)

over

QE 75 P

Emery, Kenneth O.
Geology of Bikini and nearby atolls. By Kenneth O. Emery, J. I. Tracey, Jr., and H. S. Ladd. [Bikini and nearby atolls: Part 1, Geology]

(U. S. Geological Survey Prof. Paper 260-A, 1954)

AS 36 C8

Emerton, James Henry, 1847–
... New England spiders of the family *Epeiridæ*.

(*In* Connecticut academy of arts and sciences. Transactions. New Haven, 1882-85. 25^{cm}. v. 6, p. (295)-342. pl. XXXIII-XL)

Araneae
1. (Epeiridæ) 2. Spiders—New England. I. Title.

A 17-807

Library of Congress   Q11.C9 vol. 6
Yale University   A53n.366.6

QL 345.N 6 S 24

Emery, C.
Les fourmis de la Nouvelle-Calédonie et des iles Loyalty.

Sarasin, Fritz
Nova Caledonia...A. Zoologie, Tome I, Livr. 4, 1914, No. 11

AH 20 E 53

Emery, K. O.
An international directory of oceanographers. By K. O. Emery and Mary Sears. National Academy of Sciences/ National Research Council. sm8vo. 3rd edition, 1960. 177 pp.

AS 36 C8

Emerton, James Henry, 1847–
... New England spiders of the family *Theridiidæ*.

(*In* Connecticut academy of arts and sciences. Transactions. New Haven, 1882-85. 25^{cm}. v. 6, p. 1-86. pl. I-XXIV)

Araneae
1. Theridiidæ. 2. Spiders—New England. I. Title.

A 17-801

Library of Congress   Q11.C9 vol. 6
Yale University   A53n.366.6

QL Insects Pam. 1205

Emery, Carlo
Viaggio de Lamberto Loria nella Papuasia orientale, XVIII: Formiche raccolte nella Nuova Guinea dal dott. Lamberto Loria.

(Genova, Mus. Civico, Annali, 38:546-594, 1897)

QE 1 G 3

Emery, K. O.
Lithology of the sea floor off Southern California. By K. O. Emery and F.P.Shepard.

(Bull. Geol. Soc. of America, Vol. 56, pp. 431-478, 1945)

AS 36 C8

Emerton, James Henry, 1847–
... New England spiders of the family *Thomisidæ*.

(*In* Connecticut academy of arts and sciences. Transactions. New Haven, 1888-92. 25^{cm}. v. 8, p. (359)-381. pl. XXVIII-XXXII)

Araneae
1. (Thomisidæ) 2. Spiders—New England. I. Title.

A 17-857

Library of Congress   Q11.C9 vol. 8
Yale University   A53n.366.8

QH 1 P 11

Emery, K. O.
An aerial study of Hawaiian wave patterns.

(Pacific Science, Vol. 17(3):255-261, 1963)

QE 349.M4 T 75

Emery, K. O.
Marine geology.
IN
Tracey, J. I., Jr. and others
Military geology of Guam, Mariana Islands. Parts I-II: Climate, by D. I. Blumenstock; Marine geology by K. O. Emery.
Prepared under the direction of the Chief of Engineers, U. S. Army, by the Intelligence Div. of the Office of the Engineer...with personnel of the USGS. 1959. folio. 282 pp. maps.

QE
1
G 3

Emery, Kenneth O.

Marine geology of Johnston Island and its surrounding shallows, Central Pacific Ocean.

(Bull. Geol. Soc. America, 67:1506-1520, 1956)

QE
Geol.
Pam.
1231

Emery, K. O.

Submarine topography south of Hawaii. Univ. of Southern California. (1954) 4to. 10 mimeographed pp.+ 3 figs.

DU
1
P

EMIRAU

Crago, L. P.

Spotlight on Emirau. Incidents in the patchy history of a remote island.

(Pacific Islands Monthly, Vol. 17 (10): 38, 1947)

QE
Geol.Pam.
1145

Emery, K. O.

Marine solution basins.

(Journal of Geology, Vol. 54(4):209-228, 1946)

QH
1
P 11

Emery, K. O.

Submarine topography south of Hawaii.

(Pacific Science, Vol. IX(3):286-291, 1955)

DU
1
P 18

Emma Kaleleonalani (Queen Emma)

Kamehameha I— the hero of Hawaii.

(Pan-Pacific, Vol. 3, 1939, No. 2, pp. 3-4)

QE
Geol.Pam.
1147

Emery, K. O.

Clements, Thomas

Seismic activity and topography of the sea floor off Southern California. By Thomas Clements and K. O. Emery.

(Bull. Seismological Soc. of America, Vol. 37(4):307-313, 1947)

Q
101
P 18

Emery, K. O.

Submerged marine terraces and their sediments

IN

Russell, Richard J.

Pacific Island terraces: eustatic? A symposium...(10th Pac. Sci. Congress, 1961)

(Zeit. f. Geomorphologie, Suppl. Bd. 3:17-29, 1961)

Q
Biogr.
Pam.
95

Emma: Queen of the Islands.

(The Queen's Messenger, 17(1), 1957)

QE
Geol.
Pam.
1266

Emery, Kenneth O.

Submarine geology and hydrography in the northern Marshalls. By K. O. Emery, J. I. Tracey, Jr. and H. S. Ladd

(Reprinted from International Geol. Congress Rept. of the Eighteenth Session, Great Britain, 1948, Part VIII, pp. 22-27)

GC
Oceanography
Pam. 54

and

QE
Geol.Pam.
1146

Emery, K. O.

Underway bottom sampler. By K. O. Emery and A. R. Champion.

(Jour. Sedimentary Petrology, 18 (1):30-33, 1948)

Hms
Misc. 36

Storage
Case
4

Emma, Queen

Diaries, June 22, 1865-Sept.16, 1865,- visit to London,- also clippings of that visit and diary, January 14, 1884-June 6, 1884.

— also 1866, Jan. 1 — Aug 5
—   " 1881

QE
Geol.
Pam.
1148
1152

Emery, K. O.

Submarine geology and topography in the northern Marshalls. By K. O. Emery, J.I. Tracey Jr. and H.S. Ladd.

(Trans. Am. Geophysical Union, vol. 30:55-58, 1949)

QL
754
P 36

and

QH
371
P 36

The emigrations of animals from the sea.

Pearse, A. S.

DU
Hist.
Pam. 181

EMMA, QUEEN

Cummins, John A.

Queen Emma's Tour of Oahu in 1875.

(Honolulu Star Bulletin, July 22, 1933)

QE
1
G 3

and

QE
Geol.Pam.
1140

Emery, Kenneth O.

Submarine geology of Bikini atoll.

(Bull. Geol. Soc. America, Vol. 59:855-860, 1948)

AP
2
S 35

Emiliani, C.

On paleotemperatures of Pacific bottom waters.

(Science, v. 123(3194):460-61, 1956)

Carter Coll.
12-D-8

EMMA, QUEEN

Field, Isobel

This life I've loved. New York... Longmans, Green and Co. 1937 ix + 353 pp.

QE
Geol.Pam.
1144

Emery, K. O.

Submarine geology of Ranger Bank, Mexico.

(Bull. Am. Assn of Petroleum Geologists, Vol. 32:790-805, 1948)

PL
Philo
Pam
74

Emin-Bey.

Worterverzeichnisse afrikanischer sprachen. From Zeit. f. Ethnol. 1882.

DU
Hist.
Pam. 276

EMMA, QUEEN   Jan 2,1836 —

Funeral obsequies; outline of the life of Queen Emma. (contains account of the lying in state; memorial discourse; removal of the remains of Queen Emma; ...funeral; ...Queen Emma's will). 42 pp. 8vo. n.d.

DU
623
F 95

EMMA, QUEEN

Fürer, Carl Eduard

Hawaii-nei; ein Bild aus der Inselwelt des stillen Oceans. In 6 Gesängen. Barmen. 1867. sm8vo. 75 pp.

HMS
H 44
Case 4

EMMA, QUEEN

Liliuokalani   and others

Hawaiian songs. Manuscripts, pp. 1-132. Words or music or both by Liliu. (Some incomplete: 1, 2, 13, 27, 28, 31, 32, (65 finished in pencil), 131, missing 14, 17)
     (see list with songs)

GR
885
L 72
l.c.

Photostat copies; another with manuscript.

DU
625
K 87

EMMA, QUEEN

Korn, Alfons L.

The Victorian visitors; an account of the Hawaiian kingdom, 1861-1866, including the journal letters of Sophia Cracroft, extracts from the journals of Lady Franklin, and diaries and letters of Queen Emma of Hawaii. University of Hawaii Press. Honolulu 1958. sm4to. (9) + 351 pp.

DU
625.4
B 62

Emma, Queen

Last will and testament of the late Hon. Charles R. Bishop.
     IN
Wills and deeds of trust; Bernice P. Bishop Estate; Bernice P. Bishop Museum; Charles R. Bishop Trust, Revised Edition, 1927. Compiled from the original documents and published by authority of the Trustees. Honolulu, Hawaii. 8vo. n.d. 353 pp.

DU
Hist.Pam.
214

EMMA, QUEEN

Lucas, Clorinda Low

Influences in the life of Queen Emma.

(The Queen's Hospital Bulletin, Vol. XII, 1936, Nos. 1-6, pp. 17-19)

AN
2.E
H 38

EMMA, QUEEN

(death of)

(Hawaiian Gazette, 4/19/1885; 6/13 and 6/20, 1885)

DU
Missions
Pam. 81

EMMA, QUEEN

A. I.

Queen Emma. A narrative of the object of her mission to England, by A. I. London, Day & Son, Limited. 12mo. 31 pp. n.d.

DU
Missions
Pam. 92

EMMA, QUEEN

Proceedings of the American Board of Commissioners for Foreign Missions, in relation to a recent interference with its work on the Sandwich Islands. n.d. no place. 16 pp. Heading: The Hawaiian (or Sandwich) Islands.

[entry of Reformed Catholic Church; Bishop Staley; remonstrance against unfriendly contest instead of cooperation in effort.]

Storage
Case
1

Emmert, Paul

Funeral of His late Majesty, Kamehameha III, Honolulu, January 10, 1855.   Drawn and lithographed by Paul Emmert.

2 copies, 1 in very poor condition.

DU
620
F

EMMA, QUEEN

A. I.

Queen Emma. (Review of a pamphlet by A. I., published in London, 1866)

(Friend, June 1866, pp. 41-44)

DU
620
P

EMMA, QUEEN

Smythe, Jane Kapahukalaunu

Queen Emma, the person.

(Paradise of the Pacific, Vol. 44, No. 2, 1931, pp. 5,6.)

DU
629.H7
B 16

Emmert, Paul

Baker, Ray Jerome

Honolulu in 1853- Six photographic reproductions of the lithographs made from original drawings by Paul Emmert in 1853, together with brief descriptions of occupants, owners and locations of the subjects drawn. 1950. ob8vo. 77 pp.

DU
620
H 4

EMMA, QUEEN

Korn, A. L.

Queen Emma in France, 1865-1866.

(Hawaiian Hist. Soc., 65th Rept., 1956:7-24)

DU
1
P 18

EMMA, QUEEN

Staley, Mildred

Queen Emma Kaleleonalani of Hawaii

(Pan-Pacific, Vol. 3, No. 2, 1939, p. 5-6)

Emmert, Paul

Luakaha: photo: the PALACE OF KAMEHAMEHA III

On one of the lithographs made from original drawings by Paul Emmert in 1853. No. 1, bottom, middle place.

DU
Hist.Pam.
245

EMMA, QUEEN

Judd, Albert Francis   1874-

(Note in regard to succession to the throne after Kamehameha V,- recollections of Curtis Iaukea)   1 typed sheet.

DU
620
F

EMMA, QUEEN

Visit to England (Friend, June, 1866, p.41-3.
Visit to the U. S.   "   Nov., " p.101.

Looked
case
downstairs

Emmert, Paul

Views of Honolulu.   Nos. 1-6

Engravings made from sketches made in the early 50's.   folio. (in folio folder)

DU
Hist.Pam.
241

EMMA, QUEEN

Larsen, Nils P.

On the occasion of Queen Emma's 100th Birthday anniversary.

(The Queen's Hospital Bulletin, Vol. XII, 1936, Nos. 1-6, pp. 1-9)

Hms
H2

EMMA, QUEEN.

Wyllie, R. C.

Book of instructions to Queen Emma.   (To her Majesty Queen Emma, Princess of Waiaha and Baroness of Halawa, a book of instructions for a voyage. Dated, Rosebank, May 5, 1865). Small 8vo Mss. Also 1 typed copy.

Storage
Case
4

S
451.N 5
E 54

Emmons, Ebenezer   (1799-1863)

Agriculture of New York...Volume V:Insects. Albany. C. Van Benthuysen, 1854. 4to. 272 pp. 47 plates.

AS
36
A6

Emmons, G[eorge] T[hornton]

... The basketry of the Tlingit. By G. T. Emmons ... [New York, The Knickerbocker press] 1903.

cover-title, 229–277, [1] p. illus., v–xviii pl. (1 col.) 36^{cm}. (... Memoirs of the American museum of natural history. vol. III. [Whole series, vol. III. Anthropology, vol. III])

Issued July, 1903.
Descriptive letterpress on verso of each plate.

1. Koluschan Indians. 2. Indians of North America — Basket-making.
Basketmaking. Tlingit Indians
    5–34404
Library of Congress   QH1.A43

—— Another issue.   Library of Congress GN431.E5
In the preceding, author's   name on t.-p. is followed by "U. S.
Navy;" in this issue these   words are omitted.

AS
36
A6

Emmons, George Thornton.

... The Chilkat blanket, by George T. Emmons ... With notes on the blanket designs, by Franz Boas. [New York] 1907.

1 p. l., 329–401 p., 2 l. illus., xxiv–xxvii pl. (partly col.) 36^{cm}. (... Memoirs of the American museum of natural history. Whole series, vol. III. Anthropology, vol. II)

1. Chilkat Indians. 2. Indians of North America—Weaving. I. Boas, Franz, 1858– *Weaving. Indians of North America.*
    8–19279
Library of Congress   QH1.A43

GN
2M
Pe

Emmons, George Thornton.

... The Tahltan Indians, by G. T. Emmons, illustrated by specimens in the George G. Heye collection. Philadelphia, The University museum, 1911.

120 p. illus., xix pl. (partly col.) map. 27^{cm}. (University of Pennsylvania. The Museum. Anthropological publications, vol. IV, no. 1)

Each plate accompanied by leaf with descriptive letterpress.
Errata slip at end.

1. Tahltan Indians.
    12–3429
Library of Congress   E99.T12E5

GN
2.M
A

Emmons, George Thornton.

... The whale house of the Chilkat, by George T. Emmons ... New York, The Trustees, 1916.

1 p. l., p. 1–33 incl. illus., plates. 4 col. pl. 24½^{cm}. (Anthropological papers of the American museum of natural history. vol. XIX, pt. 1)

Each colored plate accompanied by guard sheet with descriptive letterpress.

1. Chilkat Indians. 2. Indians of North America—Dwellings. I. Title.
    17–28719
Library of Congress   GN2.A27 vol. 19, pt. 1

AS
36
S1

Emmons, Samuel Franklin, 1841–1911.

Theories of ore deposition historically considered. By S. F. Emmons.

(*In* Smithsonian institution. Annual report. 1904. Washington, 1905. 23½^{cm}. p. 309–336)

"Reprinted from author's revised copy."

1. Ore-deposits. I. Title.
    S 15–1245
Library of Congress   Q11.S66 1904
Library, Smithsonian   Institution

QE
75
B

Emmons, William Harvey, 1876–

... The enrichment of ore deposits, by William Harvey Emmons. Washington, Govt. print. off., 1917.

530 p. illus., VII pl. (1 fold.) diagrs. 23½^{cm}. (U. S. Geological survey. Bulletin 625)

At head of title: Dept. of the interior.
Bibliography: p. 20–33.

1. Ore-deposits.
    G S 17–189
—— Copy 2.
Library, U. S. Geological   Survey (200) E no. 625

QL
Rept. and
Amphibia
Pam.
73

EMOIA GUAM

Smith, Albert G.

Notes on the herpetology of Guam, Marianas Islands.

(Natural History Miscellanea, Chicago Acad. of Science, No. 37, 1949)

QL
1
C 78

EMOIA MARSHALL ISLANDS

Brown, Walter C.

New Scincoid lizards from the Marshall Islands, with notes on their distribution. By Walter C. Brown and Joe T. Marshall, Jr.

(Copeia, No. 4:201–207, 1953)

AS
36
A 65 no

EMOIA NEW GUINEA

Brown, Walter C.

A review of New Guinea lizards allied to Emoia baudini and Emoia physicae (Scincidae) Results of the Archbold Expeditions, No. 69.

(Am. Mus. Novitates, No. 1627, pp. 1–25, 1953)

QL
1
L J

EMOIA NEW HEBRIDES

Baker, John R.

The seasons in a tropical rain-forest. Part 6. Lizards (Emoia).

(Journal of the Linn. Soc. of London. Zoology, Vol. 41 (no. 279):243–247, 1947)

QL
1
F 45

EMOIA SOLOMON ISLANDS

Brown, Walter C.

Notes on several lizards of the genus Emoia with descriptions of new species from the Solomon Islands.

(Fieldiana . Zoology, Vol. 34, No. 25, 1954)

GN
2.S
P 76

Emory, Kenneth P.

Additional illustrations of Tuamotuan creation.

(Journal of the Polynesian Society, Vol. 52, 1943, pp. 19–21)

GN
Ethn. Pam.
3348

Emory, Kenneth P.

Additional notes on the archaeology of Fanning Island.

(Occ. Papers, Bernice P. Bishop Museum, Vol. 15, 1939, No. 17, pp. 179–189)

GN
2.S
P 76

Emory, Kenneth P.

Additional radiocarbon dates from Hawaii and the Society Islands.

(Jour. Poly. Soc., 71(1):105–106, 1962)

AS
763
H 38

Emory, Kenneth P.

Advances in Hawaiian archaeology.

(Proceedings of the Hawaiian Academy of Science...Twenty-Seventh annual meeting...pages 8–9, 1951–1952)

DU
620
P

Emory, Kenneth P[ike]

The adz makers of Mauna Kea.

(Paradise of the Pacific, Vol. 50, No. 4, p. 21–22) 1938

DU
629 .H3
E 54

Emory, Kenneth P.

Archaeological and historical survey (of) Honokohau area, North Kona, Hawaii. By Kenneth P. Emory and Lloyd J. Soehren. Prepared by Bernice P. Bishop Museum for the Department of Land and Natural Resources, State Parks Division, State of Hawaii. Honolulu, 1961. 4to. 25 pp. (43 photos, 14 charts)

GN
Ethn. Pam.
283
268

Emory, Kenneth Pike

An archaeological survey of Haleakala.

(Bernice P. Bishop Museum, Occ. Papers, Vol. 7, No. 11, 1921, pp. 237–259)

annotated copy in St. Case 2
over

GN
2.S
H 38-n

Emory, Kenneth P.

Archaeological work in Hawaii, 1953.

(News from the Pacific, Vol. 5(1):5–6, 1954)

DU
620
P

Emory, Kenneth P.

Archaeology - in Hawaii.

(Paradise of the Pacific, Holiday Annual, pp. 38–40, 1956)

GN
2.S
T

Emory, Kenneth P[ike]

Archaeology in the Society Islands.

(In Bulletin de la Société des Etudes Océaniennes, Papeete, No. 12, pp. 29–54, 1926)

AP
2
S 35

Emory, Kenneth P.

Heyerdahl, Thor

Archaeology of Easter Island, I.

Reviewed by Kenneth P. Emory.

(Science, 138(3543):884-885, 1962)

GN
671.H2
H 23

Emory, Kenneth P(ike)

Can Hawaiian Culture Be Preserved? by E. H. Bryan, Jr., Kenneth P. Emory, and E. S. C. Handy.

Handy, E. S. C.

Ancient Hawaiian Civilization...by Handy, Emory, Bryan, Buck...and others. pp. 303-314.
1933

GN
2.S
T

Emory, Kenneth P(ike)

The Curved Club from a Rurutu Cave.

(Bulletin de la Société des Etudes Océaniennes, No. 21, 1927, pp. 304-306)

...additional note, ibid, Tome V (No. 42) 1932, pp. 12-14.

GN
Ethn.Pam.
3333

Emory, Kenneth Pike

Archaeology of Mangareva and neighboring atolls.

(Bernice P. Bishop Museum, Bull. 163, 1939. 76 pp.)

DU
620
H 41

Emory, Kenneth P.　　editor

Pukui, Mary Kawena

The canoe making profession of ancient times, translated by Mary Kawena Pukui, edited and annotated by Kenneth P. Emory.

(Hawaiian Historical Society, Papers, No.20, 1938, pp. 27-37, 1 pl.)
Also reprinted in Bernice P. Bishop Museum Occasional Paper, Vol. 15, No. 13

GN
2.S
T 12

Emory, Kenneth P.

Découverte archéologique aux Iles de la Société, par Kenneth Emory and Yosihiko Sinoto.

(Bull. Soc. d'Etudes Océaniennes, Tome 12, No. 3 (whole No. 140):126-127, 1962)

GN
875.H
E 54

AS
763
B-b

Reading
Room

Emory, Kenneth P(ike)

Archaeology of Nihoa and Necker Islands. Honolulu. 1928.

(Bernice P. Bishop Museum, Bulletin No. 53, 1928; Tanager Expedition, Publication No. 5)

GN
Ethn.
Pam.
4448

Emory, Kenneth P.

Changing hidden worlds of Polynesia.

(Paper presented before Social Science Association, Dec. 3, 1962. 6 pp.　Typed)

GN
2.S
P 76

Emory, Kenneth P.

East Polynesian relationships.

(Jour. of the Polynesian Soc., Vol. 72(2): 78-100, 1963)

GN
875
E 54

AS
763
B-b

Reading
Room

Emory, Kenneth P(ike)

Archaeology of the Pacific Equatorial Islands. Honolulu. Bernice P. Bishop Museum. 1934. R8vo. 43 pp. 5 pls. 22 figs.

(Bernice P. Bishop Museum, Bulletin 123, Whippoorwill Expedition, Pub. No. 4. 1934).

DU
620
P 22

Emory, Kenneth P.

City of Refuge.

(Paradise of the Pacific, July, 1959:66-70, 1959)

AS
36
A 5

Emory, Kenneth Pike

Every man his own Robinson Crusoe: a novel program to teach our South Sea fighters how to fare for themselves in time of need by use of ingenious native methods.

(Natural History, June, 1943, Vol. 52, No. 1, pp. 8-15)

AS
763
H 38

Emory, Kenneth Pike

Archaeology of the Phoenix Islands.

(Bernice P. Bishop Museum, Sp. Pub., 34, 1938/39, pp. 7-8. Proc. Haw. Acad. Sci., Ann. Meeting, 14th, 1938-39)

GN
2.S
P 76

Emory, Kenneth P.

Cook's comb hooded images.

(Jour. Poly. Soc., 41:66, 1932)

[see comment of Hans Damm, ibid, pp. 323-324]

GN
2.S
T

Emory, Kenneth P(ike)

Lidin, G.

Excursion dans la vallée Vaiote au Pari. Note complémentaire par Kenneth P. Emory.

(Bulletin de la Société des Etudes Océaniennes, Tome 5, No. 2, 1932, pp. 47-54)

GN
2.S
T

and

GN
Pam. 2757

Emory, Kenneth P(ike)

L'Art Tahitien.

(In Bulletin de la Societe d'Etudes Oceaniennes, No. 19, 1927) pp. 236-239

Storage
Case
3

Emory, Kenneth P(ike)

Conditions for ethnological field work in Kohala and Hamakua, Hawaii.

Typewritten manuscript 8pp, 16 photographs and a map.

Storage
Case
3

Emory, Kenneth P.

Exploration of Herbert C. Shipman cave, Keeau, Puna, Hawaii. Sept. 13-14, 1945. 9 pp. (in duplicate)

GN
Ethn.Pam.
3475

Emory, Kenneth Pike　and others

Bishop Museum lecture, Survival Training Unit, Central Pacific Base Command. March, 1945. 14 pp. mimeographed, folio.

2 copies

Emory, Kenneth P.　　editor

Current Work in Old World Archaeology [COWA Survey]

Area 21: Pacific...

No. 1, 1958 +

GN
Ethn.Pam.
3332

(2nd copy verifax)

Emory, Kenneth P.

Flying spray.

(Published in the Honolulu Advertiser and the Honolulu Star-Bulletin, weekly, December 12, 1938 to August 14, 1939,- 35 issues, under patronage of Matson Navigation Co. (Castle and Cooke))

AM
101
B 62

Emory, Kenneth P.

Flying spray: canoe building: the hull is formed.

(The Conch Shell, Vol. 1(4):44-45, 1963)

GN
Ethn.
Pam.
4179

Emory, Kenneth P.

Hawaiian archaeology: fishhooks. By Kenneth P. Emory, William J. Bonk and Yosihiko H. Sinoto.

(Bernice P. Bishop Museum Special Publication 47, 1959)

QH
1
A 88

Emory, Kenneth Pike
Investigation of material culture.
IN
Fosberg, F. Raymond
Handbook for atoll research, 2nd...ed., pp. 122.

(Atoll Research Bull., No. 17, 1953)

AM
101
B 62

Emory, Kenneth P.

Flying spray: canoe building: training of craftsmen.

(The Conch Shell, Vol. 1(3):34-35, 1963)

GN
Ethn.
Pam.
4280

Emory, Kenneth P.

Hawaiian archaeology: Oahu excavations. By Kenneth P. Emory and Yoshihiko H. Sinoto.

(Bernice P. Bishop Museum Special Publication 49, 1961)

GN
671.H2
E 55

AS
763
E-b
Reading
Room

Emory, Kenneth P(ike)

The island of Lanai, a survey of native culture. Honolulu. Bernice P. Bishop Museum. 1924. 8 vo. 129 pp. Illustrated. Map.

(Bernice P. Bishop Museum, Bulletin 12)

GN
2.S
P 76

Emory, Kenneth P.
Desmedt, G. Maurice

Les funerailles et l'expositon des morts a Mangareva (Gambier).

(Bull. Soc. des Americanistes de Belgique, Dec. 1932:128-136)

(Reviewed by K. P. Emory, in Jour. Poly. Soc. 42:125-127, 1933)   see also ibid, p. 335)

Emory, Kenneth P.

Hawaiian archaeology: fishhooks...
REVIEWS:
McCarthy, F. D. IN Oceania, 30:326, 1960

GN
2.S
P 76
also
GN
Ethn.
Pam.
3792

Emory, Kenneth P.

A kaitaia carving from south-east Polynesia?

(Jour. Poly. Soc., 40:253-254, 1931)

GN
Genealogy
Pam.
1

Emory, Kenneth P.   (compiler)

Genealogy of some Hawaiian chiefs. Ke-aka-mahana to Kamehameha, Liliha, Kiwala-o, Ke-opu-o-lani...

GN
2.S
P 76

Emory, Kenneth P.

The Hawaiian god 'Io.

(Journal of the Polynesian Society, Vol. 51, 1942, pp. 200-207)

Micro-
film
109

Emory, Kenneth P.

Kapingamarangi-Nukuoro dictionary; copy of card index.

GN
2.M
C 89
and
GN
Ethn.Pam.
3273

Emory, Kenneth P(ike)

God sticks, Hawaii

(Ethnologia Cranmorensis, 3, 1938, pp. 9-10)

GN
Ethn.Pam
3506

Emory, Kenneth Pike

Hawaiian tattooing.

(Occ. Papers, Bernice P. Bishop Museum, Vol. 18, No. 17, 1946)

GN
Ethn.Pam.
3510 a

Emory, Kenneth Pike

Kidnaped to London: being the amazing chronicle of two Hawaiians who, forced aboard a schooner off Hawaii, finally arrived safely in England after various adventures by land and sea.

(Honolulu Advertiser, Sunday, March 30, 1947)
[accounts from The Sun, London, 1820 and The New Times, London, 1820.]

GN
2.M
C 89

Emory, Kenneth P(ike)

Hawaii: notes on wooden images.

(Ethnologia Cranmorensis, No. 2, 1938, p. 3-7, 2 pl.)

GN
Eth
Pam
#581
DU
621
H3

Emory, Kenneth P(ike)

Heiaus of Lanai, ex Haw. Ann. for 1923.   p. 138

DU
620
P 22

Emory, Kenneth P.

Kilalowe was here generation after generation.

(Paradise of the Pacific, March, 1956:9-11)

Storage
Case
3

Emory, Kenneth Pike

Hawaii, Kailua. Chart of fishing grounds off Kailua; data supplied by father of T. I. Maunupau, 1933.

THIS MAY BE USED ONLY BY MEMBERS OF THE MAUNUPAU FAMILY and K.P.EMORY

AS
36
A 35

Emory, Kenneth Pike

Honolulu museums show exhibition of native lore for castaways.

(The Museum News, Vol. 20, 1943, No. 15, p. 1-2)

Storage
Case
3

Emory, Kenneth P(ike)

Kona, Hawaii, Field Notes. 1 notebook. November, 1932

GR
380.1
S 85

Emory, Kenneth P(ike)

Stimson, J. Frank

The legends of Maui and Tahaki, translated by J. F. Stimson. (Bibliography of the Tahaki legend, by K. P. Emory, pp. 89-90)

(Bernice P. Bishop Museum, Bull 127, 1934)

Storage
Case
2

Emory, Kenneth P(ike)

Museums. Notes on European and American museums. 1926. 1 bundle.

Storage
Case
3

Emory, Kenneth P(ike)

New Zealand museum. Notebooks 12,13 June, 1931.

Storage
Case
3

Emory, Kenneth P(ike)

Mangareva: field map. (U.S.H.O. chart No. 2595, with additional place names) 1935

GN
1
J

and
GN
Ethn.
Pam.
3560

Emory, Kenneth Pike

Myths and tales from Kapingamarangi, a Polynesian inhabited island in Micronesia.

(Journal of American Folklore, Vol. 62:230-239, 1949)

GN
2.S
P 76

Emory, Kenneth Pike

A newly discovered illustration of Tuamotuan creation.

(Journal of the Polynesian Society, Vol. 49, 1940, pp. 569-578)

GN
2.M
C 89

and
GN
Ethn.Pam.
3329

Emory, Kenneth Pike

Manihiki: inlaid wooden bowls.

(Ethnologia Cranmorensis, No. 4, 1939, p. 20-26)

AS
763
B-r

Emory, Kenneth Pike

Buck, Peter H. (Te Rangi Hiroa)

Native crafts have gone to war.

(Bernice P. Bishop Museum, Bull. 182, pp. 26-30, 1944; Ann. Rept. for 1943)

GN
2.S
T

Emory, Kenneth P(ike)

Note (sur la) decouverte d'une nouvelle pierre gravée.

(Bulletin de la Soc. des Etudes Océaniennes Tome 5, No. 2, 1932, pp. 53-54)

GN
2.S
T

Emory, Kenneth P(ike)

The marae at which Capt. Cook witnessed a rite of human sacrifice.

(Bull. de la Soc. des Études Océaniennes, Tome IV, 1931, pp. 195-203)

GN
Ethn.
Pam.
3422

Emory, Kenneth P.

Native lore for castaways in the South Seas. Assembled from material in the collection of the Bernice P. Bishop Museum... Honolulu Academy of Arts, Honolulu, Hawaii. 1943. mimeographed 18 pp.

2 copies

Ms
Case 4
L 19

Emory, Kenneth P.

Notes as to David Malo's "Hawaiian Antiquities." 1 typed page: after an interview with J. F. G. Stokes, Nov. 1955.

DU
620
P

Emory, Kenneth P.

Meet coconut meat- potential life saver.

(Paradise of the Pacific, Vol. 55, 1943, no. 6, pp. 20-22)

G
55
F 85

Emory, Kenneth Pike

The native peoples of the Pacific.
IN
Freeman, Otis W.
Geography of the Pacific. N.Y. 1951. pp. 44-60.

Storage
Case
3

Emory, K. P. (Kenneth Pike)

Notes on Kona Burial Caves, 1933. Russ Burial Cave, Honomalino, South Kona. Preliminary expanded notes.

Q
Biogr.
Pam. 84

Emory, Kenneth P.

Memorial for Dr. Peter H. Buck, for the Memorial Service at Kamehameha School, February 13, 1952. 2 pp. mimeographed

3 copies

DU
629.H3k
N 28

Emory, Kenneth P.

Natural and cultural history report, Kalapana Extension, Hawaii National Park.
Vol. I. Cultural history report, by Kenneth P. Emory and others.

Prepared by Bernice P. Bishop Museum for the Hawaii National Park Service, Honolulu, 1959. 4to mimeograhed.

DU
620
P

Emory, Kenneth P.

Oahu's fascinating petroglyphs.

(Paradise of the Pacific, Vol. 67(5):9-11,26, May, 1955)

Storage
Case
3

Emory, Kenneth P(ike)

Miscellaneous notes on Christmas Island, Penhryn, Fanning, Washington, Malden. Field note books. (Kaimiloa expedition)

GN
671.H2
H 23

Emory, Kenneth P(ike)

Navigation (Hawaii)

Handy, E. S. C.

Ancient Hawaiian Civilization...by Handy, Emory, Bryan, Buck...and others. pp. 237-246. 1933

GN
2.S
P 76

Emory, Kenneth Pike

Oceanian influence on American Indian culture.

(Journal of the Polynesian Society, Vol. 51, 1942, pp. 126-135)

GN
2.S
P76
Emory, Kenneth P.

Origin of the Hawaiians.

(Jour. Poly. Soc., 68(1): 29-35, 1959)

DU
1
P
Emory, Kenneth Pike

Polynesian migrations and culture; spirited defence of Dr. Buck's book.

(Pacific Islands Monthly, Vol. 13, 1942, no. 4, p. 11; see also Dr. Buck's letter, in 13:5, p. 24-25)

(answer to a letter to the editor from Stimson?)

GN
2.S
T
Emory, Kenneth P.(ike)

Recent Petroglyph Discoveries on Tahiti.

(Bulletin de la Societe des Etudes Oceaniennes, Tome 4, No. 5, Fevrier, 1931) pp. 138-143

GN
Ethn.Pam.
3881
Emory, Kenneth Pike

Origin of the Hawaiians. Summary of a talk Nov. 12, 1952. 5 mimeographed pages.

GN
2.M
P 35
Emory, Kenneth Pike

Polynesian stone remains.

IN Studies in the anthropology of Oceania and Asia...in memory of Roland Burrages Dixon, pp. 9-21

(Papers, Peabody Mus. of Am. Arch. and Ethn. Harvard Univ., Vol. 20, 1943)

GN
2.S
P 76
Emory, Kenneth P.

Report on Bishop Museum archaeological expeditions to the Society Islands in 1960 and 1961.

(Jour. Poly. Soc., 71(1):117-120, 1962)

GN
Ethn.
Pam.
4187
Emory, Kenneth P.

Origin of the Hawaiians.

(Viltis, Vol. 18, 1959)

AM
101
B 62
Emory, Kenneth P.

Prehistoric burial site, Society Islands, part I. By Kenneth P. Emory and Yosihiko Sinoto.

(The Conch Shell, Vol. 1(3):31-33, 1963)
Part II.

(The Conch Shell, Vol. 1(4):46-47, 1963)

Emory, Kenneth P.

reviews:
Stimson, J. Frank
Songs and tales of the sea kings.
(Jour. Poly. Soc. 60(4):791-794, 1958)

DU
500
T 87
Emory, Kenneth P.

The original background of the Micronesians.
IN
Trust Territory of the Pacific Islands.
Basic Information, 1 July 1951. pp. 61-69.

GN
1
A 62
Emory, Kenneth P. and others

A program for Micronesian archaeology; recommendations of the Sub-Committee on Pacific Archaeology, Nat. Research Council.

(American Anthropologist, Vol. 53:594-597, 1951)

[by Emory, Gifford, Macgregor, Osborne and Spoehr]

Emory, Kenneth P.

reviews:
Caillot, A. C. Eugene Histoire des religions de l'Archipel Paumotu... Paris. 1932. IN JPS 42:114-116, 1933
Caillot, A. C. Eugene Histoire de l'Ile de Opara ou Rapa. Paris. 1932. IN JPS 42:116-117, 1933

GN
2.S
P 76
Emory, Kenneth P.

Paepae (hockey) in Tahiti and the Austral Islands.

(Jour. Poly. Soc., 41:171-172, 1932)

GN
1
A 62
and
GN
Ethn.
Pam.
3963
Emory, Kenneth P.

A program for Polynesian archeology*.

(American Anthropologist, Vol. 55(5:1):752-755, 1953)

*Prepared at the request of the Subcommittee on Pacific Archaeology, National Research Council The Subcommittee consists of Alexander Spoehr (Chairman), Kenneth P. Emory, E. W. Gifford, Douglas Osborne, and Erik K. Reed.

GN
2.S
T 12
Emory, Kenneth P.

Le rocher des petroglyphes de Tipaerui (Tahiti). Traduit par Pierre Verin.

(Bull. Soc. d'Etudes Oceaniennes, 11: 281-287, 1961)

GN
2.S
T 12
and
GN
Ethn.Pam
2696
Emory, Kenneth P.

The petroglyph boulder at Tipaerui, Tahiti.

(Bull. Soc. d'Etudes Oceanimnnes, No. 11: 10-15, 1926)

GN
2.S
T
Emory, Kenneth P.(ike)

Un programme d'archéologie Polynésienne. Traduit de l'anglais par B. Jaunez.

(Bull. de la Société des Etudes Océaniennes, No. 110, Tome IX(9):382-387, 1955)

DU
621
H3
Emory, Kenneth P.(ike)

Ruins at Kee, Haena, Kauai (famous court of Lohiau). In Thrums Hawaiian Annual for 1929, pp. 88-94

Storage
Case
3
Emory, Kenneth P.(ike)

Polynesia, southeast. Notes, 1925-1931. 1 box.

GN
2.S
T 12
Emory, Kenneth P.

Rapport publié par le Conseil d'archéologie de l'Ancien monde, traduit de l'anglais par B. Jaunez.

(Bull. Soc. Etudes Oceaniennes, 127/128, 1959:33-41)

GN
1
C 97
Emory, Kenneth P.

Society Islands Archaeological discovery.

(Current Anthropology, Vol. 4(4):357-358, 1963)

GN
Ethn.
Pam.
3444

OVER

Emory, Kenneth P.

South Sea lore.

(Bernice P. Bishop Museum, Special Pub. 36, 1943)

[1st printing, Sept. 8, 1943; 2nd, Oct. 28, 1943; 3rd, Jan. 1944; revised ed., Sept. 1944; 2nd printing of rev. ed., Nov. 1944; final printing by U. S. Army, Apr. 26, 1945]

4th edition has appendix by Loring G. Hudson: Important ( ) plants of the Philippines and Dutch East Indies.

GN
2.S
P 76

Emory, Kenneth P(ike)

The Tahitian account of creation by Mare.

(Journal of the Polynesian Society, Vol. 47, 1938, pp. 45-63)

GN
2.S
P 76

Emory, Kenneth P.

Tuamotuan plant names.

(Journal of the Polynesian Soc., Vol. 56; 266-277, 1947)

DU
Pac. Pam.
709

Emory, Kenneth Pike

South Seas diary; Report from the South Pacific; life on Kapingamarangi; and Kapingamarangi farewell.

The Honolulu Advertiser, Sunday Polynesian, August 31, Sept. 7, Oct. 19 and November 30, 1947.

Storage
Case
3

Emory, Kenneth P(ike)

Traditional history of maraes in the Society Islands. (2 copies) ms.

GN
Ethn.Pam.
3531

Emory, Kenneth Pike

Tuamotuan religious structures and ceremonies.

(Bernice P. Bishop Museum, Bull. 191, 1947)

Reviewed by E. G. Burrows in Am. Anthropologist, 52:85, 1950

GN
671.H2
H 23

Emory, Kenneth P(ike)

Sports, Games, and Amusements (Hawaii)

Handy, E. S. C.

Ancient Hawaiian Civilization...by Handy, Emory, Bryan, Buck...and others. pp. 141-154. 1933

Storage
Case
3

over

Emory, K. P. (Kenneth Pike)

Tuamotu expedition, K. P. Emory and J. Frank Stimson. Traditional material. Books 1-6
1. S. 3rd cruise. Hikueru, Reao, Vahitahi. 1930
2. T. Anaa. (from informant Paea.) 1929-1931
3. V. 1st cruise. Raroia, Napuka, Amanu, Hao 1929.
4. W. Takaroa. 1929.
5. X. Tahiti collection.
6. Z. Anaa. (from informant Paea) 1932.

Note. Letters S-Z are ( ) merely arbitrary identifications, used by E. & S. instead of 1-6

GN
875.T
E 54

AS
763
B b

Reading
Room

Emory, Kenneth P(ike)

Tuamotuan stone structures.

(Bernice P. Bishop Museum, Bulletin 118. Honolulu, 1934). 78 pp. 10 pls. 71 figs.

GN
2.S
Po

GN
Pam
2698

Emory, Kenneth P(ike)

Stone implements of Pitcairn Island. In Polynesian Soc., Jour., v. 37, n.2, 1928. pp. 125-135

separate

GN
2.S
P 76

Emory, Kenneth P.

The Tuamotu legend of Rongo, son of Vaio.

(Journal of the Polynesian Society, Vol. 56:52-54, 1947)

AS
763
B-b

Emory, Kenneth Pike

The Tuamotuan Survey.

(Bernice P. Bishop Museum, Bull. 94:40-50, 1932)

GN
875.S
E 54

AS
763
B-b

Reading
Room

Emory, Kenneth P(ike)

Stone Remains in the Society Islands.

(Bernice P. Bishop Museum, Bulletin, No. 116 1933.)

and an annotated copy in Storage Case 2

GN
2.S
P 76

Emory, Kenneth P.

Tuamotuan bird names.

(Journal of the Polynesian Soc., Vol. 56; 188-196, 1947)

GN
1
J

and
GN
Ethn.Pam.
3559

Emory, Kenneth P.

The Tuamotuan tale of the female spirit who assumed the form of Tu's wife.

(Journal of American Folklore, Vol. 62:312-316, 1949)

GN
2.S
T 12

Emory, Kenneth P.
Verin, Pierre

Documents sur l'île de Me'etia, traduite, révisés et augmentés par P. Verin. (Extraits de "Stone Remains in the Society Islands", par K. P. Emory)

(Bull. Soc. des Etudes Océaniennes, tome 12 (2):59-80, 1962)

GN
Ethn.Pam.
3361

Emory, Kenneth Pike

Tuamotuan concepts of creation.

(Journal of the Polynesian Soc., Vol. 49, 1940, pp. 69-136)

Storage
Case
3

Emory, Kenneth P(ike)

Tuamotus. Field notebooks 1-8, 11. 1929-30.

GN
Ethn.Pam.
2836

Emory, Kenneth P(ike)

Buck, Peter H. (Te Rangi Hiroa)

Terminology for Ground Stone Cutting-Implements in Polynesia, by Peter H. Buck, Kenneth P. Emory, H. D. Skinner and John F. G. Stokes.

(Vol. 39, Journal of the Polynesian Society, pp. 174-180, 1930)

2 copies

GN
2 S
P 76

and
GN
EthnPam.
3343

Emory, Kenneth P(ike)

The Tuamotuan creation charts by Paiore.

(Journal of the Polynesian Society, Vol. 48, 1939, pp. 1-29)

Storage
Case
3

Emory, Kenneth P(ike)

Tuamotus, Napuka. 1 notebook, typed, 8vo oblong. Sent from field, via Islander. Received Oct. 30, 1934.

DU
Pacific
Pam
419

Emory,.Kenneth P(ike)

Village and house sites, Lanai. (Elsewhere than at Kaunolu) Field work, 1921-22

27 typed pages.

DU
Pac.Pam
654

EMORY, KENNETH PIKE

Rawlings, Charles

How to be healthy though shipwrecked.
(interview obtained while stalking Kenneth P.
Emory while lecturing at the Castaway" exhinit
at the Honolulu Academy of Art)

(Saturday Evening Post, Vol. 215, no. 38, pp
20-21, 109-110, March 20, 1943)

QL
401
H 1

EMPIDIDAE

Melander, A. L.

A new empidid fly in Hawaii (Dipt.)

(Haw. Ent. Soc., Proc., Vol. 10, 1938, pp.
57-58)

GN
671.H2
H23

Emory, Kenneth P.(ike)

Warfare (Hawaii)

Handy, E. S. C.

Ancient Hawaiian Civilization...by Handy,
Emory, Bryan, Buck...and others. pp. 229-236.
1933

DU
Pac.Pam
816

EMORY, KENNETH P.

Wilder, Lillian

Letters from the South Seas to Mrs. Herbert
E. Gregory. (copies)

[original typing and carbon]

QL
595.M1
I 59

EMPIDIDAE

Quate, Laurence W.

Empididae
IN
Insects of Micronesia, Vol. 13(3), 1960

DU
1
M 6

Emory, Kenneth P.(ike)

Windward Molokai: the story of a sampan trip

(The Mid-Pacific Magazine, Vol. 12, No. 5,
pp. 443-447)

QP
401
D 22

EMOTIONS   ANIMALS

Darwin, Charles

The expression of the emotions in man and
animals. With photographic and other illustrations. With a preface by Margaret Mead. Philosophical Library. New York. 8vo. xi + 372
pp. 1955c.

QL
1
A 93

EMPIDIDAE   AUSTRALIA

Hardy, G. H.

Australian Empididae.

(The Australian Zoologist, 6:237-250, 1930)

GN
671.H2
H 23

Emory, Kenneth P(ike)

Wooden Utensils and Implements (Hawaii)

Handy, E. S. C.

Ancient Hawaiian Civilization...by Handy,
Emory, Bryan, Buck, ...and others. pp.119-124.
1933

QP
401
D 22

EMOTIONS   MAN

Darwin, Charles

The expression of the emotions in man and
animals. With photographic and other illustrations. With a preface by Margaret Mead. Philosophical Library. New York. 8vo. xi + 372
pp. 1955c.

QL
461
H-1

EMPIDIDAE   HAWAII

Melander, A. L.

Drapetis insularis, a new species from
Oahu (Diptera: Empididae).

(Proc. Haw. Ent. Soc, Vol. 14(3):419-423,
1951)

GN
Ethn. Pam.
3709

EMORY, KENNETH P.

Ancient carving, with death tabu, found in
Tahiti (by Kenneth P. Emory); Polynesian 'milk
stone' full of magic figures, told of by scientist...

(Honolulu Star-Bulletin, May 9, 1925)

[Kaimiloa expedition]

QK
Pam
#601
4to

Emoto, Yoshikadzu

Uber die relative Wirksamkeit von
Kreuz-und Selbstbefruchtung bei einigen
Pflanzen, ex Jour. of Coll. of Sc.,
Imp. Univ. of Tokyo, vol. XLIII, art.
4, 1920.

DS
Asia
Pam
28

The Empire of Japan; brief sketch of the
geography, history and constitution. Published
by the Imperial Commission for the Philadelphia
International Exhibition. Philadelphia. William
P. Kildare. 1876. 42 pp.

GN
2.S
P 76

EMORY, KENNETH P.

(Visit in New Zealand)

(Jour. Poly. Soc., 40:167, 1931)

QL
537.E5
C 71

EMPIDIDAE

Collin, J. E.

British flies; Empididae. Cambridge. At
the University Press. 1961. R8vo. viii + 782
pp.

G
51
W 17

EMU

Grayson, Helen

The amazing emu.

(Walkabout, 21(2):29, 1955)

GN
662
B 29

EMORY, KENNETH P.

Lavachéry, Henri

Stèles et pierres-levées à l'Île de Pâques.
IN
Südseestudien, pp. 413-422, 1951, Basel.

[includes discussion of Emory's theory as to
history of upright monoliths of Polynesia, in
his "Tuamotuan stone steuctures", Bull. 118]

QL
468
W 99

EMPIDIDAE

Melander, Axel Leonard

Diptera, Fam. Empididae.
IN
Wytsman, P.
Genera Insectorum, Fasc. 185, 1927

PL
Phil.Pam.
237

En pol uonporen amen a kilijikau on men
kaleijia kan. Published by the Hawaiian Board.
Honolulu. Black & Auld. 1873. 8vo. 8 pp.
contains also En pol a kijilikau on Taitoj.
...1873. 4 pp.

(Galatians and Titus in Ponape dialect.)

QE 201 B

SEP - 8 19

La Encantada, Placer de Guadalupe, Estado de Chihuahua (México).—Monografía geológica y paleontológica del Cerro de Muleros, cerca de Ciudad Juárez, y descripción de la Fauna Cretácea de la Encantada, Placer de Guadalupe, Estado de Chihuahua, por el Dr. Emilio Böse.—*Boletín del Instituto Geológico de México.* Número 25. México, Imp. y Fototipia de la Secretaría de Fomento. 1910. 4º Texto 193 págs. Atlas: Carta Geológica (1:10,000), una lámina de perfiles y 48 láminas de fósiles.

QK 7 Ea E56

Encyclopédie méthodique.   15v.

Lamarck, J. B. P. A. de M. de.

(Botanique)

AS 36 S 4

ENCYRTIDAE

Timberlake, P. H.

Miscellaneous new chalcid-flies of the hymenopterous family Encyrtidae.

(In Proc. U. S. Nat. Mus., Vol. 69, Art. 3, 1926)

AE 5 E391

The Encyclopædia britannica; a dictionary of arts, sciences, and general literature. 9th ed. ... New York, C. Scribner's sons, 1878-80.

25 v. illus., plates (part col.) maps (part double) plans, diagrs. 28cm.

Ed. by T. S. Baynes.

11th edition. New York, 1910

1. Encyclopedias and dictionaries. I. Baynes, Thomas Spencer, 1823-1887, ed.

7-19448

Encyclopédie Méthodique. Insects, Entomologie.

HSPA has

Vols. IV-X, 1789-1825
Vol. XI, Part 18 (Atlas), 1797
"   "   "   24, 1818

QL 1 A 94

Endean, R.   and others

The ecology and distribution of intertidal organisms on certain islands off the Queensland coast.

(Australian Jour. of Marine and Freshwater Research, 7(3):317-342, 1956)

[a study of intertidal organisms of the continental islands off the Queensland coast]

GN 11 H 35

ENCYCLOPAEDIA OF RELIGION AND ETHICS

Hastings, James   editor

QL 7 E 56

Encyclopédie méthodique; histoire naturelle des Vers, de Lamarck, continuées par G. P. Deshayes. Texte, tomes 1-3; Planches, Tomes 1-3. Paris. Agasse. sm4to. 1792-1832.

Tome I par (J.G.)Bruguière; Tome II-III par Bruguière et de Lamarck, continuée par G. P. Deshayes.

QL 1 A 94

Endean, R.

A study of the distribution, behaviour, venom apparatus, and venom of the stone-fish.

(Australian Jour. of Marine and Freshwater Research, 12(2):177-190, 1961)

Encyclopedia Britannica, 1960 edition

E. H. Bryan, Jr. Has a copy

QL 7 E 56

Encyclopédie Méthodique.

Histoire Naturelle des Zoophytes ou Animaux Rayonnés, faisant suite a l'Histoire Naturelle des Vers de Bruguière. Par MM. Lamouroux, Bory de Saint-Vincent et Eud. Deslongchamps. Paris. Agasse. 1824. sm4to. viii + 819 pp.

(marked Tome Second, but a note in pencil states"il n'y a qu'un tome")

QL 636 A 93

ENDEAVOUR (ship)

Australia. Department of Trade and Customs.

Fisheries: Biological results of the fishing experiments carried on by the F.I.S. "Endeavour" 1909-1914. Vol. 1, 1911-   Sydney. 8vo.

H 41 S 46

Encyclopedia of the social sciences...

Seligman, Edwin R. A.

AG 5 C4

ENCYCLOPEDIAS.

... The Century dictionary and cyclopedia, with a new atlas of the world; a work of general reference in all departments of knowledge ... [Rev. and enl. ed.] New York, The Century co. [1911]

12 v. illus., plates (part col.) maps, charts. 31cm. $75.00

CONTENTS.—v. 1-10. The Century dictionary ... prepared under the superintendence of William Dwight Whitney ... rev. & enl. under the superintendence of Benjamin E. Smith.—v. 11. The Century cyclopedia of names ... ed. by Benjamin E. Smith.—v. 12. The Century atlas of the world, prepared under the superintendence of Benjamin E. Smith.

1. English language—Dictionaries. 2. Atlases. 3. Biography—Dictionaries. 4. Names. 5. Encyclopedias and dictionaries. I. Whitney, William Dwight, 1827-1894. II. Smith, Benjamin Eli, 1857-1913.

11-31934

QK 431 B 21 locked case

ENDEAVOUR (ship)

Banks, Sir Joseph

Illustrations of Australian Plants collected in 1770 during Captain Cook's Voyage round the World in H. M. S. Endeavour...London. British Museum. 1901-1905. folio. 318 plates.

AM 145.T D 55

Encyclopédie Biologique.

XX; L'art de la taxidermie au XXe siécle. Par R. Didier et A. Boudarel. 1948

QL Insects Pam. 1100

ENCYRTINAE

Ishii, Tei

Observations on the Hymenopterous parasites of Ceroplastes Rubens, Mask., with descriptions of new genera and species of the subfamily Encyrtinae.

(Bull. 3, 1923, Department of Agric. and Commerce, Imperial Plant Quarantine Station, Japan, pp. 69-114)

DU 12 B 21

ENDEAVOUR (SHIP)

Banks, Sir Joseph

Journal...during Captain Cook's first voyage in H.M.S. Endeavour in 1768-71...edited by Sir Joseph D. Hooker. London. 1896. 8vo.

QL 531 E 56

Encyclopédie Entomologique. Series B:II Diptera: Recueil d'Etudes Biologiques et Systematiques sur les Diptères du Globe, par M. Bezzi, E. Brunetti, F. W. Edwards...reunies par E.Séguy. Tome 1-5, 1924-1929. Paris. Paul Lechevalier (Editeur). 1924-29. 201, 208, 205, 204 and 189 pp. 8vo.

QL Insects Pam. 1082

ENCYRTIDAE

Timberlake, P. H.   (Philip Hunter)

Encyrtidae of the Marquesas and Society Islands (Hymenoptera, Chalcidoidea).

(Bernice P. Bishop Museum, Occ. Papers, Vol. 16, No. 9, 1941, pp. 215-230)

DU 12 B 36 locked case

ENDEAVOUR (SHIP)

Beaglehole, John C.   editor

The Endeavour journal of Joseph Banks, 1768-1771. Vol. I-II. The Trustees of the Public Library of New South Wales, in association with Angus and Robertson. 1962 R8vo. xxvii +476 pp., 40 pl; xvi + 406 pp., 40 pl.

G
161
H 15-e

ENDEAVOUR, (ship)
Beaglehole, J. C.   editor

The journals of Captain James Cook on his voyages of discovery. Edited from the original manuscripts by J. C. Beaglehole, with the assistance of J. A. Williamson...
Vol. 1. The voyage of the ENDEAVOUR, 1768-1771.

(Hakluyt Soc., Extra Ser. No. 34, 1955)

DU
12
J 86

ENDEAVOR (SHIP)

Journal of a voyage round the world, in His Majesty's ship Endeavor, in the years 1768-1771; undertaken in pursuit of natural knowledge... London. 1771. 4to. (Probably written by someone on board the ship)

DU
12
B 91

ENDERBURY ISLAND
Bryan, Edwin H., Jr.

American Polynesia; coral islands of the central Pacific. Tongg Publishing Company. Honolulu. 1941. 8vo. 208 pp.

DU
12
C 77-1

looked
case

ENDEAVOR (SHIP)
Cook, James

Captain Cook's Journal during his first voyage round the world made in H. M. bark "Endeavor" 1768-71...edited by W. J. L. Wharton... London. 1893. 4to.

DU
12
P 24

looked
case

ENDEAVOUR (SHIP)
Parkinson, Sydney

Journal of a voyage to the South Seas, in. His Majesty's ship, the Endeavour. Faithfully transcribed from the papers of the late Sydney Parkinson... London. 1773. 4to.

DU
Pac.Pam.
620

ENDERBURY ISLAND

Exchange of notes between His Majesty's Government in the United Kingdom and the United States Government regarding the Administration of the Islands of Canton and Enderbury, Washington, April 6, 1939. Treaty Series No. 21, 1939. His Majesty's Stationery Office. London. 1939. 6 pp.

DU
12
G 99

ENDEAVOUR (SHIP)
Gwyther, John

Captain Cook and the South Pacific. The voyage of the "ENDEAVOUR" 1768 - 1771. Illustrated. Houghton Mifflin Co. Boston. 1954. 8vo. xii + 269 pp.

AS
36
C 75

ENDEMISM
Cockerell, Theodore D.A.

Studies of island life.

(University of Colorado Studies, Vol.26, pp. 1-20, 1938.)

Q
115
U 58

looked
case

DU
12
U 58
looked
case

ENDERBURY ISLAND

United States Exploring Expedition...1838-1842, under the command of Charles Wilkes. Vol.III, p. 391. Philadelphia. C. Sherman. 1844 4to.

...Narrative, Vols. 1-5 and atlas. Phila. 1845. R8vo. Vol. III, pp. 370-371.

DU
12
H 39

looked
case

ENDEAVOR (SHIP)
Hawkesworth, John

An account of the voyages undertaken...for making discoveries in the Southern Hemisphere, and successively performed by Commodore Byron, Captain Wallis, Captain Carteret, and Captain Cook in the Dolphin, the Swallow, and the Endeavor... 3 vols. London. 1773. 4to.
Vols. 2 and 3.
...Fourth edition, Vol. 2, pp. 129-261; Vols. 3 and 4. Perth. 1789. 12mo.

QK
Bot.Pam.
1595

ENDEMISM
Ridley, H.N.

On Endemism and the Mutation Theory

Annals of Botany,Vol.XXX, No. CXX, 1916 8vo.

QH
138.J
S 62

Enderlein, Günther

Die Dipterenfauna der Juan-Fernandez-Inseln und der Oster-Insel.

IN
Skottsberg, Carl   editor
The natural history of Juan Fernandez and Easter Island, Vol. III. Zoology, Art. 60, pp. 643-680. Uppsala. 1940.

DU
780
H 68

ENDEAVOUR (SHIP)
Hockin, J. P.

A supplement to the account of the Pelew Islands; compiled from the Journals of the Panther and Endeavour...1790; and from the oral communications of Captain H. Wilson. London. 1803. 4to.

GC
26
H 23

ENDEMISM PACIFIC
Hartman, Olga

Endemism in the North Pacific Ocean, with emphasis on the distribution of marine annelids, and descriptions of new or little known species.
IN
Essays in the natural sciences in honor of Captain Allan Hancook...pp. 39-60. 1955. Univ. of Southern Calif. Press. Los Angeles.

QL
1
Zoo
v.20

Enderlein, Günther

Die von Herrn Prof. Dr. Friedr. Dahl im Bismarck Archipel gesammelten Copeognathen. In Zool. Jahrb. Bd.20, 1904, pp 105 - 112, Pl.vii.

AP
2
E 56

ENDEAVOUR (ship)
Holmes, Sir Maurice

Captain James Cook, R. N., F.R.S.

(Endeavour, Vol. 8:11-17, 1949)

QK
Bot.Pam.
3293

ENDEMISM THREE KINGS' ISLANDS
Cranwell, Lucy M.

Endemism and isolation in the Three Kings' Islands, New Zealand - with notes on pollen and spore types of the endemics.

(Records of the Auckland Institute and Museum, Vol. 5(5/6):215-232, 1962)

QH
11
P 11

Enders, Robert K.

Field study of rats in the Marianas and Palaus.

(Scientific Investigations in Micronesia, Report No. 3, no date)

AS
719
A 93-m

ENDEAVOUR (SHIP)
Iredale, Tom

H. M. S. "Endeavour Bark".

(The Australian Museum Magazine, Vol. 9:291-293, 1946)

DU
Pac.Pam.
624

ENDERBURY ISLAND
Arundel, John T.

The Phoenix Group and other islands. typed copy, 10 pp.

QK
490.I2
E 56

Endert, F. H.

Geslachtstabellen voor Ned.-Indische Boomsoorten naar vegetatieve kenmerken met een beschouwing over de practische en systematische waarde dezer kenmerken.

(Med. van het Proefstation voor het Boschwezen, No. 20, 1928, Dept. van Landbouw, Nijverheid en Handel in Nederlandsch Indie)

DU
600
E56

Endicott, William

    Wrecked among cannibals in the Fijis. A narrative of shipwreck and adventure in the South seas. By William Endicott, third mate of the ship "Glide" with notes by Lawrence Waters Jenkins...

    Salem, Marine Research Society, 1923. (Marine Research Society, Publication no. 3) 77 pp.

2 copies

QK
Pam.
#630
4to

Endlicher, Stephan

    Bemerkungen uber die flora der Sudseeinseln.

    Wien, 1835.

QK
11
E 58

Endlicher, Stephan

    Enchiridion botanicum exhibens classes et ordines plantarum, accedit nomenclator generum et officinalium vel usualium indicatio. Lipsiae; Viennae, 1841. 8vo. xiv + 765 pp.

QK
Pam.
630

Endlicher, Stephan

    Flora der Sudseeinseln.

QK
97
E 56

Endlicher, Stephano

    Genera Plantarum Secundum Ordines Naturales Disposita. (Includes Supplementum I) Vindobonae. Fr. Beck. 1836-1840. lx + 1483 pp. R8vo.

QK
97
E 56

Endlicher, Stephano

    Generum Plantarum. Supplementa 2-5, 1842-50. Vindobonae. Fridericum Beck. 114 + 111 + 95 + 104 pp. R8vo.

QK
97
E 56

Endlicher, Stephano

    Mantissa Botanica Altera. Sistens Generum Plantarum, Supplementum Tertium.

Endlicher, Stephano

    Genera Plantarum Supplementa 2-5, 1842-50

QK
97
E 56

Endlicher, Stephano

    Mantissa Botanica sistens Genera Plantarum Supplementum Secundum.

Endlicher, Stephano

    Genera Plantarum Supplementa 2-5, 1842-50.

QK
473.N8
E56

Endlicher, Stephano

    Prodromus florae norfolkicae sivi catalogus stirpium quae in insula Norfolk annis 1804 et 1805 a Ferdinando Bauer collectae et depictae nunc in Museo Caesareo Palatino.

    Vindobonae, Fridericum Beck Univ., 1833. 100p.

PL
48
E 56

Endo, Hiroyuki

    Script-vs.-printed-Japanese dictionary. Okura, Publisher. June, 1935. (Tokyo?) 991 pp.

AS
36
A 1

ENDODONTA

Pilsbry, Henry A.

    Hawaiian species of Endodonta and Opeas.

    (Proc. Acad. Nat. Sci., Philadelphia, 1905, pp. 783-786)

QL
401
M 23

ENDODONTIDAE

Ponsonby, J. H.

    Notes on the genus Libera.

    (Proc. Malac. Soc. London, Vol. 9, 1910, pp. 37-43)

QL
401
M 23

ENDODONTIDAE

Suter, Henry

    Notes on some New Zealand Flammulina, with the description of F. Ponsonbyi, n. sp.

    (Proc. of the Malacological Soc. of London, Vol. 2, 1896-97, pp. 284-285)

QL
401
M 23

ENDODONTIDAE

Webster, W. H.

    New Mollusca from New Zealand.

    (Proc. Mal. Soc. London, Vol. 6, 1904, pp. 106-108)

QL
401
A 67

ENDODONTIDAE   INDONESIA

Solem, A.

    Endodontide Landschnecken von Indonesien und Neu Guinea.

    (Archiv f. Molluskenkunde, Bd. 87(1/3):19-25, 1958)

AS
36
A 16 n

ENDODONTIDAE   NEW CALEDONIA

Solem, Alan

    New Caledonian non-marine snails collected by T. D. A. Cockerell in 1928.

    (Notulae Naturae, No. 338, 1960)

QL
401
A 67

ENDODONTIDAE   NEW GUINEA

Solem, A.

    Endodontide Landschnecken von Indonesian und Neu Guinea.

    (Archiv.f. Molluskenkunde, Bd. 87(1/3):19-25, 1958)

QL
Mollusca
Pam.
897

ENDODONTIDAE   SOLOMON ISLANDS

Clench, William J.

    A new genus and species of Endodontidae from the Solomon Islands.

    (Revista de la Soc. Malacologica Carlos de la Torre, 7(6):59-60, 1950)

QL
401
T 68

ENDODONTIDAE   SOLOMON ISLANDS

Clench, William J.

    A new genus and species of Endodontidae from the Solomon Islands.

    (Revista de la Soc. Malacologica "Carlos de la Torre", Vol. 7(2):59-60, 1950)

AS
36
A 65

ENDOMYCHIDAE

Strohecker, H. F.

    A new species of Encymon from the Solomon Islands (Coleoptera, Endomychidae).

    (Am. Mus. Novitates, No. 1520, 1951)

Q
115
M 46

ENDOPROCTA   ANTARCTIC

Johnston, T. Harvey

    Endoprocta, by T. Harvey Johnston and L. Madeline Angel.

Mawson, Sir Douglas   leader
    British, Australian, and New Zealand Antarctic Research Expedition, 1929-31. Reports, Ser. B., Vol. IV, Part 7, 1940.

AS 8 Car — Reading Room

ENDOWMENT OF RESEARCH
Handbook of learned societies and institutions: America. Washington, D. C., Carnegie institution of Washington, 1908.

viii, 592 p. 25½ cm. (*On verso of t.-p.:* Carnegie institution of Washington. Publication no. 39)

Introduction signed by the editor, J. David Thompson.
"List of the principal reference works on American learned societies and institutions": p. viii.

1. Learned institutions and societies. 2. America—Learned institutions and societies. 3. U. S.—Learned institutions and societies. 4. Societies—Bibl. 5. Universities and colleges—Bibl. 6. Endowment of research. 1. Thompson, James David, 1873- ed.

8—21011
Library of Congress   AS15.H2
——— Copy 2.   [s19h3]

QK 1 L

Engel, F.

Palmae novae Columbianae.

(Linnaea, XXXIII, 1865, pp. 665-754, pl. III)

QL Birds Pam. 472

Engelbach, P.

Les Oiseaux du Laos méridional.

(L'Oiseau et la Revue Francaise d'Ornithologie, No. 3, 1932)

DU 1 P

Enemies of beetle and snail sought in Africa

(Pac. Islands Monthly, 22(2):54-55, 1951)

[work of Noel L. H. Krauss]

AS 36 A 91 t

Engel, Frederic

A preceramic settlement on the central coast of Peru: Asia, unit 1.

(Trans. of the Am. Philosophical Soc., New Series, Vol. 53(3):1-139, 1963)

GN Pam 1947

Engelbrecht, Th. H.

Uber die entstehung einiger feldmassig angebauter kulturpflanzen. From Geog. Zeit. bd.22, heft 6.

DU 1 P

Enemies of the beetle; aspects of new campaign in Fiji. (Rhinoceros beetle)

(Pacific Islands Monthly, 23(11):14, 1953)

Oryctes rhinoceros

AS 145 B

Engel, H.

Asteries et Ophiures.

Van Straelen, V.
Résultats scientifiques du voyage aux Indes Orientales Néerlandaises...Léopold de Belgique. Vol. 3, Fasc. 18, 1938, pp. 1-31

(Mem. hors ser. Mus. Roy. d'Hist. Nat. Belgique)

AS 36 S1

Engelhardt, Frédéric Auguste, 1796-1874.
On the formation of ice at the bottom of the water. By M. Engelhardt ...

(*In* Smithsonian institution. Annual report. 1866. Washington, 1867. 23½ cm. p. (425)-431)

"Translated ... from the 'Annales de chimie et de physique,' Paris, 1866."

1. Ice.
S 15-202
Library of Congress   Q11.S66 1866
Library, Smithsonian Institution

QC 73 T 44

Energy For Man
Thirring, Hans

Energy for man; windmills to nuclear power. Indiana University Press. Bloomington. 1958. 8vo. 409 pp.

AS 145 B

Engel, H.

Holothuries.

Van Straelen, V.
Résultats scientifiques du voyage aux Indes Orientales Néerlandaises...Léopold de Belgique. Vol. 3, Fasc. 13, 1933, pp. 1-42

(Mem. hors ser. Mus. Roy. d'Hist. Nat. Belgique)

QK 495.C11 E 58

Engelmann, George

Cactaceae of the Boundary. United States and Mexican Boundary Survey...W. H. Emory. Vol. II, Part 1, 1859. 4to. 78 pp. 75 pl.

QK Bot.Pam. 2435

Engard, Charles J.

Habit of growth of Rubus rosaefolius Smith in Hawaii.

(American Journal of Botany, Vol. 32 (8): 536-538, 1945)

QH Nat. Hist. 138

Engel, H.

Lieven Ferdinand de Beaufort.

(Bijdragen tot de Dierkunde, Afl. 28:1-6, 1949)

Z 7402 E 57

Engelmann, Wilhelm

Bibliotheca Historico-Naturalis. Verzeichniss der Bücher über Naturgeschichte welche in Deutschland, Scandinavien, Holland, England, Frankreich, Italien und Spanien in den Jahren 1700-1846. Bd. 1. Leipzig, 1846. 8vo. //

QK 495.R68 E 57

Engard, Charles J.

Organogenesis in Rubus.

(Univ. of Hawaii Research Pub. 21, 1944)

QL Prot-Poly. Pam. 722

Engel, H.

Ophioteresis beauforti nov. spec.

(Bijdragen tot de Dierkunde, Vol. 28:140-143, 1949)

Z 7991 C 33

Engelmann, Wilhelm
Carus, Julius Victor

Bibliotheca zoologica, II Verzeichniss der Schriften uber zoologie...1846-1860... Bearbeit von J. Victor Carus and Wilhelm Engelmann. Band 1. Leipzig. 1861.

AP 2 S 35

Engel, Celeste G.

Basalts dredged from the northeast Pacific Ocean. By Celeste G. Engel and A. E. J. Engel.

(Science, Vol. 140(3573):1321-1324, 1963)

GN Pam 2637

Engel, Joseph

Ueber die gesetze der knochen entwickelung. From Sitz. d. mathem natur. classe d. k. Akad. d. Wissen. 1851.

GN 406 Z 72

Engineering of antiquity and technical progress in arts and crafts.

Zimmer, George Frederick

GN
2.S
M 26

England, Peter

 The Ramu stones: notes on stone carvings found in the Annaberg-Atemble area, Ramu Valley, New Guinea.

 (Mankind, vol. 3 (8):233-236, 1946)

DA
30
K 71

ENGLAND HISTORY

Knight, Charles

 The popular history of England: an illustrated history of society and government from the earliest period to our own times. London. 1856-1861. 8vo.

 Library has Vols. I-VII.

QK
1
E 58

Engler, A.

 Beitrage zur Flora des sudlichen Japan und der Liu-Kiu-Inseln. (Fortsetzung)

 (Bot. Jahrb. Bd. 6, 1885, pp. 49-74)

 England

DA
30 11
L93

Luce, George H.

 Our pilgrimage: A chronicle of a visit to the old world...

 Milwaukee, Wis., 1889. 302p.

ENGLAND MAN, PREHISTORIC

 see

MAN, PREHISTORIC ENGLAND

QK
1
Eng.

Engler, Adolf

 Botanische jahrbucher...

 Band I- date

     see serial file

ENGLAND ANTHROPOMETRY

see also

ANTHROPOMETRY ENGLAND

ENGLAND PETROGLYPHS

 see

PETROGLYPHS ENGLAND

QK
97
E 58

Engler, A(dolf)

 Araceae-Colocasioideae, von Engler, A. und Krause, K.

Engler, A.
 Das Pflanzenreich, Heft 71 (IV 23 E), 1920.

England-Colonies

DU
12
F94

Froude, James Anthony.

 Oceana; or England and her colonies...new ed.

 London, 1886. 342p.

ENGLAND PORIFERA

 see

PORIFERA ENGLAND

QK
97
C 21

Engler, Adolf

 Burseraceae et Anacardiaceae

Candolle, A.L.P.P. de, and Candolle, A.C.P. de

 Monographiae Phanerogamarum...Vol. 4: Burseraceae et Anacardiaceae, by Engler; Pontederiaceae, by Comite de Solms-Laubach. Paris. 1883. 8vo.

ENGLAND FILICES

 see

FILICES ENGLAND

QK
97
C 21

Engler, Adolf

 Araceae.

Candolle, A.L.P.P. de, and Candolle, A.C.P. de

 Monographiae Phanerogamarum...Vol. 2: Araceae, by Engler. Paris. 1879. 8vo. 681 pp.

Card 1

QK
97
E 58

Engler, Adolf and Prantl, K.

 Die natürliche Pflanzenfamilien nebst ihren Gattungen und wichtigeren Arten, insobesondere den Nutzpflanzen, unter Mitwirkung zahlreicher hervorragender Fachgelehrten. Leipzig. Wilhelm Engelmann. 1887-
 Teil I. Abt. 1-1b, II, III:1-2; IV; Register
 " II. Abt. I-VI (Abt. 2 has Nachtrage 1-3)
 " III. " I, Ia, Ib, II, IIa, III, IV-V, VI, VIa, VII-VIII
 Teil IV, Abt. I-II, IIIa-b, IV-V; Reg.II-IV Teil

      cont. on next cd.

ENGLAND FISHES

 see

FISHES ENGLAND

QK
97
E 58

Engler, A(dolf)

 Araceae. Pars generalis et Index familiae generalis. (IV 23 A) 1920

 Araceae-Aroideae, Araceae-Pistioideae. (IV 23 F) 1920

Engler, A.
 Das Pflanzenreich, Heft 73, 74 (IV 23 A,F)

Card 2

QK
97
E 58

Engler, Adolf and Prantl, K.

 Die natürliche Pflanzenfamilien...

 Nachtrage I zum II-IV Teil, 1897
 " II-III zum II-IV Teil, 1900

 Wilhelm Engelmann. Leipzig. R8vo

GR
Folklore
Pam. 67

England, Frank

 Maori legends, told for the children. Auckland. n.d. R8vo. 32 pp.

QK
1
E 58

Engler, A(dolf)

 Eine Aracee von Mikronesien, by A. Engler and K. Krause.

Diels, L.
 Beiträge zur Flora von Mikronesien und Polynesien. II, No.2.

 (Bot. Jahrb., Bd. 56, 1921, p. 433.)

Card 3

QK
97
E 58

Engler, Adolf and Prantl, K.

 Die natürlichen Pflanzenfamilien...zweite stark vermehrte und verbesserte Auflage.

 Bd. 1; 1b; 2; 3; 5a:1-8;5b; 6; 1928-
 7a; 8; 10; 11; 13; 14a; 14d;
 14e; 15a; 16b; 16c; 17aII;
 17b; 18a; 19a; 19bI; 19c;
 20b, d; 21

 Wilhelm Engelmann. Leipzig. R8vo.

QK
1
B

Engler, A(dolf)

      Notizen uber die Flora der Marshall-
inseln . Auf Grund einer Sammlung des
Regierungsarztes Herrn Dr. Schwabe und
dessen handschriftlichen Bemerkungen zu-
sammengestellt. In Notizbl.K.bot. Gart.
Berlin No. 7, March 24, 1897, pp 222 - 6

Card 6

QK
97
E 58

Engler, Adolf

    Das Pflanzenreich...
IV 56a. Garryaceae. 1910. (Heft 41)
    61. Betulaceae. 1904. (Heft 19)
    68. Myzodendroceae. 1914. (Heft 62)
    75. Rafflesiaceae. 1901. (Heft 5)
    76. Hydnoraceae. 1901. (Heft 5)
    83. Phytolaccaceae. 1909. (Heft 39)
    94. Menispermaceae. 1910. (Heft 46)
    101. Monimiaceae. 1901. (Heft 4) 1911.
        (Heft 49)

Card 13

QK
97
E 58

Engler, Adolf

    Das Pflanzenreich...
IV 228. Umbelliferae-Saniculoideae. 1913.
      (Heft 61)
    228. Umbelliferae-Apioideae-Ammineae-
      Carinae, Ammineae...1927. (Heft 90)
    229. Cornaceae. 1910. (Heft 41)
      (Bound with IV 56a)
    236. Myrsinaceae. 1902. (Heft 9)
    236a. Theophrastaceae. 1903. (Heft 15)
    237. Primulaceae. 1905. (Heft 22)

QK
96
T 23

Engler, Adolf

    Das Pflanzenreich.
Davis, Mervyn T.
    A guide and an analysis of Engler's "Das
Pflanzenreich"

    (Taxon, Vol. 6(6):161-184, 1957)

Card 7

QK
97
E 58

Engler, Adolf

    Das Pflanzenreich...
IV 104. Papaveraceae. 1909. (Heft 40)
    105. Cruciferae, Draba et Erophila. 1927.
      (Heft 89)
    105. Cruciferae-Brassiceae, I. 1919.
      (Heft 70) II. 1923. (Heft 84)
    105. Cruciferae-Sisymbrieae. 1924. (H. 86)
    110. Sarraceniaceae. 1908. (Heft 34)
    111. Nepenthaceae. 1908. (Heft 36)
    112. Droseraceae. 1906. (Heft 26)
    116. Cephalotaceae. 1911. (Heft 47)

Card 14

QK
97
E 58

Engler, Adolf

    Das Pflanzenreich...
IV 241. Styracaceae. 1907. (Heft 30)
    242. Symplocaceae. 1901. (Heft 6)
    243. I-II. Oleaceae... 1920. (Heft 72)
    250. Polemoniaceae. 1907. (Heft 27)
    251. Hydrophyllaceae. 1913. (Heft 59)
    252. Borraginaceae-Borraginoideae
      Cynoglosseae. 1921. (Heft 78)
    252. Borraginaceae-Borraginoideae
      Cryptantheae. 1931. (Heft 97)

Card 1

QK
97
E 58

Engler, Adolf

    Das Pflanzenreich: Regni vegetabilis conspec-
tus. Im Auftrage der Preuss. Akademie der Wissenschaften, herausgegeben von A. Engler. Fortgesetzt von L. Diels. Leipzig. Wilhelm Engelmann.
8vo.

III Sphagnales-Sphagnaceae. 1911. (Heft 51)
IV 1. Cycadaceae. 1932. (Heft 99)
" 5. Taxaceae. 1903. (Heft 18)
" 8. Typhaceae. 1900. (Heft 2)

Card 8

QK
97
E 58

Engler, Adolf

    Das Pflanzenreich...
IV. 117. Saxifragaceae I-II. 1916, 1919.
      (Heft 67 and 69)
    127. Connaraceae. 1938. (Heft 103)
    129. Geraniaceae. 1912. (Heft 53)
    130. Oxalidaceae. 1930. (Heft 95)
    131. Tropaeolaceae. 1902. (Heft 10)
    134. Erythroxylaceae. 1907. (Heft 29)
    141. Malpighiaceae. (I-III). 1928.
      (Hefte 91, 93, 94)

Card 15

QK
97
E 58

Engler, Adolf

    Das Pflanzenreich...
IV 257 C. Scrophulariaceae-Antirrhinoideae-
      Calceolarieae. 1907. (Heft 28)
    261. Orobanchaceae. 1930. (Heft 96)
    269. Plantaginaceae. 1937. (Heft 102)
    275. I. Cucurbitaceae-tevilleae et
      Melothrieae. 1916. (Heft 66)
    275. II. Cucurbitaceae-Cucurbiteae-Cucu-
      merinae. 1924. (Heft 88)

Card 2

QK
97
E 58

Engler, Adolf

    Das Pflanzenreich...
IV 9. Pandanaceae. 1900. (Heft 3)
" 10. Sparganiaceae. 1900. (Heft 2)
" 11. Potamogetonaceae. 1907. (Heft 31)
" 12. Naiadaceae. 1901. (Heft 7)
" 13. Aponogetonaceae. 1906. (Heft 24)
" 14. Scheuchzeriaceae. 1903. (Heft 16)
" 15. Alismataceae. 1903. (Heft 16)
" 16. Butomaceae. 1903. (Heft 16)
" 18. Triuridaceae. 1938. (Heft 104)

Card 9

QK
97
E 58

Engler, Adolf

    Das Pflanzenreich...
IV. 147. Euphorbiaceae-Porantheriodeae et
      Ricinocarpoideae. 1913. (Heft 58)
    147. Euphorbiaceae-Jatropheae. 1910.(H42)
    147. II. " -Adrianeae. 1910. (H. 44)
    147. III. " -Cluytieae. 1911. (H. 47)
    147. IV. " - Gelonieae.1912. (H. 52)
    147. V. " -Hippomaneae.1912.(H. 52)
    147. VI " -Acalypheae-Chrozophori-
      nae. 1912. (Heft 57)

Card 16

QK
97
E 58

Engler, Adolf

    Das Pflanzenreich...
IV 276 b. Campanulaceae-Lobelioideae, Teil
      I, 1943, pp. 1-16 only. (stock de-
      stroyed in war, to be reprinted.)
      (Heft 106)
    276 b. Campanulaceae-Lobelioideae, Teil
      II, 1953, pp. 261-813. (Heft 107)
    277, 277a. Goodeniaceae v. Brunoniaceae.
      1912. (Heft 54)
    278. Stylidiaceae. 1908. (Heft 35)
    280. Compositae. sect. 1-15;16-47.
      1921-, 1923. (Hefte 75-77,79,82)

Card 3

QK
97
E 58

Engler, Adolf

    Das Pflanzenreich...
IV 20. Cyperaceae - Caricoideae. 1909.
      (Heft 38); (Heft 101:1, 1935; (2),
      1936; (3), 1936; (4), 1936)
" 23. Araceae: A-B, 1905-1920; C, 1911;
      D-F, 1912-1920. (Heft 21, 37, 48, 55,
      60, 64, 71, 73, 74)
" 30. Eriocaulaceae. 1903. (Heft 13)
" 32. Bromeliaceae. 1934-1935. (Heft 100:
      1,2,3,4)

Card 10

QK
97
E 58

Engler, Adolf

    Das Pflanzenreich...
IV 147. VII. Euphorbiaceae-Acalypheae-Mercur
      ialinae. 1914. (Heft 63)
    147. VIII. Euphorbiaceae. Phyllanthoideae-
      Bridelieae. 1915. (Heft 65)
    147. IX-XIV. Euphorbiaceae-Acalypheae,
      Dalechampieae, Peraenae and Additamen
      tum. 1919. (Heft 68)
    147.-a. Daphniphyllaceae. 1919. (Heft 68)
    147. XV. Euphorbiaceae-Phyllanthoideae...
      1922. (Heft 81)

QK
97
E 58

Engler, Adolf

    Saxifragaceae-Saxifraga I, by Adolf Engler
und E. Irmscher.

Engler, Adolf

    Das Pflanzenreich...IV. 117. I. 1916.
(Heft 67.)

Card 4

QK
97
E 58

Engler, Adolf

    Das Pflanzenreich...
IV 36. Juncaceae. 1906. (Heft 25)
" 38. III. II, Liliaceae. 1908. (Heft 33)
" 42. Taccaceae. 1928. (Heft 92)
" 43. Dioscoreaceae. 1924. (Heft 87)
" 45. Musaceae. 1900. (Heft 1)
" 46. Zingiberaceae. 1904. (Heft 20)
" 47. Cannaceae. 1912. (Heft 56)
" 48. Marantaceae. 1902. (Heft 11)

Card 11

QK
97
E 58

Engler, Adolf

    Das Pflanzenreich...
IV 147. XVI. Euphorbiaceae-Crotonoideae...
      1924. (Heft 85)
    147. XVII. Euphorbiaceae-Additamentum 7.
      1924. (Heft 85)
    163. Aceraceae. 1902. (Heft 8)
    165. Sapindaceae. I-VIII. 1931-1934.
      (Heft 98 a-h)
    193. Cistaceae. 1903. (Heft 14)
    216. Lythraceae. 1903. (Heft 17)
    219. Barringtoniaceae. 1939. (Heft 105)

QK
97
E 58

Engler, Adolf

    Saxifragaceae-Saxifraga II, by Adolf Engler
und E. Irmscher.

Engler, Adolf

    Das Pflanzenreich...IV. 117. II. 1919.
(Heft 69.)

Card 5

QK
97
E 58

Engler, Adolf

    Das Pflanzenreich...
IV 50. Orchidaceae-Pleonandrae. 1903. (H. 12)
    50. " -Monandrae. 1922. (Heft 80)
    50. " -Monandrae-Pseudo-monopo-
      diales. 1923. (Heft 83)
    50.II.B.21. Orchidaceae-Monandrae-
      Dendrobiinae. Pars. I. 1910. (H. 45)
      and Pars II. 1911. (Heft 50)
    50.II.B.23. Orchidaceae-Monandrae-Thelasi-
      nae. 1911. (Heft 50)
    50.II.B.7. Orchidaceae-Monandrae-Coelogy-
      ninae, 1907. (Heft 32)

Card 12

QK
97
E 58

Engler, Adolf

    Das Pflanzenreich...
IV 219a. Lecythidaceae. 1939. (Heft 105)
    219b. Asteranthaceae. 1939. (Heft 105)
    220a. Nyssaceae. 1910. (Heft 41) (Bound
      with IV. 56a)
    220b. Alangiaceae. 1910. (Heft 41)
      (Bound with IV. 56a)
    225. Haloragaceae. 1905. (Heft 23)
    228. Umbelliferae-apioideae-Bupleurum
      Trinia et reliqua amminaeae hetero-
      clitae. 1910. (Heft 43)

QK
366
S 34

Engler, A(dolf)

    Siphonogamen (Phanerogamen)...

Schleinitz, Georg Emil Gustav von
    Die Forschungsreise S.M.S."Gazelle" in den
Jahren 1874 bis 1876...Theil IV:Botanik. Berlin,
1889. Siphonogamen...pp. 1-49, 15 pl.

QK
97
E 58

Engler, Adolf

　　Syllabus der Pflanzenfamilien. Eine Übersicht über das gesamte Pflanzensystem mit besonderer Berücksichtigung der Medizinal- und Nutzpflanzen nebst einer Übersicht über die Florenreiche und Florengebiete der Erde zum Gebrauch bei Vorlesungen und Studien über spezielle und medizinisch pharmazeutische Botanik. Neunte und zehnte, mehrfach ergänzte Auflage mit unterstützung von Ernst Gilg. Mit 462 Abbildungen. Berlin. Gebrüder Borntraeger. 1924. xlii + 420 pp. 8vo.

QK
Botany
Pam.
 # 1194

Engler, Adolf

　　Über die geographische Verbreitung der Rutaceen im Verhältniss zu ihrer systematischen Gliederung. Aus den Abhand. K. Preuss. Aksd. Wissens. Berlin 1896, pp 1-27.

Engler, Adolf

　　full name is

　　Engler, Heinrich G. Adolf

QK 110
H 25
1911

QK 473 N
C 66

Engler, Heinrich G. Adolf
Engler, Adolf　　and O. Drude　　editors

　　Vegetation der Erde, vol. 13: Phytographic survey of North America, by John W. Harshberger.

　　...Vol. 14: Vegetation of New Zealand, by Leonard Cockayne. 1921　also 1928 edition

PL
950.E2
E 57

and

PL
Phil.Pam.
511

Englert, P. Sebastian

　　Diccionario Rapanui-Español. Redactado en la Isla de Pascua. Prensas de la Universidad de Chile. 1938. sm8vo. 139 pp.

DU
950.E2
E 58

Englert, P. Sebastian

　　La Tierra de Hotu Matu'a. Historia, etnología y lengua de la Isla de Pascua. Imprenta y edit. "San Francisco". Padre las Casas. 1948. 4to. 533 pp. + map

GR
385.E
E 58

and

PL
950.E2
E 58

Englert, P(ater) Sebastian

　　Tradiciones de la Isla de Pascua, en idioma rapanui y castellano. Publicaciones de la Comision de Estudios sobre la Isla de Pascua, Universidad de Chile. Imprenta "San Francisco" Padre Las Casas. 1939. R8vo. 85 pp.

QL
497
E 58

English, L. L.

　　Illinois trees and shrubs; their insect enemies.

　　(Illinois Nat. Hist. Survey, Circular 47, 1958)

Z
2001
E 58

　　The English catalogue of books...works issued in Great Britain and Ireland and the principal works published in America. Vol. V, January 1890 to December 1897. London. Sampson Low, Marston & Company. 1898. R8vo. 1180 pp.

AG
5
FU
1914

ENGLISH DICTIONARY

Funk and Wagnalls New Standard Dictionary. New York, 1914. 4to.

AG
6
M

ENGLISH DICTIONARY

March, Francis Andrew, 1825-1911.

　　A thesaurus of the English language, having the functions of a dictionary in the alphabetical arrangement of the words of the English language and their definitions, supplying the word that is forgotten or not known ... giving an exhaustive list of synonyms, antonyms, idioms, phrases, etc. ... By Francis Andrew March ... and Francis Andrew March, jr. ... 1917 ed. Philadelphia, Pa., Historical publishing company [1917]

　　xvi, 1189, [3], 102 p. incl. front. (port.) illus. 4 pl. 28cm.

　　On verso of t.-p.: Educational edition.

　　Frontispiece and plates each accompanied by leaf with descriptive letterpress.

　　1. English language—Dictionaries. I. March, Francis Andrew, 1863- joint author.

Library of Congress　　PE1625.M3 1917　　18-11871

AG
5
We

ENGLISH LANGUAGE-DICTIONARIES

Webster, Noah, 1758-1843.

　　... Webster's new international dictionary of the English language, based on the International dictionary of 1890 and 1900. Now completely rev. in all departments including also a dictionary of geography and of biography, being the latest authentic quarto ed. of the Merriam series; with a reference history of the world; W. T. Harris ... editor in chief, F. Sturges Allen, general editor. Springfield, Mass., G. & C. Merriam company, 1918.

　　xcii, 2620, 153 (i. e. 188) p. front. (port.) illus., plates (part col.) maps. 31½cm.

　　(Continued on next card)　　18-11872

AG
5
We

ENGLISH LANGUAGE-DICTIONARIES

Webster, Noah, 1758-1843. ... Webster's new international dictionary of the English language ... 1918. (Card 2)

　　At head of title: Reference history edition.

　　Page 132 followed by p. 132a.

　　"A reference history of the world ... by John Clark Ridpath and Horace E. Scudder, thoroughly reedited and greatly enl. by Edwin A. Grosvenor," with special t.-p.: 153 (i. e. 188) p. at end.

　　1. English language—Dictionaries. I. Harris, William Torrey, 1835-1909, ed. II. Allen, Frederic Sturges, 1861- ed. III. Ridpath, John Clark, 1840-1900. IV. Scudder, Horace Elisha, 1838-1902. V. Grosvenor, Edwin Augustus, 1845- ed.

　　18-11872

Library of Congress　　PE1625.W3 1918a

AG
5
We
M 1915

ENGLISH DICTIONARY

Webster's Collegiate Dictionary

Merriam & Co. Publishers

Springfield, Mass, 1915. 8vo, pp 1080.

AG
5
W 38

ENGLISH DICTIONARY

Webster, Noah

　　New International Dictionary of the English Language...

　　Editions of 1926, 1928, 1930, 1932, 1933.

AG
5
C4

ENGLISH DICTIONARY

Whitney, William Dwight

　　The Century Dictionary. Prepared under the superintendence of William Dwight Whitney ... In 6 vols. (Bound in 25 parts.)

　　New York, 1889, 4to.

AG
25
Cl

ENGLISH--FRENCH DICTIONARY

Clifton, E. C. & Grimaux. A.

　　Nouveau Dictionnaire Anglais - Francais et Francais - Anglais.

　　Paris, 1914. pp 1237.

AG
25
Cl

English - French Dictionary

Clifton, E. C. & Grimaux A.

　　New Dictionary of the French and English languages. French - English.

　　Paris, 1914, pp 1080.

AG
7
Yo

ENGLISH-GREEK DICTIONARY

Yonge, C. D.

　　New York, 1870.

　　See author card

Z
246
W 25

ENGLISH GRAMMAR

Ward, C. H.

　　Grammar for Composition. Scott, Foresman & Company. 1933c. xiii + 450 pp. 8vo. Chicago.

DU
12
F 61

looked case

ENGLISH IN THE PACIFIC

(Fleurieu, C. P. C. de)

　　Discoveries of the French in 1768 and 1769, to the south-east of New Guinea, with the subsequent visits to the same lands by English navigators...Translated from the French... London. 1791. 4to.

3

Z
Bibliography
Pam.
152

English language periodicals from or about Asia in Honolulu libraries. Preliminary edition May 1960. Citizens Liaison Committee for an International Center and Pacific and Asian Affairs Council. Honolulu. 4to.

Q
101
P 18

ENHYDRA

Fisher, Edna M.
The sea otter in California.

IN Proc. Sixth Pac. Sci. Congress, 1939, (California), Vol. 4, 1940, pp. 231-240.

(Enhydra lutris nereis)

ENIWETOK GEOLOGY

See

GEOLOGY ENIWETOK

ENGLISH SPARROW

See

PASSER DOMESTICUS

QL
Mammals
Pam.
122

ENHYDRA - ALASKA

Lensink, Calvin J.

The distribution and status of sea otters in Alaska.

(Tenth Alaskan Science Conference, 1959, mimeographed, 12 pp.)

ENIWETOK GEOTHERMY

See

GEOTHERMY ENIWETOK

QL
5
B 61

ENGRAULIDAE

Hildebrand, Samuel F.

A review of the American anchovies (family Engraulidae).

(Bull. Bingham Oceanographic Collection, Peabody Mus. Nat. Hist., Yale Univ., 8: Art. 2, pp. 1-165)

QL
Mammals
Pam.
140
141

ENHYDRA ALASKA

Lensink, Calvin J.

Status and distribution of sea otters in Alaska.

(Journal of Mammalogy, 41(2):172-182, 1960)

ENIWETOK METEOROLOGY

See

METEOROLOGY ENIWETOK

QE
1
H1

ENGRAULIDAE

Jordan, David Starr and Seale, Alvin

Review of the Engraulidae with descriptions of new and rare species. Harvard Mus. Comp. Zool. Vol. 67, 1926, pp 355 - 418.

Q
101
P 18

ENHYDRA PACIFIC

Fisher, Edna M.

The sea otter, past and present.

IN Proc. Sixth Pac. Sci. Congress, 1939, (California), Vol. 3, 1940, pp. 223-236.

ENIWETOK PLANKTON

See

PLANKTON ENIWETOK

GC
1
S 43 b

ENGRAULIS

McHugh, J. L.

Meristic variations and populations of northern anchovy (Engraulis mordax mordax).

(Bull. Scripps Inst. of Oceanography, Univ. of Calif., 6(3):123-160, 1951)

QL
461
H 1

ENICOCEPHALIDAE

Usinger, Robert L.

A new genus of Pacific Island Enicocephalidae with new species from the Hawaiian and Philippine Islands (Hemiptera).

(Proc. Haw. Ent. Soc., Vol. 10, 1939, pp. 267-270)

ENIWETOK RADIOACTIVITY

See

RADIOACTIVITY ENIWETOK

QL
1
A 94

ENGRAULIS AUSTRALIA

Blackburn, M.

A biological study of the anchovy, Engraulis australis (White), in Australian waters.

(Australian Jour. of Marine and Freshwater Research, Vol. 1(1):3-84, 1950)

ENIWETOK FLORA

See

FLORA ENIWETOK

ENIWETOK RADIOBIOLOGY

See

RADIOBIOLOGY ENIWETOK

QL
628
C 15

ENHYDRA

Boolootian, Richard A.

The distribution of the California sea Otter

(California Fish and Game, 47(3):287-292, 1961)

ENIWETOK FORAMINIFERA

See

FORAMINIFERA ENIWETOK

ENIWETOK VEGETATION

See

VEGETATION ENIWETOK

ENIWETOK   WEATHER

See

WEATHER   ENIWETOK

Q
115
S 56

ENTEROPNEUSTA   DUTCH EAST INDIES

Spengel, J. W.
   Studien uber die Enteropneusten der Siboga-Expedition nebst Beobachtungen an verwanten Arten.

Weber, Max
   Uitkomsten...Nederlandsch Oost Indie, 1899-1900...Siboga...Monographie XXVI (livr. 33).
1907. 126 pp. 17 pl.

Q
Biography
Pam.
87

ENTOMOLOGISTS   PACIFIC

   List of entomologists of the Pacific area. Standing Committee on Pacific Entomology, Pacific Science Association, Bishop Museum, Dec. 1955. 4to. mimeographed. 70 + xii pp.

     Supplement, June 1958-February 1961

DU
12
E 59

Enoch, C. Reginald

   Secret of the Pacific; a discussion of the origin of the early civilisations of America, the Toltecs, Aztecs, Mayas, Incas, and their predecessors; and of the possibilities of Asiatic influence thereon. With 56 illustrations and 2 maps. London, T. Fisher Unwin, 1912. 8vo. 359 pp.

QL
Fish Pam.
143

AS
719
A-me

ENTEROPNEUSTA   ELLICE ISLANDS

Hill, J. P.

   The Enteropneusta of Funafuti.

   (Australian Museum Memoirs, Vol. III, pt. 5, pp. 336-345, 1896-97)

QL
Insects
Pam.
1725

ENTOMOLOGISTS   PACIFIC

Pacific Science Association

   List of entomologists of the Pacific area. Prepared by the Standing Committee on Pacific entomology. Bishop Museum. Honolulu. Dec. 1955. mimeographed. 4to. 70 + xii pp.

DS
646.3
E 59

Enriquez, C. M.

   Kinabalu, the haunted mountain of Borneo. An account of its ascent, its people, flora and fauna, by Major C. M. Enriquez... With photographs and a map. London. Witherby. 1927. 8vo. pp.xix+199 pp.

QL
Fish
Pam.
No.143
and
QL
1
Au

ENTEROPNEUSTA - ELLICE ISLANDS

Hill, James P.

   The Enteropneusta of Funafuti. From Australian Mus. Mem. Vol. III, 1896 -7.

   Also separate.

QL
463
B 17

ENTOMOLOGY

Balachowsky, A. S.

   Entomologie appliquée à l'agriculture. Traité publié sous la direction de A. S. Balachowsky.
     Tome I:Coleoptères, Vol. I-2, 1962-63.

   Masson et Cie,   Editeurs. Paris. R8vo.

QL
3
C2

Endman, Wilhelmine M.

Coloration in Polistes.

127 Publ. 19.

Carnegie Institution
Washington   *1904. 8°. H. 88.*
       Bound
     AUG - 1 1907

QL
Fish Pam.
143

AS
719
A-me

ENTEROPNEUSTA   FUNAFUTI

Hill, J. P.

   The Enteropneusta of Funafuti.

   (Australian Museum Memoirs, Vol. III, pt. 5, pp. 336-345, 1896-97)

AS
78
B 92-p

ENTOMOLOGY

   Curso de entomologia, organizado y dictado por la Sociedad Entomologia Argentina.
   I-X   1947- *1955*   to cont.

   (Buenos Aires. Inst. Nac. de Investigacion de las Ciencias Nat. y Museo Argentino de Ciencias Nat. "Bernardino Rivadavia", Publicaciones de Ext. Cultural y Didactica, No. 1)

QL
1
C15

ENTEROPNEUSTA.

Ritter, William Emerson, 1856-

   ... Studies on the ecology, morphology, and speciology of the young of some *Enteropneusta* of western North America. By Wm. E. Ritter and B. M. Davis. Berkeley, The University press, 1904.

   cover-title, p. [171]-210. diagr., pl. xvii-xix. 27^{cm}. (University of California publications. Zoology. v. 1, no. 5)

   "From the San Diego Marine biological laboratory of the University of California."
   Bibliography: p. 203.

   1. Enteropneusta.   I. Davis, Benjamin Marshall, 1867-   joint author.

          A 11-2273

   Title from Univ. of Calif.   Library of Congress

QL
1
Zoo

ENTEROPNEUSTA - FUNAFUTI

Spengel, J. W.

   Neue Beiträge zur Kenntniss der Enteropneusten. II Ptychodera flava von Funafuti (Ellice-Gruppe). In Zool. Jahr. Bd. 20, 1904, pp 1-18, 1 pl.

QL
463
C 98

ENTOMOLOGY

Cushing, Emory C.

   History of entomology in World War II. Smithsonian Institution. Washington, D. C. 1957. 8vo. vi + 117 pp.

AS
244
D

ENTEROPNEUSTA

Stiasny, Gustav

   Die Tornarien-Sammlung von Dr. Th. Mortensen.

   (Vid. Med. Dansk Nat. For. Kobenhavn, Bd. 73, 1922.- Papers from Dr. Mortensen's Pacific Expedition, No. 7)

QL
Fish
Pams.

ENTEROPNEUSTA - PAMPHLETS

   For convenience in shelving , papers on Enteropneusta are classed as QL Fish pamphlets .

QL
464
D 34

ENTOMOLOGY

de la Torre-Bueno, J. R.

   A glossary of entomology. Smith's "An explanation of terms used in entomology", completely revised and rewritten. Published by Brooklyn Entomological Society. The Science Press. Lancaster, Penna. 1937. 8vo. 336 pp., 9 pl.

AS
244
D

ENTEROPNEUSTA

van der Horst, C. J.

   Observations on some small Enteropneusta.

   (Vid. Med. Dansk Nat. For. Kobenhavn, Bd. 87 1929-30,- Papers from Dr. Th. Mortensen's Pacific Expedition 1914-16, No. 61).

QH
1
A 51

ENTOMOLOGISTS

Carpenter, Mathilde M.

   Bibliography of biographies of entomologists

   (The American Midland Naturalist, Vol. 33: 1-116, 1945)

QL
463
E 78

ENTOMOLOGY

Essig, E. O.

   College entomology. The MacMillan Co. New York. 1942. 8vo. vii + 900 pp.

QL
47
F 93 Frost, S. W.

Insect life and insect natural history. (formerly entitled: General entomology) Second revised edition. Dover Publications, Inc. New York. 8vo. paperbd. viii + 526 pp.

QL
474
S27 Say, Thomas

American emtomology or descriptions of insects.... illustrated by coloured figures.......

Philadelphia Museum, 1824, 3 vols.

ENTOMOLOGY   BIBLIOGRAPHY

Hawes, Ina L.

Bibliography on aviation and economic entomology. Compiled by Ina L. Hawes and Rose Eisenberg.

(U. S. Dept. of Agric., Bibliographical Bull. No. 8, 1947)

QL
464
R 51 Imms, A. D.

A general textbook of entomology, including the anatomy, physiology, development and classification of insects. Ninth edition, entirely revised by O. W. Richards and R. G. Davies. Methuen and Co., Ltd. London, R8vo. 1957 x + 886 pp.

QL
Insects
Pam.1030 Schmidt, Carl T.

ENTOMOLOGY

Musings of an armchair philosopher.

(Proc. Haw. Ent. Soc., Vol. 10, 1939, pp. 255-262)

Z
5856
H 81 Horn, Walther, und Schenkling, Sigm.

ENTOMOLOGY   BIBLIOGRAPHY

Index Litteraturae Entomologicae: Serie I: Die Welt-Literatur über die gesamte Entomologie bis inklusive 1863...Bände 1-4. Berlin-Dahlem. 1928-1929. 8vo.

QL
464
I 34 Imms, A. D.

ENTOMOLOGY

Outlines of entomology. With 96 illustrations. New York. E.P.Dutton and Company, Inc. (1942) 8vo. 184 pp.

AS
36
S2
ENTOMOLOGY.
Smithsonian institution.

... Circular to entomologists. Washington, Smithsonian institution, 1860

2 p. 24cm. (Smithsonian miscellaneous collections. vol. VIII, art. VIII)
Caption title.
Publication 178.
Signed: Joseph Henry, secretary.

I. Henry, Joseph, 1799-1878. II. Title.

16-6354

Library of Congress   Q11.S7 vol. 8, art. 8

S
17 W3
S 44
ENTOMOLOGY — BIBLIOGRAPHY
Kirkaldy, George Willis.

... A bibliography of sugar-cane entomology, by G. W. Kirkaldy. Honolulu, Hawaii, 1909.

73 p. 22½cm. (Report of work of the Experiment station of the Hawaiian sugar planters' association. Division of entomology. Bulletin no 8)

1. Entomology. Bibliography. 2. Sugar cane. Pests. Bibliography.

Agr 10-198

Library, U. S. Dept. of   Agriculture 420H31 no. 8

S
39.A
S 12 r   Isaac, John
ENTOMOLOGY

Entomology in outline.

(California, State Board of Horticulture, Annual Report, 1905/06, pp. 37-154)

QL
461
U
ENTOMOLOGY - BIBLIOGRAPHY

Banks , Nathan
A list of works on North American Entomology . U. S. Dept. of Agr. Bur. of Ent. Bull. 81, 1910.

Z
5856
U 58   U.S.Dept. of Agric. Div. of Entomology
ENTOMOLOGY - BIBLIOGRAPHY

Bibliography of the more important contributions to American economic entomology.

Parts 1-3, 5,7,8.   1890-1905.

See main entry for detail

QL
464
L97   Lutz, Frank E.
ENTOMOLOGY

Field book of insects, with special reference to those of northeastern U.S. aiming to answer common questions. 2 ed. revised and enlarged, 800 illus., many in color.

New York, Putnam, 1921, pp. 562 ix pl. 44.

Z
Bibliography
Pam. 71   Bryan, Edwin H., Jr.
ENTOMOLOGY BIBLIOGRAPHY

Bernice P. Bishop Museum entomological catalogs. (typed notes)

Z
881
U 59c   U. S. Department of Agriculture.
Library
ENTOMOLOGY   BIBLIOGRAPHY

Catalogue of publications relating to entomology in the Library of the U. S. Department of Agriculture. Prepared under the direction of the Librarian.

(Bulletin no. 55, 1906)

QH
14
C 15   Ross, Edward S. and collaborators
ENTOMOLOGY

Systematic entomology.

IN

A century of progress in the natural sciences 1853-1953. Published in celebration of the centennial of the California Academy of Sciences. California Academy of Science. San Francisco. 1955. R8vo. pp. 485-590

Z
Bibliography
Pam.
107   Bryan, Edwin H., Jr.
ENTOMOLOGY BIBLIOGRAPHY

Bibliography of Micronesian entomology. Compiled for the Pacific Science Board of the National Research Council. July, 1948. 43 pp. mimeographed.

S
399
E7

and
QL
Insect
Pam.
14
ENTOMOLOGY   BIBLIOGRAPHY   HAWAII

Van Dine, D. L.
Bibliography of Hawaiian Entomology . U. S. Dept. Agric. Office Exper. Sta. Bull. 170 (Smith) Wash. 1906. pp 52-59. (Haw. Agric. Ex. Sta. Report 1905)

QL
464
R 82   Ross, Herbert H.
ENTOMOLOGY

A textbook of entomology. Second edition. John Wiley and Sons, Inc. New York. 8vo. xi + 519 pp.

QL
Insects
Pam.
1708   Chamberlin, W. J.
ENTOMOLOGY   BIBLIOGRAPHY

Entomological nomenclature and literature. 2nd edition. (Corvallis, Oregon, Aug. 1945. Privately printed. 1948.) 4to. 135 pp. lithographed.

AS
36
S5
ENTOMOLOGY—COLLECTING
Needham, James George, 1868-

... Directions for collecting and rearing dragon flies, stone flies, and may flies. By James G. Needham ... Washington, Govt. print. off., 1899.

9 p. illus. 24½cm.
Pt. O of Bulletin of the United States national museum, no. 39.

1. Insects—Collection and preservation. 1. Entomology—Collecting
2. Neuroptera.

Agr 5-67

Library, U. S. Dept. of   Agriculture 432N28D

QL
461
D 48 c   Horn, Walther

ENTOMOLOGY. COLLECTIONS

Ueber entomologische Sammlungen (Ein Beitrag zur Geschichte der Entomo-Museologie), by
Walther Horn and Ilse Kahle.

(Entomologische Beihefte aus Berlin-Dahlem,
Bd. 2-4, 1935-1937)

QL
465
P 48   Peterson, Alvah

ENTOMOLOGY   STUDY

A manual of entomological equipment and
methods. Part I   Edwards Brothers, Inc.
Ann Arbor, 1934.   4to. (photolith). 21 pp.,
138 pl., xiii pp.

ENTOMOLOGY FIJI

Fiji. Department of Agriculture.
Agricultural Journal

Vol. 8, No. 4 -   1937-

QL
Insect
Pam.
1891   Hawes, Ina L.

ENTOMOLOGY ECONOMIC

Bibliography on aviation and economic entomology. Compiled by Ina L. Hawes and Rose Eisenberg.

(U. S. Dept. of Agric., Bibliographical Bull.
No. 8, 1947)

QL
Insect
Pam.
2027   Ericson, Ruth O.

ENTOMOLOGY TERMS

A glossary of some foreign-language terms,
in entomology.

(U.S.D.A. Agric. Handbook No. 218, Ent.
Research Division, Dec. 1961)

S
398.F
A j   Lever, R. J. A. W.

ENTOMOLOGY FIJI

Entomological services in Fiji.

(Agricultural Journal, Fiji, Vol. 14, 1943,
no. 4, pp. 92-97)

QL
595.Mi
I 59   Gressitt, J. Linsley
Insects of Micronesia, Introduction.
IN
Insects of Micronesia, Vol. I. Bernice P.
Bishop Museum. 1954. R8vo.

ENTOMOLOGY, ECONOMIC   MICRONESIA

QL
1
C 74   Musée Royal du Congo Belge
Annales

ENTOMOLOGY   AFRICA

QL
Insect
Pam
798

(2 pts.)   Takahashi, Ryoichi

ENTOMOLOGY - FORMOSA

Observations on the Coccidae of Formosa

Parts I and II - Reports 40 and 48 of the
Department of Agriculture - Government Research
Institute, Formosa, Japan

QL
464
D 34   De la Torre-Bueno, J. R.

ENTOMOLOGY GLOSSARY

A glossary of entomology. Smith's "An Explanation of terms used in entomology". Completely revised and rewritten. Published by
Brooklyn Entomological Society. Science Press.
Lancaster. 1937. 8vo. ix + 336 pp. IX pl.

Supplement A, July 1960   36 pp.

QL
461
P 11   Gressitt, J. L.

ENTOMOLOGY ANTARCTIC

Entomological investigations in Antarctica. By J. L. Gressitt, R. E. Leech and
K. A. J. Wise.

(Pacific Insects, Vol. 5(1):287-304,
1963)

QH
1
T 12   Taihoku Imperial University
Faculty of Science and Agriculture

ENTOMOLOGY FORMOSA

Memoirs
I, XIV, XVI   (nos. 1, 6-10)
and XXIV

[Note: HSPA has 1-8, 10]

ENTOMOLOGY MEDICAL

See

MEDICAL ENTOMOLOGY

DU
96
C 32   Carter, H. J.

ENTOMOLOGY AUSTRALIA

Gulliver in the bush. Wanderings of an Australian entomologist. Sydney. Angus & Robertson,
Ltd. 1933. 8vo. 234 pp., 9 pl.

DU
621
H3   Blackburn, T. (Rev.).
Hawaiian Entomology. in Haw.
Almanac + Annual for 1882, pp. 58-61.

ENTOMOLOGY HAWAII

QL
465
P 48   Peterson, Alvah

ENTOMOLOGY METHODS

A manual of entomological equipment and
methods. Part I   Edwards Brothers, Inc.
Ann Arbor, 1934. 4to. (photolith). 21 pp.,
138 pl., xiii pp.

QL
1
A 93   Musgrave, Anthony

ENTOMOLOGY AUSTRALIA

The history of Australian entomological
research.

(The Australian Zoologist, 6:189-203, 1930)

AS
763
B-r   Buck, Peter Henry

ENTOMOLOGY HAWAII

Bishop Museum and entomological research.

(Bull. Bernice P. Bishop Museum, No. 205
[Ann. Rept., 1950]:26-35, 1951)

QL
Insect
Pam.
1708   Chamberlin, W. J.

ENTOMOLOGY NOMENCLATURE

Entomological nomenclature and literature.
2nd edition. (Corvallis, Oregon, Aug. 1945.
Privately printed. 1948.) 4to. 135 pp. lithographed.

QL
461
C15   California. University of California

ENTOMOLOGY CALIFORNIA

Publications in entomology

see serial file

AS
763
B-b   Illingworth, J. F.

ENTOMOLOGY - HAWAII

Early References to Hawaiian Entomology

Bull. No. 2, Bernice P. Bishop Museum, 1923

QL
Insects ENTOMOLOGY. HAWAII
Pam.
17 Kotinsky, Jacob.
History of economic entomology in Hawaii.
and in U.S. Dept. of Agric. Bur. of Ento. Bull. 60, pp. 57-66.
QL Washington, 1906.
461
U-b

Z ENTOMOLOGY MICRONESIA
Biblio-
graphy Bryan, Edwin H., Jr.
Pam.
107 Bibliography of Micronesian entomology.
Compiled for the Pacific Science Board of the
National Research Council. July, 1948. 43 pp.
mimeographed.

QL ENTOMOLOGY - PERIODICALS
461
E61 Entomologische Mitteilungen

Organ der wanderversammlungen deutscher
entomologen herausgegeben... Walther Horn.

see serial file

S ENTOMOLOGY HAWAII
17.H3
S 3 Pemberton, C. E.

History of the Entomology Department,
Experiment Station, H. S. P. A., 1904-1945.

(Hawaiian Planters' Record, Vol. 52;53-90,
1948)

DU ENTOMOLOGY NEW SOUTH WALES
96
C 32 Carter, H. J.

Gulliver in the bush. Wanderings of an Australian entomologist. Sydney. Angus & Robertson,
Ltd. 1933. 8vo. 234 pp., 8 pl.

QL ENTOMOLOGY - PERIODICALS
461
E71 The Entomologist's Monthly Magazine

Library has

Vol. LVI, 1920

QL ENTOMOLOGY HAWAII
Insects
Pam. Zimmerman, Elwood C.
1308
Gleanings from mainland conferences and some
aspects of Hawaiian entomology.

(The Hawaiian Planters' Record, Vol. 50;
111-118, 1946)

QL ENTOMOLOGY NEW ZEALAND
487
H 88 Hudson, G. V.

Fragments of New Zealand entomology. A popular account of all the New Zealand Cicadas. The
natural history of the New Zealand glow-worm. A
second supplement to the butterflies and moths of
New Zealand and notes on many other native insects
With two plain and seventeen coloured plates.
Ferguson and Osborn, Ltd. Wellington, N. Z.
(1950) 8vo. 15-188 pp.

QL ENTOMOLOGY PERIODICAL
461
L 59 The Lepidopterist, published by Samuel E. Cassino.

For current volumes see serial file

QL ENTOMOLOGY HIMALAYA
463
M 27 Mani, M. S.
Introduction to high altitude entomology;
insect life above the timber-line in the northwest Himalaya. London. Methuen and Co. Ltd.
8vo 1962 xix + 302 pp.

QL ENTOMOLOGY NEW ZEALAND BIBLIOGRAPHY
487
M 64 Miller, David

Bibliography of New Zealand entomology.
1775-1952 (with annotations). A Cawthron Institute Monograph.

(New Zealand, Department of Scientific and
Industrial Research, Bull. 120. 1956)

QL ENTOMOLOGY - PERIODICALS
461
P94 Psyche, a journal of entomology.

see serial file

QL ENTOMOLOGY JAPAN
461
E 74 Esakia
Occasional Papers of the Hikosan Biological
Laboratory in Entomology

No. 1, 1960 +

DU ENTOMOLOGY PAPUA AND NEW GUINEA
1
A 84 Szent-Ivany, J. J. H.

Entomology in the Territory of Papua and
New Guinea.

(Australian Territories, 2(3):4-10, 1962)

QL ENTOMOLOGY - PERIODICALS
461
Z48 Zeitschrift fur wissenschaftliche insektenbiol-
gie.

see serial file

QL ENTOMOLOGY LOWER CALIFORNIA
1
C Calvert, Philip Powell, 1871-
... Odonata from Tepic, Mexico, with supplementary
notes on those of Baja California. By Philip P. Calvert
... San Francisco, The academy, 1899.
1 p. l., p. 371-418. pl. 25½cm. (Proceedings of the California academy
of sciences. 3d ser. Zoology. vol. i, no. 12)

1. Lower California. Entomology. 2. Odonata. 3. Tepic, Mexico. Ento-
mology.
Agr 5-140
Library, U. S. Dept. of   Agriculture   432C13Od

QL ENTOMOLOGY - PERIODICALS
461
C21 Canadian Entomologist

see serial file

Q ENTOMOLOGY PHILIPPINE ISLANDS
101
P 18 Otanes, Faustino A.
A survey of Philippine entomology with
special reference to applied or economic work.

IN Proc. Sixth Pac. Sci. Congress, 1939,
(California), Vol. 4, 1940, pp. 383-396.

QL ENTOMOLOGY MEXICO
1
C Calvert, Philip Powell

...Odonata from Tepic, Mexico, with supplementary notes on those of Baja California.
By Philip P. Calvert ... San Francisco, The
academy, 1899.

(California Acad. Sci., Zoology, 3rd ser.,
vol. 1, no. 12, pp. 371-418)

QL ENTOMOLOGY - PERIODICALS
461
E91 Entomological News

Published monthly by the American Entomological Society.

see serial file

QH ENTOMOLOGY REUNION
1
M 17 La faune entomologique de l'Ile de la Reunion.- 1

(Mem. Inst. Sci. de Madagascar, Tome VIII,
Ser. E, 1957)

[articles by many authors]

QL
461
D48

ENTOMOLOGY - SOCIETIES

Deutschen Entomologischen Gesellschaft

Deutsche entomologische zeitschrift.

see serial file

QL
461
T 31

ENTOMOPHAGA   PALAU ISLANDS

Ishii, Tei

Description of a new Eucharid from Palau
Islands.

(Tenthredo, Vol. III, 1941, pp. 292-294)

AS
36
S 4

ENTOMOSTRACA

Lilljeborg, W.

Contributions to the Natural History of the
Commander Islands.
No. 9: On the Entomostraca collected by Mr.
Leonhard Stejneger on Bering Island, 1882-83.

(Proc. of the U. S. Nat. Mus. Vol. 10, 1887,
pp. 154-156)

DU
96
C 32

ENTOMOLOGY   TASMANIA

Carter, H. J.

Gulliver in the bush. Wanderings of an Australian entomologist. Sydney. Angus & Robertson,
Ltd. 1933. 8vo. 234 pp., 9 pl.

AS
36
S4

ENTOMOSTRACA

Dodds, Gideon Stanhope, 1880-
Altitudinal distribution of *Entomostraca* in Colorado.
By Gideon S. Dodds ...
(*In* U. S. National museum. Proceedings. Washington, 1919. 23½ᶜᵐ.
v. 54, p. 59-87. illus. (incl. maps) pl. 13-14, fold. tab., diagrs.)
Bibliography: p. 87.

1. Entomostraca. 2. Crustacea—Colorado.

Library of Congress   Q11.U55 vol. 54   19-20009
                                    (6)

QL
Crust.Pam.
141

ENTOMOSTRACA

Lovén, S. L.

Evadne Nordmanni, ein bisher unbekanntes
entomostracon.

(K. Wet.-Akad, Handlingar, Stockholm, 1853,
pp. 143-146)

QL
Insects
Pams.
1352

ENTOMOLOGY   UNITED STATES   PACIFIC NW

Hatch, Melville H.

A century of entomology in the Pacific
northwest. University of Washington Press.
1949. 43 pp.

AS
36
S4

ENTOMOSTRACA

Dodds, Gideon Stanhope, 1880-
Descriptions of two new species of *Entomostraca* from
Colorado, with notes on other species. By G. S. Dodds ...
(*In* U. S. National museum. Proceedings. Washington, 1916. 23½ᶜᵐ.
v. 49, p. 97-102. illus.)

1. Entomostraca. 2. Crustacea—Colorado.

Library of Congress   Q11.U55 vol. 49   16-11777
———— Copy 2.   Q11.U55 vol. 49 2d set

QL
Crust.Pam.
268

ENTOMOSTRACA

Scourfield, D. J.

Entomostraca and the surface film of water.

(Jour. Linnean Soc. Zool. Vol. XXV, 1894,
pp. 1-18)

AS
36
S1

ENTOMOLOGY AND THE WAR.
Howard, Leland Ossian, 1857-
Entomology and the war. By Dr. L. O. Howard ...
(*In* Smithsonian institution. Annual report. 1919. Washington, 1921.
23½ᶜᵐ. p. 411-419)
"Reprinted ... from the Scientific monthly, February, 1919."

1. Insects, Injurious and beneficial. 2. European war, 1914-   —Science.
I. Title.

Library of Congress   Q11.S66 1919   22-318
                                    (11)

QL
Crustacea
Pam. 91

ENTOMOSTRACA

Guerne, Jules de

Canthocamptus Grandidieri, Alona Cambouei,
nouveaux Entomostracés d'eau douce de Madagascar
par Jules de Guerne et Jules Richard.

(Mem. Soc. Zool. de France, Tome 6, 1893,
pp. 234-244)

QL
Crustacea
Pam.
258
259
260

ENTOMOSTRACA

Scourfield, D. J.

The Entomostraca of Epping Forest, with
some general remarks on the group. Parts 1-4.

(Essex Naturalist, Vol. 10, pp. 193-210,
259-274, 313-334, 1898)

QL
463
Pa

Entomology for beginners
Packard, Alpheus Spring, 1839-1905.
Entomology for beginners for the use of young folks,
fruit-growers, farmers, and gardeners, by A. S. Packard
... 2d ed. rev. New York, H. Holt and company, 1889.   1894
xvi, 367 p. illus. 19ᶜᵐ.
"The entomologist's library": p. (326)-335.

1. Insects.

                                    16-17566
Library of Congress   QL463.P115 1889

QL
Crustacea
Pam. 89

ENTOMOSTRACA

Guerne, Jules de

Note sur les entomostracés d'eau douce recueillis par M. Charles Rabot dans la province
de Nordland, Norvège Septentrionale, par Jules de
Guerne et Jules Richard.

(Bull. Soc. Zool. de France, 1889, Tome 14,
p. 27-31)

QL
Crust.Pam.
263

ENTOMOSTRACA

Scourfield, D. J.

The Ephippia of the Lynceid Entomostraca.

(Jour. Quekett Micro. Club. Ser. 2, Vol.VIII
1902, pp.217-244)

Entomology in the West Indies; a summary
of the entomological work undertaken by the Imperial
Department of Agriculture, 1898-1911.

(West Indian Bulletin, Vol. 11, 1911, pp.
282-317)

QL
Crus.Pam.
126

ENTOMOSTRACA

Kernervé, L. B. de

De L'Apparition Provoquée Des Mâles Chez
Les Daphnies (Daphnia Psittacea).

(Mémoires de la Société Zoologique de
France, Tome VIII, 1895, pp-200-211)

QL
Crust.Pam.
264

ENTOMOSTRACA

Scourfield, D. J.

The Ephippium of Bosmina.

(Jour. of the Quekett Microscopical Society,
Ser. 2, Vol. 8, 1902, pp. 51-55)

S
17 H3
S 45

ENTOMOGENEOUS FUNGI

Speare, Alden True, 1885-
... Fungi parasitic upon insects injurious to sugar cane.
By A. T. Speare. Honolulu, Hawaii, 1912.
62 p. vi pl. 23ᶜᵐ. (Hawaiian sugar planters' association. Experiment
station. Pathological and physiological series. Bulletin no. 12)
Bibliography: p. 56-58.

1. Entomogeneous fungi. 2. Sugar cane. Pests.

                                         Agr 13-241
Library, U. S. Dept. of   Agriculture 464.9H31 no. 12

QL
Crust.
Pam. 132

ENTOMOSTRACA

Klocke, Eduard

Beitrage zur Cladocerenfauna der Ostschweiz
(Entomostraca).

(Aus d. Zool. Vergl. Anat. Lab. bei der Hoch-
schulen in Zürich, 1893, pp. 384-389)

QL
Crus.Pam.
261

ENTOMOSTRACA

Scourfield, D. J.

A very common Water-Flea.

(Annual of Microscopy. Oct. 1898. pp. 1-6)

QL
Crus.Pam.
326

ENTOMOSTRACA

Thorell, T.

Till kännedomen om vissa parasitiskt lefvande
Entomostraceer.

(Ofversigt af Kongl. Vetenskaps-Akademiens
forhandlingar, arg. 16, no. 8, 1859. pp. 335-362)

ENTOMOSTRACA

See also under

DAPHNIA

---

d'ENTRECASTEAUX ISLANDS   MUSACEAE

See

MUSACEAE   d'ENTRECASTEAUX ISLANDS

QL
Crust.Pam.
302

ENTOMOSTRACA

Wiegmann, A. F.

Ueber Entstehung von Entomostraceen und Po-
durellen aus der Priestleyschen grünen Materie...

(Acad. Caes. Leop., Nova Acta, X, 1821, pp.
717-722)

AS
720.T
R

Joseph Antoine
D'ENTRECASTEAUX, BRUNI

Hogg, G. H.

D'Entrecasteaux: an account of his life,
his expedition, and his officers.

(Papers and Proc. of the R. Soc. of Tasmania
1937, pp. 53-74)

QK
Botany
Pam.
1221

ENTRECASTEAUXIA MONTR.

Beauvisage , V.

Deuxieme note sur l'herbier du R.P.
Montrouzier. Le genre Entrecasteauxia
Montr. Lyons, 1897.

QL
1
C

ENTOPROCTA

Robertson, Alice, 1859-
Studies in Pacific coast *Entoprocta*, by Alice Robertson
... San Francisco, The Academy, 1900.
1 p. l., p. 323-348. pl. xvi (fold.) 25½ᶜᵐ. (Proceedings of the Califor-
nia academy of sciences. 3d ser. Zoology. vol. ii, no. 4)
"Issued December 20, 1900."

1. Entoprocta.

Library of Congress   Q11.C25 vol. 2, no. 4   16-22018
——— Separate.   QL398.E6R6

DU
12
L 11
looked
case

ENTRECASTEAUX, JOSEPH ANTOINE BRUNI d'

Labillardière, J. J. de

An account of a voyage in search of La
Pérouse...1791-1793, in the Recherche and Esper-
ande...under the command of Rear-Admiral Bruni d'
Entrecasteaux. Translated from the French...
Vols. 1-2. Second edition. London. 1802. 8vo.

GN
2.S
P 76

Enua-Manu, the land of birds.

(Jour. Poly. Soc., 20:159-161, 1952)

AS
36
S4

ENTOMOSTRACA

Sharpe, Richard Worthy, 1869-
Notes on the marine *Copepoda* and *Cladocera* of Woods
Hole and adjacent regions, including a synopsis of the
genera of the *Harpacticoida*. By Richard W. Sharpe ...
(*In* U. S. National museum. Proceedings. Washington, 1911. 23½ᶜᵐ.
vol. 38, p. 405-436. illus.)
Bibliography: p. 435-436.

1. Entomostraca. 2. Crustacea—Massachusetts.
11-15889
Library of Congress   Q11.U55 vol. 38

DU
12
L 11
looked
case

ENTRECASTEAUX, JOSEPH ANTOINE BRUNI d'

Labillardière, J. J. de

Relation du voyage a la recherche de La
Pérouse,...1791, 1792... Tomes 1-2 and atlas.
Paris. n.d. (1800 ?)   4to and folio.
(Under the command of d'Entrecasteaux)

AS
36
A25
and
QK
Pam.
190

Enumeration of Hawaiian Plants.

Mann, Horace
Enumeration of Hawaiian plants. From
Am. Acad. Arts & Sc. Proc. VII, 1866.
Cambridge, 1867.

QH
11
G 74

ENTOMOSTRACA   ANTARCTIC

Harding, J. P.

Lower Crustacea.

In British Graham Land Expedition, 1934-37,
Scientific Reports, Vol. 1, no. 6, pp. 319-322,
1941. British Museum (Natural History).

DU
12
L 47

ENTRECASTEAUX,(JOSEPH ANTOINE BRUNI d')

Lee, Ida

Commodore Sir John Hayes, his voyage and
life (1767-1831) with some account of Admiral
D'Entrecasteaux's voyage of 1792-3.

London: Longmans, 1912

QH
431
C6C75

ENVIRONMENT

Conklin, Edwin Grant

Heredity and environment in the development of men.

Princeton, 1922, 379 pp.

QL
Crustacea
Pam.
508

AS
763
B-4

ENTOMOSTRACA   HAWAII

Ueno, Masuzo

Cladocera of Mauna Kea, Hawaii.

(B.P. Bishop Mus., Occ. Papers, vol. XII,
no. 11, 1936, 9 pp., 3 figs.)

GN
2.S
P 76

ENTRECASTEAUX, JOSEPH ANTOINE D'

The visit of Dentrecasteaux to the North
Cape, New Zealand, in March, 1793.

(Journal of the Polynesian Society, 28:117-
120, 1919)

GN
320
D 62

ENVIRONMENT

Dixon, Roland B.

The building of Cultures. New York. 1928.

QH
1
M 17

ENTOMOSTRACA   KERGUELEN ISLANDS

Brehm, V.

Les Entomostracés des Kerguelen.

(Mémoires de l'Institut Scientifique de
Madagascar, Ser. A, Biologie Animale, Tome IX:41-
44, 1954)

DU
12
R 82
looked
case

ENTRECASTEAUX, JOSEPH ANTOINE BRUNI d'

Rossel, E. P. E. de

Voyage de Dentrecasteaux, envoye a la recherche de La Perouse...redige par M. de Rossel,
ancien capitaine de vaisseau. 2 vols. Paris.
1808. 4to.

AS
36
S 1

ENVIRONMENT

Kropotkin, Petr Aleksieevich

The direct action of environment and evolution.

(Smithsonian Ann. Rept., 1918:409-427)

QH
302
S 74

ENVIRONMENT

Spector, William S.   editor

Handbook of biological data. Prepared under the direction of the Committee on the Handbook of Biological Data, Div. of Biology and Agriculture, The National Acad. of Sci., The Nat. Res. Council. W. B. Saunders Company. Philadelphia and London. 4to. 1956o xxxvi + 584 pp.

GN
370
T 24

ENVIRONMENT

Taylor, Griffith

Environment, race and migration: fundamentals of human distribution, with special section on racial classification, and settlement in Canada and Australia. University of Chicago Press. Chicago. 1937. 8vo. xv + 483 pp.

QL
461
P 11

ENVIRONMENT   ANTARCTICA

Pryor, M. E.

Some environmental features of Hallett Station, Antarctica, with special reference to soil arthropods.

(Pacific Insects, 4(3):681-728, 1962)

QP
82
A 93

ENVIRONMENT   AUSTRALASIA

Australian Academy of Science

Symposium on man and animals in the tropics at the School of Physics, University of Queensland, Brisbane, May 24/25, 1956. 4to. mimeographed. 234 pp.

[Theme: The impact of the physical and biological environment on man and his domestic animals in the Australasian tropics; Purpose: To review the present position of research...needs for future develop-　　ment.]

Z
4501
S 12

ENVIRONMENT   CORAL ATOLLS

Sachet, Marie-Hélène

Island bibliographies: Micronesian botany, land environment and ecology of coral atolls, vegetation of tropical Pacific islands. Compiled under the offices of the Pacific Science Board. By Marie-Hélène Sachet and F. Raymond Fosberg.

(Nat. Acad. of Sci.-Nat. Research Council, Publication 335. v + 577 pp. 1955)

GN
386
S 52

ENVIRONMENT   HAWAII

Shapiro, Harry L.

Migration and environment: a study of the physical characteristics of the Japanese immigrants to Hawaii and the effects of environment on their descendants. With the field assistance of Frederick S. Hulse. Issued under the auspices of the University of Hawaii. Oxford University Press. London... 1939. R8vo. xi + 594 pp.

GN
Ethn.
Pam.
4207

ENVIRONMENT   MELANESIA

Bühler, Alfred

Der Platz bestimmender Faktor von Siedlungsformen in Ostindonesien und Melanesien.

(Separate: Region Basiliensis, I(2):202-212, 1960)

QP
82
A 93

ENVIRONMENT   NEW GUINEA

Australian Academy of Science

Symposium on man and animals in the tropics, at the School of Physics, University of Queensland, Brisbane, May 24/25 1956. 4to. mimeographed. 234 pp.

[Theme: The impact of the physical and biological environment on man and his domestic animals in the Australasian tropics; Purpose: To review the present position of research...needs for future develop-　　ment.]

G
112
S 97

Environment: a natural geography.

Swaine, G. R.

GN
370
T24

Environment and race

Taylor, Griffith

Q
101
P 18

ENVIRONMENT   PACIFIC

Thomas, William L. Jr.

The variety of physical environments among Pacific islands.

IN
Fosberg, F. Raymond   editor
Man's place in the island ecosystem, a symposium. pp. 7-38. Honolulu. 1963. Tenth Pacific Science Congress.

AS
763
B 62 p

Q
101
P 18

ENVIRONMENT   PACIFIC

Fosberg, F. Raymond   editor

Man's place in the island ecosystem; a symposium. Bishop Museum Press 1963. Tenth Pacific Science Congress, Honolulu, Hawaii, 1961

GN
775
M 13

Eolithic Problem

Maccurdy, G. G.

QL
461
H 38

EOPENTHES

van Zwaluwenburg, R. H.

Notes on the Elaterid genus Eopenthes Sharp (Coleoptera).

(Proc.Haw. Ent.Soc.,1958:117-125)

QK
Bot.Pam
2332

EPACRIDACEAE

St. John, Harold

New combinations in the Gleichenaceae and in Styphelia (Epacridaceae). Pacific Plant Studies, 1.

(Occ. Papers, Bernice P. Bishop Museum, Vol. 17, 1942, no. 7, pp. 79-84)

AS
36
C8

EPEIRIDAE

Emerton, James Henry, 1847-

... New England spiders of the family *Epeiridæ*.

(*In* Connecticut academy of arts and sciences. Transactions. New Haven, 1882-85. 25ᵗ. v. 6, p. 295-342; pl. XXXIII-XL)

1. [Epeiridae] 2. Spiders—New England. I. Title.

Library of Congress   Q11.C9 vol.6
Yale University   A53n.366.6   A 17-807

QL
461
P 11

EPHEMERELLIDAE

Allen, Richard K.

New and little known Ephemerellidae from Southern Asia, Africa and Madagascar (Ephemeroptera) By Richard K. Allen and George F. Edmunds, Jr.

(Pacific Insects, Vol. 5(1):11-22, 1963)

QL
512.7
H 88

EPHEMERIDAE

Hudson, George Vernon.

New Zealand Neuroptera.

London, 1904.

QL
489.M
P 11

EPHEMERIDAE   MARQUESAS

Needham, James G.
Coenagrion interruptum, new species, from the Marquesas, and nymph of *Hemicordulia assimilis* Hagen.
IN
Marquesan Insects-I, pp. 111-115. (Art. 10)

(Bernice P. Bishop Museum, Bulletin 98,1932. Pacific Entomological Survey Publication 1)

AS
720.T
R

EPHEMERIDAE   TASMANIA

Tillyard, R. J.

The trout-food insects of Tasmania, Part 1. A study of the genotype of tje mayfly genus Atalophlebia and its life history; Part 2. A monograph of the mayflies of Tasmania.

(Papers and Proc. R. Soc. Tasmania, 1933: 1-16; 1935:23-60)

AS
750
C 22 m

EPHEMEROPTERA   NEW ZEALAND

Penniket, J. G.

Notes on New Zealand Ephemeroptera, II and III.

(Records of the Canterbury Mus., Vol. 7 (5):375-388; 389-398, 1962)

QL
Insect
Pam 847

EPHEMEROPTERA   NEW ZEALAND

Phillips, J. S.

A Revision of New Zealand Ephemeroptera. Parts 1-2.

(Extract from the Transactions of the New Zealand Institute, Vol. 61, pp. 50-67, August, 1930)

AS
244
D

EPICARIDEA

Nierstrasz, H. F.

Epicaridea II, by H. F. Nierstrasz and G. A. Brender à Brandis.

(Vid. Med. Dansk nat. For. i Kobenhavn, Bd. 91, 1931-32,- Papers from Dr. Th. Mortensen's Pacific Expedition, 1914-16, No. 57)

QK
495.0 58
T 78

EPILOBIUM UNITED STATES

Trelease, William

A Revision of the American Species of Epilobium Occurring North of Mexico.

(Missouri Botanical Garden Report, 1891 (2nd) pp. 69-117, pls. 1-48)

AS
36
S4

EPHIALTINI

Cushman, Robert Asa.

The North American ichneumon-flies of the tribe *Ephialtini*. By R. A. Cushman ...

(*In* U. S. National museum. Proceedings. Washington, 1921. 23½ᶜᵐ. v. 58, p. 327-362. 1 illus., pl. 21)

1. Ichneumonidae.

Library of Congress   Q11.U53 vol. 58   21-21443

AS
36
SG

EPIDELLA

Heath, Harold.

... The anatomy of *Epidella squamula*, sp. nov., by Harold Heath ... Stanford university, Cal., 1902.

2 p. l., 109-136 p. xv-xvi fold. pl. 24½ᶜᵐ. (Contributions to biology from the Hopkins seaside laboratory of the Leland Stanford jr. university. XXVIII)

Reprinted from the Proceedings of the California academy of sciences. 3d ser., Zoology, vol. III.

"Literature cited": p. 133.

1. Epidella.

Library of Congress   QL1.L53 no. 28

——— Copy 2.   9-640
                          Library of Congress QL391.T7H4

QK
495.0
Tr

EPILOBIUM

Trelease, William

A revision of the American species of Epilobium occurring north of Mexico. In Missouri Bot. Garden Rept, 1891, pp 69-117, pls. 1-48.

GN
2.M
Le2

Ephraim, Hugo

Uber die Entwicklung der Webetechnik und ihre Verbreitung ausserhalb Europas. Leipzig Museum fur Volkerk. Band I, Heft 1. 4to. pp 72, illus., map.
Leipzig, 1905.

GN
Ethn.
Pam.
No.607

Also separate

QL
1
C

EPIDELLA

Heath, Harold, 1868-

The anatomy of *Epidella squamula*, sp. nov., by Harold Heath ... San Francisco, The Academy, 1902.

1 p. l., 109-136 p. xv-xvi (fold.). 25½ᶜᵐ. (Proceedings of the California academy of sciences. 3d ser. Zoology. vol. III, no. 4)

"Issued June 12, 1902."

"Literature cited": p. 133.

1. Epidella.

                                16-22026
Library of Congress   Q11.C25 vol. 3, no. 4

QL
513.0 2
A 79

EPIOPHLEBIA

Asahina, Syoziro

A morphological study of a relic dragonfly Epiophlebia superstes Selys (Odonata, Anisozygoptera). Japan Society for the Promotion of Science. 1954. R8vo. 153 + (70) pp.

QL
461
H-1

EPHYDRIDAE HAWAII

Wirth, Willis W.

Aphydra gracilis Packard, a recent immigrant fly in Hawaii (Diptera:Ephydridae).

(Proc. Haw. Ent. Soc., 13:141-142, 1947)

RB
601
F 23

Epidemiology of diseases of military importance in the Netherlands Indies, including the identification and distribution of arthropods of medical importance. Washington. sm8vo. 250 pp.

Farner, D. S.

AS
36
S4

EPIPHRAGMOPHORA

Bartsch, Paul, 1871-

The Californian land shells of the *Epiphragmophora traskii* group. By Paul Bartsch ...

(*In* U. S. National museum. Proceedings. Washington, 1917. 23½ᶜᵐ. v. 51, p. 609-619. pl. 114-117)

1. Epiphragmophora. 2. Mollusks—California.

                                        17-23860
Library of Congress   Q11.U55 vol. 51

——— Copy 2.   Q11.U55 vol. 51 2d set

QL
1
H-1

EPHYDRIDAE HAWAII

Wirth, Willis W.

A taxonomic study of Hawaiian Ephydridae (Diptera), related to Scatella Robineau-Desvoidy.

(Haw. Ent. Soc., Proc. 13(2):277-304, 1948)

QL
1
O 62

EPILACHNINI

Fursch, H.

Die palaearktischen und indomalayischen Epilachnini der Zoologischen Sammlung des Bayerischen Staates München (Col.Cocc).

(Opuscula Zoologica, No.26,1959)

AS
36
S4

EPIPHRAGMOPHORA

Bartsch, Paul, 1871-

Two new land shells of the *Epiphragmophora traskii* group. By Paul Bartsch ...

(*In* U. S. National museum. Proceedings. Washington, 1919. 23½ᶜᵐ. v. 54, p. 523-524. pl. 83)

1. Epiphragmophora.

                                        19-20029
Library of Congress   Q11.U55 vol. 54

AS
763
B-4

EPHYDRIDAE NEW GUINEA

Malloch, John R.

A New Chaetomosillus from New Guinea (Diptera Ephydridae). Honolulu. May 12, 1934.

QL
Insect
Pam 875

(Bernice P. Bishop Museum, Occasional Papers Vol. X, No. 17, 1934.)

Reading
Room

QL
461
P 11

EPILACHNINAE TAIWAN

Li, C. S.

The Epilachninae of Taiwan (Col. Coccinellidae). By C. S. Li and E. F. Cook.

(Pacific Insects, 3(1):31-92, 1961)

QK
1
U

EPIPHYLLUM

Britton, Nathaniel Lord, 1859-

... The genus *Epiphyllum* and its allies, by N. L. Britton and J. N. Rose. Washington, Govt. print. off., 1913.

v p., p. 255-262. p. vii. pl. 78-84. 24½ᶜᵐ. (Smithsonian institution. United States national museum. Contributions from the United States national herbarium. v. 16, pt. 9)

"Bulletin of the United States national museum: issued June 20, 1913."

1. Epiphyllum. I. Rose, Joseph Nelson, 1862-   joint author.

                                        Agr 13-1419
Library, U. S. Dept. of   Agriculture 450C76 vol. 16, pt. 9

AS
244
D

EPICARIDEA

Nierstrasz, H. F. and Brender & Brandis, G. A.

Epicaridea I.

(Vid. Med. Dansk Nat. For. Kobenhavn Bd. 87 1929-30,- Papers from Dr. Th. Mortensen's Pacific Expedition 1914-16, No. 48)

QK
495.0 58
T 78

EPILOBIUM CANADA

Trelease, William

A Revision of the American Species of Epilobium Occurring North of Mexico.

(Missouri Botanical Garden Report, 1891 (2nd) pp. 69-117, pls. 1-48)

QL
461
P 11

EPIPOMPILUS AUSTRALIA

Evans, Howard E.

The genus Epipompilus in Australia (Hymenoptera:Pompilidae).

(Pacific Insects, 4(4):773-782, 1962)

QL
401
N

EPISCYNIA

Pilsbry, Henry Augustus

    Another Pacific species of Episcynia.
By H. A. Pilsbry and Axel A. Olsson.

    (Nautilus, Vol. 60:11-12, 1946)

GC
Oceano-
graphy
Pam.
37

EQUATOR

Arrhenius, Gustaf and others

    The unimaginary equator. By Gustav Arrhenius, John Knauss, Russell Raitt and George Shor.

    (Saturday Review, Oct. 3, 1959:52-54)

QL
Prot-Poly
Pam.
749

EQUINOIDEA CUBA

Sanchez Roig, Mario

    I. La geofisica en su relacion con la paleontologia; II. Nuevos equinidos fosiles de la fauna Cubana.

    (Anales de la Acad. de Ciencias Medicas, Fisicas y Naturales de La Habana, 91(2):119-176, 1953)

    [article   on equinoids, pp. 135-176]

AS
36
S4

EPITONIUM

Dall, William Healey, 1845–
    Notes on the shells of the genus *Epitonium* and its allies of the Pacific coast of America. By William Healey Dall ...

    (*In* U. S. National museum. Proceedings. Washington, 1917. 23½ᶜᵐ. v. 53, p. 471-488)

1. Epitonium.

    18-14643

Library of Congress   Q11.U55 vol. 53

G
1
As

EQUATORIAL ISLANDS

Williams, John

    More American air bases.

    (Asia. vol.37. 1937. pp.409-413)

QK
97
Fe

EQUISITUM

Mäckel, H. G.

    Zur Kenntnis der spateren Entwicke-lungsstadien der Prothallien von Equisitum arvense . Fedde, Rep.spec.nov.reg.., Beihefte, Band XXVIII, 1924, pp 36, 1 map.

QK
211
B 74

Epling, Carl

    The Labiatae of the Yucatan Peninsula.

    IN

Botany of the Maya area, Miscellaneous Papers, No. 18, 1940.

AP
2
N 4

    Equatorial regions of the Pacific

    (Nature, Vol. 148, 1941, p. 171)

QK
495.G 74
G 69

ERAGROSTIS

Gould, Frank W.

    Grasses of southwestern United States, by Frank W. Gould; The role of grasses in the vegetation of Arizona, by Forrest Shreve; The genus Eragrostis, by LeRoy H. Harvey.

    (Univ. of Arizona Bull. 22(1), 1951,,being Biol. Sci. Bull. No. 7)

QK
Botany
Pam
1483

Epling, Carl Clawson
    Monograph of the genus monardella. From Annals of Missouri Bot. garden, v.12, 1925. pp. 1-106.

AM
101
P 35-g

EQUIDAE

Lull, Richard Swann

    The Evolution of the Horse Family.

    (Special Guide, No. 1, Peabody Museum of Natural History, Yale University, Revised Edition 1931)

Biblio-
film
24

ERAGROSTIS

Jedwabnick, E.

    Studies on species of Eragrostis.

    (Botanisches Archiv, Bd. 5, 1924, pp.?-photostat copy of a few pages only)

AS
36
S1

Epry, Charles, 1865–
    Ripple marks. By Ch. Epry ...
    (*In* Smithsonian institution. Annual report. 1913. Washington, 1914. 23½ᶜᵐ. p. 307-318. 10 pl. on 5 l.)
    "Translated ... from the Annales de l'Institut océanographique ... Paris, vol. 4, pt. 3, 1912."

1. Ripple-marks.

    15-1739

Library of Congress   Q11.S66 1913

EQUIDAE.

AS
36
A6

Osborn, Henry Fairfield, 1857–
    ... Craniometry of the *Equidæ.* By Henry Fairfield Osborn. [New York] 1912.
    cover-title, p. 55-100. illus., diagrs. 36 x 28½ᶜᵐ. (Memoirs of the American museum of natural history. n. s., vol. I, pt. III)
    1 leaf, "Addendum," inserted between p. 66 and 67.
    Bibliography: p. 100.

1. Equidae. 2. Skull.

    14-3946

Library of Congress   QH1.A43 n. s., vol. I, pt. 3

QK
Bot.Pam.
1929

AS
763
B-4

ERAGROSTIS

Whitney, Leo D.

    New species of Hawaiian Panicum and Eragrostis, by Leo. D. Whitney and Edward Y. Hosaka.

    (Bernice P. Bishop Museum, Occasional Papers, vol. XII, no. 5, 1936)

GN
1
O 15

Epstein, A. L.
    The economy of modern Matupit: continuity and change on the Gazelle Peninsula, New Britain.

    (Oceania, Vol. 33(3):182-215, 1963)

AS
36
C8

EQUILIBRIUM

Gibbs, Josiah Willard, 1839-1903.
    ... On the equilibrium of heterogeneous substances.
    (*In* Connecticut academy of arts and sciences. Transactions. New Haven, 1874-78. 25ᶜᵐ. v. 3, p. [108]-248, [343]-524. 16 illus.)

1. Equilibrium.   I. Title.

    A 17-781

Library of Congress   Q11.C9 vol. 3
Yale University   A53n.366.3

AP
2
A 5

ERBEN GUYOT

Carsola, Alfred J.

    Submarine geology of two flat-topped northeast Pacific seamounts. By Alfred J. Carsola and Robert S. Dietz.

    (Am. Jour. Sci., Vol. 250:481-497, 1952)

DU
621
H 3

Epstein, Moray (editor)

    History of Hawaii.

    (All About Hawaii, 78th Edition, pp. 275-322, 1953)

AS
36
S1

EQUILIBRIUM OF A LIQUID MASS

Plateau, Joseph Antoine Ferdinand, 1801-1883.
    Experimental and theoretical researches on the figures of equilibrium of a liquid mass withdrawn from the action of gravity, etc. By J. Plateau ...
    (*In* Smithsonian institution. Annual report. 1863-1866. Washington, 1864-67. 23½ᶜᵐ. 1863, p. [207]-285; 1864, p. [285]-369; 1865, p. [411]-435; 1866, p. [355]-289. illus., diagrs.)

1. Molecular dynamics.   I. Title: Equilibrium of a liquid mass.

    S 15-142

Library of Congress   Q11.S66 1863-1866
Library, Smithsonian   Institution

PL
Philo
Pam
126

Erbt, Wilhelm

    Tendenzgeschichte ? From Wissen. Corresp. d. Philo. Nov. Oct. 1906.

GN
537
E65

Erckert, R von

Der Kaukasus und seine völker.

Leipzig, Frohberg, 1887.   385p.   8vo.

GN
1
An

Erdland, P. A.

Die Sternkunde bei den Seefahrern der Marschallinseln.

(Anthropos. Bd. V. 1910. pp.16-26)

QK
H 78

locked
case

EREBUS (SHIP)

Hooker, J. D.

The Cryptogamic botany of the Antarctic voyage of H.M. ships Erebus and Terror in the years 1839 -1843 under the command of Captain Sir James Clark Ross by Joseph Dalton Hooker...Assistant surgeon of the Erebus and botanist of the expedition. London, 1845, 258 pp. pls. 57-80, 151-198. 4to.

GN
Pam
1292

Erckert, R von

Kopfmessungen kaukasischer völker. From Arch. f. anthrop. bd.18.

PL
647
E 66

Erdland, P. August

Wörterbuch und Grammatik der Marshall Sprache nebst ethnographischen Erlauterungen und kurzen Sprachübungen.

(Archiv f. das Studium deutscher Kolonialsprachen, Bd. 4, 1906, 248 pp.)

[see review by Arnold Burgmann, in Anthropos 50:931-934, 1955]   PL Pam. 622

G
387
590
M13

EREBUS (Ship)

M'Cormick, R.

Voyages of discovery in the Arctic and Antarctic seas ..... and of an openboat expedition.... in search of Sir John Franklin and Her Majesty's ships "Erebus and Terror..... 2 vols.

London, 1884.

GN
400
B 97

Der Erdball.

Buschan, G. ed.

Der Erdball. Illustrierte Zeitschrift für Menschen- und Völkerkunde, herausgegeben von Dr. G. Buschan und Dr. H. Kunike. Berlin-Lichterfelde. Hugo Bermühler Verlag. Jahrgang I, 1926/27. 8vo. 478 pp.

QK
658
E 66

Erdtman, G.

An introduction to pollen analysis. Foreword by Roger P. Wodehouse. Chronica Botanica Company. Waltham. 1943. R8vo. 239 pp.

QL
5
R 52

locked
case

EREBUS (ship)

Richardson, John

The Zoology of the Voyage of the H.M.S. Erebus and Terror, under the command of Sir James Clark Ross, during the years 1839-1843. Edited by John Richardson and John Edward Gray... Vols. 1-2. 1844-1875.

GN
1
An

Erdland, August

Die Eingebornen der Marschallinseln im Verkehr mit ihren Häuptlingen.

(Anthropos. Bd.VII. 1912. pp.559-565)

GN
Pam
1001

Erdweg, J

Ein besuch bei den Varopu (Deutsch-Neu-Guinea). From Globus, bd.79, n.7, 1901. 4p.

G
850
Ro

EREBUS (ship)

Ross, James Clark (Sir)

A voyage of discovery and research in the southern and Antarctic regions during the years 1839- 43 . 2 vols.

London, 1847 .

Microfilm
97

Erdland, August

Grammatik und Worterbuch der Marshall-Sprache in Mikronesien.   microfilm.

GN
Pam
1122

Erdweg, Mathias Josef

Die bewihner der insel tumleo, Berlinhafen Deutsch-Neu-Guinea. From bd.23, mitt, der anthrop. gesell. Wien.

QL
Mollusca
Pam.
935

EREMINA

Steenberg, C. M.

Etudes sur l'anatomie et la systematique du genre Eremina (Gastéropodes pulmonés)

(Kgl. Danske Videnskabernes Selskab, Biol. Meddelelser, 20(14), 1949)

GN
671.M2
E 66

Erdland, P. A.

Die Marshall-Insulaner: leben und sitte, sinn und religion eines Südsee-volkes... Mit 14 tafeln und 27 figuren im text. Münster, Aschendorff. 1914. R8vo. xii + 376 pp.

Bibliothek
(Anthropos, Band II, Heft 1, 1914).

QL
562
W 28

EREBIA

Warren, B. C. S.

Monograph of the genus Erebia. London, Oxford Univ.Press, 1936. R8vo. 407 pp., 104 pl.

QK
1
Z 96

EREMOPANAX

Baumann-Bodenheim, M. G.

Beiträge zur Kenntnis Neu-Caledonischer Pflanzen die Gattung Eremopanax.

(Mitteilungen aus dem Botanischen Museum der Universität Zürich, CXCVIII (198), 1954)

GN
1
An

Erdland, August

Die Stellung der Frauen in den Häuptlingsfamilien der Marschallinseln (Südsee).

(Anthropos. Bd.IV. 1909. pp.106-112)

QK
5
H 78

locked
case

EREBUS (ship)

Hooker, Joseph Dalton

The Botany of the Antarctic Voyage of the H.M.Discovery Ships Erebus and Terror in the years 1839-1843, under the command of Sir James Clark Ross... Vol.1-3(in 6).

AS
36
S6

EREUNIAS

Jordan, David Starr, 1851-

... Description of two new genera of fishes (Ereunias and Draciscus) from Japan. By David Starr Jordan and John Otterbein Snyder.

(In Leland Stanford junior university. Hopkins seaside laboratory. Contributions to biology. Stanford university, Cal., 1901. 24½cm. [no.] XXIV, 377-380 p. xviii-xix fold. pl.)

Reprinted from the Proceedings of the California academy of sciences. 3d ser., Zoology, vol. II.

1. Ereunias. 2. Draciscus. I. Snyder, John Otterbein, 1867- joint author.

Library of Congress   QL1.L53 no. 24   9-637
——— Copy 2.   Library of Congress QL634.J3J72

QL
1
C

EREUNIAS
Jordan, David Starr, 1851–

... Description of two new genera of fishes (*Ereunias* and *Draciscus*) from Japan, by David Starr Jordan and John Otterbein Snyder ... San Francisco, The Academy, 1901.

1 p. l., p. 377-380, pl. XVIII-XIX (fold.) 25½ᵐᵐ. (Proceedings of the California academy of sciences. 3d ser. Zoology. vol. II, no. 7)

"Issued April 24, 1901."

1. Ereunias. 2. Draciscus. I. Snyder, John Otterbein, 1867– joint author.

16-22019

Library of Congress   Q11.C25 vol. 2, no. 7

QK
Bot.Pam.
2121

AS
763
B-4

Reading
Room

ERICACEAE
Skottsberg, Carl

Ericaceae and Santalaceae of southeastern Polynesia.

(Occ. Papers, Bernice P. Bishop Museum, Vol. 14, No. 4, 1938, pp. 31-43) Mangarevan Expedition Publication 21

QL
E
M

Erichson, W. (Dr.)

Lepidoptera.

DU
12
M61

in Meyen's Beiträge zur Zoologie gesammelt auf einer reise um die Erde. pp. 237-264, pl. XII.
Breslau & Bonn, 1834, 4º.

QL
Fish Pam
329

EREUNIAS GRALLATOR
Schmidt, P.

On a rare japanese deep-sea fish, *Ereunias grallator* Jordan and Snyder.

(Comptes Rendus de l'Academie des Sciences de l'URSS, 1928, pp. 319-320)

QK
1
E 58

ERICACEAE
Sleumer, H.

Neue Ericaceen aus Malesien.

(Botanische Jahrbucher, Bd. 71, 1940, pp. 139-168)

QL
573
E 68

Erichson, Wilhelm Ferdinand

Genera et species Staphylinorum, insectorum Coleopterorum familiae. Auctore Guil. F. Erichson. Accedunt tabulae aeneae quinque. Berolini F. H. Morin. 1840. 8vo. 954 pp., 5 pl.

AS
36
S4

ERGASILIDÆ
Wilson, Charles Branch, 1861–

North American parasitic copepods belonging to the family *Ergasilidæ*. By Charles Branch Wilson ...

(*In* U. S. National museum. Proceedings. Washington, 1911. 23½ᵐ. v. 39, p. 263-400. illus, pl. 41-60)

Bibliography: p. 393-395.

1. Ergasilidae. 2. Crustacea—North America.

11-21204

Library of Congress   Q11.U55 vol. 39

QK
1
E 58

ERICACEAE
Sleumer, Herman

Revision der Ericaceae von Neu-Guinea.

(Botanische Jahrbücher... Vol.70,1939,pp.95-124)

QL
573
E 68

Erichson, Wilhelm Ferdinand

Naturgeschichte der Insecten Deutschlands. Fortgesetzt von Prof. Dr. H. Schaum...
Erste Abtheilung: Coleoptera, Zweiter Bd. bearbeitet von Gustav Kraatz. 1858.
Vierter Bd. bearbeitet von Ernst August Hellmuth von Kiesenwetter. 1863.
Berlin. Verlag der Nicolaischen Buchhandlung. 8vo.

Q
115
F 92

Ergebnisse der Frobenius-Expedition 1937-38 in die Molukken und nach Hollandisch Neu-Guinea.
Bd. IV:Felsbilder und Vorgeschichte des MacCluer-Golfes, West Neuguinea. 1959. 4to. Darmstadt. 162 pp. By Josef Röder

---

QK
Bot. Pam.
3060

ERICACEAE
Sleumer, H.

A revision of the genus Diplysocia (Ericaceae). Florae Malesianae Praecursores XIV.

(Reprint: Reinwardtia, 4(2):119-161, 1958)

QL
Insect
Pam.
2027

Ericson, Ruth O.

A glossary of some foreign-language terms in entomology.

(U.S.D.A. Agric. Handbook No. 218, Ent. Research Division, Dec. 1961)

Ergebnisse der Frobenius-Expedition 1937-1938 in die Molukken und nach Hollandisch Neu-Guinea. Vol. 2 1948 (being Die drei Ströme by A. E. Jensen)

UH has

QK
1
B 65

ERICACEAE MALAY
Smith J. J.

The Malaysian genus Rigiolepis Hooker f.
(Blumea, Vol. 1, No. 2, 1935, pp. 295-302)

DU
Hist.
Pam. 205

Eriki

The Knights of Maoriland: Carroll...Pomare, Ngata.

(The B. P. Magazine, June 1st, 1933, pp. 44-45, 75)

QK
1
A 75

ERIANDRA
van Royen, P.

Eriandra, a new genus of Polygalaceae from New Guinea. By P. van Royen and C.G.G.J. van Steenis.

(Journal of the Arnold Arboretum, 33:91-95, 1952)

QK
110
N 56

ERICALES
Small, John Kunkel   and others

Ericales.

In North American flora, Vol. 29, Part 1, 1914, pp.

QK
97
E 58

ERIOCAULACEAE
Engler, Adolf

Das Pflanzenreich...IV. 30, 1903. (Heft 13)
Eriocaulaceae, by W. Ruhland.

QK
Botany
Pam.
2777

ERICACEAE
Hansen, Irmgard

Die europäischen Arten der Gattung Erica L. (Morphologie und Systematik der europäischen Erica-Arten als Grundlage für ein neues, auf natürliche Artengruppen aufgebautes system der Gattung Erica L.)

(Sonder- Abdruck aus Botanische Jahrbücher, Band 75, Heft 1, pp. 1-81, 1950)

QL
M

DU
12
M61

Erichson, W.

Coleoptera.

in Meyen's Beiträge zur Zoologie gesammelt auf einer reise um die Erde. pp. 219-236, pl. XXVIII-XXXIX (chiefly from Philippine Islands, China & S. America)
Breslau & Bonn, 1834, 4º.

QK
211
B 74

ERIOCAULACEAE
Moldenke, Harold N.

The Eriocaulaceae, Verbenaceae, and Avicenniaceae of the Yucatan Peninsula.

IN
Botany of the Maya area, Miscellaneous Papers, No. 17, 1940.

QK
Bot.Pam.
2342
a,b

ERIOCAULACEAE

Moldenke, Harold Norman

The known geographic distribution of the members of the Verbenaceae and Avicenniaceae. Privately printed. New York. 1942. 4to. 104 pp.

also 1949 edition, which includes as well the Stilbaceae, Symphoremaceae, and Eriocaulaceae.

PL
Philo
Pam
93

Erman, Adolf v.

Bericht uber das worterbuch der Aegptischen sprache. From Sitz. d. k. Akad. d. Wissen. bd.IV, 1919.

QL
1
F

EROLIA

Conover, Boardman

The North Pacific allies of the purple sandpiper.

(Field Museum of Nat. Hist., Zool. Ser., Vol. 29, No. 11, 1944, pp. 169-179)

QK
97
E
Heft 13

Eriocaulaceae

Ruhland, W.

Pflanzenreich, Das   Heft 13 IV. 30.

Leipzig, Wilhelm Engelmann, 1903,pp294,Figs.40.

PL
Philo
Pam
95

Erman, Adolf

Die flexion des aegyptischen verbums. From Sitz. d. k. Akad. d. Wissen. zu Berlin, v.XIX, 1900.

EROMANGA

see

NEW HEBRIDES

QK
Botany
Pam.
1266

ERIOCAULACEAE -- BRAZIL

Bongard, [Heinrich Gustav]

Espèces d'Eriocaulon du Brésil, suite 1. From Acad Imp. Sc. St. Petersbourg Mem. sc.math., phys.,et nat.Vol. II, pp 221 - 237, pls xi- xviii, 1832.

PL
Philo
Pam
94

Erman, Adolf

Die mahnworte eines agyptischen propheten. From Sitz. d. k. Akad. d. Wissen. v.XLII, 1919.

AS
36
S

EROSION

Hitchcock, Edward, 1793-1864.

... Illustrations of surface geology. By Edward Hitchcock ... [Washington, Smithsonian institution, 1857]

v, [2], 155 p. illus, XII pl. (part fold, incl. maps) 33cm. (Smithsonian contributions to knowledge. (vol. IX, art. 3))

Smithsonian institution publication 90.

CONTENTS.—pt. I. On surface geology especially that of the Connecticut Valley in New England.—pt. II. On the erosions of the earth's surface, especially by rivers.—pt. III. Traces of ancient glaciers in Massachusetts and Vermont.

1. Physical geography—Connecticut Valley.   2. Erosion.   3. Glacial epoch.

S 13-40

Library, Smithsonian   Institution Q11.S68

QK
Bot.Pam.
1978

ERIOCAULACEAE DUTCH EAST INDIES

van Steenis, C.G.G.J.

Nieuwe Nederlandsch Indische waterplantens. 4. Eriocaulon setaceum L.

(Overdruk uit "de Tropische Natuur", Jrg. 25, afl. 7, 1936)

GN
Pam
1368

Erman, Adolf

Reden. Rufe und lieder auf graberbildern des alten reiches. From abh. Akad. der Wissen. jahr. 1918. phil-hist. klasse, n.15, 1919.

QM
Pam
#345
Pam
Bot

EROSION

Platania, Gaetano

Marmitte dei giganti di erosione marina. Istituto di Geografia Fisica e Vulcanologia dell R.Università di Catania. Pub. No. 2.

Roma, 1915, 8vo. pp. 7, illus.

QK
1
P 23

ERIOCAULON   NEW CALEDONIA

Lecomte, H.

Eriocaulon nouveau de la Nouvelle-Calédonie.

(Notulae Systematicae, Vol. 2, p. 380, 1913)

AS
182
H

Erneute Exploration der Viti-Inseln.

(Jour. Mus. Godeffroy, Heft XII, 1876, pp. 162-175)

AP
2
A 5

EROSION

Twenhofel, W. H.

The cost of soil in rock and time.

(Am. Journal of Science, Vol. 237, 1939, pp. 771-780)

Q
115
R 29

ERIOPHYIDAE   SAMOA

Nalepa, A.

Eriophyidae.

Rechinger, Karl
Botanische und Zoologische Ergebnisse einer Wissenschaftlichen Forschungsreise nach den Samoainseln...1905. Teil II:6, pp.139-152,1908

AS
322
Z-v

Ernst, Alfred

Das biologische Krakatauproblem.

(Vierteljahrsschrift der Naturforschenden Gesellschaft in Zurich, Jahrg. 79, 1934, Beiblatt No. 22. pp. 1-187)

QE
581
T97

EROSION

Twenhofel, William H.

Treatise on sedimentation.

Balt., Williams & Wilkins, 1926. xxv, 661p., pls.

AS
36
S4

ERISMATURA JAMAICENSIS.

Wetmore, Alexander, 1886–

On certain secondary sexual characters in the male ruddy duck, *Erismatura jamaicensis* (Gmelin). By Alexander Wetmore ...

(In U. S. National museum. Proceedings. Washington, 1917. 23½cm. v. 52, p. 479-482. 1 illus.)

1. Erismatura jamaicensis.

18-15666

Library of Congress   Q11.U55 vol. 52

QK
367
E 71

Ernst,A.   Trans. by A.C.Seward

The New Flora of the Volcanic Island of Krakatau

Cambridge: University Press,1908,pp 74

13 photos,2 Maps.

QE
Geol.Pam.
1194

EROSION

Visher, Stephen S.

Regional contrasts in torrential rainfalls help to explain regional contrasts in erosion.

(Jour. of Geology, 50(1):96-105, 1942)

QE
Geol.
Pam.1090　EROSION

Wentworth, Chester K.

　　Potholes, pits, and pans:subaerial and marine.

　　(Journal of Geology, Vol. 52, pp. 117-130, 1944)

QE
Geology
Pam
657
658　EROSION　HAWAII

Wentworth, Chester K.

　　Estimates of marine and fluvial erosion in Hawaii. From Journ. Geology, v.35, n.2, 1927.

　　2 copies

QL
696.E 7
L 14　EROTYLIDAE

Lacordaire, Jean Théodore

　　Monographie des Erotyliens, famille de l'ordre des Coléoptères. Paris. Roret. 1842. 8vo. xiv + 543 pp.

QE
75
P　EROSION　BIKINI

Revelle, Roger

　　Chemical erosion of beachrock and exposed reef rock. By Roger Revelle and K. O. Emery. Bikini and nearby atolls, Marshall Islands. A study of the solution of calcium carbonate in the intertidal zone.

　　(U. S. Geol. Survey, Prof. Paper, No. 260-T 1957)

AP
2
A 5　EROSION　HAWAII

and
QE
Geol.Pam.
1191

White, Sidney E.

　　Processes of erosion on steep slopes of Oahu Hawaii.

　　(American Journal of Science, Vol. 247:168-186, 1949)

　　Discussion of this paper by Harold St.John and the author IN Am. J. Sci., Vol. 248:508-514

QL
1
C 74　EROTYLIDAE　AFRICA

Delkeskamp, Kurt

　　Revision der afrikanischen Gattung Palaeolybas Crotch (Coleoptera Erotylidae). 17. Beitrag zur Kenntnis der Erotyliden.

　　(Zoologische Wetenschappen, Deel 44, 1956; Annalen van het K. Mus. van Belgisch-Congo, Tervuren, Ser. in 8°)

Q
101
P 18　EROSION　HAWAII

Coulter, John Wesley

　　The relation of soil erosion to land utilization in the Territory of Hawaii.

　　IN Proc. Sixth Pac. Sci. Congress, 1939, (California), Vol. 4, 1940, pp. 897-904.

QE
Geol.
Pam.
1269　EROSION　KAUAI

　　Waimea beach and Hanapepe Bay, Island of Kauai, T. H., beach erosion control study. Letter from the Secretary of the Army transmitting a letter from the Chief of Engineers, Department of the Army, dated April 25, 1956...report...cooperative beach erosion control study of Waimea Beach and Hanapepe Bay...Kauai...Section 2 of the River and Harbor Act...July 3, 1930... Washington.1957 House Doc. 432, 84th Congress, 2nd session.

QH
1
O 81　EROTYLIDAE　NEW CALEDONIA

Chûjô, Michio

　　Erotylid beetles of New Caledonia.

　　(Bull. Osaka Museum of Nat. Hist., 15:1-2, 1962)

AP
2
S 35　EROSION　HAWAII

Egler, Frank E.

　　Unrecognized arid Hawaiian soil erosion.

　　(Science, Vol. 94, 1941, pp. 513-514)

G
3
A 1　EROSION　NEW ZEALAND

Cumberland, Kenneth B.

　　Contrasting regional morphology of soil erosion in New Zealand.

　　(Geographical Review, Jan. 1944, Vol. 34, pp. 77-95)

QK
Bot.Pam.
1814　ERPODIUM DOMINGENSE

Steere, W. C.

　　The occurrence of Erpodium Domingense in the United States, with notes on its distribution.

　　(Bryologist, Vol. XXXVII, July-August, 1934, pp. 74-75)

QE
Geol
Pam.
483　EROSION　HAWAII

Judd, C. S.(Supt. of Forestry.)

　　Aeolian Erosion in Hawaii. In American Forestry, Vol. 23, No. 280. Wash.D.C. April, 1917. pp 239-240. Illus.

QE
Geol.
Pam.
1241　EROSION　MARINE

Fairbridge, Rhodes W.

　　Marine erosion.

　　(Seventh Pacific Science Congress, Vol. III, 1952)

DU
760
R64　Erromanga, the martyr isle

Robertson, H　　A

QE
Pam
835　EROSION　HAWAII

Palmer, Harold S.

　　Soil Forming Processes in the Hawaiian Islands from the Chemical and Mineralogical Points of View.

　　(Reprinted from Soil Science, Vol. XXXI, No. 4, April, 1931) pp. 253-265.

QL
461
M 98　EROTYLIDAE

Chujo, Michio

　　Descriptions of six new Erotylid-beetles from Formosa and the Marianna Islands.

　　(Mushi, Vol. 13:84-92, 1941)

Carter Coll.
2-D-22

Erskine, Charles

　　Twenty years before the mast with the more thrilling scenes and incidents while circumnavigating the globe under the command of the late Admiral Charles Wilkes 1838-1842. Boston Charles Erskine. 1890 x + 311 pp. 8vo.

QE
Geol.
Pam.
548
544
549　Erosion　Hawaii

Wentworth, Chester K.

　　The desert strip of West Molokai. From Iowa Stud nat.hist. Vol.11, No.4, 1925, pp 41-56, 3 pls.

QL
1
C 74　EROTYLIDAE

Delkeskamp, Kurt

　　Beitrag zur Kenntnis der Erotyliden. Revision der afrikanischen Gattung Palaeolybas Crotch (Coleoptera Erotylidae), 17

　　(Ann. Mus. R. du Congo Belge, s in 8, Sci. Zool., Vol. 44, 1956)

QK
1
C 22　Erskine, David S.

　　Plants of Prince Edward Island.

　　(Canada. Dept. of Agric., Research Branch, Publication 1088, Dec. 1960)

G
7
R 8
Erskine, J. E.   (John E.)

Proceedings at the South Sea Islands. (1849)

(Jour. of the R. Geogr. Soc., Vol. 21,
1851, pp. 221-240)

DU
1
P
Eruption: two days of terror in New Hebrides

(Pacific Islands Monthly, Vol. 10, 1939, p.
23-24)

GN
Ethn.Pam.
2832
Erwin, Richard P.

Indian Rock Writing in Idaho

Biennial Report of the State Historical
Society of Idaho, Twelfth Volume, 132 pp. 1929-
1930.   8vo.

DU
12
E 73

looked
case

2 copies
Erskine, John Elphinstone

Journal of a cruise among the islands of the
western Pacific, including the Feejees and others
inhabited by the Polynesian negro races, in Her
Majesty's ship Havannah, by John Elphinstone
Erskine, Capt. R.N. With maps and plates.
London.   John Murray. 1853. 8vo. vii+488 pp.

ERUPTIONS

See also

VOLCANIC ERUPTIONS

QK
Bot.Pam.
3115
ERYCIBE

Hoogland, R. D.

A review of the genus Erycibe Roxb.

(Blumea, 7(2):342-361, 1953)

AP
2
A 5
Eruption of Kilauea.

(Am. Jour. of Sci., Ser. 3, Vol. 41, 1891,
p. 516)

QE
526
Ha-v
ERUPTIONS   KILAUEA

Macdonald, Gordon A.

The eruption of Kilauea volcano in May,
1954. By Gordon A. Macdonald and Jerry P. Eaton.

(The Volcano Letter, No. 524, pp. 1-9,
April-June, 1954)

QL
1
L-j
ERYTHRAEIDAE

Womersley, H.

Additions to the Trombidiid and Erythraeid
Acarine fauna of Australia and New Zealand.

(Journal of the Linnean Soc. of London.
Zoology. vol. XL, no. 269, 1936. pp. 107-121)

G
51
W 17
Eruption of Mt. Lamington, Papua, Jan. 21,
1951. 7 photos- captions (no other text).

(Walkabout, 17(6):21-28, 1951)

QE
Geol.
Pam.
1211
ERUPTIONS   KILAUEA

Tests show heat of lava pit less than ex-
pected. (Halemaumau)

(Newspaper-which?-February 5, 1917)

includes photos by R. J. Baker

QL
Insects
Pam.
1314
ERYTHRAEIDAE   AUSTRALIA

Southcott, R. V.

Studies on Australian Erythraeidae (Acarina).

(Proc. Linn. Soc. N. S. Wales, Vol. 71 (1/2)
pp. 6-48,1946)

AP
2
A 5
Eruption of Mauna Loa.

(Am. Jour. of Sci., Ser. 4, Vol. 8, 1899,
pp. 237-238)

G
51
W 17
ERUPTIONS   MT. LAMINGTON

Photograph.

(Walkabout, 18(5):48, 1952)

QK
1
N 53
ERYTHRINA

Krukoff, B. A.

The American species of Erythrina.

(Brittonia, Vol. 3, 1939, p. 205-337)

AP
2
A 5
Eruption of Mauna Loa, Hawaii, in January.

(Am. Jour. of Sci., Ser. 3, Vol. 33, 1887,
pp.310-312)

AS
36
A 5
ERUPTIONS   NEW GUINEA

Stephens, Laura M.

The Mt. Lamington blast; one of the few survivors of an eruption unsurpassed in recent years
gives her account of the frightful day when a
cloud of incandescent gas claimed the lives of
over 3000 persons.

(Natural History, 62(5):217-223, 1953)

QK
1
A 75
ERYTHRINA

Krukoff, B. A.

Preliminary notes on Asiatic-Polynesian species of Erythrina.

(Journal of the Arnold Arboretum,Vol.XX,1939,
pp. 225-233)

QE
525.P
P 45
The eruption of Mt. Pelée 1929-1932.

Perret, Frank A.

G
51
W 17
ERUPTIONS   PAPUA

Eruption of Mt. Lamington, Papua, Jan. 21,
1951. 7 photos- captions (no other text).

(Walkabout, 17(6):21-28, 1951)

QK
1
B 15
ERYTHRINA

McClintock, Elizabeth

The cultivated species of Erythrina.

(Baileya, a Quarterly Journal of Horticultural
Taxonomy, Vol. 1(3):53-58, 1953)

QL
671
E 39   ERYTHRINA

Munro, George C.

Leahi Native Garden.

(Elepaio, Vol. XI(7):37-39, 1951)

AP
2
S 42   ERYTHROXYLUM COCA

Gutierrez-Nobriga, Carlos

The strange case of the coca leaf. By Carlos Gutierrez-Nobriga and Victor Wolfgang von Hagen.

(Scientific Monthly, 70(2):81-89, 1950)

and
GN
Ethn.Pam.
4268

QL
461
T 31   Esaki, Teiso

Die Cicadiden-Fauna der Karolinen.

(Tenthredo, Vol. 1, p. 1-8, 1936)
(Ergebnisse, Professor T. Esaki's Mikronesien-Expedition, 1936, Nr. 1)

and
QL
5
M 62

QK
Bot.Pam.
2898   ERYTHRINA

St. John, Harold

The relationship between the species of Erythrina (Leguminosae) native to Hawaii and Tahiti. Pacific plant studies 13.

(Webbia, Vol. XI:293-299, 1955)

SB
107
Ja
J24   ERZIEHUNG DER PFLANZEN

Jäger, H.

Die Erziehung der Pflanzen aus Samen: Ein Handbuch fur Gartenfreunde, Gartner und Samenhandler.

Erfurt, 1887, pp 421.

QL
5
M 62   Esaki, Teiso

Crabs injurious to crops. (Micronesian exp. reports, 2)

Esaki, Teiso
Results of the Micronesian Expedition, 1936-38, No. 17.

QK
1
W 37   ERYTHRINA   HAWAII

St. John, Harold

The relationship between the species of Erythrina (Leguminosae) native to Hawaii and Tahiti. Pacific Plant Studies 13.

(Webbia, Vol. XI:197-292, 1956)

QL
5
M 62   Esaki, Teiso

Bats of Ponape.

(source in Japanese, as well as text)

IN Esaki, Teizo Results of the Micronesian Expeditions, 1936-1940, No. 39

QL
5
M 62   Esaki, Teiso

Einige biologische Beobachtungen über die Bienen und Wespen Mikronesiens. (Mushi, Vol. 9, 1936, pp. 44-47)

Esaki, Teiso
Results of the Micronesian Expeditions, No. 4.

QK
1
W 37   ERYTHRINA   TAHITI

St. John, Harold

The relationship between the species of Erythrina (Leguminosae) native to Hawaii and Tahiti. Pacific Plant Studies 13.

(Webbia, Vol. XI:293-300, 1956)

QL
595.Mi
I 59   Esaki, Teiso   and others

Bibliography.
IN
Insects of Micronesia. Volume 2. Bibliography. By Teiso Esaki, S. H. Bryan, Jr. and J. L. Gressitt. 1955.

Published by Bernice P. Bishop Museum. R8vo.

QL
Insects
Pam.
1345   Esaki, Teiso

Curious habits of some Tipulids from the South Seas.

(Mushi, Vol. 13:80, 1941)

QK
1
C 2   ERYTHROPHYLLUM DELESSERIOIDES

Twiss, Wilfred Charles, 1868-
... *Erythrophyllum delesserioides* J. A. G. [i. e. J. Ag.] by Wilfred Charles Twiss. Berkeley, The University press, 1911.

cover-title, p. [159]-176. pl. 21-24. 27ᶜᵐ. (University of California publications in botany, vol. 4, no. 10)

"A thesis submitted in partial satisfaction of the requirements for the degree of Master of arts, University of California, May, 1910, but since amplified." p. [159]
"Publications referred to": p. 168.

1. Erythrophyllum delesserioides.

A 11-1310

Title from Univ. of Calif.   Library of Congress

QL
Insects
Pam.
1066   Esaki, Teiso

Tokunaga, Masaaki

Biting midges from the Micronesian Islands, with biological notes by Teiso Esaki.

QL
461
T 31
186)   (Tenthredo, Vol. III, No. 2, 1940, pp. 166-

PL
Phil.Fam.
568
a,b,c   Esaki, Teiso

Enumeration of native names of land and marine animals of Palao. By Teiso Esaki and Shiro Murakami.

(Kagaka Nanyo, Vol. 1(3):128-137, 1939; Vol. 2(1):9-15, 1939; Vol. 3(2):89-95, 1940)

QL
1
C 15   ERYTHROPSIS

Kofoid, Charles Atwood, 1865-
On the orientation of *Erythropsis*, by Charles Atwood Kofoid and Olive Swezy. Berkeley, University of California press, 1917.

cover-title, p. [89]-102. illus. 27½ᶜᵐ. (University of California publications in zoology. v. 18, no. 6)

"Contribution from the Zoological laboratory and the Scripps institution of biological research of the University of California."
"Literature cited": p. 101-102.

1. Erythropsis. 2. Orientation. I. Swezy, Olive, 1878- joint author. II. Title.

A 18-101

Title from Univ. of Calif.   Library of Congress

QL
595.Mi
I 59   ESAKI, T.

Chûjô, Michio

Bostrychidae.
IN
Insects of Micronesia, Coleoptera
[Insects of Micronesia, Vol. 16(2):85-104, 1958]

(note at p. 85: "This represents, in part, Results of Professor T. Esaki's Micronesian Expeditions (1936-1940), No. 93)

DU
500
U 58   Esaki, Teiso

Fauna of injurious insects of the Japanese South Sea Islands and their control. (from Botany and Zoology, theoretical and applied: Shokubatsu oyabi Dobutsu, 8(1):724-80, 1940)
IN
U. S. Commercial Company. Economic survey of Micronesia. No. 20. 1946. 20 pp. translation

---

QK
97
E 58   ERYTHROXYLACEAE

Engler, Adolf

Das Pflanzenreich...IV. 134. 1907. (Heft 29) Erythroxylaceae, by O. E. Schulz.

QL
Insects
Pam.
1075   Esaki, Teiso

Tokunaga, Masaaki

Ceratopogonidae and Chironomidae from the Micronesian Islands, with biological notes by Teiso Esaki.

(Philippine Journal of Science, Vol. 71, 1940, pp. 205-230)

QL
461
T 31   Esaki, Teiso

Die Gerroidea Mikronesiens (Hemiptera-Heteroptera).

and
QL
5
M 62   (Tenthredo, Vol. 1, pp. 351-359, 1937)
(Ergebnisse, Professor T. Esaki's Mikronesien-Expedition, 1936, Nr. 9)

QL
461
M 98

Esaki, Teiso

Hemiptera Micronesica, I-III.

(Mushi, 15:69-76, 1943; 17:29-38, 1947;
22(13):73-86, 1951)

and
QL
Insect
Pam. 1659-III

QL
Mollusca
Pam.
882

Esaki, Teiso

Introduction of the African snail, Achatina
fulica, Ferrusac into Japan, esp. Micronesia,
and subsequent developments. By Teiso Esaki
and Keizo Takahashi.

(Kagaku Nanyo (Science of the South Seas),
4(3):16-25, 1942. Translation by Toyohi Okada)

Q
101
P 18

and
QL
Insects
Pam.
1341

Esaki, Teiso

A preliminary report on the entomological
survey of the Micronesian Islands under the
Japanese Mandate, with special reference to the
insects of economic importance.

IN Proc. Sixth Pac. Sci. Congress, 1939,
(California), Vol. 4, 1940, pp. 407-416.

QL
543
E 74

Esaki, Teiso   and others

Icones Heterocerorum Japonicorum in colori-
bus naturalibus. By Teiso Esaki, Syuti Issiki
Akira Mutuura, Hiroshi Inoue, Masami Ogata,
Hiromu Okagaki and Hiroshi Kuroko. Hoikusha.
Osaka. 1957, and also 1958 edition. 8vo.

QL
Insects
Pam.
1343

Esaki, Teiso

The myrmecophilous beetles of the South
Seas.

(Mushi, Vol. 13:114, 1941)

QL
Insect
Pam.
802

Esaki, Teiso

A Remarkable Speo-halophilous Water-strider
(Heteroptera, Mesoveliidae).

(From Annals and Magazine of Natural History
Ser. 10, iv. p. 341, October 1929, 8 pages).

QL
5
M 62

and
QL
Insects
Pam.
1073

Esaki, Teiso

Injurious Arthopoda to man in Mandated South
Sea Islands of Japan (First Report). (Volumen
Jubilare pro Prof. Sadao Yoshida, Osaka, 1939, p.
230-252)

Esaki, Teiso
Results of the Micronesian Expedition, 1937-
1938, No. 16.

QL
1
T 64

Esaki, T.

A new species of the Cicadidae from Formosa (Hemiptera)

(Annotationes Zool. Japonenses, Vol. 14:29-
30, pl. 3, 1933)

Esaki, Teiso   (Temporary ca.)

Results of the Micronesian Exp., 1936-1940

Missing nos. are 8,25,40,43,45,49,56,64,73

either not yet printed or destroyed in the
war.

See next card

QL
Insects
Pam.1342

Esaki, Teiso

Injurious insects of the South Sea islands
and their control.

(Botany and Zoology, Vol. 8(1):274-280, 1940)

QL
461
T 31

and
QL
Insects
Pam.1072

Esaki, Teiso

A new species of Cicadidae from the Caroline Islands.

(Tenthredo, Vol. II, 1939, p. 231-233)

QL
5
M 62

(Esaki, Teiso)

(Results of the Micronesian Expedition,
1937-38)
1:Die Cicadiden-Fauna der Karolinen, von
Teiso Esaki.
2: Das Vorkommen der charontiden Amblypygi
auf den Palau-Inseln, von Teiso Esaki.
3: Two plume-moths of the Palau Islands collected by Professor Teiso Esaki in 1936, by
Hiroshi Hori.
4: Einige Biologische Beobachtungen über die
Bienen und Wespen Mikronesiens, von Teiso Esaki.

continued on next card.

Card 1

QL
5
M 62

Esaki, Teiso

Injurious insects to cotton in Mandated
South Sea Islands of Japan (First Report).
(Kontyu, Vol. XI, 1937, pp. 164-169)

Esaki, Teiso
Results of the Micronesian Expedition, 1937-
1938, No. 7

QL
Insect
Pam.
1656

Esaki, Teiso

Notes and records on some important pests of
Micronesia mostly introduced during the period
under Japanese mandate.

(Reprinted from Trans. Ninth Int. Congr.
Ent., Vol. 1:813-818, 1952)

QL
5
M 62

(Esaki, Teiso)

(Results of the Micronesian Expedition,
1937-38)
5: A new biting midge from the Palau Islands
with its biological notes, by Masaaki Tokunaga...
6: Some Aleyrodidae, Aphididae, Coccidae...
from Micronesia, by Ryoichi Takahashi.
7: Injurious insects to cotton in Mandated
South Sea Islands of Japan ...by Teiso Esaki.
8: Catalogue Coleoptera Japonicorum, II:
Lucanidae, by Y. Miwa... (not present in BM)

continued on next card

Card 2

QL
5
M 62

Esaki, Teiso

Insects injurious to cucurbits in Mandated
South Sea Islands of Japan (First Report)
(A ki tu, Vol. 1, No. 1, 1937, pp. 1-6)

(Esaki, Teiso)
Results of the Micronesian Expedition, 1937-
1938, No. 10.

QL
461
M 98

Esaki, Teiso

Notes on Hermatobates haddonii Carpenter.

(Mushi, Vol. 18 (7):49-51, 1947)

QL
5
M 62

(Esaki, Teiso)

(Results of the Micronesian Expedition,
1937-38)
9:Die Gerroidea Mikronesiens...by Teiso Esaki
10: Insects injurious to cucurbits...by
Tesio Esaki.
11:Sphecoidea of Micrnesia...by Keizo Yasumatsu.
12. Ein neuer, Halophiler Käfer...by Hiromichi Kono...

continued on next card

Card 3

QL
555.Mi
I 59

Esaki, Teiso

Insects of Micronesia, Bibliography.
By Teiso Esaki, E. H. Bryan, Jr. and J. L. Gres-
sitt.
IN

Insects of Micronesia, Vol. 2, 1955.
Bishop Museum Press.   Honolulu

QL
1
T 64

and
QL
Insects
Pam.
1071

Esaki, Teiso

The occurrence of a Mutillid wasp in Micronesia.

(Annotationes Zool. Japonenses, 17:431-432,
1938) Results of the Micronesian Expedition,
1937-1938, No. 15.

QL
5
M 62

(Esaki, Teiso)

(Results of the Micronesian Expedition,
1937-38)
13:Descriptions of two hispid-beetles...
by Michio Chujo.
14:Notes on decapod crustaceans collected by
Prof. Tesio Esaki...by Sadayoshi Miyake.
15:The occurrence of a mutillid wasp in
Micronesia, by Teiso Esaki.
16:Injurious Arthopoda...by Teiso Esaki.
17: Crabs injurious to crops, by Teiso Esaki.

continued on next card

Card 4

QL 5 M 62   (Esaki, Teiso)   Card 5

(Results of the Micronesian Expedition, 1937-1938)

18:Notes on Crustacea Brachyura collected by Prof. Teiso Esaki's Micronesian Expeditions... by Sadayoshi Miyake.

QL 5 M 62   Esaki, Teiso

Results of the Micronesian Expedition, 1937-1938.

20:Revision on marine craneflies (Tipulidae) with descriptions of some species. By Masaaki Tokunaga.

(Kontyû, Vol. 14, no. 4, pp. 133-148, 1940)

QL 5 M 62   Esaki, Teiso

Results of the Micronesian Expedition, 1937-1938.

32: Micronesian Desmidiaceae. By Hisanao Yamaguti.

(source in Japanese ????)

QL 5 M 62   Esaki, Teiso

Results of the Micronesian Expedition, 1937-1938.

26: A description of the adult and larval stages of a new species of Palaemonetes from the Marianne Islands. By Robert Gurney.

(Annotationes Zool. Japonenses, Vol. 18(2): 145-150, 1939)

---correction, ibid, 19:80, 1940

QL 5 M 62   Esaki, Teiso

Results of the Micronesian Expedition, 1937-1938,:

19: Injurious insects to coconut palm in the Mandated South Sea Islands of Japan, 1. Furcaspis oceanica Lindinger. By Teiso Esaki.

(Oyo-Kontyu, Vol. 2, No. 1, pp. 1-44, 1939)

QL 5 M 62   Esaki, Teiso

Results of the Micronesian Expedition, 1937-1938.

33: Sphecoidea of Micronesia, II. Crabronidae (Hymenoptera). By Keizo Yasumatsu.

(Mushi, Vol. 12:153-155, 1939)

QL 5 M 62   Esaki, Teiso

Results of the Micronesian Expedition, 1937-1938.

25: Hippoboscidae of the Caroline Islands (including the Palau Group). By Joseph Bequaert

(Mushi, Vol. 12(2):81-82, 1939)

QL 5 M 62   Esaki, Teizo

Results of the Micronesian Expedition, 1937-1938.

27:A new species of Cicadidae from the Caroline Islands.

(Tenthredo, Vol. 2(3):231-233, 1939)

QL 5 M 62   Esaki, Teizo

Results of the Micronesian Expedition, 1937-1938.

34: Apoidea of Micronesia, II: Ceratinidae. By Keizo Yasumatsu.

(Tenthredo, Vol. 2:344-347, 1939)

QL 5 M 62   Esaki, Teizo

Results of the Micronesian Expedition, 1937-1938.

24: Apoidea of Micronesia (Hymenoptera) By Keizo Yasumatsu.

(Tenthredo, Vol. 2:329-338, 1939)

QL 5 M 62   Esaki, Teizo

Results of the Micronesian Expedition, 1937-1938.

28: Polychaetous annelids collected by Prof. Teizo Esaki at Kusaie and Korror in the Carolines, South Sea Islands. By Shiro Okuda

(Annotationes Zoologicae Jponenses, Vol. 13 (3):183-184, 1939)

QL 5 M 62   Esaki, Teizo

Results of the Micronesian Expedition, 1937-1938.

35:Arrhenurus toxopeusi Viets from the Palau Islands. By Tohru Uchida.

(Annotationes Zool. Japonenses, 18:213, 1939)

QL 5 M 62   Esaki, Teizo

Results of the Micronesian Expedition, 1937-1938.

23: Vespoidea of Micronesia (Hymenoptera) By Joseph Bequaert and Keizo Yasumatsu.

(Tenthredo, Vol. 2:313-328, 1939)

QL 5 M 62   Esaki, Teizo

Results of the Micronesian Expedition, 1937-1938.

29: A new Tingitid from Palau Islands. (Hemiptera) By Carl J. Drake.

(Mushi, Vol. 12(2):102-103, 1939)

QL 5 M 62   Esaki, Teizo

Results of the Micronesian Expedition, 1937-1938.

36: On some littoral shrimps collected from Micronesia. By Ituo Kubo.

(Journal of the Imperial Fisheries Inst., Vol. 34(1):77-99, 1940)

QL 5 M 62   Esaki, Teizo

Results of the Micronesian Expedition, 1937-1938.

22: Some Aleyrodidae, Aphididae, and Coccidae from Micronesia (Homoptera). by Ryoichi Takahashi.

(Tenthredo, Vol. 3:234-272, 1939)

QL 5 M 62   Esaki, Teizo

Results of the Micronesian Expedition, 1937-1938.

30: Some earthworms from the South Sea Islands. By Shinjiro Kobayashi

(Sci. Repts, Tohoku Imp. Univ., s4, Biol. Vol 15(1):1-5, 1940)

QL 5 M 62   Esaki, Teizo

Results of the Micronesian Expedition, 1937-1938.

37: On a collection of fishes from Nanyo, the Japanese Mandated Islands. By Albert W.C.T. Herre.

(Annotationes Zool. Japonenses, Vol. 18(4): 298-307, 1939)

QL 5 M 62   Esaki, Teizo

Results of the Micronesian Expedition, 1937-1938.

21: Ceratopogonidae and Chironomidae from the Micronesian Islands, with biological notes by Teizo Esaki. By Masaaki Tokunaga.

(Phil. Jour. Sci., 71:205-230, 1940)

QL 5 M 62   Esaki, Teizo

Results of the Micronesian Expedition, 1937-1938.

31: Two Trigona bees collected by Prof. Teiso Esaki on the Palau and East Caroline Islands. By Herbert F. Schwarz.

(Mushi, Vol. 12:151-152, 1939)

QL 5 M 62   Esaki, Teizo

Results of the Micronesian Expedition, 1937-1938.

38: Odonata-Anisoptera of Micronesia. By Syoziro Asahina.

(Tenthredo, Vol. 3:1-23, 1940)

QL 5 M 62

Esaki, Teizo
Results of the Micronesian Expedition, 1936-1939.
39: Bats of Ponape. By Teiso Esaki.
(? in Japanese, Vol. pp. 762-763)

QL 5 M 62

Esaki, Teizo
Results of the Micronesian Expedition, 1936-1940.
48: Evaniidae of Micronesia (Hymenoptera) by Keizo Yasumatsu.
(source in Japanese.)

QL 5 M 62

Esaki, Teizo
Results of the Micronesian Expedition, 1936-1940.
57: Eine neue Köcherfliege, Triaenodes esakii con den Palau-Inseln. By Matsunae Tsuda
(Annot. Zool. Japon., Vol. 20(2):121-122, 1941)

QL 5 M 62

Esaki, Teizo
Results of the Micronesian Expedition, 1937-1939.
41: Thysanoptera of Micronesia. By Mikio Kurosawa.
(Tenthredo, Vol. 3:45-57, 1940)

QL 5 M 62

Esaki, Teizo
Results of the Micronesian Expedition, 1936-1940.
50: Notes on some Chalcidoids from the Micronesian Islands with descriptions of two new Eucharids. By Tei Ishii.
(Annot. Zool. Japon, Vol. 20(2):106-108, 1941)

QL 461 M 98

Esaki, Teizo
Results of Prof. Tesio Esaki's Micronesia Expeditions 1936-1940. No. 58: Sphecoidea of Micronesia, III. Family Larridae, by Keizo Yasumatsu.
(Mushi, Vol. 14:44-47, 1941)

QL 5 M 62

Esaki, Teizo
Results of the Micronesian Expedition, 1936-1939.
42: Biting midges from the Micronesian Islands, with biological notes by Teiso Esaki.
(Tenthredo, Vol. 3:166-186, 1940)

QL 5 M 62

Esaki, Teizo
Results of the Micronesian Expedition, 1936-1940.
53: Studies on the Decapod Crustaceans of Micronesia. III. Porcellanidae, by Sadayoshi Miyake
(Palao Tropical Biological Station, Studies Vol. 2(3):329-379, 1942)

QL 5 M 62

Esaki, Teizo
Results of the Micronesian Expedition, 1936-1940.
59: Chrysomelid-beetles of Micronesia. By Michio Chûjô.
(Mem. Fac. of Sci. and Agric., Taihoku Imp. Univ., Entomology No. 12, 1943) pp.281-334

QL 5 M 62

Esaki, Teiso
Results of the Micronesian Expedition, 1936-1939.
43: Dermatteri della Micronesia. By Carlo Menozzi.
(Mushi, Vol. 13:73-80, 1941)

QL 5 M 62

Esaki, Teizo
Results of the Micronesian Expedition, 1936-1940.
51: Materials of the Micronesian higher Fungi. by Rokuya Imazeki.
(The Journal of Japanese Botany, Vol. 17(3): 57-66, 1941. Also paged 175-184)

QL 5 M 62

Esaki, Teizo
Results of the Micronesian Expedition, 1936-1940.
60: Apoidea of Micronesia, III. Records of the genera Megachile, Heriades, Ceratina and Prosopis. By Keizo Yasumatsu.
(Tenthredo, Vol. 3(4):335-348, 1942)

QL 5 M 62

Esaki, Teizo
Results of the Micronesian Expedition, 1936-1939.
44: Tipulidae from the Japanese Mandated South Sea Islands (Diptera). By Charles P. Alexander.
(Annotationes Zool. Japonenses, Vol. 19: 198-221, 1940)

QL 5 M 62

Esaki, Teizo
Results of the Micronesian Expedition, 1936-1940.
52: Die Opiliones Mikroneusiens. By Seisyo Suzuki.
(Annot. Zool. Japon. Vol. 20, No. 2:98-103, 1941)

QL 5 M 62

Esaki, Teizo
Results of the Micronesian Expedition, 1936-1940.
61: Some Species of Aleyrodidae, Aphididae and Coccidae in Micronesia. By Ryoichi Takahashi
(Tenthredo, Vol. 3(4):349-358, 1942)

QL 5 M 62

Esaki, Teizo
Results of the Micronesian Expedition, 1936-1939.
46: Two interesting Scelionidae from Micronesia with biological notes by Prof. T. Esaki.
(Trnas. Nat. Hist. Soc. Formosa, Vol. 31, No. 209:76-83, 1941)

QL 5 M 62

Esaki, Teizo
Results of the Micronesian Expedition, 1936-1940.
54: Biting Ceratopogonid midges from the Caroline Islands. By Masaaki Tokunaga.
(Annot. Zool. Japon, Vol. 20(2):109-117, 1941)

QL 5 M 62

Esaki, Teizo
Results of the Micronesian Expedition, 1936-1940.
62: Beitrag zur Kenntnis der Echthromorpha-fauna Mikronesiens (Hym., Ichneumonidae). By Keizo Yasumatsu
(Ins. Mats., Vol. 15(4):141-145, 1941)

QL 5 M 62

Esaki, Teizo
Results of the Micronesian Expedition, 1936-1939.
47: Beitrage zur Kenntnis der Ameisenfauna Mikronesiens, 1. Die Ameisengattung Anochetus Mayr der Karolinen. By Keizo Yasumatsu.
(Ann. Zool. Japonenses, Vol. 19:312-315, 1940)

QL 5 M 62

Esaki, Teizo
Results of the Micronesian Expedition, 1936-1940.
55: Some species of Aleyrodidae, Aphididae, and Coccidae from Micronesia (Homoptera). By Ryoichi Takahashi.
(Tenthredo, Vol. 3(3):208-220, 1941)

QL 461 M 98

Esaki, Teizo
Results of Prof. T. Esaki's Micronesia Expeditions 1936-1940, No. 63: Coleoptera of Micronesia, I-II.
(Mushi, Vol. 14:81-86, 1942)

QL
5
M 62

Esaki, Teizo

    Results of the Micronesian Expeditions, 1936-1940.
    65: Zur Kenntnis der Aphodiiden aus Mikronesiens, (Coleoptera:Scarabaeidae). By Sizumu Nomura.

    (Mushi, Vol. 15:77-82, 1943)

QL
5
M 62

Esaki, Teizo

    Results of the Micronesian Expedition, 1936-1940.
    74: Collembola von Mikronesien. By Hajime Uchida.

    (Bull. Tokyo Science Museum, No. 17, 1944, pp. 1-24)

QL
Insects
Pam.
1093

Esaki, Teizo

Yasumatsu, Keizo

    Two interesting Scelionidae from Micronesia with biological notes by Prof. T. Esaki.

    (Trans. Nat. Hist. Soc. Formosa, Vol. 31, 1941, No. 209, pp. 76-83)

QL
5
M 62

Esaki, Teizo

    Results of the Micronesian Expedition, 1936-1940.
    66: Notes on some Micronesian Elasmidae and Eucharidae (Hymenoptera, Chalcidoidea), by Keizo Yasumatsu

    (Ins. Mats., Vol. 16(3/4):151-158, 1942)

QL
5
M 62

Esaki, Teizo

    Results of the Micronesian Expeditions, 1936-1940.
    75: Hemiptera Micronesica, II. Cicadidae. By Teizo Esaki.

    (Mushi, Vol. 17:29-38, 1947)

QL
Insects
Pam.1015

Esaki, Teiso

    Uebersicht uber die Insektenfauna der Bonin (Ogasawara)-Inseln, unter besonderer Berucksichtigung der Zoogeographischen Faunencharaktere.

    (Bull. Biogeographical Soc. of Japan, 1930, Vol. I, pp. 205-226)

QL
5
M 62

Esaki, Teizo

    Results of the Micronesian Expedition, 1936-1940.
    67/68: Hemiptera Micronesica, I. Nabidae. By Teizo Esaki and Tamotsu Ishihara.

    (Mushi, Vol. 15:69-76, 1943)

QL
5
M 62

Esaki, Teizo

    Results of the Micronesian Expedition, 1936-1940.
    76: A new tingid from Yap Island. By Carl J Drake

    (Mushi, Vol. 17(6):27-28, 1946)

QL
1
T 64

Esaki, Teiso

    Undescribed Hemiptera from Japan and Formosa.

    (Annotationes Zool. Japonenses, 13:259-269)

QL
461
M 98

Esaki, Teizo

    Results of the Micronesia Expeditions, 1936-1940, No. 69: Some Chalcidoid parasites of Saissetia nigra and S. hemisphaerica in Micronesia. (Hymenoptera), by Keizo Yasutmatsu and Seiichiro Yoshimura.

    (Mushi, Vol. 16:29-34, 1945)

QL
5
M 62

Esaki, Teizo

    Results of the Micronesian Expeditions, 1936-1940.
    77: Noctuidae of Micronesia (Lepidoptera). By Ichio Fukushima.

    (Mushi, Vol. 18(1):1-22, 1947)

QL
5
M 62

Esaki, Teizo

    Das Vorkommen der charontiden-Amblypygi auf den Palau-Inseln. (Lansania, Vol. 8, 1936, p. 79-80)

Esaki, Teizo.
    Results of the Micronesian Expedition, No.2.

QL
461
M 98

Esaki, Teizo

    Results of Prof. Teiso Esaki's Micronesia Expeditions 1936-1940. No. 70: Vespoidea of Micronesia. 2.

    (Mushi, Vol. 16:35-45, 1945)

QH
1
P 11

Esaki, Teizo

    Results of the Micronesian Expeditions, 1936-1940.
    79. Vespoidea of Micronesia. 3. By Keizo Yasumatsu.
    (Pacific Science, Vol. 4:116-117, 1950)

QL
Insect
Pam.
1657

Esaki, Teizo

    A zoogeographical consideration of the insect fauna in the Pacific Islands.

    (Eighth International Congress of Entomology, pp. 1-7, 1950?)

QL
5
M 62

Esaki, Teizo

    Results of the Micronesian Expeditions, 1936-1940.
    71: Spiders of Micronesia, by Teizo Esaki.
    (Acta Arachnologica, Vol. 8 (1/2):1-5, 1943)

QL
5
M 62

Esaki, Teizo

    Spiders of Micronesia.

    (Acta Arachnologica, Vol. 8 (1/2):1-5, 1943)

    IN Esaki, Teizo Results of the Micronesian Expeditions, 1936-1940, No. 71

AS
763
B 74

QL
Insect Pam.
927

Reading
Room

Esben-Petersen, P.

    Check list of Neuroptera Planipennia of Oceania.

    (B. P. Bishop Museum, Occ. Papers, vol. XIII, no.5. 1937. pp. 45-60)

QL
5
M 62

Esaki, Teizo

    Results of the Micronesian Expeditions, 1936-1940.
    72: Note on some Micronesian Braconidae. By Chihisa Watanabe.

    (Mushi, Vol. 16(9):47-58, 1945)

QL
Insect
Pam.
1658

Esaki, Teizo

    A tentative catalogue of Jassoidea of Japan, and her adjacent territories. By Teizo Esaki and Syusiro Ito. Published by the Japan Society for the Promotion of Science. Tokyo. 1954. 8vo. 315 pp.

AS
145
B

Esben-Petersen, P.   and others

    Neuroptera

Van Straelen, V.
    Resultats scientifiques du voyage aux Indes Orientales Néerlandaises...Léopold de Belgique, Vol. 4, Fasc. 2, 1931, pp. 1-15

    (Mem. hors ser. Mus. Roy. d'Hist. Nat., Belgique)

AS
763
B-b

Esben-Petersen, P.

Neuroptera from the Marquesas.

(Bernice P. Bishop Museum, Bull. No. 142, pp. 13-18) Issued Jan. 2, 1935. Pac. Ent. Survey Publication, 8, Art. 2.

GN
2.1
A4

Eschatology

Frazer, James G.

On certain burial customs as illustrative of the primitive theory of the soul. In Journ. Roy. Anth. Inst. XV, 1885-1886. pp 64-104.
Also separate.

ESENBECKIA.

AS
36
S2

Krause, Kurt *i. e.* Albrecht Emil Kurt, 1883-

... A new shrub of the genus *Esenbeckia* from Colombia, by Dr. K. Krause ... Washington, Smithsonian institution, 1913.

1 p. l., 1 p. 24½ᵐᵐ. (Smithsonian miscellaneous collections, v. 61, no. 16)
Publication 2243.

1. Esenbeckia. 2. Shrubs—Colombia.

Library of Congress   QK495.E85K8

——— Copy 2.   13-35783

AS
763
B-b

Esben-Petersen, P.

Neuroptera from the Society Islands.

(Bernice P. Bishop Museum, Bull. 142, pp. 137-142. Issued June 8, 1935. Pacific Ent. Survey Publication 8, Art. 11)

QE
1
G3

Escher, B. G.

Relations between the mechanism of the formation of fault troughs and volcanic activity.

(Bull. Geol. Soc. of America, Vol. 63:749-756, 1952)

[Africa, not Hawaii, discussed]

QL
627
P55

Esguerra, Ricardo S.

Enumeration of algae in Philippine bangos fishponds and in the digestive track of the fish with notes on conditions favorable for their growth.

(The Philippine Journal of Fisheries, Vol. 1(2):171-192, 1951)

QL
671
C74

Escalante, Rodolfo

Some records of oceanic birds in Uruguay.

(Condor, 61(2):158-159, 1959)

GN
1
An

Eschlimann, Henri

L'enfant chez les Kuni (Nouvelle Guinée anglaise).

(Anthropos. Bd. VI. 1911. pp. 260-275)

Am
10
A71
(5)

ESKIMOS

American museum of natural history, *New York*.

The Stokes paintings representing Greenland Eskimo. A description of the mural decorations of the Eskimo Hall given to the American museum of natural history by Arthur Curtiss James ... New York, The museum, 1909.

18 p. illus., plan. 24ᵐᵐ. (*Its* Guide leaflet series no. 30)

1. Stokes, Frank Wilbert. 2. Eskimos.

Library of Congress   E99.E7A5

12-21741

AS
36
A4

ESCENIUS HAWAII

Chapman, Wilbert M.

Review of the fishes of the Blennioid genus Escenius, with descriptions of five new species. By Wilbert M. Chapman and Leonard P. Schultz (Proc. U. S. Nat. Mus., Vol. 102:507-528, 1952)

QL
737.C4
F64

L.7.21

Eschricht Professor

v. *Flower Ed. Hy.*

Recent memoirs on the Cetacea...
Ed. by W. H. Flower.
London, 1866.

GN
673
K13

ESKIMOS

Birket-Smith, Kaj

Eskimoerne. Udgivet af Det Grønlandske Selskab med tilskud fra Carlsbergfondet og Ministeriet for Grønland. Rhodos. 1961. 301 pp. 4to.

AS
36
A4

ESCENIUS PACIFIC

Chapman, Wilbert M.

Review of the fishes of the Blennioid genus Escenius, with descriptions of five new species. By Wilbert M. Chapman and Leonard P. Schultz (Proc. U. S. Nat. Mus., Vol. 102:507-528, 1952)

DU
12
K87
locked
case

Eschscholtz, Fr

Review of the zoological collection.

Kotzebue, Otto von

A new voyage round the world, in...1823-1826 ... 2 vols. London. 1830. sm8vo. Vol. 2, pp. 325-362.

GN
550
S

GN
673
B66

ESKIMOS.

Boas, Franz, 1858-

... The central Eskimo. By Dr. Franz Boas.

(*In* U. S. Bureau of American ethnology. Sixth annual report, 1884-85. Washington, 1888. 29½ᵐᵐ. p. 399-669. illus., pl. II-X (incl. 2 fold. maps))

"Authorities quoted": p. 410-413.
"Poetry and music": p. 648-658.

separate

1. Eskimos. 2. Indians of North America—Music.

Library of Congress   E51.U55 6th

16-5502

GN
1
F

Eschatology

Holland, M. A. (Mrs.)

Influence of burial customs on the belief in a future state. In Folk-lore XXIX, 1918. pp 34-57.

QL
5
E74
locked
case

Eschscholtz, (Johann) Friedr(ich)

Zoologischer Atlas, enthaltend Abbildungen und Beschreibungen neuer Thierarten, während des Flottcapitains von Kotzebue zweiter Reise um die Welt, auf der Russisch-Kaiserlichen Kreigsschlupp Predpriaetiß in den Jahren 1823-1826. Hefte 1-5, 1829-1833. Berlin. G. Reimer. sm folio. viii + 17 + 13 + 18 + 19 + 28 pp., 25 pl.

AS
36
S3

ESKIMOS.

Bolles, Timothy Dix, *d.* 1892.

A preliminary catalogue of the Eskimo collection in the U. S. National museum, arranged geographically and by uses. By Lieut. T. Dix Bolles ...

(*In* U. S. National museum. Annual report. 1887. Washington, 1889. 23½ᵐᵐ. p. 335-365)

"... Intended ... as an introduction to a complete analysis of Eskimo art."

1. Eskimos. 2. U. S. National museum—Collections.

Library of Congress   Q11.U5 1887

——— Copy 2   14-19257

AS
750
N

Eschatology, Maori.

Best, Elsdon.

in N. Z. Inst. XXXVIII, 1905, pp. 148-239.

QL
401
N

ESCHSCHOLTZ, JOHANN FRIEDRICH

Baily, J. L.

The first Pacific conchologist.

(Nautilus, Vol. XLVIII, No. 3, Jan. 1935, pp. 73-75)

GN
2.F
W47

ESKIMOS

Collins, Henry B.

The origin and antiquity of the Eskimo.

(Smithsonian Report for 1950:423-467, 1951)

GN
Ethn.
Pam.
4036

ESKIMOS

Giddings, J. L., Jr.

Forest Eskimos, an ethnographic sketch of the Kobuk River people in the 1880's.

(The University Museum Bulletin, Philadelphia, Vol. 20, No. 2, 1956)

GF
501
S81

ESKIMOS

Steensby, H. P.

An anthropogeographical study of the origin of the Eskimo culture.

Kovenhavn, Bianco Lunos, 1916.   228p.

GN
Ethn.
Pam.
2810

ESKIMOS ALASKA

Shapiro, H. L.

The Alaskan Eskimo. A Study of the Relationship Between the Eskimo and the Chipewyan Indians of Central Canada.

(Anthropological Papers of the American Museum of Natural History, Vol. XXXI, Part VI, 1931. New York. pp. 347-384)

E
58
J 54

ESKIMOS

Jenness, Diamond

The Problem of the Eskimo.

Jenness, Diamond

The American Aborigines...pp. 371-396.

GN
673
S81

ESKIMOS

Steensby, H. P.

Om Eskimokulturens oprindelse: em etnografisk og antropogeografisk studie.

København, Salmonsens, 1905.   219p.

GN
2.M
F 45 1

ESKIMOS   PACIFIC

Quimby, George I.

Aleutian Islanders: Eskimos of the North Pacific.

(Chicago Nat. Hist. Museum, Anthropology Leaflet No. 35, 1944)

GN
Pam
2208

ESKIMOS

Kroeber, Alfred L.

The Eskimo of Smith Sound. From Bull. Amer. Mus. Nat. His. v.12, art.21, 1900.

GN
2M
A

ESKIMOS.

Stefánsson, Vilhjálmur, 1879–

... The Stefánsson-Anderson Arctic expedition of the American museum: preliminary ethnological report. By Vilhjalmur Stefánsson. New York, The Trustees, 1914.

1 p. l., 395 p. illus. fold. maps. 24½ᶜᵐ. (Anthropological papers of the American museum of natural history. vol. XIV, pt. I)

1. Eskimos.

Library of Congress   GN2.A27 vol. 14   19–14263
—— Copy 2.   E99.E7 S82
                                   J₁

ESKIMOS   ANTHROPOMETRY

see

ANTHROPOMETRY   ESKIMOS

AS
36
S5

ESKIMOS

Kumlien, Ludwig, 1853–1902.

Contributions to the natural history of Arctic America, made in connection with the Howgate polar expedition, 1877–78, by Ludwig Kumlien ... Washington, Govt. print. off., 1879.

AS
36
S2

179 p. 24ᵐᵐ. (Added t.-p.: ... Bulletin of the United States National museum. no. 15)

Issued also as vol. XXIII, art. 5, of the Smithsonian miscellaneous collections.

Smithsonian institution publication 342.

Contributions by Ludwig Kumlien and others.

1. Botany—Arctic regions. 2. Zoology—Arctic regions. 3. Eskimos. I. Howgate polar expedition, 1877–78.

S 13–124

Library, Smithsonian   Institution Q11.U6

GN
673
W 54

ESKIMOS

Weyer, Edward Moffat

The Eskimos...New Haven. Yale University Press. 1932. 8vo. xvii + 491 pp.

ESKIMOS   ART

see

ART   ESKIMOS

AS
36
S3

ESKIMOS.

Murdoch, John, 1852–

... A study of the Eskimo bows in the U. S. National museum. By John Murdoch.

(In U. S. National museum. Annual report. 1884. Washington, 1885. 23½ᵐᵐ. p. 307–316, 1 l. XII pl. (incl. map))

Descriptive letterpress on verso of each plate except the last.

Running title: Eskimo bows.

1. Bow and arrow. 2. Eskimos. 3. U. S. National museum—Collections. I. Title: Eskimo bows.

Library of Congress   Q11.U5 1884   14–19242
—— Copy 2.

ESKIMOS   ORIGINS

See

ORIGINS   ESKIMOS

GN
2.M
A

ESKIMOS--CANADA

Hrdlička, Aleš i. e. Alois Ferdinand, 1872–

... Contribution to the anthropology of central and Smith Sound Eskimo. By Aleš Hrdlička. New York, The Trustees, 1910.

1 p. l., p. 177–280. pl. IX–XXIII. 24½ᵐᵐ. (Anthropological papers of the American museum of natural history. vol. V, pt. II)

1. Eskimos—Canada. 2. Anthropometry—Eskimos.

11–18968

Library of Congress   GN2.A27 vol. 5, pt. 2

GN
673
R 64

ESKIMOS

Roberts, Helen H.

Eskimo songs: Songs of the copper Eskimos, by Helen H. Roberts and D. Jenness. Ottawa. 1925

Q
115
C 21

(Report of the Canadian Arctic Expedition, 1913–18; Southern Party-1913–16, Vol. XIV.)

GN
550
S

ESKIMOS--ALASKA.

Murdoch, John, 1852–

Ethnological results of the Point Barrow expedition. By John Murdoch, naturalist and observer, International polar expedition to Point Barrow, Alaska, 1881–1883.

(In U. S. Bureau of American ethnology. 9th annual report ... 1887–88. Washington, 1892. 29½ᵐᵐ. p. 3–441. illus., 2 maps)

List of works consulted: p. 20–25.

1. Barrow, Cape. 2. Eskimos—Alaska.

12–14314

Library of Congress   E51.U55 9th

ESKIMOS   ETHNOLOGY

see

ETHNOLOGY   ESKIMOS

GN
71
D 26

ESKIMOS

Ross, Sir John

Appendix to the narrative of a second voyage in search of a north-west passage and of a residence in the Arctic Regions during the years 1829–33, including the reports of James Clark Ross and the discovery of the Northern Magnetic Pole.

London. 1835.

Davis, J. B.

Collection of papers on craniology...Vol. 3, No. 4.

GN
550
S

ESKIMOS--ALASKA.

Nelson, Edward William, 1855–

The Eskimo about Behring Strait, by Edward William Nelson.

(In U. S. Bureau of American ethnology. Eighteenth annual report, 1896–97. Washington, 1899. 29½ᵐᵐ. pt. 1, p. 3–518. illus., CVII pl. (incl. fold. map))

1. Eskimos—Alaska. I. Title.

1-5533

Library of Congress   E51.U55 18th

ESKIMOS   FISHING

see

FISHING   ESKIMOS

ESKIMOS   FOLKLORE

see

FOLKLORE   ESKIMOS

ESKIMOS--SIBERIA.

aa
36
A6

Bogoras, Vladimir Germanovich, 1864–

... The Eskimo of Siberia, by Waldemar Bogoras.
Leiden, E. J. Brill ltd.; New York, G. E. Stechert & c°,
1913.

cover-title, p. 417–456. 36ᶜᵐ. (Memoir of the American museum of
natural history. ᵥₒₗ. xiii)

Publications of the Jesup north Pacific expedition. vol. VIII, pt. III.

Contents.—Folk-tales.—Songs.—Text: The one-who-finds-nothing.

1. Folk-lore, Eskimo. 2. Eskimos — Siberia. 3. Eskimo language —
Texts.

16–108

Library of Congress   QH1.A43 vol. 12

QL
45
E77

Esper, Eugenius Johann Christoph

Fortsekungen der pflanzenthiere in abbildungen nach der natur. Theil I, II

Nurnberg, 1797. 2v.

*Where is this? Can find only
Bd I of "Die Pflanzenthiere" at this
Shelf number, 4th Aug., it to QL 375
E 77.*

GN
Pam
2371

ESKIMOS - GREENLAND

Boas, Franz

The relationships of the Eskimos of
East Greenland. From Science, n.s. v.30,
n.772, 1909.

ESKIMOS   SOCIAL LIFE

see

SOCIAL LIFE   ESKIMOS

QL
375
E 77

Esper, Eugenius Johann Christoph

Die Pflanzenthiere in Abbildungen nach der
Natur mit Farben erleuchtet nebst Beschreibungen.
Theil I-III. Nurnberg. Raspeschen Buchhandlung.
1791-1794. 4to.

GN
2M
A

ESKIMOS--GREENLAND.

Wissler, Clark, 1870–

... Archaeology of the Polar Eskimo, by Clark Wissler
... New York, The Trustees, 1918.

1 p. l., p. 105–166 incl. illus., pl. fold. map. 24½ᶜᵐ. (Anthropological
papers of the American museum of natural history, vol. XXII, pt. III)

1. Greenland—Antiq. 2. Eskimos—Greenland. ɪ. Title.

19–6011

Library of Congress   GN2.A27 vol. XXII, pt. III
⟨5⟩

ESKIMOS   STRING FIGURES

see

STRING FIGURES   ESKIMOS

DU
12
B 75
looked
case

Bougainville, L. A. de

Journal de la navigation autour du globe de
la frégate la Thétis et de la corvette l'Espérance
pendant les années 1824-1826...2 vols. Paris.
1837. 4to.
Atlas. Folio.

L'ESPÉRANCE (SHIP)

ESKIMOS   IMPLEMENTS AND UTENSILS

see

IMPLEMENTS AND UTENSILS   ESKIMOS

DU
605
E 75

Eskridge, Robert Lee

Manga Reva: the Forgotten Islands. With
illustrations by the author. Indianapolis.
The Bobbs-Merrill Company. 1931 c. 8vo. 286pp.

DU
12
L 11
looked
case

Labillardière, J. J. de

An account of a voyage in search of La
Pérouse...1791-1793, in the Recherche and Esper-
ance...under the command of Rear-Admiral Bruni d'
Entrecasteaux. Translated from the French...
Vols. 1-2. Second edition. London. 1802. 8vo.

ESPERANCE (SHIP)

GN
550
S

ESKIMOS LANGUAGE--BIBL.

Pilling, James Constantine, 1846–1895.

Bibliography of the Eskimo language, by James Constantine Pilling. Washington, Govt. print. off., 1887.

v, 116 p. incl. facsims. 24½ᶜᵐ. (Smithsonian institution. Bureau of
ethnology. ⟨Bulletin, no. 1⟩)

Title vignette.

1. Eskimo language—Bibl.

1—13568

Library of Congress   E51.U6 no. 1
———— Copy 2.   Z7119.E7P6

GR
385.H
C 97

Curtis, Caroline

Pikoi and other legends of the island of
Hawaii. Collected or suggested by Mary Kawena
Pukui; retold by Caroline Curtis; illustrated by
Robert Lee Eskridge. Printed and published by
Kamehameha Schools Press. 1949c. 8vo. 282 pp.

Eskridge, Robert Lee

DU
12
L 11
looked
case

Labillardière, J. J. de

Relation du voyage a la recherche de La
Pérouse...1791, 1792... Tomes 1-2 and atlas.
Paris. n.d. (1800 ?) 4to and folio.

ESPERANCE (SHIP)

ESKIMOS   MUSIC

see

MUSIC   ESKIMOS

QK
Botany
Pam.
1247

Esmarch, Ferdinand

Beitrag zur Cyanophyceenflora unsrer
Kolonien. From Hamburg.Wissens.Anstalt.
Jahrb. XXVII, 1910, Beiheft 3, pp. 63-82)

QK
266
D 56

Espinosa, Reinaldo   tr anslator

Diels, Ludwig

Contribuciones al conocimiento de la vegetacion y de la flora del Ecuador. Version castellana del Reinaldo Espinosa, de la edicion de
Stuttgart, 1937. Quito. Imp. de la Univ. Central. 1939   364 pp. R8vo.

AP
2
S 35

ESKIMOS   ORIGIN

Laughlin, William S.

Eskimos and Aleuts: their origins and
evolution.

(Science, Vol. 142(3593):633-645, 1963)

G
3
A 1

Espenshade, Ada

A program for Japanese fisheries.

(Geographical Review, Vol. 39(1):76-85, 1949)

G
7
R 91

ESPIRITU SANTO (NEW HEBRIDES)

Baker, John R.

Espiritu Santo, New Hebrides: a paper read
at the evening meeting of the society on 10
December, 1934, by John R. Baker.

(Geographical Journal. Royal Geographical
Society. London. Vol. 85. No. 3. March 1935.
pp. 209-233)

GN
671.N 55
G 94

ESPIRITU SANTO

Guiart, Jean

Grands et petits hommes de la montagne,
Espiritu Santo (Nouvelles-Hébrides). Office
de la Recherche Scientifique et Technique Outre-
Mer. Institut Francais d'Océanie. (New Caledonia) 4to. mimeographed. 218 pp. 1956

QK
1
L 2

ESPIRITU SANTO

Guillaumin, A(ndré)

A florula of the island of Espiritu Santo,
one of the New Hebrides. (Prefatory note by
John R.Baker.)

(Journal of the Linnean Soc. of London,
Botany, Vol. 51, 1938, pp. 547-566)

GN
2.S
P 76

ESPIRITO SANTO

Miller, J. Graham

Naked cult in central west Santo.

(Journal of the Poly. Soc., Vol. 57:330-341
1948)

Microfilm
no. 111

ESPIRITU SANTO

Report of students' trak in the hinterland
of south Espiritu Santo, 1947.

ESPIRITO SANTO   BIRDS

See

BIRDS   ESPIRITO SANTO

ESPIRITO SANTO   CARVING

See

CARVING   ESPIRITO SANTO

PL
Phil.
pam.
206

ESPIRITO SANTO   VOCABULARY

Ray, Sidney H.

Vocabulary of the Tangoa dialect, Espiritu
Santo, New Hebrides (Bijdragen tot de Tall-
Land- en Volkenkunde van Ned. - Indie, 5e volgr.,
VIIe deel. n.d.)

Z
Bib.Pam.
39

Essai de Bibliographie Piopucienne...

Alazard, Ildefonse (Père)

DU
870
E 78

Essai sur l'isle d'Otahiti, situee
dans la Mer du Sud; et sur l'esprit
et les moeurs de ses habitans.

Avignon, 1779. 125p.

QH
9
S 77

Essays and papers in memory of late president Fu Ssu-Nien, National Taiwan University.
Taipei, Taiwan, December 1952. 4to. 575 pp.

[in Japanese with some English translations
or abstracts]

GN
22
K 93

&

GN
8
K 89

Essays in anthropology presented to A. L.
Kroeber in celebration of his sixtieth birthday
June 11, 1936. Univ. of California Press, Ber-
keley. 1936. R8vo. xxiii + 433 pp.

GC
26
H 23

Essays in the natural sciences in honor of
Captain Allan Hancock, on the occasion of his
birthday, July 26, 1955. University of
Southern California Press. Los Angeles. 8vo.
(1955) xii + 345 pp.

Q
171
F 64

Essays on museums and other subjects
connected with natural history.
Flower, William Henry
London, 1898, 8", pp. 394.

QL
1
C 15

and

QH
Nat
His
Pam #41

Essenberg, Christine Elizabeth, 1879–

...Description of some new species of *Polynoidae* from
the coast of California, by Christine Essenberg. Berkeley, University of California press, 1917.

cover-title, p. [45]–60. pl. 2–3. 27½ᶜᵐ. (University of California publications in zoology. v. 18, no. 3)

"Literature cited": p. 56.

1. Polynoidae.   I. Title.

A 17–1493

Title from Univ. of Calif.   Library of Congress

QL
1
C 15

Essenberg, Christine Elizabeth, 1879–

... The factors controlling the distribution of the *Polynoidae* of the Pacific coast of North America, by Christine
Essenberg. Berkeley, University of California press,
1918.

cover-title, p. [171]–238 incl. maps, tables. pl. 6–8 (pl. 6, fold.) 27½ᶜᵐ.
(University of California publications in zoology. v. 18, no. 11)

"Literature cited": p. 231–234.

1. Polynoidae.   I. Title.

A 18–346

Title from Univ. of Calif.   Library of Congress

QL
1
C 15

and

QH
Nat
His
Pam #42

Essenberg, Christine Elizabeth, 1879–

... New species of *Amphinomidae* from the Pacific
coast, by Christine Essenberg. Berkeley, University of
California press, 1917.

cover-title, p. [61]–74. pl. 4–5. 27½ᶜᵐ. (University of California publications in zoology. v. 18, no. 4)

"Literature cited": p. 70.

1. Amphinomidae.   I. Title.

A 17–1494

Title from Univ. of Calif.   Library of Congress

QL
1
C 15

and

QH
Nat
His
Pam #39

Essenberg, Christine Elizabeth, 1879–

... On some new species of *Aphroditidae* from the coast
of California, by Christine Essenberg. Berkeley, University of California press, 1917.

cover-title, p. [401]–430. pl. 31–37. 27ᶜᵐ. (University of California
publications in zoology. v. 16, no. 22)

"Literature cited": p. 416.

1. Aphroditidae.   I. Title.

A 17–364

Title from Univ. of Calif.   Library of Congress

QL
1
C 15

also

QH
Nat.hist
Pam.#44
(4to)

Essenberg, Christine Elizabeth, 1879–

... The pteropod *Desmopterus pacificus* sp. nov., by
Christine Essenberg. Berkeley, University of California
press, 1919.

cover-title, p. [85]–88. illus. 27½ᶜᵐ. (University of California publications in zoology. v. 19, no. 2)

"Literature cited": p. 88.

1. [Desmopteridae]   I. Title.

A 19–460

Title from Univ. of Calif.   Library of Congress
[4]

QL
Protozoa
& Poly
Pam
#22

Essenberg, Christine E.

Quantitative studies on inshore marine diatoms and dinoflagellates of
Southern California in 1920, ex Univ.
of California Pub. in Zool., vol. 22,
no. 5-6.

QH
Nat
Hist
Pam
#25

Essenberg, Christine E.

The seasonal distribution of the
appendicularia in the region of San
Diego, California, ex zoology, vol. III
no. 1, January, 1922.

ESSENTIAL OILS

See

Penfold, A. R.

GC
1
M 33

ESSEX (ship)

Cresswell, M.

Open boat voyages.

(The Marine Observer, Vol. 16, No.134, 1939, pp. 55-58)

DU
12
P 84

locked
case

ESSEX (SHIP)

Porter, David

A voyage in the South Seas, in the years 1812, 1813, and 1814. With particular details of the Gallipagos and Washington Islands. By Captain David Porter, of the American frigate, the Essex. London. 1823. 8vo.

QL
463
E 78

Essig, E. O.

College entomology. The MacMillan Co. New York. 1942. 8vo. vii + 900 pp.

QL
595.Mi
I 59

Essig, E. O.

Insects of Micronesia, Homoptera: Aphididae. IN

Insects of Micronesia, Vol. 6, No. 2, 1956. Published by the Museum. Honolulu. (Bishop Museum)

QL
473
E78

Essig, Edward Oliver

Insects of western North America.

New York, Macmillan, 1926. 1035p.

S
39.A
S 12

Essig, E(dward) O(liver)

Injurious and beneficial insects of California.

(Monthly Bull., State Commission of Horticulture, Vol. 2, nos. 1&2, 1913) California

---

AS
36
C3

Essig, Edward Oliver, 1884–
... Some Japanese *Aphididæ*, by E. O. Essig and S. I. Kuwana ... San Francisco, The Academy, 1918.

cover-title, p. [35]–112. illus. 26ᶜᵐ. (Proceedings of the California academy of sciences. 4th ser. vol. VIII, no. 3)

"Printed from the John W. Hendrie publication endowment."

1. Plant-lice. I. Kuwana, Shinkai Inokichi, joint author.
Aphididae
18-23451
Library of Congress Q11.C253 vol. VIII, no. 3

QH
Nat. Hist.
Pam.
200

Establishing a National Wilderness preservation system for the permanent good of the whole people, and for other purposes. Report together with Minority and separate views. July 27, 1961 Senate, U.S., 87th Congress, 1st Session. Report no. 635. 55 pp.

QH
431
E 79

Estabrook, Arthur Howard, 1885–
The Jukes in 1915, by Arthur H. Estabrook ... Washington, The Carnegie institution of Washington, 1916.

vii, 85 p. fold. diagrs. 29½ᶜᵐ. (On verso of t.-p.: Carnegie institution of Washington. Publication no. 240)

Paper no. 25 of the Station for experimental evolution at Cold Spring Harbor, New York.
"Historical note [sketch of Richard L. Dugdale]": p. v–vi.
"Literature cited": p. 85.

1. Defective and delinquent classes. 2. Heredity. 3. Juke family. 4. Dugdale, Richard Louis, 1841-1883. The Jukes. I. Title.
16–18515
Library of Congress HV6125.E8
———— Copy 2.

AS
540
P

Estampador, Eulogio P.

A check list of Philippine crustacean decapods.

(Philippine Journal of Science, Vol. 62, 1937, pp. 465-559)

AS
540
P

Estampador, Eulogio P.

Studies on Scylla (Crustacea: Portunidae), I. Revision of the genus.

(Philippine Jour. of Sci., Vol. 78(1):95-108, 1949)

DS
501
M 27

Estel, Leo A.

Racial origin in northern Indonesia.

(Journal of East Asiatic Studies, Univ. of Manila, II(3):1-20, 1953)

Estella, Bienvenido de

See

Bienvenido de Estella

QL
1
C15

Esterly, Calvin Olin, 1879–
Additions to the copepod fauna of the San Diego region, by Calvin Olin Esterly. Berkeley, The University press, 1906.

cover-title, p. [53]–92. pl. IX–XIV. 27ᶜᵐ. (University of California publications. Zoology. v. 3, no. 5)

At head of title: Contributions from the laboratory of the Marine biological association of San Diego. XII.
Bibliography: p. 80–81.

1. Copepoda.
A 11-2252 Revised
Title from Univ. of Calif. Library of Congress

QL
1
C 15

Esterly, Calvin Olin, 1879–
... The feeding habits and food of pelagic copepods and the question of nutrition by organic substances in solution in the water, by Calvin O. Esterly. Berkeley, University of California press, 1916.

cover-title, p. [171]–184. illus. 27½ᶜᵐ. (University of California publications in zoology, v. 16, no. 14)
"Literature cited": p. 183–184.

1. Copepoda. I. Title.
A 16-461 Revised
Title from Univ. of Calif. Library of Congress

QL
1
C1

Esterly, Calvin Olin, 1879–
... Fourth taxonomic report on the *Copepoda* of the San Diego region, by Calvin O. Esterly. Berkeley, University of California press, 1913.

cover-title, p. [181]–196. pl. 10-12. 27ᶜᵐ. (University of California publications in zoology, v. 11, no. 10)
Bibliography: p. 190.

1. Copepoda.
A 13-2602 Revised
Title from Univ. of Calif. Library of Congress

QL
1
C18

Esterly, Calvin O.

The free-swimming Copepoda of San Francisco Bay. Univ. Calif. Pub. Zool. Vol. 26, No.5, pp 81 - 129, 1924.

GC
Ocean
Pam
13

Esterly, C O

Investigations of zooplankton at the Scripps Institution of Oceanography. From Proc., Third Pan-Pacific Science Congress, Tokyo, 1926.

Q
Gen Sc
Pam
#17

Esterly, Calvin O.

Limitations of experiment in explaining natural habit, as illustrated by the diurnal migration, ex Science, vol. LII, no. 1344, Oct. 1, 1920.

QL
1
C15

Esterly, Calvin Olin, 1879–
... The occurrence and vertical distribution of the *Copepoda* of the San Diego region, with particular reference to nineteen species, by Calvin O. Esterly. Berkeley, University of California press, 1912.

cover-title, p. [253]–340. 3 fold. tab., diagrs. 27ᶜᵐ. (University of California publications in zoology, v. 9, no. 6)
Bibliography: p. 339–340.

1. Copepoda.
A 13-752 Revised
Title from Univ. of Calif. Library of Congress

QH
Nat
Hist
Pam
#40
4to

Esterly, Calvin O.

The occurrence of a rhythm in the geotropism of two species of plankton Copepods when certain recurring external conditions are absent, ex Univ. of California Pub. in Zool., vol. 16, no. 21, March 3, 1917.

QL 1 C 15 Esterly, Calvin Olin, 1879–

... The occurrence of a rhythm in the geotropism of two species of plankton copepods when certain recurring external conditions are absent, by Calvin O. Esterly. Berkeley, University of California press, 1917.

cover-title, p. [393]–400 incl. tables. 27ᶜᵐ. (University of California publications in zoology, v. 16, no. 21)

"Contribution from the Scripps institution for biological research." "Literature cited": p. 400.

1. Geotropism. 2. Copepoda.   i. Title.

A 17–269 Revised

Title from Univ. of Calif.   Library of Congress

QL 1 C15 Esterly, Calvin Olin, 1879–

... The structure and regeneration of the poison glands of *Plethodon*. By C. O. Esterly. Berkeley, The University press, 1904.

cover-title, p. [227]–268. pl. xx–xxiii (1 col. fold.) 27ᶜᵐ. (University of California publications. Zoology. v. 1, no. 7)

Bibliography: p. 255–259.

1. Plethodon. 2. Poison glands.

A 11–2255 Revised

Title from Univ. of Calif.   Library of Congress

AS 36 S Estes, L   O.

The antiquities on the banks of the Mississippi River and Lake Pepin. By Dr. L. C. Estes.

(*In* Smithsonian institution. Annual report. 1866. Washington, 1867. 23½ᶜᵐ. p. [366]–367)

1. Mounds—Minnesota.

S 15–195

Library of Congress   Q11.S66 1866
Library, Smithsonian   Institution

QL C1 Esterly, Calvin Olin, 1879–

... The pelagic *Copepoda* of the San Diego region, by C. O. Esterly. Berkeley, The University press, 1905.

cover-title, p. [113]–233. illus. 27ᶜᵐ. (University of California publications. Zoology. v. 2, no. 4)

At head of title: Contributions from the laboratory of the Marine biological association of San Diego. IV.
Bibliography: p. 227–233.

1. Copepoda.

A 11–2253 Revised

Title from Univ. of Calif.   Library of Congress

QL 1 C15 Esterly, Calvin Olin, 1879–

... The vertical distribution of *Eucalanus elongatus* in the San Diego region during 1909, by Calvin O. Esterly. Berkeley, The University press, 1911.

cover-title, 7 p. incl. tab. 27ᶜᵐ. (University of California publications in zoology, v. 8, no. 1)

Contribution from the laboratory of the Marine biological association of San Diego.
Bibliography: p. 7.

1. Eucalanus.

A 11–1862 Revised

Title from Univ. of Calif.   Library of Congress

AS 262 Tar   Esthonian Museum

See

Tartu . Eesti Rahva Muuseumi

QL 1 C 15 Esterly, Calvin O.

Preliminary statistical report on the occurrence of marine copepoda in the plankton at La Jolla, Calif. Univ. of Calif. Pub. in zoology, vol. 22, No. 10. 1923.

QL 1 C15 Esterly, Calvin Olin, 1879–

... Third report on the *Copepoda* of the San Diego region, by Calvin Olin Esterly. Berkeley, The University press, 1911.

cover-title, p. [313]–352. pl. 26–32. 27ᶜᵐ. (University of California publications in zoology, v. 6, no. 14)

Contributions from the laboratory of the Marine biological association of San Diego, XXXIII.
Bibliography: p. 338–339.

1. Copepoda.

A 11–931 Revised

Title from Univ. of Calif.   Library of Congress

GN 2.S P 76   Estimate of the Maori population in the North Island circa 1840.

(Jour. Poly. Soc., 24:72–74, 1915)

QL 1 C 15 Esterly, Calvin Olin, 1879–

... Reactions of various plankton animals with reference to their diurnal migrations, by Calvin O. Esterly. Berkeley, University of California press, 1919.

cover-title, p. [1]–83 incl. tables. 27½ᶜᵐ. (University of California publications in zoology, v. 19, no. 1)

"Literature cited": p. 81–83.

1. Phototropism. 2. Plankton.   i. Title.

A 19–348

Title from Univ. of Calif.   Library of Congress
[s19b3]

QL 1 C15 Esterly, Calvin Olin, 1879–

... A study of the occurrence and manner of distribution of the *Ctenophora* of the San Diego region, by Calvin O. Esterly. Berkeley, University of California press, 1914.

cover-title, p. [21]–38 incl. tables. 27ᶜᵐ. (University of California publications in zoology, v. 13, no. 2)

Contribution from the Scripps institution for biological research.
Bibliography: p. 38.

1. Ctenophora.

A 14–1002 Revised

Title from Univ. of Calif.   Library of Congress

GN 1 A 51   Estrada, Emilio

A complex of traits of probable transpacific origin on the coast of Ecuador. By Emilio Estrada and Betty J. Meggers.

(American Anthropologist, Vol. 63(5):913–939, 1961)

QL 1 C15 Esterly, Calvin Olin, 1879–

... Some observations on the nervous system of *Copepoda*, by C. O. Esterly. Berkeley, The University press, 1906.

cover-title, 12 p. II pl. 27ᶜᵐ. (University of California publications. Zoology. v. 3, no. 1)

Bibliography: p. 7–8.

1. Copepoda. 2. Nervous system.

A 11–2254 Revised

Title from Univ. of Calif.   Library of Congress

QL 1 C1 Esterly, Calvin Olin, 1879–

... The vertical distribution and movement of the *Schizopoda* of the San Diego region, by Calvin O. Esterly. Berkeley, University of California press, 1914.

cover-title, p. [123]–145 incl. tables. 27½ᶜᵐ. (University of California publications in zoology, v. 13, no. 5)

Contribution from the laboratory of the Scripps institution for biological research.
"Literature cited": p. 145.

1. Schizopoda.

A 14–1207 Revised

Title from Univ. of Calif.   Library of Congress

GN 2.I E 19   Estrada, Emilio

Correlaciones entre la arqueologia de la costa del Ecuador y Peru.

(Humanitas, II:2, 1961) pp. 31–73, 1961)

QL 1 C 15 Esterly, Calvin Olin, 1879–

... Specificity in behavior and the relation between habits in nature and reactions in the laboratory, by Calvin O. Esterly. Berkeley, University of California press, 1917.

cover-title, p. [381]–392 incl. tables. 27ᶜᵐ. (University of California publications in zoology, v. 16, no. 20)

"Contribution from the Scripps institution for biological research." "Literature cited": p. 391–392.

1. Heliotropism. 2. Adaptation (Biology) 3. Copepoda.   i. Title.

A 17–268 Revised

Title from Univ. of Calif.   Library of Congress

ESTERLY, CALVIN OLIN, 1881–JOINT AUTHOR

QL 1 C15 Bancroft, Frank Watts, 1871–

... A case of physiological polarization in the ascidian heart, by Frank W. Bancroft and C. O. Esterly. Berkeley, The University press, 1903.

cover-title, p. 105–114. 27ᶜᵐ. (University of California publications. Zoology. v. 1, no. 2)

Bibliography: p. 114.

1. Ascidians. 2. Heart.   i. Esterly, Calvin Olin, 1881–   joint author.

A 11–2247

Title from Univ. of Calif.   Library of Congress

GN Ethn. Pam. 4016   Estreicher, Z.

Chants et rythmes de la danse d'hommes Bororo. (Enregistrements Henry Brandt)

(reprint from Bull. Soc. Neuchateloise de Geographie, 51(5):57–93, 1954/55)

QH Nat Hist Pam #43 4to   Esterly, Calvin O.

Reactions of various plankton animals with reference to their diurnal migrations, ex Univ. of California Pub. in Zool., vol. 19, no. 1, April 4, 1919.

G 27 M   ESTEREOFOTOGRAMETRIA

R. Sociedad Geografica . Madrid

Conferencias ... Abril de 1924 . La estereofotogrametria en 1924.

Madrid, 1925, 87 pp., illus.

DU Pac Pam No.108   D'Estrey, Meyners

Deux tribus de la Nouvelle-Guinee. ex Le Tour du Monde, 1893.

GN
659.A2
E 79

Estudos etnograficos., I.

(Memorias e Trabalhos Inst. de Investigacao de Angola, 2, 1960)

GN
Ethn.Pam.
3304

ETABLISSEMENTS FRANCAIS D'OCEANIE

Villaret, Bernard

Climatologie médicale des Etablissements Francais d'Océanie. Paris, 1938. 48 pp.

2 copies

Z
Bibl.
Pam
20
21

Etheridge, R.

Catalogue of works, reports, and papers on the anthropology, ethnology, and geological history of the Australian and Tasmanian aborigines, parts 1 and 2. Sydney. 1890-1891.

(Dep't of Mines, Memoirs of the Geological Survey of New South Wales, Paleontology, No. 8)

DU
50
E 96

ETABLISSEMENTS FRANCAIS DE L'OCÉANIE

Etablissements Français du Pacifique Austral. Nouvelle Calédonie, et Dependances, Nouvelles Hébrides, Iles Wallis et Futuna. - Etablissements Français de l'Océanie...

DU
Pac.Pam.
635

Etablissements Francais de l'Oceanie. Gouvernement de Tahiti.

Lois codifiées de l'Archipel des Iles-sous-le-vent. Papeete. 1911. 19 pp.

GN
2.1
N

Etheridge R. Junr.

I.- Cylindro-conical and cornute stone implements of Western New South Wales and their significance.

II.- Warrigal, or "Dingo," introduced or indigenous?

N.S. Wales Geol. Survey. Mem. Ethn. Ser. no. 2. Sydney, 1916, 4to. pp. 54, pls. I-XII.

DU
50
E 96

Etablissements Français du Pacifique Austral. Nouvelle Calédonie et Dependances, Nouvelles Hébrides, Iles Wallis et Futuna. - Etablissements Français de l'Océanie. (Published by) Exposition Coloniale Internationale de Paris, Commissariat Generale. Paris. Societe d'Editions Geographiques, Maritimes et Coloniales. 78 + iv pp. 4to.
1931

QL
121
C 53

Etcheverry D., Hector

Nomenclatura y sistematica de las algas.

(Revista de Biologia Marina, Vol. III(3): 215-225, 1951)

GN
2.1
N

Etheridge, R. Junr.

Dendroglyphs, or "carved trees" of New South Wales. Mem. Geol. Survey of N. S. W. Ethnol. Ser. No. 3, 1918. 4to pp 104 pls.29.

QE
Geol.Pam.
1055

ETABLISSEMENTS FRANCAIS DE L'OCEANIE

Giovanelli, J. L.

Les cyclones en Oceanie Francaise: caractères généraux des cyclones tropicaux.

(Bull. Soc. des Etudes Océaniennes, No. 68, Mars, 1940, pp. 250-267)

G
51
Q

Ethell, A. L.

Across Papua's mighty delta.

(Queensland Geographical Journal, Vol. 50: 85-93, 1945/46)

AS
720.N
L-m

Etheridge, R., Jr.

A Description of some of the Weapons and Implements of the Alligator Tribe, Port Essington, North Australia.

(Macleay Memorial Volume, 1893, pp. 228-251. Linnean Society of New South Wales.)

DU
870
L433

ETABLISSEMENTS FRANCAIS DE L'OCEANIE

Le Chartier, H.

Tahiti et les colonies francaises de la Polynésie.

Paris, 1887, 228 pp.

AS
719
A

Etheridge, R., Junr. 57.28 (934.)

Additions to the Ethnological Collections, chiefly from the New Hebrides.

Rec. Austr. Mus., vi., 8, 1917.

pp. 189 - 203

GN
Pam
1893

Etheridge, R. Jr.

Descriptions of further highly ornate boomerangs from New South Wales and Queensland. From Proc. Linnean Soc. 1896, pt.1

G
153
M 49

ETABLISSEMENTS FRANCAIS DE L'OCEANIE

Megglé, Armand

Le domaine colonial de la France, ses ressources et ses besoins. Paris. 1922.

AS
719
A

Etheridge R. Junr.

Ancient Stone implements from the Gydda Valley Goldfield north-east British New Guinea

(In Rec. Aus. Mus. VII. 1908 p.24-28)

QE
Pam
#181

and

AS
719
A

Etheridge, R.

Descriptions of upper Silurian fossils from the Lilydale limestone, upper Yarra district, Victoria, ex Aus. Mus. Rec. Vol. I.

GN
1
O 16

ETABLISSEMENTS FRANCAIS DE L'OCEANIE

Sasportas, L.

Au coeur du Pacifique.

(Bull. de la Société des Océanistes, Tome 1, 1937, pp. 85-97)

AS
719
A

Etheridge, R.

The Australian museum: Fragments of its early history. Illus. pls. XVIII-XX. Rec. Australian Mus. Vol. XI, 4. 1916.

GN
Pam
2083

Etheridge, R

The game of teetotum as practised by certain of the Queensland aborigines. From Anthrop. Instit. Journ. v.25. 1896.

QH
Nat.Hist.
Pam
87

AS
719
A-me

Etheridge, R. Jr.

The general Zoology of Lord Howe Island.

(Australian Mus. Mem. No. 2, 1889.)

GN
Pam
114
and
AS
720.N
L

Etheridge, R.

Modifications of the Billetta or gnalealing womerah. From Proc. Linn. Soc. of N.S.W. Vol. VII, 2nd series, pp 399-402, 1 plate.

GN
Pam
1595

Etheridge, R. Jr.

On three highly ornate boomerangs from the Bulloo river. From Proc. Linnean Soc. N.S.W., v.9, ser.2, 1894.

DU
Pac
Pam
No.36
and
AS
719
A

Etheridge, R.

Geological and ethnological observations made in the valley of the Wollondilly River..... ex Records of Australian Museum, vol. II, No. 4. np. nd.

DU
Pam
No. 96
and
AS
720.N
L

Etheridge, R.

Note on the Bibliography of Lord Howe Island. ex. Linnean Soc. NSW 2nd ser. Vol. IV, pp. 627-631, 1889.

QE
Pam
#117
and
AS
720.N
L

Etheridge, R.

Note on the fructification of Phlebopteris Alethopteroides, Etheridge, fil. from the lower Mesozoic beds of Queensland, ex Linn. Soc. of New South Wales Proc., vol. IV. July, 1889.

GN
Pam
1718

Etheridge, R. Jr.

A highly ornate "sword" from Coburg, peninsula, North Australia. From Anthrop. Instit. Journ. 1895.

AS
719
A

130

Etheridge, R.

Notes on "rock-shelters" or gibba gunyahs at Deewhy Lagoon in Australian Mus. Records I.8, 1891, 8°. p. 171-174.

QE
Pam
#175
and
AS
720.N
L

Etheridge, R.

Note on the structure of Annularia Australis, Feistmantel, ex Linn. Soc. of New South Wales Proc., vol. V, 2d. ser., Feb. 26, 1890.

GN
Pam
1594

Etheridge, R. Jr.

The kuditcha shoes of central Australia. From Proc. Linnean Soc. N.S.W., v.9, a.s., 1894.

GN
Pam
1596

Etheridge, R. Jr.

On an aboriginal implement, believed to be undescribed, and supposed to be a hoe. From Proc. Linnean Soc. N.S.W., v.9, ser.2, 1894.

QE
Pam
#178
and
AS
720.N
1

Etheridge, R.

On additional evidence of the occurence of Plesiosaurus in the Mesozoic rocks of Queensland, ex Linn. Soc. of New South Wales Proc., vol. III, 2d. ser., April 25, 1888.

QE
Pam
#122
and
AS
720.N
L

Etheridge, R.

A large Equisetum from the Hawkesbury sandstone, ex Linn. Soc. of New South Wales Proc., vol. V, July, 1890.

AS
719
A

Etheridge R. June.

An circular and spiral incised ornament on Australian aboriginal implement and weapons.

(In Rec. Au. Mus. III. 1897-1900 p. 1-)

GN
Pam
#112
and
AS
720.N
L

Etheridge, R.

On a form of womerah or "throwing stick" presumed to be undescribed, ex Linn. Soc. of New South Wales Proc., vol. VI, Nov. 25, 1891.

AS
719
A-me

ETHERIDGE, ROBERT, jr., 1846-

Australian museum, *Sydney.*

... Lord Howe Island. Its zoology, geology, and physical characters. Printed by order of the trustees, E. P. Ramsay, curator. Sydney, C. Potter, government printer, 1889.

5 p. l., 132 p., 7 l. front. (fold. map) x pl. (part fold.) incl. 2 fold maps (1 col.) 24cm. (The Australian museum, Sydney. Memoirs, no. 2)

CONTENTS.—General zoology; by R. Etheridge, jr.— Oology; by A. J. North.— Reptiles and fishes; by J. D. Ogilby.— Insects; by A. S. Olliff.— Geology and physical structure; by R. Etheridge, jr.— Notes on rock specimens; by T. W. E. David.

1. Lord Howe Island, Oceanica. I. Etheridge, Robert, jr., 1846- II. North, Alfred J. III. Ogilby, J. Douglas. IV. Olliff, Arthur Sidney, 1865-1895. V. David, Tannet William Edgeworth, 1858-

Agr 3-695 Revised

Library, U. S. Dept. of   Agriculture 514Au7M

AS
720.N
L

Etheridge R. Jr.

On leaia mitchelli, from the upper coal measures of the NewCastle District. from Proc. Linn. Soc. N.S.W. VII, 1892. 8vo. pp. 307-310.

QE
Pam
#115
and
AS
919
A

Etheridge, R. Jr.

On further traces of meiolania in New South Wales, ex Australian Mus. Rec., vol. II, no. 4.

GN
Pam
#132
and
720.S
R

Etheridge, R.

The "mirrn-yong" heaps at the North-west bend of the River Murray, ex Roy. Soc. of South Australia Trans., 1893.

AS
719
A

Etheridge, R. Junr.

On the occurrence of the genus Palaeaster in the upper silurian rocks of Victoria. Records of Aust Mus. 1891, I, 10, pp. 199-205, pl. XXX.

QE
Pam
#119
and
AS
720.N
L

Etheridge, R. Jr.

On additional evidence of the genus Ichthyosaurus in the Mesozoic rocks ("rolling downs formation") of North-eastern Australia, ex Linn. Soc. of New South Wales Proc., vol. III, April, 1888.

GN Pam 1910 — Etheridge, R. Jr.

On five interesting shields from northern Queensland. From Proc. Linnean Soc. N.S.W. v.9, 1894.

QE Pam #56 and AS 719 A — Etheridge, R.

On the occurrence of Beekite in connection with "Fossil organic remains" in New South Wales, ex Australian Mus. Records, vol. LL, no. 5.

GN 2.1 N — Etheridge, R. Junr.

Warrigal, or "Dingo," introduced or indigenous? in N.S.Wales Geol. Survey Mem. Ethn. Ser. no. 2, pp. 43-51, pls. X-XII.

QL Pam #127 — Etheridge, R. Jr.

On Leaia Mitchelli, ... from upper coal measures of the Newcastle District, ex Proc. Linnean Soc. of New South Wales, June 29, 1892.

QE Pam #412 — Etheridge, R. Jr.

The physical and geological structure of Lord Howe Island. Aus. Mus. Mem. #2 Sydney, 1889.

QE Pam #180 — Etheridge, R. & Thorpe, J. A.

General notes made during a visit to mount Sassafras, Shoalhaven district, N.S.W.

GN 1 Ar 3 — Etheridge, R

On the ornamentation of some North Australian "Dilly-Baskets": a study in Australian aboriginal decorative art. In Archiv f. Ethnog. 1900 XIII pp 1-20

QE Pam #118 and AS 719.N L — Etheridge, R.

The silurian trilobites of New South Wales, with references to those of other parts of Australia, ex Linn. Soc. of New South Wales Proc., vol. VI, July, 1891.

QE Pam #427 and AS 719.V R — Etheridge, R. and Woodward, Arthur

On the occurrence of the genus Belonostomus in the Rolling Downs formation or Central Queensland, ex Roy. Soc. of Victoria Trans., for 1891.

GN 1 Ar — Etheridge, R.

On modifications in form + ornament of the Australian aboriginal weapon the "lil-lil" or "woggara" etc. In Archiv f. Ethn. X. 1897. pp 7-16. See Journ. Anthr. Inst. 1894 XXIII p. 317.

QE Pam #179 — Etheridge, R.

On Turrilepas and Annelid jaws, from upper Silurian, New South Wales, ex Geol. Mag., August, 1890.

AS 719 A — ETHERIDGE, ROBERT, JUNIOR

Dun, W. S.

Robert Etheridge, Junior. Obituary. In Australian Museum Rec., Vol. XV, 1926, pp 1-27, port.

[Bibliography compiled by W. A. Rainbow, pp 5-27]

QE Pam #174 and AS 720.N R — Etheridge, R. Jun.

On some Australian species of the family Archaeocyathinae, ex Roy. Soc. of N. S. Wales Trans., 1890.

QE Pam #177 and AS 719.N L — Etheridge, R.

Remarks on fossils of permo-carboniferous age, from North-western Australia, in the Macleay Museum, ex Linn. Soc. of New South Wales Proc., vol. IV, 2d. ser., April 24, 1889.

AS 36 S1 — ETHICS, JAPANESE

Suyematsu, Kencho, baron, 1843–
The ethics of Japan. By Baron Kencho Suyematsu.
(*In* Smithsonian institution. Annual report. 1905. Washington, 1906. 23½ᶜᵐ. p. 293-307)
"Reprinted ... from Journal of the Society of arts, London, no. 2729, vol. LIII, March 10, 1905."

1. Ethics, Japanese.

Library of Congress   Q11.S66 1905
Library, Smithsonian   Institution

S 15-1294

QE Pam #176 and AS 720.N L — Etheridge, R.

On the further structure of Conularia inornata, Dana, and Hyolithes lanceolatus, Morris, sp. ex Linn. Soc. of New South Wales Proc., vol. IV, 2d. ser, Sept. 25, 1889.

GN Pam #111 and AS 720.N L — Etheridge, R. Jr.

A second undescribed form of womerah from Northern Australia, ex Linn. Soc. of New South Wales Proc., vol. VII, March 30, 1892.

GN Ethn.Pam. 3312 — ETHICS   NEW GUINEA

Hogbin, H. Ian

Social reaction to crime: law and morals in the Schouten Islands, New Guinea.

(Journal of the R. Anthrop. Inst. Great Britain and Ireland, Vol. 68, 1938, pp. 223-262)

QE Pam #116 and AS 720.N L — Etheridge, R. Jr.

On the identity of Bronteus Partschi de Koninck (no barrande), from the upper silurian rocks of New South Wales, ex Linn. Soc. of New South Wales Proc. vol. V, August, 1890.

AS 719 A — Etheridge R. Junr.

Spear with incised ornament from Angledool, N.S.W.

(In Rec. Aus. Mus. III. 1897-1900. p.6-)

GN 1 O 15 — ETHICS   NEW GUINEA

Read, K. E.

Morality and the concept of the person among the Gahuku-Gama.

(Oceania, Vol. XXV(4):233-282, 1955)

[eastern highlands of New Guinea]

3

GN
670
H 71   ETHICS POLYNESIA

Hogbin, H. Ian

Law and order in Polynesia. A study of primitive legal institutions. With an introduction by B. Malinowski. London. 1934.

ETHNIC GROUPS

See also

RACE

GN
2.8
P 76   ETHNOBOTANY FIJI

Parham, (Mrs.) H. B. Richenda

Fiji plants, their names and uses.

(Memoirs, Polynesian Society, 16, 1939-)

DT
373
H 31   ETHIOPIA

Harris, W. Cornwallis

The highlands of Ethiopia. From the first London edition. J. Winchester. New York. (1843) 8vo. xii + 392 pp.

AS
36
S1   ETHNOBOTANY.

Safford, William Edwin, 1859–
Narcotic plants and stimulants of the ancient Americans. By W. E. Safford ...

(In Smithsonian institution. Annual report. 1916. Washington, 1917. 231ᵐ. p. 387-424. illus, 17 pl. on 9 l)

1. Narcotics. 2. Stimulants. 3. Indians—Soc. life & cust.

    18–3070

Library of Congress   Q11.S66 1916

AS
771
F 47   ETHNOBOTANY FIJI

Parham, B. E.

Minor food plants of the Fijian and Indian.

(Fiji Society of Sci. and Industry, Trans. and Proc., 1940, pp. 12-18)

ETHIOPIA CULICIDAE

SEE

CULICIDAE ETHIOPIA

GN
EthnoPam.
3092   ETHNOBOTANY

Sapper, Karl

Geographie der Altindianischen Landwirtschaft.

(Sonderabdruck aus Petermanns Geographischen Mitteilungen, 1934, Heft 2-4, pp. 41-44; 80-83; 118-121)

GN
EthnoPam.
3030   ETHNOBOTANY GILBERT ISLANDS

Luomala, Katharine
GN
406
L 96   Ethnobotany of the Gilbert Islands.

(Bernice P. Bishop Museum, Bulletin 213, 1953)

ETHIOPIA SIMULIIDAE

See

SIMULIIDAE ETHIOPIA

ETHNOBOTANY

See also

MEDICINAL PLANTS
FOOD PLANTS
PLANT NAMES

DU
647
G 91   ETHNOBOTANY GUAM

Sanchez, Joaquin

Guam herbs are said to be medicinal.

(Guam Recorder, Vol. 16, 1940, pp. 460)

AS
36
S3   ETHNIC DISTRIBUTION

Mason, Otis, Tufton

E. 14
and
GN
Pam.
184   Aboriginal American Harpoons: A study in Ethnic Distribution and invention.
from the Report of the U. S. Nat. Mus. for 1900, pp. 189-304 with 80 plts. Washington. 1902. 8°.

S. - Author.

GN
1
A   ETHNOBOTANY-INSTRUCTIONS, METHODS

Gilmore, Melvin R.

Importance of Ethnobotanical Investigation.

(American Anthropologist, Volume 34, 1932, pp. 320-327)

QK
473.H
D 31   ETHNOBOTANY HAWAII

Degener, Otto

Plants of Hawaii National Park illustrative of plants and customs of the South Seas. (First photo-lithoprint edition of "Ferns and flowering plants of Hawaii National Park...") * no place. 1945c. 8vo. xv + 314 pp.

*The title begins, "Illustrated guide to the more common or noteworthy ferns or flowering plants..."

GN
635.S2
E 53   ETHNIC GROUPS ASIA

Embree, John F.

Ethnic groups of northern southeast Asia. By John F. Embree and William L. Thomas, Jr. Yale Univ., Southeast Asia Studies. New Haven. 1950. 175 pp. unbd. 4to.

GN
2.I
T 89   ETHNOBOTANY ARGENTINA (Chaco, Tucuman)

Storni, Julio S.

Hortus Guaranensis: flora. Universidad Nacional de Tucuman, Gabinete de Etnologia Biologica. Tucuman, 1944. 8vo. 268 pp.

QK
Bot.Pam.
2364   ETHNOBOTANY HAWAII

Eames, Arthur J.

The botanical identity of the Hawaiian ipu nui or large gourd. By Arthur J. Eames and Harold St. John.

(American Journal of Botany, Vol. 30, no. 3, 1943, pp. 255-259)

AS
492
S 6   ETHNIC GROUPS BORNEO

Needham, Rodney

A note on ethnic classification in Borneo.

(Journal of the Malayan Branch, R. Asiatic Society, 28(1):167-171, 1955)

QK
I
U   ETHNOBOTANY CALIFORNIA

Chesnut, V. K.

Plants used by the Indians of Mendocino Co., California.
U.S. Nat. Herb., VII, 3, Wash., 1902.

QK
Bot.Pam.
2345   ETHNOBOTANY HAWAII

Fosberg, F. Raymond

Uses of Hawaiian ferns.

(American Fern Journal, Vol. 32, 1942, pp. 15-23)

GN
671.H2
H 23   ETHNOBOTANY   HAWAII

Handy, Edward Smith Craighill

    The Hawaiian planter, Volume I: his plants, methods and areas of cultivation.

    (Bulletin, Bernice P. Bishop Museum, No. 161, 1940, pp. 1-227, 21 figs, 8 pl.)

QK
Bot.Pam.
1820   ETHNOBOTANY   HAWAII

Seemann, Berthold

    Notes on the Sandwich Islands. Photostatic copy of pp. 335-341 of Hooker's Journal of Botany Vol. 4, 1852.

AS
36
M64
and

QK
194
Sm
S64   ETHNOBOTANY   MENOMINI

Smith, Huron H.

    Ethnobotany of the Menomini Indians. Milwaukee Mus. Bul. IV, 1, 1923.

QK
Bot.Pam.
2235   ETHNOBOTANY   HAWAII

Hudson, Loring

    Plants of the Kamehameha Schools Hawaiian forest. Kamehameha Schools. Honolulu. 1939. 39 pp. mimeographed.

DU
620
P   ETHNOBOTANY   HAWAII

Westervelt, William Drake

    Hawaii's heights grow rare and sturdy plants with leaves like swords of silver.

    (Paradise of the Pacific, Vol. 37, No. 8, 1924, pp. 29,30)

AS
36
M 64   ETHNOBOTANY   MESKWAKI

Smith, Huron H.

    Ethnobotany of the Meskwaki Indians.

    (Bulletin of the Public Museum of the City of Milwaukee, Vol. 4, No. 2, pp. 175-326, plates 37-46, 1928)

S
17.H3
H 38
and
QK
Bot.Pam.
521   ETHNOBOTANY   HAWAII

Judd, Charles Sheldon

    The Alahee tree.

    (Hawaiian Forester and Agriculturist, vol. 18, no. 6, 1921, pp. 133-137)

GN
2.S
P 76   ETHNOBOTANY   MANIHIKI

Linton, A. Murray

    Notes on the vegetation on Penrhyn and Manihiki Islands.

    (Journal of the Polynesian Society, 42: 300-307, 1933.)

GN
2 S
P 76   ETHNOBOTANY   MICRONESIA

Christian, F. W.

    On the distribution and origin of some plant and tree-names in Polynesia and Micronesia.

    (Journal of the Polynesian Society, Vol. 6, 1897, pp. 123-140)

S
17.H3
H 38   ETHNOBOTANY   HAWAII

Judd, Charles Sheldon

    The natural resources of the Hawaiian forest regions and their conservation.

    (Hawaiian Forester and Agriculturist, vol. 24, no. 2, 1927, pp. 40-47)

GN
2.S
P 76   ETHNOBOTANY   MAORI

Best, Elsdon

    Forest lore of the Maori; with methods of snaring, trapping, and preserving birds and rats, uses of berries, roots, fern-root, and forest products, with mythological notes on origins, karakia used, etc.

    (Mem. Poly. Soc., 19, 1942)

GN
2.S
O 15   ETHNOBOTANY   NEW CALEDONIA

Leenhardt, Maurice

    Le ti en Nouvelle-Calédonie.

    (Journal de la Soc. des Océanistes, Vol. 2: 192-193, 1946)

AP
2
P8   ETHNOBOTANY   HAWAII

MacCaughey, Vaughan

    Food plants of the ancient Hawaiians. In Scientific Monthly IV, 1917. pp. 75-80.

AS
750
N   ETHNOBOTANY   MAORI

Best, Elsdon

    Maori forest lore...

    (Trans. and Proc. New Zealand Inst., Vol. 40, 1907, pp. 185-254; 41, 1908, pp. 231-286; Vol. 42, 1909, pp. 433-481)

Q
101
P 18   ETHNOBOTANY   NEW GUINEA

Blackwood, Beatrice
Use of plants among the Kukukuku of Southeast-Central New Guinea.

    IN Proc. Sixth Pac. Sci. Congress, 1939, (California), Vol. 4, 1940, pp. 111-126.

QK
482
N 34   ETHNOBOTANY   HAWAII

Neal, Marie C.

    In gardens of Hawaii.

    (Bernice P. Bishop Museum, Special Publication 40, 1948)

GN
2.S
P 76   ETHNOBOTANY   MAORI

Hammond, T. G.

    The kumara, perei and taewa.

    (Jour. of the Poly. Soc., Vol. 3, 1894, p 237-238)

QK
1
E 58   ETHNOBOTANY   NEW GUINEA

Kärnbach, Ludwig

    Ueber die nutzpflanzen der eingeborenen in Kaiser-Wilhelmsland.

    (Bot. Jahrb. Engler, 16 (Beibl. 37):10-19, 1892)

S
17.H3
H 1   ETHNOBOTANY   HAWAII

Rocke, T. C. B.

    Report on the sweet potatoe, (Convolvulus Batata.) In Trans. R. Haw. Agri. Soc. II, 2. pp. 38 - 43.

GN
2.1
A-4   ETHNOBOTANY   MAORI

Tregear, E.

    The spirit of vegetation.

    (Journ. Anthrop. Inst. of Great Britain and Ireland, Vol. 31, 1901, pp. 157-159)

AS
720.N
L   ETHNOBOTANY   NEW GUINEA

Miklukho-Maklai, Nikolai Nikolaevich

    List of plants in use by the natives of the Maclay Coast, New Guinea. With some botanical remarks by Baron Ferd. von Mueller. (1885)

    (Linn. Soc. of N. S. Wales, Proc., 10, 1886, pp. 346-358)

QK
Bot.Pam.
2858

ETHNOBOTANY   NEW GUINEA

van Steenis, C. G. G. J.

Vegetatie en flora...

[reprint from Nieuw Guinea..., edited by W.C
Klein, Deel II, pp. 218-275, 1954]

(summary in English)

GN
Pam.613

and

AP
2
N 54

ETHNOBOTANY   POLYNESIA

Christian, F. W.

Words and races: Story of the Kumara.

(N.Z.Jour. of Sci. and Tech. Vol. VI, pp.
152-153, 1923.)

QK
1
A 75

ETHNOBOTANY   SOLOMON ISLANDS

Kajewski, S. F.

Plant collecting in the Solomon Islands.

(Journal of the Arnold Arboretum, Vol.27,
pp. 292-304, 1946)

AS
36
M 64

ETHNOBOTANY   OJIBWE INDIANS

Smith, Huron H.

Ethnobotany of the Ojibwe Indians.

(Bull. Public Museum of the City of Milwaukee, Vol. 4, pp. 327-525, Plates 46-77, 1932)

QK
Bot.Pam.
343

ETHNOBOTANY   POLYNESIA

Cook, O. F.

Polynesian names of sweet potatoes, by O. F.
Cook and Robert Carter Cook.

(Journal Washington Academy of Sciences,
Vol. 6, pp. 339-347, 1916)

AS
763
B-b

QK
473.S
W 67
Reading
Room

ETHNOBOTANY   TAHITI

Wilder, Gerrit Parmile

The breadfruit of Tahiti. (B.P. Bishop Mus.,
Bull. 50, 1928, 83 pp.)

QK
Bot.Pam.
2608

ETHNOBOTANY   PACIFIC

Carter, George F.

Plant evidence for early contacts with America.

(Southwestern Journal of Anthropology, Vol.
6(2):161-182, 1950)

GN
1
A

and
GN
Ethn.Pam.
2885

ETHNOBOTANY   POLYNESIA

Dixon, Roland B.

The Problem of the Sweet Potato in Polynesia.

(American Anthropologist, New Series,   Vol.
34, No. 1, 1932, pp. 40-66)

GN
2.S
Z 78

ETHNOBOTANY   TAIWAN

Kano, Tadao

Some cultivated plants of the Formosan aborigines, and their relation to the ethnic history of Formosa.

(Zinruigaku Zassi, Vol. 56:522-527,1941)

GN
Ethn.Pam.
3185

ETHNOBOTANY   PACIFIC

Friederici, Georg

Die Süsskartoffel in der Südsee.

(Mitteilungsblatt der Gesellschaft für Völkerkunde, 1936, No. 7, Leipzig)

GN
2.S
O 15

ETHNOBOTANY   POLYNESIA

Petard, Paul

Cordyline terminalis: ethno-botanique et
médecine polynésienne.

(Journal de la Soc. des Oceanistes, Vol. 2:
194-208, 1946)

GN
550
S

ETHNOBOTANY OF THE TEWA INDIANS.
Robbins, Wilfred William.
    ... Ethnobotany of the Tewa Indians, by Wilfred Wil-
liam Robbins, John Peabody Harrington and Barbara
Freire-Marreco. Washington, Govt. print. off., 1916.
    xii, 124 p. illus., 9 pl. (incl. fold. map) 23½ᶜᵐ. (Smithsonian institu-
tion. Bureau of American ethnology. Bulletin 55)
    "Forms a part of the results of the ethnological and archeological re-
search in the upper Rio Grande Valley of New Mexico, undertaken jointly
by the Bureau of American ethnology and the School of American arch-
ology in 1910 and 1911."—Letter of submittal, p. v.
    Bibliography: p. 119-120.
    1. Botany, Economic. 2. Tewa Indians. I. Harrington, John Pea-
body, joint author. II. Freire-Marreco, Barbara W., joint author. III.
Santa Fe, N. M. School of American research. IV. Title.
                                                    16-26846
    Library of Congress   E51.U6 no. 55
    —— Copy 2.   E99.T35R6
                                 (a20i2)

GN
2.S
P 76

ETHNOBOTANY   PENRHYN ISLAND

Linton, A. Murray

Notes on the vegetation on Penrhyn and
Manihiki Islands.

(Journal of the Polynesian Society, 42:
300-307, 1933.)

AS
36
M 64

ETHNOBOTANY - POTAWATOMI

Smith, Huron H.

Ethnobotany of the Forest Potawatomi
Indians.

(Bull. Public Museum of the City of
Milwaukee, Vol. 7, No. 1, pp. 1-230, 1933)

GN
Ethn.Pam.
3316

ETHNOBOTANY   THOMPSON INDIANS

Teit, James A.

The ethnobotany of the Thompson Indians of
British Columbia, based on field notes by James
A.Teit, edited by Elsie Viault Steedman.

(Bureau of American Ethnology, 45th Annual
Report, 1930, pp. 443-522)

DU
96
B 47

ETHNOBOTANY   POLYNESIA

Bennett, George

Gatherings of a naturalist in Australasia,
being observations principally on the animal and
vegetable productions of New South Wales, New
Zealand and some of the Austral Islands. London
1860.

QH
301
C 3

ETHNOBOTANY   SAMOA

Setchell, W. A.

American Samoa: Part II. Ethnobotany of the
Samoans. Washington. 1924. Parts I-III.

(Carnegie Institution, Dep't of Marine Biology
Vol. XX, Publ. No. 341)

GN
550
S

ETHNOBOTANY OF THE ZUNI INDIANS.
Stevenson, *Mrs.* Matilda Coxe (Evans) 1850-1915.
    Ethnobotany of the Zuñi Indians, by Matilda Coxe
Stevenson.
    (*In* U. S. Bureau of American ethnology. Thirtieth annual report,
1908-1909. Washington, 1915. 29½ᶜᵐ. p. 31-102. 3 pl.)

    1. Botany, Medical. 2. Botany, Economic. 3. Zuñi Indians. 4. Botany—
New Mexico. I. Title.
                                                    16-9898
    Library of Congress   E51.U55 30th

GN
2.S
P 76

ETHNOBOTANY   POLYNESIA

Christian, F. W.

On the distribution and origin of some plant
and tree-names in Polynesia and Micronesia.

(Journal of the Polynesian Society, Vol. 6,
1897, pp. 123-140)

GN
Ethn. Pam.
3400

ETHNOBOTANY   SOCIETY ISLANDS

Pétard, Paul

La végétation madréporique du District
de Teavaro (Ile Moorea); description et usages de
quelques plantes indigènes de Tahiti.

(Ann. de Medecine et de Pharmacie
Coloniales Tome 37, 1939, pp. 76-96. typed copy)

AS
122
B

and
GN
Ethn.
Pam.
295

ETHNOCONCHOLOGY   INDONESIA

Schmeltz, J. D. C.

On the shells used in the domestic economy
of the Indonesians.

(Report of the Meeting, Brit. Ass'n for
the Adv. Sci., Oxford, 1894, pp. 786-787.)

DU
740
T 48

ETHNOCONCHOLOGY NEW GUINEA (British.)

Hedley, C.
Uses of shells among the Papuans.

In
Thomson, J. P.
British New Guinea.   London, 1892. Appendix V, pp. 283-285.

GN
Ethn.Pam.
3135

Ethnographie, Archaeologie et Folklore en U. R. S. S.

(Recueil Periodique Illustré, Organe de la Société pour Relations Culturelles entre L'U. R. S. S. et L'Étranger, Vol. 4, 1933)

GN
Ethn.Pam.
3310

and

GN
Ethn.Pam.
3310

ETHNOGRAPHY   AUSTRALIA

Davidson, D. Sutherland

An ethnic map of Australia.

(Proceedings of the American Philosophical Society, Vol. 79, 1938, pp. 649-679)

GN
1
I 61

ETHNOCONCHOLOGY   SAMOA

Bülow, Werner von

Die Muscheln im Leben der Eingebornen. (Samoa)

(Archiv f. Ethnogr., XIII, 1901, p. 177-184)

GN
Z
v.19

Ethnographie von Hawaii

Arning, Ed.

See author card

AS
720.3
R

ETHNOGRAPHY   AUSTRALIA

Hamlyn-Harris, R.

Some anthropological considerations of Queensland and bibliography with special reference to Queensland ethnography: presidential address, in Proc. Ry. Soc. Queensland XXIX, 1917, pp 1-35. Note. Bibliography pp 36-44.

GN
Ethn.Pam.
2935

ETHNOGENETICS

Pitt-Rivers, George

Anthropological Approach to Ethnogenetics: a New Perspective.

(Human Biology, Vol. 4, 1932, pp. 239-251)

PL
Pam
#5

ETHNOGRAPHY
Brandstetter, Renward

Monographien zur Indonesischen Sprachforschung, IX, Das Verbum.

Luzern: 1912, pp 69.

GN
2.1
A-M

ETHNOGRAPHY   FIJI

Hocart, A. M.

Ethnographical sketch of Fiji.

(Man, vol. 15, 1915, no. 43, pp. 73-77)

AS
36
S 2

ETHNOGEOGRAPHIC BOARD

Bennett, Wendell Clark

The Ethnogeographic Board.

(Smithsonian Miscellaneous Collections, Vol. 107 (1), 1947)

GN
307
L 68

8vo.

2 copies

ETHNOGRAPHY

Leyburn, J. G.

Handbook of Ethnography.   New Haven. 1931.

GN
635.F1
K 16

ETHNOGRAPHY   FORMOSA

Kano, Tadao

An illustrated ethnography of Formosan aborigines. Vol. 1: The Yami. By Tadao Kano and Kokichi Segawa. Revised edition. Tokyo. Maruzen Company, Ltd. 1956. 4to. xii + 456 pp. 1 map.

AM
Mus.Pam.
290

Ethnographic collections, National Museum, Manila, 1953.   4to. mimeographed. 51 pp.

ETHNOGRAPHY

see also

ETHNOLOGY (WITH GEOGRAPHIC DIVISION)

GN
669
C 77

ETHNOGRAPHY   IFALUK

Burrows, Edwin G.

An atoll culture; ethnography of Ifaluk in the Central Carolines. By Edwin G. Burrows and Melford E. Spiro.

(CIMA, 1947-1949, Reports 16, 18. Also issued as Behavior Science Monographs, Human Relations Area Files, New Haven, 1953)

GN
32
J58

Ethnographical Album....

Jesup north Pacific expedition.
Ethnographical album of the north Pacific coasts of America and Asia. Jesup north Pacific expedition. Pt. I. New York, American museum of natural history, 1900.

5 l. 28 pl. 28 x 35½ᶜᵐ.

No more published.

1. Salishan Indians. 2. Indians of North America.   I. American museum of natural history, New York. II. Title.

12—30246

Library of Congress   E99.S21J5

GN
2.8
S 72

ETHNOGRAPHY   TECHNIQUE

Haring, Douglas G.

Comment on field techniques in ethnography illustrated by a survey in the Ryūkyū Islands.

(Southwestern Journal of Anthropology, Vol. 10(3):255-267, 1954)

AM
Mus.Pam.
360 a

ETHNOGRAPHY   INDONESIA

Guide à l'usage du corps enseignant. Musée d'Ethnographie, Neuchatel.   (exhibition) Iles des Dieux, Indonésie. 38 pp.   mimeographed.

GN
1
Ar 1

Ethnographical museums, II, the contents of the museums, IV: Australia and the South Sea Islands.

(The Archaeological Review, Vol. 2, 1888, pp. 217-225)

GN
659.A2
E 79

ETHNOGRAPHY   ANGOLA

Estudos etnograficos., I.

(Memorias e Trabalhos Inst. de Investigacao de Angola, 2, 1960)

DS
Asia
Pam.
51

ETHNOGRAPHY   INDONESIA

Kunst, J.

The peoples of the Indian Archipelago. With thirty-two illustrations and two maps. The Royal Society "Institute for the Indies", Amsterdam. E. J. Brill. Leiden. 1946. 8vo. 9 pp.

GN 668
C 89

ETHNOGRAPHY   MELANESIA

Cranstone, B. A. L.

Melanesia, a short ethnography.
Published by the Trustees of the British Museum.
London. sm4to. 1961. 115 pp.

GN 671.N5
N 53

ETHNOGRAPHY   NEW GUINEA

Wirz, P.

Ethnographie.

(Nova Guinea, Bd. XVI, Livr. 1-4, 1921-34)

GN 2.S
S 72

ETHNOGRAPHY   RYUKYU ISLANDS

Haring, Douglas G.

Comment on field techniques in ethnography
illustrated by a survey in the Ryūkyū Islands.

(Southwestern Journal of Anthropology,
Vol. 10(3):255-267, 1954)

GN 671.N4
O 66

ETHNOGRAPHY   NEW CALEDONIA

O'Reilly, Patrick

Nouvelle-Calédonie, documents iconogra-
phiques anciens. By Patrick O'Reilly and Jean
Poirier. Publications de Centenaire de la
Nouvelle Calédonie. Nouvelles Editions Latines.
Paris. R8vo. 1959. 126 pp.

GN 760.5
N 47

ETHNOGRAPHY   NEW IRELAND

Neuhaus, P. K.

Beiträge zur Ethnographie der Pala, Mittel
Neu Irland. Köln. Kölner Universitäts
Verlag. 1962. 452 pp. R8vo

GN 855.I
D 23

ETHNOGRAPHY   SANTAL

Datta-Majumder, Nabendu

The Santal, a study in culture-change.

(Department of Anthropology, Government of
India, Memoir No. 2, 1955)

GN Ethn. Pam. 4349

ETHNOGRAPHY   NEW GUINEA

Bodrogi, T.

Some notes on the ethnography of New Guinea.

(Acta Ethnographica, Acad. Sci. Hungaricae,
Tome 3(1-4), 1953)

GN 2.S
O 15

ETHNOGRAPHY   PACIFIC

Kooijman, S.

L'ethnographie et l'Océanie dans les Pays-
Bas après la seconde guerre mondiale.

(Jour. de la Soc. des Océanistes, 16:29-43
1960)

[records of exhibitions, publications, etc.]
chiefly Melanesia, New Guinea

GN 561
S 94

ETHNOGRAPHY   SOUTH AMERICA

Steward, Julian H.

Native peoples of South America. By Julian
Steward and Louis C. Faron. McGraw-Hill Book
Company, Inc. New York... 8vo. 1959. xi +
481 pp.

GN 2.S
N 67

ETHNOGRAPHY   NEW GUINEA

Fischer, H. Th.

Recent ethnographical studies on Netherlands
New Guinea*).

(Nieuw Guinea Studiën, Jaargang 1, Nr. 2:
91-105, April, 1957)

*) Paper read at the International Congress
of Anthropological and Ethnological Sciences, 1-
9 Sept. 1956, at Philadelphia.

Z 4501
T 23

ETHNOGRAPHY   PACIFIC   BIBLIOGRAPHY

Taylor, C. R. H.

A Pacific bibliography; printed matter relating to the native peoples of Polynesia, Melanesia and Micronesia.

(Memoir, Polynesian Society, No. 24, 1951)

GN Ethn. Pam. 3044
GN 855.V
C 12

ETHNOGRAPHY   VIETNAM

Cadiere, L.   and others

Vietnamese ethnographic papers. Behavior
Science Monographs. Published by Human Relations
Area Files, Inc. New Haven. 1953. 8vo. 128 pp
+ figs.

GN 1
An

ETHNOGRAPHY   NEW GUINEA

Nilles, John

The ethnographic position of the Rai Coast,
Territory of New Guinea.

(Anthropos, Vol. 50(1-3):437-438, 1955)

GN 2.1
A-M

ETHNOGRAPHY   PAPUA

Haddon, A. C.

The Agiba cult of the Kerewa culture.

(Man, vol. 18, 1918, no. 99, pp. 177-183,
pl. M, figs. 1-6)

Ethnography

See also

Ethnology

GN 1
Ar3

Ethnography -- NEW GUINEA

Parkinson, R.

Ein Beitrag zur Ethnographie der Neu-
Guinea-Kuste in Internationales Archiv
fur Ethnographie, pp.18-54, Tafel xv-xxii.
Leiden, 1900.

GN 1
An

ETHNOGRAPHY   PAPUA

Schmidt, Joseph

Die Ethnographie der Nor-Papua (Murik-
Kaup-Karau) bei Dallmannhafen, Neu-Guinea.
(Anthropos. Bd. 18-19, 1923-1924. pp.
700-732)

PL 1
B 59

ETHNOLINGUISTICS

Josselin de Jong, J. P. B.

Ethnolinguistiek.

(Bijdragen tot de Taal, Land- en Volkenkunde
Deel 107:161-178, 1951)

GN 2.1
Ar

Ethnography -- NEW GUINEA

Schmeltz, J.D.E.

Beiträge zur Ethnographie von Neu-
Guinea

See author card

DS 659
B 57

ETHNOGRAPHY   PHILIPPINE ISLANDS

Beyer, H. Otley

Population of the Philippine Islands in
1916. Philippine Education Co., Manila. 1917.

GN Ethn. Pam. 3251

ETHNOLOGICAL COLLECTIONS   AUSTRALIA
ETHNOLOGY AUSTRALIA COLLECTIONS

Bunzendahl, Otto

Der Australien-Forscher Dr. Erhard Eylmann
und seine Sammlung in Deutschen Kolonial- und
Ubersee-Museum zu Bremen.

(Veroffentl. aus dem Deutschen Kolonial-
und Uebersee-Museum in Bremen. Bd. 2, Heft 1,
1928, pp. 33-80)

GN
2.M
L 53

ETHNOLOGICAL COLLECTIONS   HAWAII

Lichtenberg, Julia

Die hawaiianischen Kollektionen in den
Sammlungen des Museums für Anthropologie und
Ethnographie.

(Jahrbuch des Museums für Völkerkunde zu
Leipzig, 19:207-238, 1962)

GN
1
Ar 1

ETHNOLOGICAL   COLLECTIONS   PACIFIC

Ethnographical museums, II, the contents of
the museums, IV: Australia and the South Sea
Islands.

(The Archaeological Review, Vol. 2, 1888,
pp. 217-225)

GN
2.S
O 15

ETHNOLOGICAL COLLECTIONS   POLYNESIA

O'Reilly, Patrick

Note sur les collections Océaniennes des
Musées d'Ethnographie de la Suisse.

(Jour. de la Soc. des Oceanistes, Vol. 2:
109-127, 1946)

GN
2.S
Po

ETHNOLOGICAL
COLLECTIONS   BRITISH MUSEUMS

Skinner, H. D.

Maori and other Polynesian material in
British museums.

(Polynesian Soc. Journal, Vol. 26, pp. 134-
137, 1917)

GN
37
C 12

ETHNOLOGICAL
COLLECTIONS   PACIFIC

Eudes-Deslongchamps, E(ugène)

Note sur la collection ethnographique du
Musée de Caen et sur deux haches en pierre polie
provenant de la Colombie.

(Bull. de la Soc. Linnéenne de Normandie.
Caen. 3d ser., vol.5. 1880-1881. pp.26-74)

GN
2.M
L 53

ETHNOLOGICAL COLLECTIONS   RUSSIA

Lichtenberg, Julia

Die hawaiianischen Kollektionen in den
Sammlungen des Museums für Anthropologie und
Ethnographie.

(Jahrbuch des Museums für Volkerkunde zu
Leipzig, 19:207-238, 1962)

GN
41
G 45

ETHNOLOGICAL COLLECTIONS   MUSEUMS

Giglioli, Enrico Hillyer

Materiali per lo studio della "eta della
pietra" dai tempi preistorici all'epoca attuale.
n.p.. Castello, 1914. 346 pp.

AM
101
F 45-n

ETHNOLOGICAL COLLECTIONS   PACIFIC

Force, Roland W.

Our Pacific exhibits are worth a brag!
(Chicago Nat. Hist. Mus. Bull., 27(10):3-4,
1956)

GN
Pam.
923

ETHNOLOGICAL COLLECTIONS   SAMOA

Marquardt, Carl

Verzeichniss einer ethnologischen sammlung
aus Samoa.

Berlin, Reimer, 1902.   21p.

GN
41
G 45

ETHNOLOGICAL COLLECTIONS   MUSEUMS

Giglioli, Enrico Hillyer

Materiali per lo studio della "eta della
pietra" dai tempi preistorici all'epoca attuale:
origine e sviluppo della mia collizione. Firenze
Lando, 1901. 248 pp. pls.

Q
101
P 18

ETHNOLOGICAL
COLLECTIONS   PACIFIC

Notes on collections from the Pacific region.
Appendix II, Fifth Pacific Science Congress,
Canada, 1933, Proceedings, Vol. 1, pp. 438-472

DU
Hist.
Pam.
278

ETHNOLOGICAL COLLECTIONS   TAHITI

Micard, Etienne

Resumé d'histoire Tahitienne depuis les
origines jusqu'à nos jours. Suivi du catalogue
de la collection royale dressé par Magdaleine
de Bellescize. Tahiti. 1941. 4to. (4) + 20 +
5 pp.

GN
2.S
O 15

ETHNOLOGICAL COLLECTIONS   MELANESIA

O'Reilly, Patrick

Note sur les collections Océaniennes des
Musées d'Ethnographie de la Suisse.

(Jour. de la Soc. des Oceanistes, Vol. 2:
109-127, 1946)

AM
Pam
#29

ETHNOLOGICAL COLLECTIONS--PACIFIC

Read, Charles H.

Account of a collection of
ethnographical specimens,
formed during Vancouver's
Voyage in the Pacific Ocean
1790-1795.

In R. Anthrop   Inst. XXI 1892
pp. 99-108.   Pl. X + XI.

GN
2.M
W 64

ETHNOLOGICAL COLLECTIONS   VIENNA

Moschner, Irmgard

Katalog der Neuseeland Sammlung (A.Reischek)
Wien.

(Archiv f. Volkerkunde, Bd.13:51-131, 1958)

GN
2.S
M 26

ETHNOLOGICAL
COLLECTIONS   PACIFIC

Catalog of Exhibits of Native Arts and Crafts
Keith Kennedy Collection.

Section 1-Objects associated with primitive
dancing.
Section 2-Primitive instruments of music.
Pacific Island currency, fishing, and other
exhibits.

(Mankind, Vol.1, No. 8, January, 1934, pp.
169-188).

GN
Ethn.Pam.
1366

ETHNOLOGICAL COLLECTIONS   PACIFIC

Schmeltz, Johannes Diedrich Eduard

Die etnographisch anthropologische Abteilung des Museum Godeffroy. By J.D.E. Schmeltz
and R. Krause.

(Archiv f. Ethnographie, Bd. 1, 1888, pp.
60-67)

GN
1
An

ETHNOLOGICAL RESEARCH   DUTCH EAST INDIES

Heine-Geldern, Robert von

Research on southeast Asia; problems and
suggestions.

(Amer. Anthropologist, 48 (2):149-175, 1946)

GN
1
Ar

ETHNOLOGICAL
COLLECTIONS - PACIFIC

Dalton, O. M.

Notes on an ethnological collection
..... Captain Vancouver ..... and now
in the British Museum. In Archiv. fur
Ethnog. X, 1897, pp 225 - 245.

(North America, Hawaii, Tahiti)

AM
101
G 47-s

GN
662
G 58

ETHNOLOGICAL COLLECTIONS   PACIFIC

Schmeltz, J. D. E.

Die etnographisch-anthropologisch Abtheilung des Museum Godeffroy in Hamburg. Ein Beitrag zur Kunde der Südsee-Völker. By J. D. E.
Schmeltz and R. Krause. Mit. 46 Tafeln und
einer ethnologischen Karte des Grossen Oceans.
Hamburg. L. Friedrichsen and Co., 1881. 8vo.
Xlviii + 687 (6) pp., 46 pl.

GN
1
An

ETHNOLOGICAL RESEARCH   MALAYSIA

Heine-Geldern, Robert von

Research on southeast Asia; problems and
suggestions.

(Amer. Anthropologist, 48 (2):149-175, 1946)

GN
1
I 61

ETHNOLOGICAL SPECIMENS

Schmeltz, Johann Diedrich Eduard

Südsee Reliquien.

(Archiv für Ethnographie, I, 1888, pp. 134-145, pl. VII-VIII)

(New Zealand, Samoa, Tonga, Fiji, Society Islands, Hawaii, Melanesia)

GN
1
A67

ETHNOLOGY

Archiv für rassen-und gesellschafts-biologie... herausgegeben von... Alfred Ploetz... v. 1-10

Berlin, Archiv-gesellschaft, 1904-1913

GN
Ethn
Pam.No.
594

ETHNOLOGY

Cartailhac, E. & Chantre, E.

Materiaux pour l'Histoire primitive et naturelle de l'Homme Dix huitième vol. (3 Série Tome I) Paris 1884. 8°. pp. 177-240. -2 1909

ETHNOLOGICAL SPECIMENS

See also

MATERIAL CULTURE
ETHNOLOGICAL COLLECTIONS

GN
22
B 15

ETHNOLOGY

Bahnson, Kristian

Etnografien: fremstillet i dens hovedtraek. Bind 1-2. Med farvetryk, kort... København. Ernst Bojesen. 8vo. 1900. 548 + 704 pp.

GN
Ethn.
Pam.
3915

ETHNOLOGY

Clark, Grahame

From savagery to civilization. Henry Schuman, Inc. New York. 1953. cr8vo. ix + (2)2-116 pp.

ETHNOLOGICAL SPECIMENS

Use this heading for objects not in museums.

remove this card after first entry is made.

GN
320
B 32

ETHNOLOGY

Bastian, Adolph

Controversen in der Ethnologie. I. Die Geographischen Provinzen in ihren culturgeschichtlichen Berührungspuncten. Berlin. 1893.

GN
320
C 85

ETHNOLOGY

Coupin, Henri

Les Bizarreries des Races Humaines. Paris. Vuibert et Nony. 1905. R8vo. 285 pp.

GN
I 61

ETHNOLOGICAL SPECIMENS   SOLOMON ISLANDS

Roth, H. Ling

Spears and other articles from the Solomon Islands.

(Archiv f. Ethnogr., Bd. XI, 1898, p. 154-161)

GN
22
B 46

ETHNOLOGY

Benedict, Ruth

Patterns of culture. Boston and New York. Houghton Mifflin Company. (1934c) 8vo. xiii + 291 pp.

AS
36
S 1

ETHNOLOGY

Davis, Edwin Hamilton, 1811-1888.
On ethnological research. A communication from Dr. E. H. Davis ...
(*In* Smithsonian institution. Annual report. 1866. Washington, 1867. 23⅓cm. p. (370)-373. tab.)

1. Ethnology.

Library of Congress   Q11.S66 1866
Library, Smithsonian   Institution

S 15-197

GN
Pam.
#138

ETHNOLOGY

D'Alviella, G.
De la Crois gammée au svastika. Etude de symbolique comparée. Bruxelles, 1889. 8o. pp. 291-346.

GN
22
B 66

ETHNOLOGY

Boas, Franz   and others

General anthropology. Boston. 1938

GN
Pam
#391

Ethnology

Davis, B. J.
On some of the bearings of ethnology upon archaeological science.
Edinburg, 1856, pp. 13. 8vo.

GN
320
A 55

ETHNOLOGY

Andree, Richard

Ethnographische Parallelen und Vergleiche. Stuttgart. 1878.

GN
22
B 66

ETHNOLOGY

Boas, Franz

Race, language and culture. Macmillan Company. New York. 1940. R8vo. xx + 647 pp.

GN
320
D 62

ETHNOLOGY

Dixon, Roland B.

The Building of Cultures. New York. 1928.

GN
Ethn
Pam.
#255

ETHNOLOGY

(The) Archaeologist A monthly magazine devoted to Archaeology Ethnology, History etc.

Vol III. no. 4 April 1895.

Columbus O. 1895.

GN
671.N 5
B 97

ETHNOLOGY

Burridge, Kenelm

Mambu: a Melanesian millennium. London Methuen and Co. Ltd. 8vo. 1960. xxiii + 296 pp

---

GN
22
F 52

ETHNOLOGY

Firth, Raymond

Human types. Thomas Nelson and Sons, Ltd. London... (1938). sm8vo. 207 pp.

GN 33 G 73	ETHNOLOGY Graebner, F. 　　Methode der Ethnologie. Mit einem vorwort des herausgebers. Heidelberg, 1911. 8vo. xvii + 192 pp.

GN 320 K 24	ETHNOLOGY Keane, A. H. 　　The world's peoples...London. Hutchinson & Co. 1908. xii + 434 pp.

GN 22 L 91	ETHNOLOGY Lowie, Robert H. 　　An introduction to cultural anthropology. New York. Farrar & Rinehart, Inc. (1934c) 8vo. xii + 365 pp.

GN 400 H 19	ETHNOLOGY Hambly, W. D. 　　Origin of education among primitive peoples ...London. 1926.

AS 36 S1	ETHNOLOGY. **Keith, Arthur,** 1866– 　　The differentiation of mankind into racial types. By Prof. Arthur Keith ... 　　(*In* Smithsonian institution. Annual report. 1919. Washington, 1921. 23½ᶜᵐ. p. 443–453) 　　"Reprinted ... from Nature, vol. 104, no. 2611, Nov. 13, 1919." 　　1. Ethnology.　2. Race. 　Library of Congress　　　Q11.S66 1919 　　　　　　　　　　　　　[10]　　　　　　22–322

GN 470 L 91	ETHNOLOGY Lowie, Robert H. 　　Primitive religion. New York. 1924.

GN 22 H 28	ETHNOLOGY Haring, Douglas G. 　　Order and possibility in social life, by Douglas G. Haring and Mary E. Johnson. New York. Richard R. Smith. 1940. R8vo. xii + 772 pp.

GN 451 L 66	ETHNOLOGY Lévy-Bruhl, Lucien 　　Primitive Mentality...London. (1923.) 2 copies

GN 451 M 32	ETHNOLOGY Marett, R. R. 　　Psychology and folk-lore. London. (1920).

GN 1 A 51	ETHNOLOGY Herskovits, Melville J. 　　Past developments and present currents in ethnology. 　　(American Anthropologist, Vol. 61(3):389–397, 1959)

GN 22 L 76	ETHNOLOGY Linton, Ralph 　　The study of man. An introduction. D. Appleton-Century Company. New York, London. 1936. 8vo. viii + 503 pp. (The Century Social Science Series).

GN Pam. 3029	ETHNOLOGY Omalius D'Halloy,(Jean Baptiste Julien d') baron 　　Manuel pratique d'ethnographie ou description des races humaines...Cinquième édition. Paris. Eugène Lacroix. 1864 　　(Bibliothèque des Professions Industrielles et Agricoles, Série I, No. 16)

GN 11 J11	ETHNOLOGY Jäger, Gustav 　　Handwörterbuch der zoologie, anthropologie und ethnologie. Bd I-VIII. Breslau, Trewendt, 1880-1900.

GN 22 L 76	ETHNOLOGY Linton, Ralph 　　The tree of culture. Alfred A. Knopf. New York. 1955. 8vo. xiv + 3-692 + xvi pp.

GN 400 O 62	ETHNOLOGY Oppel, Alwin 　　Natur und arbeit...Leipzig. 1904.

GN 320 K 24	ETHNOLOGY Keane, A. H. 　　Ethnology. In 2 parts: 1, Fundamental ethnical problems. II, The primary ethnical groups. Stereotyped edition. Cambridge. Univ. Press. 1901. 8vo. xxx + 442 pp.

GN 1 A 62	ETHNOLOGY Lowie, Robert H. 　　Ethnography, cultural and social anthropology 　　(Am. Anthropologist, 55(4):527-534, 1953)

GN 320 P 46	ETHNOLOGY Perry, W. J. 　　The children of the sun;...London. (1923)

GN 320 K 24	ETHNOLOGY Keane, A. H. 　　Man, past and present. Stereotyped edition. Cambridge. Univ. Press. 1900. 8vo. 584pp. illus

GN 17 L 91	ETHNOLOGY Lowie, Robert H(arry) 　　The history of ethnological theory.New York Farrar & Rinehart. (1937) 8vo. xi + 296 pp.

GN 320 P 47	ETHNOLOGY Peschel, Oscar 　　The races of man, and their geographical distribution. From the German. New York. Appleton. 1906. 8vo. xiv + 528 pp.

GN
325
P 68   ETHNOLOGY

Pitt-Rivers, A. Lane-Fox

    The Evolution of Culture and Other Essays. Edited by J. L. Myers, with an introduction by Henry Balfour. Twenty-one plates. Oxford. Clarendon Press. 1906. xx + 232 pp. 8vo.

GN
451
R 62   ETHNOLOGY

Rivers, W. H. R.

    Psychology and Ethnology...London...1926.

GN
22
S 52   ETHNOLOGY

Shapiro, Harry L.   Editor

    Man, culture, and society. Oxford University Press. New York. 1956. 8vo. xiii + 380 pp.

GN
22
Q 2   ETHNOLOGY

Quatrefages de Breau, Jean Louis Armand de

    Histoire Generale des races humaines: introduction a l'etude des races humaines..avec 441 gravures dans le texte, 6 planches et 7 cartes. Paris. A. Hennuyer. 1889. 8vo. xxxiii + 618pp.

GN
320
S 35   ETHNOLOGY

Schmidt, Max

    Grundriss der ethnologischen volkswirtschaftslehre.

Stuttgart, Enke, 1920-21.   2 vol.

GN
490
S 57   ETHNOLOGY

Sieber, Sylvester A.

    The social life of primitive man, by Sylvester A. Sieber and Franz H. Mueller. B. Herder Book Co. St. Louis, and London. 8vo. xiii + 566 pp.

    (based upon "Völker und Kulturen" by Pater Wilhelm Schmidt)

GN
33
R 12   ETHNOLOGY

Radin, Paul

    The method and theory of ethnology; an essay in criticism. First edition. McGraw-Hill Book Company, Inc. New York... 1933 8vo. xv + 278 pp.

GN
22
S 35   ETHNOLOGY

Schmidt, Wilhelm

    The culture historical method of ethnology, the scientific approach to the racial question. Translated by S. A. Sieber. Fortuny's, New York. 1939c. R8vo. XXX, 383 pp.

GN
400
S 64   ETHNOLOGY

Smith, G. Elliot

    Culture: the diffusion controversy...London. 1928

GN
320
R 23   ETHNOLOGY

Ratzel, Friedrich

    The history of mankind, translated from the second German edition, by A. J. Butler, with introduction by E. B. Tylor, with coloured plates maps, and illustrations. 3 vols. London. Macmillan. 1896-1898. R8vo.

GN
22
S 35   ETHNOLOGY

Schmidt, Wilhelm

    Handbuch der Methode der kulturhistorischen Ethnologie. Mit Beiträgen von Wilhelm Koppers. Münster (Westf.) 1937. 8vo. xvi + 338 pp.

GN
22
S 64   ETHNOLOGY

Smith, G. Elliot

    The Diffusion of Culture. London. Watts and Co. 1933. 8vo. x + 239 pp.

GN
320
R 23   ETHNOLOGY

Ratzel, Friedrich

    Völkerunde...Leipzig. Bibliographischen Instituts. 1886-1888. 3 vols. R8vo.

GN
490
S 35   ETHNOLOGY

Schmidt, W(ilhelm)   (Pater Wilhelm)

    Völker und Kulturen. Erster Teil: Gesellschaft und Wirtschaft der Völker. Von W. Schmidt und W. Koppers. Mit einer Karte, 30 teils farbigen Tafeln und 551 Textabbildungen. Regensburg. Josef Habbel. sm4to. (1924) xii + 793 pp.

GN
22
S 82   ETHNOLOGY

Steinmetz, S. R.

    Ethnographisce Fragesammlung zur Erforschung des sozialen Lebens der Völker ausserhalb des modernen europäisch-amerikanischen Kulturkreises...Bearbeitet und erweitert von R. Thurnwald. Berlin. R. v. Decker's Verlag. 1906. 215 pp. 8vo

---

GN
400
R29   ETHNOLOGY

Reclus, Elie

    Primitive folk; studies in comparative ethnology. London, Scott, n.d. 336 pp. pls.

GN
Pams
2798   ETHNOLOGY

Serrano, Antonio

    Primitivos habitantes del Territorio Argentino. Buenos Aires, Jaun Roldan, 1930.

GN
490
T 46   ETHNOLOGY

Thomas, William I.

    Source book for social origins...Chicago. (c1909.)

GN
Pams
2797   ETHNOLOGY

Renaud, E. B.

    Prehistoric cultures of the Cimarron valley, northeastern New Mexico and Western Oklahoma. Colorado Scientific Society Proceedings, vol.12, no.5, 1930.

GN
400
S 49   ETHNOLOGY

Service, Elman R.

    Profiles in ethnology: a revision of "A profile of primitive culture." New York. Harper & Row. 1963. xxix + 509 pp. R8vo.

GN
490
T 54   ETHNOLOGY

Thurnwald, Richard

    Die Menschliche Gesellschaft in ihren Ethno-Soziologischen Grundlagen. Bd. 1-5 Berlin u. Leipzig. Walter de Gruyter & Co. 1931-1935. 8vo.

GN
490
To
ETHNOLOGY

Tozzer, Alfred M.

Social origins and social continuitie

New York, 1925, 286 pp.

GN
406
W 54
ETHNOLOGY

Weule, Karl

Kulturelemente der menschheit: aufänge und urformen der materiellen kultur...Stuttgart. (c1910).

GN
549.M2
Z64
ETHNOLOGY

Zichy, Eugene de

La migration de la race Hongroise.

Budapest, Ranschburg, 1897. 2v. pls. (Voyages au Caucase et en Asie Centrale)

GN
2.I
W 64
ETHNOLOGY

van Bulck, Gaston

Beiträge sur Methodik der Völkerkunde.

(Wiener Beiträge, Jahrgang II, 1931)

GN
Ethn
Pam
2802

AS
763
B-4

Reading
Room
ETHNOLOGY

Whitcombe, J. D.

Notes on Tongan ethnology. Bernice P.Bishop Museum. Occasional paper, vol. IX, no. 9. 1930. 20p.

ETHNOLOGY

See also

CULTURE
MATERIAL CULTURE
ANTHROPOLOGY

GN
470
V 25
ETHNOLOGY

Van Gennep, Arnold

Religions: Moeurs et Légendes...Paris. 1908.

Deuxième série. 1909. 8vo. 318 pp.
Troisième série. 1911. 8vo. 265 pp.
Quatrième série. n.d. 8vo. 270 pp.

GN
22
W1-m
W 81
ETHNOLOGY

Wissler, Clark

Man and culture

New York, Crowell, 1923, 371 pp.

AS
36
S2
Ethnology - BIBLIOGRAPHY

Stearns, May R.

Bibliography of scientific writing of R. E. Stearns. Biographical sketch by William H. Dall. In Smith. Mis. Coll. Vol. 56. no. 18. Wash. 1911.

Note. Ethnology on p. 13.

GN
1
R 45

GN
Pam.
18
ETHNOLOGY

Van Gennep, A.

Remarques sur l'imagerie populaire.

(Revue d'ethnographie et de sociologie, Tome II, Nos. 1-2, 1911)

GN
320
W 87
ETHNOLOGY

Wood, J. G.

Natural history of man...London. George Routledge & Sons. 1868-1870. 2 vols. illus. R8vo.

GN
490
T 46
ETHNOLOGY BIBLIOGRAPHY

Thomas, William I.

Source book for social origins...Chicago. (c1909).

GN
Ethn.
Pam.
No. 676

and
AS
70
So
ETHNOLOGY

Vignati, Milciades Alejo

Contribucion al estudia de la litotecnia chapadmalense. Physis, Vol. VI, pp 238- 247, 1923.

Separate.

GN
320
W 87
ETHNOLOGY

Wood, J. G.

The uncivilized races of men in all countries of the world...In 2 volumes. Hartford. J.B.Burr. 1878. R8vo.

GN
320
W54
ETHNOLOGY - BIBLIOGRAPHY

Weule, Karl

Leitfaden der volkerkunde.

Leipzig, Bibl.Inst. 1912. 152p. pls.

Gn
Eth
Pam
2796
ETHNOLOGY.

Wood-Jones, Frederic.

Claimes of the Australian Aborigine. From Auts. Assn. Adv. Science, vol. XVIII, 1926.

AS
763
B-o
ETHNOLOGY - Collections

Brigham, William T.

Report of a journey around the world undertaken to examine various ethnological collections' 1896

In Occasional Papers, Bernice P. Bishop Museum, Vol.I, No. 1, 1898.

GN
406
W 54

GN
Pam.
2353
ETHNOLOGY

Weule, Karl

Kie kultur der kulturlofen: ein blick in die anfänge menschlicher teiftesbetätigung... Stuttgart. (c1910).

GN
451
W 96
ETHNOLOGY

Wundt, Wilhelm

Element der völkerpsychologie: grundlinien einer psychologischen entwicklungsgeschichte der menschheit. Leipzig, Kröner, 1912. 8vo. xii + 523 pp.

DU
Missions
Pam. 78
ETHNOLOGY COLLECTIONS

Catalogue des Reliques et Collections de l'Oeuvre. Oeuvre de la Propagation de la Foi. Lyon. n.d. 112 pp. 8vo.

AM
Mus.
Pam.
487

ETHNOLOGY COLLECTIONS

An exhibition of Hungarian popular art.
The Ethnographical Museum of Budapest.
1963. 27 pp.

GN
Ethnol.
Pam.
3017

ETHNOLOGY DICTIONARIES

U. S. Immigration Commission

Dictionary of races or peoples...Washington
Government Printing Office. 1911. 150 pp.

(61st Congress, 3d Session, Senate Doc.No.
662. Reports of the Immigration Commission)

GN
33
B 86

ETHNOLOGY -INSTRUCTIONS, METHODS, etc.

British Association for the Advancement of
Science.

Notes and Queries on Anthropology. Fifth
Edition. Edited for the British Association...
London. Royal Anthropological Institute. 1929.
sm8vo. xvi + 404 pp.

2 copies.

AM
Mus.
Pam. 154

ETHNOLOGY COLLECTIONS

The Hawaiian portion of the Polynesian collections in the Peabody Museum of Salem.
Special exhibition, August-November, 1920. R8vo
56 pp. Peabody Museum, Salem.

GN
33
B 86

ETHNOLOGY INSTRUCTIONS METHODS

R. Anthropological Institute of Great Britain
and Ireland.

Notes and queries on anthropology. Sixth
edition. Revised and rewritten by a Committee
of the Royal Anthropological Institute... Routledge and Kegan Paul Ltd., London. 8vo. no date
xi + 403 pp.

AS
701
A

ETHNOLOGY INTRUCTIONS, METHODS,...

Buck, Peter H.

The value of tradition in Polynesian research.

(Australian Association for the Advancement
of Science, Vol.18, 1926, pp. 552-569)

AM
101
S 86

ETHNOLOGY COLLECTIONS

Söderstrom, J(an)

A.Sparrman's ethnographical collection
from James Cook's 2nd expedition (1772-1775)

(The Ethnographical Museum of Sweden,
Stockholm (Statens Etnografiska Museum), New
Ser., Pub. No. 6, 1939)

GN
29
B 18

ETHNOLOGY INSTRUCTIONS, METHODS, ETC.

Balfour, Henry, and others.

Anthropological essays...Oxford. 1907. 4to
pp. 309-324. On the Origin of the Classificatory
System of Relationships, by.W. H. R. Rivers.

GN
Ethn.
Pam.
3028

ETHNOLOGY INSTRUCTIONS, METHODS, ETC.

Frazer, J. G.

Questions on the customs, beliefs, and
languages of savages. Cambridge. University
Press. 1916.

GN
405
Fr

1907 edition.

GN
2.1
A-4

ETHNOLOGY COLLECTORS

Braunholtz, H. J.

Ethnographical museums and the collectors
aims and methods.

(Journ. of the R. Anthrop. Inst. of Great
Britain and Ireland, Vol. 68, 1938, pp. 1-16)

GN
Ethn.Pam.
4125

ETHNOLOGY INSTRUCTIONS, METHODS

Beaglehole, Ernest

Some wider obligations of the field ethno-
logist.

(Am. Anthropologist, 38:516-519, 1936)

AS
36
S2

ETHNOLOGY--INSTRUCTIONS, METHODS, ETC.

Gibbs, George, 1815-1873.
... Instructions for research relative to the ethnology
and philology of America. Prepared for the Smithsonian
institution. By George Gibbs. Washington, Smithsonian
institution, 1863.
2 p. l., 51 p. 23½ᶜᵐ. (Smithsonian miscellaneous collections. [vol. VII,
art. XII])
Publication 160.
Appendix A, Physical character of the Indian races (p. 35-39) and B,
Numeral systems (p. 40-51), dated May, 1865.
Another issue of same date (1 p. l., 33 p.) is without the appendices.
1. Ethnology—Instructions, methods, etc. 2. Indians—Languages. 3. Numerals.
Library of Congress   Q11.S7 vol. 7, art. 11
———— Copy 2.   Q11.S7 2d set   16-5468

GN
670
B 92

ETHNOLOGY, COMPARATIVE-POLYNESIA

Buck, Peter H. (Te Rangi Hiroa)

Vikings of the sunrise...New York. 1938

GN
1
A

ETHNOLOGY INSTRUCTIONS, METHODS

Boas, Franz

The Methods of Ethnology.

(American Anthropologist, N. S.,
Vol. 22, 1920, pp. 311-321)

GN
Ethn.Pam.
2918

INSTRUCTIONS,
ETHNOLOGY -- METHODS

Guthe, Carl E.

A Method of Ceramic Description.

(Papers of the Michigan Academy of Science,
Arts and Letters, Vol. VIII, 1927, pp. 23-29)

GN
1
E 84

ETHNOLOGY - COMPARATIVE - POLYNESIA

Burrows, Edwin G.

Western Polynesia, a study in cultural differentiation.

(Etnologiska Studier, No. 7, 1938, pp. 1-
192)

GN
Pam
2373

ETHNOLOGY - INSTRUCTIONS, METHODS,ETC

Boas, Franz

Review of Graebner's "Methode der
ethnologie". From Science, n.s. v.34,
n.884, 1911.

Q
101
P 18

ETHNOLOGY-INSTRUCTIONS, METHODS

Handy, E. S. Craighill
The importance of recording native systems
of horticulture and therapeutics and the technical knowledge required therein.

IN Proc. Sixth Pac. Sci. Congress, 1939,
(California), Vol. 4, 1940, pp. 127-130.

GN
Ethnol.
Pam.
3017

ETHNOLOGY DICTIONARIES

U. S. Immigration Commission

Dictionary of races or peoples...Washington.
Government Printing Office. 1911. 150 pp.

(61st Congress, 3d Session, Senate Doc.
No. 662. Reports of the Immigration Commission.)

GN
33
B 86

ETHNOLOGY INSTRUCTIONS, METHODS, ETC.

British Association for the Advancement of Science

Notes and Queries on Anthropology, for the
use of travellers and residents in uncivilized
lands...London. 1874. sm8vo. 146 pp.

4th edition, edited by Barbara Freire-Marreco
and John Linton Myers. London. 1912. sm8vo.
288 pp.

AP
2
S 35

ETHNOLOGY - INSTRUCTIONS, METHODS

Herskovits, Melville J.

Applied anthropology and the American anthropologists.

(Science, Vol. 83, 1936, No. 2149, pp. 215-
222)

AS 36 S5

ETHNOLOGY - INSTRUCTION, METHODS, ETC

Holmes, William Henry, 1846-

... Instructions to collectors of historical and anthropological specimens. (Especially designed for collectors in the insular possessions of the United States.) By William Henry Holmes ... and Otis Tufton Mason ... Washington, Govt. print. off., 1902.

16 p. 24½ᶜᵐ. (Part Q of Bulletin of the United States National museum, no. 39)

At head of title: Smithsonian institution. United States National museum.

1. Ethnology—Instruction, methods, etc. 2. Anthropology—Instruction, methods, etc. I. Mason, Otis Tufton, 1838-1908, joint author.

S 13-154

Library, Smithsonian   Institution Q11.U6

GN Ethn. Pam.3412

INSTRUCTIONS
ETHNOLOGY METHODS etc.

Oyarzun, Aureliano

Metodo antropo-etnologico.

(Medicina Moderna, Ano XV, No. 1, 1941, 19 pp.)

AM Mus.Pam. 183

INSTRUCTIONS,
ETHNOLOGY METHODS

Ford, Clellan S.

World area files. (Cross culture survey at Yale) mimeographed. 7 pp.

GN 307 L 68

ETHNOLOGY INSTRUCTIONS, METHODS, etc.

Leyburn, James G.

Handbook of Ethnography. New Haven, Yale University Press. 1931. vii +323 pp. VI maps. 8vo.

GN 2.S Po

INSTRUCTIONS
ETHNOLOGY METHODS

Roberts, Helen H.

Suggestions to Field-workers in Collecting Folk Music and Data about Instruments.

(The Journal of the Polynesian Society, Vol. 40, No. 3, pp. 103-128, 1931)

GN 2.S S 72

ETHNOLOGY LINGUISTICS

Voegelin, C. F.

Linguistics in ethnology. By C. F. Voegelin and Z. S. Harris.

(Southwestern Journal of Anthropology, Vol. 1(4):455-465, 1945)

AS 36 N 3

ETHNOLOGY INSTRUCTIONS, METHODS

Manual for the study of food habits. Report of the Committee on Food Habits. Carl E. Guthe, Chairman; Margaret Mead, Secretary.

(Bull. Nat. Research Council, no. 111, 1945)

QE 185 M

ETHNOLOGY INSTRUCTIONS, METHODS

Sapir, Edward

Time perspective in aboriginal American culture, a study in method.

(Mem. Geological Survey, Canada, Dept. of Mines, No. 90, 1916; being no. 13, of Anthropological series)

GN 1 An

Ethnology-Periodicals

... Anthropos. Ephemeris internationalis ethnologica et linguistica. Rivista internazionale d'etnologia e di linguistica. Revista internacional de etnologia y de lingüistica. International review of ethnology and linguistics. Internationale zeitschrift für völker- u. sprachenkunde ... bd. 1- 1906- Salzburg, Oesterreich, Zaunrith'sche buch-, kunst- und steindruckerei, akt.-ges. [1906-

v. illus., plates, maps, facsim. 23½ᶜᵐ.

(Continued on next card)

7-31775

GN Ethn. Pam. 3150

ETHNOLOGY INSTRUCTIONS, METHODS

Milke, Wilhelm

Südostmelanesien: Eine ethnostatistische Analyse. (dissertation) Würzburg. Konrad Triltsch. 8vo. 60 pp.

AS 36 S2

ETHNOLOGY - INSTRUCTIONS, METHODS, ETC.

Smithsonian institution.

... Suggestions relative to objects of scientific investigation in Russian America. [Washington, Smithsonian institution, 1867]

10 p. 24ᶜᵐ. (Smithsonian miscellaneous collections. [vol. VIII, art. VII])

Caption title.
Publication 207.
"The meteorological suggestions were prepared by myself, the ethnological by Mr. George Gibbs, and those which relate to natural history by Professor Baird ..." [Signed] Joseph Henry.

1. Meteorology—Observers' manuals. 2. Ethnology—Instructions, methods, etc. 3. Natural history—Technique. I. Henry, Joseph, 1799-1878. II. Gibbs, George, 1815-1873. III. Baird, Spencer Fullerton, 1823-1887. IV. Title.

16-6886

Library of Congress   Q11.S7 vol. 8, art. 6

GN 1 An

Ethnology-Periodicals

... Anthropos ... [1906-] (Card 2)

At head of title: Revue internationale d'ethnologie et de linguistique. Im auftrage der oesterreichischen Leo-gesellschaft mit unterstützung der deutschen Görres-gesellschaft hrsg. unter mitarbeit zahlreicher missionare von P. W. Schmidt s. v. D.

Contributions in French, German, English, Italian, etc.

1. Ethnology—Period. 2. Languages—Period. I. Schmidt, Wilhelm, 1868- ed. II. Leo-gesellschaft, Vienna. III. Görres-gesellschaft zur pflege der wissenschaft im katholischen Deutschland, Bonn.

7-31775

Library of Congress   GN1.A7

GN 2.I Y 17

ETHNOLOGY INSTRUCTIONS, METHODS

Murdock, George P. and others

Outline of cultural materials. Prepared by George P. Murdock, Clellan S. Ford, Alfred E. Hudson, Raymond Kennedy, Leo W. Simmons, John W. M. Whiting.

(Yale Anthropological Studies, Vol. 2, 1945)

GN Pam 2419

ETHNOLOGY - INSTRUCTIONS, METHODS, ETC

Societe Belge de sociologie

Enquete enthographique et sociologique sur les peuples de civilisation inferieure.

Bruxelles, Polleunis, 1905.   95p.

GN 1 B92-a

ETHNOLOGY PERIODICALS

Buenos Aires, Universidad

Archivos del Museo Etnografico, Facultad de Filosofia y Letras.

Numeros 1-   1930-

Buenos Aires, Imprenta de la Universidad, 1930-   8vo
For current volumes see serial file

GN Ethn.Pam. 3877

ETHNOLOGY INSTRUCTIONS, METHODS

Murdock, George P. and others

Outline of cultural materials. 3rd revised edition. By George P. Murdock, Clellan S. Ford, Alfred E. Hudson, Raymond Kennedy, Leo W. Simmons, John W. M. Whiting. Published by Human Relations Area Files, Inc. New Haven.

(Behavior Science Outlines, Vol. 1, 1950)

GN Ethn.Pam. 2965

ETHNOLOGY INSTRUCTIONS, METHODS

Westermann, Diedrich

The Missionary and Anthropological Research, by Diedrich Westermann and Richard Thurnwald.

(International Institute of African Languages and Cultures, Memorandum VIII, 1932. 31 pp. 8vo)

GN 1 B 92-n

ETHNOLOGY PERIODICALS

Buenos Aires, Universidad

Notas del Museo Etnográfico, Facultad de Filosofia y Letras.

Numeros 2,4   1930

Buenos Aires, Imprenta de la Universidad, 1930-> 8vo For current volumes see serial file

---

GN Ethn. Pam. 3972 3973

GN 308 M 97

ETHNOLOGY INSTRUCTIONS, METHODS

Murdock, George P.

Outline of world cultures. Behavior Science Outlines. Human Relations Area Files. Yale University. New Haven. 1954. mimeographed 4to. 180 pp.

[two copies]

Q 101 P 18

ETHNOLOGY-INSTRUCTIONS, METHODS POLYNESIA

Piddington, Ralph
Methods of research in Polynesian ethnography.

IN Proc. Sixth Pac. Sci. Congress, 1939, (California), Vol. 4, 1940, pp. 81-84.

G 1 G56

ETHNOLOGY - PERIODICALS

Globus. Illustrierte zeitschrift für länder und völkerkunde... begründet 1862 von Karl Andree... herausgegeben von H. Singer... Richard Andree.

Braunschweig, 1862-1911.

Library has
Bd. LXXI-XCVIII, 1896-1911.

GN
1
Ar

ETHNOLOGY -- PERIODICALS

Internationales Archiv fur Ethnographie

Band I, 1888 -

Leiden , 4to

See serial file

QK
1
L 2

ETHNOLOGY   ADMIRALTY ISLANDS

Moseley, H. N.

Notes on the varieties of plants made use of as food and as implements, clothing, etc. by the natives of the Admiralty Islands.

(Jour. Linn. Soc. London, Botany, 15: 80-82, 1877)

GN
651
C 99

ETHNOLOGY AFRICA

Czekanowski, Jan

Forschungen im Nil-Kongo-Zwischengebiet von Dr. Jan Czekanowski: Dritter band: Ethnographisch-anthropologischer atlas. Zwischenseen-Bantu, Pygmäen und Pygmoiden, Urwaldstämme...Leipsig. 1911. 4to.

2 copies

(Wissenschaftliche Ergebnisse der Deutschen Zentral-Afrika-Expedition 1907-1908 unter führung Adolf Friedrichs, Herzogs zu Mecklenburg, Band VII.)

AS
63
M

ETHNOLOGY PERIODICALS

Mexico. Museo Nacional de Arqueologia, Historia y Etnologia.

Boletin

For current volumes see serial file

GN
663
T 44

ETHNOLOGY ADMIRALTY ISLANDS

Nevermann, Hans

Admiralitäts-Inseln

Thilenius, G.

Ergebnisse der Südsee-Expedition, 1908-1910. II. Ethnographie: A.Melanesien, Band 3. 1934.

GN
653
D 39

ETHNOLOGY AFRICA

Dennett, R. E.

Nigerian studies, or, the religious and political system of the Yoruba. London. 1910. 8vo.

GN
1
069

ETHNOLOGY - PERIODICALS

Orientalisches Archiv: illustrierte zeitschrift fur kunst, kulturgeschichte und volkerkunde der lander des Ostens. Herausgegenem von Hugo Grothe.

Leipzig, Hiersemann, 1910-

see serial file

GN
671.A2
S 41

ETHNOLOGY   ADMIRALTY ISLANDS

Schwartz, Theodore

The Paliau Movement in the Admiralty Islands, 1946-1954.   4to

(Am. Mus. of Nat. Hist., Anthropological Papers, Vol. 49(2):211-421 + plates:14-28, 1962)

GN
655
E 47

ETHNOLOGY AFRICA

Ellis, A. B.

The Yoruba-speaking peoples of the Slave Coast of West Africa, their religion, manners, customs, laws, language, etc. With an apendix containing a comparison of the Tshi, Gā, Ewe, and Yoruba languages. London. 1894. 8vo.

GN
2.S
W 96

ETHNOLOGY PERIODICALS

Württembergischen Vereins für Handelsgeographie und Förderung deutschen Interessen im Auslande E. V.

Jahresbericht

30-   1911-

For current volumes see serial file

GN
646
B 28

ETHNOLOGY AFRICA

Barth, Heinrich

Reisen und entdeckungen in nord und central Africa in den jahren 1849-1855. Gotha. Perthes 1857-1858. 5 vols. in 15 parts (each Vol. in 3 parts.) 8vo.

GN
645
F 92

ETHNOLOGY AFRICA

Frobenius, L.

Die Masken und Geheimbünde Afrikas... Halle. 1898. 4to.

(Nova Acta. Abh. der Kaiserl.Leop.-Carol. Deutschen Akademie der Naturforscher, Band LXXIV, Nr. 1, Juni 3, 1898.)

GN
E thm.Pam.
2844

ETHNOLOGY - Race Relations

Park, Robert E.

A Race Relations Survey - Suggestions for a Study of the Oriental Population of the Pacific Coast.

Reprinted from Journal of Applied Sociology Vol. VIII, pp.195-205, March-April 1924.

GN
651
B 32

ETHNOLOGY AFRICA

Bastian, Adolf

Die Deutsche Expedition an der Loango-küste, nebst älteren Nachrichten über die zu erstorschenden Länder...Erster band, Mit 1 lithographirten tafel und 1 Karte; Zweiter band, mit 2 lithographirten tafeln...Jena. 1874-1875. 2 vols. in 1. 8vo.

AS
36
S1

ETHNOLOGY--AFRICA

Frobenius, Leo, 1873-
The origin of African civilizations. By L. Frobenius.

(*In* Smithsonian institution. Annual report. 1898. Washington, 1899, 23¾ᶜᵐ. p. 637-650. fold. map, tab.)

"Translated from Sonder-abdruck aus der Zeitschr. der Gesellsch. f. erdk. zu Berlin, bd. XXXIII, 1898."

1. Ethnology—Africa. 2. Africa—Civilization.

Library of Congress   Q11.S66 1898
Library, Smithsonian   Institution

S 15-1015

GN
2.S
S 72

ETHNOLOGY   TECHNIQUE

Goodenough, Ward

Residence rules.

(Southwestern Journal of Anthropology, Vol. 12(1):22-37, 1956)

GN
651
C 33

ETHNOLOGY AFRICA

Casati, Gaetano

Zehn jahre in Äquatoria und die rückkehr mit Emin Pascha...nach der italienischen originalausgabe ins Deutsche übersekt von Professor Dr. Karl von Reinhardstöttner. Einzige autoristierte deutsche ausgabe...Erster band; Zweiter band. Hamberg. 1891. 2vols. 8vo.

GN
2.M
F 45

ETHNOLOGY AFRICA

Hambly, Wilfrid D.

Source book of African anthropology.

(Field Museum of Nat. His. Anthropological Series, Vol. 26, 1937)

AS
142
V

ETHNOLOGY   ADMIRALTY ISLANDS

Finsch, Otto

Ethnologische Erfahrungen und Belegstücke aus der Südsee...

(Ann. K. K. Naturhist. Mus., Wien, Bd. 3:83-160, 1888; Bd. 8:400, 1893)

GN
658
C 97

ETHNOLOGY AFRICA

Cunningham, J. F.

Uganda and its peoples: notes on the Protectorate of Uganda...London. 1905. R8vo.

GN
645
H 33

ETHNOLOGY AFRICA

Hartmann, Robert

Die Nigritier: Eine anthropologisch-ethnologische monographie...Erster theil...Berlin. 1876. R8vo.

GN
645
H33
ETHNOLOGY - AFRICA

Hartmann, Robert

    Die völker Afrikas. Mit 94 abbildungen in holzschnitt.
Leipzig, Brockhaus, 1879. xxii + 344 pp. 12mo.

GN
655.K2
P28
ETHNOLOGY - AFRICA,

Passarge, Siegfried

    Adamaua: bericht über die expedition des deutschen Kamerun-komitees in den jahren 1893/94...
Berlin, Reimer, 1895. 4to. 573p. pls.

GN
651
S 41

2 copies
ETHNOLOGY AFRICA

Schweinfurth, Georg

    Artes Africanae. Illustrations and descriptions of productions of the industrial arts of central African tribes...Leipzig. 1875. 4to.

GN
651
J 72
ETHNOLOGY AFRICA

Johnston, H. H.

    Der Kilima-Ndjaro:forschungsreise im östlichen Aequatorial-Afrika. Nebst einer schilderung der naturgeschichtlichen und commerziellen verhältnisse sowie der sprachen des Kilima-Ndjaro-gebietes. Autorisirte Deutsche ausgabe aus dem Englischen von W. von Freeden...Leipzig. 1886. 8vo.

GN
650
P 32
ETHNOLOGY AFRICA

Paulitschke, Philipp

    Ethnographie Nordost-Afrikas. Die materielle cultur der Danäkil, Galla und Somâl...Berlin. 1893. 4to.

GN
654
T 48
ETHNOLOGY AFRICA

Thonner, Franz

    Vom Kongo zum Ubangi: meine zweite reise in mittelafrika...Berlin. 1910. R8vo.

GN
651
J 72
ETHNOLOGY AFRICA

Johnston, H. H.

    Der Kilima-Ndjaro:forschungsreise im östlichen Aequatorial-Afrika. Nebst einer schilderung der naturgeschichtlichen und commerziellen verhältnisse sowie der sprachen des Kilima-Ndjaro-gebietes...Leipzig. 1886. 8vo.

GN
651
P 36
ETHNOLOGY AFRICA

Pechuël-Loesche, E.

    Die Loango-Expedition. Dritte abteilung, zweite hälfte. Stuttgart. 1907. 4to.

GN
Ethn.
Pam.
3939
ETHNOLOGY AFRICA

UNESCO

    Men against ignorance. Printed by Gassmann S.A. Soleure (Switzerland). 1953. 8vo. 5-81 pp.

GN
645
L 74
ETHNOLOGY AFRICA

Lindblom, Gerhard

    Jakt- och Fangstmethoder bland Afrikanska Folk. Del I-II. (with a retrospect in English) Med...textbilder. Stockholm. Victor Pettersons 1925-1926. (Etnografiska Riksmuseet). 8vo. 138 + 157 pp.

GN
653
R 84
ETHNOLOGY AFRICA

Roth, H. Ling

    Great Benin, its customs, art and horrors...Halifax. 1903. R8vo.

GN
646
W 46
ETHNOLOGY AFRICA

    Der Weltteil Afrika in Einzeldarstellungen. Leipzig. Freytag. 1883-1885. 4 vols. 12mo.

    v.1 Abyssinien...von R. Hartmann.
    v.2 Die Nilländer, von R. Hartmann.
    v.3 Afrikas Westküste...von F. Falkenstein.
    v.4 Südafrika...von Gustav Fritsch.

    (Das Wissen der Gegenwart. Deutsche Universal-Bibliothek für Gebildete, Band XIV, XXIV, XXIX, XXXIV)

GN
Ethn.
Pam.
3395
ETHNOLOGY AFRICA

Lindblom, K. G.

    The sling, especially in Africa: additional notes to a previous paper.

    (Statens Etnografiska Museum, Smarre Meddelanden, Nr. 17, 1940)

GN
Ethn.Pam.
3203
ETHNOLOGY AFRICA

Schapera, I.

    The contributions of western civilisation to modern Kxatla culture.

    (Reprint from Trans. of the Royal Soc. of South Africa, vol.XXIV. 1936. pp.221-252)

GN
Ethn.
Pam.
3407
ETHNOLOGY AFRICA

Wieschhoff, H. A.

    The Zimbabwe-Monomotapa culture in southeast Africa.

    (General Series in Anthropology, No. 8, 1941 (place?))

GN
653
M 35
ETHNOLOGY AFRICA

Marquart, Jos.

    Die Benin-Sammlung des Reichsmuseums für Volkerkunde in Leiden...

    (Veroff. des Reichsmuseums f. Völkerkunde in Leiden. Ser. II, Nr. 7, 1913)

GN
656
S 39
ETHNOLOGY AFRICA

Schultze, Leonhard

    Aus Namaland und Kalahari:Bericht an die Kgl. Preuss.Akademie der Wissenschaften zu Berlin über eine forschungsreise im westlichen und zentralen Südafrika, ausgeführt in den jahren 1903-1905 von Dr. Leonhard Schultze...Jena. 1907. 4to.

Q
W 95

looked
case
ETHNOLOGY AFRICA

Wüllerstorf-Urbair, Bernhard

    Reise der österreichischen Fregatte Novara um die erde in den jahren 1857, 1858, 1859...

    Anthropologischer Theil, Dritte Abt.: Ethnographie...Wein. 1868. 4to. pp. 91-121. von Friedrich Müller.

GN
651
M 48
ETHNOLOGY AFRICA

Mecklenburg-Strelitz,Adolf Friedrich herzog zu

    Ins innerste Afrika: Bericht über den Verlauf der deutschen wissenschaftlichen Zentral-Afrika-Expedition 1907-1908. Leipzig. 1909. R8vo.

GN
656
S 41
ETHNOLOGY AFRICA

Schwarz, E. H. L.

    The Kalahari and its native races: being the account of a journey through Ngamiland and the Kalahari, with a special study of the natives in that area...London. 1928. 8vo.

ETHNOLOGY AFRICA

    See also tribal headings under subjects, as

Religion- Bantu, etc.

GN
654
B 91
ETHNOLOGY AFRICA CONGO

(Brussells, Musée du congo)

L'Etat Indépendant du Congo. Documents sur le pays et ses habitants. Annexe aux Annales du Musée du Congo. Bruxelles. 1904. 4to.

GN
657.K2
M 95
ETHNOLOGY AFRICA, EAST

Muller, Hendrik P. N.

Industrie des Cafres du Sud-est de l'Afrique Collection recueillie sur les lieux et notice ethnographique par Hendrik P. N. Muller. Description des objects representes par Joh. F. Snelleman. Leiden. n.d. 4to.

2 copies

GN
660.B8
S 89
ETHNOLOGY AFRICA, SOUTH

Stow, George W.

The native races of South Africa, a history of the intrusion of the Hottentots and Bantu into the hunting grounds of the Bushmen, the Aborigines of the country. With numerous illustrations ...edited by George McCall Theal...London. 1905. R8vo.

GN
659.G3
F 95
ETHNOLOGY AFRICA, EAST

Fülleborn, Friedrich

Das Deutsche Njassa und Ruwama-gebiet, land und leute, nebst bemerkugen über die Schire-Länder. Mit benutzung von ergebnissen der Njassa und Kingagebirgs-Expedition der Hermann und Elise geb. Heckmann Wentzel-Stiftung verfasst von Dr. Friedrich Fülleborn...Berlin. 1906. R8vo.

Oversize
Atlas. Folio.
(Deutsch-　　　Ost-Africa, Band IX)

GN
658
R 34
ETHNOLOGY AFRICA, EAST

Rehse, Hermann

Kiziba: land und leute. Eine Monographie von Hermann Rehse. Mit einem vorwort von Prof. Dr. v. Luschan...Stuttgart. 1910. R8vo.

AS
36
S1
ETHNOLOGY - AFRICA, NORTH

Fischer, Theobald, 1846-
The Mediterranean peoples. By Theobald Fischer ...

(*In* Smithsonian institution. Annual report. 1907. Washington, 1908. 33¼ᶜᵐ. p. 497-521)

"Translated ... from the Internationale wochenschrift. Berlin, September 7, 14, 21, 28, 1907."

1. Mediterranean race. 2. Ethnology—Europe. 3. Ethnology—Africa, North.

Library of Congress　　　Q11.S66 1907
Library, Smithsonian　　　Institution
S 15-1349

GN
658
G 98
ETHNOLOGY AFRICA, EAST

Gutmann, Bruno

Dichten und denten der Dschagganeger: Beiträge zur ostafrikanischen volkskunde von Bruno Gutmann...Leipzig. 1909. 8vo.

GN
659.G3
W 42
ETHNOLOGY AFRICA, (EAST)

Weiss, Max

Die völkerstämme in norden Deutsch Ostafrikas...Berlin, Marschner, 1910. R8vo.

GN
655
E 47
ETHNOLOGY AFRICA, WEST

Ellis, A. B.

The Ewe-speaking peoples of the Slave Coast of West Africa: their religion, manners, customs, laws, languages, etc...London. 1890. 8vo.

GN
659.A
H 68
ETHNOLOGY AFRICA, (EAST)

Hobley, C. W.

Ethnology of A-Kamba and other east African tribes. Cambridge. 1910. 8vo.

GN
658
W 54
ETHNOLOGY AFRICA, EAST

Weule, Karl

Negerleben in Ostafrika: Ergebnisse einer ethnologischen forschungsreise von Dr. Karl Weule...Zweite auflage. Leipzig. 1909. 8vo.

GN
653
E47
ETHNOLOGY - AFRICA, WEST

Ellis, A. B.

The Tshi-speaking peoples of the Gold Coast of West Africa: their religion, manners, customs, laws, language, etc.

London, Chapman, 1887.　343p.　8vo.

GN
658
K 39
ETHNOLOGY AFRICA, (EAST)

Kersten, Otto

Baron Carl Claus von der Decken's reisen in Ost-Afrika in den jahren 1859 bis 1861. Bearbeitet von Otto Kersten...Die Insel Zanzibar. Reisen nach dem Niassasee und dem Schneeberge Kilimandscharo...Leipzig. 1869. R8vo. Erster band.

GN
659.G3
W 54
ETHNOLOGY AFRICA, EAST

Weule, Karl

Wissenschaftliche ergebnisse meiner ethnographischen forschungsreise in den Südosten Deutsch-Ostafrikas: Ergänzungsheft Nr. 1. Der Mitteilungen aus den Deutschen Schutzgebieten... Berlin. 1908. 4to.

2 copies
(Wissenschaftliche Beihefte zum Deutschen Kolonialblatte.)

GN
654
D 39
ETHNOLOGY AFRICA, WEST

Dennett, R. E.

At the back of the black man's mind, or Notes on the kingly office in west Africa. London. 1906. 8vo.

GN
659.A
L 74
ETHNOLOGY AFRICA, (EAST)

Lindblom, Gerhard

The Akamba in British East Africa: an ethnological monograph...P.I-III. Inaugural dissertation...Uppsala. 1916. 8vo.

GN
649
B 54
ETHNOLOGY AFRICA, NORTH

Bertholon, L.

Recherches anthropologiques dans la Berbérie Orientale: Tripolitaine, Tunisie, Algérie, par L. Bertholon et E. Chantre...2 vols. Lyon. 1912-1913. 4to.

Tome premier: Anthropométrie, Craniométrie, Ethnographie...
Tome Deuxieme: Album de 174 portraits Ethniques.

GN
Ethn.Pam.
3303
ETHNOLOGY AFRICA, WEST

Hall, H. U.

The Sherbro of Sierra Leone, a preliminary report on the work of the Univ. Museum's expedition to West Africa, 1937.

(Univ. Press, University of Pennsylvania, Philadelphia. 1938. 4to.　v+ 52 pp. index and map.)

GN
659.M3
M 56
ETHNOLOGY AFRICA, (EAST)

Merker, M.

Die Masai. Ethnographische Monographie eines Ostafrikanischen Semitenvolkes...Berlin. 1904. 2 volumes. R8vo.

GN
656
F 91
ETHNOLOGY AFRICA, SOUTH

Fritsch, Gustav

Die eingeborenen Süd-Afrika's ethnographisch und anatomisch beschrieben von Gustav Fritsch... mit zahlreichen illustrationen...zwanzig lithographischen tafeln...nebst einem Atlas enthaltend sechzig in kupfer radirte portraitköpfe. Breslau 1872. R8vo.

Atlas. Enthaltend dreissig tafeln racentypen ...4to. 7 pp. &　　　pls.

GN
655.K2
H 98
ETHNOLOGY AFRICA, WEST

Hutter, Franz

Wanderungen und forschungen im Nord-Hinterland von Kamerun...Braunschweig, Vieweg. 1902. R8vo.

GN
653
L 58 ETHNOLOGY AFRICA, WEST

Leonard, Arthur Glyn

The lower Niger and its tribes. London.
1906. 8vo.

GN
655.K2
M 28 ETHNOLOGY AFRICA, WEST

Mansfeld, Alfred

Urwald-Dokumente: vier jahre unter den cross
flussnegern Kameruns von Dr. Alfred Mansfeld...
Berlin. 1908. 4to.

GN
654
S 79 ETHNOLOGY AFRICA, WEST

Starr, Frederick

Congo natives: an ethnographic album.
Chicago. 1912. 4to.

GN
Ethn.Pam.
3229 ETHNOLOGY AINU

Batchelor, John

Echoes of doomed race. 46 typed pages.
(Ainus)

GN
635.J3
B 32 ETHNOLOGY AINU

Batchelor, John

The pit-dwellers of Hokkaido and Ainu place
names considered. Sapporo. 1925. 8vo. 48 pp.

GN
27
M 97 ETHNOLOGY AINU

Murdock, George Peter

Our primitive contemporaries.
The Macmillan Company. New York. sm8vo. xxii +
614 pp. 1934c

GN
635.J3
S 79 ETHNOLOGY AINU

Starr, Frederick

The Ainu group at the Saint Louis Exposition.
Chicago, Open Court, 1904. 118 p. pls.

GN
2.S
P 76 ETHNOLOGY AINU

Sutherland, I.L.G.

The Ainu people of northern Japan.

(Journal of the Polynesian Society, Vol.
57(3):203-226, 1948)

GN
635.J3
T 68 ETHNOLOGY AINU

Torii, R.

Etudes Archeologiques et Ethnologiques: Les
Aïnou des Iles Kouriles. Tokyo. 1919. 4to.

(Journal of the College of Science, Imperial
Univ. of Tokyo, Vol. XLII, Art. 1, Jan. 29, 1919)

G
1
As ETHNOLOGY ALASKA

Hrdlička, Aleš

Where Asia and America meet.

(Asia,Vol.39, 1939,pp.354-359)

GN
Ethn.Pam
2810 ETHNOLOGY ALASKA

Shapiro, H. L.

The Alaskan Eskimo. A Study of the Relationship Between the Eskimo and the Chippewyan Indians
of Central Canada.

(Anthropological Papers of the American
Museum of Natural History, Vol. XXXI, Part VI, 1931
New York. pp. 347-384)

GF
501
S81 ETHNOLOGY - ALASKA

Steensby, H. P.

An anthropogeographical study of the
origin of the Eskimo culture.

Kovenhavn, Bianco Lunos, 1916. 228p. pls

GN
673
S81 ETHNOLOGY - ALASKA

Steensby, H. P.

Om Eskimokulturens oprindelse: en
etnografisk og antropogeografisk studie.

København, Salmonsens, 1905. 219p.

QH
1
P 11 ETHNOLOGY ALEUTIAN ISLANDS

Bank, Theodore P.

Biological succession in the Aleutians.

(Pacific Science, Vol. VII(4):493-503, 1953)

GN
673
H 87 ETHNOLOGY ALEUTIAN ISLANDS

Hrdlička, Aleš

The Aleutian and Commander Islands and their
inhabitants. Published by The Wistar Institute
of Anatomy and Biology. Philadelphia. 1945.
R8vo. xx + 630 pp.

F
951
J 63 ETHNOLOGY - ALEUTIAN ISLANDS

Jochelson, Waldemar

History, Ethnology and Anthropology of the
Aleut.

(Carnegie Institution of Washington,
Publication No. 432. 1933. 4to. v + 91 pp.)

GN
649
V.25 ETHNOLOGY - ALGERIA

Van Gennep, Arnold

En Algerie.

Paris, Mercvre de France. 1914. 8vo. 217pp.

DU
80
A 93 ETHNOLOGY AMBRYM

Guiart, J.

Report on the native situation in the north
of Ambrym (New Hebrides).

(South Pacific, Vol. 5(12):256-267, 1952)

GN
2.S
O 15 ETHNOLOGY AMBRYM

Guiart, Jean

Societes, rituels, et mythes du Nord Ambrym.

(Journal de la Socl des Oceanistes, 7:5-103,
1951)

GN
550
B 32 ETHNOLOGY AMERICA

Bastian, Adolf

Die Culturländer des Alten America; Erster
band, Zweiter band. Berlin. 1878.

GN
2M
F1 ETHNOLOGY - AMERICA

Field museum of natural history, *Chicago.*
Publications of the Field Columbian museum; anthro-
pological series. v. 1– date
Chicago [1895–

v. illus., plates (part fold., part col.) plans (part fold.)
diagrs. (part fold.) 24½ᶜᵐ.

1. Anthropology—Societies. 2. Ethnology—America. 3. Indians.

6-20329

Library of Congress   GN2.F4

3

AS S1
ETHNOLOGY - AMERICA.
Mason, Otis Tufton, 1838-1908.
Migration and the food quest; a study in the peopling of America. By Otis Tufton Mason.
(*In* Smithsonian institution. Annual report. 1894. Washington, 1896. 23½cm. p. 523-539. pl.)

1. Man, Migrations of. 2. Ethnology—America. I. Title.
S 15-874
Library of Congress   Q11.S66 1894
Library, Smithsonian   Institution

AS 36 B 74 j
ETHNOLOGY AMERICA
Morton, Samuel G.
An inquiry into the distinctive characteristics of the aboriginal race of America.
and GN Ethn. Pam. 4281
(Boston Journal of Natural History, Vol. 4: 190-223, 1844)

AS 36 S1
ETHNOLOGY--AMERICA
Putnam, Frederic Ward, 1839-
A problem in American anthropology. By Frederic Ward Putnam.
(*In* Smithsonian institution. Annual report. 1899. Washington, 1901. 23½cm. p. 473-485)
"Printed in Science, August 25, 1899."

1. Ethnology—America.
S 15-1039
Library of Congress   Q11.S66 1899
Library, Smithsonian   Institution

AS 36 S1
ETHNOLOGY - AMERICA
Quatrefages de Bréau, Armand i. e. Jean Louis Armand de, 1810-1892.
The advent of man in America. By Armand de Quatrefages.
(*In* Smithsonian institution. Annual report. 1892. Washington, 1893. 23½cm. p. 513-520.)
Proceedings of the 8th session of International congress of Americanists. Paris, 1890. pp. 43-55.

1. Ethnology—America. I. Title.
S 15-797
Library of Congress   Q11.S66 1892
Library, Smithsonian   Institution

GN 550 S
ETHNOLOGY -- AMERICA
U. S. *Bureau of American ethnology.*
Annual report of the Bureau of American ethnology to the secretary of the Smithsonian institution. 1st-1879/80-19 to date
Washington, Govt. print. off., 1881-19
v. illus., plates (part fold., part col.) ports., maps (part fold.) plans (part fold.) 29½cm.
Some of the folded plates, maps and plans are in pockets.
Administrative report and accompanying papers.
Report year ends June 30.
Director, 1879-1902: J. W. Powell; chief, 1902-1909: W. H. Holmes; ethnologist-in-charge, 1910-1918: F. W. Hodge; 1918- J. W. Fewkes.
Reports for 1879/80-1893/94 have title: First-fifteenth annual report of the Bureau of ethnology.
1. Ethnology—America. 2. Indians. 3. America—Antiq. I. Powell, John Wesley, 1834-1902. II. Holmes, William Henry, 1846- III. Hodge, Frederick Webb, 1864- IV. Fewkes, Jesse Walter, 1850-
Library of Congress   E51.U55   7-38073
(a2013)

GN 550 S
ETHNOLOGY--AMERICA.
U. S. *Bureau of American ethnology.*
Bulletin. no. 1-
Washington, Govt. print. off., 1887-
v. in illus., plates (part fold.) maps (part fold.) plans, facsims. 24-29½cm.
Bulletins 1-24 have individual titles only, numbering and use of series title beginning with no. 25.

1. Ethnology—America. 2. Indians. 3. America—Antiq. I. Title.
Library of Congress   E51.U6   6-6657
(a20h2)

AS 36 S1
ETHNOLOGY - AMERICA
Wilson, *Sir* Daniel, 1816-1892.
... Physical ethnology. By Daniel Wilson ...
(*In* Smithsonian institution. Annual report. 1862. Washington, 1863. 23½cm. p. (240)-302. illus., tables)

1. Craniology—America. 2. Ethnology—America. I. Title.
S 15-126
Library of Congress   Q11.S66 1862
Library, Smithsonian   Institution

---

6 116 W 95
locked case
ETHNOLOGY AMERICA
Wüllerstorf-Urbair, Bernhard
Reise der Österreichischen Fregatte Novara um die erde in den Jahren 1857, 1858, 1859...
Anthropologischer Theil, Dritte Abt.: Ethnographie...Wien. 1868. 4to. pp. 122-36. von Friedrich Müller.

GN 550 S
ETHNOLOGY--AMERICA--BIBL.
U. S. *Bureau of American ethnology.*
... List of the publications of the Bureau of ethnology, with index to authors and subjects, by Frederick Webb Hodge. Washington, Govt. print. off., 1894.
2 p. l., 3-25 p. 24cm. (Its Bulletin, no. 24)

1. Indians of North America—Bibl. 2. Ethnology—America—Bibl. 3. U. S.—Government publications—Bibl. I. Hodge, Frederick Webb, comp.
Library of Congress   E51.U6 no. 24   1—2425
—— Copy 2.   Z5114.U58

GN 550 S
ETHNOLOGY--AMERICA--BIBL.
U. S. *Bureau of American ethnology.*
... List of publications of the Bureau of American ethnology with index to authors and titles. Washington, Govt. print. off., 1906.
31 p. 23cm. (Smithsonian institution. Bureau of American ethnology. Bulletin 31)

1. Indians of North America—Bibl. 2. Ethnology—America—Bibl. 3. U. S.—Government publications—Bibl. I. Title.
Library of Congress   E51.U6 no. 31   6-35297
—— (Another issue)   Z5114.U58 1906
59th Cong., 1st sess. House. Doc. 927.   (a19g3)

GN 550 S
ETHNOLOGY--AMERICA--BIBL.
U. S. *Bureau of American ethnology.*
... List of publications of the Bureau of American ethnology with index to authors and titles. Washington, Govt. print. off., 1907.
31 p. 23cm. (Its Bulletin no. 36)
59th Cong., 2d sess. House. Doc. 819.

1. Indians of North America—Bibl. 2. Ethnology—America—Bibl. 3. U. S.—Government publications—Bibl.
Library of Congress   E51.U6 no. 36   7—35274
—— Copy 2.   Z5114.U58 1907

GN 550 S
ETHNOLOGY--AMERICA --BIBL.
U. S. *Bureau of American ethnology.*
List of publications of the Bureau of American ethnology, with index to authors and titles.
(*In its* Thirtieth annual report, 1908-1909. Washington, 1915. 29½cm. p. 387-425)

1. Indians of North America—Bibl. 2. Ethnology—America—Bibl. 3. U. S.—Government publications—Bibl. I. Title.
Library of Congress   E51.U55 30th   16-9899

GN 550 S
ETHNOLOGY--AMERICA--BIBL.
U. S. *Bureau of American ethnology.*
... List of publications of the Bureau of American ethnology with index to authors and titles. (2d impression) Washington, Govt. print. off., 1911.
34 p. 23½cm. (Smithsonian institution. Bureau of American ethnology. Bulletin 49)

1. Indians of North America—Bibl. 2. Ethnology—America—Bibl. 3. U. S.—Government publications—Bibl. I. Title.
Library of Congress   E51.U6 no. 49   11—23020
—— Copy 2.   Z5114.U58 1911

GN 550 S
ETHNOLOGY--AMERICA--BIBL.
U. S. *Bureau of American ethnology.*
... List of publications of the Bureau of American ethnology, with index to titles. (2d impression) Washington, Govt. print. off., 1915.
39 p. 24½cm. (Smithsonian institution. Bureau of American ethnol-... Bulletin 58)

1. Indians of North America—Bibl. 2. Ethnology—America—Bibl. 3. U. S.—Government publications—Bibl.
Library of Congress   E51.U6 no. 58 a   16—2383
—— Copy 2.   Z5114.U58 1915

GN 550 S
ETHNOLOGY -- AMERICA -- BIBLIOGRAPHY
U. S. *Bureau of American ethnology.*
List of publications of the Bureau of American ethnology, with index to authors and titles. Washington, Govt. print. off., 1919.
40 p. 23cm.

1. Indians of North America—Bibl. 2. Ethnology—America—Bibl. 3. U. S.—Government publications—Bibl.
Library of Congress   Z5114.U58 1919   19-11879
—— Copy 2.   (3)

AS 36 S1
ETHNOLOGY - AMERICA, WESTERN
Havard, Valery, 1846-
The French half-breeds of the Northwest. By V. Havard ...
(*In* Smithsonian institution. Annual report. 1879. Washington, 1880. 23½cm. p. 309-327)

1. Ethnology—The West. I. Title.
S 15-491
Library of Congress   Q11.S66 1879
Library, Smithsonian   Institution

DS 491.A5 B 71
ETHNOLOGY ANDAMAN ISLANDS
Bonington, M. C. C.
The Andaman and Nicobar Islands. Census of India, 1931, Volume II. Calcutta, 1932. Government of India, Central Publication Branch. folio. 119 pp.

GN 635.A M 26
ETHNOLOGY ANDAMAN ISLANDS
Man, Edward Horace
On the aboriginal inhabitants of the Andaman Islands...with Report of researches into the language of the south Andaman Islands by A. J. Ellis. Reprinted from the Journal of the Anthropological Institute of Great Britain and Ireland. London...n.d. 8vo.

GN 635.A B 87
ETHNOLOGY ANDAMAN ISLANDS
Radcliffe-Brown, Alfred Reginald
The Andaman Islanders: a study in social anthropology...Cambridge. 1922. 8vo.

AS 36 S1
ETHNOLOGY--ANDAMAN ISLANDS.
Safford, William Edwin, 1859-
The Abbott collection from the Andaman Islands. By Lieut. W. E. Safford, U. S. N.
(*In* Smithsonian institution. Annual report. 1901. Washington, 1902. 23½cm. p. 475-492. VI pl.)

1. Ethnology—Andaman Islands. I. Title.
S 15-1117
Library of Congress   Q11.S66 1901
Library, Smithsonian   Institution

AS 701 A
ETHNOLOGY ANEITYUM
Lawrie, J.
Aneityum, New Hebrides.
(Austr. Ass'n for the Adv. of Sci., 4th meeting, 1892, pp. 708-717)

GN
2.8
P 76
ETHNOLOGY ANUTA

Firth, Raymond

Anuta and Tikopia: symbiotic elements in
social organization.

(Jour. Poly. Soc., 63(2):87-131, 1954)

G
7
R 9
ETHNOLOGY ARU ISLANDS

Wallace, Alfred Russell

On the Arru Islands. (sic)

(Proc. of the R. Geogr. Soc. of London, Vol.
2, Session 1857-58, pp. 163-171)

GN
625
E 53
ETHNOLOGY- ASIA - BIBLIOGRAPHY

Embree, John F.

Bibliography of the peoples and cultures of
mainland southeast Asia. By John F. Embree and
Lillian Ota Dotson. Yale University, Southeast
Asia Studies. New Haven. 1950. xxxiii + 821
+ XII pp.

GR
385.P1
W 74

and
GR
Folklore
Pam.
80
ETHNOLOGY APAYAO

Wilson, Laurence L.

Apayao life and legends. Privately printed
by the author. Baguio. 1947. sm8vo. 195 pp.

GN
625
K 16

over
ETHNOLOGY ASIA (SOUTHEAST)

Kano, Tadao

Studies in the ethnology and prehistory of
southeast Asia. Vol. I, 1946; Vol. 2, 1952.
In Japanese. illustrated. sm8vo. Yajima Shoto
and Co. Tokyo.

Vol. 2 contains the English list of contents
for Vol. 1; and introduction by H. Otley Beyer.

GN
635.I
M 65
ETHNOLOGY ASSAM

Mills, J. P.

The Ao Nagas...London. 1926.

GN
27
M 97
ETHNOLOGY ARANDA

Murdock, George Peter

Our primitive contemporaries.
The Macmillan Company. New York. sm8vo. xxii +
614 pp. 1934c

GN
635.M4
L 34
ETHNOLOGY ASIA (southeast)

Lasker, Bruno

Peoples of southeast Asia. Prepared under
the auspices of the American Council of the Institute of Pacific Relations. Alfred A. Knopf.
New York. 1945. 8vo.   viii + 288 + x pp.

GN
635.I
S 66
ETHNOLOGY ASSAM

Smith, William Carlson

The Ao Naga Tribe of Assam: a study in
ethnology and sociology...London. 1925.

GN
2.I
C 99
ETHNOLOGY ARGENTINA

Métraux, Alfred

Los Indios Manáo.

(Anales del Instituto de Etnografia Americano, Univ. del Cuyo, 1, 1940, pp. 235-244)

P
121
L 85
ETHNOLOGY ASIA

Logan, J. R.

The ethnology of eastern Asia...

(Journal of the Indian Archipelago and Eastern Asia, 1850 (?)-1856)

GN
671.A4
A 31

AS
763
B-b

Reading
Room
ETHNOLOGY AUSTRAL ISLANDS

Aitken, R. T.

Ethnology of Tubuai. Honolulu, 1930. 8vo.
iv + 169 pp. 13 pls. 40 figures.

(Bernice P. Bishop Museum, Bulletin No. 70,
Bayard Dominick Expedition, Pub. No. 19.)

GN
1
O 15
ETHNOLOGY ARNHEM LAND

Berndt, C. H.

An Oepelli monologue: culture-contact.
By C. H. and Ronald M. Berndt.
(Oceania, Vol. 22(1):24-52,1951)

GN
Ethn.
Pam.
3939
ETHNOLOGY ASIA

UNESCO

Men against ignorance. Printed by Gassmann
S.A. Soleure (Switzerland). 1953. 8vo. 5-81 pp.

GN
Ethn. Pam.
2903

ers.
8vo.
1929
ETHNOLOGY AUSTRALIA

Australian Aborigines and South Sea Island-
Implements, Weapons, and Curios. 36 pp.
(Adv. of sale, Tyrrell's Museum, Sydney,

AS
36
A 65-n
ETHNOLOGY ARNHEM LAND

Harrington, Lyn

Stone age artists of Milingimbi. A friendly
visit among the aborigines of Arnhem Land, who
are retaining the best in their culture under a
plan of government help. Photographs by Richard
Harrington.

(Natural History, Vol. LXV(3):120-217, 165,
March, 1955)

Q
115
W 95

locked
case
ETHNOLOGY ASIA

Wüllerstörf-Urbair, Bernhard

Reise der Österreichischen Fregatte Novara
um die erde in den jahren 1857, 1858, 1859...

Anthropologischer Theil, Dritte Abt.: Ethnographie...Wien. 1868. 4to. pp. 137-76. von
Friedrich Müller.

GN
665
B29
ETHNOLOGY...AUSTRALIA

Basedow, Herbert

The Australian aboriginal.

Adelaide, Preece, 1925. 422p. pls. 8vo.

G
51
W 17
ETHNOLOGY ARNHEM LAND

Thomson, Donald F.

The story of Arnhem Land.

(Walkabout, Vol. 12(10):5-22, 1946)

AS
36
S1
ETHNOLOGY--ASIA, WESTERN

Luschan, Felix von, 1854-
The early inhabitants of western Asia. By Felix v.
Luschan ...

(In Smithsonian institution. Annual report. 1914. Washington, 1915.
23½°. p. 555-577. 12 pl. on 6 l. diagrs.)

"The Huxley memorial lecture for 1911. Reprinted ... from the Journal
of the Royal anthropological institute of Great Britain and Ireland, vol. 41,
1911."

1. Ethnology—Asia, Western.

15-19949

Library of Congress   Q11.S66 1914

GN
2.1
A-4
ETHNOLOGY AUSTRALIA

Basedow, Herbert

Notes on the natives of Bathurst Island,
North Australia.

(Journ. R. Anthrop. Inst. of Great Britain
and Ireland, Vol. 43, 1913, pp. 291-323, with
pls. 7-20)

GN
2.1
A-4
ETHNOLOGY   AUSTRALIA

Bennett, M. M.

Notes on the Dalleburra tribe of Northern Queensland.

(Journ. R. Anthrop. Inst. of Great Britain and Ireland, Vol. 57, 1927, pp. 399-415, pls. 22,23)

GN
Ethn.Pam.
3104
ETHNOLOGY   AUSTRALIA

Cleland, J. B.

The natives of Central Australia.

(The Medical Journal of Australia, 1933, pp. 322-   )

AS
36
A 9
and
GN
Ethn.
Pam.3310
ETHNOLOGY   AUSTRALIA

Davidson, D. Sutherland

An ethnic map of Australia.

(Proc. Am. Philosophical Society, Vol. 79, 1938, pp. 649-679)

GN
665
B 52
ETHNOLOGY   AUSTRALIA

Berndt, Ronald M.

The first Australians. By Ronald M. Berndt and Catherine H. Berndt. A Ure Smith Publication. Sydney. 1952. 8vo. 144 pp. (illustrated)

GN
Ethn.Pam.
2902
ETHNOLOGY - AUSTRALIA

Cleland, J. Burton

Anthropological Expedition to Central Australia.

(The Medical Journal of Australia, Dec. 19, 1931, pp. 793-796)

GN
Ethn.
Pam.
4321
ETHNOLOGY   AUSTRALIA

Elkin, A. P.

The aboriginal Australians. Illustrated by Pamela Johnston. Longmans. 8vo. no date. 56 pp.

GN
665
B 52
ETHNOLOGY   AUSTRALIA

Berndt, Ronald

From black to white in South Australia. By Ronald and Catherine Berndt. With an introduction by Professor A. P. Elkin. F. W. Cheshire. Melbourne. (1951) 8vo. (1-10)11-315 pp.

DU
1
M 6
ETHNOLOGY   AUSTRALIA

Cleland, J. Burton

An Anthropological Expedition to Central Australia.

(Mid-Pacific Magazine, Vol. 44, 1932, pp. 317-327)

GN
1
O 15
ETHNOLOGY   AUSTRALIA

Elkin, A. P.

Anthropology and the future of the Australian aborigines.

(Oceania, Vol. 5, No. 1, 1934, pp. 1-17).

GN
665
B 64
ETHNOLOGY   AUSTRALIA

Bleakley, J. W.

The aborigines of Australia, their history, their habits, their assimilation. The Jacaranda Press. Brisbane. 8vo. 1961 (12) + 367 pp.

AP
2
S.35
ETHNOLOGY   AUSTRALIA

Cleland, J. B.

Field Anthropology in Australia.

(Science, New Series, Vol. 75, No. 1932, 1932, pp. 50-52)

GN
665
E 42
ETHNOLOGY   AUSTRALIA

Elkin, A. P.

The Australian aborigines, how to understand them. Angus & Robertson. Sydney and London. 1938. 8vo. xiv, 262 pp.

also Third Edition, 1954. Angus and Robertson. xvii + 349 pp.

GN
667.T
B 72
ETHNOLOGY   AUSTRALIA

Bonwick, James

Daily life and origin of the Tasmanians... Second edition. London...1898. 8vo.

GN
Ethn.Pam.
3102
ETHNOLOGY   AUSTRALIA

Cleland, J. B.

The natives of the north-west of South Australia.

(The Medical Journal of Australia, 1931, pp. 848-   )

GN
1
O 15
ETHNOLOGY   AUSTRALIA

Elkin, A. P.

The Kopara: the settlement of grievances.

(Oceania, Vol. 2, 1931-1932, pp. 191-198)

GN
6
B 97
ETHNOLOGY   AUSTRALIA

Buschan, Georg   editor

Illustrierte Völkerkunde. Unter Mitwirkung von U. Buhan and others. Stuttgart. no date.

[Australien und Ozeanien, by Georg Buschan, pp. 164-214]

GN
1
Ar
ETHNOLOGY   AUSTRALIA

Clément, E.

Ethnographical notes on the Western Australian aborigines. With a descr. catal. of a collection of ethnogr. objects from Western Australia by Schmeltz. In Archiv. f. Ethn. XVI pp. 1-29   Leiden 1904

GN
1
O 15
ETHNOLOGY   AUSTRALIA

Elkin, A. P.

The secret life of the Australian aborigines.

(Oceania, Vol. 3, 1932, pp. 119-138, pls. 1-5)

GN
665.T
C 14
ETHNOLOGY   AUSTRALIA

Calder, J. E.

Some account of the wars, extirpation, habits, etc., of the native tribes of Tasmania. Hobart Town. 1875. 12mo.

GN
665
C 95
ETHNOLOGY   AUSTRALIA

Curr, Edward M.

The Australian race: its origin, languages, customs, place of landing in Australia, and the routes by which it spread itself over that continent...In four volumes. Melbourne. 1886. 8vo

Oversize

Volume 4. Folio. 1887.

AS
720.N
L-m
ETHNOLOGY   AUSTRALIA

Etheridge, R., Jr.

A Description of some of the Weapons and Implements of the Alligator Tribe, Port Essington, North Australia.

(Macleay Memorial Volume, 1893, pp. 228-251. Linnean Society of New South Wales.)

GN 665 G 84	ETHNOLOGY AUSTRALIA Gribble, E. R. B. The Problem of the Australian Aboriginal. Sydney. Angus & Robertson Ltd. 1932. xi + 157 pp. sm8vo.
AS 720.S R	ETHNOLOGY AUSTRALIA Helms, Richard Anthropology. (Transactions of the Royal Society of South Australia. Vol. XVI, 1896, pp. 238-332)
AS 720.Q R	Ethnology, Australia Mackie, R. Cliffe Anthropological notes of 50 years ago. In Proc. R. S. of Queensland XXXVII..1 pp. 107-120.
AS 720.S S 72	ETHNOLOGY AUSTRALIA (QUEENSLAND) Hale, Herbert M. Aborigines of Princess Charlotte Bay, North Queensland, by Herbert M. Hale and Norman B. Tindale. (Records of the South Australian Museum, Vol. 5, 1933-36, pp. 63-172)
Q 115 H 81 locked case	ETHNOLOGY AUSTRALIA (Horn, W. A.) Report on the work of the Horn Scientific Expedition to Central Australia...edited by Baldwin Spencer. London. 1896. 4to. Pts.1-4. Part. IV: Anthropology.
GN 665 M42	ETHNOLOGY AUSTRALIA Mathew, John Eaglehawk and crow: a study of the Australian aborigines including an inquiry into their origines and a survey of Australian languages. London, Nutt, 1899. 288p. 8vo.
GN 2.M F 451	ETHNOLOGY AUSTRALIA Hambly, Wilfrid D. Primitive hunters of Australia. (Field Museum of Natural History, Anthropology Leaflet 32, 1936, 59 pp., 12 pl.)
GN Ethn.Pam. 322 AS 36 S1	ETHNOLOGY AUSTRALIA Howitt, A. W. Australian group relations. (Smithsonian Inst. Report for 1883. Washington, 1885, 8vo. pp. 797-824)
AS 720.N R 88	ETHNOLOGY AUSTRALIA Mathews, John Australian aborigines. (Jour. R. Soc. N. S. Wales, 23:335-449, 1889)
GN Ethn. Pam. 2811	ETHNOLOGY AUSTRALIA Hambruch, Paul Einführung in die Abteilung Australien. (Geschichte, Lebensraum, Umwelt und Bevölkerung) Hamburgishhes Museum für Völkerkunde. Hamburg, Friederichsen, de Gruyter & Co. m.b.H. 1931. 42 pp. 12mo.
GN Pam. 1935	ETHNOLOGY AUSTRALIA Klaatsch, Hermann Some notes on scientific travel amongst the black population of tropical Australia in 1904, 1905, 1906.
DU Pac. Pam. 984	ETHNOLOGY AUSTRALIA Our aborigines. Prepared under the authority of the Minister of Territories...Australia. 1957, revised 1962. (32 pp.) sm8vo.
GN 1 O 15	ETHNOLOGY AUSTRALIA Hart, C.W.M. Personal names among the Tiwi. (Oceania, Vol. 1, 1930-1931, pp. 280-290)
GN 665 L 84	ETHNOLOGY AUSTRALIA Lommel, Andreas Die Unambal, ein Stamm in Nordwest-Australien. (Monographie zur Volkerkunde, Hamburg Mus. f. Volkerkunde, No. II, 1952)
GN 1 O 15	ETHNOLOGY AUSTRALIA Piddington, Marjorie Report of field work in northwestern Australia. By Marjorie Piddington and Ralph Piddington. (Oceania, Vol. 2, 1931-1932, pp. 342-358)
GN 1 O 15	ETHNOLOGY AUSTRALIA Hart, C.W.M. The Tiwi of Melville and Bathurst Islands. (Oceania, Vol. 1, 1930-1931, pp. 165-180)
GN 665 M 11	ETHNOLOGY AUSTRALIA McCarthy, Frederick D. Australia's aborigines, their life and culture. Color-gravure Publications. Melbourne. (1958) 4to. 200 pp.
GN 453 A P 84	ETHNOLOGY AUSTRALIA Porteus, Stanley D. The Psychology of a Primitive People: A Study of the Australian Aborigine. New York. Longmans, Green & Co. 1931c. xv + 438 pp. 8vo.
GN 665 H 32	ETHNOLOGY AUSTRALIA Hart, C. W. M. The Tiwi of North Australia. By C. W. M. Hart and Arnold R. Pilling. Holt, Rinehart and Winston, Inc. New York. 8vo. 118 pp.
AS 720.S S 72	ETHNOLOGY AUSTRALIA McConnel, Ursula H. Native arts and industries on the Archer, Kendall and Holroyd Rivers, Cape York Peninsula, North Queensland. (Records of the South Australian Museum, Vol. XI:1-42, 1953)
AS 720.Q Q	Ethnology-Australia Queensland museum, *Brisbane.* Memoirs of the Queensland museum. v.1- Brisbane, 1912- v. illus., plates. 24½ᶜᵐ. Editor: 1912- R. Hamlyn-Harris. 1. Natural history—Australia. 2. Ethnology—Australia. I. Hamlyn-Harris, Ronald, 1874- ed. Library of Congress Q93.Q27 14-6073

GN
1
O 15

ETHNOLOGY AUSTRALIA

Radcliffe-Brown, A. R.

The Social Organization of Australian Tribes.

(In Oceania, Vol. 1, 1930/31, pp. 34-63, 206-246, 322-341 and 426-456)

GN
665
S 74

ETHNOLOGY AUSTRALIA

Spencer, Baldwin

The Arunta: a study of a stone age people, by Sir Baldwin Spencer and F. J. Gillen. In two volumes. London. Macmillan. 1927. 8vo. xxviii + 390; xvi + 391-646 pp.

AS
182
H

ETHNOLOGY AUSTRALIA

Virchow, Rudolph

Australier. 20 ethnographische und anthropologische Tafeln, ausgeführt nach Anweisungen und Zeichnungen des Rudolph Virchow.

(Journal des Museum Godeffroy, Heft 10, 1902)

GN
667.Q
R 84

ETHNOLOGY AUSTRALIA

Roth, Walter E.

Ethnological studies among the north-west-central Queensland aborigines. Brisbane. 1897. R8vo.

GN
665
S 74

ETHNOLOGY AUSTRALIA

Spencer, Baldwin

The native tribes of Central Australia, by Baldwin Spencer and F. J. Gillen. London. 1899. 8vo.

DU
96
W 18

ETHNOLOGY AUSTRALIA

Wallace, Alfred Russell

Australasia...With ethnological appendix by A. H. Keane...London. 1883. 8vo. pp. 86-106.

GN
655
S 61

ETHNOLOGY AUSTRALIA

Simpson, Colin

Adam in ochre; inside aboriginal Australia. Angus and Robertson. Sydney and London. 8vo (1951) 220 pp. illustrated

---

GN
1
O 15

ETHNOLOGY AUSTRALIA

Stanner, W.E.H.

The Daly River tribes. A report of field work in North Australia.

(Oceania, Vol. 3, No. 4, 1933, pp. 375-405; Vol. 3, No. 4, pp. 10-29)

GN
1
O 15

ETHNOLOGY AUSTRALIA

Warner, W. Lloyd

Malay influence on the aboriginal cultures of Northwestern Arnhem Land.

(Oceania, Vol. 2, 1931-1932, pp. 476-495)

AS
122
E

ETHNOLOGY AUSTRALIA

Smith, W. Ramsay

Notes on aboriginals of the Northern Territory of South Australia.

in Roy. Soc. Edin. Proc. XXIII, pp. 51-63, illus.

GN
4
C 33

ETHNOLOGY AUSTRALIA

Stanner, W. E. H.

Durmugam, a Nangiomeri (Australia).
IN

Casagrande, Joseph B.   editor
In the company of man. pp. 63-100.
Harper and Bros. New York. 1960. R8vo.

Q
115
W 95

locked
case

ETHNOLOGY AUSTRALIA

Wüllerstorf-Urbair, Bernhard

Reise der Oesterreichischen Fregatte Novara um die Erde...1857-1859. Anthropologischer Theil, III, pp. 1-10. Wien. 4to. 1868   by Friedrich Müller.

GN
667.V
S 66

ETHNOLOGY AUSTRALIA

Smyth, R. Brough

The aborigines of Victoria: with notes relating to the habits of the natives of other parts of Australia and Tasmania. Compiled from various sources for the Government of Victoria. 2 vols. London. John Ferres. 1878. R8vo. lxxii + 483; 456 pp. + map.

DU
1
P 12

ETHNOLOGY AUSTRALIA

Tindale, Norman B.

First Australian- the aborigine.

(Pacific Discovery, 9(5):6-13, 1956)

AS
720.N
R 88

ETHNOLOGY AUSTRALIA

Wyndham, W. T.

The aborigines of Australia.

(R. Soc. of New South Wales, Jour. 23:36-42, 1889)

AS
720.S
S 72

ETHNOLOGY AUSTRALIA

South Australian Museum. ...

Records, Vol. 1, 1918->

G
51
W 17

ETHNOLOGY AUSTRALIA

Thomson, Donald F.

The fishermen and dugong hunters of Princess Charlotte Bay.

(Walkabout, 22(11):33-36, 1956)

AS
720.N
R 88

ETHNOLOGY AUSTRALIA

Wyndham, W. T.

Australian aborigines: varities of food and methods of obtaining it.

(R. Soc. N. S. Wales, Jour. 24:112-120, 1890)

GN
665
S 74

ETHNOLOGY AUSTRALIA

Spencer, Baldwin

Across Australia, by Baldwin Spencer and F. J. Gillen. 2 volumes. With illustrations and maps. London. Macmillan. 1912. 8vo. xiv + 254; xvii + 515 pp.

QH
Nat.Hist.
Pam.
165

ETHNOLOGY AUSTRALIA

Troughton, Ellis   and others

Australian animals, birds, flowers. (pictorial, with texts taken from printed works) (28)pp) 4to. no date

---

ETHNOLOGY AUSTRALIA

see also

ETHNOLOGY QUEENSLAND

Z
Bibl.
Pam
20
21

ETHNOLOGY AUSTRALIA BIBLIOGRAPHY

Etheridge, R.

Catalogue of works, reports, and papers on the anthropology, ethnology, and geological history of the Australian and Tasmanian aborigines, parts 1 and 2. Sydney. 1890-1891.

(Dep't of Mines, Memoirs of the Geological Survey of New South Wales, Paleontology, No. 8)

GN
Ethn.Pam
4209

ETHNOLOGY BATAK

Keuning, J.

The Toba Batak, formerly and now. Translation Series, Modern Indonesia project. Southeast Asia Program, Dept. of Far Eastern Studies, Cornell University. 1958 4to.

GN
668
F 89

ETHNOLOGY BISMARCK ARCHIPELAGO

Friederici, Georg

Wissenschaftliche Ergebnisse einer Amtlichen Forschungsreise nach dem Bismarck-Archipel im Jahre 1908.
II and III.

(Mitt. aus den Deutschen Schutzgebieten, Erganzungsheft, Nrs. 5 and 7, 1912, 1913)

GN
630.M3
C 68

ETHNOLOGY - BALI

Cole, F.C.

The peoples of Malaysia. D. Van Nostrand Company, Inc. Toronto, New York... 8vo. 1945c xiv + 354 pp.

GN
2.1
A-4

ETHNOLOGY BATHURST ISLAND

Basedow, Herbert

Notes on the natives of Bathurst Island, North Australia.

(Journ. R. Anthrop. Inst. of Great Britain and Ireland, Vol. 43, 1913, pp. 291-323, with pls. 7-20)

GN
2.M
H
also
GN
Pam
#496
(4to)

ETHNOLOGY BISMARCK ARCHIPELAGO

Hambruch, Paul

Die Anthropologie von Kaniet.
in Hamburg. Mus. für Völker. Mitt. (Xㅗ), 1906, pp. 43-70. Illus.
(5 Beiheft zum Jahr. der Hamb. Wissen. Anstalten XXIV. 1906).

DS
647.B2
C 87

ETHNOLOGY BALI

Covarrubias, Miguel

Island of Bali. With an album of photographs by Rose Covarrubias. New York. Alfred A. Knopf. 1942. xxv + 417 + x pp. R8vo

---

GN
653
M 35

ETHNOLOGY BENIN

Marquart, Jos.

Die Benin-Sammlung des Reichsmuseums für Volkerkunde in Leiden...

(Veroff. des Reichsmuseums f. Völkerkunde in Leiden. Ser. II, Nr. 7, 1913)

GN
671.B5
H 19

also
GN
2.M
H 19m

ETHNOLOGY BISMARCK ARCHIPELAGO

Hambruch, Paul

Wuvulu und Aua (Maty und Durour-Inseln) auf Grund der Sammlung F. E. Hellwig aus den Jahren 1902 bis 1904 von Dr. phil. Paul Hambruch... Hamburg. 1908. 4to.

(Hamburg Mus. für Völkerkunde, Mitt. II, 1, Aus dem 4 Beiheft zum jahrbuch der Hamburgischen Wissenschaftlichen Anstalten. XXV. 1907).

GN
2.S
P 76

ETHNOLOGY BANABA

Tutuila

The Line Islanders. Notes on the raves known as the Tokelaus, or the Line Islanders, called by themselves the Kai-n-Abara, which means "People of our land".

(Journal of the Polynesian Society, Vol. 1, 1892, pp. 263-272)

GN
673
R 91

ETHNOLOGY BERING SEA

Rudenko, S. I.

The ancient culture of the Bering Sea and the Eskimo problem.

(Arctic Institute of North America, Anthropology of the North, Translations from Russian Sources, No. 1. 1961)

Translated by Paul Tolstoy.

GN
Ethn.Pam
3328

ETHNOLOGY BISMARCK ARCHIPELAGO

Krämer, Augustin

Zur Volkskunde der Matupiter und Wanderungsfragen.

(Kultur und Rasse, Festschrift zum 60 Geburtstag Otto Reches, 1939, pp. 354-363)

AS
720.V
R 88

ETHNOLOGY BANKS ISLANDS

Codrington, R. H.

Notes on the customs of Mota, Banks Islands. With remarks by Lorimer Fison.

(Trans. and Proc. R. Soc. of Victoria, 16: 119-143)   1880

GN
2.S
C 16

ETHNOLOGY BIG NAMBAS

Corlette, L.A.C.

Langue des Big Nambas: le Mallicolo (Nouvelles-Hebrides).

(Journal de la Soc. des Océanistes, Vol. 3: 57-91, 1947)

GN
662
P 24

ETHNOLOGY BISMARCK ARCHIPELAGO

Parkinson, R.

Dreissig jahre in der Südsee: Land und leute Sitten und gebräuche im Bismarckarchipel und auf den Deutschen Salomoinseln...Stuttgart. 1907. R8vo.

GN
671.N55
S 74

ETHNOLOGY BANKS ISLANDS

Speiser, Felix

Ethnographische Materialien aus den Neuen Hebriden und den Banks-Inseln...Mit 1610 abb. auf 109 tafeln und mit 1 karte. Berlin, Kreidel, 1923. vii + 457 pp. pls. 4to.

(Review by G. H. Luquet, in L'Anthropologie, Tome 34, 1924, pp. 158-160)

AS
28
E 85

ETHNOLOGY BIG NAMBAS

Guiart, Jean

La fin d'un mirage ou le ralliement des villages "Big Nambes" du nord de Malekula, Nouvelles-Hebrides.

(Etudes Melanesiennes, Numero 7, pp. 6-13, 1953)

(treats of the "legend" of the existence to this day of cannibals in Malekula- only in the minds of the   writers and movie writers, says the author)

GN
2.1
A-4

ETHNOLOGY BISMARCK ARCHIPELAGO

Pitt-Rivers, George Lane Fox

Aua Island: ethnological and sociological features of a south sea pagan society.

(Journ. R. Anthrop. Inst. of Great Britain and Ireland, Vol. 55, 1925, pp. 425-438, pls. 33-38)

GN
657.B2
R 51

ETHNOLOGY BANTU

Richards, Audrey I.

Hunger and Work in a Savage Tribe...London. George Routledge and Sons, Ltd., 1932. 8vo. xvi + 238 pp.

GN
662
F 51

ETHNOLOGY BISMARCK ARCHIPELAGO

Finsch, (Friedrich Hermann Otto)

Ethnologische Erfahrungen und Belegstücke aus der Südsee. Beschreibender Katalog einer Sammlung im K. K. Naturhistorischen Hofmuseum in Wien von Dr. O. Finsch.... Wien. 1893. R8vo.

(Annalen des K. K. Naturhistorischen Hof-Museums in Wien, Band III-VIII, 1888-1893, separat abgedruckt).

GN
668
R 62

ETHNOLOGY BISMARCK ARCHIPELAGO

Rivers, W. H. R.

The history of Melanesian society. In two volumes. Vol. 2, pp. 497-555. Cambridge. University Press. 1914. 8vo. xii + 400; 610 pp.

(Percy Sladen Trust Expedition to Melanesia)

GN
668
S 24   ETHNOLOGY BISMARK ARCHIPELAGO

Sapper, Karl

    Wissenschaftliche Ergebnisse einer Amtlichen Forschungsreise nach dem Bismarck-Archipel im Jahre 1908.
    I. Beitrage zur Landeskunde von Neu-Mecklenburg und Seinen Nachbarinseln.

    (Mitt. aus den Deutschen Schutzgebieten, Erganzungsheft, Nr. 3, 1910)

GN
671.B5
S 82   ETHNOLOGY BISMARCK ARCHIPELAGO

Stephan, Emil

    Neu-Mecklenburg (Bismarck-Archipel): Die Küste von Umuddu bis Kap St. Georg. Forschungsergebnisse bei den Vermessungsfahrten von S.M.S. Möwe im Jahre 1904. Aus dem Königlichen Museum für Völkerdunde zu Berlin mit Unterstützung des Reichs-Marine-Amtes. Herausgegeben von Dr. Emil Stephan und Dr. Fritz Graebner... Berlin. Reimer. 1907. R8vo.

GN
668
T 44   ETHNOLOGY BISMARCK ARCHIPELAGO

Thilenius, Georg

    Ethnographische Ergebnisse aus Melanesien... I. Theil... II. Theil...

    (Nova Acta, Abh. der Kaiserl. Leop.-Carol. Deutschen Akademie der Naturforscher, Band LXXX, Nr. 1-2. Halle. 1902-1903).

GN
662
V 87   ETHNOLOGY BISMARCK ARCHIPELAGO

Vogel-Hamburg, Hans

    Eine forschungsreise im Bismarck-Archipel... Hamburg. 1911. R8vo.

    (Hamburgische Wissenschaftliche Stiftung.)

GN
564
C 52   ETHNOLOGY BOLIVIA

Chervin, Arthur

    Anthropologie Bolivienne. 3 volumes. Paris. 1907-1908. 4to.

    Tome I. Ethnologie, Démographie, Photographie, Métrique. 411 pp.

    (Mission Scientifique, G. De Créqui Montfort et E.Sénéchal de la Grange.)

GR
Folklore
Pam. 69   ETHNOLOGY BOLIVIA

Métraux, Alfred

    Chipayaindeianerna: en folkspillra fran en Forgangen andinsk kultur.

    (Ymer...1932, pp. 233-271)

GN
Ethn.Pam.
3291   ETHNOLOGY BOLIVIA

Métraux, Alfred

    L'organisation sociale et les survivances religieuses des indiens Uru-Cipaya de Carangas (Bolivie). Note preliminaire.

    (XXV Congreso Int. de Americanistas, 1932, Actas, Tomo I, pp. 191-213)

GN
2.I
C 99   ETHNOLOGY BOLIVIA

Métraux, Alfred

    Los Indios Chapakura del Oriente Boliviano.

    (Anales del Instituto de Etnografia Americana, Univ. del Cuyo; Vol. 1, 1940, pp. 117-127)

GN
630.M3
C 68   ETHNOLOGY - BORNEO

Cole, F.C.

    The peoples of Malaysia.   D. Van Nostrand Company, Inc.   Toronto, New York...   8vo. 1945c   xiv + 354 pp.

DS
646.3
E 92   ETHNOLOGY BORNEO

Evans, I. H. N.

    Among primitive peoples in Borneo; a description of the lives, habits and customs of the piratial head-hunters of North Borneo, with an account of interesting objects of prehistoric antiquity discovered in the island... London. 1922. 8vo.

AM
Mus. Pam.
127   ETHNOLOGY BORNEO

    Führer durch das Museum für Völkerkunde, Basel. Borneo.

    (Buchdruckerei G. Krebs, Basel, 1932, 20 pp.

GN
2.S
P 76   ETHNOLOGY BORNEO

Harrisson, Tom

    Outside influences on the culture of the Kelabits of North Central Borneo.

    (Jour. Poly. Soc., 58(3):91-111, 1949)

GN
Pam
2358   ETHNOLOGY - BORNEO

Hein, Alois Raimund

    Malerei und technische kunste bei den Dayaks. From Annalen d. k.k. Nat. Hofmuseums, bd.4, Wien, 1889.

GN
635.B7
K 93   ETHNOLOGY BORNEO

Krohn, William O.

    In Borneo Jungles: among the Dyak headhunters London. (c1927.)

DS
646.3
L8   ETHNOLOGY- BORNEO

Lumholtz, Karl Sofus, 1851-
    Through Central Borneo; an account of two years' travel in the land of the head-hunters between the years 1913 and 1917, by Carl Lumholtz ... with illustrations from photographs by the author and with map ... New York, C. Scribner's sons, 1920.

    2 v. fronts., illus. (music) plates, ports., maps (1 fold.) diagr. 25cm.

    1. Borneo—Descr. & trav. 2. Ethnology—Borneo. 3. Natural history—Borneo.   I. Title.

    Library of Congress   DS646.3.L8
    ——— Copy 2.   20—16918
    Copyright A 576515   [a21f3]

GN
635.B7
R 84   ETHNOLOGY BORNEO

Roth, Henry Ling

    The Natives of Sarawak and British North Borneo, based chiefly on the MSS. of the late Hugh Brooke Low, Sarawak Government Service... In two vols. London. 1896. R8vo.

GN
635.B7
R 98   ETHNOLOGY BORNEO

Rutter, Owen

    The Pagans of North Borneo...London. 1929. R8vo.

GN
671.N5
C 53   ETHNOLOGY BOUGAINVILLE

Chinnery, E. W. Pearson

    Notes on the Natives of South Bougainville and Mortlocks (Taku).

    (Anthropological Report, Territory of New Guinea, No. 5, Melbourne, ND)

GN
1
B   ETHNOLOGY BOUGAINVILLE

Frizzi, Ernst

    Ein Beitrag zur Ethnologie von Bougainville und Buka mit spezieller Berücksichtigung der Nasioi.

    (Baessler Archiv, Beiheft 6:1-52, 1914)

GN
2.M
P 35   ETHNOLOGY BOUGAINVILLE

Oliver, Douglas L.

    Economic and social uses of domestic pigs in Siuai, southern Bougainville, Solomon Islands.

    (Papers, Peabody Mus. of Am. Arch. and Ethn. Harvard Univ., Vol. 29(3), 1949)

GN
2.M
P 35   ETHNOLOGY BOUGAINVILLE

Oliver, Douglas L.

    Studies in the anthropology of Bougainville, Solomon Islands.   Nos. 1-4

    (Papers of the Peabody Museum of American Archaeology and Ethnology, Harvard University, Vol. 29 (1-4), 1949.

GN 561 H 97
ETHNOLOGY   BRAZIL
Hutchinson, Jarry William

Village and plantation life in northeastern Brazil. University of Washington Press. Seattle. 8vo. ix + 199 pp. 1957

GN 660.B8 S 89
ETHNOLOGY BUSHMEN
Stow, George W.

The native races of South Africa, a history of the intrusion of the Hottentots and Bantu into the hunting grounds of the Bushmen, the aborigines of the country. With Numerous illustrations. ...edited by George McCall Theal...London. 1905. R8vo.

E 2001 R 89
ETHNOLOGY   CARIBBEAN
Rubin, Vera   editor

Caribbean studies: a symposium. The American Ethnological Society... University of Washington Press. Seattle. 1960. 8vo. viii + 124 pp.

GN 561 L 66
ETHNOLOGY   BRAZIL
Levi-Strauss, C.

Tristes tropiques.
Terre Humaine, Civilisations et Sociétés, Collection d'Etudes et de Témoignages.... Paris. Librairie Plon. (1955c) 462 pp.

AS 36 S3
ETHNOLOGY   CALIFORNIA
Holmes, William Henry, 1846–
Anthropological studies in California. By William Henry Holmes ...

(*In* U. S. National museum. Annual report. 1900. Washington, 1902. 23½ᶜᵐ. p. 155-187. 50 pl. (incl. front.))
Half-title.

1. Indians of North America—Indus. 2. Indians of North America—California.   I. Title.
Library of Congress   Q11.U5 1900
——— Copy 2.   14-19905
——— Separate.   GN560.C2H7

GN Pam 2415
ETHNOLOGY - CAROLINE ISLANDS
Barreiro, R. P. Augustino F.

El origen de la raza indigena de las islas Carolinas. From Sociedad Espanola d. antrop. etnog. y praehist. Actas y Mem. v.1, n.2-3, Madrid, 1922.

AS 80 P
Ethnology-Brazil
Pará, Brazil (City) Museu Goeldi de historia natural e ethnographia.
Boletim do Museu Goeldi (Museu paraense) de historia natural e ethnographia. t. 1–1894/96–
Pará, Brazil, 1896-19
v. illus., plates (part col.) ports., maps, plans, tables. 24ᶜᵐ.
Vols. 1-4 in 4 nos. each; v. 5 in 2 nos.; v. 6– issued in volume form.
Vols. 1-3 have title: Boletim do Museu paraense de historia natural e ethnographia.
1. Science—Societies. 2. Natural history—Brazil. 3. Ethnology—Brazil. I. Title.
Library of Congress   Q33.P2   18-7167
——— 2d set.

GN 550 S
ETHNOLOGY CALIFORNIA
Kroeber, A. L.   (Alfred Louis)

Handbook of the Indians of California Smithson. Inst. Bur. Am. Ethn. Bull. 78.

Washington, 1925.

GN 669 B 32

GN Ethn. Pam. 704
ETHNOLOGY CAROLINE ISLANDS
Bastian, Adolf

Die mikronesischen Colonien aus ethnologischen Gesichtspunkten. Berlin. A. Asher. 1899. 8vo. vii + 370 pp. Ergänzung.

Ergänzung, I. Berlin, 1900, 112pp.

GN 564 St
ETHNOLOGY - BRAZIL
Steinen, C. von den

Unter der Naturvölkern, Zentral-Brasiliens.

Berlin, 1894.

GN 2.S E 19
ETHNOLOGY CAMBODIA
Baradat, R.

Les Samre ou Pear. Population primitive de l'Ouest du Cabodge.

(Bull. de l'Ecole Francaise d'Extreme-Orient Tome 41(1), 1941)

GN 669 B 69
ETHNOLOGY CAROLINE ISLANDS
Bollig, P. Laurentius

Die Bewohner der Truk-Inseln: religion, leben und kurze grammatik eines Mikronesiervolkes. From Anthropos, v. 3, heft 1, 1927. Münster. Aschendarff. 1927. R8vo. vii + 302 pp.

(Anthropos, Band III, Heft 1.)

GN 1 B
ETHNOLOGY BUKA
Frizzi, Ernst

Ein Beitrag zur Ethnologie von Bougainville und Buka mit spezieller Berücksichtigung der Nasioi.

(Baessler Archiv, Beiheft 6:1-52, 1914)

GN 635.C1 D 36
ETHNOLOGY CAMBODIA
Delvert, Jean

Le paysan Cambodgien.

(Le Monde d'Outre Mer, Passe et Present, Ser. 1: Etudes X; Ecole Pratique des Hautes Etudes, Sorbonne; Sciences Economiques et Sociales. 1961 Paris)

GN Ethn.Pam. 3485
ETHNOLOGY CAROLINE ISLANDS
Born

Einige Beobachtungen ethnographischer natur über die Oleai-Inseln.

(Mitt. aus den Deutschen Schutzgebieten, 17:175-191, 1904)

GN 635.B9 W41
ETHNOLOGY - BURMA
Wehrli, Hans J.

Beitrag zur ethnologie der Chingpaw (Kachin) von ober Burma.

Leiden, Brill, 1904.   83p. pls.
(Suppl. bd. XVI Internat. Arch. f. ethnog

G 51 W 17
ETHNOLOGY CAPE YORK PENINSULA
Thomson, Donald F.

The masked dancers of I'wai'i; a remarkable hero cult which has invaded Cape York Peninsula.

(Walkabout, 22(12):17-20, 1956)

GN 2 S P 76
ETHNOLOGY CAROLINE ISLANDS
Christian, F. W.

Notes from the Caroline Islands.

(Journal of the Polynesian Society, Vol. 6, p. 187-200, 1897)

(Ponape gods, Yap gods, Ponape plants, varieties of breadfruit in Ponape, star names in Lamotrek, Ponape, Yap, Mortlock, calendar, etc.)

GN Pam 2423
ETHNOLOGY - BURMA
Wehrli, Hans J.

Zur wirtschafts-geographie von Ober-Burma und den Nordlichen Shan-Staaten. From Jahresbericht d. Geog-Ethnog. Gesell Zurich, 1905-1906.

AS 36 S1
ETHNOLOGY   CANARY ISLANDS
Gambier, James William, 1841–
The Guanches; the ancient inhabitants of Canary. By Capt. J. W. Gambier, R. N.
(*In* Smithsonian institution. Annual report. 1894. Washington, 1896. 23½ᶜᵐ. p. 541-553. illus.)
"From the Antiquary, nos. 49, 50, 51, new series, vol. XXIX, January, February, March, 1894."

1. Ethnology—Canary Islands.   I. Title.
                          S 15-875
Library of Congress   Q11.S66 1894
Library, Smithsonian   Institution

GN Ethn.Pam 3489
ETHNOLOGY CAROLINE ISLANDS
Fritz, G.

Eine Reise nach Palau, Sonsol, und Tobi.

(Deutsches Kolonialblatt 18: 1907, pp. 659-668)

GN
671.C3
F 98

ETHNOLOGY CAROLINE ISLANDS

Furness, W. H.

The island of stone money: Uap of the Carolines. With illustrations from photographs by the author. Philadelphia. Lippincott. 1910. 8vo. 278 pp.

GN
671.C3
K 95

ETHNOLOGY - CAROLINE ISLANDS

Kubary, J. S.

Ethnographische Beiträge zur Kenntnis des Karolinen Archipels. Veröffentlicht im auftrage der Direktion des Kgl. Museums f. Völkerkunde zu Berlin. Unter mitwirkung von J.D.E.Schmeltz. Mit 55 Tafeln. Leiden. C.F. Winter. 1889-95. R8vo. 306 + (1) pp. 55 tafeln. In 3 Hefte.

GN
663
T 44

ETHNOLOGY CAROLINE ISLANDS

Thilenius, G.

Ergebnisse der Südsee Expedition, 1908-1910. II. Ethnographie: B. Mikronesien, Bd. 9: Westkarolinen, von Anneliese Eilers. Halbband I-II, 1935-1936.

AS
142
V

ETHNOLOGY CAROLINE ISLANDS

Finsch, Otto

Ethnologische Erfahrungen und Belegstücke aus der Südsee.

(Ann. Naturhist. Mus., Wien, 8:182-383,420-422, 1893)

[Kusaie, 193-230, Ponape,231-275, Truk and Mortlock, 295-383]

Q
101
P 18

ETHNOLOGY CAROLINE ISLANDS

Lessa, William A.

An evaluation of early descriptions of Carolinian culture.

(Ethnohistory, 9(4):313-404, 1962)

GN
669
C 77

ETHNOLOGY CAROLINE ISLANDS (eastern)

Weckler, Joseph Edwin

Land and livelihood on Mokil; an atoll in the Eastern Carolines, Part I
...Part II, by Conrad Bentzen

(Coordinated Investigation of Micronesian Anthropology. Pacific Science Board. June 1949)

GN
669
F 52

ETHNOLOGY CAROLINE ISLANDS

Fischer, John L.

The eastern Carolines, by John L. Fischer with the assistance of Ann M. Fischer. Pacific Science Board, National Acad. Sci., Nat. Research Council, in association with Human Relations Area Files. 1957. xiv + 274 + (15) pp. Behavior Science Monograph

---

GN
669
M 43

ETHNOLOGY CAROLINE ISLANDS

Matsumura, Akira

Contributions to the ethnography of Micronesia... With 36 plates and 72 text-figures. Tokyo. 1918.

AS
552
T

(Journal of the College of Science, Tokyo Imperial University, Vol. XL, Art. 7, Dec. 15, 1918.)

GN
Ethn.Pam.
4093

ETHNOLOGY CARIBBEAN

Rubin, Vera

Caribbean Studies: a symposium. Publ. by Institute of Social and Economic Research, University College of the West Indies, Jamaica... (1957) 8vo. viii + 124 pp.

AN
2.E
P 78

ETHNOLOGY CAROLINE ISLANDS

Gulick, Luther H.

Lectures on Micronesia: I: The Ladrone and Caroline Islands; II: Ponapi and the Ponapian; III: Kusaie and the Kausaien...

(The Polynesian, Vol. 17, Nos. 29, 30, 32, Nov. 17, 24, Dec. 8, 1860)

GN
2.1
A-M

ETHNOLOGY CAROLINE ISLANDS

Ray, Sidney H.

The people of Greenwich Atoll, Western Pacific Ocean.

(Man, vol. 17, 1917, no. 130, pp. 187-190)

(See also note by H.G. Beasley, Man, vol. 18, 1918, no. 13, pp. 22-23, with illustration)

GN
537
E65

ETHNOLOGY - CAUCASIC RACE

Erckert, R. von
und
Der Kaukasus seine völker.

Leipzig, Frohberg, 1887. 386p.

DU
647
G 91

ETHNOLOGY CAROLINE ISLANDS

Harmon, L. McK.

Acho Yap.

(Guam Recorder, Vol. XV, No. 8, pp.7-8,1938)

GN
Ethn.Pam.
3490

ETHNOLOGY CAROLINE ISLANDS

Schneider, E.

Tagebuchblätter von Jaluit.

(Deutsche Kolonialzeitung, 8:30-4, 46-48, 56-61, 75-7, 1891)

GN
2.M
Dr

ETHNOLOGY CELEBES

Meyer, A(dolf) B(ernhard)

Celebes I: Sammlung der Herren Dr. Paul und Dr. Fritz Sarasin aus den Jahren 1893-1896, von A.B. Meyer und O. Richter. Die Bogen-, Strich-, Punkt- und Spiralornamentik von Celebes. Mit 29 Tafeln, 17 Textabbildungen, und 1 Karte.

(Publ. Kgl. Ethnographisches Museum, Dresden, Bd. XIV, 1903)

Storage
Case
3

ETHNOLOGY CAROLINE ISLANDS

Hornbostel, Hans G.

Marianas: 2 boxes of ms. notes. (notes on some Caroline Islanders in Guam)

G
1
G 56

ETHNOLOGY CAROLINE ISLANDS

Senfft, Arno

Die Bewohner der Westkarolinen.

(Globus, 90:279-283, 1906)

[Merir, Tobi, Yap, Oleai, Ululsi, Sonsol. Palau]

GN
635.M4
S 24

ETHNOLOGY CELEBES

Sarasin, Paul

Reisen in Celebes ausgeführt in den jahren 1893-1896 und 1902-1903 von Paul und Fritz Sarasin. 2 vols. Erster band, Zweiter band. Wiesbaden. 1905. 8vo.

GN
663
T 44

ETHNOLOGY CAROLINE ISLANDS

Krämer, Augustin
Zentralkarolinen.

Thilenius, G.
Ergebnisse der Südsee Exp., 1908-1910. II. Ethnographie: B. Mikronesien, Bd. 10, Halbband 1, 1937.

G
1
G 56

ETHNOLOGY CAROLINE ISLANDS

Singer, H.

Die Karolinen.

(Globus, 76:37-52, 1899)

GN
635.D9
W 68

ETHNOLOGY CELEBES

Wilken, G. A.

Handleiding voor de vergelijkende Volkenkunde van Nederlandsch-Indië. Leiden. E. J. Brill. 1893. 8vo. 669 pp.

E 58
J 54

ETHNOLOGY - CENTRAL AMERICA

Spinden, Herbert J.

Origin of Civilizations in Central America and Mexico.

Jenness, Diamond

The American Aborigines...pp. 217-246.

GN 2.I
A-4

ETHNOLOGY CHATHAM ISLANDS

Williams, J. W.

Notes on the Chatham Islands.

(Journ. Anthrop. Inst. of Great Britain and Ireland, Vol. 27, 1897-8, pp. 343-346)

DS 793.S8
Y 94

ETHNOLOGY CHINA

Yueh-hua, Lin

The Lolo of Liang Shan. (Liang-shan I-chia) Translated by Ju-shu Pan. Edited by Wu-chi Liu Human Relations Area Files Press. New Haven. 1961. 8vo. 159 pp.

AS 474
S

ETHNOLOGY CEYLON

Raghavan, M. D.

Ethnological Survey of Ceylon, No. 4-8.

(Spolia Zeylanica, 27(1):139-211, 1953)

GN 550
S

ETHNOLOGY CHEROKEE INDIANS

Royce, Charles C 1845–

...The Cherokee nation of Indians: a narrative of their official relations with the colonial and federal governments. By Charles C. Royce.

(*In* U. S. Bureau of American ethnology. Fifth annual report, 1883-84. Washington, 1887. 30ᵐᵐ. p. 121-378. pl. VII-IX (maps, 2 fold.))
Bibliographical foot-notes.

1. Cherokee Indians—Government relations. 2. Cherokee Indians—Treaties.

16-5495

Library of Congress   E51.U55 5th

GN Pam
2471

ETHNOLOGY - CONGO FREE STATE

Jonghe, Eduard de

Les societes secretes au bas-Congo. From Rev. Questions sci. Oct. 1907.

GN 635.C1
S 24

ETHNOLOGY CEYLON

Sarasin, Paul Benedict

Die Weddas von Ceylon und die sie umgebenden Volkerschaften...(Ergebnisse naturwissenschaftlicher Forschungen auf Ceylon in den Jahren 1884-1886, by P. and F. Sarasin, Bd. III) 1893. Lief. 1-6. 4to. C. W. Kreidel's Verlag. Wiesbaden.

GN Pam
2381

ETHNOLOGY - CHILE

Bienvenido de Estrella, P.

Isla de Pascua. From Mus. d. etnol. y. antrop. Chile publ. v.2, n.1, 1920.

GN 671.C 7
B 92

ETHNOLOGY COOK ISLANDS

Buck, Peter H.   (Te Rangi Hiroa)

Ethnology of Manihiki and Rakahanga.

(Bernice P. Bishop Museum, Bulletin 99, 1932)

GN 635.C1
S 46

ETHNOLOGY CEYLON

Seligmann, C. G.

The Veddas, by C. G. Seligmann and Brenda Z. Seligmann...Cambridge. 1911.

GN Pam
2585

ETHNOLOGY CHILE

Gusinde, P. Martin

La sangre en las creencias y costumbres de los antiguos araucanos. From Publ. d. Mus. d. Etnol. y antrop. d. Chile, ano 1, n.2-3, 1917.

GN 671.C7
B 92

AS 763
B-b

Reading Room

ETHNOLOGY COOK ISLANDS

Buck, Peter H.   (Te Rangi Hiroa)

Mangaian Society. Honolulu. 1934. R8vo.

(Bernice P. Bishop Museum, Bull. 122. 1934.)

GN 2 S
P 76

ETHNOLOGY CHATHAM ISLANDS

Shand, Alexander

The Morioris people of the Chatham Islands: their traditions and history.

(Journal of the Polynesian Society, Vol.3, 1894, pp. 76-92; pp. 121-133;187-198;Vol.4, 1895, pp. 33-46,89-98,160-176,209-225; Vol.5, 1896, pp. 13-32,73-91,131-141,195-211; Vol.6, 1897, pp.11-18, 145-151,161-168; Vol.7, 1898, pp. 73-88)
(also anonymous,   Ibid, Vol. 19: 206-217, 1910.)

GN 2.M
Sa

ETHNOLOGY CHILE

Latcham, Ricardo E.

La organizacion social y las creencias religiosas de los antiguos araucanos. Mus. Nac de Ethol. y antrop. de Chile, Tomo III, Nos. 2-4, 1924.

Storage Case 3

ETHNOLOGY COOK ISLANDS

Buck, Peter H.

Manihiki-Rakahanga. Three field note-books. 1929

GN 671.C5
S 62

AS 763
B-m

Reading Room

ETHNOLOGY CHATHAM ISLANDS

Skinner, H. D.

The Morioris, by H. D. Skinner and William Baucke. Honolulu. 1928. 4to.

(Bernice P. Bishop Museum, Memoir, Vol. IX, No. 5, pp. 343-384, pls. LI-LVIII. 1928).

GN Pam
2384

ETHNOLOGY - CHILE

Uhle, Max

Los aborigenes de Arica. From Mus. d. etnol. y antrop. Chile, publ. v.1, n. 4-5, 1920.

GN 2.S
M 29a

ETHNOLOGY COOK ISLANDS

Buck, Peter H.

The Material Culture of the Cook Islands.

(Memoirs of the Board of Maori Ethnological Research, Vol. 1, 1927, New Plymouth, xxv + 384 pp. 8vo)

AS 763
B-m

GN 671.C5
S 62

ETHNOLOGY CHATHAM ISLANDS

Skinner, H. D.

The Morioris of Chatham Island.

(B.P. Bishop Mus., Mem., vol. IX, no. 1, 1923)

2d copy

GN 635.C
S 82

GN 2.M
Le

ETHNOLOGY CHINA

Stenz, Georg M.

Beiträge zur volkskunde Süd-Schantungs... Leipzig. 1907. 4to.

(Veröffentlichungen des Städtischen Museums für Völkerkunde zu Leipzig, Heft 1, 1907.)

GN 2.M
C 69

and

GN Ethn.Pam. 3329

ETHNOLOGY COOK ISLANDS

Emory, Kenneth Pike

Manihiki: inlaid wooden bowls.

(Ethnologia Cranmorensis, No. 4, 1939 p. 20-26)

AS 701 A

ETHNOLOGY COOK ISLANDS

Gill, William Wyatt

Mangaia (Hervey Islands). IN Repot on the Australasian, Papuan, and Polynesian races...

(Rept. of the 2nd Meeting, Australasian Assn for the Adv. of Sci., Melbourne, 1890, pp. 323-353)

GN Ethn.Pam. 3461

ETHNOLOGY DUTCH EAST INDIES

Kennedy, Raymond

Races and peoples of the Indies. Reprinted with permission of the author from "The Netherlands",-B. Landheer, Editor. University of California Press. Berkeley and Los Angeles, 1943. 14 pp.

AS 36 S2

ETHNOLOGY-EGYPT-EL KHARGEH.

Hrdlička, Aleš i. e. Aloiš Ferdinand, 1869-

... The natives of Kharga Oasis, Egypt, with thirty-eight plates, by Dr. Aleš Hrdlička ... Washington, Smithsonian institution, 1912.

vi, 118 p. incl. tables, diagrs. 20 pl. 24½ᶜᵐ. (Smithsonian miscellaneous collections, v. 59, no. 1)

Publication 2071.
Most of the plates printed on both sides.
"Bibliography relating to or referring to the Kharga Oasis population": p. 104-105.

1. Ethnology — Egypt — El Khargeh. 2. Anthropometry — Egypt — El Khargeh.

12-35562

Library of Congress   /   Q11.S7 vol. 59, no. 1

DU Pac. Pam 144

ETHNOLOGY COOK ISLANDS

Gill, W. W.

The South Pacific and New Guinea past and present; with notes on the Hervey group, an illustrative song and various myths. Sydney. 1892. 38 pp.

GN 635.M4 L 34

ETHNOLOGY DUTCH EAST INDIES

Lasker, Bruno

Peoples of southeast Asia. Prepared under the auspices of the American Council of the Institute of Pacific Relations. New York. 1945.

GN 2.S V

ETHNOLOGY EASTER ISLAND
(P.)
Gusinde, M(artin)

Mutterrechtliche Eigentumskunde von der Osterinsel.

(Mitteilungen der Anthropologischen Gesellschaft in Wien, Bd. LX, pp. 352-355, 1930)

GN 515.C G53

ETHNOLOGY - CYPRUS

Gjerstad, Einar

Studies on prehistoric Cyprus.

Uppsala, n.p., 1926. 342p.

GN 635.D9 V 25

ETHNOLOGY DUTCH EAST INDIES

Van Eerde, J. C.

Die volken van Nederlandsch Indie. Deel 1-2. Amsterdam. Uitgevers-Maatschappij "Elsevier" 1920. sm 4tô. illustrated.

GN 2.M B 91

ETHNOLOGY EASTER ISLAND

Lavachéry, Henri

La galerie du Mercator.

(Bull. des Musées Royaux d'Art et d'Histoire Année 8, 1936, No. 5, pp. 98-106)

AS 36 S1

ETHNOLOGY--CZECHOSLOVAK REPUBLIC.

Matiegka, Jindřich.

The origin and the beginnings of the Czechoslovak people. By Jindřich Matiegka ...

(*In* Smithsonian institution. Annual report. 1919. Washington, 1921. 23½ᶜᵐ. p. 471-486. illus., 4 pl. on 3 l. (incl. fold. map))

1. Ethnology—Czechoslovak Republic.

Library of Congress   Q11.S66 1919   22-324

[9]

AS 145 B

ETHNOLOGY DUTCH EAST INDIES

Van Straelen, V. publisher

Résultats scientifiques du voyage aux Indes Orientales Néerlandaise de...Léopold de Belgique Vol. 1:Introduction, par V. VanStraelen, pp.1-222, pl. 1-91

(Mem. hors serie, Musee Roy. d'Hist. Nat. Belgique, Vol. 1, 1930)

GN Ethn.Pam. 3146

ETHNOLOGY EASTER ISLAND

Métraux, Alfred

Introduction a la connaissance de l'Ile de Pâques. Préface de Paul Morand. A propos d'une exposition au Musée d'Ethnographie du Trocadéro (Museum National d'Histoire Naturelle). 1935.

GN 668 F 74

ETHNOLOGY DOBU ISLANDS

Fortune, Raoul F.

Sorcerers of Dobu. The Social Anthropology of the Dobu Islanders of the Western Pacific. With an Introduction by Bronislaw Malinowski. London. George Routledge & Sons, Ltd. 1932. xxviii + 318 pp. 8vo.

GN Pam 2420

ETHNOLOGY - DUTCH EAST INDIES

Walden, R. v.

Die ethnographischen und sprachlichen verhaltnisse im nordlichen teile Neu-Mecklenburgs und auf den umliegenden inseln. From Korresp-blatt d. deutschen Gesell. Anthrop. Ethnol. und urgeschichte jahrg. 42, n.4, 1911.

GN 1 F

ETHNOLOGY EASTER ISLAND

Balfour, Henry

Some ethnological suggestions in regard to Easter Island.

(Folk-lore, Vol. 28, Dec. 4, 1917, pp. 356-381)

GN Ethn.Pam. 3197

ETHNOLOGY DUTCH EAST INDIES

Josselin de Jong, J. P. B. de

De Maleische Archipel als ethnologisch Studieveld. Leiden. 1935. 24 pp.

GN 635.D9 W 68

ETHNOLOGY DUTCH EAST INDIES

Wilken, G. A.

Handleiding voor de vergelijkende Volkenkunde van Nederlandsch-Indië. Leiden. E. J. Brill. 1893. 8vo. 669 pp.

GN Ethn. Pam.3222

ETHNOLOGY EASTER ISLAND

Bergman, Bengt

"Easter Island" in the Ethnographical Museum of Sweden.

(Ethnos, No. 4, 1937, pp. 102-115)

GN 2.I S 66

ETHNOLOGY DUTCH EAST INDIES

Kennedy, Raymond

Islands and peoples of the Indies.

(War Background Studies, Smithsonian Institution, No. 14, 1943)

GN 671.N5

ETHNOLOGY- E MIRA

Chinnery, E. W. Pearson

Notes on the Natives of E.Mira and St. Matthias.

(Anthropological Report, Territory of New Guinea, No. 2, Melbourne, ND)

GN Ethn.Pam. 3065 2381

GN 2.M S 23

ETHNOLOGY EASTER ISLAND

Bienvenido de Estella, P.

Isla de Pascua. Santiago de Chile. 1920.

(Publicaciones del Museo de Etnologia y antropologia de Chile, Tomo II, Num. 1, 1920, pp. 45-118).

GN
Ethn. Pam.
3116

ETHNOLOGY   EASTER ISLAND

Drapkin, I.

Contribution to the demographic study of Easter Island.

(Occ. Papers, Bernice P. Bishop Museum, Vol. XI, No. 12, 1935)

GN
2.S
B 91

French edition: Contribution...(Bull. Soc. Amer. Belgique, No. 18, 1935, pp. 137-158)

GN
Ethn.
Pam.
3146 a

ETHNOLOGY   EASTER ISLAND

Métraux, Alfred

Introduction a la connaissance de l'Ile de Paques. ... 1935. 8vo.

GN
2.S
P 76

ETHNOLOGY   EASTER ISLAND

Tregear, E(dward)

Easter Island.

(Journal of the Polynesian Society, Vol. 1, 1892, pp. 95-102)

GN
Ethn. Pam.
3122

ETHNOLOGY   EASTER ISLAND

Imbelloni, Jose

Los "Misterios" de la Isla de Pascua.

(Revista Geografica Americana, Ano I, No. 1, 1933. pp. 13-30)

GN
Ethn. Pam.
3162

ETHNOLOGY   EASTER ISLAND

Métraux, Alfred

Voyage autour de l'Ile de Pâques.

(La Revue de Paris, 42d année, no. 14, July 15, 1935, pp. 372-399)

GN
671.E 2
W 85

ETHNOLOGY   EASTER ISLAND

Wolff, Werner

Island of death: a new key to Easter Island's culture through an ethno-psychological study. J. J. Augustin. New York. R8vo. 1948c. 228 pp

---

DU
950.E2
K 72

ETHNOLOGY   EASTER ISLAND

Knoche, Walter

Die Osterinsel: eine Zusammenfassung der chilenischen Osterinselexpedition, des Jahres 1911. Concepcion. Soc. Imp. y Lit. 1925. sm8vo. (8) + 320 pp.

DU
Pao. Pam.
559

ETHNOLOGY   EASTER ISLAND

Ojeda, Carlos Chardin

Los isleños de "Te Pito Henua".

(Atenea, Santiago de Chile, March, 1934. pp. 75-85)

DU
620
H 4

ETHNOLOGY   EBON

Ae'a, H.

The history of Ebon, written by H. Ae'a, a Hawaiian missionary now living there. (1863) [a translation from the "Nupepa Kuokoa" of Feb. 7, 1863, by Mary Kawena Pukui.]

(Hawaiian Historical Soc., Ann. Rept., 56:9-19, 1948)

GN
700
A 62

ETHNOLOGY   EASTER ISLAND

Lavachéry, Henri

Easter Island, Polynesia.

(Antiquity, Vol. 10, No. 37, 1936, pp. 54-60)

GN
2.I
A

ETHNOLOGY   EASTER ISLAND

Palmer, J. Linton

Observations on the inhabitants and the antiquities of Easter Island.

(Journal of the Ethnological Society of London, N. S., Vol. 1, 1869, pp. 371-377)

AS
701
A

ETHNOLOGY   EFATE

Macdonald, D.

Efate, New Hebrides.

(Australian Ass'n for the Adv. of Sci., 4th meeting, 1892, pp. 720-735)

GN
Ethn. Pam.
3268

ETHNOLOGY   EASTER ISLAND

Lavachery, Henri

A propos d'une vue inédite de l'Ile de Paques au XVII siécle.

(Bull.Soc. des Americanistes de Belgique, No. 26, 1938, pp. 86-99)

GN
Ethn. Pam.
3147

ETHNOLOGY—EASTER ISLAND

Ropiteau, André

Une visite au Musée Missionaire des Pères des Sacres-Coeurs de Picpus à Braine-le-Comte (Belgique). Papeete. Imprimerie du Gouvernement. 1936. 8vo. 10 pp.

GN
648
C 45

ETHNOLOGY   EGYPT

Chantre, Ernest

Recherches anthropologiques dans l'Afrique Orientale: Égypte, par Ernest Chantre. Lyon. 1904. 4to.

GN
671.E 2
M 59

ETHNOLOGY   EASTER ISLAND

Metraux, Alfred

Easter Island, a stone-age civilization of the Pacific. Translated from the French by Michael Bullock. Oxford University Press. New York. 1957. 8vo. 249 pp.

GN
Ethn. Pam.
3163

ETHNOLOGY   EASTER ISLAND

Roussel, Hippolyte

Ile de Pâques.

(Annales des Sacres-Coeurs, No. 305, Feb. 1926, p. 355-360; No. 307, April-May, 1926, pp. 423-430; No. 308, June, 1926, pp. 462-466; No. 309, July, 1926, pp. 495-499)

AS
720.N
L

ETHNOLOGY   ELLICE ISLANDS

Donat

Sur quelques similitudes des langues et des coutumes des indigenes de Funafuti (Ellice Group) et des indigenes des Iles de la Société, de l'Archipel des Tuamotu, etc., par MM. Donat et Seurat.

(Proc. Linn. Soc. N. S. Wales, Vol. 28, 1903, pp. 926-931)

GN
671.E2
M 59

ETHNOLOGY   EASTER ISLAND

Métraux, Alfred

Ethnology of Easter Island.

(Bernice P. Bishop Museum, Bulletin 160, 1940)

AS
36
S3

and
DU
950.E2
T 48

ETHNOLOGY—EASTER ISLAND.

Thomson, William Judah, 1841-1909.
Te Pito te Henua; or, Easter Island. By Paymaster William J. Thomson ...

(*In* U. S. National museum. Annual report. 1889. Washington, 1891. 23½ᶜᵐ. p. 447-552. illus., pl. XII-LX (incl. front.: map))
On the written language, with translation of Easter Island tablets: p. 513-526.
Language-vocabulary: p. 546-552.

1. Easter Island. 2. Ethnology—Easter Island. 3. Rapanui language.
1. Title.

Library of Congress   Q11.U5 1889
—— Copy 2.   14-19269
—— Separate.   F3169.T48

GN
671.F8
H 45

AS
691
1959

GN-Pam
691
1959

ETHNOLOGY   ELLICE ISLANDS

Hedley, Charles

The ethnology of Funafuti.

(Mem. Aust. Mus., III, Pt. 4, pp. 229-304, 1897.)

3

GN
2.S
P76
ETHNOLOGY ELLICE ISLANDS

Kennedy, Donald Gilbert

Field Notes on the Culture of Vaitupu, Ellice Islands.

(Memoirs of the Polynesian Society, Vol. 9, 1931)

GN
2.M
B 51 v
ETHNOLOGY ELLICE ISLANDS

Koch, Gerd

Die Materielle Kultur der Ellice-Inseln.

(Veröffentlichungen des Museums für Völkerkunde, Berlin, n.f. 3, Abteilung Südsee, 1, 1961)

AS
701
A
ETHNOLOGY ELLICE ISLANDS

Newell, J. E.

Notes, chiefly ethnological, of the Tokelau, Ellice and Gilbert Islands.

(Australasian Ass'n for the Adv. of Sci., 1895, pp. 603-612)

GN
2.S
P 76
ETHNOLOGY ELLICE ISLANDS

Tutuila

The Line Islanders. Notes on the races known as the Tokelaus, or the Line Islanders, called by themselves the Kai-n-Abara ...
(Polynesian Society Journal, Vol. 1, 1892, pp. 263-272)

GN
673
B 61
ETHNOLOGY ESKIMOS

Birket-Smith, Kaj

The Eyak Indians of the Copper River Delta, Alaska. By Kaj Birket-Smith and Frederica de Laguna. København. 1938.

GN
673
B 66

GN
550
S
ETHNOLOGY ESKIMOS

Boas, Franz

The Central Eskimo. Washington. 1888. 4to.

(U. S. Bureau of American Ethnology, 6th Annual Report, 1884-85, pp. 399-669).

Q
115
C 21
ETHNOLOGY-ESKIMOS

Canadian Arctic Expedition, 1913-18.

Report... Ottawa. 1920-1928. R8vo.

Volumes XII, XIII, XIV and XV.

GN
673
R 91
ETHNOLOGY ESKIMO

Rudenko, S. I.

The ancient culture of the Bering Sea and the Eskimo problem.

(Arctic Institute of North America, Anthropology of the North, Translations from Russian Sources, No.1. 1961)

Translated by Paul Tolstoy.

G
R96
ETHNOLOGY - ESKIMOS

Russell, Frank

Explorations in the Far North.

n.p., Iowa University, 1898. 281p.

GN
673
W 54
ETHNOLOGY ESKIMOS

Weyer, Edward Moffat

The Eskimos...New Haven. Yale University Press. 1932. 8vo. xvii + 491 pp.

QH
1
N 28
ETHNOLOGY ESPIRITU SANTO

Deniker, J.

Collections ethnographiques rapportées de Mélanésie par le Dr. François.

(Le Naturaliste, Vol. 6, 1891, pp. 227-229; 245-247)

GN
Ethn.Pam.
3854
ETHNOLOGY ESPIRITU SANTO

Harrisson, Tom H.

Living in Espiritu Santo. [Oxford University New Hebrides Expedition, 1933-1934]

(Geographical Journal, 88(3):243-261, 1936)

[map of the island]

AS
36
S1
ETHNOLOGY - EUROPE

Bloch, Adolphe.

Origin and evolution of the blond Europeans. By Dr. Adolphe Bloch.

(*In* Smithsonian institution. Annual report, 1912. Washington, 1913. 23½ᶜᵐ. p. 609-630)

"Translated ... from Origine et évolution des blonds Européens ... Bulletins et mémoires de la Société d'anthropologie de Paris. 6th ser., vol. 2, nos. 1 and 2. Paris, 1911, pp. 55-79."

1. Color of man. 2. Ethnology—Europe.

Library of Congress   Q11.S66 1912   13-25699
(s21f2)

AS
36
S1
ETHNOLOGY - EUROPE

Fischer, Theobald, 1846-
The Mediterranean peoples. By Theobald Fischer ...
(*In* Smithsonian institution. Annual report. 1907. Washington, 1908. 23½ᶜᵐ. p. 497-521)
"Translated ... from the Internationale wochenschrift. Berlin, September 7, 14, 21, 28, 1907."

1. Mediterranean race. 2. Ethnology—Europe. 3. Ethnology—Africa, North.

S 15-1349

Library of Congress   Q11.S66 1907
Library, Smithsonian Institution

GN
575
R 59
ETHNOLOGY EUROPE

Ripley, William Z.

The races of Europe: a sociological study (Lowell Institute Lectures.) Accompanied by a supplementary bibliography of the anthropology and ethnology of Europe...New York. 1899. 8vo.

GN
575
S 48
ETHNOLOGY EUROPE

Sergi, G.

Europa: l'origine dei popoli Europei e loro relazioni coi popoli d'Africa, d'Asia e d'Oceania. Milano. 1908. R8vo.

GN
575
R 59

Z
5117
R 59

Reading
Room
ETHNOLOGY EUROPE BIBLIOGRAPHY

Ripley, William Z.

A selected bibliography of the anthropology and ethnology of Europe: a supplement to the Races of Europe, a sociological study...New York 1899. 8vo.

GN
Ethn.Pam.
3001
ETHNOLOGY-FIJI

Barker, G.W.

The Calendar of the Fijian. 5 typed pages.

GN
1
O 15
ETHNOLOGY FIJI

Cato, A. C.

Malolo Island and Viseisei village, western Fiji.

(Oceania, 22(2):101-115, 1951)

GN
671.F1
D 28
ETHNOLOGY FIJI

Deane, W.

Fijian Society, or the Sociology and Psychology of the Fijians. London. Macmillan. 1921. 8vo. xv + 255 pp.

GN
2.S
F 47
ETHNOLOGY FIJI

Fijian Society

Transactions, 1908- >

For current volumes see serial file.

GN 2.S P 76 ETHNOLOGY FIJI Geddes, W. R. Deuba: a study of a Fijian village. (Polynesian Society, Memoir 23, 1945-46)	AS 122 B ETHNOLOGY FIJI Im Thurn, Sir Everard A study of primitive character. (British Association for the Adv. of Sci., Report, 1914, pp. 515-524)	GN 2.I A-m ETHNOLOGY FIJI Paine, R. W. Some Rock Paintings in Fiji. (In Man: 1929, Nr. 9, pp. 149-151, 5 plates)
GN 2-I A-m ETHNOLOGY FIJI Hocart, A. M. Alternate Generations in Fiji. (Man: a Monthly Record of Anthropological Science, Vol. 31, No. 214, 1931)	AS 763 B-s GN Ethn. Pam. 3308 Reading Room ETHNOLOGY FIJI Lambert, S.M. East Indian and Fijian in Fiji: their changing numerical relation. (Bernice P. Bishop Museum, Special Publication No. 32, 1938)	GN 2.I A-2 ETHNOLOGY FIJI Pritchard, Wm. T. Viti and its inhabitants. (Mem. Anthrop. Soc. of London, Vol. 1, 1863-1864, pp. 195-209)
GN 2.1 A-4 GN Pam. 2715 ETHNOLOGY FIJI Hocart, A. M. Early Fijians. (Journ. R. Anthrop. Inst. of Great Britain and Ireland, Vol. 49, 1919, pp. 42-51, pla. I-II)	GN 2.S F 47 ETHNOLOGY FIJI Lester, R. H. A few customs observed by Fijians in connection with birth, betrothal and marriage and death. (Transactions of the Fiji Society of Science and Industry, Vol. 3(2):113-129, 1946)	GN 671.F1 Q 1 ETHNOLOGY FIJI Quain, Buell Fijian village. With an introduction by Ruth Benedict. The University of Chicago Press. Chicago. R8vo. xvii + 459 pp. 1948
GN 2.1 A-m ETHNOLOGY - FIJI Hocart, A. M. Ethnological Sketch of Fiji. (Man, Vol. 5, No. 43, 1915)	GN 662 M 27 ETHNOLOGY FIJI Mander, Linden A. Some dependent peoples of the South Pacific. Issued under the auspices of the International Secretariat, Institute of Pacific Relations. The MacMillan Co. New York. 1954. 8vo. xix + 535 pp.	GN 671.F1 R 84 ETHNOLOGY FIJI Roth, G. K. Fijian way of life. Oxford University Press. Melbourne, London... 1953. 8vo. xvi + 176 pp.
AS 763 B-b GN 671.F1 H 68 Reading Room ETHNOLOGY FIJI Hocart, A. M. Lau Islands, Fiji. Honolulu. 1929. 8vo. (Bernice P. Bishop Museum, Bull. 62. 1929.)	GN 2.1 A-4 ETHNOLOGY FIJI Mason, J. E. On the natives of Fiji. (Journ. Anthrop. Inst. of Great Britain and Ireland, Vol. 16, 1887, pp. 217-220)	GN 1 A ETHNOLOGY FIJI Thompson, Laura The culture history of the Lau Islands. (The American Anthropologist, Vol. 40, 1938 pp. 181-197)
GN 2-I A-m ETHNOLOGY FIJI Hocart, A. M. Natural and Supernatural (Man; 1932:78)	GN 1 A 62 ETHNOLOGY - FIJI Mauss, Marcel L'extension du potlatch en Mélanesie. (L'Anthropologie, Tome 30, 1920, pp. 396-397)	GN 2.S P 76 ETHNOLOGY FIJI Hart-Raven, R. A village in the Yasawas (Fiji). (Jour. of the Poly. Soc. 65(2):95-154, 1956)
GN 2.I A 4-o ETHNOLOGY FIJI Hocart, A. M. The northern states of Fiji. (Occ. Pub. No. 11, R. Anthropological Inst., 1952)	GN 2.S Po ETHNOLOGY FIJI Morey, C. J. Wrecked on the Voyage to Lau. (Fijian poem) (Journal of the Polynesian Society, Vol. 41, pp. 301-311, 1932)	GN 671.F 1 T 47 ETHNOLOGY FIJI Thompson, Laura Fijian frontier. Introduction by B. Malinowski. (Studies of the Pacific No. 4) American Council, Inst. of Pacific Relations. New York... 1940. R8vo. xxiii + 153 pp.

QK
Ethn.Pam.
3243

ETHNOLOGY FIJI

Thompson, Laura

Kulturegeschichte der Lauinseln (Fidschi-gruppe.)

(Archiv f. Anthropologie, 24:2, pp. 140-153)

Yale?   Date not given
on separate

AS
492
S 6

ETHNOLOGY FORMOSA

Dodd, John

A glimpse at the manners and customs of the Hill Tribes of North Formosa.

(Journal of the Straits Branch of the Royal Asiatic Society, No. 15, pp. 69-78, 1885)

GN
1
A

ETHNOLOGY FORMOSA

Wirth, A.

The aborigines of Formosa and the Liu-Kiu Islands.

(The American Anthropologist, 10:357-370, 1897)

GN
668
T 47

ETHNOLOGY FIJI

Thompson, Laura

Southern Lau, Fiji: an ethnography.

(Bernice P. Bishop Museum, Bull. 162, 1940)

GN
2.S
V

ETHNOLOGY FORMOSA

Haberlandt, M.

Die Eingeborenen der Kapsulan-Ebene von Formosa.

(Mitt. der Anthrop. Gesell., Wien, 24:184-193, 1894)

GN
2.S
V

ETHNOLOGY FORMOSA

Yamasaki, N.

Ein Besuch in den Köpfjägerdörfen auf Formosa.

(Mitt.Anthrop. Gesell. Wien, 31:23-37, 1901)

[head-hunters' villages]

GN
2.S
F 47

ETHNOLOGY FIJI

Tonganivalu, Deve

Ai yau kei nai yaya vakaviti. (Fijian property and gear)

(Trans. Fijian Soc., 1917:1-18)

[note in Dr. Buck's possession: perhaps most complete native estimony concerning material culture of Fiji...quite authentic, not full but more than is to be found elsewhere on masi, oil, salt. A little information on netting, basketry, coconut receptacles; primary fault, lack of completeness]

G
7
R 9

ETHNOLOGY FORMOSA

Hughes, T. F.

Visit to Tok-e-Tok, chief of the eighteen tribes, southern Formosa.

(Proceedings of the R. Geogr. Soc., 16:265-271, 1872)

GN
671.F8
H 45

AS
719
A-me

GN-Pam
691
1959

ETHNOLOGY FUNAFUTI

Hedley, Charles

The ethnology of Funafuti.

(Mem. Aust. Mus., III, Pt. 4, pp. 229-304. 1897.)

Storage
Case
3

ETHNOLOGY FIJI

Waterhouse, J. H. L.

King and People of Fiji. Vol. II.

G
13
B

ETHNOLOGY FORMOSA

Kakyo, Ino

Die Wilden Stämme von Formosa, ihre Einteilung und ihr Kulturstand.

(Zeitschrift der Gesellschaft fur Erdkunde zu Berlin, Vol. 34:63-74, 1899)

DU
604
B 76

ETHNOLOGY FUTUNA

Bourdin, Le R. P.

Vie du vénérable P.-M.-L. Chanel, prêtre de la Société de Marie, Provicaire Apostolique et premier martyr de l'Océanie. Paris. 1867. 8vo. pp. 429-472.

AS
36
S1

ETHNOLOGY-FRANCE-VÉZÈRE VALLEY

Broca, Paul *i. e.* Pierre Paul, 1824-1880.

The troglodytes, or cave-dwellers, of the Valley of the Vézère. By M. Paul Broca ...

(*In* Smithsonian institution. Annual report. 1872. Washington, 1873. 231ᵈ. p. (310):347. illus.)

"An address delivered before the French association for the advancement of science. <Translated from 'La Revue scientifique,' November 16, 1872 ...">

1. Cave-dwellers. 2. Ethnology—France—Vézère Valley.

S 15-341

Library of Congress   Q11.S66 1872
Library, Smithsonian   Institution

GN
1
Z

ETHNOLOGY FORMOSA

Müller, W.

Ueber die Wildenstämme der Insel Formosa.

(Zeitschrift f. Ethnologie, 42:228-241, 1910)

[the wild tribes...]

GN
671.F9
B 97

ETHNOLOGY FUTUNA

Burrows, Edwin G.

Ethnology of Futuna.

(Bernice P. Bishop Museum, Bulletin No. 138, 1935)

GN
1
An

ETHNOLOGY FORMOSA

Alvarez, Jose Maria

The aboriginal inhabitants of Formosa.

(Anthropos, 22:248-259, 1927)

G
3
A

ETHNOLOGY FORMOSA

Steere, J. B.

Formosa.

(Journal of the American Geographical Soc., VI:302-334, 1874)

GN
Ethn.Pam.
3223

ETHNOLOGY FUTUNA

Burrows, Edwin G.

Wallis et Futuna: Etude Ethnographique.

(Colonies Autonomes, Magazine Trimestriel, Juin, 1937. pp. 3-6)

GN
2.I
A

ETHNOLOGY FORMOSA

Collingwood, C.

Visit to the Kibalan village of Sauo Bay, northeast coast of Formosa.

(Transactions of the Ethnological Soc. of London, VI:135-143, 362-3, 1868)

G
7
R 9

ETHNOLOGY FORMOSA

Taylor, George

Formosa: characteristic traits of the island and its aboriginal inhabitants.

(Proc. R. Geogr. Soc., N.S. XI:224-239, 1889)

DU
604
G 48

ETHNOLOGY FUTUNA

Gilmore, Florence

The Martyr of Futuna. Blessed Peter Chanel of the Society of Mary. Maryknoll, Ossining P. O., New York. Catholic Foreign Mission Society of America. 1917. 8vo. 199 pp., 16 illus.

GN
2.S
P 76

ETHNOLOGY   FUTUNA

Smith, S. Percy

Futuna; or, Horne Island and its people.
Western Pacific.

(Journal of the Polynesian Society, Vol. 1,
1892, pp. 33-52)

see also Note 17 on p. 190

GN
1
I 61

ETHNOLOGY   GILBERT ISLANDS

Parkinson, R.

Beiträge zur Ethnologie der Gilbertisulaner.

(Archiv f. Ethnographie, II, 1889, pp. 31-
49, 90-106)

AS
36
S1
and
GN
1
A

ETHNOLOGY--GUAM

Safford, W. E.

Guam and its people. In Rept. Smithson.
Inst. 1902 pp 493-508. Also in Amer.
Anthrop. iv, 1902.

AS
142
V

ETHNOLOGY   GILBERT ISLANDS

Finsch, Otto

Ethnologische Erfahrungen und Belegstücke
aus der Südsee. Dritte Abt. Mikronesien (West-
Oceanien), 1. Gilberts-Inseln.
(Ann. Naturhist. Mus., Wien, 8:1-106, 417-
418, 1893)

GN
Ethn.Pam.
1366

ETHNOLOGY   GILBERT ISLANDS

Schmeltz, Johannes Diedrich Eduard

Die etnographisch anthropologische Abthel-
ung des Museum Godeffroy. By J.D.E. Schmeltz
and R. Krause.

(Archiv f. Ethnographie, Bd. I, 1888, pp.
60-67)

DU
647
T 46

ETHNOLOGY   GUAM

Thompson, Laura.

Guam and its people; a study of culture change and colonial
education, by Laura Thompson ... San Francisco, New York
[etc.] American council, Institute of Pacific relations, 1941.

xii p., 1 l., 308 p. incl. tables, 2 diagr. on fold. l. 10 pl. (incl. front.)
8 maps (2 fold.) 22½ᵐ. (Studies of the Pacific, no. 8)

"Printed in China."
Appendices: I. Merizo village journal, by Jesus C. Barcinas. II. Address by Mrs. Agueda Johnston. III. "Those who join the navy", a
modern Chamorro folk song.

1. Guam. 2. Chamorros. I. Institute of Pacific relations. American
council.

Library of Congress   DU1.87 no. 8   42-36122
                           [80]   (960.062) 919.67

GN
2.S
P 76

ETHNOLOGY   GILBERT ISLANDS

Grimble, Arthur

The migrations of a Pandanus people...

(Polynesian Society, Memoir 12, 1933)

in Journal 42, 1933 only

DU
600
T 48

ETHNOLOGY   GILBERT ISLANDS

Thomson, Basil

The Fijians: a study of the decay of custom.
Illustrated. London. William Heinemann. 1908
8vo.
    p. 210-211 pregnancy customs

GN
Ethn.Pam.
3591

ETHNOLOGY   HAINAN

Odaka, Kunio

Economic organization of the Li tribes of
Hainan Island. Yale University, Southeast Asia
Studies. Dec. 1950. mimeographed. 95pp.

ETHNOLOGY   GILBERT ISLANDS

Grimble, Sir Arthur

War finds its way to Gilbert Islands:United
States forces dislodge Japanese from enchanted
atolls which loom now as stepping stones along
South Sea route from Australia to Hawaii. With
illustrations from photographs by Dr. Raymond A.
Dillon.
(National Geographic Magazine, Vol. 83, 1942
71-92)

GN
2.S
P 76

ETHNOLOGY   GILBERT ISLANDS

Tutuila

The Line Islanders, Notes on the races
known as the Tokelaus, or the Line Islanders...
(Polynesian Society Journal, Vol. 1, 1892,
pp. 263-272)

GN
1
Z

ETHNOLOGY   HAWAII

Arning, Ed.(uard)

Ethnographie von Hawaii.

(in Zeit. fur Ethn., Bd. 19, pp.(129)-
(138). Berlin, 1887.

AN
2.E
P 78

ETHNOLOGY   GILBERT ISLANDS

Gulick, Luther H.

Lectures on Micronesia...V, The Gilbert
Islands.
(The Polynesian, Vol. 17, No. 36, Jan. 5,
1861)

DU
647
G 91

ETHNOLOGY   GUAM

Characteristics of the natives of Guam when
the first settlement was established by the
Spaniards.

(Guam Recorder, Vol. 6, 1930, No. 10, p. 188)

GN
2.M
H

ETHNOLOGY   HAWAII

Arning, Eduard

Ethnographische Notizen aus Hawaii 1883-86.

(In Mitteilungen aus dem Museum für Völkerkunde in Hamburg, XVI, Hamburg, 1931)

GN
2.S
P 76

ETHNOLOGY   GILBERT ISLANDS

Laxton, P. B.

Nikumaroro.

Journal of the Poly. Soc., 60(2/3):134-160,
1951

DU
647
G 91

ETHNOLOGY   GUAM

Planting by the moon and tide: a superstition of the Chamorro people.

(Guam Recorder, Vol. 17, No. 10, 1941, pp.
411, 437)

GN
2.I
A-m

ETHNOLOGY   HAWAII

Beasley, H. G.

A carved wooden figure from Hawaii.

(Man, Vol. 32, Feb. 1932, No. 43)

AS
701
A

ETHNOLOGY   GILBERT ISLANDS

Newell, J. E.

Notes, chiefly ethnological, of the Tokelau,
Ellice and Gilbert Islands.

(Australasian Ass'n for the Adv. Of Sci.,
1895, pp. 603-612)

GN
Ethn.Pam.
3522

ETHNOLOGY   GUAM

Repetti, W. C.

Conditions in Guam in 1678.

(The Catholic Historical Review, Vol. 32(4):
430-434, 1947)

GN
Ethn.Pam.
3934

ETHNOLOGY   HAWAII

Beckwith, Martha Warren   (collector)

[Clippings from Honolulu newspapers, undated.
Those of greatest interest cataloged separately.

[by Emerson, Alexander, etc. on kahunas,
Thomas Square, altar fires of Punchbowl, etc.]

GR
385.H
B 39

ETHNOLOGY HAWAII

Beckwith, Martha Warren

Kepelino's Traditions of Hawaii.

(Bernice P. Bishop Museum Bulletin 95, 1932)

GN
671.H2
B 91

ETHNOLOGY HAWAII

Bryan, Edwin H., Jr.

Ancient Hawaiian life. Advertiser Publishing Company. Honolulu. 1938. 8vo. (5) + 113 pp.

DU
Pac
Pam
#255

ETHNOLOGY HAWAII

Coan, Titus Munson.

Natives of Hawaii; a study of Polynesia charm. Reprint fr. Annals Am. Acad. of Political and Social Sc. July 1901. pp 9-17 Philadelphia.

JAN ... 73

GN
Ethn.Pam.
2774

ETHNOLOGY - HAWAII

Bicknell, James

Hoomanamana - Idolatry.

(Typewritten copy pp. 1-7 and printed copy, 10 pp. ND. No place. 12mo.)

GN
Ethn.Pam.
3663

ETHNOLOGY HAWAII

Bryan, Edwin H., Jr.

A check list of Hawaiian artifacts. Compiled for the Mokihana Club...with the assistance of Kenneth P. Emory. 6 pp. mimeographed. (1951)

GN
1
Ar

ETHNOLOGY HAWAII

Dalton, O. M.

Notes on an ethnological collection from the west coast of North America, Hawaii, and Tahiti formed during the voyage of Captain Vancouver , 1790 - 1795 and now in the British Museum . In Archiv fur Ethnog. X, 1897, pp 225 - 245.

GN
Ethn.Pam.
3368

ETHNOLOGY HAWAII

Bishop, Marcia Brown

Hawaiian life of the pre-European period, with a catalogue of the Marcia Brown Bishop Collection. Exhibited at the Peabody Museum of Salem. 1940. 8vo. 105 pp.

QH
198.H
B 91

ETHNOLOGY HAWAII

Bryan, William Alanson

Natural history of Hawaii... Honolulu. Hawaiian Gazette Co., Ltd. 1915. R8vo. 596 pp.

Gn
1
B

ETHNOLOGY HAWAII

Eichhorn, Aug.

Alt-Hawaiische Kultobjeckte und Kultgeräte.

(Baessler-Archiv, Bd. XIII, Heft 1, 1929, pp. 1-30)

GN
Ethn.Pam.
2925

ETHNOLOGY - HAWAII

Bishop, S. E.

Why are the Hawaiians Dying Out? Or, elements of disability for survival among the Hawaiian people. 18 pp. (Read to Honolulu Social Science Association, November, 1888.)

DU
12
C 18
looked
case

ETHNOLOGY HAWAII

Campbell, Archibald

A Voyage round the world, from 1806 to 1812 ; in which...the Sandwich Islands were visited... with an account of the present state of the Sandwich Islands... Edinburgh. 1816. 8vo. pp.120-215; 267-275.

GN
671.H2
E 55

AS
763
B-b

Reading
Room

ETHNOLOGY HAWAII

Emory, K. P.

The island of Lanai, a survey of native culture. Honolulu. Bernice P. Bishop Museum. 1924. 8vo. 129 pp. Illustrated. map.

(Bernice P. Bishop Museum, Bulletin 12)

GN
671.H2
B 85

AS
763
B-m

Reading
Room

ETHNOLOGY HAWAII

Brigham, William T.

The Ancient Hawaiian House.

(Memoirs of the Bernice P. Bishop Museum, Volume II, No. 3, 1908)

GN
Ethn. Pam
3710

ETHNOLOGY HAWAII

Case, Howard D.

The story of Hawaii and Hawaiian people.

(Honolulu Star-Bulletin, Oct. 13, 20, 27, Nov. 3, 10, 17, Dec. 1, 1923) being articles 1-5, 8, 12.

[articles 6,7,9-11 missing. Is no 12 the last?]

kumulipo,   ancient voyages, legends, Kamehameha I,   kahunas...

GN
1
A 62

ETHNOLOGY HAWAII

Elbert, Samuel H.

Hawaiian literary style and culture.

(American Anthropologist, 53(3):345-354, 1951)

GN
671.H2
B 85

AS
763
B-m

Reading
Room

ETHNOLOGY HAWAII

Brigham, William T.

Mat and Basket Weaving of the Ancient Hawaiians, described and compared with the basketry of the other Pacific islanders, with an account of Hawaiian nets and nettings by John F.G.Stokes.

(Memoirs of the Bernice P. Bishop Museum, Volume II, No. 1, 1906)

DU
12
C 51
looked
case

DU
623
C 51

ETHNOLOGY HAWAII

Cheever, H. T.

Island world of the Pacific: being the personal narrative and results of travel through the Sandwich or Hawaiian Islands, and other parts of Polynesia... New York. 1851. 8vo.

The same. 2 copies. 1 copy published in Glasgow. n.d. 12mo.

GN
Ethn.Pam.
3933

WITHDRAWN
and
placed
with
Letters
Carter
Mss Room

ETHNOLOGY HAWAII

Emerson, Joseph S.

Letters to Martha Warren Beckwith, 1913, 1914, 1921.

(various matters: breeding stones, the singing snail, sayings and riddles, comments on the new dictionary, on Lyle Dickey's string figures)

GN
671.H2
B 85

AS
763
B-m

Reading
Room

ETHNOLOGY HAWAII

Brigham, William T.

Old Hawaiian Carvings Found in a Cave on the Island of Hawaii. Figured and described by William T. Brigham.

(Memoirs of the Bernice P. Bishop Museum, Vol. II, No. 2, 1906)

G
3
A

ETHNOLOGY HAWAII

Coan, Titus Munson

Hawaiian Ethnography.

(Bulletin of the American Geographical Society, Vol. 31, 1899, pp. 24-30)

DU
620
I

ETHNOLOGY HAWAII

F. B.

Hawaiian antiquities, a note on certain relics, chiefly cave finds.

(Islander, Vol. I, 1875, p. 6)

GN
2.1
Ar

ETHNOLOGY HAWAII

Gill, Lorin Tarr

Mystery of the Northwest Islands. In Art and archaeology, vol. 29, no. 2, Feb. 1930. pp. 80-89.   pl.

DU
620
H 4

ETHNOLOGY HAWAII

Houston, Victor S. K.

Chamisso in Hawaii. Translated from the German...

(Report, Haw. Hist. Soc., 48, 1940, p. 55-82)

DU
623
L 42

ETHNOLOGY HAWAII

Lawrence, Mary Stebbins

Old time Hawaiians and their work. Ginn and Co. New York. 1912c. sm8vo. xiii, 172 pp.

3rd edition: Old time Hawaiians. Revised and enlarged edition. Patten Company, Ltd.. Honolulu. 1939. 8vo. 187 pp.

GN
1
A
and
GR
Folklore
Pam. 39

ETHNOLOGY HAWAII

Green, Laura C.

Hawaiian Customs and Beliefs Relating to Birth and Infancy, by Laura C. Green and Martha Warren Beckwith.

(American Anthropologist, N. S., Vol. 26, 1924, pp. 230-246)

DU
620
H 4

ETHNOLOGY HAWAII

Hunnewell, James

Voyage in the Brig Bordeaux Packet, Boston to Honolulu, 1817, and residence in Honolulu 1817-1818, transcribed from his journal, and edited by his son, James F. Hunnewell, 1895. (Hawaiian Hist., Soc., Papers, no. 8, 1895, pp. 3-18)

DU
620
F

ETHNOLOGY HAWAII

Lobscheid,

Ethnological and philological notes respecting Hawaiians.

(Friend, Jan., 1872, p. 4)

GN
671.H2
H 23

ETHNOLOGY-HAWAII

Handy, E. S. C.

Ancient Hawaiian Civilization. A series of lectures delivered at the Kamehameha Schools by Handy, Emory, Bryan, Buck, Wise and Others. Published and Printed by the Kamehameha Schools. 1933. 8 vo. 323 pp. Honolulu.

Storage
Case
3

ETHNOLOGY HAWAII (ISLAND)

Judd, Albert F., 1874-

Ethnologic Notes re Kapua, South Kona, Hawaii. (2 copies, each 2 typed sheets) 1932.

GN
671.H2
M 25
2 copies

AS
763
N. B.
B-s

Reading
Room

ETHNOLOGY HAWAII

Malo, David

David Malo; translated from the Hawaiian by Dr. Emerson. Honolulu. Hawaiian Gazette. 1903. 8vo. 366 pp.

Hawaiian antiquities (Moolelo Hawaii) by

(Bernice P. Bishop Museum, Spec. Pub. No. 2)

DU
623
H 23

ETHNOLOGY HAWAII

Handy, E. S. Craighill

Cultural Revolution in Hawaii. Preliminary Paper Prepared for the Fourth General Session of the Institute of Pacific Relations...Hangchow, China...1931...

GR
385.H
K 14

ETHNOLOGY - HAWAII

Kalakaua

Na Mele Aimoku, na Mele Kupuna a ma na Mele Ponoi, o ka Moi Kalakaua I., a ua Pai ia no ka la Hanau o ka Moi. Ka Kanalima Ponoi o Kona Mau Makahiki. (1886) 311 pp. 8vo.

GN
Ethn.Pam.
2926

ETHNOLOGY - HAWAII

Marques, A.

The Population of the Hawaiian Islands. Is the Hawaiian a doomed race? Present and future prospects.

(Taken from Journal Polynesian Society, Vol. I: pp.253-270. 1892. 8vo.)

Storage
Case
4

Hms K
"   L
"   M

ETHNOLOGY HAWAII

Hawaiian ethnological notes.

Vol. 1: Kahuna wisdom, lore.
  "   2: Legends, stories and historical tales.
  "   3: Meles.

Storage
Case
3

ETHNOLOGY HAWAII

Kelsey, Theodore

Ethnological notes on fishing, adze making, place names (Kona), bird-catching, names of the nights of the moon, proverbs...

DU
1
M 6

ETHNOLOGY HAWAII

Miller, Carey D.

The Foods of the Ancient Hawaiians.

(Mid-Pacific Magazine, Vol. 44, 1932, pp. 337-342)

GN
671.H2
H 23

ETHNOLOGY HAWAII

Handy, Edward Smith Craighill

The Hawaiian planter, Volume I: his plants, methods and areas of cultivation.

(Bulletin, Bernice P. Bishop Museum, No. 161, 1940, pp. 1-227, 21 figs, 8 pl.)

GN
1
A

ETHNOLOGY HAWAII

Kroeber, A. L.

Observations on the Anthropology of Hawaii

(American Anthropologist, N. S., Vol. 23, 1921, pp. 129-137)

GN
Ethn.Pam.
3002

ETHNOLOGY-HAWAII

Northwood, J. d'Arcy

The Game of Maika. 11 typed pages.

Storage
Case
4

Hms
Misc.
42

ETHNOLOGY HAWAII

Henriques, (Mrs.) Edgar

Ethnological notes, Hawaii: kapa making, names of planets and months, royal addresses to the chiefs and people, chronological events, place names from Waihee, Maui, names of fishes, birds and kinds of taro.

DU
Pac.Pam
491

ETHNOLOGY HAWAII

Kukahi, J. L.

Ka Kumulipo he Moolelo Hawaii. Buke 1-2. Honolulu. 1902. pp. 1-50 and 51-98. 8vo.

GN
671.H2
B 66

ETHNOLOGY-HAWAII

A Preliminary Catalogue of the Bernice Pauahi Bishop Museum of Polynesian Ethnology and Natural History. Part I: Kahilis, Feather Ornaments, Mats and Kapas.

(Special Publication, Bernice P. Bishop Museum, No. 1, Part I, 1892)

GN
Ethn.
Pam.
3410

ETHNOLOGY HAWAII

Pukui, Mary Kawena

Hawaiian beliefs and customs during birth, infancy, and childhood.

(Occasional Papers, Bernice P. Bishop Mus., Vol. 16, No. 17, 1942, pp. 357-381)

GN
Pam
3082

ETHNOLOGY HAWAII

Stokes, J. F. G.

Japanese cultural influences in Hawaii.

(Reprinted from the Proceedings of the Fifth Pacific Science Congress, 1933, Vancouver, pp. 2791-2803)

DU
629.H3
N 28

ETHNOLOGY HONAUNAU

The natural and cultural history of Honaunau, Kona, Hawaii.

Volume II: The cultural history, by Kenneth P. Emory, John F. G. Stokes, Dorothy B. Barrere, Marion A. Kelly. Text and plates. Bernice P. Bishop Museum. 4to. 257 pp. mimeographed. 63 plates (Photos)

GN
Ethn. Pam.
3501

ETHNOLOGY HAWAII

Pukui, Mary Kawena

The makahiki; fishing and farming. By Mary Kawena Pukui and Caroline Curtis. Kamehameha Schools, Preparatory Department. mimeographed. rec'd Aug. 1946. 50 pp. 4to.

GN
1
A

ETHNOLOGY HAWAII

Stokes, John F. G.

Spaniards and the Sweet Potato in Hawaii and Hawaiian-American Contacts.

(American Anthropologist, N.S.Vol. 34, 1932 pp. 594-600)

GN
Ethn.Pam.
3121

ETHNOLOGY HOPI

Beaglehole, Ernest

Ownership and inheritance in an American Indian tribe.

(The Iowa Law Review, Vol. 20, 1935, pp. 304-316)

DU
625
R 39

ETHNOLOGY HAWAII

Remy, Jules

Recits d'un vieux sauvage pour servir a' l'histoire ancienne de Hawaii. Notes d'un voyageur lues à la Société d'agriculture, commerce, sciences er arts du departement de la Marne... 15 decembre 1857. Chalons-sur-Marne. 1859. 8vo. 67 pp.

GN
Ethn.
Pam.
4276

ETHNOLOGY HAWAII

Taylor, Clarice B.

Hawaiian Almanac. 2nd printing, 1960. Tongg Publishing Company, Ltd. Honolulu sm8vo 64 pp.

GN
Ethn.
Pam.
3050

ETHNOLOGY HUNGARY

Jánostol, Janko and others

A Magyar nemzeti Múzeum Néprajzi Osztálya. A Múzeum Alapításának Százados Évforduloja Alkalmábol ismertetik az osztály tisztviselöi. Budapest. 1902. Folio.

GN
Pam
2809

ETHNOLOGYISLAHAWAIIETHNOLOGY

Ruggles, Samuel

From a Missionary Journal, by Samuel and Nancy Ruggles.
(In Atlantic Monthly, Vol. 134, November, 1924, pp. 648-657)

Typed copy- original in Library of Hawaiian Mission Children's Society, Missionary Extract No. 1.

DU
620
M 67

ETHNOLOGY HAWAII

Tour around Maui. (by the missionaries at Lahaina,- William Richards, Lyon Andrews and Jonathan Smith Green- in August 1828. Perhaps the first ascent of Haleakala by English travellers)
(Missionary Herald, August, 1829, pp. 246-251)

GN
671.N5
H 71

ETHNOLOGY HUON GULF

Hogbin, H. Ian

Transformation scene, the changing culture of a New Guinea village. London. Routledge and Kegan Paul Ltd. London. (1951) xii + 326 pp. 8vo. (International Library of Sociology and Social Reconstruction.

DU
12
S 52

ETHNOLOGY HAWAII

Shaler, William

Journal of a voyage between China and the northwestern coast of America, made in 1804, by William Shaler. Introduction by Lindley Bynum, illustrations by Ruth Saunders. Claremont, California. 1935. R8vo. (Reprint from The American Register...Part I for 1808, Vol. III)

DU
620
P

ETHNOLOGY HAWAII

Webb, Elizabeth Lahilahi Rogers

Hookupu of Hawaii-tribute and gift.

(Paradise of the Pacific, Vol. 51, No. 12, 1931, pp. 61-63)

GN
671.C3
B 97

ETHNOLOGY IFALUK

Burrows, Edwin Grant

Flower in my ear: arts and ethos of Ifaluk Atoll. Seattle. University of Washington Press. 1963. vii + 439 pp. R 8vo

---

DU
620
F

ETHNOLOGY HAWAII

Some traits of the old Hawaiians.

(Friend, March 1903, pp.4-5)

GN
Ethn.Pam.
2639

ETHNOLOGY HAWAII

Wichman, Juliet Rice

Hawaiian Planting Traditions. Honolulu. Honolulu Star-Bulletin. 1931c. 43 pp. 8vo

---

GN
2.S
S 72

ETHNOLOGY IFALUK

Burrows, Edwin G.

From value to ethos on Ifaluk atoll.

(Southwestern Jour. of Anthropology, Vol. 8(1):13-35, 1952)

DU
620
H 41

ETHNOLOGY HAWAII

Stokes, J.F.G.

Iron with the early Hawaiians.

(Haw. Hist. Soc. Papers, No. 18, 1931, pp. 6-14)

GN
2.I
Ar

ETHNOLOGY HAWAII

Yates, Lorenzo Gordon

Some ancient relics of the aborigines of the Hawaiian Islands.

(Records of the Past, I, 1902, pp. 115-122)

GR
385.P1
W 74

ETHNOLOGY ILONGOT

Wilson, Laurence L.

Ilongot: life and legends. (Privately printed by the author) Baguio, 1947. sm8vo. 109 pp.

and
GR
Folklore
Pam.
81

GN 562
M 48

ETHNOLOGY INCAS

Mead, Charles W.

Old civilizations of Inca Land. New York. American Museum of Natural History . 1924.

(American Museum of Natural History, Handbook Series, No. 11.)

GN 635.1
N 17

ETHNOLOGY INDIA

Nanjundayya, H. V.

The Mysore tribes and castes, by H. V. Nanjundayya and L. K. Ananthakrishna Iyer. Mysore Government press. 1930. 8vp. 4 vols.

GN 635.1
T 54

ETHNOLOGY INDIA

Thurston, Edgar

Ethnographic notes in Southern India... Madras. 1906.

GN 2.1
S 66

ETHNOLOGY INDIA

Gilbert, William H., Jr.

Peoples of India

(Smithsonian Institution, War Background Studies, No. 18, 1944)

GN 635.1
R59

ETHNOLOGY - INDIA

Risley, H. H.

Census of India, 1901. vol. I, ethnographic appendices being the data upon which the caste chapter of the report is based.

Calcutta, Gov't Print., 1903. 251p. 4 to.

ETHNOLOGY INDIA

see also

INDIA ETHNOLOGY

GN Ethn. Pam. No.645 and No. 625

ETHNOLOGY - INDIA
Hocart, A. M.

Flying through the air. Reprinted from the Indian Antiquary Vol. LII,1923 pp 80 - 82.

GN 635.T6
R 62

ETHNOLOGY INDIA

Rivers, W. H. R.

The Todas. With illustrations. London and New York. Macmillan Company, Ltd. 1906. 8vo. xviii + 755 pp.

GN 550
W 81

ETHNOLOGY INDIANS

Wissler, Clark

The American Indian; an introduction to the anthropology of the new world. New York. 1917.

GN Ethn.Pam. 2831

ETHNOLOGY INDIA

Hornell, James

The Tongue and Groove Seam of Gujarati Boat-Builders.

(Reprinted from The Mariner's Mirror, The Quarterly Journal of the Society for Nautical Research, Vol. XVI, No. 4, October, 1930)

GN 635.1
R 88

ETHNOLOGY INDIA

Roy, Sarat Chandra

The Kharias, by Sarat Chandra Roy and Ramesh Chandra Roy. With numerous illustrations and a map; & a foreword by R. R. Marett. Ranchi: "Man in India" Office. 1937. 2 vols. 8vo.

GN 560.M
P 94

ETHNOLOGY INDIANS OF MEXICO

Preuss, Konrad Theodor

Die Nayarit-Expedition...Erster band: Die Religion der Cora-Indianer...Leipzig. 1912. 4to.

AS 472
M

Ethnology-India
Madras. Government museum.
Bulletin no. 1-
Madras, 1894-

v. plates (partly col.) map, diagrs. 21½ᶜᵐ.

1. Ethnology—India.

Library of Congress   Q73.M3   9-15382†
—2d set.

GN 635.1
S 66

ETHNOLOGY INDIA

Smith, William Carlson

The Ao Naga Tribe of Assam: a study in Ethnology and sociology...London. 1925.

AS 36
S1

ETHNOLOGY INDIANS OF NORTH AMERICA
Gardner, William Henry, 1837-
Ethnology of the Indians of the valley of the Red River of the North. By Dr. W. H. Gardner ...

(In Smithsonian institution. Annual report. 1870. Washington, 1871. 23½ᶜᵐ. p. 369-373)

1. Indians of North America—Ethnology.   I. Title.

Library of Congress   Q11.S66 1870   S 15-291
Library, Smithsonian   Institution

GN 635.1
M 65

ETHNOLOGY INDIA

Mill, J. P.

The Ao Nagas...London. 1926.

AS 472
M
v.2

Ethnology-India
Thurston, Edgar.
... Anthropology. Badagas and Irulas of the Nīlgiris; Paniyans of Malabar; a Chinese-Tamil cross; a Cheruman skull; Kuruba or Kurumba; summary of results ... By Edgar Thurston ... Madras, Government press, 1897.
2 p. l., 68 p. xvi (i. e. 17) pl. 21½ᶜᵐ. (Madras government museum. Bulletin, vol. II, no. 1)

1. Ethnology—India.

Library of Congress   Q73.M3 vol. 2, no. 1   9-15381†

GN 550
Go.

ETHNOLOGY INDIANS OF NORTH AMERICA
Goddard, Pliny Earle.

Indians of the southwest, by Pliny Earle Goddard.

New York, 1913. 191p. (American museum of natural history, Handbook series, No. 2)

GN 855.1
M 68

ETHNOLOGY INDIA

Mitra, Panchanan

Prehistoric India: its place in the world's culture. Second edition, revised and enlarged. Calcutta. 1927. 8vo.

GN 635.1
T 54

ETHNOLOGY INDIA

Thurston, Edgar

Castes and tribes of southern India, by Edgar Thurston, assisted by K. Rangachari. Madras. 1909. 7vo. R8vo.

GN 550
K 91

ETHNOLOGY INDIANS OF NORTH AMERICA

Krause, Fritz

Die Pueblo-Indianer. Eine historisch-ethnographische Studie...Halle. 1907. 4to.

(Nova Acta. Abh. der Kaiserl.Leop.-Carol. Deutschen Akademie der Naturforscher, Band LXXXVII, Nr. 1. Mar. 18, 1906.)

E
77
K 93
ETHNOLOGY INDIANS OF NORTH AMERICA

Kroeber, A(lfred) L(ouis)

Cultural and natural areas of native North America. University of California Press. Berkeley. 1939. R8vo. xi + 242 pp.

GN
550
S 37
ETHNOLOGY INDIANS OF NORTH AMERICA

Schoolcraft, Henry R.

Historical and statistical information respecting the history, condition and prospects of the Indian tribes of the United States...(In 4 parts.) Philadelphia. 1851-1854. 4to.

For index, see Bull. Bur. Ethnology, Smithsonian Inst., No. 152, 1954

GN
550
W 81
ETHNOLOGY INDIANS OF NORTH AMERICA

Wissler, Clark

North American Indians of the Plains. New York. American Museum of Natural History. 1912

(American Museum of Natural History, Handbook, Series No. 1.)

GN
562
B 35
ETHNOLOGY INDIANS OF SOUTH AMERICA

Bayern, Therese, Prinsessin von

Reisestudien aus dem Westlichen Südamerika. In zwei Bänden, Band 1, Band 2...Berlin. 1908. R8vo.

GN
562
K 18
ETHNOLOGY INDIANS OF SOUTH AMERICA

Karsten, Rafael

The civilization of the South American Indians, with special reference to magic and religion...London. 1926.

GN
562
K 76
ETHNOLOGY INDIANS OF SOUTH AMERICA

Koch-Grünberg, Theodor

Anfänge der kunst im urwald. Indianer-Handzeichnungen auf seinen Reisen in Brasilien... Berlin. n.d. Ob8vo.

GN
562
K 76
ETHNOLOGY INDIANS OF SOUTH AMERICA

Koch-Grünberg, Theodor

Zwei Jahre unter den Indianern. Reisen in Nordwest-Brasilien 1903/1905. Erster band... Zweiter band...Berlin. 1909, 1910. 4to.

GN
562
N 83
ETHNOLOGY INDIANS OF SOUTH AMERICA

Nordenskiöld, Erland

The changes in the material culture of two Indians tribes under the influence of new surroundings. (Göteborg. Elanders. 1920.) 8vo.

(Comparative ethnographical studies, No. 2.)

GN
562
N 83
ETHNOLOGY INDIANS OF SOUTH AMERICA

Nordenskiöld, Erland

Eine geographische und ethnographische analyse der materiellen kultur zweier indianerstämme in El Gran Chaco (Sudamerika.)

(Göteborg, Erlander, 1918.) 8vo. xv + 305. pp.

(Vergleichende Ethnographische Forschungen, 1)

GN
562
N 83
ETHNOLOGY INDIANS OF SOUTH AMERICA

Nordenskiöld, Erland

An ethno-geographical analysis of the material culture of two Indian tribes in the Gran Chaco. (Göteborg. Elanders. 1919.) 8vo.

(Comparative ethnographical studies, No. 1).

GN
562
S 35
ETHNOLOGY INDIANS OF SOUTH AMERICA

Schmidt, Max

Indianerstudien in Zentralbrasilien...Berlin 1905. R8vo.

GN
562
S 82
ETHNOLOGY INDIANS OF SOUTH AMERICA

Steinen, Karl von den

Unter den Naturvölkern Zentral-Brasiliens... Berlin. 1894. R8vo.

E
78.S8
B 21
ETHNOLOGY INDIANS SOUTHWEST

Bandelier, A. F.

Final report of investigations among the Indians of the southwestern United States, carried on mainly in the years from 1880 to 1885. Parts I and II. Cambridge, University Press, 1890 and 1892. 8vo. 323 and 591 pp. (Papers of the Archaeological Inst. of America, American series III and IV.)

ETHNOLOGY INDOCHINA

Gourou, Pierre

Les Paysans du Delta Tonkinoise.

(Ecole Française d'Extrême-Orient, 1936)

UH

GN
2.I
I 40
ETHNOLOGY INDOCHINA

Indochine. Institut Indochinois pour l'Etude de l'Homme.

Bulletins et Travaux

Tome 2:1, 1939

GN
1
E 84
ETHNOLOGY INDOCHINA

Izikowitz, Karl Gustav

Lamet- hill peasants in French Indochina.

(Etnologiska Studier, 17, 1951)

GN
2.I
S 66
ETHNOLOGY INDOCHINA

Janse, Olov R. T.

The peoples of French Indochina.

(Smithsonian Institution, War Background Studies, No. 19, 1944)

GN
Ethn. Pam.
2815
ETHNOLOGY INDO-EUROPEAN

Hocart, A. M.

The Indo-European Kinship System.

(Reprinted from the Ceylon Journal of Science Section G.-Archaeology, Ethnology, Vol. 1, Part 4 1928) London.

GN
539
T24
ETHNOLOGY - INDO-EUROPEAN

Taylor, Isaac

The origin of the Aryans, an account of the prehistoric ethnology and civilisation of Europe. 2d ed.

London, Scott, 1892. 8vo. 339p.

GN
Ethn. Pam.
3309
ETHNOLOGY INDO-IRANIAN

Wikander, Stig

Der Arische Männerbund; studien zur indoiranischen sprach-und religionsgeschichte.

Håkon Ohlssons Buchdruckerei, Lund, 1938, 111 pp. 8vo.

P
121
L 85
ETHNOLOGY INDO-PACIFIC

Logan, J. R.

The ethnology of Eastern Aisa; the ethnology of southeast Asia... and the Indo-Pacific islands

(Journal of the Indian Archipelago and Eastern Asia, 1850 (?)-1856)

PL
1
B 59 ETHNOLOGY INDONESIA

Bijdragen tot de Taal, Land- en Volkenkunde

Deel 106, 1950+

GN
806
B 73 ETHNOLOGY IRELAND

Borlase, W. C.

Dolmens of Ireland, their distribution, structural characteristics, and affinities in other countries; together with the folk-lore attaching to them; supplemented by considerations on the anthropology, ethnology, and traditions of the Irish people...3 volumes. London. 1897. 8vo.

GN
635.J3
S79 ETHNOLOGY - JAPAN

Starr, Frederick

The Ainu group at the Saint Louis exposition.

Chicago, Open Court, 1904. 118p. pls.

GN
Ethn.Pam.
2813 ETHNOLOGY INDONESIA

Hambruch, Paul

Einführung in die Abteilung Indonesien (Geschichte, Lebensraum, Umwelt und Bevölkerung) Hamburgisches Museum für Völkerkunde.

Hamburg, Friederichsen, de Gruyter & Co. m. b.H. 1931, 47 pp. 12mo.

AS
36
S1 ETHNOLOGY - ITALY

Taylor, Isaac, 1829-1901.
The pre-historic races of Italy. By Canon Isaac Taylor.

(*In* Smithsonian institution. Annual report. 1890. Washington, 1891. 23½ᶜᵐ. p. 489-498)

"From the Contemporary review, August, 1890, vol. LVIII, pp. 261-270."

1. Ethnology—Italy.

Library of Congress   Q11.S66 1890   S 15-742
Library, Smithsonian   Institution

GN
Ethn.
Pam.
3847
and
3193 ETHNOLOGY JAPAN

Torii, Ryuzo

Ancient Japan in the light of anthropology. Kokusai Bunka Shinkokai (The Society for International Cultural Relations) Tokyo, 1937. 8vo. 22 pp. illustrated

---

GN
635.D9
D 32 ETHNOLOGY INDONESIA

De Josselin de Jong, J. P. B.

Studies in Indonesian culture. I-

(Verh. K. Akad. van Wetenschappen te Amsterdam, Afd. Letterkunde, Nieuwe Reeks, Deel 39, 1937; 50(2), 1947

AS
36
S1 ETHNOLOGY---JAPAN.

Brinkley, Frank, 1841-1912.
Primeval Japanese. By Capt. F. Brinkley.

(*In* Smithsonian institution. Annual report. 1903. Washington, 1904. 23½ᶜᵐ. p. 793-804)

Reprinted ... from "Japan. Its history, art and literature, vol. I, chapter II."

1. Ethnology—Japan. I. Title.

Library of Congress   Q11.S66 1903   S 15-1222
Library, Smithsonian   Institution

GN
635.J3
Y 20 ETHNOLOGY JAPAN

Yamamoto, Yuki editor

Approach to Japanese culture. Kokusai Bunka Shinkokai. Japan Times Company. Tokyo. 8vo. ob 1961c   109 pp.

GN
Ethn.Pam.
3494 ETHNOLOGY INDONESIA

Kennedy, Raymond

Contours of culture in Indonesia.

(The Far Eastern Quarterly, 2:5-14,1942)

GN
Ethn.Pam.
3241 ETHNOLOGY JAPAN

Campbell, Archibald Gowan

Among the hairy Ainus of Yezo.

(Popular Science Monthly, Vol. 4, No. 7, pp. 49-57, 1872 (?))

GN
630.M3
C 68 ETHNOLOGY - JAVA

Cole, F.C.

The peoples of Malaysia. D.Van Nostrand Company, Inc. Toronto, New York... 8vo. 1945c   xiv + 354 pp.

GN
Ethn.
Pam.
3916 ETHNOLOGY INDONESIA

Kennedy, Raymond

Field notes on Indonesia: South Celebes, 1949-50. Behavior Science Monographs. Published by Human Relations Area Files, Inc. New Haven. 1953. 8vo. xxiv + 269 pp.

GN
635.J3
C 44 ETHNOLOGY JAPAN

Chamberlain, Basil Hall

Things Japanese: Being Notes on various subjects connected with Japan. For the use of travellers and others. Reprint of the 1905 Fifth Edition Revised, to which two appendices have been added. London. Kegan Paul, Trench Trubner & Co., Ltd. 1927 (9) +591 pp. 1 map 8vo.

GN
635.D9
W 68 ETHNOLOGY JAVA

Wilken, G. A.

Handleiding voor de vergelijkende Volkenkunde van Nederlandsch-Indië. Leiden. E. J. Brill. 1893. 8vo. 669 pp.

GR
315
M 94 ETHNOLOGY INDONESIA

Münsterberger, W.

Ethnologische Studien an Indonesischen Schopfungsmythen. Ein Beitrag zur Kultur-Analyse Südostasiens. Haag. 1939.

GN
635.J3
E 53 ETHNOLOGY JAPAN

Embree, John F.

Suye Mura, a Japanese village. University of Chicago Press. Chicago. 8vo. xxvii + 354 pp.

Q
115
W 95
locked
case ETHNOLOGY JAVA

Wüllerstorf-Urbair, Bernhard

Reise der Oesterreichischen Fregatte Novara um die Erde...1857-1859. Anthropologischer Theil, III, pp. 72-90. Wien. 1868. 4to. by Friedrich Müller.

GN
2.M
E 85 ETHNOLOGY INDONESIA

Nutz, Walter

Eine Kulturanalyse von Kei. Beitrage zur vergleichenden Völkerkunde Ostindonesiens.

(Beiheft 2 (1959) zur Ethnologica)

GN
Ethn.Pam.
3240 ETHNOLOGY JAPAN

Hitchcock, Romyn

The Ainus of Yezo, Japan.

(Report of the U. S. Nat. Mus., 1890, pp. 429-502)

AS
763
B-r ETHNOLOGY KAPINGAMARANGI

Buck, Peter H.

Bishop Museum expedition to Kapingamarangi

(Bernice P. Bishop Museum, Bulletin 194, 1948, pp. 31-40)

GN 663 T 44 — **ETHNOLOGY KAPINGAMARANGI.**
Eilers, Anneliese
Thilenius, Georg (editor)
Ergebnisse der Südsee Expedition, 1908-1910, II. Ethnographie: B. Mikronesien, Bd. 8, 1934. Inseln um Ponape.

GN 663 T 44 tr — also translation, typed, excerpts Kapingamarangi and Nukuoro.

DS 557.L2 L 44 — **ETHNOLOGY LAOS**
LeBar, Frank M.
Laos, its people, its society, its culture. By the Staff and Associates of the Human Relations Area Files; editors: Frank M. LeBar and Adrienne Suddard. HRAF Press New Haven. 8vo. 1960 (12) + 294 pp.

DU 870 H 12 — **ETHNOLOGY LOYALTY ISLANDS**
Hadfield, E.
Among the natives of the Loyalty group. London, Macmillan, 1920. xix + 316 pp.

GN 2.M E 85 — **ETHNOLOGY KEI**
Nutz, Walter
Eine Kulturanalyse von Kei. Beitrage zur vergleichenden Völkerkunde Ostindonesiens.
(Beiheft 2 (1959) zur Ethnologica)

GN Ethn. Pam. 3939 — **ETHNOLOGY LATIN AMERICA**
UNESCO
Men against ignorance. Printed by Gassmann S.A. Soleure (Switzerland). 1953. 8vo. 5-81 pp.

GN Ethn.Pam. 3647 — **ETHNOLOGY LOYALTY ISLANDS**
Lenormand, Maurice H.
Connaissance du corps et prise de de la personne chez Melanésien de Lifou (Iles Loyalty).
(Jour. Soc. des Océanistes, 6: 33-65, 1950)

GN 673 H 87 — **ETHNOLOGY KODIAK ISLAND**
Hrdlička, Aleš
The anthropology of Kodiak Island. Published by The Wistar Institute of Anatomy and Biology. Philadelphia. 1944. R8vo. xix + 486 pp.

AS 763 B-b — **ETHNOLOGY LAU ISLANDS**
Hocart, A. M.
Lau Islands, Fiji. Honolulu. 1929. 8vo.
GN 671.F1 H 68
(Bernice P. Bishop Museum, Bull. 62. 1929)
Reading Room

GN 2.S T — **ETHNOLOGY LOYALTY IS.**
Lescure, Rey
Maré et la Polynésie.
(Bulletin de la Société des Études Océaniennes. Tome 5, 1935, pp. 443-449)

As 36 S3 — **ETHONOLOGY--KOREA.**
Hough, Walter, 1859–
The Bernadou, Allen, and Jouy Korean collections, in the U.S. National museum. By Walter Hough.
(*In* U.S. National museum. Annual report. 1891. Washington, 1892. 231½... p. 429-488. pl. II-XXXII)
Each plate accompanied by leaf with descriptive letterpress.
Running title: Korean collections in the National museum.
1. Ethnology—Korea. 2. U.S. National museum—Collections. I. Title: Korean collections in the National museum.
14-19779
Library of Congress   Q11.U5 1891
———— Copy 2.
———— Separate.   DS903.H6

GN 668 T 47 — **ETHNOLOGY LAU ISLANDS**
Thompson, Laura.
Southern Lau, Fiji: an ethnography, by Laura Thompson ... Honolulu, Hawaii, The Museum, 1940.
1 p. l., iv, (3)-228 p. illus. (incl. maps) 5 pl. on 3 l., fold. geneal. tab. 25½... (Bernice P. Bishop museum. Bulletin 162)
"Literature cited": p. 224.
1. Ethnology—Lau islands. I. Title.
42-18454
Library of Congress   GN870.B4 no. 162
———— Copy 2.   GN671.L85T5
(3)   (572.996) 572.9961

GN 1 Z — **ETHNOLOGY LOYALTY ISLANDS**
Nevermann, H.
Lifou (Loyalty-Inseln).
(Zeit. f. Ethnologie, 67, 1936, pp. 201-231)

AN 2.E P 78 — **ETHNOLOGY KUSAIE**
Gulick, Luther H.
Lectures on Micronesia...III. Kausaie and the Kusaien.
(The Polynesian, Vol. 17, No. 32, Dec. 8, 1860)

GN 645 W 52 — **ETHNOLOGY LIBERIA**
Westermann, Diedrich
Die Kpelle, ein negerstamm in Liberia. Dargestellt auf der grundlage von eingeborenenberichten, mit zwei nachträgen: text in der golasprache und Kpelle-beiträge von H. Rohde nebst einer kartenskizze von Diedrich Westermann. Göttingen. 1921. R8vo.

GN 671.N4 S 24 — **ETHNOLOGY-LOYALTY ISLANDS**
Sarasin, Fritz
Ethnologie der Neu-Caledonier und Loyalty-Insulaner. Mit einem Atlas von 73 Tafeln in Lichtdruck. München. C. W. Kreidel's Verlag. 1929. 320 pp. 73 tafeln. 4to.

GN 663 T 44 — **ETHNOLOGY KUSAIE**
Sarfert, E.
Kusae (Kusaie)
Thilenius, G.
Ergebnisse der Südsee Expedition, 1908-1910. II. Ethnographie: B. Mikronesien, Bd. 4, 1919-20

AS 701 A and GN Ethn.Pam. 341 — **ETHNOLOGY LOYALTY ISLANDS**
Creagh, S. M.
Notes on the Loyalty Islands.
(Austr. Ass'n for the Adv. of Sci., Rept. of the 4th meeting, 1892, pp. 680-688)

GN 1 A62 — **ETHNOLOGY LOYALTY ISLANDS**
Sarasin, Frtiz
Streiflichter aus der Ergologie der Neu-Caledonier und Loyalty-Insulaner und die Europaische Praehistorie. Review by Fr. de Zeltner.
(L'Anthropologie, Tome 29, 1918-1919, pp. 150-151)
(Original article is in Verhandl. der Naturforschenden Gesell. in Basel, Bd. 28, 1916, 27pp. 23 fig.)   Library has not.

GN 635.L H 19 — **ETHNOLOGY LAOS**
Halpern, Joel Martin
Aspects of village life and culture change in Laos. Special report prepared for the Council on Economic and Cultural Affairs, Inc. Pre-publication copy. Council on Economic Affairs... New York. 4to. April 1958. 146 pp. illustrated.

AM Mus. Pam. 124 — **ETHNOLOGY LOYALTY ISLANDS**
Führer durch das Museum für Völkerkunde, Basel. Neu-Caledonien und die Loyalty-Inseln. G. Krebs, Basel. 1931. 26 pp.

GN 550 S 83 — **ETHNOLOGY LUMMI INDIANS**
Stern, Bernhard J.
The Lummi Indians of Northwest Washington. New York. Columbia University Press. 1934. 8vo. 127 pp.

GN
493
K 18

ETHNOLOGY MADAGASCAR

Kardiner, Abram

The individual and his society; the psycho-
dynamics of primitive social organization.
With a foreword and two ethnological reports,by
Ralph Linton. New York. Columbia University
Press. 1939. R8vo. xxxvi + 503 pp.

GN
635.M4
E 92

ETHNOLOGY MALAYA

Evans, Ivor H. N.

The Negritos of Malaya. Cambridge. University Press. 1937. 8vo. xiii + 323 pp.

AS
719
A-m

ETHNOLOGY MALAY PENINSULA

McCarthy, F. D.

Jungle dwellers of the Malay Peninsula; the
Ple-Temiar Senoi.

(Australian Museum Magazine, Vol. 8, 1942
pp. 61-65)

GN
2.M
F 1

ETHNOLOGY MADAGASCAR

Linton, Ralph

The Tanala: a Hill Tribe of Madagascar.
Marshall Field Expedition to Madagascar, 1926.

(Field Museum of Natural History, Publication, Anthropological Series, Vol. 22, 1933)

GN
635.M4
L 34

ETHNOLOGY MALAYSIA

Lasker, Bruno

Peoples of southeast Asia. Prepared under
the auspices of the American Council of the Institute of Pacific Relations. New York. 1945.

GN
635.M4
M 38

ETHNOLOGY MALAY PENINSULA

Martin, Rudolf

Die inlandstämme der Malayischen halbinsel;
wissenschaftliche ergebnisse einer reise durch die
Vereinigten malayischen staaten...Jena. 1905.
R8vo. 1 vol. in 3 parts.

GN
Ethn.Pam.
4096

ETHNOLOGY MADAGASCAR

Mellis, J. V.

Volumena et Volafotsy, nord et nord-ouest
de Madagascar. Tananarive. 1938. 8vo. 247 pp.

GN
630.M3
W 76

ETHNOLOGY MALAY

Winstedt, Richard

The Malaysia cultural history. Philosophical
Library. New York. 1950. 8vo. vii + 198 pp.

GN
635.M4
S 62

ETHNOLOGY MALAY PENINSULA

Skeat, Walter William

Malay Magic, being an introduction to the
folklore and popular religion of the Malay Peninsula...London. 1900.

GN
Ethn.Pam.
2979

(438)

ETHNOLOGY - MALAITA

Eyerdam, Walter J.

Among the Mountain Bushmen of Malaita

(Natural History, vol. 33, 1933, pp. 430-

Q
115
W 95

locked
case

ETHNOLOGY MALAY

Wüllerstorf-Urbair, Bernhard

Reise der Oesterreichischen Fregatte Novara
um die Erde...1857-1859. Anthropologischer
Theil, III, pp. 19-45. Wien. 4to. 1868
by Friedrich Müller.

GN
635.M4
S 62

ETHNOLOGY MALAY PENINSULA

Skeat, Walter William

Pagan Races of the Malay Peninsula, by Walter
William Skeat and Charles Otto Blagden...London.
1906. 2 vols.

GN
1
O 15

ETHNOLOGY MALAITA

Russell, T.

The Fataleka of Malaita.

(Oceania, Vol. 21(1):1-13, 1950)

GN
635.M4
W 58

ETHNOLOGY MALAY ARCHIPELAGO

White, W. G.

The sea gypsies of Malaya, an account of the
nomadic Mawken people of the Mergui Archipelago
...London. 1922. 8vo.

AS
36
S1

ETHNOLOGY--MALAY PENINSULA.

Skeat, Walter William, 1866-
The wild tribes of the Malay Peninsula. By W. W.
Skeat, M. A.

(In Smithsonian institution. Annual report. 1902. Washington, 1903.
23½ᵐ. p. 463-478. illus., II pl. on 1 l.)

"Reprinted ... from Journal of the Anthropological institute of Great
Britain and Ireland, vol. XXXII, January-June, 1902, pp. 124-138."

1. Ethnology—Malay Peninsula.   I. Title.

S 15-1162

Library of Congress   Q11.S66 1902
Library, Smithsonian   Institution

GN
635.M4
B 81

ETHNOLOGY MALAY

Brandstetter, Renward

Wir Menschen der indonesischen Erde. Lusern.
1923-1933.

Library has:
III-VIII

GN
635.M4
A 61

ETHNOLOGY MALAY PENINSULA

Annandale, Nelson

Fasciculi Malayenses: Anthropological and
Zoological results of an expedition to Perak and
the Siamese Malay States, 1901-1902, undertaken
by Nelson Annandale and Herbert C. Robinson...
4 parts. Anthropology, Part 1, 180 pp. London.
1903. 4to.

Supplement, Map and Itinerary. xliv pp.

AS -
496
F

ETHNOLOGY MALAY STATES

Robinson, Herbert C. and Kloss, C. B.

Additional notes on the Semang Paya
of Ijok, Selama, Perak. In Journ. Fed.
Mal. St. Mus. V, 4, 1915, pp 187-191.

GN
635.M4
C 68

ETHNOLOGY MALAYSIA

Cole, Fay-Cooper

The peoples of Malaysia. Second printing.
D. Van Nostrand Company, Inc. New York. 1945.
8vo. xiv + 354 pp.

GN
635.M4
E92

ETHNOLOGY - MALAY PENINSULA

Evans, Ivor H   N

Papers on the ethnology and archaeology of
the Malay peninsula.

Cambridge, University Press. 1927. 8vo. x + 164
pp. pls.

GN
635.M4
W 72

ETHNOLOGY - MALAYA

Williams-Hunt, P. D. R.

An introduction to the Malayan aborigines.
With a foreword by Sir Gerald Templar. Kuala
Lumpur. Printed at the Government Press. 1952.
4to. 102 pp.

GN
630.M3
C 68

ETHNOLOGY - MALAYSIA

Cole, F.C.

The peoples of Malaysia. D. Van Nostrand Company, Inc. Toronto, New York... 8vo. 1945c xiv + 354 pp.

GN
Ethn.Pam.
3197

ETHNOLOGY MALAYSIA

Josselin de Jong, J. P. B. de

Die Maleische Archipel als ethnologisch Studieveld. Leiden. 1935. 24 pp.

GN
635.D9
W 68

ETHNOLOGY MALAYSIA

Wilken, G. A.

Handleiding voor de vergelijkende Volkenkunde van Nederlandsch-Indië. Leiden. E. J. Brill. 1893. 8vo. 669 pp.

AS
28
E 85

ETHNOLOGY MALEKULA

Guiart, Jean

La fin d'un mirage ou le ralliement des villages "Big Nambas" du nord de Malekula, Nouvelles-Hebrides.
(Etudes Mélanésiennes, Numéro 7, pp. 6-13, 1953)

(treats of the "legend" of the existence to this day of cannibals in Malekula- only in the minds of the   writers and movie writers, says the   author)

G
7
R 91

ETHNOLOGY MALEKULA

Harrisson, Tom H.

Living with the people of Malekula.

(Geogr. Journal, 88:97-127, 243-261, 332-341 1936)

AS
701
A

ETHNOLOGY MALEKULA

Leggatt, T. Watt

Malekula, New Hebrides.

(Austr. Ass'n for the Adv. of Soil, 4th meeting, 1892, pp. 697-708)

GN
Pam.
3035

ETHNOLOGY MANCHURIA

Torii, R.

Etudes Anthropologiques: Les Mandchoux. Tokyo. Imperial University. 1914. 35 pp. pls.

(Journal of the College of Science, Imperial University of Tokyo, Vol. XXVI, Art. 6, Dec. 30, 1914.)

GN
Pam.
3037

ETHNOLOGY MANCHURIA

Torii, R.

Etudes Archéologiques et Ethnologiques: Populations Prehistoriques de la Mandchourie Meridionale. Tokyo. 1915.

(Journal of the College of Science, Imperial University of Tokyo, Vol. XXXVI, Art. 8, Oct. 21, 1915)

GN
671.C7
B 92

AS
763
B-b

Reading Room

ETHNOLOGY MANGAIA

Buck, Peter H.   (Te Rangi Hiroa)

Mangaian Society. Honolulu. 1934. R8vo.

(Bernice P. Bishop Museum, Bulletin 122. 1934.)

GN
671.M1
B 92

ETHNOLOGY MANGAREVA

Buck, Peter H. (Te Rangi Hiroa)

Ethnology of Mangareva, by P. H. Buck (Te Rangi Hiroa).

(Bernice P. Bishop Museum, Bull. 157, 1938)

AN
2.E
S 22

ETHNOLOGY MANGAREVA

A glance at Gambier's Islands.

(Sandwich Island Gazette, Vol. II, No. 32, March 10, 1838)

GN
671. M1
L 39

over

ETHNOLOGY MANGAREVA

Laval, Honoré

Mangareva, l'histoire ancienne d'un peuple Polynésien. Mémoires ethnographiques conservés aux Archives de la Congrégation des Sacrés-Coeurs de Picpus. Edités et annotés par...Alfred Métraux en collaboration avec...Maurice Desmedt. Préface ...P.H.Buck...Braine-le-Comte.Maison des Pères des Sacrés-Coeurs. 1938,viii + 378pp. R8vo.

2 copies,   one being No.26 of the de luxe edition.

GN
Ethn.Pam.
3234

ETHNOLOGY MANGAREVA

Métraux, Alfred

Una antigua aristocracia en Polinesia.

(La Prensa, Buenos Aires, 22 de Agosto de 1937)

GN
2.S
P 76

ETHNOLOGY MANGAREVA

Smith, S. Percy

Notes on the Mangareva, or Gambier Group of islands, Eastern Polynesia.

(Journal of the Polynesian Society, 27: 115-131, 1918.)

GN
671.S2
M 47

AS
763
B-b

Reading Room

ETHNOLOGY MANUA

Mead, Margaret

Social organization of Manua. Honolulu. 1930. 218 pp.

(Bernice P. Bishop Museum, Bulletin 76)

GN
671.N5
M 48

ETHNOLOGY MANUS ISLAND

Mead, Margaret

Growing up in New Guinea, a comparative study of primitive education. London. George Routledge and Sons. 1931. 8vo. xi + 285 pp.

GN
671.N5
M 48

ETHNOLOGY MANUS ISLAND

Mead, Margaret

New lives for old; cultural transformation-Manus, 1928-1953. William Morrow and Company. New York. 1956. 8vo. xxi + 548 pp.

GN
2.S
P 76

ETHNOLOGY MAORI

Andersen, Johannes

Maori place-names also personal names and names of colours, weapons, and natural objects.

(Mem. Poly. Soc., no. 20, 1942)

GN
2.S
M 29

ETHNOLOGY MAORI

Andersen, Johannes C.

Maori String Figures.

(Memoirs of the Board of Maori Ethnological Research, Vol. 2, 1927. 8vo. xi +173 pp.)

AP
2
N 54

GN Pam
697
698
699
2010

ETHNOLOGY MAORI

Anderson, Johannes C.

Maori String Games.

(New Zealand Journal of So. and Tech.
Ser. 1-Vol. 3, Nos. 2,3,4. 1920.
Ser. 2-Vol. 4, Nos. 4-5. 1921.
Ser. 3-Vol. 6, Nos. 5-6. 1924.
Ser. 4-Vol. 8, No. 9. 1926.)

GN
671.N56
A 54

ETHNOLOGY MAORI

Andersen, Johannes C.

The Maori tohunga and his spirit world. Thos. Avery and Sons Ltd. New Plymouth. 1948. sm8vo. xii + 135 pp.

GN
671.N56
A 58
ETHNOLOGY MAORI

Angas, George French

l.c.
The New Zealanders, illustrated.
London. Thomas M'Lean. 1847. folio. [preface
of 1 page; general remarks, 6 pp.; 60 plates,
each with its text]

GN
670
B 87
ETHNOLOGY MAORI

Brown, J. Macmillan

Maori and Polynesian: their origin, history,
and culture. London. 1907. 8vo.

GN
Eth.
Pam.
2873
ETHNOLOGY = MAORI

Firth, Raymond

Maori Canoe-Sail in the British Museum.
Additional Notes by Te Rangi Hiroa (Peter H. Buck)

(From Journal of the Polynesian Society,
Extract from Vol. 40, No. 3, pages 129-140).1931.

GN
Ethn.Pam.
3440
ETHNOLOGY MAORI

Archey, Gilbert

South Sea folk. Handbook of Maori and
Oceanic ethnology. 1937. (Auckland?) 8vo. 59
pp., 11 pl.

GN
671.N56
B 92
ETHNOLOGY MAORI

Buck, Peter Henry

The coming of the Maori, by Te Rangi Hiroa,
Sir Peter Buck. Wellington. Maori Purposes
Fund Board. Whitcombe and Tombs Ltd. 1949.
R8vo. (xix) + 548 pp.; 24 pl.

also 2nd printing, 1950. 551 pp., 24 pl.

GN
671.N 56
F 52
ETHNOLOGY MAORI

Firth, Raymond

Primitive economics of the New Zealand
Maori. With a preface by R. H. Tawney. With
30 illustrations of 16 plates and 3 maps. E. P.
Dutton and Company. New York. 1929. 8vo. xxiv
+ 505 pp.

GN
671.N 41
N 56
ETHNOLOGY MAORI

The arts of the Maori. Department of
Education, Wellington, New Zealand. 1961. R. E.
Owen, Gov. Printer. 8vo. ob. 54 pp.

[games, carving, string games, weaving,
dances, chants]

GN
671.N 56
B 93
ETHNOLOGY MAORI

Buick, T. Lindsay

The moa-hunters of New Zealand: sportsmen
of the Stone Age. New Plymouth, 1937. 8vo.
Thomas Avery & Sons, Ltd. xiv, 260 pp.

AS
36
A 5
ETHNOLOGY MAORI

Gregory, William K.

An evolutionist looks at the Maoris.

(Natural History, Vol. 45, 1940, pp. 132-
145)

AS
750
A 89 t
ETHNOLOGY MAORI

Auckland Institute and Museum

Transactions   (Anthropology and Maori
                 Race Section)

1937, 1939-

AS
750
N
ETHNOLOGY MAORI

Colenso, William

On the Maori races of New Zealand.

(Trans. and Proc. New Zealand Institute, 1,
Part III, 1-75 pp., 1868)

GN
2.I
A
ETHNOLOGY MAORI

Grey, Sir George

On the social life of the ancient inhabitants of New Zealand, and on the national character it was likely to form.

(Journ. Ethnol. Soc. of London, N.S., Vol.
1, 1868, pp. 333-364)

GN
2.S
P 76
ETHNOLOGY MAORI

Beaglehole, Ernest

The Polynesian Maori.

(Jour. of the Polynesian Soc., Vol. 49,1940,
pp. 39-68)

GR
Folkore
Pam.
123
ETHNOLOGY MAORI

Cowan, James

The Caltex book of Maori lore. Illustrated
by Dennis Turner. A. H. and A. W. Reed. sm4to.
1959. 63 pp.

GN
2.S
P 76
ETHNOLOGY MAORI

Gudgeon, W.E.

The Maori people.

(Journal of the Polynesian Society, 13:
177-192, 1904)

GN
671.N56
B 56
ETHNOLOGY MAORI

Best, Elsdon

The Maori as he was; a brief account of
Maori life as it was in pre-European days.

(New Zealand Board of Science and Art,
Manual No. 4, 1924)

GN
2.S
M 26
ETHNOLOGY MAORI

Duff, Roger S.

The evolution of native culture in New
Zealand: Moa hunters, Morioris, Maoris.

(Mankind, Vol. 3 (10):281-291, 1947)

GN
671.N56
H 21
ETHNOLOGY MAORI

Hamilton, Augustus

The art workmanship of the Maori race in New
Zealand: a series of illustrations from specially
taken photographs, with descriptive notes and
essays on the canoes, habitations, weapons, ornaments, and dress of the Maoris, together with
lists of the words in the Maori language used in
relation to the subjects. Parts 1-5. Dunedin.
(New Zealand Institute). 1896-1900. 4to. 438 +
vii pp. 55 pls.
(Title on   back: "Maori art")

AP
2
N 54
ETHNOLOGY MAORI

Best, Elsdon

The Maori system of measurement.

(New Zealand Jour. of Sci. and Tech., vol. 1,
1918, pp. 26-32)

GN
Ethn.Pam.
3551
ETHNOLOGY MAORI

Fildes, H.

The last of the Ngati Mamoe; the wild people
of the New Zealand mountain and bush. 8vo. 1936.
15 pp.

GN
671.N56
H 96
ETHNOLOGY MAORI

Hurinui, Pei Te

King Potatau; an account of the life of
Potatau Te Wherowhero, the first Maori king.
Auckland.   The Polynesian Society. 1959.
iii + 302 pp.   R8vo.

ETHNOLOGY MAORI

GN 671.N56 J 65

Johansen, J. Prytz

The Maori and his religion in its non-ritualistic aspects. With a Danish summary. Ejnar Munksgaard. København. R8vo. 298 pp.

ETHNOLOGY MAORI

GN 671.N56 M 68

Mitchell, J. H.

Takitumu, by Tiaki Hikawera Mitira (J. H. Mitchell). A. H. and A. W. Reed, Wellington. 8vo. 271 + xxii pp. (1944)

ETHNOLOGY MAORI

GN 2.S P 76

Skinner, H.D.

Maori life on the Poutini coast, together with some traditions of the natives. (Based on notes...1897 by G. J. Roberts)

(Journal of the Polynesian Society, 21: 141-151, 1912.)

ETHNOLOGY MAORI

GN 2.S M 29

Keesing, Felix M.

The Changing Maori.

(Memoir of the Board of Maori Ethnological Research, Volume 4, 1928)

ETHNOLOGY MAORI

GN 2.M W 64

Moschner, Irmgard

Katalog der Neuseeland Sammlung (A.Reischek) Wien.

(Archiv f. Volkerkunde, Bd.13:51-131, 1958)

ETHNOLOGY MAORI

GN 2.S P76

Skinner, H. D.

The Origin and Relationships of Maori Material Culture, and Decorative Arts.

(Journal of the Polynesian Society, Vol. 33, No. 4, 1924), pp. 229-243.

ETHNOLOGY MAORI

GN 2.I A-4

Kerry-Nicholls, J. H.

The origin, physical characteristics, and manners and customs of the Maori race, from data derived during a recent exploration of the King County, New Zealand.

(Journ. Anthrop. Inst. of Great Britain and Ireland, Vol. 25, 1885-6, pp. 187-209)

ETHNOLOGY MAORI

G 161 H 15-e

Remarkable occurences in the South Seas. IN Beaglehole, J. C. editor The journals of Captain James Cook...Vol. 1 1955, pp. 154-294.

(Works of the Hakluyt Society, Extra Ser., No. 34, 1955)

ETHNOLOGY MAORI

GN 2.S P 76

Skinner, W.H.

Ancient Maori canals, Marlborough, N.Z.

(Journal of the Polynesian Society, 21: 105-108, 1912.)

ETHNOLOGY - MAORI

GN Ethn.Pam. 2893

Lehmann, F. Rudolf

Io, die höchste Gottheit der Maori (Neuseeland)

(From "Ethnologische Studien" ed. by Fritz Krause, Halle, a.s. 1931) pp. 271-292.

ETHNOLOGY MAORI

GN 2.I A-4

Robley, Horatio Gordon

(Baked heads of Maoris.)

(Journ. Anthrop. Inst. of Great Britain and Ireland, Vol. 26, 1896-97, pp. 111-112)

ETHNOLOGY MAORI

GN 2.S P 76

Smith, S. Percy

The lore of the Whare-wananga or teachings of the Maori College on religion, cosmogony, and history. Written down by H. T. Whatahoro from the teachings of Te Matorohanga and Nepia Pohuhu ... Part I, Te Kauwae-runga, or Things Celestial; Part II, Te Kauwae-raro, or Things Terrestrial. (Memoirs of the Polynesian Society, Vols. 3-4, 1913, 1915)

ETHNOLOGY MAORI

GN 662 M 27

Mander, Linden A.

Some dependent peoples of the South Pacific. Issued under the auspices of the International Secretariat, Institute of Pacific Relations. The MacMillan Co. New York. 1954. 8vo. xix + 535 pp.

ETHNOLOGY MAORI

GN 2.S P 76

Rutland, Joshua

Traces of ancient human occupation in the Pelorus district, Middle Island, New Zealand.

(Jour. of the Polynesian Soc., Vol. 3, 1894 pp. 220-231; Vol. 6, 1897, p. 77-84)

ETHNOLOGY MAORI

PL 400 S 89

Stowell, Henry M. (Hare Hongi)

Maori-English tutor and vade mecum.

London. Christchurch. 1911. 12mo.

ETHNOLOGY MAORI

GN 2.I A-4

Mason, J. E.

On the natives of Fiji.

(Journ. Anthrop. Inst. of Great Britain and Ireland, Vol. 16, 1887, pp. 217-220)

ETHNOLOGY MAORI

GN 2.S Po

Skinner, W. H.

Decorative featherwork.

(Journal of the Polynesian Society, Vol. 41, pp. 214-215, 1932)

ETHNOLOGY MAORI

GN 671.N56 S 96

Sutherland, I. L. G. editor

The Maori people today, a general survey. Wellington, 1940. 8vo.

ETHNOLOGY MAORI

AM 101.A71 (5)

Mead, Margaret

The Maoris and their arts. American Mus. Nat. His., Guide Leaflet ser. n.71, 1928.

also GN Ethn. Pam. 3705

Separate.

ETHNOLOGY MAORI

GN 2.S P76

Skinner, H. D.

Maori amulets in stone, bone and shell.

(Journal of the Polynesian Society, Vol. 41, no. 3, Sept. 1932, pp. 202-211; no. 4, Dec. 1932, pp. 302-309; Vol. 42: no. 1, Mar. 1933, pp. 1-9; no. 2, June, 1933, pp. 107-113; no. 3, Sept. 1933 pp. 191-201; no. 4, Dec. 1933, pp. 310-320; Vol. 43: no. 1, Mar. 1934, pp. 25-29; no.2, June,1934, pp.106-117; no.3, Sept.1934, pp.198-215; No. 4, Dec.1934, pp.271-279; Vol. 44, no.1 Mar. 1935, pp. 17-25; vol.45,1936,pp. 127-141

ETHNOLOGY MAORI

GN 671.N56 T 24

Taylor, Richard

Te Ika A Maui; or, New Zealand and its inhabitants. Illustration the origin, manners, customs, mythology, religion, rites, songs, proverbs, fables, and language of the Maori and Polynesian races in general; together with the geology, natural history, productions, and climate of the country. London. William Macintosh. 1870. 8vo. xv+715 pp.

GN
671.N56
W 24

ETHNOLOGY MAORI

Taylor, W. A.

Lore and history of the South Island Maori.
All photos by the author. Bascands Limited.
Christchurch. n.d. 8vo. (1-8)9-196 pp.

GN
671.N 56
W 58

ETHNOLOGY MAORI

White, John

Revenge: a love tale of the Mount Eden
tribe. (New Zealand). Edited by A. W. Reed.
A. H. and A. W. Reed. Wellington. 8vo. 1940
xviii + 290 pp.

GN
2.S
T

ETHNOLOGY MARQUESAS

Darling, David

Extrait du Journal du Révérend David Darling
à Vaitahu, Tahuata, Décembre 1834- Septembre
1835. (signed Colin Newbury- translator?)

(Bull. Soc. des Etudes Océaniennes, No.
113; Tome IX(12):476-480, 1955)

[religion, social organization, tabu...]

GN
Ethn.Pam.
3507

ETHNOLOGY MAORI

Taylor, W. A.

Waihora: Maori associations with Lake Ellesmere. Reprinted from The Ellesmere Guardian.
Leeston, Canterbury. n.d. rec'd 1946. 26 pp.

GN
2.M
Be

ETHNOLOGY MARIANAS

Fritz, G.

Die Chamorro. Eine Geschichte und Ethnographie der Marianen. Erklärungen zu den Tafeln
1-4, von Rudolf Hermann.

(Ethnologisches Notizblatt, Bd. III, Heft
3, 1904, pp. 25-110)

DU
700
D 38
35

ETHNOLOGY MARQUESAS

Delmas, le R. P. Siméon

Essai d'histoire de la Mission des Iles
Marquises, depuis les origines jusqu'en 1881.

(Extrait des Annales des Sacres-Coeurs,
1905-1911) Au Bureau des Annales des Sacres-
Coeurs, Paris, 1929, 358 pp. 8vo

GN
2.I
A-4

ETHNOLOGY MAORI

Tregear, Edward

The Maoris of New Zealand.

(Journ. Anthrop. Inst. of Great Britain and
Ireland, Vol. 19, 1889-90, pp. 97-123)

AN
2.E
P 78

ETHNOLOGY MARIANAS

Gulick, Luther H.

Lectures on Micronesia: I. The Ladrone and
Caroline Islands...

(The Polynesian, Vol. 17, No. 29, Nov. 17,
1860)

GN
Ethn.Pam.
3340

ETHNOLOGY MARQUESAS

Dodge, Ernest Stanley

The Marquesas Islands Collection in the
Peabody Museum of Salem. Salem. Peabody Museum.
1939. R8vo. vii, 38 pp., 20 pl.

GN
671.N56
T 78

ETHNOLOGY MAORI

Tregear, Edward

The Maori Race. Wanganui. A. D. Willis.
1904. 8vo. xviii + 592 pp.

GN
Ethn.
Pam.
3470

ETHNOLOGY MARIANAS ISLANDS

Thompson, Laura

The native culture of the Marianas Islands.

(Bernice P. Bishop Mus., Bull. 185, 1945)

GN
Ethn.Pam.
3323

264)

ETHNOLOGY MARQUESAS

The Marquesas and the Marquesans.

(Chamber's Edinburgh Journal, 1846, pp. 262-

GN
671.N41
W 38

ETHNOLOGY MAORI

Webster, K. Athol

The Armytage collection of Maori jade.
The Cable Press. London. 1948. 8vo. 79 pp.

GN
2.S
T

ETHNOLOGY MARQUESAS

Ahnne, E. ...

De l'usage des Echasses aux Marquises.

(Bulletin de la Société des Etudes
Océaniennes, Tome 5, No. 14, 1935, pp. 508-517)

GN
671.M3
H 23

AS
763
B-b

Reading
Room

DU
700
H 23

ETHNOLOGY MARQUESAS

Handy, E. S. Craighill

The native culture in the Marquesas.
Honolulu. 1923. R8vo. iv 358 pp.

(Bernice P. Bishop Museum, Bulletin 9;
Bayard Dominick Expedition, Pub. No. 9, 1923).

GN
2.I
A

ETHNOLOGY MAORI

Wellington (Bishop of)

Notes on the Maoris of New Zealand and some
Melanesians of the southwest Pacific.

(Journ. Ethnol. Soc. of London, N.S., Vol.
1, 1868-9, pp. 364-371)

AN
7.T
J 86

ETHNOLOGY MARQUESAS

Burnel

Les Iles Marquises.

(Messager de Tahiti, Annee 15, 1866, Nos.
9-16)

GN
498
K 18

ETHNOLOGY MARQUESAS

Kardiner, Abram

The individual and his society; the psycho-
dynamics of primitive social organization.
With a foreword and two ethnological reports, by
Ralph Linton. New York. Columbia University
Press. 1939. R8vo. xxvi + 503 pp.

GN
Ethn.Pam.
3379

ETHNOLOGY MAORI

White, John

Maori superstitions: a lecture. Delivered
June 20th, 1856. Auckland. Williamson and
Wilson. 1856. 8vo. 33 pp.

GN
671.M3
C 61

ETHNOLOGY MARQUESAS

Clavel,

Les Marquisiens...Avec figures dans le texte
Paris. Octave Doin. 1885. 8vo. 182 pp.

DU
700
R 12

ETHNOLOGY MARQUESAS

Radiguet, Max

Les Derniers Sauvages: la Vie et les Moeurs
aux Iles Marquises (1842-1859). Illustrations
inedites de l'Auteur. Avant-propos de Jean Dorsenne. Paris. Editions Duchartre et Van Buggenhoudt. 1929c. ix + 240 pp. 8vo.

GN
2.S
T

ETHNOLOGY   MARQUESAS

Rey-Lescure

Temoteitei, Marquisien.

(Bull. Soc. d'Etudes Oceaniennes, Tome 7 (3)
1945, pp. 115-124)

["these accounts are taken from an old
Revue anglaise of 1800" -which?]

GN
Ethn.Pam.
3147

ETHNOLOGY   MARQUESAS

Ropiteau, André

Une visite au Musée Missionarie des Pères
des Sacres-Coeurs de Picpus à Braine-le-Comte
(Belgique). Papeete. Imprimerie du Gouvernement. 1936. 8vo. 10 pp.

GN
671.M3
S 54

ETHNOLOGY   MARQUESAS

Sheahan, George M., Jr.

Marquesan source materials. Parts I-II.
Preliminary edition. mimeographed. 207 pp.
4to.

DU
620
P

ETHNOLOGY   MARSHALL ISLANDS

Bryan, Edwin H., Jr.

Marshall Islands stick chart.

(Paradise of the Pacific, Vol. 50, No. 7
1938, pp. 12-13)

GN
Ethn.Pam.
3487

ETHNOLOGY   MARSHALL ISLANDS

Chamisso, Adelbert von

Kadus Fahrten und die Kultur der Radaker.

IN Geographische Kulturkunde, ed. by Leo
Frobenius, Leipzig, 1904, pp. 68-80.

GN
Ethn.Pam.
3509

ETHNOLOGY   MARSHALL ISLANDS

Eisenhart, Otto

Acht Monate unter den Eingeborenen auf Ailu
(Marshalls-Gruppe).

(Aus Allen Welttheilen, XIX:207-8, 223-6,
250-2, 1888)

GN
671.M2
E 66

ETHNOLOGY   MARSHALL ISLANDS

Erdland, P. A.

Die Marshall-Insulaner: Leben und Sitte,
Sinn und Religion eines Südsee-volkes... Mit 14
tafeln und 27 figuren im text. Münster. Aschendorff. 1914. R8vo. xii + 376 pp.

(Anthropos, Band II, Heft 1, 1914).

AS
142
V

ETHNOLOGY   MARSHALL ISLANDS

Finsch, Otto

Ethnologische Erfahrungen und Belegstücke
aus der Südsee. II. Marshall-Archipel.

(Ann. Nathist. Mus., Wien, 8:119-182, 419-
420, 1893)

AN
2.E
P 78

ETHNOLOGY   MARSHALL ISLANDS

Gulick, Luther H.

Lectures on Micronesia:...IV, The Marshall
Islands.

(The Polynesian, Vol. 17, No. 34, Dec. 22,
1860)

DU
620
F

ETHNOLOGY   MARSHALL ISLANDS

Kahelemauna, Mary K.

Hawaiian missionaries on Mille Island, 1869-
1876.

(The Friend, Vol. 114, 1944, No. 5, pp. 7,8,
27 28; no. 6, pp. 14, 27,28,29; no. 7, pp. 14-
16, 29; no. 8, pp. 7-8, 27-31)

GN
663
T 44

ETHNOLOGY   MARSHALL ISLANDS

Krämer, Augustin

Ralik-Ratak (Marshall-Inseln), von Augustin
Krämer und Hans Nevermann.
IN
Thilenius, Georg
Ergebnisse der Südsee Expedition, 1908-1910,
II. Ethnographie: B.Mikronesien,XI,1938.

GN
Ethn.Pam.
1366

ETHNOLOGY   MARSHALL ISLANDS

Schmeltz, Johannes Diedrich Eduard

Die etnographisch anthropologische Abtheilung des Museum Godeffroy. By J.D.E. Schmeltz
and R. Krause.

(Archif f. Ethnographie, Bd. 1, 1888, pp.
60-67)

GN
669.M 2
S 72

ETHNOLOGY   MARSHALL ISLANDS

Spoehr, Alexander

Majuro: a village in the Marshall Islands.

(Fieldiana: Anthropology, Vol. 39, 1949)

G
13
B-v

ETHNOLOGY   MARSHALL ISLANDS

Steinbach, Erwin

Die Marshall-Inseln und ihre Bewohner.

(Verh. der Gesellschaft f. Erdkunde, Berlin,
Bd. 22, 1895, pp. 449-488)

GN
659.M3
M 56

ETHNOLOGY   MASAI

Merker, M.

Die Masai. Ethnographische Monographie
eines Ostafrikanischen Semitenvolkes...Berlin.
1904. 2 volumes. R8vo.

GN
2.M
P 35

ETHNOLOGY   MAYA

Landa, Don Fray Diego de

Relacion de las cosas de Yucatan, a translation. Edited with notes by Alfred M. Tozzer.

(Papers of the Peabody Museum of American
Archaeology and Ethnology, Harvard University,
Vol. 18, 1941)

GN
1
O 15

ETHNOLOGY   MEKEO

Belshaw, Cyril S.

Recent history of Mekeo society.

(Oceania, Vol. 22(1):1-23, 1951)

[Central Division of Papua]

GN
22
B 15

ETHNOLOGY   MELANESIA

Bahnson, Kristian

Etnografien: fremstillet i dens hovedtraek.
Bind 1-2. Med farvetryk, kort... København.
Ernst Bojeson. 8vo. 1900. 548 + 704 pp.
Bd. I: pp. 159-208.

GN
2.S
M 26

ETHNOLOGY   MELANESIA

Bell, F. L. S.

What makes life worth living for the
savage?

(Mankind, Vol. 1, No. 12, 1935, pp. 13-17)

GN
668
B 87

ETHNOLOGY   MELANESIA

Brown, George

Melanesians and Polynesians: their life-
histories described and compared. London. 1910.
8vo.

AS
701
A

ETHNOLOGY   MELANESIA

Brown, George

The Pacific, east and west.

(Australasian Association for the Adv. of
Sci., Rept. of the meeting, 1902, Hobart, pp.
458-479)

PL
738
C.56 ETHNOLOGY-MELANESIA
Churchill, William, 1859-

Sissano; movements of migration within and through
Melanesia, by William Churchill. Washington, The Carnegie institution of Washington, 1916.

3 p. l., 181 p. fold. front., maps (part fold.) diagrs. 25½ᵐᵐ. (*On verso
of t.-p.:* Carnegie institution of Washington. Publication no. 244)

"In this monograph we are to subject to intimate examination the discovery record of one new-found language ... Sissano."—p. 3.

Bibliography: p. 7.

CONTENTS.—Sources of Melanesian material.—The Sissano community.—Sissano words.—Melanesian annotations on the vocabulary.—Indonesian annotations on the vocabulary.—Geography of the migrations.

1. Sissano language. 2. Malay—Polynesian languages. 3. Ethnology—
Melanesia.

Library of Congress   PL6308.C5   16-23055
——— Copy 2.

GN
1
O 15 ETHNOLOGY MELANESIA
Groves, William C.

Tabar today: a study of a Melanesian community in contact with alien non-primitive cultural
forces.

(Oceania, Vol. 5, No. 2, 1934, pp. 224-240;
Vol. 5, No. 3, 1935, pp. 346-360, pls. 1,2; Vol.
6, No. 2, 1935, pp. 145-157)

GN
22
L96 ETHNOLOGY MELANESIA
Luschan, Felix von

Beiträge zur Völkerkunde der
Deutschen Schutzgebiete.

Berlin, Reimer, 1897.   87p. pls.

GN
668
C 67 ETHNOLOGY MELANESIA
Codrington, R. H.

The Melanesians: Studies in Their Anthropology and Folk-lore. With illustrations.
Oxford. Clarendon Press. 1891. xv + 419 pp.
8vo.

GN
2.1
A-m ETHNOLOGY MELANESIA
Ivens, W. G. (Walter G.)

The Diversity of Culture in Melanesia.

(Man, Vol. 33, 1933, No. 8)

GN
668
M 25 ETHNOLOGY MELANESIA
Malinowski, Bronislaw

Coral gardens and their magic; a study of
the methods of tilling the soil and of agricultural rites in the Trobriand Islands. With 3
maps...Vols. 1-2. New York. 1935. R8vo.

GN
Ethn.Pam.
3337 ETHNOLOGY MELANESIA
Damm, Hans

Zeremonialschemel vom Sepik (Kaiser
Wilhelms land).

(Kultur und Rasse, Festschrift 60 Geburtstag
Otto Reches, 1939, pp. 274-289)

GN
2.1
A-4 ETHNOLOGY MELANESIA
Ivens, Walter

The diversity of culture in Melanesia.

(Jour. Roy. Anthr. Inst., vol. LXIV, 1934,
pp. 45-56.)

GN
668
M 25 ETHNOLOGY MELANESIA
Malinowski, Bronislaw

The sexual life of savages in north-western
Melanesia: an ethnographic account of courtship,
marriage, and family life among the natives of
the Trobriand Islands, British New Guinea...with
a preface by Havelock Ellis. With 96 full-page
plates and figures. London. George Routledge.
1929. 8vo. xxiv + 506 pp.

QH
1
N 28 ETHNOLOGY MELANESIA
Deniker, J.

Collections ethnographiques rapportées de
Mélanésie par le Dr. François.

(Le Naturaliste, Vol.6, 1891, pp. 227-229;
243-247)

GN
Ethn.
Pam.
3694 ETHNOLOGY MICRONESIA
Krieger, Herbert W.

Island peoples of the western Pacific,
Micronesia and Melanesia.

(Smithsonian Institution War Background
Studies, No. 16, 1943)

GN
1
A 62 ETHNOLOGY - MELANESIA
Mauss, Marcel

L'extension du potlatch en Mélanesie.

(L'Anthropologie, Tome 30, 1920, pp. 396-
397)

AS
36
A 5 ETHNOLOGY-MELANESIA
Eyerdam, Walter J.

Among the Mountain Bushmen of Malaita.
Invading a Primitive Wilderness in the Cause of
Science.

(Natural History, Vol. 33, pp. 430-438, 1933)

GN
662
L 56
GN
Pam.
408 ETHNOLOGY MELANESIA
Lennier, G.

Description de la collection ethnographique
Océanienne qu'a offerte à la Ville du Havre, M.
Le Mascam, négociant à Nouméa par G. Lennier...
Havre..Museum d'Histoire Naturelle & d'Ethno-
graphie du Havre. 1896. 4to.

GN
Ethn. Pam.
3214 ETHNOLOGY MELANESIA
Métraux, Alfred

Océanie et Australie. Chapitre 5. 1936.
18 pp. (Extract from "Les Peuples sur la terre")

GN
662
F 51 ETHNOLOGY MELANESIA
Finsch, (Friedrich Hermann Otto)

Ethnologische Erfahrungen und Belegstücke
aus der Südsee. Beschreibender katalog einer
sammlung im K. K. Naturhistorischen Hofmuseum in
Wien von Dr. O. Finsch.... Wien. 1893. R8vo.

(Annalen des K. K. Naturhistorischen Hof-
Museums in Wien, Band III-VIII, 1888-1893, separat abgedruckt).

AM
101
F 45 g ETHNOLOGY MELANESIA
Lewis, Albert B.

Ethnology of Melanesia.

(Guide, Field Museum of Natural History,
Department of Anthropology, No. 5, 1932)

GN
668
M 63 ETHNOLOGY MELANESIA
Miklukho-Maklai, Nikolai Nikolaevich

Puteshchestviia (Voyages). Dnevniki pure-
shchestvii na novuiu gvinei i ostrova admiral-
teistva v 1871-1883 godakh. Moscow. 1936. 8vo.
584 pp.

GN
1
An ETHNOLOGY MELANESIA
Graebner, F.

Die melanesische Bogenkultur und ihre
Verwandten.

(Anthropos. Band IV. 1909. pp.726-780,
998-1032)

GN
668
L 67 ETHNOLOGY MELANESIANS
Lewis, Albert B.

The Melanesians: people of the south Pacific.
Chicago Natural History Museum. 1945. 8vo.
264 pp.

GN
Ethn. Pam.
3150 ETHNOLOGY MELANESIA
Milke, Wilhelm

Südostmelanesien: Eine ethnostatistische
Analyse. (dissertation) Würzburg. Konrad
Triltsch. 8vo. 60 pp. 1935.

GN
668
N 49   ETHNOLOGY MELANESIA

Nevermann, Hans

Masken und Geheimbünde in Melanesien. Mit 55 Bildern in Kupfertiefdruck und einer Landkarte. Berlin. Reimar Hobbing. n.d. 8vo. 168 pp.

GN
668
R 62   ETHNOLOGY MELANESIA

Rivers, W. H. R.

The history of Melanesian society. In two volumes. Cambridge. University Press. 1914. 8vo. xii + 400; 610 pp. pp. 497-555.

(Percy Sladen Trust Expedition to Melanesia.)

GN
663
T 44   ETHNOLOGY MELANESIA

Thilenius, Georg editor

Ergebnisse der Südsee Expedition, 1908-1910. II. Ethnographie. A. Melanesien.

GN
662
P 24   ETHNOLOGY MELANESIA

Parkinson, R.

Dreissig Jahre in der Südsee: Land und Leute Sitten und Gebräuche im Bismarckarchipel und auf den Deutschen Salomoinseln...Stuttgart. 1907. R8vo.

GN
1
O 15   ETHNOLOGY MELANESIA

Rosenstiel, Annette

Historical perspective and the study of Melanesian culture.

(Oceania, Vol. 24(3):172-189, 1954)

GN
668
T 44   ETHNOLOGY MELANESIA

Thilenius, Georg

Ethnographische Ergebnisse aus Melanesien... I. Theil...II. Theil...

(Nova Acta, Abh. der Kaiserl. Leop.-Carol. Deutschen Akademie der Naturforscher, Band LXXX, Nr. 1-2. Halle. 1902-1903).

GN
668
P 52   ETHNOLOGY MELANESIA

Pfeil, Joachim Graf

Studien und Beobachtungen aus der Südsee... Mit beigegebenen tafeln nach aquarellen und zeichnungen des verfassers und photographien von Parkinson. Braunschweig. 1899. R8vo.

GN
668
S 32   ETHNOLOGY MELANESIA

Schellong, Otto

Alte Dokumente aus der Südsee; zur Geschichte der Gründung einer Kolonie Erlebtes und Eingeborenenstudien. Königsberg i Pr. Gräfe und Unzer. 8vo. 1934c. 207 pp.

Q
101
P 18   ETHNOLOGY MELANESIA

Thurnwald, Richard

Some traits of society in Melanesia.

(Proc. of the Fifth Pacific Science Congress, Vol. 4, pp. 2805-2814, 1933)

GN
2.I
A-4   ETHNOLOGY MELANESIA

Ray, Sidney H.

Note on the people and languages of New Ireland and the Admiralty Islands.

(Journ. Anthrop. Inst. of Great Britain and Ireland, Vol. 21, 1891-2, pp. 3-13)

GN
Ethn.Pam.
1366   ETHNOLOGY MELANESIA

Schmeltz, Johannes Diedrich Eduard

Die etnographisch anthropologische Abtheilung des Museum Godeffroy. By J.D.E. Schmeltz and R. Krause.

(Archif f. Ethnographie, Bd. 1, 1888, pp. 60-67)

GN
1
O 15   ETHNOLOGY MELANESIA

Wedgwood, Camilla H.

Some Aspects of Warfare in Melanesia.

(In Oceania, Vol. 1, No. 1, pp. 5-33, 1930)

GN
Ethn.Pam.
3087   ETHNOLOGY MELANESIA

Reschke, Heinz

Linguistische Untersuchung der Mythologie und Initiation in Neuguinea. Münster. 1935.

(Anthropos; Ethnologische Bibliothek, Internationale Sammlung Ethnologischer Monographien, Band III, Heft 5, Münster, 1935. 8vo)

GN
668
S 33   ETHNOLOGY MELANESIA

Schlaginhaufen, Otto

Muliama; zwei Jahre unter Südsee-Insulanern. Zürich. Orell Füssli Verlag. 1959. 212 pp.

GN
668
W 46   ETHNOLOGY MELANESIA

Wench, Ida

Mission to Melanesia. Elek Books. London. 8vo. 1961. (7)+209 pp.

GN
2.I
A-4   ETHNOLOGY MELANESIA BIBLIOGRAPHY

Riesenfeld, A.

Tobacco in New Guinea and the other areas of Melanesia.

(Jour. R. Anthrop. Inst., Grt. Britain and Ireland, 81 (1/2):69-102, 1951)

GN
Ethn. Pam.
3128   ETHNOLOGY MELANESIA

Speiser, Felix

Über Keulenformen in Melanesien.
(Zeitschrift für Ethnologie, 64 Jahrgang. pp. 74-105) 1932.

GN
670
W 72   ETHNOLOGY MELANESIA

Williamson, Robert W.

Essays in Polynesian ethnology. Edited by Ralph Piddington. With an analysis of recent studies in Polynesian history by the editor. Cambridge. At the University Press. 1939. R8vo. xlii + 373 pp.

GN
1
An   ETHNOLOGY MELANESIA

Riesenfeld, Alphonse

Was there a Paleolithic period in Melanesia?

(Anthropos, Bd. 47(3/4):405-446, 1952)

AM
101
F 45-n   ETHNOLOGY MELANESIA

Spoehr, Alexander

The museum as custodian of Pacific cultures.
(Chicago Nat. Hist. Museum Bull. Feb. 1947, p. 7)

GN
667.M
M 92   ETHNOLOGY MELVILLE ISLAND

Mountford, Charles P.

The Tiwi, their art, myth and ceremony. With 64 plates, 2 in colour, 15 line drawings and a map. Phoenix House, London, R8vo. 185 pp. 1958.

F
1220
B 47
ETHNOLOGY MEXICO
Bennett, Wendell C.

The Tarahumara, an Indian tribe of northern Mexico, by Wendell C. Bennett and Robert M. Zingg. Chicago. University of Chicago Press. (1935c) 8vo. xviii + 412 pp.

GN
2.I
A-4
ETHNOLOGY MICRONESIA
Christian, F. W.

On Micronesian weapons, dress, implements, etc.

(Journ. Anthrop. Inst. of Great Britain and Ireland, N. S., Vol. 1, 1898-9, pp. 288-306, pls. 19-24)

GN
669
M 43
ETHNOLOGY MICRONESIA
Matsuoka, Shizuo

Taiheiyo minzokushi. (Pacific ethnology) Tokyo. 1941. 330 pp. sm8vo.

in Japanese

GN
700
A 51
ETHNOLOGY MEXICO
Contributions to American Anthropology and History. Vols. 1-

Storage
Case
5
ms
Micr. 1
ETHNOLOGY MICRONESIA
Colcord, Mrs. Andrew D.

Journal aboard the missionary brig Morning Star on a voyage to Micronesia, 1875. ms. 45 pp. [not for publication]

GN
Ethn. Pam.
3212
ETHNOLOGY MICRONESIA
Métraux, Alfred

Océanie et Australie. Chapitre 5. 1936. 18 pp. (Extract from "Les Peuples sur la terre")

F
1211
G 19
ETHNOLOGY MEXICO
Gamio, Manuel

La poblacion del valle de Teotihuacan... Mexico, 1922. 2 volumes in 3.

Introduction, syntheses and conclusion of the work, "The population of the Valley of Teotihuacan". Mexico, 1922. 2 copies.

GN
662
F 51
ETHNOLOGY MICRONESIA
Finsch, (Friedrich Hermann Otto)

Ethnologische Erfahrungen und Belegstücke aus der Südsee. Beschreibender katalog einer sammlung im K. K. Naturhistorischen Hofmuseum in Wien von Drl O. Finsch.... Wien. 1893. R8vo.

(Annalen des K. K. Naturhistorischen Hof-Museums in Wien, Band III-VIII, 1888-1893, separat abgedruckt).

GN
1
I 61
ETHNOLOGY MICRONESIA
Parkinson, R.

Zur Ethnographie der Ontong Java und Tasman Inseln.

(Archiv f. Ethnographie, X, 1897, pp. 104-118, 137-151; Nachträge, Bd. XI, 1898, p. 194-209) and figures on pp. 242, 243

E
58
J 54
ETHNOLOGY - MEXICO
Spinden, Herbert J.

Origin of Civilizations in Central America and Mexico.

Jenness, Diamond

The American Aborigines...pp. 217-246

GN
670
K 89

DU
12
K 89
ETHNOLOGY MICRONESIA
Krämer, Augustin

Hawaii, Ostmikronesien und Samoa: Meine zweite Südseereise (1897-1899) zum Studium der Atolle und ihrer Bewohner...Stuttgart. 1906. 8vo.

DU
620
P
ETHNOLOGY MICRONESIA
Riesenberg, S. H.

People in Micronesia.

(Paradise of the Pacific, 63(5):25-27, 37, 1951)

F
1211
S79
ETHNOLOGY - MEXICO
Starr, Frederick

Notes upon the ethnography of southern Mexico. 2 pts. From v.8, Proc. Davenport Acad. Nat. Sci., 1900.

AM
101
F 45 g
ETHNOLOGY MICRONESIA
Linton, Ralph

Ethnology of Polynesia and Micronesia.

(Field Museum of Natural History, Guide, Part 6. Handbook, 1926)

DU
500
T 87
ETHNOLOGY MICRONESIA
Riesenberg, Saul H.

People in Micronesia.
IN Trust Territory of the Pacific Islands, Basic Information. 1 July 1951. pp. 70-72.

GN
22
B 15
ETHNOLOGY MICRONESIA
Bahnson, Kristian

Etnografien: fremstillet i dens hovedtraek. Bind 1-2. Med farvetryk, kort... København. Ernst Bojesen. 8vo. 1900. 548 + 704 pp. Bd. I: pp. 139-158.

GN
669
M 43

AS
552
T
ETHNOLOGY MICRONESIA
Matsumura, Akira

Contributions to the ethnography of Micronesia... With 36 plates and 72 text-figures. Tokyo. 1918.

(Journal of the College of Science, Tokyo Imperial University, Vol. XL, Art. 7, Dec. 15, 1918.

GN
Ethn. Pam.
3855
ETHNOLOGY MICRONESIA
Spoehr, Alexander

Time perspective in Micronesia and Polynesia

(Southwestern Journal of Anthropology, Vol. 8(4):457-465, 1952)

GN
669
B 32

GN
Ethn.
Pam.
704
ETHNOLOGY MICRONESIA
Bastian, Adolf

Die mikronesischen Colonien aus ethnologischen Gesichtspunkten. Berlin. A. Asher. 1899. 8vo. vii + 370 pp. Ergänzung.

Ergänzung, I. Berlin, 1900, 112 pp.

GN
669
M 43
ETHNOLOGY MICRONESIA
Matsuoka, Shizuo

Micronesia minzoku-shi. (ethography of Micronesia.) Tokyo. 1938.

In Japanese

GN
663
T 44
ETHNOLOGY MICRONESIA
Thilenius, Georg   editor

Ergebnisse der Südsee Expedition, 1908-1910. II. Ethnographie. B. Mikronesien.

GN 2M FI

ETHNOLOGY - MINDANAO

Cole, Fay Cooper, 1881-

... The wild tribes of Davao district, Mindanao, by Fay-Cooper Cole ... Chicago, 1913.

1 p. l., 49-203, vii p. front. (map) illus., 75 pl. 24½ᶜᵐ. (Field museum of natural history. Publication 170. Anthropological ser. vol. XII, no. 2)

Some of the plates accompanied by guard sheets with descriptive letterpress.
"The R. F. Cummings Philippine expedition."

1. Ethnology—Mindanao.

Library of Congress   GN2.F4   13-24658
———— Copy 2.   GN671.P5C7

GN Ethn. Pam. 3271

ETHNOLOGY MORIORI

Schurtz, H.

Stein- und Knochengeräthe der Chatham-Insulaner (Moriori)

(Berlin Anthropologischen Gesellschaft Sitzung vom Feb. 15, 1902,-pp. 1-24 Zeit. f. Ethnologie, 1902)

DU 620 F

ETHNOLOGY NAURU

Delaporte, Philip H.

Nauru as it was, and as it is now, by Rev. Philip H. Delaporte.

(Friend, June 1907, pp.6-7; July, pp.13-14; Aug., pp.7-8; Sept., pp.9-11.)

GN Ethn. Pam.3583

ETHNOLOGY MOKIL

Murphy, Raymond E.

Economic geography of a Micronesian atoll. (Mokil, Eastern Carolines)

(Annals of the Association of American Geographers, Vol. XI(1):58-83, 1950)

GN 2.S P 76

ETHNOLOGY MORIORI

Williams, H. W.

The Maruiwi myth.

(Journal of the Polynesian Society, Vol.46, 1937, pp. 105-122)

GN 663 T 44

ETHNOLOGY NAURU

Hambruch, Paul

Nauru.

Thilenius, G.
Ergebnisse der Südsee Expedition, 1908-1910. II. Ethnographie: B. Mikronesien, Bd. 1, 1914-15.

GN 669 C 77

ETHNOLOGY MOKIL

Weckler, Joseph Edwin

Land and livelihood on Mokil; an atoll in the Eastern Carolines, Part I ...Part II, by Conrad Bentzen.

(Coordinated Investigation of Micronesian Anthropology. Pacific Science Board. June 1949)

GN 2.S P 76

ETHNOLOGY MORTLOCK ISLANDS

Hogbin, H. Ian

"Polynesian" colonies in Melanesia.

(Journal of the Polynesian Society,Vol. 49, 1940, pp. 199-220)

G 1 G 56

and

GN Ethn.Pam. 1014

ETHNOLOGY NAURU

Krämer, Augustin

Nauru.

(Globus, Bd. 74, No. 10, 1898, pp. 153-158)

Q 115 F 92

ETHNOLOGY MOLUCCAS

Jensen, Ad. E.

Die drei Ströme, Züge aus dem geistigen und Leben der Wemale, einem primitiv-Volk in den Molukken.

(Ergebnisse der Frobenius-Expedition 1937-39 in die Molukken und nach Hollandisch Neu-Guinea. Bd. 2, 1948)

DU 620 M 67

ETHNOLOGY MORTLOCK ISLANDS

Price, F. M.

Notes on Ruk and the Mortlook Islands.

(American Missionary Herald, Vol. 91, 1895, pp. 311-314)

GN 1 C 15

ETHNOLOGY NAURU

Stephen, Ernest

Notes on Nauru.

(Oceania, Vol. 7, 1936, pp. 34-63)

GN Pam. 3036

ETHNOLOGY MONGOLIA

Torii, R. and Torii, Kimiko

Etudes Archaeolgiques et Ethnologiques: Populations Primitives de la Mongolie Orientale, Tokyo. 1914.

(Journal of the College of Science, Imperial University of Tokyo, Vol. XXXVI, Art. 4, March 29, 1914.)

GN 2.I A-4

ETHNOLOGY MOTU

Lawes, W. G.

Ethnological notes on the Motu, Koitapu and Koiari tribes of New Guinea.

(Journ. Anthrop. Inst. of Great Britain and Ireland, Vol. 8, 1878-9, pp. 369-377)

GN 1 O 15

ETHNOLOGY NAURU

Wedgwood, Camilla H.

Report on research work in Nauru Island, Central Pacific. Part I-II

(Oceania, vol. VI, 1936, pp. 359-391; vol. VII, 1936, pp.1-33)

GN 2.I A-M

ETHNOLOGY MORIORI

Balfour, H(enry)

Some specimens from the Chatham Islands.

(Man, vol. 18, 1918, no. 80, pp. 145-148, pl. K)

GN 2.I A-4

ETHNOLOGY MOTU

Turner, William Y.

The ethnology of the Motu.

(Journ. Anthrop. Inst. of Great Britain and Ireland, Vol. 7, 1877-78, pp. 470-499)

GN 645 H 33

ETHNOLOGY NEGROES

Hartmann, Robert

Die Nigritier: Eine anthropologisch-ethnologische monographie...Erster theil...Berlin. 1876. R8vo.

GN 2.S M 26

ETHNOLOGY MORIORI

Duff, Roger S.

The evolution of native culture in New Zealand: moa hunters, Morioris, Maoris.

(Mankind, Vol. 3 (10):281-291, 1947)

GN 671.N6 A 93

ETHNOLOGY NAURU

Australia. (Commonwealth of)

Report to the Council of the League of Nations on the Administration of Nauru. Canberra. Government Printer. folio.

1914- 1937

GN 638 J .72

ETHNOLOGY NEGROES

Johnston, Harry H. (Sir Henry Hamilton Johnston)

The negro in the new world...London. (1910) R8vo.

GN
538
S 56

ETHNOLOGY NEGROES

Shufeldt, Robert Wilson

America's greatest Problem: the negro.
Philadelphia. 1915.

GN
Pam
2434

ETHNOLOGY - NEW BRITAIN.

Martegg, Ernest

Eine Forschungsreise vom Weberhafen
in das Innere der Gazellen-Halbinsel
(Neu Pommern), 1897.

GN
2.I
A-m

ETHNOLOGY NEW CALEDONIA

Brown, J. Macmillan

Notes on a visit to New Caledonia.

(Man, 1916, pp. 113-115)

GN
658
W 54

ETHNOLOGY NEGROES

Weule, Karl

Negerleben in Ostafrika: Ergebnisse einer
ethnologischen forschungsreise von Dr. Karl
Weule...Zweite auflage. Leipzig. 1909. 8vo.

GN
4
C 33

ETHNOLOGY NEW BRITAIN

Mead, Margaret

Weaver of the border (New Britian).
IN
Casagrande, Joseph B.   editor
In the company of man. pp. 175-210.
Harper and Bros. New York. 1960. R8vo.

GN
Pam
309

ETHNOLOGY NEW CALEDONIA

Foley, -

La coquette Neo- Calédonienne.
Paris, 1879 (extrait) pp 10.

MAR 28 44

AS
701
A

ETHNOLOGY NEW BRITAIN

Brown, George

Some New Britain customs.

(Australasian Association for the Adv. of
Sci., Rept. of the 8th meeting, Melbourne, 1900,
pp. 307-312)

(peace-making, duk duk, burial)

GN
Ethn.Pam.
1216

ETHNOLOGY NEW BRITAIN

Parkinson, R.   and W. Foy

Die Volkstämme Neu Pommerns.

(Abh. u. Ber. K. Zool. u. Anthrop...Mus.
zu Dresden, Festschrift, 1899, nr. 5, pp. 1-14)

AM
Mus. Pam.
124

ETHNOLOGY NEW CALEDONIA

Führer durch das Museum für Völkerkunde,
Basel. Neu-Caledonien und die Loyalty-Inseln.
G. Krebs, Basel. 1931. 26 pp.

GN
671.N5
C 53

ETHNOLOGY - NEW BRITAIN

Chinnery, E. W. Pearson

Certain Natives in South New Britain and
Dampier Straits.

(Anthropological Report, Territory of New
Guinea, No. 3, Melbourne, ND)

G
51
W 17

ETHNOLOGY NEW BRITAIN

Wallace, Jane Todd

The Bainings of New Britain.

(Walkabout, Vol. 4(8):21-24,1938)

AS
28
E 85

ETHNOLOGY NEW CALEDONIA

Guiart, Jean

L'histoire non ecrite de la Nouvelle-Caledonie.

(Etudes Mélanésiennes, No. 8, pp. 21-26,
Dec. 1954)

GN
2.M
L 53

ETHNOLOGY NEW BRITAIN

Damm, Hans

Ethnographische Materialien aus dem Küsten-
gebiet der Gazelle-Halbinsel (Neubritannien).

(Jahrbuch des Museums f. Völkerkunde zu
Leipzig, Bd. XVI: 110-152, 1959)

GN
1
F

ETHNOLOGY NEW CALEDONIA

Atkinson, J. J.

The natives of New Caledonia.

(Folklore, Vol. 14, 1903, pp. 243-260)

also note on "Totemism in New Caledonia", by
N. W. Thomas, on pp. 418-419, a comment on this
article.

GN
671.N4
G 94

ETHNOLOGY NEW CALEDONIA

Guiart, Jean

Inventaire des ressources de trois réserves
autochtones en Nouvelle-Calédonie. Par J.
Guiart et G. Teroinier. Institut Francais
d'Océanie, Laboratoires d'Ethnologie et de
Pedologie. Office de la Recherche Scientifique
et Technique Outre-Mer.   Fevrier, 1956. 4to.
83 pp. mimeographed.

AS
701
A

ETHNOLOGY NEW BRITAIN

Danks, B.

New Britain and its people.

(Austr. Ass'n for the Adv. of Sci., 1892
(2nd meeting) pp. 614-620)

GN
671.N4
B 26

ETHNOLOGY NEW CALEDONIA

Barrau, Jacques

L'agriculture vivrière autochtone de la
Nouvelle-Calédonie, précédée de... by Jean
Guiart. Commission du Pacifique Sud. Nouméa
8vo. (1956) 153 pp.

GN
2.S
O 15

ETHNOLOGY NEW CALEDONIA

Laroche, Marie-Ch.

La vie dans les tribus calédoniennes en 1954.
Notes pour une ethnologie de l'acculturation.

(Journal de la Société des Océanistes, Tome
X(10):77-90, Décembre, 1954)

AS
142
V

and

GN
662
F 51

ETHNOLOGY NEW BRITAIN

Finsch, Otto

Ethnologische Erfahrungen und Belegstücke
aus der Südsee...

(Annalen K. K. Naturhist. Mus., Wien, Bd.
3:83-160, 1888; Bd. 8:384-397, 1893)

AS
28
E 85

ETHNOLOGY NEW CALEDONIA

Belouma, Gaston

Problèmes e'conomiques et sociaux autochtones a Gomen.

(Etudes Melanesiennes, n.s. nr. 12/13:20-
31, 1958/59)

GN
1
A 62

ETHNOLOGY NEW CALEDONIA

Leenhardt, Maurice

Communication sur la fete du Pilou Pilou
en Nouvelle-Caledonie. Review by P. Rivet.

(L'Anthropologie, Tome 31, 1921, pp. 355-
356)

[see also under La Fête du Pilou...]

GR
385.N3
L 48

ETHNOLOGY   NEW CALEDONIA

Leenhardt, Maurice

Documents Néo-Calédoniens.

(Travaux et Memoires de L'Institut d'Ethnologie, Université de Paris, IX, 1932)

GN
671.N4
S 24

ETHNOLOGY-NEW CALEDONIA

Sarasin, Fritz

Ethnologie der Neu-Caledonier und Loyalty-Insulaner. Mit einem Atlas von 73 Tafeln in Lichtdruck. München. C. W. Kreidel's Verlag. 1929. 320 pp. 73 tafeln. 4to.

GN
1
An

ETHNOLOGY NEW GUINEA

Aufinger, P. Albert

Wetterzauber auf den Yabob -Inseln in Neu-Guinea.

(Anthropos, Bd. 34, 1939, pp. 277-291)

AS
28
E 85

ETHNOLOGY   NEW CALEDONIA

Leenhardt, Maurice

Le masque et le mythe en Nouvelle-Calédonie.

(Etudes Mélanésiennes, No. 8, pp. 9-20, Dec. 1954)

GN
1
A62

ETHNOLOGY   NEW CALEDONIA

Sarasin, Fritz

Streiflichter aus der Ergologie der Neu-Caledonier und Loyalty-Insulaner auf die Europaische Praehistorie. Review by Fr. de Zeltner.

(L'Anthropologie, Tome 29, 1918-1919, pp. 150-151)
(Original article is in Verhandl. der Naturforschenden Gesell. in Basel, Bd. 28, 1916, 27pp. 23 fig.)   Library has not.

GN
671.N5
A 93

ETHNOLOGY   NEW GUINEA

Australia. (Commonwealth of)

Report to the Council of the League of Nations on the Administration of the Territory of New Guinea. Canberra. Government Printer. folio.

1914- 1936/37

GN
671.N4
L 96

ETHNOLOGY NEW CALEDONIA

Leenhardt, Maurice

Notes d'Ethnologie Néo-Calédonienne. Paris. Institut d'Ethnologie. 1930. viii + 265 pp, xxxvi planches. Cartes I-II.

Travaux et Mémoires de l'Institut d'Ethnologie, Université de Paris, VIII

GN
Ethn.Pam.
3534

ETHNOLOGY NEW CALEDONIA

Speiser, Felix

Neu-Caledonien, die südlichen Neuen Hebriden und Polynesien.

(Verhandlungen Naturforschenden Gesell. Basel, Bd. 57:1-24, 1946)

GN
671.N5
B 32

ETHNOLOGY NEW GUINEA

Bateson, Gregory

Naven; a survey of the problems suggested by a composite picture of the culture of a New Guinea tribe drawn from three points of view Second edition. Stanford University Press. 8vo. xix + 312 pp. illustrated.

GN
Ethn.Pam.
3471

ETHNOLOGY   NEW CALEDONIA

Leenhardt, Maurice

La personne Mélanésienne.

(Ecole Pratique des Hautes-Etudes, Section des Sciences Religieuses, Annuaire 1940-41 et 1941-42, pp. 5-36. 1941)

GN
1
Z

ETHNOLOGY NEW CALEDONIA

Speiser, Felix

Versuch einer Kultur-Analyse von Neu-Kaledonien.

(Zeit. f. Ethnologie, 65:173-192, 1933)

GN
2.1
A-4

ETHNOLOGY   NEW GUINEA

Beardmore, Edward

The natives of Mowat, Daudai, New Guinea.

(Journ. Anthrop. Inst. of Great Britain and Ireland, Vol. 19, 1889-90, pp. 459-468)

GN
Ethnology
Pam.3225

ETHNOLOGY NEW CALEDONIA

Leenhardt, Maurice

Le temps et la personnalité chez les Canaques de la Nouvelle-Calédonie.

(Revue Philosophique de la France et de L'Etranger, Année 62, 1937, pp. 43-58)

G
51
W 17

ETHNOLOGY NEW GEORGIA

Griffiths, B. M. H.

The arts and crafts of New Georgia. (Solomon Islands)

(Walkabout, Vol. 10 (12):16, 1944)

GN
Ethn.
Pam.
3452

ETHNOLOGY   NEW GUINEA

Bearup, A. J.

The Ramu and Wahgi Valleys of New Guinea.

(The Australian Geographer, Vol. 3, no. 1, 1936, pp. 1-12)

GN
2.8
P

ETHNOLOGY   NEW CALEDONIA

Moncelon, Léon

Réponse alinéa par alinéa, pour les Néo-Calédoniens, au questionnaire de sociologie et d'éthnographie de la Société.

(Bull. de la Soc. d'Anthropologie de Paris, Ser. 3, Tome 9, 1886, pp. 345-380)

GN
671.N5
A 733

ETHNOLOGY   NEW GUINEA

Armstrong, W. E.

Rossel Island, an ethnological study. With introduction by A. C. Haddon. Cambridge. 1928. 8vo.

AS
182
S 47

ETHNOLOGY   NEW GUINEA

Behrmann, W.

Aus dem steinzeitlichen Dorfe Malu in innern Neuguineas.

(Natur un Volk, Vol. 65, No. 11, 1935, pp. 551-556)

GN
671.N4
R 23

ETHNOLOGY   NEW CALEDONIA

Rau, Eric

Institutions et coutumes Canaques. Préface de Rene Maunier. Paris. Larose, Editeur. 1944. 8vo. 199 pp.

GN
1
A 63

ETHNOLOGY   NEW GUINEA

Aufenanger, H.

Nose piercing, stone adzes and pig traps at Mundanghai (New Guinea).

(Anthropos, Vol. 56: 940-941, 1961)

AM
Mus.
Pam
69
70

ETHNOLOGY - NEW GUINEA

Berlin. k. Museum fur Volkerkunde

Catalog der ethnologischen sammlung der Neu Guinea compagnie ausgestellt im k. Museum fur Volkerkunde. Berlin, 1886.

G
3
A 1
ETHNOLOGY   NEW GUINEA (Dutch)

Brass, L. J.

Stone age agriculture in New Guinea.

(The Geographical Review, Vol. 31, 1941,
pp. 555-569, 15 figs.)

G
51
W 17
ETHNOLOGY   NEW GUINEA

Chinnery, E. W. P.

Natives of Paua and New Guinea.

(Walkabout, 18(2):29-35, 1952)

DU
1
Pa
ETHNOLOGY   NEW GUINEA

Discoveries in New Guinea. Centre of Main
Island is Rich, Temperate Densely Populated
Plateau.

(The Pacific Islands Monthly, Vol. 4, No. 5,
1933, pp. 11-15)

GN
1
O 15
ETHNOLOGY   NEW GUINEA

Brown, Paula

Chimbu land and society.   By Paula Brown
and H.C. Brookfield.

(Oceania, Vol. 30(1): 1-75, 1959)

GN
671.N5
C 53
ETHNOLOGY   NEW GUINEA

Chinnery, E. W. Pearson

Natives of the Waria, Williams, and Bailolo
Watersheds. (New Guinea)

(Anthropological Report, Territory of New
Guinea, No. 4, Melbourne, ND)

GN
1
O 15
ETHNOLOGY   NEW GUINEA

Elkin, A. P.

Delayed exchange in Wabag sub-district, Central Highlands of New Guinea, with notes on social organization.

(Oceania, Vol. 23(3):161-201, 1953)

GN
Ethn.
Pam.
4384
ETHNOLOGY   NEW GUINEA

Bühler, Alfred

The significance of colour among primitive
peoples.

(Palette, No. 9, Spring 1962:2-8, 1962)

GN
671.N5
C 53
ETHNOLOGY- NEW GUINEA (MANDATED TERRITORY)

Chinnery, E. W. Pearson

Notes on the Natives of Certain Villages of
the Mandated Territory of New Guinea visited during the Voyages of the Government Steam Yacht
"Franklin", January-March, 1925.

(Anthropological Report, Territory of New
Guinea, No. 1, Melbourne, ND)

AS
719
A 93
ETHNOLOGY   NEW GUINEA

Elkin, A. P.

Peoples of New Guinea.

(Australian Mus. Mag., 12:406-408, 1958)

AS
719
A 93 m
ETHNOLOGY   NEW GUINEA

Bulmer, Ralph

A primitive ornithology.

(Australian Museum Magazine, 12(7):224-229,
1957)

[remarkable knowledge of New Guinea people
of their remarkable birds]

GN
671.N5
C 62
ETHNOLOGY   NEW GUINEA

Clercq, F. S. A. de

Ethnographische Beschrijving van de West- en
Noordkust van Nederlandsch Nieuw-Guinea, door
F. S. A. De Clerq, met medewerking van J. D. E.
Schmeltz Mit Bijvoeging eener schets der ethno-
graphie van Duitsch en Britsch Nieuw-Guinea...
Leiden. 1893. 4to.

GN
662
F 51
ETHNOLOGY   NEW GUINEA

Finsch, (Friedrich Hermann Otto)

Ethnologische Erfahrungen und Belegstücke
aus der Südsee. Beschreibender katalog einer
sammlung im K. K. Naturhistorischen Hofmuseum in
Wien von Dr. O. Finsch.... Wien. 1893. R8vo.

(Annalen des K. K. Naturhistorischen Hof-
Museums in Wien, Band III-VIII, 1888-1893, separat abgedruckt).

GN
671.N5
B 95
ETHNOLOGY   NEW GUINEA

Burger, Friedrich

Die Küsten- und Bergvölker der Gazellehalbinsel: Ein Beitrag zur Völkerkunde von Neuguinea
unter besonderer Hervorhebung rechtlicher und
sozialer Einrichtungen... Stuttgart. 1913. 8vo

(Studien und Forschungen zur Menschen- und
Völkerkunde unter wissenschaftlichen Leitung von
Georg Buschan, XII)

DU
740
C 64
ETHNOLOGY   NEW GUINEA

Clune, Frank

Somewhere in New Guinea; a companion to
"Prowling through Papua". Illustrated by Syd
Miller. Angus and Robertson. Sydney 1951.

(excellent sketches of the people)

AS
142
V

and

GN
662
F 51
ETHNOLOGY   NEW GUINEA   (British)

Finsch, Otto

Ethnologische Erfahrungen und Belegstücke
aus der Südsee...
Zweite Abteilung: Neu-Guinea (british)

(Ann. Naturhist. Mus., Wien, Bd. 3:293-364,
1888; Bd. 6:13-36, 1891; Bd. 8:401-407, 1893)

GN
Ethn. Pam
3096
ETHNOLOGY   NEW GUINEA

Chinnery, E. W. P.

The central ranges of the Mandated Territory
of New Guinea from Mount Chapman to Mount Hagen.

(Geographical Journal, Vol. 84, 1934, pp.
398-412)

GN
2.I
A-4
ETHNOLOGY   NEW GUINEA

Comrie, Peter

Anthropological notes on New Guinea.

(Journ. Anthrop. Inst. of Great Britain and
Ireland, Vol. 6, 1877, pp. 102-119, pl. 1)

AS
142
V

and

GN
662
F 51
ETHNOLOGY   NEW GUINEA   (Dutch)

Finsch, Otto

Ethnologische Erfahrungen und Belegstücke
aus der Südsee...
Zweite Abteilung: Neu-Guinea, II. Kaiser
Wilhelms Land.

(Ann. Naturhist. Mus., Wien, Bd. 6:37-130,
1891; Bd. 8:407-413, 1893)

GN
Pam
3090

GN
2.I
A-m
ETHNOLOGY   NEW GUINEA

Chinnery, E. W. P.

Mountain tribes of the mandated territory of
New Guinea from Mt. Chapman to Mt. Hagen.

(Man, Vol. XXXIV, Art. 140, August 1934. 8pp.)

GN
671.N5
C 93
ETHNOLOGY   NEW GUINEA   (Dutch)

Crockett, Charis

The house in the rain forest. With illustrations. Houghton Mifflin Company. Boston.
1942c. 8vo.   x + 300 pp.

DU
740
F 51
ETHNOLOGY   NEW GUINEA

Finsch, Otto

Samoafahrten. Reisen in Kaiser Wilhelms-land
und Englisch-Neu-Guinea in de Jahren 1884 u.
1885... With Ethnologischer atlas. Leipzig.
Ferdinand Hirt. 1888.

2 copies of Atlas.

GN
671.N5
F 52

ETHNOLOGY NEW GUINEA

Firth, Raymond

Art and life in New Guinea. London. The Studio Ltd., 1936. 8vo. 126 pp., 83 pl.

GN
Ethn.Pam.
3379

ETHNOLOGY NEW GUINEA

Gill, William Wyatt

Notes on New Guinea.

(Leisure Hour, 1874, pp. 45-47)

ETHNOLOGY NEW GUINEA

GN
Ethn.Pam.
3713

Goodenough, Ward H.

Ethnological reconnaissance in New Guinea.

(University Museum [Pennsylvania] Bulletin, Vol. 17, No. 1, 1952) pp. 5-37

GN
1
B 14

ETHNOLOGY NEW GUINEA

Fischer, Hans

Ethnographica von den Kukukuku (Ost-Neu-guinea).

(Baessler-Archiv, 32(1):99-122, 1959)

GN
Ethn.Pam.
3380

ETHNOLOGY NEW GUINEA

Gill, William Wyatt

Torres Straits and New Guinea.

(Leisure Hour, 1874, pp. 245-248)

GN
1
O 15

ETHNOLOGY - NEW GUINEA

Groves, William C.

Anthropology and native administration in New Guinea.

(Oceania, Vol. 6, No. 1, 1935. pp. 94-104)

GN
668
F 89

ETHNOLOGY NEW GUINEA

Friederici, Georg

Wissenschaftliche Ergebnisse einer Amtlichen Forschungsreise nach dem Bismarck-Archipel im Jahre 1908.
II. Beitrage zur Volker- und Sprachenkunde von Deutsch-Neuguinea.
III. Untersuchungen uber eine Melanesische Wanderstrasse.
(Mitt. aus den Deutschen Schutzgebieten, Erganzungsheft, Nrs. 5, 7, 1912-1913.)

AS
36
A 5

ETHNOLOGY NEW GUINEA

Gilliard, E. Thomas

Exploring New Guinea for Birds of paradise.

(Natural History, 62(6):248-255, 1953)

[Wahgi valley, Bismarck range]

GN
1
O 15

ETHNOLOGY NEW GUINEA

Groves, William C.

Report of field work in the territory of New Guinea from May 1933 to August 1934.

(Oceania, Vol. 5, No. 2, 1934, pp. 218-223)

GN
671.N5
F 95

ETHNOLOGY NEW GUINEA

Fuhrmann, Ernst

Neu-Guinea: Schriften reihe Kulturen der Erde, Band XIV.

Folkwang, Hagen, 1922. 51p. pls. 4to.

AS
36
A 65 n

ETHNOLOGY NEW GUINEA

Gilliard, E. Thomas

A stone age naturalist; in a mountain valley near the center of New Guinea, an American ornithologist meets a Neolithic fellow student of birds...

(Natural History, 66(7):344-351, 1957)

GN
671.N5
H 12

ETHNOLOGY NEW GUINEA

Haddon, Alfred Cort

The decorative art of British New Guinea: a study in Papuan ethnography. Dublin. 1894. 4to. 279 pp. Plates.

AM
Mus.Pam.
.128

ETHNOLOGY NEW GUINEA

Führer durch das Museum für Völkerkunde, Basel. Neu-Guinea.

Buchdruckerei G. Krebs, Basel, 1930. 24 pp.

GN
700
A 63

ETHNOLOGY NEW GUINEA

Girard, F.

The Buang of the Snake River. (Australian New Guinea)

(Antiquity and Survival, No. 5:406-414, 1956)

GN
2.1
A-4

ETHNOLOGY NEW GUINEA

Haddon, A. C.

Migrations of cultures in British New Guinea.

(Journ. R. Anthrop. Inst. of Great Britain and Ireland, Vol. 50, 1920, pp. 237-280)

GN
671.N5
G 21

ETHNOLOGY NEW GUINEA

Gardi, René

Tambaran, an encounter with cultures in decline in New Guinea. Translated by Eric Northcote. Constable. London. R8vo. 201 pp.

[Foothills of the Maprik Mountains]

GN
671.N5
G 53

ETHNOLOGY NEW GUINEA

Gitlow, Abraham L.

Economics of the Mount Hagen tribes, New Guinea.

(Monographs of the Am. Ethnological Soc., XII, 1947c)

Q
115
G 76

ETHNOLOGY NEW GUINEA (Dutch; Utakwa River)

Haddon, Alfred Cort
Report made by the Wollaston Expedition on the ethnographical collections from the Utakwa River, Dutch New Guinea.
Grant, William R. Ogilvie
Reports on the collections made by the British Ornithologists' Union Expedition..., Vol. 2, no. 19, pp. 1-92, 8 pl.; vii pp.
(The mountain people and the coast Papuans)

GN
1
An

ETHNOLOGY NEW GUINEA

Gerstner, A.

Aus dem Gemeinschaftsleben der Wewak-Boikin-Leute, Nordost-Neuguinea.

(Anthropos, 48(3/4):413-457; (5/6):795-808, 1953)

[yam festivals]

GN
2.S
S 72

ETHNOLOGY NEW GUINEA

Goodenough, Ward H.

Ethnographic notes on the Mae people of New Guinea's western highlands.

(Southwestern Journal of Anthropolgy, Vol. 9(1):29-44, 1953)

GN
Pam
2459

ETHNOLOGY - NEW GUINEA

Hedley, C

The Cassowary figure head; Stray note on Papuan ethnology. From Proc. Linnean Soc. N.S.W. v.10, 1895, pp. 613-619).

GN
Pam
2646 Heger,

        Steinaxte aus Neu-Guinea. (From Mitth.
d. Anthrop. Gesell. Wien, sitz. n.7,
1886). pp. 65-70.

GN
1
O 15 Kienzle, Wallace

        Notes on the natives of the Fly and Sepik
River headwaters, by Wallace Kienzle and Stuart
Campbell.

        (Oceania, Vol. 8, 1938, pp. 463-481)

GN
1
A 63 Luzbetak, L. J.

        The Middle Wahgi culture: a study of first
contacts and initial selectivity.

        (Anthropos, 53(1/2):51-87, 1958)

GN
2.M
L 53 Höltker, Georg

        Aus dem Kulturleben der Kire-Puir am un-
teren Ramu (Neuguinea)

        (Jahrb. des Museums für Völkerkunde zu
Leipzig, 19:76-107, 1962)

GN
671.N5
K 92 Krieger, Maximilian

        Neu-Guinea...mit Beiträgen von Professor Dr.
A. Freiherrn von Danckelman, Professor Dr. F. von
Luschan, Kustos Paul Matschie und Professor Dr.
Otto Warburg mit Unterstützung der Kolonial-Abt-
eilung des Auswärtigen Amtes, der Neu-Guinea-
Kompagnie und der Deutschen Kolonial-Gesellschaft
Berlin. Alfred Schall. n.d.

        (Bibliothek der Länderkunde...Band 5 and 6).

G
51
W 17 Maahs, Arnold M.

        Climbing New Guinea's Finisterres.

        (Walkabout, 18(6):29-33, 1952)

GN
2.I
V 34 Höltker, Georg

        Ethnographica aus Neuguinea, mit einem
Textiltechnologischen Beitrag, von Kristin
Buehler-Oppenheim.

        (Annali Lateranensi, 9:261-320, 1945)

AM
Mus. Pam.
126

        Kult und Kunst auf Neu-Guinea. Sammlungen
von Dr. Felix Speiser und Dr. Paul Wirz.
Gewerbemuseum, Basel. 1931. 31 pp.

G
51
W 17 Maahs, Arnold M.

        Mt. Michael's fortified villages (Central
Highlands, New Guinea).

        (Walkabout, 16(7):29-32, 1950)

DU
Pac. Pam.
890 Huetz de Lemps, Alain

        La Nouvelle Guinée.

        (Les Cahiers d'Outre-Mer, Tome IX, No. 33:
5-35, Janvier-Mars 1956)

QK
1
A 75-s Lam, H. J.

        Fragmenta papuana [observations of a natur-
alist in Netherlands New Guinea.] With two maps
and thirty-two text-figures, translated from the
Dutch by Lily M. Perry.

        (Sargentia, V, 1945)

AS
36
A 65-n Maahs, Arnold

        New Guinea chiefs give to get rich.

        (Natural History, April, 1956:177-183, 223)

GN
1
O 15 Ivinskis, V.

        A medical and anthropological study of the
Chimbu natives in the central highlands of New
Guinea. By V. Ivinskis, Olga Koopizoff, R. J.
Walsh and Diane Dunn.

        (Oceania, Vol. XXVII(2):143-157, Dec., 1956)

GN
671.N5
L 26 Landtman, Gunnar

        The Kiwai Papuans of British New Guinea:
a Nature-born instance of Rousseau's ideal community...Introduction by Alfred C. Haddon.
Illustrated. London, Macmillan, 1927. 8vo.
xxxix + 485 pp.

G
51
W 17 Maahs, Arnold M.

        New Guinea's Stone-Axe Men.

        (Walkabout, 19(2):29-35, 1953)

        [live near   the Jimmi River, in the
heart of New   Guinea]

GN
2.I
A-m Joyce, T. A.

        A Ceremonial "Mask" from the Sepik River,
New Guinea.

        (In Man: 1926, p. 1-2)

GN
2.I
A-4 Lawes, W. G.

        Ethnological notes on the Motu, Koitapu and
Koiari tribes of New Guinea.

        (Journ. Anthrop. Inst. of Great Britain and
Ireland, Vol. 8, 1878-9, pp. 369-377)

GN
2.I
A-4 Macgregor, Sir William

        British New Guinea.

        (Journ. Anthrop. Inst. of Great Britain and
Ireland, Vol. 21, 1891-2, pp. 75-77; see also
pp. 482-487)

        (Extracted from Annual Report on New Guinea,
1890-1891)

GN
1
O 15 Kaberry, Phyllis M.

        The Abelam tribe, Sepik District, New
Guinea: a preliminary report.

        (Oceania, Vol. XI, 1941, pp. 345-367)

GN
671.N5
L 61 Le Roux, C. C. F. M.

        De Bergpapoea's van Nieuw-Guinea en hun woon-
gebied. Deel 1-3   Leiden. E. J. Brill.
R8vo. 1948 -1950   [Deel 3 is obfolio]

        [Translation of title: The Mountain Papuans
of New Guinea and their living-territory]

GN
662
M 27 Mander, Linden A.

        Some dependent peoples of the South Pacific.
Issued under the auspices of the International
Secretariat, Institute of Pacific Relations. The
MacMillan Co. New York. 1954. 8vo. xix + 535
pp.

GN
671.N5
M 48   Mead, Margaret

ETHNOLOGY NEW GUINEA

Growing up in New Guinea, a comparative study of primitive education. London. 1931.

DU
740
M 99   Mytinger, Caroline

ETHNOLOGY NEW GUINEA

New Guinea headhunt. New York. The Macmillan Company. 1946. 8vo. viii + 441 pp.

GN
.1
O 15   Nilles, John

ETHNOLOGY NEW GUINEA

The Kuman people: a study of cultural change in a primitive society in the central highlands of New Guinea.

(Oceania, Vol. XXIV(1):1-27, 1953; (2):119-131, 1953)

GN
2.M
A   Mead Margaret

ETHNOLOGY NEW GUINEA

The mountain Arapesh, V. The record of Unabelin with Rorschach analyses.

(Am. Mus. of Nat. Hist., Anthrop. Papers, Vol. 41(3):289-390, 1949)

GN
2.M
S 93   Nevermann, H.

ETHNOLOGY NEW GUINEA

Die Gabgab auf Südneuguinea.

(tribus, 1952/53:196-209)

GN
1
Ar 1

ETHNOLOGY NEW GUINEA

Notes from Parliamentary Papers, No. 8: Report of the special commission for 1887 on British New Guinea.

(Archaeological Review, Vol. III, 1889, pp. 276-283; 411-418)

GN
1
O 15   Meggitt, M. J.

ETHNOLOGY NEW GUINEA

The Enga of the New Guinea highlands: some preliminary observations.

(Oceania, Vol. 28(4):253-330, 1958)

GN
671.N5
N48   Neuhauss, R.

ETHNOLOGY - NEW GUINEA

Deutsch Neu-Guinea: herausgegeben mit unterstützung der Rudolf Virchow-stiftung in Berlin. In drei bänden. R8vo.

Berlin, Reimer, 1911.   3v.

GN
1
Ar 1

ETHNOLOGY NEW GUINEA

Notes from Parliamentary Papers, No. 9: Correspondence respecting New Guinea, May, 1883.

(Archaeological Review, Vol. IV, 1889-1890, pp. 147-149)

GN
1
O 15   Meggitt, M.J.

ETHNOLOGY - NEW GUINEA

The valleys of the upper Wage and Lai rivers, western highlands, New Guinea.

(Oceania, Vol. XXVII(2):90-135, Dec., 1956

GN
1
B   Nevermann, Hans

E   ETHNOLOGY NEW GUINEA

Die Jabga auf Sudneuguinea.

(Baessler-Archiv, Beitrage zur Volkerkunde, neue folge Bd. 1(26 Bd.), pp. 49-82, 1952)

southern Dutch New Guinea

GN
671.N5
N 93

ETHNOLOGY NEW GUINEA

Nova Guinea. Résultats de l'Expédition Scientifique Néerlandaise à la Nouvelle-Guinée, 1903, 1907, 1909.

Vol. 3, 7, 16   1907,1923,1924-34

GN
2.M
B 29

ETHNOLOGY NEW GUINEA

Mensch und Handwerk. Verarbeitung und Verwendung von Stein und Muschelschalen.

(Fuhrer durch das Museum f. Volkerkunde und Schweizerische Museum f. Volkskunde (Basel), Apr. 1963)

GN
663
T 44   Nevermann, Hans

St.Matthias-Gruppe

Thilenius, G.

Ergebnisse der Südsee-Expedition, 1908-1910. II. Ethnographie: A. Melanesien, Band 2, 1933.

ETHNOLOGY NEW GUINEA

GN
671.N5
O 60   Oosterwal, G.

ETHNOLOGY NEW GUINEA

People of the Tor; a cultrual-anthropological study on the tribes of the Tor territory (Northern Netherlands New Guinea) Royal van Gorcum Ltd., Assen, The Netherlands. H. J. and H. M. G. Prakke. 1961. R8vo. (v) + 293 pp., 11 plates.

.GN
2.S
P 76   Monckton, Whitmore

ETHNOLOGY NEW GUINEA

Goodenough Island, New Guinea.

(J. Poly. Soc., Vol. 6, 1897, p. 89-90)

GN
1
O 15   Niles, J.

ETHNOLOGY NEW GUINEA

Natives of the Bismarck Mountains, New Guinea.

(Oceania, Vol. 14, pp. 104-123, 1944)

GN
1
Ar2   Parkinson, R.

ETHNOLOGY NEW GUINEA

Ein Beitrag zur Ethnographie der Neu-Guinea-Kuste in Internationales Archiv fur Ethnographie, pp.18-54, Tafel xv-xxii. Leiden,1900.

GN
2 S
P 76   Monckton, Whitmore

ETHNOLOGY NEW GUINEA

Some recollections of New Guinea customs.

(Journal of the Polynesian Society, Vol. 5, 1896, pp. 184-186)

GN
1
O 15   Nilles, John

ETHNOLOGY NEW GUINEA

The Kuman of the Chimbu region, Central Highlands, New Guinea.

(Oceania, Vol. 21(1):25-65, 1950)

[social life, chiefly]

GN
Pam
788   Plischke, Hans

ETHNOLOGY - NEW GUINEA

Geistertrompeten und Geisterflöten aus Bambus vom Sepik, Neuguinea. From (Jahr. stad. des Mus. für Völkerkunde zu Leipzig, Bd. 8, 1918/21.).

PL
1
B 57

ETHNOLOGY   NEW GUINEA

Pouwer, J.

New Guinea as a field for ethnological study.

(Bijdragen tot de Taal-, Land-en Volkenkunde, Deel 117 (1):1-24, 1961)

GN
2.1
A 4

ETHNOLOGY   NEW GUINEA

Rosser, W. E.

String Figures from British New Guinea, by W. E. Rosser and J. Hornell.

(Journal of the R. Anthropological Inst. of Great Britain and Ireland, Vol. 62, 1932, pp. 39-50)

GN
2.1
A-M

ETHNOLOGY   NEW GUINEA

Seligman, C. G.

Notes on the Tugere tribe, Netherlands New Guinea.

(Man, vol. 6, 1906, no. 42, pp. 65-67, pl. E, fig. 1)

Du
1
P

ETHNOLOGY   NEW GUINEA

Pygmies in New Guinea.

(Pacific Islands Monthly, Aug. 1936, p. 57)

GN
671.N5
S 35

ETHNOLOGY   NEW GUINEA

Schmitz, Carl A.

Beiträge zur Ethnographie des Wantoat Tales, Nordost Neuguinea.

(Kölner Ethnologische Mitteilungen, I, 1960)

GN
671.N5
S 61

ETHNOLOGY   NEW GUINEA

Simpson, Colin

Adam in plumes. Angus and Robertson. Sydney. 1955. 8vo. xvii+268 pp.

[Wahgi valley; central highlands] New Guinea

G
7
R 91

ETHNOLOGY   NEW GUINEA

Rawling, C. G.

Explorations in Dutch New Guinea.
(British Ornithologists' Union Expedition, 1910-)

(The Geographical Journal, Vol. 38, 1911, pp. 233-255)

GN
671.N5
S 45

ETHNOLOGY   NEW GUINEA

Schmitz, Carl A.

Historische Probleme in Nordost-Neuguinea, Huon Halbinsel.

(Studien zur Kulturkunde, Bd. 16, 1960)

DU
740
S 74

ETHNOLOGY   NEW GUINEA

Spencer, Margaret

Doctor's wife in New Guinea. Angus and Robertson. Sydney. 1959. 8vo. (6) + 189 pp.

[everyday life in the Wahgi Valley]

GN
2.S
S 72

ETHNOLOGY   NEW GUINEA

Read, K. E.

Cultures of the Central Highlands, New Guinea.

(Southwestern Journal of Anthropology, Vol. 10(1):1-43, 1954)

GN
1
A 63

ETHNOLOGY   NEW GUINEA (NORTHEAST)

Schmitz, C. A.

Zur Ethnologie der Rai-Kuste in Neuguinea.

(Anthropos, 54:27-56, 1959)

GN
2.1
S 66

ETHNOLOGY   NEW GUINEA

Stirling, M. W.

The native peoples of New Guinea.

(Smithsonian Institution, War Background Studies, No. 9, 1943)

GN
671.N5
R 28

ETHNOLOGY   NEW GUINEA

Reay, Marie

The Kuma; freedom and conformity in the New Guinea highlands. Melbourne University Press, on behalf of the Australian National University. 8vo. 1959c. xvi + 222 pp.

G
51
W 17

ETHNOLOGY   NEW GUINEA

Schuchard, H. W. L.

Our neighbors in New Guinea; craft and craftsmen of Humboldt Bay.

(Walkabout, Vol. 8(1):29-31, 1941)

GN
2.1
A-4

ETHNOLOGY   NEW GUINEA

Strong, W. M.

Some personal experiences in British New Guinea.

(Journ. R. Anthrop. Inst. of Great Britain and Ireland, Vol. 49, 1919, pp. 292-316)

AS
36
A 91-m

OVER

ETHNOLOGY   NEW GUINEA

Reed, Stephen Winsor

The making of modern New Guinea.

(Memoirs of the American Philosophical Society, Vol. 18, 1943) Issued in cooperation with the International Secretariat, Institute of Pacific Relations.

GN
1
I 64

ETHNOLOGY   NEW GUINEA

Seligman, C. G.

The Dubu and Steeple-Houses of the Central District of British New Guinea. With 21 figures, plates 65-71

(In Ipek, 1927, pp. 177-192)

GN
1
O 15

ETHNOLOGY-NEW GUINEA (DUTCH)

Thomas, K. H.

Notes on the natives of the Vanimo coast, New Guinea.

(Oceania, Vol. 12, 1941, pp. 163-186)

AS
701
A

ETHNOLOGY   NEW GUINEA   (Papua)

Report on the Australasian, Papuan, and Polynesian races. (1.) New Guinea. Toaripi and Koiari tribes, by...James Chalmers...

(Rept. of the 2nd meeting, Australasian Ass'n for the Adv. of Sci., Melbourne, 1890, pp. 311-323)

GN
671.N5
S 46

ETHNOLOGY   NEW GUINEA

Seligmann, C. G.

The Melanesians of British New Guinea... Cambridge. 1910. R8vo.

GN
Ethn. Pam.
3158

AS
763
B 4

Reading
Room

ETHNOLOGY   NEW GUINEA

Thompson, Laura Maud

Native trade in southeast New Guinea.

(B. P. Bishop Museum, Occ. Papers, Vol. XI, No. 15, 1935, 43 pp.)

G 51
W 17

ETHNOLOGY NEW GUINEA

Thomson, Donald F.

In the head-hunter's country in Dutch New Guinea. The conquest of the swamps of the Obaa-Wildeman Rivers.

(Walkabout, 17(1):10-18, 1951)

GN 662
V87

ETHNOLOGY - NEW GUINEA

Vogel-Hamburg, Hans

Eine Forschungsreise im Bismarck-Archipel... R8vo.

Hamburg, Friederichsen, 1911. (Hamburgische wissenschaftliche Stiftung)

GN 671.N5
W 723

ETHNOLOGY NEW GUINEA

Williams, F. E.

Papuans of the Trans-Fly. Oxford. Clarendon Press. 1936. 8vo. xxxvi + 452 pp., 19 pl., 36 figs.

G 7
R 91

ETHNOLOGY NEW GUINEA

Thomson, Donald F.

War-time exploration in Dutch New Guinea.

(The Geographical Journal, Vol. 119(1):1-16, 1953)

GN 4
C 33

ETHNOLOGY NEW GUINEA

Watson, James B.

A New Guinea "opening man".
IN

Casagrande, Joseph B. editor
In the company of man. pp. 127-174.
Harper and Bros. New York. 1960. R8vo.

[the Agarabi, Highlands of New Guinea]

G 3 A

ETHNOLOGY NEW GUINEA

Winter, Francis

New Guinea natives who can scarcely walk.... in the Bulletin of the American Geographical Society, Vol.XXXVI, 1904, no.11, pp.691-692.

GN 2.M
H 19-m

ETHNOLOGY NEW GUINEA

Tischner, Herbert

Eine Ethnographische Sammlung aus dem Ostlichen Zentral-Neuguinea. (Hagen-Gebirge; Wagi-Tal-Ramu)

(Mitt. Mus. f. Volkerkunde in Hamburg, No. 21, 1939)

GN 1
O 15

ETHNOLOGY NEW GUINEA

Wedgewood, Camilla H.

Report on research in Manam Island, Mandated Territory of New Guinea.

(Oceania, Vol. 4, No. 5, 1934, pp. 373-403, pls. 1-3)

AS 182
D ≠

ETHNOLOGY NEW GUINEA

Wirz, Paul

Beiträge zur ethnographie des Papua-Golfes, Britisch-Neuguinea... Leipzig. 1934. 103 pp.

(Abh. und Ber. der Museen für Tierkunde und Völkerkunde zu Dresden, Band XIX, Nr. 2, 1934)

GN 1
O 15

ETHNOLOGY NEW GUINEA

Todd, J. A.

Report on research work in southwest New Britain, Territory of New Guinea.

(Oceania, Vol. 5, No. 1, 1934, pp. 80-101; Vol. 5, No. 2, 1934, pp. 191-213)

GN 635.D9
W 68

ETHNOLOGY NEW GUINEA

Wilken, G. A.

Handleiding voor de vergelijkende Volkenkunde van Nederlandsch-Indië. Leiden. E. J. Brill. 1893. 8vo. 669 pp.

GN 671.N5
W 79

ETHNOLOGY NEW GUINEA

Wirz, Paul

Dämon und Wilde in Neuguinea. Verlag Stuttgart. Strecker und Schröder. 1928. 8vo. XII + 385 + (2) pp.; map.

Ethnology-New Guinea

GN 671.N5
N

Van der Sande, G.A.J.

...Ethnography and anthropology, By G.A.J. Van der Sande.

Leyden, 1907. 390p. 50,pls., 216 text-figures and a map. (Nova Guinea. Resultats de l'expedition scienrifique Neerlandaise a la Nouvelle-Guinee. En 1903...Vol. III)

GN 671.N5
W 61

ETHNOLOGY NEW GUINEA

Whiting, John W. M.

Becoming a Kwoma: teaching and learning in a New Guinea tribe. With a foreward by John Dollard. Published for the Institute of Human Relations, by Yale University Press. New Haven. 1941. R8vo. xix + 266 pp.

GN Ethn. Pam. 3883

ETHNOLOGY NEW GUINEA

Wirz, Paul

Die E a, ein Beitrag zur Ethnographie eines Stammes im nordöstlichen zentralen Neuguinea.

(Zeit. f. Ethnologie, 77(1):7-56, 1952)

G 1
AS

ETHNOLOGY NEW GUINEA

Vial, Leigh G.

Knights of the stone age. (In New Guinea)

(Asia, July, 1939, p. 408-412)

GN 1
O 15

ETHNOLOGY NEW GUINEA (Papua)

Williams, F. E.

Mission influence amongst the Keveri of south-east Papua.

(Oceania, Vol. 15, No. 2, pp. 89-141, 1944)

GN 2.I
Ha

ETHNOLOGY NEW GUINEA (Dutch)

Wirz, P.

Die Marind-anim von Hollandisch-Neu-Guinea Bd. I-II.

(Hamburgische Univ., Abd. aus dem Gebiet der Auslandskunde, Bd. 10, 16, 1922,1925)

GN 671.N5
V 63

ETHNOLOGY NEW GUINEA

Vicedom, Georg F.

Die Mbowamb: die Kultur der Hagenberg-Stämme im östlichen Zentral-Neuguinea. Bde. 1-3 1943-1948. 4to. Hamburg.

reviewed by A. Capell IN Oceania, 20:166-8, 1949.

GN 2.I
A 4

ETHNOLOGY NEW GUINEA

Williams, F. E.

Plant-emblems among the Orokaiva (New Guinea)

(Journ. Roy. Anthrop. Inst. of Great Britain and Ireland, Vol. 55, 1925, pp. 405-424). illus.

ETHNOLOGY NEW GUINEA

Wirz, P.

Die Marind-Anim von Hollandisch-Sud-Neu-Guinea. vols. 1-2, 1922-1925.

UH

G
7
R 91

ETHNOLOGY   NEW GUINEA

Wollaston, A. F. R.

   An expedition to Dutch New Guinea. (1912-1913).

   (Geographical Journal, Vol. 43, 1914, pp. 248-273)

GN
Ethn.Pam.
3226

ETHNOLOGY   NEW HEBRIDES

de la Rüe, Edgar Aubert

   Les populations des Nouvelles-Hébrides et leur civilisation.

   (La Terre et la Vie, Année 7, 1937, pp. 129-158)

GN
671.N 55
G 94

ETHNOLOGY   NEW HEBRIDES

Guiart, Jean

   Grands et petits hommes de la montagne, Espiritu Santo (Nouvelles-Hébrides). Office de la Recherche Scientifique et Technique Outre-Mer. Institut Francais d'Océanie. (New Caledonia) 4to. mimeographed. 218 pp. 1956

Q
115
G 76

ETHNOLOGY   NEW GUINEA   (Dutch)

Wollaston, A. F. R.
Grant, William R. Ogilvie
Reports on the collections...British Ornithologists' Union Expedition and the Wollaston Expedition in Dutch New Guinea, 1910-1913. Vol. I-II. London. 1916.
   Introduction (and narrative of the two expeditions) by A. F. R. Wollaston, Vol. I, pp. 1-22.

QH
1
N 28

ETHNOLOGY   NEW HEBRIDES

Deniker, J.

   Collections ethnographiques rapportées de Mélanésie par le Dr. François.

   (Le Naturaliste, Vol. 6, 1891, pp. 227-229; 243-247)

GN
2.S
O 15-p

ETHNOLOGY - NEW HEBRIDES

Guiart, Jean

   Un siècle et demi de contacts culturels à Tanna, Nouvelles Hébrides.

   (Publications de la Soc. des Océanistes, No. 5, 1956)

GN
Ethn.Pam.
3226

ETHNOLOGY   NEW HEBRIDES

Aubert de la Rüe, Edgar

   Les populations des Nouvelles-Hébrides et leur civilisation.

   (La Terre et la Vie, Année 7, 1937, pp. 129-158)

GN
Pam
2457

ETHNOLOGY - NEW HEBRIDES

Edge-Partington, J.

   Note on a shell adze from Ambrym Island, New Hebrides.

   (Journ.Roy.Anthrop.Inst.Great Britain and Ireland, Vol. 30, p. 49, 1900).

GN
Ethn.Pam.
4108

ETHNOLOGY   NEW HEBRIDES

Guiart, Jean

   Unite culturelle et variations locales dans le centre nord des Nouvelles-Hebrides.

   (Jour. Soc. des Oceanistes, 12:217-225, 1956)

QH
198.NH
B 16

ETHNOLOGY   NEW HEBRIDES

Baker, John R.

   Man and animals in the New Hebrides. George Routledge and Sons, Ltd. London. 1929. 8vo. xiv + 200 pp.

AS
719
A

ETHNOLOGY   NEW HEBRIDES

Etheridge, R.

   Additions to the ethnological collections, chiefly from the New Hebrides. (In Austn. Mus. Rec. XI. pp 189-203. pls. xxxii-xxxix. 1916-1917.

GN
Ethn.
Pam.
3854

ETHNOLOGY   NEW HEBRIDES

Harrisson, Tom H.

   Living in Espiritu Santo. [Oxford University New Hebrides Expedition, 1933-1934]

   (Geographical Journal, 88(3):243-261, 1936)

   [map of the island]

GN
1
O 15

ETHNOLOGY   NEW HEBRIDES

Corlette, Ewan A. C.

   Notes on the natives of the New Hebrides.

   (Oceania, Vol. 5, 1935, pp. 474-487; Vol. 6, 1935, pp. 48-65)

AM
Mus. Pam.
-123

ETHNOLOGY   NEW HEBRIDES

   Führer durch das Museum für Völkerkunde, Basel. Die Neuen Hebriden und Santa Cruz-Inseln.

   (Buchdruckerei G. Krebs, Basel, 1929. 36 pp.)

G
7
R 91

ETHNOLOGY   NEW HEBRIDES

Harrisson, T. H.

   Living with the people of Malekula.

   (The Geographical Journal, vol.88, no.2, 1936, pp.97-127) also pp. 243-261, 332-341

GN
671.N55
D 27

ETHNOLOGY   NEW HEBRIDES

Deacon, A. B.

   Malekula, a vanishing people in the New Hebrides. Edited by Camilla H. Wedgwood. With a preface by A. C. Haddon. London. 1934. 8vo.

AS
701
A

ETHNOLOGY NEW HEBRIDES

Gray, William

   Some notes on the Tannese.

   (Aust. Ass'n for the Adv. of Sci., 4th metting, 1892, pp. 645-680)

   (districts, religion, circumcision, kava, war, a song, calendar, winds, navigation, terms of relationship).

G
7
R 91

ETHNOLOGY   NEW HEBRIDES

Harrisson, T. H.

   The New Hebrides people and culture.

   (Geographical Journal, Vol.88, 1936, pp. 332-341)

GN
2.1
A-4

ETHNOLOGY   NEW HEBRIDES

Deacon, A. Bernard

   Notes on some islands of the New Hebrides. (Edited by Camilla H. Wedgwood).

   (Journ. R. Anthrop. Inst. of Great Britain and Ireland, Vol. 59, 1929, pp. 461-515)

GN
1
Ar 3

ETHNOLOGY   NEW HEBRIDES

Gray, William

   Some notes on the Tannese. An abstract with notes and comparisons by Sidney H. Ray.

   (Archiv fur Ethnogr., Bd. 7, 1894, pp. 227-241, pl. 21)

DU
760
H 32

ETHNOLOGY   NEW HEBRIDES

Harrisson, Tom

   Savage civilisation. London. Victor Gollancz Ltd. 8vo. 461 pp., 38 pl., 35 figs. 1937.

GN
671.N55
H92

ETHNOLOGY - NEW HEBRIDES

Humphreys, C. B.

The southern New Hebrides, an ethnological record.

Cambridge, Univ. Press, 1926. 207 p.

AS
701
A

ETHNOLOGY NEW HEBRIDES

Leggatt, T. Watt

Malekula, New Hebrides.

(Austr. Ass'n for the Adv. of Sci., 4th meeting, 1892, pp. 697-708)

GN
Ethn.Pam.
3534

ETHNOLOGY NEW HEBRIDES

Speiser, Felix

Neu-Caledonien, die südlichen Neuen Hebriden und Polynesien.

(Verhandlungen Naturforschenden Gesell. Basel, Bd. 57:1-24, 1946)

GN
2.I
A

ETHNOLOGY NEW HEBRIDES

Inglis, John

Report of a missionary tour in the New Hebrides.

(Journ. Ethnol. Soc. of London, Vol. 3, 1854, pp. 53-85)

AS
701
A

ETHNOLOGY NEW HEBRIDES

Macdonald, D.

Efate, New Hebrides.

(Australian Ass'n for the Adv. of Sci., 4th meeting, 1892, pp. 720-735)

GN
671.N55
S 74

ETHNOLOGY NEW HEBRIDES

Speiser, Felix

Südsee- urwald Kannibalen, Reise eindruck aus den Neuen Hebriden.

Leipzig, Voigtlander, 1913. v + 398 pp.
pls. R8vo.

GN
2.I
A-4

ETHNOLOGY NEW HEBRIDES

Jennings, John
Notes on the exhibition of an ethnological collection from Santa Cruz and the New Hebrides.

(Journ. Anthrop. Inst. of Great Britain and Ireland, N. S. Vol. 1, 1898-9, pp. 164-165)

GN
662
M 27

ETHNOLOGY NEW HEBRIDES

Mander, Linden A.

Some dependent peoples of the South Pacific. Issued under the auspices of the International Secretariat, Institute of Pacific Relations. The MacMillan Co. New York. 1954. 8vo. xix + 535 pp.

GN
1
An

ETHNOLOGY NEW HEBRIDES

Suas, P. J. Bt.

Notes ethnographiques sur les indigènes des Nouvelles Hébrides.

(Anthropos. Bd.9. 1914. pp.241-260, 760-773)

G
3
N 27

ETHNOLOGY NEW HEBRIDES

Johnson, Irving

South Seas' incredible land divers. By Irving and Electa Johnson.

(The National Geographic Magazine, Vol. CVII(1):77-92, 1955)

DU
850
M 99

ETHNOLOGY NEW HEBRIDES

Mytinger, Caroline

Headhunting in the Solomon Islands around the Coral Sea. Illustrated. New York. Macmillan Co. 1942. 8vo ix + 416 pp.

GN
671.N 55
T 61

ETHNOLOGY NEW HEBRIDES

Titayna

Chez les Mangeurs d'Hommes (Nouvelles-Hébrides), par Titayna, Antoine, A. P. et Lugeon, R. Paris. Editions Duchartre. 1931c. 57 pp. 80 plates. 4to.

AS
701
A

ETHNOLOGY NEW HEBRIDES

Lawrie, J.

Aneityum, New Hebrides.

(Austr. Ass'n for the Adv. of Sci., 4th meeting, 1892, pp. 708-717)

GN
2.I
A-4

ETHNOLOGY NEW HEBRIDES

Somerville, Boyle T.

Notes on some islands of the New Hebrides.

(Journ. Anthrop. Inst. of Great Britain and Ireland, Vol. 23, 1893-4, pp. 2-21, pls. 1,2)

GN
2.S
M 26

ETHNOLOGY NEW HEBRIDES

Webb, A. S.

The people of Aoba, New Hebrides.

(Mankind, Vol. 2, 1937, pp. 73-80)

G
7
R 91

ETHNOLOGY NEW HEBRIDES

Layard, John W.

Atchin twenty years ago.

(Geographical Jrl., vol.88, 1936, pp.342-351)

GN
671.N55
S 74

ETHNOLOGY NEW HEBRIDES

Speiser, Felix

Ethnographische materialien aus den Neuen Hebriden und den Banks-inseln...Mit 1610 abb. auf 109 tafeln und mit 1 karte. Berlin, Kreidel, 1923. vii + 457 pp. pls. 4to.

GN
Ethn.Pam.
2712

GN
1
A An

IRELAND
ETHNOLOGY NEW MECKLENBURG

Abel, P.

Knabenspiele auf Neu-Mecklenburg (Sudsee)

(Anthropos. Bd.I. 1906. pp.818-823)

GN
671.N55
L 41

ETHNOLOGY NEW HEBRIDES

Layard, John

Stone men of Malekula: Vao. London. 1942. Chatto and Windus. R8vo. xxiii + 816 pp.

GN
1
Z

ETHNOLOGY NEW HEBRIDES

Speiser, Felix

Forschungsreisen in den Neuen Hebriden, 1910-1912.

(Zeitschrift f. Ethnologie, 46:456-465, 1914)

GN
2.I
A-m

ETHNOLOGY NEW IRELAND

Braunholtz, H. J.

An Ancestral Figure from New Ireland.

(In Man, Vol. 27, p. [217]-[219], 1 plate 1927)

GN
671.N5
C 53

ETHNOLOGY   NEW IRELAND

Chinnery, E. W. Pearson

Studies of the Native Population of the East Coast of New Ireland.

(Anthropological Report of the Territory of New Guinea, No. 6, ND)

GN
1
O 15

ETHNOLOGY   NEW IRELAND

Powdermaker, Hortense

Report on research in New Ireland.

(Oceania, Vol. 1, 1930-1931, pp. 355-365)

GN
671.N56
F 95

ETHNOLOGY - NEW ZEALAND

Fuhrmann, Ernst

Neu-Seeland. Kultur der Maori und ihr Zusammenhang mit Indien und dem Weiteren Westen. 36 Bilder auf Tafeln. Friederichssegen. Folkwang-Auriga Verlag. 1931. 112 pp. 36 plates. 4to.

(Kulturen der Erde. Band 33).

GN
2.S
M 26

ETHNOLOGY   NEW ZEALAND

Duff, Roger S.

The evolution of native culture in New Zealand.

(Mankind, Vol. 3:313-322, 1947)

GN
671.B5
S 82

ETHNOLOGY   NEW XXXXXXXXXXX

Stephan, Emil

Neu-Mecklenburg (Bismarck-Archipel): Die Küste von Umuddu bis Kap St. Georg. Forschungsergebnisse bei den Vermessungsfahrten von S.M.S.Möwe im jahre 1904. Aus dem Königlichen Museum für Volkerdunde zu Berlin mit Unterstützung des Reichs-Marine-Amtes. Herausgegeben von Dr. Emil Stephan und Dr. Fritz Graebner... Berlin. Reimer. 1907. R8vo.

GN
Pam
2472

ETHNOLOGY - NEW ZEALAND

Herz, Max

Neu-Seelands Erschliessung.   From Berliner Tageblatt, n. 632, 1903.

AS
142
V

ETHNOLOGY   NEW IRELAND

Finsch, Otto

Ethnologische Erfahrungen und Belegstücke aus der Südsee...

(Annalen K. K. Naturhist. Mus., Wien, Bd. 3:83-160, 1888; Bd. 8:397-400, 1893)

GN
4
N

Ethnology-New South Wales

New South Wales. *Geological survey.*
... Memoirs ... Ethnological series, no. 1-
Sydney, 1899-

v. plates, map. 31 x 25ᶜᵐ.

At head of title of no. 1—   Department of mines and agriculture. E. F. Pittman, government geologist.

1. Ethnology—New South Wales.

Library, U. S. Geol.   survey   G S 7-954

DU
406
M 36

ETHNOLOGY   NEW ZEALAND

Marsden, Samuel

The Letters and Journals of Samuel Marsden, 1765-1838. Edited by John Rawson Elder. Dunedin. Coulls Somerville Wilkie, Ltd. 580 pp. 8vo. 1932

GN
1
O 15

ETHNOLOGY   NEW IRELAND

Groves, W. C.

Report on field work in New Ireland.

(Oceania, Vol. 3, 1933, pp. 323-361, pls. 1-4)

GN
Ethn.Pam
2846

ETHNOLOGY - NEW SOUTH WALES

Towle,C.C.

Certain Stone Implements of the Scraper Family - Found Along the Coast of New South Wales. A brief enquiry concerning the so-called "Chipped Back Knife."

16 pp., 1930, 8vo   Privately printed

GN
671.N56
P 76

ETHNOLOGY   NEW ZEALAND

Polack, J. S.

Manners and customs of the New Zealanders; with notes corroborative of their habits, usages, etc., and remarks to intending emigrants, with numerous cuts drawn on wood... 2 volumes. London. James Madden. 1840. 8vo. pp.xxxiv + 288; xviii + 304 pp.

GN
1
An

IRELAND
ETHNOLOGY   NEW MXXXXXXXXXXX

Peekel, P. G.

Die Ahnenbilder von Nord-Neu-Mecklenburg.

(In Anthropos, Bd. 21, Nos. 5-6, 1926, pp. 806-825, and Bd. 22 Nos. 1-2, 1927, pp. 16-45)

GN
671.N56
B 12

ETHNOLOGY   NEW ZEALAND

Bachmann, Kurt Wilhelm

Die Besiedlung des alten Neuseeland. Eine anthropogeographische Studie. (mit 7 Skizzen...) Leipzig. Druckerei der Werkgemeinschaft. 1931. (7) + 111 pp. 8vo.

(Studien zur Volkerkunde, Band 4)

GN
671.N56
S 65

ETHNOLOGY   NEW ZEALAND

Smith, S. Percy

The Peopling of the North; Notes on the ancient Maori history of the Northern Peninsula and sketches of the history of the Ngati-Whatua Tribe of Kaipara, New Zealand: "Horu-Hapainga."

(Journal Polynesian Society. Vol. VI, 1896, Supplement, pp. 1-108. 8vo.)

GN
1
An

ETHNOLOGY   NEW IRELAND

Peekel, P. G.

Religiöse Tänze auf Neu-Irland (Neu-Mecklenburg).

(In Anthropos, Bd. XXVI, Heft 3/4, 1931, pp. 513-532)

GN
671.N56
B 36

ETHNOLOGY   NEW ZEALAND

Beattie, Herries

Our southernmost Maoris; their habitat; nature notes; problems and perplexities...antiquity of man in New Zealand. Otago Daily Times and Witness Newspapers Co., Ltd. Otago. 1954. sm8vo. 160 pp.

GN
2.S
Po

ETHNOLOGY   NEW ZEALAND

Teviotdale, David

The Material Culture of the Moa-Hunters in Murihiku.

(Journal of the Polynesian Society, Vol. 41, pp. 81-120, 1932)

GN
671.N 41
P 88

ETHNOLOGY   NEW IRELAND

Powdermaker, Hortense

Life in Lesu: The Study of a Melanesian Society in New Ireland.   Foreword by Clark Wissler.   New York. W. W. Norton & Company,Inc. 1933. 352 pp. 8vo.

AS
750
A 89

ETHNOLOGY   NEW ZEALAND

Fisher, V. F.

Maori decorated sinkers.

(Records of the Auckland Institute and Museum, Vol. 1, No. 3, 1932, pp. 163-167, plates 29-30)

Q
115
W 95

locked case

ETHNOLOGY   NEW ZEALAND

Wüllerstorf-Urbair, Bernhard

Reise der Oesterreichischen Fregatte Novara um die Erde...1857-1859. (Anthropologischer Theil, III, pp. 46-71. Wien, 1868). 4to. by Friedrich Müller.

GN
630.M3
C 68

ETHNOLOGY - NIAS

Cole, F.C.

    The peoples of Malaysia.   D. Van Nostrand
Company, Inc.   Toronto, New York...   8vo.
1945c   xiv + 354 pp.

GN
671.S 9
K 64

ETHNOLOGY NIAS

Kleiweg de Zwaan, J. P.

    Die Insel Nias bei Sumatra. Martinus Nijhof
Haag. R8vo.   1913-1915
    I: Untersuchungen
    II: Anthropologische Untersuchungen
    III: Kraniologische Untersuchungen

DS
491.A5
B 71

ETHNOLOGY NICOBAR ISLANDS

Bonington, M. C. C.

    The Andaman and Nicobar Islands. Census of
India, 1931, Volume II. Calcutta, 1932.
Government of India, Central Publication Branch.
folio, 119 pp.

GN
Ethn.
Pam.
4295

ETHNOLOGY NISSAN

Schlaginhaufen, Otto

    Uber Eingeborene des melanesischen Atolls
Nissan.

    (Reprint, Bull. Schweizerischen Gesell. f.
Anthropolgie und Ethnologie, Bern, 37 Jahrg.
1960/61, pp. 32-45)

GN
671.N73
L 82

AS
763
B-b

Reading
Room

ETHNOLOGY NIUE

Loeb, Edwin M.

    History and traditions of Niue. Honolulu.
1926. R8vo. 225 pp.

    (Bernice P. Bishop Museum, Bulletin 32)

GN
2.M
C 89

ETHNOLOGY NIUE

Miles, G. P. L.

    Notes on the material culture of Niue.

    (Ethnologia Cranmorensis, 3, 1938, pp. 19-
22)

GN
2.I
P 76

&

GN Pam.
333
Incomp.
Copy.

ETHNOLOGY NIUE

Smith, S. Percy

    Niue Island and its people.

    (Jour. Poly. Soc. XI, pp. 80-106, 163-178,
195-218; XII, pp. 1-31, 85-119, 1902-03)

GN
2.1
A-4

ETHNOLOGY NIUE

Thomson, Basil

    Note upon the natives of Savage Island, or
Niue.

    (Journ. Anthrop. Inst. of Great Britain and
Ireland, Vol. 31, 1901, pp. 137-145)

GN
550
G 57

ETHNOLOGY - NORTH AMERICA

Goddard, Pliny Earle

    Indians of Northwest Coast. New York. 1924.

    (American Museum of Nat. Hist., Handbook Ser.
2 copies No. 10.)

GN
2.1
C 14

ETHNOLOGY NORTH AMERICA

Kroeber, A. L.
Cultural and natural areas of native North
America.

    (University of California, Pubs. in Am.
Arch. and Ethnology, Vol. 38, 1939)

AS
36
S1

ETHNOLOGY - NORTH AMERICA

Morgan, Lewis Henry, 1818-1881.
    Suggestions relative to an ethnological map of North
America, 36 by 44 inches. By Lewis H. Morgan ...
    (*In* Smithsonian institution. Annual report. 1861. Washington, 1862.
23¹ᵐ. p. 397-398)

    1. Ethnology—North America.

                                              S 15-122
Library of Congress   Q11.S66 1861
Library, Smithsonian   Institution

AS
36
S1

ETHNOLOGY-NORTH AMERICA

Much, Matthäus, 1832-1909.
    Ancient history of North America. Communication to
the Anthropological society of Vienna, by Dr. M. Much.
    (*In* Smithsonian institution. Annual report. 1871. Washington, 1873.
23¹ᵐ. p. 425-433)
    "Translated ... by Professor C. F. Kroeh."

    1. North America—Antiq. 2. Ethnology—North America.   I. Kroeh,
Charles Frederick, 1846-   tr.

                                              S 15-329
Library of Congress   Q11.S66 1871
Library, Smithsonian   Institution

GN
550
S

ETHNOLOGY NORTH AMERICA

U. S. *Bureau of American ethnology.*
    Annual report of the Bureau of American ethnology to
the secretary of the Smithsonian institution. 1st-
1879/80-19
    Washington, Govt. print. off., 1881-19
    v.   illus., plates (part fold., part col.) ports., maps (part fold.)
plans (part fold.)   29½ᵐ.
    Some of the folded plates, maps and plans are in pockets.
    Administrative report and accompanying papers.
    Report year ends June 30.
    Director, 1879-1902: J. W. Powell: chief, 1902-1909: W. H. Holmes;
ethnologist-in-charge, 1910-1918: F. W. Hodge; 1918-   J. W. Fewkes.
    Reports for 1879/80-1893/94 have title: First-fifteenth annual report
of the Bureau of ethnology.
    1. Ethnology—America.   2. Indians.   3. America — Antiq.
I. Powell, John Wesley,   1834-1902.   II. Holmes, William
Henry, 1846-   III.   Hodge, Frederick Webb, 1864-
IV. Fewkes, Jesse Walter,   1850-
    Library of Congress   E51.U55
                             [s20i3]   7—38073

E
58
J 54

ETHNOLOGY - NORTH AMERICA

Wissler, Clark

    Ethnological Diversity in America and Its
Significance.

Jenness, Diamond

    The American Aborigines...pp. 165-216.

GN
2.8
P 76

ETHNOLOGY NUKUMANU

Hogbin, H. Ian

    "Polynesian" colonies in Melanesia.

    (Journal of the Polynesian Society, Vol. 49,
1940, pp. 199-220)

GN
663
T 44

ETHNOLOGY NUKUMANU

Sarfert, E.

    Luangiua und Nukumanu, von E. Sarfert und
H. Damm.

Thilenius, G.
    Ergebnisse der Südsee Expedition, 1908-1910.
II. Ethnographie: B. Mikronesien, Bd. 12, 1929,
1931.

GN
663
T 44

GN 663
T 44 tr

ETHNOLOGY NUKUORO

Eilers, Anneliese

Thilenius, G. (editor)
    Ergebnisse der Südsee Expedition, 1908-1910.
II. Ethnographie: B. Mikronesien, Bd. 8, 1934.
Inseln um Ponape.

    translation of excerpts, Kapingamarangi,
Nukuoro.

DU
563
K 95

DU563
K95 tr

ETHNOLOGY NUKUORO

Kubary, Johann S.

    Beitrag zur Kenntniss der Nukuoro- oder Mon-
teverde-Inseln. (Karolinen)

    (Mitt. der Geogr. Gesell. Hamburg, Bd. 16:71-
138, 1900)

    also translation, typed, 54 pp.

GN
635.O 4
G 54

ETHNOLOGY OKINAWA

Glacken, Clarence J.

    The Great Loochoo; a study of Okinawan life.
University of California Press. Berkeley and
Los Angeles. 1955. 8vo. xvi + 324 pp. illus-
trated

GN
1
Z

ETHNOLOGY ONGTONG JAVA

Finsch, Otto

    Bemerkungen uber einige Eingeborne des Atoll
Ongtong Java (Njua) [1880]

    (Zeit. f. Ethnol., 13, 1881:110-114)

ETHNOLOGY ONGTONG JAVA

Hogbin, H. Ian

    Coconuts and coral islands.

    (National Geographic Magazine, Vol. 65, 1934,
pp. 265-298)

GN Ethn.Pam. 2890	ÓNGTONG JAVA ETHNOLOGY - XXXXXXXXXXXX Hogbin, H. Ian, Education at Ongtong Java, Solomon Islands (American Anthropologist, vol. 33, no. 4.) pp. 601-614. 1931	DU B 21	ETHNOLOGY PACIFIC Banks, Sir Joseph Journal...during Captain Cook's first voyage ...1768-71...edited by Sir Joseph D. Hooker. London. 1896. 8vo. pp. 127-178.	GN Ethn.Pam. 2899 2 copies	ETHNOLOGY - PACIFIC Camps, Juan Comas Contribución al estudio antropológico de Oceanía. (Memorias Sociedad Española de Antropológico Etnografía y Prehistoria - Tomo X, 1931, pp.263- 283)
GN 2.S P 76	ÓNGTONG JAVA ETHNOLOGY XXXXXXXXXXXX Hogbin, H. Ian "Polynesian" colonies in Melanesia. (Journal of the Polynesian Society, Vol. 49, 1940, pp. 199-220)	GN 662 B 32	ETHNOLOGY PACIFIC Bastian, Adolph Inselgruppen in Oceanien. Reiseergebnisse und Studien von A. Bastian. Berlin. 1883. 8vo.	Q 116 D 89	ETHNOLOGY PACIFIC Dumoutier, Pierre Marie Alexandre Dumont d'Urville, Jules Sébastien César Voyage au Pôle Sud et dans l'Océanie sur les corvettes l'Astrolabe et la Zélée...Anthropologie Texte (in 1 tome), 1854, and Atlas, 1842-47.
GN Ethn.Pam. 2891	ÓNGTONG JAVA ETHNOLOGY XXXXXXXXXXXX Hogbin, H. Ian Tribal ceremonies at Ongtong Java (Solomon Islands). (Journal of the Royal Anthropological In- stitute, Vol. 61, 1931, pp. 27-55)	GN Ethn.Pam. 5047 GN 670 B 33	ETHNOLOGY PACIFIC Battaglia, Raffaello Le Razze e le Civiltà dell' Oceania. (Estratto dal Vol. III dell'opera "Le Razze e i Popoli della Terra, di Renato Biasutti") Torino. 1940. R8vo. 192 pp.	AP 2 N 4	ETHNOLOGY PACIFIC Early Knowledge of Iron in the Pacific. (Nature, Vol. 129, No. 3247, p. 124)
GN 1 I 61	ÓNGTONG JAVA ETHNOLOGY XXXXXXXXXXXX Parkinson, R. Zur Ethnographie der Ongtong Java und Tasman Inseln. (Archif f. Ethnographie, X, 1897, pp. 104- 118, 137-151; Nachträge, Bd. XI, 1898, p. 194- 209) and figures on pp. 242, 243	GN Ethn.Pam. 2829	ETHNOLOGY PACIFIC Breton, André Collection André Breton et Paul Eluard. Sculptures d'Afrique, d'Amérique, d'Océanie. Paris. 1931. 51 pp. XXIV plates.	GN 662 E 23	ETHNOLOGY PACIFIC Edge-Partington, James An album of the weapons, tools, ornaments, articles of dress, etc. of the natives of the Pacific Islands; drawn and described from ex- amples in public and private collections in Eng- land...Manchester. Ser. 1-Ser. 2 (in boxes). 1890;1895. Ob4to. Ser. 3...drawn and described from examples...in Australasia. 1898. Ob4to.
GN 2.1 A-M	ÓNGTONG JAVA ETHNOLOGY XXXXXXXXXXXX Woodford, C. M. Notes on Leueneuwa, or Lord Howe's Group. (Man, vol. 6, 1906, No. 89, pp. 133-135, figs. 1,2)	GN Ethn.Pam. 2917	ETHNOLOGY-PACIFIC Brown, J. Macmillan Océanie et côte d'Amerique. (Problémes polynésiens.) translated into French by Vernier. (Bulletin nº 3 de la Société d'Etudes Oceaniennes, 1918, pp. 114-126).	GN Ethn.Pam. 3422	ETHNOLOGY PACIFIC Emory, Kenneth P. Native lore for castaways in the South Seas. Assembled from material in the collection of the Bernice P. Bishop Museum... Honolulu Academy of Arts. Honolulu. 1943. 18 pp., mimeo- graphed.
GN Ethn.Pam. 3440	ETHNOLOGY PACIFIC Archey, Gilbert South Sea folk. Handbook of Maori and Oceanic ethnology. 1937. (Auckland?) 8vo. 59 pp., 11 pl.	GN 6 B 97	ETHNOLOGY PACIFIC Buschan, Georg editor Illustrierte Völkerkunde. Unter Mitwirkung von U. Buhan and others. Stuttgart. no date. [Australien und Oceanien, by Georg Buschan, pp. 164-214]	AM 101 F 45-n	ETHNOLOGY PACIFIC Force, Roland W. Discovery of the Pacific Isles... (titles of these articles vary) (Chicago Nat. Hist. Mus. Bull. 31(1-5), 1960)
GN Ethn.Pam. 2903	ETHNOLOGY PACIFIC Australian Aborigines and South Sea Island- ers. Implements, Weapons, and Curios. 36 pp. 8vo. (Adv. of sale, Tyrrell's Museum, Sydney, 1929)	DU 12 C 18 locked case	ETHNOLOGY PACIFIC Campbell, John Maritime discovery and Christian missions, considered in their mutual relations... London. 1840. 8vo. pp. 436-512.	DU 12 F 74 locked case	ETHNOLOGY PACIFIC Forster, J. R. Observations made during a voyage round the world, on physical geography, natural history, and ethic philosophy... London. 1778. 4to. pp. 285-609.

GN
Eth.Pam.
3213

ETHNOLOGY PACIFIC

Friederici, Georg

Veränderungen in der Südseekultur seit der
Zeit Mendañas.

(Petermanns Mitteilungen, Jahrg. 77, 1931,
pp. 138-143)

GN
Ethn.Pam.
2816

ETHNOLOGY PACIFIC

Hocart, A. M.

Notes on Previous Articles: India and the
Pacific.
Sect. G:Archaeology
(Ceylon Journal of Science...Vol. 1, Part 4,
1925, pp. 175-178)

GN
320
L 96

ETHNOLOGY PACIFIC

Luschan, Felix von

Zusammenhänge und Konvergenz. Wien. 1918.
117 pp. Mit 71 abbildungen im text.

(Sonderabdruck aus Band XXXXVIII (der dritter
Folge Band XVIII) der Mitteilungen der Anthropologischen Gesellschaft in Wien, 1918).

GN
2.S
F 47

ETHNOLOGY PACIFIC

Gifford, A. E.

Anthropology in Oceania.

(Transactions of the Fiji Society of Science
and Industry, Vol. 3(3):143-144, 1947)

GN
671.S6
I 94

ETHNOLOGY PACIFIC

Ivens, Walter G.

Melanesians of the South-East Solomon Islands.
London, Kegan Paul, 1927. 529p.

GN
662
M 13

ETHNOLOGY PACIFIC

MacDonald, D.

Oceania: linguistic and anthropological, by
the Rev. D. MacDonald...Melbourne. 1889. 8vo.

GN
Eth.
Pam.
2860

ETHNOLOGY - PACIFIC

Gudger, E. W.

Wooden Hooks Used for Catching Sharks and
Ruvettus in the South Seas; A Study of their
Variation and Distribution.

(From Anthropological Papers of the American
Museum of Natural History, Vol. XXVIII, Part III
Pages 212-343). 1927

DU
12
J 94
looked
case

ETHNOLOGY PACIFIC

Jukes, J. B.

Narrative of the surveying voyage of H.M.S.
Fly...in Torres Strait, New Guinea, and other
islands of the eastern archipelago, during...
1842-1846... 2 vols. London. 1847. 8vo.
Vol. 2, pp. 232-252.

DU
Pac.Pam.
721

ETHNOLOGY PACIFIC

Michel, E.

La tentative de colonisation belge aux
Nouvelles Hebrides et aux Iles Fidji et Salomon
(Mission Michel-Eloin, 1861)

(K. Belgisch Koloniaal Instituut, Bulletijn
der Zittingen, 19 (1):137-159, 1948)

GN
1
B

ETHNOLOGY PACIFIC

Haeckel, Josef

Männerhauser und Festplatzanlagen in Ozean-
ine und im östlichen Nordamerika.

(Baessler Archiv, Bd. 23, Heft 1, 1940, p.
8-18)

GN
662
K 26

ETHNOLOGY PACIFIC

Keesing, Felix M.

Native peoples of the Pacific world.
The Macmillan Company, New York. 1945. 8vo.
xv + 144 pp.

GN
Ethn.
Pam.
4077

ETHNOLOGY PACIFIC

Munsing, Stefan P. editor ...

Kunst der Südsee; Ausstellung des Staat-
liches Museums für Völkerkunde München. Text
von Andreas Lommel; fotos von Herbert List.
Prestel-Verlag München 1952 R8vo. 47 pp.

[Includes Katalog of the Pacific collections
in the State museums of Ethnology in Munich]

GN
Ethn.Pam
2812

ETHNOLOGY PACIFIC

Hambruch, Paul

Einführung in die Abteilung Südsee.
(Geschichte, Lebensraum, Umwelt und Bevölkerung)

Hamburgisches Museum für Völkerkunde. Hamburg. Friederichsen, de Gruyter & Co. m.b.H.
1931. 58 pp. 12mo

GN
Ethn.Pam.
3474

ETHNOLOGY PACIFIC

Keesing, Felix M.

Native peoples of the Pacific world.
Washington. The Infantry Journal. 1945. sm8vo.
142 pp.

GN
32
N 93

ETHNOLOGY PACIFIC

Noury, M. C.

Album Polynesien de M. C. Noury, capitaine
de vaisseau. Nantes. 1861. 15pls. 4to.

DU
1
I 59

ETHNOLOGY PACIFIC

Handy, E. S. Craighill

The Insular Pacific

(Pacific Affairs, Vol. V, pp. 487-496, 1932)

GN
Ethn.Pam.
3524

ETHNOLOGY PACIFIC

Kennedy, Raymond

The islands and peoples of the South Seas
and their cultures. Jayne Memorial Lectures, Am.
Phil. Soc., March 8 and 15, 1944, Philadelphia,
1945.

GN
671.N56
B 64

ETHNOLOGY PACIFIC

Oceanie ethnographic Bulletin.

(Works of the Ethnographic Institute,
N. N. Mikluho-Maklai, Vol. 38, 1957)
[Trudy Institut..]

GN
1
Cey

ETHNOLOGY -- PACIFIC

Hocart, A. M.

India and the Pacific. In Ceylon Journ
Sc. Sect. G. Arch., Vol. I, pp 61 - 84,
175-178, 1925.

AS
36
84

ETHNOLOGY - PACIFIC

Krieger, Herbert W.

Design Areas in Oceania, based on Specimens
in the United States National Museum.

(Proceedings of the United States National
Museum, Vol. 79, Art. 30, 1932).

GN
1
Z 67

ETHNOLOGY PACIFIC

Ozeanistische Forschungen.

(Zeitschrift f. Ethnologie, Bd. 86(2),
1953) [Special issue on the Pacific]

GN
320
P 46 — ETHNOLOGY PACIFIC

Perry, W. J.

The children of the sun:...London. (1923).
Chapter IV.

DU
12
P 11 — ETHNOLOGY - PACIFIC

Sternberg, L.

Ethnology

The Pacific: Russian Scientific Investigations.
pp. 161-188, Leningrad. 1926. R8vo.

GN
662
W 85 — ETHNOLOGY PACIFIC

Wolf, E.

Die Hanseatische Südsee-Expedition im jahre
1909. Reisebericht von Dr. E. Wolf. Mit tafel
1-12, 57 textfiguren und 1 karte. Frankfurt am
Main. 1915. 4to. pp. 111-164.

(Sonderabdruck aus den Abhandlungen der
Senckenbergischen Naturforschenden Gesellschaft
Bd. XXXVI, Heft 2: Wissenschaftliche Ergebnisse
der Hanseatischen Südsee-Expedition 1909).

GN
Ethn.Pam.
2955 — ETHNOLOGY PACIFIC

Plischke, Hans

Die Ethnographische Sammlung der Universi-
tät Göttingen, ihre Geschichte und ihre Bedeutung.
Mit 24 Lichtdrucktafeln. Göttingen. Vandenhoeck
& Ruprecht. 1931. 48 pp. 24 plates.

GN
Ethn.Pam.
3595 — ETHNOLOGY PACIFIC

Taylor, C. R. H.

The Hocart papers in the Turnbull Library.

(Jour. Poly. Soc. 59(3), 1950)

[anthropological, tales and legends, philological, genealogies, drawings, sw Pacific]
4 pages

Q
115
W 95

locked
case — ETHNOLOGY PACIFIC

Wüllerstorf-Urbair, Bernhard

Reise der Österreichischen Fregatte Novara
um die erde in den jahren 1857, 1858, 1859...

Anthropologischer Theil, Dritte Abt.: Ethnographie...Mit X photographirten tafeln une einer
karte...Wein. 1868. 4to. von Friedrich Müller

GN
2.I
A 4 — ETHNOLOGY PACIFIC

Rickard, T. A.

The Knowledge and Use of Iron Among the
South Sea Islanders.

(Journal of the R. Anthropological Inst. of
Great Britain and Ireland, Vol. 62, 1932, pp. 1-
22)

GN
662
T 61 — ETHNOLOGY PACIFIC

Tischner, Herbert

Kulturen der Südsee, einfuhrung in die Völkerkunde Ozeaniens. Hamburgisches Museum f.
Völkerkunde und Vorgeschichte. 1958. R8vo;
150 pp. 24 pl. 1 map.

Z
Biblio-
graphy
Pam.
91 — ETHNOLOGY-PACIFIC-BIBLIOGRAPHY

Brooklyn Museum reference library of art and
ethnology, Oceania and Indonesia. May, 1942
35 mimeographed pages.

GN
2.I
A-m — ETHNOLOGY PACIFIC

Rickard, T. A.

The knowledge and use of iron among the
South Sea Islanders.

(Man, Vol. 32, Feb. 1932, No. 43)

GN
2.S
O 15 — ETHNOLOGY PACIFIC

Toumarkine, D. D.

L'ethnologie océanienne en U.R.S.S.
(Situation actuelle et état des recherches)

(Jour. de la Soc. des Océanistes, Tome
18(18):1-10, 1962)

AM
101
G 57 e
GN
662
G 58 — ETHNOLOGY - PACIFIC - BIBLIOGRAPHY

Schmeltz, J. D. E.

Die ethnographisch-anthropologisch Abtheilung des Museum Godeffroy in Hamburg. Ein Beitrag zur Kunde der Südsee-Völker. By J.D.E.
Schmeltz and R. Krause. Mit 46 Tafeln und einer
ethnologischen Karte des Grossen Oceans. Hamburg.
L. Friedrichsen and Co. 1881. 8vo. xlviii +
687 (6) pp. 46 pl.

GN
Ethn.Pam.
3856 — ETHNOLOGY PACIFIC

Rousseau, Madeleine

L'art Océanien, sa présence. Introduction
de Paul Rivet; Textes de Guillaume Apollinaire et
de Tristan Tzara. Etude présentée par Madeleine
Rousseau. 215 reproductions - 4 cartes. Association Populaire des Amis des Musées. Paris
4to. 138 pp. n.d. Collection "Le Musée
Vivant".

Q
115
U 58

locked
case — ETHNOLOGY PACIFIC

United States Exploring Expedition...1838-
1842, under the command of Charles Wilkes.
Vol. 6: Ethnography and Philology by Horatio Hale
Philadelphia. 1846. 4to.

GN
Ethn.Pam
3489 — ETHNOLOGY PALAU ISLANDS

Fritz, G.

Eine Reise nach Palau, Sonsol, und Tobi.

(Deutsches Kolonialblatt 18: 1907, pp. 659-
668)

DU
12
S 14 — ETHNOLOGY-PACIFIC

St. Johnston, T. R.

The Islanders of the Pacific, or The Children of the Sun. With Maps and 32 pages of
Illustrations. London. T. Fisher Unwin Ltd.
(1921) 8vo. 307 pp.

AM
501
W 37 — ETHNOLOGY PACIFIC

Webster, W. D.

Catalog of ethnographical specimens...on sale
by W. D. Webster. Bicester. 1895-
Vol. 1, no. 1-10
Vol. 2, no. 11-17
Vol. 3, no. 18-23
" ? " 24, 25, 26, 28, 31
XXXXXX18-23 bound separately.

GN
663
T 44 — ETHNOLOGY PALAU

Krämer, Augustin

Palau

Thilenius, G.
Ergebnisse der Südsee Expedition, 1908-1910.
II. Ethnographie: B. Mikronesien, Bd. 3, 1917-29.

GN
2.I
T 89 — ETHNOLOGY PACIFIC

Speiser, Félix

Note à propos des dents de cochon deformées
dans les mers du sud et en Indonésie (1)

(Revista del Instituto de Etnologia, Universidad de Tucumán, Tomo II, 1932, pp. 441-444)

AS
122
V — ETHNOLOGY PACIFIC

Whitmee, S. J.

The ethnology of the Pacific.

(Journal of Trans. of Victoria Institute.
Vol. XIV. 1881. pp. 16-40)

GN
671.C3
K 95 — ETHNOLOGY PALAU ISLANDS

Kubary, J. S.

Ethnographische Beiträge zur Kenntnis des
Karolinen Archipels. Veröffentlicht im Auftrage
der Direktion des Kgl. Museums f. Völkerkunde
zu Berlin. Unter mitwirkung von J.D.E.Schmeltz.
Mit 55 Tafeln. Leiden. C.F.Winter. 1889-95.
R8vo. 306 + (1) pp. 55 tafeln. In 3 Hefte.

AS 182 H

ETHNOLOGY PALAU ISLANDS

Kubary, J(ohann)

Die Palau-Inseln in der Südsee.

(Mus. Godeffroy, Journal, Heft IV, 1873, pp. 179-240)

GN 2.M Dr

ETHNOLOGY PALAU IS.

Meyer, A. B.

Bilderschriften des Ost-indischen Archipels und der Südsee.

(K. Ethnogr. Mus. zu Dresden, Publikation 1, 1881)

GN Ethn. Pam. 4018

ETHNOLOGY PALAU

Plischke, Hans

Uber die Palau-Inseln um 1790.

(Zeit. f. Ethnologie, 80(2):165-169, 1955)

DU 780 W 74

looked case

DU 780 W 74

ETHNOLOGY PALAU ISLANDS

Wilson, Henry

Account of the Pelew Islands...Composed from the journals and communications of Captain Henry Wilson, and some of his officers, who...were there shipwrecked, in the Antelope...by George Keate. Second edition. London. 1788. 4to.
...Third edition. 1789. 4to.
...Fourth edition. 1789. 8vo.

GN 669 B 32

GN Ethn. Pam. 704

ETHNOLOGY PALAU ISLANDS

Bastian, Adolf

Die mikronesischen Colonien aus ethnologische Gesichtspunkten, Ergänzung I. Berlin. 1900. 112 pp.

AS 36 S2

ETHNOLOGY - PALAWAN (ISLAND)

Venturello, Manuel Hugo.

Manners and customs of the Tagbanuas and other tribes of the island of Palawan, Philippines, by Manuel Hugo Venturello ... Tr. from the original Spanish manuscript by Mrs. Edw. Y. Miller.

(*In* Smithsonian institution. Smithsonian miscellaneous collections. Washington, 1907. 24½ᶜᵐ. vol. XLVIII (Quarterly issue, vol. III) p. [514]-558)

Publication 1700.

1. Tagbanuas. 2. Ethnology—Palawan (Island) I. Miller, Mrs. Edward Young, tr.

Library of Congress   Q11.S7 vol. 48   16-11624
—— Copy 2.

GN 2.I P 21

ETHNOLOGY PAPUA

Armstrong, W. E.

Anthropology of South Eastern Division (excluding Woodlark Island), Engineer Group, Bosilai, East Cape, Normandy Island, (South Coast) and of Morima, Fergusson Island. 1: Beliefs and Customs, 2: Language.

(Territory of Papua, Anthropology Report, No. 2, 1922 ?, Part 1, pp. 1-31)

GN 2.I P 21

ETHNOLOGY PAPUA

Armstrong, W. E.

Report on the Suau-Tawala, with Notes by W. M. Strong.

(Territory of Papua, Anthropology, Report No. 1, 1921)

GN 671.N5 B 45

ETHNOLOGY PAPUA

Belshaw, Cyril S.

The great village; the economic and social welfare of Hanuabada, an urban community in Papua. Foreword by Raymond Firth. Routledge and Kegan Paul. London. 8vo. (1957) xviii + 302 pp

---

GN 2.I A-4

ETHNOLOGY PAPUA.

Chalmers, James

Toapiri. (or Motumotu tribe)

(Journ. Anthrop. Inst. of Great Britain and Ireland, Vol. 27, 1897-8, pp. 326-334)

G 51 W 17

ETHNOLOGY PAPUA

Chinnery, E. W. P.

Natives of Paua and New Guinea.

(Walkabout, 18(2):29-35, 1952)

GN 2.I A-4

ETHNOLOGY PAPUA

Guise, R. E.

On the tribes inhabiting the mouth of the Wanigela River, New Guinea.

(Journ. Anthrop. Inst. of Great Britain and Ireland, Vol. 28, 1898-99, pp. 205-219)

G 51 W 17

ETHNOLOGY PAPUA

Hall, Basil

The string-bag people (Papua, New Guinea)

(Walkabout, 22(11):15-16, 1956)

GN Pam 2075

ETHNOLOGY PAPUA

Hedley, C.

Stray notes on Papuan ethnology. From Proc. Linnean Soc. N.S.W. 1897, pt. 2.

GN 671.N5 H 47

ETHNOLOGY PAPUA

Held, G. J.

The Papuans of Waropen.

(K. Instituut voor Taal-, Land- en Volkenkunde, Translation series 2, 1957)

[east coast of Geelvink Bay]

GN 2.S Po

ETHNOLOGY PAPUA

Jenness, D.

Language, Mythology, and Songs of Bwaidoga. By D. Jenness and A. Ballantyne.

(Memoirs of the Polynesian Society, Vol. B), 1928)

GN 4 G 45

ETHNOLOGY PAPUA

Loria, Lamberto

Appunti di psicologia Papuana (Punta S.E. Nuova Guinea Britannica)

(Atti del V Congresso Internas. di Psicologia, April, 1905, 19 pp.)

GN 2.I A-m

ETHNOLOGY PAPUA

Lyons, A. P.

A Sacrificial Altar- Papua.

(In Man:1927,np. [15])

GN 2.I A-M

ETHNOLOGY PAPUA

Murray, J.H.P.

The people and language between the Fly and Strickland Rivers, Papua. Communicated with notes by S. H. Ray.

(Man, vol. 18, 1918, no. 24, pp. 40-45)

(Over)

AS 36 A 5

ETHNOLOGY PAPUA

Rand, A. L.

Papuans I have known.

(Natural History, Vol. 51, 1943, pp. 84-94)

GN 2.I A-m

ETHNOLOGY PAPUA

Strong, W. Marsh

More Rock Paintings from Papua.

(In Man: Vol. 24, pp. 97-99)

GN 2.1 A-m — ETHNOLOGY PAPUA

Strong, W. Marsh

Rock Paintings from the Central District, Papua.

(In Man: Vol. 23, No. 12, 1923)

GN 671.N5 W 72 — ETHNOLOGY PAPUA

Williams, F. E.

Orokaiva magic...Oxford University Press. 1928. 231 pp. pls.

GN 2M FI — ETHNOLOGY PERU

Dorsey, George Amos, 1868-

... A bibliography of the anthropology of Peru. By George A. Dorsey ... Chicago, U. S. A., 1898.

2 p. l., p. 55-206. 24½ᶜᵐ. (Field Columbian museum. Publication 23. Anthropological series. vol. II, no. 2)

1. Ethnology—Peru—Bibl. 2. Anthropology—Bibl. 3. Peru—Antiq.—Bibl.

Library of Congress   GN2.F4   4—12214
—— Copy 2.   Z5114.D71

GN 1 An — ETHNOLOGY PAPUA

Vormann, Frits

Das tägliche Leben der Papua (unter besonderer Berücksichtigung des Valman-Stammes auf Deutsch-Neuguinea) Anthropos, Bd. XII-XIII, 1917-1918, pp. 891-909.

GN 671.N5 W 72 — ETHNOLOGY PAPUA

Williams, F. E.

Orokaiva Society. With an Introduction by Sir Hubert Murray. London. Oxford University Press. 1930. xxiii + 355 pp. 8vo.

F 3430 O 65 — ETHNOLOGY PERU

Ordinaire, Olivier

Les Sauvages du Pérou. Paris. Ernest Leroux 1888. 58 pp. 8vo

GN 671.N5 W 72 — ETHNOLOGY PAPUA

Williams, Frances E.

Drama of Orokolo: the social and ceremonial life of the Elema. Oxford, Clarendon Press. 1940. 8vo. xxiv + 464 pp.

GN 2.1 P 21 — ETHNOLOGY PAPUA

Williams, Francis E.

Papuans of the Trans-Fly. Oxford. At the Clarendon Press. 1936. 8vo. xxxvi + 452 pp. 1 map, 19 pl.

(Anthropology Report No. 15, Territory of Papua)

GN 2.F V 69 — ETHNOBOTANY PERU

Towle, Margaret A.

The ethnobotany of pre-Columbian Peru. Foreword by Gordon R. Wiley. Aldine Publishing Company. Chicago. R8vo.

(Viking Fund Publications in Anthropology, No. 30, 1961)

GN Ethn.Pam. 3376 — ETHNOLOGY PAPUA

Williams, F. E.

The Grasslanders.

(Extract from Annual Report, 1938-39, Territory of Papua, pp. 1029, Appendix)

Q 115 W 95 locked case — ETHNOLOGY PAPUA

Wüllerstorf-Urbair, Bernhard

Reise der Oesterreichischen Fregatte Novara um die Erde...1857-1859. Anthropologischer Theil, III, pp. 11-18. Wien. 1868. 4to. by Friedrich Müller.

GN Ethn.Pam. 3576 — ETHNOLOGY PERU

Wassen, Henry

Tre foremal fran Paracas, Peru.

(Goteborgs Musei Arstryck 1949/50: 213-222)

GN 1 O 15 — ETHNOLOGY PAPUA

Williams, Francis E.

Natives of Lake Kutubu, Papua.

(Oceania, Vol. XI, No. 3, pp. 259-294; No. 4, 1941, pp. 374-401; Vol. XII, No. 1, 1941, pp. 49-74; No. 2, pp. 134-154

to be cont'.

AS 36 S1 — ETHNOLOGY - PATAGONIA

Ried, Aq.

Account of human remains from Patagonia in the Smithsonian institution. By Dr. Aq. Ried.

(In Smithsonian institution. Annual report. 1862. Washington, 1863. 23½ᶜᵐ. p. 426-429)

1. Ethnology—Patagonia. 2. Indians of South America—Patagonia.

S 15-136

Library of Congress   Q11.S66 1862
Library, Smithsonian   Institution

GN Pam. 544 — ETHNOLOGY PHILIPPINES

Barton, R. F.

Ifugao economics.

(Univ. of California Pub. in Arch and Eth., Vol. 15, April 12, 1922)

GN 2.1 A-m — ETHNOLOGY PAPUA

Williams, F. E.

The natives of Mount Hagen, Papua: further notes.

(Man, Vol. 37. no.114. 1937. pp.90-96)

GN 551 L 63 — ETHNOLOGY PAWNEE INDIANS

Lesser, Alexander

The Pawnee Ghost Dance Hand Game: a study of cultural change. New York. Columbia Univ. Press. 1933. 8vo. x+339 pp.

(Columbia Univ. Contrib. to Anthropology, XVI.)

GN 2 I Ca — ETHNOLOGY - PHILIPPINE ISLANDS

Barton, Roy Franklin, 1883-

... Ifugao law, by R. F. Barton. Berkeley, University of California press, 1919.

cover-title, p. [1]-186. front. (map) pl. 1-33 (pl. 20-21 fold.) 27½ᶜᵐ. (University of California publications in American archaeology and ethnology. v. 15, no. 1)

1. Ifugaos. 2. Law, Primitive. 3. Ethnology — Philippine Islands. I. Title. II. Title: Law, Ifugao.

A 19-193

Title from Univ. of Calif.   Library of Congress
[4]

GN 2.1 P 21 — ETHNOLOGY PAPUA

Williams, F. E.

The Natives of the Purari Delta. With Introduction by J.H.P. Murray.

(Territory of Papua, Anthropology Report No. 5, 1924)

GN 2.8 O 15 and GN Ethn. Pam. 4127 — ETHNOLOGY PENTECOST ISLAND

Lane, R. R.

The heathen communities of southeast Pentecost.

(Jour. Soc. des Oceanistes, 12:139-180, 1957)

GN 671.P5 B 29 — ETHNOLOGY PHILIPPINE ISLANDS

Barton, R. F.

The Kalingas: their institutions and custom law. With an introduction by E. Adamson Hoebel. University of Chicago Publications in Anthropology, Social Anthropological Series (no number) 1948. 8vo. xii + 275 pp.

GN
671.P5
B 29

ETHNOLOGY　PHILIPPINE ISLANDS

Barton, R. F.　(Roy Franklin)

　　　Philippine pagans; the autobiographies of
three Ifugaos. London. George Routledge and
Sons, Ltd. 1938. 8vo. xxi + 271 pp.

GN
2.I
P 55

ETHNOLOGY　PHILIPPINES

Christie, Emerson Brewer

　　The Subanuns of Sindangan Bay.

　　(Ethnological Survey,Publications, Bureau
of Science(Dept.of the Interior),Philippine Islands,Vol.6, Part 1,1909)

GN
2.M
P1
F45

ETHNOLOGY　PHILIPPINE ISLANDS

Cole, Fay-Cooper

　　The wild tribes of Davao District,
Mindanao.... in Field Mus.Nat.Hist.Anth.
Series, Vol.XII, pp.49-203,pls.LXXVI,
Chicago, 1913.

GN
2.S
P 76

ETHNOLOGY　PHILIPPINE ISLANDS

Best, Elsdon

　　Pre-historic civilization in the Philippines
I-II: The Tagalo-Bisaya tribes.

　　(Journal of the Polynesian Society, Vol. 1,
1892, pp. 118-125, 195-201)

GN
Ethn.
Pam.
1696

ETHNOLOGY　PHILIPPINE ISLANDS

Cole, Fay Cooper

　　The Bagobos of Davao Gulf.

　　(Philippine Jour. of Sci., Vol. 6, no. 3,
1911, pp. 127-136, pl. 1-4)

GN
4
C 33

ETHNOLOGY　PHILIPPINES

Conklin, Harold C.

　　Maling, a Hanunoo girl from the Philippines
IN
Casagrande, Joseph B.　editor
　　In the company of man. pp. 101-118.
Harper and Bros. New York. 1960. R8vo.

GN
2.S
P 76

ETHNOLOGY　PHILIPPINE ISLANDS

Best, Elsdon

　　The races of the Philippines.

　　(Journal of the Polynesian Society, Vol. 1,
1892, pp. 7-19)

GN
Ethn.
Pam.
4292

ETHNOLOGY　PHILIPPINE ISLANDS

Cole, Fay-Cooper

　　Cultural relations between Mindanao; regions and islands to the south. mimeographed.
19 pp. n.d.

GN
671.P5
F 51

ETHNOLOGY　PHILIPPINE ISLANDS

Finley, John Park

　　The Subanu: studies of a sub-Visayan
mountain folk of Mindanao. Part I. Ethnographical
and geographical sketch of land and people, by
Lieut.-Col. John Park Finley, Part II. Discussion
of the linguistic material, by William Churchill,
Part III. Vocabularies, Washington. Carnegie
Institution. 1913. R8vo. 236 pp. maps.

　　(Carnegie Institution of Washington, Pub.
No. 184).

DS
668
B 57

ETHNOLOGY　PHILIPPINE ISLANDS

Beyer, H. Otley

　　Philippine saga: a pictorial history of the
archipelago since time began. By Prof. H. Otley
Beyer and Prof. Jaime C. de Veyra. Published
by the Evening News, Manila, 1947. folio. 152
pp.

GN
Ethn.Pam
1435

ETHNOLOGY　PHILIPPINE ISLANDS

Cole, Fay Cooper

　　Distribution of the non-Christian tribes of
northwestern Luzon.

　　(Amer. Anthrop. Vol. 11, no. 3, 1909, pp.
329-347)

AS
540
P 55 j

and

GN
Ethn.
Pam.
2000

GN
671.P5
F 79

ETHNOLOGY　PHILIPPINE ISLANDS

Fox, Robert B.

　　The Pinatubo Negritos, their useful plants
and material culture.

　　(The Philippine Journal of Science, Vol.
81(3-4), 1952)

GN
Ethn.Pam.
3861

ETHNOLOGY　PHILIPPINE ISLANDS

Birket-Smith, Kaj

　　The rice cultivation and rice-harvest feast
of the Bontoc Igorot.

　　(Det Kongelijke Danske Videnskabernes Selskab, Hist.-fil. Meddelelser, Bd. 32, Nr. 8,1952)

GN
630.M3
C 68

ETHNOLOGY - PHILIPPINE ISLANDS

Cole, F.C.

　　The peoples of Malaysia.　D. Van Nostrand
Company, Inc.　Toronto, New York... 8vo.
1945c　xiv + 354 pp.

GN
Eth.
Pam.
2861

ETHNOLOGY - PHILIPPINE ISLANDS

Guthe, Carl

　　Distribution of Sites Visited by the
University of Michigan Philippine Expedition
1922-1925.

　　(From Papers of the Michigan Academy of
Science, Arts and Letters, Vol. X, 1928, 8 pages.)

AS
36
S1

ETHNOLOGY--PHILIPPINE ISLANDS.

Blumentritt, Ferdinand, 1853-
　　List of the native tribes of the Philippines and of the
languages spoken by them. By Prof. Ferdinand Blumentritt. ⟨Tr., with introduction and notes, by O. T. Mason.⟩

　　⟨*In* Smithsonian institution. Annual report. 1899. Washington, 1901.
23½ᵐ. p. 527-547. 9 pl., fold. map⟩

　　"Translated from Zeitschrift der Gesellschaft für erdkunde zu Berlin.
Berlin, vol. xxv, pp. 127-146."

　　1. Ethnology—Philippine Islands. I. Mason, Otis Tufton, 1838-1908,
tr.

　　　　　　　　　　　　　　S 15-1042

Library of Congress 　　　Q11.S66 1899
Library, Smithsonian　　　Institution

GN
Ethn.
Pam.
1648

ETHNOLOGY　PHILIPPINE ISLANDS

Cole, Fay Cooper

　　The Tinggian.

　　(Philippine Jour. of Sci., Vol. 3, No. 4,
1908, pp. 196-211)

GN
671.P5
J 53

ETHNOLOGY　PHILIPPINE ISLANDS

Jenks, Albert Ernest

　　The Bontoc Igorot.

　　(Ethnological Survey Publications,(Philippine Islands), Vol. 1, 1905. 266 pp. R8vo.)

GN
1
A

ETHNOLOGY　PHILIPPINE ISLANDS

Brinton, Daniel G.

　　Professor Blumentritt's Studies of
the Philippines.

　　(American Anthropologist, N. S.,
Vol. 1, 1899, pp. 122-125)

GN
635.M3
C 68

ETHNOLOGY　PHILIPPINE ISLANDS

Cole, Fay-Cooper

　　The Tinguian, social, religious, and economic life of a Philippine tribe. With a chapter
of music, by Albert Gale.

　　(Field Mus. of Nat. Hist., Anthrop. Ser.
14(2), 1922)

GN
2.I
S 78

ETHNOLOGY　PHILIPPINE ISLANDS

Keesing, Felix M.

　　The ethnohistory of northern Luzon. By
Felix and Roger Keesing.
　　(Stanford Anthropological Series, No. 4,
1962, Stanford University Press. R8vo. vi + 362
pp.)

GN
2.I
S 68

ETHNOLOGY PHILIPPINES

Krieger, Herbert W.

Peoples of the Philippines.

(Smithsonian Institution, War Background
Studies, No. 4, 1942)

GN
2.M
Dr

ETHNOLOGY PHILIPPINES

Meyer, A(dolf) B(ernhard)

Die Philippinen. II. Negritos. Mit 10 Tafeln
in Lichtdruck und 10 Holzschnitten.

(Publ. Kgl. Ethnographisches Museum, Dresden,
Bd. IX, 1893)

GN
Pam.
3033

ETHNOLOGY PHILIPPINE ISLANDS

Saleeby, Najeeb M

Origin of the Malayan Filipinos. Manila.
1912. 37 pp.

(Philippine Academy Papers, Vol. 1, Pt. 1,
1912)

GN
2M
A

ETHNOLOGY--PHILIPPINE ISLANDS.

Kroeber, Alfred Louis, 1876-
... The history of Philippine civilization as reflected in
religious nomenclature, by A. L. Kroeber ... New York,
The Trustees, 1918.
1 p. l., p. 35-67. 24½ᵐᵐ. (Anthropological papers of the American
museum of natural history. vol. XIX, pt. II)

1. Philippine Islands—Religion. 2. Ethnology—Philippine Islands.

19-6010

Library of Congress   GN2.A27 vol. XIX, pt. II
〔5〕

GN
Ethn.Pam.
3041

ETHNOLOGY PHILIPPINE ISLANDS

Miller, Edward Y.

The Bataks of Palawan.

(Department of the Interior, Philippine
Islands, Ethnological Survey Publications, Vol.
II, pp. 181-199, 1905.)

GN
2.I
P 55

ETHNOLOGY PHILIPPINES

Saleeby, Najeeb M.

Studies in Moro history, law and religion.

(Ethnological Survey Publications, Dept. of
the Interior. Philippine Islands, Vol.4, 1905,
pp. 1-107)

GN
2M
A

ETHNOLOGY--PHILIPPINE ISLANDS.

Kroeber, Alfred Louis, 1876-
... Kinship in the Philippines, by A. L. Kroeber. New
York, The Trustees, 1919.
1 p. l., p. 69-84. 24½ᵐᵐ. (Anthropological papers of the American mu-
seum of natural history. vol. XIX, pt. III)
Bibliography: p. 75.

1. Family. 2. Ethnology—Philippine Islands.

Library of Congress   GN2.A27 vol. 19, pt. 3   19-15170
——— Copy 2.   GN480.5.K7
〔6〕

GN
671.P5
M 76

ETHNOLOGY PHILIPPINE ISLANDS

Montano, J.

Rapport à M. le Ministre de l'Instruction
Publique sur une mission aux Iles Philippines et
en Malaisie (1879-1881) par M. le Docteur J.
Montano. Paris. Imprimerie Nationale. 1885.
8vo. 209 pp. + planches XXXIV + 2 maps.

(Extrait des Archives Des Missions Scientifiques et Littéraires, Troisième Série, Tome
Onzième)

GN
400
S 49

ETHNOLOGY PHILIPPINE ISLANDS

Service, Elman R.

A profile of primitive culture. Harper
and Brothers. New York. 1958. R8vo. xiv +
474 pp.

(For revision: see "Profiles in ethnology")

GN
671.P5
K 93

ETHNOLOGY PHILIPPINE ISLANDS

Kroeber, Alfred Louis

Peoples of the Philippines, by A. L. Kroeber
... New York. American museum press. 1919.

(American museum of natural history.
Handbook series, no. 8)

also 2nd edition, revised, 1928

GN
Ethn.Pam.
367

ETHNOLOGY
CLOTHING PHILIPPINE ISLANDS

Pardo de Tavera, T. H.

Las costumbres de los Tagalos en Filipinas.
Madrid. 1892.

GN
400
S 49

ETHNOLOGY PHILIPPINE ISLANDS (KALINGA)

Service, Elman R.

Profiles in ethnology: a revision of "A
profile of primitive culture." New York.
Harper & Row. 1963. xxix + 509 pp.
R8vo.

GN
63b.M4
L 34

ETHNOLOGY PHILIPPINE ISLANDS

Lasker, Bruno

Peoples of southeast Asia. Prepared under
the auspices of the American Council of the Institute of Pacific Relations. New York. 1945.

DS
501
M 27

ETHNOLOGY PHILIPPINE ISLANDS

A preliminary bibliography of Philippine
anthropology, linguistics, ethnology and archaeology.

(Journal of East Asiatic Studies, Univ. of
Manila, 2(2):55-110, 1953)

GN
2M
A

ETHNOLOGY--PHILIPPINE ISLANDS.

Sullivan, Louis Robert, 1892-
... Racial types in the Philippine Islands, by Louis R.
Sullivan. New York, The Trustees, 1918.
1 p. l., 61 p., 2 fold. maps, diagrs. (part fold.) 24½ᵐᵐ. (Anthropological
papers of the American museum of natural history, vol. XXIII, pt. I)
Bibliography: p. 57-59.

1. Ethnology—Philippine Islands. I. Title.

19-9862 Revised

Library of Congress   GN2.A27 vol. XXIII, pt. I
〔r20c2〕

GN
671.P5
M 61

ETHNOLOGY PHILIPPINE ISLANDS

Meyer, A. B.

Album von Philippinen-typen. Nord Luzon.
Negritos, Tingianen, Bánaos, Ginaanen, Silipanen,
Calingas, Apoyáos, Kianganen, Igorroten und Iloc-
anen. Ueber 600 abbildungen auf 50 tafeln in
lichtdruck. Herausgegeben von A. B. Meyer und A.
Schadenberg. Dresden. Stengel & Markert. 1891.
4to. 19 pp. + pls.

AS
540
P 55 j

ETHNOLOGY PHILIPPINE ISLANDS

Quirino, Carlos

The manners, customs, and beliefs of the
Philippine inhabitants of long ago; being chapters of "a late 16th century Manila manuscript"
transcribed, translated and annotated. By Carlos
Quirino and Mauro Garcia.

(Philippine Jour. of Science, 87(4):325-454,
1960)

DU
620
H 4

ETHNOLOGY-PHILIPPINES

Townsend, Henry S.

A letter from Prof. Townsend (concerning
some interesting coincidences between the Polynesians and the Malayans of the Philippines)

(Annual Report, Hawaiian Historical Society,
11th, 1903, pp. 10-11)

GN
2.M
Dr

ETHNOLOGY PHILIPPINES

Meyer, A(dolf) B(ernhard)

Die Philippinen. I. Nord-Luzon, von A.B.
Meyer und A. Schadenberg.

(Publ. Kgl. Ethnographisches Museum, Dresden,
Bd. VIII, 1890)

GN
2.I
P 55

ETHNOLOGY PHILIPPINE ISLANDS

Reed, William Allan

Negritos of Zambales.

(Ethnological Survey Publications, Dept. of
the Interior. Philippine Islands, Vol.II, 1904,
pp. 1-90)

GN
1
An

ETHNOLOGY PHILIPPINE ISLANDS

Vanoverbergh, Morice

Negritos of Northern Luzon again.

(In Anthropos, Bd. 25, 1931, pp. 25-71, 527-
565)

AS 36 S2 S66

ETHNOLOGY PHILIPPINE ISLANDS

Venturello, Manuel Hugo.

Manners and customs of the Tagbanuas and other tribes of the island of Palawan, Philippines, by Manuel Hugo Venturello ... Tr. from the original Spanish manuscript by Mrs. Edw. Y. Miller.

(*In* Smithsonian institution. Smithsonian miscellaneous collections. Washington, 1907. 24½ᶜᵐ. vol. XLVIII (Quarterly issue, vol. III) p. (514)-558)

Publication 1700.

1. Tagbanuas. 2. Ethnology—Palawan (Island)   I. Miller, Mrs. Edward Young, tr.

Library of Congress   Q11.S7 vol. 48

———— Copy 2.   16-11624

GN 22 B 15

ETHNOLOGY POLYNESIA

Bahnson, Kristian

Etnografien; fremstillet i dens hovedtraek. Bind 1-2. Med farvetryk, kort... Köbenhavn. Ernst Bojesen. 8vo. 1900. 648 + 704 pp. Bd. I: pp. 56-138

GN 670 B 87

ETHNOLOGY POLYNESIA

Brown, J. Macmillan

Maori and Polynesian: their origin, history, and culture. London. 1907. 8vo.

.GN 1 I 61

ETHNOLOGY PHILIPPINE ISLANDS

Venturillo, Manuel H.

The Batacs of the island of Palawan, Philippine Islands.

(Archiv f. Ethnogr., XVIII, 1908, p. 137-144)

GN 2.I A-m

ETHNOLOGY POLYNESIA

Beaglehole, Ernest

Cultural peaks in Polynesia.

(Man, Vol. 37, 1937, No. 176)

AS 701 A

ETHNOLOGY POLYNESIA

Brown, George

The Pacific, east and west.

(Australasian Association for the Adv. of Sci., Rept. of the meeting, 1902, Hobart, pp. 458-479)

AS 36 S2 S66

ETHNOLOGY--PHILIPPINE ISLANDS

Virchow, Rudolf Ludwig Karl, 1821-1902.

The peopling of the Philippines. By Rud. Virchow. ⟨Tr., with notes, by O. T. Mason.⟩

(*In* Smithsonian institution. Annual report. 1899. Washington, 1901. 23½ᵐ. p. 509-526. III pl.)

"Translated from Sitzungsberichte der Königlich preussischen akademie der wissenschaften zu Berlin. Berlin, 1897, January-June, 279-289."

1. Ethnology—Philippine Islands.   I. Mason, Otis Tufton, 1838-1908, tr. II. Title.

S 15-1041

Library of Congress   Q11.S66 1899
Library, Smithsonian   Institution

GN 2.8 P 76

ETHNOLOGY POLYNESIA

Beaglehole, Ernest

The Polynesian Maori.

(Jour. of the Polynesian Soc., Vol. 49, 1940 pp. 39-68)

GN 22 B 92

ETHNOLOGY POLYNESIA

Buck, Peter Henry

Anthropology and religion.   New Haven, 1939.

GN Ethn. Pam. 4291

ETHNOLOGY PHILIPPINES ISLANDS

Wood, Grace L.

The Tiruray, (Philippine Islands) mimeographed. 24 pp.

GN 1 O 15

ETHNOLOGY POLYNESIA

Bell, F. L. S.

A Functional Interpretation of Inheritance and Succession in Central Polynesia.

(Oceania, Vol. III, 1932, pp. 167-206)

GN Ethn.Pam. 2897

ETHNOLOGY POLYNESIA

Buck, Peter H.

Brief Report of Polynesian Material in Canadian Museums.

(Typed copy, extract from letter to Mr. A.F. Judd, September, 1932)

GN Ethn.Pam 3421

ETHNOLOGY PHILIPPINE ISLANDS

Worcester, Dean C.

Head-hunters of northern Luzon.

(National Geographic Magazine, Vol. 23, 1912 pp. 833-930)

GN 670 B64 and AS 763 B

ETHNOLOGY & POLYNESIA

Bernice Pauahi Bishop museum of Polynesian ethnology and natural history, *Honolulu*.

A preliminary catalogue of the Bernice Pauahi Bishop museum of Polynesian ethnology and natural history ... Honolulu, 1892-93.

5 v. in 1. illus. 22½ᵐ.

CONTENTS.—pt. I. Kahilis, feather ornaments, mats and kapas.—pt. II. Household implements, tools, amusements, war, worship, ornaments, medicine, fisheries and canoes, relics of chiefs.—pt. III. New Zealand, Samoa and other Polynesian islands; New Hebrides, Fiji, Solomon Islands, New Guinea, Micronesia, Australia.—pt. IV. The natural history collections.—pt. V. A list of pictures, books treating of the Pacific regions, silverware and coins.

1. Ethnology—Polynesia. 2. Natural history—Polynesia.

Library of Congress   GN670.B64   8-14643

GN 670 B 92

ETHNOLOGY POLYNESIA

Buck, Peter H.

An introduction to Polyneisan anthropology.

(Bernice P. Bishop Museum, Bulletin 187, 1945)

GN Ethn.Pam. 3419

ETHNOLOGY PHILIPPINE ISLANDS

Worcester, Dean C.

The non-Christian peoples of the Philippine Islands; with an account of what has been done for them under American rule.

(National Geographic Magazine, Vol. 24, 1913 pp. 1157-1256) (colored plates)

GN 2.I A-4

ETHNOLOGY POLYNESIA

Braunholtz, H. J.

Culture contact as a museum problem.

(Jour. R. Anthrop. Inst. Great Britain and Ireland, Vol. 72, pp. 1-7, 1942)

GN Ethn.Pam. 2836

ETHNOLOGY POLYNESIA

Buck, Peter H. (Te Rangi Hiroa)

Terminology for Ground Stone Cutting-Implements in Polynesia, by Peter H. Buck, Kenneth P. Emory, H. D. Skinner and John F. G. Stokes.

(Vol. 39, Journal of the Polynesian Society, pp. 174-180, 1930)

2 copies

DS Asia Pam. 48

ETHNOLOGY PHILIPPINE ISLANDS

Zaide, Gregorio F.

Early Philippine history and culture. Published by the author. Manila. 1937. 8vo. 54 pp.

GN 668 B 87

ETHNOLOGY POLYNESIA

Brown, George

Melanesians and Polynesians: their life-histories described and compared. London. 1910. 8vo.

(Samoa and Tonga only)

GN 670 B 92

ETHNOLOGY POLYNESIA

Buck, Peter H. (Te Rangi Hiroa)

Vikings of the sunrise. With fifty-eight illustrations from photographs. Frederick A. Stokes Company. New York. 1938. 8vo. xii + 335 pp.

GN
1
I 61
ETHNOLOGY POLYNESIA

Bülow, Werner von

Notizen zur Ethnographie, Anthropologie, und Urgeschichte der Malayo-Polynesier.

(Archiv f. Ethnogr., XVIII, 1908, p. 152-166)

DU
12
E 47

DU12E 47
locked
case

"
DU12E 47
ETHNOLOGY POLYNESIA

Ellis, William

Polynesian Researches... 2 vols. London. 1829. 8vo.

The same...1830. 2 vols. 8vo.

The same...Second edition, enlarged and improved. 4 vols. London. (1831)-1839. 18mo.
The same. (1831)-1842. 4 vols. 12mo.
Index to 2d edition. 2 copies.

GN
1
A

and

GN
Ethn.
Pam.
730
ETHNOLOGY POLYNESIA

Handy, Edward S.

Some conclusions and suggestions regarding the Polynesian problem. In Am. Anthrop. Vol. 22, 1920, pp 226-236.

GN
2.S
P 76
ETHNOLOGY POLYNESIA

Burrows, Edwin G.

Culture areas in Polynesia.

(Journal of the Polynesian Soc., Vol. 49, 1940, pp. 349-363)

GN
671.T 5
F 52
ETHNOLOGY POLYNESIA

Firth, Raymond

Primitive Polynesian economy. Illustrated. George Routledge & Sons, Ltd. London. R8vo. xi, 387 pp.

GN
1
Z 65
ETHNOLOGY POLYNESIA

Henking, Karl H.

Kultanlagen in Polynesien. Umriss einer Analyse.

(Zeit. f. Ethnologie, 86(2):250-255, 1961)

GN
1
E 84
ETHNOLOGY POLYNESIA

Burrows, Edwin G.

Western Polynesia, a study in cultural differentiation.

(Etnologiska Studier, No. 7, 1938, pp. 1-192)

GN
Ethn.Pam.
2909
ETHNOLOGY - POLYNESIA

Friederici, Georg

Malaio-Polynesische Wanderungen.

(Vortrag gehalten auf dem XIX Deutschen Geographentage zu Strassburg, 1914. 37 pp.)

GN
670
H 71
ETHNOLOGY POLYNESIA

Hogbin, H. Ian

Law and order in Polynesia. A study of primitive legal institutions. With an introduction by B. Malinowski. London. Christophers. 1934. 8vo.

DU
Missions
Pam. 78
ETHNOLOGY POLYNESIA

Catalogue des Reliques et Collections de l'Oeuvre. Oeuvre de la Propagation de la Foi. Lyon. n.d. 112 pp. 8vo.

GN
1
An
ETHNOLOGY POLYNESIA

Graebner, F.

Die melanesische Bogenkultur und ihre Verwandten.

(Anthropos. Band IV. 1909. pp.726-780, 998-1032)

GN
Ethn.Pam.
2921
ETHNOLOGY - POLYNESIA

Hogbin, H. Ian

Polynesian Ceremonial Gift Exchanges.

(Reprinted from Oceania, September 1932. Vol. III, No. 1. Sydney. Australasian Medical Publishing Company, Limited. 1932. 13-39 pp. 8vo.) Plates III.

GN
2.I
A 4
ETHNOLOGY POLYNESIA

Chadwick, Nora K.

The Kite: a Study in Polynesian Tradition.

(Journal of the Royal Anthropological Institute, 1931, July-Dec., pp. 455-491)

GN
Ethn.Pam
55
ETHNOLOGY POLYNESIA

Gregory, Herbert E.

Progress in Polynesian research.

(Science, 56:527-529, 1922)

GN
670
K 89

DU
12
K 89
2 cops.
1 in locked
case
ETHNOLOGY POLYNESIA

Krämer, Augustin

Hawaii, Ostmikronesien und Samoa: Meine zweite Südseereise (1897-1899) zum Studium der Atolle... Stuttgart. 1906. 8vo.

GN
498.C6
C6
ETHNOLOGY-POLYNESIA

Churchill, William, 1859-
Club types of nuclear Polynesia, by William Churchill. Washington (D. C.) The Carnegie institution of Washington, 1917.

v. 173 p. illus., xvii pl. (incl. front.; 1 col.) 25ᶜᵐ. (On verso of t.-p.: Carnegie institution of Washington. Publication no. 255)

1. Arms and armor, Primitive. 2. Ethnology—Polynesia. I. Title.

Library of Congress   GN498.C6C4

17-31769

—— Copy 2.

GN
470
H 23

AS
763
B-b

Reading
Room
ETHNOLOGY POLYNESIA

Handy, E. S. Craighill

Polynesian religion. Honolulu. 1927. R8vo.

(Bernice P. Bishop Museum, Bulletin 34; Bayard Dominick Expedition, Pub. No. 12. 1927.)

GN
Ethn.Pam.
3484
ETHNOLOGY POLYNESIA

Lavachery, Henri

Vie des Polynésiens. J. Lebegue and Co. Bruxelles. 1946. sm8vo. 59 pp. illustrated.

GN
446.51
D 64
ETHNOLOGY POLYNESIA

Dodge, Ernest S.

Gourd growers of the South Seas: an introduction to the study of the Lagenaria gourd in the culture of the Polynesians.

(The Gourd Society of America, Ethnographical Series, No. 2, 1943)

GN
Pam
2803
ETHNOLOGY POLYNESIA

Handy, Edward S   Craighill

Problem of Polynesian origins.   Bernice P. Bishop Museum. Occasional papers, vol. IX, no.8. 1930.   27p. map.

GN
2.S
T
ETHNOLOGY POLYNESIA

Lesoure, Rey

Maré et la Polynésie.

(Bulletin de la Société des Études Océaniennes. Tome 5, 1935, pp. 443-449)

GN
670
L 64   ETHNOLOGY POLYNESIA

Lesson, Pierre Adolphe

Les Polynesiens, leur origine, leur migration leur language...ouvrage rédigé d'après le manuscrit de l'auteur par Ludovic Martinet...
Paris. Leroux. 1880-1884... 4 volumes. 8vo. maps.

(Index-Tome 4).

ETHNOLOGY POLYNESIA

GN
32
N93   Noury, M. C.

Album Polynésien de M. C. Noury, capitaine de vaisseau. Nantes. 1861. 15 pls. 4to.

GN
668
T 44   ETHNOLOGY POLYNESIA

Thilenius, Georg

Ethnographische Ergebnisse aus Melanesien...
T. Theil... II. Theil...

(Nova Acta, Abh. der Kaiserl. Leop.-Carol. Deutschen Akademie der Naturforscher, Band LXXX, Nr. 1-2. Halle. 1902-1903).

GN
2.S
Po   ETHNOLOGY POLYNESIA

Linton, Ralph

The Degeneration of Human Figures Used in Polynesian Decorative Art.

(In Journal of the Polynesian Society, Vol. 33, Part 4, 1924)

GN
1
An   ETHNOLOGY POLYNESIA

Plischke, Hans

Gürtelinvestitur polynesischer Oberhäuptlinge.

(In Anthropos, Bd. 25, 1930, pp. 147-162)

AN
2.S
S 19   ETHNOLOGY-POLYNESIA

Turner, George

-    Ethnology of Polynesia (Samoa)

(The Samoan Reporter, Nos. 13-17, 19, 1851-1857)

AM
101
F 45 g   ETHNOLOGY POLYNESIA

Linton, Ralph

Ethnology of Polynesia and Micronesia.

(Field Museum of Natural History, Guide, Part 6. Handbook, 1926)

GN
Ethn. Pam.
3147   ETHNOLOGY POLYNESIA

Ropiteau, André

Une visite au Musée Missionaire des Pères des Sacrés-Coeurs de Picpus à Braine-le-Comte (Belgique). Papeete, Imprimerie du Gouvernement. 1936. 8vo. 10 pp. 4 figs.

DU
12
T 97   ETHNOLOGY POLYNESIA
locked
case

Tyerman, Daniel, and Bennet, George

Journal of voyages and travels...in the South Sea islands...1821-1829. Compiled from original documents by James Montgomery. London. 1831. 8vo.
...the same, in 3 vols. From the 1st London edition, revised by an American editor. Boston. 1832. 12mo.
...the same. 2d edition, corrected. London. 1841. 8vo.

GN
Ethn. Pam.
3214   ETHNOLOGY POLYNESIA

Métraux, Alfred

Océanie et Australie. Chapitre 5. 1936
18 pp. (Extract from "Les peuples sur la terre")

DU
12
R 96   ETHNOLOGY POLYNESIA

Russell, Alexander

Aristocrats of the South Seas.   London.
Robert Hale Limited.   1961.   190 pp.   8vo

GN
2.I
A-4   ETHNOLOGY POLYNESIA

Tylor, Edward B.

Notes on the Asiatic relations of Polynesia culture.

(Journ. Anthrop. Inst. of Great Britain and Ireland, Vol. 11, 1881-2, pp. 401-405)

GN
1
M 26   ETHNOLOGY POLYNESIA

Mitra, Panchan

Cultural Affinities between India and Polynesia. (A Preliminary Study)

(Man in India, Vol. XI, pp. 217-242, 1931, and Vol. XII, pp. 30-44, 1932)

GN
2.S
Po   ETHNOLOGY POLYNESIA

Skinner, H. D.

Maori and other Polynesian material in British Museums.

(Polynesian Society Journal, Vol. 26, 1917, pp. 134-137)

GN
2.I
A-4   ETHNOLOGY POLYNESIA

Wake, C. Staniland

Notes on the Polynesian race.

(Journ. Anthrop. Inst. of Great Britain and Ireland, Vol. 10, 1880-1, pp. 109-123)

DU
12
M 69   ETHNOLOGY POLYNESIA
locked
case

Moerenhout, J. A.

Voyages aux îles du grand océan...2 vols.
Paris. 1837. 8vo.

GN
Ethn. Pam.
3534   ETHNOLOGY POLYNESIA

Speiser, Felix

Neu-Caledonien, die südlichen Neuen Hebriden und Polynesien.

(Verhandlungen Naturforschenden Gesell. Basel, Bd. 57:1-24, 1946)

GN
2.I
A 4   ETHNOLOGY POLYNESIA

Whitmee, S. J.

The ethnology of Polynesia.

(Journal of the Anthropological Institute. Vol. VIII. 1878-79. pp. 261-275)

GN
Ethn. Pam.
2908   ETHNOLOGY POLYNESIA

Mühlmann, W. E.

Die Geheime Gesellschaft der Arioi; eine Studie über Polynesische Geheimbunde, mit besonderer Berücksichtigung der Siebungs- und Auslesevorgänge in Alt-Tahiti.

(Separat-Abdruck aus Supplement zu Band 32 von Internationales Archiv für Ethnographie, 1932)

GN
Ethn. Pam.
3855   ETHNOLOGY POLYNESIA

Spoehr, Alexander

Time perspective in Micronesia and Polynesia

(Southwestern Journal of Anthropology, Vol. 8(4):457-465, 1952)

GN
2.I
A-4   ETHNOLOGY POLYNESIA

Whitmee, S.J.

On some characteristics of the Malayo-Polynesians.

(Journ. Anthrop. Inst. of Great Britain and Ireland, Vol. 7, 1878, pp. 372-378)

GN
670
W 72

ETHNOLOGY POLYNESIA

Williamson, Robert W.

    Essays in Polynesian ethnology. Edited by
Ralph Piddington. With an analysis of recent
studies in Polynesian history by the editor.
Cambridge. At the University Press. 1931. R8vo.
xlii + 373 pp.

GN
2.M
Be

and

GN Ethn.
Pam.
2014

ETHNOLOGY PONAPE

Hahl, (vicegovernor of Ponape)

    Mittheilungen uber Sitten und rechtliche
Verhaltnisse auf Ponape.

    (Ethnologisches Notizblatt, Bd. II, Heft 2,
1901, pp. 1-13)

AS
720.Q
Q

and

GN
Ethn.Pam.
339

ETHNOLOGY QUEENSLAND

Hamlyn-Harris, Ronald

    On messages and "message sticks" em-
ployed among the Queensland aborigines.
In Mem. Queensland Mus. VI, 1918, pp 13-
36. illus.

GN
670
W 72

ETHNOLOGY POLYNESIA

Williamson, Robert W.

    The social and political systems of central
Polynesia... In three volumes. Cambridge.
University Press. 1924. 8vo.

GN
663
T 44

ETHNOLOGY PONAPE

Hambruch, Paul

Ponape

Thilenius, G.

    Ergebnisse der Südsee Expedition, 1908-1910.
II. Ethnographie: B. Mikronesien, Bd. 7, Halbband
1-3. 1932-1936.

AS
720.Q
Q

and

GN
Ethn.
Pam.
#299

ETHNOLOGY QUEENSLAND

Hamlyn-Harris, Ronald

    Queensland ethnological notes (2)
In Mem. Queensland Mus. VI, 1918. pp 5-12
illus.

GN
Ethn.
Pam.
3963

ETHNOLOGY POLYNESIA BIBLIOGRAPHY

Luomala, Katharine

    Bibliography in Polynesian ethnology. (9)
mimeographed pp. 1955.

2 copies

GN
Ethn.Pam.
3543

ETHNOLOGY PONAPE

Murrill, Rupert I.

    Ponape: a Micronesian culture of the Caro-
line Islands.

    (Transactions of the New York Academy of
Sciences, Ser. II, Vol. 10, No. 4:154-158,1948)

AS
720.Q
R

ETHNOGRAPHY QUEENSLAND

Hamlyn-Harris, R.

    Some anthropological considerations
of Queensland and bibliography with
special reference to Queensland ethnography: presidential address, in Proc.Ry.
Soc. Queensland XXIX, 1917, pp 1-35.
Note. Bibliography pp 36-44.

GN
663
T 44

ETHNOLOGY PONAPE

Eilers, Anneliese

Inseln um Ponape

Thilenius, G.

    Ergebnisse der Südsee Expedition, 1908-1910.
II. Ethnographie: B. Mikronesien, Bd. 8. 1934.

GN
671.P9
B 36

ETHNOLOGY PUKAPUKA

Beaglehole, Ernest

    Ethnology of Pukapuka, by Ernest and Pearl
Beaglehole.

    (Bulletin, Bernice P. Bishop Museum, No. 150,
1938)

GN
667.Q
R 84

ETHNOLOGY QUEENSLAND

Roth, Walter E.

    Ethnological studies among thenorth-west-
central Queensland aborigines. Brisbane. 1897.
R8vo.

GN
1
Z

ETHNOLOGY PONAPE

Finsch, Otto

*Ueber die Bewohner von Ponapé (östl.
Carolinē). in Zeits.für Ethno. XII. 1880,
pp. 303-332, illus.*

Storage
Case
3

ETHNOLOGY PUKAPUKA

Beaglehole, Ernest

    Pukapuka. 25 field notebooks; 3 packages
of field notes, 1 of them containing fish names.
1935.

GN
Ethn.Pam.
3051-
3058

AS719 A

ETHNOLOGY QUEENSLAND

Roth, Walter E.

    North Queensland Ethnography. Brisbane.
1901-1913.

    Bulletins Nos. 1-8. 1901-1905. 4to.

    Bulletins Nos. 9-14. 1905-1910. In
Records of Australian Museum, Vols. VI-VIII
1905-1913.

AN
2.E
P 78

ETHNOLOGY PONAPE

Gulick, Luther H.

    Lectures on Micronesia...II, Ponapi and the
Ponapian...

    (The Polynesian, Vol. 17, 1860, No. 30, Nov.
24)

GN
Ethnology
pam.
3113

AS
763
B 4

Reading
Room

ETHNOLOGY PUKAPUKA

Macgregor, Gordon

    Notes on the ethnology of Pukapuka. Honolulu
1935. 52 pp. 4 pl.

    (Bernice P. Bishop Museum, Occasional Papers,
Vol. XI, No. 6)

ETHNOLOGY QUEENSLAND

see also

ETHNOLOGY AUSTRALIA

GN
2.M
Be

ETHNOLOGY PONAPE

Hahl

    Feste und Tänze der Eingeborenen von Ponape.

    (Ethnologisches Notizblatt, Bd. III, Heft
2, 1902, pp. 95-102)

AS
720.S
S 72

ETHNOLOGY QUEENSLAND

Hale, H. M.

    Aborigines of Princess Charlotte Bay, North
Queensland, by Herbert M. Hale and Norman B.
Tindale.

    (Records of the South Australian Museum,
Vol. V, No. 1, 1933, pp. 63-116; No. 2, pp. 117-
172)

F
1435
V 71

ETHNOLOGY QUINTANA ROO

Villa R., Alfonso

    The Maya of east central Quintana Roo.
Carnegie Institution of Washington, Pub. 559,
1945. 4to. xii + 182 pp.

Storage
Case
5

Ms R 1,2

ETHNOLOGY RAIVAVAE

Stimson, J. Frank

Material collected for an ethnological study
of Raivavae...1938.

ms. two copies, one with additional notes.

GN
Ethn.
Pam.
3928

ETHNOLOGY RYUKYU ISLANDS

Smith, Allan H.

Recent anthropological research in the
Ryukyu Islands.

(Clearinghouse Bull. of Research in Human
Organization, Vol. 2(2):1-4, 1953)

GN
2.5
F 47

ETHNOLOGY ROTUMA

Eason, W. J.

Rotuma and the Rotumans.

(Transactions of the Fiji Society of Science
and Industry, Vol. 3(3):145-151, 1947)

QH
11
P 11

ETHNOLOGY RAROIA

Danielsson, Bengt

Raroia culture. By Bengt Danielsson and
Aurora Natua.
Part 1. Economy; Part 2. Native topographi-
cal terms; Part 3. Native terminology of the coconut palm; Part 4.*Bird names; Part 5. Check
list of the native names of fishes.

*by Bengt Danielsson and Aurora Natua

GN
1
A

ETHNOLOGY RIU KIU ISLANDS

Wirth, A.

The aborigines of Formosa and the Liu-Kiu
Islands.

(The American Anthropologist, 10:357-370,
1897)

DU
620
M 67

ETHNOLOGY RUK

Price, F. M.

Notes on Ruk and the Mortlock Islands.

(American Missionary Herald, Vol. 91, 1895,
pp. 311-314)

GN
671.R4
B 61

ETHNOLOGY RENNELL ISLAND

Birket-Smith, Kaj

An ethnological sketch of Rennell Island;
a Polynesian outlier in Melanesia.

(Det K. Danske Videnskabernes Selskab,
Hist.-fil. Meddelelser, Bd. 35(3), 1956)

GN
671.N5
A 73

ETHNOLOGY ROSSEL ISLAND

Armstrong, W. E.

Rossel Island, an ethnological study.
With introduction by A. C. Haddon. Cambridge.
1928. 8vo.

GN
Ethn. Pam.
3135

ETHNOLOGY RUSSIA

Ethnographie, Archaeologie et Folklore en
U. R. S. S.

(Recueil Periodique Illustré, Organe de la
Société pour Relations Culturelles entre L'U. R.
S. S. et L'Étranger, Vol. 4, 1933)

Q
115
B 91

ETHNOLOGY RENNELL ISLAND

Birket-Smith, Kaj

Ethnological studies.
IN

Bruun, Anton F. and others
The Galathea deep sea expedition, 1950-1952.
pp. 246-256, 1956

DU
802
E 11

ETHNOLOGY ROTUMA

Eason, W. J. E.

A short history of Rotuma. Printed and
published by the Govt. Printing Dept., Suva, Fiji
R8vo. ix + 127 + iii pp. nd (preface, 1951)

AS
36
S2

ETHNOLOGY--RUSSIA.

Hrdlička, Aleš, 1869-
... The races of Russia (with 1 map) by Aleš Hrdlička
... Washington, Smithsonian institution, 1919.

1 p. l., 21 p. fold. map. 24½ᶜᵐ. (Smithsonian miscellaneous collections.
v. 69, no. 11)

Publication 2532.

1. Ethnology—Russia. ɪ. Title.
ɪName originally: Alois Ferdinand Hrdličkaɪ
19-26377

Library of Congress   Q11.S7 vol. 69, no. 11
——— Copy 2.   DK33.H7
ɪ7ɪ

GN
1
O 15

ETHNOLOGY RENNELL ISLAND

Firth, Raymond

A native voyage to Rennell.

(Oceania, Vol. 2, 1931-1932, pp. 179-190)

GN
2.I
A

ETHNOLOGY ROTUMA

Gardiner, J. Stanley

The Natives of Rotuma.

(Journal of the R. Anthropological Society,
Vol. 27, 1897-1898, pp. 396-435, 457-524)

GN
Ethn.
Pam.
4085

ETHNOLOGY RYUKYU ISLANDS

[Digest of material culture. Ryukyu Government Committee on Preservation of Material Culture. 1957.]

entirely in Japanese. unbound. sm4to.

GN
2.1
A-M

ETHNOLOGY RENNELL ISLAND

Woodford, C. M.

Notes on Rennell Island.

(Man, vol. 7, 1907, no. 24, pp. 33-37, figs.
1-4)

GN
1
E 85

ETHNOLOGY ROTUMA

Howard, Alan

Land, activity systems, and decision-mak-
ing models in Rotuma.

(Ethnology, Vol. 2(4):407-440, 1963)

GN
Ethn.
Pam.
4199

ETHNOLOGY RYUKYU ISLANDS

Smith, Allan H.

The culture of Kabira, southern Ryukyu Islands.

Proc. Am. Philosophical Soc., 104(2):134-
171, 1960)

AS
36
S 1

ETHNOLOGY RIU KUI ISLANDS

Newman, Marshall T.

The Ryukyu people: a cultural appraisal.
By Marshall T. Newman and Ransom L. Eng.

(Smithsonian Report for 1947:379-405)

GN
2.S
P 76

ETHNOLOGY ROTUMA

Russell, W. E.

Rotuma, its history, traditions, and customs
Tales and notes supplied by Mr. F. Gibson, of
Rotuma.

(Journal of the Polynesian Society, Vol. 51
No. 4, 1942, pp. 229-255)

GN
2.M
F 45

ETHNOLOGY SAIPAN

Spoehr, Alexander

Saipan, the ethnology of a war-devasted island.

(Fieldiana: Anthropology, Vol. 41, 1954)

GN
671.N5
C 53
ETHNOLOGY–ST.MATTHIAS

Chinnery, E. W. Pearson

Notes on the Natives of E Mira and St. Matthias.

(Anthropological Report, Territory of New Guinea, No. 2, Melbourne, ND)

GN
1
I 61
ETHNOLOGY SAMOA

Bülow, Werner von

Ein räthselhaftes Steininstrument in Samoa.

(Archiv f. Ethnogr., XIII, 1901, pp. 55-58)

AS
701
A

DU
Pacific
Pam
281
S
ETHNOLOGY SAMOA

Ella, S. (Rev.)

Samoa &. In Aus. Assoc., Adv. Sc., Rep. Vol. IV, pp 620-645, 1892.

G
1
G 56
ETHNOLOGY ST. MATTHIAS

Parkinson, R.

Die Einwohner der Insel St. Matthias (Bismarck Archipel).

(Globus, 79, 1901, pp. 229-233)

G
1
G 56
ETHNOLOGY SAMOA

Bülow, H. von

Kenntnisse und Fertigkeiten der Samoaner.

(Globus, Bd. 72, No. 15, 1897, pp. 237-240)

Storage
Case
5
Ms Sa 2
ETHNOLOGY SAMOA

Fisher, William E.

Samoan ethnological notes:– songs, proverbs vital statistics. (received, 1934)

DU
1
C 56

and

GN
671.S2
B 32
ETHNOLOGY SAMOA

Bastian, Adolph

Einiges aus Samoa und andern Inseln der Südsee. Mit ethnographischer Anmerkungen zur Colonialgeschichte. Berlin, 1889. Ferd. Dümmlers Verlagsbuchhandlung.

(Polynesian Papers, IV)

separate. 8vo. iv + 107 pp.

GN
1
E 84
ETHNOLOGY SAMOA

Burrows, Edwin G.

Western Polynesia, a study in cultural differentiation.

(Etnologiska Studier, No. 7, 1938, pp. 1-192)

GN
671.S2
G 77
ETHNOLOGY SAMOA

Grattan, F. J. H.

An introduction to Samoan custom. Samoa Printing and Publishing Co., Ltd. Apia. 8vo. (1)2-189 pp.

Storage
Case
3
ETHNOLOGY SAMOA

Buck, Peter H.

Samoa. Seven field note-books, 1927-28, in ethnology and one note-book of artifacts.

DU
810
C 56
ETHNOLOGY SAMOA

Churchill, Llewella Pierce

Samoa 'Uma, where life is different. New York and London. n.d. 8vo. 295 pp.

GN
Ethn.
Pam.
3844
ETHNOLOGY SAMOA

Hogue, Charles E.

Cartwright ' finds native culture of Samoa dying from contact with world.

(Honolulu Star-Bulletin, May 5, 1929)

' Bruce Cartwright

GN
671.S2
B 92

AS
763
B-b
Reading
Room
ETHNOLOGY SAMOA

Buck, Peter H. (Te Rangi Hiroa)

Samoan Material Culture. Honolulu. 1930. R8vo. xi + 724 pp. LV pls.

(Bernice P. Bishop Museum, Bulletin 75)

REVIEW in (American Anthropologist, N.S. 34, pp. 347-348, 1932)

GN
671.S2
C 78
ETHNOLOGY SAMOA

Copp, John Dixon

The Samoan dance of life; an anthropological narrative. By John Dixon Copp, with the help of Faafouina I. Pula, and with a preface by Margaret Mead. The Beacon Press. Boston, 1950. 8vo. xvi + 176 pp.

Storage
Case
3
ETHNOLOGY SAMOA

Judd, A. F., 1874–

Expanded notes on the ethnology of American Samoa. 1926.

GN
1
Ar
ETHNOLOGY SAMOA

Bülow, Werner von

Beiträge zur Ethnographie der Samoa-Inseln.

(Arhiv f. Ethnogr., XII, 1899, pp. 66-77, 129-145; Bd. XIII, 1900, pp. 55-58, 59-70,177-184, 185-194.)

(tapa, whetstones, tattooing, fine mats...)

GN
Ethn.Pam.
2958
ETHNOLOGY SAMOA

Deihl, Joseph

The Position of Woman in Samoan Culture.

(Primitive Man, Vol. V, 1932, pp. 21-26)

GN
2.1
S 78
ETHNOLOGY SAMOA

Keesing, Felix M.

Elite communication in Samoa: a study of leadership. By Felix M. and Marie M. Keesing.

(Stanford Anthropological Series, No. 3, 1956)

G
1
G 56
ETHNOLOGY SAMOA

Bülow, Werner von

Die Namen der Samoa-Inseln.

(Globus, Bd. 78, 1900, pp. 31-33)

GN
1
A
ETHNOLOGY SAMOA

Densmore, Frances

The Native Music of American Samoa.

(American Anthropologist, Vol. 34, 1932, pp. 415-417).

GN
671.S2
K 89
ETHNOLOGY SAMOA

Krämer, Augustin

Die Samoa-Inseln. Entwurf einer Monographie mit besonderer Berücksichtigung Deutsch-Samoas... Stuttgart. 1902-1903. 4to.

Erster Band: Verfassung, Stammbäume und Überlieferungen...

II. Band: Ethnographie... Nebst einem besonderen Anhang: Die wichtigsten Hautkrankheiten der Südsee...

GN
Ethn.Pam.   ETHNOLOGY SAMOA
3353
a and b   Kurse, G.

                   Die Samoaner in der heidnischen Zeit: Bei-
                   träge zur Volkskunde der Samoaner nach den For-
                   schungen der Missionare G. Turner, J. B. Stair
                   und A. W. Murray.

                   (Mitt. der Geographischen Gesell. f.
                   Thuringen zu Jena, Bd. 18, 1900, pp. 1-29; Bd.
over   19, 1900/1901, pp. 1-42)

GN
27   ETHNOLOGY SAMOA
M 97   Murdock, George Peter

                   Our primitive contemporaries.
                   The Macmillan Company. New York. sm8vo. xxii +
                   614 pp. 1934c

GN
Ethn.Pam.   ETHNOLOGY SAMOA
3382   Wagner, J. H. (John Harrison)

                   The lotus land of the Pacific. (Samoa)

                   (Harpers Magazine, 1897, pp. 620-629)

GN
2.S   ETHNOLOGY SAMOA
P 76   McKay, C. G. R.

                   An introduction to Samoan custom.

                   (Jour. Poly. Soc., 66(1):36-43, 1957)

GN
Ethn.Pam.   ETHNOLOGY SAMOA
3383   O'Brien, Frederick

                   Happy days in Safune, Samoa: the simple
                   life of a joyous, peace-loving nation in the
                   South Seas.

                   (Mentor Magazine, 1925, pp. 37-52)

GN
1   ETHNOLOGY SANTA CRUZ ISLANDS
N 27   Bogese, George

                   Notes on the Santa Cruz group.

                   (Native Medical Practitioner, 3:538-543,
                   1941)

GN
671.S2   ETHNOLOGY SAMOA
M 15   McKenzie, A.

                   Samoan customs, etc. For The Administration
                   Schools. no place, no date. mimeographed. sm
                   8vo. 107 pp.

GN
Ethn.Pam.   ETHNOLOGY - SAMOA
2984   Schultz, E.

                   Samoan Laws Concerning the Family, Real
                   Estate and Succession. Translated by Father
                   E. Bellward. 29 typed pages. 1912.

AM
Mus.Pam.   ETHNOLOGY SANTA CRUZ ISLANDS
123
                   Führer durch das Museum für Völkerkunde,
                   Basel. Die Neuen Hebriden und Santa Cruz-
                   Inseln. G. Krebs, Basel. 1929. 36 pp.

GN
662   ETHNOLOGY SAMOA
M 27   Mander, Linden A.

                   Some dependent peoples of the South Pacific.
                   Issued under the auspices of the International
                   Secretariat, Institute of Pacific Relations. The
                   MacMillan Co. New York. 1954. 8vo. xix + 535
                   pp.

QH
301   ETHNOLOGY SAMOA
C 3   Setchell, W. A.

                   American Samoa, Parts I-III. Washington.
        1924.   Part II. Ethnobotany of the Samoans.

                   (Carnegie Institution, Dep't of Marine Biol-
                   ogy, Vol. XX, Publ. No. 341)

GN
2.M   ETHNOLOGY SANTA CRUZ ISLANDS
B 85   Graebner, F.

                   Völkerkunde der Santa-Cruz-Inseln.

                   (Ethnologica, 1:71-184, 1909)

GN
671.S2   ETHNOLOGY SAMOA
M 47   Mead, Margaret

                   Coming of age in Samoa, a psychological
                   study of primitive youth for western civilisation.
                   Foreword by Franz Boas. New York, Morrow, 1928.
                   8vo. xv + 297 pp.

GN
2.S   ETHNOLOGY SAMOA
P 76   Smith, S. Percy

        and   Kava drinking ceremonies among the Samoans
                   and a boat voyage around 'Upolu Island, Samoa.
        GN
        Ethn.   (Jour. Poly. Soc., Vol. 29, 1920, Suppl.
        Pam.   pp. 1-21)
        336

GN
2.I   ETHNOLOGY SANTA CRUZ
A-4   Jennings, John

                   Notes on the exhibition of an ethnological
                   collection from Santa Cruz and the New Hebrides.

                   (Journ. Anthrop. Inst. of Great Britain and
                   Ireland, N. S. Vol. 1, 1898-9, pp. 164-165)

GN
2.1   ETHNOLOGY SAMOA
A-4   Mead, Margaret

                   The role of the individual in Samoan culture.

                   (Journ. R. Anthrop. Inst. of Great Britain
                   and Ireland, vol. 58, 1928, pp. 481-495)

AS
701   ETHNOLOGY SAMOA
A   Stair, John B.

                   Early Samoan Voyages and settlements.

                   (Australasian Ass'n for the Adv. of Sci.
                   Report of the 6th Meeting, 1895, pp. 612-619)

GN
2.M   ETHNOLOGY SANTA CRUZ ISLANDS
E 65   Speiser, Felix

                   Völkerkundliches von den Santa Cruz Inseln.

                   (Ethnologica, 2(2):153-213, 1916)

GN
671.S2   ETHNOLOGY SAMOA
M47   Mead, Margaret

AS   Social organisation of Manua. Bernice P.
763   Bishop Museum, bulletin 76, 1930.   218p.
B-b

Reading
Room

GN
2.M   ETHNOLOGY SAMOA
B 51   Steubel, Otto

                   Samoanische Texte unter Beihefte von einge-
                   borenen Gesammelt und Übersetzt. Herausgegeben
                   von F. W. K. Müller.

                   (Veroffentlichungen der K. Museum f. Völker-
                   kunde, Berlin, Bd. 4, Heft 2-4, 1897)

GN
1   ETHNOLOGY SANTA ISABEL
O 15   Bogesi, George

                   Santa Isabel, Solomon Islands.

                   (Oceania, Vol. 18: 208-232, 1948)

AS 492 S 6	ETHNOLOGY SARAWAK Banks, E. The natives of Sarawak. (Journal of the R. Asiatic Soc., Malayan Branch, Vol. 18, 1940, pp. 49-54)
GN 635.B7 H 32	ETHNOLOGY SARAWAK Harrisson, Tom editor The peoples of Sarawak. Sarawak Museum. 8vo. 1959. 141 pp. [articles by the editor, A. J. N. Richards, J. F. Drake-Brookman, C. H. Southwell and others]
GN 635.B7 M 87	ETHNOLOGY SARAWAK Morris, H. S. Report on a Melanau sago producing community in Sarawak. (Colonial Research Studies No. 9, 1953. (London) 176 pp. folio mimeographed) [economic and social systems]
GN 27 M 97	ETHNOLOGY SEMANG Murdock, George Peter Our primitive contemporaries. The Macmillan Company. New York. sm8vo. xxii+ 614 pp. 1934c
GN 652.S4 B 48	ETHNOLOGY SENEGAMBIA Bérenger-Féraud, L. J. B. Les Peuplades de la Sénégambie: Histoire, Ethnographie, Moeurs et Coutumes, Legendes, etc... Paris. 1879. 8vo.
G 51 W 17	ETHNOLOGY SEPIK RIVER Clune, Frank "Drums on the Sepik": being an account of a launch journey along New Guinea's greatest river. (Walkabout, Vol. 8(4):9-14, 1942)
G 51 W 17	ETHNOLOGY SEPIK RIVER Clune, Frank Stone-age men of the upper Sepik. (Walkabout, Vol. 8(6):12-14, 1942)

GN 671.N5 G 21	ETHNOLOGY SEPIK RIVER Gardi, René Sepik, Land der sterbenden Geister. Bilddokumente aus Neuguinea. Einführender Text und Bildlegenden von Alfred Bühler. Alfred Scherz Verlag. Bern... 4to. 144 pp. 1958c.
G 51 W 17	ETHNOLOGY SEPIK RIVER Read, G. M. Tripping and trading on the Sepik River. (Walkabout, Vol. 11 (4):11-15, 1945)
GN 635.S1 G 36	ETHNOLOGY SIAM Gerini, G. E. Chulakantamangala: the tonsure ceremony as performed in Siam. Bangkok. 1893. R8vo.
GN 635.M4 L 34	ETHNOLOGY SIAM Lasker, Bruno Peoples of southeast Asia. Prepared under the auspices of the American Council of the Institute of Pacific Relations. New York. 1945.
AS 122 I	ETHNOLOGY SIERRA LEONE Berry, R. J. *Sierra Leone cannibals with notes on their history, religion and customs.* *In Proc. R. Irish Acad. XXX C. 2. Dublin 1912.*
GN 2.8 P 76	ETHNOLOGY SIKAIANA Hogbin, H. Ian "Polynesian" colonies in Melanesia. (Journal of the Polynesian Society, Vol. 49, 1940, pp. 199-220)
GN 2.8 P 76	ETHNOLOGY SIKAIANA MacQuarrie, H. Sikaiana or Stewart Island. (Jour. Poly. Soc., 61(3/4):209-221, 1952) [from a report submitted in 1924]

GN 2.1 A-M	ETHNOLOGY SIKAIANA Woodford, C. M. Some account of Sikaiana or Stewart's Island in the British Solomon Islands Protectorate. (Man, vol. 6, 1906, no. 103, pp. 164-169, figs. 1,2)
GN 671.S5 B 94	ETHNOLOGY SOCIETY ISLANDS Bunzendahl, Otto Tahiti und Europa, I. Entdeckungsgeschichte der Gesellschaftsinseln. Rassische Verhältnisse Stoffliche Kultur und deren erste Beeinflussung durch die Europäer. (Studien zur Völkerkunde, Bd. 8) Werkgemeinschaft. Leipzig. 1935. 8vo
GN 22 F 71	ETHNOLOGY SOCIETY ISLANDS Forde, C. Daryll Habitat, economy and society: a geographical introduction to ethnology. With a frontispiece and 108 other illustrations and maps. London. Methuen and Co., Ltd.; New York. E. P. Dutton and Co., Inc. 8vo. xv + 500 pp.
GN 671.S 5 H 23	ETHNOLOGY SOCIETY ISLANDS Handy, E. S. Craighill Houses, Boats and Fishing in the Society Islands. (Bulletin Bernice P. Bishop Museum, 90. 1931. 111 pp. 25 plates, 21 figures)
AS 763 B-b DU 870 H 52 Reading Room	ETHNOLOGY SOCIETY ISLANDS Henry, Teuira Ancient Tahiti. (Bernice P. Bishop Museum. Bull. 48, 1928, 651 pp.)
G 161 H 15-e	ETHNOLOGY SOCIETY ISLANDS Remarkable occurrences on board His Majesty's bark Endeavour. IN Beaglehole, J. C. editor The journals of Captain James Cook...Vol. 1 1955, pp. 118-154. (Works of the Hakluyt Soc., Extra Ser. No. 34, 1955)
GN 2.8 T	ETHNOLOGY SOCIETY ISLANDS Ropiteau, André Notes sur l'ile Maupiti. (Bulletin Soc. d'Etudes Océaniennes, Tome 5, 1932, pp. 113-129)

GN
Ethn. Pam.
3142

ETHNOLOGY — SOCIETY ISLANDS

Silverthorne, Henry

Society Islands pounders.

AS
763
B-4

(B. P. Bishop Mus., Occasional Papers, Vol. XI, No. 17, 1936, 17 pp., 5 figs.)

Reading
Room

GN
Ethn. Pam.
3341

ETHNOLOGY SOCIETY ISLANDS

Stevenson, Tom

Theater in the Society Islands

(Univ. of Washington Bull., Abstracts of Theses...Vol. 3, 1938, pp. 156-157. Typed copy. Complete volume sent to Univ. of Hawaii)

GN
2.M
C 89

ETHNOLOGY SOLOMON ISLANDS

Beasley, Harry Geoffrey

The tamar of Santa Cruz.

(Ethnologia Cranmorensis, No. 4, 1939, p. 27-30)

GN
671.S6
B 45

ETHNOLOGY SOLOMON ISLANDS

Belshaw, Cyril S.

An economic development of a Melanesian economy (A study of Gela, British Solomon Islands). Thesis presented for the degree of M.A. in the University of New Zealand, Nov. 1945. carbon copy, typed. folio. 124 pp.

GN
671.S6
B 63

ETHNOLOGY SOLOMON ISLANDS

Blackwood, Beatrice

Both sides of Buka Passage. An ethnographic study of social, sexual, and economic questions in the north-western Solomon Islands. Oxford. Clarendon Press. 1935. 624 pp., 80 pl., 30 figs., 1 map. 8vo.

GN
1
O 15

ETHNOLOGY SOLOMON ISLANDS

Blackwood, Beatrice

Report on field work in Buka and Bougainville.

(Oceania, Vol. 2, 1931-1932, pp. 199-219)

GN
1
O 15

ETHNOLOGY SOLOMON ISLANDS

Bogesi, George

Santa Isabel, Solomon Islands.

(Oceania, Vol. 18: 208-232, 1948)

GN
1
O 15

ETHNOLOGY SOLOMON ISLANDS

Capell, A.

Notes on the islands of Choiseul and New Georgia, Solomon Islands.

(Oceania, Vol. 14, 1943, pp. 20-29)

QL
617
C 46

ETHNOLOGY SOLOMON ISLANDS

Chapman, Wilbert McLeod

Fishing in troubled waters. J. B. Lippincott Company. Philadelphia and New York. 1949. 8vo. 256pp.

GN
2.I
A-4

ETHNOLOGY SOLOMON IS.

Elton, F.

Notes on natives of Solomon Islands.

(Journ. Anthrop. Inst. of Great Britain and Ireland, Vol. 17, 1887-8, pp. 90-99)

GN
Ethn. Pam.
2979

ETHNOLOGY-SOLOMON ISLANDS

Eyerdam, Walter J.

Among the Mountain Bushmen of Malaita

(Natural History, vol. 33, 1933, pp. 430-438)

QL
401
N

ETHNOLOGY-SOLOMON ISLANDS

Eyerdam, Walter J.

Collecting shells in the Solomon Islands.

(The Nautilus, Vol. 57, 1943, No. 2, pp. 41-42)

(the author saw the immense collection of material from the Solomons when he was at the Mus. of Ethnogr. at Basle.)

AS
142
V

and

GN
662
F 51

ETHNOLOGY SOLOMON ISLANDS

Finsch, Otto

Ethnologische Erfahrungen und Belegstücke aus der Südsee...

(Ann. K. K. Naturhist., Mus., Wien, Bd. 3:83-160, 1888; Bd. 8; 400, 1893)

GN
22
F 71

ETHNOLOGY SOLOMON ISLANDS

Forde, C. Daryll

Habitat, economy and society; a geographical introduction to ethnology. With a frontispiece and 108 other illustrations and maps. London. Methuen and Co., Ltd.; New York. E. P. Dutton and Co., Inc. 8vo. xv + 500 pp.

GN
668
F 79

ETHNOLOGY SOLOMON ISLANDS

Fox, C. E.

The threshold of the Pacific; an account of the social organization, magic and religion of the people of San Cristoval in the Solomon Islands. With a preface by G. Elliot Smith. With 14 plates 39 illustrations in the text, and a map. London. Kegan Paul, Trench, Trubner and Co., Ltd. New York... 1924. 8vo. xvi, 379, pp.

GN
2.S
P.78

Review by editors. (Jour. of Poly. Soc., Vol. 35: 58-62, 1926)

GN
1
A62

ETHNOLOGY SOLOMON ISLANDS

Hagen, A.

Les indigènes des îles Salomon.

(L'Anthropologie, Tome 4, 1893, pp. 1-10; 192-216)

GN
2.I
A-4

ETHNOLOGY SOLOMON ISLANDS

Harrison, H. S.

Flint Tranchets in the Solomon Islands and Elsewhere.

(Journal of the R. Anthropological Institute, Vol. LXI, 1931, pp. 425-434)

AS
28
E 85

ETHNOLOGY SOLOMON ISLANDS

Hébert, Bernard

Aperçus sur l'administration et la justice autochtones dans le Protectorat Britannique des Iles Salomon.

(Etudes Mélanesiennes, n.s. nr. 12/13:32-44, 1961)

GN
2.I
A-4

ETHNOLOGY - SOLOMON ISLANDS

Hocart, A. M.

Warfare in Eddystone of the Solomon Islands.

(Journal of the R. Anthropological Institute Vol. LXI, 1931, pp. 301-324)

GN
Ethn. Pam.
2890

ETHNOLOGY - SOLOMON ISLANDS

Hogbin, H. Ian

Education at Ongtong, Java, Solomon Islands

(American Anthropologist, vol. 33, no. 4) pp. 601-614. 1931

GN
671.S6
H 71

ETHNOLOGY SOLOMON ISLANDS

Hogbin, H. Ian

Experiments in civilization; the effects of European culture on a native community of the Solomon Islands. London. George Routledge and Sons. Ltd. (1939) 8vo. xviii + 268 pp.

GN
1
O 15

and
GN
Ethn.Pam.
3218

ETHNOLOGY SOLOMON ISLANDS

Hogbin, H. Ian

The hill people of north-eastern Guadalcanal

(Oceania, Vol. 8, 1937, pp. 62-89)

GN
Ethn.Pam.
2891

ETHNOLOGY SOLOMON ISLANDS

Hogbin, H. Ian

Tribal ceremonies at Ongtong Java (Solomon
Islands).

(Journal of the Royal Anthropological Institute, Vol. 61, 1931, pp. 27-55)

GN
662
P 24

ETHNOLOGY SOLOMON ISLANDS

Parkinson, R.

Dreissig jahre in der Südsee: Land und Leute
Sitten und Gebräuche im Bismarckarchipel und auf
den Deutschen Salomoinseln...Stuttgart. 1907.
R8vo.

GN
Ethn.Pam.
2922

ETHNOLOGY - SOLOMON ISLANDS

Hogbin, H. Ian

A Note on Rennell Island.

(Reprinted from Oceania, December, 1931.
Vol. II, No. 2. Sydney. Australasian Medical
Publishing Company, Limited. 1931. 174-178 pp.
8vo.) Plates I-IV.

GN
2.1
A-4

ETHNOLOGY SOLOMON ISLANDS

Ivens, W. G.

Flints in the South-East Solomon Islands.

(Journal of the R. Anthropological Institute
Vol. LXI, 1931, pp. 421-424)

AS
182
B 83

ETHNOLOGY SOLOMON ISLANDS

Petri, Hans-Hermann

Beitrage zur Volkerkunde von Bougainville
(Salomo-Ins ln) I

(Veroffentlichungen aus dem Ubersee-Museum
in Breman, Reihe B, Bd. 1:197-200, tf I-II,1959)

GN
Ethn.Pam.
2842

ETHNOLOGY - SOLOMON ISLANDS

Hogbin,H.I.

Primeval Life as it is Lived To-Day:
"Untainted" Existence on Rennell Island--An
Anthropologist's "Paradise".

The Illustrated London News, 1931, Apr. 4
2 pp., 8vo.

GN
668
K 69

ETHNOLOGY SOLOMON ISLANDS

Knibbs, S. G. C.

The savage Solomons as they were and are: a
record of a head-hunting people gradually emerg-
in from a life of savage cruelty and bloody customs, with a description of their manners and
ways and of the beauties and potentialities of
the islands. With illustrations and map.
London. Seeley, Service and Co., Ltd. 1929.
8vo. 282 pp.

GN
671.S6
R 48

ETHNOLOGY SOLOMON ISLANDS

Ribbe, Carl

Zwei jahre unter den Kannibalen der Salomo-
Inseln. Reiseerlebnisse und Schilderungen von
Land und Leuten von Carl Ribbe. Unter Mitwirkung
von Heinrich Kalbfus. Mit zahlreichen abbildunge
im text, 14 tafeln, 10 lithographischen beilagen
und 3 karten. Dresden-Blasewitz. Hermann Beyer.
1903. R8vo. vii + 352 pp.

GN
1
O 15

and
GN
Ethn.Pam.
3245

ETHNOLOGY SOLOMON ISLANDS

Hogbin, H. Ian

Social advancement in Guadalcanal, Solomon
Islands.

(Oceania, Vol. 8, 1938, pp. 289-305)

DU
Pac.Pam.
487

ETHNOLOGY - SOLOMON ISLANDS

Lambert, S. M.

Health Survey of Rennell and Bellona Islands

(Oceania, Vol. II, No. 2, 1931, pp.136-173)

GN
1
An

ETHNOLOGY SOLOMON ISLANDS

Riesenfeld, Alphonse

Was there a Paleolithic period in Melanesia?

(Anthropos, Bd. 47(3/4):405-446, 1952)

GN
1
A

ETHNOLOGY - SOLOMON ISLANDS

Hogbin, H. Ian

Sorcery at Ongtong Java.

(American Anthropologist, Vol. 34, pp. 441-
448, 1932)

GN
662
M 27

ETHNOLOGY SOLOMON ISLANDS

Mander, Linden A.

Some dependent peoples of the South Pacific.
Issued under the auspices of the International
Secretariat, Institute of Pacific Relations. The
MacMillan Co. New York. 1954. 8vo. xix + 535
pp.

GN
2.3
P 76

ETHNOLOGY SOLOMON ISLANDS

Russell, T.

The culture of Marovo, British Solomon Islands.

(Jour. Poly. Soc., Vol. 57:306-329, 1948)

GN
Ethn.Pam.
2833

ETHNOLOGY   SOLOMON ISLANDSY

Hogbin, H. Ian

Spirits and the Healing of the Sick in
Ontong Java.
8vo.

(Reprint from Oceania,Vol.1,No.2,pp.146-166,
8vo., 1930)

DU
850
M 99

ETHNOLOGY SOLOMON ISLANDS

Mytinger, Caroline

Headhunting in the Solomon Islands around
the Coral Sea. Illustrated. New York. Macmillan Co. 1942. 8vo ix + 416 pp.

GN
671.S6
S 29

ETHNOLOGY SOLOMON ISLANDS

Schaffrath, K. J.

Südseebilder. Nach Aufnahmen von K. J.
Schaffrath. 74 lichtdruckbilder auf 38 tafeln
nebst erläuterndem text. Berlin. D. Reimer.
1909. R8vo. (85 pp.)

GN
Ethn.Pam.
2834

ETHNOLOGY - SOLOMON ISLANDS

Hogbin, H. Ian

Transition Rites at Ontong Java

Extract from Vol. 39, Nos. 2 and 3, 1930
Journal of the Polynesian Society - 1930

GN
2.1
T 89

ETHNOLOGY SOLOMON ISLANDS

Paravicini, Eugen

Die speere der Salomons Inseln.

(Revista del Instituto de Etnologia, Universidad de Tucuman, Tomo II, 1932, pp. 481-491)

GN
Ethn.
Pam.
4295

ETHNOLOGY SOLOMON ISLANDS

Schlaginhaufen, Otto

Uber Eingeborene des melanesischen Atolls
Nissan.

(Reprint, Bull. Schweizerischen Gesell. f.
Anthropolgie und Ethnologie, Bern, 37 Jahrg.
1960/61, pp. 32-45)

GN
Ethn.Pam.
3336

ETHNOLOGY   SOLOMON ISLANDS

Thurnwald, Hilde

Ehe und Mutterschaft in Buin.(Bougainville, Salomo-Archipel).

(Archiv f. Anthropologie, N. F. Bd. 24,1938?
pp. 214-246)

GN
671.S6
T 54

ETHNOLOGY   SOLOMON ISLANDS

Thurnwald, Hilde

Menschen der Südsee, Charaktere und Schicksale. Ermittelt bei einer Forschungsreise in Buin auf Bougainville, Salomo-Archipel. Mit 32 Abbildungen auf Tafeln. Mit einem Vorwort von Richard Thurnwald. Ferdinand Enke. Stuttgart. R8vo. 1937. vi + 201 pp.

GN
671.S6
T 54

ETHNOLOGY SOLOMON ISLANDS

Thurnwald, Richard

Forschungen auf den Salomo-Inseln und dem Bismarck-Archipel... Berlin. 1912. R8vo.

Band I. Lieder und Sagen aus Buin. Nebst einem anhang: Die Musik auf den Salomo-Inseln von E. M. v. Hornbostel. Mit 14 tafeln, 3 karten und 42 notenbeispielen. xx + 538 pp. + tafeln.

Band III. Volk, Staat und Wirtschaft. Mit 1 lichtdrucktafel und 70 stammtafeln. viii + 92 pp. + tafeln.

GN
1
O 15

ETHNOLOGY SOLOMON ISLANDS

Wright, L. W. S.

Notes on the hill people of north-eastern Guadalcanal.

(Oceania, Vol. 9, 1938, p. 97-100)

GN
2.I
C 99

ETHNOLOGY SOUTH AMERICA

Cuyo, Universidad Nacional
      Instituto de Etnografia Americana.
      Anales,
      Tomo 1, 1940-

GN
2.M
Pe

ETHNOLOGY SOUTH AMERICA

Farabee, William Curtis

The Central Caribs.

(Univ. of Penn. Univ. Mus. Anthrop. Pub. No. X, 1924.)

GN
Ethn.Pam.
2915

ETHNOLOGY SOUTH AMERICA

Friederici, Georg

Die Amazonen Amerikas. Leipzig. Simmel and Co. 1910. 22 pp. 8vo.

GN
Ethn.Pam.
2927

ETHNOLOGY SOUTH AMERICA

Imbelloni, J.

Un Arma de Oceanía en el Neuquén: Reconstrucción y Tipología del Hacha del Río Limay.

(Humanidades, Tomo XX, Páginas 293-316,1929)

GN
Ethn.Pam.
2934

ETHNOLOGY SOUTH AMERICA

Imbelloni, J.

Clava-Insignia de Villavicencio. Un Nuevo Ejemplar de los "Mere" de Oceania Descubierto en el Territorio Americano.

(Anales de la Facultad de Ciencias de la Educacion, Universidad Nacional del Litoral, Paraná, República Argentina, Tomo III, 219-228, 1928)

GN
Ethn.
Pam.
4101

ETHNOLOGY   SOUTH AMERICA

Murdock, George P.

Outline of South American cultures.

Behavior Science Outlines, Vol. 2, Yale University, Human Relations Area Files, Inc.1951

F
2229
N 83

ETHNOLOGY   SOUTH AMERICA

Nordenskiöld, Erland

Origin of the Indian Civilizations in South America. (Comparative Ethnographical Studies,9) Göteborg, 1931.

GN
550
S 46

ETHNOLOGY SOUTH AMERICA

Seler, Eduard

Gesammelte Abhandlungen zur americanischen Sprach-und Altertumskunde. Bd. 3, 5, 1908,1915. Berlin. R8vo. Behrend & Co.

GN
550
S

and

F
2229
S 94

ETHNOLOGY   SOUTH AMERICA

Steward, Julian H.   editor

Handbook of South American Indians.
Vol. 1: The marginal tribes. Vol. 2: The Andean civilizations. Vol. 3: The tropical forest tribes. Vol. 4: The circum-Caribbean tribes. Vol. 5: The comparative ethnology of South American Indians. Vol. 6:Physical anthropology, Linguistics, and cultural geography of South American Indians.
(Bur. Am.   Ethnology, Bull. 143, Vols. 1-6,   1946-1950)

GN
561
S 94

and

F
2229
S 84

ETHNOLOGY SOUTH AMERICA

Steward, Julian H.

Native peoples of South America. By Julian Steward and Louis C. Faron. McGraw-Hill Book Company, Inc. New York... 8vo. 1959. xi + 481 pp.

F
2229
T 69

ETHNOLOGY SOUTH AMERICA

Torres, Luis Maria

Los primitivos habitantes del Delta del Paraná. Buenos Aires. Coni Hermanos. 1913. (Universidad Nacional de la Plata).

E
58
J 54

ETHNOLOGY - SOUTH AMERICA

Wissler, Clark

Ethnological Diversity in America and Its Significance.

Jenness, Diamond

The American Aborigines...pp. 165-216.

AS
36
S1

ETHNOLOGY - STUDY AND TEACHING

Schoolcraft, Henry Rowe, 1793-1864.
Plan for American ethnological investigation. By the late Henry R. Schoolcraft.
(*In* Smithsonian institution. Annual report. 1885. Washington, 1886. 234ᵗʰ. p. 907-914)

1. Ethnology—Study and teaching.

Library of Congress   Q11.S66 1885   S 15-641
Library, Smithsonian   Institution

GN
Ethn.Pam.
3863

ETHNOLOGY SUMATRA

Bartlett, Harley Harris

A Batak and Malay chant on rice cultivation, with introductory notes on bilingualism and acculturation in Indonesia.

(Proc. Am. Philosophical Soc., Vol. 96(6): 629-652, 1952)

GN
630.M3
C 68

ETHNOLOGY - SUMATRA

Cole, F.C.

The peoples of Malaysia.   D. Van Nostrand Company, Inc.   Toronto, New York... 8vo. 1945c xiv + 354 pp.

GN
Ethn.Pam.
3040

ETHNOLOGY SUMATRA

Hagen, Dr. B. von

Die Orang Kubu auf Sumatra. Frankfurt a/m 1908, 4to. pp. 266.

(Veröffentlichungen aus dem Städt. Völker-Museum. Frankfurt a/m, 1908)

GN
635.S
H 96

ETHNOLOGY SUMATRA

Hurgronje, C. Snouck

The Achehnese...translated by the late A. W. S. O'Sullivan...with an index by R. J. Wilkinson ...2 vols. Leyden. 1906. 4to.

GN
2.I
W 64

ETHNOLOGY SUMATRA

Loeb, Edwin M.

Sumatra: Its History and People.

(Wiener Beiträge zur Kulturgeschichte und Linguistik...Univ. Wien, Vol. III, 1935, pp. 1-303)

DU
Pac.Pam.
483

ETHNOLOGY TAHITI

Crossland, Cyril

Tahiti.

(Blackwood's Magazine, Vol. 225, pp. 126-33, January, 1929)

DU
12
M 15

ETHNOLOGY TAHITI

Mackaness, George

The life of Vice-Admiral William Bligh. Two volumes in one. Illustrated with contemporary charts and engravings. Farrar and Rinehart, Inc. New York; Toronto. R8vo. (12) + 348 + (48) pp. (no date- preface 1931)

AS
322
Z 96 v

ETHNOLOGY SUMATRA

Schneider, Gustav

Die Orang Mamma auf Sumatra.

(Vierteljahrsschrift der Naturforschenden Gesselschaft in Zürich, 103(5), 1958)

GN
1
Ar

ETHNOLOGY TAHITI

Dalton, O. M.

Notes on an ethnological collection from the west coast of North America, Hawaii, and Tahiti formed during the voyage of Captain Vancouver, 1790-1795, and now in the British Museum.

(Archiv. fur Ethnog. X, 1897, pp. 225-245)

Case
5
Ms
T 4

ETHNOLOGY TAHITI

Mare

Tahitian account of creation, of Ruahatu and the flood, of Maui, Oro, of Teriitinorua or Turi, of the Arioi and a genealogy of the chiefs of Raiatea. Translated by L. Gaussin: Cosmogonie Tahitienne, q.v.

GN
635.S
V 94

ETHNOLOGY SUMATRA

Volz, Wilhelm

Nord-Sumatra: bericht über eine im auftrage der Humboldt-stiftung der Königlich Preussischen Akademie der Wissenschaften su Berlin in den jahren 1904-1906...2vols. Berlin. 1909-1912. R8vo.

Band I. Die Batakländer...1909.
Band II. Die Gajoländer...1912.

GN
Ethn.Pam.
3217

ETHNOLOGY TAHITI

de la Condamine

Observations de Mr. de la Condamine sur l'insulaire de la Polynésie , amené de lisle de Tayti en France par Mr. de Bougainville.

(Photostat copy of ms in the Bibliothèque Nationale, Paris, with transcription by André Ropiteau. 8 pages and a map)

DU
870
M 87

ETHNOLOGY TAHITI

Morrison, James

The journal of James Morrison, boatswain's mate of the Bounty, describing the mutiny and subsequent misfortunes of the mutineers, together with an account of the island of Tahiti. With an introduction by Owen Rutter and five engravings by Robert Gibbings. Printed and made in Great Britain by The Golden Cockerel Press. 1935. sm4to. 243 pp.

GN
Ethn.Pam.
407

ETHNOLOGY SURINAM

Goeje, C. H. de

Beiträge zur Völkerkunde von Surinam.

(Festgabe an den XVI Intern. Amerikanisten Kongress in Wien, Leiden, 1908. 32 pp., 20 tafeln)

GN
2.S
T

ETHNOLOGY TAHITI

Emory, Kenneth P.

L'Art Tahitien.

(In Bulletin de la Société d'Etudes Océaniennes, No. 19, 1927)

GN
Ethn.Pam
2837

ETHNOLOGY TAHITI

Plischke, Hans

Tahitische Trauergewänder.

(Abhandlungen der Gesell. der Wiss. su Göttingen, Phil-Hist. Kl. N.F. Bd. XXIV, 2, which forms Arbeiten aus der Ethnographischen Sammlung der Univ. Göttingen, 2. Berlin, 1931)

GN
585.S
C 17

ETHNOLOGY - SWEDEN

Campbell, Ake

Akänska Bygder under Förra Hälften Av 1700 - Talet.

(Ethnographic study of the culture, agriculture development and habitations of the people). Uppsala 1928. A.-B. Lundequistska Bokhandeln.

GN
Ethn.Pam.
2883

ETHNOLOGY TAHITI

Gaussin, L.

Cosmogonie Tahitienne.

(Le Tour du Monde, 1860, pp. 10-12 and 302-304)

GN
400
S 49

ETHNOLOGY TAHITI

Service, Elman R.

A profile of primitive culture. Harper and Brothers. New York. 1958. R8vo. xiv + 474 pp.

(For revision: see "Profiles in ethnology")

GN
Ethn.Pam.
3207

ETHNOLOGY TAHITI

Agostini, Jules

Folk-lore de Tahiti et des iles voisines. Changements survenus dans les coutumes, moeurs, ...depuis soixante-dix années environ (1829-1899).

(Revue des Traditions Populaires. Tome 15, nos.2-3. Feb.-Mar. 1900)

GN
Ethn.Pam.
3381

ETHNOLOGY TAHITI

Keeler, Charles

Upon a coral strand. (Tahiti)

(Out West Magazine, 1903, pp. 491-499, 635-644).

GN
400
S 49

ETHNOLOGY TAHITI

Service, Elman R.

Profiles in ethnology: a revision of "A profile of primitive culture." New York. Harper & Row. 1963. xxix + 509 pp. R8vo.

GN
671.S5
B 89

ETHNOLOGY TAHITI

Brunor, Martin Anthony   collector

The morai at Opara, Tahiti:
London Missionary account, by Jefferson
Lt. Tobin's drawings
Capt. William Bligh's log book- second voyage for the breadfruit. ms in Mitchell Library. 80 pp. typed by Brunor

---

GN
2.S
T

ETHNOLOGY TAHITI

Lesoure, Rey

Essai de reconstitution des moeurs et des coutumes de l'ancien Tahiti.

(Bull. Soc. des Etudes Oceaniennes, no. 72 [Vol. VII(1)]:28-34, 1945)

GN
Ethn.Pam.
3324

ETHNOLOGY TAHITI

Tahitian princesses. The daughters and nieces of Pomare IV., queen of Otaheite.

(The Ladies Treasury, 1865, pp. 65-67,1 pl.)

GN
1
T 35

ETHNOLOGY TAIWAN

Achievements by Japanese researchers in the anthropological sciences concerning Formosa.

(Japanese Jour. of Ethnology, 18(1/2), 1953)

GN
Pam
2227

ETHNOLOGY TASMANIA

Noetling, Fritz

The food of the Tasmanian aborigines. Roy. Soc. Tasmania, July, 1910.

GN
635.T3
Y 72

ETHNOLOGY THAILAND

Young, Gordon

The hill tribes of Northern Thailand; the origins and habitats...together with significant changes in their social, cultural and economic patterns.

(Monograph, The Siam Society, No. 1, 1962)

GN
Ethn.
Pam.
3950

ETHNOLOGY TAIWAN

Achievements by Japanese researchers in the anthropological sciences concerning Formosa.

(Japanese Journal of Ethnology, Vol. 18, no. 1/2, 1953)

(linguistics, religion, mat. cult., prehist., physical anthrop. migration...)

GN
Pam
2088

ETHNOLOGY , TASMANIA

Noetling, Fritz

Further notes on the habits of the Tasmanian aborigines. From Royal Soc. Tasmania, papers & proc., 1911.

AS
36
S3

ETHNOLOGY-TIBET.

Rockhill, William Woodville, 1854-1914.
Notes on the ethnology of Tibet. Based on the collections in the United States National museum. By William Woodville Rockhill ...

(*In* U. S. National museum. Annual report. 1893. Washington, 1895. 23½ᶜᵐ. p. 665-747. 52 pl.)

Half-title.
Many plates accompanied by guard sheets with descriptive letterpress.

1. Ethnology—Tibet.

Library of Congress   Q11.U5 1893   14-19798
——— Copy 2.
——— Separate.   GN635.T5R8

GN
Ethn.
Pam.
4086

ETHNOLOGY TAIWAN

Kanaseki, Takeo

Checklist of library of... concerning archeology and ethnology of Taiwan.
also
List of 250 Prehistoric objects from various Formosan sites, and Hongkong.
List of the names of prehistoric sites, Formosa.
List of 38 ethnological objects from Formosa

several pages,   typed.

GN
665.T
R 84

ETHNOLOGY TASMANIA

Roth, H. Ling
The aborigines of Tasmania, by H. Ling Roth, assisted by Marion E. Butler; with a chapter on the Osteology, by J. G. Garson...Preface by Edward B. Tylor...London. Kegan Paul. 1890. 8vo. xxvii + 224 + cx pp.
Second edition, revised and enlarged, with a map. Assisted by Marion E. Butler, and Jas. Backhouse Walker...Illustrated. Halifax. F.King. 1899. R8vo. xix + 228 + ciii pp.

GN
562
F 81

ETHNOLOGY TIERRA DEL FUEGO

(France.) Ministères de la Marine et de l'Instruction Publique

Mission Scientifique du Cap Horn, 1882-1883. Tome VII. Anthropologie, Ethnographie (de Tierra del Fuego) par P. Hyades et J. Deniker. Paris. 1891. 4to.

AS
701
A

ETHNOLOGY TANNA

Gray, William

Some notes on the Tannese.

(Aust. Ass'n for the Adv. of Sci., 4th meeting, 1892, pp. 645-680)

(districts, religion, circumcision, kava, war, a song, calendar, winds, navigation, terms of relationship.)

AS
720.T
R

ETHNOLOGY TASMANIA

R. Soc. Tasmania, Papers and Proceedings

1900->

GN
2.S
P 76

ETHNOLOGY TIKOPIA

Firth, Raymond

The analysis of *mana*: an empirical approach.

(Journal of the Polynesian Society, Vol. 49, 1941, pp. 483-510)

GN
1
Ar 3

ETHNOLOGY TANNA

Gray, William

Some notes on the Tannese. An abstract with notes and comparisons by Sidney H. Ray.

(Archiv f. Ethnogr., Bd. 7, 1894, pp. 227-241, pl. 21)

GN
2.S
P 76

ETHNOLOGY TASMANIA

Skinner, H. D.

A greenstone adze or axe from northern Tasmania.

(Journal of the Polynesian Society, Vol. 45, 1936, pp. 39-42)

and
GN
Ethn.Pam.
3798

GN
2.S
P 76

ETHNOLOGY TIKOPIA

Firth, Raymond

Anuta and Tikopia: symbiotic elements in social organization.

(Jour. Poly. Soc., 63(2):87-131, 1954)

GN
1
I 61

ETHNOLOGY TASMAN ISLANDS

Parkinson, R.

Zur Ethnographie der Ongtong Java und Tasman Inseln.

(Archif f. Ethnographie, X, 1897, pp. 104-118, 137-151; Nachträge, Bd. XI, 1898, p. 194-209) and figures on pp. 242, 243

GN
667.V
S 66

ETHNOLOGY TASMANIA

Smyth, R. Brough

The aborigines of Victoria: with notes relating to the habits of the natives of other parts of Australia and Tasmania... Vol. 2. London. 1878. R8vo. 2 vols.

ETHNOLOGY TIKOPIA

Firth, Raymond

The meaning of dreams in Tikopia.

IN Essays presented to C. G. Seligman. pp. 63-74.

UH has

AS
720.V
M

ETHNOLOGY TASMANIA

Meston, A. L.

Miscellaneous notes on the culture of the Tasmanian aboriginal.

(Mem. National Mus. of Victoria, Melbourne, No. 20:191-200, 1956)

[drinking bowl, wooden implements, middens]

Z
Bibl.
Pam
20
21

ETHNOLOGY TASMANIA BIBLIOGRAPHY

Etheridge, R.

Catalogue of works, reports, and papers on the anthropology, ethnology, and geological history of the Australian and Tasmanian aborigines. Parts 1 and 2. Sydney. 1890-1891.

(Dep't of Mines, Memoirs of the Geological Survey of New South Wales, Paleontology, No.8)

GN
4
C 33

ETHNOLOGY TIKOPIA

Firth, Raymond

A Polynesian aristocrat (Tikopia).
IN

Casagrande, Joseph B. editor
In the company of man. pp. 1-40.

Harper. 1960. New York. R8vo.

GN
67LT 5
F 52

ETHNOLOGY   TIKOPIA

Firth, Raymond

Primitive Polynesian economy. Illustrated.
George Routledge & Sons, Ltd. London. R8vo.
xi, 387 pp.

GN
671. T 64
M 14

ETHNOLOGY TOKELAU ISLANDS

Macgregor, Gordon

Ethnology of Tokelau Islands

(Bernice P. Bishop Museum, Bulletin No. 146,
1937)

GN
2.I
A-m

ETHNOLOGY   TONGA

Beaglehole, Ernest

Tongan colour-vision.

(Man, Vol. 39, pp. 170-172, 1939)

GN
1
O 15

ETHNOLOGY TIKOPIA

Firth, Raymond

Report on research in Tikopia.

(Oceania, Vol. 1, 1930-1931, pp. 105-117)

AS
701
A

ETHNOLOGY TOKELAU

Newell, J. E.

Notes, chiefly ethnological, of the Tokelau,
Ellice and Gilbert Islands.

(Australasian Ass'n for the Adv. of Sci.,
1895, pp. 603-612)

GN
1
E 84

ETHNOLOGY TONGA

Burrows, Edwin G.

Western Polynesia, a study in cultural differentiation.

(Etnologiska Studier, No. 7, 1938, pp. 1-
192)

GN
671.T5
F 52

ETHNOLOGY TIKOPIA

Firth, Raymond

We, the Tikopia. A sociological study of
kinship in primitive Polynesia, by Raymond Firth,
with a preface by Bronislaw Malinowski. London.
George Allen & Unwin Ltd. 1936. 8vo.
xxv + 605 pp., 25 pl.

GN
2.S
P 76

ETHNOLOGY TOKELAU

Smith, S. Percy   translator

Notes on the Ellice and Tokelau groups.
(Translated from the "Karere Mangaia," 1899,
New Zealand paper)

(Journal of the Polynesian Society, 29:
144-148, 1920.)

GN
2.S
P 76

ETHNOLOGY TONGA

Collocott, E. E. V.

Sickness, ghosts, and medicine in Tonga.

(Journal Polynesian Soc., XXXII, 1923, pp.
136-142)

GN
668
R 62

ETHNOLOGY TIKOPIA

Rivers, W. H. R.

The history of Melanesian society. In two
volumes. Vol 1, pp. 298-362. Cambridge.
University Press. 1914. 8vo. xii + 400;
610 pp.

(Percy Sladen Trust Expedition to Melanesia.)

GN
2.S
P76

ETHNOLOGY TOKELAU

Tutuila

The Line islanders . Notes on the
races known as the Tokelaus, or Line
islanders..... In Poly. Soc. Journ.
Vol. I, 1892, pp 263 -272.

Storage
Case
5

Ms To 2

ETHNOLOGY TONGA

Fisher, William E.

Tongan notes: history, burial, legends,
marriage, cooking, omens, medicine.

GN
1
O 15

ETHNOLOGY TIMOR

Capell, A.

Peoples and languages of Timor.
(Oceania, Vol. 14, 1944, pp. 191-219)

DU
1
P

P. 5

ETHNOLOGY - TONGA

Ancient Tongan ceremony.

(Pacific Islands Monthly, Vol. V, No. 11,

GN
671.T7
G 45

AS
763
B-b

Reading
Room

ETHNOLOGY TONGA

Gifford, E. W.

Tongan Society. Honolulu. 1929. R8vo.
iv + 366 pp.

(Bernice P. Bishop Museum, Bulletin 61. 1929.
Bayard Dominick Expedition, Publication No. 16)

GN
Pam
3077

ETHNOLOGY TOKELAU

Bird, V. G.

Missionsreise im suedlichen stillen Meer:
Besuch der Fakaofo oder Bowditch-Insel.

(typed copy of this excerpt from Das Ausland,
Bd. 37, 1864, p. 415-427).

DU
Pao
Pam
294

ETHNOLOGY TONGA

Bataillon, Pierre

Oceanie, archipel de Tonga ou des Amis,
groupe d'Ouvea (Iles Wallis). ex Revue de
l'Orient Bul.,np. nd. (about 1843.)

GN
662
M 27

ETHNOLOGY TONGA

Mander, Linden A.

Some dependent peoples of the South Pacific.
Issued under the auspices of the International
Secretariat, Institute of Pacific Relations. The
MacMillan Co. New York. 1954. 8vo. xix + 535
pp.

GN
Pam
2033

ETHNOLOGY TOKELAU

Lister, Joseph Jackson

Notes on the natives of Faaofu (Bowditch
Island), Union Group.

(R. Anthrop. Inst. Grt. Brit. and Ireland,
Jour., Vol. 21, 1892, pp. 42-63)

GN
2.S
P 76

ETHNOLOGY TONGA

Beaglehole, Ernest

Pangai village in Tonga, by Ernest and Pearl
Beaglehole.

(Memoirs of the Polynesian Soc., Vol. 18,
1941)

DU
880
M 33

ETHNOLOGY TONGA

Mariner, William

An account of the natives of the Tonga Islands...with an original grammar and vocabulary of
their language. Compiled and arranged...by John
Martin. Vols. 1-2. London. 1817. 8vo.
...Second edition, with additions. London.
1818. 8vo. Vols. 1-2.
...Third edition. Vols. 1-2. Edinburgh.
1827. 12mo.

GN
Ethn.Pam.
3314

ETHNOLOGY   TONGA

Plischke, Hans

Ein Brust-Schmuck von Tonga-tabu und die
Verarbeitung von Walknochen in Polynesien.

(Nachrichten von der Gesellschaft der Wissenschaften zu Göttingen, Philologisoh-Historische
Klasse. Fachgruppe II, Neue Folge, Bd. 2, 1939,
pp. 121-138)

GN
Pam.
2069

ETHNOLOGY   TORRES STRAITS

Haddon, A. C.

Ethnology of the western tribe of
Torres Straits. (From Anthrop. Instit. Journ. V 19
1889-90, pp. 297-440, pls. 7-10)

GN
4
C 33

ETHNOLOGY   TRUK

Gladwin, Thomas

Petrus Mailo, Chief of Moen. (Truk)
IN

Casagrande, Joseph B.   editor
In the company of man. pp. 41-62.
Harper and Bros. New York. 1960. R8vo.

GN
2.3
F 47

ETHNOLOGY--TONGA

Tuipelehake Prince

Tongan customs.

(Trans. and Proc. of the Fiji Society, Vol.
5:47-50, 1953)

G
51
W 17

ETHNOLOGY   TORRES STRAITS

Hall, Basil

The eastern isles. (in the Torres Straits)

(Walkabout, 23(12):17-19, 1957)

GN
669
C 77

and

GN
2.F
V 69

ETHNOLOGY TRUK

Gladwin, Thomas

Truk: man in paradise. By Thomas Gladwin
and Seymour B. Sarason.

(CIMA, Rept. No. 32, 655 pp., 8 pls., 1953)

GN
Ethn.Pam.
2802

ETHNOLOGY TONGA

Whitcombe, J. D.

Notes on Tongan ethnology.

(Bernice P.Bishop Museum,Occasional Papers,
Vol.9, No.9, 1930, 20 pp.)

GN
2.1
A-M

ETHNOLOGY   TROBRIAND ISLANDS

Malinowski, Bronislaw

Pigs, Papuans, and police court perspective.

(Man, vol. 32, 1932, no. 44, pp. 33-38)

(See also reply by A.G. Rentoul, vol. 32,
no. 325, pp. 274-276)

GN
671.T8
H 17

ETHNOLOGY TRUK

Hall, Edward T.

The economy of the Truk Islands; an anthropological and economic survey, by Edward T. Hall
and Karl J. Pelzer. U. S. Commercial Company,
Economic Survey of Micronesia, Report No. 7,
1946. Honolulu 4to. mimeographed. 114 pp.

PL
Phil.Pam.
549

ETHNOLOGY TONGA

Whitcombe, J. D.

Tongan phrase book.   2nd edition. no place,
no date. 12mo. 43 pp.

GN
2.1
A-M

ETHNOLOGY   TROBRIAND ISLANDS

Rentoul, A. G.

Papuans, professors, and platitudes.

(Man, vol. 32, 1932, no. 325, pp. 274-276)

(See also article by Bronislaw Malinowski,
vol. 32, no. 44, pp. 33-36)

DU
620
F

ETHNOLOGY TRUK

Hanlin, Harold F.

Christmas at Tol Island, Truk Atoll.

(The Friend, Vol. 118 (4):11-16,31-2, 1948)

GN
671.T 77
B 92

AS
763
B-b
1932

Reading
Room

ETHNOLOGY TONGAREVA

Buck, Peter H. (Te Rangi Hiroa)

Ethnology of Tongareva.

(Bull. Bernice P. Bishop Museum, No. 92,
1932.

GN
400
S 49

ETHNOLOGY   TROBRIAND ISLANDS

Service, Elman R.

Profiles in ethnology: a revision of "A
profile of primitive culture." New York.
Harper & Row. 1963. xxix + 509 pp.
R8vo.

DU
620
F

ETHNOLOGY TRUK

Price, Rev. Francis M.

The work (missionary) at Ruk (Truk)

(Friend, May 1898, pp. 34-38; June 1898, pp.
44-46)

GN
1
O 15

ETHNOLOGY-TORRES ISLANDS

Durrad, W. J.

Notes on the Torres Islands.

(Oceania, Vol. X, 1940 pp. 389-403; Vol.
XI, 1940, pp. 75-109; 186-201)

GN
669
B 69

ETHNOLOGY TRUK ISLAND

Bollig, P. Laurentius

Die Bewohner der Truk-Inseln: religion,
leben und kurze grammatik eines Mikronesiervolkes.
From Anthropos, v. 3, heft 1, 1927. Münster.
Aschendorff. 1927. R8vo. viii + 302 pp.

(Anthropos, Band III, Heft 1.)

GN
663
T 44

ETHNOLOGY   TRUK

Thilenius, G.

Ergebnisse der Südsee Expedition, 1908-1910.
II. Ethnographie: B. Mikronesien, Bd. 5, 1932,
Truk, von Augustin Krämer; Bd. 6, 1935, Inseln
im Truk, Halbband 1, von Augustin Krämer, Halbband 2, von H. Damm und E. Sarfert.

GN
671.T6
C 17

ETHNOLOGY   TORRES STRAITS

Report of the Cambridge Anthropological
Expedition to Torres Straits. Vols. 1-6. 1901-
1935. Cambridge. University Press. 4to.

GN
1
E 85

ETHNOLOGY   TRUK

Fischer, Ann

Reproduction in Truk

(Ethnology, Vol. 2(4):527-540, 1963)

GN
2.3
T 12

ETHNOLOGY   TUAMOTUS

Audran, Hervé

Fakahina.

(Bull. Soc. d'Etudes Oceaniennes, No. 19:
227-235, 251-259, 1927)

Storage
Case
3

ETHNOLOGY TUAMOTUS

Emory, Kenneth P.

Tuamotus, Napuka. 1 notebook, typed, 8vo oblong. Sent from field, via Islander. Received Oct. 30, 1934.

DU
870
M 87

ETHNOLOGY TUBUAI

Morrison, James

The journal of James Morrison, boatswain's mate of the Bounty, describing the mutiny and subsequent misfortunes of the mutineers, together with an account of the island of Tahiti. With an introduction by Owen Rutter and five engravings by Robert Gibbings. Printed and made in Great Britain by The Golden Cockerel Press. 1935. sm4to. 243 pp.

GN
671.U6
B 72

AS
763
B-b

Reading
Room

ETHNOLOGY UVEA

Burrows, Edwin G.

Ethnology of Uvea (Wallis Island.)

(B.P.Bishop Museum. Bulletin 145. 1937. 8vo. 176 pp., 8pl.)

DU
890
G 39

ETHNOLOGY TUAMOTUS

Gessler, Clifford

Road my body goes. Illustrated. Reynal & Hitchcock. New York. 1937 c. 8vo. xx + 362 pp.

GN
Ethn.Pam.
2838

ETHNOLOGY TUBUAI

Aitken, Robert T.

(Tubuai Adzes). (Description published by Aitken, Bulletin B. P. Bishop Museum, No. 70) 5 typed pages.

(withdrawn from Library and turned over to Curator of Collections, 2/28/44,- filed in Acc. 34, Curator's file.)

GN
Ethn.Pam.
3223

ETHNOLOGY UVEA

Burrows, Edwin G.

Wallis et Futuna: Etude Ethnographique.

(Colonies Autonomes, Magazine Trimestriel, Juin, 1937, pp. 3-8)

GN
1
A 62

ETHNOLOGY TUAMOTUS

Seurat, L. G.

Les Engins de Pêche des Anciens Paumotu.

(L'Anthropologie, Tome 16, 1905, pp. 295-307)

GN
658
C 97

ETHNOLOGY UGANDA

Cunningham, J. F.

Uganda and its peoples: notes on the Protectorate of Uganda...London. 1905. R8vo.

GN
2.S
P 76

ETHNOLOGY UVEA

Smith, S. Percy

Uvea, or, Wallis Island and its people. Western Pacific. in Poly.Soc.Journ. I, pp. 107-117.

1892

GN
1
A 62

ETHNOLOGY TUAMOTUS

Seurat, L. G.

Les Marae des Iles Orientales de L'Archipel des Tuamotus.

(L'Anthropologie, Tome 16, 1905, pp. 475-484)

GN
669
C 77

ETHNOLOGY ULITHI

Lessa, William A.

The ethnography of Ulithi Atoll.

(CIMA Report, No. 28. Rec'd Oct. 1950)

GN
671.N 55
L 41

ETHNOLOGY VAO

Layard, John

Stone men of Malekula: Vao. London. 1942. Chatto and Windus. R8vo. xxiii + 816 pp.

ETHNOLOGY TUAMOTUS

See also

ETHNOLOGY - RAROIA

GN
Ethn.
Pam.
3737

ETHNOLOGY ULITHI

Vollbrecht, John

The "Ulithi" encyclopedia. WVTT, the Armed Forces Radio Station, Ulithi, Western Carolines. ii + 41 pp. (1945)

E
2001
R 89

ETHNOLOGY WEST INDIES

Rubin, Vera   editor

Caribbean studies: a symposium. The American Ethnological Society... University of Washington Press. Seattle. 1960. 8vo viii + 124 pp.

GN
2.S
Po

ETHNOLOGY TUAMOTU ISLANDS

Stimson, J. Frank

Songs of the Polynesian Voyagers.

(Journal of the Polynesian Society, Vol. 41, pp. 181-201, 1932)

AS
36
S1

ETHNOLOGY - U.S.
Ripley, William Zebina, 1867-

The European population of the United States. The Huxley memorial lecture for 1908. By William Z. Ripley ...

(*In* Smithsonian institution. Annual report. 1909. Washington, 1910. 23½ᶜᵐ. p. 585-606. diagr.)

"Reprinted ... from the Journal of the Royal anthropological institute of Great Britain and Ireland, London, vol. 38 ... 1908, pp. 221-240."

1. U. S.—Foreign population. 2. Ethnology—U. S.

11-12197

Library of Congress   Q11.S66 1909

GN
Ethn.Pam.
3111

ETHNOLOGY WOGEO

Hogbin, H. Ian

Native culture of Wogeo: report of field work in New Guinea.

(Oceania, Vol. 5, 1935, pp. 308-337)

GN
671.A4
A 31

AS
763
B-b

Reading
Room

ETHNOLOGY TUBUAI

Aitken, R. T.

Ethnology of Tubuai. Honolulu. 1930. 8vo. iv + 169 pp. 13 pls. 40 figures.

(Bernice P. Bishop Museum, Bulletin No. 70, Bayard Dominick Expedition, Pub. No. 19.)

DU
620
P 96

ETHNOLOGY UVEA

Bataillon,

Notice sur l'ile et la mission de Wallis, adressé au R. P. Colin...de la Société de Marie. Wallis, Juillet 1838; Mai 1839.

(Annales de la Propagation de la Foi, 1841, Tome 13, pp 5-34)

GN
1
An

ETHNOLOGY YABOB ISLANDS

Aufinger, P. Albert

Wetterzauber auf den Yabob -Inseln in Neu-Guinea.

(Anthropos, Bd. 34, 1939, pp. 277-291)

GN
671.C3
F 98   ETHNOLOGY YAP

Furness, W. H.

The island of stone money: Uap of the Carolines. With illustrations from photographs by the author. Philadelphia. Lippincott. 1910. 8vo. 278 pp.

G
P   ETHNOLOGY YAP

Senfft, Arno

Ethnographische Beiträge uber die Karolineninsel Yap.

(Petermann's Mitt., 49:49-60, 83-87, 1903)

AS
122
V   Ethnology of the Pacific

Whitmee, S. J.

The ethnology of the Pacific . In Victoria Inst. Trans. Vol. XIV, pp 16- 40, 1881. Folded map.

DU
647
G 91   ETHNOLOGY YAP

Harmon, L. McK.

Acho Yap

(Guam Recorder, Vol. XV, No. 8, pp.7-8,1938)

GN
2.M
P 35   ETHNOLOGY YUCATAN

Landa, Don Fray Diego de

Relacion de las cosas de Yucatan, a translation. Edited with notes by Alfred M. Tozzer.

(Papers of the Peabody Museum of American Archaeology and Ethnology, Harvard University, Vol. 18, 1941)

Ethnology

See also

Anthropology; Art, Primitive; Color of man; Folk-lore; Man, Prehistoric

---

GN
671.C3
K 95   ETHNOLOGY YAP

Kubary, J. S.

Ethnographische Beiträge zur Kenntnis des Karolinen Archipels. Veröffentlicht im Auftrage der Direktion des Kgl. Museums f. Völkerkunde zu Berlin. Unter mitwirkung von J.D.E.Schmeltz. Mit 55 Tafeln. Leiden. C.F.Winter. 1889-95. R8vo. 306 + (1) pp. 55 tafeln. In 3 Hefte.

GN
561
R 31   ETHNOLOGY YUCATAN

Redfield, Robert

Chan Kom, a Maya village, by Robert Redfield and Alfonso Villa R. Washington. Carnegie Institution. 1934. 4to.

(Carnegie Institution of Washington, Publication No. 448)

ETHNOPSYCHOLOGY

See

PSYCHOLOGY

GN
663
T 44   ETHNOLOGY YAP

Müller, Wilhelm

Yap.

Thilenius, G.
Ergebnisse der Südsee Expedition, 1908-10. II. Ethnographie: B. Mikronesien, Bd. 2, 1917-18.

F
1376
R 31   ETHNOLOGY YUCATAN

Redfield, Robert

The folk culture of Yucatan. University of Chicago Press. Chicago. 1941c. 8vo. xxiii + 416 pp.

ETHNOZOOLOGY OF THE TEWA INDIANS.

GN
550
S   Henderson, Junius, 1865-
    ... Ethnozoology of the Tewa Indians, by Junius Henderson and John Peabody Harrington. Washington, Govt. print. off., 1914.
    x, 76 p. 231ᵐᵐ. (Smithsonian institution. Bureau of American ethnology. Bulletin 56)
    Issued also as House doc. 1235, 62d Cong., 3d sess.
    "This memoir embodies a part of the results of the joint researches conducted in New Mexico by the Bureau of American ethnology and the School of American archæology during 1910 and 1911."—p. v.
    Bibliography: p. 69-72.
    1. Tewa Indians. 2. Indians of North America—Econ. condit. 3. Zoology—New Mexico. I. Harrington, John Peabody, joint author. II. Santa Fé, N. M. School of American archæology. III. Title.
    Library of Congress   E51.U6 no. 56   14-30139
    ———— Copy 2.   E99.T35H4
    ———— (Another issue)   E99.T35H42
    62d Cong., 3d sess.   House. Doc. 1235
    [s19g3]

GN
Ethn.Pam.
4042   ETHNOLOGY YAP

Native customs of Yap
In Japanese, illustrated: canoes, houses, stools.

GN
Pam
2417   ETHNOLOGY - YUCATAN

Seler, Eduard

Gesammelte abhandlungen zur amerikanischen sprach und alterthumskunde. From Die Ruinen von Chich'en Itza in Yucatan, bd.V, 1914.

ETHOLOGY

See

BEHAVIOR

GN
669
C 77   ETHNOLOGY YAP

Peabody Museum, Harvard University

The Micronesians of Yap and their depopulation. Report of the Peabody Museum Expedition to Yap Island, Micronesia, 1947-1948.

(Coordinated Investigation of Micronesian Anthropology, Pacific Science Board)

F
1376
S 53   ETHNOLOGY-YUCATAN

Shattuck, George Cheever

The Peninsula of Yucatan: Medical,Biological Meteorological and Sociological Studies. By George Cheever Shattuck and Collaborators. Washington. Published by Carnegie Institution of Washington. (Publication No. 431). 1933. 4to xvii +576 pp.

QL
Insect
Pam.
1445   ETIELLA

Parker, Harry L.

Parasites of the lima-bean pod borer in Europe.

(U. S. Dept. of Agriculture, Technical Bull. No. 1036, Nov. 1951)

[Etiella zinckenella (Treit.)]

GN
1
H 91   ETHNOLOGY YAP

Schneider, David M.

Typhoons on Yap.

(Human Organization, 16(2):10-15, 1957)

ETHNOLOGY OF THE KWAKIUTL.

GN
550
S   Boas, Franz, 1858-
    Ethnology of the Kwakiutl, based on data collected by George Hunt, by Franz Boas.
    (In U. S. Bureau of American ethnology. Thirty-fifth annual report, 1913-1914. Washington, 1921. 30ᶜᵐ. p. 41-794, xi. illus.)

    1. Kwakiutl Indians. 2. Indians of North America—Food. I. Hunt, George. II. Title.   21-20998
    Library of Congress   E51.U55 35th
    ———— Copy 2.   GN2.U5 35th
    [4-6]

Reference
Shelf   Etiquette and protocol; a handbook of conduct in American and International circles.

Radlovic, I. Monte

3

GN
2.S
P 76

ETIQUETTE MAORI

Downes, T. W.

Maori etiquette.

(Journal of the Polynesian Society, 38:
148-168, 1929.)

GN
1
C 37 -o

Etudes sur les techniques de pêche du Viêt-
nam.

(Inst. Oceanographique de Nhatrang, Contrib.
no. 8, 1952, being extrait du Bull. Soc. Etudes
Indochinoises, ns tome 27, No. 1, 1952)

QK
1
C15

and

QK
Bot.Pam.
3084

Eubank, Lois L.

Hawaiian representatives of the genus
Caulerpa.

(University of Calif. Publications in
Botany, Vol. 18 (18):409-432, 1946)

QE
Geol
Pam.
#344

Etna

Gregorio, Antonio de

Etna, gita sulla Madonie
e sull' Etna.

Etzel, Anton von   editor

Erdumsegelung der K. Swedischen Frigatte
Eugenie in den Jahren 1851-53. Berlin, 1856.

HHS
HMCS   (narrative only)
(Galapagos, Hawaii)

AS
36
S2

EUBELIDAE

Richardson, Harriet.
Terrestrial isopods of the family *Eubelidæ*, collected in
Liberia by Dr. O. F. Cook, by Harriet Richardson.

(*In* Smithsonian institution. Smithsonian miscellaneous collections.
Washington, 1908. 24½ᵐ. vol. L (Quarterly issue, vol. IV) p. 219-247.
illus.)

Publication 1733.
Originally published September 12, 1907.
"List of references": p. 219-220.

1. Eubelidae. 2. Crustacea—Liberia.   I. Cook, Orator Fuller, 1867-

Library of Congress   Q11.S7 vol. 50   16-11643
——— Copy 2.

QE
Geology
Pam
616

ETNA

Washington, Henry S., Aurousseau & Keyes
The lavas of Etna. From Amer. Journ.
Sci. v.12, 1926.

QE
349.T6
H 69

EUA

Hoffmeister, J. Edward

Geology of Eua, Tonga. Includes Petrography,
by Harold L. Alling; Foraminifera, by G. Leslie
Whipple.

(Bernice P. Bishop Museum, Bulletin 96, 1932)

QL
1
C15

EUCALANUS.

Esterly, Calvin Olin, 1879-
... The vertical distribution of *Eucalanus elongatus* in
the San Diego region during 1909, by Calvin O. Esterly.
Berkeley, The University press, 1911.

cover-title, 7 p. incl. tab. 27ᵐ. (University of California publications
in zoology, v. 8, no. 1)

Contribution from the laboratory of the Marine biological association
of San Diego.
Bibliography: p. 7.

1. Eucalanus.

A 11-1862 Revised

Title from Univ. of Calif.   Library of Congress

QE
Geol
Pam
142

Etna, Observations on Mt.

Langley, S. P.

Chart
Case

Eua - Map

[Gifford. E. W.]

Working sheets of island of Eua.
Chart. n. 342.

QK
Pam.
366

EUCALYPTUS

Albert, Federico

El Karri o Eucalyptus diversicolor Santiago
de Chile, 1906.

DU
12
B 75

locked
case

L'ÉTOILE (SHIP)

Bougainville, L. A. de

Voyage autour du monde, par la frégate du roi
la Boudeuse, et la flute l'Etoile; en 1776-1769.
Paris. 1771. 4to.

PL
615
E 86

also
PL
Phil.Pam
330

Euankerio ake aua, ake Mataio, Mareko, Ruka,
Ioane, ma kabaran nanoia irouni beinam. Published for the American Board of Commissioners for
Foreign Missions, Boston, by the American Tract
Society. New York. 1909. pp. 1-326. 8vo.
contains also Taekan aia Makuri tan tuatua
are koreaki iroun Ruka ... pp. 327-450.
and Te rikitianere ni Baibara ... 104 pp.
(1909 ed. of Phil. pam. 336)

(Matthew only. 131 pp. 1903)
(Gilbert Is. Bible commentary and dictionary)

QK
495.E 86
B 63

EUCALYPTUS

Blakely, W. F.

A key to the Eucalypts, with descriptions
of over 500 species and 138 varieties, and a
companion to J. H. Maiden's "Critical revision
of the genus Eucalyptus". Sydney. 1934.

DU
12
B 75

locked
case

L'ÉTOILE (SHIP)

Bougainville, L. A. de

A Voyage round the World. Performed...in ...
1766-1769, by Lewis de Bougainville...Commodore
of the Expedition, in the Frigate La Boudeuse,
and the Store-ship l'Étoile. Translated from
the French by John Reinhold Forster. London.
1772. 4to.

AS
719
A 92

EUASTACUS

Riek, E. F.

Additions to the Australian freshwater crayfish.

(Records of the Australian Museum, 24(1):1-
6, 1956)

QK
495.E86
C 32

locked
case

EUCALYPTUS

Carter, C. E.

The distribution of the more important timber trees of the genus Eucalyptus. Commonwealth
Forestry Bureau. Atlas No. 1
Government Printer. Canberra. folio. n.d.
8 pp., 34 folded plates.

GN
2.S
T

Etude sur Lisiansky.

(Bull. Soc. Etudes Oceaniennes, Vol. VI, No.
1, 1938, pp. 17-28; No. 5, 1939, pp. 196-205)

GC
63
D 61

EUBALAENA

Matthews, L. Harrison

Notes on the southern right whale, Eubalaena
australis.

Discovery Committee
Discovery Reports, Vol. 17, 1938, p. 169-182

AS
720.V
R

EUCALYPTUS

Eucalypts.

Drew, Royston, + Green, H.
Notes on some Stringy-bark Eucalypts.
in Roy. Soc. Vict., XXV, n.s. 1912, pp. 176-185.
pls. X - XI.

AS
721.V
R

EUCALYPTUS
McAlpine, D. and Ramsey, J. R.

Transverse sections of Petioles of Eucalypts
as aids in the determination of species.
in Roy. Soc. Victoria. Trans. X. Part I. 1910. pp. 1-64.
pls. I-VII, and VIIa.

AS

QK
495.EU6
S 59

EUCALYPTUS
Simmonds, J. H.

Trees from other lands for shelter and
timber in New Zealand: Eucalyptus. Illustrated
with 76 botanic plates and 28 scenic plates.
Auckland, The Brett Printing and Publishing Co.
1927. sm. folio.

S
399
A6

EUCALYPTUS -- HAWAIIAN ISLANDS
Margolin, Louis

Eucalyptus culture in Hawaii   Bd.
Agric. For. Div. Forestry, Bull. 1, 1911

QH
1
B 61

EUCALYPTUS
J., M.

Los Eucaliptos.

(Biota, Vol. II, No. 11-12, pp. 1-21, Julio
1957)

QK
Bot.Fam.
2507

EUCALYPTUS
van Steenis, C. G. G. J.

Physiologische rassen bij Eucalyptus. Een
phytochemisch-botanische controverse.

(Natuurwetenschappelijk Tijds. Ned. Indie,
deel 101, afl. 5, pp. 146-147, 1941)

QL
595.Mi
I 59

EUCHARIDAE   MICRONESIA
Watanabe, Chihisa

Eucharidae (Hymenoptera)
IN

Insects of Micronesia, 19(2), pp. 19-34,
1958

QK
485.E86
M 21

EUCALYPTUS
Maiden, Joseph Henry

A critical revision of the genus Eucalyptus.
Sydney. Government Printer. folio.

Have only
Vol. 7;8-10, 1927-28

QK
Bot.Pam.
1562

EUCALYPTUS RARIFLORA
Penfold, A. R.

The Essential Oil of Eucalyptus Rariflora
(Bailey). By A. R. Penfold, C. B. Radcliffe and
W. F. Short.

(Reprinted from the Journal and Proc. of the
Roy. Society of New South Wales, Vol. LXIV, pp.
101-114. 1930)

AS.
719
A 93-m

EUCHORISTOPUS
Whitley, G. P.

Goggle-eyed mangrove fish.

(Austr. Mus. Mag., XI(6):187-88, 1954)

AS
720.N
R

EUCALYPTUS   pts. Myrtaceae.
Maiden, J. H.

Notes on Eucalyptus, (with descriptions of new species). No. 1. in Roy. Soc.
of N. S. W. Journ. + Proc. XLVII, 1, 1913,
pp. 76-97.

AS
36
A9

EUCALYPTUS - AFRICA
Pepper, Edward

Eucalyptus in Algeria and Tunisia,
from an hygienic and climatological
point of view. In Proc. Am. Phil. Soc.
XXXV, 1896, pp 39-55.

QL
401
N

EUCIDARIS
Pilsbry, Henry A.

A gastropod domiciliary in sea urchin spines

(The Nautilus, Vol. 69(4):109-110, April,
1956)

QK
Pam
#159

1009

and

S
399
A6

EUCALYPTUS
Margolin, Louis

Eucalyptus culture in Hawaii, ex
Board of Agr. and For., Bull. no. 1,
1911.

QK
Botany
Pam.
#1211

EUCALYPTUS -- AUSTRALIA
Adamson, R. S.

The ecology of the eucalyptus forests
of the Mount Lofty ranges (Adelaide district) South Australia. From Trans. Roy.
Soc. South Australia, Vol. 48, 1924.

AS
36
A I

EUCIROA
Pilsbry, H. A.

A New East Indian Euciroa. in Proc. Acad.
Nat. Sc. Phil. Oct. 1911. pp. 523-24.

Given by author   JAN 24 1913

QK
936
T 85

EUCALYPTUS
Moulds, Frank R.

Eucalyptus and their use in semi-tropical
plantings.

(Tropical Woods, no. 91, 1947)

DU
1
P 12

EUCALYPTUS   AUSTRALIA
Beadle, N. C. W.

The eucalypt; tree of many guises.

(Pacific Discovery, 9(5):19-21, 1956)

QL
461
H-1

EUCNEMIDAE
van Zwaluwenburg, R. H.

A new Euonemid beetle from New Caledonia
(Col.:Eucnemidae)

(Proc. Haw. Ent. Soc., Vol. 11, 1942, pp.
219-220)

QK
Bot.Pam.
1560

EUCALYPTUS
Penfold, A. R.

Notes on the Essential Oils from Some Cultivated Eucalypts. Part II. By A. R. Penfold
and F.R. Morrison.

(Journal and Proc. R. Soc. of New South
Wales, Vol. LXIV, pp. 210-222, 1930-31)

QK
Bot.
Pam.
3273

EUCALYPTUS   HAWAII
LeBarron, Russell K.

Eucalypts in Hawaii; a survey of practices
and research programs. Pacific Southwest
Forest and Range Experiment Station; Forest
Service, U. S. Department of Agriculture.
Misc. Papers No. 64 1962.

QL
595.M1
I 59

EUCOILINAE
Yoshimoto, Carl M.

Hymenoptera: Eucoilinae (Cyniopoidae).
IN

Insects of Micronesia, 19(3), 1962

QE
461
P 11   EUCOILINAE HAWAII

Yoshimoto, Carl M.

Revision of the Hawaiian Eucoilinae (Hym.:
Cynipoidea).

(Pacific Insects, 4(4):799-845, 1962)

QK
Bot.Pam.
2975   EUGENIA HAWAII

Wilson, Kenneth A.

A taxonomic study of the genus Eugenia
(Myrtaceae) in Hawaii.

(Pacific Science, April 1957:161-180, Vol.
XI)

DU
12
S 62   EUGENIE (SHIP)

looked
case   Skogman, C.

Fregatten Eugenies resa aomring jorden
aren 1851-1853, under befäl af C. A. Virgin.
Stockholm. (1854.) 8vo. 2 vols. in 1. 250
and 224 pp., 27 and 18 illus.

GN
37
C 12   Eudes-Deslongohamps, E(ugène)

Note sur la collection ethnographique du
Musée de Caen et sur deux haches en pierre polie
provenant de la Colombie.

(Bull.de la Soc.Linnéenne de Normandie.
Caen. 3d ser., vol.5. 1880-1881. pp.26-74)

QK
1
P 23   EUGENIA NEW CALEDONIA

Guillaumin, A.

Revision des Eugenia cauliflores de Nouvelle-
Calédonie.

(Notulae Systematicae, Vol. 3, pp. 260-263,
1916)

DU
Pac
Pam
#313   EUGENIE (ship)

Skogman, C

The frigate Eugenie's trip around
the world 1851-1853 under the command of
C. A. Virgin. 2nd part.

[in manuscript form - 10 typewritten pp.]

AS
36
C   EUDRILIDAE

Eisen, Gustav, 1847-

... On California *Eudrilidæ*. By Gustav Eisen. San
Francisco, Cal., 1894.

cover-title, p. [21]-62. pl. xii-xxix. 30½ x 24½ᶜᵐ. (Memoirs of the
California academy of sciences. vol. ii, no. 3)

Papers referred to: p. 57.

1. Eudrilidae. 2. Worms—California.

Library of Congress   Q11.C17 vol.2, no.3   13-24575

AS
540
P   EUGENIA PHILIPPINE ISLANDS

Merrill, Elmer D.

Readjustments in the nomenclature of Philippine Eugenia species.

(Phil. Jour. Sci., 79:351-430, 1951)

DU
Pac.Pam.
841   EUGENIE (ship)

Skogman, C.

His Swedish Majesty's frigate Eugenie at
Honolulu, June 22 to July 2, 1852, being a reprint
of seventeen pages from "Fregatten Eugenies Resa
omkring jorden, aren 1851-53, under befal af
C. A. Virgin." Translated from the original
Swedish by Meiric K. Dutton. Loomis House Press.
1954. Honolulu (21) pp. 1 map.

QK
1
P 23   EUGENIA

Guillaumin, Andre

Materiaux pour la flore de la Nouvelle Calédonie. VI: Revision des Eugenia cauliflores.

(Notulae Syst., 1916:260-263)

GN
400
H19   EUGENICS

Hambly, W. D.

Origins of education among primitive
peoples: a comparative study in racial
development.

London, MacMillan, 1926.   432p.   pls.

Q
115
V 81   EUGENIE (SHIP)

looked
case   Virgin, Christian Adolf

Kongliga Svenska Fregatten Eugenies Resa omkring jorden under befal af C. A. Virgin, aren
1851-1853. Deler I-III. Stockholm. 1858-1874.
P. A. Norstedt & Fils. 4to. Pages 33-78 of Del
II, issued in 1910, are bound separately.

QK
1
S 61   EUGENIA

Henderson, M. R.

The genus Eugenia (Myrtaceae) in Malaya.

(The Gardens' Bulletin, Vol. 12(1):1-293,
1949)

GN
Ethn.Pam.
3289   EUGENICS

Huntington, Ellsworth

Season of birth and mental stability.

(American Association on Mental Deficiency,
1937, Vol. 2, pp. 7 9 pp)

AS
36
02   EUGLENOIDINA.

Walton, Lee Barker, 1871-

... A review of the described species of the order *Euglenoidina* Bloch. class *Flagellata* (Protozoa) with particular reference to those found in the city water supplies
and in other localities of Ohio, by L. B. Walton. Columbus, The Ohio state university, 1915.

1 p. l, p. 343-459. illus. 25½ᶜᵐ. (On cover: The Ohio state university
bulletin, vol. xix, no. 5. Ohio biological survey. [v. 1: Bulletin 4])

1. Euglenoidina.

A 15-783

Title from Ohio State   Univ. Printed by L. C.

QK
1
L 2   EUGENIA

Jayaweera, D. M. A.

Variation in the flower of Eugenia malaccen-
sis Linn.

(Jour. Linn. Soc. of London, Botany, 55(362)
pp. 721-728, 1957)

QH
431
K   EUGENICS

Key, *Mrs.* Wilhelmine Marie (Enteman) 1872-

Heredity and social fitness; a study of differential mating in a Pennsylvania family, by Wilhelmine E. Key ...
Washington, The Carnegie institution of Washington,
1920.

102 p. diagrs. (2 fold.) 25½ᶜᵐ. (On verso of t.-p.: Carnegie institution of Washington. Publication, no. 296)

"Paper no. 32 of the Station for experimental evolution at Cold Spring
Harbor, New York."

"References": p. 102.

1. Heredity. 2. Eugenics.   i. Title.

Library of Congress   HQ753.K4   20-12486
———— Copy 2.   [10]

QL
401
J 85   EULIMA

Dautzenberg, Ph.

Description d'un Eulimidé nouveau provenant
de Lifou.

(Jour. de Conchyliologie, Vol. 67: 260-261,
1922)

AS
36
A 25   EUGENIA

Merrill, Elmer Drew

The Myrtaceous genus Syzygium gaertner in
Borneo, by E. D. Merrill and L. M. Perry.
(dated April 13, 1938)

(Mem. American Academy of Arts and Sciences,
Vol. 18, 1939, pp. 135-202)

QL
Insect
Pam.
1982   EUGENIE (SHIP)

Kirkaldy, G. W.

Quelques mots sur les Hemiptères polynesiens du voyage de l'Eugenie.

(Annales de la Soc. Ent. de Belgique, Tome
51:120-122, 1907)

QL
Mollusca
Pam.677   EULIMIDAE

Sykes, E. R.

Notes on some British Eulimidae.

(Proc. Malac. Soc., Vol. 5, 1903, pp. 348-
353)

AS 36 S4   EULOPHIDAE

Girault, Alexandre Arsène, 1884–

Descriptions of miscellaneous North American chalcidoid *Hymenoptera* of the family *Eulophidae*. By A. A. Girault ...

(*In* U. S. National museum. Proceedings. Washington, 1917. 23½ᵐ. v. 51, p. 39-52)

1. Eulophidae.

Library of Congress   Q11.U55 vol. 51   17–23830
———— Copy 2.   Q11.U55 vol. 51 2d set

AS 36 S4   EULOPHIDAE

Girault, Alexandre Arsène, 1884–

New North American *Hymenoptera* of the family *Eulophidae*. By A. A. Girault ...

(*In* U. S. National museum. Proceedings. Washington, 1917. 23½ᵐ. v. 51, p. 125-133)

1. Eulophidae.

Library of Congress   Q11.U55 vol. 51   17–23838
———— Copy 2.   Q11.U55 vol. 51 2d set

QL 461 H–1   EULOPHIDAE   HAWAII

Fullaway, David T.

Description of a new genus and species of parasitic wasp (Hymenoptera: Eulophidae).

(Proc. Haw. Ent. Soc. for 1954, Vol. 15(3): 409-410, 1955)

QL Insects Pam. 1250   EUMASTACIDAE

Rehn, James A. G.

A contribution to our knowledge of the Eumastacidae (Orthoptera, Acridoidea) of Africa and Madagascar. Part I. By James A. G. Rehn and John W. H. Rehn.

(Proc. Acad. Nat. Sci. Philadelphia, 97:179-248, 1945)

AS 36 S4   EUMETA

Bartsch, Paul, 1871–

The west American mollusks of the genus *Eumeta*. By Paul Bartsch ...

(*In* U. S. National museum. Proceedings. Washington, 1911. 23½ᵐ. v. 39, p. 565-568. illus.)

1. Eumeta. 2. Mollusks—America.

   11–21254

Library of Congress   Q11.U55 vol. 39

QL Mammals Pam. 132   EUMETOPIAS

Mathisen, Ole A.

Studies on Steller sea lion (Eumetopias jubata) in Alaska.

(Trans. 24th N. American Wildlife Conference March 2-4, 1959:346-356)

QL Mammals Pam. 143   EUMETOPIAS   ALASKA

Mathisen, Ole A.   and others

Breeding habits, growth and stomach contents of the Steller sea lion in Alaska, By Ole A. Mathisen, Robert T. Baade and Ronald J. Lopp.

(repr. Jour. of Mammalogy, Vol. 43(4): 469-477, 1962)

EUNICE VIRIDIS

See

PALOLO

QL 1 Liv   EUPAGARUS

Jackson, H. G.

Eupagarus: Liverpool Biol. Soc. Proc. and Trans. Vol. XXVII, 1913, pp 495 - 573

GC 63 D 61   EUPHAUSIA

Baker, A. de C.

Distribution and life history of Euphausia triacantha Holt and Tattersal.

(Discovery Reports, Vol. 29:309-340, 1959)

GC 63 D 61   EUPHAUSIA

Bargmann, Helene E.

The development and life-history of adolescent and adult krill, Euphausia superba.

IN

Discovery Reports, Vol. 23, pp. 103-176, Cambridge, 1945

GC 63 D 61   EUPHAUSIA

Bargmann, Helene E.

The reproductive system of Euphausia superba.

Discovery Committee
Discovery Reports, Vol. 14, 1937, p.325-350

GC 63 D 61   EUPHAUSIA

Fraser, F. C.

On the development and distribution of the young stages of krill (Euphausia superba)

Discovery Committee
Discovery Reports, Vol. 14, 1936, p.1-192

GC 63 D 61   EUPHAUSIA

John, D. Dilwyn

The southern species of the genus Euphausia.

Discovery Committee
Discovery Reports, Vol. 14, 1936, p.193-324

GC S 43 b   EUPHAUSIA   PACIFIC

Brinton, Edward

The distribution of Pacific Euphausiids.

(Bull. of the Scripps Inst. of Oceanography, of the Univ. of Calif. La Jolla, Vol. 8(2), 1962)

QH 1 P 11   EUPHAUSIA   PACIFIC

Brinton, Edward

Variable factors affecting the apparent range and estimated concentration of Euphausiids in the North Pacific.

(Pacific Science, 16(4):374-408, 1962)

QL Crust. Pam. 553   EUPHAUSIACEA

Banner, Albert Henry

The Crustacea of the orders Mysidacea and Euphausiacea of the northeastern Pacific.

(University of Washington, Abstracts of Theses and Faculty Bibliography, 1943-44, Vol. 9, pp. 33-34, 1946)

QL Insect Pam. 1655   EUPHAUSIACEA

Banner, Albert H.

New records of Mysidacea and Euphausiacea from the northeastern Pacific and adjacent areas.

(Reprinted from Pacific Science, Vol. 8(2): 125-139, 1954)

Q 115 C 28   EUPHAUSIACEA

Einarsson, Hermann

Euphausiacea, 1. Northern Atlantic species. Dana Report No. 27, 1945.

GC 63 D 61   EUPHAUSIACEA

Boden, Brian P.

Euphausiacea of the Benguela current; first survey, R. R. S. 'William Scoresby', March 1950.

(Discovery Reports, Vol. XXVII:337-376, August, 1955)

AS 36 S4   EUPHAUSIACEA

Hansen, Hans Jacob, 1855–

The *Crustacea Euphausiacea* of the United States National museum. By H. J. Hansen ...

(*In* U. S. National museum. Proceedings. Washington, 1915. 23½ᵐ. v. 48, p. 59-114. pl. 1-4)

1. Euphausiacea.

   15–24769

Library of Congress   Q11.U55 vol. 48

EUPHAUSIACEA
AS
36
S4

Hansen, Hans Jacob, 1855-

... The euphausiacean crustaceans of the "Albatross" expedition to the Philippines. By H. J. Hansen ...

(*In* U. S. National museum. Proceedings. Washington, 1916. 23½ᶜᵐ. v. 49, p. 635-654. pl. 83)

"Scientific results of the Philippine cruise of the fisheries steamer 'Albatross,' 1907-1910.—no. 33."

1. Euphausiacea. 2. Albatross (Steamer)

Library of Congress   Q11.U55 vol. 49   16-11810
——— Copy 2.   Q11.U55 vol. 49 2d set

GC
1
S 43b

EUPHAUSIACEA   PACIFIC

Boden, Brian P.

The Euphausiacea (Crustacea) of the North Pacific. By Brian P. Boden, Martin W. Johnston, and Edward Brinton.

(Bull. of the Scripps Institution of Oceanography of the University of California, Vol. 6(8):287-400, 1955)

QK
41
B 15

EUPHORBIACEAE

Baillon, H

Nouvelles observations sur les Euphorbiacees
Adansonia, v. 11, pp. 72-138, pl.9, 1874.

QL
Crustacea
Pam.
549

EUPHAUSIACEA

Hansen, H. J.

On some Malacostracous Crustacea (Mysidacea, Euphausiacea, and Stomatopoda) collected by Swedish Antarctic Expeditions.

(Arkiv for Zoologi, 13, No. 20, pp. 1-7, 1921)

DU
Hist.
Pam.
572

EUPHEMIA (SHIP)

... Foreclosure of the hypothecation on the British brig Euphemia, Capt. John S. Nightingale. Honolulu. Govt. Press. 1845. 63 pp. 8vo.

QK
936
T 85

EUPHORBIACEAE

Croizat, Leon

New Euphorbiaceae from the Island of Mauritius.

(Tropical Woods, No. 77, 1944, pp. 13-18)

AS
36
S 2

EUPHAUSIACEA

Tattersall, W. M.

Euphausiacea and Mysidacea collected on the Presidential Cruise of 1938.

(Smith. Misc. Coll., Vol. 99, No. 13, 1941, pp. 1-7)

QK
1
B 97-b 3

EUPHORBIA

Croizat, L.

A significant new species from New Guinea: Euphorbia euonymoclada Croiz., n. sp.

(Bull. Jardin Bot., Buitenzorg, Ser. 3, Vol. 16, 1940, pp. 351-357)

QK
Bot.Pam.
2396

EUPHORBIACEAE

Croizat, Leon

Notes on Fijian Euphorbiaceae.

(Occ. Papers, Bernice P. Bishop Museum, Vol. 18, No. 3, 1944, pp. 69-71)

QH
11
G 78

EUPHAUSIACEA

Tattersall, Walter M.

Mysidacea and Euphausiacea.

IN Great Barrier Reef Expedition, 1928-29, Scientific Reports, Vol. V, No. 4, 1936, pp. 143-176. British Museum (Natural History).

QK
Bot.Pam.
2080

EUPHORBIA

Sherff, Earl Edward

Revision of the Hawaiian species of Euphorbia L.

(Annals of the Missouri Botanical Garden, Vol. 25, 1938, pp. 1-94)

QK
97
E 58

EUPHORBIACEAE

Engler, Adolf

Das Pflanzenreich...IV. 147. (I)-VII. 1913-1924.(Heft 42, 44, 47, 52, 57, 58, 63, 65, 68, 81, 85.) Euphorbiaceae, by G. Gruning, F. Pax, E. Jablonszky, Käthe Hoffman, Käthe Rosenthal.

QH
11
G 78

EUPHAUSIACEA

Tattersall, Walter M.

The occurrence and seasonal distribution of the Mysidacea and Euphausiacea [The zooplankton, V].

IN Great Barrier Reef Expedition, 1928-29, Sci. Repts., Vol. II, No. 8, 1936, pp. 277-289. British Mus. of Nat. Hist.

S
399
E82

Euphorbia Lorifolia.

McGeorge, Wm. and Anderson, W. A.

Euphorbia Lorifolia, a possible source of rubber and chicle. Haw. Agric. Exper. Sta. Press Bull. No. 37. 1912.

QK
Bot.Pam.
1980

EUPHORBIACEAE

Frey-Wyssling, A.

Over de Bloeiwijze en de Vruchtzetting van den Rubberboom.

(De Tropische Natuur, Jrg. 25, Afl. 11-12, 1936)

QL
5
M 98

EUPHAUSIACEA   INDIAN OCEAN

Tattersall, W. M.

The Euphausiacea and Mysidacea of the John Murray Expedition to the Indian Ocean.

IN The John Murray Expedition, 1933-34, Sci. Repts., Vol. V, no. 8, 1939, pp. 203-246

QK
Pam.
#675
4to

7-2

Botany, Euphorbia L

Warming, Eugene

Er Koppen hos Vortemaelken en Klimat eller en Blomstertand.

København, 1871. 8ᵗ pp. 1-104. 1-18

Note Translation or resumé in French follows Le Cyathium de l'Euphorbe (Euphorbia L.) est-il une fleure ou réellement une inflorescence. par Eugène Warming. pp. 1-18

QK
473.N2
N 93

EUPHORBIACEAE

Nova Guinea. Resultats de l'Expedition Scientifique Neerlandaise...1912-1913, Vol. XII: Botanique, Livr. V, 1917, pp. 479-486, pl. 182-192. Euphorbiaceae, by A. T. Gage.

QH
1
P 11

EUPHAUSIACEA   PACIFIC

Banner, Albert H.

New records of Mysidacea and Euphausiacea from the northeastern Pacific and adjacent areas.

(Pacific Science, Vol. 8:125-139, 1954)

QH
181.T
T 13

EUPHORBIA   TAIWAN

Keng, Hsuan

Studies in the genus Euphorbia of Taiwan.

(Quarterly Jour. of the Taiwan Mus., 4(3/4): 253-260, 1951)

QK
1
E 58

EUPHORBIACEAE

Hemsley, William Botting

(Die flora der Samoa-Inseln. Teil II. Siphonogamen.) Euphorbiaceae.

(Engler's Bot. Jahrb., 25, 1898, 658-660)

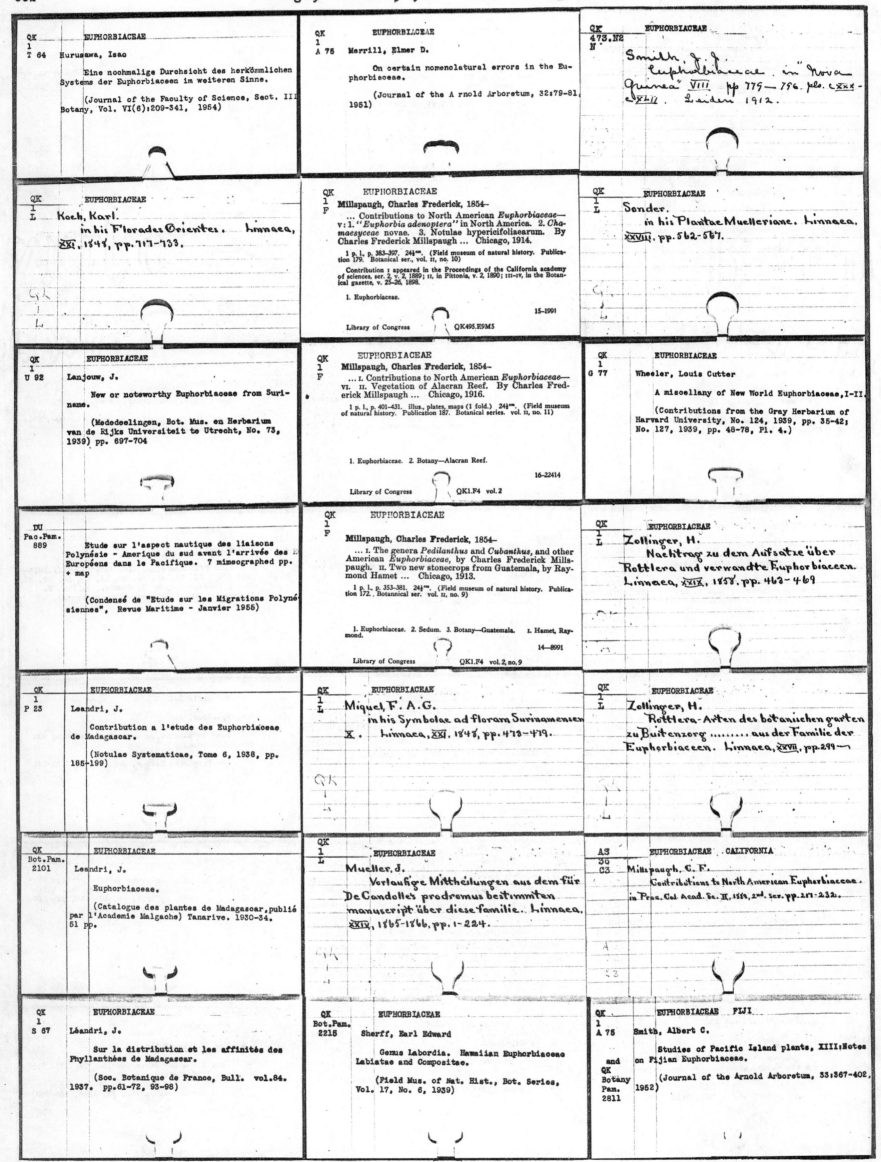

Row 1, Card 1

QK
1
T 64

EUPHORBIACEAE

Hurusawa, Isao

Eine nochmalige Durchsicht des herkömmlichen
Systems der Euphorbiaceen im weiteren Sinne.

(Journal of the Faculty of Science, Sect. III
Botany, Vol. VI(6):209-341, 1954)

Row 1, Card 2

QK
1
A 75

EUPHORBIACEAE

Merrill, Elmer D.

On certain nomenclatural errors in the Euphorbiaceae.

(Journal of the Arnold Arboretum, 32:79-81,
1951)

Row 1, Card 3

QK
473.N2
N

EUPHORBIACEAE

Smith, J.J.
Euphorbiaceae in "Nova
Guinea" VIII pp 779—796 pls. CXXX-
CXLII. Leiden 1912.

Row 2, Card 1

QK
1
L

EUPHORBIACEAE

Koch, Karl.
in his Florades Orientes. Linnaea,
XXI, 1848, pp. 717-733.

Row 2, Card 2

QK
1
F

EUPHORBIACEAE

Millspaugh, Charles Frederick, 1854–

... Contributions to North American *Euphorbiaceae*—
v: 1. "*Euphorbia adenoptera*" in North America. 2. *Cha-
maesyceae novae.* 3. Notulae hypericifoliacearum. By
Charles Frederick Millspaugh ... Chicago, 1914.

1 p. l., p. 383-397. 24½ᶜᵐ. (Field museum of natural history. Publication 179. Botanical ser., vol. II, no. 10)

Contribution I appeared in the Proceedings of the California academy
of sciences, ser. 2, v. 2, 1889; II, in Pittonia, v. 2, 1890; III-IV, in the Botanical gazette, v. 25-26, 1898.

1. Euphorbiaceae.

15–1991

Library of Congress   QK495.E9M5

Row 2, Card 3

QK
1
L

EUPHORBIACEAE

Sonder.
in his Plantae Muellerianae. Linnaea,
XXVIII. pp. 562-567.

Row 3, Card 1

QK
1
U 92

EUPHORBIACEAE

Lanjouw, J.

New or noteworthy Euphorbiaceae from Suri-
name.

(Mededeelingen, Bot. Mus. en Herbarium
van de Rijks Universiteit te Utrecht, No. 73,
1939) pp. 697-704

Row 3, Card 2

QK
1
F

EUPHORBIACEAE

Millspaugh, Charles Frederick, 1854–

... I. Contributions to North American *Euphorbiaceae*—
VI. II. Vegetation of Alacran Reef. By Charles Frederick Millspaugh ... Chicago, 1916.

1 p. l., p. 401-431. illus., plates, maps (1 fold.) 24½ᶜᵐ. (Field museum
of natural history. Publication 187. Botanical series. vol. II, no. 11)

1. Euphorbiaceae. 2. Botany—Alacran Reef.

16–22414

Library of Congress   QK1.F4 vol.2

Row 3, Card 3

QK
1
G 77

EUPHORBIACEAE

Wheeler, Louis Cutter

A miscellany of New World Euphorbiaceae, I-II.

(Contributions from the Gray Herbarium of
Harvard University, No. 124, 1939, pp. 35-42;
No. 127, 1939, pp. 48-78, Pl. 4.)

Row 4, Card 1

DU
Pac.Pam.
889

Etude sur l'aspect nautique des liaisons
Polynésie - Amerique du sud avant l'arrivée des
Européens dans le Pacifique. 7 mimeographed pp.
+ map

(Condensé de "Etude sur les Migrations Polyné-
siennes", Revue Maritime - Janvier 1955)

Row 4, Card 2

QK
1
F

EUPHORBIACEAE

Millspaugh, Charles Frederick, 1854–

... I. The genera *Pedilanthus* and *Cubanthus*, and other
American *Euphorbiaceae*, by Charles Frederick Millspaugh. II. Two new stonecrops from Guatemala, by Raymond Hamet ... Chicago, 1913.

1 p. l. p. 353-381. 24½ᶜᵐ. (Field museum of natural history. Publication 172. Botanical ser. vol. II, no. 9)

1. Euphorbiaceae. 2. Sedum. 3. Botany—Guatemala. I. Hamet, Raymond.

14–8991

Library of Congress   QK1.F4 vol.2, no.9

Row 4, Card 3

QK
1
L

EUPHORBIACEAE

Zollinger, H.
Nachtrag zu dem Aufsatze über
Rottlera und verwandte Euphorbiaceen.
Linnaea, XXIX, 1858, pp. 463-469

Row 5, Card 1

QK
P 23

EUPHORBIACEAE

Leandri, J.

Contribution a l'étude des Euphorbiaceae
de Madagascar.

(Notulae Systematicae, Tome 6, 1938, pp.
185-199)

Row 5, Card 2

QK
1
L

EUPHORBIACEAE

Miquel, F. A. G.
in his Symbolae ad floram Surinamensen
X. Linnaea, XXI, 1848, pp. 473-479.

Row 5, Card 3

QK
1
L

EUPHORBIACEAE

Zollinger, H.
Rottlera-Arten des botanischen garten
zu Buitenzorg .... aus der Familie der
Euphorbiaceen. Linnaea, XXVII, pp.299—

Row 6, Card 1

QK
Bot.Pam.
2101

EUPHORBIACEAE

Leandri, J.

Euphorbiaceae.

(Catalogue des plantes de Madagascar, publié
par l'Academie Malgache) Tananarive. 1930-34.
51 pp.

Row 6, Card 2

QK
1
L

EUPHORBIACEAE

Mueller, J.
Vorläufige Mittheilungen aus dem für
De Candolles prodromus bestimmten
manuscript über diese Familie. Linnaea,
XXIV, 1865-1866, pp. 1-224.

Row 6, Card 3

AS
36
C3

EUPHORBIACEAE . CALIFORNIA

Millspaugh, C. F.
Contributions to North American Euphorbiaceae.
in Proc. Cal. Acad. Sc. II, 1889, 2nd. ser. pp. 217-232.

Row 7, Card 1

QK
1
S 67

EUPHORBIACEAE

Léandri, J.

Sur la distribution et les affinités des
Phyllanthées de Madagascar.

(Soc. Botanique de France, Bull. vol.84.
1937. pp.61-72, 93-98)

Row 7, Card 2

QK
Bot.Pam.
2215

EUPHORBIACEAE

Sherff, Earl Edward

Genus Labordia. Hawaiian Euphorbiaceae
Labiatae and Compositae.

(Field Mus. of Nat. Hist., Bot. Series,
Vol. 17, No. 6, 1939)

Row 7, Card 3

QK
1
A 75

and
QK
Botany
Pam.
2811

EUPHORBIACEAE . FIJI

Smith, Albert C.

Studies of Pacific Island plants, XIII: Notes
on Fijian Euphorbiaceae.

(Journal of the Arnold Arboretum, 33:367-402,
1952)

QK
1
T 64

EUPHORBIACEAE   FORMOSA

Hurusawa, Isao

Eine nochmalige Durchsicht des herkömmlichen Systems der Euphorbiaceen im weiteren Sinne.

(Journal of the Faculty of Science, Sect. III Botany, Vol. VI(6):209-341, 1954)

AS
540
P

EUPHORBIACEAE PHILIPPINE ISLANDS

Merrill, E. D.
in Phil. Journ. Sc. VII.6

Euphorbiaceae-Jatropheae

QK
97
E
Heft 42

Pax, F.

Pflanzenreich, Das   Heft 42 IV.147
Leipzig, Wilhelm Engelmann,1910, pp 148, Figs.45

QK
495
H 41

EUPHORBIACEAE   JAPAN

Hayata, B.

Revisio Euphorbiacearum et Buxacearum Japonicarum. Tokyo. 1904. R8vo. 92 pp. cum tabulis 6.

(Journ. of College of Science, Imperial Univ. Tokyo, Vol. 20, Art. 3, 1904)

QK
1
T 13

EUPHORBIACEAE   TAIWAN

Keng, Hsuan

The Euphorbiaceae of Taiwan.

(Taiwania, No. 6, pp. 27-66, December, 1955)

Euphorbiaceae-Gelonieae

QK
97
E
Heft 52

Pax, F.

Pflanzenreich, Das   Heft 52 IV.147. IV
Leipzig, Wilhelm Engelmann, 1912,pp 41, Figs.11.

QK
1
B 73

EUPHORBIACEAE   HAWAII

Sherff, Earl Edward

Notes on certain members of the Amaranthaceae, Caryophyllaceae, Euphorbiaceae and Compositae.

(Botanical Leaflets, No 2, 1950. Chicago)

Euphorbiaceae-Acalypheae-Chrozophori/ae

QK
97
E
Heft 57

Pax, F.

Pflanzenreich,Das   Heft 57 IV.147.x
Leipzig, Wilhelm Engelmann, 1912,pp 142,Figs.25.

Euphorbiaceae-Phyllanthoideae-Bridelieae

QK
97
E
Heft 65

Jablonszky, E.

Pflanzenreich, Das   Heft 65 IV.147. VIII.
Leipzig, Wilhelm Engelmann,1915,pp 98, Figs.15.

QK
1
S 67

EUPHORBIACEAE - MADAGASCAR

Léandri, Jacques

Euphorbiacées malgaches nouvelles recoltées par M.R.Capuron.

(Bull. Soc. Bot. de France, Tome 103 (9/10): 604-608, 1956)

Euphorbiaceae-Acalypheae-Mercurialin

QK
97
E
Heft 63

Pax, F.

Pflanzenreich,Das   Heft 63 IV.147.VII
Leipzig, Wilhelm Engelmann,1914,pp 475,Figs.67.

Euphorbiaceae-Porantheroideae et Ricinocarpoideae (Euphorbiaceae-Stenolobeae)

QK
97
E
Heft 58

Gruning, G.

Pflanzenreich, Das   Heft 58 IV. 147
Leipzig, Wilhelm Engelmann,1913,pp 97,Figs.16.

QK
1
K 44

EUPHORBIACEAE   MALAYSIA

Shaw, H. K. Airy

Notes on Malaysian and other Asiatic Euphorbiaceae.

(Kew Bull., 16(3):341-372, 1963)

Euphorbiaceae-Adrianeae

QK
97
E
Heft 44

Pax, F.

Pflanzenreich, Das   Heft 44 IV.147.II
Leipzig, Wilhelm Engelmann,1910, pp 109, Figs.35.

QK
Bot. Pam.
1870

EUPHRASIA

Du Rietz, G. Einar

The long-tubed New Zealand species of Euphrasia (Siphonidium Armstr.).

(Svensk Botanisk Tidskrift, Bd. 25, H. 1, 1931, pp. 108-125)

QK
Bot.Pam.
2739
and
QK
1
W 37

EUPHORBIACEAE   MALAYSIA

Merrill, Elmer D.

Reductions of two Malaysian genera of Euphorbiaceae. By E. D. Merrill and C.G.G.J. van Steenis.

(Webbia, 8:405-406, 1952)

Euphorbiaceae-Cluytieae

QK
97
E
Heft 47

Pax, F.

Pflanzenreigh, Das Heft 47 IV.147. III
Leipzig, Wilhelm Engelmann, 1911, pp 124, Figs.35.

QK
Bot. Pam.
1872

EUPHRASIA

Du Rietz, G. Einar

Two new species of Euphrasia from the Philippines and their phytogeographical significance.

(Svensk Botanisk Tidskrift, Bd. 25, H. 4, 1931, pp. 500-542)

AS
720.Q
R

EUPHORBIACEAE   NEW GUINEA

Smith, L. S.

The ligneous genus Endospermum Benth. (Euphorbiaceae) in New Guinea.

(Proc. R. Soc. of Queensland for 1946, Vol. 58:51-60)

Euphorbiaceae-Hippomaneae

QK
97
E
Heft 52

Pax, F.

Pflanzenreich, Das   Heft 52 IV.147. V.
Leipzig, Wilhelm Engelmann, 1912, pp 319,Figs.58.

QL
1
Z

EUPLOEA

Carpenter, G. D. Hale

The genus Euploea (Lep. Danaidae) in Micronesia, Melanesia, Polynesia and Australia. A zoo-geographical study.

(Transactions of the Zoological Society of London, Vol. 28(1):1-184, 1953)

QL
1
C 15

EUPLOTES PATELLA

Taylor, Charles Vincent, 1885–

... Demonstration of the function of the neuromotor apparatus in *Euplotes* by the method of microdissection, by Charles V. Taylor. Berkeley, University of California press, 1920.

cover-title, p. [403]–470. illus., pl. 29–33. 27½ᶜᵐ. (University of California publications in zoology. v. 19, no. 13)

Bibliography: p. 458–461.

1. Euplotes patella.   I. Title.

A 20–1354

Title from Univ. of Calif.   Library of Congress

QL
1
C 15

EUPLOTES PATELLA

Yocom, Harry Barclay, 1888–

... The neuromotor apparatus of *Euplotes patella*, by Harry B. Yocom ... Berkeley, University of California press, 1918.

cover-title, p. [337]–396. pl. 14–16. 27½ᶜᵐ. (University of California publications in zoology. v. 18, no. 14)

"Literature cited": p. 388–390.

1. Euplotes patella.   I. Title.

A 18–2056

Title from Univ. of Calif.   Library of Congress

QL
Birds
Pam.
379

EUPODA

Walker, Lewis Wayne

Mountain plover.

(Audubon Magazine, 57(5):210-212, Sept./Oct. 1955)

[Eupoda montana, nests from n. Montana and western Nebraska south to w. Kansas and n. New Mexico and nw Texas]

QL
1
F

EUPOMOTIS

Meek, Seth Eugene, 1859–1914.

... The genus *Eupomotis*. By S. E. Meek ... Chicago, 1900.

2 p. l., 11–14 p. 24½ᶜᵐ. (Field Columbian museum. Publication 47. Zoological series. vol. III, no. 2)

1. Eupomotis.

4–10571

Library of Congress   QL1.F4

Q
115
S 56

EUPSAMMIDAE

Van der Horst, C. J.
The Madreporaria of the Siboga Expedition, Part III: Eupsammidae.

Weber, Max
Uitkomsten...Nederlandsch Oost-Indie; 1899-1900...Siboga...Monographie XVI o (livr. 92). 1922. 75 pp. 8 pl.

DK
20
S 89

EUROPE

Strahlenberg, Philip John von

An historico-geographical description of the north and eastern parts of Europe and Asia; but more particularly of Russia, Siberia, and Great Tartary...translated into English. London. 1738. 8vo.

EUROPE ANTHROPOLOGY

see

ANTHROPOLOGY EUROPE

EUROPE ARCHAEOLOGY

see

ARCHAEOLOGY EUROPE

EUROPE BOTANY

see

BOTANY EUROPE

EUROPE ECHINODERMATA

see

ECHINODERMATA EUROPE

EUROPE ETHNOLOGY

see

ETHNOLOGY EUROPE

EUROPE FLAX

see

FLAX EUROPE

EUROPE HISTORY

D
102
G96

Guizot, M.

General history of civilisation in Europe, from the Fall of the Roman empire to the French revolution ...9th American, from the 2nd English ed...

New York, 1860. 216p.

EUROPE INSECTS

see

INSECTS EUROPE

AS
36
S1

EUROPE–LANGUAGE.

Dominian, Leon.

Linguistic areas in Europe: their boundaries and political significance. By Leon Dominian.

(*In* Smithsonian institution. Annual report. 1915. Washington, 1916. 23½ᶜᵐ. p. 409–443. illus., 5 fold. maps)

"Reprinted ... Bulletin of the American geographical society, vol. 47, June, 1915."

1. Europe—Languages. 2. Nationalism and nationality.   I. Title.

16–16022

Library of Congress   Q11.S66 1915
————— Copy 2.   Q11.S66 1915 2d set

PL
Phil.Pam
176

EUROPE LANGUAGE

Friederici, Georg

Lehnwörter exotischer Herkunst in europäischen Sprachen. 26 pp.

(Zeitschrift für französische Sprache und Literatur, Band LVIII, Heft 3-4, pp. 135-156, 1934).

EUROPE LEPIDOPTERA

see

LEPIDOPTERA EUROPE

EUROPE MAN, PREHISTORIC

see

MAN, PREHISTORIC EUROPE

EUROPE MUSIC

see

MUSIC EUROPE

EUROPE PALEONTOLOGY

see

PALEONTOLOGY EUROPE

EUROPE RACE

see

RACE EUROPE

EUROPE   ZOOLOGY

see

ZOOLOGY   EUROPE

S
399
E 18

EUSCEPER POSTFASCIATUS

Sherman, Martin

The sweetpotato weevils in Hawaii; their biology and control. By Martin Sherman and Minoru Tamashiro.

(Hawaii Agric. Exp. Station, Univ. of Hawaii Technical Bull. No. 23, 1954)

QL
401
N 31

EUTOMOPSIS

Henrard, J. B.

On the green land mollusk from New Guinea.

(The Nautilus, 73(2):63-65, 1959)

AS
36
S3

EUROPE-LEARNED INSTITUTIONS AND SOCIE-
TIES
Meyer, Adolf Bernhard, 1840-1911.
Studies of the museums and kindred institutions of New York city, Albany, Buffalo, and Chicago, with notes on some European institutions. By A. B. Meyer ...
(*In* U. S. National museum. Annual report. 1903. Washington, 1905. 23½ᵐᵐ. p. 311-608. illus. (incl. plans) 40 pl.)
Half-title.
"Translation, rev. by the author, from Abhandlungen und berichte des Königlichen zoologischen und anthropologisch-ethnographischen museums in Dresden, bd. ix, 1900-1901, and bd. x, 1902-1903."
"Translation of Über museen des ostens der Vereinigten Staaten von Amerika. Reisestudien von dr. A. B. Meyer. Berlin, 1900-01": p. 321-520.
"Translation of Über einige europäische museen und verwandte insti-tute. Reiseerfahrungen von dr. A. B. Meyer. Berlin, 1902": p. 520-608.
1. Museums. 2. U. S.—   Learned institutions and societies.
3. Europe—Learned   institutions and societies.
Library of Congress   Q11.U5 1903   14-19921
———— Copy 2.

QK
524.E8
C 18

EUSPORANGIATAE

Campbell, Douglas Houghton, 1859-
The *Eusporangiatae*; the comparative morphology of the *Ophioglossaceae* and *Marattiaceae*, by Douglas Houghton Campbell ... Washington, D. C., Carnegie institution of Washington, 1911.
vi, 229 p. illus. 13 pl. 29ᶜᵐ. (*On verso of t.-p.:* Carnegie institution of Washington. Publication no. 140)
Bibliography: p. 219-222.

1. Ophioglossaceae. 2. Marattiaceae. i. Title.
                                                     11-27546
Library of Congress   QK524.E8C3
———— Copy 2.   (a19e2)

GN
1
N 27

Eva, Alokihakau

Some native beliefs and surgical procedures encountered in the Tongan group.

(The Native Medical Practitioner, Vol. 2, no. 4, 1937, pp. 383)

DK
20
St.4

Europe and Asia, Description of north and eastern part of.

Strahlenberg, Philip John von

DU
Pac.Pam.
930

Eustaquio, George C.

Legislative syntopics, written under the direction of the Fifth Guam Legislature. Office of Public Relations and Information, Guam Congress building. Agana, Guam. 4to. 1959 48 pp.

GN
1
N 27

Eva, Alokihakau

The Tongan midwife.

(The Native Medical Practitioner, Vol. 2, no. 4, 1937, pp. 366-367)

EUROPEAN CORN BORER

See

PYRAUSTA

QE
Geol.
Pam.
#567

Eustatic bench of islands of the North Pacific.
Wentworth, Chester K

PL
Phil.Pam.
500

Evanerio na Ruka Peato. V. C. I. S.
I Oomi ia Bar-le-Duc. 1883. 12mo. 129 & (1) pp.

(Gospel according to St. Luke. In Marquesan)

P
2171
P 71

The European possessions in the Caribbean
Area:
Platt, Raye R.

Q
115
C 28

EUTHYNNUS

Matsumoto, Walter M.

Descriptions of Euthynnus and Auxis larvae from the Pacific and Atlantic Oceans and adja-cent seas.
IN
Carlsberg Foundation's Oceanographical Ex-pedition...Dana Reports... No. 50, 1959.

QL
438.I
C 35

EVANIDAE   INDIA

Mani, M. S.

Evanidae.

(Catalogue of Indian Insects, Part 24, 1939)

GN
2.8
T

EUROPEANS IN TAHITI

Rey-Lescure

Les premiers Européens à Tahiti.

(Bull. Soc. des Etudes Oceaniennes, No. 105, pp. 162-175, 1953)

QH
1
P 11

EUTHYNNUS

Schaefer, Milner B.

Juvenile Euthynnus lineatus and Auxis tha-sard from the Pacific Ocean off Central America. By Milner B. Schaefer and John C. Marr.

(Pacific Science, Vol. 2:262-271, 1948)

QL
Insects
Pam.
1092

EVANIIDAE

Yasumatsu, Keizo

Evaniidae of Micronesia (Hymenoptera). Results of Professor T. Esaki's Micronesia Expeditions, 1936-1940, No. 48.

(source ?, pp. 19-21)

AS
244
D

EURYALIDAE   INDO-PACIFIC

Mortensen, Th.

Studies of Indo-Pacific Euryalids.

(Vid. Med. fra Dansk nat. For. i Kobenhavn, Bd. 96, 1933, pp. 1-75).

QL
62V
P 11

EUTHYNNUS

Uda, Michitaka

The time and duration of angling and the catch of "Katsuo", Euthynnus vagans (Lesson).

(Bull. Japanese Soc. of Scientific Fisheries Vol. 9(3):103-106, 1940)

Translation No. 46, Pacific Oceanic Fishery Investigations, by W. G. van Campen

---

QL
595.Mi
I 59

EVANIIDAE   MICRONESIA

Townes, Henry

Ichneumonidae, Stephanidae, and Evaniidae. IN

Insects of Micronesia, 19(2):35-57, 1958)

QK
556
Ev

Evans, A.

Notes on North America hepaticae.

Reprint. 1917.

Pamphlet

AS
36
C9

Evans, Alexander William, and *Nichols, George Elwood.*

The bryophytes of Connecticut. By Alexander William Evans and George Elwood Nichols. Hartford, 1908.

203 pp., 23ᶜᵐ.

(Bulletin no. 11, Connecticut geological and natural history survey.)

AS
36
C8

AND
QK
Pam.
401
406

Evans, Alexander William, 1868–

... The Hawaiian *Hepaticæ* of the tribe *Jubuloideæ.*

(*In* Connecticut academy of arts and sciences. Transactions. New Haven, 1899-1900. 25ᶜᵐ. v. 10, p. [387]-462. pl. XLIV-LIX)

(added to Pam 401 is list prepared by C. M. Cooke, Jr. of species of Hepaticae mentioned in Stephani's list. Prepared up to date of 1901)

1. Jubuloideae. 2. Hepaticae—Hawaiian Islands. I. Title.

A 17-879

Library of Congress   Q11.C9   vol. 10
Yale University   A53n.366.10

QL
694
W 75

locked
case

Evans, A. H.

Wilson, Scott B.

Aves Hawaiienses: the birds of the Sandwich Islands. London. 1890-99. 4to. xxv + 257 pp. illustrated.

QK
Botany
Pam
1493

Evans, Alexander William and Rose Myyrowitz

Catalogue of the lichens of Connecticut. Hartford. State Geological and natural history survey. Bulletin no 37. 1926. 50 p.

QK
Pam
#243

and

QK
1
T1

Evans, Alexander W.

Hepaticae of Puerto Rico, ex Torrey Club Bull., August, 1902.

G
51
W 17

Evans, A. H.

Goroka walkabout: a journey through the Central Highlands of New Guinea.

(Walkabout, 22(9):31-34, 1956)

QK
1
O 11

Evans, Alexander W.

The Cladoniae of Connecticut.

Contributions from the Osborn Botanical Laboratory, Yale University, VII. (Trans. of the Conn. Acad. of Arts and Sci. Vol. 30, pp. 357-510, June 1930)

QK
Pam
#244

and

QK
1
T1

Evans, Alexander W.

Hepaticae of Puerto Rico III, ex Torrey Bot. Club Bull., vol. 30, Oct., 1903.

QK
Pam
#683

Evans, Alexander W.

Additions to the Hepatic flora of Quebec, ex Bryologist, vol. XIX, no. 2, March, 1916.

QK
Bot. Pam.
2175
2319

Evans, Alexander W.

The classification of the Hepaticae.

(Botanical Review, 5, 1939, pp. 49-96)

QK
Pam
#242

and

QK
1
T1

Evans, Alexander W.

Hepaticae of Puerto Rico, ex Torrey Bot. Club Bull., vol. 31, April, 1904.

QK
Pam
#1005

and

QK
1
T1

Evans, Alexander W.

The air chambers of Grimaldia fragrans, ex Torrey Bot. Club Bull. vol. 45, June 15, 1918.

QK
Pam
#240

and

QK
1
T1

Evans, Alexander W.

An enumeration of the Hepaticae collected by John B. Hatcher in Southern Patagonia, ex Torrey Bot. Club Bull. vol. 25, no. 8, August, 1898.

AS
36
C8

Evans, Alexander William, 1868–

Hepaticae: Yale Peruvian expedition of 1911.

(*In* Connecticut academy of arts and sciences. Transactions. New Haven, Conn., 1914. 25ᶜᵐ. v. 18, p. [291]-345)

1. Hepaticae—Peru. I. Yale Peruvian expedition, 1911. II. Title.

A 17-940

Library of Congress   Q11.C9   vol. 18
Yale University   A53n.366.18

AS
36
C8

QK
555.M2
E 92

Evans, Alexander William, 1868–

... The American species of *Marchantia*, by Alexander W. Evans. New Haven, Conn., 1917.

p. [201]-313. illus. 24½ᶜᵐ. (Transactions of the Connecticut academy of arts and sciences, v. 21, p. 201-313)

1. [Marchantia]

Library of Congress   Q11.C9   vol. 21
Yale University   A53N.366.15

A 18-2089

QK
7

Evans, Alexander W.

An enumeration of the Hepaticae collected by John B. Hatcher in Southern Patagonia. Reprinted from the Bulletin of the Torrey Botanical Club, Vol. XXV, No. 8, Aug. 1898.

QK
Pam
#238

and

QK
1
T1

Evans, Alexander W.

The Lejeuneae, ex Memoirs of the Torrey Bot. Club, vol. VIII, no. 2, 1902.

AS
36
C8

Evans, Alexander William, 1868–

... An arrangement of the genera of *Hepaticæ.*

(*In* Connecticut academy of arts and sciences. Transactions. New Haven, 1888-92. 25ᶜᵐ. v. 8, p. [262]-280)

1. Hepaticae. I. Title.

A 17-852

Library of Congress   Q11.C9   vol. 8
Yale University   A53n.366.8

QK
Pam
#701

and

AS
36
C8

Evans, Alexander W.

The genus Riccardia in Chile, ex Connecticut Acad. of Arts and Sc. Trans., vol. 25, December, 1921.

AS
36
C 8

Evans, Alexander W.

The lobate species of Symphyogyna.

(Trans. Conn. Acad. Arts and Sci., 27:1-50, 1925)

QK
Pam
#402
403

and

QK
1
T1

Evans, AlexanderW.

A new genus of Hepaticae from the Hawaiian Islands, ex Torrey Bot. Club. Bull. vol. 27, March, 1900.

QK
Botany
Pam
1492

Evans, Alexander W

Notes on Connecticut lichens. From Rhodora, vol. 29, June 1927, pp. 97-105.

QK
Pam
#236

Evans, Alexander W.

Notes on North American Hepaticae, VIII, ex The Bryologist, vol. XXII, no. 5, September, 1919.

QK
Pam
#230
and

QK
1
B3

Evans, Alexander W.

A new Hepatic from the Eastern United States, ex The Bot. Gazette, vol. XXXIV, November, 1902.

QK
Pam
#705

and

QK
1
T1

Evans, Alexander W.

Notes on the genus Herberta, with a revision of the species known from Europe, Canada and the United States, ex Torrey Bot. Club Bull., vol. 44, April 14, 1917.

QK
Bot.Pam
2426

Evans, Alexander W,

On Cladonia polycharpia Merrill.

(The Bryologist, 47:49-56, 1944)

QK
Pam
#237

and

QK
1
T1

Evans, Alexander W.

A new Lejunea from Bermuda and the West Indies, ex Torrey Bot. Club. Bull. vol. 44, November 19, 1917.

QK
Pam
#684

Evans, Alexander W.

Notes on New England Hepaticae, XIII. ex Rhodora, Journ. of New England Bot. Club, vol. 18, 1916.

QK
Pam
#1001

Evans, Alexander W.

Preliminary list of Arizona Hepaticae ex The Bryologist, vol. XX, no. 4, July, 1917.

QK
Pam
#233

Evans, Alexander W.

A new Riccia from Peru, ex Torreya, vol. 19, no. 5, May, 1919.

QK
Pam
#228

Evans, Alexander W.

Notes on New England Hepaticae, ex Rhodora, Jour. of the New England Bot. Club, vol. 19, 1917.

AS
36
C8

Evans, Alexander William, 1868-
... A provisional list of the *Hepaticæ* of the Hawaiian Islands.
(*In* Connecticut academy of arts and sciences. Transactions. New Haven, 1888-92. 25ᶜᵐ. v. 8, p. [253]-261. pl. XXII-XXIII)

1. Hepaticae—Hawaiian Islands.   1. Title.

A 17-851

Library of Congress   Q11.C9 vol. 8
Yale University   A53n.366.8

QK
Pam
#682

Evans, Alexander W.

A new species of Metzgeria from the Galapagos Islands, ex Torreya, vol. 16, no. 3, March, 1916.

QK
Pam
#235

Evans, Alexander W.

Notes on New England Hepaticae, ex Rhodora, Jour. of the New England Bot. Club, vol. 21, 1919.

QK
Bot.Pam.
2027

Evans, Alexander W.

Recent segregates from the genera Lophozia and Sphenolobus.

(The Bryologist, Vol. 38, 1935, pp. 61-70)

QK
Pam
#693

and

QK
1
U

Evans, Alexander W.

The North American species of Asterella, ex Contributions from U. S. Nat. Herbarium, vol. 20, pt. 8, 1920.

QK
Pam
#702

Evans, Alexander W.

Notes on New England Hepaticae, XVI., ex Rhodora, vol. 23, December, 1921.

QK
534
V 48

1934

Evans, Alexander W.

A Revision of the genus Acromastigum.

(Annales Bryologici, Supplementary Vol. 3,

QK
Pam
#1003

Evans, Alexander W.

Noteworthy Lejeuneae from Florida, ex Am. Journ. of Bot., vol. V, March 1918.

QK
Pam
#229

Evans, Alexander W.

Notes on North American Hepaticae ex The Bryologist, vol. XX, no. 2, March 1917.

AS
36
C8

and
QK
Pam
241

Evans, Alexander William, 1868-
... A revision of the North American species of *Frullania*, a genus of *Hepaticæ*.
(*In* Connecticut academy of arts and sciences. Transactions. New Haven, 1899-1900. 25ᶜᵐ. v. 10, p. [1]-39. pl. I-XV)

1. Frullania. 2. Hepaticae—North America.

A 17-872

Library of Congress   Q11.C9 vol. 10
Yale University   A53n.366.10

QK
Bot.Pam.
1841

Evans, Alexander W.

Some representative species of Bazzania from Sumatra.

(Papers of the Michigan Academy of Science, Arts and Letters, Vol. VII, 1932, pp. 69-118, pl. 13-18)

QK
1
O 11

Evans, Alexander, W.

Three species of Scapania from western North America.

Contributions from the Osborn Botanical Laboratory, Yale University. X. (Bulletin of the Torrey Botanical Club, 57:87-112, Sept. 1930)

Q
115
P 29

Evans, Arthur W.

Hepaticae

Princeton University
Reports of the Princeton University Expeditions to Patagonia, 1896-1899. Vol. VIII:Part 1, pp. 1-33. 1903.

QK
Pam
#227

Evans, Alex W.

Studies among our common Hepaticae. Reprints from Plant World. II ,Vol. I, no.9, 1898, pp.133-137... III, Vol. I, no.12,1898, pp. 182-186.... IV, Vol. II, 1899, pp. 79-84.

QK
1
O 11

Evans, Alexander W.

Two species of Lejeunea from Chile.

Contributions from the Osborn Botanical Laboratory Yale University, XIII. (Reprinted from Annales Bryologici, Vol. III, 1930, pp. 83-88)

GN
550
S 66

Evans, Clifford

Archaeological investigations in British Guiana. By Clifford Evans and Betty Meggers.

(Bureau of American Ethnology, Bull. 177, 1960)

[reviewed in Humanitas, II:2, 1961, p. 87-90]

QK
Pam
#700
and
QK
1
T1

Evans, Alexander W.

Taxilejeunea pterogonia and certain allied species, ex Torrey Bot. Club. Bull., vol. 48, March 25, 1921.

QL
536
H 79

Evans, Alwen M.

Mosquitoes of the Ethiopian Region. II: Anophelini, adults and early stages. By the late Alwen M. Evans. London. Printed by order of the Trustees. 1938. R8vo. x + 404 pp.

(Vol. I is by G. H. E. Hopkins.)

QL
Prot.-
Poly.
Pam. 785

Evans, F.

Tidal streams and larval dispersal at Whitstable, by F. Evans and G. E. Newell.

(Annals and Mag. Nat. Hist., s 12, vol. X: 161-173, 1957)

QK
Pam
#232
and
QK
1
T1

Evans, Alexander W.

A taxonomic study of Dumortiera, ex Torrey Bot. Club Bull. May, 1919.

GN
22
M 32

Evans, Arthur J.

The European diffusion of primitive pictography and its bearings on the origin of script.

Marett, R. R., editor

Anthropology and the classics: six lectures ...by Arthur J. Evans and others. Oxford. 1908. pp. 9-43.

Q
115
C

Evans, Sir Frederick

Challenger Expedition.

Narrative II

G. 13. 14.   Magnetic Observations.

QH
138.J
S 62

Evans, Alexander W.

The thallose Hepaticae of the Juan Fernandez Islands.

IN
Skottsberg, Carl   editor
The natural history of Juan Fernandez and Easter Island, Vol. II. Botany, Art. 20, pp. 551-586, 1943. Uppsala.

GN
Pam
1341

Evans, Arthur J.

Mycenaean cyprus as illustrated in the British Museum excavations. From Anthrop. Instit. Journ. v. 30, 1900. 21p

---

QK
1
K 44

Evans, G.

The characteristic vegetation of recent volcanic islands in the Pacific. (near New Britain)

(Bull. Misc. Information, Kew, 1939, pp. 43-44)

QK
1
O 11

Evans, Alexander W.

The thallose Hepaticae of the Juan Fernandez Islands.

Contributions from the Osborn Botanical Laboratory Yale University, XII. (Extract from The Natural History of Juan Fernandez and Easter Island, Edited by Carl Skottsberg, Vol. II, pp.551-586)

AS
36
S1

Evans, *Sir* Arthur John, 1851-
New archeological lights on the origins of civilization in Europe. By Sir Arthur Evans ...

(*In* Smithsonian institution. Annual report. 1916. Washington, 1917. 23½ᶜᵐ. p. 425-445)

\ 1. Civilization—Hist.

18-3071

Library of Congress   Q11.S66 1916

QL
1
B 86

Evans, G. Owen

Mites of the genus Macrocheles latr. (Mesostigmata) associated with coprid beetles in the collections of the British Museum (Natural History). By G. Owen Evans and K.H. Hyatt.

(Bull., Brit. Mus. (Nat. Hist.) Zool., Vol. 9(9):(327)-401, 1963)

QK
Pam
#234
and
QK
1
T1

Evans, Alexander W.

Three South American species of Asterella, ex Torrey Bot. Soc. Bull. December 31, 1919.

AS
36
S1

Evans, Arthur John, 1851-
The palace of Minos. By Arthur J. Evans.

(*In* Smithsonian institution. Annual report. 1901. Washington, 1902. 23½ᶜᵐ. p. 425-437. VIII pl.)

Reprinted from the Monthly review, vol. II, London, January-March, 1901, pp. 115-132."

\ 1. Crete—Antiq.   I. Title: Minos, Palace of.

S 15-1113

Library of Congress   Q11.S66 1901
Library, Smithsonian   Institution

QL
458.A2
E 92

Evans, G. Owen

The terrestrial Acari of the British Isles; an introduction to their morphology, biology and classification. Vol. I: Introduction and biology. By G. Owen Evans and J. G. Sheals, and D. Macfarlane. Trustees, British Museum. London. 1961 R8vo. (6) + 219 pp.

QL
461
P 11

Evans, Howard E.

The genus Epipompilus in australia (Hymen-optera:Pompilidae)

(Pacific Insects, 4(4):773-782, 1962)

AS
496
F

Evans, I(vor) H. (N.)

Notes on the aborigines of Lenggong and Kuala Kenering, Upper Perak. In Journ. Fed. Malay States Museums, Vol. V, 2, 1914, pp 64-73.

AS
720,T
R

Evans, J. W.

Australian leaf-hoppers (Jassoidea, Homop-tera) Parts 4-5.

(Papers and Proc. R. Soc. Tasmania, 1936:37-50, 51-72)

QK
Pam
#660
4to

Evans, I; Rogers A. Marloth R; etc.

A guide to Bot. Survey work, ex Bot. Survey of South Africa, Mem. no. 4, 1922.

AS
496
F

Evans, I(vor) H. (N.)

Notes on the aborigines of the Ulu Langat and Kenabci districts of Selangor and Jelebu. In Journ. Fed. Mal. St. Mus. V, 2, 1914, pp 74-81.

AS
720.T
R

Evans, J. W.

Australian leaf-hoppers (Homoptera, Jas-soidea). Part 8.

(Papers and Proc. R. Soc. Tasmania, 1938: 1-18)

QK
395
U 58

Evans, I. B. Pole

Roadside observations on the vegetation of East and Central Africa.

(Botanical Survey Memoir 22, Union of South Africa, Dept. of Agric., 1948)

AS
496
F.

Evans, I(vor) H. N.

Notes on the Besisi of Tamboh, Kuala Langat, Selangor.

(Journ. F.M.S., Mus. V, 1914, pp. 1-14)

AS
720.T
R

Evans, J. W.

The Bythoscopidae of Australia (Homoptera, Jassoidea).

(Papers and Proc. R. Soc. Tasmania, 1935: 61-84)

DS
646.3
E92

Evans, Ivor H   N

Among primitive peoples in Borneo; a descrip-tion of the lives, habits and and customs of the piratical head-hunters of North Borneo, with an account of interesting objects of prehistoric antiquity discovered in the island. With many illustrations & a map. London. Seeley. 1922. 8vo. 318 pp.

GN
Pam
2760

Evans, Ivor H

Notes on the religious beliefs.. of the .. Dusuns of British North Borneo. From Jour. of Royal Anthropological Institute, July to Dec., 1912.

AS
720.T
R

Evans, J. W.

A contribution to the study of the Jassoidea (Homoptera).

(Papers and Proc. R. Soc. Tasmania, 1938: 19-56)

AS
522.S
R 13

Evans, Ivor H. N.

"Melanesoid" culture in Malaya.

(Bulletin of the Raffles Museum, Ser. B, Vol. 1:141-146, 1937)

GN
635.M4
E92

Evans, Ivor H   N

Papers on the ethnology and archaeology of the Malay peninsula.

Cambridge, University Press, 1927. 8vo. x + 164 pp. pls.

AS
719
A 93-m

Evans, J. W.

The life and work of Charles Darwin.

(Australian Mus. Mag., 13(4):105-114, 1959)

GN
635.M4
E 92

Evans, Ivor H. N.

The Negritos of Malaya. Cambridge. Univer-sity Press. 1937. 8vo. xiii + 323 pp.

GN
635.B7
E 92

Evans, I. H. N.

The religion of the Tempasuk Dusuns of North Borneo. The University Press. Cambridge. 1953. 8vo. xviii + (1)2-579 pp., +22 pl. and map

---

AS
720.T
R

Evans, J. W.

A Mecopterous larva from Tasmania and notes on the morphology of the insect head.

(Papers and Proc. R. Soc. Tasmania, 1941: 31-36)

AS
496
F

Evans, I(vor) H. (N.)

Notes on the aboriginal inhabitants of Ijok in the district of Selama, Perak. In Journ. Fed. Mal. St. Mus. V, 4, 1915, pp 176-186.

GN
635.M4
E 92

Evans, Ivor. H. N.

Studies in religion, folk-lore, custom in British North Borneo and the Malay Peninsula. Cambridge, University Press, 1923. 8vo. ix + 299 pp.

AS
720.T
R

Evans, J. W.

The morphology of Tettigarcta tomentosa White, (Homoptera, Cicadidae).

(Papers and Proc. R. Soc. Tasmania, 1940: 35-50)

AS
720.T
R

Evans, J. W.

The morphology of the head of the Homoptera.

(Papers and Proc. R. Soc. Tasmania, 1937:
1-20)

GN
775
E92

Evans, John

Petit album de l'age du bronze de la Grande Bretagne.

Londres, Longmans, 1876. 26 pls. 8vo.
iv + (105) pp.

AP
2
A 5

Evans, Robley D.

The radium and radon content of Pacific Ocean water, life and sediments, by Robley D. Evans, Arthur F. Kip, and E.G.Moberg.

(American Journal of Science, Ser. 5, Vol. 36, 1938, pp. 241-259)

AS
720.T
R

Evans, J. W.

New leaf-hoppers from Tasmania and Queensland.

(Papers and Proc. R. Soc. Tasmania, 1941:
27-30)

AS
36
A 5

Evans, L. Conway

A monarch and his court,- saved from white man's ravages. (kauri pine of New Zealand)

(Natural History, Vol. 50, 1942, pp. 159-162)

AS
36
S1

Evans, S   B.

Antiquities in Mexico. By S. B. Evans.

(*In* Smithsonian institution. Annual report. 1887. Washington, 1880.
23½ᶜᵐ. p. 689-691. illus.)

Archaeology - Mexico
1. Mexico—Antiq. 2. Indians of Mexico—Art.

Library of Congress   Q11.S66 1887
Library, Smithsonian   Institution

S 15-670

AS
719
A 92

Evans, J. W.

The Peloridiidae of Lord Howe Island (Homoptera, Coleorrhyncha).

(Records, Australian Museum, Vol. 25(3),
1959)

DU
Pac
Pam
455

Evans, Luther Harris.

New Guinea under Australian mandate rule. From Southwestern Political and Social Science Quarterly, vol. X, no. 1. 1929.

AS
36
S1

Evans, Samuel B   1837-

Notes on some of the principal mounds in the Des Moines Valley. By Samuel B. Evans ...

(*In* Smithsonian institution. Annual report. 1879. Washington, 1880.
23½ᶜᵐ. p. 344-349. illus. (maps))

1. Mounds—Iowa.

Library of Congress   Q11.S66 1879
Library, Smithsonian   Institution

S 15-497

AS
720.T
R

Evans, J. W.

The phylogeny of the Homoptera.

(Papers and Proc. R. Soc. Tasmania, 1941:
37-40)

DU
620
P

Evans, Margaret O.

Pele, fire goddess, as dream-bride of of King of Kauai.

(Paradise of the Pacific, Vol. 38, No. 1,
1925, pp. 4,5,6)

QL
451
B 16

Evans, T. M.

Baker, E. W.   and others

A manual of parasitic mites of medical or economic importance. A technical publication of the National Pest Control Association, Inc. New York. 1956. 8vo. (5) + 170 pp.

AS
720.Q
R

Evans, J. W.

Some new leaf-hoppers from Australia and Fiji.

(Proc. Royal Soc. of Queensland, for 1942, Vol. 54, issued 1943, pp. 49-51)

QL
Protozoa
& Poly
Pam
#16

Evans, Richard

A description of two new species of Spongilla from Lake Tanganyika, ex Quart. Journ. Micro. Sc. vol. 41, pt. 37.

QL
561.H 5
E 92

Evans, W. H.

A catalogue of the African Hesperiidae indicating the classification and nomenclature adopted in the British Museum. London. Printed by order of the Trustees, British Museum. 8vo. 1937. xii + 212 pp, 30 pl.

GN
805
E 92

Evans,(Sir) John

The ancient stone implements, weapons, and ornaments, of Great Britain. London. Longmans.. 1872. R8vo. xvi + 640 pp.

Second edition, revised. London. Longmans.. 1897. R8vo. xviii + 747 pp.

Evans, Robert Frank   Carter Coll.
7-B-24

Notes on land and sea, 1850. Boston Richard G. Badger. 1922. 140 pp. 8vo.

QL
561.H5
E 92

Evans, W. H.

A catalogue of the American Hesperidae, indicating the classification and nomenclature adopted in the British Museum (Natural History). Part I: Introduction and Group A, Pyrrhopyginae. Printed by order of the Trustees of the British Museum. London. 1951. 8vo. x + 92 pp.

Part II (Groups B,C,D) Pyrginae. Sect. 1. 1952. 178 pp.

Part III (Groups E, F, G) Pyrginae . Sect. 2 pl. 26 to 53. 1953. 246 pp.

AS
36
S1

Evans, *Sir* John, 1823-1908.

Antiquity of man. By John Evans, F. R. S.

(*In* Smithsonian institution. Annual report. 1890. Washington, 1891.
23½ᶜᵐ. p. 467-474)

"From Nature, September 18, 1890, vol. XLII, pp. 507-510."

1. Man, Antiquity of.

Library of Congress   Q11.S66 1890
Library, Smithsonian   Institution

S 15-740

AP
2
A 5

Evans, Robley D.

The radium content of marine sediments from the East Indies, the Philippines, and Japan, and of the Mesozoic fossil clays, East Indies, by R. D. Evans and Arthur F. Kip.

(American Jour. of Sci., Ser. 5, Vol. 76, 1938, pp. 321-336)

QL
561.H5
E 92

Evans, W. H.

A catalogue of the Hesperiidae from Europe, Asia and Australia in the British Museum (Natural History). London. Printed by order of the Trustees. 1949. xix + 502 pp, 53 pl.

GN 490 E 92
Evans-Pritchard, E. E.

The institutions of primitive society; a series of broadcast talks by E. E. Evans-Pritchard, Raymond Firth, E. R. Leach, J. G. Peristiany, John Layard, Max Gluckman, Meyer Fortes, Godfrey Lienhardt. Oxford. Basil Blackwell. 8m8vo. 1954. viii + 107 pp.

QL Birds Pam. 328
Everest, F. Alton

Photographs of birds of Midway Islands, presented to Bernice P. Bishop Museum. Photos taken between May 10 and May 26, 1951. 37 photos with captions. 4to.

QL Fish Pam #82
Evermann, Barton Warren

Alaska fisheries and fur industries in 1913; Bur. of Fish. Doc. no. 797.

GN 22 E 92
Evans-Pritchard, E. E.

Social anthropology. The Free Press. Illinois. 1952. 8vo. vii and 134 pp.

QK 936 T 85
The EvergreenForests of Liberia...

Cooper, G. Proctor   (and Record, Samuel J)

QL 627 U-b
Evermann, Barton Warren

Jordan, David Starr

The aquatic resources of the Hawaiian islands...Part I. The shore fishes... Part III: Miscellaneous papers...
(Bull U. S. Fish Commission, Vol. 23, 1903, Part 1, pp. xxviii + 574 and Part III, pp. x + 769-1198)

Evaporation Plants.
see
Botany, physiological and structural. Evaporation.

QK Bot.Pam. 2019
Everhart, B. M.

Ellis, J. B.

New Fungi, mostly Uredineae and Ustilagineae from various localities, and a new fomes from Alaska, by J. B. Ellis and B. M. Everhart.

(The Bulletin of the Torrey Botanical Club, Vol. 22, 1895, pp. 362-364)

QL Fish Pam #235
EVERMANN, BARTON WARREN

Jordan, David Starr.

Check list of Fishes of Hawaii. In Pan-Pac. Research Inst. Journ. vol.1, no.1. 1926.

DT Af Pam No.4
D'Evelyn, Fred W.

Terra Natalis.   ex ?, n.d.

QK Bot. Pam # 649
Everhart, B. M. & Ellis, J. B.

New Species of Fungi. Reprint from Bull. of Torrey Bot. Club, Vol. 22, No.10, pp 434-440.

AS 36 S4
Evermann, Barton Warren, 1853–
A comparison of the chub-mackerels of the Atlantic and Pacific oceans. By Barton Warren Evermann and William Converse Kendall ...

(*In* U. S. National museum. Proceedings. Washington, 1911. 23½ᵐᵐ. vol. 38, p. 327-328)

1. Mackerel.   1. Kendall, William Converse, 1861–   joint author.

11-15734

Library of Congress   Q11.U55 vol. 38

DU 625 E 93 locked case
[Eveleth, E.]

History of the Sandwich Islands: with an account of the American Mission established there in 1820.   American Sunday-School Union. Philadelphia. 1829. 12mo.   214 pp.

[a "Brief memoir of the Rev. Mr. Eveleth" is followed by"Letters on the Sandwich Islands" signed E. E.]
ALSO 1831 edition with a supplement: "embracing the history of the wonderful displays of God's power in these islands in 1837-1839."same publisher. 231 pp

---

DS Pam No.7
Everill, Henry Charles

The Malay Archipelago.

XXXXI, XXXXXXXXXXXXXXXXX

(Bulletin of the Geographical Society of California,   Vol. II, May, 1894, pp. 13-42)

Q. Gen.SC. Pam #1
Evermann, Barton Warren

The conservation and proper utilization of our natural resources, ex Scientific monthly, Oct. 1922.

DU 625 E 93 locked case
EVELETH, E.

[Eveleth, E.]

History of the Sandwich Islands: with an account of the American Mission established there in 1820. American Sunday-School Union. Philadelphia. 1829. 12mo.

also 1831 edition, with a supplement...

[contains a brief memoir of Rev. E. Eveleth]

QK Bot.Pam. 3171
Everist, S. L.

Features of the Queensland flora.

(Extract from A. N. Z. A. A. S. Handbook, 1951. pp. 1-5)

QL Mam Pam #2
Evermann, (Dr.) Barton Warren

The conservaton of the mammals and other vanishing animals of the Pacific. ex The Scientific Monthly, Mar. 1922, vol. XIV, No. 3.

QK 475 E 93
Evelyn, John

Silva; or, a discourse of forest-trees... together with an historical account of the sacredness and use of standing groves, to which is added The Terra; a philosophical discourse of earth. With notes by A. Hunter. 5th edition... In two volumes. Vols. 1-2. London. 1825. folio.

QK Geol. Pam. 1258
Everist, S. L.

Studies in the environment of Queensland. 2. The climatic factor in drought. By S. L. Everist and G. R. Moule. In collaboration with Elizabeth Baynes and Sylvia Cossins.

(Reprinted from "The Queensland Journal of Agricultural Science,", Vol. 9(3); September, 1952)

AP 2 S 35
Evermann, Barton Warren

David Starr Jordan

(Science, Vol. 74:327-329, 1931)

QL
627
U-b
Evermann, B. W. (Barton Warren)

Fishes and fisheries of Porto Rico, by B.W. Evermann and M.C. Marsh. Washington. 1900. 8vo. 350 pp. 52 pls.

QL
618
Jo
Evermann, Barton Warren, 1853-
Jordan, David Starr, 1851-

... The genera of fishes ... A contribution to the stability of scientific nomenclature. By David Starr Jordan. Stanford University, Calif., The University, 1917-20.

4 v. 25½ᶜᵐ. (Leland Stanford junior university publications. University ser. 27, 36, 39, 43₁)

CONTENTS.—pt. I₀ From Linnæus to Cuvier, 1758-1833, seventy-five years, with the accepted type of each. By D. S. Jordan, assisted by B. W. Evermann.—pt. II. From Agassiz to Bleeker, 1833-1858, twenty-six years, with the accepted type of each.—pt. III. From Guenther to Gill, 1859-1880, twenty-two years, with the accepted type of each.—pt. IV. From 1881 to 1920, thirty-nine years, with the accepted type of each.

1. Fishes—Nomenclature. I. Evermann, Barton Warren, 1853-

17-29156 Revised 2

Library of Congress   QL618.J7
———— Copy 2. pt. II-II   AS36.L5 no. 36, 39
           [21h3]

GN
775
Q 2
Everyday life in the old stone age

Quennell, Marjorie, and Quennell, C. H. B.

QL
Fish
Pam
249
Evermann, Barton Warren and Shaw, Tsen-Hwang

Fishes from eastern China, with descriptions of new species. From Proc. Cal. Acad. Sci., v.XVI, n.4, 1927.

QL
631.P
E 93
Evermann, Barton Warren

General report on the investigations in Porto Rico of the United States Fish Commission steamer Fish Hawk in 1899.

(U. S. Fish Commission Bulletin for 1900: 1-350, pl. 1-52, 1900)

Contains: The fisheries and fish trade of Porto Rico, by William A. Wilcox (pp. 29-48); The fishes of Porto Rico, by B. W. Evermann, and Millard Caleb March (pp. 49-350)

DU
1
P 10
Evidence on cargo cult outbreak in Bainings area.

(Pac. Isl. Monthly,26(1):163, 1955)

QL
Fish
Pam
#158
4to
Evermann, B. W.; Goldsborough E. L.

The fishes of Alaska, ex Bur. of Fish. Bull. vol. XXVI, doc. 624, 1907.

QL
Fish
Pam.
557
Evermann, Barton Warren

Note on the Basking Shark.

(Copeia, No. 74, pp. 77-78, Oct., 1919)

QH
366
E 92
Evolution and anthropology: a centennial appraisal. The Anthropological Society of Washington. Washington, D. C. 1959. 8vo. viii + 172 pp.

AS
36
S5
EVERMANN, BARTON WARREN, 1853 jt.au
Jordan, David Starr, 1851-

... The fishes of North and Middle America: a descriptive catalogue of the species of fish-like vertebrates found in the waters of North America, north of the Isthmus of Panama. By David Starr Jordan ... and Barton Warren Evermann ... Washington, Govt. print. off., 1896-1900.

4 v. cccxcii pl. 24ᶜᵐ. (Added t-p.: ... Bulletin of the United States National museum no. 47)

At head of title: Smithsonian institution. United States National museum.

1. Fishes—North America. I. Evermann, Barton Warren, 1853- joint author.

1—1361

Library of Congress   Q11.U6

AS
36
C 1
Evermann, Barton Warren

Jordan, David Starr

A review of the giant mackerel-like fishes, tunnies, spearfishes and swordfishes. By David Starr Jordan and Barton Warren Evermann.

(Occasional Papers of the California Acad. of Sci., XII, 1926)

QH
366
A 57
EVOLUTION

Anfinsen, Christian B.

The molecular basis of evolution. New York John Wiley. 1960. 8vo. xiii + 228 pp.

QL
631.P
E 93
Evermann, Barton Warren

The fishes of Porto Rico, by B. W. Evermann and Millard Caleb Marsh.
IN
Evermann, Barton Warren
General report on the investigations in Porto Rico of the United States Fish Commission steamer Fish Hawk in 1899.

(U. S. Fish Commission Bulletin for 1900: 49-350, pl. 1-52)

Q
Biog
Pam.
No.32
Evermann, Barton Warren

John Van Denburgh, 1872 - 1924. From Science, Vol. 61, 1925, pp 508-510.

GN
1
A67
EVOLUTION

Archiv für rassen-und gesellschafts-biologie... herausgegeben von ... Alfred Ploetz... v. 1-18

Berlin, Archiv-gesellschaft, 1904-1918

AS
36
S4
Evermann, Barton Warren, 1853-
The fishes of the Lake of the Woods and connecting waters. By Barton Warren Evermann and Homer Barker Latimer ...

(In U. S. National museum. Proceedings. Washington, 1911. 23½ᶜᵐ. v. 39, p. 121-136)

1. Fishes—Lake of the Woods. I. Latimer, Homer Barker, joint author.

11-20929

Library of Congress   Q11.U55 vol. 39

AP
2
S 35
EVERMANN, BARTON WARREN

Hanna, G. Dallas

Barton Warren Evermann

(Science, Vol. 76:317-318, 1932)

AS
36
S1
EVOLUTION.

Bailey, Liberty Hyde, 1858-
The factors of organic evolution from a botanical standpoint. By Prof. L. H. Bailey.

(In Smithsonian institution. Annual report. 1897. Washington, 1898. 23½ᶜᵐ. p. 453-475)

"Printed in the Proceedings of the American philosophical society, vol. xxxv, 1896."

1. Evolution. I. Title.

S 15-969

Library of Congress   Q11.S66 1897
Library, Smithsonian   Institution

QL
Fish
Pam
#15
Evermann, B. W. & Seale, Alvin

Fishes of the Philippine Islands, ex Bur. of Fisheries Bull. vol. XXVI, doc. no. 607, 1907.

QK
Bot.Pam
8164
Evers, Robert A.

The filmy fern in Illinois.

(Illinois Natural History Survey, Biol. Notes No. 44, 1961)

AS
36
S1
EVOLUTION

Baker, Frank, 1841-
The ascent of man. By Frank Baker, M. D.

(In Smithsonian institution. Annual report. 1890. Washington, 1891. 23½ᶜᵐ. p. 447-466)

"From Proceedings Am. assoc. adv. sci., vol. xxxix, pp. 351-373."

1. Evolution.

S 15-739

Library of Congress   Q11.S66 1890
Library, Smithsonian   Institution

EVOLUTION

QH
361
B49
Bergson, Henri

Creative evolution. Translated by Arthur Mitchell.

New York, Henry Holt, 1911.   407p.

EVOLUTION

QH
368
C 75
Conklin, Edwin Grant

The direction of human evolution.

New York, 1925, 247 pp.

EVOLUTION

QH
Nat.Hist.
Pam.
167
Dansereau, Pierre

The varieties of evolutionary opportunity.

(Reprinted from Revue Canadienne de Biologie, 11(4):305-388, 1952)

EVOLUTION

QH
366
B 87
Brown, R.   Editor

Evolution. Symposia of the Society for Experimental Biology, No. VII. Edited by R. Brown and J.F. Danielli. Academic Press Inc., Publishers. New York. 1953. xix + 448 pp.

EVOLUTION

AS
36
S1
Constantin, Julien Noël

The development of orchid cultivation and its bearing upon evolutionary theories.

(Smithsonian Inst., Annual Report, 1913, pp. 345-358)

EVOLUTION

QH
365
D 22
Darwin, Charles

Evolution by natural selection, by Charles Darwin and Alfred Russel Wallace. With a foreword by Sir Gavin de Beer. Cambridge, 1958

EVOLUTION

AS
36
S1
Candolle, Alphonse Louis Pierre Pyramus de, 1806-1893.

The probable future of the human race. From the History of science and of savants, by Alphonse de Candolle ...

(*In* Smithsonian institution. Annual report. 1875. Washington, 1876. 23½ᶜᵐ. p. 142-150)

"Translated for the Smithsonian institution."

1. Evolution.

Library of Congress   Q11.S66 1875
Library, Smithsonian   Institution

S 15-409

EVOLUTION.

AS
36
S1
Cook, Orator Fuller, 1867–

The evolutionary significance of species. By O. F. Cook.

(*In* Smithsonian institution. Annual report. 1904. Washington, 1905. 23½ᶜᵐ. p. 397-412)

"Consists principally of a revision and combination of two articles, 'Evolution not the origin of species' (Popular science monthly, March, 1904) and 'Natural selection in kinetic evolution' (Science, April 1, 1904)"

1. Evolution. 2. Species, Origin of.   I. Title.

Library of Congress   Q11.S66 1904
Library, Smithsonian   Institution

S 15-1251

EVOLUTION

QH
365
D 22
Darwin, Charles Robert, 1809-1882.

The origin of species by means of natural selection, or The preservation of favoured races in the struggle for life. By Charles Darwin ... London, J. Murray, 1897.

2 v. front. (port.) fold. diagr. 19½ᶜᵐ.

"First edition, November 24th, 1859; sixth edition, Jan. 1872."

Evolution. t

1. Species, Origin of. 2. Natural selection.

Library of Congress   QH365.O 1897

4-1283

EVOLUTION

QH
366
C 22
Cannon, H. Graham

The evolution of living things. Charles C. Thomas. Springfield. sm8vo. 1958. x + 180 pp.

EVOLUTION

QH
367
C78
Cope, E   D

The origin of the fittest: essays on evolution

New York, Appleton, 1887.   467p.

EVOLUTION

QH
367
D22
Darwin, Leonard

Organic evolution: outstanding difficulties and possible explanations. Cambridge, University press, 1921.

EVOLUTION

QH
366
C 32
Carter, G. S.

A hundred years of evolution. Sidgwick and Jackson. London. 8vo. x + 206 pp.

EVOLUTION

QH
367
C78
Cope, E. D.

Primary factors of organic evolution. Chicago, Open Court, 1896.   547p.

EVOLUTION

QH
Nat.Hist.
Pam.
179
Darwin-Wallace Centenary.

(Journal of the Linnean Society of London, Botany, Vol. 56, No. 365: pp. 1-152, 1958)

EVOLUTION.

AS
36
S1
Caullery, Maurice Jules Gaston Corneille, 1868–

The present state of the problem of evolution. By Prof. M. Caullery.

(*In* Smithsonian institution. Annual report. 1916. Washington, 1917. 23½ᶜᵐ. p. 321-335)

"Translated from the French by Mrs. C. H. Grandgent. Reprinted from Science, April 21, 1916."

1. Evolution.   I. Grandgent, Mrs. Ethel Wright (Cushing) 1863– tr.

18-3066

Library of Congress   Q11.S66 1916

EVOLUTION

AS
36
S1
Constantin, Julien Noël, 1857–

The development of orchid cultivation and its bearing upon evolutionary theories. By J. Constantin.

(*In* Smithsonian institution. Annual report. 1913. Washington, 1914. 23½ᶜᵐ. p. 345-358)

"Translation of 'Les progrès de la culture des fleurs et leur importance pour les théories transformistes' ... from Scientia ... London, no. 3, 1911."

1. Orchids. 2. Evolution.

15-1742

Library of Congress   Q11.S66 1913

EVOLUTION

QH
366
D 63
Dobzhansky, Theodosius

Evolution, genetics, and man. John Wiley and Sons, Inc. New York. 1955. 8vo. ix + 398 pp.

EVOLUTION

Q
Gen.Sci.
Pam.104
Caullery, Maurice

Present Theories of Evolution and the Problem of Adaptation. University of Pennsylvania, 1933. 8vo. 19 pp.

EVOLUTION

QH
367
C88
Crampton, Henry Edward

The doctrine of evolution; its basis and its scope.

New York, Columbia, 1924.   320p.

EVOLUTION

AP
2
A 52
Dobzhansky, Theodosius

Evolution in the tropics.

(American Scientist, Vol. 38:209-221, 1950)

QH
366
D 63

EVOLUTION

Dobzhansky, Theodosius

Genetics and the origin of species.
New York. Columbia University Press. 8vo.
xvi + 364 pp. (Columbia Biological Series, No.
XI) 1939

QH
366
F89

EVOLUTION

Friedenthal, Hans

Sonderformen der menschlichen leibes-
bildung...ein beitrag zur vergleichenden
formenlehre der menschlichen gestalt.

Jean, Fischer, 1910. 100p. pls.
(Beitrage zur Naturgeschichte des
menschen V)

QL
Mol
Pam
#192
and
QL
Mol
Pam
#128

EVOLUTION

Gulick, John T.

Divergence under the same environment
as seen in the Hawaiian snails ex Am.
Naturalist, vol. XXXVIII, Nos. 451-2,
1904.

QH
366
D 63

EVOLUTION

Dobzhansky, Theodosius

Mankind evolving: the evolution of the
human species. Yale University Press. New
Haven... 1962 8vo. xiii + 381 pp.

QH
361
G29

Evolution

Geddes, Patrick and Thomson, J   Arthur

AS
36
S1

EVOLUTION

Gulick, John Thomas, 1832–
Divergent evolution through cumulative segregation.
By Rev. John Thomas Gulick.

(*In* Smithsonian institution. Annual report. 1891. Washington, 1893.
23½cm. p. 269-336. tables)
"From the Journal of zoology of the Linnean society, September, 1888,
vol. xx, pp. 189-274."

1. Evolution.

Library of Congress   Q11.S66 1891
Library, Smithsonian   Institution   S 15-765

AP
2
A 52

EVOLUTION

Dobzhansky, Th.

On methods of evolutionary biology and an-
thropology.
Part I, Biology, by Th. Dobzhansky
" II, Anthropology, by Joseph B. Birdsell

(American Scientist, Vol. 45:381-400)

GN
Ethn.
Pam.
4312

EVOLUTION

Gerard, R. W.

Biological and cultural evolution: some
analogies and explorations. By R. W. Gerard,
Clyde Kluckhohn, and Anatol Rapoport.

(Behavioral Science, 1(1):6-34, 1956)

QL
1
L-j

EVOLUTION

Gulick, John T.

Diversity of evolution under onset of external conditions.

(Journal Linnean Society of London, XI, 1873
pp. 496-505)

Q
Gen.Sci.
Pam.
115

EVOLUTION

Dobzhansky, Theodosius

The raw materials of evolution.

(Carnegie Institution of Washington, Suppl.
Publ. No. 38, pp. 5, 1938)

AS
36
S1

EVOLUTION

Glangeaud, Philippe, 1866–
Albert Gaudry and the evolution of the animal kingdom. By Ph. Glangeaud ...

(*In* Smithsonian institution. Annual report. 1909. Washington, 1910.
23½cm. p. 417-429)
"Translated ... from Revue générale des sciences pures et appliquées,
Paris, 20th year, no. 6, March 30, 1909."

1. Gaudry, Albert *i. e.* Jean Albert, 1827-1909. 2. Evolution.

                    11-9878

Library of Congress   Q11.S66 1909

QH
408
G-97

Evolution

Gulick, John T.

Evolution, racial and habitudinal.

Carnegie inst. of Washington, 1905.
Pub.#25. 269p.

QH
368
D 92

EVOLUTION

Dunn, L. C.

Heredity and evolution in human populations
Harvard University Press. Cambridge, Mass.
1959. sm8vo. viii + 157 pp.

QH
366
G 62

EVOLUTION

Goldschmidt, Richard

The material basis of evolution. Yale
University press. New Haven. 1940. R8vo. pp.
xii + 436.

QL
Nat
Hist
Pam
#13

QL
30

EVOLUTION.

Gulick, John T.

Inconsistencies of Utilitarianism as the
exclusive theory of organic evolution.
in Am. Journ. Sci. XL, pp. 1-14.

QH
366
E 36

EVOLUTION

Eiseley, Loren

Darwin's century; evolution and the men who
discovered it. Doubleday Anchor Books. 1958.
New York. 8vo. xvii + 378 pp.

AS
36
S1

EVOLUTION.

Graff, Ludwig von, 1851–
Zoology since Darwin. By Ludwig v. Graff.
(*In* Smithsonian institution. Annual report. 1895. Washington, 1896.
23½cm. p. 477-491. pl. XXVII (port.))
"Translated from original, 'Die zoologie seit Darwin,' Graz, 1896."

1. Zoology—Hist. 2. Evolution.

                    S 15-896

Library of Congress   Q11.S66 1895
Library, Smithsonian   Institution

QL
Mol
Pam
#129
#193
and
QL
1
L-j

EVOLUTION.

Gulick, John Thomas (Rev.)

Intensive segregation or divergence
through independent transformation. ex
Linnean Society's Journal, Zoology, vol.
xxiii (about 1890).

QH
431
E

Evolution

Estabrook, Arthur H.
The Jukes in 1915.
Carnegie Inst. Wash. Pub. 240. (Experiment-
al evolution paper No. 25.)
Washington 1916.

QH
366
G92

EVOLUTION

Guenther, Konrad

Vom urtier zum menschen.

Stuttgart, Anstalt, 1909.   2v.

AS
36
B3
and
QL
Moll.
Pam.
153

EVOLUTION

Gulick, John T.

Lessons in the theory of divergent
evolution drawn from the distribution of
the land shells of the Hawaiian Islands.
Abstract of a paper read before the Boston
Society of Natural History, Jan.2, 1889.
In Bost. Soc. Nat. Hist. Proc. XXIV, pp 166
-167.

EVOLUTION

AS
36
S1
Haeckel, Ernst Heinrich Philipp August, 1834–
  On our present knowledge of the origin of man. By Ernst Haeckel.
  (*In* Smithsonian institution. Annual report. 1898. Washington, 1899. 23½ᶜᵐ. p. 461–480)
  "Translated from the author's edition in German; printed at Bonn, 1898."

  1. Evolution. 2. Man, Origin of.

Library of Congress   Q11.S66 1898   S 15–1005
Library, Smithsonian   Institution

EVOLUTION

QH
367
J92
Judd, J. W.
  The coming of evolution; the story of a great revolution in science. Cambridge, University press, 1925. 171 p.

EVOLUTION

QH
371
L97
Lutz, Frank Eugene, 1879–
  Experiments with *Drosophila ampelophila* concerning evolution. By Frank E. Lutz. Washington, D. C., Carnegie institution of Washington, 1911.
  iii, 40 p. incl. tables, diagrs. 25ᶜᵐ. (*On verso of t.-p.:* Carnegie institution of Washington. Publication no. 143)
  Bibliography: p. 40.
  Paper no. 16, of the Station for experimental evolution at Cold Spring Harbor, New York.
  CONTENTS.—The inheritance of abnormal venation.—The effect of sexual selection.—Disuse and degeneration.
  1. Evolution. 2. Heredity. 3. Drosophila ampelophila.

Library of Congress   QH371.L8   11–8151
——— Copy 2.   (s20k3)

EVOLUTION

QH
367
H 68
Hooton, Ernest Albert
  Apes, Men and Morons. New York. G.P. Putnam's Sons. 1937. 8vo. ix + 307 pp.

EVOLUTION

AS
719
A 93-m
Keast, Allen
  The role of islands in evolution.
  (Australian Mus. Mag., 13(4):128–132, 1959)

EVOLUTION

AS
36
S1
Macnamara, Nottidge Charles, 1834–
  Organic evolution: Darwinian and De Vriesian. By N. C. Macnamara ...
  (*In* Smithsonian institution. Annual report. 1911. Washington, 1912. 23½ᶜᵐ. p. 363–378)

  1. Evolution.

Library of Congress   Q11.S66 1911   13–3786

EVOLUTION

AP
2
S 35
Hooton, Ernest A.
  Homo sapiens—whence and whither.
  (Science, N. S. Vol. 82, 1935, pp. 19–31)

EVOLUTION

QH
431
K46
Kidd, Walter
  The direction of hair in animals and man.
  London, Adam, 1903. 154p. pls.

EVOLUTION

QC
1001
M 43
Matthew, William Diller
  Climate and evolution. Second edition, revised and enlarged. Arranged by Edwin Harris Colbert; preface by William King Gregory; with critical additions by the author and others and a bibliography of his scientific works...Special Publications of the New York Academy of Sciences, Vol. 1, 1939.

EVOLUTION

QH
368
H 77
Hooton, Earnest Albert
  Up from the Ape. Illustrated. New York, The Macmillan Company. 1931. xvii + 626 pp. 8vo.
  also revised edition, 1946. Macmillan Company. xxii + 788 pp.

EVOLUTION

Q
3
K86
Kosmos; zeitschrift für einheitliche weltanschauung auf grund der entwicklungslehre.
  Leipzig, Gunther, 1877–
  Library has:
  Vol. I–IX, 1877–1881

EVOLUTION

QH
366
M 47
Mayr, Ernst
  Animal species and evolution. The Belknap Press of Harvard University Press. Cambridge. 1963. 8vo. xiv + 797 pp.

EVOLUTION

QH
368
H 85
Howells, William
  Mankind in the making; the story of human evolution. Drawings by Janis Cirulis. Doubleday and Co., Inc. Garden City, New York R8vo. 382 pp.

EVOLUTION

AS
36
S1
Kropotkin, Petr Alekseevich, knîàz', 1842–
  The direct action of environment and evolution [by] Prince Kropotkin.
  (*In* Smithsonian institution. Annual report. 1918. Washington, 1920. 23½ᶜᵐ. p. 409–427)
  "Reprinted ... from the Nineteenth century and after, January 1919."

  1. Evolution.

Library of Congress   Q11.S66 1918   20–18976
                           (9)

EVOLUTION

QH
366
M 47
Mayr, Ernst
  Systematics and the origin of species from the viewpoint of a zoologist. New York. Columbia University Press. 1942. R8vo. x + 334 pp.

EVOLUTION

Q
158
N 55
Huxley, Julian
  Evolution and genetics.
  IN
  (Newman, J. R., ed. What is science? 1955. p.256–289)

EVOLUTION

GN
Ethn.
Pam.
3905
Le Gros Clark, W. E.
  History of the primates, an introduction to the study of fossil man. Third edition. British Museum (Natural History) London. 1953 8vo. 117 pp.

EVOLUTION

GN
Ethn.
Pam.
4043
Mettler, Fred A.
  Culture and the structural evolution of the neural system. James Arthur Lecture on the Evolution of the Human Brain, 1955. The American Museum of Natural History. New York. 1956 57 pp. 9 vo.

EVOLUTION

QH
366
H 98
Huxley, Julian
  Evolution, the modern synthesis. Harper and Brothers. New York and London. R8vo. 1943c 646 pp.

EVOLUTION

QH
325
L 48
Leeper, G. W.   editor
  The evolution of living organisms; a symposium to mark the Centenary of Darwin's 'Origin of Species' and of the Royal Society of Victoria ...1959. Melbourne University Press. R8vo. 1962 (8)+ 459 pp.

EVOLUTION

QH
366
M87
Morris, Charles
  Man and his ancestor. New York, Macmillan, 1900. 238p.

EVOLUTION	

QH 325
O 61

EVOLUTION

Oparin, A. I.

    Life: its nature, origin and development. London. Oliver and Boyd. 1961. xi + 207 pp. 1961 R8vo.

AS 122
L-p.

Evolution.

Poulton, E. B.

    Presidential address, Linnean Society London, Proceedings, Oct. 1913. pp. 26-45

    Note:- A review of an old American pamphlet containing an anticipation of Darwin.

QH 361
S 56

EVOLUTION

Shull, A. Franklin

    Evolution. First edition, Second impression. New York. McGraw-Hill Book Co., Inc. 1936. R8vo. x + 312 pp.

AS 36
S1

EVOLUTION

Osborn, Henry Fairfield, 1857–

    Present problems in evolution and heredity. By Henry Fairfield Osborn.

    (*In* Smithsonian institution. Annual report. 1892. Washington, 1893. 23½ᵐ. p. 313-374. tab. diagrs.)
    "From the Medical record for February 20, March 5, April 23, and May 14, 1892."

    1. Evolution. 2. Heredity. I. Title.

                                         S 15-794

Library of Congress   Q11.S66 1892
Library, Smithsonian   Institution

QL 366
R 42

EVOLUTION

Rensch, Bernhard

    Evolution above the species level. Columbia University Press. New York. 1960 R8vo. xvii + 419 pp.

G Geography
Pam. 68

EVOLUTION

Simpson, George Gaylord

    Evolution and geography; an essay on historical biogeography, with special reference to mammals. Condon Lectures. Oregon State System of Higher Education, Eugene, Oregon. 1953. R8vo. 64 pp.

Q General Science
Pam. 99

EVOLUTION

Osborn, Henry Fairfield

    Fundamental Discoveries of the Last Decade in Human Evolution.

    (From the Bulletin of the New York Academy of Medicine, 1927, Second Series, Vol. III, pp. 513-521).

GN Ethn.Pam. 2937

EVOLUTION

Ribaucourt, Edouard de

    Reflexions Philosophiques sur quelques données zoologiques pouvant être appliquées à l'Anthropologie. Privately printed. Paris. 1932 ?

QH 366
S 61

EVOLUTION

Simpson, George Gaylord

    The major features of evolution. Columbia University Press. New York. R8vo. xx+ 434 pp. 1955.

Q General Science
Pam. 98

EVOLUTION

Osborn, Henry Fairfield

    Recent Discoveries in Human Evolution.

    (From the Long Island Medical Journal, Vol. 21, 1927, No. 10, 4 pages).

GN Ethn.Pam. 67 and 26

EVOLUTION

Rotzell, W. E.

    Some vestigial structures in man.

    (The Hannemanian Monthly, June 1895) 8vo.

5 pp.

QH 361
S 61

EVOLUTION

Simpson, George Gaylord

    The meaning of evolution, a study of the history of life and of its significance for man. Yale Univ. Press. New Haven. 1952. 8vo. xv + 364 pp.

QH 371
P 36

EVOLUTION

Pearse, A. S.

    The emigrations of animals from the sea. The Sherwood Press. Dryden, N.Y. 8vo. (1950) xii + 210 pp.

QH 363
R 69

EVOLUTION

Roe, Anne

    Behavior and evolution. Edited by Anne Roe and George Gaylord Simpson. New Haven. Yale University Press. 1958. 8vo. viii + 557 pp.

AS 36
W 1-b

EVOLUTION

Simpson, George Gaylord

    A synopsis of three lectures on evolution and the history of life.

    (Bull. Wagner Free Institute of Science, Vol. 25(2):5-12, 1950)

QH 366
P45

EVOLUTION

Perrier, Edmond

    The earth before history.

    London, Kegan Paul, 1925.   345p.

GN 2.1
A-m

EVOLUTION

Schultz, Adolph H.

    Man's place among the primates.

    (Man, Vol. 53, Jan. 1953, pp. 7-8)

QH 366
S 61

EVOLUTION

Simpson, George Gaylord

    Tempo and mode in evolution. New York. Columbia Univ. Press. 1949. (1st printing 1944) xviii + 237 pp.

AS 36
S1

EVOLUTION

Petronievics, Branislav, 1875–

    On the law of irreversible evolution. By Branislav Petronievics ...

    (*In* Smithsonian institution. Annual report. 1918. Washington, 1920. 23½ᵐ. p. 429-440.)
    "Translated ... by Gerrit S. Miller, jr., from Science progress, January, 1919."
    "Literature": p. 439-440.

    1. Evolution. I. Miller, Gerrit Smith, 1869– tr.

Library of Congress   Q11.S66 1918
                    [10]   20-18977

QH 366
843

Evolution

Scott, William Berryman

Theory of evolution

    New York: Macmillan, 1917. pp 185

AS 36
S1

EVOLUTION

Smith, Grafton Elliot, 1871–

    The evolution of man. By Prof. G. Elliot Smith ...

    (*In* Smithsonian institution. Annual report. 1912. Washington, 1913. 23½ᵐ. p. 553-572.)
    "Reprinted ... from Nature, London, Sept. 26, 1912."

    1. Evolution. 2. Man, Origin of.

                                     13-25696

Library of Congress   Q11.S66 1912

AP
2
S 35

EVOLUTION

Sumner, F. B.

Is evolution inscrutable?

(Science, Vol. 93, 1941, pp. 521-522; and
Contrib. 135, Scripps Inst. of Oceanography)

QH
366
W 18

EVOLUTION

Wallace, Alfred Russel, 1823-1913.
    The world of life; a manifestation of creative power,
directive mind and ultimate purpose, by Alfred Russel
Wallace ... New York, Moffat, Yard & company, 1911.
    xvi, 441 p. illus., plates. 22½ᶜᵐ. $3.00

1. Evolution. 2. Life.   ɪ. Title.
Library of Congress   QH366.W32
———— Copy 2.   11—1767
Copyright A 280647   (s20g2)

QH
366
Z 81

EVOLUTION

Zirkle, Conway

Evolution, Marxian biology, and the social
scene. University of Pennsylvania Press.
Philadelphia. 8vo. 1959c 527 pp.

QH
325
T 23
and
QH
366
T 23
of vol.
III
only

EVOLUTION

Tax, Sol. editor

Evolution after Darwin.
    Vol. I: The evolution of life: its origin
history and future.
    Vol. II: The evolution of man: man, cul-
ture and society.
    Vol. III: Issues in evolution.
The University of Chicago Press. R8vo. 1960
Edited by Sol Tax and Charles Callender

QE
Geol.
Pam.
813

EVOLUTION.

Watson, D.M.S.

Palaeontology and the evolution of man.
Romanes lecture... May 4, 1929.

Oxford, Clarendon press.   27 p.

QH
197
S 72

EVOLUTION   AUSTRALIA

Howchin, Walter
    The building of Australia and the succession
of life: with special reference to South Australia, Part I; II:Mesozoic and Cainozoic; III:
Pleistocene and recent.

IN
South Australian Branch of the British Science
    Guild... Handbook of the flora and Fauna
    of South Australia... Adelaide, 1925-1930.

QH
Nat. Hist.
Pam.
155
and
97

EVOLUTION

Tillyard, R. J.

Tracing the dawn of life further backwards.
The Cawthron Institute Lecture 1935.

GN
Ethn.Pam.
3347

EVOLUTION

Weidenreich, Franz

The drifts of human phylogenetic evolution.

(Peking Natural History Bulletin, 1938/39,
Vol. 13, part 4, p. 227-230)

QL
Birds
Pam.
278
279

EVOLUTION   BIRDS   HAWAII

Amadon, Dean

Ecology and the evolution of some Hawaiian
birds.

(Evolution, 1:63-68, 1947)

GN
Pam
1896

EVOLUTION

Virchow, Rudolf

Descendenz und pathologie. From Arch.
f. Pathol. Anat. bd. 103, heft 1.

AS
36
S1

EVOLUTION.

White, Charles Abiathan, 1826-1910.
    The mutation theory of Professor De Vries. By
Charles A. White.
    (In Smithsonian institution. Annual report. 1901. Washington, 1902.
23½ᶜᵐ. p. 631-640)

1. Evolution. 2. Vries, Hugo de, 1848-   Die mutationstheorie.
ɪ. Title.
                                              S 15-1130
Library of Congress   Q11.S66 1901
Library, Smithsonian   Institution

QH
1
P 11

EVOLUTION   GASTROPODA

Morton, J. E.

The evolution of vermetid gastropods.

(Pacific Science, Vol. IX(1):3-15, 1955)

AS
36
S1

EVOLUTION.

Vries, Hugo de, 1848-
    The evidence of evolution. By Hugo de Vries.
    (In Smithsonian institution. Annual report. 1904. Washington, 1905.
23½ᶜᵐ. p. 389-396)

1. Evolution. ɪ. Title.
                                              S 15-1250
Library of Congress   Q11.S66 1904
Library, Smithsonian   Institution

QH
366
W 87

EVOLUTION

Wood-Jones, Frederick

Arboreal man.   New York. 1916. 8vo.

viii + 230 pp.

QL
Mammals
Pam.
126

EVOLUTION   MUS

Packard, Robert L.

Speciation and evolution of the pygmy mice,
Genus Baiomys.

(Univ. of Kansas Publ., Mus. of Nat. Hist.,
9(23):579-670, 1960)

AS
36
S1

EVOLUTION

Wallace, Alfred Russel, 1823-1913.
    The method of organic evolution. By Alfred R. Wal-
lace.
    (In Smithsonian institution. Annual report. 1894. Washington, 1896.
23½ᶜᵐ. p. 413-435)
    "From the Fortnightly review, February and March, 1895, vol. xvii,
new series, nos. 138, 139."

1. Evolution.
                                              S 15-868
Library of Congress   Q11.S66 1894
Library, Smithsonian   Institution

QH
Nat.
Hist.
223

EVOLUTION

Zangrel, Rainier

The methods of comparative anatomy and its
contribution to the study of evolution.

(Evolution, 2(4):351-374, 1948)

AS
122
L 75

EVOLUTION   PACIFIC

Pantin, C. F. A.

Geonemertes: a study in island life

(Proc. Linn. Soc. of London, Vol. 172:137-
151, 1960)

AS
122
L

EVOLUTION

Wallace, Alfred Russell

On the tendency of varieties to depart in-
definitely from the original type.

(Linn. Soc. Journ., III, 1859, Zool., pp.
53-62)

QH
Nat.Hist.
Pam.
120

EVOLUTION

Zimmerman, Elwood C.

On Wheeler's paper concerning evolution and
the nemertean Gorgonorhynchus.

(The American Naturalist, Vol. 77, 1943,
pp. 373-376)

QH
Nat.Hist.
141

EVOLUTION   TROPICS

Dobzhansky, Theodosius

Evolution in the tropics.

(American Scientist, Vol. 38:209-221, 1950)

QL
605
C 68

EVOLUTION   VERTEBRATA

Colbert, Edwin H.

Evolution of the vertebrates. A history of
the backboned animals through time. John Wiley
and Sons, Inc. New York. 1955. xiii + 479 pp.

Evolution of sex in plants

QK
980
Co
C85

Coulter, John Merle.

Evolution of sex in plants.

Chicago, 1914. 140p. illus.

QK
459
E 94

Ewart, Alfred J.

Flora of Victoria. Prepared under the authority of the Victorian Government and printed
by the Government Printer for the University
Press. 1930. 1257 pp. 8vo.

QH
365
D 22

Evolution by natural selection

Darwin, Charles and Alfred Russel Wallace

QH
408
Gu

EVOLUTION, RACIAL AND HABITUDINAL

Gulick, John Thomas, 1832–
— Evolution, racial and habitudinal. By Rev. John T.
Gulick. Washington, D.C., Carnegie institution of Wash-
ington, 1905.

xii, 269 p. III col. pl., 2 maps. 26½ᶜᵐ. (Carnegie institution of Washington. Publication no. 25)

"List of papers on evolution by John T. Gulick": p. 262.

1. Natural selection. 2. Species, Origin of.

Library of Congress   QH366.G97   5–28038
—— Copy 2.

GN
1
A 62

Ewers, John C.

Problems and procedures in modernizing
ethnological exhibits.

(Am. Anthropologist, Vol. 57:1-12, 1955)

GN
22
W 58

The evolution of culture.

White, Leslie A.

DU
620
H 4

EWA

Pukui, Mary Kawena

Ke awa lau o Pu'uloa. The many harbored
sea of Pu'uloa. (Pearl Harbor)
(Ann. Rept., Hawaiian Hist. Soc., 52nd:56-
66, 1943)

DU
Pac.Pam.
853

Ewers, J. K.

Lord Howe Island

(Walkabout, 20(6):10-16, 1954)

The Evolution of Man.   By six Yale professors. Yale Univ. Press. 1922.

LH has

QK
Bot.Pam.
2664

Ewan, Joseph

Taxonomic notes on various species of Musaceae, Marcgraviaceae, Guttiferae, and Solanaceae
of Colombia.

(Nat. Hist. Miscellanea, Chicago Acad. Sci.
No. 88, Sept. 7, 1951)

G
51
W 17

Ewers, John K.

Whaling on the west coast of Australia.

(Walkabout, Vol. 19(12):11-17, 1953)

GN
17
S 77

The evolution of man's capacity for culture.

Spuhler, J. N.   and others

QK
Bot.Pam.
2673

Ewan, Joseph

An undescribed scandent Solanum of Central
Colombia.

(Nat. Hist. Miscellanea, Chicago Acad. Sci.
No. 94, 1952)

QL
Insects
Pam 389

Ewing, H. E.

Ectoparasites of some Polynesian and Malaysian rats of the genus Rattus.

QL
Mammals
Pam 23

Miller, G. S.

Characters and probable history of the
Hawaiian rat. Honolulu. 1924. pp. 7-11.
(Bernice P. Bishop Museum, Bulletin 14)

AS
763
B-b

Reading
Room

QK
980
M41

The evolution of plant life

Massee, G

AS
720.
R

Ewart, Alfred J + Bertha Rhees

Contributions to the flora
of Australia.

In Proc. Roy. Soc. Victoria.
vol. XIX – date. Papers 5 – 27.

QL
Insect
Pam.
1172

Ewing, H. E.

The fleas of North America: classification,
identification, and geographic distribution of
these injurious and disease-spreading insects.
by H. E. Ewing and Irving Fox.

(United States Department of Agriculture,
Misc. Pub. 500, 1943)

QH
471
G 29

The Evolution of Sex.

Geddes, Patrick

QK
451
E 94

Ewart, Alfred J

Flora of the Northern territory, by Alfred J.
Ewart and Olive B. Davies ... Melbourne, McCarron, Bird & co., 1917.
387p. illus.

QK
Ins.Pam.
1005

Ewing, H. E.

A revision of the mites of the subfamily
Tarsoneminae of North America, the West Indies
and the Hawaiian Islands.

(U.S.Dept.of Agriculture,Technical Bulletin
653, 1939,(Bureau of Entomology and Plant Quarantine,Division of Insect Identification) 63 pp.)

QE
1
G 3 m

Ewing, Maurice

Long-range sound transmission, by Maurice Ewing and J. Lamar Worzel.
IN

Worzel, J. Lamar   and others
Propagation of sound in the ocean...

(Geol. Soc. America, Mem. 27, 1948)

QK
Bot.Pam.
2799

Exell, A. W.

Florae Malesianae Precursores IV. New species of Terminalia from Malaysia.

(Reprinted from Blumea, Vol. VII(2):322-328, 1953)

AM
Mus.
Pam.
487

An exhibition of Hungarian popular art. The Ethnographical Museum of Budapest. 1963.   27 pp.

AP
2
A 5

Examination of the coral-rock cores from the borings at Funafuti.

(Am. Jour. of Sci., Ser. 4, Vol. 18, 1904, pp. 239-242)

QK
Bot.Pam.
2853

Exell, A. W.

A new species of Combretum from east Borneo.

(no source given. 1 page)

DU
Pac.Pam
941

The exhibition of oil paintings by William Hodges, R. A....exhibited in New Zealand by courtesy of The Lords Commissioners of the Admiralty. Catalogue of additional material shown in the Alexander Turnbull Library, June-July, 1959. mimeogr. 9 pp.

GN
671.N5
B 52

Excess and restraint.

Berndt, Ronald M.

Excess and restraint; social control among a New Guinea mountain people.   Univ. of Chicago Press.   xxii + 474 pp. 1962. R8vo.

QK
1
N 53

Exell, A. W.

New Papuan species of Terminalia.

(Brittonia, Vol. 2, 1936, pp. 137-138)

AS
36
S1

EXHIBITIONS

Smithsonian institution.
Congresses, celebrations and expositions.

(In Smithsonian institution. Annual report. 1898-   Washington, 1899-   23¾°°. 1898, p. 16; 1899, p. 17; 1900, p. 21; 1901, p. 26; 1902, p. 16; 1904, p. 27; 1905, p. 22; 1906, p. 25; 1907, p. 27; 1908, p. 24; 1909, p. 18; 1910, p. 25; 1911, p. 15; 1912, p. 21; 1913, p. 22; 1914, p. 25)

Title varies.
Statements cover congresses, celebrations and expositions in which the Smithsonian institution participated in any way. Separate entries have been made for reports of Smithsonian exhibits at the principal expositions.

1. Science—Congresses. 2. Exhibitions. I. Title: Celebrations and expositions.

                                        S 15-981 a

Library of Congress   Q11.S66 1898-
.   Library, Smithsonian   Institution

GN
2.S
S 72

EXCHANGE   EASTER ISLAND

Ferdon, Edwin N., Jr.

Easter Island exchange systems.

(Southwestern Journal of Anthropology, Vol. 14:136-151, 1958)

QK
1
J 86

Exell, A. W.

Species of Terminalia from the Solomon Islands.

(Journal of Botany British and Foreign. May, 1935. pp. 131-134)

AM
151
F 82

Exhibitions: a survey of international designs.

Franck, Klaus

DU
Pac.Pam.
620

Exchange of notes between His Majesty's Government in the United Kingdom and the United States Government regarding the Administration of the Islands of Canton and Enderbury, Washington, April 6, 1939.   Treaty Series No. 21, 1939. His Majesty's Stationery Office. London. 1939. 6 pp.

QK
Bot.Pam.
1904

Exell, A. W.

Two new species of Terminalia from the Austral Islands and Mangareva.

(Occ. Papers, Bernice P. Bishop Museum, Vol. XI, No. 22, 1936)

AM
Pam
No. 10 + 1910
and
QL
627
U-b

EXHIBITS , EDUCATIONAL

Miner, Roy W

A plan for an educational exhibit of fishes

Reprint Bulletin of the Bureau of Fisheries Vol. XXVIII, 1908

Q
101
P 18

Excursion guides, Fourth Pacific Science Congress, Java, 1929.

(Pamphlets in a box, on Geology, Volcanology Biology, Agriculture and Anthropology of Java)

QE
Geol.
Pam
587

Exfoliation as a phase of rock weathering.

Blackwelder, Eliot

From Geol. Journ. Vol. XXXIII, 1925.

EXHIBITS HAWAII

see

HAWAII   EXHIBITS

QK
412.St
E 96

Exell, Arthur Wallis   and others

Catalogue of the vascular plants of S. Tomé (with Principe and Annobon). With three maps and twenty-six figures. Trustees of the British Museum, London, 1944. xi + 428 pp.

Supplement...1956. 58 pp.

AM
7
D 26

EXHIBIT TECHNIQUE

Davis, Helen Miles   editor

Exhibit techniques. Science Service. Washington. 1951. sm8vo. 112 pp.

Exhibits , Museum

see

Museum exhibits

AM
101
F 45 n

EXHIBITS   PACIFIC

Panorama of the Pacific for Members' night,
May 8 (1959)

(Chicago Nat. Hist. Mus. Bulletin, 30(5),
1959)

QK
1
Z 96

EXOCARPUS   HAWAII
Stauffer, Hans Ulrich

Revision Anthobolearum, eine morphologische
Studie mit "inschluss der Geographie, Phylogenie
und Taxonomie. Santalales-Studien IV.

(Mitt. Bot. Mus. der Univ. Zurich, 213,1959)

and

QK
495.S23
S 79

Hawaii, pp. 140-152

GN
1
A

EXOGAMY

Lowie, R. H.

Exogamy and the classificatory systems of
relationship.

(Amer. Anthropologist, n. s., vol. 17, 1915,
pp. 223-239).

DU
620
P

Exit the hula.

(Paradise of the Pacific, Vol. 25, 1912, No.
3, p. 8)

QL
Fish
Pam
305

EXOCOETIDAE

Breder, C(harles) M(arcus)

Field observations on flying fishes; a
suggestion of methods. From Zoologica, v. 9,
n. 7, 1929.

GN
480
M 16

EXOGAMY

McLennan, John Ferguson

Studies in ancient history, comprising a
reprint of "Primitive Marriage":...London. 1876.
pp. 109-120.

DU
1
P

Exit the sacred calabash.

(Pacific Islands Monthly, 22(7):113, 1952)

QL
5
B 61

EXOCOETIDAE ATLANTIC

Breder, C(harles) M(arcus), Jr.

A contribution to the life histories of Atlantic Ocean flyingfishes.

(Bull. Bingham Oceanographic Collection,
Vol. VI, Art. 5, 1938)

GN
480
M 16

EXOGAMY

McLennan, John Ferguson

Studies in ancient history, the second series comprising an inquiry into the origin of exogamy. Edited by his widow (Eleonora A. McLennan
and Arthur Platt. London. 1896.

QK
367
K83

Exkursionsflora von Java; umfassend die
Blutenflanzen mit besonderer berucksichtigung
der im hochgebirge wildwachsenden arton.
Jena, Fischer, 1911-1926.

Band I-III
Band IV Abt. 1-5 1913-1926
     Abt. 7, häl. 1 1926
     " 7, " 2, teil 1 1937

QL
Fishes
Pam.
A+5

EXOCETIDAE   SOCIETY ISLANDS

On the spawning of flying fish, Huahine,
Society Islands. ms.

GN
451
W 96

EXOGAMY

Wundt, Wilhelm

Element der völkerpsychologie: grundlinien
einer psychologischen entwicklungsgeschichte der
menschheit. Leipzig, Kröner, 1912. 8vo. xii +
523 pp.

QK
367
K83

Exkursionsflora von Java ,   see

Koorders, S. H.

GN
29
B 18

EXOGAMY

Balfour, Henry, and others

Anthropological essays...Oxford. 1907. 4to.
pp.51-64. Exogamy and the mating of cousins, by
A. E. Crawley.

GN
491
F 84

EXOGAMY MELANESIA

Fraser, James George

Totemism and Exogamy: a treatise on certain
early forms of superstition and society. In four
volumes. v. 2, pp. 65-118. London. 1910.

QL
1
H 53 b

Exline, Harriet

American spiders of the genus Argyrodes
(Araeas Theridiidae), by Harriet Exline and
Herbert W. Levi.

(Bull. Mus. Comp. Zool., Harvard, Vol.
127(2), 1962)

GN
29
B 18

EXOGAMY

Balfour, Henry, and others.

Anthropological essays...Oxford. 1907. 4to.
pp. 343-354. The Origin of Exogamy, by Northcote
W. Thomas.

GN
670
W 72

EXOGAMY POLYNESIA

Williamson, Robert W.

The social and political systems of central
Polynesia... Vol. 2, pp. 124-146. Cambridge.
University Press. 1924. 8vo.

QL
Anat.
Pam
1

Exner, Sigmund

Die funktion der menschlichen haare.
From Biologischen Centralblatt, bd.16,
h.12, 1896.

GN
491
F 84

EXOGAMY

Fraser, James George

Totemism and Exogamy: a treatise on certain
early forms of superstition and society. In four
volumes. London. 1910.

GN
491
F 84

EXOGAMY SUMATRA

Fraser, James George

Totemism and exogamy: a treatise on certain
early forms of superstition and society. In four
volumes, v. 2, pp. 185-97. London. 1910.

DU
620
P

Exotic birds of Hawaii.

(Paradise of the Pacific, 49 (12):29, 1907)

Q
Gen. Sci.
Pam
95

EXPEDITIONS

Aimone de Saboya-Aosta, S.A.R. El Principe

Expedición Italiana al Karakoram, 1929,
(Baltoro y valles Shaksgam y Punmah.) Conferen-
cia pronunciada...1930. Traducida al espanol por
Jose María Torroja.

Publicaciones de la Real Sociedad Geográfica,
Madrid, 1930, 32 pp. 16 láminas. 8vo

EXPEDITIONS PREPARATION

See also

CASTAWAY LORE

QL
404
S 97

Exotic Conchology

Swainson, William

QL
696
M 97

EXPEDITIONS

Murphy, Grace E. Bartow

There's always adventure: the story of a
naturalist's wife. Harper and Brothers, New
York. 8vo. [1951] xvi + 299 pp.

Q
116
B 87

EXPEDITIONS PREPARATION PACIFIC

Marshall, P.
Oceania.

Brouwer, H. A. editor
Practical hints to scientific travellers, VI.
The Hague. Martinus Nijhoff. 1929. sm8vo. 177
pp. (Chapter on Oceania, by P. Marshall, pp.
79-100.)

QK
475
H 78

Exotic flora, containing figures and descriptions of new, rare and otherwise interesting
exotic plants. 3 vols.

Hooker, William Jackson

AS
36
S2

EXPEDITIONS

Smithsonian institution.
Explorations and expeditions.
(*In* Smithsonian institution. Annual report. 1852– Washington,
1853– 23½cm. 1852, p. 58; 1854, p. 79; 1855, p. 42; 1856, p. 48; 1857,
p. 29; 1858, p. 50; 1859, p. 51; 1860, p. 47, 66; 1861, p. 39, 58; 1862, p. 39;
1863, p. 52; 1864, p. 48, 421; 1865, p. 38; 1866, p. 26; 1867, p. 41, 420; 1868,
p. 22; 1869, p. 29; 1870, p. 29, 381; 1871, p. 26; 1872, p. 43, 87; 1873, p. 37,
417; 1874, p. 36; 1875, p. 51; 1876, p. 47; 1877, p. 55; 1878, p. 65, 446; 1879,
p. 43; 1880, p. 22; 1881, p. 15; 1882, p. 11; 1883, p. 11; 1884, p. 13; 1885,
p. 7; 1886, p. 5; 1887, p. 5; 1888, p. 20; 1889, p. 8; 1890, p. 13; 1891, p. 8;
1892, p. 10; 1893, p. 7; 1894, p. 8; 1895, p. 7; 1896, p. 8; 1897, p. 10; 1898,
p. 11; 1899, p. 13; 1900, p. 15; 1901, p. 18; 1902, p. 16; 1903, p. 10; 1904,
p. 16; 1905, p. 13; 1907, p. 10; 1908, p. 7; 1909, p. 7; 1910, p. 10; 1911, p. 5;
1912, p. 7; 1913, p. 7; 1914, p. 8;
Title varies.
1. Scientific expeditions. 2. U. S.—Surveys. 3. America—Descr. &
trav.   I. Title.
S 15-6 Revised
Library of Congress   Q11.S66 1852-
Library, Smithsonian   Institution

QL
461
U-b

EXPEDITIONS AFRICA

Silvestri, F.

Report of an expedition to Africa in search of
the natural enemies of fruit flies: with descriptions, observations and biological notes
in Bd. Agric. For. Bull. 3, 1914, pp. 1-176, pls. I-XXIV,
(Division of Entomology.).

Note.- The above is a translation of his Viaggio in
Africa, etc.

QK
Bot.Pam.
3081

Exotic plants, illustrated...

Graf, Alfred Byrd

AS
36
S2

EXPEDITIONS

Smithsonian institution.
... Explorations and field-work of the Smithsonian institution ... 1910/1911–
Washington, Smithsonian institution, 1912–
v. illus., plates. 24½cm. (Smithsonian miscellaneous collections ...
Title varies: 1910/1911, Expeditions organized or participated in by the
Smithsonian institution ...
1912–   Explorations and field-work of the Smithsonian institution ...

1. Scientific expeditions.
13-35550 Revised
Library of Congress   Q11.S7
—— Copy 2.   Q11.S8A2

AS
36
O3

EXPEDITIONS ALASKA

National geographic society, *Washington, D. C.*
... Scientific results of the Katmai expeditions of the
National geographic society. I-X. By Robert F. Griggs,
J. W. Shipley, Jasper D. Sayre, Paul R. Hagelbarger
and James S. Hine ... [Columbus] The Ohio state univer-
sity, 1920.
[244] p. incl. illus., maps, diagrs. pl. 25cm. (The Ohio state university
bulletin. vol. xxiv, no. 15. Contributions in geographical exploration,
no. 1)
Reprinted from the Ohio journal of science, vol. xix.
CONTENTS.—I. The recovery of vegetation at Kodiak, by Robert F.
Griggs.—II. Are the Ten thousand smokes real volcanoes? By Robert F.
Griggs.—III. The great hot mud flow of the Valley of ten thousand smokes,
by Robert F. Griggs.—IV. The character of the eruption as indicated by
(Continued on next card)
A 21-295

QK
87
G 73

Exotica 3: pictorial encyclopedia of
exotic plants; guide to the care of plants in-
doors.... Roehrs Company. Rutherford, N.J.
1963c 4to 1011 pp.

Graf, Alfred Byrd

DU
Pac. Pam.
465

EXPEDITIONS

"Snellius" Expedition

Derde Bulletin van de Willebrod Snellius
Expeditie. Uitgezonden door de "Maatschappij
ter bevordering van het Natuurkundig Onderzoek
der Nederlandsche Kolonien" en het "Koninklijk
Nederlandsch Aardrijkskundig Genootschap".

Indisch Comité voor Wetenschappelijke Onder
zoekingen. Batavia. G. Kolff. ND 12 pp.

AS
36
O3

EXPEDITIONS ALASKA

National geographic society, *Washington, D. C.* ...
Scientific results of the Katmai expeditions ... 1920.
(Card 2)
CONTENTS—Continued.
its effects on nearby vegetation, by Robert F. Griggs.—V. The nitrogen
content of volcanic ash in the Katmai eruption of 1912 by J. W. Shipley.—
VI. The water soluble content, the ferrous iron content and the acidity of
Katmai volcanic ash, by J. W. Shipley.—VII. Ammonia and nitrous nitro-
gen in the rainwater of southwestern Alaska, by J. W. Shipley.—VIII. A
study of temperatures in the Valley of ten thousand smokes, by Jasper D.
Sayre and Paul R. Hagelbarger.—IX. The beginnings of revegetation in
Katmai Valley, by Robert F. Griggs.—X. Birds of the Katmai region, by
James S. Hine.
1. Katmai, Mount. 2. Valley of ten thousand smokes.   I. Griggs, Rob-
ert Fiske, 1881–   II. Shipley, John Wesley.   III. Sayre, Jasper Dean.
IV. Hagelbarger, Paul Rarey.   V. Hine, James Stewart, 1866–
Title from Ohio State   Univ. Printed by L. C.
A 21-295

AM
101
F 45-n

Expedition to Marianas completes work.

(Chicago Nat. Hist. Mus. Bull. 21(12):8,
1950)

Q
116
B 87

EXPEDITIONS PREPARATION

Brouwer, H. A. editor
Practical hints to scientific travellers, VI
The Hague. Martinus Nijhoff. 1929. sm8vo. 177
pp. (Chapter on Oceania, by P. Marshall, pp.
79-100)

AS
36
A 65-n

EXPEDITIONS ALASKA

Sutton, Ann

The adventures of Steller; the first expe-
dition to set foot on Alaska was organized by
Russia, led by a Dane, and described by a German,
George Wilhelm Steller. By Ann and Myron Sutton.

(Natural History, 65(9):485-491, 1956)

AM
Mus.Pam.
278

An expeditionary party to the ids. Mariana
and Caroline. (The Micronesian Expedition of
1936)

(The Museum Studies...Tokyo, Vol. 9(1):1,
1936)

Q
119
H 66

EXPEDITIONS PREPARATION

Hints to travellers. Royal Geographical
Society. London. Eleventh edition. 1935,1938
Vol. I: Survey and field astronomy, by E.A.
Reeves... 1935
Vol. II: Organization and equipment, scien-
tific observation, health, sickness, and injury,..
1938.

AS
36
S1

EXPEDITIONS ANTARCTIC

Amundsen, Roald Engelbregt Gravning, 1872–
Expedition to the South pole. By Roald Amundsen.
(*In* Smithsonian institution. Annual report, 1912. Washington, 1913.
23½cm. p. 701-716)
"Translated and reprinted from the Zeitschr. der Gesell. für erdkunde
zu Berlin, 1912, no. 7, pp. 481-498. Here reprinted ... from Bulletin of
the American geographical society, vol. 44, no. 11, November, 1912. New
York, pp. 822-838."

1. South pole.   I. Title.
13—25704
Library of Congress   Q11.S66 1912

QH
11
B86

EXPEDITIONS ANTARCTIC

British Antarctic expedition, 1907–1909.

British Antarctic expedition, 1907–9, under the command of Sir E. H. Shackleton, c. v. o. Reports on the scientific investigations ... London, W. Heinemann, 1910–16.

QE
347
Da

4 v. illus., plates (part fold.) maps (part fold.) 31 x 25ᶜᵐ.
Biology, edited by James Murray.
Geology, edited by T. W. E. David and R. E. Priestley.
The two volumes on biology were issued in parts, those of each volume paged continuously, and are without title-pages.
"No further publications in this series are contemplated."—Publisher's announcement in Geology, v. 2, 1916.

(Continued on next card)
12–29854 Revised
[r19c3]

AS
750
D 07 c

EXPEDITIONS ANTARCTIC

Cape Expedition, Scientific Results of the New Zealand Sub-antarctic Expedition, 1941–45.

Bulletins 2- 1940-

Dept. Sci. and Industrial Research, Wellington

Q
115
M 46

EXPEDITIONS ANTARCTIC

Mawson, Sir Douglas leader

British, Australian, and New Zealand Antarctic Research Expedition, 1929–1931.

Reports, Series A, B

University of Adelaide. 4to. 1937-

QH
11
B86

EXPEDITIONS ANTARCTIC

British Antarctic expedition, 1907–1909. British Antarctic expedition ... 1910–16. (Card 2)

CONTENTS.

Biology: vol. I. I. On collecting at Cape Royds, by J. Murray. 1910. II. On microscopic life at Cape Royds, by J. Murray. 1910. III. Antarctic *Rotifera*, by J. Murray. 1910. IV. *Musci*, by J. Cardot. 1910. V. *Tardigrada*, by J. Murray. 1910. VI. Rhizopodes d'eau douce, by E. Penard. 1911. VII. Fresh water *Algae*, by W. West, and G. S. West. 1911.—vol. II. I. *Mollusca*, by C. Hedley. 1911. II. Antarctic fishes, by E. R. Waite. 1911. III. Mallophages, by L. G. Neumann. 1911. IV. Asteries, ophiures, et echinides, by R. Koehler. 1900.

(Continued on next card)
12–29854 Revised
[r19c3]

QK
5
D 79
locked
case

EXPEDITIONS ANTARCTIC

Drygalski, Erich von

Deutsche Südpolar-Expedition, 1901–1903...
Bd. 8: Botanik.
Heft 1–5 1906–1928.(complete in 5 heft

Berlin. Georg Reimer. 4to.

AS
36
S1

EXPEDITION ANTARCTIQUE BELGE, 1897–1899.
Arctowski, Henryk, 1871-

The Antarctic voyage of the Belgica during the years 1897, 1898, and 1899. By Henryk Arctowski ...

(*In* Smithsonian institution. Annual report. 1901. Washington, 1902. 24½ᶜᵐ. p. 377–388. VII pl. (incl. map))

"Reprinted in abstract from the Geographical Journal, London, October, 1901."

1. Expédition antarctique belge, 1897–1899. 2. Antarctic regions. 3. Belgica (Ship)

Library of Congress
Library, Smithsonian

Q11.S66 1901
Institution

S 15–1109

QH
11
B86

EXPEDITIONS ANTARCTIC

British Antarctic expedition, 1907–1909. British Antarctic expedition ... 1910–16. (Card 3)

CONTENTS—Continued.

QH
11
B86

Geology: vol. I. Glaciology, physiography, stratigraphy, and tectonic geology of South Victoria Land, by T. W. Edgeworth David and R. E. Priestley. With short notes on palæontology by T. Griffith Taylor and E. J. Goddard. 1914.—vol. II. Contributions to the palæontology and petrology of South Victoria Land, by W. N. Benson, F. Chapman, Miss F. Cohen, L. A. Cotton (and others). 1916.

1. Scientific expeditions. 2. Antarctic regions. 3. Natural history—Antarctic regions. 4. Geology—Antarctic regions. 5. Paleontology—Antarctic regions. 6. Petrology—Antarctic regions. 7. Ice—Antarctic regions. I. Murray, James, 1865- II. David, Tannatt William Edgeworth, 1858- III. Priestley, Raymond Edward, 1886-

Library of Congress
12–29854 Revised
Q115.B84
[r19c3]

Microfilm
122
(in 4 pts)

EXPEDITIONS ANTARCTIC

Gerlache de Goméry, Adrien de

Expedition Antarctic Belge. Resultats du voyage du S. Y. Belgica, en 1897–1899, sous le commandement de A. de Gerlache de Goméry.
Zoologie (insects)

(see leading card for list)

GN
Pam
#95

EXPEDITION--ARCTIC
Nordenskiöld, A. E.
1878

Expédition polaire suédoise de 1878. Passage du nord-est. Rapports de M. le professeur Nordenskiöld à M. le Dr. Oscar Dickson, (du Septembre, 1878, au 2 Septembre, 1879). Upsala 1879. 8vo., pp. 131. Traduit du Suédois par F. Schulthess.

A.12.25.
HZ

Cd 4

QH
11
B 86

EXPEDITIONS ANTARCTIC

British Antarctic Expedition, 1907–1909

British Antarctic Expedition, 1907–9, under the command of Sir E. H. Shackleton...
Meteorology, Vols. I–III, 1919–1923

Q
115
B 42

EXPEDITIONS ANTARCTIC

Gerlache de Goméry, Adrien de

Expedition Antarctic Belge. Résultats du voyage du S. Y. Belgica, en 1897–1899, sous le commandement de A. de Gerlache de Goméry.
Rapports Scientifiques...
Zoologie
Fragments du recit de voyage...1938
Zoologie, Mallophaga, by Gordon B.
Thompson. 1938.
Anvers. 4to.

Q
115
A 74

EXPEDITIONS ARNHEM LAND

Records of the American-Australian Scientific Expedition to Arnhem Land.
I. Art, myth and symbolism, by Charles P. Mountford.

Melbourne University Press. R8vo. (1956)

QH
11
G 74

EXPEDITIONS ANTARCTIC

British Museum (Natural History)

British Graham Land Expedition, 1934–37
Scientific Reports.
Vol. 1:1- 1940-

London. Printed by order of the Trustees of the British Museum. 4to.

G
Geogr.
Pam.
79

EXPEDITIONS - ANTARCTIC

Hillary, Sir Edmund

The New Zealand Antarctic Expedition.

Thomas Cawthron Memorial Lecture, No. 33, 1958.
R. W. Stiles and Co., Ltd. Nelson, New Zealand.
8 vo. 12 pp.

Q
115
A 67

EXPEDITIONS AUSTRALIA

Archbold, Richard

Results of the Archbold Expeditions.

Nos. 1, 1935 +

[Published in the Am. Mus. Nat. Hist. issues]

Q
115
N 27

EXPEDITIONS ANTARCTIC

British museum. (Nat. hist.).

National Antarctic expedition, 1901–1904: Natural history...

London, 1907–1912. 8 vols. illus.

Q
115
M 46
1937.

EXPEDITIONS ANTARCTIC

Johnston, T. Harvey
Biological organization and station list, 1937.

Mawson, Sir Douglas leader
British, Australian, and New Zealand Antarctic Research Expedition, 1929–1931.
Reports, Series B, Vol. I, Part 1.

G
51
W 17

EXPEDITIONS AUSTRALIA

Fitzpatrick, Kathleen

The enigma of Leichhardt. (Ludwig Leichhardt, explorer)

(Walkabout, Vol. 29(10):14–15, 1963)

QH
84.2
Br

EXPEDITIONS ANTARCTIC

British museum (Nat. hist.)

Report on the collections of natural history, made in the Antarctic regions during the voyage of the "Southern Cross".

London: Printed by the order of the Trustees, 1902. 344p. pls.

Q
115
M 46

EXPEDITIONS ANTARCTIC

Mawson, Sir Douglas leader
Australasian Antarctic Expedition, 1911–14.
Scientific Reports, Ser.C., Zoology and Botany.

Vol. 1, 1916-

Sydney. Government Printer. 4to.

G
51
W 17

EXPEDITIONS AUSTRALIA

Graves, Kathleen

"The charmed spell"; Ernest Giles' explorations of the interior of Australia.

(Walkabout, 21(2):10–17, 1955)

Row 1, Column 1

AP
2
N 28

EXPEDITIONS   BORNEO

North Borneo Expedition 1961.

(Nature, Vol. 191:4785, p. 26-7, 1961)

Row 1, Column 2

AS
36
A3

EXPEDITIONS   GALAPAGOS ISLANDS

California Academy of Sciences

Expedition of the California Academy of
Sciences to the Galapagos Islands, 1905-1906.
Proc. Cal. Acad of Sc. 4th ser. I-II pts. 1907-1914.

Row 1, Column 3

QL
5
M 98

EXPEDITIONS   INDIAN OCEAN

British Museum (Natural History)

The John Murray Expedition, 1933-34.
Scientific Reports. (Indian Ocean)

Printed by order of the Trustees of the British
Museum. 4to. London.

Row 2, Column 1

GC
1
S 43 cnh

EXPEDITIONS   CAPRICORN

Shipboard report, Capricorn Expedition.
26 September 1952-21 February 1953. Sponsored
by Office of Naval Research and Bureau of Ships.

(University of California, Scripps Institution of Oceanography, SIO Ref. 53-15, pp. 1-60,
1953)
[Kwajalein, Fiji, Marquesas, Samoa, Tahiti]

Row 2, Column 2

AS
36
C3

EXPEDITIONS   GALAPAGOS

California academy of sciences, *San Francisco.*
... Expedition of the California academy of sciences to
the Galapagos Islands, 1905-1906 ...
San Francisco, The Academy, 1907–
v.   plates (part col.) diagrs. 25½ᶜᵐ. (Proceedings of the California academy of sciences. 4th ser., v. 1–
CONTENTS.—I. Preliminary descriptions of four new races of gigantic
land tortoises from the Galapagos Islands, by J. Van Denburgh. Dec.
1907. (Proceedings. 4th ser., v. 1, no. 1)—II. A botanical survey of the
Galapagos Islands, by A. Stewart. Jan. 1911. (Proceedings. 4th ser.,
v. 1, no. 2)—III. The butterflies and hawk-moths of the Galapagos Islands,
by F. X. Williams. Oct. 1911. (Proceedings. 4th ser., v. 1, no. 3)—IV.
The snakes of the Galapagos Islands, by J. Van Denburgh. Jan. 1912.
(Proceedings. 4th ser., v. 1, no. 4)—V. Notes on the botany of Cocos
Island, by A. Stewart. Jan. 1912. (Proceedings. 4th ser., v. 1, no. 5)—
(Continued on next card)

17-8550

Row 2, Column 3

QL
5
M 98

EXPEDITIONS   INDIAN OCEAN

The John Murray Expedition, 1933-34.
Scientific reports

Vol. 1-   1935-

British Museum (Natural History). Printed by
order of the Trustees of the British Museum. 4to
1935-

Row 3, Column 1

Q
115
E 37

EXPEDITIONS - CELEBES

Elbert, Johannes

Die Sunda-Expedition des Vereins für Geographie und Statistik zu Frankfurt am Main.
Fest-schrift zur Feier des 75 jahrigen Bestehens
des Vereins. Bde. I-II, 1911-1912. Frankfurt
am Main. 4to xxv + 274 pp., 29 pl., 3 maps
and xv + 373 pp., 31 pl. 7 maps. Druck und
Verlag von Hermann Minjon.

Row 3, Column 2

AS
36
C3

EXPEDITIONS   GALAPAGOS

California academy of sciences, *San Francisco.*   ... Expedition ... to the Galapagos Islands, 1905-1906 ...
1907–   (Card 2)
CONTENTS—Continued.
VI. The geckos of the Galapagos Islands, by J. Van Denburgh. Apr.
1912. (Proceedings. 4th ser., v. 1, no. 6)—VII. Notes on the lichens of
the Galapagos Islands, by A. Stewart. Dec. 1912. (Proceedings. 4th ser.,
v. 1, no. 7)—VIII. The birds of the Galapagos Islands, with observations
on the birds of Cocos and Clipperton Islands (*Columbiformes* to *Pelecani-
formes*) by E. W. Gifford. Aug. 1913. (Proceedings. 4th ser., v. 2
(no. 1)—IX. The Galapagoan lizards of the genus *Tropidurus*; with notes
on the iguanas of the genera *Conolophus* and *Amblyrhynchus*, by J. Van
Denburgh and J. R. Slevin. Sept. 1913. (Proceedings. 4th ser., v. 2
(no. 2)—X. The gigantic land tortoises of the Galapagos Archipelago, by
J. Van Denburgh. Sept. 1914. (Proceedings. 4th ser., v. 2 (no. 3)
1. Natural history—   Galapagos Islands.   I. Title. II.
Title: Galapagos Islands.   Expedition to the-
AS
36
C3
Library of Congress   Q11.C253

17-8550

Row 3, Column 3

QL
1
L-t

EXPEDITIONS   INDIAN OCEAN

Reports of the Percy Sladen Trust Expedition
to the Indian Ocean in 1905, under the leadership of Mr. J. S. Gardiner.

(Linnean Society of London, Trans., Zoology
Vols. 12-18, 1907-1922)

Row 4, Column 1

GC
1
N 56 m

EXPEDITIONS   CHATHAM ISLANDS

Biological results of the Chatham Islands
1954 Expedition.

(New Zealand Oceanographic Inst., Mem. 2-7
1957- 1960)

Row 4, Column 2

AM
Mus.Pam.
284

EXPEDITIONS   GALAPAGOS

Next stop: the Galapagos.

(Tropic Topics, Oct., 1952, Vol. 3(4):4)

Row 4, Column 3

Q
115
H 39
locked
case

EXPEDITIONS   JAPAN

Hawks, Francis L.   compiler

Narrative of the expedition of an American
squadron to the China Seas and Japan, performed
in the years 1852-1854, under the command of
Commodroe M. C. Perry. Vols. 1-3. Washington.
1856. 4to.

Row 5, Column 1

QE
502
N 56-b

EXPEDITIONS   CHATHAM ISLANDS

Knox, G. A.

General account of the Chatham Islands 1954
Expedition.

(New Zealand. Department of Scientific and
Industrial Research, Bull. 122, 1957)

Row 5, Column 2

AS
36
S 6

EXPEDITIONS   GALAPAGOS

Schmitt, Waldo L.

Hancock Galápagos expedition, 1934, by
Waldo L. Schmitt.

(Smithsonian Institution. Explorations and
field-work of the Smithsonian Institution in
1934. pp. 17-22)

Row 5, Column 3

Q
115
L 57

EXPEDITIONS - JAPAN

Lensen, G.A.

Russia's Japan Expedition of 1852 to 1855.
University of Florida Press.   Gainesville.
1955. 8vo. xxvii+208 pp.

Row 6, Column 1

Q
115
H 39
locked
case

EXPEDITIONS   CHINA

Hawks, Francis L.   compiler

Narrative of the expedition of an American
squadron to the China Seas and Japan, performed
in the years 1852-1854, under the command of
Commodroe M. C. Perry. Vols. 1-3. Washington.
1856. 4to.

Row 6, Column 2

AS
36
C 3

EXPEDITIONS   GALAPAGOS

The Templeton Crocker Expedition of the
California Academy of Sciences, 1932.

(Proceedings of the California Academy of
Sciences, Fourth Series, Vol. 21: 1-7 1932-7   )

Row 6, Column 3

DU
500
T 12

EXPEDITIONS   JAPAN

Taguchi, Ukichi

Nanto Junko-ki. (Diary of a journey through
the Southern Islands - Micronesia- 1890-1891;
Pnape to Palau.) 1923 edition. 8vo, small.
348 pp. illustrated.

Row 7, Column 1

DU
1
P

EXPEDITIONS   DENMARK

To probe Pacific's depths Danish expedition
next year.

(Pacific Islands Monthly, Vol. 20(11):11,
1950)

Row 7, Column 2

QH
11
G 78

EXPEDITION- GREAT BARRIER REEF

British Museum (Natural History)

Great Barrier Reef Expedition 1928-29.
Scientific Reports.

Vol. I-   1930-

Row 7, Column 3

Q
115
E 37

EXPEDITIONS - JAVA

Elbert, Johannes

Die Sunda-Expedition des Vereins für Geographie und Statistik zu Frankfurt am Main.
Fest-schrift zur Feier des 75 jahrigen Bestehens
des Vereins. Bde. I-II, 1911-1912. Frankfurt
am Main. 4to xxv + 274 pp., 29 pl., 3 maps
and xv + 373 pp., 31 pl. 7 maps. Druck und
Verlag von Hermann Minjon.

EXPEDITIONS LAYSAN ISLAND

QH
104
U-b
and
QL
Birds
Pam.126

Dill, Homer R. & Bryan, William Alanson

Report of an expedition to Laysan
Island in 1911.

U. S. Dept. Agric.Biol.Survey Bull 42
Washington 1911. pp 30.

EXPEDITIONS MICRONESIA (Ethnology)

GN
1
A

Embree, John F.

University of Hawaii research in Micronesia.

(American Anthropologist, n.s. 48:476-77,
1946)

EXPEDITIONS NEW GUINEA

Q
115
F 92

Ergebnisse der Frobenius-Expedition 1937-
38 in die Molukken und nach Hollandisch Neu-
Guinea.

Bd. IV*Felsbilder und Vorgeschichte des
MacCluer-Golfes, West Neuguinea. 1959. 4to.
Darmstadt. 162 pp. by Josef Röder.

EXPEDITIONS - LOMBOK

Q
115
E 37

Elbert, Johannes

Die Sunda-Expedition des Vereins für Geographie und Statistik zu Frankfurt am Main.
Fest-schrift zur Feier des 75 jahrigen Bestehens
des Vereins. Bde. I-II, 1911-1912. Frankfurt
am Main. 4to xxv + 274 pp., 29 pl., 3 maps
and xv + 373 pp., 31 pl., 7 maps. Druck und
Verlag con Hermann Minjon.

EXPEDITIONS MICRONESIA

See also

MICRONESIAN EXPEDITION

EXPEDITIONS NEW GUINEA (Dutch)

Q
115
G 76

Grant, William R. Ogilvie

Reports on the collections made by the
British Ornithologists' Union Expedition and the
Wollaston Expedition in Dutch New Guinea, 1910-
1913. Vol. I-II. London. Francis Edwards.
1916. 4to. (150 copies printed...this is Copy
1)

EXPEDITIONS MADAGASCAR

Q
115
A 67-m

Archbold, Richard

Results of the Archbold Expeditions.
(Mission Zoologique Franco-Anglo-Américaine à
Madagascar)

for full list see
Archbold, Richard

EXPEDITIONS MISSISSIPPI RIVER TO PACIFIC
OCEAN.

Q
115
U 58

U.S. War Dept.

Reports of explorations and surveys, to
ascertain the most practicable and economical
route for a railroad from the Mississippi River
to the Pacific Ocean. Made under the direction
of the Secretary of war. 12 vols.
Washington, 1855-1861. illus. maps.

EXPEDITIONS NEW GUINEA

QL
461
B 86

Kimmins, D. E.

Miss L. E. Cheesman's expeditions to New
Guinea: Trichoptera.

(Bull. British Museum(Nat. Hist.), Entomology, Vol. II(2), 1962)

EXPEDITIONS MALAYSIA

Q
115
A 67

Archbold, Richard

Results of the Archbold Expeditions.

Nos. 1-   1935-

[published in the Am. Mus. Nat. Hist. issues]

New York   8vo and 4tp

EXPEDITIONS MOLUCCASS

Q
115
F 92

Ergebnisse der Frobenius-Expedition 1937-
38 in die Molukken und nach Hollandisch Neu-
Guinea.

Bd. IV:Felsbilder und Vorgeschichte des
MacCluer-Golfes, West Neuguinea. 1959. 4to
Darmstadt. 162 pp. By Josef Röder.

EXPEDITIONS NEW GUINEA

Q
115
M 16

Macmillan, David S.

A squatter went to sea; the story of Sir
William Macleay's New Guinea expedition (1875)
and his life in Sydney. Currawong Publishing
Co. Pty. Ltd. Sydney. 8vo. (1957) X + 165 pp.

EXPEDITIONS MANGAREVA

See

MANGAREVAN EXPEDITION

EXPEDITION NETHERLANDS EAST INDIES

GN
671.N5
K 95

Kunst, J.

A Study on Papuan Music... Expedition to the
Central Mountains (Nassau-Range) in the Nether-
lands East Indies 1926.
(V. The Netherlands East Indies Committee for
Scientific Research)
Weltevreden. G. Kolff & Co. 97 pp. R8vo
1931

EXPEDITIONS NEW GUINEA

AS
719
A 93-m

Museum work in the New Guinea highlands.

(Australian Mus. Mag., 9(8):256, 1954)

EXPEDITIONS MELANESIA

Q
115
A 67

Archbold, Richard

Results of the Archbold Expeditions.

Nos. 1-   1935-

(published in the Am. Mus. Hat. Hist. issues

New York. 8vo and 4to

EXPEDITIONS NEW GUINEA

Q
115
A 67

Archbold, Richard

Results of the Archbold Expeditions.

Nos. 1-   1935-

[published in the Am. Mus. Nat. Hist. issues]

8vo. and 4to

EXPEDITIONS NEW GUINEA

Nova Guinea. Résultats des Expéditions Scientifiques à la Nouvelle Guinée, 1903, 1907, 1909.

(For fuller entry and contents see main card)

EXPEDITIONS MEXICO

AS
36
S1

France. *Ministère de l'instruction publique et des beaux-
arts.*

Scientific expedition to Mexico. A report addressed to
the emperor by the minister of public instruction.

(*In* Smithsonian institution. Annual report. 1864. Washington, 1865.
234ᵗᵐ. p. 412-415)
"Trans. for the Smithsonian institution."

1. Scientific expeditions. 2. Mission scientifique au Mexique et dans
l'Amérique Centrale.

Library of Congress   Q11,S66 1864   S 15-170 a
Library, Smithsonian   Institution

EXPEDITIONS NEW GUINEA

DU
740
B 86

Brongersma, L. D.

To the mountains of the stars. (Expedition to Central Dutch New Guinea) By L. D.
Brongersma and G. F. Venema. Translated
from the Dutch by Alan G. Readett. Garden
City, N. Y. Doubleday & Co., Inc. 1963.
xv + 17-318 pp. R8vo.

EXPEDITIONS NEW ZEALAND

AS
750
D 67 c

Cape Expedition, Scientific Results of the
New Zealand Sub-antarctic Expedition, 1941-45.

Bulletins 2, 1949-

Dept. Sci. and Industrial Research, Wellington.

EXPEDITIONS   PACIFIC

(Presidential Cruise of 1938)

See under authors: Ellsworth P. Killip, Allen McIntosh, Austin H. Clark, Olga Hartman, O. F. Cook, Isaac Ginsburg...

IN Smithsonian Misc. Coll., Vol. 98, 1939

Q
115
D 89

locked
case

EXPEDITIONS   PACIFIC

Dumont d'Urville, Jules Sebastien Cesar

Voyage au Pôle Sud et dans l'Océanie sur les corvettes l'Astrolabe et la Zélée...1837-1840... commandement de M. J. Dumont d'Urville...publié sous la direction supérieure de C.H.Jacquinot... Paris, 1841-54.
Historie du Voyage...DU12D89locked case
Anthropologie...
Zoologie...

AS
244
D

over

EXPEDITION= PACIFIC

Mortensen, Th.

Papers from Dr. Th. Mortensen's Pacific Expedition 1914-16.

(Videnskabelige Meddelelser fra Dansk naturhistorisk Forening i Kobenhavn, Bd. 69, 73,75,77, 79,81,83,85,87,89 91
1918- 1932)

QL
1
H2

EXPEDITION$ -- PACIFIC

Agassiz, Alexander

Reports on the scientific results of the expedition to the Eastern Tropical Pacific, in charge of Alexander Agassiz, by U.S. Fish Commission steamer "Albatross", from Oct. 1904 to March 1905, Lieut. Commander L.M. Garrett, U.S.N. Commanding. V. General report on the expedition. Mus. Comp. Zool. Mem. XXXIII, 1906.

AP
2
S 35

EXPEDITIONS   PACIFIC

Hornell, James and others

St. George Expedition to the Pacific. (1924)

(Science, 60(1558):423-424, 1924)

Q
115
S 97

EXPEDITIONS   PACIFIC

Pettersson, Hans

The voyage.
IN
Pettersson, Hans
Reports of the Swedish Deep-Sea Expedition, 1947-1948, Vol. 1, 1957

AP
2
N 28

EXPEDITIONS   PACIFIC

Arley, Niels

Magnetic investigations on the Galathea Expedition.

(Nature, vol. 171(4348):384-385, 1953)

QL
1
H 2

EXPEDITIONS   PACIFIC

Kendall, William Converse, 1861-
... The shore fishes. By William C. Kendall and Edmund L. Goldsborough. With seven plates ... Cambridge, U. S. A., Printed for the Museum, 1911.
1 p. l., [241]-343, [1] p. 7 pl. 28cm. (Memoirs of the Museum of comparative zoölogy at Harvard college. vol. xxvi, no. 7)
"Reports on the scientific results of the expedition to the tropical Pacific ... by the U. S. Fish commission steamer 'Albatross' from August, 1899, to March, 1900 ... XIII."
"Published by permission of George M. Bowers, U. S. commissioner of fish and fisheries."
1. Fishes—Pacific Ocean. 2. Albatross (Steamer)   I. Goldsborough, Edmund Lee, joint author. II. Title.

Title from Univ. of Chicago   QL1f.H375 vol. 26   A 21-451
Printed by L. C.
[4]

AP
2
S 35

EXPEDITIONS   PACIFIC

Scientific expeditions. (National Geographic Society and University of Virginia; Fahnestock expedition to the South Seas, American Museum of Natural History)

(Science, Vol. 90, 1939, pp. 437-438)

QK
Botany
Pam.
3272

EXPEDITIONS   PACIFIC

Bonner, C. E. B.

Exploration des petites iles de l'Ocean Pacifique.

(Musées de Genève, No. 25:15-17, 1962)

QL
1
H 2

EXPEDITIONS   PACIFIC

Kendall, William Converse, 1861-
... The shore fishes. By William C. Kendall and Lewis Radcliffe. With eight plates ... Cambridge, U. S. A., Printed for the Museum, 1912.
1 p. l., [77]-171, [1] p. 8 pl. 30cm. (Memoirs of the Museum of comparative zoölogy at Harvard college. vol. xxxv, no. 3)
"Reports on the scientific results of the expedition to the eastern tropical Pacific ... by the U. S. Fish commission steamer 'Albatross,' from October, 1904, to March, 1905 ... xxv."
"Published by permission of George M. Bowers, U. S. commissioner of fish and fisheries."
1. Fishes—Pacific Ocean. 2. Albatross (Steamer)   I. Radcliffe, Lewis, 1880-   joint author.

Title from Univ. of Chicago   QL1f.H375 vol. 35   A 21-456
Printed by L. C.
[3]

AS
36
A-1

EXPEDITIONS   PACIFIC

Stimpson, William

Prodromus descriptionis animalium evertebratorum quae in Expeditione ad Oceanum Pacificum Septentrionalem a Republica Federata missa, Cadwaladero Ringgold et Johanne Rodgers ducibus...

(Proc. Acad. Nat. Sci., Philadelphia, 1857, p. 19-31, 159-165, 216-221; 1858, pp. 31-40, 93-110 159-163, 225-252; 1860, pp. 22-47)

Q
115
C 43

EXPEDITIONS   PACIFIC

Challenger expedition.

Report on the scientific results of the voyage of H.M.S. Challenger...

London, 1881-1895.

For fuller entry see main card

DU
Pacific
Pam.
No. 224

EXPEDITION$ - PACIFIC

Krämer, Augustin

Die neuere Erforschung der Sudsee - Inseln. ex Petermanns Geogr. Mitt. 1924.

(Comments based on B.P.B.Mus. Rept . for 1922.)

GN
663
T 44

EXPEDITIONS   PACIFIC(Western)

Thilenius, Georg editor

Ergebnisse der Südsee Expedition, 1908-1910. Hamburg. Friederichsen, de Gruyter & Co. 4to. 1913- 1938

AP
2
N 4

EXPEDITIONS   PACIFIC

Chapman, S.

United States Geophysical Expedition to the Pacific Ocean.

(Nature, Vol. 144, 1939, p. 182)

QL
1
H2

EXPEDITIONS   PACIFIC

MacFarland, Frank Mace, 1869-
... The Dolabellinae. By F. M. MacFarland. With ten plates ... Cambridge, U. S. A., Printed for the Museum, 1918.
2 p. l., p. [301]-348, 1 l. 10 pl. (1 col.) 30cm. (Memoirs of the Museum of comparative zoölogy at Harvard college. vol. xxxv, no. 5)
Each plate preceded by leaf with descriptive letterpress.
"Reports on the scientific results of the expedition to the tropical Pacific ... by the U. S. Fish commission steamer 'Albatross,' from August, 1899, to June, 1900 ... XIX."
"Published by permission of H. M. Smith, U. S. commissioner of fish and fisheries."
"Literature": p. 346-348.
1. [Dolabellinae] 2. Albatross (Steamer)

Title from Univ. of Chicago   QL1f.H375 vol. 35   A 21-458
Printed by L. C.
[2]

Q
115
V 13

locked
case

EXPEDITIONS   PACIFIC

Vaillant, Auguste Nicolas

Voyage autour du monde exécuté pendant les années 1836 et 1837, sur la corvette La Bonite, commandée par M. Vaillant.
Relation du Voyage...
Zoologie...
Botanique...

DU
1
P 10

EXPEDITIONS   PACIFIC

Danish scientists in the Pacific.

(Pacific Islands Monthly, 31(12):23, 1961)

[Monnberg going to Rennell and Bellona...]

AP
2
N 55

EXPEDITIONS   PACIFIC

Mielche, Hakon

Science and the man in the street; a deep-sea expedition round the world. By Hakon Mielche and Anton F. Bruun.

(New Zealand Science Review, 10(1/2):6-8, 1952)

AS
36
A 65

EXPEDITIONS   PACIFIC

Ward, Melbourne

The Brachyura of the Second Templeton Crocker-American Museum Expedition to the Pacific Ocean.

(American Museum Novitates, No. 1049, 1939)

QL
1
F 45
EXPEDITIONS   PHILIPPINE ISLANDS

Hoogstraal, Harry

Philippine Zoological Expedition, 1946-1947.
Narrative and itinerary.

(Fieldiana: Zoology, Vol. 33(1), 1951)

Q
115
E 37
EXPEDITIONS - TIMOR

Elbert, Johannes

Die Sunda-Expedition des Verins für Geographie und Statistik zu Frankfurt am Main.
Fest-schrift zur Feier des 75 jahrigen Bestehens
des Vereins. Bde. I-II, 1911-1912. Frankfurt
am Main. 4to xxv + 274 pp., 29 pl., 3 maps
and xv + 373 pp., 31 pl. 7 maps. Druck und
Verlag con Hermann Minjon.

QL
401
H 39
EXPEDITIONS   BERNICE P. BISHOP MUSEUM

Bishop Museum - Phillipine Expedition.

(Hawaiian Shell News, Vol. 5(5):49-50, 1957)

QL
1
S 96

and

QL
Insects
Pam.
1523
EXPEDITIONS   POLYNESIA

Trägardh, Ivar

Acarina, collected by the Mangarevan expedition to South Eastern Polynesia in 1934 by the
Bernice P. Bishop Museum, Honolulu, Hawaii: Mesostigmata.

(Arkiv för Zoologi, s2, Bd 4:45-90, 1952)

Expédition Française sur les récifs coralliens de la Nouvelle-Calédonie. 1960-
1962.

See

La Fondation Singer-Polignac

GN
2.8
P 76
EXPEDITIONS - BISHOP MUSEUM

Emory, Kenneth P.

Report on Bishop Museum archaeological expeditions to the Society Islands in 1960 and
1961.

(Jour. Poly. Soc., 71(1):117-120, 1962)

AS
720.S
R
Expeditions-- South Australia.

Waite, Edgar R. and others

Results of the South Australian Mus-
eum expedition to Strzelecki and Cooper
Creeks. In Trans. & Proc. Roy. Soc. S.
Aus.. XLI, 1917. pp. 405-658. Pls. XXI-
XLIII.

AS
36
A 65 b
EXPEDITIONS AM. MUS. EXP. TO NEW GUINEA, '54

Gilliard, E. Thomas

Birds of the Victor Emanuel and Hindenburg
Mountains, New Guinea. Results of the American
Museum of Natural History Expedition to New
Guinea in 1954. By E. Thomas Gilliard and Mary
LeCroy.

(Bull. Am. Mus. Nat. Hist., Vol. 123(1),
1961)

AM
Mus.Pam.
278
BERNICE P.
EXPEDITIONS   BISHOP MUSEUM

An expeditionary party to the ids. Mariana
and Caroline. (The Micronesian Expedition of
1936)

(The Museum Studies...Tokyo, Vol. 9(1):1,
1936)

[Bishop Museum/Japanese scientists]

Q
115
V 58
EXPEDITIONS - SUMATRA

Veth, P. J.

Midden-Sumatra. Reizen en onderzoekingen
der Sumatra-Expeditie, uitgerust door het Aar-
drijkskundig Genootschap, 1877-1879.
Deel I. Reisverhal...
"   II. Aardrijkskundige beschrijving...
" III. Volksbeschrijving...
"   IV. Natuurlijke historie.
          I. Fauna
         II. Flora
Leiden. 4to.   1882-1892. (Atlas missing)

Q
115
A 67
EXPEDITIONS   ARCHBOLD

Archbold, Richard

Results of the Archbold Expeditions, by
Richard Archbold and others

1->

DU
620
P 22
EXPEDITIONS   BERNICE P. BISHOP MUSEUM

Dillingham, Harold G., Jr.

Hawaii's scientists look west.

(Paradise of the Pacific, Oct. 1957:22-23)

QK
1
L 52
EXPEDITIONS - SUNDA ISLANDS

Elbert, Johannes

Die botanischen Ergebnisse der Elbert'schen
Sunda-Expedition des Frankfurter Vereins für
Geographie und Statistik, von Hans G. Hallier.

(Mededeelingen, Rijks Herbarium, Leiden
No. 14, 22, 37, 1912-1918)

G
51
W 17
EXPEDITIONS   AUSTRALIAN NATIONAL RESEARCH
                    EXPEDITION

Law, Phillip G.

The Australian National Antarctic Research
Expedition.

(Walkabout, 18(6):10-16, 1952)

AM
Mus.Pam.
279
EXPEDITIONS   BERNICE P. BISHOP MUSEUM

Gregory, Herbert Ernest

The Bishop Museum Mangarevan Expedition.
(Being some notes by Herbert E. Gregory, '96)

(Yale Alumni Weekly, 44(11):315, 1934)

Q
115
E 37
EXPEDITIONS - SUNDA ISLANDS

Elbert, Johannes

Die Sunda-Expedition des Vereins für Geographie und Statistik zu Frankfurt am Main.
Fest-schrift zur Feier des 75 jahrigen Bestehens
des Vereins. Bde. I-II, 1911-1912. Frankfurt
am Main. 4to xxv + 274 pp., 29 pl., 3 maps
and xv + 373 pp., 31 pl., 7 maps. Druck und
Verlag con Hermann Minjon.

AM
Mus.Pam.
306
EXPEDITIONS   BERNICE P. BISHOP MUSEUM

Bernice P. Bishop Museum has participated in
the following expeditions to Pacific Islands since
1920. 2 carbon pp.

GN
2.8
T 12
EXPEDITIONS   BERNICE P. BISHOP MUSEUM

Jacquier, Henri

Le Président donne lecture de son rapport
annuel.

(Bull. de la Société d'Études Océaniennes, No. 141, Vol. 12(4):142-148, 1962)

(Mentions Dr. Emory and Dr. Sinoto)

G
51
W 17
EXPEDITIONS   TAHITI TO SOUTH AMERICA

Garcia-Palacios, Carlos

The Tahiti-nui raft expedition.

(Walkabout, 22(9):16-18, 1956)

AM
Mus.
Pam.
273
BERNICE P.
EXPEDITIONS   BISHOP MUSEUM

Bishop Museum expeditions since 1920-1938.
(Outside the main Hawaiian Islands.) 5 typewritten pages. Prepared by E. H. Bryan, Jr.

DU
Pac.Pam.
818
BERNICE P.
EXPEDITIONS   BISHOP MUSEUM

Kondo, Yoshio

Mangarevan Expedition of Bishop Museum as
related by Engineer.

(The Nippu Jiji, Honolulu, May ? - Sept. ?
1934)

QL
401
H 39

EXPEDITIONS   BERNICE P. BISHOP MUSEUM

More Sulu Sea ideas.

(Hawaiian Shell News, Vol. 5(8):79-80, 1957)

QL
461
P 11

EXPEDITIONS   GALATHEA

Yoshimoto, C. M.   and others

Airborne insects from the Galathea Expedition. By C. M. Yoshimoto, J. L. Gressitt and Torben Wolff.

(Pacific Insects, 4(2):269-291, 1962)

QH
198.Re
W 85

EXPEDITIONS   RENNELL ISLAND

Wolff, Torben

The natural history of Rennell Island, British Solomon Islands.
Vol. 1, 1958 -

Scientific Results of the Danish Rennell Expedition, 1951, and The British Museum (Natural History) Expedition, 1953. Published on behalf of the University, Copenhagen, The British Museum (Natural History), London.   Danish Science Press. Copenhagen   1958 - R8vo.

GN
2.S
T 12

EXPEDITIONS   BERNICE P. BISHOP MUSEUM

Vérin, Pierre

Travaux archéologiques en Polynésie Française pendant l'année 1961-1962.

(Bull. de la Société d'Études Océaniennes, No. 141, Vol. 12(4):167-170, 1962)

AP
2
N 4

EXPEDITIONS GEORGE VANDERBILT PAC. EQ. EXP.

Fish collection from the Leeward and Line Islands. (George Vanderbilt Pacific Equatorial Expedition of 1951)

(Nature, Vol. 168(4285):1027, 1951)

AP
2
S 35

EXPEDITIONS ST. GEORGE (ship)

Hornell, James and others

St. George Expedition to the Pacific.(1924)

(Science, 60(1558):423-424, 1924)

AM
101
F 45 n

EXPEDITIONS   BORNEO ZOOLOGICAL EXPEDITION

Inger, Robert F.

Departure of Borneo Zoological Expedition.

(Chicago Nat. Hist. Mus., Bull., 33(8):4-5, 1962)

AS
36
A 65 b

and

Q
115
A 67 m

EXPEDITIONS   MISSION FRANCO-ANGLO...

Rand, A. L.

The distribution and habits of Madagascar birds. Summary of the field notes of the Mission Zoologique Franco-Anglo-Américaine à Madagascar.

(Bull. Am. Mus. Nat. Hist., 72(5):143-499, 1936)

QL
1
T 28

EXPEDITIONS   SNELLIUS EXPEDITION

Clark, Austin H.   and others

Biological results of the Snellius Expedition, part I +

(Temminckia, Vol. 1, 1936 +)

QH
11
G 14

EXPEDITIONS   DANISH DEEP-SEA EXPEDITION

Galathea report: Scientific results of the Danish Deep-Sea Expedition round the world 1950-1952... Copenhagen. 1957-

Vol. 1 +

AS
36
A 65-b

EXPEDITIONS   NEW GUINEA

Brass, L. J.

Summary of the fourth Archbold Expedition to New Guinea (1953). Results of the Archbold Expeditions No. 75.

(Bull. Am. Mus. Nat. Hist., Vol. 111(2), 1956)

Q
115
S 97

EXPEDITIONS   SWEDISH DEEP-SEA EXPEDITION, 1947-48

Pettersson, Hans   Editor; Scientific Leader of the Expedition. Göteborgs Kungl. Vetenskaps- och Vittwrhets-Samhälle

Reports of the Swedish Deep-Sea Expedition, 1947-1948

Vol. II: Zool. Fasc. 1
" III: Physics & Chemistry, Fasc. 1

Göteborg. Boktryckeri Aktiebolag. 4to.
n.d.   rec'd July 1952

QH
31.W
S 44

EXPEDITIONS   DISCOVERY (SHIP)

Seaver, George

Edward Wilson of the Antarctic, naturalist and friend. With an introduction by Apsley Cherry-Garrard. John Murray. London. 8vo. 1936 xxxiv + 301 pp.

GC
Oceanography
Pam.
53

EXPEDITIONS   PACIFIC

Fairbridge, Rhodes W.

Basis for submarine nomenclature in the South-West Pacific Ocean.

(Reprint, Deutschen Hydrographischen Zeitschrift, Band 15, Heft 1:1-15, 1962)

AS
28
E 85

EXPEDITIONS   UNIVERSITY OF CALIFORNIA

Gifford, E. W.

Expédition archéologique de l'Université de Californie en Nouvelle-Calédonie. By E. W. Gifford et Dick Shutler, Jr.

(Études Mélanésiennes, Numéro 7, pp. 19-24, 1953)

Q
115
B 91

EXPEDITIONS   GALATHEA DEEP SEA

Bruun, Anton F.   and others

The Galathea deep sea expedition, 1950-1952, described by members of the expedition. Edited by Anton F. Bruun, Sv. Greve, Hakon Mielche and Ragnar Spärck. Translated from the Danish by Reginald Spink. New York. The Macmillan Company R8vo. 296 pp. (1956)

GN
Ethn. Pam
4141

EXPEDITIONS   PACIFIC

Stoller, Marianne L.

Te-moana-nui-o-Kiwa.

(Expedition, University Museum, Univ. of Pennsylvania, Fall 1958:15-25,34; Winter, 1959: 29-33; Spring, 1959: 26-38)

EXPEDITIONS, see also
VOYAGES & TRAVELS

QL
401
J 85

EXPEDITIONS   GALATHEA

Fischer, P. H.

Exposition à Paris des résultats scientifiques de l'Expedition danoise de la "Galathea".

(Journal de Conchyliologie, 97(1):41-43, 1957)

QH
1
A 88

EXPEDITIONS   RAROIA ATOLL EXPEDITION

Newell, Norman D.

Expedition to Raroia, Tuamotus.

(Atoll Research Bull., No. 31, 1954)

Q
Gen.Sci.
Pam.
123
a,b

An experiment in marine fish cultivation. II. Some physical and chemical conditions in a fertilized sea-loch (Loch Craiglin, Argyll). By A. P. Orr. (Proc. R. Soc. Edinburgh, Sect. B, Vol. 63:Part I, no. 2, 1947)
III. The plankton of a fertilized loch, by Sheina M. Marshall. (ibid, Vol. 63:Part 1, no. 3, 1947)

Q''
104
U-.G
... Explanation of the proposed regulations for the protection of migratory birds ... [Washington, Govt. print. off.] 1913.

5 p. 23ᶜᵐ. (U. S. Dept. of agriculture. Bureau of biological survey. Circular no. 93)

1. Bird protection.

Agr 13—1362

Library, U. S. Dept. of　　　Agriculture 1B52C no. 93

AS
763
H 38
EXPLORATION - PACIFIC OCEAN

Filatova, Zinaida

Exploration of the Pacific Ocean and its deep-sea fauna by the "Vitaz".

(Proc. Haw. Acad. Sci., 34th meeting, p. 27, 1959)

G
Geography
Pam.
85
EXPLORER SHIP

Jones, Davis

Dictionary of Hawaiian place names, including the islands of Oahu, Hawaii, Kahoolawe, Kauai, Lanai, Maui, Molokai and Niihau; also beacon lights and channels. By Major Davis Jones and Sgt. W. C. Addleman, U. S. Army Printing Plant, 2nd printing. 1942 (first issued in 1937) R8vo. 43 pp.

AS
36
S 6
EXPLORATION　PERIODICALS

Smithsonian Institution

Explorations and Field-work of the Smithsonian Institution in

1929-

For current volumes see serial file

For previous issues, see Smithsonian Miscellaneous Collections.
Smithsonian Inst. Washington. 1929- 8vo

EXPLORATION POLAR

See

POLAR EXPLORATION

DU
Pac.Pam.
914
The explorers log.　Archbold Expedition to New Guinea.

(The Explorers Journal, Vol. XXXV(1):12, Spring, 1957)

AP
2
N 28
EXPLORATION　ANTARCTIC

Mawson, Sir Douglas

Programme of Australian Antarctic exploration

(Nature, No. 4376:479, 1953)

F
592
F 86
EXPLORATION　UNITED STATES

Fremont, J. C.

Report of the Exploring Expedition to the Rocky Mountains in...1842 and to Oregon and North California, in ...1843-44. Washington,1845.

DU
12
B 92
Explorers of the Pacific: European and American discoveries in Polynesia.

Buck, Peter H.

DU
Pac.Pam.
961
EXPLORATION　AUSTRALIA

Triebel, L. A.

French exploration of Australia. By L. A. Triebel and J. C. Batt. Les Editions Courrier Australien. Sydney. 1943. 39 pp. sm8vo.

G
Geography
Pam.
78
EXPLORATION　UNITED STATES

Geographical exploration and topographic mapping by the United States Government. Catalog. 1952.

G
225
L 61
EXPLORERS

Leroi-Gourhan, André　(compiler, with others)

Les explorateurs celebres. Editions d'Art Lucien Mazenod. (Paris?, 1946 ?) 4 to.　367 pp.

G
55
F 85
EXPLORATION　PACIFIC

Manchester, Curtis A., Jr.

The exploration and mapping of the Pacific. IN

Freeman, Otis W.
Geography of the Pacific. N.Y. 1951. pp. 61-88

F
871
G 81
EXPLORATION　UNITED STATES　NORTHWEST

Greenhow, Robert

Memoir, historical and political, on the northwest coast of North America, and the adjacent territories...Washington, 1840.

EXPLORERS　POLYNESIANS

See

POLYNESIANS　EXPLORERS

EXPLORATION　PACIFIC

See also

VOYAGES　PACIFIC

AS
36
S2
Explorations and expeditions

Smithsonian institution.
Explorations and expeditions.
(In Smithsonian institution. Annual report. 1852- Washington, 1853- 23½ᶜᵐ. 1852, p. 58; 1854, p. 79; 1855, p. 42; 1856, p. 48; 1857, p. 29; 1858, p. 50; 1859, p. 51; 1860, p. 47, 66; 1861, p. 39, 58; 1862, p. 39; 1863, p. 52; 1864, p. 48, 431; 1865, p. 38; 1866, p. 26; 1867, p. 41, 420; 1868, p. 22; 1869, p. 29; 1870, p. 29, 381; 1871, p. 26; 1872, p. 43, 87; 1873, p. 37, 417; 1874, p. 36; 1875, p. 51; 1876, p. 47; 1877, p. 55; 1878, p. 65, 446; 1879, p. 43; 1880, p. 22; 1881, p. 15; 1882, p. 11; 1883, p. 11; 1884, p. 13; 1885, p. 7; 1886, p. 5; 1887, p. 5; 1888, p. 20; 1889, p. 8; 1890, p. 13; 1891, p. 8; 1892, p. 10; 1893, p. 7; 1894, p. 8; 1895, p. 7; 1896, p. 8; 1897, p. 10; 1898, p. 11; 1899, p. 13; 1900, p. 15; 1901, p. 18; 1902, p. 16; 1903, p. 10; 1904, p. 16; 1905, p. 13; 1907, p. 10; 1908, p. 7; 1909, p. 7; 1910, p. 10; 1911, p. 5; 1912, p. 7; 1913, p. 7; 1914, p. 8;
Title varies.
1. Scientific expeditions. 2. U. S.—Surveys. 3. America—Descr. & trav.　i. Title.
S 15-6 Revised
Library of Congress　Q11.S66 1852-
Library, Smithsonian　Institution

Z
Bibl. Pam.
73
Explorers' Club of America

Selected list of bibliographies of the Polar Regions, Part I. Sponsored by the Explorers' Club of America. United States Works Progress Administration, New York City. (1938) Part II.(1939) mimeographed 27 pp.

AM
101
F 45-n
EXPLORATION - PACIFIC

Force, Roland W.

South Sea isles: what led to early discoveries. Part 1

(Chicago Nat. Hist. Mus. Bull. 31:1,1960)

G
3
A
Explorations in Dutch New Guinea. Dr. Lorentz's ascent of Wilhelmina Peak.

(Bull. Amer. Geogr. Soc., Vol. 43, 1911, pp. 837-844)

DU
50
Col
Exposition Coloniale de 1889

Les colonies francaises: notices illustrées publiees par ordre du Sous-Secretaire d'Etat des Colonies.....
IV, Colonies et protectorats de l'Ocean Pacific ....

Paris,[1889], 407 pp

DU
Pac.
Pam.
782

EXPOSITONS GOLDEN GATE...1939

Pacific cultures. Official catalog, Golden Gate International Exposition, Division of Pacific cultures. San Francisco. 1939. 156 pp., illustrated. sm 4to.

pp. 114-116; pl. A-J; Islands of the Pacific by Peter H. Buck.

QH
650
E 96

Extermann, R. C. Editor

Research with radioisotopes in plant biology and some general problems.
IN
Extermann, R. C.
Radioisotopes in scientific research, IV.
Pergamon Press. New York... R8vo. xxi + 690 pp.

Q
115
V 13
locked
case

Eydoux, Joseph Fortune Théodore

Vaillant, Auguste Nicolas

Voyage autour du monde exécuté pendant les annees 1836 et 1837, sur la corvette La Bonite, commandée par M. Vaillant.
Zoologie, par MM. Eydoux et Souleyet. Tomes 1-2 and atlas, 1841-52.

DU
50
Ex
L.7

Exposition Universelle 1867

Catalogue des produits des Colonies Françaises précédé d'une Notice Statistique
DEC 24 190_ *Paris 1867*
8°. pp CXLVII. & 155.

QL
703
H 29

Extinct and vanishing mammals of the old world.

Harper, Francis

QL
697
P 78

EYE

Polyak, Stephen

The vertebrate visual system; its origin, structure and function...with and analysis of its role in the life of animals and in the origin of man...historical review of investigations of the eye, and of the visual pathways and centers of the brain. Edited by Heinrich Klüver University of Chicago Press. R8vo. xviii + 1390 pp.

DU
620
M 67

and
AM
Pams. 1,2

EXPOSITION UNIVERSELLE

Hassinger, John A.

Catalogue of the Hawaiian exhibits at the Exposition Universelle, Paris, 1889. Honolulu. 1889. 8vo. 48 pp.

(Misc. Pams. Haw. II: 263-310)

QL
703
A 4z

Extinct and vanishing mammals of the western hemisphere, with the marine species of all the ocean.

Allen, Glover M.

QK
Bot.Pam.
2834

Eyerdam, Walter J.

Alaska and Aleutian Island hepatics.

(Reprinted from The Bryologist, Vol. 55(1): 26-35, 1952)

Q
101
E 96

1915.

Exposition Universelle et Internationale de San Francisco

La Science Francaise. Vols. 1-2. Paris.

Hms
Misc
34

Steel
Storage
Case
4

Extracts from old Hawaiian periodicals

Collected by Thrum in process of preparing source book.

GN
Ethn.Pam.
2979

Eyerdam, Walter J.

Among the Mountain Bushmen of Malaita.

(Natural History, Vol. 33, 1933, pp. 430-438)

DU
620
M 67

Exposure of the villany and cowardice of Richard Charlton, in the case of his slanderous imputation upon the character of George Pelly, Esq., Honolulu. 1844. 8vo. 8 pp.

(Misc. Pams. Haw. I:277-284)

GN
673
B 61

The Eyak Indians of the Copper River Delta, Alaska.

Birket-Smith, Kaj ...

AS
36
A 5

Eyerdam, Walter J.

Among the Mountain Bushmen of Malaita. Invading a Primitive Wilderness in the Cause of Science.

(Natural History, Vol. 33, pp. 430-438,1933)

AS
36
S1

EXPRESSION
Darwin, Charles Robert, 1809-1882.

Queries about expression for anthropological inquiry. By Charles Darwin ...

(In Smithsonian institution. Annual report. 1867. Washington, 1868. 23½ᶜᵐ. p. (324])

1. Expression.

S 15-216

Library of Congress Q11.S66 1867
Library, Smithsonian Institution

GN
Ethn.Pam.
4032
1001

Eyde, David B.

A preliminary study of a group of Samoan migrants in Hawaii. (Project rendered possible by an Undergraduate Research Stipend awarded by the Social Science Research Council, University of Hawaii. June 1954.) mimeographed. 36 pp.

QL
401
N

Eyerdam, Walter J.

Collecting shells in the Solomon Islands.

(The Nautilus, Vol. 57, 1943, No. 2, pp. 41-42)

QL
461
Q 3

EXTATOSOMA

Korboot, K.

Observations on the life histories of the stick insects: Acrophila tessellata Gray and Extatosoma tizratum Macleay.

(Univ. of Queensland, Dept. of Entomology, Vol. 1(11), 1961)

DU
12
L 31
locked
case

Eydoux, Joseph Fortune Théodore

Laplace, Cyrille Pierre Théodore

Voyage autour du monde par les mers de l'Inde et de Chine, exécuté sur la corvette de l'etat La Favorite, pendant les années 1830-1832. Tome 5:(Zoologie par Eydoux) 1839. Paris. 8vo.

QL
Mollusca
Pam.
942

Eyerdam, Walter J.

A collection of mollusks from Washington Bay, Kuiu Island, southeastern Alaska.

(Minutes of the Conchological Club of Southern California, No. 114:7-11, 1951)

QK
Bot.Pam.
2924

Eyerdam, Walter J.

The genus Sphagnum in Alaska.

(Reprinted from The Bryologist, Vol. 58(3):
211-215, September, 1955)

DU
12
E 97

Eykyn, John

Parts of the Pacific, by a Peripatetic Parson. Illustrated from drawings by the author and
from photographs. London. Swan Sonnenschein and
Co., Ltd. 1896. 8vo. xii+388 pp.

F. R. D.

See

D., F. R.   (This may be Francis Rooke Day)

QK
Botany
Pam.
2833

Eyerdam, Walter J.

A giant bracket fungus found in South Eastern
Alaska.

(Reprinted from Svensk Botanisk Tidskrift,
Vol. 46(1):131-132, 1952)

DU
950.E2
R 17

EYRAUD, HERMANO EUGENIO

Ramirez, J. T.

"El Conquistador de Pascua"; biografia del
Hermano Eugenio Eyraud, de los Sdos. Corazones.
Tomo I-II. San Jose (printer), Santiago de
Chile. 1944. sm8vo.

Du
621
H3

"F-4" Disaster

Mackaye, P. L.

"F-4" Disaster

in Hawaiian Annual for 1916, pp. 131-134.

QL
401
N 31

Eyerdam, Walter Jacob

Mollusks and brachipods from Afognak and
Sitkalidak Islands, Kodiak Group, Alaska.

(Nautilus, 74(3):91-95, 1961)

DU
Pac.Pam.
596

Eyraud, H. Eugenio

(Letter (in Spanish) written in 1864 of a
sojourn in Easter Island.   Santiago de Chile,
1918. pp. 23-48)

PL
810
F 11

Faamatalaga o le Tusi Paia. Ua liliuina i
le Gagana Samoa. Lolomia i le Fale Lomi Tusi.
Avondale, Cooranbong, NSW 1910 sm8vo. 174 pp.

Samoa Bible stories

QL
401
S 72

Eyerdam, Walter J.

A remarkable endemic species of Melania
from the Solomons.

(Conchological Club of Southern Calif.,
Minutes, Feb. 1944.pp. 11-12)

DU
Hist.
Pam.
542

Eyre, Cynthia

The new PR at P.R. Dick Smart has big plans
for his big ranch...

(Beacon, Honolulu, 2(1), 1962:6-11)

GN
Ethn.Pam.
3xxx
4122

Faamausili, S.

Second book of Samoan social culture.
For the Public Schools of American Samoa. mimeographed. 13 pp. folio. rec'd Jan. 1944

QL
401
S 72

Eyerdam, Walter J.

Solomon Island Megapodes recommended as
destroyers of African snail pests.

(Minutes of the Conchological Club of Southern California, No. 121:4-5, 1952)

QL
697
E97

Eyton, Thomas Campbell, 1809-1880.
  Osteologia avium; or, A sketch of the osteology of
birds. By T. C. Eyton ... Wellington, Salop, R. Hobson,
1867.
  vi, iv, x, 229, vii p. 116 pl. 28½ x 23ᶜᵐ.
  Published in parts 1858 (or 1859) to 1867.
  Bibliography: p. (v)-vi.
  —— Supplement to Osteologia avium ... By T. C. Eyton
  ... Wellington, Salop, 1869.
    2 p. L, 18 pl. 28½ x 22½ᶜᵐ.
  —— Osteologia avium; or, A sketch of the osteology of
birds. Supplement II. pt. 1(-3) London, Williams and
Norgate; (etc., etc.) 1873-75.
    3 v. 51 pl. 28 x 22ᶜᵐ.
  Pt. 1-2 bound with his   Supplement to Osteologia avium. 1869.
  1. Birds—Anatomy.   2. Osteology.

  Library of Congress   QL697.E8   8-26817-9†

GN
1
N 27

Faatiga, Togamau

Infant feeding in native villages.

(The Native Medical Practitioner, Vol. 2,
No. 3, 1935, pp. 255-262)

QL
Mollusca
Pam.
943

Eyerdam, Walter J.

Some land shells from Japan and the maritime
province of Siberia.

(Reprinted from The Nautilus, Vol. 66(1):13-
15, July, 1952)

QL
5
D 22
locked
case

Eyton, T. C.

Darwin, Charles

The Zoology of the Voyage of H.M.S.Beagle...
during the years 1832 to 1836. London. 1839-42.
4to. Part III:Birds, by John Gould...with an
anatomical appendix by T. C. Eyton.

PL
Phil.Pam.
721

Faauta ua ia afio mai. O le toe afio mai
o Iesu Keriso. Avondale Press. Cooranbong, NSW
2nd edition, 1912. 12mo. 12 pp.

Samoa- The second advent

QK
Bot.Pam.
2923

Eyerdam, Walter J.

With Dr. Eric Ekman in southern Haiti in the
summer of 1927.

(Field and Laboratory, Vol. XXII(4):85-106,
October, 1954)

DU
620
I

F. B.

Hawaiian antiquities.

(Islander, Vol. I, 1875, p. 6)

(A note on certain relics, chiefly cave
finds)

AS
773
N 93

Faber, F.J.

The first geological expedition (1952) of the
Technical University at Delft in Netherlands New
Guinea.

(Nova Guinea, Vol. 6(1):177-183, 1955)

QK
Botany
Pam
1870

Faber, Friedrich Carl von

Die Kraterpflanzen Javas in physiologisch-okologischer Beziehung.

Buitenzorg, 1927.
[Arbeiten aus dem Treub-laboratorium]

AM
Mus.Pam.
116

Fabiani, Ramiro

L'Istituto e il Museo de Geologia della R. Universita di Palermo. 1931. 37 pp. 12mo.

QL
569
F12

Fabre, Jean Henri Casimir

Mason- Bees. New York, Dodd, 1914.

QK
101
S 33

Faber, F. C. von

Schimper, A. F. W.

Pflanzegeographie auf physiologischer Grundlage. Dritte, neubearbeitete und wesentlich erweiterte Auflage herausgegeben von F. C. von Faber. Bande 1-2. Mit Abbildungen...und ...tafeln...und 3 Karten. Jena. Gustav Fischer. 135. 1612 pp. R8vo

---

QE
Geol.
Pam.
557

Fabiani, Ramiro

Osservazioni preliminari sulle condizioni di giacitura del Permiano della valle del Sosio. Estrato Boll. Soc.Sci. Nat. ed Econ. di Palermo, n.s. Anno VII, 1925.

QL
496
F 12

Fabre, J(ean) H(enri)

Souvenirs entomologiques: études sur l'instinct et les moeurs des insectes. (Huitième Série). 8vo.

Paris, Delgrave, n.d. 378p.

QK
938.C1
F 11

Faber, Friedrich Carl von

The Crater Plants of Java In Physiological and Ecological Aspect.(Translated by Charlotte Groos, edited by Howard C. Abbott) Seattle, Economy Publishers, 1931. 150 pp. 5 plates.

QE
Geology
Pam
614

Fabiani, Ramiro

Primi risultati di nuove ricerche negli affioramenti permiani del bacino del Sosio (Palermo). From Rend. d. r. Accademia Nazionale dei Lincei, classe fis. mat. e nat. v.3, ser.6, fasc.10, 1926.

AS
36
S1

FABRE, JEAN HENRI CASIMIR, 1823-1915.

Bouvier, Eugène Louis, 1856–
The life and work of J. H. Fabre. By E. L. Bouvier ...
(*In* Smithsonian institution. Annual report. 1916. Washington, 1917. 23½ᶜᵐ. p. 587-597)
"Translated ... from Revue générale des sciences. Paris, Nov. 30, 1915."

1. Fabre, Jean Henri Casimir, 1823-1915.

18-3080

Library of Congress   Q11.S66 1916

QL
Crustacea
Pam
645

FABIA

Irvine, John

Laboratory culture and early stages of Fabia subquadrata (Dana), (Crustacea, Decapoda). By John Irvine and Harold G. Coffin.

(Walla Walla College Publ. of the Dept. of Biol. Sci., and Biol. Station, No. 28, 1960)

QE
Geology
Pam
728

Fabiani, Ramiro

A proposito d'una ricerca del carbonifero in Sicilia. From Boll. d. Assn. Mineraria Siciliana, Anno V, n.4, 1929.

PL
Phil.pam.
203
and
PL
Dict.Pam.
10

Fabre, M.

Vocabularies Polynesiens (Revue Coloniale, Juin, 1847. pp. 156-176)

GN
2.3
F

Fabiani, Adelaide

Sulla provenienza della collezione conservata nel Museo Nazionale di Antropologia e Etnologia che si ritiene raccolta dal Cook.

(Archivio per L'Antrop. e la Etnologia, Vol. 64, 1934, pp. 210-213)

QE
Geology
Pam
620

Fabiani, Ramiro

Risultati delle escursioni geologiche da me fatte in Sicilia durante il 1925 e il 1926. From Boll. d. Soc. Sci. Nat. ed Econ. di Palermo. n.s. ann.8, 1926.

QH
1
P 11

FABRICINAE PACIFIC

Hartman, Olga

Fabricinae (feather-duster Polychaetous Annelids) in the Pacific.

(Pacific Science, Vol. 5:379-391, 1951)

QE
Geol.
Pam
559

Fabiani, Ramiro

Cenni su alcune particolarita della struttura geologica del territorio di Bivona (Giggenti) in rapporto alla presenza di affioramenti petroleiferi. Estratto dal Boll. Assoc. Min. Siciliana, N. 7. 1923. Palermo.

QE
Geol.
Pam
646

Fabiani, Ramiro

Scoperta di un apparato eruttivo del Giunessesmedio in Sicilia. From Boll. d. Assn. Min. Siciliana, n.9, 1926.

Fabricius, J. C.

Entomologia systematica, I-IV, 1792-94 and supplement, 1798.

HSPA has
UH has

QE
Geology
Pam
797

Fabiani, Ramiro

Cenni sulle raccolte di Mammiferi quaternari del Museo Geologico della R. Universita di Palermo e sui risultati di nuovi assaggi esplorativi. From Boll. d. Assn. Mineraria Siciliana, Anno IV, n.5, 1928.

QE
Geology
Pam
799

Fabiani, Ramiro

Vestigia di vulcanismo e di movimenti tettonici nel Giurese di Sicilia. From Boll. Soc. Geol. Italiana, v. 47, fasc. 2, 1928.

QL
463
F 12

Fabricius, Johann Christian

Genera Insectorum, eorumque characteres naturales secundum numerum, figuram, situm et proportionem...Chilonii. (1776)

IN
Fabricius, Johann Christian
Philosophia entomologica, sistens scientiae fundamenta adiectis definitionibus... Hamburgi et Kilonii. 1778 sm8vo.

3

QL
575
C 77
Fabricius, Johann Christian
Coquebert de Montbret, Antoine Jean

Illustratio iconographica insectorum quae
in Musaeis parisinis observavit et in lucem edi-
dit Joh. Christ. Fabricius... Paris. Anno VII,
X, et XII (1799,1801, 1804) folio.

QL
520
F 12
Fabricius, Johann Christian

Systema Rhyngotorum. Secundum ordines, genera, species, adiectis synonymis, locis, observationibus, descriptionibus. Brunsvigae. 1803.
8vo.   x + 314 + (1) pp.

DU
Pac.Pam.
646
Facts and figures about the Philippines.
Information Division, Office of the Resident
Commissioner of the Philippines, Washington,
T. C., 1942. 8vo.   64 pp.

QL
463
F 12
Fabricius, Johann Christian

Philosophia entomologica, sistens scientiae
fundamenta adiectis definitionibus, exemplis, observationibus, adumbrationibus. Hamburgi et
Kilonii. 1778. sm8vo. (12)+178 pp.

(bound in with the above is "Genera Insectorum", 1776)

Card 1

QK
261
F 12
Fabris, Humberto A.   and others

La plantas cultivadas en la Republica Ar-
gentina:
Papaveraceas, by E. P. Molinari
Nictaginaceas, "   "   "
Aceraceas, by F. R. Alberti
Ramnaceas, by A. Marzocca and C.E.M. Marthi
Litraceas, by E.P.Molinari and V.A.Malano
Punicaceas, by V. A. Milano
Primulaceas, by E.P. Molinari
Apocinaceas, by Angel Marzocca

                    cont. on next cd.

GN
1
A 63
FAECES   PRESERVATION
Aufonanger, Heinrich

How children's faeces are preserved in the
Central Highlands of New Guinea.

(Anthropos, 54:236-237, 1959)

[to preserve the child's health]

QL
463
F 12
Fabricius, Johann Christian

Systema Antliatorum secundum ordines, genera,
species adiectis synonymis, locis, observationibus, descriptionibus. Brunsvigae. Apud
Carolum Reichard. 1805. 8vo.   372 + 30 pp.

Card 2

QK
261
F 12
Fabris, Humberto A.   and others

La plantas cultivadas en la Republica Argen-
tina:
Escrofulariaceas, by G. Dawson
Bignoniaceas, by Humberto A. Fabris

(Inst. de Bot. Agricola, Buenos Aires, Republica Argentina, Fasc. 82,65,115,120,141,142,155,
165,172,173,   1952-1959)

AS
162
P 23
FAGACEAE
Baumann-Bodenheim, M. G.

Fagacées de la Nouvelle-Calédonie.

(Bull. du Muséum Nat. d'Histoire Naturelle,
Tome XXV, 2 Série(4):419-421, 1953)

QL
463
F 12
Fabricius, Johann Christian

Systema Eleutheratorum, secundum ordines,
genera, species, adiectis synonymis, locis, observationibus, descriptionibus. Tomae I-II.
Kiliae. 1801. 8vo.

GN
Ethn.Pam.
4112
FACES   ASIA
Coon, Carleton S.

Faces of Asia.

(Univ. of Pennsylvania, Mus. Bull. 22(1),
1958)

QK
1
T 1
FAGACEAE
Li, Hui-Lin

Taxonomic notes on the Fagaceae of Formosa.

(Bull. Torrey Bot. Club, 80(4):317-324,
1953)

QL
463
F 12
Fabricius, Johann Christian

Systema entomologiae, sistens insectorum
classes, ordines, genera, species, adiectis synonymis, locis, descriptionibus, observationibus.
Flensburgi et Lipsiae. 1775. 8vo.   (30) + 832
pp.

DU
620
P 22
Faces of the South Pacific.
Ayres, Hester Merwin

(Paradise of the Pacific, 69th Holiday edition, for 1958; issued 1957:102-105)

PL
Phil.Pam.
781
Fagani. Mani rifunagi. Melanesian Mission
Press. 1904. 15 pp.

Solomon Islands, Florida? Wano?, hymns +

QL
542
F 12
Fabricius, Johann Christian

Systema glossatorum. Im Anhang: K. Illiger:
Die neueste Gattungs-Eintheilung der Schmetter-
linge aus den Linneischen Gattungen Papilio und
Sphinx; J. Chr. Fabricius: Rechenschaft an das
Publicum uber seine Classification der glossaten.
Herausgegeben von Felix Bryk.   REPRINT, 1938
Sammlung naturwissenschaftlicher Facsimile-
Drucke, Band 1,   Verlag Gustav Feller. Neubran-
denburg. R8vo. Original imprint, Brunovici,1807

QH
1
P 11
Facilities for research in the natural
sciences in the Hawaiian islands.

(Pacific Science, Vol. 1 (2):119-126, 1947)

QK
1
T 1
FAGARA
St. John, Harold

Dryopteris, Deschampsia, Portulaca, Lupinus,
Fagara, Stenogyne, and Dubautia.   Hawaiian
Plant Studies 12.

(Bul.. Torrey Botanical Club, Vol. 72, pp.
22-30, 1944)

QL
463
F 12
Fabricius, Johann Christian

Systema Piezatorum,secundum ordines, genera,
species, adiectis synonymis, locis, observationibus, descriptionibus. Brunsvigae. Apud Carolum Reichard. 1804. 8vo.   439 + 30 pp.

DU
Pac
Pam
#4

N.Z
Fact and fancy in New Zealand.
Cowan, Frank

Fact and fancy in New Zealand. The
terraces of Rotomahana a poem to which
is prefixed a paper on Geyser eruptions
and terrace formations by Josiah Martin.
Auckland, 1885.

AP
2
S 35
Fager, E. W.

Zooplankton species groups in the North
Pacific. By E. W. Fager and J. A. McGowan.

(Science, Vol. 140(3566):453-460, 1963)

QK
Bot.Pam.
2564

Fagerlind, Folke

Some reflections on the history of the climate and vegetation of the Hawaiian Islands.

(Svensk Botanisk Tidskrift, Bd. 43:73-81, 1949)

G
51
W 17

FAHNESTOCK EXPEDITION

Friday, H. E. L.

The Fahnestock Expedition to the South Seas.

(Walkabout, Vol. 7(2)P16-18,1940)

QL
Insect
Pam.
2103

Fain, A.

On three species of rhinonyssids described by Hirst. By A. Fain and K. Hyland.

(Annals and Mag. of Nat. Hist., Ser. 13, vol.V,pp.341-348,1962)

QH
1
H 38 b

Fagerlund, Gunnar O.

A checklist of the plants, Hawaii National Park, Kilauea-Mauna Loa Section, with a discussion of the vegetation. By Gunnar O. Fagerlund and Arthur L. Mitchell.

(Nat. Hist. Bull. Hawaii Nat. Park, No. 9, 1944)

QL
Insect
Pam.
2105

Fain, A.

Les Acariens de la famille Epidermoptidae (Sarcoptiformes) parasites des fosses nasales chez les Oiseaux au Congo belge.

(Rev. Zool. Bot.Afr.,LIV(3-4):209-222, 1956)

DU
Hist.Pam.
217

FAIR AMERICAN (SHIP)

Vancouver, George

Two manuscript letters (copies of the originals, which are in the Bishop Museum), dated March 8, 1793 and March 2, 1794, respectively, on board "Discovery", at Owhyhee, and having to do with the character of the Hawaiian chiefs, cession of the islands to Great Britain and the incident of the "Fair American".

QH
1
H 38-b

Fagerlund, Gunnar O.

The exotic plants of Hawaii National Park.

(Natural History Bulletin, Hawaii National Park, no. 10, 1947)

QL
Insect
Pam.
2107

Fain, A.

Les Acariens de la famille Rhinonyssidae Vitzthum 1935, parasites des fosses nasales des Oiseaux au Ruanda-Urundi.

(Rev. Zool. Bot. Afr., LIII(1-2):131-157, 1956)

GN
2.S
P 76

Fairbairn, Ian

Samoan migration to New Zealand.

(Jour. Poly. Soc., 70(1):18-30, 1961)

Q
115
C 28

Fage, Louis

Mysidacea Lophogastrida- I-II

Dana Report Nos. 1, 1941 and 23, 1942

AS
145
B 91 b

Fain, Alex

Chaetotaxie et classification des Speleognathinae: (Acarina: Trombidiformes).

(Bull., Institut Roy. des Sciences Nat. de Belgique, Tome 39(9):1-80, 1963)

QE
Pam.
#74

Fairbanks, Harold W.

The great earthquake rift of California, ex Cal. Phy. Geog. Club Bull. vol. I, no. 2, October, 1907.

GN
2.S
O 15

Fagot, ?

Relations familiales et coutumières entre le chefferies aux Iles Loyalty.

(Jour. Soc. des Océanistes, Vol. 5:87-96, 1950)

QL
461
P 11

Fain, A.

Insects of Macquarie Island. Acarina:Trombidiformes: Ereynetidae.

(Pacific Insects, 4(4):921-928, 1962)

QE
75
A

[Fairbanks, Harold Wellman] 1860-
... San Luis folio, California. [By H. W. Fairbanks] ... Washington, D. C., U. S. Geological survey, 1904.

cover-title, 14 p. 3 pl. 4 maps. 55 x 47ᶜᵐ. (U. S. Geological survey. Geologic atlas of the United States no. 101)

Lat. 35°-35° 30', long. 120° 30'-121°; scale 1 : 125,000; contour interval 100 ft.

1. Geology—California—San Luis Obispo Co.—Maps.   G S 7-269
——— Copy 2.
Library, U. S. Geological   (   )   Survey (200) fH no. 101
                                              (a20c1)

AS
28
E 85

Fagot

Relations familiales et coutumières entre les trois iles Loyauté (Maré, Lifou, Ouvea), et en particulier entre leurs chefferies.

(Etudes Mélanesiennes, n.s. Année 2(4):19-31, 1949)

QL
Insect.
Pam.
2104

Fain, A.

The mites parasitic in the lungs of birds. The variability of Sternostoma tracheacolum Lawrence, 1948, in domestic and wild birds. By A. Fain and K. E. Hyland.

(Parasitology (1962), Vol. 52, pp.401-424, 1962)

QE
22.P
F 16

Fairbanks, Helen R.

Life and letters of R. A. F. Penrose, Jr. By Helen R. Fairbanks and Charles P. Berkey. Geological Society of America. New York. 1952 x + 765 pp.

S
301
P

Faguirigan, Domingo B.

Notes on the manufacture of tobacco in the Philippines. Philippine Agri. Rev. v.20, n.1, 1927.

QL
Insect
Pam.
2106

Fain, A.

Note complémentaire sur les Rhinonyssidae au Ruanda-Urundi.

(Rev. Zool. Bot. Afr., LIII(3-4), pp.392-398, 1956)

GC
Oceanography
Pam.
52

Fairbridge, Rhodes W.

Alexa Bank, a drowned atoll on the Melanesian Border Plateau. By Rhodes W. Fairbridge and Harris B. Stewart, Jr.

(Reprint, Deep-Sea Research, Vol. 7(2): 100-116, 1960)

G
Geogr.
Pam.
72

Fairbridge, R. W.

     The Archipelago of the Recherche: physiography. By R. W. Fairbridge and V. N. Serventy.

     (Reprinted from Australian Geographical Society Reports, No. 1, 1954:1-19)

QE
Geol.Pam.
1332

Fairbridge, Rhodes W.

     Eustatic changes in sea level.

     (Reprint, Physics and Chemistry of the Earth, Vol. 4:99-185, 1961)

QE
Geol.
Pam.
1263

Fairbridge, Rhodes W.

     Niveaux multiples de la mer à l'âge postglacial. Tirage à part des Actes du IV Congrès International du Quaternaire, 1953.

G
51
W 17

Fairbridge, Rhodes W.

     Australia in the Indian Ocean?

     (Walkabout, Sept. 1953: 10-11)

QE
Geol.Pam
1127

Fairbridge, Rhodes W.

     The geology and geomorphology of Point Peron, Western Australia.

     (Journal of the Royal Society of Western Australia, 34:35-72, 1950)

GC
Oceanography
Pam.
71

Fairbridge, Rhodes W.

     Notes on the geomorphology of the Felsart Group of the Houtman's Abrolhos Islands.

     (Journal of the R. Soc. of Western Australia 33:1-43, 1948)

QE
651.A
F 16

Fairbridge, Rhodes W.

     Australian stratigraphy. A summary of the stratigraphical geology of Australia, with special reference to the principles of palaeogeography, stratigraphy and geotectonic evolution... for the use of university students. University of Western Australia Text Books Bords. Nedlands, Western Australia. 1953. 4to. iii+100 pp. mimeographed.

QE
Geol.Pam.
1139

Fairbridge, R. W.

     The juvenility of the Indian Ocean.

     (Scope, 1(3):29-35+(2), 1948)

QE
Geol.Pam.
1137

Fairbridge, Rhodes W.

     Our changing sea-level.

     (Scope, Vol. 1 (2):25-28, 1947)

GC
Oceanography
Pam.
53

Fairbridge, Rhodes W.

     Basis for submarine nomenclature in the South-West Pacific Ocean.

     (Reprint, Deutschen Hydrographischen Zeitschrift, Band 15, Heft 1: 15 pp., 1962)

QE
Geol.Pam.
1195

Fairbridge, Rhodes W.

     Landslide patterns on oceanic volcanoes and atolls.

     (Geographical Journal, 115:84-88, 1950)

QE
Geol.Pam.
1331

Fairbridge, R. W.

     Physiography, Archipelago of the Recherche. By R. W. Fairbridge and V. N. Serventy.

     (Reprint, Australian Geographical Society Reports, No. 1, 1954. 20 pp.)

QE
Geol.Pam.
1333

Fairbridge, Rhodes W.

     Convergence of evidence on climatic change and ice ages.

     (Reprint, Annals of the New York Academy of Sciences, Vol. 95, Article 1:542-579, 1961)

QE
Geol.Pam.
1143

Fairbridge, Rhodes W.

     The Low Isles of the Great Barrier Reef: a new analysis. By Rhodes W. Fairbridge and Curt Teichert.

     (Geographical Journal, 111:67-88, 1948)

QE
Geol.Pam
1128

Fairbridge, Rhodes W.

     Problems of Australian geotectonics.

     (Scope: Journal of the Sci. Union, Univ. of Western Australia, 1(5):22-29, 1950)

QE
Geol.Pam.
1334
and
1284

Fairbridge, Rhodes W.

     Dating the latest movements of the quaternary sea level.

     (Reprint, Transactions of the New York Academy of Sciences, Ser. II, Vol. 20(6): 471-482, 1958)

QE
Geol.
Pam.
1241

Fairbridge, Rhodes W.

     Marine erosion.

     (Seventh Pacific Science Congress, Vol. III, 12 pp.

1952)

QE
Geol.
Pam.
1260

Fairbridge, Rhodes W.

     Quaternary eustatic data for Western Australia and adjacent States.

     (Reprint from Proc. of the Pan Indian Ocean Science Congress, Perth, Aug. 1954, Sect. F. pp. 64-84)

QE
Geol.
Pam.
1283

Fairbridge, Rhodes W.

     The Dolomite question.

     (Reprinted from "Regional Aspects of Carbonate Deposition":125-178, 1957)

GC
Oceanography
Pam.
70
and
QE
Geol.
Pam.
1240

Fairbridge, Rhodes W.

     Multiple stands of the sea in Post-glacial times.

     (Seventh Pacific Science Congress, Vol. III 3 pp. unnumbered, 1952)

QE
Geol.Pam.
1135

Fairbridge, Rhodes W.

     The rampart system at Low Isles, 1928-45. by Rhodes W. Fairbridge and Curt Teichert. (Reports of Great Barrier Reef Committee, Vol. VI, Part 1, 1947)

MEG Fairbridge, Rhodes W.

      Recent and Pleistocene coral reefs of Australia.

      (Journal of Geology, Vol. 58:330-401, 1950)

QE Geol. Pam. 1285 Fairbridge, Rhodes W.

      What is a consanguineous association?

      (Journal of Geology, 66(3):319-324, 1958)

GN 2.8 P 76 Fairfield, F. G.

      Maori fish-hooks from Manukau Heads, Auckland.

      (Journal of the Polynesian Society, 42: 145-155, 1933.)

GC Oceanography Pam. 57 and 69 Fairbridge, Rhodes W.

      Report on limits of the Indian Ocean.

      (Reprint, Proc. of the Pan Indian Ocean Science Congress, Section F:18-28, 1954)

GN 2.8 P 76 Fairbrother,

      Tale of Fambumu and his wives Betinaoa and Nosonaoa. From the Eastern Solomon Islands.

      (Journal of the Polynesian Society, 34: 36-60, 1925.)

GN 2.8 P 76 Fairfield, F. G.

      Maungakiekie.

      (Journal of the Polynesian Soc., Vol. 50, 92-104; 170-172)

QE Geol. Pam. 1261 Fairbridge, R. W.

Carrigy, M. A.

      Recent sedimentation, physiography, and structure of the continental shelves of Western Australia, by M. A. Carrigy and R. W. Fairbridge.

      (Reprint, Jour. R. Soc. of Western Australia, 38:65-95, 1954)

GN 2.8 P 76 Fairbrother, H. Trevor

      The tale of the Tembu tree or the four boys and the four ogres. From the Malaita (To'a Baitá). Told by Foalandoa, and put into English by H. Trevor Fairbrother.

      (Journal of the Polynesian Society, 33: 114-120, 1924.)

AS 36 C8 Fairfax, Thomas Fairfax, *3d baron,* 1612–1671.

      ... The poems of Thomas, third lord Fairfax, from Ms. Fairfax 40 in the Bodleian library, Oxford, by Edward Bliss Reed. New Haven, Conn., Pub. under the auspices of Yale university, 1909.

      1 p. l., p. (239)–290. 24ᶜᵐ. (Transactions of the Connecticut academy of arts and sciences ... v. 14 (art. iv))

      1. Reed, Edward Bliss, 1872– ed.

Library of Congress Q11.C9 vol. 14 12–31559a
——— Copy 2.

QE Geol.Pam. 1330 Fairbridge, Rhodes W.

      Sea-level and climate.

      (Reprint, New Scientist, Vol. 15:242-245, n.d.)

QL 461 P 11 Fairchild, G. E.

Quate, Laurence W.

      Phlebotomus sand flies of Malaya and Borneo (Diptera:Psychodidae). By Laurence W. Quate and G. B. Fairchild.

      (Pacific Insects, Vol. 3(2-3): 203-222, 1961)

DU 95 F2 F14 Fairfax, William, ed.

      Handbook to Australasia; Being a brief historical and descriptive account of Victoria, Tasmania, South Australia, New South Wales, Western Australia, and New Zealand; ed. by William Fairfax...

Melbourne, 1859. 244p. map. sm8vo

GC Oceanography Pam. 44 68 Fairbridge, Rhodes W.

      Some bathymetric and geotectonic features of the eastern part of the Indian Ocean.

      (reprinted from Deep-Sea Research, Vol. 2(3) pp. 161-171, 1955)

QK 367 F 16 Fairchild, David

      Garden islands of the great east: collecting seeds from the Philippines and Netherlands India in the junk "Chêng Ho". Charles Scribner's Sons. New York. 1943. R8vo. xiv + 239 pp.

DU Pac Pam 398 Fairfax-Blakeborough, J

      The bi-centenary of Captain James Cook: an historical play.

Whitby, Horne and Son, 1928. 48p.

QE Geol. Pam. 1238 Fairbridge, Rhodes W.

      Stratigraphic correlation by micro-facies.

      (American Jour. of Science, Vol. 252:683-694, 1954)

QK 474.5 F 16 Fairchild, David

      The world grows round my door; the story of The Kampong, a home on the edge of the tropics. Charles Scribner's Sons. New York. 8vo 1947. xii + 347 pp.

GN 2.8 P 76 Fairfield, F. G.

      A necklace of human teeth,- he maioha mau-kaki.

      (Journal of the Polynesian Society, Vol. 46, 1937, pp. 130-133)

QE Geol.Pam. 1138 Fairbridge, Rhodes W.

      The study of eustatic changes of sea-level. By Rhodes W. Fairbridge and Edmund D. Gill.

      (Australian Journal of Sci., Vol. 10 (3): 63-67, 1947)

Fairchild, David G.

      The world grows round my door. 1947c.

      UH

GN 2.8 P 76 Fairfield, F. G.

      Puketutu pa on Weekes' Island, Manukau Harbor.

      (Journal of the Polynesian Society, Vol. 47, 1938, pp. 119-128)

QH
1
N 28

Fairmaire, Léon

Diagnoses de coléoptères Australiens et Polynésiens.

(Le Naturaliste, Vol.I, 1879, p.46, 70, 75-76)

DU
12
F 17

Faivre, Jean-Paul

L'expansion francaise dans le Pacifique de 1800 à 1842. Nouvelles Editions Latines. Paris 1953c 8vo. 549 pp.

QL
671
E 39

FALCO

Dunmire, William W.

Peregrine falcon in Hawaii National Park.

(The Elepaio, 21(11):80-81, 1961)

[Falco peregrinus]

QH
1
N 28

Fairmaire, Léon

Diagnoses de coléoptères de la Mélanésie et de la Micronésie.

(Le Naturaliste, Vol.I, 1881, pp.340,348,359, 372,381,389,406)

DU
720
F 17

Faivre, J. P.

La Nouvelle Calédonie; geographie et histoire, economie demographie, ethnologie. By J. P. Faivre, avec la collaboration de J. Poirier and P. Routhier. Publications du Centenaire de la Nouvelle Calédonie. Nouvelles Editions Latines. Paris. 8vo. 311 pp.

G
3
N 27

FALCON ISLAND

Hoffmeister, J. Edward

Falcon, the Pacific's newest island. By J. Edward Hoffmeister and Harry S. Ladd.

(National Geographic Magazine, 54:757-766, 1928)

QH
1
N 28

Fairmaire, L.

Diagnoses de coléoptères de la Nouvelle-Bretagne.

(La Naturaliste, Vol.2, 1883, pp. 238-239)

GN
2.S
O 15

Faivre, J. P.   editor

Un siecle d'acculturation en Nouvelle-Caledonie,1853-1953. Contributions by J. Guiart P. Metais, M. Laroch, Père Patrick O'Reilly, and others.

(Jour. Soc. des Océanistes, Vol. 9, 1953)

DU
Pacific
Pam
442
443

FALCON ISLAND

Hoffmeister, J. E., Harry S. Ladd, and Harold L. Alling.

Falcon Island. From Amer. Jour. of Sci., vol. 18, 1929. pp. 461-471.

Fairmaire, Leon

Essai sur les Coleopteres de la Polynesie. (Rev. et Mag. Zool. I, 1849: 277-291, 352-356, 410-414, 445-460, 504-516, 550-559; II: 50-64, 115-122, 181-185.)

HSPA has

reprint - repaginated

GN
Pam
2033

FAKAOFU

Lister, J. J.

Notes on the natives of Fakaofu (Bowditch island). Union group. From Anthrop. Instit. Journ. v.21.

DU
Pac.Pam
753

FALCON ISLAND

The mysterious disappearing island of the South Pacific (Falcon Island). Twice washed away by waves and storms, it again rears its volcanic head 350 feet above the ocean...

(source? newspapers)

QL
627
U-b

Fairport Fisheries Biological Station:
Coker, Robert E.
The Fairport Fisheries Biological Station: Its equipment, organization, and functions. in Bull. U.S. Bur. Fish. XXXIV, 1914, pp. 383-405. (Document 820). Washington 1916, illus.

FAKAAFO

See also TOKELAU

(UNION GROUP)

QH
431
F 18

Falconer, D. S.

Introduction to quantitative genetics. The Ronald Press Company. New York. 8vo. 1961 (reprinted, with amendments)

FAIRS HONOLULU

see

HONOLULU FAIRS

GN
2.S
T 12

Audran, Hervé

Fakahina.

(Bull. Soc. d'Etudes Oceaniennes, No. 19: 227-235, 251-259, 1927)

AS
36
S 5

FALCONIFORMES

Bent, Arthur Cleveland

Life histories of North American Birds of Prey: Order Falconiformes. (Part 1-2)

(U. S. Nat. Mus., Bull. 167, 1937)(Part 2) Bull. 170, 1938)

FAIS GEOLOGY

See

GEOLOGY FAIS

QL
Bird
Pam
#43

FALAISE COLLECTION

Catalogue des oiseaux de la collection de feu M. le Bon. de Lafresage de Falaise.

Lithograph of manuscript. Gelin & Keller n.p. n.d.

QL
117
F 18

Falcoz, Louis

Contribution a l'etude de la faune des microcavernes; faune des terriers et des nids. Lyon. Univ. of Lyon. 1914. 8vo. 187 pp.

QL
345.N 6
S 24

Falcoz, L.

Diptères Pupipares de la Nouvelle-Calédonie et des Iles Loyalty (Streblidae et Nycteribiidae)

Sarasin, Fritz

Nova Caledonia...A. Zoologie, Tome III, Livr 1, 1923. pp. 83-96

Falkland Islands

P
2936
C65

Coan, Titus.

Adventures in Patagonia...1880.

For fuller entry see main card

AS
719
A 93 m

Falk, R. A.

Antarctic birds.

(Australian Mus. Mag., 12(8):261-263, 1957)

GN
2.S
P 76

FALEMAUNGA CAVES

Freeman, J. D.

The Falemaunga caves.

(Journal of the Polynesian Soc., Vol. 53, 86-106, 1944)

QK
Bot.Fam.
2525

FALKLAND ISLANDS

Skottsberg, Carl

The Falkland Islands.

(Chronica Botanica, Vol. 7:23-26, 1942)

QL
671
E 55

Falla, R. A.

The Australian element in the Avifauna of New Zealand.

(The Emu, Vol. 53(1):36-46, 1953)

Z
Biblio
Pam.
26

Fale'ula Library

Churchill, William

Reading
Room

FALKLAND ISLANDS   BIRDS
See
BIRDS   FALKLAND ISLANDS

AS
750
C 22-m

Falla, R. A.

Bird remains from moa-hunter camps.

(Records of the Canterbury Museum, Vol. V, No. 1, , pp. 43-49)

Falk, Alfred

Trans-Pacific Sketches; tour through U.S. and Canada. 12mo, pp. 328, Melbourne, 1877.

HMCS

FALKLAND ISLANDS   BOTANY
See
BOTANY   FALKLAND ISLANDS

Q
115
M 46

and
QL
695
F 19

Falla, R. A.

Birds.

Mawson, Sir Douglas   leader
British, Australian, and New Zealand Antarctic Research Expedition, 1929-31, Reports, Ser. B, Vol. II. 1937.   xiv + 288 pp.

DU
620
P

Falke, Lucia Ripley

Oahu fish vs fish of Samoa.

(Paradise of the Pacific. vol.49, no.8, p.11)
1937.

AS
36
C3

Fall, H. C.

The chrysomelidae (coleoptera). Expedition of the California Acad. Sci. to the gulf of California in 1921. Proc. Calif. Acad. Sci. 4th ser. v.16, n.13, 1927.

AS
750
A 89

Falla, R. A.

The distribution and breeding habits of petrels in northern New Zealand.

(Records of the Auckland Inst. and Mus., Vol. 1, p. 245-259, 1934)

GN
Pam
983

Falkenburger, Fritz

Diagraphische untersuchungen an normalen und deformierten rassenschädeln. From Arch. f. Anthrop. bd.12, heft 2,1913 14p.   pls.

AS
36
C1

Fall, H. C.

List of the coleoptera of southern California with notes on habits and distribution and descriptions of new species. California Academy of Sciences, v.8, 1901.

DU
1
P 12

Falla, R. A.

Flying mammals and birds without wings. How did New Zealand get its strange fauna?

(Pacific Discovery, Vol. 7(4):8-12, 1954)

GN
645
W46

Falkenstein, F

Der Weltteil Afrika...

Leipzig, Freytag, 1883-1885.   4v.

Contents:
v.1 Hartmann, R.   Abyssinien
v.2   "   Die Nilländer
v.3 Falkenstein, F. Afrikas Weltküste
v.4 Fritsch, G. Südafrika

AP
2
N 55

Falla, R. A.

Antarctic adventure and research. Hudson Lecture 1955.

(New Zealand Science Review, 13(9/10):107-116, 1955)

QH
1
T 88

Falla, R. A.

Identification of New Zealand gulls and terns.

(Tuatara, 8(2):72-76, 1960)

GN
700
N 53

Falla, R. A.

The moa, zoological and archaeological.

(New Zealand Archaeological Association
Newsletter, 5(3):189-191, 1962)

Fallers, Margaret Chave

The changing position of the mixed-bloods
in the Marshall Islands. 1948

Doctorial dissertation in the

University of Chicago

DU
1
P 10

FALLS OF CLYDE (SHIP)

Old sailer saved. (Falls of Clyde)

(Pacific Islands Monthly, Vol. 34(1):99
and 101, 1963)

QL
Bird
Pam. 378

Falla, R. A.

New Zealand bird life past and present.

(Cawthron Lecture Series No. 29, 1955)

GN
Pam
2624

Fallmeraner, Jakob Philipp

Uber die entstehung der heutigen
Griechen. From Sitz. d. bayerschen
Akad. d. Wissen. Stuttgart, 1825.

DU
Pac.
Pam.
1015

FALLS OF CLYDE (SHIP)

Wright, John

A kamaaina to come home. (Falls of
Clyde)

(Dilco Digest, Vol. 1(1):8-9, 1963)

AS
750
A 89

and
QL
Birds
Pam.
428

Falla, R. A.

Notes on New Zealand Petrels; with descriptions of new forms and some new records.

(Rec. Auckland Inst. and Mus., 1 (4):173-
180, 1933)

G
51
W 17

Fallon, Elaine

Hanuabada, the big village of Papua.

(Walkabout, 27(2):31, 33, 1961)

DU
Pac.Pam.
1006

Falls of Clyde. 2 pages typed. 1963.
(Office of the Dillingham Company)

QL
671
E 55

Falla, R. A.

Notornis re-discovered.

(Emu, 48(4):316-322, 1949)

DT
Af
Pam
No.5

Fallot, Ernest

Histoire de la Colonie Francaise du
Senegal. n.p. n.d. (incomplete).

GN
2.S
H 38 n

The Falls of Clyde. (Arrival in Honolulu on Nov. 17, 1963)

(News from the Pacific, Vol. 14(4):5,
1963)

QL
Birds
Pam.
400

Falla, R. A. and others

The takahe; accounts of field investigations
on Notornis. Special Publication of The Ornithological Soc. of New Zealand. 1951. 8vo. 24 pp.

[notes on nesting season, food, protection,
habitat...]

QE
Geol.Pam.
1273

Fallot, M. Paul

Contribution à la connaissance de la géologie
des Etablissements francais d'Océanie. Note de
M. Edgar Aubert de La Rüe.

(Extrait des Comptes rendus des séances de
l'Académie des Sciences, t. 242, p. 2243-2245,
séance du 30 avril 1956)

DU
Pac.
Pam.
1017

The Falls of Clyde: running with the
winds of history.

(Public Employee, Vol. 3(9):12-14, 1963)

QL
671
F 71

Falla, R. A.

The turnstone.

(Forest and Bird, No. 55: 2 - and cover,
in color, 1940)

DU
Pac.Pam.
1006

FALLS OF CLYDE (SHIP)

Falls of Clyde. 2 pages typed. 1963.
(Office of the Dillingham Company)

QK
97
H 97

The Families of Flowering Plants.

Hutchinson, John

QL
693.Nz
N 91

Falla, R. A.

A wedge-tailed shearwater in New Zealand.

(Notornis, 9:278-279, 1962)

GN
2.S
H 38 n

FALLS OF CLYDE (SHIP)

Kealiinohomoku, Joann W.

85 year old ship, The Falls of Clyde,
purchased as floating museum.

(News from the Pacific, Vol. 14(3): p. 4,
1963)

GN
Ethn.
Pam.
634

FAMILY

Krämer, Augustin

Die Entstehung der Familie von totem-
istischen Standpunkte. Aus Zeitschrift
fur Ethn. 1923.

GN
490
L 26

FAMILY

Lang, Andrew

Social origins, by Andrew Lang; Primal law
by J. J. Atkinson. London. 1903. 8vo.

GN
2 S
A 22

FAMILY

Thurnwald, Richard, 1869–

... Bánaro society; social organization and kinship
system of a tribe in the interior of New Guinea, by Richard Thurnwald. Lancaster, Pa., Pub. for the American
anthropological association, the New era printing company [1916]

cover-title, 1 p. l., p. 251–391 incl. tables, diagrs. 24½ᶜᵐ. (Memoirs of
the American anthropological association. vol. iii, no. 4. Oct.–Dec., 1916)

1. Banaro tribe. 2. Tribes and tribal system. 3. Family. 19–10227

Library of Congress   GN2.A22   vol. iii, no. 4

[3]

GN
668
M 25

FAMILY MELANESIA

Malinowski, Bronislaw

The sexual life of savages in north-western
Melanesia; an ethnographic account of courtship,
marriage, and family life among the natives of
the Trobriand Islands, British New Guinea...with
a preface by Havelock Ellis. With 96 full-page
plates and figures. London. George Routledge.
1929. 8vo. xxiv + 506 pp.

GN
22
L 76

FAMILY

Linton, Ralph

The study of man. An introduction. D.
Appleton-Century Company. New York, London.
1936. 8vo. viii + 503 pp. (The Century Social
Science Series.)

GN
451
W 96

FAMILY

Wundt, Wilhelm

Element der völkerpsychologie; grundlinien
einer psychologischen entwicklungsgeschichte der
menschheit. Leipzig, Kröner, 1912. 8vo. xii +
523 pp.

GN
1
A n

FAMILY MICRONESIA

Eckert, Georg

Der Einfluss der Familienorganisation auf
die Bevölkerungsbewegung in Ozeanien.

(Anthropos, Bd. XXXI, 1936. pp. 789–799)

GN
Ethn.
Pam.
4318

FAMILY

Lowie, Robert H.

The family as a social unit.

(Reprinted, Papers of the Michigan Acad.,
Sci, Arts and Letters, 18, 1932:53–69)

GN
492.2
F 85

FAMILY BORNEO

Freeman, J. D.

The family system of the Iban of Borneo.
Dept. of Anthropology and Sociology, Australian
National University, 1957. [to be published in
Cambridge Papers in Social Anthropology, Vol. 1
1957] folio. mimeographed. 54 pp.

GN
2.I
V 34

FAMILY NEW HEBRIDES

Maconi, V.

La famiglia nelle Nuove Ebridi.

(Annali Lateranensi, Vol. 19:9–183, 1955)

GN
479
M 25

FAMILY

Malinowski, Bronislaw

Sex and repression in savage society. London.
...1927.

GN
490
M 84

FAMILY HAWAII

Morgan, Lewis H.

Ancient Society...New York. 1878. pp. 403–
446.

GN
671.N5
W 723

FAMILY PAPUA

Williams, F. E.

Papuans of the Trans-Fly, Oxford. Clarendon
Press. 1936. 8vo. xxxvi + 452 pp., 19 pl., 36
figs.

GN
490
M 84

FAMILY

Morgan, Lewis H.

Ancient Society...New York. 1878.

GN
Ethn.Pam.
3819

FAMILY MAORI

Aginsky, Bernard W.

Interacting forces in the Maori family.
By Bernard W. Aginsky and Peter H. Buck.

(Am. Anthropologist, Vol. 42(2):195–210,
1940)

GN
1
A n

FAMILY POLYNESIA

Eckert, Georg

Der Einfluss der Familienorganisation auf
die Bevölkerungsbewegung in Ozeanien.

(Anthropos, Bd. XXXI, 1936. pp. 178–799)

GN
Ethn.
Pam.
4317

FAMILY

Murdock, George Peter

Family stability in non-European cultures.

(Annals of the Am. Acad. of Political and
Social Science, 1950:195–201)

GN
2.S
P 76

FAMILY MAORI

Best, Elsdon

The lore of the Whare-Kohanga. Notes on
procreation among the Maori people of New Zealand, with some account of the various customs,
rites and superstitions pertaining to menstru-
ation, pregnancy, labour, etc. Parts I to V.

(Journal of the Polynesian Society, 14:
205–215,1905; 15: 1–26, 147–162, 183–192, 1906;
16: 1–12,1907.)

GN
480
S 79

FAMILY POLYNESIA

Starcke, C. N.

Die Primitive Familie in ihrer enstehung
und entwickelung dargestellt von Dr. Phil. C. N.
Starcke. Leipzig. 1888. pp. 95–100. 12mo.

GN
480
S 79

FAMILY

Starcke, C. N.

Die Primitive Familie in ihrer enstehung
und entwickelung dargestellt von Dr. Phil. C. N.
Starcke. Leipzig. 1888. 12mo.

GN
1
A n

FAMILY MELANESIA

Eckert, Georg

Der Einfluss der Familienorganisation auf
die Bevölkerungsbewegung in Ozeanien.

(Anthropos, Bd. XXXI, 1936. pp. 789–799)

GN
671.S6
B 63

FAMILY SOLOMON ISLANDS

Blackwood, Beatrice

Both sides of Buka Passage. An ethnographic
study of social, sexual, and economic questions
in the north-western Solomon Islands. Oxford.
Clarendon Press. 1935. 624 pp., 80 pl., 30
figs., 1 map. 8vo.

GN
671.T5
F 52

FAMILY TIKOPIA

Firth, Raymond

    We, the Tikopia. A sociological study of kinship in primitive Polynesia, by Raymond Firth, with a preface by Bronislaw Malinowski. London. George Allen & Unwin Ltd. 1936. 8vo. xxv + 605 pp. 25 pl.

DU
12
F22
F21

Fanning, Edmund (Captain)

    Voyages and discoveries in the South Seas, 1792 - 1832. Marine Research Soc. Salem, Pub. No.6, 1924.

    Salem, 1924, pp xvi, 355, illus.

Fanning Island

DU
12
896

Burnett Frank

    Through tropic seas pp 14-21.

GN
492.2
S 65

FAMILY WEST INDIES

Smith, M. G.

    West Indian family structure. A monograph from the Research Institute for the Study of Man. Seattle. Univ. of Washington Press. 1962. vii + 311 pp. 8vo.

DU
12
F 21
looked
case

Fanning, Edmund

    Voyages round the world; with selected sketches of voyages to the South Seas, north and south Pacific Oceans, China, etc., performed under the command and agency of the author. Also, information relating to important late discoveries; between the years 1792 and 1832, together with the report of the commander of the first American exploring expedition...in the brigs Seraph and Annawan, to the southern hemisphere. New York. Collins & Hannay. 1833. 8vo. xii + 499 pp.

DU
12
B 91

FANNING ISLAND

Bryan, Edwin H., Jr.

    American Polynesia: coral islands of the central Pacific. Tongg Publishing Company. Honolulu. 1941. 8vo. 208 pp.

DU
1
P

Famous Black collection of artifacts.

    (Pac. Islands Monthly, 21(3):12, 1950)

DU
Pac.Pam.
747

Fanning, Robert Joseph

    Pacific Islands nutrition bibliography. Compiled and annotated by Robert Joseph Fanning. University of Hawaii Press. Honolulu, Hawaii. 8vo. 1951. viii + 70 pp.

DU
620
F
and
DU
Missions
Pam.72

FANNING ISLAND

Damon, Samuel Chenery

    Morning Star Papers...Honolulu, 1861

    (contains an account of a visit to Fanning Island by Rev. J. Bicknell, pp. 76-78)

    (Friend, 1861: Sept:42-45, 50-55; Oct:58-63, 66-71; Nov:74-78)

DU
1
P

Famous old sailing ship; service under many names.

    (Pac. Is. Monthly, 22(11):111, 1952)

FANNING ISLAND

    [native name is TAPUAERANI. Personal communication from Harry Maude, August, 1958]

MSS
File

FANNING ISLAND

Emory, Kenneth P

    Archaeology of Fanning Island.

QK
1
T 69 b

Fan, Kung-Chu

    Studies on the life histories of marine algae I. Codiolum Petrocelidis and Spongomorpha Coalita.

    (Bull. Torrey Botanical Club, Vol. 86(1): 1-12, 1959)

DU
1
P

FANNING ISLAND

Hodges, Morwell

    The Greigs of the line atolls.

    (Pacific Islands Monthly, 18 (7):42, 1948)

DU
1
P

FANNING ISLAND

    Fanning and Washington Islands. Sold to B. P. interests.

    (Pacific Islands Monthly. Vol.VI, no.6. p.6)

1936.

G
1
As

FANGATAU

Gessler, Clifford

    "Aita Fanau"

    (Asia, Vol. 35, 1935, pp. 551-555)

FANNING ISLAND

over

    See also articles :
IN "Sydney Daily Telegraph", Aug. 14, 1908
"Graphic", May 23, 1912; Centre of the Pacific;
    the importance of Fanning Island to the Empire
Fanning Island, Limited (Prospectus)6 pp. 1912.
    contains a report on Fanning and Washington
    Islands by J. W. Hayward.
Occupation of Fanning Is. by the enemy; Report of
    the Chairman of the Pacific Cable Board,1915.

DU
12
F 21
looked
case

FANNING ISLAND

Fanning, Edmund

    Voyages round the world; with selected sketches of voyages to the South Seas, north and south Pacific Oceans...Also, information relating to important late discoveries; between...1792 and 1832... New York. 1833. pp. 222-226.

DU
1
P 12

Fanning, Edmund

Parkhurst, Joseph L., Jr.

    "Betsey's" voyage of Pacific discovery.

    (Pacific Discovery, 12(5):4-5, 1959)

DU
Pac.Pam.
521

FANNING ISLAND

    British Possessions in Oceania...(London). H. M. Stationery Office. 1920. 8vo. 126 pp.

GN
2.S
P 76

FANNING ISLAND

    Fanning Island.

    (Jour. Poly. Soc., 20:225, 1911)

DU 12 F 41 locked case	FANNING ISLAND Festetics de Tolna, Rodolphe Chez les cannibales. Huit ans de croisiere dans l'Ocean Pacifique a bord du yacht "Le Tolna". Paris. 1903. 4to. pp. 36-45.	Storage Case 3	FANNING ISLAND Rogers, George D Report on Fanning Island. 1925.		FANNING ISLAND BOTANY see BOTANY FANNING ISLAND
G 103.98 F 49	FANNING ISLAND Findlay, Alexander George A directory for the navigation of the North Pacific Ocean, with descriptions of its coasts, islands, etc., from Panama to Behring Strait, and Japan; its winds, currents, and passages. Third edition. London. Richard Holmes Laurie. R8vo. (1886) xxxii + 1315 pp. 928-930	QL Fishes Pam. 436	FANNING ISLAND Ross, S. G. Fanning Island (central Pacific):its past and present... Australasian Medical Publishing Company Ltd. Sydney 1948. pp. 1-28		FANNING ISLAND BRACHYURA see BRACHYURA FANNING ISLAND
AS 763 B-r	FANNING ISLAND Gregory, Herbert E. Report of the Director of Bernice P. Bishop Museum, 1922. (Bulletin, No. 4)	Q 115 U 58 locked case	FANNING ISLAND United States Exploring Expedition...1838-1842...Vol. 23:Hydrography...p. 271		FANNING ISLAND CORALS see CORALS FANNING ISLAND
DU 12 I 31	FANNING ISLAND Im Thurn, Sir Everard Thoughts, talks and tramps...Some less-known islands in the Pacific...pp. 237-250 (discovery, early settlement and annexation)		FANNING ISLAND Whippoorwill Expedition Publications. Nos. 1-4. 1927- 1934.		FANNING ISLAND CRUSTACEA see CRUSTACEA FANNING ISLAND
DU 1 P	FANNING ISLAND Islands for sale. Romantic story of Fanning and Washington. (Pacific Islands Monthly. Vol.V, no.12. 1935. p.5.)		FANNING ISLAND ADZES See ADZES FANNING ISLAND		FANNING ISLAND FISH POISONING See FISH POISONING FANNING ISLAND
DU 1 M 6	FANNING ISLAND Larsen, Nils P. The young coconut as substitute for mothers' milk. (Pan-Pacific Union Bulletin, no. 64, May, 1925, pp. 13-16)		FANNING ISLAND ARCHAEOLOGY see ARCHAEOLOGY FANNING ISLAND		FANNING ISLAND FISHES see FISHES FANNING ISLAND
QL 671 I	FANNING ISLAND MacFarlane, J. R. H. Notes on birds in the western Pacific, made in H. M. S. "Constance", 1883-1885. (Ibis, Ser. 5, Vol. 5, 1887, pp. 201-215)		FANNING ISLAND BIRDS see BIRDS FANNING ISLAND		FANNING ISLAND GEOLOGY see GEOLOGY FANNING ISLAND

FANNING ISLAND   ISOPODA

See

ISOPODA   FANNING ISLAND

Fanning Island

see also

Line Islands

GN
Ethn.
Pam.
4075

Far Eastern Quarterly
    Review of Eastern Asia and the Adjacent
Pacific Islands.

    Vol. IV, No. 2, February 1945
       Special Number on the Philippines:
Races and peoples in the Philippines, by
Herbert W. Krieger; Cultural trends in the ...
by Felix M. Keesing; Central Mindanao... by Fay-
Cooper Cole; The Moros in the Philippines, by
Edward M. Kuder; The shadow of unfreedom, by
Bruno Lasker...

FANNING ISLAND   ISOPTERA

see

ISOPTERA   FANNING ISLAND

AS
36
S1

Fano, Giulio, 1856–
   The relations of physiology to chemistry and morphology. By Giulio Fano.
   (*In* Smithsonian institution. Annual report. 1894. Washington, 1896.
23½ᶜᵐ. p. 377–389)
   "Translated from the Revue scientifique 1894, vol. II, 4th ser., pages
257–264."

   1. Physiology—Addresses, essays, lectures

                              S 15–866

Library of Congress   Q11.S66 1894
Library, Smithsonian   Institution

GN
2.M
Pe

Farabee, William Curtis
   The central Arawaks. Univ. Penn. Mus.
Anthrop. Pub. Vol. IX, 1918.

FANNING ISLAND   MOLLUSCA

see

MOLLUSCA   FANNING ISLAND

GR
385.P1
F 21

Fansler, Dean S.
   Filipino popular tales, collected and
edited, with comparative notes.

   (Memoirs of the American Folk-lore Soc.,
Vol. 12, 1921)

GN
2.M
Pe

Farabee, William Curtis
   The central Caribs. Univ. of Penn.
University Mus. Anthrop. Pub. No. X, 1924.

FANNING ISLAND   PANDANACEAE

see

PANDANACEAE   FANNING ISLAND

G
103.98M
F 21

Far East Command, General Headquarters...
   Preliminary gazetteer of geographic names
for Saipan. Prepared by Geological Surveys
Branch, Intelligence Division, Office of the Engineer, General Headquarters, Far East Command.
Feb. 1949. 26 pp., 10 accompanying maps. 4to.
mimeographed text.

AS
36
P1

FARABEE, WILLIAM CURTIS   [editorial]
Pennsylvania University Museum Journal /

   Dr. William Curtis Farabee. In Penn.
Univ. Mus. Journ. Vol. XVI, No.2, June, 1
1925.

   [An obituary. Bibliography on p. 80]

FANNING ISLAND   VIEWS

see

VIEWS   FANNING ISLAND

DU
Pac.Pam.
825

Far East Command, General Headquarters...
   Preliminary report on the bauxite deposits
of Babelthuap Island, Palau Group. Prepared by
U. S. Geological Survey, Military Geology Section, under direction of Office of the Engineer,
General Headquarters, Far East Command. Jan. 1948
4to. 46 pp., 11 pl., 4 maps

AS
36
S1

FARADAY, MICHAEL
La Rive, Auguste Arthur de, 1801–1873.
   Michael Faraday—his life and works. By Professor
A. de La Rive.
   (*In* Smithsonian institution. Annual report. 1867. Washington, 1868.
23½ᶜᵐ. p. [227]–245)
   "Translated from the Bibliothèque universelle, October 25, 1867, Arch.
des sci., pp. 131–176."

   1. Faraday, Michael, 1791–1867.

                              S 15–210

Library of Congress   Q11.S66 1867
Library, Smithsonian   Institution

FANNING ISLAND

Photographs.

   See albums Miscellaneous no.1, Whipporwill
Expedition, Tanager Expedition.

DS
Asia
Pam.
57

FAR EAST
Wriston, Henry M.
   The United States and the Far West. The
American Assembly, Graduate School of Business,
Columbia University. New York. Dec. 1956.
8vo. (10) + 229 pp.

   [Henry M. Wriston is Director of the American
Assembly]

AS
80
Port

Faria, José G. de
   Contribução ao estudo do
carbunculo symptomatico
Rio de Janeiro, 1908. 8º. p. 68

DU
1
P

Fanning and Washington Islands. Sold to
B. P. interests.

   (Pacific Islands Monthly. Vol.VI, no.6,
1936. p.6)

Far East

See also

East (Far East)

GN
Ethn.Pam.
3282

Faris, Ellsworth
   The superiority of race: some considerations
in approaching the study of racial difference.

   (Preliminary paper prepared for Second
General Session, July 15–29, 1927, Institute of
Pacific Relations. 13 pp.)

Faris, John T.   Carter Coll.
                                   2-E-39
    The paradise of the pacific. New York
Doubleday, Doran and Co. 1929 xvi + 367 pp.
8vo.

QK   Farlow, W.G.
617
Fa   Some edible and poisonous fungi.

        Washington, 1898.

            Pamphlet.

QH   Farner, D. S.
1.S
W 31   A new species of Aedes from the Caroline
        Islands. (Diptera, Culicidae)

            (Proc. Biol. Soc. Washington, 58:59-62,
        1945)

DU   Farley, J.K.
621
H3   Notes on the Maulili pool, Kolea.
        Thrum's Hawaiian Annual. 1907, p.92-3.

Q   Farmer, B. H.
101
P 18   Peasant and plantation in Ceylon.

            (Reprint, Pacific Viewpoint, Vol. 4(1):
        9-16, 1963)

AP   Farner, Donald S.
2
N 55   Northward transequatorial migration of birds.

            (New Zealand Science Review, 12(2):29-31,
        1954)

DU   Farley, J. K.
621
H 3   The pictured ledge of Kauai. Thrum's Hawaii-
        an Annual. 1898. pp. 119-125.

QL   Farmer, J. B.   and others
45
L 28   Introduction and Protozoa

        Lankester, Sir Edwin Ray   editor
        A treatise on zoology, Part I, Fasc. 2, 1903

QH   Farner, D. S.
1.S
W 31   Three new species of Australasian Aedes
        (Diptera, Culicidae). By D.S.Farner and R.M.
        Bohart.

            (Proc. Biol. Soc. of Washington, 57:117-
        122, 1944)

            [from Guam, New Hebrides, Solomon Is.]

QK   Farlow, William G.
Bot.Pam.
1772   Bibliographical Index of North American Fun-
        gi. Vol. I. Part I; Abrothallus to Badhamia.

            (Carnegie Institution of Washington, No. 8,
        1905)

            (All published. The work was never completed)

DU   Farmer, Sarah S.
880
F 23   Tonga and the Friendly Islands.

        London, 1855, pp 427, illus.

DU
880   2d copy
F 23

                                   Carter Coll.
Farnham, J. T.   2-B-17

            The early days of California: embracing
        what I saw and heard there, with scenes in the
        Pacific. Philadelphia John E. Potter. 1860
        vi + 314 pp. 8vo.

QK   Farlow, W. G.
Pam
#376   Edible and poisonous fungi, ex
        U.S. Dept. of Agr., Bull. no 15, 1898.

AS   Farmer, Wesley M.
36
S 19   Two new Opisthobranch mollusks from Baja
        California.

            (Trans. San Diego Soc. of Nat. Hist.,
        13(6):81-84, 1963)

F   Farnham, T. J.
852
F 23   Life, adventures, and travels in California,
        to which are added the conquest of California,
        travels in Oregon, and history of the gold re-
        gions. Nafis and Cornish. New York. 1849. 8vo.
        468 pp.

AS
36   Farlow, William Gilson, 1844-
S1   Memoir of Asa Gray. By Prof. William G. Farlow.
        (In Smithsonian institution. Annual report. 1888. Washington, 1890.
        39½ᵐ. p. 763-783)

        1. Gray, Asa, 1810-1888.

                                   S 15-690
        Library of Congress   Q11.S66 1888
        Library, Smithsonian   Institution

QL   Farner, D. S.   and others
536
F 23   The distribution of mosquitoes of medical
locked importance in the Pacific area. Prepared by
case   Lieut. D. S. Farner, Lieut. R. J. Dicke, G.Sweet,
        L. Isenhour and T.Y.Hsiao. Bureau of Medicine
        and Surgery, Navy Department, Washington. March
        1946. obfolio. 64 pp.

                                   Carter Coll.
Farnham, Thomas J.   7-B-19-20

            Travels in the great western prairies,
        the Anahuac and Rocky Mountains, and in the
        Oregon Territory. London Richard Bentley
        1843 2 volumes. 297pp. 315 pp. sm 8vo

AS   FARLOW, WILLIAM GILSON,
36
S1   Smithsonian institution.
        Botany.
        (In Smithsonian institution. Annual report. 1880-88. Washington,
        1881-90. 23½ᵐ.; 1880, p. 313-329; 1881, p. 391-408; 1882, p. 551-563; 1883,
        p. 581-598; 1888, p. 475-495)
        Contains bibliographies.

        1. Botany—Hist. I. Farlow, William Gilson, 1844- II. Knowlton,
        Frank Hall, 1860-

                                   S 15-525 Revised
        Library of Congress   Q11.S66 1880-88
        Library, Smithsonian   Institution

RB   Farner, D. S.
601
F 23   Epidemiology of diseases of military impor-
        tance in the Netherlands Indies, including the
        identification and distribution of arthropods of
        medical importance. Washington. sm8vo. 250
        pp. 1944. Government Printing Office. (Nav-
        med 133)

            [includes injurious insects, mites and ticks
        snakes, fish, mollusca]

GN   Farnsworth, Dewey   compiler
802
F 23   The Americas before Columbus. Compiled by
        Dewey Farnsworth and Edith Wood Farnsworth. 3rd.
        ed., 1952. Farnsworth Pub. Co., El Paso. 4to.
        176 pp. illustrated.

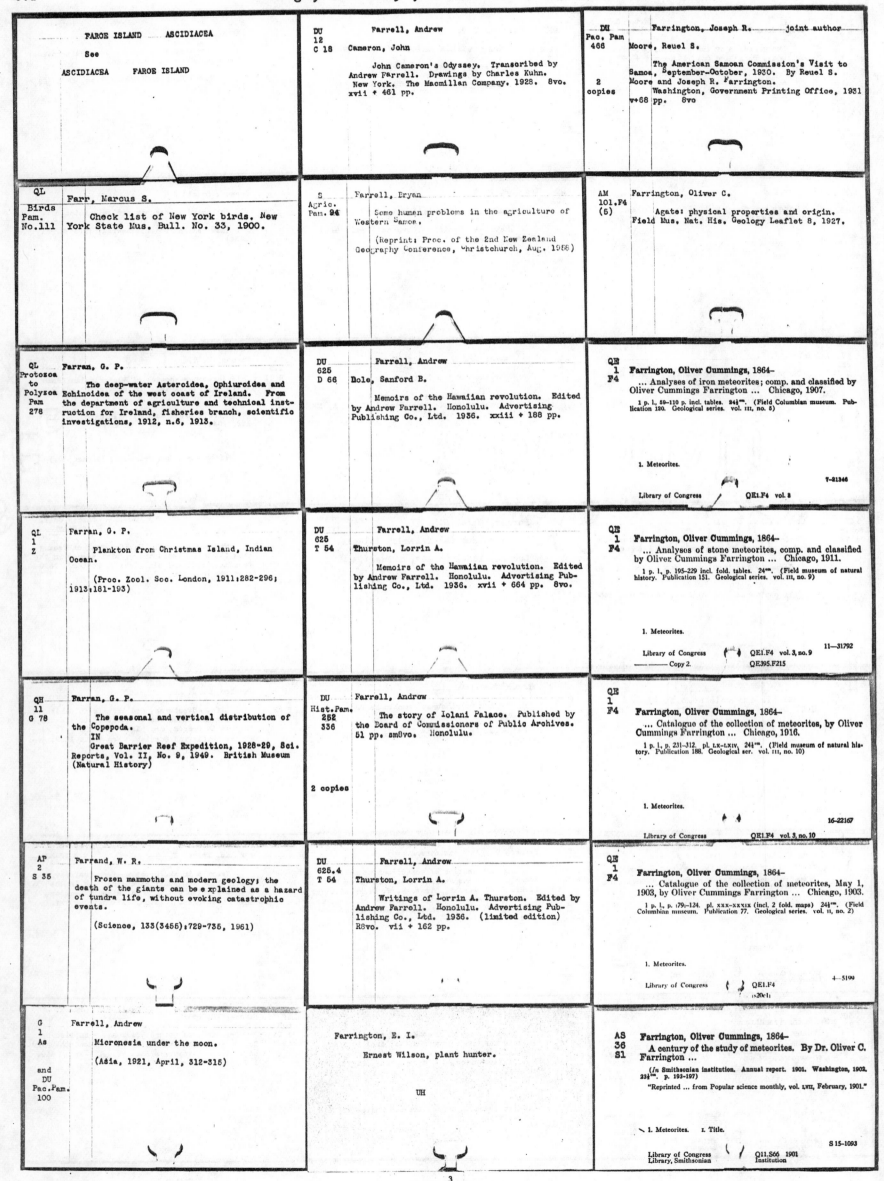

FAROE ISLAND   ASCIDIACEA

See

ASCIDIACEA   FAROE ISLAND

DU
12
C 18   Farrell, Andrew

Cameron, John

     John Cameron's Odyssey. Transcribed by Andrew Farrell. Drawings by Charles Kuhn. New York. The Macmillan Company. 1928. 8vo. xvii + 461 pp.

DU
Pac. Pam   Farrington, Joseph R.   joint author
466

Moore, Reuel S.

     The American Samoan Commission's Visit to
2   Samoa, September–October, 1930. By Reuel S.
copies   Moore and Joseph R. Farrington.
     Washington, Government Printing Office, 1931
v+68 pp. 8vo

QL
Birds
Pam.   Farr, Marcus S.
No.111

     Check list of New York birds. New York State Mus. Bull. No. 33, 1900.

S
Agric.   Farrell, Bryan
Pam. 94

     Some human problems in the agriculture of Western Samoa.

     (Reprint: Proc. of the 2nd New Zealand Geography Conference, Christchurch, Aug. 1958)

AM
101.F4   Farrington, Oliver C.
(5)

     Agate: physical properties and origin. Field Mus. Nat. His. Geology Leaflet 8, 1927.

QL
Protozoa
to   Farran, G. P.
Polyzoa
Echinoidea   The deep-water Asteroidea, Ophiuroidea and Echinoidea of the west coast of Ireland. From
Pam   the department of agriculture and technical inst-
278   ruction for Ireland, fisheries branch, scientific investigations, 1912, n.6, 1913.

DU
625
D 66   Farrell, Andrew

Dole, Sanford B.

     Memoirs of the Hawaiian revolution. Edited by Andrew Farrell. Honolulu. Advertising Publishing Co., Ltd. 1936. xxiii + 188 pp.

QE
1
F4   **Farrington, Oliver Cummings, 1864–**

     ... Analyses of iron meteorites; comp. and classified by Oliver Cummings Farrington ... Chicago, 1907.

     1 p. l., 59–110 p. incl. tables. 24½ᶜᵐ. (Field Columbian museum. Publication 120. Geological series. vol. III, no. 5)

     1. Meteorites.

     T–21346

Library of Congress   QE1.F4 vol. 3

QL
1
Z   Farran, G. P.

     Plankton from Christmas Island, Indian Ocean.

     (Proc. Zool. Soc. London, 1911:282–296; 1913:181–193)

DU
625
T 54   Farrell, Andrew

Thurston, Lorrin A.

     Memoirs of the Hawaiian revolution. Edited by Andrew Farrell. Honolulu. Advertising Publishing Co., Ltd. 1936. xvii + 664 pp. 8vo.

QE
1
F4   **Farrington, Oliver Cummings, 1864–**

     ... Analysis of stone meteorites, comp. and classified by Oliver Cummings Farrington ... Chicago, 1911.

     1 p. l., p. 195–229 incl. fold. tables. 24ᶜᵐ. (Field museum of natural history. Publication 151. Geological series. vol. III, no. 9)

     1. Meteorites.

     11–31792

Library of Congress   QE1.F4 vol. 3, no. 9
—— Copy 2.   QE395.F215

QH
11
G 78   Farran, G. P.

     The seasonal and vertical distribution of the Copepoda.
     IN
     Great Barrier Reef Expedition, 1928–29, Sci. Reports, Vol. II, No. 9, 1949. British Museum (Natural History)

DU
Hist.Pam.   Farrell, Andrew
252
336   The story of Iolani Palace. Published by the Board of Commissioners of Public Archives. 51 pp. sm8vo. Honolulu.

2 copies

QE
1
F4   **Farrington, Oliver Cummings, 1864–**

     ... Catalogue of the collection of meteorites, by Oliver Cummings Farrington ... Chicago, 1916.

     1 p. l., p. 231–312. pl. LX–LXIV, 24½ᶜᵐ. (Field museum of natural history. Publication 188. Geological ser. vol. III, no. 10)

     1. Meteorites.

     16–22167

Library of Congress   QE1.F4 vol. 3, no. 10

AP
2
S 35   Farrand, W. R.

     Frozen mammoths and modern geology; the death of the giants can be explained as a hazard of tundra life, without evoking catastrophic events.

     (Science, 133(3455):729–735, 1961)

DU
625.4
T 54   Farrell, Andrew

Thurston, Lorrin A.

     Writings of Lorrin A. Thurston. Edited by Andrew Farrell. Honolulu. Advertising Publishing Co., Ltd. 1936. (limited edition) R8vo. vii + 162 pp.

QE
1
F4   **Farrington, Oliver Cummings, 1864–**

     ... Catalogue of the collection of meteorites, May 1, 1903, by Oliver Cummings Farrington ... Chicago, 1903.

     1 p. l., p. 179–124. pl. XXX–XXXIX (incl. 2 fold. maps) 24½ᶜᵐ. (Field Columbian museum. Publication 77. Geological series. vol. II, no. 2)

     1. Meteorites.

     4–5199

Library of Congress   QE1.F4
     (s20c1)

G
1
As   Farrell, Andrew

     Micronesia under the moon.

     (Asia, 1921, April, 312–315)

and
DU
Pac.Pam.
100

Farrington, E. I.

     Ernest Wilson, plant hunter.

     UH

AS
36
S1   **Farrington, Oliver Cummings, 1864–**

     A century of the study of meteorites. By Dr. Oliver C. Farrington ...

     (In Smithsonian institution. Annual report. 1901. Washington, 1902, 23½ᶜᵐ. p. 193–197)
     "Reprinted ... from Popular science monthly, vol. LVII, February, 1901."

     1. Meteorites. I. Title.

     S 15–1093

Library of Congress   Q11.S66 1901
Library, Smithsonian   Institution

AM
101.F45
(5)
Farrington, Oliver C

Famous diamonds. Field Mus. Nat. Hist.,
Geol. Leaflet 10, 1929.

QE
1
F4
Farrington, Oliver Cummings, 1864–
... Observations on the geology and geography of west-
ern Mexico, including an account of the Cerro Mercado.
By Oliver Cummings Farrington ... Chicago, 1904.

1 p. l., 197–228 p. illus., LV–LXX pl., map. 24½ᶜᵐ. (Field Columbian
museum. Publication no. 89. Geological series. vol. II, no. 5)

1. Geology—Mexico. 2. Mexico—Descr. & trav. 3. Iron mines and
mining—Mexico. 4. Cerro Mercado, Mexico.

Library of Congress   QE1.F4   4–21574
——— Copy 2.   QE201.F24

Q
Biogra-
phy
Pam.
72
FARRINGTON, WALLACE RIDER

re   Wallace Rider Farrington.   clippings in

QE
1
F4
Farrington, Oliver Cummings, 1864–
... A fossil egg from South Dakota, by Oliver Cum-
mings Farrington ... Chicago, 1899.

1 p. l., 14 p., XX–XXI pl. (incl. front.) 25ᶜᵐ. (Field Columbian museum. Publication 35. Geological series. vol. I, no. 5)
Plate 21 preceded by guard sheet with brief explanation.

1. Birds, Fossil—Eggs. 2. Paleontology—South Dakota.

Library of Congress   QE1.F4   4–10869
——— Copy 2.   QE875.F24

QE
1
F4
Farrington, Oliver Cummings, 1864–
... The Rodeo meteorite by Oliver Cummings Farring-
ton ... Chicago, 1905.

1 p. l., 6 p. III pl., map. 24½ᶜᵐ. (Field Columbian museum. Publication 101. Geological series. vol. III, no. 1)

1. Rodeo meteorite.

Library of Congress   QE1.F4   5–26745

Farrow, John Villiers

Damien the leper.   London, 1937

(reviewed in Geogr. Journal, Vol. 91, 1938, p. 392)

QE
1
F4
Farrington, Oliver Cummings, 1864–
... Meteorite studies—I. By Oliver Cummings Farring-
ton ... Chicago, 1902.

1 p. l., p. 283–323. illus., pl. XLIII–XLVI (incl. front.). 25ᶜᵐ. (Field
Columbian museum. Publication 64. Geological series. vol. I, no. 11)
Each plate preceded by guard sheet with brief explanation.

1. Meteorites.

Library of Congress   QE1.F4   4–10874
——— Copy 2.   QE395.F26

QE
1
F4
Farrington, Oliver Cummings, 1864–
... The Shelburne and South Bend meteorites. By
Oliver Cummings Farrington ... Chicago, 1906.

1 p. l., 7–23 p. illus., pl. V–XVIII (incl. 2 maps) 24½ᶜᵐ. (Field Columbian museum. Publication 109. Geological series. vol. III, no. 2)

1. Meteorites.

Library of Congress   QE1.F4   6–16982

G
51
W 17
Farwell, Grace

Challenge of the Channel Country.

(Walkabout, Vol. 18(1):10–19, 1952)

(southwest corner of Queensland, Australia)

AS
36
C8
Farrington, Oliver Cummings, 1864–
... The nephrostomes of rana.

(In Connecticut academy of arts and sciences. Transactions. New
Haven, 1888–92. 25ᶜᵐ. v. 8, p. [309]–314. pl. XXIV)

1. Frogs.   I. Title.

Library of Congress   Q11.C9   vol. 8   A 17–854
Yale University   A53n.366.8

QE
1
F4
Farrington, Oliver Cummings, 1864–
... Zoisite from lower California, by Oliver Cummings
Farrington ... Chicago, 1906.

1 p. l., p. 55–57. pl. 24½ᶜᵐ. (Field Columbian museum. Publication
112. Geological series. vol. III, no. 4)

1. Zoisite.

Library of Congress   QE1.F4   6–34843
[s20c1]

QK
Bot.
Pam.
1603
Farwell, Oliver Atkins

Fern Notes II – Ferns in the Herbarium of
Parke, Davis and Company.

From The American Midland Naturalist.
vol. XII, no. 8, pp. 233–312, 1931).

QE
1
F4
Farrington, Oliver Cummings, 1864–
... New meteorites, by Oliver Cummings Farrington ...
Chicago, 1914.

1 p. l., 14 p. VI pl. 24ᶜᵐ. (Field museum of natural history. Publication 178. Geological ser., vol. V, no. 1)
Plates I–II, IV–VI accompanied by guard sheets with descriptive letterpress.

1. Meteorites.

Library of Congress   QB755.F3   15–1992

QL
617
F 24
Farrington, S. Kip, Jr.

Pacific Game Fishing.   Illustrated by
Lynn Bogue Hunt.   Coward-McCann, Inc.,   New
York. 1942 c.   R8vo. xii + 290 pp.

Fasciculi Malayenses: Anthropological Zool-
ogical results of an expedition to Perak and the
Siamese Malay States, 1901–1902, undertaken by
Nelson Annandale and Herbert C. Robinson...
4 parts.   1903.   London.   4to.
GN635.M4A61   Anthropology, Part 1.   180 pp.
GN635.M4A61   Supplement: Map and itinerary. xliv pp.
QL318A61   Zoology, Parts 1 and 2, pp.290; 201–307 +vii

QE
1
F4
Farrington, Oliver Cummings, 1864–
... Notes on various minerals in the museum collection,
by Oliver Cummings Farrington ... and Edwin Ward
Tillotson, jr. Chicago, 1908.

1 p. l., p. 131–163. pl. XLIV–LIV (1 col.) diagrs. 24½ᶜᵐ. (Field Columbian museum. Publication 129. Geological series. vol. III, no. 7)
Ten of the plates preceded by leaf with letterpress.

1. Mineralogy—Catalogs and collections. I. Tillotson, Edwin Ward,
jr., joint author.

Library of Congress   9–24349
Library of Congress   QE1.F4 vol. 3, no. 7

DU
Hist.Pam.
209
Farrington, Wallace Rider

The March of Progress in Hawaii. Revised
and published through courtesy of Honolulu
Chamber of Commerce.   Honolulu. 1934.

Am
101
A 71
(5)
Fassett, E C B.

Plant forms in wax, some methods employed in the
Department of preparation and installation of the Ameri-
can museum of natural history, by E. C. B. Fassett. New
York, The Museum, 1911.

28 p. incl. front., illus., plates. 25ᶜᵐ. (On cover: American museum of
natural history ... Guide leaflet no. 34)

1. American museum of natural history, New York.   2. Wax-modeling.
I. Title.

Library of Congress   QK79.N5F3   16–25240

QE
1
F4
Farrington, Oliver Cummings, 1864–
... Observations on Popocatepetl and Ixtaccihuatl, with
a review of the geographic and geologic features of the
mountains. By Oliver C. Farrington ... Chicago, 1897.

2 p. l., p. 71–120. illus., pl. VII–XVIII (part fold.; incl. front., map) 25ᶜᵐ.
(Field Columbian museum. Publication 18. Geological series. vol. I,
no. 2)
Plates 14 and 15 each preceded by guard sheet with brief explanation.
Bibliography: p. 73.

1. Popocatepetl. 2. Ixtaccihuatl.

Library of Congress   QE1.F4   4–10467
——— Copy 2.   QE523.P8F2
[s20g2]

DU
625.4
H 27
FARRINGTON, WALLACE RIDER

Hardy, Thornton Sherburne

Wallace Rider Farrington.   Honolulu.
Honolulu Star-Bulletin, Ltd.   1935.   202 pp.
8vo.

QK
916
F 24
Fassett, Norman C.

A manual of aquatic plants.   first edition
McGraw-Hill Book Company, Inc.,   New York and
London, 1940.   8vo.   vii + 382 pp.

PL
Phil.Pam.
778

Fata faatainilana na fata ni saefilolana ma saioliskiana. A gradual catechism for children and catechumens, Fiu District, Mala, Solomon Islands.[followed by one for the Lau District, Mala, Solomon Islands: Baeta ni faasonola ana ina Baela Soe-alamai. Printed at the Melanesian Mission Press. Norfolk Island. 1910 sm8vo 103 pp.

P
121
F 26

Faulmann, Carl

Das Buch der Schrift, enthaltend die Schriftzeichen und Alphabete aller Zeiten und aller Volker des Erdkreises. Zweite ... auflage. Wien. 1880. 286 pp. R8vo.

QL
401
M 23

FAUNA ATOLLS

Bullen, R. Ashington

On a new variety of Planispira zebra from Gisser Island, and a new species of Chloritis from Java.

(Proc. Mal. Soc. London, Vol. 6, 1905, pp. 191-192)

GN
1
O 15

FATALEKA

Russell, T.

The Fataleka of Malaita.

(Oceania, Vol. 21(1):1-13, 1950)

QE
1
G 3

FAULT TROUGHS

Escher, B. G.

Relations between the mechanism of the formation of fault troughs and volcanic activity.

(Bull. Geol. Soc. Of America, Vol. 63:749-756, 1952)

(Africa, not Hawaii, discussed)

QL
353
A 96

and

QH
Nat. Hist.
Pam.
196

FAUNA CLASSIFICATION

Ax, Peter

Die Entdeckung neuer Organisationstypen im Tierreich. (Die Neue Brehm Bucherei) A. Ziemsen Verlag. Wittenberg.Lutherstadt. 1960 sm8vo. 116 pp.

FATĒ

see

NEW HEBRIDES

QE
Pam
#37

FAULT TROUGHS

Taber, Stephen

The great fault throughs of the Antilles, ex Journ. of Geol., vol. XXX. no. 2, February-March, 1922.

QL
352
R 84

FAUNA CLASSIFICATION

Rothschild, Lord

A classification of living animals. Longmans. 1961 R8vo. (Great Britain) vii + 106 pp.

DU
Missions
Pam. 18

Father Damien. Many clippings from old Hawaiian newspapers.

QE
Geol.Pam.
1023

FAULTS CALIFORNIA

Benioff, Hugo

The determination of the extent of faulting with application to the Long Beach earthquake.

(Bull. of the Seismological Soc. of America, Vol. 28, 1938, pp. 77-84)

Q
101
P 18

FAUNA-DISTRIBUTION PACIFIC

Carpenter, G. D. Hale

The present status of studies of faunal distribution with reference to Oceanic islands. By G. D. Hale Carpenter and E. P. Mumford.

IN Proc. Sixth Pac. Sci. Congress, 1939, (California), Vol. 4, 1940, pp. 241-248.

DU
1
P

Father Rougier.

(Pacific Islands Monthly, Vol. 14, No. 8, 1944, pp. 32-33)

QE
Geol.Pam.
1127

FAULTS WAIMEA, OAHU

Palmer, Harold S.

Fault at Waimea, Oahu.

(Pacific Science, Vol. 1(2):85-91, 1947)

QL
1
S 99

FAUNA DISTRIBUTION PACIFIC

Gressitt, J. Linsley

Faunal distribution on Pacific Islands.

(Systematic Zoology, Vol. 5; pp. 11-32,47, 1956)

GN
451
M 25

The Father in Primitive Psychology.

Malinowski, Bronislaw

QL
3
S 89

FAUNA

Strand, Embrik

Festschrift zum 60. Geburtstage von Professor Dr. Embrik Strand. Vols. 1-5, 1936-39.

[collection of articles by many authors, on fauna, preponderantly Insecta]

QL
754
P 36

FAUNA EVOLUTION

Pearse, A. S.

The emigrations of animals from the sea. The Sherwood Press, Dryden, New York. 1950c. 8vo. xii + 210 pp.

AM
Mus.
Pam.
479

Faulkner, Douglas

Aquarium de Noumea.

(Aquarium Jour., Vol. 34(5):145-147, 1963)

FAUNA

see also

MARINE FAUNA
ZOOLOGY
FRESH WATER FAUNA
SHORE FAUNA

QL
671
E 89

FAUNA EXTINCTION

Harroy, Jean-Paul

The disappearance of zoological species.

(Elepaio, 16(3):20, 1955)
[reprinted from Bull. Int. Union for the Protection of Nature, 4(2)pt. 1, 1955]

QL
461
A 51

FAUNA-INSULAR

Bequaert, Joseph

    The folded-winged wasps of the Bermudas, with some preliminary remarks on insular wasp faunae.

    (Annals of the Ent. Soc. of America, Vol. 22, 1929, pp. 555-582)

FAUNA MARINE

See

MARINE FAUNA

AP
2
N 28

FAUNA MIGRATION

Kalmus, H.

    Sun navigation by animals.

    (Nature, 173- (no. 4406):657-658, 1954)

QL
754
L 47

FAUNA MIGRATION

Lindroth, Carl H.

    The Faunal connections between Europe and North America. John Wiley and Sons, Inc. New York. 8vo. 1957c 344 pp.

AP
2
N 58-b

FAUNA MIGRATION NEW ZEALAND

Marwick, J.

    Faunal migrations in New Zealand seas during the Triassic and Jurassic.

    (New Zealand Journal of Science and Technology, ser. B, Vol. 34(5):317-321, 1953)

QL
754
P 36

FAUNA MIGRATION

Pearse, A. S.

    The emigrations of animals from the sea. The Sherwood Press, Dryden, New York. 1950c. 8vo. xii + 210 pp.

Q
101
P 18

FAUNA MIGRATION

Simpson, George Gaylord
Antarctica as a faunal migration route.

    IN Proc. Sixth Pac. Sci. Congress, 1939, (California), Vol. 2, 1940, pp. 755-768.

QH
1
T 88

FAUNA SEA BOTTOM

Ralph, Patricia M.

    Seafloor animals from the region of Portobello marine biological station, Otago Harbour by Patricia M. Ralph and J. C. Yaldwyn.

    (Tuatara, 6(2):57-85; 1956)

QL
754
L 47

FAUNA TRANSPORT

Lindroth, Carl H.

    The faunal connections between Europe and North America. John Wiley and Sons, Inc. New York. 8vo. 1957c 344 pp.

QH
Nat.Hist.
Pam.
176

FAUNA AFRICA

Caldwell, Keith

    Report of a faunal survey in eastern and central Africa.

    (Society for the Preservation of the Empire, Occ. Paper No. 8, 1948).

GN
2.1
S 66

FAUNA ALEUTIAN ISLANDS

Collins, Henry B., Jr.

    The Aleutian Islands: their people and natural history. (With keys for the identification of the birds and plants). By Henry B. Collins, Jr., Austin H. Clark, and Egbert H. Walker.

    (Smithsonian Institution, War Background Studies, No. 21, 1945)

QK
3
P 89

FAUNA ANDAMAN ISLANDS

Prain, David
Remarks on the fauna of Narcondam and Barren Island.
(Proc. Asiatic Soc. Bengal, 1892:109-121)

IN

Prain, David
Memoirs and memoranda... pp. 253-300

AP
2
S 41

FAUNA ANTARCTIC

Llano, George A.

    The terrestrial life of the Antarctic.

    (Scientific American, 207(3):212-230, 1962)

AS
719
A 93 m

FAUNA ANTARCTIC

Pope, Elizabeth C.

Teeming life in Antarctic seas.

    (Australian Mus. Mag., 12(8):268-269, 1957)

Q
101
P 18

FAUNA ANTARCTIC

Simpson, George Gaylord
Antarctica as a faunal migration route.

    IN Proc. Sixth Pac. Sci. Congress, 1939, (California), Vol. 2, 1940, pp. 755-768.

QL
461
P11

FAUNA ANTARCTIC

Tyndale-Biscoe, C. H.

    On the occurrence of life near the Beardmore Glacier, Antarctica.

    (Pacific Insects, 2(2):251-253, 1960)

QL
461
P 11

FAUNA ANTARCTICA

Janetschek, Heinz

    On the terrestrial fauna of the Ross-Sea area, Antarctica (Preliminary report).

    (Pacific Insects, Vol. 5(1):305-311, 1963)

QH
Nat. Hist.
Pam.
226

FAUNA ANTILLES

Darlington, P. J., Jr.

    The origin of the fauna of the Greater Antilles, with discussion of dispersal of animals over water and through the air.

    (Quarterly Rev. of Biology, 13(3):274-300, 1938)

QL
Insect
Pam.
2048

FAUNA ARCTIC

Hammer, Marie

    Some aspects of the distribution of microfauna in the Arctic.

    (Arctic, Journal of the Arctic Institute of North America, Vol. 8(2):115-126, 1955)

QL
1
A 93

FAUNA AUSTRALIA

Harrison, Launcelot

    The migration route of the Australian marsupial fauna.

    (The Australian Zoologist, 3:247-263, 1924)

QL
5
B 97

FAUNA BURU

    Boeroe-Expeditie, 1921-1922: Résultats zoologiques de l'Expédition Scientifique Néerlandaise à l'île de Buru en 1921 et 1922. Vol. 1, Vertebrata, Livr. 1-3, 1925-1930; Vol. 2, Insecta, Livr. 1-9, 1924-1936; Vol. 3, Invertebrata, Livr. 1-3, 1927-1936. Buitenzorg. Archipel Drukkerij. R8vo.

    [publication occurred simultaneously in Treubia]

3

AS
36
S 1

FAUNA CENTRAL AMERICA

Clark, Austin H.

The fauna of America.

(Smithsonian Inst., Ann. Rept., 1951:287-302)

AS
720.N
L

FAUNA DUKE OF YORK ISLANDS

Ramsay, Edward Pierson

Notes of a collection of birds from New Britain, New Ireland, and the Duke of York Islands, with some remarks on the zoology of the group.

(Proc. Linn. Soc. New South Wales, 1, 1877, 369-378)

AS
36
A 65-n

FAUNA GALAPAGOS ISLANDS

Couffer, Jack C.

Galápagos adventure.

(Natural History, Vol. LXV(3):140-145, March, 1955)

QL
321.C
D 43

FAUNA CEYLON

Deraniyagala, P. E. P.

Some vertebrate animals of Ceylon. Vol. 1 1949. folio. The National Museums of Ceylon Pictorial Series.

RB
601
F 23

FAUNA DUTCH EAST INDIES

Farner, D. S.

Epidemiology of diseases of military importance in the Netherlands Indies, including the identification and distribution of arthropods of medical importance. Washington, sm8vo. 250 pp. 1944. Government Printing Office. (Navmed 133)

[includes injurious insects, mites, and ticks snakes, fish, mollusca]

Q
101
P 18

Also
AS
36
C 15 o

FAUNA GALAPAGOS ISLANDS

Kuschel, Guillermo

Composition and relationship of the terrestrial faunas of Easter, Juan Fernandez, Desventuradas, and Galápagos Islands.

(Occ. Papers of the Calif. Acad. of Sciences, No. 44:79-95, 1963)

(Presented at a symposium: Galápagos Islands. Tenth Pacific Science Congress, Honolulu, 1961)

QH
Nat. Hist.
Pam.
227

FAUNA - CEYLON

Mendis, A. S.

A guide to the freshwater fauna of Ceylon. By A. S. Mendis and C. H. Fernando.

(Ceylon, Fisheries Research Station, Bull. 12, 1962)

Q
101
P 18

Also
AS
36
C 15 o

FAUNA EASTER ISLAND

Kuschel, Guillermo

Composition and relationship of the terrestrial faunas of Easter, Juan Fernandez, Desventuradas, and Galápagos Islands.

(Occ. Papers of the Calif. Acad. of Sciences, No. 44:79-95, 1963)

(Presented at a symposium: Galápagos Islands. Tenth Pacific Science Congress, Honolulu, 1961)

QL
141
B 82

FAUNA GERMANY

Brauer, A. Editor

Die Süsswasserfauna Deutschlands:
Heft 2A, 3/4, 5/6, 7-9, 12, 19

Verlag von J. Cramer. Weinheim. 12mo. 1961

GN
2.M
R 13

FAUNA-COCOS-KEELING ISLANDS

Papers on the fauna of the Cocos-Keeling Islands. Based on material and data collected in the group by C. A. Gibson-Hill, between December 1940 and November 1941.

(Bulletin of the Raffles Museum, Singapore, No. 22, 1950)

AS
182
H

FAUNA FIJI

Erneute Exploration der Viti-Inseln.

(Jour. Mus. Godeffroy, Heft XII, 1876, pp. 162-177)

AS
122
L 75

FAUNA GOUGH ISLAND

Holdgate, M. W.

The fresh water fauna of Gough Island (S. Atlantic).

(Proc. Linnean Soc. of London, 172nd session, Part 1:8-24, 1961)

F
1761
B 23

FAUNA CUBA

Barbour, Thomas

A naturalist in Cuba. Little, Brown and Company. Boston. 1945, 8vo. x + 317 pp.

GN
2.S
F 47

FAUNA FIJI

Lever, R. J. A. W.

The origin of the fauna of Fiji.

(Trans. and Proc. of the Fiji Soc., Vol. 2, 1940-44:164-168, 1953)

QH
197
D 13

FAUNA GREAT BARRIER REEF

Dakin, William J.

Great Barrier Reef and some mention of other Australian coral reefs. Australian Travel Association. 1955 repr. Melbourne. R8vo. 133 + (2) pp.

QL
Insect
Pam.
2049

FAUNA - DENMARK

Hammer, Marie

Svingninger i mikrofaunaen i skrifter i Dansk landbrug.

(Annales Entomolgici Fennici, Supplement 14, 1949:75-80)

English summary included (acarids and collemboles)

QH
1
T 12

FAUNA FORMOSA

Taihoku Imperial University
Faculty of Science and Agriculture

Memoirs
VII, XIV, XXIII (Zoology 1-12)

QL
Prot.-
Poly.
Pam.691

FAUNA HAWAII

Brehm, V.

Notizen zur Süsswasserfauna der Hawaii-Inseln.

(Int. Revue d'Hydrobiologie, Stuttgart, Vol. 34: 331-336, 1937)

Q
101
P 18

Also
AS
36
C 15 o

FAUNA DESVENTURADAS ISLANDS

Kuschel, Guillermo

Composition and relationship of the terrestrial faunas of Easter, Juan Fernandez, Desventuradas, and Galápagos Islands.

(Occ. Papers of the Calif. Acad. of Sciences, No. 44:79-95, 1963)

(Presented at a symposium: Galápagos Islands, Tenth Pacific Science Congress, Honolulu, 1961)

QH
1
A 88

FAUNA FRENCH FRIGATE SHOALS

Svihla, Arthur

Observations on French Frigate Shoals, February, 1956.

(Atoll Research Bull., 51, 1957)

QH
198.H
B 91

FAUNA HAWAII

Bryan, William Alanson

Natural history of Hawaii... Honolulu. Hawaiian Gazette Co., Ltd. 1915. R8vo. 596 pp.

Q
101
P 18

FAUNA   HAWAII

Germain, Louis

L'origine et l'evolution de la faune de Hawaii.

(Proc. Third Pan-Pacific Sci. Congress, Tokyo, 1:973-1011, 1928)

QL
1
B 93

FAUNA   JAVA

Dammerman, K. W.

On the zoogeography of Java.

(Treubia, Vol. XI:1-88, 1929)

QH
1
M 17

FAUNA   MADAGASCAR

Inst. Scientifique de Madagascar. Memoires, Ser. A. Biologie Animale

---

QH
1
A 88

FAUNA   HERON ISLAND

Fosberg, F. Raymond and others

Heron Island, Capricorn Group, Australia. By F. R. Fosberg, R. F. Thorne, and J. M. Moulton

(Atoll Research Bulletin, No. 82, 1961)

Q
101
P 18
Also
AS
36
C 15 o

FAUNA   JUAN FERNANDEZ

Kuschel, Guillermo

Composition and relationship of the terrestrial faunas of Easter, Juan Fernandez, Desventuradas, and Galápagos Islands.

(Occ. Papers of the Calif. Acad. of Sciences, No. 44:79-95, 1963)

(Presented at a symposium: Galápagos Islands. Tenth Pacific Science Congress, Honolulu, 1961)

DT
Africa
Pam.
24

FAUNA   MADAGASCAR

Petit, G.

Contribution a l'etude de la faune de Madagascar.

(Faune des Colonies Francaises, Tome IV, Fasc. 5, 1931)

QL
Crustacea
Pam.
651

FAUNA   INDIA

Kemp, Stanley

Notes on the fauna of the Matlah River in the Gangetic Delta.

(Records of the Indian Museum, 13(4):233-241, 1917)

[fish, crustacea...]

QH
11
P 11

FAUNA   KAPINGAMARANGI

Wiens, Harold J.

The geography of Kapingamarangi atoll in the Eastern Carolines.

(Scientific Investigations in Micronesia, 1949- Report No. 21, June 1955)

[includes "The vegetation pattern" by William Niering, pp. 23-26] etc.

QL
319
T 97

FAUNA   MALAYA

Tweedie, M. W. F.

Malayan animal life. By M.W.F. Tweedie and J. L. Harrison. Longmans, Green and Co., London New York. 8vo. 1954. x + 237 pp.

QL
1
L-t

FAUNA   INDIAN OCEAN

Gardiner, J. Stanley

Concluding remarks on the distribution of the land and marine fauna, with a list of the water temperature observations.

(Trans. Linnean Soc. of London, Ser. 2. Zool., Vol. 19 (4):447-464)

AS
750
N

FAUNA-KERMADEC ISLANDS

Cheeseman, T. F.

On the flora of the Kermadec Islands; with notes on the fauna.

(Trans. and Proc. New Zealand Institute, Vol. 20, 1887, pp. 151-181)

AS
122
L

FAUNA   MALAY ARCHIPELAGO

Wallace, Alfred Russell

On the zoological geography of the Malay Archipelago.

(Journal of the Proc. of the Linnean Soc. Zool., Vol. 4, 1860, 172-184)

QL
319
D 36

FAUNA   INDONESIA

Delsman, H. C.

Dierenleven in Indonesië. N.V. Uitgeverij W. van Hoeve. 's-Gravenhage-Bandung. 1951. R8vo. 348 pp.

AS
701
A

FAUNA   KOREA

Fauna of Corea.

(Report of the Sixth Meeting of the Australian Ass'n for the Adv. of Sci., Brisbane, 1895, p. 526)

AS
750
N

FAUNA   MAORI

Best, Elsdon

Maori forest lore...

(Trans. and Proc. New Zealand Inst., Vol. 40, 1907, pp. 185-254; Vol. 41, 1908, pp. 231-286; Vol. 42, 1909, pp. 433-481)

[see Vol. 41 especially]

QH
Nat.Hist.
Pam.
125

FAUNA   JAMAICA

Natural History Society of Jamaica

Glimpses of Jamaican natural history, by members of the Nat. Hist. Soc. of Jamaica. Published by the Institute of Jamaica. 8vo. 84 pp. (1945 ?)

QH
195.M
D 29

FAUNA   MADAGASCAR

Decary, Raymond

La faune malgache, son role dans les croyances et les usages indigènes. Avec 22 figures. Payot. Paris. 1950. 8vo. 236 pp.

QH
1
P 11

FAUNA   MARCUS ISLAND

Sakagami, Shoichi F.

An ecological perspective of Marcus Island, with special reference to land animals.

(Pacific Science, Vol. 15(1):82-104, 1961)

QL
1
T 64

FAUNA   JAPAN

Annotationes Zoologicae Japonenses

Vol. 1-19, 1897-1940 and continuation

[lacking, 10:3; 11:2-3]

The Tokyo Zoological Society. Tokoy. 8vo.

AS
162
S 67

FAUNA   MADAGASCAR

Dechambre, Ed.

Origine des animaux domestiques de Madagascar.

(La Terre et la Vie, 1951(4):188-196)

QH
198.Msh
U 58

FAUNA   MARSHALL ISLANDS

Fosberg, F. Raymond

Military geography of the northern Marshalls

Prepared under the direction of the Chief of Engineers, U. S. Army, by the Intelligence Division, Office of the Engineer, U. S. Army Forces Far East, and 8th U. S. Army, with personnel of the U. S. Geological Survey. 1956. folio. mimeographed. xi + 320 pp.

3

QL
1
L-t

FAUNA   MAURITIUS

Gardiner, J. Stanley

    Concluding remarks on the distribution of
the land and marine fauna, with a list of the
water temperature observations.

    (Trans. Linnean Soc. of London, Ser. 2,
Zool., Vol. 19 (4):447-464)

AS
182
S 47

FAUNA   MELANESIA

Sternfeld, Richard

    Zur Tiergeographie Papuasiens und der pazi-
fischen Inselwelt.

    (Abh. der Senckenb. Naturf. Gesell, Bd.
36, Heft 4, pp. 375-436, pl. 31) 1918.

QH
Nat.Hist.
Pam.
129

FAUNA   MICRONESIA

Baker, Rollin H.

    Some effects of the war on the wildlife of
Micronesia.

    (Transactions of the Eleventh North American
Wildlife Conference, 1946:205-213)

DU
500
U 58

FAUNA   MICRONESIA

Gantt, Paul A.

    Livestock survey of Micronesia.
IN
U. S. Commercial Company. Economic survey
of Micronesia. No. 15. 1946.

QL
595.Mi
I 59

FAUNA   MICRONESIA

Gressitt, J. Linsley
Insects of Micronesia, Introduction.
IN
Insects of Micronesia, Vol. I. Bernice P.
Bishop Museum. 1954. R8vo.

QH
11
P 11

FAUNA   MICRONESIA

Moul, Edwin T.

    Preliminary report on land animals at Onotoa
Atoll, Gilbert Islands.

    (Scientific Investigations in Micronesia,
1949-   Report No.19, Feb. 1954. Pac. Sci.
Bd.,Nat.Research Council)

AS
182
S 47

FAUNA   MICRONESIA

Sternfeld, Richard

    Zur Tiergeographie Papuasiens und der pazi-
fischen Inselwelt.

    (Abh. der Senckenb. Naturf. Gesell, Bd.
36, Heft 4, pp. 375-436, pl. 31) 1918.

QL
1
B 93

FAUNA   MOLUCCAS

Diakonoff, A.

    Fauna buruana. Lepidoptera, Fam.Tortricidae

    (Treubia, Vol. 18:213-216, pl. 7,8, 1941)

AS
720.N
L

FAUNA   NEW BRITAIN

Ramsay, Edward Pierson

    Notes of a collection of birds from New
Britain, New Ireland, and the Duke of York Islands, with some remarks on the zoology of the
group.

    (Proc. Linn. Soc. New South Wales, 1, 1877,
369-378)

QH
Nat. Hist.
Pam.
184

FAUNA   NEW GUINEA

Brongersma, L. D.

    The animal world of Netherlands New Guinea.
J. B. Wolters. Groningen. 1958. 8vo. 71 pp.

AS
720.N
L

FAUNA   NEW GUINEA

Ramsay, Edward Pierson

    Contributions to the zoology of New Guinea.

    (Proc. Linn. Soc. New South Wales, 3, 1879,
pp. 241-305; 402-405; 4, 1880, pp. 85-102, 464-
470, 8, 1884, pp. 15-29)

QH
198.NH
B 16

FAUNA   NEW HEBRIDES

Baker, John R.

    Man and animals in the New Hebrides.
George Routledge and Sons, Ltd. London. 1929.
8vo. xiv + 200 pp.

AS
720.N
L

FAUNA   NEW IRELAND

Ramsay, Edward Pierson

    Notes of a collection of birds from New
Britain, New Ireland, and the Duke of York Islands, with some remarks on the zoology of the
group.

    (Proc. Linn. Soc. New South Wales, 1, 1877,
369-378)

DU
1
P 12

FAUNA   NEW ZEALAND

Falla, R. A.

    Flying mammals and birds without wings. How
did New Zealand get its strange fauna?

    (Pacific Discovery, Vol. 7(4):8-12, 1954)

AP
2
N 54

FAUNA   NEW ZEALAND

Hutton, Frederick Wollaston

    On the origin of the fauna and flora of New
Zealand.

    (New Zealand Journal of Science, II, 1884,
pp. 1-20; 249-274)

QH
Nat.Hist.
Pam.
224

also
QH
Nat.
Hist.
Pam.
203

FAUNA   NEW ZEALAND

Powell, A. W. B.

    Native animals of New Zealand. Auckland
Museum Handbook of Zoology. 2nd impression.
1954. 96 pp. R8vo.

AS
36
S 1

FAUNA   NORTH AMERICA

Clark, Austin H.

    The fauna of America.

    (Smithsonian Isnt., Ann. Rept., 1951:287-302)

GC
Oceano-
graphy
Pam.
83

FAUNA   PACIFIC

Filatova, Zenaida*

    Exploration of the Pacific Ocean and its
deep-sea bottom fauna. A speech given by...
of the Institute of Oceanology, Academy of Sciences, Moscow, at the Chemistry Building, University of Hawaii, February 5, 1959.

    *(scientist on board the Russian oceanogra-
phic ship Vitjaz)

QL
1
S 99

FAUNA   PACIFIC

Gressitt, J. Linsley

    Faunal distribution on Pacific Islands.

    (Systematic Zoology, Vol. 5; pp. 11-32, 47,
1956)

DU
1
M 6

FAUNA   PACIFIC

Nelson, E. W.

    The land fauna of islands in the Pacific.

    (Mid-Pacific Magazine, 23:233-240, 1922)

QH
Nat.Hist.
Pam.
124

FAUNA   PACIFIC   (southwest)

Smithsonian Institution, U. S. Nat. Museum.

    [Natural history of the southwest Pacific:
birds, butterflies, mammals, invertebrates, mollusca, plants, reptiles and amphibians, starfishes, etc., fishes.] Prepared for the use of
the armed forces, 1943?) mimeographed.

AS
182
S 47
FAUNA   PACIFIC

Sternfeld, Richard

Zur Tiergeographie Papuasiens und der pazifischen Inselwelt.

(Abh. der Senckenb. Naturf. Gesell, Bd. 36, Heft 4, pp. 375-436, pl. 31) 1918.

QL
401
S 72
FAUNA   SOLOMON ISLANDS

Eyerdam, Walter J.

A remarkable endemic species of Melania from the Solomons.

(Conchological Club of Southern Calif., Minutes, Feb. 1944, pp. 11-12)

S
181
I 59 j
FAUNA   VIRGIN ISLANDS

Beatty, Harry A.

Fauna of St. Croix, V. I.

(Jour. of Agric., Univ. of Puerto Rico, Vol. 28 (3/4):103-185, 1944.)

[Endoparasites, Arachnida, Insects, Brachyuran crabs, fresh waters fishes, Mammals]

QL
1
C 21 b
FAUNA   PACIFIC   DISTRIBUTION

Aron, William

The distribution of animals in the Eastern North Pacific and its relationship to physical and chemical conditions.

(Jour. Fisheries Res. Board of Canada, Vol. 19(2):271-314, 1962)

QH
1
P 11
FAUNA   SOLOMON ISLANDS

Lever, R. J. A. W.

Faunal speciation in New Georgia, Solomon Islands.

(Pacific Science, Vol. 7:250-251, 1953)

QH
Nat.Hist.
Pam.
243
FAUNA   WESTERN AUSTRALIA

Ride, W. D. L.

The fauna of Western Australia. By W. D. L. Ride and D. L. Serventy.

(Reprinted from the Official Year Book of Western Australia, 1960, no. 2, n.s.:159-70, 1961)

QL
638.S35
I 61-b
FAUNA   PACIFIC OCEAN (EASTERN)

Holmes, Robert W. and others

Primary production, chlorophyll, and zooplankton volumes in the tropical eastern Pacific Ocean.

(Inter-American Tropical Tuna Commission, Bull., Vol. II(4):129-169, 1957)

AS
720.N
L

and
AP
2
N 4
FAUNA SOLOMON ISLANDS

Ramsay, Edward Pierson

Notes on the zoology of the Solomon Islands.

(Proc. Linn. Soc. New South Wales, 4,1880 pp. 65-84; 6, 1882, pp. 176-181, 718-727; 7, 1883, pp. 16-43; and Nature, 20, 1879, pp. 125-126; 24, 1881, p. 277; 25, 1882, p. 282)

QL
632.B
M 67
Fauna Brasiliense

Miranda-Ribeiro, Alipio de

Fauna Brasiliense: Peixes, Vol. II, Parte 1, Fascicolo 1, 1923. Museu Nacional do Rio de Janeiro. 4to.

AS
182
S 47
FAUNA   POLYNESIA

Sternfeld, Richard

Zur Tiergeographie Papuasiens und der pazifischen Inselwelt.

(Abh. der Senckenb. Naturf. Gesell, Bd. 36, Heft 4, pp. 375-436, pl. 31) 1918.

AS
719
A
FAUNA   SOLOMON ISLANDS

Ramsay, Edward Pierson

Report on a zoological collection from the Solomon Islands. Part I.

(Australian Museum Records, 1, 1890-91, pp. 3-5)

QL
309
G 22
Fauna and geography of the Maldive and Laccadive Archipelagoes.......Expedition 1899 - 1900. Edited by J. Stanley Gardiner. Cambridge 1903-1906. 2 vols. 4to. pls.

AS
719
A 93-m
FAUNA   PORT KEATS

Keast, Allen

Port Keats.

(Australian Mus. Mag., XI(2):47-55, 1953)

AM
101
F 45-n
FAUNA   SOLOMON ISLANDS

Schmidt, Karl P.

Some Solomon Islanders. (animal life)

(Chicago Natural History Museum Bulletin, Vol. 15, no. 3-4, 1944, p. 7)

QL
336
Z 88
Die Fauna der Deutschen Kolonien...

Zoologisches Museum in Berlin.

QL
461
P 11
FAUNA   ROSS SEA

Janetschek, Heinz

On the terrestrial fauna of the Ross-Sea area, Antarctica (Preliminary report).

(Pacific Insects, Vol. 5(1):305-311, 1963)

AS
36
S 1
FAUNA   SOUTH AMERICA

Clark, Austin H.

The fauna of America.

(Smithsonian Isnt., Ann. Rept., 1951:287-302)

AS
763
B-sp.7

and
QL
345.H
S 53
FAUNA HAWAIIENSIS   Card 1

Sharp, David, 1840-   ed.

Fauna hawaiiensis; or, The zoology of the Sandwich (Hawaiian) Isles: being results of the explorations instituted by the joint committee appointed by the Royal society of London for promoting natural knowledge and the British association for the advancement of science, and carried on with the assistance of those bodies and of the trustees of the Bernice Pauahi Bishop museum at Honolulu. Ed. by David Sharp ...

(Continued on next card)

CA 6—924 Unrev'd

QH
Nat.Hist.
Pam.
130
FAUNA   ST. CROIX

Beatty, Harry A.

Fauna of St. Croix, V. I. (Virgin Islands)

(Journal of Agriculture of the University of Puerto Rico, Vol. 28:103-185, 1944)

QH
Nat.Hist.
Pam.
142
FAUNA   SOUTH AMERICA

Simpson, George Gaylord

History of the fauna of Latin America.

(American Scientist, Vol. 38:361-389, 1950)

AS
763
B-sp.7

and
QL
345.H
S 53
FAUNA HAWAIIENSIS   Card 2

Sharp, David, 1840-   ed.   Fauna hawaiiensis ... (Card 2)

Cambridge, University press; London, C. J. Clay and sons; [etc., etc.] 1899- 1913

3 v. in [8?] illus., plates (part col.) ports, maps (1 fold.) tables. 32½cm.

Contains bibliography.

see author card for contents

1. Zoology—Hawaiian Islands. I. Royal society of London. II. British association for the advancement of science. III. Bernice Pauahi Bishop museum of Polynesian ethnology and natural history, Honolulu. IV. Title.

Library of Congress   QL345.H3F2

——— Copy 2.   CA 6—924 Unrev'd

QL
Insects
Pam.
457
and

Reading
Room

FAUNA HAWAIIENSIS

General Index to Fauna Hawaiiensis.

QL
623
S 57

locked
case

Fauna Japonica   (Pisces only)

Siebold, Ph. Fr. de

QL
556.1
T 13

The Fauna of British India...

Talbot, G.

Butterflies, Vol. II.   London. 1947

QL Ins.
Pam.19
" 468

FAUNA HAWAIIENSIS

Reviewed by
Busck, August   Vol. I(5):Macrolepidoptera ONLY
(Canadian Ent., 1908:134-138)
Entomological News Editor
(Ent. News, 24, 1913, pp. ?)

Z
Biblio-
graphy
Pam.
155

Fauna of British India. List of the volumes
in Arthropoda. Typed.

AS
701
A

Fauna of Corea.

(Report of the Sixth Meeting of the Australian Ass'n for the Adv. of Sci., Brisbane,
1895, pp. 526)

Storage
Case
4

Misc.
64

FAUNA HAWAIIENSIS

Newton, Alfred

Letters to R. C. L. Perkins, 1892-1904, ab
about 91 items. In re fauna of Hawaii, "Fauna
Hawaiiensis" in process.

QL
596.C9
A 56

The fauna of British India, including Ceylon
and Burma...

Coleoptera, Carabidae, Vol. 1.-Carabinae.
By H. E. Andrewes.   London. 1929

QL
352
L 75

Fauna Svecica...

Linnaeus, Carolus

Storage
Case
4

Misc.
63

FAUNA HAWAIIENSIS

Sharp, David

Letters to R. C. L. Perkins, 1895-1910, in
re Hawaiian fauna, during preparation of "Fauna
Hawaiiensis". About 260 letters, postals, etc.

QL
592
A 77

The fauna of British India, including Ceylon and Burma...

Coleoptera, Lamellicornia.
Parts II, III, IV, 1917-1949, by G. J.
Arrow. London.

QL
444.S8
B 45

Fauna und Flora des Golfes von Neapel...

Monographie 33: Stomatopoden, Theil 1, von
Wilhelm Giesbrecht.

QH
188
F 26

Fauna Japonica:
Chalcididae, Leucospididae and Podagrio-
nidae. (Insecta: Hymenoptera) By Akinobu Habu.
1962.

Biogeographical Society of Japan. Tokyo. R8vo.

QL
531
B 89

The fauna of British India, including Ceylon
and Burma...

Diptera Brachycera. Vol. 1. By E. Brunetti.
London. 1920
Diptera. Vol. III. Pipunculidae, Syrphidae,
Conopidae, Oestridae. By E. Brunetti. London.
1923.

QL
468.A2
P 78

Fauna U. S. S. R.

Pomerantzev, B. I.

Arachnida, Vol. IV, No. 2. Ixodid ticks
[Ixodidae]. Fauna of the U. S. S. R. Translated
by Alena Bibl. Edited by George Anastos.
Published by the American Institute of Biological Sciences. Washington, D. C. R 8vo. 1959c
199 pp.

QH
188
F 26

Fauna Japonica:
Cottidae (Pisces), by Masao Watanabe,
Contributors: Yaichiro Okada and Kityomatsu
Matsubara. 1960
Serranidae (Pisces), by Masao Katayama
Contributors: Yaichiro Okada and Kiyomatsu
Matsubara. 1960

Biogeographical Society of Japan. Tokyo
R8vo

QL
666.S
.S 75

The fauna of British India, including
Ceylon and Burma.

Reptilia and Amphibia, Vol. II:Sauria, by
Malcolm A. Smith. London. 1935

QL
754
L 47

FAUNAL RELATIONSHIPS

Lindroth, Carl H.

The faunal connections between Europe and
North America. John Wiley and Sons, Inc. New
York. 8vo. 1957c 344 pp.

QH
188
F 26

Fauna Japonica:
Tabanidae (Insecta:Diptera) by Hirosi
Takahasi. Contributor, Tokuichi Shiraki.1962
Cicadidae (Insecta), by Masayo Kato.
Contributor: Tokuichi Shiraki. 1961

Biogeographical Society of Japan. Tokyo
R8vo

QL
661
S 65

The fauna of British India, including Ceylon
and Burma...

Reptilia and Amphibia, Vol. III: Serpentes
by Malcolm A. Smith.

QL
391.P9
F 27

Fauna de France

16: Polychètes sédentaires, addenda aux
Errantes, Archiannélides, Myzostomaires. Paris.
1927. By Pierre Fauvel.

Faune de l'Empire Francais

See SERIAL FILE

QH 7
F 726

FAURIE, URBAIN

Yoshimatu, Yamamoto

Père Urbain Faurie.

(Trans. of the Nat. Hist. Soc. of Formosa, Vol. 28, No. 177, 1938, pp. 218-226)

QL
Prot.
Polyzoa
Pam. 575

Faustino, Leopoldo A.

Coral Reefs of the Philippine Islands.

(Philippine Journal of Science, Vol. 44, 1931, pp. 291-305)

Faune de l'Union Française

See serial file

Sent to Univ. of Hawaii

Faust, Albert B.

Guide to the materials for American history in Swiss and Austrian archives. Carnegie Inst. of Wash., Pub. No. 220. Washington, 1916, 8vo. pp. 299.

QE
Geology
Pam.
780

Faustino, Leopoldo A

General geology and geologic history of the Philippine Islands; with preliminary geologic map of the Philippine Islands. From Mineral Resources of the Phillipine Islands for 1924-25.

QH 1
M 17

La faune entomologique de l'Ile de la Reunion.- 1

(Mem. Inst. Sci. de Madagascar, Tome VIII, Ser. E, 1957)

[articles by many authors]

QH
548
F 26

Faust, Ernest Carroll

Animal agents and vectors of human disease. 216 text figures, 9 plates... Lea and Febiger Philadelphia. R8vo. 1955c 660 pp.

QE
Geol.Pam.
887

Faustino, Leopoldo A.

General Geology and Geologic History of the Philippine Islands, with Preliminary Geologic Map of the Philippine Islands.

(Separate from the Mineral Resources of the Philippine Islands for 1924 and 1925. Bureau of Science, Manila, 1927) pp. 41-43

GN
Ethn.
Pam.
4446

Faure, Janet

Renascence in Hawaii. (Music and dance of the Far East in Honolulu.)

(Dance Magazine, August 1960, pp. 44-47)

QL
757
F 26

Faust, Ernest Carroll and others

Craig and Faust's Clinical parasitology. By Ernest Carroll Faust, and Paul Farr Russell, with the editorial assistance of David Richard Linicome. Sixth edition, thoroughly revised, 346 illustrations and 7 colored plates. Lea and Febiger. Philadelphia. R8vo. 1958. 1078 pp.

AS
540
P 55

Faustino, Leopoldo A.

Recent Madreporaria of the Philippine Islands.

(Monograph, Bureau of Science, Philippine Islands, No. 22, 1927)

QK
368
J

Faurie, U. (L'Abbé)

Copeland, Edwin Bingham
Hawaiian ferns collected by L'Abbé U. Faurie. in Phil. Journ. Sc. C. Botany IX, 5, 1914. pp. 435-441.

AS
36
I 4

Faust, Ernest Carroll, 1890-

Life history studies on Montana trematodes ... by Ernest Carroll Faust. [Urbana, Ill., University of Illinois, 1918]

120 p. illus. (map) IX pl. 27ᵐᵐ. (*Added t.-p.:* Illinois biological monographs. vol. iv, no. 1, July, 1917) $2.00

"Contributions from the Zoological laboratory of the University of Illinois ... no. 98."

Thesis (PH. D.)—University of Illinois, 1917.

Thesis note on verso of t.-p.

Bibliography: p. 96-101.

\ I. Trematoda.

Library of Congress   QL391.T7F3   18—7039

——— Copy 2.

Copyright A 494276

AS
540
P 55

Faustino, Leopoldo A.

Summary of Philippine Marine and Fresh-Water Mollusks.

(Monograph, Bureau of Science, Philippine Islands, No. 25, 1928)

QK
Bot.Pam.
1690

FAURIE, URBAIN

Kinashi, E.

Japanese plant collector.- Urbain Faurie. (translated title)

(Acta Phytotaxonomica et Geobotanica, 1:315-321, 1932)

Translated into English from the Japanese.

AS
222
G

Faust, J(ohannes)

Curculionidae. (Viaggio de Lamberto Loria nella Papuasia Orientale, XXIII)

(Ann. Mus. Civico di Storia Nat. de Genova, Ser. 2, Vol. 20, 1899, pp. 1-130)

Biblio-
film
31

Fauvel, Albert

Catalogue de Coléoptères de la Nouvelle-Calédonie.

(Bull. Soc. Linneene de Normandie, Ser. 2, Vol. 1, pp. 172-209, 1867)

QK
Bot.
Pam.
2708

FAURIE, URBAIN

Kinashi, E.

Japanese plant collector --Urbain Faurie. 3 type-written pages.

(Translated from Acta Phytotaxonomica et Geobotanica 1:315-321, 1932)

AS
222
G

Faust, J(ohannes)

Viaggio di Leonardo Fea in Birmania e regioni vicine, LX:Curculionidae.

(Annali del Mus. Civico di Storia Nat.di Genova, Ser. 2, Vol. 14 (34), May 15, 1894, pp. 153-370)

QL
Insects
Pam.
1229

Fauvel, Albert

Coléoptères de la Nouvelle-Calédonie recueillis par M. E. Deplanche, 1858-1860.

(Bull. Soc. Linneene de Normandie, Vol. 7, 1861/1862, pp. 154-163 ONLY. Pages of the complete article are 120-185)

PHOTOSTAT

also Bibliofilm 32, of the entire work, pp. 120-185

QL
Insects
Pam.
1207

Fauvel, Albert

    Les Staphylinides de l'Australie et de la
Polynésie. 2nd mémoire.

    (Genova, Mus. Civ., Annali, Tomo 13:1-134,
1878. Original pagination was pp. 465-598)

    [Mémoire 1 is LACKING - same source, Tomo
10, 1877, pp. 168-298]

AS
162
P 23

Fauvel, Pierre

    Une petite collection d'annélides polychètes
des Iles Kerguélen.

    (Bulletin du Muséum National d'Histoire
Naturelle, Tome XXV(3):307-310, 1953)

AS
36
S1

Favre, Ernest, 1845–

    Louis Agassiz: a biographical notice. By Ernest
Favre.

    (*In* Smithsonian institution. Annual report. 1878. Washington, 1879.
23½ᶜᵐ. pp. 236-261)

    "Translated ... by M. A. Henry."
    "From the 'Archives des sciences de la Bibliothèque universelle, Genève,
mai 1877, tome LXIX.'"

    \1. Agassiz, Louis *i. e.* Jean Louis Rodolphe, 1807–1873. 1. Henry,
Mary A., tr.

    S 15–480

    Library of Congress   Q11.S66 1878
    Library, Smithsonian   Institution

QL
391.P9
F 27

Fauvel, Pierre

    Annelida Polychaeta of the Indian Museum,
Calcutta.

    (Mem. Indian Museum, Vol. 12(1), 1932)

QL
391.P9
F 27

Fauvel, Pierre

    Polychètes sédentaires, addenda aux Errantes
Archiannélides, Myzostomaires. (Faune de France,
16) Paris. Paul Lechevalier. 1927. 8vo.
494 pp.

Vol. 2
may be
issued
in 1956

letter-
3/7/55

QK
229
F 27

Card 1

Fawcett, William

    Flora of Jamaica, containing descriptions
of the flowering plants known from the island, by
William Fawcett and Alfred Barton Rendle. With
illustrations.
    Vol. 1: Orchidaceae. 1910.
    "   2: not yet issued   Oct 1, 1937
    "   3: Dicotyledons:Piperaceae to Connara-
ceae. 1914.
    "   4: Dicotyledons: Leguminisae to Calli-
trichaceae. 1920.

    continued on next cd.

AS
145
B

Fauvel, Pierre

    Annélides Polychètes

Van Straelen, V.
    Résultats scientifiques du voyage aux Indes
Orientales Néerlandaises...Léopold de Belgique.
Vol. 2, Fasc. 7, 1931, pp. 1-28.

    (Mem. hors ser. Mus. Roy. d'Hist. Nat.
Belgique)

Q
115
S 56

Fauvel, Pierre

    Polychetes sedentaires de l'expedition du
"Siboga"...par Felix Lesnil et Pierre Fauvel.

Weber, Max
    Uitkomsten...Nederlandsch Oost Indie, 1899-
1900...Siboga...Monographie XXIV² (livr. 133).
1939. 42 pp.

QK
229
F 27

Card 2

Fawcett, William

    Flora of Jamaica...
    Vol. 5: Dicotyledons:Buxaceae to Umbelli-
ferae. 1926.
    "   6: not yet issued.
    Oct 1, 1937
    letter 3/7/55 - may be issued in 1956

    cont. on next card

GC
1
M 73

Fauvel, Pierre

    Annélides Polychètes des Iles Kerguelen,
recueillies par M. Patrice Paulian en 1951.

    (Bull. Inst. Oceanographique, No. 1026,
1953)

QL
406
F 27

(Favanne de Montcerville, Guil. Jac de)

    Catalogue systématique et raisonné, ou
description du magnifique cabinet appartenant ci-
devant à M. le C. de***(La Tour d'Auvergne).
Ouvrage intéressant pour les Naturalistes & pour
les Amateurs de l'Histoire Naturelle, à cause de
sa nomenclature & de la nouvelle méthode de Con-
cholyliologie...par M. de***. Paris. Quillau.
1784. 8vo. xii + 558 pp.

QK
229
F 27

Card 3

Fawcett, William & Rendle, Alfred B.

    Flora of Jamaica (continued)
    Vol. VII - Dicotyledons: Rubiaceae to Compositae.
1936.

    Brit. Mus. (Nat. Hist.) London. 8vo.

AS
162
P 23

Fauvel, P.

    Annélides polychètes recueillies aux îles
Kerguélen par le Dr. Arétas et polychètes du Museum de la même provenance.

    (Bull. Mus. Nat. d'Hist. Nat., ser. 2, Tome
24:294-301,1952)

Favanne de Montcerville

    also
    See under

Dezallier d'Argenville

DU
12
H 77
locked
case

FAWN (SHIP)

Hood, T. H.

    Notes of a cruise in H.M.S. "Fawn" in the
western Pacific in the year 1862. Edinburgh.
1863. 8vo.

QH
147.1
F 26

Fauvel, Pierre

    Annélides Polychètes de Nouvelle-Calédonie
et des Iles Gambier.

    (Faune de l'Empire Francais, VIII, 1947)

DU
98.1
F27

Faveno, Ernest.

    **The history of Australian explora-
tion from 1788 to 1888...by Ernest
Faveno.**

    Sydney, Turner & Henderson, 1888.
474p.   maps.

QL
461
H-1

Faxon, Richard

    Some phases of federal plant quarantine
work in Hawaii. (Presidential address)

    (Proc. Haw. Ent. Soc., Vol. 12:291-300,1945)

AS
552
K

Fauvel, P(ierre)

    Annelides polychaetes du Japon.

    (Mem. Col. Sci., Kyoto Imp. Univ., Ser. B.
Vol. XII, 1936, pp. 41-92)

DU
12
L 31
Locked
case

FAVORITE (ship)

Laplace, Cyrille Pierre Théodore

    Voyage autour du monde par les mers de
l'Inde et de Chine, exécuté sur la corvette de l'
etat La Favorite, pendant les années 1830-1832.
Tomes 1-5 and folio atlas. Paris, Arthus Bertrand. 1833-1839.

QL
1
H2

Faxon, Walter, 1848–

    ... Brewster's warbler (*Helminthophila leucobronchia-
lis*) A hybrid between the golden-winged warbler (*Helminthophila chrysoptera*) and the blue-winged warbler
(*Helminthophila pinus*). By Walter Faxon. Cambridge,
U. S. A., Printed for the Museum, 1913.

    1 p. l., p. (311)-316. 30½ᶜᵐ. (Memoirs of the Museum of comparative
zoölogy at Harvard college. vol. XL, no. 6)

    \1. Warblers. Brewster's warbler

    Title from Univ. of Chicago   QL1f.H375 vol. 40   A 21–466
    Printed by L. C.

QL
Crus
Pam
#73

Faxon, Walter

Notes on North American Crayfishes
Family Astacidae.

Proc. of U. S. N. Mus. Vol. XII. No. 785

pp. 619-634, 1890

Wash. 1890   8vo pp. 619-634.

AP
2
S 35

Fay-Cooper Cole, architect of anthropology.

(Science, 135(3502): 412-413, 1962)

DU
620
P 22

Bishop, Brenda

Priceless treasures return.

(Paradise of the Pacific, Dec 1958:18-19)

QL
112

Faxon, Walter, 1848–

... Notes on the crayfishes in the United States National museum and the Museum of comparative zoölogy, with descriptions of new species and subspecies, to which is appended a catalogue of the known species and subspecies. By Walter Faxon. With thirteen plates. Cambridge, U. S. A., Printed for the Museum, 1914.

2 p. l., p. [351]-427, 1 l. 13 pl. (part col.) 30½ᶜᵐ. (Memoirs of the Museum of comparative zoölogy at Harvard college. vol. XL, no. 8)
Each plate preceded by leaf with descriptive letterpress.
1. Crayfish. 2. U. S. National museum. 3. Harvard university. Museum of comparative zoölogy.

A 21-468

Title from Univ. of Chicago   QL1f.H375 vol. 40
Printed by L. C.
[4]

PL
802
F 28

Feag-hoiporakkiug foou ne os gagaja na
namauriga, Iesu Karisito.   London. Printed
for the British and Foreign Bible Society. 1884.
410 pp. 8vo.

(Rotuma,   . Bible)

GN
Ethn.
Pam.
3857

Bardwell, Francis

Perkins feather cape. n.d. (1)1-5 typewritten pages.

FEATHER CAPES   HAWAII

QL
Crus
Pam
#74

Faxon, Walter
                              Astacidae
Observations on the Astacidae
in the U. S. Nat. Museum – and in
the Museum of Comparative Zoology,
with descriptions of new species.
Proc. U. S. N. M. Vol. XX, pp. 643-694,
1898.

FEB 23 1911

Washington   1898, 8vo pp. 643-694
Plates LXII - LXX.

GN
671.H2
H 23

FEASTS   HAWAII

Handy, E. S. C., and others

Ancient Hawaiian Civilization, pp.58-65:
Feasts and Holidays, by E. S. C. Handy.

DU
620
P 22

FEATHER CAPES   HAWAII

Bishop, Brenda

Journeying feather capes.

(Paradise of the Pacific, Holiday issue,
1959:28-31)

[Issued Nov.1958]

QL
1
H1

Faxon, Walter, 1848–

... Relics of Peale's museum. By Walter Faxon. Cambridge, Mass., The Museum, 1915.

p. [117]-148. 24½ᶜᵐ. (Bulletin of the Museum of comparative zoölogy at Harvard college. vol. LIX, no. 3)

1. Peale's museum, Philadelphia.

17-31400

Library of Congress   QL1.H3 vol. 59, no: 3

DU
Pac.Pam.
856

FEASTS   KAPINGAMARANGI

Moore, W. Robert

Feast day in Kapingamarangi.

(National Geographic Magazine, Vol. 97(4):
523-537, April, 1950)

GN
2.S
P 76

FEATHER CAPES   HAWAII

Buck, Peter H.

The local evolution of Hawaiian feather
capes and cloaks.

(Journal of the Polynesian Society, Vol. 53,
No. 1, 1944, pp. 1-16)

QL
1
H2

Faxon, Walter

A revision of the Astacidae. Part 1,
the genera Cambarus and Astacus. Harvard
Mus. Comp. Zool. Mem., Vol. X, No.4, 1885
pp vi, 186, pls. 1- 10.

GN
1
A

FEASTS   NEW IRELAND

Powdermaker, Hortense

Feasts in New Ireland: the social functions
of eating.

(Am. Anthropologist, 34:236-247, 1932)

GN
Ethn.Pam.
3934

FEATHER CAPES   HAWAII

Fred Malulani Beckley Kahea's making of a
feather cape.

IN Collection of clippings gathered by
Martha W. Beckwith, p. 27

QL
1
H 2

Faxon, Walter

Agassiz, Alexander

Selections from embryological monographs...
I.- Crustacea, by Walter Faxon.

(Memoirs of the Museum of Comparative Zoology, Harvard, Vol. 9, no. 1, 1882)
---Bibliography:Bull. MCZH, Vol. IX:6

DU
620
P 22

FEATHER CAPES   BISHOP MUSEUM

Ancient Hawaiian feather work to be on display during Aloha Week.

(Paradise of the Pacific, Oct. 1958:2)

AM
101
B 52

FEATHER CAPES   HAWAII

Henking, Karl H.

Ein Königsornat von Hawaii im Bernischen
Historischen Museum.

(Jahrbuch des Bernischen Museums in Bern,
34:231-244, 1954)

QL
1
H2

Faxon, Walter, 1848–

... The stalk-eyed *Crustacea*. By Walter Faxon ... Cambridge, Printed for the Museum, 1895.

292 p. plates (part col.) fold. map. 29ᶜᵐ. (Memoirs of the Museum of comparative zoölogy at Harvard college, vol. XVIII)

... Reports on an exploration off the west coasts of Mexico, Central and South America, and off the Galapagos Islands ... by the U. S. Fish commission steamer "Albatross," during 1891 ... xv.

1. Crustacea. 2. Albatross (Steamer) I. Title.   A 19-1056

Title from Univ. of Chicago   QL1.H375 vol. 18 Printed by L. C.
[3]

DU
620
P22

FEATHER CAPES   ELGIN CAPE

Ancient Hawaiian feather work to be on display during Aloha Week.

(Paradise of the Pacific, Oct. 1958:2)

F
72.N2
N 19

FEATHER CAPES   HAWAII

Lederer, Richard M.

An Hawaiian feathered cape.

(Proceedings of the Nantucket Historical
Association, 1950:14-15)

DU 620 P

FEATHER CAPES   HAWAII

Smith, Roger M.

Crafts of ancient Hawaii.

(Paradise of the Pacific, March 1953, pp. 18, 19, 34, 40)

[cover design is a feather cape, in color]

GN 2.1 A-M

FEATHER WORK   HAWAII

Beasley, H. G.

An unrecorded feather cape.

(Man, vol. 30, 1930, no. 140, p. 197, pl. M)

GN 2.1 T 89

also GN Ethn.Pam 3735

FEATHER WORK   HAWAII

Dellenbach, Marguerite

Un manteau de plumes ancien inédit des îles Hawaï.

(Revista del Instituto de Etnologia, Universidad de Tucumán, Tomo II, 1932, pp. 539-541)

AM Mus. Pam. 293

FEATHER CAPES   HAWAII

Where are the Hawaiian feather cloaks and capes? 3 mimeographed pp. 1953

GN Ethn.Pam. 4129

FEATHERWORK   HAWAII

Bernice P. Bishop Museum, Special Aloha Week Exhibit, October 17 to December 17, 1958.

[brief description of the Elgin cloak and helmet; Kiwalao, Kalanikauikaalaneo; Kamehameha I; Kearny; Kekaulike-nui; Lady Franklin; Liliuokalani cloaks]

DU 621 H 3

FEATHERWORK   HAWAII

Emerson, Nathaniel Bright

The bird hunters of ancient Hawaii.

(Hawaiian Annual, 1895:101-111)

GN Ethn. Pam. 4464

FEATHER CLOAKS   HAWAII

Wasner, Franz

Literarische Zeugen für eine Federkrone der Päpste im Mittelalter.

(Reprint, Ephemerides Liturgicae, Vol. 74:409-427, 1960)

(Bishop Museum mentioned)

GN 671.H2 B 85

AS 763 B-m

Reading Room

FEATHER WORK HAWAII

Brigham, William Tufts

Hawaiian Feather Work.

(Memoirs of the Bernice P. Bishop Museum, Vol. 1, No. 1, 1899)

Additional Notes on Hawaiian Feather Work, (Memoirs of the Bernice P. Bishop Museum, Vol. 1 No. 5 and Vol. VII, No. 1, 1903, 1918)

GN Ethn. Pam. 3747

FEATHER WORK   HAWAII

Gill, Lorin Tarr

Featherwork of old Hawaii. Articles 1-4,6,8 (out of 1-9)

(Honolulu Star-Bulletin, no date)

Feather-stars

see

CRINOIDEA

DU 620 P

GN Pam. 3438

FEATHERWORK   HAWAII

Buck, Peter H.

The feathercapes and cloaks of old Polynesia; the feather capes and cloaks of old Hawaii.

(Paradise of the Pacific, March and April, 1943)

[a carbon copy of article sent]

GN 671.H2 H 23

FEATHERWORK   HAWAII

Handy, E. S. C., and others

Ancient Hawaiian Civilization, pp. 131-140: Featherwork and Clothing, by Lahilahi Webb.

AS 36 S 55

FEATHER WORK   AZTECS

Woodward, Arthur

Feather working among the Aztecs.

(Bull. Southern Calif. Acad. Sci., Vol. 46: 1-25, 1947)

GN 2.S P 76

FEATHERWORK   HAWAII

Buck, Peter H.

The local evolution of Hawaiian feather capes and cloaks.

(Journal of the Polynesian Society, Vol. 53, No. 1, 1944, pp. 1-16)

QH 1 N 28

12)

FEATHERWORK   HAWAII

Les manteaux de plumes aux îles Hawaii.

(Le Naturaliste, 2 série, No. 284, pp. 11-12)

AS 763 B-s

FEATHERWORK   HAWAII

Ball, Stanley, C.

Bishop Museum handbook, Part II: Clothing.

(Bernice P. Bishop Museum, Special Publication, no. 9, 1924)

DU Pac. Pam. 109

FEATHER WORK HAWAII

Christy, Miller

The rare feather work of Hawaii.

(Windsor Mag., pp. 725-730. n.d.)

GN 1 B

FEATHERWORK   HAWAII

Nevermann, Hans

Zur Geschichte des hawaiischen Federmantels.

(Baessler-Archiv, n.f., Bd. 1:83-85, 1952)

GN 2.1 A-m

FEATHERWORK   HAWAII

Beasley, H. G.

Joseph Banks' Feather Cape from Hawaii, by H. G. Beasley and H. J. Braunholtz.

(Man, Vol. 33, 1933, No. 1)

AS 36 A 5

FEATHER WORK   HAWAII

(Cover design and short description. Natural History, vol.38, Dec.1936)

AS 80 R2-b

and GN Ethn.Pam 3882

FEATHERWORK   HAWAI-I

Roquette- Pinto, Edgardo

Ummanto real de Hawaii. Rio de Janeiro, Bol. I, 1923, pp 69 - 77.

Storage Case 3

FEATHERWORK HAWAII

Stokes, John F. G.

Featherwork, Hawaii, including excerpts from accounts of old voyages in re featherwork.

GN 671.N56 R 84

FEATHER WORK MAORI

Roth, H. Ling

The Maori Mantle, and some comparative notes on N. W. American twined work. With over 250 line illustrations and diagrams and 22 collotype plates. Halifax. Bankfield Museum. 1923. R8vo. 120 pp.

GN Ethn.Pam. 3159

Q 101 P 18

FEATHER WORK POLYNESIA

Stokes, John F. G.

Notes on Polynesian feather work.

(B.P. Bishop Mus., Special Publications, no. 7, 1921, pp. 75-85.)

(Being Proc. Pan-Pacific Science Congress, 1st, Honolulu, 1920)

Storage Case 3

FEATHER WORK- HAWAIIAN ISLANDS

Stokes, J. F. G.

Notes on Hawaiian feather work.

GN 2.S Po

FEATHERWORK MAORI

Skinner, W. H.

Decorative featherwork.

(Journal of the Polynesian Society, Vol. 41, pp. 214-215, 1932)

GN 2.S P 76

FEATHER WORK POLYNESIA

Stokes, John F. G.

Notes on Polynesian feather work.

(Journal of the Polynesian Soc., Vol. 34, 1925, pp. 24-35)

Storage Case 3

FEATHER WORK- HAWAIIAN ISLANDS

Stokes, J. F. G.

1 roll colored plates on feather work.

GN Ethn.Pam. 3454

FEATHERWORK MEXICO

Garcia.Granados, Rafael

Mexican feather mosaics.

(This Week in Mexico, Dec. 4-10, 1943, pp. 25-30)

GN 2.M A

FEATHER-WORK--SOUTH AMERICA.

Mead, Charles Williams, 1845-

... Technique of some South American feather-work. By Charles W. Mead. New York, The Trustees, 1907.

1 p. l., 17 p. illus., iv pl. 24½ᶜᵐ. (Anthropological papers of the American museum of natural history. vol. I, pt. 1)

1. Feather-work—South America.

11-28859 Revised

Library of Congress   GN2.A27 vol. 1, pt. 1

Local Newspapers

In Locked Closet Upper Floor

FEATHERWORK HAWAII

Swan, James

Letter to Prof. W. D. Alexander dated Feb. 25, 1890. In Haw. Gaz. Apr. 1, 1890.

(Letter relates to the Voyage of the Columbia 1787-1790. Mentions Hawaiian prince and the feather cloak he wore in Boston, 1790).

GN 2.I A-4

FEATHERWORK NEW HEBRIDES

Beasley, Harry G.

Notes on red-feather money from Santa Cruz Group, New Hebrides.

(Journal of the Royal Anthropological Institute of Great Britain and Ireland, Vol. 66, 1936 pp. 379-391)

GN 2.S P 76

FEATHERWORK TAHITI

Buck, Peter H.

The feather cloak of Tahiti.

(Journal of the Polynesian Society, Vol. 52, 1943, pp. 12-15)

AM Mus. Pam. 293

FEATHER WORK HAWAII

Where are the Hawaiian feather cloaks and capes? 3 mimeographed pp. 1953

AS 750 D 45-3

Feather-work---New Zealand.

Te Rangihiroa.

In his Maori art of weaving. in Dom. Mus. Bul. III. pp 83-4.

AS 36 P1

FEATHERWORK -- TAHITI

Hall, H. U.

A souvenir of the great explorers. In Univ. Penn. Mus. Journ. Vol.16, 1925, pp 182 - 197.

GN 1 A

FEATHER-WORK --INDIANS OF NORTH / AMERICA

Lathrop, S. K.

American feather-decorated mats. In Am. Anthrop. Vol. 25, No.3, 1923.

GN Ethn. Pam. # 406

Feather-work. Peru

Giglioli, Henry Hillyer

QL 1 C15

FEATHERS.

Chandler, Asa Crawford, 1891-

... Modifications and adaptations to function in the feathers of *Circus hudsonius*, by Asa C. Chandler. Berkeley, University of California press, 1914.

p. ₍329₎-376. pl. 16-20. 27ᶜᵐ. (University of California publications in zoology. v. 11, no. 13)

"Literature cited": p. 366.

1. Feathers. 2. Adaptation (Biology)

A 14-858

Title from Univ. of Calif.   Library of Congress

GN Ethn. Pam. 621

FEATHER-WORK -- MAORI

Buck, P. H.

Review.. "The Maori mantel" by H. Ling Roth. Poly. Soc. Journ. Vol. XXXIII pp 1-8, 1924.

DU 620 P

GN Pam 3438

FEATHERWORK POLYNESIA

Buck, Peter H.

The feather capes and cloaks of old Polynesia; the feather capes and cloaks of old Hawaii.

(Paradise of the Pacific, March and April, 1943)

[a carbon copy of article sent]

QL 1 C 15

FEATHERS

Chandler, Asa Crawford, 1891-

... A study of the structure of feathers, with reference to the taxonomic significance, by Asa C. Chandler. Berkeley, University of California press, 1916.

cover-title, p. ₍243₎-446. illus, diagr, pl. 13-37. 27½ᶜᵐ. (University of California publications in zoology. v. 13, no. 11)

Bibliography: p. 392-396.

1. Feathers.   I. Title.

A 16-612

Title from Univ. of Calif.   Library of Congress

GN
Pam
2769

FEATHERS

Extracts from William Ellis: regarding the use and significance of feathers. Compiled by J. F. G. Stokes

26 typed pages.

GN
1
O 15

FECUNDITY

Ashley-Montagu, M. F.

The infertility of the unmarried in primitive societies.

(Oceania, Vol. 8, 1937, pp. 15-26)

AS
496
F

Federated Malay States Museums

Journal

Vol. I, 1905 -

See serial file

AS
36
S2

FEATHERS
Mascha, Ernst.

... The structure of wing-feathers, by Doctor E. Mascha.

(*In* Smithsonian institution. Smithsonian miscellaneous collections. Washington, 1907. 24½ᵐ. vol. XLVIII (Quarterly issue, vol. III) p. 1-30. pl. I-XVI)

Publication 1575.
Originally published May 6, 1905.
The original German text, with title "Über die schwungfedern," pub. in Zeitschrift für wissenschaftliche zoologie. Leipzig, 1904. bd. 77, p. 606-651.
"List of authors consulted and quoted": p. 26-27.

1. Feathers.   I. Smithsonian institution. Hodgkins fund.   II. Title.

16-11026

Library of Congress   Q11.S7 vol. 48
——— Copy 2.
——— Separate.   QL697.M4
At head of cover-title: Hodgkins fund.

Z
5351
F 29

Fedde, Friedrich

Allgemeine und spezielle Morphologie und Systematik der Siphonogamen. 1905.

(Botanischer Jahresbericht, Vol. 33, 1905, pp. 239-598)

AG
500
P 11

FEDERATION OF MALAYA

Sutter, John O.

Federation of Malaya and State of Singapore.

(Pacific Scientific Information, No. 2, 1961)

QL
1
C15

Feathers ~ Structure

Chandler, Asa C.

Study of the structure of feathers, with reference to their taxonomic significance.

Univ. of Cal. Pub. in Zool. XIII, 11, 1916, pp. 243-446, illus.

QK
11
F 29

Fedde, Friedrich and others

Novorum generum, specierum, varietatu formarumque Siphonogamarum Index. ex Just's Botanischer Jahresbericht.

Library has
Index for 1904 , Berlin, 1905
    "   1906   "   1906
    "   1908   "   1908
         1910   "   1910

GN
Pam
#459

Fedtschenko, Frau

A. Fedtschenko's Reisen in Turkestan, 1868-71, ex Petermann's Geogr. Mitt., 1874, Heft VI.

QH
104
U 58

Featurettes from the National Park Service.

(U.S.D.I. News Release for July 7, 1963)

QK
97
E 58

Fedde, Friedrich

Papaveraceae-Hypecoideae et Papaveraceae-Papaveroideae.

Engler, Adolf

... Das Pflanzenreich...IV. 104. 1909. (Heft 40.)

DU
missions
Pam.
98

Feeney, Thomas John   (-1955)   (Catholic missionary)

(Letter), Oct. 1952. 4 pp. and a map. (address: P. O. Box 197, Planetarium Station, New York 24, N.Y.)

[report on his missionary work in Micronesia]

GF
31
F28

Febvre, Lucien

A geographical introduction to history.

London, Kegan Paul, 1925. 388p.

QK
1
F-29

Fedde, Friedrich

Repertorium Specierum Novarum Regni Vegetabilis.

Band I-   1905-
Beihefte I- Band I   1914-
Sonderbeiheft A,B,C

For current volumes see serial file under "Repertorium..."

DU
500
F 29

Feeney, Thomas J., S. J., D. D.

Letters from Likiep. (Pandick Press. New York, 1952c) 8vo. vii+259 pp.

QL
1
C 15

FECES - ANALYSIS
Boeck, William Charles, 1894-

... A rapid method for the detection of protozoan cysts in mammalian faeces, by William C. Boeck. Berkeley, University of California press, 1917.

cover-title, p. [145]-149. 27½ᵐ. (University of California publications in zoology. v. 18, no. 9)

"Literature cited": p. 149.

1. Feces—Analysis.   I. Title.

A 18-114

Title from Univ. of Calif.   Library of Congress

QK
11
F 29

Fedde & Schlechter.

Siphonogamarum Index. for 1904 Berlin, 1905.

Also for 1906 , 1908, 1910.

DU
Pac.Pam.
717
a,b,c,d

Feeney, Thomas J.   S.J.

(Letters 1,4-6, 1947-1948, from the Marshall Islands)

and several issues, 1954, without series title or number.

[Catholic missionary]

QK
827
M 92

FECUNDATION IN PLANTS
Mottier, David Myers.

Fecundation in plants, by David M. Mottier ... Washington, The Carnegie institution of Washington, 1904.

viii, 187 p. illus. 26ᵐ. (On verso of t.-p.: Carnegie institution of Washington. Publication no. 15)

Bibliography: p. 181-187.

1. Botany—Embryology. 2. Plants, Sex in. 3. Karyokinesis.   I. Title.

5-4158

Library of Congress   QK827.M9
——— Copy 2.

QL
752
U 58 b

Federal aid in fish and wildlife restoration: annual report on Dingell-Johnson and Pittman-Robertson programs for the fiscal year ending June 30, 1962.

(U.S.D.I., Bur. of Sport Fisheries and Wildlife, v + 83 pp., 1963)

DU
Pac
Pam
#258

Feer, Henri

Les Iles Havaïennes, ex Annales de l'Extreme Orient et de l'Afrique, Paris, 1889.

GN
Ethn.
Pam.
3398

FEET ANATOMY

Weidenreich, Franz

The external tuberole of the human tuber calcanei.

(Am. Jour. Phys. Anthrop., Vol. 26, 1940, pp. 473-486)

DU
620
P

Feher, Joseph (artist)

Carroll, K. M.

Beyond the Hawaiian horizon. The island of Yap.

(Paradise of the Pacific, pp. 43, 104, Annual Holiday Edition 1955)

[illustrated by watercolors by Joseph Feher]

Clipping
File

FEHER, JOSEPH

Wright, Carl

New and noteworth in the arts: biography of Joseph Feher.

(Honolulu Star-Bulletin, 8/31/63)

GN
161
V 81

FEET CHINA

Virchow, Hans

Der fuss der Chinesin: anatomische untesuchung... Bonn. 1913. Ob4to.

DU
620
P

Feher, Joseph artist

(Micronesian number of the Paradise of the Pacific, Vol. 63, No. 5, May 1951)

GN
Pam
2396

Fehlinger, H

Die Juden. From Politisch-Anthrop. Revue, jahrg. X, n.1, 1911.

AP
2
N 4

FEET MELANESIA

Feet of Melanesians and Europeans.

(Nature, Vol. 145, 1940, pp. 153)

AM
101
B 62

Feher, Joseph

Portrait of Dr. Alexander Spoehr, by Feher.

(The Conch Shell, Vol. 1(3):36, 1963)

GN
Pam
2065

Fehlinzer, Hans

Kreuzungen beim menschen. From Arch. f. rassen und gesell-biol. heft 4, 1911.

GN
Pam
821

FEET JAPAN

Adachi, Buntaro

Die fussknochen der Japaner (anatomische untersuchungen an Japanern VII). From Mittheil. d. med fakultat d. k. Japanischen Univ. zu Tokyo, 1905.

Storage
Case
1

Feher, Joseph

Portraits of Charles and Bernice Bishop, by Joseph Feher, for the Trustees of the Bernice P. Bishop Estate. PRELIMINARY SKETCH.

The paintings are in the Trustees' Office, in the Bishop Estate Building, Halekauwila St.

GN
Pam
1167

Fehlinger, H.

Neues von der biologie des menschen. From Nat. Wochenschrift, n.f., bd.12, n.23, 1913.

GN
2.S
O 15

FEET PACIFIC

Palès, Léon and others

Le peid dans les races humaines. Les Melanesiens de la Nouvelle-Caledonie et des iles Loyalty, compares aux Francais, Malgaches, Melano Africains et Vietnamiens. Etude sur le vivant. Par Leon Pales, Claude Chippaux et Henri Pineau.

(Jour. de la Soc. des Oceanistes, 16:45-90, 1960)

DU
620
K 15

Feher, Joseph (artist)

Portraits of Charles Reed Bishop and Bernice Pauahi Bishop.

(Kamehameha Schools, Annual Report, 1955/56 pp. 2-3)

QK
Bot.Pam.
2471

FE'I POLYNESIA

MacDaniels, L. H.

A study of the fe'i banana and its distribution with reference to Polynesian migrations.

(B. P. Bishop Mus., Bull. 190, pp. 1-56, 10 pl., 1947)

AP
2
N 4

Feet of Melanesians and Europeans.

(Nature, Vol. 145, 1940, pp. 153)

GR
380.1
L 96

Reading
Room
R8vo.

AS 763 B 62

Feher, Joseph

Luomala, Katharine

Voices on the wind. Illustrated by Joseph Feher. Bishop Museum Press. Honolulu. (1955) 191 pp. 8 plates.

S
17.H5
H 38

FEIJOA SELLOWIANA

MacCaughey, Vaughan

The pineapple guava, a delicious subtropical fruit.

(Haw. For. and Agric., Vol. 14, 1917, pp. 366-368)

AM
101
B 62

FEHER, JOSEPH

Bishop, Brenda

Hawaii's history and the New York World's Fair.

(The Conch Shell, Vol. 1(4):39-43, 1963)

DU
620
P 22

FEHER, JOSEPH

Spoehr, Alexander

The artist as historian.

(Paradise of the Pacific, 72(10):68-71, 1960)

QL
671
I

Feilden, H. W.

On the birds of Barbadoes.

(Ibis, Ser. 6, Vol. 1, 1889, pp. 477-503)

AS
36
S1

Feilner, John, d. 1864.
Exploration in upper California in 1860, under the auspices of the Smithsonian institution. By John Feilner, U. S. A.
(In Smithsonian institution. Annual report. 1864. Washington, 1865. 23½ᶜᵐ. p. (421)-430)

1. Zoology—California.

S 15-172

Library of Congress   Q11.S66 1864
Library, Smithsonian   Institution

QH
1
P 11

FELISACUS
Woodward, T. E.

Further notes on Felisacus Distant (Heteroptera; Miridae; Bryocorinea)

(Pacific Science, 12(3):236-240, 1958)

QL
1
V 64

Fell, H. Barraclough

Deep-sea echinoderms of New Zealand.

(Zool. Publ., Victoria Univ. of Wellington, No. 24, 1958)

GR
Folklore
Pam.
83

Felbermayer, Federico
Historias y leyendas de la Isla de Pascua. (Valparaiso. 1948.) 8vo. 93 pp.

QE
Pam
#123

Felix, Johannes
Korallen aus ägyptischen Miocänbildungen, ex Zeitschr. d. Deutsch. geolog. Gesellschaft, Bd. 55, Jahrs. 1903.

QL
1
V 64

Fell, H. Barraclough

Echinoderms from southern New Zealand.

(Victoria University College, Zool. Pub. No. 18, 1952)

AS
182
P 23

Feldman, Geneviève
Sur quelques Céramiacées de Nouvelle-Zélande

(Bull. Mus. Nat. d'Hist. Nat., Paris, Vol. 22 (ser. 2); 131-141, 1950)

QL
Protozoa
to
Polyzoa
Pam
428

Felix, Johannes
Korallen aus portugisischem senon. (Abdruck a.d. Zeitschr. d. Deutsch. geolog. gessellschaft, Bd.55, 1903.)

AS
750
D 67 c

Fell, H. Barraclough

Echinoderms from the Subantarctic Islands of New Zealand: Asteroidea, Ophiuroidea, and Echinoidea.

(Cape Exp., Sci. Res. New Zealand Subantarctic Exp., 1941-45, No. 18, 1953)

QK
567
S 64

Feldmann, Jean
Ecology of marine Algae. Translated by Maxwell S. Doty.
IN
Smith, Gilbert M. editor
Manual of phycology; an introduction to the Algae and their biology. 1951. pp. 313-334.

QE
Pam
#224

Felix, Johannes
Über eine untertertiäre Korallenfaunaaus der Gegend von Barcelona, ex Palaeontographica, Bd. LVI, 1909.

AS
750
D 67 r

Fell, H. Barraclough

Echinoderms from the Subantarctic Islands of New Zealand: Asteroidea, Ophiuroidea, and Echinoidea.

(Records of the Dominion Museum, Vol. 2(2): 73-111, 1953)

DU
625.2
T 32

Feldwisch, Walter F. and others
Water resources (of Hawaii); Climate...by W. F. Feldwisch; Surface-water resources, by Max H. Carson...
Territorial Planning Board, Hawaii, First Progress Report...Honolulu, 1939, pp. 110-152.

AS
28
E 85

Felix, R. P. s.m.
Essai d'etablissement des missionaries a Yaté

(Etudes Mélanésiennes, n.s., 3rd year, no. 5: 5-39, 1951)

QL
338.N
F 31

Fell, H. B. and others

The first century of New Zealand zoology, 1769-1868, comprising abstracts from the early works on New Zealand fauna. Compiled by H. B. Fell and others, and issued from the Department of Zoology, Victoria University College, Wellington. July, 1953. mimeographed. 4to.

[Cook, Vancouver, etc.]

AM
Mus.Pam.
419

The Feleti Memorial Teacher Training College, Utulei, Tutuila, American Samoa. Bulletin No. 3, 1959-60. 18 pp.

GN
Pam
1607

Felkin, Robert W.
Notes on the Madi or Moru tribe of Central Africa. From Proc. Royal Soc. Edinburgh, 1883-84.

QH
1
T 88

Fell, H. Barraclough

A key to the sea urchins of New Zealand.

(Tuatara, 1(3):6-13, 1948) and ibid, 3(1); 42, 1950)

QL
627
U-b

Felin, Frances E.
Population heterogeneity in the Pacific pilchard.

(U. S. Dept. of the Interior, Fish and Wildlife Service, Fishery Bull. 86, 1954)

[Sardinops caerulea]

GN
Pam
2595

Felkin, Robert W.
Ueber lage und stellung der frau bei der Geburt. Inaugural dissert... Facul. Marburg, 1885.

AS
750
N 56

Fell, H. Barraclough

New genera and species of Ophiuroidea from Antarctica.

(Trans. of the R. Soc. of New Zealand, Vol. 88(4):839-841, 1961)

GN
2.1
A-m

Fell, H. Barraclough

The pictographic art of the ancient Maori of New Zealand.

(Man, Vol. 41, 1941, No. 61)

(comment on this article, Man, July-Aug., 1942, no. 55)

QL
463
F 32

Felt, Ephraim Porter

Insects affecting park and woodland trees. Vol. 1-2. 1905, 1907. Albany.

(Mem. 8, New York State Education Dept.; and 59th Ann. Rept., New York State Museum, 1905, Vol. 4)

FENI ISLAND   PHYSICAL ANTHROPOLOGY

See

PHYSICAL ANTHROPOLOGY   FENI ISLAND

QH
1
T 88

Fell, H. Barraclough

Starfishes of New Zealand.

(Tuatara, 7(3):127-142; 1959)

AS
36
S4

Felt, Ephraim Porter, 1868–

New genera and species of gall midges. By E. Porter Felt ...

(In U. S. National museum. Proceedings. Washington, 1915. 23½ᶜᵐ. v. 48, p. 195-211. illus.)

Asphondyliariae
1. Gall-gnats.

15-24776

Library of Congress   Q11.U55 vol. 48

FENI ISLAND   TATTOOING

See

TATTOOING   FENI ISLAND

QL
1
V 64

Fell, H. Barraclough

Synoptic keys to the genera of Ophiuroidea.

(Zool. Publ. Victoria University of Wellington, No. 26, 1960)

QL
461
H 1

Felt, E. P. (Ephraim Porter)

A new species of gall midge predacious on mealybugs (Dipt.)

(Haw. Ent. Soc., Proc., Vol. 10, 1938, pp. 43-)

QL
Insects
Pam.
1395

Fennah, R. G.

Fulgoroidea of Fiji.

(Bernice P. Bishop Museum, Bull. 202, 1950)

AM
Mus.
Pam.
316

Felland, Nordis

The American Geographical Society Library.

(The Professional Geographer, Jan. 1955: 6-9)

QL
Insects
Pam.
1127

Felt, Ephraim Porter

Scale insects of importance and list of the species in New York State.

(New York State Museum, Bull. No. 46, Vol. 9, 1901)

QL
Insect
Pam.
1878

Fennah, R. G.

Fulgoroidea of south-eastern Polynesia.

(Trans. R. Ent. Soc. London, 110(6): 117-220, 1958)

AG
25
Fe

Feller, F. E.

Nouveau dictionnaire de poche Francais et Anglais. Vol. II. Fr. - Ang. Leipzig. 1898. pp 311.

AS
36
S
and
QM
117
Fe
F 68

FEMUR
Foote, James Stephen, 1851–

... A contribution to the comparative histology of the femur, by J. S. Foote ... ed. by Aleš Hrdlička ... Washington, Smithsonian institution, 1916.

ix, 242 p. 19 pl. 33½ᶜᵐ. (Smithsonian contributions to knowledge. v. 35, no. 3)

Publication no. 2382.

1. Femur. 2. Bone.   i. Hrdlička, Aleš, 1869–   ed.

16-26843

Library of Congress   Q11.S68 vol. 35, no. 3

QL
461
B 86

Fennah, R. G.

A generic revision of Achilidae (Homoptera: Fulgoroidea), with descriptions of new species.

(Bull. Brit. Mus. (Nat. Hist.), Vol. 1(1): 3-170, 1950)

QE
75
W

Fellows, Abraham Lincoln, 1864–

... Water resources of the state of Colorado, by A. L. Fellows. Washington, Gov't print. off., 1902.

151 p., 1 l. illus., xiv pl. (incl. map) 23ᶜᵐ. (U. S. Geological survey. Water-supply and irrigation paper no. 74)

Subject series: I, Irrigation, 14.

1. Irrigation—Colorado.

G S 5-17

Library, U. S. Geol.   survey

GN
70
W18

FEMUR
Walkhoff, Otto

Studien uber die entwickelungsmechanik des primatenskelettes.

Weisbaden, Kreidel, 1904.   58p. pls.

QL
595.M1
I 59

Fennah, R. G.

Homoptera:Fulgoroidea
IN
Insects of Micronesia, Vol. 6(3), 1956

GN
Ethn.
Pam.
4408

FELS, WILLI

Skinner, H. D.

Willi Fels, C.M.G., 1858-1946. Otago Museum, Dunedin, 1946. 13pp.

GN
Ethn.Pam.
3228

Feng, Han Yi

The Chinese kinship system. A dissertation ...Univ. of Penn.   1937.

(Harvard Journal of Asiatic Studies, Vol. 2, No. 2, 1937, pp. 141-275)

QL
671
E 39

Fennell, Chester

At the nest of the black-tailed gull.

(The Elepaio, Vol. 11(4):19-21; (5):26-28; (6):32-33, 1950)

[in Japan]

QL
671
E 39

Fennell, Chester

    Birding in Japan (excerpted from a letter).

    (The Elepaio, Vol. 9(6):30-31; (7):33-35, 1949)

QE
Pam
#34

Fenner, Clarence N.

    The mode of formation of certain Gneisses in the highlands of New Jersey, ex Journ. of Geol., vol. XXII, Sept.-Oct; and Oct-Nov., 1914.

QL
Insect
Pam.
1438

Fenwick, E. M.

    On Macrophylla pubens Peringuey (Coleoptera, Scarabaeidae, Melolonthinae)

    (Journal Ent. Soc. of Southern Africa, Vol. 9:24-30, 1947)

QL
671
C 74

Fennell, Chester M.

    Birds of southern Korea.

    The Condor, 54(2):101-110, 1952)

QE
Pam
#475

Fenner, Clarence N.

    The origin and mode of emplacement of the great tuff deposit of the Valley of Ten Thousand Smokes, ex Nat. Geog. Soc. Katmai Ser., no. 1, 1923.

Q
115
W 95
locked
case

Fenzl, E.

Wüllerstorf-Urbair, Bernhard

    Reise der Oesterreichischen Fregatte Novara um die Erde...1857-1859.
    Botanischer Theil. Sporenpflanzen, redigirt von E. Fenzl. 1866-1870. Wien. 4to.

Reading
Room

Fennel, Eric A.

    Periodicals on medical, surgical and allied subjects in libraries of Honolulu. Honolulu, [The Clinic], 1930. 12p.

QC
801
Ca
and
QE
Pam
475

Fenner, Clarence N.

    The origin and mode of emplacement of the Great Tuff deposit of the Valley of Ten Thousand Smokes. Carnegie Inst. of Washington, Geophysical Laboratory, No. 480, 1923.

GN
Ethn.Pam.
4121

Fepulea'i (Leoso), E. R.

    Samoan culture (Mataupu Samoa). Translated into English, by the students of Feleti School. folio. mimeographed. 22 pp. rec'd 1944

G
51
W 17

Fenner, Charles

    Australian trees and shrubs.

    (Walkabout, Vol. 22(1):19-20, January, 1956)

G
159
C 15

Fenton, Edward

Callander, John

    Terra Australis Cognita...Vol. 1, pp. 378-412: Fenton's Voyage to Magellanica, written by his vice-admiral Ward. Edinburgh. 1766.

QK
81
W 27

Ferdinandsen, C.

    Studier over en hidtil upaaaget, almindelig dansk Baegersvamp, Sclerotinia scirpicola Rehm. Abstract. Some Studies on a hitherto unobserved common Danish fungus, Sclerotinia scirpicola Rehm. by C. Ferdinandsen and Ø. Winge.
    (In Biologiske Arbejder Tilegnede Eug. Warming...70 ars Fødelsdag...1911, pp. 280-298)

QE
Geology
Pam
627

Fenner, Charles.

    Major structural and physiographic features of South Australia. From Trans. Roy. Soc. South Australia, v. 54, 1930.

DU
Pacific
Pam.
163

Fenton, Francis Dart

    Suggestions for a history of the origin and migrations of the Maori people. By Francis Dart Fenton, late Chief Judge of the native lands court of New Zealand.

    Auckland, 1885, 132 pp.

GN
2.S
S 72

Ferdon, Edwin N., Jr.

    Easter Island exchange systems.

    (Southwestern Journal of Anthropology, Vol. 14:136-151, 1958)

G
51
W 17

Fenner, Charles

    Stone implements of the aborigines.

    (Walkabout, Vol. 21(7):32, 1955)

GN
Pam
1820

Fenton, S. G.

    North American Indian bead-work purse. From The Reliquary and Illustrated Archaeologist, Oct. 1905.

GN
2.S
S 72
and
GN
Ethn.
Pam.
4343

Ferdon, Edwin N., Jr.

    Notes on the present-day Easter Islanders.

    (Southwestern Journal of Anthropology, Vol. 13(3):223-238, 1957)

QC
801
Ca

Fenner, Clarence N.

    Earth movements accompanying the Katmai eruption. Gepphysical Lab.Carnegie Inst. Paper No. 562, 1925.

GN
Ethn.Pam.
3265

Fenton, William N.

    The Seneca society of faces.

    (Scientific Monthly, March, 1937, Vol. 44, pp. 215-238)

G
3
A 1

Ferdon, Edwin N., Jr.

    Pitcairn Island 1956.

    (Geogr. Review, 48(1):69-85, 1958)

QL
Ins.
Pam.
147

Fereday, R. W.

Synonymic list of the Lepidoptera
of New Zealand.

(Trans. N.Z.Inst. 1897)

QL
487
F4

Ferguson, Eustace W.

4 papers on Australian Tabanidae.
Ex Proc. Linn. Soc. N.S.W. 1919; Proc.
Roy. Soc. Vict.for 1920; Rec. S. Aus.
Mus. 1921; Linn. Soc. N.S.W. Proc.1920.

Eustace W.
QL
Ins.
Pam.
173
174

Ferguson,E.W. & Hill, G.F.

Notes on Australian Tabanidae

(Proc.Linn.Soc.N.S.W. 1920)
Same: Pt.2.   1922.

(2 copies each)

AS
182
H

FERESA

Gray, John Edward

(Jour. Mus. Godeffroy, Heft 8, 1875,p.52)

Eustace W.
QL
Ins.
Pam.
175

Ferguson, E.W.

List of the Tabanidae (Diptera)
in the S.Australian Museum ...

(Rec. S.Aust.Mus. 1921)

AS
720 N
Fe

Ferguson, Eustace W.

Notes on Australian Tabanidae Part 11
Linnean Soc. N.S.W. Proc. xlvii,3, 1922.

QL
525

Pam.Box

Also separate

GN
2.S
T

FERGUS, EDUARD

Note sur "Fergus".

(Bull. Soc. des Etudes Oceaniennes, No. 105,
pp. 142-161, 1953)

[History, Tahiti, life of Eduard Fergus]

Eustace W.
QL
Ins.
Pam.
176,

Ferguson, E.W.

New Australian Tabanidae.

New species of Corethra (Mochlonyx) from Australia.

(Proc.Roy.Soc.Victoria, 1921)

QL
Insects
Pam.
396

Ferguson, Eustace W.

Notes on the nomenclature of Australian Tabanidae: subfamily Pangoniinae.
Reprinted from Bull. Ent. Research, Vol.
XIV, Part 3, March, 1924.

QK
495. S 68
F 35

Ferguson, A. M.

All about tobacco, including practical
instructions for planting, cultivation, and
curing of the leaf, with other suitable information, from a variety of sources, referring to
the industry in Ceylon, South India, Sumatra,
Virginia, and the West Indies. Compiled and
published by A. M. and J. Ferguson of the "Ceylon Observer"... Colombo. (1889) 8vo. viii +
303 + ix pp.

QL
Ins.
Pam.
1
2
3

Ferguson, Eustace W.

Notes on Amyoterides.

Part 1. (Proc.Royal.Soc.Vict. 1914)
  "   2.   "   "   "   "   1915
  "   3.   "   "   "   "   1921

Eustace W.
QL
Ins.
Pam.
6
7
8
9
10
11
12
13

Ferguson, E. W.

Revision of the Amyoterides.

(Proc.Linn.Soc.N.S.W.)

Pt.2a & b, 1912, 1913; Pt.3, 1914;
Pt.4.a & b.1916; Pt.5, 1916;
Pt.6, 1921; Pt.7, 1921.

Eustace W.
AS
720.S
S 72

Ferguson, E. W.

A list of the Tabanidae (Diptera) in the
S. A. Museum, with descriptions of new species.

(Rec. South Australian Museum, I:365-380,
1921)

Eustace W.
QL
Ins.
Pam.
4
5.

Ferguson, E. W.

Notes on Amyoterides in the
South Australian Museum.

(Trans.Royal Soc.S.Aust.)

Pt.1, 1914; Pt.2, 1915;

Eustace W.
QL
Ins.
Pam.
177

Ferguson, E.W.

Tabanidae from Camden Haven,N.S.W.

(Proc.Linn.Soc.N.S.W. 1919)

Eustace W.
QL
1
A 93

Ferguson, E. W.

Australian ticks.

(The Austr. Zoologist, 4:24-35, 1925)

QL
487
F4

Ferguson, Eustace W

Notes on the Amyoterides in the
South Australian Museum. Ex Trans. Roy
Soc. S. Aus/ 1914- 1915   2 papers

AM
Mus.Pam.
133

Ferguson, Homer L.

The Mariners' Museum.   9 pp. 1937.

QL
1
A 93

Ferguson, Eustace W.

Fleas.   (in Australia)

(Austr. Zool. 3:114-118, 1923)

QL
487
F4

Ferguson, Eustace W

Notes on Amyoterides with description
of new species. Parts L-III. Ex. Roy.
Soc. Vict. Proc. 1913- 1921. 3 papers.

GN
Ethn.Pam.
3335

Ferguson, Homer L.

Brown, Alexander Crosby

Twin ships, notes on the chronological history of the use of multiple hulled vessels.
With an introduction by Homer L. Ferguson.

(The Mariners' Museum, Publication No. 5,
1939, 90 pp.)

Z
4011
F 35

Ferguson, John Alexander

    Bibliography of Australia.
    Vol. 1:1784-1830
    "   2:1831-1838
    "   3:1839-1845
    "   4:1846-1850
    "   5:1851-1900, A-G

    Sydney. R8vo. 1941,1945,1951,1955,1963

                 R8vo

GN
790
F 35

Fergusson, James

    Rude stone monuments in all countries; their age and uses. With 234 illustrations. London. John Murray. 1872. 8vo. xix + 559 + 32 pp.

AS
36
S5

FERNALD, CHARLES HENRY

Dyar, Harrison Gray, 1866–

    A list of the North American *Lepidoptera* and key to the literature of this order of insects. By Harrison G. Dyar ... assisted by C. H. Fernald, PH. D., the late Rev. George D. Hulst, and August Busck. Washington, Govt. print. off., 1902.

    xix, 723 p. 24½ᶜᵐ. (*Added t.-p.:* ... United States National museum. Bulletin ... no. 52)

    "List of works quoted": p. ix-xix.

    1. Lepidoptera—North America. 2. Lepidoptera—Bibl. I. Fernald, Charles Henry, 1838– II. Hulst, George D. III. Busck, August, 1870–

Library of Congress   Q11.U6   6–27693
——— Copy 2.   QL545.D98
                       (s19e1)

Z
Bibliography
Pam. 32

Ferguson, John A.

    A bibliography of the New Hebrides, and a history of the Mission Press. Part I. Aneityum, Futuna, and Erromanga. 1917; Part II. Tanna, Aniwa, Efate, 1918.   Sydney. Privately printed. sm8vo. 36 + 52 pp.

       FERGUSSON ISLAND   CANOE MAKING

       See

CANOE MAKING   FERGUSSON ISLAND

AS
36
S4

Fernald, Henry Torsey, 1866–

    Descriptions of certain species of wasps of the family *Sphecidæ*. By Henry T. Fernald ...

    (*In* U. S. National museum. Proceedings. Washington, 1912. 23½ᶜᵐ. vol. 42, p. 257-259)

    1. Sphegidae.

                        13–9530

Library of Congress   Q11.U55 vol. 42

DU
Missions
Pam. 79

Ferguson, J. A.   (John A.)

    The Rev. Samuel Marsden: his life and work. (A paper read before the Royal Australian Historical Society, Sept. 26, 1922.) 35 pp. 8vo.

QK
523
C 64

    The fern allies of North America north of Mexico.

Clute, Willard Nelson

QK
Bot. Pam.
2754

and

QH
301
Qu

Fernald, M. L. (Merritt Lyndon)

    The antiquity and dispersal of vascular plants.

    (The Quarterly Review of Biology, Vol. 1: 212-245, 1926)

AP
2
A 5

Ferguson, J. B.

    The occurence of Molybdenum in rocks with special reference to those of Hawaii.

    (Amer. Journ. of Science, Vol. 37, 1914, pp. 299-402)

DU
620
P 22

Fern, Stewart

    Historic Lahaina.

    (Paradise of the Pacific, 69(8):20-21,1957)

QK
Pam
#525

Fernald, M. L.   (Merritt Lyndon)

    Contributions from the Gray Herbarium of Harvard University, ex Am. Acad. of Arts. & Sc. Proc., vol. XXXIV, no. 19, April, 1899.

GR
16
M 99

Ferguson, John C(alvin)

    Chinese (Mythology)

    Mythology of All Races... Vol. 8, 1928, pp. 1-203...

GR
Folklore
Pam.
83

Fern, C. J., Jr.

    His collection of published sheet music, Hawaiian. 3 typed pages. LIST only

---

AS
36
A 25-p

Fernald, M. L.

    I. Eleocharis ovata and its American allies. II. Scirpus Eriophorum and some related forms.

    (Proc. Am. Acad. Arts and Sci., 34:485-503, 1899. Reprinted to be Contrib. from the Gray Herbarium, No. 15)

GR
25
F35

Ferguson, John C(alvin)

    The mythology of all races: Chinese by John C. Ferguson; Japanese by Masaharu Anesaki.

    Boston, Marshall Jones, 1928.   416p.   p 1s

QL
561.L7
F 69

Fernald, Charles H.

Forbush, Edward H.

    The Gypsy moth, Porthetria dispar (Linn.) A report of the work of destroying the insect in...Massachusetts...By Edward H. Forbush and Charles H. Fernald. Boston. 1896.

QK
53
G 77

Fernald, Merritt Lyndon

Gray, Asa

    Gray's Manual of botany. A handbook of the flowering plants and ferns of the central and northeastern United States and adjacent Canada. Largely rewritten and expanded by Merritt Lyndon Fernald, with assistance of specialists in some groups. Eighth (centennial)edition- illustrated American Book Company. New York... R8vo. 1950c lxiv + 1632 pp.

GN
2.S
P 76

Fergusson, Charles

    He Kupu poroporoaki ki te maua iwi Maori o Te Nukuroa. By Charles and Alice Fergusson.

    (Journal of the Polynesian Society, 39: 73, 1930.)

QL
Insect
Pam
726

Fernald, C   H

    The orthoptera of New England.

    Boston, Wright and Potter, 1888.   61p.

QK
117
G 77

Fernald, Merritt Lyndon   editor

Gray, Asa, 1810-1888.

    Gray's new manual of botany (7th ed.—illustrated) A handbook of the flowering plants and ferns of the central and northeastern United States and adjacent Canada, rearranged and extensively revised by Benjamin Lincoln Robinson ... and Merritt Lyndon Fernald ... New York, Cincinnati [etc.] American book company [1908]

    926 p. illus. 21½ᶜᵐ.

    1. Botany—U. S. I. Robinson, Benjamin Lincoln, 1864– ed. II. Fernald, Merritt Lyndon, 1874– joint ed.

                        8–27398

Library of Congress   QK117.G75   1908
Copyright A 210865   (s21h2)

QK
Bot.Pam.
2164

Fernald, M. L. (Merritt Lyndon)

Must all rare plants suffer the fate of Franklinia?

(Journal of the Franklin Institute, Vol. 226, 1938, pp. 383-397.)

QK
Bot.Pam.
3121

Fernandes, Rosette

Cucurbitaceae africanae novae - 1

(Boletim da Sociedade Broteriana, 33, 1959; 189-195)

AP
2
A 5

FERNANDO DE NORONHA

Williams, George H.

Geology of Fernando de Noronha.

(Am. Jour. of Sci., Ser. 3, Vol. 37, 1889, pp. 178-187)

QK
Botany
Pam
1454

Fernald, M(erritt) L(yndon), and Harold St. John.

Nymphaea variegata or N. americana? From Rhodora: Jour. of the New England Bot. club. v. 18, no.188. pp.137-141.

AS
36
S1

Fernández, León.

... The Guatuso Indians of Costa Rica. By Don Leon Fernandez ...

(In Smithsonian institution. Annual report. 1882. Washington, 1884. 23¹ᵐ. p. 675-681)

1. Indians of Central America—Costa Rica. 2. Guatuso Indians.

S 15-590

Library of Congress   Q11.S66 1882
Library, Smithsonian   Institution

FERNANDO DE NORONHA GEOLOGY

see

GEOLOGY FERNANDO DE NORONHA

AS
36
A25

Fernald, M. L. (Merritt Lyndon)

Persistence of plants in unglaciated areas of boreal America. In Am. Acad. Sc Mem. Vol. XV, No. III, 241 - 342, 1925.

AS
36
S2

FERNANDEZ de YBARRA, AUGUSTINE MARCUS
Chanca, Diego Álvares.   1857
The letter of Dr. Diego Alvarez Chanca, dated 1494, relating to the second voyage of Columbus to America (being the first written document on the natural history, ethnography and ethnology of America) ... By A. M. Fernandez de Ybarra ...

(In Smithsonian institution. Smithsonian miscellaneous collections. Washington, 1907. 24½ᵐ. vol. XLVIII (Quarterly issue, vol. III) p. 428-457. illus. (map) pl. LXVI)

(Continued on next card)

16-11622

FERNS

See

FILICES
HYMENOPHYLLACEAE

QK
Bot.Pam.
2346

Fernald, M. L.

Some historical aspects of plant taxonomy.

(Rhodora, Vol. 44, 1942, pp. 21-43)

AS
36
S2

FERNANDEZ de YBARRA, AUGUSTINE MARCUS
Chanca, Diego Álvares.   1857   The letter of Dr. Diego Alvarez Chanca ... 1907. (Card 2)

Publication 1698.
"Translated from Spanish original ... with explanatory notes, geographical and historical remarks."
First pub. by M. F. de Navarrete in his "Colección de los viajes y descubrimientos," Madrid, 1825-1837, t. 1, from a ms. preserved in the Academia real de la historia de Madrid.
A lecture delivered before the Biological section of the New York academy of sciences ... March 5, 1906.

1. America—Early accounts to 1600. 2. West Indies—Descr. & trav. I. Fernández de Ybarra, Augustine Marcus, 1857-

Library of Congress   Q11.S7 vol. 48   16-11622
———— Copy 2.

AG
41
D26

Ferrall, J   S   and Repp, T   G

A Danish-English dictionary.

Copenhagen, Gyldendal, 1845.   433p.

QK
Botany
Pam
1522

Fernald, M(erritt) L(yndon)

Some relationships of the flora of the Northern hemisphere.   From Proc. of International congress of plant sciences,   vol. 2, 1929. p. 1487-1507.

QK
359
F 36

Fernando, Dorothy

Wild flowers of Ceylon. With a foreword by His Excellency the Rt. Hon. Lord Soulbury. West Brothers. Mitcham. 1954. 4to. xvii + 86 pp.

[illustrations in color]

GN
Ethn.Pam.
2963

Ferrand, Gabriel

Un Vocabulaire Malgache-Hollandais. (no date, no source)

QK
Botany
Pam
1452

Fernald, M(erritt)L(yndon), and Harold St.John

Variations of silene acaulis.   From Rhodora: Jour. of New England Bot. club, v.23, no. 269, 1921. pp. 119-20.

QL
1
C 42

Fernando, Wilfred

Contributions to a knowledge of the insects of Ceylon, No. 1-6.

(Ceylon Journal of Science, Sect. B. Zool. Vol. 25(3):197-222, 1957)

QK
Bot.Pam.
2618

Ferris, Bernard J.

Johnson, J. Harlan

Tertiary and Pleistocene coralline Algae from Lau, Fiji. By J. Harlan Johnson and Bernard J. Ferris.

(Bernice P. Bishop Museum, Bull. 201, 1950)

QL
1
C 42

Fernand, V. S. V.

The teeth of the dugong.

(Ceylon, Jour. of Sci., Sec. B. Zoology, Vol. XXV(2):139-146, 1953)

AP
2
A 5

FERNANDO DE NORONHA

Branner, J. C.

Is the Peak of Fernando de Noronha a volcanic plug like that of Mont Pelé?

(Am. Jour. of Sci., Ser. 3, Vol. 16, 1903, pp. 442-444)

QL
595.M1
I 59

Ferris, G. F.

Anoplura.

IN
Insects of Micronesia
[Insects of Micronesia, Vol. 8(2), 1959] pp. 9-12.

AN
763
B-b

Ferris, G. F (Gordon Floyd)

    An apparently undescribed mealybug (Hemiptera: Pseudococcidae) from Tahiti.

    (Bernice P. Bishop Museum, Bull. 142, pp. 133-135. Issued May 29, 1935. Pacific Ent. Survey Publication 8, Art. 10)

QL
489.S
P 11

AS
763
B-b
Reading
Room

Ferris, G. F. (Gordon Floyd)

    Mallophaga from Tahiti.

    Society Islands Insects. Pacific Entomological Survey Publication 6, pp. 7-12 (Art. 2), 1935.

    (Bernice P. Bishop Museum, Bulletin 113)

GN
2 S
A 22

Ferris, Harry Burr, 1865-

    ... The Indians of Cuzco and the Apurimac, by H. B. Ferris. Lancaster, Pa., Pub. for the American anthropological association, the New era printing company [1916]

cover-title, 2 p. l., p. 59-148 incl. 1 illus., map, tables, diagr. LX pl. 25cm. (Memoirs of the American anthropological association. vol. III, no. 2. April-June, 1916)

"A study of the anthropometric data collected by L. T. Nelson, M. D., surgeon of the Peruvian expedition of 1912 under the auspices of Yale university and the National geographic society."

"References": p. 104.

1. Indians of South America—Peru. 2. Anthropometry—Peru. 3. Kechua Indians. I. Nelson, Luther Townsend, 1882- II. Peruvian expedition of 1912.

                   18-6196

Library of Congress   GN2.A22 vol. 3, no. 2

QL
523.C7
F 39

Ferris, Gordon Floyd

    Atlas of the scale insects of North America. Stanford University Press. Volumes 1-7, 1937-1955. 4to.

QL
489.M
P 11

Ferris, G. F. (Gordon Floyd)

    New species and other records of Mallophaga from the Marquesas.
IN
Marquesan Insects-I, pp. 53-72. (Art. 5)

    (Bernice P. Bishop Museum, Bulletin 98, 1932. Pacific Entomological Survey Publication 1)

AS
36
S72

Ferris, Roxana Stinchfield

    Preliminary report on the flora of the Tres Marias Islands. Contributions from Dudley Herbarium, Stanford Univ. v.1, n.2, 1927.

AS
36
C3

Ferris, Gordon Floyd.

    ... A catalogue and host list of the *Anoplura*, by G. F. Ferris ... San Francisco, The Academy, 1916.

cover-title, p. [129]-213. 25½cm. (Proceedings of the California academy of sciences. 4th ser. vol. VI, no. 6)

1. Anoplura.

            17-1230

Library of Congress   Q11.C253 vol. 6, no. 6

QL
461
M 62

Ferris, G. F.

    Notes on and descriptions of Cimicidae (Hemiptera). By G. F. Ferris and Robert L. Usinger.

    (Microentomology, Vol. 22(1):1-37, 1957)

QL
523.C7
F6

Ferris, Gordon Floyd.

    ... Report upon a collection of *Coccidae* from Lower California, by Gordon Floyd Ferris ... Stanford University, Calif., The University, 1921.

1 p. l., p. [61]-132. illus. 25½cm. (Stanford university publications. University series. Biological sciences, v. 1, no. 2)

1. Scale-insects. 2. Insects—California, Lower.

            21-7256

Library of Congress   QL523.C7F46
         [5]

AS
36
S7

Ferris, Gordon Floyd.

    ... A contribution to the knowledge of the *Coccidae* of southwestern United States, by Gordon Floyd Ferris ... Stanford University, Calif., The University, 1919.

. 67, [1] p. illus. 25½cm. (Leland Stanford junior university publications. University ser. [no. 35?])

1. Scale-insects.

            19-10021

Library of Congress   QL523.C7F45
         [5]

Microfilm
no.
130

Ferris, Gordon F.

    Parasitology (Cambridge, England) vol. 15: 54-58, 1923.

    (article by Ferris Observations...larve... Diptera Pupipara...)

AS
36
S6

Ferris, Gordon Floyd.

    ... Scale insects of the Santa Cruz peninsula, by Gordon Floyd Ferris ... Stanford University, Calif., The University, 1920.

57 p. illus. 25½cm. (Stanford university publications. University series. Biological sciences, v. 1, no. 1)

1. Scale-insects. 2. Insects—California.

            20-14157

Library of Congress   QL523.C7F47
         [3]

AS
36
S7

Ferris, Gordon Floyd.

    ... Contributions toward a monograph of the sucking lice ... by Gordon Floyd Ferris ... Stanford University, Calif., The University, 1919-

v. illus. 25½cm. (Leland Stanford junior university publications. University series. [no. 4])

1. Lice. Siphunculata

Library of Congress   QL503.A6F5   20-6469

——— Copy 2.   AS36.L5 no. 41
         [3]

QL
Insects
Pam
No. 375

and

QL
Insect
Pam
530

Ferris, G. F. (Gordon Floyd)

    Report upon a collection of insect ectoparasites from Australian and Tasmanian mammals. Am. Mus. Nov. No. 110, 1924.

SEP 4 '46

DU
1
P

Ferris, W. G.

    Smashed on a coral reef: description of a wreck in the Tongan Islands.

    (Pacific Islands Monthly, Vol..20(7):41-43, 1950)

QL
489.M
P 11

Ferris, G. F. (Gordon Floyd)

    Ectoparasites of Marquesan rats.
IN
Marquesan Insects-I, pp. 117-127. (Art. 12)

    (Bulletin Bernice P. Bishop Museum, No. 98, 1932. Pacific Entomological Survey Publication 1)

AS
763
B-b

Ferris, G. F (Gordon Floyd)

    Scale insects (Hemiptera: Coccidea) from the Marquesas.

    (Bernice P. Bishop Museum Bull. 142, pp. 125-131. Issued May 29, 1935. Pacific Entomological Survey Publication 8, Art. 9)

QL
671
F4

Ferry, John Farwell.

    ... Catalogue of a collection of birds from Costa Rica, by John Farwell Ferry ... Chicago, 1910.

1 p. l., p. 257-282. 24½cm. (Field museum of natural history. Publication 146. Ornithological ser. vol. I, no. 6)

1. Birds—Costa Rica.

            10-25848

Library of Congress   QL671.F4 vol. I, no. 6

QL
595.M1
I 59

Ferris, G. F.

    Usinger, Robert L.   and others

    Heteroptera
IN
Insects of Micronesia, Vol. 7(5), 1960: Enicocephalidae, by R. L. Usinger and Pedro Wygodzinsky; Reduviidae, by Pedro Wygodzinsky and R. L. Usinger; Cimicidae by R. L. Usinger and G. F. Ferris.

QL
503.A6
F 39

Ferris, G. F.

    The sucking lice. With the collaboration of Chester J. Stojanovich.

    (Memoirs of the Pacific Coast Entomological Society, Vol. 1, 1951) Calif. Acad. Sci., San Francisco

---

PL
Philo
Pam
131

Fertig, M

    Der raub der draupadi, der gattin d funs pandawas: aus dem indischen in den versmassen der urschrift, Wurzburg, 1841

GN
2.S
A 65

FERTILITY

Back, Kurt W.

The survey under unusual conditions; the Jamaica Human Fertility Investigation. By Kurt W. Back and J. Mayone Styoos.

(Soc. for Applied Anthropology, Monograph No. 1, 1959)

QP
1
C

FERTILIZATION (BIOLOGY)

Loeb, Jacques, 1859–

... Further experiments on the fertilization of the egg of the sea-urchin (*Strongylocentrotus purpuratus*) with sperm of various species of starfish and a holothurian (*Cucumaria*) By Jacques Loeb. Berkeley, The University press, 1904.

cover-title, p. [83]–85. 27ᶜᵐ. (University of California publications. Physiology. vol. 1, no. 11)

1. Fertilization (Biology) 2. Echinodermata. 3. Embryology, Experimental. 4. Sea-urchins.

A 11–1271

Title from Univ. of Calif.   Library of Congress

QP
1
C

FERTILIZATION (BIOLOGY)

Robertson, Thorburn Brailsford, 1884–

... On the extraction of a substance from the sperm of a sea urchin (*Strongylocentrotus purpuratus*) which will fertilize the eggs of that species, by T. Brailsford Robertson. [Berkeley, University of California press] 1912.

p. [103]–105. 27ᶜᵐ. (University of California publications in physiology. v. 4, no. 12)

From the Rudolph Spreckels physiological laboratory of the University of California.

Issued in single cover with v. 4, nos. 11 and 13 of the series.

1. Fertilization (Biology) 2. Sea-urchins.   I. Title.

A 12–493

Title from Univ. of Calif.   Library of Congress

QP
1
C

FERTILIZATION (BIOLOGY)

Bullot, Georges.

... Artificial parthenogenesis and regular segmentation in an annelid (*Ophelia*), by G. Bullot. Berkeley, The University press, 1904.

cover-title, p. [165]–174. illus. 27ᶜᵐ. (University of California publications. Physiology. vol. 1, no. 19)

From the Rudolph Spreckels physiological laboratory of the University of California.

Reprinted, in part, from the Archiv für entwicklungs-mechanik der organismen. vol. 18, 1904, p. 161–

1 Parthenogenesis (Animals) 2. Fertilization (Biology) 3. Embryology, Experimental.

A 11–1255

Title from Univ. of Calif.   Library of Congress

QP
1
C

FERTILIZATION (BIOLOGY)

Loeb, Jacques, 1859–

... Further experiments on heterogeneous hybridization in echinoderms ... By Jacques Loeb (tr. from Pflüger's Archiv, 1904, v. 104, p. 325, by John Bruce MacCallum) [Berkeley, The University press] 1904.

p. [5]–30. illus. 27ᶜᵐ. (University of California publications. Physiology. vol. 2, no. 2)

Issued in single cover with v. 2, no. 3–4, of the series.

1. Echinodermata. 2. Fertilization (Biology) 3. Embryology, Experimental.   I. MacCallum, John Bruce, 1876–1906, tr.

A 11–1270

Title from Univ. of Calif.   Library of Congress

QP
1
C

FERTILIZATION (BIOLOGY)

Moore, Arthur Russell, 1882–

... On the nature of the sensitization of sea urchin eggs by strontium chloride, by A. R. Moore. [Berkeley, University of California press] 1912.

p. [91]–93. 27ᶜᵐ. (University of California publications in physiology. vol. 4, no. 10)

From the Rudolph Spreckels physiological laboratory of the University of California.

Issued in single cover with vol. 4, no. 9, of the series.

1. Sea-urchins. 2. Fertilization (Biology)

A 12–401

Title from Univ. of Calif.   Library of Congress

QH
48
L72

FERTILIZATION (BIOLOGY)

Lille, Frank Rattray

Problems of fertilization.

Chicago, Univ. Press, [1919].   278p.

QP
1
C

FERTILIZATION (BIOLOGY)

Loeb, Jacques, 1859–

... On a method by which the eggs of a sea-urchin ⟨*Strongylocentrotus purpuratus*⟩ can be fertilized with the sperm of a starfish ⟨*Asterias ochracea*⟩. By Jacques Loeb. Berkeley, The University press, 1903.

cover-title, 3 p. 27ᶜᵐ. (University of California publications. Physiology. v. 1, no. 1)

1. Fertilization (Biology) 2. Echinodermata. 3. Embryology, Experimental. 4. Sea-urchins.

A 11–1275

Title from Univ. of Calif.   Library of Congress

GN
2 S
A 22

FERTILIZATION, IDEA OF.

Haeberlin, Herman Karl, 1890–

... The idea of fertilization in the culture of the Pueblo Indians, by H. K. Haeberlin. Lancaster, Pa., Pub. for the American anthropological association, The New era printing company [1916].

cover-title, 1 p. l., 55 p. 25ᶜᵐ. (Memoirs of the American anthropological association. vol. III, no. 1. Jan.–Mar. 1916)

Pub. also as thesis (PH. D.) Columbia university, 1915.

References: p. 52–55.

1. Pueblo Indians. 2. Indians of North America—Religion and mythology.   I. Title: Fertilization, Idea of.

16–25723

Library of Congress   GN2.A22 vol. 3, no. 1

QP
1
C

FERTILIZATION (BIOLOGY)

Loeb, Jacques, 1859–

... Artificial membrane-formation and chemical fertilization in a starfish (*Asterina*), by Jacques Loeb. Berkeley, The University press, 1905.

cover-title, p. [147]–158. 27ᶜᵐ. (University of California publications. Physiology. vol. 2, no. 16)

From the Rudolph Spreckels physiological laboratory of the University of California.

1. Fertilization (Biology) 2. Starfishes.

A 11–1264

Title from Univ. of Calif.   Library of Congress

QP
1
C

FERTILIZATION (BIOLOGY)

Loeb, Jacques, 1859–

... On the production of a fertilization membrane in the egg of the sea-urchin with the blood of certain gephyrean worms. ⟨A preliminary note.⟩ By Jacques Loeb. [Berkeley, The University press] 1907.

p. [57]–58. 27ᶜᵐ. (University of California publications. Physiology. v. 3, no. 8)

1. Fertilization (Biology) 2. Sea-urchins.

A 11–1283

Title from Univ. of Calif.   Library of Congress

QK
827
M94

The fertilisation of flowers

Müller, Hermann

QP
1
C

FERTILIZATION (BIOLOGY)

Loeb, Jacques, 1859–

... The chemical character of the process of fertilization and its bearing upon the theory of life phenomena, by Jacques Loeb. [Berkeley, The University press] 1907.

p. [61]–80. 27ᶜᵐ. (University of California publications. Physiology. vol. 3, no. 10)

Address delivered at the 7th International zoological congress, Boston, August 22, 1907.

1. Fertilization (Biology) 2. Life.

A 11–1266

Title from Univ. of Calif.   Library of Congress

QP
1
C

FERTILIZATION (BIOLOGY)

Moore, Arthur Russell, 1882–

... A new method of heterogeneous hybridization in echinoderms, by A. R. Moore. [Berkeley, University of California press] 1912.

p. [109]–110. 27ᶜᵐ. (University of California publications in physiology. vol. 4, no. 14)

"From the Herzstein research laboratory of the University of California, New Monterey, California."

Issued in single cover with v. 4, no. 15, of the series.

1. Hybridization. 2. Fertilization (Biology) 3. Sea-urchins.

A 12–768

Title from Univ. of Calif.   Library of Congress

AS
36
S1

FERTILIZATION OF PLANTS.

Bouvier, Eugène Louis, 1856–

Bees and flowers. By E. L. Bouvier ...

(*In* Smithsonian institution. Annual report. 1904. Washington, 1905. 23½ᶜᵐ. p. 469–484. illus.)

"An abridged translation ... from Revue générale des sciences pures et appliquées, Paris, April 15, 1904."

1. Bees. 2. Fertilization of plants.

S 15–1257

Library of Congress   Q11.S66 1904

Library, Smithsonian   Institution

QP
1
C

FERTILIZATION (BIOLOGY)

Loeb, Jacques, 1859–

... On fertilization, artificial parthenogenesis, and cytolysis of the sea urchin egg. By Jacques Loeb ... [tr. by John Bruce MacCallum from Pflüger's Archiv, v. 103, p. 257, 1904] [Berkeley, The University press] 1905.

p. [73]–81. 27ᶜᵐ. (University of California publications. Physiology. v. 2, no. 8)

From the Rudolph Spreckels physiological laboratory of the University of California.

Issued in single cover with v. 2, no. 7, of the series.

1. Fertilization (Biology) 2. Parthenogenesis (Animals) 3. Cytolysis. 4. Sea-urchins.   I. MacCallum, John Bruce, 1876–1906, tr.

A 11–1278

Title from Univ. of Calif.   Library of Congress

QP
1
C

FERTILIZATION (BIOLOGY)

Moore, Arthur Russell, 1882–

... On the nature of the cortical layer in sea urchin eggs, by A. R. Moore. [Berkeley, University of California press] 1912.

p. [89]–90. 27ᶜᵐ. (University of California publications in physiology. vol. 4, no. 9)

From the Rudolph Spreckels physiological laboratory of the University of California.

Issued in single cover with vol. 4, no. 10, of the series.

1. Sea-urchins. 2. Fertilization (Biology)

A 12–400

Title from Univ. of Calif.   Library of Congress

QK
840
D22

FERTILIZATION OF PLANTS

Darwin, Charles

The different forms of flowers on plants of the same species.

London, Murray, 1877.   352p.   pls.

QP
1
C

FERTILIZATION (BIOLOGY)

Loeb, Jacques, 1859–

... The fertilization of the egg of the sea-urchin [*Strongylocentrotus purpuratus* and *Strongylocentrotus franciscanus*] by the sperm of the starfish [*Asterias ochracea*] by Jacques Loeb. Berkeley, The University press, 1903.

cover-title, p. [39]–53. 27ᶜᵐ. (University of California publications. Physiology. vol. 1, no. 6)

"Address delivered before Sigma Xi scientific society at Stanford university, Oct. 13, 1903."

1. Fertilization (Biology) 2. Echinodermata. 3. Embryology, Experimental. 4. Sea-urchins.

A 11–1269

Title from Univ. of Calif.   Library of Congress

QP
1
C

FERTILIZATION (BIOLOGY)

Robertson, Thorburn Brailsford, 1884–

... On the cytolytic action of ox-blood serum upon sea-urchin eggs, and its inhibition by proteins (preliminary communication) by T. Brailsford Robertson. Berkeley, University of California press, 1912.

cover-title, p. [79]–88. 27ᶜᵐ. (University of California publications in physiology. v. 4, no. 8)

"From the Herzstein research laboratory and the Rudolph Spreckels physiological laboratory of the University of California."

1. Cytolysis. 2. Fertilization (Biology) 3. Sea-urchins. 4. Proteids.

A 12–402

Title from Univ. of Calif.   Library of Congress   [s19c2]

QK
1
C 2

FERTILIZATION OF PLANTS

Goodspeed, Thomas Harper, 1887–

... Controlled pollination in *Nicotiana*, by Thomas Harper Goodspeed and Pirie Davidson. Berkeley, University of California press, 1918.

cover-title, p. [429]–434. 27ᶜᵐ. (University of California publications in botany. v. 5, no. 13)

1. Fertilization of plants. 2. Tobacco.   I. Davidson, Pirie, 1892– joint author. II. Title.

A 18–900

Title from Univ. of Calif.   Library of Congress

QK
1
C 2

FERTILIZATION OF PLANTS.

Goodspeed, Thomas Harper, 1887–

... On the partial sterility of *Nicotiana* hybrids made with *N. sylvestris* as a parent. [1]— By Thomas Harper Goodspeed.

(*In* California. University. Publications in botany. Berkeley, 1913-27[--]. v. 5, p. [189]-198; plates)

1. Hybridization, Vegetable. 2. Sterility. 3. Fertilization of plants. 4. Tobacco. I. Title.

A 15-1901 Revised

Title from Univ. of Calif.   Library of Congress

S
17 H3
S 41

FERTILIZERS FOR SUGAR CANE

Eckart, Charles F.

Report on fertilization, by Charles F. Eckart, chairman of committee. Submitted to the Hawaiian sugar planters' association, November, 1901. Honolulu, Hawaiian gazette co., 1901.

1 p. l., 45 p. 22½[--].

[Reprint]

(*In* Hawaiian sugar planters' association. Experiment station. Division of agriculture and chemistry. Special bulletin B. Honolulu, H. T., 1905. 23½[--]. p. [21]-59)

1. Fertilizers for sugar cane. 2. Hawaii. Soils.

Agr 7-336-7

Library, U. S. Dept. of   Agriculture 100H31

DU
Pacific
Pam
250

Fery, F. (trans.)

Richards, William

Archipel des îles Hawaii.

in Revue de l'Orient, n.d. pp. 331-367.

QK
926
Kn
K79

Fertilization of plants

Knuth, Paul.

Handbook of flower pollination based upon Hermann Müller's work "The fertilisation of flowers by insects." 3 vols.

Oxford, 1906-1909.

S
17.H3
S 41

FERTILIZERS FOR SUGAR CANE

Eckart, Charles F.

... The action of soluble fertilizers on cane soils. By C. F. Eckart. Honolulu, Hawaii, 1909.

88 p. illus. 23[--]. (Report of work of the Experiment station of the Hawaiian sugar planters' association. Division of agriculture and chemistry. Bulletin no. 29)

1. Fertilizers for sugar cane. 2. Hawaii. Soils.

Agr 9-2782

Library, U. S. Dept. of   Agriculture 100H31B no. 29

GN
671.S5
F 41

Fesche, C. F. P.

La Nouvelle Cythère (Tahiti). Journal de Navigation Inédit. Écrit à bord de la frégate du Roy la Boudeuse, commandée par M. le Chevalier de Bougainville. Avant-propos de Jean Dorsenne. Paris. Editions Duchartre et Van Buggenhoudt. 1929o. xxx + 34 pp. 8vo.

QK
827
M94

FERTILIZATION OF PLANTS

Müller, Hermann

The fertilisation of flowers. Translated and edited by D'Arcy W. Thompson with a preface by Charles Darwin.

London, Macmillan, 1883.   669p.   pls.

QL
430.4
R 19

Ferussac, J. B. L. d'A. de

Histoire Naturelle, Generale et Particulière des Mollusques, tant des especes que l'on trouve aujourd'hui vivantes, que des dépouilles fossiles...

Rang, Paul Karel Sander
Histoire Naturelle des Aplysiens...Paris.
1828

QK
Bot.Pam.
1752

Fessenden, A. P.   (Anna Parker)

Tilden, Josephine E.

Bactophora irregularis...by Josephine E. Tilden and Anna Parker Fessenden.

(Bull. of Torrey Botan. Club, Vol. 57, pp. 381-388. pl. 20-21. June 20, 1931)

S
17.H3
S 41

FERTILIZERS

Eckart, C[harles] F.

... Lysimeter experiments, by C. F. Eckart. Honolulu, 1906.

31 p. 22½[--]. (Report of work of the Experiment station of the Hawaiian sugar planters' association. Division of agriculture and chemistry. Bulletin no. 19)

1. Fertilizers. 2. Lysimeter.

Agr 7-335

Library, U. S. Dept. of   Agriculture 100H31B no. 19

QL
403
F 41

Ferussac, (J. B. L. d'A.) de

Histoire Naturelle Générale et Particulière des Mollusques Terrestres et Fluviatiles...par D. de Ferussac et G. P. Deshayes. Accompagnée d'un Atlas de 247 Planches Gravées.   Text, Tome 1-2, Atlas, Tomes 1-2. 1820-1851. Paris. J.-B. Baillière. folio.

DU
12
F 41
locked
case

Festetics de Tolna, Rodolphe

Chez les cannibales. Huit ans de croisiere dans l'Ocean Pacifique a bord du yacht "Le Tolna." Ouvrage orne de 200 gravures et de cartes, d'apres les photographies et les documents de l'auteur. Paris. Plon-Nourrit. 1903. 4to. pp.iv+407.

S
399
E8

Fertilizers

McGeorge, William

Effect of fertilizers on the physical properties of Hawaii soil.
Haw. Agric. Exper. Station, Bull. 38, 1915.

QL
430.2
Fe
F39

Ferussac M. de et d'Orbigny, Alcide

Histoire generale et particulaire des Cephalopodes acetabuliferes, text and atlas.

Paris, 1835-48.

Tomes 1 & 2

G
51
W 17

FESTIVALS   NEW GUINEA

Maahs, Arnold M.

Festival of the pig.

(Walkabout, Vol. 15 (12):17-20, 1949)

S
17.H3
S 41

FERTILIZERS AND MANURES

Eckart, Charles Franklin.

... Fertilizer experiments, 1897-1905. By C. F. Eckart. Honolulu, H. T., 1905.

57 p. diagrs. 22½[--]. (Report of work of the Experiment station of the Hawaiian sugar planters' association. Division of agriculture and chemistry. Bulletin no. 15)

1. Fertilizers and manures. [1. Fertilizers for sugar cane] 2. Sugar growing.

Agr 6-1903 Revised

Library, U. S. Dept. of   Agriculture 100H31B no. 15

QL
406
F 41
locked
case

Ferussac, Le Baron(A.E.J.P.J.F. d'A. de)

Tableaux Systematiques des Animaux Mollusques Classés en Familles Naturelles, dans lesquels on a établi la concordance de tous les systèmes; suivis d'un prodrome général pour tous les mollusques terrestres ou fluviatiles, vivants ou fossiles. Paris. Arthus Bertrand.1820. 4to. xlvii + 110 pp.

[Last ones colonies pp. xlvii, 27, 114]

QK
1
G 68

Festskrift för Carl Skottsberg.

(Meddelanden från Göteborgs Botaniska Trädgård, XIV, 1940-1941)

S
17.H3
S 41

FERTILIZERS FOR SUGAR CANE

[Eckart, Charles F]
Fertilization.

(*In* Hawaiian sugar planters' association. Experiment station. Division of agriculture and chemistry. Special bulletin B. Honolulu, H. T., 1905. p. [10]-20)
Signed: C. F. Eckart.

1. Fertilizers for sugar cane.

Agr 7-334

Library, U. S. Dept. of   Agriculture 100H31

QL
401
M 23

FERUSSACIIDAE

Beddome, R. H.

Notes on Indian and Ceylonese species of Glessula.

(Proc. Mal. Soc. London, Vol. 7, 1906, pp. 160-172)

QK
1
U

FESTUCA

Piper, Charles Vancouver, 1867–

... North American species of Festuca. By Charles V. Piper. Washington, Govt. print. off., 1906.

vi, 48, vii-ix p. xv pl. 25[--]. (Smithsonian institution. United States national museum. Contributions from the United States national herbarium. vol. x, pt. 1)

1. Festuca.

Agr 7-1744

Library, U. S. Dept. of   Agriculture 450C76 vol. 10, pt. 1

QK
1
U

FESTUCA
Piper, Charles Vancouver, 1867–
Supplementary notes on American species of *Festuca*.
By Charles V. Piper.

(*In* Smithsonian institution. United States national museum. Contributions from the United States national herbarium. Washington, 1903–24½ᵉᵐ. v. 16, pt. 5, p. 197–199)
"Issued February 11, 1913."

1. Festuca.

Agr 13–248

Library, U. S. Dept. of ⌣ Agriculture 450C76 vol. 16, pt. 5

AS
36
S1

FEUDALISM––PERSIA
Morgan, Jacques Jean Marie de, 1857–
Feudalism in Persia: its origin, development, and present condition. By Jacques de Morgan ...

(*In* Smithsonian institution. Annual report. 1913. Washington, 1914. 23½ᵉᵐ. p. 579–605)
"Translated ... from the Revue d'ethnographie et de sociologie ... Paris, vol. 3, nos. 5–8."

1. Feudalism—Persia.

15–1755

Library of Congress ⌣ Q11.S66 1913

GN
Pam
1436

Fewkes, J. Walter
The Alosaka cult of the Hopi Indians.
From Amer. Anthrop. v.1, 1899.

QK
1
G 32

FESTUCA
Saint-Yves, Alfred
Aperçu sur la distribution géographique des
Festuca (subgen. Eu-Festuca).

(Candollea, Vol. IV, 1929–31, pp. 146–165)

AS
28
,E 85

Feugnet, Madeleine
Enquête sur la situation sociale des indigènes à Nouméa. (Enquête de la Mission Protestante de Nouvelle-Calédonie)

(Etudes Mélanésiennes, n.s., 3rd yr., No. 5: 85–116, 1951)

QL
Prot.Poly
Pam.605

Fewkes, J. Walter
The anatomy of Astrangia danae.
(5 plates only. Drawings by A. Sonrel. The explanation of the plates is by J. Walter Fewkes and is missing in the Bishop Museum copy.)

QK
1
G 32

FESTUCA
Saint-Yves, Alfred
Contribution à l'étude des Festuca (subgen.
Eu-Festuca) de l'Afrique australe et de l'Océanie.

(Candollea, Vol. IV, 1929–31, pp. 65–129)

AS
36
S1

FEVER
Wood, Horatio C., 1841–
Researches upon fever. By H. C. Wood, jr. ...

(*In* Smithsonian institution. Annual report. 1878. Washington, 1879. 23½ᵉᵐ. p. 420–426)

1. Fever.

S 15–483

Library of Congress
Library, Smithsonian ⌣ Q11.S66 1878
Institution

GN
550
S

Fewkes, Jesse Walter, 1850–
Archeological expedition to Arizona in 1895, by Jesse
Walter Fewkes.

(*In* U. S. Bureau of American ethnology. Seventeenth annual report, 1895-96. Washington, 1898. 29½ᵉᵐ. p. 519–744. illus., pl. XCI-CLXXXV (i. e. 86 pl., incl. map, plan; part col.))
Also issued separately.

1. Arizona—Antiq. 2. Pueblo Indians.

16–5532

Library of Congress ⌣ E51.U55 17th

QK
1
G 32

FESTUCA
Saint-Yves, Alfred
Festuca de la Nouvelle-Zélande.

(Candollea, Vol. IV, 1929–31, pp. 293–307)

PL
870
T 25

(Pritchard, George)
A few lessons in English, and Tahitian; with
a view to make an attempt to teach the natives the
English language. Tahiti. Mission Press. 1832.
12 + 10 pp. 8vo.

(Bound with 33 other pamphlets: Te evanelia
a to tatou ... no. 23)

AS
36
S2

... Archeological investigations in New Mexico, Colorado, and Utah (with 14 plates) by J. Walter Fewkes ...
Washington, Smithsonian institution, 1917.

1 p. l., 38 p. illus. (incl. plans) 14 pl. on 7 l. 24½ᵉᵐ. (Smithsonian miscellaneous collections. v. 68, no. 1)
Publication 2442.

1. New Mexico—Antiq. 2. Colorado—Antiq. 3. Utah—Antiq.

Library of Congress ⌣ Q11.S7 vol. 68, no. 1 17–26463
—— Copy 2. E78.S7F39

GN
Ethn.
Pam.
4435

FETISHES   BISMARCK ISLANDS
Damm, Hans
Versuch einer Deutung der sog. Fetische
von den Anachoreten-Inseln (Kaniet), Bismarckarchipel.

(Ethnologica, Neue Folge, Band 2:146–153, 1960)

(experiment in interpreting the so-called
fetishes of the Anachoreten Islands,
Bismarck Archipelago)

GN
550
S

Fewkes, Jesse Walter, 1850–
The aborigines of Porto Rico and neighboring islands,
by Jesse Walter Fewkes.

(*In* U. S. Bureau of American ethnology. Twenty-fifth annual report ... 1903-04. Washington, 1907. 29½ᵉᵐ. p. 3–220. illus., XCIII (i. e. 95) pl.)
Half-title.

1. Indians of the West Indies—Porto Rico.

7—35402

Library of Congress E51.U55 25th

AS
36
S2

Fewkes, Jesse Walter, 1850–
... Archeology of the lower Mimbres Valley, New Mexico (with eight plates) by J. Walter Fewkes ... Washington, Smithsonian institution, 1914.

1 p. l., 53 p. illus., 8 pl. 24½ᵉᵐ. (Smithsonian miscellaneous collections. v. 63, no. 10)
Publication 2316.

1. Mimbres Valley, N. M.—Antiq. *Archaeology - New Mexico*

Library of Congress ⌣ Q11.S7 vol. 63, no. 10 14–30958
—— Copy 2. E78.N65F43

GN
472
B 33

FETISHISM
Baudin, R. P.
Fétichisme et Féticheurs. Extrait des
"Missions Catholiques", se vend au profit de la
mission. Lyon...1884. 8vo.

AS
36
S2

Fewkes, J. Walter
Additional designs on prehistoric
Mimbres pottery. Smithson. Miscell. Coll.
Vol. 76, No.8, 1924.

GN
550
S

Fewkes, Jesse Walter, 1850–
Casa Grande, Arizona, by Jesse Walter Fewkes.

(*In* U. S. Bureau of American ethnology. Twenty-eighth annual report, 1906-07. Washington, 1912. 29½ᵉᵐ. p. 25–179. illus., 79 pl. (incl. plans; part fold.))

1. Casa Grande ruin.

16–5548

Library of Congress E51.U55 28th

GN
Pam
2074

Fetzer, Christian
Rassenanatomische untersuchungen an
17 Hottentottenköpfen. From Zeit. f.
morphol. und anthrop. bd 16, heft 1, 1913.

QL
1
H 2

Fewkes, J. Walter
Agassiz, Alexander and others
Selections from embryological monographs.
III. Acalephs, by J. Walter Fewkes and Polyps
by E. L. Mark.

(Mem. Mus. Comp. Zool. Harvard, Vol. 9, No. 3, 1884)
-------Bibliography:Bull. MCZH, Vol. XI, No.1C

AS
36
S1

Fewkes, Jesse Walter, 1850–
The cave dwellings of the Old and New worlds ... By
J. Walter Fewkes.

(*In* Smithsonian institution. Annual report. 1910. Washington, 1911. 23½ᵉᵐ. p. 613–634. 11 pl. on 6 l.)
"Reprinted ... from American anthropologist, vol. 12, no. 3, July–Sept., 1910."

1. Cave-dwellings.

11–31584

Library of Congress Q11.S66 1910

3

GN 550 S

Fewkes, Jesse Walter, 1850–
Certain antiquities of eastern Mexico, by Jesse Walter Fewkes.
(*In* U. S. Bureau of American ethnology. Annual report ... 1903/04. Washington, 1907. 25th, p. 221-284. illus., pl. XCIV-CXXIX)
Half-title.

Archaeology-Mexico
1. Mexico—Antiq.
7-35403
Library of Congress E51.U55

GN 560 I-C

Fewkes, Jesse Walter
Porto Rican elbow-stones in the Hehe museum, with discussion of similar objects elsewhere.
(Contrib. from the Heye museum, vol. 1, no. 4, 1913, pp. 435-459)

GN 550 I-C

Fewkes, Jesse Walter, 1850–
... Relations of aboriginal culture and environment in the Lesser Antilles, by J. Walter Fewkes ... New York, D. Taylor & co., printers, 1914.
cover-title, p. 662-678. 25½ᶜᵐ. (Contributions from the Heye museum, v. 1; no. 8)
Reprinted from Bulletin of the American geographical society, vol. XLVI, no. 9, September 1914.

1. Indians of the West Indies—Antilles, Lesser. 2. Antilles, Lesser—Archaeology—Antiq.
16-23259
Library of Congress E11.N56 vol. 1

GN 550 S

Fewkes, Jesse Walter, 1850–
Designs on prehistoric Hopi pottery, by Jesse Walter Fewkes.
(*In* U. S. Bureau of American ethnology. Thirty-third annual report, 1911-1912. Washington, 1919. 30ᶜᵐ. p. 207-284. illus., plates (1 fold.))
Part of the plates printed on both sides.
"Authorities cited": p. 284.

1. Hopi Indians. 2. Indians of North America—Pottery.
19-17498
Library of Congress E51.U55 33d

AS 36 S1

Fewkes, Jesse Walter, 1850–
A prehistoric Mesa Verde pueblo and its people. By J. Walter Fewkes ...
(*In* Smithsonian institution. Annual report. 1916. Washington, 1917. 23½ᶜᵐ. p. 461-488. illus., 15 pl. on 8 l. (incl. fold. map))

1. Mesa Verde national park. 2. Colorado—Antiq.
18-3073
Library of Congress Q11.S66 1916

QL Protozoa to Poly. Pam. #169

Fewkes, J. Walter
The Siphonophores II. The anatomy and development of Agalma (continued). From American Nat. 1880, pp 617 - .

GN 550 I-C

Fewkes, Jesse Walter, 1850–
... Engraved celts from the Antilles, by J. Walter Fewkes. New York, The Museum of the American Indian, Heye foundation, 1915.
cover-title, 12 p. illus. 25½ᶜᵐ. (Contributions from the Museum of the American Indian, Heye foundation, vol. II, no. 2)

1. Indians of the West Indies—Implements. 2. West Indies—Antiq.
16-23253
Library of Congress E11.N56 vol. 2

AS 36 S2

Fewkes, Jesse Walter, 1850–
... Prehistoric ruins of the Gila Valley, by J. Walter Fewkes ...
(*In* Smithsonian institution. Smithsonian miscellaneous collections. Washington, 1910. 24½ᶜᵐ. vol. LII (Quarterly issue, vol. V) p. 403-436 incl. illus., plans. pl. XXXVIII-XLII)
Publication 1873.
Originally published August 4, 1909.

1. Gila River Valley—Antiq.
16-12718
Library of Congress Q11.S7 vol. 52
——— Copy 2.

AS 36 S1

Fewkes, Jesse Walter, 1850–
Sun worship of the Hopi Indians. By J. Walter Fewkes ...
(*In* Smithsonian institution. Annual report. 1918. Washington, 1920. 23½ᶜᵐ. p. 493-526. illus., 11 pl.)

1. Hopi Indians—Religion and mythology. I. Title.
20-18983
Library of Congress Q11.S66 1918

AS 36 S2

Fewkes, Jesse Walter, 1850–
... Excavations at Casa Grande, Arizona, in 1906-07, by J. Walter Fewkes.
(*In* Smithsonian institution. Smithsonian miscellaneous collections. Washington, 1908. 24½ᶜᵐ. vol. L (Quarterly issue, vol. IV) p. 289-329. illus. (plans), pl. XXIII-XL (2 fold.) incl. plans)
Publication 1773.
Originally published October 25, 1907.

1. Casa Grande ruin.
16-11645
Library of Congress Q11.S7 vol. 50
——— Copy 2.

GN 550 S

Fewkes, Jesse Walter, 1850–
... Prehistoric villages, castles, and towers of southwestern Colorado, by J. Walter Fewkes. Washington, Govt. print. off., 1919.
79 p. illus., 17 pl. 24ᶜᵐ. (Smithsonian institution. Bureau of American ethnology. Bulletin 70)
Plates printed on both sides.

1. Colorado—Antiq.
19-27641
Library of Congress E51.U6 vol. 70

GN 550 S

Fewkes, Jesse Walter, 1850–
Tusayan flute and snake ceremonies, by Jesse Walter Fewkes.
(*In* U. S. Bureau of American ethnology. Nineteenth annual report, 1897-98. Washington, 1900. 29½ᶜᵐ. pt. 2, p. 957-1011. illus., pl. XLV-LXV (part col.))

1. Hopi Indians—Religion and mythology. 2. Snake-dance. I. Title.
16-5541
Library of Congress E51.U55 19th

AS 36 S2

Fewkes, Jesse Walter, 1850–
... Great stone monuments in history and geography, by J. Walter Fewkes ... Washington, Smithsonian institution, 1913.
1 p. L, 50 p. illus. 24½ᶜᵐ. (Smithsonian miscellaneous collections, v. 61, no. 6)
Publication 2229.
Presidential address delivered before the Anthropological society of Washington, February 20, 1912.

1. Megalithic monuments.
13-35692
Library of Congress Q11.S7
——— Copy 2.   GN791.F4

AS 36 S1

Fewkes, Jesse Walter, 1850–
Preliminary account of an expedition to the cliff villages of the Red Rock country, and the Tusayan ruins of Sikyatki and Awatobi, Arizona, in 1895. By J. Walter Fewkes ...
(*In* Smithsonian institution. Annual report. 1895. Washington, 1896. 23½ᶜᵐ. p. 557-588. pl. XXXV-(LXVII))

1. Cliff-dwellings—Arizona. 2. Arizona—Antiq.
S 15-901
Library of Congress
Library, Smithsonian Q11.S66 1895 Institution

GN 550 S

Fewkes, Jesse Walter, 1850–
Tusayan katcinas, by Jesse Walter Fewkes.
(*In* U. S. Bureau of American ethnology. Fifteenth annual report, 1893-94. Washington, 1897. 29½ᶜᵐ. p. 245-313. illus., pl. CIV-CXI (part col.))
Also issued separately.

1. Katcinas. 2. Hopi Indians—Religion and mythology. I. Title.
16-5524
Library of Congress E51.U55 15th

GN 550 S

Fewkes, Jesse Walter, 1850–
Hopi katcinas drawn by native artists, by Jesse Walter Fewkes.
(*In* U. S. Bureau of American ethnology. Twenty-first annual report, 1899-1900. Washington, 1903. 29½ᶜᵐ. p. 3-126. LXIII col. pl. (incl. fold. map))

1. Katcinas. 2. Hopi Indians—Religion and mythology.
16-5544
Library of Congress E51.U55 21st

AS 36 S1

Fewkes, Jesse Walter, 1850–
A preliminary account of archæological field work in Arizona in 1897. By J. Walter Fewkes.
(*In* Smithsonian institution. Annual report. 1897. Washington, 1898. 23½ᶜᵐ. p. 601-623. XXIII pl. (incl. 2 maps))

1. Arizona—Antiq.
S 15-978
Library of Congress
Library, Smithsonian Q11.S66 1897 Institution

GN 550 S

Fewkes, Jesse Walter, 1850–
Tusayan migration traditions, by Jesse Walter Fewkes.
(*In* U. S. Bureau of American ethnology. Nineteenth annual report, 1897-98. Washington, 1900. 29½ᶜᵐ. pt. 2, p. 573-633)

1. Hopi Indians. I. Title.
16-5535
Library of Congress E51.U55 19th

QL Protozoa to Polyzoa Pam 285

Fewkes, J. Walter
New invertebrata from the coast of California. From the Bull. of the Essex Institute, v.21, 1889.

AS 36 S2

Fewkes, Jesse Walter, 1850–
Preliminary report on an archeological trip to the West Indies, by J. Walter Fewkes.
(*In* Smithsonian institution. Smithsonian miscellaneous collections. Washington, 1903. 24½ᶜᵐ. vol. XLV (Quarterly issue, vol. I) p. 112-133. pl. XXXIX-XLVIII)
Plate XL incorrectly numbered LX.
Publication 1429.
An account of excavations in Porto Rico and description of specimens from Porto Rico and Santo Domingo.
Vol. 45 (Quarterly issue, v. 1) with t-p. dated 1903, was issued 4 parts in 2, with covers dated 1904.

1. Porto Rico—Antiq. 2. Haiti—Antiq.
16-11314
Library of Congress Q11.S7 vol. 45
——— Copy 2.

Fewkes, Jesse Walter, 1850–
The Tusayan ritual: a study of the influence of environment on aboriginal cults. By J. Walter Fewkes.
(*In* Smithsonian institution. Annual report. 1895. Washington, 1896. 23½ᶜᵐ. p. 683-700. pl. LXX-LXXIII)

1. Hopi Indians—Religion and mythology. I. Title.
S 15-907
Library of Congress
Library, Smithsonian Q11.S66 1895 Institution

GN 550 S

Fewkes, Jesse Walter, 1850–
Tusayan snake ceremonies, by Jesse Walter Fewkes.

(*In* U. S. Bureau of American ethnology. Sixteenth annual report, 1894–95. Washington, 1897. 29½ᵐ. p. 267–312. pl. LXX–LXXXI)

Also issued separately, Washington, 1897.
Bibliography: p. 312.

1. Hopi Indians—Religion and mythology. 2. Snake-dance. I. Title.

16–5528

Library of Congress   E51.U55 16th

S Agri Pam 47

FIBERS

Rice, George Damon Jr.

A lecture on a fibre of cotton from the bale to the finished fabric. From Technical Quarterly (sec.ser) Millbury, Mass.

S Agri Pam 56

FIBERS

Guilfoyle, W. R.

Catalogue (descriptive) of fibres, papers, carpological specimens, etc., forwarded to the Centennial Int. Exhibition, Melbourne, 1888.

GN 550 S

Fewkes, Jesse Walter, 1850–
Two summers' work in Pueblo ruins, by Jesse Walter Fewkes.

(*In* U. S. Bureau of American ethnology. Twenty-second annual report, 1900–01. Washington, 1904. 29½ᵐ. pt. 1, p. 3–195. illus. LXX pl. (incl. map, plan, part col.))

1. Arizona—Antiq. 2. Pueblo Indians—Antiq.

16–5546

Library of Congress   E51.U55 22d

QK 22 S6 S77

Fibers

Tropical fibres by W. Squier

London 1863. 8vo pp 64 pl XVI

K.13.28

QK 473.H BL and AS 763 B-o and QK Botany Pam. # 1095

FIBERS - HAWAIIAN ISLANDS

Blackman, L. G.

Fibres of the Hawaiian Islands.

in Bishop Mus. O. P. II. 1. 1902, 8vo. pp. 37-64.

Honolulu, 1902.

Also separate.

AS 36 S1

Fewkes, Jesse Walter, 1850–
Two types of southwestern cliff houses. By J. Walter Fewkes …

(*In* Smithsonian institution. Annual report. 1919. Washington, 1921. 23½ᵐ. p. 421–426. 6 pl. on 3 l.)

1. Cliff-dwellings.

22–319

Library of Congress   Q11.S66 1919
[91]

SB 240 Pam. Box

Fiber

U.S. Department of Agriculture
Division of Statistics. Fiber reports.
No.1. Flax, Hemp, Ramie, and Jute.   K9

" 3. Sisal hemp culture in United States.   K9

" 4. Flax culture for fiber in   "   "   K9

" 5. Leaf fibers of the United States.   K9

" 6. Uncultivated bast fibers of U.S.   K9

" 7. Cultivation of ramie in U.S.   K9

AP 2 S35

FIBERS -- HAWAIIAN ISLANDS

MacCaughey, Vaughan

Olona, Hawaii's unexcelled fiber-plant. In Science XLVIII, July-Dec. 1918 pp 236-238.

Also separate.

Fewkes, J. Walter, Ed.
see
Journal of American Ethnology and Arch.

SB 240 Pam. Box

Fiber

U.S. Department of Agriculture
Division of Statistics. Fiber reports.
No. 8. Culture of hemp and jute in U.S.   K9

" 9. Descriptive catalogue of useful fiber plants of the world.   K9

" 10. Flax culture for seed and fiber in Europe and America.   K9

" 11. Culture of hemp in Europe.   K9

S 17.H3 H1

FIBERS - Hawaiian Islands

Report of the Committee on the Olona. (tr. from the Hawaiian) in Trans. R. Haw. Agric. Soc., II. 1. pp 142 - 144. (Honolulu, 1854.)

AS 36 S1

Fialho, Anfriso.
Biographical sketch of Dom Pedro II, emperor of Brazil. By Anpriso [!] Fialho …

(*In* Smithsonian institution. Annual report. 1876. Washington, 1877. 23½ᵐ. p. 173–204.)

"Translated … by M. A. Henry."

1. Pedro II, emperor of Brazil, 1825–1891. I. Henry, Mary A., tr.

S 15–419

Library of Congress   Q11.S66 1876
Library, Smithsonian   Institution

S 399 E82

FIBER - Hemp

Smith, Jared G.
Manila hemp or abaca.
Haw. Agric. Exper. Sta. Press Bull. 5, p.1.

Chiefly extracts from Philippine. Farmers' Bull. 4. Gilmore.

GN 671.H2 H 23

FIBERWORK HAWAII

Handy, E. S. C., and others

Ancient Hawaiian Civilization, pp.125-130; Fiberwork, by E. H. Bryan, Jr.

QK 494 D64

FIBER

Dodge, Chas Richards

A descriptive catalogue of useful fiber plants of the World, including the structural and economic classification of fibers. U.S. Dept. Agric. Fiber Invest. Rept. No.9, 1897.

S 399 E82

FIBER - Sisal

Wilcox, E. V. + McGeorge, Wm.
Sisal and the utilization of sisal waste.
Haw. Agric. Exper. Sta. Press Bull. 35, pp. 24. 1912

QL Mollusk Pam 571

Ficalbi, Eugenio

Una pubblicazione poco conosciuta di Ruppel intitolata: "Intorno ad alcuni cefalopodi del mare di Messina (Messina, 1844)". From Monitore Zool. Italiano, anno 10, n.3, 1899.

S 17.N4 a

FIBER

Heron, E. H.
Cultivation of Agave sisalina. In Agric Gaz. N.S.W. XXVIII; 1917, pp 498-504.

S Agri Pam 59

FIBERS

Dodge, Charles Richards

A report on the uncultivated bast fibers of the United States... allied species produced commercially in the Old World. From U. S. Dept. Agri. Fiber Investigations, Rept. 6, 1894.

QL Mollusk Pam 570

Ficalbi, Eugenio

Unicita di specie delle due forme di cefalopodi pelagici chiamate "Chiroteuthis Veranyi" e "Doratopsis vermicularis". From Monitore Zool. Italiano, anno 10, n.4, 1899.

QK
495.M8
E 34

FICUS

Eisen, Gustav

The fig: its history, culture, and curing, with a descriptive catalogue of the known varieties of figs.

(U. S. Dept. of Agric., Div. of Pomology, Bull. 9, 1901.   317 pp.)

QK
Bot.Pam.
2246

FICUS

Summerhayes, V. S.

The genus Ficus (Moraceae) in southeastern Polynesia.

(Bernice P. Bishop Museum, Occasional Papers Vol. 15, 1940, pp. 227-228 (No. 21). Mangarevan Exp. Pub. 33.)

S
17.H3
H38

129)

FICUS BENGALENSIS

Pope, Willia T.

The banyan and some other closely allied species.

(Haw. For. and Agric., Vol. 6, 1909, pp. 121-

QK
1
C 14

looked
case

FICUS

King, George

The species of ficus of the Indo-Malayan and Chinese countries, Appendix (only):Some new species from New Guinea.

(Annals of the Royal Botanic Garden, Calcutta, Vol. 1, Appendix (only):1-52, 1889)

QK
Bot.
Pam.
3202

3203

FICUS   ASIA

Corner, E. J. H.

Taxonomic notes on Ficus Linn., Asia and Australasia, V. Subgen. Ficus Sect. Rhizooladus Kalosyce...

(The Garden's Bulletin, 18(1):1-69, 1960)

...sections 1-4, ibid, 17(3), 1960

DU
Pac.Pam.
884

in envelope
attached

Fiddler, Frank

Mokapu: a study of the land. By Technical Sergeant Frank Fiddler, U. S. Marine Corps. (1956) 20 pp. mimeographed. Privately issued

[installments each week from Oct. 5 through Nov. 23, 1956 from The Windward Marine newspaper. Part I missing]

QK
495.F44
S 25

FICUS

Sata, Nagaharu (Tyosyun)

A monographic study of the genus *Ficus* from the point of view of economic botany.

(Contributions from the Institute of Horticulture and Economic Botany, Fac. of Agric., Ta Taihoku Imp. Univ., No. 32, 1944)

QK
1
S 61

FICUS   AUSTRALASIA

Corner, E. J. H.

Taxonomic notes on Ficus.L. Asia and Australasia, Addendum II.

(The Gardens' Bull. 19(3):385-401, 1962)

DU
Pac.Pam.
894

Fiddler, Frank

Mokapu; a study of the land. Privately printed- mimeographed. 4to. 20 pp.

QK
1
U

FICUS

Standley, Paul Carpenter, 1884–

... The Mexican and Central American species of *Ficus*. By Paul C. Standley. Washington, Govt. print. off., 1917.

v. 35, vii-viii p. 241ᵐᵐ. (Smithsonian institution. United States National museum. Contributions from the United States National herbarium. v. 20, pt. 1)

Bibliographical foot-notes.

1. Botany—Central America. [1. Central America—Botany] 2. Ficus. 3. Botany—New Mexico. [3. New Mexico—Botany]

Agr 17–626

Library, U. S. Dept. of   Agriculture 450C76 vol.20, pt.1

QK
Bot.
Pam.
3202

3203

FICUS   MALAYSIA

Corner, E. J. H.

Taxonomic notes on Ficus Linn., Asia and Australasia, V. Subgen. Ficus Sect. Rhizooladus Kalosyce...

(The Gardens' Bulletin, 18(1):1-69, 1960)

...sections 1-4, ibid, 17(3), 1960

QL
596.C9
F 45

R8vo.

Fiedler, Karl

Monograph of the South American weevils of the genus Conotrachelus.   London. By Order of the Trustees of the British Museum. 1940.   365 pp.

QK
1
A 75

FICUS

Summerhayes, V. S.,

Additions to our knowledge of the figs of New Guinea.

(Journal of the Arnold Arboretum, Vol. 22, 1941, pp. 81-109)

QK
1
B 15

FICUS   PHILIPPINE ISLANDS

Pancho, Juan V.

Notes on cultivated species of Ficus in the Philippines.

(Baileya,6(3):129-134, 1958)

AP
2
A 5

FIEBERLING GUYOT

Carsola, Alfred J.

Submarine geology of two flat-topped northeast Pacific seamounts. By Alfred J. Carsola and Robert S. Dietz.

(Am. Jour. Sci., Vol. 250:481-497, 1952)

QK
Bot.Pam.
2228

FICUS

Summerhayes, V. S.

The genus Ficus (Moraceae) in southeastern Polynesia.

(Bernice P. Bishop Museum, Occasional Papers, Vol. 15, 1940, No. 21, pp. 227-228)

QK
495.M 8
C 74

FICUS   BIBLIOGRAPHY

Condit, Ira J.

A bibliography of the fig. By Ira J. Condit and Julius Enderud.

(Hilgardia, Vol. 25, 1956)

DS
646.5
F45

Fiedler, Hermann

Die insel Timor; mit 162 bildern und 1 kartenskizze.   Friedrichssegen, Felkwang, 1929. 87 p.   pl.   4to.

QK
Bot.Pam.
2216

FICUS

Summerhayes, V. S.

The genus Ficus in the Samoan Islands.

(Occ. Papers, Bernice P. Bishop Museum, Vol. XV, No. 9, pp. 109-118, 1939)

DU
12
G 47

looked
case

FICUS BENGALENSIS

Gill, W. W.

Jottings from the Pacific, pp. 172-75. (London). 1885. sm8vo.

QK
531
#1F45
†

K.11.3.

Field, H. C.

The ferns of New Zealand and its immediate dependencies, with directions for their collection and cultivation. London, 1890. 4to pp 164   29 Plates

'93

DU
621
H3
Field, H.G.

Game fishing in the Hawaiian waters.
Thrum's Hawaiian Annual, 1917, p.86-93.

Z
Biblio-
graphy
Pam.
134
Field, Henry

Bibliography on southwestern Asia. Univ.
of Miami Press. Coral Gables, 1953. 4to. xvi+
106 pp.

2 copies

GN
Ethn.Pam.
3533
Field, Henry

U. S. S. R. (prehistory); excerpt from the
Oriental Institute Archaeological Report on the
Near East. By Henry Field and Eugene Prostov.

(American Journal of Semitic Languages and
Literatures, Vol. 58:108-110, 1941)

DU
620
P
Field, H. Gooding

Game fishing in Hawaiian waters.

(Paradise of the Pacific, Vol. 29, 1916,
No. 2, pp. 22-23)

GN
2.M
P 35
Field, Henry

Body-marking in southwestern Asia.

(Papers, Peabody Mus. of Arch. and Ethn.,
Harvard, Vol. 45(1), 1958)

DU
1
P
Field, Isobel

Stevenson did not die from TB in Samoa.

(Pac. Is. Monthly, 21(12):63, 1951)

DU
620
P
Field, H. Gooding

The royal sport of Hawaiian game fishing.

(Paradise of the Pacific, Vol. 29, 1916,
No. 12, pp. 41-43; Vol. 33, No. 1, 1920, p. 6-8)

GN
2.M
P 35
Field, Henry

Contributions to the anthropology of the
Caucasus.

(Papers of the Peabody Museum of American
Archaeology and Ethnology, Harvard University,
Vol. 48(1), 1953)

Field, Isobel   Carter Coll.
                                       12-D-8

This life I've loved. New York...
Longmans, Green and Co. 1937 ix + 353 pp.

GN
Ethn.Pam
3671
Field, Henry

Ancient man in southwestern Asia.

(Reprinted from the "Studies presented to
David Moore Robinson", pp. 232-237. received
Dec. 1951) no date, no place

QK
Bot.Pam.
2785
Field, Henry

Notes on medicinal plants used in Tepoztlan,
Morelos, Mex.

(América Indígena, Vol. XIII(4):291-300,
1953)

QH
323
D 87
Field, Louise Randall

Sea anemones and corals of Beaufort, North
Carolina.

(Duke University Marine Station, Bull. No.
5, 1949)

GN
2.M
P 35
Field, Henry

An anthropological reconnaissance in the
Near East, 1950.

(Papers of the Peabody Museum of Archaeology
and Ethnology, Harvard University, Vol. 48(2),
1956)

GN
2.M
F 45-1

and
GN
Ethn.Pam
4208
Field, Henry

The Races of Mankind: An Introduction to
Chauncey Keep Memorial Hall. Preface by Berthold
Laufer. Introduction by Sir Arthur Keith.

(Anthropology Leaflet, 30, Field Museum of
Natural History. 1933)

QH
Nat. Hist.
Pam.
122

A field collector's manual in natural history. Prepared by members of the staff of the
Smithsonian Institution. Published by the
Smithsonian Institution, Washington, 1944. 12mo
118 pp.

GN
1
A
Field, Henry

Anthropology in the Soviet Union, 1945.

(American Anthropologist, 48 (3):375-396,
1946)

GN
Ethn.Pam.
3561
Field, Henry

Recent archaeological discoveries in the
Soviet Union. By Henry Field and Kathleen Price

(Southwestern Journal of Anthropology, Vol.
5:17-27, 1949)

QK
Pam
#172
171
164
17
FIELD EXCURSIONS
MacCaughey, Vaughan

The Botanical field excursion in
collegiate work, ex Science, N. S.
vol. XLIV, no. 1137, October 13, 1916.

Z
Biblio-
graphy
Pam.
142
Field, Henry

Bibliography: 1926-1955
       "   1926-1958

[his works concern Asia almost entirely]

GN
Ethn.Pam.
3617
Field, Henry

Reconnaissance in southwestern Asia.

(Southwestern Journal of Anthropology,
Vol. 7(1):86-102, 1951)

AS
36
S1
FIELD STUDY IN ORNITHOLOGY
Tristram, Henry Baker, 1822-1906.
    Field study in ornithology. By H. B. Tristram ...

(*In* Smithsonian institution. Annual report. 1893. Washington, 1894.
23½ᶜᵐ. p. 465-485)

"From the Zoologist, London, October, 1893, vol. XVII, pp. 361-386;
and Nature, September 21, 1893, vol. XLVIII, pp. 490."

1. Birds.   I. Title.

                                              S 15-837
Library of Congress   (Q11.S66 1893
Library, Smithsonian   (Institution

3

AS
36
N 54

Fieldes, M. and others

Mineralogy and radioactivity of Niue Island soils. By M. Fieldes, G. Bealing, G.G.C.Claridge and N. H. Taylor.

(New Zealand Journal of Science, Vol. 3(4): 658-675, 1960)

GN
1
J 86

Fife, A. E.

The legend of the three Nephites among the Mormons.

(Journal of Am. Folklore, Vol. 53:1-49, 1940)

A fight with distances

DU
623
Au2
A 33

Aubertin, J. J.

A fight with distances: The States, the Hawaiian Islands, Canada, British Columbia, Cuba, the Bahamas, by J.J. Aubertin.

London, 1888. 352p. illus., 2 maps.

RA
789
Aus

Fielding. J. W.

Australasian ticks.

(In Service Publication (Tropical Division) Commonwealth of Australia, Department of Health, No. 9, 1926)

Q
Biogr.
Pam.
105

Fifteen great names in New Zealand history. Bank of New South Wales. 8vo. 16 pp. 1957

[Tasman, Cook, Marsden, Bellingshausen, Nene, d'Urville, maning, Colenso, Grey, Mantell, Brunner, Heaphy, von Haast, Tukino, Dobson]

QL
Insect
Pam.
1631

Fighting our insect enemies. Achievements of professional entomology, 1854-1954.

(U. S. Dept. of Agric., Agric. Information Bull. No. 121, 1954)

RC
Pathol.
Pam.
44

Fielding, J. W.

Improved silver technique for Leptospirae in paraffin sections.

(Laboratory Jour. of Australasia, 1941, [2 pp])

PL
Phil.Pam.
665

Fifth anniversary report of the Summer Inst. of Linguistics, Philippine Islands.

(Philippine Social Sci. and Humanities Review, Vol. 23(2/4):369-372, 1958)

DU
1
P

Fighting rhinoceros beetle in W. Samoa: entomologists and wasps play their part.

(Pacific Islands Monthly, 22(7):116, 1952)

RC
Pathol.
Pam.
50

Fielding, J. W.

Rapid microtomy.

(Laboratory Journal of Australasia, Vol. 1, 1936, no.1) 2 pp. unnumbered.

DU
Hist.
Pam.
377

50th Anniversary of the arrival of the first Japanese immigrants in Hawaii. February 17, 1885-February 17, 1935.

(The Honolulu Advertiser, February 17, 1935)

AS
763
B-b

FIGITIDAE

Kinsey, Alfred C.

New Figitidae from the Marquesas Islands.

(Bull. Bernice P. Bishop Museum, No. 142, pp. 193-197. Issued October 20, 1938. Pac. Ent. Survey Publication 8, Art. 21)

RC
Pathol.
Pam.
48

Fielding, J. W.

Silver impregnation of Leptospirae in paraffin sections.

(Laboratory Journal of Australasia, 1940, [4 pp. unnumbered])

AS
540
P

Fig
Baker, C. F.

Study of caprification in Ficus Nota.

in Phil. Journ. Sc. D. VIII No.2, pp. 63-88. Manila, 1913.

GN
740
F 47

Figuier, Louis

L'homme primitif, par Louis Figuier: Ouvrage illustré de 30 scènes de la vie de l'homme primitif composées par Émile Bayard, et de 232 figures représentant les objets usuels des premiers ages de l'humanité. Dessinées par Delahaye. Paris. L. Hachette. 1870. 8vo. vii + 446 pp.

RC
Pathol.
Pam.
49

Fielding, J. W.

Typhus: modified Breinl method for staining Rickettsiae and other inclusions.

(Med. Jour. of Australia, 1943, p. 435-36)

AS
36
S1

Figaniere e Morão, Joaquim Cesar de, 1798-1866.

An account of a remarkable accumulation of bats. By M. Figanierre é Morao ...

(In Smithsonian institution. Annual report. 1863. Washington, 1864, 234¹ᵐ. p. (407)-409)

1 Chiroptera
1. Bats.

Library of Congress
Library, Smithsonian
Institution

Q11.S66 1863

S 15-154

Figures of molluscous animals

QL
404
Gr

Gray, Mrs. Maria Emma (Smith) 1787-1876.

Figures of molluscous animals, selected from various authors. Etched for the use of students by Maria Emma Gray ... London, Longman, Brown, Green and Longmans, 1859.

5 v. front. (port., v. 4) plates. 22½ᶜᵐ.
First issued 1842-57.
Vol. I-III and v: plates; vol. IV: Explanation of plates in vol. I-III, and list of genera.
"A list of the genera of recent *Mollusca*, their synonyma and types. By J. E. Gray ... London, Printed by R. and J. E. Taylor, 1847," vol. IV, p. 129-206, is reprinted from the Proceedings of the Zoological society for 1847.
Imperfect: v. 5 wanting.
1. Shells. I. Gray, John Edward, 1800-1875.

Library of Congress

QL404.G78

6-18748†

QL
628
C 15

Fields, W. Gordon

A preliminary report on the fishery and on the biology of the squid, Loligo opalescens.

(California Fish and Game, Vol. 36 (4): 366-377, 1950)

AM
Pam
No.11

Figgins, J. D.

New methods of preparing fishes for museum exhibit. Bul. Bur. of Fisheries.

Washington, 1908.

AP
2
S 35

FIGURES OF SPEECH   PALAU

Force, Roland W.

Keys in cultural understanding. By Roland W. Force and Maryanne Force.

(Science, 133(3460):1202-1206, 1961)

G
103.98
F1-m
Findley, A. G.

North Pacific Ocean + Japan Dictionary, 3rd. + 5th. edition.

London, 1886 – 1890

(5th ed missing (1855)

DU
600
F3
F47
Fiji.

    Handbook to Fiji, giving some information concerning the government, legislation, history, geography, land titles, religion, population, education, institutions, trade, agriculture, and climate, of the colony...1892.

Suva, Govt. printing office, 1892.
    78p. map.

S
Agric
Pam.
No.18
No.19
No.20
Fiji Legislative Council

Council Papers
No.39. Annual Report of the Dept. Of Agriculture for the year 1920.Suva, 1921
  " 56. Annual Report ... for 1921. 1922
  " 46 " " 1922. 1923.

DU
Pac.Fam
919
    Fiji. [data collected October, 1958, at Bishop Museum library] 16 pp. letterpress

---

DU
600
F1-b
F48
Fiji [Government]

    Fiji Blue Book for the year 1922, compiled from records in the Colonial Secretary's office.
Suva, 1923, 240 pp. folio.

FIJI

Adams, E. H.

    Jottings from the Pacific; life and incidents in the Fijian and Samoan islands. c1890.

UH has

DU
Pac.Pam.
740
    Fiji, British Crown Colony. Descriptive pamphlet of 24 pp. ob8vo. Fiji Publicity Board. Rec'd 1950.

DU
600
F1-c
F48
Fiji, Colony of

    Civil list and record of officers serving in the Western Pacific High Commission Service. Corrected up to Jan. 1st, 1924.

DU
12
A 21
FIJI

Adams, Henry

    Letters of Henry Adams (1858-1891). Edited by Worthington Chauncey Ford. Boston and New York. Houghton Mifflin Company. 1930. R8vo. vi + 552 pp.

see p. 491-508

DU
600
H 54
    Fiji. Handbook of the Colony. Published by Authority. Government Printer. Suva, Fiji. 1937. R8vo. 165 + iii pp.

S
398.F
F1-a
Fiji. Department of Agriculture

    Agricultural Circular

Vol. I, 1920 . Complete in 10 numbers
  " II 1921. " " 5 "
  " III 1922. " " 4 "
  " IV. 1923, No.1(Jan.-June)
  " V. 1924 No.1(Jan.- June)

AP
2
A 5
FIJI

Agassiz, Alexander

    Explorations of the Albatross in the Pacific ocean...

    (Am. Jour. Sci., Ser. 4, Vol. 9, 1900, pp. 193-98, 369-74)

DU
600
F1
Fiji (Government)

    The colony of Fiji , 1874 - 1924.

Suva, Gov't printer, 1924, pp 159, 4.

Cannot find. Feb. 1934

S
398.F
Fiji Dept of Agriculture. (Div of Entomology)

Bulletin:-
No. 3 Rhinoceros beetle in Samoa. 1912
  5 Scale Insect infesting banana in Fiji. 1913
  7 Mission to Java - Quest of natural enemies for a
      Coleopterous pest of bananas. 1914

Suva, Fiji

QL
1
H1
Fiji

Agassiz, Alexander.

    The islands and coral reefs of Fiji. Mus. Comp. Zoöl. XXXIII Bull. Cambridge 1899.

QL
1
H1

DU
600
F1
Fiji.

    ...Fiji; Report for 1915. (Colonial reports)

London, 1916. 16p.

Cannot find, Feb. 1934

S
398.F
Fiji Dept of Agriculture (Entomology)

Pamphlets:-   Rec'd
No 7 Banana spraying experiments. JAN 8 '
  16 Tour of Coconut districts of Fiji. JAN 8 '
  21 The Lantana seed fly. (Agromyzidae) JAN 8 '

DU
12
A 33
FIJI

Albert, Victor C. Edward, Prince, and George E. Frederick E. Albert, Prince of Wales.

    Cruise of Her Majesty's ship "Bacchante", 1879-1882. Compiled from the private journals, letters, and note-books... vol. 1, pp. 630-675. London. 1886. 8vo.

PL
Phil.Pam.
161
FIJI

Gabelentz, Hans Conon von der

    Die melanesischen Sprachen, nach ihrem grammatischen Bau und ihrer Verwandtschaft unter sich und mit den malaaisch-polynesischen Sprachen.

    (Abh. der phil.-hist. Classe der K. sächsischen Gesellschaft der Wissenschaften, 3, 1861; VII, 1879) 266 pp.

S
398.F
F1-b
Fiji. Department of Agriculture

    Bulletin

See serial file

GN
Pam
236
FIJI

Allardyce, W L

    The Fijians in peace and war. From Man, n. 45, 1904.

DU
Pac
Pam
208

FIJI

Allen, Percy S

Fiji and Samoa. From The Sydney Morning
Herald, Sydney, 1921.

DU
12
B 66

FIJI

Boddam-Whetham, J. W.

Pearls of the Pacific. London, Hurst and
Blackett. 1876. 362 pp. 8vo.

DU
12
B 87

FIJI

Brown, J. Macmillan

Peoples and problems of the Pacific.
London. 1927. Vol. 1, pp. 73-88.

DU
Pac.
Pam.
764

FIJI

Allen, Percy S.

The Pacific Islands: Fiji and Samoa.

(Reprinted from the "Sydney Morning Herald,"
being a series of articles contributed by its
Special Commissioner to Fiji and Samoa, Sydney,
1921. 16 pp. 8vo.

DU
600
B 81

FIJI

Branchi, Giovanni

Tre mesi alle isole dei cannibali nell'
arcipelago delle Figi. Firenze. 1878. 8vo.

DU
12
B 96

FIJI ISLANDS

Burnett, Frank

Through tropic seas. London, 1910. pp. 173
illus.

(Hawaiian Ilds. Fanning. Gilberts and Fiji.)

QK
Botany
Pam 1568

FIJI

Barnes, A. C.

Noxious Weeds and Their Control in Fiji.
Part I by A. C. Barnes. Part II by H. W. Simmonds.

(From Agricultural Journal, Department of
Agriculture, Fiji, Vol. 3, No. 2, 1930; Vol. 4,
No. 1, 1931, pp. 29-31)

DU
12
B 83

locked
case

FIJI

Brenchley, J. L.

Jottings during the cruise of H. M. S.
Curaçoa among the South Sea Islands in 1865...
London. 1873. R8vo.
pp. 143-192.

Fiji Islands

DU
600
B92

Burton, John Wear

The Fiji of to-day.

London, 1910. 364p. illus.

GN
662
B 32

FIJI

Bastian, Adolph

Inselgruppen in Oceanien. Reiseergebnisse
und studien von A. Bastian. Berlin. 1883. 8vo.
pp. 59-112.

DU
600
Br

FIJI

Brewster, A. B.

The hill tribes of Fiji... from
cannibalism to present time.

Philadelphia, Lippincoot, 1922, pp. 308
pls. 24.

DU
600
B 97

FIJI

Burton, J. W.

A hundred years in Fiji. By J. W. Burton
and Wallace Dean. London. The Epworth Press.
(1936) sm8vo. 144 pp.

DU
12
B 42

locked
case

FIJI

Belcher, Edward

Narrative of a voyage round the world, performed in Her Majesty's Ship Sulphur, during the
years 1836-1842...by Captain Sir Edward Belcher,
Commander of the Expedition. In two volumes.
Vol. II, pp.36-53. London. 1843. 8vo.

DU
600
B 84

FIJI

Brewster, A. B.

King of the cannibal isles; a tale of early
life and adventure in the Fiji Islands. London
Robert Hale and Company. 1937. 8vo. 286 pp.

DU
600
R7

FIJI ISLANDS

Calvert, James and Williams. Thomas
Fiji and the Fijians. Vol. I, the
islands and their inhabitants, by Thomas
Williams. Vol. II, mission history, by
James Calvert. Edited by George Stringer
Rowe.
London, 1858.

G
27
M-s

FIJI

Beltrán y Rospide, Ricardo

Islas Viti y Rotuma

(Boletin de la Sociedad Geografica de
Madrid, Tomo XII, pp. 177-204, 1882).

DU
Pac.Pam.
521

FIJI

British Possessions in Oceania...(London).
No. 144. H. M. Stationery Office. 1920. 8vo.
126 pp.

DU
600
C46

FIJI

Chapple, W. A

Fiji, its problems and resources.

Auckland, Whitcombe & Tombs, 1921. 189p.

DU
880
B 63

FIJI

(Blanc, Jean Marie)

Chez les Méridionaux du Pacifique. By P.
Soane Malia. Lyon, Paris. Librairie Catholique
Emmanuel Vitte. 1910. 8 vo. xv + 321 pp.

DU
Pacific
Pam.
235

FIJI

Britton, H.

Fiji in 1870. Letters of the Argus
special correspondent with a complete map
and gazetteer of the Fijian Archipelago.

Melbourne, 1870, 87 pp.

QK
Botany
Pam.
2029

FIJI

Chun, Ella

The jungle of Fiji: Dr. (Harold) St. John
conducting one-man scientific expedition enjoys
quaint hospitality among primitive people.

(Honolulu Advertiser, Nov. 21, 1937)

DU
600
C 71
FIJI

The Colony of Fiji, 1874-1929. (Second edition, revised and edited by Arthur Alban Wright). Suva. J. J. Mc Hugh. 1929. R8vo. v+198+iii pp.

also 1931 edition

Fiji Islands

DU
600
097
Cumming, C.F. Gordon.

At home in Fiji.

New York, 1882. 365p. illus. map.

DU
Pac
Pam
354
FIJI

Descriptive article on Fiji islands (British). n.p., n.d.

DU
12
C 72
FIJI

Colvocoresses, George M.

Four years in a government exploring expedition; to the Island of Madeira...Paumato Group, Society Islands, Navigator Group...Fejee Group... New York. 1852.

GN
671.F1
D 28
FIJI

Deane, W.

Fijian Society, or the Sociology and Psychology of the Fijians. London. Macmillan. 1921. 8vo. xv + 255 pp.

Fiji Islands

DU
12
D62
[Dix, William G., ed].

Wreck of the Glide, with recollections of the Fijiis and of Wallis Island.

New York & London, 1848. 203p.

DU
Pac
Pam
#231
F
FIJI
[Consul at Fiji]

A consulate amonst the Fijis. Overland monthly, 1869, pp. 325-335.

DU
Pac.Pam.
664
FIJI

Degener, Otto

The last cruise of the "Cheng-Ho". Parts 1-2.

(Journal of the New York Botanical Garden, Vol. 44, 1943, Nos. 525-526, pp. 197-213; 221-232)

FIJI
Carter Coll.
7-A-23
Dodman, G. Sutherland

A voyage round the world in 500 days, with details, compiled and arranged by G. Sutherland Dodman, giving an account of the principal parts to be visited... 2nd ed. London. Mackie, Brewinall and Co. 1880 xii + 173 pp. 8vo.

DU
12
C 79
FIJI

Cooper, H. S.

Coral lands. Vol. I, pp. 18-342. London. 1880.

looked case

DU
600
D 31
FIJI

Degener, Otto

Naturalist's South Pacific expedition:Fiji. Paradise of the Pacific, Ltd. Honolulu. 1949. 8vo. (8)+301 pp.

DU
12
D 89
FIJI

Dumont d'Urville, J. S. C.

Voyage de découvertes autour du monde et a la recherche de La Pérouse...sur la corvette l'Astrolabe...1826, 1827, 1828, et 1829. Histoire du voyage. 5 vols. in 10 pts. Paris. 1832-1834. 8vo.
Vol. 4, pts 2, pp. 397-458; 691-728.

FIJI
Carter Coll.
6-P-9
Coote, Walter, F.R.G.S.

Wanderings, south and east; with two maps and forty-seven wood engravings. London. Sampson Low, Marston, Searle, and Rivington 1882 369 pp. 8vo.

DU
600
D 43
FIJI

Derrick, R. A.

The Fiji Islands, a geographical handbook. Government Printing Department. Suva, Fiji. R8vo. xviii+334+xix pp. (1951)

DU
12
D 89
FIJI

Dumont d'Urville, J. S. C.

Voyage de la corvette l'Astrolabe...1826-1829 ...Paris. 1830-1835. 8vo.
Histoire du voyage, Tome 4, pp. 394-458.

looked case

DU
12
C 80
FIJI

Coppinger, R. W.

Cruise of the "Alert". Four years in Patagonia, Polynesian, and Mascarene waters.(1878-82) ...pp. 159-163. London. 1885. 8vo.

The same. Fourth edition. 1899. 8vo.

DU
600
D 43
FIJI

Derrick, R. A.

A history of Fiji. Vol. 1
School edition. Printed and published by the Printing and Stationery Department, Suva, Fiji. (1946). R8vo. vii + 250 + VIII + ix-xxviii pp.

G
159
D 89
FIJI

Dumont d'Urville, J. S. C.

Voyage pittoresque autour du monde; resumé général des voyages de découvertes de Magellan, Tasman, Dampier, Anson...Vols. 1-2. Paris. 1834-1835. 4to. Vol. 2, pp. 83-103.

DU
600
C 85
FIJI

Coulter, John Wesley

Fiji: little India of the Pacific. University of Chicago Press. 1942c. 8vo. xiii + 156 pp.

DU
600
D 43
FIJI HISTORY

Derrick, R. A.

A history of Fiji. Vol. 1.
Printed and published by the Printing and Stationery Department, Suva, Fiji. sm4to. 1946. vii + 250+xxviii pp.

DU
600
E 56
FIJI

Endicott, William

Wrecked among cannibals in the Fijis... Salem, 1923.

FIJI   Carter Coll.
2-D-22

Erskine, Charles

     Twenty years before the mast with the more thrilling scenes and incidents while circumnavigating the globe under the command of the late Admiral Charles Wilkes 1838-1842. Boston. Charles Erskine. 1890. x + 311 pp. 8vo.

GN
2.8
F 47   FIJI

Fijian Society

     Transactions, 1908→ >

For current volumes see serial file

FIJI   Carter Coll.
11-C-19

Freeman, Lewis R.

     In the tracks of the trades; the account of a fourteen thousand mile yachting cruise to the Hawaiis, Marquesas, Societies, Samoas and Fijis. London, William Heinemann. 1921 380 pp. 8vo.

DU
12
E 73   FIJI

locked
case   Erskine, J. E.

     Journal of a cruise among the islands of the western Pacific, including the Feejees and others inhabited by the Polynesian negro races... London 1853. 8vo. pp. 165-298; 411-477.

       Fiji Islands   λ

DU   Fison, Lorimer.
600   Tales from old Fiji.
F4F54

G
51
A 93   FIJI

Garretty, M. D.

     The Crown Colony of Fiji, by M. D. Garretty and J. Garretty.

     (The Australian Geographer, Vol. 3, 1936, pp. 23-30) No. 2

G
7
R 8   FIJI

Erskine, J. E. (John E.)

     Proceedings at the South Sea Islands.(1849)

     (Jour. of the R. Geogr. Soc., Vol. 21, 1851, pp. 221-240)

DU
12
K 54   FIJI

locked
case   Fitz-roy, Robert   and others

     Narrative of the surveying voyages of His Majesty's Ships Adventure and Beagle...1826-1836. ...3 vols. London. 1839. Vol. II, pp. 557-562.

DU
12
G 64   FIJI

Goodenough, J. G.

     Journal of Commodore Goodenough, during his last command as senior officer on the Australian station, 1873-1875... London. 1876. 8vo. pp. 205-229; 312-314.

DU
620
F   FIJI

     Feejee Islands.

     (Friend, September 1853, p.63
        October   "   p.69
        December   "   p.92)

       Fiji Islands

DU   Forbes, Litton.
600
F6   Two years in Fiji.

     London, 1875. 340p.

G
7
R 7   FIJI

Gorrie, Sir John

     Fiji as It Is.

     (Proceedings of the Royal Colonial Institute, Vol. 14, 1882-1883, pp. 160-199)

DU
12
F 41   FIJI

locked
case   Festetics de Tolna, Rodolphe

     Chez les cannibales. Huit ans de croisiere dans l'Ocean Pacifique a bord du yacht "Le Tolna" ... Paris. 1903. 4to. pp. 132-147.

DU
12
F 73   FIJI

locked
case   Forster, George

     Voyage round the world, in...Resolution, commanded by Capt. James Cook, during the years 1772-75... 2 vols. London. 1777. 4to. Vol. 2, pp. 193-95.

DU
Pacific   ~~Fiji(Islands)~~
Dam
#.234   Graeffe, Eduard.

     Reisen im Innern der Insel Viti-Levu.

DU
600
A54   FIJI.

Anderson, J   W

     Notes of travel in Fiji and New Caledonia, with some remarks on South Sea islanders and their languages.

     Lond.,Ellissen,1880. 288p.,4pls.,map.

DU
600
F75   FIJI

Foster, Harry L.

     A vagabond in Fiji.

     New York, Dodd, Mead & Co., 1927. 309p. pls

DU
600
G 84   FIJI

Grey, J. R.

     World's end: life and laughter in the South Seas. Robertson and Mullens, Ltd., Melbourne. 8vo. n.d. (about 1944)

DU
600
H 54   FIJI

     Fiji. Handbook of the Colony. Published by Authority. Government Printer. Suva, Fiji. 1937. R8vo. 165 + iii pp.

DU
Pao.Pam.
375   FIJI

and   Foye, W(ilbur) G(arland)

     The Lau Islands of Fiji. (From Geographical Rev., Vol. 4, 1917, pp. 374-386)

G5
A1

DU
600
G 86   FIJI

Grimshaw, Beatrice

     Fiji and its possibilities. New York. 1907. 8vo. xiii + 315 pp.

DU
12
G 86   Grimshaw, Beatrice

From Fiji to the cannibal islands. Thomas
Nelson and Sons, Ltd., London... sm8vo. n. d.
255 pp.

G
51
W 17   FIJI

Hanna, D.

Voyage to the Yasawas   (Fiji Islands).

(Walkabout, 22(8):33-35, 1956)

[photos of canoe, kava ceremony, women fishing]

DU
1
P   FIJI

Hillas, Julian

A wanderer in Fiji a hundred years ago.

(Pacific Islands Monthly, vol. VII, no. 6,
1937. pp. 17-18)

DU   FIJI
G 95   Guillemard, A. G.

looked   Over land and sea. A log of travel round the
case   world in 1873-1874. London. 1875. 8vo.
pp. 148-167.

G
51
W 17   FIJI

Hanna, Sarah F. T.

Life on a Fijian island.

(Walkabout, 23(9):14-16, 1957)

GN
2.I
A   FIJI

Hocart, A. M

Early Fijians. In Journ. Roy. Anthr.
Inst. xlix, 1919, pp 42-51.

DU   FIJI
600
G 97   Guppy, H. B.

Observations of a Naturalist in the Pacific
between 1896 and 1897. Volume I: Vanua Levu,
Fiji. A description of its leading Physical and
Geological characters. London. Macmillan and
Co., Limited. 1903. 8vo. xix + 392 pp.

DU   FIJI
12
H 33   Hartwig, Georg

looked   Die Inseln des grossen Oceans im Natur- und
case   Völkerleben...pp. 391-423.   Wiesbaden. 1861.
8vo.

GN   FIJI
1
Cey   Hocart, A. M.

India and the Pacific. In Ceylon Jour.
Sc. Sect. G. Vol. I, pp 61 - 84, 175-178,
1925.

[Comparison based chiefly on conditions
in Fiji]

DU   FIJI
1
M 6   H. S. F.

Up the Sigatoka River.

(Mid-Pacific Magazine, Vol. 49, No. 1,
1936, pp. 51-54)

GN   FIJI
671.F1
H 41   Hayden, Howard

Moturiki. A pilot project in community de-
velopment. Published under the auspices of the
South Pacific Commission. Oxford Univ. Press.
London... 1954. 8vo. xxiv + 180 pp.

AS   FIJI
763
B-b   Hocart, A   M

Lau Islands, Fiji.   B. P. Bishop Mus.,
GN   Bull. 62, 1929.
671.F1
H 68

Reading
Room

DU   FIJI
12
H 16   Haley, Nelson

Diary of Nelson Haley. (Excerpts only,-
complete copy is in the Library of the University of Hawaii)

PL   FIJI
600
H 43   Hazlewood, David

A Fijian and English and an English and
Fijian Dictionary...Also containing...the native
names of natural productions and notices of the
islands of Fiji...   Second edition...Reprinted,
1914. (London)
also first edition: A Feejeean and English
Dictionary...Vewa, Fiji. 1850

GN   Fiji
2-I
A   Hocart, A. M.
Meaning of "Kalou" + origin of
Fijian temples. in Roy. Anth. Inst XLII

DU   FIJI
12
H 16   Haley, Nelson Cole

Whale hunt, the narrative of a voyage...
1849-1853. Ives Washburn, Inc.   New York. 8vo.
304 pp. 1948c

pp. 180-193

DU   FIJI
600
H 53   The 'Herald' Handbook of Fiji. 1921. The
Reference book of Information and Statistics Re-
lating to the Colony of Fiji. Trade and General
Directory Guide to the Tourists. Published by
Alport Barker. Suva. Fiji Times & Herald
Office. 1921. (1922 on outside cover)

2 copies

GN   FIJI
2-I
A-m   Hocart, A. M.

Natural and Supernatural.

(Man, 1932:78)

G
51
W 17   FIJI

Hanna, D.

Housekeeping in Fiji.

(Walkabout Magazine, Vol. 22(5):18-19,
May, 1956)

DU   FIJI
Pac.
Pam.
820   Herrick, J.

Fifty trips in fair Fiji. Issued by the
Fiji Publicity Board. J. J. McHugh, Government
Printer. Suva. n.d. 8vo. (1-3)4-28, (1-2) pp.

DU   FIJI
600
H 81   Horne, John

A year in Fiji: an inquiry into the
botanical, agricultural, and economical
resources of the colony. ...

London, 1881, 297 pp.

DU   FIJI
Pac.Pam.
877   Huetz de Lemps, Alain

Les Iles Fidji.

(Les Cahiers d'Outre-Mer, No. 23, 6me Année, 1953:201-231)

Fiji (Islands)
DU
600   King, Agnes Gardner.
K52
Islands far away...1920.

For fuller entry see main card

DU   FIJI
12
L 47   Lee, Ida

Captain Bligh's second voyage to the South
Sea. (1791)   London, 1920.

FIJI   Carter Coll.
                 1-E-16
Humphrey, Seth K.

Loafing through the Pacific.   Garden
City... Doubleday, Page and Co.   1927.
x + 306 pp.   8vo.

DU   FIJI
12
L 15   La Farge, John

Reminiscences of the South Seas...pp. 393-
477.   Garden City.   1916.   8vo.

DU   FIJI
600
L 51   Legge, J. D.

Britain in Fiji, 1858-1880.   Macmillan and
Co. Ltd.   London.   1958.   8vo.   x + 307 pp.

DU   FIJI
Pacific
Pam   Hutson, Eyre
233
Fiji, 1915. Colonial annual report
No. 887, 1916.

DU   FIJI
12
L 22   Lambert, C., and Lambert, S.
looked
case   Voyage of the "Wanderer"...pp. 191-212.
London.   1883.   R8vo.

DU   FIJI
12
L 52   Le Guillou, Élie
looked
case   Voyage autour du monde de l'Astrolabe et de
la Zélée...Dumont d'Urville, pendant...1837-1840
...Vols. 1-2.   Paris.   1842.   8vo.
Vol. 1, pp. 183-202.

DU   FIJI
600
I 42   Indra, K.R.

Sudseefahrten. Schilderungen einer Reise
nach den Fidschi-Inseln, Samoa und Tonga.
Wilhelm Susserott.   Berlin. 1903. 8vo.
(2) + 226 pp

AS   FIJI
763
B-s   Lambert, S.M.

East Indian and Fijian in Fiji: their changing numerical relation.

(Bernice P. Bishop Museum, Special Publication No. 32, 1938)

DU   FIJI
12
L 57   Lenwood, Frank

Pastels from the Pacific. With illustrations in colours and in black and white.

(Oxford: Oxford Univ. Press, 1917, 8vo.
pp. xii + 224)

DU   FIJI
12
J 52   Jenkins, J. S.
looked
case   Recent exploring expeditions to the Pacific,
and to the South Seas, under the American, Englis
and French governments. London. 1854. sm8vo.
pp. 325-359.

DU   FIJI
12
L 22   Lambert, S. M.

A Yankee doctor in Paradise.
Boston, 1941.

pp. 113-130; 270-276; 315-334

DU   FIJI
620
F

Letter from a planter.

(Friend, May 1873, p. 38).

DU   FIJI
12
J 67   Johnson, Irving

Westward bound in the schooner Yankee, by
Captain and Mrs. Irving Johnson. With drawings
by Roland Wentzel. New York. W.W. Norton & Co.
1936.   8 vo.   348 pp.

Fiji (Islands)
DU
600   Lawry, Walter.
L39   Friendly and Feejee Islands.

G
161   FIJI
Lockerby, William

The journal of William Lockerby , san
dalwood trader in the Fijian islands during the years 1908 - 1909..... Hakluyt
Soc., Ser. II, Vol. LII. Issued for 1922,
pub., 1925.

[Bibliography, pp 225 - 231]

DU   FIJI
1
P 10   A key to Fiji's ancient past. (Fragments of pottery ...)

(Pacific Islands Monthly, Vol. 34(4):79,
1963)

DU   FIJI
600
L 39   Lawry, Walter

A second missionary visit to the Friendly
and Feejee Islands, in the year MDCCCL. Edited
by the Rev. Elijah Hoole, one of the General
Secretaries of the Wesleyan Missionary Society.
London. John Mason... 1851. sm8vo. viii + 217
pp.

G
3
N 17   FIJI

Marden, Luis

The islands called Fiji.

(National Geographic Mag., 114(4):526-561,
1958)

DU 880 M 33	FIJI Mariner, William An account of the natives of the Tonga Islands...with an original grammar and vocabulary of their language. Compiled and arranged...by John Martin. Vols. 1-2. London. 1817. 8vo. Vol. 1, pp. 317-347. ...Second edition, with additions. London. 1818. 8vo. Vols. 1-2. ...Third edition, Vols. 1-2. Edinburgh. 1827. 12mo.

DU Pacific Pam # 232	Fiji(Islands) Parr, William Fillingham. Slavery in Fiji: Address delivered before the Ballon Society on September 24th, 1895. By. Wm. Fillingham Parr. London, 1895. 20p.

DU 12 S 14 locked case	FIJI St. Johnston, Alfred Camping among cannibals. London. 1883. pp. 206-327.

DU 600 M39	Fiji(Islands) Mayer, Alfred G. A history of Tahiti; A history of Fiji; Papua, where the stone-age lingers; The men of the Mid-Pacific; The Islands of the mid-Pacific; Java, the exploited island. Reprinted from the Popular science monthly and The Scientific monthly, 1915-16.

DU 12 P 31	FIJI Patterson, Samuel Narrative of the Adventures and Sufferings of Samuel Patterson, experienced in the Pacific Ocean, and many other parts of the world, with an account of the Feegee, and Sandwich Islands. From the Press in Palmer. May 1, 1817. xii + 144 pp. sml2mo. also Second edition, enlarged, Providence, 1825. 164 pp. 12mo.

DU 12 S 14	FIJI St. Johnston, T. R. South Sea Reminiscences. Illustrated. London. T. Fisher Unwin Ltd. (1922) 8vo. 209 pp.

DU 400 M 48	FIJI Meade, Herbert A ride through the disturbed districts of New Zealand; together with some account of the South Sea islands. Being selections from the journals and letters of Lieut. the Hon. Herbert Meade. Edited by his brother. Second edition. With maps and illustrations from the author's sketches. London. John Murray. 1871. 8vo. xi + 375 pp.

DU 620 F	FIJI Pritchard, George Feegee and Tonga. An account of a voyage in the ship Calypso. (Friend, Dec., 1849, pp. 91-92)

DU 620 M 67	Fiji St.Julian, Charles International Status of Fiji......... Sydney, 1872, pp. 31. in Miscell. Pams. Haw. II. pp. 329-364.

DU 880 M 74	FIJI Monfat, (Le P.) A. Les Tonga ou archipel des amis, et Le R.P. Joseph Chevron, de la Société de la Marie: étude historique et réligieuse. Deuxième édition. Lyon. Librairie Générale Catholique et Classique. n.d. xvi + 473, 1 map.

DU 96 R19	Fiji(Islands) Ranken, George. The federal geography of British Australasia... Sydney, 1891. 506p. maps.

DU 12 S 32	FIJI Schenck, Earl Come unto these yellow sands. Illustrated by the author. The Bobs-Merrill Company. New York; Indianapolis. (1940s) R8vo. 372 pp.

DU 12 M 89 locked case	FIJI Moseley, H. N. Notes by a naturalist on the "Challenger", being an account of various observations made during the voyage of H.M.S. "Challenger" round the world...1872-1876...London. 1879. 8vo. pp. 293-341.

G 51 W 17	FIJI Redwood, Rosaline Lonely isles of Lau. (Walkabout, 20(2):14-16, 1954)

AP 2 A 5	FIJI Seemann, (Berthold) Fiji Islands. (Am. Jour. Sci., Ser. 2, Vol. 34, 1862, pp. 366-367)

DU 12 N98	FIJI Nutting, C. C. Fiji - New Zealand expedition. Univ. Iowa, Studies, Vol. X, No.5, 1924.

DU 12 R33	Fiji(Islands) Reeves, Edward. Brown men and women... London, 1898. 294p. illus. map.

DU 600 S 45	FIJI Seemann, Berthold Viti: an Account of a Government Mission to the Vitian or Fijian Islands in the Years 1860-61. With Illustrations and a Map. Cambridge. Macmillan and Co. 1862. 8vo. xv + 447 pp.

GN 2.1 A-m	FIJI Paine, R. W. Some Rock Paintings in Fiji. (In Man: 1929, Nr. 9, pp. 149-151, 5 plates)

DU 12 R 96 locked case	FIJI Russell, M. Polynesia: a history of the south sea islands including New Zealand, with narrative of the introduction of Christianity, etc. ...London. 1863. 12mo. pp. 414-424.

QK Bot.Pam. 2699	FIJI Selling, Olof H. Strövtag pa Fiji-öarna. (Jorden Runt, 23(7/8):351-366, Stockholm, 1951)

DU
Pac. Pam.
556   FIJI
 	
Shepherd, G. Scoresby
 	
    Levuka.
 	
    (Walkabout, Dec. 1, 1935, pp. 41-43)
	AS
	182 Fiji
	H
	    Spengel, J.W.
	
	    Beiträge zur Kenntnis der Fidsche-
	Inseln in Mus.Godeffroy Journ.,pp.241-
	254.Heft IV Tafeln 5-11. Hamburg,1873.
		DU
		600
		T 48 FIJI
		
		Thomson, Basil
		
		    The Fijians: a Study of the Decay of Custom.
		Illustrated. London. William Heinemann. 1908.
		8vo. xviii + 396 pp.

DU
510
S 44   FIJI
 	
Seddon, R. J.
 	
    The Right Hon. R. J. Seddon's (the Premier
of New Zealand) visit to Tonga, Fiji, Savage Island, and the Cook Islands. May, 1900. Government Printer. Wellington. 1900. sm8vo. 445 pp
	AS
	182 Fiji
	H
	    Spengel, J.W.
	
	    Nachtrag zu den Beiträgen zur Kenntnis
	der Fidsche-Insulaner in Mus.Godeffroy
	Journ.,pp.421-422. Hamburg,1873-4.
		DU
		Pac. Pam.
		617 FIJI
		
		Thomson, J. P.
		
		    Fiji: the islands and peoples revisited.
		
		    (Journal of the Manchester Geographical
		Society, Vol.48, 1937-38, pp. 31-37)

DU
12
S 44   FIJI
 	
locked
case   (Seddon, R. J.)
 	
    The Right Hon. R. J. Seddon's visit to Tonga,
Fiji, Savage Island, and the Cook Islands, May,
1900. Wellington. 1900. pp. 62-93.
	DU
	625.4
	S 78 FIJI
	
	Staley, Mildred E.
	
	    A tapestry of memories; an autobiography.
	Illustrated by the author from original drawings.
	Printed in Hawaii, U.S.A., by the Hilo Tribune
	Herald. 1944. 8vo. 9-232 pp.
		G
		7
		S FIJI
		
		Thomson, J. P.
		
		    The Island of Kadavu.
		
		    (Scottish Geogr. Mag. Vol. 5, 1889, pp.
		638-652)

DU
510
S 55   FIJI
 	
locked
case   Shipley, Conway (artist)
 	
    Sketches in the Pacific; the South Sea islands. London. T. McLean. 1851. folio.
Colored plates, drawn from nature and on stone;
34 pages of text.
 	
    [sketches and text concern Pitcairn, Society
Navigator, and Fiji Islands. Vessel was the
Calypso]
	DU
	96
	T 19 FIJI
	
	locked
	case Tasman, A. J.
	
	    Journal of his discovery of Van Dieman's
	Land and New Zealand in 1642 with documents relating to his exploration of Australia in 1644...
	Amsterdam. 1898. Folio.
	    (See contents at beginning for paging)
		G
		7
		S FIJI
		
		Thomson, J. P.
		
		    The Land of Viti.
		
		    (Scottish Geogr. Mag. Vol. 10, 1894, pp.
		120-140)

DU
12
S 56   FIJI
 	
Shurcliff, Sidney Nichols
 	
    Jungle Islands, the "Illyria" in the South
Seas. The record of the Crane Pacific Expedition, Field Museum of Natural History, With a
scientific appendix by Karl Patterson Schmidt.
Ninety illustrations; two maps...by Walter A.
Weber. G. P. Putnam's Sons. The Knickerbocker
Press. New York; London. 1930. R8vo. xv + 298
pp.
	DU
	96
	T 24 FIJI
	
	Taylor, Griffith
	
	    Geography of Australasia. Oxford. 1914.
		DU
		12
		T 55 FIJI
		
		Tichborne, Herbert
		
		    Noqu Talanoa:stories from the South Seas.
		By "Sundowner". London. The European Mail
		Limited. 1896. sm8vo. vii + 178 pp.

GN
668
S 61   FIJI
 	
Simpson, Colin
 	
    Islands of men. A six-part book about life
in Melanesia. Illustrated with 12 colour plates,
other photographs, and with line decorations by
Claire Simpson. Angus and Robertson. Sydney,
London... R8vo. 1955. (7)+248 pp.
	G
	7
	S FIJI
	
	Thiele, H. H.
	
	    Rewa river, Fiji. In Scottish Geog.
	Mag., Vol. VII, pp 434 - 441. 1891.
		Carter Coll.
		7-B-5
		   FIJI
		
		    Treasury of travel and adventure, in
		North and South America, Europe, Asia, and
		Africa. A book for young and old. With...
		illustrations. New York. D. Appleton and
		Company. 1865. sm8vo. 456 pp.

DU
600
S 66   FIJI
 	
Smythe, (Mrs.) S. M.
 	
    Ten Months in the Fiji Islands, with an Introduction and Appendix by W. J.Smythe. Illustrated by Chronolithographs and Woodcuts from
Sketches made on the spot. With Maps by Arrowsmith. Oxford and London. John Henry and James
Parker. 1864. 8vo. x + xviii + 282 pp.
	FIJI
	
	Thomas, Marjory C.
	
	    Copra-ship voyage to Fiji's outlying islands.
	
	    (National Geographic Magazine, July, 1950:
	121-140)
		DU
		12
		T 94 FIJI
		
		locked
		case Turnbull, John
		
		    Voyage round the world, in...1800-1804...
		Second edition, pp. 509-514. London. 1813.
		4to.

Q 115 U 58
locked case

DU 12 U 58 locked case

FIJI

United States Exploring Expedition...1838-1842, under the command of Charles Wilkes. Vol. III, pp. 47-384, 397-402, 431-454. Philadelphia. C. Sherman. 1844. 4to.
Vol. 23: Hydrography...pp. 148-245 ; 248
...Narrative, Vols. 1-5 and atlas. Phila. 1845. R8vo. Vol. III, pp. 45-364.

DU 600 W72

FIJI

Williams, Thomas and Calvert, James
Fiji and the Fijians: Vol. I, the islands and their inhabitants, by Thomas Williams. Vol. II. Mission history, by James Calvert. Ed. by George Stringer Rowe.
London, 1858.

FIJI   AGRICULTURE

see also

AGRICULTURE   FIJI

DU 12 V 56

FIJI

Verschuur, G.
Aux Antipodes. Voyage en Australie, a la Nouvelle-Zélande, aux Fidji, a la Nouvelle-Calédonie, aux Nouvelles-Hébrides et dans l'Amerique du Sud, 1888-1889... Paris. 1891. 8vo. pp. 249-285.

DU 12 W 74
3 copies 2 in locked case

FIJI

Wilson, James
A missionary voyage to the southern Pacific Ocean, performed in...1796-1798 in the ship Duff commanded by Captain James Wilson. Compiled from journals of the officers and the missionaries... London. 1799. 4to. pp. 286-292.

FIJI   ALCYONIDIA

See

ALCYONIDIA   FIJI

Fiji

Voyage to the Fijis. 17 articles. in Haw. Gazette 1868. Dec. 30 - April 17, 1869.

G 7 R 88

FIJI

Wood, Laurence
In the South Seas.
(United Empire, vol. 28, no. 1, pp. 25-27)

This file sent to the University of Hawaii

FIJI   AMPHIPODA

See

AMPHIPODA   FIJI

DU 600 W32

FIJI
Waterhouse, Joseph.
The king and people of Fiji: Containing a life of Thakombau; with notice of the Fijians, their manners, customs, and superstitions, previous to the great religious reformation in 1854. By the Rev. Joseph Waterhouse.
London, Wesleyan conference office, 1866. 435p.

FIJI   ACCULTURATION

see

ACCULTURATION   FIJI

FIJI   ANOBIIDAE

See

ANOBIIDAE   FIJI

GN 2.S M 26

FIJI

Whonsbon-Aston, C. W.
A Visit to Lavoni, Fiji.
(Mankind, Vol. I, pp. 114-115, 1933)

FIJI   ADOLESCENCE

See

ADOLESCENCE   FIJI

FIJI   ANOPHELES

See

ANOPHELES   FIJI

GN 2.S F 47

FIJI

Wilkinson, D.
Origin of the Fijian race.
(Trans. Fijian Society, 1908-1910, pp. 7-17)

FIJI   ADZES

See

ADZES   FIJI

FIJI   ANTHROPOLOGY

See

ANTHROPOLOGY   FIJI

DU 12 W 66
locked case

FIJI

Wild, John James
At anchor. A narrative of experiences afloat and ashore during the voyage of H.M.S. "Challenger" from 1872 to 1876...pp. 92-98. London. 1878. 4to.

FIJI   AEDES

See

AEDES   FIJI

FIJI   ANTHROPOMETRY

see

ANTHROPOMETRY   FIJI

FIJI   ARADIDAE

See

ARADIDAE   FIJI

Z
Bibliography
Pam.
170

FIJI
/BIBLIOGRAPHY XXXXXX

Tuinaceva, S. T.   compiler

    Land tenure in Fiji: a bibliography.
Suva.   Central Archives of Fiji and the Western Pacific High Commission.   1963.   5 pp.
Mimeographed.

FIJI   BUFO MARINUS

See

BUFO MARINUS   FIJI

FIJI   ARCHAEOLOGY

See

ARCHAEOLOGY   FIJI

FIJI   BIOLOGICAL CONTROL

See

BIOLOGICAL CONTROL   FIJI

FIJI   BURIAL

See

BURIAL   FIJI

FIJI   ARMLETS

See

ARMLETS   FIJI

FIJI   BIRDS

see

BIRDS   FIJI

FIJI   CALENDAR

see

CALENDAR   FIJI

FIJI   ARMOR

See

ARMOR   FIJI
WEAPONS   FIJI

FIJI   BIRTH CUSTOMS

See

BIRTH CUSTOMS   FIJI

FIJI   CANOES

see

CANOES   FIJI

FIJI   ART

see

ART   FIJI

FIJI   BLOOD GROUPS

see

BLOOD GROUPS   FIJI

FIJI   CARVING

See

CARVING   FIJI

FIJI   ARYIDAE

See

ARYIDAE   FIJI

FIJI   BOTANY

See

BOTANY   FIJI

PL
Phil.
Pam.
649

FIJI CATHOLIC MISSION

O'Reilly, Patrick

    Imprints of the Fiji Catholic Mission, including the Loreto Press.   1958.   8vo.   London.
Francis Edwards Ltd.   60 pp.

FIJI   BELIEFS

see

BELIEFS   FIJI
WORSHIP   FIJI

FIJI   BRONTISPA

See

BRONTISPA   FIJI

FIJI   CAVES

see

CAVES   FIJI

DU 600 Fish F18

FIJI - CENSUS

Fiji. Legislative Council

Council Ppaer No.2 . Report of the Census taken on the night of the 24th of April, 1921.

Suva, 1922, 190 pp. folio.

FIJI   CHELONIA

See

CHELONIA   FIJI

FIJI   COCOA

See

COCOA   FIJI

DU 600 F 47

FIJI   CENSUS

Fiji. Legislative Council.
Council Paper, No. 42. A report on the Fiji census, 1936, by Commander W. Burrows. Laid on the table, 23 October, 1936. Government Printer, Suva. 1936. folio. viii + 89 pp. 5 maps.

FIJI   CHIEFS

See

CHIEFS   FIJI

FIJI   COLEOPTERA

see

COLEOPTERA   FIJI

FIJI   CENTRAL MEDICAL SCHOOL

See

CENTRAL MEDICAL SCHOOL   FIJI

FIJI   CHILDREN

See

CHILDREN   FIJI

FIJI   COLLECTIONS

See

COLLECTIONS FIJI

FIJI   CEPHALOPODA

See

CEPHALOPODA   FIJI

FIJI   CIRCUMCISION

See

CIRCUMCISION   FIJI

DU Pacific Pam. No.139

Fiji. Colony of Fiji

Land and products.

Suva, Gov't Printer, 1924.

FIJI   CERAMBYCIDAE

See

CERAMBYCIDAE   FIJI

FIJI   CLOTHING

See

CLOTHING   FIJI

FIJI   CONSERVATION

See

CONSERVATION   FIJI

Chart Case Folder 15

Fiji (Islands) Chart

Compiled and drawn at the Land Department, Suva, Fiji, January 1916. Revised January, 1914. (Size, 40 x 59 3/4)

FIJI   CLUBS

See

CLUBS   FIJI

FIJI   CORAL REEFS AND ISLANDS

See

CORAL REEFS AND ISLANDS   FIJI

Chart Case Fiji

FIJI -- CHARTS

U. S./Hydrographic Office

Charts of Fiji islands and reefs Library has
U.S.H.O.Nos. 2850, 2851, 2855, 2853, 409, 2852, 109, 412, 413, 2859, 2861, 2860, 111, 411, 2858, 2863, 2865, 2864, 2862, 2856, 2857, 118, 112, 2018.

See page 166   of the Guide to Charts [Marked   copy of General Catalogue of   Mariners' charts. 1922

FIJI   COCCIDAE

See

COCCIDAE   FIJI

FIJI   CORALS

see

CORALS   FIJI

FIJI CRANIOLOGY

see

CRANIOLOGY FIJI

FIJI DACUS

See

DACUS FIJI

PL
600
C 24

FIJI DICTIONARY

Capell, A.

A new Fijian dictionary. Sydney. Australasian Medical Publishing Company limited. 1941. sm8vo. x + 464 pp.

FIJI CRUSTACEA

see

CRUSTACEA FIJI

FIJI DANCES

see

DANCES FIJI

PL
600
H 43

FIJI DICTIONARY

Hazlewood, David

A Feejeean and English Dictionary...Vewa, Feejee. Wesleyan Mission Press. 1850. sm8vo. 192 pp.

also second edition: A Fijian and English and an English and Fijian Dictionary...Reprinted, 1914. (London) 281 + 64 pp. 8vo.

FIJI CULICIDAE

See

CULICIDAE FIJI

FIJI DANCING

see

DANCING FIJI

PL
600
M67

FIJI DICTIONARY

Mission press. (pub.)

New English and Feejeean dictionary. Vewa, Mission press, n.d. 328 p.

No title page

FIJI CULTURE CHANGE

See

CULTURE CHANGE FIJI

FIJI DECAPODA

see

DECAPODA FIJI

FIJI DIPTERA

See

DIPTERA FIJI

FIJI CUNONIACEA

See

CUNONIACEA FIJI

FIJI DEFORMITIES ARTIFICIAL

see

DEFORMITIES ARTIFICIAL FIJI

G
Geogr.
Pam.
63

FIJI DISCOVERY AND EXPLORATION

Barnes, A. E.

Tracks of the discoverers of the Fiji Islands (Map) compiled and drawn by A. E. Barnes, Hydrographic Department, Admiralty, London. 1933. 30 inches by 32 inches.

FIJI CURCULIONIDAE

see

CURCULIONIDAE FIJI

FIJI DEPOPULATION

see

DEPOPULATION FIJI

DU
600
H 49

FIJI DISCOVERY AND EXPLORATION

Henderson, G. C.

The Discoverers of the Fiji Islands:Tasman, Cook, Bligh, Wilson, Bellingshausen. London. (1933).

FIJI CYRTANDRA

See

CYRTANDRA FIJI

GN
2.8
P 76

FIJI DIALECT

Raven-Hart, R.

A dialect of Yasawa Island (Fiji).

(Jour. Polynesian Soc., 62(1):33-56, 1953)

FIJI ECHINOIDEA

see

ECHINOIDEA FIJI

FIJI   ECOLOGY

See

ECOLOGY   FIJI

FIJI   EUPHORBIACEAE

See

EUPHORBIACEAE   FIJI

FIJI   FISHES

see

FISHES   FIJI

G
7
N 56   Cumberland, Kenneth B.

FIJI   ECONOMIC CONDITIONS

Problem and prospect in Fiji.

(New Zealand Geographer, 16(2):214-217, 1960)

FIJI   FAUNA

See

FAUNA   FIJI

FIJI   FISHES   NATIVE NAMES

See

FISHES NATIVE NAMES   FIJI

FIJI   EDUCATION

see

EDUCATION   FIJI

FIJI   FILARIASIS

See

FILARIASIS   FIJI

FIJI   FISHING

see

FISHING   FIJI

FIJI   ELAEOCARPUS

See

ELAEOCARPUS   FIJI

FIJI   FILICES

see

FILICES   FIJI

FIJI   FOLKLORE

see also

FOLKLORE FIJI

FIJI   ELATERIDAE

see

ELATERIDAE   FIJI

FIJI   FIRE-WALKING

see

FIRE-WALKING   FIJI

FIJI   FOOD

see

FOOD   FIJI

FIJI   ETHNOGRAPHY

See

ETHNOGRAPHY

FIJI   FISH POISONING

See

FISH POISONING   FIJI

FIJI   FOOD PLANTS

see

FOOD PLANTS   FIJI

FIJI   ETHNOLOGY

see

ETHNOLOGY   FIJI

FIJI   FISHERIES

See

FISHERIES   FIJI

FIJI   FORESTS AND FORESTRY

See

FORESTS AND FORESTRY   FIJI

FIJI   FORAMINIFERA

see

FORAMINIFERA   FIJI

FIJI   GODS

see

GODS   FIJI

PL
490.F
M 65   Milner, G. B.

     Fijian grammar. Government Press. Suva,
Fiji. R8vo. vii + 150 pp. (rec'd 1958)

FIJI   GRAMMAR

FIJI   FORMICIDAE

see

FORMICIDAE   FIJI

GN
1
A 62   Mayer, Adrian C.

     Associations in Fiji Indian rural society.

     (American Anthropologist, Vol. 58(1):97-108,
February, 1956)

FIJI   GOVERNMENT

DU
600
F5

Fiji (Islands) Handbooks

Fiji.

     Handbook to Fiji...1892.

     For fuller entry see main card

FIJI   FUNGI

see

FUNGI   FIJI

FIJI   GRAMINEAE

see

GRAMINEAE   FIJI

FIJI   HEALTH

See

HEALTH   FIJI

FIJI   GAMES

see

GAMES   FIJI

PL
600
C 56   Churchward, C. Maxwell

     A new Fijian grammar. Printed by the
Australasian Medical Publishing Company, Limited, for the Government of Fiji. Suva. 1941.
sm8vo. 94 pp.

FIJI   GRAMMAR

FIJI   HEMIPTERA

See

HEMIPTERA   FIJI

DU
Pacific
Pam
235

FIJI   GAZETTEERS

Britton, H.

     Fiji in 1870: Letters of "The Argus"
special correspondent with a complete map
and gazetteer of the Fijian Archipelago.
Melbourne 1870, 8vo, pp 87.

PL
600
H 43   Hazlewood, D(avid)

     A compendious grammar of the Feejeean lan-
guage; with examples of native idioms. Vewa,
Feejee. 1850. 16mo.

FIJI   GRAMMAR

FIJI   HIRUDINEA

See

HIRUDINEA   FIJI

FIJI   GEOGRAPHY

See

GEOGRAPHY   FIJI

PL
600
H 43   Hazlewood, David

     A Feejeean and English Dictionary...Vewa,
Feejee. Wesleyan Mission Press. 1850. sm8vo.
192 pp.

     also second edition, A Fijian and English
and an English and Fijian Dictionary...Reprinted,
1914. (London) 281 + 64 pp. 8vo.

FIJI   GRAMMAR

DU
600
B 84   Brewster, A. B.

     King of the cannibal isles; a tale of early
life and adventure in the Fiji Islands. London
Robert Hale and Company. 1937. 8vo. 286 pp.

FIJI   HISTORY

FIJI   GEOLOGY

see

GEOLOGY   FIJI

GN
2.1
A-M   Hocart, A. M.

     A point of Fijian orthography.

     (Man, vol. 10, 1910, no. 41, pp. 77-78)

FIJI   GRAMMAR

DU
1
P 10   The Cakaudrove wars.

     (Pacific Islands Monthly, Vol. XXVI(4):80-81,
1955)

FIJI   HISTORY

GN
1
O 15   Capell, A.

    FIJI   HISTORY

    Local divisions and movements in Fiji.
By A. Capell and R. H. Lester.

    (Oceania, Vol. XI, 1941, pp. 313-341; Vol.
12, 1941, pp. 21-48)

DU
1
M 6   Paske-Smith, M.

    FIJI ISLANDS   HISTORY

    Early British consuls in Hawaii. Part II:
Other Pacific Islands.

    (Mid-Pacific Magazine, vol.49, pp.262-268.
1936)

    FIJI   HOLOTHURIA

    See

    HOLOTHURIA   FIJI

GN
2.S
F 47   Derrick, R. A.

    FIJI   HISTORY

    The early days of Levuka.

    (Trans. and Proc. of the Fiji Soc., Vol. 2,
1940-44: 49-58, 1953)

GN
1
A   Thompson, Laura

    FIJI   HISTORY

    The culture history of the Lau Islands.

    (The American Anthropologist, Vol. 40, 1938
pp. 181-197)

    FIJI   HOMOPTERA

    See

    HOMOPTERA   FIJI

GN
2.S
F 47   Fijian Society

    FIJI   HISTORY

    Transactions, 1908- 7

    For current volumes see serial file

GN
Ethn.Pam.
3243   Thompson, Laura Maud

    FIJI   HISTORY

    Kulturgeschichte der Lauineseln (Fidschi-
gruppe.

    (Archiv f. Anthropologie, 24:2, pp. 140-153)

    FIJI   HOT SPRINGS

    See

    HOT SPRINGS   FIJI

GN
2.S
F 47   Garvey, Sir Ronald

    FIJI   HISTORY

    The chiefly island of Bau.

    (Trans. and Proc. of the Fiji Society, Vol.
6:157-167, 1957)

GN
2.S
F 47   Toganivalu. R. D.

    FIJI   HISTORY

    Fiji and the Fijians during the 50 years now
ending 1874-1924. A paper...translated...by
G.A.F. W. Beauclero...

    (Trans. Fijian Society, 1924, pp. 15-24)

    FIJI   HOUSES

    See

    HOUSES   FIJI

DU
1
P   Hillas, Julian

    FIJI   HISTORY

    Jackson's adventures in Fiji 100 years ago.

    (Pacific Islands Monthly. 1937. vol. VII,
no. 7. pp. 33-34)

Z
4651
T 92   Tuinaceva, S.   prepared by

    FIJI   HISTORY

    Records of the Cakobau government, the
Ad-Interim Government, and the Provisional Government. June 1871-September, 1875.

    Preliminary Inventory, No. 1. (rec'd 1961,
January)

    FIJI   HURRICANES

    See

    HURRICANES   FIJI

GN
2.S
F 47   Nadalo, Isikeli

    FIJI   HISTORY

    Old wars of Western Fiji.

    (Trans. and Proc. of the Fiji Society, Vol.
6:51-57, 1955)

DU
600
W 32   Waterhouse, Joseph

    FIJI   HISTORY

    Vah-ta-ah, the Feejeean princess: with
occasional allusions to Feejeean customs; and
illustrations of Feejeean life. London.
Hamilton, Adams and Co. 1857. 16mo. 164 pp.

    FIJI   IMAGES

    see

    IMAGES   FIJI

AS
36
A 91 ‡   Knaplund, Paul   editor

    FIJI   HISTORY   1874-1880

    Gladstone-Gordon correspondence, 1851-1896.
Selections from the private correspondence of a
British Prime Minister and a Colonial Governor.

    (Trans. American Philosophical Society, n.s.
Vol. 51(4), 1961)

DU
1
P   Wilson, Erle

    FIJI   HISTORY

    The first crossing of Na Viti Levu.

    (Pacific Islands Monthly. 1937. vol. VII,
no. 7. pp. 45-47)

    FIJI   IMPLEMENTS AND UTENSILS

    See

    IMPLEMENTS AND UTENSILS   FIJI

FIJI   IDOLS

see

IDOLS   FIJI

GN
2.S
P 76   FIJI   LABOR

Parnaby, Owen W.

    The regulation of indentured labour to Fiji, 1864-1888.

    (Jour. Poly. Soc., 65(1):55-66, 1956)

GN
2.S
F 47   FIJI   LANGUAGE

Fijian Society

    Transactions, 1908-?

For current volumes see serial file

FIJI   IMPLEMENTS AND UTENSILS

see

IMPLEMENTS AND UTENSILS   FIJI

FIJI   LAND TENURE

see

LAND TENURE   FIJI

PL
Phil.
Pam.
161   FIJI   LANGUAGE

Gabelentz, Hans Conon's von der

    Die Melanesischen Sprachen, nach ihrem grammatischen bau und ihrer verwandtschaft unter sich und mit den Malaaisch-Polynesischen Sprachen. vi + 266 pp.

    (Abh. d. K. Sachsischen Ges. d. Wiss, VIII, [1882 ?], pp. 1-266)

FIJI   INSECTS

see

INSECTS   FIJI

FIJI   LAND UTILIZATION

see

LAND UTILIZATION   FIJI

DU
12
W 681   Fiji Language

Hale, Horatio

Vitian dictionary.

in Wilkes Expedition VI, pp. 391-424.

FIJI   INSECTS INJURIOUS AND BENEFICIAL

see

INSECTS INJURIOUS AND BENEFICIAL   FIJI

GN
2.S
F 47   FIJI   LANGUAGE

Beauclerc, G. A. F. W.

    The corruptions of the Fijian language.

    (Trans. Fijian Society, 1914, pp. 7-18)

GN
1
An   FIJI   LANGUAGE

Hocart, A. M.

    Fijian and other demonstratives. Anthropos Bd. XII-XIII, 1917-1918, pp. 871-890.

FIJI ISLANDS   ISOPODA

See

ISOPODA   FIJI ISLANDS

GN
2.S
F 47   FIJI   LANGUAGE

Beauclerc, G. A. F. W.

    The Fijian language; some peculiarities of the languages of Fiji.

    (Trans. Fijian Society, 1908-1910, pp. 65-69; 72-75)

GN
2.S
F 47   FIJI   LANGUAGE

Milner, B. G.

    The language of house-building.

    (Trans. Fiji Society, 4:9-14, 1948/50)

FIJI   KAVA

see

KAVA   FIJI

PL
Phil.Pam.
XVI
523   FIJI   LANGUAGE

Chambers, Harold

    Handbook of Fijian language. A simple introduction to the grammar and construction of Fijian, with lists of useful sentences and phrases, sets of exercises, and a comprehensive vocabulary. Methodist Book Depot. Suva. sm8vo. 74 pp. (1936).

GN
2.S
P 76   FIJI   LANGUAGE

Raven-Hart, R.

    A dialect of Yasawa Island (Fiji).

    (The Journal of the Polynesian Society, Vol. 62(1):33-56, 1953)

FIJI   KINSHIP

See

KINSHIP   FIJI

Q
115
D 89

looked
case   FIJI   LANGUAGE

Dumont d'Urville, J. S. C.

    Voyage de la corvette l'Astrolabe...1826-1829...Paris. 1830-1835. 8vo. Philologie, Part 2, pp. 137-142. (French-Fijian vocabulary)

GN
1
O 15   FIJI   LANGUAGE

Tippett, A. R.

    An interesting aspect of sound movement and decay in the Fijian language.

    (Oceania, Vol. 24(3):229-233, 1954)

FIJI   LANTANA

See

LANTANA   FIJI

FIJI   MALARIA

See

MALARIA   FIJI

Chart
Case
Folder
No. 33
Fiji

U.S.Expl.

FIJI - MAPS

Map of Fiji. Ex U.S.Explor. Exped.
Atlas of charts Vol. I.

Bishop Museum Chart No. 398.

(Shows Whippy, Suva, Granby, and
Ndronga harbors).

FIJI   LAURACEAE

See

LAURACEAE   FIJI

FIJI   MAMMALS

See

MAMMALS   FIJI

Chart
Case
No.1
Fiji

FIJI - MAPS

Maps of Totoya I, enlarged from H.O.ch
chart 2852(B. Mus. Chart No. 377);of the
three Fiji islands visited by E. Bryan
to July 17, 1924(H.O.Chart 2850, B.Mus.
chart No. 378); Matuku I. (From H.O.
chart No. 413, B.Mus. chart No. 379.)

FIJI   LEGENDS

see

LEGENDS   FIJI

FIJI   MANGROVES

See

MANGROVES   FIJI

MAPS   FIJI

see

FIJI   MAPS

FIJI   LEODICIDAE

see

LEODICIDAE   FIJI

FIJI   MANNERS AND CUSTOMS

See

MANNERS AND CUSTOMS   FIJI

Chart
Case
No.1
Fiji

FIJI - MAPS

Maps of Fiji. Drawn by E.H.Bryan.
Bishop Museum charts Nos. 377 - 379.
Totoya I. Enlarged from H.O. Chart 2852
(See H.O.Chart 412) -

FIJI   LEPIDOPTERA

See

LEPIDOPTERA   FIJI

G
Geogr.
Pam.
63

FIJI   MAPS

Barnes, A. E.

Tracks of the discoverers of the Fiji Islands (Map) compiled and drawn by A. E. Barnes,
Hydro-graphic Department, Admiralty, London.
1933. 30 inches by 32 inches.

Chart
Case
Folder
15

FIJI   MAPS

Fiji Islands,compiled and drawn at the
Land Department, Suva, Fiji.

Revised Jan. 1914.

Size 40 x 59 3/4.

FIJI   LEPROSY

See

LEPROSY   FIJI

DU
Pacific
Pam 235

FIJI   MAPS

Britton, H.

Fiji in 1870...

Melbourne, 1870. 87p.

For fuller entry see main card

FIJI   MARINE FAUNA

See

MARINE FAUNA   FIJI

FIJI   MAGIC

see

MAGIC   FIJI

Chart
Case
Fiji
in
Folder33

U.S.Expl.

FIJI - MAPS

Map of Fiji. General . Ex U.S. Explo
Exped. Atlas of Charts, Vol. I.

Bishop Museum Chart No. 399.

FIJI   MASKS

See

MASKS   FIJI

FIJI MATERIAL CULTURE

see

MATERIAL CULTURE FIJI

FIJI MIGRATIONS

See

MIGRATIONS FIJI

AM
101.Fi
(5)

Fiji Museum

Catalogue, 1916. pp 44.
Suva, Fiji.

FIJI MEDICAL EDUCATION

See

MEDICAL EDUCATION FIJI

FIJI MISSIONARIES

See

MISSIONARIES FIJI

AM
Mus.Pam.
113

FIJI MUSEUM

Roth, G. K.

The Reopening of Fiji Museum.

(The Museums Journal, the Organ of the
Museums Association, Vol. 31, pp. 496-497, 1932)

FIJI MEDICAL SCHOOLS

See

MEDICAL SCHOOLS FIJI

FIJI MISSIONS

see

MISSIONS FIJI

FIJI MUSIC

see

MUSIC FIJI

FIJI MEDICINE

See

MEDICINE FIJI

FIJI MOLLUSCA

See

MOLLUSCA FIJI

FIJI MYRTACEAE

See

MYRTACEAE FIJI

FIJI MEDICINAL PLANTS

See

MEDICINAL PLANTS FIJI

FIJI MONEY

see

MONEY FIJI

FIJI MYTILOPSIS

See

MYTILOPSIS FIJI

FIJI METEOROLOGY

see

METEOROLOGY FIJI

FIJI MORDELLIDAE

See

MORDELLIDAE FIJI

FIJI NATURAL HISTORY

see

NATURAL HISTORY FIJI

FIJI MICROLEPIDOPTERA

See

MICROLEPIDOPTERA FIJI

FIJI MUSCI

See

MUSCI FIJI

FIJI NAVIGATION

See

NAVIGATION FIJI

FIJI NEMATODES

see

NEMATODES FIJI

FIJI ORYCTES

See

ORYCTES FIJI

FIJI PETROGLYPHS

See

PETROGLYPHS FIJI

FIJI NETS

See

NETS FIJI

FIJI PALEONTOLOGY

see

PALEONTOLOGY FIJI

FIJI PETROGRAPHY

see

PETROGRAPHY FIJI

FIJI OPHIDIA

See

OPHIDIA FIJI

FIJI PALMS

see

PALMS FIJI

B. Mus.
Photos
Bryan
Vol. I

Reading
Room

FIJI - PHOTOGRAPHS

Bryan, Edwin H.

Photographs of Samoa, Phoenix Isls.
Faksofo, and Fiji. Photographed by E.H.B.
Whitney South Sea Wxpedition February to
October, 1924.

FIJI OPHIUROIDAE

See

OPHIUROIDAE FIJI

FIJI PALOLO

See

PALOLO FIJI

Photo

File

Fiji

FIJI - PHOTOGRAPHS

Photographs taken by Miss Muriel
Mattocks, passenger on the S. S. Buford
in the spring of 1924. 18 views - landscapes, natives , native dances, and a
canoe.

FIJI ORCHIDACEAE

See

ORCHIDACEAE FIJI

FIJI PANDANACEAE

see

PANDANACEAE FIJI

Storage
Case
3

Fiji.

FIJI- PICTOGRAPHS

Ladd, Harry S

Notes on pictographs found in Vitilevu,
1928.

FIJI OROCHLESIS

see

OROCHLESIS FIJI

FIJI PEPEROMIA

See

PEPEROMIA FIJI

FIJI PICTOGRAPHS

see

PICTOGRAPHS FIJI

FIJI OROCHLESIS

see

OROCHLESIS FIJI

FIJI PETRELS

see

PETRELS FIJI

FIJI PIERS

see

PIERS FIJI

FIJI NEMATODES

see

NEMATODES FIJI

FIJI ORYCTES

See

ORYCTES FIJI

FIJI PETROGLYPHS

See

PETROGLYPHS FIJI

FIJI NETS

See

NETS FIJI

FIJI PALEONTOLOGY

see

PALEONTOLOGY FIJI

FIJI PETROGRAPHY

see

PETROGRAPHY FIJI

FIJI OPHIDIA

See

OPHIDIA FIJI

FIJI PALMS

see

PALMS FIJI

B. Mus.

Photos
Bryan
Vol. I

Reading
Room

FIJI - PHOTOGRAPHS

Bryan, Edwin H.

Photographs of Samoa, Phoenix Isls.
Fakaofo, and Fiji. Photographed by E.H.B.
Whitney South Sea Wxpedition February to
October, 1924.

FIJI OPHIUROIDAE

See

OPHIUROIDAE FIJI

FIJI PALOLO

See

PALOLO FIJI

Photo

File

Fiji

FIJI - PHOTOGRAPHS

Photographs taken by Miss Muriel
Mattocks, passenger on the S. S. Buford
in the spring of 1924. 18 views - landscapes; natives , native dances, and a
canoe.

FIJI ORCHIDACEAE

See

ORCHIDACEAE FIJI

FIJI PANDANACEAE

see

PANDANACEAE FIJI

Storage
Case
3

FIJI- PICTOGRAPHS

Ladd, Harry S

Notes on pictographs found in Vitilevu,
Fiji. 1928.

FIJI OROCHLESIS

see

OROCHLESIS FIJI

FIJI PEPEROMIA

See

PEPEROMIA FIJI

FIJI PICTOGRAPHS

see

PICTOGRAPHS FIJI

FIJI OROCHLESIS

see

OROCHLESIS FIJI

FIJI PETRELS

see

PETRELS FIJI

FIJI PIERS

see

PIERS FIJI

FIJI PLANARIA
See
PLANARIA FIJI

FIJI PREHISTORY
see also
PREHISTORY FIJI

FIJI RANK
See
RANK FIJI

FIJI PLANT DISEASES
See
PLANT DISEASES FIJI

FIJI PROTOZOA
see
PROTOZOA FIJI

FIJI RELIGION
See
RELIGION FIJI

FIJI PLANT NAMES
See
PLANT NAMES FIJI

FIJI PSELAPHIDAE
see
PSELAPHIDAE FIJI

FIJI RHINOCEROS BEETLE
See
RHINOCEROS BEETLE FIJI

FIJI PLANTS INTRODUCED
See
PLANTS INTRODUCED FIJI

G
51
W 17
FIJI PSYCHOLOGY
Cato, Helen D.
Sidelights on Fijian custom.
(Walkabout, Vol. 12 (9):42-45, 1946)

FIJI RIDDLES
see
RIDDLES FIJI

FIJI POETRY
see
POETRY FIJI

FIJI RACE
see
RACE FIJI

FIJI- RITES AND CEREMONIES
See
RITES AND CEREMONIES FIJI

FIJI POISONOUS FISHES
See
POISONOUS FISHES FIJI

FIJI RADIO CARBON DATING
See
RADIO CARBON DATING FIJI

FIJI ROCK SPIRALS
see also
ROCK SPIRALS FIJI

FIJI POTTERY
see
POTTERY FIJI

FIJI RAIN AND RAINFALL
See
RAIN AND RAINFALL FIJI

FIJI RUBIACEAE
See
RUBIACEAE FIJI

FIJI RUTACEAE

See

RUTACEAE FIJI

GN
2.S
F 47

FIJI SOCIETY

Parham, B. E. V.

Pacific life and the Fiji Society.

(Trans. Fiji Society, 4:47-51, 1950)

FIJI STURNUS

See

STURNUS FIJI

FIJI SACCULINA

See

SACCULINA FIJI

FIJI SOILS

See

SOILS FIJI

FIJI TAMBUA

See

TAMBUA FIJI

FIJI SALT

See

SALT FIJI

FIJI SONGS

see

SONGS FIJI

FIJI TAPA

See

TAPA FIJI

FIJI SCIENCE

See

SCIENCE FIJI

FIJI SORCERY

see

SORCERY FIJI

FIJI TARO

see

TARO FIJI

FIJI SECRET SOCIETIES

see

SECRET SOCIETIES FIJI

FIJI SPIRIT HOUSES

See

SPIRIT HOUSES FIJI

FIJI TATTOOING

see

TATTOOING FIJI

FIJI SLAVERY

see

SLAVERY FIJI

FIJI STENCILLING

see

STENCILLING FIJI

FIJI TENEBRIONIDAE

See

TENEBRIONIDAE FIJI

FIJI SOCIAL ORGANIZATION

see

SOCIAL ORGANIZATION FIJI

FIJI STRING FIGURES

see

STRING FIGURES FIJI

PL
600
A 31

FIJI TEXTS

Ai vola ni veiyalayalati vou i Jisu Karisito na noda turaga kei na nodai vakabula. Sa tabakai mai Lodoni, e Piritania. 1890. 8vo. 282 pp.

(Fiji. New Testament)

PL
600
O 20

FIJI TEXTS

Ai vola tabu, sa oolai kina na veiyalayala-
ti makawa. Kei na veiyalayalati vou. Lodoni.
Sa Tabaki me Nodre mai na Vale ni Vola Tabu e
Lodoni. 1902. 8vo. 284 pp. # 960 pp.

Bible in Fijian

PL
Phil. Pam.
765

FIJI TEXTS

Nai matai ni siga ni wiki. 1wmo. 14 pp.
no title-page.

Fiji, Bible lessons

FIJI THYSANOPTERA

See

THYSANOPTERA FIJI

PL
Phil.Pam.
250

FIJI TEXTS

(Fijiian calendar, 1886)

PL
600
N 11

FIJI TEXTS

Na raivotu Taumada I, Misisi E. G.
Waiti. Sa Tabaki e Buresala, Ovalau, Viti.
1910 8vo. 215 pp.

Fiji Bible teachings

FIJI TOTEMISM

see

TOTEMISM FIJI

PL
Phil.
Pam.
589

FIJI TEXTS

Milner, G. B.

A study of two Fijian texts.

(Bull. School of Oriental and African Studies (Univ. of London, 14(2):346-377, 1952)

PL
Phil.
Pam.
649

FIJI TEXTS

O'Reilly, Patrick

Imprints of the Fiji Catholic Mission, including the Loreto Press. 1958. 8vo. London.
Francis Edwards Ltd. 60 pp.

DU
Pacific
Pam.
No.138

Fiji Tourist Gazette.

Fiji Tourist Gazette, printed for the
Tourist Bureau by the Fiji Times and Herald. Vol. 2, No.9, May 1924.

PL
600
N 11

FIJI TEXTS

Na fisioloji kei na aijini...Sa Iaveti oqo
ki na vosa Vaka-Viti me yaga vei ira nai taukei.
Sai Vakatakarakataki. ...Avondale School Press.
Cooranbong NSW 1908 8vo. 111 + (18) pp.

PL
870
T 25

FIJI TEXTS

Sa alphabeta na vosa faka Fiji. Burder's
Point, Tahiti. Mission Press. 8 pp. 8vo.

(Bound with 33 other pamphlets; Te evanelia
a to tatou ... no. 4)

GN
2.S
P 76

FIJI TRADITIONS

Thompson, Basil

The land of our origin. (Viti, of Fiji.)

(Journal of the Polynesian Society, Vol. 1,
1892, pp. 143-146)

PL
Phil.
Pam.
766

FIJI TEXTS

Na siga ni vakacecegu. no place, no date.
32 pp. sm8vo.

Fiji, Bible stories

GN
2 S
P 76

FIJI TEXTS

Smith, S. Percy

The Polynesian sojourn in Fiji.

(Journal of the Polynesian Society, Vol.3,
1894, pp. 145-152)

FIJI TREES

See

TREES FIJI

PL
600
N 15

FIJI TEXTS

Nai balebale ni vola tabu. ...J.E. Fuli-
toni. Sa Tabaki mai Avondale Press. Cooranbong. 1911. sm8vo. 125 pp.

Fiji, Bible readings

GN
2.S
P 76

FIJI TEXTS

Thompson, Basil

The land of our origin. (Viti, of Fiji.)

(Journal of the Polynesian Society, Vol. 1,
1892, pp. 143-146)

FIJI TRUMPETS

See

TRUMPETS FIJI

PL
Phil.
Pam.
764

FIJI TEXTS

Nai katini. no title-page, no place, no
date. (Sa Tabaki e Buresala, Ovalau, Viti)
16mo. 8 pp.

Fiji, Bible lessons ?

PL
600
N 15

FIJI TEXTS

White, E. G.

Nai tukutuku ni veigauna, mai na Gauna sa
rusa kina ko Jerusalemi makawa me yacova na
Jerusalemi vou. Sa vola nai vola oqo ko Mrs.
E.G.White. Avondale Press. Cooranbong, N.S.W.
1903. 8vo. 286 pp.

FIJI VEGETATION

See

VEGETATION FIJI

FIJI   VESPIDAE

See

VESPIDAE   FIJI

AS
492
S6

FIJI   VOCABULARY

Royal Asiatic Society Straits Branch.
Fijian comparative vocabulary.
in Journ. VIII. 1881, pp. 162-169.

FIJI   WORSHIP

see

WORSHIP   FIJI

GN
1
A 93

FIJI   VOCABULARY

Biggs, Bruce G.

A vocabulary and phrases in the Nandronga
dialect of Fijian.

(Journal of Austronesian Studies, Vol. 1(1):
106-115, 1953)

FIJI   VOLCANOES

See

VOLCANOES   FIJI

DU
Pac.Pam.
752
4to.

Fiji.   Tourist Bureau, Suva, Fiji. n.d.
16 pp.

GN
1
A 93

FIJI   VOCABULARY

Biggs, Bruce G.

A vocabulary from Nailawa, Viti Levu.

(Journal of Austronesian Studies, Vol. 1(1):
118-121, 1953)

FIJI   WAR

See

WAR   FIJI

DU
600
F 47-1

Fiji fishes. (glossary of Fijian names
and English popular names)

(Fiji Information s4, No. 2, Oct. 1956, p.
55)

GN
670
B 64

FIJI   VOCABULARY

Brigham, William Tufts

Ka hana kapa, the making of bark-cloth in
Hawaii.

(Bernice P. Bishop Museum, Memoirs, Vol.III,
1911, iv + pp. 1-273, 49 plates and atlas of 27
colored plates)

FIJI   WARFARE

See

WARFARE   FIJI

DU
1
P 10

Fiji's fight against Oryctes rhinoceros will
cost more.

(Pacific Islands Monthly, 27(4):45, 51,1956)

DU
623
E 47

2 cops.

FIJI   VOCABULARY

Ellis, William, 1794-1872

Journal of a tour around Hawaii...by a deputation from the Mission on those islands.
Boston. 1825. 12mo. pp. 254-258.

FIJI   WEAPONS

see

WEAPONS   FIJI

DU
1
P

Fiji's war on Rhino beetle; definite infestation in Suva area. [followed by "Few beetles-
many larvae" and "Life history of beetle" by B.
A O'Connor.]

(Pacific Islands Monthly, Vol. 23(9):19-20,
1953)

GN
2.1
A-M

FIJI   VOCABULARY

Hocart, A. M.

On the meaning of the Fijian word Turanga.

(Man, vol. 13, 1913, no. 80, pp. 140-143)

(See also note, Man, vol. 21, 1921, no. 50,
pp. 85-86)

FIJI   WEATHER FORECASTING

See

WEATHER FORECASTING   FIJI

DU
1
P

Fiji's war on Rhinoceros beetle; South
Pacific Commission to direct research and attack.

(Pacific Islands Monthly, Vol. 23(10):19,
1953)

GN
2.8
P 76

FIJI   VOCABULARY

Raven-Hart, R.

A dialect of Yasawa Island (Fiji) by R.

(Jour. Polynesian Soc., 62(1):33-56, 1953)

FIJI   WEEDS

See

WEEDS   FIJI

PL
Phil.pam.
250

(Fijian calendar, 1886)

GN
Pam
#555

The Fijian Society, ex The Pacific
Age, Aug. 22, 1922.

QL
Insects
Pam.
1801

FILARIASIS

Na tabacakacaka ka carava na vakacaka ni
kona vakawabokotaki na vacaga. (Publication in
Fijian concerning filariasis. no place, no date
received 1943)

DU
S 72t

FILARIASIS   PACIFIC   (south)

Iyengar, M. O. T.

Distribution of filariasis in the South
Pacific region.

(South Pacific Commission, Technical Paper
No. 66, September, 1954)

DU
1
P

Fijian navigators. Memories of the great
canoes.

(Pacific Islands Monthly. Vol.VII, no.11,
1937, pp.23-24)

DU
1
S 72t

FILARIASIS   BIBLIOGRAPHY

Iyengar, M. O. T.   and others

Annotated bibliography on Filariasis and
Elephantiasis. Parts 1-3

(South Pacific Commission, Technical Papers
65, 88, 109, 1957)

[most of the credit should go to M.O.T. Iyengar, J. Kerrest, G. Loison, and Mrs. Monlau"]

QL
Insects
Pam.
1199

FILARIASIS   FIJI

Knott, James I.

Mosquito control, Suva. What you should
know about filariasis. Suva. 16 pp. 1944

GN
1
O 15

FIJIANS

Cato, A. C.

Malolo Island and Viseisei village, western
Fiji.

(Oceania, 22(2):101-115, 1951)

DU
1
S 72 t

FILARIASIS   BERAU

Rook, H. de

An investigation on filariasis in the Berau
region.

(South Pacific Commission, Technical Paper,
No. 105, 1956)

[Netherlands New Guinea]

DU
1
S 72 t

FILARIASIS   PACIFIC

Iyengar, M. O. T.

A review of the literature on the distribution and spidemiology of filariasis in the
South Pacific region.

(South Pacific Commission, Tech. Paper No.
126, 1959)

GN
2.1
C 14 a

FIJIANS   ORIGINS

Gifford, Edwin Winslow

Tribes of Viti Levu and their origin places.

(Anthropological Records, 13:5, 1952.
Univ. of California)

DU
1
S 72t

FILARIASIS   NEW CALEDONIA

Iyengar, M. O. T.

Studies on filariasis in New Caledonia.
By M.O.T. Iyengar and M.A.U. Menon.

(South Pacific Commission, Tech. Inf.
Circular No. 15, 1956)

DU
1
S 72 t

FILARIASIS   PACIFIC

Iyengar, M. O. T.

Summary data on filariasis in the South
Pacific.

(South Pac. Commission, Technical Paper,
No. 132, 1960)

GN
2.S
P 76

FILA LANGUAGE

Capell, A.

Notes on the Fila language, New Hebrides.

(Journal of the Polynesian Society, Vol.
51, 1942, pp. 153-180)

DU
1
S 72 t

FILARIASIS   NEW CALEDONIA

Lacour, M.

Enquête epidemiologique et entomologique
sur la filariose de Bancroft en Nouvelle-Calé-
sonie it dependances. By M. Lacour and J.
Rageau.

(South Pacific Commission, Tech. Paper,
No. 110, 1957)

AP
2
N 4

FILARIASIS   PACIFIC

Manson-Bahr, Philip

Filariasis in the Pacific.

(Nature, Vol. 168, no. 4279, p. 776-777,
1951)

DU
1
S 72 t

FILARIAE

Iyengar, M. O. T.

Developmental stages of Filariae in mosquitoes.

(South Pac. Commission, Tech. Pap. No. 104,
1957)

DU
1
S 72-t

FILARIASIS   PACIFIC   (south)

Annotated bibliography of filariasis and
elephantiasis. Part I: Epidemiology of filariasis
in the South Pacific region.

(South Pacific Commission, Technical Paper
No. 85, August, 1954)

DU
1
S 72

FILARIASIS   PACIFIC

Study group on filariasis, South Pacific
Commission. Report of the study group. Noumea
November 1959.

Annex II: A brief review of the epidemiology
of filariasis in the South Pacific, by M.O.T.
Iyengar; A resume of filariasis control work...
Pacific, same author.

DU
1
S 72 ti

FILARIASIS

Iyengar, M. O. T.

An investigation on filariasis in Niue.

(South Pacific Commission, Tech. Inf. Circ.
No. 30, 1958)

DU
1
S 72 t

FILARIASIS   PACIFIC

Byrd, Elon E.

Studies on the epidemiology of filariasis
on central and south Pacific Islands. By Elon
E. Byrd and Lyle S. St. Amant.

(South Pacific Commission, Technical Paper
No. 125, 1959)

DU
1
S 72 ti

FILARIASIS   PACIFIC

Summary of the report of the study group
on filariasis, Noumea, 1959.

(South Pacific Com., Tech. Inf. Cir.,
no. 42:1-4, 1960)

AP
2
N 28

FILARIASIS   POLYNESIA

Manson-Bahr,   Sir Philip

The fight against filariasis in the Pacific.

(Nature, Vol. 171(4348):368-371, 1953)

Q
115
F47

Filchner, Wilhelm

Wissenschaftliche ergebnisse der expedition... China und Tibet 1903-1905.

Bd.I.- Teil 1.

Abs.1.- Zoologische sammlungen
"   2.- Botanische sammlungen ... Diels.

Berlin, Mittler, 1908.   288p.

QK
1
C 21

FILICES

Becherer, A.

Fougères de la Nouvelle-Calédonie et des Iles Loyalty.

(Candollea, Vol. VII, 1937, pp. 217-220)

Q
101
P 18

FILARIASIS   TAIWAN

Wu, Yao-Tsing   and others

Recent advances in the studies of filariasis and its control in Taiwan. By Yao-Tsing Wu, Po-Tsung Tseng and Wan-I Chien.

(The Taiwan Public Health Journal, 1(4):1-17, 1962)

GN
Ethn.Pam.
3551

Fildes, H.

The last of the Ngati Mamoe; the wild people of the New Zealand mountain and bush. A.H. and A.W.Reed. Dundedin and Wellington. 8vo. 1936. 15 pp.

QK
525
B 87

FILICES

Broun, Maurice

Index to North American ferns, constituting a catalogue of the ferns and fern allies of North America north of Mexico, including all known forms, varieties, and hybrids. With a foreword by Charles A. Weatherby.   Orleans, Mass. 1938.   sm8vo.   217 pp.

QL
Insects
Pam.
1743

FILARIASIS   TOKELAU ISLANDS

Laird, Marshall

Notes on the mosquitos of the Gilbert, Ellice and Tokelau Islands, and on filariasis in the latter group.

(Bull. Ent. Research, 46(2):291-300, 1955)

QK
9
F 44

K.13.22

Tilet, G. Y.   (Filet, G. J.)

Plantkundig Woordenboek voor Nederlandsch-indië; met korte aanwijzingen van het geneeskundig en huishoudelijk gebruik der planten, en vermelding der verschillende inlandsche en wetenschappelijke benamingen. Amsterdam,   1888. 8vo. pp. x.348. 2nd Edit.

QK
523
C 55

FILICES

Christensen, Carl

Index Filicum... Hafniae, 1906
and Supplementum, 1906-1912, Hafniae, 1913
"   1913-1916'   1917
"   tertium, 1917-1933, Hafniae, 1934

DU
1
S 72 ti

FILARIASIS   WESTERN SAMOA

Iyengar, M. O. T.

A scheme for filariasis control in Western Samoa.

(South Pacific Com., Tech. Inf. Cir., No. 20:1-13, 1954)

QL
Crust
Pam
377

Filhol, Henri

Considerations relatifs a le faune des crustaces de la Nouvelle-Zelande.

Paris, 1885. 60p.

QK
523
C 55

FILICES

Christensen, Carl

Taxonomic fern-studies I-II.

(Dansk Botanisk Arkiv, Bind 6 (nr.3):1-99, pl. 1-13, 1929)

QL
1
A 93

FILARIOIDEA

Mackerras, Josephine

Filarial parasites (Nematoda:Filarioidea) of Australian animals.

(Australian Journal of Zoology, 10(3):400-457, 1962)

P
1440
W 66

FILIBUSTERS

Wilbur, Marguerite Eyer   tr and ed.

Raveneau de Lussan: Buccaneer of the Spanish Main and early French filibuster of the Pacific. A translation... Arthur H. Clark Company. Cleveland. 1930. R8vo. 303 pp.

QK
Bot.Pam.
1768

FILICES

Conard, Henry Shoemaker

The Structure and Life-History of the Hay-scented Fern.

(Carnegie Institution of Washington, Publication No. 94, 1908)

AS
763
H 38

Filatova, Zinaida

Exploration of the Pacific Ocean and its deep-sea fauna by the "Vitjaz".

(Proc Haw. Acad. Sci., 34th meeting, p. 27, 1959)

FILICALES

See

FILICES

AS
36
I 64

FILICES

Cooperrider, Tom S.

The ferns and other Pteridiphytes of Iowa.

(State University of Iowa Studies in Nat. Hist., 20(1), 1959?)

GC
Oceanography
Pam.
83

Filatova, Zenaida*

Exploration of the Pacific Ocean and its deep-sea bottom fauna. A speech given by... of the Institute of Oceanology, Academy of Sciences, Moscow, at the Chemistry Building, University of Hawaii, February 5, 1959.

*(scientist on board the Russian oceanographic ship Vitjaz)

DU
1
P 12

Filice, Francis P.

Tsunami: destructive oceanic waves.

(Pacific Discovery, 12(3):20-22, 1959)

QK
1
A 75

FILICES

Copeland, Edwin Bingham

Ferns of the Second Archbold Expedition to New Guinea.

(Journal of the Arnold Arboretum, Harvard University, Vol. 24, 1943, pp. 440-444)

QK
523
C 78

FILICES

Copeland, Edwin Bingham

Genera filicum: the genera of ferns.
Published by the Chronica Botanica Company.
Waltham. 1947. R8vo. xvi + 247 pp., 10 pl.
(Annales Cryptogamici et Phytopathologici, Vol.
V)

QK
523
M 82

FILICES

Moore, Thomas

Index filicum: being a synopsis of the
genera of ferns, with characters and illustrations, and an enumeration of the species, with
geographical distribution, synonyms, references
to figures... [Parts 1-20] London. Williams
and Norgate. pp. clxii + 372, pl. 1-78. sm8vo.
1857-1862

QK
110
N 56

FILICES

Underwood, Lucien Marcus and others

Filicales.

IN North American flora, Vol. 16, Part 1,
1909, pp. 25-88.

QK
1
H

FILICES

Greville, Robert Kaye

Enumeratio Filicum, by R. K. Greville and
W. J. Hooker.

(Hooker, Botan. Miscell. II, 1831, pp. 360-
403; III, pp. 104-109, 216-232, 1833)

QK
524.H9
P 93

FILICES

Presl, Karel B(oriwog)

Hymenophyllaceae. Eine botanische Abhandlung. Mit XII Kupfertafeln. Prag. 1843. sm4to
70 pp. 12 Tafeln.

QK
T 1

FILICES

Underwood, Lucien Marcus

A review of the genera of ferns proposed
prior to 1832.

(Memoirs of the Torrey Botanical Club, Vol.
6, No. 4, 1899.)

AS
36
A 5

FILICES

Hodge, Henricks

Tree ferns.

(Natural History, Vol. LXV(2):88-91, 1956)

QK
523
P 92

FILICES

Presl, Karel Bořiwog

Tentamen Pteridographiae, seu Genera Filica-
cearum, Praesertim juxta Venarum Decursum et
Distributionem Exposita. Pragae. Theophili
Haase. 1836. 290 pp. XII Tabellen. sm8vo.

FILICES

See also

PTERIDOPHYTA

QK
523
H 78

FILICES

Hooker, William Jackson

A Century of Ferns; being figures with
brief descriptions of one hundred new, or rare,
or imperfectly known species of ferns, from
various parts of the world; a selection from the
author's "Icones Plantarum". London. William
Pamplin. R8vo. 1854. (descriptive text ac-
companies plates)

QK
523
S 65

FILICES

Smith, John

Ferns: British and foreign: their history,
organography, classification, and enumeration;
with a treatise on their cultivation. London.
Edition of 1866. Robert Hardwicke. sm8vo.
Edition of 1879. Bogue.

QK
523
C 55

FILICES GEOGRAPHICAL DISTRIBUTION

Christ, Hermann

Die Geographie der Farne. Jena 1910. 8vo.
357 pp.

QK
523
H 78

FILICES

Hooker, William Jackson

Filices Exoticae; or, coloured figures and
descriptions of exotic ferns, chiefly of such as
are cultivated in the Royal Gardens of Kew. The
drawings executed by Mr. Fitch. London. Lovell
Reeve. 1859. 4to. 100 plates, with descriptions.

QK
523
S 84

FILICES

Stevenson, Greta

A book of ferns. Printed by John McIndoe,
Ltd. Dunedin. 1954. 8vo. (1-7)8-160 pp.

QK
520
A 51

FILICES LAVA FIELDS

Crookes, Marguerite

On the lava fields of Rangitoto.

(American Fern Journal, 50(4):257-263,
1960)

QK
523
H 78

FILICES

Hooker, Sir William Jackson

Garden ferns; or, coloured figures and descriptions, with the needful analyses of the
fructification and venation, of a selection of
exotic ferns adapted for cultivation in the
garden, hothouse and conservatory. The drawings
by Walter Fitch. London. Lovell Reeve & Co.
1862. R8vo. v, pp., 64 plates, with descriptive text.

QK
Bot.Pam.
2994

FILICES

Tindale, Mary D.

A preliminary revision of the genus Lastre-
opsis Ching.

(Victoria Nat. 73:180-185, 1957)

QK
Bot. Pam.
3252

FILICES TRICHOMES

Iwatsuki, Kunio

The trichomes of the thelypteroid ferns.

(Mem. College of Science, Univ. of Tokyo,
Ser. B., Vol. 29(1):103-11, 1962)

QK
523
H 78

FILICES

Hooker, William Jackson

Genera Filicum;...London. 1842...

QK
Bot.Pam.
2766

FILICES

Wagner, Warren H. Jr.

Types of foliar dichotomy in living ferns.

(Reprinted from the American Journal of
Botany, Vol. 38(8):578-592, 1952)

QK
530
S 68

FILICES AFRICA, SOUTH

Sim, Thomas R.

The ferns of South Africa, containing
descriptions and figures of the ferns and
fern allies of South Africa. 2d ed.

Cambridge Univ. Press, 1915, 384 pp, 186
pls.

FILICES   AMBON

QK
Bot.Pam.
3016
Alston, A. H. G.

Some undescribed ferns from New Guinea and Ambon.

(Nova Guinea, n.s., vol. 7(1):1-3, 1956)

FILICES.   AMERICA

AS
36
S2
Christensen, Carl Frederik Albert, 1872-
The American ferns of the group of *Dryopteris opposita* contained in the U. S. National museum, by Carl Christensen ...

(*In* Smithsonian institution. Smithsonian miscellaneous collections. Washington, 1910. 24¼ᶜᵐ. vol. LII, (Quarterly issue, vol. V) p. 365-396)

Publication 1867.
Originally published July 12, 1909.

1. Dryopteris. 2. Ferns—America. I. U. S. National museum.

Library of Congress   Q11.S7 vol. 52   16-12774 Revised
——— Copy 2.

FILICES   AMERICA

QK
1
U
Maxon, William R.

Studies of tropical American ferns. U.S. Nat. Herb. no I in Vol X p. 473-508; no 2, in Vol XIII pp 1-43; no 3 in Vol XVI 2, pp. 25-62, no 4 in Vol XVII pp 83-179, 391- 425 (no 5), pp 541-608 (no 6)

FILICES   AMERICA

AS
36
S 1
Maxon, William R(alph)

Tree ferns of North America.

(Smithsonian Inst., Rept., 1911, pp. 463-491, 15 pls.)

FILICES   AMSTERDAM ISLANDS

QH
1
M 17 b
Tardieu-Blot, Mme.

Sur les Fougères récoltées par Aubert de la Rue aux Iles Kerguelen et Amsterdam.

(Mémoires de l'Institut Scientifique de Madagascar, série B. Biologie, Tome V:59-64, 1954)

FILICES   ANTARCTICA

AS
540
P
Copeland, E. B.

Fern evolution in Antarctica.

(Philippine Journal of Science, Vol. 70, pp. 157-188, 1939. 2 Figs.)

FILICES   AUSTRALIA

QK
541
B 15
Bailey, Frederick Manson

Lithograms of the ferns of Queensland. Brisbane. Department of Agriculture. 8vo. 7 pp. and 191 plates.

FILICES   AUSTRALIA

QK
Bot. Pam.
2733
Bartram, Edwin B.

North Queensland mosses collected by L. J. Brass.

(Farlowia, 4(1):235-247, 1952)

FILICES   AUSTRALIA

AS
720.N
L
Trebeck, P. N.

Mount Wilson and its ferns.

(Linn. Soc. N.S.W., Proc., 2d ser., 1886, pp. 491-496)

FILICES   AUSTRALIA

QK
531
W 14
Wakefield, N. A.

Ferns of Victoria and Tasmania; with descriptive notes and illustrations of the 116 native species. Published by the Field Naturalists Club of Victoria. 1955. 8vo. iv(2) + 71 pp.

FILICES   BOMBAY

QK
529
B 64
Blatter, E.

The ferns of Bombay. By E. Blatter and J. F. d'Almeida. With 2 coloured and 15 black and white plates, and 43 text figures. D. B. Taraporevala Sons and Co., Bombay. sm8vo. 1922 vii + 228 pp.

FILICES   BORNEO

AS
522.B
Sa
Brooks, C. J.
The ferns of Mount Penrissen in Sarawak Mus. Journ. I, 2, Art IV, 8vo. 1912, pp. 39-51.

FILICES   BORNEO

AS
522.B
Sa
Copeland, Edwin Bingham

Keys to the Ferns of Borneo. In Sarawak Mus. Journ. II, pp 287-424, 1917.

FILICES   CELEBES

Christ, H.

Die Farnflora von Celebes.

(Annales du Jardin Botanique de Buitenzorg, Vol. 15, 1898, pp. 73-186)

HSPA

FILICES   CENTRAL AMERICA

QK
1
C a
Copeland, Edwin Bingham

Tropical American ferns.

(University of Calif., Pub. in Botany, Vol. 19, 1941, pp. 287-340)

FILICES   CENTRAL AMERICA

AS
36
S2
Maxon, William R.

Remarkable new fern from Panama. Smith. Mis. Coll. LVI, 24. Wash 1911

FILICES   CEYLON

QK
Pam.
357
Yates, Lorenzo G.

Ferns of Ceylon. Santa Barbara, Cal., 1887.

FILICES   CHINA

QK
529
H 87
Hu, Hsen Hsu

Icones Filicum Sinicarum, by Hsen Hsu Hu and Ren Chang Ching. Fascicule 1-   1930- Metropolitan Museum of Natural History, Academia Sinica, Nanking, and the Fan Memorial Institute of Biology, Peiping.   4to.

FILICES   CHINA

QK
1
H 59
Vol, Charles E. de

Ferns and fern allies of east central China.

(Musée Heude, Notes de Bot. Chinoise, 7, 1945)

FILICES   COOK ISLANDS

AS
182
H
Luerssen, Chr.

Ein Beitrag zur Farnflora der Palaos und Hervey-Inseln. In Journ. Mus. Godeffroy, Heft 1, pp 52- 62.

FILICES   EASTER ISLAND

QH
138.J
S 62
Christensen, C.
The ferns of Easter Island. By C. Christensen and C. Skottsberg.

IN
Skottsberg, Carl
The natural history of Juan Fernandez and Easter Island. Vol. 2. Botany. No. 2, pp. 47-53. Uppsala, 1920.

QK
1
J 86

FILICES   FIJI

Baker, J. G.

New ferns collected by J. B. Thurston, Esq. in Fiji.

(Jour. Bot. Brit. and For., vol. 24, pp. 182, 183, 1886)

QK
1
Ke

FILICES   FIJI

Wright, C. H.

Ferns Collected in Fiji by Sir Everard im Thurn.

(In Bull. of Misc. Information, Royal Botanic Gardens, Kew, 1930, pp. 343-348)

QK
368
J

FILICES   HAWAII

Copeland, Edwin Bingham

Hawaiian ferns collected by L'Abbé U. Faurie.

(Phil. Journ. So. C. Botany IX, 5, 1914. pp. 435-441)

QK
1
J 86

FILICES   FIJI

Baker, J. G.

On a collection of ferns gathered in the Fiji Islands by Mr. John Horne, F.L.S.

(Jour. Bot. Brit. and For., vol. 17, pp. 292-300, 1879)

QK
Bot.Pam.
2484

FILICES   FOSSIL

Palmer, Harold S.

Fern prints in lava.

(American Journal of Science, Vol. 245, 320-321, 1947)

QK
368
J

FILICES   HAWAII

Copeland, Edwing Bingham

Hawaiian ferns collected by J. F. Rock.

(Philip. Journ. of Sci. XI, 4. 1916. (C) pp. 170-173)

QK
Bot.Pam.
2179

QK
473.F
S 64

As
763
B-b

FILICES   FIJI

Christensen, C.

Pteridophyta filicales.

(Bernice P. Bishop Museum, Bulletin 141. 1936. pp.5-11)

QK
527
F-81

FILICES   GREAT BRITAIN

Francis, G. W.

Analysis of British Ferns.
London, 1855. 8vo. pp. 88. 10 pls.

DU
621
H3

FILICES   HAWAII

Derby, Charles

List of Hawaiian ferns. Thrum's Hawaiian Annual, 1875, pp.16-18.

AS
763
B-b

QK
532.F4
C78

Reading
Room

FILICES   FIJI

Copeland, Edwin Bingham

Ferns of Fiji. B. P. Bishop Mus., Bull. 59, 1929.

QK
527
L 89

FILICES   GREAT BRITAIN

Lowe, E. J.

Ferns: British and Exotic. New edition. In 8 vols.

London: George Bell & Sons. 1872.

QK
Bot.Pam
2345

FILICES HAWAII

Fosberg, F. Raymond

Uses of Hawaiian ferns.

(American Fern Journal, Vol. 32, 1942, pp. 15-23)

QK
Bot.Pam.
2213

FILICES   FIJI

Copeland, E. B.   (Edwin Bingham)

New or interesting ferns from Micronesia, Fiji and Samoa.

(Occ. Papers, Bernice P. Bishop Museum, Vol. 15, 1939, No. 7, pp. 79-92. 9 figs.)

QK
Pam
#249
and
254
248

FILICES   HAWAII

Bailey, Edward

Hawaiian Ferns, a synopsis taken mostly from Hooker and Baker, with additions and emendations, adapting it more especially to the Hawaiian Islands. 3 cop.
Honolulu, 1883.

QH
1
H 38-b

FILICES   HAWAII

Fowler, Robert L.

Key to ferns, Kilauea-Mauna Loa section, Hawaii National Park.

(Natural History Bulletin, No. 4, 1940) Hawaii National Park.

AS
771
F 47

FILICES   FIJI

Parham, B. E.

Fijian ferns and fern allies.

(Fiji Soc. of Sci. and Industry, Trans. and Proc., 1940, pp. 19-25)

QK
Bot.Pam.
250

FILICES   HAWAII

Bingham, Hiram

Artificial key to genera of Hawaiian ferns. ms. n.d.

QK
520
A 51

FILICES   HAWAII

Fowler, R. L.

Ferns of the Kilauea-Mauna Loa section of the Hawaii National Park.

(American Fern Journal, Vol. 30, 1940, p. 9-18)

QK
520
A 51

FILICES   FIJI

Smith, A. C.

Reminiscences of fern collecting in Fiji.

(American Fern Journal, Vol. 34, 1944, pp. 1-16)

QK
523
C 55

FILICES   HAWAII

Christ, Hermann

Die Geographie der Farne. Mit einem Titelbild, 129 Abbildungen...im Text und 3 Karten. Gustav Fischer. Jena. 1910. 8vo. 357 pp.

(bound in at back is English translation of pp. 239-243 on Hawaiian ferns.) See also copies at QK Bot. Pam. 247, 251.

QK
Bot. Pam
1798

FILICES   HAWAII

Hieronymus, Georg

Aspleniorum species novae et non satis notae

(Extract from Hedwigia, Vol. 60, pp.226-228 1919).

QK
520
A 51   FILICES   HAWAII

Horner, Eugene

An unusual Hawaiian population of Ophioglossum pendulum.

(American Fern Journal, 48(3):118-122, 1958)

QK
Bot.Pam.
1794   FILICES   HAWAII

Smith, Frances Grace

Diellia and its variations. Honolulu. 1934.

AS
763   (Bernice P. Bishop Museum, Occasional Papers
B-4   Vol. X, No. 16. 1934.)

Reading
Room

QK
Bot.Pam.
2990   FILICES   HAWAII

Wold, Myron L.

Tree ferns of Hawaii; a non-technical description of the three main species, their characteristics and uses. (folder) Printed and
distributed by courtesy of Hawaiian Fern-Wood,
Ltd. 1957

QH
1
H 38   FILICES   HAWAII

Hubbard, Douglass H.

Ferns of Hawaii National Park.

(Hawaii Nature Notes, Vol. V(1), 1952)

QK
1
Ca   FILICES   HAWAII

and   Wagner, Warren H., Jr.
QK
524.D5   The fern genus Diellia, its structure, affin-
W 13   ities and taxonomy.

(Univ. of California Pub. in Botany, 26(1):
1-212, pl. 1-21, 1952)

QK
Pam   FILICES   HAWAII
#252
Herb   Yates, Lorenzo G.

Notes on Hawaiian Ferns, compiled
from the works of Hooker, Baker,
Bailey & others.
Santa Barbara. 1887. 12 mo pl.

K.16.5

QK
Bot.Pam.
188   FILICES   HAWAII

Lyons, A. B.

Artificial key to the genera and species of
Hawaiian ferns.

(Hawaiian Annual, 1891:76-87)

QK
Bot.Pam.
2616   FILICES   HAWAII

Wagner, W. H. Jr.

Ferns naturalized in Hawaii.

(Bernice P. Bishop Museum, Occ. Paper, Vol.
20, No. 8, 1950)

QK
Bot.Pam.
2644   FILICES   HONGKONG

Gibbs, L.

Common Hongkong ferns. Kelly and Walsh, Ltd.
Hongkong, Shanghai, Singapore. no date. 8vo.
x + 85 pp.

DU
620
M 21   FILICES   HAWAII

locked Lyons, A. B.
case
The ferns of Hawaii. Read before the
Williams College Lyceum of Natural History, March
2, 1865.

(Maile Quarterly, Vol. 2, No. 2, Jan. 1867,
pp. 28-33)

QK
520
A 51   FILICES   HAWAII

Wagner, W. H., Jr.

A new species of Diellia from Oahu.

(American Fern Journal, Vol. 41(1):9-15,
1951)

QK
Bot. Pam
3164   FILICES   ILLINOIS

Evers, Robert A.

The filmy fern in Illinois.

(Illinois Natural History Survey, Biol.
Notes No. 44, 1961)

QK
Bot.Pam.
246   FILICES   HAWAII
253
538   Lydgate, J. M.

A short synopsis of Hawaiian ferns. 1873.
14 pp.

QK
1
T 1   FILICES   HAWAII

Wagner, Warren H., Jr.

A reinterpretation of Schizostege lidgatei
(Baker) Hillebrand.

(Bull. Torrey Botanical Club, Vol. 76:444-
461, 1949)

QK
529
B 39   FILICES   INDIA

Beddome, R.H.

Ferns of British India. vols. 1-2.
Madras, 1890. 4to.

DU
620
F   FILICES   HAWAII

Rock, J. F.

Ferns of Hawaii.

(Friend, Feb., 1913, pp. 28-30; 40)

AP
2
S 35   FILICES   HAWAII

Wieland, G. R.

A sacrifice to Pele.

(Science, 71:386, 1930)

[destruction   of flora by lava flows
not so extreme   as earlier supposed"]

QK
529
B-39   FILICES   INDIA

Beddome, R.H.

Ferns of Southern India.

Madras, 1863.

QK
Bot.Pam.
2968   FILICES   HAWAII

St. John, Harold

Notes on Hawaiian terrestrial species of
Ophioglossum.

(Reprinted, Am. Fern Journal, 47(2):74-76,
1957)

QK
Bot.Pam.
2989   FILICES   HAWAII

Wold, Myron L.

Hawaiian treeferns for landscaping and in-
door use. (folder) 1951.

QK
529
B 39   FILICES   INDIA

Beddome, R. H.

Handbook to the ferns of British
India, Ceylon and the Malay Peninsula
with supplement.

Calcutta, 1892. 8vo. pp. 110, illus.

QK
529
B 64

FILICES   INDIA

Blatter, E.

The ferns of Bombay. By E. Blatter and J.
F. d'Almeida. With 2 coloured and 15 black and
white plates, and 43 text figures. D. B. Taraporevala Sons and Co., Bombay. sm8vo. 1922
vii + 228 pp.

AS
720.N
L

FILICES   LORD HOWE ISLAND (N.S.Wales)

Watts, W. Walter

Ferns of Lord Howe Island. In Proc.
Linn. Soc. N.S.W., 1912, pp 395 - 403.

QK
529
V 27

FILICES   MALAY PENINSULA

Alderwerelt van Rosenburg, C.R.W.K. van

Malayan ferns and fern allies. Handbook to
the determination of the ferns and fern allies
of the Malayan islands (incl. those of the Malay
Peninsula, the Philippines and New Guinea).
Dept. of Agric., Industry and Commerce, Netherlands India. Batavia. 1916-1917. R8vo. 577 pp.
and supplement I of 73 pp.

AS
36
S2

FILICES   JAMAICA

Maxon, William R.

New species of fern of genus
Polypodium from Jamaica.

In Smith   Mis. Coll. Vol. 47
pp. 410-411.   1 pl. 1905.

QK
623
B 87

FILICES   LOUISIANA

Brown, Clair A.

Ferns and fern allies of Louisiana. By
Clair A. Brown and Donovan S. Correll. Louisiana
State University Press. Baton Rouge. 1942
R8vo. 1942c. xii + 185 pp.

QK
532
V 27

FILICES   MALAY ARCHIPELAGO

Alderwerelt, C.R.W.K. van Rosenburgh van

Malayan ferns. Handbook of the determination
of the ferns of the Malayan islands (including
those of the Malayan Peninsula, the Philippines
and New Guinea). Batavia, 1908. R8vo. 900 pp.

QK
367
B 12

FILICES   JAVA

Backer, C. A.

Varenflora voor Java: overzicht der op Java
voorkomende varens en varenachtigen, hare ver-
spreiding, oekologie en toepassingen, door C. A.
Backer and O. Posthumus.   's Lands Plantentuin.
Bauitenzorg. 1939. R8vo. xlvii + 370 pp.

QK
Bot.Pam.
1780

FILICES   LOYALTY ISLANDS

Bonaparte, Le Prince Roland

Filicales et lycopodiales de la Nouvelle-
Caledonie et des Iles Loyalty. F. Sarasin and J.
Roux, Nova Caledonia, Botanique, Vol. I, L, I, No.
5 and 6. Wiesbaden, Kriedels, 1914. 51 pp. pl.

QK
1
B 97 b

FILICES   MALAY ARCHIPELAGO

Alderwerelt, C.R.W.K. van Rosenburgh van

New or interesting Malayan ferns. Parts
3, 4, 5, 6, 7.

(Bull. Jardin Bot. de Buitenzorg, Ser. 2,
Nos. I, VII, XI, XVI, XX. 1911-1915)

QK
523
B 74

FILICES   JAVA

Bosch, Roelof Benjamin van den

Hymenophyllaceae Javanicae; sive Descriptio
Hymenophyllacearum Archipelagi Indici, Iconibus
Illustrata...

(Amsterdam. K. Akad. van Wetenschappen, Ver-
handel. Deel 9. 1861)

QK
Bot.Pam.
1415

FILICES   MADAGASCAR

Baker, J. G.

On a collection of ferns made by Langley
Kitching, Esq., in Madagascar.

(Jour. of Bot., Britain and Foreign, pp.
326-330, 369-373, 1880. Reprint repaged
1-8)

QK
1
S 61

FILICES   MALAY PENINSULA

Holttum, R. E.

Notes on Malayan ferns, with descriptions
of 5 new species.

(The Gardens' Bulletin, Straits Settlements.
vol.9. 1937. pp.119-138)

AS
540
P

FILICES   JAVA

Copeland, E. B.

Notes on some Javan ferns.

(Philippine Journal of Science. C, Botany.
vol.VIII. 1913. pp.139-146)

QK
Botany
Pam
1466

FILICES   MADAGASCAR

Christensen, Carl

New ferns from Madagascar.   Archiv fur
botanik, Band 14, no. 19, 1916.   8 p. pl.

QK
366
H 75

FILICES   MALAYA

Holttum, R. E.

A revised flora of Malaya; an illustrated
systematic account of the Malayan flora, including commonly cultivated plants.

Vol. II: Ferns...   (1954)

Gov't. Printing   Office. Singapore.   R8vo.

QH
1
M 17 b

FILICES   KERGUELEN ISLANDS

Tardieu-Blot, Mme.

Sur les Fougères récoltées par Aubert de la
Rue aux îles Kerguelen et Amsterdam.

(Mémoires de l'Institut Scientifique de
Madagascar, série B. Biologie, Tome V:59-64,
1954)

AS
540
P

FILICES   MALAY

Copeland, E. B.
On phyllitis in Malaya and the
supposed genera diplora and triphlebia.
In Phil. Journ. of Sc. C, Botany, VIII, 3, 1913
pp. 147-156, pls. V-VII.

QK
Botany
Pam.
3319

FILICES   MALAYSIA

Holttum, R. E.

New species of Malaysian ferns.

(Reprint, Blumea, Vol. 11(2):529-534,
1962)

QK
1
J 86

FILICES   LORD HOWE ISLAND (N. S. Wales)

Baker, J. G.

New ferns from Lord Howe Island.

(Jour. Bot. Brit. and Foreign, Vol. 11:16-17,
1873)

QK
529
V 27

FILICES   MALAY PENINSULA

Alderwerelt van Rosenburg, C.R.W.K. van

Malayan fern allies. Handbook to the
determination of the ferns and fern allies
of the Malayan islands (incl. those of the
Malay Peninsula, the Philippines and New Guinea)
Landsdrukkerij. Batavia. 1915. xvi + 261 pp.
R8vo.

QK
Bot.Pam.
2768

FILICES   MARIANAS ISLANDS

Wagner, W. H., Jr.

A new fern from Rota, Mariana Islands.

(Reprinted from Pacific Science, vol. 2(3):
214-215, 1948)

QK
Bot.Pam.
2213

FILICES   MICRONESIA

Copeland, E. B. (Edwin Bingham)

New or interesting ferns from Micronesia, Fiji and Samoa.

(Occ. Papers, Bernice P. Bishop Museum, Vol. 15, 1939, No. 7, pp. 79-92. 9 figs.)

QK
1
J 86

FILICES   NEW GUINEA

Alston, A.H.G.

Undescribed ferns from New Guinea.

(Journal of Botany, British and Foreign, Vol. 78, No. 934, 1940, pp. 225-229)

AS
540
P

FILICES   NEW GUINEA

Copeland, Edwin B.

Miscellaneous ferns of New Guinea.

(The Philippine Journal of Science, Vol. 76, 1941, pp. 23-25)

QK
1
M 65

FILICES   MINNESOTA

Rosendahl, Carl Otto, 1875-

Guide to the ferns and fern allies of Minnesota, by C. O. Rosendahl and F. K. Butters. [Minneapolis] University of Minnesota, 1909.

3 p. l., 22 p., 1 l. illus., pl. 25½ᶜᵐ. (Minnesota plant studies. III)

At head of cover-title: Geological and natural history survey of Minnesota. Frederic E. Clements, state botanist.

1. Ferns. 2. Botany—Minnesota. [2. Minnesota—Botany] I. Butters, Frederic King, 1878- joint author.

Agr 11-1199

Library, U. S. Dept. of   Agriculture 451M66M no. 3

AS
773
N 93

FILICES   NEW GUINEA

Alston, A. H. G.

Undescribed ferns from New Guinea.

(Nova Guinea, 4:109-112, pl. 4-10, 1940)

Biblio-
film 28

FILICES   NEW HEBRIDES

Kuhn, Maximilian

Filices novarum Newhebridarum.

(Verh. Zool.-Bot. Wien, Bd. 19, 1869, (Abh.) pp. 569-586)

QK
Bot.Pam.
1780

FILICES   NEW CALEDONIA

Bonaparte, Le Prince Roland

Filicales et lycopodiales de la Nouvelle-Calédonie et des Iles Loyalty. F. Sarasin and J. Roux, Nova Caledonia, Botanique, Vol. I, L, I, No. 5 and 6. Wiesbaden, Kriedels, 1914. 51 pp. pl.

QK
Bot.Pam.
2732

FILICES   NEW GUINEA

Bartram, Edwin B.

Mosses of northwest (Dutch) New Guinea, collected by Dr. Sten Bergman.

(Svensk Botanisk Tidskrift, Bd. 45(4):603-607, 1951)

QH
1
P 11

FILICES   NEW ZEALAND

Brownlie, G.

Geographical relationships of New Zealand fern flora.

(Pacific Science, 16(4):363-365, 1962)

QK
529
V 27

FILICES   NEW GUINEA

Alderwerelt van Rosenburg, C.R.W.K. van

Malayan fern allies. Handbook to the determination of the ferns and fern allies of the Malayan islands (incl. those of the Malay Peninsula, the Philippines and New Guinea) Landsdrukkerij. Batavia. 1915. xvi + 261 pp. R8vo.

QK
Bot.Pam.
2355

FILICES   NEW GUINEA

Bartram, Edwin B.

Mosses of Papua, New Guinea.

(Farlowia, Vol. 1, 1943, pp. 41-47)

QK
Bot.Pam.
2378

FILICES   NEW ZEALAND

Colenso, William

A classification and description of some newly-discovered ferns collected in the northern island of New Zealand in the summer of 1841-2. Launceston. 1845. 8vo. 29 pp. (author's copy,- published in "Tasmanian Journal of Nat. Science," Vol. II, 1844)

QK
529
V 27

FILICES   NEW GUINEA

Alderwerelt van Rosenburg, C.R.W.K. van

Malayan ferns and fern allies. Handbook to the determination of the ferns and fern allies of the Malayan islands (incl. those of the Malay Peninsula, the Philippines and New Guinea). Dept. of Agric., Industry and Commerce, Netherlands India. Batavia. 1916-1917. R8vo. 577 pp. and supplement I of 73 pp.

QK
Bot.Pam.
2354

FILICES   NEW GUINEA

Bartram, Edwin B.

Third Archbold Expedition mosses from the Snow Mountains, Netherlands New Guinea.

(Lloydia, Vol. 5, 1942, pp. 245-292)

QK
531
C 94

FILICES   NEW ZEALAND

Crookes, Marguerite

New Zealand ferns. Incorporating illustrations and original work by H. B. Dobbie. 6th edition. Auckland. Whitcombe and Tombs Ltd. 1963. xxiv + 407 pp. 8vo.

QK
532
V 27

FILICES   NEW GUINEA

Alderwerelt, C.R.W.K. van Rosenburgh van

Malayan ferns. Handbook of the determination of the ferns of the Malayan islands (incl. those of the Malayan Peninsula, the Philippines and New Guinea). Batavia, 1908, R8vo. 900 pp.

QK
520
A 51

FILICES   NEW GUINEA

Brass, L. J.

Ferns of a New Guinea gully.

(American Fern Journal, Vol. 43(4):150-158, 1953)

QK
520
A 51

FILICES   NEW ZEALAND

Crookes, Marguerite

On the lava fields of Rangitoto.

(American Fern Journal, 50(4):257-263, 1960)

QK
Bot.Pam.
3016

FILICES   NEW GUINEA

Alston, A. H. G.

Some undescribed ferns from New Guinea and Ambon.

(Nova Guinea, n.s., vol. 7(1):1-3, 1956)

AS
540
P 55 J

FILICES   NEW GUINEA

Copeland, Edwin Bingham

Grammitidaceae of New Guinea.

(Phil. Jl. of Sci., 81(2):81-120, 1953)

QK
531
F 45

FILICES   NEW ZEALAND

Field, H. C.

The ferns of New Zealand and its immediate dependencies, with directions for their collection and cultivation. London. 1890. 4to. 164 pp. illustrated.

QK
531
T 48
FILICES   NEW ZEALAND

Thomson, George M.

The ferns and fern allies of New Zealand.
With instructions for their collection and hints
on their cultivation. George Robertson. Melbourne. 1882. 8vo. viii+132 pp. + 5 pl.

QK
1
K 44
FILICES   PACIFIC

Christensen, Carl

Two new ferns from Oceania

(Kew, Bull. Misc. Information, No.1, 1939, pp.
28-29)

AS
36
S2
FILICES   PANAMA

Maxon, William Ralph, 1877-
... A remarkable new fern from Panama, with three
plates, by William R. Maxon ... Washington, Smithsonian institution, 1911.

1 p. l., 5 p. 3 pl. 24½ᶜᵐ. (Smithsonian miscellaneous collections. v. 56,
no. 24)

Publication 2055.

1. Ferns—Panama.

Library of Congress   Q11.S7 vol. 56, no. 24   12—1291
——— Copy 2.   QK524.P7M27

QK
525
E-14
FILICES   NORTH AMERICA

Eaton, Daniel Cody

Ferns of North America 1879-80.

2 vols. 4to.

AS
36
A25
FILICES   PACIFIC

Eaton, Daniel C.
Characters of some new filices, from
Japan and adjacent regions, collected by
Charles Wright in the North Pacific ex-
ploring expedition under Captain John
Rodgers. In Amer. Acad. Arts & Sc. Proc.
IV. pp. 110-111.   (1860.)

QK
1
N 53
FILICES   PAPUA

Christensen, Carl

New and noteworthy Papuan ferns. Botanical
Results of the Archbold Expedition, no. 8.

(Brittonia. Vol. 2, 1937. pp.265-317)

QK
Bot.Pam
2013

QK
445
M 21
FILICES   NEW SOUTH WALES

Maiden, J. H.

The Flowering Plants and Ferns of New South
Wales...1895-1898.

QK
Bot. Pam
1569
FILICES   PACIFIC

Hooker, W. J.

List of the Ferns in the Collection made by
Mr. Nightingale in the Pacific Isles.

(From Nightingale, Sir Thomas' Oceanic
Sketches. London, 1835 pp. 127-132)

see also the complete work, DU 12 N 68

AS
36
S2
FILICES   PERU

Maxon, William Ralph, 1877-
... *Saffordia*, a new genus of ferns from Peru (with
two plates) by William R. Maxon... Washington, Smithsonian institution, 1913.

1 p. l., 5 p. 2 pl. 24½ᶜᵐ. (Smithsonian miscellaneous collections. v. 61,
no. 4)

Publication 2183.

1. Saffordia. 2. Ferns—Peru.

Library of Congress   Q11.S7   13—35413
——— Copy 2.   QK524.S3M3

AS
36
S1
FILICES   NORTH AMERICA

Maxon, William Ralph, 1877-
The tree ferns of North America ... By William R.
Maxon.
(*In* Smithsonian institution. Annual report. 1911. Washington, 1912.
23½ᶜᵐ. p. 463-491. 15 pl. on 8 l.)
Plates printed on both sides.

1. Ferns—North America.

13-3794

Library of Congress   Q11.S66 1911

QK
1
M 68
FILICES   PACIFIC

Luerssen, Chr.

Filices Graeffeanae. Beitrag zur Kenntniss
der Farnflora der Viti-Samoa-Tonga- und Ellice's
Inseln.

(Mitteilungen aus dem Gesammtgebiete der
Botanik, Bd. 1, pp. 57-312, 1874)

QK
529
V 27
FILICES   PHILIPPINE ISLANDS

Alderwerelt van Rosenburg, C.R.W.K. van

Malayan fern allies. Handbook to the
determination of the ferns and fern allies of
the Malayan islands (incl. those of the Malay
Peninsula, the Philippines and New Guinea)
Landsdrukkerij. Batavia. 1915. xvi + 261 pp.
R8vo.

QK
1
L 75
FILICES   PACIFIC

Baker, John Gilbert

On the Polynesian ferns of the Challenger
Expedition.

(Linnean Soc. of London, Journal, 15:104-
112, 1877)

QK
520
A 51
FILICES   PACIFIC

Wagner, W. H., Jr.

Ferns on Pacific island coconut trees.
(American Fern Journal, Vol. 35, 1945, pp.
74-76)

QK
529
V 27
FILICES   PHILIPPINE ISLANDS

Alderwerelt van Rosenburg, C.R.W.K. van

Malayan ferns and fern allies. Handbook to
the determination of the ferns and fern allies
of the Malayan islands (incl. those of the Malay
Peninsula, the Philippines and New Guinea).
Dept. of Agric., Industry and Commerce, Netherlands India. Batavia. 1916-1917. R8vo. 577 pp.
and supplement I of 73 pp.

QH
1
P 11
FILICES   PACIFIC

Ballard, Francis

Pacific ferns described in Nightingale's
Oceanic Sketches.

(Pacific Science, Vol. X(3):268-270, 1956)

QK
520
A 51
FILICES   PACIFIC

Wagner, W. H., Jr.

Tree-climbing Gleichenias.

(American Fern Journal, Vol. 36,90-95, 1947)

QK
532
V 27
FILICES   PHILIPPINE ISLANDS

Alderwerelt, C.R.W.K. van Rosenburgh van

Malayan ferns. Handbook of the determination of the ferns of the Malayan Islands (incl.
those of the Malayan Peninsula, the Philippines
and New Guinea). Batavia, 1908, R8vo. 900 pp.

QH
1
P 11
FILICES   PACIFIC

Brownlie, G.

Studies on Pacific ferns, Parts I.

(Pacific Science, 14:242-245, 1960-

AS
182
H
FILICES   PALAU ISLANDS

Luerssen, Chr.

Ein Beitrag zur Farnflora der Palaos
und Hervey -Inseln.   In Journ. Mus. Godeffroy, Heft 1, pp 52-62, 1873.

AS
540
P 55
FILICES   PHILIPPINE ISLANDS

Copeland, Edwin B.

Fern flora of the Philippines. Vols. 1-3.

(Philippine Islands, Nat. Inst. of Sci. and
Technology, Monograph no. 6:1-3, 1958-60)

AS
540
P 55

FILICES   PHILIPPINE ISLANDS

Copeland, Edwin B.

New Philippine ferns. X-XI

(Philippine Jour. of Science, Vols. 83(2):97-99, 1954; 84(2):161-166, 1955)

to be continued

QK
Bot.Pam.
3158

FILICES   QUEENSLAND

Check list of North Queensland ferns.

(North Queensland Naturalists' Club, Publ. No. 3, 1946)

QK
Bot.Pam.
2213

FILICES   SAMOA

Copeland, E. B.   (Edwin Bingham)

New or interesting ferns from Micronesia, Fiji and Samoa.

(Occ. Papers, Bernice P. Bishop Museum, Vol. 15, 1939, No. 7, pp. 79-92. 9 figs.)

QK
Bot.Pam.
2908

FILICES   PHILIPPINE ISLANDS

Copeland, Edwin B.

The origin of the Philippine fern flora.

(Separate from The Philippine Journal of Science, Vol. 79(1):1-5, March, 1950)

QK
Botany
Pam.
2792

FILICES   ROTUMA

St. John, Harold

Ferns of Rotuma Island, a descriptive manual.

(Occasional Papers of B. P. Bishop Mus., Vol. XXI(9):161-208, 1954)

QK
1
M 68

FILICES   SAMOA

Luerssen, Chr.

Die Farne der Samoa-Inseln. Ein Verzeichniss der bis jetzt von den Schiffer-Inseln bekannten Gefässcryptogamen, nebst allgemeinen Bemerkungen über die Systematik dieser Pflanzengruppe. Leipzig. 1874.

(Mittheilungen aus dem gesammtgebiete der botanik, Bd. 1, pp. 345-413)

QK
Bot.Pam.
2292
941
QK
1
T 1

FILICES   PHILIPPINE ISLANDS

Underwood, Lucien Marcus

A summary of our present knowledge of the ferns of the Philippines.

(Contributions from the Dept. of Botany of Columbia University, No. 206. - Bull. Torrey Botanical Club, 30: 665-684, 1903)

QK
1
K 99

FILICES   RYUKYU ISLANDS

Nishida, M.

Notes on the ferns from the Loochoo (Ryukyu) Islands.

(Acta Phytotaxonomica et Geobotanica, Vol. 16(4):106-109, 1956)

QK
1
J 86
and
Biblio-
film 2

FILICES   SAMOA

Powell, S.

List of Samoan ferns.

(The Journal of Botany, British and Foreign, Vol. VI(70):317-319; (71):340-342, 1868)

QH
1
P 11

FILICES   PITCAIRN

Brownlie, G.

Studies on Pacific ferns, Part IV. The Pteridophyte flora of Pitcairn Island.

(Pacific Science, 15:297-300, 1961)

QK
1
J 86

FILICES   SAMOA

Baker, J. G.

On a collection of ferns made in Samoa by the Rev. S. J. Whitmee.

(Jour. Bot. Brit. and For., vol. 14, pp. 9-13, 342-345, 1876)

QK
Bot.Pam.
1585

FILICES   SAMOA

Vaupel, F.

Samoanische Farne.

(Verh. Bot. Ver. Brandenburg, Vol. 50, pp. LXXIII-LXXV, 1908)

DU
1
S 72 q

FILICES   POLYNESIA

Barrau, Jacques

Para - a former staple food plant of the Polynesians.

(South Pacific Commission Quarterly Bulletin Vol. 6(1):29, January, 1956)

[Marottia pezinoa, Sm.]

QK
1
J 86

FILICES   SAMOA

Baker, J. G.

On a second collection of ferns made in Samoa by the Rev. S. J. Whitmee.

(Jour. Bot. Brit. and For., vol. 14, pp. 342-345, 1876)

QK
529.S1
J 67

FILICES   SINGAPORE ISLAND

Johnson, Anne

A student's guide to the ferns of Singapore Island.

(Reprint: Malayan Nature Journal, Vol. 13: 99-223, 1960. University of Malaya Press.)

QK
Bot.Pam.
2119
-
AS
763
B-4
Reading
Room

FILICES   POLYNESIA

Copeland, E. B.

Ferns of southeastern Polynesia.

(Occ. Papers, Bernice P. Bishop Museum, Vol. 14, No. 5, 1938, pp. 45-101) Mangarevan Expedition Publication 22.

QK
1
B

FILICES   SAMOA

Brause, G.

Einige neue Samoa - Farne. In Notizbl K. Garten, Berlin, No 72, pp 138 - 141, 1922.

AS
540
P

FILICES   SOLOMON ISLANDS

Copeland, E. B.   (Edwin Bingham)

Solomon Island ferns.

(Philippine Jour. of Science, vol. 60, pp. 99-118. 25 pl. 1936)

QK
Bot.Pam.
2274

FILICES   POLYNESIA

Copeland, E(dwin) B(ingham)

Three Polynesian ferns.

(Occ. Papers, B. P. Bishop Museum, Vol. 16, No. 3, 1940, pp. 77-79)

Q
101
P 18

FILICES   SAMOA

Christensen, Carl
A brief analysis of the fern flora of Samoa.

IN Proc. Sixth Pac. Sci. Congress, 1939, (California), Vol. 4, 1940, pp. 655-656.

AS
36
S2

FILICES   SOUTH AMERICA

Maxon, William Ralph, 1877-
... Report upon a collection of ferns from western South America, by William R. Maxon ... Washington, Smithsonian institution, 1915.

1 p. l., 12 p. 24½ᶜᵐ. (Smithsonian miscellaneous collections. v. 65, no. 8) Publication 2366.

1. Ferns—South America.

15-26371

Library of Congress   Q11.S7 vol. 65, no. 8
———   Copy 2.   QK526.M27

AS 36 S2

FILICES   SOUTH AMERICA

Maxon, W. R.

Saffordia, a new genus of ferns from Peru. Smith. Mis. Col. LXI, 4, 1913, pp. 5, pls. I-II

QK Bot. Pam. 3162

FILICES   WEST INDIES

Proctor, George R.

Notes on Lesser Antillean ferns.

(Rhodora, 63(746):31-35, 1961)

PL Pam #32

Filippo, Pietro Amat de S.

I veri scopritori delle isole Azore.

Roma, 1892.

AS 36 S2

FILICES   SPANISH AMERICA

Christensen, Carl Frederik Albert, 1872-

... Maxonia, a new genus of tropical American ferns, by Carl Christensen ... Washington, Smithsonian institution, 1916.

1 p. l., 4 p. 24½ᵐᵐ. (Smithsonian miscellaneous collections. v. 66, no. 9)
Publication 2424.

1. Maxonia. 2. Ferns—Spanish America.

Library of Congress   Q11.S7   16-26845
——— Copy 2.   QK524.M45C5

QK 523 H 78

Filices Exoticae.

Hooker, William Jackson.

DU 1 S 72t

Film and filmstrip appraisal service. Catalogue of 16 mm. films and filmloops and 35 mm. filmstrips.

(South Pacific Commission, Technical Paper No. 71, 1954)

QK Botany Pam. 1263

FILICES   TAHITI

Greville, R. K.

Notice of a new species of Antrophyum.

(Trans. Bot. Soc. Edinburgh, Vol. III, 1850, pp. 63-64, 1 pl.)

AS 750 N

FILICINAE   NEW ZEALAND

Crookes, Marguerite W.

A revised and annotated list of New Zealand Filicinae.

(Trans. and Proc. of the R. Soc. of New Zealand, Vol. 77:209-225, 1949)

DU 1 S 72t

FILMS   PACIFIC

Film and filmstrip appraisal service. Catalogue of 16 mm. films and filmloops and 35 mm. filmstrips.

(South Pacific Commission, Technical Paper No. 71, 1954)

QK Bot. Pam. 1671

FILICES   TAHITI

Maxon, William R.

Report upon a collection of ferns from Tahiti

QK 1 CA 1924

(University of California Publications in Botany vol. 12, no. 2, pp. 17-24, plates 1-6)

S 17 H3 S7

FILIPINO STRIKE OF 1924

Hawaiian Sugar Planters' Association

A statement concerning the sugar industry in Hawaii...... By A.W.T. Bottomley. Nov. 1924. (No series number)

JAN 28

GN 2.S P 76

FILMS   POLYNESIA

Koch, Gerd

Films on Polynesian culture and the programme of the Scientific Film Institute, Goettingen.

(Jour. of the Polynesian Soc., Vol. 72(2):155-157, 1963)

QK 531 W 14

FILICES   TASMANIA

Wakefield, N. A.

Ferns of Victoria and Tasmania; with descriptive notes and illustrations of the 116 native species. Published by the Field Naturalists Club of Victoria. 1955. 8vo. iv(2) + 71 pp.

Filipinos

See

Ethnology-Philippine Islands

GN Pam 856

Filshner, W.

Plan einer Deutschen Antarktischen expedition. From Zeit. der Gesell. f. Erdkunde zu Berlin, Jahrg.1910, n.3.

AP 2 A5

FILICES   UNITED STATES

Beck, Lewis C.

Synoptical table of the ferns and mosses of the United States, in Am. Journ. of Sc. XV. Ser. I, pp. 287-297, 1829,

---

DU 1 M 6

FILIPINOS IN HAWAII

Ligot, Cayetano

The Filipinos in the Territory of Hawaii.

(Mid-Pacific Magazine, Vol. 49, No. 1, 1936, p. 27)

QK Bot. Pam. 2911

FIMBRISTYLIS

Ohwi, J.

Florae Malesianae Precursores IX. New Malaysian species of Fimbristylis.

(Reprinted from Blumea, Vol. VIII(1):96-109, 1955)

AS 36 A9

FILICES   UNITED STATES

Davenport, George E.

Some comparative tables showing the distribution of ferns in the United States of North America. In Proc. Amer. Phil. Soc. XX, 1883, pp 605-612.

QL 1 A 52 b

FILIPPIA

Reyne, A

Scale insects from Thailand with description of a Filippia, n. sp.

(Beaufortia, Vol. 10(115), pp. 29-39, 1963)

QH 1 P 11

FIMBRYSTYLIS

St. John, Harold

A new variety of Pandanus and a new species of Fimbrystylis from the Central Pacific Islands Pacific Plant Studies No. 11.

(Pacific Science, 6(2):145-150, 1952)

3

Storage Case 5 / Ms / To 3 — Finau, William (translator)

The Story of the Maui. Supplied by the Rev. Jonathan Fonua, of Neiafu, Vavau, from the account published in Koe Makasini a Koliji. Vol. -, pages -, 18--. Translated by William Finau of Neiafu, Vavau. Given to the Bishop Museum by E. W. Gifford. (University of Calif.)

QH 1 / P 11 — Finch, R. H.

The mechanics of the explosive eruption of Kilauea in 1924.

(Pacific Science, Vol. 1:237-240, 1947)

AS 36 / C 1 — FINCHES   GALAPAGOS ISLANDS

Lack, David

The Galapagos finches (Geospizinae); a study in variation.

(Occ. Papers, Calif. Acad. Sci., No. 21, 1945)

GA 105 / F 49 — Finch, J.K.

Topographic maps and sketch mapping, by J.K. Finch. 1st ed.

N.Y. Wiley, 1920. xi, 175p. illus.

AP 2 / A 5 — Finch, R. H.

Sulphate deposits in lava tubes, by R. H. Finch and O. H. Emerson.

(Am. Jour. of Sci., Ser. 5, Vol. 10, 1925, pp. 38-40)

QL 671 / I — FINCHES   GALAPAGOS ISLANDS

Lowe, Percy R.

The finches of the Galapagos in relation to Darwin's conception of species.

(Ibis, Vol. VI, 1936, pp. 310-321)

QE 75 / B — Finch, R. H.

Hawaiian volcanoes during 1950. A contribution to general geology. By R. H. Finch and Gordon A. Macdonald.

(U.S. Geological Survey Bull. 996-B, 1953)

G 142 / W 57 — Finch, V. C.

Whitbeck, R. H.

Economic geography, by R. H. Whitbeck and V. C. Finch. 1st edition. New York, 1924.

"FINCHES"   LAYSAN ISLAND

See

TELESPIZA

QE / Geol. Pam. 821 / and / AP 2 / A 5 — Finch, R H

Rainfalls accompanying explosive eruptions of volcanoes. From Amer. Jour. of science, vol. 19, Feb. 1930. p. 147-50.

QL 1 / C 15 — FINCHES   GALAPAGOS

Bowman, Robert I.

Morphological differentiation and adaptation in the Galápagos finches.

(Univ. of Calff., Pub. in Zoology, Vol. 58, 1961)

PL / Phil.Pam. 209 — Finck, Fr. N. (Frank Nicolaus)

Die samoanischen Personal - und Possessiv-pronomina.

(Sitzungsbericht der Königlich Preussischen Akademie der Wissenschaften, phil. -hist.Kl., 1907, XXXVII, 1(721)-22(742)pp.)

AP 2 / A 5 — Finch, R. H.

Jaggar, T. A.

The explosive eruption of Kilauea in Hawaii, 1924, by T. A. Jaggar and R. H. Finch.

(Am. Jour. of Sci., Ser. 5, Vol. 8, 1924, pp. 353-374)

AS 36 / A65 — FINCHES

Chapman, Frank M.

The variations and distribution of saltator aurantiirostris. Amer. Mus. Nov. no. 261, New York, 1927.

AS 36 / S1 — Finck, Hugo.

Account of antiquities in the state of Vera Cruz, Mexico. By Hugo Finck ...

(*In* Smithsonian institution. Annual report. 1870. Washington, 1871. 23½ᶜᵐ. p. 373-376. diagr.)

1. Vera Cruz (Mexico)—Antiq. 2. Indians of Mexico—Antiq.

            S 15-292

Library of Congress   Q11.S66 1870
Library, Smithsonian   Institution

QE 75 / B — Finch, R. H.

Hawaiian volcanoes during 1950. A contribution to general geology. By R. H. Finch and Gordon A. Macdonald.

(U. S. Geological Survey Bull. 996-B, 1953)

QL / Bird Pam. 483 — FINCH

Oksche, A. and others

The hypothalamo-hypophysial neurosecretory system of the Zebra Finch, Taeniopygia castanotis.

(Reprint by C.S.I.R.O. from Zeitschrift für Zellforschung, Vol. 58(6):846-914, 1963)

G 103.98 / F 49 — Findlay, Alexander George

A directory for the navigation of the North Pacific Ocean, with descriptions of its coasts, islands, etc., from Panama to Behring Strait, and Japan; its winds, currents, and passages. Third edition. London. Richard Holmes Laurie. R8vo. (1886) xxxii + 1315 pp.

QE 526 / Ha-v — Finch, R. H.

Kilauea in 1790 and 1823.

(Volcano Letter, No. 496, 1947)

QL / Birds Pam. 335 — FINCHES

de Schauensee, Rodolphe Meyer

A review of the genus Sporophila.

(Proceedings of The Academy of Natural Sciences of Philadelphia, Vol. CIV, pp. 153-196, 1952)

G 103.98 / F 49 — Findlay, Alexander George

A directory for the navigation of the South Pacific Ocean; with descriptions of its coasts, islands, etc., from the Strait of Magalhaens to Panama, and those of New Zealand, Australia, etc. its winds, currents, and passages. Fifth edition. London. Richard Holmes Laurie. (1884) R8vo. lvi + 1252 pp.

DU
406
B34

DU
Pac Pam
20

Finest walk in the world

Baughan, B. E.

The finest walk in the world.
[3rd. ed.].

Christchurch, n.d. 51p. illus.

AS
36
O3

Fink, Bruce, 1861–
... The ascomycetes of Ohio, I. Preliminary consideration of classification [by] Bruce Fink ... II. The *Colle-
maceae* [by] Bruce Fink and C. Audrey Richards. Columbus, The Ohio state university, 1915.
71 p. incl. pl. 25½ᶜᵐ. (Ohio biological survey. vol. II, no. 1. Bulletin 5)
On cover: The Ohio state university bulletin. vol. XIX, no. 28.
Contributions from the Botanical laboratory of Miami university, XI–
XII.
"List of papers consulted": p. 25–29.
"List of the titles cited": p. 62.
1. Ascomycetes. 2. Fungi—Ohio. I. Richards, C. Audrey, joint
author.
A 15–1928

Title from Ohio State   Univ. Printed by L. C.
Library of Congress   QK623.A1F6
[a21c1]

QL
Moll.
Pam.
418

and
AS
750
N

Finlay, H. J.

Additions to the recent molluscan
fauna of New Zealand.   In New Zealand
Inst., Trans., Vol. 55, pp 517- 526,
1924.

QK
1
S67

Finet, E. A.
Dendrobium nouveaux de l'herbier du
Museum. Soc. Bot. France Bull. v.50,
pp.372-383, pls.11-14, 1903.

QK
1
U

Fink, Bruce, 1861–
... The lichens of Minnesota, by Bruce Fink. Washing-
ton, Govt. print. off., 1910.
viii, 269, ix–xvii p. front., illus., 51 pl. 24½ᶜᵐ. (Smithsonian institution.
United States national museum. Contributions from the United States
national herbarium. v. 14, pt. 1)
"Special bibliography": p. 4–5.
"Bibliography. By P. L. Ricker": p. 251–269.
"Bulletin of the United States national museum. Issued June 1, 1910."

1. Lichenes. 2. Minnesota. Botany.   I. Ricker, Percy Leroy, 1878–
[Botany—Minnesota]
Agr 10–1080

Library, U. S. Dept. of   Agriculture 450C76 v. 14, pt. 1

QL
Moll.
Pam.
422

Finlay, H. J.
The family Liotiidae, Iredale, in the
New Zealand Tertiary. From New Zealand
Inst., Trans., Vol. 55, 1924, pp 526 -
531.

QK
1
S67

Finet, E. A.
Orchidees nouvelles ou peu connues
II. Soc. Bot. France Bull. v.55, pp. 333-
343, pl.2, 1908.

FINLAND   FISHING

see

FISHING   FINLAND

QL
Moll.
Pam.
420

Finlay, H. J.
The molluscan fauna of Target Gully.
From New Zealand Inst., Trans., Vol. 55,
pp 495 - 516.

QK
1
P 23

Finet, E. A.
Pelma, orchidacearum genus novum.

(Notulae Systematicae, Vol. 1, pp. 111-114,
Fig. 6, 1909.)

FINLAND   HEMIPTERA

See

HEMIPTERA   FINLAND

QL
Moll.
Pam.
419

Finlay, H. J.
New shells from New Zealand Tertiary
beds.   From New Zealand Inst. Trans. Vol.
55, 1924, pp 450 - 479.

AS
36
S1

FINGER-PRINTS

Laufer, Berthold, 1874–
History of the finger-print system. By Berthold Lau-
fer ...
(In Smithsonian institution. Annual report, 1912. Washington, 1913.
23½ᶜᵐ. p. 631–652. 7 pl. on 4 l.)
Most of plates printed on both sides.

1. Finger-prints.
13–25700
Library of Congress   Q11.S66 1912

FINLAND   HETEROPTERA

See

HETEROPTERA   FINLAND

AS
750
N

Finlay, H. J.

New Zealand Foraminifera: key species in
stratigraphy, No. 1- A

(Trans. and Proc. R. Soc. New Zealand, Vol.
68, 1938/39, pp. 504-533; Vol. 69, 1939/40, pp.
89-128, 309-329, 448 - A16)

GN
2.S
P76

FINGERS   MAORI

Maori names for fingers.

(Journal of the Polynesian Society, 36:
298, 1927.)

FINLAND   INSECTS

See

INSECTS   FINLAND

QL
Moll.
Pam.
423

Finlay, H. J.

New Zealand Tertiary rissoids. From
New Zealand Inst. Trans. Vol. 55, pp 480-
494, 1924.

G
51
W 17

FINISTERRE MOUNTAINS

Maahs, Arnold M.

Climbing New Guinea's Finisterres.

(Walkabout, 18(6):29-33, 1952)

QE
75
A

Finlay, George Irving.
... Colorado Springs folio, Colorado, by George I. Finlay. Washington, D. C., U. S. Geological survey, 1916.
cover-title, 15, [1] p. illus., II pl., 5 maps (part fold.) diagrs. 55 x 47ᶜᵐ.
(U. S. Geological survey. Geologic atlas of the United States. no. 203)
Lat. 38° 30'–39°, long. 104° 30'–105°; scale 1 : 125,000 and 1 : 48,000; contour interval 100 and 50 ft.

1. Geology—Colorado—Maps.
G S 16–650
Library, U. S. Geological   Survey (200) fH   no. 203
—— Copy 2.

QL
Moll.
Pam.
421

Finlay, H. J.

Some modern conceptions applied to
the study of the Cainozoic Mollusca of
New Zealand.   Reprint Verh. Geol. - Mij.
Genoots. Nederland en Kolonien, Geol. Ser.
Deel VIII, pp 161- 172, 1925.

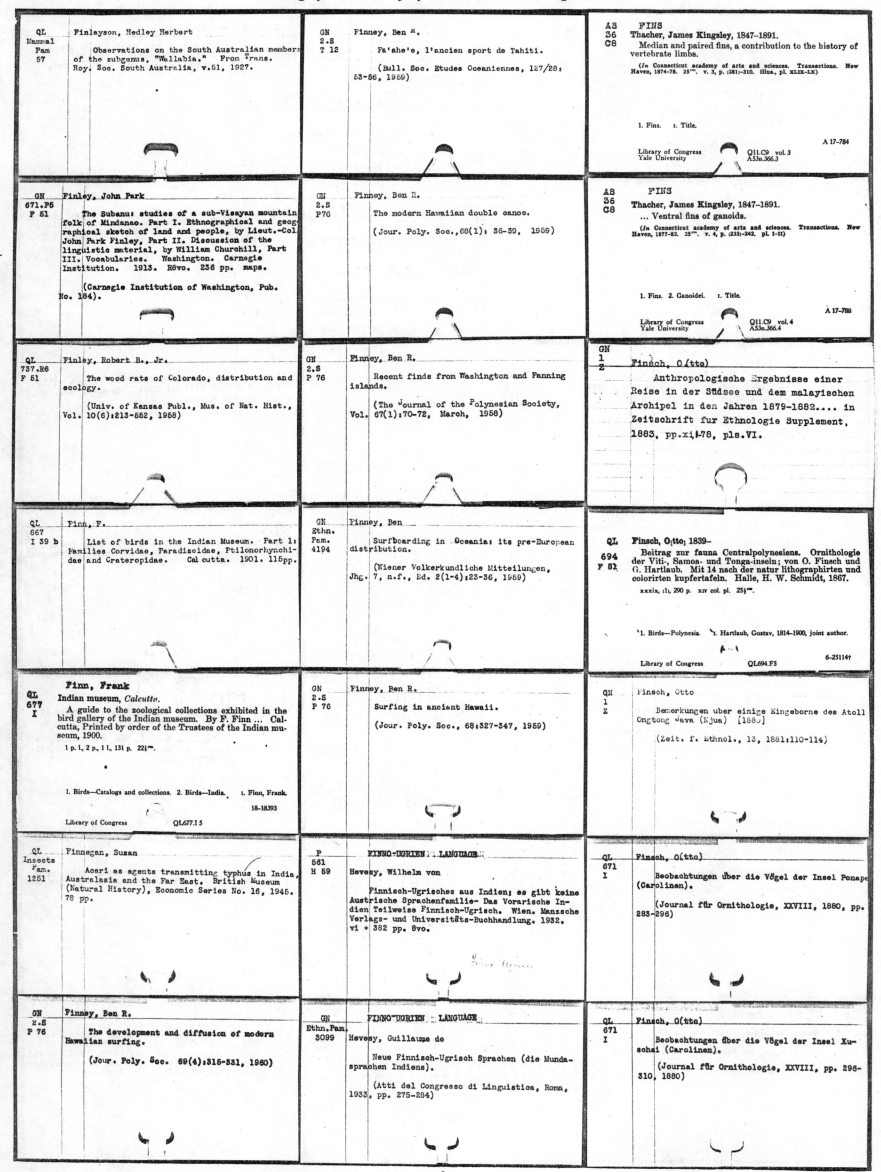

Card 1 (row 1, col 1)

QL
Mammal
Pam
57

Finlayson, Hedley Herbert

Observations on the South Australian members of the subgenus, "Wallabia." From Trans. Roy. Soc. South Australia, v.51, 1927.

Card 2 (row 1, col 2)

GN
2.S
T 12

Finney, Ben R.

Fa'ahe'e, l'ancien sport de Tahiti.

(Bull. Soc. Etudes Oceaniennes, 127/28: 53-56, 1959)

Card 3 (row 1, col 3)

AS
36
C8

FINS

Thacher, James Kingsley, 1847-1891.
Median and paired fins, a contribution to the history of vertebrate limbs.
(*In* Connecticut academy of arts and sciences. Transactions. New Haven, 1874-78. 25ᶜᵐ. v. 3, p. (281)-310. illus., pl. XLIX-LX)

1. Fins. ɪ. Title.

Library of Congress   Q11.C9 vol. 3
Yale University   A53n.366.3   A 17-784

Card 4 (row 2, col 1)

GN
671.P5
F 51

Finley, John Park

The Subanu: studies of a sub-Visayan mountain folk of Mindanao. Part I. Ethnographical and geographical sketch of land and people, by Lieut.-Col. John Park Finley, Part II. Discussion of the linguistic material, by William Churchill, Part III. Vocabularies. Washington. Carnegie Institution. 1913. R8vo. 236 pp. maps.

(Carnegie Institution of Washington, Pub. No. 184).

Card 5 (row 2, col 2)

GN
2.S
P76

Finney, Ben R.

The modern Hawaiian double canoe.

(Jour. Poly. Soc.,68(1): 36-39, 1959)

Card 6 (row 2, col 3)

AS
36
C8

FINS

Thacher, James Kingsley, 1847-1891.
... Ventral fins of ganoids.
(*In* Connecticut academy of arts and sciences. Transactions. New Haven, 1877-82. 25ᶜᵐ. v. 4, p. (233)-242. pl. I-II)

1. Fins. 2. Ganoidei. ɪ. Title.

Library of Congress   Q11.C9 vol. 4
Yale University   A53n.366.4   A 17-788

Card 7 (row 3, col 1)

QL
737.R6
F 51

Finley, Robert B., Jr.

The wood rats of Colorado, distribution and ecology.

(Univ. of Kansas Publ., Mus. of Nat. Hist., Vol. 10(6):213-552, 1958)

Card 8 (row 3, col 2)

GN
2.S
P 76

Finney, Ben R.

Recent finds from Washington and Fanning islands.

(The Journal of the Polynesian Society, Vol. 67(1):70-72, March, 1958)

Card 9 (row 3, col 3)

GN
1
Z

Finsch, O(tto)

Anthropologische Ergebnisse einer Reise in der Südsee und dem malayischen Archipel in den Jahren 1879-1882.... in Zeitschrift fur Ethnologie Supplement, 1883, pp.xi-78, pls.VI.

Card 10 (row 4, col 1)

QL
667
I 39 b

Finn, F.

List of birds in the Indian Museum. Part 1: Families Corvidae, Paradiseidae, Ptilonorhynchidae and Crateropidae. Calcutta. 1901. 115pp.

Card 11 (row 4, col 2)

GN
Ethn.
Pam.
4194

Finney, Ben

Surfboarding in Oceania: its pre-European distribution.

(Wiener Volkerkundliche Mitteilungen, Jhg. 7, n.f., Bd. 2(1-4):23-36, 1959)

Card 12 (row 4, col 3)

QL
694
F 51

Finsch, O(tto) 1839-

Beitrag zur fauna Centralpolynesiens. Ornithologie der Viti-, Samoa- und Tonga-inseln; von O. Finsch und G. Hartlaub. Mit 14 nach der natur lithographirten und colorirten kupfertafeln. Halle, H. W. Schmidt, 1867.
xxxix, (1), 290 p. xiv col. pl. 25½ᶜᵐ.

1. Birds—Polynesia. ɪ. Hartlaub, Gustav, 1814-1900, joint author.

Library of Congress   QL694.F5   6-25114†

Card 13 (row 5, col 1)

QL
677
I

Finn, Frank
Indian museum, *Calcutta.*
A guide to the zoological collections exhibited in the bird gallery of the Indian museum. By F. Finn ... Calcutta, Printed by order of the Trustees of the Indian museum, 1900.
1 p. l., 2 p., 1 l., 131 p. 22½ᶜᵐ.

1. Birds—Catalogs and collections. 2. Birds—India. ɪ. Finn, Frank.

     18-18393

Library of Congress   QL.677.I 5

Card 14 (row 5, col 2)

GN
2.S
P 76

Finney, Ben R.

Surfing in ancient Hawaii.

(Jour. Poly. Soc., 68:327-347, 1959)

Card 15 (row 5, col 3)

GN
1
Z

Finsch, Otto

Bemerkungen uber einige Eingeborne des Atoll Ongtong Java (Njua) (1880)

(Zeit. f. Ethnol., 13, 1881:110-114)

Card 16 (row 6, col 1)

QL
Insects
Pam.
1251

Finnegan, Susan

Acari as agents transmitting typhus in India, Australasia and the Far East. British Museum (Natural History), Economic Series No. 16, 1945. 78 pp.

Card 17 (row 6, col 2)

P
561
H 59

FINNO-UGRIEN LANGUAGE.

Hevesy, Wilhelm von

Finnisch-Ugrisches aus Indien; es gibt keine Austrische Sprachenfamilie- Das Vorarische Indien Teilweise Finnisch-Ugrisch. Wien. Manzsche Verlags- und Universitäts-Buchhandlung. 1932. vi + 382 pp. 8vo.

Card 18 (row 6, col 3)

QL
671
I

Finsch, O(tto)

Beobachtungen über die Vögel der Insel Ponape (Carolinen).

(Journal für Ornithologie, XXVIII, 1880, pp. 283-296)

Card 19 (row 7, col 1)

GN
2.S
P 76

Finney, Ben R.

The development and diffusion of modern Hawaiian surfing.

(Jour. Poly. Soc. 69(4):315-331, 1960)

Card 20 (row 7, col 2)

GN
Ethn.Pam.
3099

FINNO-UGRIEN - LANGUAGE

Hevesy, Guillaume de

Neue Finnisch-Ugrisch Sprachen (die Mundasprachen Indiens).

(Atti del Congresso di Linguistica, Roma, 1933, pp. 275-284)

Card 21 (row 7, col 3)

QL
671
I

Finsch, O(tto)

Beobachtungen über die Vögel der Insel Kuschai (Carolinen).

(Journal für Ornithologie, XXVIII, pp. 296-310, 1880)

GN
1
Z

Finsch, Otto

    Bericht über die Insel Oahu.

    (Verhandlungen der Berliner Gesell. f. Anthropologie, Ethn. u. Urgeschichte, Jahrg. 1879, pp.(326)-(331). IN Zeit. f. Ethn., Bd. 11, 1879)

    (for trans. see GN Ethn. Pams. 134 or 317,- by W. D. Alexander)

AS
142
V

                            Card 2

Finsch, Otto

    Ethnologische Erfahrungen und Belegstücke aus der Südsee.

    Zweite Abteilung: Neu-Guinea (British) (Ann. Nat.hist. Mus. Wien, 3:293-364, 1888)

    Zweite Abt. (cont.): Neu-Guinea (British) (ibid, 6:13-36, 1891)

    Zweite Abt., (cont.):Neu-Guinea, II. Kaiser-Wilhelms Land. (ibid, 6:37-130, 1891)

                    cont. on next cd.

GN
Ethn.Pam.
3492

Finsch, Otto

    Kriegsführung auf den Marshall-Inseln.

    (Die Gartenlaube, 29:700-703, 1881)

GN
Ethn.Pam.
3493

Finsch, Otto

    Canoes und Canoebau in den Marshall-Inseln.

    (Verhandlungen der Gesellschaft für Anthropologie, Ethnologie und Urgeschichte, 19:22-29, 1887)

AS
142
V

                            Card 3

Finsch, Otto

    Ethnologische Erfahrungen und Belegstücke aus der Südsee.

    Dritte Abt.:Mikronesian (West-Oceanien). I. Gilberts-Inseln; II Marshall-Archipel. III. Carolinen (Kuschai, Ponape).

    (Ann. Nat.hist. Mus. Wien, 8:1-106,119-275, 295-437, 1893)

QL
1
Z

Finsch, Otto

    A list of birds of the island of Kuk in the Central Carolines.

    (Proc. Zool. Soc. London, 1880, 574-577)

DU
Pac
Pam
#202

Finsch, Otto

    Carolinen und Marianen.
Hamburg, 1900. 8vo. pp. 60.

GN
662
F 51

Finsch, (Friedrich Hermann Otto)

    Ethnologische erfahrungen und belegstücke aus der Südsee. Beschreibender katalog einer sammlung in K. K. Naturhistorischen Hofmuseum in Wien von Dr. O. Finsch... Mit einem vorwort von Franz Heger. Mit 25 tafeln (davon 6 in farbendruck und 108 abbildungen im texte.) Wien. Alfred Hölder. 1893. R8vo. 675 pp.

    (Annalen des K. K. Naturhistorischen Hof-Museums in Wien, Band III-VIII, 1888-1893, separat abgedruckt)

GN
Pam
2722

Finsch, Otto

    Masks of faces of races of men from the south sea islands and the Malay archipelago, taken from the living originals in the years 1879-82. From Ward's Nat. Sci. Establishment, 1888.

QL
1
Z

Finsch, Otto

    Characters of six new Polynesian birds in the Museum Godeffroy at Hamburg.

    (Proc. Zool. Soc. London, 1875:642-644)

GN
Pam
2101
2100

Finsch, O(tto)

    Ethnologische erfahrungen und belegstücke aus der Sudsee. From Annalen k.k. Natur. Hofmuseums, bd. 3, Wien, 1888

Contents:

Abt. 1.- Neu-Guinea
   "   2.- Bismarck-archipel

DU
740
F51

Finsch, Otto

    Neu-Guinea und seine Bewohner.
Bremen 1865. 8vo pp 185 map.

QL
1
Z

Finsch, Otto

    Description of a new species of penguin: Dasyrhamphus herculis.

    (Proc. Zool. Soc., London, 1870,p.322)

QL
1
Z

Finsch, Otto

    Further remarks on some New Zealand birds.

    (New Zealand Inst. Trans., 8, 1875, pp. 200-204)

QL
1
Z

Finsch, Otto

    Notes on some Fijian birds, including description of a new genus and species:[Drymochaera radiceps].

    (Proc. Zool. Soc., London, 1876, pp. 19-20)

QL
1
Z

Finsch, Otto

    Description of a new species of penguin from New Zealand: Eudyptula albosignata.

    (Proc. Zool. Soc., 1874, pp. 207-208)

Biblio-
film
1

Finsch, O(tto)

    Hautverzierungen der Gilbert-Insulander.

    (Globus, Vol. 65, No. 17, 1894, pp. 265-279)

QL
1
Z

Finsch, Otto

    Notes on the fruit-pigeons of the genus Chrysoena.

    (Proc. Zool. Soc. London, 1876:557-558)

AS
142
V

                     Card 1

Finsch, Otto

    Ethnologische Erfahrungen und Belegstücke aus der Südsee. Beschreibenden Katalog einer Sammlung in K. K. naturhistorischen Hofmuseum in Wien. Mit einem Vorwort von Franz Heger. Erste Abteilung: Bismarck Archipel.

    (Annalen K. K. Naturhistorischen Museum, Wien, Bd. 3:83-160, 1888)

                    cont. on next card

GN
Pam
1013

Finsch, O (tto)

    Das klilt-armband der Pelauer. From Globus, bd.77, n.10, 1900. 7p.

QL
1
Z

Finsch, Otto

    On a collection of birds from Eua, Friendly Islands.

    (Proc. Zool. Soc. London, 1877:770-777)

QL 1 Z — Finsch, Otto
On a collection of birds from Niuafou Island, in the Pacific.
(Proc. Zool. Soc., London, 1877:782-787)

QL 1 Z — Finsch, Otto
On a new species of finch from the Fiji Islands: [Amblynura kleinschmidti].
(Proc. Zool. Soc. London, 1878:440)

QL 1 Z — Finsch, Otto
On Lobospiza notabilis, a remarkable new finch from the Navigator's Islands. By O. Finsch and G. Hartlaub.
(Proc. Zool. Soc. London, 1870, pp. 817-18)

QL 1 Z — Finsch, Otto
On a collection of birds from Savai and Rarotonga Islands in the Pacific. By Otto Finsch and G. Hartlaub.
(Proc. Zool. Soc. London, 1871, pp. 21-32)

QL 1 Z — Finsch, Otto
On a new species of fruit-pigeon (Ptilonopus huttoni) from the Pacific island of Rapa or Opara. [1873]
(Proc. Zool. Soc. London, 1874:92-95)

QL 1 Z — Finsch, Otto
On Pristorhamphus versteri, a new genus and species of bird from the Arfak Mountains, New Guinea.
(Proc. Zool. Soc., London, 1875:641-642)

QL 1 Z — Finsch, Otto
On a collection of birds from the Pelew Islands. By Otto Finsch and G. Hartlaub.
(Proc. Zool. Soc. London, 1868, pp. 4-9, 116-118)

QL 1 Z — Finsch, Otto
On a new species of petrel from the Fiji Islands:[Procellaria albigularis].
(Proc. Zool. Soc. London, 1877, pp. 722)

QL 1 Z — Finsch, Otto
On the birds of the island of Ponape, Eastern Carolines.
(Proc. Zool. Soc. London, 1877:777-782)

QL 1 Z — Finsch, Otto
On a collection of birds made by Mr. Hübner on Duke of York Island and New Britain.
(Proc. Zool. Soc. London, 1879:9-17)

QL 1 Z — Finsch, Otto
On a small collection of birds from the Marquesas Islands.
(Proc. Zool. Soc., London, 1877, pp. 407-410)

QL 1 L 53 — Finsch, O.(tto)
On the so-called "Sandwich-Rail" in the Leyden Museum.
(Notes from the Leyden Museum, Vol. XX, 1898-99, pp. 77-80)

QL 1 L 53 — Finsch, Otto
On a collection of birds made up by Mr. Karl Schädler at Sekru (northwest coast of New Guinea) 1900.
(Notes of the Leyden Museum, 22, 1900-1901, pp. 49-69)

QL 1 Z — Finsch, Otto
On a small collection of birds from the Tonga Islands. By Otto Finsch and G. Hartlaub.
(Proc. Zool. Soc. London, 1869:544-546)

QL 1 Z — Finsch, Otto
On two apparently new species of penguin from New Zealand:[Eudyptes vittata, Finsch; E. atrata, Hutton].
(Ibis, Vol. 5, 1875, pp.,112-114)

QL 1 Z — Finsch, Otto
On a fourth collection of birds from the Pelew and Mackenzie Islands. By O. Finsch and G. Hartlaub.
(Proc. Zool. Soc. London, 1872, pp. 87-114)

QL 1 Z — Finsch, Otto
On a very rare parrot from the Solomon Islands: Domicella cardinalis.
(Proc. Zool. Soc. London, 1869, pp. 126-129)

QL 671 I — Finsch, O(tto)
On two new species of birds from New Ireland
(Ibis, Ser. 5, Vol. 4, 1886, pp. 1-2)

QL 671 I — Finsch, Otto
On a new reed-warbler from the Island of Nawodo, or Pleasant Island, in the western Pacific.
(Ibis, Ser. 5, Vol. 1, 1883, pp. 142-144)

QL 1 Z — Finsch, Otto
On Lamprolia victoriae, a most remarkable new passerine bird from the Feejee Islands.
(Proc. Zool. Soc. London, 1873, pp. 733-735)

QL 1 Z — Finsch, Otto
On two species of pigeons from the Caroline Islands: [Ptilopus hernsheimi, n. sp.; P. ponapensis, Finsch].
(Proc. Zool. Soc., London, 1880, 577-578)

QL 671 I — Finsch, Otto

Ornithological letters from the Pacific [1879 to 1881].

(Ibis, 4, 1880, pp. 75-81, 215-220, 329-333, 429-434; 5, 1881:102-115, 245-249, 532-540; 6, 1882:391-402)

DU 740 F 51 — Finsch, Otto

Samoafahrten. Reisen in Kaiser Wilhelms-Land und Englisch-Neu-Guinea in den jahren 1884 u. 1885 an bord des Deutschen Dampfers "Samoa"...hierzu ein einzeln käuflicher "Ethnologischer Atlas, typen aus der Steinzeit New Guineas", 24 lithogr. tafeln nach originalen gezeichnet von O. und E. Finsch, met text von Dr. O. Finsch. Leipzig, Ferdinand Hirt & Sohn. 1888. 8vo. 390 pp.

Atlas. 4to. 2 copies.

QL 671 J — Finsch, Otto

Zur ornithologie der Samoa-Inseln.

(Journal f. Ornithologie, XX:30-58, 1872)

QL 671 I — Finsch, Otto

Ornithological letters etc. from the Pacific, 1879- .... in Ibis, see index, 1859-94.

GN 662 F 51 — Finsch, Otto

Südseearbeiten. Gewerbe- und Kunstfleiss, Tauschmittel und "Geld" der Eingeborenen auf Grundlage der Rohstoffe und der geographischen Verbreitung. Mit 584 Abbildungen auf 30 Tafeln (davon 2 farbig) vom Verfasser u. A. Strohmeyer. Hamburg. L. Friederichsen & Co. 1914. R8vo. xii +605 pp.

(Abhandlungen des Hamburgischen Kolonial-instituts, Band XIV).

AS 182 H — Finsch, Otto

Zur Ornithologie der Südsee-Inseln, I. Die Vögel der Palau-Gruppe; II. Ueber neue und weniger gekannte Vögel von den Viti-, Samoa-, und Carolinen-Inseln.

(Jour. Mus. Godeffroy, Heft 8, 1875, pp. 1-51; Heft 12, 1876, pp. 1-42)

G 1 G 56 — Finsch, O.

Papua-Töpferei. Aus dem Wiegenalter der Keramik.

(Globus, 84:329-334, 1903)

Z Bibl Pam #16 — Finsch, O(tto)

Systematische Uebersicht der Ergebnisse seiner Reisen und schriftstellerischen Thatigkeit. (1859-1899.

Berlin, 1899.

QH 1 P 11 — FINSCHIA — White, C. T.

Finschia- a genus of "nut" trees of the southwest Pacific.

(Pacific Science, Vol. 3:187-194, 1949)

AS 750 N — Finsch, Otto

Preliminary remarks on some New Zealand birds.

(New Zealand Inst., Trans., 7, 1874, pp. 226-236)

GN 2.S V — Finsch, Otto

Ueber Bekleidung, Schmuck, und Tätowirung der Papuas der Südostküste von Neu-Guinea.

(Mitt. der Anthropologischen Gesellschaft in Wien, 1885, pp. 12-33)

GB 454.F5 G 82 — FIORDS — Gregory, J. W.

The nature and origin of fiords. With diagrams and illustrations. London. John Murray. 1913. R8vo. xvi + 542 pp.

AS 750 N — Finsch, Otto

Remarks on some birds of New Zealand.

(New Zealand Inst., Trans., V, 1872, pp. 206-212)

GN 1 Z — Finsch, Otto

Ueber die Bewohner von Ponape (östl. Carolinen). Nach eigenen Beobachtungen und Erkundigungen.

(Zeit. f. Ethnologie, XII, 1880, pp. 303-332)

GN 416 B 29 — FIRE HAWAII — Bartlett, Harley H.

Fire in relation to primitive agriculture and grazing in the tropics: annotated bibliography. Vol. II: A-G, Tropics in general; H-J, South Asia and Oceania. Presented at the Ninth Pacific Science Congress, Nov. 1957. Ann Arbor Univ. of Michigan, Dept. of Botany, 1957. 873 pp. 4to.

QL 671 1 and AS 750 N — Finsch, Otto

Remarks on some species of birds from New Zealand.

(Ibis, V, 1869, pp. 378-381; New Zealand Institute, Trans., II, 1869, pp. 389-390)

GN 1 Z — Finsch, Otto

Ueber seine Reise nach Neu-Guinea.

(Zeit. f. Ethnologie, 14, 1882, (309)-(313))

GN 2.S P 76 — FIRE MAORI — Fowler, Leo

Some thoughts on charcoal and the generation of fire by percussion in old Maori usage.

(Jour. Poly. Soc., 66(3):264-270, 1957)

QL 1 Z — Finsch, Otto

Reports on the collection of birds made during the voyage of H. M. S. Challenger. No. IV: On the birds of Tongatabu, the Fiji Islands, Api(New Hebrides), and Tahiti.

(Proc. Zool. Soc., London, 1877: 723-742)

QK Birds Pam 284 — Finsch, Otto

Über Vögel der Südsee.

(Ornithologische Verein, Wien, Mitteilungen, 8:54-55,75-76,92-95,108-111,120-127, 1884)

GN 416 B 29 — FIRE PACIFIC — Bartlett, Harley H.

Fire in relation to primitive agriculture and grazing in the tropics: annotated bibliography. Vol. II: A-G, Tropics in general; H-J, South Asia and Oceania. Presented at the Ninth Pacific Science Congress, Nov. 1957. Ann Arbor Univ. of Michigan, Dept. of Botany, 1957. 873 pp. 4to.

GN
416
B 29   FIRE TROPICS BIBLIOGRAPHY

Bartlett, Harley H.

Fire in relation to primitive agriculture and grazing in the tropics: annotated bibliography. Vol. II: A-G, Tropics in general; H-J, South Asia and Oceania. Presented at the Ninth Pacific Science Congress, Nov. 1957. Ann Arbor Univ. of Michigan, Dept. of Botany, 1957. 873 pp. 4to.

GN
Pam
2686   FIRE-MAKING

Hough, Walter

Fire-making apparatus in the United States National Museum. From Proc. U. S. Nat. Mus., v. 73, art. 14, 1928.

GN
2.S
P 76   FIRE-MAKING MAORI SIA

Best, Elsdon

The Polynesian method of generating fire, with some account of the mythical origin of fire and of its employment in ritual ceremonies as observed among the Maori folk of New Zealand.

(Journal of the Polynesian Society, Vol. 33: 87-102, 151-161, 1924)

AS
720.V
R   Fire Ceremony - Australia

Spencer, Baldwin

and

GN
Ethn
Pam
321

An account of the Engwurra or fire ceremony of certain central Australian tribes. In Proc. Roy. Soc. of Victoria X, 1897. pp 12-21.

Also separate.

AS
36
S3   FIRE-MAKING

Hough, Walter, 1859-

The methods of fire-making. By Walter Hough ...

(*In* U. S. National museum. Annual report. 1890. Washington, 1891. 23½ᶜᵐ. p. 395-409. illus., pl. LI)

GN
Pam
768   separate

1. Fire-making.

Library of Congress   Q11.U5 1890   14-19277
—— Copy 2.
—— Separate.   GN447.F52H8

GN
Ethn.Pam
4244   FIRE-MAKING MAORI

Koskinen, Aarne A.

Hika. By Aarne A. Koskinen and Alan F. Hatfull.

(Jour. Poly. Soci, 68(4):277-283, 1959)

AS
36
S2   FIREFLY

Langley, Samuel Pierpont, 1834-1906.

... On the cheapest form of light. By S. P. Langley and F. W. Very. Washington city, Smithsonian institution, 1901.

20 p. III pl. (incl. diagrs.) 24ᶜᵐ. (Smithsonian miscellaneous collections. [vol. XLI, art. IV])

Publication 1258.
From studies at the Allegheny observatory.
"Reprinted, with additional note, from the American Journal of science, third series, vol. XL, no. 236, August, 1890."

1. Radiation. 2. Phosphorescence. 3. Firefly. I. Very, Frank Washington, 1852- joint author. II. Title: Light, On the cheapest form of.

     16-6898

Library of Congress   Q11.S7 vol. 41, art. 4
—— Copy 2. 23½ᶜᵐ.   QC475.L2
—— Copy 3.   Q11.S7 2d set

GN
1
A   Fire-making, aboriginal

Hough, Walter

Aboriginal fire-making. In Am. Anthrop. 1st Ser. III, pp 359-372.

(Washington 1890.)

DU
12
K 87

looked
case   FIRE MAKING PACIFIC

Kotzebue, Otto von

Voyage of discovery, into the South Sea and Beering's Straits...1815-1818...in the ship Rurick... (Translation of German edition...1821) 3 vols. London. 1821. 8vo.
Vol. 3, pp. 259-260.

DU
623
C97   FIRE FOUNTAINS

Cumming, C. F. Gordon

Fire fountains: the kingdom of Hawaii its volcanoes, and the history of its missions.

See author card

GN
1
B   Fire-making

Wendler, P. J.

Zur Feuer- und Nahrungsbereitung der Marshall-Insulaner (Südsee). In Baessler Archiv Band I, pp 269-276.

GN
1
An

and

GN
Ethn.Pam
3606   FIREMAKING PACIFIC

Speiser, Felix

Über Feuerzeuge in der Südsee.

(Anthropos, Bd. 35-36, 1940/41, pp. 239-263)

AS
36
S1   FIRE-MAKING

Balfour, Henry, 1863-

The fire piston. By Henry Balfour ...

(*In* Smithsonian institution. Annual report. 1907. Washington, 1908. 23½ᶜᵐ. p. 565-593. V pl.)

"Reprinted ... from Anthropological essays presented to Edward Burnett Tylor in honor of his 75th birthday, Oct. 2, 1907."

GN
Pam
1710   separate

1. Fire-making. I. Title.

     S 15-1352

Library of Congress   Q11.S66 1907
Library, Smithsonian   Institution

GN
406
W 54   FIRE MAKING

Weule, Karl

Die kultur der kulturlosen: ein blick in die anfänge menschlicher teiftesbethätigung... Stuttgart. (c1910). Chapter VII, pp. 60-93.

GN
Pam.
2353

GN
2.S
P 76   FIREMAKING PAPUA

Gill, William Wyatt   (collector)
The arrival of fire at Papua.
IN
Gill, W. Wyatt
Extracts from Dr. Wyatt Gill's papers, No. 3.

(Jour. Poly. Soc., 20:125-127, 1911)

GN
2.S
Po   FIRE-MAKING

Best, Elsdon

The Polynesian method of generating fire. Poly. Soc. Journ. Vol. XXXIII, 1924, pp 87-102;

to be continued

GN
Ethn.Pam.
3934   FIREMAKING HAWAII

Curious legend tells how secret of making fire was discovered by Hawaiians.
IN Collection of clippings made by Martha W. Beckwith, pp. 35

GN
2.S
P 76   FIRE-MAKING POLYNESIA

Best, Elsdon

The Polynesian method of generating fire, with some account of the mythical origin of fire, and of its employment in ritual ceremonies as observed among the Maori folk of New Zealand.

(Journal of the Polynesian Society, Vol. 33: 87-102, 151-161, 1924)

AS
36
S3   FIRE-MAKING.

Hough, Walter, 1859-
Fire-making apparatus in the U. S. National museum. By Walter Hough.

(*In* U. S. National museum. Annual report. 1888. Washington, 1890. 23½ᶜᵐ. p. 531-587. illus., pl. LXXIV-LXXXI)

1. Fire-making. 2. Indians of North America—Implements. 3. U. S. National museum—Collections.

     14-19263

Library of Congress   Q11.U5 1888
—— Copy 2.

GN
671.H2
K 15   FIREMAKING HAWAII

Kamakau, Samuel Manaiakalani

Mo'olelo Hawaii: Hawaii traditions. (copy of ms offered for publication. typed, bound under two covers.) Translated by Mary Pukui. Edited by Martha W. Beckwith. (received 1939)

AS
36
S1   THE FIRE WALK CEREMONY IN TAHITI.

Langley, Samuel Pierpont, 1834-1906.
The fire walk ceremony in Tahiti. By S. P. Langley.

(*In* Smithsonian institution. Annual report. 1901. Washington, 1902. 23½ᶜᵐ. p. 539-544. III pl.)

"Reprinted from Nature, London, August 22, 1901."

1. Tahiti—Soc. life & cust. I. Title.

     S 15-1122

Library of Congress   Q11.S66 1901
Library, Smithsonian   Institution

GN
2.S
Po
FIRE- WALKING CEREMONY

Young, J. L.

The Umu-ti. Ceremonial fire walking as practised in the eastern Pacific. In Polynesian Soc. Journ. Vol. XXXIV, pp 214-222, 1925.

GN
2 I
A m
FIRE-WALKING FIJI

Roth, Kingsley

A note on the Fijian 'Fire-walking' ceremony from an ethnological standpoint.

(Man, vol.36, 1936, pp.172-173)

GN
2 S
P 76
FIREWALKING RAIATEA

Henry, Teuira

Te umu-ti, a Raiatean ceremony.

(Journal of the Polynesian Society, Vol.II, pp. 105-108; Paradise of the Pacific, VI, p. 148)

DU
620
P
1893;
1893;

GN
2.S
P 76
FIRE WALKING ATIU

Large, J.T.

An Umu-ti (Fire ceremony) at Atiu island, Cook group.

(Journal of the Polynesian Society, 20: 1-3, 1911.)

AP
2
N 4
FIRE-WALKING FIJI

Thomas, Ernest S.

Fire-walking.

(Nature, Vol.137, 1936, pp. 213-215)

AS
36
A 5
FIREWALKING RAIATEA

Menard, Wilmon

Fire walkers of the South Seas.

(Natural History, Vol. 58(1):8-15,48, 1949)

AS
750
N 2
FIRE-WALKING FIJI

Fulton, Robert

An account of the Fiji fire-walking ceremony or vilavilairevo, with a probable explanation of the mystery.

(New Zealand Inst., Trans. and Proc., XXXV, 1902, pp. 187-201)

DU
Pac.Pam.
736
FIRE-WALKING FIJI

Wright, Harry B.

My South Pacific expedition of 1949, carrying Explorers Club flag no 133.

(The Explorers Journal, Vol. 28(1):5-8, 52, 1950)

GN
2.S
P 76
FIRE-WALKING SOCIETY ISLANDS

Gudgeon (W.E.)

Te Umu-Ti, or fire-walking ceremony.

(Journal of the Poly. Soc., Vol. 8:58-60, 1899)

GN
2 S
P 76
FIREWALKING FIJI

Jackson, F. Arthur

A Fijian legend of the origin of the "Vilavilairevo" or "Fire Ceremony".

(Journal of the Polynesian Society, Vol.3, 1894,pp.72-75)

AS
492
S6
FIRE - WALKING Malay Peninsula

Freeman, David

Fire-walking at Ampang, Selangor, In Royal Asiatic Society -Malayan Branch - Journal Vol. II, pp 74 - 76, 1924.

GN
2.S
P 76
FIRE-WALKING SOCIETY ISLANDS

Henry, Teuira

More about fire-walking.

(Journal of the Polynesian Society, Vol. 10: 53-54, 1901)

G
51
W 17
FIRE-WALKING FIJI

Paull, Raymond

Fire-walkers of the islands.

GN
2.S
M 26
FIRE WALKING MALAYA

Richardson, W. J.

Hindu fire-walking in Selangor.

(Mankind, Vol. 3, 1942, pp. 88-90)

AS
36
S1
and
GN
Ethn.Pam.
319
FIRE-WALKING TAHITI

Langley, Samuel Pierpont, 1834-1906.
The fire walk ceremony in Tahiti. By S. P. Langley.
(*In* Smithsonian institution. Annual report. 1901. Washington, 1902. 23½ᶜᵐ. p. 339-544. III pl.)
"Reprinted from Nature, London, August 22, 1901."

1. Tahiti—Soc. life & cust.   I. Title.

S 15-1122

Library of Congress   Q11.S66 1901
Library, Smithsonian   Institution

G
51
W 17
FIREWALKING FIJI

Ryan, F. I.

Fiji; land of many races.

(Walkabout, Vol. 1 (6):16-20,1935)

[includes discussion of firewalking, illustrated; see also article by Elizabeth Powell, idem, p. 43]

GN
671.N56
A 54
FIREWALKING MAORI

Andersen, Johannes C.

The Maori tohunga and his spirit world. Thos. Avery and Sons Ltd. New Plymouth. 1948. sm8vo. xii +135 pp.

pp. 44-56

QK
1
B 16
FIRMIANA

Kostermans, A. J. G. H.

The genus Firmiana Marsili (Sterculiaceae)

(Pengumuman (Communication) Balai Besar Penjelidikan Kehutanan Indonesia, Nr. 54, 1956)

GN
Ethn. Pam.
3117
FIRE-WALKING FIJI

Roth, Kingsley

The fire-walk in Fiji.

(Man, Vol. 33, Nos. 48-62, 1933, pp. 44-49)

G
51
W 17
FIRE-WALKING NEW GUINEA

Paull, Raymond

Fire-walkers of the islands.

(Walkabout, 27(4):14-17, 1961)

[at Nasinu, Fiji and at Gaulim, New Guinea]

QK
Bot.Pam.
3039
FIRMIANA

Kostermans, A. J. G. H.

The genus Firmiana marsili (Sterculiaceae)

(Reinwardtia, 4(2):281-310, 1957)

QK
358
C 18

Firminger's manual of gardening
Cameron, J. (ed.).
Calcutta, 1904. 5th ed. 8vo. pp. II-XIX, 1-710.

DU
Hist.Pam.
90

First Pan-Pacific Educational Conference,
Honolulu, August 11-24, 1921. ND

Program and Proceedings.
Official Bulletin, 1st. ed., August 8th.

GN
2.S
P 76

Firth, R. W.

The Korekore Pa, an ancient Maori fortress.

(Journal of the Polynesian Society, 34: 1-18, 1925)

Carter Coll.
4-B-29

First book in Hawaiian. A text book in the
Hawaiian Language. Honolulu. Star-Bulletin.
1930. 94 pp. sm8vo.

DU
1
S 72q

The first South Pacific Conference.

(South Pacific Commission Quarterly Bull.,
3(1):7-9, 1953)

[ends with a note of the 2nd to be held]

GN
2.S
P 76

Firth, R. W.

The Maori carver.

(Journal of the Polynesian Society, 34: 277-291, 1925.)

DU
Hist.Pam.
441

First Federal's first fifty years... 1904-
1954. First Federal Savings and Loan Association
of Hawaii. 4to. (46) pp.

DU
1
P

First South Pacific Conference.

(Pacific Islands Monthly, Vol. 20(11):25-27, 1950)

GN
2.S
P 76

Firth, Raymond

The analysis of mana: an empirical approach.

(Journal of the Polynesian Society, Vol.
49, 1941, pp. 483-510)

(also Mem. Poly. Soc., Vol. 17, 1941, pp.
189-216)

Map
Room

First geological map of B. S. I. P., between
1950-1961; in two sheets gummed together, and
a separate "key".

British Solomon Islands Protectorate

DU
600
M 62

First T(rust) T(erritory) flag.

(Micronesian Reporter, X(5):4-5, 1963)

GN
1
O 15

Firth, Raymond

Anthropology and native administration.

(Oceania, Vol. 2, 1931-32, pp. 1-8)

DU
12
B 39

A First Fleet Family

Becke, Louis

GN
Pam
2445

First Universal Races Congress

Record of the proceedings of the
first Universal races congress held at
The University of London, July 26-29,
1922.

GN
Ethn.Pam.
3759

Firth, Raymond

Anthropology and the study of society.

(Social Sciences, Sept. 1936, pp. 1-12)

DU
Hist.Pam.
327
437 a

The first 100 years; a report on the operations of Castle and Cooke for the years 1851-
1951. (Honolulu. Privately printed) 1952. sm
4to. 63 pp.

GN
865.N
E 32

Firth, C. M.

Egypt, Ministry of Finance. Survey Department

Archaeological Survey of Nubia.
Vol. I. Report for 1908-1909, by C. M. Firth
Plates and plans accompanying Vol. I.
...

Cairo. Government Press, 1910-1912. Folio,
4 vols.

GN
1
O 15

Firth, Raymond

Anthropology in Australia: 1926-1932 - and
after.

(Oceania, Vol. 3, No. 1, 1932, pp. 1-12)

DU
625.1
B 62

FIRST NATIONAL BANK OF HAWAII

Story of The Bank of Bishop & Co. Now
Bishop First National Bank of Honolulu.
n.p., n.d. 39 pp.

GN
2.S
P 76

Firth, R. G.

Another unknown artifact from swamp land,
with illustration.

(Journal of the Polynesian Society, Vol. 35:
70, 1926)

(cockscomb image?)

GN
2.S
P 76

Firth, Raymond

Anuta and Tikopia: symbiotic elements in
social organization.

(Journ. Poly. Soc., 63(2):87-131, 1954)

GN
671.N5
F 52

Firth, Raymond

Art and life in New Guinea. London. The Studio Ltd., 1936. 8vo. 126 pp., 83 pl.

GN
2.S
M 26

Firth, Raymond

Economics and ritual in sago extraction in Tikopia.

(Mankind, Vol. 4(4):131-142, 1950)

GN
490
F 52

Firth, Raymond ___ editor

Man and culture; an evaluation of the work of Malinowski. Routledge and Kegan Paul. London. 8vo.(1957) viii + 292 pp.

GN
490
F 73

Firth, Raymond

Authority and public opinion in Tikopia. IN

Fortes, Meyer   editor
Social structure: studies presented to A.R. Radcliffe-Brown. Oxford. Clarendon Press. 1949. pp. 168-188.

GN
490
F 52

Firth, Raymond

Elements of social organization. Josiah Mason Lectures delivered at the University of Birmingham. Watts and Co., London. (1951) 8vo. xi + 257 pp.

GN
Eth.
Pam.
2873

Firth, Raymond

Maori Canoe-Sail in the British Museum. Additional Notes by Te Rangi Hiroa (Peter H. Buck)

(From Journal of the Polynesian Society, Extract from Vol. 40, No. 3, pages 129-140).1931.

GN
2.1
A-m

Firth, Raymond

Bark-cloth in Tikopia, Solomon Islands.

(Man, Vol. 47, No. 74, 1947, pp. 69-72)

GN
Ethn.
Pam.
4015
4226

Firth, Raymond

The fate of the soul; an interpretation of some primitive concepts. The Frazer Lecture for 1955. Cambridge University Press. 12mo. 46 pp.

GN
700
A62

Firth, Raymond

Maori hill-forts. In Antiquity, v.1, n.1, 1927.

GN
Pam
2379

separate

GN
Ethn.
Pam.
4406

Firth, Raymond

Case reports: rumor in a primitive society.

(The Journal of Abnormal and Social Psychology, Vol. 53, No.1, pp.122-132, 1956)

GN
671.N5
B 45

Firth, Raymond

Belshaw, Cyril S.

The great village; the economic and social welfare of Hanuabada, an urban community in Papua. Foreword by Raymond Firth. Routledge and Kegan Paul. London. 8vo. (1957) xviii + 302 pp.

GN
2.S
P 76

Firth, Raymond

Maori material in the Vienna Museum.

(Journal of the Polynesian Society, 40: 95-102, 1931.)

GN
1
O 15

Firth, Raymond

Ceremonies for children and social frequency in Tikopia.

(Oceania, 27(1):12-55, 1956)

GN
22
F 52

Firth, Raymond

Human types.   Thomas Nelson and Sons, Ltd. London... (1938). sm8vo.   207 pp.

GN
2.1
A4

Firth, Raymond

Maori store-houses of to-day. In Roy. Anthrop. Inst. Journ. Vol. LV, 1925, pp. 363 - 372.

GN
1
O 15

and
GN
Ethn. Pam.
3811

Firth, Raymond

A dart match in Tikopia.

(Oceania, Vol. 1, 1930-1931; 64-96, pls. 1-3)

GN
2.1
A-M

Firth, Raymond

Initiation rites and kinship bonds in Tikopia.

(Man, vol. 33, 1933, no. 118, pp. 117-118)

GN
2.1
A-4

and
GN
Ethn. Pam
3838

Firth, Raymond

Marriage and the classificatory system of relationship.

(Journ. R. Anthrop. Inst. of Great Britain and Ireland, Vol. 60, 1930, pp. 235-268)

GN
2.1
A4

Firth, Raymond

Economic psychology of the Maori. In Roy. Anthrop. Inst. Vol. LV, 1925, pp 340-362.

GN
635.M4
F 52

Firth, Raymond

Malay fishermen: their peasant economy. London. Kegan Paul, Trench, Trubner and Co., Ltd. 8vo. 1946. xii + 354 pp.   2 maps.

Open

Firth, Raymond

The meaning of dreams in Tikopia.

IN Essays presented to C. G. Seligman. pp. 63-74.

UH has

GN
1
O 15

Firth, Raymond

    A native voyage to Rennell.

    (Oceania, Vol. 2, 1931-1932, pp. 179-190)

GN
490
L 43

Firth, Raymond

Leach, E. R.

    Political systems of highland Burma; a study of Kachin social structure. With a foreword by Raymond Firth. Published for the London School of Economics and Political Science. Harvard University Press. Cambridge. 1954. 8vo. xii + 324 pp.

GN
2.1
A-M

Firth, Raymond

    A Raga tale.

    (Man, vol. 30, 1930, no. 46, pp. 58-60, figs. 1-4)

GN
2.1
A-m

Firth, Raymond

    A note on descent groups in Polynesia.

    (Man, Vol. LVII, Article 2, pp. 4-8, Jan., 1957)

GN
4
C 33

Firth, Raymond

    A Polynesian aristocrat (Tikopia).
IN

Casagrande, Joseph B. editor
    In the company of man. pp. 1-40.

Harper. 1960. New York. R8vo.

GN
670
W 72

Firth, Raymond

Williamson, Robert W.

    Religion and social organization in central Polynesia. Edited by Ralph Piddington, with a preface by Raymond Firth. Cambridge. University Press. 1937. 8vo. xxix +340 pp.

GN
2.1
A 62 j

Firth, Raymond

    Offering and sacrifice: problems of organization.

    (Jour. of the R. Anthrop. Inst. of Great Britain and Ireland, 93(1):12-24, 1963)

AP
2
N 28

Firth, Raymond

    Prehistoric America and Polynesia. A review of "American Indians in the Pacific" by Thor Heyerdahl.

    (Nature, Vol. 171(4356):713-714, 1953)

GN
1
O 15

Firth, Raymond

    Report on research in Tikopia.

    (Oceania, Vol. 1, 1930-1931, pp. 105-117)

DU
Pac.Pam.
849

Firth, Raymond

Spate, O. H. K.

    Notes on New Guinea. October-November, 1951. By O. H. K. Spate, J. W. Davidson and Raymond Firth. typed, folio. 3+13+18+10 pp. (from The Australian National University)

    [studies of history, government, social and economic change, etc.]

GN
671.N 56
F 52

Firth, Raymond

    Primitive economics of the New Zealand Maori. With a preface by R. H. Tawney. With 30 illustrations on 16 plates and 3 maps. E.P. Dutton and Company. New York. 1929. 8vo. xxiv + 505 pp.

GN
23
F 52

Firth, Raymond

    Social change in Tikopia; re-study of a Polynesian community after a generation. Illustrated. The Macmillan Company. New York. R8vo 360 pp. (1958, preface)

GN
Ethn.
Pam.
4342

Firth, Raymond

    Notes on some Tikopia ornaments.

    (Jour. Poly. Soc., Vol. 60(2/3):130-133, 1951)

GN
671.T 5
F 52

Firth, Raymond

    Primitive Polynesian economy. Illustrated. George Routledge & Sons, Ltd. London. R8vo. xi, 387 pp.

GN
Ethn.
Pam.
4320

Firth, Raymond

    Social changes in the western Pacific.

    (Journal of the R. Soc. of Arts, London, Vol 101(4909):803-819, 1953)

GN
2.1
A-m

Firth, Raymond

    Notes on the social structure of some south-eastern New Guinea communities, Part I: Mailu. Part II. Koita.

    (Man, 52, Art. 99, 1952; 52, Art. 123,1952)

GN
1
O 15

Firth, Raymond

    Privilege ceremonials in Tikopia: a further note.

    (Oceania, Vol. 21:161-177, 1951; 26(1):1-13, 1955)

GN
2.1
A-4

Firth, Raymond

    Social organization and social change. Presidential address.

    (The Jour. of the Royal Anthropological Inst of Great Britain and Ireland, Vol. 84(I-II):1-20, 1954)

GN
2.M
E 85

and
GN
Ethn.
Pam.
4217

Firth, Raymond

    The plasticity of myth: cases from Tikopia.
    (Ethnologica, n.f., Bd. 2:181-188, 1960)

GN
1
F

Firth, Raymond

    Proverbs in native life, with special reference to those of the Maori.

    (Folk-lore, vol. 37, no. 2, 1926, pp. 134-153; vol. 37, no. 3, 1926, pp. 245-270)

GN
2.S
P 76

Firth, Raymond

    Social changes in the western Pacific.

    (Journal of the Royal Society of Arts, Vol. CI, No. 4909, October 1953, pp. 803-819)

    REVIEW ONLY, in Jour. Poly. Soc., 64(1): 172-73, 1955 by Ralph Piddington

GN
Ethn.
Pam.
4403

Firth, Raymond

The sociology of "Magic" in Tikopia.

(Sociologus, NF., Jahr.4, Heft 2, 1954,
pp.97-116)

GN
671.T5
F 52

Firth, Raymond

We, the Tikopia. A sociological study of
kinship in primitive Polynesia, by Raymond
Firth, with a preface by Bronislaw Malinowski.
London. George Allen & Unwin Ltd. 1936. 8vo.
xxv + 605 pp., 25 pl.

over

GN
671.M5
F 52

Fischer, Dora

Unter Südsee-Insulanern; das Leben des
Forschers Mikloucho Maclay. Mit zahlreichen
Abbildungen und mehreren Kartenskizzen. Koehler
and Amelang. Leipzig. 8vo. 466 pp. 1950

GN
2.I
A-4

Firth, Raymond

Some principles of social organization.

(Jour. R. Anthrop. Inst. Great Britain and
Ireland, 85:1-18, 1955)

GN
671.T 5
F 52

Firth, Raymond

The work of the gods in Tikopia, Vol. I -II

Monographs on Social Anthropology, No.1-2 1940,
the London School of Economics and Pol. Sci.

GN
1
A62

Fischer, E.

Anatomische Untersuchungen an den Kopfweich-
teilen zweier Papua.   Review by Dr. L. Laloy.

(L'Anthropologie, Tome 17, 1906, p. 200)

GN
2.I
A-m

Firth, Raymond

The study of values by social anthropologists
The Marett Lecture, 1953
(Man, 53:146-153, 1953)

GN
2.1
A-M

Firth, Raymond

Wharepuni: a few remaining Maori dwellings
of the old style.

(Man, vol. 26, 1926, no. 30, pp. 54-59, figs.
1,2)

G
3
A-1

Fischer, Eric

A German and English glossary of geographical terms. By Eric Fischer and Francis E. Elliott. American Geogr. Soc., Library Series 5,
1950.

GN
1
O 15

Firth, Raymond

Succession to chieftainship in Tikopia.

(Oceania, 30(3):161-180, 1960)

GN
Ethn.
Pam.
4404

Firth, Raymond

Work and community in a primitive society.

(H.R.H. The Duke of Edinburgh's Study Conference, X, 1956)   12 pp.

GN
Pam
2323

Fischer, Eugene

Anthropogenese. From Handworterbuch
der Nat. bd.1, 1912.

GN
2 I
A m

Firth, Raymond

Tattooing in Tikopia.

(Man, vol.36, 1936, pp.173-177)

GN
1
E 85

Fischer, Ann

Reproduction in Truk.

(Ethnology, Vol. 2(4):527-540, 1963)

GN
Pam
2348

Fischer, Eugen

Anthropologie. From Handworterbuch d.
Naturwissen. bd.1.

GN
2.I
A-m

Firth, Raymond

The theory of 'cargo' cults: a note on
Tikopia.

(Man, Vol. LV(142):130-132, September, 1955)

QH
11
P 11

Fischer, Ann

Role of the Trukese mother and its effect
on child training.

(Scientific Investigations in Micronesia,
No. 8, 1950)

GN
Pam
1152

Fischer, Eugen

Anthropologische aufgaben in unseren
deutschen Kolonien. From Korre-blatt
der deutschen gesell. f. anthrop. ethnol.
und urges. jahr. 42, n.8-12, 1911. 2p.

GN
1
O 15

Firth, Raymond

Totemism in Polynesia.

(Oceania; Vol. 1, 1930-1931, pp. 291-321;
377-398)

QK
Bot.Pam.
2182

Fischer, C. E. C.

Where did the Sandalwood tree(Santalum album
Linn.) evolve?

(Journal of the Bombay Natural History Society, Vol. XL, 1938, pp. 382-387, 1 plate)

GN
Pam
2533

Fischer, Eugen

Beeinflusst der M. genioglossus durch
seine funktion beim sprechen den bau des
unterkiefers? From Anatomischen Anzeiger
bd.23, 1903.

GN
Pam
1209

Fischer, Eugen

    Beobachtungen am "Bastardvolk" in Deutsch-Sudwestafrika. From jahrg. 40, n. 9-12, 1909. 3p.

GN
Pam
1231

Fischer, Eugen

    Rassen und rassenbildung. From Handworterbuch der Naturwissm, 1913.

QM
Anatomy
Pam
#6

Fischer, Eugen

    Zur frage der domestikationsmerkmale des menschen. From Zeit. f. Sexualwissen. bd.8, heft 1, 1921.

GN
Pam
1208

Fischer, Eugen

    Die destimmung der menschlichen Haarfarben. From Korresp-blatt der deutschen anthrop. gesell. jahrg. 38, n.9-12, 1907. 7p.

GN
Pam
2443

Fischer, Eugen

    Rassenkreuzung und vererbung nach beobachtungen an den bastards in Deutsch-Sudwest Afrika. From Sitz. Berichte d. Physi-med. gesell. Würzburg, 1912.

GN
Pam
2451

Fischer, Eugen

    Zur frage der Kinnbildung und Walkhoffs "Theorie". From Deutschen Monats. f. Zahnheilkunde, jahrg. 23, Bec. heft, 1905.

GN
Pam
2387

Fischer, Eugen

    Gehirn (anthropologisch). From Handworterbuch d. naturwissen. 1913.

GN
Pam
2123

Fischer, Eugen

    Die reste eines neolithischen graberfeldes am Kaiserstuhl. From Berichte der Natur. Gesell. Freiburg, bd. 13, 1903.

GN
Pam
1786

Fischer, Eugen

    Zur frage der "Kreuzungen beim menschen." From Archiv f. rassen und Gesell-biol. 1912, heft 1.

GN
Pam
1861

Fischer, Eugen

    Haar: anthropologisch. From Hand. d. Naturwissenschaften, bd.5, 1913.

GN
Pam
1862

Fischer, Eugen

    Schädellehre und skelettkehre. From Hand. der Naturwissenschaften, bd.8, 1913.

GN
Pam
1213

Fischer, Eugen

    Zum inzuchts und bastardierungsproblem beim menschen. From Korresp-blatt der deutschen gesell. f. anthrop. ethnol. und urgeschichte, jahrg. 42, 8-12, 1911.

GN
Pam
1151

Fischer, Eugen

    Die neueinrichtung eines anthropologischen laboratoriums an der Universi. Freiburg i B. From Korresp-blatt der deutschen gesellschaft f. anthrop. ethn. und urges. jahr. 41, n.5, 1910. 3p.

GN
Pam
2571

Fischer, Eugen

    Untersuchungen bezuglich der pigmentverteilung im auge melanotischer rassen. From Naturforschende Gesell. Freiburg: Deutschen Med. Wochen. 1905, n.37.

GN
Pam
1155

Fischer, Eugen

    Zur vergleichung des menschen und affenschadels in fruhen entwickelungsstadien. From Corresp-blatt der deutsche anthrop. gesell. n.11-12, 1902. 3p.

GN
Pam
1460

Fischer, Eugen

    Nochmals Walkhoffs lehre von der kinnbildung. From Anatom. Anzeiger, bd. 25, 1904.

GN
Pam
830

Fischer, Eugen

    Die variationen an radius und ulna des menschen. From Zeit. f. Morphol. und Anthrop. bd.9, 1906.

GN
Pam
854

Fischer, Eugen

    Zur vergleichenden osterlogie der menschlichen vorderarmknochen. From Correspond. Blatt der Deut. anthrop. Gesell. n.12, 1903.

GN
Pam
1873

Fischer, Eugen

    Das problem der rassenkreuzung beim menschen. From Die Naturwissenschaften, heft 42, 1918.

GN
Pam
2236

Fischer, Eugen

    Zur entwicklungsgeschichte des affenschadels. From Zeit. f. Morphol. und Anthrop. bd.5.

QL
516
F 52

Fischer, F. C. J.

    Trichopterorum catalogus.
      Vol. I:Necrotauliidae, Prosepididontidae, Rhyacophilidae. 1960
      Vol. II:Philopotamidae, Hydroptilidae, Stenopsychidae. 1961
      Vol. III:Polycentropodidae; Psychomyidae. 1962
      Vol. IV:Hydropsychidae; Arctopsychidae. 1963.
    Publ. by Nederlandsche Ent. Vereeniging.

    Amsterdam.   R8vo

QL
Crus
Pam
#75

Fischer, J.

Conspectus Classium Animalium Respectu Organisationis Eorum Habita. (?. no date, 1831 in pencil. from ?)

8vo pp. 329-362.

GN
Pam
2613

Fischer, H

Ueber den stand der kenntnis von der praehistorie Persiens. From Corresp-blatt d. Deutschen Gesell. f. Anthrop. Ethnol. und Urgeschichte, Jahrg. 16, n.3, 1885.

GN
2.S
N 67

Fischer, H. Th.

Recent ethnographical studies on Netherlands New Guinea*).

(Nieuw Guinea Studiën, Jaargang 1, Nr. 2: 91-105, April, 1957)

*) Paper read at the International Congress of Anthrpological and Ethnological Sciences, 1-9 Sept. 1956, at Philadelphia.

GN
Pam
1055

Fischer, H.

Eine altmexikanische steinfigur. From Globus, bd. 85, n.22, 1904. 4p.

GN
1
B 14

Fischer, Hans

Ethnographica von den Kukukuku (Ost-Neu-guinea).

(Baessler-Archiv, 32(1):99-122, 1959)

GN
1
T 61

Fischer, H. Th.

Some notes on kinship systems and relationship terms of Sumba, Manggarai and South Timor.

(Int. Archives of Ethnography, Vol. 48(1), 1957) pp. 1-62

GN
Ethn.Pam.
2751

Fischer, H.

L'Art dans les Îles de la Mer du Sud.

(Cahiers d'Art, Année 4, pp. 73-78, 1929)

GN
1
Z 65

Fischer, Hans

Polynesische Musikinstrumente: innerpolynesische Gliederung - ausserpolynesische Parallen.

(Zeif. f. Ethnologie, 86(2):282-302, 1961)

GN
Pam
2460

Fischer, H. W.

Een houten klopper om boombast te bewerken van het eiland Nias. From Int., Arch. f. Ethnog. bd. 17, 1905.

QL
Mollusk
Pam
612

Fischer, H

Céphalopodes. From Expéditions sci. du Travailleur et du Talisman, tome 8, 1907.

GN
468
F 52

Fischer, Hans

Schallgeräte in Ozeanien: Bau und Spieltechnik, Verbreitung und Funktion. Mit 487 Abbildungen auf 29 Tafeln. Strasbourg. 1958

(Collection d'Etudes Musicologiques, Sammlung Musikwissenschaftlicher Abhandlungen, Bd. 36)

GN
671.N5
N 93

Fischer H.W.

Ethnographica von den Pěsěchěm und aus Südwest-Neu-Guinea (Nachtrag). in Nova Guinea VII, 2, 1915, pp. 145-162, pls. XXVII-XXIX.

QL
401
J 85

Fischer, H.

Dautzenberg, Ph.

Contribution à la faune malacologique de l' Inndochine. By Ph. Dautzenberg and H. Fischer.

(Jour. de Conchyl., Tome 54:145-226, 1906)

AS
322
Z 96 n

Fischer, Hans

Die Tierwelt im Lichte der Pharmakologie.

(Neujahrsblatt, Naturforschende Gesellschaft in Zurich, 1962)

GN
671.N5
N 93

Fischer, H.W.

Ethnographica aus Süd- und Südwest-Neu-Guinea. in Nova Guinea VII, 1, 1913, pp. 37-145, pls. VII-XXVI.

QL
401
J 85

Fischer, H.

Description d'un Oliva nouveau provenant des Nouvelles Hébrides.

(Jour. de Conchyl., Vol. 50:409-411, 1902)

GN
1
Z

Fischer, H. Th.

Indonesische Paradiesmythen.

(Zeitschrift f. Ethnologie, Jahrg. 84, 1932 pp. 204-245)

GN
1
Ar3

Fischer, H.W. ed.

Internationales Archiv für Ethnographie.

QL
Mollusca
Pam
567

Fischer, H.

Dautzenberg, Ph.

Sur quelques types de Garidés de la collection de Lamarck existant au Muséum de Paris. Par Ph. Dautzenberg and H. Fischer.

(Jour. de Conchyl., 61:215-228, 1913)

GN
1
1 61

Fischer, H. Th.

Polyandry.

(Int. Archives of Ethnography, 46(1):106-115, 1952)

AM
101.
L
(5)

Fischer, H.W.

Katalog des Ethnographischen Reichsmuseums. Band X. Mittel-Sumatra (Sumatra III). Leiden, 1916, roy. 8vo, pp. 214, pls. I-XII.

GN
Pam
2622

Fischer, H. W.

Lets over de wapens uit de mentawei-verzameling van s'Rijks Ethnografisch Museum te Leiden. From Int. Arch. f. Ethnog. v.18.

GN
2.8
P 76

Fischer, J. L.

Folktales, social structure, and environment in two Polynesian outliers.

(The Journal of the Polynesian Society, Vol. 67(1):11-36, March, 1958)

Q
101
P 18

John L.
Fischer, J. L.

The retention rate of Chamorro basic vocabulary.

(Lingua, 10(3):255-266, 1961)

GN
Pam
2466

Fischer, H. W.

Mittheilungen uber die Nias Sammlung des Ethnog. Reichsmuseums zu Leiden. From Int. Arch. f. Ethnog. bd. 18, 1906.

GN
1
H 91 c

Fischer, J. L.

The Japanese schools for the natives of Truk, Caroline Islands.

(Human Organization, 20(2):83-88, 1961)

GR
Folklore
Pam.
121

Fischer, J. L.

Sequence and structure in folktales.

(Reprinted from Selected Papers of the Fifth International Congress of Anthrop. and Ethnological Sciences, Philadelphia, Sept. 1956: 442-446)

AM
101 L
(5)

Fischer, H. W. and Rassers, W. H.

Die ostlichen kleinen Sunda - Inseln: I. Sumbawa - II Flores - III Sumba. Leiden Mus. Katalog, Band XVII, 1924.

GN
1
O 15

Fischer, J. L.

Genealogical space.

(Oceania, 30(3):181-187, 1960)

GN
1
C 97

Fischer, J. L.

The sociopsychological analysis of folktales.

(Current Anthropology, Vol. 4(3):235-295, 1963)

QK
367
B 65

looked
case

Fischer, J. B.

Blume, Karel Lodewijk

Flora Javae nec non Insularum adjacentium. Adjutore J. B. Fischer. Tomus 1-4. Lugduni Batavorum. 1828-1858. folio.

GN
Ethn.Pam
3959

Fischer, John L.

Native land tenure in the Truk District. manuscript. typed copy. carbon. 24 pp.

GN
1
J 86

and

GR
Folklore
Pam.
101

Fischer, J. L.

Riesenberg, Saul H.

Some Ponapean proverbs. By Saul H. Riesenberg and J. L. Fischer.

(Journal of American Folklore, vol. 68(267): 9-18, 1955)

GN
Ethn.
Pam.
4423

Fischer, J. L.

Avunculocal residence on Losap.

(Am. Anthropologist, Vol.57, No.5, pp.1025-1032, 1955)

GN
490
Y 73

Fischer, Jack L.   (John L.)

Native land tenure in the Truk District.

Young, John de   and others
Land tenure patterns, Trust Territory of the Pacific Islands. Volume 1, 1958, Part 3

GN
Ethn.
Pam.
4210
4338

Fischer, J. L.   (John L.)

Totemism and allergy. By J. L. Fischer, Ann Fischer and Frank Mahony.

(International Jour. of Social Psychiatry, 5(1):33-40, 1959)

GN
490
Y 73

Fischer, Jack L.

Contemporary Ponape Island land tenure.

Young, John de   and others
Land tenure patterns, Trust Territory of the Pacific Islands, Vol. 1, Part 2, 1958.

Storage
Case
5

Ms C 2

Fischer, J. L.

[Notes on Ponape]   Not for general use. deposit, temporary. June 17, 1951 and 7/19/54

GN
Ethn.
Pam.
4369

Fischer, J. L.

Totemism on Truk and Ponape.

(Am. Anthropologist, 59(2):250-265, 1957)

GN
669
F 52

Fischer, John L.

The eastern Carolines, by John L. Fischer with the assistance of Ann M. Fischer. Pacific Science Board, National Acad. Sci., Nat. Research Council, in association with Human Relations Area Files. 1957 xiv + 274 + (15) pp Behavior Science Monograph

---

GN
1
J 86

Fischer, J. L.

The position of men and women in Truk and Ponape: a comparative analysis of kinship terminology and folktales.

(Journal of American Folklore, Vol. 69(271): 55-62, 1956)

QL
Prot.
te
Poly.
Pam
241

Fischer, Jules

Liste des bryozoaires. From Bull. Soc. Zool. France, v.6, 1881.

GN
Pam
1354

Fischer, Ludwig Hans

Indischer volksschmuck und die art ihn zu tragen. From Annalen des k.k. Nat. Hofmuseums, bd. 5, 1890.

QL
Protozoa
to
Polyzoa
Pam
341

Fischer, Paul

Bryozoaires, échinodermes et foraminiferes marins du departement de la Gironde et des cotes du sud-ouest de la France. From Act. Soc. Linneenne de Bordeaux, v. 27, 1870.

QL
401
J 85

Fischer, P(aul)

Notes pour servir à la faune malacologique de l'archipel Calédonien.

(Jour. de Conchyl.,7:329-342, 1858/9; 9:143-148, 1861)

also 11:49-57, 1863

GN
Pam
2647

Fischer, Ludwig Hans

Schalensteine auf Corfu. From Mitth. d. Anthrop. Gesell. Wien, sitz. h.5, 1886.

QL
Crus
Pam
#76

Fischer, Paul

Crustacés Ostracodes Marins des côtes du Sud-Ouest de la France

Ex. des Actes de la Soc. Linnéenne de Bordeaux + XXXI. 1877, 12 pp.

FEB 28 1911

Paris 1877.   pp. 1-12.

QL
Crustacea
Pam
453

Fischer, Paul

Observations sur les aplysies. Sc. Nat., Feb. 1870, n.3.

QP
1
C

Fischer Martin H.

On the Production & Suppression of Glycosuria in Rabbits through Electrolytes

FEB 23 1904   University of Cal. Publication

N.2.   Physiology Vol.1.

QL
Crustacea
Pam
458

Fischer, Paul

Crustacés podophthalmaires et cirrhipedes du departement de la Gironde et des cotes du sud-ouest de la France. From Act. Soc. Linneene d. Bordeaux, v. 28, liv.5, 1872.

QE
Geology
Pam
765

Fischer, Paul

Subdivisions des ammonites.

QL
401
J 85

Fischer, P. H.

Exposition à Paris des résultats scientifiques de l'Expedition danoise de la "Galathea".

(Journal de Conchyliologie, 97(1):41-43, 1957)

QL
Mollusk
Pam
566

Fischer, Paul

Essai sur la distribution geographique des brachiopodes et des mollusques du littoral oceanique de la France. From Soc. Linneenne de Bordeaux, v.32, 1878.

QL
Protozoa
to
Polyzoa
Pam
484

Fischer, Paul

Synascidies du département de la gironde et des Cotes du sub-ouest de la France. From Act. de la Soc. Linnéenne de Bordeaux, t.30, 1876.

AS
162
P

Fischer, P. H.

Gasteropodes marins recueillis aux Nouvelles-Hebrides par M. E. Aubert de la Rue. Par P. H. Fischer adn E. Fischer-Piette.

(Bull. Mus. Nat. Hist. Nat. Paris, Ser. 2, Tome XI, 1939, pp. 263-266)

QL
Mollusk
Pam
544

Fischer, Paul

Faune conchyliologique marine du departement de la Gironde et des cotes du sud-ouest de la France. Supplement. From Act. Soc. Linneene de Bordeaux, v.27, liv.1.

QL
Mollusk
Pam
544

Second suppl. from v.29, live.4, 1874.

QL
403
F 52

Fischer, Paul Henri, 1835-1893.

... Manuel de conchyliologie et de paléontologie conchyliologique; ou, Histoire naturelle des mollusques vivants et fossiles. Suivi d'un appendice sur les brachiopodes par D. P. Œhlert. Avec 23 planches contenant 600 figures dessinées par S. P. Woodward ... Paris, F. Savy, 1887.

xxiv, 1369, [22] p., 1 l. front., illus., 23 pl., fold. map. 24½cm.

1. Mollusks. [1. Mollusca]

Agr 18-38

Library, U. S. Dept. of   Agriculture 437F52

QL
403
F 52

Fischer, P. J.

Vie et moeurs des mollusques. Avec 180 figures. Payot, Paris. 1950. 8vo. 312 pp.

QL
401
J 85

Fischer, P.

Faune de l'ile du Lord Howe. (Océan Pacifique)

(Jour. de Conchyl., Tome 31:305-314, 1891)

QL
401
J 85

Fischer, P(aul) H(enrique)

Observations d'écologie littorale aux Iles de la Société.

(Journal de Conchyliologie, Vol. 92(4):186-194, 1952)

QL
Protozoa
to
Polyzoa
Pam
509

Fischer, Paul

Anthozoaires du departement de la Gironde et des cotes du sud-ouest de la France. From Act. Soc. Linneenne d. Bordeaux, v.30, liv.2, 1875.

QL
401
J 85

Fischer, P. H.

Mollusques terrestres de l'Indo-Chine et du Yunnan conservés dans la collection de l'Ecole des Mines de Paris.

(Journal de Conchyliologie, Vol. 103(1): 32-37, 1963)

AS
36
S1

Fischer, Paul Henri, 1835-1893.

The scientific labors of Edward Lartet. By Dr. P. Fischer.

(In Smithsonian institution. Annual report. 1872. Washington, 1873. 23½cm. p. [172]-184)

"A translation ... of 'Note sur la vie et les travaux d'Ed. Lartet ... lu à la séance générale annuelle de la Société géologique de France' from 'Vie et travaux d'Edouard Lartet' ... pp. 39-55."

1. Lartet, Édouard Amand Isidore Hippolyte, 1801-1871.

S 15-332

Library of Congress   Q11.S66 1872
Library, Smithsonian   Institution

QL
401
J 85

Fischer-Piette, E.

Mollusques terrestres de Madagascar, genre Leucotaenius.

(Jour. de Conchyliologie, Vol. 103(1):15-23, 1963)

GC
1
W 89-t

and

QL
Fish Pam
562

and

Fish, Charles J.

Noxious marine animals of the central and western north Pacific. By Charles J. Fish and Mary Curtis Cobb.

(Woods Hole Oceanographic Inst., Tech. Rept. 7, 1949)

(U.S. Fish and Wildlife Service, Research Report 36, 1954)

QL
634.In
F 81 s

FISH CULTURE   INDONESIA

Hofstede, A. E.   and others

Fish-culture in Indonesia.

(Indo-Pacific Fisheries Council, Sp. Pub. No. 2, 1953)

AS
36
S1

GN
Pam
10

Fischer, Theobald, 1846–

The Mediterranean peoples. By Theobald Fischer ...

(In Smithsonian institution. Annual report. 1907. Washington, 1908. 23½ᶜᵐ. p. 497-521)

"Translated ... from the Internationale wochenschrift. Berlin, September 7, 14, 21, 28, 1907."

separate

1. Mediterranean race. 2. Ethnology—Europe. 3. Ethnology—Africa, North.

Library of Congress   Q11.S66 1907
Library, Smithsonian   Institution

S 15-1349

QL
752
U 58

Fish, Charles J.

Noxious marine animals of the central and western Pacific ocean. By Charles J. Fish and Mary Curtis Cobb.

(U. S. Fish and Wildlife Service, Research Report 36, 1954)

QL
634.In
F 81

FISH CULTURE   JAVA

Schuster, W. H.

Fish-culture in brackish-water ponds of Java.

(Indo-Pacific Fisheries Council, Special Publications, No. 1, 1952)

AS
36
S1

Fischer, Theobald, 1846–

Morocco. By Theobald Fischer.

(In Smithsonian institution. Annual report. 1904. Washington, 1905. 23½ᶜᵐ. p. 355-372)

"Translated ... from Geographische zeitschrift, Leipzig, February, 12, 1903."

1. Morocco.

Library of Congress   Q11.S66 1904
Library, Smithsonian   Institution

S 15-1247

GC
1
W 89-t

Fish, Marie Poland

Marine mammals of the Pacific with particular reference to the production of underwater sound.

(Woods Hole Oceanographic Institution, Technical Rept. 8, Office of Naval Research, 1949)

QL
Fish
Pam
#243

FISH-CULTURE—NEW ZEALAND

Thomson, George M.

Marine Fish-Hatchery and Biological Station, Portobello. From Amn. Rept. Mar. Dept. Dunedin, 1925.

GN
Pam
2617

Fischer, Wilhelm

Ein einfaches und praktisches verfahren fur hand und fussaudrucke auf Papier. From Corresp-blatt d. Deutschen Gesell. f. Anthrop. Ethnol. und Urges. jahrg. 35, n.7, 1904.

QL
623
F 53

Fish, Marie Poland

Sonic fishes of the Pacific.

(Woods Hole Oceanographic Institution, Technical Rept. No. 2, 1948. Office of Naval Research, Contract N6 ori-195, T.O 1, NR-083-003. 144 pp. lithograph. 4to.)

AS
36
S5

AS
36
S

QL
1
H–M
Vol
22

FISH HAWK (SHIP)

Goode, George Brown, 1851–1896. ... Oceanic ichthyology ... 1896. (Card 2)

Series title also at head of t-p.
"Reports on the results of dredging ... in the Gulf of Mexico (1877–78), in the Caribbean Sea (1878–79) and along the Atlantic coast of the United States (1880), by the U. S. Coast survey steamer 'Blake' XXXVI."
"Published by permission of Carlile P. Patterson and W. W. Duffield, superintendents of the U. S. Coast and geodetic survey."
Issued also as Smithsonian contributions to knowledge (vol. XXX–XXXI; and U. S. National museum. Special bulletin no. 2.

1. Fishes, Pelagic. 2. Marine fauna—North Atlantic. I. Bean, Tarleton Hoffman, 1846-1916, joint author. II. U. S. National museum. III. Smithsonian institution.

Title from Univ. of Chicago   QL1f.H375   vol. 22

A 21-447

Printed by L. C.

GN
Pam
852

Fischer, Wilhelm

Einfaches und praktisches verfahren für hand und fussaudrucke auf Papier. From Correspond. Blatt. der Deut. anthrop Gesell. n.7, 1904.

AM
101
F 45 n

Fish collecting in Hawaii.

(Chicago Nat. Hist. Bull. 32(8):6-8, 1961)

QL
Crus
Pam.
#210

Fish Hawk expedition to Porto Rico. Benedict, J.E.

The Anomuran collections made by the fish hawk expedition to Porto Rico. (Extracted from U.S. Fish comm bul for 1900 vol. 2, pages 129 to 148).

Washington, 1901.

AS
162
P

Fischer-Piette, E.

Fischer, P. H.

Gasteropodes marins recueillis au Nouvelles-Hebrides par M. E. Aubert de la Rue. Par P. H. Fischer adn E. Fischer-Piette.

(Bull. Mus. Nat. Hist. Nat. Paris, Ser. 2, Tome XI, 1939, pp. 263-266)

DU
1
P 10

Fish cooked with coconut keeps for months.

(Pacific Islands Monthly, 26(2):63, 1955)

QL
631.P
E 93

FISH HAWK (ship)

Evermann, Barton Warren

General report on the investigations in Porto Rico of the United States Fish Commission steamer Fish Hawk in 1899.

(U. S. Fish Commission Bulletin for 1900: 1-350, pl. 1-52, 1900)

QL
401
K 85

Fischer-Piette, E.

Mollusques terrestres de Madagascar: Genre Trodiphora.

(Journal de Conchyliologie, 89(1):1-40,1949; 41-61; 111-146, 1949)

QL
627
U–b

FISH CULTURE

Markus, Henry C.

Propagation of bait and forage fish.

(U. S. Dept. of Commerce, Bu. of Fisheries, Fishery Circ., 28, 1939)

FISH HOOKS

See

FISHHOOKS

QL
Fish
Pam.
623

FISH   MACQUARIE ISLAND

Slack-Smith, R. J.

A small collection of fish from Macquarie Island.

(Mem. Nat. Mus., Melbourne, No. 25:13-16, 1962)

QL
1
C 78

FISH POISONING

Halstead, Bruce W.

Some general considerations of the problem of poisonous fishes and ichthyosarcotoxism.

(Copeia, 1953(1):31-33)

FISH POISONING

See also

POISONOUS FISHES

Fish Poisoning

(Plants used to poison fishes)

For articles on fishes that are poisonous
See

Poisonous fishes

QP
941
H 38

FISH POISONING

Hawaii Marine Laboratory

List on various aspects of biotoxicology (with emphasis on toxic fishes) in the files of the Hawaii Marine Laboratory. University of Hawaii. verifax. 63 pp. rec'd Oct. 1961.

GN
550
S

FISH POISONING   HAWAII

Heizer, Robert F.

Aboriginal fish poisons.

(Smithsonian Inst., Bur. Am. Ethnology, Bull. 151:225-284, 1953)

(Oceania, pp. 245-246; Hawaii, "kava as a bait poison for sharks", p. 246)

FISH POISONING

See also

POISONOUS FISH

QL
Fish Pam.
589

FISH POISONING

Randall, John E.

A review of Ciguatera, tropical fish poisoning, with a tentative explanation of its cause.

(Reprint: Bull. Mar. Sci. Gulf and Carib., 8(3):236-267, 1958)

AS
763
B-o
and
GN
Ethn.Pam
294
212

FISH POISONING   HAWAII

Stokes, John F   G.

... Fish poisoning in the Hawaiian Islands, with notes on the custom in southern Polynesia. By John F. G. Stokes. Honolulu, Hawaii, Bishop museum press, 1921.

17 p. pl. XVII-XIX on 2 l. 24 cm. (Occasional papers of the Bernice Pauahi Bishop museum of Polynesian ethnology and natural history. vol. VII, no. 10)

"Brief list of references": p. 232-233.

1. Fishing—Hawaiian Islands.   I. Title.

Library of Congress   GN670.B6 vol. VII, no. 10   22-1216
——— Copy 2.   GN423.S7
                                        [2]

FISH POISONING

See issues of The Queen's Hospital Bulletin; especially, Vol. II (1), pp. 1-3, June 1, 1925. Dr. Edmondson has a copy.

Storage
Case
3

POISONING
FISH NARCOTIZING

Stokes, J. F. G.

Notes on fish narcotizing.

DU
1
S 72 q

FISH POISONING   PACIFIC

Banner, A. H.

Fish poisoning in the tropical Pacific.

(South Pacific Bulletin, 11(4):18-21, 1961)

DU
12
B 39

FISH POISONING

Becke, Louis

Fish drugging in the Pacific
IN his

Yorke the adventurer and other stories. pp. 189-202. London, 1901.

QK
1
K 44

FISH POISONING

Tattersfield, F.

Some fish-poison plants and their insecticidal properties, by F. Tattersfield, J. T. Martin, and F. N. Howes.

(Bulletin of Miscellaneous Information, Kew, 1940, pp. 169-180.

GN
2.S
F 47

FISH POISONING   PACIFIC

Gatty, Harold

The use of fish poison plants in the Pacific

(Transactions of the Fiji Society of Science and Industry, Vol. 3(3):152-159, 1947)

[in Fiji, Samoa, Hawaii, New Caledonia, New Zealand, Cook Islands]

GC
1
M 73

FISH POISONING

Bourder, H.   and others

Poissons veneneux et ichtyosarcotoxisme. By H. Bouder, A. Cavallo and M. J. Bouder.

(Bull. Inst. Oceanographique, Monaco, No. 1240, 1962)

QL
Fishes
Pam.
436

FISH POISONING   FANNING ISLAND

Ross, S. G.

Preliminary report on fish poisoning at Fanning Island (central Pacific). Australasian Medical Publishing Co. Ltd.   Sydney,1948. 8vo.

GN
550
S

FISH POISONING   PACIFIC

Heizer, Robert F.

Aboriginal fish poisons.

(Smithsonian Inst., Bur. Am. Ethnology, Bull. 151:225-284, 1953)

(Oceania, pp. 245-246; Hawaii, "kava as a bait poison for sharks", p. 246)

QL
Fishes
Pam.
510

FISH POISONING

Halstead, Bruce W.

Ichthyotoxism, a neglected medical problem:

(Medical Arts and Sciences, Vol. 5(4):1-7, 1951)

QL
Fish
Pam.
412

FISH POISONING   FIJI

Barker, G. T.

Fish poisons and antidotes, Fiji Islands. ms. 2 pages. Received 1945

AS
540
P

FISH POISONING   PHILIPPINE ISLANDS

Quisumbing, Eduardo

Philippine plants used for arrow and fish poisons.

(Philippine Journal of Science, Vol. 77: 127-177, 1947)

GN
2.S
P 76
FISH POISONING   RAROTONGA

Buck, Peter Henry

    Fish-poisoning in Rarotonga, hora.

    (Jour. Poly. Soc., 37:57-66, 1928)

QL
Prot.-
Polysoa
Pam.
689
FISHPONDS   HAWAII

Abbott, Donald P., Jr.

    Some Polychaetous annelids from a Hawaiian fish pond.

    (Univ. of Hawaii, Research Pub. 23, 1946)

QL
Crustacea
Pam.
566
FISHPONDS   HONOLULU

MacKay, Donald C. G.

    A survey of the Decapod Crustacea of Wailupe, commercial fishpond near Honolulu, Hawaii.

    (reprint: Canadian Field Naturalist, Vol. 61:134-140, 1947)

GN
Ethn
Pam.
656
and
S Agric.
Pam.
No.11.
FISH POISONING - VIRGIN ISLANDS

Clarke, T. L. E.

    Some observations on fish poisoning in the Virgin Islands. In West Indian Bulletin, Vol. XVII, No 1, 1918. pp. 56-67

Also separate

DU
623
B9
Fish ponds - Hawaiian Ids.

Byron, Lord

    In his voyage H. M. S. Blonde 1824-25. pp. 120, illus.

GN
2.S
T
FISHPONDS   HUAHINE

Malardé, Yves

    Maeva, iles de Huahine.

    (Bull. de la Soc. des Etudes Oceaniennes, Vol. 7 (5):247-250, 1946)

GN
1
A 62
FISH POISONS

Quigley, Arroll

    Aboriginal fish poisons and the diffusion problem.

    (Am. Anthropologist, 58(3):508-525, 1956)

AS
763
H 38
FISHPONDS   HAWAII

Hiatt, Robert W.

    Biotic interaction in Hawaiian fish ponds.

    (Haw. Acad. Sci., Proc., 21st Ann. Meeting, 1945/46, p. 7)

QL
Fishes
Pam.
501
FISH PONDS   MOLOKAI

Carlson, Norman K.

    Fishponds inside the coral reef.   (Molokai)
ms.   26 pp.

GN
2.S
P 76
FISH POISONS   MANGAIA

Gold, Edwin

    Fish poisons at Mangaia.

    (The Journal of the Polynesian Society, Vol. 64(2):237-239, June, 1955)

QL
Fish.Pam.
471
a,b
FISH PONDS   HAWAII

Hiatt, Robert W.

    Food-chains and the food cycle in Hawaiian fish ponds. Part I. The food and feeding habits of mullet (Mugil cephalus), milkfish (Chanos chanos), and the ten-pounder (Elops machnata).

    (Reprint: Trans. Am. Fisheries Soc., Vol. 74:250-261, 1944 [published 1947])
...Part II. Biotic reaction. (Trans. Am. Fisheries Soc., 74:262-280, 1944)

GN
Ethn.Pam.
3681
FISH PONDS   MOLOKAI

Carlson, Norman K.

    Palaau and the saltwater fishponds of Molokai.

    (Manuscript:pp. 1-23)

AP
2
N 4
FISH PONDS

Hickling, C. F.

    Fish farming in the middle and far east.

    (Nature, Vol. 161:748-751, 1948)

GN
971.H2
K 15
FISHPONDS   HAWAII

Kamakau, Samuel Manaiakalani

    Mo'olelo Hawaii: Hawaii traditions. (copy of ms offered for publication. typed, bound under two covers.) Translated by Mary Pukui. Edited by Martha W. Beckwith. (received 1939)

AS
36
A 5
FISH PONDS   MOLOKAI

Carlson, Norman K.

    The vanishing fishponds of Molokai.

    (Natural History, 63(6):248-254, 1954)

GN
2.S
P 76
FISH PONDS   COOK ISLANDS

Gold, Edwin

    Netting and the pa at Mangaia.

    (Jour. Poly. Soc., 65(4):363-364, 1956)

DU
12
M61
Fish ponds Hawaiian Ids.

Meyen, F.J.F. (Dr.)

    in his Reise um die Erde. pp. 154 (in trans. by D. Alexander. p. 62)
(short reference only)

QL
5
B 61
FISHPONDS   PHILIPPINE ISLANDS

Frey, D. G.

    The pond fisheries of the Philippines.

    (Journal of Marine Research, Vol. 6:247-258, 1947)

QL
Fishes
Pam.
508 a,b
FISH PONDS   ECOLOGY

Hiatt, Robert W.

    Food-chains and the food cycle in Hawaiian fish ponds.- Part I. The food and feeding habits of mullet...milkfish...and the ten-pounder...; Part II. Biotic interaction.

    (Reprinted from Trans. Am. Fisheries Soc., Vol. 74:250-280, 1944)

Storage
Case
3
FISH PONDS - HAWAIIAN ISLANDS

Stokes, J. F. G.

    1 portfolio: charts of fish ponds.

DU
1
S 72q
FISH PRESERVATION

Van Pel, H.

    Simple methods of fish preservation.

    (South Pacific Commission, Quarterly Bulletin 5(1):13-14, 19, 1955)

Card 1 (Column 1, Row 1)

AS
540
P 55

FISH TRAPS

Hart, Donn V.

    Securing aquatic products in Siaton Munici-
pality, Negros Oriental Province, Philippines.

    (Philippine Islands, Nat. Inst. of Sci. and
Tech., Monograph no. 4, 1956)

Card 2 (Column 2, Row 1)

AS
719
A

FISH TRAPS. NEW SOUTH WALES

North, Alfred J.

    The birds of Coolobah and Brewarrina, North-
western New South Wales. pp. 123-129.

    (Records of the Australian Museum, XI, 1916-
1917, pp. 121-162)

Card 3 (Column 3, Row 1)

GN
1
B

Fish Weirs - Caroline Islands

Girschner, Max

    In his Karolineninseln Namoluk und Ihre
Bewohner, p. 155.

Card 4 (Column 1, Row 2)

Storage
Case
3

FISH TRAPS- HAWAIIAN ISLANDS

Stokes, J. F. G.

    Maps of fish traps.

Card 5 (Column 2, Row 2)

GN
2.S
P2

Fish - weirs

Deyrolle, E.

    In his "Engins de pêche des
Annamites et des Thos du
Tonquin." In Soc. d'Anthr. de
Paris. Bul. série, Tome II fasc. 1-2 pp. 12
-130. See p. 134.

Card 6 (Column 3, Row 2)

GN
1
Ar3
v. 13

FISH WEIRS -- NEW GUINEA

Parkinson, R.

    Ethnographie der Neu-Guinea-Küst

    See author card

Note. Reference fish weirs on p. 30.

Card 7 (Column 1, Row 3)

Storage
Case
3

FISH TRAPS

Stokes, J. F. G.

    Polynesian fish traps and ponds.

Card 8 (Column 2, Row 3)

G
3
A

Fish weirs

Foye, W. G.

    In his Lau Islands of Fiji. In Geog
Rev. IV, 1917, p 377.

Card 9 (Column 3, Row 3)

GN
2.I
A4

Fish Weirs New Guinea

Williamson, R. W.

    in his Customs of the Mekeo People
of British New Guinea. in Roy. Ant. Inst.
Journ. XLIII, pp. 286 and 287. London, 1913.

Card 10 (Column 1, Row 4)

GN
Pam. 292,
2794

FISH TRAPS HAWAII

Stokes, J. F. G.

    Walled fish traps of Pearl Harbor.

    (Bernice P. Bishop Museum, Occasional
Papers, Vol. IV, no. 3, 1908, pp. 199-212)

Card 11 (Column 2, Row 4)

AS
750
N

Fish - weirs

Mair, G. (Capt.)

    In his Notes on fish found in
the Piako river. In T. + P. New
J. Inst. XXXV 1902 p. 319.

Card 12 (Column 3, Row 4)

AS
750
N

NEW ZEALAND
Fish - weirs (eels)

Best, Elsdon

    In his Food products of
Tuhoe land In T. + P. New J.
Institute, XXXV. 1902. pp. 70-71.

Card 13 (Column 1, Row 5)

GN
Ethn.
Pam.
718

FISH - TRAPS -- India and Brazil

Hornell, James

    Marine fish-traps in South India
and Brazil. Reprinted from Man, April,
1924.

Card 14 (Column 2, Row 5)

Storage
Case
3

FISH WEIRS

Stokes, J. F. G.

    Fish weirs.

Card 15 (Column 3, Row 5)

AS
750
N

Fish weirs New Zealand

Downes, T. W.

    Notes on eels and eel-weirs. In Tran.
New Zealand Inst. L, 1917 pp 296-316. illus

Card 16 (Column 1, Row 6)

GN
Ethn. Pam.
3579

FISH TRAPS MARSHALL ISLANDS

Tinker, Spencer

    Some Marshall Islands fish traps.

    (Bernice P. Bishop Museum, Occ. Papers,
Vol. 20(7), 1950)

Card 17 (Column 2, Row 6)

GN
667.Q
N

Fish weirs - Australia

Roth, Walter E.

    In his North Queensland Ethnography,
Bulletin 3: Food, its search, capture,
and preparation, p. 23.

Card 18 (Column 3, Row 6)

DU
406
J 73

FISH WEIRS NEW ZEALAND

Johnstone, J. C.

    Maoria, a sketch of the manners and customs
of the aboriginal inhabitants of New Zealand.
London, Chapman and Hall, 1874. 8vo. 199pp.

Card 19 (Column 1, Row 7)

G
51
W 17

FISH TRAPS NEW GUINEA

Speck, O. L.

    Fish-traps.

    (Walkabout, Vol. 17(5):14-15, 1951)

    [Sepik River, New Guinea]

Card 20 (Column 2, Row 7)

AS
720.5
R

Fish Weirs (Stone) Australia

Stretton, W. G.

    In his Customs, rites, and superstitions of
aboriginal tribes of Gulf of Carpentaria.....
in Roy. Soc. of S. Australia, Trans. XVII, p. 241

Card 21 (Column 3, Row 7)

GN
2M
FI
53-6

Fish weirs. Philippine Islands.

Cole, Fay-Cooper

    in his wild tribes of Davao District,
Mindanao

3

GN
4
E

Fish weirs Santa Cruz Ilds

Graebner, F.

in his Völkerkunde der Santa Cruz
Inseln Ethnologica A. f. Mus. Cöln ec
pp. 103 + 106.

QH
104
U-B

FISHER, ALBERT KENRICK.

... The Death Valley expedition. A biological survey
of parts of California, Nevada, Arizona, and Utah. Part
II ... Washington, Govt. print. off., 1893.

402 p. front., illus. xiv pl., 5 maps. 23ᶜᵐ. (U. S. Dept. of agriculture. Division of ornithology and mammology. North American fauna
no. 7)

Pt. I not yet published (May 1910)
CONTENTS.—1. Report on birds. By A. K. Fisher.—2. Report on reptiles
and batrachians. By Leonhard Stejneger.—3. Report on fishes. By Charles
H. Gilbert.—4. Report on insects. By C. V. Riley.—5. Report on mollusks.
By R. E. C. Stearns.—6. Report on desert trees and shrubs. By C. Hart
Merriam.—7. Report on desert cactuses and yuccas. By C. Hart Mer-
riam.—8. List of localities. By T. S. Palmer.

1. Zoology—Pacific states. 2. Botany—Pacific states. I. Fisher, Albert
Kenrick. II. Stejneger,   Leonhard Hess. III. Gilbert, Charles
Henry. IV. Riley, Charles   Valentine. v. Stearns, Robert Edwards Carter. VI. Merriam,   Clinton Hart. VII. Palmer, Theodore Sherman.

Library, U. S. Dept. of   Agriculture   Agr 6-1192

Q
101
P 18

Fisher, Edna M.

The sea otter, past and present.

IN Proc. Sixth Pac. Sci. Congress, 1939,
(California), Vol. 3, 1940, pp. 223-236.

DU
12
C 78

FISH WEIRS   SOUTH AMERICA

Coppinger, R. W.

In his Cruise of the "Alert" 1878-82. ref.
to Aboriginal Stone Weirs near Cape Horn. pp.
125-6.

2 copies
1 copy 4th ed.   1885, 1899

S
21
A. 35

Fisher, A. K. (Albert Kenrick)

The economic value of predaceous
birds and mammals.

Reprint from the Yearbook Dep. of Agric. 118
Wash. 1909. 8°. pp. 187-194. DEC 3 1909

QK
Botany
Pam.
2718

Fisher, F. J. F.

Observations on the vegetation of screes in
Canterbury, New Zealand.

(Journal of Ecology, 40:156-167, 1952)

Fish weirs

see also
Canoes and Fishing

QL
696.A2
F53

Fisher, Albert Kenrick.

... The hawks and owls of the United States in their
relation to agriculture ... By A. K. Fisher ... Washington, Govt. print. off., 1893.

210 p. 26 pl. 23ᶜᵐ. (U. S. Dept. of agriculture. Division of ornithology and mammalogy. Bulletin 3)

1. Hawks. 2. Owls. 3. Birds—U. S.

Agr 6-826

Library, U. S. Dept. of   Agriculture

QL
401
J 25

Fischer, H. J. L.

Recherche de mollusques antarctiques.

(Journal de Conchyliologie, 101(2):81-8,
1961)

AP
2
N 4

Fish collection from the Leeward and Line
Islands. (George Vanderbilt Pacific Equatorial
Expedition of 1951)

(Nature, Vol. 168(4285):1027, 1951)

AS
36
S4

Fisher, Albert Kenrick

Report on birds recorded by the Pinchot
expedition of 1929 to the Caribbean and Pacific
by Albert K. Fisher and Alexander Wetmore

(Proc. U.S. Nat. Mus. vol. 79, Art. 10. 1931)

QL
671
Co

Fisher, Harvey I.

The avifauna of Niihau.

(Condor, 53:31-42, 1951)

GN
2 S
A 22

Fishberg, Maurice, 1872–

... Materials for the physical anthropology of the eastern European Jews, by Maurice Fishberg. Pub. under
the auspices of the American ethnological society of New
York. Lancaster, Pa., The New era printing company,
1905.

cover-title, 146 p. diagrs. 25ᶜᵐ. (... Memoirs of the American anthropological and ethnological societies. vol. I, pt. 1)

"Reprinted from the Annals of the New York academy of sciences,
vol. XVI, no. 6, pt. 2."
Bibliography: p. 141-146.

1. Jews in Europe. 2. Anthropometry—Jews.

6—2111

Library of Congress   GN2.A22

QE
75
W

Fisher, Cassius Asa, 1872–

... Geology and water resources of the Great Falls
region, Montana, by Cassius A. Fisher. Washington,
Govt. print. off., 1909.

89 p. VII pl. (part fold., incl. maps) 23ᶜᵐ. (U. S. Geological survey.
Water-supply paper 221)

Folded map in pocket.
"Bibliography of the more important papers relating to the water resources of the Great Falls region, Montana": p. 9-10.

1. Geology—Montana. 2. Water-supply—Montana. I. Title.

G S 9-55

Library, U. S. Geological   Survey (200) G no. 221

QL
671
A

Fisher, Harvey I.

Bibliography of Hawaiian birds since 1890.

(The Auk, Vol. 64:78-97, 1947)

and

QL Birds
Pam. 274

GN
Pam
1526

Fishberg, Maurice

Physical anthropology of the Jews: I– the
cephalic index. From Amer. Anthrop. n.s., v.4,
1902.

QE
75
A

Fisher, Cassius Asa, 1872–

... Nepesta folio, Colorado. By Cassius A. Fisher ...
Washington, D. C., U. S. Geological survey, 1906.

cover-title, 5, (1) p. illus., 3 maps, diagrs. 55 x 47ᶜᵐ. (U. S. Geological survey. Geologic atlas of the United States no. 135)

Lat. 38°-38° 30', long. 104°-104° 30'; scale 1 : 125,000; contour interval
25 ft.

1. Geology—Colorado—Pueblo Co.—Maps. 2. Geology—Colorado—
Otero Co.—Maps.

G S 7-303

Library, U. S. Geol.   survey

QL
671
A

Fisher, Harvey I.

Richardson, Frank

Birds of Moku Manu and Manana Islands off
Oahu, Hawaii. By Frank Richardson and Harvey I.
Fisher.

(The Auk, Vol. 67:285-306, 1950)

GN
Pam
1727

Fishberg, Maurice

Physical anthropology of the Jews:
II.– pigmentation. From Amer. Anthrop.
n.s., 5, 1903.

Q
101
P 18

Fisher, Edna M.

The sea otter in California.

IN Proc. Sixth Pac. Sci. Congress, 1939,
(California), Vol. 4, 1940, pp. 231-240.

(Enhydra lutris nereis)

AP
2
S 35

Fisher, Harvey I.

[Birds of Pacific islands, extinction of
those on Midway and Laysan islands] by Harvey I.
Fisher and Paul H. Baldwin.

(Science, Vol. 102, no. 2651, Supplement,
p. 14, 1945)

QH
1
P 11

Fisher, Harvey I.

The birds of Yap, Western Caroline Islands.

(Pacific Science, Vol. 4:55-62, 1950)

QH
1
P 11

Fisher, Harvey I.

The question of avian introductions in Hawaii.

(Pacific Science, Vol. 2:59-64, 1948)

G
51
W 17

Fisher, N. H

Rabaul's volcanic eruptions.

(Walkabout, Vol. 5 (5):13-22, 1939)

QL
671
Co

Fisher, Harvey I.

Black-footed albatrosses eating flying fish.

(Condor, 47:128-129, 1945)

QL
671
E 39

Fisher, Harvey I.

A recent trip to Midway Islands, Pacific Ocean. By Harvey I. Fisher and Paul H. Baldwin.

(The Elepaio, Vol. 6, No. 2, 1945, pp. 11-13)

QE
349.NG
A 93

Fisher, N. H.

Report on the volcanoes of the Territory of New Guinea.

(Geological Bulletin, Territory of New Guinea, No. 2, 1939.)

QH
1
P 11

Fisher, Harvey I.

Laysan albatross nesting on Moku Manu Islet, off Oahu, T. H.

(Pacific Science, Vol. 2:66, 1948)

QH
1
P 11

Fisher, Harvey I.

Utinomi's "Bibliographica Micronesica", chordate sections.

(Pacific Science, 1 (3):129-150, 1947)

G
51
W 17

Fisher, N. H.

Volcanic centres of New Guinea.

(Walkabout, 17(6):35-38, 40, 1951)

QL
1
C 78

Fisher, Harvey I.

Locality records of Pacific island reptiles and amphibians.

(Copeia, 1948:69)

QL
Birds
Pam.
267

Fisher, Harvey I.

War and the birds of Midway. By Harvey I. Fisher and Paul H. Baldwin.
(Paradise of the Pacific, Vol. 58, (1): 9 pp Jan. 1946)

Q
101
P 18

Fisher, N. H.

The volcanos of the Mandated Territory of New Guinea.

IN Proc. Sixth Pac. Sci. Congress, 1939, (California), Vol. 2, 1940, pp. 889-894.

QH
1
P 11

Fisher, Harvey I.

Notes on the Red-billed Leiothrix in Hawaii. By Harvey I. Fisher and Paul H. Baldwin.

(Pac. Sci. vol. 1(1):45-51, 1946)

QL
Birds
Pam. 265

Fisher, Harvey I.

War and the birds of Midway atoll. By Harvey I. Fisher and Paul H. Baldwin.

(Condor, 48:3-15, 1946)

AP
2
S 41

Fisher, Robert L.

The trenches of the Pacific. By Robert L. Fisher and Roger Revelle.

(Scientific American, Vol. 193(5):36-41, November, 1955)

QL
671
E 39

Fisher, Harvey I.

Oahu's offshore islets as bird refuges.

(The Elepaio, Vol. 6, No. 5, pp. 29-32, 1945)

QL
673
F 53

Fisher, James

Bird recognition, II:Birds of prey and water-fowl. With 85 illustrations by Fish-hawk; 82 maps compiled by W. B. Alexander and 71 charts compiled by the writer. Penguin Books. Harmondsworth, Middlesex, England. sm8vo. (1951) 182 pp.

AS
750
A 89

and
GN
Ethn.Pam
3775

Fisher, V. F.

Maori decorated sinkers.

(Records of the Auckland Institute and Museum, Vol. 1, No. 3, 1932) pp. 163-167, plate 29-30.

QH
1
P 11

Fisher, Harvey I.

Populations of birds on Midway and the man-made factors affecting them.

(Pacific Science, Vol. 3:103-110, 1949)

QL
677.5
F 53

Fisher, James

Watching birds. Pelican Books. New York. reprint of September 1941. sm 8vo. 192 pp.

AS
750
A 89

and
GN
Ethn.Pam
3776

Fisher, V. F.

The material culture of Oruarangi, Matatoki, Thames (New Zealand).
I. Bone ornaments and implements.
II. Fish-hooks.
III. Stone implements and ornaments.
IV. Musical instruments.

(Records of the Auckland Institute and Museum, Vol. 1, pp. 275-286, 287-300, Vol. 2:15-27, 111-118, 1934-1937)

AS
750
A 89

Fisher, Victor F.

Some notes on Maori agricultural and earth-working implements.

(Rec. Auckland Inst. and Mus., 1 (2):81-84, 1931)

also
GN
Ethn.Pam.
3779

QL
671
C o

Fisher, Walter Kenrick

The albatross dance at sea.

(Condor, 6:78, 1904)

QL
Prot. to
Poly.
Pam.
539

Fisher, Walter K(enrick)

The Holothurians of the Hawaiian Islands.

(Proc. U. S. Nat. Mus., Vol. XXXII, pp. 637-744, pls. 66-82, 1907.)

DU
1
P

FISHER, VICTOR F.

(Beattie, I. Hamilton)

Men on Pitcairn 14,000 years ago.

(Pacific Islands Monthly, 23(4):99-101, 1952)

[also rebuttal of this idea, by Victor F. Fisher]

GC
63
D 61

Fisher, Walter K.

Asteroidea.

IN
Discovery Committee...Reports, Vol. 20, 1940, pp. 71-306.

QL
671
Co

Fisher, Walter Kenrick

The home life of a buccaneer.

(Condor, 6:58-61, 1904)

[Fregata aquila on Laysan.]

AS
540
P

Fisher, W. S.

New coleoptera from the Philippine Islands.

(Phil. Jour. of Sci. Vol. XVIII, 1921, pp. 349-446)

&

QL
Ins.Pam.
125

QL
384.A8
F 53

Fisher, Walter Kenrick

Asteroidea of the North Pacific and Adjacent Waters. Part 1: Phanerozonia and Spinulosa.

(Bull. U. S. Nat. Mus., 76, 1911, Part I)

AS
36
S4

Fisher, W. K. (Walter Kenrick)

Hyalinothrix, a new genus of starfishes from the Hawaiian Ids. in Proc. of U.S. Nat. Mus. 39, 1911, pp. 659-663.

AND
QL
Prot.
& Poly.
143

QL
461
H-1

Fisher, W. S.

A new species of Trixagus from the Hawaiian Islands. (Col.:Trixagidae)

(Proc. Haw. Ent. Soc., Vol. 11, 1942, pp. 165-166)

QL
627
U-b

Fisher, Walter K(enrick)

Birds of Laysan and the Leeward Islands, Hawaiian Group. 39 pp.

QL
Bird Pam
124

(Bulletin of the United States Fish Commission, Vol. 23, 1903, Part III, 1906, pp. 767-807)

AS
36
S 4

Fisher, Walter Kenrick

Hydrocorals of the North Pacific Ocean.

(Proc. of the U. S. Nat. Mus., Vol. 84, 1938, pp. 493-554, pl. 34-76)

QL
Insects
Pam
1390

Fisher, W. S.

A revision of the North American species of beetles belonging to the family Bostrichidae.

(U. S. Department of Agric., Misc. Publ. No. 698, 1950)

AS
36
S 4

Fisher, Walter Kenrick

Echiuroid worms of the north Pacific ocean.

(Proc. U. S. Nat. Mus., Vol. 96:215-292, 1946)

AS
36.
S2

Fisher, Walter Kenrick, 1878–

Necessary changes in the nomenclature of starfishes, by Walter K. Fisher.

(In Smithsonian institution. Smithsonian miscellaneous collections. Washington, 1910. 24½ᶜᵐ. vol. LII (Quarterly issue, vol. V) p. 87-93)

Publication 1799.
Originally published May 27, 1908.

Asteroidea
1. Starfishes.

Library of Congress   Q11.S7 vol. 52   16-12705
—— Copy 2.

QL
Insects
Pam
1168

Fisher, W. S.

A revision of the North American species of Buprestid beetles belonging to the tribe Chrysobothrini.

(United States Department of Agric., Misc. Pub. 470, 1942)

AS
36
S4

Fisher, Walter Kenrick, 1878–

... Four new genera and fifty-eight new species of starfishes from the Philippine Islands, Celebes, and the Moluccas. By Walter K. Fisher ...

(In U. S. National museum. Proceedings. Washington, 1913. 23½ᶜᵐ. v. 43, p. 599-648)

"Scientific results of the Philippine cruise of the fisheries steamer 'Albatross,' 1907-1910.—no. 23."

Asteroidea
1. Starfishes. 2. Echinodermata — Philippine Islands. 3. Echinodermata—Dutch East Indies. 4. Albatross (Steamer)

13—13128

Library of Congress   Q11.U55 vol. 43

QH
Nat
Hist
Pam
#16

Fisher, Walter K(enrick)

New east Indian starfishes, ex Biol. Soc. of Washington Proc., vol. XXIX, Feb. 24, 1916.

AS
36
S 4

Fisher, Walter Kenrick

Additions to the Echiuroid fauna of the North Pacific Ocean.

(Proc. U. S. Nat. Mus., Vol. 99, No. 3248, 1949)

QL
1
H-1

Fisher, Walter K(enrick)

The Genus Blakiaster Perrier

Bull. Mus. of Comp. Zool. LIV, No. 4, 1911, pp. 161-165. Pl. 2.

QH
1
P 11

Fisher, Walter K.

A new Echiuroid worm from the Hawaiian Islands and a key to the genera of Echiuridae.

(Pacific Science, Vol. 2:274-277, 1948)

AS
36
S4

and
QL
Proto.
to
Poly.
Pam.
161

Fisher, Walter Kenrick, 1878–

... New genera of starfishes from the Philippine Islands. By Walter K. Fisher ...

(*In* U. S. National museum. Proceedings. Washington, 1911. 23½ᶜᵐ. v. 40, p. 415–427)

"Scientific results of the Philippine cruise of the fisheries steamer 'Albatross,' 1907–10—no. 10."

Asteroidea – Phil. Is
1. Starfishes. 2. Echinodermata — Philippine Islands. 3. Albatross (Steamer)

11–31526

Library of Congress   Q11.U55 vol. 40

QL
Protozoa
to
Polyzoa
Pam
224

Fisher, Walter K(enrick)

New starfishes from the Pacific coast of North America. From Proc. Washington Academy of Sciences, v. 8, 1906.

QL
627
U–b

QL
Protozoa
to
Polyzoa
Pam
222

Fisher, Walter K(enrick)

Starfishes of the Hawaiian Islands. in U.S. Fish Com Bull. XXIII Part III, pp. 987–1130, 49 pls.

separate

QL
Protozoa
to
Poly.
Pam.
180

Fisher, Walter K(enrick)

A new genus and subgenus of East-India sea-stars. From Ann. Mag. Nat. Hist. Ser. 8, Vol. 20, 1917.

AS
36
S4

Fisher, Walter Kenrick, 1878–

... New starfishes from the Philippine Islands, Celebes, and the Moluccas. By Walter K. Fisher ...

(*In* U. S. National museum. Proceedings. Washington, 1914. 23½ᶜᵐ. v. 46, p. 201–224)

"Scientific results of the Philippine cruise of the fisheries steamer 'Albatross,' 1907–1910.—no. 30."

Asteroidea
1. Starfishes. 2. Echinodermata—Philippine Islands. 3. Echinodermata—Dutch East Indies. 4. Albatross (Steamer)

14–10979

Library of Congress   Q11.U55 vol. 46

AS
36
S5

Fisher, Walter Kenrick, 1878–

... Starfishes of the Philippine seas and adjacent waters, by Walter K. Fisher ... Washington, Govt. print. off., 1919.

xi, 712 p. 156 pl. 24½ᶜᵐ. (Smithsonian institution. United States National museum. Bulletin 100, v. 3)
At head of title: ... Contributions to the biology of the Philippine Archipelago and adjacent regions.
On verso of t.-p.: Bulletin of the United States National museum.
Plates printed on both sides.
Bibliography: p. 541–546.
Report based upon a collection made by the United States Fisheries steamer Albatross, 1907–1910, in the region of the Philippine Islands, Celebes and Molucca Islands.

Asteroidea 1. Starfishes. 2. Echinodermata — Philippine Islands. 3. Echinodermata—Dutch East Indies.

Library of Congress   Q11.U6 no. 100 vol. 3 19–26691
——— Copy 2.   QL384.A8F7
(8)

AS
36
S4

QL
Bird
Pam
168
77

Fisher, Walter K(enrick)

A new Procelsterna from the Leeward islands, of the Hawaiian group. In U. S. Nat. Mus. Proc. Vol. 26. pp. 559–563. Washington, 1903.

separate

QL
Poly-Prot.
Pam
154
406
606

Fisher, Walter Kenrick

Notes on Asteroidea, I–III.

(Annals and Mag. Nat. Hist., Ser. 8, vol. 20, 1917; pp. 166–172, Ser. 9, vol. 2, pp. 103–111, 1918; Ser. 9, vol. 10, 1922, pp. 590–598)

QL
671
Co

Fisher, Walter Kenrick

Three boobies interviewed.

(Condor, 6:58–61, 1904)

[nesting and feeding of young]

QL
Protozoa
to
Polyzoa
Pam
424

Fisher, Walter K(enrick)

A new species of Echinaster, with a note on the name Othilia. (Sonderabdruck aus dem Zool. Anzeiger. Bd. 42. Nr.5, vom 4, 1913.)

QL
671
A

Fisher, Walter Kenrick

Notes on the birds peculiar to Laysan Island Hawaiian Group.

(Auk, 20:384–397, pl. 12–16, 1903)

AS
36
S4

Fisher, Walter Kenrick, 1878–

Trophodiscus, a new sea star from Kamchatka. By Walter K. Fisher ...

(*In* U. S. National museum. Proceedings. Washington, 1917. 23½ᶜᵐ. v. 52, p. 367–371. pl. 28–30)

1. Trophodiscus.

18–15655

Library of Congress   Q11.U55 vol. 52

QL
Protozoa
to
Poly.
Pam.
156

Fisher, W. K. (Walter Kenrick)

A new starfish from Hongkong. From Ann. Mag. Nat. Hist. Ser.9, Vol.X, 1922, pp 415–418, 1 pl.

QL
671
A

Fisher, Walter Kenrick

On the habits of the Laysan albatross.

(Auk, 21:8–20, pl. 2–7, 1904)

QE
75
B

FISHER, WALTER LOWRIE.

Veatch, Arthur Clifford, 1878–

... Mining laws of Australia and New Zealand, by Arthur C. Veatch, with a preface by Walter L. Fisher, secretary of the interior. Washington, Govt. print. off., 1911.

180 p. 23ᶜᵐ. (U. S. Geological survey. Bulletin 505)

1. Mining law—Australia. 2. Mining law—New Zealand. 1. Fisher, Walter Lowrie, 1861–

Library, U. S. Geol.   survey (200) E no. 505   G S 11–616
——— Copy 2.

QL
Prot.
to
Poly.
Pam
234

Fisher, W(alter) K(enrick)

New starfishes from the North Pacific. I. Phanerozonia. From Zool. Anzeiger, v.35, n.18, 1910.

QL
Protozoa
to
Polyzoa
Pam
157

Fisher, W. K. (Walter Kenrick)

A remarkable new sea star from Japan. From Proc. U. S. Nat. Mus. Vol.64, Art 3, 1924.

AS
36
S 4

Fisher, W. S.

Notes on the Rhinotragine beetles of the family Cerambycidae, with descriptions of new species. From Proc. U. S. Nat. Mus. vol. 77, art. 19, pp. 1–20.

QL
Protozoa
to
Polyzoa
Pam
310

Fisher, W(alter) K(enrick)

New starfishes from the North Pacific – II. Spinulosa. From Zool. Anzeiger, v.35, n.18, 1910.

QL
138
E 24

AS
763
B–b

Reading
Room

Fisher, Walter K(enrick)

Sea stars (Pacific)

Edmondson, C. H.   and others

Marine zoology of tropical central Pacific... pp. 63–88.

(Bernice P. Bishop Museum, Bulletin No. 27, 1925; Tanager Expedition Publication No. 1)

AS
36
S4

Fisher, Warren S.

Buprestid beetles collected by the Mulford Biological Exploration in Bolivia. U. S. Nat. Mus. Proc. Vol. 66, Art. 31, pp 1–46.

AS
36
S4 Fisher, Warren Samuel, 1878–
Five new species of ptinid beetles. By W. S. Fisher ...
(*In* U. S. National museum. Proceedings. Washington, 1920. 23½ᶜᵐ.
v. 55, p. 295–299)

\ 1. Ptinidae.

Library of Congress ⌒ Q11.U55 vol. 55
⁽⁵⁾
20–5862

QE
Pam
#208 Fisher, Willard J.
Low-sun phenomena in Luson III. Marine sunsets and the duration of sunset on Manila Bay and the China sea, ex Philippine Journ. of Sc., vol. 17, no. 6, December, 1920.

AP
2
N 4 FISHERIES
Gross, F.
Food production by fish and oyster farming.
(Nature, Vol. 148, 1941, pp. 71–74)

DU
620
P Fisher, William E.
Robert Louis Stevenson in Hawaii.
(Paradise of the Pacific, Vol. 47(3):7–12, 1935)

QE
Pam
#207 Fisher, Willard J.
Low sun phenomena–IV. The "green flash"., ex Popular Astron., vol. XXIX, nos. 5 and 7, May and Aug.–Sept. 1921.

QL
752
U 58 FISHERIES
Nakamura, Hiroshi
Tuna longline fishery and fishing grounds.
(U.S. Dept. of the Interior, Special Scientific Rept.: Fisheries No. 112, 1954)

Storage
Case
5

Ms Sa 2 Fisher, William E.
Samoan ethnological notes:– songs, proverbs, vital statistics. (received 1934)

DU
1
S 72 q Fisheries investigations in Netherlands New Guinea.
(South Pacific Commission, Quarterly Bulletin Vol. 4(4):6, 1954)

QL
752
U 58 FISHERIES
Scattergood, Leslie W.
English translations of fishery literature.
(Special Sci. Rept., Fisheries, No. 35, 1951, Fish and Wildlife Service, U.S.)
[continuation of work of Wilbert McLeod in "Translations of fisheries literature from foreign languages into English, I–II] QL Fishes Pams. 502,503

Storage
Case
5

Ms To 2 Fisher, William E.
Tongan notes: history, burial, legends, marriage, cooking, omens, medicine.

QL
705
B 54 FISHERIES
Bertram, James G.
The harvest of the sea; a contribution to the natural and economic history of the British food fishes. With fifty illustrations. London. 1865. 8vo. xv + 519 pp.

QL
Fish
Pam.
542 FISHERIES
Schaefer, Milner B.
Fisheries dynamics and the concept of maximum equilibrium catch.
(Reprinted from Proc. of the Gulf and Caribbean Fisheries Inst., Sixth Annual Session, Sept., pp. 1–11, 1954)

Storage
Case
5

Ms To 1 Fisher, William E.
Tongan tales and notes, collected by William E. Fisher, 1934.

QL
Fishes
Pam.
465 FISHERIES
Blackburn, M.
Fishery management and changes in abundance of fish.
(Australian Journal of Science, Vol. 12(1): 14–17, 1949)

QH
705
S 59 FISHERIES
Simmonds, P. L.
The commercial products of the sea; or marine contributions to food, industry, and art. New and cheaper edition. With thirty-two illustrations. E. P. Dutton and Co., New York. 8vo. viii + 484 pp.

QE
Pam
#210 Fisher, Willard J.
Low-sun phenomena in Luzon, ex Philippine Journ. of Sc., vol. 16, no. 2, Feb., 1920.

QL
Fishes
Pam.
502
503 FISHERIES
Chapman, Wilbert McLeod
Translations of fisheries literature from foreign languages unto English, I–II. Issued by the Department of Fisheries, State of Washington, Biological Research Division, 1940. mimeographed.
[This is data as to what has been translated and how it may be acquired or consulted]

OVER

Q
Gen. Sc.
Pam. No
47
and
QL
Fish
Pam.
131 FISHERIES
Smith, Hugh M.
The United States Bureau of Fisheries and its relation to the United States Coast and Geodetic Survey. Reprint from Centennial Celebration of the U. S. Coast & Geod. Survey , April 5–6, 1916.

QE
Pam
#209 Fisher, Willard J.
Low-sun phenomena in Luzon II. Zenith observations of dawn, Baguio, 1920, ex Philippine Journ., vol. 17, no. 5, November, 1920.

QL
615
G 78 FISHERIES
Great Britain. Colonial Office
Fishery Publications
Vol. 1 +   1950 +

QL
121
T 65 FISHERIES
Tomasevich, Jozo
International agreements on conservation of marine resources. Food Research Institute. Stanford University. R8vo. 1943c. xi + 297 pp.

AS
36
S5

FISHERIES

U. S. National museum.

... Catalogue of the collection to illustrate the animal resources and the fisheries of the United States, exhibited at Philadelphia in 1876 by the Smithsonian institution and the United States Fish commission, and forming a part of the United States National museum. Prepared under the direction of G. Brown Goode. Washington, Govt. print. off., 1879.

AS
36
S2

xvi, 351 p. 24ᶜᵐ. (*Added t.-p.:* Bulletin of the United States National museum. no. 14)

(Continued on next card)

[s21e1]   S 13-123

AS
36
S5

FISHERIES

U. S. National museum.   ... Catalogue ... 1879.
(Card 2)

AS
36
S2

At head of title: International exhibition 1876.
Issued also as vol. XXIII, art. 4 of the Smithsonian miscellaneous collections.
Smithsonian institution publication 326.
Part II. "Catalogue of illustrations of the economical invertebrates of the American coast. By W. H. Dall."

1. Zoology—North America. 2. Animal products. 3. Fisheries. 4. Philadelphia. Centennial exhibition, 1876. I. Goode, George Brown, 1851-1896. II. Dall, William Healey, 1845— III. U. S. Bureau of fisheries. IV. Smithsonian institution.

Library, Smithsonian   Institution Q11.U6
[s21e1]   S 13-123

QL
625
W

FISHERIES

Washington. University of Washington

Publications in Fisheries

Vol. I, 1925 -

G
113
W 95

FISHERIES

Woytinsky, W. S.

World population and production; trends and outlook. By W. S. and E. S. Woytinkky. The Twentieth Century Fund. New York. 1953. R8vo. lxxii + 1268 pp.

QL
Fish
Pam.
548

FISHERIES   ABUNDANCE OF YIELD

Tester, Albert L.

Theoretical yields at various rates of natural and fishing mortality in stabilized fisheries.

(Reprinted from Transactions of the American Fisheries Society, Vol. 82:115-122, 1952)

AP
2
S 35

FISHERIES   ATOMIC RADIATION

Oceanography, fisheries, and atomic radiation. Committee on the effects of atomic radiation on oceanography and fisheries.

(Science, Vol. 124(3210):13-16, July, 1956)

[...summary report of the Committee on the Effects of Atomic Radiation on Oceanography and Fisheries...will be published in monograph form by the NAS]

Z
5971
C 46

FISHERIES   BIBLIOGRAPHY

Chapman, Wilbert McLeod

Translations of fisheries literature from foreign languages, I- II.   1940

(notes of where the translations may be found)

QL
627
U- a

FISHERIES - BIBLIOGRAPHY

Macdonald, Rose M. E.

An analytical subject bibliography of the publications of the Bureau of Fisheries, 1871- 1920. Bur. of Fish. Doc. 899. U.S.Fish.Rept.1920, App. V.

Washington, 1921.

AS
36
S5

FISHERIES - EXHIBITIONS

U. S. Commissioner to the International fisheries exhibition, London, 1883.   ... Descriptive catalogues ... 1884. (Card 2)

CONTENTS.—A. Preliminary catalogue and synopsis of the collections exhibited by the United States Fish commission and by special exhibitors. 1883.—B. Collection of economic crustaceans, worms, echinoderms, and sponges. By Richard Rathbun. 1883.—C. Catalogue of the aquatic and fish-eating birds exhibited by the United States National museum. By Robert Ridgway. 1883.—D. Catalogue of the economic *Mollusca* and the apparatus and appliances used in their capture and preparation for market, exhibited by the United States National museum. By Lieut. Francis Winslow. 1883.—E. The whale fishery and its appliances. By James Temple Brown. 1883.—F. Catalogue of the collections of fishes exhibited by the United States National museum. By Tarleton H. Bean. 1883.—G. De-

(Continued on next card)

Card 1 is missing   S 13-132

QH
Nat.Hist.
Pam.
199

FISHERIES MARINE

Schaefer, Milner B.

Marine fisheries.

reprint from McGraw-Hill Encyclopedia of Science and Technology, p. 113, 1960.

QL
Fishes
Pam.454

FISHERIES SALMON

Brett, J. R.

The design and operation of a trap for the capture of migrating young sockeye salmon.

(Reprint-Trans. Am. Fisheries Soc., vol. 75 pp. 97-104, 1945)

G
51
W 17

FISHERIES SHARKS

Rayment, Tarlton

Vitamins from the sea.

(Walkabout, Vol. 10 (1):5-9,1943)

QL
371
Mo

and

QL
627
U -b

FISHERIES - Sponges

Moore, H. F.

The commercial sponges and the sponge fisheries. Ex Bur. Fish. Bul. XXVIII,1908. Washington, 1910.

QL
737.C4
J 52

FISHERIES - WHALES

Jenkins, J. T.

A history of the whale fisheries from the Basque fisheries of the tenth century to the hunting of the finner whale at the present date, with reproductions from photographs and old engravings.

London, Witherby, 1921.   pp. 335.

QL
638.S2
U

Fisheries—Alaska

U. S. Treasury dept. Special agents division.   Seal and salmon fisheries and general resources of Alaska ... 1898. (4 vols. Vols. 1-2 only.)

CONTENTS—Continued.
ports by W. G. Morris, I. Petroff, C. H. Townsend, F. W. True, J. J. Brice and L. Stejneger on internal resources of Alaska and the fur-seal fisheries of the North Pacific Ocean, with comments on the reports of Townsend, True, and Brice by D. S. Jordan.

I. Alaska—Econ. condit. 2. Bering Sea controversy. 3. Sealing. 4. Fisheries—Alaska. I. Jordan, David Starr, 1851— II. Elliott, Henry Wood, 1846— III. Maynard, Washburn, 1844— IV. Jackson, Sheldon, 1834— V. Morris, William Gouverneur. VI. Petrov, Ivan. VII. Townsend, Charles Haskins, 1859— VIII. True, Frederick William, 1858-1914. IX. Brice, John J. X. Stejneger, Leonhard Hess, 1851—

Library of Congress   SH361.U518
—— Another issue.   SH361.U52
Without document series   note (Bureau edition)
[a19b1]   1-15694

QL
638.S2
U

Fisheries—Alaska

U. S. Treasury dept. Special agents division.

Seal and salmon fisheries and general resources of Alaska ... Washington, Govt. print. off., 1898. 4 v. illus., plates (part col., part fold.) ports., maps (part fold.) charts. 23½ᶜᵐ. (55th Cong., 1st sess. House. Doc. no. 92, pt. 1-4)

CONTENTS.—v. 1. Reports on condition of seal life on the Pribilof Islands by special Treasury agents ... 1868 to 1895 ... by D. S. Jordan.—v. 2. Reports on seal and salmon fisheries ... and correspondence between the State and Treasury departments on the Bering Sea question ... 1895 to 1896, with comments on that portion thereof which relates to pelagic sealing by D. S. Jordan.—v. 3. Reports by H. W. Elliott and Leon W. Maynard, U. S. N., on the fur-seal fisheries, etc., of the Pribilof Islands, and by Rev. S. Jackson on "Reindeer in Alaska" and "Education in Alaska," with comments on Elliott's and Maynard's reports by D. S. Jordan.—v. 4. Re-

(Continued on next card)

[a19b2]   1-15694

QL
638.S2
U

FISHERIES—ALASKA

Jordan, David Starr

Comments on 'Seal and Salmon Fisheries and general resources of Alaska' 4 vols. & Murray Joseph.

G.14.21.
22.
Note. Library   have only Vols I + II.

QL
Fish Pam.
580

FISHERIES AMERICA

Stern, J.A.

Influence of technological advancements on utilization of fisheries in the future.

(Reprint: Trans. Amer. Fisheries Soc., vol. 87, 1957:293-298)

QL
632.A
B 92

FISHERIES ARGENTINA

Primer Congreso Nacional de Pesquerias Maritimas e Industrias Derivadas. Mar del Plata, 24-29 Octubre 1949. Tomo I: Recomendaciones; Tomo II: Trabajos presentados. Buenos Aires. 1950. R8vo.

QL
634.In
F 81

FISHERIES ASIA

Indo-Pacific Fisheries Council

Directory of Fisheries Institutions (Asia and the Far East). Edited by IPFC Secretariat, Regional Office for Asia and the Far East. Food and Agriculture Organization of the United Nations. Bangkok, Thailand. 4to. 1957.

QL
618
I 41

FISHERIES ASIA

Indo-Pacific Fisheries Council

Directory of Fisheries Institutions (Asia and the Far East). Edited by IPFC Secretariat, Regional Office for Asia and the Far East, Food and Agriculture Organization of the United Nations. Bangkok, Thailand. 4to. (1957) 4to 81 pp. unnumbered.

QL
461
I 61

FISHERIES   ATLANTIC

International Commission for the Northwest
Atlantic Fisheries.

Annual Proceedings

Vol. 6, 1955/56

Halifax, 1956.   4to

QL
1
A 93 p

FISHERIES   AUSTRALIA

Roughley, T. C.

The fisheries of Australia.

(Proc. R. Zool. Soc. New South Wales,
1934-35, pp. 9-20)

QL
Fish
Pam.
413

FISHERIES   CALIFORNIA

Van Cleave, Richard

Program of the Bureau of Marine Fisheries.

(California Fish and Game, Vol. 31 (3):81-
138)

QL
Fishes
Pam.
417

FISHERIES   ATLANTIC COAST

Carson, Rachel L.

Fish and shelfish of the middle Atlantic
coast.

(Conservation Bull. 38,1945, U. S. Dept.
of the Interior)

QL
Fishes
Pam. 425

FISHERIES   AUSTRALIA

Serventy, D. L.

A report on commercial tuna trolling tests
in south-eastern Australia.

(Reprint, Journal of the Council for Scientific and Industrial Research, Vol. 20(1):1-16,
1947)

QL
Fisheries
Pam.
475

FISHERIES   CANADA

Manchester, Lorne

Science in fisheries. Reprinted from the
Canadian Geographical Journal, n. d.   23 pp.
rec'd March 1951.

QL
636
A 93

FISHERIES   AUSTRALIA

Australia. Department of Trade and Customs.

Fisheries: Biological Results of the Fishing
Experiments carriend on by the F.I.S. "Endeavour"
1909-1914. Vols. 1-   1911   Sydney, Minister
for Trade and Customs, 1911-   8vo.

G
51
A 93

FISHERIES   AUSTRALIA

Stead, David G.

Development of Northern Australia; with
special reference to Australia's tropical fisheries.

(The Australian Geographer, Vol. 1, 1929,
pp. 3-25)   No. 2

QL
752
U 58

FISHERIES   CAROLINE ISLANDS

Ikebe, Kenzo   and others

Exploratory tuna fishing in the Caroline
Islands. Translation by W. G. Van Campen. (4
articles)

(U. S. Fish and Wildlife Service, Special
Scientific Report: Fisheries No. 46, 1951; original date 1937)

QL
1
A 93

FISHERIES   AUSTRALIA

Dakin, William John

Migrations and productivity in the sea. A
study of the factors controlling marine organisms
with some reference to New South Wales fishing
problems.

(The Australian Zoologist, 7:15-33, 1931)

QL
Fishes Pam.
424

FISHERIES   BRITISH COLUMBIA

Neave, Ferris

Biological investigations of commercial
shell-fish.

(Report of the British Columbia Fisheries
Department, 1944:pp. M64-67)

QL
752
U 58

FISHERIES   CAROLINE ISLANDS

U. S. Fish and Wildlife Service
Special Scientific Reports

G
51
W 17

FISHERIES   AUSTRALIA

Roughley, T. C.

Australian fisheries; what of the future?

(Walkabout, Vol. 16(8):10-15, 1950)

QL
Mollusca
Pam.
850

FISHERIES   BRITISH COLUMBIA

Neave, Ferris

Conditions of the butter-clam fishery in
British Columbia.

(British Columbia Fisheries Department,
Report, 1945: pp. N 67-N 74)

QL
617
C 42

FISHERIES   CEYLON

Ceylon fisheries; recommendations of
experts on fisheries development, research,
socio-economic and industrial problems. Ceylon
Sessional Papers VI.-1951. Colombo. Government
Press. April 1951. 170 pp.   8vo.

QL
636
R 85

FISHERIES   AUSTRALIA

Roughley, T. C.

Fish and fisheries of Australia. With 60
colour plates and 21 plates in black and white.
Angus and Robertson. Sydney; London. R8vo.
Revised and enlarged edition, 1951. xv + 343 pp.

QL
628
C 15 i

FISHERIES   CALIFORNIA

California. State
     Department of Fish and Game
     Marine Research Committee

California Cooperative Oceanic Fisheries
Investigations

     Reports
         Vol. 8-   Jan. 1961-

Sacramento   4to.

QH
183
H 54

FISHERIES   CEYLON

Herdman, William Abbott

Report to the government of Ceylon on the
pearl oyster fisheries of the gulf of Manaar:
with supplementary reports upon the marine biology
of Ceylon by other naturalists.

London, Royal Society., 1903-1906.   5 vol.

QL
636
R 85

FISHERIES-AUSTRALIA

Roughley, Theodore Cleveland, 1889-

... Fishes of Australia and their technology. By T. C.
Roughley ... Pub. by the authority of the government of
New South Wales. Sydney, W. A. Gullick, government
printer, 1916.

xvi, 296 p., 1 l. col. front., illus. (incl. maps) 70 col. pl. 25 cm. (Technical education series. no. 21. Technological museum, Sydney)

Pages 274 and 276, full-page illustrations accompanied by guard sheets
with outline drawings.

1. Fishes—Australia. 2. Fisheries—Australia.

A 17-1382 Revised

Title from Leland Stanford, Jr., Univ. Printed by L. C.
[r19c2]

QL
628
Ca

FISHERIES--CALIFORNIA

See also

California State Fisheries Laboratory

Q
125.NI
H 77

FISHERIES   DUTCH EAST INDIES

Herre, Albert W. C. T.

Research on fish and fisheries in the Indo-
Australian Archipelago.

Honig, Pieter   editor
     Science and scientists in the Netherlands
Indies. pp. 167-175. New York, 1945.

QL Fishes Pam. 395	FISHERIES FIJI Hornell, James Report on the fisheries of Fiji. Suva, 1940. vi + 87 pp. 8vo. Government Printer.

QL
627
U-a
 	
QL
Fish Pam.
282
	~~Fisheries - Hawaiian Islands.~~
	Cobb, John N.
	
	    Commercial fisheries of the Hawaiian
	Islands in 1903. In U. S. Bureau of Fish-
	eries report 1904. pp. 435 - 512.
	
	    See also Report 1901 (1902), pp. 442-451
	(2 copies)

DU Fish.Pam. 364	FISHERIES HAWAII Norwood, William Harvest of the sea- the story of Oahu's fishermen. (Honolulu Star-Bulletin, Dec. 18, 1937)

DU
1
U 58 g
	FISHERIES FORMOSA
	
	U. S. Navy
	    Office of the Chief of Naval Operations
	    Civil Affairs Guide, OPNAV
	    13-32: The fishing industry in Taiwan
	(Formosa). 1 Nov.1944.

GC
1
S 431
	FISHERIES HAWAII
	
	Cobb, John N.
	
	    Scientific problems of the fisheries of the
	north Pacific.
	
	    (Bull. Scripps Inst. for Biol. Research, 9,
	1919: 35-50)
	
	    pp. 47-48: Hawaiian fishery problems.

QL
627
U b
	FISHERIES HAWAII
	
	Shippen, Herbert H.
	
	    Distribution and abundance of skipjack in
	the Hawaiian fishery, 1952-53.
	
	    (U. S. Dept. Interior, Fishery Bull. 188
	of the Fish and Wildlife Service, 1961)

DU 1 S 72	FISHERIES FRENCH OCEANIA van Pel, H. The fisheries industry of French Polynesia. By H. vna Pel and L. C. Devanbez. South Pacific Commission. 1957. folio. mimeogr. 29 pp.

QL
Fishes
Pam.458
	FISHERIES HAWAII
	
	Eckles, Howard H.
	
	    Fishery exploration in the Hawaiian Islands.
	(August to October 1948, by the vessel <u>Oregon</u>
	of the Pacific Exploration Company)
	
	    (U. S. D. Int., Fish and Wildlife Service,
	Sep. No. 251. V ol. 11, No. 6, 1949)
	(Commercial Fisheries Review, June 1949:1-9)

QL
627
U-b
	FISHERIES HAWAII
	
	Yamashita, Daniel T.
	
	    Analysis of catch statistics of the Hawaiian
	skipjack fishery.
	
	    (U. S.Fish and Wildlife Service, Fishery
	Bull. 134, 1958)

GN Ethn.Pam. 305	FISHERIES HAWAII Beckley, Emma Metcalf (Mrs.) Hawaiian fisheries and methods of fishing with an account of the fishing implements used by the natives of the Hawaiian islands. Adver- tiser Steam Print. Honolulu, 1883. 21 pp.

DU
620
P
	FISHERIES HAWAII
	
	    Home fisheries. (Honolulu)
	
	    (Paradise of the Pacific, Vol. 20 (no. 9)
	pp. 16-17, 1907)

QL 634 H 77	FISHERIES HONG KONG Hong Kong Fisheries Research Station Journal Vol. 1, 1940 -

QL
627
U-I
 	
and
QL
Fish
Pam.380,
381
	FISHERIES HAWAII
	
	Bell, Frank T.
	
	    A plan for the development of the Hawaiian
	fisheries, by Frank T. Bell and Elmer Higgins.
	
	    (U.S.Dept. of Commerce, Bureau of Fisheries,
	Investigation Report No.42, 1938, pp. 1-25)

QL
Fishes
Pam.
600
	FISHERIES HAWAII
	
	    Honolulu Biological Laboratory, Hawaii
	Area.
	
	    (U. S. Bureau of Commercial Fisheries,
	Fish and Wildlife Circular 83, 1960)

QL
634.1
Ma
	FISHERIES - INDIA
	
	Madras , Fisheries Department
	    Bulletin
	
	    See serial file.

AS
763
H-38
	FISHERIES HAWAII
	
	Brock, Vernon E.
	
	    Marine and fresh-water resources.
	
	    (Proceedings of the Hawaiian Academy of
	Science, Twenty-eight Annual Meeting, pp. 2-3,
	1953)

QL 627 U-a	~~Fisheries - Hawaiian Islands.~~ Jordan, David Starr Preliminary report on an investigation of the fishes and fisheries of the Haw. Ilds. In U. S. Fish. Com. Report 1901. pp. 355- 380.

QL 634.In F 81	FISHERIES INDOCHINA Service de la pêche et de la chasse en Indo- chine. Communications presentées aux 1re et 2e sessions du Conseil Indo-Pacifique des Pêches Singapore 1949-Cronulla 1950. Haut Commissariat de France pour l'Indochine. 1950. Phnom-Penh. 115 pp.

QL
627
U -b
 	
and
QL
Fish Pam.
119
120
	~~Fisheries - Hawaiian Islands.~~
	Cobb, John N.
	
	    Commerical fisheries of the Hawaiian
	Islands. In U. S. Fish Com. Rep. 1901.
	pp. 383- 499. illus.
	
	    (Reprint in Bull. U. S. Fish Com., vol. 23,
	pp. 717-765, 1903)

QL
Fishes
Pam.
461
	FISHERIES HAWAII
	
	June, Fred C.
	
	    Preliminary fisheries survey of the Hawa-
	iian-Line Islands area. Part 1: The Hawaiian
	long-line fishery.
	
	    (Commercial Fisheries Review, Vol. 12(1):
	1-23, 1950)

QL 618 I 41	FISHERIES INDONESIA Indo-Pacific Fisheries Council Directory of Fisheries Institutions (Asia and the Far East). Edited by IFFC Secretariat, Regional Office for Asia and the Far East, Food and Agriculture Organization of the United States. Bangkok, Thailand. 4to. (1957) 4to 81 pp. unnumbered.

QL
752
U 58

FISHERIES INDONESIA

Shimada, B, M. (editor)

Exploratory tuna fishing in Indonesian waters. Trans. by SCAP translators and W. G. Van Campen. Edited by B. M. Shimada and W. G. Van Campen.

(U. S. Fish and Wildlife Service; Fsiheries No. 45, 1951. original dates 1941-42)

QL
Fishes
Pam.457

FISHERIES JAPAN

Croker, Richard S.

Glossary of Japanese fisheries terms.

(General Headquarters, Supreme Commander for the Allied Powers, Natural Resources Section Report No. 65, Tokyo, 1946)

G
3
A 1

FISHERIES JAPAN

Espenshade, Ada

A program for Japanexe fisheries.

(Geogr. Review, Vol. 39(1):76-85, 1949)

QL
627
P 11

FISHERIES JAPAN

Imamura, Yutala

The skipjack fishery.

(Suisan Koza [the text of the fishery], Vol. 6, The fishing section, pp. 17-94; published by Nippon Suisan Kai [Japan Fisheries Ass'n], Tokyo, March 5, 1949)

Pacific Oceanic Fishery Investigations, Translation No.   32 by W. G. van Campen.

QL
Fishes
Pam.
598

FISHERIES JAPAN

Japanese deep-sea fishing areas in change.

(Japan Report, 7(10, 1961)

QL
627
P 11

FISHERIES JAPAN

Report of investigations of skipjack and tuna resources, No. 1, 1947.

(Fisheries Experimental Station, March 1949)

(Pacific Oceanic Fishery Investigations, Translation No. 33, by W. G. van Campen)

QL
752
U 58

FISHERIES JAPAN

Results of encouragement for the development of Albacore fishing grounds in 1939. Published February 1940 by the Fisheries Bureau of the Ministry of Agriculture and Forestry, Japan.
Translated from the Japanese by W. G. Van Campen, Pacific Oceanic Fishery Investigations,

(Fish and Wildlife Service, Special Sci. Report, Fisheries, No. 33)

QL
Fishes
Pam.456

FISHERIES JAPAN

Shapiro, Sidney

The Japanese tuna fisheries.

(General Headquarters, Supreme Commander for the Allied Powers, Natural Resources Section, Report No. 104, Tokyo, 1948)

QL
Fishes
Pam. 450

FISHERIES JAPAN

Shapiro, Sidney

The Japanese tuna fisheries.

(U. S. Fish and Wildlife Service, Fishery Leaflet 297, April 1948)

QL
634.Inp
K 42

and

QL
634.Ma
K 42

FISHERIES MALAYA

Kesteven, G. L.

Malayan fisheries: a handbook prepared for the inaugural meeting of the Indo-pacific Council Singapore, March, 1949. Foreword by the Right Honorable Malcolm Mac Donald. Malaya Publishing House, Ltd. Singapore, 1949. R8vo. viii + 88 pp., 16 pl.

AS
492
S 6

FISHERIES MALAYA

Maxwell, C. N.

Malayan fishes.

(Journal of the Straits Branch, Royal Asiatic Society, No. 84, 1921, pp. 179-280, 72 pl.)

DU
Pac.Pam.
686

FISHERIES MARIANAS ISLANDS

Civil Affairs Guide. The fishing industry of the Japanese Mandated Islands. OPNAV 50E-20. Office of the Chief of Naval Operations. Navy Department. 15 August 1944. 4to 26 pp.

QL
752
U 58

FISHERIES MARQUESAS

Austin, Thomas S.

Summary, Oceanographic and fishery data, Marquesas Islands area, August- Sept., 1956 (EQUAPAC)

(U. S. Fish and Wildlife Service, Sp. Sci. Rept: Fisheries, No. 217, 1957)

QL
627
P 11

FISHERIES MARSHALL ISLANDS

Marshall Islands fishery investigations 1926-1927.

(Progress Report; South Seas Government-Gen. Fisheries Exp. Sta., for 1923-1935)

Translated from the Japanese by W.G. Van Campen. Pacific Oceanic Fishery Investigations, Translation No. 31

DU
Pac.Pam.
686

FISHERIES MICRONESIA

Civil Affairs Guide. The fishing industry of the Japanese Mandated Islands. OPNAV 50E-20. Office of the Chief of Naval Operations. Navy Department. 15 August 1944. 4to 26 pp.

GN
2.S
Z 78

FISHERIES MICRONESIA

Hizikata, Hizikata

Fishery in Satawal, Mikronesia.

(Zinruigaku Zassi, Vol. 56:310-326,1941)

QL
Fishes
Pam.
459

FISHERIES MICRONESIA

Smith, O. R.

Fishery exploration in the western Pacific. (January to June, 1948, by vessles of the Pacific Exploration Company). By O. R. Smith and M. B. Schaefer.

(U. S. Depat. of the Int., Fish and Wildlife Service, Sep. No. 225, - Vol. 11, No. 3, 1949)

QL
Fishes
Pam.
426

FISHERIES MICRONESIA

Smith, Robert O.

Fishery resources of Micronesia.

(Fish and Wildlife Service, U. S. Dept. Int. Fishery Leaflet 239, 1947)

DU
500
U 58

FISHERIES MICRONESIA

Smith, Robert O.

Survey of the fisheries of the former Japanese Mandated Islands.
IN
U. S. Commercial Company. Economic survey of Micronesia. No. 10. 1946

QL
627
P 11

FISHERIES MICRONESIA

U. S. Department of the Interior
Fish and Wildlife Service

Pacific Oceanic Fishery Investigations Translations from the Japanese

---

DU
1
U 58 g

FISHERIES MICRONESIA

U. S. Navy
Office of the Chief of Naval Operations
Civil Affairs Guide, OPNAV
50 E-20: The fishing industry of the Japanese Mandated Islands. 15 Aug. 1944.

DU
1
S 72 q

FISHERIES   NEW GUINEA

Fisheries investigations in Netherlands New Guinea.

(South Pacific Commission, Quarterly Bulletin Vol. 4(4):6, 1954)

QL
Fish
Pam
324

FISHERIES- NEW ZEALAND

Wellington. New Zealand.   Marine department.

Report on fisheries for the year ended March 1929.

QL
752
U 58

FISHERIES   PACIFIC

Sette, Oscar E.

Progress in Pacific oceanic fishery investigations, 1950-53.

(U. S. Fish and Wildlife Service, Special Scientific Report-Fisheries, No. 116, 1954)

DU
1
S 72-q

FISHERIES   NEW GUINEA (NETHERLANDS)

Zwollo, D. C.

Fisheries development in Netherlands New Guinea.

(South Pacific Commission, Quarterly Bull., Vol. 5(3):33-34, July, 1955)

QL
627
P 11

FISHERIES   PACIFIC

Ban, Yoshinori

On the search for southern tuna fishing grounds.

(South Sea Fisheries [Nanyo Suisan], Vol. 7 (9):10-21, 1941)

Translated from Japanese, by W. G. Van Campen, Pacific Oceanic Fishery Investigations Translation No. 13

DU
12
S 72

FISHERIES   PACIFIC

Southard, Samuel L.

Report, with S. Bill No. 176, The Committee on naval affairs, to whom was referred a memorial from sundry citizens of Connecticut, interested in the whale fishery, praying that an exploring expedition be fitted out to the Pacific Ocean and south seas, report: ...(24th Congress, 1st session, in Senate of the United States, March 21, 1836.   87 pp. 8vo.)

QL
636.5N
S 79

FISHERIES   NEW SOUTH WALES

Stead, David G.

A Brief Review of the Fisheries of New South Wales: Present and Potential. With 17 plates. Department of Fisheries, New South Wales. Sydney, 1930; sm8vo. 31 pp.

S
399
A 2

FISHERIES   PACIFIC

Brock, Vernon E.

Fisheries research in the central tropical Pacific.

(Rept. Bd. of Agric. and For., Terr. of Hawaii, 1946/1948:31-39)

DU
1
S 72-q

FISHERIES   PACIFIC

van Pel, H.

Fisheries in the South Pacific. Administrations throughout the Pacific are showing increasing interest in the development of their fisheries as this survey reveals.

(South Pacific Commission, Quarterly Bull., Vol. 5(3):2-4, July, 1955)

[New Caledonia, New Guinea, southwestern Polynesia...]

QL
Fish
Pam
#73

FISHERIES--NEW SOUTH WALES

Stead, David J.

A few facts about the fisheries of N. S. W.

Sydney 1911. 8vo pp. 11

FEB -5 1912

GC
1
S 431

FISHERIES   PACIFIC

Cobb, John N.

Scientific problems of the fisheries of the north Pacific.

(Bull. Scripps Inst. for Biol. Research, 9, 1919: 35-50)

pp. 47-48: Hawaiian fishery problems.

QL
636.5
P 11

FISHERIES   PACIFIC COAST

Pacific Marine Fisheries Commission.

Bulletin, 1, 1948+

QL
636.N
To

Fisheries-New South Wales

Tenison-Woods, Julian Edmund.

Fish and fisheries of New South Wales. By the Rev. J. E. Tenison-Woods ... Sydney, T. Richards, 1882.

1 p. l., xi, 213 p. front., plates. 25½ cm.

"Fishery laws and regulations": p. 160-181.
"Index of local names": p. 182-193.
"Works relating to fish and fisheries": p. 194-203.

1. Fisheries—New South Wales. 2. Fishes—New South Wales.

F 17-231

Library, U. S. Bur. of   Fisheries

QL
618
I 41

FISHERIES   PACIFIC

Indo-Pacific Fisheries Council

Directory of Fisheries Institutions (Asia and the Far East). Edited by IPFC Secretariat, Regional Office for Asia and the Far East, Food and Agriculture Organization of the United States. Bangkok, Thailand. 4to. (1957) 4to 81 pp. unnumbered.

QL
752
U 58

FISHERIES   PACIFIC COAST

Schaefer, Milner B.

Growth of Pacific coast pilchard fishery to 1942. By Milner B. Schaefer, Oscar E. Sette and John C. Marr.

(U.S. Dept. of the Interior, Fish and Wildlife Service, Research Report 29, 1951)

QL
Fish
Pam
#81

FISHERIES--NEW SOUTH WALES

Thompson, Lindsay G.

History of the fisheries of N. S. Wales with a sketch of the Laws by which they have been regulated.

Sydney 1893. 80 pp. 124 Maps 6. Plts.

G. 6 ½

QL
752
U 58

FISHERIES   PACIFIC

Murphy, Garth I.

Long-line fishing for deep-swimming tunas in the central Pacific, August-November 1952. By Garth I. Murphy and Richard S. Shomura.

(U. S. Dept. of the Int., Fish and Wildlife Service, Special Sci.,Rept-Fisheries, No. 137, 1955)

QL
Fishes
Pam.
451

FISHERIES   PACIFIC   (northwest)

Tester, A. L.

Results of the West Coast of Vancouver Island herring investigation, 1947-1948. By A. L. Tester and J. C. Stevenson.

(Report of the British Columbia Department of Fisheries, 1947, pp. M 41-86)

QL
Fishes
Pam.
577

FISHERIES   NEW ZEALAND

Allen, K. Radway

A New Zealand trout stream; some facts and figures.

(New Zealand Marine Department, Fisheries Bull. 10 A, 1952)

DU
620
F

FISHERIES   PACIFIC

The Pacific Cod fishery.

(The Friend, Vol. 17, no. 2, Feb. 1, 1866, p. 13)

[locality not specified]

QL
Fishes
Pam.462

FISHERIES   PACIFIC   (NW)

Thompson, William Francis

The effect of fishing on stocks of halibut in the Pacific.

(Publications of the Fisheries Research Institute, Univ. of Washington. Mr. 1950. no ser.

QL
627
P 11

FISHERIES   PACIFIC

Uehara, Tokuzō

A survey of tuna grounds in equatorial waters

(South Sea Fishery News [Nanyō Suisan Jōhō], vol. 5(3):13-17, 1941)

Translation from Japanese, Pacific Oceanic Fishery Investigations, Translation No. 14

QL
752
U 58

FISHERIES   PHILIPPINE ISLANDS

Clague, John A.

Bacteriological studies of Philippine fishery products. By John A. Clague and Crisanto Almario.

(U.S. Dept. of the Interior, Fish and Wildlife Service, Research Report 27, 1950)

BU
80
A 93

FISHERIES   SAMOA

van Pel, H.

SPC fisheries investigation in Western Samoa.

(South Pacific Bull., vol. 11(1):20-22, 1961)

QL
617
S 17

FISHERIES   PACIFIC COAST

International Pacific Salmon Fisheries Commission.

Annual Report

1943-

QL.P
634.P
F 53

FISHERIES   PHILIPPINE

Fisheries Society of the Philippines

Bulletin

QL
627
U-f

Fisheries-U.S.
Goode, George Brown, 1851-1896.

... The fisheries and fishery industries of the United States. Prepared through the co-operation of the commissioner of fisheries and the superintendent of the tenth census by George Brown Goode ... and a staff of associates ... Washington, Govt. print. off., 1884-1887.

5 sections in 7 v. plates, charts. 28ᶜᵐ.

CONTENTS.—sec. I. Natural history of useful aquatic animals, by G. B. Goode, J. A. Allen, H. W. Elliott, F. W. True, E. Ingersoll, J. A. Ryder, R. Rathbun.—sec. II. A geographical review of the fisheries industries and fishing communities for the year 1880, by R. E. Earll, W. A. Wilcox, A. H.

(Continued on next card)

F 20-35

QL
752
U 58

FISHERIES   PALAU

Shimada, B. M (ed.)

Tuna fishing in Palau waters. Edited by B. M. Shimada and W. G. Van Campen. Translated from the Japanese by SCAP translators and W. G. Van Campen.

(U. S. Fish and Wildlife Service, Special Scientific Reports Fisheries No. 42, [1951] original dates 1927-1942)

AS
540
P 55

FISHERIES   PHILIPPINE ISLANDS

Herre, Albert W.

Fishery Resources of the Philippine Islands.

(Monograph, Bureau of Science, Philippine Islands, No. 3, 1927)

QL
627
U-Of

Fisheries-U.S.
Goode, George Brown, 1851-1896. ... The fisheries and fishery industries of the United States ... 1884-1887. (Card 2)

CONTENTS—Continued.

Clark, F. Mather, J. W. Collins, M. McDonald, S. Stearns, D. S. Jordan, F. W. True.—sec. III. The fishing grounds of North America, by R. Rathbun, J. W. Collins, D. S. Jordan, T. H. Bean, L. Kumlien, F. W. True.—sec. IV. The fishermen of the United States, by G. B. Goode, J. W. Collins.—sec. v. History and methods of the fisheries, by G. B. Goode, J. W. Collins, N. P. Scudder, T. H. Bean, A. H. Clark, R. E. Earll, S. Stearns, F. W. True, M. McDonald, W. A. Wilcox, C. G. Atkins, D. S. Jordan, C. H. Gilbert, L. Kumlien, A. H. Clark, J. T. Brown, H. W. Elliott, J. G. Swan, E. Ingersoll, R. Rathbun.

(Continued on next card)

F 20-35

QL
627
P 11

FISHERIES   PALAU

U. S. Department of the Interior Fish and Wildlife Service

Pacific Oceanic Fishery Investigations Translations from the Japanese

---

QL
618
I 41

FISHERIES   PHILIPPINE ISLANDS

Indo-Pacific Fisheries Council

Directory of Fisheries Institutions (Asia and the Far East). Edited by IPFC Secretariat, Regional Office for Asia and the Far East, Food and Agriculture Organization of the United States. Bangkok, Thailand. 4to. (1957) 4to 81 pp. unnumbered.

QL
627
U-f

Fisheries-U.S.
Goode, George Brown, 1851-1896. ... The fisheries and fishery industries of the United States ... 1884-1887. (Card 3)

1. Fisheries—U. S. I. Goode, George Brown, 1851-1896. II. Allen, Joel Aseph, 1838- III. Elliott, Henry Wood, 1846- IV. True, Frederick William, 1858-1914. V. Ingersoll, Ernest, 1852- VI. Ryder, John Adam, 1852-1895. VII. Rathbun, Richard, 1852-1918. VIII. Earll, Robert Edward, 1853-1896. IX. Wilcox, William A., 1839-1908. X. Clark, Alonzo Howard, 1850- XI. Mather, Fred, 1833-1900. XII. Collins, Joseph William, 1839-1904. XIII. McDonald, Marshall, 1835-1895. XIV. Stearns, Silas. XV. Jordan, David Starr, 1851- XVI. Bean, Tarleton Hoffman, 1846-1916. XVII. Kumlien, Ludwig, 1853-1912. XVII. Scudder, Newton Pratt. XVIII. Gilbert, Charles Henry, 1859- XIX. Atkins, Charles G., 1841- XX. Brown, James Temple.

F 20-35

Library, U. S. Bur. of   Fisheries

Fisheries --- PENNSYLVANIA

QL
628.P
P

Report of the Pennsylvania State Commissioners. of the Pennsylvania.

QL 628. P
P

Gr. 4-

AS
540
P

FISHERIES   PHILIPPINE ISLANDS

Seale, Alvin

The fishery resources of the Philippine Islands. Part 1: Commercial fishes.

(Philippine Journal of Science, Vol. 3, D: 513-529, 1908)

QL
Crust.Pam.
193

FISHERIES   UNITED STATES

Rathbun, Richard

Great International Fisheries Exhibition, London, 1883. United State of America. G. Descriptive catalogue of the collection illustrating the scientific investigation of the sea and fresh waters. Washington. Government Printing Office 1883. 8vo. 109 pp.

QL
Fish Pam.
345

FISHERIES - PHILIPPINE ISLANDS

Adams, Wallace

Cultivation of Baños in the Philippines. By Wallace Adams, Heraclio R. Montalban and Claro Martin. Contribution from the Subcommittee on Fisheries Technology of the Philippine Committee on Oceanography to the Fifth Pacific Science Congress, Canada, 1932. 38 pp. 8vo.

QL
627
P 11

FISHERIES   PONAPE

An investigation of the waters adjacent to Ponape.

(Fisheries Exp. Sta. Progress Rept., No. 1, 1923-35. Pub. by the South Seas Government-General, Palao, Dec. 1937)

Translated by W. G. Van Campen, from the Japanese, Pacific Oceanic Fishery Investigations, Translation No. 12.

QL
752
U 58 s

FISHERIES   UNITED STATES

United States Department of the Interior Fish and Wildlife Serivce

Fishery Statistics of the United States

Statistical Digest, No. 1, 1939-

Gov. Printing Off.   Washington. 8vo. 1942-

QL
752
U 58

FISHERIES   PHILIPPINE ISLANDS

Avery, Arthur C.

Fish processing handbook for the Philippines.

(U.S. Dept. of the Interior, Fish and Wildlife Service, Research Rept. No. 26, 1950)

QL
752
U 58

FISHERIES   SAIPAN

Ikebe, Kenzo

Report of a skipjack bait investigation in Saipan waters. By Kenzo Ikebe and Takeshi Matsumoto. Trans. by W. G. Van Campen, and retitled Tuna bait resources at Saipan.

(U. S. Fish and Wildlife Service, Special Scientific Report: Fisheries No. 44, 1951; original date 1938)

QL
627
U

FISHERIES - UNITED STATES

See also

United States Bureau of Fisheries

FISHERIES

See also

Fishing

AS
36
A 65-b   FISHES

Clark, Eugenie

Mating behavior patterns in two sympatric species of Xiphophorin fishes: their inheritance and significance in sexual isolation. By Eugenie Clark, Lester R. Aronson and Myron Gordon.

(Bull. Am. Mus. of Nat. Hist., Vol. 103(2), 1954)

QL
Fishes   FISHES
Pam.
536   Copley, Hugh

A popular guide to some of the fishes of the coral reef. The East Africa Natural History Society. May, 1944. 8vo. 13 pp.

Q
101
P 18   Fisheries of the Pacific.
(Articles by W. E. Allen, J. Russell Smith and others)

(Pan-Pacific Scientific Congress, 1st, Honolulu, 1920, pp. 213-239)

QL
622
I 39   FISHES

Indian Museum. Calcutta.

Descriptive catalogue of the Indian deep-sea fishes in the Indian museum, being a revised account of the deep-sea fishes collected by the royal Indian marine survey ship Investigator, by A. Alcock.   Calcutta, 1898.   211 p, index 8 p.

QL
615
C 99   FISHES

Cuvier, G. L. C. F. D.

Histoire Naturelle des Poissons, by Cuvier and Valenciennes. Plates only, incomplete,—not certain the plates are from this work.

QL
627
U-d   FISHERY PRODUCTS - PRESERVATION

Taylor, Harden F.

Refrigeration of fish. Department Commerce, Bur. Fisheries, Doc. n.1016, 1927.

QL
618
I 39.   FISHES

Indian Museum.   Calcutta.

Guide to zoological collection exhibited in the fish gallery.   Calcutta, 1899.   92 p.

AS
36
S1   FISHES

Edinger, Ludwig, 1855–
Have fishes memory? By L. Edinger.

(*In* Smithsonian institution. Annual report. 1899. Washington, 1901. 23½ᶜᵐ. p. 375-394)

"Translated from the Supplement to the Allgemeine zeitung, nos. 241 and 242, October 21 and 23, 1899."

1. Memory. 2. Fishes.

Library of Congress   Q11.S66 1899
Library, Smithsonian   Institution

S 15-1035

AM
101
AU   FISHES
(5)   Australian museum, *Sydney*.
... Catalogue of the fishes in the collection of the Australian museum. Pt. I. Recent palæichthyan fishes, by J. Douglas Ogilby ...   Printed by order of the Trustees ... Sydney, F. W. White, printer, 1888.

v. 26, (2) p. 24½ᶜᵐ. (Australian museum, Sydney. Catalogue no. 14)

1. Fishes.   I. Ogilby, John Douglas.

20-11188

Library of Congress   QL618.A93

AS
619
S   FISHES

Barnard, K. H.

A monograph of the marine fishes of South Africa. In South African Mus. Ann. 1925 - .

[Part I is in Vol. XXI. See Barnard for continuation]

QL
1
C2   FISHES

Forbes, J. C.

Investigation on the tensile strength of strips of haddock muscle before and after various treatments. Can. Biol. Board Stud. no. 31.

QL
618
B 76   FISHES

Boulenger, George Albert

Catalogue of the Perciform fishes in the British Museum. Second edition. Vol. 1: Centrarchidae, Percidae, and Serranidae (part.). London. Order of the Trustees. 1895. 8vo. xix+ 394 pp.

QL
1
C2   FISHES

Battle, Helen I.

Effects of extreme temperatures on muscle and nerve tissue in marine fishes. Canada Biological Board Studies series 3. Vol............., 1926.

AS
36
A5   FISHES

Fowler, Henry W.

Description of a new Cyprinoid fish from China.

Am. Mus. Novitates, No. 83, July, 1923.

QL
Amphib.
and Rept.   FISHES
Pam. 56   British Museum (Nat. Hist.)

Guide to the galleries of reptiles and fishes in the Department of Zoology of the British Museum...1893. 3rd edition. London 8vo. 119 pp.

QL
618
V22   FISHES

Borodin, N.A.

Fishes.

Vanderbilt marine museum, 1928, v.1, art.1 37 p. 5 pl.

Scientific results of the yacht Ara expedition during the years 1926-8, while in command of William K. Vanderbilt.

AS
36
S2   Fishes

Gill, T.

Marsipobranchii, and leptocardii.

QL
G17
B 87   FISHES

(Brookes, R)

The art of angling, rock and sea-fishing... London. 1740.

QL
616
S 54   FISHES

Chute, Walter H.

Guide to the John G. Shedd Aquarium. [Chicago]. 4th edition, 1944. 8vo. 236 pp. [illustrated in black and white and in color]

AS
36
S1   FISHES

Gill, Theodore Nicholas, 1837-1914
Parental care among fresh-water fishes. By Theodore Gill.

(*In* Smithsonian institution. Annual report. 1905. Washington, 1906. 23½ᶜᵐ. p. 403-531. illus., pl.)

1. Fishes. I. Title.

S 15-1300

Library of Congress   Q11.S66 1905
Library, Smithsonian   Institution

AM
101
A 51
(5)

FISHES

Gregory, William K.

The world of fishes, by William K. Gregory and Francesca LaMonte.

(Amer. Mus. of Nat. Hist., Science Guide, No. 122, 1947)

AS
36
S6

FISHES

Jordan, David Starr, 1851–

...Notes on fishes, little known or new to science. By David Starr Jordan ... Palo Alto, Cal., Leland Stanford jr. university, 1896.

2 p. l., [201]–244 p. xx–XLIII pl., port. 24½ᶜᵐ. (Leland Stanford junior university publications. Contributions to biology from the Hopkins seaside laboratory. v)

Reprint from the Proceedings of the California academy of sciences, series 2, vol. VI.

1. Fishes.

Library of Congress   QL1.L53   7–10274

AS
36
S1

FISHES

Moore, Henry Frank, 1867–

The sea as a conservator of wastes and a reservoir of food. By H. F. Moore ...

(*In* Smithsonian institution. Annual report. 1917. Washington, 1919. 23½ᶜᵐ. p. 595–608. 8 pl. on 4 l.)

1. Ocean. 2. Fishes.

Library of Congress   Q11.S66 1917   20–5166
    (5)

QL
615
G 89

FISHES

Gudger, Eugene Willis   editor

The Bashford Dean Memorial Volume: Archaic Fishes. Article I–VIII. New York, American Museum of Natural History. 1930– 1942   4to

---

QL
5
No

Fishes

Kner, Rudolf

in Reise der Novara, Zool. I, pp. 433, pls. 16.

Wien, 1869.

QL
615
N 84

FISHES

Norman, J. R.

Field book of giant fishes. By the late J. R. Norman and F. C. Fraser. With eight plates in full color and over one hundred drawings by W. P. C. Tenison. G. P. Putnam's Sons. New York. 1949. 12mo. xxii + 360 pp.

QL
615
G 89

FISHES

Gudger, Eugene Willis

The Segmentation of the Egg of the Myxinoid, Bdellostoma stouti, Based on the Drawings of the Late Bashford Dean. By Eugene Willis Gudger and Bertram G. Smith.

(The Bashford Dean Memorial Volume: Archaic Fishes. Edited by E. W. Gudger, Article II, New York, Am. Mus. of Nat. Hist. 1931, pp. 47–57, 2 plates. 4to)

QL
618
L 12

FISHES

La Blanchère, H. de

La Peche et les Poissons. Nouveau Dictionnaire Général des Peches. Précédé d'une préface par Aug. Dumeril...1100 illustrations dessinées et coloriées par A. Mesnel. Paris. Librairie de Ch. Delagrave et Cie. 1868. R8vo. xv + 859 pp.

GC
63
D 61

FISHES

Norman, J. R.

Oceanic fishes and flatfishes collected in 1925–1927.

Discovery Committee
Discovery Reports, Vol. 2, 1930, 261–370.

QL
Fish
Pam.
337

FISHES

Gudger, E. W.

The Whale Shark off Havana Harbor by E. W. Gudger and W. H. Hoffman.

(From The Scientific Monthly, Jan. 1931, Vol. XXXII, pp. 33–36).

QL
615
L 17

FISHES

La Gorce, John Oliver   editor

The book of fishes: revised and enlarged edition, presenting the better known species of food and game fishes of the coastal and inland waters of the United States. National Geographic Society. Washington, R8vo. 367 pp. 1939c

[a compilation of various articles that have appeared in the National Geographic.]

Q
115
S 97

FISHES

Nybelin, Orvar

Deep-sea bottom-fishes.

IN
Pettersson, Hans
Reports of the Swedish Deep-Sea Expedition, 1947–1948, Vol. 2(3):250–364, 1957)

QL
615
H 53

FISHES

Herald, Earl S.

Living fishes of the world. Doubleday and Company Inc. Garden City, New York. 4to. 1961 304 pp.

QL
618
L 23

FISHES

La Monte, Francesca

Marine game fishes of the world. Illustrations by Janet Roemhild. Doubleday and Co., Inc. Garden City. 1952. 8vo. (1–4)5–190 pp.

QL
1
C2

FISHES

Simpson, W. W.

The effects of asphyxia and isletectomy on the blood sugar of myoxocephalus and ameiurus. Can. Biol. Board Stud. no.34.

QL
Fish
Pam.
336

FISHES

Hoffman, W. H.

The Second Capture of the Whale Shark, Rhineodon Typus, near Havana Harbor, Cuba.

(From Science, June 1930, Vol. LXXI, No. 1851, pp. 639–640).

QL
625
L 23

FISHES

LaMonte, Francesca

North American game fishes. Illustrations by Janet Roemhild. With a foreword by Philip Wylie. Doubleday, Doran and Co., Inc., Garden City, New York. 1945. sm8vo. xiv + 202 pp.

QL
Fish
Pam
#159
4to

FISHES

Steindachner, Franz

Fische

Frankfurt am Main 1901.

Abtheilung des Senckenberischen naturforschenden Gesellschaft. Band XXV. Heft II. pp. 2 Tafel.

QL
615
J82

FISHES

Jordan, David Starr, 1851–

A guide to the study of fishes, by David Starr Jordan ... New York, H. Holt and company, 1905.

2 v. col. fronts., illus. 26ᶜᵐ.

"The history of ichthyology": v. 1, p. 387–428.

1. Fishes. 2. Zoology—Hist. 3. Fishes—Bibl.

Library of Congress   QL615.J82   5–14970
Copyright

QL
619
M 49

FISHES

Meek, Alexander, 1865–

The migrations of fish. By Alexander Meek ... London, Edward Arnold, 1916.

xviii p., 1 l., 427 p. illus., front., XI pl. 23ᶜᵐ.

1. Fishes. 2. Fishes, Migration of.

Library, U. S. Bur. of   Fisheries

QL
Amphib
& Rept
Pam. #5

FISHES

Steindachner, Franz

Herpetologische und Ichthyologische Ergebnisse einer Reise nach Südamerica.

Wien 1902. 4to pp 60. pl 5.

g. x Dr. Steindachner.

QL
Fish
Pam
252

FISHES

Steindachner, Franz

Ichthyologische mittheilungen (IV).
From Verh. der k.k. zool-bot Gesell.
Wien, 1862.

QL
627
P 11

FISHES AGE

Aikawa, Hiroaki

Age determination of fish (preliminary report 1). By Aikawa, Hiroaki and Kato, Masuo

(Pacific Oceanic Fishery Investigations,
U. S. Fish and Wildlife Service, Dept. of the
Interior, Honolulu 1949)

QL
Fish
Pam
262

FISHES - ANATOMY

Hall, F. G.

The functions of the swimbladder of fishes.
From Biological Bull. v.47, n.2, 1924.

QL
FISH
Pam
#116

FISHES

Weber, Max

Eine neue art von Macrorhamphosus und revision dieses genus.

(From Tijdsch. d. Ned. Dierk. Vereen (2) Dl. XI
Afl. 2.)
Amsterdam. n.d. 8vo pp. 79 plate IV.

SEP 19 1911

QL
1
H2

FISHES (ALBATROSS EXPED.)

Garman, S.

"The Fishes" - Reports of albatross
Expedition 1891.　　Harvard Mus. Comp.
Zool. Mem. XXIV, 1899.

Cambridge M.S.A. 1899. 4to pp. 431. pl. 97

G. 13.91
10

27/1/20

AS
36
I 4

FISHES - ANATOMY

Kindred, James Ernest.
The skull of *Amiurus*, with eight plates, by James E. Kindred ... [Urbana, Ill., University of Illinois, ʻ1919]
120 p. VIII pl. 27½ᶜᵐ. (Added t.-p.: Illinois biological monographs, vol. v, no. 1, January, 1919)
Thesis (PH. D.)—University of Illinois.
Thesis note on verso of t.-p.
"Contributions from the Zoological laboratory of the University of Illinois under the direction of Henry B. Ward, no. 135."
Bibliography: p. 98-104.

1. Catfishes. 2. Fishes—Anatomy.

Library of Congress　　　　　QL638.S6K5　　19-13830
——— Copy 2.
Copyright A 530571　　　　　　　[5]

QL
Fish
Pam
#90

FISHES

Weber, Max

A new case of parental care among fishes.

(From K. Akad. van Wetenschappen te
Amsterdam. Proceed. Sat. Nov. 20. 1910.)

n.p. 1910. 8vo pp. 583-587.

SEP 19 1911

QL
627
U4b

FISHES - ALBATROSS EXPEDITION

Mayer, Alfred Goldsborough

Medusae of the Hawaiian Islands collected by the
Steamer Albatross in 1902.
Sep. from U.S. Fish Comm. Bull. for 1903, Part III.
pp. 1131-1143, pls. I-III.
Washington, 1906. 4to.

Proto
Pam 2

QL
1
C2

FISHES - ANATOMY

Jackson, Slater

The islands of Langerhans in Elasmobranch and Teleostean fishes.

Journ. of Metabolic Res., vol. II, 1923.

QL
Fish
Pam
#115

FISHES

Weber, Max.

Eine zoogeographische prophezeiung
aus dem Zool. Anzeiger Bd. XXXII nr. 4.
vom 10 Dezember 1907.

n. p. n. d. 8vo pp. 401-404.

SEP 19 1911

QL
Fish
Pam
257

FISHES - ANATOMY

Cramer, Rudolf

Ueber mene rhombeus (Volta sp.).
Inaugural dissertation... Friedrich-
Wilhelms Univ. zu Berlin, 1906.

QL
1
H2

FISHES--ANATOMY

Lendenfeld, Robert J edler von Lendlmayer, reichsritter von, 1858-1913.
... The radiating organs of the deep sea fishes. By Robert von Lendenfeld. With an appendix on the structure of the bud-like organs of *Malthopsis spinulosa* Garman. By Emanuel Trojan ... Cambridge, Printed for the Museum, 1905.
2 p. l., p. [169]-213. XII pl. (incl. fold. map) diagr. 31 x 26ᶜᵐ. (Memoirs of the Museum of comparative zoölogy at Harvard college, vol. XXX, no. 2)

(Continued on next card)
A 19-1061
[3]

QL
Fishes
Pam.
465

FISHES ABUNDANCE

Blackburn, M.

Fishery management and changes in abundance of fish.

(Australian Journal of Science, Vol. 12(1):
14-17, 1949)

QL
1
C15

FISHES - ANATOMY

Daniel, J. Frank and Stoker, Edith

The relations and nature of the
cutaneous vessels in selachian fishes.
Calif. Univ. Publ. Zool. v.31, n.1, 1927.

QL
1
H2

FISHES -- ANATOMY

Lendenfeld, Robert J edler von Lendlmayer, reichsritter von, 1858-1913. ... The radiating organs of deep sea fishes ... 1905. (Card 2)
Each plate accompanied by leaf with descriptive letterpress.
Reports on an exploration off the west coasts of Mexico, Central and South America, and off the Galapagos Islands ... by the U. S. Fish commission steamer "Albatross," during 1891 ... XXXI.
"Literature": p. 207, 213.

1. Fishes—Anatomy. 2. Fishes, Pelagic. 3. Phosphorescence. 4. Albatross (Steamer) I. Trojan, Emanuel.
A 19-1061

Title from Univ. of Chicago　QL1.H375　vol. 30, no. 2
Printed by L. C.　　　　　　　　　[3]

QL
Fishes
Pam.
466

FISHES ABUNDANCE

Blackburn, M.

Measures of abundance of pelagic fish in
some southeastern Australian waters. By M.
Blackburn and J. A. Tubb.

(Australia, Commonwealth Sci. and Ind. Research Organization, Bull. 251, 1950)

QL
1
C 15

FISHES - ANATOMY

Davidson, Pirie, 1892-
... The musculature of *Heptanchus maculatus*, by Pirie Davidson. Berkeley, University of California press, 1918.
cover-title, p. [151]-170. illus. 27½ᶜᵐ. (University of California publications in zoology. v. 18, no. 10)
"Literature cited": p. 170.

1. Heptanchus maculatus. 2. Fishes—Anatomy. I. Title.

A 18-455
Title from Univ. of Calif.　　　Library of Congress

QL
618
G 97

FISHES ACANTHOPTERI

Günther, Albert

Catalogue of the Acanthopterygian Fishes in
the Collection of the British Museum. Vol. 1-8
London. Order of the Trustees. 1859-1870. 8vo.

AS
36
I 4

FISHES - ANATOMY

Gutberlet, John Earl, 1887-
On the osteology of some of the *Loricati*, with five plates, by John Earl Gutberlet ... [Urbana, University of Illinois, ʻ1915]
40 p. v pl. 27ᶜᵐ. (Added t.-p.: Illinois biological monographs. vol. II, no. 2, Oct. 1915) $0.50
"Contributions from the Zoological laboratory of the University of Illinois, under the direction of Henry B. Ward, no. 56."
Bibliography: p. 29.

1. Loricati. 2. Fishes—Anatomy.

Library of Congress　　　QL638.L8G8　　16-12771
——— Copy 2.
Copyright A 427739

AS
36
S7

FISHES - ANATOMY

Starks, Edwin Chapin, 1867-
... The sesamoid articular, a bone in the mandible of fishes, by Edwin Chapin Starks ... with fifteen text figures ... Stanford University, Cal., The University, 1916.
40 p. illus. 26ᶜᵐ. (Leland Stanford junior university publications. University ser. [22])

1. Fishes—Anatomy. I. Title.

16-15309
Library of Congress　　　QL639.S73

3

QL Fish Pam 255

FISHES - ANATOMY

Tims, H. W. Marett

The development, structure, and morphology of the scales in some teleostean fish. From Quart. Journ. Micros. Sci. v.49, pt.1, 1905.

QL 1. H2

FISHES--ANATOMY
Trojan, Emanuel.

... Ein beitrag zur morphologie des tiefseefischgehirnes. Von Emanuel Trojan ... Cambridge, Printed for the Museum, 1906.

2 p. l., p. [219]-255. 6 col. pl. 31 x 26ᶜᵐ. (Memoirs of the Museum of comparative zoology at Harvard college, vol. xxx, no. 3)

Each plate accompanied by leaf with descriptive letterpress.
Reports on an exploration off the west coasts of Mexico, Central and South America, and off the Galapagos Islands ... by the U. S. Fish commission steamer "Albatross," during 1891 ... xxxvi.
"Literaturverzeichnis": p. 253-254.

1. Fishes—Anatomy. 2. Brain. 3. Fishes, Pelagic. 4. Albatross (Steamer)

Title from Univ of Chicago   QL1.H375   vol. 30, no. 3   A 19-1078
Printed by L. C.   [3]

QL 627 P 11

FISHES BAIT SAIPAN

Ikebe, Kenzo

Report of a skipjack investigation in Saipan waters. By Kenzo Ikebe and Takeshi Matsumoto.

(from South Sea Fishery News, No. 6:2-12, Jan 1938)

Pacific Oceanic Fishery Investigations, Translaton No. 30-

Q 115 C 28

FISHES BATHYPELAGIC

Ege, Vilh.

Chauliodus Schn., bathypelagic genus of fishes, a systematic, phylogenetic and geographical study. The Carlsberg Foundation's Oceanographical Exp. ...1928-1930... Dana Report No. 31, 1948.

QL 1 S 99

FISHES BATHYPELAGIC

Haffner, Rudolph E.

Zoogeography of the bathypelagic fish, Chauliodus.

(Systematic Zoology, 1(3):113-133, 1953)

GC 1 S 43b

FISHES BATHYPELAGIC

Hubbs, Carl L.

The widespread, probably antitropical distribution and the relationship of the bathypelagic iniomous fish Antopterus pharao. By Carl L. Hubbs, Giles W. Mead, and Norman J. Wilimovsky.

(Bull. of the Scripps Institution of Oceanography of the University of California, Vol. 6(5):173-198, 1953)

AS 36 A-4

FISHES BEHAVIOR

Breder, Charles M., Jr.

On the relationship of social behavior to pigmentation in tropical shore fishes.

(Bull. Am. Mus. of Nat. Hist., Vol. 94:87-106, 1949)

QL 1 Z

FISHES BEHAVIOR

Clark, Eugenie

Notes on the behavior and morphology of some West Indian Plectognath fishes.

(Zoologica, Vol. 35(3):159-168, pl.1-2,1950)

AS 472 A-m

FISHES BEHAVIOR

Gudger, E. W.

The alleged pugnacity of the swordfish and the spearfishes as shown by their attacks on vessels. [A study of their behavior and the structures which make possible these attacks.]

(Mem. R. Asiatic Soc. of Bengal, 12(2):215-315, 1940)

AS 36 A 65-b

FISHES BEHAVIOR

Tavolga, William N.

Reproductive behavior in the gobiid fish Bathygobius soporator.

(Bull. Am. Mus. of Nat. Hist., Vol. 103(5), 1954)

Z 5971 C 46

FISHERIES BIBLIOGRAPHY

Chapman, Wilbert McLeod

Translations of fisheries literature from foreign languages.- I

(notes of where translations may be found) (1940

Z 5971 D 35

FISHES-BIBLIOGRAPHY
Dean, Bashford, 1867-

A bibliography of fishes, by Bashford Dean; enl. and ed. by Charles Rochester Eastman ... New York, The Museum, 1916- 1923

3 v. 25ᶜᵐ.

Seal of the American museum of natural history on t-p.

1. Fishes — Bibl.   I. Eastman, Charles Rochester, 1868-   ed.
II. American museum of natural history, New York.

                                  17-12736

Library of Congress   Z5971.D35

QL Fish Pam. # 148

FISHES -- BIBLIOGRAPHY

Gudger, E. W.

The classified continuation card catalogue of the Bibliography of fishes. In Science , May 15, 1925, pp 516- 517

QL 615 K 99

FISHES- BIOLOGY

Kyle, Harry M.

The biology of fishes. New York. Macmillan Company. 1926. 8vo. xvi + 396 pp.

QL 750 N

FISHES BREEDING

Graham, David H.

Breeding habits of the fishes of Otago Harbour and adjacent seas.

(Trans. and Proc.R. Soc. New Zealand, Vol. 69, 1939, pp. 361-372)

QL 618 B 49

FISHES CLASSIFICATION

Berg, Leo S.

Classification of fishes both recent and fossil. English and Russian. J.W.Edwards. Ann Arbor. 1947. R8vo.

(Translated from Travaux de l'Institut Zoologique de l'Academie des Sciences de l'URSS, Tome V, livr. 2, 1940:87-517)

QL 5 B 61

FISHES CLASSIFICATION

Breder, Charles M., Jr.

An analysis of the deceptive resemblances of fishes to plant parts, with critical remarks on protective coloration, mimicry and adaptation.

(Bulletin of the Bingham Oceanographic Coll. Vol. 10 (2):1-49, 1946)

AS 36 S2

FISHES--CLASSIFICATION.
Gill, Theodore Nicholas, 1837-1914.

... Arrangement of the families of fishes, or classes *Pisces, Marsipobranchii*, and *Leptocardii*. Prepared for the Smithsonian institution by Theodore Gill ... Washington, Smithsonian institution, 1872.

xlvi, 49 p. 23½ᶜᵐ. (Smithsonian miscellaneous collections. [vol. xi, art. iii])

Publication 247.
Bibliography. A synopsis of the great standard works of descriptive ichthyology: p. 27-45.

1. Fishes—Classification.

Library of Congress   [Q11.S7 vol. 11, art. 2   16-6362
———— Copy 2. 24ᶜᵐ.   QL618.G43
———— Copy 3. 24½ᶜᵐ.   Q11.S7 2d set

QL 618 J 82

FISHES CLASSIFICATION

Jordan, David Starr

A classification of fishes, including families and genera as far as known.

(Stanford Univeristy Pub., Biol. Sci., Vol. III, No. 2, 1923, pp. 77-244)

QL 615 S 38

FISHES CLASSIFICATION

Schultz, Leonard P.

The ways of fishes. By Leonard P. Schultz with Edith M. Stern. Illustrated. D. Van Nostrand Company, Inc. New York... 8vo. xii + 264 pp.

QL Fish Pam 259

FISHES - COLLECTION & PRESERVATION

Samter, Max

Das messen toter und lebender fische fur systematische und biologische untersuchungen. From Arch. f. Hydro. u. Planktonkunde, bd.2, 1906.

AM S., P. L.
Pam
No.28
FISHES -- COLLECTION AND PRESERVATION

On collecting and preserving specimens of fishes and reptiles. Miscellanea.

n.p. n.d.

FISHES COLOR

see also

COLOR OF FISHES

QL FISHES DISEASES
Fish
Pam. Markewitsch, A. P.
390
Diseases of fresh water fishes. (In
Russian, with English abstract.) Akad. Nauk,
Kiev, 1940. 167 pp. 8vo.

QL FISHES GROWTH
Fishes
Fam. Parker, Robert R.
614
622
A concept of growth in fishes. By Robert R.
Parker and Peter A. Larkin.

(Journal Fish. Res. Bd. Canada, 16(5):721-
745, 1959)

QL FISHES COLOR CHANGES
Fishes
Pam.389 Matsushita, Kazundo

Studies on the color changes of the catfish,
Parasilurus asotus (L.)

(Science Repts. of the Tohoku Imp. Univ.,
Ser. 4, Biology, Vol. 13, 1938, pp. 171-200)

QL FISHES DISEASES AND PESTS
N 6-z Nigrelli, Ross F.

Causes of diseases and death of fishes in
captivity.

(Zoologica, Vol. 28, Part 4, 1943, pp.
203-216)

QL FISHES LARVAE
627
U-h Wade, Charles B.

Larvae of Tuna and Tuna-like fishes from
Philippine waters.

(Fishery Bulletin 57, U. S. Fish and Wildlife Service, 1951)

QL FISHES CONSERVATION
Fishes
Pam. Pritchard, A. L.
430
Fish cultural problems involved in the
conservation of anadromous fish with particu-
lar reference to salmon on the Skeena River,
British Columbia.

(Canadian Fish Culturist, Vol. 1 (2):8-13,
1947)

Q FISHES ECOLOGY
Gen.Sci.
Pam.109 Pearse, A. S.

Ecology of lake fishes.

(Reprinted from Ecological Monographs, 4:
475-480, 1934)

QL FISHES MEASUREMENT
Fish.Pam.
474 Hiatt, Robert W.

A device for measuring fish.
By Robert W. Hiatt and Christopher J. Hamre.

(Journal of Wildlife Management, Vol. 9(1):
79-81, 1945. Reprint)

QL FISHES CORAL REEF
Fishes
Pam. Copley, Hugh
536
A popular guide to some of the fishes of the
coral reef. The East Africa Natural History
Society. May, 1944. 8vo. 13 pp.

QL FISHES ECOLOGY
Fishes
Pam. Woods, Loren P.
427
Ecology and distribution of reef fishes at
Bikini Atoll.

(The American Soc. of Ichthyologists and
Herpetologists, 27th Annual Meeting, Aug. 27-30,
1947, Higgins Lake, Michigan)

GC COLLECTIONS
1 FISHES INSTITUT OCEANOGR. DE MONACO
M 73 Belloc, Gérard

Catalogue des types de poissons du Musée
Océanographique de Monaco.

(Bull. Inst. Oceanographique, Monaco,
No. 958, 1949)

AP FISHES CULTIVATION (open sea)
2
N 4 Gross, F.

Marine fish cultivation.

(Nature, Vol. 162, No. 4114:378, 1948)

FISHES—EMBRYOLOGY.
QL
959 Dean, Bashford, 1867-
B4 Chimaeroid fishes and their development, by Bashford
D28 Dean ... Washington, D. C., Carnegie institution of
Washington, 1906.

2 p. l., 194 p. illus., xi pl. (10 col., 1 fold.) 29^{cm}. (*On verso of t.-p.:*
Carnegie institution of Washington. Publication no. 32)

Each plate preceded by a leaf with descriptive letterpress.
"Literature list": p. 159-172.

1. Embryology—Fishes. 2. Chimeridae.

Library of Congress { QL959.D28 6-45312
—— Copy 2.

AS FISHES—COLOR
36
A 4 Breder, C. M., Jr.

Observations on coloration in reference to
behavior in tide-pool and other marine
shore fishes.

(Bull. Am. Mus. of Nat. Hist., Vol.92 (5),
pp. 285-311, 1948)

AP FISHES DEPTH
2
N 28 Wolff, Torben

The deepest recorded fishes.

(Nature, No. 4772, p. 283, 1961, Vol. 190)

QL FISHES, EDUCATIONAL EXHIBIT OF
627 Holder Charles J
U-b
JUN 14 1910 A plan for an educational
exhibit of fishes.
and
Reprint, Bulletin, Bureau of Fisheries
AM Vol XXVIII, 1908
Pam
No.8

AM FISHES COLLECTING
101
F 45 n Jindrich, Marilyn K.

Coral reef collecting in Tahiti.

(Chicago Nat. Hist. Mus. Bull., Vol. 34
(7):2-3,5, 1963)

QL FISHES DESTRUCTION OF
Fishes
Pam. Hubbs, Carl L.
564
Report on experiments designed to determine
effects of underwater explosions on fish life.
By Carl L. Hubbs and Andreas B. Rechnitzer.

(Reprint from California Fish and Game, Vol.
38(2):333-365, July, 1952)

[...conclusion...exploration for oil can be
continued without the undue destruction of
fish life...]

FISHES, FLYING.
AS Gill, Theodore Nicholas, 1837-1914.
36 Flying fishes and their habits. By Theodore Gill.
S1
(*In* Smithsonian institution. Annual report. 1904. Washington, 1905.
23½^{cm}. p. 495-515. illus., IV pl. on 2 L)

1. Fishes, Flying.

S 15-1259

Library of Congress { QL11.S66 1904
Library, Smithsonian Institution

Q
115
H 24-o

FISHES FOOD

Dawson, E. Yale

Marine Algae from Palmyra Island with special reference to the feeding habits and toxicology of reef fishes. By E. Yale Dawson, A. A. Aleem and Bruce W. Halstead.

(Allan Hancock Foundation Publications, Occ. Papers No. 17, 1955)

QH
1
P 11

FISHES FOOD (of)

June , Fred C.

Note on the feeding habits of the giant white marlin of the Pacific.

(Pacific Science, Vol. 5:287, 1951)

QL
627
U-b

FISHES FOOD

Reintjes, John W.

Food of yellowfin tuna in the central Pacific. By John W. Reintjes and Joseph E. King.

(U.S. Dept. of the Interior, Fish and Wildlife Service, Fishery Bulletin 81, 1953)

[Neothunnus macropterus]

QL
671
Co

FISHES FOOD

Fisher, Harvey I.

Black-footed albatrosses eating flying fish.

(Condor, 47:128-129, 1945)

QL
627
P 11

FISHES FOOD

Kishinouye, Kamakichi

The food of tunas.

(Suisan Gakkai Ho, Vol. 2(1):106-108, My 1917)

Pacific Oceanic Fishery Investigations, Translation No. 29

QL
1
J 35

FISHES FOOD

Suehiro, Y.

A study on the digestive system and feeding habits of fish.

(Japanese Journal of Zool., 10(1):1-303, 1942)

QL
Fishes
Pam.
476

FISHES FOOD

Fraser, C. McLean

Food of fishes.

(R. Soc. of Canada, Trans, Sect. 5, 1946, pp. 33-39)

QL
615
G 78

FISHES-FOOD

Kow, Tham Ah

The food and feeding relationships of the fishes of Singapore Straits.

(Fishery Publications, Colonial Office, [Great Britain], London, Vol. 1(1), 1950)

QK
Bot.Pam.
1606

FISHES FOOD

Tilden, Josephine E.

"Plant Material and Debris": The Algal Food of Fishes.

(Reprinted from Vol. 59, 1929. Transactions of the American Fisheries Society, pp. 1-10)

QL
Fishes
Pam.
508 a,b

FISHES FOOD

Hiatt, Robert W.

Food-chains and the food cycle in Hawaiian fish ponds.- Part I. The food and feeding habits of mullet...milkfish...and the ten-pounder...; Part II, Biotic interaction.

(Reprinted from Trans. Am. Fisheries Soc., Vol. 74:250-280, 1944)

QL
752
U 58 s

FISHES FOOD

Leach, Glen C. and others

Propagation and distribution of food fishes. Calendar Year 1941.

(Fish and Wildlife Service, U. S. Dept. Int. Statistical Digest No. 6, 1943)

QH
1
P 11

FISHES FOOD HAWAII

Tester, Albert L.

The food of the aholehole, Kuhlia sandvicensis (Steindachner), in Hawaiian waters. By Albert L. Tester and Shirley M. Trefz.

(Pacific Science, Vol. VIII(1):3-10, 1954)

QH
1
P 11

FISHES FOOD OF

Hiatt, Robert W.

Food and feeding habits of the nehu, Stolephorus purpureus Fowler.

(Pacific Science, Vol. 5:347-358, 1951)

QL
627
P 55

FISHES FOOD

Martin, Claro

Studies on the preparation of salted fish paste (bagoong) from dried dilis (Stolephorus indicus). By Claro Martin and Jose I. Sulit.

(The Philippine Journal of Fisheries, Vol. 3(1):39-45, 1955)

QL
627
U-b

FISHES FOOD PACIFIC

King, Joseph E.

Comparative study of food of bigeye and yellowfin tuna in the central Pacific. By Joseph E. King and Isaac I. Ikehara.

(Fishery Bulletin, Fishery Bulletin of the Fish and Wildlife Service, US, Vol. 57, 1956)

QL
627
U 58 b

FISHES FOOD

Iverson, Robert T. B.

Food of Albacore Tuna, Thunnus Germo (Lacépède), in the central and northeastern Pacific.

(Fishery Bulletin 214, U. S. Fish and Wildlife Service, Vol. 62, 1962)

AS
719
A

FISHES FOOD

McKeown, Keith C.

The food of trout in New South Wales*. 1938.1940.

(*1st paper appeared in Rec. Aust. Museum, Vol. XX(1):38-, 1937; XXIII(5):273-282, 1955)

QL
1
C 23

FISHES FOOD SOUTH AFRICA

Davies, D. H.

Preliminary investigations on the foods of South African fishes. (With notes on the general fauna of the area surveyed)

(Union of South Africa, Dept. of Comm. and Ind., Fisheries and Marine Biol. Survey Div., Investigational Report No. 11, 1949)

QL
628
C 15

and

QL
Fish
Pam.
546

FISHES FOOD

Juhl, Rolf

Notes on the feeding habits of subsurface yellowfin and bigeye tunas of the eastern tropical Pacific Ocean.

(California Fish and Game, Vol. 41(1):99-101, 1955)

QL
627
P 11

FISHES FOOD

Nakamura, Hiroshi

On the food habits of yellowfin tuna Neothunnus macropterus (Schlegel) from the Celebes Sea.

(Trans. Nat. Histo. Soc. Formosa, Vol. 26, No. 148, 1936)

Translated from Japanese by W. G. Van Campen in Pacific Oceanic Fishery Investigations, Trans. No. 17

QE
730
C3

FISHES, FOSSIL

Case, Ermine Cowles, 1871-

Revision of the *Amphibia* and *Pisces* of the Permian of North-America, by E. C. Case ... With a description of Permian insects by E. H. Sellards, and a discussion of the fossil fishes by Louis Hussakof. Washington, D. C., Carnegie institution of Washington, 1911.

vii, 179 p. illus., 32 pl. (1 fold.) 29^{cm}. (*On verso of t.-p.*: Carnegie institution of Washington. Publication no. 146)

Bibliography: p. 176-178.

1. Paleontology — Permian. 2. Paleontology — North America. 3. Batrachia, Fossil. 4. Fishes, Fossil. 5. Insects, Fossil. I. Sellards, Elias Howard, 1875- II. Hussakof, Louis, 1881-

Library of Congress   QE730.C3

———— Copy 2.   (s19g3)

12—1090

FISHES, FOSSIL.

AS 36 A6 — Dean, Bashford, 1867–

... Studies on fossil fishes (sharks, chimæroids, and arthrodires). By Bashford Dean. [Cambridge, Mass., E. W. Wheeler, printer] 1909.

cover-title, p. 209–287. illus., pl. xxvi–xli. 36ᶜᵐ. (Memoirs of the American museum of natural history. vol. IX, pt. v)

1. Fishes, Fossil.

11-14268

Library of Congress   QH1.A43 vol. 9
———— Copy 2.   QE851.D4

AS 36 S7 — FISHES, FOSSIL

Jordan, David Starr, 1851–

... Fossil fishes of diatom beds of Lompoc, California, by David Starr Jordan ... and James Zaccheus Gilbert ... Stanford University, Calif., The University, 1920.

44, [2] p. xxix pl. on 15 l. 25½ᶜᵐ. (Leland Stanford junior university publications. University series. [no. 42])

1. Fishes, Fossil. 2. Paleontology—California. I. Gilbert, James Zaccheus, 1866– joint author.

20-11392

Library of Congress   QE845.J6
   [4]

QE 349.F L 15 — FISHES FOSSIL FIJI

Ladd, Harry S.
Vertebrata. (fishes)
IN
Ladd, Harry S.
Geology of Lau, Fiji, by Harry S. Ladd and J. Edward Hoffmeister. pp. 384–385

(Bernice P. Bishop Museum, Bull. 181, 1944)

AS 36 S4 — FISHES, FOSSIL

Eastman, Charles Rochester, 1868–

Fossil fishes in the collection of the United States national museum. By Charles R. Eastman ...

(In U. S. National museum. Proceedings. Washington, 1917. 23½ᶜᵐ. v. 52, p. 235–304. illus., pl. 1–23)

1. Fishes, Fossil.

18-15652

Library of Congress   Q11.U55 vol. 52

AS 36 S7 — FISHES, FOSSIL

Jordan, David Starr, 1851–

... Fossil fishes of southern California. I. Fossil fishes of the Soledad deposits [by] David Starr Jordan. II. Fossil fishes of the Miocene (Monterey) formations [by] David Starr Jordan and James Zaccheus Gilbert. III. Fossil fishes of the Pliocene formations [by] David Starr Jordan and James Zaccheus Gilbert. Stanford University, Calif., The University, 1919.

98 p. xxxi pl. on 16 l. 25½ᶜᵐ. (Leland Stanford junior university publications. University series. [no. 38])

1. Fishes, Fossil. 2. Paleontology—California. 3. Paleontology—Miocene. 4. Paleontology—Pliocene. I. Gilbert, James Zaccheus, 1866– joint author.

20—505

Library of Congress   QE851.J6
   [s20f5]

AP 2 S 35 — FISHES FRESH WATER

Herre, Albert W. C. T.

Marine fishes in fresh water.

(Science, Vol. 123(3206):1035, June, 1956)

AS 719 A 93-m — FISHES FOSSIL

Fletcher, H. O.

Ancient armoured fishes discovered at Canowindra, N. S. W.

(The Australian Museum Magazine, Vol. XII, No. 2:37–40, June, 1956)

AS 36 S71 — FISHES, FOSSIL

Jordan, David Starr

The fossil fishes of the miocene of southern California, contribution n.IX. Stanford Univ. Publ. Biological Sci. v.5, n.2, 1927.

QL 752 U 58 — FISHES GEOGRAPHICAL DISTRIBUTION

Murphy, Garth I.

A summary of sightings of fish schools and bird flocks and of trolling in the central Pacific. By Garth I. Murphy and Isaac I. Ikehara

(U.S. Dept. of the Interior, Fish and Wildlife Service, Special Scientific Rept.-Fisheries No. 154, 1955)

AS 36 S4 — FISHES, FOSSIL

Gidley, James Williams, 1866–

Some new American pycnodont fishes. By James Williams Gidley ...

(In U. S. National museum. Proceedings. Washington, 1914. 23½ᶜᵐ. v. 46, p. 445–449. illus.)

1. Fishes, Fossil.

14-10992

   Q11.U55 vol. 46

QE 851 M 93 — FISHES FOSSIL

Moy-Thomas, J. A.

Palaeozoic fishes. With 33 diagrams. Methuen and Co., Ltd. London. 1939. sm8vo. ix + 149 pp.

G 3 A 1 — FISHES, GEOGRAPHICAL DISTRIBUTION PACIFIC

Allen, Edward W.

Fishery geography of the north Pacific Ocean.

(Geographical Review 43(4):558–563, 1953)

AS 36 S2 — FISHES, FOSSIL.

Jordan, David Starr, 1851–

... The cretaceous fishes of Ceará, Brazil, by David Starr Jordan and John Casper Branner ...

(In Smithsonian institution. Smithsonian miscellaneous collections. Washington, 1910. 24½ᶜᵐ. vol. LII (Quarterly issue, vol. v) p. 1–29. illus., pl. I–VIII)

Publication 1793.
Originally published April 29, 1908.
Bibliography: p. 7–8.

1. Fishes, Fossil. 2. Paleontology—Cretaceous. 3. Paleontology—Brazil. I. Branner, John Casper, 1850– joint author.

Library of Congress   Q11.S7 vol. 52   16-12700
———— Copy 2.

AS 36 C51 — FISHES, FOSSIL

Pittsburgh. Carnegie institute. *Museum.*

... Catalog of fossil fishes in the Carnegie museum. pt. I– ... By Charles R. Eastman. Pittsburgh, Board of trustees of the Carnegie institute, 1911–

v. illus., plates. 33½ᶜᵐ. (Memoirs of the Carnegie museum. vol. IV, no. 7 ... W. J. Holland, ed.)

Cover-title.
Publications of the Carnegie museum, serial no. 65.

1. Fishes, Fossil. I. Eastman, Charles Rochester, 1868–

11-25030

Library of Congress   AS36.P75 vol. 4, no. 7

Q 101 P 18 — FISHES-GEOGRAPHICAL DISTRIBUTION PACIFIC

Herre, Albert W.
Distribution of fish in the tropical Pacific.

IN Proc. Sixth Pac. Sci. Congress, 1939, (California), Vol. 3, 1940, pp. 587–592.

AS 36 C3 — FISHES, FOSSIL.

Jordan, David Starr, 1851–

... Description of a new fossil fish from Japan, by David Starr Jordan ... [San Francisco? 1919]

p. [271]–272. pl. 20. 25½ᶜᵐ. (Proceedings of the California academy of sciences. 4th ser. vol. IX, no. 9)

Caption title.

1. Fishes, Fossil. 2. Fishes—Japan.

Library of Congress   Q11.C253 vol. 9, no. 9   20-4831
———— Copy 2.   QE851.J6
   [5]

QE Geol. Pam 613 — FISHES, FOSSIL

Steindachner, Franz

Beitrage zur kenntniss der fossilen fischfauna Osterreichs. From Akad. d. Wissen. sit. d. math–nat. classe, bd.40, 1860.

QL 1 C 78 — FISHES GROWTH

Bonham, Kelshaw

Measurements of some pelagic commercial fishes of Hawaii.

(Copeia, 1946(2):81–84)

AS 36 S7 — FISHES, FOSSIL

Jordan, David Starr, 1851–

... The fish fauna of the California Tertiary, by David Starr Jordan ... Stanford University, Calif., The University, 1921.

2 p. l., p. [237]–300. 57 pl. on 29 l. 25½ᶜᵐ. (Stanford university publications. University series. Biological sciences, v. 1, no. 4)

1. Fishes, Fossil. 2. Paleontology—California. 3. Paleontology—Tertiary.

Library of Congress   QE851.J5   21-19592
   [3]

AS 720.V M — FISHES, FOSSIL

Woodward, Arthur Smith, 1864–

... On a carboniferous fish fauna from the Mansfield district, Victoria. By Arthur Smith Woodward ... Melbourne, Printed by Ford & son, 1906.

1 p. l., 32 p. illus., xi (i. e. 12) pl. (partly col., partly fold.) 27ᶜᵐ. (Memoirs of the National museum, Melbourne. no. 1)

1. Fishes, Fossil. 2. Paleontology—Carboniferous. 3. Paleontology—Victoria, Australia.

Library of Congress   Q93.V7   6-40199

QL 627 U-b — FISHES-GROWTH

Moore, Harvey L.

Estimation of age and growth of yellowfin tuna (Neothunnus macropterus) in Hawaiian waters by size frequencies.

(U. S. Fish and Wildlife Service, Fishery Bull. 65, 1951)

QL
1
N 6-z

FISHES   HABITS

Breder, C. M., Jr.

    Factors influencing the establishment in shells by tropical shore fishes.

    (Zoologica, Vol. 35(3):153-158, 1950)

AS
36
A 5

FISHES   INTRODUCED   HAWAII

Elliot, Edith

    Its mouth is its nursery and its adaptability is making the Largemouth Kurper a promising source of revenue in Hawaii.

    (Natural History, 64(6):330-331, 1955)

QL
752
U 58

FISHES   LITERATURE   TRANSLATIONS

Scattergood, Leslie W.

    English translations of fishery literature; additional listings. (4th issue)

    (U. S. Fish and Wildlife Service, Special Scientific Report; Fisheries No. 72, 1952)

QL
Fishes
Pam.
438

FISHES   HABITS

Gudger, Eugene W.

    Fishes that play "leapfrog".

    (Am. Naturalist, 78, pp. 451-463, 1944)

GN
2.S
T 12

FISHES   INTRODUCED   TAHITI

    Pisciculture. (introduction of fish into Tahiti: rainbow trout, carp, catfish, black bass)

    (Bull. Soc. d'Etudes Oceaniennes, No. 20: 283-284, 1927)

QL
Fish Pam.
356

QL
1
N 6 z

FISHES   LOCOMOTION

Breder, C. M., Jr.

    The locomotion of fishes.

    (Zoologia, vol. 4, no 5, Sept. 28, 1926, pp. 159-297)

QL
1
N 6-z

FISHES   HABITS

Gudger, Eugene W.

    Fishes that rank themselves like soldiers on parade.

    (Zoologica, Vol. 34(2):63-97, 1949)

S
399
A 2

FISHES   INTRODUCTION

Brock, Vernon E.

    A history of the introduction of certain aquatic animals to Hawaii.

    (Rept. Bd. of Agric. and For., 1952)

QL
Fish Pam.
357

QL
1
N 6 z

FISHES   LOCOMOTION

Gregory, William K.

    Studies on the body-forms of fishes.

    (Zoologica, vol. VIII, no. 6, Mar. 1, 1928, pp. 325-421)

QL
1
C 78

and
QL
Fishes Pam.
437

FISHES   HABITS

Gudger, Eugene W.

    Fishes that swim heads to tails in single file.

    (Copeia, 1944, pp. 152-154)

QH
1
P11

FISHES   INTRODUCTION

Murphy, Garth I.

    Introduction of the Marquesan sardine, Harengula vittata (Cuvier and Valenciennes), to Hawaiian waters.

    (Pacific Science, 14:185-187, 1960)

QH
1
P 11

FISHES   LUMINESCENCE

Haneda, Yata

    The luminescence of some deep-sea fishes of the families Gadidae and Macrouridae.

    (Pacific Science, Vol. 5:372-378, 1951)

QH
1
P 11

FISHES   HABITS   HERDING OF PREY

Hiatt, Robert W.

    On the herding of prey and the schooling of the black skipjack, Euthynnus yaito Kishinouye.

    (Pacific Science, Vol. 2:297-298, 1948)

QL
Fish Pam.
549

FISHES   JUVENAL STAGES

Rivero, Luis Howell

    Estados larvales y juveniles del bonito. Por Luis Howell Rivero und Mar Juarez Fernandez.

    (Torreia, Num. 22, 1954)

QL
Fishes
Pam.
487

also
AM
Mus.Pam.
251

FISHES   MEASUREMENTS

Hiatt, Robert W.

    A device for measuring fish. By Robert W. Hiatt and Christopher J. Hamre.

    (Jour. Wildlife Management, 9(1):79-81, 1945)

QL
615
S 38

FISHES   HABITS

Schultz, Leonard P.

    The ways of fishes. By Leonard P. Schultz with Edith M. Stern. Illustrated. D. Van Nostrand Company, Inc. New York... 8vo. xii + 264 pp.

QL
752
U 58

FISHES   LARVAE

Ahlstrom, Elbert H.

    Pacific sardine (pilchard) eggs and other fish larvae, Pacific coast, 1953. By Elbert H. Ahlstrom and David Kramer.

    (U. S. Dept. of the Interior, Fish and Wildlife Service, Special Sci. Rept.-Fisheries No. 155, 1955)

QL
628
C 15 b

FISHES   MIGRATION

Clemens, Harold B.

    The migration, age and growth of Pacific albacore (Thunnus germo), 1951-1958.

    (California. Dept. of Fish and Game, Fish Bull. No. 115, 1961)

QL
1
C 78

and
QL
Fishes
Pam.
441

FISHES   HABITS

Wiggin, Paahana

    "Fishes that swim heads to tails in single file", by Paahana Wiggin, Mary Kawena Pukui, (and other informants of Mrs. Pukui)

    (Being a note from a letter to Dr. E. W. Gudger, following his article of this title IN Copeia, 1944, pp. 152-154)

QL
752
U 58

FISHES   LARVAE

Ahlstrom, Elbert H.

    Pilchard eggs and larvae and other fish larvae, Pacific Coast, 1951.

    (U. S. Fish and Wildlife Service, Sp. Scientific Report: Fisheries, No. 102, 1953)

G
51
W 17

FISHES   MIGRATION

Ford, E. T.

    Australian sea mullet.

    (Walkabout, Vol. 8 (7):15-16, 1942)

AS
763
H 38

FISHES   MIGRATION

Graham, Joseph J.

Albacore migration in the North Pacific as shown by tagging experiments.

(Haw. Acad. Sci., Proceedings, 31:22, 1956)

QL
1
A 94

FISHES   MIGRATION

Thomson, J. M.

The movements and migrations of mullet (Mugil cephalus L.)

(Australian Jour. of Marine and Freshwater Research, 6(3):328-347, 1955)

QL
Fishes
Pam.
418

FISHES   NATIVE NAMES   MANIHIKI

Anderson, William G.

Fish names, Manihiki. ms. on cards, with scientific equivalents, by E. H. Bryan, Jr. [Evidently Mr. Anderson identified fish casts at Bishop Museum, according to the Manihiki names]

QL
Fish.Pam.
370

FISHES   MIGRATION

Hart, John Lawson

Tagging British Columbia pilchards(Sardinops Caerulea (Girard)): Insertions and recoveries for 1937/38.

(British Columbia Fisheries Department, Report, 1937, pp. T57-T63.)

QL
5
B 61

FISHES   MIMICRY

Breder, Charles M., Jr.

An analysis of the deceptive resemblances of fishes to plant parts, with critical remarks on protective coloration, mimicry and adaptation.

(Bulletin of the Bingham Oceanographic Coll. Vol. 10 (2):1-49, 1946)

GN
2.S
P 76

also
GN
Ethn.Pam.
3698

FISHES   NATIVE NAMES   MAORI

Phillipps, W. J.

A list of Maori fish names.

(Journal of the Polynesian Society, Vol. 56: 41-51, 1947)

QL
Fish.Pam.
391

FISHES   MIGRATION

Hart, John Lawson

Tagging British Columbia Pilchards (Sardinops Caerulea (Girard)): Insertions and recoveries for 1939-40.

(Rept. Brit. Columbia Fisheries Dept., 1939, K 39-K41)

AS
474
S 76

FISHES   MORTALITY

Deraniyagala, P. E. P.

Mass mortality of the fish? Lutianus marginatus.

(Spolia Zeylanica, 27(2):239-240, 1955)

QL
Fishes
Pam.
567

FISHES   NATIVE NAMES   RAROTONGA

South Pacific Commission Project B.7.- Fisheries, Rarotonga, April 1952. (native names, fish traps; lagoon bait; sea bait; off shore fishes)

QL
Fish
Pam.
392

FISHES   MIGRATION

Hart, John Lawson

The tagging of herring (Clupea Pallasii) in British Columbia: insertions and recoveries during 1939-40. By John Lawson Hart and Albert L. Tester.

(Rept. Brit. Columbia Fisheries Dept., 1939, K42-K66)

QL
1
A 93 p

FISHES   SCHOOLS OF

Whitley, Gilbert P.

Aerial observations on fish schools.

(Proc. R. Zool. Soc. New South Wales, 1945/46:17-27)

GN
2.S
T 12

FISHES NATIVE NAMES   TAHITI

Nordhoff, Charles

Some of the commoner fishes of Tahiti, with their native names.

(Bull. Soc. d'Etudes Oceaniennes, No. 20: 280-282, 1927)

QL
1
N6-Z

FISHES   MIGRATION

Hildebrand, Samuel F.

The Panama Canal as a passageway for fishes, with lists and remarks on the fishes and invertebrates observed.
                    pt. 1, No. 3
(Zoologica, Vol. 24, 1939, pp. 14-45, 2 pls.)

DU
600
F 47-i

FISHES   NATIVE NAMES   FIJI

Fiji fishes.   (glossary of Fijian names and English popular names)

(Fiji Information s4, No. 2, Oct. 1956, p. 55)

GN
2.S
T 12

FISHES NATIVE NAMES   TAHITI

Schmidt, Johannes

Poissons d'eau douce de Tahiti. (photos; names in Tahitian, with scientific equivalents)

(Bull. Soc. d'Etudes Oceaniennes, No. 20: 278-279, 1927)

AP
2
N 4

FISHES   MIGRATION

Migration of Pacific Mackerel.

(Nature,Vol.143,1939, p.903)

AS
492
S 6

FISHES   NATIVE NAMES   MALAYA.

Burdon, T. W.

Papers on Malayan fishing methods. By T. W. Burdon and M. L. Parry.

(Jour. of the Malayan Branch Royal Asiatic Society, Vol. 27(2): 1954)

[pp. 176-176]

QQL
Fishes
Pam.
457

FISHES   NOMENCLATURE

Croker, Richard S.

Glossary of Japanese fisheries terms.

(General Headquarters, Supreme Commander for the Allied Powers, Natural Resources Section Report No. 63, Tokyo, 1946)

QL
1
C 78

FISHES   MIGRATION

Myers, George S.

Usage of anadromous, catadromous and allied terms for migratory fishes.

(Copeia, 1949:89-97, 1949)

QL
634.Ma
K 42

FISHES-NATIVE NAMES   MALAYA

Kesteven, G. L.

Malayan fisheries: a handbook prepared for the inaugural meeting of the Indo-Pacific Council, Singapore, March 1949. Foreword by Malcolm MacDonald. Malaya Publishing House, Ltd. Singapore. 1949. R8vo. viii+ 88 pp., 16 pl.

QL
618
J 82

FISHES   NOMENCLATURE

Jordan, David Starr

A Classification of Fishes...

(Stanford University Publications, University Series, Biological Sciences, Vol. III, No. 2, 1923)

Fishes—Nomenclature

AS
36.7
S 71

Jordan, David Starr, 1851–
... The genera of fishes ... A contribution to the stability of scientific nomenclature. By David Starr Jordan. Stanford University, Calif., The University, 1917–20.
4 v. 25½ᶜᵐ. (Leland Stanford junior university publications. University ser. 27, 36, 39, 43.)
CONTENTS.—pt. I: From Linnæus to Cuvier, 1758–1833, seventy-five years, with the accepted type of each. By D. S. Jordan, assisted by B. W. Evermann.—pt. II. From Agassiz to Bleeker, 1833–1858, twenty-six years, with the accepted type of each.—pt. III. From Guenther to Gill, 1859–1880, twenty-two years, with the accepted type of each.—pt. IV. From 1881 to 1920, thirty-nine years, with the accepted type of each.
1. Fishes—Nomenclature. I. Evermann, Barton Warren, 1853–
17–29156 Revised 2
Library of Congress   QL618.J7
—— Copy 2. pt. II–III   AS36.L5 no. 36, 39
[r21h3]

FISHES   NOMENCLATURE

AS
719
A 93-m

Whitley, Gilbert

The common names of fishes.

(Australian Museum Magazine, Vol. 10(10): 310–315, 1952)

FISHES   NOMENCLATURE

QL
1
A 93

Whitley, Gilbert P.

Ichthyological genotypes:Desmarest's designations, 1874.

(The Australian Zoologist, 9:222–226, 1939)

FISHES   NOMENCLATURE

See also

FISHES   NATIVE NAMES

FISHES   OCEAN BOTTOM

Q
115
S 97

Nybelin, Orvar

Deep-sea bottom-fishes.

IN

Pettersson, Hans
Reports of the Swedish Deep-Sea Expedition, 1947–1948, Vol. 2(3):250–364, 1957)

FISHES   OSTEOLOGY

QL
821
S 79

Starks, Edwin Chapin

Bones of the Ethmoid Region of the Fish Skull.

(Stanford University Publications, Biological Sciences, Volume IV, No. 3, 1926)

FISHES   PARASITES

See

PARASITES   FISHES

FISHES   PELAGIC

QL
Fishes
Pam.
466

Blackburn, M.

Measures of abundance of pelagic fish in some southeastern Australian waters. By M. Blackburn and J. A. Tubb.

(Australia, Commonwealth Sci. and Ind. Research Organization, Bull. 251, 1950)

FISHES, PELAGIC

AS
36
S
AS
36
S5
sp.#2
QL
1
H-m
v.22

Goode, George Brown, 1851–1896.
... Oceanic ichthyology, a treatise on the deep-sea and pelagic fishes of the world, based chiefly upon the collections made by the steamers Blake, Albatross, and Fish Hawk in the northwestern Atlantic, with an atlas containing 417 figures. By George Brown Goode ... and Tarleton H. Bean ... Washington, The Smithsonian institution, 1895.
3 p. l., iii–xxxv, 26*, 70, [2], 71–553 p. illus., pl. and atlas of 3 p. l., iii–xxiii, 26 p., cxxiii pl. 31½ᶜᵐ. (Smithsonian contributions to knowledge. [vol. xxx–xxxi])
(Continued on next card)
4–9383 Revised

FISHES, PELAGIC

AS
36
S
AS
36
S5
sp.#2
QL
1
H-m
v.22

Goode, George Brown, 1851–1896. ... Oceanic ichthyology ... 1895. (Card 2)
Smithsonian institution publications 981, 982.
Published at the joint expense of the Smithsonian institution and the United States National museum.
Issued also as U. S. National museum. Special bulletin no. 2.

1. Fishes, Pelagic. 2. Marine fauna—North Atlantic. I. Bean, Tarleton Hoffman, 1846– joint author. II. Smithsonian institution. Publications 981, 982.
4–9383 Revised
Library of Congress   Q11.S68 vol. 30–31

FISHES, PELAGIC

QL
1
H2

Lendenfeld, Robert J   edler von Lendlmayer, reichsritter von, 1858–1913.
... The radiating organs of the deep sea fishes. By Robert von Lendenfeld. With an appendix on the structure of the bud-like organs of *Malthopsis spinulosa* Garman. By Emanuel Trojan ... Cambridge, Printed for the Museum, 1905.
2 p. l., p. [169]–213. xii pl. (incl. fold. map) diagr. 31 x 26ᶜᵐ. (Memoirs of the Museum of comparative zoölogy at Harvard college, vol. xxx, no. 2)
(Continued on next card)
A 19–1061
[3]

FISHES, PELAGIC

QL
1
H2

Lendenfeld, Robert J   edler von Lendlmayer, reichsritter von, 1858–1913. ... The radiating organs of deep sea fishes ... 1905. (Card 2)
Each plate accompanied by leaf with descriptive letterpress.
Reports on an exploration off the west coasts of Mexico, Central and South America, and off the Galapagos Islands ... by the U. S. Fish commission steamer "Albatross", during 1891 ... xxxi.
"Literature": p. 207, 213.

1. Fishes—Anatomy. 2. Fishes, Pelagic. 3. Phosphorescence. 4. Albatross (Steamer) I. Trojan, Emanuel.
A 19–1061
Title from Univ. of Chicago   QL1.H375   vol. 30, no. 2
Printed by L. C.   [3]

FISHES, PELAGIC

QL
1
H2

Trojan, Emanuel.
... Ein beitrag zur morphologie des tiefseefischgehirnes. Von Emanuel Trojan ... Cambridge, Printed for the Museum, 1906.
2 p. l., p. [219]–255. 6 col. pl. 31 x 26ᶜᵐ. (Memoirs of the Museum of comparative zoölogy at Harvard college, vol. xxx, no. 3)
Each plate accompanied by leaf with descriptive letterpress.
Reports on an exploration off the west coasts of Mexico, Central and South America, and off the Galapagos Islands ... by the U. S. Fish commission steamer "Albatross", during 1891 ... xxxvi.
"Literaturverzeichnis": p. 253–254.

1. Fishes—Anatomy. 2. Brain. 3. Fishes, Pelagic. 4. Albatross (Steamer)
Title from Univ. of Chicago   QL1.H375   vol. 30, no. 3
Printed by L. C.   [3]   A 19–1078

FISHES   PELAGIC

Q
101
P 18

Ward, H. B.

Parasitism and disease among oceanic fishes: Economic aspects and epidemics due to animal parasites.

(Proc. of the Fifth Pacific Science Congress, Vol. 5, pp. 4177–4182, 1933)

FISHES – PHYSIOLOGY

QL
Fish Pam.
342

Bond, Richard M.

A note on the blood of the hag-fish (Polistotrema stouti)(Lockington) by Richard M. Bond, M.Katherine Cary and G.E.Hutchinson.

(Jour.Experimental Bielogy Vol. IX, No. 1, pp. 12–14, Jan. 1932)

FISHES POISONOUS

See

POISONOUS FISHES

FISHES   PRESERVATION

QL
Fish Pam.
588

Stern, J. A.

Pacific coast program on the irradiation preservation of fish. By Joseph A. Stern and John A. Dassow.

(Reprint: Comm. Fish. Rev., 20(2):16–20, 1958)

FISHES   PUGNACITY

AP
2
N 28

Smith, J. L. B.

Pugnacity of marlins and swordfish.

(Nature, 178(4541):1065, 1956)

FISHES – RESPIRATION

QL
Fish Pam.
332

Kokubo, Seiji

Contribution to the Research on the Respiration of Fishes. II. Studies on the Acidosis of Fishes.

Reprinted from the Science Reports of the Tohoku Imperial University – Vol. V. No.2, 1930

FISHES   SCHOOLING

QL
Fish Pam.
625

Joseph, James

The schooling behavior of Pacific yellowfin and skipjack tuna held in a bait well. By James Joseph and Izadore Barrett. For Inter-American Tropical Tuna Commission, Scripps Institution of Oceanography, La Jolla, Calif., July, 1962.

(Reprint, California Fish and Game, Vol. 49(1), 1963)

FISHES   SCHOOLING

AP
2
S 41

Shaw, Evelyn

The Schooling of Fishes.

(Scientific American, 206(6): 128–141, 1962)

AS
36
A 4

FISHES   SCHOOLS

Breder, C. M., Jr.

Studies on the structure of the fish school

(Bull. Am. Mus. of Nat. Hist., Vol. 98(1):
1-27, 1951)

QL
627
P 11

FISHES   SPAWNING GROUNDS

A symposium on the investigation of tuna
and skipjack spawning grounds.

(From South Sea Science [Kagaku Nanyō], Vol.
4:64-75, 1941)

Translation from Japanese, Pacific Oceanic
Fishery Investigations, No. 16

QL
1
F

FISHES--AFRICA, EAST
Hubbs, Carl Levitt, 1894-
... Notes on fishes from the Athi River in British East
Africa, by Carl L. Hubbs ... Chicago, 1918.
cover-title, p. 9-16. III pl. 24½ᶜᵐ. (Field museum of natural history.
Publication 198. Zoölogical series. vol. XII, no. 2)

1. Fishes—Africa, British East. 2. Athi River.

18-13028

Library of Congress   QL1.F4 vol. 12, no 2

QL
638.S35
I 61-b

FISHES   SCHOOLS

Orange, Craig J. and others

Schooling habits of yellowfin tuna (Neothunnus macropterus) and skipjack (Katsuwonus
pelamis) in the eastern Pacific Ocean, as indicated by purse seine catch records, 1946-1955.

(Inter-tropical Tuna Commission, Bull. Vol.
2(3), 1957)

QL
627
U-b

FISHES   STUDY AND TEACHING

Reighard, Jacob

Methods of studying the habits of fishes,
with an account of the breeding habits of the
horned dace.

(Bull. U. S. Fish Commission, 28, 1908, Pt.
2, pp. 1111-1136, pl. 114-120)

QL
Fishes
Pam.
591

FISHES   AFRICA (EAST)

Williams, F.

Fishes of the family Carangidae in British
East African waters.

(Ann. and Mag. Nat. Hist., s13, vol. 1:369-
430, 1958)

QL
1
M 33

FISHES   SIZE

Nichols, John Treadwell

Remarks on size in fishes.

(Marine Life, Vol. 1 (2), 1944, pp. 3-6)

QL
Fish
Pam.
558

FISHES   TROPICAL

Nichols, J. T.

Certain marine tropical fishes as food.
By J. T. Nichols and L. L. Mowbray.

(Copeia, No. 48, pp. 77-84, Sept. 1917)

AS
36
S4

FISHES--AFRICA, WEST
Fowler, Henry Weed.
The fishes of the United States eclipse expedition to
West Africa. By Henry W. Fowler ...
(*In* U. S. National museum. Proceedings. Washington, 1920. 23½ᶜᵐ.
v. 56, p. 195-292. illus.)

1. Fishes—Africa, West.   I. Title: United States eclipse expedition to
West Africa.

Library of Congress   Q11.U55 vol. 56   20-9671
——— Copy 2.   Q11.U55 vol. 56 2d set
                          [5]

QL
627
U-b

FISHES   SPAWNING

June, Fred C.

Spawning of yellowfin tuna in Hawaiian
waters.

(United States Dept. of the Interior,
Fishery Bulletin 77, pp. 47-64, 1953)

[Neothunnus   macropterus]

QL
1
C 15

FISHES - VEINS
Daniel, John Franklin, 1873-
... The subclavian vein and its relations in elasmobranch fishes, by J. Frank Daniel. Berkeley, University
of California press, 1918.
cover-title, p. [479]-484. illus. 27ᶜᵐ. (University of California publications in zoology. v. 18, no. 16)
"Literature cited": p. 484.

1. Subclavian vein. 2. Fishes—Veins.

A 18-903

Title from Univ. of Calif.   Library of Congress

QL
Fish
Pam
#240

FISHES-AFRICA, WEST

Fowler, Henry W.

New Taxonomic Names of West African
Marine Fishes. Am. Mus. Nov. Mar. 1925

QL
Fishes
Pam.449

FISHES   SPAWNING

Schaefer, Milner B.

Spawning of Pacific tunas and its implications to the welfare of the Pacific Tuna fisheries.

(Trans. of the 13th North American Wildlife
Conference, Moh 8,9,10, 1949, pp. 365-371)

AS
36
A 4

FISHES   AFRICA

Fowler, Henry W.

Marine fishes of West Africa.

(Bull. Am. Mus. Nat. Hist., 30:1-1493, 1936)

OL
1
F

FISHES --AFRICA.
Meek, Seth Eugene, 1859-1914.
... List of fishes and reptiles obtained by Field Columbian museum East African expedition to Somali-land in
1896. By S. E. Meek ... Chicago, 1897.
1 p. l., p. 163-184. pl. 24½ᶜᵐ. (Field Columbian museum. Publication 22. Zoölogical series. vol. I, no. 8)

1. Fishes—Africa. 2. Reptiles—Africa.   I. Eliot, Daniel Giraud,
1835-1915.

Library of Congress   QL1.F4   4-10465
——— Copy 2.   QL337.M47

QL
627
U-b

FISHES - SPAWNING

Yuen, H.S.H.

Yellowfin tuna spawning in the central
equatorial Pacific. By Heeny S.H. and Fred
C. June.

(Fishery Bull.112, Fish and Wildlife Service, U.S.Dept.Int., Vol.97, 1957)

QL
Fishes
Pam.
598

FISHES - AFRICA

Morgans, J. F. C.

Three confusing species of Serranid fish,
one described as new, from East Africa.

(Annals and Mag. Nat. His., s13, vol. 1:
642-656, 1958)

AS
36
S2

FISHES--ALASKA.
Bean, Barton Appler, 1860-
Notes on certain features of the life history of the
Alaskan fresh-water sculpin, by Barton A. Bean and
Alfred C. Weed.
(*In* Smithsonian institution. Smithsonian miscellaneous collections.
Washington, 1910. 24½ᶜᵐ. vol. LII (Quarterly issue, vol. V) p. 457-460)
Publication 1876.
Originally published August 19, 1909.

1. Sculpin. 2. Fishes—Alaska.   I. Weed, Alfred Cleveland, joint
author.

Library of Congress   Q11.S7 vol. 52   16-12719
——— Copy 2.

QH
1
P 11

FISHES   SPAWNING BEHAVIOR

Morris, Robert W.

Spawning behavior of the cottid fish Clino-
cottus recalvus (Greeley).

(Pacific Science, Vol. 6:256-258, 1952)

QL
Fishes
Pam.
596

FISHES   AFRICA

Williams, F.

Marlins in British East African waters.

(Nature, 183:762-763, 1959)

QL
752
U 58 e

FISHES   ALASKA

Rhode, Clarence J.

Alaska's fish and wildlife. By Clarence
J. Rhode and Will Barker. Illustrated by Bob
Hines.

(U. S. Fish and Wildlife Service, Circular
no. 17, 1953)

QL 627 U-b   FISHES—ALASKA

Rich, Willis H.

Salmon-tagging experiments in Alaska, 1924-1925. U.S. Bur. of Fisheries Bull. doc. 1005, 1926.

GC 63 D 61   FISHES ANTARCTIC

Norman, J. R.

Coast fishes, Part I: The South Atlantic; Part II: The Patagonian region; Part III: The Antarctic zone.
Discovery Committee
    Discovery Reports, Vol. 12, 1935, p. 1-58; Vol. 16, 1937, p. 1-150; Vol. 18, 1940, pp. 3-104

QL Fish. Pam. 354   FISHES ATLANTIC

Legendre, R.

La faune pélagique de l'Atlantique au large du Golfe de Gascogne, recueillie dans des estomacs de Germons. Première Partie: Poissons, par R. Legendre.

(Annales de l'Institut Océanographique, Nouvelle Série, Tome XIV, Fasc. VI. Août 1934, pp. 249-418)

AS 36 S4   FISHES ALBATROSS (Steamer)

Radcliffe, Lewis, 1880–
... Descriptions of a new family, two new genera, and twenty-nine new species of anacanthine fishes from the Philippine Islands and contiguous waters. By Lewis Radcliffe ...

(*In* U. S. National museum. Proceedings. Washington, 1913. 23½ᶜᵐ. vol. 43, p. 105-140. illus., pl. 22-31)
"Scientific results of the Philippine cruise of the fisheries steamer 'Albatross,' 1907-1910.—no. 21."

1. Fisheries—Philippine Islands. 2. Albatross (Steamer)

    13-13110

Library of Congress   Q11.U55 vol. 43

Q 115 M 46   FISHES ANTARCTIC

Norman, J. R.
    Fishes

Mawson, Sir Douglas
    British, Australian, and New Zealand Antarctic Research Expedition, 1929-1931, Reports, Ser. B, Vol. I, Part 2, 1937, pp. 49-88.

FISHES--ATLANTIC COAST

AS 36 S4   Gilbert, Charles Henry, 1859–
Descriptions of two new fishes of the genus *Triglops* from the Atlantic coast of North America. By Charles H. Gilbert ...

(*In* U. S. National museum. Proceedings. Washington, 1913. 23½ᶜᵐ. v. 44, p. 465-468. pl. 64)

1. Triglops. 2. Fishes—Atlantic coast.

    13-20873

Library of Congress   Q11.U55 vol. 44

AS 36 S4   FISHES ALBATROSS (Steamer)

Radcliffe, Lewis, 1880–
... Descriptions of seven new genera and thirty-one new species of fishes of the families *Brotulidæ* and *Carapidæ* from the Philippine Islands and the Dutch East Indies. By Lewis Radcliffe ...
(*In* U. S. National museum. Proceedings. Washington, 1913. 23½ᶜᵐ. v. 44, p. 135-176. pl. 7-17)
"In the study of this collection the writer has been associated with Dr. Hugh M. Smith, who becomes joint author of the new genera and species herein described."
"Scientific results of the Philippine cruise of the fisheries steamer 'Albatross,' 1907-1910.—no. 24."
1. Brotulidæ. 2. Carapidæ. 3. Fishes—Philippine Islands. 4. Albatross (Steamer) ɪ. Smith, Hugh McCormick, 1865– joint author.

    13-20858

Library of Congress   Q11.U55 vol. 44

QH 11 B86   FISHES – ANTARCTIC

Waite, Edgar R.

Antarctic fishes. British Antarctic Expedition. v.II, pt.2, 1911.

QL 621.C B 83   FISHES ATLANTIC COAST

Breder, Charles M., Jr.

Field book of marine fishes of the Atlantic Coast, from Labrador to Texas. Being a short description of their characteristics and habits with keys for their identification. With 8 colored plates by W. S. Bronson and 403 other illustrations. G.P.Putnam's Sons. New York and London. 1929c. sm8vo. xxxvii + 332 pp.

AS 36 S4   FISHES ALBATROSS (Steamer)

Radcliffe, Lewis, 1880–
... New pediculate fishes from the Philippine Islands and contiguous waters. By Lewis Radcliffe ...

(*In* U. S. National museum. Proceedings. Washington, 1912. 23½ᶜᵐ. vol. 42, p. 199-214. illus., pl. 16-27)
"Scientific results of the Philippine cruise of the fisheries steamer 'Albatross,' 1907-1910.—no. 16."
"In the study of this collection the writer has been associated with Dr. Hugh M. Smith, who becomes joint author of the new genus and species herein described."

1. Fishes—Philippine Islands. 2. Albatross (Steamer) ɪ. Smith, Hugh McCormick, 1865–

    13-9524

Library of Congress   Q11.U55 vol. 42

Q 115 M 46   FISHES ANTARCTIC

Waite, Edgar R.
    Fishes

Mawson, Sir Douglas
    Australasian Antarctic Expedition, 1911-14. Sci. Reports, Series C, Vol. III, Part 1, 1916.

FISHES--ATLANTIC COAST.

AS 36 S2   Gill, Theodore Nicholas, 1837–1914.
... Catalogue of the fishes of the east coast of North America. By Theodore Gill ... Washington, Smithsonian institution, 1873.
iii, 50 p. 24ᶜᵐ. (Smithsonian miscellaneous collections. ɪvol. xɪv, art. ɪɪ;)
Publication 283.
Bibliography of east coast fishes: p. 37-44.
"Prepared ... as an Appendix to the report of the U. S. commissioner of fish and fisheries for 1871-2 ... ɪandɪ now issued as one of the publications of the Smithsonian miscellaneous collections."
"May be considered as a new edition of 'Catalogue of the fishes of the eastern coast of North America, from Greenland to Georgia,' published in 1861."
1. Fishes—Atlantic coast.

Library of Congress   Q11.S7 vol. 14, art. 2
—— Copy 2.   Q77.S7 2d set   16-6365
—— Another issue.   QL618.G436
On verso of t.-p.:   Philadelphia, Collins, printer.

AS 36 A4   FISHES – ALBERTA

Nichols, John Treadwell.

On a new race of minnow from the Rocky Mountains park. A new *Gymnachirus* from North Carolina. By John Treadwell Nichols ... New York, 1916.

cover-title, p. 69-72, illus. 24ᶜᵐ. (Bulletin of the American museum of natural history. vol. xxxv, arts. vɪɪɪ and ɪx)

1. Fishes—Alberta. 2. Fishes—North Carolina. 3. ɪCyprinidæ; 4. ɪSoleidæɪ

    F 16-97

Library, U. S. Bur. of   Fisheries

AS 540 P 55   FISHES ASIA

Brittan, Martin R.

A revision of the Indo-Malayan fresh-water genus Rasbora.

(Philippine Island, Nat. Inst. Sci. and Tech., Monograph no. 3, 1954)

AS 182 S 47   FISHES ATLANTIC

Klausewitz, W.

Fische aus dem Atlantik und Pazifik.

(Senckenbergiana, Biologica, Bd. 39:57-84, 1958)

QL Fishes Pam. 358   FISHES AMSTERDAM ISLAND

de la Rue, E. Aubert

Informations sur les pêches étrangères et coloniales: la pêche aux îles Saint-Paul et Amsterdam.

(Revue des Travaux de l'Office des Pêches Maritimes, Tome V fasc. 1, No. 17, nd, pp. 83-109)

QL Fish Pam. 363   FISHES ASIA

Mori, Tamezo

Studies on the geographical distribution of freshwater fishes in eastern asia. 1936. 4to. 88 pp.

AS 750 D 67 c   FISHES AUCKLAND ISLAND

Stokell, G.

Freshwater fishes from the Auckland and Campbell Islands.

(Cape Exp. - Sci. Res. of the New Zealand Sub-antarctic Exp., 1941-45, Bull. No. 9, 1950

QL 1 I-m   FISHES ANDAMAN ISLANDS

Herre, Albert W. C. T.

A list of the fishes known from the Andaman Islands.

(Memoirs of the Indian Museum, Vol. 13 (3): 331-403, 1941)

QL Fish.Pam. 442   FISHES ATLANTIC (SOUTH)

Carson, Rachel L..

Fish and shellfish of the South Atlantic and Gulf coasts.

(Conservation Bulletin, 37, 1944, U. S. Dept. of the Interior, Office of the Coordinator of Fisheries)

QL Fishes Pam. 467   FISHES AUSTRALIA

Blackburn, M.

Age, rate of growth, and general life-history of the Australian Pilchard (*Sardinops neopilchardus*) in New South Wales Waters.

(Australia, Commonwealth Sci. and Ind. Research Organization, Bull. 242, 1949)

QL
Fishes
Pam.
466

FISHES   AUSTRALIA

Blackburn, M.

    Measures of abundance of pelagic fish in some southeastern Australian waters. By M. Blackburn and J. A. Tubb.

    (Australia, Commonwealth Sci. and Ind. Research Organization, Bull. 251, 1950)

QL
636
M 13

FISHES   AUSTRALIA

McCulloch, Allan R.

    A check-list of the fishes recorded from Australia. Parts I-III.

    (Australian Museum, Mem. V, 1929)

QL
636
R 85

FISHES   AUSTRALIA

Roughley, T. C.

    Fish and fisheries of Australia. With 60 colour plates and 21 plates in black and white. Angus and Robertson. Sydney; London. R8vo. Revised and enlarged edition. 1951. xv + 343 pp

---

QL
636
C33

Fishes - Australia

Castelnau, F. de (Count)

    Contribution to the ichthyology of Australia. Ex Zool. & Acclim. Society of Victoria.. I, 1872. pp. 29-247.

AS
720.3
S 72

FISHES   AUSTRALIA

McCulloch, Allan R.

    Some new and little-known fishes from South Australia, by Allan R. McCulloch and Edgar R. Waite.

    (Rec. South Austr. Mus., I:39-78, 1918)

FISHES-AUSTRALIA

QL
636
Ro
R 85

Roughley, Theodore Cleveland, 1889-

    ... Fishes of Australia and their technology. By T. C. Roughley ... Pub. by the authority of the government of New South Wales. Sydney, W. A. Gullick, government printer, 1916.

    xvi, 296 p., 1 l. col. front., illus. (incl. maps) 70 col. pl. 25ᶜᵐ. (Technical education series. no. 21. Technological museum, Sydney)

    Pages 274 and 276, full-page illustrations accompanied by guard sheets with outline drawings.

    1. Fishes—Australia. 2. Fisheries—Australia.

    A 17-1382 Revised

Title from Leland Stanford, Jr., Univ. Printed by L. C.
(r19c2)

QL
Fishes
Pam.
477

FISHES   AUSTRALIA

Coates, George

    Fishing on the Barrier Reef and inshore. Printed and published by T. Willmett and Sons... Townsville, Australia. 8vo. 72 pp. n.d.

QL
1
A 93

FISHES   AUSTRALIA

McCulloch, Allan R.

    Check-list of the fish and fish-like animals of New South Wales.

    (The Australian Zoologist, Vol. 1:217-227, 1919; 2:24-68, 1921; 3:86-130, 1922)

G
51
A 93

FISHES   AUSTRALIA

Stead, David G.

    Australian food and game fishes.

    (The Australian Geographer, Vol. 1, 1932 pp. 85-92) No. 4

QL
Fish
Pam
#80

Fishes.- Australia.

Cohen Philip

    The Marine fish and fisheries of N. S. Wales, past and present, In their Commercial aspect.
Sydney. 1892. 8° pp. 30 Map.

G. 4. 5.

AS
720.N
L
5

Fishes Australia

Macleay, William

    Descriptive catalogue of the fishes of Australia.
in Linn. soc. N.S.W. Proc. II, 1823, pp. 1-174, 201-387.

QL
Fish
Pam
#74

FISHES--AUSTRALIA

Stead, David G.

    On the need for more uniformity in the vernacular names of Australian edible fishes.
N.S.W. Fisheries Branch.

Sydney, 1911. 8vo pp. 12

FEB 23 1912

QL
5
D 22

locked
case

FISHES   AUSTRALIA

Darwin, Charles

    The Zoology of the Voyage of H.M.S. Beagle, under the command of Captain Fitzroy, during the years 1832 to 1836. London. 1839-1843. 4to. Part IV: Fish, by Leonard Jenyns. 1842.

QL
Fishes
Pam.
618a,b

FISHES   AUSTRALIA

Mees, G. F.

    Additions to the fish fauna of Western Australia, 1-2

    (Fisheries Bull. No. 9:1-2, 1960)

AS
720.S
S 72

FISHES   AUSTRALIA (south)

Waite, Edgar R.

    Catalogue of the fishes of South Australia.

    (Records of the South Australian Museum, Vol. 2, 1921-1924, pp. 1-208 [published 1921])

QL
636
Q 3

FISHES   AUSTRALIA

Fowler, Henry W.

    Australian fishes obtained or observed by the United States Exploring Expedition, 1838-1842.

    (Ichthyological Notes, No. 2:11-20, 1953)

QL
Fishes
Pam.
617

FISHES   AUSTRALIA

Mees, G. F.

    The Uranoscopidae of Western Australia (Pisces, Perciformes)

    (Journal of the R. Soc. of Western Australia, Vol. 43(2):46-53, 1960)

DU
1
P

FISHES   AUSTRALIA

Waite, Edgar R.

    A catalogue of the marine fishes of South Australia.

    (Journal of the Pan-Pacific Research Institution, Vol. 3, 1928, No. 1, pp. 3-10)

QL
636
N

FISHES   AUSTRALIA

Lake, John S.

    The fresh-water fishes of New South Wales. (Research Bull, State Fisheries, N. S. Wales, No. 5, 1959)

QL
636
O 34

FISHES   AUSTRALIA

Ogilby, J. Douglas

    Catalogue of the fishes in the collection of the Australian Museum. Part I. Recent Palaeichthyan fishes. Australian Museum (Catalogue No. 14). Sydney. F. W. White. 1888. 8vo. 28 pp

---

QH
197
S 72

FISHES   AUSTRALIA

Waite, Edgar R.

    The fishes of South Australia.

    IN
South Australian Branch of the British Science Guild... Handbook of the flora and fauna of South Australia... Adelaide, 1923.

FISHES AUSTRALIA

AS
720.S
S 72   Waite, Edgar R.

Review of the Lophobranchiate fishes of
South Australia, by Edgar R. Waite and Herbert
M. Hale.

(Rec. S. Australian Mus., 1:293-324, 1921)

FISHES AUSTRALIA

QL
623
W 61   Whitley, Gilbert Percy

The fishes of Australia, Part I: The sharks,
rays, devil-fish, and other primitive fishes of
Australia and New Zealand.

Sydney. Published by the Royal Zool. Soc. of New
South Wales. Australian Zoological Handbook.
1940.

FISHES BAKER ISLAND

QL
636.5
F 78   Fowler, Henry W.

AS   Fishes of the tropical central Pacific.
763
B-b   (Bernice P. Bishop Museum, Bulletin No. 38,
1927; Whippoorwill Expedition, Publication No. 1)

Reading
Room

FISHES AUSTRALIA

QL
619
W 37   Weber, Max

Fishes of the Indo-Australian archipelago.
By Max Weber and L. F. de Beaufort. Vols. 1-10
1911-1953 E. J. Brill. Leiden. 8vo.

Vol. 1 has sub-title: Index of the ichthyol-
gical papers of P. Bleeker.
Vol. 8   by L. F. de Beaufort alone.

FISHES AUSTRALIA

QL
1
A 93   Whitley, G. P.

Ichthyological notes and illustrations.
(Australian fishes)

(The Australian Zoologist, 10:1-50, 167-187,
1941/43)

FISHES BALI

AS
36
A 65-no   Nichols, J. T.

A new blenny from Bali and a new threadfin
from New Guinea.

(American Museum Novitates, No. 1680, 1954)

FISHES' AUSTRALIA

QL
1
A 93   Whitley, Gilbert P.

The Australian devil ray.

(The Australian Zoologist, 8:164-188, 1936)

FISHES AUSTRALIA

QL
1
A 93   Whitley, G. P.

Illustrations of some Australian fishes.

(The Australian Zoologist, 9:397-428, 1940)

FISHES-BALI

AS
36
A 65   Nichols, John T.

One new, and other labroid fishes from
Bali.

(American Mus. Novitates, No. 1154, 1941)

FISHES AUSTRALIA

AS
719
A-m   Whitley, Gilbert P.

Burramundi.

(Australian Museum Mag., Vol. 7, 1941,
pp. 264-268)

FISHES AUSTRALIA

QL
1
A 93   Whitley, Gilbert P.

The lancelets and lampreys of Australia.

(The Australian Zoologist, 7:256-264, 1932)

FISHES BATAVIA

QL
Fishes
Pam.   Koumans, F. P.
420

Results of a reexamination of types and
specimens of gobioid fishes, with notes on the
fishfauna of the surroundings of Batavia.

(Zoologische Mededeelingen, 22, 1940, pp.
121-210)

FISHES AUSTRALIA

AS
720.N
L   Whitley, Gilbert P.

Ichthyological descriptions and notes.

(Proceedings of the Linnean Soc. of N. S.
Wales, 68:114-144, 1943)

FISHES AUSTRALIA

QL
1
A 93   Whitley, Gilbert P.

New names for Australian fishes.

(The Australian Zoologist, 6:310-334, 1930)

FISHES - BERMUDA ISLANDS

QL
1
F   Bean, Tarleton Hoffman, 1846-1916.

... A catalogue of the fishes of Bermuda, with notes on a
collection made in 1905 for the Field museum. By Dr.
Tarleton H. Bean ... Chicago, 1906.

1 p. l., 21-89 p. illus. 24½ᶜᵐ. (Field Columbian museum. Publication
108. Zoological series. vol. VII, no. 2)

1. Fishes—Bermuda Islands.

6-34842

Library of Congress   QL1.F4

FISHES AUSTRALIA

QL
1
A 93   Whitley, Gilbert P.

Leichhardt's sawfish.

(The Australian Zoologist, Vol. XI, 43-45,
1945)

FISHES AUSTRALIA

QL
1
A 93   Whitley, Gilbert P.

New sharks and fishes from Western Australia.

(The Australian Zoologist, Vol. 10, 1944, pp.
252-273)

FISHES BERMUDA

QL
Fish Pam.
349   Beebe, William

Deep-Sea Somiatoed Fishes: One New Genus
and Eight New Species.

(Copeia, 1933, No. 4, pp. 160-175)

FISHES AUSTRALIA

QL
1
A 93   Whitley, Gilbert P.

Ray's bream and its allies in Australia.

(The Australian Zoologist, 9:191-194, 1938)

FISHES BAHAMAS

AS
36
A 16p   Böhlke, James
and
QL   A review of the blenny genus Chaenopsis,
Fishes   and the description of a related new genus from
Pam.   the Bahamas.
575

(Proc. of the Acad. of Nat. Sci. of Phila.
Vol. CIX:81-103, 1957)

FISHES BERMUDA

QL
621.B
B 41   Beebe, William

Field book of the shore fishes of Bermuda,
by William Beebe and John Tee Van. Published
under the auspices of the New York Zoological
Society. 343 illustrations. New York. 1933.
sm8vo.

FISHES--BERMUDA ISLANDS.
AS
36
C8
Garman, Samuel, 1846-
... Additions to the ichthyological fauna of the Bermudas, from the collections of the Yale expedition of 1898.
(In Connecticut academy of arts and sciences. Transactions. New Haven, 1899-1900. 25ᶜᵐ. v. 10, p. [510]-512)

1. Fishes—Bermuda Islands.   I. Title.

Library of Congress   Q11.C9 vol. 10   A 17-882
Yale University   A53n.366.10

QL
F 45
FISHES   BORNEO

Inger, Robert F.

Report on a collection of marine fishes from North Borneo.

(Fieldiana: Zoology, Vol. 36(3):339-405, 1957)

FISHES--BRAZIL
Steindachner F
QL
Fish
Pam
#128
Über einige Fischarten aus dem Flusse Cubatao in State Santa Catharina bei Theresopolis.

AUG - 1 1907

Wei 1907.   8° Th 18. T4 1.

AS
36
S5
and
AS
36
S2
FISHES   BERMUDA

Goode, George Brown, 1851-1896.
Catalogue of the fishes of the Bermudas. Based chiefly upon the collections of the United States National museum. By G. Brown Goode ... Washington, Govt. print. off., 1876.
2, 82 p. 24½ᵐᵐ. (Added t.-p.: ... Bulletin of the United States National museum. no. 5)
Issued also as vol. XIII, art. 5 of the Smithsonian miscellaneous collections.
Smithsonian institution publication 296.

1. Fishes—Bermuda Islands.   I. U. S. National museum.

S 13-117

Library, Smithsonian   Institution Q11.U6

AS
540
P
FISHES   BORNEO

Seale, Alvin

Fishes of Borneo, with descriptions of four new species.

(Philippine Journal of Sci., V, D:263-286, 1910)

AS
80
R2
Fishes, Brazil
see publications of Museu Nacional de Rio de Janeiro.

QL
1
F 45
FISHES   BERMUDA

Kanazawa, Robert H.

More new species and new records of fishes from Bermuda.

(Fieldiana. Zoology, Vol. 34(7), 1952)

QL
321.B
W 59
FISHES   BORNEO

Vaillant, Léon

Sur les poissons des eaux douces de Borneo.

Whitehead, John
Exploration of Mount Kina Balu, North Borneo.
London. 1893.   Appendix, p. 286

AS
42
V 64
FISHES   BRITISH COLUMBIA

Carl, G. Clifford and others

The fresh-water fishes of British Columbia, by G. Clifford Carl, W. A. Clemens, and C. C. Lindsey.

(British Columbia Provincial Museum, Handbook No. 5, 1959)

AS
36
S 1
FISHES BIKINI

Schultz, Leonard P.

The biology of Bikini Atoll, with special reference to the fishes.

(Smithsonian Report, 1947:301-316, 1948)

QL
Fish
Pam
263
FISHES - BRAZIL

Borodin, N. A.
Some new catfishes from Brazil. Amer. Mus. Nov. 266, 1927.

QL
Fishes
Pam
422
FISHES   BRITISH COLUMBIA

Wilby, G. V.

Fishes collected by the Wm. J. Stewart in British Columbia waters during 1934 and 1935.

(Canadian Journal of Research, D.24:134-155, 1946)

QL
634.J
T 16
FISHES   BONIN ISLANDS

Tanaka, Shigeho

Figures and descriptions of the fishes of Japan, including Riukiu Islands, Bonin Islands... Tokyo. 1925-30 R8vo.

FISHES--BRAZIL
QL
1
H1
Eigenmann, Carl H   1863-
... Zoological results of the Thayer Brazilian expedition. Preliminary descriptions of new genera and species of tetragonopterid characins, by Carl H. Eigenmann. Cambridge, Mass. ... Printed for the museum, 1908.
p. [91]-106. 24ᶜᵐ. (Bulletin of the Museum of comparative zoology at Harvard college. vol. LII, no. 6)

1. Characinidae. 2. Fishes—Brazil.

Library, U. S. Bur. of   Fisheries   F 11-173

AS
36
C51
FISHES-BRITISH GUIANA
Eigenmann, Carl H   1863-
... The freshwater fishes of British Guiana, including a study of the ecological grouping of species, and the relation of the fauna of the plateau to that of the lowlands. By C. H. Eigenmann, PH. D. Pittsburgh, Pub. by the authority of the Board of trustees of the Carnegie institute, 1912.
cover-title, xx, 578 p. front., illus., CIII pl. (1 col., incl. 33 maps) 33½ᵐᵐ.
(Memoirs of the Carnegie museum. vol. v)
Publications of the Carnegie museum, serial no. 67.
Bibliography: p. 530-554.
1. Fishes—British Guiana. 2. Fishes—South America—Bibl.

Library of Congress   QL632.B9E5   12-23721
—— Copy 2.   AS36.P75

QL
1
F 45
FISHES   BORNEO

Inger, Robert F.

The fresh-water fishes of North Borneo. By Robert F. Inger and Chin Phui Kong.

(Fieldiana: Zoology, Vol. 45, 1962)

QL
632.B
M 67
FISHES   BRAZIL

Miranda-Ribeiro, Alipio de

Fauna Brasiliense: Peixes, Vol. II, Parte 1, Fasciculo 1, 1923. Museu Nacional do Rio de Janeiro, 4to.

QL
Fishes
Pam.
597
FISHES   BURMA

Misra, K. S.

An aid to the identification of the fishes of India, Burma and Ceylon. 1. Elasmobranchii and Holocephali.

(Records of the Indian Museum, 49(1):89-137 1952)

QL
1
F 45
FISHES   BORNEO

Inger, Robert F.

A new fish from North Borneo.

(Fieldiana . Zoology, Chicago Natural History Museum, Vol. 34(11):149-152, 1953)

AS
36
S7
FISHES - BRAZIL

Starks, Edwin Chapin, 1867-
... The fishes of the Stanford expedition to Brazil, by Edwin Chapin Starks ... with fifteen plates ... Stanford University, Cal., The University, 1913.
2 p. l., [3]-77 p. xv pl. 26ᶜᵐ. (Leland Stanford junior university publications. University ser. [12])

1. Fishes—Brazil.

13-11160

Library of Congress   QL632.B8S7

QL
1
I-r
FISHES   BURMA

Misra, K. S.

A check list of the fishes of India, Burma and Ceylon. I. Elasmobranchii and Holocephali.

(Records of the Indian Museum, Vol. 45(1): 1-46, 1947)

QL 628.C B 26

FISHES   CALIFORNIA

Barnhart, Percy Spencer

Marine fishes of Southern California. Univ. of Calif. Press. Berkeley. 1936. R8vo. iv + 209 pp.

QL 1 C 15

FISHES - CALIFORNIA

Hubbs, Carl Levitt, 1894–

... Notes on the marine fishes of California, by Carl L. Hubbs. Berkeley, University of California press, 1916.

cover-title, p. [153]-169. pl. 18-20. 27cm. (University of California publications in zoology. v. 16, no. 13)

1. Marine fauna—California. 2. Fishes—California.   i. Title.

A 16-460

Title from Univ. of Calif.   Library of Congress

AS 750 D 67 c

FISHES   CAMPBELL ISLAND

Stokell, G.

Feshwater fishes from the Auckland and Campbell Islands.

(Cape Exp.-Sci. Res. of the New Zeland Sub-antarctic Exp., 1941-45, Bull. No. 9, 1950)

QL Fishes Pam. 607

FISHES   CALIFORNIA

Baxter, John L.

Inshore fishes of California. Department of Fish and Game, State of California. 1960 sm8vo. 80 pp.

QL Fishes Pam. 601

FISHES   CALIFORNIA

Miller, Daniel J.

A field guide to some common ocean sport fishes of California, Part 1 (rev. ed.), 1959 State of California, Dept. of Fish and Game. Marine Resources Operations. 1960.

AS 42 C 41 m

FISHES   CANADA

McAllister, D. E.

List of the marine fishes of Canada.

(National Museum of Canada, Bull. 168, 1960)

QL 1 C15

FISHES--CALIFORNIA.

Daniel, John Frank, 1873–

... The anatomy of *Heterodontus francisci*, I– By J. Frank Daniel.

(*In* University of California publications in zoology. Berkeley, 1914-27. v. 13, p. [147]-166; plates)

Bibliographies.

1. Heterodontus francisci. 2. Fishes—California.   i. Title.

A 14-1336

Title from Univ. of Calif.   Library of Congress

QL 628 Ca-h

FISHES   CALIFORNIA

Roedel, Phil M.

Common marine fishes of California.

(California, Division of Fish and Game, Fish Bulletin No. 68, 1948)

QL 1 S 96

FISHES   CANARY ISLANDS

Bergenhayn, J. R. M.

Beiträge zur Malakozoologie der Kanarischen Inseln.   Die Loricaten.

(Arkiv for Zoologi, Bd. 23, no. 13, pp. 1-38 1932)

QL Fishes Pam. 602

FISHES   CALIFORNIA

Fitch, John E.

Offshore fishes of California. California Dept. of Fish and Game. Sacramento. sm8vo. 1958.

AS 36 S4

FISHES--CALIFORNIA.

Snyder, John Otterbein, 1867–

An account of some fishes from Owens River, California. By John Otterbein Snyder ...

(*In* U. S. National museum. Proceedings. Washington, 1919. 23½cm. v. 54, p. 201-205)

1. Fishes—California.

Library of Congress   Q11.U55 vol. 54

19-20016

[4]

QL 1 A 93

FISHES   CAPRICORN GROUP

Musgrave, Anthony   and others

The biology of North-west Island, Capricorn Group. Narrative, by Anthony Musgrave; Birds by P.A.Gilbert; Fishes, by Gilbert P. Whitley; Marine molluscs, by Tom Iredale; Insects, by Anthony Musgrave; Bryozoa, by A.A.Livingstone; Corals, by Charles Hedley; Botany, by C.T.White and W. MacGillivray.

(The Australian Zoologist, 4:199-255, 1926)

AS 36 C 3

FISHES   CALIFORNIA

Follett, W. H.

Annotated list of fishes obtained by the California Academy of Sciences during six cruises of the U. S. S. Mulberry conducted by the United States Navy off central California in 1949 and 1950.

(Proc. Calif. Acad. Sci. s4, Vol. 27(16); 399-432, 1952)

AS 36 S4

FISHES--CALIFORNIA

Snyder, John Otterbein, 1867–

Notes on *Ranzania makua* Jenkins and other species of rare occurrence on the California coast. [By] John Otterbein Snyder ...

(*In* U. S. National museum. Proceedings. Washington, 1913. 23½cm. v. 44, p. 455-460. pl. 63)

1. Fishes—California.

13-20871

Library of Congress   Q11.U55 vol. 44

AS 36 S4

FISHES--CELEBES

Smith, Hugh McCormick, 1865–

... Description of a new family of pediculate fishes from Celebes. By Hugh M. Smith and Lewis Radcliffe...

(*In* U. S. National museum. Proceedings. Washington, 1912. 23½cm. vol. 42, p. 579-581. pl. 72)

"Scientific results of the Philippine cruise of the fisheries steamer 'Albatross,' 1907-1910. no. 20."

1. Fishes—Celebes. 2. Albatross (Steamer)   i. Radcliffe, Lewis, 1880– joint author.

13-9546

Library of Congress   Q11.U55 vol. 42

AS 36 S4

FISHES--CALIFORNIA

Gilbert, Charles Henry, 1859–

Fishes collected by the United States fisheries steamer "Albatross" in southern California in 1904. By Charles Henry Gilbert ...

(*In* U. S. National museum. Proceedings. Washington, 1915. 23½cm. v. 48, p. 305-380. pl. 14-22)

1. Fishes—California.   i. Albatross (Steamer)

15-24779

Library of Congress   Q11.U55 vol. 48

QL 1 C15

FISHES--CALIFORNIA

Starks, Edwin Chapin, 1867–

... New and rare fishes from southern California, by Edwin Chapin Starks and William M. Mann. Berkeley, The University press, 1911.

cover-title, p. [9]-19. illus. 17cm. (Universtiy of California publications in zoology. vol. 8, no. 2)

Contribution from the laboratory of the Marine biological association of San Diego.

1. Fishes—California.   i. Mann, William M., joint author.

A 11-2117

Title from Univ. of Calif.   Library of Congress

QL 1- H2

FISHES--CENTRAL AMERICA

Garman, Samuel, 1846–

... Reports on an exploration off the west coasts of Mexico, Central and South America, and off the Galapagos Islands, in charge of Alexander Agassiz, by the U. S. Fish commission steamer "Albatross," during 1891, Lieut. Commander Z. L. Tanner, U. S. N., commanding. XXVI. The fishes. By S. Garman ... Cambridge, U. S. A., Printed for the Museum, 1899.

2 v. 97 pl. 31cm. (Harvard university. Museum of comparative zoölogy. Memoirs, vol. xxiv)

1. Fishes—Mexico. 2. Fishes—Central America. 3. Fishes—South America.

F 17-161

Library, U. S. Bur. of   Fisheries

AS 36 S4

FISHES--CALIFORNIA

Gilbert, Charles Henry, 1859–

Two cottoid fishes from Monterey Bay, California. By Charles H. Gilbert ...

(*In* U. S. National museum. Proceedings. Washington, 1915. 23½cm. v. 47, p. 135-137. pl. 11)

1. Fishes—California.

15-14947

Library of Congress   Q11.U55 vol. 47

AS 36 S4

FISHES--CALIFORNIA.

Snyder, John Otterbein, 1867–

The fishes of Mohave River, California. By John Otterbein Snyder ...

(*In* U. S. National museum. Proceedings. Washington, 1919. 23½cm. v. 54, p. 297-299. 1 illus.)

1. Fishes—California.

19-20019

Library of Congress   Q11.U55 vol. 54

[4]

QL 627 U -b

FISHES -- CENTRAL AMERICA

Hildebrand, Samuel F.

Fishes of the Republic of El Salvador, Central America. U. S. Bur. Fish. Bull. XLI, pp 237- 287, 1925.

QL 1 F
FISHES - CENTRAL AMERICA
Meek, Seth Eugene, 1859-1914.
... Description of three new species of fishes from middle America, by Seth Eugene Meek ... Chicago, 1906.
1 p. l., p. 93-95. 24½ᶜᵐ. (Field Columbian museum. Publication 116. Zoölogical series. vol. vii, no. 3)

1. Fishes—Central America.
6—34841
Library of Congress   QL1.F4

QL 1 I-r
FISHES   CEYLON
Misra, K. S.
A check list of the fishes of India, Burma and Ceylon. I. Elasmobranchii and Holocephali.
(Records of the Indian Museum, Vol. 45(1): 1-46, 1947)

QH 193.C R 32
FISHES   CHINA
Nichols, John Treadwell
The fresh-water fishes of China.
IN
Reeds, Chester A. and others   editors
Natural History of Central Asia, Vol. 9, 1943.

QL 1 F
FISHES - CENTRAL AMERICA
Meek, Seth Eugene, 1859-1914.
... Notes on fresh-water fishes from Mexico and Central America, by Seth Eugene Meek ... Chicago, 1907.
1 p. l., 133-157 p. 24½ᶜᵐ. (Field Columbian museum. Publication no. 124. Zoölogical series. vol. vii, no. 5)

1. Fishes—Mexico. 2. Fishes—Central America.
8—9040
Library of Congress   QL1.F4

QL 634.C M 96
FISHES   CEYLON
Munro, Ian S. R.
The marine and fresh water fishes of Ceylon. With a foreword by R. G. Casey. With 19 figures in the text and 56 plates in black and white. Published for Dept. of External Affairs, Canberra. 1944. sm4to. xvi + 349 pp.

DU 1 P
FISHES   CHINA
Reeves, Cora D.
A catalogue of the fishes of northeastern China and Korea.
(Journal of the Pan-Pacific Research Institution, Vol. 2, 1927, No. 3, pp. 3-16)

QL Fishes Pam. 604
FISHES   CEYLON
Ceylon. Department of Fisheries
Fisheries Research Station
Bulletin 8, 1958: A guide to the fisheries of Ceylon. Compiled by the Staff of the Dept. of Fisheries.

QL Fishes Pam. 393
FISHES   CHILE
Fowler, Henry W.
Fishes obtained in Chile by Mr. D. S. Bullock
(Proc. Acad. Nat. Sci. Philadelphia, Vol. 92 1940, pp. 171-190)

QL 619 We
Fishes-China
Weber, Max William Carl.
The fishes of the Indo-Australian Archipelago...1911.
See main card for fuller entry

QL 634.C D 42
FISHES   CEYLON
Deraniyagala, P. E. P.
A colored atlas of some vertebrates from Ceylon. Vol. 1: Fishes, Vol. 2. Tetrapod Reptilia.
Illustrated by the author. Ceylon National Museums Publication. Ceylon Government Press. 1952. ob4to. 149 pp., 34 pl.; 101 pp. 35 pl.

QL Fish Pam 249
FISHES - CHINA
Evermann, Barton Warren and Shaw, Tsen-Hwang
Fishes from eastern China with descriptions of new species. From Proc. Calif. Acad. of Sci. v. XVI, n.4, 1927.

AS 36 S4
FISHES--CHINA--SOOCHOW
Fowler, Henry Weed, 1878–
A small collection of fishes from Soochow, China, with descriptions of two new species. By Henry W. Fowler ... and Barton A. Bean ...
(In U. S. National museum. Proceedings. Washington, 1921. 23½ᶜᵐ. v. 58, p. 307-321. illus.)

1. Fishes—China—Soochow.   i. Bean, Barton Appler, 1860-   joint author.
21-21441
Library of Congress   Q11.U55 vol. 58
[5]

AS 474 S
FISHES   CEYLON
Herre, Albert W. C. T.
Fishes collected in Ceylon in April, 1934.
(Spolia Zeylanica, Vol. 24(3):173-179,1946)

QL Fish Pam #241
FISHES-CHINA
Fowler, Henry W.
Some fishes collected by the third Asiatic expedition in China. Bull. Am. Mus. Nat. His. Vol.L; Art.VII, 1924.

AS 36 A 16
FISHES   CHRISTMAS ISLAND
Fowler, Henry W.
The fishes of the George Vanderbilt South Pacific Expedition, 1937.
(Acad. of Nat. Sci., Philadelphia, Monograph No. 2, 1938)

QL Fish Pam. 534
FISHES   CEYLON
Mendis, A. S.
Fishes of Ceylon (a catalogue, key and bibliography).
(Dept. of Fisheries, Ceylon, Bull. No. 2, July, 1954)

AS 36 S4
FISHES--CHINA
Ginsburg, Isaac.
On two species of fishes from the Yalu River, China. By Isaac Ginsburg ...
(In U. S. National museum. Proceedings. Washington, 1919. 23½ᶜᵐ. v. 54, p. 99-101)

1. Fishes—China.
19-20011
Library of Congress   Q11.U55 vol. 54
[4]

QL 636.5 F 78
AS 763 B-b
Reading Room
FISHES   CHRISTMAS ISLAND (PACIFIC)
Fowler, Henry W.
Fishes of the tropical central Pacific.
(Bernice P. Bishop Museum, Bulletin No. 38, 1927; Whippoorwill Expedition, Publication No. 1)

QL Fishes Pam. 597
FISHES   CEYLON
Misra, K. S.
An aid to the indentification of the fishes of India, Burma and Ceylon. 1. Elasmobranchii and Holocephali.
(Records of the Indian Museum, 49(1):89-137 1952)

QH 1 H 76
FISHES   CHINA
Honan Museum
Bulletin (Natural History)
Vol. 1:1-2, 1933-34
Published by the Honan Museum, Kaifeng, China. R8vo

AS 522.S R 13
FISHES   CHRISTMAS ISLAND (IND. OCEAN)
Palmer, G.
Additions to the fish fauna of Christmas Island, Indian Ocean.
(Bulletin, Raffles Museum, No. 23:200-205, 1950)

QL Fish Pam. 11

FISHES   CLIPPERTON ISLAND

Snodgrass, Robert

     Shore fishes of the Revillagigedo, Clipperton, Cocos and Galapagos Islands, by Robert Snodgrass and Edmond Heller.

     (Proc. Washington Acad. Sci., Vol. 6, 1904, pp. 333-427; published Jan. 31, 1905)

QH 1 M 17

FISHES   COMORES ISLANDS

Fourmanoir, P.

     Ichthyologie et pêche aux Comores.

     (Mémoires de l'Institut Scientifique de Madagascar, Ser. A. Biologie Animale, Tome IX:187-239, 1954)

QL 634 B 64 locked case

FISHES   DUTCH EAST INDIES

Bleeker, P(ieter)

     Atlas Ichthyologique des Indes Orientales Néerlandaises. Tomes 1-9. folio. Amsterdam. 1862-1878.

QL Fish Pam. 11

FISHES   COCOS ISLAND

Snodgrass, Robert

     Shore fishes of the Revillagigedo, Clipperton, Cocos and Galapagos Islands, by Robert Snodgrass and Edmond Heller.

     (Proc. Washington Acad. Sci., Vol. 6, 1904, pp. 333-427; published Jan. 31, 1905)

QL Fish Pam #245

FISH-CONGO

Myers, G. S.

     A new poecilid fish from the Congo with remarks on Funduline genera. Am. Mus. Nat. His. Nov. #116, 1924.

AS 36 S5

FISHES--EAST INDIES

Gilbert, Charles Henry, 1859-

     ... The macrouroid fishes of the Philippine Islands and the East Indies, by Charles Henry Gilbert ... and Carl L. Hubbs ... Washington, Govt. print. off., 1920.

     1 p. l., p. 369-588. illus. 24½ᶜᵐ. (Smithsonian institution. United States National museum. Bulletin 100, v. 1, pt. 7)

     At head of title: Contributions to the biology of the Philippine Archipelago and adjacent regions.

     1. Coryphaenoididae. 2. Fishes—Philippine Islands. 3. Fishes—East Indies. I. Title.   20-26849

Library of Congress   Q11.U6   no. 100, vol. 1, pt. 7

——— Copy 2.   QL638.C7G5 [10]

GN 2.M R 13

FISHES--COCOS KEELING ISLANDS

Marshall, Norman

     Pisces.

     IN

     Papers on the fauna of the Cocos-Keeling Islands....collected...1940...1941

     (Bull. Raffles Museum, No. 22:166-205, 1950)

AS 36 A4

FISHES - CONGO BASIN

Nichols, John Treadwell, 1883-

     ... Fresh-water fishes of the Congo Basin obtained by the American museum Congo expedition, 1909-1915. By John Treadwell Nichols and Ludlow Griscom. [With field notes by the collectors, Herbert Lang and James P. Chapin. New York, 1917]

     cover-title, p. 653-756. illus., pl. LXIV-LXXXIII (part col.) 25ᶜᵐ. (Bulletin of the American museum of natural history. vol. xxxvii, art. xxv)

     1. Fishes—Congo Basin. I. Griscom, Ludlow, joint author. II. Lang, Herbert. III. Chapin, James P.

Library, U. S. Bureau of   Fisheries   F 18-754

[s19d2]

AS 145 B

FISHES   DUTCH EAST INDIES

Giltay, Louis

Poissons

Van Straelen, V.

     Résultats scientifiques du voyage aux Indes Orientales Néerlandaises...Léopold de Belgique, Vol. 5, Fasc. 3, 1933, pp. 1-129.

     (Mem. hors ser. Musee Roy. d'Hist. Nat., Belgique)

QL Fishes Pam. 403

FISHES   COLOMBIA

Eigenmann, Carl H.

     The fresh-water fishes of Panama east of longitude 80° W; The Magdalena basin and the horizontal and vertical distribution of its fishes.

     (Indiana University Studies, 47 A and B., 1920)

AS 36 C9

FISHES--CONNECTICUT

Connecticut. State geological and natural history survey. Bulletin No. 18. Triassic fishes of Connecticut. By C. R. Eastman. Hartford, 1911.

     77 pp., 11 pls., 8 figs. 23ᶜᵐ.

QL 1 N 6-z

FISHES   DUTCH EAST INDIES

Hollister, Gloria

     Young Megalops cyprinoides from Batavia, Dutch East India, including a study of the caudal skeleton and a comparison with the Atlantic species, Tarpon atlanticus.

     (Zoologica, Vol. 24, 1939, pp. 449-475)

QL Fish Pam. 402

FISHES   COLOMBIA

Eigenmann, Carl H.

     On new species of fishes from the Rio Meta, Colombia, and on albino fishes from near Bogotá.

     (Indiana University Studies, 23, 1914)

QL 1 F

FISHES--COSTA RICA.

Meek, Seth Eugene, 1859-1914.

     ... An annotated list of fishes known to occur in the fresh waters of Costa Rica, by Seth Eugene Meek ... Chicago, 1914.

     1 p. l., p. 101-134. 24½ᶜᵐ. (Field museum of natural history. Publication 174. Zoölogical ser. vol. x, no. 10)

     1. Fishes—Costa Rica.   14-8995 Revised

Library of Congress   QL1.F4 vol. 10, no. 10

Q 115 S 56

FISHES   DUTCH EAST INDIES

Leigh-Sharpe, W. Harold

The Copepoda of the Siboga Expedition, Part II: Commensal and parasitic Copepoda.

Weber, Max

     Uitkomsten...Nederlandsch Oost Indie, 1899-1900...Siboga...Monographie XXIX b (livr. 123). 1934. 43pp.

QL Fish Pam. 399 400 401

FISHES   COLOMBIA

Eigenmann, Carl H.

     Some results from an ichthyological reconnaissance of Colombia, South America.

     (Indiana University Studies, 16, 18, 20, 1912,-1914: Contributions from the Zoological Laboratory, 127, 131, 135)

QL 1 F

FISHES--COSTA RICA.

Meek, Seth Eugene, 1859-

     ... New species of fishes from Costa Rica, by Seth Eugene Meek ... Chicago, 1912.

     1 p. l., p. 69-75. 24½ᶜᵐ. (Field museum of natural history. Publication 163. Zoölogical ser. vol. x, no. 7)

     1. Fishes—Costa Rica.   13-8145

Library of Congress   QL1.F4 vol. 10, no. 7

AS 36 A 65

FISHES   DUTCH EAST INDIES

Nichols, John Treadway

     East Indian mackerel scads (Decapterus) described and differentiated. (Notes on Carangin fishes, VI)

     (American Museum Novitates, 1196, 1942)

QL Fishes Pam. 434

FISHES   COLOMBIA

Miles, Cecil

     Los Peces del Rio Magdalena. (A field book of Magdalena fishes). Republica de Colombia, Ministerio de la Economia Nacional, Seccion de Piscicultura, Pesca y Caza. 1947. Bogota. 214 + xxviii pp. R8vo.

QL Fish Pam. 334

FISHES - CUBA

     La Ciguatera, Enfermedad Producida por Peces Venenosos de Cuba.

     (Extracto de "Investigacion Y Progreso" Ano III, Nr. 11, pag. 101-107, Madrid, 1929).

AS 36 A 65

FISHES-DUTCH EAST INDIES

Nichols, John T.

     One new, and other labroid fishes from Bali.

     (American Mus. Novitates, No. 1154, 1941)

QL
Fishes
Pam.
117

FISHES   DUTCH EAST INDIES

Weber, Max

Diagnosen neuer Fische der Siboga-Expedition

(Notes from the Leyden Museum, Vol. 31,
1909, pp. 143-169)

QL
636.5
F 78

AS
763
B-b

Reading
Room

FISHES   FANNING ISLAND

Fowler, Henry W.

Fishes of the tropical central Pacific.

(Bernice P. Bishop Museum, Bulletin No. 38,
1927; Whippoorwill Expedition, Publication No. 1)

AS
36
C 3

FISHES   FIJI

Seale, Alvin

Fishes. The Templeton Crocker Expedition
to Western Polynesia and Melanesian Islands,
1933, No. 27.

(Proc. California Academy of Sciences, Ser.
4, Vol. 21, 1935, pp. 337-378)

Q
115
S 56

FISHES   DUTCH EAST INDIES

Weber, Max
Die Fische der Siboga-Expedition.

Weber, Max
Uitkomsten...Nederlandsch Oost Indie, 1899-
1900...Siboga...Monographie LVII (livr. 65).
1913. 710 pp., 12 pl.

AS
36
S 5

AS
36
S 2

QL Fish
Pam 150

FISHES   FANNING ISLAND

Streets, T. H.

Contributions to the natural history of the
Hawaiian and Fanning Islands...U. S. North Pacific surveying expedition, 1873-1875. pp. 78-94.

(U. S. Nat'l Mus., Bull. No. 7, 1877; Smithsonian Misc. Coll., Vol. XIII, art. 7, publ. no.
303)

QL
Fish
Pam
No.142

FISHES-FIJI

Steindachner, Franz und Kner, Rudolph

Uber einige Pleuronectiden, Salmoni-
den, Gadoiden und Blenniden aus der Decastris'
Bay und von Viti-Levu. From K.Akad.
Wien, Sitz. 1870.

AS
162
P

FISHES   EASTER ISLAND

Adam, G.

La faune ichthyologique de l'Ile de Pâques.

(Bull. Nat. d'Hist. Nat., Paris, Ser. 2,
Tome 17:355-394, 1945)

QL
Fishes
Pam.
537

FISHES   FIJI

Fowler, Henry W.

Archaeological fishbones collected by E. W.
Gifford in Fiji.

(Bernice P. Bishop Museum, Bulletin 214, 1959)

QL
Fish
Pam.
142
and
#360

FISHES--FIJI

Steindachner, Franz und Kner, Rudolph

Uber einige Pleuronectiden, Salmoniden,
Gadoiden und Blenniiden aus der Decastris
Bay und von Viti- Levu.   Aus K. Akad. Wi
Wien, Sitzb.Bde.LXI, Abt.1, April. 1870.

QH
136.J
S 62

FISHES   EASTER ISLAND

Rendahl, Hialmar

The fishes of Easter Island.

IN

Skottsberg, Carl   editor
The natural history of Juan Fernandez and
Easter Island. Vol. III. Zoology, pp. 59-68.
Uppsala. 1921.

AS
750
N-56

FISHES   FIJI

Fowler, Henry W.

A collection of coral-reef fishes made by
Dr. and Mrs. Marshall Laird at Fiji.

(Transactions of the Royal Society of New
Zealand, Vol. 83(2):373-381, September, 1955)

QL
Fish
Pam
247

FISHES - FIJI

Whitley, Gilbert P

A check list of fishes recorded from
Fijian waters. From Journal of Pan-Pac
Research Institution. v. 2, no.1, 1927.

QL
Fish
Pam
144

AS
719
A-m8

FISHES   ELLICE ISLANDS

Waite, Edgar

Fishes of Funafuti

(Australian Museum Memoir, Vol. III, pp. 181-
201. 1896-97).

AS
36
A 16 n

FISHES   FIJI

Fowler, Henry W.

Description of a new goby from the Fiji
Islands.

(Notulae Naturae, No. 115, 1943)

AS
36
S4

FISHES--FLORIDA

Bean, Barton Appler, 1860-
An electric ray and its young from the west coast of
Florida. By Barton A. Bean and Alfred C. Weed ...

(*In* U. S. National museum. Proceedings. Washington, 1911. 23½ᶜᵐ.
v. 40, p. 231-232. pl. 10-11)

1. Torpedinidae. 2. Fishes--Florida.   i. Weed, Alfred Cleveland, joint
author. ii. Title: Electric ray.

11--31516

Library of Congress   Q11.U55 vol. 40

QL
Fish
Pam.
#6

Howie, R.

FISHES -- ENGLAND

Catalogue of fishes of the rivers
and coasts of Northumberland and
Durham and the adjacent sea.
Nat. Hist. Soc. of Northumberland etc.
1890, 8vo, pp. 64.

AS
763
B-4

and
QL
Fish Pam.
340

FISHES   FIJI

Fowler, Henry W.

Fishes obtained at Fiji in 1929.

(Bernice P. Bishop Museum Occasional Papers,
Volume IX, Number 20, 1932)

QH
301
C 3

FISHES   FLORIDA

Longley, William H.

Systematic catalogue of the fishes of Tortugas, Florida, with observations on color, habits and local distribution, edited and completed by Samuel F. Hildebrand.

(Papers from Tortugas Laboratory, Vol. 34,
1941)

AS
36
A 15

FISHES   FANNING ISLAND

Fowler, Henry W.

The fishes of the George Vanderbilt South
Pacific Expedition, 1937.

(Acad. of Nat. Sci., Philadelphia, Monograph
No. 2, 1938)

QL
636.5 F
F 78

FISHES   FIJI

Fowler, Henry W.

Fishes of Fiji. Published by Government of
Fiji. Suva. 1959. R8vo. (6)+670.

AS
36
A4

FISHES - FLORIDA

Nichols, John Treadwell, 1883-
Ichthyological notes from a cruise off southwest Flor-
ida, with description of *Gobiesox yuma* sp. nov. By John
Treadwell Nichols. New York, 1917.

cover-title, p. 873-877. illus., pl. cxi. 24½ᶜᵐ. (Bulletin of the American
museum of natural history, vol. XXXVII, art. XXXVII)

1. Fishes--Florida.

F 18-755

Library, U. S. Bur. of   Fisheries

FISHES--FORMOSA

AS
36
C51

Jordan, David Starr, 1851-

... A catalog of the fishes of Formosa. By David Starr Jordan and Robert Earl Richardson. Pittsburgh, Board of trustees of the Carnegie institute, 1909.

cover-title, p. 159-204. illus. pl. LXIII-LXXIV. 34 x 26½ᵐ. (Memoirs of the Carnegie museum, vol. IV, no. 4. W. J. Holland, ed.)

At head of title: Publications of the Carnegie museum, serial no. 58.

1. Fishes--Formosa. I. Richardson, Robert Earl, joint author.

9-30294

Library of Congress   AS36.P75 vol. 4, no. 4

FISHES - FORMOSA

QL
834.J
T 16

Tanaka, Shigeho

Figures and descriptions of the Fishes of Japan including...Formosa...

FISHES FRENCH GUIANA

QH
147.1
F 26

Puyo, Joseph

Poissons de la Guyane Francaise.

(Faune de l'Empire Francaise, XII, 1949)

FISHES FUNAFUTI

QL
Fish
Pam
144

Waite, Edgar

Fishes of Funafuti

AS
719
A-me

201.

(Australian Museum Memoir, Vol. III, pp. 181-1896-97).

FISHES GALAPAGOS ISLANDS

QL
1
N 6-z

Beebe, William

Fishes from the tropical eastern Pacific. (From Cedros Island, Lower California, south to the Galapagos Islands and northern Peru.) I-II. By William Beebe and John Tee-Van.

(Zoologica, Vol. 26, 1941, pp. 89-92, 93-122

to be cont.

FISHES - GALAPAGOS ISLANDS

AS
36
A 16

Fowler, Henry W.

The fishes of the George Vanderbilt South Pacific Expedition, 1937.

(Acad. of Nat. Sci., Philadelphia, Monograph No. 2, 1938)

FISHES GALAPAGOS ISLANDS

AS
36
W 2

Heller, Edmund   and R.E.Snodgrass

and
QL
Fishes
Pam. 9

New fishes. (Papers from the Hopkins Stanford Galapagos Expedition, 1898-1899, XV. IN Proc. Washington Acad. Sci., V, 1903, pp. 189-230)

FISHES GALAPAGOS ISLANDS

AS
36
A 65-n

Lundy, William E.

Galapagos produces the "Thing", a grotesque member of the batfish family, unknown a few years ago...

(Natural History, 65(9):468-469, 1956)

FISHES - GALAPAGOS ISLANDS

QH
1
P 85

Morrow, J.E.

A redefinition of the subspecies of Fodiator acutus.

(Postilla, Yale Peabody Museum...No. 29, 1957)

FISHES GALAPAGOS ISLANDS

Q
115
H 23

Myers, George S.

New fishes of the families Dactyloscopidae, Microdesmidae, and Antennariidae from the west coast of Mexico and the Galapagos Islands, with a brief account of the use of rotenone fish poisonings in ichthyological collecting. By George S. Myers and Charles B. Wade.

IN Allan Hancock Pacific Expeditions, Vol. 9 (6), 1946.

FISHES GALAPAGOS ISLANDS

Q
101
P 18

Rosenblatt, Richard H.

Also
AS
36
C 15 o

The marine shore-fishes of the Galápagos Islands. By Richard H. Rosenblatt and Boyd W. Walker.

(Occ. Papers of the Calif. Acad. of Sciences, No. 44:97-106, 1963)

(Presented at a symposium: Galápagos Islands. Tenth Pacific Science Congress, Honolulu, 1961)

FISHES GALAPAGOS ISLANDS

AS
36
S 2

Schmitt, Waldo L.

List of the fishes taken on the Presidential Cruise of 1938. By Waldo L. Schmitt and Leonhard P. Schultz.

(Smithsonian Misc. Coll., Vol. 98, 1940, pp. 1-10, No. 25)

FISHES-GALAPAGOS ISLANDS

AS
36
W 2

Shultz, Leonard P.

The first record of the ophichthyid eel Scytalichthys miurus (Jordan and Gilbert) from the Galapagos Islands, with notes on Mystriophis intertinctus (Richardson).

(Journal of the Washington Acad. of Sci., Vol. 32, 1942, pp. 83)

FISHES GALAPAGOS ISLANDS

QL
Fish
Pam.
11

Snodgrass, Robert

Shore fishes of the Revillagigedo, Clipperton, Cocos and Galapagos Islands, by Robert Snodgrass and Edmond Heller.

(Proc. Washington Acad. Sci., Vol. 6, 1904, pp. 333-427; published Jan. 31, 1905)

FISHES - GILBERT ISLANDS

QL
Fish
Pam
258

Kraemer, Augustin

Der purgierfisch der Gilbertinseln. From Globus, bd.79, n.12, 1901.

FISHES GILBERT ISLANDS

QL
1
A 68

Randall, John E.

Fishes of the Gilbert Islands.

(Atoll Research Bulletin, No. 47, August, 1955)

FISHES GILBERT ISLANDS

QL
Fishes
Pam.
566

Randall, John E.

Stethojulis renardi, the adult male of the Labrid fish Stethojulis strigiventer.

(Copeia, 1955 (3):237, 1955)

FISHES GILBERT ISLANDS

AS
720.N
L

Whitley, Gilbert P.

Fishes from Nauru, Gilbert Islands, Oceania. By Gilbert P. Whitley and Alan N. Colefax.

(Proc. of the Linnean Society of New South Wales, 1938, Vol. 63, pp. 282-304)

FISHES GUAM

DU
647
G 91

Bowker, H. T.

The walking fish.

(Guam Recorder, Vol. 15, 1938, No. 2, pp. 17-18)

FISHES GUAM

DU
647
G 91

Bryan, Edwin H., Jr.

Fishes of Guam.

(Guam Recorder, Vol. XV, No. 9, 1938, pp. 7-8, 41 to be continued

---

FISHES GUAM

DU
647
G 91

Buehler, Albert R.

Walking fish. (Guam)

(The Guam Recorder, August, 1934, p. 81)

QL
Fish Pam
149

AS
763
B-b
Reading
Room

FISHES GUAM

Fowler, Henry W.

Fishes of Guam, Hawaii, Samoa, and Tahiti.
(Bernice P. Bishop Museum, Bulletin No. 22,
1925.)

AS
36
A65

FISHES - HAWAIIAN ISLANDS

Borodin, N A

A new blenny from the Hawaiian islands
Am. Mus. Nov. h. 281, 1927.

QH
1
P 11

FISHES HAWAII

Brock, Vernon E.

Some aspects of the biology of the aku,
Katsuwonus pelamis, in the Hawaiian Islands.
(Pacific Science, Vol. VIII(1):94-104,
1954)

DU
647
G 91

FISHES GUAM

(Linsley, Leonard Noel)

Curious things about Guam, by L.N.L. (the
scorpion fish and the sea centipede)
(The Guam Recorder, 1935, p. 180)

DU
620
P

FISHES HAWAII

Brigham, William Tufts

The Roosevelt fish.
(Paradise of the Pacific, Vol. 21, 1908,
No. 5, p. 17-18)

GN
Ethn.Pam.
3254

2 copies

FISHES HAWAII

Bryan, Edwin H., Jr.

Fish and fishing in Hawaii. (Castle &
Cooke booklet, No. 3). Honolulu. 1938. 10 pp.

QL
5
S 43

AS
763
B-o

AS
763
B-r

FISHES GUAM

Seale, Alvin

Report of a mission to Guam. Part I. Avi-
fauna; Part II. Fishes.
(Bernice P. Bishop Museum, Occasional Papers,
Vol. 1, No. 3, 1900, pp. 17-128. Director's
Report for 1900).

QH
1
P 11

FISHES HAWAII

Brock, Vernon E.

An addition to the fish fauna of the Hawaiian islands.
(Pacific Science, Vol. 2:298, 1948)

[Pomacanthodes imperator (Bloch)]

QL
Fish Pam.
384

FISHES HAWAII

Bryan, E. H., Jr.

Hawaiian fishes.
Published by the Chamber of Commerce of Honolulu.
7 pp.

QL
1
F

FISHES - GUATEMALA

Meek, Seth Eugene, 1859-1914.

... The zoölogy of lakes Amatitlan and Atitlan, Guatemala, with special reference to ichthyology. By Seth
Eugene Meek ... Chicago, 1908.

1 p. l., 159-206 p. illus. (incl. maps) 25cm. (Field Columbian museum.
Publication no. 127. Zoölogical series. vol. vii, no. 6)

1. Zoology—Guatemala. 2. Fishes—Guatemala.

Library of Congress   QL1.F4   8–18304

S
399
A 2

FISHES HAWAII

Brock, Vernon E.

A history of the introduction of certain
aquatic animals to Hawaii.
(Rept. Bd. of Agric. and For., 1952)

QL
Fish
Pam
20
105
108

AS
763
B-o

FISHES HAWAII

Bryan, W. A.

Three new Hawaiian fishes.
(Bernice P. Bishop Museum, Occ. Pap., Vol.
II. 1906) no. 4, pp 22-37

QL
1
C

FISHES - GULF OF CALIFORNIA

Rutter, Cloudsley, d. 1903.

... Notes on fishes from the Gulf of California, with
the description of a new genus and species. By Cloudsley Rutter. With one plate ... San Francisco, The Academy, 1904.

1 p. l., 251-254 p. pl. 25cm. (Proceedings of the California academy
of sciences. Third series. Zoology. vol. iii, no. 8)
"Issued August 17, 1904."

1. Fishes—California, Gulf of.

Library of Congress   Q11.C25   4–30943

QL
1
C 78

FISHES HAWAII

Brock, Vernon E.

The identity of the parrotfish Scarus ahula,
the female of Scarus perspicillatus. By Vernon
E. Brock and Yoshio Yamaguchi.
(Copeia, 1954, No. 2:154-155)

FISHES HAWAII   (colored pictures)

Chute, Walter H.

Net results from Oceania.
(National Geographic Magazine, Vol. 79,
1941, pp. 347-372)

QE
565
B 41

FISHES HAITI

Beebe, William

Beneath tropic seas...New York, 1928.
Appendix E: Families and number of species of
Haitian fish collected. pp. 225-227

QH
1
P 11

FISHES HAWAII

Brock, Vernon E.

A new blennoid fish from Hawaii.
(Pacific Science, 2:125-127, 1948)

[Petroscirtes]

AS
36
A 65

FISHES HAWAII

Clark, Eugenie

Notes on some Hawaiian Plectognath fishes,
including a key to the species.
(American Museum Novitates, No. 1397, Jan.
24, 1949)

QL
1
C 78

FISHES HAWAII

Bonham, Kelshaw

Measurements of some pelagic commercial
fishes of Hawaii.
(Copeia, 1946 (2):81-84)

QH
1
P 11

FISHES HAWAII

Brock, Vernon E.

A preliminary report on Parathunnus sibi in
Hawaiian waters and a key to the tunas and tuna-
like fishes of Hawaii.
(Pacific Science, Vol. 3:271-277, 1949)

DU
620
P 22

FISHES HAWAII

Cunningham, Steve

Fresh water "tropical" fish off the beaten
track, sparkling gems abound.
(Paradise of the Pacific, Sept. 1956:9-11)

QL 627 U-b   **FISHES HAWAII**

Eckles, Howard H.

Observations on juvenile oceanic skipjack (Katsuwonus pelamis) from Hawaiian waters and Sierra mackerel (Scomberomorus sierra) from the Eastern Pacific.

(Fishery Bull., U. S. Fish and Wildlife Service, Vol. 51, 1949)

QL 628 C 15   **FISHES HAWAII**

Fitch, John E.

Notes on some Pacific fishes.

(California Fish and Game, Vol. 36(2):65-73, 1948)

AS 36 A 16   **FISHES HAWAII**

Fowler, Henry W.

The fishes of the George Vanderbilt South Pacific Expedition, 1937.

(Acad. of Nat. Sci., Philadelphia, Monograph No. 2, 1938)

QL 345.H E 24   **FISHES HAWAII**

Edmondson, Charles Howard

Reef and shore fauna of Hawaii.

(Bernice P. Bishop Museum, Special Publication, 22, 1946- revised edition)

DU 620 P   **FISHES HAWAII**

Flying fish in Hawaii.

(Paradise of the Pacific, Vol. 19, 1906, No. 7, p. 9)

QL Fishes Pam.397   **FISHES HAWAII**

Fowler, Henry W.

The George Vanderbilt Oahu Survey- the fishes.

(Proc. Acad. Nat. Sci. Philadelphia, Vol. 93, 1941, pp. 247-279)

AS 36 A 5   **FISHES HAWAII**

Elliot, Edith

Its mouth is its nursery and its adaptability is making the Largemouth Kurper a promising source of revenue in Hawaii.

(Natural History, 64(6):330-331, 1955)

AS 36 A-1   **FISHES - HAWAIIAN ISLANDS**

Fowler, Henry W.

Contributions to the ichthyology of the tropical Pacific. Acad. Nat. Sci. Philadelphia, Proc. 1900, pp. 483-528.

QL Fish Pam #6 #106   **FISHES - HAWAIIAN ISLANDS**

Fowler, Henry W.

New or little-known Hawaiian fishes. B. P. B. Mus. Occ. Papers Vol. VIII, No. 7. pp. 375-392.

Storage Case 1   **FISHES HAWAII**

Emerson, Joseph S.

Fish classed as kuku. ms note

(Hawaiian ethnological notes, ms. I:728)

AS 36 A 9   **FISHES HAWAII**

Fowler, Henry W.

The fishes obtained by the Wilkes Expedition 1838-1842.

(Proc. Am. Philosophical Society, Vol. 82: 733-800, 1940)

MS Case I Oversize   **FISHES HAWAII**

Garrett, Andrew

Sketches of Hawaiian fishes. 25 pls.

DU 620 P   **FISHES HAWAII**

Falke, Lucia Ripley

Oahu fish vs fish of Samoa.

(Paradise of the Pacific. vol.49, no.8. 1937. p.11)

QL Fish Pam 149   AS 763 B-b   Reading Room   **FISHES HAWAII**

Fowler, Henry W.

Fishes of Guam, Hawaii, Samoa, and Tahiti.

(Bernice P. Bishop Museum, Bulletin No. 22, 1925.)

QL 635.5H Gm46   **FISHES HAWAII**

Gilbert, Charles Henry

The Deep-Sea Fishes. (Hawaii)

(Bull. U. S. Fish Commission, 1903, Part II, pp. 575-713: The Aquatic Resources of the Hawaiian Islands, by David Starr Jordan and Barton Warren Evorman)

4 copies

DU 620 P   **FISHING HAWAII**

Field, H. Gooding

The royal sport of Hawaiian game fishing.

(Paradise of the Pacific, Vol; 29, 1916, No. 12, pp. 41-43; Vol. 33, No. 1, 1920, p. 6-8)

QL Fish Pam. # 164 and AS 763 B-b and Reading Room   **FISHES -- HAWAIIAN ISLANDS**

Fowler, Henry W. and Ball, Stanley C.

Fishes of Hawaii, Johnston Island, and Wake Island. B. P. B. Mus. Bul. 26, Tanager Exped. Pub. No.2, 1925.

AS 36 S4   **FISHES--HAWAIIAN ISLANDS.**

Gilbert, Charles Henry, 1859-

Description of *Hymenocephalus tenuis*, a new macruroid fish from the Hawaiian Islands. By Charles H. Gilbert and Carl L. Hubbs ...

(*In* U. S. National museum. Proceedings. Washington, 1919. 23½ᶜᵐ. v. 54, p. 173-175)

1. Macruridae. 2. Fishes—Hawaiian Islands. I. Hubbs, Carl Levitt, 1894- joint author.

Library of Congress   Q11.US5 vol. 54   19-20014

(7)

AP 2 N 4   **FISHES HAWAII** (Leeward Is.)

Fish collection from the Leeward and Line Islands. (George Vanderbilt Pacific Equatorial Expedition of 1951)

(Nature, Vol. 168(4285):1027, 1951)

AS 763 B-m   QL 623 F 78   Reading Room   **FISHES HAWAII**

Fowler, Henry W.

Fishes of Oceania. Honolulu. 1928. 4to. 540 pp. Supplements 1-3. 1931-34.

(Bernice P. Bishop Museum, Memoirs, Vol. X, Plates I-XLIX; Vol. XI, Nos. 5-6) 14:4 XII: 2 1949

AS 36 S4   **FISHES HAWAII**

Gilbert, C. H. & Cramer, F.

Report on fishes dredged .... near the Hawaiian islands, ...

in Proc. of U.S. Nat. Mus. XIX, pp. 403-436, pls. XXXVI - XLVIII.

Wash., 1897.

DU
620
P
FISHES HAWAII
(Gilbert, Chas. H.)

Strange fishes of Hawaii. (Albatross survey)

(Paradise of the Pacific, Vol. 15, 1902,
No. 11, p. 19-21)

QL
1
F 45
FISHES HAWAII
Grey, Marion

Catalogue of type specimens of fishes in
Chicago Natural History Museum.

(Fieldiana: Zoology, Vol. 32 (3):109-205,
1947)

[Hawaiian types are checked in pencil]

QL
Fishes
Pam.323
FISHES HAWAII

Hawaiian names of fishes. typed sheet,
source unknown

QL
628
Ca-b
FISHES HAWAII
Godsil, H. C.

A systematic study of the Pacific tunas.
By H. C. Godsil and Robert D. Byers

(California, Division of Fish and Game, Fish
Bulletin No. 60, 1944)

QH
1
P 11
FISHES HAWAII
Grey, Marion

Fishes killed by the 1950 eruption of Mauna
Loa, Part V. Gonostomatidae.

(Pacific Science, Vol. 15(3):462-476, 1961)

QL
1
M 4
FISHES HAWAII
Hiatt, Robert W.

Effects of chemicals on a schooling fish,
Kuhlia sandvicensis. By Robert W. Hiatt, John J.
Naughton and Donald C. Matthews.

(Biological Bulletin, Vol. 104(1):28-44,
1953)

QL
636.5 H
G 67
FISHES HAWAII
Gosline, William A.

Handbook of Hawaiian fishes. By William A.
Gosline and Vernon E. Brock. University of
Hawaii Press. Honolulu. R8vo. 1960. ix + 372
pp.

QL
Fish Pam
343
376
FISHES HAWAII
Gudger, Eugene W.

The Opah or Moonfish, Lampris luna, on the
Coasts of California and of Hawaii.

(American Naturalist, Vol. 65, 1931, pp. 531-
540)

QL
Fish.Pam.
471
a,b

also

QL
Fishes
Pam.
508 a,b
FISHES HAWAII
Hiatt, Robert W.

Food-chains and the food cycle in Hawaiian
Fish ponds. PartI. The food and feeding habits
of mullet (Mugil cephalus), milkfish (Chanos
chanos), and the ten-pounder (Elops machnata).
(Reprints, Trans. Am. Fisheries Soc., Vol.
74:250-261, 1944 [published 1947])
...Part II. Biotic reaction. (Trans. Am.
Fisheries Soc., 74:262-280, 1944)

QL
1
C 78
FISHES HAWAII
Gosline, William A.

The Hawaiian fishes of the family Moringuidae
another eel problem. By William A. Gosline and
Donald W. Strasburg.

(Copeia, 1956, No. 1: pp. 9-18)

QH
1
P 11
FISHES HAWAII
Haig, Janet

Fishes killed by the 1950 eruption of Mauna
Loa. III. Sternoptychidae.

(Pacific Science, Vol. IX(3):318-323, 1955)

QL
617
H 82
FISHING HAWAII
Hosaka, Edward Y.

Sport fishing in Hawaii. One hundred and
forty-eight illustrations, including one hundred and fourteen drawings by the author. Published by Bond's, Honolulu, 1944. sm8vo. ix +
198 pp.

QH
1
P 11
FISHES HAWAII
Gosline, William A.

A new atherinid fish of the genus Iso from
the Hawaiian Islands.

(Pacific Science, 6(1):47-50, 1952)

QL
Fish
Pam.
398
FISHING HAWAII
Hamre, Christopher J.

Recommendations to improve fishing industry
in Hawaii.

(Honolulu Advertiser, May 2, 1943)

AS
36
S4
FISHES -- HAWAIIAN ISLANDS
[Flounders and soles from Japan]
Hubbs, Carl L.
in U.S. Nat. Mus. Proc. 46, 1915, pp. 449-496.

Haw. specimens on p. 457.

QH
1
P 11
FISHES HAWAII
Gosline, William A.

A new Hawaiian percoid fish, Suttonia line-
ata, with a discussion of its relationships and
a definition of the family Grammistidae.

(Pacific Science, Vol. 14(1):28-38, 1960)

DU
620
P
FISHES HAWAII

Hawaii's fish fauna.

(Paradise of the Pacific, Vol. 18, 1905, No.
10, p. 10-14)

(Review of literature and surveys)

FISHES -- Hawaiian Islands
Jenkins, Oliver P.

QL
Fish
Pam.
122

Descriptions of fifteen new
species of fishes from the Hawaiian
Island.

G. & K. (?) Washington 1901.

QH
1
P 11
FISHES HAWAII
Gosline, William A.

The scientific name of the nehu, an engrau-
lid baitfish of the Hawaiian Islands.

(Pacific Science, Vol. 5:272; 1951)

QL
636.5.H
E 59
FISHES HAWAII

Hawaiian fishes, 60 water color sketches by
an unknown artist, - from the Enriques estate.
obl2mo. (Henriques)

(attributed to Isobel Strong)

FISHES -- HAWAIIAN ISLANDS
Jenkins, Oliver P.

QL
Fish
Pam.
121

Descriptions of new species of
fishes from the Hawaiian Island
belonging to Labridae & Scaridae.

G. & K. (?) Washington 1900. 8vo.

AS 36 C2 — FISHES -- HAWAIIAN ISLANDS

Jenkins, Oliver P.

Description of a new species of Ransania from the Hawaiian Islands. In Proc. of Calif. Acad. of Sc. 2d ser. Vol. V, pt. 1, 1895, pp 779-784.

AS 36 Cbl — FISHES - HAWAII

Jordan, David Starr and Eric K. Jordan

A list of the fishes of Hawaii, with notes and descriptions of new species. Carnegie Mus. Mem. X, No.1, 1922, pp. 1-92 pl. 1-4

QL 627 U-b — FISHES HAWAII

June, Fred C.

Spawning of yellowfin tuna in Hawaiian waters.

(United States Dept. of the Interior, Fishery Bulletin 77, pp. 47-64, 1953)

[Neothunnus macropterus]

QL 627 U-b — FISHES HAWAII

Jordan, David Starr

The aquatic resources of the Hawaiian islands, by David Starr Jordan and others. Parts I-III.

(Bull. U. S. Fish Commission, Vol. 23, 1903)

AS 36 S4 — Fishes - Hawaiian Islands.

Jordan, David Starr and Snyder, John O. Notes on collections of fishes from Oahu Island and Laysan Island, Hawaii, with descriptions of four new species. In U.S. Nat. Mus. Proc. Vol. XXVII, 1904. pp. 939-948.

QL Fishes Pam. 470 — FISHES HAWAII

Kepelino

Ka mooolelo o na ia Hawaii. (The story of the fish of Hawaii)

IN Hawaiian.

DU 1 P and QL Fish Pam 235 — FISHES -- HAWAIIAN ISLANDS

Jordan, David Starr and Evermann, B.W.

A check list of the fishes of Hawaii. In Pan-Pacific Research Inst. Journ. Vol. I, No.1, Jan. 1926.

AS 36 C3 and QL Fish Pam 264 — FISHES - HAWAIIAN ISLANDS

Jordan, David Starr, Evermann, B.W., & Tanaka, S.

Notes on new or rare fishes from Hawaii. California Academy of Sci., 4 ser. v.16, n.20, 1927.

separate

AS 36 A 65-b — FISHES HAWAII

Lamonte, Francesca R.

A review and revision of the marlins, genus Makaira.

(Am. Mus. of Nat. Hist., Bull. 107(3), 1955)

AS 36 S 4 and QL Fish Pam 285 — FISHES HAWAII

Jordan, D. S., and Snyder, J. O.

Description of a new species of fish (Apogon Evermanni) from the Hawaiian Islands, with notes on other species.

(U. S. Nat. Mus. Proc., XXVIII, 1905, pp. 123-126)

AS 36 S 4 and QL Fishes Pam. 280 365 — FISHES HAWAII

Jordan, David Starr

On a collection of fishes from Fiji, with notes on certain Hawaiian fishes, by D. S. Jordan and M. C. Dickerson. (Proc. U. S. Nat. Mus., 34, 1908, pp. 603-617)

QL 617 I 61 — FISHES HAWAII

LaMonte, Francesca

Swordfish, sailfish, marlin and spearfish, by Francesca LaMonte and Donald E. Marcy.

(Ichthyological Contributions of the Int. Game Fish Association, Vol. 1, No. 2, 1941, pp. 1-24)

QL Fish Pam #242 — FISHES-HAWAIIAN ISLANDS

Jordan, David Starr

Description of deep-sea fishes from the coast of Hawaii, killed by a lava flow from Mauna Loa. From Proc. U. S. Nat. Mus. 1921. vol. 59, 1922, pp. 643-656 (date of publication, Oct. 14, 1921)

AS 36 S4 — FISHES -- HAWAII

Jordan, Eric Knight

Notes on the fishes of Hawaii with descriptions of six new species. U. S. Nat. Mus. Proc. Vol. 66, Art. 33, pp 1-43, pls 1-2, 1925.

Q 101 P 18 — FISHES-HAWAII

Larsen, Nils P.

Tetrodon poisoning in Hawaii.

(Proc. Pac. Sci. Congress, 6th, 1942, Vol. 5, pp. 417-422) (Congress took place in 1939)

QL 627 U-b U. S. MAY 30 1910 and QL Fish Pam # 125 — FISHES -- HAWAIIAN ISLANDS

Jordan, D. S. & Evermann, B.W.

Descriptions of New Genera & Species of Fishes from the Haw. Islds.

Wash. 1903. 4° p. 161-208. U.S. Fish Com. Bull for 1902 See also pp 209-210

AS 36 C 1 — FISHES HAWAII

Jordan, David Starr

A review of the giant mackerel-like fishes, tunnies, spearfishes and swordfishes. By David Starr Jordan and Barton Warren Evermann.

(Occasional Papers of the California Acad. of Sci., XII, 1926)

QH 1 P 11 — FISHES HAWAII

Matsumoto, Walter M.

Notes on the Hawaiian frigate mackerel of the genus Auxis.

(Pacific Science, 14:173-177, 1960)

QL Fish Pam. 367 — FISHES HAWAII

Jordan, David Starr

Descriptions of two new species of fishes from Honolulu, Hawaii. By David Starr Jordan and Charles William Metz.

(Proc. U. S. Nat. Mus., Vol. 42, pp. 525-527, 1912)

QL 752 U 58 — FISHES HAWAII

June, Fred C.

Common tuna-bait fishes of the central Pacific. By Fred C. June and John W. Reintjes.

(U. S. Dept. of the Interior, Fish and Wildlife Service, Research Report 34, 1953)

QL 627 U-b — FISHES-HAWAII

Moore, Harvey L.

Estimation of age and growth of yellowfin tuna (Neothunnus macropterus) in Hawaiian waters by size frequencies.

(U. S. Fish and Wildlife Service, Fishery Bull. 65, 1951)

QL
617
I 61   FISHES   HAWAII

Nichols, John Treadwell

    Differences in marlins based on weights and measurements, by J. T. Nichols and Francesca R. LaMonte.

    (Ichthyological Contributions of the International Game Fish Association, Vol. 1, no. 1, pp. 1-6, 1941)

QL
752
U 58   FISHES   HAWAII

Royce, William F.

    Observation of skipjack schools in Hawaiian waters, 1953. By William F. Royce and Tamio Otsu.

    (U.S. Dept. of the Interior, Fish and Wildlife Service, Special Sci. Rept., Fisheries No. 147, 1955)

QL
Fishes
Pam.
505   FISHES   HAWAII

Tester, Albert L.

    Distribution of nehu eggs and larvae in Kaneohe Bay.

    (Hawaii Marine Laboratory, Univ. of Hawaii, New Circular, No. 13, 1952)

QL
1
C 78   FISHES   HAWAII

Nichols, John T.

    The Hawaiian "ulua".

    (Copeia, 1935, No. 4, Dec. 31, p. 192-193)

QL
636.S34
S 33   FISHES-HAWAIIAN ISLANDS

Schindler, Otto

    Sexually mature larval Hemiramphidae from the Hawaiian Islands.

    (Bernice P. Bishop Museum Bulletin 97, 1932)

QL
121
H 38-n   FISHES   HAWAII

Tester, Albert L.

    Maomao spawning.

    (Univ. of Hawaii, Hawaii Marine Laboratory, News Circular No. 14, 1953)

AS
36
A 3   FISHES   HAWAII

Nichols, John Treadwell

    How many marlins are there? By J. T. Nichols and F. R. LaMonte.

    (Natural History, 36:327-330, 1935)

AS
36
W 2

and

QL
Fishes
Pam. 396   FISHES   HAWAII

Schultz, Leonard P.

    Kraemeria bryani, a new species of trichonotid fish from the Hawaiian islands.

    (Journal of the Washington Academy of Sciences, Vol. 31, 1941, pp. 269-272)

QH
1
P 11   FISHES   HAWAII

Tester, Albert L.

    Variation in egg and larva production of the Anchovy, Stolephorus purpureus fowler, in Kaneohe Bay, Oahu, during 1950-1952.

    (Pacific Science, Vol. IX(1):31-41, 1955)

QL
Fishes
Pam.
460   FISHES   HAWAII

Pietschmann, Victor

    Eine neue Aalfamilie aus den hawaiischen Gewässern.

    (Akad. Wissenschaften...Wien, Anzeiger, 72: 93-94, 1935)

AS
36
S 5

AS
36
S 2

QL
Fish Pam
150   FISHES   HAWAII

Streets, T. H.

    Contributions to the natural history of the Hawaiian and Fanning Islands...U. S. North Pacific surveying expedition, 1873-1875. pp. 56-77.

    (U. S. Nat'l Mus., Bull. No. 7, 1877; Smithsonian Misc. Coll., Vol. XIII, art. 7, publ. no. 303)

QH
1
P 11   FISHES   HAWAII

Tester, Albert L.

    Variation in the vertebral number of the anchovy (Stolephorus purpureus) in Hawaiian waters. By Albert L. Tester and Robert W. Hiatt.

    (Pacific Science 6(1):59-70, 1952)

QL
636.5H
P 62   FISHES   HAWAII

Pietschmann, Victor.

    Hawaiian shore fishes, by Victor Pietschmann ... Honolulu, Hawaii, The Museum, 1938.

    2 p. L, [3]-55 p. 18 pl. on 9 L, diagrs. 25½ᶜᵐ. (Bernice P. Bishop museum. Bulletin 156)

    "Literature cited": p. 53.

    1. Fishes—Hawaiian islands.   I. Title.   II. Title: Shore fishes, Hawaiian.

                         39-9912

    Library of Congress   GN670.B4 no. 156

              [3]   (572.996) 597.09969

QL
627
U-b

QL
Fish Pam
287   FISHES   HAWAII

Snyder, John Otterbein

    Catalogue of the shore fishes collected by the steamer "Albatross" about the Hawaiian Islands in 1902.

    (U. S. Fish Commission Bulletin, XXII, pp. 513-538, 1904)

QL
Fishes
Pam.
532   FISHES   HAWAII

Tinker, Spencer

    At the Aquarium.

    (various issues, Honolulu Star-Bulletin, Sept. 15, 1951-Aug. 2, 1952)

QL
Fishes
Pam.
611   FISHES   HAWAII

Randall, John E.

    A contribution to the biology of the convict Surgeonfish of the Hawaiian Islands, Acanthurus triostegus sandvicensis.

    (Pacific Science, 15(2):215-272, 1961)

QL
636.5H
E 59   FISHES   HAWAII

Strong, Isobel

    Hawaiian fishes; 60 water color sketches by an unknown artist. (from the Henriques Estate 12mo. oblong)

QL
636.5 H
T 58   FISHES   HAWAII

Tinker, Spencer Wilkie

    Hawaiian fishes; a handbook of the fishes found among the islands of the central Pacific Ocean. Honolulu, 1944

AS
763
H 38   FISHES   HAWAII

Randall, John E.

    Spawning cycle development, and growth of the convict surgeon fish or manini.

    (Proc. Haw. Acad. Sci., Ann. Meeting, 1954-55, p. 15, 1955)

QH
1
P 11   FISHES   HAWAII

Tester, Albert L.

    The distribution of eggs and larvae of the anchovy, Stolephorus purpureus Fowler, in Kaneohe Bay, Oahu, with a consideration of the sampling problem.

    (Pacific Science, Vol. 5:321-346, 1951)

GN
2.S
P 76

and

GN
671.H2
T 61   FISHES   HAWAII

Titcomb, Margaret

    Native use of fish in Hawaii. With the collaboration of Mary Kawena Pukui.

    (Mem. Polynesian Soc., No. 29, 1952)

QL
Fishes
Pam.
547

FISHES　HAWAII

Wahlert, Gerd von

Die Typen und Typoide des Übersee-Museums
Bremen, 2:Pisces.

(Veröff. Überseemuseum Bremen, Reihe A,
Band 2, heft 5:323-326, 1955)

DU
621
H3

FISHES - HAWAIIAN ISLANDS

Wetmore, Charles H.

Concerning Hawaiian fishes: prepared
expressly for the Hawaiian Annual. Thrums
Hawaiian Annual, 1890, pp. 90-7.

AS
540
P

FISHES　HONGKONG

Seale, Alvin

Fishes of Hongkong.

(Philippine Journal of Sci., IX, D:59-79,
1914)

QL
636.5
F 78

AS
763
B-b

Reading
Room

FISHES　HOWLAND ISLAND

Fowler, Henry W.

Fishes of the tropical central Pacific.

(Bernice P. Bishop Museum, Bulletin No. 38,
Whippoorwill Expedition, Publication No. 1)
1927

QL
1
F

FISHES - ILLINOIS

Meek, Seth Eugene, 1859-

... A synoptic list of the fishes known to occur within
fifty miles of Chicago. By S. E. Meek and S. F. Hildebrand ... Chicago, 1910.

1 p. l., p. 223-338. illus. 24½ᶜᵐ. (Field museum of natural history.
Publication 142. Zoölogical series. vol. VII, no. 9)

1. Fishes—Illinois. 2. Fishes—Michigan, Lake. I. Hildebrand, S. F.,
joint author.

10-16245

Library of Congress　　　QL1.F4 vol. 7, no. 9

FISHES-INDIA

QL
621
D 27

locked
case

Day, Francis, 1829-1889.
The fishes of India; being a natural history of the fishes
known to inhabit the seas and fresh waters of India,
Burma, and Ceylon ... London, B. Quaritch, 1875-78.
4 pt. cxcv (i. e. 198) pl.　32 x 26ᶜᵐ.
—— Supplement to the Fishes of India ... By Francis
Day ... London [etc.] Williams and Norgate, 1888.
1 p. l., p. 779-816. illus. 31½ x 25½ᶜᵐ.
—— One hundred and ninety-eight plates to illustrate
Francis Day's work on the Fishes of India. [London,
G. Norman and son, printers] 1889.
11 p. cxcv (i. e. 198 pl.)　32½ x 26ᶜᵐ.
Plates are the same as those issued with the work.
1. Fishes—India.

A 18-1868

Title from Harvard Univ.　　　Printed by L. C.

QL
622
I 39

FISHES　INDIA

Indian Museum. Calcutta.

A Descriptive Catalogue of the Indian Deep-Sea
Fishes in the Indian Museum. Being a Revised
Account...Fishes collected by the...Investigator.
Calcutta. 1899. 4to. 211 pp.

QL
Fishes
Pam.
597

FISHES　INDIA

Misra, K. S.

An aid to the identification of the fishes
of India, Burma and Ceylon. 1. Elasmobranchii
and Holocephali.

(Records of the Indian Museum, 49(1):89-137
1952)

QL
1
I-r

FISHES　INDIA

Misra, K. S.

A check list of the fishes of India, Burma
and Ceylon. I. Elasmobranchii and Holocephali.

(Records of the Indian Museum. Vol. 45(1):
1-46, 1947)

AS
472
A-s

FISHES　INDIA

Shaw, G. E.

The fishes of northern Bengal, by G. E. Shaw
and E. O Shebeare.

(Journal of the Royal Asiatic Soc. of Bengal,
Science, Vol. III, 1937.)

QL
5
M 98

FISHES　INDIAN OCEAN

Norman, J. R.
Fishes.

IN The John Murray Expedition, 1933-34,
Sci. Repts., Vol. VII, no. 1, pp. 1-116, 1939.

AS
36
A 16-n

FISHES　INDO CHINA

Fowler, Henry W.

A small collection of fishes from Saigon,
French Indo-China.

(Notulae Naturae, Acad. Nat. Sci. Phil.,
No. 8, 1939)

QL
Fishes
Pam.
428

FISHES　INDOCHINA

Institut Océanographique de l'Indochine.

Principaux poissons comestibles d'Indochine.
60 especes de mer et d'eaux douces. (Issued by)
Institut Oceanographique. Saigon. 1945. 71 pp.

QL
619
W 37

FISHES　INDONESIA

Weber, Max

Fishes of the Indo-Australian archipelago.
By Max Weber and L. F. de Beaufort. Vols. 1-11
1911-1962. E. J. Brill. Leiden. 8vo.

Vol. 1 has sub-title: Index of the ichthyological papers of P. Bleeker.
Vol. 8 by L. F. de Beaufort alone.

Q
115
U3

H39

FISHES - JAPAN

Brevoort, James Carson

Notes on some figures of Japanese
fish taken from recent specimens by the
artists of the U. S. Japan Expedition.
In Perry, Commodore M. C. Narrative...
Vol. II, pp 253- 258, Washington, 1856.

QL
619
We

Fishes—Japan

Day, Francis.

The fishes of the Indo-Australian
Archipelago...1911.

See main card for fuller entry

AS
36
S4

FISHES--JAPAN.

Gilbert, Charles Henry, 1859-
Report on the Japanese macrouroid fishes collected by
the United States fisheries steamer "Albatross" in 1906,
with a synopsis of the genera. By Charles Henry Gilbert
and Carl L. Hubbs ...

(In U. S. National museum. Proceedings. Washington, 1917. 23½ᶜᵐ.
v. 51, p. 135-214. pl. 8-11)

1. Macruridae. 2. Fishes—Japan. 3. Albatross (Steamer)　I. Hubbs,
Carl Levitt, 1894-　joint author.

Library of Congress　　　Q11.U55 vol. 51　　　17-23839
—— Copy 2.　　　Q11.U55 vol. 51 2d set

AS
36
C51

FISHES--JAPAN

Gilbert, Charles Henry, 1859-
... The lantern-fishes of Japan, by Charles H. Gilbert.
Pittsburgh, Board of trustees of the Carnegie institute,
1913.
cover-title, p. 67-107. pl. XI-XIV. 33½ᶜᵐ. (Memoirs of the Carnegie
museum. vol. VI, no. 2)
Publications of the Carnegie museum, serial no. 76.

1. Lantern-fishes. 2. Fishes—Japan.

13-22468

Library of Congress　　　AS36.P75

AS
36
S4

FISHES - JAPAN

Gilbert, Charles Henry, 1859-
New cyclogasterid fishes from Japan. By C. H. Gilbert and C. V. Burke ...

(In U. S. National museum. Proceedings. Washington, 1912. 23½ᶜᵐ.
vol. 42, p. 351-380. illus., pl. 41-48)

1. Fishes—Japan.　I. Burke, Charles Victor, joint author.

13-9535

Library of Congress　　　Q11.U55　vol. 42

QL
1
T 64

FISHES　JAPAN

Hatta, S.

On the lampreys of Japan together with notes
on a specimen of lamprey from Siberia.

(Annotationes Zoologicae Japonenses, Vol.
IV:21-29, 1901)

Q
115
H 39

locked
case

FISHES　JAPAN

Hawks, Francis L.
Narrative of the expedition of an American
squadron to the China Seas and Japan...1852-54.
Vol. II, pp. 255-288: Notes on figures of Japanese fish, by James Carson, Brevoort.

FISHES--JAPAN

AS 36 S4 Hubbs, Carl Levitt, 1894–

Flounders and soles from Japan collected by the United States bureau of fisheries steamer "Albatross" in 1906. By Carl L. Hubbs ...

(*In* U. S. National museum. Proceedings. Washington, 1915. 23½ᶜᵐ. v. 48, p. 449-496. pl. 25-27)

1. Flounders. 2. Soles. 3. Fishes--Japan. I. Albatross (Steamer)

Library of Congress   Q11.U55 vol. 48   15–24786

FISHES`--JAPAN

QL 1 C and AS 36 S6 Jordan, David Starr, 1851–

... Description of two new genera of fishes (*Ereunias* and *Draciscus*) from Japan, by David Starr Jordan and John Otterbein Snyder ... San Francisco, The Academy, 1901.

1 p. l., p. 377-380. pl. XVIII-XIX (fold.) 25½ᶜᵐ. (Proceedings of the California academy of sciences. 3d ser. Zoology. vol. II, no. 7) "Issued April 24, 1901."

1. Ereunias. 2. Draciscus. I. Snyder, John Otterbein, 1867– joint author.

Library of Congress   Q11.C25 vol. 2, no. 7   16–22019

FISHES--JAPAN

AS 36 S4 Jordan, David Starr, 1851–

A review of the *Serranidæ* or sea bass of Japan. By David Starr Jordan and Robert Earl Richardson ...

(*In* U. S. National museum. Proceedings. Washington, 1910. 23½ᶜᵐ. v. 37, p. 421-474. illus.)

1. Sea-bass. 2. Fishes--Japan. I. Richardson, Robert Earl, 1877– joint author.

Library of Congress   Q11.U55 vol. 37   11–9678
[a20f2]

FISHES   JAPAN

QL Fishes Pam.386 Ikeda, Hyosi

Some suggestive notes on the fauna of fresh water fishes in northern parts of Japan.

(Bull. Biogeographical Soc. of Japan, Vol. 9, 1939, pp. 81-90. Japanese and English)

FISHES--JAPAN

AS 36 S4 Jordan, David Starr, 1851–

Notes on a collection of fishes from the island of Shikoku in Japan, with a description of a new species, *Gnathypops iyonis*. By David Starr Jordan and William Francis Thompson ...

(*In* U. S. National museum. Proceedings. Washington, 1914. 23½ᶜᵐ. v. 46, p. 65-72. illus.)

1. Gnathypops iyonis. 2. Fishes--Japan. I. Thompson, William Francis, joint author

Library of Congress   Q11.U55 vol. 46   14–10968

FISHES--JAPAN

AS 36 S4 Jordan, David Starr, 1851–

A review of the *Sparidæ* and related families of perch-like fishes found in the waters of Japan. By David Starr Jordan and William Francis Thompson ...

(*In* U. S. National museum. Proceedings. Washington, 1912. 23½ᶜᵐ. v. 41, p. 521-601. illus.)

1. Sparidae. 2. Fishes--Japan. I. Thompson, William Francis, joint author.

Library of Congress   Q11.U55 vol. 41   12–17796
[19e2]

FISHES   JAPAN

QL Fishes Pam.387 Ikeda, H.

Statistical observations on the species of the genus Tribolodon in Japan and some notes on their distribution.

(Sci. Reports, Tokyo Bunrika Daigaku, No. 56, (Vol. 3, pp. 165-192), 1938)

FISHES - JAPAN

AS 36 S2 Jordan, David Starr, 1851–

On a collection of fishes made by Mr. Alan Owston in the deep waters of Japan, by David Starr Jordan and John Otterbein Snyder.

(*In* Smithsonian institution. Smithsonian miscellaneous collections. Washington, 1903. 24½ᶜᵐ. vol. XLV (Quarterly issue, vol. 1) p. 230-240. illus., pl. LVIII-LXIII)

Publication 1447.
Originally published April 11, 1904.
Vol. 45 (Quarterly issue, v. 1) with t.-p. dated 1903, was issued 4 parts in 2, with covers dated 1904.

1. Fishes--Japan. I. Snyder, John Otterbein, 1867– joint author.

Library of Congress   Q11.S7 vol. 45   16–11323
——— Copy 2.

FISHES -- JAPAN

AS 36 C51 Jordan, David Starr and Hubbs, Carl L.

Record of fishes obtained by David Starr Jordan in Japan, 1922. In Carnegie Mus. Mem. Vol. X. pp 93 - 346, pls. v-xii, 1925.

FISHES   JAPAN

QL Fish Pam 361 Inuo, Saburô

Sexual differences in the labroid fishes of Japan.

(Animal and Plant Life, Vol. 9, No. 3, 1936. 6 pp.)

Text and source in Japanese

FISHES   JAPAN

QL 1 T 64 Jordan, David Starr

A preliminary check list of the fishes of Japan, by David Starr Jordan and John Otterbein Snyder.

(Annotationes Zoologicae Japonenses, Vol. 3, nos. 2-3;31-159, 1901)

FISHES   JAPAN

QL 634.J K 15 Kamohara, Toshiji

Coloured illustrations of the fishes of Japan (I). Coloured illustrations by Hirosuke Ishizu. Revised edition. 1961. Hoikusha. Osaka. 8vo. 158 pp.

FISHES   JAPAN

QL 615 J 35 Japanese Journal of Ichthyology

FISHES--JAPAN

AS 36 C51 Jordan, David Starr, 1851–

... Record of the fishes obtained in Japan in 1911, by David Starr Jordan and William Francis Thompson. Pittsburgh, Board of trustees of the Carnegie institute, 1914.

cover-title, p. 205-313. illus., pl. XXIV-XLII. 33½ᶜᵐ. (Memoirs of the Carnegie museum. vol. VI, no. 4)

Publications of the Carnegie museum, serial no. 80.

1. Fishes--Japan. I. Thompson, William Francis, joint author.

Library of Congress   AS36.P75 vol. 6, no. 4   15–3209

FISHES   JAPAN

QL 627 P 11 Kishinouye, Kamakichi

A study of the mackerels, Cybiids and tunas.

(Suisan Gakkai, Vol. 1(1);1-24, My 1915)

[Pacific Oceanic Fishery Investigations, Translation No. 25]

FISHES--JAPAN.

AS 36 C3 Jordan, David Starr, 1851–

... Description of a new fossil fish from Japan, by David Starr Jordan ... [San Francisco? 1919]

p. [271]-272. pl. 20. 25½ᶜᵐ. (Proceedings of the California academy of sciences. 4th ser. vol. IX, no. 9)

Caption title.

1. Fishes, Fossil. 2. Fishes--Japan.

Library of Congress   Q11.C253 vol. 9, no. 9   20–4831
——— Copy 2.   QE851.J6
[5]

FISHES -- JAPAN

AS 36 S4 Jordan, David Starr, 1851–

A review of the fishes of the families *Lobotidæ* and *Lutianidæ*, found in the waters of Japan. By David Starr Jordan and William Francis Thompson ...

(*In* U. S. National museum. Proceedings. Washington, 1911. 23½ᶜᵐ. v. 39, p. 435-471. illus.)

1. Lobotidae. 2. Lutianidae. 3. Fishes--Japan. I. Thompson, William Francis, joint author.

Library of Congress   Q11.U55 vol. 39   11–21247

FISHES   JAPAN

QL 1 C 2-b Mead, Giles W.

A collection of oceanic fishes from off northeastern Japan. By Giles W. Mead and F. H. C Taylor.

(Jour. of the Fisheries Research Board of Canada, Vol. X(6):560-582, 1953)

FISHES - JAPAN

QL 1 C and AS 36 S6 Jordan, David Starr, 1851–

... Description of three new species of fishes from Japan. By David Starr Jordan and Edwin Chapin Starks. With two plates ... San Francisco, The Academy, 1901.

1 p. l., 381-386 p. xx-xxi pl. 25½ᶜᵐ. (Proceedings of the California academy of sciences. 3rd ser. Zoology. vol. II, no. 8) "Issued April 24, 1901."

Library of Congress Q11.C25
——— San Francisco, The Academy, 1901.
1 p. l., 381-386 p. xx-xxi pl. 25½ᶜᵐ. (Contributions to biology from the Hopkins seaside laboratory of the Leland Stanford junior university. xxiv)

1. Fishes--Japan. I. Starks, Edwin Chapin, joint author.

Library of Congress   QL1.L53   5–35347-8
——— Copy 2.

AS 36 S4 **FISHES -- JAPAN.** Jordan, David Starr, 1851–

A review of the sciænoid fishes of Japan. By David Starr Jordan and William Francis Thompson ...

(*In* U. S. National museum. Proceedings. Washington, 1911. 23½ᶜᵐ. v. 39, p. 241-261. illus.)

1. Sciænidae. 2. Fishes--Japan. I. Thompson, William Francis, joint author.

Library of Congress   Q11.U55 vol. 39   11–21203

FISHES   JAPAN

QL Fishes Pam. 359 Okada, Yaichiro

Preliminary note on the pearl organs in some Japanese cyprinoid fishes.

(Science Reports of the Tokyo Univ. of Literature and Science, Sec. B. Vol. 2, No. 28, 1934 pp. 29-36, pl. 3-5)

QL
Fishes
Pam.388

FISHES JAPAN

Okada, Y.

A revision of the Japanese striped loaches referred to the genus Cobitis. By Y. Okada and H. Ikeda.

(Zool. Inst., Tokyo Bunrika Daigaku, Sci., Reports, Section B., No. 69 (Vol. 4, pp. 89-104), 1939)

QL
634.J
O 41

FISHES JAPAN

Okada, Yaichiro

Studies on the freshwater fishes of Japan. Parts 1-2 (in 3)

(Jour. Fac. of Fisheries, Prefectural Univ. of Mie, Japan, 1959-60)

QL
Fish Pam
330

FISHES JAPAN

Schmidt, P.

On a rare japanese shark, Calliscyllium venustum Tanaka.

(Comptes Rendus de l'Académie des Sciences de l'URSS, 1928, pp. 65-67)

QL
Fish Pam
331

FISHES JAPAN

Schmidt, P.

On the occurrence of the eel Uroconger lepturus Richardson in Japan.

(Comptes Rendus de l'Academie des Sciences de l'URSS, 1929, pp. 189-193)

QL
Fish Pam
329

FISHES JAPAN

Schmidt, P.

On a rare japanese deep-sea fish, Ereunias grallator Jordan and Snyder.

(Comptes Rendus de l'Academie des Sciences de l'URSS, 1928, pp. 319-320)

AS
251
L 56-t

FISHES JAPAN

Schmidt, P. J.

Fishes of Japan collected in 1901 (with a summary and 30 textfigs.)

(Trans. of the Pacific Com. of the Acad. of Sci., USSR, II, 1931, pp. 1-176)

QL
623
S 57
locked case

FISHES JAPAN

Siebold, Ph. Fr. de

Fauna Japonica, sive descriptio animalium, quae in itinere per Japoniam...tenent...1823-1850 Conjunctis studiis C. J. Temminck et H. Schlegel pro vertebrata atque W. de Haan pro invertebrata elaborata. Lugduni Batavorum. folio.
Pisces only. 1842-1850. 323 pp. 160 plates
LIBRARY lack all other parts.

QL
638.094
Sm

FISHES JAPAN

Smith, Hugh McCormick, 1865-

Japanese goldfish, their varieties and cultivation; a practical guide to the Japanese methods of goldfish culture for amateurs and professionals, by Hugh M. Smith ... Washington, W. F. Roberts company, 1909.

112 p. incl. front., illus. col. plates. 19 x 25½ cm.

"Literature cited": p. 105.

1. Goldfish.   10-626

Library of Congress   SH167.G6Sm

Copyright A 253631

AS
36
S4

FISHES-- JAPAN

Snyder, John Otterbein, 1867-

Descriptions of new genera and species of fishes from Japan and the Riu Kiu Islands. [By] John Otterbein Snyder ...

(In U. S. National museum. Proceedings. Washington, 1911. 23½ cm. v. 40, p. 525-549)

1. Fishes—Japan. 2. Fishes—Riu Kiu Islands.

11-31534

Library of Congress   Q11.U55 vol. 40

AS
36
S4

FISHES--JAPAN

Snyder, John Otterbein, 1867-

Japanese shore fishes collected by the United States Bureau of fisheries steamer "Albatross" expedition of 1906. By John Otterbein Snyder ...

(In U. S. National museum. Proceedings. Washington, 1912. 23½ cm. vol. 42, p. 399-450. illus, pl. 51-61)

1. Fishes—Japan. 2. Albatross (Steamer)

13-9538

Library of Congress   Q11.U55 vol. 42

QL
Fish
Pam
#226

FISHES--JAPAN

Tanaka, Sh.

Description of one New Genus and ten new species of Japanese Fishes
Tokyo 1909. 8°. pp. 27. DEC 24 1909

QL
Fish
Pam
#225

FISHES--JAPAN

Tanaka, Sh.

Descriptions of eight new species of Fishes from Japan.
8°. pp. 27-47. DEC 24 1909

QL
634J
T 16

FISHES - JAPAN

Tanaka, Shigeho

Figures and descriptions of the fishes of Japan including Riukiu Islands, Bonin Islands, Formosa, Kurile Islands, Korea and Southern Sakhalin. Vols. 1-30, 1935. Second, revised edition.
---Vols. 31-48   1921-1930

Tokyo. Daichi Shoin. R8vo. With...plates.

QL
Fish
Pam
#224

FISHES--JAPAN

Tanaka, Sh.

Notes on freshwater fishes from the Province of Shinano Japan
8°. pp. 175-188. DEC 24 1909

QL
Fish
Pam
#223

FISHES--JAPAN

Tanaka, Sh.

Notes on some rare Fishes of Japan with Descriptions of two new genera & six new species.
8°. pp. 1-24. DEC 24 1909

QL
Fish
Pam
#220

FISHES--JAPAN

Tanaka, Sh.

On a small collection of tide-pool Fishes from Misaki, with Descriptions of two new species.
8°. pp. 17-26. DEC 24 1909

QL
Fish
Pam
#221

FISHES--JAPAN

Tanaka Shigeho

On some Fishes from Lake Biwa, with Descript. of one new species + a list of all the fish species hitherto known from that locality.
8°. pp. 15. DEC 24 1909

AS
36
A 16

FISHES JARVIS ISLAND

Fowler, Henry W.

The fishes of the George Vanderbilt South Pacific Expedition, 1937.

(Acad. of Nat. Sci., Philadelphia, Monograph No. 2, 1938)

QL
636.5
F 78
AS
763
B-b
1927
Reading Room

FISHES JARVIS ISLAND

Fowler, Henry W.

Fishes of the tropical central Pacific.

(Bernice P. Bishop Museum, Bulletin No. 38, 1927; Whippoorwill Expedition, Publication No. 1)

AS
36
S4

FISHES--JAVA

Bean, Barton Appler, 1860-

Notes on a collection of fishes from Java, made by Owen Bryant and William Palmer in 1909, with description of a new species. By Barton A. Bean and Alfred C. Weed ...

(In U. S. National museum. Proceedings. Washington, 1912. 23½ cm. vol. 42, p. 587-611. illus, pl. 73-75)

1. Fishes—Java. I. Weed, Alfred Cleveland, joint author. II. Bryant, Owen. III. Palmer, William, 1856-

13-9648

Library of Congress   Q11.U55 vol. 42

QL
Fish
Pam
253

FISHES - JAVA

Fowler, Henry W. and Bean, Barton A.

Notes on fishes obtained in Sumatra, Java and Tahiti. From Proc. U. S. Nat. Mus. v.71, art.10, 1927.

QL
1
C 78

FISHES   JOHNSTON ISLAND

Brock, Vernon E.

The identity of the parrotfish Scarus ahula,
the female of Scarus perspicillatus. By Vernon
E. Brock and Yoshio Yamaguchi.

(Copeia, 1954, No. 2:154-155)

AS
162
P 23

FISHES   KERGUELEN ISLANDS

Blanc, Maurice

Poissons recueillis aux Îles Kerguelen, par
le Dr. Aretas.

(Bull. Mus. Nat. d'Histoire Naturelle, Tome
23 (ser. 2):493-496, 1951)

QL
Fishes
Pam.
394

FISHES   KUSAIE

Herre, Albert W. C. T.

On a collection of fishes from Nanyo, the
Japanese Mandated Islands.

(Annotationes Zool. Japonenses, Vol. 18,
298-307, 1939)

AS
763
B-b

and

QL
Fish
Pam
164

Reading
Room

FISHES   JOHNSTON ISLAND

Fowler, Henry W. and Ball, Stanley C.

Fishes of Hawaii, Johnston Island and Wake
Island.

(Bernice P. Bishop Museum, Bulletin, No. 26,
Tanager Exped. Publication, No. 2, 1925)

AS
162
P 23

FISHES   KERGUELEN ISLANDS

Blanc, Maurice

Poissons recueillis aux Îles Kerguelen par
P. Paulian (1951) et M. Angot (1952).

(Paris, Bull. du Museum National d'Histoire
Naturelle, 2e serie, Tome XXVI(2):190-193, 1954)

AS
36
S4

FISHES -- LABRADOR.

Kendall, William Converse, 1861-
Report on the fishes collected by Mr. Owen Bryant on a
trip to Labrador in the summer of 1908. By William
Converse Kendall ...

(*In* U. S. National museum. Proceedings. Washington, 1911. 23½ᶜᵐ.
vol. 38, p. 503-510. pl. 30)

1. Fishes—Labrador.   I. Bryant, Owen.

11-15894

Library of Congress   Q11.U55 vol. 38

QL
636.5
F 78

AS
763
B-b

Reading
Room

FISHES   JOHNSTON ISLAND

Fowler, Henry W.

Fishes of the tropical central Pacific.

(Bernice P. Bishop Museum, Bulletin No. 38,
1927; Whippoorwill Expedition, Publication No. 1)

AS
162
P 23

FISHES   KERGUELEN ISLAND

Blanc, M.

Sur quelques poissons des Îles Kerguelen
rapportés par le Dr. Bourlaud.

(Bull. Mus. Nat. d'Hist. Nat. Paris, Tome
30, 2nd ser., 1958: 134-138)

AP
2
N 4

FISHES   LINE ISLANDS

Fish collection from the Leeward and Line
Islands. (George Vanderbilt Pacific Equatorial
Expedition of 1951)

(Nature, Vol. 168(4285):1027, 1951)

QH
1
P 11

FISHES   JOHNSTON ISLAND

Gosline, William A.

The inshore fish fauna of Johnston Island,
a central Pacific atoll.

(Pacific Science, Vol. IX(4):442-480, 1955)

AS
36
C51

FISHES--KOREA

Jordan, David Starr, 1851-
... A catalog of the fishes known from the waters of
Korea. By David Starr Jordan and Charles William
Metz. Pittsburgh, Board of trustees of the Carnegie in-
stitute, 1913.

cover-title, 65 p. illus., x pl. 33½ᶜᵐ. (Memoirs of the Carnegie museum.
vol. vi. no. 1)
Publications of the Carnegie museum, serial no. 75.

1. Fishes—Korea.   I. Metz, Charles William, joint author.

13-21895

Library of Congress   AS36.P75

QH
1
P 11

FISHES   LINE ISLANDS

Iversen, Edwin S.

Notes on the biology of the wahoo in the
Line Islands. By Edwin S. Iversen and Howard
O. Yoshida.

(Pacific Science, XI:370-379, 1957)

[wahoo: Acanthocybium solandri]

QH
138.J
S 62

FISHES   JUAN FERNANDEZ

Rendahl, Hialmar

The fishes of the Juan Fernandez Islands.

IN
Skottsberg, Carl   editor
The natural history of Juan Fernandez and
Easter Island. Vol. III. Zoology, Art. 10, pp.
49-58. Uppsala. 1921.

DU
1
P

FISHES   KOREA

Mori, Tamezo

A catalogue of the fishes of Korea.

(Journal of the Pan-Pacific Research Institution, Vol. 3, No. 3, 1928, pp. 3-8)

AS
36
S4

FISHES--LOUISIANA

Weymouth, Frank Walter.
Notes on a collection of fishes from Cameron, Louisiana.
By Frank Walter Weymouth ...

(*In* U. S. National museum. Proceedings. Washington, 1911. 23½ᶜᵐ.
vol. 38, p. 135-145. illus.)

1. Fishes—Louisiana.

11-15595

Library of Congress   Q11.U55 vol. 38

QL
Fishes
Pam.
609

FISHES   KAMCHATKA

Rass, T. C.

Deep-water fishes of the Kurile-Kamchatka
trench. Translated by Lisa Lanz and Robert R.
Rofen.

(Trud. Inst. Okeanol., Vol. 12:328-339,
1955; The George Vanderbilt News Bull.)

DU
1
P

FISHES   KOREA

Reeves, Cora D.

A catalogue of the fishes of northeastern
China and Korea.

(Journal of the Pan-Pacific Research Institution, Vol. 2, 1927, No. 3, pp. 3-16)

QL
1
A 93

FISHES   MACQUARIE ISLAND

Whitley, G. P.

A lantern fish from Macquarie Island.

(The Australian Zoologist, 10:124, 1943)

QL
5
D 22

locked
case

FISHES   KEELING ISLAND

Darwin, Charles

The Zoology of the Voyage of H.M.S. Beagle,
under the command of Captain Fitzroy, during
the years 1832 to 1836. London. 1839-1843. 4to.
Part IV: Fish, by Leonard Jenyns. 1842.

QL
634.J
T 16

FISHES - KOREA

Tanaka, Shigeho

Figures and descriptions of the
fishes of Japan including... Korea...

QH
1
M 17 a

FISHES   MADAGASCAR

Angot, M.

Aspect physique et etude ichthyologique du
recif de Soalara.

(Mem. Inst. Scientifique de Madagascar,
Ser. A. Tome 4:455-462, 1950)

Row 1, Column 1

QH
1
M 17 a   FISHES   MADAGASCAR

Angot, M.

    Poissons littoraux de Soalara.

    (Inst. Sci. de Madagascar, Mem. Ser. A, Tome 4:175-196, 1950)

Row 1, Column 2

AS
36
S 5   FISHES   MARIANAS

Schultz, Leonard P.   and others

    Fishes of the Marshall and Marianas Islands. By Leonard P. Schultz and collaborators: Earl S. Herald, Ernest A. Lachner, Arthur D. Welander, and Loren P. Woods. Vol. 1, Families from Asymmetrontidae through Siganidae.

    (Smithsonian Institution, U. S. Nat. Mus., Bull. 202, 1953)

Row 1, Column 3

AS
36
S 4   FISHES   MARSHALL ISLANDS

Schultz, Leonard P.

    A review of the labrid fish genus Wetmorella with descriptions of new forms from the tropical indo-Pacific. By Leonard P. Schultz and N. B. Marshall.

    (Proc. of the U. S. Nat. Mus., Vol. 103 No. 3327, 1954)

Row 2, Column 1

GN
71
D 26   FISHES   MALAY ARCHIPELAGO

Bleeker, Pieter

    Révision des espèces Indo-Archipélagiques du groupe des Apogonini...pp. 1-81. Révision des espèces d'Ambassis et de Parambassis de l'Inde Archipélagique...pp. 82-105. Révision des espèces insulindiennes de la Famille des Synanceoïdes.. pp.21

Davis, J. B.
Collection of papers on craniology... Vol. 2, No. 11.

    (over)

Row 2, Column 2

QL
Fish
Pam. 344   FISHES   MARQUESAS

Fowler, Henry W.

    Fresh-water Fishes from the Marquesas and Society Islands.

    (Bernice P. Bishop Museum, Occasional Papers Volume IX, Number 25, 1932. Pacific Entomological Survey Publication 4)

Row 2, Column 3

AS
763
B-m   FISHES   MELANESIA

QL
623
F 78   Fowler, Henry W.

Reading
Room   Fishes of Oceania. Honolulu. 1928. 4to. 540 pp. Supplements 1-2, 3 1931-34, 1949

    (Bernice P. Bishop Museum, Memoirs, Vol. X. Plates I-XLIX; Vol. XI, Nos. 5-6) ibid. XII:2. 1949

Row 3, Column 1

AS
472
A-j   FISHES -- MALAY ARCHIPELAGO

Cantor, Theodore

    Catalogue of Malayan Fishes. Journ. Asiatic Soc. 1849.

Row 3, Column 2

QH
1
P 11   FISHES   MARQUESAS

Murphy, Garth I.

    Introduction of the Marquesan sardine, Harengula vittata (Cuvier and Valenciennes), to Hawaiian waters.

    (Pacific Science, 14:185-187, 1960)

Row 3, Column 3

QL
1
H2   FISHES--MEXICO

Garman, Samuel, 1846–

    ... Reports on an exploration off the west coasts of Mexico, Central and South America, and off the Galapagos Islands, in charge of Alexander Agassiz, by the U. S. Fish commission steamer "Albatross," during 1891, Lieut. Commander Z. L. Tanner, U. S. N., commanding. XXVI. The fishes. By S. Garman ... Cambridge, U. S. A., Printed for the Museum, 1899.

    2 v. 97 pl. 31. (Harvard university. Museum of comparative zoölogy. Memoirs, vol. XXIV)

    1. Fishes—Mexico. 2. Fishes—Central America. 3. Fishes—South America.

                   F 17-161

Library, U. S. Bur. of   Fisheries

Row 4, Column 1

AS
496
F 29   FISHES   MALAY PENINSULA

    Report on the Gunong Tahan Expedition, May-September, 1905...Report on the Fishes, Batrachians and Reptiles, by G. A. Boulenger.

    (Jour. of the Fed. Malay States Mus., Vol. 3 1908-1909, pp. 1-11)

Row 4, Column 2

AS
36
S 5   FISHES   MARSHALL ISLANDS

Schultz, Leonard P.   and others

    Fishes of the Marshall and Marianas Islands. By Leonard P. Schultz and collaborators: Earl S. Herald, Ernest A. Lachner, Arthur D. Welander, and Loren P. Woods. Vol. 1. Families from Asymmetrontidae through Siganidae.

    (Smithsonian Institution, U. S. Nat. Mus., Bull. 202, 1953)

Row 4, Column 3

AS
36
S6   FISHES - MEXICO - SINALOA

Jordan, David Starr, 1851–

    ... The fishes of Sinaloa, by David Starr Jordan ... Palo Alto, Cal., Leland Stanford jr. university, 1895.

    2 p. l., 377[-514 p. XXVI-LV pl. on 29 l. 24½. (Leland Stanford junior university publications. Contributions to biology from the Hopkins laboratory of biology. I)

    Reprint from the Proceedings of the California academy of sciences, series 2, vol. V.

    1. Fishes—Mexico—Sinaloa.

Library of Congress   QL1.L53   7-10277

Row 5, Column 1

AS
492
S6   FISHES - MALAYA

Maxwell, C. N.
    Malayan fishes . Straits Br. Roy. Asiatic Soc. Journ. No. 84, 1921, 202 pp, 72 pls. pp. 171-280

Row 5, Column 2

AS
36
S 4   FISHES   MARSHALL ISLANDS

Schultz, Leonard P.

    Three new species of fishes of the genus Cirrhitus (family Cirrhitidae) from the Indo-Pacific.

    (Proc. U. S. Nat. Mus., Vol. 100, no. 3270, 1950)

Row 5, Column 3

QL
1
F   FISHES - MEXICO

Meek, Seth Eugene, 1859-1914.

    ... A contribution to the ichthyology of Mexico. By Seth Eugene Meek ... Chicago, 1902.

    1 p. l., 63-128 p., 1 l. XIV-XXXI pl. 24½. (Field Columbian museum. Publication 65. Zoological series. vol. III, no. 6)

    1. Fishes—Mexico.

                4-10572

Library of Congress   QL1.F4

Row 6, Column 1

QK
371
M 26   FISHES   MANCHOUKUO

Tokunaga, Shigeyasu   leader

    Report of the first scientific expedition to Manchoukuo...Sec. V,   Part I. 1934: The fresh water fishes of Jehol, by Tamezo Mori.

Row 6, Column 2

AS
36
A 16   FISHES   MARQUESAS

Fowler, Henry W.

    The fishes of the George Vanderbilt South Pacific Expedition, 1937.

    (Acad. of Nat. Sci., Philadelphia, Monograph No. 2, 1938)

Row 6, Column 3

QL
1
F   FISHES - MEXICO

Meek, Seth Eugene, 1859-1914.

    ... Notes on fresh-water fishes from Mexico and Central America, by Seth Eugene Meek ... Chicago, 1907.

    1 p. l., 133-157 p. 24½. (Field Columbian museum. Publication no. 124. Zoological series. vol. VII, no. 5)

    1. Fishes—Mexico. 2. Fishes—Central America.

                8-9040

Library of Congress   QL1.F4

Row 7, Column 1

DU
950.M3
B 91   FISHES   MARCUS ISLAND

Bryan, William Alanson

    A monograph of Marcus Island.

DU
Pac.Pam
68   (Bernice P. Bishop Museum, Occasional Papers Vol. II, No. 1, 1902, pp. 125-140) (Whole article is pp. 77-140)

QL
Birds
Pam.136

Row 7, Column 2

AS
36
A 4   FISHES   MARSHALL ISLANDS

Chapman, Wilbert M.

    Review of the fishes of the Blennioid genus Escenius, with descriptions of five new species. By Wilbert M. Chapman and Leonard P. Schultz.

    (Proc. U. S. Nat. Mus., Vol. 102:507-528, 1952)

Row 7, Column 3

QL
1
F   FISHES - MICHIGAN, LAKE

Meek, Seth Eugene, 1859–

    ... A synoptic list of the fishes known to occur within fifty miles of Chicago. By S. E. Meek and S. F. Hildebrand ... Chicago, 1910.

    1 p. l., p. 223-338. illus. 24½. (Field museum of natural history. Publication 142. Zoological series. vol. VII, no. 9)

    1. Fishes—Illinois. 2. Fishes—Michigan, Lake. I. Hildebrand. S. F., joint author.

                10-16245

Library of Congress   QL1.F4 vol.7, no. 9

AS
763
B-m

FISHES   MICRONESIA

Fowler, Henry W.

QL
623
F 78

Fishes of Oceania. Honolulu. 1928. 4to.
540 pp.   Supplements 1-2, 3 1931-34, 1949

Reading
Room

(Bernice P. Bishop Museum, Memoirs, Vol. X.
Plates I-XLIX; Vol. XI, Nos. 5-6) ibid XII :2

QL
345.N 6
S 24

FISHES   NEW CALEDONIA

Weber, Max

Les poissons d'eau douce de la Nouvelle-
Calédonie, par M. Weber and L. F. de Beaufort.

Sarasin, Fritz
Nova Caledonia...A. Zoologie, Tome II, Livr.
1, No. 2. 1915.

AS
36
A 16

FISHES   NEW GUINEA

Fowler, Henry W.

Zoological results of the Denison Crockett
South Pacific Expedition for the Academy of
Natural Sciences of Philadelphia, 1937-1938.
Part III. The fishes.

(Proc. Acad. Nat. Sci., Phil., Vol. 91, 1939,
pp. 77-96)

QL
Fishes
Pam.394

FISHES   MICRONESIA

Herre, Albert W. C. T.

On a collection of fishes from Nanyo, the
Japanese Mandated Islands.

(Annotationes Zool. Japonenses, Vol. 18,
1939, pp. 298-307)

QL
1
A 93 p

FISHES   NEW CALEDONIA

Whitley, Gilbert P.

Fishes from New Caledonia.

(Proc. R. Zoological Society of New South
Wales, 1958/59:60-65, publ. 1961)

QL
1
B 93

FISHES   NEW GUINEA

Hardenberg, J. D. F.

Fishes of New Guinea.

(Treubia, Vol. 18:217-231, 1941)

[Dutch New Guinea; fresh water and estuary]

QL
623.Mi
H 67
1.c.

FISHES   MICRONESIA

Hiyama, Yoshio   editor

[Report on the investigation of Poisonous
fishes of the South Seas. Nissan Fisheries
Research Laboratory, 1943.] 137 pp. + -; 29 col
pl.   4to.

text in Japanese

QH
104
U 58c

FISHES   NEW ENGLAND

Carson, Rachel L.

Food from the sea: fish and shellfish of
New England.

(Conservation Bulletin 33, Fish and Wildlife Service, 1943)

QL
636.5 NG
P 21

FISHES   NEW GUINEA

Munro, Iam S. R.

The fishes of the New Guinea region; a
checklist of the fishes of New Guinea incorporating records of species collected by the Fisheries Survey Vessel "Fairwind" during the years
1948 to 1950.

(Fisheries Bull., Territory of Papua and
New Guinea, No. 1, 1958)

DU
1
M 6

FISHES   MOOREA   (Society Is.)

Herre, Albert W.

A List of Fishes Collected at Moorea, One of
the Society Islands, Being the First Record from
this Island.

(Journal of the Pan-Pacific Research Institution, Vol. VI, No. 4, p. 10, IN Mid-Pacific
Magazine, Vol. 42, No. 4, 1931)

QL
1
M 33

FISHES   NEW GUINEA

Barton, Otis

Green New Guinea parrotfishes. By Otis
Barton and J. T. Nichols.

(Marine Life, Vol. 1 (4), pp. 11-13, 1946)

AS
36
A 65-no

FISHES   NEW GUINEA

Nichols, J. T.

A new blenny from Bali and a new threadfin
from New Guinea.

(American Museum Novitates, No. 1680, 1954)

AS
720.N
L

FISHES   NAURU

Whitley, Gilbert P.

Fishes from Nauru, Gilbert Islands, Oceania.
By Gilbert P. Whitley and Alan N. Colefax.

(Proc. of the Linnean Society of New South
Wales, 1938, Vol. 63, pp. 282-304)

AS
36

FISHES   NEW GUINEA

Barton, Otis

Stephanolepis (Pervagor) Septemclassiensis,
a new species of aluterine fish from New Guinea.

(American Mus. Novitates, No. 1303, Dec. 27,
1945, pp. 1-2)

AS
36
A 65

FISHES   NEW GUINEA

Nichols, John T.

New catfishes from northern New Guinea.
Results of the Archbold Expeditions, No. 30.

(American Museum Novitates, No. 1093, 1940)

QL
Fishes
Pam.
523

FISHES   NEW CALEDONIA

Legand, Michel

Etude de la croissance postlarvaire de
Sillago ciliata Cuv. dans la région de Nouméa.

(Bulletin Biologique, de la France et de la
Belgique; Tome LXXXVI (2):109-139, 1952)

QL
1
A 52-b

FISHES   NEW GUINEA

Beaufort, L. F. de

On a new and interesting globe-fish from
New Guinea.

(Beaufortia, Zoological Museum-Amsterdam,
Vol. 5, No. 48, June, 1955)

AS
36
A 65

FISHES   NEW GUINEA

Nichols, J.T.

A new fish of the genus Bostrychus from
New Guinea. Results of the Archbold Expeditions,
no. 15.

(American Museum Novitates, no.922, May 4,
1937. 2 pp.)

QL
Fishes
Pam.
525

FISHES   NEW CALEDONIA

Legand, Michel

Première liste de poissons collectés en
Nouvelle-Calédonie.

(Extrait, Bull. Soc. Zool. de France, 75(5/6)
pp. 206-207, 1950)

QL
1
Bu 93

FISHES   NEW GUINEA

Beaufort, L. F.

On a new species of Chilonycterus from New
Guinea.

(Treubia, Vol. 17, 1939, pp. 33-34)

AS
36
A 65-no

FISHES   NEW GUINEA

Nichols, John T.

A new melanotaeniid fish from New Guinea.

(American Museum Novitates, No. 1802, 1956)

AS
36
A 65-no   Nichols, John T.

FISHES   NEW GUINEA

     Two new fresh-water fishes from New Guinea.
Results of the Archbold Expeditions. No. 71

     (American Museum Novitates, No. 1735, 1955)

AS
719
A   Whitley, Gilbert P.

FISHES   NEW GUINEA

     Descriptions of some New Guinea fishes.

     (Records of the Australian Museum, Vol. 20,
pp. 223-233, 1938)

AS
720.N
L   Ramsay, Edward Pierson

FISH   NEW HEBRIDES

     Description of a new Coris from the New
Hebrides. By Edward Pierson Ramsay and J. Douglas Ogilby.

     (Proc. Linn. Soc. New South Wales, 1, 1887,
pp. 131-132; and 2, 1888, p. 1024)

AS
36
A 65   Nichols, J. T.

FISHES   NEW GUINEA

     Two new fresh-water fishes (Percesoces)
from New Guinea, by J. T. Nichols and H. C. Raven

     (American Museum Novitates, No. 755, Nov. 17,
1934. 4 pp)

AS
719
A 92   Whitley, G.P.

FISHES — NEW GUINEA

     Fishes from inland New Guinea.

     (Records of the Australian Museum, Vol.XXIV,
No. 3:23-30, 1956)

QL
1
A 93   McCulloch, Allan R.

FISHES   NEW SOUTH WALES

     Check-list of the fish and fish-like animals
of New South Wales.

     (The Australian Zoologist, Vol. 1:217-227,
1919; 2:24-68, 1921; 3:86-130, 1922)

AS
720.N
L   Ramsay, Edward Pierson

FISHES   NEW GUINEA

     A contribution to the knowledge of the fish-
fauna of New Guinea. By E. P. Ramsay and J. Douglas Ogilby.

     (Proc. Linn. Soc. of New South Wales, Vol.
1, 1887, pp. 8-20)

AS
719
A-m   Whitley, G. P.

FISHES   NEW GUINEA

     Fishes of New Guinea.

     (Australian Museum Magazine, Vol. 8, 1943
pp. 141-144)

QL
636.
N 56   Ogilby, J. Douglas

FISHES   NEW SOUTH WALES

     Catalogue of the fishes of New South Wales,
with their principal synonyms.

     (Report, New South Wales, Fisheries, for
1886, Appendix A, 1887)

AS
720.N
L   Ramsay, Edward Pierson

FISHES   NEW GUINEA

     On an undescribed Dules from New Guinea.
By Edward P. Ramsay and J. Douglas Ogilby.

     (Proc. Linn. Soc. New South Wales, Vol. 2,
1888, pp. 4-5)

AS
719
A 93   Whitley, Gilbert P.

FISHES   NEW GUINEA

     New Guinea's fishes.

     (Australian Mus. Mag., 12:398-401, 1958)

QL
1
A 93   Whitley, Gilbert P.

FISHES   NEW SOUTH WALES

     Additions to the check-list of the fishes
of New South Wales, No. 2.

     (The Australian Zoologist, 5:353-357, 1929)

Q
115
G 76   Regan, C. Tate

FISHES   NEW GUINEA

     Report on the freshwater fishes collected
by the British Ornithologists' Union Expedition
and the Wollaston Expedition in Dutch New Guinea.
Grant, William R. Ogilvie
Reports on the collections made by the
British Ornithologists Union Expedition...Vol. 1,
No. V, pp. 275-286, from the Trans. Zool. Soc.
London, Vol. 20, 1914.

AS
36
A 4   Chapman, Wilbert M.

FISHES   NEW HEBRIDES

     Review of the fishes of the Blennioid genus
Escenius, with descriptions of five new species.
By Wilbert M. Chapman and Leonard P. Schultz.

     (Proc. U. S. Nat. Mus., Vol. 102:507-528,
1952)

QL
Fish
Pam
#75
G.b.   *Stead, David G.*

FISHES--NEW SOUTH WALES

     *New Fishes from New South
Wales No. 1. Sept. 1908.
N. S. W. 1908 pp. ...*

AS
36
S 4   Schultz, Leonard P.

FISHES   NEW GUINEA

     A new genus and two new species of Percoid
fishes from New Guinea, family Centropomidae.

     (Proc. U.S. National Museum, Vol. 96:115-
121, 1945)

QL
Fishes
Pam.
440   Fowler, Henry W.

FISHES   NEW HEBRIDES

     Fishes obtained in the New Hebrides by Dr.
Edward L. Jackson.

     (Proc. Acad. Nat. Sci., Phil., Vol. 96,
1944, pp. 155-199)

QL
636.5 N
O 34   Ogilby, J. Douglas

FISHES   NEW SOUTH WALES

     Edible Fishes and Crustaceans of New South
Wales. Sydney. Charles Potter. 1893. 8vo.
212 pp. 51 plates.

QL
Fish
Pam
#114   *Weber, Max*

FISHES--NEW GUINEA

     *Neue Fische aus Niederländisch
Süd-West Guinea.*

     Notes from Leyden Mus. XXVIII & Vol. XXVIII

     n.p. n.d. 8vo   pp. 225-240 plate 3

DU
1
M 6   Herre, Albert W.

FISHES   NEW HEBRIDES

     A Check List of the Fishes Recorded from the
New Hebrides.

     (Journal of the Pan-Pacific Research Institu-
tion, Vol. VI, No. 4, pp. 11-14. IN Mid-Pacific
Magazine, Vol. 42, No. 4, 1931)

QL
636.5N
S 79   Stead, David G.

FISHES   NEW SOUTH WALES

     The Edible Fishes of New South Wales: Their
Present Importance and Their Potentialities.
With 81 plates and 1 map. Department of Fish-
eries, New South Wales. 1908. sm8vo. 119 pp.

Fishes—New South Wales

QL
635.N
B9
T 29

Tenison-Woods, Julian Edmund.

Fish and fisheries of New South Wales. By the Rev. J. E. Tenison-Woods ... Sydney, T. Richards, 1882.

1 p. l., xi, 213 p. front., plates. 25½ᶜᵐ.

"Fishery laws and regulations": p. 160-181.
"Index of local names": p. 182-193.
"Works relating to fish and fisheries": p. 194-203.

1. Fisheries—New South Wales. 2. Fishes—New South Wales.

F 17-231

Library, U. S. Bur. of   Fisheries

AS
750
N

FISHES NEW ZEALAND

Graham, David H.

Fishes of Otago Harbour and adjacent seas with additions to previous records.

(Transactions and Proceedings of the Royal Society of New Zealand, Vol. 68, 1938, pp. 399-419)

QL
636.5 N
H 98

FISHES NEW ZEALAND

Hutton, Frederick Wollaston

Fishes of New Zealand. Catalogue with Diagnoses of the Species.
Notes on the Edible Fishes, by James Hector. With twelve plates. Wellington. James Hughes. 1872. 8vo.

QL
628.N
B3

FISHES - NEW YORK

Bean, Tarleton H.

Catalogue of the fishes of New York. New York State Mus. Bull. No. 60, 1903. 784 pp.

QL
636.5N
G 73

FISHES NEW ZEALAND

Graham, David H.

A treasury of New Zealand fishes. Wellington A. H. and A. W. Reed. R8vo. 404 pp. (1953)

AS
750
D 67 r

FISHES NEW ZEALAND

McCann, Charles

Ichthyological notes, with special reference to sexual dimorphism in some New Zealand fishes.

(Records of the Dominion Museum, Vol. 2(1): 1-17, 1953)

AS
36
S1

FISHES - NEWYORK

Gill, Theodore Nicholas, 1837–1914.

On the fishes of New York. By Theodore Gill, esq.

(*In* Smithsonian institution. Annual report. 1856. Washington, 1857. 23½ᶜᵐ. p. 253-269)

1. Fishes—New York.

S 15-41

Library of Congress   Q11.S66 1856
Library, Smithsonian   Institution

AS
36
A 4

FISHES NEW ZEALAND

Gregory, William K.

Body-forms of the black marlin (Makaira nigricans marlina) and striped marlin (Makaira mitsukurii) of New Zealand and Australia. By William K. Gregory and G. Miles Conrad.

(Bull. Am. Mus. Nat Hist., Vol. 76, 1939, pp. 443-456)

QL
628.C
S 78

FISHES NEW ZEALAND

Myers, George S.

Fresh-water fishes and East Indian zoogeography.

(Stanford Ichthyological Bull., 4(1):11-21, 1951)

QL
Fish
Pam
#1

FISHES—NEW YORK

Nichols, John Treadwell, 1883-

Fishes of the vicinity of New York city, by John Treadwell Nichols, with an introduction by William K. Gregory. New York, Printed at the Museum, 1918.

118, [4] p. col. front., illus., pl. 23ᶜᵐ. (The American museum of natural history. Handbook series, no. 7)

1. Fishes—New York.

19-2681

Library of Congress   QL628.N7N6
[4]

QL
Fish
Pam.
166

FISHES -- NEW ZEALAND

Griffin, L. T.

Descriptions of New Zealand fishes. From Trans. New Zealand Inst. Vol. 56, pp 538 - 546, 1926.

QL
Fish
Pam
248

FISHES - NEW ZEALAND

Phillips, W. J.

A check list of the fishes of New Zealand. Pan-Pac. Research Inst. Journ. v.2, no.1, 1927.

AP
2
N 55

FISHES NEW ZEALAND

Allen, K. Radway

The geography of New Zealand's freshwater fish. Presidential address delivered to the Wellington Branch of the Royal Society of New Zealand, 27th July, 1955.

(New Zealand Science Review, Vol. 14(3):3-9, March, 1956)

AS
750
N

Fishes, New Zealand.

Hamilton, A

List of papers on New Zealand fishes and fishing. In T & P. New Zealand Inst. XXXIV. 1901 pp 539-548.

QL
636.5 N
P 55

FISHES NEW ZEALAND

Phillipps, W. J.

The fishes of New Zealand. Vol. 1-1940   Thomas Avery and Sons Limited. New Plymouth. 8vo.

Storage
Case
5

Ms N 3

FISHES NEW ZEALAND

Buck, Peter Henry

Notes on New Zealand fish, and fishing (anthropological).

QL
636.5 N
H 98

FISHES- NEW ZEALAND

Hector, James
Notes on the Edible Fishes.
Hutton, Frederick Wollaston
Fishes of New Zealand. Catalogue with Diagnoses of the Species. Notes on the Edible Fishes by James Hector...

AS
750
N

FISHES NEW ZEALAND

Phillipps, W. J.

New or rare fishes of New Zealand.

(Trans. and Proc. of the Royal Soc. of New Zealand, Vol. 71, 1941, pp. 241-246)

QL
750
N

FISHES NEW ZEALAND

Graham, David H.

Breeding habits of the fishes of Otago Harbour and adjacent seas.

(Trans. and Proc. R. Soc. New Zealand, Vol. 69, 1939, pp. 361-372)

QL
693
H 98

FISHES NEW ZEALAND

Hutton, Frederick Wollaston

Fishes of New Zealand...

IN:

Hutton, Frederick Wollaston
Catalogue of the Birds of New Zealand...

AS
244
D

FISHES NEW ZEALAND

Rendahl, Hialmar

Fishes from New Zealand and the Auckland Campbell Islands.

(Vid. Med. Dansk Nat. For. Kobenhavn, Bd. 81 1926.- Papers from Dr. Th. Mortensen's Pacific Expedition, 1914-16, No. 30)

Row 1, Card 1

QH
197.N
T48

FISHES - NEW ZEALAND.

Thomson, George M

The naturalisation of animals &
plants in New Zealand.

Cambridge, Univ.press, 1922.   607p.

Row 1, Card 2

AS
750
N 56

FISHES NORFOLK ISLAND

Fowler, Henry W.

On a collection of fishes made by Dr. Marshall Laird at Norfolk Island.

also
QL
Fishes
Pam.
531

(Transactions of the Royal Society of New
Zealand, Vol. 81(2):257-367, 1953)

Row 1, Card 3

AS
36
S

FISHES - NORTH AMERICA
Girard, Charles Frédéric, 1822-1895.

... Contributions to the natural history of the fresh
water fishes of North America. By Charles Girard. I. A
monograph of the cottoids ... [Washington, Smithsonian institution, 1851]

80 p. III pl. 32cm. (Smithsonian contributions to knowledge. vol. III,
art. 3)

Publication 30.
Bibliography: p. 72-74.

1. Cottidæ. 2. Fishes—North America.

F 11-103 Revised

Library, U. S. Bur. of   Fisheries Q11.S68

Row 2, Card 1

AS
750
C 22-m

FISHES NEW ZEALAND

Waite, Edgar R.
Scientific results of N. Z.
trawling expedition in 1907. Pisces
in Rec. Canterbury Mus. I.
pp. 131-25? pls XIII - XXVII .

Row 2, Card 2

QL
627
U-a

FISHES NORTH AMERICA

Jordan, David Starr

A Check-List of the Fishes and Fish-Like
Vertebrates of North and Middle America. By
David Starr Jordan and Barton Warren Evermann.

(Report Commissioner of Fisheries, 1895.
App. 5, pp. 207-584)

Row 2, Card 3

AS
36
S5

FISHES - NORTH AMERICA - BIBL.
Goode, George Brown, 1851-1896.

... The published writings of Dr. Charles Girard. By
George Brown Goode. Washington, Govt. print. off.,
1891.

vi, 141 p. front. (port.) 24cm. (Bibliographies of American naturalists. v)

Added t.-p.: Smithsonian institution. United States National museum.
Bulletin, no. 41.

1. Girard, Charles Frederic, 1822-1895-Bibl. 2. Zoology-Bibl.
3. Fishes-North America-Bibl. 4. Reptiles-North America-Bibl.

1-818

Library of Congress   Q11.U6 no. 41
———— Copy 2.   Z8344.G64

Row 3, Card 1

AS
750
N

FISHES NEW ZEALAND

Whitley, Gilbert P.

Descriptive notes on some New Zealand fishes.

(Trans. and Proc. R. Soc. New Zealand,
Vol. 69, 1939, pp. 228-236)

Row 3, Card 2

AS
36
S5

FISHES-NORTH AMERICA
Jordan, David Starr, 1851-

Contributions to North American ichthyology. Based
primarily on the collections of the United States National
museum ... Washington, Govt. print. off., 1877-78.

3 v. plates. 24cm. (Added t.-p.: U. S. National museum. Bulletin.
Washington, 1877-78. no. 9, 10, 12)
Smithsonian Inst. misc. coll. v. 13, no. 305-306; v. 23, no. 308.
Bibliography: I. p. 105-119; III, p. 221-230.
CONTENTS.—I. Review of Rafinesque's memoirs of North American
fishes.—II. A. Notes on Cottidæ, Etheostomatidæ, Percidæ, Centrarchidæ,
Aphododeridæ, Dorysomatidæ, and Cyprinidæ. B. Synopsis of the Siluridæ
of the fresh waters of North America.—III. A. On the distribution of the
fishes of the Alleghany region of South Carolina, Georgia, and Tennessee
... by D. S. Jordan and A. W. Brayton. B. A synopsis of the family Cato-
stomidæ. By D. S. Jordan.
1. Fishes—North Amer-   ica. I. Brayton, Alembert Win-
throp, joint author.
Library of Congress   Q11.U6   6-19479
Copy 2.   QL625.J81
(320g2)

Row 3, Card 3

QL
625

FISHES-NORTH AMERICA
Jordan, David Starr, 1851-

... The fishes of North and Middle America: a descriptive catalogue of the species of fish-like vertebrates found
in the waters of North America, north of the Isthmus of
Panama. By David Starr Jordan ... and Barton Warren
Evermann ... Washington, Govt. print. off., 1896-1900.

4 v. cccxcii pl. 24cm. (Added t.-p.: ... Bulletin of the United States
National museum no. 47)

At head of title: Smithsonian institution. United States National museum.

1. Fishes—North America. I. Evermann, Barton Warren, 1853-
joint author.

1-1361

Library of Congress   Q11.U6

Row 4, Card 1

QL
623
W 61

FISHES NEW ZEALAND

Whitley, Gilbert Percy

The fishes of Australia, Part I: The sharks,
rays, devil-fish, and other primitive fishes of
Australia and New Zealand.

Sydney. Published by the Royal Zool. Soc. of New
South Wales. Australian Zoological Handbook.
1940.

Row 4, Card 2

QL
Fish
Pam
#93

FISHES -- NORTH AMERICA
Jordan, David S.

Contributions to North American
Ichthyology, no. 1, ex U. S. Nat. Mus.
Bull. no. 9, 1877.

See also main entry

Row 4, Card 3

QL
625
201

Fishes-North America
Jordan, David Starr, 1851-

Synopsis of the fishes of North America. By David S.
Jordan and Charles H. Gilbert. Washington, Govt. print.
off., 1882.

lvi, 1018 p. 24cm. (Added t.-p.: ... Bulletin of the United States National museum. no. 16)

Issued also as vol. xxiv of the Smithsonian miscellaneous collections.
Smithsonian institution publication 492.

1. Fishes—North America. I. Gilbert, Charles Henry, 1859- joint
author.

S 13-125

Library, Smithsonian   Institution Q11.U6

Row 5, Card 1

AS
750
N

FISHES NEW ZEALAND BIBLIOGRAPHY

Hamilton, A.

List of papers on New Zealand fishes and
fishing.

(Trans. and Proc. New Zealand Institute,
Vol. 34, 1901, pp. 539-548)

Row 5, Card 2

AS
36
S5

FISHES - NORTH AMERICA
Jordan, David Starr, 1851-

... The fishes of North and Middle America: a descriptive catalogue of the species of fish-like vertebrates found
in the waters of North America, north of the Isthmus of
Panama. By David Starr Jordan ... and Barton Warren
Evermann ... Washington, Govt. print. off., 1896-1900.

4 v. cccxcii pl. 24cm. (Added t.-p.: ... Bulletin of the United States
National museum no. 47)

At head of title: Smithsonian institution. United States National museum.

1. Fishes—North America. I. Evermann, Barton Warren, 1853-
joint author.

1-1361

Library of Congress   Q11.U6

Row 6, Card 1

QL
1
F

FISHES - NICARAGUA.
Meek, Seth Eugene, 1859-1914.

... Synopsis of the fishes of the great lakes of Nicaragua, by Seth Eugene Meek ... Chicago, 1907.

1 p. l., 97-132 p. illus. 25cm. (Field Columbian museum. Publication
121. Zoological series. vol. VII, no. 4)

1. Fishes—Nicaragua.

7-28979

Library of Congress   QL1.F4 vol. 7

Row 6, Card 2

AS
36
S2

FISHES--NORTH AMERICA.
Jordan, David Starr, 1851-

Synopsis of the fishes of North America. By David S.
Jordan and Charles H. Gilbert. Washington, Govt. print.
off., 1882.

QL
625
J82

lvi, 1018 p. 24cm. (Added t.-p.: ... Bulletin of the United States National museum. no. 16)

AS
36
S5

Issued also as vol. xxiv of the Smithsonian miscellaneous collections.
Smithsonian institution publication 492.

1. Fishes—North America. I. Gilbert, Charles Henry, 1859- joint
author.

S 13-125

Library, Smithsonian   Institution Q11.U6

Row 6, Card 3

AS
36
A25-M

FISHES - NORTH AMERICA
Storer, David Humphreys.

A synopsis of the fishes of North America. By David
Humphreys Storer ... Cambridge, Metcalf and co., 1846.

1 p. l., 293 p. front. (port.) 29½cm. (Memoirs of the American academy. VIII)

1. Fishes—North America.

F 12-350

Library, U. S. Bur. of   Fisheries

Row 7, Card 1

AS
36
S 4

FISHES NIUAFOOU

Fowler, Henry W.

The Fishes Obtained by Lieut. H.C.Kellers
of the United States Naval Eclipse Expedition of
1930, at Niuafoou Island, Tonga Group, in
Oceania.

(Proceedings U. S. National Museum, Vol. 81,
Art. 8, 1932)

Row 7, Card 2

AS
36
C3

FISHES - NORTH AMERICA

Jordan, David Starr and Evermann, B. W.

New genera and species of North
American fishes. Proc. Calif. Acad. Sci.
4th ser. v. 16, n.15, 1927.

Row 7, Card 3

AS
36
A4

FISHES - NORTH CAROLINA
Nichols, John Treadwell

On a new race of minnow from the Rocky Mountains
park. A new *Gymnachirus* from North Carolina. By
John Treadwell Nichols ... New York, 1916.

cover-title, p. 69-72. illus. 24cm. (Bulletin of the American museum
of natural history. vol. xxxv, arts. VIII and IX)

1. Fishes—Alberta. 2. Fishes—North Carolina. 3. [Cyprinidæ]
4. [Soleidæ]

F 16-97

Library, U. S. Bur. of   Fisheries

Row 5, Card 3

QL
627
N 61

FISHES-NORTH AMERICA
Nichols, John Treadwell

Representative North American fresh-water
fishes. Illustrated by Andrew R. Janson.
New York. The Macmillan Company. 1942. 12ob.
128 pp.

QL
628.N
S64

FISHES - NORTH CAROLINA

Smith, Hugh M

The fishes of North Carolina; North Carolina Geological and Economic Survey, v.2, Raleigh, 1907.

QL
638.835
I 61-b

FISHES - PACIFIC

Alverson, F.G.

A study of the eastern Pacific fishery for Tuna baitfishes, with particular reference to the Anchoveta (Centengraulis mysticetus). By Franklin G.Alverson and Bell M.Shimada.

(Inter-American Tropical Tuna Commission, Bulletin, Vol II, No,2, 1957)

QL
628.C
S 78

FISHES PACIFIC

Bolin, Rolf L.

A review of the myctophid fishes of the Pacific coast of the United States and of lower California.

(Stanford Ichthyological Bulletin, Vol.1, 1939, pp. 89-156)

DU
1
M 62

FISHES OKHOTSK SEA

Schmidt, Peter

Strange life in the Okhotsk Sea.

(Journal of the Pan-Pacific Research Inst., Vol. 10 (2), pp. 161-176, 1935)

QL
1
N 6-z

FISHES-PACIFIC

Beebe, William

Atlantic and Pacific fishes of the genus Dixonia. Eastern Pacific Expeditions of the New York Zoological Society, XXX.

(Zoologica, Vol. 27, 1942, pp. 43-48)

AS
36
S 4

FISHES - PACIFIC

Bolin, Rolf L.

Two new Cottid fishes from the western Pacific, with a revision of the genus Stlengis Jordan and Starks

(Proceedings of the United States National Museum, vol.83, pp.325-334)

QL
1
F

FISHES - ONTARIO

Meek, Seth Eugene, 1859-

... Notes on a collection of fishes and amphibians from Muskoka and Gull lakes. By S. E. Meek ... Chicago, 1899.

1 p. l., p. 307-311. 24½ᶜᵐ. (Field Columbian museum. Publication 41. Zoological series. vol. I, no. 17)

1. Fishes—Ontario. 2. Reptiles—Ontario.

Library of Congress   QL1.F4   4-10570
———— Copy 2.   QL219.M47

QL
1
N 6-z

FISHES PACIFIC

Beebe, William

Fishes from the tropical eastern Pacific. (From Cedros Island, Lower California, south to the Galapagos Islands, and northern Peru) I-II. By William Beebe and John Tee Van.

(Zoologica, Vol. 26, 1941, 89-122

to be cont.

QL
618
V 22

FISHES PACIFIC

Borodin, N. A.

Scientific Results of the Yacht "Alva" World Cruise, July, 1931 to March, 1932, in Command of William K. Vanderbilt.
Fishes, by N. A. Borodin

(Bulletin of the Vanderbilt Marine Museum, Vol. 1, Art. 2, 1932, pp. 65-101, 2 plates)

QL
1
P 15

FISHES PACIFIC

Abe, Tokiharu

A list of the fishes of the Palao Islands.

(Palao Tropical Biological Station Studies, 4, 1939, pp. 523-583)

QL
1
N 6-z

FISHES PACIFIC

Beebe, William

Pacific Myctophidae (Fishes), by William Beebe and Mary Vader Pyl. Eastern Pacific Expeditions of the New York Zoological Society, XXXIII.

(Zoologica, Vol. 29, 59-95, 1944)

DU
12
B 83
locked case

FISHES PACIFIC

Brenchley, J. L.

Jottings during the cruise of H. M. S. Curaçoa among the South Sea Islands in 1865... pp. 409-430: Fishes, by Albert Günther. London. 1873. R8vo.

QL
627
U-b

FISHES PACIFIC

Ahlstrom, Elbert H.

Development and distribution of Vinciguerria lucetia and related species in the eastern Pacific. By Elbert H. Ahlstrom and Robert C. Counts.

(U. S. Fish and Wildlife Service, Fishery Bull. 139, 1959)

QL
1
N 6-z

FISHES PACIFIC

Beebe, William

Seven new marine fishes from Lower California. By William Beebe and John Tee Van. Eastern Pacific Expeditions of the New York Zoological Society, XV.

(Zoologica, 23, 1938, pp. 299-312).

QL
628.C
S 78

FISHES PACIFIC

Brock, Vernon E.

Contribution to the biology of the albacore (Germo alalunga) of the Oregon coast and other parts of the North Pacific.

(Stanford Ichthyological Bulletin, 2, No. 6, Dec. 1943)

QL
627
U-b

FISHES PACIFIC

Ahlstrom, Elbert H.

Eggs and larvae of the Pacific hake, Merluccius productus. By Elbert H. Ahlstrom and Robert C. Counts.

(U.S. Dept. of Interior, Fish and Wildlife Ser., Fishery Bulletin 99, 1955)

DU
12
B 47
locked case

FISHES PACIFIC

Bennett, F. D.

Narrative of a whaling voyage round the globe, from...1833 to 1836...with an account of ...the natural history of the climates visited. 2 vols. London. 1840. 8vo.
Vol. II, pp. 255-289

Q
115
C 28

FISHES PACIFIC

Bruun, Anton Fr.

A study of a collection of the fish Schindleria from south Pacific waters.

Dana Report No. 21, 1940

QL
752
U 58

FISHES PACIFIC

Ahlstrom, Elbert H.

Pacific sardine (pilchard) eggs and larvae and other fish larvae, Pacific coast - 1952.

(U. S. Dept. of the Interior, Fish and Wildlife Service, Special Scientific Rept.-Fisheries No. 123, 1954)

Q
115
C 28

FISHES PACIFIC

Bertin, Léon

Les poissons abyssaux du genre Cyema Günther (anatomie, embryologie, bionomie.)

(Carlsberg Foundation's Oceanographical Expedition round the world, 1928-30...Dana Reports...No. 10. 1937)

AS
36
S 4

FISHES PACIFIC

Chapman, Wilbert McLeod

Eleven new species and three new genera of Oceanic fishes collected by the International Fisheries Commission from the northeastern Pacific.

(Proceedings of the U.S.National Museum, Smithsonian Institution, Vol.86, No.3062, 1939, pp. 501-542)

QL
628
Ca-b

FISHES PACIFIC

Clark, Frances N.

     Measures of abundance of the sardine, Sardinops caerulea, in California waters.

     (California, State Bureau of Marine Fisheries, Fish Bulletin No. 53, 1939, pp. 1-37 + appendix, 6 charts)

AS
36
C 3

FISHES PACIFIC

Follett, W. I.

     Annotated list of fishes obtained by the California Academy of Sciences during six cruises of the U. S. S. Mulberry conducted by the United States Navy off central California in 1949 and 1950.

     (Proc. Calif. Acad. Sci. s4, Vol. 27(16): 399-432, 1952)

AS
763
B-m

QL
623
F 78

Reading
Room

FISHES PACIFIC

Fowler, Henry W.

     Fishes of Oceania. Honolulu. 1928. 4to. 540 pp. Supplements 1-2,3 1931-34, 1949

     (Bernice P. Bishop Museum, Memoirs, Vol. X. Plates I-XLIX; Vol. XI, Nos. 5-6); XII, 2, 1949

QL
628
C 15

FISHES PACIFIC

Clemens, Harold B.

     Fishes collected in the tropical Eastern Pacific, 1952-53.

     (California Fish and Game, vol. 41(2):161-166, 1955)

QL
Fish
Pam
149
and
AS
763
B-b
and
Reading
Room

FISHES -- PACIFIC

Fowler, Henry W.

     Fishes of Guam, Hawaii, Samoa, and Tahiti. B. P. Bishop Mus. Bull. 22, 1925, 38 pp.

AS
36
A 16

FISHES PACIFIC

Fowler, Henry W.

     The fishes of the George Vanderbilt South Pacific Expedition, 1937.

     (Acad. of Nat. Sci., Philadelphia, Monograph No. 2, 1938)

DU
1
S 72t

FISHES PACIFIC

Conférence des pêches, Noumea, 14-22, Mai, 1952; Rapport.

     (Commission du Pacifique Sud, Document Technique, No. 25, 1952)

QL
Fish
Pam
No.145
and
No.146

FISHES - PACIFIC

Fowler, Henry W. and Ball, Stanley C.

     Description of new fishes obtained by the Tanager Expedition of 1923 in the Pacific islands west of Hawaii. Acad. Nat Sc. Philadelphia, Proc. Vol 76, 1924, pp 269-274.

AS
763
B-b

QL
636.5
F78

Reading
Room

FISHES - PACIFIC

Fowler, Henry W.

     Fishes of the tropical central Pacific. Bernice P. Bishop Mus. Bull. n.38, 1927.

Q
115
D 89

locked
case

FISHES PACIFIC

Dumont d'Urville, Jules Sebastian César

     Voyage de la corvette l'Astrolabe, exécuté par ordre du Roi, pendant les années 1826-1829... Zoologie, Tome 3, pp. 647-720. plates. 1834. Paris. J. Tastu. 8vo and folio. (Plates are in atlas to Zoologie)

AS
36
A 16

FISHES PACIFIC (eastern)

Fowler, Henry W.

     The fishes. (eastern Pacific:Tres Marias Is. Galapagos, coast of Mexico, etc.)
IN
Results of the Fifth George Vanderbilt Expedition (1941)...
(Acad. Nat. Sci. Philadelphia, Monograph 6, 1944, pp. 57-529)

QL
Fish Pam
385

FISHES PACIFIC

Fowler, Henry W.

     Zoological results of the Denison-Crockett South Pacific Expedition of the Academy of Natural Sciences of Philadelphia, 1937-1938. Part III.- Fishes.

     (Proc. of the Acad. of Nat. Sci., Philadelphia, Vol. 91, 1939, pp. 77-96)

QL
1
Ham

FISHES PACIFIC

Duncker, Georg

     Die Fische der Südsee-Expedition der Hamburgischen Wissenschaftlichen Stiftung, 1908-1909, von Georg Duncker und Erna Mohr. Teil 1-3

     (In Mitt. Zool. Staatsinst. und Zool. Mus. Hamburg, Bd. 41:93-112, 1925; Bd. 42:126-136, 1926; Bd. 44:57-84, 1931 - ?)

AS
36
A-16n

FISHES PACIFIC

Fowler, Henry W.

     Fishes from the Pacific slope of Colombia, Ecuador and Peru.

     (Notulae Naturae, Acad. Nat. Sci., Philadelphia, No. 33, 1939)

AS
182
H

Fishes - Pacific

Garrett, Andrew

     in his Fische der Südsee beschrieben und redigirt von Albert C.L.G. Gunther. Journal des Mus. Godeffroy.Band II, IV and VI. Hamburg, 1873 - 1910.

QL
623
F 53

FISHES PACIFIC

Fish, Marie Poland

     (Woods Hole Oceanographic Institution, Technical Report, No. 2, 1948) Office of Naval Research...

AS
36
S 4

FISHES PACIFIC

Fowler, Henry W.

     The Fishes Obtained by the Pinchot South Seas Expedition of 1929, with Description of One New Genus and Three New Species.

     (Proceedings of the United States National Museum, Vol. 80, Art. 6, pp. 1-16, 1932)
(Society Is., Marquesas, Tuamotus, Galapagos Cocos Is.)

QL
Fishes
Pam.
606

FISHES PACIFIC

Gibbs, Robert H., Jr.

     Astronesthes nigroides, a new species of Stomiatoid fish from the eastern Pacific Ocean. By Robert H. Gibbs, Jr. and William Aron.

     (Copeia, 1960(2):134-316)

QL
628
C 15

FISHES PACIFIC

Fitch, John E.

     Notes on some Pacific fishes.

     (California Fish and Game, Vol. 36(2):65-73, 1948)

AS
36
A 9

FISHES PACIFIC

Fowler, Henry W.

     The fishes obtained by the Wilkes Expedition 1838-1842.

     (Proc. Am. Philosophical Society, Vol. 82: 733-800, 1940)

AS
145
B

FISHES PACIFIC

Giltay, Louis

     Poissons. Résultats scientifiques des croisières du navire-école Belge "Mercator", Vol. II. 9th croisière, 1935-36.

     (Mem. Musée R. d'Hist. Nat. Belgique, Ser. 2, Fasc. 15, pp. 39-45, 1939)

     [fishes from Tuamotus, Marquesas, Easter Island, Tahiti]

AS 36 S 2 — FISHES PACIFIC Ginsburg, Isaac Two new gobioid fishes collected on the Presidential cruise of 1938. (Smithsonian Miscellaneous Collections, Vol. 98, No.14, 1939, pp. 1-5, 2 figures)	QL 636.5 G 97 locked case — FISHES PACIFIC Günther, Albert C. L. G. Andrew Garrett's Fische der Südsee. Band 1-3. Hamburg. L. Friederichsen and Co. 1873-1881. 4to. (Journal des Museum Godeffroy, Heft 3,5,7,9,11,13,15)	QL 1 E — FISHES PACIFIC Herre, Albert W. Fishes of the Crane Pacific Expedition. (Field Museum of Natural History, Zool. Ser. Vol. 21, 1936)
AS 36 A 4 — FISHES PACIFIC Gregory, William K. Body-forms of the black marlin (Makaira nigricans marlina) and striped marlin (Makaira mitsukurii) of New Zealand and Australia. By William K. Gregory and G. Miles Conrad. (Bull. Am. Mus. Nat Hist., Vol. 76, 1939, pp. 443-456)	AS 182 H — FISHES PACIFIC Günther, Albert C. G. L. Erster ichthyologischer Beitrag nach Exemplaren aus dem Museum Godeffroy. (Jour. Mus. Godeffroy, Heft II, 1873, pp. 169-175)	QL 1 F — FISHES PACIFIC Herre, Albert W. New fishes obtained by the Crane Pacific Expedition. (Field Museum, Pull. 335, Zool. Ser., Vol. XVIII, No. 12, 1935, pp. 383-438)
QL 1 F 45 — FISHES PACIFIC Grey, Marion Catalogue of type specimens of fishes in Chicago Natural History Museum. (Fieldiana: Zoology, Vol. 32 (3):109-205, 1947)	Q 115 C 43 — FISHES PACIFIC Guenther, Albert C. L. G. Report on the shore fishes, deep-sea fishes and pelagic fishes collected by H. M. S. Challenger. IN Report on the scientific results of the voyage of H. M. S. Challenger...1873-76... Zoology, Vol. 1(part 6), 1881; Vol. 22, 1887; Vol. 31(part 78), 1889.	QL 5 H 66 locked case — FISHES PACIFIC Hinds, Richard Brinsley editor The Zoology of the Voyage of H.M.S. Sulphur under the command of Captain Sir Edward Belcher, during the years 1836-1842. London. 4to. Ichthyology, by John Richardson. Parts 1-3, 1844-1845. pp. 53-150, plates 35-64.
QL 1 C 78 — FISHES PACIFIC Grey, Marion First record of the deep-sea fish Dolichopteryx longipes from the Pacific, with notes on Ophthalmopelton macropus. (Copeia, 1952(2):87-90, 1952)	AS 182 H — FISHES PACIFIC Günther, Albert C. G. L. Zweiter ichthyologischer Beitrag nach Exemplaren aus dem Museum Godeffroy; weitere Mitteilungen uber junge Schwertfische. (Mus. Godeffroy, Jour., Heft IV, 1873, pp. 267-270)	AS 36 C 3 — FISHES PACIFIC Horsburgh, D. B. Templeton Crocker Expedition of the California Academy of Sciences, 1932, No. 19: A revision of two species of Vinciguerria, a genus of deep sea fishes. (Proc. Calif. Acad. of Sciences, 4th ser., Vol. XXI, No. 19, pp. 225-232, Feb. 6, 1935)
Q 101 P 18 — FISHES PACIFIC Guberlet, J. E. Recent advances in our knowledge of the parasites of the marine fishes of the Pacific. (Proc. of the Fifth Pacific Science Congress, Vol. 5, pp. 4165-4170, 1933)	QL 1 P 15 — FISHES PACIFIC Haneda, Yata On the luminescence of the fishes belonging to the family Leiognathidae of the tropical Pacific. (Palao Tropical Biological Station Studies, Vol. 2, 1940, pp. 29-39)	DU 1 P 11 — FISHES PACIFIC Hubbs, Carl L. Initial discoveries of fish faunas on seamounts and offshore banks in the Eastern Pacific. (Pacific Science, 13(4):311-316, 1959)
QL Fish.Pam. 375 — FISHES PACIFIC Gudger, E. W. The distribution of Ruvettus, the oilfish, throughout the South Seas, as shown by the distribution of the peculiar wooden hook used in its capture. (The American Naturalist, Vol. LXII, 1928, pp. 467-477)	QL 628.C S 78 — FISHES-PACIFIC Herald, Earl Stannard A systematic analysis of variation in the western American pipefish, Syngnathus californiensis. (Stanford Ichthyological Bulletin, Vol. 2, No. 3, 1941. pp. 49-88)	QL 752 U 58 — FISHES PACIFIC Iversen, Edwin S. Size variation of central and western Pacific yellowfin tuna. (U. S. Fish and Wildlife Service, Sp. Sci. Rept. Fisheries, No. 174, 1956) [Neothunnus macropterus]
QL 1 Z — FISHES PACIFIC Gudger, Eugene W. The natural history and geographical distribution of the pointed-tailed ocean sunfish (Masturus lanceolatus), with notes on the shape of the tail. (Proc. of the Zoological Society of London, Ser. A. Vol. 107, 1937, pp. 353-396)	Q 101 P 18 — FISHES PACIFIC Herre, Albert W. C. T. Distribution of the mackerel-like fishes in the western Pacific north of the equator. IN Proc. 6th Pac. Sci. Congress, 1939, (California), Vol. 3, 1940, pp. 211-216.	QL 1 C 78 — FISHES PACIFIC Johnson, Raymond E. Habitat of the Blennioid fish Brotula multibarbata in the southwestern Pacific. (Copeia, 1945, no. 1, pp. 55-56, 1945) [Solomon Islands, Woodlark (Murua) and Milne Bay, New Guinea]

AS 552 T
FISHES PACIFIC
Jordan, David Starr
Description of nine new species of fishes contained in museums of Japan. By David Starr Jordan and John Otterbein Snyder. (Journal of the College of Sci., Imp. Univ. Tokyo, 15, (Pt. 2):300-311, 1901)

QL 636.5 Hz K 68
FISHES - PACIFIC
Kner, R. & Steindachner, Franz
Neue Fische aus dem Museum der Herren Joh. Ces. Godeffroy & Sohn in Hamburg.
~~Vienna 1866-1868~~
For detail see author card.

QL 628.C S 78
FISHES PACIFIC
Myers, George S.
Fresh-water fishes and East Indian zoogeography.
(Stanford Ichthyological Bull., 4(1):11-21, 1951)

AS 36 C 1
FISHES PACIFIC
Jordan, David Starr
A review of the giant mackerel-like fishes, tunnies, spearfishes and swordfishes. By David Starr Jordan and Barton Warren Evermann.
(Occasional Papers of the California Acad. of Sci., XII, 1926)

QL 1 J 35
FISHES-PACIFIC
Kuronuma, Katsuzo
Cleisthenes pinetorum vs. Protopsetta herzensteini.
(Bull. Biogeographical Soc. of Japan, Vol. 9, 1939, pp. 181-192)

QL 627 P 11
FISHES PACIFIC
Nakamura, Hiroshi
Tunas and spearfishes.
(Science of the seas [Kaiyo no Kagaku], Vol. 3, No. 10, 1943)
Translation, Pacific Oceanic Fishery Investigations, No. 47, by W. G. van Campen

QL 1 H 2
FISHES - PACIFIC
Kendall, William Converse, 1861-
... The shore fishes. By William C. Kendall and Edmund L. Goldsborough. With seven plates ... Cambridge, U. S. A., Printed for the Museum, 1911.
1 p. l., (241)-343, (1) p. 7 pl. 28cm. (Memoirs of the Museum of comparative zoölogy at Harvard college. vol. xxvi, no. 7)
"Reports on the scientific results of the expedition to the tropical Pacific ... by the U. S. Fish commission steamer 'Albatross' from August, 1899, to March, 1900 ... XIII."
"Published by permission of George M. Bowers, U. S. commissioner of fish and fisheries."
1. Fishes—Pacific Ocean. 2. Albatross (Steamer) I. Goldsborough, Edmund Lee, joint author. II. Title.
Title from Univ. of Chicago   QL1f.H375 vol. 26
                               Printed by L. C.
A 21-451

DU 1 S 72-q
FISHES PACIFIC
Massal, Emile
Fish: a valuable Pacific island food.
(South Pacific Commission, Quarterly Bull., Vol. 5(3):18-19, July, 1955)

QL 636.5 N 61
FISHES PACIFIC
Nichols, John Treadwell
Fishes and shells of the Pacific world. By John T. Nichols and Paul Bartsch. The Macmillan Company. New York. 1945. 8vo. (iv) + 201 pp.

QL 1 H 2
FISHES - PACIFIC
Kendall, William Converse, 1861-
... The shore fishes. By William C. Kendall and Lewis Radcliffe. With eight plates ... Cambridge, U. S. A., Printed for the Museum, 1912.
1 p. l., (77)-171, (1) p. 8 pl. 30cm. (Memoirs of the Museum of comparative zoölogy at Harvard college. vol. xxxv, no. 3)
"Reports on the scientific results of the expedition to the eastern tropical Pacific ... by the U. S. Fish commission steamer 'Albatross,' from October, 1904, to March, 1905 ... xxv."
"Published by permission of George M. Bowers, U. S. commissioner of fish and fisheries."
1. Fishes—Pacific Ocean. 2. Albatross (Steamer) I. Radcliffe, Lewis, 1880- joint author.
Title from Univ. of Chicago   QL1f.H375 vol. 35
                               Printed by L. C.
A 21-456

QL 1 N6-z
FISHES PACIFIC
Mead, Giles W.
Tarletonbeania taylori, a new lantern fish from the western North Pacific.
(Zoologica, Vol. 39(2), No. 7:105-108, 1953)

AS 36 A 3
FISHES PACIFIC
Nichols, John Treadwell
How many marlins are there? By J. T. Nichols and F. R. LaMonte.
(Natural History, 36:327-330, 1935)

QH 1 P 11
FISHES PACIFIC
King, Joseph E.
Some unusual fishes from the central Pacific. By Joseph E. King and Isaac I. Ikehara.
(Pacific Science, Vol. X(1):17-24, Jan., 1956)

AS 720.Q Q
FISHES PACIFIC
Munro, Captain Ia S. R.
Revision of Australian species of Scomberomorus.
(Memoirs of the Queensland Museum, Vol. 12, 1943, pp. 65-95)

AS 36 A 65
and Fishes Pam. 362
FISHES PACIFIC
Nichols, J. T.
New Pacific flying-fishes collected by Templeton Crocker, by J. T. Nichols and C. M. Breder, Jr.
(American Museum Novitates, no. 821, 1935)

AS 182 S 47
FISHES PACIFIC
Klausewitz, W.
Fische aus dem Atlantik und Pazifik.
(Senckenbergiana, Biologica, Bd. 39:57-84, 1958)

QL 752 U 58
FISHES PACIFIC
Murphy, Garth I.
A summary of sightings of fish schools and bird flocks and of trolling in the central Pacific. By Garth I. Murphy and Isaac I. Ikehara.
(U.S. Dept. of the Interior, Fish and Wildlife Service, Special Scientific Rept.-Fisheries No. 154, 1955)

QL Fish Pam No.152
FISHES -- PACIFIC
Nichols, J. T.
Two new fishes from the Pacific ocean. American Mus.Nov. No. 94, Oct.19 1923, 3 pp.
[From Rapa and Mangareva]

QL 636.5 K 68
FISHES PACIFIC
Kner, Rudolf
Neue Fische aus dem Museum der Joh. Ces. Godeffroy und Sohn in Hamburg, von R. Kner u. Franz Steindachner.
(Sitz. Akad. d. Wissensch. Abth. 1, B. LIV. 1866. Berlin?)
(Bound within are two later papers, by Schmeltz and Kner, 1867, 1868)

Q 101 P 18
FISHES PACIFIC
Myers, George S.
The fish fauna of the Pacific Ocean, with especial reference to zoogeographical regions and distribution as they affect the international aspects of the fisheries.
IN Proc. Sixth Pac. Sci. Congress, 1939, (California), Vol. 3, 1940, pp. 201-210.

QL 617 I 61
FISHES PACIFIC
Nichols, John T.
Yellowfin, Allison's and related tunas. By J. T. Nichols and Francesca R. LaMonte.
(Ichthyological Contributions of the International Game Fish Association, Vol. 1, No. 3, pp. 27-32)

AS 36 A 65 — FISHES PACIFIC

Nichols, J. T.

Variation in Pacific Trachurops Crumenophthalmus.

(Am. Mus. Novitates, No. 815, 1935. 6 pp.)

QL 1 C 78 — FISHES PACIFIC

Rechnitzer, Andreas B.

Ichthyococcus irregularis, a new gonostomatine fish from the eastern Pacific. By Andreas B. Rechnitzer and James Bölke.

(Copeia, 1958(1):10-15, 1958)

["off Baja California"]

QL Fish Pam 326 — FISHES- PACIFIC

Schmidt, P

A revision of the genus Triglops Reinhardt (Pisces, Cottidae). 1929. 6 p.

QL 636 O 34 — FISHES PACIFIC

Ogilby, J. Douglas

Catalogue of the fishes in the collection of the Australian Museum. Part I. Recent Palaeichthyan fishes. Australian Museum (Catalogue No. 14) Sydney. F. W. White. 1888. 8vo. 28 pp

---

QL 1 S 96 — FISHES PACIFIC (North)

Rendahl, Hialmar

Fische aus dem östlichen Sibirischen Eismeer und dem Nordpazifik.

(Arkiv for Zoologi, Bd. 22 A, n:o 10, 1931, pp. 1-81)

AS 36 W 2 — FISHES PACIFIC

Schultz, Leonard P.

Acanthurus triostegus marquesensis, a new subspecies of surgeonfish, family Acanthuridae, with notes on related forms. By Leonard P. Schultz and Loren P. Woods.

(Journal of the Washington Adademy of Sciences, Vol. 38 (7):248-251,1948)

QH 1 P 11 — FISHES PACIFIC

Otsu, Tamio

Albacore migration and growth in the North Pacific Ocean as estimated from tag recoveries.

(Pacific Science, 14:257-266, 1960)

QL 627 U-b — FISHES PACIFIC (central)

Royce, William F.

Observations on the spearfishes of the central Pacific.

(U. S. Fish and Wildlife Service, Fishery Bulletin, (Vol. 57) no. 124, 1957)

QL 1 W 31 — FISHES PACIFIC

Schultz, Leonhard P.

Keys to the fishes of Washington, Oregon, and closely adjoining regions.

(Univ. of Washington, Pub. in Biol. Vol. 2, 1936, pp. 103-228).

QL 1 C 78 — FISHES PACIFIC

Panton, John R.

A new lanternfish (family Myctophidae) of the genus Lampadena from the Eastern Pacific Ocean.

(Copeia, 1963(1):29-33, 1963)

QL Fishes Pam. 468 — FISHES PACIFIC

Schaefer, Milner B.

Additional records confirming the trans-Pacific distribution of the Pacific saury, Cololabis saira (Brevoort). By Milner B. Schaefer and John W. Reintjes.

(Pacific Science, Vol. 4(2):164, 1950)

AS 36 W 2 — FISHES PACIFIC

Schultz, Leonard P.

Notes on the blennioid fish genera Runula (subfamily Petroscirtinae) and Tripterygion and Heloogramma (family Clinidae), of the American tropical Pacific.

(Journal of the Washington Acad. of Sci., Vol. 40:266-268, 1950)

QL 636.5 P62 — FISHES- PACIFIC

Pietschmann, Victor

Remarks on Pacific fishes. B.P. Bishop Museum bulletin no. 73, 1930.

AS 763 B-b

Reading Room

AS 36 S 2 — FISHES PACIFIC

Schmitt, Waldo L.

List of the fishes taken on the Presidential Cruise of 1938. By Waldo L. Schmitt and Leonhard Schultz.

(Smithsonian Misc. Coll., Vol. 98, 1940, pp. 1-10, No. 25)

QL 36 S 4 — FISHES PACIFIC

Schultz, Leonard P.

Redescription of the Capelin Mallotus catervarius (Pennant) of the north Pacific.

(Proc. of the U. S. Nat. Mus., Vol. 85, 1937, pp. 13-20)

QL 1 N 6-z — FISHES PACIFIC

Randall, John E.

A revision of the surgeon fish genus Ctenochaetus, family Acanthuridae, with descriptions of five new species.

(Zoologica, Vol. 40:149-166, 1955)

QL Fish Pam 328 — FISHES- PACIFIC

Schmidt, P

On the Pacific halibut. 1930. 3 p.

AS 36 S 5 — FISHES PACIFIC

Schultz, Leonard P.

Review of the parrotfishes Family Scaridae.

(U. S. National Mus., Bull. 214, 1958)

AS 36 A 4 — FISHES PACIFIC

Raven, Henry C.

On the anatomy and evolution of the locomotor apparatus of the nipple-tailed ocean sunfish (Masturus lanceolatus).

(Am. Mus of Nat. Hist., Bull., Vol. 76, 1939, pp. 143-150)

QL Fish Pam 327 — FISHES- PACIFIC

Schmidt, P

A revision of the genus crossias Jordan et Starks (Pisces , Cottidae). 1929. 2 p.

AS 763 B-o — FISHES - PACIFIC

Seale, Alvin.

... Fishes of the south Pacific. By Alvin Seale. Honolulu, H. I., Bishop museum press, 1906.

89 p. illus., fold. pl. 24½ᵐ (Occasional papers of the Bernice Pauahi Bishop museum of Polynesian ethnology and natural history. vol. IV, no. 1)

1. Fishes—Pacific Ocean.

7-3850

Library of Congress   GN670.B6 vol.4, no. 1

QL
752
U 58

FISHES   PACIFIC

Shomura, Richard S.

     Central North Pacific Albacore surveys, January 1954 - February 1955, By Richard S. Shomura and Tamio Otsu.

     (U. S. Fish and Wildlife Service, Sp. Sci. Rept- Fisheries No. 173, 1956)

     [Germo alalunga]

QL
Fish Pam.
376

FISHES   PACIFIC

Walford, Lionel A.

     Contributions from the Fleischmann expedition along the west coast of Mexico. I. New fishes of the west coast of Mexico; II. The groupers (Mycteroperca) of the Pacific Coast...; III. The Bonitos (Sarda) of the Pacific Ocean.

     (Santa Barbara Museum of Natural History, Occasional Papers, No. 4, December 1, 1936, 10 pp.)

QL
Fishes
Pam.
571

FISHES   PACIFIC   POISONOUS

Halstead, Bruce W.

     Current status of research on Pacific poisonous fishes and ichthyosarcotoxism.

     (IN Venoms, Am. Assn. for the Adv. of Sci., pp. 29-32, n.d.)

QL
627
U-b

FISHES   PACIFIC (CENTRAL)

Strasburg, Donald W.

     Estimates of larval tuna abundance in the central Pacific.

     (Fishery Bull. 167, Fish and Wildlife Service. U. S. D. I., 1960)

QL
523
W 17

FISHES   PACIFIC

Walford, Lionel A.

     Marine game fishes of the Pacific coast from Alaska to the Equator. A contribution from the Santa Barbara Museum of Natural History. Berkeley. University of California Press. 1937. 4to. xxix + 205 pp., 69 pl.

QL
1
C 2 bu

and

QL
626
C 62

FISHES   PACIFIC COAST

Clemens, W. A.

     Fishes of the Pacific coast of Canada, by W. A. Clemens, and G. V. Wilby.

     (Fisheries Research Board of Canada, Bulletin 68, 1946)

AS
244
D

FISHES   PACIFIC

Taning, A. Vedel

     Notes on Scopelids from the Dana Expeditions, I.

     (Videnskabelige Meddelelser, Bind 84, 1932-33, pp. 125-146)

QL
615
W 31-c

FISHES   PACIFIC

Welander, Arthur D.

     New and little known fishes of the eastern Pacific. By Arthur D. Welander and Dayton L. Alverson.

     (Extracted from Fisheries Research papers, Washington Dept. of Fisheries, Vol. 1(2), 1954)

QL
Fish Pam
409

FISHES   PACIFIC COAST

Eigenmann, Carl H.

     A catalogue of the fishes of the Pacific Coast of American north of Cerros Island.

     (New York Academy of Sciences, Annals, Vol. 6, 1892, pp. 349-358)

QL
1
C 78

FISHES   PACIFIC

Townsend, Lawrence D.

     Geographical variation and correlation in Pacific flounders.

     (Copeia, 1937, No. 2, pp. 92-103)

QL
615
W 31

FISHES   PACIFIC

Welander, Arthur D.

     Rare fishes from the eastern north Pacific Ocean.

     (Fishery Research Papers, Washington Dept. of Fisheries, Vol. 2(1), 1957)
     [Univ. of Washington School of Fisheries, Contribution No. 26 - reprint]

QL
1
C

FISHES - PACIFIC COAST

Gilbert, Charles H[enry] 1859-
     Notes on fishes from the Pacific coast of North America. By Charles H. Gilbert. With five plates ... San Francisco, The Academy, 1904.
     1 p. l., 255-271 p. xxv-xxix pl. 25½ᵐ. (Proceedings of the California academy of sciences. Third series. Zoology. vol. III, no. 9)
     "Issued August 20, 1904."

     1. Fishes—Pacific coast.

Library of Congress   Q11.C25   4-30947

Q
115
H 23

FISHES   PACIFIC

Wade, Charles B.

     New fishes in the collections of the Allan Hancock Foundation.

     IN Allan Hancock Pacific Expeditions, Vol. 9 (8):215-237, 1946.

AS
779
A 93-m

FISHES   PACIFIC

Whitley, Gilbert P.

     The story of Galaxias.

     (The Australian Museum Magazine, Vol. XII(1): pp. 30-34, March, 1956)

     [whitebait]

DU
1
P

FISHES   PACIFIC COAST

Hubbs, Carl L.

     A check-list of the marine fishes of Oregon and Washington.

     (Journal of the Pan-Pacific Research Institution, Vol. 3, 1928, No. 3, pp. 9-16)

Q
115
H 23

FISHES   PACIFIC

Wade, Charles B.

     Two new genera and five new species of apodal fishes from the eastern Pacific.

     IN Allan Hancock Pacific Expeditions, Vol. 9, No. 7, pp. 181-213, 1946.

QL
1
C 78

FISHES   PACIFIC

Wisner, Robert L.

     Lampanyctus hubbsi, a new myctophid fish from the East-Central tropical Pacific Ocean, with notes on the related, sympatric Eastern Pacific species, L. omostigma and L. parwicauda.

     (Copeia, 1963(L):16-23, 1963)

QL
617
S 17

FISHES   PACIFIC COAST

International Pacific Salmon Fisheries Commission.

     Annual Report,   1943-

     New Westminster, B. C.   R8vo.   1944-

Q
115
M 46

FISHES   PACIFIC

Waite, Edgar R.
Fishes

Mawson, Sir Douglas
     Australasian Antarctic Expedition, 1911-14. Sci. Reports, Series C, Vol. III, Part 1, 1916.

QL
1
C 78

FISHES   PACIFIC

Wisner, Robert L.

     A new genus and species of myctophid fish from the South-Central Pacific Ocean, with notes on related genera and the designation of a new tribe, Electronini.

     (Copeia, 1963(1):24-28, 1963)

QL
Fish
Pam. 583

FISHES   PACIFIC COAST

Kincaid, Trevor

     An annotated list of Puget Sound fishes. Prepared at the request of ...State Fish Commissioner, State of Washington, Department of Fisheries. August 20, 1919. 8vo. 51 pp.

DU 1 M 6
FISHES   PACIFIC COAST
Schultz, Leonard P.

Fishes of the American northwest: a catalogue of the fishes of Washington and Oregon, with distributional records and a bibliography. By Leonard P. Schultz and Allan C. DeLacy.

(Mid-Pacific Magazine, Vol. 49, 1936, pp. 275-290)

QL 1 P 15
FISHES   PALAO ISLANDS
Abe, Tokiharu

A list of the fishes of the Palao Islands.

(Palao Tropical Biological Station Studies, 4, 1939, pp. 523-583)

QL 636.5 F 78 / AS 763 B-b / Reading Room
FISHES   PALMYRA
Fowler, Henry W.

Fishes of the tropical central Pacific.

(Bernice P. Bishop Museum, Bulletin No. 38, 1927; Whippoorwill Expedition, Publication No. 1)

FISHES   PACIFIC COAST
Schultz, Leonard P.

Treasures of the Pacific: marine fishes and fisheries yeild vast wealth from Alaska to Baja California.

(National Geographic Magazine, Vol. 74, 1938, pp. 463-498)

QL 1 T 64
FISHES   PALAU ISLANDS
Aoyagi, Hyozi

The fishes of the family Pseudochromidae found in the waters of the Riu-Kiu Islands and the Palau Islands.

(Annotationes Zoologicae Japonenses, Vol. 20(1):41-54, 1941)

AS 36 C 3
FISHES   PALMYRA ISLAND
Seale, Alvin

Fishes. The Templeton Crocker Expedition to Western Polynesia and Melanesian Islands, 1933, No. 27.

(Proc. California Academy of Sciences, Ser. 4, Vol. 21, 1935, pp. 337-378)

QL 752 U 58
FISHES   PACIFIC COAST
Sette, Oscar E.

Studies on the Pacific pilchard or sardine (Sardinops caerulea) I-V By Oscar E. Sette and others.

(Special Scientific Reports, Fish and Wildlife Service, No. 19-24, 1943)

AS 36 S 1
FISHES   PALAU ISLANDS
Bayor, Frederick M.

Project coral fish looks at Palau. By Frederick M. Bayer and Robert R. Harry-Rofen.

(Ann. Rept. of the Smithsonian Institution for 1956; pp. 481-508)

QL Fishes Pam. 403
FISHES   PANAMA
Eigenmann, Carl H.

The fresh-water fishes of Panama east of longitude 80° W; The Magdalena basin and the horizontal and vertical distribution of its fishes.

(Indiana University Studies, 47 A and B., 1920)

QL 628 Ca-b
FISHES   PACIFIC COAST
Skogsberg, Tage

The fishes of the family Sciaenidae (croakers) of California.

(California, Division of Fish and Game, Fish Bulletin No. 54, 1939)

DU 1 M 6
FISHES--PALAU ISLANDS
Herre, Albert W. C. T.

A check list of the fishes of the Pelew Islands.

(Mid-Pacific Magazine, 1935, pp. 163-166)

AS 36 C / AS 36 S7
FISHES--PANAMA BAY
Gilbert, Charles Henry, 1859-
... The fishes of Panama Bay, by Charles H. Gilbert and Edwin C. Starks. Issued February 6, 1904. San Francisco, The Academy, 1904.
304 p. XXXIII pl. 30½cm. (Memoirs of the California academy of sciences. vol. IV)
Bibliography: p. 219-226.   QL11.C17
------- <Reprinted from the Memoirs of the California academy of sciences. vol. IV> [San Francisco] Stanford university, 1904.
1 p. l., 304 p. XXXIII pl. 30½cm. (Contributions to biology from the Hopkins seaside laboratory of the Leland Stanford jr. university. XXXII)
1. Fishes--Panama Bay. I. Starks, Edwin Chapin, joint author.

Library of Congress   QL3.L53   4-11564-5
------- Copy 2.   QL630.G46

QL 1 C15
FISHES--PACIFIC COAST.
Starks, Edwin Chapin, 1867-
... The marine fishes of southern California, by Edwin Chapin Starks and Earl Leonard Morris. Berkeley, The University press, 1907.
cover-title, p. [159]-251. pl. XXI. 27cm. (University of California publications. Zoology. v. 3, no. 11)
At head of title: Contributions from the laboratory of the Marine biological association of San Diego. XIV.
"Literature cited": p. 248-251.
1. Fishes--Pacific Ocean. 2. Marine fauna--Pacific Ocean. I. Morris, Earl Leonard, joint author.

A 11-2277
Title from Univ. of Calif.   Library of Congress

AS 540 P
FISHES   PALAU ISLANDS
Herre, Albert W. C. T.

Fishes in the Zoological Museum of Stanford University, III: New genera and species of gobies and blennies and a new Myxus, from the Pelew Islands and Celebes.

(Philippine Journal of Science, vol.59, no.2, February 1936, pp.275-286)

QL 1 F
FISHES--PANAMA.
Hubbs, Carl Levitt, 1894-
... Notes on fishes from the Athi River in British East Africa, by Carl L. Hubbs ... Chicago, 1918.
cover-title, p. 9-16. III pl. 24½cm. (Field museum of natural history. Publication 198. Zoological series. vol. XII, no. 2)
1. Fishes--Africa, British East. 2. Athi River.

18-13028
Library of Congress   QL1.F4   vol. 12, no 2

QL 628 Ca-b
FISHES   PACIFIC COAST
Walford, L. A.

Handbook of common commercial and game fishes of California.

(California Fish and Game Bull. 28, 1931)

QL 1 T 64 and QL Fishes Pam. 394
FISHES   PALAU ISLANDS
Herre, Albert W. C. T.

On a collection of fishes from Nanyo, the Japanese Mandated Islands.

(Annotationes Zool. Japonenses, 18:298-307, 1939)

QL 1 F
FISHES --PANAMA
Meek, Seth E.

The marine fishes of Panama. Field Mus.Zool. Ser. Vol. XV, 1924 -

---

AS 36 S5 / AS 36 S2
FISHES PACIFIC COAST BIBLIOGRAPHY
Gill, Theodore Nicholas, 1837-
Bibliography of the fishes of the Pacific coast of the United States to the end of 1879. By Theodore Gill. Washington, Govt. print. off., 1882.
2 p. l., 73 p. 23½cm. (Added t.-p.: ... Bulletin of the United States National museum. no. 11)
Issued also as vol. XXIII, art. 1 of the Smithsonian miscellaneous collections.
Smithsonian institution publication 463.
1. Fishes--Pacific coast--Bibl.

S 13-121
Library, Smithsonian Institution   Q11.U6

AS 36 A 16
FISHES   PALMYRA
Fowler, Henry W.

The fishes of the George Vanderbilt South Pacific Expedition, 1937.

(Acad. of Nat. Sci., Philadelphia, Monograph No. 2, 1938)

QL 1 F
FISHES--PANAMA.
Meek, Seth Eugene, 1859-
... New species of fishes from Panama, by Seth Eugene Meek ... and Samuel F. Hildebrand ... Chicago, 1913.
1 p. l., p. 77-91. 24½cm. (Field museum of natural history. Publication 166. Zoological ser. vol. x, no. 8)
1. Fishes--Panama. I. Hildebrand, Samuel Frederick, 1884- joint author.

13-8144
Library of Congress   QL1.F4 vol. 10, no. 8

FISHES - PANAMA

QL
1
F

Meek, Seth Eugene, 1859–

... Descriptions of new fishes from Panama, by S. E. Meek ... and S. F. Hildebrand ... Chicago, 1912.

1 p. l., p. 67-68. 24ᶜᵐ. (Field museum of natural history. Publication 158. Zoölogical series. vol. x, no. 6)

1. Fishes—Panama. i. Hildebrand, Samuel Frederick, 1884– joint author. 12-9942

Library of Congress QL1.F4 vol. 10, no. 6

FISHES--PANAMA

QL
1
F

Meek, Seth Eugene, 1859–1914.

... The fishes of the fresh waters of Panama, by Seth E. Meek ... and Samuel F. Hildebrand ... Chicago, 1916.

1 p. l., p. 217-374. illus. pl. vi-xxxii. 24½ᶜᵐ. (Field museum of natural history. Publication 191. Zoölogical series. vol. x, no. 15)

"Glossary of technical terms": p. 371-374.

1. Fishes—Panama. i. Hildebrand, Samuel Frederick, 1884– joint author. 17-9600

Library of Congress QL1.F4 vol. 10, no. 15

FISHES PANAMA

AS
36
A 4

Nichols, John Treadwell

A collection of fishes from the Panama bight, Pacific Ocean, by John Treadwell Nichols and Robert Cushman Murphy.

(Bull. Am. Mus. of Nat. Hist., Vol. 83, Art. 4, 1944, pp. 217-260)

FISHES PANAMA

QL
628.C
S 78

Springer, Steward

Three new sharks of the genus Sphyrna from the Pacific coast of tropical America.

(Stanford Ichthyological Bulletin, Vol. 1, No. 5, 1940, pp. 161-169)

FISHES -- PANAMA BAY

AS
36
C

Gilbert, Charles Henry, 1859–

... The fishes of Panama Bay, by Charles H. Gilbert and Edwin C. Starks. Issued February 6, 1904. San Francisco, The Academy, 1904.

304 p. xxxiii pl. 30½ᶜᵐ. (Memoirs of the California academy of sciences. vol. iv)
Bibliography: p. 219-226.

AS
36
S6

——— ⟨Reprinted from the Memoirs of the California academy of sciences. vol. iv⟩ ₍San Francisco₎ Stanford university, 1904.

1 p. l., 304 p. xxxiii pl. 30½ᶜᵐ. (Contributions to biology from the Hopkins seaside laboratory of the Leland Stanford jr. university. xxxii)

i. Fishes—Panama Bay. i. Starks, Edwin Chapin, joint author.

Q11.C17 4–11564–5

Library of Congress QL3.L53
——— Copy 2. QL630.G46

FISHES PANAMA CANAL

QL
1
N6-Z

Hildebrand, Samuel F.

The Panama Canal as a passageway for fishes, with lists and remarks on the fishes and invertebrates observed.

Pt. 1
(Zoologica, Vol. 24, No. 3, 1939, pp. 15-45, 2 pls.)

FISHES PAPUA

QL
1
A 93 p

Whitley, Gilbert P.

A new mud-skipper from Papua.

(Proc. R. Zoological Soc. of New South Wales, 1958/59:69-70)

FISHES PATAGONIA

GC
63
D 61

Hart, T. John

Report on trawling surveys on the Patagonian continental shelf.

IN Discovery Reports, Vol. 23, pp. 223-408, 1946.

FISHES PERU

AS
36
S 5

Hildebrand, Samuel F.

A descriptive catalog of the shore fishes of Peru.

(U. S. Nat. Mus., Bull. 189, 1946)

FISHES PERU

QL
5
B 61

Morrow, James E.

Studies in ichthyology and oceanography off coastal Peru. By James E. Morrow and Gerald S. Posner.

(Bull. Bingham Oceanographic Collection, Peabody Mus. Nat. Hist., Yale Univ., 16(2), 1957)

FISHES - PHILIPPINE ISLANDS

AS
36
S4

Bigelow, Henry Bryant, 1879–

... Preliminary account of one new genus and three new species of *Medusæ* from the Philippines. By Henry B. Bigelow ...

(*In* U. S. National museum. Proceedings. Washington, 1913. 23½ᶜᵐ. vol. 43, p. 253-260)

"Scientific results of the Philippine cruise of the fisheries steamer 'Albatross,' 1907-1910.—no. 22."

1. Medusae. 2. Fishes—Philippine Islands. 3. Albatross (Steamer)

13-13115

Library of Congress Q11.U55 vol. 43

FISHING PHILIPPINE IS.

AS
540
P

Domantay, Jose S.

The catching of live bait for tuna fishing in Mindanao.

(Phil. Jour. Sci., 73:337-342, 1940)

FISHES PHILIPPINE ISLANDS

AS
540
P

Domantay, Jose S.

Tuna fishing in southern Mindanao.

(Philippine Journal of Science, Vol. 73, 1940, pp. 423-436)

FISHES PHILIPPINE ISLANDS

AS
36
S 5

Fowler, Hnery W.

Contributions to the Biology of the Philippine Archipelago and Adjacent Regions: The Fishes of the Families Pseudochromidae, Lobotidae..."Albatross"...

(In Bulletin United States National Museum, No. 100, Volume XI, 1931. xi, 388 pp)

FISHES PHILIPPINE ISLANDS

AS
36
S 5

Fowler, Henry W.

Contributions to the biology of the Philippine Archipelago and adjacent regions: the fishes of the groups Elasmobranchii, Holocephali, Isospondyli, and Ostarophysi obtained by the United States Bur. of Fisheries steamer "Albatross" in 1907 to 1910, chiefly in the Philippine Islands and adjacent seas.

(U.S.National Museum, Bull. 100, vol. 13, (1941)

FISHES PHILIPPINE ISLANDS

AS
36
S 5

Fowler, Henry W.

Descriptions and figures of new fishes obtained in Philippine seas and adjacent waters by the United States Bureau of Fisheries steamer "Albatross". [Contributions to the biology of the Philippine Archipelago and adjacent regions].

(U. S. Nat. Museum, Bull. 100, Vol. 14, Part 2, 1943, pp. 53-91)

FISHES PHILIPPINE ISLANDS

AS
36
S 5

Fowler, Henry W.

Descriptions and figures of new fishes obtained in Philippine seas and adjacent waters by the United States Bureau of Fisheries steamer "Albatross".

(U. S. National Museum, Bull. 100, Vol. 14, Part 2, 1948)

FISHES - PHILIPPINE ISLANDS
Fowler, Henry W and Bean, Barton A

QL
636.5P
F78

The fishes of the families Pomacentridae, Labridae, and Callyodontidae, collected by the United States Bureau of Fisheries steamer "Albatross," chiefly in Philippine seas and adjacent waters... U.S. Nat. Mus., Bull.100, v.7, 1928.

FISHES PHILIPPINE ISLANDS

AS
36
A 4

Fowler, Henry W.

New fishes of the family Callionymidae, mostly Philippine, obtained by the United States Bureau of Fisheries Steamer "Albatross".

(Proc. U. S. Nat. Mus., Vol. 90, 1941, pp. 1-31, No. 3106)

FISHES--PHILIPPINE ISLANDS

AS
36
S5

Gilbert, Charles Henry, 1859–

... The macrouroid fishes of the Philippine Islands and the East Indies, by Charles Henry Gilbert ... and Carl L. Hubbs ... Washington, Govt. print. off., 1920.

1 p. l., p. 369-588. illus. 24½ᶜᵐ. (Smithsonian institution. United States National museum. Bulletin 100, v. 1, pt. 7)

At head of title: Contributions to the biology of the Philippine Archipelago and adjacent regions.

1. Coryphaenoididae. 2. Fishes—Philippine Islands. 3. Fishes—East Indies. i. Title. 20-26849

Library of Congress Q11.U6 no. 100, vol. 1, pt. 7
——— Copy 2. QL638.C7G5
  ₍10₎

FISHES PHILIPPINE ISLANDS

QL
752
U 58

Herre, Albert W.

Check list of Philippine fishes.

(U.S. Dept. of the Interior, Fish and Wildlife Service, Research Rept. 20, 1953)

AS
540
P 55-j   FISHES   PHILIPPINE ISLANDS

Herre, Albert W. C. T.

Eight additions to the Philippine fish fauna, including three new species.

(The Philippine Journal of Science, Vol. 82(1):9-14, 1953)

AS
540
P   FISHES   PHILIPPINE ISLANDS

Herre, Albert W. C. T.

The Philippine blennies.

(Phil. Jour. of Sci., Vol. 70, 1939, pp. 315-372)

AS
540
P 55   FISHES   PHILIPPINE ISLANDS

Jordan, David Starr

Check-List of the Species of Fishes Known from the Philippine Archipelago, by David Starr Jordan and Robert Earl Richardson.
(Monograph, Bureau of Science, Philippine Islands, No. 1, 1910)

AS
540
P 55   FISHES PHILIPPINE ISLANDS

Herre, Albert W.

Gobies of the Philippines and the China Sea.

(Monograph, Bureau of Science, Philippine Islands, No. 23, 1927)

AS
36
S 71   FISHES   PHILIPPINE ISLANDS

Herre, Albert W. C. T.

A review of the halfbeaks or Hemiramphidae of the Philippines and adjacent waters.

(Stanford University Publications, Univ. Ser., Bilogical Sciences, Vol. 9, 1944, No. 2, pp. 1-48)

AS
540
P 55   FISHES PHILIPPINE ISLANDS

Montalban, Heraclio R.

Pomacentridae of the Philippine Islands.

(Monograph, Bureau of Science, Philippine Islands, No. 24, 1927)

AS
540
P 55j   FISHES   PHILIPPINE ISLANDS

Herre, Albert W. C. T.

The guitarfishes, family Rhinobatidae, of the Philippines and adjacent seas.

(Philippine Journal of Science 83(4):381-399, 1954)

AS
540
P   FISHES   PHILIPPINE ISLANDS

Herre, Albert W.

Six additions to the Philippine fish fauna, including two new species.

(Phil. Jour. Sci., 79:341-346, 1950)

AS
36
S4   FISHES - PHILIPPINE ISLANDS

Radcliffe, Lewis, 1880-

... Descriptions of a new family, two new genera, and twenty-nine new species of anacanthine fishes from the Philippine Islands and contiguous waters. By Lewis Radcliffe ...

(*In* U. S. National museum. Proceedings. Washington, 1913. 23½ᶜᵐ. vol. 43, p. 105-140. illus., pl. 22-31)
"Scientific results of the Philippine cruise of the fisheries steamer 'Albatross,' 1907-1910—no. 21."

1. Fisheries—Philippine Islands. 2. Albatross (Steamer)

Library of Congress   Q11.U55 vol. 43   13-13110

QL
628.C
S 78   FISHES-PHILIPPINE ISLANDS

Herre, Albert W. C. T.

New and little known Phallostethids, with keys to the genera and Philippine species.

(Stanford Ichthyological Bulletin, Vol. 2, 1942. No. 5, pp. 137-156)

AS
540
P   FISHES   PHILIPPINE ISLANDS

Herre, Albert W. C. T.

Twenty-six noteworthy Philippine fishes.

(Phil. Jour. Sci., 79:137-154, 1950)

AS
36
S4   FISHES--PHILIPPINE ISLANDS

Radcliffe, Lewis, 1880-

... Descriptions of fifteen new fishes of the family *Cheilodipteridæ* from the Philippine Islands and contiguous waters. By Lewis Radcliffe ...

(*In* U. S. National museum. Proceedings. Washington, 1912. 23½ᶜᵐ. v. 41, p. 431-446. pl. 34-38)
At head of title: Scientific results of the Philippine cruise of the fisheries steamer "Albatross," 1907-1910.—no. 13.

1. Chilodipteridae. 2. Fishes — Philippine Islands.   I. Albatross (Steamer)

Library of Congress   Q11.U55 vol. 41   12-17789

QL
1
C 78   FISHES   PHILIPPINE ISLANDS

Herre, Albert W. C. T.

A new Philippine Apogonid, with notes on some rare species.

(Copeia, 1943, pp. 216-218)

QL
1
C 78   FISHES   PHILIPPINE ISLANDS

Herre, Albert W. C. T.

Two new genera and four new gobies from the Philippines and India.

(Copeia, 1945, no. 1, pp. 1-6)

AS
36
S4   FISHES- PHILIPPINE ISLANDS

Radcliffe, Lewis, 1880-

... Descriptions of seven new genera and thirty-one new species of fishes of the families *Brotulidæ* and *Carapidæ* from the Philippine Islands and the Dutch East Indies. By Lewis Radcliffe ...

(*In* U. S. National museum. Proceedings. Washington, 1913. 23½ᶜᵐ. v. 44, p. 135-176. pl. 7-17)
"In the study of this collection the writer has been associated with Dr. Hugh M. Smith, who becomes joint author of the new genera and species herein described."
"Scientific results of the Philippine cruise of the fisheries steamer 'Albatross,' 1907-1910—no. 24."
1. Brotulidæ. 2. Carapidæ. 3. Fishes — Philippine Islands. 4. Albatross (Steamer)   I. Smith, Hugh McCormick, 1865-   joint author.

Library of Congress   Q11.U55 vol. 44   13-20858

QH
1.S
W 31   FISHES-PHILIPPINE ISLANDS

Herre, Albert W. C. T.

A new species of Salarias, with a key to the Philippine species. (Notes on fishes in the Zoological Museum of Stanford University, IX.)

(Proc. Biol. Soc. of Washington, Vol. 55, 1942, pp. 1-8)

QH
1.S
W 31   FISHES   PHILIPPINES

Herre, Albert W. C. T.

Two new minute gobies of the genus Mistichthys from the Philippines.

(Proc. Biol. Soc. of Washington, 57:107-112, 1945)

AS
36
S4   FISHES- PHILIPPINE ISLANDS

Radcliffe, Lewis, 1880-

... New pediculate fishes from the Philippine Islands and contiguous waters. By Lewis Radcliffe ...

(*In* U. S. National museum. Proceedings. Washington, 1912. 23½ᶜᵐ. vol. 42, p. 199-214. illus., pl. 16-27)
"Scientific results of the Philippine cruise of the fisheries steamer 'Albatross,' 1907-1910—no. 16."
"In the study of this collection the writer has been associated with Dr. Hugh M. Smith, who becomes joint author of the new genus and species herein described."

1. Fishes—Philippine Islands. 2. Albatross (Steamer)   I. Smith, Hugh McCormick, 1865-

Library of Congress   Q11.U55 vol. 42   13-9524

AS
540
P   FISHES   PHILIPPINE ISLANDS

Herre, Albert W.

Noteworthy additions to the Philippine fish fauna, with descriptions of a new genus and species. By Albert W. Herre and Earl S. Herald.

(Phil. Jour. Sci., 79:309-338, 1950)

QL
1
C 78   FISHES-PHILIPPINE ISLANDS

Herre, Albert W. C. T.

Two new species of Petrocirtes, and a key to the Philippine species. (Contributions from the Zoological Museum of Stanford University, California, IX.)

(Copeia, 1942, pp. 111-116)

AS
36
S4   FISHES--PHILIPPINE ISLANDS

Radcliffe, Lewis, 1880-

... Notes on some fishes of the genus *Amia*, family of *Cheilodipteridæ* with descriptions of four new species from the Philippine Islands. By Lewis Radcliffe ...

(*In* U. S. National museum. Proceedings. Washington, 1912. 23½ᶜᵐ. v. 41, p. 245-261. illus., pl. 20-25)
At head of title: Scientific results of the Philippine cruise of the fisheries steamer "Albatross," 1907-10.—no. 12.

1. Amia. 2. Fishes—Philippine Islands.   I. Albatross (Steamer)

Library of Congress   Q11.U55 vol. 41   12-17775

AS 540 P

FISHING   PHILIPPINE ISLANDS

Rasalan, Santos B.

Preservation of fishing gear in Samar Province, Philippnes.

(Phil. Jl. Sci., 73:321-333, 1940)

AS 36 S5

FISHES--PHILIPPINE ISLANDS

Smith, Hugh McCormick, 1865–

... Descriptions of three new fishes of the family *Chætodontidæ* from the Philippine Islands. By Hugh M. Smith and Lewis Radcliffe ...

(*In* U. S. National museum. Proceedings. Washington, 1911. 23½ᶜᵐ. v. 40, p. 319-326. illus.)

"Scientific results of the Philippine cruise of the fisheries steamer 'Albatross,' 1907-10—no. 9."

1. Chaetodontidae. 2. Fishes—Philippine Islands. 3. Albatross (Steamer) 1. Radcliffe, Lewis, 1880– joint author.

Library of Congress   Q11.U55 vol. 40   11–31521
[s21g2]

QL 627 U-b

FISHES   PHOENIX ISLANDS

Shimada, Bell M.

Juvenile oceanic skijack from the Phoenix Islands.

(Fishery Bulletin, U. S. Dept. of the Int., No. 64, 1951)

AS 540 P

FISHES   PHILIPPINE ISLANDS

Roxas, Hilario A.

A new fish from Lingayan Gulf, Philippines, by Hilario A. Roxas and Guillermo L. Ablan.

(Philippine Journal of Science, Vol. 71, 1940, 77-78)

QL 752 U 58

FISHES   PHILIPPINE ISLANDS

Umali, Agustin F.

Key to the families of common commercial fishes in the Philippines.

(Fish and Wildlife Service, U. S. Dept. of the Interior, Research Report 21, 1950)

AS 36 A 65

FISHES   PITCAIRN ISLAND

Nichols, J. T.

New Pacific flying-fishes collected by Templeton Crocker, by J. T. Nichols and C. M. Breder, Jr.

(American Museum Novitates, no. 821, 1935)

AS 540 P

FISHES   PHILIPPINE ISLANDS

Roxas, Hilario A.

A review of Philippine Carangidae, by Hilario A. Roxas and Antolin G. Agco.

(Philippine Jour. of Sci., Vol. 74, 1941, pp. 1-82, pl. 1-12)

DU 1 S 72 q

FISHES   PHILIPPINE ISLANDS

van Pel, H.

Introduction of edible pond fish from Philippines.

(South Pacific Commission Quarterly Bulletin Vol. 6(1):17, January, 1956)

[into New Caledonia]

AS 763 B-m

QL 623 F 78

Reading Room

FISHES   POLYNESIA

Fowler, Henry W.

Fishes of Oceania. Honolulu. 1928. 4to. 540 pp.   Supplements 1-2, 3 1931-34, 947

(Bernice P. Bishop Museum, Memoirs, Vol. X. Plates I-XLIX; Vol. XI, Nos. 5-6); XII: 1947

AS 540 P

FISHES   PHILIPPINE ISLANDS

Seale, Alvin

The fishery resources of the Philippine Islands. Parts 1-4

(Philippine Journal of Sci., 3:513-531, 1908; 4A:57-64, 1909; 5, D:87-99, 1910; 6, D:283-320, 1911)

QL 627 P 55

FISHES   PHILIPPINES   BIBLIOGRAPHY

Blanco, Guillermo J.

A bibliography of Philippine fishes and fisheries. By Guillermo J. Blanco and Heraclio R. Montalban.

(The Philippine Journal of Fisheries, Vol. 1(2):107-130, 1951)

QL Fishes Pam. 394

FISHES   PONAPE

Herre, Albert W. C. T.

On a collection of fishes from Panyo, the Japanese Mandated Islands

(Annotationes Zool. Japonenses, 18:298-307, 1939)

AS 540 P

FISHES   PHILIPPINE ISLANDS

Seale, Alvin

Sea products of Mindanao and Sulu. I: Food fishes and sharks; II. Pears, pearl shells and button shells.

(Philippine Journal of Science, Vol. 11, Sect. D:235-241; 245-264, 1916)

QL 1 C 78

FISHES   PHOENIX ISLANDS

Halstead, Bruce W.

A survey of the poisonous fishes of the Phoenix Islands. By Bruce W. Halstead and Norman C. Bunker.

(Copeia, 1954 No. 1, pp. 1-11)

QH 109.P N 53

FISHES   PORTO RICO

Nichols, John Treadwell

The fishes of Porto Rico and the Virgin Islands.

IN Scientific survey of Porto Rico and the Virgin Islands. Vol. 10:2-3, 1929-1930.

AS 36 S4

FISHES--PHILIPPINE ISLANDS

Smith, Hugh McCormick, 1865–

... The chimaeroid fishes of the Philippine Islands, with description of a new species. By Hugh M. Smith ...

(*In* U. S. National museum. Proceedings. Washington, 1912. 23½ᶜᵐ. vol. 42, p. 231-232. pl. 29)

"Scientific results of the Philippine cruise of the fisheries steamer 'Albatross,' 1907-1910—no. 18."

1. Chimaeridae. 2. Fishes—Philippine Islands. 3. Albatross (Steamer)   13-9527

Library of Congress   Q11.U55 vol. 42

QL 1 C 78

FISHES   PHOENIX ISLANDS

Randall, John E.

Acanthurus rackliffei, a possible hybrid surgeon fish (A. achilles X A. glaucopareius) from the Phoenix Islands.

(Copeia, 1956, No. 1: pp. 21-25)

AS 36 S6

FISHES - PUGET SOUND

Jordan, David Starr, 1851–

... The fishes of Puget Sound, by David Starr Jordan and Edwin Chapin Starks ... Palo Alto, Cal., Leland Stanford jr. university, 1895.

2 p. l., p. [785]-855. 30 pl. 24½ᶜᵐ. (Leland Stanford junior university. Hopkins laboratory of biology. Contributions. no. III.)

"Reprint from the Proceedings of the California academy of sciences, series 2. vol. v."

1. Fishes—Puget Sound. 1. Starks, Edwin Chapin, 1867– joint author.   3-31842

Library of Congress   QL61.L53 no. 3

AS 36 S4

FISHES--PHILIPPINE ISLANDS

Smith, Hugh McCormick, 1865–

... The squaloid sharks of the Philippine Archipelago, with descriptions of new genera and species. By Hugh M. Smith ...

(*In* U. S. National museum. Proceedings. Washington, 1912. 23½ᶜᵐ. v. 41, p. 677-683. illus, pl. 51-54)

At head of title: Scientific results of the Philippine cruise of the fisheries steamer "Albatross," 1907-10—no. 15.

1. Sharks. 2. Fishes—Philippine Islands. 1. Albatross (Steamer)   12-17798* Cancel

Library of Congress   Q11.U55 vol. 41

AS 36 S 5

FISHES   PHOENIX ISLANDS

Schultz, Leonard P.

Fishes of the Phoenix and Samoan Islands collected in 1939 during the expedition of the U. S. S. "Bushnell".

(U. S. National Museum, Bull. 180, 1943)

QL Fish Pam. 385

FISHES   PUGET SOUND

Kincaid, Trevor

An annotated list of Puget Sound fishes. Prepared at the request of ...State Fish Commissioner, State of Washington, Department of Fisheries. August 20, 1919. 8vo. 51 pp.

AS 36 S6

FISHES - PUGET SOUND

Starks, Edwin Chapin, 1867-

... List of fishes collected at Port Ludlow, Wash. By Edwin Chapin Starks ... Palo Alto, Cal., Leland Stanford jr. university, 1896.

2 p. l., (549)-562 p. LXXIV-LXXV pl. 24½ᵐᵐ. (Leland Stanford junior university publications. Contributions to biology from the Hopkins seaside laboratory. VIII)

p. 553-560 misplaced.
Reprint from the Proceedings of the California academy of sciences, series 2, vol. VI.

1. Fishes—Puget Sound.

Library of Congress   QL1.L53   7-10272

QH 198.Re W 85

FISHES   RENNELL ISLAND

Wolff, Torben

The natural history of Rennell Island, British Solomon Islands.
Vol. I (Vertebrates).

Scientific Results of the Danish Rennell Expedition, 1951, and The British Museum (Natural History) Expedition, 1953. Published on behalf of the University, Copenhagen, The British Museum (Natural History)   London. Danish Science Press, Ltd. Co-   penhagen. R8vo. 1958

AS 251 L 56-t

FISHES   RIU KIU ISLANDS

Schmidt, P. J.

An additional list of the fishes of the Riu-Kiu Islands, with description of Pseudochromichtys riukianus n.g.n.sp. (with a summary and 1 textfig.).

(Trans. of the Pac. Com. of the Acad. of Sci., USSR, II, 1931, pp. 177-185)

Storage Case 3

FISHES   PUKAPUKA

Beaglehole, Ernest

Pukapuka. 25 field notebooks; 3 packages of field notes, 1 of them containing fish names. 1935.

QL Fish Pam. 11

FISHES   REVILLAGIGEDO ISLAND

Snodgrass, Robert

Shore fishes of the Revillagigedo, Clipperton, Cocos and Galapagos Islands, by Robert Snodgrass and Edmond Heller.

(Proc. Washington Acad. Sci., Vol. 6, 1904, pp. 333-427; published Jan. 31, 1905)

AS 251 L 56-t

FISHES   RIU KIU ISLANDS

Schmidt, P. J.

Fishes of the Riu-Kiu Islands (with a summary, 6 plates and 8 textfigs.)

(Trans. Pac. Com., Acad. Sci., USSR, I, 1930, pp. 19-156)

QL 636 Q 3

FISHES   QUEENSLAND

Marshall, T.C.

Know your fishes; an illustrated guide to the principal commercial fishes and crustaceans of Queensland.   By T.C.Marshall, E.M. Grant and N.M.Hayson.

(Ichthyological Notes, Vol.1(4), 1959)

QL 1 T 64

FISHES   RIU KIU ISLANDS

Aoyagi, Hyozi

The fishes of the family Pseudochromidae found in the waters of the Riu-Kiu Islands and the Palau Islands.

(Annotationes Zoologicae Japonenses, Vol. 20(1):41-54, 1941)

QL 752 U 58

FISHES   RIU KIU ISLANDS

Shapiro, Sidney

Aquatic resources of the Ryukyu area.

(U. S. Fish and Wildlife Service, Fishery Leaflet 333, 1949)

QL Fishes Pam. 539

FISHES   QUEENSLAND

Ogilby, J. Douglas

The commercial fishes and fisheries of Queensland. (First published in 1916...) Revised and illustrated by Tom C. Marshall. Fisheries Branch, Dept. of Harbours and Marine. Brisbane. 1954. sm4to. 121 pp.

QL 1 T 64

FISHES   RIU KIU ISLANDS

Aoyagi, Hyozi

The fishes of the genus Franzia found in the waters of the Riu-kiu Islands.

(Annotationes Zoologicae Japonenses, Vol. 21(1):48-53, 1942)

AS 36 S4

FISHES-- RIU KIU ISLANDS

Snyder, John Otterbein, 1867-
Descriptions of new genera and species of fishes from Japan and the Riu Kiu Islands. [By] John Otterbein Snyder ...

(*In* U. S. National museum. Proceedings. Washington, 1911. 23½ᵐᵐ. v. 40, p. 525-549)

1. Fishes—Japan. 2. Fishes—Riu Kiu Islands.

Library of Congress   Q11.U55 vol. 40   11-31534

QH 11 P 11

FISHES   RAROIA

Harry, Robert R.

Ichthyological field data of Raroia Atoll, Tuamotu Archipelago.

(Scientific Investigations in Micronesia, Report No. 16, 1953)

See also
QH 1 A 88

(Atoll Research Bulletin, No. 18, July, 1953)

QL Fishes Pam. 421

FISHES   RIU KIU ISLANDS

Fowler, Henry W.

A collection of fishes obtained in the Riu Kiu Islands by Captain Ernest R. Tinkham A.U.S.

(Proc. Acad. Nat. Sci., Philadelphia, Vol. 98:123-318, 1946)

AS 36 S4

FISHES-- RIU KIU ISLANDS

Snyder, John Otterbein, 1867-
The fishes of Okinawa, one of the Riu Kiu Islands. By John Otterbein Snyder ...

(*In* U. S. National museum. Proceedings. Washington, 1912. 23½ᵐᵐ. vol. 42, p. 487-519. pl. 62-70)

1. Fishes—Okinawa Island.

Library of Congress   Q11.U55 vol. 42   13-9542

QL 336 R 92

FISHES - RED SEA

Rüppell, Eduard

Atlas zu der Reise im nördlichen Afrika ...

Frankfurt am Main, 1826- 1828, folio

See Ruppell

QH 188 U 58

FISHES   RYU KYU ISLANDS

Hiyama, Yoshio
Systematic list of fishes of the Ryukyu Islands.

(U. S. Army, General Headquarters, Supreme Commander for the Allied Powers, Nat. Resources Section, Report No. 150. Tokyo, 1951)

QL 634.J T 16

FISHES   RIU KIU ISLANDS

Tanaka, Shigeho

Figures and descriptions of the fishes of Japan, including Riukiu Islands, Bonin Islands... Tokyo. 1925-   R8vo.

QL 1 E 32

FISHES   RED SEA

Clark, Eugenie

The fishes of the Red Sea: order Plectognathi By Eugenie Clark and H. A. F. Gohar.

(Univ. of Cairo, Publications of the Marine Biological Station Al Ghardaqa (Red Sea), No. 8, 1953)

AS 36 C 6

FISHES   RIU KIU ISLANDS

Jordan, David Starr

The fresh water fishes of the Riu-Kiu Islands, Japan, By D. S. Jordan and Shigeho Tanaka.

(Annals of the Carnegie Museums, Vol. 17, 1927, pp. 259-282)

AS 222 M

FISHES   RIU KIU ISLANDS

Tortonese, Enrico

Su alcuni pesci, anfibi e rettili dell' isola di Kiu-Shiu (Giappone). By Enrico Tortonese and Teresa Ceriana.

(Soc. Atiliana di Sci. Nat. Mus. Civico di Storia Nat. in Milano, Atti, Vol. 83:64-76, 1944)

QL
Fishes
Pam. 358

FISHES   SAINT PAUL ISLAND

de la Rue, E. Aubert

Informations sur les pêches étrangères et
coloniales: la pêche aux îles Saint-Paul et
Amsterdam.

(Revue des Travaux de l'Office des Pêches
Maritimes, Tome V, Fasc. 1, No. 17, nd, pp.
83-109)

FISHES-SAMOA

QL
636.55
J82

Jordan, David Starr, 1851-

... The fishes of Samoa. Description of the species
found in the Archipelago, with a provisional check-list of
the fishes of Oceania. (By David Starr Jordan and Alvin
Seale) ... Washington, Govt. print. off., 1906.

1 p. l., p. 173-455, xxx p. illus., pl. xxxiii-liii (partly col.) 27ᵐ.
(U. S. Bureau of fisheries. Doc. 605)

3 copies

From Bulletin of the Bureau of fisheries, vol. xxv.
At head of title: Department of commerce and labor. Bureau of fisher-
ies. George M. Bowers, commissioner.
"Glossary of principal words composing native names of Samoan fishes.
By W. E. Safford": p. 446-455.

1. Fishes—Samoa. 2. Fishes—Oceanica.   I. Seale, Alvin, 1873-
joint author.

Library, U. S. Bur. of   /   Fisheries   F-11-70

AS
36
C 3

FISHES   SANTA CRUZ

Seale, Alvin

Fishes. The Templeton Crocker Expedition
to Western Polynesia and Melanesian Islands,
1933, No. 27.

(Proc. California Academy of Sciences, Ser.
4, Vol. 21, 1935, pp. 337-378)

QL
Fishes
Pam.
411

FISHES   SAIPAN

Fowler, Henry W.

Fishes from Saipan Island, Micronesia.

(Proc. Acad. Nat. Sci., Philadelphia, Vol.
97:59-74, 1945)

DU
1
C 56

FISHES-SAMOA

Jordan, David Starr

(Samoan fishes, poisonous and edible)
With translation in Samoan. Letter to Captain
U. Sebree, August 9, 1902. 2 pp.

(Polynesian Papers, IV)

QL
615
G 78

FISHES-SINGAPORE

Kow, Tham Ah

The food and feeding relationships of the
fishes of Singapore Straits.

(Fishery Publications, Colonial Office,
[Great Britain], London, Vol. 1(1), 1950)

QL
1
T 64

FISHES   SAKHALIN

Tanaka, S.

Notes on a collection of fishes made by
Prof. Ijima in the southern parts of Sakhalin.

(Annotationes Zool. Japonenses, VI:235-254,
1908)

DU
1
P

FISHES   SAMOA

Jordan, David Starr

Shore fishes of Samoa.

(Journal of the Pan-Pacific Research Institution, Vol. 2, 1927, No. 4, pp. 3-11)

AS
36
A 1

FISHES   SOCIETY ISLANDS

Fowler, Henry W.

Description of a new long-finned tuna
(Semathunnus guildi), from Tahiti.

(Proceedings of the Academy of Natural Sciences of Phila., Vol. LXXXV, 1933, pp. 163-164.)

DU
620
P

FISHES   SAMOA

Falke, Lucia Ripley

Oahu fish vs fish of Samoa.

(Paradise of the Pacific. vol.49, no.8.
1937, p.11)

AS
36
S 5

FISHES   SAMOA

Schultz, Leonard P.

Fishes of the Phoenix and Samoan Islands
collected in 1939 during the expedition of the
U. S. S. "Bushnell".

(U. S. National Museum, Bull. 180, 1943)

AS
36
A 16

FISHES   SOCIETY ISLANDS

Fowler, Henry W.

The fishes of the George Vanderbilt South
Pacific Expedition, 1937.

(Acad. of Nat. Sci., Philadelphia, Monograph
No. 2, 1938)

QH
301
C

FISHES - SAMOA

Fowler, Henry W. and Silvester Charles F.

A collection of fishes from Samoa.
Carnegie Inst. Washington, Pub. No. 312
(Dept. Marine Biol. Vol. XVIII) 1922,
Art. VII.

AS
36
C 3

FISHES   SAMOA

Seale, Alvin

Fishes. The Templeton Crocker Expedition
to Western Polynesia and Melanesian Islands,
1933, No. 27.

(Proc. California Academy of Sciences, Ser.
4, Vol. 21, 1935, pp. 337-378)

QL
Fish
Pam. 344

FISHES   SOCIETY ISLANDS

Fowler, Henry W.

Fresh-water Fishes from the Marquesas and
Society Islands.

(Bernice P. Bishop Museum, Occasional Papers
Volume IX, Number 25, 1932. Pacific Entomological Survey Publication 4)

QL
Fishes
Pam 339

FISHES   SAMOA

Fowler, Henry W.

Fishes Obtained at Samoa in 1929.

(Occasional Paper, Bernice P. Bishop Museum,
Volume IX, Number 18, 1932)

AS
142
V-si

FISHES - SAMOA

Steindachner, Franz

Zur Fischfauna der Samoa - Inseln. In
Akad. Wissens. Wien. Bd. 115, Abt.1, pp
1369- 1425, 1906.

DU
1
M 6

FISHES   SOCIETY ISLANDS

Herre, Albert W.

A List of Fishes Collected at Moorea, One of
the Society Islands, Being the First Record from
this Island.

(Journal of the Pan-Pacific Research Institution, Vol. VI, No. 4, p. 10. IN Mid-Pacific
Magazine, Vol. 42, No. 4, 1931)

QL
Fish Pam
149

AS
763
B-b
Reading
Room

FISHES   SAMOA

Fowler, Henry W.

Fishes of Guam, Hawaii, Samoa, and Tahiti.

(Bernice P. Bishop Museum, Bulletin No. 22,
1925.)

AS
36
S 5

AS
36
S 2

QL Fish
Pam 150

FISHES   SAMOA

Streets, T. H.

Contributions to the natural history of the
Hawaiian and Fanning Islands...U. S. North Pacific surveying expedition, 1873-1875. pp. 94-102.

(U. S. Nat'l Mus., Bull. No. 7, 1877; Smithsonian Misc. Coll., Vol. XIII, art. 7, publ. no.
303)

DU
1
M 6

FISHES   SOLOMON ISLANDS

Herre, Albert W.

A Check List of Fishes from the Solomon Islands.

(Journal of the Pan-Pacific Research Institution, Vol. 6, No. 4, IN Mid-Pacific Magazine,
Vol. 42, No. 4, 1931) pp. 4-9

AS
36
C 3

FISHES   SOLOMON ISLANDS

Seale, Alvin

Fishes. The Templeton Crocker Expedition to Western Polynesia and Melanesian Islands, 1933, No. 27.

(Proc. California Academy of Sciences, Ser. 4, Vol. 21, 1935, pp. 337-378)

FISHES--SOUTH AMERICA

AS
36
C51

Eigenmann, Carl H   1863-

... The freshwater fishes of British Guiana, including a study of the ecological grouping of species, and the relation of the fauna of the plateau to that of the lowlands. By C. H. Eigenmann, PH. D. Pittsburgh, Pub. by the authority of the Board of trustees of the Carnegie institute, 1912.

cover-title, xx, 578 p. front., illus., CIII pl. (1 col., incl. 33 maps) 33½ᶜᵐ. (Memoirs of the Carnegie museum. vol. v)
Publications of the Carnegie museum, serial no. 67.
Bibliography: p. 530-554.

1. Fishes--British Guiana. 2. Fishes--South America--Bibl.

Library of Congress   QL632.B9E5   12-23721
————— Copy 2.   AS36.P75

AS
496
F 29

FISHES   SUMATRA

Regan, C. Tate
Fishes collected in Korinchi, West Sumatra..

IN Results of an expedition to Korinchi Peak, Sumatra (1914). Part II, pp. 307-309, 1920.

(Jour. of the Fed. Malay States Mus., Vol. 8, pp. 307-309, 1920)

DU
1
P

FISHES   SOLOMON ISLANDS

Whitley, Gilbert P.

A check list of the fishes of the Santa Cruz Archipelago, Melanesia.

(Journal of the Pan-Pacific Research Institution, Vol. 3, No. 1, 1928, pp. 11-13)

AS
36
S2

FISHES - SOUTH AMERICA

Eigenmann, Carl H   1863-
New genera of South American fresh-water fishes, and new names for some old genera, by Carl H. Eigenmann.

(In Smithsonian institution. Smithsonian miscellaneous collections. Washington, 1903. 24½ᶜᵐ. vol. XLV (Quarterly issue, vol. I) p. 144-148)
Publication 1431.
Vol. 45 (Quarterly issue, v. 1) with t.-p. dated 1903, was issued 4 parts in 2, with covers dated 1904.

1. Fishes--South America.

Library of Congress   Q11.S7 vol. 45   16-11316
————— Copy 2.

GN
1
Z

FISHING   TAHITI

Baessler, Arthur

Fischen auf Tahiti.

(Zeit. f. Ethnologie, Bd. 37, 1905, pp. 924-940)

AS
619
S

FISHES -- SOUTH AFRICA

Barnard, K. H.

A monograph of the marine fishes of South Africa. In South African Mus. Ann. Vol. XXI, 1925 --

See author card for detail

FISHES--SOUTH AMERICA

AS
36
C51

Ellis, Max Mapes, 1887-

... The gymnotid eels of tropical America, by Max Mapes Ellis. Pittsburgh, Board of trustees of the Carnegie institute, 1913.

cover-title, p. 109-204. illus., pl. XV-XXIII. 23½ᶜᵐ. (Memoirs of the Carnegie museum. vol. VI. no. 3)
Publications of the Carnegie museum, serial no. 77.

1. Gymnotidae. 2. Fishes--South America.

Library of Congress   AS36.P75   13-21896

AS
36
A 1

FISHES   TAHITI

Fowler, Henry W.

A New Species of Sailfish, Istiophorus brookei, from Tahiti.

(Proceedings of the Academy of Natural Sciences of Philadelphia, Volume 84, 1933, pp. 403-404)

AS
619
S

Fishes - South Africa.

Gilchrist, J. D. F.

The freshwater fishes of South Africa. 1908-1911. In Annals South African Mus. XI. 1911-

---

QL
1
H2

FISHES--SOUTH AMERICA

Garman, Samuel, 1846-

... Reports on an exploration off the west coasts of Mexico, Central and South America, and off the Galapagos Islands, in charge of Alexander Agassiz, by the U. S. Fish commission steamer "Albatross," during 1891, Lieut. Commander Z. L. Tanner, U. S. N., commanding. XXVI. The fishes. By S. Garman ... Cambridge, U. S. A., Printed for the Museum, 1899.

2 v. 97 pl. 31ᶜᵐ. (Harvard university. Museum of comparative zoölogy. Memoirs, vol. XXIV)

1. Fishes--Mexico. 2. Fishes--Central America. 3. Fishes--South America.

Library, U. S. Bur. of   Fisheries   F 17-161

QL
Fish
Pam
253

FISHES - TAHITI

Fowler, Henry W. and Bean, Barton A.

Notes on fishes obtained in Sumatra, Java and Tahiti. From Proc. U. S. Nat. Mus. v.71, art. 10, 1927.

FISHES--SOUTH AMERICA

AS
36
C51

Eigenmann, Carl H   1863-

... The *Cheirodontinæ*, a subfamily of minute characid fishes of South America, by Carl H. Eigenmann. Pittsburgh, Pub. by the authority of the Board of trustees of the Carnegie institute, 1915.

cover-title, 99 p. illus., XVII pl. (incl. fold. map) 33½ᶜᵐ. (Memoirs of the Carnegie museum. vol. VII, no. 1)
Publications of the Carnegie museum, serial no. 87.
Contributions from the Zoological laboratory of Indiana university, no. 150.

1. Chirodontinae. 2. Fishes--South America.

Library of Congress   AS36.P75 vol. 7, no. 1   16-4874

AS
36
S4

FISHES--SOUTH AMERICA

Thompson, William Francis.
Fishes collected by the United States bureau of fisheries steamer "Albatross" during 1888, between Montevideo, Uruguay, and Tome, Chile, on the voyage through the Straits of Magellan. By Will F. Thompson ...

(In U. S. National museum. Proceedings. Washington, 1916. 23½ᶜᵐ. v. 50, p. 401-476. pl. 2-6)

1. Fishes--South America. 2. Albatross (Steamer)

Library of Congress   Q11.U55 vol. 50   16-19492
————— Copy 2.   Q11.U55 vol. 50 2d set

AS
36
A 65

FISHES   TAHITI

Gudger, E. W.

A photograph and description of Masturus Lanceolatus taken at Tahiti, May, 1930. The 16th adult specimen on record.

(Amer. Mus. Novitates, No. 778, 1935. 7 pp.)

QL
632
E 34

FISHES   SOUTH AMERICA

Eigenmann, Carl H.

Fishes of western South America. I. The intercoordilleran and Amazonian lowlands of Peru; II. The high pampas of Peru, Bolivia, and northern Chile. With a revision of the Peruvian Gymnotidae, and of the genus Orestias. The University of Kentucky. Lexington. 1942. 4to. xv + 494 pp.

AS
750
D 67 c

FISHES   SUBANTARCTIC ISLAND (NZ)

Parrott, Arthur W.

Fishes from the Auckland and Campbell Islands.

(Cape Expedition, Sci. Res. of the New Zealand Subantarctic Expedition, 1941-45, Bull. No. 22, 1958)

QL
Fish Pam
149

AS
763
B-b

Reading
Room

FISHES   TAHITI

Fowler, Henry W.

Fishes of Guam, Hawaii, Samoa, and Tahiti.

(Bernice P. Bishop Museum, Bulletin No. 22, 1925.)

AS
36
C 51

FISHES   SOUTH AMERICA

Eigenmann, Carl H.

The fishes of western South America, Part I. The fresh-water fishes of northwestern South America, including Colombia, Panama, and the Pacific slopes of Ecuador and Peru, together with an appendix upon the fishes of the Rio Meta in Colombia.

(Mem. Carnegie Mus. Vol. 9(1):1-578, 39 pl. 1922)

QL
Fish
Pam
253

FISHES - SUMATRA

Fowler, Henry W. and Bean, Barton A.

Notes on fishes obtained in Sumatra, Java and Tahiti. From Proc. U. S. Nat. Mus. v.71, art.10, 1927.

AM
101
F 45 n

FISHES   TAHITI

Jindrich, Marilyn K.

Coral reef collecting in Tahiti.

(Chicago Nat. Hist. Mus. Bull., Vol. 34 (7):2-3,5, 1963)

AS
36
S4

FISHES -TAHITI

Jordan, David Starr and Snyder, John Otterbein

A list of fishes collected in Tahiti by Mr. Henry P. Bowie. Proc. U. S. Nat. Mus., v. 29, 1905.

QL
Fish
Pam
283

separate

GN
2.S
T 12

FISHES TAHITI

Rougier, Emmanuel

Essai de pisciculture. [fresh-water fishes of Tahiti]

(Bull. Soc. d'Etudes Oceaniennes, No. 11: 16-20, 1926) and note on p. 40 of No. 12, 1926

AS
720.T
R

FISHES TASMANIA

Lord, Clive E.

Additions to the fish fauna of Tasmania.

(Papers and Proc. R. Soc. Tasmania, 1924: 51-52)

GN
2.S
T

FISHES TAHITI

Lesoure, Ray

Liste de poissons de mer à identtfier.

(Bull. Soc. d'Etudes Oceaniennes, Vol. 8:3 [no. 92]:89-92, 1950)

QL
Fish
Pam
261

FISHES - TAHITI

Schmidt, John

Les anguilles de Tahiti. From La Nature, 1927.

DU
1
P

FISHES TASMANIA

Lord, Clive

A list of the fishes of Tasmania.

(Journal of the Pan-Pacific Research Institution, Vol. 2, No. 4, 1927, pp. 11-16)

AS
36
A 65

FISHES - TAHITI

Nichols, J. T.

The Tahitian black marlin, or silver marlin swordfish, by J. T. Nichols and F. R. LaMonte.

(American Museum Novitates, no. 807, May 24, 1935)

GN
2.S
T 12

FISHES TAHITI

Schmidt, Johannes

Nomenclature des poissons d'eau douce de Papeari. (Tahiti).

(Bull. Soc. d'Etudes Oceaniennes, No. 17: 176-179, 1927)

[native names given]

AS
720.T
R

FISHES TASMANIA

Lord, Clive E.

A list of the fishes of Tasmania.

(Papers and Proc. R. Soc. Tasmania, 1922: 60-73)

GN
2.S
T

FISHES TAHITI

Nordhoff, Charles

Nomenclature d'un grand nombre de poissons de Tahiti avec leurs noms tahitiens et scientifiques.

(Bull. Soc. d'Etudes Oceaniennes, No. 20: 280-282, 1927)

GN
2.S
T 12

FISHES TAHITI

Schmidt, Johannes

Poissons d'eau douce de Tahiti. (photos; names in Tahitian, with scientific equivalents)

(Bull. Soc. d'Etudes Oceaniennes, No. 20: 278-279, 1927)

AS
720.T
R

FISHES TASMANIA

Scott, O. G.

Observations on fishes of the family Galaxiidae: Parts 1-3.

(Papers and Proc. R. Soc. Tasmania, 1935: 85-112; 1937:111-143; 1940:55-70)

GN
2.S
T 12

FISHES TAHITI

Nordhoff, Charles

Some of the commoner fishes of Tahiti, with their native names.

(Bull. Soc. d'Etudes Oceaniennes, No. 20: 280-282, 1927)

QH
181.T
T 13

FISHES TAIWAN

Chen, Johnson T. F.

Check-list of the species of fishes known from Taiwan (Formosa).

(Quarterly Journal of the Taiwan Museum, 4(3/4):181-210, 1951) concluded in ibid, 6(2): 102-140, 1953

AS
720.T
R

FISHES TASMANIA

Scott, E. O. G.

Observations on some Tasmanian fishes, with descriptions of new species. Parts 1-5

(Papers and Proc. R. Soc. Tasmania, 1933: 31-53; 1934:63-74; 1935:113-130; 1936:139-160; 1941:45-54)

GN
2.S
T 12

FISHES TAHITI

Pisciculture. (introduction of fish into Tahiti: rainbow trout, carp, catfish, black bass)

(Bull. Soc. d'Etudes Oceaniennes, No. 20: 283-284, 1927)

QH
181.T
T 13

FISHES TAIWAN

Johnson, T. F. Chen

Check-list of the species of fishes known from Taiwan (Formosa).

(Quarterly Journal of the Taiwan Museum, Vol. 5(4):305-341, 1952)

AS
720.T
R

FISHES TASMANIA

Scott, E. O. G.

On a new genus of fishes of the family Galaxiidae.

(Papers and Proc. R. Soc. Tasmania, 1934: 41-46)

AS
145
B

FISHES TAHITI

Poll, M.

Les poissons de Tahiti recueillis par G. A. de Witte.

(Bull. Musée royal d'Hist. Nat. de Belgique, Tome 18, no. 61, 20 pp. 1942)

QL
752
U 58

FISHES TAIWAN

Nakamura, Hiroshi

Report of an investigation of the spearfishes of Formosan waters. Translated from the Japanese language by W. G. Van Campen.

(U. S. Dept. of the Interior, Fish and Wildlife Service, Special Sci. Rept.:Fisheries No. 153, 1955)

AS
720.T
R

FISHES TASMANIA

Whitley, Gilbert P.

R. M. Johnston's memoranda relating to the fihses of Tasmania.

(Papers and Proc. R. Soc. Tasmania, 1928: 44-68)

QL
Fishes
Pam. 382   FISHES   THAILAND

Fowler, Henry W.

     Zoological results of the third de Schauensee Siamese expedition. Part IX,--additional fishes obtained in 1936.

     (Proc. of the Acad. of Nat. Sci. Philadelphia, Vol. 91, 1939, p. 39-76, 1939)

QL
1
F   FISHES - TROPICS

Meek, Seth Eugene, 1859-1914.
     ... New species of fishes from tropical America, by Seth Eugene Meek ... Chicago, 1909.

     1 p. l., p. 207-211. 24cm. (Field Columbian museum. Publication 132. Zoölogical series. vol. VII, no. 7)

1. Fishes--Tropics.

Library of Congress   QL1.F4 vol. 7, no. 7   9—17310
                      [a20d2]

QL
1
F   FISHES--U. S.

Hay, Oliver Perry, 1846-
     ... On some collections of fishes, by O. P. Hay ... Chicago, 1896.

     1 p. l., 85-97 p. 24½cm. (Field Columbian museum. Publication 12. Zoölogical series. vol. I, no. 4)

1. Fishes--U. S.

Library of Congress   QL1.F4   4—10469
————— Copy 2.   QL.622.H42

QL
Fish
Pam.
351   FISHES   THAILAND

Pearse, A. S.

     The Gobies at Paknam.

     (Jour. of the Siam Soc., Nat. Hist. Supp., Vol. IX, No. 2, 1933.)

QL
Fishes
Pam.
595   FISHES   TROPICS

Tropical Fish Hobbyist

Summer, 1958.

Jersey City, N.J.   8vo.

AS
36
S4   FISHES--U. S.

Snyder, John Otterbein, 1867-
     Notes on a collection of fishes made by Dr. Edgar A. Mearns from rivers tributary to the Gulf of California. By John Otterbein Snyder ...

     (In U. S. National museum. Proceedings. Washington, 1916. 23½cm. v. 49, p. 573-586. 1 illus., pl. 76-77)

1. Fishes--U. S.   I. Mearns, Edgar Alexander, 1856-

Library of Congress   Q11.U55 vol. 49   16-11806
————— Copy 2.   Q11.U55 vol. 49   2d set

QL
Fish
Pam.
352   FISHES   THAILAND

Pearse, A. S.

     Parasites of Siamese Fishes and Crustaceans.

     (Jour. of the Siam Soc., Nat. Hist. Supp., Vol. IX, No. 2, 1933.)

AS
750
N   FISHES   TUAMOTUS

Albright, Harry

Death lurks in a coral lagoon.

(Honolulu Advertiser, Feb. 5, 1939)

AS
36
S6   FISHES   UNITED STATES, WESTERN

Rutter, Cloudsley, d. 1903.
     ... Notes on fresh water fishes on the Pacific slope of North America. By Cloudsley Rutter ... Palo Alto, Cal., Leland Stanford jr. university, 1896.

     2 p. l., [245]-267, [1] p., 1 l. illus. 24½cm. (Leland Stanford junior university publications. Contributions to biology from the Hopkins seaside laboratory. VI)

     Reprint from the Proceedings of the California academy of sciences, series 2, vol. VI.

1. Fishes--Western states.

Library of Congress   QL1.L53   7-10273

AS
36
S5   FISHES   THAILAND

Smith, Hugh M.

     The fresh-water fishes of Siam, or Thailand.

     (U. S. Nat. Mus., Bull. 188, 1945)

AS
36
A16   FISHES   TUAMOTUS

Fowler, Henry W.

     The fishes of the George Vanderbilt South Pacific Expedition, 1937.

     (Acad. of Nat. Sci., Philadelphia, Monograph No. 2, 1938)

AS
36
S4   FISHES--VENEZUELA

Van Cleave, Harley Jones, 1886-
     Two new genera and species of acanthocephalous worms from Venezuelan fishes. By H. J. Van Cleave ...

     (In U. S. National museum. Proceedings. Washington, 1921. 23½cm. v. 58, p. 455-466. pl. 27-28 on 1 L)

     "Literature cited": p. 464.

1. Acanthocephala. 2. Fishes--Venezuela.

Library of Congress   Q11.U55 vol. 58   21-21449
                  [5]

QL
656.5
F 78   FISHES   TONGA

Fowler, Henry W.

AS
763
B-b

     Fishes of the tropical central Pacific.

     (Bernice P. Bishop Museum, Bulletin No. 38,

Reading
Room   1927; Whippoorwill Expedition, Publication No. 1)

AS
36
A 65   FISHES   TUAMOTUS

Nichols, J. T.

     New Pacific flying-fishes collected by Templeton Crocker, by J. T. Nichols and C. M. Breder, Jr.

     (American Museum Novitates, no. 821, 1935)

QH
109.P
N 53   FISHES   VIRGIN ISLANDS

Nichols, John Treadwell

     The fishes of Porto Rico and the Virgin Islands.

     IN Scientific survey of Porto Rico and the Virgin Islands. Vol. 10:2-3, 1929-1930.

AS
36
A 16   FISHES   TONGAREVA

Fowler, Henry W.

     The fishes of the George Vanderbilt South Pacific Expedition, 1937.

     (Acad. of Nat. Sci., Philadelphia, Monograph No. 2, 1938)

FISHES   TUAMOTUS

See also

FISHES   RAROIA

AS
763
B-b   FISHES   WAKE ISLAND

Fowler, Henry W.

and
QL
Fish Pam
164

     Fishes of Hawaii, Johnston Island and Wake Island, by Henry W. Fowler and Stanley C. Ball.

     (Bulletin No. 26, Bernice P. Bishop Museum,

Reading
Room   1925; Tanager Expedition, Publication No. 2)

AS
36
A4   FISHES - TRINIDAD

Nichols, John Treadwell, 1883-
     Fishes from South Trinidad Islet. By John Treadwell Nichols and Robert Cushman Murphy ... New York, 1914.

     cover-title, p. 261-266. illus. 25cm.

     "Author's edition, extracted from Bulletin of the American museum of natural history, vol. XXXIII, art. XX ..."

1. Fishes--Trinidad.   I. Murphy, Robert Cushman.

                     F 14-49
Library, U. S. Bur. of   Fisheries

QH
104
U 58 o   FISHES   UNITED STATES

Carson, Rachel L.

     Fishes of the Middle West.

     (U. S. Fish and Wildlife Service, Conservation Bulletin 34, 1943)

QL
656.5
F 78   FISHES   WASHINGTON ISLAND

Fowler, Henry W.

AS
763
B-b

     Fishes of the tropical central Pacific.

     (Bernice P. Bishop Museum, Bulletin No. 38,

Reading
Room   1927; Whippoorwill Expedition, Publication No. 1)

QL 1 F

FISHES - WASHINGTON (STATE) - OLYMPIC/
MOUNTAINS

Meek, Seth Eugene, 1859-1914.

... Notes on a collection of cold-blooded vertebrates from the Olympic Mountains, by S. E. Meek ... Chicago, 1899.

1 p. l., 225-236 p. 24½ᵐ. (Field Columbian museum. Publication 31. Zoological series. vol. I, no. 12)

1. Fishes — Washington (State) — Olympic Mountains. 2. Reptiles — Washington (State)—Olympic Mountains.

Library of Congress   QL1.F4
———— Copy 2.   QL212.M5   4—10569

GN 2.S P 76

FISHES NATIVE NAMES HAWAII

Titcomb, Margaret

Native use of fish in Hawaii. With the collaboration of Mary Kawena Pukui.

(Mem. Polynesian Soc., No. 29, 1952)

GN 667 .Q N

FISH-'HOOKS ---Australia

Roth, Walter E.

In his North Queensland Ethnography
Bull. 7.

QL 5 B61

FISHES - WEST INDIES

Breder, C M Jr

Fishes: Bulletin Bingham Oceanographic collection, v.1, art.1, 1927.

QL 752 U 58 c

FISHES NATIVE NAMES PHILIPPINE IS.

Herre, Albert W.

English and local common names of Philippine fishes. By Albert W. Herre and Agustin F. Umali.

(U. S. Dept.of the Int., Fish and Wildlife Service, Circular 14, 1948)

GN Ethn. Pam. 3413

FISHHOOKS-CALIFORNIA

Robinson, Eugene

Shell fishhooks of the California coast.

(Occ. Papers, Bernice P. Bishop Museum, Vol. 17, 1942, No. 4, pp. 57-65)

FISHES WEST INDIES

Dunlop, W. R.

Poisonous fishes in the West Indies.

(West Indian Bulletin, Vol. 16, 1917, pp. 158-167)

UH

QL Fish Pam. 558

FISHES AS FOOD

Nichols, J. T.

Certain marine tropical fishes as food.
By J. T. Nichols and L. L. Mowbray.

(Copeia, No. 48, pp. 77-84, Sept. 1917)

GN Ethn. Pam. 4450

FISHHOOKS ECUADOR

Zevallos, Carlos

Los Anzuelos de Concha y su valor como elemento diagnóstico en las Culturas Ecuatorians. By Carlos Zevallos M. y Olaf Holm.

(Reprint, Akten des 34, Internationalen Amerikanistenkongresses, pp. 404-410, 1960)

AS 71 C 96

FISHES WEST INDIES

Fowler, Henry W.

The fishes of Hispaniola.

(Mem. Soc. Cubana de Hist. Nat., Vol. 21(1): 81-115, pl. 21-26, 1952)

AS 36 S5

AS 36 S

QL 1 H-M Vol 22

FISHHAWK (SHIP)

Goode, George Brown, 1851-1896.

... Oceanic ichthyology, a treatise on the deep sea and pelagic fishes of the world, based chiefly upon the collections made by the steamers "Blake," "Albatross," and "Fishhawk" in the northwestern Atlantic, with an atlas containing 417 figures. By George Brown Goode and Tarleton H. Bean. Pub. in connection with the National museum and the Smithsonian institution. Cambridge, U. S. A., Printed for the Museum, 1896.

3 p. l., iii-xxxv, 26*, 70, 2, 71-553 p. illus., pl. and atlas of 3 p. l., iii-xxiii, 26* o., cxxiii pl. 32ᵐ. (Memoirs of the Museum of comparative zoölogy at Harvard college. vol. XXII)

(Continued on next card)   A 21-447

GN 662 B 36

FISH HOOKS HAWAII

Beasley, Harry G.

Pacific island records: Fish hooks...London. 1928. pp. 48-53.

AS 36 S 71

FISHES-WEST INDIES

Herre, Albert W. C. T.

Notes on a collection of fishes from Antigua and Barbadoes, British West Indies.

(Stanford Univ. Pub., Biological Sciences, Vol. 7, No. 2, 1942, pp. 1-21)

GN 447.T9 M 56

FISHHOOKS

Mérite, Edouard

Les pièges: étude sur les engins de capture utilisés dans le monde, technique du piège... Avec 107 figures dans le texte dessinées par l'auteur et 16 planches hors texte. Préface de Raymond Furon. Payot, Paris, 1942. R8vo. 327 pp.

GN Ethn. Pam. 4179

FISHHOOKS - HAWAII

Emory, Kenneth P.

Hawaiian archaeology: fishhooks. By Kenneth P. Emory, William J. Bonk, and Yosihiko H. Sinoto.

(BPBM Special Publication 47; 1959)

AS 36 A4

FISHES - WEST INDIES

Nichols, John Treadwell, 1883-

Gobiosoma longum and *Rivulus heyei*, new fishes from the West Indian fauna. By John Treadwell Nichols ... New York, 1914.

cover-title, p. 143-144. illus. 25ᵐ.

"Author's edition, extracted from Bulletin of the American museum of natural history. vol. XXXIII, art. x, p. 143-144. New York, February 26, 1914."

1. Gobiidae 2. Poeciliidae 3. Fishes—West Indies.

Library, U. S. Bur. of   Fisheries   F 14-89

GN Ethn.Pam. 3156

FISH HOOKS AFRICA

Lagercrantz, S.

Fish-hooks in Africa and their distribution.

(Riksmuseets Etnografiska Avdelning, Smärre Meddelanden, Nr. 12, 1934. Stockholm)

GN 875.H M 11

FISHHOOKS HAWAII

McAllister, J. Gilbert

Archaeology of Kahoolawe.

(Bernice P. Bishop Museum, Bull. 115, 1933)

FISHES, see also

MARINE FAUNA; also names of special fishes, and of classes, orders, etc.

AS 720.V M

FISHHOOKS AUSTRALIA

Massola, Aldo

Australian fish hooks and their distribution.

(National Museum of Victoria, Melbourne, Memoirs, No. 22, Part 1, 1956)

GN 2.S P 76

FISHHOOKS HAWAII

Sinoto, Yosihito H.

Chronology of Hawaiian fishhooks.

(Jour. Poly. Soc., 71(2): 162-166, 1962)

AS
472
A83-j

FISH-HOOKS   INDIA

Sarkar, Shri Haribishnu

    Fish-hooks from the Indus Valley.

    (Journal of the Asiatic Society, 19(2): 133-140,1953)

GN
Ethn.Pam.
3781

FISH-HOOKS   MAORI

Skinner, H. D.

    Some Maori fish-hooks from Otago.

    (Trans. New Zealand Inst., Vol. 51:267-268, 1919)

QL
Fish.Pam.
375

FISHHOOKS   PACIFIC

Gudger, E. W.

    The distribution of Ruvettus, the oilfish, throughout the South Seas, as shown by the distribution of the peculiar wooden hook used in its capture.

    (The American Naturalist, Vol. LXII, 1928, pp. 467-477)

GN
2.S
P 76

FISH HOOKS   MAORI

Beckett, Peter

    Two fish hook parts from a midden in Wellington.

    (Jour. Poly. Soc., 62(2):198, 1953)

GN
2.S
P 76

FISHHOOKS   MAORI

Teviotdale, David

    Notes on stone and moa-bone fish-hook shanks in the Otago University Museum.

    (Journal of the Polynesian Society, 38: 270-280, 1929.)

GN
Ethn.Pam.
2860

FISHHOOKS   PACIFIC

Gudger, E(ugene) W(illis)

    Wooden hooks used for catching sharks and Ruvettus in the South Seas: a study of their variation and distribution.

    (Anthrop. Papers, American Mus. of Nat. Hist. Vol. 28, 1927, pp. 212-343)

GN
2.S
P 76

FISHHOOKS   MAORI

Dawson, Elliot Watson

    Excavation of a Maori burial, at Longbeach, Otago; with notes on associated artifacts.

    (Jour. Poly. Soc., Vol. 58(2):58-63, 1949)

GN
2.S
P 76

FISHHOOKS   MAORI

Teviotdale, David

    Oruarangi pa. By David Teviotdale and H.D. Skinner.

    (Journal of the Polynesian Soc., Vol. 56: 340-356, 1947)

GN
Ethn.
Pam.
3413

FISHHOOKS-PACIFIC

Robinson, Eugene

    Shell fishhooks of the California coast.

    (Occ. Papers, Bernice P. Bishop Museum, Vol. 17, 1942, No. 4, pp. 57-65)

GN
2.S
P 76

FISHHOOKS   MAORI

Fairfield, F. G.

    Maori fish-hooks from Manukau Heads, Auckland.

    (Journal of the Polynesian Society, 42: 145-155, 1933.)

GN
662
B 36

FISHHOOKS   MICRONESIA

Beasley, Harry G.

    Pacific island records: fish hooks. London. 1928.

GN
2.S
T

FISHHOOKS   PACIFIC

Stephen-Chauvet

    Enquete sur les hamecons anciens des iles du Pacifique.

    (Soc. des Etudes Oceaniennes, Bull. No. 91, (Tome 8:2) 1950:41-43)

AS
750
A 89

FISHHOOKS   MAORI

Fisher, V. F.

    The material culture of Oruarangi, Matatoki, Thames (New Zealand).
    I. Bone ornaments and implements.
    II. Fish-hooks.
    III. Stone implements and ornaments.
    IV. Musical instruments.

    (Records of the Auckland Inst. and Mus., Vol 1, pp. 275-286, 287-300; Vol. 2:15-27, 111-118, 1934-1937)

GN
2.1
A-M

FISH HOOKS   NEW GUINEA

Balfour, Henry

    Note on a new kind of fish-hook from Goodenough Island, d'Entrecasteaux Group, New Guinea.

    (Man, vol. 15, 1915, no. 9, p. 17, pl. B)

GN
2.S
P 76

FISHHOOKS   PITCAIRN ISLANDS

Green, R.C.

    Pitcairn Island fishhooks in stone.

    (Jour. Poly. Soc., 68(1):21-22, 1959)

GN
2.M
E 84

FISH HOOKS   MAORI

Phillipps, W. J.

    A collection of Maori fish-hooks, ect.

    (Ethnos, Vol. 13:44-53, 1948)

GN
2.1
A-m

FISH HOOKS   ONGTONG JAVA

Beasley, H. G.

    Notes on the fishing appliances from Ongtong Java.

    (Man, vol. XXXVII, 1937. pp. 58-60)

GN
2.S
P 76

FISHHOOKS   POLYNESIA

Lockerbie, Leslie

    Excavations at Kings Rock, Otago, with a discussion of the fish-hook barb as an ancient feature of Polynesian culture.

    (Journal of the Polynesian Society, Vol. 49, 1940, pp. 393-446)

GN
2.S
P 76

FISH-HOOKS MAORI

Skinner, H. D.

    A classification of the fish-hooks of Murihiku.

    (Journal of the Polynesian Society, Vol. 51, 1942, pp. 208-221; 256-286)

GN
662
B 36

FISH HOOKS PACIFIC

Beasley, Harry G.

    Pacific island records: Fish hooks...London 1928.

GN
2.S
M 26

FISH HOOKS   RAROTONGA

Campbell, J. D.

    The "Paru Matau" of Rarotonga.

    (Mankind, Vol. 1, pp. 112-114, 1932)

GN 2.1 A-M — FISH HOOKS SOLOMON ISLANDS

Woodford, C. M.

Fish-hooks from the Solomon Islands.

(Man, vol. 18, 1918, no. 73, pp. 130-132, figs. 1-9)

GN 423 H 81 — FISHING

Hornell, James

Fishing in many waters. Cambridge. At the University Press. 1950. R8vo. xv+210 pp, 36 pl.

Biblio-film 33 — FISHING

Radlkofer, Ludwig A. T.

Ueber fischvengiftende Pflanzen

(Münch. Akad. Sitzungsber. 16, 1887, pp. 379-416)

FISHING

see also

FISHHOOKS
FISH NARCOTIZING
FISH POISONING
FISH TRAPS
FISH WEIRS
NETS AND NETTING

GN 423 K 91 — FISHING

Krause, Eduard

Vorgeschichtliche Fischereigeräte und neuere Vergleichsstücke...Berlin. 1904

GN 799.F5 R 23 — FISHING

AS 36 S

Rau, Charles

Prehistoric fishing in Europe and North America. Wahsington. 1884.

(Smithsonian Contributions to Knowledge, 509)

GN Ethn.Pam. 3030 — FISHING

Balfour, Henry

Kite-fishing. Cambridge. University Press. 1913. 26 pp.

QL 633.G K84 — FISHING

Krünitz, J   G

Oeconomische- technologische Encyklopadie od allgemein: system der Staats., Stadt., Haus und Landwirthschaft in alphabetischer Ordnung.

Brunn, Florke, 1787-1907.
Library has v. 13, 1788.

AS 36 W 2 — FISHING-AINU

Hewes, Gordon W.

The Ainu double foreshaft toggle harpoon and western North America.

(Journal of the Washington Acad. of Sci., Vol. 32, 1942, pp. 93-104)

GN 2.S O 15 — FISHING

Bouge, L. J.

Reconstitution du harpon ancien des Îles Marquises avec flèche en os humain ou en bois dur.

(Journal de la Soc. des Océanistes, Vol. 4: 148-151, 1948)

[spear fishing]

QL 618 L 12 — FISHING

La Blanchère, H. de

La Peche et les Poissons. Nouveau Dictionnaire Général des Peches. Précédé d'une préface par Aug. Dumeril...1100 illustrations dessinées et coloricos par A. Mesnel. Paris. Librairie de Ch. Delagrave et Cie. 1868. R8vo. xv + 859 pp.

GN 1 A — FISHING ALGONQUIN INDIANS

Willoughby, Charles C.

The Virginia Indians in the seventeenth century.

(Amer. Anthrop., 1907, pp. 57-86)

QL 617 B 87 — FISHING

(Brookes, R.)

The art of angling, rock and sea-fishing... London. 1740.

GN Ethn.Pam. 3830 — FISHING

Leth, T.

Two kinds of fishing implements: 1. The plunge basket (Stulpkorb) in Africa and elsewhere 2. The circular cast-net in Africa. By T. Leth and K. G. Lindblom.

(Riksmuseets Etnografiska Avdelning, Smarre Meddelanden, Nr. 11, 1933)

AS 720.N R — FISHING -- AUSTRALIA

Matthews, R.H.

Aboriginal fisheries at Brewarrina.... in Roy. Soc. N.S.W. XXXVII, pp.146-156, illus. Sydney, 1903.

QL Fishes Pam.463 — FISHING

Clark, Denis

New worlds to explore.

(Clipper Travel, April, 1950, pp. 12-13)

[undersea fishing with a spear]

GN 447.T9 M 56 — FISHING

Mérite, Edouard

Les pièges: étude sur les engins de capture utilisés dans le monde, technique du piège... Avec 107 figures dans le texte dessinées par l'auteur et 16 planches hors texte. Préface de Raymond Furon. Payot, Paris, 1942. R8vo. 327 pp.

QL 636 Ro R 85 — Fishing - Australia

Roughley, T. C.

In his Fishes of Australia. (Tech. Mus. Sydney. Tech. Ed. Ser. 21, 1916), pp 255-272.

Note.- Stone dams pp 261-262.

NOV 1 '17

GN 423 D 86 — FISHING

Duhamel du Monceau, Henry Louis

Abhandlung von den Fischerenen und Geschichte der Fische...Leipzig und Konigsberg. 1773.

GN 421 M 88 — FISHING

Mortillet, L. L. G. de

Origines de la chasse, de la peche et de l'agriculture, par Gabriel de Mortillet...Paris. 1890.

AS 36 A 5 — FISHING BORABORA

Menard, Wilson

A South Sea fish drive.

(Natural History, Vol. 56:400-403, 1948)

QL
Fishes
Pam.
427

FISHES BIKINI ATOLL

Woods, Loren P.

Ecology and distribution of reef fishes at Bikini Atoll.

(The American Soc. of Ichthyologists and Herpetologists, 27th Annual Meeting, Aug. 27-30, 1947, Higgins Lake, Michigan)

AS
36
A 5

FISHING COOK ISLANDS

Nordhoff, Charles B.

Fishing for the oilfish: native methods of deep-sea fishing for Ruvettus pretiosus at Atiu, Hervey Group, and elsewhere in the South Seas.

also

(Natural History, Vol. 28;40-45, 1928)

QL
Fishes
Pam. 506

Separate.

GN
2.S
F 47

FISHING FIJI

Toganivalu, Deve

Fishing, Being a paper written by Deve Toganivalu, the Roko Tui Bua; and translated and read before the Fijian Society on October 10, 1914, by Mr. G.A.F.W.Beauclerc.

7-11)

(Trans. of the Fijian Society. 1914. pp.

(but there are 2 sets of pages so numbered)

AS
522.B
S 24

FISHING BORNEO

Harrisson, Tom

Fishing in the far uplands of Borneo.

(Sarawak Museum Journal, Vol. V:274-287, 1950)

GN
2.S
P 76

FISHING ELLICE ISLANDS

Turbott, I. G.

Fishing for flying fish in the Gilbert and Ellice Islands.

(Journal of the Polynesian Society, Vol. 59(4):349-367, 1951)

GN
2.S
F 47

FISHING FIJI

Toganivalu, D.

Turtle fishing. Habits and customs of the Galoa fishermen, translated by W. Hamilton Hunter ...

(Trans. Fijian Society, 1912-1913, pp. 47-51)

GN
Ethn.Pam
3423

FISHING CALIFORNIA

Hewes, Gordon W.

Economic and geographical relations of aboriginal fishing in northern California.

(California Fish and Game, Vol. 28, 1942, pp. 103-110)

GN
2.M
A

FISHING ESKIMOS

Wissler, Clark, 1870–

... Harpoons and darts in the Stefánsson collection, by Clark Wissler. New York, The Trustees, 1916.

1 p. l., p. 397-443. illus. 24½ᶜᵐ. (Anthropological papers of the American museum of natural history. vol. XIV, pt. II)

1. Eskimos—Implements. 2. Stefánsson, Vilhjálmur, 1879–   I. Title.

17-28724

Library of Congress   GN2.A27 vol. 14, pt. 2

GN
585.F
S 61

FISHING FINLAND

Sirelius, U. T.

Über die Sperrfischerei bei den Finnisch-Ugrischen Völkern... 1906.

F
870
H72

FISHING - CALIFORNIA

Holder, Charles Frederick

The channel islands of California.

Chicago, McClurg, 1910.   365p.   pls.

GN
2.S
F 47

FISHING FIJI

Deane, W.

Fijian fishing and its superstitions.

(Trans. Fijian Society, 1908-1910, pp. 57-61)

QL
Fishes
Pam.463

FISHING GILBERT ISLANDS

Grimble, Sir Arthur

Fishing for man-eating sharks.

(Clipper Travel, April, 1950, pp. 18-20)

QL
427
P 11

FISHING CAROLINE ISLANDS

Ikebe, Kenzo

A survey of tuna fishing grounds in the Marshall and Caroline Islands.

(South Sea Fishery News [Nanyō Suisan Jōhō], vol. 5(1):6-9, 1941)

Translated from Japanese, Pacific Oceanic Fishery Investigations, Translation No. 15

QL
Fishes
Pam.
395

FISHING FIJI

Hornell, James

Report on the fisheries of Fiji. Suva, 1940. vi + 87 pp. 8vo. Government Printer.

GR
Folklore
Pam.
97

FISHING GILBERT ISLANDS

Grimble, Sir Arthur

Gilbertese creation myth; Priest and pagan and The sorcerer's revenge. Fishing for man-eating sharks.

(The Listener, Jan. 12, 1950; Apr. 5, 19, 1951)

GN
2.I
A-4

FISHING COCOS-KEELING ISLANDS

Gibson-Hill, C. A.

Boats and fishing on the Cocos-Keeling Islands.

(Journal of the Royal Anthrop. Inst. Great Britain and Ireland, Vol. 76 (1):13-23, 1946)

GN
2.1
A-M

FISHING FIJI

Liversidge, A.

Vanishing customs in the Fiji Islands.

(Man, vol. 21, 1921, no. 81, pp. 133-136)

GN
2.S
P 76

FISHING GILBERT ISLANDS

Turbott, I. G.

Fishing for flying fish in the Gilbert and Ellice Islands.

(Journal of the Polynesian Society, Vol. 59(4):349-367, 1951)

QH
1
M 18

FISHING COMORES ISLANDS

Fourmanoir, P.

Ichthyologie et pêche aux Comores.

(Mémoires de l'Institut Scientifique de Madagascar, Ser. A. Biologie Animale, Tome IX:187-239, 1954)

DU
1
P

FISHING FIJI

New tuna industry for Fiji; Harold Gatty bringing modern ships and equipment into S. Pacific.

65, 1948)

(Pacific Islands Monthly, Vol. 19(4):21-24,

QL
Fishes
Pam. 477

FISHING GREAT BARRIER REEF

Coates, George

Fishing on the Barrier Reef and inshore. Printed and published by T. Willmett and Sons... Townsville, Australia. 8vo. 72 pp. n.d.

DU
647
G 91

FISHING GUAM

Thompson, Laura

Fishing in Guam.

(The Guam Recorder, Vol. 18, No. 2, 1941,
p. 54-56, 80-81)

QL
627
U-b

FISHING HAWAII

Beckley, Emma Metcalf (Mrs.)

Hawaiian fishing implements and methods of
fishing.

(U. S. Fish Commission, Bull. 6;245-250,
1886)

QL
627
U-a

FISHING -- HAWAIIAN ISLANDS

Cobb, John N.

Commercial fisheries of the Hawaiian
Islands in 1903. In U. S. Bureau of Fisheries report, 1904. pp. 435 - 512.

GN
Ethn.Pam.
3934

FISHING HANA

Huge haul of akule is made by Hawaiian fishing hui at Hana.

IN Collection of clippings gathered by
Martha W. Beckwith, pp. 31

GN
Ethn.Pam
305

FISHING HAWAII

Beckley, Emma Metcalf (Mrs.)

Hawaiian fisheries and methods of fishing
with an account of the fishing implements used
by the natives of the Hawaiian islands. Advertiser Steam Print. Honolulu, 1883. 21 pp.

QL
Fishes
Pam.
446

FISHING HAWAII

Corboy, Philip M.

Sport fishing in Hawaii.

(Honolulu Advertiser, July 25, 1948)

GN
Ethn.
Pam.
3920

FISHING HAWAII

Ackerman, Jack

Skin diving and spear fishing.

(Forecast, Outrigger Canoe Club, Vol. 12(12):
16-18, 1953)

QL
Fishes
Pam.
530

FISHING HAWAII

Benson, Jack

Briny business. Relive a day with a sampan
crew- you'll see what makes fishing for Hawaiian
tuna an exciting, picturesque and briny business.

(Hawaiian Mag. Sect., Saturday Star-Bull.
Jan. 2, 1954, pp. 6-7)

DU
620
P

FISHING HAWAII

Dole, Sanford B.

Aquamarine

(Paradise of the Pacific, Vol. 27, 1914,No.
12, p. 41-44)

DU
620
P

FISHING HAWAII

An artist of old Oahu passes.

(Paradise of the Pacific, Vol. 41, No. 4,
1928, p. 14)

QL
Fishes
Pam.
528

FISHING HAWAII

Biehl, Bert

Outdoors-Hawaii; sportsmen's guide. (Fishing) Published by Bert Biehl. Honolulu. 1953.
8vo. 80 pp.

Storage
Case
3

FISHING HAWAII

Emory, Kenneth Pike

Hawaii, Kailua. Chart of fishing grounds
off Kailua; data supplied by father of T. K.
Maunupau, 1933.

THIS MAY BE USED ONLY BY MEMBERS OF THE
MAUNUPAU family and K.P.EMORY

DU
620
P

FISHING HAWAII

Bag net fishing in Hawaii.

(Paradise of the Pacific, Vol. 21, 1908,
No. 4, p. 18-21)

DU
620
P

FISHING HAWAII

Blue sea and inshore fishing with the nets.

(Paradise of the Pacific, Vol. 21, 1908,
No. 5, p. 18-20)

DU
621
H3

FISHING - HAWAIIAN ISLANDS

Field, H. G.

Game fishing in the Hawaiian waters,
Thrums Hawaiian Annual, 1917,pp.86-93.

DU
620
F

FISHING HAWAII

Baker, Albert S.

South Point's "canoe holes".

(The Friend, Vol. 118 (4):4, 1948)

[old mooring holes for fishing canoes]

GN
Ethn.Pam.
3254

FISHING HAWAII

Bryan, Edwin H., Jr.

Fish and fishing in Hawaii. (Castle &
Cooke booklet, No. 3). Honolulu. 1938. 10 pp.

2 copies

DU
620
P

FISHING HAWAII

Field, H. Gooding

Game fishing in Hawaiian waters.

(Paradise of the Pacific, Vol. 29, 1916,
no. 2, pp. 22-23)

DU
620
P

FISHING HAWAII

Baldwin, Paul

Sea-fishing of Kauai.

(Paradise of the Pacific, Vol. 49, No. 7,
1937, pp. 13,29,30)

QL
627
U-a

QL
627
U-b

QL
Fish
Pam. 119

FISHING -- HAWAIIAN ISLANDS

Cobb, John N.

Commercial fisheries of the Hawaiian
Islands. In U. S. Fish Com. Rep. 1901.
pp. 383-499. illus.
Also reprinted in Bul. U.S. Fish Com.
XXIII, 2. pp. 717-765. 1903.

Also separate.

AM
101
F 45 n

FISHING HAWAII

Fish collecting in Hawaii.

(Chicago Nat. Hist. Bull. 32(8):6-8, 1961)

QL
Fishes
Pam.
507

FISHING HAWAII

Fishing rights of Hawaii date back to grants of kings.

(The Honolulu Advertiser, March 11, 1922)

DU
620
H 32

FISHING HAWAII

Hawaiian fishing implements and methods of fishing.

(Hawaii's Young People, Vol. 18, no. 9, 1913, pp. 257-266)

DU
Pac.Pam.
491

FISHING HAWAII

Kukahi, Joseph L.

Ke Kumulipo he Moolelo Hawaii. Honolulu. 1902. 8vo.

QL
Fishes
Pam.
530

FISHING HAWAII

Frazier, Tom

Lobsterman's paradise. Island fishermen brave needle-toothed eels and other dangers...

(Hawaiian Mag. Sect., Saturday Star-Bull. Jan. 2, 1954) pp. 4-5

DU
620
P

FISHING HAWAII

Hawaiian fishing implements and methods of fishing.

(Paradise of the Pacific, Vol. 24, 1911, No. 9, p. 12-14; No. 10, p. 18-19; Vol. 25, 1912, No. 4, p. 18-20; No. 5, p. 21-22)

QL
Fish Pam.
408

FISHING HAWAII

Lang, Freeman

A complete and accurate description of fishing in the islands.   (Hawaii) Honolulu, 1944. 71 pp. 12mo.

DU
620
P

FISHING HAWAII

Fredlund, Melvin L.

A hukilau in Hawaii.

(Paradise of the Pacific, Vol. 44, No. 4, 1931, pp. 25-27)

GN
Ethn.Pam.
3934

FISHING HAWAII

Huge haul of akule is made by Hawaiian fishing hui at Hana.
IN Collection of clippings gathered by Martha W. Beckwith, pp. 31

DU
620
P

FISHING HAWAII

Luring the octopus.

(Paradise of the Pacific, Vol. 21, 1908, No. 8, p. 21)

GN
1
A

FISHING HAWAII

Green, Laura S.

Hawaiian Household Customs, by Laura S. Green and M. W. Beckwith.

(American Anthropologist, N. S., Vol. 30, 1928, pp. 1-17)

GN
423
K 12

FISHING HAWAII

Kahaulelio, A. D.

Fishing lore.

(Ka Nupepa Kuokoa, 1902: Feb. 28, Mar. 7,14, 21,28, Apr. 4, May 2,16,23,30, June 20,27, July 4

Translated by Mary Kawena Pukui

Typed copy

GN
875.H
M 11

FISHING HAWAII

McAllister, J. Gilbert

Archaeology of Kahoolawe.

(Bernice P. Bishop Museum, Bull. 115, 1933)

DU
620
P

FISHING HAWAII

Hand fishing.

(Paradise of the Pacific, Vol. 21, 1908, No. 1, p. 8)

GN
671.H2
K 15

FISHING HAWAII

Kamakau, Samuel Manaiakalani

Mo'olelo Hawaii: Hawaii traditions.
(copy of ms offered for publication. typed, bound under two covers.) Translated by Mary Pukui. Edited by Martha W. Beckwith. (received 1939)

GN
671.H2
M 15

FISHING HAWAII

MacKellar, Jean Scott

Hawaii goes fishing. Graphic Books. New York. 1956. 8vo. ix + 13-160 pp.

GN
671.H2
H 23

FISHING HAWAII

Handy, E. S. C., and others

Ancient Hawaiian Civilization, pp. 101-108; Aku and Ahi Fishing, by Thomas Maunupau.

S
17.H3
H 38

FISHING HAWAII

Kelly, H. L.

Problems connected with the fishing industry in Hawaii.

(Hawaiian Forester and Agriculturist, vol. 27, no. 1, 1930, pp. 5-11)

DU
620
P

FISHING HAWAII

MacLeod, A. S.

The hukilau on the beach.

(Paradise of the Pacific, Vol. 48(10):13,30-31; 1936)

DU
620
P

FISHING HAWAII

Hawaii's intrepid toilers of the sea.

(Paradise of the Pacific, Vol. 21, 1908, No. 6, p. 14-16)

Storage
Case
3

FISHING HAWAII

Kelsey, Theodore

Ethnological notes on fishing, adzemaking...

GN
Ethn.Pam.
3934

FISHING HAWAII

Makapuu fish goddess again has disappeared.

IN Collection of clippings made by Martha W. Beckwith, p. 40

GN
Ethn. Pam.
744
745

FISHING HAWAII

Massee, Edward K.

Fishing rights in Hawaii. Read befor the Bar
Association of Hawaii at their annual meeting,
June 19, 1926. Honolulu. Star-Bulletin. 1926
15 pp.

DU
620
P

FISHING HAWAII

Old and new methods of deep-sea fishing.

(Paradise of the Pacific, Vol. 20, 1907,
No. 11, pp. 19-21)

AS
763
B-o

FISHING--HAWAIIAN ISLANDS.

Stokes, John F G.

... Fish poisoning in the Hawaiian Islands, with notes
on the custom in southern Polynesia. By John F. G.
Stokes. Honolulu, Hawaii, Bishop museum press, 1921.

17 p. pl. XVII-XIX on 2 l. 24ᶜᵐ. (Occasional papers of the Bernice
Pauahi Bishop museum of Polynesian ethnology and natural history. vol.
VII, no. 10)

"Brief list of references": p. 232-233.

1. Fishing—Hawaiian Islands. I. Title.

Library of Congress   GN670.B6 vol. VII, no. 10   22-1216
———— Copy 2.   GN423.S7
           [2]

QL
752
U 58

FISHING HAWAII

Matsumoto, Walter M.

Experimental surface gill net fishing for
skipjack (Katsuwonus pelamis) in Hawaiian waters.

(U.S. Fish and Wildlife, Special Sci. Rept.
Fisheries, No. 90, 1952)

DU
Pac. Pam.
840

FISHING HAWAII

1,002-pound marlin caught off Oahu; confirmation of world record sought.

(Forecast, Vol. 13(12):6-7, 1954)

DU
620
P

FISHING HAWAII

Stone, John F.

Fishing in Kona waters.

(Paradise of the Pacific, Vol. 45(7):5-8,
1933)

GN
Ethn. Pam.
2973

FISHING-HAWAII

Maunupau, Thomas K.

Notes on Off-Shore Fishing in Hawaii.

(9 typed pages)

DU
620
P

FISHING HAWAII

Opae fishing.

(Paradise of the Pacific, Vol. 20, 1907, No.
10, p. 21)

DU
621
H3

FISHING - HAWAIIAN ISLANDS

Waterhouse, Henry

Deep sea fishing; narrative of
Hawaiian method of deep sea fishing off
Kona, Hawaii. Thrum's Hawaiian Annual,
1899, pp. 104-6.

QL
Fishes
Pam.
530

FISHING HAWAII

Misumi, Ken

Spearing for thrills. Spearfishing costs
little; it pays off in table fare...

(Hawaiian Mag. Sect., Saturday Star-Bull.
Jan. 2, 1954, pp. 8-9)

GN
Ethn. Pam.
3501

FISHING HAWAII

Pukui, Mary Kawena

The makahiki; fishing and farming.
By Mary Kawena Pukui and Caroline Curtis.
Kamehameha Schools, Preparatory Department.
mimeographed. rec'd Aug. 1946 50 pp. 4to.

DU
620
P

FISHING HAWAII

Westervelt, W. D.

Ancient Hawaiian fishing.

(Paradise of the Pacific, Vol. 15, No. 12,
1902, p. 72-75)

DU
620
P

FISHING HAWAII

(Molokini)

(Paradise of the Pacific, Vol. 8, 1895, p. 19)

DU
620
P

FISHING HAWAII

Snaring eels and crawfish.

(Paradise of the Pacific, Vol. 21, 1908,
No. 9, p. 7)

DU
620
P

FISHING HAWAII

Westervelt, W. D. (William Drake)

Kai mimiki.

(Paradise of the Pacific, Vol. 15, 1902,
No. 6, p. 15)

DU
620
P

FISHING HAWAII

Nakuina, Emma Metcalf

Hawaiian sharks.

(Paradise of the Pacific, Vol. 6, 1893, p.
82)

DU
620
P

FISHING HAWAII

Stearns, Frederick

Piscatory pursuits in the "Paradise of the
Pacific".

(Paradise of the Pacific, Vol. 6, 1893,
p. 119)

DU
620
P

FISHING HAWAII

Westervelt, William Drake

The native and his ihe. (fishing spear)

(Paradise of the Pacific, Vol. 20, 1907,
No. 6, p. 18-19)

QL
Fishes
Pam.
529

FISHING HAWAII

Norwood, William

Harvest of the sea- the story of Oahu's
fishermen.

(Honolulu Star-Bulletin, Dec. 18, 1947)

DU
620
P

FISHING HAWAII

Stephenson, William

Hukilau on the reef.

(Paradise of the Pacific, Vol. 48(11):10-11,
1936)

FISHING HAWAII

see also

NETS AND NETTING HAWAII

AS
472
A -m

FISHING - INDIA

Hornell, James

The boats of the Ganges. The fishing methods of the Ganges. Asiatic Soc. Bengal, Mem. VIII, pp 171- 238, 1924.

GN
635.J3
N 82

FISHING   JAPAN

Norbeck, Edward

Takashima, a Japanese fishing community. University of Utah Press. Salt Lake City. 1954. 8vo. xi + 231(2) pp.

GN
2.S
P 76

FISHING   MANGAIA

Gold, Edwin

Netting and the pa at Mangaia.

(Jour. Poly. Soc., 65(4):363-364, 1956)

QL
634
Ma

and

QL
Fish Pam.
239

FISHING   INDIA

Hornell, James

The fishing methods of the Madras Presidency. Part 1: Madras Fisheries Bull. Vol. XVIII, pp. 59 - 110 (= Report 2 of 1924. Madras, 1925.) Part 2: The Malabar Coast Madras Fisheries Bulletin, Vol. 27, 69 pp. (Report No. 1 of 1937. Madras, 1938.)

Filed
on
Upper
Floor
of
Library

Fishing-Kauai

in Haw. Gazette. 1865, Oct. 7, pt. ("Stray Notes from Kauai")

AS
750
D

FISHING   MAORI

Best, Elsdon

Fishing methods and devices of the Maori.

(Dominion Mus. Bull. no. 12, 1929)

GN
Pam
#184
and
AS
36
S3

FISHING   INDIANS OF NORTH AMERICA

Mason, Otis Tufton

Aboriginal American Harpoons, a study in ethnic distribution and invention, ex U. S. Nat. Mus. Rept. for, 1900.

QL
Fish
Pam
#239

FISHING   MADRAS

Hornell, James

The fishing methods of the Madras Presidency. Madras Fish. Dept. 1925.

AP
2
N 54

FISHING   MAORI

Best, Elsdon

A Maori fish trap showing unusually fine workmanship.

(New Zealand Jour. of Sci. and Tech., vol. 2, 1919, pp. 35-37, illus.)

GC
1
C 37-c

FISHING   INDOCHINA

Khuong, Nguyen Luong

Les Procédés de pêche au thon des Vietnamines de Nhatrang. By Nguyen Luong Khuong and R. Serène.

(Contributions, Institut Océanographique de Nhatrang, No. 8, 1952. Reprint) pp. 5-12

DS
534
F 84

FISHING   MALAY

Fraser, Thomas M., Jr.

Rusembilan: a Malay fishing village in Southern Thailand. Cornell University Press. Ithaca. 1960. R8vo. xviii + 281 pp.

AP
2
N 54

FISHING   MAORI

Best, Elsdon

Stone-shanked Maori fish hooks.

(New Zealand Jour. of Sci. and Tech., vol. 3, 1921, pp. 295-296, figs. 1,2)

GC
1
C 37-c

FISHING   INDOCHINA

La pêche aux poissons volants. Par Le Bureau d'Etudes des Pêches de L'Institut Océanographique, Nhatrang.

(Institut Océanographique de Nhatrang, Contribution No. 8:15-24, 1952)

QL
634.Ma
K 42

FISHING   MALAYA

Akow, Tham
Methods of fishing.

IN:
Kesteven, G. L.
Malayan fisheries...Singapore, 1949, pp. 47-58

AP
2
N 54

FISHING   MAORI

Best, Elsdon

A toki titaha, or stone axe, from Taranaki.

(New Zealand Jour. of Sci. and Tech., vol. 3, 1920, p. 168, illus.)

GN
635.M4
F 52

FISHING   INDONESIA

Firth, Raymond

Malay fishermen: their peasant economy. London. Kegan Paul, Trench, Trubner and Co., Ltd. 8vo. 1946. xii + 354 pp. 2 maps.

AS
494
S 6

FISHING   MALAYA

Burdon, T. W.

Papers on Malayan fishing methods. By T. W. Burdon and M. L. Parry.

(Jour. of the Malayan Branch Royal Asiatic Society, Vol. 27(2): 1954)

AS
750
N

FISHING   MAORI

Buck, Peter H.

Maori food supplies of Lake Rotorua, with methods of obtaining them, and usages and customs appertaining thereto.

(Trans. and Proc. of the New Zealand Institute, 53:433-451, 1921)

GN
635.J3
K 97

FISHING   JAPAN

Kujukurihama; study of fishing community in Japan. Kujukuri Research Committee, based on the Rockefeller Fund, Keio University. 1958. 4to. 166 pp. mimeographed.

GN
635.M4
F 52

FISHING   MALAYA

Firth, Raymond

Malay fishermen: their peasant economy. London. Kegan Paul, Trench, Trubner and Co., Ltd. 8vo. 1946. xii + 354 pp. 2 maps

---

Storage
Case
5
Ms N 3

FISHING   MAORI

Buck, Peter Henry

Notes on New Zealand fish, and fishing (anthropological).

AS 750 N

FISHING MAORI

Downes, T. W.

Notes on eels and eel-weirs. In Trans New Zeal. Inst. Vol. L, 1917, pp 296- 316. illus.

GN Ethn.Pam. 3293

FISHING MAORI

Poata, Tamati R.

The Maori as a fisherman and his methods. W. B. Scott, & Sons, Ltd., Printers. Opotiki. 1919. 8vo. 27 pp.

QL 752 U 58

FISHING MARSHALL ISLANDS

Watanabe, Haruo

Fishing conditions south of the Marshall Islands. Translated by W. G. Van Campen.

(U. S. Fish and Wildlife Service, Special Scientific Report: Fisheries, No. 43. orig. date 1940. trans. in 1951)

AS 750 D

FISHING MAORI

Hamilton, (Augustus)

Fishing and sea-foods of the ancient Maori. Dom. Mus. Bull. 2, pp. 73, illus.

GN 2.S P 76

FISHING MAORI

Rolston, Richard

Notched fishing-line sinker.

(Jour. Poly. Soc. Vol. 57:304-305, 1948)

GN 2.S O 15

FISHING MAUPITI

Ropiteau, Andre

La pêche aux thons à Maupiti.

(Journal de la Soc. des Océanistes, 3:12-21, 1947)

DU 1 P 12

FISHING MAORI

Hobbs, Derisely F.

How they caught Tangaroa's eels.

(Pacific Discovery, Vol. 7(4):23-28, 1954)

GN 2.S P 76

FISHING MAORI

Skinner, H. D.

Maori use of the harpoon.

(Jrl. of the Polynesian Society. Vol.46, 1937. pp.63-73)

GN 1 S 93

FISHING MELANESIA

Anell, Bengt

Contribution to the history of fishing in the southern seas. Inaugural dissertation, Univ. of Uppsala, May, 1955.

(Studia Ethnographica Upsaliensia, IX, pp. xix + 249; 1955)

GN 2.S P 76

FISHING MAORI

Knapp, F. V.

Trawling customs of the Tasman Bay Maoris.

(Journal of the Polynesian Society, Vol. 49, 1940, pp. 375-381)

GN 2.S P 76

FISHING MAORI

Skinner, W.H.

PUNGATAI and its connection with the ancient Maori ceremonies of the opening of the fishing season.

(Journal of the Polynesian Society, 27: 36-37, 1918.)

GN 1 S 93

FISHING MICRONESIA

Anell, Bengt

Contribution to the history of fishing in the southern seas. Inaugural dissertation, Univ. of Uppsala, May, 1955.

(Studia Ethnographica Upsaliensia, IX, 1955)

AS 750 N

FISHING MAORI

Newman, Alfred K.

On Maori dredges.

(New Zealand Inst., Trans. and Proc., vol. 37, 1904, pp. 138-144, pls. 1 & 2.)

AS 750 N

FISHING MAORI BIBLIOGRAPHY

Hamilton, A.

List of papers on New Zealand fishes and fishing.

(Trans. and Proc. New Zealand Institute, Vol. 34, 1901, pp. 539-548)

AS 36 A 5

FISHING MICRONESIA

Clark, Eugenie

Field trip to the South Seas.

(Natural History, Vol. 60(1):8-15,46, 1951)

Micronesia: Fais, Ulithi; Palau

DU 400 T 25

FISHING MAORI

Ohia, W.

Spear fishing.

(Te Ao Hou, The New World, Vol. 4(4):36-58, 49, December, 1956)

QH 541 E 17 m

FISHES MARSHALL ISLANDS

Hiatt, Robert E.

Ecological relationships of the fish fauna on coral reefs of the Marshall Islands. By Robert W. Hiatt and Donald W. Strasburg.

(Ecological Monographs, Vol. 30(1):65-127, 1960)

QL 627 P 11

FISHING MICRONESIA

Matsumoto.

An investigation of the skipjack fishery in the waters of Woleai, with notes on the bait situation at Lamotrel and Puluwat Is.

(South Sea Fishery News [Nanyo Suisan Joho], no. 3, 1937, p. 2-6)

Translation No. 42, Pac. Oceanic Fishery Investigations, by W. G. van Campen

---

AP 2 N 54

FISHING MAORI

Phillipps, W. J.

Maori bait-trap for catching small fish.

(New Zealand Journal of Science and Technology, Vol. XVI, No. 3, Nov., 1934, pp. 165-166)

QL 427 P 11

FISHING MARSHALL ISLANDS

Ikebe, Kenzō

A survey of tuna fishing grounds in the Marshall and Caroline Islands.

(South Sea Fishery News [Nanyō Suisan Jōhō], vol. 5(1):6-9, 1941)

Translated from Japanese, Pacific Oceanic Fishery Investigations, Translation No. 15

GN 2.S V

FISHING NAURU

Kayser, A.

Die Fischerei auf Nauru. (Pleasant Island)

(Mitt.Anthropologischen Gesellschaft,Wien, Bd. 66, 1936, pp. 92-131; 149-264)

GN
1
An

FISHING NEW BRITAIN

Meyer, Otto

Fischerei bei den Uferleuten des nördlichen Teiles der Gazellehalbinsel und speciell auf der Insel Vuatam, Neu-Pommern, Südsee.

(Anthropos. vol.VIII. 1913. pp.82-109, 325-341, 1069-1103)

G
51
W 17

FISHING NEW ZEALAND

Cusco

Surf fishing on New Zealand's Ninety Mile Beach.

(Walkabout, Vol. 11, No. 12 [Oct., 1945], pp. 29-30)

DU
12
B 39

FISHING PACIFIC

Becke, Louis

'Neath austral skies. London. John Milne 1909. 8vo. 315 pp.

pp. 75-90,95-102,298-9

GN
Ethn.Pam.
3646

FISHING NEW CALEDONIA

Legand, Michel

Contribution à l'étude des méthodes fde pêche dans les territoires francais du Pacifique Sud.

(Jour. de la Soc. des Océanistes, VI:141-184, 1950)

GN
2.S
P 76

FISHING NIUAFOU

Mahony, B. G.

A method of catching fish at Niuafo'ou.

(Jour. Poly. Soc., 24:168, 1915)

DU
12
B 39

FISHING PACIFIC

Becke, Louis

By rock and pool, on an Austral shore, and other stories. London. T. Fisher Unwin. 1901. 250 pp.

sea and lagoon fishing, pp. 7-11; 45-48; 51-57; 63-65; 148-158; 167-173

Q
101
F 81

FISHING NEW CALEDONIA

Legand, M.

La pêche en Nouvelle-Calédonie.
IN

Congrès des pêches et des pêcheries dans l'Union Francaise d'Outre-Mer...pp. 256-267. 1950.

GN
2.S
Po

Fishing - Niue

Smith, S. Percy

In his Niue Island and its people. In Polyn. Soc. Journ. XI, 1902. pp. 215-216.

DU
12
B 39

FISHING PACIFIC

Becke, Louis

Wild life in the Southern Seas. New York. 1898.

[see ms. index at back of book]

AS
28
E 85

FISHING NEW CALEDONIA

Quelques renseignements sur la fabrication d'une nasse thite.

(Etudes Melanésiennes, n.s. 3rd year, No. 5: 64-68, 1951)

(included: prohibitions for the fisherman)

GN
2.I
A-m

ONGTONG JAVA
FISHING XXXXXXXXXXXXXXXX

Lazarus, D. M.

Live bait fishing in Ongtong Java, by D. M. Lazarus, with additional notes by H. G. Beasley.

(Man, vol. XXXVII, 1937. pp. 57-58)

QL
617
F 24

FISHING PACIFIC

Farrington, S. Kip, Jr.

Pacific game fishing. Illustrated by Lynn Bogue Hunt. Coward-McCann, Inc., New York. 1942c. R8vo. xii + 290 pp.

GN
1
O 15

FISHING NEW IRELAND

Groves, William C.

Fishing rites at Tabar.

(Oceania, Vol. 4, No. 4, 1934, pp. 432-457, pls. 1-3)

QL
627
U-a

Fishing - Pacific

Alexander, A. B.

Notes on the boats, apparatus and fishing methods employed by the natives of the South Sea Islands and results of fishing trials by the Albatross. In the U. S. Fish Com. Report 1901. pp. 743-829. Illus.

DU
1
P 10

FISHING PACIFIC

Fishing school for islanders.

(Pacific Isl. Monthly, 26(1):105, 1955)

[Sponsored by S. P. Commission and UN FAO]
(see also in South Pacific, 8(6):129, 1955)

G
51
W 17

FISHING NEW IRELAND

Groves, William C.

A native fish-hunt in New Ireland.

(Walkabout, Vol. 2(4):33-35, 1936)

GN
1
S 93

FISHING PACIFIC

Anell, Bengt

Contribution to the history of fishing in the southern seas. Inaugural dissertation, Univ. of Uppsala, May, 1955.

(Studia Ethnographica Upsaliensia, IX, 1955)

GN
Eth.
Pam.
2860

FISHING - PACIFIC

Gudger, E. W.

Wooden Hooks Used for Catching Sharks and Ruvettus in the South Seas; A Study of their Variation and Distribution.

(From Anthropological Papers of the American Museum of Natural History, Vol. XXVIII, Part III. Pages 212-343). 1927

GN
2.S
M 26

FISHING NEW IRELAND

Groves, W. C.

Shark fishing in New Ireland.

(Mankind, Vol. 2, 1936, pp.3-6)

DU
1
S 72 t

FISHING PACIFIC

Angot, Michel

Trolling and longlining for tuna. Two papers by Michel Angot and Rene Criou.

(South Pacific Commission, Tech. Paper No. 134, 1961)

DU
1
S 72-q

FISHING PACIFIC

Kroon, A. H. J.

Development of Pacific fisheries.

(South Pacific Commission, Quarterly Bull., Vol. 5(3):17, July, 1955)

GN
Ethn.Pam.
413

FISHING   PACIFIC

Plischke, Hans

Die Fischdrachen.

(Leipzig Stadt. Mus. f. Volkerkunde, Ver-
offen., Heft 6, 1922)

(Indonesia, Melanesia, Micronesia)

GN
1
S 93

FISHING   POLYNESIA

Anell, Bengt

Contribution to the history of fishing in the
southern seas. Inaugural dissertation, Univ.
of Uppsala, May, 1955.

(Studia Ethnographica Upsaliensia, IX, 1955)

QL
Protozoa
Poly
Pam
#19

Fishing   Rarotonga.

Gill, W. Wyatt

Zoologische Missellen aus der Südsee
.... in Geog. Gesell. zu Jena, Mittheilung-
en, VII, 2, pp. 18-37.

DU
1
P

FISHING   PACIFIC

South Pacific Commission stimulating fishing
in south Pacific.

(Pacific Islands Monthly, 22(11):23-26,
1952)

GN
2.I
A

FISHING   POLYNESIA

Beasley, Harry G.

Some Polynesian cuttlefish baits. In
Journ. Royal Anthrop. Instit. of Great
Britain and Ireland, v.51, pp. 100-114,
Jan.-June, 1921.

QL
Fishes
Pam.
567

FISHING   RAROTONGA

South Pacific Commission Project E.7.- Fisheries, Rarotonga, April 1952. (native names,
fish traps; lagoon bait; sea bait; off shore
fishes)

QL
627
P 11

FISHING   PACIFIC

Watanabe, Haruo

Fishing conditions south of the Marshall
Islands. Translated from the Japanese language
by W. G. Van Campen.

(Pacific Oceanic Fishery Investigations,
U. S. Fish and Wildlife Service, Dept. of the Int
Honolulu, 1949)

DU
12
E 47

DU 12
E 47
locked
case

FISHING   POLYNESIA

Ellis, William, 1794-1872

Polynesian Researches...2 vols. London.
1829. 8vo. Vol. 2, pp. 284-298.

The same...1830. 2 vols. 8vo.

Storage
Case
3

FISHING   RIU KIU ISLANDS

Hornbostel, Hans G.

Marianas: 2 boxes of ms. notes.
(notes on some Okinawa fishermen in Guam)

AS
540
P

FISHING   PHILIPPINE ISLANDS

Domantay, Jose S.

Tuna fishing in southern Mindanao.

(Philippine Journal of Sci., Vol. 73, 1940:
423-436)

GN
Ethn.Pam.
3378

FISHING   POLYNESIA

Gill, William Wyatt

The octopus in the Pacific.

(Leisure Hour, 1872, pp. 251-252; 1874,
pp. 638-639).

DU
1
P

FISHING   ROTUMA

"Amel"

A fish drive in Rotuma.

(Pacific Islands Monthly, Vol. 13, 1942,
p. 17)

GN
423
H 32

FISHING   PHILIPPINE ISLANDS

Hart, Donn V.

Securing aquatic products in Siaton
Municipality, Negros Oriental Province,
Philippines.

(Inst. Sci. and Technology, Philippines,
Monograph 4, 1956)

Q
101
F 81

FISHING   POLYNESIA   (SOUTHEAST)

Legand, M.

Les méthodes de pêche dans les territoires
du Pacifique Sud. Extraits du rapport.
IN
Congres des pêches et des pêcheries dans
l'Union Francaise d'Outre-Mer, pp. 268-276, 1950

GN
2.M
H

FISHING   SAMOA

Demandt, E.

Die Fischerei der Samoaner: Eine Zusammenstellung der bekanntesten Methoden des Fanges der
Seetiere bei den Eingeborenen.

(Mus. für Volkerkunde III, 1. 1913.
Hamburg. 142 pp. 4to. pls.)

AS
540
P 55

FISHING   PHILIPPINE ISLANDS

Herre, Albert W.

Fishery Resources of the Philippine Islands.

(Monograph, Bureau of Science, Philippine
Islands, No. 3, 1927)

GN
Pam
#294

FISHING -- POLYNESIA
Stokes, John F. G.

Fish Poisoning in the Hawaiian
Islands, ex Occ. Papl. B. P. Bishop
Mus., vol. VII, no. 10, 1921.

G
1
G 56

FISHING   SAMOA

Bülow, Werner von

Das Fischereirecht der Eingeborenen von
Deutsch-Samoa.

(Globus, Bd. 82, 1902, pp. 319-320)

QL
627
P 55

FISHING   PHILIPPINE ISLANDS

Rasalan, Santos B.

The basnig, a bag net for pelagic fishing
in the Philippines. By Santos B. Rasalan and D.
V. Villadolid.

(The Philippine Journal of Fisheries, Vol.
3(1):1-30, 1955)

QH
11
P 11

FISHING   RAROIA

Harry, Robert R.

Ichthyological field data of Raroia Atoll,
Tuamotu Archipelago.

(Scientific Investigations in Micronesia,
Report No. 16, 1953)

GN
671.S2
K 89

FISHING   SAMOA

Krämer, Augustin

Die Samoa-Inseln. Entwurf einer Monographie
mit besonderer Berücksichtigung Deutsch-Samoas...
Stuttgart. 1902-1903. 4to. 2 vols.

Band II: Ethnographie...pp. 187-202.

G 1 G 56	FISHING SAMOA Thilenius, Georg Bonito- und Haifang in Alt-Samoa. (Globus, Bd. 78, 1900, pp. 127-128)

QL 617 C 46	FISHING SOLOMON ISLANDS Chapman, Wilbert McLeod Fishing in troubled waters. J. B. Lippincott Company, Philadelphia and New York. 1949. 8vo. 256 pp.

GN Ethn.Pam. 3540	FISHING TAHITI Blackman, Leopold G. Fishing in Tahiti. Lagoons and streams abound with edible denizens of the sea, many of them well-known in Hawaiian waters. But in Tahiti fish sell for 15 cents a pound. (Honolulu Advertiser, Sunday Polynesian, June 27, 1948)

QH 1 T 88	FISHING SAMOA Tuitoti, Siaosi E. Shark fishing in Western Samoa. (Tuatara, 5(3):82-85; 1955)

GN 2.1 A-M	FISHING SOLOMON ISLANDS Edge-Partington, J. Fishing appliance from Ysabel Island (Bugotu) (Man, vol. 15, 1915, no. 84)

DU 1 P	FISHING TAHITI Burchett, W. G. New ways of fishing; happy hours with Natua, of Tahiti. (Pacific Islands Monthly, Vol. 10, No. 10, 1940, pp. 38-40)

AS 522.B S 24	FISHING SARAWAK Harrisson, Tom Sarawak Malay fishing cycles. By Tom Harrisson and A. K. Marican Salleh. (Sarawak Museum Journal, 9:63-73, 1959)

GN 2.1 A-M	FISHING SOLOMON ISLANDS Edge-Partington, T. W. Kite fishing by the salt-water natives of Mala or Malaita Island, British Solomon Islands. (Man, vol. 12, 1912, no. 4, pp. 9-11)

GN Ethn.Pam. 3381	FISHING TAHITI Keeler, Charles Upon a coral strand. (Tahiti) (Out West Magazine, 1903, pp. 491-499, 635-644)

DU 12 F74	Fishing—Society Islands Forster, John Reinold In his observations made during a voyage round the world, pages 461-463.

G 51 W 17	FISHING SOLOMON ISLANDS Griffiths, B. M. H. Native fishing in the Solomons. (Walkabout, Vol. 10 (3):13-14, 1944)

GN 2.S O 15	FISHING TAHITI Vernier, Charles Pêches et engins de pêche à Tahiti et aux Iles Sous-le-Vent. (Journal de la Soc. des Océanistes, 3:5-11, 1947)

GN 671.S5 H 23	FISHING SOCIETY ISLANDS Handy, E. S. Craighill Houses, Boats and Fishing in the Society Islands. (Bulletin Bernice P. Bishop Museum, 90. 1931. 111 pp. 25 plates, 21 figures).

GN 2.1 A-4	FISHING SOLOMON ISLANDS Hocart, A.M. The canoe and the bonito in Eddystone Island. (Jour. R. Anthropological Inst. of Great Britain and Ireland, Vol. 65, 1935, pp. 97-111)

QL Fishes Pam. 433	FISHING TASMANIA Blackburn, M. Recent progress with pelagic fishing in Tasmanian waters. (Journal of the Council for scientific and Industrial Research, Vol. 20 (4):434-444, 1947)

GN Ethn.Pam. 3646	FISHING SOCIETY ISLANDS Legand, Michel Contribution à l'étude des méthodes de pêche dans les territoires francais du Pacifique Sud. (Jour. de la Soc. des Oceanistes, VI:141-184, 1950)

GN 1 N 27	FISHING SOLOMON ISLANDS (bonito) Kuper, Geoffrey An initiation ceremony in the British Solomon Islands. (The Native Medical Practitioner, Vol. 2, 1937, pp. 387-398)

DU 1 P 10	FISHING TONGA How to "sweet-talk" those Tongan sharks. (Pacific Islands Monthly, 28(7):83, 1958)

GN Ethn.Pam. 2827	FISHING SOCIETY ISLANDS Nordhoff, Charles Notes on the Off-Shore Fishing of the Society Islands. (Reprinted from the Journal of the Polynesian Society, Vol. 39, Nos. 2 and 3, 1930.79pp)

GN 2.1 T 89	FISHING SOLOMON ISLANDS Paravicini, Eugen Die speere der Salomons Inseln. (Revista del Instituto de Etnologia, Universidad de Tucumán, Tomo II, 1932, pp. 481-491)

GN 2.S P 76	FISHING TONGA Vaea, Hon. Preliminary report on a fisheries survey in Tonga. By Hon. Vaea and W. Straatmans. (Jour. of the Poly. Soc., Vol. 63(3-4):199-215, 1954)

PL
Phil.Pam.
549

FISHING TONGA

Whitcombe, J. D.

Tongan phrase book. 2nd edition. no place
no date. 12mo. 43 pp.

FISHING GEAR

See

FISHING IMPLEMENTS AND APPLIANCES

GN
799.F5
R 23

FISHING PREHISTORIC

Rau, Charles

Prehistoric fishing in Europe and North
America. Washington. 1884.

AS
36
S

(Smithsonian Contributions to Knowledge, 509)

GN
2.1
A-M

FISHING TROBRIAND ISLANDS

Malinowski, Bronislaw

Fishing in the Trobriand Islands.

(Man, vol. 18, 1918, no. 53, pp. 87-92)

GN
2.M
L 52

FISHING IMPLEMENTS AND APPLIANCES

Frese, H. H.

The classification of fishing gear.

(Mededelingen van het Rijksmuseum voor Volkenkunde, Leiden, No. 15:12-25, 1962)

GN
799.F5
R 23

FISHING PRIMITIVE

Rau, Charles

Prehistoric fishing in Europe and North
America. Washington. 1884.

AS
36
S

(Smithsonian Contributions to Knowledge, 509)

GN
Ethn.Pam.
3646

FISHING TUAMOTUS

Legand, Michel

Contribution à l'étude des méthodes de
pêche dans les territoires francais du Pacifique
Sud.

(Jour. de la Soc. des Oceanistes, VI:141-
184, 1950)

FISHING--IMPLEMENTS AND APPLIANCES.
U. S. National museum.
... Classification of the collection to illustrate the animal resources of the United States. A list of substances
derived from the animal kingdom, with synopsis of the
useful and injurious animals and a classification of the
methods of capture and utilization. By G. Brown Goode
... Washington, Govt. print. off., 1876.
  xiii, 126 p. 24½ᶜᵐ. (Added t.-p.: ... Bulletin of the United States Na-
tional museum. no. 6)
  At head of title: International exhibition, 1876. Board on behalf of
United States executive departments.
  Issued also as vol. XIII, art. 6 of the Smithsonian miscellaneous collections.
Smithsonian institution publication 297.
  1. Zoology—U. S.   2. Animal products. 3. Hunting—
Implements and appliances.   4. Fishing—Implements and appli-
ances. 5. Philadelphia.   Centennial exhibition, 1876. I.
Goode, George Brown,   1851-1896.
1851-1896.
  Library, Smithsonian   Institution Q11.U6   S 13-118
    [s20g3]

AS
36
S2

AS
36
S5

AN
2.E
P 78

FISHING SHARKS

Pearl fishing and shark fishing.

(The Polynesian, Aug. 29, 1864)

GN
1
A 62

and

DU
Pac.Pam.
328

FISHING TUAMOTUS

Seurat, L. G.

Les Engins de Pêche des Anciens Paumotu.

(L'Anthropologie, Tome 16, 1905, pp. 295-
307)

AN
2.E
P 78

FISHING PEARLS

Pearl fishing and shark fishing.

(The Polynesian, Aug. 29, 1864)

QL
626
C 15

and

QL
Fish
Pam.544

FISHING TUNA

Wilson, Robert C.

Tuna longlining: results of a cruise to the
eastern tropical Pacific Ocean. By Robert C.
Wilson and Bell M. Shimada.

(California Fish and Game, Vol. 41(1):91-98,
1955)

[Japanese tuna fishing grounds]

GN
2.S
P 76

FISHING UVEA

Phillipps, W. J.

Wallis Island fishing customs.

(Jour. Poly. Soc., 62(3):263-266, 1953)

DU
1
S 72-q

FISHING POISONS

Barrau, Jacques

Fishing poisons of the South Pacific.

(South Pacific Commission, Quarterly Bull.,
Vol. 5(3):7-8, July, 1955)

QL
Fishes
Pam.
507

Fishing rights of Hawaii date back to grants
of kings.

(The Honolulu Advertiser, March 11, 1922)

GN
1
C 37-e

FISHING VIETNAM

Etudes sur les techniques de pêche du Viêt-
nam.

(Inst. Oceanographique de Nhatrang, Contrib.
no. 8, 1952, being extrait du Bull. Soc. Etudes
Indochinoises, ns tome 27, No. 1, 1952)

QL
Fish
Pam.
559

FISHING POISONS
FISHING WITH POISON

Gregory, W. K.

Fishing with poison in Africa.

(Copeia, No. 25, pp. 57-58, Dec., 1915)

GN
Ethn.
Pam.
744
745

Fishing Rights in Hawaii

Massee, Edward K.

GN
Ethn.Pam.
3830

FISHING BASKETS

Leth, T.

Two kinds of fishing implements: 1. The
plunge basket (Stulpkorb) in Africa and elsewhere
2. The circular cast-net in Africa. By T. Leth
and K. G. Lindblom.

(Riksmuseets Etnografiska Avdelning, Smärre
Meddelanden, Nr. 11, 1933)

GN
423
K 91

FISHING PREHISTORIC

Krause, Eduard

Vorgeschichtliche Fischereigeräte und neuere
Vergleichsstücke...Berlin. 1904.

DU
Hist.
Pam.
590

FISHING RIGHTS HAWAII

Bailey, C. T.

List of fishing rights, Hawaiian Islands:
not adjudicated. Honolulu. Star-Bulletin,
Ltd. 1923. 15 pp.

DU 1 P 10

Fishing school for islanders.

(Pacific Isl. Monthly, 26(1):105, 1955)

[Sponsored by S. P. Commission and UN FAO]
(see also in South Pacific, 8(6):129, 1955)

GN 2.I A-4

Fison, Lorimer

Land tenure in Fiji.

(Journ. Anthrop. Inst. of Great Britain and Ireland, Vol. 10, 1880-1, pp. 332-352)

FISSION.

QL 1 C15

Robertson, Alice, 1859–

... Embryology and embryonic fission in the genus *Crisia*. By Alice Robertson. Berkeley, The University press, 1903.

cover-title, p. 115-156. pl. XII-XIV (2 fold.) 27ᶜᵐ. (University of California publications. Zoology, v. 1, no. 3)

Thesis (PH. D.)—Univ. of Calif.

1. Crisiidae. 2. Embryology—Polyzoa. 3. Fission.

A 11-2274

Title from Univ. of Calif.   Library of Congress

FISHPONDS

SEE

FISH PONDS

GN 2.I A-4

Fison, Lorimer

The Nanga, or Sacred Stone Enclosure of Wainimala, Fiji.

(Journal of the R. Anthropological Institute of Great Britain and Ireland, Vol. 14, 1884-1885, pp. 14-30)

QE 201 P

Fisiografía.—Informe acerca de la Fisiografía, Geología é Hidrología de los alrededores de La Paz, Baja California, por el Dr. Ernesto Angermann.—*Parergones del Instituto Geológico de México*. Tomo I, nº 2, p. 3-21, 2 láms. 1904.

N.16.   OCT 10 1904

GN 2.I A-4

Fison, Lorimer

Notes on Fijian burial customs.

(Journ. Anthrop. Inst. of Great Britain and Ireland, Vol. 10, 1880-1, pp. 137-149)

AS 36 S4

Fisk, Mary.

A review of the fishes of the genus *Osmerus* of the California coast. By Mary Fisk.

(*In* U. S. National museum. Proceedings. Washington, 1914. 23½ᶜᵐ. v. 46, p. 291-297, illus.)

1. Osmerus.

14-10984

Library of Congress   Q11.U55 vol. 46

AS 720.V R 88

Fison, Lorimer

Codrington, R. H.

Notes on the customs of Mota, Banks Islands. With remarks by Lorimer Fison.

(Trans. and Proc. R. Soc. of Victoria, 16; 119-143)

AS 720.V R

Fison, Lorimer

Classificatory System of Kinship.

(Royal Society of Victoria, Trans. and Proc. Vol. X, 1874, pp. 154-179)

GN 2.I A-4

Fison, Lorimer

On Fijian riddles.

(Journ. Anthrop. Inst. of Great Britain and Ireland, Vol. 11, 1881-2, pp. 406-410)

GN 2.I A-4

Fison, Lorimer

The classificatory system of relationship.

(Journ. Anthrop. Inst. of Great Britain and Ireland, Vol. 24, 1894-5, pp. 360-371)

DU 600 F54

Fison, Lorimer.

Tales from old Fiji, by Lorimer Fison.

London, Alexander Moring, 1907. 175p. illus.

AS 701 A

Fison, Lorimer

Group Marriage & Relationship

In Aus. Assoc. Adv. Sc. Vol. IV, 1892

Hobart 1892 8vo pp. # 688-697

SEP-3 1910

P

QC Physics and Met. Pam. 44

FISSION

Cohn, S. H.

Experimental treatment of poisoning from fission products. Ability of chemical agents to alter the uptake and retention of fission products in animals exposed to radioactive fall-out. By S. H. Cohn, J. K. Gong and W. L. Milne.

(Reprinted from the A. M. A. Archives of Industrial Health, Vol. 14, pp. 533-538, December, 1956)